SUMMARY CONTENTS

PART ONE: PROPERTY
Stuart Anderson   1

PART TWO: CONTRACT
Michael Lobban   295

PART THREE: COMMERCIAL LAW
Michael Lobban   611

PART FOUR: TORT
Michael Lobban   877

TABLE OF CONTENTS

Abbreviations   xiii
Table of Cases   xvii
Table of Statutes   cxxi

PART ONE: PROPERTY   *Stuart Anderson*

I.   **Succession, Inheritance, and the Family**   3

       1. The Forms of Family Provision   3
       2. Courts as Settlors   12
       3. The Legal Framework of Successive Interests   18
       4. Wills and their Interpretation   22

II.   **Property Rights in Land: Reforming the Heritage**   47

       1. Introduction   47
       2. The World of the Real Property Commission   49

III.   **Land Transactions: Settlements and Sales**   79

       1. Introduction   79
       2. Strict Settlement   79
       3. Buying and Selling   94

IV.   **Leases, Mortgages, and Servitudes**   110

       1. Leases   110
       2. Mortgages   132
       3. Servitudes and Allied Rights over Land   159

V.   **Changing the Nature of Real Property Law**   179

       1. 'Assimilation' to 1875   179
       2. Conveyancing and Land Transfer 1875–1914   202

VI.   **Trusts and Trustees**   232

       1. The Usefulness of Private Trusts   232
       2. A Law of Private Trusts   238
       3. Trustees   268

PART TWO: CONTRACT   *Michael Lobban*

I.	**Introduction**	297
	1. The Age of Freedom of Contract	297
	2. The Impact of Legal Treatises	300
	3. The Influence of Procedure	313
	4. The Contracting Society	323
II.	**The Formation of Contracts: Offer and Acceptance**	329
	1. The Meeting of the Minds	334
	2. Communication Problems	343
	3. Unilateral Contracts	348
III.	**Consideration**	358
	1. The Rise and Fall of Moral Consideration	361
	2. Consideration and Reliance	366
	3. Adequacy of Consideration	372
	4. The Performance of Existing Duties	376
	5. Consideration and Privity of Contract	388
	6. Theories of Consideration	394
IV.	**Misrepresentation**	400
	1. Duress and Undue Influence	400
	2. Fraud at Common Law	409
	3. Fraud in Equity	414
	4. Negligent Misrepresentations	417
	5. Misrepresentation after Fusion	425
V.	**Mistake**	433
	1. Mistake in Equity	435
	2. Mistake at Common Law	445
	3. Mistake of Identity	452
	4. An Unsettled Doctrine	471
VI.	**Contractual Terms and their Performance**	473
	1. Quality Obligations in the Sale of Goods	475
	2. Conditions and Warranties	485
	3. Waiver	491
	4. Anticipatory Breach	494
	5. Frustration	508

VII.	Contractual Remedies	522
	1. Penalties and Liquidated Damages	523
	2. *Quantum Meruit* and Expectation Damages	530
	3. Remoteness of Damage	541
	4. Specific Performance	548
VIII.	Restitutionary Remedies	563
	1. An 'Equitable' Action	563
	2. Waiver of Tort	573
	3. Mistaken Payments	583
	4. Failure of Consideration	588
	5. Money Paid	595
	6. Equity, Common Law, and the Redefinition of 'Quasi-Contract'	601

PART THREE: COMMERCIAL LAW   *Michael Lobban*

I.	Joint Stock Companies	613
	1. Companies and Partnerships in the 1820s	613
	2. Reforming Company Law, 1830–1848	619
	3. The Transformation of Company Law, 1848–1862	625
	4. Companies and the Stock Market, 1862–1914	631
	5. The Birth of Companies	638
	6. Winding Up Companies	647
	7. Company Management and the Courts	652
	8. The Private Company	667
	9. Cartels	670
II.	The Law of Insurance	674
	1. The Development of Insurance	674
	2. The Principle of Indemnity and the Insurable Interest	679
	3. The Formation of Insurance Policies	696
	4. Claims on the Policy	711
III.	Negotiable Instruments	728
	1. Bills of Exchange and Promissory Notes	731
	2. Letters of Credit	754
	3. Bills of Lading	758
	4. Banks and Cheques	764

IV.   **Bankruptcy and Insolvency**   779

    1. The System of Bankruptcy in 1820   780
    2. Reforming the Law of Bankruptcy, 1825–1831   793
    3. The Law of Insolvency, 1810–1838   797
    4. Reforming Bankruptcy and Insolvency, 1838–1849   804
    5. Bankruptcy Law, 1849–1861   808
    6. Reforming Bankruptcy and Insolvency, 1861–1883   817
    7. The Law of Bankruptcy, 1883–1914   823

V.   **Consumer Credit and Debt**   834

    1. Imprisonment for Debt   836
    2. The Poor Man's Bankruptcy   844
    3. Pawnbroking   849
    4. Money Lenders   858
    5. Hire Purchase   869

PART FOUR: TORT   *Michael Lobban*

I.   **The Development of Tort law**   879

    1. The Uses of Tort Law   881
    2. The Structure of Tort Law   887
    3. The Problem of Vicarious Liability   894
    4. The Jury and Damages   899

II.   **Negligence**   903

    1. The Birth of Negligence   903
    2. Defining Negligence   921
    3. Rethinking Negligence   940

III. **Personal Injuries**   958

    1. Railway Accidents   958
    2. Accidents on the Highway   970
    3. Occupiers' Liability   976
    4. Dangerous Goods   984
    5. Damages for Personal Injury   990

IV.   **Workplace Injuries**   1001

    1. Workmen and the Common Law   1002
    2. The Employers' Liability Act 1880   1012

3. The Workmen's Compensation Act 1897   1018

V.   **Intentional and Economic Torts**   1033

1. Malice and Intent in Early Nineteenth-century Law   1034
2. Economic Torts   1039
3. Expanding Economic Torts, 1853–1887   1043
4. Rethinking Malice and Intent, 1887–1901   1049
5. Rethinking Conspiracy, 1901–1914   1060

VI. **Nuisance**   1068

1. The Right to Light   1071
2. Water Rights   1080
3. Smoke and Noise   1093
4. Remedies   1105

VII. **Property Torts**   1112

1. Wrongs to Chattels   1114
2. Wrongs to Real Property   1125

Further Reading   1151
Index of Names   1171
Index of Subjects   1177

ABBREVIATIONS

Statutes of UK Parliament: the regnal year is included in a first citation of a statute until 1853. Then the modern series published by HM Stationery Office begins, the annual volumes having reliable indices.

Law Reports: Abbreviations of series of law reports are not listed here. The names of nominate series follow standard practice for the nineteenth century, as abbreviated in *Halsbury's Laws of England* (4th and 5th eds, 2009), Consolidated Tables, Cases A–L, pp. xi–xliv. Further assistance may be found in C.W. Ringrose (ed.), *Where to Look for your Law* (14th ed., 1962) and also within D. Raistrick's very thorough *Index of Legal Citations and Abbreviations* (3rd ed., 2008).

AJLH	American Journal of Legal History
Am J. Comp. Law	American Journal of Comparative Law
Am. J. Int. Law	American Journal of International Law
Am. Soc. Int. Law	American Society of International Law
Anglo-Am. Law Rev.	Anglo-American Law Review
App.	Appendix
Att.-Gen.	Attorney-General
B.	Baron of the Exchequer
Bt	Baronet
BIHR	Bulletin of the Institute of Historical Research
Bl. Comm.	Blackstone's Commentaries on the Laws of England
BYIL	British Yearbook of International Law
CB	Chief Baron
CCC	County Courts Chronicle
CFLQ	Child and Family Law Quarterly
Ch. Chs	Chapter, Chapters
CJCP	Chief Justice of Common Pleas
CJK(Q)B	Chief Justic of King's (Queen's) Bench
CLE	Council for Legal Education
CLJ	Cambridge Law Journal
CLP	Current Legal Problems
Con. and Ch.	Continuity and Change
Cornhill Mag.	Cornhill Magazine
Crim. Law Rev.	Criminal Law Review

DC	Departmental Committee
DNB	Dictionary of National Biography
East P. C.	East, Pleas of the Crown
Econ. Hist. Rev.	Economic History Review
Edinburgh Rev.	Edinburgh Review
Eng. Hist. Rev.	English Historical Review
Hale H.P.C	Hale, History of the Please of the Crown
Hawk P. C.	Hawkins, Pleas of the Crown
Hist. J.	Historical Journal
Hist. St. Ind. Rels	Historical Studies in Industrial Relations
Holdsworth, HEL	Sir W.S. Holdsworth, History of English Law
ICLQ	International and Comparative Law Review
ILS	Independent Law Society
Int. Rev. Soc. Hist.	International Review of Social History
J., JJ.	Justice, Justices
JBS	Journal of British Studies
JCPC	Judicial Committee of the Privy Council
JEH	Journal of Economic History
J. Hist. Geography	Journal of Historical Geography
J. Hist. Ideas	Journal of the History of Ideas
J. Hist. Int. L.	Journal of the History of International Law
JLE	Journal of Law and Economics
JLH	Journal of Legal History
JLS	Journal of Legal Studies
JPOS	Journal of the Patent Office Society
JPTOS	Journal of the Patent and Trade Mark Office Society
JP	Justice of the Peace
JR	Juridical Review
J. Soc. Hist.	Journal of Social History
JSPTL	Journal of the Society of Public Teachers of Law
KC	King's Counsel
LAS	Law Amendment Society
LC	Lord Chancellor
LCO	Lord Lord Chancellor's Office
Leg. Ob.	Legal Observer
LG	Law Gazette
LJ, LJJ	Lord Justice, Lord Justices
LHR	Law and History Review

LJ	Law Journal
LM	Law Magazine
LN	Legal Notes
LQR	Law Quarterly Review
LR	Law Reporter
LS	Legal Studies
LT	Law Times (journal)
MLR	Modern Law Review
MPLA	Metropolitan and Provincial Law Association
MR	Master of the Rolls
NA	The National Archives
NAPSS	National Association for the Promotion of Social Science
NILQ	Northern Ireland Legal Quarterly
19C Fict.	Nineteenth-century Fiction
ODNB	Oxford Dictionary of National Biography
OED	Oxford English Dictionary
OJLS	Oxford Journal of Legal Studies
P &P	Past and Present
PDA	Probate, Divorce and Admiralty Division (High Court)
PRO	Public Record Office
QC	Queen's Counsel
Quart. Rev.	Quarterly Review
RC	Royal Commission
SC	Select Committee
Sjt	Serjeant
Sol.-Gen.	Solicitor-General
SJ	Solicitors Journal
SLT	Scots Law Times
SPAL	Society for Promotion of the Amendment of the Law (?)
State Tr.	State Trials
TLR	Times Law Reports
TNAPSS	Transactions of the National Association for the Promotion of Social Science
TRHS	Transactions of the Royal Historical Society
VC	Vice-Chancellor
VCH	Victoria Country History
Vict. St.	Victorian Studies
West. Rev.	Westminster Review
YLJ	Yale Law Journal

TABLE OF CASES

Note: Criminal prosecutions are indexed under the defendant's name.

A Debtor, Re (1903)...867, 868
Aaron's Reefs v. Twiss (1896) 644
Abbott v. Middleton (1858) 33
Abbott v. Sworder (1852) 549
Abbotts v. Barry (1820) 458, 574
Aberdeen Railway Co v. Blaikie Brothers (1854)................................405, 663
Abington v. Lipscomb (1841)..1120
Abraham v. Dimmock (1914) 867
Abraham v. Hannay (1843) 619
Abrath v. The North Eastern Railway Co (1883) 1037, 1038
Acey v. Fernie (1840) 704
Acheson v. Fountain (1723) 741
Ackroyd v. Smith (1850)..................................160, 165, 166, 167, 177
Acton v. Blundell (1843)...1047, 1083
Acton v. Woodgate (1833)..240
Adam v. Newbigging (1888) 426
Adams and the Kensington Vestry, Re (1884)...37
Adams v. Adams (1871) 38, 41
Adams v. Andrews (1850) 160
Adams v. Claxton (1801) 791
Adams v. Jones (1840) 742
Adams v. Lancashire and Yorkshire Railway Co (1869) 937
Adams v. Lindsell (1818)..................................303, 335, 336, 337, 342, 345
Adams v. Weare (1784)..549
Adderley v. Dixon (1823) 553
Agar v. Official Manager of the Athenaeum Life Assurance Co (1858)...........658
Aggs v. Nicholson (1856) 739
Agra Bank ex p Tondeur, Re..755
Agra Bank v. Barry (1874) 205
Agra and Masterman's Bank, Asiatic Banking Corporation, Ex p., Re 757
Agra and Masterman's Bank, Ex p. Waring, Re (1866) 766, 767
Agriculturist Cattle Insurance Co, Re (1849) 300
Ahll v. Fuller (1826) 304
Aiken v. Short (1856) 587
Ainley v. Kirkheaton Local Board (1891) 1090
Airey v. Hall (1856)...257
Akerman v. Humphrey (1823)...762
Albert Life Assurance, re. (1871) 650
Alchin v. Hopkins (1834)...384
Alder v. Keighley (1846)..539
Alderson v. Maddison (1880) 368, 369, 370
Alderson v. White (1858) 151, 152
Aldred's Case (1610)...1072
Aldridge v. Great Western Railway (1830) 919, 920
Aldridge v. Great Western Railway Co (1841) 908

Aldridge v. Johnson (1857)..478
Alewyn v. Pryor (1826)..510
Alexander v. Burchfield (1842)..765
Alexander v. Gardner (1835)..492
Alexander v. Sizer (1869)..739
Alexander v. Southey (1821) 1120
Allan v. Bower (1814) 330
Allan v. Lake (1852)..477
Allcard v. Skinner (1887) 403, 405, 407, 408
Allegheny College v. National Chautauqua County Bank of
    Jamestown (1927) 367
Allen v. Anthony (1816) 174
Allen v. Dundas (1789)..750
Allen v. Flood (1898)...1056, 1057, 1058, 1059,
                                                            1061, 1062, 1065
Allen v. Greenwood (1980) 1080
Allen v. Hayward (1845)...951
Allen v. Jackson (1875) 7
Allen v. London and South Western Railway Co (1870) 898
Allen v. Walker (1837)...735
Allenby v. Dalton (1827)...151
Alliance v. Broom (1864)...376
Allkins v. Jupe (1877) 680
Allmarch v. Walker (1898)...1016
Allnut, Re (1882) 249
Allsop, Re (1914) 293
Almada and Tirito Company, Re (1888)......................................646
Althenaeum Life Assurance Co, Re (1859)....................................629
Alton v. Midland Railway Co (1865) 960, 1042
Alvanley v. Kinnaird (1849) 440, 441
Ambler and Fawcett v. Gordon (1905).......................................1079
Ambrose Lake Tin and Copper Mining Co, Taylor, Ex p.,
    Moss, Ex p., Re (1880) 645
Ames, Re (1893)..94
Amicable Society v. Bolland (1830) 726
Amory v. Meryweather (1824)..734
Ancher v. Governor and Co of Bank of England (1781).......................742
Anderson v. Anderson (1821) 248
Anderson v. Clarke (1824)...761
Anderson v. Elsworth (1861) 406
Anderson v. Emsworth (1861)..267
Anderson v. Fitgerald (1853) 708
Anderson v. Oppenheimer (1880) 1147
Anderson v. Pignet (1872) 73
Anderson v. Royal Exchange Co (1805) 717
Anderson v. Thornton (1853)...703
Anderson v. Wallis (1813)...686, 717
Anderton and Milner's Contract, Re (1890) 127
Andree v. Fletcher (1789)..592, 680
Andrew v. Boughey (1552) 492
Andrews v. Askey (1837) 1041
Andrews v. Gas Meter Co (1897) 635

Angel v. Merchant Marine Insurance Co (1903)...717
Anglo-Australian Steam Navigation Co v. Richards (1911)...............................1031
Anglo-Danish and Baltic Steam Navigation Co, Sahlgreen and
    Carrall's Case (1868)..340
Anglo-Egyptian Navigation Co v. Rennie (1875)..515
Anglo-Italian Book v. Daview (1878)...189
Angus v. Dalton (1877)..1137, 1138
Angus v. Dalton (1878)..1138
Annen v. Woodman (1810)...701
Anon (1821)..136
Anon v. Jackson (1800)...911
Ansell v. Waterhouse (1817)..909
Antrobus v. Smith (1805)..256, 360
Appleby v. Meyers (1866)...515
Araminta , The (1854)..377
Arbouin v. Williams (1824)...789
Archard v. Horner (1828)...496
Archer v. Hudson (1844)..405
Archer v. James (1859)...300
Arden v. Pellen (1842)..117
Arkwright v. Gell (1839)..162, 1082
Arkwright v. Newbold (1880)..410, 428, 430
Armitage v. Lancashire and Yorkshire Railway Co (1902)......................1028
Armory v. Delamirie (1721)..1118
Armsworth v. South Eastern Railway (1847)..............................990, 998
Arnold v. Cheque Bank (1876)..770, 772
Arnold's Trusts, Re (1870)..38, 40
Arnsby v. Woodward (1827)..126, 491
Aronson v. Mologo Holzindustrie (1927).....................................536
Arris v. Stukely (1677)..571
Ashbury Railway Carriage and Iron Company v. Riche (1874)..............658, 659
Ashbury v. Watson (1885)...635
Ashby v. White (1703)..1036, 1046
Ashley v. Ashley (1829)..691, 692
Ashmole v. Wainwright (1842)...402, 576
Ashton v. Dakin (1859)...632
Aspden v. Seddon (1876)...167
Astley v. Reynolds (1733)...401, 403, 576
Astley v. Weldon (1801)..525, 526, 527
Aston v. Heaven (1797)...910
Atchinson v. Baker (1796)..513
Athenaeum Life Assurance Society, Re (1859)...............................705
Athenaeum Life Society, Re (1858)...658
Atkins v. Hill (1775)..361
Atkinson, Re (1911)..37
Atkinson v. Barton (1861)...45
Atkinson v. Bell (1828)...478
Atkinson v. Denby (1861)...594
Atkinson v. Macreth (1866)...665
Atkinson v. Newcastle Waterworks Co (1877)...............................1007
Atkinson v. Ritchie (1809)..511
Atkinson v. Settree (1744)..377

Atkyns v. Kinnier (1850) 527
Atlee v. Backhouse (1838). 402, 576
Attenborough v. Henschel (1895). 839
Attenborough v. London (1853) 852
Attorney General v. The Queen Anne and Gardens Mansions Co (1889) 1071, 1077
Attorney General at the Relation of the Trustees of the River
    Lee v. Metropolitan Board of Works (1863). 1080, 1110
Attorney General Barnet District Gas & Water Co (1910). 166
Attorney General of the Commonwealth of Austalia v. Adalaide
    Steamship Co (1913) 673
Attorney General of Hong Kong v. Reid (1994). 605
Attorney General v. Acton Local Board (1883) 1090
Attorney General v. Christ Church, Oxford (1862) 88
Attorney General v. Cleaver (1811). 1097, 1106
Attorney General v. Clerkenwell Vestry (1891) 1090
Attorney General v. Cole & Son (1901) 1102
Attorney General v. Colney Hatch (1868). 1110, 1111
Attorney General v. Colney Hatch Lunatic Asylum (1868). 1109
Attorney General v. Corporation of Manchester (1893) 1110
Attorney General v. Cory Bros (1921) 1148
Attorney General v. Council of the Borough of
    Birmingham (1858). 1081, 1084, 1086,
                                                                                        1089, 1106, 1109
Attorney General v. Forbes (1836) 1106
Attorney General v. Frimley and Farnborough District Water Co (1907) 165
Attorney General v. Gee (1870) 1108
Attorney General v. Grand Junction Canal Co (1909). 163
Attorney General v. Great Eastern Railway (1880). 659
Attorney General v. Guardians of Poor of Union
    of Dorking (1882) 1089, 1090, 1091,
                                                                                           1108, 1109
Attorney General v. Hardy (1851). 136
Attorney General v. Jacobs Smith (1895) 263
Attorney General v. Luton Local Board of Health (1856) 1082, 1084
Attorney General v. Mayor, Aldermen and Burgesses of the Borough
    of Kingston-upon-Thames (1865) 1082, 1110
Attorney General v. Murray (1904) 690
Attorney General v. Nichol (1809). 170, 1075, 1106, 1107
Attorney General v. Odell (1891) 224
Attorney General v. Sheffield Gas Consumers Co (1853). 972
Attorney General v. Wilson (1840) 652
Attwood v. Small (1835) 410, 415, 416
Atwood v. Sellar & Co (1879) 715
Atwool v. Merryweather (1868) 653
Aubrey v. Maze (1801) 592
Aubrey v. Walsh (1810). 592
Austerberry v. Corporation of Oldham (1885) 177
Austin v. Drewe (1816) 719
Austin v. Great Western Railway (1867) 959
Auworth v. Johnson (1832) 116
Avery v. Bowden (1855). 503
Ayles v. Cox (1852). 438

Aylet v. Dodd (1741) 115, 525
Aynsley v. Glover (1874).. 170, 1074, 1077, 1108
Ayre's Case (1858) 648
Azemar v. Casella (1867) 478

Baber v. Harris (1839)... 599
Back v. Gooch (1815)... 784
Back v. Stacey (1826).. 170, 1075
Backhouse v. Bonomi (1861) 1129, 1139, 1143
Backhouse v. Harrison (1834).. 749
Backhouse v. Whiteley (1878) 632
Bacon, Re (1907) 271
Baddeley v. Baddeley (1878)... 259
Baddeley v. Mortlock (1816) 513
Badger v. Gregory (1869) 40
Badger v. Shaw (1860)...816
Badow v. Salter (1625).. 377
Bafeild v. Collard (1646) 388
Bagge v. Slade (1616)... 387
Bagget v. Meux (1846) 8, 159, 252
Baglehole v. Walters (1811).. 479
Bagnall v. Carlton (1877) 603
Bagot Pneumatic Tyre Co v. Clipper Pneumatic Tyre Co (1901) 392
Bagshaw v. Eatern Union Railway Co (1849)... 652
Bagueley v. Hawley (1867) 484
Bahia and San Francisco Railway and Amelia Tritton, Richard Burton
    and Mary Anne Goodburn, In the matter of (1868)................................ 661
Bailey, Ex p. (1853)... 783
Bailey v. Barnes (1894).. 139
Bailey v. Bidwell (1844) 745
Bailey v. Birkenhead, Lancashire and Cheshire Junstion railway Co (1850) 653
Bailey v. Neal (1888) 981
Bailiffs of Romney Marsh v. Trinity House (1870) 935
Bain v. Fothergill (1874).. 98, 100, 539, 540
Bainbridge v. Firmstone (1838)... 374
Bainbridge v. Neilson (1808)... 717
Baines v. Baker (1752).. 1106
Baines v. Swainson (1863) 1124
Baintgoorie (Dooars) Tea Co v. British & Benington's (1921)........................ 493
Baird v. Williamson (1863) 1142, 1144
Baker v. Bolton (1808) 996
Baker v. Holtpzaffell (1811) 116
Baker v. Jones (1850)... 491
Baker v. London and South Western Railway Co (1867) 994
Baker v. Monk (1864)... 404, 865
Baker v. Paine (1750).. 435
Baker v. Walker (1845) 746
Baldey v. Parker (1823).. 331
Baldock v. Waterhouse (1819) 912
Baldwin v. Cole (1704) 574
Baldwin v. Society for Diffusion of Useful Knowledge (1838) 558
Bale v. Cleland (1864)... 654

Balfe v. West (1853) 374
Balfour v. Balfour (1919). 309, 399
Balfour v. Ernest (1859) 738
Balfour v. Sea Fire Life Assurance Co (1857) 747
Balkis Consolidated Co v. Frederick Tomkinson (1893) 661
Ball v. Coggs (1710) 558
Ball v. Harris (1839). 181
Ball v. Ray (1873) 1102
Ball v. Storie (1823) 435
Ballacorkish Silver Company v. Harrison (1873). 164
Ballard v. Tomlinson (1884) 1086
Bamford v. Baron (1788) 784
Bamford v. Turnley (1858) 1099, 1100
Bangor and Portmadoc Slate and Slab Co (1875) 636
Bank of Bengal v. Fagan (1849). 749
Bank of England v. Vagliano Brothers (1891). 771
Bank of Ireland v. Archer and Daly (1843) 734
Bank of Ireland v. Trustees of Evans's Charities (1855) .770, 929, 931
Bank Line v. Arthur Capel & Co (1919). 521
Bank of London and National Provincial Insurance
    Association, Re (1871) 629
Bank of London v. Tyrrell (1859) 602
Bank of New South Wales v. William Owston (1879). 660
Bankart v. Houghton (1859) 1100
Banner, Ex p. (1846) 376
Bantwick v. Rogers (1891) 975
Barber Surgeons of London v. Pelson (1679) 566
Barber v. Fox (1670) 362
Barber v. Meyerstein (1870). 759
Barber v. Morris (1831) 690
Barclay v. Cousins (1802). 686
Barclay v. Pearson (1893) 594, 595
Baring v. Dix (1786) 616
Barker, Re (1887) 42
Barker v. Herbert (1911) 1130
Barker v. Hodgson (1814). 511
Barker v. Janson (1868). 682
Barker v. Walters (1844). 711
Barker v. Windle (1856) 485
Barley v. Walford (1846). 413
Barnabus v. Bersham Colliery Co (1910) 1024
Barnard v. Austin (1820) 1094
Barnes Urban Council v. London General Omnibus Co (1909) 976
Barnes v. Freeland (1794). 790
Barnes v. Grant (1856) 36
Barnes v. London, Edinburgh and Glasgow Life Assurance Co (1892). 689
Barnes v. Nunnery Colliery Co (1912). 1028
Barnes v. Rowley (1797) 243
Barnes v. Ward (1850). 972
Barnett, Hoares & Co v. South London Tramways Co (1887). 660
Barnett v. Coronna (1902) 867
Barnsley v. Powel (1748) 565

Baroness Wenlock v. River Dee Co (1885) 659
Barr v. Gibson (1838).. 481, 484
Barraclough v. Cooper (1905) 37, 43
Barret v. Dutton (1815) 511
Barrett v. Hartley (1866) 139, 147, 148, 865
Barrett v. Midland Railway Co (1858) 980
Barrick v. Buba (1857)... 503
Barrow v. Arnaud (1846) 535
Barry v. Croskey (1861)... 632
Barry v. Marriott (1848)... 281, 282
Bartholomew v. Markwick (1864) 532
Bartlett v. Downes (1826)... 67
Bartlett v. Hodgson (1785) 573
Bartley v. Bartley (1855) 274
Barton, Ex p. (1734).. 782
Barton v. Briscoe (1822) 248
Barton v. Cooke (1800) 243
Barton v. Glover (1815) 525, 526, 1815
Barton v. Vanheythusen, Stone v. Vanheythusen (1853) 264
Bartonshill Coal Co v. McGuire (1856)........................... 1003, 1004, 1009
Bartonshill Coal Co v. Reid (1856).. 1003
Bartram v. Farebrother (1828).. 790
Barwick v. English Joint Stock Bank (1867) 423, 660, 899
Basely v. Clarkson (1681) 1114
Basker v. Willan (1818)... 458, 913
Basset v. Kern (1587) 349
Bastable v. Little (1907) 975
Basten v. Butter (1806).. 530
Batard v. Hawes (1852) 601, 724
Bateman v. Mid-Wales Railway Co (1866) 738
Bateman v. Pinder (1842)... 362
Bates v. Batey & Co (1913) 990
Bathurst v. Murray (1802) 13
Batson v. Donovan (1820) 914
Baud v. Fardell (1855) 279, 280, 283
Bavins v. London and South-Western Bank (1899) 778
Bawden v. London Edinburgh and Glasgow Assurance Co (1892) 706
Baxendale v. Bennett (1878) 770, 929
Baxendale v. Harvey (1859) 707
Baxendale v. McMurray (1867).................................... 163, 1084, 1085
Baxendale v. Seale (1855) 440
Baxter v. Pritchard (1834) 815
Bayfield v. Collard (1671) 389
Bayley v. Homan (1837) 383
Baylis v. Bishop of London (1913) 609
Beale v. Thompson (1804) 491
Beatson v. Beatson (1841).. 257
Beattie v. London and North Western Railway Co (1862)..................... 985
Beauclerk v. Ashburnham (1845) 234, 279
Beaulieu v. Fingham (1401).. 920
Beavan, Ex p. (1803) 147
Beavan v. Earl of Oxford (1856) 186

Bechaunaland Exploration Co v. London Trading Bank (1898)..............................637
Beck v. Evans (1812) 913
Beck v. Kantorowicz (1857) 602
Beckett v Tower Assets (1891)......................................152, 875
Beckwith v. Beckwith (1876)......................................28, 40, 42
Becquet v. MacCarthy (1831)...917
Bedford v. Bagshaw (1859) 1040
Bedford v. Brunton (1834) 615
Bedford v. Deakin (1818) 385
Beed v. Blandford (1828) 590
Beeman v. Duck (1843)..750
Begbie v. Phospahate Sewage Co (1875) 591
Behn v. Burness (1863).............................450, 485, 488, 489, 490
Behnke v. Beds Shipping Co (1927) 555
Belchier, Ex p. (1754)..289
Bell v. Carter (1853)...151
Bell v. Gardiner (1842)...585
Bell v. Great Northern Railway Co (1890) 995
Bell v. Ingestre (1848) 742
Bell v. Lever Bros (1932)...472
Bell v. Midland Railway Co (1859)......................................178
Bell v. Midland Railway Co (1861)......................................902
Bellairs v. Bellairs (1874) 6
Bellamy v. Debenham (1890) 109
Bellamy v. Marjoribank (1852) 774
Bell's Case (1856)...420
Belshaw v. Bush (1851) 746
Benn, Re (1885) 40
Bennett v. Allcott (1787)..901, 1041
Bennett v. Farnell (1807) 753
Bennett v. Womack (1828)..126
Benson v. Chapman (1843) 716
Benson v. Heathorn (1842) 405, 602, 663
Bent v. Puller (1794) 768
Bent v. Wakefield and Barnsley Union Bank (1878) 350
Bentinck v. Fenn (1887) 645
Bentley v. Craven (1853) 663
Bentley v. Mackay (1851) 258
Bentley v. Mackay (1862) 435, 438
Bentley v. Vilmont (1887)..468
Bentsen v. Taylor Sons & Co (1893) 489, 490, 492
Beresford v. Royal Insurance Co (1937).................................726
Bermingham v. Sheridan (1864)...554
Bernards's Case (1852) 420
Berndtson v. Strang (1867)...761
Berridge v. Man on Insurance Co (1887) 680
Berringer v. Great Eastern Railway Co (1879) 1042
Berrington v. Collis (1839)...144
Berthon v. Cartwright (1796) 1041
Besseler Waechter Glover and Co v. South Derwent Coal Co (1938)........494
Bethell v. Abraham (1873) 280
Bethell & Co v. Clarke & Co (1888) 761

Bettini v. Gye (1875) 488
Betts v. Burch (1859) .... .525
Bettyes v. Maynard (1883) .... .139
Beyfus and Master's Contract, Re (1888) .... .101
Bianchi v. Offord (1886) .... .154
Bibbens v. Potter (1879) 246
Bibby v. Carter (1859) 1131, 1133
Biccard v. Shepherd (1861) .... .701
Bickerdike v. Bollman (1786) .... .491, 736
Bickerton v. Burrell (1816) 454, 456, 463
Biddle v. Bond (1865) 1121
Biffin v. Bignell (1862) .... .401
Biggar v. Rock Life Assurance Co (1902) 706
Biggart v. SS Minnesota (Owners of) (1911) .... .1027
Bigge v. Parkinson (1862) .... .481
Biggers v. Owen (1887) .... .356
Biggs v. Hoddinott (1898) .... .148, 149
Bignold v. Waterhouse (1813) .... .912
Bilbee v. London and North Western Railway Co (1865) 936, 980
Bilbie v. Lumley (1802) .... .587
Bilke v. Havelock (1813) .... .377
Bill v. Bament (1841) .... .331
Bill v. Curetton (1835) 262
Billage v. Southee (1852) 403, 405, 407
Bills v. Hopkinson (1843) .... .39
Bingham v. Bingham (1748) 442
Bingham v. Stanley (1841) .... .745
Binks v. South Yorkshire Railway and River Dun (1862) .... .973
Binmer, Ex p. (1816) 786
Birch v. Depeyster (1816) 446
Birch v. Sharland (1787) .... .401
Birch v. Stephenson (1811) 115
Bird Ex p. Bourne, Re (1851) .... .751
Bird v. Great Western Railway (1858) 960
Bird v. Holbrook (1828) 977
Bird v. Jones (1845) .... .1034
Birkbeck Permanent Benefit Building Society, Re (1912) 607
Birkett v. Willan (1819) .... .458, 913
Birkley v. Presgrave (1801) .... .714
Biscoe v. Great Eastern Railway Co (1873) .... .921
Bishop v. Busse (1873) .... .383
Bishop v. Pentland (1827) .... .713
Bissell v. Bradford Tramways Co (1891) .... .637
Bissell v. Fox, Brothers & Co (1885) 778
Blaauwpot v. Da Costa (1758) .... .723
Black v. Baxendale (1847) .... .543
Blackburn Bobbin Co v. Allen & Sons (1918) .... .521
Blackburn and District Benefit Building Society v. Cunliffe,
    Brook & Co. (1883) 606, 607
Blackburn, Low & Co v. Vigors (1886) 700, 890
Blackburn v. Smith (1848) 590
Blackburn v. Stables (1814) .... .16, 24

Blackburn v. Warwick (1836) 143, 147
Blackburne, Ex p. (1804) 765
Blacker v. Lake and Elliott (1912) 989
Blackie v. Clark (1852) 409
Blacklow v. Laws (1842) 109
Blackman v. London, Brighton and South Coast Railway (1869) 980
Blacknell v. Plowman (1831) 67
Blagden v. Bradbear (1806) 333
Blairmore v. Macredie (1898) 716
Blake, Re (1885) 237
Blake v. Barnard (1840) 1035
Blake v. Head (1912) 1024
Blake v. Lanyon (1795) 1043
Blake v. Midland Railway Co 992, 998
Blake v. Mowatt (1856) 416
Blake v. Woolf (1898) 1147, 1148
Blakeley v. Muller & Co (1903) 519
Blakemore v. Bristol and Exeter Railway Co (1858) 987, 988
Blake's Case (1865) 649
Blakesley v. Whieldon (1841)..126
Blanchard v. Bridge (1835) 1072
Bland v. Ryan (1795) 732, 742
Blanshard, Re, Hattersley, Ex p. (1878) 874
Blesard v. Hirst (1770) 735
Blight v. Page (1801) 511
Bliss v. Hall (1838)..1097, 1099
Bloomer v. Bernstain (1874) 488
Bloomer v. Spittle (1872) 442
Blount v. Doughty (1747) 360
Blovelt v. Sawyer (1904)..1027
Bloxam's Case (1864) 340
Bloye's Trust (1849)..138
Bluett v. Osbourne (1816)..479
Blumenthal v. Goodall (1891) 356
Blundell v. Winsor (1837)..618
Blunden v. Desart (1842) 150
Blyth v. Birmingham Waterworks Co (1856)............................... 920, 925, 926
Blyth v. Topham (1608) 976
Board of Management of Trim Joint District School v. Kelly (1914) 1024
Board of Trade, Ex p., Martin, Re (1888) 825
Board of Trade, Stovold, Re (1889)..825
Boardman v. Scott and Whitworth (1902) 1024
Boast v. Frith (1868) 516
Boddington v. Schlencker (1833) 773
Bodenham v. Bennett (1817)..914
Bodley v. Reynolds (1846) 900
Boehm v. Bell (1799)...685
Boehm v. Combe (1813) 712
Boehm v. Wood (1820)..95
Bolch v. Smith (1862) 978
Bold v. Hutchinson (1855) 378
Bolland v. Disney (1827)..726

Bolton v. Madden (1873)...372
Bolton v. Puller (1796) 767, 768
Bonbonus, Ex p. (1803)..614
Bond v. Dickenson (1875)..36
Bond v. Gibson (1808) 614
Bone v. Ekless (1860) 592, 593
Bonnard v. Dott (1906) 868, 869
Bonner v. Tottenham etc Building Society (1899)......................................596
Bonomi v. Backhouse (1858) 164, 166, 1128, 1129
Bonzi v. Stewart (1842)...1123
Booker v. Higgs (1887)...1016
Boon v. Eyre (1779) 486, 487
Boorman v. Nash (1829)...534
Bordenave v. Gregory (1804)...495
Borradaile v. Hunter (1873)...727
Borries v. Huchinson (1865)...539
Borrowman v. Rossel (1864)...446
Bos v. Helsham (1866)..101
Boscawen v. Bliss (1813)...491
Boss v. Litton (1832) 909
Boston Deep Sea Fishing & Ice Co v. Ansell (1888) 604
Boswell v. Kilborn (1862)...304
Bottomley v. Fisher (1862)...739
Boucher v. Murray (1844) 318
Bouillon v. Lupton (1863)..701
Boulter v. Peplow (1850)...600
Boulton v. Jones (1857)...455, 456, 457, 467
Bourn v. Mason (1669)..349
Boursot v. Savage (1866) 210
Bowcher v. Noidstrom (1809) 906
Bowen v. Hall (1881) 951, 952, 1044, 1045, 1046,
                                                     1047, 1051, 1053, 1062
Bowen v. Lewis (1884) 29, 34
Bower v. Cooper (1843)...373
Bower v. Peate (1876) 898, 1133
Bowers v. Nixon (1848)...115
Bowles v. Weeks (1845)...275
Bowman, Re (1889)..40
Bowman v. Gedders (1899) 43
Bowman v. Hyland (1878) 109
Bowse v. Colby (1841)..126
Bowyer v. Bright (1824)..438
Box v. Jubb (1879)..1149
Boyce v. Edbrooke (1903)..93
Boyd v. Fitt (1862)..545
Boyd v. Hind (1857)..385
Boyd v. Siffkin (1809)...510
Boydell v. Drummond (1808)...330, 362
Boyes, Re (1884)...5
Boyle v. Tamlyn (1827)..1126
Boys v. Ancell (1839)..318
Boyson v. Coles (1817)...461

Brace v. Wehmert (1858) 551
Bracebridge v. Buckley (1816) 125
Bradburn v. Great Western Railway Co (1874) 991
Bradford Bank v. Briggs (1886) 150
Bradford Navigation Co (1865) 1088
Bradford v. Belfield (1828) 273
Bradford v. Pickles (1895) 1054, 1055, 1056, 1059
Bradford v. Romney (1862) 435
Bradford v. Roulston (1858) 365
Bradford v. Williams (1872) 489
Bradley v. Carritt (1903) 154, 155, 158
Bradley v. Cartwright (1867) 29
Bradley v. Peixoto (1797) 246
Bradley v. Waterhouse (1828) 915
Braithwaite, Re (1882) 237
Braithwaite v. Foreign Hardwood Co (1905) 488, 506
Bramah v. Roberts (1837) 738
Bramhall v. Hall (1764) 361
Brandon v. Robinson (1811) 247, 249, 250, 251, 252
Bransby v. East London Bank (1866) 768
Brass v. Maitland (1856) 986
Brassey v. Chalmers (1853) 274
Brecknock Co v. Pritchard (1796) 509
Bree v. Holbech (1781) 98, 411
Bremner v. Williams (1824) 911
Bretherton v. Davies (1830) 905
Bretherton v. Wood (1821) 909
Breton's Estate (1881) 260
Brett v. Clowser (1880) 101
Brett v. East India and London Shipping Co (1864) 559
Brewer v. Drew (1843) 1115
Brewster v. Angell (1820) 82
Briant, Re (1888) 12
Bridge v. Bridge (1852) 259
Bridge v. Cage (1605) 377
Bridge v. Grand Junction Railway Co (1838) 908, 933
Bridge v. Wain (1816) 538, 539
Bridgeman v. Green (1757) 403, 409
Bridges v. Hawkesworth (1851) 575, 1118, 1119
Bridges v. Longman (1857) 137
Bridges v. North London Railway (1874) 932, 936, 937, 938
Bridgman v. Green (1755) 565
Brierley, Re (1894) 30
Briggs v. Penny (1849) 4, 36
Bright v. Cowper (1612) 495
Bright v. Hutton (1851-2) 625
Brine v. Great Western Railway 921
Brintons v. Turvey (1905) 1025
Brisbane v. Dacres (1813) 586, 587
Bristol, Cardiff and Swansea Aerated Bread Co v. Maggs (1890) 109
Bristow v. Wood (1844) 171
Bristow v. Wright (1781) 314

Britain v. Rossiter (1879) 533
British and American Telegraph Co v. Albion Bank (1872) 639
British and American Telegraph Co v. Colson (1871). 343, 344
British and American Trustee and Finance Corporation v. Couper (1894). 635
British Colombia and Vancouver's Island Spar, Lumbar and
   Sawmills v. Nettleship (1868) 547, 758
British Industry Life Assurance Co v. Ward (1856) 703
British Mutual Banking Co v. Charnwood Forest Railway Co (1887). 423, 660
British Provident Life and Fire Assurance Society, Stanley's Case, Re (1864). 637
British Seamless Paper Box Co, Re (1881). 645
British South Africa Gold Miners v. De Beers (1910) 156
British United Shoe Machinery Co v. Somervell Bros (1907) 673
Brittain v. Lloyd (1845). 596, 597
Britton v. Great Western Cotton Co (1872) 1007, 1008
Britton v. South Wales Railway Co (1858) 990, 993
Brix v. Braham (1823) 746
Broad v. Ham (1839) 1037
Broad v. Selfe (1863) 147
Broadbent v. Imperial Gas Co (1857). 1106, 1107
Broadbent v. Ledward (1839). 1116
Brockwell's Case (1857) 420, 421
Broder v. Saillard (1876). 1102, 1130, 1146
Broderick v. London County Council (1908). 1026
Broderip v. Salomon (1895) 668, 669
Brodgen v. Metropolitan Railway (1877) 339, 341, 342,
                                                                                          343, 347, 355
Bromage v. Prosser (1825) 1038
Brook v. Brook (1858) 437
Brook v. Delcomyn (1864). 477
Brook v. Rawl (1849). 1039
Brookes, Re (1914). 292
Brooks, Ex p., in Fowler, Re (1883). 874, 876
Brooks v. Haigh (1839) 375
Brophy v. Bellamy (1873) 246
Brothers v. Hindley & Co (1913) 452
Broughton v. Hutt (1858) 442
Broughton v. Manchester and Salford Water-Works Co (1819) 738
Broughton v. Sandilands (1811). 436, 448
Brown, Re (1885) 279, 280, 283
Brown v. Brown (1858). 283
Brown v. Davies (1789). 734
Brown v. Edgington (1841) 481, 962
Brown v. Hawkes (1891) 1038
Brown v. Higgs (1800) 243
Brown v. Hodgson (1811) 598
Brown v. Hodgson (1835) 598
Brown v. Holt (1812) 617
Brown v. Kewley (1801) 767
Brown v. Mayor, Aldermen and Burgesses of Dunstable (1899). 1090
Brown v. Muller (1872). 534
Brown v. Nairne (1839). 531
Brown v. Pocock (1831). 159

Brown v. Pocock (1833). 248
Brown v. Pocock (No. 2) (1834). 248
Brown v. Robins (1859). 1134, 1136
Brown v. Royal Insurance Co (1859) 694
Brown v. Windsor (1830) 1132, 1134
Browne v. Browne (1857) 39
Browne v. Carr (1831) 792
Browne v. La Trinidad (1887) 393
Browne v. Paull (1850) 10, 244, 245
Browne v. Ryan (1902) 155
Browning v. Morris (1778) 594
Browning v. Wright (1799) 101
Brownlie v. Campbell (1880). 98, 101, 102, 417
Brownlow (1839) 996
Brudenell v. Elwes (1802). 25
Bryan v. Bancks (1821) 125
Bryan v. Lewis (1826) 99, 498
Bryant v. Herbert (1878). 1116
Bryden v. Willett (1869). 37
Brydges v. Branfill (1842). 665
Brydon v. Stewart (1855). 1005
Bryon v. Metropolitan Saloon Omnibus Company (1858) 635
Buck v. Buck (1808). 617
Buckland v. Johnson (1854). 581
Buckland v. Papillon (1866). 126
Buckle v. Mitchell (1812) 263
Buckley v. Gross (1853). 1119
Buddle v. Wilson (1795) 911
Bufe v. Turner (1815) 705
Bull v. Faulkner (1847) 61
Bull v. Pritchard (1847). 39
Bullack v. Dommitt (1796). 509
Buller v. Crips (1703). 733
Buller v. Harrison (1777) 751
Bult v. Morrell (1840) 738
Bulter v. Gray (1869). 30
Bunbury v. Winter (1820) 146
Bunker v. Midland Railway Co (1882). 1015, 1016
Bunn (1872) 1053
Burchell v. Hickisson (1880) 981
Burchfield v. Moore (1854). 750
Burdett v. Willett (1708). 572
Burdett v. Wright (1819). 67
Burgess v. Gray (1845). 973
Burke v. South Eastern Railway Co (1879) 968
Burkit v. Willan (1819) 913
Burland v. Earle (1902). 653
Burley, Re (1910) 37
Burn v. Miller (1813) 487, 531
Burnand v. Rodocanachi, Sons & Co (1882). 724
Burnby v. Bollett (1847) 482, 484
Burnell v. Brown (1820) 550

Burnes v. Pennell (1849)... 420, 421, 654, 655
Burnie Port Authority v. General Jones Pty (1994)....................................... 946
Burnie v. Getting (1845)..283
Burrough v. Philcox (1840) 30, 243
Burroughes v. Bayne (1860).. 1115, 1117, 1121, 1122
Burrowes v. Lock (1805)...417
Burrows v. Barnes (1900)...871
Burrows v. March Gas and Coke Co (1872) 951
Burrows v. Matabele Gold Reefs and Estates Co (1901) 647
Burslem v. Attenborough (1873)..854
Bush v. Steinman (1799)... 895, 896
Busk v. Davis (1814) 478
Busk v. Royal Exchange Assurance Co (1818) 713, 928
Busk v. Walsh (1812)..594
Butler v. Manchester etc Railway (1888)..161
Butler v. Wildman (1820)..712
Butler v. Withers (1860)..281
Butt v. Great Western Railway (1851)..915
Butter v. Ommaney (1827)...41
Butterfield v. Forrester (1809).. 908, 973
Butterfield v. Heath (1852)... 263, 264
Butterknowle Colliery v. Bishop Auckland Industrial
  Co-operative Society (1906)...166
Butterworth v. West Riding of Yorkshire Rivers Board (1909).....................1091, 1092
Buxton v. Lister (1746) 414, 552, 555
Buxton v. North Eastern Railway Co (1868) 964
Bwllfa & Merthyr Dare Colliery Co v. Pontypridd Water Co (1903).....................178
Byam v. Byam (1854)..274
Byrne v. Great Southern and Western Railway Co (1884)............................... 995
Byrne v. Van Tienhoven (1880)... 346
Byrne v. Wilson (1862).. 934
Bythesea v. Bythesea (1854).. 46
Bywater v. Richardson (1834) 480

Cackett v. Keswick (1902) 641
Cadell v. Palmer (1832).. 20, 62
Cadman v. Horner (1810)...415
Caerphilly Colliery Co, Pearson's Case, Re (1877) 662
Cahn v. Pockett's Bristol Channel Steam Packet Co (1899) 762
Caines v. Smith (1847) 498
Caladonian Railway Co v. Magistrates of Helensburgh (1856).........................392
Calcraft v. Thompson (1867)...170, 1077
Calico Printers Association v. Higham (1912)......................................1031
Callender v. Carlton Iron Co (1893)..1015
Callisher v. Bischoffsheim (1870)..375, 376
Calverley v. Williams (1790)..438
Calvert v. Thomas (1887)...154
Cambridge Water Co v. Eastern Counties plc (1994)................................1087
Camden v. Anderson (1794) 684
Cameron v. Charing-Cross Railway Co (1865) 1104
Cameron and Wells, Re (1887)...265
Camidge v. Allenby (1827).. 740

Campbell v. Fleming (1834)..460
Campbell v. Jones (1795) 486
Campbell v. Mersey Docks and Harbour Board (1863) 478
Campbell's Policies, Re (1877)..261
Canadian Oil Works Corporation, Re (1875)...............................662
Canavan v. Owners of the SS Universal (1910) 1027
Cann v. Cann (1721) 442
Cann v. Cann (1830)...101
Cann v. Wilson (1888) 947
Cannon v. Bryce (1819)..592
Cape Breton, Re (1885) 645, 646
Capital & Counties Bank v. Rhodes (1903)................................223
Capital & Counties Bank v. Gordon (1903) 778
Cappur v. Harris (1723) 552
Card v. Case (1848)...918, 1126
Cardiff Savings Bank, Marquis of Bute's case, Re (1892).................665
Cargill v. Bower (1878)...428
Carlen v. Drury (1812)..617
Carlill v. Carbolic Smoke Ball Co (1892) 328, 348, 354, 355
Carlisle v. Blamire (1807)..129
Carlton v. Ireland (1856) 774
Carlyon v. Lovering (1857)...1083
Carmichael's Case (1850)..339
Carpenter v. Blandford (1828)...491
Carpenter v. Heriot (1759) 405
Carpmael v. Powis (1846) 437
Carpue v. London and Brighton Railway Co (1844)........................960
Carr, Ex p. (1814)..416
Carr v. Allatt (1858)...815
Carr v. Carr (1811) 766
Carr v. Lancashire and Yorkshire Railway Co (1852).................474, 328
Carr v. Living (1860)...244
Carr v. Living (No. 2) (1864) 36
Carr v. Lord Erroll (1808) 25
Carrick's Case (1851)...624
Carrington Ltd v. Smith (1905)..868
Carr's Settled Estates, Re (1861) 88
Carson's Settlement Trust, Re (1867)....................................276
Carstairs v. Taylor (1871) 1147, 1148
Carter v. Boehm (1766) 698
Carter v. Carter (1869)...261
Carter v. Fossett (1623)..576
Carter v. Toussant (1822)...338
Casberd v. A.G. (1819)..134
Casey's Patents, Re (1892) 366
Castellain v. Preston (1882)..725
Castilia, The (1822) 377
Castillain v. Preston (1880) 693, 695
Castrique v. Buttgieg (1855)..743
Caswell v. Coare (1809) 534
Caswell v. Worth (1856)..1007
Cator v. Board of Works for the Lewisham District (1864)...............1087

Catt v. Tourle (1869) 176
Cattell v. Corrall (1839) 104
Catterall v. Kenyon (1842)...1121
Cattle v. Stockton Waterworks (1875) 1144
Cavalier v. Pope (1906).. 988
Cave v. Cave (1880)..210
Cavey v. Ledbitter (1863) 1100
Cazelet v. St Barbe (1786).. 686
Cazenove v. British Equitable Assurance Co (1859) 708
Central Railway Co of Venezuela v. Kisch (1867) 430
Chadwick v. Trower (1839) .... .1133, 1142
Chadwick v. Turner (1866) 205
Challis v. London and South Western Railway Co (1905)........1023
Chamber Colliery Co. v. Twyerould (1893) 167
Chamberlain v. Hazelwood (1839)..1041
Chamberlain v. West End of London and Crystal Palace Railway (1845).....................1104
Chambers v. Caulfield (1805) 900
Chambers v. Goldwin (1802)...145
Chandler v. Bradley (1897) 93
Chandler v. Thompson (1811) 1072
Chandler v. Webster (1904).. 519
Chanter v. Hopkins (1838)... 477, 485
Chanter v. Hopkinson (1838) 482
Chanter v. Leese (1838)... 508, 591
Chaplin, Ex p. (1839).. 279, 283
Chaplin v. Rogers (1800) 332
Chapman v. Beach (1820)...616
Chapman v. Bradley (1863) 437
Chapman v. Koops (1802) 616
Chapman v. Morton (1843) 590
Chapman v. Rothwell (1858) 978
Chapman v. Smethurst (1909) 739
Chapman v. Speller (1850)... 484
Chapman v. Walton (1833)...916
Chapman v. Westerby (1913) 561
Chappell v. Poles (1837) 588
Chappell & Co v. Harrison (1910) 874
Charitable Corporation v. Sutton (1742).................................616
Charles Semon & Co v. Bradford Corporation (1922) 1079
Charles v. Backwell (1877)... 766
Charles v. Finchley Local Board (1883).................................1089
Charles v. Marsden (1808)... 746
Charlotte v. Rendall (1853)...15
Charlton v. Fletcher (1791)..401
Chartered Mercantile Bank of India, London and China v. Netherlands
    India Steam Navigation Corp (1883)................................ 928
Chartlon v. Rendall (1853)... 15, 17
Chasemore v. Richards (1859)................ 164, 1047, 1048, 1055, 1083
Chaurand v. Angerstein (1791) 446
Chawner's Will, Re (1869)..137
Chaytor's Settled Estate Act, Re (1884)................................... 94
Cheale v. Kenward (1858).. 553

Cheater v. Cater (1918) 117
Cheese v. Keen (1908). 148
Cheesman v. Exall (1851) 853
Cheshire & Co v. Vaughan Bros & Co (1919) 681
Chester v. Urwick (No. 3) (1856). 5
Chetham v. Williamson (1804) 177
Chichester v. Cobb (1866) 379
Chichester v. Lethbridge (1738) 1069
Chidell v. Galsworthy (1859). 815
Child, Ex p. (1751) 573
Child v. Douglas (1854) 175
Chillingworth v. Chillingworth (1837) 142
Chilton v. Carrington (1855) 322
Chinery, Re (1888) 41, 42
Chinnock v. Marshioness of Ely (1865). 109, 329
Cholmondeley v. Clinton (1821) 138, 145
Christie v. Griggs (1809) 910, 919
Christie v. Secretan (1799) 701
Christopherson v. Bare (1848). 1035
Christopherson v. Naylor (1816). 40, 43
Christy v. Row (1808). 496
Church v. Brown (1808). 126
Churchill v. Evans (1809). 1126
Churchill v. Siggers (1852) 1036
Citizen's Bank of Louisiana and the New Orleans Canal and
    Banking Co v. First National Bank of New Orleans (1873). 370
City of London Brewery Co v. Tennant (1873). 1074, 1075, 1107
City of London v. Goree (1677). 566
Civil, Naval and Military Outfitters (1899) 651
Civil Service Co-Operative Society v. General Steam Navigation Co (1903) 519
Clack v. Sainsbury (1851) 144
Claflin v. Claflin (1889) 252
Clare v. Maynard (1837) 534, 537, 539
Clarence v. Marshall (1834). 571
Claridge v. Dalton (1815) 736
Claridge's Patent Asphalte Co, Re (1921) 294
Claringbould v. Curtis (1852) 555
Clark v. Chambers (1878). 952, 954, 955
Clark v. Lindsay (1902). 518
Clark v. London General Omnibus Co Ltd (1906) 998
Clark v. Malpas (1862) 404, 865
Clark v. Molyneux (1877). 1038
Clark v. Pigot (1699) 741
Clarke (1927) 351
Clarke v. Army and Navy Co-operative Society (1903) 989
Clarke v. Blything (1823) 723
Clarke v. Clark (1865). 1075
Clarke v. Clarke (1806). 367
Clarke v. Cock (1803) 734
Clarke v. Colls (1861) 33
Clarke v. Dickson (1858). 411, 649
Clarke v. Dickson (1859). 429

Clarke v. Gray (1805) 315
Clarke v. Holford (1848) 121
Clarke v. Holmes (1861) 1006, 1007, 1008
Clarke v. Price (1819) 558, 560
Clarke v. Royal Panopticon (1854) 137
Clarke v. Somersetshire Drainage Commissioners (1888) 1085
Clarke v. West Ham Corporation (1909) 969
Clarke v. Willet (1872) 263
Clarke v. Wright (1861) 263, 265, 361
Clarke's Trust, Re (1863) 45
Clarkson v. Henderson (1880) 147
Clarkson v. Musgrave and Sons (1882) 1017
Clay v. Jones (1849) 73
Clay v. Sharpe (1802) 135
Clay v. Willan (1789) 912
Clay v. Yates (1856) 331, 534
Clayards v. Dethick (1848) 931, 932
Clay's Settlement, Re (1873) 276
Clayton v. Andrews (1767) 331
Clayton v. Earl of Wilton (1813) 265
Clayton v. Hardwick Colliery (1915) 1029
Clayton v. Leech (1889) 98, 101
Cleaver v. Mutual Reserve Fund Life Association (1892) 726
Clegg, Parkinson & Co v. Earley Gas Co (1896) 1007
Clements v. Bowes (1852) 647
Clements v. Flight (1846) 1116, 1117
Clements v. Ohrly (1848) 1036
Clements v. Welles (1865) 175
Clergy Orphans Corporation, Re (1874) 286
Clerk v. Mundall (1698) 740
Clerke v. Martin (1702) 733
Cliff v. Midland Railway Co (1870) 980
Clifford, Re (1902) 92
Clifford v. Koe (1880) 44
Clift v. Schwabe (1846) 727
Clinch v. Financial Corporation (1868) 653
Clinon v. Cooke (1802) 330
Clipsham v. Vertue (1843) 489
Clitheroe Estate, Re (1885) 94
Clive v. Clive (1872) 15
Close v. Phipps (1884) 577
Close v. Wilberforce (1838) 131
Clough v. Bond (1838) 280, 282
Clough v. London and North West Railway Co (1871) 411
Clover, Clayton & Co v. Hughes (1910) 1024, 1025
Clydebank Engineering and Shipbuilding Company v. Don Jose
     Ramos Yzquierdo y Castanedo (1905) 529
Coal Economising Co, Re (1875) 643
Coates v. Nottingham Waterworks Co (1861) 634
Coats v. Chaplin (1842) 331, 338
Cobb v. Great Western Railway Cp (1894) 967
Cobban v. Downe (1803) 758

Cobbett v. Brock (1855). 406
Cobbett v. Grey (1850) 1034
Cobbold, Re (1903) 46
Cockburn v. Edwards (1881) 140
Cockburn v. Peel (1861) 281, 285
Cockburn v. Thompson (1809). 617
Cocker v. Cowper (1834) 160
Cocking v. Pratt (1749-50) 441
Cockle v. London and South Eastern Railway Co (1871) 937
Cocks v. Materman (1827). 752
Coe v. Platt (1852) 1007
Cogan v. Duffield (1875). 11, 14
Coggs v. Bernard (1703) 374, 514, 852
Coghlan, Re 261
Cohen v. Armstrong (1813) 363
Cohen v. Hale (1878). 765
Cohen v. South Eastern Railway Co (1876) 474
Colby v. Hunter (1827) 703
Cole v. Gibbons (1734) 403
Cole v. Turner (1704) 1035
Cole v. Wade (1807). 273, 274
Colebeck v. Girdlers Co (1876) 1127, 1140
Coleman v. Foster (1856) 161
Coles v. Coles (1901) 261
Coles v. Governor of the Bank of England (1839) 929, 930
Coles v. Pilkington (1874) 369
Coles v. Sims (1854). 173
Coles v. Trecothick (1804) 332, 333, 373, 404, 549, 663
Colkett v. Freeman (1787) 782
Collard v. South Eastern Railway (1861) 545
Collen v. Wright (1857). 305, 463, 657
Collett v. London and North Western Railway Co (1851) 959, 961
Collett v. Preston (1852) 409
Collingridge v. Royal Exchange Assurance Corporation (1877) 694
Collins v. Barrow (1831) 116
Collins v. Castle (1887). 176
Collins v. Godefroy (1831) 376
Collins v. Lamport (1864) 561
Collins v. Locke (1879) 1050
Collins v. Martin (1797) 768
Collins v. Middle Level Commissioners (1869). 951
Collins v. Perkins (1909) 988
Collins v. Plumb (1810). 172, 174
Collins v. Price (1828). 496
Collis v. Emett (1790) 752
Collis v. Laugher (1894) 170
Collis v. Selden (1868). 944
Colls v. Home and Colonial Stores (1904) .170, 1078, 1079
Colman v. Sarel (1789) 360
Colne Valley and Halstead Railway Bill, Re (1859). 280, 286
Colonial Trust Corporation, Bradshaw, Ex p. (1879) 637
Colson v. Williams (1889) 137, 139

Colt v. Nettervill (1725) 552
Colt v. Woollaston (1723)...565
Colyear v. Countess of Mulgrave (1836) 392
Colyer v. Clay (1843)...437
Colyer v. Finch (1856)...182
Combe, Re (1925)... 30
Coming, Ex p. (1803) 134
Comiskey v. Bowring-Hanbury (1905) 45, 245, 246
Commissioners for Special Purposes of the Income
    Tax v. Pemsel (1891) 241
Company of Feltmakers v. Davis (1797) 389
Company of Proprietors of the Rochdale Canal v. Radcliffe (1852).....................1083, 1084
Conflans Stone Quarry Co v. Parker, Public Officer of the
    National Bank (1867) 756
Congreve v. Evetts (1854)...123, 815
Connop v. Meaks (1834)...144
Conolly, Re (1910) 37
Consolidated Tea and Lands Co v. Oliver's Wharf (1910) 696
Consort Deep Level Gold Mines, Re (1897)... 647
Constantinople and Alexandria Hotels Co, Finucane's Case, Re (1869) 343
Consterdine v. Consterdine (1862) 279, 281, 283
Conway v. Wade (1909) 1065
Conybeare v. New Brunswick and Canada Railway and
    Land Company (1860).. 422
Cook, Ex p. (1728) 615
Cook v. Black (1842).. 692
Cook v. Hartle (1838) 900
Cook v. Jenkinson (1797)...496
Cook v. Wright (1853)...375
Cooke v. Chilcott (1876)...176
Cooke v. Crawford (1842) 273
Cooke v. Forbes (1867) 1070
Cooke v. Lamotte (1851)...406
Cooke v. Midland Great Western Railway of Ireland (1909) 982, 984
Cooke v. Munstone (1805)...316
Cooke v. Oxley (1790).. 329, 333, 334, 335, 345
Coombe v. Hughes (1872) 15
Coope v. Ridout (1921)...109
Cooper & Crane v. Wright (1902)...1023
Cooper v. Adams (1894).. 830
Cooper v. Chitty (1756) 1117
Cooper v. Denne (1792) 550
Cooper v. Elston (1796) 331
Cooper v. Emery (1844)...103
Cooper v. Hubbuck (1860)...1073
Cooper v. Macdonald (1866)...275
Cooper v. Macdonald (1873) 40
Cooper v. Meyer (1830) 753
Cooper v. Neil (1878) 632
Cooper v. Parker (1853) 349, 375
Cooper v. Parker (1855) 384, 385
Cooper v. Phibbs (1867) 442, 444

Cooper v. Stephenson (1852)..187
Cooper v. Straker (1888)..170, 1077
Cooper v. Trewby (1860)..184
Cooper v. Walker (1862)...972
Cooper v. Willomatt (1845)...1120
Cope, Re (1908)..43
Corbett v. Brown (1831)...411, 1040
Corbett's Estate, Re (1860)..40
Corbett's Trust, Re (1860)..40
Corby v. Hill (1858)..978
Corder v. Margan (1811)..135
Cording, Ex p. (1832)..852
Cork and Youghal Railway Co, Re (1869)..606
Cornelson v. Sun Mutual Insurance Co (1852)...356
Cornfoot v. Fowke (1840)..412
Cornish v. Abingdon (1859)...339, 367, 456, 457
Cornman v. Eastern Counties Railway Co (1859)..................................936, 980
Corporation of the City of Glasgow v. Taylor (1922)................................984
Corr v. Gole (1850)..970
Corsellis, Re (1887)...269
Cort v. Ambergate, Nottingham and Boston and Eastern
    Junction Railway Company (1851)..500
Cory v. Scott (1820)...736
Cory v. Thames Ironworks Co (1868)..547
Cory & Son v. France, Fenwick & Co (1911)..1023
Cotman v. Brougham (1918)...659
Cotterill v. Starkey (1839)...908
Cotton v. Thurland (1793)...594
Cotton v. Wood (1860)..936, 971
Cottrell v. Homer (1843)..264
Couch v. Steel (1852)..1007
Coughlin v. Gillison (1899)...988
Couldery v. Bartrum (1881)..386
Coulson v. Allison (1860)...437
Coulthard v. Consett Iron Co (1905)..1030
Coulthurst v. Carter (1856)...42
Countess of Warwick Steamship Co v. Le Nickel (1918)...............................521
County Marine Insurance Co, Rance's Case, Re..666
Coupland v. Hardingham (1813)...972
Courtauld v. Legh (1869)...170, 1077
Courtenay v. Wright (1860)..153
Cousins, Re (1886)..210
Coutts v. Acworth (1869)..267
Couturier v. Hastie (1852)...448, 449, 471
Coventry, Sheppard & Co v. Geat Eastern Railway (1883)..........................947, 952
Coverdale v. Eastwood (1872)..369
Coward v. Baddeley (1859)..1035
Cowdry v. Day (1859)..149
Cowell v. Edwards (1800)..599
Cowen, Ex p. (1867)...784
Cowie v. Goodwin (1840)...116
Cox v. Bishop (1857)..131, 174

Cox v. Burbidge (1863) 922, 981, 1126
Cox v. Champneys (1822) 146
Cox v. Hickman (1860) 627
Cox v. Muncey (1859) 580
Cox v. Prentice (1815) 449
Cox v. Troy (1822) 303, 304, 733
Coxe v. Harden (1803) 761
Cradock v. Piper 269
Crafter v. Metropolitan Railway (1866) 980
Cramer & Co (Ltd) v. Barre (1866) 870, 871
Cramer & Co (Ltd) v. Mott (1869) 870
Cramer & Co v. Carlton (1884) 871
Cramer v. Amsler (1868) 870
Cramer v. Aylen (1868) 870
Cranch v. White (1835) 1118
Crane v. London Dock Co (1864) 457
Craske v. Wigan (1909) 1029
Crawcour, Ex p., Robertson, Re (1878) 875
Crawcour v. Salter (1881) 873
Crawshay v. Maule (1818) 554
Crawshay v. Thornton (1836-37) 853
Craythorne v. Swinburne (1804) 599
Cremins v. Guest, Keen & Nettlefolds (1908) 1027
Cribb v. Kynoch Ltd (No. 2) (1908) 1022
Crick (1859) 882
Crisdee v. Bolton (1827) 527, 528
Critchlow v. Parry (1809) 751
Crockett v. Crockett (1848) 245
Croft v. Graham (1863) 148
Croft v. Lumley (1858) 125
Crofter Hand Woven Harris Tweed Co v. Veitch (1942) 1066
Crofts v. Beale (1851) 747
Crofts v. Waterhouse (1825) 910
Croockewit v. Fletcher (1857) 489
Crook v. Jadis (1834) 749
Crosbie v. M'Doual (1806) 378
Crosby v. Crouch (1809) 784
Crosby v. Wadsworth (1810) 330
Crosley v. Serby Gas-Light Co (1838) 582
Cross (1812) 1084
Cross (1826) 1096
Cross, Ex p. (1848) 784
Crosse v. Gardner (1689) 479
Crossfield v. Such (1853) 1116
Crosskill v. Bower (1863) 147
Crossley & Sons v. Lightowler (1867) 163, 167, 1084, 1085, 1087
Crossley Brothers Ltd, Ex p. (1894) 874
Cross's Charity, Re (1859) 88
Crouch v. Credit Foncier of England (1873) 637
Crowder v. Tinkler (1816) 1110
Crowe v. Clay (1854) 766
Crowhurst v. Laverack (1852) 377

Crump d. Woolley v. Norwood (1815) 31
Crump v. Lambert (1867).. 1101, 1146
Crunden and Meux's Contract, Re (1909) 178, 274
Cubitt v. Porter (1828) 1127
Cubitt v. Smith (1864).. 551
Cuckson v. Stones (1858) 512
Cud v. Rutter (1719)... 552
Cuff v. Penn (1813)... 492
Cullen v. Butler (1816) 712
Cullen v. Duke of Queensberry (1781).. 469
Cullen v. Morris (1819)...1036
Cullerne v. London etc Building Society (1890) 294, 664
Culverwell v. Eames and Billett (1823) 905, 910
Cumber v. Wane (1721)..383, 384, 385
Cumming v. Brown (1808) 760
Cumming v. Ince (1847)...401
Cunard v. Antifyre (1933) 1071
Cundy v. Lindsay (1878).. 1119
Cunliffe v. Brancker (1876) 64
Cunliffe v. Harrison (1851)..477
Cunnington v. Great Western Railway (1883) 945, 946
Curnick v. Tucker (1874) 36
Currey v. Willan (1818)...912
Currie v. Misa (1875)..359, 381, 746
Curriers Co v. Corbett (1865) 1074
Curties, Re (1852) 812
Curtis, Re (1862) 818
Curtis v. Hannay (1800)..478, 534
Curtis v. Lukin (1842)..243
Cust v. Middleton (1861) 89
Cuthbert v. Gostling (1814)... 905
Cuthbert v. Purrier (1822) 246
Cuthbertson v. Irving (1859)..129
Cutter v. Powell (1795) 485, 532
Cutts v. Thodley (1842)..106, 491

Dahl v. Nelson, Donkin & Co (1880)... 517
Daking v. Whimper (1859) 264
Dalby v. Hirst (1819) 114
Dalby v. India & London Life Assurance Company (1854)............................. 690
Dale v. Hall (1750)...911
Dalgleigh's Settlement (1876), Re (1876) 276
Dalglish v. Jarvis (1850).. 698
Dally v. Wonham (1863).. 405, 663
Dalton v. Angus (1881).. 170, 1127, 1138, 1139
Dalton v. South Eastern Railway Co (1858) 998, 999
Dalyell v. Tyrer (1858)...959
Dalzell v. Mair (1808)... 697
Dames and Wood, Re (1885)...109
Danby v. Lamb (1861)... 1116
Dance v. Goldingham (1873)... 76
D'Angibau, Re (1880) 261

Daniel v. Metropolitan Railway (1871) 965, 966, 967

Daniels v. Davison (1809) 174

Daniels v. Potter (1830). 907, 977

Danube and Black Sea Railway and Kustendie Harbour Company
    Limited v. Xenos (1861) 502

Darby, Brougham, Ex p., Re (1911) 646

Darke v. Martyn (1839). 283

Darley Main Colliery Co v. Mitchell (1886). 1129, 1130

Darrell v. Tibbitts (1880) 694, 724, 725

Dashwood v. Bulkeley (1804) 8

Dashwood v. Jermyn (1879). 369

Daubigny v. Duval (1794). 761

Daughlish v. Tenannt (1866). 784

Davenport v. Queen (1877) 125

Davenport v. Stafford (1851) 242

Davey (1805). 1096

Davey v. Durrant (1857). 139

Davey v. London & South Western Railway Co (1883). 932

David v. Ellice (1826) 385

David v. Goodman (1880) 860

Davidson v. Burnand (1868) 712

Davidson v. Foley (1787). 250

Davidson v. Tulloch (1860) 411

Davies v. Davies (1888). 116

Davies v. Hawkins (1815) 617

Davies v. Humphreys (1840) 567, 600

Davies v. London and Provincial Marine Insurance Co (1878) 410

Davies v. Mann (1842) 932, 953

Davies v. Penton (1827). 526

Davies v. Rees (1886). 861

Davies v. Rhymney Iron Co Ltd (1900). 1027

Davies v. Willan (1817). 912

Davies v. Williams (1847) 1041

Davis v. Bryan (1827) 566, 591

Davis v. Earl of Strathmore (1810) 186

Davis v. Elsam (1828) 125

Davis v. Garrett (1830) 928

Davis v. Hutchings (1907) 294

Davis v. Mason (1793). 373

Davis v. Morrison (1773) 457

Davis v. Oswell (1837). 900

Davis v. Russell (1829) 1037

Davis v. Thomas (1831). 152

Davis v. Thornycroft (1836) 248, 249

Davison v. Gillies (1879). 655

Dawkes v. Earl of Deloraine (1771). 743

Dawson v. Collins (1851) 478

Dawson v. Linton (1822). 598

Dawson v. Manchester, Sheffield and Lincolnshire Railway Co (1862). 960

Day v. Edwards (1794) 906

Day v. Newman (1788) 373

Day v. Radcliffe (1876) 33, 43

Day v. Singleton (1899).. 540
De Beers v. British South Africa Gold Mines (1912)..154
De Berdt v. Atkinson (1794) 736
De Bernardy v. Harding (1853).. 533, 534
De Francesco v. Barnum (1890)...559, 580
De Gaminde v. Pigou (1812) 697
De Hahn v. Hartley (1786)... 698, 702
De Leira v. Edwards (unreported)...1122
De Mattos v. Gibson (1858).. 176, 561, 562
De Mattos v. North (1868)... 680
De Mestre v. West (1891)..265
De Pass's Case (1859) 421
De Pothonier, Re (1900)... 292
De Vaux v. Salvador (1836)...713
Dean, Re (1889) 241
Dean v. Peel (1804) 1041
Deane v. Clayton (1817) 976, 977
Deane v. Rastron (1792) 415
Debenham v. Sawbridge (1901)..101
Deek v. Stanhope (1844)...619
Deeks v. Strutt (1794) 361
Deeley v. Lloyds Bank (1912)..150
Deffle v. Desanges (1819) 782
Deighton and Harris's Contract, Re (1898) 109
Delauney v. Barker (1819).. 790
Delegal v. Highley (1837) 1037
Dell, Ex p. (1862) 818
Dendy v. Nicholl (1858) 491
Dennett v. Atherton (1872) 174
Dennis v. A.J. White & Co (1916)...1029
Dennistoun v. Lillie (1821).. 699
Dent v. Auction Mart Company (1866) 170, 1072, 1076, 1108
Dent v. Bennet (1835) 406, 407
Dent v. London Tramways Co (1880) 655
Denton v. Great Northern Railway Co (1856) 328, 352, 757
Denton v. Richmond (1833)... 115, 525
Derry v. Peek (1888) 430, 431, 618, 644, 666,
                                                           942, 943, 947, 949, 1041
Detmold, Re (1889)..251
Devaux v. Steele (1840).. 685
Devaynes v. Noble, Sleech's Case (1816) 766
Dewhirst's Settlement, Re (1886)...276
Diamond Fuel Co, Metcalfe's Case (1880) 662
Dick, Re (1891)... 286, 287
Dickenson v. Dillwyn (1869)...261
Dickenson v. Dodds (1876) 345, 346
Dickenson v. Jardine (1868)... 716, 719, 723
Dickenson v. Valpy (1829).. 614, 738
Dickenson v. Wright (1860)..265
Dicker v. Angerstein (1874)...141
Dickinson v. Harbottle (1873).. 170, 1075, 1078
Dickonson v. North Eastern Railway Co (1863) 999

Dickinson v. Player (1838) 279, 283
Dickson v. Earl of Wilton (1859). 1038
Dickson v. Thomson (1680). 362
Diestal v. Stevenson (1906) 528
Diggle v. Higgs (1877). 595
Diggles, Re (1888) 37
Dillon v. Coppin (1840) 255, 256, 259
Dillon v. Langley (1831) 1115
Dimech v. Corlett (1858) 489
Diplock v. Blackburn (1811). 602
Directors of the Central Railway Co of Venezuela v. Kisch (1867) 649
Directors of the Imperial Gas Light and Coke Co v.
  Samuel Broadbent (1859). 1106, 1108
Ditcham v. Bond (1814) 1041
Dive, Re (1909). 292
Dix v. Burford (1854) 242
Dixon v. Bell (1816) 985
Dixon v. Heriot (1862) 491
Dixon v. Metropolitan Board of Works (1881). 1148
Dixon v. Olminius (1787). 565
Dixon v. Sadler (1839). 701, 713
Dixon v. SS Ambient (Owners of) (1912) 1027
Dixon v. Yates (1833). 478
Dobby v. Wilson Pease & Co (1909) 1032
Dobell v. Hutchinson (1835) 330
Dobell v. Stevens (1825) 409, 411
Dobson v. Blackmore (1847) 1070
Dobson v. Land (1850) 138
Dobson v. Sotheby (1827). 706
Docker v. Somes (1834). 565, 602
Dodd (1808) 617
Dodd v. Holme (1834). 1134, 1135, 1137
Dodd v. Norris (1814) 1041
Dodgson's Case (1849) 420
Doe v. Filliter (1844). 901
Doloret v. Rothschild (1824) 553
Dominion Natural Gas Co v. Collins and Perkins (1909). 988
Donaldson, Re (1884) 148
Donaldson v. Donaldson (1854) 258
Donoghue v. Stevenson (1932) 944, 988
Doogood v. Rose (1850) 486
Dornford, Re (1851). 812
Doswell v. Imprey (1823) 787
Dotzauer v. Strand Palace Hotel (1910) 1026
Dougal v. Wilson (1769). 1072
Douglas v. Culverwell (1861). 152
Douglas v. Scougall (1816) 701
Dovey v. Corey (1901). 665
Dowager Duchess of Sutherland v. Duke of Sutherland (1893) 93
Dowell v. General Steam Navigation Company 933
Down v. Fromont (1814). 912
Down v. Halling (1825). 748

Down v. Hatcher (1839) 384
Downes v. Back (1816) 535
Downes v. Grazebrook (1817) 138, 145, 404
Downman v. Williams (1845) 462
Drew v. Lockett (1863) 555
Drew v. New River Company (1834) 908
Drewe v. Hanson (1801) 440, 550
Drewell v. Towler (1832)..1114
Drielsma v. Manifold (1894) 96
Driver's Settlement, Re (1875) 276
Dronfield Silkstone Coal Co, Re (1880) 655
Drummond v. Van Ingen (1887)...483
Drysdale v. Piggott (1856) 153
Du Cros v. Lambourne (1907)..975
Dublin, Wicklow and Wexford Railway Company v.
    Slattery (1878) 939
Dubost, Ex p. (1811)...253, 255, 257, 259
Duckett v. Williams (1834) 708, 711
Duddell v. Simpson (1866)...109
Dudgeon v. Pembroke (1877) 702, 713
Dudley v. Vaughan (1808) 782
Dufaur v. Oxenden (1831) 734
Dufaur v. Professional Life Assurance Co (1858) 692
Duff v. Budd (1822) 458, 913, 914
Duff v. Great Northern Railway (1878) 968
Duff v. Mackenzie (1857) 718
Duffield v. Duffield (1829) 38
Duke of Bedford v. Marquis of Abercorn (1836) 17, 83
Duke of Bedford v. Trustees of British Museum (1822)..................................171
Duke de Cadaval v. Collins (1836) 459, 577
Duke of Devonshire v. Eglin (1853) 161
Duke of Somerset v. Cookson (1735) 552
Duke of Sutherland v. Heathcote (1891) 177
Duke v. Barnett (1846) 104
Duke v. Newcastle v. Lade Lincoln (1806) 24, 25
Dulieu v. White & Sons (1901) 996
Dumas, Ex p. (1754) 767
Duncan v. Topham (1849) 337
Duncuft v. Albrecht (1841)..553
Dungannon v. Smith (1846) 20, 21, 30
Dunlop Pneumatic Tyres Co Ltd v. New Garage and Motor Co (1915).....................529
Dunlop Pneumatic Tyres Co Ltd v. Selfridges & Co Ltd (1915) 388, 673
Dunlop v. Higgins (1848)....................................336, 337, 343, 344, 538
Dunlop v. Waugh (1792)...479
Dunn v. Flood (1885) 76
Dunne v. English (1874)..405, 663
Duppa v. Gerrard (1689) 566
Durell v. Pritchard (1865)..1074
Durrant v. Ecclesiastical Commissioners (1880).......................................586
Durrie v. Nind (1835) 264
Dutton v. Marsh (1871)...739
Dutton v. Morrison (1809-10) 784

Dutton v. Pole (1677)..388
Dutton v. Solomonson (1803)..458
Dutton v. Thompson (1833)..267
Duvergier v. Fellows (1828)..618
Dwyer v. Edie (1788)...689
Dyers' Company v. King (1870)..1078
Dynen v. Leach (1857)..1006

Eaden v. Firth (1863)..1107
Eager v. Grimwood (1847)..1041
Eaglesfield v. the Marquis of Londonderry (1876)...................... 427
Eardly v. Price (1806)... 496
Earl of Aldborough v. Trye (1840)..................................... 403
Earl of Aylesford v. Morris (1873).................................148, 404
Earl of Bristol v. Wilsmore (1823).....................................458
Earl of Chesterfield v. Janssen (1750-1)...........................404, 414
Earl of Cundonald v. Masterman (1869)................................ 665
Earl of Durham v. Legard (1865).......................................440
Earl of Falmouth v. Thomas (1832).....................................533
Earl of Harrington v. Corporation of Derby (1905)..............1089, 1109
Earl of Lindsey v. Great Northern Railway Co (1853)....................391
Earl of Lonsdale v. Church (1790).................................... 602
Earl of Lonsdale v. Littledale (1793)..................................1128
Earl of Macclesfield v. Davis (1814)...................................552
Earl of Mansfield, Ex p.. 624
Earl of March v. Pigot (1771).....................................676, 705
Earl of Radnor's Will Trusts, Re (1890)................................93
Earl of Ripon v. Hobart (1834).......................................1110
Earl of Sandwich v. Great Northern Railway Co (1878)..................164
Earl of Shrewsbury v. North Staffordshire Railway Co (1865)............392
Earl of Stamford and Warrington, Re (1912)............................11
Earl v. Lubbock (1905)... 988
Earl Vane v. Rigden (1870)..137
Earle v. Oliver (1848)...363
Early v. Garrett (1829)...411, 484
East India Co v. Tritton (1824).......................................751
East India Co v. Vincent (1740)......................................161
East-India Co v. Henchman (1791).................................... 602
East Indian Railway v. Kalidas Makerjee (1901)........................967
East London Water Works Co v. Bailey (1827)..........................738
Eastern & South African Telegraph Co v. Cape Town Tramways (1902)......1145
Eastern Counties Railway Co (1841)...................................1104
Eastern Counties Railway Co v. Hawkes (1855)........................ 549
Easton v. Pratchett (1835)...744, 745
Eastwood v. Brown (1825)..783
Eastwood v. Kenyon (1840)..364, 390
Eastwood v. Lever (1863)...175
Eaton v. Jaques (1780)...128
Eaton v. Lyon (1798)...550
Eaves v. Blaenclydach Colliery Co (1909)..............................1025
Ebbw Vale Steel, Iron, and Coal Co, Re (1877)......................641, 655
Ecclesiastical Commissioners v. Kino (1880)..........................1077

Eden v. Parkinson (1781) 701
Edgeley v. Barker (1891) 31
Edgington v. Fitzmaurice (1885)................................... 430, 1040
Edie v. East India Co (1761) 741, 742
Edmeads v. Newman (1823)..574
Edmunds v. Bushell and Jones (1865) 657
Edmunds v. Merchants' Dispatch Transportation Co (1883) 470
Edmunds v. Wallingford (1885) 596, 597
Edwards, Re (1873) 261
Edwards, Re (1906)..46
Edwards v. Bates (1844) 566
Edwards v. Baugh (1843) 375
Edwards v. Brown (1831) 400
Edwards v. Burt (1852) 403
Edwards v. Cameron's Coalbank Steam Coal and Swansea
   and Loughor Railway Co (1851) 738
Edwards v. Etherington (1825) 116
Edwards v. Footner (1808).. 699
Edwards v. Godfrey (1899) 1022
Edwards v. Grand Junction Railway Co (1836) 391
Edwards v. Harben v. (1788) 783
Edwards v. Jones (1836) 256, 257
Edwards v. Jones (1837) 745
Edwards v. London and North Western Railway Co (1870) 660, 898
Edwards v. M'Leay (1815)...100, 415, 422
Edwards v. Thompson (1868) 279, 280, 283
Edwards v. West (1878).. 695
Egerton v. Earl Brownlow (1853).. 6, 24
Ehrensperger v. Anderson (1848)...507
Ehrman v. Bartholomew (1898) 561
Eicholz v. Bannister (1864) 305, 484, 853
Eke v. Hart-Dyke (1910)..1026
Elbinger Actien-Gesellschaft v. Armstrong (1874) 539
Elderton v. Emmens (1847) 365, 496, 497
Electric Telegraph Co of Ireland, Budd's Case, Re (1861) 648
Electric Telegraph Co of Ireland, Cookney's Case (1858) 340
Eley v. Positive Government Security Life Assurance Co (1876).....................393
Eliza, The (1823)..378
Ellen v. Topp (1851) 486, 487, 497
Ellice, Ex p. (1821) 282
Elliman & Sons & Co v. Carrington & Sons (1901)......................672
Elliot v. Thomas (1838) 331
Elliotson v. Feetham (1835) 1097, 1099
Elliott v. Crutchley (1906) 518
Elliott v. Kemp (1840).. 1115
Ellis v. Eden (1857) 283
Ellis v. Ellis (1875) 36
Ellis v. Great Western Railway Co (1874) 980
Ellis v. Hamlen (1810)..531
Ellis v. Loftus Iron Co (1874)... 1125
Ellis v. Nimmo (1835) 254, 255, 258
Ellis v. Rogers (1885) 94

Ellis v. Sheffield Gas Consumer's Co (1853) 896
Ellison v. Bignold (1821) 617
Ellison v. Ellison (1802) 253, 255, 260, 262
Ellison v. Reacher (1908) 176
Ellis's Settlement, Re (1909) 261
Elmhirst v. Spencer (1849) 1106
Elmore v. Stone (1809) 332
Elphinstone v. Monkland Iron and Coal Co (1886) 528
Elsee v. Gatward (1793) 374
Elsworth v. Cole (1836) 632
Elsworth v. Woolmore (1803) 377
Elwes v. Hopkins (1906) 975
Elwes v. Mawe (1803) 118
Emanuel v. Dane (1812) 411
Emblen v. Myers (1860) 902
Embrey v. Owen (1851) 163
Embrey v. Owens (1851) 1082
Emery v. Richards (1845) 594
Emly v. Lye (1811) 615
Emma Silver Mining Co v. Grant (1879) 603
Emmerton v. Matthews (1862) 482
Empress Engineering Co, Re (1880) 392, 393
Engel v. Fitch (1868) 100, 540
England v. Curling (1843) 554
England v. Davidson (1840) 349, 377
England v. Downs (1840) 252
England v. Marsden (1866) 596
Entick v. Carrington (1765) 1125
Equitable Fire and Accident Office v. Ching Wo Hong (1907) 703
Equitable Reversionary Interest Society v. Fuller (1861) 281, 285
Erlanger v. New Sombrero Phosphate Co (1878) 416, 590, 643, 645
Ernest v. Nicholls (1857) 657
Errington v. Errington (1952) 357
Erskine v. Adeane (1871) 117
Esdaile v. La Nauze (1835) 750
Espuela Land and Cattle Co, Re (1909) 636
Estwick v. Caitlaud (1793) 783
Etches v. Etches (1856) 42
European Assurance Society Arbitration Acts and Industrial and
    General Life Assurance and Deposit Co, Cocker's Case, Re (1876) 651
European Assurance Society Arbitration Acts and Wellington
    Reversionary and Life Assurance Society, Conquest's Case, Re (1875) 651
European Life Assurance Society, Re (1869) 648
Evan v. Saunder (1855) 268
Evans, Ex p. (1852) 300
Evans, Re (1879) 189
Evans, Re (1884) 246
Evans v. Bicknell (1801) 417, 1040
Evans v. Collins (1844) 413
Evans v. Cory Brothers & Co (1912) 1032
Evans v. Dodd (1912) 1026
Evans v. Drummond (1801) 385

Evans v. Edmonds (1853) 413, 425
Evans v. Llewellin (1787) 404, 565
Evans v. Smallcombe (1868) 659
Evans v. Williams (1832) 363
Evans v. Wood (1867) 553
Evans v. Wright (1851) 573
Everett v. Desborough (1829) 709
Everett v. London Assurance (1865)... 720
Everett v. Remington (1892) 176
Everitt v. Everitt (1870)..267
Ewart v. Fryer (1901)...127
Exall v. Partridge (1799)...122, 595, 598, 599
Exchange Banking Co, Flitcroft's Case, Re (1882)............................. 654, 664
Exchange Telegraph Co v. Gregory & Co (1896)................................1065
Eyre v. Glover (1812) 686
Eyre v. Houghton Main Colliery (1910)..1031
Eyre v. Hughes (1876)..147, 148
Eyre v. Wynn-Mackenzie (1894) 148
Eyston v. Simmonds (1842) 99

Fabian v. Plant (1691) 375
Fagg v. Dobie (1838) 130
Faines v. Brown (1751).. 549
Fairclough v. Pavia (1854) 741
Fairclough v. Swan Brewery (1912)...154
Fairlee v. Herring (1826) 734
Falcke v. Gray (1859)...549, 555
Falkner v. Equitable Reversionary Society (1858) 106
Falkner v. Ritchie (1813)... 686
Fallick v. Barber (1838)... 349
Family Endowment Society, Re (1869-70) 650
Farina v. Home (1846) 764
Farmer v. Arendel (1772) 578
Farnsworth v. Garrard (1807)...530
Farnworth v. Hyde (1866) 718
Farrant v. Barnes (1862)...986, 987, 1145
Farrant v. Olmius (1820) 115, 525, 527
Farrer v. Nelson (1885) 1146
Farrer v. Nightingal (1798)..438
Farwell v. Boston and Worcester Railroad (1842)...............................1003
Faure Electric Accumulator Co, Re (1888)...........................646, 664, 666
Fawcett v. Fearne (1844)..816, 1115
Fawcett v. Whitehouse (1829) 662
Fawcus v. Sarsfield (1856).. 702
Fearon v. Bowers (1753) 759
Featherstone v. Fenwick (1784)...133
Featherstonhaugh v. Johnston (1818)...1118
Fechter v. Montgomery (1863) 560
Feilden v. Slater (1869) 174
Feise v. Parkinson (1812) 703
Fell v. Riley (1775) 401
Fellows v. Lord Gwydyr (1826) 454

Fells v. Read (1796) 552
Feltham v. England (1866). 1004
Felthouse v. Bindley (1862) 337, 338
Fenn v. Harrison (1790) 739
Fenton v. Thorley (1903). 1024, 1025
Fentum v. Pocock (1813). 746
Fereday v. Wightwick (1829) 143
Ferguson v. Carrington (1829) 411, 458, 589
Ferguson v. Wilson (1866). 664
Fergusson v. Fyffe (1841) 147
Fergusson v. Norman (1838) 852
Ferrand v. Hallas Land and Building Co (1893) 1091
Festing v. Allen (1843) 39
Fewings v. Tisdal (1847) 496
Fidgeon v. Sharpe (1814) 784
Field v. Field (1894) 292
Field v. Hopkins (1890) 148
Filburn v. People's Palace and Aquarium Co (1890). 1145
Filiter v. Phippard (1847) 917, 919
Finch, Re (1881) 39
Fine Art Society v. Union Bank (1886) 1118
Finlay v. Liverpool and Great Western Steamship Co (1870) 760
Finley v. Gardner (1827). 144
Finn v. Hutchinson (1702) 401
Firbank v. Humphreys (1886). 942, 947
Fischel v. Scott (1854) 510
Fisher v. Liverpool Marine Insurance Co (1873) 697
Fisher v. Prowse (1862). 972
Fisher v. Pyne (1840). 316
Fisher v. Samuda (1808) 478
Fisher v. Shirley (1889) 261
Fishmongers' Co v. Robertson (1843) 304
Fitch v. Snedaker. 351
Fitch v. Sutton (1804) 384
Fitzgerald Settlement, Re (1887). 241
Fitzgerald v. Clarke & Son (1908). 1028
Fitzherbert v. Mather (1785) 699
Fitzpatrick v. Kelly (1873). 881
Flanagan v. Great Western Railway Co (1868). 663
Flavell, Re (1883) 392
Fleet v. Metropolitan Asylums Board (1886) 1110
Fleetwood re. (1880) 5
Fleming v. Hislop (1886) 1146
Flemington v. Smithers (1826) 1042
Fletcher v. Dyche (1787) 525, 526
Fletcher v. Fletcher (1844) 255, 392
Fletcher v. Heath (1827) 1123
Fletcher v. Rylands (1866) 1125, 1142, 1143, 1144, 1145
Fletcher v. Tayleur (1855) 537
Flight v. Thomas (1839). 1097
Flinn v. Headlam (1829). 699
Flinn v. Tobin (1829). 411, 699

Flint, Ex p. (1818) 744
Flint v. Brandon (1803) 556
Flockton v. Hall (1849) 384
Flood v. Allen (1896) 1056
Flood v. Jackson (1895) 1054, 1055, 1056
Florence Land and Public Works Co, Moor Ex p., Re (1878) 637
Flower v. Adam (1810) 541, 908
Flower v. London and North Western Railway (1894) 969
Flower v. Peck (1830) 491
Flureau v. Thornhill (1776) 98, 99, 100, 106, 373,
539, 540, 544
Foakes v. Beer (1884) 385, 386, 387
Foe. v. Filliter (1844) 901
Foley v. Hill (1848) 764, 767
Follett v. Moore (1849) 144
Footner v. Sturgis (1852) 61
Forbes v. Cochrane (1824) 1043
Forbes v. Peacock (1846) 181
Ford v. Heely (1857) 140
Ford v. London and South Western Railway Co (1862) 961
Ford v. Olden (1867) 138, 139
Ford v. Tiley (1827) 498
Forde v. Skinner (1830) 1035
Fordham v. London, Brighton and South Coast Railway Co (1868) .938
Fordyce v. Bridges (1848) 274
Fores v. Wilson (1791) 1041
Forest of Dean Coal Mining Co, Re (1878) 665
Forget v. Ostigny (1895) 632
Forman v. Homfray (1813) 614
Formby v. Barker (1903) 177
Forsey and Hollebone's Contract, Re (1927) 108
Forshaw v. Chabert (1821) 701
Forshaw v. Welsby (1860) 267
Forster v. Clements (1809) 769
Forster v. Hale (1798) 330, 332
Forster v. Hogart (1850) 140
Fortescue v. Barnett (1834) 257, 692
Forward v. Pittard (1785) 911
Fosbrooke v. Balguy 602
Foss, Ex p. (1858) 789
Foss v. Harbottle (1843) 652, 653
Foster v. Allanson (1788) 615
Foster v. Charles (1830) 411, 1040
Foster v. Oxford, Worcester and Wolverhampton Railway Co (1853) 662
Foster v. Pearson (1835) 749
Foster v. Stewart (1814) 579, 580, 1043
Foster v. Urban District Council of Warblington (1906) 1070, 1092, 1146
Foster and Lister, Re (1877) 265
Fothergill v. Rowland (1873) 560
Fouldes v. Willoughby (1841) 1114, 1117
Foulkes v. Metropolitan District Railway Co (1879) 959, 960
Foulkes v. Sellway (1800) 513

Fountaine v. Carmarthen Railway Co (1868) 658
Fowkes v. Manchester and London Life Assurance Co (1862) 707
Fowler v. Hollins (1872) 1119
Fowler v. Padget (1798)..782
Fox v. Clifton (1830) 618, 623
Fox v. Mackreth (1788)..146, 663
Foy v. London, Brighton and South Coast Railway (1865) 937
Fragano v. Long (1825) 510
Francis v. Burton (1895)...719
Francis v. Cockrell (1870) 945, 963, 1013
Franklin v. Miller (1836) 487, 507
Franklin v. South Eastern Railway Co (1858).......................................998, 999
Franklyn, Ex p. (1848) 281
Franks v. Price (1840).. 24
Fraser v. Fraser (1814).. 242
Fraser v. Thompson (1859)..378
Frazer v. Hatton (1857)..377
Frazer v. Walker (1967)... 224
Fred Wilkins and Brothers v. Weaver (1915)...1065
Freeman v. Baker (1833) 477, 479
Freeman v. Cooke (1848) 338, 367, 451, 930, 931
Freeman v. Jeffries (1869)...570
Freeman v. Taylor (1831)...489
Freer v. Hesse (1853) 187
Freeth v. Burr (1874) 488
Freme v. Wright (1819) 104
French v. Bombernard (Tower Furnishing and Finance Co,
    Claimants) (1888) 875
French v. Underwood (1903)..1030
Frewen v. Phillips (1862) 170
Fricker v. Thomlinson (1840) 331
Fritz v. Hobson (1880) 1069, 1107
Frogley v. Earl Lovelace (1859) 161
Frost v. Knight (1872)..504, 506
Fry v. Lane (1888) 404, 865
Fuentes v. Montis (1868) 1124
Fulham v. Down (1798) 401, 576
Fuller v. Bennett (1843) 210
Fuller v. Wilson (1842) 413
Fullerton v. Provincial Bank of Ireland (1903) 376
Furtado v. Rogers (1802) 703
Fust, Re (1817) 282
Fydell v. Clark (1795)...739

Gadd v. Provincial Union Bank (1909).. 869
Gaden v. Newfoundland Savings Bank (1899)... 768
Gainsford v. Carroll (1824) 535, 538
Gainsforth v. Griffith (1666)...525, 528
Gale v. Halfknight (1821) 781
Gale v. Reed (1806) 373
Galer v. Rawson (1889)..974

Gallagher v. Piper (1864) 1004
Gallimore, Ex p. (1816) 781
Gallin v. London and North Western Railway Co (1875) 969
Gallini v. Gallini (1833) 28
Galsworthy v. Strutt (1848) 527
Gandall v. Pontigny (1816) 496
Gandy v. Gandy (1884) 255, 392
Gane v. Norton Hill Colliery Co (1909) 1027
Garbutt v. Watson (1822) 331
Gardiner, Ex p. (1812) 792
Gardiner v. Gray (1815) 480
Gardner v. London Chatham and Dover Railway Co (No. 1) (1867) 636
Garlick v. Lawson (1853) 23
Garnett v. Willan (1821) 914
Garrard of Grinling (1818) 440
Garrard v. Cottrell (1847) 595
Garrard v. Hardey (1843) 618
Garrard v. Lord Lauderdale (1830) 240
Garrards v. Frankel (1862) 442
Garrells v. Cannon (1854) 461
Garret v. Taylor (1620) 1048, 1056
Garrett v. Barclay (1826) 727
Gas Light and Coke Company v. Vestry of St. Mary (1885) 1104
Gasquoine, Re (1894) 292
Gaters v. Madeley (1840) 744
Gatty v. Field (1846) 594
Gaunt v. Hill (1815) 334
Gautret v. Egerton (1867) 923, 978
Gaved v. Martyn (1865) 1083
Gayford v. Nicholls (1854) 1133
Gayler and Pope v. B. Davies and Son (1924) 1125
Geach v. Ingall (1845) 708
Geddis v. Proprietors of Bann Reservoir (1878) 921
Gedge v. Royal Exchange Association (1900) 680
Gee v. Lancashire and Yorkshire Railway Co (1860) 545, 546
Gee v. Lucas (1867) 479
Gee v. Metropolitan Railway Company (1873) 939, 951
General Couth American, Re (1876) 637
Genese, Re, Kearsley & Co, Ex p. (1886) 827
George and Richard, (1871) 931, 934
George v. Skivington (1869) 945, 948, 988
Gerhard v. Bates (1852) 352
German Mining Co, Re (1854) 606
Gervais v. Edwards (1842) 559
Gibbins v. North Eastern Metropolitan Asylum Board (1847) 109
Gibbon v. Mendez (1818) 495
Gibbon v. Paynton (1769) 911
Gibbons v. Gibbons (1881) 34
Gibbons v. Pepper (1695) 909
Gibbons v. Proctor (1891) 350, 351, 352
Gibbons v. Vanguard Motorbus Co (1908) 975
Gibbs v. Messer (1887) 224

Giblan v. National Amalgamated Labourers' Union of Great
    Britain and Ireland (1903).. 1064, 1065
Giblin v. M'Mullen (1868) 916
Gibson, Re (1871)..570
Gibson v. Bray (1817)... 790
Gibson v. D'Este (1843)... 100
Gibson v. Hunter (1794)...753
Gibson v. Jeyes (1801) 404, 663
Gibson v. Minet (1791) 752, 753
Gibson v. Small (1853)...701, 702
Gibson v. Wells (1805) 116
Gibson v. Wilde (1848).. 100
Gilbert v. Guignon (1872) 760
Gilbey v. Rush (1906) 93
Gilding v. Eyre (1861) 1036
Giles v. Giles (1837)... 42
Giles v. Perkins (1807)...767
Gill v. Cubitt (1824)...748
Gill v. Edouin (1895)..1147
Gill v. Waterhouse (1830)...912
Gillett v. Peppercorne (1840) 416, 663
Gillett v. Rippon (1829) 599
Gillman v. Fletcher (1791) 401
Gilmour v. Supple (1858) 478
Gladstone v. Hadwell (1813)..458
Gladstone v. King (1813)... 699
Gladstone v. Padwick (1871) 303
Gladwell v. Steggall (1839)...883
Glasspole v. Young (1829) 1115
Gledstane v. Hewitt (1831) 1116
Glen v. Lewis (1853)... 707
Gloholm v. Hays (1841)... 489
Glossop v. Heston and Isleworth Local Board (1879)........................... 1089, 1090, 1091,
                                                        1092, 1093
Glover v. North Staffordshire Railway Co (1851)......................................1104
Glucksein v. Barnes (1900) 646
Glyn Mills, Currie & Co v. East and West India Dock Co (1882) 759, 763
Glynn v. Margetson (1893) 43
Godard v. Gray (1870) 528
Goddard v. O'Brien (1882).. 384, 386
Goddard v. Snow (1826)... 251
Godden v. Crowhurst (1842)...250, 251
Godefroy v. Dalton (1830) 883, 916
Godfrey, Re (1883).. 292
Godfrey v. Poole (1888) 264
Godsal v. Webb (1838) 261
Godsall v. Boldero (1807).. 689, 690, 691
Goebel v. Linn (1882)...383
Gold co, Re (1878) 645
Goldsmid v. Tunbridge Wells Improvement Commissioners (1865)............... 1085, 1090, 1111
Gomersall, Re (1875)...749
Gomery v. Bond (1814)... 492

Gompertz v. Bartlett (1853) 445, 740
Gompertz v. Denton (1832) 478
Good v. Cheeseman (1831) 384
Goodall v. Dolley (1787) 735
Goodall v. Lowndes (1844) 593
Goode v. Langley (1827) 1115
Goodman v. Harvey (1836) 749
Goodman v. Pocock (1850) 533
Goodman v. Taylor (1832) 909
Goodman v. Whitcomb (1820) 616
Goodright d. Humphreys v. Moses (1773) 264
Goodtitle d. Richardson v. Edmonds (1798) 17
Gordon (1889) 863
Gordon v. Graham (1716) 149, 150
Gordon v. Street (1899) 469, 863
Gordon v. Swan (1810) 530
Gordon (Gordon's Administrator) v. Stephen (1902) 865
Goring v. Nash (1744) 361
Gorringe, Re (1906) 43
Gorrissen v. Perrin (1857) 510, 511
Gorton v. Champneys (1823) 144
Gosbell v. Archer (1835) 588
Goss v. Lord Nugent (1833) 492
Goss v. Withers (1758) 686
Gossip v. Wright (1863) 152
Gottlieb v. Cranch (1853) 153
Gouger v. Jolly (1816) 912
Gough v. Bult (1847) 243
Gouldsworth v. Knights (1843) 130
Goupy v. Harden (1816) 733, 734, 743
Government Stock Investment and Other Securities Co v.
    Manilla Railway Co (1895) 637
Governor and Co of the Bank of England v. Vagliano (1891) 754
Governor and Co of the British Cast Plate Manufacturers v.
    Meredith (1792) 919
Govett v. Radnidge (1802) 911
Gowan v. Gowan (1880) 12
Gowland v. De Faria (1810) 403
Gowling v. Thompson (1868) 41
Grace v. Smith (1775) 614
Graham v. Chapman (1852) 636, 815
Graham v. Dyster (1816) 1122
Grainger v. Hill (1838) 1034
Grand Junction Railway Co (1839) 996, 997
Grand Trunk Railway Co of Canada v. Jennings (1888) 998
Grant v. Grant (1865) 259
Grant v. Hulton (1817) 1114
Grant v. Parkinson (1782) 686
Grant v. Vaughan (1764) 764
Graves v. Dolphin (1826) 250, 251
Graves v. Legg (1854) 477, 486
Gray v. Cox (1825) 481

Gray v. Fowler (1872) 109, 540
Gray v. Garman (1814) 41
Gray v. Lewis (1868) 639, 653
Gray v. Pullen (1864) 898
Gray v. Stanion (1836). 94, 99
Greasley v. Codling (1824). 1069
Great Luxembourg Railway Co v. Magnay (1858). 663
Great Northern Railway Co (1849) 1104
Great Northern Railway Co v. Harrison (1854). 959
Great Northern Railway Co v. Witham (1873). 348
Great Peace Shipping v. Tsavliris Salvage (International) (2002) 444
Great Western Railway Co of Canada v. Braid (1863) 960
Great Western Railway Co v. London and County Banking Co (1901) 777, 778
Great Western Railway Company v. Blake (1862). 964
Greaves v. Wilson (1858) 104, 109
Green v. Barrett (1826). 565
Green v. Beesley (1835) 614
Green v. Bridges (1830). 125
Green v. Button (1835) 1039, 1045
Green v. Duckett (1883) 401, 577
Green v. Elmslie (1794). 712
Green v. London General Omnibus Co (1859). 897
Green v. New River Company (1792). 905
Green v. Paterson (1888) 264, 265
Green v. Price (1827). 526
Green v. Price (1845). 527
Green v. Spicer (1830). 250, 251
Greene v. West Cheshire Railway Co (1871). 557
Greenhalgh v. Manchester & Birmingham Railway Co (1838). 391
Greenland v. Chaplin (1850) 544, 932, 935, 954
Greenock Corp v. Caledonian Railway Co (1917) 1148, 1149
Greenway v. Fisher (1824) 1118
Greenwell v. Low Beechburn Coal Co (1897). 1130
Greenwood v. Leather Shod Wheel Co (1900). 641
Greenwood v. Sutherland (1853). 23
Gregg v. Wells (1839). 367
Gregory v. Duke of Brunswick (1843) 1048, 1053, 1059, 1063
Gregory v. Williams (1817) 391
Gregson's Trust, Re (1864). 44
Gretton v. Howard (1815) 31
Greville v. Browne (1859). 181
Grey v. Friar (1854) 126
Grey v. Pearson (1857) 33
Grier v. Grier (1872) 16, 17
Grieve v. Grieve (1867). 37
Griffin v. Coleman (1859). 1034
Griffinhoofe v. Daubuz (1855). 596
Griffith v. Brymer (1903) 518
Griffith v. Paget (1877). 635
Griffith v. Spratley (1787). 404
Griffiths v. Earl of Dudley (1882) 1017
Griffiths v. London and North Western Railway (1866) 979

Griffiths v. Perry (1859) 764
Grill v. General Iron Screw Collier Co (1866) 923
Grimes v. Gooch (1820) 142
Grimstone v. Cunningham (1894) 561
Grindley, Re (1898) 293
Grinnell v. Wells (1844) 1041, 1042
Grissell v. Robinson (1836) 598, 600
Grizewood v. Blane (1851) 632
Grizzle v. Frost (1863) 1007
Grote v. Chester and Holyhead Railway Co (1848) 963
Groves v. Buck (1814) 331
Groves v. Hicks (1841) 16
Groves v. Wimborne (1898) 1007
Guardian Permanent Benefit Building Society, Re (1883) 607
Guardians of Halifax Union v. Wheelwright (1875) 770, 929, 930
Guest, Ex p. (1852) 647
Guichard v. Roberts (1763) 744
Guidon v. Robson (1809) 614
Guiness v. Land Corporation of Ireland (1882) 635
Gulliver v. Cosens (1845) 401
Gully v. Bishop of Exeter (1830) 361
Gully v. Cregoe (1857) 245
Gunn v. London and Lancashire Fire Insurance Co (1862) 393
Gunter v. Halsey (1739) 330
Gunter v. James (1908) 974
Gunton v. Nurse (1821) 1120
Gurford v. Bayley (1842) 318
Gurney v. Behrend (1852) 760
Gurney v. Womersley (1854) 461, 751
Gwinnell v. Herbert (1836) 735

Habergham v. Ridehalgh (1870) 30, 41, 43
Hackney Furnishing v. Watts (1912) 873
Haddington Island v. Huson (1911) 139
Haddrick v. Heslop (1848) 1038
Hadley v. Baxendale (1854) 99, 304, 319, 539, 541, 542,
                                                   543, 544, 545, 547, 714, 954, 992
Hadley v. Clarke (1799) 511
Hadley v. Taylor (1865) 973
Hadow v. Hadow (1838) 10, 245
Hadves v. Levit (1631) 388
Hadwen v. Hadwen (1847) 16
Hagedorn v. Whitmore (1816) 718
Haille v. Smith (1796) 763
Hailton Fraser & Co v. Thames and Mersey Marine Insurance Co (1886) 712
Haines v. Burnett (1859) 126
Haines v. Taylor (1847) 1110
Hale v. Hale (1876) 45
Hale v. Rawson (1858) 511
Halford v. Cameron's Coalbank Steam Coal and Swansea and
    Loughor Railway Co (1851) 738
Halford v. Kymer (1830) 689

Halhead v. Young (1856) 686
Halket v. Merchant Trader's Insurance Co (1849) 630
Hall v. Conder (1857) 445
Hall v. Dewes (1821) 273
Hall v. Duke of Norfolk (1900)...1130
Hall v. Ewin (1887) 175
Hall v. Fearnley (1842) 909
Hall v. Fuller (1826)... 769
Hall v. Hall (1872) 267
Hall v. Hayman (1912) 717
Hall v. Hollander (1825)...1042
Hall v. Johnson (1865)... 1004, 1005
Hall v. Lees (1904)...882
Hall v. May (1857) 274
Hall v. North Eastern Railway Co (1875) 969, 1016
Hall v. Smith (1824) 895, 919
Hall v. Wright (1858)... 502, 512, 513
Hallett v. Dowdall (1852) 630
Hallett's Estate, Re (1880) 604, 605, 609
Halsey v. Grant (1806) 441, 550
Hambly v. Trott (1776) 576, 577, 583
Hamilton, Fraser & Co v. Pandorf & Co (1887)...1024
Hamilton, Re (1895) 37
Hamilton v. Mendes (1761) 686
Hamlet, Re (1888) 43, 46
Hammack v. White (1862)...959, 971
Hammersley v. De Biel (1845) 368, 369
Hammersmith and City Railway Co v. Brand (1869)... 921, 1003, 1104
Hammond, Ex p. (1855) 812
Hammond v. Barker (1588) 400
Hammond v. Messenger (1838)...691
Hammond v. Neame (1818)..243
Hampshire v. Wickens (1878) 11, 126
Hampton v. Holman (1877)...23, 26, 245
Hanbury v. Ella (1834) 318
Hanbury's Settled Estates (1913)...245
Hancke v. Hooper (1835) 882
Handley v. Davies (1859) 236
Hanley v. Wood (1819) 159
Hannaford v. Hannaford (1871) 45
Hannan's Lake View Ltd v. Armstrong (1900) 779
Hansard v. Robinson (1827)... 766
Hanson v. Lancashire & Yorkshire Railway Co (1872)... 960
Hanson v. Meyer (1805) 304
Hanson v. Royden (1867) 378
Hanway v. Boulltbee (1830)...1114
Harbridge v. Wogan (1846)...267
Hardcastle v. South Yorkshire Railway and River Dun Co (1859)...973
Harding, Ex p. in Fairbrother, Re (1873)...816
Harding v. Brybddu Colliery Co (1911)...1028
Harding v. Harding (1886) 258
Hardman v. Booth (1863)... 464, 465, 466, 468, 1119, 1120

Hardy v. Central London Railway Co (1920) 984
Hardy v. Martin (1783) 524
Hare v. Groves (1796) 117
Hare v. Henty (1861) 765, 768
Hare v. Travis (1827) 702
Hargrave v. Le Breton (1769) 1039
Hargreaves v. Rothwell (1836) 210
Harley v. King (1835) 129
Harman v. Anderson (1809) 791
Harman v. Fishar (1774) 784
Harman v. Jones (1841) 1106
Harnett v. Yeilding (1805) 549
Harnor v. Groves (1855) 590
Harrington v. Harrington (1871) 24, 25
Harris v. Butler (1837) 1041
Harris v. Carter (1852) 377
Harris v. De Pinna (1886) 1077
Harris v. Great Western Railway Co (1876) 328, 475
Harris v. Harris (No. 1) (1861) 284
Harris v. Loyd (1839) 587
Harris v. Nickerson (1873) 353
Harris v. Oke (1759) 316, 531
Harris v. Pepperell (1867) 443
Harris v. Ryding (1839) 166, 1128
Harris v. Tinn (1888) 1015, 1016
Harris v. Tremenheere (1808) 403
Harris v. Tubb (1889) 266
Harris v. Watson (1791) 377
Harrison v. Armitage (1819) 614
Harrison v. Good (1871) 175
Harrison v. Great Northern Railway (1864) 951
Harrison v. Guest (1855) 404
Harrison v. Harrison (1901) 40
Harrison v. Heathorn (1843) 618
Harrison v. Jackson (1797) 737
Harrison v. London Brighton and South Coast Railway Co (1860) 474
Harrison v. Mexican Railway Co (1875) 635
Harrison v. N E Railway (1874) 980
Harrison v. Walker (1792) 457
Harrison v. Wright (1811) 528
Harrold v. Great Western Railway (1866) 937
Harrold v. Watney (1898) 982
Harse v. Pearl Life Assurance (1903) 711
Hart v. Aldridge (1774) 1042
Hart v. Alexander (1837) 385
Hart v. Herwig (1873) 555
Hart v. Lancashire and Yorkshire Railway Co (1869) 960
Hart v. Stephens (1845) 744
Hart v. Swaine (1877) 100, 425
Hart v. Tribe (1854) 244, 245, 246
Hart v. Windsor (1844) 117
Hartley v. Cummings (1847) 1043

Hartley v. Hymans (1920) 493
Hartley v. Ponsonby (1857) 377, 378
Hartshorn v. Slodden (1801) 784
Harvey v. Crickett (1816) 615
Harvey v. Mount (1845) 403
Harvey v. Ramsbottom (1822)...782
Harvey v. Towers (1851) 745
Hastlelow v. Jackson (1828) 592, 594
Hatch v. Hatch (1804)...405
Hatch v. Trayes (1840) 745
Hatfield v. Phillips (1842)...1123
Hatfield v. Phillips (1845)...1123
Hatham v. East India Co (1787) 497
Hatton v. Haywood (1874)...189
Haughton v. King (1843) 144
Hauxwell (1883)..815
Havelock v. Geddes (1809)...486, 487
Hawes v. Watson (1824) 791
Hawkes v. Saunders (1782)...361
Hawkins v. Cooper (1838) 908
Hawkins v. Powell's Tillery Steam Co Ltd (1911)...............................1024
Hawse v. Crowe (1826) 458
Haycraft v. Creasy (1801) 412, 413
Haygarth, Re (1912)...42
Hayn v. Culliford (1879)..948
Hayward v. Bennett (1846) 497
Haywood v. Cope (1858)...549, 550
Haywood v. New Brunswick Building Society (1881)........................175, 177
Hazeldine, Re (1852)..275
Head v. Gould (1898) 293
Heald v. Carey (1852) 1117
Hearne v. Garton (1859)..986
Hearne v. Rogers (1829) 367
Heartley v. Nicholson (1874) 260
Heath, Ex p. (1813)...736
Heath v. Bucknall (1869) 1074
Heath v. Lewis (1853) 7
Heath v. Sansom (1831)...745
Heath v. Wallingford (1868) 1110
Heathcote v. Crookshanks (1787)..384
Heathcote v. North Staffordshire Railway Co (1850) 561
Heathcote v. Paignon (1787)..147
Heaven v. Pender (1883) 946, 947, 948, 949,
                                           982, 988, 989, 1014
Hebdon v. West (1863) 691
Heilbutt v. Hickson (1872)...478
Helby v. Matthews (1894) 871, 872
Helsham v. Barnett (1873) 865
Hemmings v. Sceptre Life Association (1905) 707
Henderson & Co v. Williams (1895) 900
Henderson v. Lacon (1867) 426
Henderson v. Royal British Bank (1857) 649

Henderson v. Stevenson (1875) 328, 475
Heneage v. Lord Viscount Andover (1822). 35
Henkle v. Royal Exchange Assurance Co (1749) 441
Henry v. Armstrong (1881) 267, 406
Hensey v. White (1901). 1024
Henson v. Blackwell (1845) 690
Henthorn v. Fraser (1892) 346
Henty v. Wray (1882) 43
Hepburn v. Lordan (1865) 1110
Herbert v. Samuel Fox & Co (1916) 1028
Hercy v. Birch (1804) 554
Hern v. Nichols 412
Hernaman v. Coryton (1850) 337
Herne Bay Steam Boat Company v. Hutton (1903). 519
Herne v. Benbow (1813) 116
Herring v. Corell (1840). 377
Herz v. Union Bank of London (1859). 1076
Heseltine v. Simmons (1892). 861, 864
Heselton v. Allnut (1813) 703
Heske v. Samuelson (1883). 1015
Hesketh v. Birmingham Corporation (1924). 1093
Hesketh v. Gray (1755) 495
Heslop, Ex p. (1852). 816
Hewison v. Negus (1853) 265
Hewitt, Re (1918) 7
Hewitt v. Price (1842). 632
Hewlett v. Cruchley (1813) 902
Hewlins v. Shippam (1826) 160
Heyling v. Hastings (1698). 362
Heywood v. Rickering (1874) 765
Hibbert v. Carter (1787) 760
Hibblewhite v. M'Morine (1839). 99, 498
Hichens v. Congreve (1831) 602
Hickenbothom v. Groves (1826). 869
Hickes v. Cooke (1816) 138, 145, 149
Hickley, Re (1917) 41
Hickman v. Haynes (1875). 494
Hicks v. Faulkner (1878). 1037
Hicks v. Newport, Abergavenny and Hereford Railway Co (1857) 998
Hide v. Proprietors of the Trent and Mersey Navigation (1793). 912
Hide v. Thornborough (1846) 1135, 1136
Hiern v. Mill (1806) 134
Higginbottom v. Holme (1812) 251
Higgins v. Campbell & Harrison (1904). 1025
Higginson v. Barneby (1826). 17
Higginson v. Clowes (1808). 439
Higgons v. Burton (1857) 463, 464
Hilberry v. Hatton (1864) 1119
Hilder v. Dexer (1902) 647
Hill v. Barclay (1810). 124
Hill v. Buckley (1811). 438
Hill v. Hill (1834). 17

Hill v. Hill (1897)..37
Hill v. Lewis (1694)..739
Hill v. London Assurance Co (1855) 625
Hill v. New River Co (1868)......................................950, 951
Hill v. Ocean Coal Co (1909) 1032
Hill v. Perrott (1810) 578
Hill v. Secretan (1798)... 685
Hill v. Sughrue (1846)... 511, 512
Hill v. Tupper (1863)..160, 177
Hillman, Ex p. (1879) 266
Hills v. Croll (1845)..559
Hills v. London Assurance Corporation (1839)......................717, 718
Hillyer v. Governors of St Bartholomew's Hospital (1909) 882
Hilton v. Earl of Granville (1841).................................1106
Hilton v. Earl of Granville (1845)..................................166
Hilton v. Eckersley (1855).....................................1050, 1052
Hilton v. Fairclough (1811)...337
Hilton v. Woods (1867)... 900
Hinchliffe v. Earl of Kinoul (1838)................................167
Hind v. Poole (1854) 137
Hinde v. Gray (1840)..672
Hinde v. Liddell (1875) 539
Hinde v. Whitehouse (1806).....................................304, 333
Hinton v. Dibbin (1842)...915
Hiort v. Bott (1874) 1120
Hirsche v. Sims (1894) 666
Hirschfield v. Smith (1866) 741
Hitchcock v. Coker (1837)......................................373, 672
Hitchcock v. Giddings (1817).. 436
Hoare v. Cazendove (1812).......................................733, 737
Hoare v. Cazendove (1882) 303
Hoare v. Rennie (1859) 487, 488
Hoare & Co v. McAlpine (1923) 1145
Hobart v. Southend Corporation (1906)..............................1146
Hobbs v. Marlow (1978)...725
Hobbs v. Norton (1682) 416
Hobday v. Peters (No1) (1860)...................................... 406
Hobson v. Bell (1839) 106, 109, 139
Hobson v. Gorringe (1897) 874
Hochster v. De La Tour (1852).................319, 500, 501, 502, 503, 504
Hodge v. Foot (1865)... 40
Hodgens v. Hodgens (1837)...13
Hodges v. Earl of Litchfield (1835) 98
Hodges v. Hodges (1796) 362
Hodges v. Webb (1920)..1065
Hodgkinson v. Cooper (1846)...103
Hodgkinson v. Crowe (1875)...126
Hodgkinson v. Ennor (1863)...1083
Hodgson, Ex p., Re (1853)...812
Hodgson, Re (1812) 251
Hodgson v. Harris (1669)... 566
Hodsoll v. Stallebrass (1840).....................................1042

Hodson v. Terrill (1833) 594
Hoffman v. Pitt (1803) 783
Hogan v. South Eastern Railway Co (1873) 967
Hoggart v. Scott (1830) 99
Hoggins v. Gordon (1842) 349
Hoghton v. Hoghton (1852) 406
Holbird v. Anderson (1793) 523, 783
Holcombe v. Wade (1765) 401
Holder v. Durbin (1849) 275
Holdsworth v. Wise (1828) 713
Hole v. Barlow (1858) 1086, 1098, 1099, 1100
Hole v. Sittingbourne and Sheerness Railway Co (1861) 898
Holford v. Dunnett (1844) 116
Holford v. Hatch (1779) 128
Holker v. Porritt (1875) 163
Holland v. District Committee of the Middle Ward of
    Lanarkshire (1909) 983
Holland v. Eyre (1825) 334
Holland v. Hughes (1809) 282
Holliday v. Atkinson (1826) 364, 744
Hollingworth v. Brodrick (1837) 701
Hollins v. Fowler (1875) 465, 1117, 1119, 1120
Hollins v. Verney (1884) 1125
Holloway v. Headington (1837) 255
Holloway v. Holloway (1877) 261
Holman v. Johnson (1775) 593
Holmes v. Clarke (1861) 1004, 1006
Holmes v. Great Northern Railway Co (1900) 1027
Holmes v. Mather (1875) 970, 1034, 1114,
                                                                                                1125, 1145, 1150
Holmes v. Prescott (1864) 39
Holmes v. Williamson (1817) 600
Holmesdale v. West (1871) 17
Holroyd v. Marshall (1862) 555, 636
Holt v. Ely (1853) 575
Holtzapffel v. Baker (1811) 117
Homersham v. Wolverhampton Waterworks Co (1851) 531
Honck v. Muller (1881) 488
Hones v. North (1875) 1050
Honeyman v. Marryat (1855) 109
Hong Kong Fir Shipping Co v. Kawasaki Kisen Kaisha (1962) 490
Hooper v. Holme (1896) 1015, 1016
Hooper v. Smith (1763) 783
Hope, Re (1899) 93
Hope v. Cusst (1774) 614
Hope v. Cust (1800) 913
Hope's Settled Estate, Re (1910) 93
Hopgood v. Parkin 289
Hopkins v. Grazebrook (1826) 99, 100, 540
Hopkins v. Logan (1839) 365
Hopkins v. Worcester and Birmingham Canal Proprietors (1868) .637
Hopkinson v. Rolt (1861) 150

Hora v. Hora (1863)...245
Horn v. Baker (1808)..816
Horn v. Rouquette (1878)......................................735
Hornblower v. Proud (1819)...............................744, 768
Horne v. Barton (1822)......................................17, 82
Horne v. Hellard, Re (1885)...................................637
Horne v. London and North Western Railway Co (1862)...........559
Horne v. Midland Railway Co (1873)............................547
Horner v. Flintoff (1842)................................526, 527
Horner v. Graves (1831)..................................373, 672
Horner's Estate, Re (1881)..................................... 40
Horsey Estate v. Steiger (1899)...............................127
Horsfall v. Thomas (1862).....................................410
Horsley v. Bell (1778)..469
Horsnail v. Bruce (1872)......................................838
Horton v. Coggs (1691)..733
Horwood v. Smith (1788)..................................464, 465
Hosden v. Harridge (1670).....................................566
Hosking v. Phillips (1848)....................................899
Hospital v. Gibson (1814).....................................171
Hotchkiss's Trusts, Re (1869)..................................41
Hotham v. East India Co (1779)................................495
Houghton v. Bankart (1861)...................................1100
Houldsworth v. Evans (1868)...................................659
Hounsell v. Smyth (1860)......................................978
Household Fire and Carriage Accident Insurance Co v. Grant (1879)...344
Howard v. Bennett (1888).....................................1016
Howard v. Hudson (1852).......................................367
Howard v. Pickford Tool Co (1951).............................503
Howard v. Refuge Friendly Society (1886)......................711
Howard v. Shepherd (1850).....................................760
Howard v. Wood (1678)...571
Howe v. Earl of Dartmouth (1802)....................278, 281, 282
Howe v. Hunt (1862)...540
Howell v. Coupland (1874).....................................515
Howell v. Howell (1835).......................................261
Howells v. Landore Siemens Steel Co (1874)...................1004
Howells v. Vivian & Sons (1901)..............................1030
Howgrave v. Cartier (1814).....................................41
Howkins v. Bennet (1860)......................................143
Howland v. Norris (1784)......................................441
Howley v. Cook (1873)...865
Howorth v. Dewell (1860).......................................37
Hoy v. Smythies (1856)..106
Huckman v. Fernie (1838)......................................709
Hudson, Re (1882)..46
Hudson's Case (1858).....................................420, 421
Huggett v. Montgomery (1807)..................................906
Hughes and Kimber, Ex p. (Limited), Thackrah, Re (1888).......874
Hughes v. Eames (1823)...................................905, 910
Hughes v. Jones (1861)..550
Hughes v. Macfie (1863).......................................981

Hughes v. Percival (1883) 1140
Hughes v. Williams (1806) 913
Huguenin v. Baseley (1804) 262
Huguenin v. Baseley (1807) 403, 405, 407,
                                                                                    408, 409
Hulle v. Heightman (1802) 496, 532
Hulley v. Silversprings Bleaching and Dyeing Company (1922) 1092
Humberston v. Humberston (1716) 26
Humble v. Hunter (1848) 454, 595
Hume v. Bentley (1852) 104
Hume v. Lopes (1892) 286, 287
Hume v. Richardson (1862) 281, 285
Humphreys v. City of London Electric Lighting Co (1911) 1030
Humphries v. Brogden (1850) 166, 1127, 1128, 1134
Humphries v. Carvalho (1812) 333, 334
Humphries v. Cousins (1877) 1146
Hunsden v. Cheyney (1690) 416
Hunt v. Moore (1811) 31, 38
Hunt v. Peake (1860) 1134
Hunt v. Royal Exchange Association Co (1816) 717
Hunt v. Silk (1804) 590
Hunter v. Atkins (1834) 406
Hunter v. Caldwell (1847) 883
Hunter v. Canary Wharf (1997) 1071
Hunter v. Cheshire (1873) 42
Hunter v. Jeffery (1797) 753
Huntley v. Ward (1859) 1038
Hurd v. Hurd (1862) 281, 285
Hurdman v. North Eastern Railway (1878) 1146
Hurford v. Carpenter (1785) 133
Hurry v. Morgan (1866) 40
Hurst v. Hurst (1852) 141
Hurst v. Parker (1817) 362
Hurst v. Picture Theatres (1915) 161
Hurst v. Usborne (1856) 490, 512
Hurt v. Bott (1873) 1120
Hutchindon and Tenant, Re (1878) 37
Hutchinson v Copestake (1861) 1073
Hutchinson v. Bell (1809) 1040
Hutchinson v. Bowker (1839) 335
Hutchinson v. Copestake (1861) 1076
Hutchinson v. Surrey Consumers Gas Light and Coke Association (1851) 390
Hutchinson v. Sydney (1854) 597
Hutchinson v. York, Newcastle and Berwick Railway Co (1850) 1003
Hutchison v. National Loan Assurance Co (1845) 708
Huttley v. Simmons (1898) 1061
Hutton v. Cruttwell (1852) 815
Hutton v. Scarborough Cliff Hotel Co (Ltd) (1865) 634, 635
Hutton v. Sealy (1858) 141
Hutton v. Upfill (1850) 339, 625
Hutton v. Warren (1836) 114, 446
Hyde v. Dallaway (1842) 104

Hyde v. Watts (1843) 491
Hyde v. Wrench (1840) 335
Hydraulic Engineering Company v. McHaffie (1878) 547, 548
Hylton v. Hylton (1754) 405
Hyman v. Nye (1881) 963, 964
Hyman v. Rose (1912) 127

Idle v. Thorton (1812) 510
Illidge v. Goodwin (1831) 921, 973
Ilott v. Wilkes (1820) 977
Imperial Bank of Canada v. Bank of Hamilton (1903) 752, 771
Imperial Land Co of Marseilles, Harris's Case, Re (1872) 344
Imperial Land Co of Marseilles (Ltd), Vining's Case, Re (1870) 648
Imperial Merchantile Credit Association v. Coleman (1871) 602, 603
Ince Hall Rolling Mills Co, Re (1883) 646
Ince v. Reigate Education Committee (1916) 1029
Inchbald v. Barrington (1869) 1107
Indermaur v. Dames (1866) 978, 979
Inderwick v. Tatchell (1901) 40
Inderwick v. Tatchell (1903) 37
Ingham v. Primrose (1859) 770
Inglis v. Usherwood (1801) 790
Inman Steamship Co v. Bischoff (1881) 713
International Society of Auctioneers and Valuers, Baillie's case (1898) 468
Iondes v. Pender (1874) 698
Ionides v. Pacific Insurance Co (1871) 697
Irvine v. Union Bank of Australia (1877) 658
Irving v. Greenwood (1824) 513
Irving v. Manning (1847) 682, 716
Irving v. Motly (1831) 458
Irwin v. Dearman (1809) 901, 1041
Isaac Walton and Co v. Vanguard Motorbus Co (1908) 975
Isaack v. Clark (1615) 575
Isenberg v. East India House Estate Company (1863) 1074
Ismay, Imrie & Co v. Williamson (1908) 1026
Israel v. Clark and Clinch (1803) 910
Ives, Re (1876) 89
Ivimey v. Stocker (1866) 1083
Izon v. Gorton (1839) 116

Jackson and Haden's Contract, Re (1906) 109
Jackson v. Anderson (1811) 1119
Jackson v. Duke of Newcastle (1864) 170, 1075, 1077
Jackson v. Harrison (1862) 482
Jackson v. Hobhouse (1817) 247
Jackson v. Lowe (1822) 331
Jackson v. Metropolitan Railway Co (1877) 938
Jackson v. Noble (1838) 24
Jackson v. Pigott (1698) 733
Jackson v. Smithson (1846) 1126
Jackson v. Union Marine Insurance Co (1874) 489, 516, 517, 518
Jackson's Will, Re (1879) 43

Jacobs v. Hyde (1848) 807
James Baird Co v. Gimbel Bros (1933) 367
James, Ex p. (1803) 663
James Jones v. Earl of Tankerville (1909) 161, 556
James v. Campbell (1832) 909
James v. Couchman (1885) 267
James v. David (1793) 384
James v. Kerr (1887) 147
James v. Thomas H Kent Co (1951) 534
Jameson v. Stein (1855) 418
Jaques v. Golightly (1776) 594
Jarvis v. Pond (1839) 42
Jay v. Richardson (1862) 172
Jay's Furnishing Co v. Brand & Co (1914) 873
Jee v. Audley (1787) 21
Jefferson v. Tyrer (1845) 244
Jefferys v. Gurr (1831) 566, 598
Jefferys v. Jefferys (1841) 255, 259
Jeffrey v. St. Pancras Vestry (1894) 975
Jeffries v. Great Western Railway Co (1856) 1118
Jeffries v. Williams (1850) 1131
Jendwine v. Slade (1797) 479
Jenkin v. Row (1851) 136
Jenkins v. Great Western Railway (1912) 983
Jenkins v. Hutchinson (1849) 305, 462
Jenkins v. Jones (1860) 139
Jenkins v. Portman (1836) 131
Jenkins v. Power (1817) 697
Jenner v. Morris (1861) 606
Jenner v. Smith (1869) 478
Jenner v. Turner (1880) 8
Jennings v. Baddeley (1856) 616
Jennings v. Broughton (1854) 409
Jenys v. Fawler (1733) 750
Jervis v. Tomkinson (1856) 509
Jervoise v. Duke of Northumberland (1820) 13, 16, 24, 31
Jesser v. Gifford (1767) 1070
Jesson v. Solly (1811) 379
Jesson v. Wright (1820) 16, 28, 31, 32, 35
Jewry v. Busk (1814) 531
Jewson v. Gatti (1886) 981
Job v. Bannister (1856) 125
Job v. Langton (1856) 715
Jodrell, Re (1890) 37
Jodrell v. Jodrell (1851) 244
Joel v. Law Union and Crown Insurance Co (1908) 727
Joel v. Mills (1857) 30
Joel v. Morison (1834) 897
John Cowan, Ex p. (1819) 787
John Edwards and Co v. Motor Union Insurance Co (1922) 681
John v. Bacon (1870) 946, 964
Johns v. James (1877) 241

Johnson, Re (1904) 251
Johnson v. Collings (1800) 734
Johnson v. Credit Lyonnais (1877) 1124
Johnson v. Freeth (1836) 248
Johnson v. Great Southern and Western Railway Co (1874) 968
Johnson v. Johnson (1802) 98, 567
Johnson v. Legard (1817) 264
Johnson v. Macdonald (1842) 510
Johnson v. Royal Mail Steam Packet Co (1867) 597
Johnson v. Sheddon (1802) 719
Johnson v. Shrewsbury and Birmingham Railway (1853) 559
Johnson v. Smart (1860) 409
Johnson v. Windle (1836) 750
Johnson v. Wyatt (1863) 1107
Johnstone v. Milling (1886) 505
Johnstone v. Sutton (1785) 1037
Joint Stock Discount Co v. Brown (1869) 665
Joliffe v. Barker (1883) 101, 425
Jolland v. Stainbridge (1797) 205
Jolly v. Kine (1907) 1079
Jonassohn v. Young (1863) 488
Jones (No. 2), Re (1874) 874
Jones, Re (1884) 25, 94
Jones, Re (1898) 246
Jones v. Ashburnham (1804) 375
Jones v. Badley (1867) 4
Jones v. Bailey (1853) 61
Jones v. Barkley (1781) 486, 495, 499
Jones v. Bird (1822) 919, 1131
Jones v. Bowden (1813) 480
Jones v. Boyce (1816) 546, 931
Jones v. Bright (1829) 354, 481
Jones v. Carter (1845) 572
Jones v. Carter (1846) 125
Jones v. Chappell (1875) 1070
Jones v. Clarke (1858) 477
Jones v. Dowle (1841) 577, 1117
Jones v. Downman (843) 305
Jones v. Downman (1843) 462
Jones v. Dwyer (1811) 789
Jones v. Festiniog Railway Co (1868) 921, 1144
Jones v. Gooday (1841) 899
Jones v. Gordon (1877) 745, 749
Jones v. Green (1829) 115, 525, 526
Jones v. Hibbert (1817) 747
Jones v. Hill (1817) 116
Jones v. Hughes (1851) 182
Jones v. Jones (1803) 554
Jones v. Just (1868) 482, 483
Jones v. Llanrwst Urban District Council (1911) 1146
Jones v. Llanrwst Urban District Council of Warblington (1906) 1092, 1093

Jones v. Lock (1865). 256, 260
Jones v. Matthie (1847). 139, 140
Jones v. Morgan (2001). 138
Jones v. Plumer 523
Jones v. Pope (1668) 566
Jones v. Powell (1627) 1096
Jones v. Provincial Insurance Co (1857) 708
Jones v. Ricketts (1862). 403
Jones v. Ryde (1814). 589, 751
Jones v. Salter (1815) 248
Jones v. Sparrow (1793). 901
Jones v. Tapling (1862) 1073
Jordan (1683) 1096
Jordan v. Adams (1859). 29
Jordan's Trust, Re (1863) 41, 42
Jorden v. Money (1854). 307, 368, 369, 370, 371, 418, 699
Jordeson v. Sutton, Southcoates and Drypool Gas Co (1899). 1109
Josceline v. Lassere (1714) 745
Joseph, Ex p. (1811) 792
Joseph v. Pebrer (1825) 617
Joslin v. Hamond (1834). 36
Josling v. Irvine (1861) 535
Josling v. Kingsford (1863). 477
Joy v. Campbell (1804). 459
Joyce v. Swann (1864). 684
Joynes v. Stratham (1746). 439
Jull v. Jacobs (1876) 39

Kain v. Old (1824) 477
Kaltenbach v. Mackenzie (1878). 717
Kampf v. Jones (1837) 243
Kay, Re (1897). 293
Kaye v. Dutton (1844). 365, 375
Keane v. Boycott (1795). 1043
Kearley v. Thomson (1890) 592, 594
Kearney v. Lloyd (1890) 1061
Kearslake v. Morgan (1794). 746
Kearsley v. Woodcock (1843). 250
Keates v. Cadogan (1851) 117
Keates v. Lyon (1869) 175
Keeble v. Hickeringill (1706). 1048, 1056
Keech v. Sandford (1905) 240
Keen v. Milwall Dock Co (1882). 1017
Kekewich v. Manning (1851). 255, 257, 258, 259, 260, 266
Kelk v. Pearson (1871). 170, 1075
Kellard v. Rooke (1887). 1016
Kelly v. Partington (1833). 544
Kelly v. Solari (1841) 567, 584, 585, 586, 588
Kelner v. Baxter (1866). 393, 469
Kelsey v. Ellis (1878) 42
Kemble v. Farren (1829) 526
Kemble v. Kean (1829) 558, 559

Kemeys v. Proctor (1813) 333
Kemp v. Falk (1882). 762
Kemp v. Finden (1844) 600
Kemp v. Halliday (1865). 714
Kemp v. Neville (1861) 1036
Kemp v. Sober (1851). 172
Kempson v. Saunders (1826) 617, 618, 624
Kennaway v. Treveavan (1839) 349
Kennedy v. Broun (1863) 366
Kennedy v. de Trafford (1896). 139
Kennedy v. Green (1834) 210, 409, 770
Kennedy v. Lee (1817) 333, 334, 338
Kennedy v. Panama, New Zealand and Australian
    Royal Mail Company (1867). 424, 449, 450, 452
Kennerley v. Kennerley (1852). 15
Kenrig v. Eggleston (1648). 911
Kensit v. Great Eastern Railway (1884) 164
Keppell v. Bailey (1834) 159, 160, 167, 171,
                                                                                              173, 177, 252
Kern v. Deslandes (1861) 760
Kernot v. Pittis (1852) 1116
Kerr v. Kerr (1896) 862
Kerr v. Willan (1817). 912
Kerrison v. Coatsworth (1825) 905
Kerrison v. Smith (1897). 161
Kerry v. Maori Dream Gold Mines (1898) 653
Kershaw v. Kalow (1855). 139
Kettle v. Bromsall (1738) 577, 1115
Kettle v. Hammond (1767). 784
Kewley v. Ryan (1794). 702
Khorasandijan v. Bush (1993) 1071
Kickson v. Willan (1817). 905
Kidgill v. Moor (1850). 1070
Kidson v. Dilworth (1818) 743
Kidston v. Empire Marine Insurance Co (1866) 719
Kilsby v. Williams (1822). 769
Kimberley v. Jennings (1836). 549
Kincaid's Case (1867) 649
Kinderley v. Jervis (1856) 182
Kine v. Jolly (1904) 1079, 1109
King, Ex p. (1805) 792
King, Re (1879). 258
King v. King (1735) 153
King v. Marshall (1864) 637
King v. Victoria Insurance Co (1896) 723
Kings Norton Metal Company Ltd v. Edridge Merrett & Co Ltd 468, 469
Kings v. Osborne (1905). 868
Kingsbury v. Walter (1901) 37
Kingsford v. Merry (1856) 460, 461, 462, 464, 764
Kingston Cotton Mill Co, Re (1896) 652
Kinnear v. Borradaile, Kinnear v. Nicholson (1832). 727
Kirk v. Gregory (1876) 1114

Kirk v. Todd (1881) 582
Kirkheaton District Local Board v. Ainley,
    Sons & Co (1892) 1091, 1092
Kirkman v. Keast (1862) 870
Kirkpatrick v. Tattersall (1845) 363
Kirkwood v. Carrol (1903) 864
Kirkwood v. Gadd (1910) 869
Kirkwood v. Smith (1896) 864
Kirkwood v. Thompson (1865) 136
Kirwan v. Kirwan (1834) 385
Kleinwort v. Comptoir d' Escompte (1894) 1118
Kleinwort Benson v. Lincoln City Council (1999) 588
Knapp v. Salsbury (1810) 909
Knatchbull v. Grueber (1815) 438, 550
Knebell v. White 614
Knibbs v. Hall (1794) 401
Knight v. Cambers (1855) 632
Knight v. Fitch (1855) 632
Knight v. Fox (1850) 896
Knight v. Knight (1840) 35
Knight v. Marjoribanks (1849) 138
Knight v. Simmonds (1896) 176
Knight v. Wiffen (870) 339
Knowles v. Horsfall (1821) 759
Knowles v. Queen Anne and Garden Mansions (1888) 1071
Knox v. Lord Hotham (1845) 243
Knox v. Turner (1870) 143, 153
Koufos v. Czarnikow (1969) 548
Kreglinger v. New Patagonia Meat Company (1914) 149, 154, 157, 158
Krell v. Henry (1903) 518, 519
Kulen Kemp v. Vigne (1786) 679, 686
Kwei Tek Chao v. British Traders and Shippers (1954) 494

La Marquise de Ribeyre v. Barclay (1857) 665
Lacaussade v. White (1798) 592
Lacave & Co v. Credit Lyonnais (1897) 778
Lacey, Ex p. (1801) 404, 663
Lacon v. Mertins (1743) 330
Lady Arundell v. Phipps (1804) 783
Lady Langdale v. Briggs (1856) 245
Ladywell Mining Co v. Brookes (1887) 646
Lafitte v. Slatter (1830) 736
Lagunas Nitrate Co v. Lagunas Syndicate (1899) 644, 645, 666
Laing v. Fidgeon (1814) 480, 1815
Laing v. Laing (1839) 15
Laird v. Birkenhead Railway Co (1859) 161
Laird v. Pim (1841) 499
Lake v. Duke of Argyll (1844) 623
Lamb, Re (1894) 825
Lamb v. Vice (1840) 393
Lambe v. Eames (1871) 36
Lambert v. Eames (1827) 915

Lambkin v. South Eastern Railway Co (1880) .... .901
Lamine v. Dorrell (1705) 563, 571
Lampleigh v. Brathwait (1615) .... .365
Lamprell v. Guardian of Billericay Union Essex (1849) 531
Lancashire v. Kellingworth (1701) .... .495
Lancashire and Yorkshire Railway Co v. Highley (1917) .... .1027
Lancaster v. Walsh (1838) 349
Land Credit Co of Ireland, Overend Gurney & Co, Ex p. (1869) .... .658
Land Credit Co of Ireland v. Lord Fermoy (1869) 665
Lander and Bagley's Contract, Re (1892) .... .127
Lander v. Weston (1855) .... .293
Lane v. Cox (1897) 949
Lane v. Debenham (1853) .... .271
Lane v. Horlock (1846) .... .144
Lane v. Horlock (1853) .... .144
Lane v. Horlock (1856) .... .145
Lane v. Newdigate (1804) 560
Lanfranchi v. Mackenzie (1867) 170, 1076, 1077, 1078, 1079
Langdale's settlement, Re (1870) 284
Langford's Trusts, Re (1861) 185, 281
Langhorn v. Langhorn (1852) .... .275
Langridge v. Levy (1837) 411, 924, 985, 987, 1040
Langstaffe v. Fenwick (1805) .... .145
Langton v. Horton (1842) .... .152
Lanphier v. Buck (1865) 42
Lanphier v. Philpos (1838) .... .882, 916
Lantsbery v. Collier (1856) 244
L'Apostre v. Le Plaistrier (1708) .... .572
Lapsley v. Pleasants .... .716
Larkin v. Long (1915) 1064
Laroque v. Beauchemin (1897) .... .645
Lassence v. Tierney (1849) 243, 368
Latham v. R. Johnson & Nephew (1913) 983, 988
Latimer v. Brown (1825) .... .783
Lattimore v. Harsen (1817) .... .383
Laugher v. Pointer (1826) .... .895
Laughton v. Lord Bishop of Sodor and Man (1872) .... .1038
Law v. London Indisputable Life Policy Co and Another (1855) .... .691
Lawes v. Purser (1856) .... .590, 591
Lawrence v. Great Northern Railway Co (1851) .... .921
Lawrence v. Knowles (1839) 492
Lawrence's Case (1867) 649
Laws v. Rand (1857) .... .765
Lawson v. Weston (1801) .... .748
Lax and Bainbridge v. Borough of Darlington (1879) .... .932
Laythoarp v. Bryant (1836) .... .331
Laythorpe v. Bryant (1836) .... .330
Lazarus v. Artistic Photographic Co (1897) .... .1077
Le Cras v. Hughes 685
Le Lievre v. Gould (1893) 949
Le Marchant v. Le Marchant (1874) .... .36
Le Mason v. Dixon .... .577

Le Neve v. Le Neve (1747). 205
Lea v. Adams (1615). 349
Lea v. Pickford & Co (1823). 912
Leach v. Buchanan (1802). 750
Leach v. Jay (1877). 32
Leach v. Leach (1843) 244
Leach v. Thomas (1836) 116
Leadbitter v. Farrow (1816) 743
Leader v. Duffey (1888). 33, 37, 43
Leake v. Robinson (1817) 21, 22, 24, 44
Leame v. Bray (1803). 906
Learoyd v. Whiteley (1887) 292
Leather Cloth Co v. Lorsont (1869) 672
Leather Cloth Co v. Hieronimus (1875). 493
Lechmere v. Brotheridge (1863) 8
Lee v. Bayes (1856). 1118, 1120, 1121
Lee v. Butler (1893) 871
Lee v. Clutton (1876). 205
Lee v. Griffin (861). 331
Lee v. Lanchashire & Yorkshire Rail Co (1871) 994
Lee v. Muggeridge (1813) 364
Lee v. Neuchatel Asphalte Co (1889) 655
Lee v. Riley (1865) 1126
Lee v. Shore (1822). 578
Lee v. SS Bessie (Owners of) (1912) 1030
Lee v. Young (1843) 234
Leeds v. Cheetham (1827) 117
Leeds v. Cook (1803). 513
Leeds and Hanley Theatres of Variety, Re (1902) 645
Leeds Bank, Ex p. (1812). 787
Leeds Estate, Building and Investment v. Shepherd (1887). 655, 664
Lees v. Dunkerley Brothers (1911). 1023
Lees v. Nuttall (1829) 662
Leeson v. Holt (1816). 912
Legge v. Croker (1811). 414, 441
Leicester v. Rose (1803). 784
Leigh v. Hewitt (1803). 114
Leigh v. Paterson (1818) 497, 535
Leighton v. Wales (1838). 527
Leith v. Irvine (1833) 145, 146
Leith v. Pope (1779). 900
Lemaitre v. Davis (1881). 1139
Leng v. Hayes (1822). 242
Leominster Canal Navigation Co v. Shrewsbury and
    Hereford Railway (1857) 392
Leonard v. Baker (1813). 783, 1115
Leonard v. Leonard (1812) 442
Leonard v. Wilson (1834). 741
Lerry v. Goodson (1792). 577
Les Affreteurs Reunis S.A. v. Leopold Walford (London) (1919) 394
Levene v. Greenwood (1904). 868
Lever v. Heys (1599). 388

Levett v. Hawes (1599) 388
Levita's Case, Re (1867) 340
Levy v. Green (1857) 477
Levy v. Lindo (1817) 95
Lewis v. Averay (1971) 470
Lewis v. Campbell (1849) 597
Lewis v. Hillman (1852) 138, 143
Lewis v. London, Chatham and Dover Railway Company (1873) 937
Lewis v. Nicholson (1852) 305, 462, 463
Lewis v. Nobbs (1878) 279, 283
Lewis v. Peake (1816) 541
Lewis v. Price (1761) 1072
Lewis v. Rees (1856) 264
Lewis v. Rucker (1761) 681, 718, 719
Licensing Victuallers' Mutual Trading Association,
    Audain, Ex p., Re (1889) 647
Lickbarrow v. Mason (1787) 759
Lickbarrow v. Mason (1793) 791
Life Interest Corp v. Hand-in-Hand Fire & Insurance (1898) 140
Liggins v. Inge (1831) 160
Lightly v. Clouston (1808) 579, 580, 1043
Like v. Howe (1806) 367
Lilley v. Doubleday (1881) 928
Lilly v. Hays (1836) 564, 571
Lillywhite v. Trimmer (1867) 1108
Limpus v. London General Omnibus Co (1862) 897
Lindenau v. Desborough (1828) 708
Lindon v. Hooper (1776) 401
Lindon v. Sharp (1843) 815
Lindsay v. Cundy (1876) 434, 465, 466, 467,
                                                                        468, 469, 470
Lindus v. Melrose (1857) 739
Line v. Stephenson (1838) 101
Linford v. Provincial Horse and Cattle Insurance Co (1864) 703
Lingham v. Biggs (1797) 876
Lister v. Perryman (1870) 1037
Lister & Co v. Stubbs (1890) 605
Litchfield-Speer v. Queen Anne's Gate Syndicate (No. 2) (1919) 1079
Littedale v. Lonsdale (1793) 895
Littlefield v. Shee (1831) 364
Live Stock Agency v. Temperley Shipping Co (1899) 714
Liversidge v. Broadbent (1859) 571
Livesay v. Hood (1809) 790
Livie v. Janson (1810) 712
Llandover v. Homfray (1879) 582
Lloyd (1802) 1069
Lloyd v. General Iron Screw Co (1864) 928
Lloyd v. Ingleby (1846) 125
Lloyd v. Lloyd (1852) 7
Lloyd v. Loaring (1801) 552
Lloyd v. Needham (1823) 906
Lloyd v. Sigourney (1829) 742

Lloyd (Pauper) v. Grace, Smith & Co (1912) .... .661
Lloyds v. Harper (1880) .... .393, 394
Load v. Green (1845) .... .459
Loader v. Clarke (1850). .... .252
Loch v. Bagley (1867) .... .15
Lock v. Furse (1866) 540
Lockhart v. Barnard (1845) 349
Lockley v. Pye (1841). 900
Loder v. Kekule (1857) .... .534
Lodge v. Dicas (1820) .... .385
Loffus v. Maw (1862). 369
Logan v. Willan (1818) .... .458, 913
Lomax v. Ripley (1855) 4
Lomi v. Tucker (1829). 479
London & County Banking v. Ratcliffe (1881) .... .150
London & North-Western Railway Co v. Bradley (1851) .... .921
London and North Western Railway Co v. Dunham (1856). .... .474
London and North Western Railway Company v. Glyn (1859) 696
London and River Plate Bank v. Bank of Liverpool (1896) .... .752
London & South Western Railway v. Gomm (1882) 172, 176
London Assurance v. Mansel (1879) .... .708, 711
London Assurance Co v. Sainsbury (1783) .... .723
London, Brighton and South Coast Railway Co v. Truman (1885) 1104
London County Council v. Allen (1914). .... .177
London Dock Co (1836). 1104
London Freehold and Leasehold Property Co v. Baron Suffield (1897). .... .661
London Furnishing Company v. Solomon (1912) .... .873
London and General Bank (No. 2) (1895). .... .652
London and General Bank, Re (1895) .... .652
London General Omnibus Co v. Lavell (1902) .... .410
London India Rubber Co, Re (1868) .... .635
London Joint Stock Bank v. Charles James Simmons (1892). .... .749
London and Lancashire Life Assurance Co v. Fleming (1897) 704
London Pressed Hinge Co (1905). .... .637
Longchamp v. Kenny (1778) .... .566, 577
Longman v. Tripp (1805) 789
Longmate v. Ledger (1860) 404
Longmeid v. Holliday (1851) 924, 990
Longmore v. Elcum (1843). .... .36
Longridge v. Dorville (1821) .... .375
Lonrho v. Shell Petroleum (No. 2) (1982) 1067
Lord Advocate v. Countess of Moray (1905). .... .184
Lord Chedworth v. Edwards (1802). 602
Lord Deerhurst v. Duke of St. Albans (1820) .... .25
Lord Gordon v. Marquis of Hertford (1817) .... .439
Lord Irnham v. Child (1781) .... .441, 453
Lord James Stuart v. London and North-Western Railway (1852). .... .549, 557
Lord Lisles Case (1478). 349
Lord Peter v. Eastern Counties Railway (1838) .... .391
Lord Stafford's Settlement and Will, Re (1904). .... .93
Lord Strathcona Steamship Co v. Dominion Coal Co (1926). .... .561
Loring v. Thomas (1861). 42

Lorymer v. Smith (1822)...99, 498
Los Angeles Traction Co v. Wilshire (1902)...356
Loscombe v. Russell (1830) 614
Losh v. Richard Evans & Co (1903) 1028
Lovat v. Lord Ranelagh (1814)..124
Lovatt v. Hamilton (1839) 510
Lovegrove v. London Brighton and South Coast
  Railway Co (1864)..1004
Lovell v. Howell (1876)..1013
Lovelock v. Franklyn (1846) 499
Lovering, Ex p., In Jones (No.2), Re (1874)..876
Low Moor Co. v. Stanley Coal Co (1875)...177
Lowe v. Adams (1901)..161
Lowe v. Pearson (1899)..1028
Lowe v. Peers (1768) 115, 525, 527, 528
Lowery v. Walker (1911) 983
Lownes v. Lane (1789)...410, 414
Lowry v. Bourdieu (1780)..592, 680
Lowry v. Guilford (1832) 883, 916
Lows v. Telford (1876)..303
Lowther v. Lowther (1806) 373, 405, 663
Lubbock v. Tribe (1838) 596, 769
Lucas, Ex p. (1858)..816
Lucas v. Comerford (1790)..130, 131
Lucas v. De La Cour (1813)...454
Lucas v. Godwin (1837)..531
Lucas's Will, Re (1881)..38, 41
Luce v. Izod (1856)..446
Lucena v. Craufurd (1804)...684, 685, 686
Lucena v. Lucena (1877)...40
Luke v. Dennis (1877)...561
Luke v. Lyde (1759) 495
Luker v. Dennis (1877)...176
Lumley v. Gye (1853)............................950, 1043, 1044, 1045, 1046, 1049,
                                              1055, 1057, 1059, 1062, 1064, 1066
Lumley v. Palmer (1734)..734
Lumley v. Wagner (1852) 161, 173, 559, 560, 561, 1043
Lunn v. Thornton (1845)..814
Luscombe v. Steer (1867) 1108
Luxford v. Large (1833)..908
Lyddon v. Ellison (1854)...26
Lydney v. Wigpool Iron Ore Co v. Bird (1886) 646
Lygo v. Newbold (1854) 932
Lynch v. Dalzell (1729) 694
Lynch v. Knight (1861) 950, 992
Lynch v. Nurdin (1840) 921, 973
Lyon v. Morris (1887) 154
Lyon v. Tomkins (1836) 121
Lyons v. Hoffnung (1890)..761
Lyons v. Martin (1838) 897
Lysney v. Selby (1705) 409, 479

Lysons v. Andrew Knowles & Sons (1901) .... .1030
Lyth v. Ault (1853) .... .385
Lytton v. Great Northern Railway Co (1856) .... .557

Maas v. Pepper (1905)... 876
Maber v. Hobbs (1836) 248, 266
MacAndrew v. Chapple (1866) 489
Macauley v. Furness Railway Co (1872) 968
Macbeth & Co v. Maritime Insurance Co (1908) .... .717
MacCarthy v. Young (1861).. 987
McCartney v. Londonderry & Lough Swilly Railway Co (1904) 164
McCawley v. Furness Railway Co (1872).. 968
McCormick v. Grogan (1869) 4
Macdonald v. Law Union Insurance Co (1874) 708
McDonald v. Owners of the SS Banana (1908) 1027
Macdonald v. Walker (1851) .... .274
MacDougall v. Gardiner (1875).. .653
MacDougall v. Jersey Imperial Hotel (1864) 654
Mace v. Cadell (1774) 789
McEntire v. Crossley Brothers (1895) .... .874, 875
McGiffin v. Palmer's Shipbuilding Co (1882)... 1015
McGowen & Co v. Dyer (1873) 660
Macgregor v. Rhodes (1856) .... .751
Mack v. Walter (1865)... .854
Mackenzie v. Childers (1889) .... .176
Mackenzie v. Coulson (1869) .... .435
Mackett v. Mackett (1872) .... .36
Mackey, Re (1911)... 293, 294
Mackey v. Commercial Bank of New Brunswick (1874) .... .423
Mackie v. Herbertson (1884)... .265
Mackintosh v. Pogose (1895) 251
Mackworth v. Hinxman (1836).. 26
McManus v. Cooke (1887) 161
Macnab v. Whitbread (1853) .... .36
Madell v. Thomas (1891)... 152, 875
Magee v. Lavell (1874).. .528
Maggrath v. Church... .716
Magor v. Chadwick (1840).. 162, 1083
Magrath v. Morehead (1871) 10, 15
Mahony v. East Holyford Mining Co (1875).. .658
Main Colliery Co v. Davies (1900)..1030
Mainland v. Upjohn (1889) .... .148
Mainwaring v. Brandon (1818) .... .541
Mainwaring v. Newman (1800) .... .614
Mair v. Himalaya Tea Co (1865).. .559
Maitland v. Chalie (1822).. 46
Maitland v. Chartered Mercantile Bank of India,
    London and China (1869) .... .758
Malcolm v. O'Callaghan (1835)... 248
Malcolm v. Scott (1859) .... .571
Malin v. Keighley (1794) .... .36
Malins v. Freeman (1837)... .439, 441

Mallan v. May (1843)..373
Malone v. Cayzer, Irvine & Co (1908)...1025
Malone v. Laskey (1907)...988, 1070, 1071, 1146
Maltby, Re (1880)...825
Manchester Bond Warehouse v. Carr (1880)...117
Manchester Corporation v. New Moss Colliery (1906)....................................178
Manchester Royal Infirmary, Re (1889)..286
Manchester, Sheffield & Lincs Railway v. North Central Wagon (1888).....................152
Manchester, Sheffield & Railway Co v. Worksop Board of Health (1856)....................1109
Manders v. Williams (1849)...1115
Mangan v. Atterton (1866)..922, 923, 952, 981
Manico, Ex p. (1853)..810, 812
Manley v. Field (1859)..1041
Mann v. Barrett (1806)...1041
Mann v. Stephens (1846)...171, 173, 174
Manning v. Manning (1854)..275
Mansel v. Webb (1919)..974
Manser v. Back (1848)..439
Mant v. Leith (1852)...279, 280, 283
Manvell v. Thomson (1826)..1041
Mara v. Browne (1895)..292
Marchington v. Vernon (1787)...389
Marcussen v. Birkbeck Bank (1889)...771
Maredelanto Compania Naviera SA v. Berbau-Handel GmbH
   (The Mihalis Nagelos) (1917)...506
Marfell v. Atterton (1866)..923
Marfell v. South Wales Railway Co (1860)..923
Marker v. Marker (185)...173
Markin v. Aldrich (1862)..807
Marley v. Osborn (1894)..1016
Marlow v. Pitfield (1719)...606
Marquis of Bute v. Thompson (1844)..509, 512
Marquis of Bute's Will, Re (1859)...275
Marquis Townsend v. Strangroom (1808)..414, 439, 441
Marriot v. Hampton (1797)..567
Marriot v. Marriot (1726)...565
Marriott v. Brett and Beney (1911)..1028
Marriott v. East Grinstead Gas & Water Co (1908)....................................165
Marriott v. Stanley (1840) Cases..908
Marryat v. Broderick (1837)...594
Marsack v. Webber (1860)...600
Marsden v. City and County Assurance Co (1865).....................................720
Marsh and Earl Granville, Re (1883)...266
Marsh v. Keating (1834).............................419, 573, 574, 575, 604, 665
Marshall v. Barkworth (1833)...784
Marshall v. Bousfield (1817)...16, 24
Marshall v. Glanville (1917)..521
Marshall v. Lynn (1840)..492, 493
Marshall v. York, Newcastle and Berwick Railway Co (1851)............................959
M'Arthur v. Lord Seaforth (1810)..535
Martin, Ex p. (1815)...790
Martin v. Connah's Quay Alkali Co (1885)..1016

Martin v. Goble (1808)...170, 1075
Martin v. Great Northern Railway Co (1855)...........................932, 960
Martin v. Holgate (1866)...33
Martin v. Manchester Corporation (1912)..................................1026
Martin v. Morgan (1819)...751
Martin v. Porter (1839)...900
Martin v. Price (1894)...1108
Martin v. Reid (1862)...763
Martindale v. Booth (1832)...783, 814
Martineau v. Kitching (1872)..304
Martinez v. Gerber (1841)..1042
Martini v. Coles (1813)..761, 1122
Martyn v. Hind (1776)...389
Mary Ann King v. Younger (1864)...872
Marzetti v. Williams (1830)..764, 768
Maskell v. Horner (1915)..402
Mason v. Armitage (1806) 333
Mason v. Farnell (1844)..1116
Mason v. Harris (1879)..653
Mason v. Hill (1833)...1082
Mason v. Keeling (1700)..903, 1126
Mason v. Sainsbury (1782)...723
Massey v. Davies (1794)..405, 663
Massey v. Goyder (1829)..1132
Massey v. Parker (1834)...248
Masters v. Ibberson (1849)...745, 748
Masterton & Smith v. City of Brooklyn (1845)..............................537
Mather v. Lord Maidstone (1856)...750
Matthews v. Brown & Co. (1894)..778
Matthews v. West London Water Works Co (1813).............................895
Matthie v. Edwards (1846)...139
Matthiessen v. London and County Bank (1879).............................772
Matthison v. Clarke (1854)...138, 147
Maunsell v. Hedges (1854)...368
Maving v. Todd (1815)..696, 912
Mavor v. Pyne (1825)..533
Mawdsely v. West Leigh Colliery Co (1911)................................1028
Mawman v. Gillett (1809)..615
Mawson v. Blane (1854)..363
Mawson v. Fletcher (1870)...109
Max v. Roberts (1807)...911
May v. Belleville (1905)..161
May v. Burdett (1846)..1126
May v. Chapman (1847)..748, 749
May v. Platt (1900)...444
Mayhew v. Asby (1839)...125
Maynard v. Rhode (1824)...709
Mayor & cn of Merchants of the Staple of England v.
    Bank of England (1887)..770
Mayor of Exeter v. Trimlet (1759)...566
Mayor of London v. Bolt (1799)...1106
Mayor of Salford v. Lever (1891)..606

M'Carthy v. Abel (1804)...713
M'Carthy v. Decaix (1831) 442
M'Combe v. Davies (1805)..1122
Mears, Re (1914) 46
Mears v. Callender (1901)..118
Medina v. Stoughton (1701)...484
Meek v. Kettlewell (1842)...256, 257, 258
Melhado v. Porto Alegre Railway Co (1874)......................................391
Mellish v. Motteux (1792) 479
Mellish v. Rawdon (1832)...734
Mellor's Trustee v. Maas (1902) 152
Mellors v. Shaw (1861)....................................... 985, 1005, 1006
Mendizabal v. Machado (1833) 735
Menier v. Hooper's Telegrph Works (1874) 653
Merchantile Trading Co, Stringer's Case, Re (1869)........................... 655, 666
Merchants National Bank v. Curtis (1953) 34
Merchants' Trading Co v. Banner (1871)..560
Meredith v. Heneage (1824)...35
Merest v. Harvey (1814) 901
Meriel v. Wymondsold (1661)..469
Merril v. France (1812) 101
Merry v. Green (1841)...1118
Mersey Docks and Harbour Board Trustees v. William Gibbs (1864) 921
Mersey Steel and Iron Co v. Naylor Benzon & Co (1884) 488, 507
Messer v. Boyle (1856)...61
Metall und Rohstoff AG v. Donaldson Lufkin & Jenrette Inc (1990) 1067
Metcalfe v. Bruin (1810) 615, 617
Metcalfe v. Hutchinson (1875) 34
Metropolitan Asylum District v. Frederick (1881) 1104
Metropolitan Asylum District v. Hill (1881) 1104
Metropolitan Bank v. Heiron (1880) 604
Metropolitan Coal Consumers' Association v. Scrimgeour (1895) 646
Metropolitan Railway Company v. Jackson (1877)..................................938
Meux and Co v. Poole (1820)..908
Meux v. Great Eastern Railway Co (1895)...959
Meux v. Howell (1803) 523, 783
M'Ewan v. Smith (1849)...764
Meyer v. Haworth (1838) 364
Meyerstein v. Barber (1866) 763
M'Fadden v. Jenkyns (1842) 256
Michael v. Tredwin (1856) 702
Mickleston v. Brown (1801)..4
Middlemas v. Stevens (1901) 93
Middleton v. Greenwood (1864)...552
Middleton v. Magnay (1864)..551
Midland Railway Co (1846) 996
Midwood & Co v. Manchester Corporation (1905) 1146
Miles v. Harford (1879)...14, 16, 25
Miles v. New Zealand Alford Estate Co (1886) 375, 376
Millar's Karri & Jarrah Co v. Weddel, Turner & Co (1909)........................488
Millbourn v. Lyons (1914) 177
Miller v. Atlee (1849) 567

Miller v. Cook (1870) 139, 141
Miller v. Race (1758) 748, 750
Milligan v. Wedge (1840).. 896
Mills v. Barber (1836) 746
Mills v. Guardians of Alderbury Union (1849) 584
Mills v. Mills (1835).. 282, 284
Mills v. Northern Railway of Buenos Aires, Re (1870)................................655
Milman v. Dolwell (1810).. 909
Miln v. Prest (1816) 734
Milnes v. Dawson (1850) 744
Milnes v. Duncan (1827) 585, 588
Milroy v. Lord (1862) 260
Milward v. Forbes (1802)..457
Miner v. Gilmour (1858).. 163, 1146
Mines Royal Society v. Magnay (1854) 322
Minet v. Gibson (1789) 752
Minet v. Leman (1855) 86
Mitchel v. Reynolds (1711) 373
Mitchell v. Allestry (1676) 903
Mitchell v. Crassweller (1853) 897
Mitchell v. Edie (1787) 717
Mitchell v. Jenkins (1833)..1037
Mitchell v. Lapage (1816) 454, 455
Mitford v. Reynolds (1842) 241
Mixers Case (1859) 421, 649
M'Kee v. Great Northern Railway Co (1908)...1027
M'Kenzie v. British Linen Co (1881) 771
M'Kinnell v. Robinson (1839) 593
M'Lachlan v. Evans (1827)...578
M'Laughlin v. Pryor (1842)... 896
M'Lean v. Clydesdale Banking Co (1883) 746
M'Leod v. Annesley (1853)..234, 279
M'Mahon v. North Kent Ironworks (1891)...637
M'Manus v. Crickett (1800) 906
M'Manus v. Lancashire and Yorkshire Railway Co (1859) 474
M'Nab v. Robertson (1897) 165
M'Naghten's case (1843)...727
M'Neilage v. Holloway (1818) 744
M'Niece v. Singer Sewing Machine Co (1911) 1029
Moakes v. Nicolson (1865)...761
Mobile, The (1857)..378
Mocatta v. Murgatroyd (1717) 416
Mody v. Gregson (1868)..483
Moens v. Heyworth (1842) 412, 419, 698
Moffat v. Bateman (1869)..916, 959
Mogg v. Mogg (1811-15)..26, 31
Mogul Steamship Co v. McGregor, Gow & Co (1892) 671, 1050, 1051, 1052,
                                                               1056, 1058, 1061, 1062
Molton v. Camroux (1848)..591
Montague v. Flockton (1873).. 560
Montague v. Kater (1853)..263
Montefiore v. Browne (1858) 241

Montefiori v. Montefiori (1762)...378
Montgomerie v. Woodley (1800) 243
Montgomery v. Montgomery (1845) 29
Moore (Pauper) v. Manchester Liners (1910) 1027
Moore v. Greg (1848) 131
Moore v. Hall (1878) 170, 1077
Moore v. Metropolitan Railway Co (1872) 898
Moore v. Moore (1874)... 260
Moore v. Morgue (1776)... 913
Moore v. Rawson (1824)...1072, 1074
Moore v. Walter (1863)..234, 279
Moores v. Choat (1839)... 131
Moran, Galloway & Co v. Uzielli (1905) 687
More v. Manning (1718) 741
Morecroft v. Meux (1825)..491
Moreton v. Hardern (1825) 907
Morgan v. Bain (1874)... 488
Morgan v. Brundrett (1833) 813
Morgan v. Gath (1865) 477
Morgan v. Horseman (1810) 784
Morgan v. Hutchins (1890) 1015
Morgan v. Jeffreys (1910) 154
Morgan v. Malleson (1870) 259, 260
Morgan v. Owners of Steamship Zenaida (1909) 1026
Morgan v. Powell (1842)... 900
Morgan v. Price (1849)..722
Morgan v. Vale of Neath Railway Co. (1865) 1004
Morish v. Foote (1818)... 905
Morison v. Thompson (1874)..603, 605
Morisse v. Royal British Bank (1856)..625, 630
Morland v. Cook (1868) 167, 168, 176
Morley v. Boothby (1825) 359
Morley v. Clavering (1860) 549
Morley v. Cook (1842) 106, 109
Morley v. Gaisford (1795)... 906
Morley v. Loughnan (1893) 405, 408
Morris v. Baron & Co. (1918)..493, 494
Morris v. Colman (1812)...558, 560
Morris v. Nugent (1836) 1114
Morrison v. Muspratt (1827) 709
Morse v. Royal (1806)... 404
Morse v. Slue (1673)... 911
Morshead v. Frederick (1806) 441
Mortimer, Re (1905) 26
Mortimer v. Capper (1782) 373
Mortimer v. Ireland (1847) 274
Mortimer v. M'Callan (1840) 99, 632
Mortimer v. Picton (1864)..281, 285
Mortlock v. Buller (1804)..373
Morton and Hallett, Re (1880) 274
Morton v. Burn (1837)...523
Morvah Consols Tin Mining Co, McKay's Case (1875) 662

Mosely v. Virgin (1796) 557
Moses v. Macferlan (1760) 361, 566, 609
Mosley's Trusts, Re (1871) 44
Moss v. Cooper (1861) 4
Moss v. Hall (1850) 372
Moss v. Smith (1850) 716
Mosse v. Salt (1863) 147
Motherwell v. Motherwell (1976) 1070
Mott v. Shoolbred (1875) 1070
Moule, Ex p. (1808) 786
Moule v. Garrett (1872) 596
Moulton v. Edmonds (1859) 103
Mountfield v. Keene (1871) 267
Mountford, Ex p (1808) 134
Moyce v. Newington (1878) 467
Moyle v. Moyle (1831) 283
Mozley v. Alston (1847) 653
Mozley v. Tinker (1835) 349
M'Swiney v. Royal Excahnge Assurance (1849) 686
Muckleston v. Brown (1801) 4
Muilman v. D'Eguino (1795) 734
Mulchay v. Reg (1868) 1060
Muller v. Moss (1813) 816
Mumford v. Collier (1890) 154
Mumford v. Oxford, Worcester and Wolverhampton
    Railway Co (1856) 1070
Mundel's Trust, Re (1860) 276
Munro v. Butt (1858) 531
Munroe v. Perkins (1830) 383
Munton v. Lord Truro (1886) 205
Murgatroyd v. Robinson (1857) 163, 1084
Murphy v. Bell (1828) 680
Murphy v. O'Shea (1845) 405, 663
Murphy v. Phillips (1876) 1008
Murphy v. Smith (1865) 1004
Murray v. John Denholm & Co (1911) 1024
Murray v. Mann (1848) 460
Murray v. Parker (1854) 435
Murray v. Scott (1884) 607
Murrell, Ex p. (1849) 647
Musgrave v. Horner (1874) 127
Muskett v. Hill (1839) 159
Muspratt v. Gregory (1838) 122
Musther, Re (1890) 42, 43
Muston v. Gladwin (1845) 125
Mutual Reserve Fund Life Association v. New York Life
    Insurance Co and Harvey (1896) 561
Myddleton v. Lord Kenyon (1794) 359

Naish, Re (1930) 143
Nanney v. Williams (1856) 267
Nant-Y-Glo and Blaina Ironworks Co v. Grave (1879) 662

Nantes v. Corrock (1807) 403
Nash v. Birch (1836) 491
Nash v. Brown (1817)... 744, 747
Nash v. Eads (1880)... 139
Nash v. Inman (1908) 570
National Bank of Wales, Re (1899)... 656, 666
National Exchange Company of Glasgow v. Drew (1855) 420
National Funds Assurance Co, Re (1878)... 664
National Permanent Building Society, Williamson, Re (1869) 606, 607
National Phonograph Co v. Edison-Bell Consolidated
    Phonograph Co (1908).. 1065
National Savings Bank Association, Hebb's Case, Re (1867) 340, 343
National Telegraph Co v. Baker (1893) 1146
National Trustees Co of Australasia v. General Finance Co of
    Australasia (1905).. 293
Native Ore Co, Re (1876) 656
Naylor Benzen & Co v. Krainische Industrie Gesellschaft (1918) 521
Naylor v. Taylor (1829).. 717
Neate v. Harding (1851) 570, 574, 575
Nedby v. Nedby (1839) 248
Nelson v. Belfast Corporation (1908) 1027
Nelson v. Serle (1839) 747
Nelthorpe v. Holgate (1844) 453
Nerot v. Wallace (1789).. 508
Neville v. Kelly (1862).. 350
Neville v. Snelling (1880)... 865
Neville v. Wilkinson (1781) 416
New Brunswick and Canada Railway and Land Co v.
    Conybeare (1862) 422, 423
New Brunswick and Canada Railway Co v. Muggeridge (1859)...................... 430, 554, 555
New Monckton Colliery Co v. Davies (1900).. 1030
New Sharlston Colleries v. Earl of Westmoreland (1900)(1904)....................... 166
New York Life Insurance Co v. Fletcher (1885) 706
Newal v. Barnard (1611) 498
Newall v. Tomlinson (1871)... 586
Newbigging v. Adam (1886) 426
Newbury v. Armstrong (1829) 349
Newby v. Harrison (1861).. 165
Newcastle Fire Insurance Co v. Macmorran (1815).................................. 706
Newill v. Newill (1871) 38
Newlands v. National Employers Accident Association Ltd (1885) 660
Newman, Re (1876)... 528
Newman v. Newman (1885).. 692, 693
Newman v. Payne (1793) 403
Newman v. Rusham (1852) 264
Newman v. Warner (1851) 274
Newman v. Zachary (1646).. 541
Newsome v. Graham (1829).. 584
Newson v. Thornton (1805) 760, 761
Newstead v. Searles (737)... 265
Newton, Ex p. (1880) 748
Newton v. Birmingham Small Arms Co (1906) 657

Newton v. Reid (1830)... 248
Nichol v. Godts (1854) 477
Nichol v. Goodall (1804) 685
Nichol v. Martyn (1799)...1043
Nicholl v. Nicholl (1777)... 26
Nichols v. Eaton (1875)...252
Nichols v. Marsland (1876) 1148, 1149
Nicholson v. Ricketts (1860)..757
Nicholson v. Willan (1804) 912, 913
Nicklin v. Williams (1854)..1129
Nickling v. Heaps (1870) 466
Nickoll & Knight v. Ashton, Edridge & Co (1901)................ 515, 518
Nicol's Case (1859) 421, 422
Nisbet v. Rayne and Burn (1910).....................................1024
Nisbet and Potts' Contract, Re (1905)...............................177
Noakes v. Rice (1900)... 155
Noakes v. Rice (1902)...177
Noble v. Adams (1816) 458, 459
Noble v. Ward (1867) 493
Nockels v. Crosby (1825)..588, 617
Noel v. Jones (1848)..243
Noke v. Awder (1596) 129
Norbury v. Norbury (1819)...282
Nordenfelt v. Maxim Nordenfelt Guns and Ammunition Co (1894) 672
Norman v. Bell (1831).. 1115
Norman v. Great Western Railway (1915)......................... 979, 980
Norris v. Jackson (1860)..551
North British and Mercantile Insurance Co v. London,
    Liverpool and Globe Insurance Co (1877)............... 694, 696, 722,
                                                            723, 724
North British and Mercantile Insurance Co v. Moffatt (1871) 696
North of England Pure Oil-Cake Co v. Archangel Maritime
    Insurance Co (1875) 688
Northumberland Avenue Hotel Co, Re (1886) 392
North Western Salt Co v. Electrolytic Alkali Co (1914)..............673
Norton v. Pickering (1828)..736
Norton v. Relly (1764)... 403, 405
Nottidge v. Price (1860) 405
Notting Hill, (1884) 954
Nottingham Patent Brick and Tile Co v. Butler (1885)................175
Nugent v. Smith (1876)..1149
Nurse v. Barns (1663) 541
Nutbrown v. Thornton (1804)...552

Oakeley v. Ooddeen (1861)...749
Oakes v. Turquand (1867) 649
Oakes v. Wood (1837)..1034
Oates d. Wigfall v. Brydon (1766) 17
Oates v. Hudson (1851)..577
Ockford v. Barelli (1871)...376
Offord v. Davies (1862).. 355, 356
Ogden v. Battams (1855).. 147, 151

Ogden v. Benas (1874)..772
Ogden v. Rummens (1862)..1005
Ogilvie v. Foljambe (1817) 94
Ogilvie v. West Australian Mortgage and Agency
    Corporation (1896)..771
Oglander v. Oglander (1848)...275
Ogle v. Barnes (1799) 906
Ogle v. Earl Vane (1867)..493
Oglivy v. Collins (1824) 1105
Okell v. Charles (1876)...739
Oklestone v. Heap (1847)..274
Oldershaw v. King (1857)..376
Oldfield, Re (1904) 37
Oldfield v. Round (1800) 414, 415
Oldham v. Lawson (No. 1) (1976) 1071
Oliver v. Davis (1949)...747
Olley v. Fisher (1887)..439
Ollivant v. Bayley (1843).. 482
Ollive v. Booker (1847).. 489
Olympia, Re (1898) 644
Omnium Electric Palaces v. Baines (1914) 646
O'Neill v. Armstrong, Mitchell & Co (1895) 378
Onslow v. Corrie (1817) 130
Oom v. Bruce (1810) 680
Ooregum Gold Mining Co of India v. Roper (1892)............................... 646
Ormerod v. Todmorden Joint Stock Mill Co (1883) 163
Ormrod v. Huth (1845)..413
Orr v. Maginnis (1806)...736
Orr & Barber v. Union Bank of Scotland (1854) 756, 770
Osborn v. Gillett (1873) 1042
Osborne v. Jackson and Todd (1883) 1016
Osborne v. Rogers (1669)... 316, 364, 595,
                                                                        596, 600
O'Sullevan v. Dublin and Wicklow Railway Co (1870) 959
Otley v. Manning (1807) 264, 361
Oughton v. Seppings (1830)...573
Overend and Curney Co v. Gibb (1872) 666
Overseas Tankship (UK) Ltd v. Morts Dock and Engineering
    Co (The Wagon Mound) (1961) 956
Overton v. Freeman (1853)..896
Owen, Re (894) 61
Owen v. Burnett (1834)...915
Owen v. Routh (1854)...535
Owenson v. Morse (1796)... 740

Packer v. Gillies (1806)...853
Paddock v. North Eastern Railway Co (1868) 979
Pagani v. Gandolfi (1826)..496
Page v. Adam (1840)..106
Page v. Cox (1852) 392
Page v. Way (1840) 250, 251
Paget v. Marshall (1885).. 443

Paget's Settled Estates (1885). 94
Palace Shipping Co v. Caine (1907). 378
Palace Theatre v. Clensy and Hackney and Shepherd's
    Bush Empire Palaces (1909) 561
Paley v. Garnett (1885) 1015
Palmer, Re (1900) 184
Palmer v. Baker (1813). 1115
Palmer v. Fleshees (1663) 1131
Palmer v. Johnson (1884). 101
Palmer v. Simmonds (1854). 36
Palyart v. Leckie (1817) 592, 680
Panama, New Zealand, and Australian Royal Mail Co,
    Re (1870). 637
Paradine v. Jane (1647). 116, 509
Parfitt v. Hember (1867). 26
Parker v. Boulton (1835). 16
Parker v. Bristol and Exeter Railway Co (1851) 402
Parker v. Great Western Railway Co (1844). 577
Parker v. McKenna (1874) 662
Parker v. Marchant (1843) 766
Parker v. Mitchell (1840) 1125
Parker v. Patrick (1793). 457, 459, 853
Parker v. Smith (1832). 170, 1075
Parker v. South Eastern Railway Co (1877) 328, 475, 968
Parker v. Wallis (1855) 332
Parker v. Whyte (1863). 175
Parkes v. White (1805) 247
Parkinson v. Hanbury (1860) 140
Parkinson v. Lee (1802) 479
Parnaby v. Lancaster Canal Company (1839). 977
Parnell v. Hingston (1856) 257, 259
Parnell v. Parnell (1878) 246
Parrott, Re (1886) 15
Parry v. Great Ship Co (1864) 697
Parry v. Smith (1879) 1145
Parsons, Re (1890). 258
Parson v. Sexton (1847) 478
Parsons v. Bignold (1846). 706
Parsons v. Gulliford (1864) 41
Parsons v. Scott (1810) 686
Part v. Bond (1905) 868
Partridge v. Scott (1838) 1133, 1134
Pasley v. Freeman (1789) 924, 1040
Pasmore v. Oswaldtwistle Urban District Council (1898). 1091
Patchell v. Irish North Western Railway Co (1871). 960
Patching v. Barnett (1880). 39
Patent Bread Machinery Co, Valpy & Chapman, Ex p. (1872) 656
Pater v. Baker (1847). 1039
Paterson v. Murphy (1853) 262
Paterson v. Tash (1743) 761, 1122
Paterson v. Wallace (1854). 1005
Patmann v. Harland (1881) 174

Patrick, Re 255, 258
Patten v. Rea (1857) 897
Patten v. Thompson (1816) 761
Patterson v. Harris (1861) 687
Patterson v. Ritchie (1815) 717
Paul v. Paul (1880) 267
Pawle v. Gunn (1838) 595, 596, 597
Pawson v. Watson (1778) 429, 698
Payne v. Bacombe (1781) 316, 531
Payne v. Cave (1789) 329, 333, 334
Payne v. New South Wales Coal and Intercolonial Steam
    Navigation Co (1854) 390
Payne v. Wilson (1827) 376
Peace v. Brookes (1895) 154
Peachey v. Rowland (1853) 973
Peachy v. Rowland and Evans (1853) 896
Peacock v. Evans (1809) 403
Peacock v. Penson (1848) 173, 552
Peacock v. Penson (1854) 175
Peacock v. Rhodes (1781) 741, 750
Peake v. Penlington (1813) 82
Pearcy v. Walter (1834) 909
Pearks v. Moseley (1880) 45
Pearne v. Lisle (1749) 552
Pear's Case (1779) 457
Pearse v. Baron (1821) 83
Pearson v. Amicable Assurance Office (1859) 257
Pearson v. Lane (1809) 243
Pearson v. Lemaitre (1843) 902
Pearson v. Wilcock (1906) 845, 847
Pearson (a Lunatic), Re (1877) 276
Pease (1832) 919, 920, 1103
Pease, Ex p. (1812) 767, 768
Pease v. Chaytor (1863) 1036
Pease v. Gloahec-The Mary Joseph (1866) 460, 760, 761, 764
Peek v. Gurney (1871) 426, 427
Peek v. North Staffordshire Railway Co (1862-63) 474
Peel, Re (1907) 294
Peel v. Catlow (1838) 41
Peer v. Humphrey (1835) 459
Peet v. Baxter (1816) 853
Peeters v. Opie (1677) 495
Pembroke v. Thorpe (1740) 551
Pembroke v. Thorpe (1796) 551
Pender v. Lushington (1877) 653
Penfold v. Mould (1867) 258, 259
Pennell v. Alexander (1852) 476
Pennell v. Deffell (1853) 604
Pennell v. Woodburn (1835) 541
Penny v. Innes (1834) 735, 739
Penny v. Turner (1848) 30
Penny v. Watts (1849) 409

Penson v. Lee (1800) 703
Penwarden v. Ching (1829) 169, 1072
Pepper v. Burland (1791) 531
Percival v. Frampton (1835) 746
Perez v. Oleaga (1856) 447
Perionowsky v. Freeman (1866) 882
Perkins v. Ede (1852) 438
Perkins v. Smith (1752) 1118
Perrin v. Blake (1769-72) 29
Perring & Co v. Emerson (1906) 872
Perring v. Hone (1826) 618
Perrins v. Bellamy (1897) 293
Perrott and King's Contract, Re (1904) 277
Perry v. Davis (1858) 125
Perry v. Fitzhowe (1846) 160
Perry v. Meddowcroft (1841) 151
Perry v. Suffields (1916) 109
Peruvian Railways Co, Re (1867) 738
Petch v. Tustin (1846) 123
Peters v. Opie (1671) 349
Peters v. Warren Insurance Co (1838) 713
Peterson v. Ayre (1853) 537
Peto v. Brighton, Uckfield and Tunbridge Wells Railway Co (1863) 561
Pettingall v. Pettingall (1842) 241
Pettit, Ex p. (1825) 136
Peyton v. Mayor and Commonality of London as Governors of
    St Thomas' Hospital (1829) 1136
Peyton's Settlement, Re (1858) 275
Peyton's Settlement Trust, Re (1869) 234, 279, 280
Phillip v. Jones (1839) 509
Phillipo v. Munnings (1837) 242
Phillips v. Barber (1821) 712
Phillips v. Bistolli (1824) 332, 447
Phillips v. Brooks (1919) 470
Phillips v. Duke of Bucks (1683) 453
Phillips v. Homfray (1883) 580, 581, 582, 583
Phillips v. Huth (1840) 1123
Phillips v. Im Thurn (1866) 750, 753, 754
Phillips v. James (1865) 16
Phillips v. Jones (1834) 532
Phillips v. Mullings (1871) 267, 406
Phillips v. Phillips (1864) 41
Phillips v. South Western Railway Company (1879) 991, 992
Philliskirk v. Pluckwell (1814) 745
Phillpotts v. Evans (1839) 497
Philp v. Squire (1791) 1041
Phipps v. Ackers (1842) 39
Pickard v. Bankes (1810) 578
Pickard v. Sears (1837) 367
Pickard v. Smith (1861) 896, 972, 977
Pickering v. Bishop of Ely (1843) 559
Pickering v. Busk (1812) 761

Pickering v. Dowson (1813) 411, 477
Pickering v. Ilfracombe Railway (1868) 186
Pickering v. Stephenson (1872) 294
Pierce v. Provident Clothing and Supply Co (1911) 1029
Piercy v. Roberts (1832) 250, 251
Pierson v. Dunlop (1777) 734
Piggot v. Eastern Counties Railway Company (1846) 920
Piggott v. Birtles (1836) 121
Pigot v. Cubley (1864) 762
Pigott v. Thompson (1802) 389
Pike v. Street (1828) 743
Pilkington v. Scott (1846) 373, 1043
Pillans v. Van Mierop (1765) 359, 395, 734, 744
Pillot v. Wilkinson (1864) 1121
Pilmore v. Hood (1838) 1040
Pim v. Reid (1845) 706
Pimm v. Lewis (1862) 706
Pimm v. Roper (1862) 882
Pinard v. Klockmann (1863) 304
Pinchon's Case (1611) 575
Pinnel's Case (1602) 383, 385, 386, 387
Pippin v. Sheppard (1822) 883
Pitchford v. Davis (1839) 623
Pitt v. Donovan (1813) 1039
Pitt v. Jackson (1786) 20
Planche v. Colburn (1831) 501, 532, 533
Plaskynaston Tube Co, Re (1883) 646
Plevins v. Downing (1876) 494
Plimley v. Westley (1835) 739
Plimmer v. Mayor of Wellington (1884) 162
Pluckwell v. Wilson (1832) 909, 910
Plumb v. Campbell (1888) 356
Plumb v. Cobden Flour Mills Co (1914) 1028
Plumber v. Gregory (1874) 665
Plummer v. Bentham (1757) 1072
Plumptre's Settlement (1910) 261
Plyer's Trust, Re (1851) 275
Pocock, Ex p. (1849) 647
Pocock v. Reddington (1801) 282
Podmore v. Gunning (1832) 4
Pole v. Fitzgerald (1750) 681, 686
Pole v. Leask (1860) 461
Polemis and Furness-Withy and Co, Re (1921) 956
Polhill v. Walter (1832) 411, 462, 1040
Pollard v. Clayton (1855) 555, 557
Pollock v. Lester (1853) 1098
Polwart (1841) 997
Pomfret v. Ricroft (1669) 1126, 1127
Pond v. King (1748) 686
Ponicione v. Higgins (1904) 867, 868
Poole v. Adams (1864) 694
Poole v. Middleton (1861) 554

Poole's Case (1704) 118
Pooley v. Brown (1862)..752
Pope, Re (1886) 189
Pope v. Hill's Plymouth Co (1911)..1027
Pope v. Pope (1839) 36
Popewell v. Wilson (1720) 745, 747
Pophal v. Eyre (1774)..453
Popplewell v. Hodkinson (1869)...165
Pordage v. Cole (1669) 305, 485, 486
Porthouse v. Parker (1807)..750
Postlethwaite v. Parkes (1766)..1041
Pothonier v. Dawson (1816)...762
Pott v. Clegg (1847) 767
Potter, Re (1869) 37, 40, 41
Potter v. Edwards (1857)..147, 148
Potter v. Faulkner (1861) 1013
Potter v. Rankin (1868) 724
Potter v. Richardson (1855) 7
Poulton v. Kelsall (1912)..1027
Poulton v. Lattimore (1829)..478
Poulton v. London and South Western Railway Co (1867) 898
Pounder v. North Eastern Railway Co (1832)...967
Pounsett v. Fuller (1856)..100
Poussard v. Spiers (1876) 517
Powel, Ex p., in Matthews, Re (1875)...873
Powell v. Fall (1880) 920, 974
Powell v. Hellicar (1919)...40
Powell v. Hingston (1856) 259
Powell v. Jones (1793) 734
Powell v. Monnier (1737) 734
Powell v. Rees (1837) 574, 576
Powell v. Thomas (1848)...161
Powell & Thomas v. Evan Jones & Co (1905) 605
Power v. Barham (1836) 479
Power v. Butcher (1829) 697
Powles v. Innes (1843)..688
Powley v. Walker (1793) 114
Pownal v. Ferrand (1827) 596, 599
Praed v. Graham (1889) 901
Praeger v. Bristol and Exeter Railway (1871) 937
Pratt v. British Medical Association (1919)...................................1064, 1065
Pratt v. Hutchinson (1812)...617
Prehn v. Royal Bank of Liverpool (1870)......................................546, 1870
Pressley v. Burnett (1914)...976
Preston v. Grand Collier Dock Co (1840)..652
Preston v. Liverpool, Manchester and Newcastle-upon-Tyne
    Junction Railway Co (1856)...392
Preston v. Neele (1879) 153
Preston v. Strutton (1792) 615
Prevesi v. Gatti (1888)..1017
Price v. Easton (1833) 389
Price v. Jenkins (1875)..265

Price v. Jenkins (1877)..266
Price v. Ley (1863)...435
Price v. Neal (1762)..750
Price v. Penzance (1845)..557
Price v. Price (1847)..746
Price v. Severn (1831)..900, 901
Price v. Taylor (1860)..739
Price & Co v. The Al Ships' Small Damage Insurance (1889).........................719
Prickett v. Badge (1856)..534
Pride of Derby and Derby Angling Association v.
    British Celanese (1953)..1093
Prideaux v. Lonsdale (1863)...267
Priestley v. Fowler (1837)......................................925, 1002, 1003, 1008
Priestley v. Pratt (1912)...873
Prince of Wales & Association Co v. Palmer (1858)............................711, 726
Prince of Wales Assurance Co v. Harding (1858)..............................658, 704
Pringle v. Wernham (1836)...1075
Pritchard v. Merchant's and Tradesman's Mutual Life
    Assurance Co (1858)...449, 705
Pritchard v. Wilson (1864)..140
Proctor v. Harris (1830)..907, 972, 977
Prole v. Soady (1859)...369
Proudfoot v. Montefiori (1867)..700
Provender v. Wood (1630)...388
Pryce v. Belcher (1847)..1036
Pryce's Settlement, Re (1917)...261
Public Work Commissioner v. Hills (1906)..529
Puckford v. Maxwell (1794)..740
Pugh v. London, Brighton and South Coast Railway Co (1896)......................1025
PUK Samuel and Co v. Dumas (1924)...681
Puller v. Glover (1810)...686
Pulling v. Tucker (1821)..783
Pulsford v. Richards (1853)..415, 418
Pultenay v. Warren (1801)...583
Pulvertoft v. Pulvertoft (1811)...............................253, 255, 260, 360
Purvis v. Rayer (1821)..97
Pusey v. Desbouvrie (1734)..442
Pusey v. Pusey (1684)...552
Putland v. Hilder (1819)..67
Pybus v. Smith (1791)...247
Pye, Ex p (1811)...255, 257, 259
Pyer v. Carter (1857)...167
Pym v. Great Northern Railway Company (1862)...............................999, 1000

Quarman v. Burnett (1840)...896
Quartz Hill Gold Mining Co v. Eyre (1883)..................................1036, 1037
Quebec Fire Assurance Co v. St Louis (1851).......................................716
Quinion v. Horne (1906)...108, 109
Quinn v. Leathem (1901).................................1061, 1062, 1063, 1066

R v. Aickles (1784)..457, 458
R v. Aspinall (1876)..639

R v. Justice of the Central Criminal Court (1886).. 466
R v. Morrison (1859)...853
R v. Spencer (1867) 882
R v. Trebilcock (1858)...853
R v. Webb (1811)...617
R v. Wynn (1887)...871
Rackham v. Marriott (1856) 362
Radley v. London & North Western Railway Co (1883)...........................932, 934, 953
Raey v. White (1833)...385
Raffles v. Wichelhaus (1864) 446, 471
Raikes v. Wood (1842) 245
Railway and General Light Improvement Co, Marzetti's
  case (1880) 666
Ralli v. Janson (1856) 718
Ralph v. Carrick (1879).. 43, 46
Ramchurch Mullick v. Luchmeechund Radakissen (1854)..............................734, 764
Ramsbottom v. Gosden (1812) 439, 440
Ramsbottom v. Lewis (1808)..782
Ramsden v. Dyson (1866) 162
Ramsey v. Gilchrist (1892).. 266
Ramuz v. Crowe (1847)... 766
Randal v. Cockran (1748)..723
Randall v. Everest (1827) 527
Randall v. Newson (1877)..483
Randall v. Willis (1800)..435
Ranger v. Great Western Railway (1854)...420, 659
Rankin v. Acraman (1822)... 1096
Rann v. Hughes (1778) 359
Ransgate Victoria Hotel Co v. Montefiore (1866).......................................343
Raper v. Birkbeck (1811)..303, 733
Raphael v. Governor of Bank of England (1855)...749
Raphael v. Thames Valley Railway Co (1866) 557
Rapier v. London Tramways Co (1893)...1105
Rapson v. Cubitt (1841)...991
Rapson v. Cubitt (1842)... 896
Rawleins v. Lockey (1639) 387
Rawlins v. Desborough (1840) 709
Rawlins v. Wickham (1858)..410, 418, 419, 424
Rawson v. Johnson (1801) 486, 495
Rayner v. Grote (1846)..456
Rayner v. Preston (1880) 695
Rayner v. Rederiaktiebolaget Condor (1895)..528
Read v. Baker (1916) 1029
Read v. Coker (1853)...1035
Read v. Edwards (1864) 1126
Read v. Friendly Society of Operative Stonemasons of England,
  Ireland and Wales (1902)... 1064
Read v. Great Eastern Railway Co (1868) 998
Read v. Hutchinson (1813) 589
Read v. J. Lyons & Co (1947) 1145
Read v. Rann (1830)...534
Readhead v. Midland Railway Co (1867) 961, 962, 963, 964

Real & Personal Advance v. Clears (1887) 154
Rede v. Farr (1817)...125, 491
Redgrave v. Hurd (1881)..410, 425
Redman v. Wilson (1845)..713
Reece v. Rigby (1821)..883, 916
Reech v. Kennegal (1748) 565
Reed v. Braithwaite (1871) 40
Reed v. Great Western Railway Co (1909) 1028
Reed v. Royal Exchange Co (1795) 689
Reed v. White (1803)..385
Reedie v. London and North Western Railway Company (1849)..............896
Rees v. Penrikyber Navigation Colliery Co (1903) 1030
Rees v. Thomas (1899)...1028
Rees v. Warwick (1818)..734
Reese River Silver Mining Co (Smith's Case), Re (1867) 423, 424, 649
Reeve v. Lisle (1902) 154
Reeve v. Palmer (1858) 577, 1117
Reg v. Inhabitants of Slawstone (1852)....................................337
Reid v. Bickerstaffe (1909) 176
Reid v. Fenwick (1855)..261
Reid v. Hoskins (1855)..503
Reinhardt v. Menasti (1889) 1101, 1109
Reniger v. Fogossa (1550) 302
Renshaw v. Bean (1852) 1072, 1073
Rew v. Pettet (1834)...729
Rex v. Inhabitant of Bedworth (1807) 509
Rex v. Marshall (1804) 458
Reynell v. Lewis (1846)..623
Reynell v. Sprye (1852) 410, 594
Reynolds v. Bridge (1856)..527
Reynolds v. Pinhowe (1595) 348
Reynolds v. Pitt (1812)..124
Rhodes v. Bate (1865) 403, 407
Rhodes v. Rhodes (1882) 34
Rhodes v. Rhodes (1890) 570
Rhymney Railway v. Brecon and Merthyr Tydfil Junction
     Railway (1900)..507
Rice v. Reed (1900) 581
Rich v. Basterfield (1847) 1097
Rich v. Parker (1798)..702
Rich v. Pierpont (1862)..882
Richards v. Davies (1831) 614
Richards v. Delbridge (1874) 260
Richards v. Lewis (1852)... 264
Richards v. Richards (1831) 744
Richards v. Stark (1911)...633
Richardson, Re (1904) 26, 94
Richardson v. Dunn (1841) 492, 954
Richardson, Spence & Co v. Rowntree (1894) 968
Richardson v. Great Eastern Railway Co (1875) 964, 965
Richardson v. Larpent (1843) 619
Richardson v. Mellish (1824)... 886

Richardson v. Metropolitan Railway Co (1868) 938
Richardson v. Richardson (1867) 259, 260
Richmond Hill Hotel Company, Elkington's Case, Re (1867) 340
Richmond Hill Hotel Company, Pellatt's Case, Re (1867) 340
Rickards v. Lothian (1913) 1148, 1149
Ricket v. Metropolitan Railway Co (1865) 1104
Ricket v. Metropolitan Railway Co (1867) 1104
Ricketts v. Scornhorn (1898) 367
Rickford v. Ridge (1810) 765
Riddeford v. Warren (1901) 431
Ridge's Trust, Re (1872) 45
Ridgway v. Lord Stafford (1851) 121
Ridgway v. Wharton (1857) 330
Ridler, Re (1882) 266
Ridley v. Taylor (1810) 737
Ridout v. Brislow (1830) 745, 747
Rigby v. Hewitt (1850) 544, 935, 954
Right d. Shortridge v. Creber (1826) 31
Riley v. Garnett (1849) 39
Riley v. Horne (1828) 912, 914
Ring v. Hardwick (1840) 243
Ripley v. McClure (1849) 499, 500
Rippon v. Norton (1839) 250
Risbourg v. Bruckner (1858) 448
Ritchie v. Atkinson (1808) 486
Rivaz v. Gerussi (1880) 698
River Wear Commissioners v. Adamson (1877) 1125
Robarts v. Tucker (1851) 770, 771, 772, 929
Robbins v. Jones (1863) 972
Robers v. Gwrfai District Council (1899) 164
Roberts, Fereday and Smith v. Haines (1856) 1128
Roberts, Re (1863) 41
Roberts, Re (1889) 148
Roberts, Re (1903) 46
Roberts v. Bozon (1825) 136
Roberts v. Davey (1833) 126, 491
Roberts v. Eastern Counties Railway Co (1859) 994
Roberts v. Lloyd (1840) 257
Roberts v. Macord (1832) 1072
Roberts v. Security Co (1897) 703
Roberts v. Wyatt (1810) 491
Robertson v. Allan Brothers & Co (Liverpool and London) (1908) 1027
Robertson v. Hamilton (1811) 685
Robertson v. Kensington (1811) 742
Robertson v. Liddell (1808) 782
Robertson v. Norris (1858) 138, 139
Robertson v. Scott (1866) 236
Robertson v. Ware (1853) 393
Robinson v. Chartered Bank (1865) 554
Robinson v. Davison (1871) 516
Robinson v. Dickenson (1828) 437
Robinson v. Harkin (1896) 292

Robinson v. Harman (1848) 539, 540
Robinson v. Hawsford (1846) 765
Robinson v. Kilvert (1889)...1070
Robinson v. Mayor and Corporation of Workington (1897)...........................1091
Robinson v. Price (1876)..714
Robinson v. Reynolds (1841) 745
Robinson v. Robinson (1851)...279, 283
Robinson v. Waddington (1849)..872
Robinson v. Yarrow (1817) 750
Robson v. Calze (1779) 792
Robson v. Drummond (1831)..454, 595
Robson v. Flight (1864)..273
Robson v. Godfrey (1816)...315
Robson v. North-Eastern Railway Co (1876) 937
Robson v. Whittingham (1866) 1076
Rochdale Canal Co v. King (1853) 161
Rochfort v. Fitzmaurice (1842) 24
Roddick v. Indemnity Mutual Marine Insurance Co (1895)........................680, 681
Roddy v. Fitzgerald (1858) 16, 27, 28, 32, 33
Roden v. Eyton (1848)...120
Roe v. Birkenhead Lancaster and Cheshire Junction
    Railway Co (1851) 894
Rogers, Eungblut & Co. v. Martin (1911)..873
Rogers v. Boehm (1798) 602
Rogers v. Challis (1859) 540, 551
Rogers v. Hosegood (1900) 177
Rogers v. Imbleton (1806) 906
Rogers v. Langford (1833)...740
Rogers v. Macnamara (1853) 1114
Rogers v. Rajendro Dutt (1860) 1049
Rogers v. Spence (1844) 1115
Rogers v. Stephens (1788)...736
Rogers v. Taylor (1858) 1134
Rohde v. Johnson (1857) 478
Rolfe v. Harris (1816) 125
Rolfe v. Peterson (1772) 115, 525
Rolfe v. Rolfe (1846) 560
Rolin v. Steward (1854)...545
Rolland v. Hart (1871)..210
Rondeau v. Wyatt (1792) 331
Rooke v. Nowell (1813) 31, 38
Rookes v. Barnard (1964)...1067
Roper v. Greenwood & Sons (1900)...1024
Roper v. Johnson (1873) 506
Roscorla v. Thomas (1842)..365, 479
Rose Street Foundry and Engineering Co v.
    John Lewis & SOns (1917) 1065
Rose v. Buckett (1901)..1115
Rose v. Miles (1815) 1069
Rosetta v. Gurney (1851)..718
Rosevear China Clay Co, Re (1879) 762
Rosewell (1699) 1072

Roskell v. Whitworth (1870) 1107
Ross v. Fedden (1872) 1127, 1147, 1149
Ross v. Ross (1819) 243, 246
Ross v. Ross (1849) 236
Rossdale v. Denny (1921) 109
Roth, Re (1896) 286
Rotherham Alum and Chemical Co, Re (1883) 392, 393
Routh v. Thompson (1809) 685
Routledge v. Burrell (1789) 719
Routledge v. Dorril (1794) 21, 24, 26
Routledge v. Grant (1828) 303, 334
Routledge's Trust, Re (1909) 277
Roux v. Salvador (1836) 716
Rowbotham v. Wilson (1857) 1128
Rowbotham v. Wilson (1860) 166
Rowe (1859) 1118
Rowe v. Young (1820) 735
Rowland v. Morgan (1848) 25
Rowley v. Adams (1839) 130
Rowley v. London and North Western Railway Co (1873) 991, 998
Roy v. Duke of Beaufort (1741) 525
Royal Aquarium and Summer and Winter Garden Society v.
    Parkinson (1892) 1038
Royal Bank of Scotland, Ex p. (1815) 753
Royal British Bank v. Turquand (1856) 657, 658
Royal Steam Packet Co v. English Bank of Rio de Janeiro (1887) 714
Ruben v. Great Fingall Consolidation (1906) 660
Ruck v. Tooke (1829) 810
Rucker v. Hiller (1812) 736
Rudder v. Price (1791) 530
Rudge v. New (1825) 1097
Rufford v. Bishop (1829) 147
Rugg v. Minett (1809) 304, 510, 514
Ruggles v. General Interest Insurance Co (1827) 699
Rushmere v. Polsue & Alfieri (1906) 1102
Russel v. Bell (1842) 578, 579
Russel v. Langstaffe (1780) 770
Russel v. Russel (1783) 133
Russell, Ex P Temperton, In re (1893) 1053
Russell v. Jackson (1852) 4, 409
Russell v. Plaice (1854) 137
Russell v. Thornton (1859) 338
Rutherford v. Acton-Adams (1915) 550
Ruys v. Royal Exchange Association Co (1897) 717
Ryall v. Rolle (1749) 789
Ryall v. Rowles (1749) 789
Ryan v. Hartley (1912) 1031
Ryan v. Mutual Tontine Westminster Chambers Association (1892) 558
Rylands v. Fletcher 894, 895, 943, 974, 1087, 1093,
                                                                                      1112, 1126, 1140, 1150
Sackville-West v. Holmesdale (1870) 17, 18, 24
Sadler v. Belcher (1843) 767

Sadler v. Dixon (1841)..701
Sadler v. Lee (1843) 419
Sadler v. South Staffordshire and Birmingham District
   Steam Tramways Company (1889) 970, 971
Sadler and Jackson, Ex p. (1808)..78
Sadlers Co v. Badcock (1743) 694
St Aubyn v. Smart (1868)... 665
St George v. Wake (1833) 252
St Helen's Smelting Co v. Tipping (1865) 1070, 1100, 1101,
                                                        1109, 1143, 1150
Sainter v. Ferguson (1849)..528
Salaman v. Warner (1891) 1061
Sale (1868)..455, 466, 487,
                                                        489, 501, 514
Sales v. Moore (1827)...35
Salisbury v. Marshal (1829)..116
Salmon v. Bensley (1825) 1094, 1096
Salmon v. Ward (1825) 479
Salomon v. A. Salomon & Co (1897) 645, 668, 669, 670
Salt v. Marquess of Northampton (1892) 153, 154
Salusbury v. Denton (1857) 30
Salvin v. James (1805)...704
Salvin v. North Brancepeth Coal Co (1874) 1101
Sampayo v. Gould (1842)..132, 283
Sampson v. Pattison (1842) 136
Samuel v. Bell (1905).. 868
Samuel v. Jarrah Timber (1903) 154, 156
Samuel v. Miles (1903) 868
Samuel v. Newbold (1906) 868
Sanders' trusts, Re (1878)..241
Sanders v. Benson (1841) 131
Sanders v. Kentish and Hawksley (1799)...535
Sanders v. Richards (1846)...137
Sanders v. Vanzeller (1843) 760
Sanders-Clark v. Grosvenor Mansions Co and
   G. D'Allessandri (1900) 1101, 1102
Sanderson v. Brignall (1727) 566
Sanderson v. Cockermouth and Workington
   Railway Co (1849)..557
Sanderson v. Graves (1875) 533
Sanderson v. Walker (1807).. 404
Sanderson's Case (1849).. 624
Sanderson's Trust, Re (1857) 250
Sandilands v. Marsh (1819) 614
Sands v. Clarke (1849)... 497
Santley v. Wilde (1899)..154, 155, 158
Sapsford v. Fletcher (1792)..598
Sargeant, Ex p. (1810)...767
Sarquy v. Hobson (1827)...713
Saunders v. Evans (1855)...263
Saunders v. Lord Annesley (1804) 442
Saunders v. Newbold (1905) 868

Saunders v. Vautier (1841) 242, 244, 251, 252
Saunderson v. Jackson (1800) 331
Savage v. Taylor (1736) 373
Savery v. King (1856) 403, 405
Savignac v. Roome (1794) 906
Savile v. Roberts (1699) 1060
Sawmills v. Nettleship (1868) 541
Saxby v. Manchester and Sheffield Railway Co (1869) 1130
Saxton v. Hawkesworth (1872) 1006
Sayers v. Whitfield (1829) 146
Sayles v. Blane (1849) 596, 599
Scales v. Maude (1855) 256, 257
Scarborough v. Borman (1838) 248
Scattergood v. Sylvester (1850) 464
Schlencker v. Moxsy (1825) 599
Schneider v. Heath (1813) 411, 479, 480
Schofield v. Earl of Londesborough (1895) 771
Schofield v. Mayor & C of Bolton (1910) 983
Scholfield v. Spooner (1884) 249
School Dist of City of Kansas v. Stocking (1897) 367
Schotsman v. Lancashire and Yorkshire Railway Co (1867) 762
Schultz v. Astley (1836) 770
Schuster v. McKellar (1857) 760
Sclater v. Cottam (1857) 147
Scotson v. Pegg (1861) 379, 380, 381
Scott v. Brotherton (1827) 905
Scott v. Firth (1864) 1100
Scott v. Hanson (1826) 414, 415
Scott v. Langstaffe 453
Scott v. Littledale (1858) 447, 448
Scott v. London and St. Katherine Docks Co (1865) 960
Scott v. Lord Ebury (1867) 393
Scott v. Nesbitt (1808) 146
Scott v. Pape (1886) 170, 1077
Scott v. Pattison (1923) 534
Scott v. Pilkington (1862) 757
Scott v. Rayment (1868) 554
Scott v. Scott (1787) 416
Scott v. Shepherd (1773) 904, 905, 934, 952
Scott v. Steward (1859) 17
Scott v. Surman (1743) 458, 572, 790
Scrope v. Offley (1736) 442
Scurfield v. Gowland (1805) 591
Scweitzer v. Mayhew (1862) 136
Seagrave v. Union Marine Insurance Co (1866) 685
Seare v. Prentice (1807) 916
Searle v. Law (1846) 259
Searle v. Lindsay (1861) 1004, 1005
Sears v. Lyons (1818) 901
Seaton v. Mapp (1846) 105
Seaward v. Willcock (1804) 25
Seccombe v. Edwards (1860) 28, 38

Second East Dulwich 745th Starr-Bowkett Building
  Society, Re (1899) 293
Seddon v. Connell (1840)...565
Seeger v. Duthie (1860)...531
Selby v. Whittaker (1877)...33, 34
Sells v. Sells (1860)...438, 443
Selway v. Fogg (1839)..589
Selwyn v. Garfit (1888) 141
Senior v. Metropolitan Railway (1863) 1104
Senior v. Pawson (1866) 1074
Serle v. Norton (1841) 765
Seton v. Lafone (1886)..942, 947
Seton v. Seton (1789)..744
Seton v. Slade (1802)..95
Sevier v. Greenway (1815)..152
Sevin v. Deslandes (1860) 561
Sewell v. Burdick (1884)..760, 763
Sewell v. Moxsy (1852) 257
Seymour v. Greenwood (1861) 897
Shackell v. West (1859)..852
Shadwell v. Shadwell (1860)..............................378, 379, 380,
                                                     381, 389, 390
Shaffers v. General Steam Navigation Co (1883) 1016
Sharington v. Strotton (1565) 359
Sharman, Re (1901)..184
Sharp v. Grey (1833) 911, 963
Sharp v. Leach (1862) 406
Sharp v. Powell (1872)..954, 955, 956
Sharpe v. Brice (1774) 900
Shaw v. Bailey (1892)..633
Shaw v. Cates (909)..292
Shaw v. Fisher (1855)..553
Shaw v. Great Western Railway Co (1894) 474
Shaw v. Holland (1846)...535, 538
Shaw v. Jeffery (1860) 151
Shaw v. Neale (1858) 150
Shaw v. Robberds (1837)..706
Shaw v. Wigan Coal and Iron Co Ltd (1909) 1029
Shaw v. Wright (1796)..270, 275
Shawe v. Felton (1801)...682
Sheerin v. Clayton & Co (1910)......................................1026
Sheffield Gas Company Co v. Harrison (1853).........................554
Shelfer v. City of London Electric Lighting Co (1895) 1108, 1109
Shelley v. Shelley (1868) 16, 19, 25, 29,
                                                     31, 34, 35
Shelton v. King (1913) 244
Shelton v. King (1916)...252
Shelton v. Watson (1849) 16
Shenstone & Co v. Freeman (1910)....................................873
Sheperd v. Wakeman (1662) 1045
Shephard v. Harris (1905) 292
Shephard v. Keatley (1834)...104

Shepherd v. Harrison (1871) 761
Shepherd v. Johnson (1802) 535
Shepherd v. Kain (1821) 477
Shepherd v. Pybus (1842) 482
Sheppard v. Shoolbred (1841) 459
Sheppard v. Union Bank of London (1862) 1123
Sherreff v. Wilks (1800) 614
Shield, Re (1885) 260
Shillibeer v. Glyn (1836) 374
Shilling v. Accidental Death Insurance Co (1858) 708
Ship's Case (1865) 649
Shipton v. Thornron (1838) 304
Shirley v. Davis 440
Shirreff v. Wilks (1800) 614, 913
Shogun Finance v. Hudson (2004) 470
Shore v. Bentall (1828) 713
Short v. Kalloway (1839) 541
Short v. M'Carthy (1820) 362
Short v. Stone (1846) 498, 499
Shove v. Webb (1787) 591
Shovelton v. Shovelton (1863) 245
Shreiber v. Creed (1839) 171, 172, 173, 175
Shrewsbury v. Blount (1841) 409, 411, 429
Shuey v. United States (1875) 357
Sibley's Trusts, Re (1877) 34, 38, 42, 43
Sibree v. Tripp (1846) 384
Sichel v. Mosenthal (1862) 554
Siebert v. Spooner (1836) 815
Silkes v. Wild (1861) 99, 100
Sillar, Re (1871) 280, 281
Sillem v. Thornton (1854) 707
Sills v. Brown (1840) 908
Simmons v. Norton (1831) 115
Simmons v. Swift (1826) 510
Simmons v. Taylor (1857) 775
Simmons v. Woodward (1892) 864
Simon v. Metivier (1766) 333
Simons v. Great Western Railway Co (1856) 474
Simons v. Patchett (1857) 463
Simpson v. Accidental Death Insurance Co (1857) 704
Simpson v. Clarke 748
Simpson v. Clarke (1835) 746, 747
Simpson v. Crippin (1872) 488
Simpson v. Savage (1856) 1070
Simpson v. Scottish Union Insurance Co (1863) 693, 694
Simpson v. Sinclair (1917) 1029
Simpson v. Thompson (1877) 723, 724
Sims v. Bond (1833) 766
Simson v. London General Omnibus Co (1873) 971
Simson's Trust, Re (1860) 280
Sinclair v. Brougham (1914) 570, 572, 606,
                                                               607, 608, 609

Sinclair v. Stevenson (1825) 458
Siner v. Great Western Railway (1868) 937
Singer Manufacturing Co v. Clark (1879).................................853, 871
Singh v. Attenborough (1896).. 850
Singleton v. Eastern Counties Railway Company (1859)..............................981
Sjoerds v. Luscombe (1812) 511
Skeate v. Beale (1841) 373, 402
Skelton v. London and North Western Railway Co (1867) 936, 948
Skinner v. Gunton (1670)... 1060
Skinner v. London, Brighton and South Coast Railway Co (1850) 960
Skipp v. Eastern Counties Railway Co (1853).....................................1006
Skyring v. Greenwood (1825)... 586
Slater's Trust, Re 148
Sleat v. Fagg (1822) 914
Sleath v. Wilson (1839) 897
Slim v. Croucher (1860) 417
Sloane v. Cadogan...257
Sloman v. Walter (1783) 524
Small v. Attwood (1832) 590
Small v. Moates (1833).. 760
Small v. Oudley (1727) 784
Smart v. Jones (1864) 161
Smart v. Morton (1855)..1128
Smeaton v. Ilford Corporation (1954) 1093
Smee v. Huddlestone (1768)...534
Smeed v. Foord (1859)..543, 544, 545
Smethurst v. Hastings (1885)... 292
Smith, Ex p. (1813)..791
Smith, Re (1875)... 42
Smith, Re (1889).. 242
Smith, Re (1896) 283, 284
Smith, Re (1904) 273, 277
Smith v. Abbot (1741) 735
Smith v. Anderson (1879)... 664
Smith v. Baker (1873) 581
Smith v. Bickmore (1812) 594
Smith v. Braine (1851)...745
Smith v. Brandram (1841) 318
Smith v. Bromley (1760)..594
Smith v. Burlton (1801)..401
Smith v. Butcher (878) 32
Smith v. Cannan (1853) 783
Smith v. Chadwick (1881)...............................428, 429, 430, 644
Smith v. Charles Baker and Sons (1891) 1009
Smith v. Cherril (1867).. 264
Smith v. Chester (1787)..750
Smith v. Clarke (1794) 741
Smith v. Crabtree (1877)..38
Smith v. Cuff (1817) 594
Smith v. Dickenson (1804)...526
Smith v. Dowell (1862) 1005
Smith v. Garland (1817) 263

Smith v. Gibson (1871) 245
Smith v. Great Eastern Railway Company (1866) 923
Smith v. Hayward (1837) 496
Smith v. Hodson (1791) 578, 579
Smith v. Horne (1818) 912, 914
Smith v. Hughes (1871) 339, 410, 442, 451, 452, 471
Smith v. Hull Glass Co (1852) 658
Smith v. Iliffe (1875) 267
Smith v. Jeffreys (1846) 445, 446
Smith v. Jones (1842) 566
Smith v. Kenrick (1849) 1047, 1141, 1144
Smith v. Knox (1799) 746
Smith v. Lancashire and Yorkshire Railway (1899) 1028
Smith v. London and South Western Railway Co (1870) 920, 921, 934,
                                                                                      935, 936, 955, 979
Smith v. Lyne (1843) 262
Smith v. Marrable (1842) 116, 117
Smith v. Mercer (1815) 750, 752, 769
Smith v. M'Guire (1858) 657
Smith v. Monteith (1844) 375, 378
Smith v. Moore (1845) 349
Smith v. Morrison (1911) 1028
Smith v. Mullett (1809) 337
Smith v. Myers (1870) 449
Smith v. Osbourne (1857) 33, 40
Smith v. Payne (1795) 784
Smith v. Pritchard (1849) 1114
Smith v. Reynolds (1856) 680
Smith v. Richardson (1737) 1038
Smith v. Sherwood (1847) 614
Smith v. Smith (1854) 275
Smith v. Smith (1870) 44
Smith v. South Eastern Railway (1893) 991, 994
Smith v. Spooner (1810) 1039
Smith v. Surman (1829) 331, 332
Smith v. Topping (1833) 789
Smith v. Union Bank of London (1875) 776
Smith v. Vertue (1860) 735
Smith v. Wheatcroft (1878) 467, 469
Smith v. Wilson (1832) 446, 495
Smith v. Young (1818) 1118
Smout v. Ilbery (1842) 305, 462
Smyth's Settlement, Re (851) 275
Snee v. Prescot (1743) 742
Snow v. Peacock (1826) 749
Snow v. Poulden (1836) 243
Snowdon v. Dales (1834) 250, 251
Snowdon v. Davis (1808) 577
Soames v. Edge (1860) 551
Soares v. Glyn (1845) 742
Societe General v. Metropolitan Bank (1873) 770
Society v. Fuller (186) 285

Sockett v. Wray (1794) 247
Solicitor-General v. Law Reversionary Interest Society (1873) 184
Solle v. Butcher (1950) 444, 472
Sollers, Ex p. (1811) 767
Soloman v. Vintners Co (1859) 1137, 1138
Solomon (1912) 292
Soltau v. De Held (1851) 1106
Somerville v. Hawkins (1851) 1038
Somerville v. Lethbridge (1795) 25
Soper v. Arnold (1889) 98
Sorell v. Smith (1925) 1066
Souch v. Strawbridge (1846) 533
South, Re (1874) 189
South Carolina Bank v. Case (1828) 737
South Staffordshire Water Co v. Sharman (1896) 1119
South Wales Miners' Federation v. Glamorgan Coal Co (1905) 1064
South Wales Railway Co v. Wythes (1854) 557
Southcote v. Stanley (1856) 978, 1002
Southerton v. Whitlock (1726) 363
Soutler v. Drake (1834) 97
Sowerby v. Butcher (1834) 747
Spackman, Ex p. (1849) 648
Spackman v. Evans (1868) 659
Spalding v. Ruding (1843) 762
Spark's Trust, Re 258
Speake v. Richards (1617) 566
Speakman, Re (1876) 34, 38, 41
Spear v. Travers (1815) 791
Speight v. Gaunt (1883) 292, 665
Spencer v. Clarke (1878) 692
Spencer v. Harding (1870) 353
Spencer v. Marriott (1823) 174
Spencer v. Parry (1835) 596, 597, 598
Spencer's Case (1583) 127, 129
Spicer, Re (1901) 15
Spicer v. Martin (1888) 176
Spill v. Maule (1869) 1038
Spiller v. Paris Skating Rink Co (1878) 393
Spirett v. Williams (1869) 12
Spooner v. Gardiner (1824) 736
Sprat v. Agar (1658) 388
Spratt v. Hobhouse (1827) 578
Spratt v. Jeffery (1829) 104
Sprigwell v. Allen (1648) 484
Staight v. Burn (1869) 1074
Stainbank v. Fenning (1851) 687
Stainbank v. Fernley (1839) 416
Stains v. Banks (1863) 147
Stainton, Re Board of Trade, Ex p. (1887) 826
Standard Manufacturing, Re (1891) 154
Standen v. Christmas (1847) 116
Standish v. Ross (1849) 586

Staner, Ex p., Re (1852) 811
Stanhope v. Manners (1763) 148
Stanland v. North-Eastern Steel Co (No. 2) (1907) 1030
Stanley v. Chester and Birkenhead Railway Co (1838) 391
Stanley v. Powell (1891) 970, 1125
Stanley v. Western Insurance Company (1868) 720
Stannard v. Ullithorne (1834) 883, 916
Stansell v. Jollard (1803) 1131
Stansfeld v. Hellawell (1852) 393
Stansfield v. Cubitt (1858) 816
Stanton v. Collier (!852) 304
Stanton v. Richardson (1872) 489
Staples v. Eastman Photographic Materials Co (1896) 635
Stapley v. London, Brighton and South Coast Railway Co (1865) 936
Star v. Rookesby (1710) 1126
Startup v. Cortazzi (1835) 536
State Fire Insurance Co, Re (1863) 629
Stavers v. Curling (1836) 486
Stead v. Dawber (1839) 492, 493
Stead v. Mellor (1877) 37
Stedman v. Gooch (1793) 746, 766
Steel v. Cammell, Laird & Co (1905) 1025
Steel v. State Line Steamship Co (1877) 701
Steele v. Haddock (1855) 446
Stella, The (1900) 969
Stephens v. Badcock (1832) 571
Stephens v. Dudbridge Iron Works Co (1904) 1023
Stephens v. Elwall (1815) 1118
Stephens v. Myers (1830) 1035
Stephenson, Re (1888) 831
Stephenson v. Hart (1828) 458
Stevens v. Midland Counties Railway Co and Lander (1854) 899, 1038
Stevens v. Van Voorst (1853) 261
Stevens v. Woodward (1881) 1147
Stevenson v. McLean (1880) 345, 346
Stevenson v. Newnham (1853) 460
Stevenson v. Snow (1761) 703
Stewart v. Great Western Railway Co (1865) 994
Stewart v. Lee (1828) 773
Stewart v. London and North Western Railway Co (1864) 474, 968
Stewart v. Sanderson (870) 280
Stewart v. Wilsons and Clyde Coal Co. (1902) 1024
Stewart's case (1866) 649
Stilk v. Myrick (1809) 377
Stilwell v. Wilkins (1821) 549
Stirling v. Vaughan (1809) 685
Stock v. Inglis (1884) 687
Stockdale v. Dunlop (1840) 331, 338, 684
Stocken, Re (1888) 237
Stocken v. Collin (1841) 337, 735
Stocker v. Brockelbank (1851) 558, 559
Stockland v. Aldridge (1804) 4

Stockport Waterworks Co v. Potter (1861) 1086
Stockport Waterworks Co v. Potter (1864)..160, 163, 1086
Stokes, Ex p. (1802)..785
Stokes v. Cox (1856).. 707
Stokes v. Eastern Counties Railway Co (1860)......................................951, 961
Stokes v. Lewis (1785) 595
Stone v. Hyde (1889) 1017
Stone v. Lickorish (1891)..148
Stone v. Marsh (1826) 665
Stonor v. Curwen (1832)..15, 26
Stonor v. Fowle (1887).. 738, 843, 844
Storer v. Great Western Railway Co (1842) 557
Story, Ex p. (1817)..787
Stoveld v. Hughes (1811) 791
Stratford v. Twynam (1822)..147
Stratford and Moreton Railway Co v. Stratton (1831)................................367
Straton v. Rastall (1788) 566
Street v. Blay (1831) 460, 478, 589
Strickland v. Turner (1852) 448, 589
Strong v. Goff (1811) 31
Stroughill v. Anstey (1852)..181
Stroyan v. Knowles (1861) 1134, 1136
Strutt v. Smith (1834) 579, 589
Stuart v. Freeman (1903) 705
Stuart v. Nixon & Bruce (1900) 1030
Stuart v. Wilkins (1778) 479
Stubley v. London and North Western Railway Co (1865) 936
Studdert v. Grosvenor (1886) 294
Sturgeon v. Wingfield (1846)..130
Sturges v. Bridgman (1879) 163, 1103
Sturlyn v. Albany (1587).. 360
Sturtevant v. Ford (1842) 746
Styles v. Guy (1849)..283
Suffield v. Brown (1863) 167, 168
Sullivan v. Waters (1864) 978
Sunbolf v. Alford (1838) 1034
Surplice v. Farnsworth (1844)...117
Suse, Ex p. Dever, Re 755, 758
Suse v. Pompe (1860) 304
Sutherland v. Murray (1783) 1036
Sutton v. Chetwynd (1817)... 264
Sutton v. Clarke (1815) 919, 1131
Sutton v. Temple (1843) 117, 482
Sutton v. Weeley (1806) 781
Svendsen v. Wallace (1885) 715
Swaine v. Great Northern Railway (1864)...1107
Swaisland v. Dearsley (1861) 440
Swan v. North British Australasian Co (1863)................................770, 930, 931
Swan v. Steele (1806)...737
Sweenie v. Sharp (1826) 363
Swift v. Pannell (1883)..861, 875
Swift v. Winterbotham (1873) 1040

Swindon Waterworks Co v. Wilts & Berks Canal Navigation Co (1875) 163
Swire v. Leach (1865)...763
Sykes v. Dixon (1839) 580
Sykes v. North Eastern Railway (1875) 999
Syles v. Dixon (1839) 1043
Symes v. Hughes (1870) 592
Symonds v. James (1842) 104
Symonds v. Wilkes (1857) 15
Symons v. James (1882)...104
Synge v. Synge (1894) 506
Synot v. Simpson (1854)... 240
Syred v. Carruthers (1858) 852

T & J Harrison v. Knowles & Foster (1917) 490
Taaffe v. Conmee (1862)...45
Taff Vale Railway v. Jenkins (1913)... 998, 1064
Talbot v. Ford (1842).. 549
Tamplin v. James (1880).. 440
Tamplin Steamship Co v. Anglo-Mexacan Petroleum
    Products Co (1916) 520
Tamvaco v. Lucas (1861)..476, 504
Tamworth Colliery Co v. Hall (1911)..1030
Tanner v. Smart (1827) 362
Tanner v. Smith (1817) 491
Tanner v. Smith (1840) 106
Tapley v. Willan (1815) 905
Tapling v. Jones (1862) 1073, 1074, 1076
Tapp v. Lee (1803) 1040
Tappenden v. Randall (1801)..592
Tarleton v. M'Gawley (1794) 1048, 1056
Tarleton v. Staniforth (1794)... 704
Tarrabochia v. Hickie (1856)..489, 513
Tarry v. Ashton (1876) 899, 944
Tatam v. Haslar (1889) 746
Tate v. Hilbert (1793).. 744
Tate v. Hyslop (1885).. 698
Tate v. Wellings (1790) 535
Tate v. Williamson (1866) 407
Tattershall v. Groote (1800)...619
Taunton v. Royal Insurance Co (1864) 720
Tawney v. Crowther (1790) 330
Tayloe v. Merchants Fire Insurance Co (1850).. 344, 345
Taylor v. Ashton (1842)... 413, 429
Taylor v. Blacklow (1836) 883
Taylor v. Bowers (1876)..592, 593
Taylor v. Briggs (1827)... 446
Taylor v. Bullen (1850) 477
Taylor v. Caldwell (1863) 304, 513, 514,
                                                                                    516, 518, 520
Taylor v. Chester (1869) 593
Taylor v. Dunbar (1869) 712
Taylor v. Hare (1805).. 590

Taylor v. Hilary (1835)..492
Taylor v. Kymer (1832) 1123
Taylor v. London & Counties Bank (1901) 210
Taylor v. Manchester, Sheffield and Lincolnshire
    Railway Co (1895) 959
Taylor v. Meads (1865) 8
Taylor v. M'Viccar (1806) 401
Taylor v. Neri (1795) 1044
Taylor v. Neville 552, 555
Taylor v. Plumer (1815) 458, 572, 575, 604,
                                                                            605, 609, 790
Taylor v. Portington (1855) 551
Taylor v. Pugh (1842) 252
Taylor v. Salmon (1838) 662
Taylor v. Stibbert (1794)...174
Taylor v. Taylor (1875)..89
Taylor v. Waters (1816) 160, 161, 162
Taylor v. Zamira (1816)...598
Teal v. Auty (1820)..533
Teasdale v. Braithwaite (1876)..265
Teasdale v. Teasdale (1726)...416
Temperton v. Russell (1893).......................................1053, 1054, 1055, 1061, 1062
Templeman v. Haydon (1852) 971
Tempson v. Knowles (1849)..375
Tenant v. Goldwin (1704)..1083, 1126, 1141, 1143, 1150
Tennent v. Earl of Glasgow (1864) 1149
Terrell's Case (1851)..391
Tessymond's Case (1828) 985
Tetley v. Taylor (1853) 809
Thacker v. Hardy (1878)..632, 633
Thackrah, Re (1888) 870
Thames and Mersey Marine Insurance Co v. 'Gunford'
    Ship Co (1911) 681
Thatcher v. England (1846) 349, 350, 352
Thatcher v. Great Western Railway (1893) 979
Thelluson v. Woodford (1798)..250
Thellusson v. Fletcher (1780)...679, 702
Thellusson v. Rendlesham (1859) 33
Thiedemann v. Goldschmidt (1859)...745
Thom v. Bigland (1853)...414
Thomas v. Brown (1876)..456
Thomas v. Dering (1837)..109
Thomas v. Heathorn (1824)..384
Thomas v. Hewes (1834)..462
Thomas v. Kelly (1888)..154
Thomas v. Newton (1827)..745
Thomas v. Powell (1794)..98
Thomas v. Quartermaine (1887)..............................923, 946, 1008, 1014
Thomas v. Rhymney Railway Co (1871) 964
Thomas v. Thomas (1842)...364, 370, 371
Thompson v. Brown (1817)...495
Thompson v. Councell (1786) 794

Thompson v. Dominy (1845) 760
Thompson v. Fisher (1870) 16
Thompson v. Giles (1824) 768
Thompson v. Havelock (1808) 602
Thompson v. Hopper (1856) 702, 713
Thompson v. Hudson (1869) 528
Thompson v. North Eastern Railway Co (1860) 932
Thompson v. Percival (1834) 385
Thompson v. Royal Exchange Assurance Co (1812) 686
Thompson v. Universal Salvage Co (1849) 625
Thompson's Trust, Re (1854) 42
Thomson v. Weems and Others (1884) 708
Thornborow v. Whitacre (1705) 508
Thorne, Re (1917) 249
Thorne v. Heard (1894) 661
Thornton v. Hargreaves (1806) 784
Thornton v. Illingworth (1824) 362, 363
Thornton v. Kempster (1814) 445
Thorogood v. Bryan (1849) 932
Thorpe v. Owen (1842) 256
Threfall v. Giles (1822) 767
Thrussell v. Handyside & Co (1888) 1009
Thurlow v. Mackeson (1868) 140
Thurston v. Charles (1905) 1114
Tidd v. Lister (1853) 12
Tigress, Re (1863) 759
Tildesley v. Clarkson (1862) 117
Timmins v. Leeds Forge Co (1900) 1024
Tinn v. Hoffman (1873) 341
Tinsley v. Milligan (1994) 592
Tipping v. St Helen's Smelting Co (1863) 1100, 1101
Titchburne v. White (1618) 911
Titford v. Chambers (1814) 142
Titley v. Wolstenholme (1844) 274
Todd v. Gee (1810) 552
Toker v. Toker (1863) 262
Tollemache v. Earl of Coventry (1834) 25
Tomlinson v. Gill (1756) 391
Toogood v. Spyring (1834) 1038
Tooley v. Windham (1590) 375
Toomer v. Gingell (1846) 807
Toomey v. London, Brighton and South Coast Railway Co (1857) 936
Tottenham v. Bedingfield (1572) 563, 571
Touche v. Metropolitan Warehousing Co (1871) 391
Toulmin v. Hedley (1845) 478
Tourle v. Rand (1789) 913
Toussaint Martinnant (1787) 599
Touteng v. Hubbard (1802) 511
Tower Assets Co v. Weigall and Wife (1890) 875
Towers v. Barret (1786) 534
Towers v. Osbourne (1722) 331
Towns v. Wentworth (1859) 34

Townsend v. Crowdy (1860) 585, 586, 588
Townsend v. Inglis (1816). 759
Townsend v. Toker (1866) 264
Townsend v. Wilson (1818) 273
Tozer v. Child (1857). 1036
Traill v. Baring (1864). 410, 419
Train v. Gold (1827). 372
Treharne v. Layton (1875) 46
Trent v. Humber Co (1868) 537
Trevor v. Trevor (1847). 16
Trevor v. Whitworth (1887). 655
Trollope and Sons v. London Building Trades
    Federation (1895) 1053, 1054
Tronson v. Dent (1853) 760
Trower v. Chadwick (1836) 1132
Trower v. Newcome (1813) 409
Trueman v. Fenton (1777) 363
Trustee of G. Mellor v. Maas (1903). 876
Tucker v. Bennett (1887). 264, 267
Tucker v. Linger (1882). 114
Tucker v. Vowles (1893) 176
Tuff v. Warman (1857) 933
Tulk v. Moxhay (1848) 132, 159, 171, 173,
                                                                     174, 175, 252
Tullett v. Armstrong (1839) 8, 159, 248, 249, 252
Tullidge v. Wade (1768) 901
Tully v. Howling (1877) 489
Tunney v. Midland Railway Co (1865) 1004
Turberville v. Stamp (1697). 916, 918, 1135, 1141
Turley v. Bates (863) 304
Turley v. Thomas (1837) 908
Turner, Re (1897). 293
Turner, Re (1904). 829
Turner v. Ambler (1847). 1037
Turner v. Hawkins (1796). 906
Turner v. Mirfield (1865) 1083
Turner v. Mucklow (1862) 482
Turner v. Owen (1862) 378
Turner v. Sargent (1853) 15, 17
Turner v. Stallibrass (1898) 1116
Turner v. Wright (1860) 245
Turpin v. Chambers (1861) 109
Turquand v. Marshall (1869). 654, 664, 666
Turvey v. Brintons (1904) 1025
Tweddle v. Atkinson (1861) 389, 390
Twining v. Morrice (1788) 415
Twisleton v. Griffith (1716). 403
Twopenny v. Peyton (1840) 250, 251
Twycross v. Grant (1877) 643
Twyne's Case (1601) 783
Tyers v. Rosedale and Ferryhill Iron Co (1873) 493
Tyler v. Horne (1785). 703

Tyler's Trust, Re (1851) 275
Tyrie v. Fletch (1777). 703
Tytherleigh v. Harbin (1835) 42

Udall, Ex p., Mew & Thorne, Re (1862) 818
Udell v. Atherton (1861). 420, 660
Underhill v. Horwood (1804) 373
Underwood, Re (1857) 136
Underwood v. Hitchcox (1799) 373
Union Bank of Scotland v. National Bank of Scotland (1886) 150
Union Credit Bank v. Mersey Docks and Harbour Board (1899) 771
Union Lighterage Co v. London Graving Dock Co (1902) 1139
United Australia v. Barclays Bank (1941) 581
Universal Banking Corporation, Gunn's Case, Re (1867) 340
Universal Cargo Carriers Corporation v. Citati (1957) 506
Universal Non-Tariff Fire Insurance Co, Forbes & Co's claim, Re (1875). 706
Universal Stock Exchange v. Strachan (1898) 632
University of Des Moines v. Livingston (1881). 367
University of Vermont v. Buell (1829) 367
Universo Insurance Co of Milan v. Merchants Marine Insurance Co (1897) 697
Unlake v. Giles 256
Upperton v. Mickolson (1871). 104
Usher v. Noble (1810) 719, 721
USMC of Canada v. Brunet (1909). 673
Uther v. Rich (1839). 749

Vagliano Brothers v. Bank of England (1889) 753, 754
Valentine v. Hyde (1919). 1065
Valpy v. Manley (1845). 577
Valpyn v. Manley (1845). 402
Van Grutten v. Foxwell (1897) 27, 28, 29
Van Omeron v. Dowick (1809) 717
Van Sandau v. Moore (1825) 617, 618, 619
Vandenburgh v. Truax (1847) 934
Vanderplank v. King (1843). 24, 45
Vanderplank v. Miller (1828) 908
Vandyck v. Hewitt (1800) 680
Varney v. Hickman (1847). 595
Vaughan v. Cork and Youghal Railway Co (1860) 1006
Vaughan v. Matthews (1849). 571
Vaughan v. Menlove (1837) 917, 918, 919, 920
Vaughan v. Taff Vale Railway Co (1860). 920, 1103
Vaughan v. Watt (1840) 854, 1120
Vaughan v. Wilkins (1830). 1115
Vaughan v. Wood (1833). 535
Vazie v. Bretherton (1825) 905, 910
Vegelahn v. Guntner (1896). 1057
Vennall v. Garner (1832). 908
Vere v. Lewis (1789). 752
Vernede v. Weber (1856). 477
Verner v. General and Commercial Investment Trust (1894). 656
Vernon v. Keyes (1812) 409

Vernon v. Vawdry (1740) 573
Verrall v. Robinson (1835) 1121
Vertue v. Jewell (1814). 791
Vicars v. Wilcocks (1806) 305, 541, 544, 928, 1046
Vicat (a person of unsound mind), Re (1886) 276
Victor Mills Ltd v. Shackleton (1912). 1031
Victoria Dairy Co (of Worthing) v. West (1895) 875
Victoria Laundry (Windsor) v. Newman Industries (1949) 548
Victorian Daylesford Syndicate Ld v. Dodd (1905). 869
Victorian Railway Commissioners v. Coultas (1888). 995, 996
Victors v. Davies (1844) 316
Vidler v. Parrott (1864) 285
Villers v. Beaumont (1682). 402
Vincent v. Horlock (1808) 741
Viscount Canterbury v. Attorney General (1843) 919
Vogel, Ex p. (1818) 787
Vorley v. Barrett (1856). 446
Voyle v. Hughes (1854) 258, 259, 262

W. White & Sons v. Harris (1909) 1032
Waddell v. Wolfe (1874) 104
Waddington v. Naylor (1889) 1139
Wade v. Simeon (1846). 376
Wain v. Warlters (1804) 349
Wainewright v. Bland (1835) 689
Waite v. Littlewood (1872). 40, 281, 285, 286
Wake v. Harrop (1861) 446
Wake v. Lock (833) 905
Wake v. Varah (1876) 28, 40
Wakefield, Ex p. (1850). 811
Wakefield v. Maffet (1885) 33
Wakefield v. Newbon (1844) 402
Wakeman v. Duchess of Rutland (1796-7) 414
Wakeman v. Robinson (1823) 909
Walburn v. Ingelby (1833) 618
Walhampton Estate, Re (1884) 266
Walker v. Bartlett (1856) 553
Walker v. Constable (1798) 333
Walker v. Hatton (1842). 541
Walker v. Macdonald (1848) 741
Walker v. Maitland (1821) 713
Walker v. Moore (1829) 99, 100, 539, 540
Walker v. Needham (1841). 1116
Walker v. South Eastern Railway Co (1870). 898
Walker v. Walker (1740). 330
Wall v. Rederiaktiebolaget Luggude (1915). 528
Wallace, Re (1920). 6
Wallace v. King (1788) 872
Waller v. South Eastern Railway Co (1863) 1004
Walley v. Holt (1876). 1114
Wallgrave v. Tebbs (1855). 4
Wallis, Re (1890) 148

Wallis v. Harrison (1838) 160
Wallis v. Morris (1864) 188
Wallis, Son & Wells v. Pratt & Haynes (1910) 494
Wallis v. Smith (1882) 528
Walsby v. Guntner (1896) 1057
Walsh v. Lonsdale Revisted (1987) 161
Walsh v. Wason (1873) 12
Walsh v. Whiteley (1888) 1014, 1015
Walstab v. Spottiswoode (1846) 589, 623
Walter v. Selfe (1851) 1097, 1101, 1108
Walter's Case (1850) 624
Walters v. Northern Coal Mining Co (1855) 131
Walters v. Pfeil (1829) 1136
Walthew v. Mavjorani (1870) 715
Walton v. London, Brighton and South Coast Railway (1866) 934
Walwyn v. Coutts (1815) 240
Wansborough v. Maton (1836) 118
Wanstead Local Board of Health v. William Hill (1863) 1100
Want v. Blunt (1810) 704
Warburton (1870) 1061
Warburton v. Sandys (1845) 271
Ward v. Audland (1845) 257, 259
Ward v. Byrne (1839) 672
Ward v. Hobbs (1878) 479
Warde, Re (1861) 285
Warde, Re (1889) 286
Warde v. Dickson (1859) 106
Warden v. Bailey (1811) 1036
Ware and De Freville Ltd v. Motor Trade Association (1920) 1064
Ware v. Lord Egmont (1854) 409
Waring v. Cox (1808) 760, 761
Warlow v. Harrison (1859) 352, 353, 757
Warner v. Couchman (1912) 1026
Warner v. Jacob (1882) 139
Warner v. Riddiford (1858) 1034
Warner v. Willington (1856) 334
Warren v. Brown (1900) 1078
Warren v. Brown (1902) 170
Warriner v. Rogers (1873) 260
Warrington, Ex p. (1853) 144
Warwick Steamship Co v. Callaghan (1912) 1031
Warwick v. Bruce (1813) 363
Warwick v. Slade (1811) 697
Water v. Taylor (1807) 619
Waterhouse v. Brotherton v. Boswood (1825) 905
Waters v. Monarch Fire Office (1856) 695, 696
Waters v. Taylor (1813) 616
Waters v. Towers (1853) 541, 543
Watkins, Ex p. in Coulston, Re (1873) 873
Watkins v. Great Western Railway (1877) 979
Watkins v. Guest, Keen and Nettlefolds (1912) 1028

Watkins v. Reddin (1861) .... .974
Watkins v. Rymill (1883) .... .475
Watson, Ex p. (1877) .... .762
Watson, Re (1890) 152
Watson, Re, Official Receiver in Bankrupct, Ex p. (1890) .... .875
Watson v. Mainwaring (1813) 709
Watson v. Strickland (1887) 154
Watson v. Weekes (1887) .... .971
Watt's Settlement, Re (1851) .... .275
Watts v. Bucknall (1902) .... .641
Watts v. Christie (1849) .... .767
Watts v. Kelson (1871) .... .167
Watts v. Porter (1854) .... .186
Watts v. Spottiswoode (1843) .... .491
Waugh v. Carver (1793) .... .614, 627
Waugh v. Waugh (1833) .... .41
Weaver, Re (1882) .... .570
Weaver v. Boroughs (1725) 531
Weaver v. Ward (1616) .... .903, 919
Webb v. Bird (1863) .... .169
Webb v. Direct London and Portsmouth Railway Co (1852) 549
Webb v. Earle (1875) 634
Webb v. England (1860) .... .558
Webb v. Rennie (1865) 1008
Webb v. Rorke (1806) .... .145
Webb v. Shropshire Railways Co (1893) 646
Webb v. Wools (1852) .... .37, 246
Webber v. Tivill (1670) 531
Webster, Re (1883) 42
Webster v. Bosanquet (1912) .... .529
Webster v. Dillon (1857) 560
Webster v. Sharp & Co (1904) .... .1030
Webster's Case (1866) 649
Wedd v. Porter (1916) .... .114
Wedderburn v. Wedderburn (1836) .... .616
Wedgewood v. Adams (1843) 549
Wedgwood Coal and Iron, Anderson's Case, Re (1876) .... .635
Weeding v. Aldrich (1839) 1115
Weeke's Settlement, Re (1897) 30
Weiler v. Schilizzi (1856) .... .477
Weir v. Bell (1878) 425, 429, 431, 644
Welfare v. London and Brighton Railway Co (1869) 980
Weller v. Stone (1885) .... .162
Wells v. Allott (1904) 867
Wells v. Joyce (1905) 868
Wells v. Mayor etc of Kingston-upon-Hull (1875) .... .161
Wells v. Ody (1836) .... .1075
Wells v. Porter (1836) .... .632
Welman v. Welman (1880) .... .267
Wenigner's Policy, Re (1910) 692
Wennall v. Adney (1802) .... .362

Wennhak v. Morgan (1888) 1114
West of England and South Wales District Bank, Dale, Re (1879). 604
West India and Pacific Steamship Co v. Guion (1867) 986
West India Telegraph Co v. Home and Colonial Insurance Co (1880) 712, 713
West v. Houghton (1879) 394
West v. Orr (1877) 41, 42
West v. Williams (1899) 150
Westdeutsche Landesbank Girozentrale v. Islington LBC (1996) 608
Western Bank of Scotland v. Addie (1867) 423, 649
Western v. Macdermot (1866). 172
Western v. Russell (1814) 330
Westlake v. Adams (1858) 375
Weston v. Downes (1773) 496
Westover v. Chapman (844) 283
Westzinthus, Re (1843). 762
Weymouth v. Boyer (1792). 566
Whaley Bridge Calico Printing Company v. Green and Smith (1879) 642
Wharton v. Masterman (1895) 244, 252
Whatman v. Gibson (1838) 171, 172, 173, 174, 175
Wheate v. Hall (1809). 17, 82
Wheatley v. Low (1623). 374
Wheatley v. Westminster Brymbo Coal Co (1869)..................................558
Wheatley's Trustee v. H Wheatley Ltd (1901) 876
Wheeldon v. Burrows (1879). 167
Wheeler v. Van Wart (1838). 619
Wheeler v. Whiting (1840) 1034
Wheelton v. Hardisty (1857) 709, 710
Wheelwright v. Walker (1883). 93
Whelpdale v. Cookson (1747) 663
Whichcote v. Lawrence (1798) 404
Whistler v. Forster (1863). 748
Whitaker v. Bank of England (1834) 768
Whitaker v. Edmunds (1834) 745
Whitby v. Mitchell (1890) 19
White (1757) 1096
White v. Bass (1862) 167
White v. Beeton (1861) 488
White v. Bluett (1853) 371
White v. Boulton (1791) 910
White v. Briggs (1848) 15
White v. Briggs (1948) 15
White v. Damon (1802) 373
White v. Garden (1851). 459, 460
White v. Nicholson (1842) 116
White v. Spettigue (1845). 457
White v. Steadman (1913). 989
White v. White (1842). 275
White v. Wilks (1813) 478
Whitecombe v. Jacob (1710). 572, 790
Whitehead v. Bennett (1858) 118
Whitehead v. Greetham (1825) 374
Whitehead v. Harrison (1844) 1116

Whitehead v. Parks (1858) 165
Whitehead v. Reader (1901) 1028
Whitehead v. Tuckett (1812) 1122
Whiteman v. Sadler (1910) 869
White's Trust, Re (1883) 30
Whitfield v. South Eastern Railway Co (1858) 899
Whitham v. Kershaw (1885) 899
Whitlock's Case (1609) 90, 92
Whitmore v. Mackeson (1852) 418
Whitney v. Smith (1869) 269
Whittell v. Dudin (1820) 243
Whitton v. Peacock (1835) 129
Whitwood Chemical Co v. Hardiman (1891) 560
Whitworth v. Gaugain (1846) 186
Whiwill v. Scheer (1838) 318
Wickens v. Evans (1829) 1050
Wickham v. Nicholson (1854) 141
Widdowson v. Duck (1817) 282
Wiffen v. Roberts (1795) 747
Wiffin v. Kinçard (1807) 1035
Wiggett v. Fox (1856) 1009
Wilbraham v. Snow (1670) 1116, 1118
Wild v. Harris (1849) 398
Wild v. Waygood (1892) 1017
Wilde v. Gibson (1848) 420
Wilde v. Minsterley (1640) 1131
Wild's Case (1880) 44
Wilkes v. Hungerford Market Co (1835) 1069
Wilkes v. Steward (801) 283
Wilkins v. Fry (1816) 130
Wilkinson v. Byers (1834) 384
Wilkinson v. Calvert (1878) 113
Wilkinson v. Coverdale (1793) 374
Wilkinson v. Downton (1897) 995, 996
Wilkinson v. Fairrie (1862) 978
Wilkinson v. Hyde (1858) 718
Wilkinson v. Johnston (1824) 588, 589, 751
Wilkinson v. Verity (1871) 1117
Wilkinson's Case, In Madrid Bank, Re (1867) 649
Wilkis v. Wood (1848) 114
Willans v. Taylor (1829) 1037
Willetts v. Watt (1892) 1015
Williams, Re (1914) 43
Williams v. Bayley (1866) 408
Williams v. Birmingham Battery and Metal Co (1899) 1009
Williams v. Bosanquet (1819) 128
Williams v. Cardwardine (1833) 303, 349, 350, 351, 352, 757
Williams v. Currie (1845) 900
Williams v. Eady (1893) 981
Williams v. Earl of Jersey (1841) 161
Williams v. East India Co (1802) 987
Williams v. Everett (1811) 571

Williams v. Germaine (1827)...304
Williams v. Gesse (1837)..1118
Williams v. Groucott, In re (1863) 1127
Williams v. Holland (1833) 907, 908
Williams v. Lewis (1797) 1036
Williams v. Lloyds (1628)...514
Williams v. Mersey Docks and Harbour Board (1905) 998
Williams v. Moor (1843)..363
Williams v. Morris (1841) 162
Williams v. Ocean Coal Co (1907)...1030
Williams v. Owen (1840) 152
Williams v. Reynolds (1865) 538
Williams v. Richards (1852)...971
Williams v. Thorp (1828) 692
Williams v. Trye (1854) 632
Williams v. Williams (1851)..246
Williams v. Williams (1897) 37, 246
Williamson v. Allison (1802) 412
Williamson v. Goold (1823)..144
Willis, Re (1911) 284
Willis v. Bank of England (1835)..412
Willis v. Peckham (1820) 376
Willmott v. Barber (1880) 162
Willson v. Love (1896) 529
Wilmot v. Wilkinson (1827) 104
Wilson, Re (1885)...237
Wilson v. Anderton (1830)..759, 1120
Wilson v. Bennett (1852) 274
Wilson v. Brett (1843)...916
Wilson v. Duguid (1883)..30
Wilson v. Finch Hatton (1877) 117
Wilson v. Fuller (1843) 419
Wilson v. Furness Railway Co (1869) 557
Wilson v. General Iron Screw Co (1878)..537
Wilson v. Hart (1866)...174
Wilson v. Jones (1867)..687
Wilson v. Lancashire and Yorkshire Railway Co (1861)..538
Wilson v. Leonard (1840)..131
Wilson v. Martin (1856) 684
Wilson v. Merry & Cunningham (1868)..1004
Wilson v. Newport Dock Co (1866)..542, 543, 544,
                                                                                545, 546
Wilson v. Ray (1839) 402, 593
Wilson v. Royal Echange Association Co (1811) 717
Wilson v. Townend (1860)...1073
Wilton & Co. v. Osborne (1901) 867
Wimbledon Park Golf Club v. Imperial Insurance Co (1902) 694
Wing v. London General Omnibus Co (1909)..964, 975, 976
Winn v. Bull (1877)...109
Winsmore v. Greenbank (1745)...1041
Winspear v. Accident Insurance Co (1880) 1024
Winter v. Brockwell (1807) 160

Winter v. Lord Anson (1827)...210
Winter v. Perratt (1843) 28, 33
Winterbottom v. Lord Derby (1867) 1069
Winterbottom v. Wright (1837)...924, 925, 943, 963,
                                                                   987, 988, 1045
Wise v. Piper (1879)...17
Wise's Settlement, Re (1913) 11
Withers v. London, Brighton and South Coast
    Railway Co (1916) 1025
Withers v. Reynolds (1831)..487, 488, 532
Withington v. Herring (1829) 757
Withy v. Cottle (1823)..553
Wodehouse v. Farebrother (1855) 322, 447
Wolff v. Horncastle (1798) 685
Wollaston v. Tribe (1869)..267
Wolley v. Jenkins (1856)..244, 261
Wolverhampton and Walsall Railway Co v. London and North
    Western Railway Co (1873) 560
Womersley v. Church (1867)..1083
Wood, Re (1894) 42
Wood v. Abrey (1818) 404
Wood v. Bretherton (1820) 909
Wood v. Conway Corp (1914) 1108
Wood v. Downes (1811)...404
Wood v. Duke of Argyll (1844)..623
Wood v. Dwarris (1856) 710
Wood v. Governor and Co of Copper Miners in
    England (1856)...322
Wood v. Griffith (1818)...550
Wood v. Leadbitter (1845) 160, 161, 162
Wood v. Morewood (1841)..900
Wood v. Scarth (1855)..439, 440, 441
Wood v. Smith (1829) 479
wood v. Sutcliffe (1851) 1081, 1107
Wood v. Thwaites (1800) 782
Wood v. Waterhouse (1819)...912
Wood v. Waud (1849) 162, 1081,
                                                                   1083, 1087
Woodcock v. Houldsworth (1846) 337
Woodford v. Whiteley (1830) 766
Woodhouse v. Jenkins (1832)...101
Woodley v. Metropolitan District Railway Co (1877) 1008
Woodman v. Skuse (1708) 400
Woodman v. Skute (1706) 400
Woodmeston v. Walker (1831)...159, 247, 248
Woods v. Woods (1836) 246
Woodside v. Globe Marine Insurance Co (1896) 717
Woodward v. Gyles (1689)..115, 525
Woodward v. Walton (1807) 1041
Woolam v. Hearn (1802) 439
Wooley v. Batte (1826) 909
Woolf v. Beard (1838) Cases...908

Worcester Corn Exchange Co, Re (1853) 648
Wordall v. Smith (1808) 783
Wormald v. Maitland (1865) 205
Worseley v. De Mattos (1758) 783
Worsley v. Wood (1796) 495, 719
Worth, Ex p. (1859) 421
Worthington v. Curtis (1875) 689
Worthington v. Warrington (1849) 98
Wortley (1851) 59
Wright v. Atkins 245
Wright v. Bell (1818) 553
Wright v. Butler (1830) 566
Wright v. Hennessey (1895) 1054
Wright v. Horton (1887) 656
Wright v. Midland Railway Co (1873) 964
Wright v. Newton (1835) 588
Wright v. Proud (1806) 405
Wright v. Stavert (1860) 161
Wright v. Williams (1836) 163, 1083
Wright v. Woodgate (1835) 1038
Wrightup v. Chamberlain (1839) 541
Wrottesley's Settlement, Re (1911) 11
Wuild v. Holt (1842) 900
Wyatt v. Barwell (1815) 205
Wyatt v. Great Western Railway Company (1865) 932
Wyatt v. Harrison (1832) 1133
Wycherley v. Wycherley (1763) 405
Wyld v. Pickford (1841) 473
Wyndham v. Carew (1841) 125
Wynn Hall Coal Co, Re (1870) 656

Xenos v. Wickham (1866) 697

Yard v. Ward (1769) 1072
Yarmouth v. France (1887) 1009
Yates v. Eastwood (1851) 573
Yates v. Jack (1866) 170, 1076, 1077, 1110
Yates v. South Kirby &c. Collieries (1910) 1025
Yates v. Whyte (1838) 723
Yellowly v. Gower (1855) 116
Yetts v. Norfolk Railway Co (1849) 653
York and North Midland Railway v. Hudson (1845) 405, 663
York Buildings Co v. Mackenzie (1795) 663
Yorkshire Insurance v. Nisbet Shipping (1962) 725
Yorkshire Railway Wagon Co v. Maclure (1882) 870
Yorkshire West Riding Council v. Holmfirth Urban Sanitary
    Authority (1894) 1091
Young Men's Christian Association v. Estill (1913) 367
Young v. Clerk (1720) 373, 415
Young v. Cole (1837) 445, 478
Young v. Grote (1827) 770, 771, 929, 930

Young v. Peachy (1741) 405
Young v. Timmins (1831) 373
Younghusband v. Gisborne (1844). 250, 251

Zagury v. Furnell (1809) 304
Zinck v. Walker (1777) 767, 790
Zunz v. South Eastern Railway Co (1869). 328, 475

TABLE OF STATUTES

1540
Grantees of Reversions Act 1540, 32
    Hen. VIII c. 34 127
1543
Statute of Bankrupts Act 1543, 34 & 35 Hen.
    VIII c. 4 780
1571
Bankrupts Act 1571, 3 Eliz. c. 7 781
Fraudulent Convenyances Act 1571, 13 Eliz.
    c. 5 . . . . .256, 783
Letters Patent Act, 13 Eliz. I c. 6 622
1584
Fraudulent Convayances Act 1584, 27 Eliz.
    c. 4 . . . . 256, 263
1623
Bankrupts Act 1623, 21 Jac I c. 19 789
1677
Statute of Frauds 1677, 29 Cha. II c. 3 329
    s 4 . . . . 330, 349
    s 17 329
1690
Distress for Rent Act 1690, 2 Wm. & M.
    (sess 1) c. 5 120
1696
Administration of Justice Act 1696, 8 & 9
    Will. III c. 11 524
1704
Stamps Act 1833, 3 & 4 Anne c. 9
    s 4 736
1705
Private (See of Dublin) Act 1705, 4 & 5 Anne
    c. 13 524
Taxation Act 1705, 4 & 5 Anne c. 17 . . .781, 785
    s 19 781
1707
Fire Prevention Act 1707 6 Ann,
    c. 31 917
    s 6 1141
    s 7 1141
1708
Middlesex Registry Act 1708,
    7 Ann c. 20 . . . . 204, 205
Trust and Mortgage Estates Act 1708, 7 Ann
    c. 19 270

1709
Taxation etc. Act 1709, 8 Ann c. 4
    s 2 122
1718
Bankrupts Act 1718, 5 Geo. I c. 24
    s 16 781
1720
Charters for Assurance etc Act (Bubble Act)
    1720, 6 Geo. I c. 18 . . . . 617, 618, 619
1724
Adulteration of Tea and Coffee Act 1724,
    1 Geo. I c. 30 697
1725
Frivolous Arrests Act 1725, 12 Geo.
    I c. 29 . . . . 797, 803
1728
Merchant Seamen Act 1728, 2 Geo II c 36
    s 1 377
1730
Landlord and Tenant Act 1730, 4 Geo.
    II c. 28 . . . . .124, 131
Lunatics Act 1730, 4 Geo. II c. 10 270
1731
Bankrupts Act 1731, 5 Geo. II c.
    30 s 10 . . . . .781, 792
1733
Prevention of stock-Jobbing Act (Sir John
    Barnard's Act), 7 Geo. II. c. 8 632
1736
Mortmain Act 1736, 9 Geo. II c. 36 . . . . 4, 241
1737
Distress for Rent Act 1737, 11 Geo. II c. 9 . . .122
1745
Marine Insurance Act,
    19 Geo II c. 37 . . . . 678, 679
1762
Merchant Seamen Act 1762, 2 Geo. III c. 31 . . .377
1772
Metropolitan Buildings Act 1772, 12 Geo.
    III c. 73
    s 37 1141
1774
Fire Prevention (Metropolis) Act 1774, 14
    Geo III c. 78 917

Fire Prevention (Metropolis) Act 1774, 14
    Geo III c. 78 (cont.)
    s 83 694
    s 86 1141
Gambling Act 1774, 14 Geo. III .676, 679, 694
Insolvent Debtors Act 1774, 14 Geo.
    III c. 77. 798
1776
Bills of Exchange Act 1776, 17 Geo III
    c. 30 734
Insolvent Debtors Act 1776, 16 Geo.
    III c. 38. 798
1777
Grants and Life Annuities Act 1777, 17 Geo.
    III c. 26. 591
1778
Insolvent Debtors Act 1778, 18 Geo.
    III c. 52. 798
1779
Inferior Courts Act 1779, 19 Geo.
    III c. 70 . . . . 797, 803
1781
Insolvent Debtors Act 1781, 21 Geo.
    III c. 63. 798
1786
Hemp and Flax Act 1786, 26 Geo.
    III c. 43. 851
1788
Stage Coaches Act 1788, 28 Geo.
    III c. 57. 904
1790
Stage Coaches Act 1790, 30 Geo.
    III c. 56. 904
1795
Stamps Act 1795, 35 Geo. III c. 63. 697
1796
Bank of England Stock Act 1796, 36 Geo.
    III c. 90 271
1800
Accumulations Act (Thelluson Act) 1800,
    39 & 40 Geo. III, c. 98 21
Pawnbrokers Act 1800, 39 & 40 Geo.
    III c. 99 . . . . 851, 855
    s 2 851
    s 6 852
    s 15. 853
    s 16. .852, 853, 854
    s 24 852
1803
Costs Act 1803, 43 Geo. III c. 46. 803
1806
Bankrupts Act 1806, 46 Geo. III c. 135 . . . 788

Stage Coaches, etc. Act 1806, 46 Geo.
    III c. 136. 904
1807
Debts of Traders Act 1807, 47 Geo. III Sess. 2)
    c. 74. 182
1809
Bankrupts (England and Ireland)
    Act 1809, 49 Geo. III c. 121 788
    s 28 792
1810
Stage Coaches, etc. (Great Britain) Act 1810,
    50 Geo. III c. 48 904
1811
Frivolous Arrests Act 1811, 51 Geo.
    III c. 124. 797
1813
Inrolment of Grants and Annuities Act 1813,
    53 Geo. III c. 141 . . . . 143, 591
1814
Stamps Act 1814, 54 Geo. III c. 144 697
1815
Apothecaries Act 1815, 55 Geo. III c. 194. . . 882
1816
Bankrupts (England) Act 1816, 56 Geo. III c. 137
    s 1 788
Insolvent Debtors (England) Act 1816,
    56 Geo. III c. 102
    s 1 799
1817
Distress (Costs) Act 1817, 57 Geo. III c. 93. . . .122
1820
Capital Punishment Act 1820, 1 Geo.
    IV c. 15 . . . . , , 785
Insolvent Debtors (England) Act 1820,
    Geo. IV c. 119 . . . . 798, 799
    s 17. 799
    s 18. 799
1821
Lunatics Act 1821, 1 & 2 Geo. IV c. 114 271
Regulation of Acceptances Act 1821,
    1 & 2 Geo. IV c. 78 . . . . .734, 735
    s 2 734
Steam Engines Furnaces Act 1821, 1 & 2 Geo.
    IV c. 41. 1094
1822
Duties on Stage-coaches, etc. Act 1822, 3 Geo.
    IV c. 95
    s 11. 904
Insolvent Debtors (England) Act 1822, 3 Geo.
    IV c. 123. 799
Punishment for Manslaughter, etc. Act 1822,
    3 Geo. IV c. 38. 904

Sale of Bread (Metropolis) Act, Geo. IV
    c. 106 82
Warranty of Attorney Act 1822, 3 Geo.
    IV c. 39. . . . . 523, 860
1823
Factors Act 1823, 4 Geo. IV c. 83 761
Masters and Servants Act 1823, 4 Geo.
    IV c. 34, 299
1824
Insolvent Debtors (England) Act 1824,
    5 Geo. IV c. 61. 799
1825
Bankrupts (England) Act 1825, 6 Geo.
    IV c. 16
    s 2 . . . . .781, 783, 792
    s 4 793
    s 6 793
    s 15. 781
    s 59 810
    s 74 . . . . 121, 781
    s 81. 523
    s 108 523
    s 112. 785
    s 114. 794
    s 130. 811
    s 131. 363
    s 133. 794
    s 134. 794
    s 230 810
Factors Act 1825, 6 Geo. IV c. 94 . . . 1122, 1123
Infant Lunatics etc. Act 1825, 6 Geo.
    IV c. 74. . . . . .65, 271
1826
Board of Trade (President) Act 1826, 7 Geo.
    IV. c. 32 523
Country Bankers Act 1826, 7 Geo.
    IV c. 46 728
    s 9 619
    s 13. 619
    s 14 619
Insolvent Debtors (England) Act 1826, 7 Geo.
    IV c. 57. . . . . 523, 798, 799
    s 31. 121
    s 61. 363
Licensing of Stage Coaches Act 1826, 7 Geo.
    IV. c. 33. 523
1827
Imprisonment for Debt Act 1813, 7 & 8 Geo.
    IV c. 71. . . . . 800, 801, 803
Larceny (England) Act 1827, 7 & 8 Geo.
    IV c. 29
    s 57 . . . . 459, 461

Spring Guns Act 1827, 7 & 8 Geo.
    IV c. 18. 977
1828
Average Clause Act 1828, 8 Geo. IV c. 13 . . .721
Indemnity Act 1828, 9 Geo. IV c. 6 1040
Stamps on Fire Insurances Act 1828,
    9 Geo. IV c. 13. 330
    s 17. 330
Statute of Frauds Amendment Act 1828,
    9 Geo. IV c. 4
    s 15. 363
1830
Carriers Act 1830, 11 Geo. IV & 1 Will.
    IV c. 68 . . . . .458, 473, 543, 696, 915
    s 1 915
    s 6 915
Debtors Act, 1 Will IV c. 47 182
Executors Act 1830, 11 Geo. IV & 1 Will.
    IV c. 40 242
Transfer of Trust Estates Act 1830, 11 Geo.
    IV and 1 Will. IV c. 60 271
1832
Prescription Act 1832, 2 & 3 Will.
    4 c. 71. . . . . .58, 169, 363, 1077
    s 3 . . . . 1073, 1076, 1077, 1078
Tithe Act 1832, 2 & 3 Will.
    IV c. 100. .169, 170
1833
Administration of Estates Act 1833,
    3 & 4 Will. IV c. 104. 182
Bank of England Act 1833, 3 & 4 Will.
    IV c. 98 . . . . 729, 764
Bank Continuation Act (1833), 3 & 4 Will. IV
    c. 98 144
Dower Act 1833, 3 & 4 Will. IV c. 105 . . . 9, 58
Fines and Recoveries Act 1833, 3 & 4 Will.
    IV c. 74. . . . . .58, 103, 212
Inheritance Act 1833, 3 & 4 Will.
    IV c. 106. . . . . 6, 58
Payment of Debt out of Real Estate Act 1833,
    3 & 4 Will. IV c. 104. 55
Real Property Limitation Act 1833,
    3 & 4 Will. IV c. 27. 58
Stamps Act 1833, 3 & 4 Will. IV c. 23
    s 5 721
1834
Apportionment Act 1834, 4 & 5 Will.
    IV c. 22. 58
Trading Companies Act 1834, 4 & 5 Will.
    IV c. 94 619
Trust Property Escheat Act 1834,
    4 & 5 Will. IV c. 23. . . . . .58, 271

1835
Bankruptcy Act 1835, 5 & 6 Will. IV c. 29
    s 21................................ 795
1836
Bills of Exchange Act 1836, 6 & 7 Will 4
    c. 58............................737
    s 8(5)............................. 739
Bread Act 1836, 6 & 7 Will. c.37.........881
Marriage Act 1836, 6 & 7 Will.
    4 c. 85..........................55, 59
Registration of Births, Deaths and Mar-
    riages Act 1836, 6 & 7 Will. 4 c. 86 ... 59
Tithe Communication Act 1836, 6 & 7 Will.
    IV c. 71......................... 85
1837
Wills Act 1837, 7 Will. IV & 1 Vict.
    c. 26 .... 3, 6, 19, 22, 23, 44, 58, 59
    s 24 6
    s 25 6
1838
Judgments Act 1838, 1 & 2 Vict.
    c. 110......................803, 804
    s 11.....................55, 61, 144, 185,
                            186, 188, 524
    s 58 121
    s 91.............................363
    s 11..........................73, 802
    s 13.......................... 73, 144
Supply Act 1838, 1 & 2 Vict. c. 11
    s 7 185
1839
Judgment Act 1839, 2 & 3 Vict.
    c. 11........................ 144, 186
Metropolitan Courts Act 1839, 2 & 3 Vict.
    c. 71
    s 34 ....855, 858
    s 39 ....122, 124
Metropolitan Police Act 1839, 2 & 3 Vict. c. 47
    s 67 122
Usury Act 1839, 2 & 3 Vict. c. 37......144, 851
1840
Admiralty Court Act 1840, 3 & 4 Vict.
    c. 65 687
Judgments Act 1840, 3 & 4 Vict. c. 82 186
Railway Regulation Act 1840, 3 & 4 Vict.
    c. 97 985
Settled Estates Drainage Act 1840, 3 & 4 Vict.
    c. 55........................... 86
1841
Conveyance by Release without Lease Act
    1841, 4 & 5 Vict. c. 21 60
Copyhold Enfranchisement Act 1841, 4 & 5
    Vict. c. 35........................ 59

Court of Chancery Act 1841, 5 Vic.
    c. 5.............................191
    s 4 191
1842
Bankruptcy Act 1842, 5 & 6 Vict.
    c. 122.......................... 806
    ss 11–14 806
    s 36 811
    s 39 806
    s 43 363
    s 64 796
    sch Z............................811
Insolvent Deptors Act 1842, 5 & 6 Vic.
    c. 116.......................... 807
    s 4 807
1843
Copyhold Act 1843, 6 & 7 Vict.
    c. 23............................ 59
Scientific Societies Act 1843, 6 & 7 Vict.
    c. 36 860
1844
Arrangement between Debtors and
    Creditors Act 1844, 7 & 8 Vict.
    c. 70 807
Bank Charter Act 1844 7 & 8
    Vict......................... 729, 764
Bankruptcy Act 1844 7 & 8 Vict. c. 96806
Burning of Farm Buildings Act 1844,
    7 & 8 Vict. c. 62 90
Cheap Trains Act, 7 & 8 Vict. c. 85 968
Execution Act 1844, 7 & 8 Vict. c. 96
    s 57 .... 807, 836
    s 58 836
Factories Act 1844, 7 & 8 Vict. c. 15..... 1007
Joint Stock Banks Act 1844, 7 & 8
    Vict. c. 113
    s 10 630
Joint Stock Companies Act 1844,
    7 & 8 Vict. c. 110
    s 28 .... 662, 738
    ss 34-36....................... 621, 622
    s 66 ....391, 622, 623, 624,
                        625, 627, 628, 629
Joint Stock Companies Winding-Up
    Act 1844, 7 & 8 Vict.
    c. 110.................... 619, 621, 624,
                            625, 627, 630
Metropolitan Buildings Act 1844,
    7 & 8 Vict. c. 84 1071
Railway Regulation Act 1844,
    7 & 8 Vict. c. 85...................73
Transfer of Property Act 1844, 7 & 8 Vict.
    c. 76 .... 60, 61, 62, 71, 181, 182, 190

s 2 61
s 5 63
s 8 63
1845
Companies Clauses Consolidation Act 1845,
    8 & 9 Vict. c. 16. . . . . 622, 629, 636,
    646, 662
ss 29–35. 120
Conveyance of Real Property Act 1845, 8 & 9
    Vict. c. 119 . . . . 72, 90
Gaming Act 1845. . . . . 594, 595, 632,
    633, 680
Inclosure Act 1845, 8 & 9 Vict. c. 118
s 147. 86
Indemnity (Amendment) Act 1845 8 Vict.
    c. 24 836
Lands Clauses Consolidation Act 1845,
    8 Vict. c. 18 85
s 8 73
Law of Real Property Amendment Act 1845,
    8 & 9 Vict. c. 106 . . . . 61, 66, 90, 190
s 6 63
Leases Act 1845, 8 & 9 Vict. c. 124 72
Railway Clauses Act 1845, 8 & 9 Vict.
    c. 20 . . . . .163, 1104
s 105. 986
Railways Clauses Consolidation Act 1845,
    8 Vict. c. 20
s 97 120
Satisfied Terms Act 1845, 8 & 9 Vict.
    c. 12. 72
Small Debts Act 1845, 8 & 9 Vict.
    c. 127. . . . . 808, 836
1846
County Courts (England) Act 1846,
    9 & 10 Vict. c. 95. 836
s 98 . . . . 808, 836
s 99 . . . . 808, 836
Fatal Accidents Act 1846, 9 & 10 Vict.
    c. 93 . . . . 997, 998, 1001
Importation of Corn Amendment Act (Corn
    Laws) 1846 9 & 10 Vict. c. 22 779
Nuisances Removal, etc. Act 1846, 9 & 10
    Vict. c. 96 1094
Rateable Property (Ireland) Act 1846, 9 & 10
    Vict. c. 110
s 45 738
1847
Bankruptcy etc Act 1847, 10 & 11 Vict.
    c. 102. . . . . .796, 807
s 1 796
s 2 796

Harbours, Docks and Piers Clauses Act 1847,
    10 & 1 Vict. c. 27
s. 45. 120
Market and Fairs Clauses Act 1847,
    10 & 11 Vict. c. 4 120
Towns Improvement Clauses Act 1847,
    10 & 11 Vict. c. 34 1094
Trustees Relief Act 1847, 10 & 11 Vict.
    c. 96 . . . . .235, 236
Waterworks Clauses Act 1847, 10 & 11
    Vict. c. 17 .163, 287
1848
Incumbered Estates (Ireland) Act, 11 & 12
    Vict. c. 48 197
Joint Stock Companies Winding-Up Act
    1848, 11 & 12 Vict. c. 45 . . . . .619, 621, 630
Loan Societies Act 1848, 11 & 12 Vict. c. 64
s. 64. 1094
Nuisances Removal, etc. Act 1848, 11 & 12
    Vict. c. 123 1094
1849
Bankruptcy Consolidation Act 1849, 12 & 13
    Vict. c. 106. . . . . 363, 808, 816
s 125. 816
s 133. 815
s 182. 810
s 198. 813
s 201 811
s 211. 809
ss 251–254. 810
s 255. 811
s 256 . . . . .810, 813
s 257 813
ss 257-259 810
Incumbered Estates (Ireland) Act 1849,
    12 & 13 Vict. c. 77 197
Nuisances Removal, etc. Act 1849, 12 & 13
    Vict. c. 111 1094
Private Money Drainage Act 1849, 9 & 10
    Vict. c. 101. 85
Trustees Relief Act 1849, 12 & 13 Vict.
    c. 74. 236
1850
County Courts Extension Act 1850,
    13 & 14 Vict. c. 61
s 11. 570
Stamp Act 1850, 3 & 4 Vict. 97 59
Trustee Act 1850, 13 & 14 Vict.
    c. 60 . . . . 271, 274,
    275, 276
s 9 275
s 10 275

Trustee Act 1850, 13 & 14 Vict. c. 60 (cont.)
   s 32 274
   s 33. 274
   s 34 275
   s 35. 275
   s 37 274
   s 38 274
   s 39 274
   s 40 274
   s 41 274
   s 42 274
   s 43 274
   s 44 274
1851
Christ's Hospital Estate Act 1851,
   14 & 15 Vict. c. 2 113
Episcopal and Capitular Estate Acts 1851,
   14 & 15 Vict. c. 104 113
Landlord and Tenant Act 1851,
   14 & 15 Vict. c. 25
   s. 3 .... 118, 119
Steam Navigation Act 1851,
   14 & 15 Vict. c. 79 985
1852
Chancery Procedure Act 1852,
   15 & 16 Vict. c. 86 141
   s 48 141
Common Law Procedure Act 1852,
   15 & 16 Vict. c. 76 ....1116, 1117
   s 3 569
   s 27 .... 524, 888
   s 41 569
   s 49 569
   sch B..............................314
Trustee Act 1852, 15 & 16 Vict. c. 55 271
   s 6 275
   s 7 275
   s 9 275
1853
Smoke Nuisance Abatement (Metropolis)
   Act 1853 1094
Stamp Act 1853 .... 730, 772
   s 19........................ 772, 775, 777
Succession Duty Act 1853
   s 42 183
   s 44 183
   s 52 183
1854
Bankruptcy Act 1854 .... 808, 816
   s 224 809
Common Law Procedure Act 1854 ... 321, 607
   s 2 556

s 28 59
ss 50–57 321
s. 68. 321
s 78 .... 556, 1115
s. 79. 321
s. 83. 321
Episcopal and Capitular Estate
   Act 1854 113
Merchant Shipping Act 1854........ 985, 999
Railway and Canal Traffic
   Act 1854 .... 474, 967
   s 7 474
Stamp Act 1854
   s. 27
1855
Judgments Act 1855 .... 144, 186
   s 12. 185
Limited Liability Act 1855.............. 780
Metropolitan Building Act 1855.........1071
Nuisances Removal Act 1855 1094
   ss 55–56..........................1094
1856
Bankruptcy (Scotland) Act 1856
   ss 35–40 820
Companies Act 1856. 339
   s 43 738
Crossed Cheques Act. 775, 1856
Joint Stock Companies
   Act 1856 .... 629, 630, 662
   s 62 629
   s 63 629
   s 66 629
Settled Estates Act 1856........ 81, 87, 88, 193
   s 9 89
   s 10 89
   s 32 90
1857
Fraudulent Trustees Act 1857.......... 288
   ss 5–8 661
Inclosure Act 1857. 85
Joint Stock Companies Act 1857 629
   s 19. 629
Obscene Publications Act 1857.......... 883
1858
Chancery Amendment Act 1858 1108
Chancery Amendement Act (Lord Cairns'
   Act) 1858 ....322, 540, 551, 552
Copyholds Act 1858 59
Crossed Cheques Act 1858 .... 775, 776
   s 2 777
   s 10 777
   s 90 777

Joint Stock Companies Act 1858 629
Local Government Act 1858
  s 108 1094
Settled Estates Act 1858 88
Settled Land Act (1858) 49
  s 3 55
  s 4 55
Universities and Colleges Estates
  Act 1858 113
1859
County Courts Judges Act 1859 838
Law of Property Amendment and Trustees
  Relief Act 1859 188,
                           276, 284
  ss 4–9 . . . . 125, 182
  ss 14–18 189
  s 21 276
  s 23 . . . . .182, 184
  s 30 290
  s 32 284
Pawnbrokers Act 1859 855
1860
Ecclesiastical Commissioners Act 1860 . . . 113
Law of Property Further Amendment
  Act 1860
  s 1 . . . . 145, 184, 185, 188, 284
  s 2 . . . . 145, 184, 188
  s 3 184
  s 10 284
  s 11 284
  s 12 . . . . 284, 285
Nuisances Removal Act 1860 1094
Trustees and Mortgagees
  Act 1860 . . . . 90, 91, 92, 137,
                     182, 274, 276, 284
  s 2 106
  s 25 284
  s 28 . . . . 275, 276
  s 29 182
  s 53 93
1861
Bankruptcy Act 1861 . . . . 820, 837
  s 4 837
  s 116 822
  s 117 822
  s 125 821
  s 126 821
  s 127 822
  s 128 822
  s 159 816
  s 221 816

Larceny Act 1861 . . . . .463, 466, 467, 468
  s 82 661
  s 84 661
  s 85 827
1862
Chancery Regulation Act 1862 . . . . . 1107, 1108
General Companies Act 1862 . . . . 630, 631,
                634, 647, 652, 656,
              658, 659, 662, 738
  s 47 739
  s 161 648
  s 162 648
Land Registry Act 1862
  s 32 195
Merchant Shipping Act 1862 985
Transfer of Land Act 1862 . . . . 198, 200
1863
Companies Clauses Act 1863
  s 14 634
India Stock Certificates to Bearer Act 1863
  s 4 286
1864
Improvement of Land Act
    1864 . . . . 8, 82, 85, 284
  s 60 284
Judgments Act 1864 . . . . 145, 188, 189, 190
Merchantile Law Amendment
  Act 1856 . . . . .188, 556, 724
  s 2 556
Settled Estates Act Amendment
  Act 1864 88
1865
County Courts (Equity Jurisdiction)
  Act 1865
  s 1 236
Crown Suits Act 1865 188
  s 49 188
Partnership Law Amendment
  Act 1865 627
1866
Isle of Man Customs, Harbours, and Public
  Purposes Act 1866 697
Sanitary Act 1866 .1095
1867
Companies Act 1867 . . . . 641, 655, 689
  s 38 . . . . .428, 641, 642, 643
County Courts Act 1867
  s 24 236
County Courts Act Amendment
  Act 1867
  s 5 570

Investment of Trust Funds Act 1867. 284, 286
Limited Liability Act 1867. 649
Policies of Assurance Act 1867. 692
Sales of Shares and Stock in Joint Stock
    Banking Companies Act (Leeman's Act)
    1867. 638
Sales of Reversions Act 1867. 403
1868
Bankruptcy Amendment Act 1868 821
Ecclesiastical Commissioners
    Acts 1868 113
Policies of Marine Insurance
    Act 1868 689
1869
Bankruptcy Act 1869 . . . . . . 647, 820, 822, 825
   s 5 647
   s 9 266
   s 48 820
   Sch. 1. 648
Debtors Act 1869
   s 5 837
   ss 12-20. 820
Debts of Deceased Persons Act 1869. 183
1870
Bearer Act 1870
   s 29 286
Inland Revenue Repeal Act 721, 1870
Life Assurance Companies Act 1870. 630
   s 21. 648
Limited Owners Residences Act 1870. 85
Married Women's Property Act
   1870. . . . . 8, 49, 323
Stamp Act 1870 59
1871
Debenture Stock Act 1871 284
   s 1 284
Limited Owners Residences Act 1871 85
Lodgers Goods Protection Act 1871
   s 3 . . . . .123, 872
   s 4 . . . . 872, 873
Metropolitan Board of Works (Loans)
   Act 1871
   s 13. 284
1872
Borough Fund Act 1872. 164
Indian Contract Act 1872 . . . . .308, 369,
                            386, 433, 485
   s 4 345
   s 62 369
   s 63 386
   s 109 485
Life Assurance Companies Act 1872. 651

Pawnbrokers Act 1872 . . . . .853, 855, 857
   s 22 857
   s 24 857
   s 25 871
   s 29 855
   s 34 858
Railways Regulation Act 1872 1001
1873
Judicature Act 1873. . . . .161, 189, 320, 425, 693
   s 24(1) 322
   s 24(2) 322
   s 24(5) 322
   s 25(8) 189
   s 24(7) 439
1874
Infants Relief Act 1874. 363
Leases and Sales of Settled Estates
   Amendment Act 1874 88
Vendor and Purchaser Act 1874. 107
   s 5 277
1875
Agricultural Holdings Act 1875. 119
Conspiracy and Protection of Property
   Act 1875 . . . . 1060, 1063
Judicature Act 1875. 320
Land Transfer Act 1875 . . . . .179, 200, 203,
                         214, 217, 218, 220
   s 10 220
   s 48 277
   s 49 223
Local Loans Act 1875 284
   s 6 286
   s 21. 286
   s 27 284
Public Health Act 1875. . . . . . . 164, 1071, 1088,
                     1090, 1092, 1095
   s 13. 1088
   ss 15–17 1080
   s 17. 1090
   s 21. 1090
   s 299 . . . . .1088, 1091
Sale of Food and Drugs Act 1875 881
1876
Crossed Cheques Act 1876 774
   s 9 777
   s 12. 772
   s 80 777
Rivers Pollution Prevention Act
   1876. . . . . 1088, 1092
   s 3 . . . . .1080, 1090,
                              1091, 1092
   s. 4. 1092

1877
Contingent Remainders Act 1877 64
Factors Act 1877 1124
Select Committee on the Companies
    Act 1877 .641, 655
1878
Bills of Sale Act 1878 . . . . . . .637, 816, 859, 875
    s 10 860
Mercantile Law Amendment Act 1878 . . . 734
1880
Employers Liability Act 1880 . . . . 677, 1012,
    1013, 1016, 1017
Ground Game Act 1880 119
1881
Conveyancing and Law of Property
    Act 1881 . . . . .91, 107, 137, 208,
                                 209, 276, 277
    s 3(6) 107
    s 14 127
    s 19 . . . . 137, 141
    s 20 . . . . 137, 141
    s 21 . . . . 137, 141, 212
    s 25 141
    s 30 277
Solicitors Remuneration Act 1881 . . . . 211, 212
1882
Bills of Sale (Amendment) Act 1882 154,
                    156, 637, 861, 862, 875
    s 7 154
    s 9 154
Bills of Exchange Act 1882 . . . . .734, 739,
                    754, 777, 778, 864
    s 7(3) 753
    s 8(3) 741
    s 16 743
    s 19 735
    s 24 750
    s 27(1)(b) 747
    s 28(2) 748
    s 29(3) 748
    s 30(2) 746
    s 55(2) 751
    s 60 777
    s 79(2) 778
    s 82 . . . . 773, 777
    s 90 749
Boiler Explosion Act 1882 985
Conveyancing Act 1882 . . . . 91, 208
    s 2 211
    s 3 210
Married Women's Property Act 1882 . . . 8, 49
Settled Land Act 1882 . . . . 79, 81, 91,
                    92, 112, 208, 287

1883
Agricultural Holdings Act 1883 . . . . . . 119, 123
    ss 44-45 123
Bankruptcy Act 1883 . . . . 651, 827, 828,
                                 829, 830
    s 11 829
    s 13 829
    s 28 826
    s 47 266
    s 54 823
    s 121 847
    s 122 . . . . 845, 847, 848
    s 122(1) 845
    s 131 . . . . 826, 828, 831,
                                 832, 846, 861
1884
Merchant Shipping Bill 1884 683
Yorkshire Registries Act 1884 206,
                                 207, 221
1885
Bills of Lading Act 1855 760
Housing of the Working Classes
    Act 1885 94
Yorkshire Registries Amendment
    Act 1885 . . . . .207, 221
1887
Allotments and Cottage Gardens
    Compensation for Crops
    Act 1887 119
1888
County Courts Act 1888 865
    s 67 866
Indian Companies Act 1888 656
Land Charges Registration and Searches
    Act 1888 . . . . .184, 190, 213
Law of Distress Amendment Act
    1888 . . . . .123, 873
    s 4 873
    s 6 872
Trustee Act 1888 .213
    s 3 291
    s 4 291
    s 4(1) 292
    s 5292
    s 8 293
1889
Factors Act 1889 . . . . 761, 762, 871,
                                 872, 1124
    s 9 871
Trust Investment Act 1889 . . . . 286, 287
    s 3 287
    s 4 287

s 21 287

1890
　Bankruptcy Act 1890 . . . . 827, 864
　　s 23 . . . . .864, 866
　　s 25 832
　Companies Act 1890
　　s.8 651
　Companies (Winding Up) Act 1890
　　s 29 . . . . 638, 651, 652, 668
　Directors Liability Act 1890 . . . . 644, 651, 652
　Housing of the Working Classes
　　(Amendment) Act 1890 94
　Settled Land Act 1890 92
　Tenants Compensation Act 1890 119
1891
　Middlesex Registry Act 1891 206
　Mortmain and Charitable Uses Act 1891 . 241
1892
　Bettings and Loans (Infants) Act 1892
　　s 2 867
　Conveyancing Act 1892 127
1893
　Married Women's Property
　　Act 1893 . . . . 8, 49
　Sale of Goods Act 1893 . . . . 468, 485
　　s 11(1)(a) 494
　　s 11(1)(b) 490
　　s 11(c) 478
　　s 14(2) 448
　　s 19(3) 761
　　s 24(2) 470
　　s 25(2) 762
　　s 31(2) 488
　　s 47 762
　　s 51 535
　　s 52 556
　　ss 14 483
　　ss 14(1) 483
　　ss 15 483
　Trustee Act 1893 . . . . 277, 284
　　s 1 287
　　s 5 284
　　s 8(1) 292
　　s 9 292
　　s 10 277
　　s 12 277
　　s 34 277
　Voluntary Conveyances Act 1893 266
1894
　Finance Act 1894 184
　　ss 8 184
1895
　Law of Distress Amendment Act 1895 123

Market Gardeners Compensation
　　Act 1895 119
1896
　Judicial Trustees Act 1896 . . . . .237, 667
　　s 3293
　Life Assurance Companies (Payment
　　into Court) Act 1896 693
　Public Trustee Act 1896 237
1897
　Land Transfer Act 1897 . . . . 23, 184, 201,
　　　　　　　　　　　　　　220, 221, 222, 228
　　s 13 184
　Workmen's Compensation Act 1897 . . . .
　　　　　　　　　　　　　　　　　1018–1032
　　Sch. 1, para. 17 1031
1899
　Bodies Corporate (Joint Tenancies)
　　Act 1899 237
1900
　Agriculture Holdings Act 1900 . . . . . . .49, 119
　　s 6 119
　Companies Act 1900 . . . . .638, 642,
　　　　　　　　　　　　　　　　　　656, 670
　　s 10 642
　　s 14 638
　　s 38 640
　Land Charges Act 1900 190
　Money Lenders Act 1900 . . . . . . 863, 867, 869
　　s 1(1) 867
1904
　Money Lenders Act 1904 . . . . 863, 869
1906
　Agricultural Holdings Act 1906 119
　Bills of Exchange (Crossed Cheques)
　　Act 1906 778
　Marine Insurance Act 1906 . . . . 681, 685,
　　　　　　　　　　　　　　　　688, 717, 718
　　s 5(2) 688
　　s 9 679
　　s 18(1) 700
　　s 20(5) 699
　　s 27(3) 682
　　s 33(3) 703
　　s 51 688
　　s 60(2)(ii) 717
　　s 80(2) 722
　Trade Disputes Act 1906
　　s 3 1064
　　s. 6 1023
1907
　Companies Act 1907 . . . . 156, 157, 657, 667
　　s 2 657

s 14 156

s 32 667

1908

Agricultural Holdings Act 1908 119

Companies (Consolidation) Act 1908

s 63 739

s 77 739

s 279 294

Fatal Accidents (Damages) Act 1908..... 998

Law of Distress Amendment Act 1908 123

s 4 873

1909

Housing of the Working Classes
    (Amendment) Act 1909 94

Marine Insurance (Gambling Policies) Act
    1909 681

1911

Conveyancing Act 1911

s 5 140

s 8(1) 278

s 19............................. 137, 141

Money Lenders Act 1911 869

1913

Bankruptcy and Deeds of
    Arrangement Act 1913..........831, 832

s 1 829

1916

Larceny Act 1916..................... 470

1925

Administration of Estates Act 1925........23

1964

Perpetuities and Accumulations
    Act 1964....................... 48, 64

1969

Employers Liability (Compulsory
    Insurance) Act 1969...............1021

Part One

PROPERTY

I

Succession, Inheritance, and the Family

1. THE FORMS OF FAMILY PROVISION

Demand for a range of devices to facilitate family provision had long accounted
for much of property law's formidable bulk. Wills were one form, *inter vivos* settlements a portfolio of others. There is a continuity of content between them;
settlements were both models for wills and constraints upon them. The emphasis
in this chapter is on wills, but for the most part their content is treated in conjunction with settlements. In that way context is provided for one of its major
themes, which is to consider how judges approached the task of interpreting
wills—which was a major concern of the legal literature—and how that changed.
How far would judges strive to achieve for a testator the usual forms of family
provision, and how far would they let the consequences of ambiguity or error lie
where they fell?

The supposition throughout much of this chapter is that 'wealth was a family
affair', as Jim McAloon put it of one expatriate British community.[1] It need not
be so, of course. For a testator intent on making a series of independent dispositions what mattered were the rules of capacity to make a will, the rules of formal
validity, and a few traps by way of rules of interpretation for even simple gifts, if
they concerned real property. Much of that was tidied up by the Real Property
Commissioners in their report in 1833, leading to the Wills Act 1837.[2] The result
was a rational code of formal validity that lasted with only minor amendment
through to the end of our period. In one respect it did require wills of personalty
to be more formal than hitherto, but in reducing to one (and one exception) the
form of a valid will, and requiring for that one that the will be attested by two
witnesses, the Act simplified and standardized what had been markedly different
rules for wills of realty and wills of personalty.[3] That enabled property to be dealt
with in bulk more easily than before.

---

[1] J. McAloon, *No Idle Rich* (Dunedin, 2002), 75.
[2] *RC on Real Property*, 4th Report, *PP* 1833 (226), xxii, 1; 7 Will. IV & 1 Vict. c. 26.
[3] T. Jarman, *A Treatise on Wills* (1844), i, 11–26, 69–105.

Such a sharp formal line between testamentary instruments and others did not always suit the indecisive, the anxious, or the devious. Composites, where the formally attested will told only part of the story and other obligations were contained in informal documentation or perhaps transmitted merely orally, could still be valid, though many were not. Judges throughout our period applied principles established before its beginning, broadly that a will could incorporate unattested documentation provided that it existed when the will was executed and that it could be clearly identified. Documents meant to modify or supplement an existing will were treated as codicils, whatever the deceased's wishes in that respect, and must satisfy the formal requirements of a will.

On the other hand the principles of secret trusts were well established too.[4] Someone who induced a testamentary gift to him or herself by undertaking to make provision out of it for another would be held to a trust to that effect, valid, the judges said, because to insist on formal writing and witnessing for that provision would facilitate the very frauds and perjuries that formal requirements were meant to prevent. Since the fraud consisted only of denying a commitment intended to be binding, the way was open to using nominal legatees or devisees as conduits for transmission to a concealed true beneficiary. In twentieth-century presentations the suggestion is often that secret trusts primarily benefited mistresses and illegitimate children, which is perhaps how they had come to be used. While such cases certainly can be found, more often the early nineteenth-century case law concerned secret trusts of lands for charity—typically to build chapels or schools to be named after the donor—which if expressed in the will would be invalidated by the Statute of Mortmain.[5] Of course, so would the secret trust once detected, but the reasoning necessarily included that the trust bound the devisee which, while invalidating the particular instance, reinforced the principle as a whole.

The well-advised charitably intended had therefore to avoid obligation altogether, trusting both that the devisees would honour the hope and that judges would take the stern view that an heir who alleged fraud must show something unequivocal, as increasingly they did.[6] A similar strictness of proof came to be applied to family cases too, akin to the trend away from holding that merely

---

[4] T. Lewin, *A Practical Treatise on Trusts* (2nd edn, 1842), 34–42 (clarified from his 1st edn).

[5] *Podmore* v. *Gunning* (1832) 5 Sim. 485 (daughters); *Muckleston* v. *Brown* (1801) 6 Ves. 52; *Stickland* v. *Aldridge* (1804) 9 Ves. 516; *Russell* v. *Jackson* (1852) 10 Hare 204 and cases in the next note (charities).

[6] Contrast *Briggs* v. *Penny* (1849) 3 De G. M. & G. 525 with *Wallgrave* v. *Tebbs* (1855) 2 K. & J. 313; *Jones* v. *Badley* (1867) LR 3 Eq 635 (1868) LR 3 Ch App 362; and *McCormick* v. *Grogan* (1869) LR 4 HL 82. A well-advised non-obligor can be seen in *Lomax* v. *Ripley* (1855) 2 Sm. & G. 48, and for one who could not bring himself to do as he had been advised see *Moss* v. *Cooper* (1861) 1 J. & H. 352.

precatory words imposed a trust.[7] Perhaps (who can tell with something secret?) strictly private secret trusts became more vulnerable to invalidation whereas those carefully orchestrated by the testator's solicitor became more reliable. None of this was controversial in principle, judges and commentators resting content with a general jurisdiction premised upon the prevention of fraud, however difficult the occasional borderline or hybrid case might be.[8]

Inheritance could instead just be left to happen. There were significant differences between intestate succession to personalty and to realty, which had some symbolic political importance towards the end of the century. In 1829 the Real Property Commissioners took intestate succession to realty as the first topic of their first report. But the rules for intestate succession to personalty attracted little attention. Broadly, the deceased's children took that equally, unless their mother was still living, in which case she took one third. If she was living but there were no children she would take half. There were substitutionary rules for grandchildren, and then a system for working out further degrees of remoteness, which could take some pages to explain.[9]

The formal mechanism for getting in and distributing an intestate's personalty was through letters of administration issued by the ecclesiastical courts until 1858, thereafter by the Probate Court and its successor division of the Supreme Court of Judicature.[10] It did not affect large numbers of people. Only 9000 of the 210,000 adults who died in 1858 left sufficient personalty for someone to have thought it worthwhile to take out letters of administration, less than half the number who left wills admitted to probate.[11] Men's estates outnumbered women's nearly two to one, and averaged £851 as against £587 for women.[12] Numbers rose ahead of the increase in population, but in 1910 still fewer than 7 per cent of deceased adults needed someone to formally administer their personal estate under the rules of intestacy.[13]

By contrast real property descended to the heir, which in a simple case meant the eldest living son. How often that happened is unknown. The Real Property

[7] *Chester* v. *Urwick (No. 3)* (1856) 23 Beav. 407; *re Boyes* (1884) 26 Ch D 531. See pp. 35–7 below.

[8] *Re Fleetwood* (1880) 15 Ch D 594 ('Mr Jarman, it is clear, would not have approved': Jarman, *Wills* (6th edn, 1910, by C. Sweet), i, 484n.

[9] P. Lovelass, *The Law's Disposal of a Person's Estate who Dies without Will or Testament* (10th edn, 1809), 74–85.

[10] See Vol. XI, pp. 692–713, 733–42. Assets had to be worth £5, or £10 in London to qualify.

[11] *Registrar-General of Births, Deaths, and Marriages*, 22nd Annual Report, *PP* 1861 [2897], xviii, 1, 52.

[12] These would be gross valuation before deduction of debts: B. English, 'Probate Valuations and Death Duty Registers' (1984) 57 *BIHR* 80–91.

[13] Calculated from *Judicial Statistics, Civil (England & Wales), PP* 1912–13 [Cd. 6047], cx, 1, 267 and *Registrar-General of Births, Deaths, and Marriages*, 73rd Annual Report, *PP* 1911 [Cd. 5988], xi, 1, 394.

Commissioners made much of the need for a more thoroughly logical algorithm for calculating remoter degrees of heirship, which was adopted with some modifications by the Inheritance Act 1833.[14] Identification of the heir of some long-dead settlor could be important in applying ultimate dispositions in wills and settlements, but although one of the commissioners' recommendations seems calculated to ease that inquiry it does not seem to have been their primary motivation.[15] Instead their discussion of the relative merits of allowing the deceased's father (but not his mother) to inherit rather than his brother, and of the morality of choosing between a close relative of the half blood over a remoter one of the whole blood, suggest that they saw these as important issues of intestate succession. Important or not, by the time our period begins there were no strong presumptions in favour of interpreting devises so as to preserve the rights of heirs, and the commissioners' recommendation that henceforward a general devise of realty should apply to lands owned at the date of death, rather than at the date of the will, reduced an heir's expectations further.[16]

Testamentary freedom was a central fact of nineteenth-century propertied life. It had its critics, and their views would sometimes creep into lawyers' law reform tracts as an indication of cultural awareness, but they had no impact.[17] In a will 'provisions may be whimsical and capricious, and may operate cruelly in disappointing expectations of families...but there seem to be no limits to such dispositions if they do not offend against the rule as to perpetuity and are not illegal in themselves', Crompton J. advised the House of Lords in 1853.[18] In that case the Lords, against the advice of nearly all the judges that they ought not to entangle the judiciary in questions of public policy, invalidated a condition that would have divested a devisee for failure to acquire a dukedom or marquisate. The facts were unusual enough, however, for the decision to have next to no consequences for wills generally.[19] Instead testators were free to choose whom to benefit and whom to omit, and, particularly, what conditions to attach to their generosity, subject to technical rules about getting the

---

[14] *RC on Real Property*, 1st Report, *PP* 1829 (263), x, 1, 10–16; 3 & 4 Will. IV c. 106, explained in verbal and diagrammatic form in L. Shelford, *Real Property Statutes* (e.g. 4th edn, 1842, 424b–451).

[15] 'Entitlement', which was an issue of law, was substituted for 'seisin', which included questions of fact, as an element in identifying persons from whom descent was to be traced.

[16] Wills Act 1837, 7 Will. IV & 1 Vict. c. 26, s 24 ('unless a contrary intention shall appear by the will'). See also s 25, enacting that a devise of residue should henceforward include lapsed and void specific devises.

[17] e.g. C. H. Bellenden Ker, *On the Reform of the Law of Real Property* (1853), 7–8.

[18] *Egerton* v. *Earl Brownlow* (1853) 4 H.L.C. 1, 67.

[19] In 1920, shortly before the Maundy Gregory scandal helped bring down Lloyd George's coalition government, the Court of Appeal naively ruled that a condition that a devisee acquire a baronetcy did not encourage illegal behaviour and was therefore valid: *re Wallace* [1920] 2 Ch 274.

wording right and just one or two policy limitations that the judges generally found rather difficult.[20]

The most significant limitation concerned conditions that divested a legatee or devisee on marriage, or on remarriage, or on marriage to a particular person, or into a particular class of persons, or into a particular family, or to a person of a particular religion, or without consent of the testator's executors or whatever prejudice, fear, or ambition the testator harboured.[21] If the beneficiary of this solicitude was his daughter the motive seems to have been control, but if it was his widow there were often more complex strategies for early advancement of the couple's older children and protection of younger ones from the malice or indifference of a stepfather. For that reason, perhaps, all the rules agreed that a condition against *re*marriage was valid and easily accomplished.

Common law, which governed devises—gifts of land by will—invalidated general restraints on marriage, but allowed them if only partial. Even that general rule could be sidestepped by wording the gift as a limitation rather than a condition ('while unmarried' rather than 'but if she marries').[22] Legacies of pure personalty were more difficult, because along with the jurisdiction to adjudicate on them Chancery had reluctantly inherited the rules of the ecclesiastical courts, which were far more hostile to any restrictions on marriage. It was possible for an expert drafter to achieve a valid restriction, probably in any circumstances, but the pitfalls for those who wrote their own wills (or, often it seems, their own codicils) were numerous, and the result was a notoriously complex tangle of case law. Chancery judges would sometimes express dislike of their ecclesiastical court inheritance, and often criticized the technical rules that had developed as two sets of principles collided, but equally they often expressed their understanding of why testators were imposing restrictions.[23] It was natural for testators to want to map out the devolution of their estate on alternative contingencies and to express posthumously the approval or disapproval they would have done in their lifetime.

These rules, so far, were gender blind. In 1875 Hall VC refused to be the first to hold that a condition restraining a widower from remarriage was valid, but the Court of Appeal had no reservation.[24] Reported instances of women imposing

---

[20] See pp. 246–52 below.

[21] Jarman, *Wills* (1st edn), i, 836–48, (6th edn, 1910), ii, 1525–42.

[22] *Lloyd* v. *Lloyd* (1852) 2 Sim. (N.S.) 255.

[23] e.g. *Heath* v. *Lewis* (1853) 3 De G. M. & G. 954; *Potter* v. *Richardson* (1855) 24 LJ Ch 488; *Bellairs* v. *Bellairs* (1874) LR 18 Eq 510; *re Hewett* [1918] 1 Ch 458 contains a good survey.

[24] *Allen* v. *Jackson* (1875) LR 19 Eq 631, 1 Ch D 399.

restrictions are few, but when they arose they were treated no differently.[25] To exercise that freedom, however, the woman needed to have her own property and to have legal capacity to make a will in the first place. Until 1882 both were largely, though not entirely, denied to married women, as the account of legal patriarchy in Volume XIII will show.[26] At common law a married woman could leave personalty only with her husband's permission, because it was his by marital right, and by ancient statute she could not leave realty at all—that would descend to her heir subject to the husband's right to support from it during his lifetime, his estate by the curtesy.

Families with settlements could, and did, work their way around that, however, by vesting testamentary powers of appointment in married women, which then functioned as a will would have done.[27] Similarly the institution in equity of a married woman's separate property enabled her to dispose of interests created by suitably worded settlements or legacies.[28] The books recorded a lingering doubt, however, whether she could leave a fee simple (limited to her own separate use) by will, because at common law title would pass only by a fine or, after 1833, an acknowledgment, which needed her to be alive.[29] The recent cases gave little encouragement to that restriction until 1863, when Romilly MR ruled that indeed she could not, only to be overruled almost dismissively two years later by Lord Westbury.[30] It had taken a long time to give full and undisputed effect to the principle that unfettered testamentary capacity was an inherent feature of the married woman's separate estate.

Freedom of testation was not a prominent cry in the campaigns for married women's equality, which may be why judges found technical problems with the legislation that brought it.[31] There was no difficulty with the Married Women's Property Act 1870, which merely extended what counted as separate property, hence invoking the by then firmly established principle that it could be left by will. But judges picked over the general statements in the 1882 Act, which for nearly all other purposes achieved formal equality, to such a degree that a more robust enactment was needed in 1893.[32] Only then were the doubts put to rest.

---

[25] *Dashwood* v. *Bulkeley* (1804) 10 Ves. 230 (grandmother); *Jenner* v. *Turner* (1880) 16 Ch D 188 (sister).

[26] See Vol. XIII, Pt 3, Ch. 1.4–1.6.

[27] M. Lush, *The Law of Husband and Wife* (2nd edn, 1896), 74–7.

[28] For the process of granting 'limited probate', see Jarman, *Wills* (1st edn), i, 24–5.

[29] J. F. Macqueen, *The Rights and Liabilities of Husband and Wife* (1849), 295–7.

[30] *Lechmere* v. *Brotheridge* (1863) 32 Beav. 353; *Taylor* v. *Meads* (1865) 4 De G. J. & S. 597, relying especially on *Tullett* v. *Armstrong* (1839) 4 My. & Cr. 378 and *Baggett* v. *Meux* (1846) 1 Ph. 627.

[31] See Vol. XIII, Pt 3, Ch. 1.4–1.6.

[32] Married Women's Property Acts 1882, 1893; Lush, *Husband and Wife*, 138–40.

Until then selecting a path for the devolution of family wealth would often have been an attribute of male power. The Real Property Commissioners took succession to land as their first major topic in their first report, emphasizing its centrality. Their view was that restriction of testamentary freedom was a family matter, to be achieved, if at all, through *inter vivos* settlements. 'A testamentary power is given', they wrote, 'which stimulates industry and encourages accumulation; and while capricious limitations are restrained, property is allowed to be moulded according to the circumstances of every family.'[33] 'Caprice' in this rendition can refer only to dispositions reaching too far into the future, those that broke the rule against perpetuities, for there were no restrictions on preference for one child over another, no rules that protected dependants from whim, as has been seen.

Indeed the commissioners removed (or virtually removed) the last entitlement that restricted men's freedom of testation. Dower, which was a widow's entitlement to support from her deceased husband's realty under the general law, was now 'highly inconvenient', they reported.[34] It so much interfered with the free sale of land that complex conveyancing devices to avoid it had become standard, and very frequently, they said, husbands left direct provision to their widow by will on condition that she relinquished dower. With marriage settlements now so common, and with there being so much more personalty nowadays out of which widows' just claims could be satisfied, they recommended that dower be restricted to land that the husband had when he died, rather than relating back to all the land he had ever owned, and that it become voluntary. The commissioners toyed with substituting a rentcharge over land the husband owned at his death, but rejected that for conflicting with another major aim, the reduction of litigation. They generally had a benign faith in the appropriateness of leaving decisions on family inheritance to husbands and fathers.[35] The Dower Act 1833 which implemented those recommendations made dower virtually obsolete as a right, converting it, in practice, to being an aspect of intestate succession.[36]

How common, then, were wills? Estimates run at between 5 and 10 per cent of the adult population for the early years of the century, endorsed by

---

[33] *RC on Real Property*, 1st Report, 7.

[34] *Ibid.*, 16–19 at 16.

[35] *Ibid.*, 12.

[36] 3 & 4 Will. IV c. 105. Research is needed. Streamlining conveyancing would have led to disuse of old forms designed to bar dower (though it is not known how far down the social scale those went anyway). Hence if ownership of urban investment properties spread there may have been more widows claiming dower in, say, the 1890s than in the 1820s, depending also, of course, on the rate of intestacy.

a calculation by the Registrar-General of Births, Deaths, and Marriages that 21,000 of the 210,000 adults dying in 1858 had left a will that had been admitted to probate—three quarters of them men.[37] Men left more than women too, an average of £3469 as against £1793, before deduction of debts. By 1910 the proportion of adults leaving a will admitted to probate had risen, but only to 15 per cent.[38]

As for content, recent studies confirm what the conveyancers' practice books suggest, that for middle-class men the point of accumulation was usually transmission to their children, usually through some form of partible inheritance, usually with an aim to rough equality between them all, though with various possible preferences for sons over daughters.[39] But, whoever drew them, the common provision made for the middle-class family, when the husband died before his wife, was that his widow would have an income for life, the capital being reserved for the children.

In the first half of the nineteenth century the form of the widow's share may have varied from place to place. Alastair Owen's study of Stockport wills found annuities there to be the most common form, whereas in the Leeds of R. J. Morris's study annuities and life interests seem to feature about equally, and in Chantal Stebbings' Devon the most common testamentary trust was the life interest to the widow with remainders to the children.[40] Variants found in the law reports include an additional annuity or share of the income for the widow to provide for her children's maintenance and education, sometimes expressly terminating on their coming of age or, if daughters, earlier marriage.[41] Historians agree that it was unusual for a man with surviving children to leave his estate to

[37] D. R. Green and A. Owens, 'Metropolitan Estates of the Middle Class, 1800–50' (1997) 70 BIHR 294–311, 296; Registrar-General of Births, Deaths, and Marriages, 22nd Annual Report 52. Wills leaving personalty worth less than £5 (£10 in London) would not be included in these figures. Nor was realty included in the valuation, since until 1858 it was not taxed on death. Probate was nonetheless important for wills of realty because conveyancers used it as presumptive proof of a will's regularity, hence validating the link in the chain of title it constituted: T. Coventry, On Conveyancers' Evidence (1832), 91–3.

[38] Calculated from Judicial Statistics, Civil (England & Wales), PP 1912–13 [Cd. 6047], cx, 1, 267 and Registrar-General of Births, Marriages and Deaths, 73rd Annual Report 394. During the twentieth century the proportion roughly doubled: J. Finch et al., Wills, Inheritance, and Families (Oxford, 1996), 32, an exemplary study.

[39] A. Owens, 'Property, Gender and the Life-course' (2001) 26 Social History 299–317; R. J. Morris, Men, Women and Property in England 1780–1870 (Cambridge, 2005). In Magrath v. Morehead (1871) LR 12 Eq 49 the preference was to daughters.

[40] A. Owens, 'Property, Gender', 299–317; R. J. Morris, Men, Women and Property (his analysis is more concerned to distinguish limited interests from absolute interests than to consider the different forms of limited interest); C. Stebbings, The Private Trustee in Victorian England (Cambridge, 2002), 10; see also McAloon, No Idle Rich, 75–93.

[41] e.g. Hadow v. Hadow (1838) 9 Sim. 438; Browne v. Paull (1850) 1 Sim. (N.S.) 92.

his widow absolutely—whether those that did had made *inter vivos* provision for their children cannot usually be discovered.[42]

Professionally drawn wills could closely resemble the form of marriage settlements, and many did, getting ever more elaborate as draftsmen added further powers, broadened permissible investments, and negated inconvenient judicial decisions.[43] The ideal type was spelled out by the conveyancer Charles Davidson in his epitome of a standard marriage settlement of personalty or mixed property. He was important as reflecting and influencing practice, often cited to and by judges.[44] His model is no doubt typical:

SETTLEMENT *on* MARRIAGE *of a sum of* STOCK, *the property of the intended* WIFE, *with* EXTENSIVE *powers of* INVESTMENT *and* VARYING SECURITIES. *The* INCOME *during the* JOINT LIVES *of husband and wife to be paid to the* WIFE *for her* SEPARATE USE, *with a* RESTRICTION *on* ANTICIPATION, *and after the death of either of them to the* SURVIVOR *for life. After the death of the survivor, the capital and income to be for the* ISSUE *of the marriage, as the* HUSBAND *and* WIFE, *or the* SURVIVOR *shall* APPOINT, *and in default of appointment, for* SONS *attaining twenty-one and* DAUGHTERS *attaining that age or marrying* EQUALLY. HOTCHPOT, ADVANCEMENT, MAINTENANCE, *and* ACCUMULATION *clauses. In default of children the fund is given to the* WIFE, *her* APPOINTEES, *or* NEXT OF KIN, *so as to exclude the husband.* TRUSTEES' RECEIPT *clause. Power to appoint* NEW TRUSTEES. *Clauses for* INDEMNITY *and* REIMBURSEMENT *of* TRUSTEES.[45]

Where the property to be settled came from both husband and wife, the usual form instead maintained two separate income streams during marriage and stipulated two separate destinations in default of children.

By contrast the English landed elite were largely wedded to male primogeniture, impartible succession to their lands secured so far as the law allowed through the strict settlement.[46] But even strict settlements are indexed in Davidson's *Precedents* as 'family settlement of estates…', his 78 model clauses including 20 devoted to funding younger sons, endowing daughters, and jointuring wives.[47]

[42] Owens, 'Property, Gender', 305, 308, 312; Morris, *Men, Women and Property*, 101, 104; McAloon, *No Idle Rich*, 86.

[43] Stebbings, *Private Trustee*, 22, 92, 109–10, 123–5, 146–50.

[44] By the end of our period *Davidson* was often treated as persuasive authority, see e.g. *re Wise's Settlement* [1913] 1 Ch 41; *re Earl of Stamford and Warrington* [1912] 1 Ch 343; *re Wrottesley's Settlement* [1911] 1 Ch 708. In the 1860s and 1870s judges seem to have been more comfortable using it as evidence of practice and usage, as e.g. in *Hampshire* v. *Wickens* (1878) 7 Ch D 555.

[45] C. Davidson, *Precedents and Forms in Conveyancing*, iii, 533 (2nd edn, 1861). Limitations like these were described by Baggallay LJ as 'the most expedient' form of settlement: *Cogan* v. *Duffield* (1876) 2 Ch D 44.

[46] See Davidson's marriage settlement for landed property, *Precedents* (2nd edn), iii, 862.

[47] Davidson, *Precedents* (2nd edn), iii, 944.

Historians do not agree whether such superimposition of family provision on male primogeniture was burdensome enough to contribute to the eventual demise of the landed aristocracy, and none would deny that younger children's interests were secondary to the heir's, but nor does anyone dispute Davidson's classification: these were family settlements, not merely transmissions from father to eldest son.[48]

The sections that follow explore first how far judges aided, obstructed, or stood neutrally above these common patterns of transmission. They begin by asking what settlements judges thought normal and desirable when they had a free hand to construct settlements themselves, or a fairly free hand to flesh out a settlor's general instructions. Then they turn to the more complex question of how judges approached the task of interpreting wills.

2. COURTS AS SETTLORS

Chancery had jurisdictions to originate a settlement of its own choosing and also a derivative jurisdiction to complete a settlement that somebody else had begun to sketch. Each jurisdiction broke into two parts. The originating jurisdiction applied to Chancery's own wards, whose property would be under court control, usually just as they were about to marry, and also to women who married without a settlement but later sought court protection, be that from their husband or his creditors. This latter 'equity to a settlement', which applied to a restricted range of property only, is described in Volume XIII.[49] The equity was to a settlement 'in analogy to what a prudent parent would probably have done in giving a portion to a daughter', which no doubt is how Chancery saw itself in relation to its wards too.[50] The form of the settlement was closely modelled on Davidson's stereotype, this being 'the mode most beneficial to the family'.[51] Hence, in fulfilling the equity to a settlement the wife would be given a life interest for her separate use, without power of anticipation, and, usually, a joint or sole power of appointment to her children. In default the children would take equally, and if they died

---

[48] J. Habakkuk, *Marriage, Debt and the Estates System* (Oxford, 1994); the debate is summarized, and continued, in D. and S. Spring, 'Debt and the English Aristocracy' (1996) 31 *Canadian Journal of History* 377–94. Davidson's precedent includes a clause enabling the life tenant, the head of the family, to reduce or cancel portions at will (cl. 29, p. 959); whether it was habitually included, and, if so, how it was operated, is not known.

[49] See Vol. XIII, pp. 742–4.

[50] Per Lord Cranworth in *Tidd* v. *Lister* (1853) 3 De G. M. & G. 857.

[51] J. P Peachey, *A Treatise on the Law of Marriage and other Family Settlements* (1860), 178–9; *Spirett* v. *Williams* (1869) LR 4 Ch App 407; *Walsh* v. *Wason* (1873) LR 8 Ch App 482; *Gowan* v. *Gowan* (1880) 17 Ch D 778 (an executory trust case); *re Briant* (1888) 39 Ch D 471.

before their mother, their own children would take their share in substitution.[52] There would be the usual powers of accumulation and advancement.

An account of the wardship jurisdiction in 1842 said that the usual provision where the property was wholly the woman's was for her to keep four-fifths of the income as her own during marriage, protected by a restraint upon anticipation— Lord Eldon having thought that there cannot be much expectation of happiness where the wife controls the whole.[53] She could double her husband's fifth by will if she wanted (for his lifetime), and subject to that the capital would go to the children if there were any and as she chose if there were not. She would have powers to provide for children of any further marriages. Her income would be for her own disposal; her children would have no call on that, their father living.[54] There would be adjustments, of course, if the husband also brought property into the settlement. Again this is much as Davidson thought conventional for personalty or mixed settlements.

Chancery's second type of jurisdiction was derivative, the fleshing out of executory trusts. When marriage articles directed a property settlement, or a will directed the creation of a trust or settlement, courts would not regard that as an instruction void for uncertainty but would instead supervise both the scheme and the details. How far they were constrained by the words used in the articles or, especially, the will, was a controversial matter, dependent on general attitudes to interpretation of such documents. Interpretation of wills in general will be discussed below.[55] Here the concern is less with how the judges determined how free their hand should be, more with what they did when they thought it was. It is enough to record that in 1820 Lord Eldon decided that the court's power to mould executory trusts was essentially a unitary jurisdiction, but with two limbs. The difference between them was that whereas the context provided the reason for a purposive reading of marriage articles, with a will the judge needed to find some indication within it that the testator had not wanted what a literal or technical reading would produce.[56]

There was no doubt that since at least as early as the mid-eighteenth century judges had considered the main object of marriage settlements to be provision for

[52] The 'per stirpes' clause directing a grandchild to take in substitution of its deceased parent seems to have been an optional refinement. It was not part of Davidson's precedents, nor of Williams's exposition, nor is it found in all reported court-directed settlements. Its effect was to guarantee succession by the grandchild directly under the settlement rather than leaving it to depend upon the will or intestacy of its deceased parent.

[53] J. D. Chambers, *A Practical Treatise on the Jurisdiction of the High Court of Chancery over the Property of Infants* (1842), 745; *Bathurst* v. *Murray* (1802) 8 Ves. 74.

[54] *Hodgens* v. *Hodgens* (1837) 4 Cl. & F. 323.

[55] Below, pp. 22–46.

[56] *Jervoise* v. *Duke of Northumberland* (1820) 1 Jac. & W. 559.

the children.[57] If marriage articles did not accurately reflect that, and remained unexecuted, rather than executing them as they stood, judges would order preparation of the usual form of settlement, for personalty or realty, as the case may be.[58] Further, they would protect the children of the marriage by amending post-marital settlements based upon marriage articles they considered to have been too hastily drawn. If such a settlement were of realty they would set aside a fee tail taken by the husband, lest by barring the entail he should remove his children's inheritance, insisting instead upon the common form that gave him only a life estate.[59] And if it were of personalty they would make the children's interests contingent on reaching 21, because otherwise on the death of a young child its interest would be inherited by its father, rather than the common and more proper alternatives of accruing to its siblings, or going through to the grandchildren, or (if it were the wife's fund) reverting to her family.[60] If a pre-marital settlement recited that it was made to fulfil marriage articles a court could again amend it in line with what Joshua Williams called 'the equitable construction placed upon the articles'.[61] In all these situations the court was imposing the general pattern of marriage settlement upon the parties, in line with what it insisted was their general intention, an intention largely constructed from the social situation.[62]

Wills could not be stereotyped as plausibly. Sometimes a testator might just have left some gaps in a partially declared trust or settlement, sometimes he might simply have said 'these are my instructions; do your best to carry them out...', as Jessel MR put it.[63] The balance between testator and judge varied accordingly. To Thomas Jarman, writing in the 1840s when many judges were shifting towards principles of stricter construction of wills, and supporting that trend himself, this blend of paternalism and pragmatism within a framework dictated to an uncertain extent by the testator's intention defied systematic justification. Were judges simply imposing their own view of what settlement would best suit that

[57] J. Williams, *The Settlement of Real Estates* (1879), 113, 118. His lectures from 113 to 182 can be read as an exposition of Davidson's precedent, though as he was nominally lecturing on land he had to approach personalty settlements through a trust for sale.

[58] Lewin, *Trusts* (4th edn, 1861), 86–91.

[59] Williams, *Settlement*, 113–14. But not if it took both parents to bar.

[60] Williams, *Settlement*, 114–18, citing *Cogan* v. *Duffield* (1875) LR 20 Eq 789 (aff'd (1876) 2 Ch D 44); A. Underhill, *The Law Relating to Trusts and Trustees* (7th edn, 1912), 124–5.

[61] Williams, *Settlement*, 114.

[62] By contrast, a settlement made before marriage, and not reciting that it was made to fulfil marriage articles, was treated as fully executed, thus amenable only to interpretation, not to moulding.

[63] *Miles* v. *Harford* (1879) 12 Ch D 691. As ancillary powers in trusts became more complex it must have been useful for lawyers advising clients *in extremis* to know that a direction to include 'the usual powers' was all that need be said.

family? Or were they really doing what the testator meant? He found it impossible to say.[64] It remained that way throughout our period.

Unless tightly constrained by the testator's words, judges executing marriage articles or testamentary executory trusts drew a clear distinction between realty settlements and personalty. For the latter they adopted the standard two-generation model of personalty settlement, with the usual powers, children taking equally but, unless the testator said otherwise, subject to a divesting power of appointment in their parents.[65] The jurisdictions overlapped where a testator directed that a marriage settlement of personalty be made for his daughter, sometimes at any age, sometimes only if she married before reaching 21. Here again the court would require the settlement to conform to the usual pattern of the time and to contain the usual powers.[66] Words which if used directly to create a trust would have achieved less than the usual protection for her children would be modified to bring them into line. However, where the woman had been over 21 when she married, the judges seem to have been more willing to agree that her husband might take a life interest in succession to her own.[67] Nor would judges contradict a testator who gave his adult daughter the option of taking the property absolutely; whereas if the matter rested with them they would impose a restraint upon anticipation.[68]

Subject to nuances necessary to accommodate any express directions that the testator had made consistently with his general intention, these court-approved settlements of personalty were very similar to those created in pursuance of a wife's equity to a settlement. In all of them the judges took the testator's aim to be the provision of a secured income for the wife and assured transmission of the capital to the next generation by using the conventional form.

Executory trusts of realty were treated differently. One reason, given by Jessel MR in 1879, was that there were more, and more important, fixed rules of interpretation for realty, hence greater justification was needed if they were

---

[64] Jarman, *Wills* (1st edn), ii, 263–6.

[65] *White* v. *Briggs* (1848) 2 Ph. 583; *Kennerley* v. *Kennerley* (1852) 10 Hare 160; *Combe* v. *Hughes* (1872) LR 14 Eq 415.

[66] *White* v. *Briggs* (1848) 2 Ph. 583; *Turner* v. *Sargent* (1853) 17 Beav. 515; *Loch* v. *Bagley* (1867) LR 4 Eq 122; *re Parrott* (1886) 33 Ch D 274; *re Spicer* (1901) 84 LT 195.

[67] *Stonor* v. *Curwen* (1832) 5 Sim. 264; *Charlton* v. *Rendall* (1853) 11 Hare 296; *Combe* v. *Hughes* (1872) LR 14 Eq 415.

[68] *Laing* v. *Laing* (1839) 9 LJ Ch 48; *Magrath* v. *Morehead* (1871) LR 12 Eq 49, and compare *Symonds* v. *Wilkes* (1857) 23 Beav. 450 (a marriage articles case). Several of the wills litigated in executory trust cases gave the bequest to the daughter absolutely at 21, but directed trustees to make a settlement for her if she married below that age; *Laing* is one such, for further examples see *Young* v. *Macintosh* (1843) 13 Sim. 445; *Charlotte* v. *Rendall* (1853) 11 Hare 296 (28 in this case, not 21); and *Clive* v. *Clive* (1872) LR 7 Ch App 433.

to be suspended.[69] From about 1820 that had come to mean in particular that a disposition in a will to someone for life and then his 'issue' would be taken in a sense that was technical twice over. First, 'issue' would be taken to mean descendants indefinitely, and hence as indicating some sort of entail.[70] Secondly, if the words had been used to create an interest directly they would have attracted the rule in *Shelley's* case, which gave the fee tail to the taker in the first generation, irrespective of the testator's (probable) intention to give him only a life estate. Of course, the testator may have known about the rule in *Shelley's* case, and conceivably wanted its result. That was the context for Lord Eldon's ruling that a will containing an executory direction like that must be scrutinized for some positive indication that instead the testator wanted what he had said.[71]

It was not a severe scrutiny, however. Judges routinely took a testator's instruction that land be entailed, or settled, or that the first taker's issue should benefit, as capable of satisfaction only by a strict settlement, sometimes seizing on very small indications of the testator's supposed intention.[72] Sons and grandsons would thus take in fee tail in succession, unless the testator had unambiguously directed a division between them.[73] In default of males, daughters would take concurrently, as tenants in common in fee tail, because that was usual in strict settlements, and courts would readily imply cross-remainders among them so as to maximize the possibility that the land would remain in the family.[74]

There were limits to such waivers of technicality. If judges were willing to find that a testator did not intend to invoke the rule in *Shelley's* case, should they also find that he did not intend to use 'issue' in its technical sense either? He might instead have meant 'children', indicating an intention that they take concurrently and equally, as in a middle-class settlement of personalty, and that there be no fee tail at all. 'No', said Turner LJ 1865: that was not what the owner of a large landed estate would usually want, and it would be dangerous if 'different effect should be given to the same words according to the extent of the property...'.[75]

---

[69] *Miles* v. *Harford* (1879) 12 Ch D 691.

[70] *Grier* v. *Grier* (1872) LR 5 HL 688; the technical interpretation stems from the two leading cases in the House of Lords: *Jesson* v. *Wright* (1820) 2 Bli. 1 and *Roddy* v. *Fitzgerald* (1858) 6 H.L.C. 823, both cases on the rule in *Shelley's* case.

[71] *Jervoise* v. *Duke of Northumberland* (1820) 1 Jac. & W. 559.

[72] *Parker* v. *Boulton* (1835) 5 LJ Ch 98; *Groves* v. *Hicks* (1841) 11 Sim. 536; *Shelton* v. *Watson* (1849) 16 Sim. 543; *Grier* v. *Grier* (1872) LR 5 HL 688; *Thompson* v. *Fisher* (1870) LR 10 Eq 20. Contrast *Blackburn* v. *Stables* (1814) 2 Ves. & Bea. 367; *Marshall* v. *Bousfield* (1817) 2 Madd. 166; and Plumer VC's order in *Jervoise* v. *Duke of Northumberland* disapproved at (1820) 1 Jac. & W. 559.

[73] *Hadwen* v. *Hadwen* (1857) 23 Beav. 551 ('unambiguously' probably required both a presence of words of distribution and an absence of words of limitation).

[74] *Trevor* v. *Trevor* (1847) 1 H.L.C. 239.

[75] *Phillips* v. *James* (1865) 3 De G. J. & Sm. 72 (Knight-Bruce LJ diss.). This was a case of marriage articles, but the same sentiment is apparent in the leading case of the 1870s, *Grier* v. *Grier* (1872)

Settlements without management powers were sterile things, so courts willingly included the usual powers of leasing, though until the 1850s not powers of sale and exchange.[76] Thereafter, however, they abandoned caution for practicality, saying that if the testator wanted a settlement he must have wanted whatever incidents conveyancers currently considered usual.[77] That would not normally extend to court-initiated inclusion of powers of jointuring and portioning, since, lacking authority from the testator, courts would not subtract from the estates he had designated, nor had they the means to determine questions of quantum.[78] The result was that testamentary executory trusts of realty were implemented heavily in favour of eldest sons.

In 1870 the Lords departed spectacularly from this tendency by creating an elaborate settlement that included jointuring and portioning powers, where the testatrix had given at least some indication that that was what she wanted.[79] Most of the Chancery law-lords concurred, but two years later, acting as if there had been no significant change, they declined to imply powers to create portions for younger sons in a case where the will was probably more typical of the general run.[80] Jarman's editors concluded from the 1870 decision that a more liberal principle of construction may have been introduced, and at the turn of the century Underhill thought the 1872 decision would no longer be followed.[81] There are no reported cases, however, and there has been no empirical research in the area. So while it is clear that from 1820 judges had a strong preference for the strict settlement when they executed such trusts of realty, it is much less clear whether that remained confined to provision for the eldest male line for the time being, or

LR 5 HL 688, which was a testamentary executory trust. There are echoes of Lord Mansfield's failed attempt to liberalize the interpretation of devises without words of limitation. In *Oates d. Wigfall* v. *Brydon* (1766) 3 Burr. 1895 he held that a devise 'to X' could carry the fee simple, not merely the conventional life estate, if it could be inferred from the small value of the land that that was what the testatrix had intended. Though he carried the King's Bench with him on that occasion, the court did not develop the idea, which was ultimately rejected by Lord Kenyon in 1798: *Goodtitle d. Richardson* v. *Edmonds* (1798) 7 T.R. 635.

[76] *Wheate* v. *Hall* (1809) 17 Ves. 80; *Horne* v. *Barton* (1822) Jac. 437.

[77] *Turner* v. *Sargent* (1853) 17 Beav. 515, building on *Hill* v. *Hill* (1834) 6 Sim. 136; *Scott* v. *Steward* (1859) 27 Beav. 367; *Wise* v. *Piper* (1879) 13 Ch D 848.

[78] *Higginson* v. *Barneby* (1826) 2 Sim. & St. 516; *Duke of Bedford* v. *Marquess of Abercorn* (1836) 1 My. & Cr. 312 (marriage articles); contrast *Charlton* v. *Rendall* (1853) 11 Hare 296 (executory trust to make a marriage settlement on a daughter allowed to include a power by which she could appoint to her husband).

[79] *Sackville-West* v. *Holmesdale* (1870) LR 4 HL 543, implemented with difficulty in *Holmesdale* v. *West* (1871) LR 12 Eq 280.

[80] *Grier* v. *Grier* (1872) LR 5 HL 688.

[81] Jarman, *Wills* (6th edn), i, 904; Underhill, *Trusts* (7th edn), 124. Habakkuk concluded that there was greater variety in the scale of provision for younger children in the 1870s than a century earlier, which suggests good reason for judicial caution: *Marriage, Debt*, 142.

whether they broadened out to secure the full measure of family provision that was commonplace in settlements fully executed by a settlor.

Judicial practice when exercising these jurisdictions thus reinforces the assumptions found in the books of model dispositions about how a responsible family should order its property. They were gendered, of course. There was a sharp distinction between personalty and realty that corresponded roughly to a class division, so settlements of realty were based upon the practices of the very wealthy. But judges regarded these patterns as conventional and hence they were confident in their practice. So far as executory trusts and settlements were concerned equity judges did not regard the incompleteness of the disposition as a regrettable failure that must be left to bear its own consequences. Nor, when asked to fulfil a married woman's equity to a settlement, did they regard her impending destitution as a natural consequence of her improvidence in marrying without an express settlement, or her family's in allowing it. Instead in both cases they assumed a role both paternalist and creative, remedying the situation in a way that a responsible family would, so far as they were able.

Section 4 of this chapter asks whether these jurisdictions were isolated, or whether they were typical of a general approach to testamentary disposition. Were judges active in seeking solutions that would make the transmission work as they imagined the testator had wanted, or as such transmissions usually did, or were they passive in taking the words as they found them and letting the memory of the testator bear the consequences? First, however, it is necessary to sketch the major rules that framed successive interests.

3. THE LEGAL FRAMEWORK OF SUCCESSIVE INTERESTS

There was an axiom so fundamental that law books simply took it for granted, that testamentary freedom operated within a matrix of property law to which it must conform. However subtle and enabling that law was, yet it was narrower and less flexible than many a testator's imagination, particularly of those who meticulously mapped alternative contingencies for their extensive family over the next two or three generations. Their aspirations had always to be translated into dispositions within the canon of recognized property interests. Many of the major rules of common law confining the ambitions of testators concerned realty. It was here that the arcane complexity of the common law, against which all reformers railed, bit hardest. There were rules, and there were counter-rules, and there were rules for choosing between them.

First there was the (old) rule against perpetuity. Common law allowed only one generation of unborn persons to take; so if a will devised land to an unborn person for life, with a remainder to the child of that unborn person, then the remainder was void as an attempt to create a perpetuity.[82] In addition there was the rule that contingent remainders would fail unless the contingency was satisfied by the time the preceding estate ended. That rule had a twin, that a limitation that would be capable of taking effect as a remainder if events turned out favourably must have its validity determined by the rules applying to remainders, even though it would then fail because events had not turned out favourably—only limitations that could never have taken effect as a remainder could be judged instead against the less demanding rules of executory devises.[83] Taken together these three rules limited the dynastic potential of will-making and engendered considerable technicality to ensnare the poorly advised.

In addition there was a rule of interpretation that by the 1830s was regarded as quite out of keeping with testators' expectations. It was that a devise simply 'to X' would be taken as conferring a life estate only.[84] Until it was reversed, prospectively only, by the Wills Act 1837, words of limitation had to be used to confer a fee simple, preferably (though not exclusively) 'to X and his heirs'. That rule too had its twin, that if a testator did use words of limitation he would be taken to have intended their consequences. This could bite hard on gifts taking the form 'to X and his heirs/issue/children', where the testator might have intended to give directly to X's children, only to have the words (nearly always/usually/sometimes) taken instead to be describing the estate to be given to X—in the jargon, the testator may have meant the words to be words of purchase but they would be taken as words of limitation.[85] In like vein there was the 'rule in *Shelley's* case'. In its most usual application this rule converted a gift expressed to be 'to X for life and then to the heirs of his body' into an immediate fee tail to X. X could then frustrate the testator's intention by barring the entail.[86]

Finally there was the modern rule against perpetuities, that executory interests in personalty and realty must vest within a stipulated period (save for contingent remainders, to which the 'old' rule applied). There was still some uncertainty about what that period was, whether it was a lifetime of someone alive at the time the instrument took effect plus a further period of 21 years in all cases, or whether

---

[82] This was the unchallenged opinion at the start of our period, and near the end was confirmed by *Whitby* v. *Mitchell* (1890) 44 Ch D 85. In 1843 W. D. Lewis (*A Practical Treatise on the Law of Perpetuity*) argued that the rule was part of, and subsumed within, the modern rule against perpetuities, a view that was rejected by most writers but followed vigorously by J. Gray (*The Rule against Perpetuities*, (1st edn, Boston, 1886). See Jarman, *Wills* (6th edn), i, 284–8, and *HEL*, vii, 24–6.

[83] J. Williams, *The Seisin of Freehold* (1878), 190–2; Williams, *Settlement*, 22–9.

[84] Jarman, *Wills* (1st edn), ii, 194–5; Wills Act 1837, s 28, for wills made after 1 January 1838, subject to expression of a contrary intention.

[85] Jarman, *Wills* (1st edn), ii, 307–60.

[86] *Ibid.*, 241–70.

that further period was available only if the putative donee under the gift was actually a minor. In 1832 the Lords decreed that it was indeed a period in gross, available in all circumstances, largely because that seemed to have been the predominant view among conveyancers, but that the further nine months canvassed in some opinions was available only if there was a pregnancy.[87]

Part of the judges' heritage in the early nineteenth century was that many of those major rules had acquired devices or techniques that mitigated their effect, perhaps even counter-rules. The most creative was the Chancery judges' jurisdiction to model or alter executory trusts, outlined above. In addition the (old) rule against perpetuity was subject to a mitigation that, on one view at least, resembled the remodelling jurisdiction applied to executory trusts. This was the principle, or technique, or rule, of *cy-près*—even formulating it commits one to a view of what it was. Left to itself the (old) rule against perpetuity, by voiding the disposition to the second unborn generation, would in most such cases have deflected the land from a senior to a junior branch of the family or out to collaterals. Instead a *cy-près* reading interpreted (or remodelled) the will so as to give the unborn taker of the first generation a fee tail even though the will had said a life estate.[88] True, he could then bar it, so the taker in the second generation might receive nothing. But because of the rule against perpetuity he would have taken nothing anyway, and this way he had a chance. It was not what the testator had said; but it was near enough.

So what, exactly, was the basis of this jurisdiction? It was part of the heritage that in the eighteenth century there had been a relatively narrow understanding about the scope of *cy-près* but that Lord Kenyon had then significantly extended its reach.[89] Did this extension show that on principle judges could actively remodel dispositions to keep them within the rules? If so, why should not that principle apply equally to gifts infringing other rules? Was there a link to Chancery's jurisdiction over executory trusts; were they all part of one broad remodelling jurisdiction? Or was *cy-près* simply a rule, to be left where Lord Kenyon had put it, or even restored to its original and purer state?

As for contingent remainders, their vulnerability to destruction would not arise if the words creating them could instead be read as creating a vested estate—and there was a folio of interpretive rules to show how common and systemized that was.[90] But did they all flow from a general principle capable of application to all

[87] *Cadell* v. *Palmer* (1832) 1 Cl. & F. 372; *Dungannon* v. *Smith* (1846) 12 Cl. & F. 546; *HEL*, vii, 226–8.
[88] Fearne, *Contingent Remainders*, 204n; Jarman, *Wills* (3rd edn), i, 277–82; Hawkins, *Wills* (2nd edn), 223–6.
[89] *Pitt* v. *Jackson* (1786) 2 Bro. C.C. 52.
[90] Jarman, *Wills* (1st edn), i, 726–55; Hawkins, *Wills* (2nd edn), 284–90.

aspects of wills—say, 'a will should be interpreted so far as possible to give effect to the testator's intention regardless of the exact words he has used?' Or were they like rules of law in having essentially arbitrary spheres of operation? If the former, then what would become of the distinction between words of limitation and words of purchase? If the latter, how are those spheres to be defined? This too caused a tension that informed a great deal of the early and mid-nineteenth-century law of wills.

In retrospect it can be seen that the critically important question was whether and how far these mitigations or ones like them would be applied to rescue dispositions infringing the modern rule against perpetuities. Two steps would have been needed, first to extend mitigating readings from remainders to executory interests in land, secondly to all executory interests in personalty. If that happened mitigations that originated in landed settlements would have been translated into equivalents for the personalty or mixed trust dispositions of the wealthy middle class. If not they would be left just as rules bound by context, parasitic upon the unique ability of realty to be divided into successive estates.

The formative period seems to have fallen just before ours begins, say 1785 to 1820, and so forms part of the heritage to be worked with. During that time it was clearly established, so later judges accepted, that there was to be no rescue or remodelling of testamentary dispositions that infringed the modern rule against perpetuities, no extension of *cy-près* or analogy to it, and no principle of partial validity. That was the ruling of Lord Kenyon himself in one of the trilogy of decisive cases.[91] In another of the trilogy, *Routledge v. Dorril*, Arden MR had denied that *cy-près* could ever be extended to wills of personalty: *cy-près* was a principle of interpretation that worked because the testator's general intention was to favour a particular course of descent; that intention could be achieved by reading the gift to the first unborn taker as a fee tail; but there could be no fees tail in personalty; hence an equivalent reading would give absolute ownership; that would not descend as the testator had indicated, but instead would go through the first taker's executor and be subject to the testator's debts; that was too big a difference from the expressed intention.[92] This limited, context-bound, explanation became a general part of the orthodoxy, but, as will be seen, its invocation of the concept

---

[91] *Jee v. Audley* (1787) 1 Cox 324; *Routledge v. Dorril* (1794) 2 Ves. Jun. 357; *Leake v. Robinson* (1817) 2 Mer. 363. On *Jee* see Simpson, *Leading Cases in the Common Law*, 76–99, who, however, rather understates its contemporary importance: see e.g. Lord Brougham's description of it in *Dungannon v. Smith* (1846) 12 Cl. & F. 546 as a cornerstone of the law. The principle of *pro tanto* validity, rejected in these decisions, was incorporated into the Thelluson Act 1800, 39 & 40 Geo. III c. 98, that regulated the permissible period for accumulations; see P. Polden, *Peter Thelluson's Will of 1797 and its consequences on Chancery Law* (Lewiston, NY, 2002).

[92] *Routledge v. Dorril* (1794) 2 Ves. Jun. 357.

of a testator's 'general intention' left the matter more open than Arden MR may have intended.

In *Leake* v. *Robinson*, the third case of this influential trilogy, Grant MR decided that the rules giving a benevolent construction to contingent remainders did not carry over to executory interests about to be invalidated by the modern rules against perpetuities. If a testamentary gift to a class by description—say, 'to be divided between all A's children who attain the age of 25'—were interpreted as a contingent remainder would be, then each child would get a vested interest on reaching 25. Instead Grant MR ruled that in this different context the words must be interpreted literally. Only if the whole class would necessarily satisfy the contingency (attaining 25) within the time allowed by the modern rule against perpetuities would it be valid.[93]

4. WILLS AND THEIR INTERPRETATION

Testators' language was often both aspirational and dispositive. It expressed hopes and strategies, a last chance for advice and direction in the maintenance of order within the family, for the reinforcement of identities and the creation or renewal of moral obligations; and it effected those wishes by creating property interests, indirectly via executors in the case of personalty, directly by the very force of its words in case of realty.[94] Thomas Jarman, a well-respected author even before he published his monumental *Treatise on Wills* in 1844, urged practitioners to have their clients distinguish clearly between the will as a legal document and the will for family reading.[95] His editors in 1910 asserted bluntly that a 'will is a business document, in which use of diplomatic or courteous language is unnecessary'.[96] Perhaps by then it was, but for the whole of our period judges had to struggle with wills that blurred the boundaries. A great deal of litigation and many hundreds of pages of learned writing was occupied by the tension between three questions: what did the testator want, what had the testator said, and what did the law allow?

The Wills Act 1837 did not address the basic conundrum. Very significantly, however, its progenitors, the Real Property Commissioners, accepted that simplification and rationalization should not extend to subjecting wills to the same strict standards of construction that applied to deeds, even wills of realty, which operated as direct conveyances.[97] The contrary view, that increasing the efficiency

---

[93] Lewis, *Perpetuity* (2nd edn), 455–63 and supplement 154–7.
[94] For wills' exhortative function see Morris, *Men, Women and Property*, 93, 97 and *passim*.
[95] For Jarman see A. W. B. Simpson (ed.), *Biographical Dictionary of the Common Law* (1984), 273.
[96] 6th edn, by C. Sweet assisted by C. P. Sanger (1910), 879.
[97] *RC on Real Property*, 4th Report, 3.

of land transactions required a uniform standard of interpretation, hence that the rigour of interpreting deeds should extend to wills, was put by the law reformer Henry Bellenden Ker in 1853, ineffectually.[98]

The third possibility, that wills of realty should cease to operate directly as conveyances, was not available in the mid-century. For realty to pass to a 'real representative' as personalty passed to a personal representative would demean its status, and, more materially, strengthen the case for making it taxable on the same basis as personalty. The idea did become part of the stock-in-trade of advocates of title registration, but even as late as 1889 the idea of subordinating the heir to an administrator was upsetting enough to occasion the rejection of a registration bill.[99] It became mandatory only with the first compulsory title registration scheme in 1897, the line of thought being completed in 1925 when devisees' entitlements were relegated to equity and executors were given overreaching powers—so as to enable unregistered conveyancing to match the efficiency of registered.[100] All that, however, was a world away from the 1830s and the 1850s.

Accordingly the Wills Act 1837 changed a few specific rules of law and a few rules of construction, but otherwise left judges to continue their processes of interpretation as before.[101] The changes were important, successful no doubt in the commissioners' aim of bringing the law more closely into line with testators' usual intentions. There is noticeably less reported litigation on the reformed rules than the unreformed. But a great deal was left unaffected, and as the Act was prospective only, wills governed by the old rules continued to come before the courts for the rest of the century. That was not just because devises in old wills remained as links in chains of title, but also because Chancery judges refused to declare entitlements until they fell into possession.[102] Since common law remedies were also possessory, a dispute about an interest in remainder had to wait on the deaths of the preceding generation(s).[103] If standards of interpretation changed, and they did, one consequence would be that wills were being judged by criteria their drafters could not have foreseen.

---

[98] Ker, *On the Reform of the Law of Real Property*, 30–1.

[99] See pp. 216–17 below.

[100] Land Transfer Act 1897; Administration of Estates Act 1925.

[101] Sections 24–29.

[102] *Greenwood* v. *Sutherland* (1853) 10 Hare App. xii; *Garlick* v. *Lawson* (1853) 10 Hare App. xv; *Hampton* v. *Holman* (1877) 5 Ch D 183.

[103] Of the wills cases reported in vols 3 and 4 of Beavan's reports (1840–2) about a quarter concerned wills 25 years old or more. The proportion is very much the same in vol. 60 of the Law Journal Chancery series (1891), though fewer of those raised questions of interpretation (and more concerned breach).

Handling the Heritage: Executory Trusts and Cy-près

Some of the severity evident in *Routledge* v. *Dorril* and *Leake* v. *Robinson* spilled over into testamentary executory trusts cases shortly before 1820.[104] Grant MR and Plumer VC took a more literal turn, giving more importance to testators' exact words and less to the courts' own values in remodelling inappropriate dispositions than often in the past.[105] In 1820, however, Lord Eldon gave his blessing to the jurisdiction, asserting that it was essentially similar to that over marriage articles and deprecating cases that appeared to have narrowed it.[106] Thus the dual standard was retained. It was not unusual for a judge about to interpret a direct disposition in a will to say that he would have been less strict had the trust been executory.[107]

The context within which judges would find that a testamentary instruction was merely executory remained narrow, however. Apart from instructions to settle land there is significant case law only on testamentary directions to create marriage settlements for daughters. Within those contexts judges showed considerable willingness to mould dispositions to a testator's general purpose, holding back only when convinced that the testator had been his 'own conveyancer', as the expression went.[108] That lay in the eye of the beholder, of course, as, exceptionally, a strong House of Lords showed in 1870 when virtually rewriting the late Countess Amherst's meticulous but misdirected will, over the vigorous protest of Lord Hatherley.[109] New contexts were not created, however. Lord Langdale quickly rebuffed counsel who suggested that whenever a will instructed that trustees should convey an estate enough remained executory for the court to shape the terms to its liking.[110]

[104] Above, pp. 21–2.

[105] *Blackburn* v. *Stables* (1814) 2 Ves. & Bea. 370; *Marshall* v. *Bousfield* (1817) 2 Madd. 166.

[106] *Jervoise* v. *Duke of Northumberland* (1820) 1 Jac. & W. 559. His own opinion in *Duke of Newcastle* v. *Lady Lincoln* (1806) 12 Ves. 217 was part of the difficulty.

[107] See e.g. Lord Westbury in *Harrington* v. *Harrington* (1871) LR 5 HL 87. The contrary view, that there was no greater reason for doing violence to a testator's words when his trust was executory than there was when it was direct, was once voiced by Wigram VC, and by one author, but did not take root: *Vanderplank* v. *King* (1843) 3 Hare 1; J. V. Prior, *A Treatise on the Construction of Limitations in which the Words 'Issue' or 'Child' occur* (1839), 60–1 cited by Lewis, *Perpetuity*, 451. Jarman struggled to find a justification that satisfied him: *Wills*, ii, 263–6.

[108] *Jervoise* v. *Duke of Northumberland* (1820) 1 Jac. & W. 559 (Eldon); *Rochfort* v. *Fitzmaurice* (1842) 2 Dr. & War. 1 (Sugden); *Egerton* v. *Earl Brownlow* (1853) 4 H.L.C. 1 (Sugden).

[109] *Sackville-West* v. *Holmesdale* (1870) LR 4 HL 453, reversing (1866) LR 3 Eq 474 (which had been decided by Hatherley when Page Wood VC).

[110] *Jackson* v. *Noble* (1838) 2 Keen 590, 2 Jur. 251 (which has counsel's argument that ambiguous or conventional phrases should be treated as executory). *Franks* v. *Price* (1840) 3 Beav. 182 also came to be cited for rejection of the same proposition.

Ambiguous or conventional expressions were not enough to invoke the jurisdiction. The difficulty was most acute in wills that designated chattels as heirlooms, their devolution to parallel a strict settlement of the family land, or which said that leaseholds should follow the realty. Such things were not possible directly, since personalty could not be entailed, but an approximation could be achieved through trusts to the extent that the modern rule against perpetuities permitted. The orthodox understanding in the mid-nineteenth century was that Lord Hardwicke had treated such clauses as indicating an executory trust that a court would model, despite the deviation from the testator's particular intention that inevitably resulted, but that Lord Thurlow had reversed his decisions.[111] Once Lord Eldon had refused to let his personal preference for Hardwicke's decisions outweigh his duty to follow the later it became a fixed rule that something far more explicit was needed to create an executory trust of chattels. The words that Lord Hardwicke had seen as justifying an executory trust were instead treated as surplusage following a direct disposition that was to be read according to its ordinary meaning.[112]

Similarly, the sphere occupied by the *cy-près* principle was not to be extended: again Lord Eldon said so.[113] And it was to be seen as a principle of interpretation giving effect to the testator's poorly expressed intention, not as a jurisdiction to remodel. But what was that to mean? A generation or so later Thomas Jarman distilled from the cases a set of rules demanding such a precise intention from the testator before his failed disposition would be interpreted *cy-près* that the principle could be explained only on the narrowest of bases. In short, the testator must be shown to have meant exactly the outcome that the court would arrive at by simple substitution of a fee tail for a life estate, but had merely expressed himself inaccurately.[114] Writers at the end of the eighteenth century had rooted

---

[111] *Rowland* v. *Morgan* (1848) 2 Ph. 764; *Harrington* v. *Harrington* (1871) LR 5 HL 87.

[112] *Duke of Newcastle* v. *Lady Lincoln* (1806) 12 Ves. 217. Eldon was outvoted by Ellenborough and Erskine, who both supported an executory trust, but, as one more confirmation of the generally stricter approach at this time, it was Eldon's opinion that was followed in cases such as *Carr* v. *Lord Erroll* (1808) 14 Ves. 478 and *Lord Deerhurst* v. *Duke of St. Albans* (1820) 5 Madd. 232 (which on appeal was not reversed on this point, though it was on its consequential interpretation of the bequest—*Tollemache* v. *Earl of Coventry* (1834) 2 Cl. & F. 611). The series was effectively ended by Lord Cottenham's reluctant acquiescence: *Rowland* v. *Morgan* (1848) 2 Ph. 764; see also *re Johnston* (1884) 26 Ch D 538. Where the words clearly did indicate an executory trust of heirlooms or of leases judges seem to have been very willing to comply: *Shelley* v. *Shelley* (1868) LR 6 Eq 540; *Miles* v. *Harford* (1879) 12 Ch D 691.

[113] *Brudenell* v. *Elwes* (1802) 7 Ves. 382; see also *Seaward* v. *Willcock* (1804) 5 East 198, 390; *Somerville* v. *Lethbridge* (1795) 6 T.R. 213.

[114] Jarman, *Wills*, i, 260–4. Jarman's meticulous precision was exceeded by J. C. Gray, whose formulation of the rule (Gray was sure that it was a rule, not a principle) was so exact that it took a sentence of 67 words to express: *Perpetuities* (2nd edn), §643, p. 484.

the *cy-près* jurisdiction in an executory trust case, *Humberston v. Humberston*, implying that *cy-près* too invoked the court's creative role. Jarman now proffered a later, narrower, case as its true ancestor.[115] By the early twentieth century judges found even that case unacceptably loose.[116]

This severe confinement of *cy-près*, however, and the drawing of sharp distinctions between executory and executed dispositions, was insecure for as long as a theory of interpretation known as 'general intention' remained available. Arden MR's explanation of *cy-près* in *Routledge* v. *Dorril* had rested upon it, but in doing so he had introduced contradictions. The technique allowed a testator's supposed general intention to remodel particular limitations (his 'particular intention') that would otherwise fail. But as a general interpretive technique it had no boundaries. It might even outflank Arden MR's ruling that *cy-près* was unavailable to bequests of personalty, since *cy-près* could be used by analogy to support a reinterpretation based upon the testator's supposed general intention. That seems to have happened in *Mogg* v. *Mogg* in 1811.[117] As late as the 1870s Sir George Jessel's explanation of *cy-près* invoked the theory of general intention, albeit with idiosyncratic additions.[118] There was even a personalty case that used the scattergun technique of *Mogg* v. *Mogg*, and another that contradicted *Routledge* v. *Dorril*.[119] By the 1880s, however, the technique of 'general intention' had for a long time been on life support, as will be seen.

Handling the Heritage: The Disavowal of 'General Intention'

The technique of 'general intention' was purposive. It involved first finding a testator's supposed general intention—the objective and strategy of the will projected against an understanding of what testators usually do, and ought to do—and then using that general intention to 'control' particular clauses, modifying their

---

[115] *Nicholl* v. *Nicholl* (1777) 2 W. Bl. 1159 in place of *Humberston* v. *Humberston* (1716) 1 P. Wms 332; Jarman *Wills*, i 261; compare Lewis, *Perpetuity*, 450–2, and contrast Fearne, *Contingent Remainders*, 204n. Sugden, an adherent to older values and methods, stuck with the eighteenth-century explanation: *A Practical Treatise of Powers* (8th edn, 1861), 498–503.

[116] *Re Mortimer* [1905] 2 Ch 502; *re Richardson* [1904] 1 Ch 332.

[117] *Mogg* v. *Mogg* (1811–15) 1 Mer. 654 (the devise of leaseholds); 'a compound result of the influence of the *cy-près* doctrine, a respect for the testator's general intention, with an anxiety to support his disposition, as far as possible, and the rule noscitur a sociis': Lewis, *Perpetuity*, 438. Since, as was the custom, the King's Bench gave no reasons for the certificate it sent to Chancery its decision enjoyed only a form of semi-authority.

[118] *Hampton* v. *Holman* (1877) 5 Ch D 183; cf. *Parfitt* v. *Hember* (1867) LR 4 Eq 443 (Romilly MR).

[119] *Lyddon* v. *Ellison* (1854) 19 Beav. 565, 18 Jur. 1066 (Romilly MR), citing *Stonor* v. *Curwen* (1832) 5 Sim. 264, an executory trust case; *Mackworth* v. *Hinxman* (1836) 2 Keen 658 (Langdale MR).

actual words if need be.[120] It could be used to sidestep a breach of a rule; it could be used to adjust a disposition that had turned out to be foolish in the circumstances. It was often regarded as a distinctively eighteenth-century technique. Thomas Jarman associated it particularly with Lord Kenyon, and he disliked it for the laxity of construction it induced.[121] It was incoherent because its reasoning was circular, and undesirable for leading courts into writing wills for testators. His editor noted that even the shape of some of his arguments seems tacitly designed to combat Lord Kenyon's form of contextualism.[122] Lord Wensleydale dismissively sired the technique on Wilmot CJ —for a common law principle to have identifiable parentage was a disparagement (unlike a principle of equity).[123]

For these and other critics the technique was illegitimate because there was no textual basis from which the general intention could be demonstrated. It rested on notions of what testators in general might be supposed to do, or, worse, what they ought to do, when the question should be what this testator had done. It smuggled in social assumptions that were both contestable and irrelevant. Further, it encouraged judges to interpret wills backwards: to take the facts as they had turned out to be, perhaps two or three generations from the testator's death, and then ask what the testator would have wanted in these circumstances. That was speculation, conjecture, the critics said. The only acceptable method was to take the words as they were written, give them the meaning they bore at the time the will became operative, and then apply the law to that meaning regardless of whether the testator would have wanted the consequences, regardless of whether a more acceptable outcome (one conjectures) could have been achieved by twisting his words. Needless to say, a displacement like that, though it happened, could not in its nature happen evenly. It is going to be, as Lord Blackburn often said, a matter of more or less.

The issue is complicated by a sub-theme: what, in the modern way of looking at wills, was to be the role of 'rules of construction'? These were myriad— perhaps 1000 of the 1500 pages of the third edition of *Jarman* concern rules of construction in one way or another. They could be very general, or could concern the meaning of a single word, or a phrase, or a sequence of dispositions, or any stage in between. They could be refined and sub-divided almost indefinitely by the accretion of case law. Since they were only rules of construction they could be ousted by the testator, expressly, or perhaps by implication, sometimes. Then

[120] It is beyond the scope of this volume to determine how widespread the technique had actually been in the eighteenth century.

[121] *Wills*, ii, 400–5. For other criticisms of Kenyon, see *ibid.*, 295–6, 319, 339–40, 419–20, 435.

[122] Jarman, *Wills* (6th edn), ii, 1942n.

[123] *Roddy* v. *Fitzgerald* (1858) 6 H.L.C. 823; repeated by Lord Macnaghten in *Van Grutten* v. *Foxwell* [1897] AC 658.

rules of construction could grow up around what words were or were not capable of ousting which rules of construction in what circumstances.

Rules of construction were based on a supposition not often made explicit, that words that had once received a judicial interpretation should continue to bear it, hence that words not significantly different should bear it too. This had implications for what got reported—since every instance of interpretation had precedent value—and for forms of argumentation in disputed cases. Much of that was to be challenged towards the end of the nineteenth century. It came to be said that, like 'general intention', rules of construction got between the interpreter and the text, introducing values that were not to do with the testator's meaning. But, then, did not rules of construction have a compensating utilitarian value? As James LJ said in 1876, regretting the erosion of one he liked, 'with respect to wills in particular, it is far better to have settled rules which will enable the members of families to know what the law gives them, than that every variation of language used by a testator, or his lawyer, should entail on family after family the costs, the heart-burning and misery of litigation'.[124]

As a useful and appropriate tool of interpretation 'general intention' was denounced in the House of Lords by Lord Redesdale in 1820, by Lord Denman in the King's Bench in 1833 (adopting textbook criticisms by William Hayes and Thomas Jarman), by Lord Brougham in 1843, by Lord Wensleydale and Lord Cranworth in the 1850s, and by a whole battery of law-lords in the 1890s.[125] The ability of any technique to survive such opposition for so long calls for admiration. Of course, being a general technique it once flourished in a variety of habitats; eradication would follow only from its elimination from each habitat separately, that is a consequence of the combined effect of *stare decisis* and *ratio decidendi*. There seem to have been four overlapping usages, habitats as it were, some easier to cleanse than others.

The first and easiest was underpinning the *cy-près* principle, as outlined above. Since *cy-près* had become an anomaly, it need not matter that it had an anomalous explanation. Hence the usage in this context need not be generalized, and, if it were not, judges who disliked both it and *cy-près* could turn the one against the other by taking a very narrow view of what should count as a general intention.[126] That was easy.

---

[124] *Wake* v. *Varah* (1876) 2 Ch D 348, echoing Romilly MR in *Seccombe* v. *Edwards* (1860) 28 Beav. 440; and see him in *Beckwith* v. *Beckwith* (1876) 46 LJ Ch 97.

[125] *Jesson* v. *Wright* (1820) 2 Bli. 1 (but contrast Eldon); *Doe d. Gallini* v. *Gallini* (1833) 5 B. & Ad. 621, citing W. Hayes, *An Inquiry into the Effect of Limitations to Heirs of the Body in Devises* (1824) and J. J. Powell, *An Essay upon the Learning of Devises* (3rd edn 1827, by Jarman); *Doe d. Winter* v. *Perratt* (1843) 9 Cl. & F. 606; *Roddy* v *Fitzgerald* (1858) 6 H.L.C. 823; *Van Grutten* v. *Foxwell* [1897] AC 658.

[126] Gray, *Perpetuities*, §§643–60 (pp. 481–94).

The second usage of 'general intention' was as an explanation of, and justification for, the rule in *Shelley's* case. If one asked why *should* a devise to 'X for life' be in some circumstances read as giving an immediate fee tail, the answer, in this usage, was that that was the only way to give effect to the testator's general intention that the land should descend through the various branches of his family in succession. That intention could be collected from the devises that were to follow the life estate, but they could not be given effect in the way the testator had particularly said—either because to do so would break some old feudal rules about how heirs could take under wills or because the limitations would be void for remoteness (which then links to the *cy-près* usage). Alternatively one could imagine various accidents of infant mortality among the beneficiaries the testator had described, and then show how the estate given by the rule in *Shelley's* case would come closer to satisfying the testator's scheme than the words he had actually used.

This explanatory usage was accepted by Lord Cairns and Lord Fitzgerald in the House of Lords as late as 1884.[127] Its danger had always been that it would shift from being an explanation of the rule to being a purposive interpretation of the will, and that that would then shift the rule to being a mere presumption of construction rebuttable by circumstance. That was exactly what Lord Mansfield's King's Bench had wanted in *Perrin* v. *Blake* in 1769, but their heresy had been immediately rejected.[128] A decision by Sir Edward Sugden in 1845 kept that possibility alive, though not very vigorous, despite the many denunciations of the technique, until in 1897 the Lords derisively rejected the entire usage.[129] The rule in *Shelley's* case was just that, they said: a rule. It needed no explanation.

The third and fourth usages were more general. The third was to resolve demonstrable ambiguity in a will by choosing the meaning that best advanced the testator's general intention. In its strong form this involved imagining the testator knowing the facts as they had happened, and then asking which outcomes he would or would not have wanted. The fourth usage was that 'general intention' could explain and justify 'rules of construction', perhaps even create new ones.

---

[127] *Bowen* v. *Lewis* (1884) LR 9 App Cas 890; cf. Bovill CJCP in *Bradley* v. *Cartwright* (1867) LR 2 CP 511.

[128] *Perrin* v. *Blake* (1769–72), summarized 4 Burr. 2579, 1 W. Bl. 672; full reports at F. Hargrave, *Collecteana Juridica* (1791–2), i 283 (King's Bench), and 1 *Hargrave's Tracts* (1787), 487 (Blackstone J.). The conveyancers' reply to Mansfield's individualism was put most directly (and intemperately) by Fearne, *Contingent Remainders* (10th edn), esp. 167–73. For a dismissive modern view see Simpson, *Leading Cases in the Common Law*, 13–44, esp. 40–1.

[129] *Montgomery* v. *Montgomery* (1845) 3 Jo. & Lat. 47; *Jordan* v. *Adams* (1859) 6 C.B. N.S. 748 (Cockburn CJ); *Van Grutten* v. *Foxwell* [1897] AC 658; and cf. Gray, *Perpetuities*, §882 (p. 599): 'The Rule in Shelley's Case is not a rule for interpretation, it is a rule the object of which is to defeat intention.'

Lord Cottenham used it in this way, for example, to explain why a court might find a trust for a class of children or grandchildren equally, where the disposition was worded as a mere power to appoint among them but the donee of the power had failed to appoint: the court could advance the testator's general intention on the failure of his particular intention.[130] Both the principle and the explanation were rooted in a purposive, social, approach to interpretation. Similarly, rules of construction could be restricted by reference to a testator's general intention, not just by express words. The strongest statement was by James VC in 1870:

> [Counsel's reasoning] is a very good illustration of the process by which in this Court we have established a body of dogma, and developed a whole code of artificial rules, according to which a testator's will is treated as if it were written in cypher, and incapable of being construed except by those learned persons who have the key of the cypher. Nevertheless, sometimes the Court is enabled to determine questions arising upon wills according to rules of common sense; either by playing off one rule against another, or by resorting to some general rule of construction which controls the rest. One of these rules... is that the general intent is to prevail against the particular intent; and if the Court can arrive at a general result as to what the testator intended, that general result will prevail over every particular construction.[131]

The potency of general intention to justify and modulate legal change was vividly demonstrated, but not in England. In 1891 the Supreme Court of New Hampshire crafted from it a principle of partial validity for devises that infringed the rule against perpetuities—an extension, thus, of the first usage described

---

[130] *Burrough v. Philcox* (1840) 5 My. & Cr. 72; *Penny v. Turner* (1848) 2 Ph. 493. Hawkins describes it as carrying out the intention *cy-près*: *Wills* (2nd edn), 77. Page Wood VC several times spoke as though the principle had hardened into a rule: *Joel v. Mills* (1857) 3 K. & J. 458; *Salusbury v. Denton* (1857) 3 K. & J. 529; *re White's Trusts* (1860) Johns. 656; see also *Butler v. Gray* (1869) LR 5 Ch App 26. The gift in default to the class was often described as an 'implied gift', leaving conveniently vague the questions of who was doing the implying and what they were implying it from. In due course, as 'ordinary meaning' supplanted 'general and particular intention' judges turned to seeking some express words in the will from which they could infer that the testator really did mean there to be a trust in default: *Wilson v. Duguid* (1883) 24 Ch D 244; *re Weekes' Settlement* [1897] 1 Ch 289; *re Combe* [1925] Ch 210. For a characteristically dense analysis, see J. C. Gray, 'Powers in Trust and Gifts Implied in Default of Appointment' (1911) 25 *HLR* 12. He made much of *re Brierley* (1894) 43 WR 36, though there the CA explicitly did not decide whether there was a trust by implication or whether a gift over in default of appointment would take effect; its method, however, was suggestive of a rule-based approach, as Gray argued. It was brushed aside in both *re Weekes* and *re Combe*.

[131] *Habergham v. Ridehalgh* (1870) LR 9 Eq 395. No judge was wholly consistent in his approach, though most had a recognizable profile. Even Parke B., Lord Wensleydale, whose reputation as a strict constructionist is well deserved, could adopt a purposive, almost creative approach on occasion: compare his advice to the Lords in *Dungannon v. Smith* (1846) 12 Cl. & F. 546 with anyone else's (except Patteson J., who did the same). This quotation from the early James VC is less typical of him than the quotation on p. 28 above from the later James LJ, though he remained more purposive in his interpretations than most of his brethren.

above—doing exactly what Lord Kenyon, Arden MR, and Grant MR had refused to do for England a century or so earlier.[132] Its contrasting fate in England is illustrated in the next two sections.

The New Orthodoxy: Technical Meanings and Ordinary Meanings

The turn towards strict construction in the decade or two before 1820 which is outlined above had not been uniform. *Mogg* v. *Mogg* was not the only example of lax construction perpetrated by the King's Bench. In 1811 it pronounced that a devise of land to one 'at 21' would usually not be interpreted as the contingent gift it appeared to be, but as a vested estate liable to be divested by death before that age.[133] Granted that there was a sheaf of rules favouring early vesting, yet this was still an extreme example. It was important because so long as an estate remained contingent it could be squeezed out if the holder of the prior estate and the holder of a subsequent estate colluded.[134] Nor were these the only departures from strict construction. Faced with dispositions that more literally minded judges would say clearly invoked the rule in *Shelley's* case the King's Bench, and the Common Pleas also, had started accepting the argument that the testator had been employing his own particular meaning for the words used: when he said 'heirs' he had meant 'children', for example, not 'descendants'.[135]

In *Jesson* v. *Wright* in 1820 that last issue reached the Lords, where Lords Eldon and Redesdale reversed the King's Bench and halted the recent trend.[136] Lord Redesdale explained, 'There is such a variety of combination in words, that it has the effect of puzzling those who are to decide upon the construction of wills. It is therefore necessary to establish rules, and important to uphold them, that those who have to advise may be able to give opinion on titles with safety.' The rule in *Shelley's* case (and indeed any other rule) was therefore to be reinforced by a rule of construction that technical words used in a will were to be given their technical meaning. But that subsidiary rule could not operate without a further rule or, at least, without a further technique: 'It cannot at this day be argued', said

---

[132] *Edgerly* v. *Barker* (1891) 66 NH 434.

[133] *Doe d. Hunt* v. *Moore* (1811) 14 East 601; *Doe d. Roake* v. *Nowell* (1813) 1 M. & S. 327. Their broad statement was wider than necessary on the facts.

[134] See pp. 62–4, below. If a devise to a father for life and then to his children at 21 creates a vested but divestible interest, a child under 21 at its father's death may still take under the will, whereas if the interest is contingent it will not.

[135] *Doe d. Strong* v. *Goff* (1811) 11 East 668; *Gretton* v. *Howard* (1815) 6 Taunt. 94; *Crump d. Woolley* v. *Norwood* (1815) 7 Taunt. 362; *Doe d. Wright* v. *Jesson* (1816) 5 M. & S. 95 and see *Right d. Shortridge* v. *Creber* (1826) 5 B. & C. 866. In *Jervoise* v. *Duke of Northumberland* (1820) 1 Jac. & W. 559 Shadwell, in argument, said that *Gretton* had 'excited much surprize'.

[136] (1820) 2 Bli. 1.

Lord Redesdale, 'that because the testator uses in one part of his will words having a clear meaning in law, and in another part other words inconsistent with the former, that the first words are to be cancelled or overthrown.'

Technical though it is, it is worth illustrating the different outcomes these formulations had. In *Jesson* v. *Wright* the testator had said 'to W for life, and after his decease to the heirs of his body *in such shares and proportions as W by deed... shall appoint, and for want of such appointment to the heirs of his body share and share alike as tenants in common*, and for want of such issue to the heirs of the devisor' [my italics]. The King's Bench had used the italicized words to reach out to what it took to be the testator's true intention: 'heirs of his body' must mean W's children, hence W took a life estate and his children shared a fee simple. That was a construction that subordinated a technical rule to a general intention; it used all the words the testator had used in order to fashion the best outcome available. By contrast Lord Redesdale privileged words he deemed technical: they gave W a fee tail, and the italicized words must be rejected as repugnant.[137]

That technical words should be given their technical meaning became a cornerstone of nineteenth-century interpretive technique. Without addressing it, it went some way towards meeting the conveyancers' value proposed by Bellenden Ker, that standards applicable to deeds should be applied to wills.[138] Of course, it was not self-evident which words were 'technical'. *Jesson* v. *Wright* held that 'heirs' was, but 'issue' divided the judges evenly until, in the second wave of strict construction, Lords Cranworth and Wensleydale ordained in 1858 that it too was; usually.[139]

There was nothing 'technical' about the King's Bench's benevolent opinion in 1811 that a devise to one 'at 21' would create a vested (but divestible) remainder rather than a contingent remainder vulnerable to destruction before vesting. The objection was that it gave the testator's words a meaning they would not bear in ordinary discourse, and that it did that to forward a purpose that was being attributed to this testator, or perhaps to testators in general, without demonstrating that purpose from the text. But to some extent all rules of construction were vulnerable to that charge, and, as Lord Redesdale had said, any rule about land titles had a utilitarian value. A direct devise of realty automatically became the next link in a chain of title to land, and it might be decades before a purchaser in a pending sale raised doubts about its exact meaning. There was obvious virtue

---

[137] This reading achieved Eldon and Redesdale's objective: certainty of title. It vindicated the lawyer who had advised that a fee tail had been created, hence that it could be barred and the land sold.

[138] For routine applications, accompanied by routine expressions of regret, see *Leach* v. *Jay* (1877) 6 Ch D 496; *Smith* v. *Butcher* (1878) 10 Ch D 113.

[139] *Roddy* v. *Fitzgerald* (1858) 6 H.L.C. 823.

in leaving established rules alone. Nonetheless, the standard that technical words should be given technical meanings was accompanied by a standard of much broader impact, that ordinary words should be given their ordinary meaning. It can be traced through James Wigram's book, first published in 1831, and on into a series of hard-fought cases in the Lords, mostly in the 1850s.[140]

The principle that ordinary words should be given their ordinary meaning seems undramatic, and as it came with a rider that allowed testators to stipulate that they were using words in some extraordinary way it might seem indeterminate enough to allow judges to follow their preferences as they wished. Judging from the reported cases, however, which number in their hundreds, and from their scrupulous monitoring in the texts, such manipulation was very occasional. Instead judges acknowledged that there had been a step away from a purposive interpretation towards something more formal. As such it was strongly contested, especially by Lord St Leonards at the time and Malins VC later.

By the new standard a judge should first give the words in a will their ordinary meaning, or their technical meaning if they had one, without asking what consequences that brought, and then apply the law to that meaning without asking whether the result was what the testator would have wanted. The mere fact that a non-ordinary meaning would bring a result the testator might reasonably be supposed to have preferred was not a reason for concluding that that had in fact been his meaning; to do so would be conjecture or speculation. It was, Lord Halsbury said, 'arguing in a vicious circle to begin by assuming an intention apart from the language of the instrument itself, and having made that fallacious assumption to bend the language in favour of the assumption so made'. To apply one principle of interpretation to a document drawn by a blood relation of the beneficiary and a different one to a document drawn by a stranger was contrary to 'the modern view'.[141]

The new standard replaced the discredited notion that a testator's legally ineffective or socially foolish particular intention could be 'controlled' by his general intention. There were rebels who clung to the old ways, in part at least. Sir Richard Malins, a Vice Chancellor from 1867 until 1881, is the most obvious, and the last

---

[140] J. Wigram, *An Examination of the Rules of Law respecting the Admission of Extrinsic Evidence in aid of the Interpretation of Wills* (1831); see R. Kerridge and J. Rivers, 'The Construction of Wills' (2000) 116 *LQR* 287–317, esp. notes 22 and 23; *Roddy v. Fitzgerald* (1858) 6 H.L.C. 823, cf. Lord Brougham in *Doe d. Winter v. Perratt* (1843) 9 Cl. & F. 606; *Grey v. Pearson* (1857) 6 H.L.C. 61; *Abbott v. Middleton* (1858) 7 H.L.C. 68; *Smith v. Osborne* (1857) 6 H.L.C. 375; *Thellusson v. Rendlesham* (1859) 7 H.L.C. 429. Cranworth and Wensleydale parted company in *Clarke v. Colls* (1861) 9 H.L.C. 601, whereafter Cranworth drifted towards an uneasy reconciliation with rules of construction in *Martin v. Holgate* (1866) LR 1 HL 175.

[141] *Leader v. Duffey* (1888) 13 App Cas 294: contrast Lord Blackburn in *Wakefield v. Maffet* (1885) 10 App Cas 422 and see also *Day v. Radcliffe* (1876) 3 Ch D 654; *Selby v. Whittaker* (1877) 6 Ch D 239.

consistent user of the old technique.[142] He was frequently reversed or overruled. And there were sceptics. Sir George Jessel MR was fond of saying that though he was certain of a clause's ordinary meaning he expected his brethren to be equally certain it was something different.[143] Further, the third usage of the old technique outlined above, its use in handling overtly ambiguous dispositions, was not very different from its replacement: that ambiguity would be resolved by searching for the meaning most consistent with the testator's usage throughout the will. Once it was conceded that the interpreter could take into account the state of the testator's family at the time of the testator's death, a flexible judge could reintroduce notions of intention and purpose very much like those the purists rejected. Lord Blackburn is the clearest example, not just in his practice of the technique, but also in the way he gently mocked the purists' pretensions.[144] Nevertheless, judges who wanted something more flexible than the 'ordinary meaning' canon denied that their middle ground was a return to 'general intention'.[145] Jessel and Blackburn are typical of a type, but they must not be taken to be representative of the whole.

Because Malins VC and, to an extent, Kay J., kept it going, and because as late as 1884 two members of the House of Lords thought it useful in explaining the rule in *Shelley's* case, the older canon was not wholly supplanted until late in the century.[146] But supplanted it was. When the New Hampshire Supreme Court revived it there in 1891 John Chipman Gray, whose text on perpetuities was devoted to bringing meticulous rule to the indiscipline of judicial decisions, thundered against this return to the 'unspeakable quagmire' of general intention.[147] Changing his metaphor, it was a 'chase after the will o'wisp of general and particular intent which the Court of King's Bench began more than 100 years ago, and which, after long wanderings and stumblings and groanings of spirit, it has now finally abandoned'.[148] There was no similar backsliding in England.

---

[142] 'Now, with regard to the construction of wills, the view I take, a view which I have frequently expressed, is, that the first step is to be satisfied what the intention of the testator really was, and then see how far the words of the will carry that intention into effect' (*Re Speakman* (1876) 4 Ch D 620).

[143] *Metcalfe* v. *Hutchinson* (1875) 1 Ch D 591; *Re Sibley's Trusts* (1877) 5 Ch D 494; *Selby* v. *Whittaker* (1877) 6 Ch D 239.

[144] *Bowen* v. *Lewis* (1884) 9 App Cas 890 (cp Bramwell); *Rhodes* v. *Rhodes* (1882) 7 App Cas 192.

[145] *Towns* v. *Wentworth* (1858) 11 Moo. P.C. 526 shows a judge cautiously threading his way through the ideas.

[146] For a late warning not to use it see *Gibbons* v. *Gibbons* (1881) 6 App Cas 471, citing *Giles* v. *Melsom* (1873) LR 6 HL 24.

[147] Gray, *Perpetuities*, §882 (p. 599); for Gray see Simpson, *Leading Cases*, 96–8.

[148] Gray, *Perpetuities*, § 887 (p. 602). New Hampshire stuck to its guns: see e.g. *Merchants National Bank* v. *Curtis* (1953) 97 A2d 207, and generally, J. Quarles, 'The *cy-près* rule: its application to cases involving the rule against perpetuities and trusts for accumulation' (1946) 21 *NYULQ* 384–99.

Precatory Trusts

The most conspicuous example of the general shift to an ordinary meaning standard concerned precatory or recommendatory trusts, as they were called. At the start of our period it was well established that testators did not have to use technical legal expressions to subject recipients of their property to legal obligations. If their words were clearly imperative courts would import a trust—to sell land, for example, or to pay legacies out of realty—since trusts were the only way most obligations could be made to affect the property and the recipients be held accountable.[149] The difficulty came with bequests to close family members, often the widow, accompanied by words of request, recommendation, hope, confidence, or some such term, that they would (typically) maintain and educate the testator's children, and/or (typically) that they would leave the property to the children, or among the family. There were many variations.

Given the social context outlined earlier, and the 'general intention' standard of interpretation, it is unsurprising that courts had for a long time leant in favour of finding such words obligatory. Broadly speaking, the cases up to about 1820 were seen as supporting a rule of construction that if the property and the beneficiaries were clearly indicated courts would take any expression of desire as importing a trust, but, benevolently, if the property and objects together were *not* clear—themselves matters of interpretation—then despite the testator's words of desire he could not have intended a trust.[150] The accretion of interpretive precedents to the primary rule had become so dense that in 1822 Graham B. spoke of being 'enslaved by the cases', and Richards CB refused to go one further step in turning precatory words into trusts.[151]

Despite these hints Lords Eldon and Redesdale seem to have declined to tighten up precatory trusts in the way they had lately tightened up the rule in *Shelley's case*.[152] In the 1840s, however, commentators were remarking upon a recent tendency to find absolute gifts where previous judges would have found trusts.[153] One catalyst was Lord Langdale's judgment in *Knight* v. *Knight*, subsequently treated as authority that to be valid a trust must display 'the three certainties', which was important because it treated the requirements as independent of each other, and

---

[149] Lewin, *Trusts* (1st edn), 77.

[150] Jarman, *Wills* (1st edn), i, 334; J. Hill, *A Practical Treatise on the Law Relating to Trustees* (1845), 32. For the rules as they appeared to be in 1863, see Hawkins, *Wills* (2nd edn), 196–206.

[151] *Heneage* v. *Lord Viscount Andover* (1822) 10 Price 230, *sub nom. Meredith* v. *Heneage* (1824) 1 Sim. 542.

[152] *Meredith* v. *Heneage* (1824) 1 Sim. 542, 10 Price 306. Compare *Jesson* v. *Wright* (1820) 2 Bli. 1.

[153] Lewin, *Trusts*, 82 (rather an afterthought); Jarman, *Wills* (1st edn), i, 338, 344; Hill, *Trustees*, 33–5; E. B. Sugden, *A Treatise on the Law of Property, as Administered by the House of Lords* (1849), 375; cf. *Sale* v. *Moore* (1827) 1 Sim. 534.

of equal weight.[154] It led to a restatement by Lord Truro in 1851 that if property and objects were clear the question was whether the recipient had been 'deprived of all option or discretion' not to do as the testator desired, which considerably weakened the earlier presumption.[155] Nevertheless, the shift was very gradual, and judges were still reported holding that precedent obliged them to find for a trust, though they themselves did not believe that that was what the testator intended.[156] Judges rarely gave social or policy reasons, on either side of the argument, but Malins VC's doubt in 1874 that a testator meant to empower his widow on remarriage to leave his family's property to her new husband rings true.[157] R. J. Morris's study finds that the trusts in his sample were risk-spreading mechanisms to achieve secure rentier income for the family as a whole, with preference to the close family.[158] Treating ambiguously worded gifts to widows (especially) as creating trusts fits well with that.[159]

From the 1870s it became orthodox that precatory words did not create trusts. It was often said that *Lambe* v. *Eames* in 1871 turned the tide, though one would not have guessed that from its immediate mixed reception.[160] James LJ's famous outburst that Chancery's kindness in finding trusts was officious and sometimes cruel, while memorable as a value statement in an area given to dry textual analysis, seems remote from the facts in hand and difficult to reconcile with the vast majority of reported cases.[161] Nevertheless, from the late 1870s a line of appellate

---

[154] (1840) 3 Beav. 173.

[155] *Briggs* v. *Penny* (1851) 3 Mac. & G. 546 (an easy case, as precatory trusts went). The cases were so many that any significant restatement could quickly be supplied with a pedigree; in this case it was a similar statement by Lord Alvanley in *Malim* v. *Keighley* (1794) 2 Ves. Jun. 335.

[156] *Palmer* v. *Simmonds* (1854) 2 Drew. 221; *Barnes* v. *Grant* (1856) 2 Jur. (N.S.) 1127; contrast Lord Langdale in *Macnab* v. *Whitbread* (1853) 17 Beav. 299.

[157] *Le Marchant* v. *Le Marchant* (1874) LR 18 Eq 419, compare *Joslin* v. *Hamond* (1834) 3 My. & K. 110 (Leach MR). Malins VC cannot have meant this as a general policy, since he reached the same result as the Court of Appeal in what came to be seen as the decisive modern case upholding absolute interests, *Lambe* v. *Eames* (1870) LR 10 Eq 267, (1871) 6 Ch App 597; see the discussion below. There might also have been something of a policy of protecting the widow/trustee's children from her creditors if she became insolvent, though, if so, it was not articulated; for examples of the situation see *Carr* v. *Living (No. 2)* (1864) 33 Beav. 474 and *re Booth* [1894] 2 Ch 282.

[158] Morris, *Men, Women and Property*, 57, 275, 372–3.

[159] As does finding Malins VC resisting change; cf. *Longmore* v. *Elcum* (1843) 2 Y. & C. Ch.Cas. 363, where Knight-Bruce VC construed a precatory maintenance trust in the way he thought most likely to preserve the 'union of the family', which he thought was the testator's intent.

[160] (1871) 6 Ch App 597; *Mackett* v. *Mackett* (1872) LR 14 Eq 49; *Curnick* v. *Tucker* (1874) LR 17 Eq 320; *Le Marchant* v. *Le Marchant* (1874) LR 18 Eq 414, ; *Ellis* v. *Ellis* (1875) LJ Ch 225; cf. *Bond* v. *Dickinson* (1875) 33 LT 221. The metaphor itself became common from the late 1870s.

[161] Compare *Pope* v. *Pope* (1839) 10 Sim. 1, where a testator recited 'the constant abuse of trustees I daily witness among men' as the reason for leaving his property to his widow with only a list of his hopes, some of them very specific; Shadwell VC found the will sufficiently 'untechnical and obscure' to warrant interpretation as the testator had said he wanted.

cases turned strongly against construing precatory words as trusts, some of them openly acknowledging that a change was being made.[162] There was next to no discussion of context or policy beyond the topical concern for the literal meaning of words. It is impossible to tell whether judges were influenced by contemporary discussion of the status of women (more confidence that they were meant to be absolute owners? less confidence they could assume a trusteeship?), or contemporary concern to simplify conveyancing (for two of the leading cases arose in that context, where the issue was whether a vendor was really a trustee and hence unable to give good title).

Instead judges simply insisted that there was an easily discernible difference between mandatory and recommendatory language, that previous cases could not be authority for the construction of the will in hand, and that the test was in large measure semantic: had the testator by the first part of his sentence given an absolute gift for the recipient's own benefit? If he had, then words that purported to cut it down were of no legal effect. It is easy enough to find a pedigree for such a test, but that would be to miss the point: it was accepted as ushering in a new standard.[163]

The Problem of Rules of Construction

At root the 'ordinary meaning' standard is antipathetic to rules of construction beyond those of the most general orienting nature. Lord Halsbury made much of this at the end of the century, coming close to arguing that rules of construction were superfluous.[164] His polar opposite was Malins VC, whose dogged adherence to what by then had become a distinctively old-fashioned purposive approach to interpretation earned him mockery from Lord Halsbury and a reputation as an indifferent judge.[165] Most judges stood between these poles. A LEXIS computer

---

[162] *Re Hutchinson and Tenant* (1878) 8 Ch D 540; *re Adams and the Kensington Vestry* (1884) 27 Ch D 394; *re Diggles* (1888) 39 Ch D 253; *re Hamilton* [1895] 2 Ch 370; *Hill v. Hill* [1897] 1 QB 483; *Williams v. Williams* [1897] 2 Ch 12; *re Atkinson* (1911) 103 LT 860; and see *Stead v. Mellor* (1877) 5 Ch D 225.

[163] Pedigree: e.g. *Webb v. Wools* (1852) 2 Sim. (N.S.) 267; *Howorth v. Dewell* (1860) 29 Beav. 18; Jarman, *Wills* (6th edn, 1910), i, 868 saw the change as being gradual 'since the early part of the eighteenth century'. All rules of construction had instances of displacement, of course, so pedigrees for new standards could easily be constructed. New standard: *re Hamilton* [1895] 1 Ch 373; *re Oldfield* [1904] 1 Ch 549; *re Burley* [1910] 2 Ch 215; *re Conolly* [1910] 2 Ch 219.

[164] *Re Jodrell* (1890) 44 Ch D 590; *Leader v. Duffey* (1888) 13 App Cas 294; *Inderwick v. Tatchell* [1903] AC 120. He once begrudgingly accepted the utilitarian defence of rules of construction: *Kingsbury v. Walter* [1901] AC 187.

[165] *Barraclough v. Cooper* (1905) [1908] 2 Ch 121n.; ODNB, 'his judgments did not add much to the law of England'; Simpson, *Leading Cases*, 98 quoting Gray, *Perpetuities*, §215a. For an appreciation of Malins's values see *Grieve v. Grieve* (1867) LR 4 Eq 180; *re Potter* (1869) LR 8 Eq 52; *Bryden v. Willett*

search of the *Law Reports* combining 'rules of construction' with 'judgmentsby' for the post-1865 judges will demonstrate that rules of construction remained as necessary interpretive scaffolding to the end of our period. Judges generally accepted, as Lord Redesdale and James LJ had claimed, that rules of construction had utilitarian value, many no doubt agreeing with Romilly MR's observation that professionals drafting wills needed to rely on them.[166] But even Jessel MR said that rules of construction were arbitrary, when he was about to disregard one.[167] 'Arbitrary' and 'artificial' came to be common descriptions.

From that starting point, two major questions arise. First, given that over the course of a century the content of some rules of construction is bound to have changed, was there a pattern to the change? This would be exceedingly difficult to chart. Unlike rules of law, rules of construction were presumptive by their nature, hence were subject to a quiet erosion through non-application that one immersed in the legal culture of the day would sense well enough, but which has not yet been recaptured by modern research. The complex tissue of rules spun by Jarman and his peers is largely unexplored territory.[168] Three examples will be offered below, chosen because they stand in different relations to the ascendant canon of construction, and also because they affected common forms of testamentary settlement. How typical they were will have to be left open. They suggest an answer to the second major question, however, which is whether judges at the end of our period used rules of construction in the same way that their predecessors had done.

The first example tracks the fate that befell the King's Bench's opinion in 1811 that a devise to one 'at 21' would create a vested (but divestible) remainder rather than a contingent remainder.[169] That benevolent ruling first came under pressure in 1829, in the House of Lords. There Lord Eldon's view, and, perhaps more importantly, the opinion of the judges called upon to advise, was that the words should instead be taken according to their grammar and that judges should not conjecture what the testator's intentions may have been. Best CJ, giving the judges advice, did add, however, that holding children's interests to be contingent was also the better policy option, since it increased parental control.[170]

(1869) LR 7 Eq 472; *re Arnold's Trusts* (1870) LR 10 Eq 252; *Newill* v. *Newill* (1871) LR 12 Eq 432; *Adams* v. *Adams* (1871) LR 14 Eq 246; *re Speakman* (1876) 4 Ch D 620; *Smith* v. *Crabtree* (1877) 6 Ch D 591; *re Lucas's Will* (1881) 17 Ch D 788.

[166] *Seccombe* v. *Edwards* (1860) 28 Beav. 440.
[167] *Re Sibley's Trusts* (1877) 5 Ch D 494.
[168] For a beginning, see Kerridge and Rivers, 'The Construction of Wills'.
[169] *Doe d. Hunt* v. *Moore* (1811) 14 East 601; *Doe d. Roake* v. *Nowell* (1813) 1 M. & S. 327; see p. 31–2, above.
[170] *Duffield* v. *Duffield* (1829) 3 Bli. (N.S.) 260.

That decision never became the leading case that Lord Eldon hoped it would, however, and when the issue returned to the Lords in 1842 only Lord Brougham would unequivocally have applied a modern standard of interpretation.[171] Lords Lyndhurst and Campbell were quite unmoved by it, so Brougham had to fall back on recommending that the existing cases be limited to their common facts— which he could make out to be rather narrow. His hint was quickly followed by the Exchequer of Pleas, Rolfe B.—the future Lord Cranworth—leading that court to find a new distinction in the facts, freeing up an area within which it could apply the 'ordinary meaning' standard of which he was to become a leading exponent.[172]

Most judges welcomed this move, which, they said, halted a 'violent' construction that had wrongly conflated two different intentions a testator might have.[173] The opposition, Malins VC and, earlier, Stuart VC at his urging, subjected this change of direction to the most outspoken criticism.[174] They did not get it reversed; to most judges the new sub-rule harmonized with modern standards. But nor was it used to begin an outright reversal of the King's Bench's original ruling in 1811, because that would have undermined land titles. In a compromise between the competing values, the rule the old cases had generated continued to apply to wills worded as they had been, while the new principle of 'ordinary meaning' hemmed that rule in, curtailed and ossified it, prevented its expansion.

The context for the second and third examples is a middle-class will, usually of personalty or of mixed realty and personalty. In general legal terms it concerns a gift to a class, but with substitutions.[175] There were many variants on the theme, but for the first suppose a will leaving property to the testator's children for life, or perhaps to the testator's nephews and nieces for life, and then to their children. Suppose further, that if one of the original class were to die without children his or her share was to go over to the survivor or survivors. This seems to have been a common formulation in wills from the late eighteenth to the mid-nineteenth

---

[171] *Phipps* v. *Ackers* (1842) 9 Cl. & F. 583; this was seven years after an abortive first hearing of this aspect of this case in the Lords (1835) 3 Cl. & F. 702.

[172] *Festing* v. *Allen* (1843) 12 M. & W. 279. By contrast the Queen's Bench continued as before, but perhaps because its equivalent decision was virtually unreasoned it had much less impact: *Doe d. Bills* v. *Hopkinson* (1843) 5 Q.B. 223. The contrast is between 'to my children at 21' (with a gift over) and 'to my children who reach 21' (with a gift over); the former may be vested, the latter must be contingent.

[173] *Bull* v. *Pritchard* (1847) 5 Hare 567; *Holmes* v. *Prescott* (1864) 33 LJ Ch 264; *Re Finch* (1881) 17 Ch D 211 (Cotton LJ); Jarman, *Wills* (6th edn), ii, 1382–4.

[174] *Browne* v. *Browne* (1857) 3 Sm. & G. 568; *Jull* v. *Jacobs* (1876) 3 Ch D 703; *Patching* v. *Barnett* (1880) 49 LJ Ch 665. Malins was successful counsel in *Browne* v. *Browne*, and losing counsel in *Festing* v. *Allen*. Knight Bruce VC also seems to have disregarded *Festing* v. *Allen*: *Riley* v. *Garnett* (1849) 3 De G. & Sm. 629.

[175] Jarman, *Wills*, ii, 609–58; (6th edn), ii, 2100–43.

centuries, if the law reports are an appropriate guide. Now suppose one of the class dies leaving children. Clearly those children take their parent's share, which if the will is well drafted will include any existing accruals to that share; but do they also take a share in the share of an uncle or aunt who dies subsequently and leaves no children of their own? Are they 'survivors'?

In the eyes of James LJ, used to the notion that each branch of a family should get its equal share, 'no plain man, not a lawyer, would have had the slightest doubt... that the real intention of the testator' was that the children of the deceased member of the class should take the share their parent would have taken had he or she survived.[176] Accordingly, at the start of our period there was generally thought to be a rule of construction that 'survivors' was to be read as 'others' so as to achieve that general intention.[177] But from sometime in the 1850s it crumbled, because it was too great a contradiction of 'ordinary meaning'.[178] Malins VC and Kay J., sympathetic to older ways, tried to stem the tide by erecting new rules from the debris of the old, but failed for the same reason.[179]

Just one subtle attempt succeeded, perhaps because its originator was the great Lord Selborne. This was that 'survivor' might sometimes mean survival of the line, of the share, not survival of the person who originated the line or would have first taken the share.[180] What words were apt to invoke this new possibility then became a matter of fine art, turning on variations thought plausible, as Younger J. later said, only because they 'served as a useful corrective to the excesses of literal interpretation'.[181] The unmistakable trend, however, was towards a literal interpretation, one that cast sole responsibility for arbitrary or whimsical results upon testators and their advisors, which it was not the courts' business to rectify. It was sealed by the House of Lords in 1903.[182]

---

[176]   *Wake v. Varah* (1876) 2 Ch D 348.

[177]   Jarman, *Wills*, ii 609; *In re Corbett's Trusts* (1860) Johns. 591 (Page Wood VC).

[178]   Jarman, *Wills* (3rd edn), ii, 648. Several cases in the 1850s and 1860s speak of the change, though often only then to say that their testator really did mean 'other': e.g. *Smith* v. *Osborne* (1857) 6 H.L.C. 392; *Hodge* v. *Foot* (1865) 34 Beav. 349; *Hurry* v. *Morgan* (1866) LR 3 Eq 152; and see *re Corbett's Estate* (1860) Johns. 591 and *Wake* v. *Varah* (1876) 2 Ch D 348. *Lucena* v. *Lucena* (1877) 7 Ch D 255 may be the last of this type. The change was embedded with *Beckwith* v. *Beckwith* (1876) 46 LJ Ch 97; *re Horner's Estate* (1881) 19 Ch D 186; and *re Benn* (1885) 29 Ch D 839, then *Harrison* v. *Harrison* [1901] 2 Ch 136, and finally *Inderwick* v. *Tatchell* [1901] 2 Ch 738 (CA), [1903] AC 120 (HL).

[179]   *Re Arnold's Trusts* (1870) LR 10 Eq 252 (Malins VC), and compare *Re Potter's Trust* (1869) LR 8 Eq 52 and *Reed* v. *Braithwaite* (1871) LR 11 Eq 514; *Re Bowman* (1889) 41 Ch D 525 (Kay J.), and compare *re Hudson* (1882) 20 Ch D 406. See also *Badger* v. *Gregory* (1869) LR 8 Eq 78 (James VC). For disavowal see *Harrison* v. *Harrison* [1901] 2 Ch. 136 and *Inderwick* v. *Tatchell* [1901] 2 Ch 738 (CA), [1903] AC 120 (HL).

[180]   *Waite* v. *Littlewood* (1872) 8 Ch App 70, 73; *Cooper* v. *Macdonald* (1873) LR 16 Eq 258; Jarman, *Wills* (6th edn), ii, 2107–10.

[181]   *Powell* v. *Hellicar* [1919] 1 Ch 138.

[182]   *Inderwick* v. *Tatchell* [1903] AC 120.

The third example is the converse of the second, where a rule of construction accorded with what many judges thought anyway was the ordinary meaning of the testator's words. The context is similar: a bequest of personalty, typically for life, then to a class, with a substitution—say, 'to my widow for life, and then to my brother's sons, but if any shall be dead leaving issue, such issue to take in his place'.[183] Suppose now that one of the brother's sons had died before the testator made the will, but had left children; do they take as issue under the will? In a decision typical of his approach, Grant MR decided in *Christopherson* v. *Naylor* in 1816 that they did not.[184] Their gift was substitutionary, he held; as a matter of logic one can only substitute for one who would himself have qualified; the son could not have qualified because a dead person cannot take a gift; therefore his children cannot take either.[185] The report of the case reads as though Grant MR was laying down a rule, not just interpreting this will, and that is how he was taken. Judges, especially later in the century, conceded that the rule probably did thwart testators' intentions, but that did not diminish its authority in their eyes.[186]

Like any rule of construction, however, it could be displaced by something express in the will showing that deceased members of the primary class were meant to be included, or by necessary implication, but not by pleas to 'general intention'.[187] By the mid-1860s instances of its displacement were numerous enough to encourage Stuart MR to criticize the rule itself, stimulating in turn a frontal attack on the rule by Malins VC under the banner that rather than thwarting testators' intentions 'justice requires that a liberal interpretation should be put on the language of a will'.[188] He got no direct support at all; even James VC, who strongly objected to some aspects of the rule's logic, thought it too well established to question.[189] Jessel MR put his great weight to ignoring the rule,

---

[183] There was a good deal of law too on 'shall be dead', 'shall have died', 'if not then living' and so forth: Jarman, *Wills* (3rd edn), ii, 169, 703–12.

[184] *Christopherson* v. *Naylor* (1816) 1 Mer. 320; adopted in *Butter* v. *Ommaney* (1827) 4 Russ. 70; *Waugh* v. *Waugh* (1833) 2 My. & K. 41; *Peel* v. *Catlow* (1838) 9 Sim. 372; *Gray* v. *Garman* (1843) 2 Hare 268. Grant MR, however, was also responsible for the purposive 'rule in *Howgrave* v. *Cartier*' ((1814) 3 Ves. & Bea. 85); see Hawkins, *Wills* (2nd edn), 263–4.

[185] The circularity of the reasoning is pointed out best in *re Hickey* [1917] 1 Ch 601.

[186] *West* v. *Orr* (1877) 8 Ch D 60; *re Chinery* (1888) 39 Ch D 614; *re Roberts* (1885) 30 Ch D 234.

[187] Judges in cases where (sometimes slight) indications in the will did displace the rule generally emphasized that they were not challenging the rule: see e.g. *re Jordan's Trusts* (1863) 8 LT (NS) 307; *Gowling* v. *Thompson* (1868) LR 11 Eq 366n.

[188] *Parsons* v. *Gulliford* (1864) 10 Jur. (N.S.) 231; *Phillips* v. *Phillips* (1864) 10 Jur. (N.S.) 1173 (Stuart MR); *re Potter's Trust* (1869) LR 8 Eq 52, which Malins VC followed himself in *Adams* v. *Adams* (1872) LR 14 Eq 246; *re Speakman* (1876) 4 Ch D 620; and *re Lucas's Will* (1881) 17 Ch D 788.

[189] *Re Hotchkiss's Trusts* (1869) LR 8 Eq 643, compare *Habergham* v. *Ridehalgh* (1870) LR 9 Eq 395; Jarman, *Wills* (6th edn), ii, 1342n.

but he made as little impression as Malins VC.[190] A steady flow of cases through to the end of the century reasserted the rule's authority.[191] One could see this easily enough as reinforcement of a rule requiring a strict interpretation of wills, and rejection of attempts at something more purposive.

To stop there, however, would be misleading. The rule depended on characterizing the gift to the issue as substitutionary: standing in the place of one who got nothing (because he was dead) gets them nothing either. But the rule itself does not say when a gift is substitutionary. It cannot say 'always', because then it would be a rule of law not a rule of construction. So it must turn on something in the words used. First Shadwell VC in the mid-1830s, and then Kindersley VC from 1861, probed that possibility. In Kindersley's version, which was technically superior to Shadwell's, the search was for words apt to convey not that the issue should stand in the shoes of their deceased ancestor but that they should take the share that their ancestor would have taken had he survived.[192] Quite probably both judges disliked the rule, but their technique had to accept that decisions applying rules of construction themselves made rules.[193] Judges interpreting wills would compare the will in hand minutely with wordings that had already been held to fall one way or the other; this was the standard mid-Victorian method.[194] Since the rule itself had a head start, and since it embodied an ordinary meaning ethic that was in the ascendancy, an alternative analysis was available only where a judge could be persuaded that there was a plausible difference. The result, then, was one rule of construction, two sub-rules, and an increasingly complex tangle of precedents on which words invoked which.

These examples support three tentative observations. First, Malins VC and Kay J.'s attempts to modernize and reformulate rules of construction failed because there was no longer a place for such purposive endeavour.[195] The meaning of a will was an individual matter, not one for generalization. 'The modern authorities show', said Jessel MR in 1877, 'that you are not to strain arbitrary rules of

---

[190] *Re Smith* (1875) 5 Ch D 494n; *re Sibley's Trusts* (1877) 5 Ch D 494. For Jessel's failure see Jarman, *Wills* (6th edn), ii, 1337; *re Webster* (1883) 23 Ch D 737; *re Chinery* (1888) 39 Ch D 614.

[191] In addition to those already cited see *Hunter* v. *Cheshire* (1873) 8 Ch App 751; *West* v. *Orr* (1877) 8 Ch D 60; *Kelsey* v. *Ellis* (1878) 38 LT 471; *re Barker* (1887) 47 LT 38; *re Musther* (1890) 43 Ch D 569; *re Wood* [1894] 3 Ch 381.

[192] *Tytherleigh* v. *Harbin* (1835) 6 Sim. 329 (and see *re Haygarth* [1912] 1 Ch 510); *Loring* v. *Thomas* (1861) 1 Dr. & Sm. 497. Shadwell's analysis delayed vesting until the time of distribution.

[193] For Shadwell VC see also *Giles* v. *Giles* (1837) 8 Sim. 360; *Jarvis* v. *Pond* (1839) 9 Sim. 549, disowned in *re Thompson's Trust* (1854) 2 WR 28 as subsequently elaborated in *re Jordan's Trusts* (1863) 8 LT (NS) 307. For Kindersley VC see also *Etches* v. *Etches* (1856) 3 Drew. 447; *Lanphier* v. *Buck* (1865) 2 Dr. & Sm. 484.

[194] As always, there were occasional exceptions: *Coulthurst* v. *Carter* (1852) 15 Beav. 421 is one.

[195] Contrast James LJ's hopes for a new rule with the judgments of the other members of the court in *Beckwith* v. *Beckwith* (1876) 46 LJ Ch 97.

construction: there are some rules fixed in the law which must be abided by, but you are not to make new ones.'[196] Lord Halsbury agreed, of course.[197] It is inconceivable that if Grant MR's decision in *Christopherson* v. *Naylor* had been given in 1876 rather than in 1816 it would have generated a 'rule'.

Secondly, James VC's meta-rule, '... if the Court can arrive at a general result as to what the testator intended, that general result will prevail over every particular construction', was already being replaced by its end of century equivalent: that rules of construction were but guidelines that must yield to the ordinary meaning of words.[198] Put differently, the proper over-arching rule of construction was that words be given their ordinary meaning, or technical meaning if they had one.[199]

Thirdly, if rules of construction are deprived of their purposive element the cases that applied them become mere jumbles of instances—anyone who doubts this should read the relevant pages of *Theobald on Wills*.[200] Judges can then cleanse the stables without feeling that anything of value is being lost. The correct method of interpretation, they often came to say, was to apply the rule of construction directly to the will rather than mediating it through the accumulated case law.[201] At most a judge should use old cases as a final check that he was not about to do something forbidden, or for reassurance if he felt a need. As a concession to the past a case that had been the first to apply a particular meaning was often retained, to be cited as a symbol of the possibility. The tone, the texture, the purpose of the exercise, were becoming quite different.

Finally, did judges change rules of construction concerning realty less readily than they changed rules concerning personalty? The present state of scholarship does not enable a confident answer to be given. Unwillingness to undermine certainty of title was an additional factor for land, and there are dicta aplenty that great caution was needed. But, as was illustrated above, change in rules concerning personalty was itself a complex process, so one cannot simply leap from the dicta to a conclusion. Occasionally a venerable but mysterious rule of construction concerning realty came up for revision or confirmation, as the 'rule

---

[196] *Re Sibley's Trusts* (1877) 5 Ch D 494; see also *Ralph* v. *Carrick* (1879) 11 Ch D 873.

[197] *Leader* v. *Duffey* (1888) 13 App Cas 294; *Barraclough* v. *Cooper* (1905) [1908] 2 Ch 121n.

[198] *Habergham* v. *Ridehalgh* (1870) LR 9 Eq 395; *Bowman* v. *Geddes* [1899] AC 518 is a good contrast.

[199] For particularly clear statements see *Glynn* v. *Margetson* [1893] AC 351; *re Hamlet* (1888) 38 Ch D 183; and *Henty* v. *Wray* (1882) 21 Ch D 332 (a settlement case).

[200] H. S. Theobald, *A Concise Treatise on the Law of Wills* (5th edn, 1900), 586–93.

[201] For typical examples, see *re Jackson's Will* (1879) 13 Ch D 189; *re Musther* (1890) 43 Ch D 569; *re Gorringe* [1906] 2 Ch 347 (especially Romer LJ, whose judgment was upheld on appeal: [1907] AC 225); *re Cope* [1908] 2 Ch 1; *re Williams* [1914] 2 Ch 61; and compare Jessel MR in *Day* v. *Radcliffe* (1876) 3 Ch D 654.

in *Wild's* case' did in 1880, when the Lords treated it as an honorary rule of law to be left quite untouched.[202] Similarly Jarman relates how one settled rule of construction was reversed in four steps over a period of 26 years, but for personalty only.[203] There followed a period of acceptance of the new rule, and warnings in the textbooks that it might some day be adopted for realty—and thus that drafters of wills should take care to address the point—before the lord justices did bring realty into line in just one step, 45 years after the change had been made for personalty.[204] But clear examples like those are rare. The interaction of legislative change of the underlying rules of law and the need for rules of construction may have differed between realty and personalty, but more research is needed before clear conclusions can be drawn.

Finale (Diminuendo)

Judges made their preference for the usual forms of family settlement clear enough, when they had a free or reasonably free hand to create one. But they drew an increasingly clear line between their executory and their interpretive functions. Whereas their executory functions were necessarily purposive, their shift to a more formal, literal mode of interpretation included displaying indifference to the consequences. If a gift was invalidated by the modern rule against perpetuities a partial intestacy would often result, but, so judges said, the obvious fact that that was not what testators would have wanted could not alter a plain interpretation of the words. Making a benevolent choice when a testator had been ambiguous was quite a different matter; but it needed a genuine ambiguity. Malins VC did try to reopen *Leake* v. *Robinson*, by deciding that the valid part of a contingent class gift could be saved by severing it from the invalid, winning sympathy from James LJ and, perhaps unexpectedly, Bramwell LJ.[205] But

---

[202] *Clifford* v. *Koe* (1880) 5 App Cas 447; Jarman, *Wills* (6th edn), ii, 1906–18. The rule said that a devise of land to X and his children is interpreted as giving X a fee tail if he had no children at the time the will was made. If when the will was made the devisee did have children, a pre-Wills Act will was usually interpreted as giving X a life estate jointly with those children, though some judges flirted with estates in succession, to Jarman's disapproval. There is a succinct account in Hawkins, *Wills* (2nd edn), 243–6.

[203] Jarman, *Wills*, ii, 640–51. The question was this: in a bequest to X for life, remainder to named persons as tenants in common or the survivors of them, do interests vest in those named persons living at the testator's death, or only in those living at X's? The change was from the former to the latter.

[204] *Re Gregson's Trusts* (1864) 2 De G. J. & Sm. 428.

[205] *Leake* v. *Robinson* (1817) 2 Mer. 363; *Re Moseley's Trusts* (1871) LR 11 Eq 499; *Smith* v. *Smith* (1870) 5 Ch App 342; *re Moseley's Trusts* (1879) 11 Ch D 555.

the Lords—Selborne, Penzance, and Blackburn—would have none of it, and nor would Jessel MR.[206]

Thus the shift also entailed a reduced willingness by judges to strive to keep a testator's property within his family.[207] The transformation of precatory trusts clearly had that effect, but it was inherent in the general shift from a 'general intention' standard of interpretation to one of 'ordinary meaning'. It must also be true of many situations where 'artificial' rules of construction were dismantled or restricted, because most such rules were based upon generalized, idealized, notions of testators' purposes, which almost necessarily involved some concept of family provision.[208] To the extent of these shifts, judges laid more responsibility on testators and their advisors, and accepted less themselves.

Not all rules of construction were curtailed, however, so any general conclusion must be qualified. The difficulty is in knowing how far. Two examples may be offered of rules of construction evolving as though nothing had changed. The first concerns a well-known form of testamentary settlement in which land was left to a class of children equally, but as tenants in tail, with a gift over on ultimate expiry of that fee. The usual form was that the children took as tenants in common, but, to emphasize the family aspect of the disposition, there would be cross-remainders between them. That ensured that as each line died out the benefit would accrue to the other lines, so the land would not go over until all lines had expired. As Jarman explained, this pattern of cross-remainders was so common that judges would readily imply it into a will from which it was absent.[209]

It was a rule of construction, not of law; it needed some context to trigger it, and it could be displaced. But context was easy to find, displacement unusual, and, in Page Wood VC's words, the doctrine was by degrees carried forward throughout the nineteenth century.[210] Restrictions on its operation were removed, some by Lord Kenyon before our period starts, others in the mid-century, and there were some extensions to other forms of limited shared interests followed by gifts over.[211] In this context judges clearly were writing words into a will, though they were doing it to fill a silence left by the testator, which is not the same as contradicting an express provision. Even so, they seem to have had no misgivings until,

---

[206] *Pearks* v. *Moseley* (1880) 5 App Cas 714; *Hale* v. *Hale* (1876) 3 Ch D 643.

[207] Except for the deceased Minister of Agriculture, writer of a homemade will, whose widow had remarried a little too quickly, perhaps: *Comiskey* v. *Bowring-Hanbury* [1905] AC 84.

[208] Those that did not were regarded as hangovers with feudal or early-modern origins.

[209] Jarman, *Wills*, ii, 457–80; Hawkins, *Wills*, 247–9.

[210] *Re Clarke's Trusts* (1863) 32 LJ Ch 525; *Taaffe* v. *Conmee* (1862) 10 H.L.C. 64; and *Hannaford* v. *Hannaford* (1871) LR 7 QB 116.

[211] *Vanderplank* v. *King* (1843) 3 Hare 1; *Atkinson* v. *Barton* (1861) 3 De G. F. & J. 339; *re Clark's Trusts* (1863) 32 LJ Ch 525; *re Ridge's Trusts* (1872) LR 7 Ch App 665.

perhaps, the very end of our period.[212] Kay J. was even allowed to restate the cases as a set of rules.[213]

A second example of continuity again concerns situations where the testator's first set of instructions is said to have run its course and his reserve set come into play. Suppose a gift 'to my daughter for life, and then to her children equally; but if she should die without leaving children, then over...'. The daughter has children who all die before her, some of them leaving children of their own. If the words are read literally the grandchildren take nothing, and in James LJ's graphic words they may go to the workhouse while the family property goes over to a stranger.[214] To avoid that, in 1822 Leach VC had imported a rule of construction from marriage settlements that read 'leaving children' as 'having had children'.[215] Non-literal, purposive, though that rule was, it stuck. Judges of the 'ordinary meaning' school made assaults on it in the 1850s and again in the 1880s, but it survived more or less intact through into the twentieth century.[216]

In the present state of scholarship it is not evident why 'without leaving children' could go on being read as 'without having had a child' when 'survivors' could not go on being read as 'others'. The trend certainly was towards an ordinary meaning standard of interpretation, and the effect of that certainly was to reduce creative readings based upon what judges presumed to be the needs of the family, or of families in general. But how far the trend went cannot be determined until the area has been more systematically studied.

---

[212] *Re Mears* [1914] 1 Ch 694.

[213] *Re Hudson* (1882) 20 Ch D 406.

[214] *Ralph* v. *Carrick* (1879) 11 Ch D 873, adopted in *re Roberts* [1903] 2 Ch 200.

[215] *Maitland* v. *Chalie* (1822) 6 Madd. 243; Hawkins, *Wills*, 260–1; Jarman, *Wills* (3rd edn), ii, 747–50. For the use of similar principles when interpreting marriage settlements, see Williams, *Settlement*, 118–23.

[216] Assaults: *Bythesea* v. *Bythesea* (1854) 23 LJ Ch 1004; *re Hamlet* (1888) 38 Ch D 183. Survival: *Treharne* v. *Layton* (1875) LR 10 QB 459; *re Cobbold* [1903] 2 Ch 299, but contrast the statement in *re Edwards* [1906] 1 Ch 200.

II

Property Rights in Land:
Reforming the Heritage

1. INTRODUCTION

It may be helpful to introduce this and the next three chapters with the verdict of two commentators on nineteenth-century land law (one would have said the law of real property). In 1909 Thomas Cyprian Williams addressed a royal commission. He was a conveyancing barrister, an author, a teacher, and successor in those interests to a famous father. Surveying a long run of statutes he concluded that 'each enactment has merely introduced some practical reform suited to the immediate necessities of the moment...in substance the English law of real property has been adapted to the exigencies of the life of the present day. But this change has been so accomplished that, in point of form, the English law of real property is a disgrace to a country which aspires to be numbered amongst civilised nations'.[1]

The ways of real property law were arcane, its mysteries impenetrable, its exposition interminable, but it produced workable results. A great deal of professional effort went into improving those results and modifying the means of achieving them to meet new ends. In one sense that made the law more knowable, but in another it multiplied complexity. For example, much of the law of sales was recast by contractual conditions, which were knowable if one wrote them, or had a localized set to hand, but which existed in derogation of the general norms implied by the common law. In due course statute law might catch up, pulling the general norms into line with practice, but the lag might be long or the catching up incomplete. Mortgages were reformulated in a similar way. An understanding of how the law worked needs to encompass all this.

The second commentator is Albert Venn Dicey. In his 'Paradox of the Land Law', written in 1905 but best read as a commentary on the politics of the 1880s, he identified five fundamental features of English land law, each one of them, he claimed, unaltered in its essence despite the passage of upwards of 100

---

[1] *RC on Land Transfer*, 2nd Report, *PP* 1911 [Cd. 5483], xxx, 1, 434.

relevant statutes since 1830.[2] Primogeniture, the rule against perpetuities, strict settlements, the private conveyancing of land, and freedom of testamentary disposition—the choice may seem idiosyncratic and the verdict questionable, but all of them are functions of a private property regime centred on family provision across the generations. Seen externally, that survived, and then Dicey's point is not very different from Williams's: it was the operational level that had changed, the level only of the practising lawyers. They met new needs; old ones continued, or faded, but the law that enabled them continued.

One theme of these chapters is that there were always voices calling for something better, be that on a grand scale or the most mundane. Often decades would elapse from the time of a reformulation some thought apt for the moment to its legislative achievement. To take an extreme case, the most important change made by the Perpetuities and Accumulations Act 1964 was recommended by the Real Property Commissioners in 1832.

With changes of a technical nature, and most of them were, it is rarely if ever possible to relate them in some simple way to the social conditions of the time— the lens would have to encompass three volumes of this series, one of them not yet commissioned. Yet it was the small changes that mattered to the lawyers whose skill lay in satisfying the new needs of their clients. For nineteenth-century real property lawyers there was truth, though not the whole truth, in Milsom's claim about the medieval law:

How can a system of law, a system of ideas whose hypothesis it is that rules are constant, adapt itself to a changing world? It has not been the ordered development of the jurist or the legislator, of men thinking about law for its own sake. It has been the rough free enterprise in argument of practitioners thinking about nothing beyond the immediate interest of each client; ...[3]

It applied with only a little adaptation to some of their legislation too. As Dicey and Williams have indicated, the legislator may be neither statesman nor jurist, just the practitioner honing the argument.

The nineteenth-century profession is less anonymous to us than Milsom's is to him. An exuberant and often very personal literature guided its steps—though with what results we usually do not know. Its authors had an authority in other contexts accorded to judges. Williams was almost a part of that, a little too late perhaps; his father, Joshua, had been, though not in the first rank. He, and Powell, Preston, Jarman, Hayes, Sugden, generations of Sweets, Davidson, Dart, and Wolstenholme left a print on their world that can be used to interpret it today.

---

[2] (1905) 21 *LQR* 221–32.
[3] S. F. C. Milsom, *Historical Foundations of the Common Law* (1969), p. xi.

Of course, that is not the whole story. The Settled Land Act, the Married Women's Property Act, and the Agricultural Holdings Acts were unthinkable in the 1820s. It may be significant that all came in the 1880s. That decade was something of a watershed.[4]

One further theme is that the sum of small changes may have added up to something qualitatively different. Where once there was a law of real property into which statutory change had to be fitted there came to be statutory laws that probably did not need any supplement, but if they did it was as background. That is offered more tentatively.

The order of topics is designed to allow these themes to unfold while allowing at least some independent reading by topic. This chapter is lawyers' law reform—the Real Property Commissioners, their vision and, indirectly, their description of what real property meant and encompassed. These themes are picked up again explicitly in Chapter V by which time the influence of national politics is inescapable. The intermediate chapters are topic-based, in a sequence reflecting roughly their proximity to the concerns of the old landed order: settlements, sales (the great landowners would have said purchases), leases, mortgages, and servitudes. Much that would interest lawyers has had to be omitted.

2. THE WORLD OF THE REAL PROPERTY COMMISSION

Competing Visions of Real Property Reform in the 1820s

The season opened in 1821 with an article in the *Edinburgh Review* by Henry Bellenden Ker which encapsulates the reform agenda for a generation.[5] The mechanisms of land transfer needed urgent modernization, he wrote, but the substance of real property law need not be affected at all. Codification was neither required nor desirable, because the shift to a new vocabulary would generate a flood of new disputes. He singled out fines and recoveries, the lease necessary for conveyancing by lease and release, and the intricacies and irrationalities of contingent remainders as particularly needing attention. Personally undecided about the merits of deeds registration, he regretted there was no public interest in the question or indeed in the deficiency of conveyancing law generally. If James Humphreys had never published his *Observations* the conventional narrative

---

[4] cf. R. Price, *British Society, 1660–1880* (Cambridge, 1999).

[5] (1821) 35 *Edin. Rev.* 190–213. The *Wellesley Index* deleted its attribution of this anonymous article to Bellenden Ker, but his authorship seems beyond doubt: M. Lobban, 'How Benthamic was the Criminal Law Commision?' (2000) 18 *JLH* 427–32, 429n.

would surely be that the trajectory from Bellenden Ker through the Real Property Commission to the ameliorative legislation of the 1830s and 1840s was straight-forward, even preordained.[6]

Humphreys, a Chancery barrister of some 25 years' standing, published his book in 1826.[7] It showed how the rot was far more extensive than Bellenden Ker had made out—there was actually rather little dissent from that. The cure, he argued, was to start again with a code that summarized and prescribed the substance of the whole of the modern law of real property, in short order, simple language, logically arranged. His book demonstrated how that could be done, bringing him praise in the Reviews, from Jeremy Bentham, from radicals in the Commons, and an invitation from the newly established London University.[8] In retrospect, ameliorative legislation has looked a distant second best, modest and piecemeal, compared with Humphreys's all embracing *tour de force*.[9]

The birth of the Real Property Commission was not entirely the outcome of a drive for law reform originating in the journals, nor even in Brougham's celebrated law-reform speech in February 1828. In 1826 Lord Eldon's self-protective Chancery Commission had suggested that litigation clogging his court might be reduced by commissioning some competent persons to recommend safe improvements to the law respecting the transfer of property.[10] The idea was picked up in the Commons by Sir Robert Peel, perhaps only tactically to defend Eldon, but looked to have lapsed until Brougham so dramatically forced law reform on to the political agenda as a general issue the following year.[11] By then Peel was back in office, and since royal commissions were ministerial appointments rather than parliamentary it was he who determined the composition of the Real Property Commission.

Contrary to his initial inclination that 'gentlemen conversant with the subject' would merely assist such a commission, Peel now approved a commission wholly

---

[6] Bellenden Ker himself claimed that his article anticipated the commissioners' recommendations: *SC on General Register of Deeds*, Report, *PP* 1831–2 (609), xviii, 365, 517; H. Bellenden Ker, *On the Reform of the Law of Real Property* (1853), 93.

[7] J. Humphreys, *Observations on the Actual State of the English Laws of Real Property with the Outlines of a Code* (1826); B. Rudden, 'A Code Too Soon', in P. Wallington and R.M. Merkin (eds), *Essays in Memory of Professor F. H. Lawson* (1986), 101–16; M. Lobban, *Common Law*, 195–201.

[8] 'Bentham on Humphreys' Property Code' (1826) 6 *Westminster Rev.* 446–507; *PD* 1827 (s2) 17: 88; 1828 19: 1526; 1830 25: 289; *The Times*, 10 July 1828. Note too Campbell's invocation of his support when introducing his deeds registration bill, *PD* 1830 (s3) 1: 1234.

[9] 'Modest and piecemeal' is Lobban, *Common Law*, 201; cf. A. W. B. Simpson, *A History of the Land Law* (2nd edn, Oxford, 1986), 256; A. H. Manchester, *Modern Legal History* (1980), 302–5.

[10] See Vol. XI, pp. 652–5.

[11] *PD* 1827 (s2) 16: 749–50; 17: 92. M. Lobban, 'Henry Brougham and Law Reform' (2000) 115 *EHR* 1184–1125.

of experts—hence politically dependent.[12] He vetoed Humphreys and Bellenden Ker—too obviously partisans for particular reforms, he said—and offered the conservative Edward Sugden the chairmanship, notwithstanding Sugden's having published a letter in opposition to Humphreys.[13] Sugden declined, to be replaced with the much less knowledgeable but more open-minded John Campbell. Likewise Peel's conception of the inquiry as limited to matters of land transfer was belied in the event by much wider terms of reference.[14] Nonetheless Peel's shade as the commission's patron was real enough for Bentham to use it as at least a pretext for keeping his own association with the commission well hidden.[15] Reduction of litigation, particularly chancery litigation, was an important theme in the commission's deliberations, its combined urgency and mundanity an antidote to the wildness of theory.[16]

Modern scholarship has tended to deny that what Humphreys proposed was truly a 'code'. Michael Lobban has pointed out that it was not Benthamic in conception, and Bernard Rudden has written that Humphreys's mistakes in presenting and labelling his scheme were merely tactical, even though fatal to his success.[17] Yet after two years reflecting on the very deep opposition he had aroused, and something of a retreat in his second edition, Humphreys still urged changes that cut right across legal and political culture.[18] His preference was that there be 'no law out of the code'.[19] To reconcile that with the law-making inherent in English adjudicative method he would designate the Exchequer Chamber the only court capable of making definitive rulings. For the common lawyers to recapture authority from Chancery was a strong theme among the commissioners' respondents, but only Humphreys would have institutionalized Chancery's subordination. Further, as he thought it wrong for litigants to bear the burden of

[12] Initial inclination: *PD* 1827 (s2) 17: 92.

[13] C. Carr, *A Victorian Law Reformer's Correspondence* (1955), 5; *PD* 1828 (s2) 19: 1524–6; M. Sokol, 'Jeremy Bentham and the Real Property Commission of 1828' (1992) 4 *Utilitas* 225–45. Peel likewise declined Charles Butler's offer to lead (or be) such a commission: *PD* 1827 (s2) 17: 92.

[14] Compare Sokol, 'Jeremy Bentham' at 236 with the commission's warrant: *Copy of commission*, *PP* 1828 (397), ix, 209.

[15] Sokol, 'Jeremy Bentham', 241–2. Campbell found Peel sympathetic: J. Campbell, *Life of John, Lord Campbell*, edited by Mrs Hardcastle (2nd edn, 1881), i, 462, and see also ii, 5–6.

[16] 'Wildness of theory' is Ker to Bentham, quoted by Lobban, 'How Benthamic?', 429n.

[17] Lobban, *Common Law*, 195; Rudden, 'Code too far'.

[18] E. B. Sugden, *A letter to James Humphreys, esq., on his Proposal to Repeal the Laws of Real Property, and Substitute a New Code* (1826); G. D. B. Beaumont, *Observations on the Code for Real Property Proposed by James Humphreys* (1827); J. J. Park, *A Contre-projet to the Humphreysian Code and the Projects of Redaction of messrs. Hammond, Uniacke and Twiss* (1828). See also J. Humphreys, *A Letter to Edward B. Sugden, Esq.* (1827). His second edition was published in 1827, and he was first examined by the commissioners in October 1828.

[19] *RC on Real Property*, 1st Report, *PP* 1829 (263), xi, 1, 248–9; his evidence, from which this paragraph is drawn, is at 248–70.

clarifying the law he would also have had a permanent law commission, not merely to weigh the need for amendments and receive the Exchequer Chamber's rulings, but to enact them directly, seemingly without passage through Parliament.

This would all necessitate consequential changes to the way the legal profession operated. Law reporting would diminish greatly, though not quite disappear, he thought, and there would be much less room for the semi-authoritative textbooks on which practitioners currently relied. Under examination by the commissioners Humphreys was willing to dilute the purity of his vision, but it would have taken extraordinary political bravado for the commissioners to believe that the cultural and institutional obstacles to even his reduced species of code could be overcome in the England of 1829.[20]

The Real Property Commission: Methods and Objectives

To maximize their chance of success the commissioners aimed for professional consensus. Probably the Institute, the dining and discussion club of elite Lincoln's Inn conveyancers, acted as a reference group for the commission.[21] Two members of the Institute, Bellenden Ker and John Tyrrell, made substantial submissions, supporting the commission's general direction, endorsing its priorities, and rejecting the concept of a code.[22]

The commissioners' method, however, was notably open and inclusive, from their open-ended invitation to submit suggestions, through their consultation on outline proposals, their lengthy and detailed questionnaires, and their oral examination of witnesses. Respondents on technical questions of real property law came predominantly though not exclusively from the commissioners' own milieu—conveyancers and specialized sub-sets of the common law and equity bars.[23] On questions concerning deeds registration the range was much wider,

[20] Rudden, 'Code Too Soon', shows how much more acceptable Humphreys' ideas were in New York, where the law of real property had already been simplified and partly digested into statute. Even so, the revisers who adopted them disguised what they were doing: *ibid.*, 105.

[21] Sokol, 'Jeremy Bentham', 238–9, drawing on J. S. Vaizey (ed.), *The Institute: Memoirs of Former Members* (1895).

[22] Tyrrell's lengthy submission, subsequently published privately as a book, was quoted by several later respondents to the commission; J. Tyrrell, *Suggestions sent to the Commissioners Appointed to Inquire into the Laws of Real Property: With Minutes of the Evidence Given Before Them* (1829). In August 1829 he, Lewis Duval, and F. W. Sanders were appointed additional members of the commission at a salary of £1200 each: *The Times*, 7 August 1829.

[23] Retrospect conceals how difficult it was to form an overall view of the law in the detail the commissioners thought warranted. Charles Butler, for example, the leading conveyancer, declined to answer detailed questions on limitation because he thought only someone with a court practice sufficiently expert: *RC on Real Property*, 1st Report, 120. There is a long exposition of the difficulties

including country solicitors, provincial barristers, Scottish lawyers, and officials from the existing registries. The commissioners received much information about overseas law and practice, some of which they used in a generalized way. Responses were published as appendices to the commissioners' reports, transcripts of oral examinations being first submitted to the respondents for correction. Finally their first tranche of bills was published, to provide one further opportunity for professional comment.[24]

In their detailed questionnaires the commissioners were clearly leading their respondents. They had made their diagnosis, reached provisional conclusions on the prescription, and were seeking now to test and validate their opinions.[25] Nevertheless, they opened their first questionnaire with the Humphreys question: is it desirable to abolish that rule or fiction of the law known as tenure? Answer 'yes' to that and seisin would fall too, bringing down the structure of future and contingent estates built upon the Statute of Uses and necessitating a restatement of interests in land, its transfer, and its inheritance.[26] Indeed if the main differentiating feature of real property were thus abolished there would be no logical reason why a new code should not encompass all forms of property. That was the line Bentham took in his consideration of the commissioners' first questionnaire, though it led far outside the commission's terms of reference.[27]

Humphreys himself saw no need to codify personal property law, save for sake of completeness, since it lacked the complexity that afflicted realty.[28] By 1829, however, he had concluded that abolition of tenure was politically impossible, and so he joined the great majority of the commissioners' respondents in answering 'no' to their first question.[29] He still wanted a code in simple language, but the fear that that would stimulate litigation rather than reducing it led most respondents to reject the idea, some of them vehemently. The commissioners pointedly

caused by divided jurisdictions and professional specialization in Tyrrell's *Suggestions*, 370–81, *RC on Real Property*, 1st Report, 563–6.

[24] [J. Tyrrell] *Proposed Statute of Limitations relating to Real Property* (1831), [J. Tyrrell] *Proposed Bills for Amending the Laws relating to Inheritance, Dower, and Curtesy* (1831); Campbell, *Life*, ii, 29.

[25] Some respondents commented on this, e.g. T. Tomlinson, *RC on Real Property*, 1st Report, 188–9, noting that the retention of primogeniture had been kept off the agenda.

[26] They made this explicit in their 3rd Report, *PP* 1831–2 (484), xxiii, 321, 324.

[27] M. Sokol, 'Bentham and Blackstone on Incorporeal Hereditaments' (1994) 15 *JLH* 287–305. Tyrrell came close to this position in his *Suggestions*, 66–7, *RC on Real Property*, 1st Report, 490. The Commissioners' 2nd Report similarly suggests the gradual expansion of the deeds registry into a general repository for all manner of property transfers.

[28] *RC on Real Property*, 1st Report, 250.

[29] Serjeant Lawes was tempted by the idea, and J. J. Park would have been too, had he seen a way of assimilating copyhold: *RC on Real Property*, 1st Report, 110, 167.

concluded that the law's existing vocabulary be retained, confident that the 'use of terms of no defined legal import, or the use of known terms in a new sense' would produce 'disastrous effects'.[30]

Commentators have criticized the commissioners for undue caution when recommending reform of the substantive law, extending perhaps even to complacency.[31] Campbell's great eulogy to its excellence represents, for them, an opportunity missed. 'When the object of transactions respecting land is accomplished, and the estates and interests in it which are recognized are actually created and secured', he wrote, 'the Law of England, except in a few comparatively unimportant particulars, appears to come almost as near to perfection as can be expected in any human institutions.'[32] Yet the criticism underestimates the commissioners' ambition, which reached much further than their legislative achievement. The latter, of course, was not under their control. It misses also that there was a major change in values from soon after the commissioners' reports, rather overtaking their priorities. When more is understood about the uses of property law from, say, the 1780s, it is likely that the commissioners' recommendations will be seen as a culmination of a period of innovation, rather than as a failure to foresee the concerns of the next generation.

That said, the commissioners did aim to avoid obvious controversy. They kept primogeniture off their official agenda, though they discussed it with several respondents—whose opinions varied. Similarly they were adamant that assimilation of real property to personal by having all property administered by an executor or administrator on death would be 'far too great an interference with the present law of real property'.[33] It would shift control away from the heir, imply that realty should be equally subject to the deceased's debts, and hence affect landowners' substantive interests.

The commissioners' method was ill-adapted to justify controversial change. Their questionnaires and subsequent discussions were bound to uncover disagreement, which, they seem to have thought, would deprive their recommendations of legitimacy. They asked, for example, whether the 'usual' powers that well drafted settlements and private Acts of Parliament gave life tenants to grant building and long occupation leases should now be made a statutory incident of life estates, to be available to all life tenants save where their settlement excluded them. Respondents even from within the charmed circle provided four irreconcilable answers, so the

---

[30] *RC on Real Property*, 1st Report, 9.

[31] Simpson, *History*, 279; A. H. Manchester, *Modern Legal History* (1980), 302–5; A. Offer, *Property and Politics 1870–1914* (Cambridge, 1981), 28.

[32] *RC on Real Property*, 1st Report, 6; Campbell, *Life*, i, 459.

[33] *RC on Real Property*, 4th Report, PP 1833 (226), xxii, 1, 57. As late as 1889 Lord Halsbury lost a bill on this issue: see pp. 216–17, below.

commissioners made no recommendation.[34] It was a similar story with the civil registration of births, marriages, and deaths. The commissioners hoped that they might find an improvement on Anglican parish records, which were both approximate (in recording christenings and burials) and incomplete in providing evidence that was often vital to conveyancers.[35] But their respondents could not agree on the critical details, so again the commissioners abandoned the question.[36] Leaders of the Protestant dissenters, lobbying hard for civil registration and for recognition of the validity of their own marriage services, had to turn elsewhere for support.[37]

It may have been sound political judgment, however, rather than timidity that induced the commissioners to hold back when recommending institutional change or change to substantive law save where grounded on professional consensus, for those recommendations the commissioners did make did not succeed like their technical, modal proposals did. Abolition of aberrant local customs of intestate succession—Borough English in some ancient cities, gavelkind in Kent— appealed to the commissioners and most of their respondents both as making land transfer simpler, cheaper, and more certain, and also as a step towards unifying land law, removing a barrier to sensible law reform.[38] But their proposals to that end were not enacted. Similarly, whereas they succeeded with their proposal that copyholders' interests be as liable to seizure for debt as tenants' in socage, their parallel proposal that copyholders' leasing powers be extended failed.[39] The latter threatened the interests of lords of the manor, the former did not. Similar examples can be found from the recommendations in their reports.

The commissioners' approach was client-centred.[40] What clients wanted could be inferred from what their lawyers habitually did for them. Complexity of disposition was not a problem. Thus, for example, landowners wanted settlements, but, for the most part, did not quarrel with the rules against perpetuities that

[34] Humphrey and Tyrrell: yes (*RC on Real Property*, 1st Report, 264, 317); Christie: no (*ibid.*, 176); Coote: a few of them (*ibid.*, 343); Bellenden Ker: all, but subject to approval by a Master in Chancery (*ibid.*, 304). The Commission's response was to list it as a topic for future investigation—'a matter of much delicacy' (*ibid.*, 57).

[35] *RC on Real Property*, 1st Report, 59.

[36] *RC on Real Property*, 2nd Report, *PP* 1830 (575), xi, 1, 64.

[37] M. J. Cullen, 'The Making of the Civil Registration Act of 1836' (1974) 25 *Journal of Ecclesiastical History* 39–60 at 43. They found their support from medical men and from Edwin Chadwick, in his role as secretary to the Poor Law Commission.

[38] *RC on Real Property*, 3rd Report, 325–34 and App. to 1st Report, *passim*.

[39] *RC on Real Property*, 3rd Report, 338; Leases and Sales of Settled Estates 1856, s 43 (the Settled Estates Act 1858, ss 3 and 4, empowered lords to licence leases, but still denied copyholders the direct powers enjoyed by tenants in socage); Judgments Act 1838, 1 & 2 Vict. c. 110, s 11 (see also Payment of Debts out of Real Estate Act 1833, 3 & 4 Will. IV c. 104.)

[40] This and the following two paragraphs are drawn mainly from *RC on Real Property*, 1st Report and, on wills, the 4th Report.

limited their permissible duration. By contrast they did not want their wives to claim dower according to the ancient common law principles still extant but nowadays universally avoided. As Bellenden Ker had foreshadowed in 1821 and Peel had assumed when agreeing to a commission, the problems lay with means, not with ends. Means, the commissioners said, should be simple and expeditious, and should be direct rather than circuitous, as they then were. Perhaps they should even be uniform, so that one document would do for all. Actions at law that mimicked and substituted for conveyances should be abolished. The law should be pruned of outdated clutter that either compelled circuity or needed careful checks to avoid; the law should be that which was necessary to achieve what today's landowners wanted, freed from feudal leftovers.

Thirdly, the law of real property should be internally standardized. Tenures should be unified. That might not be possible very quickly for copyhold, where conflicts of economic interests between lord and tenant were complex and persistent, but even there, they hoped, standardization of rules of inheritance could be achieved, and some modest increments to tenants' powers (subject, of course, to some proper compensation to the lords). The commissioners trod carefully. Everyone knew that the intermingling of copyhold and freehold land within the same estate caused conveyancing difficulties—different processes were needed for each, different documentation, hence great care was needed in identifying boundaries—but 'gradual enfranchisement' was the best the commissioners could foresee.

On questions of rules, however, they were more confident. Limitation periods should be unified by detaching them from legal forms and attaching them instead to the cause of action. The serious reforms that wills needed would necessitate some modest assimilation of realty with personalty. There were ten different rules for the formal validity of wills, depending on the sort of property concerned. They should be reduced to one new rule and, reluctantly, one small exception for the armed forces—but both must apply to all forms of property. Old and 'artificial' rules of interpretation of testamentary gifts of realty should be dragged as close as possible to the equivalent for personalty, because the latter accorded with what an unaided testator would expect. There should be just one rule stipulating an age for acquiring testamentary capacity, just one set of rules about revocation of wills, just one time for determining which property is included in a will, and so on.

Above all else, the commissioners concluded, landowners sought security in their transactions. That could be inferred from the lengthy process of investigating title, the high standard to be met before Chancery would declare a title marketable, and from the ingenious contrivances learned men used to protect their clients from adverse claims. But despite the expense incurred peace of mind was commonly unattainable. Extensive change was needed. At its centre would be compulsory registration of deeds—compulsory in the sense that an unregistered document would lose priority to a later transaction. That was such an important recommendation that it, and the reasons why it was not implemented, will be discussed separately below.[41] Other changes necessary to bring security were institutional—better means of proving pedigree, for example (though, as noted above, the commissioners could not find one to recommend), and reduction of the current 380 ecclesiastical and prerogative courts able to grant probate to just one.[42] That was another of their substantive recommendations that did not succeed at the time. Other desirable changes were difficult because they would affect the Crown. Crown debts were a 'very serious impediment' to land transfer.[43] Stamp duty was so complex that questions frequently arose whether documents in a title had been correctly stamped, and there was no way of determining them short of litigation.[44] The commissioners' respondents were forthright on these matters, but despite the commissioners' intention to formulate proposals the difficulties were such that none eventuated.

Many more of the desirable changes concerned merely the fabric of lawyers' law, within the commissioners' areas of expertise, attainable by statutes they could themselves draft. Thus a widow's dower should no longer be an entitlement incident to her husband's property, but should instead depend upon his voluntary act.[45] Her ancient claim to a life estate in one-third of his lands should apply only if he died intestate, only to lands he had at his death, and only to the extent that he had not barred her claim by a formal declaration to that effect during his lifetime or in his will. Almost universally, the commissioners thought, conveyances were structured to evade dower, hence there no longer was any real question of general common law protection for married women. Instead, the custom of the times was that women relied upon their fathers for a marriage settlement. But the intricacies required to bar dower could trip unskilled practitioners and, as dower

---

[41] See pp. 64–71, below.

[42] *RC on Real Property*, 4th Report, 38–65. The validity of a probate could affect a title when, for example, a personal representative discharged a mortgage or directed the assignment of an attendant term.

[43] *RC on Real Property*, 1st Report, 59.

[44] *RC on Real Property*, 1st Report, 60; Tyrrell, *Suggestions*, 303–6; *RC on Real Property*, 1st Report, 547. Compare W. Hayes, *The Concise Conveyancer* (1830), xiii: 'There is no branch of the statute law from whose partial, vexatious, and uncertain operation, legislative relief is more urgently demanded'. Joseph Chitty was given access to the Board of Stamps' archives for the writing of his *Practical Treatise on the Stamp Laws* (1829) and Hugh Tilsley's *Treatise on the Stamp Laws of Great Britain and Ireland* (1847) was written from within the Board; both books must have eased the uncertainty, though the Board had no adjudicative jurisdiction: see Solomon Atkinson's third (and recast) edition of *Chitty*, published in 1850 under the title *Chitty's Stamp Laws*, p. iv.

[45] *RC on Real Property*, 1st Report, 16–19.

attached to all land of which the husband had been seised during the marriage, a mistake would leave a purchaser from him vulnerable to a claim by his widow. To the expense and complexity of the initial conveyance was thus added the expense of subsequent verification of the title. Better far to remove dower as a legal incident. As with dower, so too fines and recoveries were doubly objectionable.[46] They were conveyances masquerading as actions, and the intricacy of their arcane procedures could lead unskilled practitioners into error needing expensive correction on a later sale, or even rendering a title unmarketable.

Achievement and Disappointment

The Fines and Recoveries Act 1833 not only substituted new, direct conveyances for the old actions the commissioners had condemned but also retrospectively cured a directory of oversights that might afflict current titles.[47] Likewise the Real Property Limitation Act 1833 not only reduced the actions a landowner might face and the period within which they must be brought, but its removal of many common law complications was effectively retrospective, clearing doubts off existing titles.[48] These Acts, plus the Dower Act 1833, the Inheritance Act 1833, and the Wills Act 1837 were the commissioners' obvious and direct achievements.[49] Lord Tenterden's Prescription Act 1832 was loosely related to the commissioners' work and consistent with their recommendations.[50] At much the same time the Apportionment Act 1834 and the Trust Property Escheat Act 1834 eased land transactions in further, though minor, ways, adding to the general drift of the commissioners' proposals.[51]

In the 1840s the Law Amendment Society quarried the commissioners' reports, and some of those revived proposals made it through into legislation, though not always with happy results, as will be seen. Thus by 1850 much that the commissioners and their respondents had wanted had been enacted, though far from

---

[46] RC on Real Property, 1st Report, 20–38.

[47] 3 & 4 Will. IV c. 74.

[48] 3 & 4 Will. IV c. 27.

[49] 3 & 4 Will. IV c. 95, 3 & 4 Will. IV c. 106, 7 Will. IV & 1 Vict. c. 26.

[50] 2 & 3 Will. IV c. 71. This Act and the Real Property Limitation Act risked significant opposition from the Church for introducing limitation periods for ecclesiastical claims to land, especially at a time when introducing them for claims to tithes was very contentious. See e.g. immediate Church hostility to Tenterden's bill, PD 1831 (s3) 3: 442 et seq. and Campbell's comment at 7: 910. There was opportunistic opposition from the ultra-Tory Charles Wetherell too: The Times, 17 October 1831, reporting proceedings in the Commons on the 15th. The Real Property Commissioners circulated a questionnaire to the bishops (Campbell, Life, i, 461) and devoted much of their 3rd Report to these questions. It is easy to underestimate the commissioners' achievement in bringing ecclesiastical claims into the mainstream of the law.

[51] 4 & 5 Will. IV caps 22 and 23.

all. In that year even stamp duty was simplified and a process introduced for allowing the Commissioners of Inland Revenue to adjudicate, attempts at similar reform having failed in 1836.[52] The general cause of greater security of title was aided from 1836 by the introduction of civil registration of births, marriages, and deaths, not that that owed anything to the lawyers.[53] And the long process of voluntary enfranchisement of copyholds, which the commissioners had somewhat limply hoped for, was boosted in the early 1840s by giving the tithe commissioners a statutory jurisdiction to that end.[54] All these changes eased land transfer, either by simplifying the rules or by making more reliable information more easily accessible.

Yet none of the commissioners' original legislation came easily, even under the most favourable conditions. However useful and uncontentious their bills appeared to be, they generally took three parliamentary sessions to pass. The 1833 Acts were delayed by protracted crises and debates over parliamentary reform, but even the Wills Act, which was not launched until those were over, took three years to negotiate Parliament as the lawyers in each House picked it over. Then, five months after its passage, Sugden belatedly moved to suspend its coming into force, though his virtuoso display of petulance brought him mockery rather than success.[55]

To pass bills so complex needed the determination of the leading parliamentary lawyers and consensus among the rest. The determination came from Campbell, the commission's chairman, who entered Parliament in 1830 and

---

[52] Stamp Act 1850, 13 & 14 Vict. 97; Stamp Duties Bill, *PP* 1836 (288), v, 513. The new jurisdiction was improved by the Stamp Act 1870. In 1854 the bar on receiving unstamped instruments as evidence was effectively removed, first by Stamp Act 1854, s 27 and then by Common Law Procedure Act 1854, s 28. Previously it had been applied reasonably strictly by common law judges and less so in equity. For a narrative, see S. Dowell, *A History and Explanation of the Stamp Duties* (1873), esp. 108–14. He credits Lord Campbell CJ with the change in 1854, citing his remarks *R v. Wortley* (1851) 15 Jur. 1137.

[53] Marriage Act 1836 and Registration of Births, Deaths and Marriages Act 1836, 6 & 7 Will. IV. caps 85 and 86 respectively.

[54] C. Stebbings, *Legal Foundations of Tribunals in Nineteenth-century England* (Cambridge, 2007), 94–7; Copyhold Enfranchisement Act 1841, 4 & 5 Vict. c. 35; Copyhold Act 1843, 6 & 7 Vict. c. 23. Compulsion was introduced in 1853, but the mechanism became really effective only with the Copyholds Act 1858. J. Cuddon, *A Succinct Treatise on the Copyhold Acts* (1865), 7, thought that nine-tenths of the greatly increased number of enfranchisements in this 'new era' were initiated by lords of the manor.

[55] *PD* 1837 (s3) 39: 521–30; mockery: 'H', 'The Law of Wills' (1838) 19 *LM* 132–50, esp. 141–9; Campbell (gently) *PD* 1837 (s3) 39: 530–7. Sugden thought well enough of his speech to publish it: *Speech of the Right Honourable Sir Edward Sugden in the House of Commons on Monday the 4th of December 1837 upon the Law of Wills Bill* (1838.) The openness and inclusiveness of the commissioners' procedure, coupled with Sugden's decision to stand aloof from the process, made him an easy target.

presented the commission's bills in person.[56] By the time of their passage in 1833 he was solicitor-general and Brougham was Chancellor. Those were unusual circumstances, as was the public funding that had allowed Peter Brodie and John Tyrrell to neglect their practice while working on the commission's projects.[57] This combination of authority, thoroughness, and inclusiveness did not recur.

After the commission was disbanded, preparation of legislation to reform real property law reverted to the previous pattern—shorter bills, less methodical, less open. The commission's wish lists provided ample opportunity for reformers, particularly for the Law Amendment Society, whose founding treasurer, James Stewart, was himself a conveyancer.[58] Not every snippet from that golden treasury was successful however. It became a common complaint in the legal press that without a continuing commission to prepare bills thoroughly and present them to the relevant public there would be only suspicion of enactments originating with individuals whose chief merit was their ability to command parliamentary time.

It took four attempts to institute the simple deed of transfer as the basic conveyancing document in place of the lease and release. A bill to that end introduced in 1834 collated various semi-developed proposals from the commissioners' first report, but did not progress beyond committee stage.[59] In 1841 the Conveyance by Release without Lease Act abolished the need for the lease, as Bellenden Ker had urged 20 years earlier.[60] It was widely used but made only a limited difference, since the lease-for-a-year stamp duty remained chargeable on the now nonexistent lease.[61] Nor did the Act remedy the old difficulty that corporations could not convey by the standard form bargain and sale/ lease and release. Then in 1844 Lord Lyndhurst revived much of the 1834 bill.[62] This turned out to be an embarrassing failure, but one from which much can be learned.

Lyndhurst put his bill out only to private consultation, and, after a long delay caused by the failure of several of his consultants to respond, he proceeded with only the small part of it that did not meet criticism, pushing it through all its parliamentary stages in barely a fortnight.[63] Reaction to its content from the profession

---

[56] This had been his ambition since appointment to the commission: Campbell, *Life*, i, 457, 466.

[57] Tyrrell and Brodie: J. S. Anderson, *Lawyers and the Making of English Land Law 1832–1940* (Oxford, 1992), 13.

[58] 'Conveyancing Reform' (1845) 2 *Law Rev.* 405–35; 'The Conveyancing Acts of 1845' (1845–6) 3 *Law Rev.* 175–211; Anderson, *Lawyers*, 57–63.

[59] A Bill to Facilitate the Transfer of Property by Deed, *PP* 1834 (324, 461), iv, 427, 431.

[60] 4 & 5 Vict. c. 21; Anderson, *Lawyers*, 7–8.

[61] C. Davidson, *Concise Precedents in Conveyancing* (9th edn, 1874), 11–12.

[62] Transfer of Property Act 1844, 7 & 8 Vict. c. 76; Anderson, *Lawyers*, 17; J. S., 'The Transfer of Property Act' (1844) 1(s2) *LM* 154–65.

[63] First introduced into the Lords it had its second reading there on 19 July, and received royal assent on 6 August. The only public attention it received was a brief note in *The Times* on 2 August.

was so severe that Lyndhurst had then to refer his Act for revision to a troika of leading conveyancers—Bellenden Ker, Hayes, and Christie.[64] Their verdict was damning on nearly all of it; two of the 12 sections were to be repealed outright, and the rest re-enacted either in appropriate language or, for many of them, in a very much reduced form. The Law of Real Property Amendment Act 1845 was the result.

One section of the 1844 Act included a clause from the 1834 bill that cut directly to the point: land could be conveyed by deed with the same effect as if it had been conveyed by lease and release.[65] This looks in retrospect to be admirably clear, but to contemporary practitioners it was a poor fit with the conceptual basis of real property law, quite apart from a difficulty about stamp duty that made the section too risky to use at all, so it was said.[66] The replacement section certainly did the job, but unlike the version originating in 1834 it disdained an instrumental approach and instead aimed to amend what the drafters saw as a defect in the governing principle: 'all corporeal hereditaments shall, as regards the conveyance of the immediate freehold thereof, be held to lie in grant as well as livery'.[67] That was language worthy of great lawyers, one commentator wrote.[68]

This conservative professional concern that solutions to practical problems should be consistent with the conceptual structure of real property law is an important feature of mid-century legal thinking. On a grand scale it underlay the horror at Humphreys's proposal for an entirely new vocabulary. On a small scale it limited and channelled instrumental reform. Campbell's Judgments Act 1838 contains an example. It created a new property right (or perhaps a remedy) for judgment creditors: a charge over their debtor's lands. But rather than detailing the consequences in a statutory code Campbell instead had statute confer a charge (invoking the general law of charges) and enacted that it could be enforced as if it were a mortgage (invoking the general law of mortgages). But what sort of charge? A specific charge or a general lien? The consequences differed. What sort of mortgage? Charges are equitable, so an equitable mortgage? What are the remedies to enforce that? There followed a long period of argument and uncertainty about whether the proper order should be sale or foreclosure.[69]

---

[64] H. Bellenden Ker, 'Letter to the Lord Chancellor', reprinted in C. Davidson, *Concise Precedents in Conveyancing* (3rd edn, 1848).

[65] 7 & 8 Vict. c. 76, s 2.

[66] Ker, 'Letter' in Davidson, *Concise Precedents* (3rd edn), 25–9. Contrast Davidson's own opinion: 'a good deal of unfounded cavilling' (*loc. cit.* 56).

[67] 8 & 9 Vict. c. 106, s 2; Ker 'Letter', in Davidson, *Concise Precedents* (3rd edn), 29. A further section (originating in the 1834 bill) was needed to explain that 'grant' did not imply covenants for title.

[68] W. F. Cornish, *Cornish's Treatise on Purchase Deeds*, new edn by G. Horsey (1855), 13–14.

[69] *Bull* v. *Faulkner* (1847) 1 De G. M. & G. 685; *Footner* v. *Sturgis* (1852) 5 De G. M. & G. 736; *Jones* v. *Bailey* (1853) 17 Beav. 582; *Messer* v. *Boyle* (1856) 21 Beav. 559; *re Owen* [1894] 3 Ch 220.

Concern that statutory change should have a seamless fit with the law of real property thwarted the real property commissioners' ambitious proposal to assimilate contingent remainders with executory interests, which Lyndhurst's Act had also taken up in 1844.[70] This was esoteric stuff, but important to the fabric of the law and vital to the flexibility of family settlements. In those settlements it was commonplace for limitations to have the logical form 'if…then…but if not, then…' as settlors reached out to foresee and control the future. The difficulty as the commissioners saw it was that there were (broadly) two codes of law dealing with the same idea. Under one code, contingent remainders, if the contingency attaching to the estate was not satisfied during the continuance of the previous estate the contingent estate failed. Thus if the limitation was to A for life, remainder to the eldest son of B in fee tail, remainder to C in fee simple, the second gift would fail unless B's son was born before A's estate ended. Furthermore, it did not matter whether such a failure was 'natural' or 'premature', even if it had been contrived by A and C for the very purpose of defeating the possibility that B's line would inherit. Contrivance was not difficult: A would surrender his estate to C; the two estates would merge, squeezing out the unborn son of B. For that reason settlements usually inserted an estate between A and B's son, vesting it in trustees to preserve the contingent remainder. This lengthened settlements, and, the commissioners thought, was a major cause of uncertainty and delay in subsequent transactions.

None of this learning applied to limitations that counted as executory interests or executory devises. However, those in turn were valid only if they were certain to vest within the perpetuity period—the lifetime of somebody alive when the instrument takes effect plus a further period of 21 years.[71] To avoid outright conflict between the two codes there was a rule that if a limitation could be interpreted as a contingent remainder then it must be, even though the outcome was that it then failed. Copious rules of interpretation followed these distinctions through. Fearne's *Essay* on the subject ran to over 700 pages when the commissioners wrote and to over 1000 in its last edition in 1844.[72]

The commissioners thought that throughout all the variations there was really only one broad idea, and that it should be governed by just one set of rules. Since executory estates, executory devises, springing and shifting uses, had a pliability 'adapted to every kind of provision which can be required in a family arrangement',

---

[70] *RC on Real Property*, 3rd Report, 343–64, 388–91.

[71] The rule that the extra 21 years need not be related to an actual infancy was settled finally only in 1833 (*Cadell v. Palmer* 1 Cl. & F. 372), but the decision rested on long practice. The commissioners disliked it (see below) and Humphreys thought it a perversion of principle (*Observations*, 33).

[72] C. Fearne, *An Essay on the Learning of Contingent Remainders and Executory Devises* (8th edn, 1824, by Charles Butler), (10th edn, 1844 by Josiah Smith).

they should be the model.[73] Three propositions followed. The first was easy enough: the various technical difficulties in transferring all these contingent or future interests should be removed so that all could easily pass by will or by deed. The second—which is the one that ran into trouble—was that henceforward a limitation that would fail as a contingent remainder should henceforward take effect as if it were an executory interest.[74] That would have the further simplifying advantage of subjecting those limitations to the modern rule against perpetuities, which was also a desirable policy objective. And as a third proposition that rule itself should be amended. It should no longer be possible to measure the perpetuity period by lives 'arbitrarily' chosen for the purpose, but, on the other hand, a set of wait-and-see rules should be adopted. Those would prevent a gift failing if in fact it vested during the perpetuity period, replacing the present rule that it would fail if by any imaginable possibility it might not so vest. Taking all this together rationality would be advanced, intentions better achieved, some simplification accomplished, and trustees to preserve contingent remainders would become obsolete. Transactions would be simplified and costs reduced. It was a formidable set of proposals. Sadly it was not accompanied by a detailed draft bill.

Lord Lyndhurst's hurried, semi-secret, Transfer of Property Act 1844 included a version of the commissioners' second proposition as its section 8. It was clumsily expressed, conceptually almost impossible, critics said.[75] Bellenden Ker, Hayes, and Christie duly reported that it should be retrospectively repealed and only a small part re-enacted, which is what happened.[76] Without even alluding to its origins in the broad scheme of the commissioners' third report they concluded that the only immediate problem needing remedy was the premature destruction of contingent remainders. That was justified because '[e]ven the most cautious of judges had long since pronounced a strong opinion, and the removal of this reproach upon the law had been contemplated at a former period'.[77] But saving contingent remainders from natural destruction, which the Real Property

---

[73] *RC on Real Property*, 3rd Report, 348.

[74] This was a little narrower than the discussion in the text of the report: compare 3rd Report, 345 and Proposition 1 on p. 388.

[75] 7 & 8 Vict. c. 76, s 8; 'The Transfer of Property Act' (1844) 1(s2) *LM* 154–65 at 159–61; Ker 'Letter' in Davidson, *Concise Precedents* (3rd edn), 36–47. It seems to have been based in part on the text of the 3rd Report, rather than on the 'propositions'.

[76] Ker 'Letter' in Davidson, *Concise Precedents* (3rd edn), 36–47. Section 5 of the 1844 Act implementing the commissioners' proposals to make all these future interests easily transferable was re-enacted in improved form as s 6 of the 1845 Act (8 & 9 Vict. c. 106); see *ibid.*, 34–6.

[77] Ker 'Letter' in Davidson, *Concise Precedents* (3rd edn), 46. The reference is presumably to the bill prepared by Mr Shadwell in 1783: *RC on Real Property*, 3rd Report, 345.

Commissioners had wanted, opened up such a 'very wide field' that it should be left to another occasion.

As it happened, that day arrived only in 1877, after the Court of Appeal regretfully declared that the necessary change was beyond judicial power.[78] A single-section Act then passed into law something very like the commissioners' proposition, unaccompanied by any field, wide or narrow.[79] As for reform of the rule against perpetuities, wait-and-see provisions like those proposed by the commissioners were not enacted until 1964.[80] The narrowness of conveyancing experts' vision in the 1840s contrasts with the ambition of the Real Property Commissioners and emphasizes the combination of circumstances that brought the commissioners even the success they had. Piecemeal legislation courted failure because the lawyers who had to apply it would try to integrate it with their understanding of existing principle. If the fit was poor they would reject it. Authority and expertise could together produce comprehensive legislation, but there was no institutional support for it.

Registration of Deeds

THE NEED

The Real Property Commissioners' success did not extend to their central proposal: the compulsory registration of deeds, which they advanced as their primary solution to the overriding problem of insecurity of title.[81] Only registration of all conveyancing instruments would provide adequate protection from the risk of hidden transactions that currently threatened title, they said. That would enable the present expensive and inadequate indirect protections to be abandoned, bringing substantial costs savings. Because documents would always be available for inspection at the registry there would also be no need for the elaborate, expensive, and only partly effective covenants to produce deeds, which were currently needed when the owner of a large estate retained his title deeds on sale of just a part of it. Recitals in title deeds were currently used as long narratives of all the preceding deeds, since they were accepted as secondary evidence if the recited deeds were subsequently lost.[82] But the whereabouts of registered deeds would be certain, so recitals could henceforth be shortened and more costs saved. As the commissioners developed their ideas they found more and

[78] *Cunliffe* v. *Brancker* (1876) 3 Ch D 393.
[79] Contingent Remainders Act 1877; (1875–6) 20 *Sol. J.* 916.
[80] Perpetuities and Accumulations Act 1964.
[81] *RC on Real Property*, 2nd Report.
[82] T. Coventry, *On Conveyancers' Evidence* (1832), 315–19, and see 299–304 for their use in proving events.

more possible benefits from, and uses for, deeds registration, so much so that one respondent cautioned them to begin with what was central.[83] The commissioners had no doubt what that was: registration was a necessary cure for chronic insecurity of title.

Much of this insecurity was associated with mortgages and, in various ways, with the mismatch between their form and their function. Functionally a security, in form a mortgage was an improvised use of common law possessory estates. The common law could perhaps be manipulated to produce a security that terminated automatically when the underlying obligation was fulfilled, but, it was said, difficulty in proving repayment could sometimes cause problems when the once-mortgaged land came up for sale years later, and there were difficulties too for a mortgagee wishing to assign the mortgage.[84]

So the 'more eligible mode' had come to be that the mortgagee undertook to reconvey the fee simple on repayment, or to surrender the term of years, as the case may be. But often that step was neglected, so it was said. Parties, particularly in the country, treated the mortgage as what it functionally was, a mere security that was now spent, returned the title deeds to the borrower and regarded the transaction as over. So, strictly, when the now former mortgagor contracted with a purchaser to sell the formerly mortgaged land, he did not have the title he was promising to transfer. He could get it, of course, which was not usually difficult if the mortgagee was alive and could be found. If the mortgagee had died, however, the fee simple, if that had been the security, would have descended to his heir, who would hold it on trust for the mortgagee's personal representatives, who alone could properly direct a reconveyance. So they also must be found; and if they had died, their personal representatives too.[85] If the security had been a term of years the heir could be omitted from the hunt, because terms were personalty, but not the personal representatives. 'Getting in' these shells of former transactions could be tedious and expensive, but it was necessary if the former mortgagor was to have a title Chancery would regard as 'marketable', one that it would force on to a buyer by an order for specific performance.

Several of the Real Property Commissioners' respondents said that country solicitors had their own solution to this problem: they regarded the original mortgage deed as surplusage and suppressed it.[86] What Chancery did not

---

[83] *RC on Real Property*, 2nd Report, 336 (Radford).

[84] H. Lewis, *Principles of Conveyancing* (1863), 250–1.

[85] Piecemeal legislation allowing substitutes was consolidated in 1825 (6 Geo. IV c. 74) and extended from time to time thereafter: see p. 271 below.

[86] *RC on Real Property*, 2nd Report, 299 (Clay); 262 (Tompson); 418 (Rolfe); 431–2 (Turner); 438 (Hayes); 451 (Senior); cf. W. M. Bythewood and T. Jarman, *A Selection of Precedents in Conveyancing* (1833), vii, 360.

know, Chancery would not worry about. Naturally, the Lincoln's Inn conveyancers regarded suppression of deeds as a vice, a danger, and a major problem. It is possible that their influence on standards and on general practice was increasing. One country respondent grumbled that there were now far more conveyancers than there used to be, and that they had brought nothing but complication.[87] Thomas Farrer, a London solicitor, said that any large transaction now came under investigation in London, and that solicitors there habitually referred to counsel in any case of 'intricacy or considerable amount', for fear of personal liability.[88] The consequent increase in punctiliousness would explain how lawyers could maintain that so many titles were perfectly safe yet also 'unmarketable'.

Fulfilled but formally extant mortgages were simply a nuisance. Much more serious was the possibility that there might be an unfulfilled mortgage that was not disclosed by the title deeds.[89] Men who on their marriage had settled their land might likewise subsequently suppress the settlement and purport to sell a fee simple.[90] Conveyancers in the 1820s thought these risks serious enough to have persevered with the eighteenth-century protective device known as 'attendant terms', though its costs in time and money were severe and its usefulness not guaranteed.

The device originated from the peculiar form adopted for English mortgages and similar securities, noted above. Its classic usage would begin in a marriage settlement with a term of several hundred years vested in trustees as security to raise a widow's jointure or a child's portion. The settlement itself would say what should happen when that purpose was fulfilled: the term should continue, the trustees to hold it for the person who would have been entitled to the lands if the term had expired.[91] Alternatively a commercial mortgage by demise would be kept alive after repayment by having the term transferred to trustees to 'attend the inheritance'.[92] Equity judges interpreted that to mean that the trustees held for the person for the time being entitled to possession of the land. When the land came to be sold the term would be assigned to new trustees for the purchaser.

---

[87] *RC on Real Property*, 2nd Report, 283 (Alington).

[88] *RC on Real Property*, 2nd Report, 487. Country solicitors sometimes took nice points unaided: 1st Report, 622 (Dawson).

[89] *RC on Real Property*, 2nd Report, 167 (Blanchard).

[90] *RC on Real Property*, 2nd Report, 153 (Adlington); 165 (Bird); 203 (Wilkins & Kendall); 431 (Turner); 451 (Senior); 462 (Christie).

[91] e.g. C. Davidson, *Precedents and Forms in Conveyancing*, iii, 868, 878 (2nd edn, 1861). In derivative settlements made under powers contained in parent settlements it was usual to declare that terms to secure jointures and the like would cease on fulfilment: *ibid.*, 1132, 1142.

[92] Davidson was still providing a short form for this in 1874, for fear that the Act of 1845 automatically ending satisfied terms might have a loophole: *Concise Precedents* (9th edn, 1874), 38n, 247.

If it turned out that at sometime between the creation of the term and the purported transfer of the fee to the purchaser there had been a settlement or a mortgage that still continued, the term came into play. On the face of it, it also would be held for that true but hidden legal owner. But the term was a legal estate, which had now been bought by the purchaser through his nominees. And the interest of the true but hidden owner was merely equitable. So if the purchaser had bought without notice (which he would have to prove) he would extinguish the true but hidden owner's interest and could therefore possess the land safely for the duration of the term—several hundred years. It was not the fee; but it was a reasonable substitute. Thus the true legal owner was squeezed out, and the purchaser achieved the functional equivalent of what had been intended in his deal with someone who had turned out merely to be an apparent owner.

Respondents to the Real Property Commissioners worried about the expense of this device. If the term had been assiduously assigned and reassigned on each resettlement it would have acquired a lengthy paper title that would need examining and proving along with the title to the freehold. And if it had not been assigned and reassigned the legal term would likely have come to rest somewhere among the personal representatives of the original trustees, or their personal representatives...and would need retrieving and verifying...which would include confirming that any probates that had been granted came from the correct ecclesiastical court. Family settlements usually contained two trust terms, one for the jointure and the other for portions, each with its own trustees, and sometimes more. If both, or all, were worded so as to keep them alive on fulfilment, and if the purchaser was buying land that had been settled and resettled within a family for two or three generations, the titles to these attendant terms could be much bulkier than the title to the fee.

There were various practices for keeping all this paperwork down, but no uniformity. Further, the safety of the device had recently been seriously undermined by the King's Bench, and although its decisions were subsequently to be disavowed after rejection by other courts and by Sugden in his text, the episode showed how vulnerable these intellectual constructs were to unheralded judicial mutilation, how delicately courts of common law and equity needed to co-operate.[93] Charles Butler, the conveyancers' father figure, wrote briefly to the commissioners that

---

[93] *Doe d. Burdett* v. *Wright* (1819) 2 B. & Ald. 710; *Doe d. Putland* v. *Hilder* (1819) 2 B. & Ald. 782; *Bartlett* v. *Downes* (1826) 3 B. & C. 616. Disavowal: *Doe d. Blacknell* v. *Plowman* (1831) 2 B. & Ad. 573. Opposition: the decisions are reported and analysed in Sugden, *Vendor and Purchaser*, e.g. 10th edn (1839), iii: 26–67; he published his arguments at greater length in E. B. Sugden, *A Letter to Charles Butler: On the Doctrine of Presuming a Surrender of Terms Assigned to Attend the Inheritance* (1819). For the practical consequences see *RC on Real Property*, 2nd Report, 104 (Harrison); 468 (Shaw Lefevre); 472 (Hodgkin); 488 (Farrer).

their proposal for deeds registration had his unqualified approval, and that he had been 'considerably induced' to that conclusion by the King's Bench decisions.[94] The commissioners adopted the commonly held view. The use of attendant terms showed that protection against hidden transactions was needed, they concluded, but the device itself was expensive, dilatory, and unreliable. Anyway, it merely distributed loss. The better solution was to ensure that nothing remained hidden. The way to do that was through requiring all deeds to be registered if they were to affect subsequent parties.

THE MEANS

The commissioners' conception of deeds registration was far-reaching and in some respects original. There were already some regional deeds registries in Middlesex and the Yorkshire ridings, all of them dating from the very early 1700s and scarcely touched by legislation since. As recently as 1816 Serjeant Onslow's bills for compulsory registration had adopted their model—registration by county, and of memorials only.[95] He further copied the Yorkshire precedent in putting these county registries under Quarter Sessions control.

The commissioners' proposal was quite different. Whereas the Yorkshire system was constructed to disclose the existence of a deed but to conceal its nature, the commissioners wanted registration of the whole document and at a central registry in London, though as an afterthought they added that their scheme was equally well suited to district registries.[96] But now that postal services were so speedy and reliable, delay for country transactions would be trivial and loss rare, they said. They included registration of wills and bankruptcies in their scheme; mere county registration for those obviously would not meet the point. Besides, London was the centre for transactions, even for many sales of lands in distant parts. Landowners, they thought, would not be exposed to publicity through whole-document registration, and if in the case of country bankers the public did become aware of how little land supported their apparent credit, then so much the better. Country solicitors' fears that central registration would force them into reliance upon London agents were mistaken. The commissioners acknowledged that their scheme would upset the basis on which solicitors' charges were regulated, but the tariff was already badly out of date and should be revised to secure solicitors a liberal remuneration under modern conditions. This analysis accurately anticipated where opposition would arise.

---

[94] *RC on Real Property*, 2nd Report, 232.
[95] *PP* 1814–15 (346), ii, 717, 1816 (233) i, 237.
[96] *RC on Real Property*, 2nd Report, 110; J. E. Dibb, *A Practical Guide to the Registration of Deeds and Wills in the West Riding of Yorkshire* (1846), pp. viii, 18–23, 38.

The commissioners described in detail how a central registry might be organized and administered. They provided costings; they analysed at length suitable principles of liability for error and for fraud. Their crowning intellectual achievement was Lewis Duval's invention of a classification and indexing system both precise and user-friendly, in contrast to indexation at the Middlesex deeds registry and the dockets of judgments, which were crude to the point of being unusable.[97]

In addition the commissioners addressed the legal functions of registration. It would not be necessary for validity between parties to a transaction for value, but it would be required for an action by a volunteer against the grantor. Similarly, though a voluntary deed even when registered would not have priority over a subsequent purchaser for value (continuing the existing law), the purchaser would have to register his transaction before bringing an action against the volunteer.[98] Registration would be necessary to give priority against a purchaser for value, even (they concluded after a long analysis) one with actual notice, though not in case of fraud.[99] In consequence equitable mortgage by deposit of title deeds would no longer be effective. But since it was but a recent invention by Lord Thurlow that contradicted general principle, and, since all that would be required instead was registration of a simple memorandum or a caveat, its removal from the law would be no loss.[100] Similarly, sellers would no longer automatically have a lien for unpaid purchase money, but could obtain one by some appropriate entry 'on the register'.[101]

There are features in these proposals more easily associated with registration of title than with registration of deeds, and so too in Duval's index, which was organized by root of title—the commissioners even refer to it as 'the index to the roots of registered titles'.[102] So though registration of deeds was an old idea, the commissioners' was by far its most sophisticated restatement.

[97] Judgments: see e.g. R. Preston, *An Essay in a Course of Lectures on Abstracts of Title* (1818–19), iii, 336–9, quoted by one respondent to the commission: *RC on Real Property*, 2nd Report, 104 (Lowndes).

[98] *RC on Real Property*, 2nd Report, 117. The status quo resulted from the Statute of Elizabeth (see pp. 263–6, below). Many, but not all, of the commissioners' respondents wanted it changed. It was characteristic of the commissioners to avoid controversy on an issue that was not central to their objective.

[99] *RC on Real Property*, 2nd Report, 117–25. They recommended also that the general equitable jurisdiction to relieve from mistake ought to continue: *loc. cit.*, 125.

[100] *RC on Real Property*, 2nd Report, 111.

[101] *Ibid.*, 111.

[102] *Ibid.*, 129–30; J. Howell, 'Deeds Registration in England: A Complete Failure?' (1999) 58 *CLJ* 366–98 at 396–7. The commissioners' analysis of 'mistake' and 'invalid registration' (*RC on Real Property*, 2nd Report, 141–2) similarly raises, and resolves, issues that will be familiar to anyone acquainted with the Torrens system of title registration.

THE OPPOSITION

The commissioners' registration bill was introduced into the Commons five times between 1830 and 1833 but never passed a second reading.[103] Its first introduction was merely for discussion, Campbell said, but it was immediately opposed by Sugden and by the ultra-Tory former attorney-general, Sir Charles Wetherell.[104] Their hostility never relented.[105] Soon opposition to centralization arose from Yorkshire, which spread to the other northern counties.[106] Campbell attributed the unprecedented deluge of hostile petitions from all parts of England to fomentation by country solicitors, whose emoluments would be reduced by the commissioners' scheme.[107] That sounds true, and northern law societies subsequently claimed credit for defeating the proposal, but the petitions' signatories included very many landowners, commercial men, and yeoman farmers. Viscount Morpeth, whose credentials as a moderate reformer are not in doubt, pleaded for Yorkshire (and later the whole northern circuit) to be dropped from the bill.[108] When that was refused he opposed the bill outright, though he approved its principle.

In 1834 Yorkshire MPs produced a rival bill resembling Onslow's and their own local acts—county registration, registration of memorials only, simple alphabetical index—proudly basing it, they said, upon the principle of locality.[109] The debates voiced dislike of London taking everything over, of London being in possession of country documentation.[110] There was dislike of London diagnoses of what was a problem and what was not: insecurity was far less a worry than

[103] *PP* 1830–1 (85), ii, 297; 1831 (249), iii, 197; 1831–2 (3), iv, 1; 1833 (273), iii, 489; 1834 (121), iii, 591.

[104] *PD* 1830 (s3) 1: 1233–68.

[105] *PD* 1831–2 (s3) 9: 125, 563; 1832 10: 664–6; E. B. Sugden, *Cursory Observations on a General Register* (1834). Similarly Richard Preston, a leading conveyancer of his day, and MP from 1812 to 1816, had opposed Onslow's bills and reappeared to oppose the commissioners': *SC on General Register of Deeds*, Report *PP* 1831–2 (609), xviii, 365, 579–89. His 'zeal for innovation is well known to stand below zero': (1845) 9(2) *Jurist* 197.

[106] *PD* 1832 (s3) 9: 563, 1186–92; 10: 667; Dibb, *Practical Guide*, p. viii. 'What possible objection could be made to a system of Registration, it was not easy to divine. It all, however, lay in one word—Yorkshire': *PD* 1845 (s3) 80: 508 (Brougham). Compare reform of probate jurisdiction, where the divisions were much the same: see Vol. XI, pp. 701, 706, 712–13.

[107] Campbell, *Life*, ii, 12–13; *PD* 1832 (s3) 9: 1189, 1191; *The Times*, 27 August 1832; Anderson, *Lawyers*, 41–2.

[108] *PD* 1831 (s3) 9: 125–6; 1833 (s3) 18: 1004; and see 17: 1063 (Duncombe). Brougham subsequently claimed that in 1831/2 he had found vastly more public notices displayed in Yorkshire opposing centralized registration than those concerning reform of Parliament: *PD* 1845 (s3) 80: 508.

[109] *PP* 1834 (119), iii, 563; *PD* 1834 (s3) 23: 705. It differed also in requiring formal authentication before the registrar as a precondition of registration. The commissioners had reasoned at length that the sort of fraud that this requirement deterred was so difficult to perpetrate that such a step was unnecessary—it is difficult to see how their centralized register could have worked had authentication on oath been required.

[110] *PD* 1832 (s3) 9: 1186–92; 1833 17: 1056–63; 18: 1001–10; 1834 23: 696–740.

the commissioners made out; mortgages by deposit of title documents might be unprincipled, but they were useful to farmers in sudden need. Even the select committee on Campbell's bill worried that small country transactions would be made more expensive.[111]

When the final parliamentary votes came, in 1834, both the commissioners' and the Yorkshire bill lost by big majorities. Only a score or so members voted for both, believing the principle to be more important than the mechanism.[112] It is unclear whether landowners were unconvinced of the personal benefits the commissioners said deeds registration would bring them, feared a loss of privacy, or saw centralized deeds registration as diminishing their ties with their locality. The failure of the Yorkshire bill suggests, as Campbell feared, that it was the first.[113]

Whatever their reason, there was no strong pressure from landowners to counter the opposition the bills induced. *The Times*, a steady supporter of the bill, was bemused at the irrationality of much of the debate.[114] It reminded its readers of Peel's gibe during debate on the Reform Bill: would your reformed House of Commons vote for a measure of such obvious common honesty and common sense as a general registration bill?[115] Sugden had objected that bills of this significance should be government measures, but far from adopting Campbell's bill Earl Grey made Campbell's appointment as solicitor-general conditional upon his not introducing a general measure of deeds registration.[116]

1840S AND 1850S: SHIFTING AGENDA

From the point of view of James Stewart, conveyancer, leading light of the Law Amendment Society, for a few years a Liberal MP, the 1840s were largely barren.[117] To the debacle of Lyndhurst's Act he added embarrassment over two LAS-inspired bills that Lord Brougham ushered into law in 1845.[118] Dead letters from the start, they had been intended to shorten conveyances and leases by including in a statute a full version of conventional clauses that could then

[111] *SC on General Register*, 375. It saw graduated office fees as the solution.

[112] *PD* 1834 (s 3) vol. 23, cols 740–1; *The Times*, 8 May 1834. Pepys (Cottenham) and Rolfe (Cranworth) voted for both.

[113] Campbell: *PD* 1834 (s3) 23: 729.

[114] *The Times*, 31 March 1834, and cf. 27 August 1832, 1 February 1833, 20 May 1833, 2 April 1834, 23 April 1834.

[115] *The Times*, 31 March 1834; cf. Campbell, *Life*, ii, 5–6.

[116] Sugden: *PD* 1830 (s3) 1: 1262 (and note his opinion that the commissioners' task had been only to inquire into old laws, not propose new ones). Campbell: Campbell, *Life*, ii, 30. William Brougham, who had chaired the select committee on Campbell's second bill, introduced the bills in 1833 and 1834.

[117] Stewart, *Suggestions* (2nd edn, 1851), pp. viii–ix.

[118] *Ibid.*, p. xi.

be invoked by reference.[119] 'No one...dreams of paying the slightest attention' to them, proclaimed *The Jurist*, not, it seemed from objection to the principle, but because their wording was inept.[120] Brougham had no repute as a property lawyer, and since he would not disclose which were the 'most skilful conveyancers in the country' who had drafted his forms they came without the prestigious endorsements that had characterized the commissioners' work.[121] One consequence, however, was that the conveyancer Charles Davidson published his own collection of concise conveyances to show how the job should be done.[122] It must have supplied some sort of demand, since it reached its 3rd edition within three years and did not expire until its 21st in 1926.

Further, and with the same motivation, Davidson was responsible for a third act introduced by Brougham in 1845, one that despite initial uproar did succeed in reorienting elite conveyancing.[123] In consequence the question of deeds registration was revived, but with results that showed that the real property commissioners' priorities no longer held. This section of this chapter will introduce this reassessment, which was perhaps the most significant theme of the 1840s and early 1850s.

Davidson's statute was the Satisfied Terms Act 1845, which declared that in future all satisfied terms becoming attendant on the inheritance should thereupon absolutely determine, rather than being kept alive as a backup against defects of title.[124] Existing satisfied terms should also cease, save for providing personal

---

[119] 8 & 9 Vict. caps 119, 124.

[120] (1846) 10 *Jurist* 101–2; Dart, *Vendors and Purchasers* (1st edn, 1851), 247 ('either unnecessary or mischievous'); Davidson, *Concise Precedents* (1st edn, 1845), 2 ('wholly needless, and, if compulsory, would be a most fearful evil'); P. B. Brodie, *Tax on Successions and Burdens on Land* (1850), 69–70. James Stewart accepted some responsibility for proceeding with the bills, but disclaimed having drafted them: *Suggestions as to Reform in Some Branches of the Law* (2nd edn, 1852), p. xi (n). For their provenance in Law Amendment Society reports, see 'Conveyancing Reform' (1845) 2 *Law Rev.* 403–35 and Brodie, above.

[121] *PD* 1845 (s3) 80: 505.

[122] C. Davidson, *Concise Precedents*. He was not the first: Hayes, *Concise Conveyancer* (1830); G. Sweet, *Concise Precedents in Conveyancing* (1845; first published in part in 1844 as a supplement to the 9th volume of the 3rd edn of Bythewood and Jarman's *Precedents*); and see W. F. Cornish, *A Treatise on Purchase Deeds* (1828). I have not traced 'Coventry, Concise Forms in Conveyancing, first published in 1827' referred to by Sweet, *Concise Precedents*, vi.

[123] *The Times*, 28 July, 2 September, and 17 October 1845; (1845) 9(2) *Jurist* 334, 358–60 (contrast (1846) 10(2) *Jurist* 101–2); Brodie, *Tax on Successions*, 68–9 (answered equally abrasively by [James Stewart] 'What the Landowner may demand and obtain (part 2)' (1850) 11 *Law Rev.* 440–8). By contrast the Act was greeted with approval in (1845) 9(2) *Jurist* 183–4 and (1846) 3 *Law Rev.* 395–406.

[124] 8 & 9 Vict. c. 112. Davidson had J. H. Christie revise his clauses and then sent them unsolicited to Brougham in 1844. When Brougham did not proceed with them Davidson published them in the introduction to the first edition of his *Concise Precedents*. Brougham then had them enacted with slight amendments in 1845. See Davidson, *Concise Precedents* (1st edn), 45–7, (3rd edn, 1848), 73–80, and (for Christie) [Stewart] 'What the Landowner may demand', 446. The Law Amendment Society

protection for their present holder. He took a conscious risk with its drafting, which would have crippled his Act if a very narrow reading soon propounded by the Queen's Bench had been generally adopted.[125] But, unlike Brougham's short-form Acts, Davidson's did win prestigious endorsement, so when Sugden, Dart, and Sweet backed Davidson's own broad reading of it the profession was willing to follow.[126] The Act was treated as a general instruction that the practice of keeping attendant terms alive as a form of title insurance should now stop.[127] Davidson's inspiration was the 'universal practice' adopted in railway Acts, his objective the reduction of cost and trouble, and he reckoned to have saved the landed interest £250,000 a year in conveyancing costs.[128]

Attendant terms had only ever given qualified protection against infirmities of title, and even that had been reduced by the Judgments Act 1838.[129] Still, they were said to have been common, so their removal before introduction of deeds registration alarmed some. Of the surviving commissioners, Brodie and Lord Campbell thought the sequence wrong, and the latter at once reintroduced the commissioners' registration bill.[130] Then James Stewart and others persuaded a House of Lords select committee on burdens on land, which was looking for recompense for the repeal of the corn laws, that both deeds registration and a general revision of conveyancing law were urgent social needs.[131] The result was the appointment of a royal commission in 1847, its terms of reference confined

endorsed the idea: 'Report on Attendant Terms' (1845–6) 3 *Law Rev.* 183, reprinted in *Reports etc by the Law Amendment Society HLP* 1851, xvi, 349.

[125] *Concise Precedents* (3rd edn), 76; *Doe d. Clay* v. *Jones* (1849) 13 Q.B. 774, 13 Jur. 824. Brodie thought the decision both fair and technically correct: *Tax on Successions*, 69. It was ultimately approved by the Court of Appeal in *Anderson* v. *Pignet* (1872) 8 Ch App 180, whose dicta gave an even narrower meaning to 'satisfied', the key concept, and hence to the act's ambit, but by then the practice of keeping attendant terms alive had ended.

[126] E. B. Sugden, *An Essay on the New Statutes*… (1st edn, 1852), 290–4, (2nd edn, 1862, *sub. nom. A Practical Treatise on the New Statutes Relating to Property*), 276–82; J. H. Dart, *A Compendium of the Law and Practice of Vendors and Purchasers of Real Estate* (1851), 248–9; G. Sweet, *Recent Statutes Relating to the Practice of Conveyancing* (1850), 314–20; Davidson, *Concise Precedents* (6th edn, 1865), 38–40; see also the similar opinions expressed in (1849) 13 *Jurist* 381, 382–4 (G. Sweet), and 401.

[127] See e.g. F. Prideaux, *Precedents in Conveyancing* (8th edn, 1876), i, 195–6.

[128] Davidson, *Concise Precedents*, 45–6; *ibid.* (3rd edn), 74n. Railway act practice was generalized in the Lands Clauses Consolidation Act 1845, 8 Vict. c. 18, s 81. As Davidson acknowledged, the situations were not the same.

[129] Judgment Act, ss 11, 13; Sugden, *Vendors and Purchasers* (9th edn), ii, 399–403.

[130] Brodie, *Tax on Successions*, 68–9; *PD* 1845 (s3) 80: 516. Henry Sewell, a pioneer proponent of title registration also thought attendant terms should not have been abolished without providing alternative means for doing their good: H. Sewell, *A Letter to the Earl of Yarborough on the Burdens Affecting Real Property, with Reasons in Favour of a General Registry of Titles* (1850—a revised version of his *Letter to Lord Worsley*, 1846), 52.

[131] Anderson, *Lawyers*, 60–3; *SC of HL on Burdens on Land*, Report, *PP* 1846 (HC 411), vi, 1, 12–13.

to deeds registration. It took three years to recommend a scheme for enactment however, and then only by a majority.[132]

The Whig government adopted that proposal in 1851, the first time a government had done so, and, against some opposition, pushed it through the Lords. But time had been lost re-examining whether tithe commutation maps and the nascent ordnance survey could be used as the means of indexation. The royal commission had said yes, but in the end the Lords thought no. With every prospect of renewed opposition from Yorkshire and other country solicitors, the bill was not risked in the Commons. When it next was, in 1853, a select committee reported brusquely that the many petitions against it were well-founded, that rather than deeds registration there should be registration of title, and that a commission should be established to devise a practicable bill to that end instead.[133]

That was not quite the last word on deeds registration, since Osborne Morgan's select committee in 1878 rather tepidly recommended it as a safeguard against fraud and there was a half-hearted flicker of interest in the mid-1880s.[134] Despite those revivals, however, and an occasional wistful glance by property lawyers such as Joshua Williams, as a serious legislative proposition centralized deeds registration died in 1853.

Such an abrupt end to such a major project, and one so easily accepted in so many other jurisdictions, requires some explanation.[135] The most immediate, the political explanation, would be that a weak bill was overcome by self-interested opposition from solicitors. The 1853 bill was vulnerable because the long wrangle between reformers about how to structure the register had cast doubt on the viability of Duval's root-of-title index, but then the better idea, a map-based index, turned out not to be feasible at all.[136] Everyone (outside Yorkshire) thought an index of names hopelessly inefficient, but transformation of the eighteenth-century practice of registration of memorials in local registries into a single, modern, centralized depositary of complete texts required technical support that was proving easier to imagine than to provide. The widespread use of card indexes to tame the alphabet lay 50 years ahead.

On the other hand the opposition, which originated from a region with its own deeds registries to lose by the proposed reform, could unite around the principle of locality. That was well calculated in the aftermath of the widely disliked centralization effected by the Poor Law Commissioners and the Board of Health.

---

[132] *RC on Registration and Conveyancing*, Report, *PP* 1850 [1261], xxxii, 1.

[133] *SC on Registration of Assurances Bill*, Report, *PP* 1852–3 (889), xxxvi, 397.

[134] See pp. 203–7, below.

[135] Howell, 'Deeds Registration'; Anderson, *Lawyers*, 77–84.

[136] *RC on Registration and Conveyancing*, Report, 12–19; E. T. Wakefield, *The Feasibility of Constructing a New System of Registering Title Deeds* (1853); Anderson, *Lawyers*, 75–6.

Yorkshire solicitors' address to landowners drew attention to the proposal's reliance on centralized executive discretion and to central government's patronage over appointments.[137] Promoters of deeds registration saw this as a screen for narrow self-interest, the fear of loss of emoluments, a claim that was never detailed or quantified and remains very difficult to assess. Solicitors were subject to price regulation in a form widely felt to be archaic—payment per approved task at a rate of so much per so many words. But how this related to actual costs to real clients is not known, nor did anyone publish a demonstration of how deeds registration would change things. Proponents of short-form documentation, which met the same obstacle, asserted that in practice solicitors could easily switch to a different mode of charging, but again we have no quantification.[138]

Perhaps the most likely element of self-interest in provincial solicitors' opposition to centralized registration was the prospect of having to share fees with the London agents needed to search the register and extract the relevant documents.[139] Like the increased risks of delay and loss of documents, such a drift of local professional wealth and status to London could be presented as an inevitable concomitant of centralization, one that would hurt the locality as a whole.

More fundamentally, however, positive support for deeds registration had become much weaker. To an increasingly significant strand among reformers it had become an irrelevance that addressed an obsolete problem, a distraction from what had become the modern agenda. There were two limbs to their argument. First, they said, the Real Property Commissioners had exaggerated either the extent that titles were uncertain or the degree to which clients cared. The *Law Review* grumbled about conveyancing counsels' propensity to raise 'fanciful and hypercritical' objections to titles.[140] James Stewart suggested that the risk was so small that it would be insurable, and worked out a scheme to entice insurance companies, though nothing came of it.[141] The Law Amendment Society declared in 1851 that 'the greater part of the existing titles in England are, in fact, safe; and that much the larger proportion of those which, from some doubt either as to the facts or the law which constitute the strict proof of title, may, for the time, be unmarketable, are nevertheless really free from all risk of being

---

[137] *The Times*, 29 April 1851.

[138] G. Sweet, *Concise Precedents* (2nd edn, 1845), p. vi. Sewell, *A Letter* (2nd edn, 1850), 15 implies that some sort of *ad valorem* charge was common. Brougham's short-form Acts explicitly provided for a different mode of remuneration; for commentary in the solicitors' press see (1845) 30 *Leg. Ob.* 369 and 409, cf. E. V. Neale, *The Real Property Acts of 1845* (1845), 70–1.

[139] *RC on Real Property*, 2nd Report, 109, flatly denied that agents would be needed.

[140] 'Conveyancing Reform—Ireland (1847)' 5 *Law Rev.* 398–427 at 406.

[141] Anderson, *Lawyers*, 70–2, 136. It is unclear why the idea was not revived later; perhaps the answer lies in lenders' willingness to make loans on mortgage without further security.

successfully assailed in a court of law'.[142] Railway companies habitually disregarded Chancery's 'marketable title' standard, accepting a 'good holding' title instead.[143] Though remnants of the old claim continued on occasion to serve a useful rhetorical purpose, by the end of the 1850s the preponderant view among the cognoscenti was that titles were 'practically' secure.[144]

The generous among these critics could credit the ameliorative legislation initiated by the Real Property Commissioners, continued in different styles through the 1840s and pursued in his inimitable way by Lord St. Leonards in the 1850s. Another reason, more double-edged but said to be indicative of the public's true priority, lay in the widespread insertion of special conditions into contracts of sale.[145] They might stipulate that a purchaser must accept a title going back less than the legal period, or forgo proof of some specified event, or inspect a title prior to a partition only at his own expense, or, if buying an assignment of a lease, not require proof of the landlord's title, and so on. Such conditions indicating an uncertainty in the title ought to have discounted the price, but generally did not, so it was said.[146] The true conclusion may have been that conditions of sale merely shifted the locus of argument, for they generated considerable litigation.[147] The conclusion generally urged, however, was that the common acceptance of

---

[142] Society for the Promotion of the Amendment of the Law, *On Loans on Land* (1851), reprinted in Reports etc by the Law Amendment Society, 1851 *HLP* xvi 349. See also [J. Moore] *Observations on the Proposed Registration of Deeds with Reference More Particularly to the Pamphlet by William Hazlitt, Esq., by a Country Solicitor* (1851), 4–6.

[143] Stewart, 'A Plan for a Register of Titles' (1848) 7 *Law Rev.* 386, 396; Stewart, 'A Second Letter to the Members of Agricultural Societies and Others Interested in Land', *The Times*, 30 October 1846. According to H. T. Frend and T. H. Ware, *Precedents of Conveyances and Other Instruments Relating to Railway Companies* (2nd edn, 1866), 121 the originator of this statement was John Clutton, who gave evidence to the *SC of HL on Compensation to Owners of Lands Compulsorily Taken for Building Railways*, PP 1845 (HC 420), x, 417, 445. His very brief explanation was that railway companies did not require a marketable title because they were not going to market the land. Frend and Ware disapproved.

[144] See the analysis of evidence to the 1857 royal commission in F. V. Hawkins, *The Title to Landed Estates Bills and the Solicitor-General's Speech Considered* (1859), 4–7. The commission itself adhered to the older view, though only to point the superiority of title registration: *RC on Registration of Title*, Report, PP 1857 sess. 2 [2215], xxi, 245, 257.

[145] Bythewood and Jarman, *Precedents*, vii, 353.

[146] Bythewood and Jarman, *Precedents*, vii, 354; 'On the Law Relating to Conditions of Sale' (1845) 2 *Law Rev.* 81–114 at 86. This continued to be the usual view; see e.g. F. E. Farrer, *Precedents of Conditions of Sale* (1902), 7. Chancery judges deciding whether clauses inserted by trustees as vendors were unnecessarily depreciatory took a different view: *Dance* v. *Goldingham* (1873) 8 Ch App 902; *Dunn* v. *Flood* (1885) 28 Ch D 586.

[147] Bythewood and Jarman, *Precedents*, vii, 354–93, which is the basis of S. Atkinson, *An Essay on Marketable Titles* (1833), 633–46; W. Hughes, *A Practical Treatise of the Laws Relative to the Sale and Conveyance of Real Property* (1840), i, 43–51; 'On the Law Relating to Conditions of Sale' (1845) 2 *Law Rev.* 81–114.

restrictive conditions showed that purchasers were not worried about supposedly defective titles.

The second aspect of the shift in reformers' thought was that cost and delay in effecting land transactions, which the commissioners had acknowledged as one of the problems, became the paramount evil to be addressed. This shift was important and long lasting. It is visible in the mid-1840s, in the legislation abolishing attendant terms and introducing short-form conveyancing, and also in the work of James Stewart to gain political support for reform of real property law—in no other way could he present the unreformed or semi-reformed law as a 'burden' in the sense then employed.[148] Commentators who acknowledged that conditions of sale conferred sufficient security sometimes added that the cost of drawing individualized conditions was significant. High transaction costs reduced land's value relative to other investments, unfairly affecting the landed interest and deterring small investors, it was said.[149] When land was being acquired for investment a very common objective was to make some form of family provision. But the broad freedom settlors had to settle their land, which was part of its attraction, resulted in settlements that made exit difficult and expensive, thus reducing the attraction and deterring entry. An unfavourable contrast with the ease of settling and transferring pure personalty, particularly consols, became almost mandatory among reformers, a constant theme for 30 years or more.[150]

There was at best a peripheral place in that comparison for deeds registration. Such registration might perhaps have brought a net saving of time and money if purchasers had been as meticulous in their search for security as the Real Property Commissioners made out. But for those many purchasers who accepted sale conditions restricting the inquiries they could make it was now said that the reform would be at best neutral and more likely an expense.[151] A conservative reformer such as J. H. Christie could remain strongly attached to deeds registration

[148] Anderson, *Lawyers*, 60–3; 'Conveyancing Burdens on Land' (1846) 4 *Law Rev.* 384–411; J. Williams, *Principles of the Law of Real Property* (3rd edn, 1852), 342, resiling from (2nd edn, 1849), 396 *et seq.* Ker may also have shared this view (*Suggestions*, 9, 53).

[149] e.g. evidence of Nassau Senior to the *SC of HL on Burdens on Real Property*, Report, 471–3.

[150] R. Wilson, *Outlines of a Plan for Adopting the Machinery of the Public Funds to the Transfer of Real Property* (1844); 'Burdens on Land—Conveyancing' (1846) 4 *Law Rev.* 164–83; Cobden (1849) quoted by D Martin, 'Land Reform', in P. Hollis (ed.), *Pressure from Without in Early Victorian England* (1974), 131–58 at 153; *The Times*, 28 June 1851; Stewart, *Suggestions* (2nd edn, 1852), p. ix; W. S. Cookson, 'On the Registration of Transfers of Land' (1852) 16 *Law Rev.* 361–78; *SC on Registration of Assurances Bill*, Report, 424–7 (Field), 463 (Webster), 468 (Bullar); *RC on Title Registration*, Report, 245, 274–5, 288–90, 303; (contrast Christie at 579: Parliament and the public in a fools' paradise if they think land can be sold like railway stock).

[151] Cookson, 'On the Registration', 363–4; *RC on Title Registration*, Report, 263–4; Cairns, *PD* (s3) 1859 152: 298–9; E. P. Wolstenholme, 'Simplification of Title Preferable to Introduction of Novel Modes of Assurance' in *Papers Read before the Juridical Society* (1862), ii, 533–52 at 543.

on principle while conceding that it would do nothing immediate to meet the new agenda.[152] Bellenden Ker wavered between wanting to support reformers who thought it still worthwhile and urging instead that it be postponed until the last step, after a comprehensive digest of real property law had been first constructed and then simplified.[153] The digest was his personal preference, a search for principle that would remove the disfiguring effect of so much piecemeal legislation. It would remove too the need for the professional self-help that had created special conditions in contracts, which he disliked for putting the making of the operative law in the hands of a 'far inferior class of law-makers'.[154] But this suggestion, like deeds registration, was at best an indirect way of satisfying the demand for quicker and cheaper land transactions.

[152] *RC on Registration and Conveyancing*, Report, 554, 569.

[153] *On the Reform of the Law of Real Property; Shall we Register our Deeds?* (both 1853). (On the need for a digest see Stewart, *Suggestions*, first written in 1842.) Note too *The Times*, hitherto a supporter of deeds registration, which greeted the Lords' passage of the 1851 bill by declaring that 'it is simplification of the principles of the law affecting real property, rather than in the publicity of conveyances, that the relief to the landowner from the antiquated and complicated system under which he is the principal sufferer is to be sought' (28 June 1851).

[154] *On Reform of the Law of Real Property*, 21.

III

Land Transactions:
Settlements and Sales

1. INTRODUCTION

The first part of this chapter tracks the decline of the strict settlement, the device used by wealthy landed families to tie the hands of each generation so that the patrimony would be preserved. It lasted in something like its historic shape until the Settled Land Act 1882 reconciled the continuing desire to preserve family wealth, on the one hand, with the market freedom of individual ownership, on the other, by investing all limited owners with a set of management powers that included the power of sale. In the 1820s that was unthinkable to the Real Property Commissioners; even the lesser proposition that limited owners should have standardized leasing powers brought too much disagreement for them to make a recommendation. For them an owner's ability to settle his land on successive generations was a given.

The commissioners were concerned, however, that the mechanics of buying and selling should become easier. Settlement was often presented as an impediment to sale. The second part of this chapter burrows beneath the rules of substantive law that the commissioners saw as obstacles to consider the workaday process of conveyancing. Individualism manifested itself here too, this time through the increasing use of contractual terms to shift obligations away from sellers. In due course the general law caught up with that, and was at least partly recast to accord with what had become usual practice.

2. STRICT SETTLEMENT

Over the last 60 years or so historians have become very familiar with the ways in which the strict settlement enabled wealthy families to pass possession of their landed patrimony intact to the eldest male of each generation while simultaneously providing endowments out of it for younger siblings and incomes for dowagers. Because the device relied on entails, and entails could be barred by a tenant in tail in possession, class culture ensured a voluntary pre-emptive barring on the coming of age of each heir apparent, to be followed immediately by a resettlement that tied the land up for the next generation—at the end of which the process would be repeated. Not all great estates were held under this regime, but most were, and many lesser ones. Landownership in England was highly concentrated, and the strict settlement played a part in keeping it so.

For a lawyer at the start of our period the interest would come from the small print—the big picture had long since been established. Forms of settlement could vary, since variation within the limits allowed by law was the essence of freedom of property, and exploiting it was the lawyer's art. In 1861 Charles Davidson epitomized his 'settlement upon marriage of real estate with usual clauses' thus:

SETTLEMENT *upon* MARRIAGE *of* FREEHOLDS *in* FEE SIMPLE *and* COPYHOLDS *of* INHERITANCE *the property of the intended* HUSBAND, *as to the* FREEHOLDS *to the use of the* HUSBAND *for* LIFE *subject to an annuity to the wife for her* JOINTURE, *to the first and other* SONS *of the marriage successively in* TAIL MALE, *remainder to the* HUSBAND *in* FEE. TRUSTS *of* TERMS *for raising* PIN MONEY, *to secure* JOINTURE, *and for raising* PORTIONS *for* YOUNGER CHILDREN. DECLARATION *as to receipt and application of* RENTS *during* MINORITIES. POWERS *of* JOINTURING *and* CHARGING PORTIONS. POWERS *to* LEASE *for twenty-one years, to grant* BUILDING LEASES *and to grant* MINING LEASES. *Powers of granting* LICENCES *to* COPYHOLDERS *and of* ENFRANCHISEMENT. POWER *of* SALE *and* EXCHANGE. TRUSTS *of* COPYHOLDS *to correspond with* USES *of* FREEHOLDS. TRUSTEE CLAUSES *adapted to the case of* SEVERAL *sets of* TRUSTEES. COVENANTS *for* TITLE.[1]

Conventionally, land in a strict settlement such as that would be resettled on the eldest son's coming of age. The father would retain his life estate, the son would surrender his fee tail for a life estate plus an allowance secured on the land, the unborn grandson would be given a fee tail, a set of trustees would be inserted to preserve that contingent remainder from premature destruction, and provisions would be made for portioning and jointuring the next generation, with their own set or sets of protective trustees. There was much room for variation in resettlement too, of course.

It can be seen from Davidson's headings that the general pliability of property concepts that allowed the wealthy to adopt a form of family ownership that in some measure protected its future generations from misfortune simultaneously allowed considerable leeway for a family minded to increase its fortune through capital development. It took a coincidence of forethought, good drafting, and opportunity, since resettlement, which was the usual opportunity, would occur only once each generation. Still, as his sketch shows, the law of estates that limited what life tenants could do was complemented by a law of powers that could

---

[1] C. Davidson, *Precedents in Conveyancing*, iii, 862 (2nd edn, 1861).

expand it. In the hands of a skilled draftsman a family could have, if not the whole of both worlds, at least a large part of them.

It would be a compromise, expensive in its legal running costs, always with the potential for disappointment if the balance turned out not to be quite right, but from a lawyer's point of view the question was less what was possible, more how far prudence required resting with the conventional model.[2] Nor could the lawyer doubt what that was. The supposition contained in the precedent books, running through into the Settled Estates Act 1856 and the Settled Land Act 1882, was that owners of settled land would not normally fund development directly themselves by mortgaging the inheritance, but would instead lease to capitalists. The tenants would be allowed terms of years long enough to make a profit on their investment in the mining or building operations concerned, with the long-term increase in capital value accruing to the family when the reversion fell in. The model could be adapted to local or family circumstance.

Settlements did allow the inheritance to be mortgaged to raise family portions and annuities—that was probably universal—but mortgage powers for commercial purposes were not part of the standard package.[3] Instead a life tenant who was willing to gift capital development to his successor might borrow against his life interest, if his life was insurable.[4] Alternatively, families might leave some land out of settlement to provide collateral for borrowing, or they might delay resettlement, sometimes for many years. Davidson considered that powers to mortgage for unspecified purposes but up to a fixed amount were proper and not uncommon on *re*settlement, for the benefit of the incumbent life tenant, his successor, or both.[5] Historians remark that by one means or another mortgages of the fee were much more common than the theory of strict settlement suggests.[6]

Nevertheless, the primary modern purpose of strict settlement was to protect future generations from the unrestrained borrowings of the family's current head. The precedent books did not insert mortgage powers into their standard

---

[2] For the pitfalls of poor communication between lawyers, see D. Cannadine, *Lords and Landlords: The Aristocracy and the Towns 1774–1967* (Leicester, 1980), 143.

[3] Davidson's model adopts the usual technique. Rather than allowing mortgages of the fee simple directly, it vests long terms of years in trustees prior to the life estate. The settlement allows the terms to be charged for specified purposes and provides for their cesser when the purposes are fulfilled. For an earlier example see W. M. Bythewood and T. Jarman, *A Selection of Precedents in Conveyancing* (1833), ix, 212n.

[4] Alternatively he would grant an annuity for his lifetime, especially if borrowing for consumption: see pp. 142–4, below.

[5] Davidson, *Precedents* (2nd edn), iii, 215n, 926n, 950–1; and see F. Prideaux, *Precedents in Conveyancing* (10th edn, 1881), ii, 316.

[6] J. V. Beckett, 'Landownership and Estate Management', in *The Agrarian History of England and Wales*, vol. vi (ed. G. E. Mingay, Cambridge, 1989), 545–640 at 551; B. English and J. Saville, *Strict Settlement: A Guide for Historians* (Hull, 1983), 58, 62, 82.

examples parallel to the elaborate clauses permitting various sorts of lease or regulating relations with copyhold tenants and manorial lords, until Prideaux began to copy statutory jurisdictions in the 1870s.[7] Similarly the standard models permitted outright sale only for the purposes of reinvestment in land—usually the power is referred to compendiously as 'sale and exchange', which nicely captures the context envisaged.[8] It was a power so sensitive that usually its exercise needed assent of both the life tenant and a set of trustees, and even in that form it was not one that judges in the 1820s would treat as impliedly authorized by an executory settlement without some prompting by the settlor.[9] Again, one would expect to find more flexibility on a resettlement than on a settlement resulting from a marriage treaty.

In eighteenth-century London and in some provincial towns a system of building leases had evolved that accommodated builders' economic interests as well as it suited families' ambitions both to retain and exploit their patrimony.[10] 'System' needs stressing. The capitalist—the builder or the developer—had to take his profit out of the project before the family could enjoy the full value of the developed land. Originally these building leases were about 60 years long, but well before 1820 they had conventionally become 99, during which time the family would take only a ground rent. Usually that was calculated at about one-fifth of a full rack rent. It was important, therefore, that when the reversion fell in, three or four generations hence, the family should be left with valuable buildings and not with slums that would need expensive clearing and redevelopment.

So, for a start, the landowner would normally sign merely an agreement to grant a lease, executing separate leases for each house only as each was completed to a stipulated standard. Usually just a peppercorn rent would be payable during the building period. If the builder/developer chose to take the lease himself

---

[7] Prideaux, *Precedents* (6th edn, 1870), ii, 281 (trustees may mortgage to lay out streets etc), (9th edn, 1879), ii, 314–15, 331 (powers parallel to Land Improvement Act 1864). For typical statements by lawyers see Bythewood and Jarman, *Precedents* (1833), ix, 212–13n; N. T. Lawrence, *Facts and Suggestions as to the Law of Real Property* (1880), 5–6.

[8] J. Habakkuk, *Marriage, Debt and the Estates System* (Oxford, 1994), 390–4, 638–42.

[9] E. B. Sugden, *A Practical Treatise of Powers* (4th edn, 1826), 142–4; T. Lewin, *A Practical Treatise on the Law of Trusts and Trustees* (3rd edn, 1857), 164–7; *Wheate* v. *Hall* (1809) 17 Ves. 80; *Horne* v. *Barton* (1822) Jac. 437 (continuing *Brewster* v. *Angell* (1820) 1 J. & W. 625); contrast *Peake* v. *Penlington* (1813) 2 Ves. & B. 311. An executory settlement was one created in outline by a will or marriage articles and left for detailed implementation under court supervision; see pp 13–16, above.

[10] C. W. Chalklin, *The Provincial Towns of Georgian England* (1974); D. J. Olsen, *Town Planning in London: The Eighteenth and Nineteenth Centuries* (New Haven, 1964). In some provincial towns the corporation was the prime mover and in others building leases seem simply to have been a fashion, so it cannot definitely be said that strict settlement was the cause, or the only cause, of the system. For a lawyer's statement of the early twentieth century system, little changed in its essentials, see H. Cubitt, *Building in London* (1911), 269–78.

he could then mortgage it on more favourable terms than he could mortgage a mere building agreement, and hence raise finance for the next stage of the project. Alternatively the lease would be granted to the builder/developer's nominee, being the person who had purchased the house from him. In that case the builder/developer would normally add an increment to the original ground rent reserved by the landowner—an 'improved ground rent', payable by the new tenant—which could be capitalized and sold, often back to the landowner himself. Early purchase of improved ground rents by the landowner, or purchase at a premium, functioned as a form of credit provided to the builder/developer, and could be part of the original deal. Finally, when the reversion was due to fall in the landowner would grant a repairing lease, preferably to the current occupier, to restore or further improve the property, with a full rent being charged on the improved value within a few years. The style and density of building, and the subsequent uses to which the houses could be put, were regulated by covenants that could be minutely detailed.

The powers necessary for limited owners to operate this system had to be expressly conferred, just as powers to grant mining leases did. None of them were incident to life estates at common law. In the eighteenth century that seems usually to have required a private enabling statute, the cost of which does not seem to have been an obstacle.[11] Occasional examples of empowering clauses creep into the published collections of model settlements in the 1780s, and by the 1830s and 1840s the books treat them as uncontroversial.[12] Even as late as 1833, however, Thomas Jarman thought it doubtful whether an instruction in an executory settlement to include all 'usual' powers would stretch to authorizing building leases.[13] So private statutes continued to be necessary for families whose settlements proved too cautious, or whose lawyers misjudged the terms that local developers would find acceptable, or who failed to anticipate a neighbour's project that opened possibilities for themselves.[14] They might be needed too if the landowner were putting in infrastructure requiring mortgage finance—roads, sewers, sea walls,

[11] M. Reed, 'The Transformation of Urban Space 1700–1840', in *The Cambridge Urban History of Britain*, vol. ii (ed. P. Clark), 615–40 at 619; Chalklin, *Provincial Towns*, 71.

[12] *Original Precedents in Conveyancing* (1788), iv, 1586–1652 at 1624 (none other in this collection contains power for more than 21-year occupation leases); *Bythewood's Precedents* (James Stewart's edn, 1833), viii, 434–5; *Martin's Practice of Conveyancing* (by Davidson) (1840), iv, 532–5.

[13] Bythewood and Jarman, *Precedents*, ix, 59–60 (his own precedents treated it as optional and were old-fashioned in giving merely 60 years: 237–41, 269); *Pearse* v. *Baron* (1821) Jac. 158. In 1836 Lord Cottenham said it would turn on proof of local circumstance: *Duke of Bedford* v. *Marquess of Abercorn* (1836) 1 My. & Cr. 312.

[14] Cannadine, *Lords and Landlords*, 143; R. Dennis, *English Industrial Cities of the Nineteenth Century* (Cambridge, 1984), 149 (and compare J. Springett, 'Landowners and Urban Development: the Ramsden Estate and Nineteenth Century Huddersfield' (1982) 8 *J. Hist. Geography* 129–44 at 130). Cannadine's Gilbert family failed to anticipate Lord Devonshire's expansion of Eastbourne, but by

for example.[15] In parts of the country where the leasehold system had not taken hold developers would expect to acquire the freehold outright or, in some places, subject to an annual fee farm rent, or sometimes a very long term of years that functioned in much the same way. Families whose lands were in settlement would need express powers to enter those transactions, so if their deed of settlement proved inadequate they too would petition Parliament to make good the deficiency.[16]

None of this law was new to the 1820s, neither in its content nor in its twin routes to acquisition of appropriate legal powers through family settlements and private statutes. The details in settlements might change—the usual length of leases, what did or did not need spelling out in them—but the menu of possibilities did not. Similarly the application process for a private statute continued much as before. Each bill was referred to two judges for their approval, consents were required from all parties affected, and particular attention was given to the details of sales and exchanges.[17] In 1843 the role of the judges was eased a little, but only to the extent that matters previously requiring proof before them would henceforward be proved before a committee in the Lords.[18] The process was tedious, it may have become more expensive in the late eighteenth or early nineteenth century, but it was also conventional and predictable.[19] Only one application of a policy filter is known, the House of Commons' consistent rejection of Sir Thomas Maryon Wilson's bills seeking power to grant building leases on his Hampstead estate, for fear that it would reduce the amenity value of the heath.[20]

Powers that were not usually built into settlements could instead arise externally, from legislation general in its nature even if sometimes technically private in its parliamentary procedure. It can be seen as a response to or a means of fending off political criticism that land in fetters harmed the economy, or just as the rich seizing an opportunity.[21] The fact that much land was vested in limited owners without power of sale was not going to stand in the way of railway or other statutory utility companies wanting to buy it for construction, nor was it

then they could acquire the necessary powers from Chancery (*op. cit.* 244). For earlier examples, see Chalklin, *Provincial Towns*, 97–8.

[15] Landowners could sometimes pass these costs on to the future occupiers by sponsoring a bill to create local paving commissioners: Cannadine, *Lords and Landlords*, 126, 288.

[16] Davidson, *Precedents* (2nd edn), iii, 966–7.

[17] *Practical Instructions on the Passing of Private Bills through both Houses of Parliament by a Parliamentary Agent* (1825), 146–65.

[18] F. Clifford, *A History of Private Bill Legislation* (1885–7), ii, 769.

[19] Clifford, *Private Bill Legislation*, ii, 734–45.

[20] F. M. L. Thompson, *Hampstead: Building a Borough, 1650–1964* (1974), 132–66.

[21] Railway companies acquiring land may on average have had to pay twice its value: R. J. Irving, 'The Capitalisation of Britain's Railways 1830–1914' (1984) 5 *Journal of Transport History* (3rd ser.), 1–24 at 14–15; R. W. Kostal, *Law and English Railway Capitalism 1825–1875* (Oxford, 1994), 144–80.

going to undermine a general measure such as the Tithe Commutation Act 1836.[22] Accordingly, the 1836 Act and the private statutes that created and empowered the companies contained formulae identifying a wide range of limited owners and long leaseholders who would be treated as owners for their purposes, in the one case to enable purchase of the fee simple (on payment of the purchase money into court), and in the other to enable land to be charged for some period beyond the life of the present possessor. Thus social identification of an individual 'owner' could easily be reconciled with the various forms of family ownership achieved through settlements if the will were there.

In 1845 the formula in the utility companies' Acts was generalized in the Lands Clauses Consolidation Act, which enacted a template for local and private legislation, and in the same year the definition in the Tithe Commutation Act was carried over into the Inclosure Act.[23] That year too a House of Lords select committee reported that limited owners were unable to take advantage of new technology for draining fields because their tenants could not afford it and they themselves usually lacked the power to mortgage the fee for such purposes.[24] So when, in 1846, the government offered landowners Treasury loans for invest- ment in field drainage as solace for repeal of the corn laws, care was taken to include the broad class of limited owners defined in the Tithe and Inclosure Acts.[25] Though that fund was quickly exhausted the scheme's infrastructure was continued into the Private Money Drainage Act 1849 and into a series of pri- vate statutes establishing loan companies, all enabling limited owners to secure loans for drainage against the land itself.[26] By the time of their consolidation in the Improvement of Land Act 1864 the list of permissible improvements had greatly expanded.[27]

Significantly, however, these statutory loans processes always required external mediation; the life tenant could not access their powers unaided. Even the Lords select committee worried that if life tenants could mortgage for farm buildings they might lavish money on something fanciful.[28] The first general drainage Act, in 1840, had empowered Chancery to approve secured loans to life tenants, but, its promoter said, such was the opposition to its principle that he had had to make

[22] 6 & 7 Will. IV c. 71.
[23] 8 Vict. c. 18, s 7; Improvement of Land Act 1864.
[24] SC of HL on Entailed Estates, Report, PP 1845 (490), xii, 111.
[25] Public Money Drainage Act, 9 & 10 Vict. c. 101.
[26] D. Spring, The English Landed Estate (Baltimore, 1963), Ch. 5; Cornish and Clarke, Law and Society, 144–5.
[27] 12 & 13 Vict. c. 100; SC of HL on Charging of Entailed Estates for Railways, Report, PP 1863 (209), vii, 73. The process continued with the Limited Owners Residences Acts 1870 and 1871.
[28] SC of HL on Entailed Estates, 240 and passim.

the process very cautious, hence dilatory and expensive.[29] So instead the 1846 Act and its successors channelled applications through the Inclosure Commissioners, on whose approval the loan would be secured by a 20-year rent charge payable by whoever was entitled to the income from the land for the time being. By this route a limited owner could mortgage land for any of the permitted purposes. Such was the clarity and finality of the statutory process that Davidson thought reliance on it preferable to creating express powers in a settlement.[30]

There was a similar modernity to another of the Inclosure Commissioners' useful facilities, the power to effect exchanges of land. They had had that since their inception in 1845, even for land not subject to an application for inclosure.[31] Settlors and their lawyers thought exchange important for rationalizing and consolidating the family estates, but the drafting necessary to empower a limited owner had become 'in its most improved form, a somewhat complex and elaborate piece of mechanism …'.[32] Instead the commissioners' process did what no private document could do, take land off one private title and attach it to another, obviating any need for a formal conveyance or prior investigation of title. It was not difficult for lawyers to dream up combinations of different types of settlement with lands of different tenures such that the exercise of that power might alter entitlements. But when it was litigated in 1855 Romilly MR and Turner LJ declined to read the Act narrowly, trusting instead that the commissioners would use their statutory discretion to refuse applications to avoid unfairness.[33] The power was steadily improved by statutory amendment, resulting in a process so simple, inexpensive, and conclusive that, Davidson wrote, it was 'very largely practised'.[34] A very similar process enabled co-owners to partition their land through the commissioners' good offices, and that too earned the conveyancers' recommendation.[35]

At first sight it is surprising to see an administrative agency with such functions in relation to purely private transactions. But the Inclosure Commission differed from many others in losing, not gaining, political accountability. When it merged with the Tithe and Copyhold Commission in 1851 it acquired the formal

---

[29] 3 & 4 Vict. c. 55; Philip Pusey in giving evidence to the *SC of HL on Entailed Estates*, 239. The report contains details of the applications made under that Act.

[30] Davidson, *Precedents*, iv, 439n (2nd edn, 1864).

[31] 8 & 9 Vict. c. 118, s 147. The Lords select committee (*PP* 1845, xii, 111) had suggested that some such route be made available.

[32] Davidson, *Precedents*, iii, 556 (3rd edn, 1873).

[33] *Minet v. Leman* (1855) 20 Beav. 269, 7 De G. M. & G. 340.

[34] Davidson, *Precedents*, ii, 94–101 at 95n (4th edn, 1877); W. Hayes, *The Concise Conveyancer* (2nd edn, 1864), 331–3. Amendment by the Inclosure Act 1857 was especially important, enabling exchanges to be equalized by money, up to one-eighth of the value.

[35] Davidson, *Precedents*, iii, 553–7 (3rd edn, 1873).

and functional autonomy the Tithe Commission had had from its beginning. It reported to Parliament through the Home Secretary, but he disavowed political responsibility for it.[36] Its blend of adjudicative, administrative, and supervisory functions was not so very different in principle from that of a Chancery judge or master in chambers, though its processes were much slicker—which is why it had been chosen. Since applications to it were voluntary the question became one of confidence, and as outlined above the conveyancers, who one supposes would be as sceptical as anyone, certainly had that. By the end of 1882 the commissioners had processed 6500 applications for exchange of lands and 223 for partition.[37]

By contrast the Settled Estates Act 1856 was a conservative measure.[38] It was intended to end, or partially end, the steady if unspectacular trek of limited owners to Parliament in search of private statutes to enlarge their powers. If the Irish and Scottish petitioners are excluded, and if English institutional owners are treated separately, the resulting private estate Acts usually numbered about a dozen a year in the period from 1830, but with a spike in 1853 that intensified in 1854.[39] Some were occasioned by the infancy or lunacy of the life tenant, some undid tangles that did not concern management powers, but latterly there does seem to have been an increasing demand for powers to grant mining or building leases. The process of checking the requisite consents was routine, the powers granted were more or less conventional, and it seemed to the Lord Chancellor, Lord Cranworth, that there was no need for the expense when Chancery could do the same job more cheaply (how times had changed!).[40]

The Settled Estates Act was therefore essentially a transfer of jurisdiction.[41] The powers to grant mining and building leases it enabled Chancery to confer were those that the House of Lords habitually approved for inclusion in private Acts, and their baselines were no more than Davidson had thought usual for well-drafted settlements in 1840, indeed for mining leases it was less.[42] It did enable Chancery to authorize sale, which had worried Conservatives in the Lords when the bill was first proposed, but the power was hedged with restrictions.

[36] Spring, *English Landed Estate*, 138, 171–1; C. Stebbings, *Legal Foundations of Tribunals in Nineteenth-century England* (Cambridge, 2007), 86–7. No minister would accept a Question in the Commons, though occasionally accountability was approached through a discussion on going into Supply: *PD* 1865 (s3) 179: 1124–30. The sequel that time was formal publication, not an explanation to the House: *PP* 1865 (451), xlvii, 429.

[37] *Inclosure Commissioners*, 38th Annual Report, *PP* 1883 [c. 3491], xxi, 529.

[38] 19 & 20 Vict. c. 120.

[39] *Chronological Table of the Private and Personal Acts.*

[40] *PD* 1855 (s3) 138: 397–401, 872–3; for the vote on granting a power of sale see *ibid.*, 1774–5.

[41] Section 32 enabled limited owners to grant up to 21-year occupation leases without intervention of courts or trustees, a routine power in settlements but one that might inadvertently be omitted from wills.

[42] *Martin's Practice* (1840), iv, 524–36.

In deference to freedom of property, settlors could opt out of the jurisdiction, and when exercising it Chancery was instructed not to authorize anything the settlor might not have done—a caution of unclear legal meaning perhaps, but one that set a tone.[43] The only major controversy in its passage came when the self-appointed guardians of Hampstead Heath insisted that a formula be found to block Sir Thomas Maryon Wilson from achieving through Chancery what he had been denied for so long in the Commons.[44]

Chancery's administration of the new Act confirmed Lord Cranworth's assurance that a strict watch would be kept on applications.[45] It required much the same consents that the Lords had done, and it quickly developed a requirement that even after it granted a leasing power each lease must individually be submitted to it for approval or, if the number was especially large, that they must conform to an approved template.[46] But gradually statutory amendment broadened its powers. The 1856 Act had allowed building leases to extend beyond the 99 years conventional in London and many other cities on proof that local custom required a longer term—useful in places where developers expected to acquire the freehold.[47] In 1858 that ability to lengthen terms to fit local usage was extended to all leases except agricultural.[48] In 1864 another amendment forbade Chancery from stipulating for individual or template approval of leases in its conferral of powers, and empowered it to strike that requirement out of powers already granted.[49] Saving of time and expense seem to have been the reasons. A decade later came a change of greater symbolic importance whereby Chancery was for the first time permitted to dispense with consents in some cases or override refusals.[50] A threat to the sanctity of settlements, thought the Marquess of Bath; just a means of preventing small or remote interests having an influence

---

[43] 19 & 20 Vict. c. 120, ss 26, 27.

[44] Thompson, *Hampstead*, 172–4; 19 & 20 Vict. c. 120, s 21, barring Chancery if a bill had been 'rejected on its merits', a class believed to contain only Maryon Wilson. An amendment to remove this *ad hominem* section briefly threatened the 1858 amendment bill. Bills by his supporters to remove s 21 failed in 1858, 1860, and 1863.

[45] *PD* 1855 (s3) 138: 872–3; Habakkuk, *Marriage, Debt*, 640–5.

[46] Davidson, *Precedents*, iii, 532 (3rd edn, 1873), citing M. I. F. Brickdale, *The Leases and Sales of Settled Estates Act* (1856), 38–9; *Re Procter's Settled Estates* (1857) 3 Jur. (N.S.) 534; *A.G. v. Christ Church, Oxford* (1862) 3 Giff. 514. The practice probably developed from a natural reading of s 3.

[47] e.g. *re Cross's Charity* (1859) 27 Beav. 592 (St. Helen's: 600 years); *re Carr's Settled Estates* (1861) 7 Jur. (N.S.) 1267 (Leeds: 999 years at a fee farm rent); J. A. Yelling, 'Land, Property and Planning', in *The Cambridge Urban History of Britain*, vol. ii (ed. M. J. Daunton, Cambridge 2000), 467–93 at 473–5.

[48] Settled Estates Act 1858.

[49] Settled Estates Act Amendment Act 1864. The purpose is taken from the preamble; no debate is reported.

[50] Leases and Sales of Settled Estates Amendment Act 1874.

beyond their worth, replied Lords Westbury and Chelmsford, whose cautious expectation of the new power was the one soon adopted by the judges.[51]

These Settled Estate Acts were on any reading a rescue provision for limited owners whose settlements inadvertently omitted the powers usual in their locality. If the omission was deliberate then, one supposes, the settlor would take the step the Acts allowed him of vetoing their application. Nor were the Acts as sophisticated as an express settlement crafted by an expert. They did not enable manipulations of ground rents that were quite usual in building leases in London, nor did they provide adequate powers for granting leases during minorities, Davidson thought.[52] The demand was there, however; annual applications rose from a base of about 45 in the early years, to some 75 in the early 1870s, leaping to over 100 in every year after 1872–3 bar one, as the agricultural depression began to bite.[53] So there was room for an alternative approach, one that injected the usual powers directly into settlements that lacked them.

There were two ways of doing that, and the difference was important to lawyers. To appreciate it one must understand that 'a power' was a property concept in just the same way that a trust, or a lease, or a mortgage was. Powers had their own dense and technical literature in the treatises by Sugden and by Chance, which were continued in epitomized form into the twentieth century by Farwell.[54] They had their own rules about creation, devolution, and consequences—a lease granted by a power holder did not take effect in exactly the same way as one granted by an estate holder, for example, and the difference would sometimes matter. There was great art in getting powers given to persons who did not have an estate to work exactly as was wanted. And since a power given to an estate holder did not merge into the estate or enlarge the estate, but instead remained a separate property even though annexed, it had to be crafted so that the two entities devolved together. A statute that gave someone 'a power' invoked this law; it meshed with the common law in just the same way that a judicial decision changing the law would have done. Thus Davidson admired the drafter's skill in aligning sections 9 and 10 of the Settled Estates Act 1856 with conventional doctrine.[55] Chancery's new power to grant leases worked perfectly congruently, he said, with

---

[51] *PD* 1874 (s3) 220: 855–7. *Taylor* v. *Taylor* (1875) 1 Ch D 426, aff'd (1876) 3 Ch D 145; *Daniell's Chancery Practice* (6th edn, 1884), 2295. See also *re Ives* (1876) 3 Ch D 690, reversing a trend towards a narrow interpretation of the sections defining whose consent was required.

[52] *Cust* v. *Middleton* (1861) 3 De G. F. & G. 33; Davidson, *Precedents*, iii, 535–6n (3rd edn, 1873).

[53] *PP*, Judicial Statistics: Civil, annual.

[54] Sugden, *A Practical Treatise of Powers* (8 edns, 1806–61); H. Chance, *A Treatise on Powers* (1831, 1841); G. Farwell, *Concise Treatise on Powers* (3 edns, 1874–1916). Sugden wished it never to be forgotten that J. J. Powell was the first who attempted it, in *An Essay on the Learning Respecting the Creation and Execution of Powers* (1787, 2nd edn, 1791, enlarged in 1799).

[55] Davidson, *Precedents* (3rd edn), iii, 530n.

the principle established in *Whitlock's case*, 1609. By contrast he worried about section 32, which enabled life tenants to grant 21-year leases, because it was not 'clear upon principle' how it did its work, though he did not deny that it did.[56]

This was a common way of thinking about reform of property law in the mid-century, that the new stitches must match the old fabric. It underlay the rejection in 1845 of the previous year's enactment that said simply that conveyances might be made by deed, replacing it with the seemingly indirect provision that henceforward corporeal hereditaments would lie in grant as well as in livery.[57] The latter was principled whereas the former, being merely pragmatic, might cause unforeseen difficulties. So too Lord Brougham's Acts in 1845—which enabled drafters to include statutory formulae in conveyances and leases merely by referring to the statute—were rejected because new words to be used in an old situation would be judged by the doctrine that surrounded them and hence might be unsafe.[58] Lord St. Leonards personified this thinking, which is memorialized in his many well-received but very precisely targeted reforming statutes. But it was not the only way to conceive of law reform.

The alternative was to change the 'incidents' of a concept. Thus the Real Property Commissioners in 1829 asked the profession whether powers to cut timber, open mines, and enfranchise copyholds should become incidents of a life estate, but dropped the idea for lack of consensus.[59] A New Zealand Conveyancing Ordinance of 1842 that Davidson saw as anticipating later English legislation did its work by altering the incidents of deeds.[60] A statute creating a modern power bearer like the Inclosure Commissioners, or a railway company, or—getting close to home—an 'owner' would work in something like that way; they need not be principled in Davidson's sense. Indeed they could not be, since these power bearers were without common law equivalents. So a much more direct and economical mode was available, one that instead of integrating with the old law of powers changed the way in which powers were understood.

The transition began with Lord Cranworth's Trustees and Mortgagees Act 1860, which, as its name suggests, touched only incidentally on strict settlements. Its importance is not so much in its content as in its method. Its administrative clauses for appointing new trustees and enabling trustees to give receipts were well received, but the only directly relevant dispositive power, a power to

[56] *Ibid.*, 536n.

[57] 7 & 8 Vict. c. 62, s 2; 8 & 9 Vict. c. 106, s 2; see p. 61, above.

[58] 8 & 9 Vict. caps 119, 124; see pp. 71–2, above.

[59] *RC on Real Property*, 1st Report, 57.

[60] *Ibid.*, 91–2; *Ordinances of the Legislative Council of New Zealand* 5 V. No. 10; Davidson, *Precedents*, iv, 269n (2nd edn, 1864).

effect exchanges of land, was not.[61] That was true of the Act's dispositive powers generally. There were shortcomings, the elite conveyancers thought, with the
powers it gave mortgagees, the powers it gave trustees to maintain infants, its
provisions regulating trustees' sales of land, and with what by then must surely
have been a little-needed provision for renewals of leases for lives vested in trustees. When N. T. Lawrence delivered the presidential address to the Incorporated
Law Society in 1879, an analysis that led reasonably directly to both the Settled
Land Act 1882 and the Conveyancing Acts 1881–2, he brushed aside Cranworth's
Act as valuable in principle but defective in detail.[62]

Davidson shared these doubts but pointed to the novelty of the Act's conception, more particularly its impact upon the drafting of mortgage contracts:

> [It] aimed at the comprehensive application, with a view to brevity and economy, of a
> principle the resources of which had previously been tried by the Legislature on a limited
> scale, and in special departments only (chiefly with reference to public works and the
> constitution of joint-stock companies). That principle is to annex, as incidents to con-
> tracts, such powers and provisions as are found to be convenient adjuncts, and as such
> to be habitually incorporated with the contract by the contracting parties, or, in other
> words, to imply those additional and subsidiary provisions which are by general practice
> expressly inserted. By skilful and careful alteration in this sense of the implied incidents
> of contracts, it is obvious that much of what gives rise to the length of instruments may
> be spared.[63]

Brougham's acts had had the same objective but a different method, for all that
superficially they look similar. They invoked existing learning; Cranworth's
method, if done skilfully, would replace it.

That replacement came with the Settled Land Act 1882. Much of its content
had been proposed in Lawrence's presidential address, which the Incorporated
Law Society presented in more detailed form to Lord Cairns, the then Lord
Chancellor.[64] Lawrence also proposed the technique that should be used: the new
powers should be made incident to all settlements, the technique, therefore, of
Cranworth's Act writ large, its ancestry to be found in Davidson's 'public works
and constitutions of joint-stock companies'. The proposal was worked into a bill

---

[61] For conveyancers' reaction, see Hayes, *Concise Conveyancer* (3rd edn, 1869), 551n; Prideaux,
Precedents (6th edn, 1870), ii, 175; H. W. Elphinstone, *A Practical Introduction to Conveyancing*
(1871), 156, 169, 289–90, 350–2, 399; Davidson, *Precedents*, ii, 355n (4th edn, 1877), iii, 176–8, 275,
560–70, 622–4, 633 (3rd edn, 1873).

[62] Lawrence, *Facts and Suggestions*, 9.

[63] Davidson, *Precedents*, ii, 755 (3rd edn, 1869); compare Prideaux, *Precedents* (6th edn, 1870),
i, 428 (the new powers become 'incident to the office and estate of the mortgagee', echoing the
Act's preamble).

[64] Lawrence, *Facts and Suggestions*; Anderson, *Lawyers*, 148–9.

under the guidance of E. P. Wolstenholme, who was posthumously to be the guiding spirit of the 1925 legislation.

The result was a statute as remarkable for its form as its content, the more so for with hindsight seeming natural and obvious. It differed from the Settled Estates Acts, consolidated as recently as 1877, by vesting its powers directly in tenants for life, for the most part to be exercised without need for consent by trustees, remaindermen, or courts, and irrespective of the settlor's intention. These abilities were now general incidents of estates, not dependent on cues from settlors or on local circumstance, nor did they depend for their understanding on the pre-existing law of powers conferred by settlors. 'Tenant for life' had a statutory definition, linked to a compendious definition of 'settlement' reaching well beyond strict settlements, hence not tied to any particular form. The role of trustees under the Act was likewise defined.

This significant shift in legal form was continued into the Trustee Acts of the 1880s and 1890s, culminating in the codified default powers of the 1925 legislation. After it there was no need for the old learning about powers, and so there was a long gap between Farwell's final edition in 1916 and Thomas's treatise in 1998.[65] By then the thinking is quite different. Davidson, opting out of the 1860 Act, would fall back on the old law of powers as property concepts, *Whitlock's case* and all. Thomas has no entry for *Whitlock's case*; when his settlors modify a statutory power it is as though they are writing a new one all for themselves, as if the statute empowered them to change the incidents of interests and offices for their individual case. There is not just an economy of words, but a far greater simplicity and directness of thought also.

Socially, for contemporaries and historians alike the Settled Land Act's most important innovation was that the life tenant could now sell the inheritance, without need for anyone's consent. Trustees were relegated to being generally passive recipients of funds. The exceptions were small. Sale of the principal mansion house or the heirlooms did need agreement from trustees or the court, and it should be noted that the 1882 Act contained no powers of mortgage save in connection with exchange or partition.[66] Capital money resulting from a sale or otherwise would be held on the trusts of the settlement, but the life tenant could direct whether, for example, it was to be invested in consols, or used to pay off encumbrances, or to fund improvements.

Politically this shift of direction remains an enigma. The Act was bipartisan, in that the Liberals allowed Lord Cairns to proceed with it after the Conservatives'

---

[65] G. W. Thomas, *Thomas on Powers* (1998).

[66] Power to mortgage to pay off encumbrances was given by the Settled Land Act 1890; see *re Clifford* [1902] 1 Ch 87 for interpretation.

election defeat, but the details of that negotiation and, particularly, how the Act came to confer an inalienable power of sale on life tenants are unknown.[67] Contexts are clearer, and the Act fits well within all of them: a deepening agricultural depression in southern and eastern England, an intensifying political attack on the magnates' 'land monopoly' and its accompanying institutions of 'primogeniture' and 'entail', a long-term loosening of the constraints of strict settlements, and even, though surely sounding in a lesser register, Lord Cairns's belief that it was the complication of real property law manifested in successive ownership that was thwarting his plans for title registration.[68] Applications for powers under the Settled Estates Acts had risen to over 160 a year.[69]

To put such 'very extensive powers in the hands of a person who had previously only been looked upon as a usufructuary' had created a revolution, said Chitty J., voicing only slightly more colourfully an opinion held generally by the Chancery judges to whom questions of the Act's interpretation and application went.[70] But his conclusion was not that he must approach it with caution, rather that he must not read it 'with a mind imbued strongly with the prejudices of old doctrine, and by the means of such prejudices to cut down and impair the utility of the Act'. That too was typical. Habakkuk's observation that the judges' favourable decisions on sales of mansion houses contributed a great deal to the fulfilment of the Act can be extended to their other decisions as well.[71]

They did not make the obstacle that they could have done from the section constituting life tenants trustees of their statutory powers, and when exercising their own discretion to approve sale of heirlooms they required life tenants to demonstrate no more than ordinary good faith and judgment—though sometimes they did find that lacking.[72] Similarly they gave broad readings to the section

---

[67] E. Spring, 'Landowners, Lawyers, and Land Reform in Nineteenth-century England' (1977) 21 *AJLH* 40–59, 52–3.

[68] H. J. Perkin, 'Land Reform and Class Conflict in Victorian Britain', in J. Butt and I. F. Clark (eds), *The Victorians and Social Protest* (1973), 177–217, 235–9; Habakkuk, *Marriage, Debt*, 629–49.

[69] *PP*, Judicial Statistics: Civil, annual (for years 1880–1, 1881–2).

[70] *Re Duke of Marlborough's Settlement* (1885) 30 Ch D 127; for similar statements see e.g. Lindley LJ in the same case on appeal (1886) 32 Ch D 1, and North J. in *re Wortham's Settled Estates* (1896) 75 LT 293.

[71] Habakkuk, *Marriage, Debt*, 647–8; *re Brown's Will* (1884) 27 Ch D 179; and, famously, *re Marquis of Ailesbury's Settled Estates* [1892] 1 Ch 506 (CA), [1892] AC 356.

[72] Section 53: contrast *Wheelwright* v. *Walker* (1883) 23 Ch D 752 and *Gilbey* v. *Rush* [1906] 1 Ch 11 with cases of collateral motive, bribery, and other self-interest: *Dowager Duchess of Sutherland* v. *Duke of Sutherland* [1893] 3 Ch 169; *Chandler* v. *Bradley* [1897] 1 Ch 315; *Middlemas* v. *Stevens* [1901] 1 Ch 574; *Boyce* v. *Edbrooke* [1903] 1 Ch 836. Heirlooms: *re Earl of Radnor's Will Trusts* (1890) 45 Ch D 402; *re Hope* [1899] 2 Ch 679 (but the family did not oppose the life tenant's re-application: R. Kurin, *Hope Diamond* (New York, 2006), 160–72); *re Lord Stafford's Settlement and Will* [1904] 2 Ch 72; *re Hope's Settled Estates* (1910) 26 TLR 413.

defining 'settlement', so as to advance the Act's policy of concentrating powers in the life tenant ahead of trustees, and to the section prohibiting deterrents against exercise of the powers.[73] In other words they treated the legislation as a code to be interpreted in accordance with the policy visible on its face and in light of what they knew to be the context of its enactment. No doubt they were aware too that if they had found difficulty Parliament would quickly have removed it; there were statutory amendments in 1884, 1887, 1889, and 1890, plus an amendment in the Housing of the Working Classes Act 1885, itself amended in 1890 and again in 1909.

3. BUYING AND SELLING

Throughout our period the law of land sales rested on an assumption that a purchase would proceed in two stages. The first, contract, must identify parties, property, and price, but beyond that it need do no more than commit the parties to a process of good faith, the steps in which could be left entirely to the general law if that is what the seller wanted. Buyers and sellers could comfortably get that far by themselves, provided that they wrote their agreement down. The second stage was a process of title investigation leading to conveyance of the estate. That was necessarily a technical task undertaken by experts. To anticipate, the two-stage process itself remained substantially unaltered through to 1914. It was underpinned by important common law rules, different from those applying to other contracts, and those too were reaffirmed during our period.

Two views were held about the relation between the two steps, though it was not often that they mattered and for the most part they went unexamined. One was that though the contract occasioned the subsequent process, what resulted was a matter of common right.[74] The other saw the parties' rights and obligations as being implied in their contract, as being something that they willed.[75] The first was not held in a strong form in our period. The contrast is visible, however, in Sugden's report that Lord Thurlow, who was Lord Chancellor at the very end of the eighteenth century, thought that parties to a sale of real property could not make time of the essence (just as times stipulated in a mortgage were not of the

---

[73] 'Settlement': see particularly *re Clitheroe Estate* (1885) 31 Ch D 135, also *re Chaytor's Settled Estate Act* (1884) 25 Ch D 651. Section 51: *re Jones* (1884) 26 Ch D 736; *re Paget's Settled Estates* (1885) 30 Ch D 161; *re Ames* [1893] 2 Ch 479; *re Richardson* [1904] 2 Ch 777.

[74] *Ogilvie* v. *Foljambe* (1817) 3 Mer. 53; *Ellis* v. *Rogers* (1885) 29 Ch D 661; E. Fry, *A Treatise on the Specific Performance of Contracts* (1858), 101.

[75] *Doe d. Gray* v. *Stanion* (1836) 1 M. & W. 695; E. B. Sugden, *Vendors and Purchasers* (10th edn, 1839), 42–3; T. C. Williams, *Vendor and Purchaser* (1903), i, 27n.

essence in equity), whereas by 1820 Lord Eldon had ruled that they could.[76] The result was that from early in our period sellers commonly used contractual terms to reduce their obligations, so much so that in due course some of the more usual modifications became generally applicable through statute. That reduced the length, difficulty, and cost of title investigation, just as reform of the substantive law removed many of the complexities that had needed investigating.

Conveyancing books through into the 1820s treat the initial contract of sale and purchase lightly. Often they assume that parties would consult a lawyer only after entering a contract.[77] The precedent books do contain examples of contracts directed to practitioners, but at the beginning they are either relatively stereotyped, not straying far beyond the obligations the law would anyway supply, or they are designed for obviously special occasions.[78] There is no indication that the lawyers for whom these books were intended would find themselves bargaining over contractual terms, though the Real Property Commissioners mention that sometimes a purchaser would require the vendor to get the title approved by a conveyancer before the contract was signed.[79]

In the 1820s sellers' solicitors may often have had the conduct of a sale by auction, attending it to answer questions before the bidding started and to minimize liability to auction duty where possible.[80] Their involvement may have extended to drafting the particulars (that is, the physical and legal description of the thing being sold) and the conditions of sale, though there is some evidence that auctioneers were still drafting particulars themselves.[81] Much later, in the 1880s, it came to matter how professional labour was divided between solicitors and auctioneers, because eligibility for one element in the new national pro-rata fees for solicitors turned on it. In the northern cities then solicitors were conducting

---

[76] *Vendors and Purchasers* (9th edn, 1839), i, 431–2; *Seton v. Slade* (1802) 7 Ves. 273; *Levy v. Lindo* (1817) 3 Mer. 84; *Boehm v. Wood* (1820) 1 Jac. & W. 419.

[77] e.g. E. B. Sugden, *A Concise View of the Law of Sales [etc] in a Series of Letters* (4th edn, 1821), 34–47 (advice to purchasers assumes contract already entered); *Martin's Precedents* (by Davidson), iii, 98; his discussion of solicitors' duties in vol. 1 likewise assumes that a contract has already been signed.

[78] J. J. Powell, *Original Precedents in Conveyancing* (1802), i, 43–88; W. M. Bythewood, *A Selection of Precedents* (1828; Stewart edn), i, 78–88; the Jarman edn (1829) adds a further general example: i, 99–109. The Jarman edn will be a better indicator of contemporary practice: see (1849) 13 *Jurist* pt 2, 478–80.

[79] *RC on Real Property*, 2nd Report, *PP* 1830 (575), xi, 1, 17.

[80] J. H. Howard, *The Duties of Solicitors in Sales by Auction, or Private Contracts* (1827), 5, 6, 14.

[81] T. Williams, *The Law of Auctions* (4th edn, 1826), 49–50; J. Bateman, *A Practical Treatise on the Law of Auctions* (1st edn, 1838), 19n; Sugden, *Concise View* (4th edn, 1821), 28; Sugden, *Vendors and Purchasers* (6th edn, 1822), 11. Bateman's urging that auctioneers consult lawyers became more explicit: 3rd edn (1846), 42n. Sugden (*Vendors and Purchasers*) shifted from saying auctioneers very commonly prepared the particulars to saying it was usual, before dropping that passage entirely in 1851 (11th edn, 1846), 10.

far more of the pre-contract work than their counterparts in London and the south, a difference that so far as Liverpool was concerned can be traced back into the mid-1860s.[82] How far this affected the process of contract formation and the content of contracts is not known, but probably there was considerable regional variety through into the 1880s even over particulars of sale.[83] Nor is much known about the relative frequency of sales by auction and sales by private treaty, save that land first offered at auction was often bought in and then sold privately.[84] The lawyers' books sometimes assert that in those cases the contract would adopt the conditions prepared for the auction.[85] To these general uncertainties must be added the possibility of regional differences in practice. They run through the later controversies about title registration, for example, where one of the persistent themes from Northern and Midland law societies was that their methods already handled small land sales more efficiently than title registration would.[86]

By the time of the Real Property Commissioners' investigations 'special' conditions of sale were becoming more elaborate. The causes are unclear, but may include a reaction against increased punctiliousness in title investigation. The point is by no means proved, but there are indications both that conveyancing counsel were becoming more influential in setting the standard at which a title was deemed good and that they thought conveyancing practices previously had sometimes been rather careless.[87] If, as seems plausible, they were finding titles 'unmarketable' that previously had slipped through—perhaps because previously the experts were not consulted—then one logical consequence was for those same experts to draft special conditions that would reduce the seller's obligation so that it matched the reduced proof of title he would be able to offer. Solicitors who failed to persuade their clients to get their title checked over by conveyancing counsel before offering it for auction could at least pre-empt some difficulties by having auctioneers use generic special conditions that removed purchasers'

---

[82] *Drielsma v. Manifold* [1894] 3 Ch 100; J. S. Anderson, *Lawyers and the Making of English Land Law 1832–1940* (Oxford, 1992), 25, 157.

[83] (1883) 27 *Sol. J.* 545, 555, 565, 741, 748, 753.

[84] F. M. L. Thompson, 'The Land Market in the Nineteenth Century' (1957) 9 *Oxford Economic Papers* 285–308.

[85] S. Atkinson, *A Practical Treatise on Conveyancing* (1829), ii, 51.

[86] Anderson, *Lawyers*, 128–9, 132–4.

[87] *RC on Real Property*, 1st Report, PP 1829 (263), xi, 1, 41 (abstracts getting longer); 2nd Report, 283 (Alington: conveyancing counsel cause of present costs), 487 (Farrer: fear of negligence actions drives solicitors to use conveyancing counsel); *The Times*, 4 February 1830, letter (conveyancing counsel cause of present costs) (denied in J. J. Park's reply, 6 February); W Hayes, *The Concise Conveyancer* (1830), 2 ('titles, safe to hold by, but otherwise utterly unmarketable, have been disposed of, under proper conditions, without loss, and without delay'; *Martin's Practice*, iii, 49 (purchasers' lawyers making unreasonable requisitions because cost falls on vendor); Bythewood and Jarman, *Precedents*, i, 103n (costs caused by having to remedy former lax practices).

ability to raise some of the more common objections to titles.[88] If the books are a fair guide this was happening during the 1820s and 1830s, as sellers' lawyers took increased control over the sale process.[89] *The Jurist* in 1842 summed it up well: special conditions were 'of very modern origin, having arisen out of the dangerous state into which it was found most titles had fallen, and the incapacity of vendors, generally speaking, to support their titles by such evidence as a prudent purchaser would call for'.[90]

Without such special conditions the process favoured the buyer. In 1820 an 'open' contract—one specifying merely parties, property, and price, such as might be concluded by private exchange of letters—obliged the seller of a freehold to prove a 'good title' stretching back at least 60 years. Conventionally that had come to mean supplying an abstract of the title that detailed the operative words from all the relevant deeds and recited all the relevant events with sufficient nicety for a conveyancing counsel to judge whether the seller had traced the devolution of the relevant interest, accounted for all outstanding interests and all possible adverse claims, an abstract that must then be verified against the original deeds, or certified copies, plus all the ancillary records of births, deaths, and marriages. Even the proof of facts could be complex enough for a conveyancer to write a book on it, though it did not go beyond its first edition.[91] If the abstract disclosed possibilities that yet more remote interests might be extant, the buyer could require the seller to disprove them by producing even older documentation. Buyers also needed to guard against adverse equitable interests. Chancery deemed buyers to have read the title documents produced to them and hence to be bound by equitable interests the documents disclosed or which would have been disclosed if proper inquiries had then been made. Hence buyers could require production of any further documents mentioned within the documents of title already produced. If the property sold was leasehold the seller had to deduce title to the lease in the ordinary way and in addition prove the lessor's title to grant it. That controversial question was authoritatively decided only in 1821, Richards CB opting for buyers' safety rather than sellers' practicality, for it was generally agreed that lessees were often in no position to provide the information required.[92]

[88] Bythewood and Jarman, *Precedents*, i, 104–5.

[89] Atkinson, *Practical Treatise*, ii, 38–9 describes the practice of getting counsel's opinion on an abstract before putting land up for sale as recent. See also Sugden, *Concise View* (4th edn, 1821), 28–9.

[90] (1842) 6 *Jurist* 526.

[91] T. Coventry, *On Conveyancers' Evidence* (1832).

[92] Sugden, *Vendors and Purchasers* (5th edn, 1818), 280–6; *Purvis* v. *Rayer* (1821) 9 Price 488, followed at common law in *Souter* v. *Drake* (1834) 5 B. & Ad. 992.

The costs of this process fell heavily on the seller, for though each side paid for its own lawyers the seller had to pay for production or copying of documents and was obliged to answer all reasonable and usual requisitions made by the buyer. A seller who at the end of it all did prove title could compel the buyer to complete. Speed was an objective only if the contract expressly said so, a convergence of law and conveyancers' practice typical of the process.

Essentially this was an open-ended process that would take as long as was needed, moderated principally by judges' view of what was reasonable. It was underpinned by two very important rules. The first, the rule in *Flureau v. Thornhill*, was that if a seller proved unable to make good title the buyer was confined to restitutionary remedies.[93] That allowed recovery of any deposit, interest on it, sometimes even interest on the purchase money left lying idle pending completion, and always, of course usual and reasonable expenses.[94] But it particularly excluded expectation damages for loss of bargain, and all anticipatory expenditure that judges thought jumped the gun on the title investigation process, such as purchasers' repairs or improvements ahead of completion, or a survey of the land.

The second underpinning rule was that a purchaser who accepted a conveyance of a title that later turned out to be inadequate could not then sue for breach of the contract of sale.[95] *Caveat emptor*: the time for objecting to title was between contract and conveyance. There was an equivalent for chattels, that rescission was not normally available after possession had been accepted, but the rule for land extended to barring most actions for compensation as well. These were robust rules, each emphatically reasserted by the House of Lords when challenged directly or when exceptions threatened their erosion.[96] Together they secured the space after contract for the conveyancers on each side to interrogate the title offered by the vendor.

In *Flureau v. Thornhill* Blackstone J. had said that land sales were understood as being conditional on the vendor's ability to make out title. Twentieth-century writers found that difficult to reconcile with contract theory as it had by then evolved, but early nineteenth-century conveyancers did not.[97] Powell's and

---

[93] (1776) 2 W. Bl. 1078. The contrast is with unwillingness, which did incur expectation damages.

[94] For this and the next sentence see *Bratt v. Ellis* (1805): Sugden, *Vendors and Purchasers* (10th edn, 1839), App. VII; *Hodges v. Earl of Litchfield* (1835) 1 Bing. (N.C.) 492; *Worthington v. Warrington* (1849) 8 C.B. 134; Dart, *Vendors and Purchasers* (2nd edn, 1852), 166, 226, 500–1.

[95] *Bree v. Holbech* (1781) 2 Doug. 654; *Thomas v. Powell* (1794) 2 Cox 394; *Johnson v. Johnson* (1802) 3 Bos. & P. 162.

[96] *Bain v. Fothergill* (1874) LR 7 HL 158; *Clayton v. Leech* (1889) 41 Ch D 103, based on opinions expressed in *Brownlie v. Campbell* (1880) 5 App Cas 925; *Soper v. Arnold* (1889) 14 App Cas 429.

[97] For a good modern summary see New South Wales Law Reform Commission, *Damages for Vendor's Inability to Convey Good Title: The Rule in Bain v Fothergill*, LRC 64 (Sydney, 1990).

Bythewood's collections of precedents both contained contracts intended for general use which explicitly conditioned the vendor's obligation on the opinion of the purchaser's counsel that satisfactory title had been proved, making explicit what Blackstone J. had said was commonly assumed.[98] So because an open contract neither warranted that the seller had a good title nor bound the buyer to take whatever bad one the seller had, sellers could market their estate without disclosing any information about their title, indeed they could safely conclude their contract without going near a lawyer. Provided sellers steered clear of deliberate misrepresentation they would be free from tortious liability. If their title turned out to be defective their liability was limited to the transaction costs. If, on the other hand, they did make some sort of contractual warranty, the buyer's acceptance of a conveyance would usually supersede it according to the second rule.

In 1826 Lord Tenterden unexpectedly announced that the rule in *Flureau* v. *Thornhill* should be reconsidered, though he gave no particular reason.[99] The case, *Hopkins* v. *Grazebrook*, concerned a seller who auctioned land when all he possessed himself was a recently acquired contract to buy it, a speculative enterprise that in Tenterden's eyes merited expectation damages for the disappointed sub-buyer when the head contract fell through. Much later Blackburn J., who was orthodox on *Flureau* v. *Thornhill*, drew attention to another decision by Lord Tenterden, almost contemporaneous, in which he condemned speculative grain contracts for causing popular distress, showing, Blackburn thought, a general proposition in Tenterden's mind that one should sell only what one actually possessed.[100] That idea ran so contrary to City and general mercantile practice that it was firmly rejected a decade later, with the result that *Hopkins* v. *Grazebrook* was stranded as an exception to *Flureau* v. *Thornhill* rather than becoming a new beginning.[101]

Then *Flureau* v. *Thornhill* survived *Hadley* v. *Baxendale* too, the decision establishing a general rule for expectation damages for breach of contract.[102] There Alderson B. treated it not as an exception but as a limb of the rule itself: expectations could be governed by 'known special circumstances' and, it seems to have been generally agreed, often by reference to the writings of Sir Edward

---

[98] Powell, *Precedents*, i, 53; Bythewood, *Precedents* (Stewart edn), i, 81; and see *Doe d. Gray* v. *Stanion* (1836) 1 M. & W. 696.

[99] (1826) 6 B. & C. 31.

[100] *Sikes* v. *Wild* (1861) 1 B. & S. 587; *Bryan* v. *Lewis* (1826) Ry. & Moo. 380. See also *Lorymer* v. *Smith* (1822) 1 B. & C. 1, and Littledale J. in *Walker* v. *Moore* (1829) 10 B. & C. 416, 420. Davidson picked up the same point: *Martin's Practice*, i, 46–7.

[101] *Hibblewhite* v. *M'Morine* (1839) 5 M. & W. 462; *Mortimer* v. *M'Callan* (1840) 6 M. & W. 58; and compare *Hoggart* v. *Scott* (1830) 1 Russ. & My. 293; *Eyston* v. *Simmonds* (1842) 1 Y. & C.Ch.Cas. 608.

[102] (1854) 9 Ex. 341.

Sugden, the circumstances of land sales were that performance was conditional on proof of title.[103] Misrepresentation was an exception generating liability, but, consistently with the general rule, it had to be an active misrepresentation, not a mere mistaken assumption. So *Hopkins* v. *Grazebrook* survived only as an exception based on 'blame', an exception penalizing vendors who could not reasonably have thought that they would eventually make good title.[104]

There were a few judges in the 1860s who probably thought *Flureau* v. *Thornhill* an unprincipled anomaly, but when the attack on it finally came, in *Bain* v. *Fothergill* in 1874, the House of Lords decisively reaffirmed it.[105] Though a variety of reasons was given, the one that runs most strongly through the cases was best expressed by Blackburn J. in 1861: expectation damages for failure to deliver good title would run contrary to the usage of this particular business.[106] The dissenters tended to see it instead as a concession to the poor state of real property law.

The second underpinning rule, that a purchaser who had accepted a conveyance (or an assignment of a lease) was barred from suing on the antecedent contract, was vulnerable to attacks using notions of fraud, misrepresentation, or mistake, all of which could plausibly describe both positive misstatements and concealments of defects of title. But despite shifts in the general law judges usually held to the rule. In 1848 the House of Lords ruled that concealment needed to have been deliberate and to be brought home to the vendor, not merely the vendor's agent, if it were to warrant setting aside a completed conveyance.[107] Lord Campbell, in particular, stressed the difference from rescinding a contract before completion. Nearly 30 years later Fry J. prised the rule open by deciding that to sell and subsequently convey land as freehold when it was actually copyhold was 'legal fraud' even when done innocently.[108] But his decision was quickly confined

[103] *Pounsett* v. *Fuller* (1856) 17 C.B. 660, esp. Williams J.; *Sikes* v. *Wild* (1861) 1 B. & S. 587. In 1857 Sugden shifted from saying the exception in *Hopkins* v. *Grazebrook* was unstable to saying it was wrong: *Vendors and Purchasers* (8th edn, 1830), 222–3, (13th edn, 1857), 301–2.

[104] *Robinson* v. *Harman* (1848) 1 Ex. 850; *Pounsett* v. *Fuller* (1856) 17 C.B. 660; *Sikes* v. *Wild* (1861) 1 B. & S. 587, (1863) 4 B. & S. 421.

[105] *Bain* v. *Fothergill* (1874) LR 7 HL 158, overruling *Hopkins* v. *Grazebrook*. For dissenting voices, see Cockburn CJ in *Sikes* v. *Wild* (1861) 1 B. & S. 587, he and Kelly B. in *Engel* v. *Fitch* (1868) LR 3 QB 314, (1869) LR 4 QB 659, and, more muted, Denman J.'s advice to the Lords in *Bain* v. *Fothergill* itself.

[106] *Sikes* v. *Wild* (1861) 1 B. & S. 587, relying particularly on Parke J. in *Walker* v. *Moore* (1829) 10 B. & C. 422, the KB case signalling that its decision in *Hopkins* v. *Grazebrook* was not to consume the general rule.

[107] *Gibson* v. *Wilde* (1848) 1 H.L.C. 605, reversing Knight Bruce VC in *Gibson* v. *D'Este* (1843) 2 Y. & C.Ch.Cas. 542, whose opinion based on *Edwards* v. *M'Leay* (1815) G. Coop. 308 would have allowed reopening of conveyances for merely constructive knowledge by the vendor.

[108] *Hart* v. *Swaine* (1877) 7 Ch D 42. It is unclear why suing on the covenant of right to convey, which was one of the usual covenants for title, would not have been an adequate remedy.

to its own facts, the notion of 'legal fraud' disavowed, and the integrity of the basic rule restored.[109]

Judges were likewise careful to give a narrow construction to contractual terms that allowed purchasers to claim compensation for 'errors, omissions, or misdescriptions', a form that was standard throughout our period, as will be explained shortly. The clause clearly could be intended to apply even after conveyance, unless (as came to be the case) it was expressly limited to defects discovered before then, and it could have been interpreted to include defects of title. But it was not. Judges used a variety of interpretive techniques to confine the clause to misstatements about the physical thing or about the rents the tenants paid— matters not discoverable from scrutiny of the title deeds—and disallowed claims for defects that ought to have been uncovered by the ordinary perusal of title.[110]

There was a further reason for insisting upon the second underpinning rule. Common law had once implied warranties of title into its conveyances upon sale, but, in the nineteenth-century view of it, in Coke's time the judges had obligingly ruled that express covenants for title ousted them.[111] Those had then become the norm, indeed part of a buyer's entitlement on an open contract. They could be tailored for the occasion, but generally they had fallen into conventional form, regrettably verbose, Davidson thought in 1839.[112] Their gist was to reduce the seller's liability below what the common law had once implied. They were not guarantees of title but, broadly, undertakings that the seller had not left the title worse than he found it.[113] They only supplemented the work of conveyancers, Lord Eldon explained in 1799.[114] Conveyancers relied upon their own investigations of title, not upon the existing covenants, he said; clients then relied upon their conveyancer's opinion on the historic title, supplemented by a limited covenant from the vendor to cover his own conduct. Buyers wanting more must bargain for it. Therefore judges should interpret covenants in a conventional and restricted way unless absolutely sure that something different was meant. Davidson had a precedent showing Eldon's point exactly: a seller of an advowson who was not in a

[109] *Brownlie* v. *Campbell* (1880) 5 App Cas 925; *Brett* v. *Clowser* (1880) 5 CPD 376; *Joliffe* v. *Barker* (1883) 11 QBD 255; *Clayton* v. *Leech* (1889) 41 Ch D 103; *Debenham* v. *Sawbridge* [1901] 2 Ch 98.

[110] Rents: *Cann* v. *Cann* (1830) 3 Sim. 447; *Bos* v. *Helsham* (1866) LR 2 Ex 72; *re Turner and Skelton* (1879) 13 Ch D 130; *Palmer* v. *Johnson* (1884) 13 QBD 351; title: *Clayton* v. *Leech* (1889) 41 Ch D 103; *Ex p Riches* (1883) 27 Sol. J. 313; *re Beyfus and Masters's Contract* (1888) 39 Ch D 110; *Debenham* v. *Sawbridge* [1901] 2 Ch 98; Dart, *Vendors and Purchasers* (7th edn, 1905), ii, 812–13.

[111] Cruise, *Digest*, iv 77–99; Davidson, *Concise Precedents* (3rd edn, 1848), 64–7; *Browning* v. *Wright* (1799) 2 Bos. & P. 13; HEL, iii, 163.

[112] *Martin's Practice*, iii, 203–5.

[113] For an example see *Woodhouse* v. *Jenkins* (1832) 9 Bing. 431, and for a general account see Dart, *Vendors and Purchasers* (4th edn, 1871), 711–30.

[114] *Browning* v. *Wright* (1799) 2 Bos. & P. 13; see also *Merrill* v. *Frame* (1812) 4 Taunt. 329; *Line* v. *Stephenson* (1838) 5 Bing. (N.C.) 183.

position to prove his title offered instead an absolute covenant for title, which the buyer accepted in lieu of a conveyancer's report.[115] So since restricted covenants were the norm for continuing obligations arising from the conveyance, it would have been difficult and inconsistent for judges to find that the parties had meant a broader set to arise from the preceding contract.[116] 'Intention' was to be constructed against a background of conveyancing practice.

So the intregrity of the title investigation process was supported by rules restricting the consequences of breach of contract, and judges used the fact that the process was conventional as an aid to interpretation. But within that process relations between seller and buyer were changing, largely because sellers were able to use the contract to stipulate for reduced performance. According to all the conveyancing practice books, special conditions of sale became usual at auctions in, say, the first 30 years of the century, becoming ever more favourable to sellers as time went on. From auction they spread into private contracts for sale. When Davidson first treated the topic systematically in an elite conveyancing text in 1839 his exposition and sample clauses together occupied 70 pages.[117] By 1874 he needed well over 200.[118] These new contractual terms can be seen as a professional response to complaints about the delays, costs, and uncertainty of title investigation that flowed from lawyers, clients, and politicians throughout our period, made possible because (for unknown reasons) sellers were able to impose their terms on buyers. They parallel the law reform trajectory that sought to remove the problems of complexity of title by amending the underlying law.

The function of special conditions was to reduce the obligations a seller would have under an open contract. Broadly speaking, there were two sorts. One was individualized, specific to the title a particular seller thought could be proved; the other related to the process of proof and could be generalized to any sale. The first modified in various ways the requirement that the seller show a root of title at least 60 years old. Nobody was certain why 60 years was the requirement under an open contract, but one reason was thought to be an analogy with the limitation period for the real actions, the medieval remedies for specific recovery of real property at common law.[119] So when, as a result of the Real Property Commissioners' labours, the real actions were abolished and a new relatively streamlined limitation period introduced that ordinarily would not exceed

[115] *Martin's Practice*, iii, 300–1.
[116] In *Brownlie v. Campbell* (1880) 5 App Cas 925 Lord Selborne drew attention to the express covenant in *Hart v. Swaine* (n. 108, above).
[117] *Martin's Practice*, iii, 27–97.
[118] Davidson, *Precedents*, i, 505–606 for exposition, 607–729 for clauses (4th edn, 1874).
[119] Sugden, *Vendors and Purchasers* (10th edn, 1839), ii, 132–40; Hayes, *Introduction to Conveyancing* (3rd edn, 1837), 193–202.

40 years, some conveyancers thought that only a 40-year root of title should now be required.[120] They were disappointed. The commissioners had not explicitly linked the two, one of them gave his opinion that 60 years remained the rule, and other conveyancers pointed out that reversioners and remaindermen could sometimes retain their claims even after 40 years' peaceful possession by the putative seller.[121] In 1844 Lord Lyndhurst laconically ruled in favour of safety, and so the 60-year (minimum) rule remained.[122]

Some other parts of the commissioners' work, particularly the Fines and Recoveries Act, did remove technical difficulties that would previously have led a cautious conveyancer to find fault with a title. Likewise the Real Property Limitation Act may not have reduced the root of title required but it did bar some claims that would have shown the title to be bad. Some of those changes were retrospective, but much of the simplifying work was prospective only. For the many difficulties that a conveyancer might think remained, special conditions of sale were the only antidote. These individualized special conditions might stipulate, for example, that the purchaser accept a particular document as the root of title, or accept particular facts as proved, or be content with a title dating back only so many years. The precedent books came to include many variants.

Of course, special conditions affected only the buyer's relations with the seller. By accepting them buyers signed away the possibility of discovering adverse common law rights, and in equity they remained liable to whatever adverse equitable interests a careful scrutiny of a full 60-year abstract would have revealed. Dart thought that such conditions were used to pass off 'seriously defective and unsafeholding titles' far more often than was commonly supposed.[123] Davidson could only assume that buyers accepted them because they did not understand them, so obviously imprudent they were to his professional eye.[124] So to some extent—an unknown extent—their proliferation and acceptance illustrated a gulf between the conveyancers' ideal and a reality that saw many titles as 'safe' even though falling short of the 60-year marketable title standard.

Safe or not, courts throughout our period would order specific performance of these contracts, even for something as potentially insubstantial as 'the title the vendor has', provided only that there had been no misrepresentation or knowing

[120] 3 & 4 Vict. c. 27 (1833); Sugden, *Vendors and Purchasers* (10th edn, 1839), ii: 132–40; *Hodgkinson* v. *Cooper* (1846) 9 Beav. 304.

[121] Hayes, *Introduction* (3rd edn, 1837), 193–202 and (for Peter Brodie's opinion), 239–41; Bythewood and Jarman, *Precedents* (1833), ix, 416–18.

[122] *Cooper* v. *Emery* (1844) 1 Ph. 388; see also *Moulton* v. *Edmonds* (1859) 1 De G. F. & J. 246.

[123] *Vendors and Purchasers* (4th edn, 1874), 161. See also Tyrrell's *Suggestions*, 310–11, and (1842) 6 *Jurist* 22–3.

[124] *Martin's Practice*, iii, 27–8; Davidson, *Precedents*, i, 505–6 (4th edn, 1874).

concealment.[125] Initially they grumbled—'scarcely practicable to carry them into execution consistently with settled principles of equity', said Lord Langdale in 1842.[126] And because special conditions deprived buyers of matters of common right they interpreted them strictly.[127] But they enforced them nonetheless. As *The Jurist* put it, traders in land should be taken to know their own business, just like traders in cotton, iron, or any other commodity.[128] That shifted the *caveat emptor* principle forward in time, forestalling objections by the purchaser's counsel. Dart thought that if the conditions proposed were 'very special' it might be prudent to allow potential bidders to inspect an abstract of title before the sale, but his implication is that that was not usual.[129]

In addition to such bespoke terms the books suggest that it became routine for auctioneers' conditions of sale to reverse or modify the standard incidents of an open contract. At the start of our period it was 'invariable' to require a deposit from the successful bidder, to be forfeited for non-completion if the purchaser withdrew without good legal reason.[130] It was commonplace when auctioning a lease to stipulate that the purchaser could not require proof of the lessor's title or, in the strong version, that objections to the lessor's title were inadmissible.[131] And because Chancery generally declined specific performance if the advertised quantity of the land turned out to differ from that encompassed by the title deeds, a vendor's condition at auction would usually say that errors or omissions in description should be the subject of compensation and not annulment of the contract.[132]

---

[125] *Freme* v. *Wright* (1819) 4 Madd. 364; *Cattell* v. *Corall* (1839) 4 M. & W. 734, 3 Y. & C. Ex. 413; *Duke* v. *Barnett* (1846) 2 Coll. 337; *Upperton* v. *Nickolson* (1871) 6 Ch App 436; and see *Wilmot* v. *Wilkinson* (1827) 6 B. & C. 506 for the same position at common law. Inevitably there was room for dispute about what the seller had actually undertaken, but that could be pre-empted by accurate drafting: *Southby* v. *Hutt* (1837) 2 My. & Cr. 207; *Shepherd* v. *Keatley* (1834) 1 C. M. & R. 117; *Hume* v. *Bentley* (1852) 5 De G. & Sm. 520; Dart, *Vendors and Purchasers* (3rd edn, 1856), 96–9.

[126] *Hyde* v. *Dallaway* (1842) 4 Beav. 606.

[127] *Symons* v. James (1842) 1 Y. & C.Ch.Cas. 487; *Morley* v. *Cook* (1842) 2 Hare 106; *Rhodes* v. *Ibbetson* (1853) 4 De G. M. & G. 787; *Greaves* v. *Wilson* (1858) 25 Beav. 290; 'On Restrictive Conditions of Sale' (1842) 6 *Jurist* 526–7; (1843) 7 *Jurist* 341–3.

[128] (1842) 6 *Jurist* 22–3; see also *ibid.*, 29–30.

[129] *Vendors and Purchasers* (1st edn, 1851), 68–9, (4th edn, 1874), 140.

[130] Howard, *Duties of Solicitors*, 6–7, 18 (recommending it for private sales too); Powell, *Precedents*, i, 53; Atkinson, *Practical Treatise*, ii, 39–42. Auction conditions also routinely modified auction law, particularly in stipulating how the seller might use a representative bidder.

[131] F. C. Jones, *The Attorney's and Solicitor's New Pocket book and Conveyancer's Assistant* (5th edn, 1826), i, 254; R. Babington, *A Treatise on the Law of Auctions* (1826), 237 (described as a usual term); Bateman, *Practical Treatise*, 25; *Spratt* v. *Jeffery* (1829) 10 B. & C. 249; *Hume* v. *Bentley* (1852) 5 De G. & Sm. 520; *Waddell* v. *Wolfe* (1874) LR 9 QB 515.

[132] Babington, *Treatise*, 23; Howard, *Duties of Solicitors*, 13; Jones, *Pocket Book*, 244; Bateman, *Practical Treatise*, 27n ('almost universal'); Atkinson, *Practical Treatise*, 39–42 (very bullish, even denying compensation).

Other clauses systematically shifted costs from seller to buyer. The books suggest that reallocating copying costs was particularly necessary when an estate was being sold in lots, but by 1839 Davidson was suggesting it as a general provision.[133] If the books are an accurate guide to practice, the shift seems to have occurred by the late 1830s and is treated as usual a decade later.[134] It applied to a wide range of costs that the common law otherwise put on the seller. To the scorn of *The Jurist*, Birmingham Law Society urged local solicitors to eschew such clauses themselves and resist their use by auctioneers, so harmful were they to clients' interests and professional emoluments alike.[135] Then, sometime, these clauses and ones building on them spread into private sales. At the turn of the century Cyprian Williams thought the 1850s had been the critical time.[136] That was when exceptional prosperity had brought such a brisk property market that private sellers were able to impose on private buyers the stringent conditions that had previously been usual only at auctions, he said.

Davidson thought the cost-shifting clauses necessary to deter buyers' advisers from pressing requisitions that would bring their clients no real benefit.[137] Far more direct deterrents were being developed, however, ones that went a long way to reversing the common law's assumptions. Davidson disliked them, thinking it enough to include a simple stipulation that if completion did not occur on the nominated day the purchaser must pay interest on the purchase price.[138] That would have preserved conveyancers' fees, while the cost-shifting clauses redistributed their burden. But the clauses he disliked went much further, certainly forcing speed on to the buyer and at least tending to reduce aggregate costs—assuming itemized charging remained the norm.

Generally there were two provisions, often run together in one clause. The first created a timetable for the buyer's requisitions: if requisitions did not meet the deadlines the buyer was deemed to have waived all objections and to have accepted the title as it stood. 'Binding the purchaser by a cable and the vendor by a skein of silk', complained Knight Bruce VC in 1846.[139] The second seems to have evolved from stipulations enabling the seller to cancel the contract if the

---

[133] *Martin's Practice*, iii, 47n.

[134] Compare Hayes, *Concise Conveyancer*, 18–24; Jones, *Pocket Book*, 249–50, 254 (assignment of lease); Atkinson, *Practical Treatise*, 39–42; Bateman, *Practical Treatise*, 128–36; W. Hughes, *The Practice of Sales of Real Property* (2nd edn, 1849), i, esp. 31–3. For later versions, see F. Prideaux, *Precedents in Conveyancing* (6th edn, 1870), i, 7, 29; T. Key and H. W. Elphinstone, *A Compendium of Precedents in Conveyancing* (1878), i, 188.

[135] (1842) 6 *Jurist* 2, 22–3 (recanting a little).

[136] *Vendor and Purchaser* (1903), i, 65.

[137] *Martin's Practice*, iii 49; cf. (1842) 6 *Jurist* 2.

[138] Davidson, *Precedents* (4th edn), i, 538–40.

[139] *Seaton* v. *Mapp* (1846) 2 Coll. 556.

purchaser's counsel was dissatisfied with the seller's response to a requisition, or if the purchaser's counsel raised an objection that could be answered only from documents not in the seller's possession.[140] A tough variant would also modify the principles of *Flureau* v. *Thornhill* by obliging the seller merely to return the deposit, not paying interest or the buyer's costs. Within about a decade a reasonably standard simplified form had evolved: sellers finding themselves unable *or unwilling* to answer a requisition could cancel the contract and return the deposit (with or without interest and costs, as the drafter chose).[141] Anything more unjust there could not be, protested Lord Cottenham on first meeting such a clause in 1840.[142] 'Very peculiar conditions which are becoming customary in these times, which in previous times we never heard of', grumbled Kindersley VC in 1859.[143]

These contractual terms are important because they evolved just as the most vociferous advocates of law reform were promoting speed and cheapness as cardinal values in land transactions. They forced both on buyers, with a concomitant risk that buyers might be hurried into accepting an insecure title. There may have been some resistance from buyers' lawyers, especially when the clauses were proposed in a private sale, but by 1870 they are being described as 'common and proper'.[144] Indeed even in the mid-1850s judges regarded them as so commonly used by ordinary sellers that they could not treat them as depreciatory (and hence improper) when used in mortgagees' sales.[145] In 1857 Lewin reported that trust deeds now commonly allowed trustees to use special conditions, a facility that was made general by statute three years later.[146]

In 1870 a royal commission took purchasers' acquiescence in this pattern of special conditions to prove that they valued speed and reduced transaction costs over the safety given by an open contract.[147] One route from that thinking led to a new (and voluntary) system of title registration achieved in 1875 after much

[140] *Martin's Practice*, iii, 62–3; Bateman, *Practical Treatise*, 132n.

[141] Hughes, *Practice of Sales* (1st edn, 1840), 334n, (2nd edn, 1849), i, 30; W. Hughes, *The Practice of Conveyancing* (1856), i, 39; Bateman, *Practical Treatise*, 101–3; Prideaux, *Precedents* (6th edn), i, 10–11, 29; Dart, *Vendors and Purchasers* (4th edn, 1871), 144–8; Key and Elphinstone, *Compendium*, i, 190–1.

[142] *Tanner* v. *Smith* (1840) 4 Jur. 310; see also *Tanner* v. *Smith* (1840) 10 Sim. 410 (Shadwell VC); *Page* v. *Adam* (1841) 4 Beav. 269; *Cutts* v. *Thodey* (1842) 6 Jur. 1027; *Morley* v. *Cook* (1842) 2 Hare 106.

[143] *Warde* v. *Dickson* (1859) 5 Jur. (N.S.) 698.

[144] Hughes, *Practice of Conveyancing*, i, 11, Davidson, *Concise Precedents* (6th edn 1865), 56; Prideaux, *Precedents* (6th edn, 1870), i, 9–10, 29; and see Key and Elphinstone, *Compendium* (1878), i, 7, 190–1.

[145] *Hobson* v. *Bell* (1839) 2 Beav. 17; *Hoy* v. *Smythies* (1856) 22 Beav. 510; *Falkner* v. *The Equitable Reversionary Society* (1858) 4 Jur. (N.S.) 1214.

[146] Lewin, *Trusts* (3rd edn, 1857), 423; Trustees and Mortgages Act 1860, s 2 (subject to contrary instructions in the deed).

[147] *RC on Land Transfer Act*, Report, PP 1870 [c. 20], xviii, 595; Anderson, *Lawyers*, 112–18.

argument, another to the Vendor and Purchaser Act 1874, both of them the work of Lord Cairns.[148] The latter provided that the main common features of special conditions should become the new rules for open contracts.[149] Thus it reduced the root of title required on an open contract to 40 years, enacted that on sale of a lease the lessor's title need not be produced, made recitals in documents more than 20 years old presumptive proof of their contents, and barred purchasers in various other ways that had become commonplace.

Stage two of this thinking was realized in the Conveyancing and Law of Property Act 1881, which likewise owed its enactment to Lord Cairns. It was a thorough overhaul of common law conveyancing which its originator, the Incorporated Law Society, intended as a demonstration that modernization could be achieved without title registration. One small part of it brought many of the cost-shifting clauses standard in special conditions into the general law as the new terms for open contracts, though not the timetable and rescission clauses.[150] These new rules under both statutes were subject of course to express contrary terms in the contract, but they were significant concessions to vendors nonetheless.

One consequence was that an open contract became less attractive to buyers than before, giving both sides something to bargain for. Cyprian Williams and the Court of Appeal thought the new costs presumptions harsh to be forced on buyers who innocently entered an open contract.[151] Williams urged negotiation, but it is not known whether or not that increased to meet the new rules. No doubt developers of large estates would insist upon a common contract, and no doubt at auction sales sellers dictated conditions as they had always done. Towards the end of his life Lord St. Leonards became alarmed by them, urging potential buyers to consult their solicitor before joining the bidding.[152] A less unworldly writer in the 1890s thought that those who did usually went ahead and bid anyway.[153] Generally, he thought, buyers at auction approached a solicitor only after the contract was concluded.[154] Private agreements arrived at without lawyers were still common too, but that writer, thinking from a seller's point of view, urged that

---

[148] (1884–5) 29 *Sol. J.* 382.

[149] Joshua Williams thought its provisions justifiable only on the grounds that buyers commonly accepted such terms: *Principles of Real Property* (1875), 443.

[150] Section 3(6).

[151] Williams, *Vendor and Purchaser*, 63n, 66–7; *Re Stuart and Olivant and Seadon's Contract* [1896] 2 Ch 328. The precedent books suggested more appropriate clauses for inclusion in a more equal bargain: compare the clauses in Prideaux, *Precedents* (20th edn, 1911), 233 and 233n.

[152] *Handy Book of Property Law* (8th edn, 1869), 39–40; his alarm over special conditions was new to this edition.

[153] E. F. Turner, *The Duties of Solicitor to Client as to Sales, Purchases and Mortgages of Land* (2nd edn, 1893), 50; but he thought consultation frequent: 26–7.

[154] Turner, *Duties*, 53.

once approached a solicitor's first step should be to lead the buyer's side away
from assuming that an open contract had already been concluded and into a reasonably standard 'formal' agreement instead, though he recognized the delicacy
needed.[155]

If, however, a contract mediated by solicitors was sought, this writer was sure
that buyers could negotiate terms less exacting than vendors habitually used at
auction.[156] So negotiation over contractual terms in sales by private treaty must
have been reasonably common, though its focus is unknown. Nor is its relation
known to the standard conditions produced for some areas by their local law
societies.[157] Manchester, for example, included timetable and rescission clauses in
its standard set, with a concluding note that cautioned solicitors against striking
out any of its provisions.[158] Birmingham's law society had a byelaw requiring use
of its uniform conditions.[159]

If onerous clauses were used in private sales there might be pressure for a
buyer's solicitor to begin to probe the seller's title before contract. Eventually that
did happen, but only in the mid-twentieth century, with pre-contract inquiries becoming standard practice, their subject-matter overlapping with requisitions on title. That was part of a transition that for some sorts of property saw
the exchange of contract as the significant part of the transaction, preceded by
extensive legal work, with the subsequent deduction and transfer of title as little more than a routine formality. But there is little sign of that even at the end
of our period. Pre-contract inquiries are thought to have gained their urgency
from an interpretation of the 1925 legislation that deemed buyers to know about
registered encumbrances even before contract.[160] The law books up to the end of
our period have buyers' solicitors advising whether a proposed root of title would
be acceptable in principle, and sometimes seeking informal explanation of an

---

[155] Turner, *Duties*, 58, 63; see also G. W. Greenwood, *Manual of the Practice of Conveyancing* (9th edn, 1897), 44. For open contracts still being common, see e.g. H. Seaborne, *Vendors and Purchasers* (7th edn, 1908) pp. lxxxi–lxxxii.

[156] Turner, *Duties*, 64. Timetable and rescission clauses were common enough to be thinkable in private contracts: *Quinion* v. *Horne* [1906] 1 Ch 596; Prideaux, *Precedents* (20th edn), 214–15, 233–4; F. E. Farrer, *Precedents of Conditions of Sale* (1902), 67–72, 264 (cl. 14 of Birmingham Law Society's common form conditions).

[157] There are many references in Greenwood, *Manual* (9th edn, 1897), to the desirability of using the conditions that are standard in the district.

[158] Farrer, *Precedents* (2nd edn, 1909), 326, 328. Birmingham's rescission clause was a little softer: *ibid.*, 320. Cyprian Williams noted that local standard conditions about costs were often less unfa-vourable to buyers than those codified in the Conveyancing Act: *Vendor and Purchaser*, 63n.

[159] (1894–5) 39 *Sol. J.* 287.

[160] *Re Forsey and Hollebone's Contract* [1927] 2 Ch 379; *Emmet on Title* (17th edn, 1978, by J. T. Farrand and J. G. Smith), 4–5.

unusual contractual term, but there is no sign of any more formal or systematic inquiry into title before contract.[161]

So although statute and common practice had combined to reduce a seller's obligations on a contract for sale, and hence to severely curtail investigation of title, the old two-stage process had not been undermined. Judges had helped maintain it. As Davidson had remarked, conditions of sale were always open to interpretation, and when doing that judges showed much the same contextual understanding that they had always done.[162] When a condition set a timetable they took it to run only from delivery of a perfect abstract; when a condition allowed a seller to rescind if 'unwilling' to respond to a requisition they interpreted that as a reasonable unwillingness, an unwillingness experienced by one who conscientiously intended to follow the usual conveyancing path so far as practicable, not one who had simply changed his mind or was seeking to cover up a misrepresentation.[163] It was cat and mouse, as conveyancers proffered new clauses to evade the latest interpretation, but through to the end of our period contextual interpretation was the norm.

Nor did judges see formal contracts as so universal as to be sceptical of arguments that the parties had concluded their own open contract unaided.[164] There was no practice of 'exchange' that might grow into a convention that the parties' own dealings would be presumed to be pre-contractual. Instead, judges remained content to apply a formal offer-and-acceptance analysis to parties' private dealings. If that meant that an open contract had been agreed, so be it; they were not uncommon, and the title investigation stage would sort out where that left the parties, as it always had.

[161] Turner, *Duties*, 57, 65; Seaborne, *Vendors and Purchasers* (7th edn, 1908), pp. lxxxi–lxxxii.

[162] Davidson, *Precedents* (4th edn), i, 538–40.

[163] *Hobson* v. *Bell* (1839) 2 Beav. 17; *Blacklow* v. *Laws* (1842) 2 Hare 40; *Morley* v. *Cooke* (1842) 2 Hare 106; *Greaves* v. *Wilson* (1858) 25 Beav. 290; *Turpin* v. *Chambers* (1861) 29 Beav. 104; *Duddell* v. *Simpson* (1866) 2 Ch App 102; *Mawson* v. *Fletcher* (1870) 6 Ch App 91, *Gray* v. *Fowler* (1872) LR 8 Ex 265 (contrast Bramwell B. and Blackburn J.); *Bowman* v. *Hyland* (1878) 8 Ch D 588; *re Dames and Wood* (1885) 29 Ch D 626; *re Deighton and Harris's Contract* [1898] 1 Ch 458; *re Jackson and Haden's Contract* [1906] 1 Ch 412; *Quinion* v. *Horne* [1906] 1 Ch 596.

[164] *Bellamy* v. *Debenham* (1890) 44 Ch D 481; *Perry* v. *Suffields* [1916] 2 Ch 187, disapproving *Bristol, Cardiff and Swansea Aerated Bread Co* v. *Maggs* (1890) 44 Ch D 616; cf. *Thomas* v. *Dering* (1837) 1 Keen 729; *Gibbins* v. *North Eastern Metropolitan Asylum Board* (1847) 11 Beav. 1. Similarly, agreements 'subject to contract' seem to have been analysed in the same way throughout, though the range of circumstances was wide enough to throw up some marginal applications: for a small selection see *Honeyman* v. *Marryat* (1855) 21 Beav. 14; *Chinnock* v. *Marchioness of Ely* (1865) 4 De G. & J. 638; *Winn* v. *Bull* (1877) 7 Ch D 29; *Rossdale* v. *Denny* [1921] 1 Ch 57; *Coope* v. *Ridout* [1921] 1 Ch 291.

IV
Leases, Mortgages, and Servitudes

1. LEASES

Introduction

Most land in England and Wales was occupied by leaseholders. Late nineteenth-century rates of owner occupation of urban houses reached as high as 20 per cent in some areas but nationally the average was half that.[1] By then the average for agricultural land was much the same, a long period of decline being accentuated by agricultural depression from the mid-1870s.[2] In the country leasehold was in large measure a consequence of aggregation of land into few hands through the mechanisms of settlement, though it is not the case that all small owners occupied their land themselves. Leasing one's land was a way of life, and until the mid-1870s it was seen as a secure investment. In the cities leasehold again sometimes reflected the ascendancy of a few large owners who held their domains together across the generations by use of settlement. That was particularly true of London. But it was also very common for small investors to own a few houses for leasing; that was a common pattern for family trusts, for example.

Yet for all its ubiquity the law of landlord and tenant attracted little attention. The institution of landlordism did of course, often heatedly, being advanced from time to time as either a cause or a symptom of all that was wrong with both agriculture and city life. But these were not criticisms that saw worthwhile change through tinkering with the details of landlord and tenant law. It was not like conveyancing law, where a common cry was for a better law to do the same job. Drafting leases was not generally a preserve of the elite London practitioners.[3] The Real Property Commissioners produced a brief but radical proposal to

---

[1] C. G. Pooley, 'Patterns on the Ground', in *The Cambridge Urban History of Britain*, vol. iii (ed. M Daunton, Cambridge 2000), 429–65 at 444.

[2] J. V. Beckett, 'The Decline of the Small Landowner in England and Wales 1660–1900', in F M. L. Thompson (ed.), *Landowners, Capitalists and Entrepreneurs* (Oxford, 1994), 89–112.

[3] *Martin's Practice of Conveyancing* (by Davidson) (1840), iv, 1; C. Davidson, *Precedents in Conveyancing* , v, 85 (2nd edn, 1864).

simplify and extend the reach of leasehold covenants, but nothing came of it.[4] Generally, unless one disapproved of landlordism one would conclude, on the whole, that the law worked reasonably well.

One reason perhaps was that leases were malleable to many different contexts. Not much about a lease was prescribed by law; most of it would be contractual. Just how contractual will be one of the themes of this section, as will be the efforts judges made to ensure that the contractual aspects of leases worked. It follows that the lawyers' categories of 'lease' or 'term of years', of 'landlord' and 'tenant', their conception of the lawful and usual remedies for parties in dispute, were protean, too broad to align with social analysis.[5] Nineteenth-century judges did inherit some differentiation in the common law as it came down to them. Tenants taking premises for 'trade' or 'manufacture' had greater rights to remove fixtures at the end of their lease than other tenants did, and could promise their customers greater immunity from landlords' powers to distrain. There were also some rules (though that is perhaps too strong a word) applying only to agricultural tenancies. But judges during our period did not develop those categories or create others. Instead the tendency was towards a contractarianism that left individuals to craft their own bargain. Such new differentiation as there was came from statute, the disjoined result of pressure groups. Not until the 1880s was there broad change. It left the contractual structure of leasehold intact, save for agricultural tenancies, but severely reduced landlords' freedom to exercise the remedies for breach that they had long enjoyed. It was the beginning of a period of disdain for private landlords that lasted well into the twentieth century.

Of Types of Lease, and the Power to Grant Them

In the towns of the 1820s every variety of building, repairing, and occupation lease could be found, with durations from a century or more down to weekly lets of tenement rooms. In the country agricultural tenancies might still in some places take the form of a lease for lives or some other 'beneficial lease', species that carried a low annual rental but a periodic liability to a fine—a capital payment—for renewal.[6] Those had been developed originally to encourage

---

[4] *RC on Real Property*, 3rd Report, PP 1832 (484), xxiii, 321, 366–71.

[5] See e.g. the very different histories in D. J. Olsen, *The Growth of Victorian London* (1976); M. J. Daunton, *House and Home in the Victorian City* (1983); D. Englander, *Landlord and Tenant in Urban Britain 1838–1918* (1983).

[6] For this paragraph, see J. V. Beckett, 'Landownership and Estate Management', in *The Agrarian History of England and Wales*, vol. vi (ed. G. E. Mingay, Cambridge, 1989), 545–640; M. E. Turner, J. V. Beckett, and B. Afton, *Agricultural Rent in England, 1690–1914* (Cambridge, 1997), 7–32; C. A. M. Duncan, 'Legal Protection for the Soil of England: The Spurious Context of Nineteenth

tenants to invest in permanent improvements to the land, but from at least as early as the mid-eighteenth century landowners and tenants alike had generally preferred fixed terms of years, usually 21, sometimes 14, usually at a rack rent. The general assumption underlying those was that the landowner would provide the fixed capital needed for improvements while the tenant put in the working capital, though there were many variants. Latterly, in response to the uncertainties of war and its aftermath terms had become shorter, and in many places mere yearly tenancies had become common. Nineteenth-century writers on scientific agriculture often urged landowners to persevere with terms of years, because a secure and lengthy term could be offered in conjunction with a regime of husbandry covenants, the combination, they said, most conducive to sound and innovatory cultivation. Practice varied with place, time, and person, of course, but the historians' consensus is that short or yearly tenancies predominated and that this was generally because it suited both parties, not particularly because it increased landowners' political control at election times (though it did).

Limited owners, those whose lands were tied up in family settlements that gave them only life estates, lacked power at common law to grant leases that would outlast their lifetime. The solution, of course, was to include powers expressly in the settlement, something that had to be done at the outset or on the occasion of resettlement, which usually meant just once in every generation. In John Powell's collection of precedents published in 1802 the model strict settlement included ample powers to grant occupation leases either for lives or for years.[7] In 1833 Thomas Jarman thought power to grant occupation leases for up to 21 years a matter of course.[8] It is less clear that powers to grant building, rebuilding, and repairing leases were standard practice in settlements in the 1820s, but where they were not, and a family saw an opportunity that ought not to be passed by, recourse to Parliament for a private enabling Act was readily available, as the chapter above on settlements has shown. In outline, the 'usual' powers became progressively easier to acquire, and in 1882 the Settled Land Act made them part of every limited owner's estate by right.

Institutional owners might be more severely limited by archaic constitutions, particularly if they needed to buy out leaseholders for lives. Then a private statute would be the only solution. Those were much more frequently needed to empower urban building leases than agricultural, but, for example, among

---

Century "Progress"' (1992) 66 *Agricultural History* 75–92; J. A. Perkins, 'Tenure, Tenant Right, and Agricultural Progress in Lindsey, 1780–1850' (1975) 23 *Ag. Hist. Rev.* 1–22.

[7] J. J. Powell, *Original Precedents in Conveyancing* (1802), vi, 31–2, 43.

[8] W. M. Bythewood and T. Jarman, *A Selection of Precedents in Conveyancing* (1833), ix, 59, 236–7, 269.

the 313 transactions retrospectively validated by Christ's Hospital Estate Act in 1851 there are several 14-year farming leases.[9] The Church and the Oxford and Cambridge colleges, whose capacity to lease was regulated by a web of statutes and whose access to free capital was limited, certainly shifted away from beneficial leases later than private owners had done.[10] For the Church, the 'minor revolution' that moved it out of beneficial leases was conducted under statutory powers by the Church Estates Commissioners and their successors, starting in the late 1830s and ending by the 1880s.[11] The universities' modernizing statute was passed in 1858, and again the shift was substantially completed by the 1880s, with just a few beneficial leases surviving to 1913.[12]

Thus gradually all these limited owners were freed from archaic prescriptive forms and enabled to exploit their land with something approximating to the contractual freedom of the paradigm unencumbered owner. They were often still restricted to the 'usual' forms, however, though those could be expanded by the settlement or other constitutive instrument. By the same token, however, restrictions could be added, and there were enough of those in settlement documents and in the general law for a lease's conformity to its enabling power to remain a risk for tenants taking from limited owners, albeit one that was diminishing.[13]

Giving the Relationship Content

Before 1820, probably long before, the continuing obligations of landlord, tenant, and their successors had come to depend upon the covenants contained in the lease rather than upon the default provisions of the common law. When the default terms did apply they could be exacting, as parties to oral tenancies sometimes discovered. There was some nicety, for example, in calculating the half-year's notice needed to end a yearly tenancy, which only the legally naive would believe was always going to be exactly the same thing as six months.[14] Some

---

[9] 14 & 15 Vict. c. 2 (private).

[10] W. Woodfall, *Law of Landlord and Tenant* (3rd edn, 1811), 81–5.

[11] G. F. A. Best, *Temporal Pillars: Queen Anne's Bounty, The Ecclesiastical Commissioners and the Church of England* (Cambridge, 1964), 369–80. The Church Estates Commissioners became the Estates Committee of the Ecclesiastical Commissioners, but operated autonomously. See particularly the Episcopal and Capitular Estate Acts 1851 and 1854 (14 & 15 Vict. c. 104, 17 & 18 Vict. c. 116) and the Ecclesiastical Commissioners Acts 1860 and 1868. Some sees had obtained extended powers by private statutes.

[12] Universities and Colleges Estates Act 1858; J. P. D. Dunbabin, 'Oxford and Cambridge College Finances, 1871–1913' (1975) 28 *Econ. Hist. Rev.* 631–47. Some colleges had obtained extended powers by private statute.

[13] *Wolstenholme's Conveyancing and Settled Land Acts* (10th edn, 1913), 385–94, 489, 492–4.

[14] G. W. Cooke, *A Treatise on the Law and Practice of Agricultural Tenancies* (1850), 26; *Wilkinson v. Calvert* (1878) 3 CPD 360.

default terms were still uncertain—it was unclear exactly which tenants were liable for which forms of waste at common law. That, however, was the sign of a law that was archaic, not one that was contested. The issue seems usually to have arisen indirectly, where a settlement stipulated that leases it empowered must forbid the tenant from committing waste, and the question was whether the lease actually granted complied. Whenever tenancies were put into writing, regulation of notice, of the use of leased property, of the tenant's power to assign the lease, and of the landlord's power to forfeit for breach were far more often controlled by covenants, to the point that arguments about whether judges should supply some new default rule tended to be couched in terms of whether they should imply a covenant.

In agricultural tenancies the line between covenants and obligations that judges would imply as default terms could become blurred.[15] The judges' default rule was that all husbandry leases and tenancies impliedly incorporated the 'custom of the country' save as expressly modified by covenant.[16] 'Custom' in this context did not mean some immemorial usage to be proved with certainty and without exception, but rather the established good practice of the locality. It was therefore something of a collective standard, its existence as a norm a matter for local witnesses and juries. Moderated only by a test of reasonableness that was easily satisfied, it allowed ample room for variation of weather and soil type, and it could confer entitlements on either side of the relationship.[17]

Importantly, custom need not be static; accounts of the well-known Lincolnshire tenant-right custom, which allowed outgoing tenants compensation for unexhausted improvements, show it originating in some districts in the eighteenth century, spreading to others after 1815, and undergoing frequent modification in response to changing agricultural conditions and techniques.[18] But it was regarded as binding, not just as good practice. In the opinion of the most specialized legal writers on agricultural tenancies through into the 1880s custom was still the most important determinant of rights and obligations.[19] It could be excluded by covenant, but judges would not strain covenants to do that.[20] Even when covenants were used they might often do no more than incorporate local

---

[15] *Wedd* v. *Porter* [1916] 2 KB 91 maintained that there was a difference over transmission to successors.

[16] *Powley* v. *Walker* (1793) 5 T.R. 373; *Wilkins* v. *Wood* (1848) 17 LJ QB 319.

[17] *Leigh* v. *Hewitt* (1803) 4 East 155; *Dalby* v. *Hirst* (1819) 1 Brod. & Bing. 224; *Hutton* v. *Warren* (1836) 1 M. & W. 466; *Tucker* v. *Linger* (1882) 21 Ch D 18.

[18] Perkins, 'Tenure'; T. W. Beastall, *A North Country Estate* (Chichester, 1975), 95–9. Contrast Glamorgan, where a well-intentioned codification ossified the custom: A. W. Jones, 'Glamorgan Custom and Tenant Right' (1983) 31 *Ag. Hist. Rev.* 1–14.

[19] Cooke, *Agricultural Tenancies* (2nd edn, 1882), p. vi; cf. Jones, 'Glamorgan Custom', 8–9.

[20] *Hutton* v. *Warren* (1836) 1 M. & W. 466; *Tucker* v. *Linger* (1882) 21 Ch D 18.

custom, be that in detail or by general reference.[21] It is noticeable that the reported case law on breach of husbandry covenants often concerned exploitive behaviour by tenants that would probably have breached local custom anyway, instances, therefore of covenants' functioning more as an easier method of proving obligation. On the other hand landlords could have their leases drafted to subject their tenants to obligations of the most minute particularity. The lawyers' precedent books had examples a-plenty.[22]

In other contexts, however, even in other contexts within agricultural tenancies, judges were responding to the prevalence of covenants and encouraging their further use by declining to intervene between landlord and tenant where once they might have done. An example from agricultural leases concerns a well-established form of words allowing landlords to stipulate for an additional rent for each acre of land farmed in a particular way, most usually for ploughing and cropping established pastures.[23] Originally such terms were regulatory, intended to encourage the periodic exploitation of the enhanced fertility long pasturing brought, conditional upon sharing the profits.[24] But they could be used penally as a deterrent, and frequently were.[25] Even so, by the mid-eighteenth century judges had ruled that in law their true substance was that they were liquidated damages clauses, not penalties, and nineteenth-century judges willingly followed suit.[26] Juries must not temper law with justice by confining the landlord to compensation for damage to the reversion, ruled Abbott CJ, but must award the full over-rent covenanted.[27] Nor would Chancery give relief.[28] Eighteenth-century cases suggested an exception to this abstention of equity, that relief would be granted if the clause had the logical form of a penalty, but that was quietly dropped sometime in the 1820s.[29] That was part of a general retreat by Chancery judges, as will be seen.

[21] E. Kerridge, *The Agricultural Revolution* (New York, 1968), 224; Davidson, *Precedents*, v, 197 (2nd edn, 1864); *Woodfall's Law of Landlord and Tenant* (9th edn, 1867, by W. R. Cole), 499.

[22] Even the elite texts contained them, though Davidson cautioned that his precedents of leases were not drafted by the coterie of London conveyancers and hence came without his usual stamp of authority: *Martin's Practice* (by Davidson) (1840), iv, 1; Davidson, *Precedents* (2nd edn), v, 85.

[23] Davidson tried his hand at a modern version: *Precedents* (2nd edn), v, 195.

[24] Kerridge, *Agricultural Revolution*, 191–2. Without some such covenant ploughing ancient meadow would usually be actionable waste: *Simmons* v. *Norton* (1831) 7 Bing. 640.

[25] Duncan, 'Legal Protection'.

[26] *Aylet* v. *Dodd* (1741) 2 Atk. 238; *Lowe* v. *Peers* (1768) 4 Burr. 2225, 2228; *Woodfall's Landlord and Tenant* (9th edn, 1867), 353–6.

[27] *Farrant* v. *Olmius* (1820) 3 B. & Ald. 692; see also *Birch* v. *Stephenson* (1811) 3 Taunt. 469; *Bowers* v. *Nixon* (1848) 18 LJ QB 35.

[28] *Woodward* v. *Gyles* (1690) 2 Vern. 119; *Rolfe* v. *Peterson* (1772) 2 Bro. P.C. 436; H. Maddock, *A Treatise on the Principles and Practice of the High Court of Chancery* (3rd edn, 1837), i, 47–55.

[29] *Jones* v. *Green* (1829) 3 Y. & J. 298; *Denton* v. *Richmond* (1833) 1 Car. & M. 734 (in argument).

It was a similar story for urban leases. They had no room for 'custom', so complex were urban environments, so diverse and so rapidly changing. Nor was there any longer much room for implied obligations or implied immunities. In the very early nineteenth century judges seem to have thought that occupation tenants, even tenants for years, were impliedly immune from the ancient statutory liability for 'permissive waste', that is, that they were not liable to repair ordinary dilapidations occurring during their tenure.[30] By the mid-century that had changed. Parke B. insisted that by Coke's interpretation the statutes clearly imposed liability with no exceptions for context, though he acknowledged that judges had recently 'much limited' the repairs required.[31] But save for interpreting leasing powers in settlements the point was academic. As a lecturer in 1855 said, there was scarcely any law on the question, so ubiquitous were obligations by covenant.[32] The same was true of a supposed implied obligation to use the premises in a 'tenant-like way'. It was said to exist, but the only instances the standard text could muster show it being excluded by express covenants.[33]

To be strictly accurate, there never was an implied obligation upon the landlord that a house let for occupation would be fit for habitation, in the sense that the tenant could sue if it was not. But up until the early 1840s there was a functional equivalent: if the house was uninhabitable the tenant was impliedly released from paying rent.[34] In *Smith* v. *Marrable* in 1842, the last case of this line and the only one to survive, Abinger CB thought the rule simply 'plain good common sense'.[35] There was a distant lurking problem, however, that the rent did remain payable if a house *became* uninhabitable, in the classic case because it was destroyed by fire.[36] That rule was well established, and well entrenched in legal theory, being a consequence of the principle that while use of property might be frustrated by subsequent events the estate created by the lease remained intact.[37] Once, it seems, judges with jurisdiction in equity would have protected a tenant in such a case by issuing an injunction to stop the landlord proceeding at law, but

---

[30] *Gibson* v. *Wells* (1805) 1 Bos. & P. (N.R.) 290; *Herne* v. *Benbow* (1813) 4 Taunt. 764; *Jones* v. *Hill* (1817) 7 Taunt. 392.

[31] *Yellowly* v. *Gower* (1855) 11 Ex. 274; *Davies* v. *Davies* (1888) 38 Ch D 499; *Auworth* v. *Johnson* (1832) 5 Car. & P. 239; *Leach* v. *Thomas* (1836) 7 Car. & P. 327.

[32] J. W. Smith, *The Law of Landlord and Tenant* (1855), 196.

[33] *Woodfall's Landlord and Tenant* (6th edn, 1849), 435; *Holford* v. *Dunnett* (1844) 7 M. & W. 349; *Standen* v. *Christmas* (1847) 16 LJ QB 265; *White* v. *Nicholson* (1842) 4 Man. & G. 95.

[34] *Edwards* v. *Etherington* (1825) Ry. & M. 268; *Salisbury* v. *Marshal* (1829) 4 Car. & P. 65; *Collins* v. *Barrow* (1831) 1 Man. & Ry. 113; *Cowie* v. *Goodwin* (1840) 9 Car. & P. 378; J. Reynolds, 'Statutory Covenants of Fitness and Repair: Social Legislation and the Judges' (1974) 37 *MLR* 377–98.

[35] (1842) Car. & M. 479, aff'd (1843) 11 M. & W. 6.

[36] *Baker* v. *Holtpzaffell* (1811) 4 Taunt. 45; *Izon* v. *Gorton* (1839) 5 Bing. (N.C.) 501.

[37] *Paradine* v. *Jane* (1647) Aleyn 26 is the best known case.

first Macdonald CB and then Lord Eldon had disavowed the practice.[38] As leases had become more contractual those judges found it hard to justify adding to the terms that parties had expressly agreed.

Similarly the first incursion into the common sense of *Smith* v. *Marrable* came in a case where the lease did contain quite detailed covenants, just not one that would excuse the tenant from paying the rent when the property became uninhabitable for lack of landlords' repairs.[39] Nor would judges frame the question as being just about houses, rather it was about fitness for purpose generally.[40] If there were such a rule as had been supposed it would have to apply equally to leases for building, or for agriculture, said Parke B., who was the prime mover in this revision.[41] Nor would it sit well with other sorts of contracts, such as those for the sale of goods, where judges had been busy denying that similar conditions could be implied. Thus the question was conceived as 'contract' and the old rule was reversed.

Anomalously, *Smith* v. *Marrable* itself was kept as an exception, a special rule for furnished lets—the facts happening to suit such an analysis. And thanks to the Dowager Countess of Winchelsea, forced by problems with the drains to abandon her three-month lease of a furnished house at the height of the season, the anomaly was still good law at the end of our period.[42] But the main principle itself quickly became firm. Judges declined, for example, to let it be outflanked by claims that the landlord was liable for deceit for remaining silent about the true state of the property.[43] Caveat lessee; prospective tenants should have the property surveyed and should get leases that spelled out their entitlements exactly. How this worked in practice is not recorded.

One default rule that caused some difficulty was that tenants' improvements or additions to the property fell immediately into the landlord's ownership, even if they had begun as chattels. They became 'fixtures'. Out of a rather confused body of law a policy-based exception had emerged in 1704, that at the end of their tenancy tenants could remove trade and manufacturing fixtures they

---

[38] *Hare* v. *Groves* (1796) 3 Anst. 687; *Holtzapffel* v. *Baker* (1811) 18 Ves. 115; followed on extreme facts in *Leeds* v. *Cheetham* (1827) 1 Sim. 146.

[39] *Arden* v. *Pullen* (1842) 10 M. & W. 322; cf. *Surplice* v. *Farnsworth* (1844) 7 Man. & G. 576.

[40] *Sutton* v. *Temple* (1843) 12 M. & W. 52; cf. *Erskine* v. *Adeane* (1871) 8 Ch App 756; *Cheater* v. *Cater* [1918] 1 KB 247 (leases of pasture with overhanging yew trees).

[41] *Hart* v. *Windsor* (1844) 12 M. & W. 68; Parke B. left it open whether Chancery should specifically enforce a contract for a lease of a house that turned out to be uninhabitable. In due course Romilly MR (predictably) ruled that it would not: *Tildesley* v. *Clarkson* (1862) 30 Beav. 419.

[42] *Wilson* v. *Finch Hatton* (1877) 2 Ex D 336; *Manchester Bond Warehouse* v. *Carr* (1880) 5 CPD 507; *Woodfall's Landlord and Tenant* (19th edn, 1912), 203–4. *Smith* v. *Marrable* was also a high-class let—a short stay at Brighton.

[43] *Keates* v. *Cadogan* (1851) 10 C.B. 591.

had installed, an exception that worked well for such obvious manufacturing investments as steam engines and brewing vats.[44] One of the clines out of that principle led to difficult intermediate cases between 'trade' and 'agriculture', such that in the 1790s it would have seemed likely that Lord Kenyon's King's Bench would extend the exception to farming leases too. But in 1803 Kenyon's successor, Lord Ellenborough, instead led the court to deny agricultural tenants the right that trade and manufacturing tenants enjoyed.[45] Though his rule reflected the general assumption that it was the landlord who ought to be responsible for the capital investment, and though, like any other rule, it could be altered by contract, respected law writers criticized Ellenborough's decision on grounds both of policy and precedent.[46] It was reversed by statute in 1851, a consolation prize for Philip Pusey and his allies who were agitating, unsuccessfully at the time, for a broader right that would compensate agricultural tenants for lasting improvements they made to the land.[47]

The new rule was not seriously prescriptive. The Landlord and Tenant Act 1851 applied only to fixtures, which in the common law understanding were accessions retaining a discrete chattel identity even after being fixed to the soil. They did not include items like brick buildings or improvements to the soil demonstrable only by chemical analysis. Moreover, the Act was only a partial reversal of the 1803 decision, applying the traders' rule only to fixtures for which landlords had given their prior written permission. Many farmers were yearly tenants, and though their tenancies often rolled over for years on end they still had no guarantee that they would recover the full value of the artificial fertilizers and other

[44] *Poole's case* (1704) 1 Salk. 368; A. Amos and J. Ferard, *A Treatise on the Law of Fixtures* (1827), 13–39.

[45] *Elwes* v. *Mawe* (1803) 3 East 38; J. R. Fisher, 'The Farmers' Alliance: An Agricultural Protest Movement of the 1880s' (1978) 26 *Ag. Hist. Rev.* 15–25 at 15; J. R. Fisher, 'Landowners and English Tenant Right, 1845–1852' (1983) 31 *Ag. Hist. Rev.* 15–25 at 25. The contrast was reduced a little by fuzziness on both sides. Brick buildings were not usually held to be trade fixtures, a convenient 'mixed' category treated nursery and market gardening activity as trading, and quite substantial timber structures that might be held to be removable trade fixtures were, in the agricultural context, held not be fixtures at all: *Whitehead* v. *Bennett* (1858) 27 LJ Ch 474; *Wansbrough* v. *Maton* (1836) 4 Ad. & El. 884; *Mears* v. *Callender* [1901] 2 Ch 388; Amos and Ferard, *Fixtures* (3rd edn, 1883), 62–7, 99–104. These were only default rules, of course, subject to exclusion or modification by covenant.

[46] Amos and Ferard, *Fixtures* (1827), 46–60; J. W. Smith, *A Selection of Leading Cases on Various Branches of the Law* (1838), ii, 116–17; contrast S. G. Grady, *The Law of Fixtures* (1845), 63–84.

[47] Fisher, 'Landowners'; Landlord and Tenant Act 1851, 14 & 15 Vict. c. 25, s 3. Fisher is right that Pusey, whose select committee recommended the change, did not introduce the bill, but he had introduced its predecessor containing the same clause the previous year: *PP* 1850 (97), iii, 475.

expensive off-farm inputs they now expected (and were often required) to employ to increase the soil's productivity.[48]

In the good times of the 1860s this tenants' disability seems not to have mattered, but tension grew in the late 1870s when farmers in the south and east suffered poor harvests, and it became critical when unprecedented availability of imports prevented them from raising prices in response. Pressure on Disraeli's government brought legislation in 1875 enabling outgoing tenants to claim compensation for unexhausted improvements from their landlords, but it came with an opt-out clause, anything more prescriptive offending conservative sentiment in the Lords.[49] Similarly, although the Act doubled the notice required to end a yearly agricultural tenancy, from a half-year to a whole, that provision was again subject to contrary stipulation in the agreement. A narrow reading of such legislation was appropriate, Baggallay LJ said, because it interfered with the 'prima facie right of contract'.[50]

Displacement of freedom of contract began with the Liberals' election victory in 1880, and affected agricultural tenancies more than others. In 1883 the Liberals' Agricultural Holdings Act remodelled the 1875 Act and removed its opt-out clause. Like the Lincolnshire Custom, on which this Act was based, and like the Landlord and Tenant Act 1851, disputes were to be resolved in the first instance by arbitrators and umpires, an intervention of third parties into landlord and tenant relations that commentators thought significant. Taken together with some general restriction of landlords' remedies against defaulting tenants, to be discussed below, this legislation was a significant step away from freedom of contract, followed by others of similar character through to the end of our period.[51] It included in 1900 the abolition of penal rents in agricultural leases, though, with a nuance typical of agricultural tenures, penal rents remained permissible for breaking up pasture, as they had been used for centuries.[52]

---

[48] For the following account, see J. R. McQuiston, 'Tenant Right: Farmer against Landlord in Victorian England 1847–1883' (1973) 47 *Ag. Hist. Rev.* 95–113; Fisher, 'Farmers' Alliance'; see also Beckett, 'Landowners', 616–17, and Jones 'Glamorgan Custom'.

[49] Agricultural Holdings Act 1875. Opting out was so common that the Act was generally regarded as a dead letter; see for example J. M. Lely and W. H. Aggs, *Agricultural Holdings: The Agricultural Holdings Acts 1883 and 1900* (1901), 8–9. Contrast *RC on the Depressed Condition of Agricultural Interests*, Report, *PP* 1882 [C. 3309], xiv, 1, 14, which nonetheless recommended compulsion (at 30–1).

[50] *Barlow* v. *Teal* (1885) 15 QBD 501, speaking of its re-enactment in the Agricultural Holdings Act 1883.

[51] Allotments and Cottage Gardens Compensation for Crops Act 1887, Tenants Compensation Act 1890, Market Gardeners Compensation Act 1895, Agricultural Holdings Acts 1900, 1906, 1908. Politically the Ground Game Act 1880, allowing tenants in possession to kill rabbits and hares as of right, would have been the most important.

[52] Agricultural Holdings Act 1900, s 6. There were a few other exceptions.

Remedies

In addition to suing for the rent landlords had one remedy that was wholly a matter of self-help—distress—and often another in which the courts' role was essentially to enforce a decision taken in the landlord's discretion—ejectment for breach of covenant. Neither was unique to landlords. Distress, the ability to seize and sell goods in payment of a debt without first getting a court judgment, had long been available for recovery of tolls. That use of it was brought into the modern world in the 1840s as a standard term for inclusion in the local and private Acts establishing railway, harbour, and market companies.[53] Shares in companies could be forfeited and sold for non-payment of calls.[54] But taken together landlords' remedies put them into an unusually powerful position. Until the 1870s that position went unquestioned; it was seen partly as a matter of continuity of the ancient law, partly a matter of freedom of contract. Judges were comfortable enforcing sometimes quite elaborate contractual provisions that mimicked these remedies in situations where for technical reasons they would have been unavailable or restricted under the general law.[55]

In 1820 distress already had a 500-year history of legislative amendment. As one writer observed, when distress was a remedy enjoyed particularly by feudal lords and their manorial institutions the legislative trend was towards restriction and safeguards, but once it became primarily a commercial landlords' remedy for non-payment of rent the trend was towards expansion and the removal of technicality.[56] While that is true, the important shift in 1690 from distress as a security for payment to distress as a prelude to a forced sale of the distrained goods had been accompanied by what at the time would have looked like a safeguard.[57] Prior to sale the goods had to be valued by appraisers, who had to be sworn by the sheriff, under-sheriff, or constable. There were formal requirements too—notices, signatures, and a grace period between seizure and sale. By the beginning of the nineteenth century, however, it was common for appraisers to buy the goods themselves, at their own valuation, and there was no requirement that they be professional valuers; mere reasonable competence sufficed.[58] In 99 cases out of 100, wrote Thomas Platt, it was better for a tenant to raise the rent by selling the

---

[53] Railways Clauses Consolidation Act 1845, 8 Vict. c. 20, s 97; Markets and Fairs Clauses Act 1847, 10 & 11 Vict. c. 14, s 38; Harbours, Docks and Piers Clauses Act 1847, 10 & 11 Vict. c. 27, s 45.

[54] Companies Clauses Consolidation Act 1845, 8 Vict. c. 16, ss 29–35.

[55] *Kavanagh* v. *Gudge* (1844) 7 Man. & G. 316; *Anderson* v. *Midland Railway* (1861) 30 LJ QB 94.

[56] J. Bradby, *A Treatise on the Law of Distresses* (1808), 1–17.

[57] Distress for Rent Act 1690, 2 Will. & Mar. (sess. 1) c. 5.

[58] W. Impey, *The Law and Practice of Distress and Replevin by the Late Lord Chief Baron Gilbert* (4th edn, 1823), 235; *Woodfall's Landlord and Tenant* (1831 edn, by Harrison), 370; *Roden* v. *Eyton* (1848) 6 C.B. 427.

chattels himself than to have them sold on a distress.[59] It is easy to paint distress as inherently oppressive, particularly if the focus is on the urban poor.[60]

It is easy, too, to contrast the summary and extensive nature of distress with the much more restricted rights of 'ordinary' creditors and thereby to magnify the peculiar privilege enjoyed by landlords.[61] There were other creditors, however, who were out of the ordinary. Many middle-class professionals enjoyed a general lien over whatever of their debtor's property and documents of title they held in their possession—attorneys, bankers, factors, insurance brokers, and stock-brokers all enjoyed that right.[62] So too did a motley of trades that had established general liens by custom, sometimes just for particular localities. One step back along the spectrum leads to the specific liens of all manner of warehousemen, carriers, and repairers. Lien-holders could not usually sell to recoup their debt, but their security took an absolute priority in bankruptcy proceedings. By contrast, from 1825 distress after an act of bankruptcy lay for a maximum of just one year's rent.[63] Further there were the developments of bills of sale and, later, hire purchase, as suppliers of durables sought ways to neutralize the advantages hitherto enjoyed by those select suppliers of services. With this broad middle ground restored, landlords' powers in relation to other creditors seem less extraordinary.

Nor was the law of distress intrinsically one-sided. There was an almost embarrassingly long list of actions available to a tenant who suffered a distress that was in some way defective, and another long list of possible defects.[64] The 1881 edition of the standard text, the last before a succession of statutes remodelled distress, takes 12 pages to guide the reader through the pitfalls facing landlords and their agents.[65] Replevin, trespass, and trover were all available to tenants on general principle, and in addition judges allowed declarations 'on the equity' of the statute of 1690—declarations for not selling at the best price, for example, or for not returning the surplus to the sheriff's custody.[66] With up to 90 per cent of

---

[59] *Leases*, ii, 343.

[60] Englander, *Landlord and Tenant*, 22–32.

[61] Cornish and Clark, *Law and Society*, 135.

[62] J. Cross, *A Treatise on the Law of Lien, and Stoppage in Transitu* (1840); L. E. Hall, *Possessory Liens in English Law* (1917). A general lien authorizes retention of the goods as security for all money their owner owes the retainer; a specific lien for merely the money owed on the transaction by which the retainer came to have possession.

[63] 6 Geo. IV c. 16, s 74; and, for insolvency, 7 Geo. IV c. 57, s 31; 1 & 2 Vict. c. 110, s 58. The roots of the one-year rule can be traced even further back, to disputes between distraining landlords and judgment creditors: 8 Ann. c. 14.

[64] J. Chitty, *A Treatise on the Parties to Actions* (4th edn, 1825), 717–32.

[65] *Woodfall's Landlord and Tenant* (12th edn, 1881), 425–33, 443–7.

[66] Chitty, *Parties*, 725–6; *Piggott* v. *Birtles* (1836) 1 M. & W. 441; *Lyon* v. *Tomkies* (1836) 1 M. & W. 603; *Clarke* v. *Holford* (1848) 2 Car. & K. 540; *Ridgway* v. *Lord Stafford* (1851) 6 Ex. 404.

England's land being tenanted it would be a mistake to think that all tenants were poor and downtrodden.

The poor tended to put their goods on a cart and flee, a folk custom of debt avoidance that had attracted counter-legislation since 1709.[67] The penalties blended the civil and the criminal, using justices of the peace as the enforcement agency if the goods concerned were not worth more than £20. Similarly, however, from 1817, in an attempt to reduce oppression against poor tenants, brokers' costs were regulated.[68] Again the cut-off was £20, again there were stiff penalties, and again the justices were the enforcement agency. And the notion that magistrates might act as protectors of the lower class was extended in 1839, for London only, by giving the Metropolitan Police Courts a jurisdiction to remedy unlawful or defective distress.[69] It encapsulated in a single section the various causes of action available to tenants who could afford to launch an action in the royal courts. The difficulty lay less in the adequacy of these laws than in the practical inability of the poor to access them.

In principle landlords could distrain upon any goods found on the leased premises irrespective of their ownership, making the remedy unusually broad. Common-law judges had carved out exceptions protecting third parties who left their property with traders, manufacturers, and factors, but it is not known whether this complex and to some extent uncertain body of law deterred land-lords.[70] Nor is it known how often innocent outsiders found themselves unwill-ingly acting as surety for a defaulting tenant.[71] Not often enough, it seems, to raise public concern. The common law exception did not stretch to protecting occupants of lodging houses from the depredations of the lodgings' keeper's landlord, and although Lord Denman CJ saw no reason in justice why it might not, there was no possibility that the judges would stretch the principle that far.[72] Relief for this vulnerable group did not come until 1871, when a typically brief and precisely targeted private member's Act added their goods to the protected list, against the opposition of the Liverpool Householders' Association and the

---

[67] 8 Ann. c. 14, s 2; 11 Geo. II c. 19 (1737). The Metropolitan Police Act 1839, 2 & 3 Vict. c. 47, s 67, which gave constables power to stop and search carts found out at night, was thus an extension of existing legislation.

[68] 57 Geo. III c. 93. Mr Lockhart, seeking leave to introduce it, pointed out that the great oppres-sion targeted brought no advantage to the landlord: *The Times*, 20 June 1817.

[69] Englander, *Landlord and Tenant*, 16–17, 25; Metropolitan Courts Act 1839, 2 & 3 Vict. c. 71, s 39, applying to tenancies with rents not more than £15 a year.

[70] E. Bullen, *A Practical Treatise on the Law of Distress for Rent* (1842), 95–100; A. Oldham and A. L. T. Foster, *The Law of Distress* (1886), 115–24.

[71] Surety: *Exall* v. *Partridge* (1799) 8 T.R. 308.

[72] *Muspratt* v. *Gregory* (1838) 3 M. & W. 677.

misgivings of some noble lords.[73] Confirming their fears, Professor Daunton finds that by making identification of eligible goods more difficult the act significantly curtailed urban landlords' resort to distress, though Dr Englander is more sceptical.[74]

That Act aside, there seems not to have been much change to the law during the mid-century, nor much call for it. Change began in the 1880s, stemming in part from agricultural depression, which focused legislative attention on relations between landlord and tenant in the country, and in part from the Liberals' election victory in 1880, which promised more rigorous reform of the land laws generally. In 1882 a royal commission on agricultural depression and a Commons select committee on distress (with special reference to agricultural tenancies) reached very similar conclusions: distress in this context should not be abolished, but should be restricted to just one or two years' worth of rents in arrears.[75] Interesting themes were raised—whether abolishing distress would lead to landlords requiring payment of rent in advance, whether that would produce a better class of farming tenant, and where the advantage lay in providing landlords with a form of security which, in particular, the seedsman could not emulate.[76] But the political urgency was too great to allow their pursuit.

Instead the result replicated the rule in bankruptcy (without saying so), limiting agricultural landlords' power to levy a distress to a single year's rent. Further, and in the long run more importantly, it removed their power to seize stock agisted by third parties, likewise machinery held on hire purchase, abolished appraisal as an unnecessary expense, and required bailiffs executing distresses to be licensed by a county court judge.[77] These procedural changes and the restrictions on taking third parties' goods were then generalized to all tenancies in 1888, but not the restriction to a year's rent, with further refinements in 1895 and 1908.[78] Though one could argue that these Acts were extensions of policies already long visible in the law, cumulatively they looked like a new beginning. Together they

---

[73] Englander, *Landlord and Tenant*, 25–6; Lodgers Goods Protection Act; *PD* 1871 (s3) 208: 840–1; *The Times*, 9 August 1871. Like the legislation listed in the previous paragraph this act used the justices as the enforcement agency.

[74] Daunton, *House and Home*, 157; Englander, *Landlord and Tenant*, 26.

[75] *RC on Depressed Condition of Agricultural Interests*, Report, 12, 31–2; *SC on the Law of Distress*, Report, *PP* 1882 (284), viii, 269.

[76] Liens over future crops to be grown from present seeds could be effected at common law (*Petch v. Tustin* (1846) 15 M. & W. 110; J. P. Benjamin, *A Treatise on the Law of Sale of Personal Property* (6th edn, 1920), 153–9), but in the absence of some statutory or common law exception distrainors need not respect third-party interests. Perhaps for this reason crop liens were an undeveloped corner of English law; see also *Congreve v. Evetts* (1854) 10 Ex. 298.

[77] Agricultural Holdings Act 1883, ss 44–5.

[78] Law of Distress Amendment Acts 1888, 1895, 1908.

severely limited what the 1690 statute had once grandly declared to be 'the most ordinary and ready way for recovery of arrears of rent'.

Eviction and Forfeiture

According to Professor Daunton, urban landlords would have traded distress for a truly rapid process for removing tenants from the premises after their let expired.[79] Until 1838 there was only the cumbrous legal procedure of ejectment, as inappropriate for urban tenement landlords as trover and replevin were for their tenants. But in that year landlords of premises rented at no more than £20 a year acquired a summary, almost discretion-free, eviction procedure through magistrates, a one-sided measure that upset traditionalists such as Lord St. Leonards. It was necessary, urban landlords said, to reduce the mayhem and property damage protracted litigation was encouraging.[80] By all accounts, however, the measure was a disappointment, proceedings generally taking two (effectively rent-free) months to complete. In Scotland, where relations between landlord and tenant could be even more fraught than they were in the English cities, landlords did eventually acquire an even more summary procedure, but in England the 1838 Act was the most they were able to achieve.[81]

To seek eviction the landlord must first terminate the lease. For the ubiquitous weekly tenement lets that was obviously not difficult. For tenancies measurable in years, however, the lease needed to have reserved a power of re-entry for breach of condition or covenant, forfeiture not being inherent to demises at common law. All the model leases did, of course, but the fact that they needed to gave judges an opening for interpretation. Almost always this was an exercise in common law, not equity. Just as statute had widened distress as a landlord's remedy in the late seventeenth and early eighteenth centuries, so too it had made forfeiture easier. Importantly, it had confined equity's jurisdiction to relieve against forfeiture to cases of non-payment of rent since remedied.[82] That, at least, was how the majority of equity judges saw it in the decisive litigation shortly before 1820, a denial of a general relieving jurisdiction that went unquestioned through into the 1870s.[83]

---

[79] For this paragraph, see Daunton, *House and Home*, 148–54, and Englander, *Landlord and Tenant*, 12–21.

[80] Englander recounts that it was the proposing of this measure that provoked the London magistrates and the Home Office to procure the passage of Metropolitan Courts Act 1839, s 39 (n. 69, above) as a balance: *Landlord and Tenant*, 16–17, 25.

[81] For Scotland, see Daunton, *House and Home*, 153–4.

[82] 4 Geo. II c. 28.

[83] *Hill* v. *Barclay* (1810) 16 Ves. 402, (1811) 18 Ves. 55 (Lord Eldon, overruling a contrary decision by Lord Erskine); *Lovat* v. *Lord Ranelagh* (1814) 5 Ves. & B. 24, 30; *Reynolds* v. *Pitt* (1812) 2 Price 212n;

Any other rule would come 'really to doing away with the covenant', said Thomson CB.[84]

Similarly common law judges denied that they had power to stay proceedings for ejectment.[85] That was severe, said Patteson J., but the 'general effect [was] no doubt beneficial by teaching all that they must fulfil their obligations, and by giving them certainty in their mutual relations'.[86] His was indeed a shocking case— forfeiture for a minor transgression of a covenant to insure that had never exposed the property to risk—but 14 years passed before Lord St. Leonards penned a reform to give equity jurisdiction to relieve.[87] Even then it was narrowly limited to insurance covenants and beset by conditions. Not only had the breach to have been inadvertent and inconsequential but, to emphasize the generosity of this departure from contractual principle, judges could indulge a tenant only once and must endorse the lease when they did—branding it on remitting its death sentence.

Thus with the exception of non-payment of rent, and the late addition of breach of insuring covenants, drafters need only word their covenants and their provisos for re-entry accurately for landlords to be able to evict defaulting tenants as they thought expedient, whatever the hardship to the tenant or windfall gain to the landlord. The standard text discerned a shift in interpretive values, away from the strict construction formerly applying to breach of condition to a more relaxed standard that treated breach of covenant like breach of any other contract.[88] Not all judges in the formative period of the 1840s agreed with that, but it was anyway a matter that could be met by more precise drafting.[89]

There was one instance of a shift away from strict interpretation where judges seem to have been motivated by more than just according business sense to an agreement. Faced with clauses saying that on breach of covenant the lease became 'void' judges persistently read them as meaning only 'voidable', even in the teeth of long explanations in the lease that 'void' was exactly what the landlord meant.[90] It was a reading that required landlords to make some positive,

---

Rolfe v. *Harris* (1816) 2 Price 206n; *Green* v. *Bridges* (1830) 4 Sim. 96; *Job* v. *Bannister* (1856) 2 K. & J. 374. There was a relict exception for accident and surprise.

[84] *Bracebridge* v. *Buckley* (1816) 2 Price 210 (the decisive case). Wood B. dissented on the grounds that the jurisdiction would be obviously equitable and quite easily practicable.

[85] *Doe d. Mayhew* v. *Asby* (1839) 10 Ad. & El. 72.

[86] *Doe d. Muston* v. *Gladwin* (1845) 6 Q.B. 953.

[87] Law of Property Amendment and Trustees Relief Act 1859, ss 4–9.

[88] *Woodfall's Landlord and Tenant* (by Harrison, 1831), 256; 9th edn, 367; *Doe d. Davis* v. *Elsam* (1828) Mood. & M. 189; *Perry* v. *Davis* (1858) 3 C.B. N.S. 769; *Croft* v. *Lumley* (1858) 6 H.L.C. 672.

[89] See e.g. *Doe d. Lloyd* v. *Ingleby* (1846) 15 M. & W. 465, Parke B. diss.; *Doe d. Wyndham* v. *Carew* (1841) 2 Q.B. 317.

[90] *Rede* v. *Farr* (1817) 6 M. & S. 121; *Doe d. Bryan* v. *Bancks* (1821) 4 B. & Ald. 664 (pointing out that landlords would sometimes benefit from this interpretation); *Jones* v. *Carter* (1846) 15 M. & W. 718 (Parke B.: 'perfectly well settled'); *Davenport* v. *The Queen* (1877) 3 App Cas 115. Wigram VC, an

overt election to terminate the lease, hence reducing surprise. Most importantly, it preserved the twin rules that a breach might be waived and that waiver was irrevocable.[91] Presumably it was those rules that landlords were trying to negate when they used the language of voidness and automatic termination, perhaps also the remnant equitable jurisdiction to relieve. However, judges had developed 'implied waiver' as an important common law device to limit the rigour of forfeiture clauses, finding an irrevocable waiver in such acts as accepting rent after learning of a breach, and they were unwilling to see it outflanked.[92] In this instance, therefore, Patteson J.'s objective of providing parties with 'certainty in their mutual relations' required departure from ordinary principles of interpretation and some disciplining of landlords' discretion.

According the parties freedom of contract did not entail approving of how they commonly exercised it. Parties signing an agreement for a lease seem often to have said merely that it was to contain the 'usual' covenants, and if subsequently they disagreed over what those should be the dispute would end up in Chancery in a suit for specific performance. It was not altogether an easy question, because Lord Eldon had introduced a normative element; 'usual', he held, meant 'usual and proper'.[93] Generally, though perhaps with less clarity in the mid-century, judges took a narrow view and declined to force upon tenants covenants against assigning without licence or permitting re-entry for all breaches.[94] It was in this context that in 1875 James LJ denounced general rights of re-entry as most odious stipulations, offensive and oppressive beyond measure.[95] He thought rights of re-entry conditioned only upon non-payment of rent acceptable, because Chancery had a jurisdiction to relieve from them. Almost immediately bills were introduced into Parliament to enable Chancery to relieve in all cases, if it saw fit.[96] They stalled in the Lords but the idea was then taken up and extended by the Law Society, then

exponent of 'ordinary' interpretation, was clearly unhappy about this convention: *Bowse* v. *Colby* (1841) 1 Hare 109; see also the differences of opinion in *Grey* v. *Friar* (1854) 4 H.L.C. 565.

[91] *Arnsby* v. *Woodward* (1827) 6 B. & C. 519; *Roberts* v. *Davey* (1833) 4 B. & Ald. 664, and the cases cited in the previous note.

[92] T. Platt, *A Treatise on the Law of Leases* (1847), ii 468–74; *Woodfall's Landlord and Tenant* (12th edn, 1881), 298–302. Conventionally, though still riskily, purchasers of leases accepted a recent rental receipt as evidence that there were no outstanding breaches of covenant.

[93] *Church* v. *Brown* (1808) 15 Ves. 258.

[94] *Blakesley* v. *Whieldon* (1841) 1 Hare 176; *Buckland* v. *Papillon* (1866) 1 Eq 477; *Hodgkinson* v. *Crowe* (1875) 10 Ch App 622; *Hampshire* v. *Wickens* (1878) 7 Ch D 555; Davidson, *Precedents*, v, 47–50 (3rd edn, 1873); contrast *Bennett* v. *Womack* (1828) 7 B. & C. 627 and *Haines* v. *Burnett* (1859) 27 Beav. 500, which are less normative and more empirical.

[95] *Hodgkinson* v. *Crowe* (1875) 10 Ch App 622.

[96] Forfeiture Bills, *PP* 1876 (259), ii, 379; 1877 (60), ii, 275; *PD* 1876 (s3) 231: 963–4.

by the leadership of both parties, and enacted in 1881.[97] Henceforward landlords intending to forfeit a lease for breach of covenant must first give the tenant notice and an opportunity to remedy the breach, and courts now had a greatly extended jurisdiction to relieve against forfeitures they regarded as unfair. These provisions could not be curtailed by contract.

This was a sudden and significant shift of emphasis. It generated some difficult technical questions, some of which needed addressing by further legislation, but two key holdings by courts maximized protection for tenants.[98] The first was that service of a valid notice was a prerequisite to forfeiture, judges to be the arbiters of what was valid, and the second was that courts had a free discretion to award relief, which they were not to confine by self-made rules.[99] It was a jurisdiction to be exercised generously. The result was similar to the progressive tightening of distress that began at the same time and to the changes introduced for agricultural tenants. Taken together, the law of the 1880s was markedly different from that of even a decade earlier.

Covenants

It was central to the practical operation of leases that the covenants they contained should operate for the full duration of the lease and not just between the original parties. Courts of equity tended to withdraw from direct enforcement; they would not order performance of building or repair covenants, for example, nor husbandry covenants in agricultural leases, but so long as landlords reserved a right to re-enter for breach they had the remedy in their own hands.[100] It was critical, then, that covenants should 'run'. This was old law. The books conventionally based their analysis on *Spencer's case* (1583) and a statute of Henry VIII.[101] Covenants were either collateral, in which case they bound only the original parties to the lease, or they concerned the land, in which case they would bind the parties' successors too.

---

[97] *Woodfall's Landlord and Tenant* (12th edn, 1881), 304n; Leases Bills, *PP* 1880 (30, 177), iv, 23, 27; 1881 (108), iii, 121; Conveyancing and Law of Property Act 1881, s 14.

[98] Conveyancing Act 1892; *Woodfall's Landlord and Tenant* (19th edn, 1912), 385–93.

[99] *Horsey Estate* v. *Steiger* [1899] 2 QB 79; *Hyman* v. *Rose* [1912] AC 623; cf. *Ewart* v. *Fryer* [1901] 1 Ch 499 (aff'd [1902] AC 187). See too *re Anderton and Milner's Contract* (1890) 45 Ch D 476 and *re Lander and Bagley's Contract* [1892] 3 Ch 41, holding that the new jurisdiction did not allow landlords to claim that general rights of re-entry were any more proper than they were before.

[100] Daniell, *Treatise on the Practice of the High Court of Chancery* (1841), iii, 341; *Musgrave* v. *Horner* (1874) 31 LT 632.

[101] (1583) 5 Co. Rep. 16a; 32 Hen. VIII c. 34; A. W. B. Simpson, *A History of the Land Law* (Oxford, revised edn, 1966), 255–6.

The difference was one of substance and subject-matter. Its application could be difficult at the margins, and the Real Property Commissioners would like to have got rid of it.[102] It was 'obviously just', they said, that successors should take the land on the same terms that it had been granted. There would be no hardship, because successors could always ask to inspect the documents. Nothing came of this directly, but there is a clear parallel with the resurgence of equitable jurisdiction in the mid-century through an expanded law of notice. So far as common law was concerned, however, the old test remained, and even without reform it was well established by 1820 that landlords could prohibit assignment without their prior consent and, subject to a heavily contested borderline, could control the use tenants and their successors made of the land.

These covenants ran to successors who had the same estate in the land as the original landlord or the original tenant had had, constituting the common law relationship of privity of estate. There were some blemishes to this formal legal structure, but even so it could be presented in 1820 as having a pleasing geometry.[103] In particular, in 1779 Lord Mansfield had pronounced that although there had once been great doubts it was now settled that sub-tenants were not liable to the landlord on the tenant's covenants, here the covenant to pay rent—there was no privity of estate.[104] But in the following year his court intruded a functional test: a tenant's assignee (with privity of estate) should not be liable if the assignment were by way of mortgage and the assignee had not taken possession.[105] That rule was necessary, he said, to protect lenders who funded house-building by taking the building lease as security. True, they could follow the usual practice of taking a sub-lease for the term less a day, but that was a difference lacking substance. In 1819, however, the judges of all the common law courts, meeting solemnly in Serjeants' Inn to hear a case of such importance, rejected this exception outright and restored the law's formal symmetry.[106] It was completed by the ruling in 1835 that even at common law a tenant by assignment who assigned on to another

---

[102] *RC on Real Property*, 3rd Report, 366–71.

[103] Covenants that touched and concerned the land were divided into two sub-classes, one of which ran even though assignees were not stipulated in the lease and the other of which did not. Nobody thought that sensible: see e.g. Bythewood and Jarman, *Precedents* (1831), iv, 386; T. Platt, *A Practical Treatise on the Law of Covenants* (1829), 471–2, 480. Simpson's difficulty (*History of Land Law*, 255–6), that conditions attached to the reversion were not severable, did not apply to covenants, so in practice was not a problem in the nineteenth century: see *Smith's Leading Cases* (1837), i, 28.

[104] *Holford* v. *Hatch* (1779) 1 Doug. 183.

[105] *Eaton* v. *Jaques* (1780) 2 Doug. 435.

[106] *Williams* v. *Bosanquet* (1819) 1 Brod. & Bing. 238; *Bythewood's Precedents* (by Stewart), v, 385n.

did not free himself from 'vested liabilities', only from future performance of the obligations contained in the lease.[107]

Reality was messier. Not all leases were granted by estate owners; those that were granted by power holders might need careful wording to ensure that the covenants would attach to an appropriate reversion.[108] That was an inconvenience, but can be treated as one of the management costs of putting land into settlement. It could always be met by appropriate drafting. Much more serious were the difficulties caused by landowners who mortgaged their land. Suppose two cases. In the first a landowner mortgages, then he leases, then the tenant sells the lease. In the second the landowner leases, then he mortgages, then he dies leaving his land by will, or perhaps he sells his land subject to the mortgage. It would be uncontroversial in the first case to say that the lease does not bind the mortgagee, but the effect of making liability on covenants depend on privity of estate was far more threatening. Mortgages usually took the form of an out-and-out transfer of the estate, so at the time of the lease the supposed landowner did not have an estate to which the covenants could attach. In the second case the landowner did have an estate at the beginning, but his devisee or purchaser does not now: the mortgagee has it. In neither case would covenants run to the person who, functionally, is the successor. The same was true of owners who had their newly purchased land conveyed to trustees to bar dower, a practice common before reforms initiated by the Real Property Commissioners did away with the need. Sugden found this truly alarming, because no manipulation of words would get over the objection, and his opinion was endorsed by Thomas Platt in his treatise on covenants in 1829.[109]

The solution had roots as venerable as *Spencer's case* itself, though it did not emerge (with its ready-made history) until the 1840s, to be finally confirmed in 1860.[110] It was the very antithesis of formal reasoning. In each of the cases outlined above the parties and their successors were simply estopped from denying the existence of the requisite estate. Judicially its proponent was the perhaps unlikely figure of Parke B., though the argument was presented in greatest detail

---

[107] *Harley* v. *King* (1835) 2 Cr. M. & R. 18. Previously recourse to equity had been necessary: Platt, *Covenants*, 495.

[108] Platt, *Covenants*, 461–2.

[109] Sugden, *Vendors and Purchasers* (6th edn, 1822), 544–5; Platt, *Covenants*, 462–3.

[110] *Cuthbertson* v. *Irving* (1859) 4 H. & N. 742, aff'd (1860) 6 H. & N. 135. Until then it was blocked by the conventional understanding of *Noke* v. *Awder* (1596) Cro. Eliz. 436 and *Whitton* v. *Peacock* (1835) 2 Bing. N.C. 411: Platt, *Leases*, i, 60–1, *Smith's Leading Cases* (1837), i, 38. See also *Mayor etc of Carlisle* v. *Blamire* (1807) 8 East 487.

as commentary in *Smith's Leading Cases*.[111] Its authors struggled a little with the morality:

An estoppel does not necessarily involve a falsehood. On the contrary, facts are ascertained through the medium of estoppel without reference to the question whether really true or false; and it would be sheer fallacy to assume, that a fact established by estoppel has *therefore* no real existence. For judicial purposes it ought to be dealt with as if it really existed.[112]

There was just enough formal veneer to keep the pretence credible: if at the time of taking the lease the tenant knew the landlord had no estate estoppel was not available. That might be one reason for the contractual term so common on grants or sales of leases, that the prospective tenant or purchaser must not ask for proof of the freehold title.

Privity of estate by estoppel was a solution from within common law; common law's own equity, as it were. Chancery judges generally regarded landlord and tenant as a common law relation; they would aid the common law but they would not extend it. For example if a tenant by assignment assigned the lease over to some impoverished pauper simply to be rid of future liability (say as the fag-end of the tenancy approached and brought repairing obligations uncomfortably close), Chancery would not intervene to stop him save in the rarest case of a purely fictitious assignment.[113] Indeed in 1839 Lord Cottenham held executors of a tenant by assignment personally liable for losses on a lease that they could, and should, have avoided by assigning on to a man of straw.[114] However, despite this insistence that the relation was solely legal, in the 1820s equity seems not always to have been following the law. The difficult case is *Lucas* v. *Comerford* in 1790, where a landlord sought to enforce a rebuilding covenant against the tenant's equitable assignee, that is against someone who in law did not have the lease, merely an agreement with the tenant that equity would regard as a contract for its acquisition.[115] Lord Thurlow required the assignee to take a legal lease at the landlord's behest so as to make him liable on it at law. His ruling was all the more

---

[111] *Gouldsworth* v. *Knights* (1843) 11 M. & W. 337; *Sturgeon* v. *Wingfield* (1846) 15 M. & W. 224; *Smith's Leading Cases* (3rd edn, 1849), i, 38a–g.

[112] *Smith's Leading Cases* (3rd edn, by H. S. Keating and J. S. Willes, 1849), i, 38b–c.

[113] *Wilkins* v. *Fry* (1816) 1 Mer. 244; *Onslow* v. *Corrie* (1817) 2 Madd. 330; *Fagg* v. *Dobie* (1838) 3 Y. & C. Ex. 96; cf. *Taylor* v. *Shum* (1797) 1 Bos. & P. 23. There may sometimes have been a functional justification, because such an assignment was sometimes the only way assignees in bankruptcy could avoid indefinite liability on their debtor's covenant to pay rent: B. Montagu and S. Ayrton, *The Law and Practice in Bankruptcy* (1837), i, 234–6; R. H. Eden, Baron Henley, *A Digest of Bankrupt Law* (2nd edn, 1832), 237–41.

[114] *Rowley* v. *Adams* (1839) 4 My. & Cr. 534.

[115] (1790) 3 Bro. C.C. 166.

forceful for the equitable assignment having been merely a mortgage by deposit of documents. The books noted the decision without criticism, but neither they nor the case law seem to have addressed the proposition necessarily entailed, that by this route all equitable assignees were liable to the landlord on all the covenants in the lease.[116] In the absence of a detailed study it is difficult to know how far the implications were taken, but *Lucas* v. *Comerford* was still being followed in the mid-1830s.[117]

Shortly afterwards, however, Shadwell VC changed his mind.[118] It was perplexing, he said, that someone extraneous to a contract could insist upon its specific performance. Very quickly Lord Thurlow's ruling was abandoned, first for mortgages by deposit, then for outright equitable assignments.[119] Romilly MR held out against that latter step, arguing that an equitable assignee who had entered and enjoyed the land should therefore shoulder the burdens.[120] But the orthodoxy of the 1850s was formal, not functional. Liability was relational, so possession was irrelevant. Equitable assignments were a single category, with no distinction between those that were outright and those that were mortgages. Contracts to assign were conceptually quite different from a conveyance at law.

Judges involved in this revision stressed that landlord and tenant should remain a legal, not equitable, relationship.[121] It was the final stage of a disavowal of equitable jurisdiction traceable back into the 1790s. That unravelled in the 1880s, as has been shown, when equity judges took willingly to the new statutory power to relieve against forfeiture, turning the clock back 150 years.[122] More paradoxically, however, just as they were abandoning *Lucas* v. *Comerford* equity judges were developing a new tool that would make major inroads into the formal symmetry of the common law. It was acceptable, it seems, because it had its own independent moral spring that just coincidentally reshaped relationships that Chancery had been busy ceding to common law. This was the law of notice,

---

[116] Platt, *Covenants*, 483 (contrast his view in 1847 that it was 'truly alarming': *Leases*, i 424); *Woodfall's Landlord and Tenant* (1831), 196. The cases that came closest involved claims by an original tenant suing an equitable assignee to recover money the original tenant had had to pay to the landlord in respect of the assignee's breaches. Each of them assumes that the original tenant has had to discharge a liability primarily belonging to the assignee, though each could instead have rested the claim on an express or implied promise by the assignee to the tenant to observe the covenants: *Close* v. *Wilberforce* (1838) 1 Beav. 112; *Willson* v. *Leonard* (1840) 3 Beav. 350; *Sanders* v. *Benson* (1841) 4 Beav. 350.

[117] *Flight* v. *Bentley* (1835) 7 Sim. 149; *Jenkins* v. *Portman* (1836) 1 Keen 435.

[118] *Moores* v. *Choat* (1839) 8 Sim. 508.

[119] *Robinson* v. *Rosher* (1841) 1 Y. & C.Ch.Cas. 7; *Moore* v. *Greg* (1848) 2 Ph. 717; *Walters* v. *Northern Coal Mining Co* (1855) 5 De G. M. & G. 629; *Cox* v. *Bishop* (1857) 8 De G. M. & G. 815.

[120] *Cox* v. *Bishop* (1856) 26 LJ Ch 390n.

[121] *Moore* v. *Greg* (1848) 2 Ph. 717; *Walters* v. *Northern Coal Mining Co* (1855) 5 De G. M. & G. 629.

[122] 4 Geo. II c. 28.

which blossomed after *Tulk* v. *Moxhay* in 1848. It, and its impact on tenants, will be described in section 3, below.

2. MORTGAGES

Well before the start of our period, mortgages had become the conventional form of secured borrowing by landowners and were often used by urban house owners too.[123] They had become respectable. They were common investments for trustees. A power to invest in mortgages of freeholds was a conventional element in marriage settlements even in the eyes of otherwise cautious Chancery judges, though statutory powers became available only in 1860.[124] Any property could be mortgaged, so mortgage law was not specific to land, though at the start of our period land was regarded as the paradigm.[125] There is an argument that by the end it was not, and that the imperatives of commercial property dictated at least part of its shape.[126] Similarly, an increasing conception of mortgages as just another sort of contract informs many of the changes after the repeal of the usury laws in 1854, though this is less of a novelty than is sometimes thought. Significant changes before then were contractually based too.

Before 1854 there was also a concern to differentiate mortgages from other devices with similar function but different form, sometimes regarded as rather less respectable. Awareness of their use and relationship with mortgages is important to a full appreciation of secured lending. This chapter considers those forms and what may be called the internal law of mortgages, with land as its major focus. Chattel mortgages by bill of sale and company borrowing by debentures or debenture stock are discussed elsewhere in this volume, though the latter is important to the final section of this chapter and is discussed there too.[127]

Mortgages had an external face too, the relation between a mortgagee and a purchaser or subsequent mortgagee. Suppression of legal mortgages was a risk to purchasers sometimes to subsequent mortgagees—that was one concern that

---

[123] D. Cannadine, 'Aristocratic Indebtedness in the Nineteenth century: The Case Re-opened' (1977) 30 *Econ. Hist. Rev.* 624–50 at 627–8; R. J. Morris, *Men, Women and Property in England, 1780–1870* (Cambridge, 2005).

[124] *Sampayo* v. *Gould* (1842) 12 Sim. 426; see pp. 283, 285, below.

[125] J. J. Powell, *A Treatise on the Law of Mortgages* (1785, 6 edns to 1826) set the initial form. He said a little about mortgages of ships and public stock. Only with the 2nd edn of W. R. Fisher, *The Law of Mortgage* in 1868 was there a comprehensive text about the proprietary incidents of secured lending.

[126] D. Sugarman and R. Warrington, 'Land Law, Citizenship, and the Invention of Englishness', in J. Brewer and S. Staves (eds), *Early Modern Conceptions of Property* (1995), 111–43.

[127] See pp. 155–8, above; 636–8, below.

led the Real Property Commissioners to propose that all deeds be registered.[128] Similarly the superiority equity accorded to legal estates over equitable disrupted pure temporal priority of competing mortgages and generated litigation over the niceties of the law of notice. It was common for reformers to seek to replace that complexity with an ordered registration system.

Further, apparent temporal priority could be upset by the doctrines of consolidation and tacking. The first, based upon old equitable principle, allowed a mortgagee who had been repaid to retain the land as additional security for some other mortgage he had made to the same borrower but which was still outstanding. That would prejudice a second mortgagee of the first land who had not known about that apparently unrelated mortgage. The second principle, tacking, was based upon the superiority equity accorded to legal estates. It permitted (say) a third mortgagee, who at the time of making the loan had not known about the second, to buy up the legal interest of the first and thereby leapfrog the second. Alternatively it allowed a first (legal) mortgagee who had made a further loan to the mortgagor to squeeze out intermediate secured lenders, provided, again, that the first had had no notice at the time of the additional loan. Reduction of these rules to something simpler and less haphazard was a primary objective of advocates of registration in its various forms, correspondingly a challenge to reformers who sought to mimic the results of registered conveyancing without the reliance on officialdom that registration entailed. That theme will be considered more in Chapter V.

Modernizing Mortgages: Form and Substance from the Late Eighteenth Century

Two eighteenth-century inventions shaped mortgage practice in the nineteenth. The first owed nothing to the usual developmental cycle of professional experiment and judicial response. Instead, out of nowhere, so it seemed to later lawyers, Lord Loughborough and Ashhurst J., sitting as Lords Commissioners, decided that a mere deposit of title deeds with a lender as security could create an equitable mortgage, even when unaccompanied by any writing.[129] This startling novelty was quickly confirmed by Lord Thurlow.[130]

---

[128] See pp. 64–6, above.

[129] *Russel* v. *Russel* (1783) 1 Bro. C.C. 269. Whether the parties' purpose was to create a security was a jury question on which there was much litigation.

[130] Thurlow's decisions in *Featherstone* v. *Fenwick* (1784) and *Hurford* (or *Harford*) v. *Carpenter* (1785) were known in print only through a note to *Russel* v. *Russel*: see *Ex p Mountfort* (1808) 14 Ves. 606.

To critics such casual informality was an outrageous flouting of the Statute of Frauds and a pernicious evasion of the stamp duty that was properly leviable on written transactions concerning land.[131] All it took to satisfy the Act was two lines of writing, complained Richards CB.[132] The bar's considerable surprise at the original decision had been justified by every subsequent decision upon the point, said Lord Eldon, as he found himself reluctantly obliged by precedent to apply and sometimes even extend a development he would himself not have countenanced.[133] After a quick canvass of reputable bankers and merchants in London the Real Property Commissioners persuaded themselves that nothing of substance would be lost by its abolition, a necessary consequence, they thought, of their proposals for deeds registration.[134]

By the 1830s, however, the practice was well established.[135] The loans in some of the early cases may have been made in circumstances of urgency, secrecy, and confusion, as bankers stepped in to prevent someone's financial collapse. Latterly, however, more routine justifications had developed for these 'bankers' mortgages', as they were sometimes known, that they facilitated short-term credit to farmers and generally reduced transaction costs.[136] There were 'vast numbers' of these transactions, said the conveyancer J. H. Christie, 'in which the borrower is accommodated at little expense, and in which the lender fancies himself secure'.[137] Nor was any substantive principle of mortgage law threatened, because in equitable theory the deposit operated as an unwritten, partly-performed contract for a legal mortgage—so the parties could be deemed to have intended the standard incidents. It is not even clear how much the practice added to the risks run by subsequent lenders, because in an unregistered system taking possession of the

---

[131] For lawyers' disapproval, see R. H. Coote, *A Treatise on the Law of Mortgages* (1821) 206; *RC on Real Property*, 1st Report, PP 1829 (263), x, 1, 530 (J. Tyrrell, being pp. 234–6 of his *Suggestions*). Question 100 of the Real Property Commissioners' questionnaire about deeds registration asked whether equitable mortgages by deposit should lose priority once deeds became registered; of the 40 or so respondents giving a clear answer about a dozen wanted them abolished altogether, a further half-dozen replied that they would abolish themselves in a registered world, and a further 20 agreed with the commissioners that they should lose priority to any registered transaction: 2nd Report, *PP* 1830 (575), xi, 1, App. Several carefully distinguished equitable mortgages with a written memorandum (which they would like to see registered) from those without any accompanying writing.

[132] *Casberd* v. *A.-G.* (1819) 6 Price 411, 459.

[133] *Ex p Mountfort* (1808) 14 Ves. 606, a sentiment all judges at this time shared. For the cases to 1819 see the note to *Ex p Coming* (1803) 9 Ves. 115, 117. *Hiern* v. *Mill* (1806) 13 Ves. 114 (purchaser of the legal estate with notice bound by such a mortgage) and *Casberd* v. *A.-G.* (1819) 6 Price 411 (such a mortgagee takes priority over crown debts) were particularly important.

[134] *RC on Real Property*, 2nd Report, 111.

[135] For usage see responses of R. Radford, J. H. Christie, and T. Farrer to the Real Property Commissioners' questionnaire: 2nd Report, 253, 387, 409.

[136] Anderson, *Lawyers and the Making of English Land Law 1832–1940* (Oxford, 1992), 46.

[137] *RC on Real Property*, 2nd Report, 498.

title deeds gave the clearest warning possible to subsequent would-be lenders of the risk they would run. So rather than becoming an obvious and unmourned casualty of progress, bankers' mortgages persisted as an obstacle to law reformers through to the end of our period, particularly to proponents of registration.[138]

The second innovation was intellectually ambitious, obvious, even inevitable, though it appeared with hindsight. This was the mortgage with a power of sale attached. It was crafted at the end of the eighteenth century to meet what the conveyancer and writer Charles Barton described as the 'very desirable object of enabling a lender to regain his principal without having to suffer the delay and inconvenience of a foreclosure decree'.[139] During the French war money was tight, opportunities for profit were many, and leaving money out on mortgage was correspondingly short-sighted, so at least thought the witnesses to a select committee in 1818 bent on repealing the usury laws.[140] Borrowers who could neither repay nor refinance could be foreclosed, but Chancery, the witnesses said, indulged them with generous extensions of time (though, as Sir Samuel Romilly added, during that time the lender might have the debtor locked up on his bond to repay). How much better not to have to trouble the court.

Around 1800, however, neither Barton nor John Joseph Powell, author of the major text on mortgages, thought it would work.[141] The maxim 'once a mortgage always a mortgage' seemed to them to prohibit a mortgagor from signing away his equity of redemption. Therefore, they reasoned, a sale by the mortgagee must be just a sale of the secured loan, leaving the mortgagor still with the power to redeem. Instead Barton suggested an elaborate contingent trust for sale, which he cautiously claimed might meet the need by avoiding the initial characterization: it was never a mortgage.

Even as Barton wrote, however, Lord Eldon was validating the simpler method, though his decision went unreported until Grant MR followed it in 1811.[142] The decisions seem to have been easy; no detailed reasoning is reported for either, nor for the cases that soon followed them.[143] Yet the result was striking, not just for bypassing the ancient process of foreclosure, but for the intellectual nicety

---

[138] Anderson, *Lawyers*, 197–9, 203, 259, 295.

[139] C. Barton, *Elements of Conveyancing* (1803), iii, 349.

[140] *SC on Usury Laws*, Report, PP 1818 (376), vi, 139, 147 (Frere), 149 (Romilly), 177 (Preston), 193 and 196 (Kaye).

[141] Barton, *Elements*, iii, 338, 345–9; Powell, *Mortgages* (4th edn, 1799), i, 13–19 (the possibility, but not the doubt, first appears in his 3rd edn, 1791, 12).

[142] *Clay* v. *Sharpe* (1802) (usually cited from Sugden, *Vendors and Purchasers* (e.g. 4th edn, 1813, App. 13); *Corder* v. *Morgan* (1811) 18 Ves. 344.

[143] Sugden *Vendors and Purchasers* (9th edn), ii, 189. The technical point litigated seems usually to have been whether a purchaser was safe taking title from the mortgagee without the mortgagor's concurrence.

involved. The power itself was proprietary—it had to be if it were to free a purchaser from the mortgagor's equity of redemption. But the restriction on its exercise that required the mortgagor to concur in the conveyance was held by Grant MR to be merely contractual, hence not one on which a purchaser could insist. One commentator anticipated great consequential changes to the law if, as he hoped and predicted, the new form ousted the old.[144]

Twenty years later the mortgage with power of sale was the usual form.[145] The safer and more marketable the security, wrote Charles Davidson, the greater the facility for borrowing, the greater the advantage to lenders and borrowers alike.[146] Because the power worked more efficiently if the mortgagee already had the full legal estate it also became usual for mortgagees of freeholds to take a transfer of the estate as the security, rather than the long term of years that had previously been common.[147] Text writers had abandoned their experiments with trusts for sale.[148] They thought it unclear whether such hybrids entitled mortgagors to foreclose or to tack, doubts that subsequent case law amply confirmed.[149] They worried that trustees might owe duties of even-handedness unwelcome to mortgagors, though this time the later case law showed that judges were not keen to visit on trustees in this context all the fiduciary restrictions attaching to regular family trustees.[150] And they found it cumbrous to have to provide in mortgage deeds for such matters as the replacement of trustees. Intermediate forms constituting the mortgagee a trustee for sale were discouraged by Lord Eldon, who found the conflict of interest unpalatable.[151] The simplest version worked best.

A conception so bold needed considerable technical development. When considering the uncertainty there was over mortgagees' powers during the mid-century, the novelty of this form of mortgage needs to be borne in mind. 'The

[144] T. Coventry, *Mortgage Precedents* (1826), 150–4n; Coventry had produced the 5th edn of Powell's text (1822).

[145] Bythewood and Jarman, *Precedents* (1832), v, 232; *Martin's Practice* (by Davidson) (1840), i, 478–9n.

[146] Davidson, *Precedents*, ii, 533 (2nd edn, 1858).

[147] Bythewood and Jarman, *Precedents*, v, 232 (not suggesting that this was the only reason for the shift).

[148] Coventry, *Mortgage Precedents*, 153–4n, 176–215; Bythewood (Stewart edn), *Precedents*, v, 301n; Bythewood and Jarman, *Precedents*, v, 233–5; Davidson, *Precedents*, ii, 551 (2nd edn, 1858).

[149] *Ex p Pettit* (1825) 2 Glyn & J. 47; *Sampson v. Pattison* (1842) 1 Hare 533; *Jenkin v. Row* (1851) 5 De G. & Sm. 107; *re Underwood* (1857) 3 K. & J. 745; *Scweitzer v. Mayhew* (1862) 31 Beav. 37. 'Tacking' enabled a mortgagee whose first loan had been paid off to retain his security and his original priority so long as subsequent loans he had made secured on the same property remained outstanding. This applied even though the mortgagor had granted other persons mortgages on that property in between. For its importance see Anderson, *Lawyers*, 147.

[150] *Anon* (1821) 6 Madd. 10; *A.-G. v. Hardy* (1851) 1 Sim. (N.S.) 338; *Kirkwood v. Thompson* (1865) 2 H. & M. 392, aff'd 2 De G. J. & Sm. 613.

[151] *Roberts v. Bozon* (1825) 3 LJ Ch 113; Coventry, *Mortgage Precedents*, 152–3n.

skill of successive generations of conveyancers,' wrote Charles Davidson, 'has been tasked to frame such a power as will give the greatest possibility for realising the mortgage debt consistently with proper protection of the mortgagor against surprise and hardship.'[152] Broadly, three aspects needed close attention.

First the relation between mortgagor and mortgagee had to be addressed: the circumstances in which the power could be exercised, the period of notice required, how the sale could be conducted. Secondly, purchasers had to be immunized from the mortgagee's breach of those conditions (or any others), such that they could be confident of getting good title and stopped from raising difficulties after they had agreed to buy. Thirdly, the power had to be got to devolve to the right person if the mortgagee should die, since on an intestacy the debt would go to the personal representative (who should have the power) but the security to the heir (who should not). At this time the power was not seen as 'intrinsic' to the mortgage; it was an additional equitable property of rather uncertain quality but essentially contractual in content.[153] According to Davidson the shift from seeing powers as adjuncts to seeing them as incidents began with Cranworth's Act in 1860, which gave all mortgagees a statutory power of sale save so far as it was excluded by their mortgage deed.[154] That was an important conceptual simplification, but its impact was delayed because the elite conveyancers rejected Cranworth's power of sale as inferior to what by then had become the standard model.[155] So express powers of sale continued to be used until the Conveyancing Act 1881 made a much better job of realigning the law with practice.[156]

Although the mortgage with power of sale became the usual form in the 1840s, for a further decade some more cautious judges declined to hold that fiduciary mortgagors—trustees, say, or executors—were entitled to confer a power of sale upon their mortgagee unless expressly authorized by their settlor or testator.[157] The fear, present from the beginning, was that mortgagees would not strive to achieve the best price, a risk, therefore, that only beneficial owners should be

---

[152] Davidson, *Precedents* (2nd edn), ii, 555.

[153] For rather different explanations, see *Hind* v. *Poole* (1854) 1 K. & J. 383 (Page Wood VC) and *Colson* v. *Williams* (1889) 58 LJ Ch 539 (Kekewich J.).

[154] Trustees and Mortgagees Act 1860, ss 11–24; Davidson, *Precedents*, ii, 755 (3rd edn, 1869). For the significance of the conceptual shift, see pp. 89–92, above.

[155] Davidson, *Precedents* (3rd edn), ii, 638; Davidson, *Concise Precedents* (10th edn, 1877), 9; Prideaux, *Precedents* (8th edn, 1876), 488–9; Dart, *Vendors and Purchasers* (5th edn), i, 55.

[156] Conveyancing Act 1881, ss 19–21 (amended by Conveyancing Act 1911, s 19); Davidson, *Concise Precedents* (12th edn, 1882), 58; Prideaux, *Precedents* (14th edn, 1889), 489, 538.

[157] *Sanders* v. *Richards* (1846) 2 Coll. 568; *Clarke* v. *Royal Panopticon* (1854) 4 Drew. 26. Contrast Romilly MR (*Russell* v. *Plaice* (1854) 18 Beav. 21; *Bridges* v. *Longman* (1857) 24 Beav. 27), whose view prevailed after Cranworth's Act created a statutory power of sale: *re Chawner's Will* (1869) LR 8 Eq 569; *Earl Vane* v. *Rigden* (1870) 5 Ch App 663.

free to choose.[158] As Thomas Jarman wrote, optimistically, it is now 'not only necessary for a mortgagee to take care that he lends to a solvent and honourable man, but it is equally incumbent on a mortgagor, to satisfy himself that he intrusts the power over his estate to a person who will not exercise it in a manner oppressive and detrimental to him...'.[159]

Yet if equity judges had truly found such powers of sale objectionable they could easily have used Powell and Barton's reasoning to invalidate them. The conceptual argument that powers of sale impermissibly changed the nature of a mortgage would not have been out of line with other uses of the maxim 'once a mortgage always (and only) a mortgage' or the general principle against clogs on the equity of redemption. Options to purchase were, and still are, clogs on the equity.[160] Instead judges saw them as manifestations of contract.

There were difficulties here. Aspects of the exercise of the power of sale attracted judicial scrutiny, which needed a justification. If it were that the mortgagee was trustee of the power of sale much of the utility of an autonomous power would be lost. Some things were clear: after sale the mortgagee held any surplus on trust; mortgagees could not sell to themselves. Both Lord Eldon and Lord Cottenham based the latter rule on trusteeship of the power.[161] Yet neither espoused a general principle that mortgagees were trustees.[162] Lord St. Leonards based the rule on the principle that contracts are by definition bilateral: *nobody* can sell to himself, adding, however, that the rule was necessary to protect holders of beneficial interests.[163] This hesitancy over the basis of rules pervades the mid-century decisions about mortgagees' powers generally, even when the rules themselves were well accepted.[164] The extent to which mortgagees should be treated as trustees was quite unsettled, with little obvious pattern to the various judicial pronouncements.

In the context of powers of sale, however, the two sub-rules noted above were not generalized into an onerous standard. In 1846 Knight Bruce VC found fault

---

[158] Coventry, *Mortgage Precedents*, 151–2n.

[159] Bythewood and Jarman, *Precedents*, v, 234.

[160] *Jones* v. *Morgan* [2001] EWCA Civ 995.

[161] *Downes* v. *Grazebrook* (1817) 3 Mer. 200; *re Bloye's Trust* (1849) 1 Mac. & G. 488.

[162] *Cholmondeley* v. *Clinton* (1821) 4 Bli. P.C. 1; *Knight* v. *Marjoribanks* (1849) 2 Mac. & G. 10.

[163] *Lewis* v. *Hillman* (1852) 3 H.L.C. 607 (on appeal from *re Bloye's Trust*); Sugden, *Vendors and Purchasers* (10th edn, 1839), iii, 227–9.

[164] e.g. W. W. Kerr, *A Treatise on the Law of Fraud and Mistake* (1868), 113n presents *Knight* v. *Marjoribanks* (1849) 2 Mac. & G. 10 and *Dobson* v. *Land* (1850) 8 Hare 220, which required relatively gross misconduct before a court would intervene, as the dominant rule, with a 'but see' for *Hickes* v. *Cooke* (1816) 4 Dow P.C. 16; *Downes* v. *Grazebrook* (1817) 3 Mer. 200; *re Bloye's Trust* (1849) 1 Mac. & G. 488; *Robertson* v. *Norris* (1858) 4 Jur. (N.S.) 155; and *Ford* v. *Olden* (1867) LR 3 Eq 461, which asserted more ready intervention. He could have added *Matthison* v. *Clarke* (1854) 3 Drew. 3 to the 'but sees'.

with the harshness of a power to sell without notice, the use of depreciatory terms of sale, the concealment of the true value of the property sold, and the way in which the mortgagee overrode objections from the mortgagor; these together, he reasoned, justified setting aside a sale on grounds of oppression.[165] On appeal, however, Lord Cottenham took quite a different view, that since the power was contractual mere harshness of exercise was not justiciable; only fraud would justify intervention.[166] With only occasional departures, that remained the standard throughout our period.[167]

The most important exception came from Stuart VC, who seems generally to have favoured comparing mortgagees to trustees and to have adopted a broad view of equity's jurisdiction to reform oppressive bargains.[168] His ruling in 1858 (on extreme and unusual facts) that a collateral motive for exercising the power of sale vitiated it without more was adopted uncritically by Davidson and the two major texts, despite the easy availability of two other grounds on which to base the decision.[169] Even after Jessel MR subjected Stuart to vigorous assault for misinterpreting Eldon's cases, one of the texts signalled its reservations about departing from his principle, and the other continued just as before, despite a definitive ruling from the Court of Appeal in 1896 that mortgagees were not trustees and never had been.[170] Clearly, therefore, there was continuing ambivalence about the circumstances in which a mortgagee's sale could be reopened, but equally clearly the possibility was remote enough not to detract from the general utility of the new-style mortgage with power of sale.

A contractual power to sell would necessarily have contractual preconditions—the debt must be due, perhaps notice must have been given—and under the general principles of conveyancing those would bind a buyer, who would necessarily have actual or constructive notice of them.[171] Considerable

---

[165] *Matthie* v. *Edwards* (1846) 2 Coll. 465.

[166] *Jones* v. *Matthie* (1847) 11 Jur. 504.

[167] *Kershaw* v. *Kalow* (1855) 1 Jur. (N.S.) 974; *Davey* v. *Durrant* (1857) 1 De G. & J. 535; *Warner* v. *Jacob* (1882) 20 Ch D 220; *Bettyes* v. *Maynard* (1883) 49 LT 391; *Colson* v. *Williams* (1889) 58 LJ Ch 539; *Kennedy* v. *de Trafford* [1896] 1 Ch 762 (aff'd [1897] AC 180); *Haddington Island* v. *Huson* [1911] AC 722.

[168] *Jenkins* v. *Jones* (1860) 2 Giff. 99; *Barrett* v. *Hartley* (1866) LR 2 Eq 789; *Ford* v. *Olden* (1867) LR 3 Eq 461; *Miller* v. *Cook* (1870) LR 10 Eq 641.

[169] *Robertson* v. *Norris* (1858) 1 Giff. 421; Davidson, *Precedents*, ii, 624 (3rd edn, 1869); Fisher, *Mortgage* (3rd edn, 1876), i, 489; Coote, *Mortgages*, (4th edn, 1880), 251–2. Stuart VC's alternative ground was that the mortgagee sold to himself, while on appeal Lord Cranworth held that the proof of sale was fraudulent: (1858) 4 Jur. (N.S.) 443.

[170] *Nash* v. *Eads* (1880) 25 Sol. J. 95; Fisher, *Mortgage* (4th edn, 1884), 457, hardening in the 5th edn, 1897 (by Underhill) 450; Coote, *Mortgages* (7th edn, 1904), 921; *Kennedy* v. *de Trafford* [1896] 1 Ch 762 (aff'd [1897] AC 180).

[171] *Hobson* v. *Bell* (1839) 2 Beav. 17; *Bailey* v. *Barnes* [1894] 1 Ch 25.

law developed on how to interpret these conditions in the different contexts in which mortgages might be taken or subsequently come to be held.[172] Further, a buyer who subsequently resold would need to prove to the new buyer that the conditions had been satisfied, unless a suitable condition of sale precluded that inquiry, which itself might bring a cost. The resulting tension between, on the one hand, ease of sale and subsequent conveyancing, and, on the other, protection of mortgagors was resolved by creation of purchaser protection clauses that 'to a great extent neutralized' mortgagors' ability to prevent or subsequently challenge mortgagees' sales.[173]

This was not a simple matter. Davidson himself aimed to maintain the balance by requiring fair notice of sale to the mortgagor, but immunizing a purchaser from the consequences of breach. There are instances, though, where less scrupulous mortgagees took powers that seem not to have required anything beyond a notice to repay.[174] Similarly, although Davidson, Dart, and Sugden all expressed some doubt when Stuart VC took literally a clause immunizing a purchaser from even express notice that preconditions had not been met, by the 1870s other texts were recommending such provisions without comment.[175] Davidson had misgivings too about Romilly MR's interpretation of the clause restricting the mortgagor to a remedy in damages, a clause that had become common. In Davidson's eyes drafters had meant only that a completed sale would cure irregularities, whereas Romilly had interpreted the clause more literally to bar an injunction against making a sale in breach of condition.[176] How far there was real bargaining over these clauses is quite unknown.

Thus although there were cases where judges held that an imperfectly drafted clause did not confer immunity on a purchaser, just as there were a few where they ruled that a sale had been oppressive, the trend from early on was towards clauses giving blanket protection to purchasers and towards judicial interpretation

---

[172] Coote, *Mortgages* (8th edn, 1912), ii, 912–24.

[173] *Ibid.*, 925.

[174] *Jones* v. *Matthie* (1847) 11 Jur. 504; *Thurlow* v. *Mackeson* (1868) LR 4 QB 97; *Cockburn* v. *Edwards* (1881) 18 Ch D 449.

[175] *Ford* v. *Heely* (1857) 3 Jur. (N.S.) 1116; Davidson, *Precedents*, ii, 627 (3rd edn, 1869); Sugden, *Vendors and Purchasers* (14th edn, 1862), 67; Dart, *Vendors and Purchasers* (4th edn, 1871), i, 64. Contrast T. Key and H. W. Elphinstone, *A Compendium of Precedents in Conveyancing* (1878), ii 706 ('express notice'); Prideaux, *Precedents* (9th edn, 1879), i, 516, 521 ('notice'). The 'usual condition' favoured by Davidson and Sugden said only that purchasers need not inquire, which a consistent chain of authority interpreted as neither preventing them from inquiring nor immunizing them from actual notice: see for example *Forster* v. *Hogart* (1850) 15 Q.B. 154; *Parkinson* v. *Hanbury* (1860) 1 Dr. & Sm. 143; *Life Interest Corp.* v. *Hand-in-Hand Fire & Insurance* [1898] 2 Ch 230. That was reversed by Conveyancing Act 1911, s 5, retrospective to 1882.

[176] *Prichard* v. *Wilson* (1864) 10 Jur. (N.S.) 330; Davidson, *Precedents*, ii, 624–5n (3rd edn, 1869).

that held mortgagors to their contractual word.[177] There is a suggestion in the way Davidson constructed his commentary and in his reactions to judges' decisions that contract had undermined what he saw as the proper relation between mortgagor and mortgagee. His notion that there be litigable safeguards between the parties but that they should not affect purchasers was outflanked by contractual regimes putting a defaulting mortgagor at the lender's mercy.

The effect of this contractualizing of the relationship was to secure the utility of the mortgage with power of sale. How far private sale actually ousted court process for foreclosure is unknown. That was the reason for its invention at a time when foreclosure was dilatory and expensive, but there would always have been mortgagees who could not use it. For them—say for subordinate mortgagees—the Chancery courts' acquisition in 1852 of a power to order sale in a foreclosure suit was particularly useful.[178] Thereafter little is heard about cost or difficulty of court process, a combined committee of the Incorporated Law Society and the Metropolitan and Provincial Law Association even committing itself to the view that an ordinary redemption and foreclosure suit could be conducted 'at very small expense'.[179] In the late 1870s, however, it was said that Chancery judges' exercise of the power in the 1852 Act was more restrictive than it could have been, and in 1881 the power was extended as part of the radical overhaul of conveyancing promoted by the Incorporated Law Society, described in Chapter V.[180] Nonetheless, the Conveyancing Act also wrote improved powers of private sale into all mortgages (unless excluded), and there are no signs that the popularity of the mortgage with power of sale waned.[181]

Conceptually the result was startling. Writing of a decision in 1874 that had protected a purchaser even though there had been no loan outstanding at the time of the (supposed) mortgagee's sale, the author of a standard text noted that 'the implication of equity that the mortgage was intended only as security for the debt [had been] overridden by the form of the contract'.[182] That was the very opposite of equity's traditional learning.

---

[177] For a simple exoneration clause, see for example W. Hughes, *The Practice of Mortgages of Real and Personal Estate* (1848), i, 94–5; in addition to cases already cited, see *Miller* v. *Cook* (1870) LR 10 Eq 641; *Selwyn* v. *Garfit* (1888) 38 Ch D 273.

[178] Chancery Procedure Act, 15 & 16 Vict. c. 86, s 48; *Hurst* v. *Hurst* (1852) 16 Beav. 372; *Wickham* v. *Nicholson* (1854) 19 Beav. 38. Stuart VC thought the previous lack of such a power generally oppressive and unjust to mortgagees: *Hutton* v. *Sealy* (1858) 4 Jur. (N.S.) 450.

[179] *RC on Judicature*, 2nd Report, vol. 2, *PP* 1872 [C. 631–1], xx, 245, 370. It was arguing against extension of county court jurisdiction.

[180] *Wolstenholme's Conveyancing Acts* (9th edn, 1905), 87, citing G. O. Morgan, *The Statutes... relating to the Court of Chancery* (5th edn, 1876), 196–7; Conveyancing Act 1881, s 25.

[181] Sections 19–21 (amended by Conveyancing Act 1911, s 19).

[182] *Dicker* v. *Angerstein* (1874) 3 Ch D 600; Fisher, *Mortgage* (4th edn, 1884), 467.

Not a Mortgage: How to Evade the Usury Laws

It would be easy to assume that once the mortgage with power of sale catered for the formal end of loans secured on land and the equitable mortgage by deposit of documents met the demand for a reasonably safe informal security, there would be neither need nor room for further experiment. That is true from soon after the mid-century, until the logic of title registration spawned serious proposals that all mortgages should be recast as statutory charges, but it was not true until then. The reason was the stability of one element in the central definition of the mortgage. In Davidson's opinion mortgages of freeholds were generally rather stereotyped, the more so because of the 'cardinal rule' that a mortgagee must get nothing beyond return of the principal plus interest and costs.[183] Until the repeal of the usury laws in 1854 that rule capped interest rates at 5 per cent, so at times when money was scarce or risk high lenders looked to their lawyers for something better. In the final years of the French war government itself was borrowing at about 5 per cent, and would-be borrowers offering mortgages could find no takers, it was said.[184]

Unsurprisingly some twilight forms were tried. There is a cluster of cases in which lenders advanced money to builders for the construction of new houses on the strength of their building lease, where there are sales of the lease to the lender at an inflated value, leases back to the builder at an inflated rent, options to repurchase at the original price, rentcharges for a fixed period…anything but a loan on mortgage.[185] In each case jury or judge found the transaction on its facts to be a usurious loan, but the forms are no doubt typical.

More attractive, because eighteenth-century judges had ruled it not to be usurious in law, was the life annuity. When connected with land an annuity usually operated as a rentcharge: it was a periodic payment of money arising out of an estate in land. It worked because formally it was a purchase, whereas only loans invoked the rules against usury. Typically the annuity would last for the lifetime of the grantor if the annuity was to issue out of a life estate, or for longest of three, sometimes four, nominated lives if it was to issue out of a freehold.[186] During the French war Sugden believed that house-building was being financed by annuities for lives charged on building leases.[187] There had once been doubts whether a life

---

[183] *Precedents*, ii, 533 (2nd edn, 1858).

[184] S. Homer and R. Sylla, *A History of Interest Rates* (3rd edn, New Brunswick, 1991), 181–215; *SC on Usury Laws*; E. B. Sugden, *A Cursory Inquiry into the Expediency of Repealing the Annuity Act* (1812), 48.

[185] *Doe d. Titford* v. *Chambers* (1814) 4 Camp. 1; *Doe d. Grimes* v. *Gooch* (1820) 3 B. & Ald. 664; *Chillingworth* v. *Chillingworth* (1837) 8 Sim. 404 (transaction 1812).

[186] *SC on Usury Laws* contains many examples.

[187] Sugden, *Cursory Inquiry*, 36; *SC on Usury Laws*, 151.

annuity redeemable (strictly, repurchasable) by the grantor/borrower retained the immunity from the usury laws, but once again judges were obliging, as they were too when lenders began coupling their advance with a life assurance policy that guaranteed their repayment.[188] Since the criterion for a transaction falling outside the usury laws had been that the advance was put at hazard this now near certainty of repayment made the form a mere cloak. Nineteenth-century judges insisted, however, that as there was still *some* risk it was a valid cloak—the life assurance company might fail, for example.[189] 'Usury is a creature of law', said Alderson B. in 1836, 'which in that respect must be obeyed, nothing more'.[190] 'Parties are entitled to evade the law', said Williams J. in 1860.[191]

Because formally annuities were sales of rentcharges there was no obligation to repay anything, hence no security could be taken for repayment of capital. But commonly lenders would secure payment of the annual sum by having a term of years vested in a trustee for them, usually containing extensive powers to exploit the estate if they were to take possession, plus powers of distress.[192] One example in Jarman's edition of Bythewood's collection, published in 1829, contains a trust for sale of the land, and another drawn in 1840 has a power of sale, both tracking trends in the style of mortgages.[193] In practice these life annuities functioned as semi-secured loans, an alternative to a mortgage when money could not be had at the legal rate.[194] The range and complexity of documentation was much the same for both; annuities occupy about 700 pages of Jarman's edition, mortgages 800.[195]

From 1813 there was some similarity of judicial control too. The Annuities Act of that year, drafted by Sugden, brought regulation primarily through a greatly improved system of registration, one that had no respect for the privacy of either lender or borrower, but in addition it contained fierce provisions limiting ancillary costs.[196] These paralleled the rule for mortgages that a mortgagee could recover only his principal, interest, and costs, those to be vetted by a court if necessary. For annuities the rule now was that reasonable costs could be

[188] W. G. Lumley, *A Treatise upon the Law of Annuities and Rentcharges* (1833), 184–91. Fixed-term annuities at above legal interest were treated as usurious because the principal was secure: *Fereday v. Wightwick* (1829) 1 Russ. & M. 45.

[189] *Re Naish* (1830) 7 Bing. 150; *Howkins v. Bennet* (1860) 7 C.B. N.S. 507.

[190] *Blackburn v. Warwick* (1836) 2 Y. & C. Ex. 92.

[191] *Howkins v. Bennet* (1860) 7 C.B. N.S. 507, 554.

[192] F. Blayney, *A Practical Treatise on Life Annuities* (1817), 1–20.

[193] Bythewood and Jarman, *Precedents*, ii, 137–49; *Lewis v. Hillman* (1852) 3 H.L.C. 607.

[194] Lord Hatherley had difficulty seeing how this could be so: *Knox v. Turner* (1870) 5 Ch App 515; contrast *re Duty on the Estate of Col. G. A. Vernon* [1901] 1 QB 297.

[195] Bythewood and Jarman, *Precedents*, i, 330–668 and ii, 1–370 (annuities); v, 232–587 and vi, 1–487 (mortgages).

[196] 53 Geo. III c. 141; *Lewis v. Hillman* (1852) 3 H.L.C. 607 (Sugden's authorship).

charged, but that brokerage fees were limited to 10s per £100. Importantly, no part of the consideration was to be retained by the grantee/lender or his agent—overstating the amount actually paid was a common way of disguising the real return to the annuitant. Courts policed that with enthusiasm, if the question came before them.[197] As Jarman put it, 'if any unfairness or extortion be practised the court...will not be baffled in its authority to set aside the securities by any technical or colourable compliance with the terms of the act'.[198]

One further form of semi-secured loan was developed in the late 1830s, showing again that the restriction of mortgages to loans at legal interest could be irksome. It was constructed from the conjunction of two otherwise unrelated law reforms. The first, which itself came in two stages in 1833 and 1839, began by exempting from the usury laws promissory notes and bills of exchange payable at up to three months from issue, and then, as the second stage, extended the exemption to bills (and loans on them) payable at up to 12 months save when secured on land.[199] The second reform was Campbell's Judgments Act of 1838. As an unsuccessful bait to induce the Lords to agree to the abolition of imprisonment for debt, that Act extended judgment creditors' rights against their debtors' lands so that hence-forward a judgment would create an immediate charge over lands in which the debtor had any interest.[200] After expiry of a 12-month grace period the judgment creditor could enforce the charge as though it were a mortgage. Adding the two together, therefore, a lender could extract a bill or promissory note from the bor-rower at interest exceeding the 5 per cent allowed on mortgages, take a power of attorney from him to confess judgment, enter judgment and thereupon get the statutory charge, and after a year enforce it as a mortgage against any interests in land the judgment debtor had—unless the proviso to the 1839 Act stopped that.

As with any novelty, especially one as opportunistic as this, professional judg-ment on how to construct an appropriate form varied and initial judicial reaction was very mixed.[201] Retrospectively, however, for the decisive case came after the repeal of the usury laws made such intricacy unnecessary, it became clear that a way had been found, one moreover that worked as a matter of law and did not depend upon a favourable jury finding that the landed security was merely

---

[197] This was a common law jurisdiction; see for example *Williamson* v. *Goold* (1823) 1 Bing. 234; *Gorton* v. *Champneys* (1823) 1 Bing. 287; *Finley* v. *Gardner* (1827) 6 B. & C. 165.

[198] Bythewood and Jarman, *Precedents*, i, 335.

[199] Bank Continuation Act 1833, 3 & 4 Will. IV c. 98; Usury Act 1839, 2 & 3 Vict. c. 37.

[200] 1 & 2 Vict. c. 110, s 13. The consequences for conveyancing were serious enough to provoke two amending Acts in the next two years: 2 & 3 Vict. c. 11, 3 & 4 Vict. c. 82. See also Judgments Act 1855.

[201] *Connop* v. *Meaks* (1834) 2 Ad. & El. 326; *Berrington* v. *Collis* (1839) 5 Bing. (N.C.) 322; *Lane* v. *Horlock* (1846) 4 Dow. & L. 408; *Doe d. Haughton* v. *King* (1843) 11 M. & W. 333; *Follett* v. *Moore* (1849) 4 Ex. 410, *Clack* v. *Sainsbury* (1851) 11 C.B. 695; *Ex p Warrington* (1853) 17 Jur. 430; *Lane* v. *Horlock* (1853) 1 Drew. 576.

collateral.[202] It came to nothing only because after 1854 regular mortgagees could have the best of both worlds.[203] The brief realization of the possibility that a judgment might function as an ersatz mortgage is a reminder of the contingency of all legal forms, for in Ireland there was a decisive shift that way; there from 1850 the judgment coupled with a registered memorandum identifying particular land became a standard form of mortgage.[204]

The Decline and Fall of the Cardinal Rule: Contractualism Enlarged

These opportunistic devices emphasize how right Davidson was to see the rule confining mortgagees to recovery of principal, interest, and costs as cardinal. Perhaps for that very reason there is little direct litigation on it reported from the early nineteenth century, nor was analysis of it consistent. Lord Redesdale was utterly certain that mortgagees in Ireland should not be allowed to take leases from their mortgagors—the ones he was faced with were very long, though their terms were not unfair—but he offered every explanation that there can be.[205] They were necessarily oppressive, he said, as a matter of law and without need for a jury verdict; they were usurious; and they clogged the borrower's right to redeem by preventing recovery of the full fee he had mortgaged. Lord Eldon was inclined to think fairness a defence.[206]

It was the same with the rule that a mortgagee in possession could not charge the mortgagor a fee for personally collecting the rents, or take a commission. The rule was clear, but what was its reason? Eldon was inclined to see mortgagees in possession as being like trustees—an analogy that was usually rejected when other questions about mortgagees' powers arose.[207] Lord Brougham agreed with that in some circumstances, but for mortgagees in possession after a default he gave exactly the opposite explanation: they were legal owners acting in their own interest, though he added the further reason that the rule is necessary to check what would otherwise be 'almost uncontrolled management' by the mortgagee.[208]

[202] *Lane* v. *Horlock* (1856) 5 H.L.C. 581.

[203] Freed from this secondary use, judgments law was then reconfigured to achieve a better fit with conveyancing law: Law of Property Further Amendment Act 1859, ss 1–2; *SC on the Judgments Law Amendment Bill*, Report, PP 1864 (396), v, 617; Judgments Act 1864.

[204] D. H. Madden, *A Practical Treatise on the Registration of Deeds, Conveyances, and Judgment-mortgages* (Dublin, 1868), 88–168. For earlier use in England, see Cruise, *Digest*, ii, 66.

[205] *Webb* v. *Rorke* (1806) 2 Sch. & Lef. 661; *Hickes* v. *Cooke* (1816) 4 Dow. P.C. 16. Sugden said that his successors (of whom he was one) had not been inclined to go so far: *Vendors and Purchasers* (10th edn, 1839), iii, 227.

[206] *Hickes* v. *Cooke* (1816) 4 Dow. P.C. 16.

[207] *Chambers* v. *Goldwin* (1802) 9 Ves. 254; *Langstaffe* v. *Fenwick* (1805) 10 Ves. 405 (for the rule); *Downes* v. *Grazebrook* (1817) 3 Mer. 200; *Cholmondeley* v. *Clinton* (1821) 4 Bli. P.C. 1.

[208] *Leith* v. *Irvine* (1833) 1 My. & K. 277.

Coote's analysis in 1837 was short and unsystematic, and he too twice drifted into seeing mortgagees as trustees, 'in some sort' at least.[209]

Whatever its basis, the strength of the cardinal rule can be seen in Brougham's hostile reaction to the exception Eldon had created for mortgages of West Indian plantations. It was notorious that plantation land's only value was for producing sugar, equally notorious that the only people who would lend on it were the London sugar merchants, and obvious that its attraction to them lay in securing a dedicated supply on which they could earn commission, preferably ahead of the market.[210] Hence it was customary for these mortgages to include consignments of future sugar from the estate in addition to legal interest.[211] More controversially, it was convenient to the merchants to ship provisions to the estates on the outward journey, charging a commission, which they continued to do even after the failure of their mortgagors had led to the merchant/consignee/supplier/ mortgagee taking possession of the estate. Fully conscious of the exceptions being made, first Eldon and then the Privy Council validated the consignments and the commissions; needs must; the slaves cannot be left to starve.[212] Brougham maintained that before these concessions the rule had been clear and admitted no exceptions, whatsoever the device or disguise.[213] Unlike Eldon, he declared, he would not be found altering the law so as to accommodate it to the varying circumstances of society; only Parliament could do that.

When Parliament did, in 1854, its move was in one sense decisive—the centuries old usury laws were repealed—but in another it was rather unhelpful. Apart from saving the existing statutory regulation of pawnbrokers the repealing legislation was silent about the implications. Into the early nineteenth century usury had had an aura that provided judges with an extra reason for disallowing additional charges and side deals mortgagees had claimed, beyond the narrow calculation of interest rates and strict application of the formula that mortgagees could claim only principal, interest, and costs. 'By profession he dealt in the distresses of mankind', said Lord Thurlow of a moneylender in 1788, 'I make neither better or worse of his conduct than that of a common annuity-monger'.[214] So the rule that Lord Redesdale had developed for Irish mortgages, that the mortgagee could not take a lease in addition to the mortgage, was explained by Plumer MR in 1822 as resting on the courts' refusal to allow one man to take advantage of the

---

[209] Coote, *Mortgages* (2nd edn, 1837), 419, 440–9 esp. at 444, 446. His citations were mostly old.

[210] R. W. Beachey, *The British West Indies Sugar Industry in the Late 19th Century* (1957).

[211] Bythewood and Jarman, *Precedents*, v, 533–43.

[212] *Bunbury v. Winter* (1820) 1 Jac. & W. 255; *Cox v. Champneys* (1822) Jac. 576; *Sayers v. Whitfield* (1829) 1 Knapp 133; see also *Scott v. Nesbitt* (1808) 14 Ves. 438.

[213] *Leith v. Irvine* (1833) 1 My. & K. 277.

[214] *Fox v. Mackreth* (1788) 2 Cox 320. For Mackreth, see *ODNB*.

necessities of another.[215] Necessity was inherent to mortgagors generically, quite apart from individual factors that in any particular case might add up to oppression.[216] It would have been surprising if that sort of thinking had survived the repeal of the usury laws, given the support judges had shown for the contractually based power of sale. Nonetheless in the first reported decision on the point, in 1863, Romilly MR held that the rule against collateral advantages survived because it had not been based entirely on the prohibition of usury, and his decision was explicitly adopted by Kay J. in 1889.[217]

These decisions were at odds with the more general trend. Before 1854 a common, crude, and wholly unlawful way of evading the usury laws was to recite a sum as the principal in the mortgage deed but in fact advance less. In *Potter* v. *Edwards* in 1857 Kindersley VC saw no difficulty now in enforcing such a deed according to its terms.[218] In 1880 Bacon VC treated the rule against compound interest as ancient history, though it had been applied vigorously up to 1854.[219] Similarly in 1876 he thought the rule that a mortgagee in possession could not charge a fee or commission for collecting the rents himself 'perfect justice and good sense', bearing in mind the 'enormous power' such a mortgagee possessed, but he was clear that a mortgagor could contract out of it.[220] Before 1854 that could not have been done in and at the time of the mortgage deed because such a fee was not a 'cost', hence to reserve it infringed the cardinal rule against collateral advantages.

However, this new insistence upon the primacy of free contract came with very important riders. The first was that whatever advantage it was that was being claimed beyond the law's allowance of principal, interest, and costs must actually be in the contract.[221] Many of the 'just and wholesome' decisions applying this principle, to use the words of Lopes LJ in 1890, prevented solicitor-mortgagees charging profit costs in excess of actual disbursements when they foreclosed or took possession of the mortgaged estate, unless their mortgage explicitly allowed

---

[215] *Stratford* v. *Twynam* (1822) Jac. 418; Fisher, *Mortgage* (8th edn, 1912), i, 17 traced this explanation back to Lord Hardwicke.

[216] Annuities could be set aside for oppression, on terms, following *Heathcote* v. *Paignon* (1787) 2 Bro. C.C. 167.

[217] *Broad* v. *Selfe* (1863) 11 WR 1036; *James* v. *Kerr* (1887) 40 Ch D 449.

[218] (1857) 26 LJ Ch 468.

[219] *Clarkson* v. *Henderson* (1880) 14 Ch D 348; *Ex p Beavan* (1803) 9 Ves. 223; *Fergusson* v. *Fyffe* (1841) 8 Cl. & F. 121; *Mosse* v. *Salt* (1863) 32 Beav. 269. There was an interesting exception for mortgages securing running bank accounts (*Rufford* v. *Bishop* (1829) 5 Russ. 346; *Crosskill* v. *Bower* (1863) 32 Beav. 86), and the rule did not prevent capitalization of interest following default upon an actual demand for repayment (*Blackburn* v. *Warwick* (1836) 2 Y. & C. Ex. 92).

[220] *Eyre* v. *Hughes* (1876) 2 Ch D 148.

[221] *Matthison* v. *Clarke* (1854) 3 Drew. 3; *Ogden* v. *Battams* (1855) 1 Jur. (N.S.) 791; *Sclater* v. *Cottam* (1857) 3 Jur. (N.S.) 630; *Stains* v. *Banks* (1863) 9 Jur. (N.S.) 1049; *Barrett* v. *Hartley* (1866) LR 2 Eq 795.

it: profits could not be a 'cost'.[222] Then, as the second rider, those mortgagees who stood in a fiduciary relationship with their mortgagor could rely on these special, and, to the mortgagor, specially disadvantageous, terms only if they had particularly drawn them to the mortgagor's attention, perhaps even advised the mortgagor to take independent advice.[223] Thirdly, a mortgage contract would be reopened if its terms were oppressive, an inquiry combining elements of status—an especial tenderness to youthful expectant heirs and the possessors of reversionary interests more generally—and the circumstances of the agreement.[224] Contract required 'assent', which must not be 'imperfect', Stuart VC explained in one of the first cases in this line.[225] This ability to investigate 'oppression' counterbalanced the formal contractualism of *Potter* v. *Edwards*. In 1879 Bacon VC looked behind a recital that £500 was owing as principal on an actual advance of only £250 and found a story of exploitation of a relatively humble family by a local solicitor-mortgagee.[226] Accordingly he ordered an account based only upon the amount in fact lent, not the amount the borrowers had promised to pay.

All of this brought mortgages into line with equitable jurisdiction over contracts generally, shorn of special rules attributable to the usury laws.[227] A strong theme that contracts must be honoured runs through what became the definitive restatement, *Biggs* v. *Hoddinott* in 1898.[228] That was a publican's mortgage to a brewer, with echoes, therefore, of the West Indian plantation mortgages. In the post-1854 world Lindley MR now approved and generalized that line; Lord Brougham's indignation was forgotten. The mortgage combined a tie to buying the brewer's products (less stipulated exceptions) with a provision for continuance of the mortgage for a minimum period of five years. Clauses postponing redemption had been uncontroversial throughout our period, with or without provision for repayment by instalments, the only discussion they generated being as to how best to word them consistently with preserving mortgagees' remedies on default of interest payments.[229] Again the contractual bias was clear, and again it could be

---

[222] *Re Wallis* (1890) 25 QBD 176 (Lopes LJ); *re Roberts* (1889) 43 Ch D 354; *Field* v. *Hopkins* (1890) 44 Ch D 524; *Stone* v. *Lickorish* [1891] 2 Ch 363; contrast *re Donaldson* (1884) 27 Ch D 544. Liverpool Incorporated Law Society promoted a bill to reverse this application of the principle, succeeding against 'severe odds', it reported: Mortgagees' Costs Act 1895, (1895–6) 40 *Sol. J.* 100.

[223] *Eyre* v. *Wynn-Mackenzie* [1894] 1 Ch 218 (aff'd [1896] 1 Ch 135); *Cheese* v. *Keen* [1908] 1 Ch 245.

[224] *Croft* v. *Graham* (1863) 2 De G. J. & Sm. 155; *Eyre* v. *Hughes* (1876) 2 Ch D 148; *James* v. *Kerr* (1889) 40 Ch D 449; *Mainland* v. *Upjohn* (1889) 41 Ch D 126; and see *Earl of Aylesford* v. *Morris* (1873) 8 Ch App 484.

[225] *Barrett* v. *Hartley* (1866) LR 2 Eq 789.

[226] *Re Slater's Trusts* (1879) 11 Ch D 227.

[227] See pp. 400–409, below.

[228] [1898] 2 Ch 307.

[229] Coventry, *Mortgage Precedents*, 90–1 (citing *Stanhope* v. *Manners* (1763) 2 Eden 197); Davidson, *Precedents*, ii, 510, 535–6 (2nd edn, 1858).

displaced by proof of oppression. Stuart VC rejected a 20-year postponement in a mortgage to the borrower's solicitor, worrying about the lack of proper advice given and the consequences of tying the mortgagor to one lawyer for so long.[230] But in *Biggs* v. *Hoddinott* no judge saw anything other than an ordinary business agreement; it would be an affront to render it unenforceable on arguments they regarded as merely technical.

Casting the relationship as contractual, however, involved more than holding freely contracting parties to their bargain. Sometimes judges framed rules explicitly to maximize mortgagors' ability to remain in the market, thereby avoiding dependency upon their mortgagee. There were two instances. First was their explanation of the difference between a mortgagee buying up the mortgagor's equity of redemption and buying the land itself. Conceptually the two could be made to look the same, but, courts said, economically they were quite different. In the first the mortgagor had free choice to select a buyer, whereas the mortgagee exercising a power of sale could achieve the second without entering a market.[231] The first was therefore unobjectionable, the second prohibited.

The second instance where ability to enter a market was important concerned priorities of mortgages and, in particular, the principle of tacking. Suppose a first mortgage secured both present and future advances; normally it would be to a bank. Suppose then that the mortgagor granted a second mortgage to a different lender who knew about the first and its terms. Suppose the second lender notified the first—as every sensible second mortgagee would do—and that subsequently the first lender made a further advance to the borrower. Eighteenth-century authority was taken to have decided that the first lender could refuse to relinquish its security until not only the first loan was repaid but the further advance too.[232] It was the second lender's folly; by hypothesis he lent with his eyes open.

Until Coventry's edition of *Powell on Mortgages* in 1822 this rule seems to have been accepted uncritically.[233] Even then Coventry expressed his doubts with extreme diffidence, he failed to persuade all his contemporaries that the rule was mistaken, and through to 1855 Joshua Williams can be found standing by it.[234] The rule had its practical uses as well as its moral justification, especially that it enabled continuous small advances by mortgagees to builders, similarly it enabled

[230] *Cowdry* v. *Day* (1859) 1 Giff. 316.

[231] *Hickes* v. *Cooke* (1816) 4 Dow. P.C. 16; Powell, *Mortgages* (5th edn), i, 122–4n; cf. *Kreglinger* v. *The New Patagonia Meat Company* [1914] AC 25, 50–1.

[232] *Gordon* v. *Graham* (1716) 2 Eq. Ca. Abr. 598.

[233] Powell, *Mortgages* (4th edn, 1799), i, 544–5; Barton, *Elements*, iii, 536; Cruise, *Digest* (2nd edn), ii, 205; J. Patch, *A Practical Treatise on Mortgages* (1821), 287.

[234] Powell, *Mortgages* (5th edn), i, 534–5n; contrast Bythewood and Jarman, *Precedents*, v, 427n; Cornish, *Deeds* (2nd edn, 1855, by G. Horsey), 82n; Williams, *Principles of Real Property* (4th edn), 458.

mortgagees of houses to tack the cost of repairs to their original advance.[235] Against it stood Coventry's tentative doubts, an even less confident reservation by Davidson, and a warning by Sugden while Lord Chancellor of Ireland that the rule should be revisited, subsequently repeated.[236] Conceptually those doubts could be supported by characterizing the further advance as an attempt to gain an extra security out of a property interest known to have belonged to someone else—the second mortgagee—which is contrary to general equitable principle, though there is some circularity to the reasoning (as there is in the allocation of folly).

These considerations were balanced finely enough for a policy reason to make the difference when the House of Lords split on the matter in 1861.[237] By the old rule, Lord Chelmsford said, a mortgagee 'may effectively preclude a mortgagor from afterwards raising money in any other quarter'. More clumsily, but aiming for the same point, Lord Campbell thought it important that a mortgagor 'be entitled to do what he pleases with his own'. The new rule denying the first mortgagee priority for the further advance in these circumstances was thus based on maximizing borrowers' ability to remain in the market, these judges believing that bankers would then adapt.[238] This rationale gained as firm acceptance as the new rule did itself.[239]

The Limits of Contractual Freedom: Clogs on the Equity

All property concepts have definitions beyond the will of individuals; property is always to some extent a given. How big an extent, or, rather, how tolerant judges were of attempts by individual owners or contracting parties to subvert definitions is one of the recurrent themes through the property section of this volume.

---

[235] See Stewart's edition of Bythewood, *Precedents*, v, 233n, and his *Principles of the Law of Real Property* (1837), 89; Coventry himself had such an example (*Mortgage Precedents*, 371). The first mortgage would state a maximum amount available for further advances, otherwise a £25 stamp had to be paid for an indefinite liability.

[236] *Martin's Practice*, iii, 598n; *Blunden* v. *Desart* (1842) 2 Dru. & War. 405; *Shaw* v. *Neale* (1858) 6 H.L.C. 581.

[237] *Hopkinson* v. *Rolt* (1861) 9 H.L.C. 514. The majority dug deep into the archives and concluded that *Gordon* v. *Graham* had not decided what it was reported to have done. Lord Cranworth dissented, believing the rule well established and the better rule for facilitating further advances from banks.

[238] Bethell, successful counsel, argued that cautious bankers already ruled off accounts on learning of a subsequent mortgage, a practice that was said to have become standard by the end of our period: *Deeley* v. *Lloyds Bank* [1912] AC 756.

[239] *London & County Banking* v. *Ratcliffe* (1881) 6 App Cas 726; *Bradford Bank* v. *Briggs* (1886) 12 App Cas 29; *Union Bank of Scotland* v. *National Bank of Scotland* (1886) 12 App Cas 53; *West* v. *Williams* [1899] 1 Ch 132.

In some contexts some judges worried about idiosyncrasy, describing it as a burden that impeded the efficiency of land transfer. That was not the case with mortgages, where the dynamic was the other way about: ancient definitions were seen at the end of the nineteenth century as unjustifiable impediments to contract. There *were* concerns about the impact of mortgages on the efficiency of land transfer—they were one of the prime causes of the push for deeds registration— but they were concerns about the detection of hidden mortgages, not about the content of mortgages once detected.

The principle that became strongly contested from the 1890s was expressed variously as 'once a mortgage always and only a mortgage' and 'mortgagees cannot fetter (sometimes "clog") their mortgagor's equity of redemption'. Either formulation empowered a mortgagor to disregard a contractual term, even as against the original mortgagee who had bargained or stipulated for it, and even in the absence of oppression or other factor vitiating the mortgagor's supposed agreement. If the books are a fair guide, for a long time there had been little call for analysis of the principle's content. They present it as old but static. Their accounts are stereotyped, and remain that way until prompted by the end of century litigation.[240] Their case citation jumps from early foundations to just a few more recent scraps. There is no indication of the continuous development and exposition that one might expect from an area of living law. Once the mortgage with power of sale had been declared valid the books quickly forgot its infraction of the 'once a mortgage …' principle, so much so that in all the litigation at the turn of the century it was never once mentioned. The power to postpone redemption for a reasonable period, which must also be an infraction of the principle, was not recited in the books in this context. Counsel in the Edwardian cases repeated the pattern found in the books: they proffered foundation cases, an occasional recent application, and usually nothing to bridge the two. Everyone agreed that commercially the issues were important, but the materials thought available to resolve them gave very little help.

This is not to say that the principle was being disregarded. On the contrary it operated as a background axiom that would be decisive if the transaction were classified as 'mortgage'. One recurrent situation concerned apparent outright sales, or apparent outright sales with power to repurchase by a date now passed, where the seller alleged that because the transaction was really a mortgage he could now redeem: once a mortgage, always a mortgage.[241] There were variants in

---

[240] Powell, *Mortgages* (5th edn), 122–5 and notes; Coote, *Mortgage* (2nd edn), 26–41; Fisher, *Mortgages*, 83–4 (4th edn, 1884), 685–7.

[241] *Allenby* v. *Dalton* (1827) 5 LJ KB 312; *Perry* v. *Meddowcroft* (1841) 4 Beav. 197; *Bell* v. *Carter* (1853) 17 Beav. 11; *Ogden* v. *Battams* (1855) 1 Jur. (N.S.) 791; *Alderson* v. *White* (1858) 4 Jur. (N.S.) 125; *Shaw* v. *Jeffery* (1860) 13 Moo. P.C. 432.

which a mortgagor sold the equity of redemption to the mortgagee, again either outright or subject to a power to repurchase by a particular day, perhaps in consideration of existing debts.[242] Heavy indebtedness was a feature of many of these sellers, and often there had been a long sequence of dealings between the parties. Sometimes the purchaser/mortgagee was stepping in to complete some project concerning the land which he had already been financing, lest both parties lose their investment. The transaction, whatever it was, was a last resort. If it were truly what the documentation represented it to be the right to reacquire had been lost, whereas a mortgage could be redeemed at any time before foreclosure whatever the paperwork said.

In those cases equity courts allowed proof of the circumstances in a search for what they described as the true substance of the transaction, being willing to disregard even the most watertight drafting if need be. The substance they sought was a loan, a debt for which the supposed purchaser might sue. Penetrating disguises to detect loans that infringed the usury laws was part of the seventeenth-century heritage, and a finding that the parties had intended to create a debt would still lead to the conclusion in the nineteenth that an apparently outright transfer of a property interest was merely a security for its payment. With land transactions, however, judges did not strain to find loans. Instead Lord Cranworth's ruling in 1857 was typical, typical of interpretation in the mid-century generally too.[243] Reversing a more contextual approach by Stuart VC he held that the documents should be left to speak for themselves unless there was very clear evidence to the contrary. Even Lord Macnaghten, who was to become a strong defender of the old principles, acknowledged that legal form should be respected: 'As regards their legal incidents, there is all the difference in the world between a mortgage and a sale with a right of repurchase', he said, '[b]ut if the transaction is completed by redemption or repurchase as the case may require there is no difference in the actual result'.[244] Significantly, he was speaking in a chattels mortgage case (or not, as the House of Lords held), where courts retained a keen eye to detect disguises that might evade the Bills of Sale Acts.[245] That external value, they said, justified them in looking behind the face of an apparently regular commercial contract. With land transactions it was much less obvious what that value might be.

There was a similar analysis in the assurance policy cases. If the parties had agreed to a loan there was a mortgage, and the policy taken out on the borrower's

---

[242] *Sevier* v. *Greenway* (1815) 19 Ves. 413; *Davis* v. *Thomas* (1831) 1 Russ. & M. 506; *Williams* v. *Owen* (1840) 5 My. & Cr. 303; *Douglas* v. *Culverwell* (1861) 3 Giff. 251; *Gossip* v. *Wright* (1863) 32 LJ Ch 648.

[243] *Alderson* v. *White* (1858) 4 Jur. (N.S.) 125, reversing 3 Jur. (N.S.) 1316. See pp. 31–4, above.

[244] *Manchester, Sheffield & Lincs Rwy* v. *North Central Wagon* (1888) 13 App Cas 554.

[245] *Langton* v. *Horton* (1842) 5 Beav. 9; *re Watson* (1890) 25 QBD 27; *Madell* v. *Thomas* [1891] 1 QB 230; *Beckett* v. *Tower Assets* [1891] 1 QB 638; *Mellor's Trustee* v. *Maas* [1902] 1 KB 137.

life would normally be treated as the borrower's, whosever name it was in and whoever nominally paid the premiums.[246] Therefore the lender held it merely as a security and must make it over to the borrower on repayment of the loan even though the contract said nothing about that. But if the transaction was a purchase, typically a repurchasable annuity, then the policy was the purchaser's, even though everybody knew that functionally these people were borrower and lender not seller and buyer, and that the cost of the premiums would have been an element in calculating the price.[247]

This association of mortgages with loans was very strong. 'Every mortgage implies a loan, and every loan a debt', Lord Talbot had ruled in 1735.[248] The existence of a loan, or, sometimes more generally a debt, was the 'substance' that invoked the 'once a mortgage always a mortgage' maxim, just as its absence validated repurchasable annuities. Virtually every model form for a mortgage provided in the 1858 edition of *Davidson* or the 1873 edition of *Prideaux* concerned loans of money, and the very few that did not were only technical exceptions.[249] Coote defined a mortgage as a debt, albeit with a little hesitation; Fisher defined a security as a debt or a charge.[250] Davidson, it will be recalled, wrote that mortgages were stereotyped, attributing that to the cardinal rule confining mortgagees to repayment of principal, interest, and costs. The maxim 'once a mortgage always and only a mortgage' might then mean 'once a security for a loan (or other quantified debt) always and only a security for a loan (etc)'. So it is plausible to suggest that the repeal of the usury laws removed the constraint. While they had operated lenders who would advance money only if they received in return both interest and some other benefit had had to use other devices, perhaps some variant on the sale and conditional repurchase. But after their repeal a manufacturer turning to a supplier or major customer for a loan in hard times could now offer both a mortgage and a supply contract directly. Similarly a lender might now be attracted by a mortgage plus a share of profits, which would offer security but not expose the lender to the liabilities that would attach to a more conventional partnership agreement. These would have been new, more efficient, legal possibilities; whether there were external stimuli as well is unknown.

---

[246] *Drysdale* v. *Piggott* (1856) 8 De G. M. & G. 546; *Courtenay* v. *Wright* (1860) 2 Giff. 546; *Salt* v. *Marquess of Northampton* [1892] AC 1.

[247] Sugden, *Cursory Inquiry*, 57–8, *Gottlieb* v. *Cranch* (1853) 4 De G. M. & G. 440; *Knox* v. *Turner* (1870) 5 Ch App 515; *Preston* v. *Neele* (1879) 12 Ch D 760.

[248] *King* v. *King* (1735) 3 P. Wms. 358.

[249] Davidson, *Precedents*, ii, 736–1088 (2nd edn, 1858); Prideaux, *Precedents* (7th edn, 1873), i, 471–663. The apparent exceptions are Davidson's forms xxxii–xxxv, which secure payment of bills of exchange and retransfers of stock. Both of those devices, however, were simply means of providing credit.

[250] Coote, *Mortgage* (4th edn, 1880), 1; Fisher, *Mortgages* (2nd edn, 1868), pp. lxxi–lxxvi.

When cases of those general descriptions came to be litigated in the very early twentieth century, lawyers therefore had little to work with. There was little continuous doctrine on the meaning of and justification for the 'once a mortgage…' or 'no fetters' principle. The principle is very general, but the books' analysis narrowly rule-oriented. For a long time mortgages had been so strongly associated with loans that, for all that Lord Parker was to say to the contrary in the *Kreglinger* litigation in 1913, there was no evidence of any substantial use in any other context.

On the other hand there was sometimes impatience with grandmotherly intervention by equity, a preference for enforcement of commercial contracts.[251] That must not be overstated, partly because not all judges did think that way, partly because in the related context of the Bills of Sale Act lenders were prohibited from enforcing additional covenants by taking possession of the chattels used as security unless the covenants were necessary to maintain their security.[252] There was tangled case law on that, some of it disallowing enforcement on facts similar to the collateral advantage cases.[253] However, judges usually attributed that Act's restrictions to a policy of preventing one creditor fraudulently gaining priority over others, rather than the more general explanation advanced by Lord Fitzgerald that saw them also as protecting borrowers from 'the exercise of oppressive powers on the part of the lender'.[254] In any event late nineteenth-century judges treated statutes as independent laws, neither needing integration with the common law nor offering analogy to it, so those cases were not seen as concerning mortgage law.

The sequence of mortgage cases can be followed through any modern textbook. They began with *Santley* v. *Wilde* in 1899, ran on through *Noakes* v. *Rice*, *Reeve* v. *Lisle*, *Bradley* v. *Carritt*, *Morgan* v. *Jeffreys*, *Samuel* v. *Jarrah Timber*, *British South Africa Gold Mines* v. *De Beers*, and *Fairclough* v. *Swan Brewery* before climaxing in *Kreglinger* v. *The New Patagonia Meat Company* in 1913.[255] There was judicial disagreement in many of them, much of it provoked by Lindley MR's

[251] Note (1900) 16 *LQR* 8; and see Lord Bramwell's attribution of the whole jurisdiction to equity's 'piety or love of fees': *Salt* v. *Marquess of Northampton* [1892] AC 1.

[252] Bills of Sales Act 1882, ss 7, 9; see pp. 859–63, below.

[253] e.g. *Bianchi* v. *Offord* (1886) 17 QBD 484; *Lyon* v. *Morris* (1887) 19 QBD 139; *Calvert* v. *Thomas* (1887) 19 QBD 204; *Real & Personal Advance* v. *Clears* (1887) 19 QBD 304; *Watson* v. *Strickland* (1887) 19 QBD 391; *Peace* v. *Brookes* [1895] 2 QB 451. The Act disallowed only the proprietary effect of the covenant, not its enforcement as a contract.

[254] *Thomas* v. *Kelly* (1888) 13 App Cas 506; for more usual statements, see *Mumford* v. *Collier* (1890) 25 QBD 279; *re Standard Manufacturing* [1891] 1 Ch 627.

[255] *Santley* v. *Wilde* [1899] 2 Ch 747; *Noakes* v. *Rice* [1902] AC 24; *Reeve* v. *Lisle* [1902] AC 461; *Bradley* v. *Carritt* [1903] AC 253; *Morgan* v. *Jeffreys* [1910] 1 Ch 620; *Samuel* v. *Jarrah Timber* [1904] AC 323; *De Beers* v. *British South Africa Gold Mines* [1912] AC 52; *Fairclough* v. *Swan Brewery* [1912] AC 565; *Kreglinger* v. *The New Patagonia Meat Company* [1914] AC 25.

reformulation in *Santley* v. *Wilde*, the first of its kind, the boldest, and the one with the shallowest foundation.

In that case Wilde had financed theatre manager Kate Santley's purchase of the remaining ten years of a lease on the Royalty Theatre. It was a building she had already renovated as subtenant but which needed further work to meet safety standards and which brought her only a precarious return—successes commonly transferring to bigger establishments after their opening run.[256] After four years she tendered repayment and claimed redemption, though her agreement had stipulated that in addition to interest at 6 per cent the lender should have a one-third share of the net profit rent for the remainder of the term. She argued that the provision for profits fettered her right to redeem, and succeeded before Byrne J., as on all previous understanding of the law one would expect her to, given that the transaction was classified as 'mortgage'.[257]

On appeal, however, unguided by anything other than a sense that this was a commercial bargain untainted by oppression, Lindley MR simply redefined a mortgage as a security for whatever obligation the parties stipulated, such that if any part of it remained unperformed the time for redemption had not yet arrived.[258] Initially he won little support, indeed the opinions expressed against him were sufficiently strong for *Prideaux* to treat *Santley* v. *Wilde* as 'virtually overruled'.[259] Lord Macnaghten denounced the restatement as enabling any mortgage to be made irredeemable simply by appropriate drafting; 'the method of the judgment [was] questionable and the effect subversive of a settled doctrine of equity', he said. For as long as he and Lord Davey sat in the Lords the principle was not to be cut back, rather the opposite, for in *Bradley* v. *Carritt* they extended it to invalidate an obligation which, technically, did not run with the property after redemption but only bound the former borrower personally.[260]

The question might have rested there were it not for doubts about the impact of the principle on debentures issued by incorporated companies. Often this specialized and by then very common form of loan was secured by a charge worded to allow the company to sell its stock-in-trade in the ordinary way as if unencumbered.[261] Only on default or something like an act of bankruptcy would the charge bite on that sort of asset, though commonly the documents would also

---

[256] F. H. W. Sheppard (ed.), *Survey of London* (1966), xxxiii, 215–21.

[257] [1899] 1 Ch 747.

[258] As author of *Treatise on the Law of Partnership* (1860; current edn, 2002) perhaps that is how he saw the parties' true relationship.

[259] *Noakes* v. *Rice* [1900] 2 Ch 445 (CA), [1902] AC 24 (HL); *Browne* v. *Ryan* [1902] 2 IR 653; *Bradley* v. *Carritt* [1903] AC 253 (by a majority); Prideaux, *Conveyancing* (18th edn, 1904), i, 541.

[260] [1903] AC 253, Lords Shand and Lindley dissenting.

[261] See pp. 636–8, below.

create an ordinary mortgage over fixed assets from the beginning. There were different ways of achieving this flexibility, but neither the theory nor the relation to other aspects of securities law was settled. In 1882 they were exempted from the requirements of the new Bills of Sale Act, but initial judicial interpretation was so narrow that the continuing viability of company charges over fluctuating assets was doubted.[262] In 1890, however, courts decided that company debentures had fallen outside the legislation anyway—the mischief targeted by the legislation was fraud on creditors by taking secret securities, which was not a course open to incorporated companies, they now said.[263] That left open the more general question whether debentures were subject to the 'once a mortgage...' and 'no fetters' principle. Gore-Browne wrote that for a long time lawyers thought that that principle might make issue of perpetual debentures and debenture stock impossible, which would be inconvenient.[264] Buckley J. reduced that doubt in 1905 by characterizing irredeemable debenture stock not as a loan but as purchase of an annuity—a nice example of legal history repeating itself—and it was eliminated altogether by a statutory declaration of validity in 1907, on the recommendation of a committee of which Gore-Browne himself was a member.[265]

These changes did not touch the general issue. In *Samuel* v. *Jarrah Timber* in 1903 the Court of Appeal ruled that the full force of the 'no fetters' principle applied to companies as much as to anyone else, hence a company mortgaging its debenture stock could not in the same transaction confer an option to purchase that stock on the lender/investor: once a mortgage, always a mortgage.[266] When challenged directly counsel had been unable to suggest any reason for his submission that companies were different. With obvious reluctance the House of Lords, including Lord Macnaghten, dismissed the appeal, and the committee of which Gore-Browne was a member duly recommended that legislation should do the job instead.[267] 'No doubt the rule was originally adopted to prevent oppression', it reported, 'but we think that as applied to a company with a Board of Directors it is entirely out of date'. A clause to that effect was included in the Companies Bill 1907, only to be rejected by a standing committee without

---

[262] R. Gregory and P. Walton, 'Fixed Charges over Changing Assets' (1998) 2 *Company Financial and Insolvency LR* 68–87.

[263] G. E. Lyon, *Lyon and Redman's Law of Bills of Sale* (4th edn, 1896), 188–9; *Read* v. *Joannon* (1890) 25 QBD 300; *re Standard Manufacturing* [1891] 1 Ch 627.

[264] F. Gore-Browne, *Concise Precedents under the Companies (Consolidation) Act 1908* (4th edn, 1913), 710–11. These debentures were perpetual on one side only; the company could redeem/repurchase them if it chose.

[265] *Re Southern Brazilian Railway* [1905] 2 Ch 78; Companies Act 1907, s 14; *Companies Law Amendment Committee*, Report, PP 1906 (Cd. 3052), xcvii, 199, 227.

[266] [1903] 2 Ch 1; *British South Africa Gold Mines* v. *De Beers* [1910] 2 Ch 502.

[267] [1904] AC 323; *Companies Law Amendment Committee*, 227.

reporting its reasons.[268] A second bill brought from the Lords that year would have permitted companies to issue debentures redeemable 'in certain circumstances', which looks designed to allow companies to include the sorts of restriction that would be invalid as clogs in a mortgage.[269] The bill lapsed, presumably because it was essentially duplicated by the longer bill that the standing committee generally approved, and which became the Companies Act 1907. For whatever reason, however, it is clear that the opportunity to make debentures immune from the principle of 'once a mortgage always a mortgage' and 'no fetters on the equity of redemption' had fairly arisen but had been rejected.

It was to test that issue in the Lords that counsel agreed to fast track *Kreglinger* v. *The New Patagonia Meat Company* through the lower courts.[270] Kreglingers, wool and sheepskin traders since 1797, had in 1910 lent money secured by a floating charge to a fledgling enterprise in Patagonia which was just moving into the refrigerated meat export business. Two years later, with the defendant's undercapitalized business collapsing, the American firm Swift Beef Co bought a controlling interest and resuscitated it. Although Kreglingers had undertaken not to call in the loan for five years it was repayable at any time by the borrower, and in January 1913 it was repaid at Swift's direction. The agreement had also given Kreglingers a right of pre-emption for five years over sheepskins produced at the plant, which Swift, their competitor and a pioneer of the 'thorough and scientific' exploitation of meat by-products, now claimed had ended with repayment of the loan: otherwise their equity of redemption would have been fettered.[271] Kreglingers responded that that rule did not apply to debentures securing company charges. In case that should fail, as it quickly did, they argued for a revision of the 'no fetters' rule as it applied to mortgages generally, and succeeded.[272]

The decision remains a part of modern law. That might well have disappointed Viscount Haldane, whose speech is an argument for finding a method to allow adaptation in particularized modern contexts. Mortgage law for him must retain its principles, but they must be adapted to meet new varieties of property being mortgaged in new ways. Sensitivity to context is one key; understanding that it is the principles that matter and not their application in former cases is the other. Old cases need not be discussed; they are fact dependent. That is the same technique used by Chancery judges interpreting wills in the 1880s: break away

[268] *Report from Standing Committee C on the Companies Bill*, PP 1907 (310), v, 837.

[269] Companies (Debenture and Debenture Stock) Bill, PP 1907 (301), i, 477.

[270] *The Times*, 21 March 1913; (1913) 29 TLR 393, 464.

[271] J. T. Critchell and J. Raymond, *A History of the Frozen Meat Trade* (1912), 412 (but not listing sheepskins); see also 88.

[272] [1914] AC 25.

from established patterns of decision by moving straight from the general to the document in hand.[273] So in this case he would rule that because a floating charge allows free rotation of stock-in-trade the sheepskins were not the same property as the enterprise that was charged, hence an agreement about them was no fetter and must be honoured like any other commercial contract.

Lord Parker's opinion, by contrast, is more canonical, and is frequently used as a foundation by the books today. It is more difficult to understand, as revisions often are, because it glosses over difficulties and rewrites history. He had much in common with Haldane, however. Both thought *Santley* v. *Wilde* right and *Bradley* v. *Carritt* wrong, both supported Lord Lindley's attempts at redirection. Both thought that, on the contractual plane, upholding commercial bargains was important. Haldane's observation that Lord Davey and Lord Lindley represented divergent tendencies, of which Lindley's was better suited to modern transactions, probably sums them both up well enough for this account.

It was a conscious attempt at redirection, and significant for that reason. But the direction chosen was not new, as Lord Haldane himself pointed out. Contractual provisions postponing redemption had been accepted without demur throughout most of the nineteenth century, subject to a requirement of reasonableness. There were at least two contextual exceptions to basic principle, both mentioned from time to time during the litigation of the early twentieth century. One, the exception for West Indian plantation mortgages was based on supposed commercial necessity. The other, used by Lord Haldane in *Kreglinger*, allowed a mortgage to become irredeemable if it formed part of a family transaction intended as a type of settlement. It survived into the nineteenth-century treatises, though the supporting case law was all very old.[274]

Most significant of all, however, was the mortgage with power of sale, which had become so natural that nobody seems any longer to have noticed how its contractual values had subverted what had once been standard equitable principle. Those same contractual values had also been manifested in the devices that served as functional equivalents to mortgages, not quite so good as a reformed mortgage law would have provided, but a reasonable equivalent. So the changes to mortgage law equate only approximately to changes in opportunity for borrowers and lenders. They enabled things to be done more directly and more completely, but the ingenuity of lawyers had found serviceable ways around the limitations of mortgage law for a long time before that.

---

[273] See pp. 42–3, above.
[274] Powell, *Mortgages* (6th edn, 1826), 129a–b; Fisher, *Mortgage*, 12–13; H. A. Smith, *A Practical Exposition of the Principles of Equity* (2nd edn, 1888), 241.

3. SERVITUDES AND ALLIED RIGHTS OVER LAND

One might expect that increasing intensity of land use in the nineteenth century would generate conflict and competition that might resolve itself through increased sales of use rights, licences, and so forth, and that that would test the boundaries of existing legal categories. In 1839 the authors of a new book, subsequently much cited in court, observed that in many respects the English law of easements was but thinly supported by case law, and that indeed only the law of watercourses could be regarded as settled with precision.[275] Easement was not the only legal category available; rights to extract and remove minerals, timber, and the like could be granted as *profits à prendre*. The ancillary rights of access needed to support such a profit would be analysed as a licence coupled with a grant, and the pair together would act as a common law servitude against the burdened land into whosoever hands that land came.[276] There is a question, therefore, of how far these categories expanded, or came under pressure to expand.

There is a question too about whether they were by-passed, one that is easily answered. On the one hand, some activities that in another common law jurisdiction might rely on easements for their fulfilment in England instead relied upon statute. On the other hand, equity's remedial jurisdiction to grant injunctions gave birth to the restrictive covenant, regarded from the 1880s as being a new form of servitude. It did not begin that way, but as an expression of equitable principle. To describe it as a servitude, to name it, to define it, was also to limit it, to prevent more widespread use of principle that would further undermine the logic of property categories. The process is very similar to the invention of the married woman's restraint on anticipation, which reached its end point when Lord Lyndhurst labelled it a 'new species of estate', not an equitable manifestation of owners' freedom to dispose of property as they liked.[277] There is a coincidence of time and personnel too, since both these equities seem to have come into more than occasional use in the last couple of decades of the eighteenth century, both were denounced by Lord Brougham in the 1830s in the interests of freeing property from burdens, whose opinions were in both cases decisively rejected by Lord Cottenham.[278]

---

[275] C. J. Gale and T. D. Whatley, *A Treatise on the Law of Easements*, p. v (in subsequent edns known as 'Gale on Easements'). They were wrong about watercourses: J. Getzler, *A History of Water Rights at Common Law* (Oxford, 2004), 207–327.

[276] *Doe d. Hanley* v. *Wood* (1819) 2 B. & Ald. 724; *Muskett* v. *Hill* (1839) 5 Bing. N.C. 694; W. Bainbridge, *A Practical Treatise on the Law of Mines and Minerals* (3rd edn, 1867), 300–10; R. F. MacSwinney, *The Law of Mines, Quarries, and Minerals* (1884), 249–55.

[277] *Bagget* v. *Meux* (1846) 1 Phil. 627; see pp. 247–8, below.

[278] *Woodmeston* v. *Walker* (1831) 2 Russ. & M. 197; *Brown* v. *Pocock* (1831) 2 Russ. & M. 210; *Keppell* v. *Bailey* (1834) 2 My. & K. 517; *Tullett* v. *Armstrong* (1839) 4 My. & Cr. 390; *Tulk* v. *Moxhay* (1848) 1 H. & Tw. 105.

Common Law: Easements and Licences

Common law judges did not set out to make expansion of servitudes easy. Instead they adhered generally to three principles that required landowners to conform to common law categories. First, they generally set their faces against deviation from the traditional canon of use rights that could be acquired as incorporeal hereditaments—heritable and transferable property interests over the lands of another. Counter-indications that could be gleaned from reported case law, some of it quite recent, were disavowed.

There were three strands to the reasoning. First, in a line that has as its land-marks *Keppell* v. *Bailey* in 1834—Lord Brougham's paeon to common law values though delivered in Chancery—*Ackroyd* v. *Smith* in 1850 and *Hill* v. *Tupper* in 1863, they held that 'incidents of a novel kind' could not be attached to land.[279] As Pollock CB put it in the last of those, 'the whole question depends on whether a new species of property can be created or whether the alleged right merely exists in covenant'. This principle particularly denied the status of property rights to easements held in gross—those which imposed a burden on specified land but which were assignable from person to person rather than being anchored to possession of a plot of benefited land.[280]

Secondly, judges held firm to the rule that an incorporeal hereditament could be created only by deed, and though, under the rules of prescription, a deed would be presumed from appropriate facts of long user, other exceptions were pruned back.[281] There had been a possibility that capital expenditure in reliance upon a contract for an easement would create an entitlement at common law—the principle of executed licences—but that became restricted to situations where licensees invested the money in works on their own land in derogation of some easement or privilege of the licensor.[282] The more common situation where a licensee did works on the licensor's land, say by building a watercourse across it, was held to require a deed if the right was to be irrevocable.

The third principle, the *Wood* v. *Leadbitter* principle, was that a 'mere' licence is always revocable, overruling *Tayler* v. *Waters*, a decision from 1816 to the

---

[279] *Keppell* v. *Bailey* (1834) 2 My. & K. 517; *Ackroyd* v. *Smith* (1850) 10 C.B. 164; *Hill* v. *Tupper* (1863) 2 H. & C. 122.

[280] *Hill* v. *Tupper* (1863) 2 H. & C. 122; *Stockport Waterworks* v. *Potter* (1864) 3 H. & C. 300; M. F. Sturley, 'Easements in Gross' (1980) 96 *LQR* 557–68.

[281] *Hewlins* v. *Shippam* (1826) 5 B. & C. 221; *Wood* v. *Leadbitter* (1845) 13 M. & W. 838.

[282] *Winter* v. *Brockwell* (1807) 8 East 308; *Liggins* v. *Inge* (1831) 7 Bing. 682; *Hewlins* v. *Shippam* (1826) 5 B. & C. 221; *Cocker* v. *Cowper* (1834) 1 C. M. & R. 418; *Wallis* v. Harrison (1838) 4 M. & W. 538; *Perry* v. *Fitzhowe* (1846) 8 Q.B. 757; *Adams* v. *Andrews* (1850) 15 Q.B. 284.

contrary.[283] At its narrowest that meant only that repudiation of a contract is effective even when done in breach, hence that damages lie in contract for the breach and not in tort for the ejection, eviction, demolition, or whatever.[284] Reversal of that consequence, to hold that a purchased 'leave and licence' remains effective against a licensor who reneges on it in breach of contract, followed from an infusion of equity in the early twentieth century. Put shortly, whereas common law judges had held that one needed an incorporeal hereditament in order to sustain (or defeat) an action in tort, a Chancery view that one should need only an enforceable contract prevailed.[285] Chancery judges saw that as a consequence, first, of their general jurisdiction to grant injunctions against breach of contract, which by then was well established even though lack of mutuality did sometimes limit its application, and, secondly, of the priority the Judicature Acts gave to equitable principle.[286]

Similar reasoning from Chancery undermined the second principle. There are few reported cases of straightforward applications for specific performance of contracts to grant easements or other incorporeal hereditaments, but the ones there are treat the principle as unexceptionable.[287] This may be because there were several closely related cases where Chancery issued injunctions against interference with easements enjoyed after capital expenditure in reliance on an agreement, where the argument was put more on the defendant's knowing acquiescence in the expenditure than on any underlying contract.[288] In some such cases relief was given only on terms that compensated the defendant as the parties had originally envisaged, thus blurring any line between acquiescence and the enforcement of contracts. Either way there was no deed, but either way a purchaser of the burdened land with notice would be bound. The realization that equitable principles and jurisdiction greatly reduced the importance of these common law rules crept

[283] *Wood* v. *Leadbitter* (1845) 13 M. & W. 838; *Tayler* v. *Waters* (1816) 7 Taunt. 374; *Coleman* v. *Foster* (1856) 1 H. & N. 37.

[284] Counsel quite frequently argued against even contractual liability, but unsuccessfully: *Wright* v. *Stavert* (1860) 2 El. & El. 721; *Smart* v. *Jones* (1864) 15 C.B. N.S. 717; *Wells* v. *Mayor etc of Kingston-upon-Hull* (1875) LR 10 CP 402; *Butler* v. *Manchester etc Railway* (1888) 21 QBD 207; *Kerrison* v. *Smith* [1897] 2 QB 445.

[285] *Lowe* v. *Adams* [1901] 2 Ch 598; *Hurst* v. *Picture Theatres* [1915] 1 KB 1.

[286] *Lumley* v. *Wagner* (1852) 1 De G. M. & G. 604; *Frogley* v. *Earl Lovelace* (1859) Johns. 333; *James Jones* v. *Tankerville* [1909] 2 Ch 440; S. Gardner, 'Equity, Estate Contracts and the Judicature Acts: *Walsh* v *Lonsdale* Revisited' (1987) 7 *OJLS* 60–103.

[287] *Frogley* v. *Earl Lovelace* (1859) Johns. 333; *McManus* v. *Cooke* (1887) 35 Ch D 681; *May* v. *Belleville* [1905] 2 Ch 605.

[288] *East India Co* v. *Vincent* (1740) 2 Atk. 83 (explained in *McManus* v. *Cooke* (1887) 35 Ch D 681); *Williams* v. *Earl of Jersey* (1841) Cr. & Ph. 91; *Powell* v. *Thomas* (1848) 6 Hare 300; *Duke of Devonshire* v. *Eglin* (1853) 16 Beav. 530; *Rochdale Canal Co* v. *King* (1853) 16 Beav. 630; *Laird* v. *Birkenhead Railway Co* (1859) Johns. 500.

into *Gale on Easements* in 1862, and then only as a footnote.[289] It had been *Gale* that alerted Parke B. to the unsoundness of *Tayler* v. *Waters*, hence opening the way to *Wood* v. *Leadbitter*, but while it had always been deeply learned in Roman, French, and American authorities hitherto it had been almost blind to equity.[290]

The eclipse of *Wood* v. *Leadbitter* was only partial, however. It did not entail that whatever was contained in a contract would bind third parties; in this instance the first of the three common law principles was not compromised. It could have been. 'Acquiescence' has the potential to subvert definitions of property rights. That may be why in the leading mid-century case on acquiescence, *Ramsden* v. *Dyson*, Lords Cranworth and Wensleydale, who had both sat in *Wood* v. *Leadbitter*, preferred tighter formulations grounded on implied contracts (for common law rights) or mistake (as to common law rights), as against Lord Kingsdown's looser principle based upon satisfying expectations generated by promises and conduct.[291] In the 1880s it was Lord Cranworth's statement that was turned by Fry J. into his well-known rule-based rendition of the principle.[292] Even when the looser formulation was preferred, as in *Plimmer* v. *Mayor of Wellington*, it could easily be presented as just another way of acquiring an 'interest', rather than as a freestanding value capable of binding third parties.[293] So the common law's categorical approach was not greatly threatened.

Prohibition of new species of property allowed for new mutations within an existing species, but within the category of 'easement' the mutation rate seems to have been rather modest. Lists of valid easements beyond the established categories of ways, watercourses, and light disclose little to meet new demands from an industrializing and urbanizing society.[294] The major exception occurred within the sub-category of watercourses, where rights concerning artificial channels—to continued flow, to pure flow, or to interrupt or pollute the flow—were analysed as easements capable of acquisition by express grant or prescription, hence as capable of serving a range of industrial purposes.[295] By contrast bank-side proprietors' appropriation of naturally flowing water for 'extraordinary' purposes was

---

[289] 3rd edn (by W. H. Willes), 71–2n; cf. MacSwinney, *Mines*, 251.

[290] *Williams* v. *Morris* (1841) 8 M. & W. 488.

[291] *Ramsden* v. *Dyson* (1866) LR 1 HL 129; Cranworth (Rolfe J.) was trial judge and member of the full bench in *Wood* v. *Leadbitter*; Wensleydale (Parke B.) was present for just part of the argument: 9 Jur. 187.

[292] *Willmott* v. *Barber* (1880) 15 Ch D 96, and see Fry LJ's overt reliance on Cranworth in *Weller* v. *Stone* (1885) 54 LJ Ch 497.

[293] *Plimmer* v. *Mayor of Wellington* (1884) 9 App Cas 699; F. Pollock, *Law of Torts* (2nd edn, 1890), 325–6 ('an interest which may be made good by way of equitable estoppel'); S. Moriarty, 'Licences and Land Law' (1984) 100 *LQR* 376–412.

[294] e.g. J. L. Goddard, *A Treatise on the Law of Easements* (3rd edn, 1884), 105n.

[295] Getzler, *Water Rights*, 232–45, relying especially on *Arkwright* v. *Gell* (1839) 5 M. & W. 203; *Magor* v. *Chadwick* (1840) 11 Ad. & El. 572; *Wood* v. *Waud* (1849) 3 Exch. 748.

treated as an incident of ownership, but was limited to uses that had no significant impact on the quantity or quality of the flow reaching downstream properties.[296] In principle greater rights could be acquired by easement, so again by grant or prescription, but the books contain few litigated cases compared with the many on other aspects of riparian law.[297]

Similarly, the books and a handful of cases acknowledged that there may be easements to legalize nuisances, which, had they been common would have raised issues of extent, definition, and perhaps social utility.[298] But the supposition seems always to have been that express grants were rare, hence that acquisition would be by prescription. As a companion to their prohibition of novel incidents that might burden servient property, common law judges had a principle that long use in itself did not create rights. So time started running not when some new industrial practice began, but only when it became an actionable nuisance in relation to the plaintiff's land.[299] Since 20 years' infraction was required for a prescriptive easement, successfully litigated examples are unusual.[300]

As for easements in gross, their prohibition was important for doctrine, less so for practice. In the United States easements in gross were found useful 'for railroads, for telephone and telegraph and electric power lines, for pipelines...', but in England all of those were accomplished instead through statute, whether by compulsory acquisition of land or by regimes of statutory powers.[301] Much of that law is found in local and private legislation, some of it in the Clauses Acts, and only a little in general legislation; accounts are found in specialist literature, not in works on real property law.[302] So too with water rights; riparian owners could use the natural flow only for activities on their bank-side property. Judges denied them power to licence off-tenement users to the detriment of downstream proprietors, whether the licensed use was for industrial purposes or for watering towns.[303] Again legislation was the answer, especially local legislation, which could address conflicting issues specifically.

[296] *Embrey* v. *Owen* (1851) 6 Exch. 353; *Miner* v. *Gilmour* (1858) 14 Moo. P.C. 131; *Swindon Waterworks Co* v. *Wilts & Berks Canal Navigation Co* (1875) LR 7 HL 697; Getzler, *Water Rights*, 282–96.

[297] Gale, *Easements* (6th edn, 1888), 212–86; H. J. W. Coulson and U. A. Forbes, *The Law Relating to Waters, Sea, Tidal and Inland* (1880), 239–61; *Holker* v. *Porritt* (1875) 10 Ex 59 and *A.-G.* v. *Grand Junction Canal Co* [1909] 2 Ch 505 are examples of prescriptive rights.

[298] Gale, *Easements* (6th edn), 275–95 (but mostly concerns definitions of nuisance).

[299] *Murgatroyd* v. *Robinson* (1857) 7 El. & Bl. 391; *Crossley & Sons* v. *Lightowler* (1867) 2 Ch App 478; *Sturges* v. *Bridgman* (1879) 11 Ch D 852.

[300] *Wright* v. *Williams* (1836) 1 M. & W. 77; *Baxendale* v. *McMurray* (1867) 2 Ch App 790 stand out; see pp. 1083–5, below.

[301] R. R. Powell and P. J. Rohan, *Powell on Real Property* (New York, 1969), §34.16.

[302] Railway Clauses Act, 8 & 9 Vict. c. 20, Waterworks Clauses Act, 10 & 11 Vict. c. 17.

[303] *Stockport Waterworks Co* v. *Potter* (1864) 3 H. & C. 300; *Swindon Waterworks Co* v. *Wilts & Berks Canal Navigation Co* (1875) LR 7 HL 697; *Ormerod* v. *Todmorden Joint Stock Mill Co* (1883) 11 QBD 155.

For some local authorities wishing to establish waterworks, however, expense could be a significant obstacle until the Borough Fund Act 1872 allowed their costs of promoting local bills to be charged to the rates irrespective of the success of the application.[304] From 1875 they also had power to acquire *land* compulsorily by provisional order process under the Public Health Act, a much cheaper option, but a select committee of the House of Lords decided that restrictions in the Act ruled out its use for mere water rights.[305] Rural district councils, whose originating legislation did not incorporate the Borough Fund Act, complained into the twentieth century that they were squeezed between a common law prohibiting riparian owners from licensing off-tenement use of water and a legislative process too risky for them to broach.[306] Unsympathetic judges declined to bend the Public Health Act in their favour and Parliament declined to amend it.[307]

Watercourses aside, there is less sign than one would expect in the books and the reported case law of tension between, on the one hand, commercial or industrial pressure to acquire rights over neighbouring land that would outlast the licensor's possession and, on the other, judicial unwillingness to see the list of permitted servitudes expanded. One area that came near it concerned ability to abstract subsurface waters. In *Chasemore v. Richards* in 1859 judges opted by a majority for an absolute right in the freehold owner, not to be limited by principles of reasonable on-tenement user.[308] This was not an easement but an incident of property. Nor could a downhill owner acquire a pre-emptive easement by prescription to block abstraction by uphill owners. These were rules motivated in large part by principles of legal efficiency: fear of broad and indeterminate liability, dislike of leaving the extent of rights to turn on jury verdicts and hydrologists' evidence.[309]

See Getzler, *Water Rights*, 316–24, whose conclusion, however, that there was a right to reasonable off-tenement user seems overstated. *Earl of Sandwich* v. *Great Northern Railway Co* (1878) 10 Ch D 707, which did apply that principle, was overruled in *McCartney* v. *Londonderry & Lough Swilly Railway Co* [1904] AC 301, leaving *Kensit* v. *Great Eastern Railway* (1884) 27 Ch D 122 as the only successful case of the type. There, however, the plaintiff conceded that the flow to which he was entitled was wholly unaffected in either quantity or quality by the off-tenement licensee's use.

[304] See Vol. XI, pp. 441–2.

[305] *Return Showing as Regards Every Water Undertaking [etc]* 1914, *PP* (395), lxxix, 543 at p. xxvi, reporting that the Law Officers confirmed that reading.

[306] *Joint SC on Water Supplies (Protection) Bill*, Report, *PP* 1910 (226), vi, 653.

[307] *Roberts* v. *Gwyrfai District Council* [1899] 2 Ch 608; *Joint SC on Water Supplies (Protection) Bill*.

[308] *Chasemore v. Richards* (1859) 7 H.L.C. 349; Getzler, *Water Rights*, 302–15. There was an exception, narrowly applied, for underwater streams flowing in a defined channel the existence of which was notorious.

[309] *Ballacorkish Silver Company* v. *Harrison* (1873) LR 5 PC 49; Getzler, *Water Rights*, 307n; cf. *Bonomi* v. *Backhouse* (1858) El. Bl. & El. 646 (aff'd 9 H.L.C. 503).

They look the sort of sharp-edged rules ideal for generating a trading regime. An owner wishing to sell subsurface water off site could grant an abstractor the right to drill wells (and remove the soil) plus a licence to remove the water. That would operate as a 'licence coupled with a grant', which if granted by deed could be made perpetual and irrevocable. The difficulty would be in securing continuity of supply as against someone intercepting the water from an estate higher up the slope. The principle of non-derogation from grant might sometimes apply, if there had been a subdivision. It could be used to prevent an owner who had sold a lower-lying section of his estate for a purpose known to require the subsurface waters from subsequently interrupting their flow.[310] If so, the disability would run with the servient land, creating an *ad-hoc* servitude. Judges accepted non-derogation and 'licence coupled with a grant' as part of the common law canon, though both can undermine the austere principles of *Ackroyd* v. *Smith*.[311] But without such a subdivision there seems nothing in the common law cupboard that might aid a downhill owner seeking security of supply.

In this instance, however, that potential conflict was not explored, because the focus shifted instead to Parliament. From about the early 1870s bulk water supply concentrated into the hands of public local authorities, who took to selling to commercial as well as to domestic consumers; groundwater extraction increased.[312] Nearly all this activity was conducted under local statutory powers. By the early years of the twentieth century promoters of local bills frequently met opposition in Parliament from rival water extractors and from landowners whose land would be left desiccated and subsiding.[313] In form the judges' baseline common law rules survived, but in practice once a bill was opposed deals had to be done, the most usual being insertion of a clause that the promoters must compensate groundwater users within a defined area from the new borehole by supplying them with water free.[314] Judges seem to have sympathized, interpreting local authorities' enabling legislation as not allowing them to bypass such parliamentary or governmental control by simply acquiring land and then exercising a private landowner's power of extraction.[315] Even when the House of

---

[310] *Whitehead* v. *Parks* (1858) 2 H. & N. 870; cf. *M'Nab* v. *Robertson* [1897] AC 129.

[311] For links between the two principles, see *Newby* v. *Harrison* (1861) 1 John. & H. 393 (aff'd (1861) 4 LT 424).

[312] J. A. Hassan, 'The Growth and Impact of the British Water Industry in the Nineteenth Century' (1985) 38 *Econ. Hist.* Rev. 531–47; *Return Showing as Regards Every Water Undertaking [etc]*.

[313] *Joint SC on Water Supplies (Protection) Bill.* Liability for this form of subsidence was denied in *Popplewell* v. *Hodkinson* (1869) LR 4 Ex 248 but partially reinstated by *Jordeson* v. *Sutton, Southcoates & Drypool Gas Co* [1899] 2 Ch 217.

[314] *Joint SC on Water Supplies (Protection) Bill*, Evidence, esp. at 40–6, 60–1, 73, 236.

[315] *Marriott* v. *East Grinstead Gas & Water Co* (1908) 99 LT 958; *A-G* v. *Frimley and Farnborough District Water Co* [1907] 1 Ch 727.

Lords put a stop to that strained construction in 1910, the Lord Chancellor urged Parliament to ensure that all local legislation did contain adequate protection for private interests.[316] So there was something of a bargaining process, and it did operate within something of a normative framework, but it did not engage the common law.

A clearer instance of bargaining within a common law framework concerned surface subsidence from mining.[317] From around 1800 methods of coal extraction became more aggressive.[318] In some districts pillars which customarily had been left to support the surface were now removed entirely at the end of a seam's life. Other districts began to adopt the longwall system in which subsidence of upper levels was inherent, indeed desirable. Common law judges responded by reasserting the surface owner's right to support from subjacent strata, unqualified by notions of local custom or the reasonableness of the mining methods used.[319] Similarly, time ran for mining operators only from when their works caused damage to the surface, not from when the mines were opened—so there could be no hidden servitude against the surface owner.[320] Coal owners therefore had every incentive to seek express provision.

Some judges would have denied altogether the validity of express grants to let down the surface, on grounds of repugnancy or on *Ackroyd* v. *Smith* principles—working steadily through the common law canon they found nothing in it that fitted the required description.[321] The majority, however, took the commercial view that separation of surface and mining rights would usually originate in some formal consensual transaction, thence that an adjusted principle of non-derogation was appropriate: the right to let down the surface could be granted or reserved, but that needed to be done expressly, with especial clarity in the latter instance.[322] Perhaps that principle was sufficient in itself, perhaps it generated an easement, or perhaps this was an example of an irrevocable licence coupled with a grant; the judges did not agree, but nor did they think it mattered.

---

[316] *A-G* v. *Barnet District Gas & Water Co* (1910) 102 LT 546 (Loreburn).

[317] See pp. 1127–40, below.

[318] *The History of the British Coal Industry* (by M. W. Flinn, Oxford, 1984), ii, 82–90; (by R. Church, Oxford, 1986), iii, 328–40.

[319] *Humphries* v. *Brogden* (1850) 12 Q.B. 739; *Butterknowle Colliery* v. *Bishop Auckland Industrial Co-operative Society* [1906] AC 313; *New Sharlston Collieries* v. *Earl of Westmoreland* (1900) [1904] 2 Ch 443n (HL); cf. *Harris* v. *Ryding* (1839) 5 M. & W. 60; *Hilton* v. *Earl Granville* (1845) 5 Q.B. 701.

[320] *Bonomi* v. *Backhouse* (1861) 9 H.L.C. 503.

[321] *Hilton* v. *Earl Granville* (1845) 5 Q.B. 701; *Rowbotham* v. *Wilson* (1857) 8 El. & Bl. 123 (Cresswell J. and Watson B., diss.).

[322] *Rowbotham* v. *Wilson* (1860) 8 H.L.C. 348. The ruling generated considerable litigation on the interpretation of old deeds and inclosure Acts, as did the relation between canal and railway companies' statutory power of compulsory acquisition and the underlying mineral owners' powers to work their mines.

In some districts reservations of mining rights conventionally allowed surface damage subject to a formula for compensation, usually in the shape of a covenant, which worried the editor of *Bainbridge on Mines and Minerals*.[323] How could such a thing run to successors at common law, given the principle of *Ackroyd v. Smith*? Judges, however, just reached for another useful principle, that someone claiming under a grant must honour all of it, and from there concluded that the right to let down the surface was a licence coupled with a grant, the covenant really a condition attached to the licence.[324] Common law had flexibility when needed.

Like 'acquiescence', therefore, the principle that a grantor may not derogate from his grant had potential to subvert a categorical approach to property concepts. But like acquiescence it could be subordinated to it, treated as a reason for or against implying interests into grants that were not explicit. In that different context it was used as an aid to a broader line of reasoning found in *Keppell* v. *Bailey*, that restrictions on land use should be both standardized and reduced in the interests of commerce. The question arose on subdivision of land. *Gale on Easements* had argued that English law conformed to a principle of French law (*destination du père de famille*) that a permanent and obvious pattern of usage by the common owner who was subdividing the whole or part of the land changed the incidents of the plots relative to each other.[325] On a subdivision the former sole owner's patterns of access ways, watercourses, drainage, and so forth would harden into rights. Some judges found this principle common sense when applied to subdivisions of house property, at least so as to continue existing access and drainage uses; implied rights to light were more difficult.[326] For subdivision of land it was more difficult still, since to make radical changes from existing uses might have been the point of the purchase.

Strong judicial opinions were pronounced on both sides of the argument, but as late as 1877 Davidson wrote that the conveyancing profession thought Gale's principle broadly correct.[327] Two years later the Court of Appeal ruled definitively otherwise: non-derogation from grant was the dominant principle, and it applied differentially.[328] If an owner sold part of an estate the purchaser could claim as

[323] 4th edn (1878), 260–8.

[324] *Aspden* v. *Seddon* (1876) 1 Ex D 496; *Chamber Colliery Co* v. *Twyerould* (1893) [1915] 1 Ch 268n (HL).

[325] 1st edn, pp. vi and 49–71. Davidson thought Gale the last word on easements: *Precedents*, ii, 548n (4th edn, 1877).

[326] *Hinchliffe* v. *Earl of Kinnoul* (1838) 5 Bing. N.C. 1; *White* v. *Bass* (1862) 7 H. & N. 722.

[327] *Pyer* v. *Carter* (1857) 1 H. & N. 916; *White* v. *Bass* (1862) 7 H. & N. 722; *Suffield* v. *Brown* (1863) 9 Jur. (N.S.) 999 (Romilly MR); (1864) 4 De G. J. & Sm. 185 (Lord Westbury); *Crossley* v. *Lightowler* (1867) 2 Ch App 478; *Morland* v. *Cook* (1868) LR 6 Eq 252; *Watts* v. *Kelson* (1871) 6 Ch App 166; Davidson, *Precedents*, ii, 550n (4th edn, 1877).

[328] *Wheeldon* v. *Burrows* (1879) 12 Ch D 31.

implied easements the prior usages that benefited the part bought, provided that they met tests of visibility and continuity, but the owner of the retained portion could not claim to have impliedly retained rights against the sold-off plot unless without them the retained land could not be used at all. The ruling thus reduced the factual inquiries the purchaser would have to make ahead of the conveyance, though it did nothing to aid future purchasers of the retained land. Implicitly the usages must be capable of existing as easements, that is they must conform to the common law definition. Even judges who found Gale's principle attractive accepted that.[329]

The implication was that easements owed their origin to an act of will by the servient owner, an express grant of a right to a neighbour, though they might sometimes be implied into grants to do justice in the circumstances. When implied, however, they took their colour from what could (or should) have been formally granted. In theory all easements began thus, since prescription—the acquisition of easements by use and passage of time—rested on the fiction that the uninterrupted use shows that there must once have been a grant. For some sorts of easement, however, this analysis is fictitious in a further sense, that nearly all instances were prescriptive; in practice they never (or hardly ever) resulted from acts of will by the servient owner. Thus usually the so-called easements of light, air, and support of buildings were legal constructions by judges to ground a conclusion that a proprietor must not, by activity on his own land, reduce those amenities *de facto* enjoyed by buildings on his neighbour's land.[330] Functionally this exercise in the identification of interests to be protected is most usefully analysed as part of the law of torts, which is where it will be found in this volume.[331] 'Easement' in this context is a vehicle through which judges express principles of liability.

It is possible, however, that the right to light, the most important of this class of easement, was for a time affected by technicalities concerning the law of prescription. At the start of our period that was not an area of law that drew much praise. Technically, as the Real Property Commissioners no doubt enjoyed relaying, use of the easement back to 1189 had to be proved, that being the period of legal memory.[332] Of course, proof for a shorter period sufficed in practice, but could be displaced by proof that the easement could not or did not exist at some intermediate date. That in turn had been displaced by another fiction, that the easement

---

[329] Romilly MR is the best example; his broad use of 'notice' as a justification did not extend to challenging the definition of what it was that was noticed: *Suffield* v. *Brown* (1863) 9 Jur. (N.S.) 999, explained in *Morland* v. *Cook* (1868) LR 6 Eq 252.

[330] There are no precedents for express grants in the collections, nor reported litigation.

[331] See below, Part Four, Chapter VI.

[332] *RC on Real Property*, 1st Report, *PP* 1829 (263), xi, 1, 51–2.

was modern, that it had been granted by deed, but that the deed had been lost. By the start of our period it was accepted that 20 years' use had shifted from raising a mere presumption of a lost grant to being 'in practice and effect' a bar to the servient owner.[333] There were conditions, especially that for some of that time somebody able to make a grant must have been in possession (or, perhaps, just to have known about the use). A limited owner or a mere tenant did not count, because functionally acquisition was based upon acquiescence by the owner of the inheritance. Nonetheless, if the conditions were satisfied proof of use for 20 years operated very much like a rule, though in law it was a presumption of fact requiring a jury's verdict—which at least one writer thought might tax jurors' conscience.[334] He and the Real Property Commissioners were at one in recommending that statute should replace fiction with positive law.

It is not known how the resulting statute, Prescription Act 1832, came to be drafted.[335] It was introduced by Lord Tenterden and seems not to have emanated from the Commission, though its provisions broadly follow the pattern the Commission proposed. It was ambitious, containing a series of periods of use graded according to different sorts of servitude and with different legal effect— some rebuttable, some conclusive—and with complex provisions about limited owners and owners under a legal disability. As a bill it underwent some bargaining with the Church, resulting in excision of provisions about moduses for tithes— replacement of the obligation to pay in kind by a fixed cash payment, hence tending to diminish tithe's value with the passage of time.[336] And it suffered generally from postponement to make room for debates over the Reform Bill. Perhaps for these reasons its main provisions had little public discussion, resulting in a text denigrated as 'one of the worst drafted Acts on the Statute Book'.[337] Its provisions were poorly co-ordinated, leaving judges struggling to identify its policies, some of its distinctions seemed arbitrary, and it contained a gross typographical error in one section. It soon became conventional that, in general, the Act did not replace existing methods of claiming easements by prescription.[338]

Rights to light, however, were something of an exception. Section 3 gave an 'absolute and indefeasible' right after uninterrupted enjoyment for 20 years, a

[333] T. Starkie, *A Practical Treatise on the Law of Evidence* (1824), iii, 1214; Gale, *Easements* (1st edn), 95.

[334] *Penwarden* v. *Ching* (1829) Mood. & M. 400 (prescription for light to window 22 years old good); Starkie, *Evidence*, iii, 1215n.

[335] 2 & 3 Will. IV c. 71.

[336] Moduses got their own legislation: Tithe Act 1832, 2 & 3 Will. IV c. 100.

[337] *Law Reform Committee*, 14th Report, *PP* 1966–7 (Cmnd. 3100), xxxix, 309, 322; Gale, *Easements* (1st edn), 97.

[338] Gale, *Easements* (1st edn), 97, Starkie, *Evidence* (3rd edn, 1842), iii, 911n, *Webb* v. *Bird* (1863) 13 C.B. N.S. 841.

rule that in its simplicity contrasted with the complexities and preconditions found elsewhere in the Act. From the 1860s there was a trend to reading it not merely as giving a right absolutely but as giving an absolute right.[339] That envisaged the dominant owner having a right to a 'cone' (sometimes 'pencils') of light to the particular window, irrespective of whether it was needed for the dominant owner's projected use. Previously not every reduction of light would be a breach, only those that made an appreciable difference or prevented normal usage—a nuisance standard allowing some adjustment for circumstance, one that had been adopted by equity as much as by common law.[340] The new reasoning tended to be formal, with an emphasis upon rights and upon the statute, but the consequence was to make rebuilding more difficult, or, at least, more expensive (there are no studies of the relative incidence of damages and injunctions, nor on what parties did consequent upon issue of an injunction). It was not endorsed by all judges, Malins VC and James LJ were among those adhering to the older standard, but it was the more usual.[341] In 1904, however, the House of Lords emphatically returned the law to the old nuisance standard, motivated by dislike of the additional burden rights-based reasoning placed on servient owners and the opportunity it gave dominant owners to extract windfall payments.[342]

Though there were these difficulties there was very little sign of the outright hostility to prescriptive rights to light common in American law at this time.[343] Nor were judges hostile to prescription generally; if they had been it would not have been difficult to read the 1832 Act as replacing common law prescription and the lost modern grant and then interpreting it narrowly. On the contrary, in *Dalton* v. *Angus* the Lords, supported by a majority of the judges, held that the lost modern grant survived, that it should operate in a simple form with few means of rebuttal, and that it applied to the easement of support of buildings.[344] That

---

[339] *Frewen* v. *Phillips* (1862) 11 C.B. N.S. 449; *Yates* v. *Jack* (1866) LR 1 Ch App 295; *Dent* v. *Auction Mart* (1866) LR 2 Eq 238; *Calcraft* v. *Thompson* (1867) 15 WR 387; *Aynsley* v. *Glover* (1874) LR 18 Eq 548 (aff'd LR 10 Ch App 283); *Moore* v. *Hall* (1878) 3 QBD 178; *Scott* v. *Pape* (1886) 31 Ch D 554; *Warren* v. *Brown* [1902] 1 KB 15. This approach fitted well with the cases holding that even a window to an unused building acquired the right: *Courtauld* v. *Legh* (1869) LR 4 Ex 126; *Cooper* v. *Straker* (1888) 40 Ch D 21; *Collis* v. *Laugher* [1894] 3 Ch 659.

[340] *Martin* v. *Goble* (1808) 1 Camp. 320; *A.G.* v. *Nichol* (1809) 16 Ves. 338; *Back* v. *Stacey* (1826) 2 Car. & P. 465; *Parker* v. *Smith* (1832) 5 Car. & P. 438; *Jackson* v. *Duke of Newcastle* (1864) 3 De G. J. & Sm. 275.

[341] *Lanfranchi* v. *Mackenzie* (1867) LR 4 Eq 421; *Kelk* v. *Pearson* (1871) LR 6 Ch App 809; *Dickinson* v. *Harbottle* (1873) 28 LT 186.

[342] *Colls* v. *Home and Colonial Stores* [1904] AC 179.

[343] M. Horwitz, *The Transformation of American Law 1780–1860* (Cambridge, Mass., 1977), 43–7; Gale, *Easements* (8th edn, 1908), 337. The nearest is Lord Cranworth in *Yates* v. *Jack* (1866) LR 1 Ch App 295.

[344] (1881) 6 App Cas 740. See pp. 1137–40, below.

easement aside, however, which the division of opinion among the lower court judges showed to be a marginal case, negative easements could not be acquired by prescription—again aside from the well-established rights to light and to air in a defined channel.[345] Since prescription rested upon acquiescence there had to be some plausible means by which the servient owner could interrupt acquisition of the right, which was difficult, sometimes practically impossible, for negative easements. Theory probably required that if they could not be acquired by prescription they could not be granted expressly either, but that was not strenuously contested. Instead the development in equity of the restrictive covenant amply met whatever needs there were, as will be seen in the next section.

Equity: From Principle to Rules

Lord Brougham's analysis in *Keppell* v. *Bailey* explicitly included that equity should follow the law.[346] The list of permissible legal estates and interests was closed, social utility lay in reducing burdens on land, and equity should know its place. Chancery judges disagreed. Though Brougham's analysis was argued before them with various emphases during the next decade they brushed it aside.[347] The conscience of a third party purchaser could be bound, mimicking a property right, even though no such property right existed at law. In particular purchasers who bought land knowing that a previous owner had entered covenants affecting its permissible use could be enjoined from acting contrary to them, even though the covenants fell outside the narrow range enforceable at law.

The range and force of argument in *Tulk* v. *Moxhay* in 1848 suggests that that case was a showdown on those issues, not the exercise in innovation that was later portrayed.[348] Lord Cottenham rooted injunctions to enforce covenants against third party purchasers in what he saw as conventional and well-established equity. This he based on his own long experience and on interpretation of Lord Eldon's practice and assumptions, an approach and a conclusion shared by Sugden and, more cautiously, by the Real Property Commissioners.[349] For Cottenham the analogy was not with easements or common law covenants, as Jessel MR

[345] Gale, *Easements* (8th edn), 202n, 236–7.

[346] *Keppell* v. *Bailey* (1834) 2 My. & K. 517.

[347] *Whatman* v. *Gibson* (1838) 9 Sim. 196; *Schreiber* v. *Creed* (1839) 10 Sim. 9; *Mann* v. *Stephens* (1846) 15 Sim. 377; cf. *Bristow* v. *Wood* (1844) 1 Coll. 480.

[348] 11 Beav. 571, 18 LJ Ch 83, 1 H. & Tw. 105, all of them superior to the more usually cited 2 Ph. 774; S. I. George, '*Tulk v Moxhay* Restored—to its Historical Context' (1990) 12 *Liverpool LR* 173–93.

[349] *Tulk* v. *Moxhay* (1848) 1 H. & Tw. 105, using *Duke of Bedford* v. *Trustees of British Museum* (1822) 2 My. & K. 552 and *Feoffees of Heriot's Hospital* v. *Gibson* (1814) 2 Dow. P.C. 301; Sugden, *Vendors and Purchasers* (10th edn, 1839), ii, 494–506, using the *British Museum* case and the otherwise unknown case of the Old Steyne, Brighton; *RC on Real Property*, 3rd Report, PP 1831–2 (484), xxiii, 321, 373–5.

was later to assert, but with contracts to grant leases.[350] Equity conventionally enforced those against purchasers of the fee with notice, showing at one and the same time that equity did not always simply follow the law and that contracts concerning land did generate equitable rights. To allow a purchaser with notice to disregard the burdensome equity that had enabled him to acquire the land for a lesser price would be most inequitable, unjust, and unconscientious; and why, he asked, should a landowner not be able to contract in a way beneficial to his neighbour? Reasoning such as that is obviously antipathetic to a categorical approach.

Lord Cottenham had been 40 years practising or adjudicating in Chancery so it is surprising that legal historians have generally given only tepid credence to his assertion of continuity.[351] That later judges should choose to view his ruling as innovative is of course readily understandable, because that makes its curtailment so much the easier.[352] But without some such understanding as Cottenham's and Sugden's what looks like a widespread, confident, and nuanced use of covenants to regulate the development of building land is explicable only on the basis of collective wishful thinking.[353] True, some early sets, such as those from Bath in the 1760s and Joseph Pitt's Pittville set from 1827, reserve a rentcharge to the vendor/covenantee, which in common law theory would be enough to support a covenant.[354] But others do not, and Pitt's seem to use the rentcharge to finance maintenance of the infrastructure of his proposed new township rather than to ground the covenants restricting the style and use of the covenantors' buildings.[355] In some schemes—Kemp Town in Brighton was one—the covenants were initially leasehold. Developers granted 99-year building leases containing options to purchase the freehold, which, when exercised would carry the covenants over.[356] These variations on the common theme seem contemporaneous rather than sequential, there being little or nothing in the texts to bring uniformity; the process will not be fully understood, however, until there has been empirical research.

---

[350] *London & South Western Railway* v. *Gomm* (1882) 20 Ch D 562.

[351] *HEL*, xiii, 634 (see also xvi, 34); Simpson, *History of the Land Law* (2nd edn), 256–60. Contrast A. H. Manchester, *Modern Legal History* (1980), 321. Holdsworth's use of *Collins* v. *Plumb* (1810) 16 Ves. 454 to show that Eldon knew nothing of an equitable jurisdiction to enforce covenants against successors ignores the very first line reported from him. The case seems obviously to turn on the difficulty of determining what was a breach of that particular covenant, which may be why it did not feature in the subsequent arguments.

[352] Particularly as they had come to rely on the truncated report in *Phillips* rather than the much longer opinion in *Hall and Twells*.

[353] George, '*Tulk v Moxhay* Restored'.

[354] *Western* v. *Macdermot* (1866) 2 Ch App 72; *Schreiber* v. *Creed* (1839) 10 Sim. 9.

[355] *Whatman* v. *Gibson* (1838) 9 Sim. 196 (Ramsgate, 1799).

[356] *Kemp* v. *Sober* (1851) 1 Sim. (N.S.) 520; and cf. *Jay* v. *Richardson* (1862) 30 Beav. 563.

Analytically, however, there was no sign in the 1840s of a sharp distinction between 'individual' covenants and 'building scheme' covenants. Commentators later found their operation so distinct that *Tulk* v. *Moxhay* became regarded as the progenitor of the former, *Whatman* v. *Gibson* the latter. At the time, however, both were enforced because they were contracts of which the successor had notice.[357] The only difference was whether the promisee intended promisors to be able to enforce the covenants between themselves, which in turn depended upon whether he intended them to be enforceable against himself.[358]

Tulk v. *Moxhay* was important for settling the issue, not particularly for its own facts, which were unusual.[359] Lord Cottenham addressed continuity and change, law and equity, obligation and property, and theory and social utility; it is untrue that 'the wider issues were simply not appreciated'.[360] Nor were he and his contemporaries unaware of the lack of 'privity' between the parties.[361] The combination of 'contract', 'intention', and 'notice' that they deployed validated the schemes land developers had been using to protect investors in their new housing from at least some aspects of market-driven change. Covenants would commonly stipulate housing styles, site densities, and proscribed uses, thus encouraging the general respectability of neighbourhoods and hence the security of the investment.[362] Lord Brougham had worried about the breadth of obligation that contract could impose. Content would be individual, even whimsical, detracting from the marketability that he saw as the primary value.[363]

Though Lord Cottenham said nothing to limit his own broad principle Chancery already had a built-in restriction, a general self-denying ordinance that it would not make orders if it could not superintend their execution.[364] That was its reason for not specifically enforcing building or husbandry covenants in leases. It was not a pure positive/negative distinction, because Chancery would order specific performance of covenants to renew the lease or ones giving the

---

[357] *Whatman* v. *Gibson* (1838) 9 Sim. 196; *Coles* v. *Sims* (1854) 5 De G. M. & G. 1.

[358] *Schreiber* v. *Creed* (1839) 10 Sim. 9; *Whatman* v. *Gibson* (1838) 9 Sim. 196.

[359] The covenant taken in 1808 for the preservation of Leicester Square, London, as a garden for the residents was probably meant to fulfil the obligation imposed on the Tulk family by a partition decree in 1788; see S. Anderson, 'Tulk v Moxhay', in P. Cane and J. Conaghan (eds), *New Oxford Companion to Law* (Oxford, 2008), 1197–8.

[360] Simpson, *History of the Land Law* (2nd edn), 259.

[361] *Mann* v. *Stephens* (1846) 15 Sim. 377.

[362] All three reports of *Whatman* v. *Gibson* are needed: (1838) 9 Sim. 196, 2 Jur. 273, 7 LJ Ch 160; *Mann* v. *Stephens* (1846) 15 Sim. 377; *Tulk* v. *Moxhay* (1848) 1 H. & Tw. 105; *Peacock* v. *Penson* (1848) 11 Beav. 355.

[363] *Keppell* v. *Bailey* (1834) 2 My. & K. 517.

[364] *Marker* v. *Marker* (1851) 9 Hare 1; *Lumley* v. *Wagner* (1852) 1 De G. M. & G. 604.

tenant an option to buy the freehold, even against third parties.[365] It was not even that those positive undertakings did not need superintending, since a good deal of judicial chambers work involved settling their terms. Nonetheless the practice was clear. These freehold covenants came with the limitation taken to be general in the exercise of equitable jurisdiction, that performance of positive obligations other than the granting or transferring of estates would not be ordered, nor would injunctions be granted that required assessment of matters of degree.[366] These restrictions go part way to explaining why another of Lord Brougham's fears did not materialize: that an equity to enforce covenants where there was no legal right would displace the common law rule of leasehold covenants that only those touching and concerning the land would bind successors.

Lord Cottenham's 'equity attached to the property' did affect tenants, however, a fact that was to influence its development. Tenants with notice were bound by freehold covenants just as their landlords were; with so much land tenanted it would have made little sense for them not to be.[367] The critical question was what was to constitute notice. There tenants were held to the full rigour of a conveyancing law that treated all acquirers of legal property interests as members of a single class, be they a purchaser of the freehold, a mortgagee or merely a short-term tenant. Each was entitled under the general law to inspect the full title of the vendor (or whoever), hence each was bound by constructive notice of what they would have found had they exercised that right.[368] It made no difference that in practice the right was not accessible to would-be tenants, whether because landlords simply denied it or, where the lease was preceded by a contract, because it was common practice for the contract to remove it. Common law judges expressed distaste for this 'new burden' Chancery was imposing on tenants, but at the same time declined to interpret the standard leasehold covenant for quiet possession to make a landlord liable to a tenant for an undisclosed covenant attached to the freehold.[369] Further, the logic of Lord Cottenham's equity

---

[365] *Taylor* v. *Stibbert* (1794) 2 Ves. Jun. 437; *Daniels* v. *Davison* (1809) 16 Ves. 249; *Allen* v. *Anthony* (1816) 1 Mer. 283.

[366] *Tulk* v. *Moxhay* (1848) 11 Beav. 571 (Langdale MR); *Mann* v. *Stephens* (1846) 15 Sim. 377; *Collins* v. *Plumb* (1810) 16 Ves. 454; compare Knight-Bruce LJ's assumption in *Cox* v. *Bishop* (1857) 8 De G. M. & G. 815 that *Tulk* v. *Moxhay* was about negative obligations.

[367] *Whatman* v. *Gibson* (1838) 9 Sim. 196; *Cox* v. *Bishop* (1857) 8 De G. M. & G. 815, 821.

[368] *Wilson* v. *Hart* (1866) 1 Ch App 463; *Feilden* v. *Slater* (1869) 7 Eq. 523; *Patman* v. *Harland* (1881) 17 Ch D 353.

[369] *Dennett* v. *Atherton* (1872) LR 7 QB 316; cf. *Spencer* v. *Marriott* (1823) 1 B. & C. 457. The usual covenant against encumbrances might stretch that far, but since it was conventionally limited to encumbrances created by the covenantor and the covenantor's ancestors it would not reach back to previous vendors: see W. A. Jolly, *Seabourne's Vendors and Purchasers* (6th edn, 1904), 438 for the suggestion.

coupled with the rigour of constructive notice extended to sub-tenants.[370] All of this increased the control promisees had over their investment, but it burdened buildings, particularly, with restrictions on commercial use that tenants had few means of discovering in advance. The ability of Lord Cottenham's equity to reach out even to mere yearly tenants was Lindley LJ's especial reason for limiting it in 1881 to covenants that did not require expenditure—to restrictive covenants, as they were becoming categorized.[371]

Whereas a *Tulk* v. *Moxhay* covenant usually created obligations that were unilateral, those in a development scheme might sometimes be mutual. Equity judges thought 'intention' the key, seeking to identify which schemes were advanced merely as a tool of estate management for the benefit of the vendor/covenantee/developer and which were commitments to a plan meant to bind all. The former were flexible, could be waived by the developer as the circumstances of the estate changed, and accordingly created only a set of unilateral obligations running back from the purchasers and their successors to the developer and his retained land; formation of a colony must have a governor, counsel successfully argued of Joseph Pitt's grandiose plans for Pittsville.[372] The latter, by contrast, created a local law for the estate binding in equity upon the developer as well, and hence allowed purchasers and their successors to enforce the obligations between themselves too.

The typology was present from the earliest cases but initially the types were not wholly separate, Shadwell VC indicating willingness to enjoin a (hypothetical) developer whose covenants were of the former sort but whose threatened change of direction perverted the original purpose.[373] It was a flexible equity responsive to the circumstances, but therefore one requiring evidence of the context not just of the formal documentation. It turned out that there were many variants of scale, timing, and documentation, differences between what was said, what was drawn on plans, what was written into prospectuses, differences between occasional waivers of obligation and their use as a tool of estate development. A complicated body of reported case law developed, centred still on 'intention' but with an ever more elaborate set of judicial instructions about how to find it.[374]

---

[370] *Parker* v. *Whyte* (1863) 1 H. & M. 167; *Clements* v. *Welles* (1865) LR 1 Eq 200; *Hall* v. *Ewin* (1887) 37 Ch D 74.

[371] *Haywood* v. *New Brunswick Building Society* (1881) 8 QBD 403.

[372] *Schreiber* v. *Creed* (1839) 3 Jur. 625, 627; P. Borsay, 'Health and Leisure Resorts 1700–1840', in *The Cambridge Urban History of Britain*, vol. ii (ed. P. Clark, Cambridge, 2000), 775–803 at 798.

[373] *Schreiber* v. *Creed* (1839) 10 Sim. 9; and see *Whatman* v. *Gibson*, n. 362 above, for the other type; *Peacock* v. *Penson* (1848) 11 Beav. 355.

[374] *Child* v. *Douglas* (1854) Kay 560 (LJJ); (1856) 2 Jur. (N.S.) 950 (Wood VC); *Eastwood* v. *Lever* (1863) 4 De G. J. & Sm. 114; *Keates* v. *Lyon* (1869) 4 Ch App 218; *Harrison* v. *Good* (1871) LR 11 Eq 338; *Nottingham Patent Brick and Tile Co* v. *Butler* (1885) 15 QBD 268 (aff'd 16 QBD 778); *Collins* v. *Castle*

In the early twentieth century some judges preferred to condense out those factors into a set of rules that applied as legal preconditions, independently of the original parties' actual intentions. One formulation by Parker J. in *Elliston* v. *Reacher* in 1908 became particularly influential later, even though on appeal in the same case Cozens-Hardy MR had doubted that facts should be disciplined in that way.[375] But Parker J.'s rule-based approach had two attractions. First, sheer passage of time could make a search for context and original intention illusory.[376] To expect purchasers to inquire into materials extraneous to the deeds anyway ran contrary to the late nineteenth-century drive to streamline conveyancing. An analysis based on rules and on reading the deeds fitted that value better than one based upon principle and circumstance.[377] Secondly, from the 1880s judges were reconceptualizing covenants as property interests rather than as occasions for the exercise of a remedial, principle-based jurisdiction, and it is of the essence of a property interest that it has a definition.

The reconceptualizing came very suddenly. Equity judges played a part, but the arena was the new Court of Appeal, where common lawyers predominated. There is a strong common law structure to the critique. The reasoning supporting Lord Cottenham's equity had always had two strands. One made notice a positive reason for holding someone to observance of a covenant, where disregarding it would be presumed to bring a windfall profit at the expense of the original seller or the successor to the benefited land. That was potentially a very broad principle. Shortly before the reconceptualizing there had been a flutter of expansion, not very definite, but suggesting that it might extend to positive covenants and to covenants in gross.[378] It is no surprise to find Romilly MR and Malins VC among the judges attracted to that use of equitable principle. In the 1880s, however, that reasoning was discarded. Instead, after Jessel MR's analysis in *London & South Western Railway Company* v. *Gomm*, purchasers were bound not by notice itself

---

(1887) 36 Ch D 243; *Spicer* v. *Martin* (1888) 14 App Cas 12; *Mackenzie* v. *Childers* (1889) 43 Ch D 265; *Everett* v. *Remington* [1892] 3 Ch 148; *Tucker* v. *Vowles* [1893] 1 Ch 195; *Knight* v. *Simmonds* [1896] 1 Ch 653.

[375] [1908] 2 Ch 374 (Parker J.), 665 (CA).

[376] See *Reid* v. *Bickerstaffe* [1909] 2 Ch 305, esp. Kennedy LJ.

[377] See the analysis by S. J. Bailey, 'The Benefit of a Restrictive Covenant' (1938) 6 *CLJ* 339–66 at 362–3. He quotes G. C. Cheshire, *Modern Law of Real Property*, and is in turn quoted by R. E. Megarry and H. W. R. Wade, *Law of Real Property* (e.g. 4th edn, 1975, 769n). For the importance of textbooks in transmitting conveyancers' values see J. S. Anderson, 'Land Law Texts and the Explanation of 1925' [1984] *CLP* 63–83.

[378] *Morland* v. *Cook* (1868) LR 6 Eq 252; *Cooke* v. *Chilcott* (1876) 3 Ch D 694; *Luker* v. *Dennis* (1877) 7 Ch D 227; *Catt* v. *Tourle* (1869) 4 Ch App 654; cf. *De Mattos* v. *Gibson* (1859) 4 De G. & J. 276; Dart, *Vendor and Purchaser*, 5th edn, 767–70, Davidson, *Precedents*, ii, 510n (4th edn, 1877); Kerr, *Injunctions* (1867), 531.

but by a form of servitude, unless they could show an absence of notice.[379] The servitude had definition: it must be restrictive, transferring the requirement of negativity from Chancery's rules about the sorts of orders it would make into this new property construct.[380] A little later courts held that covenants in gross fell outside the definition, to the regret of some of them, but aided by a strong judicial aversion to their use by breweries and the like to extend their range of tied outlets.[381] The benefit of a restrictive covenant was conceived of as a property, capable of assignment or annexation, the latter very similar to the privity of estate used to determine the running of leasehold covenants.[382] Formulating rules for development scheme covenants fitted this new mood well.

Synthesis

Thus there was something of a convergence between law and equity. Restrictive covenants became law-like servitudes with definition, not the by-product of the exercise of a broad remedial jurisdiction. Acquiescence became a way of conceding an interest; an equity might arise, but it would not be satisfied until shaped into something known to law. On the other hand the categories of the common law were more flexible than the forbidding creed of *Keppell* v. *Bailey, Ackroyd* v. *Smith*, and *Hill* v. *Tupper* suggested. There could be no easements in gross, but mining and quarrying rights could be created as *profits à prendre* if the grantor did not want to lease, and such profits could be held in gross. Bare licences were revocable at will, but, again, mining and quarrying rights could be created by licences coupled with a grant. That type of licence was irrevocable, could be made exclusive, despite strong dicta to the contrary by Lord Ellenborough and, by the 1870s, would at least sometimes support an action in trespass.[383] For some industries private legislation gave more comprehensive and more reliable pow-

---

[379] (1882) 20 Ch D 562; *re Nisbet and Potts' Contract* [1905] 1 Ch 391 (Farwell J) [1906] 1 Ch 386 (CA); *London County Council* v. *Allen* [1914] 3 KB 642; and compare Dart, *Vendor and Purchaser* (5th edn, 1876), 767–70 with (6th edn, 1888), 863–9.

[380] *Haywood* v. *New Brunswick Building Society* (1881) 8 QBD 403; *Austerberry* v. *Corporation of Oldham* (1885) 29 Ch D 750.

[381] *Formby* v. *Barker* [1903] 2 Ch 539; *Millbourn* v. *Lyons* [1914] 2 Ch 231; *London County Council* v. *Allen* [1914] 3 KB 642 (see Scrutton J. for regrets), *Noakes* v. *Rice* [1902] AC 24 at 32, 35, 36 (aversion).

[382] *Rogers* v. *Hosegood* [1900] 2 Ch 388.

[383] Ellenborough's dictum in *Chetham* v. *Williamson* (1804) 4 East 469 was taken uncritically in Bythewood and Jarman, *Precedents* (1831), iv, 243, but the specialist literature always asserted that mining licences could be made exclusive by appropriate wording: Bainbridge, *Mines and Minerals* (1st edn, 1841), 168–9; R. M. Collier, *A Treatise on the Law relating to Mines* (2nd edn, 1855), 10. That was eventually confirmed in *Duke of Sutherland* v. *Heathcote* [1891] 3 Ch 504. For trespass, see *Low Moor Co* v. *Stanley Coal Co* (1875) 33 LT 436 (though on appeal the instrument was construed as a tenancy at will: (1875) 34 LT 186).

ers, albeit at a cost, and where railway, canal, and waterworks Acts gave powers that mimicked or extended property concepts, judges seem to have been content to take them as they found them, without trying to assimilate them with the common law.[384]

So the system as a whole provided some flexibility, even though the parts of it worked separately. The beneficiaries were the well-established—mining brought its flexibility with it from an earlier period—and the large-scale newcomers who needed to go to Parliament anyway. The Real Property Commissioners found restrictive covenants puzzling, but accepted that they were important and of frequent occurrence, so they and the Chancery courts can be seen as finding a way to validate a practice that had already become widespread.[385]

The transformation of Lord Cottenham's principled approach into a defined servitude, like the reduction of his principled explanation of the married woman's restraint on anticipation to a 'new species of estate', then prevented the principle of property owners' autonomy from undermining a categorical approach to property law. Its potential for doing that can be seen in the expansive decisions of the late 1860s that suggested that positive covenants and covenants in gross also bound purchasers with notice. Equity judges' turn to rules and definitions can thus be seen as a belated concession to Lord Brougham's worries about indeterminate burdens on land, a signal to their common law colleagues in the post-Judicature Act world that they would not subvert the common law.[386]

---

[384] e.g. *Bell* v. *Midland Railway Co.* (1859) 3 De G. & J. 673; *Bwllfa & Merthyr Dare Colliery Co* v. *Pontypridd Water Co* [1903] AC 431; *Manchester Corporation* v. *New Moss Colliery* [1906] 1 Ch 278.

[385] *RC on Real Property*, 3rd Report, 375.

[386] Cf. Gardner, 'Equity, Estate Contracts'.

V

Changing the Nature of Real Property Law

1. 'ASSIMILATION' TO 1875

Assimilating the law of real property to that of personalty was a common theme among reformers during our period but, as Maitland pointed out, it was 'the one steady tendency of our law' for centuries past, nothing new.[1] What was new was a feeling that the process was near its end. It became feasible to propose without risking ridicule that the concept of the law of real property should be abolished, or that freeholds be converted to million-year leaseholds—so that real property law would no longer have anything to attach to—or, tamely in comparison, that a new land law be drafted that would take its features from the ways in which transactions concerning personalty were commonly constructed.

When ease of conveyancing was the major driver of that process the comparison was sometimes with ships but most often with the most abstract of all forms of personal wealth, the 'funds'—government stock. That austere regime of transfer by book entry at the Bank was the inspiration of the most durable models of land title registration in England and their rival, the simplification of land law finally enacted in 1925. Its influence through to the Land Transfer Act 1875 will be considered in the second section of this chapter.

Assimilation, however, was not always directed to improving land transfer. Removal of land's privileges was a major cry in nineteenth-century politics, one that had its counterpart in more mundane law reform. Some aspects of the cry hardly touched day-to-day law. Those were the big political gestures that would either result in a wholly new statute or not at all—intestate primogeniture should stay or it should go; entail should be possible or it should not. But others cut across the drive for easier and cheaper conveyancing. To treat land as just one form of wealth sometimes meant exposing it to liabilities from which it had previously been immune. If a new liability were then attached to the land itself, not

---

[1] 'The Law of Real Property', in *Collected Papers* (ed. H. A. L. Fisher), i, 162, 195, reprinted from *Westminster Rev.* 1879.

merely to the landowner personally, purchasers would be put at risk. Examples of this more mundane, piecemeal set of changes will be considered in the first part of this chapter, and particularly their impact on land transfer.

Removing Land's Privileges

LIABILITY FOR DEAD LANDOWNERS' DEBTS

Opening up deceased debtors' realty to claims by their creditors was one of the more obvious steps towards assimilation in the early nineteenth century. From 1807, with significant extension in 1833, first some deceased debtors' lands, then all, were made available to creditors by statute, building on well-established principles that allowed testators to reach the same result voluntarily. Apart from the political symbolism, however, there was a practical difficulty. By the general law realty descended automatically to heir or devisee without interposition of an executor or administrator. For creditors to have effective access to the realty they needed some mechanism for charging it, ultimately for it to be sold, which necessarily would attach after that automatic devolution of title. Suppose, then, that the heir or devisee had sold the land and kept the proceeds before the creditor caught up with what had happened. Would the liability still attach to the land? It was a feature of this particular assimilation of realty to personalty that purchasers were well protected.

Until 1807 the general law had been that deceased persons' simple contract debts were payable only out of their personalty, which included their leaseholds. Only specialty debts, those created by formal instrument such as a deed or bond, became the liability of the heir or devisee succeeding to the deceased debtor's realty. How many testators let the law take its course is unknown, but drafting a will to reach a different result was easy and judicial encouragement strong.[2] The realty would then become equitable assets, meaning not only that Chancery could order its sale to pay the testator's debts but also that if the proceeds were insufficient Chancery would abate all debts proportionately rather than paying them off in rank order of category like common law did.[3]

The straightforward way for professionally advised testators to make their land available to creditors was to devise it on trust for sale to pay their debts. Much of the case law, however, concerned less formal phrases that merely charged debts upon land, or upon the whole estate, or simply instructed trustees, executors, or devisees to pay debts, or spoke unhelpfully in the passive voice, not designating

---

[2] T. Jarman, *A Treatise on Wills* (1st edn), ii, 520; W. Cruise, *Digest of the Laws of England Respecting Real Property* (1804), ii, 472.

[3] Jarman, *Wills* (1st edn), ii, 543–53.

who should pay or how. Strictly, those words would give Chancery the necessary jurisdiction only if they created a trust. Eighteenth-century judges, however, had established a rule treating this species of charge as a trust and then, as Thomas Jarman remarked, had 'allowed their anxiety to prevent moral injustice...to carry them beyond the limits prescribed by established principles of construction' by conjuring charges out of words that were often little more than aspirations.[4] Once a phrase had received such an interpretation its meaning became a rule to be applied to all other wills.[5]

The logic of testamentary trusts for sale and charges for debts ought to have threatened purchasers. Chancery's jurisdiction was necessarily proprietary, so if the heir or devisee sold the land without honouring the trust/charge/instruction to pay debts out of it the creditors' property right should have bound purchasers who had notice—which they normally would have had, the will being a document of title. That possibility would throw a burden of inquiry on to all buyers and mortgagees. But having established the jurisdiction the draftsmen and the judges together stripped their property concepts of the features that affected purchasers. Draftsmen habitually neutralized trusts for sale by express clauses stipulating that the trustees' receipt for the proceeds immunized (and precluded) the purchaser from having to see that the money was properly paid over to the creditors. That clause was just a particular application of a device that was used for trusts for sale and powers to sell in a wide range of circumstances, removing the general duty equity otherwise imposed.

The technique was so common that statutory enactment of it as a rule was included in Lord Lyndhurst's Transfer of Property Act in 1844, only to be repealed the next year when Bellenden Ker, Christie, and Hayes took strong exception to its generality.[6] Christie's view on principle was that it was for settlors to decide the attributes of the equitable interest enjoyed by the beneficiary.[7] In the context of explicit powers to sell to raise debts and legacies, however, decisions by Lyndhurst and St. Leonards in 1846 and 1853 respectively restored judicially what had been withdrawn legislatively.[8] Purchasers or mortgagees from someone with such a power could rely on appearances, whether or not there was a receipt clause, and even after a lapse of many years, provided only that they had no actual knowledge that the transaction was for an improper purpose. Narrower versions

---

[4] Jarman, *Wills* (1st edn), ii, 520; *Ball* v. *Harris* (1839) 4 My. & Cr. 264.

[5] *Greville* v. *Browne* (1859) 7 H.L.C. 689, which concerned the parallel rule for charges of legacies on real estate, where the moral policy was weaker but the interpretive rule was just as strong.

[6] 7 & 8 Vict, c. 76, s 10; H. C. Bellenden Ker, *Letter to the Lord Chancellor*, in Davidson, *Concise Precedents* (3rd edn, 1848), at 21–4.

[7] *RC on Registration and Conveyancing*, Report, *PP* 1850 [1261], xxxii, 1, 558–60, 567, 570–1.

[8] *Forbes* v. *Peacock* (1846) 1 Ph. 717; *Stroughill* v. *Anstey* (1852) 1 De G. M. & G. 635.

of the section from the 1844 Act were re-enacted without difficulty in 1859 and 1860.[9]

Mere charges for the payment of debts were tamed without relying on such ancillary clauses, and even more robustly. They were trust-like, perhaps even trusts, in that they opened Chancery's doors to creditors seeking orders for the administration of equitable assets, but for conveyancing purposes they were virtually invisible.[10] Legal title to the deceased's lands passed directly to the heir or devisee, who might sell or mortgage free from the charge, on the reasoning that anyone dealing with them was entitled (and bound) to assume either that there were no debts needing paying or that the transaction was being undertaken to pay them.[11] Thus the immediate purchaser was required to trust appearances and excused from liability if they turned out to be deceptive (unless he knew that at the time). Purchasers further on down the chain were prevented from making difficulties retrospectively. Elastic principles of drafting and interpretation were therefore matched by elastic concepts of property in a way that allowed creditors to access their deceased debtors' lands without adding cost or complexity to land transactions, provided that the testator had provided a cue.[12]

Protection for purchasers was carried across into the statutes that gave creditors access to their deceased debtors' realty as of right. When Sir Samuel Romilly tried in the early years of the nineteenth century to create that right he was strongly opposed by conservatives fearing the impact on family land. His Debts of Traders Act of 1807 succeeded in establishing the rule only for deceased debtors who had been traders, to parallel the principle of bankruptcy.[13] A generation later, in 1833, John Romilly pushed his father's original design through Parliament without controversy, indeed without discussion he said, so obvious the moral principle had become that all a person's debts should be recoverable from their estate, whatever the debtor's station or the estate's composition.[14]

Both Acts addressed purchasers' interests directly. Realty would become equitable assets, but if the heir or devisee sold or mortgaged it without paying the debts the creditor could not pursue the land through into the hands of the purchaser or mortgagee. This statutory jurisdiction explicitly applied only to wills that did not themselves charge realty with debts, and commentators recommended that

---

[9] Law of Property and Trustees Relief Amendment Act 1859, s 23 (St. Leonards); Trustees and Mortgagees Act 1860, s 29 (Cranworth.)

[10] J. Williams, *On the Power of an Executor to Sell Real Estate under a Charge of Debts* (1857), esp. 21–3; Davidson, *Precedents*, ii, 992 (4th edn, 1877).

[11] *Doe d. Jones* v. *Hughes* (1851) 6 Exch. 223; *Colyer* v. *Finch* (1856) 5 H.L.C. 923.

[12] Compare the similar treatment of *inter vivos* trusts for the payment of debts, pp. 240–1, below.

[13] 47 Geo. III (s. 2) c. 74; Debtors Act 1830, I Will IV c. 47.

[14] 3 & 4 Will. IV c. 104; *Kinderley* v. *Jervis* (1856) 22 Beav. 1, 20.

in some circumstances the old way would continue to be the better.[15] Still, both ways protected purchasers.

TAX: LIABILITY TO THE STATE

Where the state itself had an interest, accommodation with the value of efficient land transfer was less, though it was not entirely lacking. The Crown's ease of access to its debtors' lands for recouping what it was owed was never less than an ordinary citizen's and often very much more. That could put an irksome burden of inquiry on to purchasers. It will be considered further below. In addition there came to be questions about the recovery of tax, especially inheritance duties.

Before 1853 there was legacy duty, which fell only on movable personalty that passed on death by will or intestacy, and there was probate duty, payable on wills and letters of administration, which were necessary only for personalty.[16] The differential taxation of land and personal property raised considerable political heat in the 1840s, adjusting or removing the imbalance a matter of high politics. In 1853 succession duty became payable on realty and settled personalty that was not otherwise liable to legacy duty. For its efficient collection a charge for unpaid duty was expressly annexed to the land, to be enforceable against alienees, which at once created a cost to be borne somewhere in the land transfer process.[17] The situation arose, typically, if a life tenant and a remainderman jointly sold a fee simple. On the death of the former life tenant a liability to succession duty became due, which would fall on the purchaser, or the purchaser's purchaser perhaps. From the beginning, however, the statute gave defences to *bona fide* purchasers for value who did not know that their title included a succession that would become taxable or who relied on an official certificate of discharge that subsequently turned out to be revocable.[18]

The defence would principally benefit purchasers whose vendor had concealed the full title to the land while making the sale. If the vendor had been open, however, there were now new costs in negotiating a contractual allocation of the duty as between vendor and purchaser (and the covenants to secure it), or the cost of acquiring a commutation from the Commissioners of Inland Revenue. That was enough to set Lord St. Leonards grumbling that such an obstacle to

---

[15] W. Hayes and T. Jarman, *Concise Forms of Wills* (2nd edn, 1838), 33–5. The statutory preference for specialty debts was removed by Debts of Deceased Persons Act 1869, usually referred to as Hinde Palmer's Act.

[16] J. Tiley, 'Death and Taxes' [2007] *BTR* 300–19; M. J. Daunton, *Trusting Leviathan* (Cambridge, 2001), 228–33.

[17] Succession Duty Act 1853, ss 42, 44; Dart, *Vendors and Purchasers* (5th edn, 1876), i, 275–8, 292–4.

[18] Succession Duty Act 1853, s 52.

cheap and simple land transfer should not have been permitted.[19] In 1859 he had
a clause passed in the Lords worded so that (among a list of other encumbrances)
a charge to tax would not bind a purchaser or mortgagee unless the Crown had
begun execution process before the transaction in question.[20] In the Commons,
however, Sir Stafford Northcote, Conservative financial secretary to the Treasury,
objected that the bill would cause considerable difficulty and embarrassment to
the revenue departments, and when it finally passed into law in stages over the
next year that provision had disappeared.[21]

    That rejection of further accommodation with the value of efficient land trans-
fer was final. The Liberals carried much the same regime over into collection of
the new estate duty created by the Finance Act 1894, though the dynamic of that
tax was rather different.[22] The Act gave the state a charge against land for unpaid
duty, but provided also that a limited owner who paid the duty should thereby
have a charge as though he had raised the money by mortgage. These liabilities
were subsequently integrated reasonably easily with the Land Transfer Act 1897,
which brought compulsory title registration to the London area, but conveyancers under the deeds system had now to make additional inquiries and require
additional documentation.[23]

Creditors' rights against their (living) debtor's land

Far more complex, far less stable, was the question of what recourse unsecured
creditors should have against their debtors' lands, assuming that the creditor
had obtained a judgment that validated and quantified the debt and ordered the
debtor to pay.[24] A strong commercial policy to give creditors effective remedies
clashed with a strong commercial policy to streamline land transactions. At the
start of our period there was a sharp contrast between the Crown and an ordinary citizen as a creditor. The Crown's ready ability to satisfy itself from land

---

[19] W. Brown, *A Practical Treatise on Succession Duty* (1864), 343–63; *Cooper* v. *Trewby* (1860) 28
Beav. 194; *Solicitor-General* v. *Law Reversionary Interest Society* (1873) LR 8 Ex. 233; Sugden, *Vendors
and Purchasers* (14th edn, 1862), 556. A committee of the Bar Council was still complaining in 1886:
Anderson, *Lawyers*, 177.

[20] Law of Property and Trustees Relief Amendment Bill, *PP* 1859 (sess. 1) (45), ii, 37, cl. 25.

[21] *PD* 1859 (s3) 153: 1594; Law of Property and Trustees Relief Amendment Act 1859; Law of
Property Further Amendment Act 1860, ss 1–3.

[22] Finance Act 1894, ss 8, 9; *re Palmer* [1900] WN 9; *re Sharman* [1901] 2 Ch 250.

[23] Land Transfer Act 1897, s 13; C. F. Brickdale, *Land Transfer Acts* (1899), 280, 367–8, 383;
Wolstenholme's Conveyancing Acts (10th edn, 1913, by B. L. Cherry, A. E. Russell, and C. V. Rawlence),
217 (these charges not registrable under Land Charges Act 1888); *Lord Advocate* v. *Countess of Moray*
[1905] AC 531; Williams, *Vendor and Purchaser* (2nd edn, 1910), i, 174; ii, 1323.

[24] For a succinct account, see J. Williams, *Principles of the Law of Real Property* (15th edn, 1885),
107–18.

that had once belonged to its debtor was a serious impediment to land purchases, so respondents to the Real Property Commissioners' questionnaire told it and so the commissioners reported.[25] By contrast ordinary unsecured creditors' remedies were noticeably less effective against realty than against personalty. But that could hardly be changed without throwing a cost on to the land transfer process, because creditors' rights had at some point to attach to the land itself if they were to be effective. Thereupon they would necessitate an extra search, becoming a clog on sales in general.

The usual early-Victorian answer to such conflicts was that there should be a register to record the claim that created the risk. Registration had an authenticating function, but whether in itself it conferred priority over subsequent claims was more difficult. Often it did not; notice was needed for that, which could be constructive notice. Even lawyers who rejected the Real Property Commissioners' prescription of a deeds register as the universal source of information saw an important role for such lesser forms of registration. Sir Edward Sugden, later Lord St. Leonards, always opposed the former, but successfully introduced bills establishing registers for Crown debts (1839), *lites pendentes* (also 1839), commercial annuities (1855), and writs of execution of judgment (1860), all located at the office of the Court of Common Pleas in London.[26] Some of that law was new, some an improvement of older, less efficient forms of recording. Similarly, from 1846 a succession of statutes, public and private, began facilitating loans to limited owners for agricultural improvement, allowing lenders to charge the loan on the inheritance, but requiring the charge to be registered.[27]

Accordingly, it was through registration that John Campbell, the Whigs' Attorney-General from 1834, sought to reconcile the interests of purchasers and mortgagees with the new range of remedies he was creating for judgment creditors against their debtors' realty. He intended them as an inducement to Parliament to abolish imprisonment for debt.[28] The Lords gave him only half his policy, just the abolition of imprisonment on mesne process, but fully accepted his inducement.

Before his reform, Judgments Act 1838, judgment creditors who issued a writ of *fieri facias* could get their debtor's personalty seized and then sold by the sheriff—personalty in this case being broad enough to include leaseholds. For

---

[25] *RC on Real Property*, 1st Report, *PP* 1829 (263), x, 1, 59.

[26] 2 & 3 Vict. c. 11, ss 7, 8; Judgments Act 1855, s 12; Law of Property Further Amendment Act 1860. *Lis pendens*: any suit in equity, still in progress, that affected entitlement to the land (for the previous tangle see Powell, *Mortgages* (6th edn, 1826), i, 540a–551a).

[27] H. W. Elphinstone and J. W. Clark, *On Searches* (1887), 109–14, 117–19.

[28] See particularly *PD* 1837 (s3) 36: 146–51; Cornish and Clark, *Law and Society in England*, 226–30.

realty, however, they had only the writ of *elegit*. That was a possessory remedy, so it did not enable the land to be sold, and it necessarily applied only to estates in possession. It enabled the sheriff to put the judgment creditor into legal possession to recoup the debt from the rents, but only to the extent of half the debtor's land.[29] Now the Judgments Act increased *elegit's* reach from half to whole and, more significantly, provided that a judgment would create an immediate charge over lands in which the debtor had any interest.[30] The charge was enforceable as a mortgage after expiry of a 12-month grace period. In keeping with the general direction set by the Real Property Commissioners, whose chairman Campbell had been, these remedies were to apply to lands of all tenures, which was a major consolidation in itself. Until the debt was paid the charge (new law) and the vulnerability to elegit (old law) attached to all a debtor's present and future lands, into whosoever hands they came, hence the need for integration with the land transfer system. Consistently with the imperatives of the Real Property Commissioners, Campbell achieved that by requiring judgment creditors to register their judgment at the Common Pleas Office if it was to bind purchasers or mortgagees from the debtor.

Reaction from the conveyancing interest was immediate. Its success is a sign of its importance. The Judgments Act clearly aimed to make registration necessary to bind purchasers, but it could also be read as making it sufficient—that would have suited Campbell's original purpose.[31] If so, a search of the register in London was now essential, and every purchaser or mortgagee could henceforward expect to be billed for one.

Reconciling these interests was difficult. It took amendments in 1839 and 1840 to settle that registration was (in most circumstances) necessary to bind a purchaser but not sufficient; lack of notice remained the defence that it had been under the old law of *elegit*.[32] That was Sir Edward Sugden's initiative, and his 1839 Act included two further provisions to ease conveyancing: registration would lapse after five years unless renewed, and a register of Crown debts and accountantships was created, though they were not subjected to re-registration.[33]

---

[29] See Cruise, *Digest*, ii, 70–2 for a full list of interests extendible by *elegit*. In executing the writ the sheriff was to give priority to seizing the debtor's goods and chattels.

[30] 1 & 2 Vict. c. 110.

[31] In 1854 Campbell, as CJ, took an expansive view of the charge's proprietary effect rather against the previous judicial trend: *Watts* v. *Porter* (1854) 3 E. & B. 743, contrast *Whitworth* v. *Gaugain* (1846) 1 Ph. 728. Subsequent courts adopted Erle J.'s dissent instead: *Beavan* v. *Earl of Oxford* (1856) 6 De G. M. & G. 507; *Pickering* v. *Ilfracombe Railway* (1868) LR 3 CP 235.

[32] 2 & 3 Vict. c. 11, 3 & 4 Vict. c. 82. See also Judgments Act 1855. Commentators thought actual notice of an executed but unregistered *elegit* probably did bind a purchaser: *Davis* v. *Earl of Strathmore* (1810) 16 Ves. 419.

[33] 2 & 3 Vict. c. 11.

The practical result was that purchasers could now buy certainty by paying for a search, or they could take a risk, which they might perhaps be able to pass on to their solicitor through a negligence action.[34] The books warned that it was unsafe to forgo searching, since notice might be inferred from slight circumstances, and, besides, on a subsequent sale the lack of notice might have to be proved to the new purchaser, which would be next to impossible.[35]

It was an uncomfortable compromise, where purchasers and their solicitors who did search usually got a nil result and felt that the expense had been unnecessary.[36] Until 1854 there was a complication, that moneylenders were manipulating the statutory charge to create a form of secured lending at rates of interest that might lawfully exceed those permitted by the usury laws.[37] So cutting back on Campbell's Act would involve more than the relation between judgment creditor and purchaser. Once the usury laws were repealed, however, north-country solicitors in particular began complaining that the cost and difficulty of searching in London for judgment creditors' charges was a significant clog on free trade in land, especially on the small dealings in urban land that were becoming so common in their regions.

That was not an uncommon theme in the 1850s and later. Registers suited a conception of efficient land transfer which combined freedom of disposition, documentation that dealt directly with the property interests concerned, and perfect access to information concerning the state of the title. They were less welcome once saving of time and costs became the important objectives. The loan registers were scattered, some being with the Inclosure Commissioners, some at the lending company's office, some, later, at the Land Registry, some even at Chancery. Sugden's were at the Common Pleas. From his first edition in 1851 the conveyancing writer J. H. Dart reported disagreement among the elite over which of the many registers should always be searched, proposing himself that inquiries between solicitors would probably uncover most of what was needed.[38] By his fourth edition in 1871 he thought that the list of searches was now 'formidable, almost prohibitive' but he was confident that the practice of inquiry between solicitors had become usual, in effect inviting solicitors to foreshorten the official mechanism.[39]

---

[34] Dart, *Vendors and Purchasers* (1st edn, 1851), 229–31; *Cooper* v. *Stephenson* (1852) 21 LJ QB 292.

[35] e.g. Sugden, *Vendors and Purchasers* (11th edn, 1846), 668; Dart, *Vendors and Purchasers* (1st edn), 230–1; *Freer* v. *Hesse* (1853) 4 De G. M. & G. 495.

[36] The information and argument in the rest of this paragraph are drawn from the evidence to the *SC on the Judgments etc Amendment Bill*, Report, PP 1864 (396), v, 617.

[37] See pp. 142–4, above.

[38] Dart, *Vendors and Purchasers* (1st edn), 227 and Ch. 11 *passim*.

[39] Dart, *Vendors and Purchasers* (4th edn, 1871), i, 418, 413.

The north-country solicitors argued that the balance of public utility now lay in reducing the risks and costs of land transfers by curtailing the charge the Judgments Act 1838 had created. Sugden, recently ennobled as Baron St. Leonards, agreed. In 1860 he returned to the issue with the new reforming strategy of shifting the binding effect away from the judgment itself and on to its execution process. Tortuously his Law of Property Further Amendment Act required judgment creditors not only to register their judgments but also to register a writ of execution. Only then would the judgment bind a purchaser or mortgagee, and even then only provided that the judgment creditor actually implemented the writ of execution within three months of its registration.[40] The motivation for the shift, as Romilly MR put it, was solely 'to enable vendors to sell their land at less expense than formerly'.[41] The same principle, less the requirement of three-month implementation, was even extended to Crown debts and accountantships in 1865, a sign of how far the values of smooth land transfer could reach.[42]

Taking the same idea much further, a measure introduced in 1864 by George Hadfield MP, a retired Manchester solicitor once active in the Anti-Corn Law League, boldly announced the solution to the northern solicitors' concerns to be the assimilation of realty with personalty.[43] In 1856 the Mercantile Law Amendment Act had provided that a *fieri facias* should no longer bind goods from the time of the writ's delivery to the sheriff, but only from its execution by seizure or attachment, an event said to be easily discoverable by local inquiry.[44] Accordingly Hadfield's Judgments Act 1864 instituted the general rule that no future judgment should affect land until it too had been actually delivered in execution by '*elegit* or other lawful authority'.[45] The consequence, left unsaid in what was first introduced as a single-section bill, was to abrogate the charge created by the 1838 Act while leaving it formally unrepealed. Registration of judgments was no longer

---

[40] Sections 1–2.

[41] *Wallis* v. *Morris* (1864) 12 WR 997.

[42] Crown Suits Act 1865, s 49. Most office holders whose duties included collecting money for the Crown were Crown accountants. On appointment their lands became liable for their future debts to the Crown, giving the Crown a lien that, until limited by s 49, could be asserted against even those subsequent purchasers who had bought when the accountant was clear of debt. Complaints about the breadth of the Crown's rights were commonplace from the evidence to the Real Property Commissioners through to the select committee on Hadfield's bill in 1864 (above) and later (Anderson, *Lawyers*, 177). The Crown was not persuaded to adopt five-year re-registration until 1859 (Law of Property Amendment Act) and withdrew that concession in the Crown Suits Act. For a brief statement of the law, see L. Shelford, *Real Property Statutes* (7th edn, 1863), 596–8.

[43] *SC on Judgments Bill*, Report; enacted as Judgments Act 1864.

[44] Mercantile Law Amendment Act 1856, s 1 (provided the purchaser had no notice of the unexecuted writ).

[45] Judgments Act 1864.

necessary, but registration of writs of execution was retained, to the puzzlement of judges.[46]

This exercise in assimilation was a failure. With some misgivings judges eventually explained away the Act's retention of registration of writs of execution as being connected with a new remedy of summary sale tacked on to the bill during its passage, and hence as necessary only to that end.[47] In consequence the interest of a judgment creditor who took legal possession on *elegit* to recoup the debt from the rents would bind a purchaser even though nothing was registered. Hadfield might have tolerated that, because solicitors' evidence to his select committee was that local inquiry to discover execution was easy. Unfortunately, however, he had envisaged assimilation operating on common law principles. Realty would be like chattels—hence the use of 'delivery' as the central concept. He made no allowance for 'equitable execution', because at that time it was essentially parasitic upon *elegit*, not a substitute for it. After the Judicature Act 1873 judges took to appointing receivers as a remedy for judgment creditors in broader circumstances than hitherto and as an originating remedy without need for prior issue of an *elegit*.[48] Their focus was simply on aiding judgment creditors while eliminating unnecessary formal or administrative steps. When they ruled, in 1886, that appointment of a receiver was 'other lawful authority' for the purposes of the Judgment Act 1864, they were sanctioning in effect a new form of execution, one that would bind the land but which would often be undiscoverable by any reasonable inquiry.[49]

As on other occasions when judges did things that seemed sensible in relation to the parties before them, there was reaction from the conveyancing interest, this time particularly solicitors.[50] The resulting legislation remodelled charges

[46] The measure's opponents did not miss the irony of advocates of assimilation dismantling a modern registration system: *PD* 1860 (s3) 158: 93–102.

[47] *Re Pope* (1886) 17 QBD 743.

[48] Judicature Act 1873, s 25(8); *Hatton* v. *Haywood* (1874) 9 Ch App 229; *re South* (1874) 9 Ch App 373; *Anglo-Italian Bank* v. *Davies* (1878) 9 Ch D 975; *re Evans* (1879) 13 Ch D 252.

[49] *Re Pope* (1886) 17 QBD 743.

[50] (1887) 31 *Sol. J.* 631; H. W. E[lphinstone] 'Executions as a Risk to Purchasers of Land' (1886) 2 *LQR* 519–21. In the 1850s decisions by Romilly MR that executors lacking an interest in a deceased person's realty nonetheless sometimes had power out of court to sell it to pay his debts provoked an uproar ended only by a characteristically meticulous but face-saving statute penned by St. Leonards: Law of Property Amendment and Trustees Relief Act 1859, ss 14–18; J. Williams, 'On the Power of an Executor to Sell Real Estate under a Charge of Debts' (1856) 2 *Jurist* (N.S.), 68–71, expanded into a booklet of the same title in 1857, and further expanded in *An Essay on Real Assets* (1861); Lewin, *Trusts* (3rd edn, 1857), 440–8; Hayes and Jarman, *Concise Forms of Wills* (8th edn, 1863), 462–8; R. Watters, *A Practical Treatise on the Law as affected by the Statutes for the Amendment of the Law of Real Property and Relief of Trustees* (1862), 237–47; Dart, *Vendors and Purchasers* (4th edn), ii 568–70; Davidson, *Precedents* (4th edn), ii, 988–94.

registration—where it was situated, who should manage it, how searches were conducted, what searches would cost.[51] Only legislation with government backing could achieve that. That had become generally true of assimilation. Being instrumental and purposive it needed legislation. That could be poorly conceived, and sometimes was—Hadfield's Act demonstrates that amply. But judges' role was always secondary; the issues were too complex for individual decision and the political or professional interest too great for anyone to wait patiently until an accumulation of precedents resolved the problem.

Thinking Big: From Amending the Law of Real Property to Facilitating Land Transfer

In 1905 J. E. Hogg, the most profound of the barristers to analyse title registration systems, claimed that 'transfer' was a usage carried over from personalty and was thus itself a symbol of assimilation, likewise 'land' as an equivalent to 'estate in fee simple'.[52] While that was an exaggeration—Hogg did not have computer searches available to him to scan entire libraries for patterns of usage—there is truth enough in his observation for it to stand as a symbol. It may be recalled that the repeal of Lord Lyndhurst's Transfer of Property Act 1844, the measure that so irritated conservative reformers for its lack of principle, was achieved by the staid and conventional Law of Real Property Amendment Act 1845.[53]

Comparison of land transfer with the transfer of public stock—consols—began in the 1840s and became a staple. It was an extraordinary comparison by the standards of the aristocracy and gentry. An exchange of stock is an exchange of so much value. To suppose land to be the same is to suppose land simply for investment, ignoring questions of management and much else besides. For some observers it would have had connotations of speculation. Comparisons with goods were sometimes made, but only at the superficial level that possession of goods usually connoted title. The complexities of the separation of ownership and possession that gave rise to the Factors Acts and the Bills of Sale Acts, and which goods shared with land, were not part of the discourse. Ships got an occasional mention, but never in detail—perhaps because mortgages of ships notoriously

[51] Land Charges Registration and Searches Act 1888, completed by the transfer of the judgments register to the Land Registry: Land Charges Act 1900. The latter extended the 'official search' process to judgments, enabling the repeal of the 1864 Act.

[52] J. E. Hogg, *Australian Torrens System* (1905), 889–90.

[53] See pp. 60–4, above. Apart from references to the 1844 Act the contemporaneous edition of Davidson, *Concise Precedents* (3rd edn, 1848) confines 'transfer' almost entirely to transfer of mortgages and shares. The 1851 edn of Sugden's *Vendors and Purchasers* is more varied, but still reasonably within Hogg's observation; 'transfer' of seisin is the biggest exception.

caused problems belying the proposition that registration brought simplicity.[54] Instead the comparison focused on the ability to fragment ownership of realty into estates, which differentiated it from all forms of personalty.

It was usually a simple two-stage contrast. First, whereas title to consols was constituted by a simple entry in a public register and transferred by just another simple entry, title to land was a matter of inference from its history. Thus a conveyance of land needed cumbrous private deeds plus associated collateral proofs— probates, pedigrees, extracts from parish registers and the like. Secondly, whereas the complexities of family settlements appeared on the face of the documents transferring land, such that each sub-interest had to be explained and accounted for if the land were now being sold in fee simple, settlements of consols remained hidden. As personalty, consols could be settled only by vesting them in trustees, but the Bank of England's register concealed trusts' existence, treating trustees simply as co-owners. The effect, as far as purchasers were concerned, was that trustees of consols had full overreaching powers. Purchasers therefore did not need to make expensive and time-consuming inquiries before buying. Writers drawing this comparison usually concluded that the benefit of easy negotiability that the system brought to the great mass of stock far outweighed the occasional losses to individual beneficiaries from trustees' fraud.

A means had been devised, however, to protect those beneficiaries of trusts of consols who wanted it. They could issue a *distringas* out of the equity side of the Court of Exchequer. Once served on the Bank it entitled them to a few days' notice of a pending transfer, during which time they could make their case that the transaction would be a breach of trust or that their, or someone else's, consent to the sale was necessary. Edwin Field, the city solicitor whose analysis of costs and practices in Chancery provoked the abolition of the Six Clerks in 1842, drew special attention to the efficiency of the *distringas*, which he credited with creating 'a value and a marketable character for life interests and reversions in stock, which could not be had without'.[55] His very accurate estimate that upwards of 700 were issued each year represented about 6 per cent (annually) of the number of joint accounts at the Bank, accounts therefore which might perhaps be held by fiduciaries.[56] That was large enough for Field's argument that official protection created value to look plausible, but small enough for proponents of assimilation

---

[54] T. A. Trollope, *A Treatise on the Mortgage of Ships* (1823).

[55] E. W. Field, *Observations of a Solicitor on Defects in the Offices, Practice and System of Costs of the Equity Courts* (1840), 91–2. When the equity side of Exchequer was abolished in 1841 *distringas* was streamlined and modernized as a Chancery procedure by Court of Chancery Act, 5 Vict. c. 5, s. 4, and Orders made under it: J. S. Smith, *A Treatise on the Practice of the Court of Chancery* (3rd edn, 1844), i, 790–3.

[56] *Writs of Distringas etc; Returns from the Bank of England*, PP 1852–3 (286), lxxviii, 481.

to argue that in practice most beneficiaries were content for their trustees to have unfettered overreaching powers.

The broadest of the new thinking focused on title registration. In the mid-1840s two reasonably detailed schemes were proposed independently by solicitors Robert Wilson and Henry Sewell, neither making an immediate impression.[57] Wilson, however, pressed his idea through an anonymous review in the Benthamite *Westminster Review*, gaining impetus enough to turn the Law Amendment Society away from deeds registration and into backing a version of his scheme sketched by another solicitor, William Strickland Cookson.[58] The momentum propelled the Commons select committee in 1853 into abandoning deeds registration and calling for a royal commission to settle a scheme for title registration.[59] It was appointed in the following year, with both Wilson and Cookson among its membership. It took three years to produce its report, and even then its members agreed only on the core; details divided them as they had divided proponents of title registration from the beginning.[60] None the less the core agreement, based substantially on the values of assimilation, turned out to be much more influential than the divisions.

With the general shift from the 1840s towards regarding speed and cheapness of land sales as primary objectives, the general attraction of a register of legal conclusions, rather than a register of data from which conclusions still remained to be drawn, was obvious enough. A once-and-for-all validation by the state of a property's historic root of title would eliminate for ever the wasteful process of re-examination on every transaction.

The challenge of the Wilson/Cookson scheme, however, lay less in this rather obvious facet of title registration than in the aggressive middle-class understanding of property it embodied. Registration would be of ownership in the personalty sense only: beneficial or nominal but not divisible into successive interests. Family settlements would of course be possible behind trusts, but in relation to a purchaser all registered owners would have a general power of sale, whatever any trust deed might say. As with consols the trust would have no external application, save that a *distringas* or something like it could be lodged to prevent a sale being undertaken at all, or to allow it only with someone's consent. Some variants added that on the death of the registered proprietor the land should not

---

[57] R. Wilson, *Outlines of a Plan for Adapting the Machinery of the Public Funds to the Transfer of Real Property* (1844); H. Sewell, *A Letter to Lord Worsley on the Burthens affecting Real Property* (1846); W. D. McIntyre, *Sewell, Henry 1807–1879*, in Dictionary of New Zealand Biography, updated 7 April 2006, URL: http://www.dnzb.govt.nz/.

[58] 'W.R.', 'Transfer of Real Property' (1845) 43 *Westminster Rev.* 373; *Reports etc by the Law Amendment Society*, HLP 1851, xvi, 349; 'Papers of the Society for Promoting the Amendment of the Law' (W. S. Cookson) (1852) 16 *Law Rev.* 361–78.

[59] SC on Registration of Assurances Bill, Report, PP 1852–3 (889), xxxvi, 397. See pp. 71–4, above.

[60] RC on Registration of Title, Report, PP 1857 (sess. 2) (2215), xxi, 245; Anderson, *Lawyers*, 84–95.

pass directly to the heir or devisee as it would at common law, but should instead descend only through a 'real representative'. So far as a good faith purchaser was concerned any disposition by a real representative would be unimpeachable. Thus wills, like trusts, would be put 'behind' the register, as the metaphor went.

The class implications of this form of title registration are immediately apparent: it had no place for strict settlements. Those did have a role for trustees, albeit limited, and best practice would even endow them with a limited power of sale, though usually only for the purposes of exchange or consolidation.[61] From 1856 Settled Estates Acts enabled Chancery to authorize sales where previously application for a private statute would have been needed, but they were cautious, and so too was the courts' application of them.[62] That was far different from vesting the fee in trustees, enacting that their power of disposal was inherent, and limiting it only by *caveat*. Predictably, J. H. Christie and other conservative reformers rejected the very concept of fee simple registration and the standardization it brought as 'wholly impossible'.[63] Bellenden Ker asserted that England was not a commercial country but instead enjoyed a mixed commercial and aristocratic constitution; title registration was too inconvenient to win landowners' acceptance, he said.[64]

Intellectually and institutionally too these early versions of title registration differed radically from the premises Bellenden Ker and the Real Property Commissioners had accepted.[65] Those sought to restore a common law, albeit in modern statutory form, but one that aimed to preserve the possibilities of the common law of real property. Their strategy had been to minimize equity and (not the same thing) the role of Chancery. By contrast the strong version of fee simple registration created a fictitious or nominal ownership, a façade for outward purposes.[66] Intergenerational enjoyment would be conducted through trusts, because only equity could achieve the 'infinitely varied modification of enjoyment' characteristic of an advanced society in the only way consistent with

---

[61] Davidson, *Precedents*, iii, 456–80 (3rd edn, 1873).

[62] See pp. 87–9, above.

[63] The words are Christie's: *RC on Registration and Conveyancing*, Report, 561 (and see his reply to the 1857 commissioners: *RC on Registration of Title*, Report, 578–9); for others see Anderson, *Lawyers*, 74. The standardizing effect of registration and its consequences are elaborated by A. Pottage, 'The Originality of Registration' (1995) 15 *OJLS* 371–401.

[64] *On the Reform*, 6, 89–90. He flirted vaguely with a 'simplification' that would keep all the standard elements of a strict settlement; *ibid.*, 28–9. By 1857 he was temporizing: *RC on Registration of Title*, Report, 609–10. Compare J. Williams, *Letters to John Bull, Esq, on Lawyers and Law Reform* (1857), 48–53.

[65] 'W.R.' [Robert Wilson], 'Transfer of Real Property'; [Cookson] 'Papers'.

[66] This can be seen as a profound change: A. Pottage, 'Evidencing Ownership', in S. Bright and J. Dewar (eds), *Land Law* (Oxford, 1998), 129–50.

its free alienation.[67] The greater role envisaged for equity both presupposed and required Chancery reform.

Proponents of the change justified it by analogies that were mostly modern and treated realty as just another form of wealth.[68] Thus, it was said, trusts for sale of mixed realty and personalty were common. So too were leasehold investments, which, on death, would devolve to an executor who could sell the property to a purchaser despite what the will might say, courts having immunized purchasers from having to check that the sale really was necessary to pay debts or legacies.[69] Similarly with the recently developed but now very common form of mortgage—from early in its inception the mortgage with power of sale had been worded so as to immunize purchasers from having to see that notices had been properly served, that surplus proceeds were paid to the mortgagor, and even that there had been any lawful occasion for the sale at all.[70] Overreaching powers were everywhere.

Supporters of title registration could differ sharply over details and methods. Whether registration should be local or centralized divided them, and remained a critical issue through to the 1890s. How to get land on to the register in the first place also seemed difficult to the more conservative, who preferred scrutiny by a landed estates court or possibly a court-appointed conveyancer to that of a mere administrator. That thinking led to a distinction between absolute or guaranteed title, which would need authoritative certification before being issued, and mere possessory title. The latter would simply record what the present owner claimed (on usual conveyancing standards), require all future dealings to be registered, and rely on lapse of time to cure any defects holding over from before the time of first registration. The members of the royal commission that reported in 1857 divided on some of these issues but were broadly united on the basic assimilationist model.[71] Commercial principles, reinforced by the ubiquity of overreaching powers, demonstrated the need for a land title registration system based upon the analogy with consols.

Though this thinking was particularly associated with title registration the two were severable. Wilson himself shifted to a more individualized form of title registration in the 1850s, the Law Amendment Society also compromised, though to a lesser extent, and in 1862 Lord Westbury based his registration statute on a

[67] 'W.R.', 'Transfer of Real Property', 383.

[68] [Cookson] 'Papers'; Wilson, *Outlines*; *RC on Registration of Title*, Report; E. P. Wolstenholme, 'Simplification of Title Preferable to Introduction of Novel Modes of Assurance', in *Papers Read before the Juridical Society* (1862), ii, 533–52.

[69] Sugden, *Vendors and Purchasers* (10th edn, 1839), iii, 176–81.

[70] See pp. 137–41, above.

[71] *RC on Registration of Title*, Report; Anderson, *Lawyers*, 90–5.

different principle altogether.[72] On the other hand, standardized, streamlined, fee simple ownership could be projected as the proper solution to the problems of cost and delay without any form of registration. Critics of title registration pointed to its many institutional difficulties, to problems of location, publicity, patronage, staff expertise, official discretion, expense, maps and indexing, and, later, the provision of guarantees and indemnities. In addition title registration suffered from the inescapable logical problem that the very concept of indefeasibility used to lure a proprietor on to the register also threatened his removal by forgery.[73] So there were proposals that accepted the challenge to make land sales as straightforward as sales of consols, but did it by remodelling the deeds system.[74]

Their most usual basis was that if registration worked it would not be because of the register itself but because of the underlying changes registration made, perhaps tacitly, to the substantive law—to the ordering of priorities between competing interests. That could be achieved without the bureaucracy and publicity of a registry. These proposals tended to be much less visible, because their inventors tended to work alone—unlike deeds and title registration, which were causes that attracted adherents. They tended to be counter-proposals, a response to pressure for title registration rather than measures advanced in their own right.

The most complete of such mid-century analyses, however, did eventually attract institutional support, and became the basis of English land law by instalments between 1882 and 1925, though it too was ignored when first advanced. This was the prescription advanced by the conveyancing barrister Edward Parker Wolstenholme to a meeting of the Juridical Society in March 1862.[75] It was radical in three ways. First, it was general, in the sense that though it would not have produced a code of land law it would have provided at least the core of one. Secondly, it integrated aristocratic settlements with middle-class trusts within a framework designed to achieve ease of sale. Thirdly, though it left landowners some room for choice the framework itself was compulsory.

Wolstenholme's technique was to formulate as direct norms the results reached by registration of consols, discarding the means by which they had been achieved.

---

[72] R. Wilson, *A Letter to the Right Honourable Lord John Russell on the Transfer of Landed Property* (1853) and *Registration of Title to Land; what it is, why it is needed, and how it may be effected* (1863); *Reports etc by the Law Amendment Society* HLP 1851, xvi, 349; Land Registry Act 1862, s 32.

[73] Similarly there were worries that removal of a *distringas* could be achieved by impersonation, making theft of consols a possibility: *RC on Chancery*, First Report, *PP* 1852 [1437], xxi, 1, 263–4; Wolstenholme, 'Simplification'.

[74] E. N. Ayrton, 'Title Books versus Title Deeds; or Public Registration of Titles superseded' (1858) 5 (s3) *LM&LR*. 67–88; F. V. Hawkins, *Optional Mobilisation of Land* (1869); G. J. Johnson (1870–1) 15 *Sol. J.* 159, (1873–4) 18 *Sol. J.* 943, (1874–5) 19 *Sol. J.* 215.

[75] Wolstenholme, 'Simplification'.

Thus 'after a certain date no person entitled to a fee simple should be allowed to make any disposition thereof except to the extent of the whole fee, or for a term of years absolute', the latter a necessary concession, he thought, to a fundamental difference between consols and land. It followed that legal settlements of the sort used by the aristocracy would simply be prohibited, legal life estates, fees tail, and conditional estates all being abolished. Wolstenholme himself accepted the whole case for structuring family settlements through trustees with overreaching powers, but should that prove unattractive he offered a novel refinement. Instead of vesting the fee simple in trustees it could be vested in the (now equitable) life tenant, who would then have all the management and overreaching powers that trustees would have under the general law. However, their exercise could be made conditional upon obtaining consent from trustees—who would thus retain the essentially passive but occasionally supervisory role they usually had in contemporary strict settlements. Leases for lives would be abolished, because they put a difficult burden of inquiry on purchasers. Mortgages would continue to be made by transfer of the fee, because in that way a purchaser would need to know only where the fee was and would always be able to take a title safely from that person. This was common law lite, a common law stripped of everything that made for expense and delay but retaining the advantages of privacy and security from forgery that Wolstenholme thought the deeds system of conveyancing held over title registration. Deeds registration he thought an expensive waste of time.

In due course Wolstenholme's prescription came to look less radical as it was outflanked by more daring variations on the same theme. Political support for it, and for schemes like it, was always very weak, evident only from the Law Society from the late 1890s as a last ditch attempt to stop compulsory, centralized registration of title, and then only with misgivings. That will be discussed in the final part of this chapter. It is significant, however, that by that time the principles of the Wolstenholme scheme were endorsed by several high-ranking barristers specializing in conveyancing or property law generally. They were to be influential in shaping the law in the first quarter of the twentieth century—though often in rivalry with each other.

First Fruits: Title Registration to 1875

At its most aggressive, assimilationist thinking could adduce fee simple ownership as a moral necessity. In the late 1820s the Real Property Commissioners had based their prescriptions upon the interests of landowners. Their strategy had been to determine what landowners wanted and then to devise the most efficient way to achieve it. The 1857 royal commission on title registration, writing well after the general swing towards free trade that characterized politics from the mid-1840s, sought justification instead in 'the spirit of commerce'. The fee simple should always be 'in the possession of persons capable of fulfilling those new duties and offices which the ownership of land in the present state of society entails or involves'.[76] As a critic more bluntly put it, 'land shall always be saleable by some person or other at a day's notice'.[77]

In 1859 a substantial measure for assimilation looked set to pass the Commons, only for the minority Conservative government to fall before its third reading was reached. This was a twin measure for a landed estates court and a title register devised by the Solicitor-General, Sir Hugh Cairns.[78] He adopted fee simple registration as his model but, following recent Irish precedent, required the landowner first to have had his title declared by this proposed new court. The link Cairns saw was that although encumbered estates courts had been instituted in Ireland as a means of wiping debt-laden estates clear of their past, a measure not needed in England, the resulting 'parliamentary title' had proved so attractive that the process had been extended to even debt-free applicants.[79]

The idea harked back to the concerns of the 1820s and 1830s that insecurity of title was the primary concern, hence that getting titles on to a register would be a complex business needing expert and authoritative adjudication. It was a concern particularly of the elite. Lord Cranworth was particularly attracted to it, offering bills to declare title as part of, or in opposition to registration proposals.[80] One was passed in 1862, but was 'so completely a dead letter' that *Dart on Vendors and Purchasers* disdained to detail its provisions.[81]

If that was a minority concern, assimilation of landownership with the ownership of stock, and of ships, which were thought to operate in much the same way, was a major theme in the debates on Cairns's bills. The Liberal MP Robert Lowe was speaking for many when he said that whatever the differences between those

---

[76] *RC on Registration of Title*, Report, 28; see also [Cookson], 'Papers'.

[77] *RC on Registration of Title*, Report, 28; F. V. Hawkins, *The Title to Landed Estates Bills and the Solicitor-General's Speech Considered* (1859), 34.

[78] Title to Landed Estates Bill, *PP* 1859 (sess. 1) (19), ii, 803; Registry of Landed Estates Bill, *PP* 1859 (sess. 1) (20), ii, 595; Anderson, *Lawyers*, 95–107.

[79] 12 & 13 Vict. c. 77 replacing the ineffective 11 & 12 Vict. c. 48, which had used the Irish High Court of Chancery instead; P. Gray, *Famine, Land and Politics: British Government and Irish Society, 1843–50* (Dublin 1999), 196–224; P. G. Lane, 'The Encumbered Estates Court, Ireland, 1848–1849' (1971–2) 3 *Economic and Social Review* 413–53. In 1854 a similar measure was adopted for the West Indies, where the British move to free trade had ruined many sugar plantations: West Indian Incumbered Estates Act (to be operative within a colony only after adoption by the local legislature); A. Howe, *Free Trade and Liberal England 1846–1946* (Oxford, 1997), 51–3; R. W. Beachey, *The British West Indies Sugar Industry in the Late 19th Century* (1957), 1–39.

[80] Anderson, *Lawyers*, 96, 108, 111.

[81] (5th edn, 1876), ii, 1149; cf. Williams, *Principles of Real Property* (11th edn, 1875), 458 ('does not appear to have been repealed').

things 'they were all capable of being represented before the public by a person clothed with all the attributes of ownership, for the purpose of transferring them, while the beneficial ownership did not appear before the public, and might be subject to any modifications which persons chose to impose'.[82] Adoption would have been voluntary, Cairns seeing his measures as merely facilitative. Demand for them was shown, he thought, both by the evidence given to the 1857 royal commission that simplification of land transfer would increase sale prices and by the Irish experience. In essence he would have given landowners the choice of treating their land very much as though it were personalty.

By contrast, and quite unexpectedly, the Liberals' Transfer of Land Act 1862, the first to institute title registration in England, rejected that model. It was equally individualistic, a facility for those who wanted to use it, but it rejected the personalty model. Denouncing reliance on 'fictitious title', denying that land could be transferred like stock or ships, Lord Westbury and his spokesmen intended instead to offer the benefits of title registration to those whom he regarded as the real owners, that is to the possessors of interests under settlements.[83] Thus although only those with, or entitled to, a fee simple could initially register, once land was on the register they could deal with it as they could have done before, and have the resulting fragmentation registered. This was registration for realty, an obvious and risky change of tack from what had looked like a settled bipartisan course associating registration with the voluntary adoption of the modes of personalty.[84] By discarding the 'fiction' that involved, Westbury must have hoped to give registration a broader appeal.

Critics of his bill objected that it would lead to the quagmire of deeds registration, for unless transactions were standardized the incidents of every registered estate were necessarily individualized, hence dependent on the terms of their constitutive settlement. So it turned out, though the commission appointed in 1870 to inquire into the Act found other reasons for its failure too.[85] In its first six years of operation the new registry had received just 507 applications for first registration, of which about half had been successfully processed.[86] Registrar Follett despairingly told the commissioners that in some instances he was reduced to copying the deed into the register.[87] Whereas transfers of the fee simple were very

[82] *PD* 1859 (s3) 152: 310.

[83] *PD* 1862 (s3) 165: 351–66 esp. 361–2; 167: 238–45 esp. 241.

[84] Robert Wilson, originator of the title registration movement, had latterly stressed that registration did not presuppose any particular underlying structure of law: *Registration of Title to Land.* It is not known whether that influenced Westbury, who said little about his reasons.

[85] *RC on Land Transfer Act*, Report, *PP* 1870 [C. 20], xviii, 595; *SC on Land Titles and Transfer*, 2nd Report, *PP* 1878–9 (244), xi, 1, 185 (Lord Cairns); Anderson, *Lawyers*, 112–18.

[86] Anderson, *Lawyers*, 112.

[87] *RC on Land Transfer Act*, Report, 650–1.

easy, once land became subject to complicated limitations and charges his office became 'helpless', 'the whole motion proceeds from the office instead of from the parties', causing delay, frustration, and expense. The commissioners linked this reason to Westbury's provisions that indefeasible title would be given only if the claimant met Chancery's 'marketable title' standard and that boundaries be definitively ascertained. Rather than just modifying that standard, however, they reiterated that title registration should be based upon commercial values and accordingly prescribed a return to the principles of the report of the royal commission in 1857.

Unanimous affirmation of fee simple registration by this commission of lawyers and lawyer-politicians mostly without prior connection to title registration, suggests that by 1870 a middle-class conception of land as merely a form of wealth had become unexceptionable, to the extent that the state should provide simple mechanisms for landowners who themselves saw land that way. The version they approved was particularly strong because it included a form of real representative for registered land. Still there was no compulsion, save for a suggestion that since common law settlements without powers of sale were an obstacle to ready transfer, courts might perhaps be entrusted with a broader jurisdiction to approve a sale than was presently available under the Settled Estates Act.

The shift towards seeing a combined registration and assimilation scheme as compulsory came in the early 1870s with the political revival of the land question.[88] It was not a complete novelty—Robert Wilson's original proposal had envisaged a parochial inspector who would bring the more reluctant landowners into line. But once others had taken up his scheme as a serious proposal it had instead been developed as a facility for landowners, not an imposition upon them. In their bills of the early 1870s, however, the Liberals proposed that on every sale of land (but only on sale) registration would be compulsory, if only of a mere possessory title.[89] They saw that as a necessary measure of free trade to meet commercial needs and to quiet demands for some more coercive means of redistribution. It would be, Lord Selborne said, the beginning of a general reconstruction of the 'whole system' of land titles.[90] Voluntary and compulsory registration were different systems, he said, 'wide as the poles asunder'.

At first the Conservatives followed suit but in the end they abandoned compulsion, under pressure from provincial solicitors. They agreed with the Liberals

---

[88] Anderson, *Lawyers*, 118–30; Cornish and Clark, *Law and Society*, 166–72; T. A. Jenkins, *Gladstone, Whiggery and the Liberal Party* (1988), Chs 1–3; F. M. L. Thompson, *English Landed Society in the Nineteenth Century* (1963), Ch. 10.

[89] This idea originated from Cookson in the 1840s, its logic being that defects existing prior to registration would eventually be cured by expiry of the limitation period.

[90] *PD* 1873 (s3) 215: 1116–34; 1875 222: 744; Anderson, *Lawyers*, 120, 171.

that for compulsion to be fair and workable there would have to be local registries not just one centralized office in London, but they did not agree that the
expense would be worthwhile. Lord Cairns was persuaded that there were so
many small transfers in the provinces that registration—perhaps in any form—
would make conveyancing more expensive.[91] Hence his Land Transfer Act 1875,
an adaptation of the 1857 commission's proposals, was to function as an invitation to landowners to treat their land as the middle class treated their consols,
not as a requirement.

From political conception to actualization was not easy, however, and not
just because of solicitors' opposition to the combination of compulsion and
centralization. Once compulsion was dropped, Westbury's Act could be left
standing; there was room for two voluntary systems, one offering certainty of
title to those who wished to exploit the full range of possibilities real property
law provided, the other offering to facilitate the transactions of those willing
to settle for something simpler.[92] But the two major commercial activities of
leasing and mortgaging had to be integrated with fee simple registration, which
raised practical and conceptual difficulties acute enough to divide even sympathetic lawyers.[93]

Leases needed dividing by nature and duration into those that were a form
of ownership (beneficial leases), those that needed noting on the register (long
leases), and those that a purchaser should find for himself by inspecting the
site (short leases in possession). There was considerable regional variation in
leasehold practice and in other devices for extracting rent or taking security.
Rentcharges and chief rents were common and elaborate in some places, scarcely
used in others. Some regions had their own ways of structuring mineral rights.
Everywhere there were different forms of mortgage for different purposes. In
working out how much of this could be accommodated within a system of fee
simple registration, how much first needed modification, how much required
greater elasticity of the register, and how much was just incompatible, the analogy
with ownership of consols, or even ships, was useless.

The 1875 Act settled for a relatively simple commercial outcome: substantive registration for mortgages and for leases with more than 21 years to run.
Proprietors of those interests were regarded as owners of something that could
be transferred through the registry, not as mere encumbrancers. To preserve the
integrity of fee simple registration, however, mortgage was to be by charge not

[91] SC on Land Titles and Transfer, 2nd Report, 186, 193.
[92] Compulsory registration under the assimilation model necessarily excluded registration under
the 1862 Act: Land Titles and Transfer Bill, PP 1874 (136), iii, 19 cll 27, 151.
[93] Anderson, Lawyers, 117–19, 134.

by transfer or demise, the charge invoking a list of statutory powers, some of which the parties could alter. The difficult question of reconciling registration with automatic transmission of land on death was solved not by instituting a real representative but by giving the Registrar power to choose the appropriate successor, with appeal to a court.

When compulsion returned to the political agenda a decade later the shortcomings of this Act as a basis for a more thorough assimilation, or even for compulsory registration, were probed in very great detail—which continued through into the royal commission of 1908–11 that investigated the successor that grew out of it, the Land Transfer Act 1897. As of 1875, however, both political parties were willing to see a major measure of assimilation for those landowners who wanted it and, if the political situation made it expedient, they were prepared to force it on those who did not.

This reasonably broad intellectual consensus supports Bernard Rudden's analysis that:

What has happened is that the objects of the law of property have become divided into two great classes. The first comprises all tangible things…and all discrete intangible things…The second consists of *funds*. A fund is an abstract segment of wealth whose identity is distinct from the objects in which it is invested.…The modern law applies to the first class a relatively simple regime of ownership, possession, and security devices. It is to the second class—the fund—that the older learning has been transferred; it is there that we find flourishing the whole complex of estates, powers, perpetuities, and (it will be argued) tenure. The pivot between the two classes is provided by the trust.[94]

Manipulation of 'the trust' to provide Rudden's pivot was itself a long and complex transition. It involved extensive amendments easing succession among trustees, annexation of powers to their office, and internalization of the trust relationship by use of parallel deeds and receipt clauses to remove purchasers' duties to check that trustees were behaving lawfully.[95] The theory and the details were regarded as unsettled in the 1840s, and J. H. Christie told the 1847–50 royal commission that some conveyancers sometimes challenged the practice.[96] By the 1870s, however, it had been largely completed. So the idea that the law should provide a relatively simple regime for ownership and transfer of land had become orthodox, possibly as a general measure, but if not at least as an option for landowners who found the law of real property unappealing.

---

[94] B. Rudden, *The New River* (Oxford, 1985), 214. For his 'tenure' argument see *ibid.*, 246–7.

[95] See pp. 181–2, above; 269–82, below.

[96] G.[eorge] S.[weet?] 'On seeing to the application of purchase-money for property charged with the payment of debts and legacies' (1847) 11(2) *Jurist* 110–14, 124–7 at 110; Dart, *Vendors and Purchasers* (1st edn, 1851), 283. Christie: *RC on Registration and Conveyancing*, Report, 559.

2. CONVEYANCING AND LAND TRANSFER 1875–1914

The focus of this final section is legislation, its making and its consequences. In his 'Paradox' Dicey listed among his five fundamentals of English land law the private conveyance of land, which he saw as offering landowners the privacy they treasured ahead of the ease and certainty of title registration.[97] It was part of his political analysis of 'opinion', his argument being that his tipping point in the 1860s from Benthamite individualism to collectivism was less evident in land law than one would expect. His identification of private conveyancing as a fundamental accurately reflects the political attention it received, though the label of collectivism fits registered conveyancing badly. It might, peripherally from time to time, have linked to purposes of state control, though that aspect of it was always tenuous and did not materialize in our period. It might have a redistributive effect, a shift of employment away from solicitors and into the hierarchies of the public service—this is the foundation of Avner Offer's writing.[98] But redistribution was not a primary objective, aside perhaps for Sir Charles Fortescue-Brickdale, land registrar from 1900, more a consequence, and an uncertain one at that.

It brought a bitterness between the rivals, however, and one that could bemuse bystanders. There were elite conveyancing barristers who saw no difficulties, and considerable advantage, in a comfortable *ménage à trois*. They were always influential because at any time some of them would have easy access to the Lord Chancellor and a parity of respect in his presence, based upon mutual recognition of professional achievement. Their verdict mattered. For them there was less an economic struggle than a competitive wooing of the public with rival promises of utilitarian advantage.

Registration of title brought an intellectual challenge that affected all who worked with it but which was rarely articulated. Is it 'registered conveyancing' or is it 'land transfer'? The former implies fidelity to and integration with an underlying law, the same law that applies to unregistered conveyancing. The latter need not; its application can be an exercise in statutory interpretation complete in itself. The former implies that registration should accommodate transactions that are normal in the unregistered system. The latter does not. This difference of perception and its implications will surface from time to time in the account that follows. It could bring discomfort. Benjamin Cherry, a conveyancing barrister

---

[97] A. V. Dicey, 'The Paradox of the Land Law' (1905) 21 *LQR* 221–32.
[98] 'The Origins of the Law of Property Acts 1910–1925' (1977) 40 *MLR* 505–22; *Property and Politics, 1870–1914* (Cambridge, 1981).

who ended up being the one to frame the 1925 legislation, introduced 'transfer' and 'proprietor' in inverted commas in his book on the Land Transfer Acts, as though he needed rubber gloves to handle them.[99] The former was inelegant, he wrote, and the latter was one of several terms that seemed 'to have been adopted in order to shock conveyancers'.

Deeds Registration: Digging up the Corpse

The Land Transfer Act 1875 offered the advantages of title registration to land-owners willing to accept its restrictions—mortgages by charge, settlements by trusts. There turned out to be very few of them. That caused difficulty for anyone of liberal inclination who could see a social problem in the existing methods of land transaction but who was disinclined to compulsion. The dilemmas are well illustrated in the report of George Osborne Morgan's select committee on land titles and registration in 1879, which asserts a deep but ultimately stultify-ing respect for individual choice.[100] The committee was established after serious and well-publicized forgeries by a solicitor showed how easy it was to exploit the trust that underlay deeds-based conveyancing. The shortening of titles in the interests of speed and economy, the ubiquity of contractual terms block-ing inquiry into inconvenient but usually trivial inadequacies of title, meant that solicitors *had* to trust each other not to be hiding something sinister. Correspondence to *The Times* following the solicitor's conviction argued that something less personal, perhaps more regulatory, was required, and the com-mittee agreed.[101]

It was clear, however, not only that Cairns's Land Transfer Act had stalled—a mere 48 registrations in three years—but that Cairns himself lacked enthusiasm for it.[102] He had wanted a landed estates court to cleanse title and a purely minis-terial registry to record it, but 'finding the state in the possession of the Office of Registry, which could not be displaced, and must be utilised, I did not consider at the time that I had any choice but to endeavour to do the best I could with it'.[103] He agreed that 'public expectation was raised to a much greater height than was legitimate' by analogies with stock.[104] He could not see a way of making title registration compulsory, whereas the registrar and his deputy told the committee

---

[99] B. L. Cherry and H. W. Marigold, *The Land Transfer Acts* (1899), 11.

[100] *SC on Land Titles and Transfer*, 2nd Report, PP 1878–9 (244), xi, 1.

[101] *The Times*, 19, 23, 28 January, 23, 27 (Torrens) May 1878.

[102] *Land Registry*, Returns of All Titles, PP 1878–9 (134), lix, 281. 12 more were pending.

[103] *SC on Land Titles and Transfer*, 2nd Report, 185, and see 195–6. Westbury had given the regis-trar and his deputy judicial tenure, hence their inability to be removed.

[104] *Ibid.*, 198.

that they could see no way of making a merely voluntary system popular.[105] The committee disagreed only on that last analysis, George Shaw-Lefevre arguing that an amended system might be given an aggressive trial in London, where data from the deeds registry showed a 'practice to treat house property, and even small landed properties, as personalty, in marriage settlements and other family arrangements'.[106]

The committee was broadly agreed, however, that a system of fee simple registration could not be forced upon people. If the power to 'tie up or charge' the land were abolished, then the 'registration of titles would be as easy as the title itself would be simple', but 'such changes would be so opposed to the general feeling of the country, that, for the present, at least, it would be idle to consider them seriously'.[107] This was a dilemma for Liberals generally. Looking back in 1889, when the political environment was quite different and the Conservatives were being altogether more aggressive, Sir Henry James explained how, as Gladstone's attorney-general, he had tried to devise a solution but failed. A system good for large estates may be 'very inapplicable to house property or building plots in the neighbourhood of towns', he wrote.[108]

The only route left for the committee was to recommend deeds registration. It was a futile cause. The Liberals would not take it up, nor would Cairns for the Conservatives.[109] Not even a modest start would be allowed by reform of the Middlesex deeds registry as a pilot measure. In the last days of the Conservative administration, Osborne Morgan floated a bill to that effect but after he became a junior minister in Gladstone's new administration he joined his colleagues in discouraging similar proposals.[110]

It was not that the Middlesex deeds registry did not need it. It had scarcely been touched by legislation since its creation in 1708.[111] The registrar paid its expenses, performed his duties by deputy, and kept the surplus. In the late 1870s that ran at about two-thirds of the takings, to be shared equally between Lord Truro, surviving sinecurist, and the Crown (in reversion after the deaths of the other sinecurists).[112] The registry's operation was customary, which is to say that officials were free to devise its process as they thought best, charging as

[105] *Ibid.*, 6.

[106] *Ibid.*, 32.

[107] There must be a suspicion of dissembling here, since both Osborne Morgan and Shaw-Lefevre wanted the abolition of entail.

[108] (1888–9) 33 *Sol. J.* 539.

[109] Cairns: *SC on Land Titles and Transfer*, 2nd Report, 189.

[110] Middlesex Land Registry Bill, *PP* 1880 (sess. 1) (189), v, 323; *PD* (s3) 1880 153: 680–2. But he chaired the Commons SC on the Yorkshire Registries Bill recounted below.

[111] 7 Ann. c. 20.

[112] *Middlesex Registry*, Return showing receipts 1877–81, *PP* 1882 (316), liv, 175.

they thought appropriate. Some London solicitors took exception to that in the 1880s, but Mathew and A. L. Smith JJ held the fees challenged to be reasonable, less than formerly had been charged, validated by passage of time, and hence lawful.[113]

There was dissatisfaction with the law too. The 1708 Act and the almost contemporaneous statutes establishing the three Yorkshire registries had not been drafted with the precision that judges had come to expect. Though it had come to be regretted in the nineteenth century, from soon after the Acts' passage judges had held that they did not oust the equitable principles of notice.[114] Registration was not of itself notice and notice of an unregistered instrument bound a purchaser. These rules did not deprive registration of all its advantages, but they did limit them. They also caused uncertainty, both because they encouraged litigation over facts and because doubt remained over exactly which forms of notice were binding in which circumstances. In 1868 Madden's text, predominantly on the Irish legislation, was reasonably confident that only actual notice of an unregistered instrument bound, not constructive notice.[115] That was in line with the general run of English cases, which tended to equate actual notice with fraud, though Stuart VC upset that for a short time by holding that constructive notice bound as well.[116] In Yorkshire too that broader view was said to have prevailed, until Jessel MR ruled in 1876 that actual notice was required.[117]

There was room therefore for both institutional and substantive change. The Liberals, however, were unwilling to commit themselves to reform that might be thought to pre-empt more general legislation. Members' bills from both sides of the House were blocked.[118] From a different point of view the Treasury sought double advantage from shifting Middlesex deeds registration into the Land Registry, abolishing the embarrassing sinecure offices and diverting their profits to shore up the moribund, loss-making business of title registration.[119] Sensible

[113] Anderson, *Lawyers*, 170n; *Munton v. Lord Truro* (1886) 17 QBD 783.

[114] *Le Neve v. Le Neve* (1747) Amb. 436; *Jolland v. Stainbridge* (1797) 3 Ves. Jun. 477; *Wyatt v. Barwell* (1815) 19 Ves. 434; *RC on Real Property*, 2nd Report, *PP* 1830 (575), xi, 1, 36–40.

[115] D. H. Madden, *A Practical Treatise on the Registration of Deeds, Conveyances, and Judgment-Mortgages* (Dublin, 1868), 210–29.

[116] *Wormald v. Maitland* (1865) 35 LJ Ch 69, contrast *Chadwick v. Turner* (1866) 1 Ch App 310. Orthodoxy was restored by *Agra Bank v. Barry* (1874) LR 7 HL 135.

[117] H. Barker, *A Manual on the Registration of Deeds and Other Assurances in Yorkshire* (1885), 32–9, 125–6, 162–3; *Lee v. Clutton* (1876) 24 WR 106.

[118] Middlesex Land Registry Bill, *PP* 1880 (sess. 2) (142), v, 335; 1881 (87), iv, 161; 1882 (184), iv, 95; *PD* 1880 (s3) 153: 680–2; 1881 (s3) 180: 825–34. Middlesex Land Registry Bill, *PP* 1884 (91), v, 329; *PD* 1884 (s3) 184: 778–87, 1672–8.

[119] Registry of Deeds (Middlesex) Bill, *PP* 1882 (22), vi, 23; Middlesex Registry of Deeds Bill, *PP* 1884 (169), v, 339; *PD* 1884 (s3) 288: 787–8; 289: 1740–9.

housekeeping though that may have been, the proposal united too many strands of opposition and was allowed to lapse. Conservatives, always less squeamish, made the shift in 1891, on Lord Truro's death.[120]

Yorkshire was a different case, because there the three registries fell under the suzerainty of their respective riding's quarter sessions; there was not even an indirect Crown interest. It was allowed to modernize them in 1884, though Yorkshire hopes that the exercise would provoke emulation nationally were disappointed.[121] The resulting legislation, Yorkshire Registries Act 1884, provided for priority by date of registration, extirpating the principles of notice from questions of priority while leaving an exception for cases of 'actual fraud'. This had the important consequence of abolishing 'tacking'.[122] That was a principle that allowed a third mortgagee to leapfrog a second by buying up the first, legal, mortgage and treating the two as one, provided that at the time of his loan he had not known about the second. It worked because legal estates trump equitable (subject to modification for notice), but being based neither upon simple temporal priority nor upon the morality of postponement for fault it came to be regarded as a 'great severity' to the intermediate lender.[123] The Real Property Commissioners had regarded it as one of the evils of the present system, to be superseded by their system of deeds registration.[124]

In addition the Yorkshire Registries Act implicitly required registration of all mortgages by deposit of documents, whether accompanied by a written memorandum or not. It introduced for the first time a system of caveats, which were designed to operate as priority notices for purchasers and mortgagees after contract.[125] There is considerable convergence throughout the Act between deeds registration and registration of title, showing why it might have been a model for emulation, were there not already a land registry in place. These were not altogether easy choices, however; there were bankers who disliked the added formality short-term mortgages now needed, and there were both bankers and solicitors who regretted the abolition of actual notice as a standard of liability.[126]

[120] Middlesex Registry Act 1891.

[121] The best source, written from a law society's angle, is Barker, *Manual*.

[122] It had been abolished once before in 1874 in anticipation of compulsory title registration, only to be reinstated retrospectively the following year when the Land Transfer Act introduced merely a voluntary system.

[123] Fisher, *Mortgage* (1st edn), 356–7; cf. *RC on Real Property*, 2nd Report, PP. 1830 (535) xi, 1, 143–4 (Bacon). It worked just as well if the first and third mortgages were taken by the same person.

[124] *RC on Real Property*, 2nd Report, 15, 35.

[125] Barker, *Manual*, 137–8.

[126] (1884–5) 29 *Sol. J.* 307; Barker, *Manual*, 40–6.

Almost immediately serious defects were found, necessitating two remedial statutes.[127] The most illuminating concerns a section that had been inserted only because law societies had asked for it. Addressing a complaint that had often been made, it said simply that registration was notice for all purposes. That, however, had the potential for a most unfortunate effect on mortgagors who repaid their mortgagees not knowing that they had transferred the mortgage, likewise on trustees dealing with beneficiaries who had transferred or encumbered their interests.[128] The general law required the incoming interest holder to notify the vulnerable mortgagor or trustee, but the effect of the section was to make registration of a memorial notice, creating a potential liability to pay a second time. Similarly, lenders whose mortgage secured further advances would lose priority for money they furnished after a subsequent mortgagee registered a memorial, even if they knew nothing of it, which would make mortgages to secure current accounts practically impossible. The offending section was repealed outright.

The episode is significant for two reasons. First, it points to the weakness of legislative process. The original bills—there were two rivals—were launched into Parliament without systematic prior consultation, the select committee on them (chaired by Osborne Morgan) declined to take oral evidence, and so lobbying was hurried and amendment was corridor work. Law-making on the run produced bad law.[129] Secondly, the difficulty primarily concerned mortgages. It is easy to conflate lawyers' cries for simplification, either for its own sake or as a precursor to registration, with the political cries for abolition of entail, settlement, and primogeniture. Yet often it was the intellectual and practical problems of mortgages that made efficient registration difficult and impeded schemes for assimilating real property with personal.

The Conveyancing Acts

Conscious of the costs and delays associated with deeds registration the Osborne Morgan committee had sought means of mitigation. Like the Real Property Commissioners they wanted documents shortened, which they thought could be done compulsorily by statute, and like the Real Property Commissioners they thought solicitors should be paid for the valuable work they did, which meant instituting a statutory *ad valorem* scale. Mortgages should be by charge, which would aid filing and searching, and realty should descend through a real representative, which

---

[127] Yorkshire Registries Act (1884) Amendment Act 1884; Yorkshire Registries Amendment Act 1885.

[128] Barker, *Manual*, 164–7.

[129] Barker, *Manual*, 153 has another example.

would ensure a dedicated paper trail. Some of these ancillary recommendations would succeed despite rejection of the committee's main proposal.

The successful impetus for legislation, however, owed more to the presidential address of N. T. Lawrence to the Incorporated Law Society in October 1879, though his focus and his values are similar.[130] His context was different, not urban fraud but growing fear of rural depression in southern and eastern England.[131] A golden age of rural prosperity looked as though it were ending. For the first time in a generation there was need to promote investment in land. Hence, for Lawrence, there needed to be a general law to equip mortgagors, mortgagees, and limited owners under settlements with the necessary powers to exploit the land fully. Well-drafted documents already did that, but too many did not, especially mortgages, he said. Accordingly, current best practice should become standard legal incidents of those transactions, reinforced by a few rule changes where it was the general law rather than practice that was at fault. To give mortgagees the security the law's structure now denied them, tacking should be abolished and all mortgages should be registered, taking their priority strictly by date of registration irrespective of whether they were legal or equitable.[132] This was an unusual recommendation from a solicitor outside Yorkshire, a sign of how serious things were.

The part of Lawrence's analysis concerning settlements became the foundation for the Settled Land Act 1882, with the addition of the life tenant's inalienable power of sale of the land, which was political. The remainder became part of the Conveyancing Acts 1881–2, save for registration of mortgages, which was presumably held over pending decision of the larger question. The process from suggestion to enactment is known in outline only. The Incorporated Law Society took up its president's paper, briefing E. P. Wolstenholme to draft bills that were then submitted to the Lord Chancellor, Lord Cairns. Somewhere—it is not known by what process—a great deal more material was added that removed many pitfalls from conveyancing, niceties which, if previously they had been assiduously attended to by the conveyancer, would have been adding delay and expense to transactions. The Conservative administration fell soon after Cairns presented the bills, and at first the incoming Liberal Chancellor, Lord Selborne, would not

---

[130] N. T. Lawrence, *Facts and Suggestions as to the Law of Real Property* (1880).

[131] The scale, duration, and distribution of agricultural depression are contested; see for example T. W. Fletcher, 'The Great Depression of English Agriculture 1873–1896' (1961) 13 *Econ. Hist. Rev.* 417–32; E. H. Hunt and S. J. Pam, 'Prices and Structural Response in English Agriculture, 1873–1896' (1997) 50 *Econ. Hist. Rev.* 477–505, and for a general account F. M. L. Thompson, *English Landed Society in the Nineteenth Century* (1963), 292–326.

[132] *Facts and Suggestions*, 23–4. Note that he envisaged registration of the whole, not merely a memorial.

let them proceed. Then over the next two years the Liberal block was lifted. It is not known how or why, but the inability of the Liberals to formulate their own policy must be part of it.

Together the Settled Land Act and the Conveyancing Acts are the culmination of a long process of modification of land transfer law by conveyancing practice. An obituary notice for Wolstenholme noted the paradox of the Settled Land Act, 'one of the most drastic and, at the same time, conservative pieces of law reform of recent times', it said.[133] Drastic for its unfettered power of sale, breaking the habits of generations; conservative in offering mere facilitation, not inducement, far less coercion; 'pre-emptive', one historian calls it.[134] That was true of the Conveyancing Acts too; they aimed to make the deeds-based system of private land transfer the best it could be—the yardstick being the best that could be found in current practice, reinforced by rule changes to make it safe. But again, facilitative.

Much of the Conveyancing Act 1881 took up the call from Osborne Morgan's committee to shorten documents.[135] It contained formulae for what a conveyance should be taken to contain (unless altered), some of which Davidson had been urging for decades.[136] Conveyancers could now simply omit covenants for title and the difficult and complex provisions ensuring future production of deeds for inspection, where a seller was retaining them because he was selling only a part of a larger estate.

The Act also equipped mortgagors and mortgagees with a set of statutory powers, which could be taken as they were or amended, but which no longer needed spelling out. Consolidation of mortgages was abolished, as a legal principle, as Lawrence had thought so self-evident that it scarcely needed justification.[137] That meant that now a second mortgagee could rely on inspection of the first mortgage deed without having to inquire from the first mortgagee whether he held a mortgage over other property—if he had, then under the old law the first mortgagee could use the land as security for both loans, reducing its value to the second mortgagee.[138] Similarly, several sections entitled purchasers to rely on documentation without inquiring into facts it recorded—whether money really had been paid, for example, or whether a power of attorney had still been extant at the time of its exercise. All this was designed to enable greater reliance on documents and

---

[133] *The Times*, 9 May 1908.

[134] H. Perkin, *The Origins of Modern English Society 1780–1880* (1969), 452.

[135] It included relief against forfeiture of leases, which had been the subject of several unsuccessful bills shortly before, including one from Davey.

[136] *Concise Precedents* (3rd edn, 1848), 6–7 (and successive editions); (12th edn, 1882), 45–8.

[137] *Facts and Suggestions*, 23.

[138] Consolidation was permitted by contract, that is, if the mortgage itself stipulated for it.

at the same time to reduce their length. Ancillary measures to ease transactions included better provisions for replacing trustees and for ensuring succession between them.

Some clauses held back in committee when the Conveyancing Bill made its first passage through the Commons were reintroduced successfully the following year. Section 3 of the 1882 Act provided a statutory definition of notice. While conveyancers regarded its statement of actual and constructive notice as declaratory, they welcomed its restriction of the circumstances in which a purchaser would be bound by the actual or constructive notice attributed to his agent, usually his solicitor.[139] The basic rule had been that only notice the agent acquired during the transaction in hand would be attributed to the principal, but there had been a substantial gloss for prior transactions 'so close' that the agent must be taken to have recalled them.[140] Now the rule was cut back to probably the narrowest it had ever been, certainly the narrowest in the nineteenth century: to bind the principal the solicitor had to have acquired his knowledge (or put himself in a situation where he ought to have acquired it) in his capacity as the principal's agent and in the transaction in hand.[141] Again, it was being made safer to rely upon appearances.

More significant for the long-term structure of conveyancing was an adaptation of a recommendation by Osborne Morgan's committee that registry officials should be empowered to conduct searches on request and issue conclusive certificates of the result, a device the committee found to be already working well in Scotland.[142] No one relying on such a certificate would be liable for any error in it. The recommendation had been geared to mitigating the costs implications of deeds registration. An official search certificate bearing the date of the search would be conclusive evidence of the state of the register at that time, in effect an ancillary document of title.[143] There was no place for deeds registration in the Conveyancing Acts but the idea was adapted to the registration of charges, which had previously caused conveyancers such uncertainty.[144] Henceforward

---

[139] Dart, *Vendors and Purchasers* (6th edn, 1888), ii, 988–92; Williams, *Vendor and Purchaser* (1903), i, 258–65.

[140] *Winter* v. *Lord Anson* (1827) 3 Russ. 488; *Hargreaves* v. *Rothwell* (1836) 1 Keen 154; *Fuller* v. *Bennett* (1843) 2 Hare. 394. This formulation may have been a restriction of an older, broader principle. For its ramifications, see *Kennedy* v. *Green* (1834) 2 My. & K. 699; *Boursot* v. *Savage* (1866) LR 2 Eq 134; *Rolland* v. *Hart* (1871) 6 Ch App 678; *Cave* v. *Cave* (1880) 15 Ch D 639.

[141] *Re Cousins* (1886) 31 Ch D 671; *Taylor* v. *London & Counties Bank* [1901] 2 Ch 231.

[142] *SC on Land Titles and Transfer*, 2nd Report, 11. For its subsequent importance when combined with a priority period see A. Pottage, 'The Originality of Registration' (1995) *15 OJLS* 371–401.

[143] Dart, *Vendor and Purchaser* (7th edn, 1905), 1196 regretted that conveyancers had not adopted the habit of including official search certificates in abstracts of title.

[144] See pp. 185, 187, above.

the custodians of those registers at the Central Office of the Supreme Court of Judicature, the renamed Office of Common Pleas, could search on behalf of inquirers and issue conclusive certificates.[145] Provincial solicitors could now requisition a search directly without having to fee a London agent, perhaps saving money, perhaps encouraging a search where previously a risk would have been taken.

How far all this empowerment and streamlining saved money is problematic because at the same time the basis of solicitors' fees was changed. Previously the general practice was that most fees had to be itemized; they were task-based and dependent on the number and length of documents being read, copied, or created. In 1864 and 1865 Lord Westbury had introduced bills to allow freedom of contract between solicitor and client, partly because that was right on principle, partly as an inducement to eliminate delay and prolixity.[146] Such exposure of lambs to wolves had alarmed Conservatives in the Lords, however, and Westbury lost his bill. Now solicitors' remuneration was to be calculated as a percentage of the transaction's value, on a sliding scale to be worked out in regulations by a committee including representatives of law societies.[147]

How far that clear shift of principle made a practical difference is a different matter. Previous practice is not well known. 'Itemized' was a generality; some charges could be made on an hourly basis and some could be adjusted for difficulty.[148] It is not known how often charges were adjusted upwards or downwards to reflect the value of the transaction. Further, there were already a Law Society scale, a general provincial scale, and some local scales operating before 1882, so, on the one hand the change may already have been made, and, on the other, some parts of those scales may have continued.[149] Law societies had persuaded Lord Cairns, whose Act this was, that contracting out of the new scale should be permitted subject to a test of reasonableness and fairness—substantially the freedom that Westbury had sought in the 1860s.[150] So, again, there will have been some instances where the new scale was disregarded, but there is no way of knowing how common that was.

---

[145] Conveyancing Act 1882, s 2. Without a priority period searches had to be made as late as possible: Dart, *Vendor and Purchaser* (7th edn, 1905), 1227.

[146] Attorneys and Solicitors Remuneration Bill; *PD* 1864 (s3) 176: 5–18; Attorneys and Solicitors Costs Bill; *PD* (s3) 177: 1463–74.

[147] Solicitors Remuneration Act 1881; Anderson, *Lawyers*, 151, 153, 157.

[148] W. Hughes, *The Practice of Conveyancing* (1856), i, 157; T. Farries, *A Guide to Drawing Bills of Costs* (1860), 193–5, G. W. Greenwood, *Manual of the Practice of Conveyancing* (4th edn, 1876), 405–7.

[149] (1879–80) 24 *Sol. J.* 591.

[150] *Ibid.*, at 692.

After 1882 some local law societies reported that for small sales and purchases solicitors in their area charged less than the scale allowed, sometimes just for building societies or in cases of building estates, sometimes generally.[151] Data that small transactions were handled very inexpensively was regularly offered to inquiries into land registration throughout our period. Whether the scale was always, or usually, charged in larger transactions was not often addressed, nor how that compared with similar transactions before 1882—if 'similar' does not beg too many questions. The effects of local competition are quite unknown.[152] Two solicitors, formerly presidents of their county law societies, wrote that the new scale's purpose was to enable clients to know their costs in advance, which argues that aggregate charges may not have been greatly affected, but that the scale introduced degrees of cross-subsidy between clients.[153] It is possible that the Conveyancing Act and Solicitors Remuneration Act did reduce costs, but equally that they combined to increase the speed and reliability of land transactions leaving costs much as they were.[154]

So far as the practice of conveyancing was concerned, however, commentary on the Conveyancing Act saw it as completing a phase change. It signalled, after many smaller changes of both law and practice, a final shift from bespoke conveyances to ready-made. It was a source of pride to the Incorporated Law Society for proposing it.[155] It and the Settled Land Act were enduring monuments to the genius of E. P. Wolstenholme, said his editors and successors in the business of drafting property legislation.[156] Lord Cairns wrote to Wolstenholme that his bills were 'the most remarkable efforts of legislation since the Fines and Recoveries Act', a comparison echoed by others.[157] The reduction in the length of documents achieved by the Conveyancing Act was revolutionary, it was claimed; 57 lines of text reduced to 15.[158] The editor of Davidson's *Concise*

---

[151] (1887) 32 *Sol. J.* 226, 243, 259, 324, 632; cf. (1888) 33 *Sol. J.* 14. These returns were in response to a general canvass by the Law Society: (1887) 32 *Sol. J.* 3.

[152] See Vol. XI [Pt 4, Ch IV. p. 6] for solicitors' continuing attempts to reduce price competition through enforcement of scales. *RC on Land Transfer Acts*, 2nd Report, *PP* 1911 [Cd. 5483], xxx, 1, 37 reported 'acute professional competition', especially in the North of England.

[153] (1884–5) 29 *Sol. J.* 692.

[154] e.g. (1882–3) 27 *Sol. J.* 143, 254.

[155] (1881–2) 26 *Sol. J.* 752.

[156] *Wolstenholme's Conveyancing and Settled Land Acts* (10th edn, 1913), p. vii. One of the editors, B. L. Cherry, was subsequently chief architect of the 1925 property legislation; another, A. E. Russell, was a member of the drafting committees and was responsible, jointly with Cherry, for the first drafts of the Trustee Bill and Settled Land Bill: Anderson, *Lawyers*, 284–313.

[157] *Wolstenholme's Conveyancing and Settled Land Acts* (10th edn, 1913), p. vii; (1880–1) 25 *Sol. J.* 768; A. Underhill, *A Concise Exposition of the New Conveyancing Act* (2nd edn, 1882), 1.

[158] (1882–3) 27 *Sol. J.* 798; (1880–1) 29 *Sol. J.* 664; the calculation is from J. Williams, *Principles of the Law of Real Property* (15th edn, 1885), 571–4, 581–2; Prideaux, *Precedents* (11th edn, 1882), pp. iii–iv.

Precedents assured his readers that the Conveyancing Act was 'the work of several gentlemen of great learning and professional eminence and seems to the writer of these observations to be worthy of their reputation'.[159] His readers would be safe relying on the new statutory formulae in substitution for the clauses previously employed.[160] A persistent critic writing for *The Solicitors' Journal* found sustained fault with the Act, but was met, in his own words, by a 'continuous cannonade' of rebuttal.[161]

Compulsory Title Registration: Parturiunt Montes[162]

Insistence that limited owners should have a power of sale, and restriction in Yorkshire of the facility to create undocumented mortgages, introduced an element of coercion, of reduction of choice, that had generally been lacking in real property legislation. Abolition of attendant terms was an exception, but for the most part the aim of legislation had been to improve the means without restricting choice as to ends. Of course, improvement of the operation of the law continued. The Incorporated Law Society procured a Trustee Act in 1888, which added to trustees' powers and eased their liabilities. In the same year it promoted the unification of all the statutory registers of land charges, broadening the requirement of registration at the same time.[163] It was most disappointed when the government insisted that the Land Registry be the new venue, but the combination of a single site and the facility for requisitioning an official search by post continued the theme of simplifying traditional conveyancing. But generally there was a shift in the mid-1880s towards bills that were more programmatic, more coercive, less inclined to adopt a facilitative rhetoric, more antagonistic towards the institutions of wealthy landowners.

Of course, that was not wholly new either. In 1873 Lord Selborne had seen compulsory registration of title as just the beginning of a reconstruction of the 'whole system' of land titles.[164] What was new was that that opinion suddenly seemed orthodox; even Conservatives espoused it. It turned out that the rhetoric, the promise, the effort, were all a good deal more than the achievement. Indeed, it would be plausible to argue that achievement was delayed until 1925.

---

[159] 12th edn, 1882, 41n; this passage was removed from later editions.

[160] Davidson, *Precise Precedents* (12th edn, 1882), 41–50, 58, 69–70.

[161] (1881–2) 26 *Sol. J.* 254.

[162] Horace, *Ars Poetica*, 1.139 (Rome, c. 18BC): 'The mountain labour'd with prodigous throes,/ And, lo! a mouse, ridiculous arose' (A. Carlyle: *The Carlyle Letters Online*, 2007).

[163] Land Charges Registration and Searches Act 1888; Anderson, *Lawyers*, 186. The ILS worked in conjunction with Sir Howard Elphinstone: (1887) 31 *Sol. J.* 475, 631.

[164] See p. 199, above.

The corollary, however, is that the legislative overhaul of land law in 1925 embodies the ideas of the 1880s, and rather little else.

The watershed was the third Reform Act, 1884. One minor consequence of the great shift it brought was to suggest—to lawyers, at least—a new middle ground. 'Free trade in land', had been a radical cry in the 1840s and again in the 1860s, but in comparison with what was truly radical in the 1880s it was now tame enough to attract some Conservatives. That common ground can be seen best in the bills Lord Halsbury presented for the Conservatives from 1887 to 1889, confident that they would produce consensual legislation. The details were his but the shape originated from letters to *The Times* by the Liberal MP and Chancery barrister Horace Davey in September 1885.[165] The Liberal government of 1880–5 had not been able to produce its own proposals, and neither did its short-lived successor in 1886. But Liberal members kept some of the ideas alive in their own bills, showing in the process the variety of detail that was possible.[166]

In the first theme of this programme the Land Transfer Act 1875 would be strengthened by a statement of principle, revised in a few details, modernized to allow for the Settled Land Act and the Married Women's Property Act, reinforced by very extensive rule-making powers, and made compulsory. There would be an optional procedure for guaranteeing boundaries. There would be an insurance fund to compensate transferees if the register turned out to be mistaken. For registration to function smoothly land must devolve through executors or representatives, so, secondly, Halsbury's bills would make that compulsory too.

Thirdly, his bills would abolish intestate primogeniture. On an intestacy widows and widowers alike would take a life estate in the whole of their deceased spouse's realty. That would be a simplification for men (there was no longer a requirement that a child of the marriage should have been born) and a levelling up for women.[167] Not all Liberals would have gone as far; some would have levelled the husband down (faster inheritance for children), some would have kept the inequality.[168] Subject to that life estate, however, the residue of the intestate's real estate would be divided as though it were personalty. In the most common case that would mean equal division between the children of the marriage; that was the political point. The heir at law would be abolished.

Fourthly, entail would be abolished too. Possession of a great estate was no longer the sole route to society's pinnacles, and the Settled Land Act had already

---

[165] *The Times*, 23, 25, 30 September 1885.
[166] Devolution of Estates Bill, *PP* 1884 (103), ii, 497 (Davey); Land Tenure and Transfer Bill, *PP* 1886 (83), iii, 49 (Ince, Courtney, and Kenny); Accumulation Bills, *PP* 1890 (171), i, 5; 1890–1 (125), i, 5.
[167] See Vol. XIII, Part 4, Ch. I.6.
[168] Levelling down: Devolution of Estates Bill 1884 and (probably) Herschell, *PD* 1888 (s3) 323: 1768. Inequality: Land Tenure and Transfer Bill 1886.

provided an exit, in law at least, for those whose finances could not bear the continued strains of agricultural depression.[169] So this in itself would be just a symbolic step, recognizing a change that had already happened, though its simplification of the law would have indirect benefits in facilitating registration. Hence Halsbury proposed that as existing tenants in tail reached the age of 21 their estate would automatically enlarge to a fee simple. Any disposition written in the future as a fee tail would be read as a fee simple. Again, he was taking the simplest option available. Liberal proposals sometimes made enlargement of future fees tail conditional too, while, on the other hand, they often also included abolition of life estates, contingent interests and trusts for accumulation—with exceptions for children during infancy.[170] The moment looked right for a measure that would simultaneously cut back the dynastic principle, free land for the market, and ease its transfer. That was what both parties were promising the new electorate in the mid-1880s, albeit that their emphasis differed.

As for the general scheme of title registration, voices against using the 1875 Act as the template were few and uninfluential. Sir Robert Torrens, after years of promoting the Australasian system bearing his name, persuaded the Social Science Association and the eighth Duke of Marlborough that it would provide a superior solution, but professional opinion was uniformly dismissive.[171] Some evidence about it had been gathered in 1872 as part of the inquest into the failure of Bethell's Act, and again in 1881, but having been rejected in 1872 it was never again examined seriously.[172] Shaw-Lefevre used it as an analogy in his draft report for the select committee in 1879, but not as a model to be adopted.[173] English professional opinion had it that its success turned on the conclusiveness of the Crown grants that originated title in the colonies, absence of complex family settlements plus, sometimes, the certainty that official surveying brought to boundaries there.[174] Marlborough outspokenly attributed registration's failure in England to solicitors' greed and obstruction, which brought a nod of agreement

---

[169] Thompson, *English Landed Society*, 298–326.

[170] Davey's letter, *The Times*, 23 September 1885; Land Tenure and Transfer Bill 1886; G. O. Morgan, *Land Law Reform in England* (1880), 24, cf. Joshua Williams's suggestion to Morgan's Committee: *SC on Land Titles*, 1st Report, PP 1878 (291), xv, 467, 584–5.

[171] Anderson, *Lawyers*, 170–1, 176. Torrens died in 1884. J. E. Hogg, writing in the early 1900s, was the only obvious champion of the Torrens system in England; see pp 223–4, below.

[172] *Registration of Title (Australian Colonies)*, PP 1872 (190), xlii, 499; *Registration of Title (British Colonies)*, PP 1881 (211) (211–1), lxiv, 601, 789.

[173] *SC on Land Titles and Transfer*, 2nd Report, 30–2; Brickdale used it this way too: *RC on Land Transfer*, App. to 1st Report, PP 1909 [Cd. 4510], xxvii, 733, 772.

[174] Joshua Williams, *SC on Land Titles*, 1st Report, 490 (Crown grants and absence of settlements); Wolstenholme, 1st Report, 592 (Crown grants; new country so people take it as it is); Bar Committee, *Land Transfer* (1886), 84, 89 (ditto); *SC on Land Titles and Transfer*, 2nd Report 5; Wolstenholme, *SC on Land Transfer Bill*, Report, PP 1895 (364), xi, 1, 57–8 (maps); E. Rogers,

from the deputy registrar but which at that time, September 1885, was not a cry senior politicians were willing to take up.[175] His Torrens bill made no progress.

Solicitors aside, who mobilized to resist it, there was political convergence on compulsion. Nobody proposed compulsory registration with absolute title—that would have been an impossibly onerous obligation requiring an army of judicial-style examiners of title. Instead, registering a possessory title was seen as sufficient, with provision to upgrade it to an absolute title after a process of advertisement, inquiry, and confirmation—effectively a shortening of the limitation period after which adverse claimants would be barred. In Halsbury's bills that period was five years from the date of advertisement. Coupled with the insurance fund its aim was to induce a rapid expansion of a form of absolute title rendered safe from risk, bringing relief from the necessity of re-examination of the historical title whenever the land was sold or mortgaged. Halsbury attributed the insurance fund to the Torrens system, though its historians now credit Torrens's use of it to the 1857 royal commission.[176] In Davey's early Liberal model compulsion would be nationwide, though the system would be operated through local registries. Halsbury likewise accepted the principle of locality, envisaging branch offices responsible to an overarching Land Transfer Board. But unlike the Liberals he would roll out compulsion only district by district, reasoning that more expert work would have to be done than there were staff to do it, were the whole country to shift to the new system at once.

There was initial convergence too, though it was misleading, over the occasion when compulsion should bite. The maximum, suggested by Davey and to be found in Halsbury's first two bills, would require title to the whole of an estate to be registered before even the smallest part of it could be sold, settled, mortgaged, or leased for longer than 21 years. Land would pass automatically to executors and administrators but neither they nor any heir or devisee to whom they released the land would be able to deal with it until its title was registered. The implications of that startled the Lords in 1888, to Halsbury's surprise after the quiet reception his bill had had the year before, causing him to delay a further year.[177] Under pressure he shifted the duty to register on to the transferee. Executors need not register if

---

'The Impact of the Australian Torrens System on the Land Transfer Debate in the UK, 1858–1914' [2006] *ANZLH E-Journal* Refereed Paper No. 4.

[175] *The Times*, 22 September 1885; responses 24 September, 5, 6, 7 (Deputy Registrar Holt) 8 October.

[176] Land Transfer Bill, Memorandum, *PP* 1887 (328), iii, 89, 90; D. J. Whalan, 'The Origins of the Torrens System and its Introduction to New Zealand', in G. W. Hinde (ed.), *The New Zealand Torrens System Centennial Essays* (Wellington, 1971), 1–32 at 7–9; G. Taylor, 'Is the Torrens System German?' (2008) 29 *JLH* 253–85 at 257, 272.

[177] Congestion in the Commons over reform of county government would likely have delayed him anyway.

they did not wish, but the fee for registration would be collected along with the succession duty nonetheless.

Coupled with the largely symbolic abolition of entail and intestate primogeniture, however, and the insistence that land devolve through executors or representatives, with concomitant expense, enough remained for conservative peers to feel that they were being made to pay in one way or another for changes from which only others would benefit, if anyone. Their lordships may have needed solicitors to point these consequences out to them, but they were compelling enough once grasped. In 1889 they defeated Halsbury's bill on an amendment to delete the clause requiring landed inheritance to pass through executors or representatives, though that was a surrogate for all the succession provisions.[178] Halsbury did not try again. When Lord Herschell did take up the model for the Liberals he too was unable to get substantive change to landed succession through the Lords, for all his protests that his bill 'did not contain any novel proposal and could scarcely be regarded as of a party character'.[179] Lord Salisbury was not going to let the Liberals have what the noble backwoodsmen had denied their natural party.[180]

Their lordships' resistance did not extend to compulsory registration, at least not in the diminished form in which Lord Herschell reintroduced it. To fend off opposition he reduced compulsion to its minimum: when land in a designated area passed by sale the transferee must register at least a possessory title to what had been bought. He dropped the provision accelerating upgrades to absolute title, likewise that for guaranteeing boundaries. He reduced the proposed rule-making powers, the statement of principle disappeared, only the most essential revisions remained. In that form the Lords passed his bills with bored acquiescence. They accepted compulsory transmission through executors and representatives too; there was no political point to be made resisting that following Harcourt's unification of death duties in 1894.

Solicitors' opposition to Herschell's registration proposals was strong enough to push his bill into a full select committee inquiry in 1895, which was wound up prematurely when the government unexpectedly resigned after a defeat in the Commons. Picked up again by Halsbury on the Conservatives' return, modified on points of detail as a result of the committee, it finally passed in 1897. It made application of a lightly revised version of the Land Transfer Act 1875 compulsory on sale, but only within localities to be designated by Order in Council with

[178] *PD* 1889 (s3) 337: 1558.
[179] *PD* 1893 (s4) 9: 1201; cf. 23: 1386.
[180] *PD* 1893 (s4) 9: 1212–17; 1894 23: 1393–6.

agreement from the local county council. London became that chosen area.[181] The Act also established that all realty, wherever situated, must descend through real representatives. That would have seemed a meagre return from all the effort, just fragments of the optimistic beginnings in Davey's letters and Halsbury's first bill.[182] The rest was not enacted until 1925.

The Trials of Compulsory Title Registration

Compulsory registration of title had been achieved over strenuous opposition from solicitors. That had grown steadily from the time of Halsbury's first bill in 1887 and it would continue beyond into battles over further extension that culminated in the royal commission of 1909–11. Its most immediate effect, however, had been to stunt the legislation.

Solicitors' opposition was a complex mix of utilitarian, ideological, and self-interested factors. If registration was designed to hasten the diffusion of landed property down the social scale, to increase the number of small proprietors (for whatever political reason) then, the law societies said, there was simply no evidence that the costs and processes of conveyancing were a hindrance. They were adept at producing quantities of raw data to show that small transactions cost little in lawyers' fees. Secondly, they said, the traditional system of private deeds operated by solicitors (with recourse to counsel in difficult cases) brought both a flexibility and a privacy that a state-run publicly open register could not. Thirdly, if the Registrar should respond—as he always did—that giving him a broad rule-making and rule-waiving discretion would provide ample flexibility, they replied that property should not depend upon officialism but upon open rules known to all in advance. On principle property should not have to be negotiable; and having to negotiate it would eat up costs.

Fourthly, however, their opposition was based on a general fear that the only way title registration could bring cost savings was by reducing solicitors' fees, perhaps directly or perhaps by removing their conveyancing monopoly. Solicitors knew that in South Australia, birthplace of the Torrens system, land brokers were licensed to use the registry on behalf of clients. In England, where solicitors were taxed heavily on their articles of clerkship and had to pay a steep annual charge

---

[181] The Act was applied parish by parish in six stages to November 1900, the City following acrimoniously in July 1902.

[182] A private members' measure in 1890 gave childless widows the right to the first £500 from their intestate husband's estate—useful, unthreatening, and circumscribed as private members' acts had to be: Intestates Estates Act 1890. It was promoted by William Ambrose QC, a Conservative, with support from Sir Henry James, a Liberal.

for their practising certificate, they would be sure to be undercut by any less expensively qualified rivals—their own clerks, for example.

Registry officials were no neutral bystanders. When the Liberal banker and historian Frederic Seebohm wrote to *The Times* in 1897 to complain of the inadequate provision Halsbury's bill made for mortgages by deposit he attributed the 'pertinacity with which one bill after another has been pressed' partly to 'the desire of disappointed officials in charge of the present Land Registry to make it pay its way'.[183] There had been embarrassing losses for many years, mitigated in 1888 by transfer of the charges registers from the Supreme Court Office, and then reversed by acquisition of the Middlesex deeds registry in 1891.[184] Though dealings with registered titles showed some increase in the 1890s, the registry's financial health then still depended upon other business. Even after 1897 there were difficulties, because the Treasury insisted that the registry recover the full costs of its new building through fees, to the concern of the royal commission in 1911 and the pain of its junior staff.[185] It might have been different if some public purpose could be found for registration, because then a public subsidy might be made, but for all the registrar's attempts to latch on to state expansion none could be found.[186] Lawyers from time to time argued that compulsion must itself imply a public purpose, but the Treasury was impervious to that.[187]

In pressing for expansion of registration senior registry officials habitually claimed that it could be made so simple, adaptable, and reliable that nobody of average business ability would need a lawyer at all.[188] It was a claim pressed particularly energetically by Brickdale, who was the registry's dominant proselytizer from his first appointment there in 1888 until he retired in 1923. Barristers assessing the boast thought it absurd, and hindsight gives it no credence—the London builders and land-dealers who were the sort of men who might have responded to that invitation conspicuously did not support further extension when asked to do so by the royal commission, and building societies were

---

[183] *The Times*, 8 June 1897. His long-winded evidence to the 1895 select committee about mortgages by deposit rather tried its members' patience: *SC on Land Transfer Bill*, Report, 210–16.

[184] *Land Registry*, Returns [various titles], PP 1888 (263), lxxxii, 415; 1890 (240 and 199), lix, 195, 197; 1895 (377 and 463), lxxxi, 339, 343.

[185] *RC on Land Transfer Acts*, 2nd Report, PP 1911 [Cd. 5483], xxx, 1, 55; *RC on the Civil Service*, 6th Report, Evidence, PP 1914–16 [Cd. 8130], xii, 91, 486–95.

[186] (1903–4) 48 *Sol. J.* 747, 757; Offer, *Property and Politics*, 76.

[187] *SC on Land Titles and Transfer*, 2nd Report 191 (Cairns); *RC on Land Transfer Acts*, 2nd Report 54–5; St Aldwyn (chairman of the 1909–11 RC): *PD* 1911 (s5 HL) 9: 565; 1913 14: 1668.

[188] *SC on Land Titles and Transfer*, 1st Report, 517, 521, 525, 525 (assistant registrar Holt); *The Times*, 11 April 1885 (letter from G. Abbott); 15 June 1887 (letter from C. F. Brickdale); 1 February 1889 (notice of new fee structure). Much of Brickdale's evidence to the 1909–11 RC was premised upon enabling owners to do their own work; there are reasonably explicit statements at *RC on Land Transfer Acts*, 1st Report, App., PP 1909 [Cd. 4510], xxvii, 733, 746–7, 770–1, 815.

equivocal.[189] But solicitors took it and all lesser threats seriously. Accordingly, in their political campaigns they spoke just as much about title registration being an experiment which, when it failed, would be closed down entirely as registry officials did about ousting solicitors wholly from the business of land transfer.

That the Land Transfer Act 1897 had passed at all was due to two last-minute concessions by the government. One provided that the only agents allowed to charge for lodging documents and searching at the registry would be barristers and solicitors—so, no South Australia here.[190] The other postponed further extensions beyond an initial designated area for three years and greatly strengthened county councils' veto when that moment came.[191] That gave the Act the character of an experiment, though the law societies and the government, urged on by the registry, were subsequently to differ greatly over what that meant. In the long run solicitors' faultfinding may have produced better law, but the immediate result of their opposition in the 1890s was that Herschell and Halsbury shrunk their bills to the minimum and structured them as amendments to the 1875 Act rather than as self-contained sets of rules and principles. It was an example of the very worst kind of parliamentary drafting, T. C. Williams would tell the royal commission.[192] It was to be an experiment, therefore, not of the best measure proponents of title register could muster but only of what had been achievable in the teeth of prolonged opposition.

The legislative process lent itself to outcomes like that. Serious initiatives had to emanate from government and to be worked by the whips, but the Commons, in particular, was chronically congested. 'Law reform' did often start in the Lords. It would be a form of departmental legislation, save that the Lord Chancellor's Office was obviously not equipped to create it.[193] Instead, this sort of legislation would be primarily the Lord Chancellor's personal responsibility, to be created with the aid of whichever conveyancing barristers he could recruit—Howard Elphinstone, who later became a reluctant critic of the Land Transfer Act, drafted the inheritance and entail provisions in Halsbury's first bill; R. B. Haldane, a member of the 1895 select committee and later Liberal Lord Chancellor, was a member of a small departmental committee established by Halsbury on his 1897 bill.[194]

[189] Anderson, *Lawyers*, 89, 176, 242.
[190] *The Times*, 17 July 1897; Land Transfer Act, s 10.
[191] *PD* 1897 (s4) 52: 294–320.
[192] *RC on Land Transfer Acts*, 2nd Report, Evidence, *PP* 1911 [Cd. 5495], 65, 435.
[193] See Vol. XI, pp. 785–7.
[194] (1887) 31 *Sol. J.* 373; *PD* 1897 (s4) 50: 939.

The culture was that a bill resulting from such a closed process would need testing against professional opinion. Thus it was not uncommon to introduce a bill towards the end of one session with the intention of reintroducing it in the next. If that consultation period was intended to give room to doubters of the bill's wisdom, then after it was over a government might legitimately press on regardless. But if the problems that were raised at a later stage went to its technical accomplishment complaints that they should have been raised earlier were somewhat beside the point—as Halsbury discovered in 1888, when the bill that he had introduced the previous year to what seemed like broad approval met such difficulties in the Lords that it was saved only by shunting it into a select committee.

That course was always open, in either House or both, but if the committee took evidence it might become confrontational—the Commons select committee in 1895 is a good example. Usually select committees did not take evidence, but then the result might be like that for the Yorkshire Registries legislation in 1884, which needed two remedial Acts within 12 months.[195] Delay, compromise, and backtracking were built into the legislative system for proposals like these, giving ample opportunity for true opposition to pick its moment. Nor did the Lord Chancellor have a junior minister in the Commons, instead having to rely on the law officers for the progress of his bills, which introduced a further element of independent (or semi-independent) judgement into the process.[196] With such weak departmental backing the enterprise was at risk of being sidelined by something of greater political priority, even without sustained opposition.[197] The success rate in the Commons of bills beginning in the Lords fell steadily from the late 1880s through into the late 1890s.[198] The Land Transfer Act 1897 was subject to higgling over amendments to the very end of the parliamentary session, completing its passage with just two days to spare.

So when the trial came it was of a reduced statute and in an atmosphere of mutual recrimination. Blame and accusation were frequent, propaganda normal. Assessment of the reality of registration remains difficult, much of the claim and counterclaim being so obviously self-interested. The great surge of experience, quite unlike the idle days of voluntary registration, brought a rash of practical difficulties, the more so because of the thin revision that had been the only thing

[195] One error was so urgent that an immediate amendment had to be passed: Yorkshire Registries Act (1884) Amendment Act 1884. Barker, *Manual*, 153 has another example stemming from hurried legislative process.

[196] See Vol. XI, pp. 787.

[197] In 1888 *The Times* was worrying about slow progress as early as 1 May. That was the year of local government reform for the counties.

[198] See Vol. XI, pp. 317.

possible in 1897. Solicitors and the elite conveyancers emphasized the difficulties, many of them to be vindicated in due course by the royal commission, but how significant they were quantitatively is a more open question. The royal commission noted that in nine years there had been some 260,000 applications to the registry of one sort or another—but externally commissioned consumer satisfaction surveys to assess such things lay in the future.[199] Nevertheless, rule changes were frequent and extensive as deficiencies in the Act were revealed. The rule revision in 1903 was so far-reaching that its introduction had to be postponed to allow time for familiarization.[200] In addition fundamental choices needed to be made about the extent (if at all) that parties could modify registry documents to meet their own circumstances.

At root Brickdale's difficulty was that the benefit of registration would accrue only to proprietors with absolute title: after that once-and-for-all state investigation of the root of title it need never be done again. However, the ill will between him and the law societies ensured instead merely the sullen compliance of registration with possessory title.[201] It could easily be made out that that increased costs.[202] The process that Davey and Halsbury had envisaged for inducing a smooth and rapid transition from the one to the other had been stripped out of the 1890s' bills, and when Brickdale tried to reintroduce it through rule changes in 1902 and again in 1908 he was beaten back, in part at least, by claims that they were *ultra vires*.[203] The very broad rule-making powers in Halsbury's original bill had likewise been slimmed down to cabin baggage, and while that still left the registrar with considerable latitude there were doubts that it spread far enough to validate even some of his technical rules, let alone the broad reconfigurations he sometimes attempted.[204]

The elite conveyancers also found fault with numerous technical matters. Even Howard Elphinstone, a supporter of title registration, found its shortcomings in relation to mortgages and the running of covenants and easements in building schemes too serious for the Act to be recommended as it stood.[205] The mortgage problem ran deep because it affected common transactions. It arose because aside from informal mortgages by deposit of title certificates (which bankers had insisted be specifically preserved in the 1897 Act) the only statutory way to

---

[199] *RC on Land Transfer Acts*, 2nd Report, 36.

[200] 1903 SR&O No. 181, postponed by 1903–4 SR&O 48/137.

[201] Cf. J. E. Hogg, 'Amendment of the Land Transfer Acts' (1908) 24 *LQR* 290–6 at 291.

[202] *PD* 1903 (s4) 122: 1382–99; (1903–4) 48 *Sol. J.* 547 (Edward Wood, President of the Building Societies Association).

[203] Anderson, *Lawyers*, 216–17, 230–1.

[204] Anderson, *Lawyers*, 241.

[205] Elphinstone, 'On the Land Transfer Acts'; (1905–6) 50 *Sol. J.* 70, 91; 'The Law Society on Officialism' (1906) 22 *LQR* 27–33 at 31.

mortgage registered land was by charge.[206] That seemed more straightforward than mortgage by transfer, with its airs of fiction and improvisation, but, led by Wolstenholme, the writers of the thick books found circumstances in which it failed to provide the full range of remedies available via the traditional form.[207] The underlying cause was the failure to integrate the statute with common law by giving the mortgagee a legal estate, they said.[208] What would previously have been a simple transaction, a purchase and simultaneous mortgage, should now, in an area of compulsory registration, be expressed through four separate documents, they recommended, if the full effect was to be achieved.

These critics were aided by a judicial opinion that the Land Transfer Acts were regimes of powers only, hence that the legal estate could still be conveyed off register.[209] Double documentation thus became possible, and was sometimes desirable to achieve maximum safety, they said, with obvious consequences for costs. The registrar told the royal commission that 'barely half' the mortgages of registered land did this, which suggests a significant number.[210] There had been a statement of principle in Halsbury's first bill explicitly directed to blocking the transmission of legal estates off the register, but it had been one of those dropped in the interests of legislative economy.[211] Who knows—with such a professionally attractive device unavailable perhaps closer analysis would have cast doubt on the problem itself.

Just one writer persevered with that analysis deeply enough to find a new statutory logic in the Land Transfer Acts, one that discarded old learning on legal estates and the inherent nature of charges, favouring instead statutory replacements that take their colour from the imperatives of registration. This is a profound intellectual shift, much easier to grasp a century later, because it requires seeing the statute as constitutive of property rights rather than as declarative of transactions taking their validity from an underlying common law.[212] The writer was James Edward Hogg, a barrister whose professional experience in New South

[206] (1896–7) 41 *Sol. J.* 554, 600, 633; *The Times*, 9 July 1897, reporting amendments in Standing Committee (cf. *PD* 1897 (s4) 50: 936). Various accommodations with the principles of title registration had been proposed in previous bills.

[207] H. W. Elphinstone, 'On the Land Transfer Acts 1875 & 1897 – I' (1905) 21 *LQR* 23–9, citing also *Prideaux* and *Key & Elphinstone*. The reasoning is explained in Williams, *Principles of Real Property* (20th edn, 1906), 657–9.

[208] This thinking persisted in 1925, hence the curious revival of mortgages by long lease: see Anderson, *Lawyers*, 285–6.

[209] *Capital & Counties Bank* v. *Rhodes* [1903] 1 Ch 631; J. E. Hogg, 'The Breakdown of the Land Transfer Acts System in England' (1904) 20 *LQR* 74–80.

[210] *RC on Land Transfer Acts*, Evidence, *PP* 1911 [Cd. 5494], xxx, 65, 610 (on qq. 3618–19).

[211] Land Transfer Bill 1887, cl. 9, explaining Land Transfer Act 1875, s 49.

[212] The next to develop the argument in England was David Jackson: 'Registration of Land Interests—the English Version' (1972) 88 *LQR* 93–137; 'Security of Title in Registered Land' (1978)

Wales sensitized him simultaneously to the possibilities of title registration, the dangers of reading its legislation through the lens of traditional conveyancing, and the distorting effect of allowing the deeds system to continue alongside its replacement.[213] Conveyancers' difficulties, he concluded lay in the English habit 'of treating jurisprudence rather as an art than a science, and refusing to recognize the utility of novel methods of presenting legal facts'.[214] But even he had found the reasoning difficult—it took him three articles in the *Law Quarterly Review* to get there.[215] The traditional view came more naturally. It underlay, for example, the decision in *Attorney-General* v. *Odell*, restricting the circumstances in which the victim of a forged mortgage could claim against the insurance fund, and its Torrens Acts equivalent, *Gibbs* v. *Messer*, where the Privy Council scarcely bothered to open the statute.[216]

Hogg also, in the end, came round to arguing that a reformulation of the underlying law on lines similar to those Wolstenholme had been urging since 1862 was necessary if registration with absolute title were to become easy and popular (or, for his preference, compulsory).[217] That lined him up with other conveyancing barristers, those who supported registration, like Elphinstone, those who were equivocal, like Benjamin Cherry—who became Wolstenholme's successor—and those who, like T. C. Williams, sought an opportunity for recasting the law of real property in truly simplified mode.[218] All of them sought new legislation. Brickdale and the Conservative government had hoped it was unnecessary, because then merely internal administrative inquiry into the necessary rule changes would suffice before extending compulsion beyond the area initially designated.[219] But the failure of their rule revisions to stem criticism and

94 *LQR* 239–54. Similar assumptions are made by Nicola Jackson, 'Overreaching in Registered Land Law' (2006) 69 *MLR* 214–41.

[213] *RC on Land Transfer Acts*, 1st Report, App., 872. After taking his MA at Oxford he practised in Sydney, first as a solicitor then a barrister, where he also wrote conveyancing texts. After returning to England he became a prolific and thoughtful writer of texts and articles on title registration. Brickdale built him up as an important witness for the commission to interview, but his evidence consisted mainly of an argument for rapid compulsory registration with absolute title, which marginalized him.

[214] J. E. Hogg, 'The "Mortgage Charge" of the Land Transfer Acts' (1907) 23 *LQR* 68–82.

[215] Hogg, 'Breakdown', 'On the Land Transfer Acts 1875 & 1897 – II' (1905) 21 *LQR* 29–34, 'Mortgage Charge'.

[216] [1906] 2 Ch 47 (reversing Kekewich J., whose interpretation was more purposive), [1891] AC 248 (contrast Webb J., *Messer* v. *Gibbs* (1887) 13 VLR 854, whose reading is almost identical to the modern orthodoxy in *Frazer* v. *Walker* [1967] 1 AC 569).

[217] Hogg, 'Amendment' (he did not acknowledge Wolstenholme).

[218] *Wolstenholme's Conveyancing Acts* (9th edn, 1905, by Cherry and Russell), p. vi. B. L. Cherry and H. W. Marigold, *The Land Transfer Acts* (1899), preface; Williams, *Principles of Real Property* (20th edn, 1906), 664–6.

[219] *PD* 1903 (s4) 122: 1382–99.

spread absolute title persuaded Brickdale otherwise, and the incoming Liberal government agreed.[220] Solicitors, of course, had always wanted a public inquiry. The outcome was a royal commission, which reported in 1911 after three years of minutely detailed examination of what the system actually did, what it might be made to do, what might take its place (in rather less detail) and what might supplement it.

Assimilation Resumed

The alternative line of assimilationist thinking, the one that disdained both registration and piecemeal adjustment of real property law, also persisted into the 1880s. As the royal commission was to observe, there were two separate strands.[221] The revolutionary, as they put it, sought to abolish real property and all its feudal accoutrements, substituting a modified version of the law of personal property. That would be true assimilation—there would be simply a law of property. The more conservative sought merely instrumental assimilation, a streamlined form of land transfer that operated through the deeds system with just the same results, speed, economy, and processes that title registration had, or should have, but without the publicity, official discretion, or cumbrousness of the registry. Instead of a folium of a register telling a purchaser all that needed to be known, a privately held deed (in short form) would do precisely the same.

The revolution was proposed in February 1886 by Sir James Fitzjames Stephen, then a High Court judge.[222] All property should simply be deemed personal, he wrote, and he sketched (for discussion only) a three-clause bill that would achieve the removal of tenure, estates, uses and all other feudal remnants. Codification would be needed—he was not a man to let that opportunity slip—together with some consequential changes to personal property law to accommodate some of the differences of land.

Stephen's was a more sophisticated version of a suggestion attributed to Nassau Senior that all land be deemed to be held on very long lease, say 100,000 years, a proposal that itself still had currency enough in 1886 for a Bar Committee to think it worth condemning.[223] 'As dangerous and complex a device as could be adopted', they protested, because there would at once need to be a long statute saying which rules deduced from the thing abolished should be kept. Without it the evils of codification would result but not the benefits. Joshua Williams had

[220] *Registrar of the Land Registry*, Report for the Years 1902–5, *PP* 1906 [Cd. 3132], xcix, 279, 291–5.

[221] *RC on Land Transfer*, 2nd Report, 57–61.

[222] J. F. Stephen, 'The Laws Relating to Land' (1886) 6 *The National Review* 729–44.

[223] *SC on Land Titles and Transfer*, 2nd Report, 192; Bar Committee, *Land Transfer* (1886), 94.

persuaded Osborne Morgan's committee to recommend repealing the Statute of Uses, substituting a modern restatement, but again conservatives worried at the unsettling effect that might have.[224] Despite appearances not a great deal had changed since Humphreys published his *Outlines* in 1826. Both proposals were revived later, however, with T. C. Williams playing the part of Stephen before the royal commission, and Arthur Underhill that of Senior a little later.[225]

The father of the merely reformist tendency was E. P. Wolstenholme, who revived his assimilation and overreaching proposal from 1862 in evidence to Osborne Morgan's committee in 1878, and again to the select committee in 1895.[226] In 1897, after considerable hesitation, the Incorporated Law Society adopted a version of Wolstenholme's bill co-drafted with Cherry as its great hope, its alternative to compulsory nationwide registration of title.[227] Thereafter it promoted the idea assiduously. By this time Wolstenholme had trimmed, adding a register of caveats to his scheme for political reasons. Instrumental assimilation lent itself to that.[228] The addition was discarded in 1925.

As it turned out these strands of thought became important in the aftermath of the royal commission's report. It need not have been so. The commission's conclusion, in essence, was that the trial intended of title registration had yet to begin. There had been a false start because so few registrations had been made with absolute title. Londoners had certainly been disadvantaged by the expense and inadequacies of registration with possessory title, but that was not a reason for not trying again. The commissioners suggested ways for shifting to absolute title, especially that limitation periods be shortened, fees reduced and restructured, and the validation necessary to demonstrate a good title be made easier. There would need to be extensive change to the way mortgages, settlements, and servitudes were handled too. On principle the system should rely less on the registrar's discretion. One day, T. C. Williams had said to them in evidence, 'official demeanour may sink to the level of that of those ladies in the Post Office whose

---

[224] *SC on Land Titles and Transfer*, 2nd Report, 9; 1st Report, 501–2 (Williams). Unsettling effect: 2nd Report, 192 (Cairns); Lawrence, *Facts and Suggestions*, 29.

[225] Underhill's *Line of Least Resistance* was presented to the committee restructuring land law in 1919: Anderson, *Lawyers*, 283–5, 292. See also M. H. Box, 'The Division of Property into Real and Personal Estate' (1887) 3 *LQR* 406–18, unusual for not concentrating on conveyancing.

[226] See pp. 195–6, above; *SC on Land Titles and Transfer*, 1st Report, 591–603, from 593. *SC on Land Transfer Bill*, Report, 46, 48, 74–5. He gave the committee a summary of his 1862 paper: *ibid.*, 248. For similar proposals see Anderson, *Lawyers*, 121–2 (where 'Owen' college should be read as 'Queen's'), 174–5; C. E. Thornhill, 'How to simplify our Titles' (1889) 5 *LQR* 11–14.

[227] Conveyancing Bill, *HLP* 1897 iii 99, reprinted as an appendix to Cherry and Marigold, *Land Transfer Acts*, 423–69.

[228] His thinking evolved as the general law and political expediency changed: see Anderson, *Lawyers*, 254–6.

rebuffs we have all encountered…'.[229] Only when all these reorientations were achieved would the trial be ready to start. Then the regime would have to be observed in operation for a reasonable time before conclusions could be drawn about its suitability as a compulsory system nationwide.

There was an important subtext too. Everything in the report was consistent with acceptance of the theoretical superiority of title registration. At the same time nothing in the report was consistent with Brickdale's crusade to oust solicitors. Across hundreds of pages of evidence, recording thousands of questions, answers, interrogations, arguments, and speculations, there is an emphasis on handling the complexity of everyday commercial transactions in all their luxuriance. Though sometimes a lay member protested that some such complexity should not be allowed, the lawyer members, who drove much of the examination, did not doubt that that was how the commercial world really was. Of the six barristers on the commission, five had a Chancery practice; one of them took the major lead in the questioning.[230] These were not men whose experience encouraged them to let lay clients loose on complexity, and the report reflects that.[231]

Subtly, without parading it, the report portrays an ideal registration system as one in which much of the work of mortgaging and settling land, and the granting of servitudes, is done 'off register', the registry to have merely a recording function. Similarly with statutory land charges imposed by local authorities under their improvement powers, they should be wholly outside the register.[232] There was a considerable literature on how to word contracts to allocate their risk appropriately, so the commission's implication is both that expert drafting would continue to be needed and that someone knowledgeable would be needed to make the requisite local inquiries.[233] In that conception of registration there would remain a lot for solicitors to do.

If, however, a more thoroughgoing conception were adopted, and if it were coupled with a more benign appreciation of the merits of official discretion, then much of that analysis could be rejected while leaving intact the numerous

---

[229] *RC on Land Transfer Acts*, Evidence, 453.

[230] The exception was Sir Samuel Evans, who had a practice in South Wales. The lead was Philip Gregory. Sir (Cornelius) Marshall Warmington died before the Commission began its second, and longer, round of evidence-taking.

[231] And compare e.g. T. C. Williams on the dangers of home-made wills: *RC on Land Transfer Acts*, Evidence, 450.

[232] *RC on Land Transfer Acts*, 2nd Report, 49.

[233] *Re Ford and Hill* (1879) 10 Ch D 365; Elphinstone and Clark, *Searches*, 3–4, 151; Dart, *Vendors and Purchasers* (7th edn, 1905), 163, 1191; Williams, *Vendor and Purchaser* (2nd edn, 1910), 135, 176–9. F. E. Farrer, *Precedents of Conditions of Sale* (1902), 261 (Birmingham Law Society's standard term). His 2nd edn, 1909, repeats that clause but also shows that Manchester Law Society's standard terms dealt only with liability arising between contract and conveyance.

detailed points for improvement it offered. That was Brickdale's view, and he had allies in Lord Halsbury and in the then Liberal Lord Chancellor, Lord Loreburn. As attorney-general, Loreburn he had been in charge of Herschell's bills in the Commons, the precursors of the 1897 Act, and had been pleased to support the Conservatives in finally getting it passed.[234] Further, in 1911 there was still a political prospect of a grand Domesday Office that would facilitate Liberal land taxation by uniting a cadastral survey and systematic valuation of land with a complete record of title. Whether the stance, then, were Halsbury's or radical Liberal, the commission could largely be written off as an exercise in flushing out the overblown opposition of solicitors in order finally to discredit it. That done, extension of compulsory registration could proceed. In anticipation, Loreburn authorized internal promotions in the Land Registry, ready to move those men out into the country as District Registrars in a new national system.[235]

It is not known why Loreburn's successor as Lord Chancellor, Lord Haldane, abandoned that path; interpretations vary.[236] If nothing else the abrupt change of direction suggests a relative lack of political importance to the issue and underscores the freedom Lord Chancellors had to make their own policy. Haldane, with a Chancery practice, seems to have shared the dislike of compulsion and respect for legal principle that characterized the lawyer-members of the commission. To be sure, Brickdale would get all his amendments, many of them more sympathetic to his expansive view of registration than the commission's had been. But trial of those would come before decisions were made about extending compulsion. 'The best way of making progress was not by driving people but by persuading them', Haldane told the Lords in 1913.[237] Perhaps more important to him was the lesser theme in the commission's report, that at the same time there should be a reformulation of the underlying law. Seeing how that worked would be part of the trial too.

The commission had not taken the idea far, seeing it as beyond its brief. But it had heard at length from Cherry and Williams, and from others in roughly similar vein. Its report was generally encouraging. Cherry had urged his and Wolstenholme's bill once again. Williams was adamant that the only true solution was to assimilate realty with personalty at doctrinal level. They had different objectives. Cherry's was to show that a modernized land law could bring the advantages of registration without its disadvantages; the modernization need

---

[234] *PD* 1903 (s4) 122: 1397; *PD* 1911 (s5 HL) 9: 557.

[235] *RC on the Civil Service*, 6th Report, Evidence, 486–95. The Treasury refused permission for them to have the full salary rise their new status might have entailed, and there was much pain and discontent when the planned expansion stalled.

[236] Offer, 'Origins'; Anderson, *Lawyers*, 249–66.

[237] *PD* 1913 (s5 HL) 14: 1661.

extend no further than that need. Williams, drawing heavily on his experience as a teacher, wished for the law to be understandable. The effect of the Land Transfer Acts and their Rules was, he said, 'to impose upon a land law, which is already so complicated that few lawyers really understand it, a new body of legal rules expressed in terms of great obscurity and founded upon principles entirely at variance with those of the previous law'.[238] By that he meant that title at common law was always relative, whereas with registered land it could be absolute, or, putting it another way, that registered land had no place for the hallowed maxim *nemo dat quod non habet*—the title one gives is no better than the title one has. Only by confronting this contradiction at the level of principle could a body of law be constructed that was complete, rational, and comprehensible.

In the legal press there was perhaps more support for Williams than for Cherry, and from Viscount St Aldwyn too, who had chaired the royal commission.[239] Haldane, however, saw no need for systematic assimilation if the bad consequences of real property law's feudal base could one by one be identified and neutralized by a precisely worded section.[240] Instead, we should settle for making the selling of land as much like the selling of stock as could be done, he said.[241] The owner of a 'proprietary estate' would be able to sell it clear of conflicting interests, subject to a list of exceptions (which would override the register too, under the other system), and subject to a system of caveats in a public register. Proprietary estates would include only the legal fee simple and the legal term of years absolute plus their equitable equivalents—to keep mortgage by transfer, let in the equity of redemption, and also to prevent avoidance. This was Wolstenholme's scheme writ large, accompanied by code-like statements of what sorts of disposition owners of proprietary estates could make, how, and then how the various sorts of subordinate interests would play out. But, that aside, it was conservative. Mortgages would continue to be made by transfer, not by statutory charge, and Haldane would even retain the Statute of Uses.

There would be a companion bill amending the Land Transfer Acts, the Settled Land Acts, the Conveyancing Acts and much else—'arrears of legislation', the *Solicitors' Journal* called it.[242] In 1914 the two bills in revised form were amalgamated into a nine-part monster, retaining the Wolstenholme-like core in a

---

[238] *RC on Land Transfer Acts*, Evidence, 447.

[239] Anderson, *Lawyers*, 251n, 254; *PD* 1913 (s5 HL) 14: 1664–5. St. Aldwyn, formerly Sir Michael Hicks Beach, sometime Conservative Chancellor of the Exchequer, had sold out of much of his ancestral lands in the 1880s: *ODNB*. Not known for any association with the registration question before chairing the commission he was a loyal and forthright defender of its recommendations.

[240] *PD* 1913 (s5 HL) 14: 1657–8; see also his explicit rejection of T. C. Williams's proposal, ibid., 1673.

[241] *PD* 1913 (s5 HL) 14: 1651–4.

[242] Conveyancing Bill 1913; Real Property Bill 1913; (1912–13) 57 *Sol. J.* 713.

principled Haldane-like setting, but with much amending and consolidating material too. It would also have abolished copyhold and special tenures, and extinguished any remaining manorial incidents. It was not a code, but it had some code-like qualities in explaining what interests fitted into which categories, which did not, what owners of them may and may not do, and so on—to be applicable equally whether an owner's title was registered or unregistered.[243]

As usual the flow of critique and amendment into the Lord Chancellor's office brought delay, so that measures first unveiled in July 1913 with a view to enactment in the following session reappeared only in August 1914, with a view to enactment in the next session. It was at about this point that Arthur Underhill, conveyancing barrister, author, and an influential witness to the royal commission, flung up his arms at so much complication and wished for the enactment instead of Nassau Senior's simple solution of converting all freeholds into very long leases. That did not happen, though for a short period after the war Underhill was allowed to think that it might.[244]

By then Cherry was firmly in control. The war stopped all official activity, but Cherry and his chosen professional associates had worked quietly on their own amending and consolidating bills, which they were able to present as improved versions of some of the parts of Haldane's monster. But the core of Haldane's bill had had its code-like parts removed, restoring a purer version of Wolstenholme's original vision, instrumental assimilation slimmed down to its essentials.

The passage of those bills began in 1922 and ended in 1925, which is well outside the scope of this book. The story has been told, and argued over, elsewhere.[245] The fruits are visible in any textbook. Stable divisions of work between the solicitors and the registry were sorted out in the 1930s, in a world of owner-occupation of houses and of farms quite different from anything in the nineteenth century.[246] In the sense in which he meant it, Dicey's fundamental remained intact.

Institutionally too there is a sort of continuity. Faced with a choice between instrumental reform and conceptual, Haldane chose the former: Wolstenholme and Cherry over Williams, just as in the 1830s it was Brodie over Humphreys. The process was not very different either. In each case a cabal of elite conveyancers worked under state patronage, amending their proposals in response to professional criticism but expecting each either to pass as a whole or not at all.[247]

Intellectually, however, there may have been a significant change, though it will have come as a result of what Wolstenholme and Haldane began and Cherry

---

[243] There are explanatory memoranda at *HLP* 1913 (170), vii, 439, (119), ix, 45.

[244] Anderson, *Lawyers*, 291–2.

[245] Offer, 'Origins'; Anderson, *Lawyers*, 207–313.

[246] Anderson, *Lawyers*, 323–9; Pottage, 'Originality'.

[247] Anderson, *Lawyers*, 282–92.

completed in 1925. In 1909 T. C. Williams told the royal commission, earnestly but incoherently, that real property law was incomprehensible apart from its history. Colonials 'such as Hindus, Australians, and French Canadians' found that so difficult, and consequently were failing their English bar exams so frequently, that instead of a paper on real property the Council of Legal Education now allowed them to substitute 'either Hindu and Mahometan law, or Roman Dutch law'.[248] Taking his point rather than his examples, that would no longer be true. Book titles have given way from 'real property' to 'land law'. Their principles are essentially statutory, their history is explanatory of concepts in only the very broadest sense, an alibi for quaintness rather than a necessary step to understanding. That, however, would be a theme for a history of the twentieth century.

[248] *SC on Land Titles and Transfer*, Evidence, 435.

VI

Trusts and Trustees

1. THE USEFULNESS OF PRIVATE TRUSTS

There is consensus that trusts became widespread during the nineteenth century as the middle classes became wealthier.[1] Testamentary trusts were common, and though there are no quantitative estimates of marriage settlements they feature often enough in litigation to suggest that, though less frequent, they too were numerous.[2] Family trusts of various sorts might be created in a wide range of other situations, and, as will be seen, these 'voluntary' *inter vivos* trusts caused some difficulty in the first three decades of our period.[3] In addition the trust mechanism could be used for property holding in other contexts—for clubs, for example, or for trade unions, or as a mechanism for paying off creditors. That last example had features worth mentioning as a contrast to the standard incidents of a trust, but for the most part this section will follow the example of the nineteenth-century professional literature and concentrate upon express family trusts. It was those that gave the law its shape.

Modern writing on private trusts seems often to assume that the nineteenth-century expansion came in trusts of personal property, and that there was a clear contrast in purpose and structure between trusts on the one hand and settlements of land on the other.[4] That distinction is supported by the structure of Lewin's treatise on trusts law, first published in 1837, where 'investment' is

---

[1] C. Stebbings, *The Private Trustee in Victorian England* (Cambridge, 2002); G. W. Keeton, 'The Changing Conception of Trusteeship' [1950] *CLP* 14–29; P. Polden, 'The Public Trustee in England 1906–86' (1989) 10 *JLH* 229–55; L. Davidoff and C. Hall, *Family Fortunes* (revised edn, 2002), 209–11.

[2] R. J. Morris, *Men, Women and Property in England, 1780–1870* (Cambridge 2005); A. Owens, 'Property, Gender and the Life-course: Inheritance and Family Welfare Provision in Early Nineteenth-century England (2001) 26 *Soc. Hist.* 290–371; H. Horwitz and P. Polden, 'Continuity or Change in the Court of Chancery in the Seventeenth and Eighteenth Centuries?' (1996) 35 *J. British Studies* 24–57.

[3] In the samples of Chancery proceedings taken by Horwitz and Polden for their paper *Continuity or Change?*, however, marriage settlements were the only statistically significant form of *inter vivos* trust.

[4] Stebbings, *Private Trustee*; M. R. Chesterman, 'Family Settlements on Trust: Landowners and the Rising Bourgeoisie', in G. R. Rubin and D. Sugarman (eds), *Law, Economy and Society, 1750–1914* (Abingdon, 1984), 124–67 plus xii pages of notes. Contrast P. Polden, *Peter Thelluson's Will of 1797*

discussed almost wholly in terms of money, loans, and intangibles. Settlements of land were of course usually achieved through fracturing the legal estate, rather than vesting it in trustees, and though trustees often did have their place in such landed settlements it was generally a 'formal and quiescent' place as trustees to preserve contingent remainders, secure portions and such like.[5] In the classical strict settlement, possession and management rested with the life tenant, the head of the family, while other family members received incomes from the land, or had capital sums charged contingently upon it.[6] The aim was land retention, to be achieved by periodic termination and renewal of the settlement as the heir of each life tenant came of age, each rebirth prolonging the settlement by a generation.

It has become a commonplace, however, that within this model there was room for much variety.[7] There are instances in the law reports of testamentary settlements from the later eighteenth century where the aim of family retention of the land was combined with a wish that the family of each child should have an equal share. They were cumbersome, requiring the children to take estates in tail as tenants in common with cross-remainders, but they were still being outlined as a possible form of marriage settlement by Joshua Williams to his students in 1876.[8] They still did involve primogeniture, after the first generation, though it need not have been male primogeniture. They were just one of four forms of marriage settlement Williams treated as being in common use. In addition to the strict settlement he described two others. One was a trust for sale, the other dispensed with active trustees and instead gave the spouses life estates, with power to appoint to their children, remainder in default of appointment to the children equally.[9] Little is known about how these different forms of settlement functioned in families who intended to keep their land for the time being.

By contrast the stereotypical nineteenth-century private trust is usually assumed to be one intended to provide an income for a generation, sometimes two, and then to distribute the capital. Again there was room for much variety, and it was a model that could accommodate land as easily as pure personalty.

---

and its Consequences on Chancery Law (Lewiston, NY, 2002), who sees that will as a deliberate attempt to straddle the two categories.

[5] H. Grant, *Advice to Trustees and to Those who Appoint to that Office* (London, 1830), 33. In times of family stress they might have an important veto, and hence a mediating role: J. Habakkuk, *Marriage, Debt, and the Estates System* (Oxford, 1994), 275.

[6] J. P. Peachey, *A Treatise on the Law of Marriage and other Family Settlements* (1860), 717n ('the management of trust property is generally left to the parties beneficially interested'—speaking of a pre-marital strict settlement by a noblewoman.)

[7] Habakkuk, *Marriage, Debt* demonstrates this at length.

[8] J. Williams, *The Settlement of Real Estates* (1879), 202–5.

[9] *Ibid.*, 124–211.

In their researches on patterns of urban inheritance in the early decades of the nineteenth century, R. J. Morris and Alastair Owens have shown how easily testamentary trusts for the provision of widows and children could include portfolios of urban land and houses.[10] Often they were kept together for many years after the testator's death, ultimately being sold along with the testator's other assets to provide capital for the next generation. Morris and Owens do not report the precise legal form of the trusts they found, but elite conveyancers recommended use of trusts for sale if an estate was intended for ultimate division.[11] The difficulty that a trust for sale put the powers in the wrong hands, in the trustees rather than in the life tenant, was met by specifying that during the lifetime of the life tenant (and his wife) the trustees were to sell or lease only on receiving his (or their) written request. That sort of restriction was common in many forms of marriage settlement, retaining considerable control for the spouses and relieving trustees from some of their responsibility.[12] Similarly, a testamentary trust for sale could be tailored to the situation described by Morris and Owens by either including a power to postpone the sale or by stipulating that the duty to sell arose only on the widow's death.[13]

Further, one of Davidson's precedents shows how a marriage settlement of funds could be adapted to include a power to buy land, again at the spouse's request, which would then be held on trust for sale.[14] His clauses are wide enough to give spouses the choice of gentrifying themselves by purchase and retention, or of making successive uses of the power to buy land for investment.[15] Similarly, broad investment clauses might be inserted into any trust, even one beginning with only pure personalty. Many judges would no doubt have shared Kindersley VC's opinion that 'you cannot have a worse or more objectionable investment' than freehold houses, but they had to take specific investment clauses as they found them, even if that did mean interpreting them to empower purchase of such risky things as leaseholds and ground rents.[16] There were important limits to trusts' flexibility, as will be seen, but, despite those, trusts gave settlors abundant

---

[10] Morris, *Men, Women and Property*; A. Owens, 'Inheritance and the Life-cycle of the Family Firms in the Early Industrial Revolution' (2002) 44 *Business History* 21–46 at 35.

[11] C. Davidson, *Davidson's Precedents and Forms in Conveyancing*, iii (2nd edn, 1861), 43–4, 700–5; Williams, *Settlement*, 124–7. Peachey, *Settlements*, 765n mentions partible inheritance as the only motive.

[12] Davidson, *Precedents*, iii (2nd edn), 546, 560, 584–5, 623, and so on; Peachey, *Settlements*, 765–73.

[13] The precedent in Peachey, *Settlements*, 765–73, allows for variation along these lines.

[14] Davidson, *Precedents*, iii (2nd edn.) 584–6, 636–7.

[15] Compare *Lee* v. *Young* (1843) 2 Y. & C.Ch.Cas. 532 and *Beauclerk* v. *Ashburnham* (1845) 8 Beav. 322.

[16] *Moore* v. *Walter* (1863) 8 LT (NS) 448; *Beauclerk* v. *Ashburnham* (1845) 8 Beav. 322; *M'Leod* v. *Annesley* (1853) 22 LJ Ch 633; *re Peyton's Settlement Trust* (1869) LR 7 Eq 463.

control over the devolution of family wealth and its management for a generation or two ahead.

Flexibility and ambition came with a price, however. Willing and competent trustees must be found, a matter that Chantal Stebbings has shown to have been of continuing concern throughout the century, as investment opportunities for trusts, beneficiaries' expectations, and the risk of error all increased.[17] Solicitor-trustees became common, and may be seen as filling the gap between settlors' aspirations for their family and their assessment of the business ability of their kin and acquaintances. Unlike a family trustee, solicitors' defaults and peculations made newspaper headlines, and their public portrayal was rarely sympathetic. Corporate trustees and public trustees were proposed as alternatives from as early as the 1850s.[18] The former gained some short-lived traction at the time, but did not last.[19] Lord St Leonards' rhetoric in 1857, that trustee companies perverted trusteeship into a mere trade, mirrored his perception of trustees as holders of a sacred office, kin or friends of a settlor whose trust was itself the performance of a social and moral obligation, but it spoke also for a wider public dislike of speculation with trust money, which is how corporate trustee investment for profit was commonly viewed through into the 1880s.[20]

Chancery itself administered trust funds on a large scale. The Chancery Fees Commission in 1864 heard that 'funds belonging to individual suitors' totalled more than £50 million, contained in some 25,000 separate accounts and steadily growing.[21] These funds were quite distinct from those known collectively as the 'suitors' funds'. Many were long-term deposits, with Chancery acting as a ministerial trustee. Some had arrived in Chancery when railway companies and the like acquired land compulsorily and needed an easy discharge. Some were there because of a genuine dispute. Some, an unknown amount, were there either because the regular trustees had voluntarily put them there or because their beneficiaries had insisted. Lord Cottenham's Trustees Relief Act 1847 had made payment into Chancery easy for trustees who wished to relieve themselves of their obligations, and in 1859 Stuart VC ruled that although that act was not compulsory trustees should heed their beneficiaries' request that they use it to

---

[17] Stebbings, *Private Trustee*, 34–42.

[18] D. R. Marsh, *Corporate Trustees* (1952), 30–1; 'Public Trusteeships' (1851) 15 *LM* 173–81.

[19] Marsh, *Corporate Trustees*, 23–48.

[20] Stebbings, *Private Trustee*, 57–9.

[21] *RC on Constitution of Accountant General's Department of the Court of Chancery*, Report, *PP* 1864 [3280], xxix, 1, 19–20, 22–5, 46. The Lisgar Commission reported in 1874 that the funds stood at over £63 million, in over 30,000 accounts: *RC on the Administrative Departments of the Courts of Justice*, 2nd Report, *PP* 1874 [C. 1107], xxiv, 583, 641.

pay the trust fund into court.[22] If they declined, forcing beneficiaries to begin an action, then the trustees must pay the costs. If beneficiaries did begin proceedings Daniell, in the 1840s, says they could compel payment into court as of right, without having to show cause.[23] Then Lord Langdale MR instituted a practice of requiring cause—we do not know what causes he accepted—only for Stuart VC to shift back again.[24]

This was largely a ministerial jurisdiction, that of a custodian, relatively passive, hence not one requiring supervision by a master. It seems to have been immune from the more common perception of Chancery administration as dilatory and expensive, the last redoubt of old corruption. Even after the Trustee Relief Act, however, the cost of getting money in and out of Chancery was substantial enough to generate a good deal of secondary law about who should have to pay it.[25] Getting capital out could be cumbrous even after reforms of the Chancery offices in the 1860s.[26] On the other hand, once an account was established administration was free.[27] The standard order accompanying payment in was that trust funds be invested in government securities, usually the 3 per cent consols, which were the standard conservative trustee investment.[28] Dividends could be paid to order. In 1895 a chief clerk of the Chancery Division reported that dividends could be paid by post, though he admitted that payments out had been more laborious in the 1860s, sometimes requiring powers of attorney.[29] Payments contingent on the maintenance of a state of affairs—from remaining unmarried to, he said, the continuing survival of a testator's pet animal—needed certification before they could safely be made.[30] It was second best to administration by 'proper family trustees', he accepted, but a good second best. Understandably, he doubted that any different form of public trustee would be more efficient.

It is difficult to know what to make of this jurisdiction. Modern research has not investigated its use, nor the question whether judges' changing experience of

---

[22] 10 & 11 Vict. c. 96, extended by 12 & 13 Vict. c. 74 (1849); *Handley* v. *Davies* (1859) 5 Jur. (N.S.) 190. County court jurisdiction to accept and administer sums below £500 became available from 1865: County Courts (Equity Jurisdiction) Act, s 1; County Courts Act 1867, s 24.

[23] E. R. Daniell, *Chancery Practice* (2nd edn, 1845), ii, 1636–53.

[24] T. Lewin, *A Practical Treatise on the Law of Trusts and Trustees* (6th edn, 1875), 823 (he mistakenly says Kindersley rather than Stuart); *Ross* v. *Ross* (1849) 12 Beav. 89; *Robertson* v. *Scott* (1866) 14 LT (NS) 187.

[25] Lewin, *Trusts* (6th edn), 840–2.

[26] See Vol. XI, pp. 682–91.

[27] *RC on Accountant General's Dept.*, Report, 23–5; *SC on Trusts Administration*, Report, *PP* 1895 (248), xiii, 403, 578.

[28] H. Ayckbourn, *Practice of the High Court of Chancery* (1870), 444–59.

[29] *SC on Trusts Administration*, Report, 576–82.

[30] This could be tedious, requiring in the 1850s a certificate from a minister or churchwarden: D. G. Begg, *The Country-Solicitor's Practice* (5th edn, 1857), 409–11.

approving payments and decisions concerning funds in court influenced their opinions on the general management of trusts. In the 1880s the presumption that beneficiaries were entitled to the security of court administration, should they want it, seems to have lapsed. Hall VC reverted to requiring beneficiaries to show cause before he would compel trustees to pay their fund into court, and in 1895 the chief clerk was equating the ability of beneficiaries to get the fund paid into court with their ability to get a general administration order, which had explicitly been made discretionary by a change to the Chancery Rules in 1883.[31] He said that general administration orders, once a matter of course, were now rare. Judges, he thought, were worried by the expense to Chancery and saw their modern role as limited to settling disputed points of construction. They must also have thought that beneficiaries whose families could not provide trustees could find alternative services. The chief clerk's audience and inquisitor was the select committee on trusts administration, whose interest lay in modern public trusteeships, not in persuading the public that the Dickensian fog had lifted from Chancery. Consequently it brushed him aside with a remark about expense, content that judges had already made the decision that mattered.[32]

A public trustee was not instituted until 1906, after the half-way house of 'judicial trustees' based upon a Scottish model had been tried and had failed.[33] At much the same time banks moved sharply into the trustee business, some 20 years after a few insurance companies had tentatively introduced 'trustee departments'.[34] Before then the partners of private banks had not uncommonly acted as trustees for their monied clients, but the organization of the joint stock banks into branches and their structure of salaried managers had deflected them away from making trusts their business—which, anyway, they had thought was too different from the proper business of banking to be worth the effort. There were legal difficulties in the way of corporate trustees too, but again the nuisance those caused was not felt sufficiently to pressure Parliament into remedying them until the late 1890s, though the lobbying began a decade earlier.[35]

Thus, for all the difficulties, private trusteeship augmented by solicitor-trusteeship was the norm for most of our period, and was certainly the model

---

[31] *Re Braithwaite* (1882) 21 Ch D 121; *SC on Trusts Administration*, Report, 576; Order LV rule 10, on which see *re Wilson* (1885) 28 Ch D 457; *re Blake* (1885) 29 Ch D 913; *re Stocken* (1888) 38 Ch D 319.

[32] *SC on Trusts Administration*, Report, 409.

[33] Public Trustee Act; Judicial Trustees Act 1896; Polden, 'The Public Trustee'; Stebbings, *Private Trustee*, 61–2.

[34] For this and what follows, see Marsh, *Corporate Trustees*, 69–80, 93–106.

[35] Stebbings, *Private Trustee*, 57–9; Bodies Corporate (Joint Tenancies) Act 1899. The initial rules promulgated to give effect to the Judicial Trustees Act 1896 needed almost immediate amendment to allow companies to enter an employee as judicial trustee by his designation rather than by name: *Additional Rule by Lord Chancellor under Judicial Trustees Act*, PP 1899 (172), lxxix, 261.

that was assumed when judges and Parliament had occasion to consider trustees' duties and liability. As will be seen, standards of liability were relaxed a little, away from ones requiring personal attention and imposing strict liability towards ones allowing delegation and providing a defence of reasonable and honest conduct. That may have made trusteeship a more attractive business for institutions to enter. But, if so, it was a consequence; there was no pressure from businesses.

2. A LAW OF PRIVATE TRUSTS

In one sense nineteenth-century trusts law was young law to meet new demands. Sir John Baker has pointed out that the appearance of books such as Lewin's *Trusts and Trustees* signifies a shift away from perceiving trusts as principally an adjunct to the conveyance of land and towards an institution in their own right.[36] These general texts by Lewin (1837) and Hill (1845) were a new start, basing their organization on the assumption that trusts were vehicles for the management of wealth in general, where the type of property involved and the type of transaction originating the trust might affect the detail but were immaterial to the basic conceptual structure.[37] They were immediately preceded by a literature on the nature of trusteeship that likewise reflected a shift away from the relatively passive office ancillary to landed settlements towards a more generalized conception.[38] By contrast, though John Walpole Willis's text, published in 1827, promises to be a general work on trusts and trustees he based it upon what he took to be authoritative statements from the previous land-based treatises.[39] His blend of eighteenth-century structure with nineteenth-century addenda failed to explain or present trusts as a whole, and did not survive the publication of Lewin and Hill, either in England, where Lewin was dominant, or in the United States, where Lewin was republished and Hill went into four editions.[40]

---

[36] *An Introduction to English Legal History* (3rd edn, 1990), 352. The contrast is with G. Gilbert, *The Law of Uses and Trusts* (1734, 3rd edn by E. Sugden, 1811); F. W. Sanders, *An Essay on the Nature and Laws of Uses and Trusts, including a treatise on conveyances at common law and on those deriving their effect from the Statute of Uses* (1791); J. de G. Fonblanque, *A Treatise of Equity* [by H Ballow], *with the addition of marginal references and notes* (1793).

[37] T. Lewin, *Practical Treatise on the Law of Trusts and Trustees* (1837); J. Hill, *Practical Treatise on the Law relating to Trustees* (1845).

[38] G. F. Hampson, *Short Treatise Endeavouring to Point Out the Means by Which Those Who Accept the Situation of Trustees may Perform their Duty Without Incurring Responsibility* (1825); Grant, *Advice to Trustees*.

[39] J. W. Willis, *A Practical Treatise on the Duties and Responsibilities of Trustees* (1827).

[40] Lewin was first published in the USA in 1839; Hill went into four American editions, but did not go beyond a first edition in England; Willis had first, and only, editions in England in 1827 and America in 1835.

Lewin dominated the English texts until his death in 1877.[41] By the end of the century his treatise, then in the hands of editors, was rivalled by Underhill's, but that had begun as a concise introduction to the law as arranged by Lewin, and though it had quickly grown to twice its original length it did not contain radically different insights. It remains difficult to see past Lewin. When we do it is usually only as far as Lord Eldon, Lord Chancellor for an almost unbroken reign between 1801 and 1827.

Practitioners seeking authority could nearly always find it in Lord Eldon, and modern scholarship has tended to follow that lead by attributing much of the shape of nineteenth-century trusts law to him.[42] But we know little about the practice of trusts during his time, so attribution and comparison need caution. Lord Eldon himself presented the basic structure of trusts law as mostly well settled. Modern scholarship has not explored how much of that was artifice. Lewin likewise based his propositions on as wide a range of authority as he could, using eighteenth-century cases copiously. If these sources are taken at face value trusts law was old law, though increasingly to be applied to new forms of middle-class wealth. The most conspicuous result of that shift of context was to be an elaboration of the law of trusteeship, covering in particular trustees' duties of investment and their powers to act by delegates or agents. That will be discussed later. First the reception of Lord Eldon's structure and its place within a general law of trusts need to be explored.

The Legal Structure of Private Trusts

Lewin's work presupposed, or asserted, a conceptual unity to the law of trusts. It was, so far as he could make it, a unity of outcome: a trust was a property relation of a certain sort, irrespective of how it had come about. Maitland later gently took issue with the ambiguity of Lewin's category of implied trusts but, at least in his lectures to his students, he did not see it as a matter of great moment.[43] Right through until the end of our period English analytical jurisprudence was much more occupied with finding a watertight definition that would encompass

---

[41] There were six English editions in his lifetime. A. Underhill's *Concise Manual of the Law relating to Private Trusts and Trustees* and H. Godefroi's *Digest of the Principles of the Law of Trusts and Trustees* first appeared in 1878 and 1879 respectively. In subsequent editions Underhill's text became *Practical and Concise Manual* etc, before settling to be simply *The Law relating to Trusts and Trustees*. Maitland's lectures, posthumously collected and published as *Equity* (various editions from 1909), use Lewin as their starting point.

[42] G. Alexander, 'The Transformation of Trusts as a Legal Category, 1800–1914' (1987) 5 *Law & Hist. Rev.* 303–50.

[43] Maitland's lectures are discussed by Alexander, 'Transformation of Trusts', who, like many others, perhaps overlooks that they were meant for a student audience, not for publication.

all trusts and distinguish them from contracts and bailments than it was with probing conceptual differences between express, implied, resulting, and constructive trusts.[44] That latter became the concern of American writers interested in sharp lines between intention-based and regulatory legal institutions, confident also of their own importance in reorienting judicial law-making.[45] In England our period ended instead with a characteristic analysis in the Law Quarterly Review of the question—vexed among writers of analytical jurisprudence—of whether a trust is *ius in rem* or *ius in personam*.[46] Equally characteristically, Sir Frederick Pollock used his editorial prerogative to add a deflating endnote reading, 'Why is Trust not entitled to rank as a head *sui generis*?'[47]

None of this expository jurisprudence had any discernible impact on case law or legislation. Specialist literature remained professionally based. Arthur Underhill's text (from 1878), which aimed for a rule-based, scientific, layout still treated resulting and constructive trusts as catalogues of instances, the latter based loosely upon breach of fiduciary duty, with no depth of analysis of their conceptual basis.[48] Essentially English writers treated trusts law as the law of express private trusts, with add-ons.

The law of express private trusts Lewin portrayed was unequivocally a branch of property law. It presupposed a concept of property existing externally to the settlor. Judges defined property and set their limits on its possibilities. Similarly, Lewin conceived of the relation between beneficiary and trustee as proprietary, and of the relation between settlor and beneficiary as one of donation. That explained how obligations ran. As Underhill wrote, it is a feature of English law, in his experience one difficult for French courts to grasp, that a trust is not a mandate; settlors, lacking a property interest, have no legal capacity to enforce their trust.[49]

The exception illustrated the point well: from at least Lord Eldon's time judges held that debtor-initiated trusts *inter vivos* for the payment of creditors did not vest interests in them.[50] Even the most formal of such deeds were routinely held

[44] The English definitions were collected and critiqued by W. G. Hart, 'What is a Trust?' (1899) 15 *LQR* 294–302. Some of them anticipate J. Langbein, 'The Contractarian Basis of the Law of Trusts' (1995) 105 *Yale LJ* 625–75.
[45] G. Costigan, 'The Classification of Trusts as Express, Resulting, and Constructive' (1914) 27 *HLR* 437, discussed at length by Alexander, 'Transformation of Trusts'.
[46] W. G. Hart, 'The Place of Trust in Jurisprudence' (1912) 28 *LQR* 290–7.
[47] *Ibid.*, 297. For Pollock as editor, see N. Duxbury, *Frederick Pollock and the English Juristic Tradition* (Oxford 2004), 287–8, 309–22.
[48] Underhill, *Private Trusts and Trustees* (7th edn), 147–86; see also W. G. Hart, 'The Development of the Rule in *Keech v Sandford*' (1905) 21 *LQR* 258–64.
[49] Underhill, *Private Trusts and Trustees* (7th edn), 3.
[50] *Walwyn* v. *Coutts* (1815) 3 Mer. 707; *Garrard* v. *Lord Lauderdale* (1830) 3 Sim. 1, (1831) 2 Russ. & My. 451; *Acton* v. *Woodgate* (1833) 2 My. & K. 492; *Synnot* v. *Simpson* (1854) 5 H.L.C. 121; *Montefiore* v.

to create mere authorities that gave a creditor no rights until actual payment, the so-called trust being seen as merely a revocable device resting between the debtor and his administrative agent. This was such a contrast with the ordinary run of trusts that Lewin found himself unable to explain the precise nature of such an oddity.[51] That was a mild embarrassment for him since, as Underhill was to observe, it was conventional for writers defining trusts in the early years of Victoria's reign to emphasize their proprietary aspect; it was only later, after a prolonged period of concern about the extent of trustees' liability, that writers put the weight of their definitions on the beneficiary's relation with the trustee.[52]

The much bigger exception that charitable trusts made to this conception merited no mention at all in Lewin's first edition, though he had things to say about charitable trustees. In his second he provided a simple definitional stop: private trusts are proprietary, which is why beneficiaries can enforce them, whereas charitable trusts are public and non-proprietary.[53] Throughout our period their validity was approached through the catalogue in the preamble to the statute of Elizabeth as extended through analogical reasoning, as it still was well into the twentieth century.[54] That generated a much wider range of valid, perpetual, public purpose trusts than (judges sometimes supposed) the popular meaning of 'charity' conveyed—not always with validity the result if the subject of the trust were land, since the statute of mortmain limited charitable holdings of land and made such gifts by will next to impossible.[55] In principle the question could have arisen whether there could be private purpose trusts valid within a perpetuity period, but it seems not to have been explicitly addressed. On the rare occasions something like one appeared before a judge they seem to have escaped particular notice in the welter of more complex issues.[56]

Browne (1858) 7 H.L.C. 241; *Johns* v. *James* (1877) 8 Ch D 744. Such an analysis was much less likely if the arrangement was to take effect only after the debtor's death, and it did not apply if the creditor concerned had signed the deed or been expressly informed of it: *re Sanders' trusts* (1878) 47 LJ Ch 667; *re Fitzgerald's Settlement* (1887) 37 Ch D 18.

[51] e.g. 4th edn, 356, carried through to 10th edn, 588.

[52] *Law of Trusts and Trustees* (7th edn, 1912), 1–5.

[53] *Trusts* (2nd edn), 25.

[54] L. Shelford, *A Practical Treatise of the Law of Mortmain and Charitable Uses and Trusts* (1836), 59; O. D. Tudor, *The Law of Charitable Trusts* (2nd edn, 1862), 5.

[55] Mortmain Act 1736, 9 Geo. II c. 36 (its sting was removed by the Mortmain and Charitable Uses Act 1891). In *Commissioners for Special Purposes of the Income Tax* v. *Pemsel* [1891] AC 531 the House of Lords, by a majority and against the rulings in lower courts, held that *prima facie* words such as 'charity' or 'charitable' in a statute invoke this broad technical meaning, and not a narrower one limited to relief of poverty.

[56] *Mitford* v. *Reynolds* (1842) 1 Ph. 185, (1848) 16 Sim. 105; *Pettingall* v. *Pettingall* (1842) 11 LJ Ch 176. See *re Dean* (1889) 41 Ch D 552.

Lewin's law of express private trusts was a coalescence of two strands of law, still incomplete at the time he first wrote. One concerned testamentary trusts, the other voluntary *inter vivos* trusts. If John Austin had completed the lectures he planned to give at University College in 1832 he would have included trusts as a branch of testamentary succession.[57] This strong association of trusts with wills was buttressed by the well-established rule that even executors who were not expressly designated trustees would become trustees of legacies once those were ascertained, and by the weaker attempts of equity courts to rebut the common law rule that executors took unallocated residue beneficially. Thus where equity courts could find something in the words to suggest that the testator meant only to create an office of executor it would enforce that intention through a trust, a principle that became the general rule in 1830, when a statute promoted by Thomas Spring Rice made executors trustees of unallocated residue for the next of kin unless the will said otherwise.[58] Again, the residue needed to be ascertained before the more exacting rules of trusteeship took over from those of executorship, so the equation was not complete.[59] Nonetheless, in lawyers' eyes the association was strong. Of the 17 concise forms of will published by William Hayes and Thomas Jarman in 1835 all but the three most simple used trusts in one way or another, several from the very start nominating representatives to be simultaneously executors and trustees.[60]

It was on that testamentary side of the family that the strong proprietary basis of trusts was most conspicuously displayed. It originated perhaps the most distinctive element of the proprietary conception of private trusts, the ability beneficiaries have collectively to override any restrictions the settlor may have ordained and insist instead upon dividing the trust property between themselves. Modern writers trace it to Lord Cottenham's decision in *Saunders* v. *Vautier* in 1841, but in its context of testamentary trusts it was neither a novelty nor an isolated point.[61] There are cases from 1814 and 1822 that treat the principle as already well established, being reported only for an ancillary detail they raised.[62] Lord Cottenham's

---

[57] J. Austin, *Lectures on Jurisprudence* (3rd edn, by R. Campbell, 1869), 60–1; Hart, 'Place of Trust', 290–1.

[58] E. V. Williams, *A Treatise on the Law of Executors* (1832), ii, 898–904; Executors Act 1830, 11 Geo. IV & 1 Will. IV c. 40; *The Times*, 11 March 1830.

[59] *Davenport* v. *Stafford* (1851) 14 Beav. 319; *re Smith* (1889) 42 Ch D 302; see also *Phillipo* v. *Munnings* (1837) 2 My. & Cr. 309; *Dix* v. *Burford* (1854) 19 Beav. 409 for overlapping relationships resolved by applying trusts rules.

[60] W. Hayes and T. Jarman, *Concise Forms of Wills* (1835).

[61] Cr. & Ph. 841; Chesterman, 'Family Settlements'; Alexander, 'Dead Hand'; Alexander, 'Transformation of Trusts'. The case itself was fought on the issue of whether the interests were in fact vested, the point for which it subsequently became famous being treated as established practice.

[62] *Fraser* v. *Fraser* (1814) Jac. 586n; *Leng* v. *Hayes* (1822) Jac. 585. They were applications by a female life annuitant and the remaindermen to dispose of a testamentary trust fund as they collectively

ruling is typical of litigation about wills of personalty in the early nineteenth century. Trusts and legacies are intertwined in many reports of cases, the office of executor and trustee likewise. Thus the issue might be whether a legatee could override an instruction in a will that an annuity be bought for her and take the money instead, or what should happen when a condition attached to a legacy became impossible, or whether the legatee could disregard an uncongenial condition, or whether someone's interest was vested so as to satisfy the rule against perpetuities, or whether a legacy held on trust to maintain a child was merely a fund to be dipped into or one that must be invested to earn full annual interest.[63]

To all these instances judges brought a proprietary disposition. They showed a strong tendency to hold that a will created absolute interests in the property, and that a testator's qualifying words merely expressed motive, or concerned administration, or, if all else failed, should be disregarded as contradictory.[64] All this sat comfortably with the proprietary culture of *Brown* v. *Higgs* and *Burrough* v. *Philcox*, that a power to appoint among children will be interpreted where possible as an implied trust in default for them all equally, so as to give them an interest, and also with the various rules of construction that favoured early vesting.[65]

None of this seems to have been new or controversial in principle, though its application in the individual case might be. Judges and writers seem to have seen the primary function of testamentary trusts to be the transmission of interests— still conveyancing, as it were, but of personal or mixed property on death. Lewin made a link to just one similar principle concerning *inter vivos* trusts, that beneficiaries of a trust for sale of land could insist on taking the land unsold.[66] From this conjuncture he deduced a principle for trusts as a whole, that the beneficiaries acting together may override 'the modifications of the estate the settlor may have contemplated', because they are the absolute beneficial proprietors.[67] There is also a parallel with cases holding that a power given to trustees to sell

wished, but where there was a very small risk that the woman might subsequently have a child who would have been entitled in place of the remaindermen. The question was what security the remaindermen should have to give against that risk materializing, the court settling for just their personal recognizances.

[63] *Barnes* v. *Rowley* (1797) 3 Ves. 305; *Barton* v. *Cooke* (1800) 5 Ves. 461; *Montgomerie* v. *Woodley* (1800) 5 Ves. 522; *Hammond* v. *Neame* (1818) 1 Swans. 35; *Ross* v. *Ross* (1819) 1 Jac. & W. 154; *Whittell* v. *Dudin* (1820) 2 Jac. & W. 279; *Snow* v. *Poulden* (1836) 1 Keen 186, *Kampf* v. *Jones* (1837) 2 Keen 756; *Ring* v. *Hardwick* (1840) 2 Beav. 352; *Knox* v. *Lord Hotham* (1845) 15 Sim. 82; *Noel* v. *Jones* (1848) 16 Sim. 309; *Gough* v. *Bult* (1847) 16 Sim. 45; *Lassence* v. *Tierney* (1849) 1 Mac. & G. 551.

[64] For a particularly lucid exposition of this pattern of thought, see Alexander, 'Dead Hand', 1224–7.

[65] *Brown* v. *Higgs* (1800) 5 Ves. 495, (1803) 8 Ves. 561; *Burrough* v. *Philcox* (1840) 5 My. & Cr. 72.

[66] Lewin, *Trusts* (4th edn, 1861), 447; *Pearson* v. *Lane* (1809) 17 Ves. 101.

[67] Lewin, *Trusts* (4th edn, 1861), 447; compare Lord Langdale's description in *Curtis* v. *Lukin* (1842) 5 Beav. 147.

trust land impliedly ends when a sole beneficiary becomes entitled in equity to the fee.[68] In all of this law there is a sense of mission accomplished: a new cycle of property ownership has begun, propertied adults can now make their own way, so remaining details from the trust may safely be disregarded as surplus.[69]

Precatory trusts provide a second example of coalescence, this time a coalescence of obligation. The chapter above on wills and their interpretation has shown how at the start of our period gifts by will to close family members accompanied by words of request, recommendation, hope, or confidence that they would maintain and educate the testator's children, and/or that they would leave the property to the children were interpreted by judges as creating a trust.[70] The 'ordinary meaning' canon of interpretation rooted that out in the 1870s, but before it did such obligations might sit heavily on the supposed trustee, who was often the testator's widow. There is a suggestion, however, that judges saw precatory trusts as creating diluted obligations. In 1845 Hill wrote that the words creating precatory trusts were 'insufficient to impress the gift with the character of a trust *generally*.'[71] 'And if a trust be created', wrote Lewin, 'it does not follow that it shall be equally restrictive as where the trust is properly such.'[72]

The difference is a little elusive, but probably it had two limbs. The first concerned precatory trusts imposed upon a parent, usually the widowed mother, for the maintenance of her children. A trustee would normally expect to have to account to her beneficiaries for the expenditure of the trust fund, but in this situation courts consistently held that no account could be demanded so long as the mother/trustee was in fact maintaining the children.[73] Analogies were drawn to guardians and to the committees of lunatics, who were likewise subject to a good faith standard rather than to strict accounting.[74] Similarly, words such as 'maintenance' and 'bringing up' were interpreted to mean maintenance in the mother/trustee's own household. Since strict accounting was not to be required, some of the supposedly trust money could be used on general household expenses. If the

[68] *Jefferson* v. *Tyrer* (1845) 9 Jur. 1083; *Wolley* v. *Jenkins* (1856) 23 Beav. 53 (affirmed (1857) 3 Jur. (N.S.) 321); *Lantsbery* v. *Collier* (1856) 2 K. & J. 709.

[69] A similar contextual explanation of *Saunders* v. *Vautier* seems to have been used by Lord Herschell in *Wharton* v. *Masterman* [1895] AC 186. The US Supreme Court, rejecting *Saunders* v. *Vautier* and *Wharton* v. *Masterman*, traced the rule in *Saunders* v. *Vautier* in England to a policy of favouring creditors, but it is difficult to support that from the texts: *Shelton* v. *King* 229 US 90 (1913).

[70] See pp. 35–7, above.

[71] Hill, *Trustees*, 32 (his emphasis).

[72] Lewin, *Trusts* (1st edn), 81.

[73] *Leach* v. *Leach* (1843) 7 Jur. 273 (a better report than 13 Sim. 304); *Browne* v. *Paull* (1850) 1 Sim. (N.S.) 92; *Hart* v. *Tribe* (1854) 18 Beav. 215; *Carr* v. *Living* (1860) 28 Beav. 644; Lewin, *Trusts* (4th edn, 1861), 106.

[74] Lewin, *Trusts* (4th edn, 1861), 106; *Jodrell* v. *Jodrell* (1851) 14 Beav. 39.

mother could keep the surplus, which seems implied in many of the cases, then as Lord Cranworth pointed out, the obligation was being treated as a charge on a bequest rather than as a trust.[75]

The second practice concerned precatory trusts requesting the recipient/ trustee, again often the testator's widow, to leave the property at her death to the children, or to a designated class of kin, often with a power of selection. Here Chancery's usual refusal to declare the extent of rights in remainder limited it to holding simply that the recipient/trustee was not entitled absolutely.[76] The consequence seems to have been to sidestep the duties of conversion of the property, apportionment of income, and so forth, that trustees holding for a life tenant and remaindermen had usually to observe.[77] It is not that the rules clearly did not apply, rather that the occasion was denied for insisting that they did.[78]

If this is what Hill and Lewin meant, their analysis did not survive. At its strongest it was a difference only of degree. Even where the precatory trustee for maintenance was the children's widowed mother the court would sometimes rule on specific proposals.[79] Further, the reduced standard of accountability supposedly attaching to precatory maintenance trusts became applied to all parent/ trustees, whether express or precatory.[80] Then that reduced standard itself faded from sight. There seem to be no reported cases after 1863, and though the relevant passage continued unamended in the later editions of Lewin, no trace can be found of it in the more modern treatise by Underhill.[81] As for precatory trusts

[75] *Browne* v. *Paull* (1850) 1 Sim. (N.S.) 92.

[76] *Gully* v. *Cregoe* (1857) 24 Beav. 185; *Smith* v *Gibson* (1871) 25 LT 559; *Hampton* v. *Holman* (1877) 5 Ch D 183; cf. *Raikes* v. *Wood* (1842) 1 Hare 445; *Crockett* v. *Crockett* (1848) 2 Ph. 553.

[77] Stebbings, *Private Trustee*, 67–77.

[78] There is a link here, also rather elusive, to the question of what were the rights of one who had a fee simple subject to an executory devise—to my wife 'absolutely in full confidence that she will make such use of it as I should have made myself and that at her death she will devise it to such one or more of my nieces as she may think fit ...' was the limitation interpreted that way in *Comiskey* v. *Bowring-Hanbury* [1905] AC 84. The cases are few, but show that the court would either decline to rule during the lifetime of the first taker, or would hold generally that the executory gift over did not reduce the first taker to the status of a mere life tenant. Since the words in the first such case were precatory, Lewin, *Trusts* (1st edn), 81–2, used this situation as the foundation for his general statement that precatory trusts were a category of their own. The difficulty flowed from the inconclusive case of *Wright* v. *Atkins*, where the rulings by the House of Lords were reported only, and belatedly, by Sugden in his *Law of Property*. See, however, the report at (1823) 1 Turn. & R. 143, and *Turner* v. *Wright* (1860) Johns. 740 for a full discussion; see also *Lady Langdale* v. *Briggs* (1856) 8 De G. M. & G. 391; *Shovelton* v. *Shovelton* (1863) 32 Beav. 143; *Smith* v. *Gibson* (1871) 25 LT 559; *re Hanbury's Settled Estates* [1913] 2 Ch 357.

[79] *Hart* v. *Tribe (No. 2)* (1854) 19 Beav. 149.

[80] *Hadow* v. *Hadow* (1838) 9 Sim. 438; *Hora* v. *Hora* (1863) 33 Beav. 88.

[81] Lewin, *Trusts* (10th edn, 1898), 150; Underhill, *Trusts* (7th edn, 1912), 34, cites Lewin's latest case, *Hora* v. *Hora* only for whether there was a trust, not for the standard of accountability. The standard generally was low: unless there was evidence of some serious breach trustees could account in

for disposal on death, the courts would accord the putative class of beneficiaries standing to complain of a clear breach, and some judges were uneasy at allowing a widow/precatory trustee possession of the fund during her lifetime, at least without giving security for due performance of the obligation.[82] If the widow was not fully obligated, then nearly always her interest was held to be absolute.[83] So the notion that words of semi-obligation might be satisfied by a semi-trust seems to have died a quiet death, probably sometime in the 1860s. By the 1890s the proposition was sternly denied: words may be precatory, but trusts are trusts.[84]

Trusts as Property: The Limits of Settlors' Autonomy

Nobody denied that settlors could modify their trustees' duties—that is how trusts became suited to the management of family wealth. The logic, especially of testamentary trusts, had rather been the other way around, starting with an obligation, say to sell land and distribute the proceeds, or to pay creditors out of designated assets, and enforcing it as a trust. The law supplied a default set of duties, but settlors could tailor them to suit. Similarly, settlors could stipulate that their trustees be paid, notwithstanding equity's conception of the office as voluntary. Probably settlors could also modify the consequences of a breach, though the logic was seen as difficult and the idea seems not to have been taken far. But the property law matrix within which trusts operated was not negotiable.

Beneficiaries had interests in the trust property, and it was part of the origin of trusts in real property law that interests had 'natures' that could not be gainsaid. A fee tail could not be made unbarrable, a fee simple could not be made inalienable, nor could settlors achieve such forbidden ends by limiting estates to trustees and then attaching repugnant conditions to the equitable interests. So too with legacies: testators could not attach conditions that judges thought contradicted the essential nature of ownership.[85] From there it had been an easy step to invalidating conditions in trusts that made personalty inalienable, just

general terms—what was a reasonable sum to have allowed for maintenance—rather than in detail: re Evans (1884) 26 Ch D 58, and compare Brophy v. Bellamy (1873) LR 8 Ch App 798, where a power to maintain was seen as wholly discretionary.

[82] Woods v. Woods (1836) 1 My. & Cr. 401; Williams v. Williams (1851) 1 Sim. (N.S.) 358; Webb v. Wools (1852) 2 Sim (N.S.) 267; cf. Hart v. Tribe (1854) 18 Beav. 215.

[83] Parnall v. Parnall (1878) 9 Ch D 96; Bibbens v. Potter (1879) 10 Ch D 733; re Jones [1898] 1 Ch 438. The combination of a precatory trust and an executory devise found in Comiskey v. Bowring-Hanbury was very rare. In the case itself the analysis seems to emerge during argument in the CA: [1904] 1 Ch 415, [1905] AC 84 (HL).

[84] Williams v. Williams [1897] 2 Ch 12.

[85] Bradley v. Peixoto (1797) 3 Ves. 324; Ross v. Ross (1819) 1 Jac. & W. 154; Cuthbert v. Purrier (1822) Jac. 415.

as it had been an easy step to apply the modern rule against perpetuities to equitable interests in pure personalty. Throughout our period English judges abided uncritically by this legal structure. On the other hand, property law being a technical rather than a moral science, they saw no difficulty in settlors manipulating the approved catalogue of interests to approximate to results that could not be reached directly.

In the 1830s judges even considered winding back the one established exception to the principle that property interests could not be made inalienable: the married woman's restraint on anticipation that Lord Thurlow had insinuated into the law in the early 1790s.[86] Equity had long allowed a married woman's property to be limited to her separate use, which contradicted a swathe of common law principles, but that had still left her the choice of turning her property over to her husband, and his creditors. By contrast, Lord Thurlow's innovation operated as a simple prohibition on alienation, such a stark affront to principle that in Sugden's view the 'general opinion of the Profession' was at first that it could not be valid.[87] The understanding in the 1830s was that it had been inspired by instances where married women's access to property limited to their separate use had brought them ruin; it was irreconcilable with property theory, nonetheless.[88]

The question then was how wide the restraint on anticipation should be, hence which of a married woman's property should be removed from active circulation and for how long. The paternalist maximum, supported by Leach MR in 1831, was that it should apply to any property so designated by a settlor, donor, or testator, and should endure throughout the woman's lifetime, married or single—so that the property should be her endowment when, if, she married, or remarried, as the case may be.[89] Orthodoxy had been that the restraint bound a woman only

---

[86] The standard legal folklore as taught by Lord Eldon was that Lord Thurlow had not done this by decision but by forceful dicta, by letting it be known that he had drafted Miss Watson's marriage settlement with such a restraint in it, and by impressing on the future Lord Eldon that a principled basis could be found: *Parkes v. White* (1805) 11 Ves. 209; *Brandon v. Robinson* (1811) 18 Ves. 429; *Jackson v. Hobhouse* (1817) 2 Mer. 483. In Eldon's rendition Thurlow's principle amounted only to saying that as equity invented the separate use, equity could do what it liked with it, and what it liked was to protect married women from possible coercion by their husbands. This narrative was then reiterated in the pages of the Law Magazine: 'On the wife's separate estate, and the established restriction upon alienation of it by anticipation' (1829) 1 *LM* 565–74; 'Clause against anticipation, in wills and settlements' (1834) 11 *LM* 83–6; 'The law of separate estate—restraint upon alienation' (1843) 30 *LM* 129. Nobody could find any details of Miss Watson and her settlement, or knew whether there had been litigation. The first known decision validating the restraint was by Lord Alvanley in 1794: *Sockett v. Wray* (1794) 4 Bro. C.C. 483.

[87] *A Practical Treatise of Powers*, (1st edn, 1808), 114, repeated through to (8th edn, 1861), 169.

[88] Particularly *Pybus v. Smith* (1791) 3 Bro. C.C. 340; see Belt's note to that case, in the English Reports reprint: 29 ER 573–4.

[89] *Woodmeston v. Walker* (1831) 2 Russ. & M. 197.

during a period of marriage, so it is unsurprising that Lord Brougham, as Lord Chancellor, should promptly reverse Leach MR's decision.[90] Lord Brougham's reasoning swung to the other extreme, however. Regarding any fetter on property as contrary to principle, and an on-again, off-again restraint on anticipation as particularly lacking justification, he would apply the restraint only to gifts received by women while married, and then for the duration of that marriage only.[91]

Brougham's suggestions seem quickly to have taken root. For a few years it was possible that Lord Thurlow's innovation would unravel and proprietary purity be restored, socially surprising though that would have been.[92] Pepys MR was one of those to follow Lord Brougham's lead, but when Lord Langdale, newly appointed to replace him as Master of the Rolls, forcefully held out for the previous orthodoxy, Pepys, who had moved up to become Lord Chancellor, Lord Cottenham, agonized for 12 months and then changed sides.[93] The resolution he ordained in *Tullett* v. *Armstrong* was not subsequently challenged: the restraint could validly be attached to a woman's property whether she was married or single at the time, it would bind her during any marriages she might have (unless worded to apply just to one), but she (and her creditors) could disregard it whenever she was single. He based his decision on the twin policies of forwarding the settlor's intention and protecting married women, in sharp contrast with Lord Brougham, with the general rule, and with his own decision in *Saunders* v. *Vautier*.

[90] *Ibid.*; 'Of the validity of gifts to the separate use of unmarried women in case of future coverture' (1835) 13 *LM* 135–55; *Barton* v. *Briscoe* (1822) Jac. 603; *Jones* v. *Salter* (1815) 2 Russ. & M. 208.

[91] *Woodmeston* v. *Walker* (1831) 2 Russ. & M. 197; *Brown* v. *Pocock* (1833) 2 Russ. & M. 210; in each case it was his reasoning rather than the result that caused the alarm; cf. *Newton* v. *Reid* (1830) 4 Sim. 141.

[92] 'For some time all was confusion': J. Williams, *Letters to John Bull Esq, on Lawyers and Law Reform* (1857), 40; he credits professional writers, particularly Jarman and Hayes, with applying the pressure to bring the law back to what it had been. The cases are *Brown* v. *Pocock (No. 2)* (1834) 5 Sim. 663; *Massey* v. *Parker* (1834) 2 My. & K. 174; *Malcolm* v. *O'Callaghan* (1835) 5 LJ Ch (NS) 137; *Davis* v. *Thornycroft* (1836) 5 LJ Ch (NS) 140; *Johnson* v. *Freeth* (1836) 5 LJ Ch (NS) 143, and the cases reported in G. Sweet, *Cases on a Wife's Separate Estate and Equity to a Settlement out of her Equitable Property* (1840). See too the reporters' note to *Maber* v. *Hubbs* (1836) 2 Y. & C. Ex. 317, 324n.

[93] *Tullett* v. *Armstrong* (1838) 1 Beav. 1, (1839) 4 My. & Cr. 390; *Scarborough* v. *Borman* (1838) 1 Beav. 34; (1839) 4 My. & Cr. 378; 'Lord Chancellor Cottenham' (1851) 15(s2) *LM* 280–8, at 284; 'Sketch of Lord Cottenham as a Judge' (1869) 27(s3) *LM&LR.* (s3), 264–72 at 265, 269. See also Sweet, *Cases on a Wife's Separate Estate*, and *Nedby* v. *Nedby* (1839) 4 My. & Cr. 367. Lord Eldon's decision in *Anderson* v. *Anderson* (unreported, 1821), which is discussed in *Tullett* v. *Armstrong* (1839) 4 My. & Cr. 390, is recounted at length in 'Of the validity of gifts to the separate use of unmarried women in case of future coverture' (1835) 13 *LM* 135–55. It suggests that Eldon's view of the restraint was like Cottenham's, and not like Brougham's.

Property lawyers, true to type, had at once recognized that the breach of property principle made by the married woman's restraint on anticipation might be exploitable in other contexts. If settlors and testators could effectively add the words 'but without power of anticipation' to an otherwise absolute disposition perhaps they could instead add 'but so as not to be available to creditors by way of execution'? The conveyancer William Hayes recounted that his fellow practitioners, who included the great Charles Butler, thought that something like that should now be possible.[94] If property were vested in trustees for a man for his lifetime, but with a duty on them to apply the income for his support, and with a prohibition on anticipation, then by parity of reasoning with the married women's restraint he would have no interest creditors could seize. Famously, that was too much for Lord Eldon. In *Brandon* v. *Robinson* he ruled that whatever social expectations justified retaining Lord Thurlow's exception, they did not warrant further infraction of general principle.[95] Many years later Page Wood VC flirted with the notion that a rider added to a legacy 'but not so as to be bound by her marriage settlement' would be effective, but once again proprietary orthodoxy soon prevailed.[96]

Lord Eldon's ruling was not that the policy of making property available to creditors overrode all others. Perhaps it should have been, the property lawyer George Sweet thought. He regretted Lord Eldon's 'dry technical rule' that 'equity cannot deprive property of its legal conclusions' because it encouraged avoidance and fine distinctions.[97] Modern commentators inclined to an instrumentalist view of judge-made law might agree.[98] Something of the same reasoning can be seen in a further strand of Lord Cottenham's ultimate validation of the restraint on anticipation.[99] It would be unfair to upset the arrangements of today's married women, he hinted, when drafters would soon find their younger sisters an indirect means to a similar end. The more usual view was that property was neutral: if its forms could be used to achieve a social end, then all well and good; but the forms should not be distorted to make it possible. So at least some of the objectors

---

[94] W. Hayes, *An Introduction to Conveyancing, and the New Statutes concerning Real Property* (2nd edn, 1835), 83, quoted also in a footnote to *Davis* v. *Thornycroft* (1836) 5 LJ Ch (NS), 140.

[95] *Brandon* v. *Robinson* (1811) 18 Ves. 429.

[96] *Re Mainwaring's Settlement* (1866) LR 2 Eq 487 (criticized by Davidson, *Precedents*, vol. iii (3rd edn), 199–200); *re Allnut* (1882) 22 Ch D 275; *Scholfield* v. *Spooner* (1884) 26 Ch D 94. The moral was quickly drawn: since such future property could be caught only by a covenant, the covenant could be drafted so as to exclude legacies expressing an intention that they *should* be excluded—*re Thorne* [1917] 1 Ch 360.

[97] Sweet, *Cases on a Wife's Separate Estate*, 7.

[98] Chesterman, 'Family Settlements', 152–3; G. Moffat and M. Chesterman, *Trusts Law: Text and Materials* (1988), 264–6.

[99] *Tullett* v. *Armstrong* (1839) 4 My. & Cr. 390.

to Lord Thurlow's innovation had conceded, or at least not opposed, the general proposition that a woman's property should be safe from her husband's importuning. They attacked only the contradiction involved in her having an interest but not having the alienability inherent in it—the contradiction that Lord Eldon had refused to countenance for anti-creditor devices in *Brandon* v. *Robinson*.[100] It followed that there was nothing amiss with avoidance, if a way could be found. The theory was easy enough: if 'property' could not be doctored so as to immunize its beneficiary from his creditors, then matters had to be arranged so that what the beneficiary had was not property, alternatively that his property lawfully terminated before his creditors' rights to it accrued.

One possibility was to construct a discretionary trust such that from the beginning the person to be protected did not have an interest but instead received benefits at the trustees' discretion.[101] The theory seems to have been taken for granted, perhaps because the validity of discretionary trusts was a consequence of the structure of the rule against perpetuities, the same reason that nobody challenged trusts for accumulation until Peter Thellusson's will showed their alarming potential.[102] Making discretionary trusts effective against creditors was not easy, however. Through the 1830s and into the early 1840s judges often interpreted such a discretionary beneficiary as the owner in equity—a nice example of their proprietary conception of trusts— construing the rest as mere machinery that could be disregarded, and sometimes expressing their disapproval of attempts to renege on debts.[103] To avoid that interpretation discretionary trustees had to be given real control, including, critically, power to withhold income from the beneficiary as it became due.[104] Such dependency contradicted notions of full adulthood, and undermined the link between manhood, property, and civic personality.[105] Further, for active discretionary trusts to become widespread would require a reservoir of trustees willing to exercise intrusive control over the

---

[100] 'The law of separate estate—restraint upon alienation' (1843) 30 *LM* 129, 133.

[101] For an early attempt that failed, see *Davidson* v. *Foley* (1787) 2 Bro. C.C. 203.

[102] *Thelluson* v. *Woodford* (1798) 4 Ves. 117, (1805) 11 Ves. 112; Polden, *Peter Thellusson's Will*.

[103] *Graves* v. *Dolphin* (1826) 1 Sim. 66; *Green* v. *Spicer* (1830) 1 Russ. & M. 395; *Piercy* v. *Roberts* (1832) 1 My. & K. 4; *Snowdon* v. *Dales* (1834) 6 Sim. 524; *Younghusband* v. *Gisborne* (1844) 1 Coll. C.C. 400, (1846) 15 LJ Ch 355.

[104] *Twopeny* v. *Peyton* (1840) 10 Sim. 487; *Godden* v. *Crowhurst* (1842) 10 Sim. 642; *Page* v. *Way* (1840) 3 Beav. 20; *Younghusband* v. *Gisborne* (1846) 15 LJ Ch 355; and note the intermediate analysis, that the beneficiary had a proportionate interest, or an interest in the surplus: *Rippon* v. *Norton* (1839) 2 Beav. 63; *Kearsley* v. *Woodcock* (1843) 3 Hare 185.

[105] Which is why *Re Sanderson's Trust* (1857) 3 K. & J. 497 was often cited as the paradigm—it was a discretionary trust for maintenance of the settlor's mentally ill brother. The nearest precedent for a discretionary trust in Peachey, *Settlements*, 890–6, is a semi-protective trust for a bachelor 'subject to fits of weakness', in anticipation that should he marry and have children a trustee might be needed to safeguard their welfare.

families of their relatives and friends, this at a time when there was chronic worry that the supply would dry up even for the ordinary range of trusts.[106]

Instead the usual form for a protective trust came to be that a man should have a life interest until he should attempt to alienate his interest, commit some act of bankruptcy, or some such. Until that determining event the trustees would be passive and might even delegate receipt of the income to him. On the determining event discretionary trusts for him and his family would come into operation, saving them from ruin by relegating him to dependence upon active trustees.[107] Because the structure of this device did no more than work out the logic of interest theory it did not call for policy approval from the judges. If there was going to be resistance or enthusiasm it would come when construing the words of individual schemes, and here one can discern a modest shift from doubt to acceptance, complete probably in the early 1840s.[108]

Judges validated protective trusts only to the extent that settlors parted with their property on trusts protective of others, however. Trusts created by a man protective of himself were a fraud on his creditors, even if he had been solvent at the time of the settlement.[109] A parallel principle in the 1820s suggested that while it was valid for a donor to impose a restraint on anticipation when making a gift to an unmarried woman, it might be fraud on her future husband for a woman to settle property on herself subject to a restraint intended to become effective on marriage.[110] Later in the century courts in the United States took this privileging of donors' freedom much further. There both *Brandon* v. *Robinson* and *Saunders*

---

[106] Stebbings, *Private Trustee*, 34 and *passim*; for what a mid-century discretionary trust might involve see *Davidson's Precedents*, vol. iii (2nd edn 1861), 849–53, so carefully crafted that the only person to have a vested interest until actual distribution is the settlor himself. Peachey's precedent mentioned in the previous note ends with a footnote on the propriety of remunerating the trustee of such a trust.

[107] *Ex p Hodgson* (1812) 19 Ves. 206; for the hallmarked versions see *Davidson's Precedents*, iii (2nd edn, 1861), 640–86 (marriage settlements), 849–53 (voluntary settlement) and his general exposition at 85–108. Note the breadth of his clauses triggering a shift from a vested interest to a discretionary trust, protecting the family from improvements in mechanisms for debt collection too. The risk, as Davidson's long footnote at pp. 645–8 indicates, was that such a shift was automatic and brought an irrevocable change of status for the beneficiary, thus should not be triggered without good cause.

[108] *Graves* v. *Dolphin* (1826) 1 Sim. 66; *Green* v. *Spicer* (1830) 1 Russ. & M. 395; *Piercy* v. *Roberts* (1832) 1 My. & K. 4; *Snowdon* v. *Dales* (1834) 6 Sim. 524; *Twopeny* v. *Peyton* (1840) 10 Sim. 487; *Godden* v. *Crowhurst* (1842) 10 Sim. 642; *Page* v. *Way* (1840) 3 Beav. 20; *Younghusband* v. *Gisborne* (1844) 1 Coll. C.C. 400, (1846) 15 LJ Ch 355.

[109] *Higginbotham* v. *Holme* (1812) 19 Ves. 88; Peachey, *Settlements*, 219–20. Its basis was a long-standing judicial extrapolation from Elizabethan legislation. There seems to have been some softening of the principle in the later cases, but by then it had become a fall-back principle applicable only if the more direct provisions in the reformed Bankruptcy Acts could not be used: *re Detmold* (1889) 40 Ch D 585; *Mackintosh* v. *Pogose* [1895] 1 Ch 505; *re Johnson* [1904] 1 KB 134.

[110] *Goddard* v. *Snow* (1826) 1 Russ. 485.

v. *Vautier* were rejected as unprincipled, the former in the 1870s the latter from
the 1880s, culminating in a Supreme Court decision in 1916.[111] Donors' freedom
to give on their own terms should prevail over donees' freedom to enjoy property
unrestrained, unless, the courts said, there was some policy reason to the contrary. Lord Cottenham cannot be claimed as a consistent adherent to this general
line of thought, because *Saunders* v. *Vautier* was his decision, but there are signs
of it nonetheless in both *Tullett* v. *Armstrong* and in his well-known decision in
Tulk v. *Moxhay*, the more so because in each case he was disagreeing with earlier
judgments of Lord Brougham explicitly based upon the opposite principle.[112]

Generally, though, English judges did not take the American road. They steered
away from policy and adhered to the basic premise that all dispositions must conform to an externally imposed register of property interests. The policy-based
prohibition against creating protective trusts for oneself could be treated as statutory, notwithstanding that its absolute nature clearly originated as a judicial gloss
on the ancient Act concerned. Lord Lyndhurst explained the married woman's
restraint not as respect for donors' freedom—which might then be generalized—
but as equity creating 'a new species of estate'.[113] There could then be no objection to an unmarried woman creating one for herself, provided only that she
did not actively misrepresent her situation to a would-be husband with intent to
deceive.[114] So in England *Brandon* v. *Robinson* remained orthodox, and although
Lord Herschell acknowledged in 1895 that *Saunders* v. *Vautier* rested more upon
assumption than upon decision he and the rest of the House of Lords thought it
too deeply entrenched to be open to review.[115]

Trusts as Transmissions: The Mechanics and Consequences of Giving

Settlors change their minds; circumstances change, favoured relatives disappoint,
the worthiness of others belatedly impresses. Wills are revocable, so trusts declared
by will bind only upon the settlor's death. But trusts constituted *inter vivos* are

---

[111] *Nichols* v. *Eaton* 91 US 716 (1875); *Claflin* v. *Claflin* (1889) 149 Mass. 19, 20 N.E. 454; *Shelton* v.
King 229 US 90 (1916); Alexander, 'Dead Hand'.

[112] (1839) 4 My. & Cr. 390, (1848) 2 Ph. 774, contradicting *Keppell* v. *Bailey* (1834) 2 My. & K. 517.
In *Tullett* v. *Armstrong* Cottenham anticipated *Tulk* v. *Moxhay* when reasoning that the only other
party directly affected, the husband, could justifiably be bound by the restraint because he must be
taken to have come to the marriage knowing of it. That proposition also subverts the principle that
the validity and definitional content of property interests is independent of the will of the parties.
See pp. 170–5, above.

[113] *Bagget* v. *Meux* (1846) 1 Phil. 627.

[114] Peachey, *Settlements*, 142–55; Davidson, *Precedents*, iii (2nd edn, 1861), 543–5n; *St. George* v.
Wake (1833) 1 My. & K. 610; *Taylor* v. *Pugh* (1842) 1 Hare 608; *England* v. *Downs* (1840) 2 Beav. 522;
Loader v. *Clarke* (1850) 2 Mac. & G. 382.

[115] *Wharton* v. *Masterman* [1895] AC 186.

beyond recall—absent an express power of revocation—however much a settlor and his creditors might come to regret them, though, the creditors might sometimes have recourse to overriding statutory provisions. This finality, qualified though it was, resulted in some tough law, putting a premium on precise legal technique and accurate expression of intention. If an intended *inter vivos* trust is not properly constituted it fails from the beginning. The settlor must effectively declare himself trustee or he must effectively transfer the trust property to trustees. If the settlor intended one mode but fails, he is unlikely to have unwittingly succeeded with the other.

All this was articulated by Lord Eldon in the two decades before our period begins and in its essence it survived unchanged well into the twentieth century.[116] But the apparent continuity is misleading; basic propositions were contested until the mid-century, and for a further generation judges felt the need to reiterate Lord Eldon's principles in case they should still be doubted. Nor is it easy to find the canon so well articulated before Lord Eldon's time. Various explanations have been proposed, but all must be seen as provisional until we know more about how trusts worked in the eighteenth century.[117] It is possible that voluntary *inter vivos* trusts, those, that is, for which there was no return, were uncommon then, or it may be that they were conceptualized differently.[118]

Whether or not the question was new, one tool for enforcing voluntary *inter vivos* trusts had been discarded during the eighteenth century. Equity judges had for long regarded contracts that they would specifically enforce as the functional equivalents of declarations of trust, but during the eighteenth century they stopped treating some sorts of promise as creating such a contractual obligation. Lewin wrote that where 'there is valuable consideration, and a trust is intended to be created, formalities are of minor importance, since if the transaction cannot take effect by way of trust executed, it may be enforced by a Court of equity as a contract'.[119] By 'formalities' he meant what we would now call constitution, the initial transfer of the property to the trustees. Had he written a century earlier he would not have said that valuable consideration was needed.

As Lewin explained, eighteenth-century equity judges generally thought that merely 'meritorious' consideration was sufficient, and some had treated a deed

---

[116] *Ellison* v. *Ellison* (1802) 6 Ves. 662; *Ex p Pye, Ex ·p Dubost* (1811) 18 Ves. 140; *Pulvertoft* v. *Pulvertoft* (1811) 18 Ves. 99.

[117] See particularly, Alexander, 'Transformation of Trusts', and the literature he cites.

[118] Horwitz and Polden's samples show that up to the start of our period litigation over *inter vivos* trusts was significant, but it was limited to marriage settlements: 'Continuity or Change?', 34.

[119] *Trusts* (3rd edn), 55.

under seal as automatically importing consideration.[120] That was a continuation and generalization of long-established doctrine determining what consideration was adequate to raise a use of land, a broader concept than the exchange-based consideration adopted in other contexts.[121] Hence Lewin bracketed promises to earmark property on trust for existing creditors—whose valuable consideration lay in the past—with promises for the benefit of close family as promises that had once been specifically enforceable. Wives and children had certainly been thought to provide meritorious consideration, though how far beyond them the concept had stretched was unclear. Nor was it altogether agreed whether such intended beneficiaries could always enforce the covenant against the promisor/settlor himself or only against subsequent voluntary transferees or devisees from him.[122] Whatever the reason for that, there was much less need for deep analysis of constitution of trusts if judges would specifically enforce promises made to fulfil these social and moral obligations, especially if they were generous in what they would treat as a promise.

Well before 1837, when Lewin first wrote, equity judges had reduced their concept of consideration to overt exchange obligations, in this context at least.[123] He relates a consensus that the consideration required must always be 'valuable', that is, be money or money's worth, and that equity should not specifically enforce a promise simply because it was made under seal.[124] Covenants in marriage settlements were unaffected by the shift. In reality marriage settlements were treaties between families, necessarily enforceable by the wife and children if the institution were to work—as it always had worked, irrespective of theories of contract. So entering marriage was a valuable consideration, and, to make marriage settlements work as everyone intended they should, the children of the marriage were likewise treated as being 'within the marriage consideration'. That applied, however, only to settlements on marriage. Outside that context a man's unreciprocated promise to settle property on his wife, or his unmarried partner, or his children, would not be enforceable in equity, however formally it was made.

---

[120] *Trusts*, (3rd edn), 62–3; W. Roberts, *A Treatise on the Construction of the Statutes 13 Eliz. c. 5 and 27 Eliz. c. 4 relating to Voluntary and Fraudulent Conveyances* (1800), 660–8; Hill, *Trustees*, 46n.

[121] D. J. Ibbetson, 'Consideration and the Theory of Contract in Sixteenth Century Common Law', in J. Barton (ed.), *Towards a General Law of Contract* (Berlin, 1990), 67–123; A. W. B. Simpson, *History of the Common Law of Contract* (Oxford, 1975), 327–74; Fonblanque, *Treatise of Equity* (5th edn, 1820), ii, 25–32; see also i, 279n; *Ellis* v. *Nimmo* (1835) Lloyd & Goold temp. Sugd. 333.

[122] Lewin, *Trusts* (3rd edn), 62–3.

[123] Meritorious consideration survived as a justification for equity judges to cure defective executions of powers: Sugden, *Powers* (8th edn, 1861), 530–5; G. Thomas, *Thomas on Powers* (1998), §§10–36 to 10–40.

[124] Lewin, *Trusts* (3rd edn), 62–4. Hill, *Trustees* (1845), 46n treats meritorious consideration as an historic curiosity.

In 1833 Sir Edward Sugden, during his brief first spell as Lord Chancellor of Ireland, attempted to undo the damage. The old law, he said in *Ellis* v. *Nimmo*, had not been completely dislodged; enough remained of meritorious consideration to justify him ordering performance of a father's otherwise voluntary promise to make a settlement on his daughter.[125] His successor quickly found alternative reasoning, counsel condemned him as antiquarian, Shadwell VC expressed his doubts, and in 1841 Lord Cottenham rejected the decision outright, never to be revived.[126] The simple law of obligations could no longer be used to enforce such promises. It is in this context that Wigram VC decided that sometimes a deed poll could be construed as creating a trust of the benefit of the covenant it contained, a proposition that was regarded as sound in theory though it was one that called for some imaginative application in practice.[127] Not many cases are reported as having followed this lead, perhaps because of judges' increasing concern that documents should be given their ordinary meaning, perhaps because the device depended upon the tenuous proposition that substantial damages for breach were available at common law. Whatever the reason, what would once have been easy was now precarious, at best.

As the law of obligation receded, so the need for clear rules for the initial validity of property dispositions as acts of will increased. From 1851 it could confidently be said that Lord Eldon had provided them— though he himself claimed merely to be restating established law.[128] In the 1830s and 1840s, however, it seems to have become unclear what it took to create an irrevocable trust *inter vivos* in favour of volunteers, even trusts for close family. There are two possible explanations, but no obvious way of choosing between them. One is that, where possible, some judges still saw voluntary *inter vivos* trusts as a species of obligation, broadly unenforceable because obligations to volunteers are only moral.[129] The second is more instrumental, that, where possible, they thought that a man's property should not be treated as having been put beyond reach of his creditors.

Creditors' interests had clearly been important to judges' limited validation of protective trusts, though even there judges often spoke as though they were

---

[125] *Ellis* v. *Nimmo* (1835) Lloyd & Goold temp. Sugd. 333; see also Sugden, *Powers* (8th edn), 534.

[126] *Ellis* v. *Nimmo* (1835) Lloyd & Goold temp. Sugd. 333n; *Holloway* v. *Headington* (1837) 8 Sim. 324, 6 LJ Ch 199 (NS); *Jeffreys* v. *Jeffreys* (1841) Cr. & Ph. 139; his (Cottenham's) ruling may also have been implicit in *Dillon* v. *Coppin* (1839) 4 My. & Cr. 647; Hill, *Trustees*, 46n; Peachey, *Settlements*, 242.

[127] *Fletcher* v. *Fletcher* (1844) 4 Hare 67; *Gandy* v. *Gandy* (1885) 30 Ch D 57; *re Patrick* [1891] 1 Ch 82; Underhill, *Trusts* (7th edn, 1912), 46–54.

[128] *Kekewich* v. *Manning* (1851) 1 De G. M. & G. 176, 16 Jur. 625, 21 LJ Ch 577, relying on *Ellison* v. *Ellison* (1802) 6 Ves. 662, *Ex p Pye, Ex p Dubost* (1811) 18 Ves. 140; and *Pulvertoft* v. *Pulvertoft* (1811) 18 Ves. 99.

[129] There is no discussion in the cases or the texts of the contemporaneous difficulties common law courts were experiencing with 'moral consideration'; see pp. 361–5, below.

merely neutral adjudicators of a property game. But when they determined the core of trusts law, the rules providing how an *inter vivos* trust might be created, the issue never surfaced, nor did it in the subsequent analysis in the textbooks. The matter is complicated by the two Elizabethan statutes that protected creditors, one directly the other indirectly. Both applied only to settlements that were 'voluntary'. First, the statute 13 Eliz. c. 5 enabled creditors to treat as fraudulent and void any voluntary settlement made at a time when the settlor was insolvent. It did not reach settlements made before his debts became that serious. Secondly, judges had long interpreted the Statute of Frauds of 1585 as rendering voluntary settlements of land void against a subsequent purchaser or mortgagee from the settlor.[130] The latter statute, particularly, affected some common forms of family settlement, as will be seen, but did not reach trusts of pure personalty. Whether either of them affected the way the judges viewed the general requirements for constituting a voluntary trust is quite unclear.

The doubts concerned both methods of constituting a trust. First, the text writers make out that some lawyers thought that a simple voluntary declaration of oneself to be trustee would not be effective. Thus Lewin was at pains to dispel the 'erroneous but not unfrequent supposition' that a voluntary trust required a 'Transmutation of possession, i.e., the legal interest must be divested from the settlor, and transferred to some third person'.[131] He did not elaborate whose supposition this was, when and in what context, but counsel can be found urging the point as late as 1842.[132] Nor did he say whether the false supposition was premised on some notion of ostensible ownership as a protection for creditors or on disbelief that such a bare declaration manifested an irrevocable intention. Hill thought a selection of cases from 1805 through to 1843 might plausibly support the supposition Lewin denied—though to modern eyes he seems to be stretching them.[133] Hill and Lewin, however, agreed that both principle and the better precedents supported Lord Eldon's opinion that a property owner could declare himself trustee of property—seemingly of any sort—that the trust would

---

[130] 27 Eliz. c. 4; Roberts, *Voluntary and Fraudulent Conveyances*; H. W. May, *A Treatise on the Statutes of Elizabeth Against Fraudulent Conveyances; and the Law of Voluntary Dispositions of Property* (2nd edn, by S. W. Worthington, 1887); Davidson *Precedents*, iii, (2nd edn, 1861), 832–7; Sugden, *Vendors and Purchasers* (10th edn, 1839), iii, 279–311, (14th edn, 1862), 712–22; Dart, *Vendors and Purchasers* (5th edn, 1876), ii, 889–904.

[131] Lewin, *Trusts* (3rd edn), 55.

[132] *Thorpe* v. *Owen* (1842) 11 LJ Ch 129 (a fuller report than 5 Beav. 224).

[133] Hill, *Trustees*, 48–9, citing esp. *Antrobus* v. *Smith* (1805) 12 Ves. 39; *Dillon* v. *Coppin* (1840) 4 Jur. 427; *Uniake* v. *Giles* 2 Moll. 267; *Edwards* v. *Jones* (1836) 1 M. & Cr. 264; *Meek* v. *Kettlewell* (1851) 1 Hare 472. See also *M'Fadden* v. *Jenkyns* (1842) 1 Hare 458 (Wigram VC); *Scales* v. *Maude* (1855) 6 De G. M. & G. 433 (Lord Cranworth), withdrawn (in some bewilderment that he had ever said it) in *Jones* v. *Lock* (1865) LR 1 Ch App 28.

be binding, and that it would be enforceable by the beneficiary even though a volunteer. [134] After *Kekewich* v. *Manning* in 1851 this became an axiom, if it had not been before.

It had never been doubted that if the owner of legal property adopted the second method of constituting a trust, transferring the property to trustees, the beneficiaries could enforce the trust even if they were volunteers. In 1808 Grant MR had probably held that even an equitable interest in pure personalty could likewise be assigned to trustees.[135] From the mid-1830s, however, the latter proposition was strongly denied and Grant MR's authority discredited. This was important, because the forms of property concerned were common: a would-be settlor's interest in property already held on trust for him, and his interest in debts and similar choses in action that were not assignable at common law or by statute.[136] Thus trust interests under wills and marriage settlements were affected, as were some forms of investment by loan on personal security. The argument was that because the would-be settlor could not transfer those sorts of asset at law, anyone seeking to enforce a purported transfer must come to equity. But equity would not assist a volunteer. It would treat those things as if assignable property only at the behest of a promisee for value, not now a promisee who was merely meritorious. It followed that purported transfers of such property to trustees for volunteer beneficiaries were simply ineffective. So held Lord Cottenham in 1836 in a ruling that was followed by a reasonably steady line of decisions, notably by Wigram VC.[137]

The decision of Knight Bruce LJ and Lord Cranworth in *Kekewich* v. *Manning* is significant not just for restoring what they presented as being the purity

---

[134] Hill, *Trusts*, 49; Lewin, *Trusts* (3rd edn), 55. In the much-discussed case of *Ex p Pye, Ex p Dubost* (1811) 18 Ves. 141— a case treated as far more significant later than it was at the time—Lord Eldon thought a letter sufficient to declare a trust of stock.

[135] *Sloane* v. *Cadogan*, reported only as an appendix to Sugden, *Vendors and Purchasers* through to its eleventh edition. Roberts, *Voluntary and Fraudulent Conveyances*, 662, is consistent with Grant MR's decision.

[136] The contrast was with shares and promissory notes, which were also choses in action but which were assignable

[137] *Edwards* v. *Jones* (1836) 1 My. & Cr. 225; *Beatson* v. *Beatson* (1841) 12 Sim. 281; *Ward* v. *Audland* (1845) 8 Beav. 201; *Meek* v. *Kettlewell* (1842) 1 Hare 464 (aff'd (1843) 1 Ph. 342) (that Wigram VC saw his decision in this light can be inferred from the accounts of his decision in *Kekewich* v. *Manning*, as reported in the arguments before the Lord Justices); *Scales* v. *Maude* (1855) 6 De G. M. & G. 43; *Sewell* v. *Moxsy* (1852) 2 Sim. (N.S.) 189. Contrast *Fortescue* v. *Barnett* (1834) 3 My. & K. 37 (a life assurance policy; sometimes explained as being assignable by convention); *Roberts* v. *Lloyd* (1840) 2 Beav. 376; *Pearson* v. *Amicable Assurance Office* (1859) 27 Beav. 229. Lewin, *Trusts* (6th edn, 1875), 62n, also cited *Airey* v. *Hall* (1856) 2 Jur. (N.S.) 658 and *Parnell* v. *Hingston* (1856) 2 Jur. (N.S.) 854 as decisions that such voluntary assignments were possible; but the former concerned consols and the latter notes and deposit notes, all of which were assignable, and the decisions seem anyway to turn on Stuart VC's willingness to hold that the assignor did enough to declare himself a trustee.

articulated by Lord Eldon and Grant MR, but also for shifting the focus away from the supposed inabilities of voluntary recipients.[138] Instead they grounded the law firmly upon the essential prerogatives of property owners. Those necessarily included the ability to give voluntarily and irrevocably, they said, and so the law must provide a way. That way, as completed by Page Wood VC shortly afterwards, was very easy: a clear written statement assigning an equitable interest in property held on trust was to be effective without necessity for notice to the trustee, far less the trustee's agreement.[139] Knight Bruce and Cranworth's appeal to Eldon and Grant, justified though it was by the conventions of legal reasoning, did not disguise from all commentators the modernity of their doctrine.[140] Their 'liberal and enlightened' decision was part of law's progress as a science, said Stuart VC, necessary to maximize an owner's right of alienation and hence 'the value to its owners of the enormous and increasing amount of reversionary personal property'.[141]

The axiom established by *Kekewich* v. *Manning*, and that might well have been held also by Lord Eldon, was circular no doubt, but important nonetheless: anything that counts as property can be transferred to trustees on a voluntary trust by one means or another. Functionally the decision created a property law to achieve what Sir Edward Sugden had sought in his unsuccessful revival of an obsolete law of obligation, and it is probably significant that Knight Bruce LJ raised Sugden's decision in *Ellis* v. *Nimmo* during argument in *Kekewich* v. *Manning*. There were important differences between the two approaches. For one thing, by not denying that these settlements were voluntary Knight Bruce LJ and Lord Cranworth did not immunize them from subsequent attack by creditors in an insolvency. More technically, it followed from *Kekewich* v. *Manning* that what was not 'property' could not be assigned nor made the immediate subject of a voluntary trust. It could only be promised, and the promise would now be enforced only under the modern law of consideration. Anticipated legacies, 'mere expectancies', were the major example of real-life assets consigned to that category.[142]

---

[138] *Kekewich v Manning* (1851) 1 De G. M. & G. 176, 16 Jur. 625, 21 LJ Ch 577.

[139] *Kekewich* v. *Manning* (1851) 1 De G. M. & G. 176, 16 Jur. 625, 21 LJ Ch 577; *Donaldson* v. *Donaldson* (1854) Kay 711. See also *Bentley* v. *Mackay* (1851) 15 Beav. 12 and *Voyle* v. *Hughes* (1854) 2 Sm. & G. 18. These new cases did not explicitly hold that voluntary assignments of choses in action should likewise be valid in equity, but subsequently they were taken to establish that principle too: *re King* (1879) 14 Ch D 179; *Harding* v. *Harding* (1886) 17 QBD 442; *re Patrick* [1891] 1 Ch 82; *re Spark's Trusts* [1904] 1 Ch 457.

[140] See esp. Davidson, *Precedents*, iii, (2nd edn, 1861), 846–8.

[141] *Voyle* v. *Hughes* (1854) 2 Sm. & G. 18, which was an assignment of a woman's one-fifth share, as next of kin, in the residuary interest arising under her deceased sister's marriage settlement. Stuart VC must have meant social value.

[142] This became the accepted explanation for *Meek* v. *Kettlewell* (1842) 1 Hare 464, (1843) 1 Ph. 342; *Penfold* v. *Mould* (1867) LR 4 Eq 564; *re Parsons* (1890) 45 Ch D 51; Lewin, *Trusts* (10th edn), 75.

A significant practical difficulty remained. It was now true that anything that counted as property could be transferred to a voluntary trust by one means or another; but the means mattered, and they varied with the sort of property concerned. The settlor must accomplish the transfer in the appropriate way. If the law had remained a law of obligation, then, as Lewin had said, 'formality' of this sort would often have been a mere matter of performance, not of initial validity. Within the family a single promise in a single deed poll would have been tantamount to a declaration of trust concerning whatever assortment of property the promisor chose to list. That would be convenient, because settlors who regarded their wealth as fungible might easily, but erroneously, think that a comprehensive deed of assignment to trustees would carry it all, just as a will would.[143]

Rescue might sometimes be possible through finding that the settlor had had, and expressed, two intentions: to transfer property to trustees, and meanwhile to hold the property on trust while the technicalities of the transfer were worked out. Perhaps what looked like a purported transfer had really been meant as a trust. Lord Eldon had once decided something like that, and judges such as Romilly MR and Malins VC would happily follow suit.[144] But most judges stressed the difference between the two sorts of intention, and hence, given the sway of the 'ordinary meaning' school of construction, the necessity of finding something express in a document ostensibly establishing others as trustees if it was also to function as a declaration of the transferor as an interim trustee.[145]

In 1867 Page Wood VC used the ethos of *Kekewich* v. *Manning* in an imaginative attempt to simplify matters further. Faced with an omnibus assignment that was ineffective as regards some promissory notes, because they needed either endorsement or delivery, he extrapolated a general proposition that 'an instrument executed as a present and complete assignment (not being a mere covenant to assign on a future day) is equivalent to a declaration of trust'.[146] This would

Contrast Hill's uncertainty whether this or the general principle better explained *Meek*: *Trustees*, 49, 51.

[143] For examples, see *Dillon* v. *Coppin* (1839) 4 My. & Cr. 647; *Ward* v. *Audland* (1845) 8 Beav. 201; *Bridge* v. *Bridge* (1852) 16 Beav. 315; *Powell* v. *Hingston* (1856) 2 Jur. (N.S.) 854; and cf. *Jefferys* v. *Jefferys* (1841) Cr. & Ph. 139.

[144] *Ex p Pye, Ex p Dubost* (1811) 18 Ves. 141; *Grant* v. *Grant* (1865) 34 Beav. 623; cf. *Morgan* v. *Malleson* (1870) LR 10 Eq 475 (Romilly); *Baddeley* v. *Baddeley* (1878) 9 Ch D 113 (Malins).

[145] *Dillon* v. *Coppin* (1839) 4 My. & Cr. 647; *Searle* v. *Law* (1846) 15 Sim. 95; *Bridge* v. *Bridge* (1852) 16 Beav. 315; *Voyle* v. *Hughes* (1854) 2 Sm. & G. 18; *Parnell* v. *Hingston* (1856) 2 Jur. (N.S.) 854.

[146] *Richardson* v. *Richardson* (1867) LR 3 Eq 686, reiterated in *Penfold* v. *Mould* (1867) LR 4 Eq 562. Gregory Alexander argues that Lord Eldon held this position in *Ex p Pye, Ex. p Dubost* and that the retreat from it later in the nineteenth century is an important element in a transformation of trusts from being a relatively general to a highly specific and differentiated concept: 'Transformation of Trusts'. There seem to me to be three difficulties with this part of his argument: (1) Lord Eldon did

have been a significant change. But he carried only Romilly MR with him; all other reaction was hostile.[147] It was in this context that Jessel MR gave the well-known reiteration of orthodoxy that has survived down into modern textbooks.[148] Intended transfers that failed for technical reasons must instead be assimilated to mere promises, hence unenforceable by volunteers, rather than to declarations of trust. Page Wood VC's proposition would have introduced a new form of voluntary transfer that would have superseded all others, and hence seemed like equity contradicting the common law.[149] It would also have contradicted the ordinary meaning of words, said Jessel MR.

One final aspect of the constitution of trusts remained to be modernized. It arose from a refinement of marriage settlements, the covenant to settle after-acquired property on the trusts of the settlement.[150] This was a potent device. Because the wife and children gave marriage consideration the trusts in their favour were treated as attaching automatically to the after-acquired property when it fell into possession, without need for formal transfer to the trustees. Secondly, by stretching the marriage consideration forward in time the covenants effectually obliged the husband/father to make a settlement that had he made merely voluntarily would have been vulnerable to his creditors. But such covenants were usually mutual, and that brought a risk to the wife that they would overshoot. If her promise had not been carefully qualified, and her marriage was short, and she inherited property from her own family after her husband died, then the trustees of her marriage settlement might still call on her to perform her covenant—for the benefit of a child perhaps, or even, depending on how the settlement was worded, for her next of kin. She would still enjoy her life interest, but would have lost the capital.

not purport to lay down a general rule, merely to interpret the letter concerned; (2) to read him as laying down such a general principle contradicts the other evidence of his thought expressed in *Ellison* v. *Ellison* (1802) 6 Ves. 565 and *Pulvertoft* v. *Pulvertoft* (1811) 18 Ves. 99, whereas taking him at face value does not; (3) the report gives us neither Eldon's reasons for interpreting the letter as a trust nor the text that he was interpreting. In these circumstances to attribute possible reasons to him and to analyse what other judges would have made of the (unknown) text seems unduly speculative. In fairness, Page Wood VC in *Richardson* v. *Richardson* also thought he knew what the letter must have said.

[147] *Morgan* v. *Malleson* (1870) LR 10 Eq 475; contrast *Warriner* v. *Rogers* (1873) LR 16 Eq 340; *Richards* v. *Delbridge* (1874) LR 18 Eq 11; *Moore* v. *Moore* (1874) LR 18 Eq 474; *Heartley* v. *Nicholson* (1874) LR 19 Eq 233; re *Breton's Estate* (1881) 17 Ch D 416; re *Shield* (1885) 56 LT 5.

[148] *Richards* v. *Delbridge* (1874) LR 18 Eq 11. Both judges who decided *Kekewich* v. *Manning* had already explicitly endorsed this orthodoxy: *Milroy* v. *Lord* (1862) 4 De G. F. & J. 264 (Knight Bruce LJ); *Jones* v. *Lock* (1865) LR 1 Ch. App. 25, 11 Jur. 913 (Lord Cranworth).

[149] *Milroy* v. *Lord* (1862) 4 De G. F. & J. 264; *Richards* v. *Delbridge* (1874) LR 18 Eq 11.

[150] Davidson, *Precedents*, iii (2nd edn), 142–60, 569–72; Peachey, *Settlements*, 523, 828n, and examples at 787–9, 807–10, 875–7.

In the 1830s Lord Langdale's solution was to concede the possibility—rather contrary to the general principle against aiding volunteers—but to avoid it by reading the covenant as impliedly limited to the duration of the marriage, on the ground that the spouses would not have intended to benefit the wife's next of kin.[151] The next two stages in the development were unsurprising: doubts in the 1850s as the 'ordinary meaning' principle labelled such an overtly purposive approach speculative, followed by enthusiastic revival in the hands of Malins VC.[152] In the later cases the trustees were suing on behalf of a child, not the next of kin, but, as Hall VC explained, freeing up the capital for a young widow facilitated a second marriage.[153] The ordinary Victorian course would have been for the Court of Appeal to impose a more literal reading in the 1870s or 1880s, but James LJ got in first. Fortified by an informal consultation with the Lord Chancellor (Selborne), he announced that Lord Langdale's interpretation was a rule to be applied generally to all such covenants to settle after-acquired property.[154] Jessel MR could only grumble at this departure from general interpretive principle.[155] It survived undamaged until 1909, indeed being applied in an ever more purposive manner, until Swinfen Eady J. flicked it aside and insisted on application of the conventional standard.[156] Modern legal science asserted itself almost immediately however. As these were covenants they could be directly enforced only by persons who gave value. Indirect enforcement should be no different. Hence trustees could sue on behalf of children of the marriage but not on behalf of next of kin.[157] If spouses wanted something different they should make it explicit in the settlement.

The result of all this was a precise, differentiated structure. It distinguished assignments on trust from declarations of trust, and both from promises. It necessitated a further distinction between existing property and future property, and sometimes it distinguished between the constituent subcategories of property. Which concepts had been used in any particular disposition depended on the

---

[151] *Howell* v. *Howell* (1835) 4 LJ Ch 242; *Godsal* v. *Webb* (1838) 2 Keen 99. For an example of an express limitation, see Davidson, *Precedents*, vol. iii (2nd edn), 659–70. Compare *Wolley* v. *Jenkins* (1856) 23 Beav. 53, affirmed (1857) 3 Jur. (N.S.) 321, where the trustees' power to sell land contained in a marriage settlement was held to be limited to the duration of the (childless) marriage.

[152] *Stevens* v. *Van Voorst* (1853) 17 Beav. 305, contrast *Reid* v. *Fenwick* (1855) 24 LJ Ch 503; *Dickinson* v. *Dillwyn* (1869) LR 8 Eq 546; *Carter* v. *Carter* (1869) LR 8 Eq 551.

[153] *Re Campbell's Policies* (1877) 16 Ch D 686.

[154] *Re Edwards* (1873) LR 9 Ch App 97, overruling *Stevens* v. *Van Voorst*.

[155] *Holloway* v. *Holloway* (1877) 25 WR 575.

[156] *Re Ellis's Settlement* [1909] 1 Ch 618, followed in *re Plumptre's Settlement* [1910] 1 Ch 609; *re Pryce's Settlement* [1917] 1 Ch 234. For earlier development, see *Fisher* v. *Shirley* (1889) 43 Ch D 290; *re Coghlan* [1894] 3 Ch 76 and *Coles* v. *Coles* [1901] 1 Ch 311.

[157] *Re Plumptre's Settlement* [1910] 1 Ch 609; *re Pryce's Settlement* [1917] 1 Ch 234; see also *re D'Angibau* (1880) 15 Ch D 228.

disponer's intention as demonstrated by the words he or she had used. Intention was sufficient if it was that the disponer become the trustee himself, but must be coupled with action if it was that someone else be trustee. As Stuart VC put it, this was the essence of the modern, liberal, science of law.[158] It focused on the individual act of will, manifested with the sort of precision that benefited from early resort to specialized lawyers. Sugden's attempted revival of meritorious consideration had instead looked backwards to an older world in which the focus was on acknowledgment of social obligation. Meritorious consideration thus had something in common with the 'general intention' method of interpreting wills, and it went the same way, though earlier.[159] It had some of the same appeal to judges such as Romilly MR and Malins VC, but they were distinctly in a minority.

Revoking a Trust

True to his proprietary model Lord Eldon had been very clear that once a settlor had constituted a trust it was beyond recall, however voluntary its inception.[160] Property settlements were not provisional performance of continuing social obligations. So judges routinely resurrected trusts that settlors, mistakenly believing them to be intrinsically revocable like wills, had purported to terminate by scissors or mere say-so.[161]

Important though the principle was, it was formal. To be lawful, revocation merely required the appropriate tool from the property lawyer's kit bag. Hence Davidson recommended that voluntary settlements should always contain express powers of revocation or of appointment paramount to the trusts, in recognition of their 'quasi-testamentary' operation.[162] Likewise his marriage settlements provided that if the marriage was childless a woman who survived her husband should regain her fund absolutely, and, in case she should not survive him, she should have a testamentary power of appointment in priority to the default trust for her next of kin.[163] Appointments made under a power of appointment could

[158] *Voyle* v. *Hughes* (1854) 2 Sm. & G. 18.

[159] See pp. 26–31, above.

[160] *Ellison* v. *Ellison* (1802) 6 Ves. 565. He insisted upon this despite knowing that the settlement would shortly be overridden by a transaction under the Statute of Frauds 1585. Peachey thought this 'one of his most important judgments': *Settlements*, 245.

[161] *Huguenin* v. *Baseley* (1804) 14 Ves. 273; *Bill* v. *Cureton* (1835) 2 My. & K. 503; *Smith* v. *Lyne* (1843) 2 Y. & C.Ch.Cas. 345; *Paterson* v. *Murphy* (1853) 11 Hare 88; *Toker* v. *Toker* (1863) 3 De G. J. & S. 487. Contrast cases where judges held the trust never came into effect at all.

[162] Davidson, *Precedents*, iii, (2nd edn), 823–5n. Appointments could be revocable. The theory and use of powers was of considerable importance, and would merit detailed research.

[163] Davidson, *Precedents*, iii, (2nd edn), 713–14, 812–13.

themselves be made revocable, unless the power was worded to exclude that or unless the appointment had been acted upon by a distribution.

This law of powers was carried over from the eighteenth century and, technical details aside, it raised very little controversy—though its exposition ran to hundreds of pages.[164] The flexibility of property settlements of all sorts rested upon its workings, which were taken for granted by nineteenth-century practitioners and which have remained largely unexplored.[165] The most notable decision during our period aided that flexibility by holding, contrary to ancient authority, that if a revocable appointment is indeed revoked the original power to appoint is presumptively revived, and hence may be exercised again.[166] Text writers can be found reminding their professional readers of their duty to raise these possibilities with their clients when drafting settlements.[167]

Further, in a functional sense only settlements of pure personalty were truly irrevocable. Voluntary settlements of land were revocable by the settlor, whether or not he had included an express power of revocation, provided he regarded the land as fungible. This flowed from the long-standing judicial interpretation of the Statute of Frauds 1585 that rendered such settlements void against a subsequent purchaser or mortgagee of the settlor; not revocation in the strict sense, but near enough.[168] The Act seemed not to say any such thing, and judges were sometimes perplexed by the breadth and consequences of its received interpretation that allowed a settlement to be overridden even if the settlor had made the settlement in good faith and while fully solvent, and even if the purchaser knew of the settlement before purchase.[169] But they loyally took their cue from a decision of Lord Ellenborough's King's Bench in 1807, that surprising and even unjust though the received interpretation was, for a court to change it now would shake land

[164] H. Chance, *A Treatise on Powers* (1831, 1841) E. Sugden, *Practical Treatise of Powers* (1808, to 8th edn, 1861); G. Farwell, *Concise Treatise on Powers* (1874, 1893, 1916).

[165] The modern text by G. Thomas, *Thomas on Powers* notices many historical details in passing.

[166] *Saunders* v. *Evans* (1855) 6 De G. M. & G. 654 (LJJ), (1861) 8 H.L.C. 721; the same conclusion had already been reached by the Exchequer in *Montague* v. *Kater* (1853) 8 Exch. 507.

[167] For example Dart, *Vendors and Purchasers* (5th edn, 1876), ii, 903.

[168] 27 Eliz. c. 4; Roberts, *Voluntary and Fraudulent Conveyances*; May (by Worthington), *Statutes of Elizabeth*; Davidson *Precedents*, iii (2nd edn) 832–7; Sugden, *Vendors and Purchasers* (10th edn, 1839), vol. iii, 279–311, (14th edn, 1862), 712–22; Dart, *Vendors and Purchasers* (5th edn, 1876), ii, 889–904. The statute applied to 'land', not just realty, and the term was interpreted broadly.

[169] *Buckle* v. *Mitchell* (1812) 18 Ves. 110 (Grant MR); *Clarke* v. *Wright* (1861) 6 H. & N. 849 (Cockburn CJ); *AG* v. *Jacobs Smith* [1895] 2 QB 341 (Lindley LJ); cf. Williams, *Settlement*, 356. For distaste for the rule, and the limits on what distaste could achieve, see *Smith* v. *Garland* (1817) 2 Mer. 123; *Clarke* v. *Willett* (1872) LR 7 Ex 313; Dart, *Vendors and Purchasers* (5th edn), ii, 999, 1046; Sugden, *Vendors and Purchasers* (14th edn), 720; but contrast *Butterfield* v. *Heath* (1852) 15 Beav. 408. Judges would also sometimes find that an apparently voluntary settlement had in fact been made for consideration: Sugden, *Vendors and Purchasers* (14th edn), 720.

titles.[170] Nor would judges accept as good law an eighteenth-century authority that had softened the rule by providing that the purchase money was to be held on the trusts of the settlement. That had been an isolated decision, they said, contrary to the ethos of the statute.[171] These rules were applied to settlements on trust just as they were to settlements at law. A settlor who conveyed land to trustees on voluntary trusts could subsequently pass good title to a purchaser or mortgagee even if they had notice, and even though the settlor had retained no legal estate for himself.[172] He or his creditors could then keep the money.

Moreover beneficiaries were not usually allowed to argue that a settlement was to be taken as a whole, such that a valuable consideration 'ran through' it. Instead, the King's Bench and the Master of the Rolls confirmed in 1817, each disposition in a settlement of land was to be tested individually for voluntariness.[173] In marriage settlements this worked to keep the wealth within the spouses' control. Usually those settlements gave collateral relatives interests in default of children of the marriage. But collateral relatives fell outside the marriage consideration and so were volunteers. The spouses to a childless marriage, or the surviving spouse, could therefore override their interests by sale or mortgage.[174] Similarly, when a widow remarried, the limitations of her land in her second marriage settlement in favour of her husband and their future children would automatically cancel limitations in favour of collateral relatives in her first.[175]

'Voluntary' had come to mean any settlement other than for money or money's worth. Thus post-nuptial settlements of land by a father on his children, or by a husband on his wife, were now seen as 'voluntary' and hence revocable by his subsequent sale or mortgage.[176] Until the 1850s that was true even when the

---

[170] *Doe d. Otley* v. *Manning* (1807) 9 East 59. This sentiment did not stop them holding, contrary to a seventeenth-century decision, that the statute worked only in favour of transactions by the settlor, not by his heir or devisees claiming under him. It would be quite contrary to policy, said Williams J. and Lord Campbell CJ, if a settlor's eldest son could subvert a voluntary settlement made by the father on his younger children by selling the land and keeping the proceeds: *Doe d. Richards* v. *Lewis* (1852) 11 C.B. 1035; *Doe d. Newman* v. *Rusham* (1852) 17 Q.B. 723; *Lewis* v. *Rees* (1856) 3 K. & J. 132; cf. *Godfrey* v. *Poole* (1888) 13 App Cas 497.

[171] *Daking* v. *Whimper* (1859) 26 Beav. 568; *Townend* v. *Toker* (1866) LR 1 Ch App 446; cf. re *Walhampton Estate* (1884) 26 Ch D 391. Again, one reason was that to do so might have imposed a duty on the purchaser to see to the proper application of the money.

[172] *Cotterell* v. *Homer* (1843) 13 Sim. 506; *Townend* v. *Toker* (1866) LR 1 Ch App 446.

[173] *Johnson* v. *Legard* (1817) 6 M. & S. 60, (1818) 3 Madd. 283, (1822) Turn. & R. 295 (Eldon). Contrast e.g. *Tucker* v. *Bennett* (1887) 38 Ch D 1, a rectification case.

[174] *Johnson* v. *Legard* (1817) 6 M. & S. 60, (1818) 3 Madd. 283, (1822) Turn. & R. 295; *Sutton* v. *Chetwynd* (1817) 3 Mer. 249; *Cotterell* v. *Homer* (1843) 13 Sim. 506. The principle is explained well in *Smith* v. *Cherrill* (1867) LR 4 Eq 390.

[175] May (by Worthington), *Statutes of Elizabeth*, 223.

[176] *Goodright d. Humphreys* v. *Moses* (1773) 2 W. Bl. 1019; *Currie* v. *Nind* (1835) 1 My. & Cr. 17; *Butterfield* v. *Heath* (1852) 15 Beav. 408; *Barton* v. *Vanheythusen, Stone* v. *Vanheythusen* (1853) 11 Hare 126; *Green* v. *Paterson* (1888) 13 App Cas 497.

husband's settlement on his wife was of an interest in land that had come to him only by virtue of his marriage to her. Then judges began to hold that adjustments of each spouse's rights in a wife's after-acquired property were contractual rather than voluntary, and thus secure against purchasers.[177] This was a modern contractualism, not a revival of meritorious consideration. It did not extend to securing the children's interests.

Curiously, however, a second example suggests both that the policy of meritorious consideration did still appeal to some judges— though by a narrow margin—perhaps also that men's voluntary dispositions were distrusted more than women's. It arose when a woman with interests in land made provision in a marriage settlement for children she had already had, by a previous husband perhaps, or out of wedlock. By no modern understanding had those children given 'value'; hence they should have been vulnerable to a subsequent sale or mortgage by their mother, instigated perhaps by their new stepfather. They were lucky. Long ago Lord Hardwicke had ruled that policy required that they be treated as having given consideration, and though some mid-nineteenth judges (and some text writers) found his decision perplexing and unjustifiable, other judges approved and declined to overrule it.[178] It limped through the 1860s, tottered in the 1880s, but was not finally overtaken by orthodoxy until 1891.[179]

By then the long-standing reading of the Elizabethan Statute of Frauds that allowed settlors to override their settlements of land had lost any justification. From 1869 general bankruptcy statutes had introduced priority rules that addressed all these issues. One catalyst had been lawyers' reaction to the vulnerability of post-nuptial settlements of land on wives and children. By inserting into marriage settlements a covenant to settle after-acquired property drafters enabled a subsequent settlement to be construed as performance of an obligation supported by the marriage consideration, hence as not being 'voluntary'. The logic, however, though compelling was socially undiscriminating. While

---

[177] *Hewison* v. *Negus* (1853) 16 Beav. 594, 22 LJ Ch 655, 657; *Teasdale* v. *Braithwaite* (1876) 4 Ch D 85, (1877) 5 Ch D 630; *re Foster and Lister* (1877) 6 Ch D 87; *Green* v. *Paterson* (1888) 13 App Cas 497.

[178] *Newstead* v. *Searles (or Searle)* (1737) 1 Atk. 265, West t. Hard. 287; cf. *Clayton* v. *Earl of Wilton* (1813) 6 M. & S. 67n. *Clarke* v. *Wright* (1861) 6 H. & N. 849, and, earlier, *sub. nom. Dickenson* v. *Wright* (1860) 5 H. & N. 401. May (by Worthington), *Statutes of Elizabeth*, 342–53; Dart, *Vendors and Purchasers* (5th edn), ii, 894–7.

[179] *De Mestre* v. *West* [1891] AC 264 (PC). Lord Selborne held that there was no such categorical exception, merely a principle that volunteers whose interests had been so entangled in the settlement with those of the children of the marriage that to disentangle them would give the latter significantly more or less than the settlement intended. The decision was foreshadowed in *Mackie* v. *Herbertson* (1884) 9 App Cas 303 (a Scottish appeal); *Price* v. *Jenkins* (1875) 4 Ch D 483 (reversed on other grounds (1877) 5 Ch D 619). See also *re Cameron and Wells* (1887) 37 Ch D 32, where Kay J. refused to extend *Newstead* v. *Searles* to marriage settlements by widowers.

it protected the wife's future property it could be used equally well to shield the husband's from his creditors. So in due course there was legislation, which enacted a set of compromises.[180] It kept the framework judges had developed, but introduced distinctions between executed and executory covenants that judges probably would not have been able to, even if they had wanted to, and stipulated time limits for the challenging of voluntary settlements, which judges certainly could not have done. With the extension of bankruptcy from traders to all debtors in 1883 this provision left the longstanding judicial reading of the Elizabethan Statute of Frauds unnecessary for the protection of creditors and at odds with the modern liberal view of property and individual agency. It was abrogated by statute in 1893, uncontroversially and almost unnoticed, probably because a Privy Council decision had shown up anomalies that could not honourably be left unaddressed.[181]

Given that for most of our period voluntary settlements of land were functionally revocable and that any settlor could reserve an express power of revocation, it is unsurprising that some settlors of personalty whose lawyers had not had such foresight should feel that they were victims of a principle honoured usually in the breach. In the mid-century two related types of settlor, each technically adult, did manage to persuade judges that the consequences of making an irrevocable settlement were so serious that they should be allowed to set theirs aside. It is unclear what if anything there was before then, hence whether these settlors' applications were a response to the hardening of the proprietary canon in *Kekewich* v. *Manning*. Some were unmarried women who, on coming of age or coming into money, had made pre-emptive settlements to trustees on trust for themselves for life, then to any future husband and children, much as in a marriage settlement, with ultimate limitations over to their next of kin.[182] The others were spendthrift young men cajoled into settlements for their own good and their family's peace of mind. Both classes of voluntary settlor might soon chafe under their settlement's restrictions if it contained no powers of revocation or of general appointment and if the ultimate limitations were tightly drawn.

---

[180] Bankruptcy Act 1869 s 91; Bankruptcy Act 1883 s 47; Williams, *Settlement*, 363–5. Davidson had worried that protecting a husband in this way was an abuse: *Precedents*, iii (2nd edn), 571–2n.

[181] Voluntary Conveyances Act 1893, introduced by Lord Macnaghten. See (1892) 36 *Sol. J.* 536, (1893) 37 *Sol. J.* 318; *Ramsay* v. *Gilchrist* [1892] AC 412; *Price* v. *Jenkins* (1877) 5 Ch D 619 (and compare *Ex p Hillman* (1879) 10 Ch D 622; *re Ridler* (1882) 22 Ch D 74; *re Marsh and Earl Granville* (1883) 24 Ch D 11; *Harris* v. *Tubb* (1889) 42 Ch D 79); *re Walhampton Estate* (1884) 26 Ch D 391. The Act provided that *bona fide* voluntary settlements were not to be defeated by a subsequent purchase for value, quietly ending 300 years of judicial interpretation. It was retrospective, except for saving existing transactions.

[182] In addition to the cases cited below, see *Maber* v. *Hobbs* (1836) 2 Y. & C. Ex. 317. Protection from fortune hunters was the accepted explanation.

Mid-century judges were sympathetic to their claims that the impact of the settlement on their property had not been fully explained to them, and that had it been they would not have signed.[183] At its high point in 1870 this willingness to set dispositions aside strayed close to attaching to any voluntary settlement that did not contain a power of revocation, extended to limitations in favour of volunteers in marriage settlements, and, in the hands of Malins VC, to a re-settlement that omitted the usual powers.[184] Judicial descent was gradual, but definite both in its rhetoric and its results.[185] It was, emphatically, not enough, said Jessel MR, that a voluntary settlement did not take the usual form; the only thing that mattered was whether settlors understood what they were doing.[186] Predictably, then, when Malins VC pronounced in *Paul* v. *Paul* that any voluntary settlement should be deemed revocable for good reason—in this case to enable a separated married woman to clear her debts and rebuild her life—the Court of Appeal was abruptly dismissive.[187]

Thus Lord Eldon's simple proprietary model was complete. The state might in some circumstances annul a voluntary settlement (of any form of property) in the interests of creditors, who would thus have priority over the beneficiaries' property interests, but the settlor himself could retract the settlement, or revoke an interest conferred by it, only if he had reserved a power to do so. The implication of Malins VC's bid in *Paul* v. *Paul* and of Davidson's precedents is that powers of revocation were common in voluntary settlements. They demonstrate very clearly how formal the system was. The building blocks of property law were there to be used, manipulated, and worked around by lawyers whose technical knowledge could be acquired from comprehensive professional texts readily, if expensively, available to all. Everyone could work from the same templates. All they needed was to express their variations in the correct idiom. As Knight Bruce LJ tetchily complained when struggling with a point of law that could so easily

[183] *Nanney* v. *Williams* (1856) 22 Beav. 452; *Forshaw* v. *Welsby* (1860) 30 Beav. 243; *Anderson* v. *Emsworth* (1861) 7 Jur. (N.S.) 1047; *Prideaux* v. *Lonsdale* (1863) 1 De G. J. & S. 433; cf. *Harbridge* v. *Wogan* (1846) 5 Hare 258 (marriage settlement); *Welman* v. *Welman* (1880) 15 Ch D 570. In some cases there are undertones of undue influence.

[184] *Coutts* v. *Acworth* (1869) LR 8 Eq 558; *Wollaston* v. *Tribe* (1869) LR 9 Eq 44 (clause in marriage settlement); *Everitt* v. *Everitt* (1870) LR 10 Eq 405; *Mountford* v. *Keene* (1871) 19 WR 708; see also *Smith* v. *Iliffe* (1875) LR 20 Eq 666.

[185] *Phillips* v. *Mullings* (1871) LR 7 Ch App 244; *Hall* v. *Hall* (1872) LR 14 Eq 365, (1873) LR 8 Ch App 430; *Henry* v. *Armstrong* (1881) 18 Ch D 668; *Dutton* v. *Thompson* (1883) 23 Ch D 278.

[186] *Dutton* v. *Thompson* (1883) 23 Ch D 278. North J. completed the transition by shifting the usual remedy to a limited rectification rather than setting aside: *James* v. *Couchman* (1885) 29 Ch D. 212; and compare *Tucker* v. *Bennett* (1887) 38 Ch D 1, a marriage settlement case, where *Wollaston* v. *Tribe* and *Smith* v. *Iliffe* were disapproved.

[187] *Paul* v. *Paul* (1882) 20 Ch D 742 confirming Fry J. (1881) 19 Ch D 547 and overruling *Paul* v. *Paul* (1880) 15 Ch D 580 (Malins VC).

have been avoided if the solicitor had just spelled out his client's intention one step further than he had, 'what are lawyers for?'[188] Policy could come in over the top, as it were, from statute.

3. TRUSTEES

It has also become conventional that trusteeship became more difficult. This is asserted less of trusts of land or houses, where trustees' management duties and their potential personal liability on leasehold covenants must always have been onerous, than it is about trusts of funds. Trusts, even of funds, remained devices for *holding* property—preservation remained trustees' primary obligation—but decisions in the aftermath of the South Sea bubble had established both a general duty to produce a secure income and a prohibition on trustees' use of the property for their own benefit.[189] The result was a differentiation from beneficial ownership sharp enough to inspire two books in the 1820s warning would-be trustees of the perils of office.[190] As trusts became so commonly used to facilitate a staged transmission of wealth between succeeding generations, a rich variety of circumstance and personality induced, as one writer soberly described, 'a probability of conflicting opinion as to [their] management'.[191] The basic conflict between capital preservation and income production intensified as capital markets developed, multiplying choice of investments that varied in their safety and in their impact on the relationship between life tenant and remaindermen.

In the 1820s an ideal trustee might sit at the intersection of family and local business networks, his knowledge and influence highly desirable trust assets in the placing of loans on mortgage, which was the primary trust investment aside from government securities.[192] Depending on how ambitious settlors were for their trustees, however, that local expertise soon came to need supplementing, or even replacing, with knowledge and understanding of the impersonal workings of regional and national capital markets. That shift provoked subtle changes in the nature of trusteeship. Trusteeship always was a personal confidence requiring personal attention to the performance of its fiduciary duties, but by the end of the century reliance on expert advice became much more acceptable— though trustees needed to plead it, of course, only when the advice had turned out to be mistaken or the advisor dishonest. The shift in attitude on that question complemented shifts that made for more efficient continuity in trust administration.

---

[188] *Evans* v. *Saunders* (1855) 6 De G. M. & G. 654.
[189] On the persistence of the primary obligation see e.g. Underhill, *Trusts* (7th edn), 279.
[190] Hampson, *Short Treatise*; Grant, *Advice to Trustees*.
[191] Grant, *Advice to Trustees*, 38.
[192] Morris, *Men, Women and Property*, 264–317.

It became easier for trustees to retire, easier for them to be replaced, and the mechanics of those transitions became easier too. Trusteeship became a little less personal and a little more in the nature of a transmissible office.

Chantal Stebbings, the historian of trustees in Victorian England, writes that issues of delegation and investment exceeded all others in importance, save for the overarching and critical question of how trustees' liability for breach should be formulated.[193] Her thesis, that inadvertent breach was too easy, liability too severe, and that the resulting deterrent effect produced a trustee shortage intermittently throughout the century, is supported by contemporary texts. It was always possible for settlors to offer a douceur, usually in the form of a small legacy as a reward, or even stipulate that their trustees be paid for their time and trouble, but judges discouraged the latter and the general culture was against it too.[194] So the market could provide only indirectly, which it did through the emergence of the solicitor-trustee as a common figure, paid not for his work as trustee but for the legal services the trust required or, at least, generated. Notoriously, judges found that a difficult line to patrol, such that express authorization was needed save for litigation costs.[195] Importantly, however, access to trust funds enabled solicitors to generate business from other clients—as for example when they lent trust funds on mortgage to a site developer and then did his conveyancing work for him. Such fees, the courts ruled, were too remote a profit for the trust to claim as trust property.[196] Solicitors thus acquired a stake in trusteeships, which in due course spilled over into law reform proposals, and into some collective antipathy to suggestions that corporate or public trustees be instituted.

Achieving Continuity

To be an effective tool for intergenerational property management, a trust needed administrative continuity, especially a trust where the management was meant to be active. During our period three interlocking developments ultimately ensured that continuity. They arose piecemeal and were not always greeted wholeheartedly by the judges. One was that appointment of new trustees to fill a vacancy or to enable a retirement became easier. The second was that it became the incontrovertible general rule that successor trustees acquired the powers of the original trustees, whether appointed by a court or privately under the trust instrument. A settlor who wanted

---

[193] Stebbings, *Private Trustee*, 18.

[194] In Peachey's precedents he suggests payment—rather that the settlor might appropriately consider the propriety of payment—only for his active discretionary trust: *Settlements*, 890–6.

[195] C. Stebbings, 'The Rule in Cradock v. Piper' (1998) 19 *JLH* 189–202 and *Private Trustee*, 37–42. For an optimistically simple precedent for such a charging clause, see Peachey, *Settlements*, 692n.

[196] *Whitney* v. *Smith* (1869) LR 4 Ch App 573; *re Corsellis* (1887) 34 Ch D 675.

it otherwise must say so explicitly. Thirdly it became easier to vest trust property in new trustees, or to their order. That involved two different processes: property had to be got out of trustees who were still the legal owners but for one reason or another were unable to function, and then it had to be got into the new ones.

Taken together these changes effected and reflected a change in the underlying conception of trusteeship, modest because it did not encompass all aspects, but a change nonetheless. At the beginning of our period the appointment of a new trustee was more like a substitution of a new personal confidant for an old. It was as though the trust was being constituted anew, perhaps with some subtraction if it was thought that the settlor had meant to rely particularly on the personal qualities of his first-chosen trustee. By 1914 trusteeship was much more like an office to which both property and powers were annexed; for the man who stepped into the office both would accrue automatically, or as near to it as could be managed.

The need to vest the assets in the appropriate person is the best place to start, because it had been identified as a problem in the eighteenth century and a response developed. Then the context would often have been a passive land-holding trust, where the trustee acted more as a security than as a manager. Someone in the incapacitated trustee's stead might be needed to pass the property on to a new trustee, but more likely the trust was ending and the transfer would be to an ultimate devisee, a beneficiary entitled to a distribution, or perhaps to a purchaser. Even some more active trusts, probably many at the start of our period, could function passably for a while without continuing intervention by the trustees. Trustees might delegate receipt of income to the life beneficiary; investments need not be varied; tenancies could roll over informally. Hence it need not matter immediately that one or more of the trustees had wandered away or become disabled. But even that sort of trust would eventually reach its terminus, be that a simple distribution of property or a sale and consequent distribution of proceeds. That destiny would be frustrated if a trustee was incapable or missing but presumed alive.

Appointment of a replacement would not meet the need, since there was no private or judicial mechanism for retrieving the outstanding title. Statute was the only solution, and in the nature of eighteenth and early nineteenth-century legislation it addressed particular problems rather than creating general jurisdictions. Since what was wanted was a transfer of title, and no more, that is what the legislation provided. Each statute carefully delimited the situations in which Chancery might now authorize someone to make a conveyance, or a transfer— each form of property was individually addressed—in lieu of the trustee in whose name the assets stood.[197]

---

[197] Infant trustees were the subject of the statute 7 Ann. c. 19, then insane trustees were covered by 4 Geo. II c. 10. In *Shaw* v. *Wright* (1796) 3 Ves. Jun. 22, Lord Loughborough suggested that these

There was enough of this statute law to be worth a consolidation in 1825, and enough more for a second consolidation and amendment in 1850.[198] Even then, as the property lawyer George Sweet complained, the jurisdiction stood as a list of instances.[199] It was longer and more complex with each addition, but not formulated as a general principle that could be moulded to new variations. Consequently it soon needed yet further amendment.[200] Nevertheless, though the Trustee Act 1850 merely tinkered with the substantive law, it caught the wave of Chancery reform that introduced extensive summary procedures in the interests of economy and dispatch of business.[201] Henceforward Chancery judges could themselves make vesting orders to transfer some forms of trust property directly, instead of going the long way around through an approved conveyancer.[202] That was a significant innovation.[203]

The mechanisms of the Trustee Act provided a solution particularly apt for enabling a terminating trust to complete its final stages. For an absent or incapable trustee it substituted a judge. The mere death of a trustee would often cause much less of a problem, if there were co-trustees surviving. So far as property ownership was concerned the joint tenancy between them would continue, unaffected by the diminution of numbers, or it would simplify into a sole trusteeship. So far as the duties were concerned those too would continue, as would the powers, provided that the continuing trustees had property and not merely status.[204] That had not been altogether uncontested, because one could argue that a testator/settlor who conferred discretion upon his trustees meant it to be available only so long as they could bring a collective mind to bear upon it. But it was established before our period begins that that was too inconvenient an outcome to be the general rule.[205] Earlier nineteenth-century cases to the contrary were conveniently explained away on the basis that they had concerned mere powers, not powers annexed to an estate.[206] This difference between trusts and mere

statutes be used as a precedent for a new one, to cover an absconding trustee of bank stock. That generated the statute 36 Geo. III c. 90. Further provision for insane trustees and mortgagees (where the problem of retrieving land was essentially the same) was made in 1 & 2 Geo. IV c. 114. There is an outline in Willis, *A Practical Treatise*, 91–5.

[198] 6 Geo. IV c. 74 (consolidation); then 11 Geo. IV and 1 Will. IV c. 60, 4 & 5 Will. IV c. 23, 1 & 2 Vict. c. 69; Trustee Act 1850, 13 & 14 Vict. c. 60.

[199] G. Sweet, *Recent Statutes Relating to Conveyancing* (1850), 1–6.

[200] 15 & 16 Vict. c. 55 (1852).

[201] See Vol XI, pp. 665–7.

[202] Stock transferable only by book entry needed a different procedure.

[203] The Law Amendment Society claimed it originated the proposal in 1844, and hence that it deserved the credit: 'The Law Amendment Society' (1851) *LM* 90–3, at 92.

[204] *Lane* v. *Debenham* (1853) 11 Hare 188; *Warburton* v. *Sandys* (1845) 14 Sim. 622.

[205] Lewin, Trusts (4th edn, 1861), 198–200, 298, 393–4.

[206] *Lane* v. *Debenham* (1853) 11 Hare 188; *re Bacon* [1907] 1 Ch 475; Farwell, *Powers* (1st edn), 372–5.

powers held by trustees over property vested in others was axiomatic. Exactly why such categorization should make such a big difference was never satisfactorily explained, unrelated as it was to the extent of the discretion.[207]

Trustees' survivorship to both property and powers provided adequate continuity for an efficient trust where the business was conducted quickly or the trustees' numbers were kept up (more will be said about that below). But a testator's hope for a multiple trusteeship could easily be thwarted if some of his nominees renounced—a common feature in litigated cases—or if his lawyers had omitted a power to appoint new ones, or if it was not exercised. Then the property would devolve upon a single trustee, whose death would break the chain. A trust was not a species of ownership, a tenure all to itself; it was a set of obligations attaching to ownership. It followed that trust property would devolve according to the general rules of inheritance. On an intestacy, which was the simplest case, the trust personalty would go to the deceased trustee's administrator and the realty to his heir. Those recipients would be bound by the trust in that they could not claim beneficial enjoyment, but were they also trustees in the sense that they could perform the trust obligations, execute the trust? Or did somebody first have to secure the appointment of a new trustee?

There was old law to hand, well-suited to passive trusts of realty. In such a case there was no difficulty in saying that the heir of the last trustee was entitled and obliged to convey the legal estate to the person beneficially entitled. Then, one step further, if the beneficial owner directed instead that the land be sold, the heir could make title directly to the purchaser. But, coming closer to the modern world, what if it were the trust deed rather than the beneficial owner that directed a sale? At this point Lewin began to worry that the line between passive and 'ministerial' trusts on the one hand and 'discretionary trusts' on the other was being crossed.[208] It was an important question not just for the economical winding up of trusts but also for the subsequent security of land titles.

The rule that in some circumstances the heir could pass legal title free from the trust—that is, that he succeeded to the office of trustee at least to the extent that he could properly sell the land—could be reconciled with the notion of a trust as a personal confidence by a fortunate coincidence. To vest a fee simple in his trustees a testator/settlor would usually have employed the standard words of limitation: to X and Y and their heirs. That mention of heirs was enough to rationalize the conclusion that the testator had foreseen that the trust might outlast his choice of trustees and had made provision for it, especially if his lawyers had repeated the

---

[207] The standard explanation was that mere powers divested, hence needed strict construction. But distributive powers held by trustees divested too.

[208] *Trusts* (4th edn, 1861), 17–18; and see the tortuous analysis at 397–401; (10th edn, 1898), 16–17.

word in other parts of the will where it was not strictly needed, particularly in receipt clauses.[209] As a rationalization it served its purpose, but as a general principle it both went too far and invited some very intricate textual analysis. It went too far in that it constituted the heir a trustee for all purposes, not just for sale. Faced with more active trusts, judges cut the rule back by holding that some powers were too confidential or discretionary for the original testator to have meant them to descend in this way—though somehow that had to be done in a way that allowed similar powers to accrue to replacement trustees regularly appointed by the court or under an express power.[210] The line was necessarily arbitrary.

A conscientious sole trustee alert to the difficulties might seek continuity for the trust by instead devising the trust property specifically to new trustees in his place. That would be particularly sensible if the trust fund were of mixed realty and personalty. The trustee's devisees get legal title, and they cannot take a personal benefit, but can they execute the trust? Thomas Jarman argued strongly that they could; that that was both the practical and the principled answer—it was justifiable for the trust to follow the estate however it descended, and such a rule would provide easy assurance to purchasers of land with such a link in their title.[211] That was rather a narrow view of what was entailed, but in due course he won outspoken support from Jessel MR.[212] They were a minority, however.

Orthodoxy began with Shadwell VC's equally outspoken decision in *Cooke* v. *Crawford* in 1842 that saw such a devise as a breach of trust.[213] For Shadwell VC trusteeship was a much broader enterprise than Jarman's view implied, but it was also, and pre-eminently, a personal confidence. He made links with the early nineteenth-century cases denying that surviving trustees could exercise discretionary powers after the death of one of their number; he thought the devise a breach because it was a delegation, and trustees cannot delegate; he thought the devisees could not be trustees, because the original testator had not said they could.[214] Hence the intricate textual analysis, as judges perused wills of varying vintages for indications that testators had implicitly authorized such devises, their willingness to attach meaning to phrases such as 'and their assigns' depending in part on deep analysis of the text and in part on their opinion of Shadwell VC's

[209] e.g. *Cole* v. *Wade* (1806) Ves. Jun. 27; and cf. *Robson* v. *Flight* (1864) 34 Beav. 110 (Romilly MR) rev'd (1864) 4 De G. & J. 608.

[210] *Robson* v. *Flight* (1864) 4 De G. & J. 608; *re Smith* [1904] 1 Ch 139.

[211] Jarman, *Wills* (1st edn), ii, 716–17.

[212] *Osborne to Rowlett* (1880) 13 Ch D 774; and see Sugden, *Vendor and Purchaser* (14th edn, 1862), 666.

[213] *Cooke* v. *Crawford* (1842) 13 Sim. 91, also *Bradford* v. *Belfield* (1828) 2 Sim. 264.

[214] Discretionary powers: *Townsend* v. *Wilson* (1818) 1 B. & Ald. 608, (1818) 3 Madd. 261, reluctantly acquiesced in by Lord Eldon, *Hall* v. *Dewes* (1821) Jac. 189.

conception of trusteeship.[215] The only theory there could be was that it all turned on what the testator had wanted, with a presumption strong enough against his wanting devisees to succeed to the trusteeship that even judges who disagreed felt obliged to hold that land titles depending on sales by such devisees were too doubtful to force on purchasers.[216]

As court-authorized conveyances and descent of (some) trustees' powers to the last trustee's heir were essentially ways of terminating a trust without undue formality, and as it was doubtful when a last surviving trustee might lawfully choose his successors by devise, long-term continuity had to be achieved through formal appointment of new trustees. Chantal Stebbings has found that by the early nineteenth century professionally drafted trust deeds provided for that as a matter of course.[217] In addition, Chancery claimed an inherent jurisdiction to appoint trustees to prevent a trust failing, so by one route or the other there was always a mechanism. Here again the Trustee Act 1850 eased court process by generalizing the jurisdiction to appoint 'new trustees' (though the phrase was to cause some difficulty later) and streamlining the procedure.[218]

In themselves, however, these processes were not enough. For true continuity the incoming trustees needed to have the same powers as the continuing trustees, and the property needed vesting in them in a way that maintained the joint tenancy. Express powers of appointing new trustees could be worded to achieve that first objective, but if it fell to a court to appoint new trustees the situation was not so clear. The 1850 Act said only that they got the powers they would have got under the previous more long-winded court process, not that those were the same as the original.[219] Instead it all depended, judges said, on the nature of the power, and on whether the trust instrument had envisaged a succession.[220]

This lingering judicial perception that one must start from the presumption that trustees' discretion was a personal gift imparted personally by a settlor to his personally selected confidential friends was not explicitly contradicted until Lord Cranworth's Act in 1860. As a footnote to implying into all future trust deeds the usual power to appoint new trustees (unless expressly excluded) it unequivocally

---

[215] *Titley v. Wolstenholme* (1844) 7 Beav. 425; *Mortimer v. Ireland* (1847) 11 Jur. 721; *Oklestone v. Heap* (1847) 1 De G. & Sm. 640; *Macdonald v. Walker* (1851) 14 Beav. 556; *Wilson v. Bennett* (1852) 5 De G. & Sm. 475; *Hall v. May* (1857) 3 K. & J. 585.

[216] To the cases in the previous footnote add *In re Morton and Hallett* (1880) 15 Ch D 143; *In re Crunden and Meux's Contract* [1909] 1 Ch 690.

[217] *Private Trustee*, 47; Willis, *A Practical Treatise*, 144–5.

[218] 13 & 14 Vict. c. 60, ss 32, 37–44.

[219] Trustee Act 1850, s 33.

[220] Lewin, *Trusts* (4th edn, 1861), 397–8; *Cole v. Wade* (1807) 16 Ves. 27; *Fordyce v. Bridges* (1848) 2 Ph. 510; *Newman v. Warner* (1851) 1 Sim. (N.S.) 457; *Byam v. Byam* (1854) 19 Beav. 58; *Brassey v. Chalmers* (1853) 4 De G. M. & G. 528; *Bartley v. Bartley* (1855) 3 Drew. 384.

added that court-appointed trustees acquired all the powers the original trustees had had.[221] Even then judges seem to have maintained their opinion that that could not have been meant to give court-appointed trustees power to appoint new trustees themselves, even if the settlor had given his original trustees such a power.[222] In the 1840s Lord Langdale had seen no harm in court-appointed trustees succeeding to such a power, but had retreated when opposed by his brethren.[223]

Private appointment of new trustees would more readily endow the new trustees with all the powers of the old—because the trust instrument could say so—but it needed complementing by private transfer of all the trust's assets into the names of the new set of trustees. In that respect court appointment of trustees may have become more attractive after 1850, for the Trustee Act not only streamlined the application process but also enabled the judge to vest at least some sorts of trust property directly in the new trustees without need for further formality.[224] Since the documentation needed to re-establish the joint tenancy on appointment of new trustees could be tedious these direct orders could effect a significant cost saving.[225] For Turner VC, however, mere cost was not an 'inconvenience' that would warrant his using the new order, which he declined to do in ordinary cases.[226] The Bank of England, administrator of the public funds that were the main outlet for trust investment other than land and mortgages, likewise made its usual difficulties over any change that might impact upon its bookkeeping methods.[227] The other judges soon shouldered Turner VC's objections aside, however, an amending statute put the Bank firmly in its place (but indemnified it for any consequent losses), and the new orders became standard practice.[228]

---

[221] Powers of Trustees, Mortgagees Act 1860, s 28.

[222] *Cooper* v. *Macdonald* (1866) 35 Beav. 504; Farwell, *Powers*, 524; Lewin, *Trusts* (6th edn, 1875), 693.

[223] *White* v. *White* (1842) 5 Beav. 221; *Holder* v. *Durbin* (1849) 11 Beav. 594; for other judges see *Oglander* v. *Oglander* (1848) 2 Drew. 381; *Bowles* v. *Weeks* (1845) 14 Sim. 591.

[224] Section 34 (lands), s 35 (stock and choses in action—which needed a less direct mechanism); see also ss 9 and 10.

[225] Sweet, *Recent Statutes*, 8; 'Public Trusteeships' (1851) *LM* 173–81 at 180.

[226] *Langhorn* v. *Langhorn* (1852) 21 LJ Ch (NS) 860; *re Watts's Settlement* (1851) 9 Hare 106; *re Plyer's Trust* (1851) 9 Hare 220. He also worried that in some circumstances the orders might sever the joint tenancy. He seems to have brought a generally narrow interpretation to the 1850 Act: compare *re Hazledine* (1852) 16 Jur. 853 with the 'reasonable latitude' employed by Parker VC in *re Tyler's Trust* (1851) 15 Jur. 1120 on a point that had to be resolved by statutory amendment (in Parker VC's favour): 15 & 16 Vict. c. 55, s 9.

[227] *Re Smyth's Settlement* (1851) 4 De G. & Sm. 499. For other instances, see *Shaw* v. *Wright* (1796) 3 Ves. Jun. 22; *re Peyton's Settlement* (1858) 25 Beav. 317 (MR), 2 De G. & J. 290 (LJJ).

[228] *Smith* v. *Smith* (1854) 3 Drew. 72; *Manning* v. *Manning* (1854) Kay App. xxviii; *re Marquis of Bute's Will* (1859) Johns. 15; Trustee Extension Act 1852, 15 & 16 Vict. c. 55, ss 6, 7.

It is rather typical of mid-century law reform that having started down this path the next steps changed direction. Technical property law reform depended on the enthusiasms and tactical ability of a tiny group of rivals in the Lords— the Chancellor, former and would-be Chancellors— and a few legal practitioners in the Commons lucky and determined enough to grab time for a private member's bill.[229] How well the changes would fit together was rather haphazard. The first relevant change was a section in Lord St Leonards' Law of Property and Trustee Relief Amendment Act 1859 which, decoded, meant that a trustee of personalty could henceforward vest the trust property in himself and a new trustee as joint tenants by one deed instead of two.[230] Then, as mentioned above, in 1860 Lord Cranworth's Act aimed to facilitate out-of-court appointment of new trustees by implying the usual clause into trust instruments.[231] That was fine so far as it went, but the section stopped with a mere exhortation that it then became someone's duty to procure the necessary transfer of property, with the attendant cost—reduced though that had been by St Leonards' Act. For a while some judges obligingly blended jurisdictions by reappointing in court as 'new trustees' under the Trustee Act those who had already been appointed out of court under Lord Cranworth's Act (or an express power), and then vesting the property in them by judicial order; it is no surprise to find Stuart VC, Malins VC, and James LJ taking that attitude.[232] Jessel MR would not, however, and in the 1880s his view prevailed as judges of sterner calibre insisted on giving the Trustee Act 1850 a literal reading: judges could only appoint, they said, not reappoint.[233] It was not for judges, they said, to remedy the deficiencies of legislation.

By then their scruple mattered less. Through the 1860s and 1870s there were still loose ends to these various strands of law, but they were spliced into a coherent whole by the Conveyancing and Law of Property Act 1881 and the Trustee Act 1893, both initiatives of the Incorporated Law Society.[234] One aspect of that modernization was to bring together the ideas in the Trustee Act 1850 and Lord Cranworth's Act, but in the converse way. From 1882 the appointor of new trustees out of court could simply vest the trust property in them by appending a suitable vesting declaration to the deed of appointment, which was the

---

[229] J.S. Anderson, *Lawyers and the Making of English Land Law* (Oxford, 1992) 1–22, 77–84; J. Getzler, 'Chancery Reform and Law Reform' (2004) 22 *LHR* 601–8 at 602–3.

[230] Section 21.

[231] Powers of Trustees, Mortgagees Act 1860, s 28; Stebbings, *Private Trustee*, 54–5.

[232] *Re Mundel's Trust* (1860) 2 LT (NS) 653; *re Carson's Settlement Trusts* [1867] WN 32; *re Clay's Settlement* [1873] WN 129; *re Dalgleish's Settlement* (1876) 4 Ch D 143; *re Pearson (a Lunatic)* (1877) 5 Ch D 982.

[233] *Re Driver's Settlement* (1875) LR 19 Eq 352; *re Vicat (a person of unsound mind)* (1886) 33 Ch D 103; *re Dewhirst's Settlement* (1886) 33 Ch D 416.

[234] Anderson, *Lawyers*, 146–56, Stebbings, *Private Trustee*, 19.

most efficient solution of all, though, as always, it came with exceptions.[235] Still, the whole process could now usually be conducted out of court, with minimal expense.

The 1881 Act also put an end to the old rules allowing limited devolution of trusts to the last surviving trustee's heir. It was not the first attempt, indeed it was the third in seven years—reforms that Underhill castigated as 'even more half-hearted and complex than is usual with attempts of Parliament to amend our law of property'.[236] The result was a mandatory succession of trust property on the death of a sole or last surviving trustee to his personal representatives, who were to have the powers of the original trustees.[237] Such *ex officio* trustees need only be temporary; their status did not foreclose the appointment and substitution of more suitable new trustees by whoever possessed that power under the trust instrument, or they could themselves exercise the statutory power.[238] Then the Trustee Act 1893 explicitly gave court-appointed trustees the power to appoint new trustees themselves, finally removing, it seemed, the remnant perception that there were some types of power too personal in their nature to be exercised other than by a court as a last resort or by a person who could trace his pedigree to express designation by the settlor.[239]

Provision for continuity of management was thus complete, by statute. The textbooks contain a residual nervousness that judges might still find gaps. Lewin's editors worried that a decision by North J. giving a broad effect to vesting declarations might not stick.[240] Underhill cautioned that the provision giving new trustees all the powers of the originals applied only to powers 'incident to the office of trustee', and that that left room—small room, he implied—for an argument that particular powers had been personal to the original trustees.[241] Though both doubts turned out to be groundless they were nonetheless born of long experience of the now rather occasional but still unpredictable judicial tendency to see trusteeship as a form of succession to a personal confidence. Thus in 1909 Parker J. held that the provision devolving full powers on the personal representatives of a sole trustee applied only if the original testator had given *some* indication that

---

[235] Section 34; becomes s 12 of the Trustee Act 1893. See Lewin, *Trusts* (10th edn), 772–4.

[236] *Trusts* (7th edn, 1912), 368. The statutes were Vendor and Purchaser Act 1874 s 5, Land Transfer Act 1875 s 48. For commentary, see Underhill, *Trusts* (7th edn, 1912), 367–9; Jarman, *Wills* (6th edn), 982–5.

[237] Conveyancing Act 1881, s 30.

[238] *In re Routledge's Trusts* [1909] 1 Ch 280.

[239] Section 10. Settlors could opt out, but must do so explicitly.

[240] *Trusts* (10th edn), 773–4, of *London & County Banking* v. *Goddard* [1897] 1 Ch 642.

[241] Underhill, *Trusts* (7th edn, 1912), 366; *re Smith* [1904] 1 Ch 139; *re Perrott and King's Contract* (1904) 90 LT 156.

he meant the trusteeship to devolve *ex officio*.[242] It took a further statute in 1911 to reverse his holding and make *ex officio* succession universal.[243] It had been a very long and difficult transition.

Investment

Following the eighteenth-century decisions, investment became the primary active management duty of trustees of personalty and mixed settlements. Those settlements had first to be identified, of course, and distinguished from trusts where the settlor intended his trustees to retain (and perhaps to manage) the property as he had left it. This process was complicated by judges' assumption that testator/settlors who created intergenerational trusts intended intergenerational equity, hence that the capital should not be depleted for the advantage of the life tenant. That disposed them towards treating trust property as a fund rather than as specific assets to be retained, but a fund in which successive beneficiaries were intended to have interests immune from the indirect adjustment exercise of trustees' discretion might bring. The resulting rules required executor/trustees first to sell a testator/settlor's specific assets and then to invest the proceeds in something more suitable, which usually meant the 3 per cent consols. Further, the income received from specific assets that ought to have been sold under the primary rule had to be reallocated to accord with what would have been produced if they had been. As Stebbings has shown, all this became very elaborate in its ramifications.[244]

The general idea, however, was not out of line with testators' wishes. In Morris's sample of wills proved in Leeds between 1830 and 1834 liquidation was the dominant strategy explicitly adopted by testators, recognizing that a different stage of the family property cycle had now been reached, requiring different uses for what had once been their property.[245] Importantly, the rule could be excluded by apt words in the will, so the case law reflects not so much an obstacle for the professionally-aided as a pitfall for the unwary, and one more reason for a will to be regarded as a business document. The resulting tangle of interpretive law added complexity of its own, as was the early nineteenth century way, as each instance was treated as part of the rule and not merely as an application.

---

[242] *In re Crunden and Meux's Contract* [1909] 1 Ch 690.

[243] Conveyancing Act 1911 s 8(1). Section 8(2) allowed a testator to opt out, but required an explicit statement to do so.

[244] It became known as the rule in *Howe* v. *Earl of Dartmouth* (1802) 7 Ves. 150; see Stebbings, *Private Trustee*, 68–77, Lewin, *Trusts* (4th edn), 227–32.

[245] Morris, *Men, Women and Property*, 130–41, 264–75. Sometimes testators qualified the duty to sell, and where they were leaving urban houses they often allowed sales to be staggered.

Stebbings concludes from the volume of reported cases that judges' assumptions were increasingly out of line with testators' probable preference for a modicum of trustee discretion.[246]

Similar tensions affected the judges' determination of the legality of investments. Because the court of Chancery had a duty to manage funds that had been paid into it, its judges created investment rules for themselves, rules which then became applied to trustees generally.[247] They were narrow, cautious, and slow to change. These general rules create a difficulty for analysts, however, because in their application to trustees in general they were merely default rules, operative only if the settlor had not specified otherwise. Throughout our period it was common for trust deeds to broaden the permissible range of investment.[248] Models are easily found in the practice books, be they Davidson's careful examples from the 1860s or the graduated clauses in *Cracroft's Trustee's Guide* in 1876, the most comprehensive of which would have been serviceable for a century.[249] Yet, as Stebbings shows, periodical and newspaper comment on judicial decisions and legislative proposals, and parliamentary debate itself, seem usually to have assumed that the default rules applied generally.

One explanation may be that judges made the legal environment for application of settlor-initiated investment clauses too risky for trustees, forcing them back to the safety of the default rules. That would be consistent with Stebbings' argument that the severity of the liability rules was a prime cause of a chronic shortage of men willing to become trustees in the first place, though there is no direct evidence for it and the argument rather exaggerates judicial antipathy to investment clauses.[250] It is noticeable, however, that the cases that were reported of trustees seeking court advice tended to be those where the question was couched in rather general terms: judges were asked whether an investment

---

[246] Stebbings, *Private Trustee*, 71.

[247] *Ibid.*, 128–62. 'This obligation is not the result of any positive law, but has been imposed on trustees by the Court as a convenient rule…', Peachey, *Settlements*, 668n (a good general account).

[248] Grant, *Advice to Trustees*, 95–7; Stebbings, *Private Trustee*, 80, 135–6, 145; Morris, *Men, Women and Property*, e.g. at 134, 255–6, 261.

[249] Davidson, *Precedents*, iii (2nd edn, 1861), 13–51, 190–2, 546–50, 582–6; *Cracroft's Trustee's Guide* (1876), 14–17.

[250] Stebbings, *Private Trustee, passim*, but esp. 166. Judicial construction of investment clauses is discussed below; the cases include *Dickonson v. Player* (1838) C. P. Coop. 178; *Ex. p. Chaplin* (1839) 3 Y. & C. Ex. 397; *Beauclerk v. Ashburnham* (1845) 8 Beav. 322; *Robinson v. Robinson* (1851) 1 De G. M. & G. 257; *Mant v. Leith* (1852) 21 LJ Ch 719; *M'Leod v. Annesley* (1853) 22 LJ Ch 633; *Baud v. Fardell* (1855) 7 De G. M. & G. 628; *Consterdine v. Consterdine* (1862) 31 LJ Ch 807; *Moore v. Walter* (1863) 8 LT (NS) 448; *Edwards v. Thompson* (1868) 38 LJ Ch 65; *re Peyton's Settlement Trust* (1869) LR 7 Eq 463; *Lewis v. Nobbs* (1878) 8 Ch D 591; *re Brown* (1885) 29 Ch D 889.

would be proper, not merely whether it was authorized by the trust instrument.[251] When answering the former question judges introduced notions of prudence, and prudence, moreover, from the position of a judge investing funds in court. They tended to conclude that the trustees 'ought' not to make the investment proposed—which has all the appearance of a general norm.[252]

Similarly, when trustees in disputed cases were directed to bring their funds into court the judges would order sale of their wide range investments for reinvestment in court-authorized securities. That did not imply that trustees had been in breach to acquire them, and judges sometimes went out of their way to say so, but commentators tended to ignore this nuance.[253] Jessel MR's decision in *Bethell* v. *Abraham* in 1873, for example, which drew wide criticism for refusing to allow investment in American stocks, when the trust instrument clearly permitted it, was treated as being of general application, although on its face it was a decision only about what the courts would do with funds under their control.[254] Judges' pronouncements had a moral authority wider than their jurisdiction, so their caution may have had a general chilling effect.

Judges' perception of what was appropriate investment began with safety. The settlor's fund was treated as a discrete property; it could be loaned, provided that its return was guaranteed either by the government or, if the settlor allowed, by taking adequate security. But (in the absence of the clearest authority from the settlor) it could not be exchanged for something thought to be of equivalent value, since that was speculation, not investment at all.[255] Counsel for a wronged beneficiary put it nicely in 1838 when he argued that 'the property has been deprived of its due protection …'.[256]

Judges' ethic that safety was an end in itself fits comfortably with Morris's conclusion that family trusts in early nineteenth-century Leeds held property 'with the medium-term aim of securing income under the terms of the trust rather

---

[251] There were exceptions, of course, e.g. *Edwards* v. *Thompson* (1868) 38 LJ Ch 65; *re Peyton's Settlement Trust* (1869) LR 7 Eq 463.

[252] *Mant* v. *Leith* (1852) 15 Beav. 524, 21 LJ Ch 719; *re Simson's Trust* (1860) 1 J. & H. 89 (*sub. nom.* re *Timson's Trust* (1860) 2 LT 170); Lewin, *Trusts* (4th edn, 1861), 242–5.

[253] *Baud* v. *Fardell* (1855) 7 De G. M. & G. 628; *re Brown* (1885) 29 Ch D 889; and cf. *Stewart* v. *Sanderson* (1870) LR 10 Eq 26 and *re Colne Valley and Halstead Railway Bill* (1859) 29 LJ Ch 33. In *re Sillar* [1871] WN 3 Stuart VC declined to exercise the power to invest in railway shares or Indian Government stock that the settlor had given his trustees, but offered to appoint new trustees and transfer the fund to them so that they could do so.

[254] (1873) LR 17 Eq 24; Lewin, *Trusts* (6th edn, 1875), 282; Stebbings, *Private Trustee*, 149–50. See esp. *re Brown* (1885) 29 Ch D 889, where Pearson J. rejected the broad reading of *Bethell* v. *Abraham*.

[255] See generally, D. C. Itzkowitz, 'Fair Enterprise or Extravagant Speculation: Investment, Speculation, and Gambling in Victorian England' (2002) 45 *Vict. St.* 121–47.

[256] *Clough* v *Bond* (1838) 3 My. & Cr. 490.

than maximising revenue in the broader sense'.[257] Likewise the judicial assertion that intergenerational equity required preservation of the capital fits well with the notion developed recently by Morris and other social historians that middle-class families operated a sort of property cycle.[258] In this model capital—it may be borrowed or inherited—is first put to active work, at risk, by the adult males of each generation, then there follows a transitional period as those men retire to live off a rentier income, then, sometimes, a passive interlude when the property provides income for widows and underage children, before the cycle begins again with a capital distribution. The judges' default rule that trustee investment must not reduce the capital facilitated that cycle.

The judges adopted as their own practice that trust funds paid into court for general administration should be invested only in government securities, and within that class usually only in permanent funded debt, particularly the 3 per cent consols. That practice hardened into a rule by the very early nineteenth century, and was applied strictly even when a testator/settlor had given his trustees a much broader power.[259] Consols offered easy management, an unvarying return, relatively little fluctuation of capital value, and could be readily liquidated when the remainderman required the capital.[260] It would not be irrational for some sorts of beneficiary to want only the narrow investment the general rule permitted.

The paradigm private trust was inter-generational, where choice and change of an investment might have a distributive effect. Judges worried greatly about this in the 1860s when asked to approve a switch of investment from consols to high interest bearing East India stock.[261] The latter could be bought only at a premium, but came with the possibility of relatively early redemption at par. A shift therefore would buy higher income for the life tenant at the possible expense of a capital reduction for the remaindermen. Shadwell VC once voiced a similar concern when ruling that 'public stocks' excluded Bank of England stock, because the directors' ability to declare bonuses would affect relations between life tenant

---

[257] Morris, *Men, Women and Property*, 275; cf. Davidoff and Hall, *Family Fortunes*, 215. A similar analysis has been made of family firms: Owens, 'Inheritance and the Life-cycle of Family Firms'.

[258] Morris, *Men, Women and Property*, 142–77, esp. 148–9; Owens, 'Property, Gender and the Life Course'; Owens, 'Inheritance and the Life-cycle of Family Firms'.

[259] *Howe v. Earl of Dartmouth* (1802) 7 Ves. 150; *Ex p Franklyn* (1848) 1 De G. & Sm. 528; *Barry v. Marriott* (1848) 2 De G. & Sm. 491; *Butler v. Withers* (1860) 1 J. & H. 332; *Consterdine v. Consterdine* (1862) 31 LJ Ch 807; *re Sillar* [1871] WN 3.

[260] For their attractiveness, see D. R. Green and A. Owens, 'Gentlewomanly capitalism?' (2003) 56 *Econ. Hist. Rev.* 510–15–36 at 519–23.

[261] *Equitable Reversionary Interest Society v. Fuller* (1861) 1 J. & H. 379, ; *Cockburn v. Peel* (1861) 3 De G. F. & J. 170; *re Langford's Trusts* (1861) 2'J. & H. 458; *Hurd v. Hurd* (1862) 11 WR 50; *Hume v. Richardson* (1862) 6 LT (NS) 624; *Mortimer v. Picton* (1864) 10 Jur. (N.S.) 83; *Vidler v. Parrott* (1864) 10 LT (NS) 686; *Waite v. Littlewood* (1872) 41 LJ Ch 636.

and remaindermen.[262] Judges did not want such discretions for themselves, nor did they think trustees should have them unless expressly endowed by the settlor. Hence trustees must invest only as the court itself would (unless the settlor had said otherwise), and to invest in something different would bring strict liability, should loss result.[263]

When Chancery's own investment practice had hardened in the war years of the early nineteenth century the 3 per cents had been plentiful and high yielding. Limiting investment to them then was no hardship. But the attraction of consols waned, both absolutely as supply diminished and yields fell, and relatively as capital markets expanded and diversified. The range of public investments broadened, successive railway booms generated new forms of investor securities, yet the judges stuck to their rules.[264] So settlors wishing their trustees to take advantage of the new opportunities had to empower them expressly. Such clauses needed interpretation of course, and Stebbings argues that judges were unnecessarily begrudging about it.[265] They made, perhaps, two sorts of difficulty.

The first applied to very general authorizations of the sort more likely to be found in legally naïve wills, hence more common at the beginning of our period and before the railway boom changed the nature of capital investment, an authorization, say, to lay money 'out in the funds or on such other good security as [the trustees] could procure and think safe'. Typically the question then was whether that allowed loans on a personal bond or promissory note, and the answer was

---

[262] *Mills* v. *Mills* (1835) 7 Sim. 501.

[263] *Howe* v. *Earl of Dartmouth* (1802) 7 Ves. 150; *Holland* v. *Hughes* (1809) 16 Ves. 111; *Clough* v. *Bond* (1838) 3 My. & Cr. 490. Despite Lord Alvanley's dictum to the contrary in *Pocock* v. *Reddington* (1801) 5 Ves. 794 it seems to have been well settled that trustees could not invest in mortgages unless authorized by their trust deed: *re Fust* (1817) Coop. T. Cott. 160n; *Widdowson* v. *Duck* (1817) 2 Mer. 494; *Norbury* v. *Norbury* (1819) 4 Madd. 191; *Ex p Ellice* (1821) Jac. 234; *Barry* v. *Marriott* (1848) 12 Jur. 1043, 2 De G. & Sm. 491. C. P. Cooper in his long note at Coop. T. Cott 157 relates the tightening of this rule to the creation of the post of Accountant-General, which made custody of suitors' money much safer than it had been. But that occurred in 1726, and the change was more usually attributed to Lord Thurlow.

[264] For an account of the attractiveness of railway company debentures to institutional trustees (whose investments can be more easily discovered from company records than private trustees), see M. C. Reed, *Investment in Railways in Britain 1820–1844* (Oxford, 1975), 240–56. During periods of railway construction, investment in railway company *shares* was highly problematic for trustees, partly because no dividend was payable until the completed line moved into profit, and partly because trustees usually lacked ready cash for paying calls. Critics of railway fraud often portrayed poor widows and orphans as primary victims of rash speculation in shares, but empirical evidence of trustee investment is lacking; see S. A. Broadridge, 'The Sources of Railway Share Capital', in M. C. Reed, (ed.), *Railways in the Victorian Economy* (Newton Abbot, 1969), and Reed's own paper in that volume, 'Railways and the Growth of the Capital Market'.

[265] *Private Trustee*, 147–50.

always no.[266] Judges understood words like 'invest' and 'security' to have legal meanings, and not to take their colour from the local context, which no doubt was that local circulation of capital to trustworthy individuals was entirely proper.[267] Put differently, to say that someone was to be a trustee but that he was also to be the testator's alter ego, doing as the testator would have done, was the sort of contradiction that needed very careful enunciation in the will. Without it judges would simply plump for the interpretive option that gave the beneficiaries maximum safety, holding that trustees' discretion extended only to choice within the court-authorized list.

Stebbings sees these rulings as setting a standard for the interpretation of general discretions through until 1896, when Kekewich J. signalled a change.[268] There are decisions similar to his from 1878, however, and it seems that part of the change may be attributed to a difference in legal context: these later broad discretions had clearly been drafted by professionals as part of detailed trust instruments, leaving much less room for the ambiguity that judges found in the skeletal, almost informal, provisions in issue in the earlier cases.[269]

Drafters seem to have aimed for specific authorization more usually than broad discretion. That too might need interpretation, and it was difficult to predict whether a judge would bring a broad or a narrow view to bear—but it is untrue to say that judges were always strict.[270] Some clauses were particularly common. In 1842 Shadwell VC ruled that powers to invest by loan on mortgage were so usual that one must be included in a court-supervised marriage settlement.[271] He

---

[266] *Wilkes* v. *Steward* (1801) G. Coop. 6; *Westover* v. *Chapman* (1844) 1 Coll. 177 (a particularly hard case); *Styles* v. *Guy* (1849) 1 Mac. & G. 422; and compare the country bank loan cases *Moyle* v. *Moyle* (1831) 2 Russ. & M. 710; *Darke* v. *Martyn* (1839) 1 Beav. 525; Peachey, *Settlements*, 668n at 670.

[267] Contrast Lord Langdale's sensitive decision that a will that as to one fund said trustees must 'invest' and as to another allowed them to 'employ' it 'in any manner they saw fit' must be taken to have meant a difference, hence that the latter allowed them to leave the fund on loan to the settlor/testator's business: *Dickonson* v. *Player* (1838) C.P. Coop. 178. Lewin thought the distinction unsafe: *Trusts* (4th edn, 1861), 239. For the importance of local loans, see Morris, *Men, Women and Property*.

[268] *Re Smith* [1896] 1 Ch 71; Stebbings, *Private Trustee*, 150.

[269] *Lewis* v. *Nobbs* (1878) 8 Ch D 591; *re Brown* (1885) 29 Ch D 889; and compare *Dickonson* v. *Player* (1838) C.P. Coop. 178. There is always an exception: see *re Hazeldine* [1918] 1 Ch 433.

[270] See e.g. *Robinson* v. *Robinson* (1851) 1 De G. M. & G. 257; *Mant* v. *Leith* (1852) 21 LJ Ch 719; *Baud* v. *Fardell* (1855) 7 De G. M. & G. 628; *Ex p Chaplin* (1839) 3 Y. & C. Ex. 397; *Consterdine* v. *Consterdine* (1862) 31 LJ Ch 807; *Edwards* v. *Thompson* (1868) 38 LJ Ch 65. There are not many reported cases; Lewin padded out his analysis by including decisions interpreting words describing assets the testator left at his death, which was not necessarily the same issue: *Burnie* v. *Getting* (1845) 2 Coll. 324; *Ellis* v. *Eden* (1857) 23 Beav. 543; *Brown* v. *Brown* (1858) 4 K. & J. 704.

[271] *Sampayo* v. *Gould* (1842) 12 Sim. 426. All 13 of Peachey's precedents in 1860 for settlements that contemplated investment (there are nine that for one reason or another did not) authorized investment in mortgages or in 'real securities'.

thought the settlement should also empower investment in 'government securities', which would be wider than merely the 3 per cent consols, but, significantly,
not in 'public securities', thus excluding such common investments as East India
Company stock.[272] Settlor-initiated clauses were often much more extensive but,
and herein lay the second major problem, by being specific they risked obsoles-
cence. As capital markets matured types of security evolved beyond those known
to the testator. But, for judges, the question was what the testator had said in his
will, not what he would have wanted if he had known what would happen. Judges
would not say that because a testator had authorized investment in a security of
one description he would now have meant to include a recently evolved form that
everyone agreed was very like it; to do so would be to adopt a form of purposive
interpretation no longer in fashion.[273]

  Statute could of course make just such a change, and from the end of the 1850s
through to 1875 several did.[274] Some of them, including the earliest, were products
of a somewhat diluted law reform mentality.[275] Others were driven by the borrowers, anxious not to jeopardize their market as their stocks evolved into newer
forms, or, in the case of municipal authorities, anxious to tap the trustee market
in the first place.[276] Some did allow that if trustees might by their deed invest in
one form of security they might now invest also in the ones the Act specified—
enlargements of express powers, as an 1893 consolidation Act termed it.[277] Others
extended to trustees generally some of the powers usually contained in well-
drafted (but conservative) trust deeds, unless the trust deed specifically said not,
of course.[278] Significantly, in 1860 one of these statutes prodded Chancery into
extending its own powers of investment and added that henceforward all trustees
could invest in whatever the court's list were to authorize.[279]

---

  [272] See also *Mills* v. *Mills* (1835) 7 Sim. 501.
  [273] *Harris* v. *Harris (No. 1)* (1861) 29 Beav. 107; *Re Langdale's Settlement* (1870) LR 10 Eq 39; *re Smith*
[1896] 2 Ch 590; *re Willis* [1911] 2 Ch 563.
  [274] Stebbings, *Private Trustee*, 134–45.
  [275] Law of Property Amendment Act 1859; Law of Property Amendment Act 1860; Powers of
Trustees, Mortgages, etc Act 1860; Investment of Trust Funds Act 1867. For the context of 'law
reform' see Anderson, *Lawyers*, 21–2.
  [276] Improvement of Land Act 1864 s 60; Debenture Stock Act 1871 s 1; Metropolitan Board of
Works (Loans) Act 1871, s 13. Before the Local Loans Act 1875 municipal authorities secured clauses
in their local Acts to empower trustee investment in their loans: J. S. Vaizey, *The Law Relating to the
Investment of Trust Money* (1890), 72.
  [277] Law of Property Amendment Act 1860 s 11; Improvement of Land Act 1864 s 60; Debenture
Stock Act 1871 s 1; Metropolitan Board of Works (Loans) Act 1871, s 13; Local Loans Act 1875 s 27;
Trustee Act 1893 s 5. The Trustee Act 1893 was a consolidation introduced at the request of the
Incorporated Law Society.
  [278] Law of Property Amendment Act 1859 s 32; Law of Property Amendment Act 1860 s 12; Powers
of Trustees, Mortgages, etc Act 1860 s 25; Investment of Trust Funds Act 1867.
  [279] Law of Property Amendment Act 1860 ss 10 and 11.

With one exception all these Acts were cautious. That exception marked what was probably the only significant divergence between Parliament's assessment of the propriety of trust investment and the judges'. It came when George Hadfield MP ambushed a bill introduced by Lord St Leonards in 1859, adding to it a clause empowering trustees to invest in Bank of England and East India Company stock and also in real securities—mortgages.[280] Judges had previously held that whereas it was valid, of course, for settlors to empower trustees to lend on the strength of private property, the general rule should restrict them to investments guaranteed by Parliament or government. St Leonards' attempt in the following year to induce Parliament to have second thoughts resulted only in its strengthening Hadfield's section by making it retrospective.[281]

In 1860 the equity judges loyally followed Parliament's intentions and generated a new, and characteristically cautious, list of securities in which they were willing to see funds in court invested, though there is a note of regret in Page Wood VC's account of this development.[282] Now they had a discretion, and could not avoid considering how it should be used. They certainly would not automatically approve applications to shift from consols into the higher interest-earning securities now authorized by statute. It was in this context that they doubted the suitability of East India stock, since the possibility that those might soon be redeemed at less than their purchase price would enable life tenants to throw the cost of their higher income on to the remaindermen. But case by case they developed criteria for exercising their own discretion, looking for some special reason beyond the mere (and probably universal) wish of the life tenant for a higher income, indicating that they expected trustees to behave likewise, but saying also that they would protect trustees who exercised their discretion *bona fide*.[283] In 1861 Page Wood VC ruled that Hadfield's section applied only if the trust deed already gave *some* power to vary investments, a ruling that Lewin's editors seem to have approved.[284] Romilly MR and Malins VC seem to have followed a less restrictive line in the 1870s, however, and in due course the Court of Appeal and the House of Lords could agree unanimously that the more explicit wording of

[280] *Ibid.*, s 32; Stebbings, *Private Trustee*, 136–8.

[281] Law of Property Amendment Act 1860 s 12; Stebbings, *Private Trustee*, 137–8.

[282] *Equitable Reversionary Interest Society* v. *Fuller* (1861) 1 J. & H. 379. The judges' Order is reprinted as an appendix to Lewin, *Trusts* (4th edn, 1861), 699 together with a note showing how difficult they found its application in the first year or so.

[283] *Equitable Reversionary Interest Society* v. *Fuller* (1861) 1 J. & H. 379; *Cockburn* v. *Peel* (1861) 30 LJ Ch 575; *re Langford's Trusts* (1861) 2 J. & H. 458; *Hurd* v. *Hurd* (1862) 11 WR 50; *Hume* v. *Richardson* (1862) 6 LT (NS) 624; *Mortimer* v. *Picton* (1864) 10 Jur. (NS) 83; *Vidler* v. *Parrott* (1864) 10 LT (NS) 686. Even Romilly MR, who took a wide view of the 1859 Act, would not approve investment in redeemable securities at a premium: *Waite* v. *Littlewood* (1872) 41 LJ Ch 636.

[284] *Re Warde* (1861) 2 J. & H. 191; Lewin, *Trusts* (6th edn, 1875), 271.

the Trust Investment Act 1889 superseded Page Wood's decision, though they did not all agree that Malins VC's had been the better reading all along.[285] It was a serious matter even for a statute to impliedly contradict a settlor, however advantageous to beneficiaries it would be.

It would be a mistake, however, to conclude that there was generally a significant difference between the judges' attitudes and Parliament's. Hadfield's intervention did not start a move towards a new general model for trustee investment. When, for example, the court of appeal in Chancery decided that the extension of investment powers to include East India Stock probably meant stock of that name in existence when the Act passed, and not the New East India Stock created very shortly afterwards (which Parliament had deliberately not guaranteed), Parliament had an almost immediate opportunity to set the record straight.[286] But an amendment to that effect was dropped in the Commons because agreement could not be reached, and was not passed until six years later.[287] Similarly, statutes extending trustees' investment powers remained painstakingly specific about what they allowed, and usually explicitly allowed settlors to exclude their provisions. There was a recurring provision too, that if an older form of security was being converted into one payable to bearer, even trustees authorized to purchase the old form were not to purchase the new one unless their deed positively permitted investment in bearer securities.[288] That was so much taken for granted that opposition from municipal authorities to a clause in the Local Loans Bill 1875 converting all their securities into bearer bonds would have sunk the bill, had not the Chancellor of the Exchequer at the last moment agreed that municipalities might also create nominal debentures suitable for trustee investment.[289] Similarly, judges' worries about possible capital losses when redeemable stock

[285] *Waite v. Littlewood* (1872) 41 LJ Ch 636 (Romilly MR); *re Clergy Orphans Corporation* (1874) LR 18 Eq 280 (Malins VC); *Hume v. Lopes* [1892] AC 112, on appeal from, and affirming, *re Dick* [1891] 1 Ch 423. Earlier, North J. had generalized and followed *re Warde* in *re Manchester Royal Infirmary* (1889) 43 Ch D 420. There has been no research on the day-to-day practice.

[286] *Re Colne Valley and Halstead Railway Bill* (1859) 29 LJ Ch 33. See Stebbings, *Private Trustee*, 137, who finds greater conflict between Parliament and judiciary.

[287] *PD* 1860 (s3) 158: 104–7; Investment of Trust Funds Act 1867.

[288] India Stock Certificates to Bearer Act 1863 s 4; Stock Certificates to Bearer Act 1870 s 29; Local Loans Act 1875 s 21. There was a well-known formula trusts draftsmen used for allowing purchase of bearer securities, modifying the more usual form that investments be in the names of the trustees jointly: Davidson, *Precedents*, iii (2nd edn, 1861), 22–3, 546–7; *Re Roth* (1896) 74 LT 50.

[289] *The Times*, 19 June 1875, p. 6, col. f.; Local Loans Act 1875, s 6. The Act was a by-product of a move by the Treasury for greater control over local borrowing and for easier access to private savings via the savings bank; see *The Times*, 8 June 1875 p. 9, col. a; 19 June p. 6, col. f; and generally, M. Schulz, 'The Control of Local Authority Borrowing by Central Government', in C. H. Wilson (ed.), *Essays on Local Government* (Oxford, 1948), esp. 169–87.

was bought over par were answered not by overriding them, but by a careful detailed code of the sort only statute can provide.[290]

So although cumulatively legislation added significantly to trustees' investment powers, it generally kept within the accepted conservative model. Even the Trust Investment Act 1889, passed after pressure by and on behalf of trustees smarting from the government's reduction of interest on consols to a miserly 2½ per cent, stayed within the fold of public and real property securities, with the marginal exception of the loan stock of water companies established by special Act or royal charter.[291] The proceedings on it in Select Committee are marked by the care members took to ascertain the extent of central government supervision of local authority loans, the means available for assessing the credit-worthiness of the less populous local authorities, and the true nature and exact extent of the reputed public guarantee of stock in Irish light railways.[292]

The Settled Land Act 1882 did allow trustees to invest 'capital money'—the proceeds of sale of land held on settlement—in railway company debentures, but this breach of the general principle was not finally extended to all trustees until 1893, though such an express power had been common for at least a generation.[293] There was never a suggestion that the law should provide trustees with a general power to invest in shares, however hedged about with qualifications. Shares were seen as having market rather than intrinsic value, hence needing skilled, knowledgeable, and active engagement in the market to sustain their worth.[294] Only the settlor could expose his family to the risk that involved.

[290] Trust Investment Act 1889 (on which see Stebbings, *Private Trustee*, 140–5), s 4; and see *re Dick* [1891] 1 Ch 423 (aff'd [1892] AC 112, *sub nom. Hume* v. *Lopes*).

[291] Section 3. Water companies, like municipal authorities, raised their income from rates; most of them were regulated via the Waterworks Clauses Act, 10 & 11 Vict. c. 17 and its successors; and see B. Rudden, *The New River* (Oxford 1985), 114–19, 176–8.

[292] *SC on Trust Funds Investment Bill*, Report PP 1889 (200), xv, 499. It stipulated a minimum population of 50,000, if an English or Welsh local authority's stock was to be available as a trustee investment under the general law, and rejected shares in Irish light railways on the chairman's casting vote.

[293] Settled Land Act 1882, s 21, Trustee Act 1893, s 1, with the proviso that the company had paid a dividend on its ordinary stock and shares for ten years.

[294] A. Preda, 'The Rise of the Popular Investor' (2001) 42 *Sociological Quarterly* 205–32. Two of Peachey's precedents in 1860 suggested that settlors might consider authorizing investment in shares in railway companies or public utility companies: *Settlements*, 775 and 867; see too the broad (though problematic) clause in the trust for the man subject to fits of weakness, p. 891. Prideaux, *Precedents in Conveyancing*, contained a recommendation against investments 'of a speculative character and fluctuating value such as ordinary stocks and shares of railway companies' until the 14th edn (1889), when it shifted to providing such a clause for those daring enough; compare 8th edn (1876), ii, 210n with 14th edn, ii, 271.

Delegation and the Standard of Liability

Diversification of investment opportunity, be it from settlors' ambition or the general law, demanded greater knowledge and expertise from trustees. Even with the most usual form of settlor-permitted investment, the loan on mortgage, not all trustees had the information necessary to match their funds to an appropriate borrower. They could hire information and expertise for the occasion, of course, and in prudence might have to; but since personal judgement was an indispensable element of their 'sacred and private' office, they needed constant awareness of the boundary between lawful delegation and improper abdication of responsibility.[295]

Excessive delegation was not a risk new to trustees in the nineteenth century. Practicality already dictated the use of agents to collect rents, solicitors to collect debts, and bankers to receive capital repayments. Eighteenth-century judges had policed its necessity, anxious always that trustees should not undermine the personal and gratuitous nature of their office by sloughing off trust management to a hired hand, nor even to the best-informed or most amenable co-trustee among them. But, it is thought, as trusts became more widespread so the number of trustees in need of expert help increased, and as investment opportunities increased so too did the occasions on which help might be sought. Judges, however, tended rather to tighten the rules against delegation, with liability resulting for trustees in breach.[296]

Stebbings argues that this severity was an increasing problem that deterred reasonable men from becoming trustees.[297] But if, as she says, most members of Parliament would have been trustees, one would expect to see some informed interest there in favour of a change. That seems not to have happened. Generally the matter lay quiet, save in the late 1850s and the late 1880s, when the property owning public was moved by anxiety over well-publicized revelations of trustee fraud, more often than not by solicitor trustees, whose misdeeds could be generalized to suggest an institution in crisis. This was a serious matter for a society where middle-class insecurity was endemic.[298] In 1857 Lord Brougham, with government support, responded with a bill to extend criminal law against trustee fraud.[299]

That new liability for the dishonest in turn provided an opening for Lord St Leonards to propose reducing the harshness with which trustee liability law could

[295] St Leonards, *PD* 1857 (s3) 145: 1553; quoted by Stebbings, *Private Trustee*, 18.

[296] Stebbings, *Private Trustee*, 115–20.

[297] *Ibid.*, esp. 173–8.

[298] G. Best, *Mid-Victorian Britain 1851–75* (rev. edn, 1973), 97, 281; H. Perkin, *The Rise of Professional Society* (1989), 95–6.

[299] Fraudulent Trustees Act 1857.

impact on honest (but mistaken) trustees, to encourage a better class of men to put themselves forward for the role.[300] The crux of the problem was that when a trustee's duty was cast in terms of rules or prohibitions, and much of it was, then judges saw breach as ineluctably triggering personal liability to make good any loss that resulted. Once a breach had been proved, a trustee's honesty, reasonableness, and best endeavours were irrelevant save, sometimes, peripherally, to the rate of interest he must pay on the reparation the court ordered.[301] At all times there had been judges who regretted such strictness; but they all applied it.

However, not all trustees' duties consisted of adherence to rules and avoidance of prohibitions, so not all liability need have been strict in the sense just outlined. Judges further controlled trustees by requiring them to meet a standard of business prudence when performing acts that were either not prohibited by the general rules or were expressly permitted by settlors.[302] The lawfulness of delegation had been subjected to that test by Lord Hardwicke in the leading eighteenth-century case.[303] The choice of an appropriate mortgage, where such investment was allowed by the trust instrument, is another easy example. In principle this eighteenth-century formulation of the standard left room for adaptation to changing pressures and changing values. Stebbings argues, however, that, operating without juries to keep them in touch with day-to-day middle-class expectations, Chancery judges rarely showed lenience.[304] Further, there was a long-term tendency for judicial applications of the prudent businessman standard to crystallize out into specific rules, more particularly into prohibitions. Much of the law of delegation developed in that way, and it can be seen too in the quasi-rule that a loan on a mortgage should not exceed two-thirds of the property's value, if it was freehold land, or half if the security was buildings.[305] Rules brought greater certainty than standards, but that included greater certainty of liability for breach.

So the centrepiece of Lord St Leonards' proposal was that judges should be able to excuse trustees who had been acting in good faith when they inadvertently breached their trust. That was unacceptably paradoxical for the Lord Chancellor, Lord Cranworth, who primly rejected it outright.[306] Practicable law reform, he thought, could extend only to revising outdated rules that trapped trustees

---

[300] Stebbings, *Private Trustee*, 182–3; PD 1857 (s3) 145: 1551–62.

[301] Stebbings, *Private Trustee*, 179–81.

[302] *Ibid*, 107–9, 117–19, 175–8.

[303] *Ex p Belchier* (1754) Amb. 218.

[304] Stebbings, *Private Trustee*, 107–21.

[305] Lewin, *Trusts* (4th edn, 1861), 242. For the tendency see e.g. Underhill, *Trusts* (7th edn, 1912), 281–7, 292–304, esp. his agonizing about *Hopgood* v. *Parkin* at 298–9.

[306] PD 1857 (s3) 145: 1561–2.

into breach in the first place, not to the logic of liability. St Leonards failed. In cases lacking an obvious public interest rule revision depended on support from elite lawyer-politicians, in this case the Chancery maestri in the Lords and the Attorney-General in the Commons.[307] Even after the return of his party to government he achieved only a small part of what he had proposed, a part that on its own gave the reform rather a different complexion. This was a streamlined procedure enabling trustees to avoid breach by first taking court advice, a much-welcomed and much-used facility, though one with a sting in its tail for trustees who failed to take their doubts to court.[308] His Act also contained a short list of other very specific rule revisions, plus a general statutory version of the standard form indemnity clause. That latter reform might seem to contradict Lord Cranworth's principle, but its effect was solely educational; the clause merely reiterated the basic premises of liability, giving no additional protection.[309]

The lawyers in Parliament were evidently unwilling to dispute the judges' rigorous standards for trustees' conduct and liability. Nor, so far as we know, were they lagging behind the general legal culture. Peachey's near-contemporaneous treatise on settlements does say that something a little more elaborate than St Leonards' provision is usually needed, but his suggested clauses retain its general standard and merely add specific exonerations for such faults as failing to make inquiry into the validity of shares and debentures. Only his precedent for a trust delegating management to the beneficiaries contains an indemnity for trustees couched in broad terms.[310]

In the 1880s the impetus was very much the same, with the added element that there were now serious proposals that settlors whose circle of acquaintance might not run to providing both security and expertise should not have to turn to the ever-willing but (it seemed) rather unreliable figure of the local solicitor to be their family's trustee.[311] Corporate trustees might be better, or even a public trustee. Revived by Howard Vincent in 1886, that latter idea sat well with notions of the expanding role of the state, eventually winning support from

---

[307] For Sir Richard Bethell's caustic rejection of his specific proposals see *The Times*, 18 August 1857, p. 6 col. c, and St. Leonards' hurt protest at *PD* 1857 (s3) 147: 1773. On law reform cf. Anderson, *Lawyers*, 77–80.

[308] Law of Property and Trustees Relief Amendment Act 1859 ss 30, 31; Stebbings, *Private Trustee*, 183–5. Other sections enabled executors to wind up estates with more confidence and protected trustees who unwittingly relied on powers of attorney that had lapsed.

[309] Grant, *Advice to Trustees*, 92–4; they were described as 'mere nullities' by G. Harris, *Reasons for Urging the Necessity of, and Suggestions for Framing, an Act 'to Provide for the Due Administration of Trust Estates and the Relief and Protection of Trustees'* (1854), 6, and cf. 13–14; see also Stebbings, *Private Trustee*, 114, 124–5.

[310] Peachey, *Settlements*, 88on (on St Leonards), 724–5, 732n, 883n, 717n (general indemnity).

[311] Polden, 'The Public Trustee'. Nine bills to establish a public trustee were introduced into the Commons from 1887 to 1894, though not all were read.

Lord Chancellors of both political parties in much the same way as the more far-reaching proposition that the state conduct land transfer business through a public land registrar.[312] Solicitors resisted, for fear of losing the paid legal work associated with trusts management to corporations or a new official.[313]

Opposition was one thing, constructing a plausible alternative much more difficult. Law societies from the later 1880s did adopt rules for the separation of clients' money from the solicitor's own, but they lacked legal power to enforce them.[314] A compulsory mutual indemnity fund was but the dream of a few.[315] A commercial alternative, the provision of fidelity bonds for trustees, was offered by one company established by elite solicitors but not, it seems, with marked success.[316] They also promoted the notion of custodian trustees as passive depositaries.[317] Their main thrust, however, against the twin problems of insecurity and trustee shortage, was to secure a reform of the substantive law much as St Leonards' prescription 30 years earlier

Even with this incentive to produce an efficient and modern restatement, the need to address rules one by one, the absence of direction by any department of state, and shortage of Parliamentary time, meant that details had to be negotiated hurriedly among the lawyer-politicians.[318] So the Law Society-sponsored Trustee Act 1888 had to be kept short to ensure its passage, and has a somewhat *ad hoc* look about it. Nonetheless it achieved a major shift of emphasis by providing that trustees should not be liable 'only' because they had breached various judicially created rules or quasi rules; instead they should be judged by a standard of prudence.[319]

This was significant because judges had already responded to renewed fears that the law's severity deterred reasonable men from being trustees. While formally maintaining the 'prudent businessman' standard for lawful delegation they were applying it more generously than in the mid-century, self-consciously

---

[312] Polden, 'The Public Trustee'; Marsh, *Corporate Trustees*, 62–6, 73–5.

[313] Marsh, *Corporate Trustees*, 38–48, 57–82; Anderson, *Lawyers*, 187–8, 230, and cf. 319–20.

[314] Anderson, *Lawyers*, 210, 230.

[315] Anderson, *Lawyers*, 210; H. Kirk, *Portrait of a Profession* (1976), 104.

[316] Anderson, *Lawyers*, 319–20; Marsh, *Corporate Trustees*, 60, 66, 70, 86. Judicial trustees might have become a source of business, since they were required to provide security (at the expense of the trust): Judicial Trustees Rules 1897, r 9. But only 49 judicial trustees were appointed between 1897 and 1909, and the experiment was regarded as a total failure: Polden, 'The Public Trustee', 232.

[317] Marsh, *Corporate Trustees*, 60, 78, 266.

[318] SC on Law, *Report on Liability of Trustees Bill*, PP 1888 (323), xii, 449.

[319] Trustee Act 1888, s 4, and compare s 3.

so in the leading case, *Speight* v. *Gaunt* in 1883.[320] A businessman might know which municipal bonds could be bought in a market (and how to access it) and which should be bought directly from the municipality (and how to do that), said Lindley LJ, but it was unreasonable to expect such specialized knowledge from trustees. Hence it was reasonable for them to use a broker, and, having chosen one prudently, they could not be expected to watch over his actions with the alertness to small signs of impending fraud that an expert might detect. There would still be cases where naïve or casual trustees were held to have put their faith and the trust's money where a prudent man would not, or, having been reasonable in the first place, to have remained satisfied with their delegate's excuses beyond the limits of prudence, but judges increasingly declared themselves anxious to give honest trustees the benefit of the doubt.[321]

Judges brought similar sympathy to the application of another section in the new Trustee Act, one that enabled trustees to rely on a valuer when lending on mortgage, not just for his valuation, but also on the question whether the security offered would be good for the loan proposed.[322] By the end of our period they were interpreting this to protect trustees even where the security was of the speculative or wasting sort they would never previously have condoned, provided only that the trustees had acted in good faith, taken care in choosing and briefing their surveyor, and that he was independent of the mortgagor.[323] Such exoneration applied only if they lent no more than two-thirds of his valuation, but if they did exceed that fraction, and the security was otherwise suitable, then they would be liable for the excess only.[324] That was another significant shift in trustees' favour, because, faced with a report that a property would be good security for a sum less than they wished to loan, trustees would often, perhaps usually, have looked for a different security for the whole sum rather than splitting their funds into two, and hence might have avoided the loss altogether.

---

[320] (1883) 22 Ch D 727 (CA), 9 App Cas 1 (HL). It was recognized as a significant step by the Select Committee on Trusts Administration, 1895 *PP* (248), xiii, 403, 406, by textbooks, and by modern commentators. *Learoyd* v. *Whiteley* (1887) 12 App Cas 727 was a reminder to trustees that investment in over-valued and wasting properties would still be penalized, cf. *Smethurst* v. *Hastings* (1885) 30 Ch D 490.

[321] Naïve trustees: *Robinson* v. *Harkin* [1896] 2 Ch 415, and cf. *re Brookes* [1914] 1 Ch 588; defiant (solicitor) trustee: *Mara* v. *Browne* [1895] 2 Ch 69; typical cases: *re Godfrey* (1883) 23 Ch D 483; *re Gasquoine* [1894] 1 Ch 470; *Field* v. *Field* [1894] 1 Ch 425, *re de Pothonier* [1900] 2 Ch 529; *Shephard* v. *Harris* [1905] 2 Ch 310.

[322] Trustee Act 1888, s 4(1); Trustee Act 1893 Act, s 8(1).

[323] *Shaw* v. *Cates* [1909] 1 Ch 389, *re Solomon* [1912] 1 Ch 261 (compromised on appeal, [1913] 1 Ch. 200]). Underhill was disapproving: *Trusts* (7th edn, 285). For poor choice of a valuer, see *re Dive* [1909] 1 Ch 328.

[324] Trustee Act 1888, s 5; Trustee Act 1893, s 9.

In addition the legislation the Law Society promoted reduced the occasions for breach. It conferred various management powers, especially powers relating to land and houses, it specifically allowed trustees to use solicitors for some stipulated tasks, and it greatly extended the ability of trustees and their executors to plead lapse of time against beneficiaries, doing much to remove the nightmare of trustees' families who previously had been vulnerable to suits for long-distant breaches.[325]

Unsurprisingly, none of this activity stemmed demands for a public trustee. But when the Select Committee that Howard Vincent had won to assess the difficulties of trusts administration recommended establishment of at least some sort of official trusteeship, it scrupulously added two further relaxations of trustees' liability to make private trusteeship more palatable. One, that judges should be able to vary a trust instrument if it had become outdated and to do so would be to the advantage of the beneficiaries, was too radical to make progress.[326] In its company the second recommendation, the one had been unacceptable to Lord Cranworth in 1857, now seemed almost mundane.

Thus in 1896 it was enacted without difficulty that judges might henceforward relieve trustees from the consequences of breach if they had acted honestly, reasonably, and ought fairly to be excused.[327] Some judges still felt uncomfortable with the notion that someone could be in breach but then be excused the consequences, and some would have liked some statutory guidance on when 'ought fairly to be excused' should be invoked. But after a firm steer from Lindley and Chitty LJJ they settled down to rescuing the conscientious while still condemning the casual and cavalier.[328] In particular they developed the notion best described as the reasonable error of law—where trustees had made a payment or transferred property reasonably believing they had power to do so but where, on the true reading of the trust instrument, they did not. Where judges in the mid-century would have insisted that because the trustees could always have asked a court for prior approval their breach could not be condoned, their successors regarded failure to seek court advice as merely one factor to be weighed with others.[329]

---

[325] Trustee Act 1888, s 8. For the operation of the previous law, see Grant, *Advice to Trustees*, 39; Lewin, *Trusts* (6th edn, 741), and for an example, *Lander* v. *Weston* (1855) 3 Drew. 389, where a claim was brought against a trustee's estate 31 years after his death, 40 years after the breach.

[326] *SC on Trusts Administration*, Report 406. Strictly, it was a power to give advance sanction to what would otherwise have been a breach; functionally it was a power to vary.

[327] Judicial Trustees Act 1896, s 3; Stebbings, *Private Trustee*, 188–91.

[328] *Re Grindey* [1898] 2 Ch 593. Earlier reported appeals for relief under s 3 were unsuccessful: *re Turner* [1897] 1 Ch 536; *Head* v. *Gould* [1898] 2 Ch 250; *In re Second East Dulwich 745th Starr-Bowkett Building Society* (1899) 68 LJ Ch 196.

[329] *Perrins* v. *Bellamy* [1897] 1 Ch 797; *re Kay* [1897] 2 Ch 518; *National Trustees Co of Australasia* v. *General Finance Co of Australasia* [1905] AC 373; *re Mackay* [1911] 1 Ch 300; *re Allsop* [1914]

Conclusions are difficult because there are elements of contradiction in these changes. Stebbings is no doubt correct that the stereotype trustee was now less of an 'honourable friend' and more of a business manager, but that does not explain why standards of liability should be reduced.[330] Professionals can make their own terms, as they did in the twentieth century. The new standard, with its increased range of powers to delegate and its defence of honest and reasonable conduct, fits better with a model of trusteeship that is still individual, gratuitous, and altruistic but which recognizes that increased complexity has brought greater risk. If that is right then the conclusion is perhaps that the new standard was based upon assumptions which, while not quite out of date the moment it was introduced, would soon become so.

1 Ch 1; contrast *Davis* v. *Hutchings* [1907] 1 Ch 365. In *re Mackay* Parker J. stretched this idea so that he did not have to decide the difficult question whether a trustee could be (subjectively) 'reasonable' under s 3 so as to be relieved from having (objectively) unreasonably delegated one of his functions. In 1872 Wickens VC had allowed a similar, though non-statutory, defence to company directors making *ultra vires* payments in good faith, but his ruling had been eroded and finally explained away, prompting passage of a statutory defence parallel to that for trustees: *Pickering* v. *Stephenson* (1872) LR 14 Eq 322; *Studdert* v. *Grosvenor* (1886) 33 Ch D 528; *Cullerne* v. *London etc. Building Society* (1890) 25 QBD 485; *re Peel* [1907] 1 Ch 5; Companies (Consolidation) Act 1908, s 279, as interpreted in *re Claridge's Patent Asphalte Co* [1921] 1 Ch 543.

[330] *Private Trustee*, 196–7.

Part Two

CONTRACT

I
Introduction

1. THE AGE OF FREEDOM OF CONTRACT

Historians of English contract law have in general agreed that the nineteenth century saw the rise of a new general conception of contract. This conception, it is argued, was based on a will theory which defined contracts in terms of obligations which parties making an agreement voluntarily imposed on themselves. The corollary of the will theory was freedom of contract, which allowed parties to engage in whatever obligations they chose to, and held them to their contracts, however unfair they seemed. Historians have been divided, however, over the ideas which predominantly lay behind this new approach. Two kinds of explanation have been put forward, one of which stresses the influence of ideas external to law, and one of which stresses the influence of legal ideas.

The first approach has been most associated (for English law) with P. S. Atiyah's *The Rise and Fall of Freedom of Contract*, which argues that a major shift occurred in thinking about contract law in the period between 1770 and 1870. According to Atiyah, eighteenth-century courts were concerned primarily with ensuring the fairness of transactions between parties. Contract theory was 'largely based on the idea that obligations were created by the acceptance of benefits, or by acts of reasonable reliance'.[1] The paradigm contract in this era was the executed one, with the court ensuring that the performing party was given a just remuneration for his trouble. This view of 'contract as performance' was replaced in the nineteenth century by a theory of 'contract as agreement', in which the mutual exchange of promises came to be seen as the basis of the contract. In this world, rights to future performance were generated by the mere will of the parties. The executory contract became the paradigm.

Atiyah explains the shift in the law as a response by the judiciary and jurists to changing political and economic theories. Until the 1830s, the approach of the

---

[1] P. S. Atiyah, *The Rise and Fall of Freedom of Contract* (Oxford, 1979), 419. See also the debates over American developments in M. Horwitz, *The Transformation of American Law, 1780–1860* (Cambridge, MA, 1977), challenged by P. Karsten, *Head versus Heart Judge-made Law in Nineteenth Century America* (1997).

judges was influenced by the ideas of a pre-industrial moral economy; after 1830, they were increasingly sympathetic to the approach of new political economists and utilitarian thinkers, which sought to encourage commercial enterprise, and free market individualism. Jurists who embraced the will theory did so because it suited the needs of modern industrial and commercial society so well. The law, according to this view, was tailored to be most suitable to a growing industrial economy, and reflected the dominant political ideology of the age, which championed freedom of contract. The dominance of this model began in turn to wane after 1870 (the argument goes) as classical economics came under attack; though it was only well into the twentieth century that state interference, in the form of consumer protection legislation, became more extensive.

Atiyah's views have been criticized by scholars who have stressed the importance of legal ideas whose genealogy is not linked to industrialization. Before considering their views, however, it is worth considering the impact of 'extra-legal' debates on the development of contract law. Mid-nineteenth-century English political debate was certainly suffused with the language of freedom of contract. Sir Henry Maine spoke for a generation in 1861 when he wrote that '[t]he movement of the progressive societies has hitherto been a movement *from Status to Contract*'.[2] Freedom of contract was a central tenet of Victorian Liberalism. For J. S. Mill, the very right of property entailed 'the freedom of acquiring by contract', since '[t]he right of each to what he has produced, implies a right to what has been produced by others, if obtained by their free consent'.[3] Equally, it was generally agreed in public debate that the science of political economy had proven that, with state interference removed, and free competition and exchange encouraged, the economy would work in a more efficient manner.

Despite the pervasiveness of this language in politics and economics, it was not the driving force which led lawyers to rethink their subject. To begin with, it was primarily a language which was invoked when calls were made to reduce government interference, or when governments threatened interventionist legislation.[4] 'Freedom of contract' and 'laissez-faire' were phrases about the role of government, not about the nature of contract. The phrase 'freedom of contract' came into circulation largely through the debates in the 1850s on whether to grant limited liability to joint stock corporations. Its use in this context was perhaps paradoxical, since the aim of reformers here was to give 'limited' companies a particular status. Their aim was not so much to enhance the power of the individual to contract, as to remove the notion that limited liability was a privilege

---

[2] H. S. Maine, *Ancient Law: Its Connection with the Early History of Society and its Relation to Modern Ideas* (1861), 170. On the wider intellectual and economic contexts, see XI, Pt 1, Chs IV and VI.

[3] J. S. Mill, *Principles of Political Economy*, 2 vols (1848), i, 256.

[4] See its use (in the late 1860s) when new proposals were made to reform Irish agricultural tenancies, *The Times*, 22 April 1867, col. 6e.

conferred by the state. It was also a political language used by employers against trade unions, which were accused of interfering with the worker's freedom of choice.[5] In the eyes of the working classes, it was a hypocritical language, for (as J. M. Ludlow pointed out) employers sought 'such freedom of contract as that they shall be and remain masters in the bargain'.[6] It was doubly hypocritical since the Master and Servant Act of 1823—which was enforced with gusto—allowed magistrates to imprison workmen for breach of contract.[7]

Secondly, the golden age of the public vocabulary of 'freedom of contract' only lasted between 1850 and 1880. It came to ascendancy in an era which (notably with the repeal of the Corn Laws in 1846) saw the triumph of the laissez-faire assumptions of classical political economy over mercantilist protection.[8] By the 1880s, the language of 'freedom of contract', and the tenets of classical economics in general were coming in for serious criticism and arguments in favour of state intervention became more commonplace.[9] In an age of an increased awareness of poverty, a moral dimension was reintroduced into economics, and economists sought to divorce their science from the advocacy of particular policies of laissez-faire. Those who cried loudest for freedom of contract in this era—such as the Liberty and Property Defence League, a pressure group founded in 1882, presided over by Lord Bramwell[10]—were no longer mainstream, but were swimming against a strong tide. The notion of 'freedom of contract' by the 1880s was as likely to invoke rebuttals, such as T. H. Green's 1881 essay 'Liberal legislation and freedom of contract', which asked liberals to rethink their very notion of freedom.

Whether used opportunistically or hypocritically, the public discourse of freedom of contract was not addressed to the bread-and-butter issues of contract law.[11] Politicians who invoked this discourse already associated 'contract'

---

[5] 'What makes combination illegal', *Liverpool Mercury*, 26 August 1842.

[6] J. M. Ludlow, *The Master Engineers and their Workmen* (1852), 32.

[7] See R. J. Steinfeld, *Coercion, Contract and Free Labour in the Nineteenth Century* (Cambridge, 2001). On the wider history of labour law, see XIII, Pt 3.

[8] More broadly, G. R. Searle, *Morality and the Market in Victorian Britain* (Oxford, 1998), 4 points out that 'the spread of the ideology of "political economy" was associated with the reforms of the 1840s and 1850s, such as the repeal of the Corn Laws and Usury laws'.

[9] See T. W. Hutchison, 'Economists and Economic Policy in Britain after 1870' (1969) 1 *History of Political Economy*, 231–55; J. W. Mason, 'Political Economy and the Response to Socialism in Britain, 1870–1914' (1980) 23 *Historical Journal*, 565–87.

[10] See N. Soldon, 'Laissez-faire as Dogma: The Liberty and Property Defence League, 1882–1914' in K. D. Brown, *Essays in Anti-Labour History* (1974), 208–33; E. Bristow, 'The Liberty and Property Defence League and Individualism' (1974) 18 *Historical Journal*, 761–89; and E. J. Bristow, *Individualism versus Socialism in Britain, 1880–1914* (1987).

[11] As Searle points out (*Morality and the Market*, 28), 'all the political economists took it for granted that market competition would take place within a framework of law, ensuring that certain kinds of anti-social conduct would be discouraged and punished'.

with the ability of the parties to make their own agreements. Judges were used to dealing with freely negotiated contracts long before free trade ideology displaced mercantilism. They would continue to deal with such contracts when government interference came back into fashion. The development of contract doctrine did not simply mirror broader ideological developments. Nor did judges look to the texts of economists or social theorists to help them develop law. Only on rare occasions did the bench enter into economic disquisitions and quote economists.[12] But they did not make use of the detailed learning of these scholars, whose macroeconomic theories were generally of little help in resolving the issues which came before the courts. When economists were cited, it was more usually to obtain definitions for economic terms found in legislation.[13]

Although we need to be cautious in drawing too close a connection between broad political theories and legal doctrine, it should also be borne in mind that judges were also citizens, aware of the needs of the social, economic, and political communities around them.[14] Many nineteenth-century judges had been active politicians, Members of Parliament and Cabinet ministers before promotion to the bench; some were active polemicists engaging in public debate. As shall be seen in what follows, novel cases were not resolved by the simple application of doctrinal solutions. Cases which came before the courts often involved significant fractures in the economic system, for which no solution had been anticipated by the legislature. Judges had, of necessity, to be social and economic policy makers, with policy made through the artificial prism of the case before them. But in making policy, they did not simply translate ideas borrowed from others into the law, any more than Members of Parliament did, when legislating. They applied their own views, views which were often refined by debate in court.

2. THE IMPACT OF LEGAL TREATISES

If political ideas did not transform thinking about contract law, did new legal ideas have that effect? Some scholars have suggested that the nineteenth century saw a 'reception' of ideas taken from civilian writers in the natural law tradition. This occurred, it is claimed, once writers began to explain English contract law

---

[12] *Archer v. James* (1859) 2 B. & S. 67 at 96. See further, XI, Pt 1, Ch. VI, pp. 166–7.

[13] *In re Agriculturist Cattle Insurance Co* (1849) 1 De G. & S. 599 at 602; *Ex parte Evans* (1852) 2 De G. M. & G. 948 at 951.

[14] Margot Finn has argued that county court judges, aware of the growth of a consumer market, applied their own conception of a moral economy when dealing with female consumers who needed protection from merchants: 'Working-class Women and the Contest for Consumer Control in Victorian County Courts' (1998) 161 *P&P* 116–54.

as a coherent set of principles, rather than as a collection of remedies.[15] In seeking to define contracts in the abstract, English judges and writers borrowed the natural lawyers' idea that a contract was an agreement of two wills, making a *consensus ad idem*. From this initial definition, they sought to discover conclusions which followed logically from it.[16] Thus, English lawyers began for the first time to articulate the notion that contracts were made by offer and acceptance. They began to rethink the doctrine of consideration. And they began to develop doctrines relating to factors vitiating consent, such as mistake and fraud.

Judges and jurists in the late eighteenth and early nineteenth century clearly began to look for principles underlying contract law. Since English law did not provide them either with statutes providing a foundation for doctrine, or ancient texts summarizing custom (as it did in property law), they argued that the rules had to be derived from universal principles, or 'the science of morals'.[17] If contract law was found in reason, rather than in any positive source, what better place to look than Roman law as mediated by the natural lawyers of the Enlightenment? Those writers who were most theoretically minded certainly felt this was the best source. One of these was William David Evans, a reformist lawyer, who wanted to set out a coherent and connected system of private law, based on 'principles of substantive justice' rather than 'the subtilties of artificial reasoning'. Realizing that any work of his own would have limited influence, he chose instead to translate Robert-Joseph Pothier's *Traité des Obligations*, hoping that the general jurisprudential principles it contained would inspire the English.[18] Evans's edition would be widely read and very influential. Another scholar, Henry Colebrooke, did write his own work in 1818, a *Treatise on Obligations and Contracts*, which sought to set out the general principles of contract derived from civilian writers, supplemented by references to the French Code Civil and Scots law. It was not a success. Privately printed, and never completed, it never achieved significant influence, though it stands testament to the keenness of jurists to introduce English lawyers to general principles derived from continental sources.

The early nineteenth century saw something of a flourishing literature on contract law.[19] 1826 saw the publication of the first edition of the younger Joseph Chitty's *Practical Treatise on the Law of Contracts not under Seal*, which would

[15] A. W. B. Simpson, 'Innovation in Nineteenth Century Contract Law' in his *Legal Theory and Legal History: Essays on the Common Law* (1987), 171–202.

[16] J. Gordley, *The Philosophical Origins of Modern Contract Doctrine* (Oxford, 1991), 175–80.

[17] J. J. Powell, *Essay upon the Law of Contracts and Agreements* 2 vols (1790), i, v–vi. See also the Aristotelian view, expressed by Abraham Hayward in *LM* 1 (1829), 527.

[18] R. J. Pothier, *A Treatise on the Law of Obligations or Contracts*, 2 vols (trans. W. D. Evans, 1806), Introduction, 98.

[19] S. Comyn, *A Treatise of the Law Relating to Contracts and Agreements not under Seal* (Dublin, 1807); E. Lawes, *A Practical Treatise on Pleading in Assumpsit* (1810).

receive a more extensive and more scholarly second edition in 1834 and remain highly influential (in numerous editions) throughout the nineteenth and twentieth centuries. Two further treatises were published on contract law before the mid-century by William Fox and C. G. Addison.[20] In 1845, Colin Blackburn's more specialized treatise on the contract of sale appeared. In addition, other specialist works aimed at particular contracts continued to appear, such as Edward Sugden's 1805 *Vendors and Purchasers*, which went through numerous editions through to the mid-century. In these works, the authors sought to present treatises on the principles of law, capable of reconciling conflicting decisions and revealing decisions which were unsupportable. However, they also wanted their works to be practical *nisi prius* books, for their target audience was one of practitioners.[21] These books were not the vehicle of a reception of civilian ideas: their authors were themselves practitioners, whose aim was not to import a new theoretical model based on will theory.

These works did generally begin with the premise that contracts rested on mutual assent. As one writer put it in 1829, 'in order to constitute an agreement, there must not only be an assent of the understanding, but an exercise of the will'.[22] Moreover, Pothier's treatise was much quoted by these writers, to support the proposition that contracts were founded on the agreement of the parties.[23] However, it was not a new thing for English lawyers to define contract in terms of agreements.[24] Equally, eighteenth-century writers had often borrowed, consciously or unconsciously, from the elegant vocabulary of civilian works, when giving definitions of contract,[25] though this did not mean that the ideas they expressed were themselves imports. John Comyns' eighteenth-century *Digest*, for instance, had declared that '[a]n agreement is *aggregatio mentium, viz.* when two or more minds are united in a thing done, or to be done'.[26] Significantly, Comyns' reference for this proposition was not a civilian one, but the arguments of counsel in a common law case of 1550.[27]

---

[20] W. Fox, *A Treatise on Simple Contracts* (1842), C. G. Addison, *A Treatise on the Law of Contracts* (1847).

[21] Chitty, *Contracts* (2nd edn, 1834), preface.

[22] [A. Hayward], 'Mercantile Law', *LM* (1829) 1: 538. See also Comyn, *Treatise*, 2; H. T. Colebrooke, *A Treatise on Obligations and Contracts* (1818), 2; Chitty, *Contracts* (1st edn, 1826), 3.

[23] For Pothier's influence, see W. Swain, 'The Will Theory of Contract in the Nineteenth Century: Its Influence and its Limitations', in A. Lewis, P. Brand, and P. Mitchell, *Law in the City* (Dublin, 2007), 162–80.

[24] e.g. *Comms.* ii, 442; Powell, *Contracts*, pp. vi–vii.

[25] P. A. Hamburger, 'The Development of the Nineteenth-Century Consensus Theory of Contract' (1989) 7 *Law and Hist. Rev.* 265–9. See also [Henry Ballow], *A Treatise of Equity* (1737).

[26] J. Comyns, *A Digest of the Laws of England*, 6 vols (4th edn, 1800), i, 400 (tit. Agreement A1).

[27] *Reniger* v. *Fogossa* (1550) 1 Plowd. 1 at 17a.

Early nineteenth-century English writers did not use Pothier to develop a general theory of contract. They borrowed from Pothier, as and when they needed to, to explain developments in the case law. For example, in the second edition of his book, Chitty quoted at length from Pothier's *Traité du contrat de vente* in the chapter on 'the assent of the parties', to draw a distinction between unaccepted promises (which were not binding) and accepted offers (which were).[28] This was a relevant issue since litigation had recently occurred, raising the problem of when offers and acceptances could be retracted.[29] The quotation taken from Pothier (on contracts by correspondence) did not in fact shed light on the precise question at issue in the cases discussed,[30] but seems to have been included for its insights into the broader doctrine. His theory was not analysed or discussed by the author, but was simply inserted alongside principles digested from English case law. The fact that the quotation remained in later editions of the text, even after legal decisions made it clear that Pothier's position was not English law, suggests that it was not a driving influence on the understanding or shaping of English law. Where a subject had not yet come up before the courts, it was neglected by English treatise writers, even though it received full treatment in civilian works. For instance, the doctrine of mistake, which had received considerable analysis in civilian works such as Pothier's, was not mentioned by Chitty in his second edition.[31]

If they did not attempt to import will theory wholesale, English lawyers did borrow from foreign treatises when the occasion suited, though it was generally the French, rather than the German jurists, who were cited.[32] As new areas of law were mapped out, it was natural for judges to debate questions which they found discussed in legal literature. Pothier's more specialist works on bills of exchange,[33]

---

[28] Chitty, *Contracts* (2nd edn, 1834), 10–11. He also quoted Pothier on contracts made through correspondence, which suggested the need for subjective agreement.

[29] That Chitty's discussion was issue-driven is seen from the fact that the question was raised in his 2nd, fuller edition, but not in the first: *Routledge* v. *Grant* (1828) 3 Car. & P. 267; 4 Bing. 653. He may have also been influenced by the discussion in the recent case of *Williams* v. *Carwardine* (1833) 5 Car. & P. 566, 4 B. & Ad. 621, which was cited in a note to his discussion. See also *Cox* v. *Troy* (1822) 5 B. & Ald. 474, where his father was counsel.

[30] Chitty's quotation from Pothier when discussing the case of *Adams* v. *Lindsell* (1818) 1 B. & Ald. 681 did not address the question raised in the case whether acceptance had to be communicated.

[31] Chitty discussed mistaken payments when dealing with the action for money had and received; and he spoke briefly of errors in statements of particulars of sale in real property transactions (*Contracts*, 2nd edn, 1834, 238), but without mentioning civilian sources.

[32] F. C. von Savigny, *Treatise on Possession* (trans. E. Perry, 1848) was occasionally mentioned in late nineteenth-century courts (e.g. *Gladstone* v. *Padwick* (1871) LR 6 Ex 203 at 208 and *Lows* v. *Telford* (1876) 1 App Cas 414 at 418), but his great *System des heutigen römischen Rechts*, 8 vols (Berlin, 1840–9) was not cited in courts. For continental influences on international law, see XI, Pt 1, Chs VIII and IX.

[33] e.g. Lord Ellenborough quoted from Pothier's treatise on bills of exchange (*Traité du Contrat de Change*, Paris, 1773) in *Raper* v. *Birkbeck* (1811) 15 East 17 at 20; in *Hoare* v. *Cazenove* (1812) 16 East

insurance, or the contract of sale,[34] as well as works by other writers such as Pardessus[35] were often quoted to elucidate particular points, as were the French codes and commentaries on them.[36] English jurists were not uncritical towards these foreign sources. For instance, in discussing rules relating to the vesting of property in the sale of goods, Colin Blackburn noted that Lord Ellenborough had laid down rules 'in terms nearly equivalent to' the rules in the *Digest*.[37] Having laid out the rules, he proceeded to quote at length from Pothier. However, he cautioned readers that Pothier's 'positions are not always to be considered as universally true of the Civil Law, and far less to be taken as authorities for English law'.[38] He also criticized the incorporation of these rules as illogical and out of place in the common law. Nonetheless, his formulation of them was repeatedly quoted by judges in the second half of the century, as a canonical formulation of rules which could be traced via Pothier to the civil law.[39]

In a number of areas, the formulation of particular doctrines of contract law can be traced to the influence of writers such as Pothier, sometimes via the filter of other treatises,[40] sometimes through direct citation.[41] However, ideas derived from continental jurisprudence were not simply translated direct into English law. General propositions from foreign jurists were sometimes mentioned in court, setting out clear positions on issues which English courts would come to adopt in later years, but which made little impact when first mentioned. If the doctrine did not directly address the problem, it would not be embraced,[42] for judges were primarily concerned with answering specific questions before them, rather than building new areas of law. Equally, where continental doctrines were

---

391 at 395–6. See also counsel's arguments in *Hall* v. *Fuller* (1826) 5 B. & C. 750 and in *Williams* v. *Germaine* (1827) B. & C. 468.

[34] R. J. Pothier, *Treatise on the Contract of Sale* (trans. L. S. Cushing, Boston, 1839).

[35] *Cox* v. *Troy* (1822) 5 B. & Ald. 474 (cited by Chitty the elder); *Suse* v. *Pompe* (1860) 8 C.B. N.S. 538; *Pinard* v. *Klockmann* (1863) 3 B. & S. 388 at 395.

[36] e.g. *Shipton* v. *Thornton* (1838) 9 Ad. & El. 314; *Pinard* v. *Klockmann* (1863) 3 B. & S. 388.

[37] C. Blackburn, *A Treatise on the Effect of the Contract of Sale* (1845), 151; cf. 122–3, referring to D.18.6.8. Although he spoke (at 154) of the rules as 'adopted directly from the civil law', no mention was made of the Roman sources or civilian jurisprudence in the cases he had in mind: *Hanson* v. *Meyer* (1805) 6 East 614; *Hinde* v. *Whitehouse* (1806) 7 East 558; *Rugg* v. *Minett* (1809) 11 East 210; *Zagury* v. *Furnell* (1809) 2 Camp. 240.

[38] Blackburn, *Sale* (1845), 172.

[39] e.g. *Boswell* v. *Kilborn* (1862) 15 Moo. 309; *Turley* v. *Bates* (1863) 2 H. & C. 200 at 209. His formulation could also be cited via other works, such as J. P. Benjamin's treatise on the sale of goods: see *Martineau* v. *Kitching* (1872) LR 7 QB 436 at 445.

[40] *Hadley* v. *Baxendale* (1854) 9 Exch. 341. On this case, see pp. 541–5.

[41] e.g. Blackburn J's judgment in *Taylor* v. *Caldwell* (1863) 3 B. & S. 826.

[42] e.g. *Stanton* v. *Collier* (1852) 3 E. & B. 274 on the remoteness of damages; *Fishmongers' Co* v. *Robertson* (1843) 5 M. & G. 131 at 176, where Maule J. discussed Pothier's views on promises accepted by performance, or what would later be seen as 'unilateral' contracts.

at odds with English precedent, courts were sometimes content not to follow the foreign views quoted by counsel.[43]

English courts were as likely to adopt formulations from writers in English as from continental jurists. The works of the American Joseph Story, who was himself familiar with the civilian jurists, and who wrote important works in a large range of areas, including bills of exchange, bailments, agency, and equity jurisprudence, were especially influential. Particular passages could become favourites for the courts. For instance, Story's statement that a party acting without authority as agent of another 'will be personally responsible [...] to the person, with whom he is dealing for or on account of his principal'[44] was quoted repeatedly in English cases,[45] and was effectively endorsed in 1857 by the Exchequer Chamber.[46] Anglophone writers were able to exert more influence on the courts than foreign ones, since they discussed rules which were articulated in case law, or could be teased out of them. In some areas, the most influential discussions were not those of treatise writers but other legal authors. For instance, perhaps the most widely quoted text in the mid-nineteenth century was J. W. Smith's *A Selection of Leading Cases in Various Branches of the Law*, which was first published in 1837, and which was edited after Smith's premature death in 1845 by H. S. Keating and J. S. Willes, both of whom were to sit for many years in the Common Pleas.[47] They digested large amounts of case law in their extensive notes, and set out rules and principles derived from the cases as clearly as possible. They were also prepared to be critical of positions established by the case law, and to suggest new formulations. They were influential precisely because they remained strongly engaged with the technical forms out of which the common law developed, but were also aware of foreign learning which could illuminate principle. In their notes to *Vicars* v. *Wilcocks*, for instance, they discussed the learning on the remoteness of damages found in Theodore Sedgwick's American treatise (itself discussing civilian sources), and thereby helped to explain and propagate a set of principles which would be highly influential. In the same way, notes made by law reporters could also exert a great influence. For example, the rules set out in Serjeant Williams's notes to Saunders's reports on conditions were as influential on judicial conceptions of performance obligations in the first half of the century as any treatise formulation.[48]

---

[43] *Eicholz* v. *Bannister* (1864) 17 C.B. N.S. 708.

[44] J. Story, *Commentaries on the Law of Agency* (4th edn, Boston, 1851), § 264.

[45] *Smout* v. *Ilbery* (1842) 10 M. & W. 1 at 5; *Jones* v. *Downman* (1843) 4 Q.B. 235 at 239, *Jenkins* v. *Hutchinson* (1849) 13 Q.B. 744 at 751; *Lewis* v. *Nicholson* (1852) 18 Q.B. 503 at 513.

[46] *Collen* v. *Wright* (1857) 8 E. & B. 647, where (at 654) Willes J. intimated that the principle it articulated derived from Roman law and was restated in the French Civil Code.

[47] The 4th (1856) edition of this work was especially influential. The 5th (1862) edition was prepared by F. P. Maude and T. E. Chitty.

[48] On conditions, see e.g. Sjt Williams's notes to *Pordage* v. *Cole* (1669) 1 Wms. Saund. 319.

In the second half of the nineteenth century, a number of new treatises were written which were more theoretically informed. Writers now sought to apply will theory, and the lessons of continental jurisprudence, in a more thorough way. Treatise writers after 1860 were writing in a new intellectual environment. The reforms of legal education in the mid-nineteenth century, which saw a Council of Legal Education established by the Inns of Court in 1852, encouraged a more theoretical approach to law. The same era saw a revival of interest in Roman law learning,[49] and a growing desire by many English scholars to discover the work of German Pandectist jurists who had so clearly influenced John Austin. By the 1870s, reforms in university legal education had led to the revival of academic law learning, notably at Oxford.

These new treatise writers were, moreover, writing in an age of reform, which encouraged them to think of law in terms of general principle. The promise of law reform made the theorization of law a potentially practical matter. By the 1860s, there was growing interest in codification. David Dudley Field, whose procedural reforms so inspired the English in the 1850s, presented a civil code, based on existing common law, to the New York legislature in February 1865. Though never enacted, it did attract some interest in England.[50] At the same time, the third Indian Law Commission, appointed in 1861, turned its attention to contract law. This body, which sat in London, included Sir John Romilly, Sir William Erle, and James Shaw Willes, himself a devotee of codification.[51] In November 1866, it produced a report with a draft bill. Like Field's code, this one aimed to codify English contract law, stripped of local peculiarities.[52] It was designed to be systematic, setting out rules clearly, and illustrating them by examples, in the Benthamite style pioneered for India by Macaulay.

The bill began with a set of rules on the subject of contract in general, before setting out rules for particular areas (sale of goods, indemnity and guarantee, bailment, agency, and partnership). Rather than being strongly influenced by foreign theories, it was largely a digest of English case law, though it proposed modifying a large number of common law rules, often very significantly.[53] The

---

[49] M. Graziadei, 'Changing Images of the Law in Nineteenth Century English Thought (the Continental Impulse)' in M. Reimann (ed.), *The Reception of Continental Ideas in the Common Law World, 1820–1920* (Berlin, 1993), 115–63. For the mid-century reforms in legal education, see XI, Pt 4, ch. V.

[50] T. L. Murray Browne, 'The Civil Code of New York' (1870) 29 *Law Magazine and Law Review* 3rd ser. 1–23. For further discussion of codification, see XI, Pt 1, Ch III, pp. 55–9, XIII, Pt 1, Ch. VI, pp. 187–216.

[51] See his dissent in the Second Report of the Royal Commission to inquire into the Expediency of a Digest of Law, *PP* 1870 [c. 121], xviii, 231 at 7.

[52] W. Stokes (ed.), *The Anglo-Indian Codes*, 2 vols (Oxford, 1887), i, xxviii.

[53] For instance, it sought to modify the doctrine of consideration to allow gratuitous promises to be enforced, if they were registered, and to allow the payment of smaller sums to discharge larger

drafters were clearly influenced not only by Field's example, but sometimes by his formulations.[54] But their draft proved controversial in India, in part because of the proposal that all India was to be regarded in effect as a market overt, which was included to protect *bona fide* buyers of stolen property. When the legislative council in India objected and the Government of India stalled, the commissioners resigned. James Fitzjames Stephen, the new Law Member for India, then redrafted many of the early clauses of the bill, in order to get a clearer statement of the fundamental terms,[55] before securing the enactment of the legislation in 1872.

The example of the Indian code was important for English writers. In writing his treatise in 1876, Frederick Pollock said he kept the act in view 'almost constantly', using it as an 'instructive example of what can be done to consolidate and simplify English case-law'.[56] Other English writers also aimed to produce preparatory works for a digest. One such writer was S. M. Leake. A prominent member of the Juridical Society in the 1850s, he set out to write a systematic and scientific treatise on the *Elements of the Law of Contracts*, which appeared in 1867. By the second edition of the work (in 1878), Leake declared that his aim was to advance the law in the direction of a code. This treatise (Leake told his readers) dealt only with the 'general part' of contract law, 'the ground work common to all species of contract', rather than covering the details of specific contracts.[57] His treatment was in many ways pioneering: Leake was, for instance, the first writer to devote serious discussion to the doctrine of mistake. In the event, the movement to codify the general principles of English contract law failed to get anywhere,[58] though some areas were codified. Thanks in large part to the enthusiastic backing of the Institute of Bankers, the law relating to bills of exchange was codified in 1882 in a bill drafted by Mackenzie Chalmers (on the basis of a digest he had written in 1878). Eleven years later, a bill drafted by the same jurist codified the

---

debts. It sought to overturn the rule in *Jorden* v. *Money* (1854) 5 H.L.C. 185 that misrepresentations of intention were not actionable; and to allow damages for negligent misrepresentations. It also sought to abolish the distinction between liquidated damages and penalties. Not all these proposals found their way into the final act. Papers showing the Present Position of the Question of a Contract Law for India, *PP* 1867–8 (239), xlix, 601.

[54] For instance, Field's general definition of a contract in s. 744 of his code—'A contract is an agreement to do or not to do a certain thing'—was echoed by the opening clause of the commissioners' draft: 'A contract is an agreement between parties whereby a party engages to do a thing or engages not to do a thing.' See also C. Ilbert's comment: 'Many gobbets of undigested Field went out to India in the Contract Bill; too many of them still remain in the Contract Act': 'Sir James Stephen as a Legislator' (1894) 10 *LQR* 222–7 at 223.

[55] *Minutes and notes by the Hon Sir James Fitzjames Stephen, 1869–1872* (Simla, 1898), 149.

[56] F. Pollock, *Principles of Contract at Law and in Equity* (1876), vii.

[57] S. M. Leake, *An Elementary Digest of the Law of Contracts* (2nd edn, 1878), ix.

[58] By the 3rd (1892) edition, Leake re-presented his work more as a manual for practitioners.

law relating to the Sale of Goods. Instead of using the Indian Contract Act as his example, Chalmers digested the English rules, making use of English treatises on the subject by Blackburn and Benjamin.[59] By the 1890s, Parliament was prepared to countenance codes of various specific areas of commercial law, but no attempts were made to codify a 'general part'.

The general part of contract law was left, instead, to the jurists. From the 1880s, two other academic writers, both Oxford professors, had come to dominate the field. Frederick Pollock and William Anson both wrote treatises in the 1870s setting out the general principles of law, while engaging in theoretical discussion of the foundations of law. Pollock in particular sought to set forth ideas taken from Roman law, as well as comparative law, which he felt were not then readily available to students.[60] It was evident to both men that their task was a complex one. '[T]he law is still unsettled even on rudimentary points', Anson told Alfred Thesiger, when sending him a copy of the first edition of his book in 1879, 'and in such matters one feels the excitement of an explorer.'[61] Over the next decades, these writers would rethink and revise their texts, reordering chapters and explanations as new cases were decided and new theories emerged.[62] These scholars responded to two intellectual impulses. The first was their reading of F. C. von Savigny's *System des heutigen römischen Rechts* and his *Obligationenrecht*. The second was the revolution in private law scholarship occurring across the Atlantic ocean at Harvard, which led to the publication of C. C. Langdell's *Summary of the Law of Contracts* in 1880, by far the most thorough and sophisticated theoretical discussion of the bases of the common law of contracts which had hitherto been written. Langdell's approach to the teaching and study of law sparked prolonged debates over contract theory and doctrine, conducted for the greater part by American law professors and in the pages of American law journals. Pollock and Anson, as academic lawyers (and in Pollock's case, the editor of the main English law journal, the *Law Quarterly Review*), sought to participate in these debates, and to incorporate their findings in their work.

Frederick Pollock's *Principles of Contract at Law and in Equity* was published in 1876, before Langdell's work appeared. Its author borrowed much of his theory from Savigny.[63] The book began with a short discussion of the concept of the will,

---

[59] Chalmers wrote *The Sale of Goods* in 1890, two years after his first draft Sale of Goods Bill.

[60] Pollock, *Principles of Contract* (1876), preface.

[61] Letter 20 March 1879, bound into the copy of W. R. Anson, *Principles of the English Law of Contract* (Oxford, 1879), Library of the Institute of Advanced Legal Studies, University of London.

[62] Anson completed the 11th edn of his work in 1906. The 12th (1910) edn was by M. L. Gwyer. The last edition of Pollock's treatise to appear in his lifetime was the 10th, in 1936.

[63] Anson also drew on Savigny's definitions of agreement for his concept, though less extensively. Anson, *Contract* (3rd edn, Oxford, 1884), 2–3.

borrowed from Savigny, whose genius he lavishly praised.[64] Pollock's general definition focused on two features which were borrowed—'almost literally', as he put it—from Savigny. The first element was the consent of the parties; the second was that their intention was directed to legal consequences.[65] But Pollock's use of the will theory was not very deep.[66] In contrast to the German's lengthy, subtle, and sophisticated analytical discussion of concepts derived from Roman law, Pollock's general discussion of contract ran to only seven pages, one of which was devoted to quoting the definition given in the Indian Contract Act. Having translated Savigny's definition of contract, Pollock wrote that it was 'one of the things which look very obvious when they are once stated', possibly 'too obvious to be worth making much of'.[67] His use of Savigny's general definition, focusing on the will, did not take matters very much further forward theoretically than the earlier writers' simple invocation of Pothier. Moreover, the one aspect of Savigny's will theory which did look novel to English eyes—the need for parties to have an intention to create legal relations—was not developed in the text.[68]

Although Pollock had read and was influenced by Savigny's work, he did not seek to develop a systematic jurisprudential treatise of obligations based on the German's work. Rather, he sought to explain the principles in English case law, and so borrowed from Savigny as and when he was useful. For instance, Pollock's handling of the doctrine of mistake relied much on Savigny. The doctrines set out in the appendix to the third book of the *System*, he said, 'appear to be in the main applicable to the law of England'[69] and Savigny's discussion of the categories of mistake proved very influential both on Pollock's organization of his material and on his articulation of the rules.[70] Nonetheless, his discussion was largely devoted to ranging the English case law materials into the headings borrowed from

---

[64] Pollock, *Contract* (1876), 1–2.

[65] Pollock gave his own translation of Book III, § 104 of the *System*, where Savigny defined contract as 'the agreement of several people on a common declaration of will designed to regulate their legal relations'.

[66] Pollock was not a very deep thinker: see Gordley, *Philosophical Origins*, 216. See also N. Duxbury, *Frederick Pollock and the English Juristic Tradition* (Oxford, 2004), esp. 191–201.

[67] Pollock, *Contract* (1876), 2n.

[68] The need for parties to intend legal relations was only articulated in case law later (such as *Balfour* v. *Balfour* [1919] 2 KB 571). Pollock himself did not use the term 'intention to create legal relations', and commented on the difficulty of translating *Rechtsverhältniss*: *Contract* (1876), 2n.

[69] Pollock, *Contract* (1876), 337.

[70] For instance, discussing mistakes of quality, Savigny said that in determining whether an essential or actionable error had been made, one had 'to consult the general opinion taken in commerce' regarding the nature or purpose of the object, *System*, iii § 137. Pollock, *Contract*, p. 393 noted that the error had to be that 'according to the ordinary course of dealing' it amounted to a difference in kind. He did not, however, discuss Savigny's distinction between the external declaration of one's will, and of the internal will, *System*, iii § 134.

Savigny, while noting that the German's 'conclusions in detail are not always the same as in our law'.[71] Moreover, in many areas of English law, Savigny's analysis provided no tools to assist the English jurist. For instance, the doctrine of consideration, which remained central in contract law, could not be explained in terms of will theory. In this area, English jurists like Pollock engaged in transatlantic debates, with the likes of Langdell and his students, Ames and Williston, which often centred on the principles behind the forms of action as they had developed in early modern England.

A bigger problem for will theory lay in the fact that an objective, rather than a subjective, view of contract formation had become embedded in English contract doctrine.[72] Treatise writers such as Pollock did not dwell on the theoretical problem this posed for will theory.[73] However, T.E. Holland, author of a textbook on *The Elements of Jurisprudence*, did raise objections to a theory which required a subjective union of the parties' wills. Holland argued, against Savigny, that the law did not look at the will itself, but at the 'will as voluntarily manifested'. As he put it, a man who had induced another to enter into a contract with him, while himself never intending to perform his obligations, would not be permitted to argue in court that he was not contractually bound, on the ground that there had been no true meeting of the wills. When the state enforced contracts, he argued, it did so 'to prevent disappointment of well-founded expectations which, though they usually arise from expressions truly representing intentions, yet may occasionally arise otherwise'.[74]

Anson attempted to defend Savigny's view from Holland's attacks but in so doing he conceded much. He admitted that a party was bound by an apparent expression of his intent, and could not be excused on the ground that he subjectively meant something different. Nonetheless, he felt that it could not be argued

---

[71] Pollock, *Contract* (1876), 394n.   [72] For a discussion, see pp. 338–9.

[73] Langdell noted that 'mental acts or acts of the will are not the materials out of which promises are made', but that they rather required a physical act, *A Summary of the Law of Contracts* (Boston, 1880) § 180. Langdell did not, however, use this insight to attack will theory. Indeed, it was not inconsistent with Savigny's distinction between the will itself and declarations of the will (see e.g. *System*, iii § 114).

[74] T. E. Holland, *The Elements of Jurisprudence* (2nd edn, Oxford, 1882), 194–5. In later editions (e.g. 7th edn, 1895) at 229–30n), Holland invoked Adam Ferguson's *Institutes of Moral Philosophy* (1800), 155, which stated, 'An action of any kind performed with a view to raise expectation, or by which it is known that expectations are naturally raised, is sufficient to constitute a contract'. Holland's argument was not, however, that courts should only ever look at the external manifestation of the will (which might prevent them from vitiating contracts entered into through fraud or mistake). Hence, at the same time that he modified Savigny's general definition, Holland accepted the Pandectist argument that 'juridical acts' (*Rechtsgeschäfte*), or acts directed at legal consequences, required the outward manifestation of the will to reflect the inner intention: *Jurisprudence*, 2nd edn, at 86–7.

that one person was bound whenever another person had changed his position, in reliance on expressions which had been made. The party who was to be held bound 'must have acted as though he intended to raise an expectation in the mind' of the other. For Anson, contract law still had to be seen as based on the notion of a *consensus ad idem*, but 'the Court will assume its existence as a necessary sequence of certain overt acts of the parties'.[75] In later editions, Anson merely observed that for 'all practical purposes', the disagreement between himself and Holland was 'immaterial'. Each theorist in effect was seeking to take on board the fact that contracts were not based on a real subjective meeting of minds, without developing a theory according to which obligations could be generated merely by conduct reasonably relied on.

A second, more radical, challenge to will theory came from Oliver Wendell Holmes. Holmes was sceptical about the kind of technical and logical definitions which were to be found both in the work of the Pandectists and of his Harvard colleague, Langdell. He was ready to agree that the obligation incurred in contract law had to be a voluntary one (unlike obligations in tort). But he pointed out that it was wrong to think that all the details of a contractual obligation were filled out by the will of the parties. Much of the detail in any contract was still left to the courts to flesh out, and this they did, not according to some logical theory, but according to the requirements of convenience.[76] In deciding, for example, whether a term in a contract was a condition or not, courts did not determine what had been the will of the parties, but decided 'by reference to the habits of the community and to convenience'.[77] Equally challenging was Holmes's denial of the view that a contractual promise generated rights which could be enforced by the innocent party. A contracting party did not give a promise to perform, he suggested, but only promised to pay the cost of non-performance. The law left anyone free to break his contract; it only forced him to pay in the event of breach. In effect, entering into a contract was simply a matter of assuming a risk, which might have to be paid for.

Although Holmes's theory offered useful insights into how to quantify damages, his notion that parties were in effect free to break contracts provided they paid did not convince English treatise writers. Anson simply dismissed the idea that contract law only generated obligations to pay, and not obligations to perform. People entering contracts thought mainly about the performance, not about the consequences of breach.[78] Holland also dismissed Holmes's view as unrealistic.[79] Pollock more charitably referred to his friend's thesis as a 'brilliant paradox', but observed that it

---

[75] Anson, *Contracts* (2nd edn, 1882), 12–13.
[76] O. W. Holmes, *The Common Law* (Boston, 1881), 302.
[77] Holmes, *Common Law*, 337.
[78] Anson, *Principles* (2nd edn, 1882), 8–9.
[79] Holland, *Jurisprudence* (2nd edn, 1882), 193–4.

was not consistent with the doctrine of specific performance, according to which parties were indeed forced to perform.[80] After the publication of *The Common Law*, Pollock responded to Holmes that '[a] man who bespeaks a coat of his tailor will scarcely be persuaded that he is only betting with the tailor that such a coat will not be made and delivered to him within a certain time. What he wants and means to have is the coat, not an insurance against not having a coat.'[81]

Nevertheless, Pollock modified his own views in the first edition to be published after *The Common Law*. Having noted Holmes's challenge to the 'current [view] that the essence of obligation is the partial subjection of one free agent's will to another', he sought to answer Holmes by shifting his own position. 'The risk', he noted, 'is in most cases not part of the promise at all; it arises from the liability imposed on the promisor by the State.'[82] The law of contract, he now said, was 'the endeavour of the State [...] to establish a positive sanction for the expectation of good faith which has grown up in the mutual dealings of men of average right-mindedness'.[83] As his ideas developed (and having encountered Holland's ideas), Pollock came to stress the expectations which had been reasonably generated in the mind of the plaintiff by the conduct of the defendant, rather than the defining contractual obligations solely in terms of the wills of the parties. 'He who has given the promise', Pollock wrote, 'is bound to him who accepts it, not merely because he has expressed a certain intention, but because he so expressed himself as to entitle the other party to rely on his acting in a certain way.'[84] This was a way of amending his will-based definition to take account of the objective theory. Having modified his definition, however, Pollock did not seek to recast his vision of contract law in general to fit with it.[85]

---

[80] Pollock, *Contract* (7th edn, 1902), 183n.

[81] Pollock, *Contract* (3rd edn, 1881), xix.   [82] *Ibid.*

[83] Pollock first devised this formulation in the introduction to the 3rd edn of *Contract* (1881, xx), when countering Holmes's view, and expanded it in the preface to the 4th (1885) edn and promoted it to the text in the 5th edn (Oxford, 1889) 1. Cf. A. L. Goodhart, 'Introduction' to F. Pollock, *Jurisprudence and Legal Essays* (1961), x–xi. See also S. Waddams, 'What *Were* the Principles of Nineteenth-Century Contract Law,' in A. Lewis, P. Brand, and P. Mitchell, *Law in the City: Proceedings of the Seventeenth British Legal History Conference* (Dublin, 2007) 304–18 at 312–13.

[84] This sentence came from the preface of the 4th (1885) edn, the first to appear after Holland had developed his point about expectations in the 2nd edn of his *Jurisprudence*. See his subsequent claim that he had seen 'reasonable expectation as the real fundamental conception in contract' in his 3rd edn: M. D. Howe (ed.), *The Pollock-Holmes Letters: Correspondence of Sir Frederick Pollock and Mr Justice Holmes 1874–1932*, 2 vols, (Cambridge, 1942), ii, 48.

[85] The lack of importance to Pollock of the overarching theory for the explanations offered can be seen from his statement (relating to contracts voided for mistake, misrepresentation, and fraud) that '[i]n substance Mr Holmes has enunciated in a more thoroughgoing and concise form the same principles by means of which, having been guided to them in Roman law by Savigny, I endeavoured in this book to introduce some rational order into' English doctrines: *Contract* (3rd edn, 1881), xviii.

In fact, English contract writers at the end of the nineteenth century and at the start of the twentieth were largely pragmatic when it came to theory. They were prepared to borrow from foreign theories when they felt it would help their expositions of particular areas of English law. But they did not strive to create logical and coherent systems of law. Pollock therefore shared Holmes's scepticism of efforts to reduce the common law to logical consistency, a trait he associated particularly with James Barr Ames. Legal rules, he said, existed not for their own sake, but 'to further justice and convenience in the business of human life'.[86] Where American scholars such as Ames, Langdell, and Williston sought in their textbooks and in law review articles to tease out logical distinctions, and figure out the philosophical foundations of numerous doctrines, common lawyers in England were often content to attempt to make the best sense of the doctrine they were given by the courts, not worrying too unduly if at moments its foundations could not be rigorously explained. There remained much in the common law—not least the doctrine of consideration—which could not adequately be explained in terms of will theory. However, for the most part, English theorists remained content with will theory as a workable tool for distinguishing contractual from non-contractual obligations.

English contract law in 1914 thus remained largely untheoretical, despite the injection of German and American ideas. The development of contract doctrine in the nineteenth century was not driven by theory, domestic or foreign. Moreover, although Pollock and Anson's texts became dominant in the student market, the early nineteenth-century works by Chitty and Addison were not superseded: they continued to be produced by new editors, in ever lengthier volumes which aimed at comprehensive coverage of the latest legal developments in court. So busy were they in digesting new case law and statute, that the new editors of old works often wholly missed out on new doctrinal developments which more recent texts discussed. Thus, despite being very substantial in length, Wyatt Paine's 1909 (15th) edition of *Chitty on Contracts* and W. E. Gordon and John Ritchie's 1911 (11th) edition of *Addison on Contracts* almost entirely omitted discussion of mistake. These works may have suggested that practitioners felt able to get on well enough without the refinements of will theory.

3. THE INFLUENCE OF PROCEDURE

At the start of our period, in 1820, there was no single procedure for dealing with contractual actions. Rather, there were numerous different kinds of remedy and numerous different courts. In 1914, there was a single Supreme Court of Judicature, and a simplified system of pleading which allowed parties to put

---

[86] Pollock *Contract* (9th edn, 1921), x. Cf. F. Pollock, 'The Methods of Jurisprudence,' in his *Oxford Lectures and Other Discourses* (1890), 1–36 at 33.

the facts of their dispute to the court. This was the result of two developments. First, the fragmented system of common law forms of action and the technical system of special pleading was first reformed (in 1852), and then abolished (in 1875). Secondly, the separate jurisdictions of common law and equity were fused in 1875. The question is therefore raised whether these procedural changes contributed to a new general conceptualization of contract law in place of a view of fragmented and disparate remedies for particular breaches.[87]

Parties seeking pecuniary compensation for breaches of contract at common law had a choice of three main forms of action.[88] The action of covenant, which was used to obtain damages, required the parties to have drawn up a formal deed. The action of debt could be used where the contract was a formal one, on a bond, or an 'informal' one, without any specialty. Unlike the other contractual actions, it was used where the plaintiff sought to recover a specific sum owed, rather than unliquidated damages. The action of assumpsit was used only for informal contracts, where damages were sought. Unlike the action of debt, it could be used both for executed contracts (using a general *indebitatus* count) or for executory ones (using a 'special' count).

This fragmentation of remedies should not, however, lead us to assume that lawyers had no general concept of contract until their abolition.[89] The actions of assumpsit, covenant, and debt were seen as procedural forms through which contractual disputes were brought to court, not as substantive categories of their own. While it is true that the distinction between contract and tort became more clearly articulated in legislation after the establishment of the county courts (which had different cost regimes for each),[90] pleaders had long been aware of the distinction between contractual and delictual actions,[91] and the established procedural rules which differentiated between them. First, plaintiffs in actions founded on contract were required to prove the contract as laid, even if the contractual question was brought to court in a delictual form.[92] They would lose (on the doctrine of variance) if they failed to prove every allegation. By contrast, in tort, it was only necessary to prove so much as left the plaintiff a good cause of

---

[87] On the procedure of the courts and their reform, see further XI, Pt 3, Ch III.

[88] The actions of annuity and account also existed but were rarely used.

[89] William Blackstone, for instance, had given a general definition of contracts in Book 2 of his *Commentaries*, when discussing how people acquired rights in things. His discussion of the fragmented remedies followed in Book 3, discussing remedies available when rights were invaded.

[90] Moreover, the 1852 Common Law Procedure Act grouped tortious and contractual forms of pleading: 15 & 16 Vict. c. 76, Sch. B.

[91] 'Personal actions are in form *ex contractu* or *ex delicto*, or, in other words, are for breach of contract or for wrongs unconnected with contract', J. Chitty, *A Practical Treatise on Pleading and on the Parties to Actions*, 2 vols (1809), i, 87.

[92] See *Bristow* v. *Wright* (1781) 2 Doug. 665.

action.[93] Secondly, the rules as to the joinder of parties differed in contractual and tort actions.[94] Thirdly, contractual actions could be brought against executors, whereas torts died with the tortfeasor.

However, the particular rules of contract law which developed were shaped by the forms of action. The most important of these was *assumpsit*, the commonest contractual action used.[95] This action was founded on the notion of a promise, which bound because it was backed by consideration. The form of pleading in this action focused attention not on any meeting of the minds, but on consideration.[96] At first glance, this form seems to support Atiyah's view of a legal system which looked to compensate for benefits received rather than to enforce the mere will of the parties. It might suggest that it was only when the concept of consideration was emptied of content as the nineteenth century went on, and as will theory developed, that a concept of contract centred on consent could develop. But in fact, the action of *assumpsit* did not mask the essentially consensual nature of contractual transactions. It was not simply an action to compensate for benefits conferred. This can be seen by looking both at how the action was used in executed and in executory contracts. Where a defendant had failed to pay for benefits he had received, the general *indebitatus* count was used. Under this count, the plaintiff was required to prove only the debt, rather than the promise, since the law implied a promise consequent on the debt.[97] However, even when parties sued on executed contracts, the court's attention was primarily focused on the contract which the parties had agreed, rather than on any broader notions of justice in the transactions. This form was generally used by parties who had made detailed contracts, which were proved in court. 'There are', Lord Ellenborough observed in 1805, 'a great variety of agreements not under seal, containing detailed provisions regulating prices of labour, rates of hire, times, and manner of performance, adjustment of differences, &c. which are every day declared upon in the general form of a count for work and labour.'[98] Although the

[93] Chitty, *Pleading* (1809), i, 373.

[94] In delictual actions, the omission of a party who ought to have been joined could only be taken by a plea in abatement or by apportioning damages at the trial, whereas in contract actions, it could be taken advantage of as the ground of a nonsuit. Chitty, *Pleading* (1809), i, 53.

[95] W. Tidd, *The Practice of the Courts of King's Bench and Common Pleas in Personal Actions*, 2 vols (6th edn, 1817), i, 2.

[96] See S. Williston, 'Freedom of Contract' (1921) 6 *Cornell Law Quarterly* 365–80 at 368: 'the basis of the action [of assumpsit] was conceived to be consideration rather than the mutual will of the parties. That the plaintiff had parted with something in reliance upon the defendant's promise, and that the defendant had made his promise in return for something requested by him, were the essential facts on which the earlier cases were decided'.

[97] In these cases, a promise was implied to pay for the benefits received; the promise was itself not traversable.

[98] *Clarke v. Gray* (1805) 6 East 564 at 569. See also *Robson v. Godfrey* (1816) 1 Stark. 275 at 277.

contract was executed, judges and juries were still expected to look to the terms agreed in determining liability. If the parties had deviated from their agreement, but work had been done and accepted, then the plaintiff could still recover on the common counts where the evidence was sufficient to support it.[99] But the mere receipt of benefits was not sufficient to generate an obligation. Rather, as the words of the pleadings in assumpsit showed, the work had to be done at the defendant's *request*. The general counts in assumpsit using the request form[100] were not a form to restore unjust enrichments:[101] the action was known to be a contractual one. By contrast, in executory contracts, where a purchaser of goods refused to accept them, or where a vendor refused to deliver goods, the agreement had to be specifically set out in the declaration.[102] The form of action in assumpsit thus did not disguise the fact that the jury was looking for an agreement between the parties.

Where assumpsit was crucial in shaping understandings of contract in England was in its focus on the need for consideration.[103] The presence of consideration was not a universal contractual requirement. It was not necessary to show any consideration in actions of covenant, nor in debt on bond. Explaining this, the elder Joseph Chitty noted that 'in general the circumstances under which the deed was made are immaterial, and a consideration is seldom essential, or at least it is to be presumed'.[104] But as the last comment indicates, consideration was regarded as important for conceptions of contract. Blackstone was again typical of late eighteenth-century writers in including it as a central element, stating that in all

---

[99] *Harris* v. *Oke* (1759) in F. Buller, *An Introduction to the Law Relative to Trials at Nisi Prius* (5th edn, 1790), 139–40; *Payne* v. *Bacomb* (1781) 2 Doug. 651. As Sir James Mansfield CJ pointed out in *Cooke* v. *Munstone* (1805) 1 B. & P.N.R. 351, for this to apply, the special contract had to have been terminated.

[100] Contrast the form of *indebitatus assumpsit* for money had and received, which did not allege a request. This is discussed further below, p. 564.

[101] In the early nineteenth century, plaintiffs were expected to aver a request whenever the consideration was executed; though as Manning Sjt noted in 1840, such an averment was unnecessary 'if the act stated as the consideration cannot, from its nature, have been a gratuitous kindness', Manning's note to *Fisher* v. *Pyne* (1840) 1 M. & G. 265. This view was endorsed by Parke B. in *Victors* v. *Davies* (1844) 12 M. & W. 758 at 760. See also the notes to *Osborne* v. *Rogers* (1669) 1 Wms. Saund. 264.

[102] See e.g. J. Wentworth, *A Complete System of Pleading*, 10 vols, (1797–9), ii: 128ff.

[103] In assumpsit, the consideration for the promise had to be stated in the declaration. 'In debt on simple contract, express or implied, to pay money in consideration of a precedent debt or duty, the subject matter of the debt is to be described precisely as in the common counts in assumpsit': Chitty, *Pleading* (1809), i, 344–5. In debt, however, no promise needed to be alleged.

[104] Chitty, *Pleading* (1809), 346. See also [Ballow], *A Treatise of Equity*, ed. J. Fonblanque (Dublin, 1793–5), i, 338.

contracts, 'something must be given in exchange'.[105] The centrality of consideration in the minds of nineteenth century lawyers was further reinforced by the fact that the 'informal' contract, based on the notion of an exchange or bargain between the parties, and associated with the action of assumpsit, became the paradigm contract. It is not insignificant that the most influential early nineteenth-century treatise was the younger Joseph Chitty's, on contracts not under seal. However strong the will theory became, it was not able to dislodge the centrality of consideration.

If the fragmented forms of action did not prevent English jurists from developing a general conception of contract, did the system of pleading hinder the development of doctrine? It has often been pointed out that issues which would later become questions of law were often dealt with as questions of fact in the early nineteenth century. This was either because defendants pleaded the general issue, leaving all questions for the jury's consideration,[106] or because they were masked by the doctrine of variance. This rule stated that if a party's evidence did not fully prove the facts alleged in his declaration, the case was lost. This might suggest that in many cases, courts would never be called on to discuss substantive issues about what degree of consensus was required to generate contractual obligations, since the defendant could simply argue that the contract declared on in the pleadings was different from the one proven in court, leaving it to the jury to find the variance.[107] This might suggest that the development of a principled law of contract would only commence when reforms in the third quarter of the nineteenth century had significantly simplified the system of pleading and allowed lawyers to think beyond the old categories dictated by the traditional forms of action.

However, the reforms of the 1830s, which tightened up the rules of pleadings to such a degree that they provoked severe criticism within a decade, were designed precisely to refine questions for legal development. The problem faced by the Common Law Commissioners of 1830 was not that plaintiffs were losing good cases by simple errors of pleading. Rather, the current system encouraged pleaders put in too many counts and pleas,[108] which added unnecessarily to the

---

[105] *Comms.* i, 444. He was also typical in claiming that consideration had the same function as *causa* in Roman law.

[106] J. H. Baker, 'From Sanctity of Contract to Reasonable Expectation?' (1979) 32 *Current Legal Problems*, 17–39 at 20.

[107] Hamburger, 'Nineteenth-Century Consensus Theory', 277–82.

[108] It was from a fear of the doctrine of variance that pleaders before 1834 inserted so many counts. They did this because the facts or the law were often ambiguous and they wanted enough counts to ensure that at least one would be put to a jury. J. Chitty, *The Practice of the Law in all its Departments*, 3 vols (1835), iii, 475.

expense of litigation.[109] The cost was multiplied by defendants pleading the general issue, which forced the plaintiff to prove everything contained in the allegation and allowed the defendant to put in any facts which might answer the claim. The commissioners did not argue that this system made it impossible to raise the relevant legal points: for if the trial failed 'to accomplish the purposes of justice', the defeated party applied for a new trial.[110] The problem caused by the general issue was that it imposed too great a burden on the judge at trial, by expecting him to extract the true issue between the parties from the proofs, and to separate out questions of law from fact, before presenting the factual question for the jury. This was an extremely difficult task for a single judge, without access to authorities, to perform at *nisi prius*. The pleading reforms of the 1830s were thus designed to raise the legal questions more precisely. Defendants were no longer to plead the general issue. In contractual actions, the general plea—'non assumpsit'—was only to be used where the fact of the promise was denied (or in the *indebitatus* counts, the facts on which the debt was said to accrue). Otherwise, every matter in confession or avoidance, including all matters which showed the contract to be void or voidable, was to be specially pleaded.[111]

The reforms of the 1830s also addressed the question of variances. It was proposed that plaintiffs should only be non-suited when there was a failure of proof, but not where there was a discrepancy between allegation and proof in some minor particulars.[112] It was to be made easier both to amend pleadings, in cases where the plaintiff had made an error, and to allow the defendant to plead a variance in cases where the contract was significantly different from that alleged by the plaintiff. In such a case, plaintiffs would be able to take issue on the variance claimed, or to admit the variance but show that it was not relevant to the claim.[113] These proposals were implemented in 1833.[114] The fact that the parties were invited to take issue on the variance by these changes invited them to ask new *legal* questions. The pleading reforms of 1834 thus did encourage lawyers to raise new legal points. Indeed, in a number of areas, the new doctrines said to have transformed contract law dated from the early 1850s, before effects of the mid-century changes

---

[109] Second Report made to His Majesty by the Commissioners appointed to inquire into the Practice and Proceedings of the Superior Courts of Common Law, *PP* 1830 (123), xi, 547 [henceforth cited as Common Law Commission 1830 Report], pp. 34–5. For the recommendations in summary, see pp. 85 *et seq.*

[110] Common Law Commission 1830 Report, 46.

[111] *Ibid.*, 48.   [112] *Ibid.*, 37–8.   [113] *Ibid.*, 40–1.

[114] According to one treatise, judges were at first reluctant to make amendments, but by the late 1830s were doing so more regularly. Chitty, *Pleading* (7th edn, by H. Greening, 1844), i, 328 n. For examples of amendments, see *Hanbury* v. *Ella* (1834) 1 Ad. & El. 61; *Whiwill* v. *Scheer* (1838) 8 Ad. & El. 112; *Boucher* v. *Murray* (1844) 6 Q.B. 362; *Boys* v. *Ancell* (1839) 5 Bing. N.C. 390; *Smith* v. *Brandram* (1841) 2 M. & G. 244; *Gurford* v. *Bayley* (1842) 3 M. & G. 781.

in pleading could be felt.[115] The fact that some doctrines—such as mistake—developed later cannot be attributed to any masking by the pleadings. By mid-century, it was apparent to many that the cost of these reforms far outweighed their benefit to litigants, since an increasing number of cases were lost on purely technical grounds, and costs had not diminished. Nonetheless, it is noteworthy that when the rules were relaxed, there was some concern in the profession that the development of the law would be left in the hands of mere *nisi prius* advocates, rather than learned lawyers, which might damage the law.[116]

The rules of pleading were significantly simplified in 1852. Commissioners who reported in 1851 sought to achieve the certainty and distinctness in pleading which had been desired by their predecessors, while avoiding the inconveniences of a highly technical system, by making the parties focus on substance instead of form. Their proposals—which were implemented by legislation and new rules—recommended removing many rules which made it easy for a party to lose for technical reasons.[117] Two changes were central. First, parties were no longer to be required to mention the forms of action in pleading. It was sufficient if the facts which constituted the cause of action were sufficiently set forth in the declaration, for it was the facts, and not the form, which determined whether there was a cause of action.[118] Secondly, it was recommended that parties be permitted to join different forms of action together in one proceeding. The theory behind the rule which prevented parties from doing this—that it kept dissimilar causes of action distinct—was shown to be false, since the boundaries created by the old forms of action allowed often incongruous claims to be brought together, while substantively compatible ones were kept apart.[119] Pleading was simplified, rather than revolutionized by these reforms. The common counts continued to be used for executed contracts, without the parties needing to specify whether they were using debt or assumpsit. Under the rules of 1853, particulars of demand had to be supplied by the plaintiff where *indebitatus* forms were used.[120] Special counts continued to be used (for executory contracts), in which the plaintiff had to set

---

[115] e.g. *Hochster* v. *De La Tour* (1852) 2 E. & B. 678, *Hadley* v. *Baxendale* (1854) 9 Exch. 341.

[116] (1852) 20 *LT* 74.

[117] Thus, where the right of a party depended on the performance of conditions precedent, it was proposed he should be able to aver performance generally, so that his adversary would be obliged to focus on the substantive issue between them. In general, see XI, Pt 3, Ch III. pp. 585–91.

[118] In coming to this conclusion, the commissioners noted that the forms of action did not coincide with substantive distinctions, since essentially contractual matters could be framed as torts, while tort disputes could be pleaded in assumpsit. First Report, RC on the Process, Practice and System of Pleading in the Superior Courts of Common Law, *PP* 1851 [1389], xxii, 567 at 33.

[119] The example they gave (at pp. 31–2) was the inability to join actions on a bond (which was sued on either in debt or covenant) with one on a bill of exchange (which was sued on in assumpsit).

[120] E. Bullen and S. M. Leake, *Precedents of Pleadings* (2nd edn, 1863), 46n.

out the substance of the contract. Matters in confession and avoidance continued
to have to be specially pleaded, just as under the 1834 rules.[121] A further step was
taken with the union of jurisdictions in the Judicature Acts of 1873/5 and the rules
of the Supreme Court promulgated under it. The old common law forms of action
were now finally abolished. Pleadings were to be as brief as possible, containing only a summary statement of the material facts on which the plaintiff relied.
In contract cases, parties had to state when the contract was written, and were
permitted to set out the contract verbatim. In all cases where the party pleading
relied on any misrepresentation, fraud, wilful default, or undue influence, this
had to be stated in the pleadings.[122] Equally, where the performance of a condition precedent was intended to be contested, it had to be distinctly specified in
the pleas.

These changes made pleading in contract cases simpler and more coherent,
and proved a great practical advantage. How far they contributed to changes
in thinking about contract law in general may be doubted. To begin with, the
rules relating to the most commonly used forms in the first half of the century—
assumpsit and debt on simple contract—were largely the same, and the same
view of contract underlay both actions. Moreover, it had already been settled
that questions of breaches of warranty or pre-contractual fraud—which in the
eighteenth century could only be sued on in the tortious action on the case for
deceit—could be raised using the action of assumpsit, to allow the plaintiff to join
the common counts. Unlike those seeking to find a conceptual unity in the law
of torts, those seeking a conceptual unity for the law of contract did not have to
attempt to knit together a disparate set of remedies after 1852.

Although pleading was significantly simplified after 1852, and although the
forms of action were abolished in 1875, the categories of pleas and defences
included in manuals of pleading after 1883 were the same as those used earlier
in the century, since they were derived from them. The fact that the changes in
pleading did not revolutionize contract law is perhaps most amply shown by
the fact that new editions of the early nineteenth century treatises by Chitty
and Addison continued to be published, with new material added. The reforms
did, however, have a significant impact on how contract cases were tried. For at
the same time that pleading in contract was simplified, so the role of the jury
in these cases diminished dramatically. The old system of pleading had been
designed to isolate questions of fact for the jury, and to identify questions of law
for the judge to resolve. After 1883, the jury was the exception in contractual

---

[121] Rule 8 of the Rules of Pleading of Trinity Term 1853, in Bullen and Leake, *Precedents of
Pleadings* (2nd edn, 1863), 731, and the editors' comments at p. 396.
[122] RSC 1883, Ord. XIX r. 6.

disputes, rather than the rule, and the judges were left to decide both questions of fact and law.[123]

A more important impediment to the development of a unified view of contract law before 1875 was the separation of law and equity. The system of common law pleading, and the rule (which remained until 1851) forbidding parties to testify, restricted the range of questions which the court could consider. By contrast, the Court of Chancery, with its flexible bill procedure which allowed the court to probe the conscience of the parties, was a much more suitable venue for exploring questions concerning the parties' intentions. Its machinery allowed it to root out fraud and undue influence and to discover mistakes in a way the common law judges could not. The Chancery could be used as an auxiliary to common law courts, as where parties already engaged in a common law dispute commenced a suit in equity to obtain the discovery of information. But equity also offered a different set of remedies—notably injunction and specific performance—and had a concurrent jurisdiction in a number of areas of contract law. This created space for different understandings of contract law to develop in the different courts.

By the mid-nineteenth century, law reformers were beginning to look to fuse the two jurisdictions of law and equity. They first sought to give each court the power to get at the truth and the merits in each case, and to allow complete justice to be done in the court where the case commenced. One aspect of this was to allow parties in suits, as well as interested persons, to be competent witnesses at common law. In 1851, legislation passed to permit the evidence of parties. A second aspect was to give the common law some of the remedies available in equity, and vice versa, so that parties would not be required to go to different tribunals. Various Acts in the 1850s sought to give the one court powers derived from the other. The 1854 Common Law Procedure Act gave to common law courts the power of compelling the discovery of documents and facts. It also empowered the common law courts to grant specific performance and injunctions, and it allowed defendants to enter equitable pleas.[124] Common law courts thereby obtained part of the auxiliary jurisdiction of equity, though the foundation of the dispute still had to be one over which the common law courts had jurisdiction. The common law judges were a little reluctant to make use of these powers, and it was soon settled that they would only allow pleadings on equitable grounds where they could by their judgment do complete and final justice and settle all the equities between

---

[123] M. Lobban, 'The Strange Life of the English Civil Jury, 1837–1914', in J. W. Cairns and G. McLeod (eds), *The Dearest Birthright of the People of England: The Jury in the History of the Common Law* (Oxford, 2002), 173–215 at 191.

[124] Common Law Procedure Act 1854 (17 & 18 Vict. c. 125), ss. 50–7, 68, 79, 83. The reforms are discussed in detail in XI, Pt 3, Chs III and IV.

the parties, since they lacked the machinery to enforce terms and conditions in the way the Chancery could. Only if equity would grant a perpetual, unqualified injunction would the common law allow such a plea.[125] The Chancery was also given some common law powers, including the power to use juries, and to award damages. Like their common law colleagues, the lawyers and judges in this court were cautious in making use of their new powers.[126] Common law and equity courts were finally fused in 1875 into one High Court of Justice. Since law and equity were now administered in the same court, equitable defences were put on the same footing as legal ones.[127] This meant that the judges of the common law divisions of the new court would no longer take the restrictive approach of their pre-fusion brethren. The Judicature Act also stated that in cases where there was a conflict between the rules of equity and those of the common law, the equitable rules were to prevail.[128]

How great an impact did these changes have on thinking about contract? Writers after 1876, led by Pollock, clearly sought to write treatises on contract in law and equity, setting forth a unified view. But fusion remained imperfect and far from complete. The shadows of the earlier jurisdictional divisions continued to be cast. For example, the equitable rules which had developed—after 1854—to allow rescission of contracts for non-fraudulent misrepresentations were not extended to the common law action for damages. Damages for misrepresentation, it was decided in 1889, could only be obtained where there had been actionable fraud. The old tort of deceit continued to shape thinking here. Similarly, the doctrine of duress, which had been articulated on the common law side, remained limited in scope, and was treated as distinct from that of undue influence, which was more expansive and owed its doctrine to equity. Lawyers did not, either in 1852 or 1875, begin to rethink their subject, setting it out anew for a new procedural age. Rather, they continued to look to the genealogies of particular doctrines, which were often very strongly shaped by the paternity of earlier technical forms, in order to make sense of them.

---

[125] *Mines Royal Societies* v. *Magnay* (1854) 10 Exch. 489; *Wodehouse* v. *Farebrother* (1855) 5 E. & B. 277; *Wood* v. *Governor and Co of Copper Miners in England* (1856) 17 C.B. 561. This narrow approach was at first controversial: see *Chilton* v. *Carrington* (1855) 25 LT 69.

[126] 21 & 22 Vict. c. 27. See Lobban, 'Strange Life', 182. On the doctrinal difficulties raised by equity's jurisdiction to give 'damages in equity' experienced after the passing of the Judicature Acts, see J. A. Jolowicz, 'Damages in Equity—A Study of Lord Cairns's Act' (1975) 34 *CLJ* 224–52; J. Getzler, 'Equitable Compensation and the Regulation of Fiduciary Relationships', in *Restitution and Equity: vol. I. Resulting Trusts and Equitable Compensation*, ed. P. Birks and F. Rose (2000), 235–57; see also P. M. McDermott, 'Jurisdiction of the Court of Chancery to Award Damages', 108 (1992) *LQR* 652–73.

[127] See Judicature Act 1873, s 24(1), (2).

[128] Judicature Act 1873, s 24(5).

4. THE CONTRACTING SOCIETY

To understand the nature and development of nineteenth-century contract law, we need also to look at the broader social and economic context of contracting. It needs to be borne in mind that England was very much a contracting society, at the beginning as well as at the end of our period. Contract law was not discovered in the nineteenth century. But the law did develop, as it responded to the needs of different economic actors. In this development, the law was driven not by theory but by the response of judges to new problems which involved them seeking a solution which would best reflect their inherited legal materials, in the most intellectually coherent way, while addressing the needs of convenience. In considering the changing nature of contract law, four contexts and four kinds of economic actor need to be considered, two of whom were familiar figures by 1820, and two of whom were not.

The first context is the use of law by the landed families, whose dealings with their wealth raised important contractual questions. If England's nineteenth-century hallmark was that she was a commercial society, the traditional values of the landed aristocracy continued to exert a very strong pull. Indeed, most nineteenth-century large fortunes ended up being invested in land, as businessmen sought to gentrify themselves. Family wealth was traditionally invested in landed property. For many families, the most important contracts were those entered into for the purchase and sale of real property. If the common law courts saw relatively few of these cases, they were the staple of the Court of Chancery. In 1818/19, 30.8 per cent of Chancery suits concerned land questions.[129] Chancery judges, in determining questions involving vendors and purchasers, or landlords and tenants, had to deal with core issues of what it meant to contract. If lawyers on the common law side took longer to articulate contractual principles in their own jurisdiction, it is therefore not to be assumed that they were irrigating a doctrinal desert. The security of aristocratic and middle-class families also often depended on their making settlements on the marriage of their children. Marriage settlements, whereby parents and relatives settled land or income on a couple, or settled an income separately on a wife, were ideal means to provide for the security especially of younger children and of daughters. They ensured that the couple would survive, and—where money was settled for the separate use of the wife—even insured the new family against the potential business losses of a foolhardy husband.[130] Such settlements were a classic aristocratic form of

[129] H. Horwitz and P. Polden, 'Continuity or Change in the Court of Chancery in the Seventeenth and Eighteenth Centuries?' (1995) 34 *J. British Studies* 24–57 at 33.

[130] See R. J. Morris, 'Men, Women and Property: The Reform of the Married Women's Property Act, 1870', in F. M. L. Thompson (ed.), *Landowners, Capitalists, and Entrepreneurs: Essays for Sir John Habakkuk* (Oxford, 1994), 171–91.

planning, but it was also a method adopted in the nineteenth century by the commercial and industrial middle classes. The early and mid-nineteenth century saw continuing litigation among families on marriage settlements, and promises to grant money to young couples which were akin to settlements. In these cases, courts—notably of equity—had to explore questions which were to be of wider ramification for contractual doctrine, including such issues as what made a binding contractual promise, and what kind of consideration was necessary to support such a promise.

The second context is commercial. England was in 1820 a very highly commercialized society, with sophisticated global business networks. Her merchants imported consumer goods such as tea and spices from the East, paid for largely in gold and silver, and sugar and tobacco from its colonies in the west, paid for by the export of new industrial products, such as cotton and iron.[131] This trading system had grown under a policy of mercantilism, which protected English merchants from continental competitors, but left them free to negotiate their own contracts under the shelter of this umbrella. By 1820, London had a series of sophisticated commodity markets and a developed insurance market. In places such as the Baltic Exchange or the Royal Exchange, merchants conducted business with speed and facility, using standardized forms of commercial documents. The division of labour which Adam Smith had lauded was clearly in operation in London, and its smooth operation required the use of settled legal forms, such as the charterparties used by merchants who hired ships from their owners to import and export their goods; or the bills of lading which were used when only part of the ship was hired, and which could be negotiated to pass property in the goods being transported. Imported goods were housed, from the turn of the nineteenth century, in the newly developed docks in 'bonded warehouses', where goods could be stored for re-exportation without import duties being paid on them, and where property in them could be transferred by the passing of dock warrants. Importers and exporters had of necessity to work through mercantile agents in buying and selling goods. The agents who obtained possession of goods for the principal (often at a distance) were known as factors. They dealt with the goods in their own name—arranging their purchase, transportation, and so forth—and were paid by commission. If they guaranteed the sales they effected for their principals they were known as *del credere* agents, and received a higher commission.[132] By contrast, brokers were intermediaries, who did not get

---

[131] C. K. Harley, 'Trade: Discovery, Mercantilism, and Technology', in R. Floud and P. Johnson (eds), *The Cambridge Economic History of Modern Britain: Vol. I: Industrialisation, 1700–1860* (Cambridge, 2004), 175–203.

[132] See in general the description of these functions in [A. Hayward], 'Mercantile Law: II', (1828–9) 1 *LM* 242–65.

possession of the goods but entered into contracts for the sale and purchase of goods in the form of 'bought' and 'sold' notes. Trade in turn depended on credit. Buyers of commodities paid for them with bills of exchange or promissory notes. Bills of exchange allowed for the easy transfer of money over great distance, and so were vital instruments to oil the wheels of foreign trade.

These complicated trade arrangements required settled legal rules governing the sale of goods, agency relationships, insurance, and negotiable instruments. It had to be clear, for instance, whether purchases had been made on the basis of a consignment system, according to which exporters sending goods to the London market retained property in the goods until they were sold by commission agents in London, or whether the London merchants became owners of the goods as soon as they were ordered by their factors on the spot.[133] In many respects, law had to follow commercial practice. Questions relating to when property passed were not abstract legal ones, but reflected the organization of each particular trade and the intention of the participants. It was not a world where merchants went to court to ask them to settle disputes fairly between them, or to implement a moral economy of trade. If the law needed to set out clear rules for the working of commerce, it also had to have a machinery for resolving problems when they arose. For instance, when goods were imported, the bulk remained in the bonded warehouse, unseen by the buyer, who would only see a sample.[134] In many cases, the bulk when delivered would not correspond to the sample.[135] In this world, rules needed to be developed to provide solutions when merchants found themselves unable to resolve their conflicts.

Many of these rules were settled in the first three decades of the nineteenth century. The expansion of commerce in the late eighteenth century coincided with a revival of litigation rates in the superior courts of common law,[136] which helped to settle the rules of commercial law, and shaped early nineteenth-century views of contract in general. In considering how the law was shaped in this era, two points need to be borne in mind. First, litigation remained so expensive that cases which went to trial generally involved substantial pecuniary claims.[137] It was only when parties had very large sums at stake that it was worth going to trial.

[133] K. Morgan, *Bristol and the Atlantic Trade in the Eighteenth Century* (Cambridge, 1993), 165. See also T. M. Devine, *The Tobacco Lords: A Study of the Tobacco Merchants of Glasgow and their Trading Activities, c. 1740–1790* (Edinburgh, 1975).

[134] J. R. McCulloch, *A Dictionary, Practical, Theoretical and Historical, of Commerce* (1832), 337–8.

[135] Report from the Select Committee on Means of Improving and Maintaining Foreign Trade (W. India Docks), PP 1823 IV (411) 489, at p. 369 (evidence of F. Kemble).

[136] See C. W. Brooks, *Lawyers, Litigation and English Society since 1450* (1998), 31.

[137] C. Francis, 'Practice, Strategy and Institution: Debt Collection in the English Common Law Courts, 1740–1840' (1986) 80 *Northwestern University LR*, 807–955 at 858.

The law which was set out by the common law courts in this era was thus largely one for commercial parties, or large propertied interests. The superior courts did not seek to arbitrate disputes between ordinary citizens; they aimed to map out rules to facilitate commerce, generally in cases brought in assumpsit. Secondly, it should be noted that the cases they handled were not necessarily representative of business, and the solutions they gave were not always best for business. As Mackenzie Chalmers pointed out at the start of the twentieth century, 'lawyers see only the pathology of commerce and not its healthy physiological action'.[138] Businessmen only went to court when things went seriously wrong. Two things took them to court most often: bankruptcy and fraud. When merchants failed, and assignees sought to recover their property, questions were invariably raised regarding the passing of property. Business failure threw into sharp relief questions whether mercantile practices would be upheld by courts, and whether legal views of ownership reflected business ones. On occasion, the rules laid down in cases arising from bankruptcies or frauds dismayed the business community, rather than reassuring it. Nineteenth-century judges, facing commercial failure or sharp practice, were often far more worried about fraud than businessmen, who were prepared to countenance a small measure of bad practice, provided the general rules of law were simple and facilitated commerce.

The third context to consider is the rise of a mass consumer market. If contract law was the sport of the commercial and landed classes in 1820, it democratized as the century went on. Between 1820 and 1914 a consumer revolution took place, which drew a growing proportion of the population into an ever-expanding range of contractual relations. The most significant change came after 1850, when working-class real incomes began to rise.[139] The Great Exhibition of 1851, coming after a decade of political instability, unemployment, and economic depression, in many respects signalled the start of a new consumer age for a mass market. New products, new production techniques, and new retail outlets helped transform consumerism. For instance, the clothing industry was transformed by the arrival of the sewing machine, first seen at the Great Exhibition. By 1890, Singer was selling 150,000 machines annually.[140] Modern cigarette manufacture began in England with the opening of Robert Gloag's Walworth factory in 1856; and the mass marketing of this product took a further step forward when W. D. and H. O. Wills began to sell machine-made cigarettes in 1884.[141] Just as the range of

---

[138] *The Sale of Goods Act* (5th edn, 1902), 129.

[139] J. Mokyr, 'Accounting for the Industrial Revolution' in Floud and Johnson, *Cambridge Economic History*, 1–27.

[140] W. H. Fraser, *The Coming of the Mass Market, 1850–1914* (1981), 179–80.

[141] Fraser, *Mass Market*, 70. See also H. Cox, *The Global Cigarette: Origins and Evolution of British American Tobacco, 1880–1945* (Oxford, 2000).

consumer goods increased, ranging from frozen meat to bicycles, so the methods of selling were transformed. The second half of the nineteenth century saw the decline of street sellers, barrow sellers, and costermongers, and their gradual replacement by retail shops. From the 1870s, multiple branch grocery stores began to develop, as well as new department stores for the middle classes. The new mass market was also accompanied by the rise of advertising. Advertising was not new to the second half of the nineteenth century, but it grew dramatically after 1855, when the stamp duty on newspaper advertising was removed.[142] Just as the second half of the nineteenth century saw an expansion in the consumption of goods, so it became much more of a service economy. The most obvious manifestation of this came with the rise of the railways. Middle-class commuters came to rely on this mode of transport for daily travel. The working classes also used trains, travelling third class for holiday excursions, an idea pioneered by Thomas Cook of Leicester in the 1840s. Railway companies themselves also began to open hotels at stations, situated at the edges of large towns.[143] From the early nineteenth century, an increasing proportion of the middle classes began to take out life assurance and fire insurance for their homes, entering into annual contracts on which the fortunes of their families might depend.

Consumer transactions thus increased dramatically in the second half of the nineteenth century. At the same time, access to courts increased, thanks to the establishment in 1846 of the new county courts, which generated a large amount of new litigation. The impact of the county courts should not be exaggerated. Much of the litigation in these courts remained simple debt recovery, often brought by old fashioned shopkeepers who operated by granting credit, which was something not given by the modern retail traders. Nonetheless, the creation of the county courts did give the opportunity for smaller litigants to bring new kinds of contractual disputes before the courts, whose judgments could be appealed to the superior courts. Moreover, the cost of bringing larger cases in the superior courts fell.[144] Costs were no longer the radical disincentive they had been on the eve of the age of reform, in 1820. This new consumer era generated new questions for courts. For instance, in an age when contracts were not individually negotiated but were issued on standard forms, courts had to decide when and if consumers were bound by terms printed on tickets or displayed on notices. Were

---

[142] See T. R. Nevett, *Advertising in Britain: A History* (1982), 42–9; D. Hindley and G. Hindley, *Advertising in Victorian England, 1837–1901* (1972).

[143] J. Simmons, 'Railways, Hotels and Tourism in Great Britain 1839–1914' (1984) 19 *J. Contemp. Hist.* 201–22.

[144] In 1893, Macdonnell estimated, the average sum recovered in 2529 actions in the Queen's Bench Division was just over £210. Plaintiffs' costs in these cases averaged in his view about £80. Judicial Statistics 1894, *PP* 1896 [c. 8263], xciv, 207 at 51.

passengers bound to read, or even be aware of the contract they had engaged in?[145] Questions of contract formation were also generated by advertising. Did a promise held out in a printed advertisement amount to a contractual offer, on which a deceived consumer could sue?[146]

The final context to consider for its influence on contract law is the rise of the investor society. One of the main areas of 'consumption' through which the middle classes came into contact with the courts was not the simple sale and purchase of goods, but through their investment in joint stock companies. The rise of a consumer society was accompanied by the rise of new forms of collective enterprise, which sought to supply a growing mass market with new goods and services. These suppliers of goods were also consumers of investment. The Victorian middle class were increasingly keen investors on the Stock Market, both in the era of the Railway Mania and after the coming of limited liability. The nineteenth century saw several waves of company promotions, when promoters issued seductive prospectuses which enticed middle-class savers to part with their money. All too often, the companies failed, and when they were wound up investors sought to escape their liability, or recoup their investment, by claiming either that they had never entered into a final contract to buy the shares, or that they had been induced into buying by fraud, and so should be relieved of liability. This was a richer source for much contract doctrine than ordinary consumer transactions, for liquidators had no choice in pursuing those who owed money to the company, while the investor seeing his life savings put at risk was likely to seek a defence. When it came to the development of contract law in the 1860s and 1870s, much doctrine was thus driven as much by litigation between the projectors of companies and their investors as by disputes between the buyers of goods and their suppliers.

---

[145] See *Carr* v. *The Lancashire and Yorkshire Railway Co* (1852) 7 Exch. 707; *Zunz* v. *South Eastern Railway Co* (1869) LR 4 QB 539; *Henderson* v. *Stevenson* (1875) LR 2 HL Sc 470; *Harris* v. *Great Western Railway Co* (1876) 1 QBD 515; *Parker* v. *South Eastern Railway Co* (1877) 2 CPD 416.

[146] *Denton* v. *Great Northern Railway Co* (1856) 5 E. & B. 860; *Carlill* v. *Carbolic Smoke Ball Co* [1892] 2 QB 484.

II

The Formation of Contracts: Offer and Acceptance

In two late eighteenth-century cases, common law judges seemed for the first time to discuss the necessary requirements for contract formation in terms of offer and acceptance. This has been taken as a sign of the arrival of a new concept of contract, centred on a meeting of minds, which would then be elaborated by treatise writers.[1] For while eighteenth-century English jurists did include discussions on the need for assent in their texts,[2] they did not discuss the kinds of issues which had intrigued civilian lawyers since the middle ages, such as the principles governing when an offer could be revoked.

The notion that contracts were produced by negotiations leading to agreement was hardly new. Eighteenth-century courts had not, however, looked for precise moments when the parties' minds met, since the contracts most likely to generate litigation in the superior courts—those involving land and family settlements, or the commercial sale of goods—were generally set down in writing, in order to comply with the Statute of Frauds of 1677. Under section 4 of the statute, no action could be brought on any contract for the sale of land or in consideration of marriage, or for a guarantee, unless the agreement or a memorandum of it had been signed by the party being sued. Under section 17, no contract for the sale of goods worth over £10 was good, unless the buyer accepted part of the goods, or gave something in earnest to bind the bargain, or 'there be some note in writing of the bargain made, and signed by the parties to be charged with such contract'. Written memoranda were regarded as evidence of the parties having entered into consensual agreements.[3] Since the contract itself did not

---

[1] *Payne* v. *Cave* (1789) 3 T.R. 148; *Cooke* v. *Oxley* (1790) 3 T.R. 653, A.W.B. Simpson, 'Innovation in Nineteenth Century Contract Law', in his *Legal Theory and Legal History: Essays on the Common Law* (1987), 171–202; D.J. Ibbetson, *Historical Introduction to the Law of Obligations* (Oxford, 1999), 222–3.

[2] J. J. Powell, *Essay upon the Law of Contracts and Agreements*, 2 vols (Dublin, 1796), i, 131 *et seq.*

[3] Cf. the remark of Westbury LC in *Chinnock* v. *Marchioness of Ely* (1865) 4 De G. J. & S. 638 at 643: 'An agreement is the result of the mutual assent of two parties to certain terms, and if it be clear that there is no consensus, what may have been written or said, becomes immaterial'.

have to be in writing to comply with the Act, but only needed to be evidenced in writing,[4] questions arose as to what kind of writings would suffice. Any number of documents could be put together to evidence the agreement, but it had to be clear from the documents alone that a binding agreement had been concluded.[5] It also had to be clear that the parties had an intention to be bound, and had fully committed themselves to the contract.[6] In practice, courts looking for contracts to be pieced together from correspondence were looking to see whether offers had been accepted.[7]

Land and marriage agreements which had not been reduced to writing could still be enforced. Although section 4 did not contain a provision for partly performed agreements, the courts held that the statute did not apply where there had been part performance of an agreement.[8] But before the Chancery would decree specific performance, it had to be sure that there had been an agreement, what the terms of the agreement were, and that the part performance could only be explained in terms of fulfilling it.[9] The idea that the contractual obligation derived from the agreement of the parties, rather than from the formalities required by the statute was confirmed by Lord Ellenborough. Although, he said, section 4 of the Act stipulated that non-compliant contracts would not be enforced, it 'does not expressly or immediately vacate such contracts, if made by parol'.[10] Tindal CJ confirmed this view in 1836: 'The agreement, in truth, is made before any signature.'[11]

Where land was sold or marriage settlements made, parties entered into long-term negotiations before concluding agreements. Few would have doubted that such contracts were the product of proposals which had been accepted. But what of the sale of goods? Such sales did not usually generate the formal kinds of documentation found in family settlements, or extensive pre-contractual negotiations. For instance, travelling salesmen might receive orders from customers which would be noted down in order books, which were not the kind of documentation

---

⁴ *Forster* v. *Hale* (1798) 3 Ves. Jun. 696.

⁵ *Boydell* v. *Drummond* (1809) 11 East 142; *Western* v. *Russell* (1814) 3 V. & B. 187; *Dobell* v. *Hutchinson* (1835) 3 Ad. & El. 355; *Ridgway* v. *Wharton* (1857) 6 H.L.C. 238.

⁶ See Lord Thurlow's approach in *Tawney* v. *Crowther* (1790) 3 Bro. C.C. 161, and the criticism of it by Lord Redesdale in *Clinon* v. *Cooke* (1802) 1 Sch. & L. 22 at 33–4. See also Redesdale's comments quoted in *Allan* v. *Bower* (1790) 3 Bro. C.C. 149 at 153n.

⁷ *Western* v. *Russell* (1814) 3 V. & B. 187 at 191.

⁸ The Act also did not apply where there had been fraud, which took the case out of the statute altogether: see *Walker* v. *Walker* (1740) 2 Atk. 98 at 99.

⁹ *Gunter* v. *Halsey* (1739) Amb. 586; *Lacon* v. *Mertins* (1743) 3 Atk. 1. Cf. E. G. Atherley, *A Practical Treatise of the Law of Marriage and other Family Settlements* (1813), 88.

¹⁰ *Crosby* v. *Wadsworth* (1810) 6 East 602 at 610.

¹¹ *Laythoarp* v. *Bryant* (1836) 2 Bing. N.C. 735 at 744.

to satisfy the statute.[12] This had caused some eighteenth-century courts to feel uneasy. To prevent possible injustice, the King's Bench in 1767 ruled that executory contracts were not within the statute, and that a plaintiff could sue for the non-delivery of corn on a parol contract.[13] Had this rule survived, space would have been opened for courts to discuss the requirements of offer and acceptance in parol executory contracts for the supply of commercial goods. However, in 1792 the Common Pleas distinguished between contracts for the sale of goods (where the statute applied) and those involving work and labour (where it did not).[14] The matter was finally settled by Lord Tenterden's Act in 1828, which held that the Act applied where goods were to be delivered in future.[15]

As with land and marriage cases, courts looked for documentation which showed a precise agreement as to the terms.[16] For instance, in *Smith* v. *Surman*, Bayley J. held that two letters containing different statements about the quality of goods to be sold did not satisfy the statute,[17] for they could not be put together to make an agreement. Judges also considered whether the memorandum was merely evidence of an underlying contract, or whether it constituted the contract itself. The wording of section 17 suggested that non-compliant contracts were void, rather than merely unenforceable, suggesting that the writing made the agreement.[18] It was accordingly held in the Exchequer in 1841 that the statute could not be complied with by making a written memorandum after an action on the purported contract had begun.[19] But the Common Pleas disagreed in 1861, holding that a subsequent letter which stated that the contract had not been complied with was sufficient writing. The court accepted that there was a prior oral contract which was merely evidenced by the writing.[20]

---

[12] See e.g. *Elliott* v. *Thomas* (1838) 3 M. & W. 170.

[13] *Clayton* v. *Andrews* (1767) 4 Burr. 2101. Cf. *Towers* v. *Osborne* (1722) 1 Stra. 506. Cf. J. P. Benjamin, *A Treatise on the Sale of Personal Property* (1868), 69.

[14] *Rondeau* v. *Wyatt* (1792) 2 H. Bl. 63. See also *Cooper* v. *Elston* (1796) 7 T.R. 14; *Groves* v. *Buck* (1814) 3 M. & S. 178; *Garbutt* v. *Watson* (1822) 5 B. & Ald. 613. Lord Tenterden's Act in 1828 (9 Geo IV c 13) extended the operation of the Act to cases where goods were to be made.

[15] It did not apply to contracts for work and labour. But the courts had some difficulty distinguishing the two: see *Clay* v. *Yates* (1856) 1 H. & N. 73; *Lee* v. *Griffin* (1861) 1 B. & S. 272.

[16] See e.g. *Saunderson* v. *Jackson* (1800) 2 B. & P. 238; *Jackson* v. *Lowe* (1822) 1 Bing. 9.

[17] *Smith* v. *Surman* (1829) 9 B. & C. 561 at 569: 'It is clear [...] that the vendee did not consider it a binding bargain'.

[18] See *Laythoarp* v. *Bryant* (1836) 2 Bing. N.C. 735 at 747; *Baldey* v. *Parker* (1823) 2 B. & C. 37.

[19] See Parke B.'s comments in *Bill* v. *Bament* (1841) 9 M. & W. 36; and contrast *Fricker* v. *Thomlinson* (1840) 1 M. & G. 772. See also C. Blackburn, *A Treatise on the Effect of the Contract of Sale* (1845), 66.

[20] Nonetheless, property did not pass until the statute was complied with, *Coats* v. *Chaplin* (1842) 3 Q.B. 483. Nor could the purchaser insure goods bought under a contract which did not comply with the statute, as the sale would be void: *Stockdale* v. *Dunlop* (1840) 6 M. & W. 224.

Section 17 of the statute could be complied with if the goods were 'accepted'. However, 'acceptance' was not simply a receipt of goods, generating an obligation to pay for benefits received. Rather, there had to be an intention to accept goods in fulfilment of the contract.[21] For instance, in *Phillips* v. *Bistolli*, where a bidder at an auction claimed to have mistaken the price, the court had to determine if he had accepted the goods, having handled them for three to four minutes before returning them. The court held that to satisfy the statute, there had to be a delivery by the vendor 'with an intention of vesting the right of possession in the vendee; and there must be an actual acceptance by the [purchaser], with an intention of taking to the possession as owner'.[22] Acceptance—which included taking 'indicia of property' such as warehouse keys[23]—was evidence of contractual intent, sufficient to take the case out of the statute. Determining whether the purchaser intended to accept the goods did not require the courts to consider their subjective state of mind, which could hardly be explored at common law, given its rules of evidence. Rather, if the purchaser had treated the goods as if he was their owner, acting in such a way which would be inconsistent with the refusal to accept, it could be inferred that he had accepted them.[24]

There was little doubt in the minds of lawyers in 1820 that contracts required offers which had been accepted. This was as true of equity as of law. In a note to the 1798 case of *Forster* v. *Hale*, Francis Vesey noted that where a party sought specific performance of an agreement found in correspondence, he had to show

not merely a treaty—still less, a proposal—for an agreement, but a treaty with reference to which mutual consent can be clearly demonstrated, or a proposal met by that sort of acceptance which makes it no longer the act of one party, but of both.[25]

Lord Eldon had reiterated the rules in 1817, holding that 'if a correspondence is of such a nature as, according to the rules of sound legal interpretation, would amount to an agreement', it would be specifically enforced. He was not concerned with whether the parties had a perfect subjective agreement, but only with whether they had outwardly bound themselves. It was not necessary that

---

[21] See Blackburn, *Sale* (1st edn, 1845), 22–3.

[22] *Phillips* v. *Bistolli* (1824) 2 B. & C. 511 at 513. At trial, Abbott CJ said that there was sufficient evidence of an intention to accept, provided the jury was satisfied (as it was) that he had made no mistake. In banc, the court felt that the jury should have considered evidence showing that there was no intention to pass possession until a deposit had been paid. The case is also notable for generating a question about the needs of the Statute, rather than a question about the mistake. See also *Elmore* v. *Stone* (1809) 1 Taunt. 458; *Smith* v. *Surman* (1829) 9 B. & C. 561.

[23] *Chaplin* v. *Rogers* (1800) 1 East 192 at 194.

[24] See the arguments of counsel and Erle J in *Parker* v. *Wallis* (1855) 5 E. & B. 21.

[25] *Forster* v. *Hale* (1798) 1 Ves. Jr. Supp. 418. See also Vesey's comments in *Coles* v. *Trecothick* (1804) 2 Ves. Jr. Supp. 164.

the 'parties really meant the same precise thing, but only that both actually gave their assent to that proposition which [...] *de facto* arises out of the terms of the correspondence'.[26]

Payne v. *Cave* and *Cooke* v. *Oxley* cannot, therefore, be credited with introducing a new concept of offer and acceptance to English law. *Payne* v. *Cave*[27] is significant as a rare case concerning the formation of a parol contract. It settled the rule that a bidder at auction could withdraw his bid at any stage before the hammer fell, since it was only at that point that the offer was accepted and a contract made. In fact, no one doubted before 1789 that auction sales were concluded by the hammer,[28] but there was considerable uncertainty whether sales at auction were within the Statute of Frauds.[29] The dilemma was resolved in the early nineteenth century, when it was decided that the auctioneer was to be construed as agent of both parties, and that he complied with the statute when he noted down the details.[30] *Payne* v. *Cave* was heard precisely at a moment when courts doubted whether auctions fell within the statute, and so the case discussed the issue of offer and acceptance more explicitly than was usually the case when it was masked by the statute.

Cooke v. *Oxley*[31] also raised novel issues about how parol contracts were formed. Here, the defendant offered to sell tobacco to the plaintiff, who asked to be given until later in the day to accept. The defendant gave him until 4 pm, but in the meanwhile sold the goods to another. The plaintiff, who thought he had accepted in time, sued for non-delivery. Although this was a case involving the sale of goods worth more than £10, the Statute of Frauds was not mentioned, perhaps because, in 1790, the King's Bench judges still felt that it did not apply to executory contracts. Counsel for the plaintiff regarded this as a conditional sale, which had taken place in the morning, but subject to the plaintiff's right to rescind.[32] The court rejected this view, but considered that the defendant's promise to keep the offer open was a *nudum pactum* and not binding.[33] The case was much discussed by later treatise writers, on the question of whether a promise to keep an

---

[26] *Kennedy* v. *Lee* (1817) 3 Mer. 441 at 450–1.

[27] (1789) 3 T.R. 148.

[28] In *Simon* v. *Metivier* (1766) 1 W. Bl. 599 at 601, Lord Mansfield said '[t]he contract is executed when the hammer is knocked down'. See also the discussion in [Anon.], *Cases with Opinions of Eminent Counsel, in Matters of Law, Equity and Conveyancing*, 2 vols, (1791), i, 142.

[29] See *Simon* v. *Metivier* (1766) 1 W. Bl. 599; *Coles* v. *Trecothick* (1804) 9 Ves. 234; *Walker* v. *Constable* (1798) 1 B. & P. 306 at 307.

[30] See *Blagden* v. *Bradbear* (1806) 12 Ves. 466; *Hinde* v. *Whitehouse* (1806) 7 East 558; *Kemeys* v. *Proctor* (1813) 3 V. & B. 57; *Mason* v. *Armitage* 2 Ves. Jr. Supp. 312.

[31] *Cooke* v. *Oxley* (1790) 3 T.R. 653.

[32] Such sales were upheld by the courts, where there had been sold notes which had been passed: see *Humphries* v. *Carvalho* (1812) 16 East 45.

[33] *Cooke* v. *Oxley* (1790) 3 T.R. 653 at 653–4.

offer open was binding,[34] a question settled by *Routledge* v. *Grant* in 1828, which held that an offeror who promised to keep an acceptance open for six weeks could retract it at any stage prior to acceptance.[35] But *Cooke* v. *Oxley* also seemed to suggest that if an offer was not instantly accepted, it lapsed. Bayley J.'s comments on the case in *Humphreys* v. *Carvalho*—that there had been only a proposal by one party and no acceptance by the other—also suggested that the transaction in the late afternoon had to be seen as a wholly new one.[36] This was not a view of the formation of contracts which would later be embraced. But it was perhaps not illogical for a court seeking a meeting of minds not set down in writing to want the meeting of minds to have occurred at one precise moment.

1. THE MEETING OF THE MINDS

Payne v. *Cave* and *Cooke* v. *Oxley* raised the novel problem of whether the acceptance had to be simultaneous with the offer. This was a question which had not generally troubled courts dealing with written contracts. In dealing with this question in 1817, Lord Eldon explained his common sense approach. He understood Chancery practice to be that

if a person communicates his acceptance of an offer within a reasonable time after the offer being made, and if, within a reasonable time of the acceptance being communicated, no variation has been made by either party in the terms of the offer so made and accepted, the acceptance must be taken as simultaneous with the offer, and both together as constituting such an agreement as the Court will execute.[37]

Instead of looking at the precise time when a contract came into existence, courts dealing with written contracts looked to see whether the parties had come to a firm mutual agreement, which could be found in their communications with each other. Judges were in no doubt that an offer which had not been accepted could not generate a contract,[38] or that the acceptance had to mirror the offer.[39]

---

[34] W. W. Story argued that the promise was not a gratuitous one, since consideration could be found in 'the expectation or hope, that the offer will be accepted, and this is sufficient legally to support the promise', *Treatise on the Law of Contracts*, 2 vols (4th edn, Boston 1856), § 382, i, 470. This view was also adopted by G. J. Bell, *Inquiries into the Contract of Sale of Goods and Merchandise as Recognised in the Judicial Decisions and Mercantile Practice of Modern Nations* (Edinburgh, 1844), 33. But Benjamin regarded this view as 'more fanciful than serious': *Sale* (1868), 47.

[35] *Routledge* v. *Grant* (1828) 4 Bing. 653.

[36] *Humphries* v. *Carvalho* (1812) 16 East 45 at 48.

[37] *Kennedy* v. *Lee* (1817) 3 Mer. 441 at 454–5.

[38] *Gaunt* v. *Hill* (1815) 1 Stark. 10.

[39] See *Holland* v. *Eyre* (1825) 2 Sim. & St. 194 at 195. Cf. *Warner* v. *Willington* (1856) 3 Drew. 523 at 533.

If the court construed letters between the parties as referring to different things, it would find no contract formed, for the offer would not have been accepted.[40] In 1840, Lord Langdale confirmed (in another case on the Statute of Frauds) that a letter containing a counter-offer had to be read as rejecting an original offer, which could then not be revived and accepted.[41]

Early nineteenth-century courts dealing with written contracts did not worry about looking for the precise moment when the parties' minds had met, since the writings they looked for were to serve as confirmation of a fixed agreement. But this issue, which had been raised for oral contracts in *Cooke v. Oxley*, was soon considered in the case of a contract made in writing. In *Adams v. Lindsell*, the parties had negotiated a contract for the sale of wool by correspondence, which satisfied the requirements of the Statute of Frauds. However, the defendants claimed that no contact had been concluded. When offering to sell the wool, they had asked the plaintiff buyers to reply by return of post. But since they had addressed their letter to the plaintiffs incorrectly, it was delayed. On its arrival, the plaintiffs wrote back accepting the offer, but before the letter arrived, the defendants sold the material. When sued for non-delivery of the wool, the defendants argued that since the acceptance had not arrived at the time expected, they were free to sell the wool on the following day: '[t]ill the plaintiffs' answer was actually received, there could be no binding contract between the parties; and before then, the defendants had retracted their offer, by selling the wool to other persons'.[42] This was to argue that the plaintiffs had to communicate their acceptance before the sellers had changed their mind; but that the sellers were not bound to communicate their retraction. The King's Bench rejected this argument, and accepted the plaintiffs' view that the contract was concluded when the acceptance was posted.

In doing so, the court rejected the defendants' view that communication was essential. If that were correct, it held, no contract could ever be made by post, as both sides would have to keep notifying each other, continuing to make offers and acceptances *ad infinitum*. For the court, what mattered was to find a moment when the parties' minds met subjectively: '[t]he defendants must be considered in law as making, during every instant of the time their letter was travelling, the same identical offer to the plaintiffs; and then the contract is completed by the acceptance of it by the latter'.[43]

---

[40] *Hutchison* v. *Bowker* (1839) 5 M. & W. 535.

[41] *Hyde* v. *Wrench* (1840) 3 Beav. 334. Pollock did not mention this case until his 7th edn of *Contract* (Oxford, 1902), 29. Cf. Benjamin, *Sale*, 30.

[42] *Adams* v. *Lindsell* (1818) 1 B. & Ald. 681 at 682–3.

[43] *Adams* v. *Lindsell* (1818) 1 B. & Ald. 681 at 683.

Although several scholars have assumed that a civilian view—according to which contracts were made at the moment when the parties minds met[44]—informed the court in *Adams* v. *Lindsell*,[45] no civilian learning was alluded to in the report of the case. The court's formulation was also significantly different from Pothier's (soon to be preferred)[46] version, that where contracts were made at a distance, the initial will of the offeror was presumed to continue, so that the single offer remained open until accepted. Nonetheless, the principle of *Adams* v. *Lindsell* did seem to fit Pothier's wider view of the need for a subjective meeting of minds, regardless of communication. In his view, if a merchant making an offer by post changed his mind before his letter arrived, and put a second letter into the post retracting it, then the offeree could not accept the offer when the first letter arrived. For there would no longer be a meeting of the wills of the parties, even though the offeree had no way of knowing then of the change of mind.[47] By contrast, if the offeree posted an acceptance before the second letter was sent, the contract would be concluded, for the minds would have met. Pothier's view was quoted approvingly by Joseph Chitty[48] and endorsed in America by W. W. Story.[49]

Adams v. *Lindsell* appeared to introduce a general principle that what mattered in contract formation was not communication, but a subjective meeting of the minds. However, courts soon reiterated the need for communication, and narrowed the general rule in that case to a particular exception, known as the 'postal rule'.[50] The first step on this path was taken by the House of Lords in 1848 in the Scottish case of *Dunlop* v. *Higgins*. The litigation involved a firm of Liverpool merchants, who had sent a letter accepting an offer for iron from a firm in Glasgow.

[44] Civilians debated whether there had to be a communication of acceptance: see e.g. Barbeyrac's note in H. Grotius, *The Rights of War and Peace* (ed. J. Barbeyrac, 1738), 290 (cf. W. Story, *A Treatise on the Law of Contracts*, 2 vols (4th edn, Boston, 1856), i, 475n which approvingly quotes the view of Christian Thomasius (misattributed to Barbeyrac) requiring a manifestation of assent). See also Samuel Pufendorf, *Of the Law of Nature and Nations* (3rd edn, trans. B. Kennet, 1717), 71–2.

[45] Simpson, 'Innovation in Nineteenth Century Contract Law' at 261 compares the judgment quoted above with Pothier's view from his *Treatise on the Contract of Sale* (trans. L. S. Cushing, 1839), 18, commenting that it looks 'suspiciously like a borrowing'. On Pothier's influence, see also J. M. Perillo, 'Robert J. Pothier's Influence on the Common Law of Contract' (2004–05) 11 *Texas Wesleyan LR* 267–90 at 278.

[46] C. G. Addison, *A Treatise on the Law of Contracts* (4th edn, 1856), 25.

[47] Pothier, *Sale* (Cushing edn, 1839), 18. Pothier added that there would be an equitable obligation on the offeror to indemnify the offeree for any loss caused by reliance on the first letter.

[48] See J. Chitty, *A Practical Treatise on the Law of Contracts not under seal* (2nd edn, 1834), 12. This was reiterated in later editions: see e.g. the 9th edn (1871, by J. A. Russell), 12.

[49] Story, *Contract*, i, 476n. His father also quoted Pothier's views approvingly: J. Story, *Commentaries on the Law of Agency* (1839), § 493n.

[50] For a discussion, stressing the importance of confidence in the Post Office, see S. Gardner, 'Trashing with Trollope: A Deconstruction of the Postal Rules in Contract' (1992) 12 *OJLS* 170–94.

In part because of a severe frost, the letter arrived later than expected, and as the price of iron had risen, the sellers refused to proceed. They claimed that no contract had come into existence since, by the usage of the trade, orders had to be sent by return of post, and the letter had not arrived in time. In giving the judgment of the Lords, Lord Cottenham held that, although the buyer was required to reply on the day the offer was received, it was not necessary for him to guarantee that the letter arrived on time. By putting his letter in the post, the buyer had complied with the seller's request. This view was consistent with the approach taken by Burrough J. in *Adams* v. *Lindsell*. However, since in the later case the defendants were not themselves responsible for the delay, Cottenham had to explain why the defendant, rather than the plaintiff, ran the risk of the post.

In contrast to the court in *Adams* v. *Lindsell*, Cottenham acknowledged the need for communication. But he neutralized this requirement by holding that notice to the Post Office was equivalent to notice to the party. This was an idea borrowed from a rule regarding bills of exchange, that a holder of a bill who posted a notice to the drawer that it had been dishonoured by the acceptor did not lose his remedy if his letter was delayed in the post.[51] For Cottenham, 'common sense tells us that transactions cannot go on without such a rule'.[52] In his view, it was immaterial to the contract's existence whether the letter ever arrived or not. This obiter comment was soon repeated by Cresswell J., who told a jury at *nisi prius* (in another commercial sale of goods case) that posting an acceptance completed a contract even if the letter never arrived.[53] It was also adopted by Addison in his textbook.[54]

The notion that it was the subjective meeting of the minds which mattered was further undermined by the 1862 Common Pleas decision of *Felthouse* v. *Bindley*. In this case, a man had come to a verbal agreement to buy his nephew's horse, though without settling whether the price was to be in pounds or guineas. The horse was mistakenly sold to a different buyer by the nephew's auctioneer, who was later sued by the uncle for the price of the beast. The defendant claimed that property in the horse had not passed to the uncle, since the requirements of the Statute of Frauds had not been complied with. The only correspondence relating to the sale prior to the auction was a letter from the uncle offering to split

---

[51] The rule was that the holder who posted his notice in due time could not be guilty of laches, *Stocken* v. *Collin* (1841) 7 M. & W. 515 at 516. See also *Smith* v. *Mullett* (1809) 2 Camp. 208; *Hilton* v. *Fairclough* (1811) 2 Camp. 633; *Woodcock* v. *Houldsworth* (1846) 16 M. & W. 124. See also the rule applied in different contexts in *Reg* v. *Inhabitants of Slawstone* (1852) 18 QB 388 and *Hernaman* v. *Coryton* (1850) 5 Exch. 453.

[52] *Dunlop* v. *Higgins* (1848) 1 H.L.C. 381 at 400.

[53] *Duncan* v. *Topham* (1849) 8 C.B. 225.

[54] Addison, *Contract* (4th edn, 1856), 25.

the difference between the price in pounds and guineas, in which the uncle said he would consider the horse his at the compromise price, if he heard no more. The nephew did not reply, but after the horse had been sold, wrote a letter which spoke of his having sold the animal to his uncle. However, since this was sent after the auction, the court held that no property had passed at the time of the auction, as the statute had not then been complied with.[55] As Willes J. explained, at that point, the nephew 'had not communicated [...] his intention to his uncle, or done anything to bind himself'.[56] These comments were taken by later jurists as the basis of a doctrine that silence could not constitute acceptance,[57] since communication was necessary.[58]

Treatise writers in the first half of the century had not stressed the need for the acceptance to be communicated.[59] The first theorist to do so was Leake in 1867. He started with the premise that the parties' intentions were to be gauged by their outward acts, not by their innermost thoughts. The question whether a court was to look 'subjectively' or 'objectively' at the parties' intentions had often been hidden before 1851, when parties to suits were unable to testify. Nevertheless, the idea that the court was to look at how the parties expressed their intent was not new.[60] J. J. Powell had even suggested that a man's assent might in some cases be presumed from inaction: 'a man by his silence, in case he be present, and acquainted with what is doing, is supposed to give his assent to what is then done'.[61] When making this statement, Powell had in mind situations where parties were held to make good representations during negotiations for family settlements that they had no claims on the property in question. In the nineteenth century, this principle was applied as a rule of evidence in other cases involving misrepresentations, that a person who had by his conduct induced another to believe a certain set of affairs was later estopped from disputing that this state of affairs existed.[62] This principle of estoppel was extended to contract cases, so that a man who appeared from his conduct to have become a party to a contract

[55] He cited *Stockdale* v. *Dunlop* (1840) 6 M. & W. 224. Counsel for the defence also contended that the Statute of Frauds could not be regarded as complied with here by a constructive acceptance of the horse by the uncle: *Carter* v. *Toussant* (1822) 5 B. & Ald. 855.

[56] *Felthouse* v. *Bindley* (1862) 11 C.B. N.S. 869 at 876.

[57] S. M. Leake, *The Elements of the Law of Contracts* (1867), 13. This author cited as support of his proposition *Russell* v. *Thornton* (1859) 4 H. & N. 788, though in fact Bramwell B. had there observed (at 798) that 'where there is a duty to speak, and the party does not, an assent may be inferred from his silence'.

[58] Willes J. suggested that the nephew could have sued the auctioneer, using the principle of *Coats* v. *Chaplin* (1842) 3 Q.B. 483.

[59] See e.g. Addison, *Contracts* (2nd edn, 1849), 29; Chitty, *Contracts* (2nd edn, 1834), 8 *et seq.*

[60] Cf. Eldon's remarks in *Kennedy* v. *Lee* (1817) 3 Mer. 441 at 450–1.

[61] Powell, *Contracts*, i, 131–2.

[62] *Freeman* v. *Cooke* (1848) 2 Exch. 654 at 663.

could be held liable on it.[63] It was from these cases that Leake teased the general principle that the law imputed to a person's mind 'the rational and honest meaning of his words and actions'.[64] The classic judicial expression of it was made by Blackburn J. in 1871:

> If, whatever a man's real intentions may be, he so conducts himself that a reasonable man would believe that he was assenting to the terms proposed by the other party, and that other party upon that belief enters into the contract with him, the man thus conducting himself would be equally bound as if he had intended to agree to the other party's terms.[65]

For Leake, the corollary of the objective rule was 'that there should be a mutual communication between the parties of their intentions to agree'.[66] Leake presented his opinion as a common sense view, backed by English case law. Nine years later, when asserting that the parties 'must be assured by mutual communication that a common intention exists', Frederick Pollock proclaimed as his starting point Savigny's notion that a contract required a common declaration of their agreed will.[67]

At the same time that theorists began to stress the importance of communication, it became an important matter for the courts. When in the late 1860s, numerous companies began to fail, and liquidators tried to recover calls from shareholders, investors who had applied for shares disputed having become members of the company, claiming that they could not be held liable unless they had been notified of their status as shareholders.[68] This was not a new problem; but when it had arisen in the 1850s, courts had looked at the letters between the parties to see if a 'definite agreement' to become a shareholder had been concluded,[69] rather in the way courts had traditionally dealt with Statute of Frauds questions. However, after the 1856 Companies Act enacted that the question of who was a contributory was to be settled by the company's register of shareholders, companies began simply to enter the names of share applicants on the register once an

---

[63] *Cornish* v. *Abington* (1859) 4 H. & N. 549. On the issue of estoppel, see pp. 336–7, 451.

[64] Leake, *Elements* (1867), 8.

[65] *Smith* v. *Hughes* (1871) LR 6 QB 597 at 607. The definition was a modification of the formulation found in J. P. Benjamin's treatise: *Sale*, 39. Benjamin's definition—which was formulated in terms of an estoppel (suggesting that the parties in such a case had not agreed, but the defendant was estopped from raising this argument)—was cited in court before Blackburn J., *Knights* v. *Wiffen* (1870) LR 5 QB 660 at 663. Blackburn later reformulated it to show that the parties had entered into an agreement, without referring to the estoppel.

[66] Leake, *Contracts* (1867), 8.

[67] Pollock, *Contract* (1876), 4. This (Savigny inspired) definition proceeded: 'The mutual communication which makes up an expression of common intention for the purposes of legal agreement consists of proposal and acceptance.' Pollock's treatise (p. 26) was in fact cited by Cockburn CJ in *Brodgen* v. *Metropolitan Railway, The Times*, 19 February 1877, col. 10b.

[68] See further, Gardner, 'Trashing with Trollope', 184–8.

[69] e.g. *Carmichael's Case* (1850) 17 Sim. 163 at 166. See also *Hutton* v. *Upfill* (1850) 2 H.L.C. 674.

allotment had been made. In turn, liquidators took the view that anyone whose name was on the register counted as a shareholder. Once companies began to fail, those whose names were on the register raised the question whether a contract could be concluded without the company communicating to the shareholder that his application had been accepted. The matter raised considerable public debate— with some calling for the appearance of a name on the register of shareholders to be as conclusive as the indorsement of a name on a bill of exchange[70]—and a select committee was appointed to look at company law.

In resolving the problem of whether a contract to buy shares had been concluded, courts almost never cited treatises. When it was first presented to courts of equity—in cases where deposits had been paid—the view was taken that once shares were allotted, the applicant was liable even if he had not been informed of the allotment.[71] Where no deposit had been paid, a different view soon emerged. In *Pellatt's Case* in 1867, Lord Cairns said that 'where an individual applies for shares in a company, there being no obligation to let him have any, there must be a response by the company, otherwise there is no contract'.[72] In *Gunn's Case*, in the same year, Sir John Rolt LJ ruled that the ordinary principles of offer and acceptance applied to companies as much as to contracts between individuals. If the acceptance did not have to be in writing, there had to be 'something which satisfies the Court, either by words or conduct, that the offer has been accepted to the knowledge of the person who made the offer'.[73] The rule began to be articulated that unless notification of the allotment arrived, the applicant for shares would not be liable. In *Hebb's Case*, an applicant for shares in the National Savings Bank Association was held not to be a contributory, since he had withdrawn his application before being informed that shares had been allotted. Lord Romilly MR explained it on general contractual principles that a party could withdraw his offer at any point before the acceptance reached him.[74]

---

[70] *The Times*, 18 April 1867, col. 6f. *The Times* also suggested that the penalties for putting a name on the register to be the same as those for falsely indorsing a bill.

[71] See *Electric Telegraph Co of Ireland, Cookney's Case* (1858) 26 Beav. 6; *Bloxam's Case* (1864) 33 Beav. 529.

[72] By contrast, Turner LJ stated that a shareholder who made an unconditional application for shares would be liable simply on allotment. The disagreement was moot here, since Pellatt's application was part of a wider agreement between the applicant for shares and the company which had not been concluded. *In re Richmond Hill Hotel Company, Pellatt's Case* (1867) LR 2 Ch App 527 at 531, 535. Contrast *In re Richmond Hill Hotel Co, Elkington's Case* (1867) LR 2 Ch App 511. For another case where an agreement to allot shares was part of another broader contract, see *In re Anglo-Danish and Baltic Steam Navigation Co, Sahlgreen and Carrall's Case* (1868) 3 Ch App 323.

[73] *In re Universal Banking Corporation, Gunn's Case* (1867) 3 Ch App 40 at 45. See also *Levita's case* (1867) LR 3 Ch 36 at 44.

[74] *In re National Savings Bank Association, Hebb's Case* (1867) LR 4 Eq 9. See also *In re Anglo-Danish and Baltic Steam Navigation Co* (1868) 3 Ch App 323.

The need for communication was also discussed by the Exchequer Chamber in 1873 in *Tinn* v. *Hoffman*, a commercial sale of goods case. In this case, the courts had to decide whether a contract had been made during the course of a correspondence. During their deliberations, the judges considered (the obiter point) whether a contract could be formed by identical offers, which crossed each other in the post. Honyman J. (echoing the views of Bramwell B. in the court below) felt that 'if two letters are posted so that they are irrevocable with respect to the writers, why should not that constitute a good contract? The parties are *ad idem* at one and the same moment.'[75] Blackburn J. by contrast felt that cross-offers could not make a contract. It was not enough that the parties had a *consensus ad idem*. The problem was resolved in his mind neither by authority nor by theory. Rather, he noted that '[s]uch grave inconvenience would arise in mercantile business if people could doubt whether there was an acceptance or not, that it is desirable to keep to the rule that an offer that has been made should be accepted by an acceptance such as would leave no doubt on the matter'.[76] Businessmen required the certainty of communication.

The need for assent to be communicated in some objective form was confirmed by the House of Lords in 1877 in *Brogden* v. *Metropolitan Railway*. This was another case involving the commercial supply of goods. From 1870, John Brogden & Sons had supplied coal as and when required to the Metropolitan Railway. Towards the end of 1871, they proposed entering into a regular annual contract. After lengthy negotiations between an agent of the coal merchant and the company's locomotive engineer, Burnett, the latter sent a draft contract to Alexander Brogden, the head of the coal firm. Brogden filled in the blanks on the form (which included the names of the partners and the arbitrator who was to settle disputes), made some minor alterations, wrote the word 'approved' on the document, and sent it back. Instead of formally executing it, however, Burnett placed it in a drawer. Coal continued to be supplied at the contract price, but at the end of 1872 (when the coal price was rising and a strike was threatened in the South Wales coalfields), the parties fell into dispute, and Brogden ceased delivering coal. The railway company sued for breach of contract, whereupon the suppliers claimed that no contract for an annual supply had ever been entered into, since the company had never communicated their acceptance of the document sent to them by Brogden.

The railway company won at each stage, though Cockburn CJ dissented strongly in the Court of Appeal. In Cockburn's view, Brogden had no intention of binding his firm 'until he had a corresponding agreement to bind the

---

[75] *Tinn* v. *Hoffmann & Co* (1873) 29 LT 271 at 275.
[76] *Tinn* v. *Hoffmann & Co* (1873) 29 LT 271 at 279.

company', while Burnett thought it inexpedient to bind his company as long as he was satisfied that the coal supply would continue. Nothing in the subsequent correspondence convinced Cockburn that the parties were acting on the proposed agreement.[77] The other judges disagreed. In the Court of Appeal, Bramwell LJ (speaking for the majority) admitted that Burnett's draft sent to Brogden was 'not quite an offer'. Though Brogden 'accepted it as near as could be', in law this was an offer, not an acceptance. Bramwell found no fault in Burnett's not returning the approved draft, seeing this as a common cost-saving short cut in business life. But it was clear to him that the plaintiffs accepted the offer, and that the defendants understood that it was accepted, since the company ordered coal at the contract price, which was delivered (at a time when prices were rising) at the contract price. How, he asked, 'is the conduct of the parties to be explained unless there was a contract?'

The House of Lords in 1877 upheld the verdict for the plaintiffs. It confirmed that some form of communication was needed. The court was particularly keen to reject the comment of Brett J. in the Common Pleas that the contract was complete once 'it can be shewn by sufficient evidence' that the offeree had 'accepted those terms in his own mind',[78] insofar as this comment was interpreted to mean that 'mere mental consent [...] followed up neither by communication nor by action' would suffice.[79] Lord Blackburn noted that some form of 'extraneous act' was needed.[80] In support of this, he cited a dictum (which he had earlier put into his own book on *Sale*) of the fifteenth-century chief justice of the Common Pleas, Sir Thomas Bryan,[81] which suggested that what was required was either communication or factual evidence of the intention to be bound.[82] Merely putting

---

[77] *The Times*, 19 February 1877, col. 10b. He cited Pollock on contract (p. 24) in accepting that the parties might have proceeded on the draft informal agreement: 'But it must be clear that the parties have both waived the execution of the formal instrument and have agreed expressly, or as shown by their conduct, to act on the informal one.'

[78] Quoted by Lord Blackburn in *Brogden* v. *Metropolitan Railway Co* (1877) 2 App Cas 666 at 691. The Common Pleas hearing is reported in the *Western Mail* and *Birmingham Daily Post* 28 May 1875. In his judgment, Lord Coleridge is also reported to have said that the rule in *Adams* v. *Lindsell* 'was that a contract was complete when the minds of the parties were at one, as shown by acceptance in terms'.

[79] *Brogden* v. *Metropolitan Railway Co* (1877) 2 App Cas 666 at 688 (per Lord Selborne). Selborne doubted whether Brett meant that such a subjective view would suffice; in fact, he did not.

[80] *Brogden* v. *Metropolitan Railway Co* (1877) 2 App Cas 666 at 692.

[81] Blackburn, *Sale* (1845), 193: 'it seems to me that the plea is not good without showing that he had certified the other of his pleasure; for it is trite learning that the thought of a man is not triable, for the devil himself knows not the thought of man; but if you agreed that if the bargain pleased you then you should shew it to such a one, then I grant you need not have done more for it is a matter of fact', (from YB 17 Edw. 4, pl. 2, fol. 2).

[82] W. R. Anson, *Principles of the English Law of Contract* (6th edn, Oxford, 1891), 19 used this dictum to argue that there had to be communicated, rather than mere mental, acceptance.

a document into a drawer was not a sufficient manifestation of assent; but if the parties 'indicate by their conduct that they accept it, the contract is binding'.[83] Blackburn's judgment indicated that the court would not merely look for object-ive evidence of the offeree's intention to accept, but would require some conduct which could be taken as a form of communication to the other party of assent. He also ruled that if an offer was made with an express or implied request to the offeree to 'signify his acceptance by doing some particular thing', then he would be bound as soon as he did that thing. The premise behind this statement was that the offeror could waive actual communication by requesting action.

2. COMMUNICATION PROBLEMS

In *Brogden*, the Lords confirmed the centrality of communication, rejecting Pothier's notion that the contract was formed at the moment when the parties' wills subjectively met. At the same time, however, the postal rule was confirmed.[84] The question was raised in a number of cases whether a contract for shares was formed where a letter of allotment had gone missing. Courts initially seemed sym-pathetic to share applicants in these cases.[85] In *British and American Telegraph Co* v. *Colson*, an applicant disputed an action to recover calls on shares, claim-ing that his letter of allotment had gone missing.[86] In finding for Colson, Kelly CB in the Exchequer interpreted *Dunlop* v. *Higgins* as establishing that where an acceptance was posted, the contract was effective from the time that the letter was put into the post. But he also held that the offeror could not be bound until he was notified of its acceptance, unless the failure to deliver the letter was his fault. The contract would not be 'complete' until the letter arrived; though once it arrived there would a relation back to the moment of posting.[87] Kelly's argu-ments were rooted in his perceptions of commercial convenience rather than in a developed system of doctrine: he felt that it would be unjust to allow suppliers to be sued for their failure to send goods, in cases where they had never received

[83] *Brogden* v. *Metropolitan Railway Co* (1877) 2 App Cas 666 at 693.

[84] The continuing relevance of the postal rule was confirmed by Romilly MR in *Hebb's* case. Fortunately for Hebb, it did not apply to him as the company had not addressed its letter to the appli-cant, but had informed its agent (who dealt with the applicant) that the shares had been allotted. *In re National Savings Bank Association, Hebb's Case* (1867) LR 4 Eq 9 at 12.

[85] See *In re the Constantinople and Alexandria Hotels Co, Finucane's Case* (1869) 17 WR 813, where a letter of allotment did not arrive, and the applicant was not considered a contributory.

[86] In this case a duplicate letter of allotment was sent out two weeks later, but the trial judge (on the authority of *Ramsgate Victoria Hotel Co* v. *Montefiore* (1866) LR 1 Ex 109) directed the jury that an allotment must be made within a reasonable time, and the jury found that the second letter was not mailed in time.

[87] *British and American Telegraph Co* v. *Colson* (1871) LR 6 Ex 108 at 111.

letters accepting their offer to supply. Bramwell B. concurred, seeking to narrow the rule in *Dunlop*, to mean only that 'where the post may be used between two parties, it must be subject to such delays as are unavoidable'.[88] This was to suggest that an uncommunicated act of assent could not make a contract binding.

However, the tide of judicial opinion soon turned against *Colson*, as judges became more conscious of the dangers of allowing applicants for shares to evade liability simply by claiming that letters of allotment had never arrived:[89] in an age of repeated company failures, judges were aware that generosity to share-holders shifted losses onto creditors.[90] In 1872, in *Harris's Case*, the Lord Justices expressed disapproval of Kelly's judgment in language which indicated their doubts about the need for communication in general. James LJ drew from *Dunlop* v. *Higgins* the broad conclusion that 'the moment one man has made an offer, and the other has done something binding himself to that offer, then the contract is complete, and neither party can afterwards escape from it'.[91] Sir George Mellish LJ drew attention to the 'extraordinary and mischievous consequences' which would follow if an offer could be revoked at any time before the acceptance had arrived. It would allow purchasers in a falling market to revoke offers, imposing a loss on a supplier who might already have gone to market. In *Harris's Case*, the letter actually arrived; but in *Household Fire and Carriage Accident Insurance Co* v. *Grant* in 1879, it did not. In this case, the Court of Appeal resolved the issue by confirming both the postal rule and the need for communication. Applying *Dunlop* v. *Higgins*, a majority of the court held that a contract was complete once the letter of allotment was posted, and that the contract was binding notwith-standing the non-arrival of the letter. Thesiger LJ pointed to two principles of law relating to the formation of contracts. The first was that to make a binding contract, the minds of the parties had to be 'brought together at one and the same moment'. This moment could only occur when the offer was accepted. The second was that acceptance had to be communicated to the offeree. In his view, the two positions could be reconciled in the case of correspondence made by the post by presuming that the Post Office acted as common agent of the parties.[92] Those who did not wish the Post Office to act as agent could specify this in their agreement. Bramwell dissented, focusing squarely on the need for assent to be

---

[88] *British and American Telegraph Co* v. *Colson* (1871) LR 6 Ex 108 at 118, 120.

[89] See *Wall's Case* (1872) LR 15 Eq 18 at 22–3, quoted in Gardner, 'Trashing with Trollope', 188.

[90] See pp. 424, 649.

[91] *In re Imperial Land Co of Marseilles, Harris's Case* (1872) LR 7 Ch 587 at 592. It was this case which informed Brett's view of the law in *Brogden*. It may be noted that Sir Richard Malins VC took a different view of the law at the first hearing: *In re Imperial Land Company of Marseilles, Harris's Case* (1871) LR 13 Eq 148 at 152.

[92] *Household Fire and Carriage Accident Insurance Co* v. *Grant* (1879) 4 Ex D 216 at 220. Thesiger also cited the US case of *Tayloe* v. *Merchants Fire Insurance Co* (1850) 9 Howard SCR 390.

communicated. If there were to be an exception to this rule, according to which a communication to the Post Office sufficed, it would have to be applied to all communications made by post. This, he felt, would have absurd consequences.

The English courts in this era also considered for the first time whether there had to be communication of the revocation of offers. The implication in *Cooke* v. *Oxley* that there did not need to be may have influenced the King's Bench in *Adams* v. *Lindsell* to conclude that the contract was made when the letter of acceptance was posted—before the defendant had sold the wool to other buyers—rather than when it arrived. In the case of oral contracts, it was not until the 1880s that jurists confirmed that the tacit revocation of verbal offers needed communication.[93] In the case of contracts by correspondence, the principle that a revocation needed communication obtained learned consensus earlier. Pothier's views in this area were soon rejected. In 1850, the US Supreme Court held that a letter retracting an offer would only be effective if it arrived before an acceptance was posted.[94] The court's opinion was shaped by what it felt was the object of the parties in entering into correspondence. Since the offeror had chosen to use the post, the offeree had to be entitled to regard it as a continuing offer until it reached him. Leake,[95] Benjamin,[96] and Pollock[97] agreed that Pothier's views on revocation were flawed, and that a letter of revocation could only be effective on arrival. English courts also came to agree that a revocation was only effective once the offeree became aware of it. But according to the Court of Appeal in 1876, in *Dickinson* v. *Dodds*, it was not necessary for the offeror himself to communicate the withdrawal of an offer, provided the offeree had become aware of it. In this case, the defendant sold property which he had offered to the plaintiff to another buyer, without formally revoking his offer. On hearing that Dodds was negotiating to sell to someone else, Dickinson gave him a formal written acceptance, and claimed to have completed a contract. Overturning Bacon VC's decree in his favour, the Court of Appeal held that no express retraction was necessary. As Mellish LJ put it:

[I]f it be the law that, in order to make a contract, the two minds must be in agreement [...] at the time of the acceptance, how is it possible that when the person to whom the offer has been made knows that the person who has made the offer has sold the property

---

[93] See Pollock, *Contracts* (3rd edn, 1881), 29. This was as a result of in *Stevenson* v. *McLean* (1880) 5 QB 346 at 351. Anson, *Contract* (1879), 17 distinguished between verbal offers and offers by correspondence.

[94] *Tayloe* v. *Merchants Fire Insurance Co* (1850) 9 Howard SCR 390.

[95] Leake, *Elements* (1867), 20n.

[96] Benjamin, *Sale* (1868), 53–4.

[97] Pollock, *Contracts* (1876),10, which followed the position on postal revocations of K. A. von Vangerow, *Lehrbuch der Pandekten*, 3 vols (Marburg, 1869), § 603 (pp. 248 *et seq*). He also cited the Indian Contract Act, which enacted (s 4) that the revocation was only effective against the offeree when it arrived.

to someone else, and that, in fact, he has not remained in the same mind to sell it to him, he can be at liberty to accept the offer?[98]

Although this seemed to indicate that what mattered was the offeree's knowledge, and not the fact of communication by the offeror, jurists such as Pollock argued that it was still necessary to have communication by conduct: so that an offeree who was unaware that an offeror had put it out of his power to perform, could still sue for breach of contract.[99]

The need for letters of revocation to arrive before they were effective was confirmed in the Common Pleas Division in 1880 in *Byrne* v. *Van Tienhoven*. In his judgment, Lindley LJ (citing the English treatise writers) dismissed Pothier's view, holding that 'a state of mind not notified cannot be regarded in dealings between man and man'.[100] In his view, the agency principle behind the postal rule could not be applicable to a letter revoking an offer.[101] This view was endorsed in 1892 in *Henthorn* v. *Fraser*, which confirmed that a letter of acceptance posted after the dispatch, but before the arrival, of a letter of revocation, concluded a contract.[102]

The development of the rules of offer and acceptance in England was thus experimental, and tended to follow judicial views of commercial convenience. Courts rejected Pothier's will theory, which focused on a subjective meeting of the minds, and instead stressed the need for communication. They did this for entirely pragmatic reasons. Parties to contracts had to know when they could act on them. Once the offeror knew that his offer had been accepted, he could act on it; once the offeree knew that the offer was no longer open, he was not entitled to rely on it. This pragmatic view may have reflected a different theory—one where reliance was more central than the will—but it was not a theory which was articulated by the judges. In the meantime, and paradoxically, the courts retained and extended the postal rule, which had its roots in a different conception, where what mattered was the moment of a subjective meeting of the minds. The judges retained it because they assumed that it was commercially convenient. It was an assumption not grounded in commercial practice.

The result of the case law left a messy theory. The most theorized discussion of offer and acceptance was not English, but American: Langdell's *Summary*. The discussion in this work owed little to either Pothier or Savigny, but much to his own theories of consideration. His theory was coherent, but did not reflect English

---

[98] *Dickinson* v. *Dodds* (1876) 2 Ch D 463 at 474.

[99] Pollock, *Contract* (3rd edn, 1881), 27–8. See also Anson's objections in *Contract* (2nd edn, 1882), 31–4 (also developed in later editions).

[100] *Byrne* v. *Van Tienhoven* (1880) 5 CPD 344 at 347.

[101] This view was endorsed by the Queen's Bench Division in *Stevenson* v. *McLean* (1880) 5 QB 346.

[102] *Henthorn* v. *Fraser* [1892] 2 Ch 27 at 31.

practice, since he did not see communication as an essential element. Langdell distinguished between two kinds of contracts: 'unilateral' ones, where the promise of the offeror was accepted by performance; and 'bilateral' ones, where the promise was met with by a counter promise. In the former case, the acceptance of an offer required only a mental act, and not communication.[103] For Langdell,

the question whether an offer has been accepted can never in strictness become material in those cases in which a consideration is necessary; and for all practical purposes it may be said that the offer is accepted in such cases by giving or performing the consideration.[104]

Langdell was therefore prepared to accept that applications for shares were offers which could be accepted by the performance of the act of allotment.[105] By contrast, in executory—or 'bilateral'—contracts, where one promise was given for another, it was a matter of logic that acceptance had to be communicated. In such contracts, the offeree, when accepting, made a counter-promise to the offeror, thereby providing the necessary consideration for the first promise. Since the acceptance in bilateral contracts was also a counter-offer, it had to arrive before it could bind. Once the counter-offer arrived, consideration was provided for the first offer and the contract was complete without waiting for acceptance to be sent to the other party.[106] The need for communication in such cases was merely the 'accidental' consequence of the fact that the contract was only made when the counter-offer was made known to the original offeror. In his view, to apply the postal rule in such cases and regard the contract as made when the acceptance—or 'counter-offer'—was put in the mail was simply incorrect, and he dismissed arguments from commercial convenience as 'irrelevant'.[107]

Langdell's view was not adopted by English scholars. For Pollock, *Brogden* v. *Metropolitan Railway* confirmed the 'obvious' point that 'an uncommunicated

---

[103] A promise of a gift, made under seal, would thus be binding without communication of acceptance. But in the common law, where consideration was needed for informal contracts, the performance of the consideration implied acceptance of the offer.

[104] C. C. Langdell, *A Summary of the Law of Contracts* (Boston, 1880), 1–2.

[105] However, he thought the allottee was entitled to notice, if only because the process of allotment itself was a secret transaction. The allotment fixed the rights and liabilities of the parties, which could not be altered without their consent, 'yet the passing of the title to the shares and the applicant's liability for the purchase-money are suspended until the condition of giving notice is either performed or waived' Langdell, *Summary*, 7.

[106] '[T]he contract is made the moment the counter-offer is made, and the counter-offer is made the moment the letter of acceptance comes to the knowledge of the original offeror', Langdell, *Summary*, 19. Langdell felt (p. 17) that *Hebb, Harris* and *Colson* were not relevant to the problem since they were 'unilateral' (or executed) contracts.

[107] Langdell, *Summary*, 21. Langdell's Harvard colleague Holmes challenged his logic and argued that the question should be settled by reference to convenience. O. W. Holmes, *The Common Law* (Boston, 1881), 305.

mental assent' could not make a contract.[108] In 1889, he referred to Langdell's 'ingenious distinction', but said he could find no authority for it.[109] However, Pollock had difficulties in explaining why, in some cases, actual communication was not necessary. In the 1894 edition of his treatise, he quoted Langdell, and (adopting the Dean's terminology) observed that the reason why in 'unilateral' contracts communication was not needed was because the offeror intended to dispense with the need for it.[110] By the 1902 edition, he adapted Langdell's distinction for his own purposes in the text, filling the American's categories with rules taken from the cases. While communication was normally required, he said, the offeror could 'dispense with express communication' in two situations. First, where the acceptance was to consist of an act (as dispatching goods ordered by post), performance would constitute acceptance. Secondly, where the acceptance was to consist of a promise, 'any reasonable means of communication prescribed or contemplated by the proposer are deemed sufficient'.[111] In effect, the offerer could waive the right to communication. This latter point could explain the postal rule. Nonetheless, it was a rule which he found troubling, and he advised all practical men to specify that the letter of acceptance had to arrive.[112] If Langdell offered Pollock categories, he took his explanations from the judges.

3. UNILATERAL CONTRACTS

If I say to another, 'if you will go to York, I will give you £100,' that is in a certain sense a unilateral contract. He has not promised to go to York. But if he goes, it cannot be doubted that he will be entitled to receive the £100. His going to York at my request is a sufficient consideration for my promise.[113]

Brett J's example of a 'unilateral' contract raised a number of questions about contract formation which late nineteenth-century jurists would consider. What made such an offer binding? Did the offeree have to communicate acceptance? Could the offer be revoked? In the late nineteenth century, these questions were raised in the context of advertising. But such kinds of contract had a longer history.

---

[108] Pollock, *Contract* (6th edn, 1894), 32.

[109] Pollock, *Contract* (5th edn, 1889), 663.

[110] Pollock, *Contract* (6th edn, 1894), 664, citing *Carlill* v. *Carbolic Smoke Ball* [1893] 1 QB at 262, 269.

[111] Pollock, *Contract* (7th edn, 1902), 33.

[112] Pollock, *Contract* (6th edn, 1894), 37. He was also unconvinced by the judicial theory of the common agency of the post office: p. 34.

[113] *Great Northern Railway Co* v. *Witham* (1873) LR 9 CP 16 at 19.

Brett's example of the journey to York was a very old and often-repeated one.[114] It was the classic example of a one-sided promise, contrasted with a recipro-cal one. In such cases, the contractual obligation to pay was generated by the promise, or request, by the defendant to the plaintiff to perform.[115] However, early modern authority suggested that no obligation arose until the stipulated condition was fully performed.[116] In the nineteenth century, one common form of 'unilateral' contract was the promise by one party to guarantee the debts of another.[117] Another was the unilateral offer made not to a specified individual (which the parties generally could have recast into a bilateral one) but to the world at large. The classic example of this was the offer of a reward. In the absence of an organized police force and with no system of public prosecution, this was a vital form of crime detection in early nineteenth-century England. Courts were keen for rewards to be paid where appropriate, since it encouraged the discovery of crimes.[118] Disputes occasionally arose as to who could claim them. Although plaintiffs generally declared that they had 'confided in the promise' of the defend-ant, courts were not generally interested in asking whether the claimant had accepted an offer. Nor did the courts look at the motives of the claimant, but rather asked whether the requested action had been performed.[119] Where infor-mation leading to the conviction of a criminal was required when a reward was offered, the courts asked whether it was the claimant's information, rather than anyone else's, which led to the conviction.[120]

The question whether a person could claim who did not act in response to the offer was first raised in 1833 in *Williams* v. *Carwardine*. Mary Ann Williams was a young prostitute who had witnessed the murder of one of her brothel-keeper's clients.[121] Two suspects (including Mary's employer) were tried for the murder, and acquitted. Although Mary knew who the real culprits were, she did not

---

[114] *Lord Lisles Case* (1478) YB 18 Edw.4. pl. 15, fol. 17b; *Basset* v. *Kern* (1587) 1 Leon. 69. For nine-teenth-century examples, see *Hoggins* v. *Gordon* (1842) 3 Q.B. 466 at 469; *Cooper* v. *Parker* (1853) 14 C.B. 118 at 121.

[115] *Bourn* v. *Mason* (1669) 2 Keb. 457. Where a performance had been accepted, the promise was implied.

[116] See *Lea* v. *Adams* (1615) 3 Bulst. 35 at 36; *Peters* v. *Opie* (1671) 1 Vent. 177.

[117] *Kennaway* v. *Treleavan* (1839) 5 M. & W. 498 at 501, cf. *Newbury* v. *Armstrong* (1829) 6 Bing. 201; *Mozley* v. *Tinkler* (1835) 1 C.M.&R. 692. Section 4 of the Statute of Frauds required the guarantee, or a memorandum of it, to be in writing, in which the consideration for the promise had to be shown: *Wain* v. *Warlters* (1804) 5 East 10.

[118] *England* v. *Davidson* (1840) Ad. & El. 856.

[119] e.g. *Fallick* v. *Barber* (1813) 1 M. & S. 108.

[120] *Lancaster* v. *Walsh* (1838) 4 M. & W. 16; *Lockhart* v. *Barnard* (1845) 14 M. & W. 674; *Smith* v. *Moore* (1845) 1 C.B. 438; *Thatcher* v. *England* (1846) 3 C.B. 254.

[121] See *The Times*, 8 August 1831, col. 6d, 27 March 1832, col. 4a. See P. Mitchell and J. Phillips, 'The Contractual Nexus: is reliance necessary?' (2002) 22 *OJLS* 115–34.

disclose this at the trial. After the trial, she fell into an argument with one of the culprits, who beat her up. She then went to one of the city's magistrates, and made a voluntary statement, naming the murderers. Although she claimed in her deposition that she believed she did not have long to live and wished to ease her conscience, there were suggestions that she wanted revenge against her assailants, who were convicted and executed as a result of her testimony.[122] She later sued for the reward offered by the deceased man's brother for information leading to a conviction. For the defence, it was argued that since the handbill offering the reward was published in April, and she gave her information in August, she had not acted 'in consequence of the handbill [but] from other and quite different motives'. This was, Curwood said, 'a case of what in the civil law is called policitation, that is, an offer by one party not accepted by the other'. Although Parke regarded the matter of motive as irrelevant, he permitted the defence to move for a new trial, on the basis of a finding by the jury that 'she did not give that information, for the sake of the £20 reward, nor in consequence of the handbill, but from stings of conscience'.[123] In the King's Bench, Mary succeeded once more. By giving the information, Denman CJ ruled, she 'brought herself within the terms of the advertisement, and therefore is entitled to recover'.[124]

Since the handbill had been distributed throughout Hereford in April, it might have been presumed that Mary was aware of it when giving the information. Nonetheless, the words of the judgment suggested that a reward could be claimed by a person who had not been aware of the offer when providing the information. This was an approach which mid-century courts endorsed. In *Neville* v. *Kelly*, in 1862, a policeman who had arrested a boy who had absconded with his master's horse and gig claimed a reward later offered by the master for information leading to a conviction. The defendant demurred to the declaration, pointing out that the arrest had taken place before the reward was offered. But the Common Pleas seemed most concerned with whether the information given had led to the arrest and conviction of the boy: the fact that the boy had already been arrested was not enough for the demurrer to succeed.[125] In 1878, in *Bent* v. *The Wakefield and Barnsley Union Bank*, the Common Pleas Division, when denying a reward to a policeman who arrested a criminal who gave himself up, looked at the question of causation, not at whether there had been an offer accepted by the claimant.[126] These issues were raised again in 1891 in *Gibbons* v. *Proctor*. Here, a police officer

---

[122] This was also suggested by Shee Sjt in *Thatcher* v. *England* (1846) 3 C.B. 254 at 260.

[123] *Williams* v. *Carwardine* (1833) 5 Car. & P. 566 at 571, 573.

[124] *Williams* v. *Carwardine* (1833) 4 B. & Ad. 621 at 623.

[125] The case never went to trial, since the defendant became insolvent, *Neville* v. *Kelly* (1862) 12 C.B. N.S. 740.

[126] *Bent* v. *The Wakefield and Barnsley Union Bank* (1878) 4 CPD 1.

claimed a £25 reward offered for information leading to the conviction of a person who had committed a criminal assault. The handbill offering the money was printed on 29 May 1890, and was sent to Supt Penn, to arrive on the morning of 30 May. On 29 May, when given a description of the offender being sought, Gibbons told another policeman, Coppin, that the man was already in custody. He told him to inform Penn. Penn received this information by letter on the morning of the 30 May, when the handbills were also delivered. Although there was no dispute that Gibbons's information led to the conviction, he lost in the county court, on the grounds that the reward had only been offered after the information had been given. The Divisional Court, however, found for the plaintiff. According to one report, Day J. said, 'The information ultimately reached Penn at a time when the plaintiff knew that the reward had been offered. I think this fulfilled the condition on which the reward was offered, the information being given after the offer was made.'[127] This comment was taken by twentieth-century judges and jurists as satisfying the need for the person claiming the reward to know of the offer when performing.[128] But in fact the court was more concerned with establishing that the offer of the reward had preceded the receipt of the information than with Gibbons' actual knowledge of the offer: accepting that the notice was 'published' on 29 May, it could find that the information was communicated subsequently.

English courts throughout the century remained content to give rewards to those who supplied the requisite information in ignorance of the offer. By contrast, American courts held this to be inconsistent with the contractual requirement of offer and acceptance. For them, a claim to a reward could only be based on a contract; and for a contract to exist, there had to be mutual consent, which required an intention to accept an offer.[129] English treatise writers were also troubled by *Williams* v. *Carwardine* and *Gibbons* v. *Proctor*. Pollock cast doubt on both cases.[130] Anson drew the conclusion that Mary Ann Williams had known about the reward, so that the case was solely one about whether motives were relevant. By the sixth edition of his book in 1891, he had discovered the American case of *Fitch* v. *Snedaker*, which he used to settle the point that a person acting in ignorance of an offer of a reward could not claim it.[131] Thus emboldened, early

---

[127] *Gibbons* v. *Proctor* (1891) 55 JP 616 at 617, but cf. 64 LT 594 at 595. See also A. H. Hudson, 'Gibbons v. Proctor Revisited' (1968) 84 *LQR* 502–12.

[128] *R* v. *Clarke* (1927) 40 CLR 227; G. H. Treitel, *Law of Contract* (12th edn, by E. Peel, 2007), 38–9.

[129] *Fitch* v. *Snedaker* (1868) 38 NY 248. See also Holmes, *The Common Law*, 294.

[130] In the 3rd edn of *Contracts* (1881), 19, Pollock wrote that: 'The decision (*Williams* v. *Carwardine*) sets up a contract without any *animus contrahendi*.' By the 5th edn (having read Langdell) he added that it was 'without any real consideration' and that the doctrine could not now be received (1889, p. 21).

[131] *Fitch* v. *Sndeaker*, which had drawn its analysis from Chitty, whose inspiration was Pothier, had not been cited in the English courts. The case had been mentioned by Langdell.

twentieth-century treatise writers felt confident enough, in all absence of English authority, to proclaim that *Williams* and *Gibbons* were not law.

The decision to grant rewards to those who complied unknowingly reflected a policy choice to encourage the payment of rewards as an incentive to solving crime. But in the second half of the century, as a consumer society developed, courts had to consider the effect of other kinds of advertisements. In 1852, the purchaser of bearer shares in a mining company conducted on the Société Anonyme principle sued its directors for breach of contract, after they had failed to pay the 33 per cent annual dividend 'guaranteed' to shareholders. Drawing a parallel with reward cases, counsel for the plaintiff argued that, '[t]he defendant, by the general announcement, puts himself in the position of a party agreeing on these terms with any individual who in pursuance of the announcement accedes to it'.[132] The Queen's Bench was not convinced. Lord Campbell said that, in the reward cases, a distinct promise had been made and consideration was found either in the benefit to the promisor (resulting from the information given) or a detriment to the promisee. He could see neither a promise nor consideration in the case before him. He felt the reward cases were 'somewhat anomalous', best seen as cases were the plaintiff might be allowed to sue for work and labour done at the promisor's request.[133]

Having been hostile to an attempt to make a contract from an advertisement in 1852, Lord Campbell took a different view in 1856. In *Denton* v. *Great Northern Railway Company*, he held that a railway timetable was a promise 'to any one who would come to the station and tender the price of the ticket', which became a binding contract when the passenger came to buy his ticket.[134] Crompton J. disagreed with this interpretation of the law. He felt that while reward cases could be explained on the basis of work and labour done at the request of the defendant, a person coming to a station—or to a shop—having seen an advertisement could not be said to have provided a requested consideration. Despite his doubts, Campbell's view was acted on in 1859 in *Warlow* v. *Harrison*, where an auctioneer had advertised a sale 'without reserve' but had then allowed the owner of goods auctioned to bid. The majority judgment in the Exchequer Chamber held that 'the auctioneer who puts the property up for sale upon such a condition pledges himself that the sale shall be without reserve; or, in other words, contracts that

---

[132] *Gerhard* v. *Bates* (1852) 2 E. & B. 476 at 484.

[133] The sum stated was to be seen as evidence of what might be due on a *quantum meruit*, *Gerhard* v. *Bates* (1852) 2 E. & B. 476 at 488. Contrast Maule J. in *Thatcher* v. *England* (1846) 3 C.B. 254 at 264: 'It is difficult to put a value on information: it is not like work and labour, which has been accepted, and is to be paid for on a quantum meruit'.

[134] *Denton* v. *Great Northern Railway Co* (1856) 5 E. & B. 860 at 865–6.

it shall be so; and that this contract is made with the highest bona fide bidder'.[135] Again, the court was not unanimous in its reasons, Willes and Bramwell JJ preferring to rest their judgment on the ground that the auctioneer had warranted when he put the items up for sale that he had power to sell without reserve.

In the 1870s, courts began again to doubt whether advertisements could constitute offers. In *Spencer* v. *Harding*, the Common Pleas Division considered whether an advertisement inviting tenders for the purchase of a stock in trade amounted to a contractual offer to sell to the highest bidder. Willes J. accepted that advertisements for rewards were offers: although they appeared to be offers to the whole world, they were in fact offers to the first person who gave the information requested, which were accepted when that person fulfilled the contract. But since the advertisement in this case did not specify that the highest bidder would be chosen, the advertisement was to be seen as a mere proclamation that the sellers were ready to receive offers.[136] A similar view of advertisements was taken in 1873 in *Harris* v. *Nickerson*, where the Queen's Bench Division rejected a claim from a commission broker, who had seen an advertisement stating that furniture was to be auctioned in Bury St Edmunds, for his loss of time and expenses when the lots were withdrawn. The judges rejected the 'startling proposition' that a contract was made when he travelled, aware of the inconvenience both of requiring advertisers to notify the public of the revocation of their 'offers', and of holding them responsible for the costs of anyone who came.[137]

When Pollock published his treatise in 1876, he had also come to the conclusion that contracts could not be formed on the basis of advertisements, by rejecting two theories explaining how they could. According to the first, an offer in an advertisement was accepted simply by performance. Pollock rejected this, since he was troubled by the problem of how to set limits to the doctrine. According to the second (borrowed from Savigny), an advertisement was a 'floating' or 'anomalous contract with the uncertain person who shall fulfil the condition'. Here, instead of an offer, there was 'a conditional obligation arising at once from the announcement made by the promisor'. Such a promise could never be retracted, since that would amount to a refusal to perform an existing contract.[138] Pollock rejected this theory by drawing on German ideas on intention. Using K. A. von Vangerow's distinction between proposals and invitations to make proposals, Pollock said that courts should consider whether there was an *animus contrahendi*. In his

---

[135] *Warlow* v. *Harrison* (1859) 1 E. & E. 309 at 316–17.

[136] *Spencer* v. *Harding* (1870) LR 5 CP 561.

[137] *Harris* v. *Nickerson* (1873) LR 8 QB 286.

[138] Pollock noted that, having seen this consequence, Savigny argued that offers of rewards should not be enforced by law, F. C. von Savigny, *Das Obligationenrecht*, 2 vols (Berlin, 1851–3), ii, 90 (§ 61). See also Anson's dismissal of Savigny's view in *Contract* (6th edn, 1891), 35n.

view, '[t]he proposal of a definite service to be done for reward, which is in fact a request' was 'quite different in its nature from declaration to all whom it may concern that one is willing to do business with them'.[139] According to this view, advertisements in general could not constitute offers.

Case law once again unsettled doctrine in 1892 when the question of advertising again came before the courts in *Carlill* v. *Carbolic Smoke Ball Company*.[140] The case was unusual. It was brought against a company which promised in its advertisements to pay a £100 'reward' to anyone who contracted influenza after using its smoke ball in the directed manner. Mrs Louisa Carlill, a particularly tenacious litigant, brought the case having bought a smoke ball and contracted the illness. Patent medicine advertisements had long been regarded with suspicion. Vast sums were spent by the suppliers of pills on advertising products which they claimed could cure any and all ailments. The reward offered by the company in this case was huge: if the 10 shilling smoke ball did not work, they proclaimed, a sum would be paid sufficient to rent a 150 acre farm in East Anglia for a year or buy the goodwill of a small business in London.

Although the advertisement was designed to make the public think that the effectiveness of the smoke ball was guaranteed, no such guarantee was incorporated into the contract of sale. The defendants therefore said that this proclamation, aimed at 'all users' was puff. Lawyers had long argued that purchasers of quack medicine who had been imposed on by advertisements—'which all the world recognises as a puff'—should not recover.[141] But both the trial judge in Mrs Carlill's case, Hawkins J., and the Court of Appeal upheld the plaintiff's claim that she had a contractual right to recover the £100. Counsel for the company claimed there could be no contract, since there was no promise or request from the defendants and no consideration provided by the plaintiff. However, the advertisement was interpreted to be an offer, and not 'mere puff', since £1000 had been deposited as proof that they were serious. Bowen LJ finessed the need for a request by pointing to cases which confirmed that where consideration had been provided, a request did not need to be averred. The crucial question was therefore whether Mrs Carlill had provided consideration. This was found, first, in the fact that the use of the smoke ball by the public would increase sales and, secondly, in the inconvenience Mrs Carlill sustained in using the ball according to the instructions. The court's reasoning was inventive. In previous cases, courts

---

[139] Pollock, *Contract* (1876), 172–80. In the 3rd edn of 1881, at p. 18, Pollock explained that Savigny had 'strangely' missed the explanation that floating agreements could not bind since there was no *animus contrahendi*.

[140] See A. W. B. Simpson, 'Quackery and Contract Law: the Case of the Carbolic Smoke Ball' (1985) 14 *JLS* 344–89.

[141] *Jones* v. *Bright* (1829) 5 Bing. 533 at 541 (Ludlow Sjt).

had insisted that performance—however trivial—had to have followed a request, or been accepted. Here, while a request to use the ball in the specified way might be implied from the wording of the advertisement, there was no 'request' to catch influenza; yet that was the 'performance' which was to be paid for. In its keenness to punish bad advertising, the court failed to tie up the doctrinal loose ends.

The court also addressed the issue of whether communication was necessary in such cases. This had not been discussed in the earlier reward cases, whose thinking was largely untouched by will theory. But this was a question which could not be avoided by the 1890s, for it went to the heart of the nature of the agreement. It was held that notification of acceptance did not have to precede performance. For Bowen LJ, 'performance of the condition is a sufficient acceptance without notification'. For Lindley LJ, the offeror 'shows by his language and from the nature of the transaction that he does not expect and does not require notice of the acceptance apart from notice of the performance'.[142] Notification of acceptance was only required for the benefit of the offeror, who could choose to dispense with it.[143] The Court of Appeal here was self-consciously following the Lords' decision in *Brogden* v. *Metropolitan Railway*.[144]

In Mrs Carlill's case, the Court of Appeal went out of its way in an unusual case to punish dishonest advertisements in order to protect a consumer. It was a decision which the public and the profession were not unhappy with.[145] Pollock and Anson both saw in the decision of the Court of Appeal a recognition of the distinction between the willingness to consider offers, and offers to be bound, contemplating legal relations.[146] However, the recognition that advertisements could constitute offers, which could be accepted by uncommunicated conduct raised the issue of when and whether the offer could be revoked. This issue, not discussed in *Carlill*, had not received much discussion in earlier case law. In *Offord* v. *Davies* in 1862, the Common Pleas considered whether a guarantee could be revoked. In argument, Williams J. asked whether a man who guaranteed the price of a carriage being built for a third party could withdraw the guarantee on discovering that person's insolvency. James QC for the plaintiff argued that once the coach builder had commenced building the carriage, the guarantee could not be withdrawn. Erle J. interjected, 'Before it ripens into a contract, either party may withdraw, and so put an end to the matter. But the moment the coach-builder has prepared the materials, he would probably be found by the jury

---

[142] *Carlill* v. *Carbolic Smoke Ball Co* [1893] 1 QB 256 at 270, 262–3.

[143] *Carlill* v. *Carbolic Smoke Ball Co* [1893] 1 QB 256 at 269 (per Bowen LJ).

[144] *Brogden* v. *Metropolitan Railway Co* (1877) 2 App Cas 666 at 691.

[145] See e.g. *Pall Mall Gazette*, 8 December 1892, 2; *Daily News*, 8 December 1892, 5. Pollock also approved: 8 *LQR* (1892), 270.

[146] Pollock, *Contract* (7th edn, 1902), 19n; Anson, *Contract* (8th edn, 1895), 40.

to have contracted.' In his judgment, however, he ruled that 'until the condition has been at least in part fulfilled, the defendants have the power of revoking it'.[147] This left it unclear whether the offer could be revoked at any time prior to complete performance, or whether it could not be revoked at all, once performance had commenced.

This issue was more broadly debated in America, both in case law[148] and juristic literature. The issue was discussed by Theophilus Parsons's treatise on contract. Although, Parsons noted, it was true that where one party promised to pay another if he performed some action, the latter was not bound to act, it was not true to say that such contracts lacked mutuality. For the party promising was not bound to do anything until the promisee had either 'engaged to do, or else does or begins to do, the thing which is the condition of the first promise'. In Parsons's view, the promisor could revoke at any stage before the promisee acted on it (as there was no consideration for the promise); but 'if the promisee begins to do the thing, in a way which binds him to complete it, here also is a mutuality of obligation'.[149] Parsons's view was followed by the Illinois Supreme Court in 1888, which held that 'performance, or part performance in such a way as to compel the promisee to complete it, is sufficient' to constitute a contract.[150] In 1902, the California Supreme Court held, in a case where the appellants promised to pay the respondent railway company a sum of money on the completion of their railway, that once the company had acted on the unilateral contract by buying a franchise (to build the line on the agreed route), the 'promised consideration had then been partly performed, and the contract had taken on a bilateral character'.[151] American jurists reacted in a number of different ways to this problem. Williston felt the best view was that the unilateral offer could be revoked at any point prior to complete performance, since an offer conditional on the performance of an act did not become a contract by part performance; and since the offeree could not be held bound to complete performance once he had begun.[152] Clarence Ashley also rejected the idea that a unilateral contract became bilateral once performance had

---

[147] *Offord* v. *Davies* (1862) 12 C.B. N.S. 748 at 753, 757.

[148] *Biggers* v. *Owen* (1887) 79 Ga 658, 5 SE 193, holding that where an offer of reward was withdrawn, a party acting on it could not recover; contrast Preston J.'s view in *Cornelson* v. *Sun Mutual Insurance Co* (1852) 7 La Ann 345, 347.

[149] T. Parsons, *The Law of Contracts*, 3 vols (5th edn, 1864), i, 450–1.

[150] *Plumb* v. *Campbell* (1888) 129 Ill 101, 107–9, 18 LE 790. In *Blumenthal* v. *Goodall* (1891) 89 Cal 251, 26 Pac 906, the Supreme Court of California refused to allow a defendant to revoke his real estate agent's authority to find a buyer for his property, since 'prior to its revocation, [t]he agent had placed the matter in the position that success was practically certain and immediate' (at 257).

[151] *Los Angeles Traction Co* v. *Wilshire* (1902) 135 Cal 654, 67 Pac 1086 at 658.

[152] F. Pollock, *Principles of Contract at Law and in Equity* (3rd American edn from the 7th English edn, by G. H. Wald and S. Williston, New York, 1906), 34, n39. See also I. M. Wormser, 'The True Conception of Unilateral Contracts' (1916) 26 *Yale LJ* 136–42.

begun. Drawing on the comments of the courts that it would be unjust to allow offerors to revoke in such cases, he argued instead that there was an estoppel, preventing the revocation once performance had begun.[153] D. O. McGovney rejected this as stretching the notion of estoppel too far, and suggested instead that courts should find a collateral contract, not to revoke the original offer once performance had begun.[154]

The issue was not debated as fully in England. In the earlier editions of his treatise, Pollock had taken the view that if 'unilateral' offers in advertisements were seen as conditional promises, then the promisor could not revoke them; whereas if they were seen as offers accepted by conduct, then they could be revoked prior to complete performance.[155] In the second edition, Pollock cited an American decision of 1875[156] that an offer by an advertisement could be revoked by another advertisement; though from the third edition, he began to refer to the decision as 'a rather strong piece of judicial legislation'.[157] It was only in the eighth edition (of 1911) that he turned to the 'speculative' question, 'at what point in time acceptance by an act is complete'. Pollock now said that 'the acceptance is complete as soon as [the offeree] has made an unequivocal beginning of the performance requested'. The offer in such a case was a promise 'conditional on the work being done'. It was 'wholly different from a revocable offer'.[158] But in Pollock's view, since 'acceptance is one thing and consideration quite another', it was not necessary for the requested performance to be complete for the offer to be accepted.

Pollock's solution was not theoretically satisfying, for it failed to explain on what principle the 'conditional promise' had been accepted. The problem of the revocation of unilateral offers continued to intrigue judges and jurists on both sides of the Atlantic. In America, section 45 of the First Restatement of the Law of Contracts stated that where the offeree performed part of the consideration requested, the offeror could no longer revoke, but would be bound to pay on full performance of the condition. In England, the Law Revision Committee recommended a similar provision being enacted.[159] None was enacted, and twentieth-century judges sought to introduce the rule themselves, albeit on the basis of theories which the committee had found unconvincing.[160]

---

[153] C. D. Ashley, 'Consideration other than a Counter Promise' (1910) 23 *Harvard LR* 159–68.
[154] D. O. McGovney 'Irrevocable Offers' (1914) 27 *Harvard LR* 644–63.
[155] Pollock, *Contract* (4th edn, 1885), 17–18.
[156] *Shuey* v. *United States* (1875) 92 US 73.
[157] Pollock, *Contract* (2nd edn, 1878), 180; (3rd edn,1881), 20.
[158] Pollock, *Contract* (8th edn, 1911), 26.
[159] Law Revision Commitee 6th Interim Report (Statute of Frauds and the Doctrine of Consideration) [Cmd 5449] 1937, para. 39.
[160] *Errington* v. *Errington* [1952] 1 KB 290.

III

Consideration

THE fact that the courts did not enforce gratuitous promises, or 'bare pacts'[1] unless made by deed, was a cornerstone of English contract law. In order to be binding as a contract, any 'informal' promise, made without a deed, had to be given for some 'consideration'.[2] In theory, consideration was 'the material cause of every contract or agreement, or that thing in expectation of which each party is induced to give his consent to what is stipulated reciprocally between both parties'.[3] In practice, it was something 'for the Benefit of the Defendant, or to the Trouble or Prejudice of the Plaintiff'.[4] Any benefit had to move from the plaintiff or promisee, for a stranger to the consideration could not sue on it.[5]

The requirement for consideration, and definitions of what constituted consideration, dated from centuries before the beginning of our period. The definitions given by nineteenth-century treatise writers of consideration were hence

---

[1] Although the Roman terminology of *nuda pacta*, was used, jurists realized that the concept of consideration was not taken from Rome. [H. Ballow], *A Treatise of Equity* 2 vols (2nd edn, 1799), 335n.

[2] For the background history, see A. W. B. Simpson, *A History of the Common Law of Contract: The Rise of the Action of Assumpsit* (Oxford, 1975), Ch. 7. For discussion of the doctrine of consideration in the nineteenth century, see W. Swain, 'The Changing Nature of the Doctrine of Consideration, 1750–1850' (2005) 26 *Journal of Legal History* 55–72; D. J. Ibbetson, *Historical Introduction to the Law of Obligations* (Oxford, 1999), 236–41; P. S. Atiyah, *The Rise and Fall of Freedom of Contract* (Oxford, 1979), Ch. 6 and 448–54; J. Gordley, *The Philosophical Origins of Modern Contract Doctrine* (Oxford, 1991), 171–5.

[3] G. Jacob, *A Law Grammar* (6th edn, 1792), 211. J. J. Powell, *Essay upon the Law of Contracts and Agreements,* 2 vols, (1790), i, 330 also used the phrase 'material cause'. Cf. W. Sheppard, *A Touch-Stone of Common Assurances* (1641), 19, quoted in Simpson, *History*, 485.

[4] J. Comyns, *A Digest of the Laws of England,* 5 vols (1762–7), i, 149 (tit: Assumpsit, B1). This definition was followed by others, including John Fonblanque, editor of Ballow's *Treatise of Equity* (2nd edn, 1799), 344–5n. See also W. Selwyn, *An Abridgment of the Law of Nisi Prius,* 2 vols (8th edn, 1831), i, 47; Simpson, *History*, 486.

[5] See W. Selwyn, *An Abridgement of the Law of Nisi Prius* (6th edn, 1824), 52–3; *Barber v. Fox* (1682) 2 Wms. Saund. 134n (e). V. V. Palmer, *The Paths to Privity: The History of Third Party Beneficiary Contracts at English Law* (San Francisco, 1992), 160–1 suggests that early nineteenth-century treatise writers spoke of consideration having to move from the 'plaintiff'; and that it was only from the 1840s that greater stress was laid on the consideration moving from the 'promisee'.

variations on an old theme.[6] The one which was most favoured, by the end of the century, was that given by Lush J., who had taken it verbatim from Joseph Story's treatise on bills of exchange:[7]

A valuable consideration, in the sense of the law, may consist either in some right, interest, profit, or benefit accruing to the one party, or some forbearance, detriment, loss, or responsibility, given, suffered, or undertaken by the other.[8]

Jurists frequently argued that consideration was necessary to ensure that promises were seriously intended,[9] and to protect 'weak and thoughtless persons from the consequences of rash, improvident, and inconsiderate engagements'.[10] But since Lord Mansfield's attempts to invoke documentary evidence as another means to establish the seriousness of a promisor's intentions were rejected,[11] jurists argued that consideration was also required to show that there had been a bargain involving an exchange.[12] Consideration served to distinguish contracts from promises to make gifts, and thereby to draw a line between legally binding obligations and moral ones.[13]

The centrality of consideration in English law can be seen from equity's approach to the doctrine. Had the function of consideration been merely to provide evidence of the seriousness of the party's intent, then it would have been less important in equity than in common law, since equity had the machinery for probing the conscience of the parties to a suit in a way which was not true of the common law courts until the second half of the nineteenth century. Yet courts of equity would not enforce specific performance of agreements or settlements

---

[6] See R. J. Pothier, *A Treatise on the Law of Obligations or Contracts*, 2 vols (trans. W. D. Evans, 1806), ii, 22 (Evans' Appendix); J. Chitty, *A Practical Treatise on the Law of Contracts* (2nd edn, 1834), 24–5; C. G. Addison, *A Treatise on the Law of Contracts* (4th edn, 1856), 11; S. M. Leake, *The Elements of the Law of Contracts* (1867), 323.

[7] J. Story, *Commentaries on the Law of Bills of Exchange* (2nd edn, Boston, 1847), § 183, p. 212.

[8] *Currie v. Misa* (1875) LR 10 Ex 153 at 162. Lush's quotation omitted the point (made by Story and others) that the benefit might accrue not to the promisor, but to a third party, benefited by the promisee at the promisor's request.

[9] Leake, *Elements*, 10. See also Powell, *Contracts*, i: 330. Cf. *Sharington v. Strotton* (1565) 1 Plowd. 298 at 309.

[10] Addison, *Contracts* (4th edn, 1856), 11; Chitty, *Contracts* (2nd edn, 1834), 23; cf. *Morley v. Boothby* (1825) 3 Bing. 107 at 111.

[11] *Pillans v. Van Mierop* (1765) 3 Burr. 1663 at 1669, 1671, overruled in *Rann v. Hughes* (1778) 4 Brown. P.C. 27.

[12] *Myddleton v. Lord Kenyon* (1794) 2 Ves. Jr. 391 at 408. See also [A. Hayward], 'Mercantile law' (1829) 2 *LM* 237–55 at 249. See also M. Graziadei, 'Changing Images of the Law in XIX Century English Legal Thought (the continental impulse)', in M. Reimann (ed.) *The Reception of Continental Ideas in the Common Law World, 1820–1920* (Berlin, 1997), 115–64 at 133.

[13] Pothier, *Obligations*, ii, 19 (Evans' Appendix).

at the instance of volunteers, that is, those who had given no consideration.[14] As Powell pointed out, this was so even where the agreement was by deed.[15] As Lord Eldon put it in 1805, equity would not compel someone to make perfect a gift, 'which in the mode of making it he has left imperfect'. For the grantor was still entitled to change his mind about making the gift.[16]

The doctrine of consideration did not sit easily with will theory.[17] However, in the nineteenth century, neither judges nor jurists who favoured will theory were prepared to argue that the doctrine of consideration was unnecessary. Instead, they continued to argue for its centrality to the English law of contract. Their defence of the doctrine of consideration, and their enthusiasm for a doctrine of privity of contract, which emphasised the need for mutuality and stressed that only parties to a contract could sue on it, led them to use language appropriate to a bargain theory. As Frederick Pollock put it, '[a]n act or forbearance of the one party, or the promise thereof, is the price for which the promise of the other is bought, and the promise thus given for value is enforceable'.[18] The fact that contracts were bargains did not, however, mean that they had to be equal or fair: as W. D. Evans put it, '[t]he extent and adequacy of a consideration in relation to the engagement with which it is connected, is allowed to be immaterial'.[19]

This bargain theory sat uncomfortably with the fact that English contract law did permit gratuitous promises, if they were embodied in deeds, which could provide evidence of a serious intent. As Powell put it, where a contract had been made by deed, 'there is a sufficient consideration apparent, namely, the deliberate will of the party that made the deed'.[20] Yet the fact that one could make a binding gratuitous promise by deed did not prevent jurists from maintaining a bargain theory of contract, seeing the rule regarding deeds as an exception which did not call for theoretical discussion.[21]

---

[14] See *Colman* v. *Sarel* (1789) 3 Bro. C.C. 12, 1 Ves. Jr. 50 at 55.

[15] Powell, *Contracts* (1790), i, 341.

[16] *Antrobus* v. *Smith* (1805) 12 Ves. 39 at 46; cf. *Pulvertoft* v. *Pulvertoft* (1811) 18 Ves. 84 at 99.

[17] See Ibbetson, *Historical Introduction*, 236–8. For a contrasting interpretation, see R. Kreitner, *Calculating Promises: The Emergence of Modern American Contract Doctrine* (Palo Alto, 2006), which argues that late nineteenth-century jurists who put consideration at the heart of their doctrine did so in order to privilege 'a conception of contracting individuals as knowing and willful, as taking on obligations in measured, calculable increments, exchanging their obligations for precise values' (17).

[18] F. Pollock, *Principles of Contract at Law and in Equity* (3rd edn, 1881), 179. Anson also wrote that 'Consideration … is something done, forborne, or suffered, or promised to be done, forborne, or suffered by the promisee in respect of the promise' (W. R. Anson, *Principles of the English Law of Contract* (6th edn, Oxford, 1891), 72).

[19] Pothier, *Obligations*, ii: 21 (Evans' Appendix). Powell, *Contracts* (1790), i, 343, citing *Sturlyn* v. *Albany* (1587) Cro. El. 67. See also *Blount* v. *Doughty* (1747) 3 Atk. 481 at 484. Contrast the view of Atiyah, *Rise and Fall*, 170.

[20] Powell, *Contracts* (1790), i, 332.

[21] While Powell's comments suggested that the act of the will was itself a consideration, he proceeded to argue that the deed bound without looking into the consideration, for the giver was estopped

1. THE RISE AND FALL OF MORAL CONSIDERATION

At the beginning of our period, 'a mere moral obligation to [...] perform a duty' was regarded as 'sufficient consideration for an express promise', for '[t]he law allows a man effectually to promise to do that which justice clearly demands from him'.[22] This notion had been fathered by Lord Mansfield. Although he was well known for his desire to introduce equitable notions into the common law, and although the idea of natural obligations was to be found in equity's approach to consideration, Mansfield did not borrow his idea from Chancery practice, for that jurisdiction's use of natural obligations was a very limited one.[23] Instead, the concept owed much to Mansfield's own ideas on preventing unjust enrichment. He developed the idea in two cases brought against executors who had promised to pay legacies, but had then failed to do so. Drawing on the notion he developed in *Moses* v. *Macferlan*,[24] that the law implied a promise whenever 'a man is under a legal or equitable obligation to pay', he held that any legal or equitable duty could constitute a consideration to support an express promise:

Where a man is under a moral obligation, which no Court of Law or Equity can inforce, and promises, the honesty and rectitude of the thing is a consideration [...] the ties of conscience upon an upright mind are a sufficient consideration.[25]

Mansfield's aim was not to introduce a new rule, analogous to equity's meritorious consideration, that mere love could constitute consideration. Rather, a person was

from denying it after delivery (Powell, *Contracts* (1790), i, 340). His arguments that Blackstone had mistaken the law were echoed by Fonblanque: [Ballow], *Equity* (2nd edn, 1799), 343n. Chitty, *Contracts* (2nd edn, 1834), 23 regarded deeds as an exception permitted by analogy with the Roman *stipulatio*.

[22] Chitty, *Contracts* (2nd edn, 1834), 40.

[23] In determining whether settlements were void for being 'voluntary', the Chancery regarded a settlor's wife and children as purchasers for valuable consideration, 'by reason of the natural obligation of parents to provide for their children' (*Goring* v. *Nash* (1744) 3 Atk. 186 at 191). When it came to other relations, the notion of 'meritorious' consideration, such as closeness of blood, or natural love and affection, could be invoked to uphold settlements as against the grantor or his heirs; but it could not be invoked against subsequent purchasers for value. See J. Gilbert, *The History and Practice of the Court of Chancery* (1758), 308–10; E. G. Atherley, *A Practical Treatise of the Law of Marriage and other Family Settlements* (1813), 177. See also *Bramhall* v. *Hall* (1764) 3 Eden 220; *Clarke* v. *Wright* (1861) 6 H. & N. 849 at 875; *Doe d. Otley* v. *Manning* (1807) 9 East 59; *Gully* v. *Bishop of Exeter* (1830) 10 B. & C. 584 at 606.

[24] *Moses* v. *Macferlan* (1760) 2 Burr. 1005. For Mansfield's approach to unjust enrichment, and the early nineteenth century response to it, see pp. 566–7.

[25] *Hawkes* v. *Saunders* (1782) 1 Cowp. 289 at 290. Cf. *Atkins* v. *Hill* (1775) 1 Cowp. 284. The King's Bench attempt to assume jurisdiction in legacy cases was controversial since plaintiffs already had a remedy in ecclesiastical and equity courts, whose machinery was far better suited to examining the issues. In 1794, the King's Bench accordingly held that it did not, after all, have jurisdiction in these cases: *Deeks* v. *Strutt* (1794) 5 T.R. 690. For a discussion of the cases, see Swain, 'The Doctrine of Consideration', 53–6.

to be contractually liable to pay for benefits received in the past, if he later made an express promise to pay.[26] This new doctrine also suggested a new means of avoiding the pitfalls of the 'past consideration' rule, according to which an executed consideration could not support a subsequent express promise to pay, unless there had been a precedent request, express or implied, for the consideration.[27]

At the start of the nineteenth century, the law reporters Bosanquet and Puller, in a note to *Wennall* v. *Adney*, examined the cases from which Mansfield drew his wide principle, and suggested a narrower interpretation of the rule to be teased from them. They pointed out that in the examples given by Mansfield, 'the party bound by the promise had received a benefit previous to the promise', on which he would have been contractually liable, but for a rule of positive law barring recovery, such as infancy or the Statute of Limitations. From this, they drew the principle that:

An express promise [...] can only revive a precedent good consideration which might have been enforced at law through the medium of an implied promise, had it not been suspended by some positive rule of law, but [it] can give no original right of action if the obligation on which it is founded never could have been enforced at law, though not barred by any legal maxim or statute provision.[28]

The cases in question fell into three categories. Each case presented problems for jurists, who disagreed over whether the new promise created a new obligation or merely ratified an old one. The first group consisted of cases where one party's promise to pay a debt which had been barred by the Statute of Limitations was held to revive it.[29] This rule seemed an anomaly,[30] for in cases not involving a debt, the party in breach could not merely waive the operation of the statute, or renew his original promise, and allow his adversary to sue, unless new consideration had been given for the promise.[31] The second group of cases involved discharged

---

[26] The fact that a party was not to be liable for benefits conferred by way of gift was shown in the consensus among judges and jurists that the doctrine of moral consideration could not be used to sustain implied promises to pay for benefits received. See *Barber* v. *Fox* (1670) 2 Wms. Saund. 136 n 2. See also Chitty, *Contracts* (2nd edn, 1834), 44; *Hodges* v. *Hodges* (1796) Peake Add. Cas. 79, where Lord Kenyon said that the provision for children was a duty of imperfect obligation which could not be enforced in law by an implied promise to pay.

[27] Chitty, *Contracts* (2nd edn, 1834), 52.

[28] *Wennall* v. *Adney* (1802) 3 B. & P. 247 at 249 note (a). Their analysis was adopted by the treatise writers, e.g. Chitty, *Contracts* (2nd edn, 1834), 43.

[29] *Heyling* v. *Hastings* (1698) 1 Ld. Raym. 389; *Heylin* v. *Hastings* (1699) Holt K.B. 427. For the nineteenth-century discussions, see *Thornton* v. *Illingworth* (1824) 2 B. & C. 824 at 825–6; *Tanner* v. *Smart* (1827) 6 B. & C. 603; *Bateman* v. *Pinder* (1842) 3 Q.B. 574; *Rackham* v. *Marriott* (1856) 1 H. & N. 234. See also *Dickson* v. *Thomson* (1680) 2 Show. K.B. 126; *Hurst* v. *Parker* (1817) 1 B. & Ald. 92 at 93.

[30] See Leake, *Elements* (1867), 542.

[31] *Boydell* v. *Drummond* (1808) 2 Camp. 157; see also *Short* v. *M'Carthy* (1820) 3 B. & Ald. 626.

bankrupts who promised to repay their creditors.[32] The rule was analogous to that regarding the revival of debts. In such cases, Parke B. held in 1848, the new promise to pay was 'supported by the past consideration' of the prior debt.[33] This anomalous rule was preserved for bankrupts by legislation in the 1820s and 1840s, which specified that any ratification had to be made in writing;[34] but it was not applied to insolvents, who were prevented by statute from reviving antecedent debts.[35]

The third group involved cases where adults promised to pay debts which they had contracted during infancy. It was a settled rule that such debts could be ratified at adulthood,[36] but jurists were unclear from when the obligation dated. In 1824, it was held that the infant made a new promise when he came of age, which 'binds him on the ground of his taking upon himself a new liability, upon a moral consideration existing before; it does not make it a legal debt from the time of making the bargain'.[37] But since contracts made by infants were not void, but voidable by the infant,[38] this was a debatable view; and Lord Tenterden's Act, which required the ratification to be in writing,[39] seemed to imply that the adult was ratifying an existing obligation and not creating a new one.[40] As late as 1843, Parke B. remained unsure on this issue, though he noted that the law permitted the infant to 'give validity to contracts entered into during his infancy', since he now had the power to decide whether it was 'one of a meritorious character, by which in good conscience he ought to be bound'.[41] By 1854, he held that a ratification was an admission in writing of actual liability.[42] The rule lasted until 1874, when the Infants Relief Act[43] enacted that all contracts entered into by children were to be held void, unless for necessaries, and that no action could be

[32] Mansfield himself (applying his own rule) held that such a promise was not a *nudum pactum*, since 'all the debts of a bankrupt are due in conscience, notwithstanding he has obtained his certificate', *Trueman* v. *Fenton* (1777) 2 Cowp. 544 at 548.

[33] *Earle* v. *Oliver* (1848) 2 Exch. 71 at 89–90. See also *Kirkpatrick* v. *Tattersall* (1845) 13 M. & W. 766.

[34] 6 Geo. IV, c. 16, s. 131, 5 & 6 Vict. c. 122, s 43. However, promises to pay debts barred by bankruptcy were deprived of any effect by s 204 of 1849 Bankruptcy Consolidation Act, 12 & 13 Vict. c. 106.

[35] 7 Geo. IV, c. 57, s. 61, 1 & 2 Vict. c. 110, s 91. See also *Evans* v. *Williams* (1832) 1 C. & M. 30. Before the statute, insolvents could bind themselves to pay old debts with new promises: *Sweenie* v. *Sharp* (1826) 4 Bing. 37.

[36] *Southerton* v. *Whitlock* (1726) 2 Stra. 690.

[37] *Thornton* v. *Illingworth* (1824) 2 B. & C. 824 at 826. Cf. *Cohen* v. *Armstrong* (1813) 1 M. & S. 724 at 725.

[38] *Warwick* v. *Bruce* (1813) 2 M. & S. 205.

[39] 9 Geo. IV c. 14, s 15.

[40] Infant contracts were held ratified even where there was no new promise: *Harris* v. *Wall* (1847) 1 Exch. 122.

[41] *Williams* v. *Moor* (1843) 11 M. & W. 256 at 264–5.

[42] *Mawson* v. *Blane* (1854) 10 Exch. 206.

[43] 37 & 38 Vict. c. 62.

brought on a contract ratified at majority by the infant, whether or not there had been fresh consideration given.

In spite of Bosanquet and Puller's doubts, some judges sought to apply the doctrine more broadly, in a way which suggested that any moral obligation could be sufficient consideration.[44] In 1834, Joseph Chitty therefore asserted that it was 'now settled, that a mere moral obligation will sometimes be a sufficient consideration to support an express promise, although no legal responsibility *ever* existed'.[45] But by then, judges like Lord Tenterden had already begun to have doubts. In 1826, he made it clear that gratitude or affection alone could not constitute consideration for a contract;[46] and five years later, he observed that 'the doctrine that a moral obligation is a sufficient consideration for a subsequent promise, is one which should be received with some limitation'.[47] Mansfield's broad doctrine of moral consideration was finally overruled in 1840. In *Eastwood* v. *Kenyon*,[48] the Queen's Bench regarded as a *nudum pactum* a promise by a husband to repay to his wife's father's executor money spent during her infancy on her upbringing and on the estates which she later inherited, and of which her husband obtained the benefit. In Lord Denman's view, the 'moral consideration' invoked by the plaintiff was simply a past consideration conferred without a request. All the cases where a 'moral consideration' had been allowed, he felt, were ones where there had been a request, express or implied.[49] Early nineteenth-century jurists had argued that 'where a party derives benefit from the consideration it is sufficient, because [it is] equivalent to a previous request'.[50] But as Denman pointed out, in this case, the husband could not be construed to have made the request during his wife's childhood. He was also troubled by the very idea of moral consideration, since '[t]he doctrine would annihilate the necessity for any consideration at all, inasmuch as the mere fact of giving a promise creates a moral obligation to perform it'.[51] Such a doctrine would have negative consequences to society, since just creditors might be prejudiced if their debtors gave voluntary undertakings to others.

---

[44] *Lee* v. *Muggeridge* (1813) 5 Taunt. 36; Swain, 'Doctrine of Consideration', 58.

[45] Chitty, *Contracts* (2nd edn, 1834), 41.

[46] e.g. *Holliday* v. *Atkinson* (1826) 5 B. & C. 501. The issue was discussed in *Thomas* v. *Thomas* (1842) 2 Q.B. 851. But in this case, neither party sought to uphold the contract on the grounds of natural love and affection; rather, the dispute centred on whether the contract in question was supported by any other form of consideration. See also Chitty, *Contracts* (2nd edn, 1834), 43–4.

[47] *Littlefield* v. *Shee* (1831) 2 B. & Ad. 811 at 813. See also *Meyer* v. *Haworth* (1838) 8 Ad. & El. 467.

[48] *Eastwood* v. *Kenyon* (1840) 11 Ad. & El. 438.

[49] The similar case of *Cooper* v. *Martin* (1803) 4 East 76 could be explained on these lines. Denman also sought to fit *Lee* v. *Muggeridge* (1813) 5 Taunt. 36 into this interpretation.

[50] Note 1 to *Osborne* v. *Rogers* (1669) 1 Wms. Saund. 264. See also Chitty, *Contracts* (2nd edn, 1834), 53.

[51] *Eastwood* v. *Kenyon* (1840) 11 Ad. & El. 438 at 450.

In the 1840s, Lord Denman also took a firmer line on the question of what kind of prior request could support a subsequent promise to pay. In *Roscorla* v. *Thomas*, the purchaser of a horse sued the vendor for the breach of a warranty given after the sale. The plaintiff stated in his declaration that in consideration that he had bought the horse at the defendant's request, the defendant promised that it was free from vice. For Denman, the purchase of the horse was clearly a past consideration, insufficient to support the subsequent express promise as to its quality.[52] Nor could the subsequent promise be held to be supported by a prior request. Although the law would raise a promise to pay for benefits where the consideration was executed and accepted, the promise had to be commensurate with the consideration. Here, the only promise raised by the consideration was to deliver a horse, not a sound one . Other courts confirmed the view of Bosanquet and Puller that executed considerations would only support a promise which the law would itself have implied, not a broader promise expressly made.[53]

In explaining how a requested past consideration could support a subsequent promise, some jurists spoke of the request 'coupling itself' with the subsequent promise, so that the promise 'related back to the original request'.[54] But others found this notion troubling. Writing in 1879, Anson observed that there was only one Irish authority for the proposition since *Lampleigh* v. *Braithwait*,[55] and that the rule was 'open to question'.[56] In his view, a prior request constituted an offer to pay a sum to be fixed subsequently, if the consideration were performed. His conclusion was that

unless the *request* is virtually an offer of a promise the precise extent of which is hereafter to be ascertained; or unless it so clearly contemplates a subsequent promise to be given by the maker of the request that such a promise may be regarded as a part of the same transaction, the rule in *Lampleigh* v. *Braithwait* has no application.[57]

Langdell was the most sceptical about the doctrine of request. He argued that 'the allegation of a request has no effect except in those cases in which […] it constitutes one of the elements of a debt'.[58] Pollock ignored the issue in his early editions, but after reading Langdell noted that it was 'not free from uncertainty'

---

[52] *Roscorla* v. *Thomas* (1842) 3 Q.B. 234 at 237.

[53] *Kaye* v. *Dutton* (1844) 7 M. & G. 807 at 815. Cf. *Hopkins* v. *Logan* (1839) 5 M. & W. 241; *Elderton* v. *Emmens* (1847) 4 C.B. 479 at 496 (and the editor's note).

[54] Leake *Elements* (1867) 315; cf. Leake, *Elementary Digest of the Law of Contracts* (1878), 53. Chitty, *Contracts* (2nd edn, 1834), 52-3.

[55] *Lampleigh* v. *Brathwait* (1615) Hob. 105. That authority was *Bradford* v. *Roulston* (1858) 8 Ir. C.L. 468.

[56] Anson, *Contract* (1st edn, 1879), 87.

[57] Anson, *Contract* (1st edn, 1879), 89–90.

[58] Langdell, *Summary*, § 91.

whether a past benefit could ever be a good consideration. He felt the very doctrine of request was too closely linked to the 'exploded ground that moral consideration is a sufficient consideration'.[59] By the turn of the century, his scepticism
had receded, and he argued that the later promise might be seen as providing
evidence of what the parties thought the service was worth, suggesting that they
had in fact entered a contract at the moment of the request.[60]

Pollock's change of mind followed the decision in *Re Casey's Patents* in 1892,
when the Court of Appeal provided a new authority for the past consideration
rule. In that case, Bowen LJ noted that 'some scientific students of law' held that a
past service could not support a future promise. But, he added, 'the fact of a past
service raises an implication that at the time it was rendered it was to be paid
for'. In these circumstances, a subsequent promise to pay 'may be treated either
as an admission which evidences or as a positive bargain which fixes the amount
of that reasonable remuneration on the faith of which the service was originally
rendered'.[61] This was to acknowledge that there was a prior contractual obligation
whose details were fleshed out by the later promise. In this way, courts and jurists
concurred that every promise had to be supported by consideration: the bargain
element of a contract could not be finessed out.

2. CONSIDERATION AND RELIANCE

Consideration remained the primary test for the enforceability of informal
contracts. Mid-nineteenth-century courts did not follow the civilian route suggested by Mansfield's approach, that an obligation could be derived simply from
the exchange of seriously intended promises. At the same time that Mansfield's
approach to moral consideration was rejected, however, two other doctrinal developments, in law and equity, seemed to offer the possibility that an obligation might
be generated by injurious reliance on a gratuitous promise. But by the 1850s, it had
become clear that these doctrines did not dispose of the need for consideration.

The first one to pose a challenge was the common law doctrine of estoppel by
representation, according to which a party who had admitted certain facts was
later estopped from denying them. According to this principle,

where one by his words or conduct wilfully causes another to believe the existence of
a certain state of things, and induces him to act on that belief, so as to alter his own

---

[59] Pollock, *Contract* (4th edn, 1885), 170.

[60] Pollock, *Contract* (7th edn, 1902), 181. Cf. Erle CJ in *Kennedy v. Broun* (1863) 13 C.B. N.S. 677
at 740.

[61] See *In re Casey's Patents* [1892] 1 Ch 104 at 115. This case also suggested that the subsequent
promise might, however, be a positive bargain.

previous position, the former is concluded from averring against the latter a different state of things existing at the same time.[62]

The doctrine was primarily developed in non-contractual situations.[63] In these cases, it was considered as a form of fraud for the party making the representation to go back on it. To generate an estoppel, the representation had to be as unambiguous as a contractual offer, or 'such as to amount to the contract or licence of the party making it'.[64] The courts looked for 'a wilful intent' on the part of the one party to make the other act on the faith of the representation,[65] and not mere negligence.[66] Applied to contract, the doctrine might have raised the question whether a seriously intended promise (or offer) which had been acted on (or accepted) might have bound without consideration,[67] by virtue of a 'promissory' estoppel.[68]

The second was the equitable doctrine of forcing parties to make good their representations.[69] Where a family member had misstated his own claims on family property, for instance during negotiations for a settlement, and thereby misled others who relied on the truth of the statement, that party was forced by equity to make good his misrepresentation by postponing his claims. This was equity's older equivalent to estoppel by representation. Equity also held parties to make good their promises, in cases where a family member promised to make a settlement on a marriage, and then failed to take the steps necessary to comply with

---

[62] *Pickard* v. *Sears* (1837) 6 Ad. & El. 469 at 473.

[63] It was mainly developed in trover: *Clarke* v. *Clarke* (1806) 6 Esp. 61; *Like* v. *Howe* (1806) 6 Esp. 20; *Hearne* v. *Rogers* (1829) 9 B. & C. 577; *Stratford and Moreton Railway Co* v. *Stratton* (1831) 2 B. & Ad. 518. It was also discussed in the unusual contract case of *Cornish* v. *Abingdon* (1859) 4 H. & N. 549, where the defendant was estopped from denying that he had entered a contractual relationship with the plaintiff, since he had acted in such a way as to induce the plaintiff to believe that he had contracted with him. For a discussion of the case, see p. 456.

[64] *Freeman* v. *Cooke* (1848) 2 Exch. 654 at 664 (per Parke B.), cf. *Cornish* v. *Abingdon* (1859) 4 H. & N. 549 at 555–6.

[65] *Howard* v. *Hudson* (1852) 2 E. & B. 1 at 10.

[66] See also *Freeman* v. *Cooke* (1848) 2 Exch. 654, explaining *Gregg* v. *Wells* (1839) 10 Ad. & El. 90.

[67] The question was raised in American case law: e.g. *University of Vermont* v. *Buell* 2 Vt 48 (Vt 1829); *University of Des Moines* v. *Livingston* 57 Iowa 307, 10 NW 738 at 739–40 (Iowa 1881); *School Dist of City of Kansas* v. *Stocking* 138 Mo 672, 40 SW 656 (Mo 1897); *Ricketts* v. *Scorhorn* 57 Neb 51, 77 NW 365 (Neb 1898); *Young Men's Christian Association* v. *Estill* 140 Ga 291, 78 SE 1075 (Ga 1913); *Allegheny College* v. *National Chautauqua County bank of Jamestown* 159 NE 173 (NY 1927); *James Baird Co* v. *Gimbel Bros* 64 F 2d 344 (CA 2 1933).

[68] Williston had first suggested the recognition of a doctrine of promissory estoppel to enforce gratuitous promises which had been relied on: H. W. Ballantine, 'Is the Doctrine of Consideration Senseless and Illogical?' (1913) 11 *Michigan LR* 423–34 at 425. A. L. Corbin, 'Comment: Part Payment of a Debt as Consideration for a Promise' (1908) 17 *YLJ* 470–3 at 472.

[69] Indeed, the doctrine of estoppel by representation was a common law response to this equitable doctrine. See M. Lobban, 'Contractual Fraud in Law and Equity, c.1750–c.1850' (1997) 17 *OJLS* 441–76 at 453–5, 469.

the Statute of Frauds. In such cases, equity would hold the party to his promise, if it was convinced that it was seriously intended to be a binding promise, or the promisor had been guilty of fraud.[70] In these cases, as with those on estoppel, the requirements of a serious 'offer' and 'acceptance' were maintained. The issue of consideration was not raised in them, since it was long established in equity that the marriage of a couple was consideration for a settlement.

Drawing on these doctrines, a number of mid-century cases explored whether a party who did not have a strictly contractual right might recover, after he had relied on the statement of another. This issue was examined in a number of cases where pre-nuptial representations had been made, on the faith of which marriages had been transacted. In *Hammersley* v. *De Biel*, Lord Cottenham LC stated as a broad principle that '[a] representation made by one party for the purpose of influencing the conduct of the other party, and acted on by him, will in general be sufficient to entitle him to the assistance of this Court for the purpose of realizing such representation'.[71] Although such a broad statement was not necessary for the resolution of the case before him,[72] it was endorsed by Lord Lyndhurst in the House of Lords.[73] Drawing on this statement, Sir Richard Bethell sought to argue in *Maunsell* v. *Hedges* in 1854 that a representation either of past fact or present intention, created 'an engagement which cannot be revoked'.[74] According to his argument, once a statement had been relied on, it bound the speaker. Bethell's argument failed to persuade the Lords, since in this case the party making the representation had made it explicitly clear that he did not intend to bind himself. More broadly, Lord Cranworth held that words which were not uttered with a contractual intent did not become contractually binding merely by virtue of their having been relied on.[75]

Several months later, the House of Lords confirmed in *Jorden* v. *Money* that a party could only be bound if she had made a contractual promise, or had made a fraudulent statement on a matter of fact, which had been relied on. In this case, Louisa Jorden had told William Money, before his marriage, that she would

---

[70] See M. Lobban, 'Foakes v. Beer' in C. Mitchell and P. Mitchell (eds) *Landmark Cases in the Law of Contract* (Oxford, 2008), 223–67 at 248–9.

[71] *Hammersley* v. *De Biel* (1845) 12 Cl .& F. 45 at 62n. In a later case, Cottenham seemed to root his decision more specifically in the fact of part performance by the baron, in settling the jointure: *Lassence* v. *Tierney* (1849) 1 M. & G. 551 at 572.

[72] See Lobban, 'Foakes v. Beer' at 249–51.

[73] *Hammersley* v. *De Biel* (1845) 12 Cl. & F. 45 at 78–9.

[74] *Maunsell* v. *Hedges* (1854) 4 H.L.C. 1039 at 1049.

[75] *Maunsell* v. *Hedges* (1854) 4 H.L.C. 1039 at 1057. In his view, in none of the cases where pre-nuptial statements were held to bind the party making them had the party making them left himself the option to change his mind. See also *Maunsell* v. *Hedges* (1854) 4 H.L.C. 1039 at 1051 (per St Leonards). See also Stephen J. in *Alderson* v. *Maddison* (1880) 5 Ex D 293, 299.

never enforce bonds which he had given her. Relying on this statement, William married. At issue was whether her statement of intent was legally binding, given that she had persistently refused to give up or destroy the securities. The Lords confirmed that it was not. In Lord Cranworth's view, Mrs Jorden had not contracted to discharge the debt, in consideration of the marriage, since she had only intended her statement to be binding 'in honour'.[76] Nor was she obliged in equity to make her representation good, since this doctrine rested 'on the principle of fraud, not at all on contract'. For Cranworth, there could only be fraud where there was a misrepresentation of fact.[77]

As Cranworth's comments showed, the key point at issue in *Jorden* v. *Money* was not whether a relied-on promise, unsupported by consideration, was binding. It was whether a representation made without contractual intent could bind when acted on. For the court, a mere representation of intention was not binding, since a person could always change her mind: she could only bind herself to future action by making it clear that her representation was meant to be contractually binding. And as the Lords well knew, a contract needed not merely an exchange of promises, but consideration as well. The decision in *Jorden* v. *Money* did not please all lawyers. For some time after, a number of judges continued to assume that the position enunciated in *Hammersley* v. *De Biel* applied[78] and in 1867, the Indian Law Commissioners proposed a rule which would reverse *Jorden* v. *Money*.[79] Some judges were especially keen to use Cottenham's notion as a means to avoid the strict rule of the Statute of Frauds.[80] However, this attempt was frowned on by the House of Lords, which confirmed in *Maddison* v. *Alderson* in 1883 that a representation of future intent was only binding if it was contractual;

---

[76] '[I]f Mrs Jordan did, before and in consideration of the marriage, bind herself not to enforce the bond or judgment, the Plaintiff might be entitled to relief on the head of contract' (*Money* v. *Jordan* (1852) 2 De G. M. & G. 318 at 334–5).

[77] *Money* v. *Jordan* (1852) 2 De G. M. & G. 318 at 332; *Jorden* v. *Money* (1854) 5 H.L.C. 185 at 214–15.

[78] e.g. *Prole* v. *Soady* (1859) 2 Giff. 1; *Loffus* v. *Maw* (1862) 3 Giff. 592; *Coles* v. *Pilkington* (1874) LR 19 Eq 174. In none of these cases did the promisor assert he was leaving himself free to change his mind. See also Bacon VC's views in *Coverdale* v. *Eastwood* (1872) LR 15 Eq 121, 42 LJ Ch 118 and *Dashwood* v. *Jermyn* (1879) 12 Ch D 776.

[79] Papers showing the Present Position of the Question of a Contract Law for India: PP 1867–8 (239), xlix, 601, p. 20: 'If one person makes a deliberate statement as to his own future conduct to another, with the intent that it should be acted upon, and the other acts upon the faith of such assurance, the person who made the statement must make it good' (s 62). The illustration given was based on the facts of *Jorden* v. *Money*. The proposal did not find its way into the 1872 Indian Contract Act.

[80] *Loffus* v. *Maw* (1862) 3 Giff. 592 at 603. As Pollock put it, Stuart 'appears … to have held that, inasmuch as these were not properly cases of contract, it was immaterial to consider whether the Statute of Frauds applied to them', *Contract* (7th edn, 1902), App. K, 716.

and if it was contractual, then (in marriage and land cases), it had to comply with the requirements of the Statute of Frauds.[81]

Academic commentators agreed that there could be no contractual obligation generated by mere representations. Frederick Pollock was persuaded by Stephen J.'s ruling in *Alderson* v. *Maddison* of the correctness of the position taken by *Jorden* v. *Money*.[82] He explicitly denied that there were 'two distinct kinds of obligation, by contract and by "representation"':[83]

There is no middle term possible. A statement of opinion or expectation creates, as such, no duty. If capable of creating any duty, it is a promise. If the promise is enforceable, it is a contract.[84]

Although the giving of seriously intended promises from both parties was a prerequisite of contractual liability, it was not sufficient to make the contract binding. Instead, it was the presence of consideration which did this.

In the marriage cases where these issues were discussed, the presence of consideration was not an issue, since a marriage had long been held sufficient consideration for a settlement in equity. In such cases, moreover, it was hardly appropriate to regard the presence of consideration as showing that there had been some kind of bargain between the parties. The focus of attention in *Jorden* v. *Money* on the nature of the promisor's intention, and the relative unimportance in the case of the question of consideration, might therefore have encouraged jurists keen on will theory to develop the notion that contractual liability depended more on the parties' intention to create legal relations, than on the presence of consideration. However, the doctrine of consideration was too well-rooted to be dislodged so easily.

Moreover, in seeking a consideration sufficient to uphold the promise, the courts did not look to the parties' subjective intentions, but attempted to find something which was objectively of value in the eyes of the law, whether or not the parties themselves valued it. This can be seen from *Thomas* v. *Thomas*. The case arose from a promise made by the executors of the estate of John Thomas, to carry out his wish, declared orally on the day before his death, to allow his widow to live in the house they inhabited for the rest of her life. An agreement was entered into by which Eleanor Thomas was to be allowed possession of

---

[81] *Maddison* v. *Alderson* (1883) 8 App Cas 467. For another example of the Lords reasserting *Jorden* v. *Money*, see *Citizen's Bank of Louisiana and the New Orleans Canal and Banking Co* v. *The First National Bank of New Orleans* (1873) LR 6 HL 352.

[82] Pollock, *Contract* (3rd edn, 1881), 497–8 and App. L.

[83] Pollock, *Contract* (7th edn, 1902), App. K, 717. This was repeated in later editions: e.g. the 12th edn by P. H. Winfield (1946), 568.

[84] Pollock, *Contract* (7th edn, 1902), 525. Pollock added a note (repeated in his twentieth-century editions), 'No such doctrine, I understand, has ever become current in America'.

the house, provided she paid an annual £1 ground rent to the executors. It was argued for the executors that this was a mere 'gift cum onere'; for the consideration for the contract was only the moral feeling which induced the executors to enter it. But the Queen's Bench upheld the contract: in the court's view, the moral feeling could not be consideration, but the payment of £1 could. In so doing, the judges rejected E. V. Williams's attempt to define consideration in terms of the 'cause or inducement' of making the promise. As Patteson J. saw it, such an argument confused motive and consideration: '[c]onsideration means something which is of value in the eye of the law, moving from the plaintiff'.[85] The fact that the parties had not contemplated the ground rent as cementing their bargain did not matter: it was the courts, not the parties, which looked for the element of bargain. Coleridge J. added that the judges could look to any part of the agreement for the consideration; while the mere motive did not have to be stated.

The need to show something of value in the eyes of the law can also be seen in the case of *White* v. *Bluett*. In this case of 1853, a man sought to defend an action by his father's executors on a promissory note he had given to his father, by claiming that the father had promised not to sue on the note, in return for the son ceasing to complain about the father's distribution of his property. As with *Jorden* v. *Money*, had the father falsely told the son he had destroyed the security, then he would have been estopped from suing on it. Instead, he had made a seriously intended promise—unlike Mrs Jorden—which had been relied on. However, the Exchequer refused to uphold the agreement, finding that it lacked consideration. As Pollock CB put it, the father had every right to distribute his property as he saw fit. Since the son had no right to complain, his 'abstaining from doing what he had no right to do can be no consideration'.[86] Later commentators, drawing on Parke B.'s question in argument—'Is an agreement by a father in consideration that his son will not bore him a binding contract?'[87]—stressed that there was no consideration here because the promise was too indefinite.[88]

Twentieth-century jurists argued that *White* v. *Bluett* was better explained as a case where the court decided that the parties had not intended to create legal relations.[89] But this notion—which was introduced to English audiences by Pollock's borrowing from Savigny—was not available to the judges in *White* v. *Bluett*. Nor did Pollock (or his contemporaries) seek to use this doctrine as

---

[85] *Thomas* v. *Thomas* (1842) 2 Q.B. 851 at 859.

[86] *White* v. *Bluett* (1853) 23 LJ Ex 36 at 37.

[87] *White* v. *Bluett* (1853) 23 LJ Ex 36.

[88] Pollock, *Contract* (1st edn, 1876), 157; Anson, *Contract* (1st edn, 1875), 75.

[89] See R. A. (Lord) Wright, 'Ought the Doctrine of Consideration to be Abolished from the Common Law?' (1936) 49 *Harvard LR* 1225–53.

an alternative to consideration.[90] Pollock invoked Savigny's notion primarily
to distinguish between agreements which were intended to be dealt with in
the courts, and those—such as agreements to go for a walk—which were not.
Although he realized that social usage and the trifling sums any dispute might
involve kept such cases out of court, he felt that 'Savigny's view' was the better
explanation. On the eve of the First World War, Williston rejected the need
for Savigny's doctrine, thinking it unnecessary in a system which had consideration. The American pointed out that parties did not think through the
legal consequences of their agreements. In his view, it was for the courts—using
the doctrine of consideration—to determine whether agreements were legally
binding.[91] Between these two views sat Holmes's view. Like Pollock, Holmes
felt that the parties' intentions were relevant, but he saw this as a means of
establishing, rather than circumventing, consideration. As he saw it, whether
something constituted consideration or not depended on the party's motive in
doing it: 'the same thing may be a consideration or not, as it is dealt with by the
parties'.[92] But in Holmes's view, as in Pollock's, it was still essential to have a
bargain. Savigny's doctrine was not seen as one to displace the need for consideration. The courts still needed to find the element of bargain.

3. ADEQUACY OF CONSIDERATION

One of the paradoxes of contract law was that, while the courts required the parties to have made a bargain, they did not judge its fairness. Since the common
law courts had no means of deciding on the adequacy of consideration, it was
felt wiser to leave parties to the free exercise of their own judgments.[93] Judges
and jurists agreed that it was not for the courts to decide whether a bargain was a
good one.[94] In Pollock's view, the idea that parties should be left to measure their
own bargains was one which could be traced to the political thought of Thomas
Hobbes.[95]

The rule that consideration had to be 'sufficient' but not 'adequate' was
embraced in equity as well as in law. Although eighteenth-century equity courts
often refused to award specific performance where the price for which property

---

[90] Nor did Pollock himself ever seek to interpret this case in this way: see e.g. *Contract* (10th edn,
1936), 181.

[91] S. Williston, 'Consideration in Bilateral Contracts' (1914) 27 *Harvard LR* 503–29 at 506–7n.

[92] Holmes, *The Common Law*, 292.

[93] Chitty, *Contracts* (2nd edn, 1834), 26.

[94] *Moss* v. *Hall* (1850) 5 Exch. 46 at 49–50; *Bolton* v. *Madden* (1873) LR 9 QB 55 at 57. Addison,
Contracts (4th edn, 1856), 17. For a striking American example, see *Train* v. *Gold* 5 Pick. 380, 22 Mass.
380 (1827) at 389–90.

[95] Pollock, *Contract* (5th edn, 1889), 171–2.

was to be sold was unreasonably small, leaving parties to their (inadequate) legal remedy,[96] Lord Eldon felt that inadequacy of price alone should not be sufficient to prevent specific performance in equity. For it would undermine the practice of land sales by auction if specific performance were denied without at least some evidence of fraud, surprise, or mistake.[97] Equally, for a contract to be set aside in equity for lack of consideration, the undervalue had to be such as would be evidence of fraud.[98]

At common law, the most trifling consideration sufficed, provided that it was not 'utterly worthless in fact and in law'.[99] The fact that the courts were not concerned with the adequacy of consideration was reiterated in the 1830s, in cases involving contracts in restraint of trade. It had been established in the eighteenth century that a person could make a contract restraining him from trading in a particular area—as when he sold his business to another—provided that it was 'made upon a good and adequate consideration, so as to make it a proper and useful contract'.[100] When looking at such agreements, the courts asked whether the consideration was 'fair' or adequate.[101] But in *Hitchcock* v. *Coker* in 1837, a new approach was taken. The court distinguished between the reasonableness of the restraint, which could be examined, and the adequacy of the consideration, which could not.[102] The courts felt able to judge whether the restraint was reasonable since this was a matter of public policy.[103] By contrast, '[i]t is impossible for the Court, looking at the record to say whether, in any particular case, the party restrained has made an improvident bargain or not'.[104]

---

[96] *Young* v. *Clerk* (1720) Prec. Ch. 538; *Savage* v. *Taylor* (1736) Cas. Temp. Talb. 234; *Underwood* v. *Hitchcox* (1749) 1 Ves. Sr. 279; *Day* v. *Newman* (1788) 2 Cox 77. *Flureau* v. *Thornhill* (1776) 2 W. Bl. 1078 settled that expectation damages would not be awarded in land cases.

[97] *White* v. *Damon* (1802) 7 Ves. 30. See also *Mortimer* v. *Capper* (1782) 1 Bro. C.C. 156; *Coles* v. *Trecothick* (1804) 9 Ves. 234 at 246; *Mortlock* v. *Buller* (1804) 10 Ves. 292. However, equity might still refuse specific performance if the consideration was uncertain: see E. B. Sugden, *Vendors and Purchasers* (8th edn, 1830), 243; *Bower* v. *Cooper* (1843) 2 Hare 408. Sugden noted (242) that, in practice, it was difficult to obtain specific performance of unreasonable executory contracts: 'few contracts can be enforced in equity where the price is unreasonable, because contracts are not often strictly observed by either party; and if an unreasonable contract be not performed by the vendor, according to the letter in every respect, equity will not compel a performance *in specie*'.

[98] *Underhill* v. *Horwood* (1804) 10 Ves. 209; *Lowther* v. *Lowther* (1806) 13 Ves. 95 at 103.

[99] Chitty, *Contracts* (2nd edn, 1834), 27.

[100] *Mitchel* v. *Reynolds* (1711) 1 P. Wms. 181 at 186.

[101] *Davis* v. *Mason* (1793) 5 T.R. 118 at 120; *Gale* v. *Reed* (1806) 8 East 80; *Horner* v. *Graves* (1831) 7 Bing. 735; *Young* v. *Timmins* (1831) 1 Tyrw. 226.

[102] *Hitchcock* v. *Coker* (1837) 6 Ad. & El. 438. Earlier courts had also looked at these as distinct questions, but had looked for both an adequate consideration and reasonableness: *Horner* v. *Graves* (1831) 7 Bing. 735.

[103] See *Mallan* v. *May* (1843) 11 M. & W. 653; *Pilkington* v. *Scott* (1846) 15 M. & W. 657.

[104] *Hitchcock* v. *Coker* (1837) 6 Ad. & El. 438 at 457. He later ruled in *Skeate* v. *Beale* (1841) 11 Ad. & El. 983 at 992 that '[t]he consideration not being unlawful, we cannot enter into its adequacy'.

If the adequacy of consideration was a matter for the parties, the court had to be persuaded that it was legally sufficient. This was not difficult to do. In *Bainbridge* v. *Firmstone*, the plaintiff sued a defendant who had taken away his boilers to weigh them, and had returned them in pieces, for a breach of contract to return them in a perfect condition. Since it did not appear from the record that the defendant was to be paid, he claimed there was no consideration for his promise. Nonetheless, the Queen's Bench found for the plaintiff. In Patteson J.'s view, the defendant felt he received a benefit from obtaining the boilers, and there was 'a detriment to the plaintiff from his parting with the possession for even so short a time'.[105] As Addison perceived, this case was one of a gratuitous loan or bailment,[106] on which the courts had long allowed bailors to recover in contract, even when the bailment was at the bailor's request and for his benefit. For instance, it was settled that the mere delivery of money to another person constituted a consideration for a promise by that party to pay it over.[107] Similarly, where property had been handed over, and the recipient promised to handle it in a particular way, he could be sued in contract for failure to perform as promised.[108] Early nineteenth-century jurists, such as Story, found consideration in the mere parting with a present right in something.[109] But jurists at the end of the nineteenth century, who sought a more careful theorization of consideration, were much more troubled by the cases of gratuitous bailments[110] as well as those on gratuitous employment.[111] For, as Pollock pointed out, in such cases, 'for the most part, the bailor does not deliver possession at the bailee's request, but requests the bailee to take it'.[112]

In the mid-nineteenth century, the very judges who had been hostile to Mansfield's approach to moral consideration took an increasingly broad view of what constituted a benefit or a detriment. In 1839, the Queen's Bench upheld

---

[105] *Bainbridge* v. *Firmstone* (1838) 8 Ad. & El. 743 at 744.

[106] Addison, *Contract* (4th edn, 1856), 534.

[107] *Wheatley* v. *Low* (1623) Cro. Jac. 668; *Shillibeer* v. *Glyn* (1836) 2 M. & W. 143.

[108] See *Whitehead* v. *Greetham* (1825) 2 Bing. 464.

[109] Story, *Bailments* (5th edn, 1851), § 171a. Cf. Chitty, *Contracts* (2nd edn, 1834), 32: 'The *intrusting* a person with property is a consideration, *in itself*, for his promise that, if he act upon the trust, he will faithfully discharge it.' The fact that the mere delivery of property constituted consideration for the bailee's promise was traced to Holt CJ's decision in *Coggs* v. *Bernard* (1703) 2 Ld. Raym. 909.

[110] Langdell, *Summary*, § 68, noted and accepted by Pollock, *Contract* (5th edn, 1889), 178n; Anson, *Contract* (6th edn, 1891), 81. Pollock said it stretched the law to breaking point. Pollock had previously accepted Holmes's view (*Common Law*, 291) seeing the delivery as consideration.

[111] Those who had promised to work gratuitously could be sued in tort for misfeasance once performance had commenced, although they could not be sued for nonfeasance. Anson, *Contract* (6th edn, 1891), 82 called this 'an anomaly in the English law of contract'. See *Elsee* v. *Gatward* (1793) 5 T.R. 143; *Wilkinson* v. *Coverdale* (1793) 1 Esp. 75; *Balfe* v. *West* (1853) 13 C.B. 466.

[112] Pollock, *Contract* (6th edn, 1894), 171n.

an agreement whereby the plaintiff gave up an unenforceable letter of guarantee in exchange for a new promise. Even though the letter might have been unenforceable,[113] 'the plaintiffs were induced by the defendant's promise to part with something which they might have kept, and the defendant obtained what he desired by means of that promise'.[114] In Lord Denman's view, nothing short of fraud—such as the plaintiffs deceiving the defendant as to the effects of the letter—would make the court think that 'a party was not bound by a promise made upon any consideration which could be valuable; while of its being so the promise by which it was obtained from the holder of it must always afford some proof'.[115]

A similarly broad view of what might count as detriment can be seen in the courts' approach in cases involving a promise to forbear from suing. The courts had regarded such a promise as constituting consideration if it was evident that there was an actionable claim for which the promisee might be liable.[116] How certain did the claim have to be? In 1821, it was decided that it was enough if there was a doubtful question of law between the parties, which they settled by agreement.[117] On the other hand, a promise to forbear from pursuing a claim utterly without foundation was not actionable. The fact that one person accused another of owing money was not enough, Abinger CB ruled in 1843, since '[a] man may threaten to bring an action against any stranger he may happen to meet in the street'.[118] In exploring the terrain between these two positions, mid-nineteenth-century courts held that a promise to forbear could be upheld, even if there was no claim in fact, provided the party acted *bona fide*, in the belief that he had a right.[119] The promisor lost his (possibly ultimately pointless) right to go to court,[120] while the promisee obtained the advantage of escaping

---

[113] The Exchequer Chamber, finding that the enforceability of the guarantee was at least ambiguous. *Brooks* v. *Haigh* (1839) 10 Ad. & El. 323.

[114] *Haigh* v. *Brooks* (1839) 10 Ad. & El. 309 at 320.

[115] See also *Westlake* v. *Adams* (1858) 5 C.B. N.S. 248.

[116] See *Jones* v. *Ashburnham* (1804) 4 East 555. See also *Tooley* v. *Windham* (1590) Cro. El. 206; *Fabian* v. *Plant* (1691) 1 Show. K.B. 183. See also *Kaye* v. *Dutton* (1844) 7 M. & G. 807.

[117] *Longridge* v. *Dorville* (1821) 5 B. & Ald. 117.

[118] *Edwards* v. *Baugh* (1843) 11 M. & W. 641 at 646.

[119] *Smith* v. *Monteith* (1844) 13 M. & W. 427 at 439; *Tempson* v. *Knowles* (1849) 7 C.B. 651 at 653; *Cooper* v. *Parker* (1853) 14 C.B. 118; *Cook* v. *Wright* (1861) 1 B. & S. 559; *Callisher* v. *Bischoffsheim* (1870) LR 5 QB 449.

[120] He did not necessarily lose a chance, since consideration was present even if the promisor had objectively no chance to win. See further, G. Treitel, *The Law of Contract* (12th edn by E. E. Peel, 2007), 96. However, as Bowen LJ pointed out in *Miles* v. *New Zealand Alford Estate Co* (1886) 32 Ch D 266 at 291, '[i]t is a mistake to suppose it is not an advantage, which a suitor is capable of appreciating, to be able to litigate his claim, even if he turns out to be wrong. It seems to me to be equally a mistake to suppose that it is not sometimes a disadvantage to a man to have to defend an action even if in the end he succeeds in his defence'.

the vexations incident to being sued.[121] However, if the promisor knew that he had no cause of action, then the promise would be held without consideration.[122] Although Brett LJ in 1881 attempted to question the authorities which said that the 'mere belief of the parties that there was [a cause of action] would support the compromise',[123] his view was not taken up.[124] By then, the courts were aware that there was commercial value in parties being able to make compromises to avoid litigation.

The fact that the courts were not concerned with the value of the consideration is also seen in their holding that any forbearance would suffice, however short. In *Alliance Bank* v. *Broom*, a promise by the defendant to give the bank an additional security for an existing debt (which the bank was seeking to recover) was held not to be a bare pact. Although the bank had not promised not to sue for the debt, the fact that they gave the defendants some degree of forbearance was sufficient.[125] For Anson, this case showed that forbearance to sue 'for however short a time' constituted consideration.[126] Some judges sought to qualify this by speaking of forbearance for a reasonable time,[127] but they did not elaborate on what such a reasonable time would be. Courts invoking this notion may have had in mind such a period of time as to evidence that there had been a forbearance in response to the request of the promisor.

4. THE PERFORMANCE OF EXISTING DUTIES

If courts were prepared to uphold contracts without weighing the value of the consideration, it was agreed that every contractual promise had to be supported by a fresh consideration. Where a party was already under a legal duty to do something—whether it arose from contract, the general law,[128] or the duties of public office—a promise to perform that duty could not constitute

---

[121] Per Cockburn CJ in *Callisher* v. *Bischoffsheim* (1870) LR 5 QB 449 at 452.

[122] *Wade* v. *Simeon* (1846) 2 C.B. 548.

[123] *Ex p Banner* (1881) 17 Ch D 480 at 490, questioning *Callisher* v. *Bischoffsheim* (1870) LR 5 QB 449 and *Ockford* v. *Barelli* (1871) 20 WR 116.

[124] See *Miles* v. *New Zealand Alford Estate Co* (1886) 32 Ch D 266.

[125] *Alliance Bank* v. *Broom* (1864) 2 Dr. & Sm. 289. In *Miles* v. *New Zealand Alford Estate Co* (1886) 32 Ch D 266 at 291, Bowen LJ pointed out that the actual forbearance had to be at the request, implied or express, of the promisor.

[126] Anson, *Contract* (6th edn, 1891), 80.

[127] Lord Macnaghten in *Fullerton* v. *Provincial Bank of Ireland* [1903] AC 309 at 313. See also *Oldershaw* v. *King* (1857) 2 H. & N. 517; *Payne* v. *Wilson* (1827) 7 B. & C. 423.

[128] For instance, promises to pay witnesses to attend court also lacked consideration, since they were already legally bound to come: *Willis* v. *Peckham* (1820) 1 B. & B. 515; *Collins* v. *Godefroy* (1831) 1 B. & Ad. 950.

consideration.[129] Although this was a bedrock of contract doctrine, there were a number of attempts to weaken its effects.

The first qualification was the articulation of a principle that a promise to do something more than one was already bound to do constituted consideration.[130] Although promises to pay public officers to perform their duties had long been regarded either as bribes or extortion, and lacking consideration,[131] Lord Denman in 1840 permitted a constable to claim a reward for having given information leading to the conviction of a suspect. This was on the ground that 'there may be services which the constable is not bound to render, and which he may therefore make the ground of a contract'.[132] Although paying rewards to policemen was controversial, courts continued to regard it as a good policy. The principle was also applied where private individuals performed something beyond their legal duty. In 1852, the Exchequer held a promise by a mother to support her illegitimate child in return for a payment from the father void for lack of consideration—as she was already bound to bring up the child—but upheld the agreement on her promise to abstain from seeking an affiliation order.[133] It was also applied to sailors, who performed more than their contractual duty. It had been settled in turn of the century cases that promises to pay sailors additional wages, in return for greater exertions during emergencies, lacked consideration.[134] Given that seamen's contracts had to be written and were subject to regulation,[135] it is not surprising that courts were unwilling to allow their modification mid-voyage. However, this rule was qualified in 1857. In *Hartley* v. *Ponsonby*, the jury found that so many of a ship's hands had deserted that proceeding with the voyage might endanger life; and that the master had entered into the new agreement with the remaining men voluntarily and without coercion. Under the circumstances of danger, the court held, the men were released from their obligation to continue,[136] and could make a new agreement agreeing to

---

[129] Equally, a promise by one party to pay for something the promisee was already bound to do lacked consideration: *Atkinson* v. *Settree* (1744) Willes 482; *Herring* v. *Dorell* (1840) 8 Dowl. P.C. 604.

[130] Pollock, *Contract* (6th edn, 1894), 174.

[131] See *Bridge* v. *Cage* (1605) Cro. Jac. 103; *Badow* v. *Salter* (1625) W. Jones 65. See also *Bilke* v. *Havelock* (1813) 3 Camp. 374.

[132] *England* v. *Davidson* (1840) 11 Ad. & El. 856. See Anson, *Contract* (6th edn, 1891), 83; Pollock, *Contract* (6th edn, 1894), 174; Leake, *Elements* (1st edn, 1867), 320.

[133] *Crowhurst* v. *Laverack* (1852) 8 Exch. 208.

[134] *Stilk* v. *Myrick* (1809) 2 Camp. 317, 6 Esp. 129. Cf. *Harris* v. *Watson* (1791) Peake 102. See also *Harris* v. *Carter* (1852) 3 E. & B. 559; *The Araminta* (1854) 1 Sp. Ecc. & Ad. 224; *Frazer* v. *Hatton* (1857) 2 C.B. N.S. 512.

[135] 2 Geo. II. c. 36, s. 1, 2 Geo. III. c. 31. See also *The Isabella* (1799) 2 C. Rob. 241; *Elsworth* v. *Woolmore* (1803) 5 Esp. 84. On these contracts, see also C. Abbott, *A Treatise of the Law Relative to Merchant Ships and Seamen* (2nd edn, 1804), 382 *et seq.*

[136] It was agreed that refusal to serve on an unseaworthy ship did not constitute desertion. Sailors were also permitted to quit ships if the master refused to supply provisions: *The Castilia* (1822) 1

undergo life-threatening danger.[137] The idea that danger terminated a contract was repeated in other cases, but by 1867, the rule was said to be that in emergencies, sailors were bound to perform any duties required, but that in other circumstances, if they performed duties not ordinarily required, they could recover more.[138]

The second qualification of the principle was the rule, settled in mid-century, that the performance of a contractual duty owed to one party could constitute the consideration for a promise by another.[139] This was held in two cases in the 1860s. The first was *Shadwell* v. *Shadwell*. In this case, Charles Shadwell promised to pay his nephew Launcelot £150 a year after his marriage, either until Charles died or until the nephew earned £600 a year. After the death of Charles (who had paid for 12 years), Launcelot sought to recover six years' worth of unpaid money from his uncle's estate. The executors resisted the action, saying that this was a mere voluntary kindness, not intended to be binding; and that there was no consideration for the promise. This dispute, arising from a promise by a relative to make a settlement on a marriage, was of a kind familiar enough in Chancery. Finding consideration in marriage settlements was not a problem in equity, since '[m]arriage is the most valuable of all considerations'.[140] However, since Shadwell was seeking damages for non-performance, rather than specific performance, he came to the common law. This jurisdiction was troubled by the idea that young Shadwell's marriage could constitute the consideration for a promise by his uncle, since the engagement had preceded the promise, had not been requested by the uncle, and bound the promisee to perform the very act which was to constitute the consideration for the promise. The plaintiff's counsel, William Harcourt, sought to invoke the equitable doctrine that a party who made a representation, on the faith of which a marriage took place, was bound to make it good.[141] He also invoked Chitty's distinction (also drawn from equity cases) between a 'mere gratuitous promise' and a 'promise on the faith of which one party is induced to do some act which, but for such promise, he would not have done'.[142] However, the Common Pleas did not wish to develop a

Hagg. Adm. 59 or if he changed the terms of the contract: *The Eliza* (1823) 1 Hagg. Adm. 182. See also *O'Neill* v. *Armstrong, Mitchell & Co* [1895] 2 QB 418; *Palace Shipping Co* v. *Caine* [1907] AC 386.

[137] *Hartley* v. *Ponsonby* (1857) 7 E. & B. 872, *The Times*, 5 June 1857, col. 11e. For further litigation on this, see *The Mobile* (1857) Swab. 256. See also *Turner* v. *Owen* (1862) 3 F. & F. 176.

[138] See *Hanson* v. *Royden* (1867) LR 3 CP 47 at 49.

[139] In 1844, Crompton had observed in argument that '[i]f A. agrees with B. that if B. will go to York, A. will pay him a certain sum, it is no answer to an action on this agreement, that B. has already contracted with some other person to go to York, which A. did not know, and that he will be there at all events', *Smith* v. *Monteith* (1844) 13 M. & W. 427 at 436.

[140] *Fraser* v. *Thompson* (1859) 4 De G. & J. 659 at 661.

[141] *Montefiori* v. *Montefiori* (1762) 1 W. Bl. 363; *Bold* v. *Hutchinson* (1855) 20 Beav. 250.

[142] Chitty, *Contracts* (6th edn, by J. A. Russell, 1857), 52, drawing from the headnote to *Crosbie* v. *M'Doual* (1806) 13 Ves. 148. This case was one in equity, and raised the question whether a party

rule which would jettison the need for consideration altogether. The majority, who nonetheless wanted to uphold the settlement, looked inventively for consideration. For Erle CJ and Keating J., the marriage could be seen as 'a loss sustained by the plaintiff at the uncle's request'. While marrying the woman of one's choice hardly constituted a loss, the groom might thereby 'have incurred pecuniary liabilities' he would not otherwise have done. From the viewpoint of the uncle, there was a benefit, since such a marriage was 'an object of interest to a near relative'.[143] Byles J. dissented, finding no evidence that the marriage had been at the uncle's request nor that he gained any benefit from it. In his view, the young man's doing what he was already bound to could not count as consideration. Lancelot's death and the executors' decision to compromise the claim prevented further litigation, but in 1866, the Queen's Bench permitted a couple to recover on a pre-nuptial promise, holding it a contract to pay in consideration of the marriage.[144]

The second case was *Scotson* v. *Pegg*. The defendant, who had failed to unload coal from the plaintiffs' ship within the period set by the contract, was sued for demurrage. He resisted by stating that he had bought the coal from a third party, who had contracted with the plaintiffs to deliver the coal to him. Since the plaintiffs were already bound to deliver the coal, its delivery could not constitute consideration for the defendant's promise to unload it. The defendant's argument was an attempt to evade the rule that consignees who accepted goods under a bill of lading stating the time for unloading were bound to pay demurrage;[145] and it failed. A fresh consideration could be found in the fact that the plaintiffs had agreed to an immediate delivery of the coal, thereby losing their right to detain the goods for any demurrage claims which might have been had against the consignor.[146] But in any event, the court felt that the performance of an existing duty could constitute consideration for a new contract. For Martin B., the fact that the plaintiffs already had a duty to the consignor to deliver the coals was irrelevant, as the defendant 'was a stranger to that contract'. In his view, 'any act done whereby the contracting party receives a benefit is a good consideration for a promise by him'.[147] For Wilde B., 'if a person chooses to promise to pay a sum of money in order to induce another to perform what he has already contracted

---

could be held to make good a representation that he would pay for a house for the plaintiff. Erskine did look for a consideration in this case, however.

[143]   *Shadwell* v. *Shadwell* (1860) 9 C.B. N.S. 159 at 173–4.

[144]   *Chichester* v. *Cobb* (1866) 14 LT 433.

[145]   *Jesson* v. *Solly* (1811) 4 Taunt. 52.

[146]   Wilde B also noted 'it is well known as an every-day occurrence that obtaining immediate possession of goods is a great advantage to a merchant, and one which he is often willing to pay a considerable sum to secure', *Scotson* v. *Pegg* 3 LT 753 at 754.

[147]   *Scotson* v. *Pegg* (1861) 6 H. & N. 295 at 299. See also 3 LT 753 at 754.

with a third person to do, I confess I cannot see why such a promise should not be binding'.[148] For the plaintiffs might choose to break their contract with the consignor, which would leave the defendant with no remedy if he had not made his own contract for the performance.

Wilde's explanation that since a man might have an interest in the performance of another party's contract, he could contract for his own right to insist on its performance was adopted by Pollock in the first edition of his treatise. As he saw it, a 'new and distinct right' was created, which was always 'of some value in law, and may be of appreciable value in fact'.[149] Anson, writing three years later, was unconvinced by this argument, for it 'assume[d] that a right is created, which would not be the case if the consideration for the promise were bad'. He found consideration for *Scotson* and *Shadwell* in the fact that, by promising a new party that he would perform his existing contract, the promisor gave up the right he had to agree with the original promisee to terminate the agreement.[150] Pollock adopted this explanation after reading Anson, though he later rejected it.[151]

In the year after Anson's treatise was published, C. C. Langdell put forward a new view. Rejecting Martin B.'s comment that a benefit could constitute consideration, he argued that since it had to move from the promisee, detriment to that party was the 'universal test' of its sufficiency.[152] The premise that the legal value of a consideration consisted only in the detriment to the promisee—which was soon accepted by English jurists[153]—led Langdell to distinguish between valid and invalid promises to perform existing duties to others. Where a contract was 'bilateral'—with both parties exchanging promises of performance—a promise to perform an existing duty to a third party could constitute consideration, for the detriment incurred was the granting of a new right to compel performance.[154] But where the contract was 'unilateral'—with a promise in exchange for the

---

[148] *Scotson* v. *Pegg* (1861) 6 H.& N. 295 at 300.

[149] Pollock, *Contract* (1st edn, 1876), 158–60. Cf. Leake, *Elements* (1st edn, 1867), 321, which Pollock later (8th edn, 1921, 199n) claimed made the same point. Pollock added that the law should recognize such a right on grounds of public policy.

[150] Anson, *Contract* (1st edn, 1879), 80–1.

[151] This explanation was mentioned by Pollock in the 3rd (1881) edition of his treatise on *Contract* in a footnote (195n), promoted into the text as the most convincing one between the 4th (1885) edition at p. 179 and the 6th (1894) edition at p. 177. He abandoned it in the 7th edition (1902) at p. 186, having rethought consideration.

[152] Langdell, *Summary*, 81–2. Langdell pointed out that, in contrast to debt, the benefit in assumpsit need not inure to the promisor, but could go to a third party, or no one at all.

[153] See Pollock's comments in *The Revised Reports*, vol. 123, v. Anson wrote in *Contract* that 'Consideration … is something done, forborne, or suffered, or promised to be done, forborne, or suffered by the promisee in respect of the promise' (6th edn, 1891), 72.

[154] Langdell, *Summary*, p. 105, § 84. For a discussion, see R. Bronaugh, 'A Secret Paradox of the Common Law' (1983) 2 *Law and Philosophy* 193–232.

performance of an existing duty—there could be no new detriment. According to this reasoning, *Scotson* v. *Pegg* and *Shadwell* v. *Shadwell* were wrongly decided, since they were 'unilateral'. Having read Langdell's *Summary*, Pollock modified his views once more. Accepting the centrality of detriment,[155] he now argued that while 'the *performance* of an existing obligation' involved no detriment and hence no consideration, 'a new *promise* to a stranger to perform it' satisfied the requirement.[156]

Anson maintained his views. Although in the sixth edition, he modified his definition of consideration to stress that it must move from the promisee,[157] he repeated the passages from his original text, where he had argued that to say that the consideration for the promise to perform an existing duty was the detriment of the promisee granting the promisor a right to enforce it was to assume that an action would lie on the second promise. It simply begged the question: in principle, neither the performance nor the promise to perform an outstanding contract with a third party could be consideration for a promise.[158] Anson's objection was taken up by the American, Samuel Williston. He argued that the objection applied to all contracts in which one promise was consideration for another: unless the promise imposed an obligation, it could not be a detriment.[159] There were only two ways in which the promise could be seen as binding. The first solution—to assume that mutual promises were always binding—was unsatisfactory, since it would allow a promise to receive a pure benefit or a gift to be seen as providing consideration.[160] The second more satisfactory solution was to look for the detriment not in the promise, but at whether the performance of the thing promised would be a detriment.[161] Taking this view, Williston agreed with Anson

[155] Pollock read Langdell between writing the 4th and 5th editions, but had already begun to stress detriment before reading his book. In the first two editions he had quoted W. D. Evans's definition (in appendix 2 to his edition on Pothier): 'Any act by which the person making the promise has benefit, or the person to whom it is made has any labour or detriment', Pollock, *Contract* (1st edn, 1876), 147. In the 4th edition, he added that '[c]onsideration means not so much that one party is profited as that the other abandons some legal right in the present, or limits his legal freedom of action in the future' (4th edn, 1885), 167.

[156] Pollock, *Contract* (5th edn, 1889), 178 (emphasis added). Cf. the 4th edn (1885) (where this sentence is omitted), 6th edn (1894), 176; 8th edn (1911), 197–8.

[157] Anson, *Contract* (6th edn, 1891), 72. In earlier editions, he had simply cited Lush's dictum from *Currie* v. *Misa* without adding this rider: 1st edn, (1879), 69; 5th edn (1888), 70.

[158] Anson, *Contract* (1st edn, 1879), 81; (6th edn, 1891), 89–90). Anson's later editor, M. L. Gwyer, changed the text to follow Langdell's view (16th edn, 1923), 119.

[159] 'It is, therefore, assuming the point in issue to say a promise is a detriment because it is binding', S. Williston, 'Successive Promises of the same Performance' (1894) 8 *Harvard LR* 27–38 at 35.

[160] Cf. Holmes, *Common Law*, 304.

[161] This (as Williston later pointed out) was the view taken by Leake: Williston, 'Consideration in Bilateral Contracts', 524. Leake wrote (*Elements*, 1st edn, 1867), 312, 'whatever matter, if executed, is

that 'neither performance, nor promise of performance of what one is already bound to perform is a valid consideration'.[162]

A third view was put forward by James Barr Ames. While accepting the view that consideration required a detriment to be incurred by the promisee, he gave the notion of 'detriment' a very wide meaning, including 'any change of position, that is, any act or forbearance given in exchange for a promise'.[163] For Ames felt that all promises should be enforced unless there were reasons of public policy not to do so. According to this view, the performance of existing duties (as well as the promise of performance) could therefore constitute consideration. In his last pre-war edition, Pollock noted the three divergent positions associated with himself and Langdell; Anson and Williston; and Ames and Beale. Although he did not endorse Ames's wider views of consideration, he concluded that on the grounds of convenience, there would be no great harm, were such cases common, in allowing the performance, as well as the promise, of existing duties to suffice.[164] In 1914, Williston modified his view, offering a new position. He now argued that when parties entered contractual negotiations, they were not bargaining over *rights*, but only asked each other for promises in fact. It was the factual promise, rather than its legal consequence, which provided the consideration, though it still remained for the court to decide on its sufficiency. Since the factual promise might constitute a benefit to the promisee, Williston now contended, this could be regarded as sufficient consideration.[165] Pollock, however, took no notice of Williston's modified view, and continued to treat detriment to the promisee as crucial.[166]

Late nineteenth-century jurists also considered whether the promise to perform existing duties owed to the promisee could count as consideration. This was not an issue much discussed by the English writers since, in Anson's words, it was 'an obvious result of the doctrine of consideration' that it could not.[167] For Pollock, it was also obvious that a promise by A to perform for B what A was

---

sufficient to form a good executed consideration, if promised, is sufficient to form a good executory consideration'.

[162] Williston, 'Successive Promises', 36, 38. In Anson's 10th edn (1903), 106n, he rejected the point that, according to his arguments, a promise could never be consideration for a promise by giving a similar solution to Williston's: 'Each promise is a consideration for the other if, and only if, it offers to the promisee something which the promisor is not otherwise bound to do or to forbear.'

[163] J. B. Ames, 'Two Theories of Consideration. 1. Unilateral Contracts' (1899) 12 *Harvard LR* 515–31 at 520.

[164] Pollock, *Contract* (8th edn, 1911), 200n; cf. 9th edn (1921), 202n; 10th edn (1936), 187n.

[165] Williston, 'Consideration in Bilateral Contracts', 506.

[166] See Wright, 'Ought the Doctrine of Consideration to be Abolished', 1227. Pollock, *Contract* (9th edn, 1921), 201–2 repeated the views of the 1911 edition. See also the 10th (1936) edn, 171–2.

[167] Anson, *Contract* (6th edn, 1891), 84.

already bound to do 'can (at any rate in contemplation of law) produce no fresh advantage to B or detriment to A'.[168] In England, this question had not arisen outside of the context of cases involving seamen. By contrast, a number of American jurisdictions had allowed plaintiffs to recover in such cases,[169] and it was a question discussed by American jurists. On the one side, Williston rejected arguments which found consideration in a practical benefit to the promisee, such as arguments that an actual performance might be worth more than the damages which would otherwise be obtained.[170] On the other hand, Ames felt that an 'act or forbearance already due from the promisee by reason of some pre-existing legal obligation' would suffice.[171] For his view, any act or forbearance by the promisee could count as consideration (provided it was not against public policy); and since a promise was an act, any promise could count.

In fact, as Ames perceived, 'the question, whether the performance of a pre-existing contractual duty to the promisor will support a promise, seldom arises, except in the case of a promise in consideration of the payment of part of the whole of a debt'.[172] At common law, this had traditionally been dealt with as an issue of 'satisfaction', rather than consideration. Debts could be waived by the creditor, but only by deed, or by an 'accord and satisfaction' with the debtor. Though distinct from consideration, satisfaction was treated by the courts in the same way. There would only be satisfaction if something of value had been given to the party owed the debt;[173] but the courts did not look into its adequacy, leaving this to the parties to determine.[174] Logic decreed that part payment of a debt could never be satisfaction of the whole debt: £10 could never be £20. There would hence only be satisfaction—as the rule in *Pinnel's Case* put it—if the payment was made early or if the creditor accepted 'the gift of a horse, hawk, or robe', which he might regard as more beneficial than the money'.[175] In the early and mid-nineteenth century, the leading case on this doctrine was thought to be *Cumber* v. *Wane* (1721) where Pratt CJ held that a promissory note for £5 could

---

[168] Pollock, *Contract* (1st edn, 1876), 157. Cf. the fuller discussion in Leake, *Elements* (1st edn, 1867), 318–20. Pollock's later editions did not discuss this point more deeply, though in the 5th edn, having read Langdell, he added that 'the performance of an existing obligation, as distinct from a new promise to a stranger to perform it, can in any view not involve any legal detriment, and therefore cannot be a consideration' (1889), 178.

[169] *Lattimore* v. *Harsen* 14 Johns 330 (NY Sup 1817); *Munroe* v. *Perkins* 26 Mass (9 Pick) 298 (Mass 1830); *Bishop* v. *Busse* 69 Ill 403 (1873); *Goebel* v. *Linn* 47 Mich 489, 11 NW 284 (Mich 1882).

[170] Williston, 'Successive Promises', 30.

[171] Ames, 'Two Theories of Consideration. 1. Unilateral Contracts', 515.

[172] Ames, 'Two Theories of Consideration. 1. Unilateral Contracts', 530.

[173] See *Bayley* v. *Homan* (1837) 3 Bing. N.C. 915.

[174] Chitty, *Contracts* (6th edn by J. A. Russell, 1857), 668. Cf. Leake, *Elements* (1867), 468; Anson, *Contract* (1st edn, 1879), 307.

[175] *Pinnel's Case* (1602) 5 Co. Rep. 117a at 117b.

not discharge a contractual claim for £15, and observed that the satisfaction 'must appear to the Court to be a reasonable' one.[176]

Judges and jurists in the mid-nineteenth century were unhappy with the rule in *Cumber* v. *Wane* and sought ways to limit it. First, it was decided in *Sibree* v. *Tripp* in 1846 that a negotiable security could satisfy a liquidated debt of a larger amount, since it was equivalent to giving a chattel in satisfaction of a debt, whose value the courts had never questioned.[177] Secondly, it was held that payment of a lesser sum was satisfaction of an unliquidated debt, since it avoided the uncertainty and costs of the litigation.[178] By the mid-nineteenth century, it was evident that the doctrine of *Cumber* v. *Wane* also raised questions about the nature of consideration. For in dealing with composition agreements with insolvents and agreements by creditors to release retiring partners from partnership debts, the courts began to ask not whether the debt (or part of it) had been satisfied, but whether there had been consideration for the creditor's promise not to sue for the whole debt.[179] In so doing, they took a creative approach to consideration to get around the restrictions of the doctrine of satisfaction.

In these two commercial contexts, and generally for pragmatic business reasons, the courts which had initially been reluctant to find consideration for the promise later changed their views. At the start of the nineteenth century the courts had held composition agreements between creditors and insolvents made without a deed to be void. As Lord Ellenborough put it, a smaller payment could never satisfy a larger debt, and any agreement to accept a lesser sum had to show some 'consideration for the relinquishment of the residue'.[180] By 1831, the King's Bench had located the consideration. Although there was no accord and satisfaction between the debtor and creditor in composition agreements, it was held that they were new contracts supported by consideration. As Parke J. put it, 'each creditor entered into a new agreement with the defendant, the consideration of which, to the creditor, was a forbearance by all the other creditors who were parties, to insist upon their claims'.[181] Other courts upheld composition deeds on

---

[176] *Cumber* v. *Wane* (1718) 1 Stra. 426 at 426–7. See also the report in 11 Mod. 342.

[177] *Sibree* v. *Tripp* (1846) 15 M. & W. 23 at 32. See also *Goddard* v. *O' Brien* (1882) 9 QBD 37 where a cheque for a smaller sum was held valid. Contrast the earlier view in *Thomas* v. *Heathorn* (1824) 2 B. & C. 477 at 481.

[178] *Wilkinson* v. *Byers* (1834) 1 Ad. & El. 106 at 113, drawing on *Reynolds* v. *Pinhowe* (1595) Cro. El. 429. See also *Cooper* v. *Parker* (1855) 15 C.B. 822, where Parke B. criticised the position taken in *Down* v. *Hatcher* (1839) 10 Ad. & El. 121.

[179] Courts regarded the issues of whether there had been satisfaction and whether there was a new agreement as separate. Since it was settled by the nineteenth century that a contractual right given to the promisee could constitute satisfaction (*James* v. *David* (1793) 5 T.R. 141; *Flockton* v. *Hall* (1849) 14 Q.B. 380), they might have been linked.

[180] *Fitch* v. *Sutton* (1804) 5 East 230 at 232. Cf. *Heathcote* v. *Crookshanks* (1787) 2 T.R. 24.

[181] *Good* v. *Cheesman* (1831) 2 B. & Ad. 328 at 335. Cf. *Alchin* v. *Hopkins* (1834) 1 Bing. N.C. 99 at 102.

the ground that each creditor bound himself to the others.[182] At the same time, the courts also began to allow retiring partners to be released from partnership debts. In the 1820s, the view had been taken that a mere agreement[183] only to look to the remaining partner lacked consideration.[184] But in 1834, the King's Bench suggested that such an agreement might not be a bare pact, since 'the sole liability of one of two debtors may be more beneficial than the joint liability of two [...] whether it was actually more beneficial in each particular case, cannot be made the subject of enquiry'.[185] In 1853 in *Lyth* v. *Ault*, Parke B. noted that a sole liability was a different kind of security from a joint one. In his view, 'the sole responsibility of one of many partners may be of greater value than that of all'. For instance, the sole debt of an elderly man who might die soon, leaving a claim on his estate, might be worth more than a joint liability with a younger man.[186] This came close to developing a view of consideration as a practical benefit.

Decisions such as these prompted judges and jurists to take an increasingly critical view of *Cumber* v. *Wane*. Criticising Pratt's view, the editors of *Smith's Leading Cases* argued that a court 'should rather strive to give effect to the engagements which persons have thought proper to enter into, than cast about for subtle reasons to defeat them upon the ground of being unreasonable'. They therefore took a very generous view of what could constitute consideration: 'if there be any benefit, or even any legal possibility of benefit, to the creditor thrown in, that additional weight will turn the scale, and render the consideration sufficient to support the agreement.'[187] Martin B. similarly observed in 1855, 'I shall always be ready to concur in such a judgment as tends to allow parties to contract for themselves what engagements they please.'[188] Such dicta suggested a desire by judges not to allow technical doctrines to impede freedom of contract.

When *Pinnel's Case* came to be re-examined by the House of Lords in 1884 in *Foakes* v. *Beer*, the doctrine of consideration was at something of a crossroads. On the one hand, the courts had in many areas eroded the requirement of consideration, by finding sufficient consideration in the slenderest of benefits. There

---

[182] *Reay* v. *White* (1833) 1 C. & M. 748 at 751; *Boyd* v. *Hind* (1857) 1 H. & N. 938 at 947.

[183] If a creditor took a fresh security from the continuing partner, this replaced the earlier one and was valid: see *Evans* v. *Drummond* (1801) 4 Esp. 89; *Reed* v. *White* (1803) 5 Esp. 122, and the comments of Bayley J. in *Bedford* v. *Deakin* (1818) 2 B. & Ald. 210 at 216.

[184] *Lodge* v. *Dicas* (1820) 3 B. & Ald. 611 at 614. See also *David* v. *Ellice* (1826) 5 B. & C. 196.

[185] *Thompson* v. *Percival* (1834) 5 B. & Ad. 925 at 933. See also Parke B.'s comments in *Kirwan* v. *Kirwan* (1834) 2 Cr. & M. 617 at 624. It became settled in the mid-nineteenth century that in these cases of novation, all that had to be shown was the agreement of the creditor to accept the liability of the new partnership: see *Hart* v. *Alexander* (1837) 2 M. & W. 484.

[186] *Lyth* v. *Ault* (1852) 7 Exch. 669 at 671, 673.

[187] J. W. Smith, *A Selection of Leading Cases on Various Branches of the Law*, 2 vols (4th edn, 1856, ed. J. S. Willes and H. S. Keating), i, 252–3.

[188] *Cooper* v. *Parker* (1855) 15 C.B. 822 at 828.

was also much dissatisfaction at the 'very singular state of the law' whereby a debt could be discharged by anything of inferior value, as long as it was not money.[189] It was a rule which Pollock regarded as an 'absurd paradox',[190] and one which the Indian Law Commissioners abrogated for the subcontinent.[191] On the other hand, jurists like Pollock had no desire to abolish or neutralize the doctrine of consideration. His solution to the dilemma presented by *Pinnel's Case* was to argue that the doctrine of consideration should apply only to the formation, and not to the discharge of contracts. But this was simply to ignore the problem that £99 could never be a satisfaction of £100, and that any promise to accept a lesser sum would be a new agreement.[192] Langdell (who like Pollock felt the law should recognize agreements to compromise debts), attempted a more sophisticated solution. Admitting that mutual promises to give and receive a smaller sum in settlement of a larger debt would be void, since the smaller sum could not satisfy the larger debt, he argued that if the debtor promised to pay in exchange for a promise by the creditor never to sue for the debt, both would be valid promises, backed by consideration.[193] But Langdell's solution also assumed that the promise to pay the smaller sum provided consideration. In effect, the question resolved itself into whether a promise to perform an existing duty to the promisee could be consideration.

In its judgment in *Foakes* v. *Beer*, the Lords rejected this position and confirmed the rule in *Pinnel's Case*. At issue was whether a promise by a creditor to waive the payment of interest due on a judgment debt, in exchange for a promise on the debtor's part to pay an initial £500 and regular payments thereafter until the original debt was repaid, was void for lacking consideration. As the Lords realized, since Dr Foakes did not bind himself to pay the instalments, the only consideration for Mrs Beer's promise to waive the interest was his promise to pay £500 of the £2090 originally owed.[194] Although the judgment was unanimous, Lord Blackburn came very close to dissenting. He argued that Coke's observation in *Pinnel's Case* that a lesser sum could not discharge a larger debt was *obiter*

---

[189] Grove J. in *Goddard* v. *O' Brien* (1882) 9 QBD 37 at 39. Cf. Jessel MR in *Couldery* v. *Bartrum* (1881) 19 Ch D 394 at 400.

[190] Pollock, *Contract* (1st edn, 1876), 160. Fortunately, 'modern decisions have confined this absurdity within the narrowest possible limits'. Anson by contrast argued that the rule was 'the necessary result of the doctrine of consideration': *Contract* (1st edn, 1879), 77. He continued to defend it: *Contract*, (6th edn, 1891), 86.

[191] PP 1867–8 (239), xlix, 601 at 13. See also Indian Contracts Act 1872, s. 63 illustration (b).

[192] Pollock admitted the logic grudgingly in the 5th (1889) edition of *Contract* (179n), and less grudgingly after the 7th (1902) edn: 190n.

[193] Langdell, *Summary*, §88, p. 108. If a 'defendant promised to pay the plaintiff any sum, however small, in consideration of a promise by the plaintiff to release the debt, there would have been a binding accord' (110–11).

[194] This was because he was not, under the agreement, bound to pay the instalments.

and was open to be revisited. It was, he felt, based on an incorrect notion that it could never be of benefit to a party to accept a smaller sum in settlement of a larger debt; for 'all men of business, whether merchants or tradesmen, do every day recognize and act on the ground that prompt payment of a part of their demand may be more beneficial to them than it would be to insist on their rights and enforce payment of the whole'.[195] However, Lord Selborne held that there had to be 'some independent benefit, actual or contingent, of a kind which might in law be a good and valuable consideration for any other sort of agreement not under seal'.[196] Even though Mrs Beer might have obtained practical benefit from the arrangement—since she secured a payment from someone who could have kept her at arm's length—this was not sufficient.

Foakes v. *Beer* entrenched a rule which commentators assumed that merchants found inconvenient, though there was little evidence that they were actually inconvenienced. Its importance lay not in its impact on the world of business—where the decision passed by completely unnoticed—but in its impact on the development of doctrine, for it was a strong reassertion by the Lords of the need for consideration. In this case, the Lords in effect reasserted a bargain theory.[197] Pollock, who continued to be troubled by the rule in *Pinnel's Case* regarding discharge,[198] described the decision in *Foakes* as 'the strictly logical result of carrying out a general principle beyond the bounds to which it is reasonably applicable'.[199] Unlike Anson, he seems not to have perceived that a contrary decision would have undermined the very need for consideration in the formation of a contract which he endorsed. But he accepted that the decision was authoritative and binding.

The biggest attack on *Foakes* v. *Beer* came from Ames. In his view, the decision in *Foakes* not only confounded the reasonable expectations of businessmen, it was 'an exception contrary to principle'[200] and flew in the face of seventeenth-century case law overlooked by the Lords.[201] He argued that the doctrine that a £10 payment could never satisfy a £20 debt was 'older than the doctrine of consideration, and is simply the survival of a bit of formal logic of the mediaeval lawyers'.[202]

---

[195] *Foakes* v. *Beer* (1884) 9 App Cas 605 at 622.

[196] *Foakes* v. *Beer* (1884) 9 App Cas 605 at 614.

[197] See also J. O'Sullivan, 'In defence of *Foakes v. Beer*' (1996) 55 *Cambridge LJ*, 219–28.

[198] Pollock, *Contract* (6th edn, 1894), 177.

[199] Pollock, *Contract* (4th edn, 1885), 180n. See also (1885) 1 *LQR* 134.

[200] Ames, 'Two Theories of Consideration. 1. Unilateral Contracts', 531. Ten American states altered the rule in *Pinnel's Case* by statute, and others had decisions hostile to the doctrine.

[201] He gave as authority *Bagge* v. *Slade* (1616) 3 Bulst. 162; 1 Roll. Rep. 354; and *Rawlins* v. *Lockey* (1639) in C. Viner, *A General Abridgment of Law and Equity*, 24 vols (Aldershot, 1741–58), i: 308. In his view, *Pinnel's Case* was about satisfaction, not consideration.

[202] Ames, 'Two Theories of Consideration. 1. Unilateral Contracts', 521.

While part payment could not, as a matter of logic, be satisfaction, he argued (like Langdell) that it could be consideration for a promise to cancel a debt. He also thought that (unlike Langdell) he had a theory to show consideration for the new promise: his theory that any act, forbearance, or promise sufficed.

5. CONSIDERATION AND PRIVITY OF CONTRACT

Since those who were strangers to the consideration could not sue on a contract, the doctrine of consideration was linked to the doctrine of privity. Just as the former doctrine, which sat uneasily with will theory, was increasingly defended and articulated in the nineteenth century, so the doctrine of privity, which was also at odds with the civilian tradition, became ever more firmly rooted.[203] In 1915, Viscount Haldane LC observed that the doctrine of privity was based on two foundations. One was the principle that a party could only enforce an informal contract if he had provided consideration. The other was that only a person who was party to the contract could enforce it, regardless of the issue of consideration.[204] In the case before him, *Dunlop Pneumatic Tyre Co Ltd* v. *Selfridge & Co Ltd*, it was therefore held that a retailer of tyres, bought at a discounted rate from a wholesaler, was not bound by an agreement with the original suppliers not to sell under a certain price, since no consideration moved from them to those suppliers. Lord Dunedin famously observed that the case was apt to 'nip any budding affection' he had for consideration, since it allowed 'a person to snap his fingers at a bargain deliberately made'.[205]

Early modern case law was unsettled on the question whether only those who had provided consideration could sue on a contract made for their benefit. There was some authority that where third party beneficiaries were family members, they could sue, with judges being influenced by a notion of meritorious consideration, which did not extend to strangers.[206] According to some decisions, marrying couples who were to be the beneficiaries of agreements made between their fathers to pay them money could sue the defaulting parent,[207] since they were held to have an interest in the cause.[208] Nonetheless, the matter was regarded in

---

[203] See Palmer, *Paths to Privity* (1992) and R. Flannigan, 'Privity—the End of an Era (Error)', (1987) 103 *LQR* 564–93.

[204] 'Our law knows nothing of a jus quaesitum tertio arising by way of contract', *Dunlop Pneumatic Tyre* v. *Selfridge* [1915] AC 847 at 853.

[205] *Dunlop Pneumatic Tyre* v. *Selfridge* [1915] AC 847 at 855.

[206] See *Dutton* v. *Pole* (1677) 3 Keble 814 at 815, 1 Vent. 332, 2 Lev. 210 at 211–12.

[207] *Lever* v. *Heys* (1599) Moore 550; *Provender* v. *Wood* (1630) Het. 30; *Sprat* v. *Agar* (1658) 2 Sid. 115; *Bafeild* v. *Collard* (1646) Aleyn 1 (holding that either parent or child could sue). See also *Levett* v. *Hawes* (1599) Cro. El. 652 (where it was held that the father could not sue, but only the son).

[208] *Hadves* v. *Levit* (1631) Het. 176.

the eighteenth century as open to doubt.[209] Outside family relationships, there were also some dicta by later eighteenth-century judges that 'if one person makes a promise to another for the benefit of a third, that third person may maintain an action upon it'.[210] But most judges were reluctant to allow third parties to sue on contractual promises given to promisees, unless there was a relationship of agency or trust between that person and the third party, which could overcome the consideration problem.[211] In 1833, the King's Bench confirmed that where one party promised a debtor to pay money to a third party creditor, that third party could not sue the promisor, since no consideration moved from him.[212]

Given the contradictory authorities, early nineteenth-century treatise writers were hesitant. In the early editions of his treatise, Joseph Chitty favoured the rule which disallowed an action by strangers to the consideration, unless one of the parties to the contract could be seen as their agent.[213] His mid-century editor confidently dismissed the older cases as 'of questionable authority', and omitted discussion of the family cases.[214] By contrast, the mid-century edition of Addison's treatise, while admitting that some consideration had to move from the third party, sought to find it in '[v]ery slight circumstances'. In family arrangements, he felt, where promises were exchanged by the parents, the children 'performed the meritorious act forming the consideration for the promise'.[215] The difficult question of family arrangements was revisited in the Queen's Bench in 1861 in *Tweddle* v. *Atkinson*. The facts revealed a run-of-the-mill marriage settlement, of the kind which could normally be enforced by the groom in equity and also (as *Shadwell* v. *Shadwell* had just shown) at law. Unfortunately for the groom, he could not sue his father-in-law's executors on the settlement himself, since it had failed to comply with the Statute of Frauds. He therefore brought an action on the contract made between the two fathers after the marriage had taken place. This contract did not mention that their mutual promises to pay were in consideration of the marriage, though it did state that the groom should have full power to sue on it. William Tweddle lost, with the Queen's Bench judges agreeing that no stranger to the consideration could sue on the contract, even though it was made for his benefit. The judges also rejected counsel's argument that there was an exception in the case of contracts made for the benefit of children. In Crompton's

---

[209] *Bayfield* v. *Collard* (1671) in Viner, *Abridgment*, i: 334.

[210] *Marchington* v. *Vernon* (1787) 1 B. & P. 101n. Cf. Mansfield's views in *Martyn* v. *Hind* (1776) 2 Cowp. 437.

[211] *Company of Feltmakers* v. *Davis* (1797) 1 B. & P. 98 at 102; *Pigott* v. *Thompson* (1802) 3 B. & P. 147 at 148–9.

[212] *Price* v. *Easton* (1833) 4 B. & Ad. 433.

[213] Chitty, *Contracts* (2nd edn, 1834), 46.

[214] Chitty, *Contracts* (5th edn, 1853), 63.

[215] Addison, *Contracts* (4th edn, 1856), 941.

view, such an argument was no longer tenable, since it had been settled (by *Eastwood* v. *Kenyon*) that natural love and affection was no consideration. The court was clearly content not to support the kind of marriage settlement it had upheld in *Shadwell* v. *Shadwell*, because it was alarmed at the prospect of reviving a consideration based on natural love.[216] For Anson, the case illustrated the need for a distinction to be made between motive and consideration:[217] if the family relationship might provide a motive for the contract entered into by a father, it could not be a consideration for it. By this view, what equity regarded as meritorious consideration would be seen by the common law as mere motive.[218] Judges who sought to settle the rule of privity in the mid-nineteenth century were thus seeking to put the doctrine of consideration onto solid foundations.[219]

The case was also taken to confirm the point that only parties to a contract could sue on it.[220] This was to displace the older view that a plaintiff who had provided consideration could sue, even if the defendant's promise had been made to another.[221] The reason why only parties to the contract could sue was because '[w]here a consideration is required there must be mutuality'. In Crompton J.'s view, it would be 'monstrous' to allow a party to sue on a contract who could not be sued on it.[222] Frederick Pollock, who was particularly influenced by Savigny's will theory, stated baldly that the agreement of contracting parties could not confer any right to enforce the contract on a third person. He also insisted on the corollary of the rule, that obligations could only be imposed on parties by their own will, or by the law, but not by the contracts of others.[223]

If *Tweddle* v. *Atkinson* helped settle the doctrinal reasons which underpinned privity of contract, there was still room to discuss whether such a doctrine was desirable, as a matter of policy. The issue was particularly pressing when considering the liability of newly formed companies for agreements made by their promoters.[224] Some judges clearly felt that suppliers had claims against the

---

[216] *Tweddle* v. *Atkinson* (1861) 1 B. & S. 393 at 396.

[217] Anson, *Contract* (1st edn, 1879), 72.

[218] See also *Thomas* v. *Thomas* (1842) 2 Q.B. 851.

[219] But as Samuel Williston pointed out in 1902, there was no necessary reason why consideration had to entail a doctrine of privity. 'The rule that consideration must move from the promisee is somewhat technical, and in a developed system of contract law, there seems no good reason why A should not be able for a consideration received from B to make an effective promise to C', as was done with promissory notes: S. Williston, 'Contracts for the Benefit of a Third Person' (1902) 15 *Harvard LR* 767–809 at 771.

[220] Leake, *Elements* (1st edn, 1867), 222.

[221] Palmer, *Paths to Privity*, 163, 171–4. Cf. Flannigan, 'Privity', 570–1.

[222] *Tweddle* v. *Atkinson* (1861) 1 B. & S. 393 at 396, 398.

[223] Pollock, *Contract* (6th edn, 1894), 190.

[224] For applications of the rule, see *Hutchinson* v. *Surrey Consumers Gas Light and Coke Association* (1851) 3 C. & K. 45; *Payne* v. *New South Wales Coal and Intercolonial Steam Navigation*

company which should be enforceable,[225] and looked for ways to offer solutions. Chancery judges had offered two ways to avoid the privity rule. The first was Lord Cottenham's, which he articulated in the 1830s, when holding statutory companies liable on agreements made by their promoters to do work for landowners in return for their withdrawing their opposition to parliamentary bills incorporating the company. The solution was an equitable one: the fact that the company obtained its statutory powers in part thanks to an agreement made between its promoters and third parties meant that it could only exercise its legal rights 'upon the terms of adopting and giving effect to the contract which has been entered into by other parties'.[226] The company was treated in effect as an assignee of the promoter's rights and duties.[227] The second was seen in Lord Hatherley's judgment in *Touche* v. *Metropolitan Warehousing Company*, where work was done by the plaintiffs under a contract made with promoters for the benefit of a company to be formed. After the company was formed, it agreed with the promoters to pay the sums due to the suppliers. Allowing the suppliers to sue, Hatherley flatly contradicted the rule of privity. 'The case', he said, 'comes within the authority that where a sum is payable by AB for the benefit of CD, CD can claim under the contract as if it had been made with himself.'[228] He cited as authority Sir William Grant MR's judgment in *Gregory* v. *Williams*, where a third party beneficiary who provided no consideration was permitted to be joined as plaintiff in an action against the promisor. In that case, the promisee had been treated as a trustee, with the third party beneficiary deriving an equitable right through the mediation of the promisee's contract.[229]

In the event, neither of these routes to evade the doctrine of privity was regarded favourably by the courts, which began to express a greater concern to protect shareholders. The strict rule of privity was seen to generate commercial results which were not undesirable. As Lord Cranworth pointed out in 1856, those who invested in statutory companies looked at the legislation to see what their liabilities were, and it would be unfair to bind them to contracts not in

Co (1854) 10 Exch. 283; *Terrell's case* (1851) 2 Sim. N.S. 126 (dealing with the companies formed under the 1844 Joint Stock Companies Act).

[225] *Melhado* v. *Porto Alegre Railway Co.* (1874) LR 9 CP 503 at 505 (Lord Coleridge).

[226] *Greenhalgh* v. *Manchester & Birmingham Railway Co* (1838) 3 Myl. & Cr. 784 at 791; Cf. *Edwards* v. *Grand Junction Railway Co* (1836) 1 Myl. & Cr. 650 at 672.

[227] See *Stanley* v. *Chester and Birkenhead Railway Co* (1838) 3 Myl. & Cr. 773. See also *Earl of Lindsey* v. *Great Northern Railway Co* (1853) 10 Hare 664 at 681; *Lord Petre* v. *The Eastern Counties Railway* (1838) 1 Rail. Cas. 462.

[228] *Touche* v. *Metropolitan Warehousing Co* (1871) 6 Ch App 671 at 677.

[229] *Gregory* v. *Williams* (1817) 3 Mer. 582 at 590. In this case, both Gregory and Williams were owed money by Parker. Parker agreed to assign property to Williams, in exchange for Williams agreeing to pay his debt to Gregory. See also *Tomlinson* v. *Gill* (1756) Amb. 330.

the statute.[230] Mid-century judges also began to look closely to see whether the contract entered into by the promoters was one which would be within the company's powers, holding that a company could not be bound by any contract which would have been *ultra vires*. They also held that corporations would only be bound by the contracts made by promoters if they adopted them.[231] Cottenham's decisions were not overruled, but they were widely disapproved of, and the doctrine of *ultra vires* in effect allowed courts to sidestep it. If they wanted to sue the company, suppliers had to ensure they had made a contract with the company.[232] Nor were judges keen to follow Hatherley's example in invoking ideas of the trust to bind companies to pay for work ordered by their promoters. Although there were signs throughout the mid-century, in cases not involving companies, that equity judges would find trusts in order to enforce agreements for the benefit of third parties,[233] there were doubts about how far this could be done,[234] and by the 1880s a much tougher approach was taken to this question. As Jessel MR observed in 1880, the simple fact that a person promised to pay a debt owed by his promisee to a third party did not make that third party a *cestui que trust*.[235] In order for a trust to be created, the contracting parties had to be seen to have intended to create a beneficial right in the third party through their contract.[236] As a result, late nineteenth-century equity judges confirmed that they applied the same doctrine of privity as the common law, which meant that those who did work for a company at the request of its promoters could not, when they were not parties to the articles of association, have any claim on the company for the work done.[237]

Common law courts strictly upheld the privity rule in company cases. Promoters could not be seen as the agents of the company, making contracts on its behalf, since the company had no power to ratify contracts made prior to

---

[230] *Preston* v. *Liverpool, Manchester and Newcastle-upon-Tyne Junction Railway Co* (1856) 5 H.L.C. 605 at 619.

[231] *The Caledonian Railway Co* v. *Magistrates of Helensburgh* (1856) 2 Macq HL 391. See also *Leominster Canal Navigation Co* v. *Shrewsbury and Hereford Railway* (1857) 3 K. & J. 654 at 669; *Earl of Shrewsbury* v. *North Staffordshire Railway Co* (1865) LR 1 Eq 593.

[232] Equally, if companies wished to sue third parties, who took the benefit of rights given to the company's promoter, they had to show a contractual relationship with that party. *Bagot Pneumatic Tyre Co* v. *Clipper Pneumatic Tyre Co* [1901] 1 Ch 196, [1902] 1 Ch 146 (CA), following *In re Northumberland Avenue Hotel Co* (1886) 33 Ch D 16.

[233] *Fletcher* v. *Fletcher* (1844) 4 Hare 67; *Page* v. *Cox* (1852) 10 Hare 163; *In re Flavell* (1883) 25 Ch D 89.

[234] *Colyear* v. *Countess of Mulgrave* (1836) 2 Keen 81.

[235] *In re Empress Engineering Co* (1880) 16 Ch D 125 at 127, 129 (CA).

[236] *Gandy* v. *Gandy* (1884) 30 Ch D 57 at 67 (CA).

[237] See *In re Empress Engineering Co* (1880) 16 Ch D 125 (CA), and *In re Rotherham Alum and Chemical Co* (1883) 25 Ch D 103 (CA).

its coming into existence.[238] Attempts to overcome the rule regarding ratification through clauses in articles of association authorizing payment to suppliers fell foul of the privity rule: since the articles constituted a contract between the subscribers, any third party who did not subscribe could not sue the company on the agreement contained in them.[239] Many judges were content with these rules, considering that those who undertook work in the formation of companies should look for payment to the promoters, who were well enough paid from their contracts with the companies formed. Cotton LJ likened the situation to that of a house builder selling his houses to purchasers: the builder could sue the purchaser for payment, but his labourers could only look to him.[240] It was the promoters and not the company who were to be liable on their contracts.[241] Judges were equally aware of the danger of promoters and their friends binding the company to employ them on favourable terms, in effect tying the hands of the company to be formed.[242]

At the same time, judges were prepared to ignore certain implications of the doctrine of privity. Unlike their twentieth-century counterparts, nineteenth-century judges and jurists were not troubled by the notion that a promisor who breached his contractual obligation to confer a benefit on a third party would only be liable for nominal damages when sued by the promisee. In 1880, in *Lloyds* v. *Harper*, Lush LJ commented 'I consider it to be an established rule of law that where a contract is made for A. for the benefit of B., A. can sue on the contract for the benefit of B. and recover all that B. could have recovered if the contract had been made with B. himself.'[243] To justify this, judges invoked the trust. There was mid-century authority for viewing the plaintiff as trustee. Mid-century cases showed that where court officers had taken bonds, they did so for the benefit of suitors to the court, and could therefore recover as trustees for them for breaches.[244] More importantly, in *Robertson* v. *Ware* in 1853, the charterers of a vessel, who had included a clause in their charterparty entitling their consignees to procure the homeward freight, were allowed by the court to sue as trustees on behalf of the consignees when the shipowners breached that clause.[245] In *Lloyds*

---

[238] See *Kelner* v. *Baxter* (1866) LR 2 CP 174; *Gunn* v. *London and Lancashire Fire Insurance Co* (1862) 12 C.B. N.S. 694. A contrary view was taken in *Spiller* v. *Paris Skating Rink Co* (1878) 7 Ch D 368, but held erroneous in *In re Empress Engineering Co* (1880) 16 Ch D 125 at 130.

[239] *Eley* v. *Positive Government Security Life Assurance Co* (1876) 1 Ex D 88.

[240] *In re Rotherham Alum and Chemical Co* (1883) 25 Ch D 103 (CA).

[241] *Scott* v. *Lord Ebury* (1867) LR 2 CP 255.

[242] See *Eley* v. *Positive Government Security Life Assurance Co* (1876) 1 Ex D 88; *Browne* v. *La Trinidad* (1887) 37 Ch D 1 (CA).

[243] *Lloyds* v. *Harper* (1880) 16 Ch D 290 at 321 (CA).

[244] *Lamb* v. *Vice* (1840) 6 M. & W. 467; *Stansfeld* v. *Hellawell* (1852) 7 Exch. 373.

[245] *Robertson* v. *Ware* (1853) 8 Exch. 299.

v. *Harper*, Fry J. therefore explained that where a contract was made for the benefit of a third party, there was an equity in the contracting party to sue for that
party and he could be treated as a trustee for that purpose.[246] The court here
was not particularly worried in looking at what was required to constitute them
as trustees: it simply took it for granted that they could be so regarded, at least
where they were expressly named in the contract.[247] The notion of trust invoked
by the courts to overcome the damages problem was thus a very loose one. It
was one which merely required the promisee to allow his name to be used in an
action, rather in the way that assignees sued in the names of their assignors.[248]
This approach was indeed endorsed in 1919 by the House of Lords.[249] But as courts
became increasingly tough on the requirements for finding a trust, so the 'black
hole' in damages caused by the rule in privity extended.

6. THEORIES OF CONSIDERATION

Pollock began his discussion of consideration by looking not at its purpose, but
at its history. Influenced by Maine, he noted that ancient law recognized only
formal contracts, and that informal ones were only recognized as exceptions,
over a period of time. In his first edition, he argued that the doctrine as it developed in the fifteenth and sixteenth centuries might have been a direct descend-
ant of the Roman concept of *causa*, which had developed in a unique form in
England (he argued) since only here had 'the common elements in the various
sets of facts which under the name of *causa* made various kinds of contracts
actionable' been generalized into a simple principle.[250] Holmes was impressed,
regarding Pollock's as the best account of consideration he had seen.[251] Holmes
shared Pollock's desire to trace the doctrine through history, and his belief that
there was nothing essential about the form in which modern contract doctrine
had descended, though the American preferred to stress the Germanic, rather

---

[246] *Lloyds* v. *Harper* (1880) 16 Ch D 290 at 309 (CA).

[247] In this case, the plaintiff had given a lease of sporting rights over his land to a lessee who in
breach of the agreement had damaged the land. But since the land was not occupied by the plaintiff and he was under no obligation to indemnify the occupier, he was held unable to recover, for he
would be under no obligation to pay the money over: *West* v. *Houghton* (1879) 4 CPD 197 at 200. In
Lloyds v. *Harper* (1880) 16 Ch D 290 at 311, James and Cotton LJJ doubted the decision, feeling that
the landlord might have been seen as trustee.

[248] See A. L. Corbin, 'Contracts for the benefit of third persons' (1930) 46 *LQR* 12–45 at 26.

[249] *Les Affréteurs Réunis S.A.* v. *Leopold Walford (London)* [1919] AC 801. The application of the
doctrine was artificial here: for the charterers were held as having contracted as trustees for the broker, even though it was the broker, who, as agent for the charterers, had negotiated the agreement.

[250] Pollock, *Contract* (1st edn, 1876), 149.

[251] M. D. Howe (ed.), *The Pollock-Holmes Letters: Correspondence of Sir Frederick Pollock and Mr
Justice Holmes 1874–1932*, 2 vols (Cambridge, 1942), i, 15.

than Roman, roots of English law. Pollock's use of history led him largely to eschew discussion of its purpose. Indeed, he argued that if Mansfield's approach in *Pillans* v. *van Mierop* had been taken 200 years earlier, English contract law might have been assimilated to Scots.[252] From the fourth edition onwards, Pollock relegated his historical discussions to an appendix which discussed the latest debates, and by the fifth edition admitted that he was 'as time goes on, rather less than more disposed to make Roman elements bear up any substantial part of the structure of common law'.[253]

Anson also believed that consideration was an essential element in contract law, though he had no theoretical explanation for it besides history. He noted that all legal systems required certain marks to be present to identify legally binding agreements, since a mere intention to create an obligation could not make one.[254] In England, this mark was supplied by consideration; but 'it is no easy matter' to explain how this came to be so. Indeed, 'so silent' was its development and 'so marked was the absence of any express authority for it' that Mansfield could question its basis.[255]

Holmes provided a fuller theoretical discussion. For him, the essence of informal contracts was that there had to be a bargain, at its root a 'relation of reciprocal conventional inducement, each for the other, between consideration and promise'. Holmes did not approve of judges hunting for artificial considerations. In his view, it was 'of the essence of consideration, that, by the terms of the agreement, it is given and accepted as the motive or inducement of the promise'.[256] Courts should ask whether parties intended something to be a consideration. Holmes was well aware that the common law also enforced gratuitous promises by deed. But he argued that the requirement of consideration 'has a foundation in good sense, or at least falls in with our common habits of thought', whereas the deed was 'a survival from an older condition of law, and is less manifestly sensible'.[257]

That Pollock also conceived of informal contracts requiring a bargain can be seen from his definition of consideration, introduced in his third edition, as being the 'price' of a promise. In editions of his work published after the turn of the twentieth century, Pollock underlined the point that English law required, for

[252] Pollock, *Contract* (1st edn, 1876), 151.
[253] Pollock, *Contract* (5th edn, 1889), 698. However, Pollock doubted the details of Holmes's theory having seen Maitland's work: F. Pollock and F. Maitland, *The History of English Law before the time of Edward I* (2nd edn, Cambridge, 1911), ii: 214.
[254] Anson, *Contract* (1st edn, 1879), 29.
[255] Anson, *Contract* (1st edn, 1879), 34; cf. 14th edn (1917) by M. L. Gwyer, 64–5.
[256] Holmes, *Common Law*, 293–4.
[257] *Ibid.*, 273.

informal contracts, 'not merely agreement or deliberate intention, but bargain'.[258]
In the editions published after the publication of both Ames's essays on consideration (with which he disagreed) and his essay on the history of assumpsit (which
he drew on), Pollock reintroduced his historical discussions into the body of
the text. The history served to make the point that 'we have both in debt and in
assumpsit the notion of some kind of value received as an element in the defendant's liability', though 'what a man chooses to bargain for must be conclusively
taken to be of some value to him'.[259]

The biggest challenge to the bargain theory at the end of the nineteenth century came from Ames's view that any 'change of position'—even the uttering
of words—would suffice. Although this theory effectively diminished consideration to vanishing point, Ames argued that only his theory could explain why
a promise had always been regarded as consideration for another promise at
common law.[260] Earlier jurists, such as Chitty, had explained that a mere promise given for a promise was backed by consideration since 'it subjects the party
to a charge and obligation which he would not otherwise have incurred'.[261] But
as Ames pointed out, this risked falling into the error Anson had identified, of
assuming the promise to be binding.[262] Since the law enforced voidable contracts
in which one party's promise was held unenforceable, he concluded that 'it is the
promise and not the legal obligation of each party that forms the consideration
for the promise of the other'.[263] The mere fact of making the promise constituted
the consideration, since the promisor was thereby performing an act he was not
obliged to perform. This, in Ames's view, explained why a promise to perform
what one was already bound to should be seen as binding. 'If B thought it sufficiently for his interest to give a counter promise in exchange for A's promise,
and the mutual agreement is open to no objections on the grounds of public policy', Ames observed, 'why should not the court give effect to this bargain as fully
as to any other?'[264] Ames's contention that consideration did not lie in the performance promised opened the way for others to argue that consideration was
wholly unnecessary. Once it was established that there had been offers accepted
by parties intending to enter into legal relations, it seemed unclear whether the

---

[258] Pollock, *Contract* (7th edn, 1902), 10. This phrase was not included in the 6th (1894) edition,
and may have been a response to Ames's new theory of consideration.

[259] Pollock, *Contract* (7th edn, 1902), 172, 176.

[260] Comyns, *Digest* (1752–7), i: 152 (tit. Assumpsit B7.)

[261] Chitty, *Contracts* (5th edn, 1853), 45.

[262] J. B. Ames, 'Two Theories of Consideration. II. Bilateral Contracts' (1899) 13 *Harvard LR* 29–42
at 31; cf. Samuel Williston, 'Consideration in Bilateral Contracts', 509.

[263] Ames, 'Two Theories of Consideration. II. Bilateral Contracts', 33.

[264] Ames, 'Two Theories of Consideration. II. Bilateral Contracts,' 39–40.

doctrine of consideration performed any additional function.[265] 'I believe that an able judge might', Clarence Ashley wrote in 1913, 'by an authoritative statement, overrule the entire doctrine, and declare that the common-law rule of consideration is not now enforced.'[266] In his view, the reality of daily life showed that gratuitous promises were upheld, for, when the requirement for consideration became too inconvenient, the courts simply 'refuse to enforce it, dodging the issue by pure fictions or by illogical and perfectly absurd reasoning'.[267]

But Pollock did not go down this road. Having read Ames,[268] he did begin to worry about how to explain why one promise could be consideration for another. He agreed that the promise itself, rather than the obligation created, was the consideration.[269] But he insisted (against Ames) that 'the value of the act does not consist in the act of promising, ... but in the assurance of the performance to which the promisor obliges himself'.[270] In 1911, he expanded the point, by noting that while 'the mere utterance of words of promise' might be regarded as 'trouble enough to be a consideration', this was 'not the nature of the business'. It was not the mere movement of lips which the parties offered and accepted. Having rejected Ames's solution, Pollock was at a loss to explain how mutual promises could be consideration for each other when 'neither of them, before it is known to be binding in law, is in itself any benefit to the promisee or burden to the promisor'.[271] This led him in the end to 'deny plainly that there is any logical

---

[265] See also A. Corbin, 'Does a pre-existing duty defeat consideration?—Recent noteworthy decisions' (1918) 27 *Yale LJ* 362–81 at 376. Discussing why return promises made a first promise binding, Corbin wrote that it was unnecessary to say the return promise was a sufficient consideration because it was a detriment: 'It is much better to answer: because the parties have expressed their mutual assent in conventional form'. According to Street, bilateral (executory) contracts were not 'based upon consideration in the sense of detriment, but ... solely upon consent, and when we say that mutual promises are considerations for each other we use the term "consideration" in the broad sense of reason, cause or equivalent': T. A. Street, *Foundations of Legal Liability*, 3 vols (Northport, NY, 1906), ii, 57.

[266] See C. D. Ashley, 'The Doctrine of Consideration, (1913) 26 *Harvard LR* 429–36 at 436. Ashley was a follower (though not a pupil) of Langdell's, and (like Ames) derived his critique from Langdell's analysis of consideration in bilateral contracts. Like Ames, he still struggled to speak the language of consideration, rather than that of intent to create legal relations. Nonetheless, the drift of his argument was evident in statements such as: 'It is contended that the two propositions, the offer and acceptance, can fertilize one another at the same instant and thus each then become an obligation', 'Consideration in Bilateral Contracts' (1915) 3 *Virginia LR* 201–13 at 206.

[267] Ashley, 'Consideration in Bilateral Contracts', 211.

[268] In his early editions, he explained that reciprocal promises could be consideration for each other, provided that the thing promised was possible and the promisor legally competent to perform it: Pollock, *Contract* (1st edn, 1876), 156.

[269] He accepted the 'masterly' views of Langdell, who defended this idea against Williston, in 'Mutual Promises as Consideration for Each Other' (1901) 14 *Harvard LR* 496–508 at 504.

[270] Pollock, *Contract* (7th edn, 1902), 183.

[271] Pollock, *Contract* (8th edn, 1911), 191.

reason, or any other reason than convenience, for holding mutual promises to be good consideration for one another'.[272] It was, he now said, 'one of the secret paradoxes of the Common Law'.[273] Pollock acknowledged the logic of Ames's position; but he saw that it led 'by a highly artificial road to the modern civilian conception that the giving and acceptance of any serious promise whatever suffice to create an obligation'.[274]

The academic debates between Williston, Langdell, and Ames on how a promise could be consideration for another promise cast serious doubts on the nature of consideration. Williston's early view, derived from Leake, which held that consideration was found in the promise of a legally binding performance, was arguably the strictest defence of a traditional view of consideration. Langdell and Ames's view that it was the promise alone which was consideration for counterpromise may have been problematic,[275] but if it was correct, then (as Ames saw) it was the mere fact of the promise which was consideration. The alternative was to argue (with Williston) that the consideration was the factual benefit which the parties had promised each other. Throughout his published work, Pollock refused to take any of the three positions, but restated the view he first outlined in his 7th edition in all his subsequent editions. Only at the end of his life in 1936 did he admit privately that the time might have come to abolish the need for consideration.[276]

While American contract law teachers debated the function of the doctrine in university law reviews, the English left it largely unquestioned. Later editions of Addison and Chitty largely ignored theoretical questions, while Anson and Pollock left consideration in place as a settled doctrine not to be uprooted. Pollock's *Law Quarterly Review* did not engage in this issue, Pollock devoting

---

[272] Pollock, *Contract* (8th edn, 1911), ix. Holmes, who regarded Ames's view as absurd, felt there was 'no answer' to Pollock's point (i, 177). W. S. Holdsworth, 'Debt, Assumpsit and Consideration' (1913) 11 *Michigan LR* 347–57, argued that a promise was only consideration for a counter promise by virtue of a positive rule of law.

[273] 30 *LQR* (1914) 129. Cf. 28 *LQR* (1912) 101.

[274] Pollock, *Contract* (9th edn, 1921), xi.

[275] According to this view, mutual promises constituted consideration, even though one party's performance could not be secured. Langdell and Ames both gave examples of cases involving promises of marriage (e.g. *Wild* v. *Harris* (1849) 7 C.B. 999), as well as discussing those involving fraud and infancy. In such cases, the mutual promises appeared valid on the face of it, although one party was allowed to give evidence to show that his promise was not in fact binding. Langdell, 'Mutual Promises', 504. See also Ames, 'Two Theories of Consideration. II. Bilateral Contracts', 33. In fact, in these cases, the unenforceable promise was not void because the obligation was void: rather, it could not be enforced because of some other vitiating factor.

[276] He wrote that '[t]he doctrine might have worked out rationally but for the rule—of obscure origin—that there must be a definite moment when the promise is exchanged for consideration'. Quoted in N. Duxbury, *Frederick Pollock and the English Juristic Tradition* (Oxford, 2004), 204.

his own contributions to occasional passing remarks in reviews. Despite having introduced English audiences to Savigny's argument that it was essential for parties to have an intention to be bound, Pollock did not develop this as an alternative to consideration.[277] The first English assault on consideration was not made until 1936.[278] In it Lord Wright rejected the old view that consideration acted as the test of contractual intention, invoking recent cases which had shown that even where consideration was present, a contract might be unenforceable if parties did not intend to enter into legal relations.[279] Despite the calls for its abolition, the doctrine survived, and twentieth-century judges and jurists continued to debate why consideration was needed and what its function might be. That they had to do so was in large part due to the fact that their Victorian and Edwardian predecessors had defended the doctrine so stoutly, but without giving it a solid theoretical grounding.

[277] The doctrine was only explored judicially after the first world war: *Balfour* v. *Balfour* [1919] 2 KB 571; *Rose and Frank Co* v. *Crompton* [1925] AC 445. Pollock mentioned the latter case in his last edition, but without altering the theory of the work.

[278] Wright, 'Ought the Doctrine of Consideration to be Abolished', 1225.

[279] *Balfour* v. *Balfour* [1919] 2 KB 571; *Rose and Frank Co* v. *Crompton* [1925] AC 445.

IV

Misrepresentation

IF the mid-Victorian generation was devoted to an idea of freedom of contract, Victorian values also deplored deception. This raised the question of how far parties entering into agreements could be protected against fraud or imposition, and how far the courts could or would ensure that one man's contractual consent had not been obtained by trickery. Courts had to tread a fine line, for the same approach was not suitable to every situation. While merchants could be trusted to look after their own interests—and did not want a legal regime which allowed buyers to escape unprofitable bargains by fixing on any minor misstatements made during negotiations—impecunious heirs and poor old men clearly needed more protection from being fleeced by opportunists. If *caveat emptor* was a principle which merchants could live happily with, was it one which was suitable for buyers of landed estates, or for widows and vicars looking for a safe joint stock investment for their savings? As the nineteenth century went on, the courts attempted to develop rules suitable for the public using them; but when doctrine which had developed in response to particular problems was generalized, it often lacked coherence.

1. DURESS AND UNDUE INFLUENCE

Both common law and equity gave some relief to parties who had suffered pre-contractual pressure through their respective doctrines of duress and undue influence. Since 'free assent' was essential, contracts were regarded as voidable if entered into by force or violence.[1] Such duress was seen as depriving a party of his free agency as much as fraud.[2] In the first half of the nineteenth century, the commonest duress cases were brought by people who had been imprisoned

---

[1] A man who acknowledged or enrolled a deed which had been procured by duress could not later avoid it: *Hamond* v. *Barker* (1588) Cro. El. 88. A similar rule applied in equity: in *Woodman* v. *Skute*, the defendant, having found the plaintiff naked in bed with his wife, threatened to cut him to pieces with an axe. The terrified plaintiff gave him a £500 security, but was later denied relief in Chancery, 'for he continued in the same mind when he was in cool blood'. *Woodman* v. *Skute* (1706) Prec. Ch. 266 sub. nom. *Woodman* v. *Skuse* (1708) Gilb. Rep. 9.

[2] M. Bacon, *A New Abridgment of the Law*, 5 vols (1736–66), ii, 155 (tit. Duress). See also Bayley J.'s comments in *Edwards* v. *Brown* (1831) 1 C. & J. 307 at 313.

for debt, and who claimed that the imprisonment had been used as a means to extort money. They invoked the long-established doctrine that deeds obtained by threats to kill, maim, or imprison could be voided. Wherever duress might be presumed, vulnerable debtors were protected. Warrants of attorney given by debtors in custody on mesne process to the creditors who arrested them would only be regarded as valid if executed in the presence of an attorney.[3] If the arrest had been at another creditor's behest, however, no attorney was required, since the imprisonment could not be regarded as the vehicle of duress.[4] These rules lost their importance with the ending of arrest on mesne process in 1838, but the courts still heard periodic cases of deeds obtained through the duress of imprisonment—as when relatives were committed to lunatic asylums to induce them to make over property—and gave relief.[5]

The common law did not regard a threat to take away or destroy property as duress.[6] The reason for this (according to Sir Edward Coke) was that such harms— unlike loss of life or limb—could be compensated for adequately in damages.[7] Despite this view, in 1733, in *Astley* v. *Reynolds*, a plaintiff, who paid a pawnbroker more interest than was legally owed in order to redeem his goods, was allowed to recover the sum overpaid in an action for money had and received, as the payment had been made by compulsion. Although the plaintiff could have recovered his goods in trover, the court held that the latter action 'would not do his business', since the plaintiff might have wanted his goods immediately.[8] The new remedy was not permitted where money had been paid to recover distrained cattle or goods, since money had and received was considered an inappropriate action to try the issues of right raised in such cases.[9] But in other cases, the courts were happy to allow it.

In the nineteenth century, judges had to figure out a way of making the rule in *Astley* v. *Reynolds* cohere with the view of duress set out by Coke and Sheppard. Parke B. suggested the following:

[3] *Finn* v. *Hutchinson* (1702) 2 Ld. Raym. 797; *Holcombe* v. *Wade* (1765) 3 Burr. 1792. See also *Gillman* v. *Hill* (1774) 1 Cowp. 141.

[4] *Charlton* v. *Fletcher* (1791) 4 T.R. 433; *Smith* v. *Burlton* (1801) 1 East 241. Equally, where the warrant of attorney was executed by debtors in gaol on final process—where the imprisonment followed a judgment—an attorney was only required if the debtor gave a warrant for more than what was really due: *Fell* v. *Riley* (1775) 1 Cowp. 281; *Birch* v. *Sharland* (1787) 1 T. R. 715.

[5] *Cumming* v. *Ince* (1847) 11 Q.B. 112. Contrast *Biffin* v. *Bignell* (1862) 7 H. & N. 877, where a husband's threat to have his wife recommitted was not held to amount to duress.

[6] W. Sheppard, *The Touch-stone of Common Assurances* (5th edn by E. Hilliard, 1784), 58–9.

[7] E. Coke, *The Second Part of the Institutes of the Laws of England* (1797), 483.

[8] *Astley* v. *Reynolds* (1733) 2 Str. 915 at 916. See also the observations of Lord Kenyon in *Fulham* v. *Down*, cited in *Taylor* v. *M'Viccar* (1806) 6 Esp. 27n.

[9] In these cases, the plaintiff was expected to recover in replevin: *Lindon* v. *Hooper* (1776) 1 Cowp. 414; *Knibbs* v. *Hall* (1794) 1 Esp. 84; *Gulliver* v. *Cosens* (1845) 1 C.B. 788. But contrast *Green* v. *Duckett* (1883) 11 QBD 275.

If my goods have been wrongfully detained, and I pay money simply to obtain them again, that being paid under a species of duress or constraint, may be recovered back; but if, while my goods are in possession of another person, I make a binding agreement to pay a certain sum of money, and to receive them back, that cannot be avoided on the ground of duress.[10]

A party who promised to pay money to obtain his goods would later be held to his promise; while one who simply paid money would be able to recover it. The idea behind this proposition—that a contract was a sign of consent, which precluded duress—was reiterated in 1841 in *Skeate* v. *Beale*. This was a dispute arising out of a distress, but here it was the party making the distraint, who had been promised money, who sued, rather than the party seeking to recover his goods. Denman CJ's judgment, rejecting the defence of duress of goods, was couched in general terms: 'the fear that goods may be taken or injured does not deprive any one of his free agency who possesses that ordinary degree of firmness which the law requires all to exert'.[11]

Throughout the mid-century, the courts continued to allow parties to recover money paid under duress of goods. Typical examples included those where railways refused to deliver goods unless additional charges were paid, or where lawyers retained title deeds in order to force clients to pay more. These were not cases where plaintiffs were denied other remedies (such as trover or detinue), but they were distinguished by the fact that the party had paid under protest and not made a voluntary agreement, or promise to pay—or, in other words, a contract.[12] The crucial question for the courts was thus to determine whether payments had been made voluntarily, for money not paid voluntarily—either as a result of a mistake or from duress—could be recovered in an action for money had and received.[13]

Equity policed pre-contractual pressure through the doctrine of undue influence. It did this to protect vulnerable parties who were at risk of being taken advantage of. The doctrine was applied primarily where large gifts were made (whether testamentary or *inter vivos*), and the donor and donee were so situated that undue

---

[10] *Atlee* v. *Backhouse* (1838) 3 M. & W. 633 at 642, 650. See also his comment in argument in *Parker* v. *Bristol and Exeter Railway Co* (1851) 6 Exch. 702 at 705, 'The mere duress of the goods does not avoid a contract; but where a person has to pay a certain sum in order to recover his goods, such payment is involuntary.'

[11] *Skeate* v. *Beale* (1841) Ad. & El. 983 at 990. He also said that the defendant here could not have recovered the money he had already paid. This was not to criticise *Astley* v. *Reynolds*, but to follow the earlier distraint cases.

[12] *Ashmole* v. *Wainwright* (1842) 2 Q.B. 837; *Wakefield* v. *Newbon* (1844) 6 Q.B. 276 at 281; *Parker* v. *Great Western Railway* (1844) 7 M. & G. 253. Contrast *Wilson* v. *Ray* (1839) 10 Ad. & El. 82.

[13] See e.g. *Valpy* v. *Manley* (1845) 1 C.B. 594. This view was reiterated in *Maskell* v. *Horner* [1915] 3 KB 106.

influence might have been exerted. Just as equity would not overturn contracts merely for being unequal, so it did not object to the most improvident donations possible, provided advantage had not been taken of the donor.[14] Where the parties were in a confidential relationship, equity required the recipient to show that the gift had been entirely voluntary.[15] The burden of proof lay on the party benefiting to show that the grantor 'fully understood what he was doing; that no artifice or contrivance was made use of to induce him to do the act complained of, and that [he] had competent means of forming an independent judgment'.[16] The donor had to have obtained independent advice prior to making the gift.[17] Where parties were in such a relationship, the law presumed undue influence had been exerted on a rule of public policy, to prevent such relationships being abused.[18] This was a rule as relevant in the world of commerce—where abuses of an agency relationship were to be policed—as in the world of gifts between friends.

Equity was also willing to undo contracts which had been obtained by undue influence where there was no confidential relationship. The Chancery had long set aside contracts made with expectant heirs who sold their inheritance at undervalue in order to get ready money. In doing so, it aimed to protect not only naive young heirs, who might be taken advantage of, but also the family as a whole, whose fortune might be lost in this way by sons seduced to a dissolute life.[19] Where the family was unaware of the transaction, equity would set aside a contract with an expectant heir on the grounds of inadequacy of price alone, with the onus being put on the purchaser to show he had paid a fair price.[20] The Chancery's very strict rule here was modified in 1867 by legislation which enacted that sales of reversions otherwise 'bona fide and without fraud or unlawful dealing' could not be set aside merely for being undervalue.[21] But in 1873 Lord Selborne held that this legislation did not prevent the courts from considering undervalue as a material element in determining whether there had been an 'unconscientious use of power' by one party over another. Quoting Lord Hardwicke's view that a presumption that this

[14] See the comments of Lord Commissioner Wilmot in *Bridgeman v. Green* (1757) Wilm. 58 at 60–2. See also *Nantes v. Corrock* 2 Ves. Jun. Supp. 159.
[15] *Huguenin v. Baseley* (1807) 14 Ves. 273 at 300.
[16] *Savery v. King* (1856) 5 H.L.C. 627 at 657; *Billage v. Southee* (1852) 9 Hare 534.
[17] *Harvey v. Mount* (1845) 8 Beav. 439; *Rhodes v. Bate* (1865) LR 1 Ch App 252 at 257.
[18] *Huguenin v. Baseley* (1807) 14 Ves. 273 at 300; *Allcard v. Skinner* (1887) 36 Ch Div 145, 171. Cf. *Newman v. Payne* (1793) 2 Ves. 199; *Harris v. Tremenheere* (1808) 15 Ves. 34; *Norton v. Relly* (1764) 2 Eden 286.
[19] See M. Lobban, 'Contractual Fraud in Law and Equity, c. 1750–c.1850' (1997) 17 *OJLS* 441–76 at 451–2; *Twisleton v. Griffith* (1716) 1 P. Wms. 310; *Cole v. Gibbons* (1734) 3 P. Wms. 290.
[20] *Peacock v. Evans* (1809) 16 Ves. 512; *Gowland v. De Faria* (1810) 17 Ves. 20; *Earl of Aldborough v. Trye* (1840) 7 Cl. & F. 436; *Edwards v. Burt* (1852) 2 De G. M. & G. 55; *Jones v. Ricketts* (1862) 31 Beav. 130.
[21] 31 Vict. c. 4.

had occurred could arise from 'the circumstances or conditions of the parties contracting', he held that in such a case 'the transaction cannot stand unless the person claiming the benefit of it is able to repel the presumption by contrary evidence, proving it to have been in point of fact fair, just and reasonable'.[22]

In cases not involving expectant heirs, while inadequacy of price alone was no ground for setting aside a purchase,[23] the Chancery would do so if it was shown that the vendor was simple-minded[24] or poor and distressed,[25] and thus incapable of taking care of his own interests. Eighteenth-century courts inferred that the buyer had taken undue advantage of the seller from the inadequacy of price coupled to poverty, surprise, or weakness of mind. Where a 'party is in a situation, in which he is not a free agent, and is not equal to protecting himself, this Court will protect him'.[26] In such cases, once the party seeking to set aside the transaction had shown that there were vitiating factors, it lay on the other party to show that independent advice had been taken. Some nineteenth-century judges, such as Stuart VC, were prepared to intervene even if the purchaser had not 'used any arts to induce the vendor' into the contract, if it was shown there was no 'reasonable degree of equality between the contracting parties'.[27] Similarly, in 1888, Kay J. held that a court of equity would set aside a purchase from a poor and ignorant man made at considerable undervalue, if he had been given no independent advice, unless the purchaser could show that the purchase was fair.[28]

There was some debate in the mid-century as to when the courts could presume undue influence, casting the burden of proof on the recipient to show none had been used. Transactions between parties in certain fiduciary relationships were clearly frowned on. Equity was particularly suspicious of purchases by trustees from their *cestuis que trustent*. For such sales to be upheld, the trustee relationship had either to be dissolved and the parties put back into the position of being strangers to each other or the trustee had to have been given an express authority by the *cestui*.[29] Equity was similarly suspicious of purchases by solicitors,[30]

---

[22] *Earl of Aylesford* v. *Morris* (1873) LR 8 Ch App 484 at 490–1, quoting *Earl of Chesterfield* v. *Janssen* (1750–1) 2 Ves. Sr. 125 at 157.

[23] *Griffith* v. *Spratley* (1787) 1 Cox CC 383.

[24] *Longmate* v. *Ledger* (1860) 2 Giff. 157 at 165, 163.

[25] *Evans* v. *Llewellin* (1787) 1 Cox C.C. 333; *Wood* v. *Abrey* (1818) 3 Madd. 417; *Clark* v. *Malpas* (1862) 4 De G. F. & J. 401; *Baker* v. *Monk* (1864) 4 De G. J. & S. 388; *Fry* v. *Lane* (1888) 40 Ch D 312 at 321.

[26] *Evans* v. *Llewellin* (1787) 1 Cox C.C. 333 at 340.

[27] *Longmate* v. *Ledger* (1860) 2 Giff. 157 at 165, 163. Contrast *Harrison* v. *Guest* (1855) 6 De G. M. & G. 424, where a poor vendor rejected the chance to obtain advice.

[28] *Fry* v. *Lane* (1888) 40 Ch D 312 at 322.

[29] See *Whichcote* v. *Lawrence* (1798) 1 Ves. Jun. Supp. 422; *Ex p Lacey* (1801) 6 Ves. 625 at 626; *Coles* v. *Trecothick* (1804) 9 Ves. 234 at 246; *Morse* v. *Royal* (1806) 12 Ves. 355; *Sanderson* v. *Walker* (1807) 13 Ves. 601; *Downes* v. *Grazebrook* (1817) 3 Mer. 200 at 208.

[30] *Gibson* v. *Jeyes* (1801) 6 Ves. 266; *Wood* v. *Downes* (1811) 18 Ves. 120.

stewards, or agents and those in analogous positions.[31] An agent could buy property from his principal only if the latter was fully informed and the transaction was fair.[32] An agent could also sell his own property to his principal. However, if there had not been a full disclosure, the principal could rescind the contract on discovering the agent's interest, on restoring the property to the agent.[33] A presumption of undue influence was also raised when parties were in other fiduciary relationships recognized in law, where one was in a superior position to exert control over the other, such as that between parent and child,[34] guardian and ward,[35] and spiritual adviser and pupil.[36]

There was some uncertainty over whether the presumption extended to other situations. In 1834, Lord Brougham distinguished between three kinds of relations. First, where the parties stood in fiduciary relationships known to the law (as guardians, attorneys, or trustees), the burden of proof lay on the party benefiting to show 'that he has dealt with the other party [...] exactly as a stranger would have done, taking no advantage of his influence or knowledge'. In such cases, lack of independent advice was alone a ground for setting aside the transaction. Secondly, where the parties were in a confidential relationship, but one 'of a sort less known and definite', then the law's jealousy was diminished: 'A confidential adviser—one who has been generally consulted in the management of the person's affairs, though he may also have been employed specially in his business—does not lie under the same suspicion with an attorney or a steward,

---

[31] They included the keeper of a lunatic asylum: *Wright* v. *Proud* (1806) 13 Ves. 136, or medical advisors: *Billage* v. *Southee* (1852) 9 Hare 534.

[32] See *Lowther* v. *Lowther* (1806) 13 Ves. Jun 95; *Murphy* v. *O'Shea* (1845) 2 J. & Lat. 422, *Dunne* v. *English* (1874) LR 18 Eq. 524. Even if the principal was perfectly willing to sell, the agent still had to show that the transaction had been fair: see *Dally* v. *Wonham* (1863) 33 Beav. 154. Unlike cases involving trustees, the positive assent of the principal did not have to be shown.

[33] Moreover, since an agent was supposed to work for the exclusive benefit of his principal, he had to disgorge any profits he made in the course of the agency. Thus, where he bought goods in the market and sold them on to his principal, the agent had to hand over any profit made on the transaction, even if the second transaction had been perfectly fair: see *Massey* v. *Davies* (1794) 2 Ves. Jr. 318; *York and North Midland Railway* v. *Hudson* (1845) 16 Beav. 485; *Benson* v. *Heathorn* (1842) Y. & C.C.C. 326. See also *Aberdeen Railway Co* v. *Blaikie Brothers* (1854) 1 Macq. 451 at 471.

[34] See *Carpenter* v. *Heriot* (1759) 1 Eden 338; *Young* v. *Peachy* (1741) 2 Atk. 254; *Wycherley* v. *Wycherley* (1763) 2 Eden 175; *Archer* v. *Hudson* (1844) 7 Beav. 551; *Savery* v. *King* (1856) 5 H.L.C. 627; J. Story, *Commentaries on Equity Jurisprudence as Administered in England and America*, 2 vols (Boston, Mass., 1836) § 310, p. 306.

[35] *Hylton* v. *Hylton* (1754) 2 Ves. Sr. 547; *Hatch* v. *Hatch* (1804) 9 Ves. 292.

[36] *Norton* v. *Relly* (1764) 2 Eden 286; *Huguenin* v. *Baseley* (1807) 14 Ves. 273; *Nottidge* v. *Prince* (1860) 2 Giff. 246; *Allcard* v. *Skinner* (1887) 36 Ch D 181; *Morley* v. *Loughnan* (1893) 1 Ch 736. R. J. Pothier (*Traité des Donations entre Vifs* (s 1, art II, § VIII) in *Oeuvres de Pothier* 18 vols (Paris, 1821–4), xiii: 246 had said that spiritual advisers could not take gifts from those they advised. See also C. Smith, 'Allcard v Skinner (1887)' in C. Mitchell and P. Mitchell (eds), *Landmark Cases in the Law of Restitution* (Oxford, 2006), 183–211.

or anyone who has a general management.' In such cases, 'care must be taken that no undue advantage shall be made of the influence thus acquired'; but at the same time the party benefiting 'shall not be put upon his defence upon vague suggestions' and 'shall not be assumed to have swerved from the right path without sufficient and positive proof'. Thirdly, where there was no confidential relationship, then the gift was good unless the donor was misled by some fraud, including misrepresentation or suppression of facts, or if he was of unsound mind when the deed was made.[37] Brougham's test gave greatest protection to a limited number of defined fiduciary relationships, but allowed gifts or contracts procured in other situations to be set aside on proof of undue advantage being taken.

By contrast, Sir John Romilly took the view that whenever a large pecuniary gift was questioned, the burden lay on the beneficiary to show that the gift was voluntary, and that the donor fully understood what he was doing. He worried that 'a principle of high morality'[38] might be 'frittered away by technicality' if the court only policed the recognized fiduciary relationships.[39] Romilly's view was not adopted. White and Tudor's *Leading Cases in Equity* noted that in the case of transactions with a stranger, the onus of proof to show that it had been obtained by fraud or undue influence lay on the donor.[40] In 1881, in a case on a voluntary deed, Kay J. held that where a man of full age and sound mind denuded himself of his property and later sought to set it aside, the onus lay on him to give a 'substantial reason' for setting it aside.[41] Romilly's view was also rejected by the textbook writers.[42]

Nor did the courts accept Brougham's idea that, in cases where the relationship did not fall within a recognized category, gifts or contracts would only be set aside if the donor proved undue influence. Numerous transactions were set aside where confidential relationships existed outside the defined 'fiduciary' ones. In 1835, Shadwell VC gave relief against an agreement between a medical attendant and his client, whereby the latter promised £125,000 after his death, treating the relationship as akin to that between attorney and client.[43] Upholding the decision, Cottenham LC refused to ground his judgment on a ruling that this relationship belonged to a defined class to be watched with jealousy, since

---

[37] *Hunter* v. *Atkins* (1834) 3 Myl. & K. 113 at 133–40.

[38] *Cooke* v. *Lamotte* (1851) 15 Beav. 234 at 241. See also *Hoghton* v. *Hoghton* (1852) 15 Beav. 278 at 298–300; *Cobbett* v. *Brock* (1855) 20 Beav. 524 at 530; *Sharp* v. *Leach* (1862) 31 Beav. 491. Stuart VC took the same approach in *Anderson* v. *Elsworth* (1861) 3 Giff. 154 at 169.

[39] *Hobday* v. *Peters (No. 1)* (1860) 28 Beav. 349 at 351. Cf. Lord Hatherley's view in *Phillips* v. *Mullings* (1871) LR 7 Ch App 244 at 246.

[40] F. T. White and O. D. Tudor, *A Selection of Leading Cases in Equity* 2 vols (2nd edn, 1858), ii: 487, citing *Villers* v. *Beaumont* (1682) 1 Vern. C.C. 100.

[41] *Henry* v. *Armstrong* (1881) 18 Ch D 668 at 669.

[42] F. Pollock, *Principles of Contract at Law and in Equity* (6th edn, 1894), 584.

[43] *Dent* v. *Bennett* (1835) 7 Sim. 539.

this would run a risk of fettering the discretion of the court in exercising this jurisdiction. Adopting Samuel Romilly's words, he held 'the relief stands upon a general principle, applying to all the variety of relations in which dominion may be exercised by one person over another'.[44] Similarly, in 1852, Sir George Turner (in another medical case) said that the court's jurisdiction 'is founded on the principle of correcting abuses of confidence [… and] it ought to be applied, whatever may be the nature of the confidence reposed or the relation of the parties between whom it has subsisted'. In his view, the 'defined' relationships were 'merely instances of the application of the principle'.[45] In these cases, the transactions which were set aside were large improvident ones; but in 1865, the Lord Justices refused to set aside a trifling gift to a professional adviser, holding that in such cases some *mala fides* had to be shown.[46]

One year later, Chelmsford LC described as 'fiduciary' a relationship between two cousins, where one was asked by the other to advise on how to deal with his debts. The Lord Chancellor held that a 'fiduciary' relationship had been established between them:

Wherever two persons stand in such a relation that, while it continues, confidence is necessarily reposed by one, and the influence which naturally grows out of that confidence is possessed by the other, and this confidence is abused, or the influence is exerted in order to obtain an advantage at the expense of the confiding party, the person so availing himself of his position will not be permitted to retain the advantage.[47]

This was again to suggest that, once the donor had shown that a confidential relationship existed, the onus of proof shifted to the donee.

In 1887, the Court of Appeal attempted to restate the rules in *Allcard* v. *Skinner*. In this case, a woman who had joined a religious sisterhood which bound its members to poverty and obedience sought to undo a transfer she had made to it of her property, after she left the order. Miss Allcard's decision to give her money derived from her willing submission to the rules of the order: she had not been imposed upon to make over her money. However, she had not received any independent advice before doing so, and the rules of the order forbad her from seeking such advice. The Court of Appeal held that, in such a situation, the court could offer relief.

The court distinguished between two classes of cases. In the first, the gift came about as a result of 'influence expressly used by the donee for the purpose'.[48] In

[44] *Dent* v. *Bennett* (1839) 4 Myl. & Cr. 269 at 277. Romilly's point was made in *Huguenin* v. *Baseley* (1807) 14 Ves. 273.

[45] *Billage* v. *Southee* (1852) 9 Hare 534 at 540.

[46] *Rhodes* v. *Bate* (1865) LR 1 Ch App 252.

[47] *Tate* v. *Williamson* (1866) LR 2 Ch App 55 at 61.

[48] *Allcard* v. *Skinner* (1887) 36 Ch D 145 at 171, per Cotton LJ.

the formulation of Lindley LJ, in these situations 'there has been some unfair and improper conduct, some coercion from outside, some form of cheating, and generally, though not always, some personal advantage obtained by a donee placed in some close and confidential relation to the donor'. This had not occurred in Miss Allcard's case. In the second, the relation between the parties was such as to raise a presumption that the donee was in a position to exert influence. For Lindley, this occurred where 'the position of the donor has been such that it has been the duty of the donee to advise the donor, or even to manage his property for him'. In these cases, the donee had the burden of showing that the gift had not been obtained by undue influence, and that the donor had been independently advised.[49] Stressing that the plaintiff had been 'absolutely in the power' of the defendants, he held that Miss Allcard fell into this class. Lindley's formulation suggested that it was not enough for the parties to be in any close relationship for the presumption to arise: rather, the donee had to be in a position to exert power over the donor, or have control of her affairs. If this suggested that Lindley had in mind only the recognized fiduciary relationships—which included religious superiors—this notion was dispelled by Wright J. in 1893, when he suggested that the rule would embrace relationships where one person allowed another to exercise dominion over him.[50] Later editions of *White and Tudor* summarized the rules in this way: '[w]here a relation of confidence is shown to exist, or is presumed from the position of the parties, then the law on grounds of public policy presumes that the gift was the effect of influence induced by these relations', with the burden being thrown on the donee to show the donor did not act under the influence. Listing the 'special relations', they added that it was not exhaustive, but intended for illustration. Where no special confidential relationship existed, 'fraud or undue influence *must be proved* against the donee'.[51]

As with common law duress, it was settled in the nineteenth century that such contracts were voidable and not void; and that they could therefore be affirmed by subsequent conduct.[52] The right to rescind could be lost through positive affirmation or delay such as to amount to proof of acquiescence, as occurred in Miss Allcard's case. The right to rescind could also be lost if third party rights intervened. Equity's protection of those who had parted with their property as a result of undue influence was not as strong as its protection of those who had been defrauded. It had been settled in the eighteenth century that where a gift had

---

[49] *Allcard* v. *Skinner* (1887) 36 Ch D 145 at 181. He cited as authority *Huguenin* v. *Baseley* (1807) 14 Ves. 273, where the plaintiff had given the defendant control over her affairs.

[50] *Morley* v. *Loughnan* [1893] 1 Ch 736 at 752.

[51] White and Tudor, *A Selection of Leading Cases in Equity* 2 vols (7th edn by T. Snow and W. F. Phillpotts, 1897), 269, 281. As an example, see *Williams* v. *Bayley* (1866) LR 1 HL 200 at 212.

[52] *Allcard* v. *Skinner* (1887) 36 Ch D 145 at 186.

originated in fraud, no one could claim under the gift, even if they were not party to or aware of the fraud. For it would be against conscience to retain a benefit derived from the fraud of another. Those who acquired such tainted property by gift or inheritance had to restore it.[53] But these rules did not apply where the property had been acquired for value from someone who had been induced to sell it by the undue influence of another. Here, the transaction could only be impeached if the purchaser had notice, actual or constructive,[54] of the influence.[55]

2. FRAUD AT COMMON LAW

Besides seeking to police pre-contractual pressure, both common law and equity sought to prevent frauds. At common law, the rules regarding fraud were developed primarily in the context of commercial sales. In this area, courts had long supported the principle of *caveat emptor*, for lawyers were no keener than businessmen to allow contracts to be avoided on the basis of statements made during negotiations. Although there was a duty not to defraud or deceive, there was no duty to bargain in good faith.[56] Moreover, purchasers were expected to use their experience of the world to tell them which kinds of statement could be relied on and which could not.[57] Courts therefore distinguished between misrepresentations which were material and induced parties into the contract, and those which were either so vague that they should not have been relied on,[58] or which were too trivial to amount to a substantial misdescription.[59] The misstatement had actually to have been relied upon by the other party,[60] for if the purchaser relied on his own judgment, then he could obtain no relief.

In the sale of goods, the principle of *caveat emptor* was taken to mean that a vendor had a duty only to disclose latent defects of which he was aware. Early nineteenth-century courts translated this duty into an implied warranty, where a fraudulent purpose need not be proved. But if there were patent defects which a

---

[53] In *Bridgeman* v. *Green* (1757) Wilm. 58 at 65, Wilmot CJ said, '[l]et the hand receiving [the benefit] be ever so chaste, yet if it comes through a corrupt polluted channel, the obligation of restitution will follow it'. See also *Huguenin* v. *Baseley* (1807) 14 Ves. 273 at 289; *Collett* v. *Preston* (1852) 15 Beav. 103. See also Turner's own comments in *Russell* v. *Jackson* (1852) 10 Hare 204 at 212.

[54] Notice could be constructive if the purchaser had sufficient knowledge to have induced a reasonable man to make further inquiries. See *Kennedy* v. *Green* (1834) 3 Myl. & K. 699; *Penny* v. *Watts* (1849) 1 M. & G. 150; *Ware* v. *Lord Egmont* (1854) 4 De G. M. and G. 460.

[55] In such cases, the burden of proof lay on the seeking to set aside the transaction to show that there had been undue influence: *Blackie* v. *Clark* (1852) 15 Beav. 595.

[56] See the comments of Mansfield CJ in *Vernon* v. *Keyes* (1812) 4 Taunt. 488 at 493.

[57] See Tindal CJ's comments in *Shrewsbury* v. *Blount* (1841) 2 M. & G. 475 at 504.

[58] *Trower* v. *Newcome* (1813) 3 Mer. 704; *Jennings* v. *Broughton* (1854) 5 De G. M. & G. 126.

[59] *Johnson* v. *Smart* (1860) 2 Giff. 151.

[60] *Lysney* v. *Selby* (1705) 2 Ld. Raym. 1118 at 1120; *Dobell* v. *Stevens* (1825) 3 B. & C. 623 at 626.

buyer could see, the vendor had no duty to draw attention to them. This principle was taken to controversial lengths in 1862, in *Horsfall* v. *Thomas*, where the purchaser of a cannon refused to pay for it, after it exploded thanks to a defect in the chamber, which had been covered with a metal plug. Quoting a letter from the plaintiffs asserting that the gun was made of the best metal and had no defects the vendors were aware of, Thomas claimed he had been defrauded. However, the Exchequer was unsympathetic. Since he had not inspected the gun, he could not have been misled. Nor was there a duty to disclose. According to Bramwell B., it would be no fraud for a vendor to say there were no weak points in a cannon, when he knew of one, if it was something which could be seen by the purchaser.[61] If the extent of Bramwell's statement was controversial, the idea that the plaintiff had to have been deceived was generally accepted.[62]

While there was no general duty to disclose in English contract law, the rule developed that parties who had made certain statements of fact—in all innocence—had to correct them, if circumstances changed. As Lord Cranworth put it in 1852, '[i]f after the error has been discovered, the party who has innocently made the incorrect representation suffers the other party to continue in error and act on the belief that no mistake has been made, this, from the time of the discovery, becomes, in the contemplation of this Court, a fraudulent misrepresentation, even though it was not so originally'.[63] Nor did the representee have a duty to check facts which were asserted. In *Redgrave* v. *Hurd* in 1881, the Court of Appeal, developing principles set out in *Attwood* v. *Small*, held that it was no defence to say that the representee was given the means of checking the accuracy of statements made, and had failed to do so. Rather, the defendant had to show that the representee actually knew facts which revealed the statement to be untrue, and did not rely on the statement in entering into the contract.[64] Indeed, while eighteenth-century courts had expected buyers to notice where exaggerated statements were made,[65] it was accepted that a representee only had a duty to check for himself if there was something to raise his suspicions.[66]

---

[61] *Horsfall* v. *Thomas* (1862) 1 H. & C. 90. Cockburn CJ disapproved of the decision in *Smith* v. *Hughes* (1871) LR 6 QB 597 at 605. The case was cited in contract law textbooks, but was generally ignored in nineteenth-century case law.

[62] See *London General Omnibus Co* v. *Lavell* [1902] 1 Ch D 135 (CA).

[63] *Reynell* v. *Sprye* (1851) 1 De G. M. & G. 656 at 709. See also Turner LJ's judgment in *Traill* v. *Baring* (1864) 4 De G. J. & S. 318; *Davies* v. *London and Provincial Marine Insurance Co* (1878) 8 Ch D 469, 475 (both of which were insurance cases). However, in *Arkwright* v. *Newbold* (1881) 17 Ch D 301 (CA) at 325, Cotton LJ doubted whether this applied to directors who discovered new facts after a prospectus had been issued.

[64] *Redgrave* v. *Hurd* (1881) 20 Ch D 1.

[65] *Lowndes* v. *Lane* (1789) 2 Cox 363.

[66] *Rawlins* v. *Wickham* (1858) 3 De G. & J. 304.

If there had been an actionable fraud, the buyer was permitted to rescind the contract, once he became aware of it, whether the statement had become a term of the contract or not,[67] and sue for money had and received or trover.[68] However, this right was lost if the innocent party had made a clear election to affirm the contract,[69] or if he was no longer in a position to restore the goods, making a complete *restitutio in integrum*.[70] Where the right to rescind was lost, the only remedy remaining was an action for damages in the tortious action of deceit. In contractual actions, if a party claimed there was a mere misrepresentation without fraud, parol evidence would not be allowed to vary the written contract.[71] But in cases where fraud was alleged, evidence could be given of deceitful representations which were not embodied in the contract.[72] Positive deception stood at the root of the action. Since the gist of the action was that the innocent party was 'draw[n] ... into a snare',[73] it had to be shown that there had been an intention to deceive.[74]

Early nineteenth-century courts regarded misrepresentations as either fraudulent or innocent. A seller would be liable for fraudulent concealment or misrepresentation,[75] but not for inaccurate statements honestly made, even if he could have discovered the truth.[76] Juries were to consider whether the party himself believed the statement to be true, not whether he had been negligent in making a statement others would not believe was true.[77] A malicious motive was not necessary in an action of deceit. It was sufficient if the defendant said something which was false to his knowledge.[78] This kind of fraud was sometimes dubbed 'legal fraud' to distinguish it from the more popular sense of a corrupt motive.[79]

---

[67] *Ferguson* v. *Carrington* (1829) 9 B. & C. 59.

[68] *Emanuel* v. *Dane* (1812) 3 Camp. 299.

[69] If no election was made, then the issue remained open until such time as he had notice of the fraud: *Clough* v. *London and North West Railway Co* (1871) LR 7 Ex 26, 34–5. But it was also noted that lapse of time might be taken as evidence of an intention to affirm.

[70] As Crompton J. put it in 1858, '[i]f you are fraudulently induced to buy a cake you may return it and get back your price; but you cannot both eat your cake and return your cake': *Clarke* v. *Dickson* (1858) E. B. & E. 148, 152–4. See also *Davidson* v *Tulloch* (1860) 2 LTR 97 at 98.

[71] See *Flinn* v. *Tobin* (1829) M. & M. 367; *Pickering* v. *Dowson* (1813) 4 Taunt. 779 at 786.

[72] *Dobell* v. *Stevens* (1825) 3 B. & C. 623.

[73] *Foster* v. *Charles* (1830) 6 Bing. 396 at 403.

[74] *Langridge* v. *Levy* (1837) 2 M. & W. 519 at 531.

[75] For a concealment case, see *Schneider* v. *Heath* (1813) 3 Camp. 506.

[76] See *Early* v. *Garrett* (1829) 9 B. & C. 928 at 932. See also *Bree* v. *Holbech* (1781) 2 Doug. 654.

[77] Although some mid-century judges spoke of the defendant being absolved if he made statements 'under a belief, reasonably well-grounded, of their truth' (*Shrewsbury* v. *Blount* (1841) 2 M. & G. 475 at 507), juries were not required to look at how well grounded the defendant's belief was, but whether he in fact held it.

[78] *Foster* v. *Charles* (1830) 6 Bing. 396, 7 Bing. 105; *Corbett* v. *Brown* (1831) 8 Bing. 33.

[79] *Polhill* v. *Walter* (1832) 3 B. & Ad. 114 at 123.

A number of unsuccessful attempts were made from the late eighteenth century onwards to modify the position that damages could only be awarded in cases of actual fraud. In *Haycraft* v. *Creasy*, Lord Kenyon suggested that if a person affirmed something as true which he did not know to be so, it was fraudulent, 'not perhaps in that sense which affixes the stain of moral turpitude on the mind of the party, but falling within the notion of legal fraud'.[80] This was to hold that a person making a positive assertion warranted the truth of his statements. Kenyon's view did not prevail in his era; but in the 1840s, a further attempt was made to modify the law, to give relief for non-fraudulent misrepresentations. In *Cornfoot* v. *Fowke*, during negotiations for the lease of a furnished house, the plaintiff's agent had told the defendant that there was nothing objectionable about it. In fact, as the plaintiff himself (though not his agent) knew, it was next to a brothel. Since the agent had acted in good faith, speaking from his own knowledge, while the plaintiff had never made any statements about the house, neither of them had made assertions of fact which were false to their knowledge. Yet the defendant—who refused to perform the agreement—had clearly been misled. In a dissenting judgment, Abinger CB admitted that neither the plaintiff nor his agent had committed any kind of moral fraud. But he did not feel this was decisive. Just as it was not necessary to prove a *scienter* in actions for breach of warranty, he said, so it was not necessary in cases of deceit to show actual knowledge.[81] For Abinger, what was known to the principal must also be held to be known to the agent.[82] He concluded that 'the concealment or misrepresentation, whether by principal or agent, by design or by mistake, of a material fact, however innocently made, avoids the contract on the ground of a legal fraud'.[83] According to this view, moral turpitude was not needed in deceit.[84] By contrast, the majority said that while the principal would have been bound by any contract entered into by his agent, he could only be bound by non-contractual misrepresentations if the fraud could be brought home to him, or if there had been fraud in the agent, for which Parke B. admitted he would be responsible.[85] As Parke B. saw it, if both principal and agent were innocent of fraud, they could not be guilty of fraud when combined.

---

[80] *Haycraft* v. *Creasy* (1801) 2 East 92 at 103, developing the rule in *Pasley* v *Freeman* (1789) 3 T.R.51, discussed below, p. 1040.

[81] *Williamson* v. *Allison* (1802) 2 East 446.

[82] Authority for this was sought in the banking case of *Willis* v. *Bank of England* (1835) 4 Ad. & El. 21.

[83] *Cornfoot* v. *Fowke* (1840) 6 M. & W. 358 at 379.

[84] In *Moens* v. *Heyworth* (1842) 10 M. & W. 147 at 155, he stated, 'In the case of a contract for the sale of a public-house, if the seller represent by mistake that the house realised more than in fact it did, he would be defrauding the purchaser, and deceiving him; but that might arise from his not having kept proper books, or from non attention to his affairs'.

[85] *Cornfoot* v. *Fowke* (1840) 6 M. & W. 358 at 362. There was some discussion of *Hern* v. *Nichols* 1 Salk. 289, where a merchant was held liable (on a contract) for the deceit of his factor in this case.

Although rejected by the Exchequer, Abinger's view that moral fraud was not needed was followed in the Queen's Bench. In *Fuller* v. *Wilson*, Lord Denman held that the principal and agent were to be completely identified, and that 'whether there was moral fraud or not, if the purchaser was actually deceived in his bargain, the law will relieve him from it'.[86] But the Exchequer judges held to their view. In *Taylor* v. *Ashton* in 1843, Parke B. reiterated his view that liability in deceit did not attach where there was gross negligence but no fraud. During argument, he answered Denman's position by stating that '[i]f the party *bona fide* believes the representation he made to be true, though he may not know it, it is not actionable'.[87] Denman reiterated his position in 1844. In *Evans* v. *Collins*, the plaintiff was a sheriff who sued two attorneys for falsely identifying a person as one against whom an execution process had been issued. The sheriff thereupon took the wrong man into custody and was sued for his pains. In Denman's view, the sheriff was not at fault 'but the party who caused his loss, though charged neither with fraud nor with negligence, must have been guilty of some fault when he made a false representation'.[88] Echoing Kenyon, he took the view that the defendants need not have spoken at all, and having taken it on themselves to speak, they were liable if what they said was not true. Like Kenyon, Denman seemed prepared to extend the tort of deceit to innocent misstatements. This case went to the Exchequer Chamber, where Denman's holding was overturned. Tindal CJ pointed out that the defendants had entered a plea that they had reason to believe their statement to be true. This raised the question whether a 'representation, which is false in fact, but not known to be so by the party making it, but on the contrary made honestly and in the full belief that it is true, affords a ground of action'.[89] Reaffirming the rule in *Pasley* and in *Haycraft*, he held there was none. The Exchequer Chamber confirmed its view of the rule in 1845 in *Ormrod* v. *Huth*, where Tindal CJ held that a false representation honestly made by a party believing it to be true was not actionable.[90] Although occasional dicta to the contrary could be found,[91] Parke B. felt it safe to assert in 1853 that it was 'settled

But it is not clear whether that action of deceit was for a breach of warranty made by the factor, or for a mere misrepresentation.

[86] *Fuller* v. *Wilson* (1842) 3 Q.B. 58 at 67. The case was overturned in the Exchequer Chamber (3 Q.B. 1009), on the grounds that there had in fact been no misrepresentation.

[87] *Taylor* v. *Ashton* (1842) 11 M. & W. 401 at 413.

[88] *Evans* v. *Collins* (1844) 5 Q.B. 804 at 819.

[89] *Collins* v. *Evans* (1844) 5 Q.B. 820 at 827.

[90] *Ormrod* v. *Huth* (1845) 14 M. & W. 651. See also the Queen's Bench's capitulation in *Barley* v. *Walford* (1846) 9 Q.B. 197.

[91] In 1853, Maule J. restated Kenyon's position, albeit *obiter*, when holding that a man who asserted something he knew nothing about 'does so at his peril' if it was done 'either with a view to secure some benefit to himself, or to deceive a third person [...] for, he takes upon himself to warrant his own belief of the truth of that which he so asserts': *Evans* v. *Edmonds* 13 C.B. 777 at 786.

law that, independently of duty, no action will lie for a misrepresentation, unless the party making it knows it to be untrue, and makes it with a fraudulent intention to induce another to act on the face of it, and to alter his position to his damage'.[92] There could be no 'legal fraud' committed by a person who said something he subjectively believed to be true.[93]

3. FRAUD IN EQUITY

Besides the common law remedy, parties could go to equity for relief in cases of fraud. The Chancery's procedure and its rules of evidence[94] were much better adapted to rooting out fraud than the common law. Chancery judges had also long resisted defining fraud, preferring to keep their jurisdiction flexible, in the knowledge that it was infinitely variable.[95] If this suggests that the Chancery would intervene more willingly than the common law courts, it is not to be assumed that the court did so lightly. The differences between common law and equity in this area are as much to be explained by the remedies sought and the kind of cases entertained as any deeper divergence of views about the nature of fraud.

The Chancery's rules regarding frauds in sales developed largely in the context of sales of land, rather than in the sale of goods. Although equity was willing to give greater relief in cases of land sales, the maxim of *caveat emptor* was also held to apply where there had been no 'positive representation essentially material to the subject in question, and which, at the same time, is false in fact'.[96] As at common law, the misrepresentation had to be material and relied on. Purchasers were not to rely on the loose opinions of vendors or their auctioneers.[97] However, equity's approach differed significantly from the common law's, when the remedy sought was specific performance of the contract of sale of land.[98] In these cases, equity would not assist a plaintiff who had behaved in an unconscionable manner.[99] According to Francis Vesey, the Chancery would refuse specific performance even if a vendor made an incorrect statement in the belief it was true.[100]

---

[92] *Thom* v. *Bigland* (1853) 8 Exch. 725 at 731.

[93] S. M. Leake, *The Elements of the Law of Contracts* (1867), 187.

[94] Chancery judges admitted parol evidence which contradicted written contracts: *Townsend* v. *Stangroom* (1801) 6 Ves. 328.

[95] See e.g. *Earl of Chesterfield* v. *Janssen* (1750–1) 2 Ves. Sr. 125 at 155–6.

[96] *Lowndes* v. *Lane* (1789) 2 Cox 363. See also E. B. Sugden, *A Practical Treatise on the Law of Vendors and Purchasers* 2 vols (9th edn,1834), i, 307.

[97] *Scott* v. *Hanson* (1826) 1 Sim. 13.

[98] This remedy was not generally used for sale of chattels or merchandise: *Buxton* v. *Lister* (1746) 3 Atk. 383.

[99] Lobban, 'Contractual Fraud', 448.

[100] *Oldfield* v. *Round* (1800) 1 Ves. Jr. Supp. 528 at 529; *Wakeman* v. *Duchess of Rutland* (1796–7) 1 Ves. Jr. Supp. 368. However, after the conveyance of a lease, the contract could not be set aside on the grounds of a non-wilful misrepresentation: *Legge* v. *Croker* (1811) 1 Ball & Beat. 506.

They thereby left the parties to their remedy at law for the non-performance of the agreement.[101] In the case of sales of land, such a remedy was generally useless for the purchaser, who after all sought to obtain the property and not merely nominal damages. Practically speaking, then, equity was generous in its relief where contracts were unexecuted.[102]

Parties also went to equity to have executed agreements for the sale of property set aside. Where in the sale of goods, parties who had been defrauded could simply return the goods, rescinding the contract by their own acts, land sales could only be undone through a court order. Equity was less generous to the party who claimed to have been misled when it came to setting aside executed agreements than it was in refusing specific performance: they were only rescinded if they had been obtained by fraud.[103] As Vesey put it, if a vendor 'makes a representation which he knows to be false, but the falsehood of which the other party had no means of knowing,' equity would rescind the contract.[104] But if, 'without entering into an express and formal warrant, [he] has made a representation which he, on reasonable grounds believed to be accurate', then the purchaser could obtain no relief after the completion of the contract.[105] In 1840, Lord Brougham summed up the rule for when both law and equity gave a remedy for misrepresentation in an executed agreement: 'the materiality as well as the falsehood of the statement, and the knowledge of the party making it that it was untrue, must concur in order to give relief in equity, and to give an action for damages at law'.[106] Nevertheless, equity's perception of fraud was broader than that of the common law in one important respect, for in land cases, parties were expected to bargain with a certain amount of good faith. If a purchaser of property knew that the price at which it was sold did not represent its real value, and wilfully concealed this from the vendor, this concealment was regarded as amounting to fraud which would justify rescission. As the Exchequer put it in 1792, 'parties to a contract are supposed, in equity, to treat for what they think a fair price'.[107]

---

[101] *Young* v. *Clerk* (1720) Prec. Ch. 538. See the very broad view of unconscionability taken by Lord Kenyon in *Twining* v. *Morrice* (1788) 2 Bro. C.C. 326.

[102] At common law, a plaintiff could sue on an unexecuted agreement in an action for non-acceptance of goods. But here it was open to the defendant merely to say that the goods offered were not those he had been promised.

[103] See the reporter's note to *Cadman* v. *Horner* (1810) 2 Ves. Jr. Supp. 499. See also *Attwood* v. *Small* (1835–40) 6 Cl. & F. 232 at 330 and 395 (where Lord Lyndhurst said equity would rescind an executed contract in the same circumstances in which the common law courts would give an action for deceit), and Lyndhurst's comments in *Scott* v. *Hanson* (1829) 1 Russ. & Myl. 128 at 131.

[104] This was the phrase of Lord Eldon in *Edwards* v. *M'Leay* (1818) 2 Swanst. 287 at 289, affirming *Edwards* v. *M'Leay* (1815) G. Coop. 308 at 312.

[105] *Oldfield* v. *Round* (1800) 1 Ves. Jr. Supp. 528 at 529.

[106] *Attwood* v. *Small* (1840) 6 Cl. & F. 232 at 444; *Pulsford* v. *Richards* (1853) 17 Beav. 87 at 96.

[107] *Deane* v. *Rastron* (1792) 1 Anst. 64. But if neither party knew the real price, the fact that it was sold at undervalue was not enough to disturb the agreement, since there would be no sign of bad faith.

As at common law, the Chancery only rescinded where it was satisfied that a *restitutio in integrum* could be effected. However, this requirement was less strict in equity. In cases involving the purchase of real property[108] as well as shares,[109] the Chancery was prepared to rescind contracts where part of the property had been consumed by the party seeking relief, provided he accounted for the profits made.[110] Equity was able to be more flexible, since it had the machinery to ensure counter-restitution in a way that was not possible at common law. When equity rescinded contracts obtained by fraud, it might also require the party who made the representation to indemnify the innocent party for any liabilities he might have sustained by entering into the agreement. This was done particularly in those cases where a person had been induced by a misrepresentation to enter into a partnership.[111]

The Chancery also offered a third remedy to those who had been misled: it would hold the party to make his representation good. This remedy was sought, generally, in disputes arising from family settlements. This doctrine was not used for pre-contractual representations. It was instead used in two different situations. The first was where a speaker had misled an inquirer about his own claims on a fund in which the inquirer was about to acquire an interest. This occurred typically where family property was involved, as where family members misled prospective husbands about the extent of their own claims. In these cases, the person who made a false statement was required to make good his representation by postponing his claims, even if he had been unaware of his own rights when making the assertion.[112] In Lord Eldon's view, where a person was induced to advance money to another as a result of a representation by a third party that he had no claim on that person, 'the Mouth of the Person, who made that Misrepresentation, was shut; that he should never utter a Contradiction to what he had so asserted, thereby misleading others'.[113] As this comment shows, this was equity's equivalent to the doctrine which developed later at common law, that a party was estopped from going back on a representation concerning his right to property.

The doctrine was also applied, secondly, in cases where one party made a statement about the financial position of another, to a person who entered into

---

[108] *Small* v. *Attwood* (1832) You. 407, 506.

[109] *Gillett* v. *Peppercorne* (1840) 3 Beav 78; *Blake* v. *Mowatt* (1856) 21 Beav. 603. See M. Lobban, 'Erlanger v. New Sombrero Phosphate Co (1878)', in C. Mitchell and P. Mitchell (eds), *Landmark Cases in the Law of Restitution* (Oxford, 2006), 123–62.

[110] See also *Erlanger* v. *New Sombrero Phosphate Co* (1878) 3 App Cas 1218 at 1278–9.

[111] See *Stainbank* v. *Fernley* (1839) 9 Sim. 556 at 567.

[112] *Hobbs* v. *Norton* (1682) 1 Vern. 136; *Hunsden* v. *Cheyney* (1690) 2 Vern. 150; *Mocatta* v. *Murgatroyd* (1717) 1 P. Wms. 393; *Teasdale* v. *Teasdale* (1726) Sel. Cas. temp. King 59; *Neville* v. *Wilkinson* (1781) 1 Bro. C.C. 543; *Scott* v. *Scott* (1787) 1 Cox C.C. 366.

[113] *Ex p Carr* (1814) 3 V. & B. 108 at 111.

a contract as a result of the statement. This occurred typically where the person making the representation was a trustee, making comments about the financial position of a beneficiary. In such cases, the representor would be financially liable to make up a shortfall, in effect giving an equitable remedy equivalent to common law damages. In these cases, equity looked for stronger evidence of fraud. For Lord Eldon, the party making the statement would be liable 'if he knows it to be false' or if there were such 'gross negligence' as to be evidence of fraudulent intent.[114] This meant that a party who made a positive statement on a matter which he had forgotten about would be liable. As Grant MR put it in 1805, a plaintiff had only to show:

1st, that the fact, as represented, is false; 2dly, that the person, making the representation, had a knowledge of a fact, contrary to it. The Plaintiff cannot dive into the secret recesses of his heart: so as to know, whether he did or did not recollect the fact; and it is no excuse to say, he did not recollect it.[115]

This was close to the common law position which did not require a fraudulent motive, but a false statement of a matter within the party's knowledge. Throughout the first half of the nineteenth century, the courts of common law and equity took a similar approach to such claims. It was only later that they diverged. One early sign of the divergence was *Slim* v. *Croucher* in 1860. Here, the Chancery Court of Appeal held a defendant liable to make good a representation where he had known the truth but forgotten it. Instead of calling this gross negligence which was equivalent to fraud, Lord Campbell acknowledged that he had been guilty of no moral fraud.[116] In holding him to make good the representation, the court continued to assert that their jurisdiction here was equivalent to that exercised by the common law in cases of deceit, despite the fact that the common law courts were now asserting the need for moral fraud. This point—made by a Lord Chancellor who had spent his career in the common law courts—helped to lay the foundations of what seemed to the later nineteenth-century courts as divergent views of deceit in law and equity.

4. NEGLIGENT MISREPRESENTATIONS

In the second half of the nineteenth century, a new approach developed among equity judges to the rescission of executed contracts for non-fraudulent misrepresentations. This new remedy was developed in a new context: that of investors

---

[114] *Evans* v. *Bicknell* (1801) 6 Ves. 174 at 183, 190.

[115] *Burrowes* v. *Lock* (1805) 10 Ves. 470 at 476. See also the analysis of Lord Selborne LC in *Brownlie* v. *Campbell* (1880) 5 App Cas 925 at 935–6.

[116] *Slim* v. *Croucher* (1860) 1 De G. F. & J. 518 at 524.

in new joint stock companies seeking to rescind their contracts to buy shares in companies which turned out to be failures. In these cases, doctrine was driven by a small number of Chancery judges, who were particularly concerned to protect vulnerable investors, by upholding a moral vision of equity.

A first step was taken by Sir John Romilly, who felt that equity went further than common law in ensuring good faith dealing. No one felt more strongly than he 'the necessity of enforcing the equity [...] of compelling a man to make good his word'.[117] In 1852, in *Money* v. *Jorden*, he held that while common law only held parties liable for statements they knew to be false, equity compelled parties to make good any statements which they asserted to be true, if the party to whom the statement had been made had entered into engagements on the faith of it.[118] Romilly's view about the effect of non-contractual misrepresentations would not be followed by the House of Lords in *Jorden* v. *Money*. But he reiterated his views in 1853 in *Pulsford* v. *Richards*, when considering pre-contractual misrepresentations. Equity, he said, would hold a party to make good a representation 'where statements, false in fact, were made by persons who believed them to be true, if in the due discharge of their duty, they ought to have known, or if they had formerly known and ought to have remembered the fact which negatives the representation made'.[119] Drawing on land cases—though going well beyond what the cases established[120]—he held that where such representations could not be made good, the contract would be set aside. In *Pulsford*, the plaintiffs who sought to rescind a contract to buy shares in a railway company lost on the facts; but the Master of the Rolls had taken the chance to set down his broad view of the law of misrepresentation in a company case.

Another step was taken in *Rawlins* v. *Wickham* in 1858, where the Chancery Court of Appeal held that a silent partner in a firm could be held liable for 'legal' fraud, even where there was no moral fraud. The plaintiff had become a partner in the Winchester and Hampshire Bank, after being shown accounts, prepared by the managing clerk, which understated the bank's liabilities to the tune of

---

[117] *Jameson* v. *Stein* (1855) 21 Beav. 5 at 10. He remained careful not to contradict the common law in respect of the awarding of damages for misrepresentation: see *Whitmore* v. *Mackeson* (1852) 16 Beav. 126.

[118] *Money* v. *Jorden* (1852) 15 Beav. 372 at 377.

[119] *Pulsford* v. *Richards* (1853) 17 Beav. 87 at 94.

[120] Romilly stated 'if a man misrepresent the tenure or situation of an estate, as if he sell an estate as freehold which proves to be copyhold or leasehold, or if he describes it as situate within a mile of some particular town, when, in truth, it is several miles distant, such a misrepresentation, as it cannot be made true, would, at the option of the party deceived, annul the contract': *Pulsford* v. *Richards* (1853) 17 Beav. 95–6. But as Sugden (*Vendors*, 8th edn, 1830, 305) put it, 'The right to a good title is a right not growing out of the agreement between the parties, but which is given by law'. In effect, equity's intervention here was for a breach of a term.

£13,000. On discovering that the clerk was plundering the bank, and that the accounts were false, Rawlins sued the managing partner for fraudulent representation. Although he was awarded £11,800 damages, he was only able to recover £300 from the now impecunious partner, and so sought to recover from the estate of the now-deceased inactive partner, James Wickham. Rawlins went to Chancery both to rescind his agreement to become a partner (thereby shedding his liabilities) and to hold Wickham's estate liable to indemnify him for the liabilities he incurred by becoming a partner. The Lord Justices held the estate liable.[121] Although Wickham had no knowledge of the matter, Turner LJ held that by delivering the inaccurate account to Rawlins, he had made a representation 'of a fact of the truth or falsehood of which he knew nothing'. While there was no moral fraud, there was a legal fraud, for which he was liable.[122] He said:

> If upon a treaty for purchase one of the parties to the contract makes a representation materially affecting the subject-matter of the contract, he surely cannot be heard to say that he knew nothing of the truth or falsehood of that which he represented, and still more surely he cannot be allowed to retain any benefit which he has derived if the representation he has made turns out to be untrue.[123]

This was so even though Rawlins knew that Wickham took no part in the business. Turner LJ also rejected the argument that the estate should only be liable to make good the original representation, rather than rescinding the contract. '[I]f a contract is obtained by fraud', he ruled, having already stated that there had been no moral fraud on Wickham's part, 'it is for the party defrauded to elect whether he will be bound.'[124]

In the mid-nineteenth century, equity judges became increasingly concerned about parties retaining benefits which had been obtained as a result of someone else's fraud, a particular problem in company and partnership dealings. The approach of common law and equity began to diverge here. Although common law judges in the early 1840s had conceded that a principal would be liable for the frauds of his agents in negotiating a contract,[125] in 1848 the House of Lords held that a principal would only be liable if he had personal knowledge of the fraud. As Lord Campbell LC observed, '[i]n an action upon contract, the representation of an agent is the representation of the principal; but in an action on the

---

[121] Stuart VC had found for the plaintiff, on the principles of agency which applied to partnerships: *Rawlins* v. *Wickham* (1858) 1 Giff. 355 at 361. For the partnership rules, see *Marsh* v. *Keating* (1834) 2 Cl. & F. 250; *Sadler* v. *Lee* (1843) 6 Beav. 324.

[122] See also *Traill* v. *Baring* (1864) 4 De G. J. & S. 318 at 328.

[123] *Rawlins* v. *Wickham* (1858) 3 De G. & J. 304 at 316–17.

[124] *Ibid.*, 322.

[125] In these cases, it was assumed that the principal would be liable for the frauds of his agent. See e.g. *Wilson* v. *Fuller* (1843) 3 Q.B. 68 at 77; *Moens* v. *Heyworth* (1842) 10 M. & W. 147 at 157.

case, for deceit, the misrepresentation or concealment must be proved against the principal'.[126]

This raised the question of whether contracts procured by the frauds of agents—such as those procured by deceitful company directors or promoters— could be rescinded. Equity judges at first seemed to have the same approach as the common lawyers, refusing to allow a rescission unless the fraud could be seen as the fraud of the company. In 1849, Knight Bruce VC refused relief to a share-holder who had been induced to buy shares by the fraud of the directors. For the shareholder to get relief, it had to be shown that the company as a whole had adopted the fraud.[127] But there was some discomfort that companies could take the benefit of the frauds of their directors, and a number of judges soon sought to argue that any report issued for the company by its directors had to be seen as binding the company. For instance, Lord Campbell made an *obiter* observation in the House of Lords in 1849 that a shareholder who had invested on the faith of false statements made by directors could rescind his purchase.[128] Drawing on the principle that a principal who adopted the fraud of his agent would be liable,[129] Lord Cranworth declared in *National Exchange Company of Glasgow* v. *Drew*, that if a company received a fraudulent report from its directors and published it to the world, it had to be taken to be a misrepresentation by the company, and those buying shares on the faith of it could rescind their contracts.[130] This view was acted on in 1857 in *Brockwell's Case* by Sir Richard Kindersley VC to remove a shareholder from the list of contributories after the directors of a bank had issued a false prospectus. In his view, a directors' report submitted to the company was to be regarded as the report of the company if it later got into circulation.[131]

Not all judges were happy with this new approach. In *Hudson's Case* in 1858, Lord Chelmsford pointed out that as directors were required by law to lay accurate

---

[126] *Wilde* v. *Gibson* (1848) 1 H.L.C. 605 at 515. He also said (at p. 623), 'there can be no personal fraud without intention'. In this case, however, the Chancery bill alleged personal fraud. The question of the liability of the principal still divided the court of Exchequer in 1861, in a case where goods were sold after the defendant's agent made a fraudulent misrepresentation of their quality: *Udell* v. *Atherton* (1861) 1 H. & N. 172.

[127] *Dodgson's Case* (1849) 3 De G. & S. 85; *Bernard's Case* (1852) 5 De G. & S. 283. See also *Bell's Case* (1856) 22 Beav. 35.

[128] *Burnes* v. *Pennell* (1849) 2 H.L.C. 497 at 522.

[129] See *Ranger* v. *Great Western Railway* (1854) 5 H.L.C. 72 at 86.

[130] 'When, therefore, the Directors, in the discharge of their duty, fraudulently (for I assume this to be so) for the purpose of misleading others as to the state of the concerns of the Company, represent the Company to be in a different state from that which they know it to be, and the persons to whom the representation is addressed act upon it in the belief that it is true, I cannot think that society can go on without treating that as a misrepresentation by the Company': *National Exchange Co of Glasgow* v. *Drew* (1855) 2 Macq. 102 at 124–5.

[131] *Brockwell's Case* (1857) 4 Drew. 205.

reports before the company twice a year, they could hardly be seen as agents of the company if they made fraudulent reports which deceived both the public and the shareholders themselves.[132] In *Nicol's Case*, in January 1859, he treated Cranworth's comment in *National Exchange Company of Glasgow* as *obiter*.[133] Anyone dealing with a company, he said, had notice by the legislation which gave them corporate status that directors had a limited authority, the extent of which could be ascertained. Shareholders should not be bound if they acted *ultra vires*. He held, therefore, that if directors made fraudulent representations to their shareholders, and then made an 'unauthorized circulation' of the report, then those who bought on the faith of the representation could only sue the directors for deceit.[134] One month later, Kindersley himself seemed to qualify the view he had articulated in *Brockwell* in February 1859, explaining that the company would only be bound where a report was *adopted* at a general meeting of shareholders.[135] Five months later, in *Mixer's Case*, the Chancery Court of Appeal again cast doubt on *Brockwell's Case*. In a case (like *Brockwell* and *Mixer*) arising from the failure of the Royal British Bank, Lord Campbell seemed to move away from the position he had taken in *Burnes* v. *Pennell*, stating that although there were clear frauds made by the directors in reports presented to the company, they could not be attributed to the company.[136] Thus, by 1860 a number of judges took the view that a contract to buy shares could only be rescinded if the misrepresentation had been made with the authority of the company. This was to square the equity approach with the common law approach of holding the principal liable for the frauds of the agent which had been adopted.

In this context, a distinctly equitable solution was proposed by Turner LJ in *Nicol's Case*.[137] Although directors were not agents of the company to commit fraud, he ruled, shareholders were 'responsible for and are not entitled to derive benefits under false and fraudulent representations made by their directors'.[138] It was clearly settled in equity that even innocent parties could not derive benefits

---

[132] *Hudson's Case* (1858) 2 De G. & J. 275. He was clear that no relief could be given if a party had bought shares on the false representations of other shareholders.

[133] *Nicol's Case* (1859) 3 De G. & J. 387 at 426. In *National Exchange Co of Glasgow*, the pursuers sought to recover a loan given to the defender to purchase more shares in a failing company. The Lords having held that no loan was made, the other comments were *obiter*.

[134] *Nicol's Case* (1859) 3 De G. & J. 387 at 431.

[135] *Ex p Worth* (1859) 4 Drew. 529. The company was also, he said, only bound if the shares were bought from the company on the faith of the misrepresentation, not from third parties.

[136] *Mixer's Case* (1859) 4 De G. & J. 575 at 586.

[137] Turner concurred in the decision here, holding Nicol was to be a contributory since the false report was not addressed to purchasers in the market, such as himself, but only to the shareholders. He took a similar view in *Mixer's Case*. See also his judgment in *De Pass's Case* (1859) 4 De G. & J. 544.

[138] *Nicol's Case* (1859) 3 De G. & J. 387 at 438.

from the frauds of others. This principle had often been applied where property had been obtained by fraud, where courts took the view that it was against conscience to hold a benefit derived from the fraud of another, even where one was unaware of the fraud.[139] Turner LJ restated his views in 1860 in *Conybeare v. New Brunswick and Canada Railway and Land Company*, where he suggested that the contract could be rescinded even if the directors' misrepresentations were not sufficiently fraudulent as to sustain an action of deceit. In this case, the plaintiff had bought shares in a company after he had (wrongly) been led to believe that it had an indefeasible title to land on which the railway was to be built. While Turner admitted that no fraud was intended when the documents were given by the directors to Conybeare, he ruled (overturning Stuart VC's decision) that it fell within the rule that where one party made a statement known to be false, which the other had no means of contradicting, the contract was to be rescinded.[140] Applying the view he expressed in *Nicol's Case*, he held that directors were in the position of trustees, whose *cestui que trust*—the company—'cannot be permitted by this Court to retain moneys acquired by means of a sale made by the directors, which in the eye of this court is fraudulent'.[141] But while the company was bound to refund the purchase money with interest, he added 'there is no sufficient case for a decree against the directors'. This was to suggest that the directors' conduct was not sufficiently morally blameworthy to make them personally liable (as if for deceit), but it was sufficiently misleading to amount to such a fraud as in the eye of equity justified rescission. It was to suggest that the company—but not its directors—was liable for their negligent misstatements.

When the case went to the House of Lords, Lord Westbury conceded Turner's point that a company could not retain benefits obtained by fraud. Where at common law, there could be liability only for misrepresentations the falsehood of which the principal was aware of, in equity it would be regarded as 'be inconsistent with natural justice to permit property so acquired through the medium of these representations to be retained by the company'.[142] But Westbury was baffled by Turner's decision to 'acquit the directors altogether, but find an immaterial being, namely, an incorporated company, guilty of fraud'.[143] In his view, while companies had to disgorge benefits obtained by fraud, the level of fraud needed remained that which would subject directors to an action of deceit at common

---

[139] See above, p. 409.
[140] *Conybeare v. New Brunswick and Canada Railway Co* (1860) 1 De G. F. & G. 578 at 595, citing *Edwards v. M'Leay* (1818) 2 Swanst. 287.
[141] *Conybeare v. New Brunswick and Canada Railway Co* (1860) 1 De G. F. & G. 578 at 596.
[142] *New Brunswick and Canada Railway and Land Co v. Conybeare* (1862) 9 H.L.C. 711 at 726.
[143] *Ibid.*, at 735.

law.[144] Concurring, Lord Cranworth reiterated his view that a contract entered into with a company as a result of the frauds of its directors could be rescinded, though he noted at the same time that the principle could not be carried to the 'wild length' of making the company liable for deceit where directors had done an act which might make them liable to such an action, for the fraud had to be personal or impliedly authorized.[145] This was to accept Turner's view that a company could not retain the benefits acquired by a fraud, while maintaining that this only applied where the director's fraud amounted to the tort of deceit. This meant that Conybeare could not undo the contract, since there was not here a sufficient degree of fraud.

This view was confirmed in 1867 by the House of Lords in *Western Bank of Scotland* v. *Addie*, when it held that a shareholder who had been induced to buy shares by the fraudulent misrepresentation of the directors could not be held to the contract, since the misrepresentations were imputable to the company, which could not retain benefits obtained through its agents' frauds. At the same time, it held that an action for damages in deceit could only be brought against the directors personally.[146] If this judgment seemed to confirm that a different approach (derived from equity) would be taken with respect to rescission from the approach (derived from common law) taken with respect to damages, a few months later a decision of the Court of Exchequer helped to reconcile the approaches, when it was held that a principal was vicariously liable for his agent's frauds. This was to render companies liable in damages for their directors' frauds.[147]

However, just when the approaches of law and equity were reconciled in one area, they diverged again in another. Courts of equity, led by Turner, began to give relief where the misstatement had not been fraudulent. In *Smith's Case*, the name of a shareholder who had bought shares on the faith of a misleading prospectus was removed from the list of contributories, even though the directors did not know that the representation they made was untrue. They had themselves been deceived by the vendor of the mines bought, and had informed the shareholders of this fact as soon as it was discovered.[148] When the case came before the Lord

---

[144] For in taking the shares, Conybeare was held to have executed the deed of association which recited the very statute making the grants defeasible which he claimed to have been suppressed.

[145] *New Brunswick and Canada Railway and Land Co* v. *Conybeare* (1862) 9 H.L.C. 711 at 740.

[146] *Western Bank of Scotland* v. *Addie* (1867) LR 1 Sc & Div 145 at 157–8.

[147] *Barwick* v. *English Joint Stock Bank* (1867) LR 2 Ex 259; *Mackay* v. *Commercial Bank of New Brunswick* (1874) LR 5 PC 394. However, the agent had to be working for the general benefit of the company and not his own private ends: see *British Mutual Banking Co* v. *Charnwood Forest Railway Co* (1887) 18 QBD 714. The director's authority to bind the company is discussed further, below, pp. 657–60.

[148] Lord Romilly MR held the misrepresentation was not one for which relief could be given. He held it was not material, since there were other mining speculations the company was engaged with: *The Times*, 7 June 1867, col. 11a.

Justices, Turner LJ stressed that the prospectus had contained a factually untrue, material statement. '[I]f a company will take upon itself to assume the authenticity of, and give credit to, the reports which are made to it', he stated, 'and represent as facts the matters stated in those reports, it must take the consequences.'[149] He found authority in his own partnership decision of *Rawlins* v. *Wickham*. The case was appealed to the Lords in 1869, where Lord Cairns (who had concurred with Turner) restated the position he had already taken: 'I apprehend it to be the rule of law', he said, 'that if persons take upon themselves to make assertions as to which they are ignorant whether they are true or untrue, they must, in a civil point of view, be held as responsible as if they had asserted that which they knew to be untrue.'[150] But at the same time that equity judges were developing a remedy for negligent misrepresentations in company cases, Blackburn J. in *Kennedy* v. *Panama, New Zealand and Australian Royal Mail Company* held that in the absence of the moral fraud necessary to support an action of deceit, a contract (in a going concern) could not be rescinded, unless the misrepresentation was such as to induce a mistake which made the purchaser believe that he was buying something wholly different from what had been agreed.[151] In making this decision, Blackburn may have been seeking to forestall a flood of litigants coming into the common law courts seeking to rescind bad share purchases, and throwing all the losses onto creditors; for at the same time that equity courts were giving greater remedies to those who suffered from negligent misrepresentations, they were also setting limits to the rights of shareholders to rescind, in order to protect creditors, in a way which could not be done by a common law court.[152] Blackburn's approach, which made the law relating to rescission for non-fraudulent misstatements seem doctrinally inconsistent between the courts of law and equity, may have been intended to ensure that the courts could develop a consistent practical approach when it came to dealing with failing companies.

By 1875, the courts of equity had, in the context of company cases, significantly extended their willingness to rescind executed contracts. First, they forced companies to disgorge any benefit obtained by fraud; and secondly, they began to allow rescission where the original misstatement had not been fraudulent, but made in good faith. The equity judges who developed this doctrine wished to make companies effectively warrant the truth of statements which were made in their prospectuses. This was a doctrine which could be useful. Nor was it revolutionary as an approach. After all, in other areas, such as agency, rules had developed that

---

[149] *In re Reese River Silver Mining Co (Smith's Case)* (1867) LR 2 Ch App 604 at 611.
[150] *Reese River Silver Mining Co* v. *Smith* (1869) LR 4 HL 64 at 79–80.
[151] *Kennedy* v. *Panama, New Zealand and Australian Royal Mail Co* (1867) LR 2 QB 580 at 587.
[152] On the developments in company law, see below, p. 649.

parties were held to warrant the truth of their representations. But this was not a rule which was to be limited to companies. Once it was established in company cases that executed contracts could be set aside for innocent misrepresentations, judges in equity applied the rule elsewhere. In 1877, Fry J. rescinded a contract for the purchase of land completed after the vendor made a *bona fide* but incorrect statement.[153] He found that a party could be liable for 'legal' frauds, even without moral fault. In his view, by speaking, the defendant took it on himself to warrant the truth of his assertion. It is ironic that the doctrinal backing he gave his decision came not from the company cases in equity, but from a contested and doubtful interpretation of common law cases. The following decade would see much debate over whether the same approach was to be taken when damages were sought in common law actions. As shall be seen, common law judges in this era were not prepared to use the idea of 'legal fraud' to give damages in deceit in similar land cases involving innocent misrepresentations.[154]

5. MISREPRESENTATION AFTER FUSION

In 1881, Jessel MR noted that common law and equity had different approaches to rescission. Where at common law, a contract could only be rescinded if the statement inducing it had been made recklessly, in equity it was not necessary to show that the representor knew his statement was false when he made it. Equity would rescind any contract which rested on a misrepresentation since it would be against conscience for the speaker to retain benefits obtained by misrepresentations whose falsehood he ought to have discovered.[155] As Jessel observed, since the Judicature Act made equity's rules prevail, rescission was now to be given wherever there was a misrepresentation of any sort.

This raised the question of what pecuniary compensation was available to a party who had acted on a non-fraudulent misrepresentation. Equity's two pecuniary remedies were requiring the defendant to make good his representation, and giving an indemnity, when a contract was rescinded, for obligations incurred by the plaintiff as a consequence of entering into the contract. Litigants in company cases did not often invoke the former of these, not least because in the case of false prospectuses, the representation could not be made good. More usually, they looked to rescind their contracts and obtain indemnities. Indemnity was a corollary of rescission. As Cotton LJ observed in 1886, if the plaintiff were not

---

[153] *Hart* v. *Swaine* (1877) 7 Ch D 42 at 47, citing *Evans* v. *Edmonds* (1853) 13 C.B. 777, 786.

[154] *Joliffe* v. *Baker* (1883) 11 QBD 255. On legal and moral fraud, see the comments of Bramwell LJ in *Weir* v. *Bell* (1878) 3 Ex D 238, 243.

[155] *Redgrave* v. *Hurd* (1881) 20 Ch D 1 at 13.

indemnified from the obligations which he had obtained under the contract which was to be set aside, he would not be restored to his pre-contractual position.[156]

The post-1867 equitable approach to rescission presented a new problem. As long as equity only set aside executed contracts on the grounds of the kind of fraud recognized at common law, the remedy of giving an indemnity was not inconsistent with the measure of damages at common law. But once equity undid contracts on the basis of even innocent misrepresentations, the question arose whether the principles on which indemnities were given were to be different from those on which damages at common law were awarded. Resting the two remedies on distinct principles had significant consequences. Where rescission was possible, a party would be freed by the indemnity from all the adverse consequences of the non-fraudulent misrepresentation. If rescission was no longer possible, the party would have no remedy at all, if the common law continued to require actual fraud in cases where the misrepresentation was not fraudulent. A party's remedy might therefore turn on the chance outcome of whether a company had entered into liquidation, or disposed of its assets in a voluntary liquidation, making restoration of the *status quo ante* impossible.

Opinions continued to differ, even among equity judges, over whether liability for misstatements required actual fraud. For instance, in December 1867, Page Wood VC stated that to make directors liable for misrepresentations—so that they would personally have to repay investors the sums invested—'you must fix them also with a guilty knowledge of the misrepresentation'. Since it was the company, and not the directors, who received the money paid by virtue of the misrepresentations, he felt that directors could not be liable for statements made in good faith.[157] This seemed to apply a 'common law view' to the equitable doctrine of indemnity. But a different approach was taken in 1871 by Lord Romilly MR in *Peek* v. *Gurney*, where he sought to apply an equitable approach to what was in essence a common law problem. The case arose from the failure of Overend, Gurney & Co, whose directors had concealed material facts—about the extent of the firm's debts—in their prospectus when the firm was turned into a limited company. The directors had subsequently been acquitted in a criminal trial for conspiracy. Shareholders who had been unable to rescind their contracts prior to the winding up of the company now sought an 'indemnity' from the directors—in effect damages. Romilly stated that, in principle, the directors were liable to indemnify the purchasers. Reiterating his moral view, he said that equity 'requires the truth, the whole truth and nothing but the truth to be told ... It is the *suppressio veri*

---

[156] *Newbigging* v. *Adam* (1886) 34 Ch D 582 at 589. However, the House of Lords did not decide the question of indemnity: *Adam* v. *Newbigging* (1888) 13 App Cas 308.

[157] *Henderson* v. *Lacon* (1867) LR 5 Eq 249 at 262. In this case, they were held liable.

or the *suggestio falsi* which is the foundation of the right to relief in equity, and this exists whether it were fraudulently or mistakenly done.'[158] The fact that the directors sincerely and honestly believed in the probable success of the company did not exonerate them from liability for concealing a fact which was material for investors to know.

Romilly refused the indemnity, however, on the grounds that the misrepresentations had not been addressed to the plaintiffs, and that a deceived party was barred from relief if he did not act in a reasonable time. '[T]hough no technical rule, as in the case of the cancellation of shares, applies as regards the liability of directors', he said, 'yet morally, and as far as equity is concerned, the same principle applies to both cases.'[159] The latter point made little doctrinal sense, unless it was assumed that the indemnity would in fact come out of the company's coffers.[160] Where directors had acted deceitfully, the common law only imposed the time bar of the statute of limitations. Having a shorter time bar for non-fraudulent misstatements, and linking it to the timing required for rescission of shares—which by 1871 had to be done before the company had begun to wind up—did suggest that the indemnity was not expected by Romilly to come from the directors' own pockets. This case was appealed to the House of Lords, which also found for the defendants on the grounds that the misstatements had not been addressed to the plaintiffs. But the Lords rejected Romilly's approach to the law. They rejected the idea that they should consider the moral obligations of the directors. Instead (there being no issue of rescission), they regarded this action as 'precisely analogous' to the common law action of deceit, whose principles should be applied. This meant that the same limitation rules applied, so that Romilly's contention that the plaintiff's rights could be lost by delay was also dismissed.[161] Having come to the conclusion that, although a mere concealment of information could not be a misrepresentation, there was sufficient fraud here to be actionable, the Lords did not ask whether equity's doctrine of making representations good would offer a distinct approach.

Three years later, Sir George Jessel MR did just that. In *Eaglesfield* v. *the Marquis of Londonderry*, a railway company's directors had made an issue of preference stock, under a *bona fide* but incorrect belief as to its ranking. When a

[158] *Peek* v. *Gurney* (1871) LR 13 Eq 79 at 113.

[159] *Peek* v. *Gurney* (1871) LR 13 Eq 79 at 120. Romilly clearly wanted to prevent people speculating on the success of a venture.

[160] Romilly's notion of the need to act in a timely way was derived from the requirement that a party's right to rescind was lost by affirmation, which might be inferred from lapse of time. This reasoning would apply to indemnities insofar as they were linked to rescission; but here Romilly treated an indemnity in effect as equivalent to damages.

[161] *Peek* v. *Gurney* (1873) LR 6 HL 377 at 402 (Lord Cairns).

purchaser of the stock sought to hold the company and its directors to make the representation good (by either issuing the relevant preference stock or refunding the money), Jessel found for the plaintiffs. He held both the company and directors liable to make good the representation, even though the directors had acted under the advice of solicitors. Although (he said) an action of deceit might not be maintained against them, 'in a civil court ... the man who either through carelessness or negligence so misleads another as to induce him to part with valuable property' had to be held liable. For Jessel '[t]he whole doctrine of equity depends on this'.[162] His judgment was overturned by the Court of Appeal, which found that the parties were all under a shared mistake of law. At the same time, Jessel's application of the doctrine of making representations good was rejected. In his judgment, James LJ restated the common law approach, that for an action of misrepresentation to be brought against the directors, the representation had to be wilful and fraudulent.[163]

The idea that the rules of deceit had to be applied when directors were to be made personally responsible was reiterated in 1880 in *Arkwright* v. *Newbold*. In this case, Fry J. had held the promoters of a company liable in deceit to individual shareholders—who wished to hold on to their shares—for failing to disclose in their prospectus the remuneration the directors were to receive. Although this was not required by section 38 of the 1867 Companies Act (which created a statutory fraud), he felt there was a common law liability. The judges in the Court of Appeal overturned his decision, observing that he had failed to draw the necessary distinction between an action of deceit and an action to set aside a purchase, either on the grounds of a breach of fiduciary duty or of a misrepresentation. In the words of Cotton LJ, '[a]n action of deceit is a common law action, and must be decided on the same principles, whether it be brought in the Chancery Division or any of the Common Law Divisions; there being ... no such thing as an equitable action for deceit'.[164]

The meaning of deceit was discussed in another appeal from a decision of Fry's which reached the Lords in 1884. In *Smith* v. *Chadwick*, the prospectus of a company which subsequently failed stated that the 'present value' of the turnover of some ironworks was over £1 million. It was not clear whether this

---

[162] *Eaglesfield* v. *Marquis of Londonderry* (1876) 4 Ch D 693 at 704–5.

[163] *Eaglesfield* v. *Marquis of Londonderry* (1876) 4 Ch D 693 at 711. Fry J. acted on James LJ's view in *Cargill* v. *Bower* (1878) 10 Ch D 502, holding that a director could not be held liable for fraudulent statements made by an agent of the company which were not specifically authorized by him, even if he had been negligent in allowing the statements to be made, since to be liable he had to have been aware of or authorized the fraud.

[164] *Arkwright* v. *Newbold* (1880) 17 Ch D 301 at 320. The share purchaser here had kept the shares and, after they fell in value, sued the promoters. Fry J. had based his decision on the common law and not on s 38 of the Companies Act.

referred to present or potential turnover. In Fry's view, the statement respecting turnover could only be read in the sense of present turnover, and he found that the prospectus contained several untrue statements.[165] He thereupon held the defendants liable in deceit. In his view, if a man made a statement about something he had no knowledge of, to induce another to enter a contract, he was liable for making the false statement.[166] Fry's decision was overturned in the Court of Appeal, which reiterated the older common law view requiring 'moral fraud'. Lindley LJ—a Chancery man by background—noted '[t]he action is one based entirely on fraud', and it had to be shown that the statement was false to the knowledge of the defendants 'or at all events that they did not believe the truth of it'.[167] Cotton LJ, another equity man, said that it had to be shown that the statements made were made either in the knowledge that they were false, or 'recklessly'.[168] The Lords affirmed this judgment, stressing the need to show 'actual fraud'.[169]

By the mid-1880s, it was thus clear that there was no distinct equitable approach to the granting of pecuniary remedies against those who had made misrepresentations, different from that taken at common law. But there was at the same time some uncertainty about the precise ambit of the common law action. In *Weir* v. *Bell*, where a director unaware of falsehoods in a prospectus was sued in deceit, two rival views were taken by the judges. On the one hand, Bramwell LJ, applying a rule found in numerous mid-nineteenth-century cases where directors were not held liable for negligent misstatements,[170] ruled that 'to make a man liable for fraud, moral fraud must be proved against him'.[171] On the other hand, Cotton LJ stated that deceit would lie for statements made 'without any reasonable grounds for believing them to be true'. In his view, directors were under a duty to ascertain whether the statements made were true or false.[172] In taking this position, Cotton was in effect translating an evidentiary question—whether the defendants could have believed the truth of their assertions—into a substantive duty. Although Cotton wished to make directors liable for constructive frauds, he did not wish to make them strictly liable, in a way which would make the remedy in deceit parallel rescission for innocent

---

[165] *Smith* v. *Chadwick* (1881) 20 Ch D 27 at 38 (Ch D).

[166] *Smith* v. *Chadwick* (1881) 20 Ch D 27 at 42. Fry cited the insurance case of *Pawson* v. *Watson* (1778) 2 Cowp. 785 as his authority.

[167] *Smith* v. *Chadwick* (1881) 20 Ch D 27 at 75.

[168] *Smith* v. *Chadwick* (1881) 20 Ch D 27 at 69.

[169] *Smith* v. *Chadwick* (1884) 9 App Cas 187 at 190.

[170] *Taylor* v. *Ashton* (1843) 11 M. & W. 401 at 415; *Shrewsbury* v. *Blount* (1841) 2 Man. & G. 475; *Clarke* v. *Dickson* (1859) 28 LJ NS 225 at 227.

[171] *Weir* v. *Bell* (1878) 3 Ex D 238 at 243.

[172] *Weir* v. *Bell* (1878) 3 Ex D 238 at 242.

misrepresentation. He only wished to impose a duty of care, rather than apply-ing equity's requirement of 'strict and scrupulous accuracy' in prospectuses.[173] It was for that reason alone that, in 1881, he seemed to state a view of law closer to Bramwell's.[174]

It remained unclear until 1889 whether deceit would lie only where someone with a full power to acquire knowledge wilfully abstained from doing so, acting 'in a gambling spirit … without caring sufficiently whether it is true or false',[175] or whether it lay where the speaker was 'careless' in making assertions 'which he ought to have known were not true'.[176] The issue was only settled in *Derry* v. *Peek*. In this case, the directors of a tramway company were sued in deceit for stating in their prospectus that they had secured certain legal rights, which they had reasonable grounds to believe would be granted, but which had not yet been granted. In the High Court, Stirling J. avoided settling the legal ques-tion. Regarding the defendants to be honest mercantile men, he found that they believed they had the rights stated, and that their belief was not unreasonable. In the Court of Appeal (which reversed the decision), Cotton LJ reiterated his view that when statements were to be circulated to the public, a director had the duty 'to take care that he has reasonable ground' for his belief.[177] The decision was welcomed by Pollock, who noted that the decision confirmed that the 'absence of reasonable ground for believing in the truth of one's assertion is a substantive ground of liability', which—whether or not it reflected past law—he regarded as 'more scientific'.[178]

However, the decision was overturned in the House of Lords. The Lords reaf-firmed that while the absence of reasonable grounds for a statement might be evidence that the party making it did not believe in its truth, it was not itself conclusive of fraud. In Lord Herschell's view, Cotton LJ was wrong to conflate

---

[173] *New Brunswick and Canada Railway Co* v. *Muggeridge* (1860) 1 Dr. & Sm. 363 at 381 (a case where specific performance was refused); a statement endorsed by the Lords in *Central Railway Co of Venezuela* v. *Kisch* (1867) LR 2 HL 99 113 (a case of rescission).

[174] While, he said, a contract could be rescinded 'although the misrepresentation was innocent'. for deceit to succeed, 'the action must not be innocent, that is to say, it must be made either with knowledge of its being false, or with a reckless disregard as to whether it is or is not true': *Arkwright* v. *Newbold* (1880) 17 Ch D 301 at 320.

[175] *Edgington* v. *Fitzmaurice* (1885) 29 Ch D 459 at 465–6.

[176] *Smith* v. *Chadwick* (1882) 20 Ch D 27 (CA) at 44; Cf. *Smith* v. *Chadwick* (1884) 9 App Cas 187 at 201.

[177] *Peek* v. *Derry* (1888) 37 Ch D 541 at 568. Sir James Hannen said (at p. 578) 'if a man takes upon himself to assert a thing to be true which he does not know to be true, and has no reasonable ground to believe to be true in order to induce another to act upon the assertion …. the person so damnified is entitled to maintain an action for deceit'. Lopes LJ (at p. 585) held that a man was liable for false statements he believed to be true, but without reasonable grounds for the belief.

[178] (1888) 4 *LQR* 369.

recklessness with the absence of care. 'To make a statement careless whether it be true or false, and therefore without any real belief in its truth', he noted, 'appears to me to be an essentially different thing from making, through want of care, a false statement, which is nevertheless honestly believed to be true.' [179] In his judgment, Lord Bramwell followed the approach he had taken in *Weir* v. *Bell*, requiring moral fraud. As he saw it, the phrase 'legal fraud' was only used

when some vague ground of action is to be resorted to, or, generally speaking, when the person using it will not take the trouble to find, or cannot find, what duty has been violated or right infringed, but thinks a claim is somehow made out. [180]

To have an action for misrepresentation, there had either to be a breach of contract (where the misrepresentation, however innocent, had become a warranty) or actual fraud.

Frederick Pollock was outraged by the decision, which 'all Lincoln's Inn' thought was wrong. [181] Pollock's real objection to it was that it hindered the development of the tort of negligence. Had the House of Lords affirmed the Court of Appeal, he noted, a new rule would have emerged that a man volunteering information intended to be acted on would be bound 'to use the ordinary care of a reasonable man to see that his assertion is warranted by the fact'. Though this had never been decided before, it would be quite in accordance with the lines of development which the common law had followed in regard to actions and undertakings affecting the safety of others in person and property. [182] As Bramwell's comment showed, the Lords were quite aware that they were resisting importing a broad principle of negligence as Pollock desired.

The law of misrepresentation was left in a state of some confusion by 1890. To begin with, it was unclear how far equity's remedy of rescission for innocent misrepresentation went. There was some debate over whether contracts for the sale of goods could be rescinded for innocent misrepresentations, with the New Zealand Court of Appeal deciding against this. [183] No English case settled this in the period covered in this volume, though treatise writers took the view that any contract could be rescinded for innocent misrepresentations. [184]

---

[179] *Derry* v. *Peek* (1889) 14 App Cas 337 at 361.

[180] *Derry* v. *Peek* (1889) 14 App Cas 337 at 346.

[181] See M. D. Howe (ed.), *The Pollock-Holmes Letters: Correspondence of Sir Frederick Pollock and Mr Justice Holmes 1874–1932*, 2 vols (Cambridge, 1942), i, 215, cf. i, 49, 13; see also F. Pollock, *The Law of Torts* (2nd edn, 1890), 254.

[182] F. Pollock, 'Derry v. Peek in the House of Lords' (1889) 5 *LQR* 410–23 at 422–3.

[183] *Riddiford* v. *Warren* (1901) 20 NZ LR 572.

[184] W. R. Anson, *Principles of the English Law of Contract* (14th edn by M. L. Gwyer, Oxford, 1917), 188.

This was a view which was hard to reconcile with the law as it developed on the distinction between conditions and warranties. A misrepresentation could of course become incorporated into the contract and become a term. Normally, the contract could only be terminated if the term breached could be classified as a condition, and not as a warranty. But if it had not been incorporated, then however minor the misrepresentation, the contract could be rescinded, not on the grounds that there had been a *fraud* but merely on the grounds of a misrepresentation.

V

Mistake

IT has generally been accepted that there was very little discussion of the effect of mistake on the consent of the parties to a contract until the second half of the nineteenth century.[1] Since parties were not allowed to give evidence until 1851, and since it was left to juries to decide what had been agreed, there seemed to be little scope for the development of legal rules regarding mistake. Changes in the law of evidence and procedure opened the way for new doctrinal developments, since courts could hear from the parties what they had meant. At the same time, it has been argued that treatise writers, influenced by will theory, turned to Pothier and Savigny to help formulate a new doctrine. Where early nineteenth-century treatise writers had ignored the topic of mistake—so central in civilian jurisprudence since the middle ages—a new theoretical interest in mistake can be traced from William Macpherson's work on the Indian law of contract in 1860,[2] and the English treatises of Leake, Benjamin, Pollock, and Anson. Of these, Pollock's was the most theoretically informed discussion, owing much to Savigny. For these writers, a contract was vitiated if the parties were at cross purposes, if there had been a mistake of identity as to one of the parties to the contract, and if the parties were both in error as to the essence of the subject-matter of the contract.[3] Treatise writers are said to have effected a reception of civilian ideas, as they took

[1] See A. W. B. Simpson, 'Innovation in Nineteenth Century Contract Law' (1975) 91 *LQR* 265–9; J. Gordley, *The Philosophical Origins of Modern Contract Doctrine* (Oxford, 1991), 140–6; D. J. Ibbetson, *Historical Introduction to the Law of Obligations* (Oxford, 1999), 225–29; C. MacMillan, 'Mistaken Arguments: The Role of Argument in the Development of a Doctrine of Contractual Mistake in Nineteenth Century England', in A. Lewis and M. Lobban (eds), *Law and History* (Oxford, 2004), 285–315. For a definitive treatment of the subject, see C. MacMillan, *Mistakes in English Law* (forthcoming, Oxford). I have benefited greatly from many conversations with Catharine MacMillan on this subject; and am grateful both for her comments on this chapter, and for allowing me to read her forthcoming work.

[2] W. Macpherson, *Outlines of the Law of Contracts as Administered in the Courts of British India* (1860).

[3] F. Pollock, *Principles of Contract at Law and in Equity* (1876), 373. The principle behind mistake of identity—that a contract was vitiated 'at least in all cases where it is material for the one party to know who the other is'—was taken from Savigny's discussion of D.12.1.32. The principle behind errors as to the subject matter was taken from D.18.1.9 and D.18.1.14.

the material of English case law and arranged it into new headings, which were then fed back into the case law by counsel who had read the treatises.[4]

In fact, notions of mistake in contract formation were not new to English law in the second half of the nineteenth century. The Court of Chancery had long dealt with mistakes relating to the subject-matter of contracts, when handling cases of land sales and family settlements. This court, with its inquisitorial machinery, was prepared to intervene not only where a contract failed to express the true agreement of the parties, but also when either one or both of the parties was mistaken as to the subject-matter of the contract. This was not simply a feature of equity's desire to ensure fairness, but was rather part of its desire to establish consent. By contrast, common law courts—which dealt more typically with commercial sales cases—were much less prepared to void contracts on the grounds that one or both parties had been mistaken. Allowing parties to evade contractual obligations by invoking mistake threatened to unsettle the stability of commercial relations.

When, in the second half of the century, writers like Leake and Pollock resorted to Roman law, it was in part to assist them in putting together the rules of equity and common law, to fashion a single law at a time of fusion. Yet if they sought to push the law in the direction of equity, they did not succeed. The common law courts remained reluctant to avoid contracts for common mistake, either as to the existence, or the quality of the subject-matter of a contract. They also reasserted that an objective view of the contract should prevail in the absence of fraud. Despite the best efforts of some treatise writers, common lawyers on the eve of the First World War therefore remained uninterested in vitiating contracts for mistakes as to the substance.

By contrast, in the second half of the century, common law courts did develop a new doctrine of mistake of identity, though one which by 1914 was very unstable and left much room for judicial discretion. In this area, the need for commercial stability and certainty was qualified by a judicial desire to protect property owners from frauds. This was not a new problem. In the first half of the nineteenth century, courts sought to deal with it by holding that fraud rendered contracts void. By the mid-century, judges seeking to protect innocent third party buyers restated the rule that fraud only rendered a contract voidable. Just as this rule was settled, a new approach was taken to protect the owners of goods from being defrauded by swindlers purporting to be their agents, which was developed (with the assistance of treatise writers) into a rule of mistake of identity. Nor was

---

[4] See C. MacMillan, 'Rogues, Swindlers and Cheats: The Development of Mistake of Identity in English Contract Law' (2005) 64 *CLJ* 711–44 at 726 (on how Benjamin's treatment of mistake was used by counsel in *Lindsay* v. *Cundy* (1876) 1 QBD 348 at 350), and 'Mistaken Arguments', 315.

this concern to prevent the owners of goods from being misled limited to cases involving criminal swindlers: for in two cases from the late 1850s, the Exchequer judges seemed to stretch the rules relating to contract formation in a way to protect a contracting party from what would otherwise have seemed an inequitable result. In fashioning these rules, judges were not seeking to develop doctrinal elegance, but were reacting to failures in the world of commerce, deciding which innocent party should bear the loss. The doctrine which they developed was far from consistent. If the doctrine of mistake could be invoked with success, then the innocent third party purchaser lost out; if it could not, he did not. Moreover, the commercial world was often exasperated with the approach of the courts. Consequently, businessmen tended to avoid solving these problems by litigation. Mistake of identity cases very rarely came to court, yet swindles perpetrated by fraudsters assuming a false identity were extremely common. Many followed the examples of pawnbrokers, who simply divided the loss with the owner of goods fraudulently obtained and pledged, rather than litigating.

1. MISTAKE IN EQUITY

Relief for fraud, surprise, and mistake had long been a staple of equity jurisprudence. The Chancery's concern was not with general commercial transactions, but with landed property and family settlements. Where a document did not reflect the real agreement between the parties, the Chancery would rectify it;[5] but before doing so, the court had to be satisfied that the mistake had been common to both parties, and that they had intended something different.[6] In Sir John Romilly MR's words, the court looked for 'the real agreement between the parties'.[7] Where a written agreement which failed to express the real terms of the contract had been executed, it could also be set aside.[8]

The Chancery also had the power to rescind contracts where the parties had been in agreement, but were both mistaken as to the subject-matter of the contract. Drawing on civilian examples, Joseph Story wrote that if a man contracted to buy

---

[5] See *Baker* v. *Paine* (1750) 1 Ves. Sr. 456; *Ball* v. *Storie* (1823) 1 S. & S. 210. Although it was a settled rule that courts could not draw on extrinsic evidence to help it construe the meaning of the words, they would admit evidence which showed that the written document did not reflect the parties' agreement.

[6] 'Under this head of *Mistake*, Settlements of *Real* or of *Personal* Estate will be reformed, if the Settlement be not according to the intention of the *Articles* upon which it is founded', H. Maddock, *A Treatise on the Principles and Practice of the High Court of Chancery*, 2 vols, (1815), i, 50, citing *Randall* v. *Willis* (1800) 5 Ves. 262.

[7] *Murray* v. *Parker* (1854) 19 Beav. 305 at 308. Cf. *Bentley* v. *Mackay* (1862) 31 Beav. 143 at 151; *Bradford* v. *Romney* (1862) 30 Beav. 431; *Mackenzie* v. *Coulson* (1869) LR 8 Eq 368 at 375.

[8] *Price* v. *Ley* (1863) 4 Giff. 235.

a house, which (unknown to both parties) had already been wholly destroyed, the contract would be vitiated for mistake, since 'both parties intended the purchase and sale of a subsisting thing, and implied its existence as the basis of their contract'.[9] For Story, both parties had to have been innocently mistaken as to a matter which was 'an efficient cause' of the contract. The case law confirmed that a sale of property was avoided in equity if the thing being sold did not exist. For instance, in *Hitchcock* v. *Giddings*, a purchaser bought the vendor's interest in a remainder in fee expectant on an estate tail, where, unknown to both parties, the tenant in tail had already suffered a recovery and barred the estate in remainder. Richards CB ruled, '[i]f contracting parties have treated while under a mistake, that will be sufficient ground for the interference of a Court of Equity.' He continued:

Suppose I sell an estate innocently, which at the time is actually swept away by a flood, without my knowledge of the fact; am I to be allowed to receive £5000 and interest, because the conveyance is executed, and a bond given for that sum as the purchase-money, when, in point of fact, I had not an inch of the land, so sold, to sell?[10]

This was in effect a case of total failure of consideration before the execution of the contract, but since there had been a conveyance and a bond, equity's intervention was needed to rescind the agreement, and adjust equities between the parties.

The problem of mistake was also raised in cases examining the validity of settlements made on marriages which turned out to be void. In these cases, marriages had been celebrated, and settlements made, without the permission of a parent, who had mistakenly been presumed to be dead. In 1811, the Common Pleas judges held that a settlement which had been executed under such a mistake was valid, since there had been an actual conveyance; though they also felt that if the matter had still rested in contract, it would have been voided for mistake.[11] By contrast, in 1828, Lyndhurst LC held that an executed settlement could be pronounced void by the Chancery, since that court could settle the equities between the parties in a way not possible at common law. The Chancery 'will not hold that a transaction, founded entirely on mistake and on the misapprehension of

---

[9] J. Story, *Commentaries on Equity Jurisprudence as administered in England and America*, 2 vols (Boston, Mass., 1836), §§ 141–2, pp. 156–8, alluding to D.18.1.57. See also R. J. Pothier, *Treatise on the Contract of Sale*, trans. L. S. Cushing (Boston, 1839), 3–4.

[10] *Hitchcock* v. *Giddings* (1817) 4 Price 135 at 141. Although this seemed to ignore the recent pronouncements which said that the purchaser assumed the risk of destruction, Richards may have had in mind the sale of a house already destroyed before the articles of sale were drawn up, and thus before any equitable property passed.

[11] *Broughton* v. *Sandilands* (1811) 3 Taunt. 342.

the parties, ought to be considered as binding'.[12] The question of marriage settlements executed on void marriages was revisited in the second half of the century, in the context of marriages celebrated overseas between men and their deceased wife's sister.[13] When in these cases, courts set aside the settlement, it was not on the basis that they were void for mistake, but that they were executed on a void consideration.[14]

Equity also intervened where the mistaken assumption on which the contract was premised did not result in a total failure of consideration, but led to a vendor selling property at an erroneous price. In *Colyer* v. *Clay* in 1843, a man holding a joint life interest with his cousin in a trust fund worth £2000, the whole of which was to go to the survivor of the two, sold his reversionary interest for £490, the sum at which an actuary had fixed its value. The valuation was premised on the assumption that the cousin was still alive, but at the time of the sale, and unknown to the parties, the cousin had already died, so that the vendor was entitled to the full sum. It was agreed on all sides that the contract had been entered into on a common mistake, and that it could not stand. The court also rescinded a contract based on a shared mistake regarding the price in *Carpmael* v. *Powis* in 1846. Here, the defendant sold property to the plaintiff for £1800, which was to be paid by way of an annuity. It was agreed that Miss Powis should be paid £18 more than an annuity purchased for £1800 from the government would pay. Information was obtained from the National Debt Office about the rates paid on government annuities, and an agreement was made based on these figures. The annuity was paid for four years before the plaintiff discovered that the figure quoted was higher than what the government would actually have paid. On discovering this, he sought to have the contract rectified or rescinded. Lord Langdale refused to rectify it, since he was not sure that Miss Powis would have gone ahead with an agreement for an annuity at a lesser rate. He therefore rescinded the contract, requiring her to account for the money she had received, and him to account for what was due in respect of the £1800.[15]

The Chancery also intervened where the parties had never come to a proper agreement, despite the existence of a written contract. In such cases, rectification was not possible, for if 'the parties took different views of what was intended, there would be no contract between them which could be carried into effect

[12] *Robinson* v. *Dickenson* (1828) 3 Russell 399 at 414.
[13] Such marriages were held void in *Brook* v. *Brook* (1858) 3 Sm. & Giff. 481.
[14] *Coulson* v. *Allison* (1860) 2 Giff. 279; *Chapman* v. *Bradley* (1863) 33 Beav. 61.
[15] *Carpmael* v. *Powis* (1846) 10 Beav. 36.

by rectifying the instrument'.[16] Rather, relief would be given. The principle was stated in this way by Thurlow LC in 1790:

if one party thought he had purchased *bona fide*, and the other party thought he had not sold, that is a ground to set aside the contract, that neither party may be damaged; as it is impossible to say, one shall be forced to give that price for part only, which he intended to give for the whole, or that the other shall be obliged to sell the whole, for what he intended to be the price of part only.[17]

In such cases, it could not simply be said that, since there had been no meeting of the minds, a contract had never come into existence. The parties had, after all, drawn up a formal document. Intervention by the Chancery was therefore required, either in the form of refusing specific performance (where this was sought) or rescission of the contract.

The most usual form of mistake in sales of land came when a vendor mistakenly thought he had title to all the property he had agreed to sell. Such cases were settled simply by looking at the terms of the contract. If the vendor could not make a title to all the land contracted for, 'the purchaser may consider the contract at an end, and bring an action for money had and received, to recover any sum of money which he may have paid'.[18] The vendor could seek specific performance if he could offer substantial performance, for the Chancery allowed him to give compensation for any minor shortfall.[19] However, if the part of an estate to which no title could be made was essential to its enjoyment—however small it was—specific performance would not be decreed.[20] Parties generally included clauses in their contracts for land sales stating that errors or misstatements in the particulars should not vitiate the sale, but be subject to compensation. But the courts set limits on how far compensation could be allowed. As Sir John Romilly MR saw it, if the misdescription was such that it would be imposing on the purchaser something of a different nature from what he expected—a leasehold rather than a freehold, for instance—then specific performance would not be granted, notwithstanding any compensation clause.[21]

More problematic for the Chancery were cases where the mistake was not one about one's ability to perform, but where a mistake had been made by one party

---

[16] *Bentley* v. *Mackay* (1862) 31 LJ Ch 697, 709, 4 De G. F. & J. 279 at 287. See also *Sells* v. *Sells* (1860) 1 Dr. & Sm. 42.

[17] *Calverley* v. *Williams* (1790) 1 Ves. Jr. 210 at 211.

[18] E. B. Sugden, *A Practical Treatise on the Law of Vendors and Purchasers* 2 vols (9th edn, 1834), i, 287; *Farrer* v. *Nightingal* (1798) 2 Esp. 639.

[19] *Hill* v. *Buckley* (1811) 17 Ves. 395.

[20] *Knatchbull* v. *Grueber* (1815) 1 Madd. 153. Cf. *Bowyer* v. *Bright* (1824) 13 Price 698 at 703; *Perkins* v. *Ede* (1852) 16 Beav. 193.

[21] *Ayles* v. *Cox* (1852) 16 Beav. 23 at 25. See also above, p. 104.

about the price, or about the subject of the sale, as where mistaken bids were made at auction, or where an agent mistakenly included land in an instrument which the vendor did not wish to sell. In such cases, it was claimed that the written contract did not reflect a real agreement, since it was premised on a mistake. Parties seeking specific performance were not allowed to give evidence of a mistake in the written agreement, in order to obtain performance on their understanding of the contract.[22] For as Grant MR put it, '[i]f the one might intend to sell upon one set of terms, as he conceives them, and the other intend to buy according to a different set of terms, there is in reality no agreement.'[23] They had first to rectify the contract in a separate proceeding, to show that there had been a real agreement mistakenly recorded.[24] But a defendant to a suit of specific performance was permitted to give evidence of mistake[25] to show that he had not intended to sell what was claimed, showing in fact that there was no agreement. As Wood VC put it, 'a person shall not be compelled by this court specifically to perform an agreement which he never intended to enter into, if he has satisfied the Court that it was not his real agreement'.[26]

Specific performance would be refused if the defendant could show that he mistakenly bid at an auction for property he did not intend to buy, or if he inadvertently included in the particulars of sale items not intended to be sold.[27] Where defendants resisting specific performance showed that the written contract did not reflect an agreement the parties had previously come to, the court would offer the plaintiff the choice to accept specific performance of that contract. As

---

[22] *Woollam* v. *Hearn* (1802) 7 Ves. 211.

[23] *Higginson* v. *Clowes* (1808) 15 Ves. 516 at 524.

[24] Though early nineteenth-century judges defended the rule as upholding the Statute of Frauds, later jurists also stressed the importance of avoiding disputes in a suit for specific performance about the nature of the agreement. As Dart put it, a plaintiff could not obtain specific performance on terms different from those stated in the written contract, unless 'by mistake, an agreement not expressing the real intention of the parties, is entered into, and the mistake is admitted by the answer, or, not being denied by the answer, is proved by unexceptionable evidence': J. H. Dart, *A Treatise on the Law and Practice relating to Vendors and Purchasers of Real Estate* (5th edn by Dart and W. Barber (1876)), ii, 1035. E. Fry, *A Treatise on the Specific Performance of Contracts* (1858), 227, felt that as a matter of justice, the courts should allow the plaintiff to have mistakes in the contract corrected and a specific performance obtained in the same bill, but noted that as the law stood, 'by two bills, one for reform and the other for specific performance, the plaintiff's end may now be attained'. In the third edition of his work (1892), 375, Fry noted that the matter had been resolved by s 24(7) of the Judicature Acts, as held by North J. in *Olley* v. *Fisher* (1887) 34 Ch D 367. See further, MacMillan, *Mistakes in Contract Law.*

[25] The defendant was permitted to give evidence to challenge the alleged agreement. See *Joynes* v. *Statham* (1746) 3 Atk. 388; *Ramsbottom* v. *Gosden* (1812) 1 V. & B 165; *Lord Gordon* v. *Marquis of Hertford* (1817) 2 Madd. 106.

[26] *Wood* v. *Scarth* (1855) 2 K. & J. 33 at 42, per Wood VC.

[27] *Malins* v. *Freeman* (1837) 2 Keen 25. See also *Marquis Townshend* v. *Stangroom* (1801) 6 Ves. 328; *Manser* v. *Back* (1848) 6 Hare 443.

Sir Thomas Plumer put it, 'the Court can only decree performance of the actual contract between the parties'.[28] In the mid-nineteenth century, Chancery judges began to extend this remedy by offering plaintiffs specific performance on the defendant's terms, when the latter showed he had acted under a mistake, and to leave them to their remedy at law if they refused.[29] This was in effect using the court as the forum to make a new agreement.

Equity judges had to be convinced that the party resisting specific perform-ance had made a genuine mistake. As Page Wood VC observed, 'it would be of the utmost danger to allow a person to escape from the consequences of his agreement, of which he repents, possibly thinking that he has not asked enough, upon slight parol evidence'.[30] Sir John Romilly similarly ruled in 1861 that it was not enough for the party simply to claim to have been mistaken. Rather, there had to be something in the description of the property 'on which a person might *bona fide* make a mistake'.[31] The Court of Appeal confirmed in 1880 that if a party had made a mistake from mere carelessness, as in not checking the particulars of a sale, he could not resist specific performance.[32]

If a party could resist specific performance by showing he had not intended to enter the contract in question, could he resist if he had made an error as to the quality of the property he had bought? A number of early authorities suggested he could not. The classic example given was *Shirley* v. *Davis*, where a purchaser bought property on the north side of the Thames, with the intention of becoming thereby a freeholder of Essex. Although the fragment of land in question turned out to be in Kent, he was held to the purchase.[33] The case was later explained as showing that where a party had entered an agreement, he could not avoid it because his motive in entering the contract was mistaken.[34] Another explan-ation, more popular in the late eighteenth and early nineteenth centuries, was that where the error was to an attribute, it was open to compensation. If this explained why a man who could only sell 99 acres rather than the 100 promised should be permitted to give compensation for the last acre, it did not well explain for many judges and jurists why a man who wanted a property for a particular purpose should be compelled to go ahead with the purchase if that purpose could

---

[28] *Garrard* v. *Grinling* (1818) 1 Wils. C.C. 460 at 464. For the plaintiff's option, see *Ramsbottom* v. *Gosden* (1812) 1 V. & B. 165.

[29] See Lord Cottenham's comments in *Alvanley* v. *Kinnaird* (1849) 2 M. & G. 1 at 8. See also Sir John Romilly's approach in *Baxendale* v. *Seale* (1855) 19 Beav. 601; *Earl of Durham* v. *Legard* (1865) 34 Beav. 611.

[30] *Wood* v. *Scarth* (1855) 2 K. & J. 33 at 39–40.

[31] *Swaisland* v. *Dearsley* (1861) 29 Beav. 430 at 433.

[32] *Tamplin* v. *James* (1880) 15 Ch D 215.

[33] The case was discussed in *Drewe* v. *Hanson* (1801) 6 Ves. 675 at 678.

[34] S. M. Leake, *The Elements of the Law of Contract* (1867), 170.

not be fulfilled.[35] A number of judges therefore felt that a party should not be compelled to perform, even if his mistake had been one of motive or of quality.

Where specific performance was refused, the parties were left to their remedy at law, unless a court of equity rescinded the contract. As Thurlow's comments showed, George III's Lord Chancellors were sometimes prepared to relieve on the grounds of one party's mistake.[36] In 1806, in *Morshead* v. *Frederick*, Erskine LC (following the opinion of Eldon) rescinded a contract for the purchase of a lease, since the purchasers had been mistaken as to the rent which was to be paid for it. But by the 1830s there was some unease with this view. Edward Sugden, who reported *Morshead* in his treatise on *Vendors and Purchasers*, did not approve of the decision,[37] and in later editions of his work restated Thurlow's view in a more qualified way, that in case of such errors, 'that is a ground to set aside the contract, or at least not to execute it'.[38] Mid-century judges who refused specific performance because of mistake left the parties to their legal remedies, rather than rescinding the contract.[39] By 1867, S. M. Leake therefore stated it as a simple proposition that 'a Court of Equity will not rectify or rescind a contract merely on the ground of a mistake of one of the parties'.[40]

However, despite Leake's general statement, equity did rescind contracts for unilateral mistake where a party was mistaken as to his own rights, and had entered into an agreement giving up property under a misconception.[41] Equity did not interfere lightly in these cases, but required very strong evidence of the mistake.[42] It did not relieve where parties made a mistake of law—for everyone

---

[35] See Lord Thurlow LC's comments in *Howland* v. *Norris* (1784) 1 Cox C.C. 59 and Lord Erskine LC's in *Halsey* v. *Grant* (1806) 13 Ves. 73. See also Sugden, *Vendors and Purchasers* (5th edn, 1818), 262.

[36] Contrast the approach in *Legge* v. *Croker* (1811) 1 Ball & Beat. 506, where Manners LC refused to set aside a lease drawn up after the lessor had mistakenly said the property was not subject to a right of way, but where the parties had not included any covenants to this effect in the deed. He compared the case with that of a horse sold without a warranty.

[37] Sugden, *Vendors and Purchasers* (9th edn, 1834), i: 72, ii, 320.

[38] Cf. E. Sugden, *A Concise and Practical Treatise of the Law of Vendors and Purchasers of Estates* (13th edn, 1857), 260.

[39] *Malins* v. *Freeman* (1837) 2 Keen 25 at 34; *Alvanley* v. *Kinnaird* (1849) 2 M. & G. 1 at 8; *Wood* v. *Scarth* (1855) 2 K. & J. 33 at 44. See also *Legge* v. *Croker* (1811) 1 Ball & Beat. 506, where Manners LC refused to set aside a lease drawn up after the lessor had mistakenly said the property was not subject to a right of way, but where the parties had not included any covenants to this effect in the deed. He compared the case with that of a horse sold without a warranty.

[40] Leake, *Elements* (1867), 170.

[41] In *Cocking* v. *Pratt*, where a daughter made an agreement as to the distribution of her father's personal estate under a mistake as to the amount to which she was entitled, the Chancery set aside the agreement on the ground of her lack of knowledge: *Cocking* v. *Pratt* (1749–50) 1 Ves. Sr. 400.

[42] See *Lord Irnham* v. *Child* (1781) 1 Bro. C.C. 92 at 93; *Marquis Townshend* v. *Stangroom* (1801) 6 Ves. 328 at 333; *Henkle* v. *Royal Exchange Assurance Co* (1749) 1 Ves. Sr. 317.

was presumed to know the law—but it was regarded as against conscience for one party to take advantage of another's mistake of his legal rights.[43] Relief on these grounds was akin to relief for fraud or undue influence and, on some occasions, the mistake was accompanied by undue influence or fraud.[44] But relief could also be given absent knowledge by the benefiting party, since it would still be against conscience to retain such benefits. One class of such cases was those where a party purchased what already belonged to him.[45]

In the mid-century, Sir John Romilly MR began to develop a more interventionist approach where one of the parties had made a mistake to the other party's knowledge. In *Garrard v. Frankel*, the parties negotiated a lease of a house for £230 a year. When the agreement was drawn up, the lessor by mistake entered the rental as £130. This was not a mistake of his rights, but a slip of the pen. It was also an error of which the lessee was clearly aware, and which she was happy to take advantage of. The lessor sought to have the agreement rectified, but Romilly agreed that this remedy was not available, since this was not a case of the parties mistakenly expressing a real agreement. However, he felt that where one party to a contract was aware that the other was acting under a mistake, she should not be permitted to take advantage of this. Although he believed that the lessee would have taken the house at the higher rate, he did not feel he could compel her to be bound by a rectified agreement for a higher price, which was inconsistent with the document she had signed. He therefore gave the defendant a choice. She could either accept a rectified agreement, or give up the lease altogether, on payment of a rent for the time she had occupied the premises, at the rate of £230 a year, which was the rate paid by the previous tenant.[46] Romilly's decision to regard this unilateral mistake as an operative one reflected his moral approach to equity's jurisdiction.[47] His manipulation of equity's power of rectification, which could usually only be used where both parties made the same mistake, was equally novel.

---

[43] See the comments of Lord Macclesfield in *Cann v. Cann* (1721) 1 P. Wms. 723 at 727; *Pusey v. Desbouvrie* (1734) 3 P. Wms. 315.

[44] *Scrope v. Offley* (1736) 1 Bro. P.C. 276; *M'Carthy v. Decaix* (1831) 2 R. & Myl. 614. See also *Broughton v. Hutt* (1858) 3 De G. & J. 501.

[45] *Bingham v. Bingham* (1748) 1 Ves. Sr. 126; *Saunders v. Lord Annesley* (1804) 2 Sch. & Lef. 73 at 101 (where Lord Redesdale held that if a plaintiff, having the fee simple, was induced by fraud to accept a chattel interest, equity would intervene, and added that where the plaintiff acted out of ignorance, he inclined to think the court might intervene: 'yet, after looking a little into the subject, I find great difficulty in holding that a court of equity could interfere'); *Leonard v. Leonard* (1812) 2 Ball & Beat. 171 at 183; *Cooper v. Phibbs* (1867) LR 2 HL 149. Sugden, *Vendors and Purchasers* (5th edn, 1818), 222.

[46] *Garrard v. Frankel* (1862) 30 Beav. 445. See also *Bloomer v. Spittle* (1872) LR 13 Eq 427.

[47] W. R. Anson, *Principles of the English Law of Contract* (Oxford, 1879), 127 suggested that this case applied the same doctrine articulated at common law in *Smith v. Hughes* (1871) LR 6 QB 597, whereby a contract would be vitiated by a mistake as to the quality of the thing promised, known to the party promising.

Romilly took a similarly interventionist approach in 1867 in *Harris* v. *Pepperell*, where a plan on the conveyance of some property—sent by the purchaser's solic-itor—included land which the vendor had not intended to sell. After the convey-ance was executed, the vendor sought to rectify it, to reflect the original proposal. Romilly pointed out that, in general, contracts could not be rectified unless it was evident that the parties had come to a real agreement which had not been accu-rately reflected in the deed. Nor would the contract be set aside on the ground of one party's mistake, if the parties could not be put in the same position as they had been before it had been made. It was for this reason, Romilly held, that equity acted with great caution in granting relief when it was called to rectify marriage settlements on the ground of mistake. Since 'it is impossible to undo the marriage, or to remit the parties to the same position they were in before', the court would only rectify on obtaining 'proof of the exact contract which the parties intended to enter into'.[48] However, where—as in cases involving vendors and purchasers—the court could put the parties into the *status quo ante*, then the court could give the defendant the option to have the whole contract annulled, or to take it in the form in which the plaintiff intended it. This was effectively to use equity's procedure to negotiate a new contract between the parties, as a way of saving them the expense which would be entailed by starting again. The principle behind the decision was stated by Bacon VC in 1885: where parties exe-cuted a conveyance under a common mistake, it was to be rectified in accordance with their true intentions. Where the mistake was of one party only, the contract could be rescinded (on the grounds that there had been no agreement); but an option could be given to the party not in error to take what the mistaken party intended, in lieu of rescission.[49] The decisions were controversial. To begin with, the notion that a contract could be rescinded for unilateral mistake in equity, where 'the true intention of one of the parties was to do one thing, and he by mistake has signed an agreement to do another',[50] entailed a considerably more generous approach towards mistaken parties than had been taken by courts of equity earlier in the century. Furthermore, critics pointed out that if there had been no contract to begin with (because of the unilateral mistake), it was for the parties (and not the court) to make a new one.[51]

The approach of Romilly and Bacon thus sought to expand equity's assistance to the mistaken parties significantly. It built on the Chancery's jurisdiction to relieve parties who acted under a mistake of their rights, allowing rescission

---

[48] *Harris* v. *Pepperell* (1867) LR 5 Eq 1 at 4. Cf. *Sells* v. *Sells* (1860) 1 Dr. & Sm. 42.

[49] *Paget* v. *Marshall* (1885) 28 Ch D 255.   [50] *Paget* v. *Marshall* (1885) 28 Ch D 255 at 263.

[51] J. Dart, *A Treatise on the Law and Practice relating to Vendors and Purchasers of Real Estate* (6th edn, by W. Barber, R. B. Haldane, and W. R. Sheldon, 1888), 839, stated that if there had originally been a contract, the court could not make a new one, and if there was none, there was nothing to enforce.

without fraud or undue influence being shown. But these judges applied the doctrine where there had been no mistake about rights, and where there had been no clear proof of fraud or undue influence. By the end of the century, some judges therefore sought to qualify Romilly's view by asserting that there had to be some kind of fraud by the party who was not mistaken.[52]

In the mid-twentieth century, in *Solle* v. *Butcher*, Lord Denning sought to revive and extend Romilly's approach. In so doing, he generated the notion that, three-quarters of a century after fusion, there were distinct approaches taken to mistake at common law and in equity, the former rendering a contract void, and the latter rendering it voidable.[53] Denning's decision rested on two foundations. The first was the expansive view of unconscionable advantage taking which had informed Romilly's approach. The second was his interpretation of equity's intervention in *Cooper* v. *Phibbs*, a case where the plaintiff leased property from his cousins which (through a family settlement) in fact belonged to him. In this case, the House of Lords held the plaintiff entitled to have the lease set aside on terms.[54] Equity's intervention was required to set aside the deed, and also to adjust equities to effect a proper *restitutio in integrum*, since part of the property occupied by the plaintiff was owned by the defendants, who had also spent money on what turned out to belong to their cousin. Denning interpreted the case as saying that the mistake was only such as to render the contract voidable, and on terms which the court sought fit to impose. In fact, *Cooper* was seen by later nineteenth-century jurists as a classic example of a contract which was set aside owing to a mistake as to the subject-matter.[55] These jurists did not speak of equity only setting aside contracts induced by mistake where it was fair to do so.[56] Indeed, Denning's idea that 'this lease can be set aside on such terms as the court thinks fit'[57] had no basis in nineteenth-century authority. Rather, he was seeking, as Romilly did, for a fair outcome in the circumstances of a hard case.[58]

---

[52] *May* v. *Platt* [1900] 1 Ch 617 at 623.

[53] For modern attempts to deal with this dilemma, see *Great Peace Shipping* v. *Tsavliris Salvage (International)* [2002] EWCA Civ 1407, [2003] QB 679.

[54] *Cooper* v. *Phibbs* (1867) LR 2 HL 149.   [55] Pollock, *Contract* (1876), 400.

[56] J. P. Benjamin, who argued in general that the effect of a mistake in agreement rendered the contract void, as never having come into existence, did say that if it had been carried into effect under a continuance of mistake, it was only voidable. In these circumstances, either party 'may set aside the sale on discovering the truth, unless he has done something to render impossible a *restitutio in integrum* of the other side': Benjamin, *A Treatise on the Law of Sale of Personal Property* (1868), 303. However, he did not regard this as a specifically equitable doctrine, and later jurists (such as Anson, *Contracts*, 6th edn, 1891, 125–6) seem to have regarded this kind of discussion as confusing mistake issues with those arising from failure of consideration.

[57] *Solle* v. *Butcher* [1950] 1 KB 671 at 695.

[58] See C. MacMillan, 'Solle v. Butcher', in C. Mitchell and P. Mitchell, *Landmark Cases in the Law of Restitution* (Oxford, 2006), 325–60.

In doing so, he generated a divergent approach to common law and equitable mistake which did not exist in the nineteenth century.

2. MISTAKE AT COMMON LAW

The common law lacked the machinery to probe the consciences of the parties and explore their true intentions. It also lacked equity's powers to rectify agreements or set them aside on terms. In the common law courts, questions about mistake of subject-matter or quality were therefore generally translated into disputes about whether there was a contract and what had been contracted for. Dealing, as they did, with a large volume of commercial disputes, common lawyers expected businessmen to take care to allocate their own risks when drawing up their contracts.

Sometimes it was easy to argue that no contract had been concluded. For instance, if bought and sold notes delivered by a broker described the goods differently, it was evident that the parties had not agreed to buy and sell the same thing, and so no contract was concluded.[59] At other times, issues of mistake resolved themselves into questions of contractual performance. Where a purchaser contracted to buy a thing, and the vendor delivered something which he mistakenly assumed to correspond to the thing wanted, the purchaser could simply return it and recover his payment in an action for money had and received.[60] The risk lay on the seller to supply what had been promised. Disagreements over quality were also resolved by looking at the terms of the contract. As Williams J. put it, 'a party is not bound to accept and pay for chattels, unless they are really such as the vendor professed to sell, and the vendee intended to buy'.[61] A buyer could not reject goods because he had mistaken that they would serve his purposes; but he could reject goods which did not comply with his contract.

Some contacts were ambiguous, with terms open to being interpreted in one sense by one party, and in another by the other party. This often occurred when a general phrase had been used to describe a commodity of which various kinds were available. Where a supplier delivered goods which matched the general phrase used in the contract—such as 'potato'—the buyer was not permitted to offer evidence that he understood the contract in a different sense—such as 'kidney potatoes'—since that would violate the rule that written contracts could not be varied by parol evidence.[62] But where a term used in the contract was so

---

[59] *Thornton* v. *Kempster* (1814) 5 Taunt. 786.
[60] *Gompertz* v. *Bartlett* (1853) 2 E. & B. 849; *Young* v. *Cole* (1837) 3 Bing. N.C. 724 at 730.
[61] *Hall* v. *Conder* (1857) 2 C.B. N.S. 22 at 41.
[62] *Smith* v. *Jeffryes* (1846) 15 M. &. W 561.

ambiguous that it could mean a variety of different things, evidence was allowed to show in what sense the parties had used the term.[63] This occurred where there was a 'latent' ambiguity, which was 'not apparent on the face of the contract, but arises from the application of the words to the objects to which they refer'.[64] As Alderson B. put it, if 'the words apply equally to two different things or subject matters [...] then evidence is admissible to shew which was the thing or subject matter intended'.[65]

Evidence was admitted to show not what the individuals subjectively meant by a term, but what any person in their position would understand by the contract, in order to assist the court in construing the contract. However, the rule could also be used to show that the parties had been at cross-purposes, without coming to an agreement. This occurred where there was such a degree of ambiguity that it could not be cured by evidence. This happened in *Raffles* v. *Wichelhaus*, where the plaintiff sold the defendant a cargo of cotton to arrive on a ship named the *Peerless*, sailing from Bombay. In fact, two ships of the same name sailed from that port, one in October and one in December. When sued for non-acceptance of the goods shipped, the defendant pleaded that the ship in the agreement was the October ship, whose cargo he was willing to accept, and not the December ship, which carried the plaintiff's cargo. The court of Exchequer held the plea good on demurrer. In the court's view, there was here sufficient ambiguity to allow parol evidence to explain the contract, as a result of which it would be for the jury to say whether the parties meant the same ship. If they did not, there would be no consensus *ad idem* and no contract concluded.[66]

The rule forbidding parol evidence to be introduced to vary written contracts was relaxed in 1854, when equitable pleas were allowed to be raised at common law. Such pleas were used to allow a defendant to claim that the contract as drawn up did not reflect the true agreement of the parties.[67] A buyer of goods could now defend an action for his failure to accept them by raising the equitable plea that the contract of sale mistakenly omitted a term with which the plaintiff had failed to comply;[68] but he would not be able to sue on the 'true' contract without first

[63] e.g. *Birch* v. *Depeyster* (1816) 1 Stark. 210. See also *Chaurand* v. *Angerstein* (1791) Peake 61; *Taylor* v. *Briggs* (1827) 2 C. & P. 525. Evidence could also be given to explain how the terms used were customarily understood: *Smith* v. *Wilson* (1832) 3 B. & Ad. 728; *Hutton* v. *Warren* (1836) 1 M. & W. 466.

[64] C. G. Addison, *A Treatise on the Law of Contracts* (4th edn, 1856), 848.

[65] *Smith* v. *Jeffryes* (1846) 15 M. & W. 561.

[66] *Raffles* v. *Wichelhaus* (1864) 2 H. & C. 906 at 907. A. W. B. Simpson, *Leading Cases in the Common Law* (Oxford, 1995), 158 attributes the interest contract lawyers had in this case to Judah Benjamin's 1868 treatise on sale. In fact, the case had already been discussed in Leake's *Elements* (1867), 179.

[67] See *Luce* v. *Izod* (1856) 1 H. & N. 245; *Vorley* v. *Barrett* (1856) 1 C.B. N.S. 225.

[68] e.g. *Borrowman* v. *Rossel* (1864) 16 C.B. N.S. 58. See also *Steele* v. *Haddock* (1855) 10 Exch. 643; *Wake* v. *Harrop* (1861) 6 H. & N. 768.

going to Chancery to have it rectified. The common law courts only allowed such pleas where the contract was executed. It was considered by the common lawyers that admitting the plea in an executory agreement would in effect entail claiming a power to rectify agreements, which was the preserve of equity.[69] This meant that the equitable plea could only be used where courts of equity would grant an absolute and perpetual injunction. 'In this last case, no difficulty occurs; for the plea is a simple bar to the action' Lord Campbell observed, '[b]ut, if the injunction is to be temporary or conditional in equity, at common law we have no such judgment, and we have no analogous judgment. We could not attempt to do justice between the parties without pronouncing, instead of a common law judgment, an equitable decree'.[70]

The common law offered very little scope for one party to argue that no contract had been concluded since he had made a unilateral mistake. On the few occasions when courts accepted a plaintiff's argument that no contract had been concluded, it was not done on the grounds of mistake. In *Phillips* v. *Bistolli*, a man who had been Empress Josephine's jeweller defended an action of assumpsit for goods sold. Though far from fluent in English, he had made a bid for some earrings at an auction. He claimed that he thought his bid was for £48, but the lot was knocked down for £88. He did not pay the deposit demanded, and returned the jewels after three or four minutes. This being a contract which had to comply with the Statute of Frauds, it had to be decided whether this constituted sufficient 'acceptance' of the goods. In his summing up, Abbott CJ told the jury that Bistolli's taking of the goods would constitute such an acceptance, provided they were convinced that he had not mistaken the price. The jury found for the plaintiff, for it was noticed that he had returned the goods only after inspecting them.[71] The King's Bench overturned this, not on the ground that there had been a mistake, but because it felt his retaining the goods for such a short time could not constitute an acceptance.[72]

Nor did the arrival of equitable pleas help defendants in this area. In *Scott* v. *Littledale* in 1858, the plaintiffs sued for the non-delivery of a cargo of tea, to be delivered from the ship *Star of the East*. The sale had been by sample, but the sample shown had been one from a totally different tea, which had not been put on the named ship. An equitable plea was therefore entered that there had been a common error of fact on a matter material to the contract, and that it was impossible for the defendants to perform according to the contract. But the

---

[69] See *Perez* v. *Oleaga* (1856) 11 Exch. 506 at 512.
[70] *Wodehouse* v. *Farebrother* (1855) 5 E. & B. 277 at 288–9.
[71] *The Times*, 19 April 1823, col. 3d.
[72] *Phillips* v. *Bistolli* (1824) 2 B. & C. 511.

court found for the plaintiff on demurrer, considering that this was not a case where the Chancery would grant simple relief. The plea, Lord Campbell asserted, 'is founded on the assumption that in equity this contract would be void at the option of the vendor. But we are of opinion that the contract would be held to be still subsisting, and that the relief in equity, if any, would be partial or conditional.'[73] The judges felt that equity would not rescind the contract at the mere option of the vendors, but might, for instance, have given the purchasers the option to take what was offered.[74]

Common law courts also had to consider issues of shared mistakes regarding the subject-matter of the contract. Early nineteenth-century common law judges seemed to assume that (like equity) the common law would regard as void contracts erroneously premised on the existence of something.[75] A flurry of mid-century cases clarified the common law's approach. In 1852, in *Strickland* v. *Turner*, the Exchequer judges held that a plaintiff, who had bought an annuity on the life of a person who at the time of contracting was already dead, could recover in an action for money had and received, since there had been a total failure of consideration.[76] Five months later, the same court considered a case where the seller of goods which had perished sought to recover the price. In *Couturier* v. *Hastie*, the plaintiffs, who were merchants at Smyrna, shipped a cargo of Indian corn, and through their London agent employed the defendant corn factors to sell it under a *del credere* commission, under which the latter guaranteed the solvency of the ultimate purchaser. The factor sold the corn to a purchaser on 15 May, but by then the cargo had already been sold en route, having begun to deteriorate from overheating. The purchaser repudiated the contract, and subsequently became bankrupt, leaving the plaintiffs to sue the factors on their guarantee. Each court which heard the case treated the question as one of contractual construction. The Exchequer judges accepted that there was an implied term in contracts of sale that the goods existed, but held that in this case the purchaser bought the adventure, and not merely the goods, and so assumed the risk.[77] The Exchequer Chamber and House of Lords overturned the judgment on the latter point and confirmed the general proposition that a vendor of goods undertook that they existed, and could be transferred. Lord Cranworth told the Lords 'that the whole question turns upon the construction

---

[73] *Scott* v. *Littledale* (1858) 8 E. & B. 815 at 821.

[74] Similarly, at common law, while a sale by sample implied a warranty that the bulk would confirm to sample, it was always open to the purchaser to waive the breach and accept inferior goods. *Scott* v. *Littledale* (1858) 8 E. & B. 815.

[75] *Broughton* v. *Sandilands* (1811) 3 Taunt. 342 at 368.

[76] *Strickland* v. *Turner* (1852) 7 Exch. 208. See also *Risbourg* v. *Bruckner* (1858) 3 C.B. N.S. 812.

[77] *Couturier* v. *Hastie* (1852) 8 Exch. 40 at 54.

of the contract'.[78] It was also confirmed in the 1850s that a contract for life assurance was void if the person whose life was assured had died prior to the contract being made or renewed. As Willes J. put it, life assurance was 'a contract for the payment of a certain sum upon the future death of a person then in being'.[79] The court in that case treated the existence of the person whose life was assured as a term of the contract.

The early nineteenth-century common law did not offer a remedy where there was a shared mistake of quality.[80] However, in the second half of the century, as jurists began to develop a theory of mistake, they became ever more interested in exploring this idea. Following Savigny, Frederick Pollock argued that a contract could be vitiated where there was an error as to the quality of the thing contracted for. He stated that if, unknown to both parties to the contract, the thing contracted for lacked an attribute which—'according to the ordinary course of dealing'—was so important that without it the thing was different in kind from what it was thought to be, then the contract was void.[81] Thus (using an example from the *Digest*), if a bar was sold as gold, but was in fact brass, then, both parties being ignorant of the truth, the contract would be void for mistake.[82]

Pollock found the principle most clearly expressed in Blackburn J.'s judgment in *Kennedy* v. *Panama, New Zealand and Australian Royal Mail Company*, one of the many company cases brought in the late 1860s by share purchasers who had invested in companies on the basis of misleading prospectuses.[83] The case was untypical since, rather than going to the Chancery, the plaintiff used an action for money had and received to recover deposits paid, while at the same time resisting a claim by the company for payment of calls on shares. Lord Gilbert Kennedy had applied for shares in the defendant company, on the faith of a prospectus which wrongly (but innocently) stated that company had entered into a contract with the New Zealand government. Having rejected the

[78] *Couturier* v. *Hastie* (1856) 5 H.L.C. 673 at 681; cf. *Hastie* v. *Couturier* (1853) 9 Exch. 102. See also *Smith* v. *Myers* (1870) LR 5 QB 429. Although Pothier's *Traité de Vente* was cited in the Lords, the civilian formulation that a contract was void if it had no object was not taken up.

[79] *Pritchard* v. *The Merchant's and Tradesman's Mutual Life Assurance Co* (1858) 3 C.B. N. S. 622 at 644.

[80] However, in *Cox* v. *Prentice* (1815) 3 M. & S. 344, the King's Bench permitted a plaintiff to recover the difference between the price paid for a bar of silver and its real value, since the assayer who was to determine the price had erred in his calculation. Lord Ellenborough here made a creative use of the action for money had and received, allowing the recovery of an overpayment, to enforce what he considered the parties' real agreement. See Pollock's critical view in *Principles of Contract* (1876), 396.

[81] Pollock, *Contract* (1876), 393, quoting F. C. von Savigny, *System des heutigen römischen Rechts*, 8 vols (Berlin, 1840–9) vol. 3, § 137.

[82] See the example repeated in *Gompertz* v. *Bartlett* (1853) 2 E. & B. 849 at 854.

[83] *Kennedy* v. *Panama, New Zealand and Australian Royal Mail Co* (1867) LR 2 QB 580.

plaintiff's arguments that the contract could be set aside for misrepresentation,[84] Blackburn J. had to address George Mellish QC's argument that the money could be recovered, since it had been a condition of the undertaking that the contract mentioned in the prospectus existed, the failure of which meant 'that the object of the contract failed'.[85] Blackburn agreed that a contract could be rescinded if there was 'a complete difference in substance between what was supposed to be and what was taken, so as to constitute a failure of consideration'. In explaining what this meant, he referred to the Roman principle that 'where the parties are not at one as to the subject of the contract there is no agreement', and cited the examples from the *Digest* which formed the foundation of discussions of mistake in the civilian literature. English law, he proceeded, was the same as Roman law,

and the difficulty in every case is to determine whether the mistake or misapprehension is as to the substance of the whole consideration, going, as it were, to the root of the matter, or only to some point, even though a material point, an error which does not affect the substance of the whole consideration.[86]

Civilian scholars had found it notoriously difficult to determine what was a material attribute, and Blackburn did not discuss this civilian literature in rejecting the plaintiff's claim. Although he did invoke a distinction found in Pothier (echoed by later English treatise writers)[87] in commenting that Kennedy's misapprehension was one relating to his motive in asking for the shares, rather than being one about the substance of the shares, it was not a line of argument he developed. Instead, he explored English analogies in a way which confirmed how little room the common law left for mistakes of quality. He admitted that the mid-century cases cited by Mellish whereby parties were permitted to terminate contracts for breaches of condition[88] provided some analogy, 'as the question in such cases very much depends on whether the stipulation goes to the root of the matter'. But he seemed reluctant to apply the thinking behind these cases (which developed the rule that contracts could be terminated without there being a *total* failure of consideration) here. Instead, he found a better analogy by comparing the approach to cases where horses, erroneously presumed to be sound, were sold without a warranty. In such cases, the mistaken buyer had no remedy.

---

[84] See the discussion above, p. 424.   [85] *The Times*, 3 June 1867, col. 10d.

[86] *Kennedy v. Panama, New Zealand and Australian Royal Mail Co* (1867) LR 2 QB 580 at 587–8, citing D.18.1.9–11.

[87] R. J. Pothier, *A Treatise on the Law of Obligations or Contracts*, 2 vols (trans. W. D. Evans, 1806), i, 12–13. This distinction was invoked, though with references to English case law rather than civilian notions, by Leake, *Elements* (1867), 170 and Benjamin, *Sale* (1868), 39.

[88] *Behn v. Burness* (1863) 3 B. & S. 751. For a discussion, see pp. 489–70.

Blackburn's essentially English solutions to the contractual problems considered in civilian texts was further in evidence four years later in *Smith* v. *Hughes*. In this case, the seller did not share the buyer's mistake. Having seen a sample of oats, a racehorse trainer offered to buy some from a farmer. During the negotiations, the buyer assumed they were old oats (suitable for feeding to horses), whereas the seller knew they were new. When new oats were delivered, the trainer refused to accept them, and was sued by the farmer. The county court judge told the jury that if the plaintiff thought the defendant believed he was contracting for old oats, they should find for the defendant, which they did. But the Queen's Bench ordered a new trial. While Cockburn CJ's judgment was largely based on the principle of *caveat emptor*, he also dismissed the defendant's argument that the parties had never been *ad idem*, thanks to the buyer's mistake, for in his view the parties had agreed on the essential subject-matter of the contract. Invoking the language of Leake and Benjamin, he said the error of the buyer was one of motive, or one as to a 'collateral' fact, which could not be taken into account. Blackburn and Hannen JJ also agreed there should be a new trial. But their approach to the issue differed from Cockburn's, for they were keener to explore how a collateral error could be distinguished from an essential one. Although this was a question discussed in the civilian (though not in the English) literature, the answer they came up with turned out to be very English rather than Roman.

Citing Parke's dictum in *Freeman* v. *Cooke*,[89] Blackburn J. endorsed the objective theory of contract formation discussed by the English writers. But like Benjamin, he rooted it in estoppel:

[I]f one of the parties intends to make a contract on one set of terms, and the other intends to make a contract on another set of terms, or, as it is sometimes expressed, if the parties are not ad idem, there is no contract, unless the circumstances are such as to preclude one of the parties from denying that he has agreed to the terms of the other.[90]

Hannen J. agreed with this notion that a party to 'an apparent contract may, by his own fault, be precluded from setting up that he had entered into it in a different sense' from that understood by the other party. But both judges felt this rule could be qualified. As Hannen put it, if the party not in error discovered that the other was in error, then the latter could show that he had not intended to enter into the apparent contract: he was no longer estopped. If

the plaintiff knew that the defendant, in dealing with him for oats, did so on the assumption that the plaintiff was contracting to sell him old oats, he was aware that the defendant

---

[89] *Freeman* v. *Cooke* (1848) 2 Exch. 654.
[90] *Smith* v. *Hughes* (1871) LR 6 QB 597 at 607. See also the discussion above, p. 339.

apprehended the contract in a different sense to that in which he meant it, and he is thereby deprived of the right to insist that the defendant shall be bound by that which was only the apparent, and not the real bargain.'[91]

Blackburn J. went further, stressing that for the mistake to vitiate the contract, the buyer had to have regarded the quality of the oats as having been warranted by the vendor. It is significant that Blackburn's doctrine was not derived from civilian ideas of which characteristics were essential and which accidental, but from the common law's language of warranties.[92] Moreover, the solution was (as Pollock realized) one unknown to Roman law, and one which was very difficult to apply.[93]

The decisions in *Smith* and *Kennedy* confirmed that the common law was not receptive to the development of the kind of doctrine of mistake to be found in the writings of will theorists. Despite the best efforts of writers like Pollock to show that there was a general doctrine of mistake which could be explained on civilian lines, it would not be until after the First World War that the English judiciary would accept that a contract could be set aside for a mistake of quality. When it did so, it imported a doctrine which would cause twentieth-century judges and jurists no small amount of trouble.

3. MISTAKE OF IDENTITY

In the later nineteenth century, a new doctrine of mistake of identity was identified and discussed by treatise writers in response to a number of common law decisions. The issue had attracted considerable attention from civilian jurists, and treatise writers took from them the idea that if the identity of the promisee was important to the promisor, then the contract would be void for the mistake. Pothier argued that 'wherever the consideration of the person with whom I contract is an ingredient of the contract which I intend to make, an error respecting the person destroys my consent [...but if] I should equally have made the contract with any other person, the contract would be valid'. Thus, no contract of loan would arise if a lender gave money to Peter, mistaking him for Paul, to whom he intended to lend. But a bookseller selling a book to Peter, thinking him

---

[91] *Smith* v. *Hughes* (1871) LR 6 QB 597 at 610, quoting W. Paley, *The Principles of Moral and Political Philosophy* (1785), 107.

[92] His solution may have owed something to Mellish's argument in *Kennedy* v. *Panama, New Zealand and Australian Royal Mail Co* (1867) LR 2 QB 580. See also Leake's comments in *Elements* (1867), 172.

[93] Pollock, *Contract* (1876), 395n pointed out that this 'somewhat refined' distinction did not exist in Roman law. See also the application of the rule in *Scriven Brothers* v. *Hindley & Co* [1913] 3 KB 564.

to be Paul, would be held to his contract.[94] Savigny also argued that a contractual obligation was void if the party contracting thought he was dealing with someone else.[95]

These learned texts were not discussed by English writers until the 1870s. But the problem of mistaken identity was hardly a new one. Rogues had since time immemorial swindled people out of their property by pretending to be someone else. Equally, people selling their property had often been choosy about the individuals they wished to deal with. Disputes over all these issues could end up in court. When they did, English courts in the early nineteenth century held people to the contracts they had made, only setting them aside where they perceived there had been fraud. When, in the later nineteenth century, a series of decisions laid the foundations for a newly identified doctrine, it was equally driven by the common lawyer's desire to root out frauds in ways not done before.

In the early nineteenth-century Chancery, if a purchaser obtained a property at a lower price than he would otherwise have done, because the vendor mistook him for someone he wanted to favour, the court would refuse to enforce the agreement, since the vendor had been prejudiced.[96] But where there was no fraud, the Chancery upheld contracts entered into under a mistake as to the vendee. In the court's view, since the intended vendee could the next day sell it to the undesirable vendee, it made little difference to the vendor whether the purchaser was buying for himself or for another.[97] In 1826, the Chancery judges upheld a contract where the purchaser claimed to be acting on behalf of a different intended vendee, since it had not been shown that the vendor had been prejudiced by it. The case arose from the sale of the decorations in Westminster Hall for George IV's coronation. W. D. Fellowes bought them from Lord Gwydyr, the Deputy Great Chamberlain, for £1000, and sold them to a builder, Samuel Page, for £1575, who was to remove them and repair any damage. During the negotiations for the sale to Page, Fellowes pretended to be Gwydyr's agent, in order (as he later claimed) to give the nobleman security that the work would be done properly. Page discovered that Fellowes was not acting for Gwydyr, and determined to cancel the contract. But when he found that Fellowes had sold on the note for £535 which he had been given in part payment, he sold the decorations, which netted him £596 beyond the value of the note. Fellowes thereupon sued him in Chancery

---

[94] Pothier *Obligations* (trans. Evans), i, 13.   [95] Savigny, *System*, vol. 3, § 136.

[96] *Phillips* v. *Duke of Bucks* (1683) 1 Vern. C.C. 227. See also *Scott* v. *Langstaffe*, quoted in *Pophal* v. *Eyre* (1774) Lofft 786 at 797–8. See also Sugden, *Vendors and Purchasers* (5th edn, 1818), 191.

[97] See *Lord Irnham* v. *Child* (1781) 1 Bro. C.C. 92 at 95. See also *Nelthorpe* v. *Holgate* (1844) 1 Coll. 203. But see *Popham* v. *Eyre* (1774) Lofft 786, where specific performance was refused in a case where the vendor was misled as to the purchaser. In this case, however, the sale did not comply with the Statute of Frauds.

to compel him to pay the money due under the agreement.[98] In his defence, Page argued that Fellowes had used Gwydyr's name to get a better deal than he would otherwise have got. However, Sir John Leach gave a decree for Fellowes. '[I]f the Plaintiff, by the use of Lord Gwydyr's name, really desired to conceal the speculative bargain which he had made with Lord Gwydyr', he noted, 'it would afford no principle upon which the Defendant could escape from the contract without special circumstances.'[99] Lord Lyndhurst LC agreed.[100] The Chancery judges clearly did not regard this contract as being void *ab initio*, on the ground that the vendor's offer had not been accepted by the purchaser. Rather, they took the view that the agreement was valid, and would only have been vitiated if the purchaser had been prejudiced by the deception (as giving a lower price). Later jurists would criticize the decision for being inconsistent with the rule of agency, that an agent could not sue in his own name on a contract made for the principal, which the latter refused to act on.[101] But it reveals the reluctance of the early nineteenth-century Chancery to vitiate contracts for mistake of identity.

Early nineteenth-century common law judges were clear that a party could only sue the person with whom he had contracted. This meant, for instance, that if one partner contracted as a sole owner of goods, his partners could not later sue on the contract.[102] But common law courts had few opportunities to consider the question of mistake of identity in cases which did not involve fraud. If a seller of goods claimed to have a contract with a purchaser who refused to accept them, the latter would simply plead *non assumpsit*, and give evidence that he had not entered the contract. If the goods had been delivered to the wrong party, but retained by him, he would be liable on an implied contract, and the seller could recover with an *indebitatus assumpsit* count.

Since commercial sales were generally effected via brokers using bought and sold notes, there was often little scope for disputing the identity of the contracting parties. On occasion, disputes about who had been contracting did arise. This happened in 1816 in *Mitchell* v. *Lapage*, where the purchase of a cargo of hemp had been effected through a broker, who had mistakenly issued a bought note giving the name of the sellers as the firm of Todd, Mitchell & Co. In fact, three months before the contract, two of the partners in the old firm had retired and been replaced by two new men. When sued for non-acceptance of the goods, the purchasers argued that no contract had come into being, since the agreement

---

[98] For this detail, see *The Times*, 5 November 1824, col. 3c.
[99] *Fellowes* v. *Lord Gwydyr* (1826) 1 Sim. 63 at 66.
[100] *Fellowes* v. *Lord Gwydyr* (1829) 1 R. & M. 83 at 90.
[101] *Bickerton* v. *Burrell* (1816) 5 M. & S. 383. Pollock, *Contract* (1876), 436.
[102] *Lucas* v. *De La Cour* (1813) 1 M. & S. 249; *Humble* v. *Hunter* (1848) 12 Q.B. 310; *Robson* v. *Drummond* (1831) 2 B. & Ad. 303.

was made with the old firm, and not the new one; and '[e]very man had a right to deal with whom he will.' But Gibbs CJ held that as the buyers had conferred with the broker after they had received notice of the change in the firm, and had treated the contract as subsisting, they were bound by it, and could be sued for non-acceptance. Gibbs conceded, however, that there would have been a defence 'if, owing to the broker, he has been prejudiced, or excluded from a set-off'.[103] The case indicated that a person might lose his right to claim there had been no contract, if acceptance of the contract could be inferred from his behaviour.

The question of mistaken identity was raised in two unusual cases in the Exchequer in the 1850s, one of which came to be seen as foundational for the doctrine of mistake. They were unusual since both involved bad business practices falling short of criminal fraud. In both cases, the Exchequer used doctrine creatively to protect the innocent party. The first case was *Boulton* v. *Jones*, where the defendant was sued for money owed for goods which he had ordered from a pipe hose manufacturing business on 13 January 1857. On the same day, before the order arrived, Boulton had bought the business from Brocklehurst, whose manager and foreman he had been. Jones was an established customer of the business, who regularly placed his orders through Boulton. Significantly, he had a credit balance with Brocklehurst, who was declared bankrupt in March. When Jones received an invoice from Boulton, he refused to pay, claiming to have no contract with him. Boulton recovered his debt in the Liverpool Court of Passage, but Jones sought to overturn this decision, arguing that he 'had a debt against Brocklehurst which they could set off against any action by him, but could not use against the plaintiff'. Jones complained that Boulton was attempting to put himself 'secretly in the place of the party' with whom he meant to contract.[104] The argument succeeded. Bramwell B. stressed the importance of the identity of the contracting party where right of set-off might be lost.[105]Martin B. simply said that '[i]f a man goes to a shop and makes a contract, intending it to be with one particular person, no other person can convert that into a contract with him'.[106]

'As to the difficulty that the defendants need not pay anybody', Bramwell observed, 'I do not see why they should, unless they have made a contract either express or implied'.[107] At first glance, it seems odd that the plaintiffs should have been allowed to retain the goods, and not pay for them on an implied contract. It

---

[103] *Mitchell* v. *Lapage* (1816) Holt 253 at 254–5.

[104] *The Times*, 26 November 1857, col. 8e.

[105] See Benjamin's discussion in *Sale* (1868), 41, 303–6, holding that the plaintiff should have recovered any sum beyond the set off. Pollock, *Contract* (1876), 428–9 disagreed with Benjamin, considering the set-off issue not important.

[106] *Boulton* v. *Jones* (1857) 2 H. & N. 564 at 566. See also the report in (1857) 27 LJ Ex 117.

[107] The set-off point was the one most stressed by counsel: see MacMillan, 'Rogues', 715.

was well established that a party who retained goods not intended as a gift had to pay for them. Equally (as the plaintiff argued), a man who contracted as agent for a third party was entitled to sue in his own name, provided he gave notice to the defendant before the action commenced that he was the interested party.[108] The decision of the Exchequer may be explained by the fact that the judges knew that Jones had already paid Brocklehurst the price of the goods, and that he would not be able to recover this sum, in light of Brocklehurst's bankruptcy. The court seems to have regarded the circumstances of Boulton's purchase as sufficiently prejudicial to Jones to prevent Boulton suing. The decision came to stand for Pollock CB's proposition that 'if a person intends to contract with A, B cannot give himself any right under it',[109] a proposition that one was not bound by a contract entered into under a mistake of identity.[110] But its effect was to affirm that a contract had come into existence between Jones and Brocklehurst, whereby the former paid for the goods delivered by the latter's business.

The second case was *Cornish* v. *Abingdon* in 1859. Here, the foreman of the plaintiff, a printer, wished to issue books and maps on his own account, and agreed to supply the defendant with works which would be published on commission. The foreman placed orders for the works to be printed on his behalf in the plaintiff's books as orders coming from the defendant. The defendant questioned the foreman about this, but was assured that this was only a mistake. Nonetheless, he was held liable to the plaintiff for the cost of printing the books and maps put in his name, since he was estopped from denying the contract. 'If any person, by a course of conduct or by actual expressions, so conducts himself that another may reasonably infer the existence of an agreement or licence, whether the party intends that he should do so or not', Pollock CB ruled, 'it has the effect that the party using that language, or who has so conducted himself, cannot afterwards gainsay the reasonable inference to be drawn from his words or conduct.'[111] In contrast to *Boulton* v. *Jones*, the judges found that the party whose identity had been mistaken was bound to a contract he had not assented to. What united the two cases was the court seeking to prevent a party who had allowed another to be misled from casting a loss on that party.

These cases determined that a party was not bound at common law by any contract entered into with a bona fide person whose identity he mistook—since he had not entered into an agreement with that party—unless he had done something which estopped him from denying the contract. They were atypical, however, and

---

[108] *Bickerton* v. *Burrell* (1816) 5 M. & S. 383; *Rayner* v. *Grote* (1846) 15 M. & W. 359.

[109] *Boulton* v. *Jones* (1857) 2 H. & N. 564 at 565.

[110] See Pollock, *Contract* (1876), 381.

[111] *Cornish* v. *Abingdon* (1859) 4 H. & N. 549 at 556. This dictum was cited with approval in *Thomas* v. *Brown* (1876) 1 QBD 714 at 722.

if *Boulton* was later seen as stating something of a truism, the doctrine suggested in *Cornish* was not later taken up in case law or literature. Much more common, throughout the century, were the cases where goods had been sold to an impostor. When dealing with such cases, courts were driven less by a clear understanding of the dictates of doctrine, than a desire not to throw the loss on the least innocent party. This approach often entailed doctrinal inconsistency.

In the first half of the nineteenth century, the question was dealt with as one of fraud, rather than mistake. The key question courts considered was whether property passed in such a sale. It was settled that where goods were feloniously taken—by theft—property did not pass, save in cases of sale in market overt.[112] Even then, it revested in the original owner, if he prosecuted the felon to conviction.[113] However, if goods were obtained by false pretences, it was only a misdemeanour. Eighteenth-century cases showed that if goods were fraudulently obtained by a buyer assuming another's identity, property passed, provided the vendor intended to sell to the person impersonated. Property passed wherever the owner had intended it to pass.[114] But if the owner only intended to pass possession to a recipient who had a preordained plan to steal them, a felony was committed, known as larceny 'by trick'.[115] With these distinctions in mind, Lord Kenyon held that a pawnbroker who had in good faith acquired goods which had been obtained from their owner by false pretences could maintain an action of trover against the original owner, since property in them had passed.[116]

But early nineteenth-century judges were troubled by the idea that property could pass where there had been fraud in a purchase.[117] Seeking to protect the

---

[112] See E. Coke, *The Second Part of the Institutes of the Laws of England* (1797), 713, and also *Crane* v. *London Dock Co* (1864) 5 B. & S. 313. Victims of theft could not sue the thief in trover for the goods—they had to prosecute for the theft—but they could sue third parties who had not bought in market overt for trover, since no property passed: *White* v. *Spettigue* (1845) 13 M. & W. 603.

[113] 21 H. 8 c. 11. See also MacMillan, 'Rogues', 718–20, and W. Swadling, 'Rescission, Property and the Common Law' (2005) 121 *LQR* 123–53 at 143–4.

[114] E. H. East, *Pleas of the Crown*, 2 vols (1803), ii, 668. *R* v. *Parks* in *Old Bailey Sessions Papers*, online edn: http://www.oldbaileyonline.org/, ref: t17940115-17; *R* v. *Catherine Coleman* in East, *Pleas of the Crown*, ii, 672.

[115] *Pear's case* (1779) in East, *Pleas of the Crown*, ii, 685. *Old Bailey Sessions Papers*, online edn, ref. t17790915-22. See also *R* v. *Aickles* (1784) 1 Leach 294.

[116] *Parker* v. *Patrick* (1793) 5 T.R. 175. Cf. *Davis* v. *Morrison* (1773) Lofft 185. See also *Milward* v. *Forbes* (1802) 4 Esp. 171 at 173, where Ellenborough held that the assignees of a bankrupt trader were able to recover the goods from a seller who claimed to have been defrauded (since the purchaser claimed he would be able to pay), since, thanks to the contract, 'there is a sufficient change of property to sustain the action'.

[117] This was also evident in bankruptcy proceedings: where a seller sought to recover bills of exchange from the assignees of a vendee who had obtained the goods by fraud, common law courts applied the equitable view that '[t]he assignment under the commission passes only such property as the bankrupt is conscientiously entitled to' (per Kenyon CJ in *Harrison* v. *Walker* (1792) Peake 150

defrauded owners, judges determined to look not at 'what the seller means to do, but what are the intentions of the customer'.[118] Instead of asking whether the fraudster's act amounted to a felony, they asked if it amounted to an indictable crime.[119] In 1820, Dallas CJ observed 'that a sale effected by fraud, works no change of property'.[120] Other cases confirmed that where goods were bought by a person who paid with a bill he knew would never be paid, no property could pass.[121] Judges were sometimes concerned that this rule should not extend to catch all insolvent traders who bought goods they could not pay for, given that innocent third parties might be forced to bear the loss.[122] But where there had been fraud, the contract was void.

In the 1820s, the victims of swindlers who ordered goods under a false identity often sought to recover their money by suing the wealthy carriers who transported the goods, claiming that the carrier had been grossly negligent in delivering to the impostor.[123] This was a successful approach in an age—before the passing of the Carriers Act in 1830—when the courts were often hostile to carriers. Faced with such suits (either for negligence or trover), carriers tried to invoke the rule that where goods were dispatched for delivery, property in them passed to the consignee.[124] But the courts responded by holding (in Park J.'s words) that the rule 'does not apply to a case bottomed in fraud, in which there has been no sale'.[125]

at 151), so that the original owner could recover them. See also *Gladstone* v *Hadwen* (1813) 1 M. & S. 517 at 526; *Scott* v. *Surman* (1743) Willes 400 at 402. See also L. D. Smith, 'Tracing in *Taylor v Plumer*: Equity in the Court of King's Bench' [1995] *Lloyds Maritime and Commercial Law Quarterly* 240–268 at 244 and P. Watts, 'Birks and Proprietary Claims, with Special Reference to Misrepresentation and to Ultra Vires Contracts', in C. Rickett and R. Grantham (eds), *Structure and Justification in Private Law: Essays for Peter Birks* (Oxford, 2008), 361–78 at 369–70.

[118] *Stephenson* v. *Hart* (1828) 4 Bing. 476 at 483. He drew on *R* v. *Aickles* (1784) 1 Leach 294. See also *Rex* v. *Marshall* (1804) R. & R. 75.

[119] See also *Earl of Bristol* v. *Wilsmore* (1823) 1 B. & C. 514 at 521. Cf. the approach of Gibbs CJ at trial in *Noble* v. *Adams* (1816) 7 Taunt. 59, 2 Marsh 366, Holt N.P. 248.

[120] *Abbotts* v. *Barry* (1820) 2 B. & B. 369 at 371. See also Lord Tenterden's view in *Ferguson* v. *Carrington* (1829) 9 B. & C. 59 at 59–60.

[121] 21. *Hawse* v. *Crowe* (1826) R. & M. 414; *Irving* v. *Motly* (1831) 7 Bing. 543 at 553. See also J. Chitty, *A Practical Treatise on the Law of Contracts* (2nd edn, 1834), 321.

[122] *Irving* v. *Motly* (1831) 7 Bing. 543 at 551. See also Best CJ's view in *Sinclair* v. *Stevenson* (1825) 2 Bing. 514 at 517: 'if a person purchase a house and the utensils of a trade, knowing that he is not able to pay for them; if possession be delivered to him, does not the property in these utensils pass to him, and will they not become the property of his creditors in the event of his bankruptcy?'

[123] *Birkett* v. *Willan* (1819) 2 B. & Ald. 356. The course of the litigation can be followed in *Logan* v. *Willan, The Times*, 7 July 1818, col. 3e; *Basker* v. *Willan, The Times*, 9 November 1818, col. 3c; *Burkit* v. *Willan, The Times*, 11 November 1819, col. 3c.

[124] The general rule was that where goods were dispatched to a carrier, property in them passed to the purchaser on delivery to the carrier: see *Dutton* v. *Solomonson* (1803) 3 B. & P. 582; C. Blackburn, *A Treatise on the Effect of the Contract of Sale* (1845), 132.

[125] *Duff* v. *Budd* (1822) 3 B. & B. 177 at 183.

At the same time that civil courts sought to protect the original owner, the criminal law followed suit. In 1827, legislation was passed to allow the recovery after sale in market overt of property acquired by false pretences.[126] In light of these developments, Lord Denman in 1835 cast doubt on Kenyon's approach, suggesting there existed no difference between fraud and felony, and that in neither case did property pass.[127]

The cases of the 1820s, which treated fraudulent sales as void, did not involve third parties who had acquired an interest in the goods.[128] In the 1840s, judges changed their approach to protect third parties. In doing so, they began to assert the view that fraud only rendered a contract voidable. In 1841, Lord Abinger agreed in *Sheppard* v. *Shoolbred* that while a vendor could sue a fraudulent vendee in trover, since no property passed to the vendee, yet if the original owner consented to the transfer, and the third party purchaser was unaware of the fraud, then the property would pass.[129] Similarly, in 1845, in *Load* v. *Green*, Parke B. defended the much-criticized judgment of *Parker* v. *Patrick* on the ground that in cases of fraud, 'the transaction is not absolutely void, except at the option of the seller: he may elect to treat it as a contract, and he must do the contrary before the buyer has acted as if it were such, and resold the goods to a third party'.[130] *Load* v. *Green* did not involve an innocent third party. Rather, in an effort to protect an innocent victim of fraud, the court held a contract voidable to prevent the plaintiff falling foul of the bankruptcy law's reputed ownership provisions.[131]

Parke's view was acted on in *White* v. *Garden*, where a bona fide purchaser of goods obtained by fraud was permitted to retain them. During the case, Cresswell J. observed, 'The distinction between fraud and felony is this, in the one case, the man who parts with the property makes a contract in fact; in the other, he does

---

[126] 7 & 8 G. 4 c. 29, s 57.

[127] *Peer* v. *Humphrey* (1835) 2 Ad. & El. 495. Note also *Duke de Cadaval* v. *Collins* (1836) 4 Ad. & El. 858, where Lord Denman held property did not pass in a case of fraud.

[128] In *Noble* v. *Adams* (1816) 7 Taunt. 59 at 61 Shepherd Sol.-Gen. did suggest that matters might be different if third party rights intervened.

[129] *Sheppard* v. *Shoolbred* (1841) C. & M. 61.

[130] *Load* v. *Green* (1846) 15 M. & W. 216 at 219. Swadling, in 'Rescission and the Common Law', argues that this case was the *locus classicus* of the rule that a defrauded party can rescind a contract and thereby revest title to property in himself, and that it was a 'complete inversion of the then existing case law' (125). This view is questioned by Watts, 'Birks and Proprietary Claims'.

[131] If the contract was voidable, not void, the bankrupt trader could be said to have had real ownership at the time of his failure, taking the case out of the statute. In fact, Parke B.'s judgment confirmed that the plaintiff would not be prevented from recovering by the reputed ownership provisions, not having consented to the bankrupt's possession (following *Joy* v. *Campbell* (1804) 1 Sch. & Lef. 328). See also B. Häcke, 'Rescission of Contract and Revesting of Title: A Reply to Mr Swadling' (2006) 14 *Restitution LR* 106–11.

nothing'.[132] Where one of two innocent people was to suffer, it was better to place the loss on those 'who were guilty of negligence in parting with their goods upon the faith of a piece of paper which a little inquiry would have shewn to be worthless'. Parke reiterated his view in 1853, when holding that fraud only rendered a contract voidable at the option of the innocent party. 'The fraud only gives a right to rescind', but '[i]n the first instance, the property passes in the subject-matter'. This meant that '[a]n innocent purchaser from the fraudulent possessor may acquire an indefeasible title to it, though it is voidable between the original parties'.[133]

The result of these doctrinal developments was that, by the 1850s, it had become clear that, rather than 'destroy[ing] the contract altogether',[134] any fraud which resulted in a contract only rendered it voidable. The innocent party lost the right to rescind if third party rights intervened (where the plaintiff had sold goods to a fraudster) or if they had affirmed the contract by dealing with the goods which were the subject-matter of the contract (where they had purchased goods from a fraudster).[135] But just as this rule was put in place to protect innocent buyers, so another one was found to protect sellers. The mid-century cases which generated a new doctrine of mistake of identity focused on the question of contract formation, rather than fraud. But they did this in order to root out what were perceived as bad business practices, and protect the morally innocent from loss. The first case which paved the way for this development was *Kingsford* v. *Merry* in 1856, which arose out of the actions of a notorious commercial fraudster. The plaintiffs sold a cargo of acid via a broker to the rogue trader, William Anderson, who falsely told the broker that he was acting in this transaction as factor to J. & C. Van Notten & Co, a firm for which he often acted as agent. He subsequently obtained delivery orders for the goods from the plaintiffs, telling them that while the purchase had been in Van Notten's name, he had really bought them for himself. He then pledged the goods with the defendants, the produce brokers Thomas Merry and Son, as security for a loan of £2000. Anderson's business was failing, and he was able to keep trading only by paying for goods with forged bills of exchange from Van Notten. It was not a game he could maintain. His frauds were soon discovered and he was arrested. In 1854, he was convicted at the Old Bailey

---

[132] *White* v. *Garden* (1851) 10 C.B. 919 at 924. For Talfourd J., where goods were obtained by felony the owner had no intention to part with his property; where they were obtained by fraud, he did.

[133] *Stevenson* v. *Newnham* (1853) 13 C.B. 285 at 302.

[134] Lord Tenterden in *Street* v. *Blay* (1831) B. & Ad. 456 at 462.

[135] *Campbell* v. *Fleming* (1834) 1 Ad. & El. 40, where the goods in question were shares. See also Parke B.'s observations in *Murray* v. *Mann* (1848) 2 Exch. 538 at 541; Pollock CB's much quoted statement in *Kingsford* v. *Merry* (1856) 11 Exch. 577 at 579; *Pease* v. *Gloahec—The Marie Joseph* (1866) 3 Moore N.S. 556 at 570–1.

of forgery and was sentenced to eight years' penal servitude.[136] Those who had given up their property to him for these false bills now sought to recoup their losses, in actions for trover,[137] among whom were the plaintiffs. The defendants, who had sold the acid after Anderson's bankruptcy, and paid over the surplus to his assignees, resisted.

Following the by-now established views on fraud, the trial judge and the Exchequer both held that property had passed to Anderson by his fraudulent purchase, and had then been acquired by an innocent transferee.[138] At the trial, Pollock CB went so far as to say that if such transactions were impeached, business could not be conducted. The Exchequer Chamber endorsed the lower courts' views of the law of fraud, but found that the plaintiffs had to win, as property had never passed, since the plaintiffs and Anderson had never been in the relation of vendor and vendee. The court treated the broker, Leask, as the vendee, rather than Anderson, who had instructed him to buy in the name of Van Notten.[139] The delivery orders were given to Anderson only on the false assumption that he had bought them from the broker; but since he had no authority from the broker to receive them, no property could pass from the plaintiffs to Anderson.[140] In Coleridge's view, Leask only gave Anderson authority to inspect the goods, and not to receive them.

The court's treatment of Leask as the real buyer was a creative way for the court to protect the original sellers. This broker regularly bought and sold commodities for Van Notten, under the supervision of Anderson, who had a general authority to act as the latter's agent. Such was the very wide authority given by Van Notten to Anderson that the firm failed in its attempt to recover payments made by Leask to Anderson in his capacity as agent for the firm, which had never been passed on.[141] The Exchequer Chamber in *Kingsford* v. *Merry* took a clearly creative approach, to protect a firm which had been defrauded by a notorious cheat, and throw the loss on lenders who should have taken greater care to secure the creditworthiness of their borrowers. But the mercantile community was soon up

---

[136] See *The Times*, 22 December 1853, col. 9c; 30 December 1853, col. 9d; 2 March 1854, col. 9e; *Old Bailey Sessions Papers*, online edn, ref. t18540227-380.

[137] e.g. *Garrells* v. *Cannan*, *The Times*, 22 December 1854, col. 9c. There was also litigation over the forged bills of exchange: see *Gurney* v. *Womersley* (1854) 4 E. & B. 133.

[138] *Kingsford* v. *Merry* (1856) 11 Exch. 577.

[139] Hugh Hill for the defendant had drawn on *Boyson* v. *Coles* (1817) 6 M. & S. 14 for authority for the view that where there was no relationship of vendor and vendee between the owner and a pawnor, the pawnee could have no title. But there, the swindler was the broker who claimed to be acting on behalf of a non-existent client.

[140] *Kingsford* v. *Merry* (1856) 1 H. & N. 503.

[141] *Pole* v. *Leask* (1860) 28 Beav. 562 at 579–80, affirmed by the House of Lords: *Pole* v. *Leask* (1862) 33 LJ Ch 155.

in arms at the decision, feeling that such delivery orders should be considered as secure as bank notes for the lender.[142] Questions were raised in Parliament, where Robert Lowe admitted that it was clear that substantial justice had not been done. In this case, where there were two innocent parties, he felt the loss should fall on the one who had made the loss possible.[143] Public meetings were called, but no reform was passed, and subsequent judges pointed to the inability of the merchants to agree to a change to show that they must have been right.[144]

Kingsford v. *Merry* opened the way for a distinction to be drawn between frauds which induced a voidable contract, and frauds which did not result in a contract at all. In the following decade, the Exchequer developed this idea in a number of other cases involving frauds by men who claimed to be agents of another. These cases established that where a person meant to sell goods to one party, and another obtained them by pretending to be that party's agent, no contract came into existence, and no property passed. These decisions echoed the approach taken more generally in this era in the law of agency. In the early nineteenth century, there had been some uncertainty whether an agent who contracted in the name of a real principal, but without authority, could be personally liable on the contract. Bayley B. took the view that he could.[145] By contrast, in 1832, the King's Bench held that the agent could not be sued on a bill of exchange—since only those to whom it was addressed could be liable—but only for deceit.[146] Courts were also reluctant to hold bona fide agents liable in contract when exceeding their authority.[147] Accordingly, in 1849, the Queen's Bench confirmed that a person contracting only as an agent could not be liable on the contract.[148] This view, in turn, raised the problem that the agent might escape all liability if he had not been guilty of the fraud necessary to sustain an action of deceit. This problem was solved in 1857

---

[142] The case caused some consternation in the city: see *The Times*, 24 December 1856, col 5a, 'Commerce v. Law' (1857) 3 *Saturday Review* 99.

[143] *Morning Chronicle*, 11 February 1857, col. 2e.

[144] The case caused some consternation in the city: see *The Times*, 24 December 1856, col. 5a; 27 December, col. 5c; 3 January 1857, col. 5a; 7 January, col. 4b; 17 January, col. 6a; 12 February, col. 2a; 13 February, col. 4a; 19 February, col. 7b.

[145] *Thomas* v. *Hewes* (1834) 2 C. & M. 519 at 530 n. (a). This was also the position of Pothier, *Obligations* (1806, trans. Evans), i: 45–6. See also *Jones* v. *Downman* (1843) 4 Q.B. 235 at 239. In this case, it was found that the words of the contract were enough to render the agent contractually liable. The decision was overturned (on the issue of whether there was evidence of want of authority) in *Downman* v. *Williams* (1845) 7 Q.B. 103.

[146] *Polhill* v. *Walter* (1832) 3 B. & Ad. 114.

[147] *Smout* v. *Ilbery* (1842) 10 M. & W. 1 at 5.

[148] *Jenkins* v. *Hutchinson* (1849) 13 Q.B. 744 at 752. The agent here (who had made a charterparty for his principal) knew he had no authority, but did not seem to have acted *mala fides*. See also *Lewis* v. *Nicholson* (1852) 18 Q.B. 503 at 511 and J. W. Smith, *A Selection of Leading Cases on Various Branches of the Law*, 2 vols (4th edn, by J. S. Willes and H. S. Keating, 1856), ii, 299–300.

in *Collen* v. *Wright*, where it was held that a party who had innocently exceeded his authority—so that he could not be held liable in deceit—could be sued for a breach of an implied contract whereby he warranted his authority to enter into the contract as agent.[149] This solution, whereby the Exchequer Chamber resisted the temptation to return to the notion that the agent could be held liable on the contract he brokered,[150] was bold and innovative, for through it the court sought to give the misled contracting party an effective contractual remedy against the agent—allowing him to recover damages[151]—without giving the agent any rights to enforce the contract himself.[152] The result of these developments was to confirm that where an agent of a real principal acted without authority, no contract came into being with the agent, by which property could pass. This rule would certainly have been present in the minds of the Exchequer who heard the mid-century cases which paved the way for a doctrine of mistake of identity.

All of the nineteenth-century cases on mistake of identity induced by fraud involved suppliers being misled about the identity of the firm which had ordered goods. The second half of the century saw the flourishing of what were known as 'long firm' frauds. They typically involved swindlers writing to distant suppliers ordering goods for a firm which was either fictitious, or which could easily be confused with a known respectable firm. Often, a small quantity of goods was ordered and paid for, to establish trust, after which a larger quantity would be ordered, which would be sold on, without having been paid for.[153] Swindlers involved in such frauds were regularly prosecuted for obtaining goods by false pretences,[154] and thanks to the Larceny Acts of 1827 and 1861, the court convicting could make an order to revest property in the original owner after such convictions.

Only on rare occasions did defrauded parties to seek to recover their property in the civil courts from third party purchasers. The first two cases in which this occurred were not typical long firm frauds, insofar as the fraudsters had some connection with the company on whose behalf they purported to order the goods. In both cases, all the transactions had been conducted in face-to-face meetings in London. The first case was *Higgons* v. *Burton* in 1857. In this case, Henry Dix, who had been a clerk in the firm of Fitzgibbon & Co of Cork, ordered textiles from the

---

[149] *Collen* v. *Wright* (1857) 7 E. & B. 301, 8 E. & B. 647. This idea had been raised by Lord Campbell in *Lewis* v. *Nicholson* (1852) 18 Q.B. 503.

[150] This seems to have been Cockburn CJ's preferred idea: *Collen* v. *Wright* (1857) 8 E. & B. 647 at 660. See also F. R. Y. Radcliffe, 'Some Recent Developments of the Doctrine of *Collen* v. *Wright*' (1902) 18 *LQR* 364–75 at 375.

[151] *Simons* v. *Patchett* (1857) 7 E. & B. 568.

[152] *Bickerton* v. *Burrell* (1816) 5 M. & S. 383.

[153] See e.g. *The Times*, 5 May 1875, col. 13e; 10 March 1877, col. 12a; 19 March 1877, col. 9d.

[154] The term 'long firm' seems to have been coined in the early 1860s.

plaintiffs, falsely pretending to act on behalf of the firm. When the goods arrived, he sent them to the defendant's auction house to be sold, and then disappeared with over £170 of proceeds. When the plaintiffs sought to recover the value of the goods from the defendants, the Exchequer held that there had been no sale to Dix, since the vendors had intended to deliver and sell the goods to Fitzgibbons and not to Dix.[155] There was therefore no sale, but merely an obtaining possession of goods by false pretences. As in *Kingsford*, the court was clearly worried about controlling fraudulent agents, for as Bramwell B. commented, had the latter case been decided differently, 'it would have established a principle dangerous to trade, *viz* that wherever a party was intrusted with goods for any purpose, even as a mere warehouseman, he might dispose of them'.[156]

Six years later, *Hardman* v. *Booth* came before the Exchequer.[157] In the spring of 1860, the plaintiffs, who intended to sell goods to Gandell & Co, were misled by Edward Gandell, the son of the proprietor, into thinking that he was a partner in the concern. In fact, Edward conducted business on his own account, with H. J. Todd. The goods were sent to Edward, who pledged them with the defendant, an auctioneer, as security for a £300 loan. Gandell and Todd went bankrupt in November 1860, whereupon the auctioneer sold the goods, some of which were bought back by the plaintiffs. Gandell was charged with forgery and obtaining property by false pretences.[158] He pleaded guilty to the latter charge in February 1861, and was also convicted in March of an offence against the bankruptcy laws.[159] A year later, in July 1862, the Hardmans sued the defendants in trover to recover the value of their goods.[160]

Trover was available to those whose goods had been obtained from them by deception, provided they prosecuted the offender to conviction, whereupon property automatically revested in the original owner.[161] However, trover did not lie against the party who acquired them bona fide in market overt if he had sold them on before the conviction.[162] Since Booth had sold the goods back to Hardman before Gandell's conviction, Hardman could not argue that property had revested under the Larceny Act.[163] He had, therefore, to argue that it had never passed in the first place. Counsel for Hardman pointed out that 'they only

---

[155] *Higgons* v. *Burton* (1857) 26 LJ Ex 342 at 344.

[156] *Ibid.*   [157] *Hardman* v. *Booth* (1863) 1 H. & C. 803.

[158] *The Times*, 26 February 1861, col. 11c.

[159] *The Times*, 16 January 1861, col. 11d; 26 February 1861, col. 11c; 28 February 1861, col. 11d; 1 March 1861, col. 11d; *Old Bailey Sessions Papers*, online edn, ref. t18610225-258.

[160] *Hardman* v. *Booth*, in *The Times*, 7 July 1862, col. 11d.

[161] *Scattergood* v. *Sylvester* (1850) 15 Q.B. 506. See also MacMillan, 'Rogues', 719.

[162] *Horwood* v. *Smith* (1788) 2 T.R. 750.

[163] See the detailed discussion of these issues in MacMillan, *Mistakes in English Law*.

intended to sell to Gandell & Co through their agent, Edward Gandell',[164] but not to Edward himself. Pollock CB duly found that there had been no contract between Hardman and Gandell, since the plaintiffs thought they were dealing with the father's firm rather than the son. The fact was, he said, 'that Edward Gandell was not a member of that firm and had no authority to act as their agent. Therefore at no period of time were there two consenting minds to the same agreement'.[165] Since Gandell had no property in the goods, he could not pass it to the auctioneer. The principle of *Hardman* v. *Booth* was endorsed in 1875 by the House of Lords in *Hollins* v. *Fowler*, another case where a fraudster pretended to be the agent of another existing person.[166]

Three years later, the Lords were asked to consider a classic long firm fraud, where agency issues were less evident. In *Cundy* v. *Lindsay*, a swindler, Alfred Blenkarn, deceived a supplier of goods based in Belfast into thinking that they were dealing with a respectable, existing London firm, A. Blenkiron & Co, by taking premises in the same street. The plaintiffs duly sent a consignment of handkerchiefs, which Blenkarn sold to the defendant. Blenkarn was convicted in April 1874 of obtaining the handkerchiefs by false pretences,[167] but before his conviction, the defendants had resold the goods to their customers. The case raised the question whether property in the goods had transferred to Blenkarn in the initial sale, and whether property in the goods revested after his conviction in the plaintiffs. When the case was tried before Blackburn J. at the Guildhall sittings, the jury found that Blenkarn had fraudulently intended that he should be taken as a partner in the firm of Blenkiron & Co. Blackburn J., however, thought that '[i]t was a contract, though obtained by fraud, and was voidable, not void'.[168] He refused to enter judgment for either party and allowed both to move for judgment in the Queen's Bench Division.

The Queen's Bench judges found for the defendants. First, they held that Lindsay had intended to deal with the firm at the address to which they sent them—Blenkarn's rather than Blenkiron's—and that a contract had therefore been entered into, albeit one obtained by fraud. Blackburn distinguished these facts from *Hardman*, where the rogue had pretended to act as agent for the party with whom the sellers intended to contract. Secondly, following *Horwood* v. *Smith*,[169] the court held that trover could not be brought on the grounds that property in

---

[164] *Hardman* v. *Booth* (1863) 1 H. & C. 803 at 806.

[165] *Ibid.*, at 807.   [166] *Hollins* v. *Fowler* (1875) LR 7 HL 757 at 763.

[167] See *The Times*, 10 March 1874, col. 11e.

[168] *The Times*, 16 February 1874; *Belfast Newsletter*, 16 February 1876; *Freeman's Journal and Daily Commercial Advertiser*, 4 December 1876.

[169] *Horwood* v. *Smith* (1788) 2 T.R. 750.

the goods had revested.[170] The decision was overturned by the Court of Appeal. This court agreed with Blackburn's statement of the law but not with his view of the facts, for it was swayed by the fact that Blenkarn had been convicted. The very fact of the conviction demonstrated that he had 'falsely pretended that the firm writing the letters was the well-known firm of Blenkiron & Sons' and that the sellers had intended to deal with that firm, and not with the residents of 37 Wood Street.[171] The decision was confirmed by the Lords. Lord Cairns, drawing on the verdict of the jury in the original proceedings—rather than Blenkarn's criminal jury—observed that the plaintiffs were led to believe that they were dealing with Blenkiron & Co, and never intended to deal with the rogue: 'as between him and them there was no *consensus* of mind which could lead to any agreement or any contract whatever'.[172] Lord Hatherley, who felt the case fell squarely within the principle of *Hardman* v. *Booth*, observed that 'the sale, if made out upon such a transaction as this, would have been a sale to the Blenkirons of Wood Street, if they had chosen to adopt it, and to no other person whatever'.[173] This was to restate a rule from the law of agency, whereby a real principal could affirm a contract entered into by his unauthorized agent.

In the cases we have discussed, there was very little theoretical analysis of the problems at issue. Indeed, the very notion of mistake was not discussed.[174] Developing ideas derived from the law of agency, the courts looked at whether the parties intended to contract with the party before them, or someone else. They did not cite or discuss civilian works, which argued that consent could be vitiated by errors as to the person. English treatise writers were also slow to take up the civilian texts. Leake did not include errors of identity in his section on mistake, but dealt with *Hardman* v. *Booth* in his discussion of fraud and agency.[175] Although Benjamin did talk of this case in a passage marked 'Mistake as to person, caused by fraud',[176] he did not refer to Pothier's distinction here. But

---

[170] *Lindsay* v. *Cundy* (1876) 1 QBD 348, overruling *Nickling* v. *Heaps* (1870) 21 LT 754. The court also rejected an argument based on the interpretation clause of 24 & 25 Vict. c. 96 that the defendants were liable since they retained financial proceeds derived from the sale at the time of the conviction, if not the goods themselves. It was confirmed in *R* v. *The Justices of the Central Criminal Court* (1886) 17 QBD 598, 18 QBD 314 that only an agent of the swindler—such as a commission agent to whom the goods had been passed to sell on behalf of the swindler—could be held liable under the 1861 Act and ordered by a criminal court to revest the financial proceeds of a sale to the original owner. Such an agent was liable regardless of whether he had notice of the fraud.

[171] *Lindsay* v. *Cundy* (1877) 2 QBD 96 at 100 (Mellish LJ).

[172] *Cundy* v. *Lindsay* (1878) 3 App Cas 459 at 465.

[173] *Cundy* v. *Lindsay* (1878) 3 App Cas 459 at 467. Counsel for the defendant, including J. P. Benjamin, denied that Blenkarn purported to act as agent, and so said that property passed to him.

[174] This point is strongly argued in MacMillan, 'Rogues', 732.

[175] Leake, *Elements* (1867), 306. He also mentioned it while discussing contract formation (at 16) and fraud (at 197).

[176] Benjamin, *Sale* (1868), 41.

in 1876, drawing on Savigny's analysis, Frederick Pollock declared that where it was material for one party to know who the other was, an error as to identity prevented the contract coming into existence.[177] In 1879, Anson similarly stated (though without the civilian allusions) that a mistake as to the person with whom a contract was made avoided it, but only where the mistaken party 'has in contemplation a definite person with whom he desires to contract'.[178]

Pothier's distinction entered English case law in June 1878, a few months after *Cundy* v. *Lindsay*, when it was quoted by Fry J., in *Smith* v. *Wheatcroft*.[179] But the reach of his influence may be doubted. When his ideas were quoted, it was generally through Fry's abbreviated version, rather than from the original.[180] Equally, many English treatise writers continued to ignore the civilian distinctions. In Leake's third edition, for example, he simply stated that 'a mere mistake as to the identity' of the party, in the absence of misrepresentation, was immaterial to its validity. But if the contract was not 'in fact offered to the party in question, so that there was an original variance' between the person who was offered the contract and the one who accepted, there would be no contract.[181] Even Pollock, who began his discussion of error as to the person with the civilian sources, only spoke of such errors vitiating contracts in cases where one party meant to deal with a different, known party (as in *Boulton* v. *Jones*), or in cases where a buyer pretended to act as agent of another known party.[182]

Moreover, if the treatise writers had identified a new doctrine, it was one which made very little impact. This is surprising. After the decision in *Cundy* v. *Lindsay*, the *Belfast Newsletter* proclaimed that it struck 'an effective blow against the very injurious ramifications of swindling in London', where swindlers had found a market for their goods 'through the law having been perhaps imperfectly understood'. Henceforth, it declared, London houses would be more careful in their purchases, since they would be liable to the original owners.[183] Shortly thereafter, in *Moyce* v. *Newington*, the Queen's Bench Division interpreted the 1861 Larceny Act to mean that property in goods obtained by false pretences did not

---

[177] Pollock, *Contract* (1876), 381.   [178] Anson, *Contract* (1879), 118.

[179] In this case, specific performance of a contract to sell land to the plaintiff was granted, even though he had (after entering into the contract) decided not to buy the land for himself but as agent for the Butterley Colliery Co. Fry J. held the defendant had not shown 'that any personal considerations entered into this contract': *Smith* v. *Wheatcroft* (1878) 9 Ch D 223 at 230.

[180] See J. C. Smith and J. A. C. Thomas, 'Pothier and the Three Dots' (1957) 20 *MLR* 38–43.

[181] S. M. Leake, *A Digest of the Principles of the Law of Contracts* (3rd edn, 1892), 278.

[182] It was not until the 9th (1921) edition (p. 510) that he spoke of cases where one party specifically did not want to contract with a particular person.

[183] *Belfast Newsletter*, 25 January 1877.

revest, once goods had come into the hands of bona fide purchasers.[184] With this remedy denied, one might have expected businessmen defrauded by long firm frauds to seek the remedy offered by the new doctrine of mistake of identity. But in fact, *Cundy* v. *Lindsay* was not followed by a spate of cases where victims of long frauds sought to recover their property. Instead, it was the decision in *Moyce* which was challenged in 1887. *Bentley* v. *Vilmont* arose from another long firm fraud, where convicted swindlers had ordered goods from France, using names resembling those of respectable firms.[185] But rather than arguing that the initial sale was void (so that no property passed), the plaintiff (who had prosecuted the swindlers) successfully sought a declaration that the criminal court should have made an order for restitution. The judges in this case regarded the sale as voidable for fraud, rather than void for mistake, but held that on conviction, property revested in the original owners.[186]

It was not until 1897 that a victim of a long firm fraud again attempted to invoke the doctrine of mistake. By then, the remedy under the Larceny Act, restored in *Bentley*, had been removed once more, when an amendment to the Sale of Goods Act in 1893 enacted that bona fide purchasers of goods obtained by deception could retain them.[187] In *King's Norton Metal Company Ltd* v. *Edridge, Merrett & Co Ltd*, a rogue named Wallis ordered a small quantity of iron from the plaintiffs, in the name of a fictitious company, Hallam & Co. He then sent a good cheque (in the name of the firm) to pay for them, and then ordered more, which were sold on without being paid for. Wallis seems not to have been prosecuted, but the suppliers sought to recover their goods from two firms who had bought them, invoking *Hardman* v. *Booth* and *Cundy* v. *Lindsay* as authority for their proposition that the contract with Wallis was void for mistake. A. L. Smith LJ did not agree, seeing this as a case of a contract voidable for fraud, but not void for mistake. He held that the case would only have come within the rule of *Cundy* v. *Lindsay* if there had been a distinct firm of Hallam & Co, which the plaintiffs had thought they were contracting with.[188] He asked, '[d]id anyone ever hear of an attempt being made by a person who had delivered his goods to a long firm to get them back on the ground that he made no contract with the long firm?', without realizing that this was precisely what had happened in *Cundy* v. *Lindsay*. 'The

---

[184] *Moyce* v. *Newington* (1878) 4 QBD 32. This case did not involve any deception about the purchaser's identity.

[185] *Reynold's Newspaper*, 20 September 1885; *Pall Mall Gazette*, 24 September 1885.

[186] *Bentley* v. *Vilmont* (1887) 12 App Cas 471, affirming *Vilmont* v. *Bentley* (1886) 18 QBD 322 (CA).

[187] See MacMillan, 'Rogues', 736–7.

[188] See also *In re International Society of Auctioneers and Valuers, Baillie's case* [1898] 1 Ch 110, where the rule in *Cundy* v. *Lindsay* was applied where a man's contract with one incorporated society was held void as it was shown that he intended to deal with another.

indictment against a long firm', he proceeded—effectively undermining another pillar on which *Cundy* was decided—'was always for obtaining the goods by false pretences, which supposed the passing of the property.' In his view, there was hence a contract 'with the person who wrote the letters', and the property passed to him.[189]

While the result was to make the law relating to mistaken identity look similar to the rule in agency, where those contracting as agents for non-existent persons were held liable on the contract,[190] A. L. Smith LJ saw his decision simply as the corollary of the rule from *Cundy* v. *Lindsay*, and did not articulate an agency-like rule according to which the validity of a contract with a rogue would turn on the existence of his purported principal.[191] *King's Norton* was not even mentioned in the textbooks of Pollock or Anson. These writers were more interested in another of A. L. Smith LJ's decisions, *Gordon* v. *Street*, which was decided two years later. Here, the swindler was not pretending to act on behalf of someone else, but had used a false name. In this case, a man who had taken a loan from the notorious Isaac Gordon successfully resisted an action brought by the money-lender on a promissory note, on the grounds that he had been induced to take the loan by a fraudulent misrepresentation by Gordon of his identity. While it was clear that the defendant could avoid all liability on the grounds of the plaintiff's fraud, Smith LJ added that the contract could be avoided even if there were no fraud. Citing the passage from Pothier quoted in *Smith* v. *Wheatcroft*, he held that Street had entered into the contract because 'George James Addison', the supposed lender, had advertised that he charged far less interest than other lenders did. For Smith, this meant that 'consideration of the person did enter into the contract' and on that ground, as well as that of fraud, the contract could not stand.[192] This seemed

---

[189] *King's Norton Metal Co* v. *Edridge, Merrett & Co* (1897) 14 TLR 98–9.

[190] J. Story, *Commentaries on the Law of Agency* (1839), §§ 280–1. See also W. Paley, *A Treatise on the Law of Principal and Agent* (1812), 251; J. Chitty, *A Treatise on the Laws of Commerce and Manufacture*, 4 vols (1824), iii: 211; Smith, *Leading Cases* (4th edn, 1856), ii, 298.

[191] The rule in agency derived from cases where improvement commissioners, or people contracting on behalf of clubs or parishes, were held personally liable on their contracts (*Meriel* v. *Wymondsold* (1661) Hardres 205; *Horsley* v. *Bell* (1778) Amb. 770; *Cullen* v. *Duke of Queensberry* (1781) 1 Bro. C.C. 101), and was later applied to hold liable promoters who purported to act as agents for companies which had not been formed, and which had no capacity to ratify contracts entered into prior to their existence: *Kelner* v. *Baxter* (1866) LR 2 CP 174 at 185. See also W. Bowstead, *A Digest of the Law of Agency* (3rd edn, 1907), 379. In these cases, courts saw a benefit in upholding, rather than undermining the contract, and so applied the maxim *ut res magis valeat quam pereat*. This maxim was hardly applicable in long firm fraud cases, however.

[192] *Gordon* v. *Street* [1899] 2 QB 641 at 648. Smith evidently did not take his law from the treatises: for he did not cite Pollock's note, citing D.12.1.32 that if a loan was taken from A, the borrower thinking that A was B's agent to lend, when he was in fact C's, no contract was formed. Pollock, *Contract* (6th edn, 1894, 449n).

hard to square with his view in *King's Norton*, since Addison had been a fabrication of Gordon's, just as Hallam & Co had been Wallis's invention.

The decision did little to secure cohesion in the doctrine.[193] It was further confused in 1919, by *Phillips* v. *Brooks*, when the King's Bench Division (citing Pothier) held valid a sale in a shop to a man claiming to be a well-known race horse owner on the grounds that the vendor intended to deal with the person in front of him, and did not regard his identity as material.[194] In making this decision, the court abandoned the rule of *Cundy* v. *Lindsay*, and replaced it with a presumption that a vendor always intended to contract with the person in front of him, and that an error as to a person's attributes—such as his wealth—was not one going to the root of the contract. The distinction between dealings *inter praesentes* (where the presumption was in favour of a contract) and those conducted by correspondence (where the presumption went the other way) was regarded by some as specious,[195] and found its parentage in the brief report of an American decision, rather than in civilian doctrine.[196] The distinction between mistake of identity and of attributes could more easily be traced to Pothier,[197] but it was one which left a good deal of discretion to the courts to make differing judgments on the facts. In 1920, for instance, McCardie J. could refer to Pothier's principle as one 'broad' enough to deny admission to a theatre a *persona non grata* who had bought a ticket through the medium of a friend.[198] With the rule in *Cundy* v. *Lindsay* thus qualified, twentieth-century scholars regarded the law of mistake of identity as being in something of a mess, leading some judges to seek to replace it with the principle that any contract entered into with a rogue as a result of a fraud as to his identity was a valid, but voidable one.[199]

---

[193] The confusion it could engender can be seen from the note in Anson's 10th (1903) edn, 146n (in a section on mistake of identity) that '[w]here the personality of one party may be important to the other, the assumption of a false name is fraudulent and makes the contract voidable'.

[194] *Phillips* v. *Brooks* [1919] 2 KB 243, following *Edmunds* v. *Merchants' Dispatch Transportation Co* 135 Mass 283 (1883). MacMillan, 'Rogues' (at 737–9) and E. C. S. Wade, 'Mistaken Identity in the Law of Contract' (1922) 38 *LQR* 201–6 (at 205) both suggest that the case is to be explained by the change in the law (in s 24(2) of the Sale of Goods Act 1893, and the Larceny Act 1916), according to which property in goods obtained by deception no longer revested in the original owner on conviction of the party deceiving.

[195] Wade, 'Mistaken Identity', 204.

[196] However, it came to be accepted throughout the twentieth century. E.g. *Shogun Finance* v. *Hudson* [2004] 1 AC 919, para. 170 (Lord Phillips of Worth Matravers).

[197] Though, as was pointed out by Smith and Thomas in 'Pothier and the Three Dots', it rested on a reading of Pothier which omitted his examples which suggested the approach here attributed to *Cundy* v. *Lindsay*.

[198] *Said* v. *Butt* [1920] 3 KB 497.

[199] See Lord Denning's judgment in *Lewis* v. *Averay* [1971] 3 WLR 603 and the dissenting judgments in *Shogun Finance* v. *Hudson* [2004] 1 AC 919.

4. AN UNSETTLED DOCTRINE

As Frederick Pollock pointed out, '[t]he whole topic [of mistake] is surrounded with a great deal of confusion in our books'.[200] He felt that the insights of Savigny could cut through the confusion, and that a general principle could be found. For him, the uniting feature behind cases where contracts were vitiated by mistakes was that the parties had made a 'fundamental error', either as to substance or identity.[201] But not all treatise writers shared Pollock's views. The pioneer of discussions of mistake, S. M. Leake, eschewed theoretical discussion of the subject. He made no reference in his chapters on mistake to the civilian literature, and looked for no overarching principle. Instead, he dealt with the topic in a matter-of-fact way suitable for practitioners. He argued that if there was a latent ambiguity in a contract, and extrinsic evidence showed the parties were at odds, the contract would be void. Equally, if it was conditional on a set of facts which turned out not to exist, there would be no contract.[202] Writing after Pollock, his Oxford colleague, W. R. Anson, took a much narrower view of mistake. In the first edition of his treatise, Anson agreed that a mistake would be operative if it went 'to the root of the contract, and is such as to negative the idea that the parties were ever *ad idem*'; but he applied this view only to a narrow range of circumstances.[203] By 1888, his doubts regarding the doctrine had grown, and in 1891 he chided other scholars (including Pollock) for including in their discussion of mistake topics which rather related to the interpretation and performance of contracts. '[O]perative mistake is very rare', he noted, while 'the cases of genuine mutual mistake are rarer still.'[204] Moreover, the editors of texts dating from before 1850 continued to omit discussion of mistake.

For most of our period, questions of mistake were most likely to be discussed in courts of equity rather than at common law. The Chancery's approach to the problem reflected the view of its practitioners that contracts were based on mutual consent. In locating the agreement of the parties, equity did not look to the subjective meanings of the parties, but to what (if anything) they had objectively agreed. Equity's approach to mistake was discussed in some detail by

---

[200] F. Pollock, *Contract* (1876) 357; in the 7th edn (1902), 440, Pollock spoke of the confusion which 'formerly' surrounded the subject.

[201] Pollock, *Contract* (1876), 374, 386.

[202] Leake, *Digest* (3rd edn, 1892), 277, 283. Leake spent little time on mistakes of identity.

[203] Anson, *Contract* (1879), 116. In his view, a mistake as to the subject-matter of the contract was only operative if it was a mistake as to the existence of the subject-matter, amounting to impossibility of performance (as in *Couturier* v. *Hastie*), a mistake as to the identity of the subject-matter of a contract (as in *Raffles* v. *Wichelhaus*), or if there was a mistake as to the quality of the thing promised, known to the promisee (as suggested in *dicta* in *Smith* v. *Hughes*).

[204] Anson, *Contract* (6th edn, 1891), 126.

Leake.[205] By contrast, and despite his professed desire to write a treatise for the age of fusion, Pollock spent rather less time on how Chancery lawyers dealt with the topic. For Pollock, the core of the subject lay in how the common law dealt with errors of substance and errors of quality. In fact, such questions were generally irrelevant for nineteenth-century common lawyers. The doctrine of common mistake developed in the twentieth century in no small part because judges and lawyers manipulated it in an often opportunistic manner to resolve unusual cases.[206] On the other hand, by 1914, the notion that a contract could be void for mistake of identity had become entrenched, though the principles of its application remained unclear. Judges and jurists developed this doctrine in order to protect the owners of goods who had been defrauded out of them, and avoid the rule that sales effected by fraud were only voidable, and not void. This path was opened by the judiciary, but treatise writers embraced it. Pollock's desire to protect the innocent owner of goods sometimes left him in a muddle. Although he argued that the general effect of a mistake was to render a contract void,[207] he wished to give the victims of misrepresentations the option of affirming the non-existent contract. He consequently continued to argue both that the contract between the innocent party and the guilty was only voidable, and that it was in fact void, but the guilty party was estopped from asserting its nullity.[208] If he showed confusion over whether the effect of mistake was to render a contract void or merely voidable, it was not the same confusion which was to dog judges and jurists in the second half of the twentieth century.

---

[205] It was also discussed in detail in E. Fry, *A Treatise on the Specific Performance of Contracts* (1858).

[206] On the crucial cases of *Bell* v. *Lever Bros* [1932] AC 161 and *Solle* v. *Butcher* [1950] 1 KB 671, see C. MacMillan, 'How Temptation led to Mistake: An Explanation of *Bell v. Lever Bros Ltd*' (2003) 119 *LQR* 625–59, and *ibid.*, 'Solle v Butcher'.

[207] Pollock, *Contract* (1876) 357. Cf. Anson, *Contract* (1879), 127–8.

[208] Pollock, *Contract* (1876), 394, 403; 9th edn, 526, 539.

VI

Contractual Terms and their Performance

DESPITE the pervasive language of freedom of contract in mid-nineteenth-century England, consumers had little bargaining power over the terms of the contracts they entered into for goods or services. While there were some moves towards developing consumer protection in the nineteenth century— with controls over the quality of food,[1] or utilities such as gas[2]—the common law developed its rules on the implied obligations of sellers and suppliers largely in commercial contexts. The relative weakness of consumers is reflected in the fact that they were more likely to find themselves faced with claims that they were prevented by express terms in a standard form contract from recovering for contractual misperformance by a powerful adversary.

For consumers, the development of standard terms is to be associated with the rise of mass transportation. Road transport carriers had long sought to limit their liability for loss or damage to goods by notice.[3] Their ability to do so was regulated by the Carriers Act 1830, which imposed on customers the duty to disclose the nature of goods above a certain value, and allowed carriers to charge different rates to carry them. Although the Act forbad carriers otherwise to limit their liability by notice, it permitted them to do so by 'any special contract'. This provision was treated by the courts in a way which was favourable for the carriers, for they were prepared to find special contracts in situations where the customer could be said to have assented to the terms of the notice by sending the goods.[4] In 1852, the Exchequer held that a customer who sent a horse via a railway

---

[1] J. Burnett, *Plenty and Want: A Social History of Diet in England from 1815 to the Present Day* (1979); J. Phillips and M. French, 'Adulteration and Food Law, 1899–1939' (1998) 9 *Twentieth Century History*, 350–69.

[2] M. Daunton, 'The Material Politics of Natural Monopoly: Consuming Gas in Victorian Britain', in M. Daunton and M. Hilton (eds), *The Politics of Consumption: Material Culture and Citizenship in Britain and America* (Oxford, 2001), 69–88.

[3] See pp. 912–16, and J. N. Adams, 'The Standardization of Commercial Contracts' (1978) 7 *Anglo-American LR* 136–54.

[4] *Wyld* v. *Pickford* (1841) 8 M. & W. 443 at 458.

was bound by the terms on the ticket, which threw the entire risk on the sender. As Parke B. saw it, 'it is very reasonable that carriers should be allowed to make agreements for the purpose of protecting themselves against the new risks and dangers of carriage to which they are in modern times exposed'.[5] Such decisions caused great disquiet, and in 1854 the Railway and Canal Traffic Act sought to give customers greater protection. Section 7 of the Act stated that companies would be liable for losses caused by their negligence, notwithstanding any notice to the contrary. It also stated that companies could impose conditions respecting the carriage, so long as they were reasonable, and that any special contract between customer and company had to be in writing. It was soon a matter of dispute between the court of Exchequer and the judges of the other common law courts whether attempts to limit the company's liability only bound if there was both a special signed contract to that effect, and it was reasonable. In Erle J.'s view of the statute, customers were to be held bound by the terms of any special contract they had signed, regardless of the judges' views of its reasonableness.[6] Where Erle's position was premised on the view that it would be iniquitous to prevent the railways from being able to limit their liability, Jervis CJ in the Common Pleas felt that the statute had intended to put the whole railway system under the control of the court, with judges being given the power to decide if a special contract was just and reasonable.[7] The matter was finally resolved by the Lords in 1863, deciding that the condition had both to be in a signed contract, and reasonable.[8]

In the aftermath of this decision, courts had to determine when the Act applied, and how to decide whether a contract had been made when it did not. In 1864, the Exchequer held that the Act did not apply to special tickets issued at reduced prices, and that the passenger whose luggage was lost was bound by the terms on the ticket he was given;[9] but where the ordinary fare was paid, the passenger obtained the protection of the Act.[10] However, the Act did not apply to loss or damage to luggage which was not in transit. A passenger who left items at a left luggage office was therefore not protected by the Act. It was in the context of

[5] *Carr* v. *Lancashire and Yorkshire Railway Co* (1852) 7 Exch. 707 at 712.

[6] *M'Manus* v. *Lancashire and Yorkshire Railway Co* (1859) 4 H. & N. 327 at 335–48. His interpretation of the statute was that it permitted carriers to impose 'reasonable' conditions by notice. See also his view in *Harrison* v. *London Brighton and South Coast Railway Co* (1860) 2 B. & S. 152.

[7] *Simons* v. *Great Western Railway Co* (1856) 18 C.B. 805 (affirmed 2 C.B. N.S. 620); *London and North Western Railway Co* v. *Dunham* (1856) 18 C.B. 826 at 829.

[8] *Peek* v. *North Staffordshire Railway Co* [1862–63] 10 HLC 473. However, at the end of the century judges found ways of removing the protection given by the Act: in *Shaw* v. *Great Western Railway Co* [1894] 1 QB 373 Wright J. held that the requirements of statute only applied where loss was caused by negligence.

[9] *Stewart* v. *London and North Western Railway Co* (1864) 3 H. & C. 135. On such exclusion clauses, see further, pp. 967–9.

[10] *Cohen* v. *South Eastern Railway Co* (1876) 1 Ex D 217.

cloakroom cases that later nineteenth-century courts explored how much notice had to be given of an exemption clause for it to be regarded as incorporated in a contract. Numerous rules were put forward to explain when a customer would be bound by the company's terms. If conditions were printed on the front of a ticket, the recipient was held bound by them, regardless of whether he read them or not;[11] but if conditions were printed on the back, and they had not been sufficiently drawn to the customer's attention, he would not be bound by them.[12] If the case law seemed inconsistent, a consensus emerged among writers 'that the taking of the ticket is nowise conclusive evidence of the passenger assenting to all or any of its conditions. *Prima facie* evidence of such assent will vary in strength with the clearness with which the conditions are printed on the ticket and other circumstances, such as the degree of publicity given by general notices.'[13] Outside the defined area of statutory protection for railway passengers, the courts therefore allowed powerful parties to limit their liability for breaches: provided they could show that the term had been accepted as a part of the contract.

1. QUALITY OBLIGATIONS IN THE SALE OF GOODS

The majority of cases where parties disputed the meaning of contractual terms at common law did not involve individual consumers, but large-scale commercial contracts for the sale of goods. In such sales, disputes often arose on the question of the quality of goods supplied. Buyers needed to be sure that goods met the standard they required, while sellers needed to prevent buyers from taking advantage of minor blemishes to get out of bad bargains. Both sides needed clear rules as to what could be done, given the expense of litigation. The common law courts, in part drawing on commercial custom, did help elaborate many rules regarding the performance obligations of parties selling goods. However, a great deal of commercial rule-making remained a matter of trade custom and private contract.

In the first half of the nineteenth century, sales in many sectors were effected without elaborate documentation. For instance, in the London corn market in the 1830s, factors sold corn on behalf of farmers at the corn exchange in Mark

---

[11] *Zunz* v. *South Eastern Railway Co* (1869) LR 4 QB 539 at 544; *Harris* v. *Great Western Railway Co* (1876) 1 CPD 515, cf. *Watkins v Rymill* (1883) 10 QBD 178.

[12] *Henderson* v. *Stevenson* (1875) LR 2 HL (Sc) 470; *Parker* v. *South Eastern Railway Co* (1877) 2 CPD 416.

[13] W. Hodges, *A Treatise on the Law of Railways* (6th edn by J. M. Lely, 1876), 617. Contrast the much less certain approach in J. H. Balfour Browne and H. S. Theobald, *The Law of Railway Companies* (4th edn by J. H. Balfour Browne and H. Conacher, 1911), 317.

Lane by giving a ticket stating the quantity of grain sold, and a delivery order addressed to the warehouse keeper. The purchaser would accept the ticket having inspected a sample. In such cases of spot sales, there was little room for disputes about quality, since the sale note stated that the buyer could reject the goods within a defined period. London grain dealers did not see the need for detailed written contracts; indeed, they admitted routinely ignoring the requirements of the Statute of Frauds.[14] Outside London, corn was traded at market entirely through verbal agreements.[15] Grain was also sold for future delivery, as where farmers corresponded directly with purchasers, or where brokers made 'time-sales' for future delivery.[16] Here, there was greater room for disputes to arise between the buyer and seller.

In many areas, market customs regulated what had to be disclosed and when goods could be rejected. These customs could be imperfect, however, and did not guarantee that disputes would be minimized. By the mid-century, trade associations were formed in a number of areas, which sought to codify these rules in their contracts. This was done by the Liverpool Corn Trade Association, formed in 1853, which aimed to ensure that 'every contract for the purchase and sale of grain or flour [...] be carried out in all its original integrity and full meaning'.[17] Many of the trade associations which flourished in the second half of the century developed standard forms of contracts, which included rules that any disputes were to be settled by arbitration, rather than litigation. These standard terms were negotiated between different interest groups—including buyers, sellers and, sometimes, insurers—and sought to minimize disputes over the quality of goods sold.

In the first half of the century, disputes over quality generally centred on whether the bulk corresponded with a sample which had been sent to market in advance, by mail coach or train. But with the development of longer distance grain imports, where the sale was not by sample, contract notes began to specify that the grain was to be of 'fair average quality' of the type sold, or of the season's harvest, at the time of dispatch.[18] Other trades followed suit, leaving it to arbitrators to settle

---

[14] Report from the Select Committee on the Sale of Corn, *PP* 1834 (517), vii, 1, at pp. 79–80.

[15] *Ibid.*, 165.

[16] W. G. Fearnside told the 1834 Select Committee, at p. 80, 'Time-sale is a term applied to purchasing a quantity of grain deliverable at a certain period; at the expiration of a month; then if not delivered, whatever the difference of price is in the market, of course it must be made good.'

[17] *Liverpool Mercury*, 22 March 1853, 7 April 1854. On the importance of trade associations for the rise of standard form contracts, see R. Cranston, 'The Rise and Rise of Standard Form Contracts: International Commodity Sales 1800–1970', in R. Cranston, J. Ramberg, and J. Ziegler (eds), *Commercial Law Challenges in the 21st Century: Jan Hellner in memoriam* (Stockholm, 2007), 11–71.

[18] See e.g. the notes in *Pennell* v. *Alexander* (1852) 3 E. & B. 283 at 287; *Tamvaco* v. *Lucas* (1861) 1 B. & S. 185. Contracts were also divided according to the condition of goods on arrival: those using the

disputes.[19] To overcome the risk of the buyer rejecting goods which had arrived in a port from a distance—and perhaps been sold to the buyer by an intermediate purchaser from the shipper—clauses were often included in contract notes that if the goods proved not to be of fair average quality, they were to be taken with a fair allowance to be assessed by arbitrators.[20] As trades became more organized, so the standard form contracts became more elaborate and more specialized, according to route and product.[21] In this way, the rules of the market were set and policed by the participants, leaving resort to the law as the exception. The role of the common law was to establish a set of ground rules, on the basis of which contracts could be made. It was not a system expected to regulate the market.

In determining disputes over quality, the common lawyers began by looking at the contract. In determining whether a buyer was free to reject goods, the courts looked at whether the seller had supplied the very thing promised, according to the contract.[22] As Lord Abinger put it in 1838, 'if a man offers to buy peas of another, and he sends him beans, he does not perform his contract'.[23] Thus, a contract for the sale of a copper-fastened vessel was held not to have been performed by the delivery of a vessel which was only partially copper-fastened.[24] Goods sold by description had to answer to what commercial parties understood by the description. Where a jury decided that the goods could not pass in the market under the description given, the seller was held not to have performed his contract.[25] In laying down strict performance obligations on sellers, the courts imposed significant risks on them.[26]

term 'tale quale' meant that the buyer had to take the goods as found (provided they were shipped in good condition); 'rye terms' meant that it had to arrive in good condition: Cranston, 'Rise and Rise', 23.

[19] For a disputed arbitration, see *In re Brook* v. *Delcomyn* (1864) 16 C.B. N.S. 403. Disputes could also arise as to the meaning of the commodity described: see e.g. *Jones* v. *Clarke* (1858) 2 H. & N. 725.

[20] e.g. *Graves* v. *Legg* (1854) 9 Exch. 709.

[21] See London Corn Trade Association, *Forms of Contracts in Force 1896* (1896), discussed in Cranston, 'Rise and Rise'.

[22] If the wrong quantity of goods were delivered, the buyer could reject the consignment, since the vendor had not delivered according to the contract: *Cunliffe* v. *Harrison* (1851) 6 Exch. 903 at 906; *Levy* v. *Green* (1857) 8 E. & B. 575. The buyer could, however, accept the tender of fewer items: *Morgan* v. *Gath* (1865) 3 H. & C. 748.

[23] *Chanter* v. *Hopkins* (1838) 4 M. & W. 399 at 404. See also *Allan* v. *Lake* (1852) 18 Q.B. 560.

[24] *Shepherd* v. *Kain* (1821) 5 B. & Ald. 239 at 241. Here the ship was sold with all faults, but the court held that this expression 'must mean with all faults which it may have consistently with its being the thing described'. Contrast *Taylor* v. *Bullen* (1850) 5 Exch. 779. See also *Freeman* v. *Baker* (1833) 5 B. & Ad. 797; *Pickering* v. *Dowson* (1813) 4 Taunt. 779; *Kain* v. *Old* (1824) 2 B. & C. 627.

[25] *Wieler* v. *Schilizzi* (1856) 17 C.B. 619; *Vernede* v. *Weber* (1856) 1 H. & N. 311. This applied even where a buyer had taken samples of the goods, which complied with the bulk, but which were not the kind of goods contained in the contract note: *Nichol* v. *Godts* (1854) 10 Exch. 191.

[26] See e.g. *Josling* v. *Kingsford* (1863) 13 C.B. N.S. 447.

What were the buyer's remedies if the goods were faulty in quality? Much turned on whether property in them had passed. Where unspecified goods were sold— such as sacks of corn—no actual sale was complete until the specific parcels which were the subject of the sale had been identified by an appropriation, assented to by the buyer. Until that moment, there was no certain agreement as to the precise goods being sold.[27] In such cases, the buyer could simply reject the goods if they did not comply with the required quality, as was the case if they did not correspond to the sample, since property in the goods had not yet passed.[28] But if the buyer accepted delivery, and kept the goods for a longer period than was necessary to check them, property passed, and he could no longer reject the goods.[29]

Where specific goods were sold, property passed at the time of the agreement, unless the contract stipulated the contrary, since the subject-matter of the contract was certain.[30] Where specific goods were sold with a warranty, early nineteenth-century opinion suggested that the purchaser could, on discovering the defect, return the object and recover the price.[31] But by the 1830s, judges ruled that the buyer of a specific warranted chattel could not return it once it had been received and property passed,[32] unless the seller agreed, or had been guilty of fraud.[33] He had rather to sue for a breach of warranty, or set up the breach in reduction of damages when sued for the price.[34] English law had no equivalent to the Roman redhibitory action, under which the vendor could be compelled to take back defective goods and refund the price.[35] Unless there had been a total failure of consideration, the breach of warranty was regarded only as the breach of a collateral engagement, which led to damages and not rescission.[36]

[27] See *White* v. *Wilks* (1813) 5 Taunt. 176; *Busk* v. *Davis* (1814) 2 M. & S. 397; *Dixon* v. *Yates* (1833) 5 B. & Ad. 313 at 340. See also *Rohde* v. *Thwaites* (1827) 6 B. & C. 388; *Atkinson* v. *Bell* (1828) 8 B. & C. 277 at 283; *Aldridge* v. *Johnson* (1857) 7 E. & B. 885; *Campbell* v. *Mersey Docks and Harbour Board* (1863) 14 C.B. N.S. 412 at 414; *Jenner* v. *Smith* (1869) LR 4 C 270 at 278.

[28] *Azémar* v. *Casella* (1867) LR 2 CP 431, 677.

[29] *Fisher* v. *Samuda* (1808) 1 Camp. 190; *Heilbutt* v. *Hickson* (1872) LR 7 CP 438 at 451; Sale of Goods Act 1893, s 11(c). See also *Toulmin* v. *Hedley* (1845) 2 Car. & K. 157.

[30] *Gilmour* v. *Supple* (1858) 11 Moore 551 at 566.

[31] See Eldon's view in *Curtis* v. *Hannay* (1800) 3 Esp. 82; T. Starkie, *A Practical Treatise on the Law of Evidence*, 3 vols (1824), ii, 645.

[32] *Street* v. *Blay* (1831) 2 B. & Ad. 456 at 462–3. See also *Poulton* v. *Lattimore* (1829) 9 B. & C. 259.

[33] *Gompertz* v. *Denton* (1832) 1 Car. & M. 207.

[34] *Street* v. *Blay* (1831) 2 B. & Ad. 456; *Parson* v. *Sexton* (1847) 4 C.B. 899; *Dawson* v. *Collins* (1851) 10 C.B. 523.

[35] D.21.1.21.27. See C. G. Addison, *Treatise on the Law of Contracts* (4th edn, 1856, 272–3); J. L. Barton, 'Redhibition, Error and Implied Warranty in English Law' (1994) 62 *Tijdschrift voor Rechtsgeschiedenis* 317–29.

[36] J. W. Smith, *A Selection of Leading Cases on Various Branches of the Law*, 2 vols (4th edn, 1854), ii, 23; citing Williams J.'s comments in *Dawson* v. *Collins* 10 C.B. 523 at 530, drawing on *Young* v. *Cole* (1837) 3 Bing. N.C. 724.

When it came to written contracts, it was easy enough to determine what had been warranted, since oral warranties not included in the document were not binding.[37] In the case of oral contracts, an affirmation made at the time of sale constituted a warranty.[38] Although it was not necessary to use any particular form of words for a statement made at the time of the contract to be a warranty,[39] the jury had to be satisfied that the statement was intended as such, and not merely be a statement of opinion.[40]

If the seller had not warranted the quality of the goods, and had committed no fraud, *caveat emptor* applied. The mid-eighteenth-century notion that a fair price implied a warranty of quality[41] was regarded by the early nineteenth century as 'exploded'.[42] *Caveat emptor* was defended in the commercial community as preventing litigation, since it was often unclear whether a fault was latent or patent, and whether or not it made goods unmerchantable.[43] If a purchaser chose to buy without an express warranty, then (absent fraud) he took the risk of latent defects.[44] Vendors could also avoid the rule that a failure to disclose undiscoverable latent defects known to them amounted to fraud,[45] by passing the risk to the buyer in the contract. When goods were sold 'with all faults', the seller would only be liable if he had actively concealed the defect.[46] Where ships or horses were sold, sellers took care to limit their liability in this way. It was in the interest of shipowners to sell their vessels 'with all faults', since the ship being sold might

[37] Nor were guarantees given subsequently binding, unless paid for with new consideration: *Lysney* v. *Selby* (1705) 2 Ld. Raym. 1118 at 1120; *Roscorla* v. *Thomas* (1842) 3 Q.B. 234.

[38] *Crosse* v. *Gardner* (1689) Comb. 142, Carth. 90; *Wood* v. *Smith* (1829) 4 Car. & P. 45. See also the cases involving the statements attributing paintings to old masters: *Lomi* v. *Tucker* (1829) 4 Car. & P. 15; *Power* v. *Barham* (1836) 4 Ad. & El. 473 at 476. Contrast Kenyon's approach in *Jendwine* v. *Slade* (1797) 2 Esp. 572. See also the comments on this case in *Gee* v. *Lucas* (1867) 16 LT 357 at 358.

[39] *Salmon* v. *Ward* (1825) 2 Car. & P. 211.

[40] *Dunlop* v. *Waugh* (1792) Peake 167.

[41] See R. Wooddeson, *A Systematical View of the Laws of England*, 3 vols (1792–3), ii: 415, iii: 199. According to A. Hayward, 'Mercantile Law: Of the Contract of Sale' (1830) 3 *Law Magazine* 180–99 at 191, '[i]t became an established maxim, applied for the most part, if not solely, to sales of horses, but in principle applicable to every other sale, that if the price paid were equal to the worth of a good and perfect commodity, the seller *must be understood* to have warranted it such'.

[42] In *Stuart* v. *Wilkins* (1778) 1 Doug. 18. See J. Chitty, *A Treatise on the Laws of Commerce and Manufactures and the Contracts relating thereto*, 4 vols (1824), iii, 303.

[43] Mercantile Law Commission, 2nd Report, *PP* 1854–5 [1977], xviii, 653, at p. 10.

[44] *Parkinson* v. *Lee* (1802) 2 East 314 at 322; *Bluett* v. *Osborne* (1816) 1 Stark. 384.

[45] [Hayward], 'Mercantile Law' 3 *LM* 191. W. W. Kerr, *A Treatise on the Law of Fraud and Mistake as Administered in Courts of Equity* (2nd edn, 1883), 66. See H. Rolle, *Un Abridgment des Plusieurs Cases et Resolutions del Common Ley* (1668), 90 (tit. Action sur case, P); *Stuart* v. *Wilkins* (1778) 1 Doug. 18 at 20; *Parkinson* v. *Lee* (1802) 2 East 314 at 323.

[46] *Baglehole* v. *Walters* (1811) 3 Camp. 154 at 156. See also *Schneider* v. *Heath* (1813) 3 Camp. 506; *Freeman* v. *Baker* (1833) 5 B. & Ad. 797; *Ward* v. *Hobbs* (1878) 4 App Cas 13. Contrast the view of Lord Kenyon, holding that good faith still required disclosure: *Mellish* v. *Motteux* (1792) Peake 156.

be in a different port, or at sea, when the sale was made, with its exact condition unknown to the seller.[47] Similarly, with the sale of horses, since so many maladies could amount to unsoundness and thereby violate a warranty, horse dealers were advised not to sell with a warranty, unless they were sure of the soundness and high value of the beast.[48] But since buyers were often reluctant to purchase without any kind of warranty, sales made at horse repositories were often accompanied by warranties which would expire after a very short period.[49] Courts, aware of the fact that quality was reflected in price, were happy to enforce such stipulations.

Although *caveat emptor* was the basic principle of the law of sales, in a number of areas, early nineteenth-century judges developed implied warranties of merchantability.[50] In doing this, the courts were not engaged in consumer protection, but in interpreting the parties' contractual intent.[51] In 1815, in *Gardiner v. Gray*, Lord Ellenborough held that '[w]here there is no opportunity to inspect the commodity, the maxim of *caveat emptor* does not apply'. Although a buyer of waste silk, sold by description, could not 'without a warranty insist that it shall be of any particular quality', it had to be 'saleable in the market under the denomination mentioned in the contract', since no purchaser bought 'goods to lay them on a dunghill'.[52] In the same year, the Common Pleas held a manufacturer of saddles for export liable for breach of contract, when the goods supplied were inferior to the pattern exhibited when the order was placed, and turned out to be 'quite unsaleable without being restuffed and relined'.[53] Although there was no express warranty of quality, and the price paid was low, the court held that 'it resulted from the whole transaction that the article was to be merchantable'.[54] The decision was taken to mean that 'in every contract to furnish manufactured

---

[47] e.g. in *Schneider* v. *Heath* (1813) 3 Camp. 506, where the sale was completed at Lloyds Coffee House in London, but the vessel was in Hull.

[48] See P. Mitchell, 'The Development of Quality Obligations in Sale of Goods' (2001) 117 *LQR* 643–63 at 649.

[49] *Bywater* v. *Richardson* (1834) 1 Ad. & El. 508 at 513.

[50] Warranties were implied where it was the custom of a trade to do so: *Jones* v. *Bowden* (1813) 4 Taunt. 846. See also [Hayward], 'Mercantile Law', 3 *LM* 194.

[51] S. J. Stoljar (suggesting that the judges 'pretended' to be giving effect to a contractual intention) points out that 'whether or not such was the actual contractual intention, the warranty implied-by-law constituted a completely new obligation upon the seller', 'Conditions, Warranties and Descriptions of Quality in Sale of Goods' (1952) 15 *MLR* 425–45 at 434.

[52] *Gardiner* v. *Gray* (1815) 4 Camp. 144 at 145.

[53] *Laing* v. *Fidgeon* (1814) 4 Camp. 169 at 170. Thomas Fidgeon of Birmingham subsequently went bankrupt and was jailed for not answering questions to the satisfaction of the commissioners: *Caledonian Mercury*, 12 October 1816.

[54] *Laing* v. *Fidgeon* (1815) 6 Taunt. 108 at 109.

goods, however low the price, it is an implied term, that the goods should be merchantable'.[55]

In the 1820s, a rule also developed that goods sold for a particular purpose were warranted as reasonably fit for such purpose.[56] In 1829, Best CJ said, 'if a man sells generally, he undertakes that the article sold is fit for some purpose; if he sells it for a particular purpose, he undertakes that it shall be fit for that particular purpose'.[57] Best's broad principle that every sale contained an implied term of merchantability startled some writers, who felt it tended towards introducing the civilian rule of implied warranties into English law in a way which could only encourage litigation.[58] But the principle was endorsed in 1841 by the Common Pleas, where Tindal CJ said that if a person bought an article 'upon his own judgment', he could not later hold the vendor responsible if it proved unfit for the purpose for which it was required. By contrast, if he told the seller of the use for which it was needed and relied on the seller's judgment 'the transaction carries with it an implied warranty, that the thing furnished shall be fit and proper for the purpose for which it was designed'.[59] This suggested that where the seller knew of the buyer's purpose, and made or selected the goods for the buyer, he would be held not to have performed his promise if he sent unsuitable goods.

However, the courts declined to go further, and imply a term that existing goods sold without a warranty were in general fit for purpose. In 1838, the Exchequer refused to imply a warranty of quality in a case where a ship, sold for £4200, turned out to be worth only £10, having run aground. Where a chattel was sold 'as being of a particular description', there was an implied contract only that 'the article sold is of that description'.[60] Provided the thing sold could be described as a ship (as Parke B. felt it could), then the contract had been fulfilled. If the parties wanted to provide for any particular condition of the ship, they had to 'introduce an express stipulation to that effect'. In the same year, the court also held that where 'a defined and well-known machine' had been ordered from a manufacturer, which the buyer wanted for a particular purpose, there was no implied warranty that it would serve that purpose, and that the seller performed

---

[55] These words, taken from the headnote of *Laing* v. *Fidgeon* (1815) 6 Taunt. 108, were quoted by Best CJ in *Jones* v. *Bright* (1829) 5 Bing. 531 at 546.

[56] *Gray* v. *Cox* (1825) 4 B. & C. 108 at 115, per Abbott CJ. He admitted that 'some of my learned brothers think differently'.

[57] *Jones* v. *Bright* (1829) 5 Bing. 533 at 544–6.

[58] [Hayward] 'Mercantile Law' 3 *LM* 196.

[59] *Brown* v. *Edgington* (1841) 2 M. & G. 279 at 290; *Bigge* v. *Parkinson* (1862) 7 H. & N. 955. Tindal's distinction was taken up by treatise writers: J. Chitty, *A Practical Treatise on the Law of Contracts not under seal* (4th edn by J. A. Russell, 1850), 392.

[60] *Barr* v. *Gibson* (1838) 3 M. & W. 390 at 399–400 (per Parke B.).

all that was required of him by sending the machine. Only if an order was 'given for an undescribed and unascertained thing, stated to be for a particular purpose, which the manufacturer supplies' could the buyer resist an action for the price, since it did not 'answer the purpose for which it was supplied'.[61]

The rule that *caveat emptor* applied to the sale of existing chattels was applied even in the sensitive area of the sale of carcasses of meat.[62] As Pollock CB pointed out in 1862, there was no reason to assume, in an age when large quantities of slaughtered meat arrived from all over the country, that a middleman would have the kind of knowledge on the basis of which a term could be implied.[63] Pollock was not an enthusiast for implied warranties where the seller had no particular knowledge of the qualities of the product sold. In *Jackson* v. *Harrison*, he held there was no implied warranty of quality when a seed crusher sold refuse oil cake to a farmer, to feed his cattle. Here, the defendant did not profess to manufacture and sell cattle feed, but merely sold his waste: in these conditions, it was for the farmer to decide if it was fit for his cattle.[64] This same approach was applied in *Turner* v. *Mucklow*, where a plaintiff was able to sue for the price of spent madder—a by-product of calico printing—even though it was not suitable for the buyer's purposes.[65] The Exchequer judges were aware that the distinction between specific goods and non-specific goods might in practice be difficult to make,[66] and they seem—in these waste cases—to have wished to diminish the role of implied terms of quality where there was no reason for the seller to be assumed to have special knowledge.

Nonetheless, the distinction between specific goods, which the buyer could check, and non-specific ones, which he could not, was reaffirmed in 1868 by the Queen's Bench in *Jones* v. *Just*. The plaintiff had purchased a cargo of Manila hemp to arrive from Singapore, from a dealer who had purchased the cargo en route.[67] The hemp had been damaged, though without losing its character as hemp, and the plaintiffs sold it 'with all faults' at 75 per cent of the price it would have obtained without the damage.[68] At trial, where it was proved that the goods

---

[61] *Chanter* v. *Hopkins* (1838) 4 M. & W. 399 at 406 (per Parke B.). See also *Shepherd* v. *Pybus* (1842) 3 M. & G. 868; *Sutton* v. *Temple* (1843) 12 M. & W. 52 at 64; *Ollivant* v. *Bayley* (1843) 5 Q.B. 288.

[62] See *Burnby* v. *Bollett* (1847) 16 M. & W. 644, where the vendor was not a dealer in meat.

[63] *Emmerton* v. *Mathews* (1862) 7 H. & N. 586 at 594.

[64] *Jackson* v. *Harrison* (1862) 2 F. & F. 782.

[65] *Turner* v. *Mucklow* (1862) 8 Jur. ns 870, 6 LT 690.

[66] As Martin B. put it, 'it often happens that cases come near the line, and it is difficult to say whether the subject of the contract is a *specific* article or not': *Turner* v. *Mucklow* (1862) 6 LT 690 at 692.

[67] *The Times*, 5 November 1868, col. 9b.

[68] *The Times*, 18 February 1868, col. 9a: 'as the market price had risen, this was not very much lower than the contract price'.

were not of 'fair current quality', Blackburn J. told the jury that the contract was for the buyer to receive 'hemp such as fair and honest merchants would expect on a contract for Manila hemp'.[69] In the Queen's Bench, Mellor J. (affirming the decision) said that *caveat emptor* had been applied in no case 'where there has been no opportunity of inspection, or where that opportunity has not been waived'. He ruled that where a person 'undertakes to supply goods, manufactured by himself, or in which he deals', which the buyer had no opportunity to inspect, there was an implied term that the goods be merchantable. Since the hemp in this case was sold by a sold note which did not specify that it was to be of 'fair current quality', the Queen's Bench was effectively implying into the contract the specification regarding quality which merchants themselves habitually used. Merchantable in this context meant neither merely saleable, nor perfect, but what merchants expected. As for the argument that the seller here had no means of knowing the quality of the goods sent by the Singapore shippers, Mellor J. ruled that he 'had recourse against them for not supplying an article reasonably merchantable'.[70]

As Brett JA ruled in 1877, in sale of goods cases, 'the fundamental undertaking is, that the *article offered or delivered shall answer the description of it contained in the contract*', as understood in 'the real mercantile or business' sense.[71] Only if the buyer had a chance to inspect, and consequently chose to buy goods of inferior quality, was the risk of defects thrown on him. This meant that even in the case of sales by sample, where bulk complied with the sample, the courts held there was an implied warranty that the goods were merchantable as to such matters as could not be judged by the sample.[72] In 1893, when the law relating to the sale of goods was codified, these rules were digested by M. D. Chalmers into sections 14 and 15 of the new Sale of Goods Act, which (he noted) 'probably narrows the already restricted rule of *caveat emptor*'.[73] Section 14(1) enacted that there was an implied term, where the buyer made known to the seller the purposes for which the goods were required 'so as to show that the buyer relies on the seller's skill or judgment', and the goods were of a description which it was in the

---

[69] *The Times*, 15 January 1867, col. 9b.

[70] *Jones* v. *Just* (1868) LR 3 QB 197 at 203–7.

[71] *Randall* v. *Newson* (1877) LR 2 QBD 102 at 109 (emphasis in original).

[72] The buyer was 'bound by what he actually recognizes in the sample, and by what he might by due diligence…have ascertained': *Mody* v. *Gregson* (1868) LR 4 Ex 49 at 52, 58. See also *Drummond* v. *Van Ingen* (1887) 12 App Cas 284.

[73] M. Chalmers, *The Sale of Goods Act* (2nd edn, 1894), 30. See also Mitchell, 'Quality Obligations', 656–61. For criticism of Chalmers' approach to codification (digesting cases without reconciling their inconsistencies), see S. J. Stoljar, 'Conditions, Warranties and Descriptions of Quality in Sale of Goods II', (1953) 16 *MLR* 174–97 at 177.

course of the seller's business to supply,[74] that the goods would be reasonably fit for purpose. This did not apply to the sale of specified articles under their patent or trade names. Section 14(2) enacted that where goods were sold by description from a seller dealing in such goods, there was an implied condition of merchant-able quality, 'provided that if the buyer had examined the goods, there shall be no implied condition as regards defects which such examination ought to have revealed'. This section in effect removed the distinction between the sale of exist-ing goods and the sale of non-specific goods. In place of Parke B.'s rule in *Barr* v. *Gibson* that where chattels were sold by description, there was an implied term that they fitted the description, the rule was now substituted that they had to be merchantable.

In the same way that the courts and legislature became more sympathetic to implied warranties of quality in the later nineteenth century, so they adopted the notion that warranties of title could be implied. Despite some eighteenth-century authorities suggesting the reverse, it was accepted in the early nineteenth century that there was no implied warranty of title in sales of goods.[75] Only if the buyer could show that the vendor had known of his lack of title and been fraudulent could he recover.[76] This meant, at least in the case of specific chattels, that the vendor only transferred such an interest as he had.[77] But the courts in mid-century began to narrow the rule: 'if the vendor of a chattel by word or con-duct gives the purchaser to understand that he is the owner', Erle CJ ruled, 'that tacit representation forms part of the contract'.[78] In his view, *caveat emptor* only applied where it was clear—as with pawnbrokers or sheriffs—that the vendor had no knowledge of the title to the goods.[79] Other judges were also unhappy with the view that *caveat emptor* might apply respecting the vendor's title, but courts continued to hold that a warranty of title could not be implied by law.[80]

In this context, Judah Benjamin proposed that the rule of law should be restated in the following way: 'a sale of personal chattels implies an affirmation by the vendor that the chattel is his, and therefore he warrants the title, unless

---

[74] The idea that implied terms only applied to such sellers can be seen in *Burnby* v. *Bollett* (1847) 16 M. & W. 644. For other views, see Mitchell, 'Quality Obligations', 658; Barton, 'Redhibition', 329; R. Zimmermann, *The Law of Obligations* (1996), 336.

[75] A number of eighteenth-century sources suggested that if a person in possession of goods affirmed they were his, this amounted to a warranty: *Medina* v. *Stoughton* (1701) 1 Salk. 210. See also Blackstone, *Comms*, ii, 451.

[76] *Early* v. *Garrett* (1829) 9 B. & C. 928 at 932; *Sprigwell* v. *Allen* (1648) Aleyn 91, 2 East 448n.

[77] *Morley* v. *Attenborough* (1849) 3 Exch. 500 at 509. See also *Chapman* v. *Speller* (1850) 14 Q.B. 621 at 624.

[78] *Eicholz* v. *Bannister* (1864) 17 C.B. N.S. 708 at 721.

[79] *Eicholz* v. *Bannister* (1864) 17 C.B. N.S. 708 at 723.

[80] *Bagueley* v. *Hawley* (1867) LR 2 CP 625 at 629.

it be shown by the facts and circumstances of the sale that the vendor did not intend to assert ownership, but only to transfer such interest as he might have in the chattel sold'.[81] This formulation attracted the attention of the Indian Law Commissioners,[82] as well as Mackenzie Chalmers. It had the advantage of preserving the rule that no warranties of title were given by sheriffs selling the goods of an execution debtor, while putting in place what had come to be the accepted norm that a seller held himself out to have title to goods. The 1893 Sale of Goods Act duly enacted that there was an implied term that the seller had the right to sell the goods, unless the circumstances of the sale were such as to show a different intention. Chalmers adopted Benjamin's suggestion that in the case of breach of this term, the buyer should be able to sue for unliquidated damages, and not merely for the price paid.

2. CONDITIONS AND WARRANTIES

By 1893, when the Sale of Goods Act passed, jurists drew a distinction between 'major' terms in a contract—conditions—whose breach entitled the innocent party to terminate a contract, and 'minor' terms—warranties—whose breach only sounded in damages. By contrast, early nineteenth-century lawyers distinguished between different kinds of terms by looking at the order in which the parties were to perform their obligations, rather than at their weight.[83] They distinguished between conditions precedent, 'the non-performance of which by one of the contracting parties is set up as a reason for the non-fulfilment of the contract by the other' and terms which were 'collateral to the express object', which could be remedied by an action for damages and which were sometimes referred to as 'warranties'.[84]

In the earlier period, contractual terms were defined as either dependent covenants (where one party's obligation depended on the other's prior performance of a condition precedent), mutual covenants (where both had to perform at the

---

[81] J. P. Benjamin, *A Treatise on the Law of Sale of Personal Property* (1868), 476. By contrast, S. M. Leake, *The Elements of the Law of Contracts* (1867), 198 was largely content with restating the old rule.

[82] The Indian Contract Act 1872, s 109 enacted that 'If the buyer, or any person claiming under him, is, by reason of the invalidity of the seller's title, deprived of the thing sold, the seller is responsible to the buyer, or the person claiming under him, for loss caused thereby, unless a contrary intention appears by the contract'.

[83] See e.g. the first two rules in Williams's notes to *Pordage* v. *Cole* (1669) 1 Wms. Saund. 319, discussed in the notes to *Cutter* v. *Powell* in Smith, *Leading Cases* (4th edn, 1856), ii, 11. See also G. Treitel, 'Conditions and Conditions precedent', (1990) 106 LQR 185–92.

[84] *Barker* v. *Windle* (1856) 6 E. & B. 675 at 679 (per Williams J.); *Chanter* v. *Hopkins* (1838) 4 M. & W. 399 at 404 (per Lord Abinger CB); see also *Behn* v. *Burness* (1862) 1 B. & S. 877 at 888.

same time),[85] or independent covenants (where one party's obligation to perform did not depend on the other's performance).[86] A number of rules of construction helped identify which of these the parties had intended when making their contract. These rules determined whether a plaintiff could sue without having performed his own obligations, and whether a party who had not performed his contractual duties perfectly could be paid.[87]

The two most important rules, taken by Serjeant John Williams from Lord Mansfield's decision in *Boone* v. *Eyre*,[88] were that where 'mutual covenants go to the whole consideration on both sides, they are mutual conditions, and performance must be averred', but that where 'a covenant goes only to part of the consideration on both sides', and its breach could be paid for in damages, it was an independent covenant.[89] *Boone* v. *Eyre*, where one party had conveyed a title to property in a plantation, but was unable to perform his covenant to convey property in its slaves, was an example of the latter. In this case, the purchaser, who had obtained property in the plantation, was held unable to claim that he need not pay the purchase money on the ground of a failure of a condition precedent. As Williams put it:

where a person has received a part of the consideration for which he entered into the agreement, it would be unjust that because he has not had the whole, he should therefore be permitted to enjoy that part without either paying or doing any thing for it. Therefore the law obliges him to perform the agreement on his part, and leaves him to his remedy to recover any damage he may have sustained in not having received the whole consideration.

According to the rule, once any consideration had passed, the innocent party could no longer claim to be discharged of his own obligations,[90] but was bound to perform them and sue for damages.[91] Thus, in *Havelock* v. *Geddes*, Lord

---

[85] Where conditions were concurrent, the plaintiff had to aver his readiness to perform: see *Rawson* v. *Johnson* (1801) 1 East 203; *Doogood* v. *Rose* (1850) 9 C.B. 132 at 137–8.

[86] *Jones* v. *Barkley* (1781) 2 Doug. 684 at 690–1.

[87] e.g. *Ritchie* v. *Atkinson* (1808) 10 East 295; *Stavers* v. *Curling* (1836) 3 Bing. N.C. 355.

[88] *Boone* v. *Eyre* (1779) 2 W. Bl. 1312 at 1314n. See also *Campbell* v. *Jones* (1795) 6 T.R. 570. See also Williams's discussion in *Pordage* v. *Cole* (1669) 1 Wms. Saund. 319.

[89] *Pordage* v. *Cole* (1669) 1 Wms. Saund. 319 note.

[90] Contrast the detailed discussion of *Boone* v. *Eyre* by T.A. Baloch, *Unjust Enrichment and Contract* (Oxford, 2009), 106–11, who rejects this interpretation, and sees the case as helping establish a principle that 'a substantial failure of consideration would excuse counter-performance' (at p. 111). For Baloch (at p. 107), under the principle developed here, '[A's] ability to recover on B's counter-performance depends on the extent of the part-performance and materiality of the breach'.

[91] As Pollock CB pointed out, this meant that 'the construction of the instrument may be varied by matter ex post facto; and that which is a condition precedent when the deed is executed may cease to be so by the subsequent conduct of the covenantee in accepting less': *Ellen* v. *Topp* (1851) 6 Exch. 424 at 441. See also *Graves* v. *Legg* (1854) 9 Exch. 709 at 716–17.

Ellenborough held that while a charterer could have refused to take a ship which was not 'tight, staunch and strong', once he had made any use of her, he could not argue that there had been a failure to perform a condition precedent, sufficient to discharge him of his obligations. Since 'the consideration has not wholly failed', he said, 'the covenant cannot be looked upon as having raised a condition precedent, but merely gives the defendants a right, under a counter-action, to such damages as they can prove they have sustained from this neglect'.[92]

This approach was also taken in continuing contracts. Once performance had begun, consideration passed, and the innocent party was no longer able to claim a breach of a condition precedent. Thus, in *Franklin* v. *Miller*, the King's Bench held that since a contract could only be rescinded by agreement, one party could not take advantage of a failure 'in the slightest degree' by the other to perform his part to terminate it. Only if the party in breach absolutely refused to proceed in the way required by the contract would it be regarded as 'a total failure' of the contract to justify rescission.[93] In *Hoare* v. *Rennie*, Pollock CB held that a buyer was in his rights in repudiating a continuing contract where the first instalment was faulty, and was rejected, since no consideration passed; but '[w]here a person has derived a benefit from a contract, he cannot rescind it because the parties cannot be put in statu quo'.[94]

However, by the mid-century, many judges were unhappy with the idea that the right to terminate was lost if any consideration had been given. Pollock was himself unconvinced that a person who might have rejected a performance which did not meet a condition precedent when tendered lost the right to terminate later, when the performance turned out to be substantially inadequate.[95] In his view, the rule in *Boone* v. *Eyre* 'cannot be intended to apply to every case in which [...] the residue of the consideration has been had by the defendant. That residue must be a substantial part of the contract.'[96] This was to suggest that the right to terminate was lost only if one accepted substantial performance. The mere fact that the defendant had commenced performance and given consideration did

---

[92] *Havelock* v. *Geddes* (1809) 10 East 549 at 562, 564. See also the rule that where faulty work was done, but inferior performance was accepted, then the buyer would have to pay for the work done on an *indebitatus assumpsit* count: *Burn* v. *Miller* (1813) 4 Taunt. 745 at 748.

[93] *Franklin* v. *Miller* (1836) 4 Ad. & El. 599 at 606, citing *Withers* v. *Reynolds* (1831) 2 B. & Ad. 882. The idea that a contract was terminated by the refusal of one contracting party to proceed was endorsed by Pollock CB in argument in *Hoare* v. *Rennie* (1859) 5 H. & N. 19 at 25, where he observed that '[t]he principle of *Boone* v. *Eyre* applies to the partial breach of a single contract, but surely not to a breach of a continuing contract, as to supply goods from day to day or from week to week, where during the contract one party becomes wholly incapable of performing his part'.

[94] *Hoare* v. *Rennie* (1859) 5 H. & N. 19 at 27–8.

[95] Benjamin, *Sale* (1868), 422 agreed that the right to rescind was lost where the innocent party 'has received and accepted a substantial part of that which was to be performed'.

[96] *Ellen* v. *Topp* (1851) 6 Exch. 424 at 442.

not mean that the plaintiff could no longer treat the breach as one of a condition, discharging him of his further obligations. What mattered in determining this was not the order of performance, but the weight of the term.

In deciding whether a term was a condition, the courts began to look at whether the parties had expressly declared it to be one, or whether its breach would be so great as to deprive the plaintiff substantially of the benefit of the contract.[97] If 'statements in a contract descriptive of the subject-matter' were 'intended to be a substantive part of the contract', Williams J. held in 1863, they constituted conditions, for failure of which repudiation was possible. But if the innocent party had 'received the whole or any substantial part of the consideration for the promise on his part', then only damages were available.[98] Blackburn J. noted in 1875 that a term was to be regarded as a condition if it went 'to the root of the matter, so that a failure to perform it would render the performance of the rest of the contract by the plaintiff a thing different in substance from what the defendant has stipulated for'.[99]

This new approach also influenced the courts' treatment of contracts involving work to be done or goods to be supplied over a period of time. The mid-century position, outlined in *Hoare* v. *Rennie*,[100] that the innocent party could only terminate where the first instalment had not been made, unless the refusal amounted to a repudiation of the whole contract, was endorsed by the Court of Appeal as late as 1881.[101] However, some jurists contended that if the failure went to the root of the contract, the innocent party could terminate. As Anson saw it, this came down to a question of fact, 'whether one party has so far made default that the consideration for which the other gave his promise has wholly failed?'[102] This view was taken by the House of Lords in 1884 in *Mersey Steel and Iron Co* v. *Naylor Benzon & Co*.[103] It was subsequently codified in section 31(2) the Sale of Goods Act, which enacted that if a seller by instalments made defective delivery, or the buyer refused an instalment, 'it is a question in each case, depending on the terms of the contract and the circumstances of the case, whether the breach of contract is a repudiation of the whole contract'.[104]

[97] *White* v. *Beeton* (1861) 7 H. & N. 42 at 49–51.   [98] *Behn* v. *Burness* (1863) 3 B. & S. 751 at 755
[99] *Bettini* v. *Gye* (1875) 1 QBD 183 at 188.   [100] *Hoare* v. *Rennie* (1859) 5 H. & N. 19.
[101] *Honck* v. *Muller* (1881) 7 QBD 92 at 100; *Freeth* v. *Burr* (1874) LR 9 CP 208. See also *Bloomer* v. *Bernstain* (1874) LR 9 CP 588; *Morgan* v. *Bain* (1874) LR 10 CP 15; *Mersey Steel and Irton Co* v. *Naylor, Benzon & Co* (1884) 9 App Cas 434; *Braithwaite* v. *Foreign Hardwood Co* [1905] 2 KB 543. These cases followed the rule established in *Withers* v. *Reynolds* (1831) 2 B. & Ad. 882. The fact that not all judges were happy at Pollock's treatment of the perfect first tender as a condition precedent can be seen in *Jonassohn* v. *Young* (1863) 4 B. & S. 296 at 300; *Simpson* v. *Crippin* (1872) LR 8 QB 14.
[102] Anson, *Contract* (6th edn, 1891), 296.
[103] *Mersey Steel and Iron Co* v. *Naylor Benzon & Co* (1884) 9 App Cas 434 at 444.
[104] See also *Millar's Karri & Jarrah Co* v. *Weddel, Turner & Co* (1909) 100 LT 128, where it was held that if, looking at the nature of the instalment not delivered, the buyer had reasonable grounds for

In determining whether parties intended a term to be a condition or not, courts were often influenced by what they felt would be best for commercial convenience. This could lead to inconsistencies, as in the case of the construction of charterparties, where the approach of the courts made it difficult for lawyers to advise clients.[105] In practice, the courts came to treat certain stipulations systematically as conditions precedent, but others not. Stipulations as to the time of loading or sailing, or as to the position of a vessel, were regarded as conditions precedent, since they affected 'the very foundation of the adventure',[106] being crucial information on which a charterer calculated the voyage.[107] By contrast, other matters, such as the stipulation that a ship should set sail with all convenient speed, were not regarded as conditions precedent, since it was assumed this related to a risk which the charterer could run.[108]

From the 1830s, a number of judges, hearing charterparty cases, suggested that whether a term was a condition or a warranty was to be decided by considering whether the breach had deprived the party of the benefit of the contract or frustrated the object of the voyage. In *Tarrabochia* v. *Hickie*, the Exchequer held that a term which stipulated that a ship was seaworthy was not to be regarded as a condition precedent, unless the breach was such as to frustrate the object of the voyage.[109] In 1862, Cockburn CJ stated in *Behn* v. *Burness* that if a contractual statement about the place of a ship or the time of sailing turned out to be wrong, 'and in consequence of it the charterer finds himself in a position where his speculation and enterprise may be frustrated', this would justify a repudiation of the contract. By contrast, if 'there is no real frustration of the objects of the charterer, and little or no damage has been done to him, he should be left to his action'.[110] 'Not arriving with due diligence, or at a day named, is the subject of a cross action only', ruled Bramwell B. in 1874; 'not arriving in time for the voyage contemplated, but at such a time that it is frustrated, is not only a breach of contract, but discharges the charterer.'[111] This approach allowed innocent parties

supposing that the goods taken as a whole would be substantially different from those he contracted to buy, then the breach would entitle the other party to terminate the contract.

[105] Benjamin, *Sale* (1868), 422.

[106] Bowen LJ in *Bentsen* v. *Taylor Sons & Co* [1893] 2 QB 274 at 282.

[107] See also *Glaholm* v. *Hays* (1841) 2 M. & G. 257; *Ollive* v. *Booker* (1847) 1 Exch. 416, *Croockewit* v. *Fletcher* (1857) 1 H. & N. 893.

[108] Benjamin, *Sale* (1868), 420.

[109] *Tarrabochia* v. *Hickie* (1856) 1 H. & N. 183 at 186–7; cf. *Clipsham* v. *Vertue* (1843) 5 Q.B. 265; *Freeman* v. *Taylor* (1831) 8 Bing. 124; *Dimech* v. *Corlett* (1858) 12 Moore 199 at 227; *MacAndrew* v. *Chapple* (1866) LR 1 CP 643. In *Tarrabochia* v. *Hickie* and *Freeman* v. *Taylor*, these questions had been put to a jury.

[110] *Behn* v. *Burness* (1862) 1 B. & S. 877 at 887. See also *Stanton* v. *Richardson* (1872) LR 7 CP 421. See also *Tully* v. *Howling* (1877) 2 QBD 182 (CA); *Bradford* v. *Williams* (1872) LR 7 Ex 259.

[111] *Jackson* v. *Union Marine Insurance Co* (1874) LR 10 CP 125 at 148. See also *MacAndrew* v. *Chapple* (1866) LR 1 CP 643.

to treat as repudiatory not only any breach of a term defined by the parties or the courts as a condition, but also any breach which frustrated the venture or went to the substance of the contract.

However, this approach, of looking at the effect of the breach, troubled other judges. Cockburn's decision in *Behn* v. *Burness* was overruled by the Exchequer Chamber, which stressed that it was for the court to construe the meaning of a contract 'with reference to the intention of the parties at the time it was made, irrespective of the events which may afterwards occur'. If, at that point, it 'was manifest that the object of the charterparty would in all probability be frustrated' if the vessel was delayed, then this could be construed as a condition. But the frustration of a voyage could not 'convert a stipulation into a condition, if it were not originally intended to be one'.[112] This approach was followed by Bowen LJ in 1893, when holding that it was for the court to decide if a term was a warranty or a condition. He admitted that the court had, in deciding this, to look at how any breach would affect 'the substance and foundation of the adventure', and noted that in cases of charterparties, it might be necessary to refer to the jury. But in his view, the jury was not to be asked about the effect of the actual breach which had taken place, but only about the likely effect of 'any such breach of that portion of the contract'.[113] In the same year, section 11(1)(b) of the Sale of Goods Act, following the approach of *Behn* v. *Burness*, enacted that whether a term was a condition or a warranty 'depends in each case on the construction of the contract'. Later judges in cases involving the sale of chattels sought to lay down rules of construction to determine whether a term was a warranty or a condition.[114] Nonetheless, by the middle of the twentieth century, courts dealing with charterparties were once more prepared to consider the effects of a breach in determining whether it justified termination.[115]

---

[112] *Behn* v. *Burness* (1863) 3 B. & S. 751 at 757–8 (per Williams J.). Cf. Baloch, *Unjust Enrichment and Contract*, 120, emphasizing the importance of will theory in focusing the courts' attention on the parties' intentions.

[113] *Bentsen* v. *Taylor Sons & Co* [1893] 2 QB 274 (CA) at 281.

[114] See e.g. Bailhache J.'s approach in *T & J Harrison* v. *Knowles & Foster* [1917] 2 KB 606 at 610, stating that where the lack of a quality 'makes the thing sold different in kind from the thing as described in the contract', a condition had been breached (though the Court of Appeal in [1918] 1 KB 608 were unconvinced by this view).

[115] *Hong Kong Fir Shipping Co* v. *Kawasaki Kisen Kaisha* [1962] 1 All ER 474 (CA). In this case, Diplock LJ held (bearing in mind the development of the doctrine of frustration) 'that it is the event and not the fact that the event is a result of a breach of contract which relieves the party not in default' (at 487). But in mid-nineteenth-century cases, the innocent party could only terminate if the purpose of the contract had been frustrated as a result of a breach: see *Hurst* v. *Usborne* (1856) 18 C.B. 144, where a ship arrived so late that no corn was left to load, but the charterer was still held liable. In this case, however, the court found no breach, since the ship had proceeded with all reasonable speed, but been delayed by conditions at sea.

3. WAIVER

If a condition precedent was not performed, the promisee could waive the performance of the condition, and proceed with the contract.[116] The principle that breaches of conditions rendered a contract voidable at the option of the party not in breach was familiar from land law. As Lawrence J. put it in 1810, 'it would be a monstrous construction if either party could vitiate the agreement by refusing to perform his part of it'.[117] An innocent party could waive breaches which would permit him to cancel a contract of sale,[118] or breaches of covenant which justified forfeiture,[119] without thereby extinguishing the obligations under the covenant.[120] An employer could similarly dispense with his right to terminate a contract of employment, if he took the servant back after he had wrongfully absented himself.[121] For, as Ashhurst J. put it (when referring to a waiver of giving a notice of dishonour of a bill of exchange), 'every rule may be waived by the person for whose benefit it is introduced'.[122]

Where a grant was voidable, the grantor had to do some act amounting to an exercise of his option to terminate.[123] If the grantor treated the contract as subsisting—as where a landlord received rent knowing of the breach—'he could not afterwards insist upon a forfeiture previously committed'.[124] Similarly, in shipping cases, if a ship arrived after the appointed time, 'if the merchant do not discharge the ship, he shall be deemed by his silence to have consented to the delay'.[125] In 1893, Bowen LJ held that where a shipper had failed to perform a condition precedent, the charterers might be seen to have waived it, if by 'their acts or conduct' they led the other party 'reasonably to suppose that they did not intend to treat

[116] As Benjamin put it, 'a party in whose favour the condition has been imposed may expressly waive it': Sale (1868), 423.

[117] Roberts v. Wyatt (1810) 2 Taunt. 268 at 277. See also Rede v. Farr (1817) 6 M. & S. 121 at 124.

[118] e.g. Cutts v. Thodey (1842) 13 Sim. 206; Tanner v. Smith (1840) 10 Sim. 410.

[119] Doe d Morecroft v. Meux (1825) 4 B. & C. 606; Doe d Nash v. Birch (1836) 1 M. & W. 402; Dendy v. Nicholl (1858) 4 C.B. N.S. 376.

[120] See e.g. Doe d Boscawen v. Bliss (1813) 4 Taunt. 735; Doe d Flower v. Peck (1830) 1 B. & Ad. 428; Doe d Baker v. Jones (1850) 5 Exch. 498.

[121] See e.g. the comments of Lord Ellenborough in Beale v. Thompson (1804) 4 East 546 at 565.

[122] Bickerdike v. Bollman (1786) 1 T.R. 405 at 409.

[123] Roberts v. Davey (1833) 4 B. & Ad. 664 at 672–3. On the duty to inform the party in breach of the election in cases concerning real property, see also Carpenter v. Blandford (1828) 8 B. & C. 575. See also Hyde v. Watts (1843) 12 M. & W. 254 at 270, where the bringing of an action was sufficient notice of election to terminate a continuing breach.

[124] Arnsby v. Woodward (1827) 6 B. & C. 519, 524. If a breach of contract continued, the innocent party could again elect to terminate. See Hyde v. Watts (1843) 12 M. & W. 254 at 269–70. For further background, see Watts v. Spottiswoode, The Times, 24 June 1843, col. 8a.

[125] E. Lawes, A Practical Treatise on Charter-parties of Affreightment, Bills of Lading, and Stoppage in Transitu (1813), 51. See also Dixon v. Heriot (1862) 2 F. & F. 760 at 763.

the contract for the future as at an end'.[126] But where a breach caused damage, the innocent party did not lose his right to damages by waiving it, since this right could only be waived by accord and satisfaction or by a deed.[127]

Executory agreements could be altered or abandoned. Although lawyers sometimes spoke of this in terms of one party 'waiving the contract', juries were asked in effect to find an agreement between the parties to vary their obligations.[128] In doing so, early nineteenth-century courts sometimes stretched the rules of contract formation. For instance, in *Richardson* v. *Dunn* in 1841, the defendant had ordered 200 to 300 tons of coal to be shipped on a vessel from Stockton on Tees. The supplier, who was only able to ship 152 tons on the vessel, sent a letter indicating this with the invoice, which also stated that a bill had been drawn on the buyer for the amount of the coals. After the vessel was lost at sea, the seller sought to recover the price from the buyer, who claimed that a condition had not been complied with. The King's Bench rejected this, finding that he had 'waived the objection'. Lord Denman accepted that since an invoice had been sent and a bill drawn, it became the buyer's duty without delay to inform the plaintiff that he dissented from this mode of executing the order: '[s]ilence for a week, and until he knew of the loss, was tantamount to assent'.[129]

Buyers commonly 'waived' a condition that the seller had to dispatch goods at a stated time. Since the waiver of terms yet to be performed was seen as constituting a new agreement, parties were faced with the problem that unless the new agreement had been evidenced in writing, it would not comply with the Statute of Frauds.[130] Lord Ellenborough's solution to this problem was to hold that where the parties verbally agreed to delay delivery, they did not change the original contract, but only modified its performance.[131] But this view was overruled by the Queen's Bench in 1839 in *Stead* v. *Dawber*. 'Independently of the statute, there is nothing to prevent the total waiver, or the partial alteration, of a written contract not under seal by parol agreement', Lord Denman held, 'but the

---

[126] *Bentsen* v. *Taylor Sons & Co* [1893] 2 QB 274 at 283.

[127] Addison, *Contracts* (4th edn,1856), 1094–8; *Andrew* v. *Boughey* (1552) 1 Dyer 75a at 75b. See p. 383 above for accord and satisfaction.

[128] See *Gomery* v. *Bond* (1814) 3 M. & S. 378, where the plaintiff was held to have 'waived the contract' to sell goods to the defendant, by asking the latter to try to sell them on, after he refused to accept delivery and *Lawrence* v. *Knowles* (1839) 5 Bing. N.C. 399.

[129] *Richardson* v. *Dunn* (1841) 2 Q.B. 218 at 224. In this case, delivery of the goods on board the ship was held to vest property in the buyer, so the risk of loss was theirs.

[130] For the rule, see *Goss* v. *Lord Nugent* (1833) 5 B. & Ad. 58 and *Marshall* v. *Lynn* (1840) 6 M. & W. 109. But cf. *Taylor* v. *Hilary* (1835) 1 C. M. & R. 741, where it was held that the new agreement did not fall within the statute's provisions, and *Alexander* v. *Gardner* (1835) 1 Bing. N.C. 671, where a bill of lading having been accepted on a parol agreement, the court ignored the Statute of Frauds altogether.

[131] *Cuff* v. *Penn* (1813) 1 M. & S. 21.

statute intervenes, and, in the case of such a contract, takes away the remedy by action.'[132] The waiver of an obligation to deliver on a certain day constituted the formation of a new agreement which needed to be evidenced in writing.[133]

This strict interpretation of the requirements of the statute, which was plainly inconvenient to commerce, troubled judges, who began in the second half of the nineteenth century to develop new approaches to the notion of waiver. This is evident from *Ogle* v. *Earl Vane*, where a purchaser entered into negotiations with his supplier, who was unable to deliver iron on time, to supply it at a later date. No iron was ultimately delivered, and the purchaser bought in the market. When sued for breach of contract, the supplier claimed that damages should be measured from the earlier time of breach, since the plaintiffs could only claim their loss at the time they went to market on the basis of a new agreement to delay delivery, which would have to comply with the Statute of Frauds. This argument was rejected. In the Queen's Bench, Blackburn J. said this was 'a case of voluntary waiting, and not of alteration in the contract', which would need to be in writing. He distinguished merely waiting (as was done here), and binding oneself to wait[134] (as was done in *Stead* v. *Dawber*[135]). In the Exchequer Chamber, the judges also felt that since the plaintiff had forborne to exercise his rights at the defendant's request, he was not to be 'tied down to the strict letter of the rule as to the measure of damages'.[136]

Judges in the 1870s continued to seek ways to avoid the Statute of Frauds being invoked unjustly by buyers who had asked for alterations in the manner of performance. In 1875, Blackburn J. in the Queen's Bench distinguished between alterations in the terms of a contract, which needed to be in writing, and agreeing 'a substituted mode of performing one of the terms of a contract', which need not.[137] Though adopted by some textbook writers,[138] this was a controversial view.[139] Judges and jurists were more happy to accept a principle that if there was a voluntary forbearance by one party to insist on delivery according to strict

---

[132] *Stead* v. *Dawber* (1839) 10 Ad. & El. 57 at 65. See also *Marshall* v. *Lynn* (1840) 6 M. & W. 109.

[133] See also *Noble* v. *Ward* (1867) LR 2 Ex 135, holding that the plaintiff could still sue on the original contract. But see the explanation of this case in *Morris* v. *Baron & Co* [1918] AC 1 at 17.

[134] *Ogle* v. *Earl Vane* (1867) LR 2 QB 275 at 283.

[135] *Stead* v. *Dawber* (1839) 10 Ad & El 57.

[136] *Ogle* v. *Earl Vane* (1868) LR 3 QB 272 at 279 (per Kelly CB). Willes J. by contrast (at 279–80) found a contract to buy forbearance, which was not covered by the Statute of Frauds. See also Martin B.'s dissenting view in *Tyers* v. *Rosedale and Ferryhill Iron Co* (1873) LR 8 Ex 305 at 319, which was approved in the Exchequer Chamber: (1875) LR 10 Ex 195

[137] *Leather Cloth Co* v. *Hieronimus* (1875) LR 10 QB 140 at 146.

[138] Benjamin, *Sale* (3rd edn by A. B. Pearson and H. F. Boyd, 1883), 183; Leake, *Digest of the Law of Contracts* (2nd edn, 1878), 272.

[139] See the critical comments of McCardie J. in *Hartley* v. *Hymans* [1920] 3 KB 475 at 493 and *Baintgoorie (Dooars) Tea Co* v. *British & Benington's* (1921) 8 LL. L. Rep. 219 at 224.

terms of the contract, in response to a request by the other, the original obligation remained intact, and no new writing was needed; whereas if they agreed
to alter their original contract, it had to be in writing.[140] In Brett J.'s view, if a
defendant buyer requested the plaintiff seller to delay delivery, and the latter
had consequently forborne from delivering according to the original contract
although willing to do so, 'the original contract is unaltered' and 'the arrangement has reference only to the mode of performing it'. But if the plaintiff seller
had asked for the delivery time to be postponed, he would not be able to show
that he was willing to deliver according to the original contract, and would be
bound to rely on the assent of the vendee to a substituted time of delivery, which
amounted to a new contract.[141] These decisions established a principle that the
party not in default could forbear to perform the contract according to its strict
letter, at the request of the other.[142]

Section 11(1)(a) of the Sale of Goods Act sought to codify the rules on waiver by
enacting that the innocent party could waive the condition altogether, or treat its
breach as if it were a breach of warranty, keeping the contract open, but recovering damages. Although the wording of the statute suggested that the innocent
party could simply waive the breach of condition, thereby abandoning the right
to damages, judges held that where the right to treat the breach as one of a condition was lost, the innocent party retained the right to treat it as a breach of a
warranty.[143] In the twentieth century, the Queen's Bench Division confirmed that
in order to show that a waiver of a breach constituted an 'abandonment of a claim
to relief' as opposed to turning a condition into a warranty, the party claiming
that such a waiver had occurred had to 'show a separate agreement, binding on
the buyer, by which he had agreed to surrender the right to damages which automatically vested in him at the time of the breach'.[144]

4. ANTICIPATORY BREACH

Where conditions were dependent, the plaintiff's right to recover was generally conditional on his having performed his part. However, if one party simply
refused to proceed, the other could sue, without actually performing, provided

[140] *Hickman v. Haynes* (1875) LR 10 CP 598 at 606.

[141] *Plevins v. Downing* (1876) 1 CPD 220 at 225–6. See the rule stated in Addison, *Contracts* (11th edn, by W. E. Gordon and J. Ritchie, 1911), 545.

[142] See also *Morris v. Baron & Co* [1918] AC 1 at 31 (per Lord Atkinson); *Besseler Waechter Glover and Co v. South Derwent Coal Co* [1938] 1 KB 408 at 416 (per Goddard J.).

[143] See also the approach of Fletcher Moulton LJ (dissenting) in *Wallis, Son & Wells v. Pratt & Haynes* [1910] 2 KB 1003 at 1013 (CA), endorsed in the House of Lords: *Wallis, Son & Wells v. Pratt & Haynes* [1911] AC 394.

[144] *Kwei Tek Chao v. British Traders and Shippers* [1954] 2 QB 459 at 467, 477.

he averred that he was ready and willing to do so.[145] This was the case both where the refusal had the effect of preventing the innocent party's performance, and where his performance, although possible, would amount to a 'nugatory act'.[146] Early nineteenth-century courts nonetheless insisted that the innocent party do everything in his power to be 'ready and willing' to perform.[147] This was a high hurdle: he could only recover if the only thing which could prevent his performance (other than the defendant's refusal) would be his own death.[148] Thus, in *Smith* v. *Wilson*, the plaintiffs failed to recover against defendants, who had renounced a charterparty. Payment of freight being conditional on delivery,[149] the plaintiffs argued that the condition was dispensed with by the defendants' refusal to give instructions, and that they should recover as if the ship had arrived. But Lord Ellenborough rejected the argument, holding that mere readiness to perform was not equivalent to performance, since the performance was 'liable to be disappointed by the act of God, and all the various other accidents to which marine adventures are subject'. Courts were strict in actions of covenant brought on charterparties not to allow the plaintiff to recover on it unless he had performed the whole agreement,[150] to prevent the shipper being able to recover freight without having incurred the costs of the voyage. Where the voyage had not been completed according to the charterparty, but the charterer had obtained a benefit, the shipowner had to sue for freight in *indebitatus assumpsit*,[151] treating the original contract as terminated, and suing on a new contract, evidenced by

---

[145] Chitty, *Contracts* (2nd edn,1834), 570–1. See also E. Sugden, *A Practical Treatise of the Law of Vendors and Purchasers of Estates* (11th edn, 1846), 260–1. See also *Peeters* v. *Opie* (1677) 2 Wms. Saund. 350; *Rawson* v. *Johnson* (1801) 1 East 203 at 208. By contrast, where the performance of the condition precedent was made impossible by the act or omission of a third party, the plaintiff could not recover, for the contract put on him the onus of procuring the act to be done which constituted the condition precedent. See *Hesketh* v. *Gray* (1755) Sayer 185; *Worsley* v. *Wood* (1796) 6 T.R. 710 at 718–19.

[146] *Jones* v. *Barkley* (1781) 2 Doug. 684 at 694 (per Lord Mansfield). The plaintiff here was not required to assign an equity of redemption of stock which the defendant had refused to pay for. Cf. the maxim *lex neminem cogit ad vana seu inutilia peragenda* discussed in E. Coke, *The First Part of the Institutes of the Laws of England, or A Commentary upon Littleton* (15th edn by F. Hargrave and C. Butler, 1794), 197b and C. C. Langdell, *A Summary of the Law of Contracts* (Boston, 1880), § 171.

[147] *Lancashire* v. *Kellingworth* (1701) 1 Comyns 116 at 117. See also *Bordenave* v. *Gregory* (1804) 5 East 107.

[148] *Smith* v. *Wilson* (1807) 8 East 437 at 444.

[149] See C. Abbott, *A Treatise of Law relative to Merchant Ships and Seamen* (2nd edn, 1804), 259.

[150] *Bright* v. *Cowper* (1612) 1 Brownl. 21 (on which see also C. Molloy, *De Jure Maritimo et Navali*, 2 vols (9th edn, 1769), ii: 373); *Cook* v. *Jennings* (1797) 7 T.R. 381. Contrast the approach taken by Lord Mansfield's King's Bench in *Hotham* v. *East India Co* (1779) 1 Doug. 272, a case disapproved of in *Thompson* v. *Brown* (1817) 7 Taunt. 656. On the drafting of charterparties (to avoid such problems), see *Gibbon* v. *Mendez* (1818) 2 B. & Ald. 17.

[151] *Luke* v. *Lyde* (1759) 2 Burr. 882, 1 W. Bl. 190; Abbott, *Treatise* (2nd edn, 1804), 290.

the receipt of the cargo by the freighter.[152] This was so even where performance had been prevented by the fault of the defendant.[153]

Although courts were unwilling in charterparty cases to allow plaintiffs to recover on contracts where they had not been required to perform work, they were content to allow employees who had been wrongfully dismissed prior to the end of their period of service to recover. There was, however, some controversy in the early nineteenth century about which form of action to use, after Lord Ellenborough allowed a servant to recover all the wages due for his period of hire in an *indebitatus assumpsit* count. 'Having served a part of the quarter and being willing to serve the residue', he ruled in 1816, 'in contemplation of law he may be considered to have served the whole.'[154] The idea that one could sue for 'constructive service' came in for criticism from those jurists who held that the correct remedy was not to sue on the implied contract for work done, but to sue on the special contract which had been breached.[155] In 1828, Lord Tenterden refused to allow a plaintiff to recover for more than the time actually served in an *indebitatus* count.[156] This view was followed in 1837 in *Smith* v. *Hayward* by the Queen's Bench, where Williams J. said that an *indebitatus* count could not be used for lost wages after the dismissal since the work might never have been performed.[157] Judges were by this time concerned lest the law encourage idleness. It was felt that employees who had been wrongfully dismissed should sue at once for breach of the special contract,[158] rather than waiting in idleness until the end of their period of employment. As Parke B. explained in *Emmens* v. *Elderton*, where an employee was 'retained and employed' for a certain period, he had 'an immediate remedy the moment he is dismissed without lawful cause, for a breach of the contract to retain and employ'. In such a case, he recovered damages for the breach, 'which may be less than the stipulated wages payable at the end of the term, if it happens that he has the opportunity of employing his time beneficially in another way'.[159] Crompton J. agreed that a dismissed employee should find other work to mitigate his damages. If the employee 'has obtained, or is likely to, obtain, another

---

[152] See Lawrence J.'s comments in *Cook* v. *Jennings* (1797) 7 T.R. 381 at 385.

[153] *Christy* v. *Row* (1808) 1 Taunt. 300.

[154] *Gandall* v. *Pontigny* (1816) 4 Camp. 375 at 376. See also *Eardly* v. *Price* (1806) 2 B. & P. N.R. 333; *Collins* v. *Price* (1828) 5 Bing. 132.

[155] *Hulle* v. *Heightman* (1802) 2 East 145, following the rule in *Weston* v. *Downes* (1773) 1 Doug. 23. But see the distinction drawn between these cases in Smith, *Leading Cases* (4th edn, 1856), ii, 14.

[156] *Archard* v. *Hornor* (1828) 3 C. & P. 349.

[157] It was also felt that using the special count would focus the attention of the court on whether the defendant had any excuse for breaching the contract: *Smith* v. *Hayward* (1837) 7 Ad. & El. 544. See also *Fewings* v. *Tisdal* (1847) 1 Exch. 295.

[158] *Pagani* v. *Gandolfi* (1826) 2 C. & P. 370. See also *Hulle* v. *Heightman* (1802) 2 East 145.

[159] *Emmens* v. *Elderton* (1852–53) 4 H.L.C. 624 at 668–9.

situation, the damages ought to be less, or nominal, according to the real loss', he held, 'and in such case the servant need not remain idle, in readiness to give services which cannot be wanted'.[160]

Judges in the first half of the century maintained that an executory contract could not be breached by one party merely renouncing it. As Dallas CJ observed in 1818, '[t]he contract being mutually made, could only be dissolved by the consent of both parties'.[161] There was no duty on an innocent party to go to market to buy goods he did not yet want, or to sell goods he had agreed to sell to a defendant, merely because that party announced he did not wish to proceed. As Parke B. put it in *Phillpotts* v. *Evans*, in 1839, a declaration by a buyer that he would refuse to accept goods when they were delivered was 'a mere nullity'. Since his only promise was to accept the goods when they were due for delivery, this promise could not be broken by a previous declaration.[162] The corollary of this rule that a contract could only be terminated by agreement was that the innocent party was bound to remain willing to perform, in case the other side changed his mind. He had to wait until the due time for the performance of his contract, and then tender it; but could not treat the contract as terminated at the moment of repudiation and sue then.

Although renouncing a contract was not regarded as a breach, early nineteenth-century authority suggested that if the defendant had made it impossible to perform his obligations, this constituted a breach, for which the plaintiff was entitled to sue at once. This derived from the rule relating to conditional bonds, which could be sued on as soon as the obligor disabled himself from performing the condition defeating the bond. The disablement had the effect of cancelling the condition,[163] allowing an immediate action, even where the condition was to be performed in future, by which time the obligor might once again be able to perform.[164] In the early nineteenth century, this rule seemed to have been

---

[160] *Emmens* v. *Elderton* (1852–53) 4 H.L.C. 624 at 645.

[161] *Leigh* v. *Paterson* (1818) 8 Taunt. 540 at 541.

[162] *Phillpotts* v. *Evans* (1839) 5 M. & W. 474.

[163] Similarly, '[i]f an obligee prevents the performance of the condition of the bond, it is, as against him, equivalent to performance': H. Rolle, *Abridgment* (1668), 455 (quoted by Wilde CJ in *Hayward v. Bennett* (1846) 3 C.B. 404 at 423). See also Coke, *Commentary upon Littleton*, 206b. For the rule that a defendant who disabled himself from performing was held to have dispensed with the performance of conditions precedent by the plaintiff, see *Sands* v. *Clarke* (1849) 8 C.B. 751 at 762–3; *Ellen* v. *Topp* (1851) 6 Exch. 424 at 442. Where the defendant made it impossible for the plaintiff to perform, the latter's readiness was to be considered as 'equal to performance': *Hotham* v. *East India Co* (1787) 1 T.R. 639 at 645.

[164] Rolle, *Abridgment* (1668) 445; C. Viner, *A General Abridgment of Law and Equity*, 24 vols (Aldershot, 1741–58), v: 224: 'If a day be limited to perform a condition, if the obligor once disables himself to perform it, though he be enabled again before the day, yet the condition is broken. As if the condition be to infeoff before Michaelmas; if, before the feast, he infeoff another, though he after

extended to allow plaintiffs to sue in assumpsit for breach of contract before the time when performance was due. In *Ford* v. *Tiley*, the defendant, who had promised the plaintiff a future lease of a public house, granted it to another. Although, Bayley J. ruled, he might have put himself in a position to grant it to the plaintiff at the time he had promised, 'the authorities are, that where a party has disabled himself from making an estate he has stipulated to make at a future day, by making an inconsistent conveyance of that estate, he is considered as guilty of a breach of his stipulation, and is liable to be sued before such day arrives'.[165] In fact, although later judges quoted Bayley's words as a statement of the general rule, the plaintiff won his verdict on a count that he had 'run from the agreement', suggesting that he had broken a present, not a future obligation.[166]

The notion that one could sue for breach of a contract even though the promisor might later put himself back in a position to perform was also applied in cases of breach of promise of marriage. In *Short* v. *Stone* (1846), the Queen's Bench held that by marrying another, the defendant had disabled himself from performing his obligation of marrying the plaintiff, and that she could sue him without first requesting him to marry her. Although it was conceivable that the defendant's new wife might die before his prior fiancée requested marriage, Lord Denman CJ held that when the promise was made, the parties' intentions were to marry in the state they were then in: '[i]f either party puts himself out of that state, he must be taken to dispense with the contract so far that the other may have an action against him without a request to marry'.[167]

Although both *Ford* and *Short* in fact involved breaches of present obligations, the dictum from *Ford* v. *Tiley* suggested to treatise writers that a promisor could be sued in respect of a future obligation as soon as he had completely disabled himself from performing the very thing he had promised.[168] However, by the 1840s, a number of judges and jurists were unhappy at extending beyond cases on bonds the rule that a promisor might be sued as soon as he disabled himself from future performance. By now, it was accepted—overcoming the earlier doubts of Abbott CJ[169]—that a vendor could sell goods not yet in his possession, which he might acquire in the market prior to the time of delivery.[170] Lord Denman CJ

---

re-purchases, yet he cannot perform the condition.' See also Coke, *Commentary upon Littleton*, 356; *Newal* v. *Barnard* (1611) 1 Bulst. 116 at 117n; M. Mustill, 'Anticipatory Breach of Contract: The Common Law at Work', *Butterworth Lectures 1989–1990* (1990), 16–18.

[165]   *Ford* v. *Tiley* (1827) 6 B. & C. 325 at 327.
[166]   Mustill, 'Anticipatory Breach', 21–2, drawing on *Ford* v. *Tiley* (1827) 5 LJ (OS) 169.
[167]   *Short* v. *Stone* (1846) 8 Q.B. 358 at 369. See also *Caines* v. *Smith* (1847) 15 M. & W. 189.
[168]   See Addison, *Contracts* (4th edn, 1856), 1128–9; Chitty, *Contracts* (2nd edn, 1834), 565.
[169]   *Lorymer* v. *Smith* (1822) 1 B. & C. 1; *Bryan* v. *Lewis* (1826) R. & M. 386.
[170]   *Hibblewhite* v. *M'Morine* (1839) 5 M. & W. 462.

therefore observed in *Lovelock* v. *Franklyn* in 1846 that '[w]here a party agrees to sell, or to lease, on a given future day, he may have all the intermediate time open to him for acquiring the means of performing his contract'.[171] This case, like *Short* v. *Stone*, was one where the defendant's obligation was not merely one to perform a promise at a future date, but one to remain ready to perform his obligation whenever requested by the plaintiff. In such cases, the defendant's disabling himself—which constituted the breach of a present and not of a future obligation—discharged the plaintiff of the obligation to make a request prior to suing.

At the same time that they became sceptical on the rules on disablement—which ill-fitted a commercial world of futures markets—the courts also began to perceive the commercial inconvenience of the rule which stated both that the one party could not be sued until the time for his performance had arrived, and that the other party had to remain 'ready and willing' to perform his part until that moment arrived. This seemed as wasteful in commercial situations as it was in employment situations. Judges began to look for ways to modify the rule. This can be seen, first, in *Ripley* v. *McClure* in 1849 where the plaintiff, who had contracted to deliver a cargo of tea in September, was told in July by the defendant that he would not accept it. When subsequently sued for breach of contract, the defendants argued that they were not liable, as no tea had been tendered.[172] Parke B. admitted that a letter of refusal sent before the cargo's arrival could not constitute a breach, since it was a mere expression of an intention to break the contract, which might have been retracted. But since the defendant had never retracted the letter refusing the cargo, but continued with the refusal to the moment of delivery, he was held to have waived the plaintiff's performance of the condition precedent to deliver.[173] Parke's approach—stressing waiver—was a modified version of that taken in *Jones* v. *Barkley*, that a plaintiff was not required to tender a pointless performance. Parke was not happy with the idea, suggested by the latter case, that an innocent party who remained willing to perform his obligations should be taken to have performed them, since that might allow him to obtain payment while avoiding the costs of his own performance.[174] Rather than

[171] *Lovelock* v. *Franklyn* (1846) 8 Q.B. 371 at 378.

[172] The parties had engaged in a joint speculation to import tea, but when the prices fell, M'Clure declined to take the tea. He subsequently alleged a fraud on him by Ripley, claiming that the latter had been aware that the contract had been disadvantageous; but he failed to persuade the Lord Chancellor of fraud: *M'Lure* v. *Ripley* in *Daily News*, 17 March 1849, *The Times*, 30 January 1850, col. 6c.

[173] *Ripley* v. *McClure* (1849) 4 Exch. 345 at 359. There was a dispute between the parties over the terms of the contract for the tea, which replaced an earlier agreement.

[174] See his approach in *Laird* v. *Pim* (1841) 7 M. & W. 474 at 478. See also Langdell, *Summary*, § 176.

adopting a fiction of actual performance, the defendant was to be held to have waived the performance.

Two years later, in *Cort* v. *Ambergate, Nottingham and Boston and Eastern Junction Railway Company*, the Queen's Bench held that a manufacturer of railway seats could sue the company for breach of contract in cancelling an order, without first making and tendering the seats. Averring readiness and willingness to perform the contract only meant that the non-completion of the contract was not the plaintiff's fault, and that they were disposed to perform the contract had it not been renounced by the defendant. In answer to the defendant's argument that the plaintiff was only discharged from making a tender where performance had been prevented in fact, Lord Campbell CJ held that the innocent party could be said to have been prevented from completing the contract when it was renounced by the other party. In any event, no benefit could accrue to the defendant from a 'useless waste of materials and labour, which might possibly enhance the amount of damages to be awarded against them'. The chief justice pointed out that in this case, as in *Ripley*, the refusal was never retracted, 'and therefore there was a continuing breach down to the time when this action was commenced'.[175]

In *Cort*, the Queen's Bench took a much more general view of the 'ready and willing' averment than had been found in the earlier charterparty cases. Where those cases had suggested that the plaintiff could only recover without performing his obligations if his ability to perform them on the due day was so certain that only his own death could have prevented it, the courts were now ready to allow him to disable himself from performing, by taking the guilty party's repudiation at his word. This approach was taken one step further in *Hochster* v. *De la Tour*, where—in contrast to the previous cases—the plaintiff sued prior to the time for performance of the defendant's obligations, so that there could be no question of a waiver at the moment of performance. Albert Hochster had been hired in April 1852 to serve as Edgar de la Tour's courier on a three-month tour of Europe, beginning in June. Soon after entering into the agreement, the defendant wrote that he would not require the plaintiff's services. The latter found alternative employment, to begin in July, and commenced an action in May for damages caused by the breach of contract. He sought to recover the loss of earnings he would have received from the employment, rather than any expenditure he had incurred in preparing for the journey. This squarely raised the question of whether a contract could be broken before its performance was due, or whether a party who repudiated before the time of performance was entitled to change his

---

[175] *Cort* v. *Ambergate Nottingham and Boston and Eastern Junction Railway Co* (1851) 17 Q.B. 127 at 144, 148.

mind, so that the non-repudiating party had to remain 'ready and willing' up to the point of performance.

According to the plaintiff's argument, a repudiation could not be retracted if it had been given 'in order that the other side might act upon [it] in such a manner as to incapacitate himself from fulfilling [the contract]'.[176] Although Hochster would have been bound to 'keep himself disengaged' and prepare for the trip with de la Tour so long as the engagement subsisted, once it was repudiated, he was entitled to treat it as a breach, and seek alternative employment. This argument derived from the treatment of damages in wrongful dismissal cases, where the employee might be expected to look for alternative work. By contrast, counsel for the defendant argued that the plaintiff had only two choices. The first choice was to accept what was in effect an offer from the defendant to rescind the contract, which would discharge any obligations on both sides. The second was to remain ready and willing—in practice, idle—until the time for performance arrived.[177] During argument, Crompton J. suggested a third position. According to this view, the innocent party should be allowed to take the repudiator 'at his word and rescind the contract', something that implied 'that both parties have agreed that the contract shall be at an end as if it had never been'. At the same time, the innocent party's consent to the termination should be treated as conditional on his being able to hold the repudiator liable for damages, which he would use his liberty to mitigate.[178]

The judgment of the court was given by Lord Campbell CJ. Campbell agreed that that a plaintiff who accepted a termination of the contract should not be limited to a remedy on an implied contract for work done, but should be able to sue for expectation damages.[179] However, he did not develop Crompton's suggestion. Instead, he held that a party could break a contract simply by renouncing it, provided the renunciation was deliberate enough.[180] He searched for a present obligation which had been breached, and derived one by analogy with the marriage and labour cases. '[W]here there is a contract to do an act on a future day, there is a relation constituted between the parties in the meantime by the contract', and 'they impliedly promise that in the meantime neither will do any thing to the

---

[176] Hochster v. De La Tour (1852) 2 E. & B. 678 at 683. For a detailed discussion of the case and the doctrine of anticipatory breach, see P. Mitchell, 'Hochster v De La Tour (1853)' in C. Mitchell and P. Mitchell (eds), Landmark Cases in the Law of Contract (Oxford, 2008), 135–66.

[177] Hochster v. De La Tour (1852) 2 E. & B. 678 at 686.

[178] Hochster v. De La Tour (1852) 2 E. & B. 678 at 685.

[179] Lord Campbell's interpretation of Planché v. Colburn supported this. He held that in Planché v. Colburn (1831) 8 Bing. 14, the plaintiff had recovered on the special contract, rather than the quantum meruit counts. Hochster v. De La Tour (1852) 2 E. & B. 678 at 693.

[180] Hochster v. De La Tour (1852) 2 E. & B. 678 at 689. See also Benjamin, Sale (1868), 423–4.

prejudice of the other inconsistent with that relation'.[181] The analogy with labour cases further supported his contention that the plaintiff should be at liberty to seek alternative employment which would help mitigate the damages. However, the fact that Campbell was not placing too much weight on an implied obligation breached by the renunciation can be seen from his comment that it was 'reasonable to allow an option to the injured party, either to sue immediately, or to wait till the time when the act was to be done, still holding it as prospectively binding for the exercise of this option'.[182]

Hochster v. De La Tour was soon recognized as establishing that an anticipatory repudiation of a contract constituted a breach which could be sued upon at once.[183] The decision was clearly innovative. It confirmed that the innocent party had a present right in a future performance which could be sued on. The judges were clearly unhappy with the economic consequences of regarding the anticipatory repudiation merely as an offer to rescind the whole contract. On the one hand, if the innocent party accepted the offer to rescind, and cancelled the contract, he might not be able to make a new agreement at a price which was as good as the first. On the other, forcing him to wait until the time of breach, and offer performance which was not desired was clearly commercially wasteful. The new doctrine was soon defended for its practical good sense. In *Danube and Black Sea Railway and Kustendjie Harbour Company Limited v. Xenos*, the Common Pleas allowed a shipper to recover from a carrier who had repudiated a charterparty the added expense he had incurred in finding an alternative carrier. Erle J. held that there would be 'intense inconvenience' if the parties were 'left in doubt down to the very last moment as to whether [the contract] is to be performed or not'. Where (as here) a plaintiff had goods which needed to be transported, he could not be expected to wait, having been told by the carrier of his intention not to comply, in order to discover if the carrier would perform after all.[184]

It was soon settled that an anticipatory repudiation did not constitute a breach unless it was accepted by the innocent party.[185] This became clear in a number of

---

[181] *Hochster* v. *De La Tour* (1852) 2 E. & B. 678 at 689.

[182] *Hochster* v. *De La Tour* (1852) 2 E. & B. 678 at 691. Mitchell, 'Hochster', 156–7, argues that the judges were influenced in this case by classical economic ideas, favouring freedom of contract. Cf. Atiyah, *The Rise and Fall of Freedom of Contract* (Oxford, 1979), 426–7.

[183] Leake, *Elements* (1867), 462. However, there were some doubts expressed: e.g. in *Hall* v. *Wright* (1859) E. B. & E. 765 at 783, Bramwell B. suggested that the case turned on the relation of master and servant and was not generally applicable.

[184] *Danube and Black Sea Railway and Kustendjie Harbour Co* v. *Xenos* (1861) 11 C.B. N.S. 152 at 177.

[185] Contrast the view of J. D. Mayne, *A Treatise on the Law of Damages* (1856), 82, holding that damages were calculated from the moment a party renounced it: '[s]uch a refusal leaves no further *locus poenitentiae* to himself, and of course the plaintiff cannot treat the agreement as any more subsisting'. This statement was repeated in the second edition of 1872, edited by Lumley Smith: p. 122.

charterparty cases brought after the outbreak of the Crimean War. It had long been settled that if a ship was hired to go to a port to load, but the charterer failed to load within the stipulated time, the master could (having made protest) sail away, and claim payment—damages for dead freight—under the charter.[186] It was also settled that 'a failure as to a complete loading will end the contract, unless afterwards *affirmed by consent*'.[187] Charterparties also had standard terms terminating the contract in case of war. In the Crimean cases, a number of ship-owners sought to avoid the war clause, by claiming that there had been a breach of the obligation to load prior to the outbreak of war. Since war had broken out before the lay-days had expired, this required the shipowners to claim, following *Hochster*, that there had been an anticipatory repudiation. But in both the test cases brought in 1855, the masters of the ships had remained in port after being told that no goods would be loaded. In *Avery* v. *Bowden*, Lord Campbell there-fore held that although the master might have treated the freighter's statement 'as a breach and renunciation of the contract', he could no longer do so having continued to insist on having a cargo.[188] Similarly, in *Reid* v. *Hoskins*, the court insisted that the innocent party was given an option by the other party's repudi-ation, which had to be exercised: 'they could not both hold the defendant to the prospective performance of the contract and at the same time say that it was renounced'.[189]

This was to apply the charterparty rules relating to waiving breaches of condi-tion to anticipatory repudiation, in a way to prevent the shipowners from using the rule in *Hochster* opportunistically to avoid the war clauses. It was to treat the failure to accept an anticipatory repudiation as analogous to affirming a contract where there had been a breach of condition.[190] However, there were limits to the analogy: the judges assumed that a refusal to accept a repudiation entailed that it was not a breach in the first place.[191] As Blackburn J. observed in 1861, 'a repudiation

---

[186] Lawes, *Charter-parties*, 117; 'though should the master not wait the time stipulated, or omit to make his protest, he will lose his freight': W. Beawes, *Lex Mercatoria Rediviva*, 2 vols (Dublin, 1795), i, 134.

[187] D. Steel, *The Ship-Master's Assistant and Owner's Manual* (10th edn, 1803), 187, quoting C. Molloy, *De Jure Maritimo et Navali* 2 vols (9th edn, 1769), i, 366 (emphasis in original).

[188] *Avery* v. *Bowden* (1855) 5 El. & Bl. 714 at 727–8.

[189] *Reid* v. *Hoskins* (1855) 5 El. & Bl. 729 at 746. See also *Barrick* v. *Buba* (1857) 2 C.B. N.S. 563 at 579.

[190] Contemporary jurists (Q. Liu, 'Claiming Damages upon an Anticipatory Breach: Why Should an Acceptance be Necessary?' (2005) 25 *Legal Studies* 559–77 at 566; F. Dawson, 'Metaphors and Anticipatory Breach of Contract' (1981) 40 *CLJ* 83–107 at 102) explain the requirement of acceptance by suggesting that it makes future performance impossible, and a future breach inevitable, by reason of the innocent party's change of position in reliance on the repudiation. But while this might be a reason for estopping the guilty party from seeking performance of those obligations, it does not render the guilty party's own future performance impossible.

[191] Asquith LJ held in *Howard* v. *Pickford Tool Co* [1951] 1 KB 417 at 421 '[a]n unaccepted repudi-ation is a thing writ in water'.

of a contract before the time for fulfilment can be treated as a breach only at the option of the other contracting party'.[192] The doctrinal result of the cases was summarized by Leake: 'A refusal to perform the contract made by a party at any time before the performance on his part is due, if not treated by the other party as a breach of the contract, is, in effect, merely an expression of an intention to break the contract, and may be retracted'.[193]

The new rule seemed commercially convenient in a world where parties were increasingly making contracts to be performed in future, and where developing communications made it easier to predict whether such contracts would be fulfilled. But the fact that some judges remained uneasy with the doctrinal basis of the rule is evident from *Frost* v. *Knight* in 1872, where the defendant, who had promised a servant that he would marry her after his father's death, broke off the engagement while his father was still alive.[194] In the Exchequer, Kelly CB was clearly troubled by the approach of *Hochster*, and felt that a better approach would have been to develop a special action for damages to be used when one party renounced.[195] His ruling for the defendant was overturned in the Exchequer Chamber. Cockburn CJ explained that a promisee had a choice. He could treat the defendant's renunciation as inoperative and wait until the time of performance before suing, leaving in place his own obligations; or he could treat the repudiation 'as a wrongful putting an end to the contract,' and sue at once for damages.[196] Cockburn agreed that there was no actual breach before the time of performance. But he held that '[t]he promisee has an inchoate right to the performance of the bargain, which becomes complete when the time for performance has arrived. In the meantime, he has a right to have the contract kept open as a subsisting and effective contract'. Cockburn regarded the contract itself as something of value: its unimpaired efficacy might be essential to the promisee's interests, and the rights acquired under it could be dealt with for his benefit. That being so, an announcement of repudiation 'amounts to a violation of the contract *in omnibus*', which permitted the promisee to treat it at once as 'a breach of the entire contract'.[197] Cockburn's analysis was clearly problematic, arguing as it did that the inchoate right given by the 'entire' contract was breached, without the actual contract being breached.[198] A further attempt to explain the doctrinal basis

---

[192] *Tamvaco* v. *Lucas* (1861) 1 B. & S. 185 at 194.   [193] Leake, *Elements* (1867), 464.

[194] *Frost* v. *Knight* (1872) LR 7 Ex 111.

[195] *Frost* v. *Knight* (1870) LR 5 Ex 322 at 336. This approach was in some ways similar to Crompton J.'s analysis in *Hochster*, discussed above. But Kelly also spoke of an action for a tort of renouncing the contract.

[196] *Frost* v. *Knight* (1872) LR 7 Ex 111 at 113.

[197] *Frost* v. *Knight* (1872) LR 7 Ex 111 at 114.

[198] As Williston pointed out, Cockburn's reasoning depended on the breach of an implied promise to keep the contract open. See S. Williston and G. J. Thompson, *Selections from Williston's Treatise on the Law of Contracts* (rev. edn New York, 1932), § 1320.

of this area of law was made by the Court of Appeal in *Johnstone* v. *Milling* in 1886. Lord Esher held here that a refusal by one party to perform did not amount to a breach of contract itself, but it could be adopted by the other 'as a rescission of the contract as to give an immediate right of action'. By making a renunciation, one party 'entitles the other party, if he pleases, to agree to the contract being put an end to, subject to the retention by him of his right of action in respect of such wrongful rescission'.[199]

English jurists in the later nineteenth century held that the promisee could treat an anticipatory repudiation as 'as an immediate breach of the contract'. Different explanations were put forward for this. Addison referred the plaintiff's right to sue on the Roman law principle that the party who was willing to perform, but was prevented by the other, 'has done that which is equivalent to performance'.[200] By contrast, his later editors argued that the promisor 'impliedly covenants to do nothing which must necessarily have the effect of preventing him from performing his covenant'.[201] Anson also considered that the breach was one of a current obligation. 'If X makes a binding promise to A', he argued, 'the obligation comes into existence at once, and consists in X's promise as well as in his performance of the promise'.[202] However, the idea that a present obligation was breached had its critics. Samuel Williston thought it 'fanciful' to imply an obligation in ordinary commercial contracts to keep them open, by analogy with marriage cases.[203] He also pointed to the problem in identifying what was the exact obligation breached. Even if one could imply a promise not to hinder performance, no such hindrance would occur until the time for some performance had arrived. The term to be implied would instead have to be a duty not to repudiate or announce an intention not to perform.[204]

The idea that the repudiator breached the contract at the moment of repudiation was also hard to square with two other features of the doctrine. First, damages were not assessed at the moment of renunciation, for the breach of a present right in the expectation of future performance.[205] Rather, the plaintiff 'claim[ed] prospectively such damages as would be caused by a breach at the appointed time, subject to any circumstances which may operate in mitigation

[199] *Johnstone* v. *Milling* (1886) LR 16 QBD 460 at 467.
[200] Addison, *Contracts* (4th edn, 1856), 436, citing D.50.17.1.161. Addison used this as an authority for the doubted doctrine of constructive employment.
[201] Addison, *Contracts* (11th edn by W. Gordon and J. Ritchie, 1911), 141.
[202] Anson, *Contract* (1879), 272.
[203] He pointed out this was not done in cases of bills and notes, where it might have been most expected. S. Williston, 'Repudiation of Contracts. II' (1901) 14 *Harvard LR* 421–41 at 438.
[204] See Williston and Thompson, *Selections from Williston's Treatise on the Law of Contracts*, § 1318. The basis of the doctrine (as Williston pointed out) was its practical convenience rather than its doctrinal logic.
[205] See Mustill, 'Anticipatory Breach', 46.

of damages'.[206] The fact that damages were to be assessed from a different time from that of the breach raised theoretical problems about the nature of the breach. Brett J. tried to solve the problem by explaining that the questions of damages and breach were distinct. Since damages were to put the innocent party into the position he would have been in had the contract been performed, damages were to be assessed from the time of performance, not from the time of the breach.[207] But this analysis depended on there being a breach of the principal contract, rather than of any implied or express term not to impede its execution.[208] Later judges therefore spoke of the innocent party's right being on to sue in anticipation of an inevitable future breach.[209] Moreover, there were difficulties in estimating what damage the plaintiff might have suffered at the distant time when performance would have been due.[210] The artificiality of the damages awarded was compounded by the decision in 1905 that since the innocent party's obligations were discharged by the anticipatory breach by the other party, his own prospective inability to perform could not be taken into account when estimating damages.[211]

Secondly, jurists were troubled by the idea that whether the repudiation was a breach depended on its acceptance by the innocent party. 'The conception that a breach of contract is caused by something which the promisee does', Williston noted, 'is so foreign to the notions not only of lawyers but of businessmen that it cannot fail to make trouble.'[212] The need for the innocent party to accept the breach certainly looked odd, since if there had been a breach, it did not need to be accepted; whereas if the repudiation was to be treated as an offer to rescind, which was accepted, there would be no breach. Williston thought that English judges continued to look for acceptance of the repudiator's intention to rescind, under the influence of dicta suggesting that there had to be mutual assent for a contract

---

[206] Leake, *Digest* (3rd edn, 1892), 751.

[207] *Roper* v. *Johnson* (1873) LR 8 CP 167 at 180.

[208] Keating J. also said 'here the breach occurred before the end of the period over which the contract extended': *Roper* v. *Johnson* (1873) LR 8 CP 167 at 176.

[209] *Universal Cargo Carriers Corporation* v. *Citati* [1957] 2 QB 401 at 438; *Maredelanto Compania Naviera SA* v. *Bergbau-Handel GmbH (The Mihalis Nagelos)* [1971] 1 QB 164 at 178–9. This was to draw on Cockburn CJ's comment in *Frost* v. *Knight* (1872) LR 7 Ex 111 at 114 that 'the eventual non-performance may [...] by anticipation be treated as a cause of action, and damages be assessed and recovered in respect of it, though the time for performance may yet be remote'.

[210] See Kelly CB's doubts in *Frost* v. *Knight* (1870) LR 5 Ex 322 at 336; but contrast the more confident approach in *Synge* v. *Synge* [1894] 1 QB 466 at 472.

[211] *Braithwaite* v. *Foreign Hardwood Co* [1905] 2 KB 543 (CA).

[212] Williston, 'Repudiation of Contracts. II', 439.

to be rescinded.[213] In the end, rather than seeing the doctrine as logical, jurists came to argue that 'the really decisive ground' for the rule was 'convenience'.[214] Not everyone was convinced by the arguments of convenience. As Williston pointed out, it could lead to uncertainty and inconvenience. 'When A repudiates his promise, what is more natural or reasonable than for B to write urging him to perform', he noted, 'yet if B does so, it seems not only does he lose his right of immediate action, but he is bound to perform his own promise, though he has reason to expect A will not perform his'.[215]

The convenience of the rule was also thrown in question as the doctrine of anticipatory repudiation became mingled with the new doctrines on performance and breach in general, and the courts began to take a looser view of what amounted to a renunciation. Jurists in the 1860s insisted that the doctrine only applied where the defendant 'expressly renounced' or 'wholly refused' to perform.[216] Since the defendant had proclaimed that he would perform none of his obligations, the other party could be held released. But with the development of new ideas on conditions, this view was modified. By the end of the century, it was established that a party could be held to have repudiated not only where he distinctly refused to perform, but also 'where the conduct of the party who has broken the contract is such that the other party is entitled to conclude that the party breaking the contract no longer intends to be bound by its provisions'. In determining this, the innocent party had to decide if the breach went to the root of the contract.[217] This was to regard the distinct refusal of one party in future to perform any part of the contract as an anticipatory breach, while leaving it to the other to take the risk of electing to treat it as a breach major enough to justify termination. Once it was accepted that a repudiatory breach could occur without an express renunciation of the whole contract, it was not possible to conceive of the termination of the contract in terms of a mutually agreed rescission. Rather, the innocent party was faced with a present breach of a major term, giving him a right to terminate the contract, a right which could be waived by affirmation. If he

[213] *Franklin* v. *Miller* (1836) 4 Ad. & El. 599 at 606; *Ehrensperger* v. *Anderson* (1848) 3 Exch. 148 at 158. S. Williston, 'Repudiation of Contracts' (1901) 14 *Harvard LR* 317–31 at 324–5 challenged this idea, stating that 'rescission is imposed *in invitum* by the law at the option of the injured party'.

[214] F. Pollock, *Principles of Contract at Law and in Equity* (9th edn, 1921, the first edition in which he discussed the doctrine), 293

[215] Williston, 'Repudiation of Contracts. II', 440.

[216] Chitty, *Contracts* (7th edn by J. A. Russell, 1863), 643; Leake, *Elements* (1867), 462.

[217] *Rhymney Railway* v. *Brecon and Merthyr Tydfil Junction Railway* (1900) (CA) 69 LJ NS Ch 813 at 818–19. This drew on Lord Blackburn's discussion of breaches going to the root of the contract in *Mersey Steel and Iron Co* v. *Naylor, Benzon & Co* (1884) 9 App Cas 434 at 443.

miscalculated, treating a minor breach as a major one as justifying termination, he would himself be in breach.

5. FRUSTRATION

Early nineteenth-century jurists were not eager to permit parties to avoid their contractual obligations by claiming they were impossible to perform.[218] Jurists agreed that if the thing promised was not 'impossible of itself',[219] the promisor assumed the risk of its occurring.[220] Although a number of dicta suggested that a contract was void where, at the time the contract was made, it was not in the power of the promisor to carry it into effect,[221] writers like Chitty insisted that where performance was merely difficult, or impossible for the party himself to perform, he assumed the risk. 'It is the duty of the contracting party in such cases', he suggested, 'to provide against contingencies'.[222] There was some disagreement over how to treat contracts to perform impossible things, such as travelling to Rome within three hours. On the one side, Joseph Chitty, following William Sheppard, suggested that such a contract would be void for impossibility.[223] On the other, Sheppard's nineteenth-century editor said that an action could be brought even on such a covenant, 'though the damages may be merely nominal'.[224] The argument was largely academic, since parties did not sue for failure to perform contracts which were in their nature impossible to perform. The impossibility which attracted more litigation was where performance of the contract was physically possible, but illegal.[225]

The problem of impossibility was more generally raised in cases where subsequent events interfered with performance. According to Addison, 'whenever a party enters into an absolute and unqualified contract to do some particular act, the impossibility of performance occasioned by inevitable accident, or some

---

[218] For a discussion of the early nineteenth-century case law, and the development of the doctrine of frustration, see esp. C. MacMillan, 'Taylor v Caldwell' (1863), in C. Mitchell and P. Mitchell (eds), *Landmark Cases in the Law of Contract* (Oxford, 2008), 167–203 at 180–9.

[219] Viner *Abridgment*, v, 111–12. (tit. Condition (D a)).

[220] Chitty, *Contracts* (2nd edn, 1834), 49–51.

[221] *Nerot v. Wallace* (1789) 3 T.R. 17 at 23; *Chanter v. Leese* (1838) 4 M. & W. 295 at 311.

[222] Chitty, *Contracts* (2nd edn, 1834), 51.

[223] Coke, *Commentary upon Littleton*, 206b. Cf. W. Sheppard, *The Touch-Stone of Common Assurances* (5th edn, 1784), 160 (giving the example as a three-day voyage to Rome). See also A. W. B. Simpson, *A History of the Common Law of Contract* (Oxford, 1975), 525. Chitty, *Contract* (2nd edn, 1834), 49.

[224] Sheppard, *Touch-Stone of Common Assurances* (7th edn by R. Preston, 1820), 164. Cf. *Thornborow v. Whitacre* (1705) 2 Ld. Raym. 1164 at 1165.

[225] Contracts were discharged where English law rendered the contract illegal, but not where foreign law did so. See MacMillan, 'Taylor v Caldwell', 186–7.

unforeseen occurrence over which he had no control, will not release him from the obligation of his contract'.[226] This rule derived from a ruling of Rolle J. in the seventeenth-century case of *Paradine* v. *Jane*,[227] where a tenant was held liable for the rent due under a lease, even after the land had been seized by enemy action in the civil war. The courts remained consistently averse to attempts by lessees to avoid their obligations by invoking the effect of an inevitable accident. If a lessee wanted to protect himself from having still to pay rent, after a fire or flood, he had to make provision for this in the lease.[228] Nor were courts keen to imply terms which might assist a lessee for whom things had turned out badly. This can be seen from mid-nineteenth-century mining cases, where lessors of mines sought to avoid their liability to pay rent when mines became unworkable, either as a result of accidents or exhaustion of seams. Judges looked closely at what provisions the parties had made in their contracts. This meant that if a mine unexpectedly turned out to have less coal than was anticipated, but the parties had not included an express term permitting termination of the lease in that event, the lessee was held liable to pay rent for the duration of the lease. If it was the intention of the parties that rent should only be paid in case coal could be mined, Pollock CB observed in 1844, 'they should so have expressed it'.[229] This judge took an equally tough approach in a case of 1856, where a salt mine turned out to be unworkable because of flooding. The flooding had commenced when shafts were first sunk. This occurred before the execution of a lease (which included a termination clause), although after it was drawn up. Pollock held that the lessees could not cancel the contract, but were in breach for not paying rent, although they were never able to mine any salt. They had entered into the contract 'knowing of the then state of the mine', and 'positively covenanted to get the quantity of 2000 tons in every year, or pay for the deficiency at the end of it; and whether they could be got easily or with difficulty, or even whether they existed at all, is immaterial in this case of an absolute unqualified covenant'.[230]

Contractual terms also determined who bore the risk in cases of sale and carriage of goods. Since property in specific or ascertained goods passed with the

---

[226] Addison, *Contracts* (4th edn, 1856), 1123; cf. 473; Chitty, *Contracts* (2nd edn, 1834), 568.

[227] *Paradine* v. *Jane* (1647) Aleyn 26 at 27: 'when the party by his own contract creates a duty or charge upon himself, he is bound to make it good, if he may, notwithstanding any accident by inevitable necessity, because he might have provided against it by his contract'. On this case, see D. Ibbetson, 'Absolute Liability in Contract: The Antecedents of *Paradine v. Jayne*' in F. D. Rose (ed.), *Consensus ad Idem: Essays in the Law of Contract in Honour of Guenter Treitel* (1996), 3–37.

[228] e.g. *Brecknock Co* v. *Pritchard* (1796) 6 T.R. 750 at 752; *Bullock* v. *Dommitt* (1796) 6 T.R. 650 at 651.

[229] *Marquis of Bute* v. *Thompson* (1844) 13 M. & W. 487 at 494. Cf. *Rex* v. *Inhabitants of Bedworth* (1807) 8 East 387 at 389.

[230] *Jervis* v. *Tomkinson* (1856) 1 H. & N. 195 at 208. Cf. *Phillips* v. *Jones* (1839) 9 Sim. 519.

contract of sale, rather than on delivery, it was the buyer who bore the risk of the goods perishing,[231] and who insured against loss.[232] Litigants often disputed whether there had been a sufficient ascertainment of goods for property to pass. While most of these disputes arose from bankruptcy proceedings, when sellers sought to argue that no property had passed to a bankrupt buyer, the question was also raised occasionally when goods had been destroyed in natural accidents.[233] In the case of non-specific goods, in which property did not pass before delivery, it was the supplier who insured the goods against accidents of carriage. The supplier also generally stipulated in the contract of sale that it was conditional 'on the arrival' of goods at a port on board a ship. This protected the seller of goods not only from liability to supply goods which might have been lost at sea, but against losses which might be caused by his supplier's failure to send goods.[234] If a contract specified that goods were to be sold on arrival of a particular ship, but the ship came with no cargo, the buyer was unable to sue for a failure to deliver the contracted goods.[235] It was held in the first half of the century that such contracts were subject to a double condition precedent: that the vessel arrived, and that the goods were on board the vessel.[236] In 1854, the further question was raised whether there was also a condition precedent that the goods on board belonged to the vendor. If a ship arrived with the goods which had been described, but which had not been consigned to the vendor, who was therefore unable to deliver them to the buyer, could the buyer sue for non-delivery? In *Fischel* v. *Scott*, the Common Pleas held that he could. The court refused to imply a condition that the goods should be at the seller's disposal, the judges taking the view that a vendor might contract to sell goods expected to arrive without warranting his title to sell them.[237] But three years later, Cockburn CJ in the same court expressed doubts on this point, considering that he should only be liable if he had dealt with the goods as if they were his.[238] Judah Benjamin sought to reconcile the cases by suggesting that the vendor would be liable if goods arrived on board which he had intended to sell, expecting them to be consigned to him; but he would not be liable if

---

[231] *Rugg* v. *Minett* (1809) 11 East 210.

[232] It was confirmed in *Fragano* v. *Long* (1825) 4 B. & C. 219 that the buyer had an insurable interest in the goods.

[233] *Simmons* v. *Swift* (1826) 5 B. & C. 857.

[234] The parties could also specify in their contract that if the ship did not arrive, the contract would be void: see *Idle* v. *Thornton* (1812) 3 Camp. 274; *Johnson* v. *Macdonald* (1842) 9 M. & W. 600.

[235] *Boyd* v. *Siffkin* (1809) 2 Camp. 326. The same applied if the goods arrived late: *Alewyn* v. *Pryor* (1826) R. & M. 406. See also *Lovatt* v. *Hamilton* (1839) 5 M. & W. 639.

[236] *Johnson* v. *Macdonald* (1842) 9 M. & W. 600.

[237] *Fischel* v. *Scott* (1854) 15 C.B. 69.

[238] *Gorrissen* v. *Perrin* (1857) 2 C.B. N.S. 681 at 701. This was to say he would not be liable if he sold certain specific goods, and a different though similar cargo arrived.

similar goods arrived not consigned to him, and which he did not intend to deal
with. In all these cases, much depended on the wording of the contract of sale.
If the wording were interpreted as a warranty, or guarantee, that the goods to be
sold were on board, then the vendor would be liable for non-delivery. Williams J.
expressed the rule thus in 1858, where there was an agreement to deliver goods on
a certain condition, and the condition never occurred, the vendor was not liable
for non-delivery, if not at fault. But where the agreement was absolute, the vendor
was liable for a breach even if he could not help it, 'for, it is his own heedlessness,
if he runs the risk of undertaking to perform an impossibility, when he might
have provided against it by his contract'.[239]

In similar fashion, early nineteenth-century courts looked closely at the terms
of charterparties to see whether non-performance was excused due to unforeseen
events. It had been held in numerous cases during the Napoleonic wars that charterparties were not discharged because of an embargo which prevented the vessel
proceeding with the voyage. Just as parties could make provision in their contracts against risks such as perils of the sea, so they could provide against embar-
goes; if they did not, they bore the risk of their contractual promise.[240] As Lord
Ellenborough put it, the parties' claims on each other were 'conclusively fixed
and defined by the terms of their own written contract', and no exception could
'be engrafted upon it by implication, as an excuse for its non-performance'.[241]
The relative allocation of risk in charterparties can be seen from the 1815 case of
Barret v. *Dutton*. Here, because of the freezing over of the Thames, a freighter
failed to load ship within the running days given by the charterparty. The vessel
was loaded 18 days too late. She then failed to obtain clearance for a further 12
days because the customs house burned down. Gibbs CJ at *nisi prius* held that
the freighter was liable for not loading in time, the state of the weather being
immaterial to his absolute obligation to load. However, the owner had to bear the
cost of the further delay, since it was his contractual duty to obtain clearances.[242]
The same strict contractual view was taken in the mid-century, where a charterer found himself unexpectedly unable to supply a cargo. In *Hills* v. *Sughrue* in
1846, the owner of a ship contracted to sail to Ichaboe (one of the guano islands
off the west coast of Africa) and load a cargo of guano. In fact, no guano was to
be had there, but the charterer was nonetheless held liable for failure to perform

[239] *Hale* v. *Rawson* (1858) 4 C.B. N.S. 85 at 95. See also *Gorrissen* v. *Perrin* (1857) 2 C.B. N.S. 681.
[240] *Hadley* v. *Clarke* (1799) 8 T.R. 259 at 267; *Blight* v. *Page* (1801) 3 B. & P. 295; *Touteng* v. *Hubbard*
(1802) 3 B. & P. 291 at 299.
[241] *Atkinson* v. *Ritchie* (1809) 10 East 530 at 533. See also *Sjoerds* v. *Luscombe* (1812) 16 East 201;
Barker v. *Hodgson*, (1814) 3 M. & S. 267.
[242] *Barret* v. *Dutton* (1815) 4 Camp. 333 at 335.

his positive contract.[243] Ten years later in *Hurst* v. *Usborne*, the defendants had undertaken to load a cargo of grain at Limerick. Because of bad weather, the ship arrived after the season and no grain was to be had. The Common Pleas, however, rejected the defendant's argument that this constituted an act of God (which was excepted by the charterparty). Instead, it was held that 'the person who is to ship the goods takes the risk, unless he stipulates that the other party shall take it'.[244]

Up to the 1850s, then, the courts looked closely at the parties' contracts, and allocated the risk of the failure of a venture accordingly. But not all jurists were happy with a doctrine according to which a party was not excused from performance by the occurrence of an event disabling it.[245] In the late 1850s, the courts began to reconsider whether a party's promise could be nullified if unforeseen events occurred which made it impossible to perform. The issue was discussed in *Hall* v. *Wright*, an unusual breach of promise of marriage case, where the prospective groom, suffering from a lung disease, claimed that marriage would endanger his life. The case divided both the Queen's Bench and the Exchequer Chamber. The judges favouring the plaintiff looked at the question from the viewpoint of settled contractual doctrine. In the Queen's Bench, Crompton J. conceded that impossibility of performance would terminate a contract, as if a painter were struck blind.[246] But he stressed that it had not been claimed that it was impossible for the defendant to marry or to procreate, only that it might result in his death. In these circumstances, he held that while the groom might be able to rescind the contract of marriage, he would remain liable for damages.[247] In the Exchequer Chamber, Martin B. agreed that the settled rule should be followed: 'To admit exceptions of this kind utterly destroys the certainty of the law, and in my opinion is inconvenient.'[248] The judges favouring the defendant looked instead at the purpose of the contract of marriage. In the Queen's Bench, Erle J. pointed to numerous instances where the law permitted an engagement to be broken off where one party's conduct was such as to undermine the purpose of

---

[243] *Hills* v. *Sughrue* (1846) 15 M. & W. 253 at 262. Parke B. invoked *Marquis of Bute* v. *Thompson* (1844) 13 M. & W. 487 as authority.

[244] *Hurst* v. *Usborne* (1856) 18 C.B. 144 at 155.

[245] In his work on bailments, Joseph Story suggested that performance should be excused where the act stipulated became impossible to be performed by any one, by inevitable accident, or an act of Providence; but that it should not be excused where the act became impossible to be performed by the party promising, though it could be performed by another: J. Story, *Commentaries on the Law of Bailments* (5th edn, 1851), § 36n.

[246] There was no case authority for the proposition that physical disability discharged a contract, though Lord Campbell CJ suggested in 1858 that an employer could discharge a contract if his employee became permanently disabled: *Cuckson* v. *Stones* (1858) 1 El. & El. 248 at 257.

[247] *Hall* v. *Wright* (1858) E. B. & E. 746 at 749.

[248] *Hall* v. *Wright* (1858) E. B. & E. 765 at 789.

marriage, which was to provide mutual comfort.[249] Bramwell B., who felt that this should not be dealt with as if it were a contract for the sale of goods or a business transaction, protested that the law could, where it was necessary, imply terms. Not only was it implied in contracts for personal service that the promisor would remain mentally and physically able to perform, but '[t]his very contract to marry has an implied condition that the woman shall continue chaste'.[250] Bramwell invoked the authority of Pothier's *Traité du Mariage*, as well as English dicta which suggested that a change in the parties' condition would be regarded as a good reason to break off an engagement.[251] 'No doubt, if a contract made by parties is unconditional, death or disease is no excuse', he ruled, 'but the question in this case is, whether the contract is not conditional on the continuance of life and health'.[252] In both courts, the 'traditionalists' won, holding the defendant's plea insufficient.

The question of whether the performance of a contract was conditional on the continued existence of a particular state of affairs was considered further in 1863 in *Taylor* v. *Caldwell*, the case generally credited with introducing the doctrine of frustration into English law.[253] The plaintiffs had hired the Surrey Gardens and Music Hall for four nights in the summer of 1861 to stage grand concerts. Before the day of the first concert, the hall was destroyed by fire,[254] and the plaintiffs sued for breach of contract, seeking to recover the expenses incurred in preparing for the concerts. The defendants pleaded a general custom of the trade that, in the event of a fire, such a contract would be rescinded, but failed to prove the custom at the trial. It was agreed, however, that the defendants would have allowed the plaintiffs to have used the gardens and hall in their ruined state, had they chosen to do so.[255] The plaintiffs failed in their action, with the judgment of the Queen's Bench departing significantly from the approach it had taken in the cases on leases.[256]

---

[249] *Hall* v. *Wright* (1858) E. B. & E. 746 at 754, citing *Foulkes* v. *Sellway* (1800) 3 Esp. 236; *Irving* v. *Greenwood* (1824) 1 Car. & P. 350; *Atchinson* v. *Baker* (1796) 2 Peake N.P.C. 103; *Leeds* v. *Cook* (1803) 4 Esp. 256; *Baddeley* v. *Mortlock* (1816) 1 Holt N.P.C. 151.

[250] *Hall* v. *Wright* (1858) E. B. & E. 765 at 778. Pollock CB took a similar view, holding that the continuance of the groom's heath was a condition to be implied.

[251] *Atchinson* v. *Baker* (1796) Peake Add. Cas. 103 at 104.

[252] *Hall* v. *Wright* (1859) E. B. & E. 765 at 781.

[253] Cf. S. J. Stoljar, *A History of Contract at Common Law* (Canberra, 1975), 192, noting that *Taylor* v. *Caldwell* was a case about 'supervening impossibility': the notion of 'frustration' 'originated in charter parties, where it at first referred to the failure of the charterer's expectation caused by an inordinate delay in the loading of a ship'. Cases include *Tarrabochia* v. *Hickie* (1856) 1 H. & N. 183, discussed above, p. 489.

[254] *Taylor* v. *Caldwell* (1863) 3 B. & S. 826. See further C. MacMillan, 'Taylor v Caldwell', 167–80.

[255] *The Times*, 19 December 1861, col. 10f.

[256] Blackburn J. ruled that there was no letting here, though he added that '[n]othing however, in our opinion, depends on this': *Taylor* v. *Caldwell* (1863) 3 B. & S. 826 at 833.

In his judgment, Blackburn J. confirmed that where there was a positive contract to do something, the contractor was bound to perform or pay damages, even though unforeseen accidents had made performance impossible or more burdensome. However, where it appeared from the nature of the contract that the parties must have known that the contract could not be performed unless 'some particular specified thing continued to exist', then, 'in the absence of any express or implied warranty that the thing shall exist', it was to be construed 'as subject to an implied condition that the parties shall be excused in case, before breach, performance becomes impossible from the perishing of the thing without default of the contractor'.[257] To help elucidate the principles on which the common law was based, Blackburn turned to Roman law.[258] He also invoked Pothier for the notion that where a thing contracted for perished, the obligation was discharged. These sources strongly influenced his thinking. His stress that an absolute liability was only imposed in cases of warranty echoed Pothier's position (discussed in Blackburn's own treatise on sale) that impossibility discharged contracts for the supply of specific things unless the supplier specifically assumed the risk.[259] Blackburn also invoked English authorities, though they offered imperfect support for his position. He first invoked the rule that a man's executors were not liable when his death prevented the performance of personal services he had contracted for, as well as the dicta which stated that a man who was physically disabled from performing services was discharged. Secondly, he pointed to the rule that when specific goods had been sold, and property had passed, the vendor's obligation to deliver them was discharged if they perished.[260] Thirdly, he pointed out that bailees of goods were not liable for losses caused by inevitable accident or the king's enemies.[261] On the basis of these arguments, Blackburn discharged the owners of the Music Hall from their liability, since he found them to have contracted on the basis of the continued existence of the chattel.

---

[257] *Taylor* v. *Caldwell* (1863) 3 B. & S. 826 at 833–4.

[258] *Taylor* v. *Caldwell* (1863) 3 B. & S. 826 at 834, citing D.45.1.23. On the weakness of Blackburn's use of Roman law, see MacMillan, 'Taylor v Caldwell', 193–4.

[259] R. J. Pothier, *A Treatise on the Law of Obligations or Contracts*, trans. W. D. Evans, 2 vols (1806), 438 said that 'the debtor of a specific thing is discharged from his obligation, when the thing is lost, without any act, default, or delay, on his part' unless he expressly took the risk on himself in the contract. His *Contract of Sale* (quoted by C. Blackburn, *A Treatise on the Effect of the Contract of Sale* (1845), 173) rooted this principle 'in the nature of things' for 'when the thing ceases to exist, the obligation can no longer exist, not being capable of existing without a subject'.

[260] He cited *Rugg* v. *Minett* (1809) 11 East 210, as well as his own translation from Pothier's *Traité du Vente* in his treatise on *Sale* (1845), 171 *et seq*. Pothier said the vendor's obligation to deliver the goods was discharged by the destruction of the subject of the sale.

[261] Blackburn invoked *Williams* v. *Lloyd* (1628) W. Jones 179, to show that the rule did not merely derive from Holt's civilian approach in *Coggs* v. *Bernard* (1703) 3 Ld. Raym. 163.

Blackburn J. continued to develop the doctrine whose midwife he had been. In *Appleby* v. *Meyers*, he overturned a decision of the Common Pleas, which allowed the plaintiffs to recover in an action arising from work done on a building which was destroyed by fire before its completion.[262] Rejecting the Common Pleas' position that there was an implied term in the contract that the defendants would provide the building—and the Roman law principles invoked by the plaintiffs in support of it[263]—he held that where premises were destroyed through no fault of either party, 'it is a misfortune equally affecting both parties; excusing them both from further performance of the contract, but giving a cause of action to neither'.[264] In his view, there was rather an implied term that the contract would be ended if the building was destroyed, which had the same effect as an express 'excepted perils' clause in a charterparty. The effect of the decision was to confirm that all the loss in such cases would lie where it fell. As this was an entire contract, with the plaintiffs not entitled to be paid until the work was complete, they could not recover any money.[265]

Blackburn J. continued his development of this doctrine in 1874 in *Howell* v. *Coupland*, where the defendant had failed to deliver a full crop of potatoes, when blight ruined the crop. Since the contract was for the purchase of a crop to be grown on particular land, he considered it to be a contract for specific goods, governed by the principle of *Taylor* v. *Caldwell*, that 'where there is a contract with respect to a particular thing, and that thing cannot be delivered without any default in the seller, the delivery is excused'.[266] This was to hold that the subject-matter whose existence was the precondition of the contract did not have to exist at the time the contract was made. By the end of the century, courts were prepared to discharge parties of their contractual duties where the physical impossibility of performance was temporary. In *Nickoll & Knight* v. *Ashton, Edridge & Co*, the Court of Appeal discharged the supplier of cotton seeds from his obligation to deliver goods to a buyer in Egypt within a specified time, when the ship they were contracted to be delivered by was stranded through perils of the sea.[267]

---

[262] *Appleby* v. *Meyers* (1866) LR 1 CP 615 at 622. The court accepted the plaintiff's argument that the materials installed became the buyer's property and were at his risk; and that the sellers were not bound by the 'entire obligations' rule, since they were prevented from completing the work by the fire.

[263] *Appleby* v. *Meyers* (1867) LR 2 CP 651 at 660.

[264] *Appleby* v. *Meyers* (1867) LR 2 CP 651 at 659.

[265] To overcome this, contractors began to ensure that interim payments would be made, which could not be recovered in case the subject-matter of the contract was destroyed: *Anglo-Egyptian Navigation Co* v. *Rennie* (1875) LR 10 CP 271.

[266] *Howell* v. *Coupland* (1874) LR 9 QB 462 at 465. Lord Coleridge CJ endorsed the notion that there was an implied condition in the Court of Appeal: *Howell* v. *Coupland* (1876) 1 QBD 258 at 261.

[267] *Nickoll & Knight* v. *Ashton, Edridge & Co* [1901] 2 KB 126.

In this case, the contract had provided for the cancellation of the contract in case of blockades or hostilities, but did not include an excepted perils clause. Despite Vaughan Williams LJ's dissenting doubts, the majority held that here the parties must have known that the contract would be impossible if the ship ran aground.

In the later nineteenth century, the courts also extended the principle of *Taylor* v. *Caldwell* to cases where illness prevented a party performing. In 1868, the Common Pleas held that the father of an apprentice was not liable for his son's inability to remain at work, after he had become permanently ill. The court held that, since the contract could only be performed if the young man remained healthy, the parties must have contemplated when they made the contract that such an illness should excuse non-performance.[268] Three years later, the Exchequer held a pianist discharged from her obligation to play, when she became unable to perform through illness.[269]

Seeds were also sewn for a further expansion of the doctrine, to embrace the notion that a contract might be terminated if its commercial purpose was frustrated. The root of this notion is to be traced to *Jackson* v. *Union Marine Insurance Company* in 1874, where a shipowner sued his insurer to recover for freight lost when his charterer cancelled a charterparty, after the ship ran aground on its way to collect the goods. Since the event fell under one of the 'excepted perils' in the charterparty, the insurers disputed their liability by denying the charterers' right to terminate the contract. In the Common Pleas, Brett J. found for the shipowners. In his view, a term had to be implied in the charterparty that neither side could compel performance by the other 'where the injury is caused by a peril excepted in the charterparty [...] without default of the ship-owner [...and] where the injury is so great as to prevent the arrival of the ship [...] within any time which could have been at the time of making the contract in the contemplation of either the charterer or ship-owner as a time in any way applicable to the commercial speculation of either of them'.[270] The decision was problematic, insofar as it implied a term in order to qualify an express term—the 'excepted perils' clause, which took away the charterer's right to treat the contract as breached. But Brett explained his view that, 'where a contract is made with reference to certain anticipated circumstances, and where, without any default of either party, it becomes wholly inapplicable to or impossible of application to any such circumstances, it ceases to have *any* application; it cannot be applied to other circumstances which could not have been in the contemplation of the parties when the

---

[268] *Boast* v. *Frith* (1868) LR 4 CP 1 at 7.
[269] *Robinson* v. *Davison* (1871) LR 6 Ex 269 at 277.
[270] *Jackson* v. *Union Marine Insurance Co* (1873) LR 8 CP 572 at 577–8.

contract was made'.[271] This was to suggest that where the commercial purpose of the venture was frustrated, the 'excepted perils' clause could no longer have any application. The Exchequer Chamber endorsed the decision of the Common Pleas, though Bramwell's leading judgment was significantly different. As has been seen, in his view, the event which frustrated the commercial purpose of the contract did not void the 'excepted perils' clauses, and the charterer remained unable to sue the owner for the late arrival of the ship.[272] But since the shipowner had not complied with an implied condition precedent that the ship arrive in time for the voyage to make commercial sense, the charterer retained his right to terminate the contract.[273]

Bramwell B.'s ruling in *Jackson* v. *Union Marine Insurance Company* was based on an interpretation of the contractual obligations of charterers. Treatise writers such as Anson accordingly discussed it as an example of the discharge of a contract by breach, rather than by impossibility of performance. But its reasoning was extended in 1876 by Blackburn J. to an employment case, *Poussard* v. *Spiers*, where there had been no breach. The plaintiff's wife had been engaged to play in an opera bouffe at the Criterion Theatre, beginning on 14 November 1874. But she caught a cold while being fitted for her costume, and was unable to perform. Instead, Miss Catherine Lewis was hired to perform, if needed, until 25 December. On 4 December, when Mme Poussard felt better, she offered her services, but they were declined. Having refused an alternative engagement at the Philharmonic Music Hall, she now sued for breach of contract. At the trial, Field J. left it to the jury to consider whether the agreement had been mutually rescinded, or whether the theatre managers had authority to alter it themselves. The jury returned a verdict of £83 damages. But the Queen's Bench Division took a different view. Blackburn J. held for the defendants by invoking *Jackson*. That case had shown that, where there was a delay occasioned by excepted perils, the shipowner was excused his breach; but if the delay went to the root of the matter, the charterer was discharged from furnishing a cargo. In this case, since Mme Poussard had become ill, and had not therefore breached her contract, she was not liable for not performing. But since her failure to appear on the opening night was so important as to go to the root of the consideration, the defendants were discharged.[274] Blackburn did not here mention implied terms, but it is clear that the premise of his decision, borrowed from *Jackson*, was that where the

---

[271] *Jackson* v. *Union Marine Insurance Co* (1873) LR 8 CP 572 at 581.

[272] *Jackson* v. *Union Marine Insurance Co* (1874) LR 10 CP 125 at 145.

[273] The case was soon approved of by judges (e.g. *Dahl* v. *Nelson, Donkin & Co* (1880) 6 App Cas 38 at 53) and treatise writers (T. E. Scrutton, *The Contract of Affreightment as Expressed in Charterparties and Bills of Lading* (5th edn by T. E. Scrutton and F. D. MacKinnon, 1904), 81).

[274] *Poussard* v. *Spiers* (1876) 1 QBD 410.

commercial purpose of a contract was undermined, the parties were discharged, regardless of whether either was in breach.

Jackson v. *Union Marine Insurance* helped pave the way for a doctrine of frustration of purpose. But it was a spate of cases caused by the postponement of Edward VII's coronation—thanks to an attack of appendicitis—which entrenched this idea. The coronation was due to take place on 26 June 1902, and was to be followed on subsequent days by a royal progress and a naval review. Since many contracts were entered into in anticipation of these events going ahead, its cancellation raised the question whether those who bought tickets could recover their money, or whether those who had spent large sums in preparing for the event could share their losses with the buyers of tickets.[275] In the aftermath of the cancellation, those who had let out their rooms to view the procession sued to be paid the hire, and those who had paid money in advance sued to recover it.[276] The leading case was *Krell* v. *Henry*, where the plaintiff sued the defendant for an outstanding payment of £50 for the hire of his rooms on Pall Mall, and the defendant counter-claimed, seeking the return of a £25 deposit. Henry had responded to a notice advertising windows to view the coronation processions.[277] Although the correspondence through which the contract was made did not mention the coronation, both Darling J. and the Court of Appeal held that both parties regarded the taking place of the processions to be the foundation of the contract, and that Krell could not recover the outstanding £50.[278] In his judgment, Vaughan Williams LJ saw the rule as an importation into English law of an expanded version of a Roman doctrine. In his view, *Nickoll & Knight* v. *Ashton, Edridge & Co* showed that the doctrine of *Taylor* v. *Caldwell* applied 'where the event which renders the contract incapable of performance is the cessation or non-existence of an express condition or state of things, going to the root of the contract, and essential to its performance'.[279] If it could be seen from extrinsic evidence that a particular state of things was regarded as the foundation of the contract, its non-occurrence could discharge the parties. The court had to ascertain from all the circumstances 'what is the substance of the contract, and then to ask the question

---

[275] See G. H. Treitel, *Frustration and Force Majeure* (2nd edn, 2004), 314 *et seq.*

[276] Litigation also ensued between parties who had made express provision in their contracts for liabilities in the event of cancellation (e.g. *Elliott* v. *Crutchley* [1906] AC 7); and where parties had entered inadvertently into contracts after the cancellation (*Griffith* v. *Brymer* (1903) 19 TLR 434. See also *Clark* v. *Lindsay* (1902) 88 *LT* 198), which were in effect cases of mistake.

[277] *The Times*, 12 August 1902, col. 5b.

[278] *Krell* v. *Henry* [1903] 2 KB 740.

[279] *Krell* v. *Henry* [1903] 2 KB 740 at 748. This was perhaps more an articulation of the notion behind *Jackson* v. *Union Marine Insurance*, a case not discussed in *Nickoll* v. *Ashton*, perhaps because the defendant there was not a shipowner who had contracted to supply the ship which ran aground, but a shipper who relied on its availability. Vaughan Williams LJ did, however, invoke *Jackson*.

whether that substantial contract needs for its foundation the assumption of the existence of a particular state of things'.[280] Vaughan Williams LJ's approach seemed to go against the rule that written contracts could not be varied by parol evidence, and the *Law Times* noted that the decision was not in accordance with the general expectation of lawyers. But it endorsed the decision as a correct one.[281] At the same time as deciding *Krell v. Henry*, the Court of Appeal heard *Herne Bay Steam Boat Company* v. *Hutton*,[282] where the plaintiffs sued for money owed for the hire of a steamship let to the defendants for the purpose of viewing the naval review. The fleet did remain at Spithead for the days in question, but there was no naval review by the king. The Court of Appeal held that the sole purpose of the contract was not to see the naval review, and that it was not frustrated.[283]

The notion that losses lay where they fell was endorsed in *Chandler* v. *Webster*, which held that moneys paid out prior to the frustrating event could not be recovered. As Collins MR saw it, the effect of impossibility was not to wipe out the contract altogether but only to discharge both parties from further perform-ance. This rule was an 'arbitrary' one, but was adopted because it was impossible in such cases to work out the rights of the parties with certainty.[284] The Court of Appeal endorsed the earlier decision of *Blakeley* v. *Muller & Co*, where the Queen's Bench Division rejected the idea that in such cases, the contract was to be regarded as rescinded *ab initio*. For Lord Alvanley CJ, this would be unjust, since it would throw all the loss on the defendants, who had spent much money preparing for the event. In so deciding, it also rejected the idea that the court was to look at what the parties would have agreed had they contemplated that per-formance would be rendered impossible. As Channell J. put it, '[i]t is impossible to import a condition into a contract which the parties could have imported and have not done so'.[285] This was to move away from Blackburn's notion that there was an implied term of the parties that the contract would remain possible, or be terminated.

Treatise writers considering the developing doctrine of impossibility of per-formance were unsure how to view it. Some, such as Leake, argued that whether an event subsequent to the making of a contract discharged it depended on 'the intention of the parties, as collected from their agreement'.[286] This was to endorse

---

[280] *Krell* v. *Henry* [1903] 2 KB 740 at 749.

[281] (1903) 116 LT 79.

[282] *Herne Bay Steam Boat Co* v. *Hutton* [1903] 2 KB 683.

[283] See also Anson, *Contract* (13th edn by M. L. Gwyer, Oxford, 1912), 375 noting that the doctrine did not apply where the existence of a thing was merely the motive or inducement of the contract.

[284] *Chandler* v. *Webster* [1904] 1 KB 493 at 497, 499.

[285] *Blakeley* v. *Muller & Co* (1903) 88 LT 90, [1903] 2 KB 760n. See also *Civil Service Co-Operative Society* v. *The General Steam Navigation Co* [1903] 2 KB 756.

[286] Leake, *Elements* (1867), 361.

the approach of Blackburn J. in *Taylor* v. *Caldwell*. By contrast, Anson's discussion of subsequent impossibility did not invoke an implied term, but rather noted that the 'acts of God' which excused from performance did so because *'they are not within the contract'*. Since neither party contemplated their performance, 'neither excepts them specifically, nor promises unconditionally in respect of them'.[287] In his early editions, Pollock dealt with the issue in a chapter on impossible agreements, which also included those entered into under a mistake. He held that the rule imposing absolute liability was qualified in two cases, by an implied condition: where performance depended on the existence of a specific thing; and where it depended on a person's health or life.[288] By the eighth edition of his text, published after the coronation cases, he began to doubt that 'impossible agreements' constituted a legal category, preferring now to think of the cases in terms of conditional agreements.[289] But it was not until the next—post-war—edition of his text that he recast his chapter. He now argued that the category of impossibility was unsatisfactory, since no man of ordinary sense would enter into an impossible contract; while 'sheer impossibility' was only an extreme instance of the situation recognized by the court where, thanks to some intervening event, the agreement could not subsequently be performed according to the parties' true intention. In the aftermath of wartime cases, which saw the rapid development of the notion of 'frustration of the adventure', he felt the language needed recasting.[290] He now spoke of four exceptions to the general rule of absolute liability: death or disablement of the promisor of personal services; destruction of the subject-matter; 'failure of [an] assumed essential state of facts'; and 'external interference of an extraordinary nature'.[291]

By the time Pollock wrote this edition, the number of 'frustration' cases had grown significantly because of the wartime events. These cases showed an ambiguity over whether the doctrine was to be rooted in the implied intention of parties to the contract, or in a judgment by the court that the continuing performance of the contract had been rendered impossible by external events. When the matter was considered by the House of Lords in 1916, it was held that the doctrine was rooted in 'an implied condition in the contract which operated so as to release the parties from performing it'. As Earl Loreburn put it, in a case involving a charterparty for a requisitioned steamer, the court had no power to absolve the parties, but it could infer from the surrounding circumstances that 'a condition which is not expressed was a foundation on which the parties contracted'.[292] In his view, if

[287] Anson, *Contract* (1879), 315. Emphasis in original.

[288] Pollock, *Contract* (1876), 336–44.   [289] Pollock, *Contract* (8th edn, 1911), ix.

[290] Pollock, *Contract* (9th edn, 1921), x.   [291] Pollock, *Contract* (9th edn, 1921), 316.

[292] *F A Tamplin Steamship Co* v. *Anglo-Mexican Petroleum Products Co* [1916] 2 AC 397 at 404.

the commercial adventure was frustrated, then it could be assumed that the parties did not intend it to continue to be binding. The court thus had to consider the event which the parties had not provided for: 'Were the altered conditions such that, had they thought of them, they would have taken their chance of them, or such that as sensible men they would have said "if that happens, of course, it is all over between us"?' However, rather than looking at what the parties would have provided for, Loreburn in resolving the case looked more at whether the court should imply a term. He felt it should not, as the interruption was not such as to make it unreasonable to require the parties to carry on.[293]

[293] See also *Countess of Warwick Steamship Co* v. *Le Nickel* [1918] 1 KB 372; *Bank Line* v. *Arthur Capel & Co* [1919] AC 435; *Naylor Benzen & Co* v. *Krainische Industrie Gesellschaft* [1918] 2 KB 486; *Marshall* v. *Glanvill* [1917] 2 KB 87; *Blackburn Bobbin Co* v. *Allen & Sons* [1918] 1 KB 540.

VII
Contractual Remedies

CONTRACT litigation in the nineteenth century was largely concerned with questions of business planning, rather than finding fair outcomes to disputes. The bulk of the litigation in the superior courts, which generated legal doctrine, involved commercial parties, rather than ordinary consumers. Juries were not asked to weigh what were the just deserts between the parties. The legal experience of the 'ordinary consumer' was typically quite different from that of the commercial litigant. He or she was most likely to experience the process of litigation as a defendant in a county court claim for a small debt. Approximately half of all plaints entered in these courts in the second half of the nineteenth century resulted in a judgment, the overwhelming majority being decided without the intervention of a jury. While it is true that county court judges were able on occasion to manipulate rules of law—such as the rule according to which a husband or father was only liable for necessaries supplied to his wife or children—to give paternalistic protection to the needy,[1] most suits in these fora involved straightforward debt recovery.

Commercial parties who sued for breach of contract in the superior courts were far less likely to get to a trial. But they did wish to have clear rules which would give certainty as to the sums which could be recovered. Throughout our era, they wanted rules appropriate for a trading economy, not for a moral economy. But these rules did not stay static. In the mid-nineteenth-century period of commercial optimism and economic growth, as business began to be conducted in ever expanding markets using increasingly sophisticated machinery, new rules developed to promote business efficiency, by allowing contracting parties both to recover profits anticipated from their contracts, and to limit their losses to those likely to arise from a breach. In an era in which they sought to control the power of juries over damages, judges and jurists became more sophisticated in their analyses, applying civilian ideas to current questions. Just as the common lawyers developed their rules to fit the law to the expectations of the commercial

---

[1] M. C. Finn, *The Character of Credit: Personal Debt in English Culture, 1740–1914* (Cambridge, 2003); P. Polden, *A History of the County Court, 1846–1971* (Cambridge, 1999).

community, so Chancery judges began to be more creative—sometimes controversially so—in awarding specific performance, from a desire to hold parties to their contractual liabilities.

1. PENALTIES AND LIQUIDATED DAMAGES

Litigation was a notoriously expensive business. On average, costs far exceeded the amount in dispute.[2] Businessmen did not go to law to ask fellow citizens to assess fair prices for their contracts, but went to recover their debts in the most efficient way. They wished to avoid trials. The best way to do this was to have the debt secured by an instrument allowing summary judgment. Many debts were therefore secured by a warrant of attorney, where the debtor authorized an attorney named by his creditor to confess an action of debt on his behalf, and to suffer judgment to be entered against him.[3] Although affluent tradesmen were suspicious of instruments which gave such great power to creditors, they were commonly taken out,[4] and were regularly enforced.[5] Those on the verge of bankruptcy used them to prefer certain creditors.[6] They were also given by debtors arrested on mesne process, who made arrangements to pay off the debt in instalments, for they allowed the creditor to obtain summary judgment on the whole debt on failure of any instalment.[7] They could equally be used at any other

[2] C. W. Francis, 'Practice, Strategy, and Institution: Debt Collection in the English Common Law Courts, 1740–1840' (1986) 80 *Northwestern University LR* 807–954, App. 37.

[3] The warrant was based on a fiction, for no action had been commenced, and no writ issued. J. Chitty, *The Practice of the Law in all its Departments* (2nd edn,1834), Pt 4, p. 334.

[4] It has been calculated that, in 1830, nearly 10,000 warrants of attorney and *cognovits* were filed under legislation requiring registration to make the instrument valid against assignees in bankruptcy. Francis, 'Debt Collection', 828–9.

[5] Thus, in the 1820s, 26% of final judgments were on warrants of attorney. The proportion of final judgments which were on warrants of attorney remained significant: in 1859, 35% of final judgments were on a judge's order to stay proceedings (because of a warrant of attorney, or the certificate on an arbitrator). In 1874, the proportion was 18%. Between 1894 and 1898, 13% of final judgments (excluding summary judgments under Order XIV) were on such an order.

[6] Such transactions were not in the late eighteenth century seen as being fraudulent within the meaning of 13 Eliz. c. 5, being made for good consideration: *Holbird* v. *Anderson* (1793) 5 T.R. 235; *Meux* v. *Howell* (1803) 4 East 1. Compare Lord Ellenborough's approach in *Jones* v. *Plumer* as reported in *The Tradesman; or, Commercial Magazine* (1812), 478–9. In the 1820s, legislation was passed to prevent frauds on creditors being committed by secret warrants of attorney: 3 Geo. IV c. 39, 6 Geo. IV c. 16, ss 81 and 108, 7 Geo. IV c. 57, c. 32, c. 33. However, there remained concern that arrest for debt was needed because of the persistent use of warrants of attorney to prefer favoured creditors: see the evidence of R. Burnet, Fourth Report made to his Majesty by the Commissioners Appointed to Inquire into the Practice and Proceedings of the Superior Courts of Common Law, PP 1831–2, xxv, (239) 1, at p. 183B.

[7] *The London Tradesman; A Familiar Treatise on the Rationale of Trade and Commerce, as carried on in the Metropolis of the British Empire* (2nd edn, 1820), 217. See also *Morton* v. *Burn* (1837) 7 Ad. & El. 19.

stage in the process of litigation to secure a settlement.[8] Besides giving warrants of attorney, parties seeking a settlement could also confess the action, by using a *cognovit actionem*. In such cases judgment would only be entered in case of default by the defendant in paying.[9]

Cautious creditors also continued to make use of formal sealed bonds to secure the payment of money. Debts on bond were regarded as preferable where the debt was large, and where any doubts existed regarding the consideration.[10] They rarely went to trial, since the formal nature of the bond made proof of the debt easy.[11] Where judgment was by default, the amount due did not have to be assessed by a jury on a writ of inquiry,[12] as it did in actions of assumpsit before 1852.[13] Moreover, bonds bound the obligor's heirs and estate, so that, unlike simple contract debts, they subjected a person's real estate to execution.[14] For these reasons, they remained a significant proportion of cases in the first half the century on which judgments were pronounced.[15]

Conditional bonds were given to secure either the payment of debts, or the performance of a promise. The person giving the bond formally bound himself to pay a penal sum, habitually double the sum really due, with the condition annexed that the bond would be void on performance of the condition. The Chancery had long given relief from penalties, ordering the party in breach to pay only what was due in conscience. It did so by regarding the condition as the agreement,[16] with the penalty being only a security for such damages as were really suffered by the breach.[17] The Chancery would therefore set aside penalties, and direct an issue, to determine the quantum of damages. By the eighteenth century, legislation ensured that the common law would also only require the obligor to pay the sums really due, rather than the penalty.[18]

---

[8] They were also used by the Insolvent Debtors' Court on releasing prisoners as a means to secure access to the debtor's future property, to pay off his debts. E. Cooke, *An Inquiry into the State of the Law of Debtor and Creditor in England, with reference of the expediency of allowing Arrest for Debt* (1829), 60.

[9] No further assessment of the sum due by a jury was needed. W. Tidd, *The Practice of the Court of King's Bench in Personal Actions* 2 vols (2nd edn, 1799), i, 474–5.

[10] Chitty, *Practice*, i, 113.

[11] In 1859, only 1.6% of cases which went to trial involved bonds; in 1874, only 0.83% did.

[12] Francis, 'Debt Collection', 814.

[13] Under the Common Law Procedure Act 1852 (15 & 16 Vict. c. 76, s 27), the sheriff's jury only had to be used where damages were unliquidated and could not be submitted to a master for calculation.

[14] 1 W 4 c. 47 subjected a trader's real estate to simple contract debts; while 1 & 2 Vict. c. 110, s 11 (1838) allowed the creditor to take all the debtor's land under an elegit.

[15] Francis records that 9% of judgments in the Queen's Bench and 16% in the Exchequer in 1840 were on debt *sur* obligation: Francis, 'Debt Collection', Apps 5, 9.

[16] *Hardy* v. *Martin* (1783) 1 Cox 26.   [17] *Sloman* v. *Walter* (1783) 1 Bro. C.C. 418 at 419.

[18] 8 & 9 W III c. 11 s. 8, 4 & 5 Ann c. 16 s. 13, Francis, 'Debt collection', 853–4.

In dealing with bonds, the eighteenth-century Chancery distinguished between penal sums, which could not be recovered, and assessed damages, which could. Where the sum was considered as forming part 'of the essence of the agreement', rather than merely securing 'the enjoyment of a collateral object',[19] the Chancery would not relieve.[20] As Lord Mansfield explained, although relief would be given on a penalty, 'where the covenant is "to pay a particular liquidated sum", a Court of Equity cannot make a new covenant for a man; nor is there any compensation or relief'.[21] Thus, landlords were able to recover very high sums stipulated in leases, to be paid if the tenant used the land in prohibited ways:[22] having made use of the land in the way described, the defendant had to pay according to the contractual rate.[23] By 1800, thanks to statute, equity's approach to distinguishing penalties and liquidated damages was incorporated into the common law's approach in all cases of debt on bond. The plaintiff could recover the stipulated sum only if it was not regarded as a penalty.

Prima facie, the distinction between penalties and assessed damages should not have applied to informal contracts, since stipulated sums included in these contracts were part of the obligation, rather than a penalty liable to be defeated by the performance of a condition. However, early nineteenth-century common law courts did begin to apply the distinction derived from the cases on bonds in assumpsit, albeit in an experimental way and without referring to the statute of 1698. 'It seems as if', Bramwell B. observed in 1859, 'by some singular instinct, the Courts have been right, though without referring to the statute by which they ought to have been governed.'[24]

Following the approach of equity, common lawyers argued that it was not the greatness of the stipulated sum which determined whether a sum was penal, since parties were free to choose to contract at whatever price they liked,[25] but rather whether the parties intended to impose an obligation, or provide security for damages. They began to seek tests for establishing this intention. In 1787, Buller J.

---

[19] This formulation is taken from Mansfield's dicta in *Lowe* v. *Peers* (1768) 4 Burr. 2225 at 2228, which were restated in F. L. Holt's notes to *Barton* v. *Glover* (1815) Holt 43 n, rules 1 and 6.

[20] The essence of the agreement being found in the condition, the court would enforce the payment of sums which could be seen as part of that condition. See e.g. *Fletcher* v. *Dyche* (1787) 2 T.R. 32.

[21] *Lowe* v. *Peers* (1768) 4 Burr. 2225 at 2228.

[22] *Rolfe* v. *Peterson* (1772) 2 Bro. P.C. 436.

[23] *Farrant* v. *Olmius* (1820) 3 B. & Ald. 692. See also *Jones* v. *Green* (1829) 3 Y. & J. 298 at 304; *Denton* v. *Richmond* (1833) 1 C. & M. 734. Cf. *Aylet* v. *Dodd* (1741) 2 Atk. 238 at 239; *Woodward* v. *Gyles* (1689) 2 Vern. 119.

[24] *Betts* v. *Burch* (1859) (1859) 4 H. & N. 506 at 511. He cited *Gainsforth* v. *Griffith* (1666) 1 Wms. Saund. 51 at 58 note (1) as authority for his view. In fact, the statute was not easy to translate to assumpsits.

[25] *Roy* v. *Duke of Beaufort* (1741) 2 Atk. 190 at 193; *Astley* v. *Weldon* (1801) 2 B. & P. 346 at 351.

held that where 'it is impossible to ascertain precisely what damages the party has really sustained', the contracting parties could agree to pay a stipulated sum.[26] In 1801, more tests were suggested in *Astley* v. *Weldon*. According to Heath J.,

[w]here articles contain covenants for the performance of several things, and then one large sum is stated at the end to be paid upon breach of performance, that must be considered as a penalty. But where it is agreed that if a party do such a particular thing such a sum shall be paid by him, there the sum stated may be treated as liquidated damages.[27]

Chambre J. added that where a smaller sum was secured by the payment of a larger one, it would always be a penalty.

Early nineteenth-century courts sometimes felt that the language used by the parties determined the question. If a contract used the phrase 'liquidated damages', it would be upheld;[28] if the word 'penalty' was used, it would be struck down,[29] as being inserted as a security for damages.[30] By the 1820s, however, the courts realized that they could not trust the wording used by the parties, but had to look to the whole agreement to see if the term was to be regarded as a penalty.[31] In *Kemble* v. *Farren*, where a theatre proprietor sought to recover a sum stated in the contract to be liquidated damages and not a penalty, the Common Pleas disregarded the wording, and ruled it to be a penalty, since the sum was to be paid by either party for any breach, even ones which could be quantified. According to the agreement, £1000 would have been payable had the plaintiff failed on any night to pay the defendant his £3–6–8 fee. As Tindal CJ ruled, 'that a very large sum should become immediately payable, in consequence of the nonpayment of a very small sum, and that the former should not be considered as a penalty, appears to be a contradiction in terms'.[32]

The fact that judges were not hostile to pre-estimations of damages can be seen from Tindal's comments that there was nothing illegal or unreasonable in agreeing damages for 'breaches which were of an uncertain nature and amount', for 'in all cases, it saves the expense and difficulty of bringing witnesses to that point'.[33] Judges who favoured such a power of pre-estimation began to move away from Heath's formulation of the rule regarding multiple breaches. In 1842, Parke B.

---

[26] *Fletcher* v. *Dyche* (1787) 2 T.R. 32 at 37. In this case, the stipulated sum was upheld as part of the contract; but it should be noted that the sum in question was included in the terms of a conditional defeasance of a penal bond taken out by the employer of the builder.

[27] *Astley* v. *Weldon* (1801) 2 B. & P. 346 at 353.   [28] *Barton* v. *Glover* (1815) Holt N.P.C. 43.

[29] *Smith* v. *Dickenson* (1804) 3 B. & P. 630 at 632.

[30] *Barton* v. *Glover* (1815) Holt 43, note, rule 3.

[31] *Davies* v. *Penton* (1827) 6 B. & C. 216 at 222–3. See also *Jones* v. *Green* (1829) 3 Y. & J. 298 at 304; *Green* v. *Price* (1845) 13 M. & W. 695 at 701.

[32] *Kemble* v. *Farren* (1829) 6 Bing. 141 at 147; cf. *Horner* v. *Flintoff* (1842) 9 M. & W. 678.

[33] *Kemble* v. *Farren* (1829) 6 Bing. 141 at 148.

ruled that if parties had contracted 'in clear and express terms, that for the breach of each and every stipulation contained in the agreement a sum certain is to be paid', the court would hold them to their contract, 'although the stipulations are of various degrees of importance'.[34] In his view, whether a clause was penal or not depended on whether the damage could be valued. '[I]f a party agrees to pay £1000 on several events, all of which are capable of accurate valuation, the sum must be construed as a penalty', he said in 1850, '[b]ut if there be a contract consisting of one or more stipulations, the breach of which cannot be measured, then the parties must be taken to have meant that the sum agreed on was to be liquidated damages.'[35] Provided the damages could not accurately be measured, parties were permitted to put very high prices on breaches,[36] or to 'assign such limits as they please to their own liability'.[37] Indeed, in restraint of trade cases, they were permitted to provide for payments which they 'considered...as something more than compensation'.[38] But if any one of the breaches could be measured, then the whole clause had to be held a penalty.[39] As a result, in 1856, Coleridge J. said that Heath's view could no longer be regarded as law.[40]

When the parties had agreed stipulated sums, juries were considered to be bound to award them, even in assumpsit.[41] Abbott CJ's ruling at *nisi prius* in 1827, that a jury could assess its own damages, even though a stipulated sum had been agreed to be paid in case of non-performance,[42] was not regarded as correct either by other judges or by treatise writers.[43] As Best CJ pointed out, parties used liquidated damages clauses when no evidence was available which 'would enable juries to do complete justice'. More broadly, he ruled that '[a] Court of Justice has no more authority to put a different construction on the part of an instrument ascertaining the amount of damages, than it has to decide contrary to any other

---

[34] *Horner* v. *Flintoff* (1842) 9 M. & W. 678 at 680.

[35] *Atkyns* v. *Kinnier* (1850) 4 Exch. 776 at 783. See also his approach in *Galsworthy* v. *Strutt* (1848) 1 Exch. 659. See also *Reynolds* v. *Bridge* (1856) 6 E. & B. 528.

[36] As Alderson B. put it in the same case, '[i]f the parties choose to measure the breach of any one of the stipulations by £10,000, we cannot say that they are wrong, inasmuch as the damages are uncertain': *Atkyns* v. *Kinnier* (1850) 4 Exch. 776 at 784. Parke noted that this might have been an imprudent contract for the defendant to enter into, but that was not a matter for the court. See also *Green* v. *Price* (1845) 13 M. & W. 695.

[37] Per Erle J. in *Reynolds* v. *Bridge* (1856) 6 E. & B. 528 at 544.

[38] *Crisdee* v. *Bolton* (1827) 3 C. & P. 240 at 243. See also *Leighton* v. *Wales* (1838) 3 M. & W. 545 at 551.

[39] *Reynolds* v. *Bridge* (1856) 6 E. & B. 528 at 541.

[40] In *Reynolds* v. *Bridge* (1856) 6 E. & B. 528 at 540.

[41] *Lowe* v. *Peers* (1768) 4 Burr. 2225 at 2229; *Astley* v. *Weldon* (1801) 2 B. & P. 346 at 354.

[42] *Randall* v. *Everest* (1827) 2 Car. & P. 577. He had taken a different approach where parties had stipulated a sum to be paid where a defendant had turned land into tillage in violation of the terms of a lease: *Farrant* v. *Olmius* (1820) 3 B. & Ald. 692.

[43] T. Sedgwick, *A Treatise on the Measure of Damages* (2nd edn, New York, 1852), 410.

of its clauses'.[44] In 1849, Wilde CJ added that to allow the jury to award damages according to their discretion would allow them to decide whether the clause was a penalty or a liquidated damages clause, which would allow them to encroach on the judge's function of construing the contract.[45] By the mid-century, then, courts were keen to allow parties to make contractual provisions which would fix the damages.[46]

In the second half of the century, however, at a time when the jury's role particularly in contract cases was diminishing,[47] Parke's approach to distinguishing between penalties and liquidated damages began to come under attack from judges who sought to focus on whether the stipulated sum was excessive or disproportionate. In 1869, Lord Westbury said, 'if the sum described as liquidated damages be a large sum, and the title to that sum is to arise upon some very trifling consideration, then it follows plainly that the large sum never could have been meant to be the real measure of damages'.[48] In 1874, Coleridge CJ sought to reformulate Heath's rule: 'where the contract contains a variety of stipulations of different degrees of importance, and one large sum is stated at the end to be paid on breach of performance of any of them, that must be considered as a penalty'.[49] Not all judges agreed with this approach. Sir George Jessel MR, that great champion of freedom of contract, declared that courts should not overrule any terms on the ground that they 'know the business of the people better than the people know it themselves'. He dismissed Heath's view as overruled by *Kemble* and Coleridge's modification as 'irreconcilable with principle'.[50] But despite Jessel's doubts, the new notion of proportionality was soon confirmed.[51] Only

---

[44] *Crisdee* v. *Bolton* (1827) 3 Car. & P. 240 at 242.   [45] *Sainter* v. *Ferguson* (1849) 7 C.B. 716.

[46] Nor could plaintiffs ignore the stipulated damages clause and sue for greater damages. Early nineteenth-century authorities on charterparties suggested that a plaintiff could 'ground his action upon the other clauses or covenants', and recover more than the penalty: C. Abbott, *A Treatise of the Law Relative to Merchant Ships and Seamen* (5th edn, by J. H. Abbott, 1827, 170), drawing on *Harrison* v. *Wright* (1811) 13 East 343; see also *Lowe* v. *Peers* (1768) 4 Burr. 2225 at 2228; *Gainsford* v. *Griffith* (1668) 1 Wms. Saund. 51 at 58 n(1)(d); *Barton* v. *Glover* (1815) Holt 43; *Godard* v. *Gray* (1870) LR 6 QB 139 at 147. But in practice, it was for the court to decide whether a clause in a charterparty was to be regarded as a penalty, and if it was not, the jury was bound by the contractually stipulated damages. See *Rayner* v. *Rederiaktiebolaget Condor* [1895] 2 QB 289; *Diestal* v. *Stevenson* [1906] 2 KB 345; *Wall* v. *Rederiaktiebolaget Luggude* [1915] 3 KB 66.

[47] M. Lobban, 'The Strange Life of the English Civil Jury, 1837–1914', in J. Cairns and G. McLeod (eds), *The Dearest Birthright of the People of England: The Jury in the History of the Common Law* (Oxford, 2002), 173–215 at 190–1.

[48] *Thompson* v. *Hudson* (1869) LR 4 HL 1 at 30.

[49] *Magee* v. *Lavell* (1874) LR 9 CP 107 at 111. Other judges continued to endorse Heath's view: see *In re Newman* (1876) 4 Ch D 724 at 731.

[50] *Wallis* v. *Smith* (1882) 21 Ch D 243 at 266.

[51] See *Elphinstone* v. *Monkland Iron and Coal Co* (1886) 11 App Cas 332 (Sc) at 342.

where the payments were proportionate to potential losses was the sum not to be seen as penal.[52]

Turn of the century cases continued the focus on whether the stipulated sum was a genuine pre-estimation of damages, and was a reasonable sum. In *Clydebank Engineering and Shipbuilding Company v. Don Jose Ramos Yzquierdo y Castaneda*, Lord Halsbury saw the question as being whether the sum was 'simply a penalty to be held over the other party in terrorem' or whether it was an agreed sum in damages. This was to be determined by asking both whether the sum was 'extravagant or unconscionable' and whether the parties determined on a sum because proof of the quantum of actual damage would be very hard to secure.[53] In April 1906, the Privy Council followed a similar approach, in setting aside a 'liquidated damages' clause which permitted the retention of deposit moneys in case work contracted for was not performed. For Lord Dunedin, the court was to ask whether the sum was a genuine pre-estimate of the creditor's probable interest in the performance of the principal obligation.[54] Finally, in 1914, the House of Lords set down a definitive set of rules for distinguishing penalties and liquidated damages clauses. Lord Dunedin, who gave the leading judgment, laid down four tests. The first test was that taken from the *Clydebank* case: if the sum was 'extravagant and unconscionable', it would be a penalty. The second test—which Dunedin associated with *Kemble*—was that where the sum stipulated was higher than the money sum which should have been paid, this was a penalty. The third test was that where a single sum payable for a multiplicity of breaches, it was to be *presumed* to be a penalty, but not conclusively so. Finally, he noted that it was no obstacle to the sum being liquidated damages that a genuine pre-estimation was impossible.[55] This formulation was to dominate twentieth-century ideas. It reflected a notion that courts were to police the quantum of damages, to ensure that the plaintiff only covered losses. This change in direction, dating from the 1870s, may have followed the development of rules on contract damages in the mid-century, which made the courts look more closely at determining which losses flowed from a breach of contract; and they may have been linked to a greater control of contract damages by judges rather than juries. In either case, they were a clear departure from the early nineteenth-century model.

---

[52] See also *Willson v. Love* [1896] 1 QB 626 at 631.
[53] *Clydebank Engineering and Shipbuilding Co v. Don Jose Ramos Yzquierdo y Castaneda* [1905] AC 6 at 10.
[54] *Public Works Commissioner v. Hills* [1906] AC 368 at 376. See also *Webster v. Bosanquet* [1912] AC 394.
[55] *Dunlop Pneumatic Tyre Co v. New Garage and Motor Co* [1915] AC 79 at 87.

2. *QUANTUM MERUIT*
AND EXPECTATION DAMAGES

Commercial parties who arrived in court had no desire for their disagreements to be settled according to the moral economy of a jury. Nor was there much room for juries to exercise their discretion. Instead, in assessing damages, they were to look at what parties had been led to expect under the contract. Where contracts had been executed, as where goods had been sold, work done or money paid, the contractual sum became a debt to be recovered, using the common counts in either debt sur contract or assumpsit.[56] Although the details of the contract were not set out in these counts, evidence was given of their agreement, on the basis of which juries were expected to award damages. Any scope the jury had to exercise its discretion was further limited by the rules of pleading, which defined the questions it was to consider,[57] and the developing rules of evidence, which defined what it could hear.[58] As a result, the awarding of contractual damages was largely a matter of calculation. Nor could juries exercise discretion in favour of plaintiffs by awarding interest in addition to contractual damages.[59]

Besides the common *indebitatus* counts, plaintiffs could also use the *quantum meruit* and *quantum valebat* counts, when work was done under a contract where no price had been stipulated or where benefits were accepted under a contract which had not been properly performed. These counts gave juries greater discretion in some circumstances. In its form, the *quantum meruit* count was distinct from the *indebitatus* count. Since it was not possible to have a *debt* for so much money as the plaintiff reasonably deserved to have,[60] a plaintiff using a *quantum meruit* count did not state that the defendant was indebted to him, but rather that he had promised to pay a reasonable sum, in consideration of work done or

---

[56] The old notion that a plaintiff using the action of debt could not recover any sum less than that demanded—a rule which discouraged the use of actions of debt—was no longer accepted as law by the 1820s. J. Chitty, *A Practical Treatise on Pleading and on the Parties to Actions*, 2 vols (1809), i, 107. See Lord Loughborough's comments in *Rudder* v. *Price* (1791) 1 H. Bl. 547 at 550.

[57] Until the early nineteenth century, strict rules of pleading meant that defendants sued for the price of goods sold could not to give evidence of inferior quality to reduce the damages, but would have instead to bring a cross-action for a breach of warranty, having paid the full contract price: *Basten* v. *Butter* (1806) 7 East 479; *Farnsworth* v. *Garrard* (1807) 1 Camp. 38. Even when the rule was relaxed, the defendant still had to prove a breach of warranty before damages could be reduced.

[58] New trials could be granted if the judge had wrongly allowed evidence to be given, or if the jury had made an erroneous conclusion on the basis of the evidence. See G. T. Washington, 'Damages in Contract at Common Law' (1931) 47 *LQR* 345–79 and (1932) 48 *LQR* 90–108. See also M. Lobban, 'Contractual Fraud in Law and Equity, c.1750–c.1850' (1997) 17 *OJLS* 441–76 at 459.

[59] *Gordon* v. *Swan* (1810) 12 East 419.

[60] D. Ibbetson, 'Implied Contracts and Restitution: History in the High Court of Australia' (1988) 8 *OJLS* 312–27 at 315–16.

goods sold.[61] This formal distinction had significant substantive implications for early eighteenth-century litigants, when plaintiffs using the *indebitatus* counts were required to prove the contractual price which fixed the debt, and could not recover for such sums as the goods or work were reasonably worth, if they failed to do so.[62] But in the later eighteenth century, the courts relaxed the boundary and allowed damages to be awarded under those counts on a *quantum meruit* basis.[63] Once the strict division between recovery on the *indebitatus* and the *quantum meruit* counts had been eroded, there seemed little point in continuing to use a separate count for the latter claim, and in 1831, new pleading rules effectively abolished it as a distinct count. *Quantum meruit* claims would henceforth be treated as *indebitatus* claims, arising from executed contracts.[64] The relaxation of these rules made life easier for litigants suing on a contract whose price they could not prove.

The jury had greatest discretion in *quantum meruit* claims when compensation was sought for goods delivered or work done which was not according to the contract, but which was accepted.[65] The mere receipt and retention of goods delivered raised an implied contract to pay for them. Since the goods delivered were different from those specified by the contract, the contracted price could not guide the damages. As with cases where no price had been agreed, it was for the jury to assess a reasonable recompense,[66] by following evidence of what the work was customarily regarded as worth.[67] Things were more complicated where building work had been done on the defendant's land, for he had no choice over whether to accept or reject it. In these cases, the courts ruled that plaintiffs should get no recompense, if the landowner had not acted in a way as to assent to the change of performance.[68] Nor could plaintiffs sue for additional work done for parties—such as corporations—who could not have contracted for it.[69]

---

[61] Chitty, *Pleading* (1809), i, 335: 'stating the subject matter of the debt according to the fact, and usually as in the indebitatus count'.

[62] *Weaver* v. *Boroughs* (1725) 1 Stra 648. See also J. L. Barton, 'Cutter v. Powell and Quantum Meruit' (1987) 8 *JLH* 48–63. In effect, plaintiffs had to choose which count they would proceed on, and could not use evidence from one count to support a claim on another. This was later relaxed: *Harris* v. *Oke* (1759); F. Buller, *An Introduction to the Law Relative to Trials at Nisi Prius* (1772), 137; *Payne* v. *Bacomb* (1781) 2 Doug. 651.

[63] *Webber* v. *Tivill* (1670) 2 Wms. Saund. 121 at 122 n2.

[64] J. Chitty, *A Treatise on Pleading*, 3 vols (6th edn, 1836), i, 342; ii, 27.

[65] See *Pepper* v. *Burland* (1791) Peake 139 (where additional work was remunerated on a *quantum meruit* basis); *Burn* v. *Miller* (1813) 4 Taunt. 745; *Lucas* v. *Godwin* (1837) 3 Bing. N.C. 736; Erle CJ's comments in *Seeger* v. *Duthie* (1860) 8 C.B. N.S. 45 at 56.

[66] See *Jewry* v. *Busk* (1814) 5 Taunt. 302.   [67] *Brown* v. *Nairne* (1839) 9 Car. & P. 204.

[68] *Ellis* v. *Hamlen* (1810) 3 Taunt. 52; *Munro* v. *Butt* (1858) 8 E. & B. 738.

[69] *Lamprell* v. *Guardian of Billericay Union Essex* (1849) 3 Exch. 283; *Homersham* v. *Wolverhampton Waterworks Co* (1851) 6 Exch. 137.

In other situations where *quantum meruit* claims were brought, juries often followed contractual measures. Such claims were often made for proportionate payment where the contractual performance had been interrupted. In these cases, the plaintiff could not sue on the contract—for it had not been completed—but had to sue on a contract implied from the fact that the defendant had accepted benefits. Before this could be done, however, it had to be clear that the plaintiff had no subsisting obligations under the original contract. This rule could create problems. According to *Cutter* v. *Powell*, if a seaman, who was to be paid on arrival in port, died during the voyage, his estate could not recover any payment for the labour he had done, since the express contract remained unperformed. '[W]herever there is an express contract the parties must be guided by it', Ashhurst J. ruled, 'and one party cannot relinquish or abide by it as it may suit his advantage.'[70] This rule was applied in 1802 in *Hulle* v. *Heightman* to prevent a seaman who had been wrongfully dismissed during the voyage from recovering any wages on an *indebitatus* count, when the court rejected Gibbs's suggestion that the special contract should be considered to have been terminated by the wrongful act of the defendant preventing the plaintiff's performance.[71]

By 1831, however, the courts were beginning to recognize that an innocent party could be discharged of his obligations if the other party repudiated, or prevented his performance.[72] In this context, judges were prepared to allow plaintiffs to recover on a *quantum meruit* basis for work done prior to the repudiation. This was settled in 1831 in *Planché* v. *Colburn*. In this case, an author who had completed part of a volume commissioned for publication by the defendants for inclusion in a series called the 'Juvenile Library' was told by them that the series had been abandoned. Under the contract, he was to have been paid £100. He sued both for breach of the special contract and on a *quantum meruit*, and was awarded £50 by the jury. The defendants sought to set aside the verdict, arguing that the plaintiff could not succeed on the special contract without a tender of the work, and could not sue on the general count while the contract remained open. However, the Common Pleas held that the contract had been abandoned by the defendants; and that '[u]nder these circumstances, the Plaintiff ought not to lose the fruit of his labour'.[73] Over 20 years later, when the rules on anticipatory

---

[70] *Cutter* v. *Powell* (1795) 6 T.R. 320 at 325.

[71] *Hulle* v. *Heightman* (1802) 2 East 145. Le Blanc J. thought the plaintiff should sue for breach of contract.

[72] *Withers* v. *Reynolds* (1831) 2 B. & Ad. 882. For the link between thinking on the *quantum meruit* counts and the issue of repudiatory breaches, see Erle CJ's comments in *Bartholomew* v. *Markwick* (1864) 15 C.B. N.S. 711 at 716.

[73] *Planché* v. *Colburn* (1831) 8 Bing. 14 at 16. See also *Phillips* v. *Jones* (1834) 1 Ad. & El. 333. Although in this case, Tindal CJ laid stress on the fact that the plaintiff could recover on the *quantum meruit* count, as opposed to the count for work and labour, the pleading reforms of 1831 rendered this

breach had become clearer, Alderson B. noted that '[w]here one party has abso-lutely refused to perform, or has rendered himself incapable of performing, his part of the contract, he puts it in the power of the other party either to sue for a breach of it, or to rescind the contract and sue on a *quantum meruit* for the work actually done'.[74]

Quantum meruit claims were also brought on implied contracts to pay a rea-sonable remuneration in cases where real contracts failed, for not complying with the Statute of Frauds. If such contracts had been fully executed, Tindal CJ said in *Souch v. Strawbridge*, the plaintiff could sue in *indebitatus assumpsit* for the con-tractual sum, since the statute had no application to actions founded on an exe-cuted consideration.[75] Moreover, it was suggested in *Mavor* v. *Pyne*, that if such a contract had not been fully executed, the plaintiff could nevertheless recover for the work which had been done, according to the agreed rate.[76] Subsequent courts indicated that in such situations, plaintiffs could recover on an implied contract for goods sold or work done, recovering not the contractual price, but such a sum as the goods or work were reasonably worth.[77] This overlooked the fact that, although it was unenforceable, the special contract still existed;[78] and seemed to ignore the principle that a *quantum meruit* claim could not be brought so long as the plaintiff had outstanding obligations on an existing contract. The problem was largely theoretical, since plaintiffs could simply sue for the debt where the contract was fully executed, or sue for a *quantum meruit* on a contract which had been terminated, as where an employee had been dismissed. Only if the contract remained open would a remedy be denied. Twentieth-century jurists sought to overcome this dilemma by holding that the *quantum meruit* claim was

---

distinction unimportant. On *Planché*, see C. Mitchell and C. Mitchell, '*Planché v. Colburn* (1831)', in C. Mitchell and P. Mitchell (eds), *Landmark Cases in the Law of Restitution* (Oxford, 2006), 65–95. See also the contrasting doctrine interpretations of the case in A. Kull, 'Restitution as Remedy for Breach of Contract' (1993–4) 67 *Southern California LR* 1456–1518 at 1487–8; T. A. Baloch, *Unjust Enrichment and Contract* (Oxford, 2009), 137–9.

[74] *De Bernardy* v. *Harding* (1853) 8 Exch. 822 at 824. The plaintiff seeking to sue under an *indebita-tus* count had to terminate the contract first: *Goodman* v. *Pocock* (1850) 15 Q.B. 576.

[75] *Souch v. Strawbridge* (1846) 2 C.B. 808 at 814. This was because the action was brought on a debt arising out of the contract: see Ibbetson, 'History', 319–20 and Bramwell B.'s comments in *Sanderson* v. *Graves* (1875) LR 10 Ex 234 at 238.

[76] *Mavor* v. *Pyne* (1825) 3 Bing. 285, *The Times*, 10 November 1825, col. 3d. In this case, where the assignees of a bankrupt writer were seeking to recover payments from his brother for eight volumes of a series of 24 he had received, the judges were clearly going out of their way not to take a decision which would affect such publications. While holding that the statute was irrelevant, Best CJ also seemed to feel the defendant had put an end to the contract, while Burrough J. felt it could not be taken for granted that the case fell within the statute.

[77] *Teal* v. *Auty* (1820) 2 B. & B. 99 at 100; *Earl of Falmouth* v. *Thomas* (1832) 1 Car. & M. 89 at 109.

[78] See the recognition of this point in *Britain* v. *Rossiter* (1879) 11 QBD 123.

a restitutionary one, rather than a contractual one.[79] But in the nineteenth century, while some judges did speak of *quantum meruit* claims as deriving from an
obligation imposed by law rather than deriving from any form of consent,[80] most
continued to regard it as based on a contract implied from the circumstances,[81]
particularly given that after 1831 such claims were brought under the *indebitatus*
counts.

In awarding damages for breach of contract, there was a general premise that
a party whose contract had been breached was entitled to be placed in the position he would have been in had the contract been performed. Juries were guided
by judges on how to measure this. In some areas, debate was generated among
judges and jurists over what the law required. For instance, there was some disagreement in the early nineteenth century over whether buyers suing for breach
of warranty should recover the difference between the price paid for the goods,
and their real value, or the difference between their value with and without the
warranty.[82] By the mid-century, the latter view—which benefited the purchaser
would had bought cheaply—prevailed. But it was a problem settled by juristic
discussion, and not simply left to the discretion of the jury.

Where goods had not been accepted, the seller was expected to mitigate his
loss by taking them to market. It was settled in the eighteenth century that a
seller, who had managed to dispose of his goods, could not sue the original
buyer for the full price, but only for his losses.[83] The opportunity to mitigate was
soon regarded as a duty, for it was settled by the early nineteenth century that
damages were to be measured by the market. As Lord Tenterden put it in a case
where a buyer refused to accept oil, the seller was to be awarded 'the difference
between the price which the defendant contracted to pay, and that which might
have been obtained for the oil on the days when the contract ought to have been
completed'.[84] Equally, where a seller refused to deliver, the buyer was expected

---

[79] *James* v. *Thomas H. Kent Co* [1951] 1 KB 551 at 556. In fact, in the rare cases (like this one) regarding employment which came to court, the contract had been terminated. Nothing stood in the way
of a *quantum meruit* claim, with the damages being assessed according to what would have been due
under the contract. See *Scott* v. *Pattison* [1923] 2 KB 723.

[80] *Clay* v. *Yates* (1856) 1 H. & N. 73 at 80. See also *Prickett* v. *Badger* (1856) 1 C.B. N.S. 296, where
the Common Pleas held that it was for the court, rather than a jury, to say whether a contract was
to be implied.

[81] *Read* v. *Rann* (1830) 10 B. & C. 438 at 441 (per Parke J.); *De Bernardy* v. *Harding* (1853) 8 Exch.
822 at 824.

[82] See *Towers* v. *Barrett* (1786) 1 T.R. 133 at 136; *Curtis* v. *Hannay* (1800) 3 Esp. 82 at 83; *Caswell* v.
Coare (1809) 1 Taunt. 566; *Clare* v. *Maynard* (1837) 7 C. & P. 741 at 743, 6 Ad. & El. 519; *Loder* v. *Kekule*
(1857) 3 C.B. N.S. 128. See also Sedgwick, *Damages* (2nd edn, 1852), 287ff; Addison, *Contracts* (4th
edn, 1856), 1147–8.

[83] *Smee* v. *Huddlestone* (1768) in J. Sayer, *The Law of Damages* (1770), 49.

[84] *Boorman* v. *Nash* (1829) 9 B. & C. 145 at 152. See also *Brown* v. *Muller* (1872) LR 7 Ex 319.

immediately to seek an alternative supplier in the market. Since a buyer who had not paid for the goods had money to go to market, if he suffered additional loss by not going to market on the day of delivery, then the increased loss was his own fault.[85] This rule, developed in the context of commodities, was applied in the mid-century to contracts for the sale of shares.[86] The rule was codified in section 51 of the 1893 Sale of Goods Act which enacted that, where there was an available market, the damages were *prima facie* to be the difference between the contract price and the time when the goods were to have been delivered; or if no time was fixed, when the seller refused to deliver.

Things were more complicated if, having paid in advance, the buyer did not have the money to go to market. The problem was familiar to jurists from cases involving loans of stock, one of the early nineteenth-century means of evading the restrictions of the usury laws.[87] Under these agreements, a lender would transfer stock to a borrower, which he could sell to raise money; and the borrower would contract to replace the stock (with dividends and interest) at a specified period.[88] Such agreements raised the question as to the measure of damages if the borrower failed to replace the stock on the due day. Since the borrower effectively had the lender's money, the latter was unable to go to market and buy new stock. Because of this, the courts took the view that damages were not to be assessed by the value of the stock on the day of breach. Since the lender only obtained the money to buy the replacement stock after the trial, damages could be assessed according to the price on the day of the trial, if the price of stock had risen since the time of the breach.[89] However, if the value of stock had fallen, the lender was permitted to recover its value on the date of breach, effectively making a gain.[90] The plaintiff was thus allowed to choose either the value on the day of the trial, or that at the time of breach. But he was not allowed to choose the highest price it had reached in between, since that was to assume he would have sold out then.[91]

---

[85] *Gainsford* v. *Carroll* (1824) 2 B. & C. 624 at 625. See also *Leigh* v. *Paterson* (1818) 8 Taunt. 540, holding that the buyer was not required to go to market to purchase the goods until the time he had contracted to receive them. See also *Barrow* v. *Arnaud* (1846) 8 Q.B. 605 at 609 and *Josling* v. *Irvine* (1861) 6 H. & N. 512.

[86] *Shaw* v. *Holland* (1846) 15 M. & W. 136.

[87] *Tate* v. *Wellings* (1790) 3 T.R. 531.

[88] There were variations of this kind of agreement: for instance, the lender might sell his stock to raise the loan, rather than transferring it; and the borrower might agree to pay interest and dividends either at the end or during the period of the loan.

[89] *Shepherd* v. *Johnson* (1802) 2 East 211; *Downes* v. *Back* (1816) 1 Stark. 318; *Owen* v. *Routh* (1854) 14 C.B. 327.

[90] *Sanders* v. *Kentish and Hawksley* (1799) 8 T.R. 162.

[91] *M'Arthur* v. *Lord Seaforth* (1810) 2 Taunt. 257. The lender did recover all additional bonuses which had been granted while the borrower held the stock: *Vaughan* v. *Wood* (1833) 1 Myl. & K. 403.

Mid-century treatise writers debated whether these rules should also apply to the sale of goods, when the buyer had parted with his money. The issue was raised in 1835 in *Startup* v. *Cortazzi*, where the buyers of linseed had paid part of the purchase price to the seller. Before delivery was due, the seller indicated his inability to supply the goods, but he did not return the deposit until after the action was commenced. However, the Exchequer held that the plaintiffs were not entitled to the difference between the contract price and the price on the day of the trial, but only the difference between the contract price and the price on the day when delivery was due, with interest for the detention of the money. Alderson B. accepted that damages could not be measured according to the price on the day when the seller indicated he would not supply the goods, for the buyer did not then have the money to go to market. They were to be measured according to the price on the day they would have been delivered, for the plaintiffs would then have resold them. Not having shown any special damage, they were not entitled to further profits beyond interest on the money which had been kept out of his hands. Lord Abinger agreed that the plaintiffs could not recover for any speculative profits they might have made by holding on to the goods.[92]

The American jurist Theodore Sedgwick approved of this approach.[93] In his view, unless it was shown that both parties knew that the goods were to be delivered for some specific object, the damages should be assessed from the time of the breach, for any other measure would be too speculative. Indeed, he felt the same rule should apply to loans of stock. John D. Mayne, who agreed with the result of *Startup* v. *Cortazzi*, argued that the rule regarding the replacement of stock was too settled to be altered, and felt it could be distinguished. It was to be presumed that stock would remain in the investor's hands down to the time of trial, since stock was bought for investment and not for resale. By contrast, since goods were presumed to be purchased for immediate resale, the moment of breach was the last moment they could be presumed to remain in the plaintiff's hands.[94] But Mayne did not regard the rule as settled; and later judges and jurists regarded it as an open question whether a plaintiff who had parted with his money should get a higher measure of damages.[95]

The general principle that the buyer was to go to market and seek an alternative supply explained the rule that the common law gave no damages for lost

---

[92] *Startup* v. *Cortazzi* (1835) 2 C. M. & R. 165. Sedgwick, *Damages* (2nd edn, 1852), 271 suggested that this case threw doubt on the English rule that 'if the price be paid in advance, the vendee is entitled to the highest value up to the date of the trial', without noting that this rule only applied to loans of stock.

[93] Sedgwick, *Damages* (2nd edn, 1852), 273 *et seq.*

[94] J. D. Mayne, *A Treatise on the Law of Damages* (1856), 87.

[95] See the comments of Lord Atkin in *Aronson* v. *Mologo Holzindustrie* (1927) 28 Ll L Rep 81.

profits on a resale; for the plaintiff was simply expected to go to market to buy in the goods required to fulfil any further contracts.[96] The question of lost profits was sometimes raised in cases involving breaches of warranty, where the buyer of goods had lost an opportunity to resell them at a higher price. The courts were unsympathetic to such claims,[97] regarding potential lost profit as too speculative. However, in the mid-nineteenth century, judges began to show more sympathy for claims for lost profits, and began to look for principles on which lost profits could be recovered. From the mid-century, plaintiffs were permitted to recover the profits which would have been earned by the use of profit-earning goods they had bought, since that was not regarded as a speculative gain.[98] In *Fletcher* v. *Tayleur* in 1855, where a ship had been delivered late, the Common Pleas upheld a jury verdict which awarded damages for the loss suffered by the fact that the ship had been unable to earn freight during a profitable season. But rather than leaving the assessment of lost earnings to the discretion of the jury, Willes J. said that 'these matters should be based upon certain and intelligible principles', and proposed a rule. Just as the measure of damages for non-payment of money was the payment of interest, no matter what inconvenience had been suffered by the plaintiff, so in cases for the non-delivery of a chattel, the measure should 'by analogy' be 'the average profit made by the use of such a chattel'.[99] His mechanical suggestion did not, however, fall on fertile ground.

A second approach to the issue of damages for lost profits was to be found in Sedgwick's treatise. This question had been addressed in New York in 1845 in *Masterton & Smith* v. *City of Brooklyn*, where the plaintiffs contracted to supply marble for the construction of a City Hall, and then entered into a contract with a supplier to obtain the marble. After some marble was delivered, the defendants refused to receive any more, and the plaintiffs successfully sued for the profit they would have made on the resale to the defendants of the undelivered marble, at a higher price than that which they paid for it.[100] The New York court rejected the contention that such damages would be too contingent and speculative. Citing Pothier and Domat, Nelson CJ distinguished between uncertain and contingent profits, such as arose from 'dependent and collateral engagements entered into on the faith of and in expectation of the performance of the principal contract', and those which were the direct and immediate fruits of the contract. For Nelson, the principle that one could get damages for the profit one should have made from

[96] *Peterson* v. *Ayre* (1853) 13 C.B. 353 at 365.
[97] See e.g. *Clare* v. *Maynard* (1837) 6 Ad. & El. 519 at 524.
[98] *In re Trent & Humber Co* (1868) LR 6 Eq 21; *Wilson* v. *General Iron Screw Co* (1878) 47 LJ QB 23.
[99] *Fletcher* v. *Tayleur* (1855) 17 C.B. 21 at 29. Jervis CJ suggested (at 27) awarding in such cases the 'average percentage of mercantile profits'.
[100] *Masterton & Smith* v. *City of Brooklyn* (1845) 7 Hill (NY) 61 (42 Am. Dec. 38).

the contract explained the rule that the buyer of goods was to have his damages measured by the market price on the day of delivery. Sedgwick felt that the analysis in this case laid down a clear distinction between those profits which were speculative and those which were not.[101] Central to the distinction was Pothier's notion that

the parties are deemed to have contemplated only the damages and interest which the creditor might suffer from the nonperformance of the obligation, in respect to the particular thing which is the object of it, and not such as may have been incidentally occasioned thereby in respect to his other affairs.[102]

A third approach was endorsed by Lord Cottenham LC. In 1848, in *Dunlop* v. *Higgins*, the House of Lords applied Scots law in holding the purchasers of goods entitled not merely to the difference between the contract and market price on the day of breach, but for all profits to be made on their resale. In so holding, Lord Cottenham LC observed that this rule was better calculated to do justice than English law.[103] Cottenham's dictum was much discussed. But it was the line taken by Sedgwick, derived from Pothier, which attracted most support. Critical of Cottenham's position, Mayne therefore wrote:

The question is not, what profit the plaintiff might have made, but what profit he professed to be purchasing. Not what damage he actually suffered, but what the other contemplated and undertook to pay for.[104]

Loss of profit on a resale was wholly contingent, and incapable of valuation. Mayne's criticism was echoed by subsequent courts, which took the view that a loss of profit on resale could not be the 'natural consequence' of a breach of contract and thus could not be recovered (unless special notice had been given).[105]

Lost profits were however awarded where there was no alternative market in which the goods could be bought and sold. In such cases, damages were calculated according to the price at which the purchaser had contracted to resell them, rather than according to the price at which he had agreed to buy them. Although this effectively secured the anticipated profits on a resale,[106] it was seen as an

---

[101] Sedgwick, *Damages* (2nd edn, 1852), 73.

[102] R. J. Pothier, *A Treatise on the Law of Obligations or Contracts*, 2 vols (trans. W. D. Evans, 1806), i, 91.

[103] *Dunlop* v. *Higgins* (1848) 1 H.L.C. 381 at 402–3. Cottenham did not mention the cases he had in mind: counsel, however, cited *Gainsford* v. *Carroll* (1824) 2 B. & C. 624 and *Shaw* v. *Holland* (1846) 15 M. & W. 136, which both confirmed that the plaintiff could only recover the value of goods at the time of breach and not according to subsequent prices.

[104] Mayne, *Damages* (1856), 18.

[105] *Wilson* v. *Lancashire and Yorkshire Railway Co* (1861) 9 C.B. N.S. 632; *Williams* v. *Reynolds* (1865) 6 B. & S. 495.

[106] *Bridge* v. *Wain* (1816) 1 Stark. 504 at 506.

application of the rule that expectation damages were to be awarded. Thus, in 1865, in *Borries* v. *Hutchinson*, where the plaintiffs had contracted to buy caustic soda from the defendants, for export to Russia (where it was not readily available), they were able to recover damages on the basis of the price at which they had contracted to sell it on to a Russian buyer. However, the defendants were not liable for the lost profit suffered by that buyer, arising from his inability to perform a contract to sell the goods on, even though the plaintiff had compensated him for this loss.[107] Not all lawyers were happy with this approach. Some tried to argue that where there was no available market, and goods were to be manufactured for the purchaser, only nominal damages could be awarded. This was because there would be no way to estimate the difference in value, and if the cost of the raw materials from which the goods were to be made had not risen, the plaintiff could claim no damages. But the Queen's Bench gave short shrift to such views. In *Elbinger Actien-Gesellschaft* v. *Armstrong*, Blackburn J. drew on Willes J.'s view that in such cases the court had to establish what the goods would have been worth to the plaintiff at the time they were due to be delivered.[108] One year later, in 1875, he reiterated the view in *Hinde* v. *Liddell*, which held that the buyer should in such cases seek the best available substitute in the market.[109]

There was an exception to the general principle that where a party sustained loss by virtue of a breach of contract, 'he is, so far as money can do it, to be placed in the same situation, with respect to damages, as if the contract had been performed'.[110] According to the 1776 decision of *Flureau* v. *Thornhill*, the buyer of land, who was disappointed when the vendor failed to make out his title, was to receive only the costs he had incurred in making the agreement, but no damages for the loss of the bargain.[111] This was because the sale was regarded as conditional on the vendor having a good title, there being always some uncertainty as to whether an effective title could be made to the property.[112] The rule of *Flureau* was sometimes seen as reflecting the rule that damages were not to be given for lost profits.[113] Where a purchaser had contracted for the purchase of property,

---

[107] The court considered the issue through the lenses of the rule in *Hadley* v. *Baxendale*, discussed below. *Borries* v. *Hutchinson* (1865) 18 C.B. N.S. 445 at 464: 'it is not to be assumed that the parties contemplated that he was to be held responsible for the failure of any number of sub-sales'.

[108] *Elbinger Actien-Gesellschaft* v. *Armstrong* (1874) LR 9 QB 473, 476–7, drawing on *Borries* v. *Hutchinson* (1865) 18 C.B. N.S. 445 at 465. He also cited *Bridge* v. *Wain* (1816) 1 Stark. 504.

[109] *Hinde* v. *Liddell* (1875) LR 10 QB 265.

[110] *Robinson* v. *Harman* (1848) 1 Exch. 850 at 855. Cf. *Alder* v. *Keighley* (1846) 15 M. & W. 117 at 120.

[111] *Flureau* v. *Thornhill* (1776) 2 W. Bl. 1078. See also above, pp. 98–100.

[112] *Bain* v. *Fothergill* (1874) LR 7 HL 158 at 210–11. Cf. the remarks of Littledale J. in *Walker* v. *Moore* (1829) 10 B. & C. 416 at 422.

[113] Subsequent commentators pointed to this fact, e.g. *Bain* v. *Fothergill* (1874) LR 7 HL 158 at 202; Sedgwick, *Damages* (2nd edn, 1852), 69. Counsel in *Clare* v. *Maynard* (1837) 6 Ad .& El. 519 at 521

and had entered into further contracts to resell the property at a higher price, he could hence only recover the expenses attending the initial purchase, but nothing for the loss of his subsequent bargain. As Bayley J. ruled in 1829, 'if premises for which a party has contracted are by him offered for resale too soon, that is at his own peril, and the damage, if any, resulting from such offer, arises from his own premature act, and not from the fault of his vendor'.[114]

The rule being an exception to the general common law, judges sought to qualify it. In 1826, in *Hopkins* v. *Glazebrook*, expectation damages were awarded where a party contracted for the sale of property to which he had yet to acquire title.[115] Such cases were distinguishable on the ground that the vendor's positive assertion of his title took away the implied condition mentioned in *Flureau* v. *Thornhill*.[116] Any assertion of title could be taken to restore the general rule, and allow the plaintiff to recover the market value of the property.[117] At the same time, some plaintiffs sought to evade the common law's refusal to give damages, by attempting to use Sir Hugh Cairns's Act, which allowed equity to award damages in lieu of specific performance.[118] Nonetheless, the rule in *Flureau* was too firmly established to be dislodged, and in 1874 it was reaffirmed by the House of Lords in *Bain* v. *Fothergill*, which overruled *Hopkins* v. *Glazebrook*.[119] Lord Chelmsford ruled that where a party entered into a contract for the sale of real estate, knowing he had no title and had no means of acquiring one, the purchaser could only recover his expenses. Any further damages he sought would have to be recovered in an action of deceit.[120] Any exception to *Flureau* had to be rooted in fraud, not contract, and had to be sued for accordingly. Such an action would of course allow the vendor to bring evidence that the purchaser had been aware of the defect of title.[121] The House of Lords overruled *Hopkins* in part because, the vendor there having an equitable title, they considered the contract to have been made *bona fide*. However, the rule in *Bain* was not unqualified: it did not apply, for instance, where a vendor, who knew he had title, refused to proceed.[122]

referred to the case as suggesting that in an action for breach of warranty, there could be no recovery for loss of bargain.

[114] *Walker* v. *Moore* (1829) 10 B. & C. 416 at 421.

[115] *Hopkins* v. *Grazebrook* (1826) 6 B. & C. 31.

[116] This was the interpretation of Cockburn CJ in *Engel* v. *Fitch* (1867) LR 3 QB 314 at 329.

[117] See also *Lock* v. *Furze* (1866) LR 1 CP 441, holding that the exception did not apply where a lease with a covenant for quiet enjoyment had been granted.

[118] However, equity judges refused to allow plaintiffs who knew they could not obtain specific performance to get damages: *Howe* v. *Hunt* (1862) 31 Beav. 420; *Rogers* v. *Challis* (1859) 27 Beav. 175.

[119] *Hopkins* was followed by the court in *Robinson* v. *Harman* (1848) 1 Exch. 850.

[120] *Bain* v. *Fothergill* (1874) LR 7 HL 158 at 207.

[121] See Blackburn J.'s comments in *Gray* v. *Fowler* (1873) LR 8 Ex 249 at 282. In *Robinson* v. *Harman* (1848) 1 Exch. 850, the defendant had not been allowed to give such evidence.

[122] As in cases such as *Engel* v. *Fitch* (1867) LR 3 QB 314. See also *Day* v. *Singleton* [1899] 2 Ch 320.

3. REMOTENESS OF DAMAGE

If damages were to put a party in the position he would have been in had the contract been performed, did this mean that a person who had been given faulty goods or received faulty services should be compensated for all losses which followed the breach?[123] In answering this question, early nineteenth-century jurists looked at the matter through the lens of causation. Joseph Chitty declared that in assessing damages for non-performance of contractual obligations, 'the jury may take into their consideration any consequential injury the plaintiff has sustained; if such injury be the fair and natural result of the defendant's violation of his agreement'.[124] Judges looked at whether the loss had been caused by the beach. Thus, purchasers of warranted goods, who had sold them on with a warranty, were permitted to recover from the original vendor the costs of lawsuits brought against them by disappointed vendees,[125] where such costs were seen as 'sufficiently consequential upon the breach of the defendants' warranty'.[126] By contrast, where the purchaser might have discovered the faults on reasonable inspection, he was unable to recover the costs of suit brought against him by his vendee, for it was his failure to inspect which caused the loss.[127]

As late as 1853, the court of Exchequer allowed damages to be awarded for money lost, when a defendant had failed to complete work on the plaintiffs' bobbin mill, rendering them unable to fulfil a contract made with a third party.[128] But in 1854, in *Hadley* v. *Baxendale*, a different approach was taken by the court. In this case, the owners of a flour mill in Gloucester sent a broken crankshaft for repair in Greenwich. The shaft was to be transported by Pickford's, who contracted to deliver it to be repaired within two days. However, the carriers took a week to deliver the shaft, and the owners subsequently claimed £300 damages for lost profits, for the five days when the mill had been unable to function. At the trial, Crompton J. instructed the jury in terms which invited them to look at causation. 'They should', he said, 'give their damages for the natural consequences of the defendant's breach of contract', and would thus have to consider whether

---

[123] Seventeenth-century authority suggested that he could: *Nurse* v. *Barns* (1663) T. Raym. 77, cited in Sayer, *Damages* (1770), 52. See also the case alluded to by Willes J. in *British Columbia Sawmills* v. *Nettleship* (1868) LR 3 CP 499 at 508.

[124] Chitty, *Contracts* (2nd edn,1834), 683. He cited tort authorities in support of this, including *Vicars* v. *Wilcocks* (1806) 8 East 1. He also cited *Flower* v. *Adam* (1810) 2 Taunt. 314 and *Newman* v. *Zachary* (1646) Aleyn 3.

[125] *Lewis* v. *Peake* (1816) 7 Taunt. 153; *Mainwaring* v. *Brandon* (1818) 8 Taunt. 202.

[126] *Pennell* v. *Woodburn* (1835) 7 Car. & P. 117 at 118 (per Tindal CJ). See also the language of causation in *Short* v. *Kalloway* (1839) 11 Ad. & El. 28.

[127] *Wrightup* v. *Chamberlain* (1839) 7 Scott 598; *Walker* v. *Hatton* (1842) 10 M. & W. 249.

[128] *Waters* v. *Towers* (1853) 8 Exch. 401. In so doing, the court rejected Hugh Hill's argument that the plaintiff's loss 'was not a necessary consequence' of the breach.

the stoppage of the mill 'was one of the probable and natural consequences' of the breach.[129] The jury found a verdict for £50—double the amount paid into court— and the defendant sought to have a new trial, on the ground of misdirection by the judge. The Exchequer judges ordered a new trial, with Alderson B. laying down a new rule:

Where two parties have made a contract which one of them has broken, the damages which the other party ought to receive in respect of such breach of contract should be such as may fairly and reasonably be considered either arising naturally, i.e. according to the usual course of things, from such breach of contract itself, or such as may reasonably be supposed to have been in the contemplation of both parties, at the time they made the contract, as the probable result of the breach of it.[130]

Where there were unusual circumstances which would increase the loss to one party in case of breach, they had to have been communicated to the other party in order to make him liable for the loss. The judges took three weeks to consider their judgment after legal argument was given, for they were clearly keen to lay down a new rule.[131]

The rule which was laid down was clearly influenced by civilian writings.[132] Both judges and counsel drew heavily on Sedgwick's recent treatise on damages. He discussed a rule, found in Pothier,[133] and in the French Civil Code,[134] according to which defendants in contract cases were 'liable for those damages only which both parties may be fairly supposed to have contemplated at the time they entered into the agreement, as likely to result from it'.[135] Sedgwick's text was clearly influential on the court,[136] as well as on subsequent English writers.[137] The

[129] Quoted in R. Danzig, 'Hadley v. Baxendale: A Study in the Industrialization of the Law' (1975) 4 *JLS* 249–284 at 252.

[130] *Hadley v. Baxendale* (1854) 9 Exch. 341 at 354.

[131] Pollock later pointed out that Parke and Alderson had supplied them with extensive knowledge of the case law, and Martin had given them his business knowledge: *Wilson v. Newport Dock Co* (1866) LR 1 Ex at 189.

[132] See A. W. B. Simpson, 'Innovation in Nineteenth Century Contract Law' (1975) 91 *LQR* 246–78 at 275–6. J. Chitty had written in 1820 that the rule was that 'only such damages are recoverable as are naturally incidental to the non-performance, or at least were pointed out to the contracting party at the time the contract was made as the certain result of his breach': *Treatise on the Law of Commerce and Manufactures*, 4 vols (1820), iii, 628. Chitty's references were to English cases (which did not fully bear out the proposition), but he made no mention of civilian sources. It is unclear whether this work would have influenced the judges here.

[133] Pothier, *Obligations* (trans. Evans), i: 91. See J. M. Perillo, 'Robert J. Pothier's Influence on the Common Law of Contract' (2004–5) 11 *Texas Wesleyan LR* 267–90 at 272.

[134] Code Civil, art. 1150. [135] Sedgwick, *Damages* (2nd edn, 1852), 58.

[136] When Willes, one of the counsel for Pickford's, produced the 4th edition of J. W. Smith's *A Selection of Leading Cases on Various Branches of the Law* in 1856, he cited Sedgwick's discussion, and observed that it agreed with the judgment in *Hadley v. Baxendale*: *Leading Cases*, ii, 431.

[137] Addison, *Contracts* (4th edn, 1856), 1140–1 talked of the change in the law brought about by the case, and cited Pothier and Toullier, quotations from both of which he took from Sedgwick.

influence of civilian ideas on the judgment was pointed out by Lord Campbell in 1859, when noting that it agreed with the view of law set out by Pothier, the French Code and Chancellor Kent's Commentaries.[138]

The fact that the judges should have chosen to implement a rule derived from Pothier in *Hadley* v. *Baxendale* can best be understood by considering the nature of the case. Mid-century judges were generally content, in cases involving losses consequential on breach of contract, as in tort, to leave the damages simply to the good sense of a jury. As Pollock CB observed in 1866, cases of damage differed as much as the leaves of different trees. Juries, who were apt to 'come to some compromise among themselves', generally produced results 'more just and equitable than any mere rule of law could arrive at'.[139] But if trusting to the jury was felt appropriate for general torts, it was not an approach which appealed to carriers, who had long sought to limit their general liability for lost or delayed items by contractual terms, and who had received legislative sanction for this practice in the Carriers Act of 1830. Carriers would only accept liability for losing expensive goods if the sender gave notice of their value and paid a higher fee. However, if the law relating to lost goods was clear enough, things were less clear when financial losses were caused by delayed delivery, for carriers did not explicitly exclude liability for such losses.

This issue had been raised before. In 1847, the Exchequer had heard a case involving Pickford's—*Black* v. *Baxendale*—where the jury awarded damages for losses arising from the late delivery of goods sent to market. As counsel for the carrier, Samuel Martin argued that they were not responsible for the loss, since they had not been given notice of the purpose for which the goods were sent. The argument cut some ice with Pollock CB, who passed a comment which anticipated the holding in *Hadley* v. *Baxendale*.[140] But the court felt it was entirely for the jury to decide what were the 'reasonable consequences' of the breach. In *Hadley*, Pickford's counsel sought to counter such an approach, by arguing that the company should not be held liable for risks which had not been paid for.[141] While they admitted that the firm's clerk had been told that the mill was

---

[138] *Smeed* v. *Foord* (1859) 1 E. & E. 602 at 613. The Exchequer judges had also been exposed to Kent's similar definition in *Waters* v. *Towers* (1853) 8 Exch. 401 at 403 (J. Kent, *Commentaries on American Law*, 4 vols, 5th edn, New York, 1844), ii, 480n. Kent's note referred the reader to C. B. M. Toullier, *Le Droit Civil Français suivant l'Ordre du Code*, 13 vols (4th edn, Paris, 1824–28), vi (*Des Contrats et Obligations Conventionelles*), 294–9 (§ 286). Toullier's discussion of liability for only the immediate consequences of breach, however, focused more on the fault of the party in breach, than the question of what they had contemplated.

[139] *Wilson* v. *Newport Dock Co* (1866) LR 1 Ex 177 at 190.

[140] 'If the carriers had had distinct notice that the goods would be required to be delivered at a particular time, perhaps they would have been liable for those expenses, for which, without notice, they would not otherwise be liable': *Black* v. *Baxendale* (1847) 1 Exch. 410 at 412.

[141] Danzig, 'Hadley', 264.

stopped and that the shaft had to be sent immediately, they argued that since the clerk's duty was merely to enter the article and take the payment, 'a mere notice to him [...] could not make the defendants, as carriers, liable as upon a special contract'.[142] Counsel devoted more time to discussing whether the loss was foreseeable, arguing that contracting parties could only assume such risks as they were acquainted with, and could not be liable for losses 'beyond all human foresight'.[143] They also argued that the lost profits could not be seen as 'natural result' of the breach of contract, citing *Flureau* v. *Thornhill* as a case establishing that lost profits were not recoverable.

Giving the judgment of the court, Alderson B. accepted that where special circumstances arose which might increase the damages, parties should be allowed to make provisions 'for the breach of contract by special terms as to the damages'. But he held that in this case, no notice had been given to Pickford's of the consequential loss.[144] Although an incorrect statement of the facts, this may have reflected the court's acceptance of Pickford's argument that notice to the clerk had no contractual significance; and it permitted the court to focus squarely on the issue of foreseeability of loss. In addressing this, in a case concerning the liability of a carrier, which lay on the borders of contract and tort, the court would also have been mindful of its recent discussions about the remoteness of damages in tort cases, where the question of foreseeability was raised. In 1850, Pollock CB had expressed his view that defendants in negligence should only be liable for consequences which could reasonably be expected to result from the negligent act, rather than every possible consequence.[145] Applied to contractual situations, this approach meant a defendant would only be liable for what would reasonably be within his contemplation as the amount of injury which would arise in case of breach. Pollock's thinking was in part influenced by his attempts to rethink the rules of causation in general,[146] and Alderson's language may in turn have been influenced by this.

The courts spent some time in the aftermath of *Hadley* figuring out the ambit of the rule, and numerous judges sought to qualify it. In 1859, in *Smeed* v. *Foord*, where late delivery of a threshing machine led to wheat becoming water-damaged

---

[142] *Hadley* v. *Baxendale* (1854) 9 Exch. 341 at 352.

[143] The slander case of *Kelly* v. *Partington* (1833) 5 B & Ad 645 was cited, along with Bacon's maxim, *in jure non remota causa sed proxima spectatur*.

[144] *Hadley* v. *Baxendale* (1854) 9 Exch. 341 at 355.

[145] *Rigby* v. *Hewitt* (1850) 5 Exch. 240 at 243; *Greenland* v. *Chaplin* (1850) 5 Exch. 243 at 248. See below, p. 935.

[146] In *Wilson* v. *Newport Dock Co* (1866) LR 1 Ex 177 at 189, he observed that the decision was not a 'new discovery in jurisprudence' but put in clearer light a principle recognized in prior cases, which could be found collected in the notes to the case of *Vicars* v. *Willcocks* in the 4th (1856) edition of Smith's *Leading Cases*, ii, 423 *et seq.*

in the field, and consequently being sent late to a falling market, the Queen's Bench awarded damages for the cost of stacking and drying the wheat and for the depreciation in its value; but refused to allow damages to cover the fall in the market price during the period of delay. In his judgment, Crompton J. considered that the 'doctrine of *Hadley* v. *Baxendale*'—by which he appeared to mean the requirement of notice of potential damages—was appropriate for carriers, where only one party knew the purpose for which goods were sent, but should not be extended to other cases. Since the supplier knew the purpose of the threshing machine, damages which were 'reasonably contemplated' were simply those which were 'naturally arising', and all the judge need ask the jury was whether the damages were the natural consequences of the breach.[147] Lord Campbell, who regarded the rule in *Hadley* as equivalent to imposing liability for 'natural' consequences, felt that the fall in market price could simply not be the 'natural result of the defendant's breach of contract'. When, two years later, the Exchequer held that a Kentish hop-grower could recover the loss he suffered from late delivery of his goods by a carrier to a falling market, it was because, unlike *Smeed*, the loss was 'a direct, immediate and necessary consequence of the defendant's breach of duty'; and the carrier 'must have known' the purpose for which they were sent.[148]

Scepticism about *Hadley* persisted. In 1860, Wilde B. observed that the rule could not be applied to all cases, and wondered whether it was possible to formulate any rule as to the measure of damages.[149] Fortified by these comments, the Irish Court of Exchequer held it sufficient for a jury to be asked to consider whether the damages claimed were the natural consequence of the breach of contract.[150] This was to reiterate the view that the court should look at questions of the causation of the loss, and not at what risks had been bargained for.[151] Martin B., himself one of the judges in *Hadley* and a former counsel for Pickford's, shared in the scepticism. He expressed his doubts regarding the rule in 1866, in a dissenting judgment in *Wilson* v. *Newport Dock Company*. Admitting that a rule limiting damages to what was within the parties' reasonable contemplation might be

---

[147] *Smeed* v. *Foord* (1859) 1 El. & El. 602 at 616.

[148] *Collard* v. *South Eastern Railway* (1861) 7 H. & N. 79 at 86, per Martin B.

[149] *Gee* v. *Lancashire and Yorkshire Railway Co* (1860) 6 H. & N. 211 at 221.

[150] *Boyd* v. *Fitt* (1862) 14 Ir CLR 43. In this case, the court upheld a verdict which awarded damages to a Dublin trader for loss of agency business for an Australian firm, which resulted from the bad reputation he acquired after his Glasgow agent (the defendant) had failed to honour a cash order. The Glasgow agent was unaware of the Australian business.

[151] Pigot CB's judgment was also influenced by *Rolin* v. *Steward* (1854) 14 C.B. 595, where (in a case against a bank for dishonouring a cheque), Williams J. held that the jury could take into consideration the natural and necessary consequences of the breach, in the same way as they would in slander cases.

appropriate for carrier cases, he argued that it had no application in the bulk of contracts. Since parties contemplated contractual performance, rather than breach, they did not take into account possible losses.[152] He was equally unhappy with the notion that courts should award damages which 'naturally' followed 'according to the usual course of things', since in many cases of loss, there was no usual course. For Martin, the question was to be decided by looking at causation as a tort lawyer would:[153] '[t]he rule is that the damage must be proximate (not immediate), and fairly and reasonably connected with the breach of contract or wrong'.[154]

Martin's view did not gain acceptance. However, even those judges who endorsed the rule in *Hadley* remained unclear whether the risk had to be bargained for, or whether it was sufficient merely for notice to be given. This question was raised in another carrier case. In *Gee* v. *Lancashire and Yorkshire Railway Company*, the plaintiffs' new cotton mill remained closed for several days, because of the defendants' delay in transporting raw cotton from Liverpool. The company had not been informed, when the cotton was dispatched, that the mill had no cotton on site, but they were informed of this on the day when it was due to arrive. The county court judge hearing the case told the jury to award damages for losses 'naturally and immediately' arising from the stoppage, and £15—representing the wages and lost profits during the time the mill was idle—was awarded. But the Exchequer ordered a new trial. Following *Hadley*, Pollock CB held that the carrier was not responsible for consequential losses, unless a distinct notice had been given when the goods were sent, for then it could have charged a higher rate. But Bramwell B. wondered whether 'in the course of the performance of the contract one party may give notice to the other of any particular consequences which will result' from a breach, and recover those losses in case of breach.[155] Bramwell—not a judge when *Hadley* was decided—was able to fly this kite, since the judgment in the earlier case had not made it explicitly clear that the risks to be paid for were those bargained for. The judgment seemed to leave it open to argue, on analogy with the tort measure which Pollock CB himself was attempting to establish, that the defendant should be liable for any losses he could foresee, prior to breach. By such a view, the breach of contract could be regarded as a wrong, the foreseeable consequences of which had to be paid for.

---

[152] *Wilson* v. *Newport Dock Co* (1866) LR 1 Ex 177 at 185.

[153] He thus felt the case should be determined by applying the test used by Lord Ellenborough in *Jones* v. *Boyce* (1816) 1 Stark. 493.

[154] *Wilson* v. *Newport Dock Co* (1866) LR 1 Ex 177 at 186. Martin restated his views in *Prehn* v. *Royal Bank of Liverpool* (1870) LR 5 Ex 92 at 100.

[155] *Gee* v. *Lancashire and Yorkshire Railway Co* (1860) 6 H. & N. 211 at 218.

The point that mere notice of a potential loss was not sufficient to attract contractual liability was made by J. S. Willes—one of the counsel in *Hadley*—in notes to *Smith's Leading Cases* written in 1856. In *Hadley*, he wrote:

it was not perhaps intended to lay down that the amount of damages should depend on the MERE knowledge or ignorance of the defendant of the surrounding circumstances, apart from contract express or implied to be liable for the extraordinary amount of damages to which those circumstances might arise.[156]

Willes reiterated the point judicially in 1868. 'Bare knowledge will not do', he ruled in *British Columbia Sawmills* v. *Nettleship*, 'it must be a knowledge which forms the basis of the contract'.[157] This did not mean that only losses which were explicitly bargained for were recoverable, for those consequences which could be reasonably expected were implied into the contract. In the same year, the Queen's Bench rejected an attempt by counsel to argue on the basis of *Hadley* that where two contracting parties had different ideas about what the use newly invented goods sold were to be put to, only nominal damages could be awarded for breach. In such cases, according Cockburn CJ, the measure of damages had to be 'the profit which would result from the ordinary use of the article for the purpose for which the seller supposed it was bought'.[158]

Judges continued to debate whether the losses had to be specifically contracted for, or whether notice at the time of contracting would suffice. In carrier cases, the courts looked for a contractual agreement. This is evident from the 1873 decision of *Horne* v. *Midland Railway Company*, where the plaintiffs sought to recover damages for lost profits on an unusually profitable sale of boots to the French army, on a contract which had been lost owing to the failure of the defendant company to deliver them on time. The station master at Kettering had been given notice that the plaintiffs had a contract to sell the boots, and that they would lose it were they to be delivered late. A majority of the Exchequer Chamber held that the company was not liable, since the loss fell within neither branch of *Hadley*. For the majority, mere notice of loss would not do. As Martin B. put it, if notice was sufficient in the case of carriers to impose exceptional liability, then 'they would be laid open to imposition without end'. It was, in his view, dangerous to impose on carriers any liability 'beyond the ordinary and natural consequences of his breach of duty, in the absence of something equivalent to contract'.[159] By contrast, in the 1878 case of *Hydraulic Engineering Company* v. *McHaffie*, the Court of Appeal held a supplier of a part for a machine to be sold to a third party

[156] Smith, *Leading Cases* (4th edn, 1856), ii, 432.
[157] *British Columbia Sawmills* v. *Nettleship* (1868) LR 3 CP 499 at 505.
[158] *Cory* v. *Thames Ironworks Co* (1868) LR 3 QB 181 at 189.
[159] *Horne* v. *Midland Railway Co* (1873) LR 8 CP 131 at 139–40.

liable for the profits to be made on that resale, since they were aware that the part had to be ready for the resale by a fixed date. Bramwell LJ here ruled that the defendant 'does not enter into a kind of second contract to pay damages, but he is liable to make good those injuries which he is aware that his default may occasion to the contractee'. Brett LJ concurred, holding that the party had to be given notice at the time of the contract, but rejecting the idea that they contracted to pay the damages which would result.[160]

The notion that the damages for which the defendant was to be held liable had to be something which had been bargained for recommended itself to numerous jurists,[161] including O. W. Holmes, in whose opinion '[t]he only universal consequence of a legally binding promise is, that the law makes the promisor pay damages if the promised event does not come to pass'.[162] But the matter remained controversial. Holmes's friend Pollock disagreed, telling him in 1905 that while one might make special provision in a contract for liquidated damages, the 'contract-theory' of damages was 'a superfluous fiction'. Pollock restated the idea that a man was 'answerable for such consequences as would appear probable to a reasonable man in his place: and consequences made probable by knowledge of special facts which he happens to possess are probable enough to *him*'.[163] Pollock, who shared his grandfather's view of how tort damages should be measured, clearly felt the damages for breach of contract should be seen in terms of foreseeability, not bargained-for losses. Pollock's view would thus have sought to establish a similar test of remoteness in contract as in tort. Such a view was for some time accepted in twentieth-century England, but was dislodged by the 1960s.[164]

4. SPECIFIC PERFORMANCE

Oliver Wendell Holmes famously wrote that '[t]he only universal consequence of a legally binding promise is, that the law makes the promisor pay damages if the promised event does not come to pass'.[165] A contracting party was free to break any contract, for all he did in contracting was to assume a certain risk. Holmes's critics (like Pollock) pointed to the equitable remedy of specific performance to show that his theory was flawed. Judges and jurists agreed that every contract

---

[160] *Hydraulic Engineering Co* v. *McHaffie* (1878) 4 QBD 670 at 674.

[161] Mayne, *Damages* (1856), 6.

[162] O. W. Holmes, *The Common Law* (Boston, 1881), 301.

[163] M. D. Howe (ed.), *The Pollock-Holmes Letters: Correspondence of Sir Frederick Pollock and Mr Justice Holmes 1874–1932*, 2 vols (Cambridge, 1942), i, 120.

[164] *Victoria Laundry (Windsor)* v. *Newman Industries* [1949] 2 KB 528; *Koufos* v. *C. Czarnikow* [1969] 1 AC 350.

[165] Holmes, *The Common Law*, 301.

generated an obligation of performance.[166] But it was clear that the courts did not habitually enforce performance. The equitable remedy was only available where the common law measure of damages was not seen as adequate. The primacy of the monetary measure of damages was explained in historical terms.[167]

Specific performance was a discretionary remedy. Courts of equity would therefore not enforce contracts which resulted from unfair, unconscionable, or fraudulent dealing. Although inadequacy of consideration alone was not a ground for refusing to award specific performance,[168] disparities in price so great as to shock the conscience might lead the court to refuse its assistance.[169] If the bargain was on the face of it a reasonable one, and consciously entered into, it would be upheld even if it turned out to be valueless to one party.[170] When judges in equity refused specific performance on the ground that it would impose great hardship, it was generally because the terms of the contract generated other risks for the defendant (such as the forfeiture of other property), of which the parties might not have been aware when contracting.[171] But it had to be clear from the contract itself that its effect was such as to impose such a hardship that the parties could not have intended it when making the contract.[172]

Despite these apparently tough rules, some mid-century equity judges were unwilling to give their help to private landowners who had contracted to sell land at high prices to railway companies, when the companies refused to go ahead with the purchase having discovered that they had no use for the land.[173] Leaving these landowners to their legal remedy effectively destroyed their financial ambitions. However, the railway cases were anomalous, and judges hearing them tended to look for other reasons to deny specific performance than merely the hardship of the bargain. The point that equity's discretion had to be governed by rules was restated by Sir John Romilly MR in 1858. He declared that he could not exercise his

---

[166] E. Fry, *A Treatise on the Specific Performance of Contracts* (2nd edn, by E. Fry and W. D. Rawlins, 1881), 2–3.

[167] E. Fry, *Specific Performance* (3rd edn, 1892), 4.

[168] *Coles* v. *Trecothick* (1804) 9 Ves. 234; *Stilwell* v. *Wilkins* (1821) Jac. 280.

[169] *Abbott* v. *Sworder* (1852) 4 De G. & Sm. 448. See also Kinderley VC's approach in *Falcke* v. *Gray* (1859) 4 Drew. 651 at 658. See also *Wedgwood* v. *Adams* (1843) 6 Beav. 600 at 605; *Kimberley* v. *Jennings* (1836) 6 Sim. 340.

[170] *Haywood* v. *Cope* (1858) 25 Beav. 140 at 150–1; *Adams* v. *Weare* (1784) 1 Bro. C.C. 567; *Morley* v. *Clavering* (1860) 29 Beav. 84.

[171] *Faine* v. *Brown* (1751) cited in 2 Ves. Sr. 307.

[172] *Talbot* v. *Ford* (1842) 13 Sim. 173 at 175. Lord Redesdale held in *Harnett* v. *Yielding* (1805) 2 Sch. & Lef. 549 at 554 that the court would not compel a party to do 'an act which he is not lawfully authorized to do' and which would expose him to liability.

[173] See *Webb* v. *Direct London and Portsmouth Railway Co* (1852) 1 De G. M. & G. 521 at 529; *Lord James Stuart* v. *London and North-Western Railway* (1852) 1 De G. M. & G. 721. Contrast *Eastern Counties Railway Co* v. *Hawkes* (1855) 5 H.L.C. 331.

'discretion by merely considering what, as between the parties, would be fair to be done', since 'what one person may consider fair, another person may consider very unfair'. In his view, if a bargain turned out to be bad, while it might be proper for one party 'to make an abatement in respect of it', that was a matter for 'the forum of his own conscience, but not one which I can notice judicially'.[174] Commentators in the second half of the nineteenth century agreed that parties should be left free to contract at whatever prices they chose, and that equity should uphold their agreements. Not only was it difficult to decide what was an inadequate price or a hard bargain, but it was better for property owners to be able to sell at less than the 'real' value of their land, than not to be able to sell at all.[175] Equity had no more paternalistic a vision of contractual remedies than common law.

Land

In an era when common law courts refused to award expectation damages for the sale of real property, specific performance was in practice the only effective remedy. In any event, money was not regarded as a sufficient remedy for a failure to convey land, for (as Edward Fry wrote in 1858), 'one landed estate, though of precisely the same market value as another may be vastly different in every other circumstance that makes it an object of desire'.[176] Although equity normally only granted specific performance where it could decree performance in its entirety, in the case of property sales, if the vendor was unable to make a title to all the property, the purchaser could obtain specific performance of whatever title could be conveyed, subject to compensation for the shortfall in the form of a proportionate reduction in price. Equity distinguished between major and minor breaches in cases involving land sales, denying specific performance only where there was substantial deviation from the contract.[177] The Chancery was more willing to intervene against vendors—who were not to be permitted to take advantage of their own failure to make a perfect title to avoid their obligations[178]—than against purchasers, given the difficulty of establishing what was essential.[179]

---

[174] *Haywood* v. *Cope* (1858) 25 Beav. 140 at 151, 153.

[175] Fry, *Specific Performance* (2nd edn, 1881), 195.

[176] E. Fry, *A Treatise on the Specific Performance of Contracts* (1858), 5.

[177] *Eaton* v. *Lyon* (1798) 3 Ves. 690; *Halsey* v. *Grant* (1806) 13 Ves. 73.

[178] *Wood* v. *Griffith* (1818) 1 Swans. 43 at 54. The purchaser could waive defects, and thereby lose the right to any compensation: *Burnell* v. *Brown* (1820) 1 J. & W. 168. Cf. *Hughes* v. *Jones* (1861) 3 De G. F. & J. 307.

[179] See *Knatchbull* v. *Grueber* (1815) 1 Madd. 153, (1817) 3 Mer. 124 at 146; *Cooper* v. *Denne* (1792) 1 Ves. Jr. Supp. 206, n 5; *Drewe* v. *Hanson* (1801) 6 Ves. 675 at 678. See also *Rutherford* v. *Acton-Adams* [1915] AC 866 at 869–70 for Lord Haldane's explanation of the doctrine.

Where a vendor or lessor agreed to put the property 'in good repair' prior to the granting of a lease, the court would not grant specific performance if unspecified work remained to be done, since it would not be clear exactly what the agreement required.[180] In 1858, the court thus refused to make a decree for the specific performance of an agreement to grant a lease as soon as the defendant had built a house on the property, since it could not supervise the building, or tell what was a suitable house.[181] The question was reconsidered after the passing of Cairns's Act in 1858, which allowed the Court of Chancery to award damages. Since damages could only be awarded under the Act in cases where specific performance could have been awarded,[182] the question was raised whether a plaintiff who had stipulated for work to be done prior to the granting of a lease could recover damages under the Act, when the work had not been done.

In *Soames* v. *Edge*,[183] Page Wood VC allowed a plaintiff to recover damages under the Act where he had agreed to grant a lease to the defendant once the latter had built a new house on the land. Although the Vice Chancellor conceded that a decree of specific performance for the building would not have been appropriate, he held that since (prior to the Act) the plaintiff could have obtained specific performance by waiving the condition to build the property, he had sufficient jurisdiction both to grant specific performance of the lease and damages for the failure to do the work. By contrast, in *Norris* v. *Jackson*, where the defendant had agreed to grant a lease once work had been done, Wood VC refused any relief. In this case, he said that the plaintiff could have no right for specific performance of the lease until he had waived the condition to repair; and that if he did so, then 'he would have no claim for damages for the non-performance of the repairs'. The cases looked inconsistent in respect of the award of damages. But Wood may have felt that *Soames*, where the defendant had failed to do the work, and was refusing the lease, was akin to cases where a purchaser could take so much of a title as the vendor could make, with compensation for the defect; while in *Norris* work was to be done by a mutual agreement which had not yet reached fruition, but which had not been refused.[184] This was to see

---

[180] *Taylor* v. *Portington* (1855) 7 De G. M. & G. 328.

[181] *Brace* v. *Wehnert* (1858) 25 Beav. 348; see also *Norris* v. *Jackson* (1860) 1 J. & H. 319. Contrast the eighteenth-century cases where specific performance was granted: *Pembroke* v. *Thorpe* (1740) 3 Swanst. 437n. There were some dicta which suggested that specific performance would be given to build or repair houses where it was certain what work was to be done: *Pembroke* v. *Thorpe* (1796) 3 Swanst. 437n. See also *Cubitt* v. *Smith* (1864) 10 Jur. N.S. 1123.

[182] *Rogers* v. *Challis* (1859) 27 Beav. 175; *Middleton* v. *Magnay* (1864) 2 H. & M. 233 at 236.

[183] *Soames* v. *Edge* (1860) Johns. 669.

[184] *Norris* v. *Jackson* (1860) 1 J. & H. 319 at 330.

the damages awarded under Cairns's Act as equivalent to compensation.[185] A
similar approach seemed to be taken in *Middleton* v. *Greenwood* in 1864, where
specific performance was granted for the lease of a public house, with damages
awarded for failure to instal a spirit vault. Turner LJ argued here that 'these
matters are mere incidents of the agreement, not affecting its substance, and I
have no doubt of the power of the Court to provide for them, otherwise than by
directing the work to be done'.[186] Although commentators had difficulty in reconciling these cases on Cairns's Act,[187] it is clear that their approach was influenced by the earlier cases on compensation.

Goods

It was settled in the eighteenth century that specific performance would not be
granted for sales of goods which could be found in the market, since the loss could
be covered by common law damages.[188] Lord Hardwicke distinguished between
contracts for real property, which was 'of a permanent nature', and contracts for
merchandise and stock, which varied 'according to time and circumstance'.[189]
The early eighteenth century Chancery therefore refused specific performance
of contracts to transfer stock, for (as Lord Parker LC put it), 'there can be no
difference between one man's stock and another's'.[190] At the start of the nineteenth century, it was generally agreed that only if the goods were unique—such
as heirlooms—would specific performance be ordered.[191]

---

[185] See also *Peacock* v. *Penson* (1848) 11 Beav. 355, where compensation was given for road building
works not done.

[186] *Middleton* v. *Greenwood* (1864) 2 De G. J. & S. 142 at 145. Equity's compensation was not the
same as common law damages: see *Todd* v. *Gee* (1810) 17 Ves. 274.

[187] Fry, *Specific Performance* (6th edn, by G. R. Northcote, 1921), 394–5, argued 'that wherever the
thing which the Court cannot enforce is a condition inserted for the plaintiff's benefit in respect of
which the defendant is in default, and where the Court would, before the passing of the Act, have
had jurisdiction to enforce the contract on the plaintiff's waiver of the condition for his benefit, there
the court can now grant specific performance of the contract so far as it is enforceable specifically,
and direct the defendant to pay damages...for his non-performance of the condition which the
Court cannot specifically enforce'.

[188] See *Pearne* v. *Lisle* (1749) Amb. 75, where this was applied to slaves.

[189] *Buxton* v. *Lister* (1746) 3 Atk. 383 at 384.

[190] *Cud* v. *Rutter* (1719) 1 P. Wms. 570 at 571. See also *Cappur* v. *Harris* (1723) Bunb. 135. See also C.
Viner, *A General Abridgment of Law and Equity*, 24 vols (2nd edn, 1791–5), v, 540. Some eighteenth-
century authorities did, however, suggest that specific performance would be awarded for chattels or
stock: *Colt* v. *Nettervill* (1725) 2 P. Wms. 304; *Taylor* v. *Neville*, cited in *Buxton* v. *Lister* (1746) 3 Atk.
383 at 384. But in 1804, Lord Eldon considered it settled that the court would not enforce specific
performance of a transfer of stock: *Nutbrown* v. *Thornton* (1804) 10 Ves. 159 at 161.

[191] e.g. *Pusey* v. *Pusey* (1684)1 Vern. 273; *Duke of Somerset* v. *Cookson* (1735) 3 P. Wms. 390; *Fells*
v. *Read* (1796) 3 Ves. 70; *Lloyd* v. *Loaring* (1801) 6 Ves 773; *Earl of Macclesfield* v. *Davis* (1814) 3 V. &
B. 16.

Some equity judges sought to soften this rigid distinction during the first half of the nineteenth century. In 1818, Richards CB criticized Hardwicke's distinction between land and chattels, which assumed that the value of the latter was far more fluid than that of the former. 'We all know very well', he observed, 'that the same quantity of land was worth very considerably more four years ago, than it is at the present time.' He was therefore prepared to decree a specific performance of a contract for the purchase of a debt.[192] Sir John Leach VC gave a similar decree in 1823. In his view, specific performance could be given for the sale of chattels where the sale was by instalments, and the future price of the goods could not be estimated, or where the damages were conjectural, and in respect of potential future earnings.[193] For in neither case would damages be adequate. Leach seemed to take the jurisdiction of the court much further in 1824, in comments in a case where a plaintiff, the holder of scrip in a Neapolitan loan, sought specific performance of the granting of stock certificates. '[I]nasmuch as this bill prays a delivery of the certificates which would constitute the Plaintiff the proprietor of a certain amount of stock, the bill in equity will hold', he ruled, 'because a Court of law could not give the property but could only give a remedy in damages, the beneficial effect of which must depend upon the personal responsibility of the party.'[194] The latter point seemed to offer a very wide power to award specific performance, as no plaintiff could ever be certain of the liquidity of a defendant.

Mid-nineteenth-century judges also refused to extend the rule that specific performance would not be given for the purchase of stock to shares. In 1841, Shadwell VC decreed the specific performance of a contract to sell railway shares, holding that they, unlike government stock, were limited in number and not always available in the market.[195] Although one investor who agreed to sell his shares to another could have the agreement enforced,[196] and require the purchaser not only to register his interest, but to indemnify the seller from liability for calls,[197] it was not always an easy remedy to obtain in practice. To begin with, if the shares were sold on by the purchaser to a third party, to whom the shares were conveyed, the original seller would no longer be able to seek specific performance of his agreement, if the third party buyer refused to register a transfer.[198] Equally, if

---

[192] *Wright* v. *Bell* (1818) 5 Price 325 at 329.

[193] *Adderley* v. *Dixon* (1823) 1 Sim. & Stu. 607 at 611. See also *Withy* v. *Cottle* (1823) 1 Sim. & Stu. 174.

[194] *Doloret* v. *Rothschild* (1824) 1 Sim. & Stu. 590 at 598.

[195] *Duncuft* v. *Albrecht* (1841) 12 Sim. 189 at 199.

[196] *Cheale* v. *Kenward* (1858) 3 De G. & J. 27.

[197] See *Evans* v. *Wood* (1867) LR 5 Eq 9. The common law also implied an indemnity: *Walker* v. *Bartlett* (1856) 18 C.B. 845.

[198] This was because privity of contract no longer existed between buyer and seller: *Shaw* v. *Fisher* (1848) 2 De G. & Sm. 11; *Shaw* v. *Fisher* (1855) 5 De G. M. & G. 596.

the directors of the company had the power to refuse to register a transfer, it was decided (after some hesitation) that the vendor would not be able to enforce the sale.[199]

Equity judges also had to puzzle whether agreements by subscribers to take shares in companies could be specifically enforced, when some defendants sought to invoke the principle that the Chancery would not enforce contracts to enter into partnerships, since such a decree would be in vain,[200] as any partner could immediately dissolve the association.[201] At first, there were signs that this argument would succeed. In 1853, Sir John Romilly MR refused a decree in a case where a company's deed of settlement permitted the shareholder to transfer his holding within 14 days. Regarding this as a contract to enter a partnership, which could be dissolved within 14 days, he said that '[t]o specifically perform a contract of this description would be merely nugatory'.[202] Later courts, however, distinguished shareholders from partners. Sir Richard Kindersley pointed out in 1859 that in a joint stock partnership, the partner could not end the association, but only his own status as a shareholder. On retiring, he would have to find another shareholder to take them on. 'The effect of decreeing him to perform his agreement', the Vice Chancellor noted, 'would be that the company would obtain the benefit of having someone liable to it for calls on so many shares, and that is a benefit of which it is not in the power of the Defendant to deprive the company by retiring from the concern.'[203]

In the second half of the nineteenth century, English equity courts began to award specific performance for the sale of specific goods, even where they had no sentimental value to the purchaser, and there were no issues of trust raised. According to White & Tudor's *Leading Cases in Equity*, there was no fundamental difference between real and personal property, save that in the latter case, damages were more often likely to be adequate.[204] In 1852, specific performance of a

---

[199] See *Poole* v. *Middleton* (1861) 29 Beav. 646 and *Bermingham* v. *Sheridan* (1864) 33 Beav. 660. The court could compel the directors to accept the transfer, if their refusal to do so was unreasonable: *Robinson* v. *Chartered Bank* (1865) LR 1 Eq 32.

[200] See *Jones* v. *Jones* (1803) 12 Ves. 188.

[201] This was the view of Lord Eldon in *Hercy* v. *Birch* (1804) 9 Ves. 357. He was later said to have doubted it: H. Maddock, *A Treatise on the Principles and Practice of the High Court of Chancery*, 2 vols (2nd edn, 1820), i, 411n, and it was questioned by Swanston in his note to *Crawshay* v. *Maule* (1818) 1 Swanst. 495. But the general rule was endorsed in *Sichel* v. *Mosenthal* (1862) 30 Beav. 371; *Scott* v. *Rayment* (1868) LR 7 Eq 112. But where the partnership agreement was for a specified time, or where the partners had already commenced business, equity would intervene: *England* v. *Curling* (1843) 8 Beav. 129 at 137; *New Brunswick &c Co* v. *Muggeridge* (1859) 4 Drew. 686 at 698.

[202] *Sheffield Gas Consumers' Co* v. *Harrison* (1853) 17 Beav. 294 at 297.

[203] *New Brunswick & Co* v. *Muggeridge* (1859) 4 Drew. 686 at 700.

[204] F. T. White and O. D. Tudor, *A Selection of Leading Cases in Equity*, 2 vols (4th edn, 1872), i, 791.

contract for the sale of a barge was thus decreed.[205] In 1859, Sir Richard Kindersley confirmed that the court would exercise its jurisdiction in contracts for the sale of chattels, where damages were not an adequate remedy, as where the contract was for the purchase of 'articles of unusual beauty, rarity and distinction'.[206] Four years later, Sir John Romilly MR decreed specific performance of a contract to sell the plaintiff stone from the old Westminster Bridge.[207] Later nineteenth-century courts of equity also suggested they would enforce contracts for the sale of ships, on the ground that damages were not an adequate remedy.[208]

Some equity judges were prepared to go even further. In 1862, Lord Westbury stated that '[t]he buyer may maintain a suit in equity for the delivery of a specific chattel when it is the subject of a contract'. In his view, this principle would apply to 'a contract to sell five hundred chests of the particular kind of tea which is now in my warehouse in Gloucester', though not to a contract to sell any tea.[209] Westbury's comments were controversial.[210] Nor did they seem to reflect mid-century practice. In 1855, in *Pollard* v. *Clayton*, Page Wood VC refused to enforce a contract between a colliery and an iron works to supply coal for its furnaces. Despite Lord Hardwicke's reference in *Buxton* v. *Lister* to the obscure case of *Taylor* v. *Neville* (involving specific performance of a contract to supply iron), Wood noted that he could not find any case where specific performance had been awarded for the supply of goods to be delivered in instalments.[211] He also pointed out that the plaintiffs had delayed in seeking specific performance: 'during the interval which has elapsed there may have been every possible variety of price' of coal, 'and the parties are not now in the same position'.[212] For Wood, the fact that the coal was conveniently located next to the iron works was not significant, for it was something which could be taken into account in damages. It was clearly important to his judgment that the goods were not unique, and that the buyer could and should have obtained an alterative supply as soon as possible, mitigating his loss.

The increased willingness of some courts to widen the scope of specific performance beyond goods of sentimental value to other specific goods may have

---

[205] *Claringbould* v. *Curtis* (1852) 21 LJ (Ch) 541.

[206] *Falcke* v. *Gray* (1859) 4 Drew. 651. See also his comments in *New Brunswick & Co* v. *Muggeridge* (1859) 4 Drew. 686 at 698.

[207] *Drew* v. *Lockett* (1863) 32 Beav. 499.

[208] See *Hart* v. *Herwig* (1873) LR 8 Ch 860, 866. Such a contract was specifically enforced in *Behnke* v. *Bede Shipping Co* [1927] 1 KB 649.

[209] *Holroyd* v. *Marshall* (1861–2) 10 H.L.C. 191 at 209–10.

[210] His position was doubted by Sir Edward Fry, who noted that the records of Chancery were not filled with suits relating to specific chattels such as tea: Fry, *Specific Performance* (2nd edn, 1881), 29–30.

[211] *Pollard* v. *Clayton* (1855) 4 K. & J. 462 at 477.

[212] *Pollard* v. *Clayton* (1855) 4 K. & J. 462 at 480.

been influenced by legislative changes giving the common law courts the power
to order chattels to be delivered up. Until 1854, where property had passed in
the goods, the buyer was able to sue at common law in an action of detinue or
conversion, and obtain damages. The Common Law Procedure Act of that year
enacted that in such cases, a common law court could order that execution should
issue for the return of the chattel, without the defendant having the option of
retaining them and paying damages.[213] The following year, the Mercantile Law
Commission recommended that a buyer of goods should be entitled to specific
performance of the contract, as was the case under Scots law. This recommendation was followed by legislation which empowered the common law court to
order the delivery under execution of specific goods, contracted to be bought
for a price in money.[214] With the fusion of law and equity in 1875, the same powers were to be exercised by both courts, which confirmed that equity had the
same powers. The provisions of the 1856 Mercantile Law Amendment Act were
later incorporated into the 1893 Sale of Goods Act (s 52), confirming that in any
action to deliver specific or ascertained goods, the court could direct a specific
performance.[215] The wording of the Act suggested that the court had jurisdiction
to award specific performance for any ascertained goods or chattels, regardless
of whether they were unique or of emotional value to the plaintiff. Thus, in 1909,
Parker J. ruled that he could award specific performance of a contract to permit
the plaintiff to enter the defendant's land and saw timber, holding that timber
constituted goods within the statute.[216] By the First World War, in part thanks to
the wording of the statute, the scope of specific performance in the sale of chattels had broadened considerably.

Services

Equity was cautious when it came to enforcing contracts to do work. If it was
evident that damages would provide an adequate remedy—where money would
pay for work to be done—then the court would decline to interfere.[217] Where
damages were inadequate, the Chancery would intervene only if it was clear what
was to be done. Thus, in 1842, Knight Bruce LJ decreed specific performance of a
contract by a railway company to build an arch under its line, to join up land of

[213] 17 & 18 Vict. c. 125, s 78.
[214] 19 & 20 Vict. c. 97, s 2. Royal Commission on Assimilation of Mercantile Laws in United
Kingdom, PP 1854–5 [1977], xviii, 653, at p. 10.
[215] The Act reproduced the section of the 1856 Mercantile law Amendment Act, as modified by the
Judicature Acts and Rules which gave all judges the power to administer all remedies.
[216] James Jones & Sons v. Earl of Tankerville [1909] 2 Ch 440 at 445.
[217] Flint v. Brandon (1803) 8 Ves. 159.

the plaintiff's which had been divided by the line.[218] Three years later, Sir James Wigram VC contemplated granting specific performance of an agreement by the corporation of Penzance, to build a market.[219] The courts were willing to interfere even at the cost of public inconvenience. In 1862, the owner of Kempton Park Estate agreed with the Thames Valley Railway Company to withdraw his opposition to their parliamentary bill, in exchange for their agreement to make a road and approach to the estate in a particular way. The railway then altered its plans and, after the bill was filed, completed the work and built an elevation rendering it impossible to comply with their agreement. The railway was then opened to the public. Lord Romilly MR refused to grant specific performance, taking into account the needs of the public; but the Chancery Court of Appeal overturned the decision and granted the decree.[220]

However, it refused to intervene where it was unclear exactly what work was to be done or where the work would require supervision.[221] It was on this principle that the court was unwilling to order specific performance of covenants to repair.[222] It also applied to agreements to build. Thus, in 1854 the South Wales Railway Company failed to obtain a decree against a firm which had contracted to build 22 miles of its line. It was clear that this was the kind of work which would require constant references to the court to see that it was being adequately performed. In making his decision, Page Wood VC noted 'the enormous inconvenience which would attend the operations of the Court, if it were to take upon itself, as between contractors and railway companies, the making...half the railways in the kingdom'.[223] Similarly, in *Pollard* v. *Clayton* in 1855, Page Wood VC refused specific performance of a contract to supply coal in part because it would have required him to have ordered that the mine continue to be worked in a sufficient manner to raise the coal, which would have required too much supervision.[224] The court's unwillingness to enforce contracts to mine was reiterated by

---

[218] *Storer* v. *Great Western Railway Co* (1842) 2 Y. & C.C.C. 47 at 53. See also *Sanderson* v. *Cockermouth and Workington Railway Co* (1849) 11 Beav. 497; *Lytton* v. *Great Northern Railway Co* (1856) 2 K. & J. 394; *Wilson* v. *Furness Railway Co* (1869) LR 9 Eq 28; *Greene* v. *West Cheshire Railway Co* (1871) LR 13 Eq 44.

[219] No decree was in the end required, as the work was done: *Price* v. *Penzance* (1845) 4 Hare 506.

[220] *Raphael* v. *Thames Valley Railway Co* (1866) LR 2 Eq 37, LR 2 Ch App 147.

[221] See also *Mosely* v. *Virgin* (1796) 3 Ves. 184, where Lord Loughborough stressed that specific performance would not be given where the agreement was uncertain as to exactly what was to be done.

[222] The court was unwilling to intervene unless the repairs were incidental to a contract to grant a lease which would ordinarily be granted specific performance. After 1858, the court could under Lord Cairns's Act direct an inquiry as to damages for the failure to repair.

[223] *South Wales Railway Co* v. *Wythes* (1854) 1 K. & J. 186 at 200. See also *Lord James Stuart* v. *London and North-Western Railway* (1852) 1 De G. M. & G. 721 at 735.

[224] *Pollard* v. *Clayton* (1855) 4 K. & J. 462 at 476.

Malins VC in 1869, laying stress on the fact that the court could not be expected 'to give every direction as to how all things were to be done'.[225]

Early nineteenth-century judges were also unwilling specifically to enforce contracts of personal service.[226] In 1819, William Clarke, publisher of George Price's Exchequer reports, brought an action against the author and his new publishers, Brooke and Sweet, seeking to enforce his own contract with the writer. But Lord Eldon held that he did not have the means to force Price to write.[227] This alluded to the Chancery's inability to intervene where it could not ensure that the work would be done.[228] In another action brought by Charles Kemble, the proprietor of Covent Garden, to prevent the actor Edmund Kean performing at Drury Lane, in breach of his contract with Kemble, Sir Lancelot Shadwell VC in 1829 stated that specific performance would not be granted to force actors to perform. '[S]upposing Mr. Kean should resist', he said, 'how is such an agreement to be performed by the Court? Sequestration is out of the question; and can it be said that a man can be compelled to perform an agreement to act at a theatre by this Court sending him to the Fleet [prison] for refusing to act at all?'[229] Even where an employee could be returned to work, it would be impossible for the court to supervise the work, and ensure it was adequately done.[230] As Sir John Romilly put it in 1860, '[t]his Court cannot compel an apprentice to work, nor can it compel a master to instruct, and therefore it cannot compel the specific performance of the contract on either side'.[231]

Just as the courts refused to force one party to do personal work promised for another, so they refused to hold employers to their contracts to employ plaintiffs. In 1843, in refusing to give relief to a solicitor who claimed the right to exercise the office of receiver for the Bishop of Ely, Knight Bruce VC ruled that as the nature of the duties to be exercised by the plaintiff were such that the court would never

---

[225] See *Wheatley* v. *Westminster Brymbo Coal Co* (1869) LR 9 Eq 538 at 551.

[226] Eighteenth-century courts of equity did specifically enforce contracts of service, where this did not entail supervising the work to be done. See *Ball v. Coggs* (1710) 1 Bro. P.C. 140, where the plaintiff was granted specific performance of articles under which he was to be paid certain sums for his life, while employed as manager of the defendants' brass works.

[227] *Clarke* v. *Price* (1819) 2 Wils. Ch. 157 at 164–5. He also noted that in *Morris* v. *Colman* (1812) 18 Ves. 437, he had no power to compel a writer to write pieces for one theatre, though he could prevent him by injunction from breaching an agreement not to write for another.

[228] See also *Baldwin* v. *Society for Diffusion of Useful Knowledge* (1838) 9 Sim. 393.

[229] *Kemble* v. *Kean* (1829) 6 Sim. 333 at 338.

[230] In *Stocker* v. *Brockelbank* (1851) 3 Mac. & G. 248 at 260, where the plaintiff sought reinstatement to a position, John Rolt invoked the principle that the court could not supervise performance, arguing that 'though the Court might decree the Defendants to admit the Plaintiff into the manufactory, it could not enforce on them his directions as to the management and conduct of the business'. See also at *Ryan* v. *Mutual Tontine Westminster Chambers Association* [1892] 1 Ch 116 at 127.

[231] *Webb* v. *England* (1860) 29 Beav. 44 at 54.

compel him specifically to perform, so the court would not issue such a decree against the bishop. For equity would not intervene in the absence of mutuality.[232] In 1851, Truro LC ruled that he knew of no instance where specific performance had been given against an employer dismissing an employee.[233] A further argument against enforcing contracts of personal services was raised in 1853. This was that, where the parties were in a relationship whereby one party was the confidential servant of the other, so that there had to be 'the most entire harmony and spirit of co-operation between the contracting parties',[234] it would be inappropriate to force the continuance of the relationship. By the 1860s, these justifications could all be rolled into a general principle that contracts for personal services could not be enforced in equity.[235] By 1890, Fry LJ expressed his unwillingness to compel people to maintain personal relations which they wished to end , noting that 'Courts are bound to be jealous, lest they should turn contracts of service into contracts of slavery'.[236]

At the same time, it was accepted in mid-century that equity could intervene by injunction to prevent a party from working for others, where she had specifically agreed not to do so. Shadwell VC had taken the view, in *Kemble* v. *Kean*, that the court would not grant an injunction in any case where it would not award specific performance. In 1845, Cottenham LC confirmed that equity would not interfere to enforce part of a contract where it could not decree specific performance of the whole contract;[237] and so it would not restrain a defendant by injunction from obtaining a supply of acid from another source, since it could not have ordered the plaintiff to manufacture it.[238] But St Leonards LC took a different view in *Lumley* v. *Wagner*, where the manager of Her Majesty's Theatre, Haymarket, was granted an injunction to prevent the singer Johanna Wagner from performing at the rival Royal Italian Opera, Covent Garden, in breach of her contract with him. 'It is true that I have not the means of compelling her to sing', he ruled, 'but she has no cause of complaint if I compel her to abstain from the commission of an act which she has bound herself not

---

[232] *Pickering* v. *Bishop of Ely* (1843) 2 Y. & C. C. C. 249 at 267.

[233] *Stocker* v. *Brockelbank* (1851) 3 Mac. & G. 248 at 266.

[234] *Johnson* v. *Shrewsbury and Birmingham Railway Co* (1853) 3 De G. M. & G. 914 at 926.

[235] *Mair* v. *Himalaya Tea Co* (1865) LR 1 Eq 411 at 415. See also *Horne* v. *London and North Western Railway Co* (1862) 10 W.R. 170; *Brett* v. *The East India and London Shipping Co* (1864) 12 W.R. 596.

[236] *De Francesco* v. *Barnum* (1890) 45 Ch D 430 at 438.

[237] His authority was *Gervais* v. *Edwards* (1842) 2 Dr. & W. 80, where Sugden LC said (at 81–2) 'The Court acts only, when it can perform the very thing, in terms specifically agreed upon; but when we come to the execution of a contract, depending upon many particulars, and upon uncertain events, the Court must see, whether it can be *specifically* executed; nothing can be left to chance; the Court must itself execute the whole contract'.

[238] *Hills* v. *Croll* (1845) 2 Ph. 60.

to do, and thus possibly cause her to fulfil her engagement'.[239] In so ruling, St Leonards sought to maintain good faith in contracts, binding parties to 'a true and literal performance of their contracts'. St Leonards claimed to follow Eldon's approach in *Morris* v. *Colman*,[240] where the latter had expressed himself content that actors should bind themselves only to perform in one theatre, and where an injunction had been issued.[241] St Leonards made it clear that injunctions could indeed be granted even where specific performance would not be.[242] In making the decision, he stressed the fact that there was a distinct negative stipulation not to work for another theatre. Later, Vice Chancellors Wood and Malins granted injunctions where there had been no negative stipulations, feeling that the negative promise was implied by the contract to perform at one theatre.[243] However, the decision was later said to have carried Chancery's power of granting injunctions to extreme limits,[244] and some judges expressed themselves unable to draw the line between cases where specific performance would not be given, but an injunction would be granted to prevent breach of one of the stipulations, and those where the court would not intervene at all.[245] By the end of the century, the Court of Appeal was very uncomfortable with the idea of implying negative stipulations in service contracts.[246] As Lindley LJ saw it, *Lumley* v. *Wagner* was 'an anomaly to be followed in cases like it, but an anomaly which it would be very dangerous to extend'. In his view, more harm than good could come of specifically enforcing contracts of personal service, whether directly or indirectly.[247] Judges therefore began to insist once more on

[239] *Lumley* v. *Wagner* (1852) 1 De G. M. & G. 604 at 619. On this case and its context, see S. M. Waddams, 'Johanna Wagner and the Rival Opera Houses' (2001) 117 *LQR* 431–58.

[240] *Morris* v. *Colman* (1812) 18 Ves. 437. Shadwell VC treated this case (as Eldon himself had suggested it should be so treated, in *Clarke* v. *Price* (1819) 2 Wils. Ch. 157 at 164) as turning on the fact that the parties were partners. St Leonards rejected this.

[241] See also *Lane* v. *Newdigate* (1804) 10 Ves. 192 where Eldon issued an injunction in a case where specific performance would not have been granted.

[242] Shadwell VC himself had moved away from his earlier views in *Rolfe* v. *Rolfe* (1846) 15 Sim. 88 at 89.

[243] *Webster* v. *Dillon* (1857) 3 Jur. (N.S.) 432; *Montague* v. *Flockton* (1873) LR 16 Eq 189. In the latter case, Malins VC cited as support the reading of such a contract by Sir John Romilly MR in *Fechter* v. *Montgomery* (1863) 33 Beav. 22 at 26. But note Romilly's view of *Lumley* v. *Wagner*, in *Merchants' Trading Co* v. *Banner* (1871) LR 12 Eq 18 at 23.

[244] *Whitwood Chemical Co* v. *Hardman* [1891] 2 Ch 416 at 431.

[245] See Jessel MR in *Fothergill* v. *Rowland* (1873) LR 17 Eq 132 at 141.

[246] See also the comments of Lord Selborne LC in *Wolverhampton and Walsall Railway Co* v. *London and North Western Railway Co* (1873) LR 16 Eq 433 at 440 and Fry, *Specific Performance* (2nd edn, 1881), 375–6.

[247] *Whitwood Chemical Co* v. *Hardman* [1891] 2 Ch 416 at 428.

the need for clear negative terms.[248] Moreover, they began to hold that where the negative terms were not confined to 'special services' but would prevent the party from engaging in any business of any kind, they were not to be enforced.[249] A general prohibition of work was not to be permitted, and the jurisdiction was to be used sparingly.

There were signs in the mid-century that the rule in *Lumley* v. *Wagner* might be extended more broadly. In *De Mattos* v. *Gibson* in 1858, Lord Chelmsford LC applied similar reasoning to that developed by St Leonards in personal service cases to charterparties. The plaintiff here sought specific performance of a charterparty, as well as an injunction to prevent the vessel from being used inconsistently with the agreement, by a mortgagee who had notice of a charterparty effected prior to the mortgage. It was argued for the defendant that an injunction could only be granted in cases where specific performance would be given. Lord Chelmsford admitted that specific performance could be not granted, since the court would never be able to ensure that the ship was furnished with a skilful master or a competent crew or that it was fit to sail.[250] But he was willing to countenance the idea of restraining the inconsistent use of the ship. Rejecting the argument that a plaintiff could be adequately compensated by damages,[251] he held that a 'vessel engaged under a charter-party ought to be regarded as a chattel of particular value to the charterer'.[252] Moreover, he felt that the negative stipulation not to use the ship inconsistently with the charter, could be implied. Though controversial in personal service cases,[253] the implied negative term continued to be followed in charterparty cases.[254] This approach was also extended to cases where brewers sought injunctions to restrain the purchase of beer from other sources.[255] However, just as judges and jurists were beginning to criticize the approach of *Lumley* in personal service cases, so in extending the doctrine to charterparties

---

[248] Lindley LJ's approach was somewhat ambiguous on how express the term had to be. However, see *Mutual Reserve Fund Life Association* v. *New York Life Insurance Co and Harvey* (1896) 75 LT 528 at 529.

[249] *Ehrman* v. *Bartholomew* [1898] 1 Ch 671 at 674. See also *Palace Theatre* v. *Clensy and Hackney and Shepherd's-Bush Empire Palaces* (1909) 26 TLR 28; *Chapman* v. *Westerby* [1913] WN 277. See also *Grimstone* v. *Cunningham* [1894] 1 QB 125.

[250] *De Mattos* v. *Gibson* (1858) 4 De G. & J. 276 at 297.

[251] As suggested by *Heathcote* v. *The North Staffordshire Railway Co* (1850) 2 M. & G. 100 at 112.

[252] *De Mattos* v. *Gibson* (1858) 4 De G. & J. 276 at 299.

[253] See also *Peto* v. *Brighton, Uckfield and Tunbridge Wells Railway Co* (1863) 1 H. & M. 468 at 486 where Page Wood VC said that the court only inferred negative agreements in 'very few and special' cases.

[254] *Le Blanch* v. *Granger* (1866) 35 Beav. 187; *Sevin* v. *Deslandes* (1860) 30 LJ Ch 457; see also *Collins* v. *Lamport* (1864) 11 LT 497; *Lord Strathcona Steamship Co* v. *Dominion Coal Co* [1926] AC 108.

[255] *Catt* v. *Tourle* (1869) LR 4 Ch App 654; *Luker* v. *Dennis* (1877) 7 Ch D 227.

and breweries, judges moved away from asking whether this was a roundabout way of enforcing a contract of personal service, preferring analogies more with restrictive covenants regarding the use of land. Injunctions were issued not to enforce personal performance, but to prevent the use or enjoyment of property in way inconsistent with prior contracts.[256]

---

[256] Courts therefore cited Knight Bruce LJ's approach in *De Mattos* v. *Gibson* (1858) 4 De G. & J. 276 at 282, which focused on the proprietary aspects. He noted that 'reason and justice' dictated that a man who acquired property with notice of a previous contract to use the property for a certain purpose could not use it inconsistently with that purpose, to the damage of the third party.

VIII
Restitutionary Remedies

1. AN 'EQUITABLE' ACTION

The contractual forms of action, debt and assumpsit, could also be used to recover sums of money which were not due under a contract.[1] Both debt and assumpsit included counts for 'money had and received by the defendant for the use of the plaintiff' and 'money laid out by the plaintiff for the defendant's business'.[2] The first of these had developed to provide an alternative to the action of account, a remedy which was originally available to make bailiffs account for money collected on behalf of their lords, but which grew to allow plaintiffs to recover sums of money obtained for their use by parties not in a prior relationship with them. By the start of the seventeenth century, the action of account could be used to recover deposits paid on failed transactions, money paid by mistake, and money which had been entrusted to the defendant to pay over to the plaintiff.[3] However, since this action was 'difficult, dilatory and expensive',[4] it fell out of use in the seventeenth century, when common law courts allowed the recovery of such claims on a count for money had and received in *indebitatus assumpsit*.[5] This remedy went further than account when it was settled in 1705 that where a defendant had tortiously obtained goods and sold them, the owner could 'waive the tort' and sue for the proceeds in an action for money had and received.[6]

---

[1] I am grateful to Charles Mitchell for his helpful comments on the subject of this chapter.

[2] They were described by J. F. Schiefer as 'species' of the genus *assumpsit: An Explanation of the Practice of Law* (1792), 123–4.

[3] J. H. Baker, *Introduction to English Legal History* (4th edn, 2002), 363–4.

[4] M. Bacon, *A New Abridgment of the Law*, 5 vols (1736–66), i, 16.

[5] S. J. Stoljar, 'The Transformations of Account' (1964) 80 *LQR* 203–24 at 215–18. See in general, J. H. Baker, 'The Use of Assumpsit for Restitutionary Money Claims 1600–1800', in E. J. H. Schrage, *Unjust Enrichment* (2nd edn, Berlin, 1999), 31–57.

[6] *Lamine* v. *Dorrell* (1705) 2 Ld. Raym. 1216. Account did not lie against tortfeasors: *Tottenham* v. *Bedingfield* (1572) 3 Leon 24; J. H. Baker and S. F. C. Milsom, *Sources of English Legal History: Private Law to 1750* (1986), 295.

The count for money had and received was significantly different from the other common counts, where the plaintiff had to allege that goods had been sold or work done at the defendant's request. In these counts, the originating debt was seen to have arisen from a contractual transaction, which could be implied from the fact of the defendant's request and receipt. By contrast, in the count for money had and received, the very wording of the declaration showed that the originating debt did not arise from a contractual transaction. In this count, the plaintiff did not aver a request, but stated that the defendant was 'indebted to the plaintiff for money had and received to his use, and being so indebted promised to pay'. Although it was essential, in *indebitatus assumpsit*, to allege that a promise had been made, proof of mutual assent and consideration were not necessary to sustain this action.[7] The promise was implied by the existing debt, and was not traversable,[8] and a plea of *non assumpsit* only put in issue whether there was a subsisting debt, or cause of action, at the time of commencing the suit[9]—that is, whether the defendant had money to the plaintiff's use.

Unlike the money had and received count, that for money paid did (like the other common counts) describe the originating obligation in contractual terms. It alleged that money had been laid out at the special instance and request of the defendant. When the count was first used in the seventeenth century, it was necessary to show that an actual request had been made; but by the end of the century, it was accepted that a request could be implied by law in some situations.[10] The request could not be implied from the acceptance of an executed consideration (as it was in the other common counts)—for the defendant had not himself received the money—but it could be implied where the plaintiff had no option but to pay money on behalf of the defendant.

Restitutionary remedies were also available in equity. Thanks to its more extensive inquisitorial machinery, the Chancery offered a much better account jurisdiction than was available at common law. Equity's jurisdiction over accounts was used both between parties to contractual relationships—such as settling accounts between partners or between principals and factors—and to take accounts from trustees and other fiduciaries. Equity made those in fiduciary positions hand over

---

[7] While the debt was regarded as the consideration for the implied promise, in practice, '[i]n an action for money had and received, a direct consideration moving from the plaintiff is seldom shewn': *Lilly v. Hays* (1836) 5 Ad. & El. 548 at 550 (Patteson J.). See also J. B. Ames, 'History of Assumpsit: II. Implied Assumpsit' (1888) 2 *Harvard LR* 53–69 at 63.

[8] R. M. Jackson, *The History of Quasi-Contract in English Law* (Cambridge, 1936), 44.

[9] W. Tidd, *The Practice of the Court of King's Bench and Common Pleas in Personal Actions*, 2 vols (6th edn, 1817), i, 686.

[10] Baker, 'Use of Assumpsit', 42.

both the proceeds of trust property and any money made by breaches of their duty, even where there had been no injury to the trust estate. It also held those not in fiduciary relationships accountable where they had wrongfully acquired assets belonging to another. A bill could therefore be brought in Chancery to recover money acquired by defendants by fraud, or as a result of undue influence.[11] Where deeds for the transfer of property had been obtained by undue means, and were accordingly set aside, defendants were further required to account for the profits they had obtained from the use of that property, the court in effect treating the defendant as trustee of the property.[12]

There was little in the way of theory to unite these various remedies. Despite occasional indications that equity lawyers might develop a doctrine of the constructive trust[13] whereby a person who obtained property at the expense of another would be regarded as a trustee of the property,[14] equity's approach to trusts remained focused on the express trust as the paradigm. Where equitable remedies were given which might have been explained in terms of giving remedies for unjust enrichment—as when secret trusts or oral trusts of land which violated the writing requirements of the Statute of Frauds were upheld—Chancery judges did so by invoking their jurisdiction against fraud.[15] Where those in fiduciary relationships were held to account, it was on the grounds of breaches of trust; where those not in such relationships were held to account, it was on the ground of equity's jurisdiction over fraud.

Common lawyers were no more prone to theorize. They were not deceived by the use of the contractual forms of debt and assumpsit into assuming that all restitutionary claims were contractual. They were well aware that claims in assumpsit or debt could be brought for non-contractual debts. The action of debt had long been used to recover money due by custom, or awarded by court judgments.[16] As *indebitatus assumpsit* became available wherever debt would

---

[11] *Colt* v. *Woollaston* (1723) 2 P. Wms. 154; *Bridgman* v. *Green* (1755) 2 Ves. Sr. 627. Such claims were often regarded as an equitable equivalent to money had and received. *Green* v. *Barrett* (1826) 1 Sim. 45; *Seddon* v. *Connell* (1840) 10 Sim. 58 at 74.

[12] *Evans* v. *Llewellin* (1787) 1 Cox C.C. 333. See G. Jones, 'The Role of Equity in the English Law of Restitution', in E. J. H. Schrage, *Unjust Enrichment* (2nd edn, Berlin, 1999), 149–69 at 155.

[13] e.g. in 1834, Lord Brougham said that 'where one not expressly a trustee has bought or trafficked with another's money[,] [t]he law raises a trust by implication, clothing him, though a stranger, with the fiduciary character, for the purpose of making him accountable': *Docker* v. *Somes* (1834) 2 Myl. & K. 655 at 665.

[14] There were some eighteenth-century suggestions in this direction which were not taken up: *Marriot* v. *Marriot* (1726) Gilb. Rep. 204; *Barnsley* v. *Powel* (1748) 1 Ves. Sr. 119; *Dixon* v. *Olmius* (1787) 1 Cox C.C. 414. See G. E. Palmer, 'History of Restitution in Anglo-American Law', in *International Encyclopedia of Comparative Law*, vol. X, ch. 3 (Tübingen, 1989), 9–30 at 19.

[15] *Reech* v. *Kennegal* (1748) 1 Ves. Sr. 123 at 125.

[16] A. W. B. Simpson, *A History of the Common Law of Contract* (Oxford, 1975), 73–4.

lie, so non-contractual debts, such as customary dues,[17] customs,[18] or fines could also be recovered using this form. Whether brought in debt or assumpsit, such claims were seen as 'quasi-contractual' claims,[19] where 'the law gives an action of debt, although there is no contract between the parties'.[20] However, there was no attempt to provide a theory of quasi-contract. The first attempt to theorize the subject was Lord Mansfield's attempt to explain the scope of the action for money had and received, in his decision in 1760 in *Moses* v. *Macferlan*. In a comment frequently quoted by nineteenth-century writers, he explained that this was an 'equitable action, to recover back money, which ought not in justice to be kept'.[21]

Mansfield's statement is regarded as the *locus classicus* for the notion that the common law could recognize unjust enrichment as a source of obligation distinct from contract or tort,[22] analogous to the Roman law principle that no man should be enriched to the detriment of another.[23] His dictum that the action was rooted in conscience was routinely repeated by treatise writers in the first half of the nineteenth century,[24] and his moral language was often invoked by judges.[25] One friend of the action, Tindal CJ, commented in 1844 that '[t]he ground and principle upon which this form of action is maintainable is, that the defendant has received money which, *ex aequo et bono*, belongs to the plaintiff'.[26] Some judges also echoed Mansfield's notion that the action was an equitable one, offering a common law equivalent to remedies available in Chancery.[27]

---

[17] *City of London* v. *Goree* (1677) 3 Keb. 677, 1 Vent. 298; *Barber Surgeons of London* v. *Pelson* (1679) 2 Lev. 252; *Duppa* v. *Gerrard* (1689) 1 Show. K.B. 78; *Saunderson* v. *Brignall* (1727) 2 Stra. 747.

[18] *Mayor of Exeter* v. *Trimlet* (1759) 2 Wils. K.B. 95.

[19] *Speake* v. *Richards* (1617) Hob. 206.

[20] *Hosden* v. *Harridge* (1670) 1 Wms. Saund. 64 at 66. Saunders had himself unsuccessfully sought to argue that an action of debt for the escape of one in execution was within the statute of limitations since 'although it is not founded upon a *lending* or *contract* properly, yet the law has made a contract': *Jones* v. *Pope* (1668) 1 Wms. Saund. 37. See also *Hodgson* v. *Harris* (1669) 1 Lev. 273.

[21] *Moses* v. *Macferlan* (1760) 2 Burr. 1005 at 1012. See also *Longchamp* v. *Kenny* (1778) 1 Doug. 137 at 138.

[22] P. Birks, *An Introduction to the Law of Restitution* (Oxford, 1989), 32. See also R. Goff and G. Jones, *The Law of Restitution* (7th edn by G. Jones, 2007, 8–9, quoting J. H. Baker 'The History of Quasi-Contract in English Law', in W.R. Cornish, R. Nolan, J. O'Sullivan, and G. Virgo, *Restitution: Past, Present and Future*, 37–56 at 54).

[23] See W. D. Evans, *Essay on the Action of Money Had and Received* (1802), 3. On the Roman law background, see P. B. H. Birks, 'English and Roman Learning in *Moses* v. *Macferlan*' [1984] *Current Legal Problems*, 1–28.

[24] J. W. Smith, *A Selection of Leading Cases on Various Branches of the Law*, 2 vols (4th edn by J. S. Willes and H. S Keating, 1856), ii, 328; S. Comyn, *The Law of Contracts and Promises* (1824), 266. See also J. Chitty, *A Practical Treatise on the Law of Contracts not under Seal* (2nd edn, 1834), 475 noting criticism but quoting it.

[25] e.g. *Davis* v. *Bryan* (1827) 6 B. & C. 651 at 655; *Jefferys* v. *Gurr* (1831) 2 B. & Ad. 833 at 841.

[26] *Edwards* v. *Bates* (1844) 7 M. & G. 590 at 597. Cf. *Smith* v. *Jones* (1842) 6 Jur. 283 at 284.

[27] *Straton* v. *Rastall* (1788) 2 T.R. 366 at 370 (Buller J.), cf. *Weymouth* v. *Boyer* (1792) 1 Ves. Jr. 416 at 424. See also *Wright* v. *Butler* 6 Wend 284, 21 Am Dec 323 (1830). See also J. Chitty, *A Practical*

But despite such language, early nineteenth-century jurists—with the sole exception of W. D. Evans—were unwilling to develop Mansfield's broad theory. Instead, they took a more restrictive view of the scope of the action. First, they rejected the idea that it offered a common law equivalent to a Chancery bill. The idea that it was an equitable action, Pollock CB said in 1849, 'is exploded in modern practice—it is a perfectly legal action, and no good can result from calling it an equitable one'.[28] Judges were aware that the common law could not simply imitate equity's jurisdiction, since it did not have the power to adjust the equities between all interested parties.[29] The common law courts had to decide for themselves when to apply the action, rather than simply imitating the Chancery. Secondly, common law courts rejected the idea that they needed to look at the conscience of the claimant in the way that equity did. This was made clearest in *Kelly* v. *Solari*,[30] when the Exchequer decided that it should not take into account any negligence or fault in the plaintiff in deciding whether she could recover money paid by mistake. The plaintiff could recover if the defendant had no right to retain the money. Whether the plaintiff had been careless, or whether repaying the money would cause hardship to the defendant, was not relevant. Thirdly, it did not take long for the courts to reject Mansfield's notion that a plaintiff could recover using this action whenever the defendant had money which he was morally obliged to return.[31] Mansfield's view of the scope of the action was the corollary to his approach to 'moral consideration', an approach which went out of fashion in the first half of the nineteenth century. In determining where a liability to repay money existed, early nineteenth-century judges therefore did not use Mansfield's dictum as a general principle of unjust enrichment. Rather, they allowed the action only to be used when a plaintiff's case fell within one of the situations in which the common law judges determined that the retention of money was unconscionable. This was a matter of positive law and not of an institution's sensitivity to morality.

Throughout the nineteenth century, judges and jurists seemed happy enough to get by without a theory. In contrast to contract and tort law, 'quasi-contract' did not attract the attention of any English treatise writer. It was not that jurists failed to recognize the distinct character of the subject. In *Ancient Law*, for

Treatise on the Law of Contracts not under Seal (4th American edn, by J. C. Perkins, Springfield, 1839, 475n).

[28] *Miller* v. *Atlee* (1849) 13 Jur. 431.

[29] *Davies* v. *Humphreys* (1840) 6 M. & W. 153 at 169. Cf. *Johnson* v. *Johnson* (1802) 3 B. & P. 162 at 169.

[30] *Kelly* v. *Solari* (1841) 9 M. & W. 54.

[31] In 1797, in *Marriot* v. *Hampton* (1797) 7 T.R. 269, the King's Bench overruled the decision in *Moses* v. *Macferlan* that a plaintiff could recover money which a court had ordered him to pay.

instance, Henry Maine commented that while the use of the word 'quasi' indicated that there was an analogy to be drawn with contract, it 'did not denote that the two conceptions are the same, or that they belong to the same genus'. In quasi-contract, he noted, the law, 'consulting the interests of morality, imposes an obligation on the receiver to refund, but the very nature of the transaction indicates that it is not a contract, inasmuch as the convention, the most essential ingredient of contract, is wanting'.[32] Austin's very cursory treatment of quasi-contract also distinguished between genuine and quasi-contracts.[33] He wrote that 'quasi-contract' denoted 'any incident by which one party obtains an *advantage* he ought not to retain'.[34] If such comments were hints towards developing a theory, neither Austin nor Maine gave much help in developing the principles which underlay the obligation.[35]

Some contract treatise writers included chapters on the matter dealt with by the *indebitatus* counts. In contrast to early nineteenth-century writers who treated these counts as merely another aspect of assumpsit, later authors like S. M. Leake made it clear that 'contracts implied in law'—as he entitled his chapter dealing with this subject—had nothing to do with real contracts.[36] Leake rooted the obligation in the fact that there was some 'undue pecuniary inequality' between the parties which 'justice and equity require should be compensated,

[32] H. S. Maine, *Ancient Law: Its Connection with the Early History of Society and its Relation to Modern Ideas* (1861), 344.

[33] 'Wherever there is a promise, express or implied (i.e. to be inferred from the words, or from the position, or conduct of the obligor, previous to the completion of the obligatory incident), that incident is not a quasi-contract, but a genuine contract': J. Austin, *Lectures on Jurisprudence, or the Philosophy of Positive Law* (4th edn, R. Campbell (ed.), 1873), 946.

[34] Austin, *Lectures* (4th edn, 1873), 944. He noted (at 947), '[n]either a quasi-contract nor a quasi-delict is like either a contract or a delict but the *consequences* of *either* of the former, are like the consequences of *either* of the latter, i.e. in begetting *jura ad rem*'.

[35] Austin was perhaps more confusing than helpful. For instance, he said that the term 'quasi-contract' should be limited to incidents where the obligee had been provided with a service for which it could be presumed that he would have contracted, had he been conscious and capable of doing so—the classic case of *negotiorum gestio*. Moreover, he noted that some cases seen as quasi-contractual were really properly contractual. For instance, in cases of failure of consideration, where money was to be repaid, 'there is a breach of accessory contract'. Austin argued that cases which were not like *negotiorum gestio* should be put under the heading of quasi-delict. Yet he treated these cases as in effect delictual. For example, he wrote that the refusal to pay money received under a mistake constituted a delict, since there was intentionality. The fact of *receiving* the money under a mistake was not a delict, he noted, though it begat an obligation to repay it. But this obligation was only generated at the moment the claimant made a demand for the money, and if the repayment was then refused, the 'refusal . . . to repay is the immediate cause of action: i.e. is a delict': Austin, *Lectures* (4th edn, 1873), 946.

[36] This area of law concerned 'those transactions affecting the two parties, other than agreement between them, upon which the law operates by imposing a contract, that is, a liability on the one side and correlative right on the other': S. M. Leake, *The Elements of the Law of Contracts* (1867), 38.

and upon which the law operates by creating a debt to the amount of the required compensation'.[37] But rather than saying more on the theoretical underpinnings of the doctrine, he proceeded simply to list the situations in which the law implied a promise to pay. Later writers said less. In a brief chapter on the relation between contract and quasi-contract, W. R. Anson suggested that '[i]t is not improbable that the relation which we call quasi contract or "contract implied in law", and the genuine contract arising upon consideration executed, sprang alike from [the same] notion of the readjustment of proprietary rights', which had historically been made when one party had acquired a benefit at the expense of another.[38] For Anson, it was only after the ideas of offer, acceptance, and agreement had been applied to executed contracts that a distinction was made between contracts arising from agreement, and legal relations which did not come from agreement. The fact that the assumpsit form was used for both only generated confusion. '[T]he obligation to which the action of *Assumpsit* conveyed a false air of agreement continues to furnish a cause of action', he explained, 'though that cause of action is now to be stated as it really exists'[39]—albeit not in his textbook.[40] The pattern of writers briefly acknowledging a distinction between contractual obligations and those arising *quasi ex contractu*, and largely omitting discussion of the latter, was repeated throughout the late nineteenth and early twentieth centuries.[41] Only in America at the end of the nineteenth century, when theoretical analysis of private law flourished at Harvard, did the law of quasi-contract get its first full treatise.[42]

In the absence of theoretical guidance, judges were often unsure about the nature of the obligation. The mid-century reforms in procedure did little to clarify judicial thinking. On the one hand, the broad reform of the forms of action might have encouraged judges to abandon all talk of implied contract, since they removed the need to allege a fictitious promise, and allowed the joining of counts.[43] But on the other hand, rules relating to costs, which had hitherto distinguished according to the form of action brought (grouped into broadly

[37] Leake, *Elements* (1867), 38–9.

[38] W. R. Anson, *Principles of the English Law of Contract* (Oxford, 1879), 321–2.

[39] Anson, *Contract* (1879), 324.

[40] Frederick Pollock's treatise on contract said even less, though he pointed to the Indian Contract Act as dealing more clearly with the matter than English law. Pollock, *Principles of Contract at Law and in Equity* (6th edn, 1894), 12–13.

[41] e.g. C. G. Addison, *A Treatise on the Law of Contracts* (9th edn by H. Smith assisted by A. P. P. Keep, 1892), 416–17. But Chitty, *Contracts* (10th edn by J. A. Russell, 1876), 55, which showed no understanding of the distinction of contracts implied in law and in fact.

[42] W. A. Keener, *A Treatise on the Law of Quasi-Contracts* (New York, 1893). Cf. F. C. Woodward, *The Law of Quasi-Contracts* (Boston, 1913). See also A. Kull, 'James Barr Ames and the Early Modern History of Unjust Enrichment' (2005) 25 *OJLS* 297–319.

[43] Common Law Procedure Act 1852 (15 & 16 Vict. c. 76), ss 3, 41, 49.

contractual and broadly delictual ones) now simply distinguished between tortious and contractual actions.[44] This led some judges to see the law of obligations in equally binary terms. Martin B. accordingly declared in 1869 that he only knew two kinds of common law actions, 'one for injury to person or property, and the other for breach of contract'.[45] Such thinking encouraged an assumption that 'quasi-contractual' remedies were fully contractual. In 1882, Jessel MR accordingly observed that he found it 'difficult to see how there can be an implied contract with a lunatic, if he is incompetent to make an express contract'.[46] But not all judges shared this assumption. For instance, in 1890, Cotton LJ held that an obligation could be imposed on a lunatic who had no contractual capacity: 'what the law implies on the part of such a person is an obligation, which has been improperly called a contract, to repay money spent in supplying necessaries'. In his view, the use of the phrase 'implied contract' was 'erroneous and very unfortunate'.[47]

These uncertainties about the basis of the remedy were settled in favour of the former view by the House of Lords in *Sinclair* v. *Brougham* in 1914.[48] Their judgment distinguished between equitable claims to trace property, and personal claims for money had and received. The latter were held to be contractual in nature, which meant that they could only be brought if the parties could have entered into a genuine contract. Though sometimes seen as confirming a view taken by jurists throughout the century,[49] this case was in fact innovative, both in its treatment of the common law action and of the equitable claim. For most of the nineteenth century, common law judges granting restitutionary remedies looked neither to any kind of genuine contract between the parties, nor to a broad principle of moral conscience or unjust enrichment. Rather, the action for money had and received was used to recover money belonging to the plaintiff which the defendant had acquired without having any right to retain it. For it to succeed, judges needed to be convinced that the defendant had received the money for the use of the plaintiff.

---

[44] Contrast the language of the 1850 County Courts Extension Act (13 & 14 Vict. c. 61), s 11 and the 1867 County Courts Act Amendment Act (30 & 31 Vict. c. 142), s 5.

[45] *Freeman* v. *Jeffries* (1869) LR 4 Ex 189 at 199. This was not a new approach for him: in 1851 he declared that the action for money had and received 'is an action on a contract', adding that 'torts and contracts are of a very different nature': *Neate* v. *Harding* (1851) 6 Exch. 349 at 352.

[46] *In re Weaver* (1882) 21 Ch D 615 at 619. See also Brett LJ's comments at 620. Contrast Mellish LJ's views in *In re Gibson* (1871) LR 7 Ch App 52 at 53–4.

[47] *Rhodes* v. *Rhodes* (1890) 44 Ch Div 94 at 105. See also Fletcher Moulton LJ's comments (about contracts with infants) in *Nash* v. *Inman* [1908] 2 KB 1 at 8 and in *In re J* [1909] 1 Ch 574 at 577.

[48] *Sinclair* v. *Brougham* [1914] AC 398.

[49] e.g. D. J. Ibbetson, *Historical Introduction to the Law of Obligations* (Oxford, 1999), 287.

This meant that there had to be some form of privity between the parties. In some situations, as where money was paid by mistake or on a consideration which had failed, there was no difficulty in finding the privity necessary to regard the defendant as holding for the use of the plaintiff. But in other situations where the action was used, finding privity could be more difficult. One area of potential difficulty was when a plaintiff brought an action for money had and received to recover the proceeds of a tort, since 'wrongs are always done without privity'.[50] Beginning with cases against parties who had usurped the profits of offices or lands, courts found privity in the subsequent assent of the plaintiff, adopting the act of the tortfeasor, and constituting him an agent.[51] This principle could also be used to allow the plaintiff to adopt the tortious act of the defendant, committed against a third party, as when he falsely pretended to be the plaintiff's agent in order to obtain the payment of a debt.[52]

Privity was harder still to establish where money was paid to the defendant by a third party, to pay over to the plaintiff. In the early modern period, courts considered the recipient in such cases to be a trustee of the money, who could simply be sued by the beneficiary.[53] But early nineteenth-century common law judges preferred the language of agency,[54] and sought to be certain that such a relationship had been created between plaintiff and defendant. This meant that where money was sent to a banker to pay over to a third party, it would not be regarded as money held to the latter's use until it had been appropriated in the banker's hands as his agent. If the remitter retained any right to countermand the order, the action of money had and received could not be used, unless the banker could be shown to have entered into a distinct contract to pay the money to the intended recipient.[55] Judges and jurists seeking an agency relationship between plaintiff and defendant sometimes spoke of the need for 'privity of contract' between them.[56] Without such privity, it was said in 1845,

[50] *Tottenham* v. *Bedingfield* (1572) 3 Leon 24.

[51] *Arris* v. *Stukely* (1677) 2 Mod. 260, B. & M. 466; *Howard* v. *Wood* (1678) 2 Show. K.B. 21, 1 Freem. 473, B. & M. 478; *Lamine* v. *Dorrell* (1705) B. & M. 470 at 471.

[52] *Clarance* v. *Marshall* (1834) 2 Car. & M. 495 at 502–3. See also the approach taken in *Vaughan* v. *Matthews* (1849) 13 Q.B. 187 at 189, and the criticism of this case in Keener, *Quasi-Contract*, 168–70.

[53] Where money as paid by A to B to pay to C, C could in the sixteenth century bring an action of debt or account against B, since 'a trust was created by the delivery "to the use" of the third party': Simpson, *History of the Common Law of Contract*, 483.

[54] *Lilly* v. *Hays* (1836) 5 Ad. & El. 548. In the early nineteenth century, it was settled that the action for money had and received would not lie to enforce a specific trust, which could only be enforced in equity. Baker, 'Use of Assumpsit', 48n.

[55] *Williams* v. *Everett* (1811) 14 East 582; *Malcolm* v. *Scott* (1850) 5 Exch. 601; *Liversidge* v. *Broadbent* (1859) 4 H. & N. 603.

[56] *Stephens* v. *Badcock* (1832) 3 B. & Ad. 354 at 362; Chitty, *Contracts* (2nd edn, 1834), 479. Certainly, in the early twentieth century, some writers were troubled by the use of the notion of privity in these

a plaintiff could not recover even where 'it is admitted that the defendant held for the benefit of the plaintiff'.[57] But the function of such contractual talk was only to establish the fact that the money in the defendant's hands was held to the plaintiff's use.[58]

In *Sinclair* v. *Brougham*, the House of Lords took the view that all claims for money had and received were personal contractual claims, clearly distinguishable from equitable proprietary ones. However, for much of the nineteenth century, common lawyers were much less clear over whether claims for money had and received rested on the defendant's personal obligation to pay, or derived from the plaintiff's proprietary rights in assets which had come into the defendant's hands. *Prima facie*, an action for money had and received appeared to have all the hallmarks of a personal claim. After all, the plaintiff was suing in an action founded in a claim of debt, for money, a commodity which 'had no earmark' and in which property passed.[59] Nevertheless, in some situations, the claim was treated as if it was proprietary.[60] For instance, it was suggested in the mid-eighteenth century by Willes J. that where the monetary proceeds of goods which had been entrusted to an agent could be identified, they could be recovered from his assignees in bankruptcy either in an action for money had and received, or by a bill in Chancery. Such money was to be regarded as the plaintiff's property, rather than as a debt which had to be proved in bankruptcy.[61] Provided it could be identified,[62] this money remained just as much his property as his goods, which could be recovered from assignees in trover.[63] In other situations, the claim could not be seen as proprietary at common law. If a principal voluntarily handed over cash to his agent, to use in a particular way, property in it would pass, and a

---

cases, feeling that this made the action for money had and received look too contractual, e.g. P. H. Winfield, *The Province of the Law of Tort* (Cambridge, 1931), 136–7.

[57] *Jones* v. *Carter* (1845) 8 Q.B. 134 at 138. Here, the holder of a Derby lottery ticket (bought from the original subscriber to a lottery) failed in his action to recover his prize from the treasurer of the lottery, since the defendant was neither a stakeholder for the plaintiff, nor his agent, nor in a contract with the plaintiff. Since the ticket was a chose in action, it could not be assigned at common law.

[58] Thus, where a tort was waived, and a sale by the defendant adopted, the plaintiff was not suing on the contract of sale, but suing his 'agent' for the proceeds.

[59] *Whitecomb* v. *Jacob* (1710) 1 Salk. 160.

[60] Cf. S. J. Stoljar's analysis of claims for money: the action 'is not in rem but ad rem [...] whereas the *right* to money is proprietary, the *action* by which we enforce it is personal': *The Law of Quasi-Contract* (2nd edn, 1989), 7.

[61] *Scott* v. *Surman* (1743) Willes 400 at 405. Willes J. also held, *obiter*, that where the legal property had passed to a factor who became bankrupt, equitable property remained in the principal, and did not pass to the bankrupt's assignees.

[62] According to *Taylor* v. *Plumer* (1815) 3 M. & S. 562, this could be done so long as such money was not mingled with other money.

[63] *L'Apostre* v. *Le Plaistrier* (1708) cited in 1 P. Wms. 318. Cf. *Burdett* v. *Willett* (1708) 2 Vern. C.C. 638.

personal debt would be generated. In this situation, equity would raise a trust, generating an equitable proprietary claim against the agent, although only a personal claim might be available at common law.[64]

Common lawyers continued to view the remedy as proprietary in some situations, and personal in others, seeing it as proprietary in cases where trover might have been brought against the defendant. It was only towards the end of the century that judges made it clear that the action was to be regarded as generally a personal one. Until then, even in cases where the action looked clearly personal, judges did not treat it as if it were based on a contract claim. Rather they regarded it as an action to ensure repayment of the plaintiff's money.

2. WAIVER OF TORT

Where a defendant had obtained money belonging to the plaintiff through tortious[65] conduct, such as conversion or deceit, the plaintiff could either sue in tort or 'waive the tort' and use the action for money had and received to recover these proceeds. As Park J. put it in *Marsh* v. *Keating*, if property was wrongfully taken, the plaintiff could 'elect to consider him as his agent, [...] adopt the sale, and maintain an action for the price'.[66] That this remedy was not seen as properly contractual, or based on any actual agency, however, is evident from *Oughton* v. *Seppings*, where the plaintiff successfully sued a sheriff for money had and received after he had seized and sold a pony she had lent to her lodger, under an execution against him. Since her husband had been the owner of the pony, it was claimed that even if she could maintain an action in tort (arising from her possession of it), she could not maintain a contractual action of *indebitatus assumpsit*, unless she could show that she was suing as his executrix or administratrix. This argument cut no ice with the court. 'If she was in possession at the time when it was seized, she might clearly have maintained trespass against a wrongdoer', Lord Tenterden CJ ruled, 'and if she might maintain trespass, she may waive the tort, and maintain this action to recover the money which was produced by the

---

[64] Where no trust was raised, and the money owed was not the proceeds of identifiable property, claims for money had and received had to be along with other creditors in bankruptcy: *Ex p Child* (1751) 1 Atk. 111. At the same time, not all trust claims were proprietary: although trust property which had been misused by a trustee could be followed, money due for breaches of trust were 'a simple contract debt, and can only fall upon the personal estate of a trustee': *Vernon* v. *Vawdry* (1740) 2 Atk. 119. Cf. *Bartlett* v. *Hodgson* (1785) 1 T.R. 42.

[65] See *Yates* v. *Eastwood* (1851) 6 Exch. 805, which held that where there was no wrongful act done by a landlord in distraining too many goods, an action for money had and received could not lie. See also *Evans* v. *Wright* (1857) 2 H. & N. 527.

[66] *Marsh* v. *Keating* (1833–4) 2 Cl. & F. 250 at 285.

sale of the horse.'[67] The notion that the sheriff had actually sold the horse on her behalf did not suggest itself to the court.[68]

Judges sometimes explained this remedy in proprietary terms. In 1820 in *Abbotts* v. *Barry*, the plaintiff recovered the proceeds of the sale of goods which the defendant had fraudulently induced him to sell to an impecunious third party buyer, while himself pocketing the proceeds. Observing that a sale effected by fraud 'works no change of property', Dallas CJ ruled that the property remained in the original owner, and the profit from the resale was 'money had and received by the defendant, to the use of the plaintiffs, who were the original proprietors'.[69] In *Powell* v. *Rees*, the Queen's Bench took a similarly proprietary view in permitting the plaintiffs to recover from the estate of an intestate the value of coal he had wrongfully extracted from their land. '[T]he money which has been produced by the sale of that which had been wrongfully severed from the plaintiffs' [land], and converted into chattels', Denman CJ held, 'is traced into the pocket of the intestate [...] His personal estate has come to the hands of the defendant, by so much increased.'[70]

Where money itself was tortiously obtained, a proprietary analysis was harder to sustain. Nonetheless, in such cases, the courts did not look at the dispute in contractual terms, but in terms of whether the defendant had wrongfully acquired money 'belonging to the plaintiff'. Thus, in *Edmeads* v. *Newman* in 1823, the plaintiff bankers were permitted to use the action to recover money wrongfully obtained by the provisional assignee of a bankrupt bank, who had obtained the payment of securities given by the plaintiffs' bank, when no debt was in fact outstanding on a balance of securities held on both sides. In Bayley J.'s view, 'the defendant was never entitled to receive the money in question, and therefore cannot, by obtaining it in the manner described in the case, be placed in a better situation than before'.[71] On occasion, judges in these cases used more explicitly proprietary language. In *Marsh* v. *Keating*, the House of Lords, on the advice of the common law judges, permitted one of the victims of Henry Fauntleroy's frauds to recover the proceeds of stock, which he had paid into the defendants' account. They were his partners, who 'had no knowledge that the money was the property of the Plaintiff'.[72] In *Neate* v. *Harding* in 1851, the plaintiff recovered

---

[67] *Oughton* v. *Seppings* (1830) 1 B. & Ad. 241.

[68] She could have sued in trover: the fact that she had recovered the goods did not remove her right to sue in trover, for as Holt CJ put it 'the having of the goods after would go only in mitigation of the damages': *Baldwin* v. *Cole* (1704) 6 Mod. 212.

[69] *Abbotts* v. *Barry* (1820) 2 B. & B. 369 at 371.   [70] *Powell* v. *Rees* (1837) 7 Ad. & El. 426 at 428.

[71] *Edmeads* v. *Newman* (1823) 1 B. & C. 418 at 423.

[72] *Marsh* v. *Keating* (1834) 1 Bing. N.C. 198 at 220, 2 Cl. & F. 250 at 289. On this case, see J. Edelman, 'Marsh v Keating (1834)' in C. Mitchell and P. Mitchell, *Landmark Cases in the Law of Restitution* (Oxford, 2005), 97–122.

money taken by poor law overseers from his mother's house and paid into their bank account. According to Pollock CB, '[t]he owner of property wrongfully taken has a right to follow it, and, subject to a change by sale in market overt, treat it as his own, and adopt any act done to it'.[73] Pollock cited *Taylor* v. *Plumer* as authority for his position, although in that case Lord Ellenborough had stated that property ceased to be identifiable and could no longer be followed in trover 'when the subject is turned into money, and mixed and confounded in a general mass of the same description'.[74] Parke B. also saw the issue in proprietary terms, holding it 'competent for the plaintiff either to bring trover or trespass for taking the particular coin, or to waive the tort and sue for money had and received'.[75] Only Martin B. put forward a contractual analysis of the defendants' obligation; and it was an extremely confused one. 'If the case had stood simply upon the taking of the money out of the house, I should have had some doubt whether the action for money had and received would lie', he said, 'for that is an action on a contract; and torts and contracts are of a very different nature.' But since the defendants had paid the money into a bank, 'that makes them both responsible as upon a contract, for they enter into a contract with the bank in respect of the money; and therefore I think that the action for money had and received is maintainable'.[76] Quite what the defendants' contract with the bank had to do with their liability to the plaintiff was unexplained.

Where plaintiffs chose to use the contractual action of *indebitatus assumpsit*, rather than trover, to recover the proceeds of the tort, it was because the former action offered two procedural advantages. First, the plaintiff did not have to prove the value of the items taken and converted, but only the sum received by the defendant. There was therefore little scope for the jury to award such damages as it saw fit. Secondly, since the action sounded in contract, and not in tort, it could be brought against executors.[77] Eighteenth-century judges, who held that

---

[73] *Neate* v. *Harding* (1851) 6 Exch. 349 at 351. Cf. the comment of Erle J. in *Holt* v. *Ely* (1853) 1 E. & B. 795 at 800 that 'where the money has been paid through the tort of the defendant, the action for money had and received has many of the incidents of an action of trover'.

[74] *Taylor* v. *Plumer* (1815) 3 M. & S. 562 at 575. Nevertheless, as has been seen, in *Marsh* v. *Keating*, the House of Lords did allow such a claim. For a discussion of Ellenborough's approach, see L. D. Smith, 'Tracing in *Taylor* v. *Plumer*: Equity in the Court of King's Bench' [1995] *Lloyds Maritime and Commercial Law Quarterly* 240–68. See also L. D. Smith, *The Law of Tracing* (Oxford, 1997), 169–74.

[75] *Neate* v. *Harding* (1851) 6 Exch. 349 at 351. Trover was maintainable to recover specific banknotes or cash: *Isaack* v. *Clark* (1615) 2 Buls. 306; *Bridges* v. *Hawkesworth* (1851) 21 LJ QB 75.

[76] *Neate* v. *Harding* (1851) 6 Exch. 349 at 352.

[77] Although actions of debt could not originally be brought against executors, since the defence available to the testator of waging his law would not have been available to his executors, it was settled in the seventeenth century that assumpsit could be brought against executors: *Pinchon's Case* (1611) 9 Co. Rep. 86b.

the maxim *actio personalis moritur cum persona* should not apply in contractual actions, also felt that a remedy should be available against executors to recover the value of property wrongfully obtained by the deceased. In explaining the maxim, Lord Mansfield said in 1776 in *Hambly* v. *Trott* that 'where, besides the crime, property is acquired which benefits the testator, there an action for the value of the property shall survive against the executor'.[78] During argument, the court pondered whether a plaintiff should be allowed to recover such proceeds in an action of trover,[79] but rejected this solution, since it was bound by 'express authorities' to the contrary.[80] But Mansfield felt that 'no mischief is done' by denying the plaintiff a remedy in trover, since wherever the cause of action arose, not *ex delicto*, but from 'a duty, which the testator owes the plaintiff; upon principles of civil obligation, another form of action may be brought, as an action for money had and received'.[81] In *Powell* v. *Rees*, the Queen's Bench confirmed that the action for money had and received could be brought against an executor to recover the value of property wrongfully taken by an intestate, even though the foundation of the action was a tort, for which the administrator could not be held liable.[82] This was to use a contractual form to trace the proceeds of property wrongfully acquired, in order to evade the rule preventing recovery for wrongs against an estate.

The action for money had and received could also be used to recover money paid under duress to recover goods wrongfully detained by a defendant who could have been sued in trover. This had been decided in 1732 in *Astley* v. *Reynolds*, where the plaintiff recovered £4 charged in excess of legal interest by a pawnbroker, which he was obliged to pay to recover his goods. The plaintiff's payment here was not induced by mistake or deceit, for the plaintiff knew what he was doing. But the court held that the money had to be repaid: because it had not been paid voluntarily, the defendant had no right to the money.[83] The principle was followed in the nineteenth century.[84] The key issue was whether the payment had been freely made or not,[85] which turned on whether the party making the payment intended to part with his rights or not. 'I am not aware that there is any difficulty or impropriety in laying it down, that, where money is voluntarily paid, with full knowledge of all the circumstances, the party intending to give up his

---

[78] *Hambly* v. *Trott* (1776) 1 Cowp. 371 at 376.

[79] This could be done if trover were to be regarded as a form of action to try title to property—as 'a substitute of the old action of detinue'—rather than being seen in substance as an action *ex maleficio*. *Hambly* v. *Trott* (1776) 1 Cowp. 371 at 373–4.   [80] *Carter* v. *Fossett* (1623) Palm. 329.

[81] *Hambly* v. *Trott* (1776) 1 Cowp. 371 at 377.

[82] *Powell* v. *Rees* (1837) 7 Ad. & El. 426 at 428.   [83] *Astley* v. *Reynolds* (1732) 2 Stra. 915.

[84] See *Atlee* v. *Backhouse* (1838) 3 M. & W. 633 at 650; *Ashmole* v. *Wainwright* (1842) 2 Q.B. 837 at 846.

[85] See also *Fulham* v. *Down* (1798) 6 Esp. 26 n.

right, he cannot afterwards bring an action for money had and received', Tindal CJ said in 1845, 'but that it is otherwise, where, at the time of paying the money, the party gives notice that he intends to resist the claim, and that he yields to it merely for the purpose of relieving himself from the inconvenience of having his goods sold.'[86] It was similarly held in 1836 that, where money had been paid to obtain the plaintiff's release from an unlawful (and malicious) imprisonment for debt, the plaintiff could recover using this action. In Lord Denman's view, the cash handed over to obtain the release was 'still the plaintiff's money', for 'property in the money [...] never passed from the plaintiff, who parted with it only to relieve himself from the hardship and inconvenience of a fraudulent arrest'.[87] As these comments indicate, where a defendant had acquired property without right, which could have been recovered in trover, common law courts would give a remedy, without pretending the repayment was made under any kind of contract.[88]

The nature of the action—which could only be used to recover money—made things more problematic where property was taken, which had not been converted into money. This had been the case in *Hambly* v. *Trott*, where, despite Mansfield's confidence, the count for money had and received could not have been used.[89] In other cases, Mansfield attempted to stretch the action for money had and received to allow the recovery of the value of goods taken.[90] But subsequent judges were hesitant to extend his presumption that goods had been converted into cash, in a way to allow the action to be brought systematically against executors.[91] Although Best CJ stated in 1827 that 'if a party gives another what may be readily turned into money, it may be treated as such in an action for

---

[86] *Valpy* v. *Manley* (1845) 1 C.B. 594 at 603. See also *Snowdon* v. *Davis* (1808) 1 Taunt. 359;, *Green* v. *Duckett* (1883) 11 QBD 275. For other cases of money obtained by duress, see *Parker* v. *Great Western Railway Co* (1844) 7 M. & G. 253; *Close* v. *Phipps* (1844) 7 M. & G. 586; *Oates* v. *Hudson* (1851) 6 Exch. 346. See also the discussion at pp. 401–2.

[87] *Duke de Cadaval* v. *Collins* (1836) 4 Ad. & El. 858 at 864–5.

[88] e.g. *Green* v. *Duckett* (1883) 11 QBD 275.

[89] His confidence may have rested in the fact that the plaintiff could obtain a remedy through the action of detinue, which could be brought against the executor, provided the goods were still in existence. As Sjt Williams wrote, 'if the goods, &c. taken away, continued still in specie, in the hands of the wrong-doer, or of his executor, replevin or detinue would lie for or against the executor to recover back the specific goods; Sir W. Jones, 173, 174 [*Le Mason* v. *Dixon*]; or in case they were consumed, an action for money had and received to recover the value. Cow. 377 [*Hambly* v. *Trott*]': 1 Wms. Saund. 217 note (1). See also *Kettle* v. *Bromsall* (1738) Willes 118, and J. Chitty, *A Practical Treatise on Pleading and on the Parties to Actions*, 2 vols (1809), i: 119–20. See also E. V. Williams, *A Treatise on the Law of Executors and Administrators*, 2 vols (1832), ii: 1065. In general, detinue could be brought even if the goods had gone out the defendant's hands: *Jones* v. *Dowle* (1841) 9 M. & W. 19; *Reeve* v. *Palmer* (1858) 5 C.B. N.S. 84.

[90] *Longchamp* v. *Kenny* (1778) 1 Doug. 137.

[91] See the comments of the court in *Leery* v. *Goodson* (1792) 4 T.R. 687.

money had and received',[92] he was only referring to financial instruments (such as country banknotes or bank drafts) which were treated by the parties as equivalent to money, rather than goods.[93] In order to bring the action, it had to be clear either that the parties had treated the securities as equivalent to money or that it could be reasonably presumed that the defendant had converted the goods into cash.

To overcome the problem that the action for money had and received could not be used to recover the value of goods retained, some judges began to use the common counts, such as goods sold, to provide a remedy, seeking a contract implied in fact between the parties. This can be seen firstly in *Hill* v. *Perrott*,[94] where the defendant was held liable to pay for goods he had obtained by fraud, having by a swindle procured the plaintiff to sell them to an insolvent, who handed them over. The court held that 'the law would imply a contract to pay for the goods, from the circumstance of their having been the plaintiff's property, and having come to the defendant's possession' in a way which could not legally be accounted for.[95] A similar approach was taken by Lord Abinger in 1842, in *Russell* v. *Bell*,[96] when the plaintiffs recovered on a count for goods sold.[97] '[I]f a stranger takes my goods, and delivers them to another man', he said, 'no doubt a contract may be implied, and I may bring an action of trover for them, or of assumpsit.'[98] In this case, the assignees of a bankrupt sought to recover the value of yarn, which had been delivered to the defendants after an act of bankruptcy to meet an accommodation bill. Since this was a fraudulent act, the assignees were entitled either to affirm the contract made by the bankrupt and sue in assumpsit on a contract of sale, or to disaffirm it (for fraud) and sue in trover.[99] According to the defence, since the assignees had chosen to affirm the contract, they were bound by its

---

[92] *Spratt* v. *Hobhouse* (1827) 4 Bing. 173 at 178.

[93] e.g. *Pickard* v. *Bankes* (1810) 13 East 20. Cf. *M'Lachlan* v. *Evans* (1827) 1 Y. & J. 380.

[94] This case was usually cited as authority for the proposition that the tort of deceit could be waived, and money recovered in the contractual form, e.g. Chitty, *Contracts* (2nd edn, 1834), 496.

[95] *Hill* v. *Perrott* (1810) 3 Taunt. 274 at 275.

[96] For a discussion, see Keener, *Quasi-Contract*, 193 *et seq.*

[97] In *Lee* v. *Shore* (1822) 1 B. & C. 94, a plaintiff sought to recover the value of spar taken from land, in an action for goods sold. There being no express contract, the King's Bench refused to entertain the action, since the plaintiff had not proved his property in the spar. Although an action in tort could be maintained for disturbing possession, it was held, where the plaintiff sued on an implied undertaking to pay, the plaintiff had to prove property and possession. Otherwise, Best J. held (at 98), 'after a defendant had paid for the goods, he might be sued in trespass for taking them by another party'. Abbott CJ also said that 'where the owner of property which has been taken away by another, waives the tort, and elects to bring an action of assumpsit for the value, it is incumbent on him to show a clear and indisputable title to that property'.

[98] *Russell* v. *Bell* (1842) 10 M. & W. 340 at 352.

[99] *Smith* v. *Hodson* (1791) 4 T.R. 211. The advantage of the latter method was that the defendant could not set off his debt.

terms, under which the cost of the goods was to be set off against bills due.[100] However, Abinger rejected the argument that the assignees were affirming a contract made through the bankrupt's agency. Instead, he considered the property to have been wrongfully acquired by the defendants via the bankrupt's act, so that the plaintiffs were to be permitted to sue on a different implied contract 'for goods sold and delivered by the assignees'.[101]

In the early nineteenth century, there were other signs that judges were willing to use the common contractual counts to force defendants to pay for benefits obtained by torts. Judges allowed counts for work and labour to be used to recover the value of work done, where the defendant had committed the tort of seduction of an apprentice or servant. In *Lightly* v. *Clouston*,[102] the Common Pleas allowed the master of an apprentice who had been seduced to work on board the defendant's ship to recover the value of his services in an action for work and labour. The court rejected the defendant's argument that the labour was obtained, not as a result of a contract with the plaintiff, but thanks to one with the apprentice. In doing so, it was partly influenced by the bankruptcy cases, where assignees were permitted to waive the defendant's fraud and adopt his contract with the bankrupt. But instead of explicitly stating that the plaintiff was to be taken to have adopted the apprentice's contract, the judgments of Mansfield CJ and Heath J. treated the case as if it (and the assignee cases) were ones for money had and received. They appeared to consider that, where the plaintiff waived a tort, the counts for work and labour and goods sold could be applied on the same principle as money had and received.[103]

This decision was followed in *Foster* v. *Stewart* in 1814, though with some reluctance on Lord Ellenborough's part.[104] Le Blanc J. was less reluctant. Not only was he willing to find for the plaintiff on the ground that there was a contract by the apprentice, which could be adopted by the master, but he said more generally that, 'inasmuch as the defendant has had a beneficial service of the apprentice, the plaintiff may waive the tort and require of him the value of the benefit'. In his

---

[100] For the proposition that a party affirming a contract was bound by its terms, see *Strutt* v. *Smith* (1834) 1 C. M. & R. 312.

[101] Alderson B. rested the matter on a simple contract for the sale of the goods which had been delivered, rejecting the defendant's evidence about the terms. This allowed the assignees to adopt the bankrupt's contract of sale, without permitting the complicit creditor to set up special terms. *Russell* v. *Bell* (1842) 10 M. & W. 340 at 354.

[102] *Lightly* v. *Clouston* (1808) 1 Taunt. 112.

[103] Thus, Mansfield CJ treated *Smith* v. *Hodson* (1791) 4 T.R. 211 as an action for money had and received, although it was an action for goods sold and delivered.

[104] *Foster* v. *Stewart* (1814) 3 M. & S. 191 at 198. As Scarlett put it in argument, 'as well might it be said that if a man take the goods of another, the owner of the goods may have assumpsit against him for goods sold': *Foster* v. *Stewart* (1814) 3 M. & S. 191 at 196.

view, the example of the action of money had and received showed that the contractual form could be used to recover for claims which were not contractual.[105]
Although, in these cases, it was possible to find a real contract made between
plaintiff and defendant through the agency of the intermediary, early nineteenth-
century judges and textbook writers regarded them as situations 'in which the
law raises a promise even from the wrongful acts of a party, and in which the
Courts will not admit of evidence of his intention to commit a tort in disavowal
of such tacit promise'.[106] This was to see the implied promise simply as a formality, a vehicle to reverse the unjust enrichment. These two cases were unusual,
and in subsequent cases masters generally sued for the tort of seduction, rather
than waiving the tort.[107] These attempts to use the 'properly' contractual common
counts for claims to obtain restitution for wrongs were controversial, since the
counts for goods sold or work and labour at the defendant's request were—unlike
the action for money had and received—premised on the existence of a 'proper'
contract, either express or implied in fact. Although textbook writers continued
to state that the law would imply a promise to pay the original employer for the
services of a servant wrongfully enticed to work for the defendant, [108] Bowen LJ
in 1883 referred to *Lightly* v. *Clouston* as '[o]ne of the most remarkable instances
of a waiver of tort', and chose to lay greater stress on the contractual aspects of
the obligation.[109] Any suggestion from these cases that a wider principle of unjust
enrichment might be developed alongside obligations derived from breaches of
contract or tort was not taken up.

In the second half of the century, judges continued to regard the remedy
given in 'waiver of tort' cases as concerned with recovering the value of property
wrongfully obtained, rather than seeing it as either a contractual remedy or one
more broadly to reverse unjust enrichments. In the aftermath of the mid-century
reforms in pleading, when parties were no longer required to mention the form
of action, the election made by a plaintiff between suing for damages or seeking
an account of the proceeds of the tort was one between different remedies arising

---

[105] *Foster* v. *Stewart* (1814) 3 M. & S. 191 at 201. He stated (at 200), that '[i]n the cases which have
decided that money had and received may be maintained without any privity between the parties,
though it has been truly said that those decisions are founded upon the principle that the money
belongs in justice and equity to the plaintiff, yet in order to attain that justice, the law raises a promise to the plaintiff as if the money were received to his use, which in reality was received by a tortious
act'.

[106] Chitty, *Contract* (4th edn, by J. A. Russell, 1850), 22. Chitty's editor added the word 'wrongful'.
Addison, *Contracts* (4th edn, 1856), 54 treated it as a contract implied in fact.

[107] 107. e.g. *Sykes* v. *Dixon* (1839) 9 Ad. & El. 693; *Cox* v. *Muncey* (1859) 6 C.B. N.S. 375; *De Francesco*
v. *Barnum* (1890) 45 Ch D 430.

[108] Addison, *Contracts* (11th edn, by W. E. Gordon and J. Ritchie, 1911), 453.

[109] *Phillips* v. *Homfray* (1883) 24 Ch D 439 at 462.

from the tort. In this context, the concept of 'waiver of tort' worked to prevent a party from seeking separate remedies for the same harm. It meant, for practical purposes, that a plaintiff, who had recovered in an action arising from the tort against one defendant, could not recover on a different basis from another. Thus, in *Buckland* v. *Johnson*, the plaintiff, who had obtained a judgment in trover against the defendant's son (who had tortiously sold his goods before passing the proceeds to his father) could not sue the father for money had and received, on finding that the original judgment could not be satisfied thanks to the son's insolvency.[110] Similarly, in *Smith* v. *Baker* in 1873, a trustee in bankruptcy who had recovered the proceeds of a bill of sale declared void by the Court of Bankruptcy was not permitted to sue the holder of the bill in trover for the difference between the value of the goods and the proceeds of the sale. '[I]f an action for money had and received is so brought', Bovill CJ held, 'that is in point of law a conclusive election to waive the tort; and so the commencement of an action of trespass or trover is a conclusive election the other way.'[111] This dictum, according to which a conclusive election was made when an action was brought, which would bind even if that action was discontinued, was taken in the twentieth century to suggest that the election transformed the obligation from a tortious to a contractual one. Yet Bovill's judgment did not suggest (as counsel in the case argued)[112] that by bringing the claim for proceeds, the plaintiff was affirming a real contract. His concern was focused on whether by seeking one remedy for the wrong, the plaintiff was precluded from seeking another.[113]

When parties sued in the second half of the nineteenth century to obtain restitution of benefits acquired by tort, they did not need to 'waive the tort' and sue in a 'contractual' action. They were able to sue simply for the tort, and recover whatever property had been lost as a result of the wrong. This can be seen from *Phillips* v. *Homfray* in 1883.[114] The case was brought by the owners of a farm against the partners in the Tredegar Iron Company, which owned a coal mine surrounding the farm. During negotiations for the sale of the farm to the firm, the vendors

---

[110] *Buckland* v. *Johnson* (1854) 15 C.B. 145. Jervis CJ ruled (at 161) 'if two jointly convert goods, and one of them receives the proceeds, you cannot, after a recovery against one in trover, have an action, against the other for the same conversion, or an action for money had and received to recover the value of the goods, for which a judgment has already passed in the former action'. He explained that by the judgment in the trover case, property in the goods themselves passed to the tortfeasor.

[111] *Smith* v. *Baker* (1873) LR 8 CP 350 at 355.   [112] *Smith* v. *Baker* (1873) LR 8 CP 350 at 353.

[113] See also *Rice* v. *Reed* [1900] 1 QB 54, where the plaintiff, having brought a first action with counts in trover and for money received which was compromised, was permitted to sue another tortfeasor for trover. The issue was finally settled in *United Australia* v. *Barclays Bank* [1941] AC 1, which held that a plaintiff was only barred if he had received satisfaction from an alternative remedy.

[114] On this case, see also W. Swadling, 'The Myth of *Phillips* v. *Homfray*', in W. Swadling and G. Jones (eds), *The Search for Principle: Essays in Honour of Lord Goff of Chieveley* (Oxford, 1999), 277–94.

discovered that the purchasers had been mining coal from under it for years, and using the workings to transport coal from their outlying workings to the pithead. Abandoning the sale, they filed a bill in Chancery in September 1866 for an account of the value of the coal extracted and compensation for the use of the land, and for an injunction to prevent further work. In 1871, the plaintiffs obtained a decree for an account of the coals obtained against the two surviving partners of the firm and against the estate of the third; and a decree for compensation for the use of the underground passages against the two surviving partners only. An inquiry was ordered into the sums due, but this was delayed until 1881, pending the outcome of further litigation to decide whether the plaintiffs, as copyholders, were entitled to the minerals.[115] By then, a second partner had died, and the question was raised whether the estate of this deceased partner could be held liable to pay for the trespassory use of the land, as well as being liable for the minerals taken.

The Court of Appeal held that it could not, since such claims were barred by the maxim *actio personalis moritur cum persona*. As Bowen LJ put it, although the deceased defendant may have saved expense by the trespass, he did not bring to his estate 'any additional property or value belonging to another person'.[116] Endorsing the view of Jessel MR that at common law, executors could not be sued for wrongs for which only unliquidated damages could be claimed,[117] he ruled that while estates could be made to return property wrongfully obtained, they were not liable for damages arising from personal wrongs. This was to suggest that restitution for wrongs was essentially proprietary, requiring only a return of property taken from the plaintiff; and that any other claim could only be one for unliquidated damages. It may be noted that Messrs Phillips' claim was brought in a court of equity, and treated as one concerned with compensation due for a tort.[118] In an era after the passing of the forms of action, the claim was not treated as contractual,[119] nor was there any suggestion that the plaintiffs' problems could be overcome by treating it as such.[120] Unfettered by the constraints which had

---

[115] *Llandover* v. *Homfray* (1879) 13 Ch D 380, (1881) 19 Ch D 224 (CA).

[116] *Phillips* v. *Homfray* (1883) 24 Ch D 439 at 463.

[117] *Kirk* v. *Todd* (1881) 21 Ch D 484 at 488.

[118] See Lord Hatherley LC's comments at *Phillips* v. *Homfray* (1871) LR 6 Ch App 770 at 780–1. Equity had long assessed damages for wrongs, when asked to issue injunctions: see e.g. *Crosley* v. *Derby Gas-Light Co* (1838) 3 Myl. & Cr. 428.

[119] As Pearson J. pointed out in the High Court, the inquiries which were directed were not aimed to determine a price to be paid by the wrongdoers for use and occupation: *Phillips* v. *Homfray* (1883) 24 Ch D 439 at 445–7.

[120] Goff and Jones, *Restitution* (7th edn, 2007), 806 demonstrates the difficulties of this approach: 'there remains the objection that no contract can be implied between the parties because the deceased was a trespasser who, by setting up an adverse title, negatived the implication of a contract'.

prevented the King's Bench from giving a remedy in tort in *Hambly* v. *Trott*, the Court of Appeal used the principles evolved in the 'contractual' form of *indebitatus assumpsit* for money had and received simply as a measure for damages available in tort against the estates of tortfeasors.

The case came in for criticism in the twentieth century since it limited restitution for wrongs to cases of 'positive' rather than 'negative' enrichments.[121] In fact, two of the judges who heard the case, Pearson J. in the High Court, and Baggallay LJ in the Court of Appeal, argued that the estate should be liable for the 'negative' enrichment. As Pearson put it, '[i]t is really and truly paying back to the Plaintiffs part of the profit which the Defendants themselves received from using the wayleave instead of raising their coal by a more expensive and difficult way'.[122] Like Pearson, a Chancery barrister by background, Baggallay LJ suggested that equity would give relief against the estate of a deceased party 'if the wrongful act has resulted in a benefit capable of being measured pecuniarily'.[123] These judges not only took a different view of Mansfield's approach in *Hambly* v. *Trott*, but felt that equity's jurisdiction to order an account for profits might offer a remedy here. But theirs was a suggestion which was not acted upon.

3. MISTAKEN PAYMENTS

Besides recovering money acquired by the defendant through a tort, plaintiffs could use the action for money had and received to recover money paid under a mistake. In these cases, provided the donor had not intended to make a gift, but had made the payment under the mistaken assumption that he was liable to the defendant for the sum, he was able to recover on the ground that the donee had no right to retain the money. Where plaintiffs sought to recover general sums of money paid by mistake, the courts did not draw an analogy with recovering chattels which had been converted. Nonetheless, in ordering restitution of the money, they were motivated by the notion that the defendant had obtained money belonging to the plaintiff, and focused their analysis on the defendant

---

[121] See A. S. Burrows, *The Law of Restitution* (2nd edn, 2002), 473–5. Swadling argues that the case was not 'anti-restitutionary' since it was only concerned with the *actio personalis* bar, and (given its later abolition) 'tells us nothing of the restitutionary liability of living wrongdoers' ('Myth', p. 294). He suggests that the case is an authority in favour of restitutionary awards for both positive and negative benefits. But for nineteenth-century judges, it was precisely the existence of the *actio personalis* rule which made plaintiffs bring the restitutionary ('quasi-contractual') claim, rather than a claim in tort. They had yet to explore whether damages for torts were to be calculated on restitutionary principles or other ones.

[122] *Phillips* v. *Homfray* (1883) 24 Ch D 439 a 446.

[123] *Phillips* v. *Homfray* (1883) 24 Ch D 439 at 476. See also *Pulteney* v. *Warren* (1801) 6 Ves. 73 at 86–7.

having no right to the money, rather than seeing his obligation to restore as being derived from either an obligation in conscience, or an implied contract.

The doctrine was most commonly used in cases where the payer mistakenly thought he was contractually liable to the payee,[124] though it could also be used where the presumed source of the plaintiff's liability was not contractual.[125] It was also used in cases of 'overpayment', where one party paid money which he mistakenly thought he was obliged to pay under an existing contract. The classic case of this was *Kelly* v. *Solari*. The defendant had been paid money on a life assurance claim, arising from the death of her husband, Angelo Solari, who had failed to pay the last instalment due on one of three policies taken out on his life. Although it had been written on this policy that it had lapsed, the directors paid his widow her claim on it of £197–10s. At the trial of an action to recover this sum, in July 1841, two directors stated that they had entirely forgotten that the policy had lapsed, when making the payment. A nonsuit was entered, since Lord Abinger CB held they could not claim to have paid under a mistake, having had the means of knowing that the policy had lapsed. By the time a motion for a new trial was heard, facts had emerged which may have influenced the judges to take a less sympathetic view of the claimant. In October 1841, it became apparent that Solari had been involved in fraudulent transactions using forged Exchequer bills, whose value exceeded £400,000,[126] and that Mrs Solari was herself implicated in these matters.[127] In November, when the case came back to the Court of Exchequer, the newspapers were full of stories about the 'Exchequer Bill Frauds'. Henry Beaumont Smith, a clerk in the Exchequer Bill office, was tried in November and sentenced in December for life imprisonment for his part in the affair,[128] and a royal commission was later set up to investigate the matter.[129]

In ordering a new trial, Parke B. laid down the following general proposition:

where money is paid to another under the influence of a mistake, that is, upon the supposition that a specific fact is true, which would entitle the other to the money, but which fact is untrue, and the money would not have been paid if it had been known to the payer that the fact was untrue, an action will lie to recover it back, and it is against conscience to retain it; though a demand may be necessary in those cases in which the party receiving may have been ignorant of the mistake.[130]

---

[124] e.g. *Newsome* v. *Graham* (1829) 10 B. & C. 234.

[125] *Mills* v. *Guardians of Alderbury Union* (1849) 3 Exch. 590

[126] See *The Times*, 30 October 1841, col. 5b; 4 November 1841, col. 5b; 5 November 1841, col. 2e; 1 January 1842, col. 5c.

[127] *The Times*, 10 August 1842, col. 5f; 14 February 1843, col. 2c.

[128] *The Times*, 30 November 1841, col. 6b; 9 December 1841, col. 6e.

[129] Royal Commission on Exchequer Bills, *PP* 1842 (1), xviii, 1.

[130] *Kelly* v. *Solari* (1841) 9 M. & W. 54 at 58.

He rejected the notion that the plaintiffs might be precluded from recovering because of their own laches in not availing themselves of their means of knowledge. The fact that they may have been careless did not give the recipient any greater right to the money. For the court, the jury had to look at the case again to see if the directors had genuinely forgotten the facts, or had initially decided to pay out, in order to avoid the bad publicity which resistance might entail. The court also took a narrow view of how far it could take into account whether it was unconscientious in the other party to retain the money. Rolfe B. said he had great difficulty in envisaging 'under what possible circumstances it can be otherwise than unconscientious to retain money paid under a mistake of facts'. For Parke B., the fact that Mrs Solari thought she was entitled to the money only meant that she should be given notice that she was not. '[I]f the case be one of a nature where the retaining the money would be an unconscientious act on the part of the payee, he ought at once to return it', he observed, 'but, if it be under such circumstances, that he may, at first sight, conceive himself in fairness and reason entitled to it, notice of the mistake ought to be given him by the opposite party.'[131]

This decision overturned a dictum of Bayley J.'s in *Milnes* v. *Duncan*, that if a party 'pay money under a mistake of the real facts, *and no laches are imputable to him* (in respect of his omitting to avail himself of the means of knowledge within his power), he may recover [it] back'.[132] The Common Pleas endorsed *Kelly* v. *Solari* a few months later in *Bell* v. *Gardiner*, while admitting that *Kelly* had changed what was thought in the profession to be the rule. It was clearly 'hard upon the party receiving the money that he should be obliged to refund it, after a long period has elapsed, and when the situation of the parties may have been entirely changed', when the person making the mistake could have found out the truth using the most ordinary diligence.[133] But the judges felt that the possession of the means of knowledge was only evidence for the jury that the party might have had actual knowledge. The result of *Kelly* was that the courts were asked simply to look at whether an overpayment had been made to which the defendant was not entitled. Thus, in *Townsend* v. *Crowdy*, where the plaintiff had paid an inflated sum for a share of a partnership as a result of mistaken calculations as to its profitability, Willes J. said, '[t]his is the simple case of one paying another money which both at the time suppose to be due, but which afterwards turns out in consequence of a mistake of fact on the part of the payer, not to have

[131] *Kelly* v. *Solari* (1841) 6 Jur. 107 at 109.

[132] *Milnes* v. *Duncan* (1827) 6 B. & C. 671 (emphasis added). Here the plaintiff was able to recover paid in error on a bill of exchange mistakenly thought to be invalid.

[133] *Bell* v. *Gardiner* (1842) 4 M. & G. 11 at 20: per Channel Sjt.

been really due. In such a case the law clearly is that the money may be recovered back.'[134]

Modern lawyers contend that the strict view taken in *Kelly* that a defendant must restore what he has no right to is counterbalanced by a broad defence of change of position by the defendant. Some early nineteenth-century cases did hold that it would not be against conscience for a defendant to retain money where he had changed his position. For instance, in *Skyring* v. *Greenwood* in 1825, the paymaster of the Royal Artillery had in error credited the account of a major with an increased level of pay, to which he was not entitled. The King's Bench allowed his administratrix to recover the sums in an action for money had and received, since the defendants had failed in their duty to inform the major that he was not entitled to the raised pay. Although counsel for the plaintiff argued the defendants were estopped from arguing that they had not received money on behalf of the officer, after they had represented 'by an account rendered, that he has received money on his account', the chief justice did not rest his judgment on the estoppel.[135] 'Every prudent man accommodates his mode of living to what he supposes to be his income', Abbott CJ ruled, 'it therefore works a great prejudice to any man, if after having had credit given him in account for certain sums, and having been allowed to draw on his agent on the faith that those sums belonged to him, he may be called upon to pay them back.' In his view, 'justice requires' that the defendants could not retain this money.[136] But in the 1840s, the courts were less sympathetic to a change of position argument, particularly when there was no representation on which to raise an estoppel. Where money was paid by a mistake of fact, Parke B. observed in 1849, 'it could not be any bar to the recovery of it, that the defendant had applied the money in the meantime to some purchase which he otherwise would not have made, and so could not be placed in statu quo'.[137] Courts following this decision in the second half of the nineteenth century agreed that money to which the recipient was not entitled had to be repaid, even if the recipient had changed his position as a result of receiving the money.[138]

Certain kinds of mistakes did not generate a duty to repay. First, if the plaintiff would not have been liable to the defendant had the facts mistaken been true, he

---

[134] *Townsend* v. *Crowdy* (1860) 8 C.B. N.S. 477 at 494–5.

[135] *Skyring* v. *Greenwood* (1825) 4 B. & C. 281 at 287–8. Bayley J. laid greater stress on the fact that the officer had relied on representations made to him.

[136] *Skyring* v. *Greenwood* (1825) 4 B. & C. 281 at 289–90. Cf. *Brisbane* v. *Dacres* (1813) 5 Taunt. 143 at 162.

[137] *Standish* v. *Ross* (1849) 3 Exch. 527 at 534.

[138] *Durrant* v. *Ecclesiastical Commissioners* (1880) 6 QBD 234. Cf. *Newall* v. *Tomlinson* (1871) LR 6 CP 405. It is notable that in neither of these cases did the defendant change his position in reliance on any representation from the plaintiff.

could not recover. Common law courts in the mid-century regarded such payments as voluntary: only if the payer thought he was under a legal obligation (contractual or otherwise) was it regarded as involuntary. If the plaintiff paid while making a mistake as to a collateral matter, rather than mistaking his liability to pay the defendant, he could not recover. Thus, in *Harris* v. *Loyd*, the plaintiffs, who were assignees under a composition agreement among creditors, paid a sheriff £57 to release goods of the debtor which he had seized under a *fieri facias*. It subsequently turned out that the debtor had already committed an act of bankruptcy, which took away their right to the goods. The Exchequer judges were unmoved by the argument that the mistake entitling them to repayment was their assumption that no act of bankruptcy had been committed, and held that they were mere volunteers: 'the money was not paid under a mistake of fact, but upon a speculation, the failure of which cannot entitle the plaintiffs to recover it back'.[139] The plaintiffs were not labouring under any impression that they were obliged to pay the sheriff. They simply assumed mistakenly that by paying him, they would acquire title to the property.[140]

Secondly, it was settled in the nineteenth century that there could be no recovery if the mistake was one of law. This derived from Lord Ellenborough's decision in *Bilbie* v. *Lumley*, where insurers, who were aware of all the relevant facts, paid out on a claim which they were not legally obliged to pay. 'Every man must be taken to be cognizant of the law', he said, 'otherwise there is no saying to what extent the excuse of ignorance might not be carried'.[141] Ellenborough's approach reflected that of Pothier, though not that of other civilians.[142] In 1813, the Common Pleas in *Brisbane* v. *Dacres* confirmed Ellenborough's approach that money paid under a mistake of law could not be recovered. As Gibbs J. saw it, 'it would be most mischievous and unjust, if he who has acquiesced in the right by such voluntary payment, should be at liberty, at any time within the statute of limitations, to rip up the matter, and recover back the money'.[143] The decision was not unanimous, for Chambre J. considered it a 'dangerous doctrine, that a man getting possession of money, to any extent, in consequence of another's ignorance of the law, cannot be called on to repay it'.[144] But in 1827, Bayley J. in the King's Bench confirmed

---

[139] *Harris* v. *Loyd* (1839) 5 M. & W. 432 at 436. Alderson B. agreed that they paid not under a mistake, but under a bad bargain.

[140] See also *Aiken* v. *Short* (1856) 1 H. & N. 210 at 215.

[141] *Bilbie* v. *Lumley* (1802) 2 East 469 at 472.

[142] W. D. Evans was critical of this view, feeling that money paid under mistake of law should be recoverable, provided there was no natural obligation to pay it. Evans, *Essay*, Ch. 1, section 1. See also De Grey CJ's *obiter* comments in *Farmer* v. *Arundel* (1772) 2 W. Bl. 824 at 825.

[143] *Brisbane* v. *Dacres* (1813) 5 Taunt. 140 at 152–3.

[144] *Brisbane* v. *Dacres* (1813) 5 Taunt. 140 at 159.

that if a party paid money under a mistake of the law, it could not be recovered.[145] The rule was accepted as settled in the nineteenth century.[146] The justifications, that all people were expected to know the law, and that to presume otherwise would encourage uncertain litigation, came in for criticism from Keener,[147] but the rule remained in place until the end of the twentieth century.[148]

4. FAILURE OF CONSIDERATION

The action was also used to recover money deposited on a contract before any part of the contract was performed by the other party, or any benefit had been received.[149] Where a contract for the purchase of an estate was abandoned, the buyer could recover his deposit in this form.[150] Similarly, where a project for a tontine was abandoned, subscribers were able to use it to recover their deposits.[151] Equally, the father of a bastard child who paid money for its maintenance could recover the money remaining in the parish officers' hands on the death of the child.[152] The action was also used when a contract had been entered into for the purchase of a non-existent thing. Instead of suing for damages for breach of contract, the plaintiff could elect to rescind the contract, and to recover the money paid for failure of consideration.

In the second half of the nineteenth century, when doctrinal writers began to develop the doctrine of contractual mistake, the notion developed that contracts which were founded on an error as to the existence of a thing were void *ab initio*. With such a doctrine in place, restitution could be justified on the basis that the payer had been under the mistaken belief that he was contractually liable to pay the defendant, when no such contractual obligation existed. But the early nineteenth-century cases, where the payer recovered for total failure of consideration, began with the premise that there had been a valid contract, which could be rescinded on total failure of consideration. Thus, in *Wilkinson v. Johnston*, a plaintiff who had taken up dishonoured bills for the honour of the indorsees

---

[145] *Milnes v. Duncan* (1827) 6 B. & C. 671 at 677.

[146] e.g, Willes J. in *Townsend v. Crowdy* (1860) 8 C.B. N.S. 477 at 495 said '[t]he only distinction is between error or mistake of law, for which the payer is responsible, and error or mistake of fact, for which he is not', and Lord Abinger's statement in *Kelly v. Solari* (1847) 9 M. & W. 54 at 57.

[147] Keener, *Quasi-Contract*, 85–92.

[148] *Kleinwort Benson v. Lincoln City Council* [1999] 2 AC 349, where (at 368) the court took into account W. D. Evans's views.

[149] Chitty, *Contracts* (2nd edn, 1834), 487.

[150] He could not get any damages, since they could only be recovered on the contract which had been abandoned: *Gosbell v. Archer* (1835) 2 Ad. & El. 500. See also *Wright v. Newton* (1835) 2 C. M. & R. 124.

[151] *Nockels v. Crosby* (1825) 3 B. & C. 814.   [152] *Chappell v. Poles* (1837) 2 M. & W. 867.

was able to recover the money paid on discovering that the bills were forgeries. As Abbott CJ put it, 'money paid under a mistake of facts may be recovered back, as being paid without consideration'.[153] Similarly, in *Strickland* v. *Turner* in 1852, a plaintiff who had purchased an annuity on a mistaken assumption by both parties that the person on whose life the annuity depended was still alive, was able to recover, since the money 'which was paid, was paid wholly without consideration'.[154]

Where the action for money had and received was used, the plaintiff was not suing on the contract,[155] but for money remaining in the defendant's hands on its failure. To recover in this action, the contract had to be regarded as rescinded, with both parties returning to the *status quo ante*. The fact that the action by which this sum was recovered was contractual in form did not mean that courts imagined it was in any sense contractual in substance.[156] This can be seen by the contrasting approach taken to this count and the other common counts. Where a plaintiff had been induced by fraud to buy goods, he could rescind the contract by returning the goods. As Lord Tenterden put it, the fraud here 'destroyed the contract altogether', allowing the buyer to recover his money in an action for money had and received.[157] By contrast, where goods were sold on credit to a fraudulent buyer, or where work was done for a customer who had lied about the amount of work to be done, the plaintiff could not ignore the terms of the contract, and sue on the common counts for goods sold or work and labour. If the contract gave a period of credit to a buyer who had no intention of ever paying, the plaintiff could not sue in assumpsit until the credit period had expired.[158] For by bringing a contractual action, the plaintiff was held to have affirmed the contract, and so was bound by its terms. As Lord Abinger CB put it, 'a party cannot be bound by an implied contract, when he has made a specific contract, which is avoided by fraud'.[159] To recover, such a plaintiff had to treat the contract as void on the ground of fraud, and sue in trover or deceit. Courts which allowed the party to sue for money had and

---

[153] *Wilkinson* v. *Johnston* (1824) 3 B. & C. 428 at 434. See also *Jones* v. *Ryde* (1814) 5 Taunt. 488.

[154] *Strickland* v. *Turner* (1852) 7 Exch. 208 at 219.

[155] See *Walstab* v. *Spottiswoode* (1846) 15 M. & W. 501 at 514.

[156] For instance, the notion was not articulated that there was an implied term in the contract which had failed to restore money.

[157] *Street* v. *Blay* (1831) 2 B. & Ad. 456 at 462.

[158] *Ferguson* v. *Carrington* (1829) 9 B. & C. 59. See also *Read* v. *Hutchinson* (1813) 3 Camp. 352. In *Strutt* v. *Smith* (1834) 1 C. M. & R. 312 at 315, Parke B. ruled in another case involving a period of credit that the plaintiffs might 'have maintained trover, on the ground that the fraud vitiated the contract; but, if they treat the transaction as a contract at all, they must take the contract altogether, and be bound by the specified terms'.

[159] *Selway* v. *Fogg* (1839) 5 M. & W. 83.

received after rescinding a contract for fraud thus regarded it as an alternative to bringing an action of deceit or trover.

Although a contract could be rescinded for fraud after performance had begun, where a party terminated for failure of consideration, the failure had to be total, with no consideration having passed.[160] Once any performance had been accepted, it was considered impossible to place the parties back to the *status quo ante*,[161] and the plaintiff lost his right to terminate and sue for money had and received. Instead, he had to sue on the contract.[162] The strict approach of the common law, which did not allow rescission unless there had been total failure of consideration, contrasted with the approach of the Chancery, where contracts could be rescinded even where a complete *restitutio in integrum* was no longer possible, since that court could order an account of profits.[163]

Total failure of consideration could be hard to establish, for courts were willing to find consideration even where the parties seemed to have acted under a serious mistake. This can be seen in patent cases, where the plaintiff had paid money for the use of patent rights, only to discover subsequently that the defendant did not have the exclusive rights claimed. In *Taylor* v. *Hare*, the defendant agreed to allow the plaintiff to use his invention (for preserving the oil of hops used in brewing) for 14 years at an annual fee. In fact, the invention was not new, but had been in public use before he obtained his patent, and so the patent was void. It was clear that both parties had been mistaken; but the plaintiff was unable to recover his money, for the Common Pleas held that the plaintiff had obtained the enjoyment of what he had stipulated for. The plaintiff had used the patent-right during a period of time when it was thought to be valid. By analogy, Heath J. observed, '[i]t might as well be said, that if a man lease land, and the lessee pay rent, and afterwards be evicted, that he shall recover back the rent, though he has taken the fruits of the land'.[164] This view was reiterated in 1856 in *Lawes* v. *Purser*. Here, Wightman J. observed that the parties might only have discovered the invalidity of the patent at the time of the litigation: 'it is clear to me that

---

[160] *Hunt* v. *Silk* (1804) 5 East 449 at 452. See also *Blackburn* v. *Smith* (1848) 2 Exch. 783. See also W. Swain, 'Cutter v Powell and the Pleading of Claims of Unjust Enrichment', *Restitution Law Review* 11 (2003) 46–56; but contrast T. A. Baloch, *Unjust Enrichment and Contract* (Oxford, 2009), 123–4.

[161] *Beed* v. *Blandford* (1828) 2 Y. & J. 278.

[162] *Harnor* v. *Groves* (1855) 15 C.B. 667. Cf. *Chapman* v. *Morton* (1843) 11 M. & W. 534.

[163] *Small* v. *Attwood* (1832) You. 407 at 506; *Erlanger* v. *The New Sombrero Phosphate Co* (1878) 3 App Cas 1218.

[164] *Taylor* v. *Hare* (1805) 1 B. & P. N.R. 260 at 262. Cf. Chambre J.'s comments at 263: 'In the case of Arkwright's patent, which was not overturned till very near the period at which it would have expired, very large sums of money had been paid [. . .] for the privilege of using the patent-right, but no money ever was recovered back which had been paid for the use of that patent'.

enjoyment by permission of the patentee, whilst the patent was supposed to be valid, is consideration'.[165]

In the early nineteenth century, questions were often raised about payments made under annuities, which were void because they had not been registered according to the Annuity Act.[166] Late eighteenth-century litigation determined that where an annuity was voided as a result of a mistake or omission in form, the seller of the annuity had to return the consideration given for it, as it was 'unconscientious in the party to retain it'.[167] Since the contract on which the payment was made had failed, the money had to be repaid.[168] However, if annuity payments had been made, the fact that the security was later voided on the grounds of not having been correctly registered did not entitle the purchaser to recover the money paid for the annuity. In *Davis* v. *Bryan*, where the executors of the recipient of an annuity attempted to recover the money after his death, Bayley J. held that there was no conscience in the claim. Having begun from Mansfield's equitable principle, he went on to suggest that, in such cases, the annuity was to be regarded not as void but 'voidable only at the will of the party'.[169] Holroyd J. by contrast felt that the court could not now set it aside, since the contract had been fully executed. Similarly, in *Molton* v. *Camroux*, the administratrix of a lunatic was unable to recover premiums he had paid for annuities received from the defendants, either on the grounds of his incapacity to contract or for want of an enrolment of the annuity. '[W]e may safely conclude', Pollock CB ruled, 'that when a person, apparently of sound mind, and not known to be otherwise, enters into a contract for the purchase of property which is fair and bona fide, and which is executed and completed, and the property, the subject-matter of the contract, has been paid for and fully enjoyed, and cannot be restored so as to put the parties in statu quo, such contract cannot afterwards be set aside, either by the alleged lunatic, or those who represent him.'[170] Such an approach was to consider the defect in the contract cured by its execution.

Contracts founded on an illegal consideration were void. Parties who had paid money on such contracts could recover it for total failure of consideration,

---

[165] *Lawes* v. *Purser* (1856) 6 E. & B. 930 at 935. This was an action to recover the money promised. Contrast *Chanter* v. *Leese* (1838) 4 M. & W. 295, where the patent was not used. For another case where the court found a consideration in the grant of a non-existent patent, see *Begbie* v. *The Phosphate Sewage Co* (1875) LR 10 QB 491.

[166] An Act for registering the grants of life annuities, 1777 (17 Geo. III, c. 26), repealed and replaced in 1813 (53 Geo. III, c. 141).

[167] *Shove* v. *Webb* (1787) 1 T.R. 732 at 735. Cf. *Scurfield* v. *Gowland* (1805) 6 East 241.

[168] See the debate over whether there was a failure of contract between Powell and Evans: Evans, *Essay*, 48ff. Cf. F. Plowden, *A Treatise upon the Law of Usury and Annuities* (1797), 444 et seq.

[169] *Davis* v. *Bryan* (1827) 6 B. & C. 651 at 656.

[170] *Molton* v. *Camroux* (1848) 2 Exch. 487 at 503.

provided they did not rely on the illegal transaction. The distinction arose from a dictum of Buller J. in the marine insurance case of *Lowry* v. *Bourdieu*, where it was held that the assured could not recover his premium on a policy in which he had no insurable interest after the ship had arrived safely.[171] In his judgment, Buller J. distinguished between executed and executory contracts, suggesting that the plaintiffs might have succeeded had they rescinded the contract, and brought their action before the risk was run.[172] Although some early nineteenth-century judges toyed with drawing a different distinction—between immoral and illegal transactions, or *mala in se* and *mala prohibita*[173]—this approach was rejected by 1820.[174] Instead, Buller's distinction was accepted in the nineteenth century.[175] Littledale J. confirmed in 1828 that '[i]f two parties enter into an illegal contract, and money is paid upon it by one to the other, that may be recovered back before the execution of the contract, but not afterwards'.[176] Parties were thus permitted to repent of their illegal contracts.[177]

The principle was acted on in 1860 in *Bone* v. *Ekless*, where the defendant, who wished to sell a ship to the Turkish government, authorized his agent to bribe officials. £500 of the purchase price was earmarked for bribes, though only £300 was actually paid over. When sued by his agent for arrears of salary, the defendant sought to set off the amount of the bribe still in the agent's hands. He was permitted to do so: for the illegal contract had not been fully executed, and it was still open to him to countermand the order to pay the £200 bribe. As Bramwell B. put it, '[t]he law is in favour of undoing or defeating an illegal purpose, and is

---

[171] This was simply the case of one party making a bet, Evans explained, and seeking to recover his stake when he saw he had lost: Evans, *Essay*, 36–42.

[172] *Lowry* v. *Bourdieu* (1780) 2 Doug. 468 at 471. The principle was acted on in *Andree* v. *Fletcher* (1789) 3 T.R. 266, where the party paying the premiums had in fact won the bet—his ship had been captured—but had not been paid by the insurer. The decision was therefore criticized by Evans who felt that it was against conscience for the insurer to retain the premiums. As he pointed out, the 'winner' of a bet was able to recover his deposit after the 'loser' refused to pay in the badly reported case of *Lacaussade* v. *White* (1798) 7 T.R. 535. The report suggested that 'whereever money has been paid upon an illegal consideration, it may be recovered back again by the party who has thus improperly paid it'. The authority of the latter case was regarded as shaken in *Aubert* v. *Walsh* (1810) 3 Taunt. 277.

[173] *Tappenden* v. *Randall* (1801) 2 B. & P. 467 at 471.

[174] *Aubert* v. *Maze* (1801) 2 B. & P. 371 at 374; *Cannan* v. *Bryce* (1819) 3 B. & Ald. 179 at 183–4.

[175] *Tappenden* v. *Randall* (1801) 2 B. & P. 467 at 471. See also *Aubert* v. *Walsh* (1810) 3 Taunt. 277 and Lord Ellenborough's reluctant endorsement in *Palyart* v. *Leckie* (1817) 6 M. & S. 290.

[176] *Hastelow* v. *Jackson* (1828) 8 B. & C. 221 at 226.

[177] Twentieth-century judges (following the view of Mellish LJ in *Kearley* v. *Thomson* (1890) 24 QBD 742 (CA)) regarded this as unsettled until the later nineteenth century cases of *Taylor* v. *Bowers* (1876) 1 QBD 291 and *Symes* v. *Hughes* (1870) LR 9 Eq 475, 479: e.g. *Tinsley* v. *Milligan* [1994] 1 AC 340. See also Goff & Jones, *Restitution* (7th edn, 2007), 619, discussing marriage brokerage cases in equity.

therefore in favour of the recovery of the money before the illegal purpose is fulfilled, not afterwards'.[178] Similarly, in *Taylor* v. *Bowers* in 1876, a plaintiff who had agreed to assign goods to his nephew to defeat his creditors was able to recover the goods, since he had never executed the fraudulent agreement by making a formal assignment. As Cockburn CJ explained, 'The action is not founded upon the illegal agreement, nor brought to enforce it, but, on the contrary, the plaintiff has repudiated the agreement, and his action is founded on that repudiation.'[179] Mellish LJ explained, '[t]o hold that the plaintiff is enabled to recover does not carry out the illegal transaction, but the effect is to put everybody in the same situation as they were before the illegal transaction was determined upon, and before the parties took any steps to carry it out'.[180]

By contrast, where the illegal consideration had been executed, no recovery was possible. In such cases, the courts did not regard the contract as valid—for it was vitiated by the illegality—but they would not assist someone who had to rest their right to recovery on an illegality to which they were party.[181] The principle was invoked by Lord Denman CJ in 1844 in refusing to allow the plaintiff to recover money paid on an illegal compromise with poor law guardians of a suit for the maintenance of a bastard child. '[I]f the transaction was wrong', he said, 'the parties are *in pari delicto*, and one of them cannot, after voluntarily paying his money, repent and then sue the other.'[182] If a party to an illegal contract refused to pay money, his adversary could not obtain it in an action which rested on the illegality. But once the money was voluntarily paid, it could not be recovered.[183] As Lord Abinger CB put it in 1839, 'the repayment of money lent for the express purpose of accomplishing an illegal object, cannot be enforced'.[184]

An exception to this rule had been developed in the eighteenth century. If the parties were not *in pari delicto*, but money had been paid under some kind of oppression or compulsion, the more innocent party was entitled to recover. The distinction derived from a dictum of Mansfield:

If the act is in itself immoral, or a violation of the general laws of public policy, there, the party paying shall not have this action; for where both parties are equally criminal against such general laws, the rule is, *potior est conditio defendentis*. But there are other

---

[178] *Bone* v. *Ekless* (1860) 29 LJ Ex 440, 5 H. & N. 925.
[179] *Taylor* v *Bowers* (1876) 1 QBD 291 at 295.
[180] *Taylor* v. *Bowers* (1876) 1 QBD 291 at 300.
[181] The result of this approach, which was rooted in public policy, was that property could pass by an illegal contract. See Mansfield's judgment in *Holman* v. *Johnson* (1775) 1 Cowp. 341. See also *Taylor* v. *Chester* (1869) LR 4 QB 309.
[182] *Goodall* v. *Lowndes* (1844) 6 Q.B. 464 at 467.
[183] *Wilson* v. *Ray* (1839) 10 Ad. & El. 82.
[184] *M'Kinnell* v. *Robinson* (1839) 3 M. & W. 434 at 441.

laws, which are calculated for the protection of the subject against oppression, extortion, deceit, &c. If such laws are violated, and the defendant takes advantage of the plaintiff's condition or situation, there the plaintiff shall recover.[185]

Thus, where a creditor, who refused to sign a bankrupt's certificate unless he was paid, demanded money from a bankrupt's family, it could be recovered.[186] Similarly, illegal insurance premiums paid to lottery office keepers could be recovered, since the laws which forbad such insurances were designed to protect the public.[187] This notion that a party to an illegal contract could sue when the illegality derived from the breach of a statute designed to protect the plaintiff remained in place throughout the century.[188]

By the nineteenth century, particular rules had also developed about the circumstances in which money could be recovered from stakeholders, deposited for illegal wagers. In the case of legal wagers, only the winner was entitled to recover the money in the stakeholder's hands, and the loser was not permitted to rescind the contract prior to the money being paid over.[189] But where the bet was illegal, both parties were permitted in law to recover their money from the stakeholder before he had paid it over to the winner. This meant that the loser of a bet could still recover his stake. It was decided in 1795 that the stakeholder could not in conscience retain the money, even if the contract between the parties was illegal: '[A]s long as the money remains in his hands, he is answerable to some one for it.'[190] At the same time, Lord Kenyon expressed the view that if the money had been paid over, no action would lie against the stakeholder. But in *Hastelow* v. *Jackson* in 1828, the King's Bench permitted the plaintiff to recover his stake from a stakeholder who had paid it to the winner of a bet on a boxing match, since he had warned him not to pay the money over. Littledale J. in this case regarded it as an instance of the plaintiff rescinding the illegal agreement before its execution. It was clear enough that if the event had happened and the money paid over, 'that is considered as a complete execution of the contract, and the Money cannot be reclaimed'. But where the stakeholder had not yet paid the money over, although the event had taken place, 'the contract is not completely executed until the money has been paid over, and therefore the party may retract at any time before that has been done'.[191] Although the 1845 Gaming Act enacted

---

[185] *Smith* v. *Bromley* (1760) 2 Doug. 696 n.

[186] See also *Smith* v. *Cuff* (1817) 6 M. & S. 160; *Atkinson* v. *Denby* (1861) 6 H. & N. 778 at 798.

[187] *Jaques* v. *Golightly* (1776) 2 W. Bl. 1073; *Browning* v. *Morris* (1778) 2 Cowp. 790.

[188] See *Reynell* v. *Sprye* (1852) 1 De G. M. & G. 660 at 678; *Kearley* v. *Thomson* (1890) 24 QBD 742 at 747; *Barclay* v. *Pearson* [1893] 2 Ch 154.

[189] *Marryat* v. *Broderick* (1837) 2 M. & W. 369; *Emery* v. *Richards* (1845) 14 M. & W. 728.

[190] *Cotton* v. *Thurland* (1793) 5 T.R. 405 at 409. See also *Smith* v. *Bickmore* (1812) 4 Taunt. 474.

[191] *Hastelow* v. *Jackson* (1828) 8 B. & C. 221 at 226–7. See also *Hodson* v. *Terrill* (1833) 1 C. & M. 797 at 804; *Gatty* v. *Field* (1846) 9 Q.B. 431; *Busk* v. *Walsh* (1812) 4 Taunt. 290.

that no suit could be brought to recover money or thing deposited in the hands of a person to abide the result of wager, the Act was interpreted not to apply when the wager was repudiated while the stake money remained in the stakeholder's hands.[192] The general rule that moneys deposited in the hands of a stakeholder could be recovered prior to its being paid over on a void contract remained in place throughout the century.[193]

5. MONEY PAID

Besides using the count for money had and received, money could also be recovered through the *indebitatus* count for 'money paid by the plaintiff for the use of the defendant at his request'. As the formulation of the pleadings—with the averment of a request—shows, this was seen as more contractual in nature than the count for money had and received. According to Bullen and Leake, in this count, a request had to be averred, 'as otherwise no contract would be shown'.[194] Where an actual request had been made, and a benefit conferred, the result was clearly contractual.[195] For instance, if agents had been requested by their principals to lay out money for them, they could recover from their principals using this count.[196] In other cases, where no actual request had been made, the courts looked for something which would justify the implication of a request. A request was not inferred merely because a benefit had been received: voluntary payments could not be recovered. It was well established that 'where a person pays money to another upon my account without my request, assumpsit will not lie without an express promise to repay it for I may have a good reason to resist the payment of the money, and another person shall not pay it for me, whether I will or not'.[197] A party who paid another's debt against his express instructions could thus not recover.[198]

---

[192] *Varney* v. *Hickman* (1847) 5 C.B. 271.

[193] *Diggle* v. *Higgs* (1877) 2 Ex D 422 (CA); *Barclay* v. *Pearson* [1893] 2 Ch 154.

[194] E. Bullen and S. M. Leake, *Precedents of Pleadings* (3rd edn, 1868), 37.

[195] A contract could also be implied as a matter of fact: *Garrard* v. *Cottrell* (1847) 10 Q.B. 679.

[196] *Pawle* v. *Gunn* (1838) 4 Bing. N.C. 445.

[197] *Osborne* v. *Rogers* (1669) 1 Wms. Saund. 264, note (1). See also Kenyon's observation in *Exall* v. *Partridge* (1799) 8 T.R. 308 at 310: 'It has been said, that where one person is benefited by the payment of money by another, the law raises an assumpsit against the former; but that I deny: if that were so, and I owed a sum of money to a friend, and an enemy chose to pay that debt, the latter might convert himself into my debtor, nolens volens'.

[198] *Stokes* v. *Lewis* (1785) 1 T.R. 20. At common law, a debtor could not assign his liabilities under a contract, since the promisee could not be compelled to accept another person's performance (*Robson* v. *Drummond* (1831) 2 B. & Ad. 303; *Humble* v. *Hunter* (1848) 12 Q.B. 310); though the parties could by consent end their agreement and substitute a new one to be performed by a different person. A creditor could not at common law assign his rights, though equity did permit the

Plaintiffs seeking to recover in the money paid count had to establish a nexus—or 'privity'[199]— which allowed the inference of request or authority. This could be done either by showing that the defendant had authorized the plaintiff's spending,[200] or by showing that the plaintiff had been compelled to pay a debt for which the defendant was liable.[201] As Sjt Williams put it, 'if the payment made by the plaintiff be compulsory, the law raises an implied promise on the part of the defendant to repay him; and the compulsion is evidence of the request'.[202] It was clear enough that plaintiffs could not recover if the payment had not truly been compulsory.[203] It was less clear whether the action could only be used where the payment had been made to discharge a debt for which the defendant was liable. In *Spencer* v. *Parry* in 1835, a landlord failed to recover money paid, after his goods were distrained for taxes which his tenant was required by his lease to pay. According to the Queen's Bench, the plaintiff should have sued on his contract with the defendant, which transferred the landlord's liability for the charges to the tenant, rather than on the general count.[204] Some counsel took this decision to mean that the money count could never be used unless the debt paid was one for which the defendant was legally liable.[205] But this proposition was denied in 1845 in *Brittain* v. *Lloyd*, when an auctioneer sought to recover the

assignment of contractual rights (such as debts), which bound the debtor once he was given notice of the assignment.

[199] In *Griffinhoofe* v. *Daubuz* (1855) 5 E. & B. 746 at 755, Parke B. held there was not 'any privity entitling the plaintiff to recover in any form of action'.

[200] See the formulation of Platt in *Lubbock* v. *Tribe* (1838) 3 M. & W. 607 at 611: 'To support the count for money paid, there must have been either an express authority directly given by the defendant for the payment, or an implied authority for that purpose, as in the instance of a surety paying a debt for his principal, or where a man becomes a party as indorser of a bill of exchange, and so has authority to pay it for the drawer and acceptor.'

[201] Thus, Coleridge J. explained, 'the count for money paid proceeds on one of two suppositions: either that the plaintiff has paid the money for the defendant at his request; or that he has been compelled to pay money for which the defendant was liable to the person receiving it, as in the case of a surety paying the debt of his principal': *Sayles* v. *Blane* (1849) 14 Q.B. 205 at 206. See also the comments of Tindal CJ in *Pawle* v. *Gunn* (1838) 4 Bing. N.C. 445 at 448.

[202] *Osborne* v. *Rogers* (1669) 1 Wms. Saund. 264 at 265n. According to Leake (*Elements*, 1867, 41): '[t]his contract is created in law upon an implied request without any request existing in fact, where the plaintiff has been compelled by law to pay, or being compellable by law has paid money which the defendant was ultimately liable to pay'. See also *Pownal* v. *Ferrand* (1827) 6 B. & C. 439 at 443–4. The rule stated by Leake was adopted in *Moule* v. *Garrett* (1872) LR 7 Ex 101, 104 and *Bonner* v. *Tottenham etc Building Society* [1899] 1 QB 161 at 173.

[203] See *Griffinhoofe* v. *Daubuz* (1855) 5 E. & B. 746, where the plaintiff failed to recover money paid after wheat he had left on a farm after the end of his lease was distrained for a tithe-charge payable by his landlord, since it was not clear that he had not left it there for his own convenience. See also *England* v. *Marsden* (1866) LR 1 CP 529. This reasoning was criticized by the late nineteenth century: see *Edmunds* v. *Wallingford* (1885) 14 QBD 811 at 816 and *Ex p Bishop* (1880) 15 Ch D 400 at 417.

[204] *Spencer* v. *Parry* (1835) 3 Ad. & El. 331.

[205] *Lubbock* v. *Tribe* (1838) 3 M. & W. 607.

excise duties he had paid on the sale of the defendant's estate. Since the statute imposing the duties made the auctioneer primarily liable for them—though it allowed him subsequently to recover them from the vendor—it was argued that he could not recover in an action for money paid. However, the Exchequer barons allowed the action. As Pollock CB put it, if one person asked another to pay money to a stranger on his behalf, 'with an express or implied undertaking to repay it', it made no difference to his liability whether the money had been paid to discharge a debt, or had simply been a loan or gift: '[t]he request to pay, and the payment according to it, constitute the debt; and whether the request be direct, as where the party is expressly desired by the defendant to pay, or indirect, where he is placed by him under a liability to pay, and does pay, makes no difference'.[206] According to this view, it was the fact that the plaintiff had been put in a position by the defendant whereby he was compelled to pay a sum, which generated the implied request and hence the debt.[207] Where the plaintiff was compelled to pay money to discharge a debt owed by the defendant, the facts themselves showed that the latter had been put into the position by the former. Where he was compelled to pay money which did not discharge the defendant's debt, more evidence was needed to show that the latter had put the former into this position, and that the plaintiff had acted under his authority.[208]

Pollock's approach was one which viewed the use of the action to recover moneys paid by compulsion in essentially contractual terms. This did not, however, mean that there had to be an actual contract, such as a contract of indemnity.[209] This was confirmed in 1885, when in *Edmunds* v. *Wallingford*, a plaintiff was allowed to recover in a count for money paid although the promise of the defendant to indemnify was found not to be legally binding. 'The right to indemnity or contribution in these cases exists', Lindley LJ ruled, 'although there may be no agreement to indemnify or contribute, and although there may be, in that sense, no privity between the plaintiff and the defendant.'[210] Similarly, Willes J. held in 1867 that a person who was compelled to pay a claim for which another was liable was entitled to reimbursement 'independent of contract'.[211]

---

[206] *Brittain* v. *Lloyd* (1845) 14 M. & W. 762 at 773. Cf. Tindal CJ in *Pawle* v. *Gunn* (1838) 4 Bing. N.C. 445 at 448–9: 'If a person were to request another to pay money to a charity, a payment which could not be enforced by law, could it be contended that an action would not lie against him for money paid?'

[207] This was not seen as inconsistent with *Spencer* v. *Parry*: see Wilde CJ's explanation in *Lewis* v. *Campbell* (1849) 8 C.B. 541 at 549.

[208] See the use of the notion of authority in *Lewis* v. *Campbell* (1849) 8 C.B. 541 at 550.

[209] Parties with contracts to indemnify often inserted the money counts as alternatives: *Lewis* v. *Campbell* (1849) 8 C.B. 541; *Hutchinson* v. *Sydney* (1854) 10 Exch. 438.

[210] *Edmunds* v. *Wallingford* (1885) 14 QBD 811 at 815.

[211] *Johnson* v. *Royal Mail Steam Packet Co* (1867) LR 3 CP 38 at 45.

The action for money paid was used typically in three kinds of situations where the payment had not been pursuant to an actual request. The first was where the plaintiff had been obliged to pay money legally owed by the defendant. For instance, in 1811, in *Brown* v. *Hodgson*, a carrier was permitted to recover the money he had paid to the consignee of goods which he had delivered in error to the defendant, after the defendant had kept and sold the goods. The Common Pleas accepted that the defendant could have been sued by the consignee—so that this was properly a debt owed by him (on an implied contract for goods sold and delivered)—and that this was not a voluntary payment.[212] Although in some cases, judges spoke of this duty to repay as one rooted in a moral obligation, the analysis was more usually contractual.[213] Thus, explaining the reasoning behind the decision in *Brown* v. *Hodgson* in 1835, Lord Denman CJ said that since the payment was made in discharge of the defendant's debt to the consignee 'it may be fairly said to have been paid at his instance, because he knew that the plaintiff's mistake, in delivering the goods to him, made the plaintiff liable to pay the price to the true owner'. For Denman, the resulting obligation derived from an implied authorization. For the defendant's receipt of the goods from the plaintiff, he said, 'may be considered as equivalent to saying, "If you pay him (as you may be compelled to do) for the goods, I will reimburse you"'.[214]

The second situation was where the plaintiff paid money to recover goods distrained for a debt owed by the defendant. This had been established in 1799 in *Exall* v. *Partridge*, when a plaintiff recovered the price he paid to recover his coach, which had been taken in distraint by the landlord of the defendant coachmaker.[215] More common was the case when a tenant's property was distrained for debts owed by his landlord. In such cases, it was settled by the early nineteenth century that the tenant could deduct such sums from the rent which he had to pay to the landlord.[216] These cases were often treated as contractual, given that the relationship between the landlord and tenant was a contractual one. Moreover, where there was a contract in place, which provided for the matter in dispute, then the plaintiff could not sue on the general count, but had to sue on the contract, since '[p]romises in law only exist where there is no express stipulation

---

[212] *Brown* v. *Hodgson* (1811) 4 Taunt. 189: it was 'not the case of a man officiously and without reason paying money for another'.

[213] *Jefferys* v. *Gurr* (1831) 2 B. & Ad. 833 at 841, where Lord Tenterden spoke of the plaintiff's claim in terms of moral justice. But contrast *Grissell* v. *Robinson* (1836) 3 Bing. N.C. 10, where the obligation was treated as entirely contractual, since the parties were in a contractual relationship.

[214] *Spencer* v. *Parry* (1835) 3 Ad. & El. 331 at 338.

[215] *Exall* v. *Partridge* (1799) 8 T.R. 308 at 311. See also *Dawson* v. *Linton* (1822) 5 B. & Ald. 521.

[216] *Sapsford* v. *Fletcher* (1792) 4 T.R. 511; *Taylor* v. *Zamira* (1816) 6 Taunt. 524.

between the parties'.[217] Thus, in *Schlencker* v. *Moxsy* in 1825, a sub-tenant who sought to recover against his landlord, after the superior landlord distrained for rent due from the lessor, was told that he could not use the money paid count, but had to sue in covenant, having a deed which secured him quiet enjoyment of his tenancy.[218]

The third situation where the money count was used was when sureties sought to recover from their principals and from their co-sureties. In this area, judges were less certain as to the basis of the obligation. In the case of actions brought against principals, eighteenth-century judges suggested that the principle on which recovery was based was rooted in equity.[219] However, early nineteenth-century judges treated it as another example of the law requiring the defendant to reimburse the plaintiff who had been compelled to pay money for him,[220] with the law raising 'a promise on the part of the person whose debt I pay to reimburse me'.[221] Similarly, when common law courts allowed the action to be used against co-sureties, to obtain a contribution,[222] early nineteenth-century judges seemed unsure on what to ground the doctrine. In 1804, Lord Eldon said that the surety's right rested 'either upon a principle of equity, or upon contract', though he favoured the former.[223] The dilemma whether it was equitable or contractual persisted. Parke B. suggested in 1840 that the action was 'founded not originally

---

[217] *Toussaint* v. *Martinnant* (1787) 2 T.R. 100 at 105. Here a surety was not permitted to sue his principal on the common count, having taken a bond.

[218] 'The parties effected an express contract by deed; that excludes any implied contract': *Schlencker* v. *Moxsy* (1825) 3 B. & C. 789 at 792. See also *Baber* v. *Harris* (1839) 9 Ad. & El. 532.

[219] Buller J. said in *Toussaint* v. *Martinnant* (1787) 2 T.R. 100 at 105 '[i]n ancient times no action could be maintained at law, where a surety had paid the debt of his principal: and the first case of the kind, in which the plaintiff succeeded, was before Gould, J. at Dorchester, which was decided on equitable grounds'.

[220] *Pownal* v. *Ferrand* (1827) 6 B. & C. 439 at 443–4. See also Lord Kenyon's dictum in *Exall* v. *Partridge* (1799) 8 T.R. 308 at 310: 'where one person is surety for another, and compellable to pay the whole debt, and he is called upon to pay, it is money paid to the use of the principal debtor, and may be recovered in an action against him for money paid, even though the surety did not pay the debt by the desire of the principal'. See also Coleridge J.'s dictum in *Sayles* v. *Blane* (1849) 14 Q.B. 205 at 206.

[221] *Pownal* v. *Ferrand* (1827) 6 B. & C. 439 at 443–4. The question of compulsion was important in these cases, since the surety was not permitted to recover from the principal for any unnecessary expenses incurred in defending actions, unless specifically at the principal's request: *Gillett* v. *Rippon* (1829) M. & M. 406.

[222] *Cowell* v. *Edwards* (1800) 2 B. & P. 268 at 269. The Chancery was considered a more appropriate court since it could adjust the proportions to be paid in case one or more sureties was insolvent; whereas at common law, payment was strictly proportionate.

[223] 'I think, that right is properly enough stated as depending rather upon a [principle] of equity than upon contract unless in this sense that the principle of equity being in its operation established, a contract may be inferred upon the implied knowledge of that principle by all persons': *Craythorne* v. *Swinburne* (1804) 14 Ves. 160 at 164.

upon contract, but upon a principle of equity'[224] which did not depend on the
fictional imputation of a promise to repay. But others saw it as contractual. 'In
all cases where one of two joint sureties pays money which either of them may
be called on to pay', Tindal CJ observed in 1836, 'a special contract by the co-
surety to repay him might be stated in an extended form; but in a compressed
shape, the moiety is money paid to the use of the co-surety.'[225] By 1844, Parke
had changed his mind, observing that 'where several are jointly liable, there is an
implied request to each of them to pay in discharge of each of the others',[226] which
gave it a more contractual flavour.

Similarly, where parties were engaged in a joint venture, courts enforced contributions against each other in a way which suggested that they did see a contract, arising from the very joint venture.[227] In 1817, it was taken for granted 'that
if one of several contractors has been compelled to pay the whole, he might seek
contribution from the others, and might recover for money paid'.[228] In 1850, in
Boulter v. *Peplow*, one member of a committee which had been set up to form a
gas company sued the other two members for contributions to the rent he had
had to pay on premises they had jointly contracted for. 'Prima facie', Maule J.
ruled, 'where one of three joint-contractors who are jointly sued, pays the whole
debt, he is entitled to receive contribution from the other two. Each was liable
in solido to the original demand: and from that arises an implied contract that
the one who pays the whole shall be reimbursed, in their respective proportions,
by the other two.'[229] This was a contract implied in fact. Two years later, while
holding that provisional committeemen were liable to make contributions, Lord
Campbell CJ stated that

we must look to the implied engagement of each, to pay his share, arising out of the joint
contract when entered into.... Each [contractor] may be considered as becoming liable
for the share of each one of his co-contractors at the request of such co-contractor;
and, on being obliged to pay such share, a request to pay it is implied as against the
party who ought to have paid it, and who is relieved from paying what, as between

[224] *Davies* v. *Humphreys* (1840) 6 M. & W. 153 at 168.
[225] *Grissell* v. *Robinson* (1836) 3 Bing. N.C. 10 at 16. See also Williams's comments in *Davies* v.
Humphreys (1840) 6 M. & W. 153 at 163, and the notes to *Osborne* v. *Rogers* (1669) 1 Wms. Saund. 264
at 265n to support the proposition that 'where two or more persons are sureties for another, and one
of them is compelled to pay the whole debt, an action for money paid lies against the co-sureties for
their respective proportions, on the implied request and promise'.
[226] *Kemp* v. *Finden* (1844) 12 M. & W. 421 at 423.
[227] But see Martin B.'s wording in *Marsack* v. *Webber* (1860) 6 H. & N. 1 at 6.
[228] *Holmes* v. *Williamson* (1817) 6 M. & S. 158 at 159.
[229] *Boulter* v. *Peplow* (1850) 9 C.B. 493 at 507. See also Talfourd J.'s judgment at 509: '[t]he contract
out of which this cause of action arises, is entirely collateral to the partnership: and the defendants
are liable to contribution irrespectively of the state of accounts amongst the partners'.

himself and the party who pays, be ought himself to have paid according to the original arrangement.[230]

6. EQUITY, COMMON LAW, AND THE REDEFINITION OF 'QUASI-CONTRACT'

Equity also offered restitutionary remedies. When the Chancery rescinded contracts, it ordered the restitution of moneys paid under the failed contract. Having a concurrent jurisdiction with the common law over fraud, it also could order an account of money obtained fraudulently. With its jurisdiction over trusts, equity could also order restitution from trustees who acted in breach of trust. In the mid-century, some jurists went as far as to suggest that, whenever a person obtained property in violation of 'some established principle of equity', the court would 'raise a constructive trust, and fasten it upon the conscience of the legal owner'.[231] However, Chancery lawyers were no less reluctant than common lawyers to develop a general principle of unjust enrichment, and constructive trusts continued to be treated as species of express trusts.[232] Instead of developing a general principle of unjust enrichment, equity, like common law, limited its remedies to existing recognized situations. The fusion of jurisdictions might have given an opportunity for judges and jurists to generalize the remedies offered in law and equity into a larger theory of unjustified enrichment. In fact, in the four decades after fusion, rethinking the bases of the restitutionary remedies available in law and equity served more to fragment than to unify the law.

Prime among equity's remedies was to hold fiduciaries liable for breaches of their fiduciary duties. It was settled by the end of the seventeenth century that all property acquired by a trustee in breach of trust was itself held on trust.[233] Trustees were not to be permitted to derive any advantage from the administration of trust property.[234] Equity's intervention extended beyond trustees to all those owing fiduciary duties, holding them accountable in equity for money made in breach of their obligations. Any property which came into the hands of

---

[230] *Batard v. Hawes* (1852) 2 El. & Bl. 287 at 296–7.

[231] J. Hill, *Practical Treatise on the Law relating to Trustees* (1845), 116, quoted in Ibbetson, *Historical Introduction*, 281.

[232] 'A constructive trust is properly a trust declared by a party, but indirectly, and therefore construed by the Court': T. Lewin, *A Practical Treatise on the Law of Trusts and Trustees* (1837), 44n. Lewin contrasted trusts by operation of law (not declared by the party but arising from a rule of law): these arose 'where a trust already in existence is created *de novo*, by operation of law, against this particular property'. (201). See Ibbetson, *Historical Introduction*, 282–3.

[233] D. E. C. Yale (ed.), *Lord Nottingham's Chancery Cases, vol. II* (Selden Society, 1961, vol. 79), 124–8.

[234] Lewin, *Practical Treatise*, 288.

someone acting in a fiduciary capacity was held to come into his hands in trust for the beneficiary, to whom he had to account for any profit. Agents were held to account for unauthorized profits they had made in the exercise of their duties. Where an agent or trustee made a profit out of the use of the principal's money, or that of the trust, he was held liable to account for it, since it was regarded simply as the latter's property.[235] Equally, where an agent made a profit by selling to his principal something the agent had already bought, equity regarded the original purchase to have been made in his capacity as agent, and held him liable to account for any profit.[236] This approach was adopted in early nineteenth-century cases where the purchase was made by an agent of a company which had not yet been formed at the time of the purchase. In *Hichens* v. *Congreve* in 1831, the promoters of the Arigna Iron and Coal Company were thus held liable to repay a £15,000 profit they had made on the purchase of mines they had acquired for resale to the company. Since the mines were to be paid for with money later subscribed by members of the company, the directors had to refund any surplus which they had kept. The agency relation could thus be held to exist even before a company was fully formed, rendering the agent liable for any profits made on the purchase of property for the company.[237] In these situations, principals or *cestuis que trustent* had a proprietary claim to recover their property or its proceeds.

In the first half of the nineteenth century, the cases dealt with in equity largely concerned trustees or agents who had wrongfully acquired trust property or sought to sell their property to the trust. In the second half of the century, in an era of increasing joint stock activity and growing commercial firms, the courts increasingly encountered cases of agents making a profit from commissions secretly paid to them by suppliers or customers of their employer. In these cases, none of their employer's property had come into the agents' hands, but they had acted in breach of their fiduciary duties. In dealing with these cases, equity judges began to distinguish more clearly than had hitherto been done between proprietary claims and personal ones arising from a breach of obligation. In *Imperial Mercantile Credit Association* v. *Coleman*, in 1871, a proprietary approach was taken when defendants were held liable to repay commission earned on the sale of stock to the plaintiff company. The defendants ran a firm of brokers, which

---

[235] *Earl of Lonsdale* v. *Church* (1790) 3 Bro. C.C. 41; *Lord Chedworth* v. *Edwards* (1802) 8 Ves. 46. See also *Fosbrooke* v. *Balguy* (1833) 1 Myl. & K. 226; *Docker* v. *Somes* (1834) 2 Myl. & K. 655. Such sums could also be recovered in an action for money had and received: *Rogers* v. *Boehm* (1798) 2 Esp. 702; *Thompson* v. *Havelock* (1808) 1 Camp. 527;, *Diplock* v. *Blackburn* (1811) 3 Camp. 43.

[236] See *East-India Co* v. *Henchman* (1791) 1 Ves. Jr. 287 at 289; *Benson* v. *Heathorn* (1842) 1 Y. & C. C.C. 326.

[237] *Hichens* v. *Congreve* (1831) 4 Sim. 420. See also *Bank of London* v. *Tyrrell* (1859) 27 Beav. 273; *Beck* v. *Kantorowicz* (1857) 3 K. & J. 230.

had agreed (on commission) to place a new issue of debentures in a railway company. This stock was sold to the plaintiff firm, of which Coleman was a director. Discussing the principle on which a remedy was to be granted, Sir Richard Malins VC treated the acquisition of the stock by Coleman 'as a purchase of them on behalf of the company'.[238] In the higher courts, the judges did not speak of Coleman's having purchased the shares as an agent, but Hatherley LC (on appeal) noted that he had derived a profit 'from the employment of the funds of the company', while acting in a fiduciary capacity,[239] while Lord Cairns (in the Lords) spoke of the profit as 'so much money taken by him from the association'.[240]

A similar view was taken at this time in the common law courts. In *Morison v. Thompson*, the plaintiff sought (in an action for money had and received) to recover a secret £225 profit made by his broker in negotiating the purchase of a ship. The defendant obtained a motion to enter a verdict for him, on the grounds that the action should have been brought for breach of duty, rather than for money had and received. Cockburn CJ rejected the argument, holding that an agent was bound to account to his principal for all profits made by him in the course of his employment. Not only could he be compelled in equity to pay this money, but there was also a legal duty 'whenever any profits so made have reached his hands [...] to pay over the amount as money absolutely belonging to his employer'.[241] This was to treat the equitable claim as proprietary, and the action for money had and received as a common law method of enforcing it.

Judges soon sought to draw a distinction between money gained by breach of duty and property acquired in the capacity of agent. In 1879, in *Emma Silver Mining Co v. Grant*, Sir George Jessel MR held a company promoter liable to repay a secret profit he had made in buying a mine for the company. Since the promoter had been guilty of a breach of a fiduciary duty, it was considered that it would not be enough for him simply to repay the difference in price between what the company paid and what the real vendor received. For even if the company had lost no money on the transaction—as would occur if the vendor (who paid the illicit commission) agreed to drop the sale price when this was discovered—the purchasing company could still recover any profit made by its agent. For it would be allowed to say, 'You made a profit by that position of trust and confidence which was reposed in you as agent, you cannot hold that profit as against me'.[242]

---

[238] *Imperial Mercantile Credit Association* v. *Coleman* (1871) LR 6 Ch App 558 at 563n.

[239] *Ibid.*, at 566.

[240] *Imperial Mercantile Credit Association* v. *Coleman* (1873) LR 6 HL 189 at 204.

[241] *Morison* v. *Thompson* (1874) LR 9 QB 480 at 486.

[242] *Emma Silver Mining Co* v. *Grant* (1879) 11 Ch D 918 at 938. The idea that a company was entitled to all profits made by those acting in fiduciary capacity, without taking into account money recovered by agreement with a true vendor, was also seen in *Bagnall* v. *Carlton* (1877) 6 Ch D 371.

The distinction was made clearer one year later, in *Metropolitan Bank* v. *Heiron*, when the Court of Appeal considered the case of a director who had received a bribe from his company's debtor, to induce the company to make a favorable compromise of his debt. The issue at stake was whether the claim of the company against the director was barred by the Statute of Limitations, since they had known of the matter since 1872. The defendant's plea succeeded when the court distinguished between proprietary claims against trustees, which could not be time-barred, and claims for breaches of duty, which could. In the court's view, where money was obtained by an agent by fraud, it could not be considered as the principal's property. Instead, the principal only had an equitable right to recover it. Where a defendant acquired money by a breach of duty, it was 'in no sense the money of the company' until it was vested in them as a result of a suit for the breach of duty.[243] The distinction between proprietary claims and those arising from breach of duty was reiterated in *Boston Deep Sea Fishing & Ice Co* v. *Ansell*, where the plaintiffs recovered from the defendant money he had received as a result of a breach of his fiduciary duty, which the company itself could never have obtained. As Bowen LJ saw it, the plaintiffs could recover not because 'the money ought to have gone into the principal's hands in the first instance', but rather 'because it is contrary to equity that the agent or the servant should retain the money so received without the knowledge of his master.' Consequently, 'there is an equitable right in the master to receive it'.[244] In *Boston Deep Sea Fishing*, Bowen LJ treated this equitable right as equivalent to the common law right which arose where the law implied a contract or a use. Both were personal rights arising from a breach of an obligation, and contrasted with proprietary rights. This obligation did not, however, depend on the existence of a contract in any real sense.

The courts continued to develop the distinction between claims which were proprietary and those which arose from breaches of obligation when discussing the tracing of property and its proceeds. Despite Lord Ellenborough's comments in *Taylor* v. *Plumer* that such proceeds could no longer be traced after being mixed with other money, equity judges in the mid-century were prepared to trace money into mixed funds,[245] just as the common law judges had in *Marsh* v. *Keating*. However, in 1880 in *In re Hallett's Estate*, the Court of Appeal appeared to draw a distinction between equitable and legal approaches, when confirming that money given to a person acting in a fiduciary capacity could be traced into an account which mixed different sums. In his judgment, Sir George Jessel MR explained

---

[243] *Metropolitan Bank* v. *Heiron* (1880) 5 Ex D 319 at 325.

[244] *Boston Deep Sea Fishing & Ice Co* v. *Ansell* (1888) 39 Ch D 339 at 367–8. The defendant had been paid bonuses as a shareholder in another company for having supplied them with business.

[245] e.g. *Pennell* v. *Deffell* (1853) 4 De G. M. & G. 372. But contrast *In re West of England and South Wales District Bank, Ex p Dale* (1879) 11 Ch D 772.

that Ellenborough's explanation of the limits on tracing in *Taylor* v. *Plumer*, 'only ceases to be correct because Lord Ellenborough's knowledge of the rules of Equity was not quite commensurate with his knowledge of the rules of Common Law'.[246] This was to suggest that the common law's approach to tracing was different from equity's. In his judgment, Thesiger LJ stated the general proposition that the proceeds of property given to a fiduciary could be traced; but he significantly added that the doctrine did not apply where a 'relationship of debtor and creditor had been constituted, instead of the relation either of trustee and *cestui que trust*, or principal and agent'.[247] This was to say that equity had no power to trace money which was not held in trust, but which only constituted a debt.

The distinction between rights in property which could be traced, and rights arising from a breach of duty was taken up in 1890 in *Lister & Co* v. *Stubbs*, where the plaintiff company sought to recover from their foreman not only the bribes he had received from a supplier, but also the profit he had made from investing those bribes. It was accepted that if the money which Stubbs had received from the supplier could be seen as the plaintiff's property, then the plaintiffs would have a proprietary claim to all the proceeds of the property. In his judgment, Stirling J. applied the test derived from *Morison* v. *Thompson*. 'Is this a case in which the suit is founded on a breach of duty or fraud by a person who was in the position of a trustee', he asked, 'or it is a case of a *cestui que trust* seeking to recover money which was his own before any act wrongfully done by the trustee?'[248] Adopting the former view, he held the plaintiffs were not entitled to follow the money. The decision was upheld by the Court of Appeal. In his judgment, Lindley LJ held that the defendant was liable to pay to his employer all moneys he had received from the supplier, which he had acquired in breach of his duty; but he was not liable to pay over his profits. '[T]he relation between them', he observed, 'is that of debtor and creditor; it is not that of trustee and *cestui que trust*.' In Lindley's view, the consequences of holding him a trustee would be startling. It could not be right, he said, that he should be accountable for the profits he might have made with the money.[249] Equally, he felt it would be wrong, in the case of insolvency, to allow any profit made by the deceitful agent to be taken away from the general

---

[246] *In re Hallett* (1880) 13 Ch D 696 at 717. See also Smith, 'Tracing'.

[247] *In re Hallett* (1880) 13 Ch D 696 at 724.

[248] *Lister & Co* v. *Stubbs* (1890) 45 Ch D 1 at 9.

[249] *Lister & Co* v. *Stubbs* (1890) 45 Ch D 1 at 15. See also *Powell & Thomas* v. *Evan Jones & Co* [1905] 1 KB 11, which held an agent not to be a trustee, but to owe a debt arising from a breach of fiduciary duty, with the result that he could not be compelled to enforce his agreement with the supplier offering him a secret commission on behalf of the principal. Contrast the modern approach, holding that moneys earned were held in a constructive trust, in *Attorney General of Hong Kong* v. *Reid* [1994] 1 AC 324.

fund.[250] This was to take a policy-driven view of how far a party in breach of duty should be accountable for his wrong.[251]

It was this distinction which lay at the root of the House of Lords' thinking in *Sinclair* v. *Brougham*. The case arose from the failure of Birkbeck Permanent Benefit Building Society. The business had been formed in 1851, but had started acting as a bank in the 1870s. The Birkbeck Bank was a significant institution, holding more than £10 million in deposits. By mingling its building society and its banking accounts, it offered generous interest rates to primarily small investors.[252] However, a run on the bank in November 1910 led to its collapse several months later. It was soon apparent that the society had exceeded its legal powers in conducting business as a bank. As a result, the shareholders claimed that they and the creditors should be paid out in full, with the depositors looking only to any surplus.[253] The shareholders were aware that, if the depositors were to have priority over them, no money would be left to meet their claims. In making their argument, they drew on the rules regarding the liability of companies for *ultra vires* acts of their directors which had developed since the mid-nineteenth-century growth of joint stock enterprise.

On the one hand, it was settled that where directors borrowed money in order to pay for benefits which were accepted by the company, the lender could recover, on the ground that his money had been used to discharge a debt owed by the firm.[254] This was said to be on the same principle according to which a person who lent money to a person legally incapable of borrowing—such as a child or a married woman—could sue for such of the money as was used to purchase necessaries for that person. Although the contract of loan was unenforceable, the lender was permitted 'to stand in the shoes of the tradespeople who furnished the necessaries'.[255] As Lord Hatherley LC observed in 1869, once money had been applied *de facto* to the legitimate purposes of the company, it was not to be allowed to 'derive the benefit of all the expenditure which has been thus incurred, and claim the surplus for the benefit of the shareholders'.[256] On the

---

[250] The fraud in this case was one which attracted much attention and led to Francis Stubbs being imprisoned for nine months with hard labour: *Leeds Mercury* 17, 23, 28, 30 April, 5, 6 May 1890; *The Times*, 22 May 1890. The criminal proceedings took place at the same time as the civil suits to prevent Stubbs disposing of the property.

[251] The Court of Appeal was, however, prepared to hold the agent liable in tort for any loss suffered by the principal: *Mayor of Salford* v. *Lever* [1891] 1 QB 168.

[252] *The Times*, 9 June 1911, col. 9e.

[253] *The Times*, 25 July 1911, col. 4c; 9 November 1911, col. 24c.

[254] See *In re German Mining Co* (1854) 4 De G. M. & G. 19 at 41.

[255] *Jenner* v. *Morris* (1861) 3 De G. F. & J. 45 at 52. Cf. *Marlow* v. *Pitfeild* (1719) 1 P. Wms. 558, explained in *In re National Permanent Building Society, Ex p Williamson* (1869) LR 5 Ch App 309.

[256] *In re Cork and Youghal Railway Co* (1869) LR 4 Ch App 748. See also *Blackburn and District Benefit Building Society* v. *Cunliffe, Brooks & Co* (1883) 22 Ch D 61, (1884) 9 App Cas 857.

other hand, where money was borrowed *ultra vires* by directors which was not used to pay the debts of the firm, lenders had no remedy against the company, but only against those directors who had exceeded their powers.[257]

The rules were applied in the context of a failed building society in 1882 in the case of the Guardian Permanent Benefit Building Society. In the view of the Court of Appeal, this society had borrowed money in an unauthorized way, albeit under a mistake that their activity was lawful. Such a loan, it was held, could not create a debt, legal or equitable, to the lender, since the company had no power to incur such a debt. This meant that such lenders had to give up any securities they had, and could not make a claim in competition with the other claimants, who were creditors or society members. However, Sir George Jessel MR held that if any surplus existed, after those claimants were paid, it had to be returned to the lenders 'on the plainest principles of equity'. 'Nobody can have a claim upon it except those whose money it is', he held, although the 'actual money cannot be traced'.[258] The House of Lords ultimately decided in this case that the borrowing was not *ultra vires*, so that the lenders were entitled to be paid out first.[259] Jessel's exposition of the law was thus not discussed by the highest court. In *Sinclair v. Brougham*, however, the Lords did take the opportunity to rethink the law, rejecting Jessel's view, which had been applied by the Court of Appeal.[260]

The Lords contrived a solution which allowed the shareholders and the depositors to rank equally, but which presented a controversial and innovative view of the law. The Lords distinguished between proprietary remedies *in rem*, where property remained in the original owner and could be traced, and those *in personam*, where a debt arose which the recipient of the money owed to the plaintiff. In the earlier cases, judges in equity had treated the action for money had and received, where the law implied a promise, as the common law corollary to equitable debts arising from a breach of a fiduciary duty. This approach acknowledged that the obligation to repay did not arise contractually. But 62 years after the Common Law Procedure Act, the House of Lords held that the action of money had and received was a contractual remedy. The common law, Lord Haldane held, only recognized two classes of actions for claims *in personam*: those founded on contract and those founded on tort. When the law 'speaks of actions arising *quasi ex contractu*', such as the action for money had and received, he proceeded, 'it refers merely to a class of action in theory based on a contract which is imputed to the defendant by a fiction of law. This can only be set up with effect if such a

---

[257] *Blackburn and District Benefit Building Society* v. *Cunliffe, Brooks & Co* (1885) 29 Ch D 902; *In re National Permanent Building Society, Ex p Williamson* (1869) LR 5 Ch App 309.

[258] *In re Guardian Permanent Benefit Building Society* (1883) 23 Ch D 440 at 451.

[259] *Murray* v. *Scott* (1884) 9 App Cas 519.

[260] *In Re Birkbeck Permanent Benefit Building Society* [1912] 2 Ch 183.

contract would be valid if it really existed.'[261] Since any contract entered into by the company would be *ultra vires*, it could not be held to have promised to repay the money unjustly acquired. This was to confirm that no distinct obligation arose at common law from an unjust enrichment.[262]

At the same time, the Lords were aware that it would be unconscionable for the building society to take advantage of the misapplication by its directors of other people's money.[263] The judges were keen to develop a remedy to prevent unjust enrichment, but felt that this could only be done in equity via the proprietary solution of tracing. Lord Haldane said that, at common law, money could be traced so long as property in it had not passed—as where it was given to an agent for a specific purpose or where it had been wrongfully obtained—and the money could be earmarked. But equity could go further, and follow the money, even when it had lost its earmark. Since it had never been converted into a debt, there was (in his view) a resulting trust.[264]

The court was creative and controversial in finding a proprietary remedy to obtain a fair result in the case.[265] At the same time, its characterization of the common law's 'quasi-contractual' remedies as 'properly' contractual was not simply an affirmation of a view long held by common lawyers, but was a contentious affirmation of a partisan view. Why the court should have chosen to take this path can be answered from two of the judgments. The first reason, seen in Lord Haldane's judgment, was that the court feared that any other decision would undermine the doctrine of *ultra vires*. As Haldane saw it (following Thesiger's judgment in *Hallett*) any claim which was not proprietary could only arise if the defendant had become a debtor to the plaintiff. But since, in the case of the Birkbeck Bank, this could only occur through the *ultra vires* action of the directors, to allow an *in personam* claim based on this debt would 'strike at the root of the doctrine of *ultra vires*'. This latter doctrine thus excluded any personal claim, even one based on 'the circumstance that the defendant has been improperly enriched at the expense of the plaintiff'.[266] The Lord Chancellor seems to have

---

[261] *Sinclair* v. *Brougham* [1914] AC 398 at 415.

[262] Lord Wright, 'Sinclair v. Brougham' (1938) 6 *CLJ* 305–26 at 315. Wright's article argued that the fiction of a contract implied in law had been adopted for procedural reasons of convenience, and had not deceived previous generations of lawyers as to the 'true nature of the concept'; and that 'the ghost of this fiction' should be forgotten.

[263] See per Lord Parker in *Sinclair* v. *Brougham* [1914] AC 398 at 444. See also per Lord Sumner at 457, and Lord Dunedin at 431.

[264] See also P. B. H. Birks, 'Restitution and Resulting Trusts', in S. Goldstein, *Equity and Contemporary Legal Developments* (Jerusalem, 1992), 335–73 at 353–4; W. Swadling, 'A New Role for Resulting Trusts?' (1996) 16 *Legal Studies* 110–31 at 124–5.

[265] See the *Westdeutsche Landesbank Girozentrale* v. *Islington LBC* [1996] AC 669 at 709 *et seq*.

[266] *Sinclair* v. *Brougham* [1914] AC 398 at 414–15.

feared that since any (non-proprietary) unjust enrichment claim would constitute a 'debt', a decision allowing its recovery would open the way for directors to
incur debts for the company beyond their powers. His way to prevent this was to
reinterpret the scope of the common law action.

The second reason is seen from Lord Sumner's judgment. Sumner clearly feared
the expansion of the action of money had and received into a general doctrine
to reverse unjust enrichments. He rejected Mansfield's assertion that the action
for money had and received was 'equitable', stating that there was 'no ground left
for suggesting as a recognizable "equity" the right to recover money *in personam*
merely because it would be the right and fair thing that it should be refunded'.[267]
This was not the first time that he expressed his concern about a doctrine which
promised 'to administer that vague jurisprudence which is sometimes attract-
ively styled "justice as between man and man"'.[268] He seems to have feared that
allowing the common law remedy in this case would open the way to its expansion. It was true that basing the plaintiffs' claim on the payment of money having
been made by mistake, or on a consideration which had totally failed, presented
problems; for the money had been paid voluntarily, under a contract with the
directors, with no error as to their legal obligation. The court may have felt that
treating the claim as one for the recovery of money which had wrongfully found
its way into the company's hands would have left the action open-ended. But by
endorsing a notion derived from *Taylor v. Plumer* and *In re Hallett* that equity
could trace property further than the common law, and granting an equitable proprietary remedy, the Lords reinforced the separation of equitable and
common law approaches and fragmented thinking about the remedy. As H.C
Gutteridge put it, 'the theory of unjustified enrichment received its death blow in
Sinclair v. Brougham'.[269]

A number of commentators clearly approved of the Lords' view. Notes in the
Law Quarterly Review, perhaps by Pollock, indicated general approval of Sumner's
'masterly exposition of the foundation of the action for money had and received'.[270]
A decade later, in an article approving of the approach in *Sinclair v. Brougham*, H.
G. Hanbury attacked Mansfield's fallacy from *Moses v. Macferlan*, noting that he
had 'crossed the all too narrow bridge which leads from the sound soil of implied
contract to the shifting quicksands of natural equity'. For Hanbury, the action for

---

[267] *Sinclair v. Brougham* [1914] AC 398 at 456.

[268] *Baylis v. Bishop of London* [1913] 1 Ch 127 at 140.

[269] H. C. Gutteridge and R. J. A. David, 'The Doctrine of Unjustified Enrichment', 5 *CLJ* 204–29
at 224.

[270] 29 *LQR* (1913) 120, 30 *LQR* (1914) 385–6. See also M. D. Howe (ed.), *The Pollock-Holmes Letters:
Correspondence of Sir Frederick Pollock and Mr Justice Holmes 1874–1932*, 2 vols (Cambridge, 1942),
i, 215.

money had and received only lay 'where there is a relation of debtor and creditor, the debt sounding in clear contract; or where there is a debt, and the law does not forbid the implication of a contract'.[271] Others continued into the 1930s to reiterate that the common law knew only contract and tort.[272] But a general notion of unjust enrichment had its adherents in England. Percy Winfield, who disliked the term 'quasi-contract', feeling that it disguised the fact that it had nothing to do with contract law, defined the obligation in question as 'liability, not exclusively referable to any other head of the law, imposed upon a particular person to pay money to another particular person on the ground of unjust benefit'.[273] He rejected the criticisms of Mansfield's dictum as being too vague by stating that, in modern law, the heads of quasi-contractual obligations had been well settled by decisions, so that there was less room for the exercise of judicial discretion. Nonetheless, in his view judges might still have to resort to the pure fountains of natural justice in developing the law. In many ways, this reflected Winfield's view of tort, and it was perhaps not insignificant that his discussion of quasi-contract was included as a chapter in a book on torts.

[271] H. G. Hanbury, 'The Recovery of Money' (1924) 40 *LQR* 31–42 at 35–6.

[272] P. A. Landon, review of 'The Province of the Law of Tort' by Percy H. Winfield, *Bell Yard* 8 (1931), 19–32.

[273] Winfield, *Province*, 119.

Part Three

COMMERCIAL LAW

I
Joint Stock Companies

1. COMPANIES AND PARTNERSHIPS IN THE 1820s

In 1820, corporate enterprise was the exception, not the rule. Corporate status, which gave the firm a legal personality distinct from that of its members, who could buy and sell their shares simply as investors, was a privilege obtained by Royal Charter or Act of Parliament. It was conferred only on large public enterprises which could not be conducted by individuals.[1] From the middle of the eighteenth century, this status was routinely sought by firms engaged in building public utilities, such as canal companies. These firms had usually to seek parliamentary authorization in any event, given their desire to acquire land compulsorily: but the financial scale of the undertaking, the large number of investors, and the potentially high level of liability also made it essential to seek corporate status. The statutes which authorized their activities regulated them. The amount of capital which could be raised would be determined by the statute, which could name the original proprietors, and those (such as riparian landowners) with the right to acquire shares, and state how the shares were to be transferred.

The more typical form of enterprise was the small partnership or individual entrepreneur, raising capital largely from family, religious, or local social networks. Such firms were often run by trusted family members in partnership, who ploughed profits back into the firm to allow its expansion.[2] Such small enterprises

---

[1] For histories of corporate enterprise, see B. C. Hunt, *The Development of the Business Corporation in England 1800–1867* (Cambridge, MA, 1936); A. B. Dubois, *The English Business Company after the Bubble Act* (New York, 1938); C. A. Cooke, *Corporation, Trust and Company: An Essay in Legal History* (Manchester, 1950); J. B. Jefferys, *Business Organisation in Great Britain, 1856–1914* (New York, 1977); R. Harris, *Industrializing English Law: Entrepreneurship and Business Organization, 1720–1844* (Cambridge, 2000); J. Taylor, *Creating Capitalism: Joint Stock Enterprise in British Politics and Culture, 1800–1870* (Woodbridge, 2006). See also the collection of primary sources in R. Pearson with J. Taylor and M. Freeman, *The History of the Company: The Development of the Business Corporation 1700-1914*, 8 vols (2006). Important shorter studies include P. L. Cottrell, *Industrial Finance 1830–1914: The Finance and Organization of English Manufacturing Industry* (1980), Ch. 3; P. Ireland, 'The Triumph of the Company Legal Form, 1856–1914', in J. Adams (ed.), *Essays for Clive Schmitthoff* (Abingdon, 1983), 29–58;

[2] P. Hudson, 'Industrial Organisation and Structure', in R. Floud and P. Johnson (eds), *The Cambridge Economic History of Modern Britain, vol. I Industrialisation, 1700–1860* (Cambridge, 2004), 28–56; D. A. Farnie, *The English Cotton Industry and the World Market 1815–1896* (Oxford, 1979), 209–10;

were generally regarded not only as the most moral form of business, but as the most efficient, for the partnership form assumed that all members would be active in the business and would share liability.[3] The defining feature of a partnership was the fact that members shared the profits of a business.[4] However, if a person allowed his name to be held out to the world as a partner, he obtained the consequent liabilities, regardless of whether he received any profits.[5] Although no document was needed to constitute a partnership, most partnerships were created by deeds which set out how the firm would be managed, and which regulated how shares in the partnership could be disposed of.[6] Partners could also make their own arrangements regarding the apportionment of liabilities between themselves, though they remained mutually liable to third parties.

The fact that the partnership was merely the aggregate of the individuals making it up, without any distinct corporate personality, could generate problems within the firm, particularly in cases of misconduct by any partner. First, any partner might bind the firm in any transaction relating to its business, even if he went against an express arrangement made between the partners.[7] Even if the acting partner was seeking to cheat his fellows, the other partners would be liable for the fraudulent transaction, as long as the person he dealt with was not acting in collusion with him.[8] Secondly, no partner could sue his fellows at common law: since he was a partner, he would be suing himself. Indeed, if a man was a partner in two firms, they could not sue each other at law.[9] Disputes between partners had to be resolved by arbitration, or by a suit in Chancery for a dissolution and accounts.[10] Some of these disabilities could be overcome in the partnership deed.

R. Boyson, *The Ashworth Cotton Enterprise: The Rise and Fall of a Family Firm 1818–80* (Oxford, 1970), 24 *et seq*; S. Shapiro, *Capital and the Cotton Industry in the Industrial Revolution* (Ithaca, NY, 1967).

[3] See e.g. J. R. McCulloch, *Considerations on Partnerships with Limited Liability* (1856), 4–5.

[4] *Grace* v. *Smith* (1775) 2 W. Bl. 998; *Waugh* v. *Carver* (1793) 2 H. Bl. 235; *Green* v. *Beesley* (1835) 2 Bing. N.C. 108.

[5] Equally, employees who were held out as partners obtained that status: *Guidon* v. *Robson* (1809) 2 Camp. 302; *Smith* v. *Sherwood* (1847) 10 Jur. (o.s.) 214.

[6] M. Lobban, 'Corporate Identity and Limited Liability in France and England, 1825–67' (1996) 25 *Anglo-Am. L. Rev.* 397–440 at 402; *Ex p Langdale* (1811) 18 Ves. 301.

[7] *Sandilands* v. *Marsh* (1819) 2 B. & Ald. 673 at 679; *Hope* v. *Cust* (1774) 1 East 53. However, a partner could not bind the others in a matter unconnected with the partnership, nor could one partner bind another for debts incurred prior to his joining: *Dickenson* v. *Valpy* (1829) 10 B. & C. 128; *Shirreff* v. *Wilks* (1800) 1 East 48.

[8] *Bond* v. *Gibson* (1808) 1 Camp. 185; *Ex p Bonbonus* (1803) 8 Ves. 540; *Shirreff* v. *Wilks* (1800) 1 East 48.

[9] *Mainwaring* v. *Newman* (1800) 2 B. & P. 120.

[10] *Forman* v. *Homfray* (1813) 2 V. & B. 329; *Loscombe* v. *Russell* (1830) 4 Sim. 8; *Knebell* v. *White* 2 Y. & C. 15. The question whether the partner had to seek a dissolution was controversial, with Sir John Leach taking the view that no dissolution was needed (*Harrison* v. *Armitage* (1819) 4 Madd. 143; *Richards* v. *Davies* (1831) 2 Russ. & M. 347). However, the contrary view was generally taken to prevail.

For instance, if it contained covenants to account periodically, an aggrieved partner was entitled to sue the defaulters at common law under this covenant.[11]

The lack of corporate personality also generated problems when it came to dealing with outsiders. Since all partnership contracts were the joint contracts of the partners, they all had to be joined as parties in any litigation.[12] Where the partnership was a large one, this could produce such problems as to amount to 'an absolute denial of justice'.[13] Moreover, since a debt was a *chose in action* which was not assignable, there was a danger if the membership of a company changed that the debt would not be recoverable at all.[14] In practice, this inconvenience was often mitigated by the use of trustees acting for the fluctuating body of partners; while in smaller partnerships the problem was less evident.[15]

Although a partnership lacked a distinct legal personality, its assets and liabilities were clearly distinct from those of its members.[16] This provided a certain degree of security to individual partners and their own separate creditors. Partnership debts were paid out of its joint assets: any partner who had suffered an execution against his private property by a partnership creditor could therefore obtain a contribution from the others. If a partner became bankrupt, and the partnership had to be dissolved, the partnership creditors would be paid from the joint estate, while the bankrupt partner's separate creditors were paid from his separate estate. Any surplus remaining in the joint estate after the joint creditors had been fully paid was allotted proportionally to the separate estates of the various partners, while any surplus from a partner's separate estate after his separate creditors were paid was allotted to the joint debts.[17] Despite the lack of corporate status or limited liability, this system effectively protected the separate creditors of the individual partners, for a partner's private debts were to be paid from his private assets ahead of his business debts.[18] At the same time, since they were partly his property, partnership assets could be seized in execution of a judgment

---

[11] *Foster* v. *Allanson* (1788) 2 T.R. 479; *Preston* v. *Strutton* (1792) 1 Anst. 50; *Bedford* v. *Brunton* (1834) 1 Bing. N.C. 399; A. Bissett, *A Practical Treatise on the Law of Partnership* (1847), 130.

[12] This did not apply to a secret partner, not a party to the contract: *Mawman* v. *Gillett* (1809) 2 Taunt. 325 n.

[13] Report on the Law of Partnership (henceforth cited as Ker Report), *PP* 1837 (530), xliv, 399 at p. 4. See also John George, *A View of the Law Affecting Unincorporated Companies*, (2nd edn, 1825), 15.

[14] Lobban, 'Corporate Identity', 403.   [15] *Metcalf* v. *Bruin* (1810) 12 East 400.

[16] Debts which were contracted privately by one partner did not become partnership debts: *Emly* v. *Lye* (1811) 15 East 7.

[17] *Ex p Cook* (1728) 2 P. Wms. 55, discussed in J. Getzler and M. Macnair, 'The Firm as an Entity before the Companies Acts', in P. Brand, K. Costello, and W. N. Osborough (eds), *Adventures of the Law: Proceedings of the Sixteenth British Legal History Conference, Dublin* (Dublin, 2005), 280.

[18] The system came in for much criticism in the later eighteenth century where it was felt that it was prejudicial to the joint creditors, but continued to be applied: see Getzler & Macnair, 'The Firm as an Entity', 281; Robert Henley Eden, *A Practical Treatise on the Bankrupt Law* (2nd edn, 1826), 169–74. See also *Harvey* v. *Crickett* (1816) 5 M. & S. 336.

against any individual partner, with the creditor becoming a joint owner of the property with the other partners.[19] Given the natural disruption this caused to any business, it was advisable for partners to buy the share when sold in execution of judgment.

The existence of the partnership depended on the continued will of its members. Unless the partnership deed specified its term of duration, the partnership continued so long as the partners were alive, capable, and willing to continue. A partnership could be dissolved at the will of any partner, or by his death, or by events rendering him incapable of being a partner, including bankruptcy and felony. Where a partnership was created for a fixed time, it could only be dissolved prior to that moment by mutual consent or a court order, which would be granted if the business was impractical to run,[20] or if there were problems[21] or fraud in the management of the concern.[22] Partnerships could also be dissolved by arbitrators, if the deed of partnership provided for disputes to be referred to them. This meant that there was a lack of legal continuity for the partnership: it had to be reconstituted on the retirement of any partner, with accounts being taken and settled between interested parties. This involved frequent recourse to lawyers to recast the deed of partnership.[23] Moreover, where surviving partners continued to trade with partnership assets, complex questions could later be raised about the entitlement of the retired or deceased partner's descendants to the property.[24] Given all these complexities, partners were well advised to avoid resorting to law if at all possible.

Besides partnerships and corporations, the eighteenth century had seen the emergence of an increasing number of unincorporated joint stock associations, which were common law partnerships which imitated the corporate form. For example, the Phoenix Assurance Company, which had been refused a charter in 1783, operated under a deed of settlement, which put the capital and finances of the firm in the hands of a small number of trustees whose powers were defined by the deed.[25] Unlike corporations, such firms could not limit the liability of their members, nor could they sue in the name of the firm without obtaining statutory

---

[19] *Chapman* v. *Koops* (1802) 3 B. & P. 289.

[20] *Baring* v. *Dix* (1786) 1 Cox 213; *Jennings* v. *Baddeley* (1856) 3 K. & J. 78.

[21] *Waters* v. *Taylor* (1813) 2 Ves. & Bea. 299, cf. *Goodman* v. *Whitcomb* (1820) 1 Jac. & W. 589 at 592–3.

[22] *Chapman* v. *Beach* (1820) 1 Jac. & W. 594.   [23] Harris, *Industrializing English Law*, 142.

[24] See *Wedderburn* v. *Wedderburn* (1836) 2 Keen 722.

[25] C. Trebilcock, *Phoenix Assurance and the Development of British Insurance, vol. I 1782–1870* (Cambridge, 1985), 69–73. The duties of such trustees had been set out in *Charitable Corporation* v. *Sutton* (1742) 2 Atk. 400.

authority to do so.[26] However, many preferred the unincorporated form, since it gave them greater freedom to diversify.

In the early nineteenth century, when there were speculative booms in the stock market, the question was raised whether such companies were illegal under the Bubble Act 1720.[27] This statute, which made it illegal to presume to act as a corporate body by raising transferable stock without a charter or statute, had lain dormant in the statute book until 1808, when it was invoked by rival traders against two new joint stock enterprises. Although Lord Ellenborough did not grant an information under the Act, he took the occasion to warn people against engaging in 'mischievous and illegal' speculative projects.[28] These comments created alarm that established unincorporated firms would be prosecuted; but it was soon accepted that the Act only applied to those companies which had 'a tendency to the common grievance, prejudice, or inconvenience' of the public.[29] The legislation was used primarily where plaintiffs sought to use the courts to support stock market speculations;[30] and with the decline of the boom, and the abating of the danger, courts were able to take a more benevolent view of the Act.

The Act was invoked again during another boom, in 1824–5, when some 624 companies were formed, mainly for speculative purposes.[31] In this era, the King's Bench applied the Act in a way which would punish speculating dealers. Refusing a remedy to a stockbroker, Lord Tenterden condemned the 'gaming and rash speculation' which had occurred on the Stock Exchange and spoke of the need for 'fair mercantile transactions' where each party would 'reap a profit in his turn'.[32] In Chancery, Lord Eldon also announced that if a deed of settlement contained any provision contrary to the Bubble Act, he would give no relief.[33] With so many companies in danger of being pronounced illegal—and with Parliament overwhelmed with more than 400 applications for statutory incorporation in 1825—the Bubble Act was repealed. But judicial suspicion of joint stock

[26] Insurance companies did, however, manage to sue in the name of their trustees: *Metcalfe* v. *Bruin* (1810) 12 East 400. See also Lord Eldon's generous approach to the Philanthropic Annuity Association in *Cockburn* v. *Thompson* (1809) 16 Ves. 321.

[27] 6 Geo. I c. 18. On this statute, see Harris, *Industrializing English Law*, 73–8.

[28] *R.* v. *Dodd* (1808) 9 East 516 at 528.

[29] See *R.* v. *Webb* (1811) 14 East 406 at 412, cf. *Pratt* v. *Hutchinson* (1812) 15 East 511; *Brown* v. *Holt* (1812) 4 Taunt. 587; *Carlen* v. *Drury* (1812) 1 Ves. & Bea. 155; *Davies* v. *Hawkins* (1815) 3 M. & S. 488.

[30] *Buck* v. *Buck* (1808) 1 Camp. 547.

[31] H. English, *A Complete View of the Joint Stock Companies Formed During the Years 1824 and 1825* (1827), 10–26.

[32] *Josephs* v. *Pebrer* (1825) 3 B. & C. 639 at 644. Contrast *Nockels* v. *Crosby* (1825) 3 B. & C. 814. See also *Kempson* v. *Saunders* (1826) 4 Bing. 5.

[33] *Van Sandau* v. *Moore* in *The Times*, 7 March 1825. See also his comments in *Ellison* v. *Bignold* (1821) 2 Jac. & W. 503.

speculation continued, and, despite the legislation, some judges continued to view companies with freely transferable shares as illegal at common law.[34] Over time, however, this position was retreated from.[35]

Judges who condemned speculative brokers and merchants aimed to protect investors. If the company was successfully launched, a purchaser of scrip was held to be a partner, liable for partnership debts, even if he had never signed the deed, for he was not permitted to speculate by holding the shares while they were profitable, and then disposing of them to a pauper.[36] But if the investor had bought scrip in an abortive firm, it was held that no partnership was formed for whose debts he was liable.[37] Equally, where an investor had been induced by fraud to join a partnership, he could recover his money from the other partners without naming them all, provided he could convince the court that the enterprise was a mere bubble.[38]

Although there were calls for greater regulation of unincorporated companies, the 1825 Act merely abolished the relevant parts of the Bubble Act, and gave the Crown the discretion to issue charters without limited liability, thus taking pressure off Parliament.[39] The law left companies to run themselves. So did the courts. As Lord Eldon put it:

as they were usually governed by some moral principle, which was found sufficient for all their purposes, and as they took care to do justice for themselves to all persons who were in a situation to claim anything from them, they went on without inconvenience.[40]

Taking an unincorporated company to court could be tricky. Given the need for all members to be joined in any contractual action, it was difficult for creditors to recover from a company which offered stout resistance.[41] Investors had equal difficulty in holding the directors to account. In the absence of covenants to account in their deed, this could only be done in Chancery, in a suit seeking a dissolution of the partnership, in which every shareholder had to be made a party. Since each one was permitted to file his own answer, this could make legal proceedings

---

[34] *Duvergier* v. *Fellows* (1828) 5 Bing. 267, discussed in Hunt, *Business Corporation;* 42; Harris, *Industrializing English law*, 245–6. This was accepted by Shadwell VC in equity: *Blundell* v. *Winsor* (1837) 8 Sim. 601.

[35] *Garrard* v. *Hardey* (1843) 5 M. & G. 471; *Harrison* v. *Heathorn* (1843) 6 M. & G. 81 (common law); *Walburn* v. *Ingelby* (1833) Myl. & K. 61.

[36] *Perring* v. *Hone* (1826) 4 Bing. 28.

[37] *Fox* v. *Clifton* (1830) 6 Bing. 776; *Kempson* v. *Saunders* (1826) 4 Bing. 5.

[38] M. Lobban, 'Nineteenth Century Frauds in Company Formation: *Derry* v. *Peek* in Context', (1996) 112 *LQR* 287–334 at 295.

[39] Harris, *Industrializing English Law*, 261.

[40] *Van Sandau* v. *Moore* in *The Times*, 16 August 1826, col. 2f.

[41] See First Report of the Select Committee on Joint Stock Companies, PP 1844 (119), vii, 1 (cited henceforth as Gladstone Committee, 1844) at p. 172, q. 2084 (Evidence of John Duncan).

impossible.[42] Some companies sought to overcome these problems by including provisions in their deeds referring disputes to arbitration. But if any partner
refused arbitration, there was little which could be done, since courts of law only
gave nominal damages in these cases, while equity ignored the agreement.[43]

At the same time that the Bubble Act was repealed, legislation was passed to
permit joint stock country banks to incorporate, with unlimited liability. These
companies were to be able to sue or be sued in the name of an officer, who obtained
a personal indemnity, with execution of judgment being available against any
member. If the plaintiff failed to obtain payment from such persons, he could (by
leave of the court) obtain execution against those who had been members for up
to three years previous to the action.[44] These banks were obliged before trading to
deliver to the stamp office in London a return containing the names of all members along with the name of the person who was to litigate for the company.[45]

2. REFORMING COMPANY LAW, 1830–1848

From the 1830s, steps were taken to give better recognition to unincorporated
associations. In an era when an increasingly large number of companies were
being formed, which attracted money from an investing public, rather than
active traders, judges and policy makers became ever more aware that the hostile environment created by the common law and equity needed to be changed.
The need to rethink company law was especially pressing at a time of regular
stock market booms and slumps. A number of measures were accordingly taken
in the 1830s to remove some of the disabilities which derived from partnership
status. In 1834, the Trading Companies' Act empowered the Crown to confer
some of the privileges which chartered corporations had—such as the power to
sue and be sued in the name of a principal officer—on bodies which were not
incorporated. Further legislation in 1837 allowed the Board of Trade to confer
limited liability on petitioners, without fully incorporating them. Nonetheless,
the Crown remained cautious in its approach, deciding in 1834 that the privileges
associated with incorporation were only to be granted where the business was

---

[42] *Van Sandau* v. *Moore* (1826) 1 Russ. 441. See also *Wheeler* v. *Van Wart* (1838) 9 Sim. 193;
Abraham v. *Hannay* (1843) 13 Sim. 581; *Deeks* v. *Stanhope* (1844) 14 Sim. 57. But the rule was relaxed
in *Richardson* v. *Larpent* (1843) 2 Y. & C.C.C. 507. See also the comments in J. M. Ludlow, *The Joint-
Stock Companies Winding-Up Act, 1848* (1850), xxiv.

[43] Ker Report, 3–4. Cf. *Tattershall* v. *Groote* (1800) 2 B. & P. 131 at 135. The Chancery expected parties to go first to arbitration: *Waters* v. *Taylor* (1807) 5 Ves. 10.

[44] 7 Geo. IV c. 46, ss 9, 13, 14.

[45] On these banks, see T. L. Alborn, *Conceiving Companies: Joint Stock Politics in Victorian
England* (1998), Ch. 4.

hazardous, required large capital, or involved large numbers of parties.[46] In its view, 'facilities should not be afforded to Joint Stock Partnerships which may interfere with private enterprise'.[47] Between 1837 and June 1854, 164 applications were made for such charters allowing limited liability, of which 93 were approved, or less than six a year.[48]

The broader question of company law was investigated in two official reports. In 1836, the Board of Trade asked Henry Bellenden Ker to look at the law of partnership. To overcome the problems presented to companies by their status as partnerships, Ker proposed that they should be given the power to sue and be sued in the name of an officer, with execution of judgment being available against the property of all members. All firms with more than 10 members should be required to have a deed in writing, which would be enrolled in the Chancery with the names of the shareholders; and no shares should be allowed to be traded in unregistered companies. He also proposed the creation of a system of official arbitrators and accountants, to improve the taking of partnership accounts. Although Ker surveyed the arguments for and against granting firms limited liability, he made no firm proposals on this question.[49]

The matter was investigated once again in the early 1840s, by a select committee chaired by William Gladstone. The initial appointment of a select committee in 1841 was prompted by concern about fraudulent company formations, felt in the aftermath of another series of failures, notably in insurance and banking.[50] The Committee reported in 1844, and was followed by the enactment of legislation to regulate all companies which operated on the joint stock principle, including insurance and utility companies. The only companies omitted were joint stock banks (which were excluded from the remit of the Gladstone Committee), which were regulated by a different Act passed in the same year. In its investigations, the Committee had been primarily concerned with how to control fraud, and to prevent the flotation of bubble companies formed for share speculation. It rejected the assumption which had hitherto guided policy, that the best way to regulate corporate enterprise was through the state's use of its discretionary power to grant charters to those companies which it felt were suitable. Instead, there was to be a mechanical form of registration, with sufficient information to allow the investor to make a sound judgment.[51] All joint stock companies would be required to register, and would obtain a distinct legal personality from their members. The Committee spent some time debating what test to use to differentiate such companies from partnerships. Some witnesses took the view that companies were

---

[46] Harris, *Industrializing English Law*, 272; Hunt, *Business Corporation*, 56.

[47] Hunt, *Business Corporation*, 57.   [48] Cottrell, *Industrial Finance*, 43.

[49] Ker Report, 19–24.   [50] Taylor, *Creating Capitalism*, 137.   [51] *Ibid.*, 141.

defined by the fact that they had freely transferable shares. Others felt that the question was a matter of size. The Act adopted both views: under it, the term 'company' included any partnership whose capital was divided into freely transferable shares, as well as any partnership with more than 25 members.[52]

The Act also aimed to draw a clear distinction between those officers who ran the company and the investors, and to give the latter the means to supervise and control the former.[53] The Act specified that the shareholders had to appoint at least three directors to manage the ordinary concerns of the firm. No director was to have any office of profit in the company, nor could they vote on matters in which they had an interest. Although there were some calls for directors to be subjected to a more stringent law of fraud,[54] this was rejected since it might deter men of ability and standing from accepting posts.[55] Under the Act, the directors were required to keep accounts, which had to be balanced, and made available to shareholders.[56] Auditors had to be appointed annually. While these provisions were designed to help shareholders supervise the management of the company, it was soon realized that 'without some more stringent regulations as to the mode of auditing the accounts' than those required by the Act, 'the accounts themselves rather facilitate than prevent mismanagement and fraud'.[57]

The Gladstone Committee heard much evidence regarding limited liability from those who felt that it would improve commercial morality by attracting prudent investors in the place of mere speculators.[58] But many (including Ker) remained unconvinced that limited liability was suitable for firms not engaged in tasks requiring large capital or involving high risk.[59] The unlimited liability of shareholders was therefore not removed by the Act. Creditors were to seek execution first against the corporate assets, but if due diligence had been used to get satisfaction of the judgment against a company, it could be had against the person or property of any current shareholder, or any person who had held shares at the time the debt was outstanding. Shareholders whose property had been taken would have to seek contributions from others. The Act also settled the problem of the continuing liability

---

[52] The Act did not extend to banks, cost-book mines, or to associations such as friendly societies.

[53] Paddy Ireland has argued that, in this era, the notion that the corporation's personality was distinct from that of its members was developed by common law courts considering whether shares were to be regarded as real or personal property: 'Capitalism without the Capitalist: The Joint Stock Company Share and the Emergence of the Modern Doctrine of Separate Corporate Personality' (1996) 17 JLH 40–72.

[54] See e.g. Ker's evidence, Gladstone Committee, 1844, q. 2199, p. 195.

[55] Gladstone Committee, 1844, q. 148, p. 13 (evidence of Peter Laurie).

[56] 7 & 8 Vict. c. 110, ss 34–36. See also Gladstone Committee, 1844, at v, xiii.

[57] A. Pulling, The Law of Joint Stock Companies' Accounts (1850), 30.

[58] Gladstone Committee, 1844, q. 2090, p. 174 (evidence of John Duncan).

[59] Ibid., q. 2148, p. 185.

of shareholders. At common law, a partner's liability continued until he gave notice of the dissolution of the partnership, typically in the *Gazette*. While in theory the same principle applied to the liability of a person selling his shares in a joint stock company,[60] in practice, joint stock companies did not dissolve when shares were sold, and in the absence of a public register, it had been easy enough to unload shares—typically onto a straw man—when liabilities loomed. Borrowing from banking legislation, the Act held former shareholders liable for three years after the transfer of their shares (section 66), with the provisions relating to the registration of shareholders helping to render the identification of shareholders possible.

The primary method devised by the Gladstone Committee to protect investors was through the double system of registration. The first stage was a provisional registration, when the name and purpose of the business would be registered, together with details of its promoters, directors, and subscribers, as well as the prospectus. This was to be accompanied by a declaration whether the company was to seek incorporation by statute, under the Letters Patent Act or by charter, which in effect meant limited liability. The second stage was complete registration, when details would be deposited with the Registrar of the prospectus, deed of settlement, the nominal capital and the amount paid up, the number and amount of each share, and the names and addresses of shareholders and officers. Shares could be allotted when the firm was provisionally registered, and costs necessary for the company's formation could then be incurred. But no shares could be transferred, and no operations could be commenced, until registration was complete. The thinking behind this proposal was that the public would be given an opportunity to discriminate between sound and unsound firms, and that only those which were solid would proceed to the second stage.

In the following year, Parliament passed the Companies Clauses Consolidation Act to codify the clauses usually inserted in statutes authorizing railway and canal companies to raise capital and undertake public works. Such statutes had generally provided for the complete subscription of the company's capital before its powers could be exercised, and regulated the structure and management of the company. By the 1830s, the procedure of passing statutes to authorize such firms had become increasingly complex, as legislators discovered new defects in the form of earlier Acts, which needed to be provided for in the latest effort. The 1845 Act created a set of standard clauses to be inserted in any Act authorizing a statutory company to operate. It regulated the raising of capital, the means of transferring shares, the borrowing powers of the company, the qualification, powers, and liabilities of directors, and the keeping of accounts. The Act specified that every person whose name was on the register was to be considered a

---

[60] *Ibid.*, qq. 213, 222, p. 69 (evidence of Peter Laurie).

shareholder; and that shareholders were to be liable for the company's debts only to the extent of unpaid calls on their shares. It provided for the management of the company by directors, who were immune from personal liability if they lawfully exercised the powers they held. The statute provided that accounts were to be kept and be balanced, and that no dividend could be paid so as to reduce the capital of the firm. The constitution of these companies was thus not a matter of choice or determination by its members, but was defined by Parliament.

If legislators felt any confidence in 1845 that they had created a firm regulatory structure which would ensure the stable growth of sound companies, they were soon to receive a shock. For rather than capping speculation, the 1844 legislation was followed by another speculative boom in companies seeking statutory power. In 1845—a year of 'railway mania'—1520 companies were registered provisionally.[61] The fact that they were provisionally registered gave the public confidence in their *bona fides*; but most failed without getting to final registration, or securing the legislation needed to proceed. In this context, it was soon found that, rather than clarifying the status of the joint stock company, the system of double registration confused it. For when provisional companies failed, the common law courts had to sort out the liabilities of provisional committeemen, allottees of scrip, and those who had bought the scrip in the market. As in the 1820s, judges went out of their way to protect the investing public, throwing much of the cost of failed enterprise on the creditors. After some uncertainty, it was settled by 1846 that provisional committee members were not partners, since they lacked the crucial attribute of sharing the profits of the concern.[62] The fact that a man's name was on a list of provisional committeemen did not itself impose liability on him: to be liable for expenses, a jury had to be convinced that the committeeman had himself authorized the spending, or had held himself out as acting for the company.[63] Nor were allottees liable to creditors, since they only agreed to become partners at a future date, when all the conditions needed for forming the company had been fulfilled.[64] They could also recover their deposits,[65] without contributing to the expenses incurred, provided they had not had signed the deed of subscription. Even scrip holders were protected. To begin with, the provisions of the 1844 Act forbidding trading in shares was held not to apply to railway

---

[61] Lobban, 'Nineteenth Century Frauds', 297. Between November 1844 and September 1856 only 910 companies were fully registered in England: H. A. Shannon, 'The First Five Thousand Limited Companies and their Duration' (1932) 3 *Econ. Hist. Rev.* 396–424.

[62] *Reynell* v. *Lewis* (1846) 15 M. & W. 17; Lobban, 'Nineteenth Century Frauds', 301. See also R. W. Kostal, *Law and English Railway Capitalism, 1825–1875* (Oxford, 1994), Ch. 2.

[63] *Wood* v. *Duke of Argyll* (1844) 6 M. & G. 928; *Lake* v. *Duke of Argyll* (1844) 6 Q.B. 477.

[64] This rule derived from *Bourne* v. *Freeth* (1829) 9 B. & C. 632; *Fox* v. *Clifton* (1830) 6 Bing. 776; *Pitchford* v. *Davis* (1839) 5 M. & W. 2.

[65] *Walstab* v. *Spottiswoode* (1846) 15 M. & W. 501.

scrip. Furthermore, it was held that a purchaser of scrip in a projected company which had been abandoned could recover his purchase price from his vendor in an action for money had and received (having bought 'a nothing'), while the vendor could sue the original projector for his money.[66] Those who had lost out in trading scrip were potentially insured from their losses, while those who had gained could keep their profits.

The failures which resulted from the railway mania also raised questions about how to dissolve failed companies. Alongside the Joint Stock Companies Act, a Winding Up Act was passed in 1844, which allowed any creditor to take proceedings in the bankruptcy courts, if any company—provisionally or completely registered[67]—committed any act of bankruptcy. It was soon evident that the system it created was faulty, as far as company members were concerned. Since it was designed to satisfy creditors, the machinery was unsuitable for settling the contributions of shareholders.[68] If a company was insolvent—as so many of the provisionally registered companies were—creditors simply sued the wealthier shareholders, who would have to use the expensive Chancery to recover contributions from the other shareholders. Proposals were soon made to give the Chancery jurisdiction over the winding up of companies, on the petition of any shareholder to dissolve a company. Legislation followed in 1848, allowing persons interested in a company to have its affairs wound up, with calls being made on contributories and accounts settled. The official manager made out a list of company members and the extent of their interest, and the Chancery master settled the list of contributories who might be made to contribute in proportion to their responsibility for the losses.[69] Contributions were to be obtained from all shareholders, which included all those who had undertaken such an agreement to buy shares as could be specifically enforced.[70] After the passing of this Act, attempts were made by the promoters of companies which had failed during the Railway Mania to recover money from the committeemen and allottees in Chancery.[71] They did not succeed, for equity endorsed the approach taken by the common law courts, that provisional

---

[66] *Kempson* v. *Saunders* (1826) 4 Bing. 6; Lobban, 'Nineteenth Century Frauds', 299, 302.

[67] For Lord Cranworth's criticism over the inclusion of provisional companies in the statutes, see *Carrick's case* (1851) 1 Sim. N.S. 505 at 514.

[68] Ludlow, *Winding Up Act*, xxx. Under the 1844 Act, the creditors' assignees could be directed to apply to the Chancery if questions relating to the contribution of shareholders arose.

[69] *Ex p the Earl of Mansfield* (1850) 2 Mac. & G. 57 at 67; *Ex p Weiss* (1852) 5 De G. & Sm. 402. The *Law Times* despaired of this doctrine, asking 'How is a call to be made, when every contributor has a different degree of liability? To determine the precise liability of each will be the work of a lifetime' (1850) 14 *LT* 385.

[70] *Sanderson's case* (1849) 3 De G. & Sm. 66. See also *Walter's case* (1850) 3 De G. & Sm. 149.

[71] They also sought the fees associated with winding-up proceedings (1850) 14 *LT* 385. It noted that the masters had pronounced them intolerable and commented that a select committee would be called to look into it.

committeemen and allottees were not partners. In Parke B.'s view, '[t]hese inchoate undertakings have generally no joint estate, effects or credits, of which there can be a manager; no person can have a judgment or decree against the whole body, except in the rare case that all the projectors have jointly contracted'.[72]

The purpose of the Winding Up Act was simply to sort out the respective liabilities of company members, and creditors continued to be able to obtain execution of judgment against individual members.[73] The courts initially took the view that since creditors were bound use due diligence to recover their debt from company assets before seeking execution against individual shareholders, they were obliged to prove their debts before the master if the company was being wound up.[74] But this view was soon questioned. 'The real of object' of the Act, Martin B. ruled in 1855, 'was to compel the shareholders to contribute and pay equally according to their interests. It does not affect creditors, but leaves them free to pursue their common law remedies',[75] which included execution of judgment against the assets of the shareholder. In effect, if the 1844 Act gave companies a distinct corporate personality at its formation, its members were treated as partners when the firm failed.

3. THE TRANSFORMATION OF COMPANY LAW, 1848–1862

By the early 1850s, it was evident that the regime introduced in 1844 needed reform. The Joint Stock Companies Act appeared to do both too much and too little: it lulled investors into a false sense of security without providing adequate mechanisms through which they could exert control. It seemed that either more government interference was required, or less.[76] At the same time, there was renewed debate over whether joint stock companies should be given limited liability. The view that it was immoral or against natural justice to allow people to limit their liability was countered by the argument—put by men like Robert Lowe and George Bramwell—that it was a matter of right, based on the notion of freedom of contract.[77] In their view, the ability to limit one's liability

---

[72] *Bright v. Hutton* (1851–2) 3 H.L.C. 341 at 368. This case overruled Lord Brougham's attempt in *Hutton v. Upfill* (1850) 2 H.L.C. 674 at 691 to hold a provisional committeeman liable.

[73] A proposed clause that such execution should not issue without leave of the Chancery was heavily defeated: *PD* 1848 98: 1415.

[74] *Thompson v. The Universal Salvage Co* (1849) 3 Ex. 310 at 319.

[75] *Hill v. The London Assurance Co* (1855) 1 H. & N. 398 at 401. He added (at 402) 'It is a great misfortune that it has ever been supposed that shareholders are in a different position from ordinary partners'. See also *Morisse v. Royal British Bank* (1856) 1 C.B. N.S. 67.

[76] Report from the Select Committee on Assurance Associations, *PP* 1852–3 (965), xxi, 1, at para. 7.

[77] Mercantile Law Commission, First Report, *PP* 1854 [1791], xxvii, 445, at p. 29 ('Opinion of Mr Bramwell'); Report from the Select Committee on the Law of Partnership (henceforth cited as Partnership Law Committee), *PP* 1851 (509), xviii, 1, q. 525 (Evidence of Cecil Fane).

should not depend on a special privilege given by the state, acting 'as a nurse or a guardian'.[78] They argued that allowing traders to limit their liability would improve commercial morality and stability, for it was unlimited liability which encouraged the reckless credit which fed speculation.[79] A system in which investors were expected to look after their own affairs, and in which creditors would be expected to assess the level of risk for themselves, charging for credit accordingly, would provide stability and growth. While admirers of political economy such as Lowe and Bramwell—who were not businessmen—saw in limited liability the logical extension of Free Trade,[80] it took rather longer for a consensus in favour of this principle to develop among businessmen.[81]

The question was discussed by a number of bodies in the early 1850s: a select committee of the Commons on the savings of the middle and working classes in 1850, a select committee on the law of partnership in 1851, and a Royal Commission on the mercantile laws in 1854. Like Henry Bellenden Ker, they also considered whether the continental principle of *commandite* partnerships should be introduced, whereby sleeping partners had limited liability, and managing partners retained full liability. Each body took a cautious approach to reform, considering that the 'privilege of limited liability' should still be conferred by charters. However, there was a consensus that charters should be obtained more cheaply and on fixed criteria.

By the middle of the decade, criticisms of the Board of Trade's power to grant privileges increased. Its competence to evaluate which firms required limited liability was questioned,[82] particularly since it permitted rival companies to oppose charters to protect their own interests. The continued role of discretion in granting limited liability was a matter of concern. By the middle of 1854, the Board of Trade therefore ceased to grant charters, anticipating a change in the law. At the same time, the repeal of the usury laws generated further calls for reform of the law of partnership, from those pointing to the inconsistency of allowing creditors to lend to partners at any rate they wished, while not allowing them to lend in proportion to profits without incurring unlimited liability.[83]

---

[78] Partnership Law Committee, q. 522, pp. 72–82 (Cecil Fane).

[79] J. Saville, 'Sleeping Partnerships and Limited Liability, 1850–1856' (1956) 8 *Econ. Hist. Rev.* (2 s) 418–33 at 427.

[80] Political economists were also divided: J. R. McCulloch strongly opposed limited liability: *Considerations*, 11–12, 25.

[81] See G. R. Searle, *Entrepreneurial Politics in Mid-Victorian Britain* (Oxford, 1993), 187–93. For an interpretation seeking to link changes in this law to changing moral views, see B. Hilton, *The Age of Atonement: The Influence of Evangelicalism on Social and Economic Thought, 1785–1865* (Oxford, 1988), 259–67.

[82] *PD* (s3) 139: 325. By 1855, 204 applications had been made for charters since the power was given to the board, of which 113 had been granted. See *PP* 1854 (299), lxv, 611.

[83] Saville, 'Sleeping Partnerships', 429.

Many reformers now felt the old regime was unsustainable. As J. M. Ludlow pointed out, there were only two ways to ensure sound commercial enterprise. One was to hold the people who controlled businesses fully responsible for its losses. This method was suitable for partnerships, where each member shared equally in the management and the risk. The other was to ensure that a due proportion existed between the capital of a business and its engagements. This method was suitable for large corporations, which limited the liability of their members. The problem with the 1844 Act was that it fell between the two stools. Shareholders retained the liability of partners; but since they lacked the ability to exert control which partners enjoyed, the Act provided creditors with the additional security (associated with corporations) of a subscribed capital. The result was that creditors invested not on the faith of the capital alone (as they did with chartered corporations), but on the faith of the shareholders' unlimited liability, which meant that 'the unlimited liability company has the dangerous privilege of retaining the individual credit of the private partnership system, whilst deprived of its checks upon the abuse of that credit'.[84] For Ludlow, the obvious solution was to allow limited liability companies with a defined capital base, and with regularly published balance sheets.[85]

In this atmosphere, two bills were introduced in 1855, one to allow *commandite* partnerships, and the other to grant limited liability to large companies as a matter of course. The first bill, allowing sleeping partners to limit their liability, failed to pass, despite widespread dissatisfaction with the rule that those who lent in return for a proportion of the profits were fully liable.[86] The second bill passed, having undergone a number of amendments in Parliament. The original proposal that limited companies were to have a minimum capital of £20,000, with 20 per cent paid up, was dropped.[87] The Commons, which wanted limited liability to be available to all joint stock companies, and not merely ones with large capitals, amended the bill to grant this status to any firm of six or more.[88] However, the Lords felt that firms of that size would generally be considered as partnerships, all of whose members were active, and it increased the figure to 25, the number used in the 1844 Act. Companies with limited liability were still subject to the regulations imposed by the 1844 Act, save that execution of judgment could only be had against the effects of a shareholder in respect of his unpaid calls.

This regulatory regime was replaced in the following year by a new Joint Stock Companies Act. The Act was piloted by Robert Lowe, who felt that the attempts

---

[84] Mercantile Law Commission, First Report, 146.   [85] *Ibid.*, 148.

[86] The rule in *Waugh* v. *Carver* was disapproved of by the Lords in *Cox* v. *Hickman* (1860) 8 H.L.C. 268, and repealed in Bovill's Partnership Law Amendment Act 28 & 29 Vict. c. 86.

[87] PD 1855 (N.S.) 139: 1457.

[88] PD 1855 139: 1518 (Hugh Cairns). This number was chosen as 'there were seldom so many as six in an ordinary partnership'.

of earlier legislation to protect the investor were flawed. While the 1844 Act appeared to offer protection against frauds, in reality none was offered. The publicity given by the system of double registration had not prevented investors from being seduced into unsustainable speculations. The rules regulating the amounts which had to be subscribed were easily evaded, as were those which forbad the sale of shares prior to complete registration. In Lowe's view, it was in any case impossible for governments to 'attempt, by a system of artificial restraints, to test the worth of any commercial undertaking'.[89] Now that investors were given the protection of limited liability, it was to be left to them to ensure that their companies were properly controlled.[90]

The new Act required all partnerships of more than 20 to register, and permitted any partnership of more than six to do so. As soon as seven shareholders signed a memorandum of association specifying the name, objects, and number of shares in the company, and deposited it with the Registrar, the company became entitled to registration and corporate status. The company could choose whether or not to have limited liability. In contrast to the 1844 Act, regulation was kept to a minimum. The register of shareholders, detailing what calls had been made on the shares, was to be housed at the company's offices, and not with the Registrar of Joint Stock Companies. The compulsory accounting and audit provisions included in 1844—which had been of limited effectiveness, given the limited number of accountants—were abandoned.[91] The new Act did not even require the company to appoint directors, but left all matters of internal management to be decided by the firm, in articles of association which were to accompany the memorandum. At the same time that it left the proprietors free to determine the shape of the company, the legislature created a model form of articles (in Table B) which was to apply if the company failed to formulate one of its own. This model was detailed, and made extensive provisions for accounting and auditing, and a century later were still regarded as being 'remarkably modern'.[92]

The Act also reformed the procedure of winding up companies. The regime introduced in 1848 was perceived to be flawed since creditors were able to pick individual shareholders to sue, or proceed against the company in bankruptcy, even if a winding-up order had been issued, but they could not obtain an order for winding up the company themselves. The regime was also criticized since it did not allow shareholders to wind up their own affairs without the costly intervention of

---

[89] *PD* 1855 (s3) 140: 123.

[90] Taylor, *Creating Capitalism*, 164–5.

[91] The original proposal that annual balance sheets be deposited with the Registrar on a uniform method was also abandoned: *PD* 1856 (s3) 140: 134.

[92] H.C. Edey and Prot Panitpakdi, 'British Company Accounting and the Law, 1844–1900', in A. C. Littleton and B. S. Yamey (eds), *Studies in the History of Accounting* (1956), 356–79 at 366.

the Chancery.[93] A series of Acts from 1856 to 1858 rectified these defects. Creditors were henceforth compelled to use the statutory winding-up procedure set out in the Act, without being able to seek execution directly against the property of individual members. The question of who was a contributory was to be settled by reference to the register.[94] Petitions for winding up could be made by the company, by contributories, or by creditors. The winding up itself could be conducted either in Chancery (under the control of an official liquidator) or in Bankruptcy (under the control of an official assignee, or an official liquidator chosen by the creditors). Besides such compulsory windings up, companies could also be voluntarily wound up if a general meeting passed a special resolution to this effect.[95]

If the 1856 Act created the most liberal and unregulated company law regime in Europe, it did not extend to the biggest companies with the widest shareholder basis, or to those dealing with the most economically important business. It was not the herald of a new age of unregulated, limited liability corporate entities. Not only were the largest companies—those regulated by the Companies Clauses Act—excluded, but so too were the economically sensitive insurance and banking companies. It was agreed that insurance companies needed greater regulation than other firms, since those who had invested premiums in a life policy over many years were not generally in a position simply to withdraw their custom in the way traders could.[96] In fact, the 1856 Act created some problems for insurance companies, since its repeal of the 1844 statute suggested that new companies could no longer register at all, but were to be treated as mere partnerships. The loophole was plugged in 1857, which reinstated the 1844 Act's provisions for insurance companies.[97] Insurance companies did not need legislation to limit their liability to policyholders, since courts upheld terms in their policies which specified that the assured could only look to the company's funds.[98] Terms limiting the liability

[93] H. Thring, *The Joint Stock Companies Act 1856* (1856), 18; N. Lindley, *Treatise on the Law of Companies*, (5th edn, 1889), 612–13.

[94] The Act provided that shareholders in limited liability companies remained liable for up to a year after the transfer of their shares; while the period for holders of shares in unlimited liability companies was three years; though the transferees were to indemnify the shareholder: 19 & 20 Vict. c. 47, ss 62–63, 66. The amending Acts were 20 & 21 Vict. c. 14 and 21 & 22 Vict. c. 60.

[95] Legislation in 1857 allowed a hybrid form of voluntary winding up, under court supervision. Under this system, the administrative business was conducted by the liquidator in a voluntary liquidation, with an appeal being given to any creditor or contributory who felt it was unjust: 20 & 21 Vict. c. 14, s 19, extended by 21 & 22 Vict. c. 60.

[96] Report from the Select Committee on Assurance Associations, *PP* 1852–3 (965), xxi, 1, at p. v.

[97] 20 & 21 Vict. c. 80. For its effect on companies formed in the interim, see *In re Bank of London and National Provincial Insurance Association* (1871) LR 6 Ch App 421. See also C. Crawley, *The Law of Life Insurance* (London, 1882), 164.

[98] *Re State Fire Insurance Co* (1863) 1 De G. & S. 634 at 640; *In re Athenaeum Life Assurance Co* (1859) 3 De G. & J. 660; *In re the Athenaeum Society* (1859) Johns 80.

of members of incorporated insurance companies were read as precluding the policyholder from suing shareholders who had not paid up their shares fully, considering that it was for the company to enforce the payment.[99]

Banks continued to be governed by the 1844 Joint Stock Banks Act. This legislation preserved unlimited liability for bank shareholders, who could be proceeded against directly if the assets of the bank were insufficient to satisfy judgment.[100] In fact, shortly after the passing of the 1856 Joint Stock Companies Act, proceedings over the failed Royal British Bank revealed the chaotic nature of the regime under which banks operated. At the same time that shareholders were attempting to wind up the bank in Chancery, under the 1848 Act, creditors were permitted not only to seek execution of judgments against individual shareholders,[101] but also to use the provisions of the 1844 Winding Up Act to recover sums owing to them in the courts of bankruptcy.[102] The result was that one court handled the assets of the firm for the creditors, while another enforced calls against the shareholders, driving the costs of the dissolution up enormously. The banking crisis prompted legislation in 1857 allowing banks to register under the 1856 Act. In the following year, legislation was passed allowing banks to limit their liability.

In 1862, a general Companies Act was passed to consolidate the law. This Act created the basic framework of company law for the next half-century. It left in place the liberal regime of 1856, for it re-enacted the 'default' set of articles, now renamed Table A. Although the Board of Trade was empowered to alter the rules, no new regulations were introduced until 1906. Where the 1856 Act had enacted that shareholders in limited companies were only to be liable for the uncalled amount on their shares, the 1862 Act also allowed limited liability by guarantee: the amount each agreed to pay in the memorandum of association. It also applied the winding-up provisions of the 1856 Act to all partnerships of more than seven, whether incorporated or not. The 1862 Act was also extended to include not only banks and insurance companies, but other associations such as mutual societies, and other associations which did not derive their capital from shares. However, they were subjected to greater regulation than other joint stock companies. Banks, insurance companies, and benefit societies were obliged to make statements twice yearly giving details of their capital and liabilities, in every place where they did business. Moreover, by 1870, it was apparent (after another wave of failures) that life insurance companies needed greater regulation than other joint stock firms, and the Life Assurance Companies Act passed, which required

[99] *Halket* v. *The Merchant Trader's Insurance Co* (1849) 13 Q.B. 960; *Lord Talbot's case* (1852) 5 De G. & Sm. 386. For the approach in unincorporated companies, see *Hallett* v. *Dowdall* (1852) 18 Q.B. 2.
[100] 7 & 8 Vict. c. 113, s 10.
[101] *Morisse* v. *Royal British Bank* (1856) 1 C.B. N.S. 67.
[102] Lobban, 'Nineteenth Century Frauds', 314.

such companies to deposit £20,000 with the Accountant General of the Court of Chancery, until they had accumulated a fund of £40,000 from premiums; and which imposed more detailed accounting duties on such companies.

4. COMPANIES AND THE STOCK MARKET, 1862–1914

In the second half of the nineteenth century, the investing public became increasingly well informed by the financial press and were increasingly confident to invest on the stock market.[103] While over 70 per cent of the securities quoted on the London Stock Exchange in 1853 were government securities, almost 16 per cent were shares in UK railways. At this time, less than 2 per cent of investments were commercial or industrial.[104] Such investments were slow to develop, for the coming of general limited liability was not followed by a mass conversion of firms into limited liability companies seeking to raise capital on the stock market. Most businesses continued to obtain their capital from reinvesting profits, from loans, or from capital injections from local connections. In contrast to utilities and railways, which needed to raise large sums on a formal capital market, the majority of manufacturing, retail, and shipping firms did not need to raise money on the Stock Exchange or have shares quoted there.[105] In the first two decades after the 1862 Act was passed, private partnerships therefore continued to be the dominant business form.[106]

This era did, however, see a number of speculative booms, with new companies frequently floated on the stock market, often promising lucrative gains from foreign operations. In 1865, 1064 companies were registered, while the years 1872–4 saw an average of 1014 companies founded annually.[107] The common practice in this era of issuing shares of high denomination, only a small proportion of which was paid up, was designed to benefit creditors who had a large fund of unpaid capital to draw on.[108] But it proved disastrous for the many investors who

---

[103] See M. Poovey, 'Writing about Finance in Victorian England: Disclosure and Secrecy in the Culture of Investment' (2002) 45 *Vict. St.* 17–41. Legal works aimed at the public were published, including A. Emden, *The Shareholder's Legal Guide* (London, 1884), reprinted in Pearson et al., *History of the Company*, 199–375.

[104] R. C. Michie, *The London Stock Exchange: A History* (Oxford, 1999), 88–9. For the development of the stock exchange, see also R. C. Michie, *The London and New York Stock Exchanges, 1850–1914* (London, 1987); D. Kynaston, *The City of London. Volume I: A World of its own 1815–1890* (London, 1994); E. Victor Morgan and W. A. Thomas, *The Stock Exchange: Its History and Principles* (London, 1962).

[105] Michie, *The London and New York Stock Exchanges*, 105–6.

[106] In 1885, there were some 100,000 'important partnerships', compared with less than 10,000 limited companies. Jefferys, *Business Organisation*, 104–5.

[107] Shannon, 'The First Five Thousand Limited Companies'; H. A. Shannon, 'The Limited Companies of 1866–83' (1933) 4 *Econ. Hist. Rev.* 290–316; PP 1907 (257), lxxvi, 549.

[108] J. B. Jefferys, 'The Denomination and Character of Shares, 1855–85' (1946) 16 *Econ. Hist. Rev.* 45–55 at 45.

bought large numbers of shares in the hope of high profit, if the firm failed. High-profile failures in this era generated considerable suspicion both about those who promoted joint stock companies and those who invested in them, who were often regarded as speculators and gamblers.[109]

Share speculation was not itself regarded as unlawful. The Prevention of Stock Jobbing Act (Sir John Barnard's Act) of 1733, which had made illegal contracts for the sale of stock not actually in the possession of the seller, was repealed in 1860. It had in any case been narrowly construed by the courts, which held it to apply only to transactions in public stocks and securities,[110] rather than investments in joint stock companies. The Act was held not to apply where the sale was *bona fide*, but only in cases of 'illegal trafficking in the funds, by selling fictitious stock merely by way of differences'.[111] In the mid-century, there was some question whether share speculation would be caught by the 1845 Gaming Act. In 1852, the Common Pleas held that this Act rendered time bargains unlawful, where a speculator agreed to sell shares to a broker and buy them back at a later date, with the intention only of paying the difference in the prices, rather than transferring the shares.[112] But when investors attempted to use this decision to repudiate bad investments made by their brokers, the courts proved unsympathetic.[113] By the late 1870s, the Court of Appeal had come to the view that unenforceable time-bargains would almost never be found on the Stock Exchange, since the jobber could always insist that the broker take the shares.[114] Such contracts were hence enforceable, and brokers could recover their commissions.[115] Only if it was shown that the parties had agreed that no stocks were ever to be delivered and that only differences in price were to be paid for, would the transaction be regarded as void under the Gaming Act.[116] Nor

---

[109] See G. R. Searle, *Morality and the Market in Victorian Britain* (Oxford, 1998), 78–86; D. C. Itzkowitz, 'Fair Enterprise or Extravagant Speculation: Investment, Speculation, and Gambling in Victorian England' (2002) 45 *Vict. St.* 121–47; J. Taylor, 'Company Fraud in Victorian Britain: The Royal British Bank Scandal of 1856' (2007) *English Hist. Rev.* 700–24; *ibid.*, 'Commercial Fraud and Public Men in Victorian Britain' (2005) *Historical Research* 230–52.

[110] *Wells* v. *Porter* (1836) 2 Bing. N.C. 722; *Elsworth* v. *Cole* (1836) 2 M. & W. 32; *Hewitt* v. *Price* (1842) 4 M. & G. 355; *Williams* v. *Trye* (1854) 18 Beav. 366.

[111] *Mortimer* v. *M'Callan* (1840) 6 M. & W. 58 at 70.

[112] *Grizewood* v. *Blane* (1851) 11 C.B. 526. Where there was a *bona fide* intention to transfer, the Act did not apply: *Ashton* v. *Dakin* (1859) 7 W.R. 384; *Barry* v. *Croskey* (1861) 2 J. & H. 1 at 29; *Cooper* v. *Neil* (1878) WN 128.

[113] Brokers were permitted to recover from their principals for work and labour done, even if the contract made with the jobber for shares was unenforceable: *Jessopp* v. *Lutwyche* (1854) 10 Ex. 614; *Knight* v. *Cambers* (1855) 15 C.B. 562; *Knight* v. *Fitch* (1855) 15 C.B. 566.

[114] See also *Forget* v. *Ostigny* [1895] AC 318 (PC).

[115] *Thacker* v. *Hardy* (1878) 4 QBD 685 at 688. See also *Backhouse* v. *Whiteley* in *The Times*, 25 November 1878, col. 11c.

[116] In *Cooper* v. *Neil* (1878) WN 128, the Court of Appeal, however, did feel there was such a contract. See also *The Universal Stock Exchange* v. *Strachan* [1896] AC 166.

did the courts do much to stamp out the unrespectable practices of the 'bucket shop' dealers, who were not members of the Stock Exchange, but advertised in the press for customers to speculate in share dealings on payment of a deposit.[117] Since their agreements included a clause by which the investor acknowledged his duty to take the shares, they managed to satisfy the test of *Thacker* v. *Hardy*.[118] Only when they invited subscriptions to trust funds, which guaranteed either profits or a return of the investor's money, did the courts regard the transaction as violating the Gaming Act.[119] In effect, the courts' response to the question of share speculation was pragmatic: for they had little purchase over the jobbers, who were members of the London Stock Exchange, which had its own code of conduct and enforced its own rules, ignoring such rules of law as were inconvenient.[120]

The market for commercial and industrial stocks and shares grew dramatically after 1880. By 1903, the proportion of securities quoted on the London Stock Exchange represented by such investments had risen to nearly 10 per cent. Where in 1883, £43 million was invested in such securities, in 1893 it had risen to £172.6 million, and in 1903 it reached £690.9 million.[121] The period after 1880 saw a growing desire by many companies to limit their liability. Over the next 15 years, more than 2000 new registered companies were formed on average each year, while in the next decade the annual average exceeded 4000.[122] The turning point, which made many companies seek limited liability, was the failure in 1878 of the unlimited City of Glasgow Bank, most of whose shareholders were bankrupted by the £2750 liability they incurred for every £100 share held.[123] The failure was followed by legislation allowing unlimited liability banks to convert to limited liability. Companies now began to issue shares of smaller denomination with a larger proportion paid up. This meant that shareholders could be confident that the limitation of their liability was not merely theoretical, while creditors had to trust to the company's liquidity rather than its capital for security.

Not all firms which adopted the corporate form with limited liability wished to raise money on the Stock Exchange. Some preferred to remain 'private',

---

[117] According to E. C. Grant, they 'brought disgrace upon the Stock Exchange by causing the ruin of ladies and gentlemen in the country', *The Times*, 25 February, 1897, col. 11a.

[118] See e.g. *Shaw* v. *Bailey* in *The Times*, 5 November 1892, col. 6d.

[119] e.g. *Richards* v. *Starck* [1911] 1 KB 296, cf. *The Times*, 24 October 1910, col. 3a.

[120] Morgan and Thomas, *The Stock Exchange*, 148.

[121] R. C. Michie, *The London Stock Exchange: A History* (Oxford, 1999), 88–9.

[122] Shannon, 'The First Five Thousand Limited Companies'; *ibid.*, 'The Limited Companies of 1866–83' (1933) 4 *Econ. Hist. Rev.* 290–316; *PP* 1907 (257), lxxvi, 549.

[123] Jefferys, *Business Organisation*, 102. Only 250 out of 1819 investors in the bank remained solvent: M. Anderson, J. R. Edwards, and D. Matthews, 'A Study of the Quoted Company Audit Market in 1886' (1996) 6 *Accounting, Business and Financial History* 363–87 at 381.

raising their own capital.[124] Many limited companies were formed in the wave of amalgamations at the end of the century, when smaller firms joined forces, often as a defensive measure, to shield the participants from foreign competition.[125] Historians have long debated whether Britain's relative industrial decline at the end of the nineteenth century is to be attributed to the failure of the capital markets to finance domestic industry, and their preference for overseas investment. In fact, the predominance of overseas investment resulted from the lack of demand from British industry for funding. Where a demand for fresh capital was needed—as in new industries, such as in the electrical or chemical fields—there was indeed a market of eager investors to be drawn on. By the end of the century, British investors were increasingly keen to find profitable investments. Joint stock investment became more popular, thanks in part to a decline in the yields from consols and railway investments.[126] It has been estimated that the number of investors in joint stock companies, excluding utilities, grew from around 50,000 in 1860 to half a million in 1910.[127] Besides investing directly in newly quoted kinds of company, they could also put their money into investment trusts, which began to multiply in the late 1880s.[128]

Those who did want to raise capital on the markets often did not wish to relinquish control of their companies. This could be achieved firstly by issuing preference shares,[129] which gave investors a priority in the payment of dividends, but limited voting rights. They were desirable for shareholders, since their dividends could be made good out of future profits, if no profit was made in any particular year.[130] Although preference shares had long been issued by railway companies, there was uncertainty over whether companies set up under the 1862 Act could do so. It was held in 1865 in *Hutton* v. *Scarborough Cliff Hotel Co (Ltd)* that if

---

[124] This was encouraged by lawyers such as Francis B. Palmer, *Private Companies; Or, How to Convert your Business into a Private Company, and the Benefit of So Doing* (1877).

[125] 'Between 1898 and 1900 alone, 650 firms valued at a total of £42 million were absorbed in 198 separate mergers': L. Hannah, *The Rise of the Corporate Economy* (1976), 21.

[126] J. Armstrong, 'The Rise and Fall of the Company Promoter and the Financing of British Industry', in J. J. Van Helten and Y. Cassis (eds), *Capitalism in a Mature Economy: Financial Institutions, Capital Exports and British Industry 1870-1939* (Aldershot, 1990), 115–38 at 119; Cottrell, *Industrial Finance*,166.

[127] Michie, *The London and New York Stock Exchanges*, 119.

[128] Y. Cassis, 'The Emergence of a New Financial Institution: Investment Trusts in Britain, 1870–1939', in Van Helten and Cassis (eds), *Capitalism in a Mature Economy*, 139–58.

[129] See Jefferys, *Business Organization*, 218, 458.

[130] *Webb* v. *Earle* (1875) LR 20 Eq 556. The rule had first been established for statutory companies: *Henry* v. *The Great Northern Railway Co* (1857) 1 De G. & J. 606 at 637; see also *Corry* v. *The Londonderry and Enniskillen Railway Co* (1860) 29 Beav. 263; *Coates* v. *The Nottingham Waterworks Co* (1861) 30 Beav. 86. Section 14 of the Companies Clauses Act 1863 (26 & 27 Vict. c. 118) changed the rule for statutory companies.

a company's memorandum and articles of association made no provision for preference shares, they could not subsequently be issued.[131] Attempts to alter the company's constitution to permit such shares to be issued were frowned on.[132] By the 1880s, however, some judges were becoming critical of this approach, which presumed that all shareholders were entitled to equal dividends, unless the memorandum had specified to the contrary.[133] In 1897, in *Andrews v. Gas Meter Company*, the Court of Appeal finally overruled *Hutton*, holding that a company which had no authority under its memorandum or original articles, could by special resolution subsequently alter its articles so as to empower it to issue preference shares.[134] Preference shareholders' rights depended on the wording of the memorandum or articles which authorized the issue, and which specified the nature of the holder's entitlements.[135] By the 1880s, companies had begun to offer a variety of different kinds of preference share, only some of which paid dividends out of future profits. After the turn of the twentieth century, new forms of preference share were developed, which gave the holder an ordinary as well as a preference dividend.

Those who converted their business had other ways to protect their interests. 'Founders Shares' were also sometimes given to those who sold their business or assets to the new company. Such shareholders postponed their participation in profits until the other investors had received a dividend. Although often designed to show the *bona fides* of those who were behind the formation of a company, they could prove highly lucrative. For after the cash investors had been paid their fixed dividend, the surplus might be divided equally between the two classes of shareholders, with the small number of founders profiting equally with a mass of investors.[136] They would also rank equally with cash investors, when the company was wound up.[137] However, companies could by their articles give preference shareholder priority over the capital as well, to enable them to rank ahead

---

[131] *Hutton v. Scarborough Cliff Hotel Co* (1865) 2 Dr. & Sm. 514, 521, 4 De G. J. & S. 672. See also *In re South Durham Co* (1885) 31 Ch D 261. However, a company could by special resolution authorize borrowing on debentures: *Bryon v. The Metropolitan Saloon Omnibus Company* (1858) 3 De G. & J. 123.

[132] See *Harrison v. Mexican Railway Co* (1875) LR 19 Eq 358; *In re Wedgwood Coal and Iron, Anderson's case* (1876) 7 Ch D 75; *Ashbury v. Watson* (1885) 30 Ch D 376; *Guinness v. Land Corporation of Ireland* (1882) 22 Ch D 349 at 375.

[133] See e.g. *Guinness of Land Corporation of Ireland* (1882) 22 Ch D 349 at 377; *In re South Durham Brewery Co* (1885) 31 Ch D 261 at 270–1; *British and American Trustee and Finance Corporation v. Couper* [1894] AC 399 at 417.

[134] *Andrews v. Gas Meter Co* [1897] 1 Ch 361 at 371.

[135] The articles might stipulate that there was to be no payment out of future profits: *Staples v. Eastman Photographic Materials Co* [1896] 2 Ch 303.

[136] See Jefferys, *Business Organization*, 234–5.

[137] *In re London India Rubber Co* (1868) LR 5 Eq 519; *Griffth v. Paget* (1877) 6 Ch D 511.

in any winding up.[138] Moreover, it was decided in 1909 that after such preferential shareholders had been paid out preferentially from a surplus in winding up, they could still rank equally with the other shareholders for the remaining surplus, unless the articles stipulated to the contrary. While their rights to dividends might be limited, when the company was wound up, they were held to rank as equal partners.[139]

A second device to raise money without sacrificing control was through the issue of debentures.[140] Debenture holders were in law lenders rather than investors, whose loans were secured by a floating charge on the company's current assets.[141] These forms of investments were popularized by railway companies.[142] The 1845 Companies Clauses Consolidation Act permitted statutory companies to assign the 'undertaking' and all the earnings of the company to mortgagees, which allowed them to mortgage present and future assets. Creditors with such securities did not have the power to seize any particular asset of the company, which might entail breaking up the enterprise. Rather, they had a charge on the company as an entire going concern, which gave them a priority when the company was wound up.[143] The Companies Acts did not give other kinds of companies the power to create floating charges, but some companies did issue them, imitating the example of the railways.[144] The judiciary was at first ambivalent towards this device. Although, in 1862, the House of Lords had allowed a creditor who had secured a loan to a manufacturer by taking a mortgage covering equipment which might be acquired later to have priority over an unsecured creditor,[145] judges in the 1860s held that companies had no power to charge their

[138] See the comments of Malins VC in *In re Bangor and Portmadoc Slate and Slab Co* (1875) LR 20 Eq 59 at 64.

[139] *In re Espuela Land and Cattle Co* [1909] 2 Ch 187.

[140] For a discussion of the use of such devices, see J. Getzler, 'The Role of Security over Future and Circulating Capital: Evidence from the British Economy circa 1850–1920', in J. Getzler and J. Payne (eds), *Company Charges: Spectrum and Beyond* (Oxford, 2006), 227–51.

[141] For a history, see R. R. Pennington, 'The Genesis of the Floating Charge' (1960) 23 *MLR* 630–46; R. Gregory and P. Walton, 'Fixed and Floating Charges—A Revelation' (2001) *Lloyds Maritime and Commercial Law Quarterly* 122–149; R. C. Nolan, 'Property in a Fund' (2004) 120 *LQR* 108–36 at 117–30; J. Armour, 'The Chequered History of the Floating Charge' (2004) 13 *Griffith Law Review* 25–56.

[142] See C. Stebbings, 'Statutory Railway Mortgage Debentures and the Courts in the Nineteenth Century' (1987) 8 *JLH* 36–47.

[143] *Gardner* v. *London Chatham and Dover Railway Co (No. 1)* (1867) 2 Ch App 201.

[144] Gregory and Walton, 'Fixed and Floating Charges' argue that companies adopted this form in order to evade the rule in *Graham* v. *Chapman* (1852) 12 C.B. 85, that the mortgage of present and future property constituted an act of bankruptcy. They show that judges interpreted s 10 of the 1875 Judicature Act favourably to companies to ensure that floating charges were not caught by bankruptcy legislation.

[145] *Holroyd* v. *Marshall* (1862) 10 H.L.C. 191.

future assets.[146] But in 1870, the Chancery Court of Appeal held that a debenture holder did have priority in the winding up of a company over its unsecured creditors.[147] Once it was confirmed that debentures were 'a security on the property of the company as a going concern, subject to the powers of the directors to dispose of the property of the company while carrying on its business in the ordinary course',[148] they became ever more popular.[149] They were attractive for companies, since they were cheaper than bank loans, and could be liquidated or renewed on terms dictated by the company. Unlike ordinary shares, they could be issued at a discount, so that money could be raised when shares were trading below par. They were also attractive for investors. Besides having the security of the floating charge, they obtained a higher return from such holdings than could be acquired from government funds; and they were regarded in the commercial community as negotiable.[150] Debenture holders' interests were also strongly protected by their power to appoint receivers. If the company was solvent, a receiver could be used to obtain payment of moneys due, without trade being suspended.[151] If it was insolvent, debenture holders could secure the appointment of a receiver, even if there was no arrear either in the principal or the interest due.[152]

In the 1890s, some concern was expressed over the use of debentures secured by floating charges, since they were felt to encourage fraud. Some feared that holders of floating charges with access to inside information could apply for a receiver if there was any danger of unsecured creditors seeking to obtain payment.[153] The Inspector General who dealt with liquidations, John Smith, felt that

---

[146] *King* v. *Marshall* (1864) 33 Beav. 565; *Re British Provident Life and Fire Assurance Society, Stanley's case* (1864) 4 De G. J. & S. 407.

[147] *In re Panama, New Zealand, and Australian Royal Mail Co* (1870) 5 Ch App 318. Cf. *In re General South American* (1876) 2 Ch D 337. Debenture holders' claims were postponed to those of subsequent incumbrancers, such as mortgagees without notice. *Government Stock Investment and Other Securities Co* v. *Manila Railway Co* [1895] 2 Ch 551; *In re Colonial Trusts Corporation, Ex p Bradshaw* (1879) 15 Ch D 465 at 472; *In re Horne and Hellard* (1885) 29 Ch D 736.

[148] *In re Florence Land and Public Works Co, Ex p Moor* (1878) 10 Ch D 530 at 541.

[149] The floating charge was threatened by the provisions of the Bills of Sale Act (1878) Amendment Act 1882, but were eventually shielded by judicial decisions: see R. Gregory and P. Walton, 'Fixed Charges over Changing Assets—The Possession and Control Heresy' [1998] *Company Financial and Insolvency Law Review* 68–87.

[150] The courts were slow to recognize this: *Crouch* v. *The Credit Foncier of England* (1873) LR 8 QB 374. But by the end of the century, they accepted commercial custom: *Bechuanaland Exploration Co* v. *London Trading Bank* [1898] 2 QB 658.

[151] See e.g. *Hopkins* v. *Worcester and Birmingham Canal Proprietors* (1868) LR 6 Eq 437.

[152] See *M'Mahon* v. *North Kent Ironworks* [1891] 2 Ch 148; *Bissill* v. *Bradford Tramways Co* (1891) WN 51.

[153] See the comments of Buckley J. in *London Pressed Hinge Co* [1905] 1 Ch 576, discussed in the Report of the Company Law Amendment Committee in PP 1906 [Cd 3052], xcvii, 199 (henceforth cited as Loreburn Committee) at p. 15.

the power to issue debentures charging future assets was a fraud on creditors and shareholders, since it enabled directors to continue trading when the firm was doomed to fail. He felt that there should be a public register of debentures to indicate to creditors the real nature of the share capital.[154] The Davey Committee in 1895 also felt that floating charges to secure debentures, and any charges on unpaid capital, should be entered at the Registrar's office; and that failure to do so should render them ineffective against the claims of a creditor or a liquidator. Provisions to this effect were included in the 1896 bill, and were passed in the 1900 Companies Act.[155] Some argued that the use of floating charges should not be permitted at all; but the Loreburn committee in 1905–6 rejected as too drastic a proposal to abolish a system of finance which had developed over 40 years, and which was extremely popular in business.[156] But it did propose to tighten the law, by rendering invalid (save to the amount of any cash paid) any floating charge made within three months of the commencement of a winding-up proceeding unless the company was solvent at the time of its issue. This was to prevent firms issuing debentures at a heavy discount when they were on the verge of failure.

5. THE BIRTH OF COMPANIES

In the 1860s and 1870s, there was great concern about the ease with which fraudulent company promoters were able to float bubble companies, and seduce the public to part with their money.[157] The regulation of share flotations was left largely to the Stock Exchange, which applied its own rules.[158] Under its rules, a prospectus had to have been issued, which agreed with the articles of association; the company was not permitted to use its capital to buy its shares; and it had to provide accounts annually to its shareholders. The Stock Exchange did, however, allow scrip to be traded prior to the allotment of shares, as long as two-thirds of the company's issued nominal capital had been subscribed for, and the company had no power to buy its own shares.[159]

[154] Seventh General Annual Report by the Board of Trade under s 29 of the Companies (Winding-Up) Act 1890, *PP* 1898 (337), lxxxiv, 179, at p. 22. See also the comments of S. Brice, *A Treatise on the Doctrine of Ultra Vires*, (3rd edn, 1893), xii.

[155] Companies Act 1900 (63 & 64 Vict. c. 48), s 14.   [156] Loreburn Committee, 15.

[157] See G. Robb, *White Collar Crime in Modern England: Financial Fraud and Business Morality, 1845–1929* (Cambridge, 1992).

[158] It was the policy of the Stock Exchange to enforce all bargains, and by its rules no member could enforce a claim against another by law. Moreover, the Sales of Shares and Stock in Joint Stock Banking Companies (Leeman's Act), which passed in 1867 to regulate the trading of shares in joint stock banks, was generally ignored by brokers: Morgan & Thomas, *Stock Exchange*, 147.

[159] Report of the Commissioners appointed to inquire into the Origin, Objects, Present Constitution &c of the London Stock Exchange, *PP* 1878 [c 2157], xix, 263, p. 13 (henceforth cited as Stock Exchange Commission Report).

Many companies sought to ensure a successful flotation by dealing in the shares prior to their allotment. Such dealings were notoriously engaged in by unscrupulous promoters who aimed to make quick profits from share dealings in companies they formed, which had little chance of long-term success. While the Stock Exchange was found to be less than thorough in rooting out such practices,[160] they were hard to control. When the Stock Exchange attempted to counter these frauds in 1864 by banning all dealings before allotment, the transactions were continued by dealers who were not its members, and the new rule was abandoned. The only sanction against bad practice was therefore the refusal of a settlement day; but since there had to be a complaining party opposing its grant, promoters and brokers who settled their differences privately could continue with the flotation. These practices were of particular concern in the 1860s and 1870s. By the end of the nineteenth century, when opinion on the Stock Exchange had turned against pre-allotment bargains, their use had declined sharply.[161]

In practice, the Stock Exchange's rules proved a flimsy barrier to fraud. It was not uncommon for company promoters to evade the rules relating to the necessary subscription, by borrowing money from a bank, which was then lent to a company guaranteeing the subscription. The money would be paid by them back to the promoters, as a deposit on shares to be allotted, and would be returned by the promoters to the bank, with the Stock Exchange being informed that the necessary shares had been subscribed and paid for. Only when the company failed would the trick be revealed, whereupon it was left to the courts to sort out the mess.[162] In particularly bad cases—such as with the flotation of the Eupion Gas and Fuel Company—the committee of the Stock Exchange insisted on a criminal prosecution of those who had obtained a settlement by fraudulent means.[163] But the fact that the company had been able to deceive the committee with a very crude scheme is testimony to the laxity of the investigations made in this era.[164] So concerned was the government with the frauds which had been permitted that a Royal Commission was set up to examine the rules of the Stock Exchange. Despite collecting a mass of evidence, its recommendations were slight; and the exchange was left to regulate itself.[165]

Since self-regulation proved so inadequate as a means to protect the investor, some steps were taken in the 1860s to provide a stronger legislative regime.

---

[160] Stock Exchange Commission Report, p. 17.

[161] Morgan & Thomas, *Stock Exchange*, 149.

[162] See the history of the flotation of Charles Laffitte & Co Ltd, in *Gray* v. *Lewis* (1868–9) LR 8 Eq 526.

[163] *R.* v. *Aspinall* (1876) 1 QBD 730; *R.* v. *Aspinall* (1876) 2 QBD 58. For Bramwell's view of the criminality of a device to deceive the Stock Exchange committee, see also *The British and American Telegraph Co* v. *The Albion Bank* (1872) LR 7 Exch 119 at 122.

[164] Robb, *White Collar Crime*, 83.   [165] D. Kynaston, *The City of London. Vol. I*, 275–85.

Even before the calamitous failure of Overend, Gurney & Co in 1865, the Stock Exchange submitted proposals to the Registrar of Joint Stock Companies calling for greater regulation before a company could commence business.[166] After the crash provoked by its failure, a select committee was appointed to investigate the operation of the limited liability legislation. Witnesses to the committee suggested various regulatory devices relating to the issuing of prospectuses and the allotment and payment of shares. There were also calls for general meetings to be held prior to commencement of business, where allottees could check the viability of the company, and for balance sheets to be filed regularly with the Registrar.[167] Some witnesses argued that the liability of directors should be unlimited, though others felt that such a rule would deter good directors, and leave knaves in control.[168]

In the face of strong opposition from businessmen, the regulatory proposals made before the committee were not taken up. Legislation was passed in 1867 allowing firms to be formed whose directors would have unlimited liability, though few chose to follow this path. During the passage of the bill, a new clause was introduced, in response to a problem revealed during the litigation over the failure of Overend, Gurney & Co. The problem was that the prospectus issued when the firm sought to convert to limited liability was not strictly speaking untrue, but was misleading since it concealed from potential purchasers the truly parlous state of the firm, which resulted from unmentioned contracts binding the firm. To address this, a new provision—section 38—enacted that any prospectus which failed to give information regarding 'any contract entered into by the company, or the promoters, directors or trustees thereof' before its issuing was to be deemed a fraud on shareholders who purchased shares on the faith of the prospectus. Those held liable under it for non-disclosure would be as liable as they would be for fraudulent misrepresentations in the prospectus.

Within a decade, a new raft of failed speculative company formations led policy-makers to seek stronger controls. In 1876, a bill was brought by David Chadwick, which required information to be published in the prospectus about the vendors to a company, as well as the details of every contract entered into by the company's promoters. Chadwick's bill also required disclosure of the particulars of anyone who received fees for issuing the company's capital. Moreover, half the capital would have to be subscribed before the company could begin operations.[169] The bill, reintroduced in 1877, also proposed that every limited liability

---

[166] Cottrell, *Industrial Finance*, 57.

[167] Select Committee on Limited Liability Acts, *PP* 1867 (329), x, 393.

[168] Select Committee on Limited Liability Acts 1867, q. 2074, p. 130; H. S. Thring, *The Law and Practice of Joint Stock and Other Companies*, (5th edn, ed. by J. M. Rendel, 1889), 351–2.

[169] P. L. Cottrell, *Industrial Finance*, 62–3.

company should be required to publish its accounts.[170] The bill was referred to a select committee, chaired by Robert Lowe. Witnesses before the committee were divided over whether increased regulations were necessary, or whether intervention was mischievous, in creating a false sense of security among investors who should inquire carefully into the character and credit of those they were dealing with.[171] Its report did, however, recommend a return to a two-stage registration process, with provisional registration to allow the issuing of a prospectus and the receipt of applications for shares, and a final registration when the capital had been subscribed for, and the proportion of it which had been stipulated to be paid on allotment had been paid up. But the report was not acted on, and only minor amendments were made to the 1867 Act.[172] The suggestions to increase the regulatory framework of company formation were not taken up.

The question of whether to impose more controls on company formation continued to be debated to the end of our period.[173] A bill embracing some of the regulatory ideas which had been in the air for 20 years was introduced in 1888, though it foundered in the face of opposition from commercial interests. Six years later, the Board of Trade appointed a departmental committee chaired by Lord Davey to reconsider the question. This committee rejected the notion that the principle of *caveat emptor* could apply to the purchase of shares, and recommended that prospectuses should 'disclose everything which could reasonably influence the mind of an investor of average prudence'.[174] The committee shared the widespread disquiet with section 38 of the 1867 Act, which had proved 'absolutely incapable of a correct interpretation',[175] and which had been evaded by the insertion of waiver clauses in prospectuses.[176] The Davey Committee recommended replacing section 38

---

[170] See Chadwick's explanation of his accounting proposals in the Report from the Select Committee on the Companies Acts 1862 and 1867, *PP* 1877 (365), viii, 419 (henceforth cited as Select Committee on Companies Act, 1877) , q. 1947, p. 112.

[171] Select Committee on Companies Act, 1877, iii.

[172] The amendment was a technical one in response to the decision in *In re Ebbw Vale Steel, Iron, and Coal Co* (1877) 4 Ch D 827 at 831.

[173] See e.g. Final Report of the Royal Commission on Depression of Trade and Industry, *PP* 1886 [C 4893], xxiii, 507 at pp. xviii, xxv.

[174] Report of the Departmental Committee appointed by the Board of Trade to inquire what amendments are necessary in the Acts relating to joint stock companies incorporated with limited liability under the Companies Acts 1862–1890, *PP* 1895 [c 7779], lxxxviii, 151, at p. vi (henceforth cited as Davey Committee Report).

[175] *PD* (s3) 328: 1506. J. M. Rendel observed in 1889 that the meaning of section 38 'remains to be settled by the House of Lords': Thring, *Joint Stock and Other Companies* (5th edn, 1889), 355.

[176] The courts often struggled to decide whether they were valid or not. See F. B. Palmer, *Company Precedents in Relation to Companies Subject to the Companies Acts, 1862 to 1890*, 2 Parts (7th edn, 1897–8), i, 125–34. See also the comments of Lindley MR regarding 'tricky' waiver clauses in *Greenwood* v. *Leather Shod Wheel Co* [1900] 1 Ch 421 at 435–5. See also *Cackett* v. *Keswick* [1902] 2 Ch 456; *Watts* v. *Bucknall* [1902] 2 Ch 628.

with one requiring disclosure of defined matters, including the name of the real vendor to the company, and details of moneys paid to every promoter. Failure to disclose was to give a right of action in damages against any person party to issuing the prospectus, but not the right to rescind against the company.[177]

When a bill based on these recommendations was introduced in 1896, there was alarm at the detail required of the prospectus, and the level of liability for non-compliance.[178] As Romer LJ commented, 'no reasonable director, so far as I can see, could prudently issue any prospectus whatever if this provision stands'.[179] It had to be watered down. The legislation which finally passed in 1900 required information on the founders' shares, the directors' qualification shares and details of shares and debentures issued as paid up; it had to detail the amount payable to vendors where the purchase was not complete at the time the prospectus was issued; and it had to distinguish the cost of the goodwill and give dates and parties to all material contracts which were not contracts entered into for the ordinary business of the company. The 1900 Act also rendered void any clause in the prospectus under which applicants were held to waive the duty to disclose imposed by section 10 of the Act. The 1900 Act did not specify penalties for directors who violated these clauses, though Walter B. Lindley, editor of *Lindley on Companies*, claimed that any director would be liable in tort for a breach of a statutory duty, with the measure of damage the same as in the tort of deceit.[180] The Act also repealed and replaced section 38, though the provisions of the new Act only applied to companies formed after 1901. Waiver clauses were also outlawed after 1900, though the purchaser still had to persuade the court that he would not have subscribed had he known of the facts omitted.[181] Although the Act gave much detail on what was to be included in a prospectus, companies were not required to issue one. Many now chose not to do so. Instead, promoters allotted shares to themselves, and sold them on the Stock Exchange. To cure this problem, legislation was passed in 1907 requiring all public companies—those whose shares were traded—to file a preliminary statement containing the same information.[182]

In the absence of detailed legislative regulation of company promotions, it was left largely to the courts to figure out the duties of promoters.[183] In the early 1870s, thanks to the frauds of men such as Albert Grant, promoters were regarded with

---

[177] Davey Committee Report, para. 36.   [178] 40 (1896) *Sol. J.* 414.

[179] Select Committee of the House of Lords on the Companies Bill, *PP* 1897 (384), x, 97 (henceforth cited as Companies Bill Select Committee 1897), q. 192, p. 18.

[180] N. Lindley *A Treatise on the Law of Companies* (6th edn by Walter B. Lindley, 1902), i, 126.

[181] See F. B. Palmer, *Company Law: A Practical Handbook for Lawyers and Businessmen* (9th edn, 1911), 347.

[182] This followed the recommendations of the Loreburn Committee, 7.

[183] There was no clear legal definition of what a promoter was, since it was a term of business, and not of law, which summed up a number of different business operations which brought a company into existence. *Whaley Bridge Calico Printing Company* v. *Green and Smith* (1879) 5 QBD 109 at 111.

much suspicion, as men apt to fleece a gullible public investing in hopeless speculations. It was clear that the interests of promoters were not the same as those of shareholders, for the professional promoter was often more concerned with whether the company could be floated, rather than whether it would be sound.[184] Promoters sought to maximize their own profits from launching companies, and as a result often bought out firms whose financial assets were much smaller than its capitalization. While the promoter took his profit, the company might be unable to generate adequate dividends for the large capital. Besides ensuring low yields, promoters might additionally cause the share price to fall when they unloaded their shares onto the market.

In the 1870s, the courts took a tough approach towards promoters. They did this firstly through their interpretation of section 38 of the 1867 Act. Its wording had left it unclear whether promoters were under a duty to disclose any contract whose existence might influence the judgment of investors, or only those which bound the new company. It was initially held that promoters were under no duty to disclose details of prior contracts by which they acquired assets which they later sold on to the firm, since a person buying an asset owed no duty to a company which he might launch in future.[185] But in *Twycross* v. *Grant*, a majority of the Court of Appeal held that company promoters were required to disclose the details of any contract entered into, which might affect the judgment of potential shareholders.[186] The decision was controversial, but was regarded by the majority of the court as an essential protection for investors.

The courts also developed a remedy for those shareholders who were unable to rely on section 38, since they had bought shares in the market, rather than on the faith of the prospectus. They did this by developing the principle that the promoter owed a fiduciary duty to the company, which resulted from the control which he had over its formation.[187] Using this approach, the House of Lords in 1878 held that promoters had a duty to disclose their interest in any property they sold to the company.[188] If they failed to do this, the company could rescind the contract and recover the full purchase price, even if a pure *restitutio in integrum* of the asset could not be made, as where a mine had been worked.[189] At a time when the legislature was unsure about how far to proceed in protecting investors,

---

[184] Palmer, *Company Precedents* (7th edn, 1897–8), i, 58.

[185] *In re Coal Economising Co* (1875) 1 Ch D 182. This was the position of Bacon VC: the Court of Appeal which upheld his decision was more divided in its reasoning.

[186] *Twycross* v. *Grant* (1877) 2 CPD 469.

[187] Palmer, *Company Precedents* (7th edn, 1897–8), i, 61–8.

[188] *Erlanger* v. *New Sombrero Phosphate Co* (1878) 3 App Cas 1218 at 1269, 1277. Cf. Jessel MR's remarks in *New Sombrero Phosphate Co* v. *Erlanger* (1877) 5 Ch D 112.

[189] See further, M. Lobban, 'Erlanger v New Sombrero Phosphate Company', in C. Mitchell and P. Mitchell (eds), *Landmark Cases in the Law of Restitution* (Oxford, 2006), 123–62.

equity judges sought to develop remedies to throw the loss as far as possible on the unscrupulous promoter.

Equity judges now also allowed shareholders who had invested on the faith of misleading prospectuses to rescind their share purchase, even where there had been no fraud committed; and some opined that a remedy should be available to shareholders in damages in such cases.[190] However, after much debate in the 1880s, it was settled by the House of Lords in *Derry* v. *Peek* that the action of deceit could not be used for negligent misstatements.[191] The decision created some consternation, both from those who desired to see an expansion of the law of negligence, and from those who wanted to impose a greater standard of care on those issuing prospectuses. To satisfy the latter lobby, a Directors Liability Act was passed in 1890, which defined the duties of promoters and directors with respect to prospectuses. When the original bill proposed they should warrant the accuracy of the prospectuses, the financial press expressed concern that it might deter respectable men from engaging in business.[192] Faced with such opposition, the bill was watered down. Directors and promoters would henceforth be liable for damage resulting from any untrue statement in a prospectus, unless they could show reasonable grounds for their belief in the statement. The act threw the onus on directors to take care, to keep evidence of correspondence to prove it, and publicly to dissociate themselves from any dubious prospectuses.[193]

The figure of the fraudulent promoter remained a familiar one in the 1890s and 1900s, thanks to the activities of men such as E. T. Hooley and Whittaker Wright. Nonetheless, in an age when more companies were turning to limited liability, and when merchant banks showed little interest in domestic industrial securities, both judges and public opinion became increasingly aware that they could fulfil a useful function. Equity judges exploring the nature of the fiduciary relationship between the promoters and the company began to be more sympathetic to the *bona fide* businessman. Led by Lord Lindley, the author of one of the leading texts on company law, they began to take a lighter touch. It was now accepted that promoters did not have to set out in the prospectus the full details of profits they had made, provided that they had disclosed the fact, and made the contracts available for inspection.[194] According to Lord Lindley, whether sufficient disclosure had been made was to be decided from the common sense viewpoint of a businessman.[195]

---

[190] *Smith* v. *Chadwick* (1882) 20 Ch D 27 at 44; *Weir* v. *Bell* (1878) 3 Ex D 238 at 242. See pp. 425–31.

[191] *Derry* v. *Peek* (1889) 14 App Cas 337.   [192] *Economist*, 19 July 1890, p. 919.

[193] See W. F. Hamilton with K. G. Metcalfe, *A Manual of Company Law for the Use of Directors and Promoters* (1891), 309.

[194] See *Aaron's Reefs* v. *Twiss* [1896] AC 273 at 287; *Lagunas Nitrate Co* v. *Lagunas Syndicate* [1899] 2 Ch 392 at 428–31. But see Wright J.'s doubt in *Sale Hotel & Co* 78 LT 368, doubting that investors ever checked.

[195] *In re Olympia* [1898] 2 Ch 153 at 166.

Judges had also to consider whether a company could set aside a purchase ratified by a board of directors which was not independent, but was composed of nominees of the promoters. Some judges and jurists, drawing on the decision in *Erlanger*, held that companies could avoid any contracts entered into by such a board.[196] However, in *Lagunas Nitrate Company* v. *Lagunas Syndicate*, a majority of the Court of Appeal held that the promoters of a company had no duty to provide an independent board of directors. Provided the company was informed of the connections between the directors and the promoters, it would be bound by their decisions.[197] At the same time, promoters had a duty to disclose their interest to the whole company, and not merely to the directors they nominated. Where a company was formed which intended to sell shares to allottees, the fiduciary duty was owed not merely to the seven original signatories of the memorandum of association, but also to the future allottees of shares.[198] By contrast, if the original signatories were to be allotted all the shares, and they were aware of the vendor's interest, the company would be bound.[199] If shares were subsequently issued to the public, they would not be able to complain.[200]

A distinction was now drawn between those promoters who had acted in good faith, and those who had not. The rule regarding rescission put forward in *Erlanger* v. *New Sombrero* was qualified in *Lagunas Nitrate Company* v. *Lagunas Syndicate*, when the Court of Appeal ruled that the equitable remedy to grant a rescission on terms, where *restitutio in integrum* was no longer possible, was only available if the vendors had acted fraudulently.[201] Nor were promoters held to account for the profit they had made in selling an asset they had previously acquired to the company they formed, where they had acted *bona fide*. It was regarded as unfair to make the promoter account for his profit in such cases, since that would be to allow the company to acquire the asset at its original price, when its market value might have risen by the time that the company acquired it.[202] By contrast, if the court felt that the promoter intended at the time the asset was purchased to form a company to buy it, and if he subsequently used the company's money to pay for the purchase, then he was taken to have been an agent for the company in the transaction, and be liable to account for the profit, unless

---

[196] Palmer, *Company Precedents* (7th edn, 1897–8), i, 64–5.

[197] *Lagunas Nitrate Co* v. *Lagunas Syndicate* [1899] 2 Ch 392 at 425.

[198] *In re British Seamless Paper Box Co* (1881) 17 Ch D 467 at 471; *In re Leeds and Hanley Theatres of Variety* [1902] 2 Ch 809.

[199] *Salomon* v. *A. Salomon & Co* [1897] AC 22 at 37. Cf. *Larocque* v. *Beauchemin* [1897] AC 358 at 364.

[200] *In re British Seamless Paper Box Co* (1881) 17 Ch D 467 at 477–8. See also *In re Ambrose Lake Tin and Copper Mining Co, Ex p Taylor, Ex p Moss* (1880) 14 Ch D 390; *In re Gold Co* (1878) 11 Ch 701.

[201] *Lagunas Nitrate Co* v. *Lagunas Syndicate* [1899] 2 Ch 392 at 433–4.

[202] Nor were courts prepared to speculate over what that correct price might be, for to do so would entail making a bargain for the parties. In re Cape Breton (1885) 29 Ch D 795, aff'd in *Bentinck* v. *Fenn* (1887) 12 App Cas 652.

the company had ratified the transaction.[203] In drawing the distinction between cases where the promoter was an agent and where he was not, much depended on the judgment of the court on his conduct.[204] If all seemed to have been done in good faith, then the decision could be in the promoter's favour, even where the period between the acquisition and formation of the company was very short, and even where there had been a continuing intention to form a company.[205] But where the entire project was clearly a device to make profits at the company's expense, courts made him account for profits.[206]

In the decades around the turn of the twentieth century, judges and legislators also turned their minds to the practice of paying brokers' commissions to place the shares of a newly floated company, and of having issues underwritten by those who would guarantee to buy the shares at a preferential price. In 1883, Chitty J. held that it was lawful to issue shares at a discount, where a company's articles made provision for it. This allowed a company to dispose of shares which it might not be able to place at par.[207] But five years later, in *Re Almada and Tirito Company*, the Court of Appeal held the practice *ultra vires* under the 1862 Act, since it amounted to an alteration in a company's capitalization and the return of part of it to the allottee.[208] Flotations continued to be underwritten, but thanks to this rule it had to be arranged by those who sold their assets to the company, rather than by the company itself.[209] In 1888, Kay J. held that payments of brokerage out of subscribed capital was also *ultra vires*. He felt that such payments were only made by unsound companies.[210] This view was overturned by the Court of Appeal in 1895. It held that the rule that shares could not be issued at a discount meant only that shareholders had to pay their full price: it did not mean that the company could not pay a broker.[211] Nonetheless, many judges remained

---

[203] See *In re Cape Breton* (1885) 29 Ch D 795 at 811.

[204] See Sargant J.'s comments in *Omnium Electric Palaces* v. *Baines* [1914] 1 Ch 332 at 347.

[205] e.g. *Ladywell Mining Co* v. *Brookes* (1887) 35 Ch D 400.

[206] See *Gluckstein* v. *Barnes* [1900] AC 240; *In re Darby, Ex p Brougham* [1911] 1 KB 95 at 101.

[207] *In re Ince Hall Rolling Mills Co* (1883) 23 Ch D 545n; *In re Plaskynaston Tube Co* (1883) 23 Ch D 542.

[208] *In re Almada and Tirito Co* (1888) 38 Ch D 415. It was confirmed by the House of Lords in *Ooregum Gold Mining Co of India* v. *Roper* [1892] AC 125 that a company whose shares were trading well below par could not issue preference shares with three-quarters of the nominal sum as paid up. The rule regarding issuing shares at discount did not apply to statutory companies under the Companies Clauses Consolidation Act: *Webb* v. *Shropshire Railways Co* [1893] 3 Ch 307 at 329.

[209] See Select Committee of the House of Lords on the Companies Bill, *PP* 1896 (342), ix, 171 (henceforth cited as Companies Bill Select Committee 1896), q. 147, p. 10. See also J. W. Budd, at q. 187, p. 12.

[210] *In re Faure Electric Accumulator Co* (1888) 40 Ch D 141 at 154–5. See also *Lydney and Wigpool Iron Ore Co* v. *Bird* (1886) 33 Ch D 85, where Lindley LJ said that a company could not use part of its capital to pay for the issue of its own shares.

[211] *Metropolitan Coal Consumers' Association* v. *Scrimgeour* [1895] 2 QB 604 at 606.

uneasy at the way promoters could use commissions effectively to issue shares at a discount.[212] The result was that in the late 1890s it was agreed to be lawful to pay brokerage for placing shares, but not to pay a commission to a person underwriting an issue of shares.[213] When the departmental committee examining the Companies Acts chaired by Lord Davey considered the question, it reported that businessmen recognized the propriety of payments for underwriting flotations.[214] Legislation in 1900 accordingly legalized the underwriting of shares offered to the public, provided that it was authorized by the articles and disclosed in the prospectus, so that investors would obtain accurate information as to the true capitalization of the firm.[215] The rule remained in place that the company could not sell ordinary or preference shares at a discount in the market when its share price had fallen below par.[216]

6. WINDING UP COMPANIES

The 1862 Act determined the procedure for winding up companies. After the passing of the 1869 Bankruptcy Act, companies registered under the 1862 Act could no longer be declared bankrupt, but had to be wound up under the provisions of that statute, or under the general jurisdiction of the Chancery.[217] Registered companies could be wound up if they passed a resolution calling for it, if they suspended business for a year, if they fell to fewer than seven members, or if they were unable to pay their debts. A petition to wind up the company could also be granted if the court considered it just and equitable to do so.[218] Courts were not keen to use this latter power extensively. They refused to intervene if there were no outstanding liabilities, and shareholders were seeking the return of relatively small sums;[219] or where a company whose assets exceeded its liabilities was in the process of winding up itself.[220] Judges generally needed firm proof that a company was insolvent, and would not enter into fine accounting calculations

---

[212] See the comments of Rigby LJ in *In re Consort Deep Level Gold Mines* [1897] 1 Ch 575 at 598.

[213] The law was, however, ambiguous for in *In re Licensed Victuallers' Mutual Trading Association, Ex p Audain* (1889) 42 Ch D 1, the Court of Appeal held that an underwriting agreement was not one to buy shares at a discount, but to buy shares with a commission being paid. The transaction was not held *ultra vires*, and the underwriters were held to be contributories.

[214] Davey Committee Report, xii.

[215] See H. B. Buckley's comments to the 1898 select committee: *PP* 1898 (392), ix, IX 19 at q. 1168, p. 82.

[216] Although there was initially some doubt, the notion of issuing shares at a discount referred to a discount from the par value of the shares, rather than the market value: see *Hilder* v. *Dexter* [1902] AC 474 overruling *Burrows* v. *Matabele Gold Reefs and Estates Co* [1901] 2 Ch 23.

[217] Bankruptcy Act, 32 & 33 Vict. c, 71, s 5. *Clements* v. *Bowes* (1852) 17 Sim. 167.

[218] Unregistered companies could also make use of the compulsory provisions of the Act.

[219] *Ex p Pocock* (1849) 1 De G. & Sm. 731; *Ex p Murrell* (1849) 3 De G. & Sm. 4.

[220] *Ex p Guest* (1852) 5 De G. & Sm. 458.

to determine if the business would in the future be able to meet its liabilities.[221] It was on this principle that James LJ refused to use his power to grant a petition to wind up the tottering European Life Assurance Company in 1869, since he felt that the future profitability of the company was a matter for its customers and investors, and not for the court.[222]

The winding up itself was conducted by official liquidators appointed by the court, who were often professional accountants, such as William Turquand. When a company was wound up, it had to cease trading, except so far as was necessary for winding it up. The liquidators could (with the sanction of the company) make an arrangement with the creditors of the firm, and might sell the business (or part of it) to another company.[223] The principal job of these men was to ascertain who was liable to contribute to the funds out of which creditors were to be paid, though the court had the power to rectify the register of members, as where shareholders had transferred their holdings to impecunious straw men, simply to avoid their liability.[224] Only debts incurred by the firm would be provable: if individual shareholders had incurred debts—even if the money they obtained was used for the company—or if directors exceeded the powers they had by the articles of association, then the debt was not one for which the company's assets would be liable.[225]

Although shareholders no longer faced the threat of company creditors seeking execution of judgment against their personal property, and could no longer be made personally bankrupt,[226] in the 1860s, when many bubble companies failed, leaving large liabilities, the prime worry for the investor was whether his name was on the list of contributories who would be required to pay uncalled amounts on their shares. Under the legislation, anyone who had 'agreed to become a member of a company' and whose name was entered on the register was held to be one. This generated much litigation over whether an applicant for shares had made a binding contract.[227] It also raised the question whether those who had bought shares on the faith of misleading prospectuses could rescind the contract. Equity judges were often sympathetic to duped investors.[228] In Lord Cairns's view, creditors using the register had to run the risk that the list might include the

---

[221] See Lord Cottenham's observations in *Ex p Spackman* (1849) 1 Mac. & G. 170.

[222] *In re European Life Assurance Society* (1869) LR 9 Eq 122 at 128. This was overturned by s 21 of the Life Assurance Companies Act 1870.

[223] Companies Act 1862, ss 161–162. Shareholders could dissent from the sale of their interest to another firm, and require the liquidators to purchase their interest in the company. While this absolved the dissentient shareholder of any liability for the new company, he retained his liability as a contributory to the old one: *Re the Imperial Land Co of Marseilles (Ltd), Vining's case* (1870) 19 WR 173.

[224] e.g. *In re Electric Telegraph Co of Ireland, Budd's case* (1861) 3 De G. F. & J. 297.

[225] *In re Worcester Corn Exchange Co* (1853) 3 De G. M. & G. 180.

[226] This was confirmed by the 1869 Bankruptcy Consolidation Act, 32 & 33 Vict. c. 71, Sch. 1.

[227] See pp. 339–40.   [228] *Ayre's case* (1858) 25 Beav. 513.

names of those who had not properly consented to be members.[229] Parties were therefore allowed to rescind their contracts to buy shares, and have their names removed, where there had been misrepresentations in the prospectus, or where the memorandum of association differed from the prospectus,[230] provided they could make a full *restitutio in integrum* of their shares.[231]

At the same time that they sought to protect the duped investor, equity judges who were aware of the interests of creditors began to stress the point that the right to rescind a voidable contract could be lost by delay or where third party interests intervened.[232] Investors misled by prospectuses were not to be allowed the luxury of keeping the shares if all turned out well, and rejecting them if they did not.[233] A shareholder who allowed his name to remain on the register held himself out to the world to be a partner. Whatever the position was between such partners *inter se*, once a shareholder had held himself out to creditors as a member of the firm, he was bound to contribute to the payment of the creditors.[234] At a time when both duped investors and creditors were pressing their claims, the courts had to find a solution which would balance their interests. In 1869, the Lords settled the point that a shareholder could rescind his contract, provided that he took steps to do so before the winding-up proceedings had commenced.[235]

The law relating to the liabilities of misled investors was largely set by the decisions of equity judges in the late 1860s. The problems relating to shareholder liability caused by the company failures of this decade were not generally replicated thereafter, for the experience of 1866 'strengthened most materially the repugnance entertained by prudent people to invest in shares with a large uncalled liability'.[236] By the 1880s, it had become the norm to have smaller share denominations with shares fully paid up, which made for *de facto* as well as *de jure* limited liability.

---

[229] *In re Reese River Silver Mining Co, Smith's case* (1867) LR 2 Ch App 604 at 616; aff'd in *Reese River Silver Mining Co* v. *Smith* (1869) LR 4 HL 64. The Companies Act did allow for names wrongfully inserted to be removed.

[230] *Ship's case* (1865) 2 De G J & S 544; *Blake's case* (1865) 34 Beav 639; *Western Bank of Scotland* v. *Addie* (1867) LR 1 HL Sc 145; *Directors of the Central Railway Co of Venezuela* v. *Kisch* (1867) LR 2 HL 99. See the discussion above, pp. 420–4.

[231] *Clarke* v. *Dickson* (1858) E. B. & E. 148; *Mixer's case* (1859) 4 De G. & J. 575; *Western Bank of Scotland* v. *Addie* (1867) LR 1 HL Sc 145.

[232] *Oakes* v. *Turquand* (1867) LR 2 HL 325 at 350.

[233] *Ship's case* (1865) 2 De G J & S 544; *Webster's case* (1866) LR 2 Eq 741; *Stewart's case* (1866) 1 Ch App 574. See also *Lawrence's case* (1867) 2 Ch App 412; *Kincaid's case* (1867) 2 Ch App 426. See also *Wilkinson's case, In re Madrid Bank* (1867) 2 Ch App 536.

[234] *Oakes* v. *Turquand* (1867) LR 2 HL 325, applying the rule of *Henderson* v. *Royal British Bank* (1857) 7 E. & B. 356.

[235] *Reese River Silver Mining Co* v. *Smith* (1869) LR 4 HL 64.

[236] Evidence of W. R. Drake, Select Committee on Limited Liability Acts 1867, q. 614, p. 40.

The problems generated by the failure of bubble companies floated by speculators were not the only ones which needed judicial resolution. The failures of the Albert Life Assurance Company (in 1869) and the European Assurance Society (in 1871) presented the courts with difficulties of a different kind, owing to the size and complexity of the firms. The failure of these companies proved traumatic for a community which had come to accept that life assurance was essential for any professional middle-class man without a fortune. Both firms were the product of a series of amalgamations over a period of 30 years with smaller insurance companies; and in both cases, the companies had extensive liabilities to policy-holders. When these firms had taken over smaller insurance companies, using the powers of amalgamation granted in their deeds of association, they failed formally to wind up the old firm. This meant that when they became insolvent, policy-holders began to seek out shareholders in the companies which had been taken over, in order to make them liable for the losses. The strategy proved successful. In 1869, the Lord Justices found in favour of a plaintiff whose original policy was with the Family Endowment Life Assurance Company, which had merged with the Albert in 1861, and had disappeared as a commercial entity, but not, unfortunately for its shareholders, as a legal entity.[237] The petition to wind up the Albert was therefore accompanied by a flood of petitions at the same time to wind up the satellite companies whose only value lay in their shareholders' wallets. The avalanche of litigation also ensured that a voluntary restructuring of the failed firm, with the sanction of the court, was impossible to arrange, since there were so many companies involved with so many shareholders that it was impossible to discover whether the requisite majorities had been achieved in each case.

The failure of these two large insurance companies proved that the Chancery's winding-up procedure was simply unable to cope when faced with a plethora of claims against a set of interlocking companies. '[I]t is a difficulty so vast', James LJ noted, when dealing with the failure of the Albert Life Assurance Company, 'that I can see no way of extricating them from the ruinous process of liquidation in this Court, except an application to Parliament; and I sincerely hope that Parliament will find some means of accomplishing that object.'[238] Parliament did step in, passing legislation which gave full power to settle all the claims in this litigation to an arbitrator. Lord Cairns was appointed to arbitrate over the Albert claims. Similar legislation was later passed for the European, and Lord Westbury was appointed as arbitrator. However, these judges, each of whom had absolute power to determine as they saw fit, took different views of the law. Lord Cairns

---

[237] *In re Family Endowment Society* (1869–70) 5 Ch App 118. The decision turned on whether the plaintiff had accepted the liability of the new company in lieu of the old.

[238] *In re Albert Life Assurance* (1871) LR 6 Ch App 381 at 387.

in effect protected the shareholders, by considering that policy-holders who received payments from the amalgamated company had thereby accepted that they would only look to that company for payment of their claims. In contrast, Lord Westbury rejected that there could be such novation by conduct—with the new firm substituted for the old—and therefore imposed greater liabilities on the shareholders of the firms which had been taken over. The confusion was compounded when Westbury died, and was replaced by Lord Romilly, who opted to follow Cairns's view, but also died before completing the arbitration. For the parties interested in the Albert and European firms, the matter was ultimately resolved when the Court of Appeal (which had been given jurisdiction to hear appeals on the matter) opted for Cairns's approach.[239] The issue had already been rendered redundant for the future by the Life Assurance Companies Act 1872, which held that a policy-holder would only lose his claim against the original company with which he had taken a policy if he had abandoned his claim in writing. In future, insurance companies made sure they complied with this.

The law relating to the winding up of companies was further reformed in 1890, by a statute which brought the principles of the 1883 Bankruptcy Act to company proceedings. First, it simplified the procedure of winding up, which was now taken out of the courts and put in the hands of a liquidator named either by the Board of Trade or by a committee of investigation set up by the company and its creditors. Secondly, it facilitated the investigation of any misfeasances committed during the creation or running of the company, applying to companies the investigative provisions introduced in bankruptcy in 1883. The Act gave the Official Receiver power to investigate frauds in the formation or direction of the company, and to obtain a public examination of any director or officer.[240] Great hopes were held out that this might improve commercial morality;[241] though the courts interpreted the Official Receiver's powers restrictively, to prevent the public examination—which was regarded as penal—from being used for the purposes only of investigation.[242] The Act also allowed the court to award damages against delinquent directors, and there was some speculation that it would be a more effective tool against bad officers than the Directors' Liability Act.[243] However,

---

[239] See e.g. *In re European Assurance Society Arbitration Acts and Industrial and General Life Assurance and Deposit Co, Cocker's Case* (1876) 3 Ch D 1. See also *In re European Assurance Society Arbitration Acts and Wellington Reversionary and Life Assurance Society, Conquest's case* (1875) (1875) 1 Ch D 334 (where no novation had occurred as there was no notice to the policy holder).

[240] Companies Act 1890, s 8.

[241] For the number of examinations made, see Eighth General Annual Report by the Board of Trade under section 29 of the Companies (Winding-Up) Act 1890, PP 1899 (331), lxxxviii, 307, at p. 21.

[242] *Ex p Barnes* [1896] AC 146. See also *In re Civil, Naval and Military Outfitters* [1899] 1 Ch 215 at 234–5.

[243] (1890) 90 LT 4.

the courts using this section did not extend the principles of directors' liability which had been elaborated over the previous decades.[244]

The 1890 Act also permitted voluntary liquidations without court control, as well as voluntary liquidations under court supervision. In the latter case, the liquidator had to obtain the sanction of the court if a debt was compromised or a scheme of arrangement entered into; but such a method of winding up avoided both any investigation of the conduct of the concern and any official audit of liquidators' accounts, as was required when winding up was compulsory. Businesses continued to prefer voluntary liquidations, and tried to avoid the intrusive investigations offered by compulsory winding up. As a result, the proportion of windings-up which were compulsory fell from 14 per cent in 1892 to only 7 per cent in 1898.[245]

7. COMPANY MANAGEMENT AND THE COURTS

The 1862 Act did little to regulate the internal management of companies, beyond making provision for an annual general meeting, specifying how the company could alter its articles of association, and permitting shareholders to request inspections by the Board of Trade, for which they would have to pay. Shareholders were expected to exert their own controls over companies. This policy of non-regulation was echoed in the courts. Attempts by individual shareholders to use the courts to sort out internal disputes were frowned on. This non-interventionist approach dated from before the passing of the first Joint Stock Companies Act. In *Foss* v. *Harbottle*, Sir James Wigram VC refused to hear a claim brought by two shareholders in the Victoria Park Company, who claimed that the company's directors had acted in breach of their fiduciary duties, by selling their own land to the company.[246] He held that since the company might in its corporate capacity elect to affirm the purchase, it was not appropriate for the court to act on the initiative of individual dissenters.[247] Had the directors acted *ultra vires*, any dissenting shareholder might have invoked the court's assistance,[248] but where

---

[244] They did, however, use this section to sketch out the duties of auditors to take reasonable care in certifying accounts: *In re London and General Bank* (1895) 2 Ch 166; *In re London and General Bank (No. 2)* [1895] 2 Ch 673; *In re Kingston Cotton Mill Co* [1896] 1 Ch 6 at 683.

[245] Eighth General Annual Report by the Board of Trade under section 29 of the Companies (Winding-Up) Act 1890, *PP* 1899 (331), lxxxviii, 307.

[246] *Attorney General* v. *Wilson* (1840) Cr. & Ph. 1 showed that the corporation could get a remedy if it were the plaintiff.

[247] *Foss* v. *Harbottle* (1843) 2 Hare 461. See also this principle of ratifiability stated by Wigram VC in *Bagshaw* v. *Eastern Union Railway Co* (1849) 7 Hare 114 at 130.

[248] *Foss* v. *Harbottle* at 493; he cited *Preston* v. *The Grand Collier Dock Co* (1840) 11 Sim. 327 as authority. Later in the judgment (at 505) he noted that the rule from that case was 'that if a

they acted *intra vires*, 'it is for the company to judge how they will punish the directors'.[249] The rule was extended in 1847 in *Mozley* v. *Alston*, where Cottenham LC held that a complaint that defendants were illegally exercising the powers of directors was one which alleged an injury to the company and not to individual shareholders, and that it was the company which should sue.[250] The courts did not permit directors to use their control of majority shareholding to ratify sales of their own property to the company in a way which would effectively defraud the minority.[251] But they would not give any assistance where a minority share-holder's complaint was only that he had been denied the right to call for a vote at a company meeting. For if the courts interfered whenever something irregular had been done at a meeting, Mellish LJ observed, 'then if there happens to be one can-tankerous member, or one member who loves litigation, everything of this kind will be litigated'.[252] Summarizing the law in 1902, Lord Davey said that 'no mere informality or irregularity which can be remedied by the majority will entitle the minority to sue, if the act when done regularly would be within the powers of the company and the intention of the majority of the shareholders is clear'.[253]

Accounting

Despite this concern not to become involved in the internal affairs of companies, judges were often called upon to examine how companies were run. In particular, they were often called upon to consider how the company kept its accounts. In contrast to statutory companies, which were required by law to produce accounts on a uniform system, joint stock companies were left free to determine how to keep their accounts. Most companies which sought to raise capital from the

---

transaction be void, and not merely voidable, the corporation cannot confirm it, so as to bind a dis-senting minority of its members' who would therefore have standing to sue alone.

[249] Per Wood VC in *Clinch* v. *Financial Corporation* (1868) LR 5 Eq 450 at 482. It was held in *Gray* v. *Lewis* (1868) LR 8 Eq 526 that where the directors' acts were *ultra vires*, the individual shareholders could take action, but the decision was overturned in *Gray* v. *Lewis* (1873) 8 Ch App 1035. See also *Yetts* v. *Norfolk Railway Co* (1849) 3 De G. & Sm. 293; *Bailey* v. *Birkenhead, Lancashire and Cheshire Junction Railway Co* (1850) 12 Beav. 433.

[250] *Mozley* v. *Alston* (1847) 1 Ph. 790.

[251] *Atwool* v. *Merryweather* (1868) LR 5 Eq 464n at 468n. See also *Menier* v. *Hooper's Telegraph Works* (1874) LR 9 Ch. 350; *Mason* v. *Harris* (1879) 11 Ch D 97; *Kerry* v. *Maori Dream Gold Mines* (1898) 14 TLR 402.

[252] *MacDougall* v. *Gardiner* (1875) 1 Ch D 13 at 25, overturning *MacDougall* v. *Gardiner* (1875) LR 20 Eq 383. On the need for the rule to avoid litigiousness, see the comments of James LJ in *Gray* v. *Lewis* (1873) 8 Ch App 1035 at 1050–1. Once a vote had been called, courts enforced the plaintiffs' right to have their votes counted, since a vote was regarded as a property right which had 'nothing to do with the question like that raised in *Foss* v. *Harbottle*': *Pender* v. *Lushington* (1877) 6 Ch D 70 at 81.

[253] *Burland* v. *Earle* [1902] AC 83 at 93–4.

public did provide information for their shareholders. While few went as far as adopting Table A, since they preferred a higher degree of confidentiality than was found there, most adapted its recommendations, creating articles which required the company to provide balance sheets and directors' reports.[254] Indeed, the legislation of 1856 proved to be a stimulus for the growing accountancy profession, whose services were increasingly required to deal with the accounts of going concerns, as well as constructing accounts in cases of insolvency.[255]

Judges had to look into the company's accounts when petitions were brought to wind it up on the grounds of its insolvency, and when promoters or directors were accused of issuing prospectuses with misleading information about the company's profitability.[256] In these cases, they had to consider what kinds of accounting practices were acceptable.[257] In deciding this, professional opinion was often taken into account. For instance, in 1864, Martin B. observed that the practice of treating preliminary expenses as part of capital expenditure had been regarded as objectionable in the past; but since it was now generally adopted by auditors, no director who did this could be held liable for fraud.[258] Judges also had to consider company accounting methods when shareholders sought to restrain directors from paying dividends out of capital, or when liquidators sought to hold company directors to account for having done so. Such payments were forbidden under the companies clauses legislation which applied to railway companies and utilities. They were also forbidden in the model articles of Table A, and by the articles of many companies which had adopted their own form. But even if the company's articles were silent on the matter, the judiciary held that the payment of dividends not justified by profits was *ultra vires*, since it would diminish the capital fund set out in the memorandum to which creditors looked for security.[259] This meant

---

[254] J. R. Edwards and K. M. Webb, 'Use of Table A by Companies Registering under the Companies Act 1862' (1985) 15 *Accounting and Business Research* 177–97. See also J. R. Edwards and K. M. Webb, 'The Influence of Company Law on Corporate Reporting Procedures, 1865–1929: An Exemplification' (1982) 24 *Business History* 259–79.

[255] M. Anderson, J. R. Edwards, and R. A. Chandler, '"A Public Expert in Matters of Account": Defining the Chartered Accountant in England and Wales' (2007) 17 *Accounting, Business and Financial History*, 381–423 at 384. See also T. Boyns and J. R. Edwards, 'The Construction of Cost Accounting Systems on Britain to 1900: The Case of the Coal, Iron and Steel Industries' (1997) 39 *Business History* 1–29.

[256] See J. M. Reid, 'Judicial Views on Accounting in Britain before 1889', (1987) 17 *Accounting and Business Research* 247–58.

[257] See Lord Campbell's approach to insurance accounts in *Burnes* v. *Pennell* (1849) 2 H.L.C. 497 at 525–7.

[258] *Bale* v. *Cleland* (1864) 4 F. & F. 117 at 144. In *Turquand* v. *Marshall* (1869) 4 Ch App 376 at 383–4 Lord Hatherley held that preliminary expenses could not be regarded as capital assets.

[259] *Macdougall* v. *Jersey Imperial Hotel* (1864) 2 H. & M. 528 at 535–6; *In re Exchange Banking Co, Flitcroft's case* (1882) 21 Ch D 519 at 533–4. In *Burnes* v. *Pennell*, Lord Campbell had called the practice

that if a director knowingly included as an asset something which he knew to be a bad debt, and declared a dividend on a purported profit, he was liable to repay it. Directors were also held liable if they had been negligent in drawing up the accounts, or had not acted sufficiently as 'prudent men of business' when having the accounts drawn up.[260] But if the directors acted *bona fide* in valuing assets which were in danger of being lost, they were not held liable if they were lost.[261]

In deciding whether dividends had been paid out of capital, the courts had to determine what constituted capital and what constituted profit.[262] In 1879, Jessel MR held that in determining whether a profit had been made, the company had to take into account any depreciation in the value of its fixed assets, since 'no commercial man' would 'calculate net profits until he has provided for all the ordinary repairs and wear and tear occasioned by his business'.[263] For Jessel, no dividend could be paid unless the entire share capital was preserved intact.[264] In taking this view, Jessel was following the views of the accounting profession. However, by the end of the decade, the judiciary changed its approach to the question of how profits were to be calculated. In *Lee* v. *Neuchatel Asphalte Co*, the Court of Appeal held that it was not necessary for a company to make provision in its accounts for the depreciation of its fixed assets, as where a mine lost value by being worked. Ever sensitive to the needs of businessmen, Lindley LJ took the view that to require companies to maintain their original assets before any dividend could be paid would 'paralyze the trade of the country'.[265] In his view, it was not for the law to determine how accounts were to be kept: that was a matter for businessmen. Nor did it matter to any creditor whether an item was counted as capital or revenue, provided that the company retained money sufficient to pay its debts. Since the liquidity of a company was far more important to creditors than its capital base, so long as income exceeded expenditure, there was nothing in the law to prevent a dividend being paid. While a company could not pay dividends by selling off its fixed capital, it was permitted to pay a dividend from profits generated by the

---

of paying dividends from capital 'nefarious', and observed that to do so to drive up the price of shares would be actionable as a conspiracy: *Burnes* v. *Pennell* (1849) 2 H.L.C. 497 at 524–5.

[260] *Leeds Estate, Building and Investment* v. *Shepherd* (1887) 36 Ch D 787 at 804.

[261] *In re Mercantile Trading Co, Stringer's case* (1869) 4 Ch App 475.

[262] See E. A. French, 'The Evolution of Dividend Law in England', in W. T. Baxter and S. Davidson, *Studies in Accounting* (1977), 306–31. See Lord Hatherley LC's distinction between capital and revenue in *Mills* v. *Northern Railway of Buenos Aires* (1870) 5 Ch App 621 at 631.

[263] *Davison* v. *Gillies* (1879) 16 Ch D 347n at 349n. See also *Dent* v. *London Tramways Co* (1880) 16 Ch D 341. In these cases, an injunction was granted against the payment of dividends.

[264] Jessel also held that the capital of the company could not be reduced either by its buying back shares (*In re Dronfield Silkstone Coal Co* (1880) 17 Ch D 76; *Trevor* v. *Whitworth* (1887) App Cas 409) or by writing off a loss by using powers given by the 1867 Companies Act to reduce its capital (*In re Ebbw Vale Steel, Iron & Coal Co* (1877) 4 Ch D 827, overturned by the 1877 Companies Act).

[265] *Lee* v. *Neuchatel Asphalte Co* (1889) 41 Ch D 1 at 19.

circulating capital.[266] The Court of Appeal in a series of decisions changed the direction taken in the previous decade, to allow companies greater scope to declare dividends. The decisions were not well received by the accounting profession.[267]

Reformers continued to express concern about the adequacy of company accounting. In 1895, the Davey Committee recommended that it be compulsory to give shareholders annual accounts and balance sheets, containing much information.[268] Some reformers went further, arguing that it was not the shareholders who needed protection—since most companies did keep balance sheets which were made available to them—but the creditors, who had far less information on the basis of which to make judgments about lending. The 1862 Act did contain some provisions aimed to protect creditors, such as the requirement to keep a register of its mortgages. But the effectiveness of this control was limited, since only current creditors had the right to inspect the register.[269] In a minority report in 1895, Vaughan Williams therefore proposed that yearly balance sheets be deposited with the registrar of companies, for he regarded it as a necessary condition to attach to limited liability that companies give such information to the traders from whom they obtained credit.[270]

The 1896 bill, modelled on the Indian Companies Act of 1888, adopted Vaughan Williams's approach. But it attracted so much opposition from legal and commercial interest groups that it was dropped from the version enacted in 1900.[271] Parliament was, however, convinced of the need for the law to require better accounts to be kept by the company. A requirement to appoint auditors annually, who had to sign the balance sheet and report to the shareholders on the accounts, was therefore included in the 1900 Act. Under these provisions, it was not in the power of a company to make regulations to provide for secret funds to be used

[266] *Verner* v. *General and Commercial Investment Trust* [1894] 2 Ch D 239 (CA); *In re National Bank of Wales* [1899] 2 Ch D 629 (CA).

[267] See B. S. Yamey, 'The Case Law Relating to Company Dividends', in W. T. Baxter and S. Davidson (eds), *Studies in Accounting Theory* (1962), 428–42 at 434–5 for the reaction. However, some companies were happy not to include depreciation charges in their accounts: see Edwards and Webb, 'Influence of Company Law', pp. 264–5.

[268] This was to include the amount of share capital issued and how much had been paid on it; the debts due to the company, including debentures and floating charges, and taking into account a proper deduction for doubtful or bad debts; and details of any provision made for the depreciation of assets.

[269] See *Wright* v. *Horton* (1887) 12 App Cas 371 at 376. Earlier judges held that unregistered debentures held by directors were invalid as against creditors, since creditors looked to the register to see whether they could trust the company (*In re Wynn Hall Coal Co* (1870) LR 10 Eq 515; *In re Patent Bread Machinery Co, Ex p Valpy & Chaplin* (1872) 7 Ch App 289; *In re Native Ore Co* (1876) 2 Ch D 345.

[270] Davey Committee, xxii–xxiii.

[271] Companies Bill Select Committee 1896, qq. 576, 599–600, p. 3, q. 626, p. 37; Companies Bill Select Committee 1897, q. 285, p. 28; Select Committee of the House of Lords on the Companies Bill (henceforth cited as Companies Bill Select Committee 1898), PP 1898 (392), ix, 19 q. 22, p. 4.

for undisclosed purposes.[272] Proposals to improve company accounting continued. In 1906, the Loreburn Committee recommended that every public company should be required to file balance sheets, containing its capital, liabilities, and assets, though not its profit and loss. This led to a provision in the 1907 Act requiring the annual filing with the registrar of a balance sheet.[273]

Ultra Vires

Judges were also able to develop a set of rules regarding a company's powers by looking at the powers given to a company under its constitution, and asking whether actions had been *ultra vires*. By 1874, Seward Brice described the doctrine as 'a species of Frankenstein',[274] which allowed companies to evade their liabilities, by shifting them onto their officers who had acted improperly.

In determining how far the company was bound by the acts of its directors, the courts had to examine the nature of the director's agency. According to law of agency, a principal was bound by the acts of his general agent—or one held out as such[275]—acting within the scope of the agency, even if he exceeded the instructions he had been given.[276] By contrast, where the agency was a particular one, with the agent having a defined and limited authority, the principal was not bound by an act exceeding it, but could repudiate it,[277] leaving the agent personally liable.[278] It was settled early that unlike partners, who had the powers of a general agent to bind the partnership in any matter within the scope of its business, directors were particular agents with powers defined and limited by the company's constitution.[279] Since the company's deed of settlement (unlike partnership deeds) provided public information which creditors could consult, they were expected to know the limited nature of the directors' agency. The rule that directors were particular agents whose unauthorized actions could be disavowed was developed in an age when shareholders had unlimited liability, in order to give them a measure of protection.[280] However, it continued to be applied once they had

---

[272] *Newton* v. *Birmingham Small Arms Co* [1906] 2 Ch. 378. But Buckley also noted that it might be sufficient if the auditors merely reported the existence of such a fund and that it had been used in accordance with the company's rules.

[273] Companies Act 1907, s 21.   [274] Brice, *Ultra Vires* (1st edn, 1874) preface.

[275] *Smith* v. *M'Guire* (1858) 3 H. & N. 554.

[276] A principal could not evade liability for one acting as his agent by a secret reservation of authority: *Edmunds* v. *Bushell and Jones* (1865) LR 1 QB 97.

[277] On the distinction between special and general agency, see J. Story, *Commentaries on the Law of Agency* (9th edn, by C. P. Greenough, Boston, 1882), § 17, p. 17.

[278] *Collen* v. *Wright* (1857) 7 E. & B. 301, 8 E. & B. 647.

[279] Thring, *Joint Stock and other Companies* (5th edn, 1889), 110.

[280] *Royal British Bank* v. *Turquand* (1856) 6 E. & B. 327; *Ernest* v. *Nicholls* (1857) 6 H.L.C. 401.

obtained limited liability, which permitted companies to protect themselves from claims from creditors who had failed to scrutinize the constitution of companies they dealt with, by claiming that directors had acted *ultra vires*.

The creditor's duty to look after himself was not unlimited, however. Although he was expected to know the extent of the powers which the directors might have, he was not required to check that they had complied with the internal procedures of the company, since he had a right to presume that all matters internal to the firm had been correctly done.[281] For instance, if under the company's constitution, the directors were given the power to borrow money if a general resolution to that effect had been passed, lenders did not have to check that these internal procedures had been complied with.[282] Nor were they bound to check that each individual dealing for the company had been given an express delegation of the company's authority to act.[283]

In the 1870s, the question was raised whether a joint stock company could ratify acts by its directors which exceeded its powers as defined in its memorandum of association, in the same way that a principal could ratify the unauthorized act of his agent. The question arose in *Ashbury Railway Carriage and Iron Company* v. *Riche*, where the directors had purchased a foreign concession which the company had no power to acquire. The shareholders initially agreed amicable settlement with the directors, but subsequently repudiated it, claiming that they could not ratify an *ultra vires* transaction. The judges who heard the case were divided on the question of whether contracts beyond the scope of the memorandum of association could be ratified. In Blackburn J.'s view, joint stock companies were not in the position of statutory companies, where any act beyond the powers given by the legislation was unlawful and unenforceable. In his view, when companies were given corporate status under the 1862 Act, they acquired the powers corporations had of binding themselves to anything which a natural person could.[284] This meant that although the actions of directors beyond the memorandum of association were unauthorized, they could subsequently be ratified.[285] But this view was

---

[281] *Mahony* v. *East Holyford Mining Co* (1875) LR 7 HL 869 at 894. In the case of railway companies, governed by the Companies Clauses Act, creditors needed to look further when directors sought to exercise borrowing power: as Page Wood VC put it, this was to protect the company against undue acts by the directors: *Fountaine* v. *Carmarthen Railway Co* (1868) LR 5 Eq 316 at 322–3.

[282] *Royal British Bank* v. *Turquand* (1856) 6 E. & B. 327. See also *In re Land Credit Co of Ireland, Ex p Overend Gurney & Co* (1869) LR 4 Ch 460. See further the distinction in *Irvine* v. *Union Bank of Australia* (1877) 2 App Cas 366. See also *Agar* v. *Official Manager of the Athenaeum Life Assurance Co* (1858) 3 C.B. N.S. 735; *Prince of Wales Insurance Co* v. *Harding* (1858) E. B. & E. 183; *Re Athenaeum Life Society* (1858) 4 K. & J. 549.

[283] *Smith* v. *The Hull Glass Co* (1852) 11 C.B. 897 at 927.

[284] *Riche* v. *Ashbury Railway Carriage Co* (1874) LR 9 Ex 224 at 263–4, 271–84.

[285] Moreover, Blackburn argued that in the cases in equity (arising from the failure of the Agricultural Assurance Company), where the acts of directors allowing shareholders to retire from

rejected by the House of Lords. Since the 1862 Act spoke of 'the company being incorporated with reference to a memorandum of association', they could not be considered as the same as ordinary corporations, but were limited by their constitution.[286] The decision sought to protect the public—which included future shareholders and creditors—by allowing them to rely on the information given by the memorandum of association.[287] This document was the company's charter, which (unlike the articles dealing with internal matters) could not be altered.

By the late nineteenth century, companies began to find that the fact that they were limited by their memorandum to be a serious hindrance. Many now sought to draw the memorandum as broadly as possible. While the registrar of companies had the power to refuse to register one whose objects were not clear, in practice memoranda became longer and aimed 'to bury beneath a mass of words the real object or objects of the company with the intent that every conceivable form of activity shall be found included somewhere within its terms'.[288] Moreover, in 1890, the Companies (Memorandum of Association) Act permitted them to change their memoranda of association by special resolution with the consent of the court. The result was that neither investors nor creditors obtained reliable information from the memorandum about what their money would be used for.[289]

Companies could not disown all the acts of their directors which they regretted. For *Ashbury Railway Carriage and Iron Company* v. *Riche* confirmed that where directors exceeded the powers they had been given by the company, but acted within the powers of the company—acting '*extra vires*'[290]—it could ratify the acts, for instance by acquiescence.[291] It had also been settled by then that a company could be vicariously liable for the wrongs of its agents, committed in the course of their employment. It had been accepted in 1854 that the simple fact that a corporation could not itself commit a fraud—having no soul—did not absolve it of liability for the frauds of its agents.[292] Although some judges continued to

the firm had been held *ultra vires*, it was because it had not been proved that the shareholders had unanimously assented: *Spackman* v. *Evans* (1868) LR 3 HL 171; *Evans* v. *Smallcombe* (1868) LR 3 HL 249; *Houldsworth* v. *Evans* (1868) LR 3 HL 263. In these cases, however, the issue was not whether the company had powers to allow shareholders to withdraw, but whether directors had properly exercised their powers.

[286] *Ashbury Railway Carriage and Iron Co* v. *Riche* (1875) LR 7 HL 653 at 668.
[287] *Ashbury Railway Carriage and Iron Co* v. *Riche* (1875) LR 7 HL 653 at 684 (Hatherley).
[288] Lord Wrenbury in *Cotman* v. *Brougham* [1918] AC 514 at 523.
[289] See also Report of the Company Law Amendment Committee, *PP* 1918 [Cd 9138], vii, 727, at p. 10.
[290] See Lord Cairns's distinction between acts *ultra vires* and acts '*extra vires* the directors, but *intra vires* the company': *Ashbury Railway Carriage and Iron Co* v. *Riche* (1875) LR 7 HL 653 at 668. See also Lord Cranworth's comments in *Houldsworth* v. *Evans* (1868) LR 3 HL 263 at 276–7.
[291] See also the application of the doctrine to statutory companies in *Attorney General* v. *Great Eastern Railway* (1880) 5 App Cas 473 and *Baroness Wenlock* v. *River Dee Co* (1885) 10 App Cas 354.
[292] *Ranger* v. *Great Western Railway* (1854) 5 H.L.C. 72 at 86.

doubt whether a principal could be held liable for his agent's frauds,[293] in 1867, the Exchequer Chamber confirmed that a principal—in this case a bank—was liable for the fraudulent misrepresentations made by its employees in the course of their employment. As Willes J. put it, 'The general rule is, that the master is answerable for every such wrong of the servant or agent as is committed in the course of the service and for the master's benefit, though no express command or privity of the master be proved.'[294]

This decision did not generate a blanket liability for companies. Much hinged on whether the agent had acted in the course of his employment. The courts determining what were the duties of company secretaries or bank managers tended to take a narrow view.[295] For instance, it was held in 1879 that since arresting and prosecuting offenders was not 'within the ordinary routine of banking business', a bank would not be liable for a malicious prosecution brought by its manager. Though the Privy Council admitted that managers might have such a power in some cases, it was for the plaintiff to show what those powers were.[296] In 1885, when in *Newlands* v. *The National Employers Accident Association Ltd*, a shareholder claimed he had been falsely led to believe by the company secretary that he would be appointed their solicitor, if he bought the shares, Brett MR told him that he had no more right to listen to the secretary than any stranger. 'A secretary is a mere servant', he said, 'his position is that he is to do what he is told.' The plaintiff should have asked the directors for confirmation: if he trusted the secretary, it was at his own risk.[297] Two years later, he took the same view in a case where a company secretary had misled a supplier into giving more credit to the company's subcontractor than would otherwise have been done.[298] In these cases, plaintiffs were given no remedy against the company, but only against the miscreant. Courts also took into account whether the act was done for the company's benefit. In *The British Mutual Banking Co* v. *The Charnwood Forest Railway Co*,[299] a company secretary had fraudulently issued debenture certificates beyond the amount authorized, and had told the plaintiffs, when asked by them, that certain transfers in the shares were valid. In this case, a jury explicitly found that the secretary was authorized to answer inquiries about the validity of transfers. But

[293] *Udell* v. *Atherton* (1861) 7 H. & N. 172.
[294] *Barwick* v. *English Joint Stock Bank* (1867) LR 2 Ex 259 at 265.
[295] See e.g. *McGowan & Co* v. *Dyer* (1873) LR 8 QB 141 at 145.
[296] Sir Montague Smith, *Bank of New South Wales* v. *William Owston* (1879) 4 App Cas 270 at 289ff. See also *Edwards* v. *The London and North Western Railway* (1870) LR 5 CP 445 for the same principle in a different context.
[297] 54 LJ QB 428 at 430.
[298] *Barnett, Hoares & Co* v. *The South London Tramways Co* (1887) 18 QBD 815. See also *Ruben* v. *Great Fingall Consolidated* [1906] AC 439, where a company secretary issued fraudulent share certificates.
[299] (1887) 18 QBD 714.

the Master of the Rolls found the company not to be liable: for in his deceit, the secretary was acting for his own benefit, and not for the benefit of the company.[300] The rule that a company could only be liable if the act had been for its benefit was only overturned on the eve of the First World War.[301] Nonetheless, companies could be estopped from denying their liability for frauds, if by their conduct they had misled innocent parties.[302]

The Duties of Directors

In the aftermath of the failure of the Royal British Bank in 1856, Parliament passed a Fraudulent Trustees Act to facilitate the prosecution of corrupt company directors. The Act made it a misdemeanour for any director to receive any of the company's money otherwise than for a just debt, to destroy or alter the books, or to circulate material about the company which was false.[303] However, before a director could be convicted, it had to be proved that he had acted with an intention to defraud; and in practice, the legislation proved weak. Criminal prosecutions were rare, and when they were instituted, the success rate was not high. For instance, the directors of Overend, Gurney & Co were acquitted in December 1869, since the jury was unconvinced that they had intended to defraud the public. Some of the most notorious figures, such as Albert Grant—the model for Trollope's Augustus Melmotte in *The Way We Live Now*—escaped prosecution, if not ruin. Corrupt directors and promoters often escaped prosecution, as shareholders and creditors were not keen to spend what little assets remained in a company to finance a prosecution. As those in the City defrauded by the flamboyant promoter Whittaker Wright discovered, the Law Officers were not keen to step in and institute their own proceedings. Unlike Grant, Wright himself was eventually prosecuted, but only after one set of creditors persuaded Buckley J. to direct the Official Receiver to institute criminal proceedings.[304] He was convicted under the Larceny Act for having concealed losses in a set of interlocking companies he had created by false accounting; and committed suicide by taking cyanide

---

[300] See also *Thorne v. Heard* [1894] 1 Ch 599 [CA].

[301] *Lloyd (Pauper) v. Grace, Smith & Co* [1912] AC 716.

[302] A share certificate in effect was a warranty of title to the shares which the company could not deny. See *In the Matter of the Bahia and San Francisco Railway, and Amelia Trittin, Richard Burton, and Mary Anne Goodburn* (1868) LR 3 QB 584; *The Balkis Consolidated Co v. Frederick Tomkinson* [1893] AC 397; *London Freehold and Leasehold Property Co v. Baron Suffield* [1897] 2 Ch 608 at 623.

[303] Fraudulent Trustees Act, 20 & 21 Vict. c. 54, ss 5–8, consolidated in the Larceny Act of 1861: 24 & 25 Vict. c. 96, ss 82, 84.

[304] See *The Times*, 29 December 1902, col. 7c, 11 March 1903, col. 2e, 14 November 1903, col. 6c, 27 January 1904, cols 3d, 7c–f. For Wright, see Robb, *White Collar Crime*, 108–9.

while waiting to be taken to Brixton prison. Suicide was not an uncommon end for notorious swindlers; prosecution was.

Company statutes did not make provision for how directors were to manage the firm. In the absence of legislative regulation, judges in the second half of the nineteenth century had to develop a code of conduct for directors. They imposed a strict liability for breaches of a director's fiduciary duties to the company, where the director made private profits for himself. They were unsympathetic towards 'guinea pig' directors, who lent their names to companies in return for shares. Where a director had been given qualification shares which were effectively paid for by the company, he was liable 'to account either for the value at the time of the present he was receiving, or to account for the thing itself and its proceeds if it had increased in value'.[305] So much did the courts disapprove of this practice that they held those who had received free shares in companies which failed liable to the highest value they had reached in the market.[306] Directors dealing in shares which belonged to the company were held to be trustees for any profit made, and had to account for it with interest.[307]

Directors' dealings with company property were controlled firstly by the company's constitution. Under the Companies Clauses Consolidation Act 1845, no person interested in a contract with a company could be a director.[308] Table A of the 1862 Act included a similar provision disqualifying directors who participated in the profits of any contract with the company.[309] Absent such provisions, directors were in any event (like promoters) subject to the rules of agency. All agents had to look solely to the interests of their principals, who had bargained 'for the exercise of the disinterested skill, diligence and zeal of the agent for his own exclusive benefit'.[310] If an agent bought property during his agency, intending to keep it for himself, he would be treated as a trustee of the property for his principal.[311] Any agent who made any secret profits from his agency was bound to restore them to his principal, whose property such profits were considered to be. The property of

---

[305] *In re Caerphilly Colliery Co, Pearson's case* (1877) 5 Ch D 336 at 341.

[306] *Nant-Y-Glo and Blaina Ironworks Co* v. *Grave* (1879) 12 Ch D 738. See also *In re Canadian Oil Works Corporation* (1875) LR 10 Ch 592; *Fawcett* v. *Whitehouse* (1829) 1 Russ. & M. 132; *In re Morvah Consols Tin Mining Co, McKay's Case* (1875) 2 Ch D 1; *In re Caerphilly Colliery Co, Pearson's case* (1877) 5 Ch D 336; *In re Diamond Fuel Co, Metcalfe's case* (1880) 13 Ch D 815.

[307] *Parker* v. *McKenna* (1874) LR 10 Ch 106.

[308] 8 & 9 Vict. c. 16, s 85. For its effect see *Foster* v. *The Oxford, Worcester and Wolverhampton Railway Co* (1853) 13 C.B. 200.

[309] The 1844 Joint Stock Companies Act (s 28) rendered void all contracts made between companies and their directors unless sanctioned by the shareholders. This provision was omitted in the 1856 Act.

[310] See Story, *Commentaries on the Law of Agency* (7th edn by I. F. Redfield and W. A. Herrick, 1869), § 210.

[311] *Lees* v. *Nuttall* (1829) 1 Russ. & My. 53; *Taylor* v. *Salmon* (1838) 4 My. & Cr. 134.

the principal could only be purchased by the agent if he made a full disclosure of his position and revealed all the information he possessed. In addition, the transaction had to be fair.[312] Unlike in cases of trust,[313] the agent did not need to prove the positive assent of his principal, but he did have to show that the principal was given sufficient information to imply consent. The principal was also protected where he bought property from his agent.[314] If an agent purchased goods for his principal, but attempted to make a personal profit by purchasing the goods himself and selling them on to the principal at a profit, he would be treated by the court as having been an agent all along, and would be required to return the profit he had made.[315] In such cases, the court was not interested in whether the price at which the principal had bought the item was a fair one; it simply made the agent repay his profit.[316] Thus, in 1845, Sir John Romilly ruled that George Hudson was not permitted to keep the profit he had made by purchasing iron in the market himself, and selling it on to the company of which he was chairman.[317] This approach was also taken in 1853 in *Bentley* v. *Craven*, where the defendant was both managing partner in a firm of sugar refiners, and a sugar dealer in his own capacity. After one of his partners objected to his engaging in speculative purchases for the partnership, he continued to do so, selling the sugar onto the partnership when it was needed, and taking himself the £853 profit when the sugar price rose. Romilly ruled that this money had to be paid to the partnership, for 'an agent employed to purchase cannot legally buy his own goods for his principal' since it 'would tempt a man to do that which is not the best for his principal'.[318]

Besides being held to account for making private gains from their position as directors, they were also accountable for acting *ultra vires*. Even if they acted

---

[312] See *Lowther* v. *Lowther* (1806) 13 Ves. Jun. 95; *Murphy* v. *O'Shea* (1845) 2 J. & Lat. 422; *Dunne* v. *English* (1874) LR 18 Eq 524. Even if the principal was perfectly willing to sell, the agent still had to show that the transaction had been fair: see *Dally* v. *Wonham* (1863) 33 Beav. 154.

[313] For the position of trustees, see *Gibson* v. *Jeyes* (1801) 6 Ves. 266 at 277. See also *Coles* v. *Trecothick* (1804) Ves. Jun. 234 at 246–7; *Fox* v. *Macreth* (1788) 2 Bro. C.C. 400; *Ex p Lacey* (1802) 6 Ves. 625. See also *Whelpdale* v. *Cookson* (1747) 1 Ves. Sr. 9; *York Buildings Co.* v. *Mackenzie* (1795) 8 Brown P.C. 42; *Ex p James* (1803) 8 Ves. Jun. 337.

[314] See *Massey* v. *Davies* (1794) 2 Ves. Jun. 318 at 331–2, *Gillett* v. *Peppercorne* (1840) 3 Beav. 78 at 84.

[315] Thus, in *Benson* v. *Heathorn*, (1842) Y. & C.C.C. 326 the defendant, employed to buy a vessel for a partnership, who had bought it for £1350 himself and sold it on for £1500 was thus forced to return the profit made to the partners.

[316] See the comments in *Aberdeen Railway Co* v. *Blaikie Brothers* (1854) 1 Macq. 451 at 471. Nor could such contracts be specifically enforced by the director: *Flanagan* v. *Great Western Railway Co* (1868) LR 7 Eq 116.

[317] *The York and North Midland Railway* v. *Hudson*. The case was reported on a different point—that Hudson could not keep the profit on shares sold, which had been allocated by the company to be 'at the disposal of the directors': (1845) 16 Beav. 485. The unreported point was discussed by Romilly MR in *Great Luxembourg Railway Co* v. *Magnay* (1858) 25 Beav. 586 at 595.

[318] *Bentley* v. *Craven* (1853) 18 Beav. 75 at 76–7.

in good faith and with the support of the shareholders, directors were held personally liable if they parted with money which belonged to the company without having the power under the company's constitution to do so.[319] This problem most usually arose where directors had paid dividends out of capital. If such payments had diminished the capital available to creditors, directors were held liable to repay them to company liquidators; though if shareholders themselves sought to recover the dividends they had already received, the courts were less sympathetic.[320] The liability of directors who had paid dividends *ultra vires* was not strict: where they had relied on statements made by auditors and managers, rather than on their own knowledge, they would not be held liable if they had taken such care as prudent businessmen or those conducting their own private affairs would have done.[321]

Where a director had neither acted *ultra vires* nor made a private profit, the courts took a lenient approach, refusing to impose rigorous standards on directors. It was well known that many took little part in running the companies on whose boards they sat. Even judges and cabinet ministers admitted that they never attended board meetings.[322] This fact caused some disquiet. 'If this be how our best men treat fiduciary obligations voluntarily entered into', one lawyer wrote in 1899, 'what may not be the notions and the conduct of men less under public observation who hold themselves out as directors?'[323] Nevertheless, there remained a great reluctance to impose on directors the same level of liability which was imposed on trustees. Although directors had great power and were subject to little control,[324] they were not legal owners of the corporate property subject to equitable obligations to account, but were rather paid servants of the company, acting as its agents.[325] Distinguishing between directors and trustees,

---

[319] *Cullerne* v. *The London and Suburban General Permanent Building Society* (1890) 25 QBD 485 at 490.

[320] *In re Exchange Banking Co, Flitcroft's case* (1882) 21 Ch D 519 at 534. Contrast *Turquand* v. *Marshall* (1869) LR 4 Ch 376 where Hatherley LC felt that directors could not be made to repay to the company (and hence shareholders) dividends already paid to shareholders. See also *In re National Funds Assurance Co* (1878) 10 Ch D 118, where the Court of Appeal held that directors could recover from the shareholders who had benefited.

[321] *Leeds Estate, Building and Investment Co* v. *Shepherd* (1887) 36 Ch D 787 at 804; drawing also on *In re Oxford Benefit Building and Investment Society* (1886) 35 Ch D 502. See also the comments of Bacon VC in *London Financial Association* v. *Kelk* (1883) 26 Ch D 107 at 146.

[322] Companies Bill Select Committee 1897, at q. 169, p. 16 (Evidence of Romer J.). See also the debate in Parliament over whether ministers should be permitted to hold directorships: PD 1899 (s4) 66: 996.

[323] *The Times*, 24 February 1899, col. 15e.

[324] *In re Faure Electric Accumulator Co* (1888) 40 Ch D 141 at 150–1.

[325] *Smith* v. *Anderson* (1879) 15 Ch D 247 at 275–6; *Leeds Estate, Building and Investment Co* v. *Shepherd* (1887) 36 Ch D 787 at 798; *In re Faure Electric Accumulator Co* (1888) 40 Ch D 141 at 150–1. Some judges did draw an analogy with trustees: *Ferguson* v. *Wilson* (1866) LR 2 Ch 77 at 89–90.

Jessel MR therefore urged that one should 'not to press so hardly on honest directors as to make them liable for these constructive defaults, the only effect of which would be to deter all men of property ... from becoming directors'.[326]

Unlike trustees or partners, directors were not held liable for the acts of other directors. Every partner was liable for all acts of the others done in the course of business, whether he was aware of them or not.[327] Partners were expected to keep their eyes open, or pay the price.[328] In Sir John Romilly's view, it was considered essential 'for the transaction of the business of mankind' that this rule be upheld.[329] In 1869, he tried to apply the same approach to a board of directors, holding that they were under a duty to find out what the others were doing.[330] However, his ruling was overturned. 'Whatever may be the case with a trustee, a director cannot be held liable for being defrauded', Lord Hatherley LC ruled, 'to do so would make his position intolerable.'[331]

The courts also endorsed the commercial view that there was no duty on directors to attend board meetings. '[A]n ordinary director, who only attends at the board occasionally', Jessel explained, 'cannot be expected to devote as much time and attention to the business as the sole managing partner of an ordinary partnership.'[332] Since directors were not to manage the business themselves, but to superintend 'other people's carrying on the business',[333] they had no duty to verify the statements of officers on whom they relied. If directors were to be called upon to guard against fraud by their subordinates, Lord Halsbury opined, it would 'render anything like an intelligent devolution of labour impossible'.[334]

Ironically, in an era which imposed on private trustees the duty to use the degree of care expected of a reasonable, prudent businessman, a lower standard was imposed on directors.[335] Provided they acted within the powers they had by the

---

[326] *In re Forest of Dean Coal Mining Co* (1878) 10 Ch D 450.

[327] They were liable if they could have known 'if they had used the ordinary diligence of men of business': *Marsh v. Keating* (1834) 1 Bing. N.C. 198, 220. See also *Stone v. Marsh* (1826) 6 B. & C. 551.

[328] This rule of partnership liability was applied in a number of cases to firms of solicitors: *Brydges v. Branfill* (1842) 12 Sim. 369; *Atkinson v. Macreth* (1866) LR 2 Eq 570; *St Aubyn v. Smart* (1868) LR 3 Ch App 646; *Earl of Dundonald v. Masterman* (1869) LR 7 Eq 504; *Plumer v. Gregory* (1874) LR 18 Eq 621.

[329] *La Marquise de Ribeyre v. Barclay* (1857) 23 Beav. 107 at 117–18.

[330] *Land Credit Co of Ireland v. Lord Fermoy* (1869) LR 8 Eq 10 at 11–112.

[331] *Land Credit Co of Ireland v. Lord Formoy* (1870) LR 5 Ch 763 at 772. Cf. *Joint Stock Discount Co v. Brown* (1869) LR 8 Eq 381 at 401.

[332] *In re Forest of Dean Coal Mining Co* (1878) 10 Ch D 450 at 452. Cf. *In re Cardiff Savings Bank, Marquis of Bute's case* [1892] 2 Ch 100 at 109.

[333] Companies Bill Select Committee 1897, at q. 160, p. 14 (Evidence of Romer J.).

[334] *Dovey v. Cory* [1901] AC 477 at 485.

[335] *Speight v. Gaunt* (1883) 22 Ch D 727. In fact, the imposition of this duty of care on trustees was itself a way of limiting their liability: see J. Getzler, 'Duty of Care', in P. Birks and A. Pretto (eds), *Breach of Trust* (Oxford, 2002), 41–74 at 63–7.

memorandum and articles of association, they were only liable for misfeasance.[336] '[I]n the absence of any fraudulent intent as against the shareholders, or as against the creditors or the public', Sir Charles Selwyn LJ ruled in 1869, 'the Court ought not to be astute in searching out minute errors in calculation, in an account honestly made out and openly declared.'[337] It was on this principle that the estate of T. A. Gibb was absolved from any liability arising from the failure of Overend, Gurney & Co. For Gibb had neither exceeded his powers as a director, nor been aware of such facts as would have dissuaded any prudent man from buying the firm.[338] He would only have been liable for gross negligence, rather than for mere imprudence.

In company cases, it was left to judges, rather than juries, to determine what amounted to such negligence as would make a director liable.[339] They were generous. In *Lagunas Nitrate Company* v. *Lagunas Syndicate*, Romer J. observed that 'directors have always been held by the Courts as being in a very favourable position as compared with other agents in respect of the degree of negligence which will make them liable to an action'.[340] They were exonerated if they were honestly careless, and accountable only where they had acted improperly.[341] Lindley LJ agreed that '[t]heir negligence must be, not the omission to take all possible care; it must be much more blameable than that: it must be in a business sense culpable or gross'.[342] This was a higher threshold than mere negligence, but a lower one than fraud.[343]

The common law position was therefore very generous to directors; and this caused some concern to reformers. Some attempts were made in the late nineteenth century to reform the law relating to directors' duties. The Companies

---

[336] See *In re Faure Electric Accumulator Co* (1888) 40 Ch D 141 at 152; *In re Railway and General Light Improvement Co, Marzetti's case* (1880) 28 WR 540 at 542, 543; *Turquand* v. *Marshall* (1869) LR 4 Ch 376 at 386.

[337] *In re Mercantile Trading Co, Stringer's case* (1869) LR 4 Ch App 475 at 493. Contrast the views of the *mala fides* of directors in *In re County Marine Insurance Co, Rance's case* (1870) LR 6 Ch App 104.

[338] *The Overend and Gurney Co* v. *Gibb* (1872) LR 5 HL 480.

[339] See the evidence of F. B. Palmer: Companies Bill Select Committee 1898, q. 345, p. 24.

[340] *Lagunas Nitrate Co* v. *Lagunas Syndicate* [1899] 2 Ch 392 at 418. See also *Hirsche* v. *Sims* [1894] AC 654 (PC) where the Privy Council ruled that directors were to repay the discount allowed on shares issued below par, but were not liable any further, since no fraud had been proved against them. See also Romer's comments in 1897 to the Select Committee on the Companies Bill, q. 150, p. 13: 'he is not liable for ordinary mere negligence, if it is of a simple kind'. See also q. 175, p. 16, where he commented that the decision in *Overend Gurney* v. *Gibb* was that a director was not liable for the absence of reasonable care and prudence. ,

[341] Companies Bill Select Committee 1897, q. 150, p. 14 (Romer J.). Cf. the view of H. B. Buckley QC in Companies Bill Select Committee 1898, q. 1257, p. 89.

[342] *Lagunas Nitrate Co* v. *Lagunas Syndicate* [1899] 2 Ch 392 at 435. See also *In re National Bank of Wales* [1899] 2 Ch 629 at 672.

[343] As Lindley noted, directors might be liable to a company for issuing a prospectus which caused loss to a company, when (thanks to *Derry* v. *Peek*) they would not be liable to outsiders, in the absence of fraud: [1899] 2 Ch 437.

Bill introduced in Parliament in 1896 sought to enact that '[e]very director shall be under an obligation to the company to use reasonable care and prudence in the exercise of his powers, and shall be liable to compensate the company for any damage incurred by reason of neglect to use such care and prudence'. The reasonable care which would be required was that of a director who was by his business experience qualified to hold the position. Although this seemed merely to give directors the same liability as other professionals, it attracted much hostility. H. B. Buckley argued that since 'a director does not warrant skill', he should only be held liable for dishonesty. Judges like Romer agreed that the law should only prevent dishonesty or fraud: to attempt more would be to deter good directors and might drive business abroad.[344] The Davey Committee's recommendation that directors should incur liability (as insolvents did) for incurring debts in the knowledge that the company had no reasonable expectation of being able to pay them, for giving undue preferences to particular creditors, or for pledging property obtained on credit otherwise than in the ordinary course of business, also attracted much opposition.[345] These proposals were also dropped. Parliament remained keen to avoid strict regulations which would be punitive and potentially offputting to directors. Drawing on the policy of the Judicial Trustees Act 1896, the Loreburn Committee recommended that the court should have the power to relieve any director or promoter from liability for breach of any duty imposed on him by the Companies Acts 'provided that the breach has been occasioned by honest oversight, inadvertence, or error of judgment on his part'. It also recommended giving courts the power to relieve a director from liability in any action of negligence or breach of trust, where it was satisfied he had acted honestly and reasonably.[346] A provision was duly introduced into the 1907 Act.[347]

8. THE PRIVATE COMPANY

The most striking development in corporate practice after 1880 was the development of the private limited company, which did not sell shares to outside investors, but which could raise money by debentures.[348] Many of Britain's largest and best known firms adopted this form. It allowed them to trade in the manner of private partnerships, without disclosing details of their business in the

---

[344] See also the view of Lindley: Companies Bill Select Committee 1897, p. 10. Cf. F. B. Palmer's views at p. 24.

[345] Companies Bill Select Committee 1898, q. 1272–3, p. 90; q. 350, p. 24.

[346] Loreburn Committee, *PP* 1906 [CD 3052], xcvii, 199, at p. 10.

[347] Companies Act 1907, s 32.

[348] Such firms had existed since the 1850s: but from 1880–4, 560 such companies were formed: Cottrell, *Industrial Finance*, 65.

way expected of companies whose shareholders included a wider public. Some concern was expressed in the 1890s that private companies provided much less information regarding their creditworthiness than those which issued a prospectus, and traded shares on the Stock Exchange. Vaughan Williams in particular wanted reform which would impose greater duties of disclosure.[349] However, defenders of the private form successfully argued that requiring such companies to disclose information would give an undue advantage to their competitors, who were often private partnerships; and their privacy continued to be protected.

The mid-1890s saw concern over the use of this form by 'one-man' companies, which sought to shield the proprietor of the business from his creditors. A trader seeking to do this could form a company, comprising himself and six relatives, which would buy his business in exchange for shares and debentures secured by a floating charge on the company's assets.[350] No new capital was brought in, and if the firm failed, the trader would both avoid bankruptcy and salvage some assets from the firm from his status as a preferred creditor. The legality of such companies was considered by the House of Lords in 1896 in *Salomon* v. *A. Salomon & Co.*[351] When the limited company set up by the bootmaker Aron Salomon was wound up, he claimed the £1055 surplus left in the company, by virtue of his debentures. The company's liquidator disputed his right, claiming that he had committed a fraud on his creditors—who were owed over £7700—by forming the company, that he had failed to fulfil the fiduciary duties he owed to the company, and that his contract with the firm should be rescinded. Both Vaughan Williams J. and the Court of Appeal agreed that Salomon should indemnify the creditors, though for different reasons. Vaughan Williams held that the company was an agent for Salomon, which had to be indemnified for liabilities incurred in carrying on his business. The Court of Appeal by contrast held that the formation of the company had been a fraud on the Companies Act. Although all the legal requirements of the legislation had been complied with, the Act had intended that there should be seven *bona fide* members of the company. In Lindley's view, the company formed was merely a trustee for Salomon. [352]

The Court of Appeal's decision was welcomed both by John Smith[353] and by the members of the Davey Committee, which reported that where a company was 'a mere device to defraud creditors', the law would look behind 'legal machinery,

---

[349] Davey Committee, Addendum.   [350] Ireland, 'Company Legal Form', 50.

[351] *Salomon* v. *A. Salomon* [1897] AC 22. For the background, see G. R. Rubin, 'Aron Salomon and his Circle', in J. Adams (ed.), *Essays for Clive Schmitthoff* (Abingdon, 1983), 99–120.

[352] *Broderip* v. *Salomon* [1895] 2 Ch. 323 at 338.

[353] Fourth Annual General Report by the Board of Trade under the Companies (Winding Up) Act 1890, *PP* 1895 (453), lxxxviii, 371 at p. 23.

and hold the persons who are the beneficial owners of the business liable to indemnify the company'. The committee recommended that a company should be able to be wound up if the certificate of incorporation had been 'obtained by fraud, misrepresentation, or mistake, or by a wilful violation of any provision of the Companies Acts' or if the court was satisfied that the company was formed to defraud creditors or for any fraudulent or illegal purpose. In such a case, the court should be able to declare unlimited liability in the members. But it rejected as unworkable the proposal that liability should be unlimited where any one of seven company members held as trustee for another.[354] At the same time, there was considerable unease in the business community at a decision restricting the right of traders to limit their liability, which threatened so many firms formed in the 1890s.[355] Since the Court of Appeal's decision rested on the particular facts of this case,[356] it created a climate of uncertainty over which companies might be regarded as fraudulent and which might not. There was also concern about the Davey Committee's winding-up proposals, since it was feared that the courts might in retrospect consider that the business of a firm had been carried on in such a way as to delay its creditors, when this might not have appeared to participants at the time to be the case. The courts might then impose unlimited liability after the event in an unfair way.[357]

It was in this context that the House of Lords upheld Salomon's appeal. It held that where the statutory requirements had been met, a court could consider neither the motives of those setting up a company, nor the *bona fides* or degree of beneficial interest which any individual shareholder had. Once the firm was set up according to the provisions of the Act, it became a distinct legal entity with its own rights and liabilities, and could not be seen as an agent for the person who set it up. The Lords also dismissed the arguments that Salomon had breached a fiduciary duty to the company, by selling his own overvalued assets to it, since every member of the company—Salomon and his relatives—was aware of the value of the assets.[358] In such a situation, the company could not rescind the purchase. The creditors had to look out for themselves. As Lord Watson put it, '[w]hatever may be the moral duty of a limited company and its share-holders, when the trade of the company is not thriving, the law does not lay any obligation upon them to warn those members of the public who deal with them on credit that they run the risk of

---

[354] It was considered to be impossible to lay down any minimum 'substantial' interest which had to be held in any company which would not exclude *bona fide* small investors. In any event, the original signatories of a memorandum of association were often trustees for the promoters. Davey Committee Report, ix.

[355] 'The Resuscitation of the One Man Company' (1896) 41 *Sol. J.* 60.

[356] *Broderip* v. *Salomon* [1895] 2 Ch 323 at 338. [357] (1896) 40 *Sol. J.* 454 at 456.

[358] *Salomon* v. *A. Salomon & Co* [1897] AC 22 at 32–3, 36–7.

not being paid'.[359] The decision was welcomed in the legal and general press, for the decision of the Court of Appeal was seen to have been hard to reconcile with the words of the legislation, and based on no clear principle. Given the endorsement of one-man companies by *Salomon* and opposition to the winding-up proposals made by the Davey Committee, the 1900 Companies Act did not include these new provisions. Nor was there legislation introduced to control vendors taking debentures, though in 1906, Ernest E. Williams suggested that it should be a penal offence for a vendor or his nominees to hold debentures in a firm.[360]

It was generally agreed that in small private companies, which operated in practice like limited liability partnerships,[361] the shareholders did not need the same level of protection expected in public companies where shares were freely traded. Concern grew, however, that 'public' companies might evade the legislative provisions which determined what information was to be given to the public by commencing as private firms and then selling their shares on the market, gradually expanding in size. Charles Woolley, the president of the Institute of Secretaries, thus proposed in 1897 that private companies should give to the Registrar the details of those who were to be eligible to be shareholders in the firm in question, so that if anyone were admitted a shareholder who was not a member of that class, the company would be compelled to re-register as a public firm.[362] His idea was not taken up. Instead, the distinction which emerged between private and public companies in the 1900 Act was one not of definition but of default: for many of the regulations of the 1900 Act regarding disclosure of information only applied to firms issuing prospectuses. The provision proved ineffective as a way to control public companies, since it was easy enough not to issue a prospectus, but to sell shares on in the market. Legislation in 1907 plugged this loophole for companies which issued shares to the public. As a consequence, a legal definition was given to private companies: it was one which restricted the right to transfer its shares, which limited the number of its members to 50, and which prohibited any invitation to the public to subscribe for its shares.

9. CARTELS

Besides seeing the growth of private limited companies, the period from the 1880s saw the growth of larger corporations. From the late 1880s, Britain saw mergers in many industries, as partnerships merged into larger units, with limited liability. From 1888 to the First World War, an average of 67 firms disappeared each year in

---

[359] *Salomon* v. *A. Salomon* (1896) [1897] AC 22 at 40.   [360] (1906) 121 *LT* 359.

[361] Companies Bill Select Committee 1896, q. 10, p. 3 (evidence of J. W. Budd).

[362] Companies Bill Select Committee 1897, q. 639, pp. 55–6.

this process, with the turn of the twentieth century seeing a significant number of mergers.[363] Many of these firms sought economies of scale in response to a downturn in prices which accompanied the Great Depression, and in response to overseas competition. But mergers were not the only way for a company to defend itself. Instead of surrendering control to a new form of managerial capitalism, many British firms entered into cartels and price-fixing agreements, seeking to obtain stability for their firms by restricting competition. Price fixing agreements were made both horizontally, across businesses, and vertically, between suppliers, manufacturers, and retailers. In contrast to the United States, where antitrust legislation encouraged firms to amalgamate into large centralized firms controlling every branch of the business, English law, which permitted such restrictive practices, allowed traditional smaller business units to survive, often under the control of the founding families.[364]

'Horizontal' cartel agreements were found in many industries, including textiles, chemicals, soap, tobacco, and coal mining.[365] At a time when competition was feared, they were created to allow stronger members to ensure that prices remained high, while allowing weaker members a reduced share of the business. They were well organized, with the cartel having its own officers who would partition the business and police compliance with its rules.[366] In some industries, such as shipping, a high level of integration was achieved without individual firms losing their separate identity. Such cartels were able to flourish in Britain thanks to the benign attitude of the courts towards them. In the first major case brought against a cartel which used a predatory pricing policy to undermine a competitor, the House of Lords held that, although the cartel's agreement might be unenforceable *inter se*, it was not itself actionable as a tort. Among all the judges who heard the case, only Lord Esher held it to be unlawful. The others felt that it was no part of a court's task to set what prices businessmen should charge. Defending their position in the market was, in Lord Watson's view, 'an object which is strenuously pursued by merchants great and small in every branch of commerce; and it is, in the eye of the law, perfectly legitimate'.[367] The case showed that while an agreement to restrain one's own trade might be unenforceable as a contract against public policy, an agreement which had the effect of impeding a rival's interests was legitimate.

---

[363] Cottrell, *Industrial Finance*, 176.

[364] T. Freyer, *Regulating Big Business: Antitrust in Great Britain and America, 1880–1990* (Cambridge, 1992), 11–42.

[365] Final Report of the Committee on Commercial and Industrial Policy after the War', PP 1918 [Cd 9035], xiii, 239 at p. 35.

[366] Freyer, *Regulating Big Business*, 21–2.

[367] *Mogul Steamship Co v. McGregor, Gow & Co* [1892] AC 25 at 42. See pp. 1050–2 on this case.

How far one trader was able to restrain his own trade was considered by the Lords two years later in *Nordenfelt* v. *Maxim Nordenfelt Guns and Ammunition Co.* The defendant was the Swedish patentee of military equipment, who had sold his business to the plaintiff company, agreeing at the same time not to compete with the firm in this business anywhere in the world for a period of 25 years. When he re-entered the armaments trade with a rival Belgian firm, the plaintiffs sought an injunction, which he attempted to resist by claiming that the contract had been in restraint of trade. It had been settled early in the nineteenth century that it was for the court to determine whether a restraint was reasonable, as a matter of public policy.[368] Earlier authorities suggested that where the restraint was a general one, then it would be void;[369] but the Lords rejected this definition as unsuitable on the modern age. In determining whether the restraint was valid, the court had to ask if it was necessary for the protection of the person who bought the business. In the case of a business like that sold by Thorsten Nordenfelt, worldwide restraint was acceptable. The policy of the common law did not prevent parties from putting fetters on economic competition. As Lord Watson observed, 'I venture to doubt whether it be now, or ever has been, an essential part of the policy of England to encourage unfettered competition in the sale of arms of precision to tribes who may become her antagonists in warfare.'[370]

British businessmen also entered into 'vertical' agreements, which aimed to tie the middleman to terms set by the supplier or the cartel. Retail price agreements allowed manufacturers to control the market, without creating their own sales outlets. Courts allowed manufacturers to impose terms on wholesalers not to sell their goods to retailers below a set price. This was regarded not as a restrictive practice which needed control by the court, but as a matter of freedom of contract between the parties.[371] Courts continued to ask whether a restraint was reasonable; but unless there was a strong countervailing public interest, they left it to the commercial parties to decide what was to be seen as reasonable.[372] In 1906, the Chancery Division therefore upheld a lease granted by the American-based United Shoe Machinery Company to a British manufacturer, which required the latter to use only its equipment for a period of 20 years. The USMC, which was unable to defend such restrictive agreements in the United States, was able to

---

[368] *Horner* v. *Graves* (1831) 7 Bing. 735; *Hitchcock* v. *Coker* (1837) 6 Ad. & El .438.

[369] J. W. Smith, *A Selection of Leading Cases on Various Branches of the Law*, 2 vols (4th edn, ed. J. S. Willes and H. S. Keating, 1856), , 301–3, citing *Ward* v. *Byrne* (1839) 5 M. & W. 548; *Hinde* v. *Gray* (1840) 1 M. & G. 195. In 1869, James VC treated the rule regarding space as less rigid, upholding a restraint which extended throughout Europe: *Leather Cloth Co* v. *Lorsont* (1869) LR 9 Eq 345.

[370] *Nordenfelt* v. *Maxim Nordenfelt Guns and Ammunition Co* [1894] AC 535 at 554.

[371] *Elliman & Sons & Co* v. *Carrington & Son* [1901] 2 Ch 275.

[372] P. S. Atiyah, *The Rise and Fall of Freedom of Contract* (Oxford, 1979), 699–702.

enforce them not only in England, but also—thanks to the Privy Council, which enforced the English approach—in Canada as well.[373] Adopting a non-interventionist approach, the courts regarded it as a matter for the legislature to intervene, if it chose to. In 1913, when dealing with an Australian antitrust statute, the Privy Council once more reiterated its view that cartels were permissible, where they acted to protect their own interests. It upheld a cartel of coal producers which had strengthened their position by stabilizing prices, and had as a consequence improved labour relations. Instead of being detrimental to the public, it was considered to be in the public interest for collieries to continue to operate at a profit, allowing workmen to be paid above the minimum.[374] On the eve of the First World War, the House of Lords took the same view. It was for the parties to a cartel agreement to decide whether its terms were reasonable for themselves. As for the public interest, it was best served by a system which allowed firms to stay in business, and workers to continue in employment.[375] There were, however, limits to how far the courts would enforce cartel agreements, for in 1915 the House of Lords, bound by its understanding of the doctrine of consideration, held that a manufacturer could not enforce his restrictive price agreement with a wholesaler by suing the retailer who had sold at his own prices; for the retailer only had an agreement with the wholesaler, and not with the manufacturer.[376]

[373] *British United Shoe Machinery Co v. Somervell Bros* (1907) 95 *LT* 711; *USMC of Canada v. Brunet* [1909] AC 330. See also W. R. Cornish, 'Legal Control over Cartels and Monopolization, 1880–1914: A comparison', in N. Horn and J. Kocka, *Law and the Formation of the Big Enterprises in the 19th and early 20th centuries* (Göttingen, 1979), 280–305.

[374] *Attorney-General of the Commonwealth of Australia v. the Adelaide Steamship Co* [1913] AC 781.

[375] *North Western Salt Co v. Electrolytic Alkali Co* [1914] AC 461.

[376] *Dunlop Pneumatic Tyre Co v. Selfridge & Co* [1915] AC 847.

II

The Law of Insurance

1. THE DEVELOPMENT OF INSURANCE

The business of insurance in Great Britain was, from its beginnings, a fragmented one, with separate markets for marine, fire, and life assurance.[1] Of these, marine insurance was by far the oldest, with medieval roots. The London marine insurance market developed significantly in the late seventeenth century, with the expansion of foreign trade engaged in by British shipping. In 1720, Parliament gave a monopoly to two corporations, the Royal Exchange and the London Assurance, when it forbad any other company or partnership to provide marine insurance. But the Act did not prevent individuals from offering insurance, and for the most part, marine insurance remained in the hands of individual merchants, who did their business at Lloyd's Coffee House, which had more than 1000 subscribers by 1810. A number of attempts were made to abolish the monopoly enjoyed by the two corporations, to allow new joint stock entrants into the market to take some of the business enjoyed by the Lloyd's traders. Although the monopoly was removed in 1824,[2] Lloyd's underwriters continued to dominate the market. New marine companies only emerged in the 1860s, thanks both to a favourable market for marine insurance and reforms in company law which encouraged company promotion.

---

[1] For the history of insurance, see C. Wright and C. E. Fayle, *A History of Lloyds* (1928); H. Raynes, *A History of British Insurance* (1948); P. G. M. Dickson, *The Sun Insurance Office, 1710–1960* (Oxford, 1960); B. Supple, *The Royal Exchange Assurance: A History of British Insurance 1720–1970* (Cambridge, 1970); O. M. Westall (ed.), *The Historian and the Business of Insurance* (Manchester, 1984); C. Trebilcock, *Phoenix Assurance and the Development of British Insurance, vol. 1: 1782–1870* (Cambridge, 1985); G. Clark, *Betting on Lives: The Culture of Life Insurance in England, 1695–1775* (Manchester, 1999); R. Pearson, *Insuring the Industrial Revolution: Fire Insurance in Great Britain, 1700–1850* (Aldershot, 2004); T. L. Alborn, *Regulated Lives: Life Assurance and British Society, 1800–1914* (Toronto, 2009). I am grateful to Charles Mitchell for his helpful comments on the subject of this chapter.

[2] Supple, *Royal Exchange Assurance*, 188, 198; Wright & Fayle, *History of Lloyds*, 71, 84, 217; C. Kingston, 'Marine Insurance in Britain and America, 1720–1844: A Comparative Institutional Analysis' (2007) 67 *JEH* 379–409.

The eighteenth century also saw the establishment of a number of fire insurance companies.[3] In the early part of the century, most business was concentrated on domestic property, involving relatively small risks. Industrialization brought a new kind of risk in the form of the factory, which led to a number of provincial firms being founded, using local knowledge to win a large share of the new business. The early nineteenth century saw a rapid growth in the number of fire offices, from 30 in 1800 to 70 in 1850. It was an era of intense competition in fire insurance. The old firms responded to new market entrants by attempting to drive them out of business or take them over.[4] By the mid-century, fire insurers began to realize that there was greater security in co-operation than in competition. A Fire Offices Committee was set up in 1860, which had obtained a constitution and set of rules by the end of the century.[5]

The nineteenth century saw a significant expansion in the volume of business handled by the fire offices. The proportion of insurable property covered grew from just under 30 per cent in 1800 to 41 per cent in 1820, and was 56 per cent by mid-century.[6] The 1870s saw another spurt in insurance, fuelled both by the growth in building projects at home, and in the growth of fire insurance overseas. Companies expanded their markets by the extensive use of advertising, and by the establishment of branches. They maximized their profits by carefully distinguishing particular risks covered by the policy, and by adjusting their rates. Much attention was paid to fire prevention, with premiums reduced according to the precautions taken. Risks were also spread from the early nineteenth century by reinsurance. Given the complexity of claims, by the 1870s a number of fire insurers began to turn to specialist loss adjusters, who could give more expert advice on the validity of claims.[7] However, until the end of the nineteenth century, fire offices did not diversify into other areas of insurance, such as accident insurance. Instead, they expanded their businesses by covering risks overseas, and by reinsurance. Indeed, it was often outsiders who provoked the fire insurers to offer more innovative cover in their own fields: such as providing (from the

[3] The most important were the Sun Insurance (an unincorporated company founded in 1710), the Royal Exchange (chartered in 1720), and the Phoenix Assurance, founded under a deed of settlement in 1782 by a group of sugar refiners.

[4] Pearson, *Insuring the Industrial Revolution*, 184. See also Robin Pearson, 'Taking Risks and Containing Competition: Diversification and Oligopoly in the Fire Insurance Markets of the North of England during the Early Nineteenth Century' (1993) 46 *Econ. Hist. Rev.* 39–64 and 'Towards an Historical Model of Services Innovation: The Case of the Insurance Industry, 1700–1014' (1997) 50 *Econ. His. Rev.* 235–56.

[5] Dickson, *Sun Insurance Office*, 149–56.

[6] Pearson, *Insuring the Industrial Revolution*, 32.

[7] See E. F. Cato Carter, *Order out of Chaos: A History of the Loss Adjusting Profession. Part I: Evolution and Early Developments* (1984).

later nineteenth century) insurance for loss of profit, as well as for damage to property.

The business of life assurance also developed in the early eighteenth century. For much of the century, the life assurance market was dominated by gamblers, who sought to make speculative gains rather than prudent investments or indemnification from loss.[8] Wagers would be made on the duration of the lives of strangers, with the parties effectively betting on the health of a prominent person.[9] At the same time, the lack of accurate demographic data and the rudimentary nature of actuarial practice were disincentives for the development of a prudent insurance market, while the habit among the wealthy to seek insurance was slow to develop. Two developments facilitated the growth of a sounder market. First, Parliament outlawed betting on lives in 1774, when the Gambling Act rendered void any life insurance policy in which the insured had no interest. Secondly, in 1781, Dr Richard Price compiled a set of mortality tables which allowed for a more scientific actuarial practice than had existed before. These developments paved the way for a significant growth of life assurance.

The number of life offices grew rapidly, from six in 1800, to 150 by the 1850s. The volume of business handled by these firms also grew sharply: where about £10 million was insured in 1800, by 1852 the figure had grown to £150 million. After the middle of the century, the number of firms fell back, to 85 at the turn of the century, and 94 on the eve of the First World War. Nonetheless, the volume of business they handled grew dramatically, with premium income tripling between 1870 and 1914.[10] Life assurance was used as a vehicle for thrift and credit, largely for the middle classes.[11] Insurance companies offered an increasingly large range of policies to such savers.[12] The simplest provided for a lump sum to be paid on a person's death to his executors. By the mid-century, deposit insurance was also available, which allowed the assured to put an end to his insurance

---

[8] See Clark, *Betting on Lives*.

[9] Nor were courts hostile to such wagers: see *Earl of March* v. *Pigot* (1771) 5 Burr. 2802, discussed in Clark, *Betting on Lives*, 53

[10] Supple, *Royal Exchange Assurance*, 111–12, 220. For a comprehensive study of life assurance in the nineteenth century, see Alborn, *Regulated Lives*.

[11] The working classes used friendly societies and benefit clubs for savings. Friendly Societies could insure lives up to £100. Some commercial firms did begin to offer forms of industrial insurance aimed at the working classes (often to provide for funeral expenses) from the 1850s, as well as life assurance. See pp. 1010–11.

[12] In the early nineteenth century, an increasingly large number of firms began to offer policies paying bonuses, which allowed them to charge higher premiums than were necessary to cover their risks, investing the fund at a higher profit than individuals could obtain, and then to return the profit periodically to the investor: T. Alborn, 'The First Fund Managers: Life Insurance Bonuses in Victorian Britain' (2002) 45 *Vict. St.* 65–92.

contract at a time of his choosing, and receive back the premiums paid.[13] By the later nineteenth century, endowment policies were popular, paying an annuity or a lump sum after a certain period during which the life was insured. Besides offering savings for the middle classes, insurance offices also offered credit facilities for those in debt. Insurance policies could be taken out as security for personal loans, to protect one partner's interest in a firm against another partner's death, or to guarantee family settlements. Policies were similarly taken out by creditors on the lives of their debtors.[14] Such policies were assets which could be bought and sold, with the purchaser of a policy on another life able to maintain it by continuing to pay the premiums, and becoming entitled to the benefits of the policy.

These three forms of insurance dominated the market. From the mid-century, a number of other kinds of insurance company emerged, although they remained small in scope. Of these, the most important was accident insurance, which began in the 1840s. These companies were a development of the railway age, designed to provide cover for railway accidents. In the period from 1845 to 1850, 13 companies were provisionally registered for railway accident insurance, although only two were actually formed. These included the Railway Passengers Assurance Company (formed in 1849), which was taken over by the Accidental Death Insurance Company, formed in 1850, which in turn amalgamated with a number of other companies. Significant growth in the personal accident market had to await the 1880s, particularly the passing of the Employers Liability Act 1880, which prompted a development of insurance against industrial accidents.

The law of insurance was rooted both in the customs and practices of merchants, and in eighteenth-century legislation. Its principles were developed by treatise writers from the late eighteenth century onwards. Although treatise writers and judges often drew on the works of continental jurists, especially R. J. Pothier and B. M. Émérigon,[15] their conclusions were not accepted uncritically. The principles of insurance law were also debated by English and American treatise writers,[16] the various editions of whose work digested and analysed case law on both sides of the Atlantic and engaged in ongoing debate, since textbook

---

[13] See J. H. James, *A Treatise on Life and Fire Assurance: Annuities and Reversionary Payments* (1851), 30.

[14] Thus, in the period between 1824 and 1842, just over half the policies issued by the Law Life Assurance Society were issued in another interest, while in the decade before 1846, 38 per cent of the Legal and General's policies were so issued. R. Pearson, 'Thrift or Dissipation? The Business of Life Assurance in the Early Nineteenth Century' (1990) 43 *Econ. Hist. Rev.* 236–54 at 241.

[15] B. M. Émérigon, *Traité des Assurances et des Contrats á la grosse* (Marseilles, 1783), tome 1, p. 3; R. J. Pothier, *Traité des contrats aléatoires* (Paris, 1767), s. 2.

[16] These included J. A. Park, *A System of Marine Insurances* (1787); S. Marshall, *A Treatise on the Law of Insurance*, 2 vols (1802); Sir Joseph Arnould, *Treatise on the Law of Marine Insurance and*

writers disagreed about the nature of many of the doctrines on insurance law and how they should be applied. Judges and jurists remained aware that insurance was not an abstract law, but one designed to facilitate commerce. To that end, they sought to develop rules which would be the most coherent and efficient for commercial society. In doing so, the courts took into account the developing customary practices of insurers and those taking out insurance. Lawyers were far from being the only organized professional group seeking to understand the principles of effective insurance. The mid-nineteenth century saw the development of professional average adjusters (with an association formed in 1869) in marine insurance, and a literature by average adjusters on the principles behind their practice.[17] Similarly, the actuarial principles behind life insurance generated a vast literature in the nineteenth century.[18] The principles developed in court could not be out of step with those developed by the insurance industry: but at the same time, the courts did not merely mirror the practices of the profession.

Judges and jurists agreed that the '*fundamental Principle* of Insurance' was simply, 'INDEMNITY; i.e. *an Obligation on the Part of the Insurer, for a Consideration received, to* reinstate *the Insured in the Value of the Property he may lose or be damnified, according to the* Terms *and* Intent *of the Contract'*.[19] The contract was to cover losses, and not to provide gains.[20] This was rooted not only in the custom of merchants, but also in legislation.[21] For marine policies, the key legislation was an Act of 1746, designed to prevent gaming contracts on shipping. The legislation arose as a result of concern over the practice whereby people insured large sums on ships not carrying any of their goods ('interest or no interest' policies), or insuring their goods many times over, which in effect turned the insurance into a gambling policy. To curb this, the Act rendered it illegal to make any policy of insurance 'interest or no interest, or without further proof of interest than the policy, or by way of gaming or wagering, or without benefit of salvage

Average, 2 vols (1848); Willard Phillips, *A Treatise on the Law of Insurance*, 2 vols (Boston, 1823–34); John Duer, *The Law and Practice of Marine Insurance*, 2 vols (New York, 1845–6).

[17] e.g. R. Stevens, *An Essay on Average* (1822); R. Lowndes, *The Law of General Average, English and Foreign* (1873).

[18] See e.g. E. Baylis, *The Arithmetic of Annuities and Life Assurance, or Compound Interest Simplified* (1844). See also T. L. Alborn, 'A Calculating Profession: Victorian Actuaries among the Statisticians', in M. Power (ed.), *Accounting and Science: Natural Enquiry and Commercial Reason* (Cambridge, 1994), 81–119.

[19] J. Weskett, *A Complete Digest of the Theory, Laws, and Practice of Insurance* (1781), viii–ix. Cf. Park, *Marine Insurances*, 1.

[20] Émérigon, *Traité des Assurances*, tome 1, 14–15; Pothier, *Traité des contrats aléatoires*, tome 1 n. 31, 35.

[21] Insurances on births and marriages was forbidden by statute in 1711, while in 1734 it was forbidden to take out insurance on the public funds.

to the insurer'.[22] However, the Act only applied to insurances on British vessels, so that policies without proof of interest—later known as 'p.p.i. policies'—could still be enforced on foreign insurances.[23] The Act also forbad reinsurance on marine policies, save where the insurer was insolvent or died, since it was considered to encourage speculation.[24] Speculation in other forms of insurance came under the control of the Gambling Act 1774, which did not extend to insurances on ships, goods, or merchandises. Under the Act, the insurer had to have an interest in the matter insured; policies had to insert the names of those interested in them; and 'no greater Sum shall be recovered or received from the Insurer or Insurers than the Amount or Value of the Interest of the Insured in such life or Lives, or other Event or Events'.[25]

Apart from the foundational eighteenth-century statutes, legislation played a relatively minor role in the development of the law of insurance in the nineteenth century. In 1906, however, a codifying Marine Insurance Act drafted by Mackenzie Chalmers was passed, to summarize and clarify this area of law, just as Chalmers had done with codifying Acts for Bills of Exchange and the Sale of Goods. It took a long time to reform the law. Lawyers in the 1890s were often sceptical about the possibility of codification, fearing that disputes over wording would distort what should be principled discussions.[26] But commercial men, who were less worried than the lawyers about theoretical perfection, wanted a set of clear rules which would prevent the need for litigation.[27] After more than ten years of debate, the Act eventually passed. It set out to express the existing law, and made only minor amendments to clear up doubtful questions.[28]

2. THE PRINCIPLE OF INDEMNITY AND THE INSURABLE INTEREST

Marine Policies

The nineteenth-century courts remained consistently hostile to wager policies. Even if the contract was a *bona fide* one for insurance rather than a wager, and the parties had an insurable interest, if they dispensed with the need to show it, the

---

[22] 19 Geo. II c. 37.

[23] *Thellusson* v. *Fletcher* (1780) 1 Doug. 315; *Kulen Kemp* v. *Vigne* (1786) 1 T.R. 304.

[24] In the 1860s, this provision was repealed and marine reinsurance became lawful. See 27 & 28 Vict. c. 56, s 1, 30 & 31 Vict. c. 23, and s 9 of the Marine Insurance Act 1906.

[25] Gambling Act 1774, 14 G. 3, c. 48, s 3.

[26] See M. D. Chalmers and D. Owen, *A Digest of the Law relating to Marine Insurance* (1901), x.

[27] See the debates of the Liverpool Underwriters' Association: *The Times*, 9 January 1902, col. 4e.

[28] *The Times*, 28 May 1895, col. 6a.

courts would not uphold the policy,[29] since to do so might encourage fraud.[30] The courts remained equally strict on voiding policies which (contrary to the statute) were made without benefit of salvage to the insurer.[31] As Grove J. put it in 1877, 'an insurance contrary to the direction of the statute is so unlawful in all its incidents that the law will not countenance any part of it'.[32] This meant that those who had paid premiums on p.p.i. policies could not recover them, since this would require them to disclose the illegal nature of their bargain.[33] But despite the strict legal rule, p.p.i. policies continued to be widely used among merchants, their enforcement being a matter of honour rather than law. Such policies were in general used for *bona fide* purposes, and not for speculation or fraud.[34] Underwriters issued them where a business interest existed, which might not admit of legal proof as an insurable interest, or which might not be easily susceptible to proof.[35] Underwriters were not prone to raise objections against p.p.i. policies, nor did they invoke the provisions of the Gaming Act 1845 against an insurance policy disclosing no interest. Indeed, according to Winston Churchill (speaking in 1909), underwriters were 'so careful of their reputations' that such policies were 'in practice never repudiated'.[36]

However, there remained concern that such policies were effected by those who had nothing to gain by the safe arrival of the ship, but who might benefit if it did not. In 1887, a Royal Commission appointed to investigate the loss of life at sea proposed that penalties should be imposed on those who gave and took such policies, and that the presence of an honour policy should also vitiate any other policy

---

[29] See e.g. *Smith* v. *Reynolds* (1856) 1 H. & N. 221; *Berridge* v. *The Man on Insurance Co* (1887) 18 QBD 346.

[30] *Murphy* v. *Bell* (1828) 4 Bing. 567 at 570.

[31] *De Mattos* v. *North* (1868) LR 3 Ex 185, where the policy was to insure for lost profits, which could not be salvaged; *Allkins* v. *Jupe* (1877) 2 CPD 375.

[32] *Allkins* v. *Jupe* (1877) 2 CPD 375 at 388. See also *Andree* v. *Fletcher* (1789) 3 T.R. 266; *Vandyck* v. *Hewitt* (1800) 1 East 96.

[33] Early nineteenth-century insurance judges only accepted with reluctance Buller J.'s view (*Lowry* v. *Bourdieu* (1780) 2 Doug. 468 at 471) that parties to illegal executory contracts should be permitted to recover money paid prior to any performance, provided they did not rely on the illegal contract: see *Oom* v. *Bruce* (1810) 12 East 225. Cf. Lord Ellenborough's comments in *Palyart* v. *Leckie* (1817) 6 M. & S. 290 at 293. On the rule, see pp. 591–3.

[34] See the comments of Kennedy J. in *Gedge* v. *Royal Exchange Association* [1900] 2 QB 214 at 222.

[35] See Arnould, *Marine Insurance* (9th edn, by E. L. De Hart and R. I. Simey, 1914), 427. 'For instance, if a cargo of grain rises in value in crossing the sea, a P.P.I. policy may be taken out as the most convenient method of insuring the increased value of the venture': *PD* 1909 (s5) 3: 1677 (W. Churchill, 22 April 1909). See also the discussion of such policies in *Gedge* v. *Royal Exchange Assurance Corporation* [1900] 2 QB 214 at 217 (Commercial Court); *Roddick* v. *Indemnity Mutual Marine Insurance Co* [1895] 1 QB 836, 2 QB 380.

[36] *PD* 1909 (s5) 3: 1676.

on the ship.[37] This proposal was designed to ensure that parties would not evade planned new regulations for marine policies; and when the wider project failed, the plan to stiffen the penalties against honour policies fell with it. In contrast to this tough proposal, the Marine Insurance Act 1906 softened the law on honour policies by making them void rather than illegal, which allowed the assured to recover his premium. But concern about such policies remained live, particularly when it was found that £12,000 of insurance had been taken out on the *Albion*, which was lost in 1908, by those with no interest. As a result, the Marine Insurance (Gambling Policies) Act 1909 was passed, making it a criminal offence to effect a contract of marine insurance without having any *bona fide* interest in the safe arrival of a ship or the prospect of acquiring one. Judicial hostility to p.p.i. remained strong, not least because parties were often able to overinsure their property by taking out an honour policy without disclosing the fact.[38] In 1911, Lord Shaw of Dunfermline, who regarded such policies as 'illegitimate, dangerous, and unenforceable' went so far as to say that 'wherever owners enter into gambling transactions of this kind, these transactions themselves are not only invalid, but they infect and invalidate the entire insurances which the same assured have made upon vessel, freight, or cargo'.[39] Other judges also continued to condemn p.p.i. policies, on the grounds that they were not contracts of indemnity but wagers.[40]

At the same time, the principle that the assured should only recover an indemnity for actual losses was qualified by the court's beneficent attitude towards valued policies. The practice of allowing the parties to state the value of the interest protected in their contract emerged in the mid-eighteenth century.[41] They were not regarded as wagers by the courts, for 'it must be taken that the value was fixed in such a manner as that the assured only meant to have an indemnity'.[42] Nonetheless, jurists admitted that 'a valued policy frequently partakes of the nature, both of a policy on interest, and of a wager'.[43] In cases where there was

[37] Final Report of the Royal Commission on Loss of Life at Sea, *PP* 1887 [c. 5227], xliii, 1, at p. 23.

[38] See *The Times*, 29 June 1911, col. 19e. Non-disclosure vitiated the policy: *Thames and Mersey Marine Insurance Co* v. *'Gunford' Ship Co* [1911] AC 529 at 539.

[39] *Thames and Mersey Marine Insurance Co* v. *'Gunford' Ship Co* [1911] AC 529 at 545. De Hart and Simey, editors of the 14th edition of Arnould on *Marine Insurance* (p. 429) observed that there was no direct authority besides this dictum for the proposition that insurances otherwise valid were vitiated by the gambling nature of an independent transaction entered into by the assured. See also *Rooddick* v. *Indemnity Mutual Marine Insurance Co* [1895] 2 QB 380 and *PUK Samuel and Co* v. *Dumas* [1924] AC 431 where the existence of an honour policy did not vitiate the larger contract.

[40] See *John Edwards and Co* v. *Motor Union Insurance Co* [1922] 2 KB 249; *Cheshire & Co* v. *Vaughan Bros & Co* (1919) 25 Com Cas 51, 57, [1920] 3 KB 240.

[41] See Nicholas Magens, *An Essay on Insurances*, 2 vols (1755), i, 35.

[42] *Lewis* v. *Rucker* (1761) 2 Burr. 1167 at 1171. Contrast Willes J.'s hostility to them in *Pole* v. *Fitzgerald* (1750) Willes 641 at 647.

[43] S. Marshall, *A Treatise on the Law of Insurance* (3rd edn by C. Marshall, 2 vols (1823)), 293.

a total loss, the assured recovered the sum stipulated in the policy, unless the insurer could show that 'the plaintiff had a colourable interest only, or that he has greatly overvalued the goods'.[44] In such policies, the value of a ship was generally estimated by looking at the ship's worth to the owner at the outset of the voyage, including in that sum the cost of stores, outfit, and even money advanced for seamen's wages. The assured would recover this sum, even if he had not had to incur these costs.[45] There was more debate over whether courts were to disregard the valuation in cases of partial loss ('opening' the policy), or whether they were to establish how much damage was done, and award a sum proportionate to the valued sum (so that if 25 per cent of the goods were lost, the sum would be 25 per cent of the valued loss). Section 27(3) of the Marine Insurance Act 1906 settled that the latter was the correct rule by enacting that the valuation in the contract was conclusive whether the loss was total or partial.[46]

Since the parties could fix the value of the subject assured in advance, by way of liquidated damages, judges had to admit that '[a] policy of assurance is not a perfect contract of indemnity'.[47] The courts would uphold such contracts even where the assured was plainly recovering more than his actual loss, provided he was *bona fide*.[48] In doing so, they followed the practice of the insurance industry, which did not regard the overvaluation of an interest as turning the contract into a wager.[49] Valued policies were regarded as commercially efficient; and it was felt that any rule allowing the courts to reopen such policies would merely drive clients into foreign insurance markets. However, in the 1870s, valued policies came in for strong criticism, since they were thought to encourage negligent shipowners to put unseaworthy ships to sea.[50] For shipowners who inserted exemption clauses in bills of lading, and who insured their freight, stood to profit by the early loss of the ship, since they would receive the sums insured without having to pay the costs of the voyage. Although the Royal Commission on Unseaworthy Ships concluded in 1874 that valued policies did not give rise to any serious evil,

[44] Park, *Marine Insurances* (2nd edn, 1790), 111. If the property were underinsured, then the merchant ran his own risk.

[45] See e.g. *Shawe* v. *Felton* (1801) 2 East 109 .

[46] See Arnould, *Marine Insurance* (9th edn, 1914), § 340. Marshall, *Treatise on the Law of Insurance* (3rd edn, 1823), 295 said that in cases of partial loss, the policy had to be opened.

[47] *Irving* v. *Manning* (1847) 1 H.L.C. 287 at 307.

[48] *Barker* v. *Janson* (1868) LR 3 CP 303 at 306–7. See also Willes J.'s views (dating from 1867) in App. LVII of Royal Commission on Unseaworthy Ships. Final Report of the Commissioners, *PP* 1874 [c. 1027], xxxiv, 1 (henceforth cited as Final Report of the Royal Commission on Unseaworthy Ships), pp. 426–9.

[49] See e.g. the evidence of B. C. Stephenson, Preliminary Report of the Commissioners Appointed to Inquire into the Alleged Unseaworthiness of British Registered Ships, *PP* 1873 [c. 853, c. 853-I], xxxvi, 315, 355. qq.7198ff, at pp. 247 *et seq.*

[50] Final Report of the Royal Commission on Unseaworthy Ships at 258, q.16846.

the government drafted a bill in 1876 to amend the law.[51] In the following decade, the Board of Trade again expressed concern that the nature of marine insurance meant 'the loss of a ship is in very many cases a profitable transaction',[52] and worried that its presence contributed to the growing number of deaths at sea.[53] Though the government's primary response to this problem was to improve the imperfect system of inspecting ships, proposals were also made to reform the law of insurance, so that it would give no more than an indemnity. In 1884, a Merchant Shipping bill was brought to make insurance policies valid only to the extent of the actual value of the subject-matter of the insurance, which was to be calculated as in the case of an open policy.[54] The bill was also extended to cover 'honour' policies, despite the fact that they were void at law. The proposals drew strong opposition from underwriters and the shipping interests, who argued that the measure would increase litigation. They also argued that an agreed value was essential to owners of ships and others in dealing with their bankers, who lent on the security of the insurance policies.[55] They were also worried that the proposals endangered 'cost, freight and insurance' policies, and would prevent the shipper insuring his profits. The matter was referred to a Royal Commission, which recommended that (to prevent overinsurance) every shipowner should retain an uninsured interest in his ship (which should be 3 per cent of the value he chose to put on it); that in cases of constructive total loss, the assured should only recover the cost of repairing his vessel; and that there should only be recovery for net freight.[56] In the end these proposals came to nought, and by the time a committee was set up by Lord Herschell LC in 1894 to look at the law of marine insurance, the focus of attention had shifted away from reforming the law with a view to improving safety at sea, to creating a coherent and settled code, acceptable to business interests. The failed attempt at reform revealed, however, that if in theory the contract of marine insurance was one of indemnity, where the amount to be recovered should be measured by the assured's interest, the practice of insurers and shipowners had gone far beyond this. Both mercantile interests and the

---

[51] It failed to make progress. See *The Times*, 15 January 1876, col. 6f: Letter to the Editor from J.L.W.

[52] *The Times*, 5 November 1883, col. 4b: Proposals for Establishing Local Marine Courts and Merchant Shipping Commissioners.

[53] *The Times*, 14 March 1884, col. 4d; 16 August 1886, col. 9b.

[54] *The Times*, 25 February 1884, col. 9d; 14 March 1884, col. 4d. The bill also provided that the costs of wages, stores, or outlay incurred in sending a ship to sea to earn freight would not be recoverable and that only net freight could be insured. If shipowners insured expenses or outlays, they were to enumerate the nature of the expenses they were insuring, so that checks could be made when claims were submitted.

[55] *The Times*, 28 February 1884, col. 10e.

[56] *The Times*, 12 August 1887 col. 3c; 13 August 1887, col. 9d.

courts accepted that if an insurer had accepted a premium for a contract to pay out a certain sum in the event of a loss, he should be held to the contract agreed, unless there was such a sign of fraud or bad faith to undo the contract.

In order to recover on a valued policy, the assured nonetheless had still 'to prove *some interest*, to take it out of the statute'.[57] In discussing what constituted an insurable interest, jurists drew on two definitions which had been made in the 1804 case of *Lucena* v. *Craufurd* by Lawrence J. and Lord Eldon.[58] According to Lawrence J., to have an interest it was not necessary for the assured to have a present right to the thing insured. Instead, he had to have such a relation to the thing insured 'as to have a moral certainty of advantage or benefit' from it, 'but for those risks or dangers' insured against. 'To be interested in the preservation of a thing', he noted, 'is to be so circumstanced with respect to it as to have benefit from its existence, prejudice from its destruction.'[59] By contrast, Lord Eldon rejected the 'moral certainty' test since it would allow any person, down to the warehouse keeper or porter who stood to gain by the arrival of property, to be able to insure. In his view, the interest had to 'be a right in the property, or a right derivable out of some contract about the property, which in either case may be lost upon some contingency affecting the possession or enjoyment of the party'.[60]

Nineteenth-century judges and jurists argued that those who had either a legal or an equitable right in the property had an insurable interest.[61] One could not insure a mere expectation: only if the assured could be shown to have risked a loss would the courts find an insurable interest to have existed.[62] A purely verbal but unenforceable agreement to buy goods on a ship therefore gave the intended purchaser no insurable interest in the goods, since he was not certain to lose if they were lost.[63] At the same time, it was not necessary to have a vested right to be able to insure. Although 'naked consignees'—who had no legal or beneficial interest—had no insurable interest of

---

[57] Marshall, *Treatise on the Law of Insurance* (3rd edn, 1823), 292.

[58] *Lucena* v. *Craufurd* (1802) 3 B. & P. 75. The House of Lords consulted the judges on the question whether commissioners authorized by statute to take possession of captured enemy ships once they had arrived in port had an insurable interest in them, before property in them had vested in the Crown, by virtue of a proclamation of reprisals.

[59] *Lucena* v. *Craufurd* (1804) 2 B. & P. N.R. 269 at 302. For Lawrence, the commissioners did not pass this test, since they could not show that they would be prejudiced by the non-arrival of the vessels which had been seized. See also *Camden* v. *Anderson* (1794) 5 T.R. 711, where Lawrence J. held that the assured needed to have a legal or equitable interest.

[60] *Lucena* v. *Craufurd* (1804) 2 B. & P. N.R. 269 at 321. The plaintiffs succeeded on a new trial, having averred an interest in the king: *Lucena* v. *Craufurd* (1808) 1 Taunt. 325.

[61] e.g. *Wilson* v. *Martin* (1856) 11 Exch. 684. See also Arnould, *Marine Insurance* (9th edn, 1914, by E. L. De Hart and R. I. Simey), i, 415. Marshall, *Treatise on the Law of Insurance* (3rd edn, 1823), 101 said anyone with an absolute or qualified property had an insurable interest.

[62] See Willes J.'s comments in *Joyce* v. *Swann* (1864) 17 C.B. N.S. 84 at 104.

[63] *Stockdale* v. *Dunlop* (1840) 6 M. & W. 224.

their own,[64] consignees who had made advances or accepted bills on the credit of the goods consigned did have an insurable interest, even though their right to the goods was not perfected until their arrival.[65] A party with any legal or equitable rights in respect of property could insure against the loss of those rights.[66]

There were nevertheless some exceptional cases involving captures, where parties were held to have an insurable interest, even though they had no vested or contractual rights to the property, and had no liens over it. According to an eighteenth-century rule, captors had an insurable interest in prizes taken at sea, even though the legal interest remained in the King, who could deny the captor any benefit by releasing the prize prior to condemnation. In such cases the assured had only 'the bare contingency of a future grant from the crown'.[67] Although Lord Eldon disapproved of the doctrine,[68] it was a settled rule that captors had an insurable interest once a prize had been taken.[69] In 1840, in *Devaux* v. *Steele*, Tindal CJ went so far as to suggest that the expectation of a bounty from the French government might be an interest which could be insured, if the plaintiff gave 'the most cogent and indubitable evidence of the actual and uniform allowance of the bounty'.[70] This was to suggest that a 'moral certainty', rather than any kind of legal or equitable right, would suffice. Given these cases, Lawrence's definition continued to be quoted, both by American[71] and English jurists.[72]

---

[64] In *Lucena* v. *Craufurd (1804)* 2 B. & P. N.R. 269, both Lawrence and Eldon felt the consignee could insure by averring the interest of those on whose account the insurance was made. Duer, however, felt that a consignee without any interest and with no lien could not insure, even on behalf of the consignor: Duer, *Marine Insurance*, s. 9, 2: 106. Commercial practice, in such cases, was for the consignor to insure.

[65] *Hill* v. *Secretan* (1798) 1 B. & P. 315; *Wolff* v. *Horncastle* (1798) 1 B. & P. 316; *Robertson* v. *Hamilton* (1811) 14 East 522. The interest was commensurate with the loss they would sustain by the loss of the goods: W. Phillips, *A Treatise on the Law of Insurance*, 2 vols (2nd edn, Boston, 1840), i, 114. See also the comments of Willes J. in *Seagrave* v. *The Union Marine Insurance Co* (1866) LR 1 CP 305 at 320.

[66] In Buller J.'s words, 'a debt which arises in consequence of the article insured, and which would have given a lien on it, does give an insurable interest. The case is not at all altered by the goods not having arrived': *Wolff* v. *Horncastle* (1798) 1 B. & P. 316 at 323.

[67] *Le Cras* v. *Hughes* (1782) in Park, *Marine Insurances* (1st edn, 1787), 307.

[68] *Lucena* v. *Craufurd* (1804) 2 B. & P. N.R. 269 at 323; but he also acknowledged the rule: *Nichol* v. *Goodall* (1804) 10 Ves. 155 at 157.

[69] See Lord Ellenborough's explanation, attempting a parallel with consignees of goods under a bill of lading in *Stirling* v. *Vaughan* (1809) 11 East 619 at 628. Cf. *Boehm* v. *Bell* (1799) 8 T.R. 154. Where ships had been taken prior to a declaration of war, the courts held there was no insurable interest, but a mere expectation of a gift from the Crown, since such captures were not under the Prize Acts: *Routh* v. *Thompson* (1809) 11 East 428 at 432.

[70] *Devaux* v. *Steele* (1840) 6 Bing. N.C. 358 at 371. He held that this would bring it within the rule of *Le Cras* v. *Hughes*, which (despite the doubts of Eldon which he quoted) he held still applicable.

[71] See e.g. Phillips, *Insurance* (2nd edn, 1840), i, 67–8.

[72] Arnould, *Marine Insurance* (9th edn, E. L. De Hart and R. I. Simey, 1914). Chalmers and Owen, in their notes to the 1906 Act, noted that Lawrence's definition 'cannot be improved upon': M. D. Chalmers and D. Owen, *The Marine Insurance Act 1906* (2nd edn, 1913), 13.

Nineteenth-century courts often took an expansive view of the insurable inter-est, moving away from the narrow view, that insurance existed only to indemnify for the loss of specific property, which had been articulated in the mid-eighteenth century. By the start of the nineteenth century, Willes J.'s 1750 opinion that one could not insure for loss of profit[73] had been rejected.[74] Provided the policy was worded correctly, one could recover for loss of profits even if the goods in question had yet to be loaded onto the ship.[75] As long as it was certain that a profit would be made if the goods arrived, there was an insurable interest.[76] Eighteenth-century judges like Willes had also insisted that one could not insure a voyage,[77] but only things, such as a ship or goods. This meant that where an owner of goods had insured not the goods, but the safe arrival of the ship carrying them—in which he had no interest—he was held unable to recover.[78] Despite Lord Mansfield's efforts to establish a contrary doctrine,[79] the courts also remained hostile to attempts by those who had insured ships in which they had an interest to recover for the loss of a voyage, when the ship itself was not lost.[80] However, by the early nineteenth century, it was accepted that, provided the policy was correctly drafted, mer-chants consigning goods could insure against the loss of the adventure, and not merely the loss of the goods.[81]

---

[73] *Pole* v. *Fitzgerald* (1750) Willes 641 at 645.

[74] *Grant* v. *Parkinson* (1782) in Park, *Marine Insurances* (1st edn, 1787), 305; *Barclay* v. *Cousins* (1802) 2 East 544.

[75] *Halhead* v. *Young* (1856) 6 E. & B. 312 at 324.

[76] *M'Swiney* v. *The Royal Exchange Assurance* (1849) 14 Q.B. 634 at 645. The rule that it had to be certain that a profit would have been made derived from *Barclay* v. *Cousins* (1802) 2 East 544 at 551, quoted in William Benecke, *A Treatise on the Principles of Indemnity in Marine Insurance* (1824), 31. *Eyre* v. *Glover* (1812) 16 East 281 at 220 confirmed that it did not have to be certain what those profits would be when the insurance was taken out, but that one could insure for profits on an open policy.

[77] *Pole* v. *Fitzgerald* (1750) Willes 641 at 646, overruling *Pond* v. *King* (1748) 1 Wils. K.B. 191. Cf. W. Beawes, *Lex Mercatoria Rediviva*, 2 vols (5th edn by Joseph Chitty, 1813), i, 446.

[78] *Kulen Kemo* v. *Vigne* (1786) 1 T.R. 304.

[79] Mansfield felt that a policy-holder could abandon the ship as a total loss, and recover, where the voyage had been lost, but not the ship itself: *Goss* v. *Withers* (1758) 2 Burr. 683; *Hamilton* v. *Mendes* (1761) 2 Burr. 1198 at 1209; cf. *Cazalet* v. *St Barbe* (1786) 1 T.R. 187 at 191. The rule applied only to those with an interest, since only they could abandon the property in which they had an interest.

[80] It was confirmed that one could only abandon and recover for a total loss where the ship was lost: *Parsons* v. *Scott* (1810) 2 Taunt. 363; *Falkner* v. *Ritchie* (1813) 2 M. & S. 290 at 293. Cf. *Anderson* v. *Wallis* (1813) 2 M. & S. 240 (taking the same approach to goods insured). The judges knew that if parties could abandon goods for the failure of a voyage, this might undermine clauses in insurance policies excluding liability for particular losses: *Thompson* v. *Royal Exchange Assurance Co* (1812) 16 East 214.

[81] *Puller* v. *Glover* (1810) 12 East 124; Marshall, *Treatise on the Law of Insurance* (3rd edn, 1823), i, 104. See also Lawrence J.'s comments in *Lucena* v. *Craufurd* (1804) 2 B. & P. N.R. 269 at 301–2, sug-gesting that according to Willes, 'the impossibility of valuing, and not the want of property, was the reason why that voyage could not be the subject-matter of this contract'.

The fact that the courts were willing to permit parties to insure their interest in an adventure, rather than in specific property, was seen in a number of mid-century cases, where shareholders were allowed to insure for losses they might suffer if the company's ventures failed. The question was raised in a number of cases arising as a result of the Atlantic Telegraph Company's failure to lay a transatlantic cable between Ireland and Newfoundland. In *Paterson v. Harris* in 1861, the Queen's Bench held that an individual shareholder, who had no legal or equitable title or charge over the cable owned by the company, nor any contractual liability in respect to it, did have an insurable interest in it. '[O]n the true construction of this policy', Cockburn CJ ruled, 'the underwriters contract to indemnify the owner of that share against any losses arising to his interest in the cable, which interest is, by agreement, valued at £1100.'[82] The question was revisited in 1867 in *Wilson v. Jones*, when the Exchequer Chamber ruled that a shareholder had an insurable interest, not in the cable, but in the adventure. As Willes J. put it, the shareholder's interest was in the profits to be made by the company, and it was the profit which would be made once the cable was laid (rather than the cable) which was insured.[83]

In 1884, Brett MR declared that the court should always 'lean in favour of an insurable interest, if possible', since there was 'no real merit' in underwriters, who had received premiums, raising the objection after the event that there was no insurable interest.[84] How far some judges were prepared to go can be seen from *Moran, Galloway & Co v. Uzielli* in 1905.[85] Here, the UK agents of a foreign ship, who were owed money for advances for the ship's disbursements, took out insurance on the ship to cover the debt. Since debts could not be lost by perils of the sea, it had been laid down in 1851 that a 'mere debt ... for repairs and disbursements could not legally be made the subject of an insurance'.[86] Nevertheless, the divisional court found for the plaintiffs. The court recognized that the assured would only recover his debt if the vessel arrived, since it was the main asset of the debtor. The court also found that the plaintiffs had a present interest in the ship, since they had a right under the Admiralty Court Act 1840 to arrest the ship, insofar as the advances had been made for necessaries. The decision proved controversial, with many in the legal community feeling that the court had developed the notion of insurable interest too liberally.[87]

---

[82] *Paterson v. Harris* (1861) 1 B. & S. 336 at 355. This insured sum represented the value of the plaintiff's shares.

[83] *Wilson v. Jones* (1867) LR 2 Ex 139.   [84] *Stock v. Inglis* (1884) 12 QBD 564 at 571.

[85] *Moran, Galloway & Co v. Uzielli* [1905] 2 KB 555.

[86] *Stainbank v. Fenning* (1851) 11 CB 51 at 89.

[87] The decision was controversial: see the criticisms in Arnould, *Marine Insurance* (9th edn by E. L. De Hart and R. I. Simey, 1914), 345.

In drafting the Marine Insurance Bill, Mackenzie Chalmers took a narrower approach: '[a] prospect or possibility of loss or gain, which, at the time of loss, is not founded on any right or liability in, or in respect of, the subject-matter, insured, is not insurable'. This proved too narrow a definition and a committee of the Commons broadened the definition so that the final Act stated that a person had an interest if 'he stands in any legal or equitable relation to the adventure, or to any insurable property at risk therein' (s 5(2)). In their notes to the Act, Chalmers and Owen noted that:

[t]he definition of insurable interest has been continuously expanding, and dicta in some of the older cases, which would tend to narrow it, must be accepted with caution. The essence of interest is (a) that there should be a physical object exposed to sea perils, and (b) that the assured should stand in some relationship, cognizable by law, to that object, in consequence of which he either benefits by its preservation, or is prejudiced by its loss, or mishap thereto.

Endorsing Lawrence's definition, they noted that insurable interest could not be defined exhaustively, and argued for an expansive rather than a restrictive view, which would uphold insurances where the assured was seeking to indemnify himself from a real loss.[88] Nonetheless, the stress on the need for a physical object in which the assured had an interest showed a reluctance to allow the insurance of purely economic interests. This continued to be seen as a form of wager.

Just as the original assured had to have an interest in the adventure, so too did any assignee of the policy. If goods were sold during a voyage, any insurance covering them could be assigned at the same time. However, the policy did not automatically follow the goods: it had to be specifically assigned, and the assignee had to have an insurable interest in the goods covered at the time of the loss. If a person taking out the insurance sold his interest, without handing over the policy with the bill of sale, he could not sue on the insurance on behalf of the new owner of the goods; and nor could the latter sue in her own interest.[89] Equally, it was settled in 1875 that if the party assigning the policy lost his interest in the goods before he made the assignment, the policy lapsed for want of interest.[90] However, if there was a complete sale of floating cargo at sea, the policy followed the bill of sale. The courts were happy to allow the assignment in such cases, as it facilitated the sale of goods at sea, and avoided the inconvenience to the

---

[88] Hence, they asked, 'Suppose A is offered an appointment abroad on condition that his acceptance of the offer is received by return of post. Why shall he not insure the safe arrival of the letter, although he has no legal rights in respect of it after it is posted': Chalmers and Owen, *The Marine Insurance Act 1906* (2nd edn, 1913), 12–13.

[89] *Powles* v. *Innes* (1843) 11 M. & W. 10.

[90] *The North of England Pure Oil-Cake Co* v. *The Archangel Maritime Insurance Co* (1875) LR 10 QB 249 at 253, codified in s 51 of the Marine Insurance Act 1906.

purchaser of seeking a new insurance while the goods were at sea. This meant that (unlike in cases of fire insurance), there was no need for the consent of the insurer to the assignment of the policy. Moreover, legislation in 1868 permitted assignees of marine policies to sue in their own names, without requiring any of the safeguards included in the 1867 Act regarding life assurances.[91]

Life Insurance Policies

What constituted an insurable interest in a life? While every person clearly had an insurable interest in his own life, to any amount he chose,[92] those who insured the lives of others had to demonstrate that they had some pecuniary interest in the life assured.[93] It was easy enough for creditors to show that they had an insurable interest in the debt owed by the assured life,[94] but parents who insured the lives of their children in the expectation of being paid money by them found the courts sceptical to claims that this constituted an insurable interest.[95]

Did the requirement of a pecuniary insurable interest mean that a contract of life assurance was one of indemnity? This question could hardly be raised where the assured had taken a policy on his own life,[96] but it was one which was relevant when creditors insured the lives of their debtors. If insurance was to be seen as indemnification, could creditors recover on a policy after they had already been indemnified for their loss? In *Godsall* v. *Boldero* in 1807, the King's Bench held that since the plaintiffs (who had supplied William Pitt with a coach, and insured his life for £500 lest he die before paying his debt) had been paid the money owed out of a parliamentary grant voted to pay off the former Prime Minister's creditors, they could not recover from the insurers.[97] The court was clearly worried lest the assured be paid twice, which seemed to contradict the principles of the law of insurance, as it had been developed in marine cases. The decision proved controversial, not least because premiums were calculated on the risk to the assured's

---

[91] 31 & 32 Vict. c. 86.

[92] *Wainewright* v. *Bland* (1835) 1 Moo. & R. 481.

[93] There was, however, a legal presumption that a wife had an insurable interest in her husband's life: *Reed* v. *Royal Exchange Co* (1795) Peake Add. Cas. 70.

[94] See *Dwyer* v. *Edie* (1788) in Park, *Marine Insurances* (2nd edn, 1790), 332; Marshall, *Treatise on the Law of Insurance* (3rd edn, 1823), ii, 779.

[95] See *Halford* v. *Kymer* [1830] 10 B. & C. 724; *Worthington* v. *Curtis* (1875) 1 Ch D 419. By contrast, in *Barnes* v. *The London, Edinburgh and Glasgow Life Assurance Co* [1892] 1 QB 864, it was held that where a relative spent money on the upbringing of a child she had no legal responsibility for, she did have 'a pecuniary insurable interest to the extent of each sum of money as it was successively expended by her for the child's benefit'.

[96] Here, the language of indemnity was hardly appropriate, unless the 'indemnification' was for the loss of the value put on his own life in the policy by the assured.

[97] *Godsall* v. *Boldero* (1807) 9 East 70.

life, and not on the (smaller) risk that his estate would end up unable to pay.[98] In practice, *Godsall* had little effect, for insurance offices remained aware that their business would suffer if they were perceived to use legal quibbles to avoid payment. They did not probe the nature of the claimant's insurable interest provided that premiums had been paid.[99] Equally, if insurers chose to pay out where there was no legal insurable interest, the courts would not interfere.[100]

In reality, life policies were entirely different in nature from marine and fire policies, since they were primarily used as a form of saving and investment which continued over a long period. A life policy was a valuable asset, representing an investment in terms of premiums paid over a prolonged period of time. This commercial reality was recognized in 1854, when *Godsall* was overruled in *Dalby* v. *India & London Life Assurance Company*. This case was brought by the Anchor Life Assurance Company, which sold four insurance policies to the Rev. John Wright on the life of the Duke of Cambridge, valued at £3000. The company had taken out a reinsurance policy with the India & London Life for £1000. In December 1848, Wright surrendered his policies in return for an annuity, but the Anchor Life continued its own insurance on the duke's life. When the duke died, the India & London challenged its liability to pay, on the grounds that the Anchor no longer had the liability in respect of which the policy had been taken out. Whereas in *Goldsall*, the life assurance contract had been seen through marine eyes, it was now acknowledged that life policies were of a different nature. As Parke B. put it:

> The contract commonly called life-assurance, when properly considered, is a mere contract to pay a certain sum of money on the death of a person, in consideration of the due payment of a certain annuity for his life [...] This species of insurance in no way resembles a contract of indemnity.[101]

The court also rejected the idea (found in marine cases) that the plaintiff's recovery was limited to the amount of his actual interest at the time the action was brought,[102] since this was inconsistent with the nature of a life insurance contract.

---

[98] See C. A. Babbage, *A Comparative View of the Various Institutions for the Assurance of Lives* (1826) in D. Jenkins and T. Yoneyama, *History of Insurance*, 8 vols (2000), iv, 245–83 at 336, 335.

[99] See the evidence as to the insurers' practices in *Barber* v. *Morris* (1831) 1 Moo. & Rob. 62.

[100] In *Henson* v. *Blackwell* (1845) 4 Hare 434, Wigram VC felt that there was an insurable interest where the defendant had insured the life of his debtor's wife. Dismissing a case brought by the debtor, he added that even if there had been no interest, and the insurance company had paid out wrongly, this would have nothing to do with the plaintiff. See also *Worthington* v. *Curtis* (1875) 1 Ch D 419; see also *AG* v. *Murray* [1904] 1 KB 165.

[101] *Dalby* v. *India & London Life Assurance Co* (1854) 15 C.B. 365 at 387.

[102] It was clear that since the Anchor's interest in the life of the duke was for the £1000 they would be liable to pay Wright on his death, the interest ended when the policies were surrendered.

For if it were so limited, the assured would pay a fixed set of premiums determined by the extent of his interest at the time the insurance was effected, but would only receive a varying sum depending on the nature of his interest at the time of death. This was to recognize the objection to *Godsall* that insurers might be paid without having to pay in their turn. Instead, the assured in life policies was to recover the value of his interest at the time the insurance was effected. In *Law* v. *The London Indisputable Life Policy Company* in 1855, the plaintiff (who had bought from his son a legacy of £3000 contingent on his attaining the age of 30) was therefore able to recover on a two-year policy on the son's life for £2999, even though the son's death occurred after he had turned 30, and the father had received the money.[103] However, the assured could not recover more than the amount of his interest at the time the insurance was taken out, which meant that if he was paid out fully by one insurer, he could not recover once more from another.[104]

Unlike marine and fire policies, life assurance policies were traded. Since the surrender value of policies might be small compared with the sums insured for, many of those who were unable to maintain premium payments preferred to sell their policies, with the purchaser continuing to pay the premiums, and obtaining the benefit on the death of the life covered. Given that a policy was a valuable financial asset, assignees in bankruptcy often auctioned the life insurance policy taken out by their bankrupt, as a way of raising money for his creditors. Life assurance companies were happy to allow policies to be transferred and did not require the assured to seek permission for this: after all, allowing policies to be sold and circulated added to their value, and increased the market. When a policy was sold, the rights under it were assigned to the buyer.[105]

While purchasers of such policies clearly had no interest of their own in the life of the assured, it was not in the interest of insurance companies to raise this question, since it could only diminish the value of their policies. The question was raised in 1829, however, in *Ashley* v. *Ashley*, when the purchaser of a policy disputed his liability to pay for it, by claiming that he had no insurable interest. This argument was rejected by Sir Launcelot Shadwell VC, who noted that the Gambling Act said nothing about the assignment of policies. Since assignees of choses in action could bring actions in the name of the assignor, the assignee who

---

[103] *Law* v. *The London Indisputable Life Policy Co and Another* (1855) 1 K. & J. 223.

[104] *Hebdon* v. *West* (1863) 3 B. & S. 579 at 591–2.

[105] Being a chose in action, an insurance policy could not be assigned at common law. However, since common law courts allowed assignees to sue in the name of the assignor, it was only necessary for the assignee to seek the aid of equity in case the assignor refused co-operation: see e.g. *Hammond* v. *Messenger* (1838) 9 Sim. 327.

bought an insurance policy in the market could be regarded as substituting him-self for the vendor, effectively removing the problem of his lack of interest.[106]

Nor was it necessary for there to have been a formal assignment of the policy for the purchaser to be able to recover on it. The question was raised in a num-ber of cases where assignees were permitted under the policy to recover even though the assignor had breached a condition of the insurance. Since many pol-icies allowed assignees to recover where the person whose life was insured had committed suicide, but not his executors, the life office's liability to a claimant sometimes turned on whether there had been a valid assignment. Mid-century Chancery judges did not require a formal assignment to have been made: all that had to be shown was an intention to assign, which would generate an equit-able right in the assignee.[107] Assignments could therefore be made without the assignor handing over the policy, or informing the office that an assignment had been made.[108] In such cases, the assignor was regarded as trustee for the assign-ees, liable to account for all moneys recovered under the policy.

Many insurance offices stated in their policies that they did not require any notice of assignment. This generated risks for them when it came to making pay-ments. In 1828, Shadwell VC held that a person who purchased an insurance pol-icy was to be deemed to have left it in the possession of the assignor unless he gave notice to the insurer. This meant that it remained within the 'order and disposi-tion' of a bankrupt assignor, and that his assignees in bankruptcy could claim it, having a prior equity.[109] Where policy-holders used their insurance as security for a large number of loans, it was often safe for the insurer to pay out the first assignee who presented himself to the office, since such a person would be the first to bring notice of his assignment to the office. While the party who had recovered first might subsequently have to account to an assignee with a prior equity, the insurer would not be liable.[110] Nonetheless, insurers were well advised not to pay out the assignee without confirmation from the original assured, for (unless the assignee had a formal assignment and the policy in his hands), the validity of the assignment might be disputed by others. In any event, until 1867, if the assignee wished to sue an insurer, he had to do it in the original policy-holder's name.

The law regarding the assignment of life policies was modified in 1867 by the Policies of Assurance Act. Under this Act, an assignee could sue in his own name

[106]   *Ashley* v. *Ashley* (1829) 3 Sim. 149.
[107]   *Cook* v. *Black* (1842) 1 Hare 390; *Dufaur* v. *The Professional Life Assurance Co* (1858) 25 Beav. 599.
[108]   This could be hard on the assignor: see *Fortescue* v. *Barnett* (1834) 3 My. & K. 36.
[109]   *Williams* v. *Thorp* (1828) 2 Sim. 257 at 263.
[110]   See *Newman* v. *Newman* (1885) 28 Ch D 674; *Spencer* v. *Clarke* (1878) 9 Ch D 127; *In re Weniger's Policy* [1910] 2 Ch 291.

if he had an equitable right (by virtue of the assignment) to receive the policy moneys from the company at the time of the action. To sue in his own name, he had to have obtained the assignment either by way of endorsement on the policy or by a separate instrument in words set out in the Act and to have given written notice of the assignment to the insurer. The Act 'was intended to give a simpler remedy against an insurance office, and also to give facilities to insurance offices in settling claims by enabling them to recognise as the first claim the claim of the person who first gave such notice as required by the statute'.[111] The fact that the assignee had to have the right in equity to receive such moneys suggested that the court would take into account prior equities between assignees, and might have suggested continued caution on the part of insurers in paying out such assignees, if a prior equitable assignment had been brought to their notice. However, the law was again modified in the Judicature Act 1873, which enacted that any absolute assignment in writing of any chose in action of which express notice was given to the debtor was to be deemed effectual in law to transfer the legal right from the date of the notice, regardless of whether at the time of action the plaintiff had the equitable right. The insurer was thus safe in paying whoever had the absolute assignment. Insurers continued to have some doubt, however, over whether it was safe to pay out where there were multiple assignees. As a result, the Life Assurance Companies (Payment into Court) Act 1896 was passed, which allowed companies to pay into the high court 'any moneys payable by them under a life policy in respect of which, in the opinion of their board of directors, no sufficient discharge can otherwise be obtained'. The receipt from an officer of court was to be a discharge to the company of moneys paid.[112]

Fire Policies

Any person in possession of a building, or with a proprietary interest in it, had an insurable interest, and could insure its full value.[113] However, the question whether the policy was to indemnify the assured against the loss actually caused by the fire (as in marine insurance), or to pay the sum specified in the event of a fire, regardless of actual loss to the assured (as in life assurance), remained unsettled until the later nineteenth century. *Prima facie*, it looked like a contract of

---

[111] *Newman* v. *Newman* (1885) 28 Ch D 674 at 681.

[112] It was promoted by the Life Offices Association, to avoid the companies being involved in protracted litigation when more than one assured person claimed the sum: *Post Mag.* 57 (1896) 582.

[113] *Simpson* v. *Scottish Union Insurance Co* (1863) 1 H. & M. 618 at 628, Page Wood VC observed, 'that a tenant for year to year, having insured, would have a right to say that the premises should be rebuilt for him to occupy, and that his insurable interest is not limited to the value of his tenancy from year to year'. See also *Castellain* v. *Preston* (1880) 11 QBD 398–401.

indemnity. This principle lay behind the Fire Prevention (Metropolis) Act 1774, under which insurance companies were obliged to use the money due under the policy to rebuild, or reinstate, the property, on the request of anyone interested in it, or if there was any suspicion that the owner had wilfully set the house on fire.[114] Equally, the Gambling Act 1774 stated that the assured could only recover the value of his interest at the time of the loss.

The question was explored in the late 1870s in cases considering whether the assured could retain money paid out on a policy, if it turned out that he suffered no actual financial loss. In 1877, Jessel MR held that the principle elaborated in marine insurance, that an insured person whose losses were caused by another person's wrongdoing could either sue the wrongdoer or recover from his insurer, but not both, applied in fire policies as well.[115] In such cases, the insurer, who had paid out, obtained the rights of the assured against the third parties. But in the same year, the divisional court held insurers liable to pay out on a policy, despite the fact that the destroyed property was to have been acquired by the Metropolitan Board of Works under compulsory powers. Although Mellor J. considered that the plaintiff might be held to be a trustee of the money for the Board, rather than being allowed to retain it for himself, he did not suggest its return to the insurers.[116]

The issue was further explored in cases where a property which the owner had contracted to sell was damaged by fire before the sale had been completed. It had been settled in the eighteenth century that fire insurance did not attach on the realty, but was a special agreement with the person insuring to indemnify him against losses sustained to property in which he had a current interest.[117] This meant that where insured property was sold, and was subsequently damaged

---

[114] 14 Geo. III c. 78, s 83. It was settled in *Ex p C. B. Gorely* (1864) 4 De G. J. & S. 477 that the provision applied nationally. Insurers often inserted reinstatement options in the policy, since the cost of rebuilding might be lower than paying the cash sum. Once they had elected to reinstate, they were obliged to do so, even if subsequent unrelated events made it more expensive: *Brown* v. *The Royal Insurance Co* (1859) 1 E. & E. 853. By contrast, insured householders faced great procedural difficulties in using the legislative provision against companies unwilling to reinstate (see *Simpson* v. *Scottish Union Insurance Co* (1863) 1 H. & M. 618; *Wimbledon Park Golf Club* v. *Imperial Insurance Co* [1902] 18 TLR 815).

[115] *North British and Mercantile Insurance Co* v. *London, Liverpool and Globe Insurance Co* (1877) 5 Ch D 569 at 576. It was on this principle in *Darrell* v. *Tibbitts* (1880) 5 QBD 560 that the Court of Appeal ordered the insured party to repay money received from his insurer, after he had received money from a local authority to rebuild the property. On subrogation, see below.

[116] *Collingridge* v. *The Royal Exchange Assurance Corporation* (1877) 3 QBD 173 at 177.

[117] *Lynch* v. *Dalzell* (1729) 4 Bro. P.C. 431, *Sadlers Co* v. *Badcock* (1743) 2 Atk. 554. Although some such as James (*Treatise on Life and Fire Assurance*, 74) argued that the policy should run with the property, the eighteenth-century view was confirmed in the nineteenth century: *Poole* v. *Adams* (1864) 12 W.R. 683.

by fire, neither the vendor, nor the new purchaser could take the benefit of the policy, unless it had been assigned with the consent of the insurer. But what was to happen to the insurance money if the fire occurred while the vendor still had a legal interest? In *Rayner* v. *Preston*, in 1880, a purchaser claimed that he should be permitted to recover the payment received by the vendor, even though the parties had not made provision in their contract for him to do so. The Court of Appeal rejected his claim, confirming the view that the insurance did not attach to the property, and rejecting the idea that the vendor should be regarded as trustee for the purchaser of the insurance money.[118] Three years later, in *Castellain* v. *Preston*, the court confirmed that, in such cases, the vendor could not keep the money himself, after he had been paid the purchase money, but had to hand it back to the insurance company. In so deciding, the Court of Appeal confirmed that the principle of indemnity stood at the root of fire insurance contracts. As Bowen LJ put it, 'What is it that is insured in a fire policy? Not the bricks and the materials used in building the house, but the interest of the assured in the subject-matter of insurance, not the legal interest only, but the beneficial interest'.[119] When it came to the insurance of fixed property, the courts therefore adopted a policy which was favourable to the insurers.

When it came to the insurance of goods, the courts had a more flexible policy which aimed to provide the most efficient outcome for the purchasers of insurance. It was not only owners who had an insurable interest in goods: bailees who were liable for losses to goods in their possession—such as common carriers and innkeepers who were strictly liable for losses to goods in their possession—could also insure them.[120] With the development of the fire insurance market, carriers, consignors, and consignees were all in a position to effect their own insurance. Furthermore, wharfingers and railway companies generally used 'floating' policies, which insured any goods which happened to be in their warehouses at the time of a fire. In this situation, tricky problems were raised about the extent of each party's insurable interest.

In *Waters* v. *The Monarch Fire Office* in 1856, where wharfingers had taken out a floating policy without their customers' knowledge, the insurers claimed that their liability was limited to the extent of the wharfingers' own property, and to the value of their lien on their customers' goods. The argument was rejected by the Queen's Bench, where Lord Campbell CJ ruled that '[i]t would be most inconvenient in business if a wharfinger could not, at his own cost, keep up a floating policy for the benefit of all who might become his customers'. Since it was clear from the

---

[118] *Rayner* v. *Preston* (1881) 18 Ch D 1 at 15. See also *Edwards* v. *West* (1878) 7 Ch D 858.
[119] *Castellain* v. *Preston* (1883) 11 QBD 380 at 397.
[120] Other bailees were not liable for losses by fire.

policy that all damage was covered, the plaintiffs could recover in full: '[t]hey will be entitled to apply so much to cover their own interest, and will be trustees for the owners as to the rest'.[121] This approach was endorsed in 1859 in *The London and North Western Railway Company* v. *Glyn*, where the Queen's Bench pointed out that any other construction would make it necessary 'that several policies should be effected on the same goods, and thus insurance companies would obtain several premiums instead of one in respect of what, to them, is the same risk'.[122] If insurers wished to prevent wharfingers recovering for the losses of their customers, the court stated that they should amend the wording of their policies to make this clear.[123] While insurers took the hint and amended the wording, by covering only goods for which the wharfingers were responsible,[124] the decisions showed that wharfingers could cover the losses of all those who goods they held, irrespective of their own legal liability in respect of these goods.[125] Business efficiency meant that they were not merely indemnifying against their own losses.

3. THE FORMATION OF INSURANCE POLICIES

Marine Policies

Those who took out insurance policies with Lloyd's underwriters had security both from the unlimited liability of its members, and from the fact that the risk was spread, with a large number of underwriters sharing it. The link between the assured and the underwriters was the insurance broker, who would prepare a brief memorandum of the risk, which was then circulated at Lloyd's. Any underwriter prepared to take a share of the risk would initial this 'slip'. Once the slip was full, a formal policy would be prepared. In practice, the slip was the basis of the contract of marine insurance from the eighteenth century, being found the most convenient way to conduct business: it was considered 'the complete and final contract' between the parties, the terms of which could not unilaterally be

---

[121]   *Waters* v. *The Monarch Fire Office* (1856) 5 E. & B. 870 at 880–1.

[122]   *The London and North Western Railway Co* v. *Glyn* (1859) 1 E. & E. 652 at 661.

[123]   See (for the effect of an amended policy) *The North British and Mercantile Insurance Co* v. *Moffatt* (1871) LR 7 CP 25.

[124]   *North British Insurance Co* v. *Moffatt* (1871) 7 LR CP 25.

[125]   It was unclear whether wharfingers were to be regarded as having a strict liability, analogous to that of carriers: contrast *Maving* v. *Todd* (1815) 1 Stark. 72; *North British and Mercantile Insurance Co* v. *London, Liverpool and Globe Insurance Co* (1877) 5 Ch D 569 at 574; *Consolidated Tea and Lands Co* v. *Oliver's Wharf* [1910] 2 KB 395 at 400. In *Waters* v. *Monarch Fire Office*, Lush argued that the wharfingers as bailees were not liable for fire; while in *The London and North Western Railway* v. *Glyn*, the company's strict liability was removed by the failure of the customer to make the declaration required by the Carriers Act 1830.

altered 'without a breach of faith, for which [the party in breach] would suffer severely in his credit and future business'.[126] But in law it was problematic, since it was regarded as a device to evade paying stamp duties.[127] The agreement on the slip was therefore not itself enforceable, but had to be written up into a policy.[128]

In theory, payment of the premium was a condition precedent to the effectiveness of the policy. In practice, premiums were not paid until long after the policy was effected, under a system of running accounts between brokers and underwriters. Despite this practice, underwriters formally acknowledged payment of the premium in the policy, which meant that the assured's claim could not be defeated by an argument that the premium had not in fact been received, unless there was a taint of fraud by the assured.[129] Under this system, the underwriter considered the premium as having been already paid by the assured, and looked for payment to the broker, who could rely on any defence the assured might have, such as that the insurance was illegal.[130] The broker in turn looked to the assured for his payment. Parke B. explained it thus in 1829:

By the course of dealing, the broker has an account with the underwriter; in that account the broker gives the underwriter credit for the premium when the policy is effected, and he, as the agent of both the assured and the underwriter, is considered as having paid the premium to the underwriter, and the latter as having lent it to the broker again, and so becoming his creditor. The broker is then considered as having paid the premium for the assured.[131]

This rule, which originated in the express acknowledgment of payment in a Lloyd's policy, was by the end of the nineteenth century generalized to all marine policies and grounded on mercantile custom, so that it was accepted as a matter of law that the broker was liable for the premium.[132]

The assured also had to disclose to the insurer all information which was likely to affect his judgment. It was settled by the eighteenth century that an insurance policy was a contract which required the utmost good faith from the contracting

---

[126] *Ionides* v. *Pacific Insurance Co* (1871) LR 6 QB 674 at 684–5.

[127] The use of slips was prohibited by numerous revenue statutes dating from the eighteenth century: 11 Geo. I c. 30, 35 Geo. III c. 63. 54 Geo. III c. 144 made the use of stamped slips legal and the law was reformed by 30 Vict. c. 23.

[128] This meant that if the policy were never drawn up, the assured could not sue on the slip: *Fisher* v. *Liverpool Marine Insurance Co* (1873) LR 8 QB 469, (1874) LR 9 QB 418. See also *Warwick* v. *Slade* (1811) 3 Camp. 127; *Parry* v. *The Great Ship Co* (1864) 4 B. & S. 556. See also the observations in *Xenos* v. *Wickham* (1866) LR 2 HL 296 at 315. See also Arthur Cohen, 'Notes on Marine Insurance Law' 30 LQR (1914) 29 at 34.

[129] *Dalzell* v. *Mair* (1808) 1 Camp. 532 at 533. See also *De Gaminde* v. *Pigou* (1812) 4 Taunt. 246.

[130] *Jenkins* v. *Power* (1817) 6 M. & S. 282.   [131] *Power* v. *Butcher* (1829) 10 B. & C. 329 at 347.

[132] *Universo Insurance Co of Milan* v. *Merchants Marine Insurance Co* [1897] 2 QB 93.

parties,[133] since the insurer did not have the same information about the nature of the risk as the assured, and had to rely on the truth of the latter's representations in setting the premium and accepting the risk.[134] Although the language of good faith was used, the courts were not concerned with the subjective good intentions or honesty of the parties. Since the aim was to protect the vulnerable insurer, the assured was required to disclose material matters within his knowledge, and was held to some implied warranties in the contract of insurance. Failure to comply with either undermined the contract, however *bona fide* the assured had been.

There was, firstly, a duty on the assured to disclose at the outset all known facts which were 'material' to the insurance as a matter of fact, and not merely those which he thought were material. As Baron Rolfe put it in 1850:

If he conceals anything that he knows to be material, it is a fraud: but besides that, if he conceals anything that may influence the rate of premium which the underwriter may require, although he does not know that it would have that effect, such concealment entirely vitiates the policy.[135]

Any fact was material which would affect the judgment of a rational insurer.[136] Since the question of materiality was one for the jury, any person seeking insurance ran a risk of losing his policy if he withheld information on the assumption either that it was not material or that it was already known to the other party.[137] However, if a representation had been substantially, though not strictly, complied with, or if it was immaterial, the policy remained valid.

There was some uncertainty about the doctrinal basis for vitiating an insurance contract for misrepresentation or non-disclosure. One approach was to examine the issue in contractual terms. This was to say that there was an implied term of the contract that full disclosures should be made and all representations be accurate,[138] their accuracy being a condition precedent to the contract.[139] An alternative approach was to say that the notion of 'good faith' in contract extended the reach of fraud, so that non-fraudulent misrepresentations would be seen as 'constructive' frauds. As J. J. Park put it, 'If there be misrepresentation, it will avoid the policy as a fraud, not as part of the agreement'.[140] The advantage of

---

[133] Émérigon, *Traité des Assurances*, tome 1, ch. 1, sect. 5, pp. 18–21

[134] *Carter* v. *Boehm* (1766) 3 Burr. 1905 at 1909.

[135] *Dalglish* v. *Jarvie* (1850) 2 Mac. & G. 231 at 243.

[136] *Ionides* v. *Pender* (1874) LR 9 QB 531 at 537–9, *Rivaz* v. *Gerussi* (1880) 6 QBD 222; *Tate* v. *Hyslop* (1885) 15 QBD 368.

[137] *Pawson* v. *Watson* (1778) 2 Cowp. 785. Cf. *De Hahn* v. *Hartley* (1786) 1 T.R. 343.

[138] See Duer, *Marine Insurance*, 2: 646; *Moens* v. *Heyworth* (1842) 10 M. & W. 147 at 157–8.

[139] Phillips, *Insurance* (4th edn, 1854), i, p. 289, § 537.

[140] Park, *Marine Insurances* (1st edn, 1787), 222; Marshall, *Treatise on the Law of Insurance* (3rd edn, 1823), 1, 450. Arnould wrote that English courts took this approach, although he preferred Duer's: Arnould, *Marine Insurance* (2nd edn, 1857), 548 (s. 196).

this view was that it avoided the problem faced by the 'contractual' approach of explaining how pre-contractual parol statements could (in violation of the general rule) be used to vary the meaning of a written contract.

The dilemma was illustrated particularly in two areas, where doctrinal disagreements produced different outcomes. First, early nineteenth-century courts were divided over whether an insurance contract was vitiated because of misrepresentations regarding future events, such as the date a vessel would sail.[141] Those who favoured making the assured liable for such representations, such as Arnould, based their arguments on the idea that the accuracy of statements about things under their control or within their knowledge was a condition precedent to the underwriter's liability.[142] The counter-argument focused on the fact that representations about future events concerned mere expectations, and that if the insurer wanted guarantees about them, he could so stipulate in his contract. This was to consider misrepresentations about future events not to be a breach of good faith, as misrepresentations about present ones were. Arnould's argument became harder to sustain after it was decided in *Jorden* v. *Money* that misrepresentations concerning future matters were not actionable in the general law of contract.[143] The insurance question was only definitively resolved in 1906, when the Marine Insurance Act enacted (s 20(5)) that misrepresentations about matters of expectation were only actionable if they had not been made in good faith.[144]

The problem was seen secondly in the context of insurances effected by agents. It had long been established that a principal was bound by the misrepresentations or concealments of an agent in effecting the policy, since what was known to the agent was deemed to be known to the principal.[145] There was some disagreement, however, over whether a contract of insurance was vitiated if an agent who took no part in effecting the insurance—such as the captain of a vessel—failed to inform his principal about something material to the insurance. American jurists were divided on the matter. Joseph Story felt that a policy should not be vitiated under these circumstances,[146] but John Duer felt that where the insurer

---

[141] *Dennistoun* v. *Lillie* (1821) 3 Bligh. 202; *Edwards* v. *Footner* (1808) 1 Camp. 530 at 531. Contrast the approach in *Flinn* v. *Tobin* (1829) M. & M. 367 at 369. See also *Flinn* v. *Headlam* (1829) 9 B. & C. 693.

[142] Arnould, *Marine Insurance* (2nd edn, 1857), 557 (s. 200). His view was shared by a number of mid-century treatise writers, looking at American decisions, who held that both 'affirmative' and 'promissory' representations had to be accurate. The terms were coined by Marshall, *Treatise on the Law of Insurance* (4th edn, by W. Shee, 1861), 345. See also Duer, *Marine Insurance* 2: 657; Phillips, *Insurance* (2nd edn, 1840), 1: 232.

[143] *Jorden* v. *Money* (1854) 5 H.L.C. 183. On this case, see pp. 368–9.

[144] A. Cohen noted that this was an alteration in the law: 'The Marine Insurance Bill' 19 *LQR* (1903) 367 at 375.

[145] *Fitzherbert* v. *Mather* (1785) 1 T.R. 11 at 16; *Gladstone* v. *King* (1813) 1 M. & S. 35 at 38.

[146] *Ruggles* v. *General Interest Insurance Co* 4 Masons Rep. 74, aff'd in *General Interest Insurance Co* v. *Ruggles* 25 US (12 Wheat) 408 (1827).

and assured were equally morally innocent, 'the loss must be borne by him who employed and trusted the person, from whose act or default it proceeded'.[147] Mid-century English courts took Duer's approach, voiding policies where the owner of the goods had been misled by his agents. In *Proudfoot* v. *Montefiori*, the Queen's Bench held that '[t]he insurer is entitled to assume, as the basis of the contract between him and the assured, that the latter will communicate to him every material fact which the assured has, or, in the ordinary course of business, ought to have knowledge'.[148]

The question was revisited by the Court of Appeal and House of Lords in 1886 in *Blackburn, Low & Co* v. *Vigors*. In this case, the plaintiffs had instructed a broker to effect a policy of reinsurance on an overdue ship. While unsuccessfully seeking to do so, the broker received news that the ship had been lost. The plaintiffs, who were unaware of the loss, subsequently effected a 'lost or not lost' policy through another broker, who was equally unaware of the loss: and the question was raised whether the plaintiffs' policy should be vitiated on the ground that the uncommunicated knowledge of first agent was to be imputed to the principal. In the Court of Appeal, a majority held that the plaintiffs could not recover.[149] Although the plaintiffs were guilty of no moral wrong, the majority felt that an approach needed to be taken to induce all agents to act in perfect good faith. The tool to achieve this was in effect to make an implied term of the insurance contract that the assured would communicate all material information within the knowledge of his employees. Lord Esher dissented, rejecting and criticizing the rule in *Proudfoot*. He accepted that it was a condition precedent in insurance contracts that all material matters within the knowledge of the person taking out the insurance should be communicated. But he did not feel that there was a condition precedent that the principal would guarantee that all his employees kept him fully informed of everything in the business.

Although the Court of Appeal's decision was overturned, the Lords did not accept Esher's views, and instead endorsed the rule in *Proudfoot*.[150] This rule was codified in 1906 in the Marine Insurance Act which declared that the assured 'is deemed to know every circumstance which, in the ordinary course of business, ought to be known by him' (s 18(1)). Even if the agent took no part in negotiating the insurance, if it was ordinarily his duty to communicate information to his principal, the latter would be deemed to have knowledge of the matter. As a

---

[147] Duer, *Marine Insurance*, vol. ii, 419, 422. See also Phillips, *Insurance* (4th edn, 1854), ii, § 549, p. 294.

[148] (1867) LR 2 QB 511 at 521–1.   [149] *Blackburn, Low & Co* v. *Vigors* (1886) 17 QBD 553 at 577.

[150] The Lords held that this broker only had a limited agency (which had lapsed by the time the insurance was effected). In this case, the nature of his agency did not require him to make the disclosures to his principal. *Blackburn, Low & Co* v. *Thomas Vigors* (1887) 12 App Cas 531.

result, the basis of this rule seemed to be where an insurance policy was voided for misrepresentation or concealment, it was not as a result of a moral fault or breach of good faith by the assured, but as a result of his failure to fulfil a condition precedent, which cast certain duties on him.

If a term was incorporated into a policy, it was regarded as a warranty, which had to be strictly complied with, regardless of its materiality or of the assured's knowledge.[151] Policies included express warranties, such as the day of sailing of the ship, or a warranty of neutrality. There were also warranties implied by law, which sought to promote good faith between the parties. One such was the warranty of seaworthiness,[152] which meant that the ship had to be reasonably fit for the particular voyage insured.[153] This condition attached at the moment the policy was made. If the ship was unseaworthy at that moment, the policy was vitiated even if it was repaired before the voyage and was lost for other reasons.[154] By contrast, if the ship became unseaworthy during the voyage, this did not vitiate the policy.[155] If an insurer wished to have a warranty of continued seaworthiness, this had to be explicitly stated in the policy. The courts also distinguished between the degrees of seaworthiness required for different stages of a particular voyage. Thus, a policy 'at and from' a port would not be vitiated if a ship, lost in port, was not yet in a fit state to go to sea, but was sufficiently seaworthy in port.[156]

Mid-century judges were divided over whether a warranty of seaworthiness should be implied in time policies (where the assured took out insurance for a period of time) as well as in voyage policies. In 1837, the Queen's Bench rejected an argument that the assured should be held responsible for seaworthiness throughout the voyage, holding that it was enough if the ship had been seaworthy at the commencement of the risk.[157] In 1853, the House of Lords went further, holding that there as no implied condition in time policies of seaworthiness at the time the risk commenced. The judges advising the Lords felt that different principles applied to time policies: in contrast to those insuring particular voyages, those taking out time policies were often unaware of the position or condition of

---

[151] *Douglas* v. *Scougall* (1816) 4 Dow. 269 (the assured unaware that a ship was unseaworthy).

[152] For 'if the ship be incapable of performing her voyage, there is no possibility of the underwriter's gaining the premium' (Lawrence J): *Christie* v. *Secretan* (1799) 8 T.R. 192 at 198.

[153] *Gibson* v. *Small* (1853) 4 H.L.C. 352 at 384; *Steel* v. *State Line Steamship Co* (1877) 3 App. Cas. 72 (Sc) at 77.

[154] *Forshaw* v. *Chabert* (1821) 3 B. & B. 158.

[155] See *Eden* v. *Parkinson* (1781) 2 Doug. 732 at 735; *Dixon* v. *Sadler* (1839) 5 M. & W. 405 at 415. Cf. *Sadler* v. *Dixon* (1841) 8 M. & W. 895 at 899.

[156] *Annen* v. *Woodman* (1810) 3 Taunt. 299. See also *Dixon* v. *Sadler* (1839) 5 M. & W. 405 at 414; *Biccard* v. *Shepherd* (1861) 14 Moo. P.C. 472 at 491; *Bouillon* v. *Lupton* (1863) 33 L.J. C.P. 37; *The Vortigern* [1899] P 140.

[157] *Hollingworth* v. *Brodrick* (1837) 7 Ad & El. 40 at 47.

the ship, and had no power to effect repairs. This meant that it would be unreasonable for the law to impose a condition which the assured could not fulfil.[158] Some judges, such as Sir William Erle, continued to argue that a warranty of seaworthiness should be implied in time policies—for modern communications could help overcome the problem of knowledge—but he failed to convince his brethren. As Campbell CJ saw it, underwriters could judge the condition of the ship as well as the assured; they could always seek express warranties; and they could charge higher premiums without them. If a shipowner wilfully and knowingly sent a bad ship to sea, he could not recover, but absent such signs of fraud, there was no warranty.[159]

What was the effect of misstatements by the assured? According to Lord Mansfield, since the accuracy of a warranty was a condition precedent to the contract, the policy was void *ab initio* if it was not complied with.[160] However, this view was controversial. Nineteenth-century treatise writers argued that the contract would only be discharged by the breach of warranty, and that the insurer's liabilities prior to the breach remained in place.[161] This issue was explored in cases of deviation. It was an implied term of the policy that the ship should not deviate from the route. Early nineteenth-century courts held that breach of the condition not to deviate only terminated a contract at the point of deviation, and did not render the policy void *ab initio*. If a captain intended to sail from and to the ports mentioned in the policy, but planned in addition to make an intermediate voyage not contemplated in it, then the policy would not be vitiated 'until the vessel arrives at the dividing point of the two voyages'.[162] If any loss occurred prior to that point, the assured could recover. On the other hand, if the captain intended from the outset to sail to a different port from that indicated in the policy, he would be regarded as never having commenced the voyage insured, so that the policy would not come into effect. Whether the policy was void *ab initio* therefore turned on whether, prior to departure, the assured had an intention to abandon, or only to deviate, which turned on whether the ultimate destination

---

[158] *Gibson* v. *Small* (1852–3) 4 H.L.C. 352 at 405, affirming *Small* v. *Gibson* (1849) 16 QB 141.

[159] See Erle's views in *Gibson* v. *Small* (1852–3) 4 H.L.C. at 383; *Thompson* v. *Hopper* (1856) 6 E. & B. 172 at 185; for the majority view see *Thompson* v. *Hopper* (1856) 6 E. & B. 172 at 188; *Fawcus* v. *Sarsfield* (1856) 6 E. & B. 192; *Michael* v. *Tredwin* (1856) 17 C.B. 551; *Dudgeon* v. *Pembroke* (1877) 2 App. Cas. 284.

[160] *De Hahn* v. *Hartley* (1786) 1 T.R. 343. See also *Rich* v. *Parker* (1798) 7 T.R. 705.

[161] Phillips, *Insurance* (4th edn, 1854), i, p. 434, § 771. Mansfield's view was reiterated in Arnould, *Marine Insurance* (2nd edn, 1857), i, p. 629, § 224. See also Arnould, *Marine Insurance* (10th edn, 1921), § 634.

[162] *Hare* v. *Travis* (1827) 7 B. & C. 14 at 17–18. An intention to deviate would not vitiate a policy: *Kewley* v. *Ryan* (1794) 2 H. Bl. 343 at 348. See also *Thellusson* v. *Ferguson* (1780) 1 Doug. 361.

had been changed.[163] In 1906, the Marine Insurance Act confirmed (s 33(3)) that if a warranty was not complied with, the insurer was only discharged from liability from the date of the breach of warranty, without prejudice to prior liabilities.

The fact that misrepresentations and breaches of warranty did not void the policy *ab initio* was also seen from the fact that underwriters were not always obliged to return the premium in such cases. Although it was settled that premiums could not be recovered where there had been fraud,[164] a 'mere misrepresentation without fraud' did not prevent the assured recovering his premium 'where the risk never attached'.[165] If the risk had been run, the premium could not be recovered.[166] Thus, if the assured breached a warranty that the ship would sail on a specified day, he could recover premiums, as the risk was never run; but if he breached a warranty by a deviation, he could not recover the premiums as the risk had been run.[167]

Fire and Life Policies

Both fire and life offices generated their business through insurance agents.[168] In fire and life insurances, premiums had to reach the office before the policy was effective.[169] If the insurance company's agent defrauded the customer, by retaining the premiums paid for himself, or by issuing a false policy, it was the policy-holder, rather than the company, who bore the loss. This was because insurance agents were not regarded as having authority to make contracts for the company.[170] This also meant that if an agent accepted late payment of a premium, or allowed a policy-holder to revive a policy by accepting back payments,[171] the company would not be bound, even if it had debited the agent's accounts for the

---

[163] See *Heselton v. Allnutt* (1813) 1 M. & S. 46.

[164] See *Tyler v. Horne* (1785) in Marshall, *Treatise on the Law of Insurance* (3rd edn, 1823), 661.

[165] *Feise v. Parkinson* (1812) 4 Taunt. 640 at 641; *Anderson v. Thornton* (1853) 8 Ex. 425; *Penson v. Lee* (1800) 2 B. & P. 330; *Colby v. Hunter* (1827) 3 C. & P. 7.

[166] *Tyrie v. Fletcher* (1777) 2 Cowp. 666 at 668. If there were distinct risks, part of the premium could be returned: *Stevenson v. Snow* (1761) 3 Burr. 1237.

[167] Equally, if a risk began when the insurance was legal and then became illegal (due to the outbreak of war), the premium could not be returned, as the risk had begun: *Furtado v. Rogers* (1802) 3 B. & P. 191 at 201.

[168] In 1850, there were 13,000 agents working for fire offices. Pearson, *Insuring the Industrial Revolution*, 19.

[169] In 1896 the Court of Appeal allowed a claim where the premium had not yet been paid, since the wording of the policy indicated that the payment had already been made. *Roberts v. Security Co* [1897] 1 QB 111. But this approach was not later followed: *Equitable Fire and Accident Office v. The Ching Wo Hong* [1907] AC 96.

[170] *Linford v. The Provincial Horse and Cattle Insurance Co* (1864) 24 Beav. 291.

[171] See *The British Industry Life Assurance Co v. Ward* (1856) 17 C.B. 644.

premium. As Parke B. explained in a case of 1840, insurance companies only debited agents' accounts 'to keep their agents right' by being able to penalize them, 'but they did not mean thereby to make themselves liable for the amount of the policy'.[172]

Both fire and life offices allowed 'days of grace' to renew insurance, by including terms in their policies that they would not be voided if the event insured against occurred within a certain period (15 or 30 days) after the end of the year, provided that the premium was paid during that time. After a decision in 1794, when the King's Bench held that no claim could be made for a fire during the days of grace, if the premium had not been paid,[173] insurance offices made it clear that anyone with a policy of one year or more should be taken to be covered for an extra 15 days. However, the King's Bench confirmed in 1805 that this did not mean that the policy was for a year plus 15 days; and that the office retained the right to decline to insure the policy-holder at the end of the year.[174] Judges were also unsympathetic to policy-holders who sought to recover on policies after making payments during the days of grace when the event insured against had already occurred. Where the assured died in the period of grace, his executors could not tender the premium due. As Cresswell J. put it in 1857, '[t]he policy was to continue provided he, the assured, paid the premium within the twenty-one days; and this, we think, did not give his executors the right to pay it after his death'.[175]

Given the serious financial consequences of a failure to keep a life policy alive, insofar as the benefits accrued would be lost, insurance companies were generally prepared to allow the assured to revive policies. A condition was included in policies allowing its revival on payment of a specified penalty, and provided the assured remained in good health. The meaning of such conditions was discussed in a number of cases arising from the death of R.P.H. Jodrell, the dissolute and drunken heir of Sir Richard Jodrell who had borrowed large sums anticipating an inheritance of over £13,000 a year. Those who lent money to Jodrell took out insurance on his life. In turn, the insurers protected themselves by reinsuring, so that by the time of his death in November 1855, there were some 50 policies of insurance on his life, running to over £100,000.[176] In *Pritchard* v. *The Merchant's*

---

[172] *Acey* v. *Fernie* (1840) 7 M. & W. 151 at 156. See also *London and Lancashire Life Assurance Co* v. *Fleming* [1897] AC 499 (PC).

[173] *Tarleton* v. *Staniforth* (1794) 5 T.R. 695 at 700.

[174] *Salvin* v. *James* (1805) 6 East 571 at 581. In this case, the policy-holders, who had declined to pay a higher premium for a second year of insurance, attempted to obtain the benefit of it by tendering the higher sum within the days of grace, after a fire had destroyed their cotton mill.

[175] *Simpson* v. *The Accidental Death Insurance Co* (1857) 2 C.B. N.S. 257 at 295. Cf. *Want* v. *Blunt* (1810) 12 East 184.

[176] In *Prince of Wales Assurance Co* v. *Harding* (1858) E. B. & E. 183, the official manager of the Athenaeum Life Assurance Society sought to resist a claim for £6500 after the death of Jodrell, on a

and Tradesman's Mutual Life Assurance Society, the plaintiffs (an insurance company which had reinsured Jodrell's life) paid the premium the day after Jodrell's death, and one day after the expiry of the days of grace. The defendants, who were (like the plaintiffs) unaware of his death, accepted the cheque. This led the plaintiffs to claim that the policy had been revived, with the insurers waiving any need for proof of Jodrell's health or the payment of a fine. The fact that the subject of the insurance was dead, it was argued, was not relevant.[177] However, the Common Pleas found for the defendants. As Willes J. saw it, life assurance required the subject to be alive: 'The renewals, like the original policy, clearly are only for the future assurance of a living person.'[178] The decision created much anxiety,[179] and many insurance companies responded with advertisements that all claims would be admitted for deaths occurring during the days of grace, provided that the premiums were fully paid by the time this expired.[180] The fact that a payment could not be made on an annual policy within the days of grace when the life had dropped was confirmed by the Court of Appeal in 1902, when Collins MR held that 'the person on whose life the matter turns must be alive, and [...] if he is dead and cannot come within the given time to ask for a future insurance, no one else can'.[181] According to the law, those who were assured therefore had to be sure to remember to pay within the days of grace; and those who insured on the lives of third parties needed to be sure to pay before the life dropped.[182] But it was open to insurers to specify in their policies that they would pay out during the days of grace; while from the mid-nineteenth century, many insurers sought to reassure their customers that they would regard the life as covered during the days of grace.

Those seeking fire and life insurance also had a duty to disclose information which might influence the insurer, prior to the making of the contract.[183] The fact that policies were effected via agents induced some courts to take a more generous approach to the policy-holder's duty to disclose information. This was

policy of reinsurance taken out by the plaintiffs. They claimed that the premiums due had been paid after the days of grace, when running accounts were settled. But the Queen's Bench ruled that the fact that the defendants had been credited with the sums due within the period of grace represented payment. See further, *In re Athenaeum Life Assurance Society* (1859) 3 De G. & J. 660.

[177] It was argued that *Earl of March* v. *Pigot* (1771) 5 Burr. 2802 had shown that parties could insure on someone already dead, while marine policies 'lost or not lost' were allowed.

[178] *Pritchard* v. *The Merchant's and Tradesman's Mutual Life Assurance Society* (1858) 3 C.B. N.S. 622 at 643–4.

[179] See *The Times*, 18 February 1858, col. 7f.   [180] (1858) 19 *Post Mag.* 140.

[181] *Stuart* v. *Freeman* [1903] 1 KB 47 at 52. This did not, however, apply when the payments were in quarterly instalments.

[182] For continuing anxieties, suggesting that insurers would insist on prompt payment, see *The Times*, 21 January 1878, col. 10d.

[183] *Bufe* v. *Turner* (1815) 6 Taunt. 338.

particularly the case where statements in a proposal had been filled out by the company's agent, as often occurred in fire cases. If the agent did more than merely report back to his employers the information he had been given, such as where he surveyed the property or described the condition of the subject of insurance, then the misrepresentation would not be attributed to the policy-holder.[184] Similarly, if an agent had seen a property, some judges held that the assured was not required to disclose to the insurers such facts as he could presume they already knew.[185] Moreover, where representations were made about the property, it was sufficient if they were substantially, though not strictly, accurate.[186]

In fire cases, the mid-century courts also took a pro-client approach when dealing with warranties in the contract concerning the condition of the property. They rejected the arguments of the fire offices that any change in the use of a building was analogous to a deviation in a marine policy, and constituted a breach of the warranty.[187] In 1837, Lord Denman held that a condition stating that the insurance would be forfeited unless the building and the trades carried on in it were accurately described in the policy only applied to its state at the commencement of the policy; while the condition that the policy would be voided if changes were made to the use of the building without notice referred only to permanent alterations.[188] In taking this view, some judges revealed their limited understanding of the business of insurance. '[O]n general principles, a policy of insurance is not avoided by an alteration in the trade carried on upon the premises', Tindal CJ pronounced in 1845, adding, 'how can an alteration in the business after the policy has been effected be material to be made known to the company, to enable them to judge of the risk they have undertaken?'[189] Nine years later, the Queen's Bench took a more informed view, when holding that a policy-holder could not recover, after having added a storey to the insured building without telling his insurer. As Lord Campbell put it, 'the description in the policy amounts to a warranty that the assured would not, during the time specified in the policy, voluntarily do any thing to make the condition of the

---

[184] See *In re Universal Non-Tariff Fire Insurance Co, Forbes & Co's claim* (1875) LR 19 Eq 485. Contrast *Parsons v. Bignold* (1846) 15 L.J. Ch. 379. Contrast also the pro-client approach taken in *Bawden v. London, Edinburgh and Glasgow Assurance Co* [1892] 2 QB 534 with the tough approach in *Biggar v. Rock Life Assurance Co* [1902] 1 KB 516 at 523 (following *New York Life Insurance Co v. Fletcher* (1885) 117 US 519), where the policy-holder signed the statement.

[185] *Pimm v. Lewis* (1862) 2 F. & F. 778 at 780.

[186] J. W. Smith, *A Compendium of Mercantile law* (7th edn by G.M. Dowdeswell, 1865), 412. However, if in the policy the assured warranted the condition of the property insured, then the policy would be void if it were not strictly accurate, regardless of whether this made any difference to the risk: *Newcastle Fire Insurance Co v. Macmorran* (1815) 3 Dow. 255 at 262.

[187] See Manning Sjt's argument in *Pim v. Reid* (1845) 6 M. & G. 1 at 14.

[188] *Shaw v. Robberds* (1837) 6 Ad. & El. 75 at 82. See also *Dobson v. Sotheby* (1827) M. & M. 90.

[189] *Pim v. Reid* (1845) 6 M. & G. 1 at 19–20.

building vary from this description, so as thereby to increase the risk or liability of the underwriter'. In insurance against fire, there was an implied engagement that the assured would not alter the premises in a way to increase the risk.[190] In 1856, the Exchequer Chamber explained the position by stating that '[a]ll that an insurer [i.e. policyholder] is called upon to do, is, in the event of an increase of the risk—and in that event only, to give notice to the insurance company of the alteration of the risk'.[191] These cases suggested that if insurers wished to make it a condition precedent that there would be no alteration whatever in the use of a building, they had to make that distinctly clear. Many insurers did not need this hint, but had already redrafted their policies to cover themselves in the event of a change in use. Thus, the West of England Fire & Life began to require notice to be given not only of the introduction of steam engines, but of any other form of fire-heat. A cabinet maker who had brought a small steam engine onto his premises to test it, to see whether it was worth purchasing, but without telling his insurers, thereby lost the benefit of the insurance, regardless of whether its presence caused the fire.[192]

Life insurance generated the most frequent litigation over concealment and non-disclosure. The relevant information here was the health and habits of the life assured. Insurers sought to find out about the nature of the risk firstly by asking the person whose life was to be assured to fill out a proposal which would answer questions about his health. The 'life' might also be required to submit other documents, such as a personal statement answering specific questions about his health; and he might be seen by the insurer's medical representative and asked questions. In addition, there would be reference to the 'life's' medical practitioners and friends to give information about his health. As a result of these inquiries, the insurers would classify the life differently, charging different rates of premium. There was much room for dispute, not merely on factual questions, such as whether the 'life' was a drunkard or diseased. First, questions put by insurers by the middle of the nineteenth century were often very specific, asking detailed questions about health which might be answered *bona fide* but incorrectly. Secondly, many creditors insured the lives of third parties and were apt make *bona fide* statements about the 'life' which turned out to be false.

[190] *Sillem* v. *Thornton* (1854) 3 E. & B. 868 at 882, 888.
[191] *Stokes* v. *Cox* (1856) 1 H. & N. 533 at 540. In this case, the holder of a policy which stated that no steam engines were employed on the premises had installed a steam boiler without telling the office. The Exchequer Chamber held the policy not vitiated, as the risk was not increased. Where an alteration increased the risk, courts held there was a duty to communicate the fact: *Baxendale* v. *Harvey* (1859) 4 H. & N. 445; *Fowkes* v. *The Manchester and London Life Assurance Co* (1862) 3 F. & F. 441; *Fowkes* v. *The Manchester and London Life Assurance and Loan Co* (1863) 3 B. & S. 917 at 930; *Hemmings* v. *Sceptre Life Association* [1905] 1 Ch. 365.
[192] *Glen* v. *Lewis* (1853) 8 Ex. 607.

Where the policy made it clear on its proper construction that statements made in the proposal formed the basis of the insurance contract, they had to be strictly true; and so the policy was voided even if the matter omitted was not material or had been omitted without bad faith.[193] Thus, one policy was voided where the assured, who had shown symptoms of consumption, failed to disclose them in the erroneous belief that they were not such symptoms;[194] while in another, an erroneous statement by a man about his medical treatment, which a jury found immaterial, was held to void a policy. The rule applied even where the assured made a *bona fide* statement according to his knowledge. 'A statement is not the less untrue', Lyndhurst CB ruled in 1834, 'because the party making it is not apprized of its untruth.'[195] In 1884, the House of Lords confirmed that a person made a warranty about his health at his peril, and that a policy would be vitiated even if the disease was latent and unknown to the sufferer. As Lord Blackburn put it, competent contracting parties could 'make the actual existence of anything a condition precedent to the inception of any contract'.[196] Those taking out life assurance policies were therefore best advised to write in that the statements made were 'to the best of their knowledge'.[197] Indeed, where the assured had been permitted to make a declaration that he was not aware of any disorder, the insurers were held to have limited their right to disclosure 'to that of being informed of what is in the knowledge of the assured, not only as to its existence in point of fact, but also as to its materiality'.[198]

If the statement in the policy was found not to be a warranty, but only a representation, it was for the jury to say whether it was material, as a matter of fact.[199] As Bayley J. pointed out, if juries were permitted to take into account the policy-holder's belief regarding the materiality of the information, people might be tempted to suppress information, since it would be difficult to prove in any trial what the assured believed to be material.[200] Nonetheless, where the matter was not warranted, the courts were satisfied with less information than was

[193] *Anderson* v. *Fitzgerald* (1853) 4 H.L.C. 484. Some judges, such as Lord St Leonards, regretted the harshness of the rule: see at pp. 510–11, 513–14. See also *Cazenove* v. *The British Equitable Assurance Co* (1859) 6 C.B. N.S. 437 at 452. See also *Macdonald* v. *Law Union Insurance Co* (1874) LR 9 QB 328.

[194] *Geach* v. *Ingall* (1845) 14 M. & W. 95.   [195] *Duckett* v. *Williams* (1834) 2 C. & M. 348 at 351.

[196] *Thomson* v. *Weems and Others* (1884) 9 App Cas 671 at 683–4, overruling *Hutchison* v. *National Loan Assurance Co* (1845) 7 Court of Sess. Cas. 2nd ser. 467.

[197] Charles John Bunyon., *The Law of Life Assurance* (3rd edn by C. J. Bunyon and J. V. Vesey Fitzgerald (1891), 40.

[198] *Jones* v. *The Provincial Insurance Co* (1857) 3 C.B. N.S. 65 at 86.

[199] The jury had to consider whether it was material to the insurance effected, and would influence the rate of premiums to be set: see *Shilling* v. *The Accidental Death Insurance Co* (1858) 1 F. & F. 116; *London Assurance* v. *Mansel* (1879) 11 Ch D 363.

[200] *Lindenau* v. *Desborough* (1828) 8 B. &. C. 586 at 592.

required in cases of warranty. In *Watson v. Mainwaring* in 1813, the Equitable Insurance Office refused to pay the executors of a man who had died of a dyspepsia, having failed to make a declaration that he had a 'disorder tending to shorten life'. It was left to the jury to say whether the disease he had was one which had a tendency to shorten life. When the insurers argued that the fact he had died of the disease was conclusive proof that he had a disease tending to shorten life, the Common Pleas dismissed the argument. As Chambre J. put it, 'All disorders have more or less a tendency to shorten life'.[201]

Perhaps the most contentious problems were raised when creditors took out insurance on their debtors. In such a situation, the information about the life assured had to come from the person whose life was assured or his friends. In the early nineteenth century, the courts held to the view that the statements made by such people bound the person taking out the policy. For instance, in *Everett v. Desborough* in 1829, the plaintiff effected a life policy with the Atlas Insurance Company on the life of James House. Although he appeared to be 'a remarkably handsome athletic man, bearing all the external indications of rude health', House was in fact a binge drinker, who could be drunk for ten days at a time, 'swallowing any thing and every thing that came in his way'. Neither the plaintiff, nor the Atlas's agent, Lye, who had suggested this insurance, was aware of this fact. However, the King's Bench held the policy void, holding that the plaintiff had made House his agent for effecting the insurance, and so was responsible for his misrepresentation.[202]

But it was soon clear that some judges were unhappy with this result and began to modify the law. In 1838, in *Huckman v. Fernie*, the plaintiff took out an insurance on his wife, who failed to disclose information about her health (which was unknown to her husband) when examined at the insurance office. The Exchequer judges held that she was only to be regarded as his agent for the purpose of answering the questions put to her; and since none of them raised the issue, his insurance was not vitiated by her non-disclosure.[203] The principle was taken further by the Exchequer Chamber in *Wheelton v. Hardisty* in 1857, one of the cases arising on the many policies of insurance taken out on Jodrell's life. Jodrell had been less than frank about his habits, claiming that he had been temperate since his marriage and was now a man of regular habits. Because of this, a number of insurers sought to dispute their liability. They got little sympathy

---

[201] *Watson v. Mainwaring* (1813) 4 Taunt. 763 at 764.

[202] *Everett v. Desborough* (1829) 5 Bing. 504 at 508. See also *Maynard v. Rhode* (1824) 1 Car. & P. 361 at 363; *Morrison v. Muspratt* (1827) 4 Bing. 60.

[203] *Huckman v. Fernie* (1838) 3 M. & W. 505. See also the reporters' note to *Rawlins v. Desborough* (1840) 2 Moo. & Rob. 328, suggesting that the policy-holder should not be liable for falsehoods which came from referees.

from the public, not least where they had proclaimed their policies to be indisputable.[204] In *Wheelton* v. *Hardisty*, the Exchequer Chamber showed that the
courts would be no more sympathetic to the insurer. The case was brought by the
Norwich Union Reversionary Company, which had taken out a policy with the
Westminster and General Life Association on Jodrell's life. Although Jodrell's
answers to the questions put by the insurance company had been fraudulent and
false—as had those given by his doctor and his friend—no fraud had been perpetrated by the policy-holder. When the case came to trial, Lord Campbell CJ
rejected the defendants' argument that Jodrell was the agent for the plaintiffs in
answering the questions put to him, and bound them by his frauds. Admitting
that life policies were of *uberrima fides*, just as marine policies were, Campbell
took the view (accepted by his brother judges in the Queen's Bench) that 'there is
no analogy between the statements of the "life" or the referees in the negotiation
of a life insurance and the statements of an insurance broker to underwriters,
by which he induces them to subscribe the policy'.[205] However, a verdict for the
defendants was entered on the plea that the declaration made in the policy by
the plaintiffs that he had no diseases tending to shorten his life was a warranty
which was false in fact. The Queen's Bench upheld the verdict on these grounds.
In the view of the majority,[206] the declaration was a positive warranty of a matter
of fact, which bound the policy-holder. Nor could this be challenged by an equitable replication, that the insurers had stated in their prospectus that the policy
would be indisputable,[207] since there was no evidence that they had been influenced by it. In turn, the Exchequer Chamber reversed this decision. The argument that the statement by the policy-holders was a warranty was rejected, since
there was no stipulation in the policy that it was to be the basis of the contract.
The accuracy of the statement was not a condition precedent to the effectiveness
of the policy; instead, the policy would only be vitiated by fraud on the part of the
policy-holders. As Willes J. put it, 'unless it were untrue to the knowledge of the
plaintiffs, and therefore fraudulent, the mere untruth of it would not avoid any
policy in which it was introduced, the policy containing no express stipulation
to that effect'.[208] In this case, the Exchequer Chamber went out of its way to assist
those who had insured the lives of third parties. In life insurance cases, the accuracy of statements was not to be a condition precedent to the policy attaching,
and the policy could only be vitiated by 'moral fraud' on the part of the assured.

---

[204] See (1856) 17 *Post Mag.* 194, 195.   [205] *Wheelton* v. *Hardisty* (1857) 8 E. & B. 232 at 270.
[206] Erle, Wightman and Compton JJ, Lord Campbell CJ dissenting.
[207] It was held in *Wood* v. *Dwarris* (1856) 11 Ex. 493 that where a policy-holder acted on the prospectus, the company was bound by it, even where they made the insurance declaration the basis of
their contract.
[208] *Wheelton* v. *Hardisty* (1857) 8 E. & B. 232 at 299.

To protect the assured, the standard of disclosure required thus appeared to be lower than in marine cases.[209]

If a life policy was void for failure to disclose information, could premiums be returned? This was a crucial question in life assurance, where premiums had been paid over a long period of time, since the value of a forfeited policy would be high. Insurance companies often made provision for this, by inserting in the policy a term that if any initial statement were false, or if the assured behaved in ways forbidden by the policy, the company would have the right to retain any premiums paid. In upholding such clauses in the contract,[210] the courts in effect rejected the view that accurate disclosure was a condition precedent to the policy coming into operation at all, which might have prevented the company relying on the clause in the contract allowing them to retain the premiums. In practice, companies were often willing to return premiums.[211] Life insurers were only too well aware of the loss of business they could incur if they disputed paying out on policies, and sought to retain premiums they had received from *bona fide* customers. Nonetheless, the law gave them the leeway to decide when to appear generous, and when to make an example. While courts of equity when cancelling life insurances were usually asked to restore any moneys received by the assurers seeking to cancel the policy,[212] where the assured had been guilty of fraud, the court would refuse to return premiums.[213] Equally, where the person making the insurance had no insurable interest, he could not repudiate the contract and recover his premiums for failure of consideration.[214]

4. CLAIMS ON THE POLICY

Marine Policies

The policy issued by Lloyd's underwriters developed into a standard form in the eighteenth century. It covered perils of the sea, fire, enemies, pirates, jettison, takings at sea, and barratry and 'all other perils, losses, and misfortunes that have or shall have come to the hurt, detriment, or damage' of the ship or goods. When a claim was made on a policy, it had to be determined whether it was for one of the risks covered, and whether the risk covered was the cause of the loss.

---

[209] See the hostile reaction to the case in (1858) 31 *LT* 213.
[210] e.g. *Duckett* v. *Williams* (1834) 2 Car. & M. 348.
[211] See e.g. *London Assurance* v. *Mansel* (1879) 11 Ch D 363.
[212] e.g. *Barker* v. *Walters* (1844) 8 Beav. 92.
[213] *The Prince of Wales &c Association Co* v. *Palmer* (1858) 25 Beav. 605.
[214] *Howard* v. *Refuge Friendly Society* (1886) 54 LT 644; *Harse* v. *Pearl Life Assurance* (1903) 2 KB 92.

In the early nineteenth century, judges took a narrow interpretation of the meaning of the words 'all other perils'. In 1816, Lord Ellenborough held that these words did not cover any kind of damage whatever, but 'other cases of marine damage of the like kind with those which are specially enumerated and occasioned by similar causes'.[215] In 1820, Best J. ruled similarly that the general words were designed 'to enlarge the construction of the terms by which particular losses are before mentioned, and to extend them to cases coming very near, but not precisely within the specified losses'.[216] To fall under this clause, the event which had occurred had to be *ejusdem generis* as the enumerated perils. This meant, for instance, that where goods were spoiled because the vessel was delayed by bad weather, there was no loss within the terms of the policy.[217] In the later nineteenth century, when ships were damaged by boiler explosions at sea, some attempts were made to qualify the *ejusdem generis* rule, to allow 'the general phrase [to] cover all those things, without exposure to the risk of which navigation cannot take place'.[218] But in 1887, the House of Lords held that any departure from the *ejusdem generis* would unsettle the interpretation of marine policies. The marine policy was regarded as a document whose meaning was settled over time: and if insurers wanted to provide new forms of cover, it had to be specified.[219]

Underwriters were only liable for losses which had directly resulted from the peril insured against. In insurance cases, the courts strictly applied the maxim that *causa proxima et non remota spectatur*. If the loss had been caused by any intervening event, then the policy-holder could not claim. If a ship ran aground on enemy territory because of the perils of the sea, and was undamaged, but was then captured by local troops, the loss would not be attributed to perils of the sea.[220] Similarly, if a ship which was driven ashore suffered a partial loss, but was then condemned by coastal authorities for the breach of an embargo, the insurers would be liable neither for the total loss (which had not been caused by a peril insured against), nor for the partial loss, since the assured could 'have no claim to indemnity where there is ultimately no damage to him from any peril insured against'.[221] Insurers were also protected by the rule that they were not liable for losses following any voluntary act by the assured, as where a ship was abandoned during an embargo which was later

---

[215] *Cullen* v. *Butler* (1816) 5 M. & S. 461 at 465.

[216] *Butler* v. *Wildman* (1820) 3 B. & Ald. 398 at 406. Cf. *Boehm* v. *Combe* (1813) 2 M. & S. 172; *Phillips* v. *Barber* (1821) 5 B. & Ald. 161; *Davidson* v. *Burnand* (1868) LR 4 CP 117.

[217] *Taylor* v. *Dunbar* (1869) LR 4 CP 206.

[218] *West India Telegraph Co* v. *Home and Colonial Insurance Co* (1880) 6 QBD 51 at 60 (Brett LJ summarizing Cockburn CJ's view). See also *Hamilton, Fraser & Co* v. *The Thames and Mersey Marine Insurance Co* (1886) 17 QBD 195.

[219] *The Thames and Mersey Marine Insurance Co* v. *Hamilton, Fraser & Co* (1887) 12 App Cas 484.

[220] *Green* v. *Elmslie* (1794) Peake N.P.C. 279.   [221] *Livie* v. *Janson* (1810) 12 East 648 at 654.

lifted.[222] Judges sometimes took the doctrine to controversial lengths. In 1836, for instance, the King's Bench held that a loss to the policy-holder, who was ordered by an arbitrator to pay compensation to the owner of a vessel after a collision at sea, was not proximately caused by the perils of the sea.[223]

These narrow rules of causation could also benefit policy-holders. In numerous early nineteenth-century cases, the assured recovered where the proximate cause had been a loss insured against, but where there had been prior negligence by one of the crew.[224] In 1821, Abbott CJ observed that to excuse underwriters where losses were remotely caused by the negligence of the crew would 'introduce an infinite number of questions, as to the quantum of care which, if used, might have prevented the loss'.[225] The assured was also covered if a ship had become unseaworthy at sea because of the negligence of the crew, since the proximate cause of loss was the unseaworthiness and not the negligence.[226] In 1856, Lord Campbell attempted to modify this rule, holding the policy-holder liable where he had knowingly sent an unseaworthy ship to sea. Campbell sought to apply the view of causation which was developing in tort law into insurance, by considering the key question to be 'not whether the wrongful act or neglect of the assured was the proximate cause or causa causans of the loss, but whether it was a cause without which the loss would not have happened'.[227] His attempt failed, for the Exchequer Chamber restated the old rule that the insurers were liable, if the proximate cause was the peril of the sea.[228] Insurers could not evade liability by attributing the loss to a remote cause without which the loss would not have occurred.[229]

Once it was shown that the peril insured against had caused the loss, the question was raised what sum the assured could recover. Insurers limited their liability

---

[222] *M'Carthy* v. *Abel* (1804) 5 East 388; *Inman Steamship Co* v. *Bischoff* (1881) 6 QBD 648, (1882) 7 App Cas 670. See also the voluntary acts in *Powell* v. *Gudgeon* (1816) 5 M. & S. 431; *Sarquy* v. *Hobson* (1827) 4 Bing. 131.

[223] In Denman CJ's view, since the policy-holder might have been required to pay more than the loss to his vessel, the excess sum was 'neither a necessary nor a proximate effect of the perils of the sea; it grows out of an arbitrary provision in the law of nations', *De Vaux* v. *Salvador* (1836) 4 Ad. & El. 420 at 432. Contrast Story J.'s approach in *Peters* v. *Warren Insurance Co* (1838) 3 Sumner's Mass. Rep. 389; 14 Peters SCR 99. Denman's decision was out of step with commercial needs, and policies were duly altered to give cover in case of collision.

[224] *Busk* v. *The Royal Exchange Assurance Co* (1818) 2 B. & Ald. 73. For other cases involving the negligence of crew, see *Bishop* v. *Pentland* (1827) 7 B. & C. 219; *Holdsworth* v. *Wise* (1828) 7 B. & C. 794 and *Shore* v. *Bentall* (1828) 7 B. & C. 798n; *Redman* v. *Wilson* (1845) 14 M. & W. 476.

[225] *Walker* v. *Maitland* (1821) 5 B. & Ald. 171 at 174.

[226] *Dixon* v. *Sadler* (1839) 5 M. & W. 405.

[227] *Thompson* v. *Hopper* (1856) 6 E. & B. 937at 951–2. On causation in tort law, see pp. 928–34.

[228] *Thompson* v. *Hopper* (1858) E. B. & E. 1038.

[229] See *The West India and Panama Telegraph Co* v. *The Home and Colonial Marine Insurance Co* (1880) 6 QBD 51; *Dudgeon* v. *Pembroke* (1874) LR 9 QB 581.

in the standard 'memorandum' in the Lloyd's policy, which stated that:

Corn, Fish, Fruit Flower, and Seed are warranted free from Average,[230] unless general, or the Ship be stranded; Sugar, Tobacco, Hemp, Flax, Hides and Skins are warranted free from Average under Five Pounds per Cent; and all other Goods, also the Ship and Freight, are warranted free from Average under Three Pounds per Cent, unless general, or the Ship be stranded.[231]

In the late eighteenth and nineteenth centuries, an elaborate set of rules developed on the basis of this apparently fixed and simple policy. Many of these rules derived from long-established mercantile practices, which themselves developed with commerce.

Under the memorandum, insurers were liable for 'general average'. The principle of general average, which predated insurance law, could be traced to the Rhodian laws. The notion was that if drastic steps had to be taken in an emergency to save a ship from being wrecked, which could entail jettisoning cargo, or cutting down a mast, then every one who was interested in the voyage had to contribute to pay for the sacrifice being made.[232] Whether a loss was covered by general average depended on the motivation of the parties at the time the action was taken. For instance, if a vessel were grounded, and goods were taken from it when it was unclear whether she could be refloated, the determination whether the cost of unloading could be recovered as general average turned on whether the aim of the parties when unloading had been to rescue the goods or the ship.[233] General average claims were not governed by the same rules of causation as other claims, since the loss did not depend only upon events, but upon the motivation of the actors faced with those events. By the later nineteenth century, it was thus agreed that losses covered included not merely those which were the *direct* consequence of the event, but those which were *natural* consequences of it.[234]

---

[230] 'Average' meant 'loss', and 'warranted free from average' meant that the item was excluded from the insurance.

[231] Thus memorandum was standardised in 1749 and revised in 1779 in response to attempts made to vary the customary policy in the interest of the assured; and by 1795, it had become compulsory to use this form. Wright and Fayle, *History of Lloyds*, 143. Though the clause was settled in the eighteenth century, other clauses were added to it, to clarify the extent of the cover. See e.g. the clause added in July 1883, quoted in William Gow, *Marine Insurance: A Handbook* (2nd edn, 1900), 187.

[232] See *Birkley* v. *Presgrave* (1801) 1 East 220 at 228. Gow, *Marine Insurance* (2nd edn, 1900), 283ff. It had to be extraordinary: see the comments of Lush J. in *Robinson* v. *Price* (1876) LR 2 QB 91.

[233] Equally, those who removed their goods to preserve them, when a ship ran aground, would not be held liable if other goods were later jettisoned to refloat it: *Royal Steam Packet Co* v. *English Bank of Rio de Janeiro* (1887) 19 QBD 362. Cf. *Kemp* v. *Halliday* (1865) 34 LJ NS QB 233 at 243.

[234] Charles McArthur, *The Contract of Marine Insurance* (2nd edn, 1890), 167–8n. This rule followed the development in *Hadley* v. *Baxendale*. See also *Anglo-Argentine Live Stock Agency* v. *Temperley Shipping Co* [1899] 2 QB 403, 410.

While the European practice was to regard as general average all spending incurred before the safe completion of the common venture, in England the obligation to contribute ceased as soon as the vessel was safe.[235] This divergence of approach caused some debate in the 1870s and 1880s, when the courts debated the liability of parties for spending incurred for the common benefit after an emergency at sea. For most of the nineteenth century, English average adjusters had accepted that the expense of discharging cargo from a ship which came into port in an emergency was general average, but did not regard the costs of warehousing, reshipment, and port charges as such, since the common danger was over once the goods were unloaded. However, by the 1870s, it was becoming increasingly common to insert into contracts of carriage a provision that general average questions were to be settled in accordance with agreed international rules. This was particularly the case after a conference of the Society for the Reform and Codification of the Law of Nations issued a revised set of rules in 1877 first drawn up in 1864, which came to be known as the York-Antwerp rules.[236] It was in this context, in 1879, that the test case of *Atwood* v. *Sellar & Co* was brought, after an eminent adjuster stated that the old practice was wrong. The case decided that the customary practice of English average adjusters contradicted 'the fundamental principle on which the whole doctrine of general average rests'; and that the continental rule should be followed.[237] However, four years later, in *Svendsen* v. *Wallace*, the House of Lords reiterated the English approach, that general average applied only to acts done to preserve the ship and the cargo, and not those done to ensure the success of the adventure.[238] These cases hardly left the law clear. In this context, the Association of Average Adjusters resolved to clarify their practice.[239] While the York-Antwerp rules were never legislated, they were incorporated into shipping contracts.

Liability for general average contribution existed independently of insurance. Nonetheless, with the development of insurance, those who were liable for general average contributions could recover from their insurers. For much of the nineteenth century, however, the question remained moot whether the party whose goods had been sacrificed could recover their entire value from his insurer

---

[235] See *Job* v. *Langton* (1856) 6 E. & B. 779, where it was held that once the cargo was safe, the cost of repairing a damaged ship fell on the ship alone. See also *Walthew* v. *Mavjorani* (1870) LR 5 Ex 121; *Svendson* v. *Wallace* (1885) 10 App Cas 404.

[236] Richard Lowndes, *The Law of General Average* (5th edn by E. L. De Hart and G. R. Rudolf, 1912), 788–802.

[237] *Atwood and Others* v. *Sellar & Co* (1879) 4 QBD 342 at 354, (1880) 5 QBD 286 (CA).

[238] *Svendsen* v. *Wallace* (1885) 10 App Cas 404, (1884) 13 QBD 69 at 77, overruling (1883) 11 QBD 616.

[239] Lowndes, *Law of General Average* (5th edn, 1912), 250–1; § 49.

(leaving him to chase the others for their contribution) or whether he could only recover the value of his contribution from the insurer. Treatise writers were divided.[240] The question was not settled until 1868, when the Common Pleas confirmed that the assured could claim in the first instance from his insurers, who in turn would be able to recover from the other contributors.[241]

In practice, general average payments were intimately connected with insurance by the nineteenth century. Once it had become clear that insurers would have to pay on these claims and recover from other contributors—in effect other insurers—the committee of Lloyd's began to seek to abolish the doctrine of general average in cases of voluntary sacrifice. It was felt that since insurers in any event paid general average claims, it would be more efficient when goods were jettisoned to have the insurer of the goods pay the loss, rather than requiring various insurers to sort out proportionate payments between themselves. According to Douglas Owen, secretary of the Alliance Company, the system added 12 per cent to the costs of claims. However, there was resistance to this idea from those who felt that it would allow shipowners too much power to limit their liability, and in effect encourage them to jettison goods to speed voyages. It was also opposed by those who felt that it would unsettle the law of insurance, since goods jettisoned might not be covered by the particular average. Although the idea was revived in the 1890s, it failed to take root.[242]

In contrast to 'general average' stood 'particular average', which comprised those losses caused by the perils insured against to particular interests, namely the shipowner or owners of the cargo. Such losses fell on the particular owner (or his insurer) alone. Under the Lloyd's policy, policy-holders could recover fully if they had suffered a total loss. Such losses could be 'actual', where the property had been destroyed, or 'constructive', where the loss was so great that no prudent uninsured owner would spend any more money in trying to rescue it.[243] In practice, this meant that the policy-holder had a right to abandon if the property could not be

---

[240] Contrast Marshall, *Treatise on the Law of Insurance* (3rd edn, 1823), 2: 552 and Willard Phillips, *Treatise on the Law of Insurance* (4th edn, 1854), ii, p. 120, §1348. See also Émérigon, *Traité des Assurances*, tome 1, 659 (citing Pothier *Traité des contrats aléatoires*, n. 52), holding that the claim may be made first against insurers. A contrary view was put by Roccius [Francesco Rocco], *De Navibus et Naulo* (Amsterdam, 1708), n. 62. American cases were also inconsistent: contrast *Lapsley* v. *Pleasants* 4 Binn. 502 (Pa. 1812) (following Roccius) and *Maggrath* v. *Church* 1 Caines 196 (NY 1803).

[241] *Dickenson* v. *Jardine* (1868) LR 3 CP 639. See also *Quebec Fire Assurance Co* v. *St Louis* (1851) 7 Moore PC 286 at 316–17, where Parke B. (using Émérigon and Pothier) stated that 'in the case of general average, the assurer, after having indemnified the assured against the losses sustained for the common benefit, ought to be subrogated to the rights of the assured'.

[242] See 'General Average Reform', *Economist*, 26 May 1894 (p. 634).

[243] *Roux* v. *Salvador* (1836) 3 Bing. N.C. 266 at 286. See also *Benson* v. *Chapman* (1843) 6 M. & G. 810; *Irving* v. *Manning* (1847) 1 H.L.C. 287; *Moss* v. *Smith* (1850) 9 C.B. 94 at 103; *SS Blairmore* v. *Macredie* [1898] App Cas 603.

rescued without spending more on it than it was worth. In such cases, the policy-holder could choose to abandon the property to his insurer, and claim for a total loss.[244] He was not permitted both to retain the goods and obtain an indemnity,[245] nor was he permitted to wait and see whether it was worth his while abandoning, but had to notify the insurer at once.[246] Moreover, if before the action was brought, the property was in a state to be restored, his right to abandon was lost.[247] The late nineteenth century saw much debate over how the calculation of the 'prudent uninsured man' was to be made. Since policies on vessels were often valued ones, valuing the vessel more highly than its market price, it was generally in the interest of the policy-holders to abandon for a constructive loss. They accordingly argued that, in deciding whether the cost of the repairs exceeded the value of the vessel, the court should take into account the value of the wreck, which tipped the calculation in their favour.[248] The judiciary was divided on whether this was the correct approach, but it was held in 1911 that the wording of the Marine Insurance Act 1906 made it clear that the value of the wreck was not to be taken into account.[249]

Besides recovering for vessels, policy-holders could recover for goods insured 'free of average' in case of total loss. If the loss made it impossible to bring them to their port of destination, the assured could claim for a constructive total loss. In such cases, the master of the ship could sell the goods in the nearest market, with the policy-holder abandoning them and claiming from his insurer. But where goods could be forwarded, without being spoiled, the assured had no right to abandon.[250] As in the case of damaged ships, whether there was a constructive

---

[244] If he chose not to abandon, he could claim for a partial loss; and if a subsequent total loss occurred under another policy, the second insurers could not claim that there had already been a constructive total loss. *Woodside* v. *Globe Marine Insurance Co* [1896] 1 QB 105.

[245] According to R. V. Richards (in *Hills* v. *London Assurance Corporation* (1839) 5 M. & W. 569 at 573), the doctrine of abandonment had been taken to 'an absurd length' before *Roux* v. *Salvador*, which defined and limited it by holding that where the goods could not be rescued, there was a total loss without need for notice of abandonment. By contrast, in *Anderson* v. *Royal Exchange Co* (1805) 7 East 38, where the plaintiffs attempted unsuccessfully to preserve corn which was underwater, it was held too late to abandon when they got it on shore and found that it did not serve their purpose. See also *Mitchell* v. *Edie* (1787) 1 T.R. 615.

[246] See *Kaltenbach* v. *Mackenzie* (1878) 3 CPD 480.

[247] *Bainbridge* v. *Neilson* (1808) 1 Camp. 240; *Patterson* v. *Ritchie* (1815) 4 M. & S. 393; *Naylor* v. *Taylor* (1829) 9 B. & C. 718; *Ruys* v. *Royal Exchange Association Co* [1897] 2 QB 135.

[248] If the cost of repairing a ship was £10,000, and its value after repairs was £12,000, a prudent uninsured man would spend the money, for he would gain £2000. But if the wrecked vessel could be sold for £3000, he would not effect the repairs.

[249] *Hall* v. *Hayman* [1912] 2 KB 5, referring to s 60(2)(ii) of the Act. For earlier divergent views, see *Angel* v. *Merchants Marine Insurance Co* [1903] 1 KB 811 and *Macbeth & Co* v. *Maritime Insurance Co* [1908] AC 144.

[250] See *Anderson* v. *Wallis* (1813) 2 M. & S. 240, and *Hunt* v. *Royal Exchange Association Co* (1816) 5 M. & S. 47; *Van Omeron* v. *Dowick* (1809) 2 Camp. 42; *Wilson* v. *Royal Exchange Association Co* (1811) 2 Camp. 623.

total loss depended on whether the cost of forwarding the goods exceeded their value at the port of destination,[251] which was a question for the jury.[252]

If the goods shipped were warranted 'free from average'—as 'corn, fish, fruit, flower and seed' were in the Lloyd's policy—the policy-holder could only recover in case of total loss. If he rescued a portion of his damaged goods, he would therefore not recover anything from his insurer. In the late eighteenth and early nineteenth centuries, the King's Bench helped policy-holders to recover where not all the goods shipped had been lost, by regarding goods shipped in separate packages to have been separately insured.[253] In 1856, the Exchequer Chamber tried to check this development, by holding that 'the ordinary memorandum exempts the underwriters from liability for a total loss or destruction of part only, though consisting of one or more entire package or packages', unless these packages were separately valued or insured.[254] But one year later, the Common Pleas held that where distinct kinds of goods were insured on a single policy, the loss of the whole of one kind of goods allowed the assured to claim the entire value of it, as a total loss of part of the goods. This was to allow what was effectively a partial loss to be recoverable on a policy free of all average.[255]

Where goods were warranted free from average under 3 per cent (as all goods not specified in the Lloyd's memorandum were), underwriters would not pay out on claims amounting only to 3 per cent of the sum insured. Since this could amount to a considerable sum where the cargo was large, shippers again sought to overcome the hurdle by dividing the cargo into a series of enumerated parcels, each of which would be considered separately insured. In such cases, the 3 per cent hurdle applied to each individual parcel, rather than to the cargo as a whole.[256] There were also attempts to overcome the 3 per cent hurdle by adding together smaller losses. The courts allowed separate losses which could be added together to meet the percentage, provided they were all particular average losses;

---

[251] *Rosetta* v. *Gurney* (1851) 11 C.B. 176.

[252] It was held that juries could not take into account the cost of freight, which would have had to be paid in any case: *Rosetto* v. *Gurney* (1851) 11 C.B. 176; *Farnworth* v. *Hyde* (1866) LR 2 CP 204 at 225. This a rule was effectively insurer-friendly, and proved controversial among commentators: McArthur, *Marine Insurance* (2nd edn, 1890), 151n and Arnould, *Marine Insurance* (9th edn, 1914) 1437–9 (sect. 1156). The wording of the 1906 Act appeared to many to correct this, allowing for the inclusion of freight.

[253] See *Lewis* v. *Rucker* (1761) 2 Burr. 1167 at 1170; *Davy* v. *Milford* (1812) 15 East 559 at 563; *Ralli* v. *Janson* (1856) 6 E. & B. 422 at 426.

[254] *Ralli* v. *Janson* (1856) 6 E. & B. 422 at 446. See also *Hills* v. *London Assurance Co* (1839) 5 M. & W. 569 at 576, where Lord Abinger held 'that where the insurance is upon each package separately, it is to be treated as a total loss upon each package lost; but when it is an insurance upon the bulk, unless the total exceed a certain value upon the particular article, there is no average loss'.

[255] *Duff* v. *Mackenzie* (1857) 3 C.B. N.S. 16. See also *Wilkinson* v. *Hyde* (1858) 3 C.B. N.S. 30.

[256] See *Hagedorn* v. *Whitmore* (1816) 1 Stark. 157.

but would not allow the policy-holder to add in different kinds of charges (such as the cost of rescuing goods) to make the sum reach the 3 per cent hurdle.[257] Nor would they allow general average claims to be added to particular average ones to make up the higher sum.[258]

Where there was a total loss of the goods, the assured recovered the value of the property insured. Where the goods arrived, but in a deteriorated condition, juries were asked to calculate the proportion between the sum the goods would have sold for at the market of destination and the sum they actually raised, and apply that proportion to the sum insured. Thus, if the price had fallen by half, the assured would recover half the sum he had insured.[259] This system was used in order to ensure that insurers would pay for the deterioration in the goods, and would not be insuring against price fluctuations. The calculation was to be made on gross market prices, not the net price which would factor out the costs of getting the goods to market. While this gave the policy-holder a smaller sum, it prevented him from profiting if the market fell.[260] A merchant who insured against partial loss was therefore well advised to insure additionally for his freight and charges.[261]

Fire and Life Policies

In the case of fires, many insurers required evidence in support of the claim, that the assured was not responsible for the conflagration, something generally seen as unnecessary in the case of marine losses.[262] Once satisfied that there was a fire which was not attributable to the assured, insurers looked at whether the loss had been proximately caused by fire.[263] As in marine cases, the courts took a narrow approach to the question of causation. Thus, in 1865, a shopkeeper failed

---

[257] *Kidston* v. *The Empire Marine Insurance Co* (1866) LR 1 CP 535, (1867) LR 2 CP 357.

[258] *Price & Co and Others* v. *The A1 Ships' Small Damage Insurance* (1889) 22 QBD 580 at 585–6. The case clarified an issue which had remained unclear since *Dickenson* v. *Jardine*, that where goods were jettisoned for the safety of the ship, this was a general average claim for which the insurer was liable, and 'that the direct liability of an underwriter for such a loss is consequently unaffected by the memorandum or any other warranty respecting particular average': Rule of Association of Average Adjusters confirmed in 1891 quoted in Gow, *Marine Insurance* (2nd edn, 1900), 313.

[259] *Lewis* v. *Rucker* (1761) 2 Burr. 1167.

[260] The rule settled by Lawrence J. in *Johnson* v. *Sheddon* (1802) 2 East 581 was followed throughout the nineteenth century: see Mathew J. in *Francis* v. *Burton* (1895) 65 LJ QB NS 153 at 156.

[261] See McArthur, *Marine Insurance* (2nd edn, 1890), 249–50. See e.g. *Usher* v. *Noble* (1810) 12 East 639 at 646.

[262] In the eighteenth century, the Phoenix required certificates attesting to the claimant's character: see *Worsley* v. *Wood* (1796) 6 T.R. 710; *Routledge* v. *Burrell* (1789) 1 H. Bl. 254.

[263] e.g. in *Austin* v. *Drewe* (1816) 6 Taunt. 436. It was held that damage caused by excessive heat caused by a furnace was not covered by a fire policy.

to recover on a policy insuring his plate glass window, after a fire at the back of his shop attracted a mob, which smashed the window to loot the premises. For Erle CJ, the proximate cause of the loss was the action of the mob and not the fire, which was only the remote cause of their assembling.[264]

Whether damage resulting from gunpowder explosions was covered by fire policies was a more tricky question, which was raised by two large explosions in 1864. After an explosion on the Mersey on board the *Lotty Sleigh*, which caused considerable damage to nearby buildings,[265] the Royal Insurance Company paid out on 81 claims, though they were not obliged to, since their policies specified that they would only pay for explosions caused by gas.[266] But when an even larger explosion occurred at a gunpowder depot near London,[267] the fire offices decided not to pay,[268] a decision condemned in the press as illiberal and ungenerous.[269] In the resulting test case, it was ruled that the companies were not liable. 'We are bound to look to the immediate cause of the loss or damage, and not to some remote or speculative cause', Willes J. ruled. 'Speaking of this injury, no person would say that it was occasioned by fire. It was occasioned by a concussion or disturbance of the air caused by fire elsewhere.'[270]

In interpreting the policy, the courts read the words according to their ordinary meaning, considering what the parties could be understood to have agreed. In *Stanley* v. *The Western Insurance Company*, the plaintiff's fire insurance policy covered gas explosions. His business entailed extracting oil from shoddy, and in the process an inflammable vapour was produced, which escaped and exploded, destroying the roof and causing a fire which did more damage. The Court of Exchequer held that the policy did not cover this accident. As Kelly CB put it, 'in the ordinary language, not only of men of business, and the owners of property (the subject of insurance), but even of scientific men themselves, the explosion in the present case would not be said to have been caused by *gas*'.[271] Those who wished to insure for such risks therefore had to have them specified in the policy, paying an appropriate premium for the risk. Insurers could in their policy definitions determine what meaning the word 'fire' was to bear in the policy, and could extend its cover to explosions.

---

[264] *Marsden* v. *The City and County Assurance Co* (1865) LR 1 CP 232.

[265] *The Times*, 18 January 1864, col. 9e.

[266] One of their shareholders unsuccessfully tried to challenge the company's decision: *Taunton* v. *Royal Insurance Co* (1864) 2 H. & M. 135.

[267] *The Times*, 3 October 1864, col. 7b; 4 October 1864, col. 7e; 5 October 1864, col. 9d; 6 October 1864, col. 7e; 8 October 1864, col. 9e; 12 October 1864, col. 8c, 13 October 1864, col. 6e.

[268] *The Times*, 7 October 1864, col. 5f.   [269] *The Times*, 12 October 1864, col. 8c.

[270] *Everett* v. *The London Assurance* (1865) 19 C.B. N.S. 126 at 133.

[271] *Stanley* v. *The Western Insurance Co* (1868) LR 3 Ex 71 at 73.

The amount of money the assured would recover depended on the nature of his policy. If the policy was a 'specified' one, insurers would be liable to pay to the full extent of the sum insured, even where the property as a whole had been under-insured. The insurer would make no claim to salvage the damaged goods, which remained the property of the assured. Such policies in effect encouraged under-insurance. This was as much a concern for the government as for insurers, insofar as it allowed the assured to pay smaller duties on the policy. To protect the duty, the Average Clause Act was passed in 1828, which required a separate specification of each risk setting out distinct sums insured. This also protected insurers incidentally.

In the mid-nineteenth century, the fire offices settled an 'average' clause, which was generally included in floating policies, to ensure that payments on losses would be proportionate to the sum insured. The use of this clause became more widespread after the repeal of the fire duty in 1869.[272] Under 'average' policies, the insurer would pay the same proportion of the value of the goods lost as the sum insured bore to the value of all the goods insured. Where there were goods to be salvaged, the insurer and assured would share the proceeds in like proportion.[273] These average policies did not initially apply to farm insurances, so that farmers were able in effect to under-insure and recover the full sum of any items entirely consumed by fire. But legislation in 1870 closed this loophole.[274]

Unlike marine policies, fire policies were not valued. Instead, property was valued according to its worth on the day before the fire. Where goods were insured, the assured obtained the market price on the day before the fire, not (as in unvalued marine insurance)[275] the original cost of the goods. Where goods were sold but not yet delivered, and property remained in the seller, insurers did not pay the value on the day of the fire, but the value on the day of the sale.[276] Where machinery or fixed property had been damaged, insurers were wary of replacing old with new, which would be more valuable. Insurers thus paid the value of the old building, not the cost of putting up a new one. Again, they had the option of reinstating, that is repairing the building or the machine, rather than paying cash. In fire cases, the assured could not elect to abandon the goods as a total loss to the insurers, as was possible in marine cases. Total annihilation of the entire

---

[272] D. Jenkins and T. Yoneyama, *The History of Insurance* 7 vols (2000), ii, 163.

[273] Richard Atkins, *On the Settlement of Losses by Fire under Average Policies* (1853) in Jenkins and Yoneyama, *The History of Insurance* (2000), ii, 163.

[274] See 3 & 4 W. 4 c. 23 s 5, repealed by 33 & 34 Vict. c. 99.

[275] The rule in marine insurance derived from the fact the it was often impossible to know the precise day when the goods were lost, and so impossible to know the market value on that day.

[276] C. J. Bunyon, *The Law of Fire Insurance* (5th edn by R. J. Quin and F. E. Colenso (1906), 242. See *Usher* v. *Noble* (1810) 12 East 639.

property was rare, and so there would usually be some property to salvage and sell at a reduced rate. In such a situation, it was not permitted to the assured to throw the remaining goods on the insurer, and request a complete indemnity in exchange for abandoned goods.[277]

In fire insurance, by the mid-nineteenth century, many of the most complex disputes centred on how to spread losses between various insurers. Where goods were kept in warehouses, there might be a multiplicity of insurances. The owner of goods might have different policies insuring goods in different warehouses, while the wharfinger might also have insured the goods in his warehouse. The goods might be covered both under specified and average policies. For instance, in October 1849, Gooch & Cousens's wool warehouse at London Wall burned down. It contained 3606 bales of wool owned by 73 different parties. Some of the wool was covered by specified policies, some by floating average policies, and some was uninsured. Much of the wool was salvaged, some of which could be identified by trade marks and some not. After the fire, the many claims which ensued were settled without litigation.[278] The insurers accepted a rule that where a person had taken out both a specified policy on goods in a particular warehouse, and an average policy on goods in a number of warehouses, the first policy was to be paid in full, and if there was any further loss beyond the sum insured on the specified policy, the average policy would pay.[279] Furthermore, where there were numerous average policies covering the same goods, those policies with the narrowest extent should be treated as specified policies and be called on first. In the following decade, the fire offices settled the principles to use in settling contributions between them, in case of multiple insurance, with each being expected to contribute in proportion to the cover he gave.[280]

Insurers henceforth included in their policies the statement that the assured had to disclose any other policies he had effected, and also that if any other policy existed, the insurers would only pay ratably and not for the full loss. This meant that the same person could not take out two insurances on the same goods and be compensated twice. Where there were two insurances on the same goods, the courts held that the claim of the assured was discharged by the payment of the first policy, and that the insurer who had paid out could have a remedy for a contribution from the one who had not, 'for they are co-sureties'.[281] However, it

---

[277] Bunyon, *Fire Insurance* (5th edn, 1906), 244 *et seq.*

[278] Jenkins and Yoneyama, *History of Insurance*, ii, 189. For the fire, see *The Times*, 8 October 1849, col. 4f; 9 October 1849, col. 8c.

[279] Jenkins and Yoneyama, *History of Insurance*, ii, 166.   [280] *Ibid.*, 228–9.

[281] *Morgan* v. *Price* (1849) 4 Exch. 615 at 612; *North British and Mercantile Insurance Co* v. *London, Liverpool and Globe Insurance Co* (1877) 5 Ch D 569. In 1906, the Marine Insurance Act provided (s 80(2)) that if any insurer paid more than his proportion of the loss, he could bring an action for contribution against the other insurers, and was entitled 'to the like remedies as a surety who has

was decided in 1877 that if two different parties took out insurance on the same goods, as when a wharfinger and an owner both insured the owner's goods under separate policies, the wharfinger's insurer could not recover a contribution from the owner's insurer. Not only was it well settled that a party liable for a loss could not take the benefit of another party's insurance,[282] but since the wharfinger remained liable to the owner for the loss, the latter's insurer would always be able to recover from the wharfinger (or his insurer) if he had paid the owner's claim.[283] This decision proved unpopular with the insurers, who amended their policies accordingly to allow rateable contribution where another party had insured 'on behalf' of the policy-holder.[284] In March 1882, the Tariff Association agreed that, in future, in insurances not covering merchandise, where more than one insurance was effected, the insurers should settle their contributions rateably without looking at the liabilities of the parties *inter se*.

Where insurers had paid on policies, they also sought to recover any further sums which the assured had received in respect of the loss, to prevent the policy-holder from obtaining a double indemnity. Rules dating from the eighteenth century made it clear that where there was a constructive total loss, the insurer obtained the property rights over the thing insured from the moment of abandonment. Having been assigned the property at that moment, the insurer could sue any wrongdoers responsible for the harm in the name of the assured.[285] It was also settled in the eighteenth century that if the assured himself sued after being paid his loss by an insurer,[286] then he would stand 'as a trustee for the insurer, in proportion for what he paid', whether or not the property had been abandoned to the insurer.[287]

In most fire cases, the insurer's ability to recover did not derive from a property right acquired through an abandonment by the assured, for in most cases

---

paid more than his proportion of the debt'. See also Charles Mitchell, *The Law of Contribution and Reimbursement* (Oxford, 2003), paras 14.22–14.23.

[282] See e.g. *Yates* v. *Whyte* (1838) 4 Bing. N.C. 272.

[283] *North British and Mercantile Insurance Co* v. *London, Liverpool and Globe Insurance Co* (1877) 5 Ch D 569.

[284] Bunyon, *Fire Insurance* (5th edn, 1906), 278.

[285] *Mason* v. *Sainsbury* (1782) 3 Doug. 61; cf. *London Assurance Co* v. *Sainsbury* (1783) 3 Doug. 245 at 253. Although the insurer could only sue in respect of a right held by the assured (*Simpson* v. *Thomson* (1877) 3 App Cas 279 (Sc)), after the passing of the Judicature Acts he could sue in his own name: *King* v. *Victoria Insurance Co* [1896] AC 250. It was on the same principle that the insurer could recover general average payments from other parties to the voyage: *Dickenson* v. *Jardine* (1868) LR 3 CP 639 at 644.

[286] *Clark* v. *Blything* (1823) 2 B. & C. 254.

[287] *Randal* v. *Cockran* (1748) 1 Ves. Sr. 98. See also *Blaauwpot* v. *Da Costa* (1758) 1 Eden 130, where insurers obtained money paid under a Royal Commission for distributing prizes to the assured, who had been paid by the insurers. Here the court regarded this as salvage.

payment was made on a partial loss, with no assignment of the property. Later nineteenth-century judges made it clear that the insurer's right to recover rested on a different principle, whereby the insurer 'subrogated' to the rights which the assured had against others.[288] The general principle behind the doctrine elaborated by the judges was that the assured should not get a double indemnity. This meant firstly that the insurer paying the indemnity was 'entitled to succeed to all the ways and means by which the person indemnified might have protected himself against or reimbursed himself for the loss'.[289] He thereby acquired the assured's rights against third parties by subrogation. Secondly, it meant that 'if anything which diminishes the loss comes into the hands of the person to whom he has paid it, it becomes an equity that the person who had already paid the full indemnity is entitled to be recouped by having that amount back.'[290]

In discussing both of these remedies, judges used the language of subrogation, which had hitherto been unfamiliar to English lawyers.[291] This doctrine, according to which one party acquired another party's rights, in effect being substituted for him, was not easily applied to cases such as *Darrell* v. *Tibbitts*, where the insurer recovered money paid to his assured, after the latter's tenant—who had a duty to repair the building—received funds from a local authority to reinstate a damaged house.[292] In this case, it was evident enough that the assured had not suffered any loss; but at the same time it was unclear to which rights of the assured the insurer could be subrogated, since all of the tenant's obligations had already been fulfilled.[293] Brett LJ's solution to the problem was to say that

---

[288] See *Potter* v. *Rankin* (1868) LR 3 CP 562 at 573; *Simpson* v. *Thompson* (1877) 3 App Cas 279 (Sc) at 292.

[289] *Simpson & Co* v. *Thomson* (1877) 3 App Cas 279 (Sc) at 284. The principle was endorsed in the same year by the Court of Appeal in *North British and Mercantile Insurance Co* v. *London, Liverpool and Globe Insurance Co* (1877) 5 Ch D 569.

[290] *Burnand* v. *Rodocanachi, Son & Co* (1882) 7 App Cas 333 at 339. In this case, it was held that compensation given by the US government did not diminish the loss, since it was in respect of uninsured items.

[291] While the principle of subrogation was well developed in continental treatises (see e.g. R. J Pothier, *Coutume d'Orleans*, in *Oeuvres de Pothier*, ed. M. Siffrein, Paris 1821, vols 15–17, titre xx, s. 5, para. 66, vol. 17, p. 278), it was not found in the English case law of the first half of the century. Although it was well settled in English law that a surety who paid a debt to a creditor was entitled to recover the debt from the debtor, this was not analysed in terms of the surety being subrogated to the creditor's rights. Instead, sureties recovered in an action for money paid, on the basis of an implied request by the principal that the surety pay: see e.g. *Batard* v. *Hawes* (1852) 2 E. & B. 287 at 296. But in 1856, Parliament passed a Mercantile Law Amendment Act which introduced to England the Scottish principle that a surety who paid a guaranteed debt could demand an assignment of all the creditor's rights against the debtor. See further, Charles Mitchell, *The Law of Subrogation* (Oxford, 1994), 56–7.

[292] *Darrell* v. *Tibbitts* (1880) 5 QBD 560.

[293] See also Thesiger LJ's suggestion that the plaintiff was entitled to recover in an action for money had and received on the ground that the money was paid on the basis that the defendant had suffered a loss, when in fact he had not, 5 QBD 560 at 567–8 discussed in Mitchell, *Subrogation*, 70.

'we have a right to imply a promise on the part of the landlord to the insurance company at the time of the payment by them, that if the loss should be afterwards made good by the tenants, he would repay the money which he received from the insurance company'.[294]

Three years later, the Court of Appeal gave a similarly broad interpretation of the doctrine in *Castellain* v. *Preston*, where the insurer sought to recover moneys paid out to a policy-holder on a fire policy, for damage done to property after a contract had been made to sell it, but prior to completion of the contract. In the divisional court, Chitty J. took the view that the insurer could not bring a subrogated action, since there were no rights of the assured *vis-à-vis* any third party to which the insurer could be subrogated.[295] However, the Court of Appeal upheld the insurer's claim. In his judgment, Brett LJ held that the principle of subrogation had to be interpreted broadly to prevent the assured receiving more than an indemnity. The principle of subrogation meant that:

as between the underwriter and the assured the underwriter is entitled to the advantage of every right of the assured, whether such right consists in contract, fulfilled or unfulfilled, or in remedy of tort capable of being insisted on or already insisted on, or in any other right, whether by way of condition or otherwise, legal or equitable, which can be, or has been exercised or has accrued, and whether such right could or could not be enforced by the insurer in the name of the assured by the exercise or acquiring of which right or condition the loss against which the assured is insured, can be, or has been diminished.[296]

The doctrine of subrogation was thus founded on the idea that the insurer had a right to any money received by the assured which diminished the loss. The decision has been criticized for 'distorting the definition of subrogation', by putting under one category distinct remedies.[297] Moreover, it left unclear the precise doctrinal basis for allowing the insurer recovery.[298] If the Court of Appeal's doctrinal solution was inelegant, it nevertheless confirmed that contracts of fire insurance, like marine contracts, were contracts for indemnity only. Because insurers were promising to pay in case of an event which caused loss, rather than promising

---

[294] *Darrell* v. *Tibbitts* (1880) 5 QBD 560 at 563.

[295] *Castellain* v. *Preston* (1882) 8 QBD 613 at 623–4.

[296] *Castellain* v. *Preston* (1883) 11 QBD 380 at 388.

[297] Philip S. James, 'The Fallacies of *Simpson* v. *Thomson*' (1971) 34 *MLR* 148–62 at 154; Mitchell, *Subrogation*, 72–3; Charles Mitchell and Stephen Watterson, *Subrogation: Law and Practice* (Oxford, 2007), 316–20. The distinct remedies are the action for money had and received, subrogation (allowing the insurer to claim the assured's rights), and the equitable duty to account.

[298] It could be seen as based on an implied term of the insurance contract (see e.g. Lord Diplock's approach in *Hobbs* v. *Marlow* [1978] AC 16 and *Yorkshire Insurance* v. *Nisbet Shipping* [1962] 2 QB 330; or on broader equitable principles, which did not rest on contract. Modern writers have derived the obligation to repay from the principle of unjust enrichment.

(as in life assurance) to pay in any event, it was felt to enrich the assured unjustly if he was paid on a policy when suffering no loss.

In life assurance, the insurer was liable to pay out the sum for which the insurance was taken out. Disputes over the sum due to be paid did not turn on the nature of the loss, but on whether the 'life' had breached the terms of the policy. Under a standard mid-nineteenth century policy, the company would not pay if the deceased assured had travelled outside Europe without the insurers' consent, or entered into military service without paying an increased premium. It was also settled early in the century that no one could recover on an insurance policy if to do so would allow him to benefit by his own felony.[299] The rule derived from litigation after the execution of Henry Fauntleroy for forgery in 1824, when the House of Lords confirmed that his assignees in bankruptcy could not recover the £6084-7-6 due under the policy.[300] Insurance companies also successfully challenged policies which had been taken out by murderers on the lives of their victims.[301] Nevertheless, in 1891 the Court of Appeal permitted the executors of James Maybrick to recover on a policy, which stipulated that his wife Florence was to be paid £2000 in the event of his death, even though she had been convicted of his murder.[302] In the court's view, since Mrs Maybrick was barred from benefiting as a result of her conviction, there was no policy against allowing the money to be paid to the estate of the deceased, to be used to pay his creditors or give an inheritance to his children.[303]

Insurance companies also refused to pay in cases of suicide, arguing that if they paid out in such cases, it would encourage people to kill themselves to benefit their families. Difficult questions were raised where the deceased had committed suicide when of unsound mind. In such cases, juries could be persuaded to

---

[299] Where the assured had assigned the policy, or where he died as a result of non-felonious suicide, this rule was not breached: and it was only in 1937 that the Court of Appeal held that where a sane man committed suicide, his representatives could not recover on the policy, as it would assist him in reaping the fruits of his crime: *Beresford* v. *Royal Insurance Co* [1937] 2 KB 197.

[300] *Amicable Society* v. *Bolland* (1830) 4 Bligh. N.S. 194, 2 Dow. & Cl. 1, overturning *Bolland* v. *Disney* (1827) 3 Russ. 351.

[301] *The Prince of Wales &c Association Co* v. *Palmer* (1858) 25 Beav. 605. For other cases of murders committed to claim on insurances, see the case of William Youngman who took out a policy for £100 on his sweetheart's life before killing her, as well as his brothers and his mother: *The Times*, 6 August 1860, col. 5g; 7 August, col. 12e; 17 August, cols 7a, 9c.

[302] On her case, see G. Robb, 'The English Dreyfus Case: Florence Maybrick and the Sexual Double Standard', in G. Robb and N. Erber, *Disorder in the Court* (Basingstoke, 1999), 57–77; H. B. Irving, *The Trial of Mrs Maybrick* (Edinburgh, 1912).

[303] *Cleaver* v. *Mutual Reserve Fund Life Association* [1892] 1 QB 147 (CA). After the decision, the Crown laid a claim to the proceeds of the policy. Instead of appealing to the Lords, the insurers paid the money into court to let the executors and Crown dispute the proceeds, while showing its own willingness to pay claims made on it: *The Times*, 17 February 1892, col. 6e.

find against the insurers, by finding that the death was not by suicide.[304] Insurers responded by requiring judges to put more precise questions to the jury, to help raise questions of law. In *Borradaile* v. *Hunter* in 1842, a jury returned a verdict that the deceased had voluntarily thrown himself into the Thames, at a time when he was incapable of telling right from wrong.[305] The Common Pleas, which felt that insurers needed protection from overly generous juries, found for the defendants on this verdict, holding that 'a man who drowns himself voluntarily may do it to found a claim on a policy, though he may not think it wrong to do so'.[306] A similarly tough approach was taken in 1846 by the Court of Exchequer in *Clift* v. *Schwabe*. Counsel for the family argued that for a man to be held to have committed suicide within the meaning of the policy, the act had to amount to a *felo de se*, or self-murder. But the majority held that it was suicide for a man to kill himself by a voluntarily act, of whose consequences he was aware, whether or not he was acting under a delusion as to its moral quality. 'In ordinary parlance', Parke B said, 'every one would so speak of one who had purposely killed himself, whether from taedium of life, or transport of grief, or in fit of temporary insanity.'[307] Since Schwabe had been in a state of depression, rather than delusion, when he killed himself, the company might have felt that if a verdict of insanity could be taken in this case, they would always be held liable in future cases of suicide. Nonetheless, the decision led to much alarm among those taking out life insurance, and companies responded by altering their policies to allow families to recover notwithstanding suicide, after a certain interval. Policies were soon drafted to include terms that would allow the directors, after five years of payments had been made, to pay the family any sum up to the surrender value of the policy on the day before the suicide of the assured. Throughout the late nineteenth century, insurance companies continued to resist claims where the assured life had committed suicide,[308] though where the death occurred after an interval, the company only resisted if there were other grounds, such as concealment of material information by the deceased.[309]

---

[304] See *Garrett* v *Barclay* (1826) 5 M. & G. 643n; cf. *Kinnear* v. *Borradaile, Kinnear* v. *Nicholson* (1832) 5 M. & G. 643n.

[305] This was the usual way judges presented the question of insanity to juries: though in *M'Naghten's case* (1843) 10 Cl. & F. 200, the House of Lords made the rules more specific.

[306] *Abraham Borradaile* v. *Sir Claudius Stephen Hunter, Bart* (1843) 5 Man. & G. 639 at 654. For discussion, see T. Alborn, 'Dirty Laundry: Exposing Bad Behavior in Life Insurance Trials, 1830–1890', in J. Bourne Taylor, M. Finn, and M. Lobban (eds), *Legitimacy and Illegitimacy in Law, Literature and History* (Basingstoke, forthcoming).

[307] *Clift* v. *Schwabe* (1846) 3 C.B. 437 at 471.

[308] See the *Lotinga* case, discussed in Alborn, 'Dirty Laundry', and *The Times*, 3 July 1885, col. 9c

[309] *Joel* v. *Law Union and Crown Insurance Co* [1908] 2 KB 863.

III
Negotiable Instruments

Engla nd's pre-eminent position as a commercial power owed much to the strength of her financial system. From the late seventeenth-century, a financial revolution had paved the way for the development of a 'fiscal-military' state, funded by a sophisticated system of government borrowing on the strength of paper securities. Besides helping to fund an expanding state, new forms of banking and credit also provided the means through which commerce and industry could expand. If money was the life-blood of commerce, new forms of bank notes and negotiable instruments helped keep its circulation healthy, by allowing both for more efficient transfers of wealth and for the provision of secure credit.

Bank notes were the most important form of commercial paper. In 1820, the Bank of England, which had been given a charter in 1696 to make short-term loans to the state in the form of circulating notes, was still the only joint stock bank permitted to issue them. But notes could also be issued by private banks run by up to six partners, of which there were more than 600 at the end of the Napoleonic wars. Country banks raised money from their customers by taking coin in exchange for bank notes which they issued. These were a kind of promissory note, in which the bank promised to pay the bearer the sum stated in specie. Since gold left at banks earned no interest, private bankers passed on as much of it as they dared to the Bank of England (which was the main depositary of the nation's reserves), leaving enough to cover anticipated demands made on them by the customers. Since their stability depended on their customers' confidence that they would be able to honour their notes, country bank notes tended to circulate only locally, where the partners were well known.[1]

The structure of banking changed in the nineteenth century in response to periodic financial crises. As a result of the crash of 1825 in which a run on the banks caused 43 of them to fail, legislation was passed to permit unlimited liability joint stock banks to be created beyond a 65 mile radius of London.[2] It was

---

[1] T. L. Alborn, *Conceiving Companies: Joint Stock Politics in Victorian England* (1998), 54; W. T. C. King, *History of the London Discount Market* (1936), 6; M. Collins, *Money and Banking in the UK: A History* (1988), 27, 93.

[2] 7 Geo. IV c. 46.

felt that country banks would be better able to withstand runs on their reserves if they had greater capital than could be provided by six partners.[3] This opened the way for the development of a national system of banking.[4] However, the issuing of notes by these banks declined, particularly after the passing of the Bank Charter Act in 1844, which sought to link the quantity of bank notes in circulation with the amount of specie held at the Bank of England, and accordingly imposed restrictions on the issuing of notes by other banks. As a consequence, the quantity of notes not issued by the Bank of England fell steadily.

Promissory notes were also given by private parties when lending money to each other, or when settling debts, with the maker promising to pay the holder a stipulated sum.[5] Merchants also used these 'two-party' instruments, as well as bills of exchange, which directed a third party to pay the holder. Bills of exchange allowed merchants to arrange payments over a distance, and to extend credit. Sellers would take payment for goods shipped by receiving a bill of exchange, in which the buyer acknowledged his liability to pay at a specified future date. The seller could use this document to obtain cash at once, by indorsing it to another person. Since that person could in turn indorse it to another, bills of exchange could be used to pay for goods in the same way as bank notes. Bills of exchange were used both internationally and nationally, a distinction being made between 'foreign' bills, which were either drawn, or were made payable abroad, and 'inland' bills, which were drawn and payable in England.

In the nineteenth century, much banking business involved dealing with bills of exchange. Bills could be 'discounted' by their holders either with banks, or with specialist discount houses, such as Overend, Gurney & Co. The trader who needed cash could indorse his bill to a bank or discount house, which would charge the seller a sum representing interest on the time remaining before the bill was due to be paid, as well as a commission.[6] Since there was an element of risk, a prudent banker or broker would only discount bills with relatively short terms before maturity, and ones in which they could reasonably repose confidence. The bank or broker could in turn sell the bill on to another bank, by 'rediscounting' it. Profit could be made by selling the bill (whose security was increased by the bank's indorsement) to a rediscounter charging a lower rate of interest.

---

[3] B. Hilton, *Corn Cash Commerce: The Economic Policies of the Tory Governments 1815–1830* (Oxford, 1977), Chs 7–8.

[4] S. E. Thomas, *The Rise and Growth of Joint Stock Banking* (1934); Collins, *Money and Banking*, 52; L. Newton and P. L. Cottrell, 'Joint Stock Banking in the English Provinces 1826–1857' (1998) 27 *Business and Economic History*, 115–28 at 116. See also D. Ziegler, *Central Bank, Peripheral Industry: The Bank of England in the Provinces, 1826–1913* (Leicester, 1990).

[5] e.g. *Rew* v. *Pettet* (1834) 1 Ad. & El. 196 (money lent to parish).

[6] The interest chargeable was limited by the usury laws; but in 1833, the Bank Charter Act exempted from the usury laws dealings in bills and notes which had less than three months to run.

In the first half of the nineteenth century, this process of rediscounting bills was widely used. It was economically efficient, since it allowed money to be channelled from areas of the country with surpluses (such as agricultural counties) to areas with a high demand for credit (such as industrial areas). However, after the failure of Overend, Gurney & Co in 1865, country banks became more wary of sending bills to London to be rediscounted, since the crisis had undermined confidence in the City's ability to come up with cash when it was needed. They began to hold on to the bills they had until maturity, and the number of inland bills of exchange traded on the London discount market fell sharply.[7] Instead of discounting, banks now increasingly encouraged the accumulation of deposits at the bank, a development facilitated by the growth of branch banking.[8] With a net influx of deposits, banks now lent more of their money in the form of overdrafts, which could be balanced against deposits. For the borrower, overdrafts were more desirable than bills, since they were more flexible. In this era, commercial banking became a cautious and conservative enterprise, largely untouched by the periodic crises which continued to befall the City, such as the Baring Crisis of 1890.

The rise of deposit banking also saw increasing use of cheques. Although printed cheques and cheque books had existed since the eighteenth century, their use was limited by the high stamp duties imposed on negotiable instruments payable otherwise than on demand. Only cheques payable to bearer were exempt from the duty, provided the drawee operated within 10 miles of the place of issue of the cheque.[9] In 1853, a Stamp Act reformed the duties payable, imposing a 1d charge for cheques payable to order, rather than the previous *ad valorem* fee, which was more costly. This change opened the way for the widespread use of cheques payable to order, something given greater encouragement when in 1858 all bearer cheques were required to pay the same duty. The use of cheques was further facilitated in 1854 when the London joint stock banks (led by the London and Westminster) were given access to the London Clearing House, which had hitherto remained the preserve of the private bankers. At the Clearing House, the different London banks settled the accounts on the various cheques paid through them, cancelling debts and paying outstanding accounts on a daily basis. A country clearing system was in place by 1860, which was joined by the Bank of England

---

[7] S. Nishimura, *The Decline of Inland Bills of Exchange in the London Money Market, 1855–1913* (Cambridge, 1971), 25: he shows that in the 1860s, the volume of inland bills was equivalent to 83% of the national income, whereas in 1904–13 it had fallen to 29%.

[8] By 1914, the total number of deposits in banks had reached £ 1 billion. F. Crouzet, *The Victorian Economy* (1982, trans. A Forster), 335.

[9] J. M. Holden, *The History of Negotiable Instruments in English Law* (1955), 219.

in 1862.[10] Moreover, provincial clearing houses were set up in larger cities such as Newcastle, Manchester, Leeds, Birmingham, Bristol, and Liverpool.[11] From the 1860s, English banking began to assume its modern character of corporate branch deposit banking.[12] The collecting of deposits from clients by joint stock banks, which invested the money elsewhere gradually replaced the old private banks whose business was centred on note issue.

1. BILLS OF EXCHANGE AND PROMISSORY NOTES

Much of the law relating to bills of exchange had been settled by the start of our period. Eighteenth-century England was already a highly commercialized society, and many of the rules relating to negotiable instruments had been settled by the founders of English commercial law, Holt and Mansfield. There was also a more extensive range of treatise literature in this area than was the case with contract law in general. The first eighteenth-century treatise on bills of exchange was published in 1760.[13] While this (and others) did not survive into the nineteenth century, succeeding editions of John Bayley's 1789 treatise and Joseph Chitty's 1799 treatise continued to be published in the nineteenth century,[14] and new influential works were published by John Barnard Byles and Joseph Story.[15]

The law relating to bills of exchange was codified in 1882, when the Bills of Exchange Act drafted by Mackenzie Chalmers was passed. In 1878, Chalmers produced a *Digest of the Law of Bills of Exchange*, in the form of a code with a commentary, following the form used by J. F. Stephen's 1876 *Digest of the Law of Evidence* and Frederick Pollock's 1877 *Digest of the Law of Partnership*.[16] Two years later, he read a paper on the question of codifying the law of negotiable instruments to the Institute of Bankers, and was subsequently invited by them and the Associated Chambers of Commerce to draft a bill. Chalmers aimed to

---

[10] Newton and Cottrell, 'Joint Stock Banking', 126.

[11] H. Hart, *The Law of Banking* (2nd edn, 1906), 333.

[12] Newton and Cottrell, 'Joint Stock Banking', 126.

[13] T. Cunningham, *The Law of Bills of Exchange, Promissory Notes, Bank-Notes, and Insurances* (1760).

[14] J. Bayley, *A Short Treatise on the Law of Bills of Exchange* (1789); J. Chitty, *A Treatise on the Law of Bills of Exchange* (1799).

[15] J. B. Byles, *A Practical Treatise of the Law of Bills of Exchange* (1834); J. Story, *Commentaries on the Law of Bills of Exchange* (Boston and London, 1843).

[16] J. F. Stephen, *Digest of the Law of Evidence* (1876); F. Pollock, *A Digest of the Law of Partnership* (1877); M. D. Chalmers, 'On the Codification of Mercantile Law, with Especial Reference to the Law of Negotiable Instruments' (1881) 2 *Journal of the Institute of Bankers* 113–31. See also M. D. Chalmers, 'An Experiment in Codification' (1886) 3 *LQR* 125–34; R. B. Ferguson, 'Legal Ideology and Commercial Interests: The Social Origins of the Commercial Law Codes' (1977) 4 *Brit. J. of Law and Soc.* 18–38.

reproduce the existing law as exactly as possible, though bridging occasional gaps when he found them. Since the bill had significant commercial backing, its progress through Parliament was smooth. At the end of the process, Chalmers could state with some satisfaction that '[m]erchants and bankers say that it is a great convenience to them to have the whole of the general principles of the law of bills, notes and cheques contained in a single Act of 100 sections'.[17]

The premise behind the working of bills of exchange was that the person who drew the bill (the *drawer*) was owed or had left money in the hands of the person to whom it was addressed (the *drawee*), who was directed to pay the money stipulated to a *payee*. The payee might be the drawer himself—for he might simply want his money back—or someone else who was owed money by the drawer. Before the drawee had any liability on the bill, he had to have accepted it (whereupon he was called the *acceptor* of the bill). Bills could be made payable 'at sight', or at any future date, as indicated on the bill. They could therefore be used to extend credit, as where a purchaser of goods accepted a bill of exchange drawn on him payable at a future date. Bills were also negotiable. If the bill was made payable to the payee 'or bearer', the payee could transfer it by delivery to any third party, who would then have a claim against the acceptor. If it was made payable to the payee 'or order', the payee could only transfer his rights in the bill by indorsing it to a third party (*indorsee*). There was no limit to the number of indorsements which could be made on a bill; and if no space remained on the bill, then they could be put onto an attached *allonge*. Anyone who had possession of the bill, with a legal entitlement to it, was known as the *holder*.

Besides bills which represented 'real' financial transactions, as where they were used to pay for goods sold, bills were also often drawn to 'accommodate' the needs of the drawer, providing him with credit. The drawee of an 'accommodation bill' would accept a bill payable at a certain date, with the drawer in turn undertaking to provide him with funds to cover the amount in the bill before the due date. The drawer of the bill would indorse the bill, and use it to raise short-term credit in the market. Bills could be made for the accommodation either of the drawer or drawee. Thus, a bill drawn by one merchant for acceptance by another might be indorsed by the merchant drawing it, and returned to the 'accepting' merchant, to use for the purpose of obtaining credit. Although the 'accepting' party was himself primarily liable on the bill, the indorsement acted as a guarantee of any money later raised on the bill.[18]

Besides bills of exchange, commercial parties (and private individuals) also used promissory notes as a form of payment. The note contained a written

---

[17] Chalmers, 'An Experiment in Codification', 128.
[18] For an example, see *Bland* v. *Ryan* (1795) Peake Add. Cas. 39.

promise by its *maker* to pay a specified sum of money to the person named (the *payee*). The maker of a note was the primary debtor (standing in a similar position to the acceptor of a bill), and the person entitled to payment was the payee. As with bills of exchange, notes could be made payable to the payee or to his order, or to a bearer. Although widely used from the late seventeenth century by merchants as negotiable instruments, promissory notes were not recognized at common law, and it required legislation in the reign of Queen Anne to declare that such notes could be assigned and sued on.[19]

Bills and notes were an exception to the common law rule that no chose in action (such as a debt or other obligation) could be assigned. Their assignability derived from the custom of merchants, which established that the holder of a bill of exchange could recover on it in his own name. As with other areas of commercial law, English law drew on a body of doctrine which had been expounded on the continent over a number of centuries to explain instruments which had been used since the middle ages. In elaborating the common law's rules, early nineteenth-century judges and jurists sometimes drew on the works of these continental writers,[20] as well as English works commenting on the *lex mercatoria*.[21] The courts—notably in the era of Mansfield—also resorted to the evidence of merchants in establishing what the common law should recognize as the rules.

Acceptance

Since the drawee was only liable if he had accepted the bill drawn on him, any holder needed to present the bill to the drawee for acceptance. Acceptance could be made before or after the bill circulated. Although it might seem prudent to obtain an acceptance as soon as possible, once a bill was put into circulation and indorsed by intermediate holders, its credit grew (since these indorsers bore a liability in case the bill was not accepted).[22] If bills were payable at a certain future date, they did not have to be presented for acceptance until they were due; though it was advisable to get bills accepted since the added security of an acceptance made them easier to negotiate.[23] Where the bill was payable at a certain time 'after sight', the holder had to present it for acceptance to the drawee in order to

---

[19] Holden, *History of Negotiable Instruments*, 79–94. See also *Horton* v. *Coggs* (1691) 3 Lev. 299; *Clerke* v. *Martin* (1702) 2 Ld. Raym. 757; *Buller* v. *Crips* (1703) 6 Mod. 29.

[20] They included in particular R. J. Pothier's treatise on bills of exchange (*Traité du Contrat de Change*, Paris, 1773): see e.g. Lord Ellenborough's references to Pothier in *Raper* v. *Birkbeck* (1811) 15 East 17 at 20; *Hoare* v. *Cazenove* (1812) 16 East 391 at 398. See also *Cox* v. *Troy* (1822) 5 B. & Ald. 474.

[21] e.g. W. Beawes, *Lex mercatoria rediviva: or, the merchant's directory* (1st edn, 1751).

[22] *Goupy* v. *Harden* (1816) 7 Taunt. 159.

[23] A bill could also be accepted after the time for payment had passed, whereupon it was regarded as payable on demand: *Jackson* v. *Pigott* (1698) 1 Ld. Raym. 364.

fix the period at which the bill was to be paid.[24] Although this gave the holder the choice of the time from which the bill would begin to run, the courts required him to put it into circulation or present it for acceptance within a reasonable time.[25] Where no time was mentioned on the bill, it was regarded as payable on demand.[26] Bills could still be negotiated when it was overdue or had been dishonoured; though the fact that it was overdue was regarded as notice to the holder of all infirmities in the bill.[27]

Eighteenth-century judgments had held that acceptances could be made verbally,[28] and that a promise to accept a bill might be sufficient to constitute an acceptance.[29] Disquiet about these rules led to the passing of the Regulation of Acceptances Act 1821, under which acceptances of inland bills had to be made in writing on the bill.[30] However, foreign bills were not covered by the Act, and debate continued over whether an agreement to accept a bill (whether already drawn or not) constituted an acceptance.[31] These debates were rendered redundant by legislation in 1856, which required acceptances for foreign bills to be in writing as well.[32] The person promising to accept a bill might be liable to the person promised, if the promise to accept was contractually binding; but he was not liable to the holder as acceptor.[33]

If he chose to accept, the drawee could give either an unqualified acceptance to the bill or a qualified one, which bound him to pay only according to the tenor

---

[24] Chitty, *Bills* (4th edn, 1812), 176.

[25] *Muilman* v. *D'Eguino* (1795) 2 H. Bl. 565 (per Buller J.); *Goupy* v. *Harden* (1816) 7 Taunt 159; *Mellish* v. *Rawdon* (1832) 9 Bing. 416; *Ramchurn Mullick* v. *Luchmeechund Radakissen* (1854) 9 Moore 46.

[26] Notes and bills under £5 had to be payable within 21 days, but larger notes had no time limit. 17 Geo. III c. 30.

[27] See *Brown* v. *Davies* (1789) 3 T.R. 80 at 82–3; *Amory* v. *Meryweather* (1824) 2 B. & C. 573 at 587; Byles, *Bills* (4th edn, 1843), 123.

[28] *Lumley* v. *Palmer* (1734) 7 Mod. 216. See also *Powell* v. *Monnier* (1737) 1 Atk. 611 at 612; *Clarke* v. *Cock* (1803) 4 East 57 at 67. Cf. *Fairlee* v. *Herring* (1826) 3 Bing. 625.

[29] See *Pillans* v. *Van Mierop* (1765) 3 Burr. 1663 at 1669; cf. *Pierson* v. *Dunlop* (1777) 2 Cowp. 571 at 573–4; *Johnson* v. *Collings* (1800) 1 East 98 at 103; *Clarke* v. *Cock* (1803) 4 East 57 at 73. It was unclear precisely what words or conduct were sufficient to constitute a promise: *Powell* v. *Jones* (1793) 1 Esp. 17; *Rees* v. *Warwick* (1818) 2 B. & Ald. 113.

[30] 1 & 2 Geo. IV c. 78, s 2. A signature was not necessary: it was sufficient to write 'accepted' on it: *Dufaur* v. *Oxenden* (1831) 1 M. & R. 90.

[31] Byles, *Bills of Exchange* (4th edn, 1843), 142–3; Chitty, *Bills* (9th edn by Chitty and J. W. Hulme, 1840), 295, Story, *Bills*, § 249, p. 275. Where the bill had not been drawn, the courts debated whether the drawee was bound if a third party had relied on the promise: *Miln* v. *Prest* (1816) 4 Camp. 393; *Bank of Ireland* v. *Archer and Daly* (1843) 11 M. & W. 383.

[32] Mercantile Law Amendment Act, 19 & 20 Vict. c. 97. An Act of 1878 clarified the law, to confirm that a signature alone would constitute acceptance; and these rules were then codified in the Bills of Exchange Act 1882.

[33] Story, *Bills*, § 113, p. 128; Chitty, *Bills* (8th edn, 1833), 308–9.

of his acceptance. A drawee who had fewer funds of the drawer in his hands than was specified in the bill might limit his acceptance to such a sum, making a partial acceptance. A bill might be accepted to be paid on a different date from that drawn; or at a different place.[34] It might be accepted conditionally, as where a drawee accepted to pay a bill when goods consigned to him (for which the bills were drawn) were sold,[35] or when a bill of lading for the goods was received,[36] or when funds were received to pay the bills.[37] The holder of the bill had the right to insist on an unconditional acceptance, and to resort to his remedy against the drawer if one was not forthcoming from the drawee. But he could also take the qualified acceptance, and the acceptor would be bound to pay on fulfilment of the condition.[38]

If the drawee refused to accept the bill, or refused to pay, the bill was regarded as *dishonoured*. Where this occurred, the holder had to seek recourse against prior indorsers of the bill and the drawer, who were treated as sureties for the drawee. Since every indorser of a bill was regarded as being in the nature of a new drawer—in effect contracting to pay the indorsee, if the drawee failed to[39]—indorsees could take action directly against the indorser, without looking first to the drawer.[40] However, before action could be taken against these parties, the holder had to give them notice of the bill's dishonour within a reasonable time, using 'due diligence'.[41] The reason for this rule was that it was presumed that the money represented by the bill was a debt due from the drawee to the drawer, and that if the drawee refused to pay it as directed, the holder was obliged to inform the drawer—the original creditor—as soon as possible in order to permit him

---

[34] Before 1821, there was much debate over whether an acceptance payable at a particular bank was a 'qualified' one, which would require the holder to prove in any action that he had presented the bill at the bank in question. The House of Lords held in *Rowe* v. *Young* (1820) 2 B. & B. 165, 2 Bligh. P.C. 391 that it was qualified, but the rule was changed by 1 & 2 Geo. IV, c. 78, which held that acceptances payable at a bank would normally be regarded as unconditional.

[35] *Smith* v. *Abbot* (1741) 2 Stra. 1152.   [36] *Smith* v. *Vertue* (1860) 9 C.B. N.S. 214.

[37] *Mendizabal* v. *Machado* (1833) 6 Car. & P. 218. These rules were later codified in s 19 of the Bills of Exchange Act 1882.

[38] According to the treatise writers, the holder taking a qualified acceptance had to give notice of this to any prior holders, who (without this) would be absolved from any liability on the bill 'for it may materially change their whole relations to, and responsibilities on, the Bill': Story, *Bills*, § 240, p. 267, and Chitty, *Bills* (5th edn, 1818), 238.

[39] See *Horn* v. *Rouquette* (1878) 3 QBD 514 at 519 (per Brett J.).

[40] *Penny* v. *Innes* (1834) 1 C. M. & R. 439; *Allen* v. *Walker* (1837) 2 M. & W. 317. Given the different nature of promissory notes (where the prime debtor was the maker), the holder of the note had to sue the maker first, rather than proceeding first against the indorsees. See *Gwinnell* v. *Herbert* (1836) 5 Ad. & El. 437 at 440.

[41] *Blesard* v. *Hirst* (1770) 5 Burr. 2670; *Goodall* v. *Dolley* (1787) 1 T.R. 712. It was held that putting a notice in the post was sufficient: *Stocken* v. *Collin* (1841) 7 M. & W. 515.

to take steps to recover the money in the hands of his debtor.[42] Since any delay by the holder of the bill in informing him of the dishonour might prejudice the drawer, he lost his remedy against him for failing to act in time.

In 1786, the King's Bench held in *Bickerdike* v. *Bollman* that there was no need to give notice of dishonour in cases where the drawee never had any funds belonging to the drawer: 'for it is fraud in itself, and if that can be proved, the notice may be dispensed with'.[43] The rule was aimed largely at those who drew accommodation bills for their own benefit: they hardly needed the protection of the notice, since there was no one against whom they could seek a remedy in case of non-payment. However, many judges were unhappy at the eroding of the rule that notice of dishonour had always to be given,[44] particularly where the person accommodated was the indorsee of the bill or the acceptor, and not the drawer, who might himself have a remedy against one of the other parties.[45] Despite *Bickerdike* v. *Bollman*, it was therefore agreed by the 1820s that if a drawer of a bill had a reasonable expectation that a bill would be paid, and if he had a remedy over against the person expected to pay, then he was entitled to notice of dishonour, even if the acceptor had no funds of the drawer in his hands.[46] Only if the drawer had no expectation that the bill would be paid, and would not be in any way prejudiced by the lack of notice, as where he drew the bill for his own accommodation, was it dispensed with.[47]

If a foreign bill was dishonoured, it also needed to be *protested*. This entailed making a formal declaration of any loss (typically before a notary). Although a formality, it was required as evidence of dishonour which would be accepted by all foreign courts.[48] The requirement of a protest was maintained to keep English law in line with international custom. Although eighteenth-century statute law made provision for protesting inland bills,[49] it was not necessary to do so, and was generally not done.

If a drawee refused to accept a bill, or if he had absconded and could not be found, another party could accept the bill 'for the honour' of the drawer or indorser. This was done to give the bill greater security and hence negotiability.

---

[42] See the comments of Buller J. in *Bickerdike* v. *Bollman* (1786) 1 T.R. 405.

[43] *Bickerdike* v. *Bollman* (1786) 1 T.R. 405 at 408 (per Ashhurst J.). See also *Rogers* v. *Stephens* (1788) 2 T.R. 713. See also the discussion of the case in J. W. Smith, *A Selection of Leading Cases on Various Branches of the Law*, 2 vols (4th edn by J. S. Willes and H. S. Keating, 1856), ii, 39 *et seq.* In *De Berdt* v. *Atkinson* (1794) 2 H. Bl. 336, the same rule was applied to promissory notes.

[44] *Orr* v. *Maginnis* (1806) 7 East 359 at 362.

[45] *Ex p Heath* (1813) 2 V. & B. 240 at 241; *Cory* v. *Scott* (1820) 3 B. & Ald. 619. Cf. *Norton* v. *Pickering* (1828) 8 B. & C. 610; *Spooner* v. *Gardiner* (1824) R. & M. 84 at 85.

[46] *Lafitte* v. *Slatter* (1830) 6 Bing. 623. See also *Rucker* v. *Hiller* (1812) 16 East 43.

[47] Story, *Bills*, § 311, p. 351. See also *Claridge* v. *Dalton* (1815) 4 M. & S. 226 at 231–2.

[48] Chitty, *Bills* (4th edn, 1812), 228; (8th edn, 1833), 361–2.   [49] 3 & 4 Anne c. 9, s 4.

A person might accept for the drawer's honour if the drawee was liable to fail, in order to keep the bill in circulation, and maintain the credit it represented.[50] Such acceptances were called acceptances *supra protest*, because they could only be made when the bill had been refused acceptance by the drawee, and been protested. As Story put it, the reason for the requirement of the protest was that the drawer and indorsers could say that the bill was not originally drawn on the acceptor for honour 'and the only proper proof of the refusal of the original Drawee is by a protest, that being the known instrument, by the custom of merchants, to establish the fact'.[51] The acceptor for honour had to stipulate in his acceptance who the parties were for whose honour he accepted, since (if he later paid the bill) he would be entitled to recourse for payment to that person (and any who were liable to him). The acceptor for honour would declare before a notary that he accepted the protested bill for the honour of the person named. This acceptance was in effect only a conditional promise to pay if the original acceptor did not. Therefore, where the acceptor had refused to accept and it had been accepted by another *supra protest*, the holder still had, at the time the bill was due, to present it for payment to the drawee. If he refused to pay, it was to be presented to the acceptor *supra protest*.[52]

Bills of Exchange and Corporate Bodies

Bills of exchange were used by businesses as well as by individual merchants. Any partner could bind his partnership by drawing a bill of exchange in the name of a firm, since all partners had authority to bind the others.[53] If the partnership traded in the name of one partner only, he was able to bind the firm by drawing in his own name.[54] But when it came to joint stock companies, matters were more complex. It was accepted that corporations could enter into simple contracts made by their agents (not using the company's seal), provided it was within the proper scope of their charter, Act or deed of settlement. Although the courts were prepared to imply powers which were necessary to accomplish a company's

---

[50] The drawee himself—if his creditworthiness was in question—might decline to accept the bill on account of the person in whose favour it was drawn, but might instead accept only for the honour of the drawer. Chitty, *Bills* (8th edn, 1833), 375.

[51] Story, *Bills*, § 256, p. 284. See also Chitty, *Bills* (8th edn, 1833), 377.

[52] See *Hoare* v. *Cazenove* (1812) 16 East 391. The statute 6 & 7 W. 4 c. 58 clarified that the presentment to the second could be made on the day after presentment to the first.

[53] In *Harrison* v. *Jackson* (1797) 7 T.R. 207 at 210, Lord Kenyon noted '[t]he law of merchants is part of the law of the land; and in mercantile transactions, in drawing and accepting bills of exchange, it never was doubted but that one partner might bind the rest'. See also *Swan* v. *Steele* (1806) 7 East 210; *Ridley* v. *Taylor* (1810) 13 East 175.

[54] *South Carolina Bank* v. *Case* (1828) 8 B. & C. 427.

objects, nineteenth-century judges repeatedly held that statutory companies, whose main purpose was not trade, only had the power to issue bills and notes if conferred in their constitution.[55] Reiterating this approach, Byles J. observed in 1866 that 'if we intimated any doubt upon the matter, the market would in a short time be inundated by acceptances by railway companies'.[56] In 1867, the Chancery Court of Appeal confirmed that companies were not given the power to issue and accept bills of exchange, by virtue of their incorporation. Rather, the Companies Act 1862 left 'the power of a company so incorporated, with regard to negotiable securities, to be determined upon the proper construction of the memorandum and articles of association'.[57] The result of these decisions was that those dealing with companies had to take care.[58] Holders of bills were bound to know the contents of a deed of settlement, and so could not complain if the securities they took were worthless.

Even if a company had the power to draw and accept bills, questions remained as to the authority of its directors. Before 1844, in an age of unincorporated joint stock companies, judges protected shareholders by requiring proof that the company's agents had been given a power to bind it, before holding the firm liable on bills drawn or accepted by the directors.[59] If a director had not been given authority to draw or accept bills, then only he, and not the company, would be liable on it.[60] Matters improved with the passing of the Joint Stock Companies Act 1844, which made it much easier to establish the powers of the directors. However, the Act still left some room for disputes to arise. According to section 45, where companies authorized their directors to draw or accept bills, it had to be done by two directors, who had also to express that it was done for the company.[61] This clause caused some difficulties, since companies could dispute their liability if the directors had failed to express themselves correctly.[62] To overcome this problem, the Companies Act 1856 (s 43) omitted the need for the directors to 'express' their authority on the document, and instead allowed a bill or note to be made, accepted, or indorsed in the name of the company 'by any person acting

---

[55] Byles, *Bills* (4th edn, 1843), 48; Story, *Bills*, § 79, p. 94; Chitty, *Bills* (8th edn, 1833), 17–21. See *Broughton* v. *Manchester and Salford Water-Works Co* (1819) 3 B. & Ald. 1; *East London Water Works Co* v. *Bailey* (1827) 4 Bing. 283 at 287.

[56] *Bateman* v. *The Mid-Wales Railway Co* (1866) LR 1 CP 499 at 510.

[57] *In re Peruvian Railways Co* (1867) LR 2 Ch App 617 at 623.

[58] e.g. *Balfour* v. *Ernest* (1859) 5 C.B. N.S. 601.

[59] *Dickinson* v. *Valpy* (1829) 10 B. & C. 128 at 137.

[60] *Bramah* v. *Roberts* (1837) 3 Bing. N.C. 963; *Bult* v. *Morrell* (1840) 12 Ad. & El. 745.

[61] 9 & 10 Vict. c. 110, s 45.

[62] See *Halford* v. *Cameron's Coalbrook Steam Coal and Swansea and Loughor Railway Co* (1851) 16 Q.B. 442; *Edwards* v. *Cameron's Coalbrook Steam Coal and Swansea and Loughor Railway Co* (1851) 6 Exch. 269.

under the express or implied authority of the company'. Under this rule, any bill or note had to bear the full and correct name of the company; but if it did, and it was signed in fact on behalf of the company by a person authorized to do so, then the company was bound by it.[63] The legislation did not remove the risk run by directors that they would be personally liable on bills drawn or accepted by them. Directors were held personally liable if they did not make it explicitly clear that they were acting for the company[64] and were not taking any liability themselves.[65] There was even debate over whether the very use of the phrasing 'I promise to pay' rendered the director personally liable; though both the Exchequer in 1869[66] and the Court of Appeal in 1909 held that it did not.[67]

Negotiability and Indorsement

The principal utility of bills and notes for commerce lay in the fact that they were negotiable, or freely transferable. Before 1882, bills and notes were only negotiable if they included wording which indicated that they were so: typically, either the words 'or order' or 'to bearer'. If they did not, the drawer and acceptor of a bill, or the maker of a note, was liable only to the payee.[68] The Bills of Exchange Act 1882 removed the need to include these words to render a bill negotiable, though a bill could be made non-negotiable by including the appropriate restrictive language.[69]

Bills which were payable 'to bearer' could be transferred by mere delivery. If the seller of a bearer bill did not indorse it, he incurred no liability to the buyer if it turned out to be a bad bill.[70] In such a situation, the purchaser had to look for any remedy against those whose names were on the bill.[71] This rule worried late

---

[63] See *Lindus* v. *Melrose* (1857) 27 L.J. Ex. 326. See also *Okell* v. *Charles* (1876) 34 *LT* 822, a case on s 47 of the Companies Act 1862. These sections were consolidated in the 1908 Act as ss 63 and 77.

[64] *Price* v. *Taylor* (1860) 5 H. & N. 540; *Bottomley* v. *Fisher* (1862) 1 H. & C. 211. Contrast the wording in *Aggs* v. *Nicholson* (1856) 1 H. & N. 165.

[65] *Dutton* v. *Marsh* (1871) LR 6 QB 361.   [66] *Alexander* v. *Sizer* (1869) LR 4 Ex 102.

[67] *Chapman* v. *Smethurst* [1909] 1 KB 927 (CA), overruling [1909] 1 KB 73 KBD.

[68] At common law, a payee of a non-negotiable bill could indorse it, and any subsequent indorsee might look for payment to that payee, though not to the earlier parties. However, it was debatable whether such an indorsement could make the instrument negotiable, for by the Stamp Acts, a second stamp was needed to charge the indorser, as it would be considered to be the drawing of a new bill. See *Hill* v. *Lewis* (1694) 1 Salk. 132 for the position before the Stamp Acts, and *Plimley* v. *Westley* (1835) 2 Bing. N.C. 249 for the later position. Where the bill was already negotiable, no new stamp was needed: *Penny* v. *Innes* (1834) 1 C. M. & R. 439. For comment, see Chitty, *Bills* (9th edn by Chitty and J. W. Hulme, 1840), 196–7.

[69] Bills of Exchange Act, s 8(5). See also Byles, *Bills* (17th edn by W. B. Byles and E. R. Watson, 1911), 108–9, 166.

[70] *Fenn* v. *Harrison* (1790) 3 T.R. 757 at 759.

[71] Byles, *Bills* (4th edn, 1843). See also *Fydell* v. *Clark* (1795) 1 Esp. 447.

eighteenth-century judges, when dealing with cases in which a seller of goods was paid by a bearer bill which turned out to be worthless. It had been held at the turn of the eighteenth century that if the bill or note was given in payment of a pre-existing debt, then the receiver could recover what he was owed from the party paying it, if it turned out to be worthless; but if a seller accepted a bill or note at the time of a sale, then he was held to have taken it in full payment, as part of the contract.[72] This strict view was softened towards the end of the century, when it was held that the purchaser of goods could recover if the note were worthless, unless he had *expressly* agreed to assume the risk.[73] But in the 1820s, it was felt that this generous approach, aimed at protecting the sellers of goods, threatened to undermine the use of negotiable instruments. The view was now taken that a seller of goods who had been paid by a bad bill had to return it promptly to allow the transferor to recover on it. Thus, in *Camidge* v. *Allenby* in 1827, the seller of corn who was paid for it with notes of a Huddersfield bank which had stopped payment earlier in the day was unable to recover the value of the notes. '[A]lthough bills and notes, delivered as satisfaction of a debt, do not in general operate as a satisfaction, unless they turn out to be valuable', Holroyd J. noted, 'yet the case is otherwise if due steps are not taken to obtain payment from the party who is in the first instance bound to pay them.'[74] Since the payee here had not presented them for payment at the bank, and returned them to the transferor on their dishonour, he was guilty of laches which barred his recovery.[75] Vendors of bills and notes did not warrant the solvency of those whose names were on them. They did, however, warrant that they were what they purported to be, so that if (for instance) something sold as a foreign bill (not liable to stamp duty) was in fact an inland bill (and therefore void for want of a stamp), then the purchaser could return it to the vendor who had not indorsed it. As Lord Campbell pointed out in 1853, '[i]f, being what was sold, the bill was valueless because of the insolvency of the parties, the vendor would not be answerable; but he is answerable if the bill be spurious'.[76]

Bills which were payable 'to order' had to be indorsed. This could be done 'in full' with the indorser writing in the name of the person in whose favour the indorsement was made.[77] Property in the bill passed by such indorsement

---

[72] See *Clerk* v. *Mundall* (1698) 12 Mod. 203; *Ward* v. *Evans* (1703) 2 Ld. Raym. 928 at 930. See also Chitty, *Bills* (4th edn, 1812), 157–8.

[73] *Owenson* v. *Morse* (1796) 7 T.R. 64 at 66; see also *Puckford* v. *Maxwell* (1794) 6 T.R. 52.

[74] *Camidge* v. *Allenby* (1827) 6 B. & C. 373 at 384.

[75] See also *Rogers* v. *Langford* (1833) 1 Car. & M. 637.

[76] *Gompertz* v. *Bartlett* (1853) 2 E. & B. 849 at 854.

[77] It was settled in the eighteenth century that a bill which was at its outset negotiable, did not lose its negotiability if indorsed to another party without also including the words 'or order'. *More*

to the new holder, who could in turn only pass it on by an indorsement of his own, which made him liable on the bill. It was much more common, however, to indorse 'in blank', by merely signing the bill without stating in whose favour the indorsement was made. It was settled by the early nineteenth century that such an indorsement in blank constituted the bill one payable to bearer, with property in the bill consequently being transferred by delivery.[78] A subsequent holder of a bill indorsed in blank could in turn make a special indorsement, writing above the indorser's name that the bill should be payable to a certain person or his order.[79] The named person thereupon obtained the right to the bill,[80] though the person who filled in the blank with the new name did not himself become liable on the bill, unless he also indorsed it.[81] In business practice, the same bill could be indorsed on numerous occasions, in blank or to order. Thus, a bill which was indorsed specially by the first payee to a second holder might then be indorsed in blank, and passed on to other holders, each of whom might in turn indorse it in blank to increase its creditworthiness. Subsequent holders might once more seek to indorse it specially, directing it to be paid to a certain payee.[82]

Before 1882, if a bill which had been indorsed in blank was then specially indorsed to a named payee, subsequent *bona fide* holders were not required to trace their title through that person, but could simply strike out the name[83] and have a remedy against the previous indorsers.[84] For it was established in the eighteenth century that once a bill had been sent into the world as negotiable—as occurred when the payee indorsed it in blank—its negotiability could not be restricted.[85] However, section 8(3) of the Bills of Exchange Act 1882 enacted that a bill would only be regarded as payable to bearer, if it was expressed to be so

---

v. *Manning* (1718) 1 Comyns. 311; *Acheson* v. *Fountain* (1723) 1 Stra. 557; *Edie* v. *East India Co* (1761) 1 W. Bl. 296.

[78] *Peacock* v. *Rhodes* (1781) 2 Doug. 633 at 636; Chitty, *Bills* (11th edn by J. A. Russell, 1878), 173.

[79] But he was not permitted to alter the liabilities of the acceptor in so doing: see *Hirschfield* v. *Smith* (1866) 1 LR CP 340 at 353.

[80] Thus, if a man sent a bill, indorsed in blank, to his agent to get accepted, he would himself be able to sue the acceptor on it while it remained in blank; but if the agent filled in his own name, he would thereby become the indorsee: *Clark* v. *Pigot* (1699) 1 Salk. 126.

[81] *Vincent* v. *Horlock* (1808) 1 Camp. 442. If he chose to indorse the bill, and thereby to increase its credit, he assumed a risk.

[82] For an example, see the life of the bill in *Leonard* v. *Wilson* (1834) 2 Car. & M. 589.

[83] Those whose names were struck out were discharged from any liability on the bill: *Fairclough* v. *Pavia* (1854) 9 Exch. 690.

[84] Byles, *Bills* (4th edn, 1843), 111 (a view quoted by Pollock CB in *Walker* v. *Macdonald* (1848) 2 Exch. 527 at 531. Cf. Chitty *Bills* (9th edn by Chitty and J. W. Hulme, 1840), 231; Bayley, *Bills* (6th edn by G. M. Dowdeswell, 1849), 132–3, Chitty, *Bills* (11th edn by J. A. Russell, 1878), 173–4. Compare M. D. Chalmers, *A Digest of the Law of Bills of Exchange* (2nd edn, 1881), 107.

[85] *Smith* v. *Clarke* (1794) 1 Esp. 180; *Walker* v. *Macdonald* (1848) 2 Exch. 527. This rule may have been related to the anxiety of judges to prevent holders of accommodation bills drawn in blank from

payable, or if its last indorsement was in blank. This was designed 'to bring the law into accordance with custom by making a special indorsement control a previous indorsement in blank',[86] and had the effect of requiring holders subsequent to the special indorsement to trace their title through the earlier holders.

Holders could also make *restrictive* indorsements, by making it 'for my use', or 'for my account', so that indorsees and later holders held the bill or its proceeds in trust for the restraining party.[87] The theory behind this was that a holder who made a restrictive indorsement was not selling the bill, or transferring ownership in it, but was only authorizing a particular person to receive it for him and for his own use.[88] Merchants receiving bills of exchange in payment for goods often indorsed them restrictively to their factors, to hold them 'for their use'. Banks who paid factors on these instruments ran great risks if they did not take care to check that the factor was not paying the money to his own account. For, as was revealed in *Sigourney* v. *Lloyd*, if the factor went bankrupt, the bank would remain liable to the merchant, who retained his property in the bill. As Best CJ put it in the Exchequer Chamber, 'we see no inconvenience to commercial interests from such a limitation of the effect of the indorsement so expressed; the only result will be, to make parties open their eyes and read before they discount'.[89]

Indorsements could also be *conditional*, for instance with the indorser directing money to be paid on the happening of a specified event. If the terms of the condition were not performed, property in the bill reverted to the indorser, who could recover on it;[90] though once the conditions were complied with, the transfer was complete, even if the indorsee's situation later changed so that he no longer complied with the conditions.[91] The doctrine of conditional indorsements was controversial. Treatise writers in the early nineteenth century suggested that they only bound the acceptor if they were made prior to acceptance.[92] The whole doctrine came in for strong criticism from Mackenzie Chalmers, who pointed out that no foreign code recognized such indorsements, and that Pothier had noted that the indorser had to conform to the same conditions as the drawer in his draft. It was in

attempting to evade liability by writing in names of payees. See e.g. *Bland* v. *Ryan* (1795) Peake Add. Cas. 39.

[86] Chalmers, *The Bills of Exchange Act* (6th edn,1900), 6.

[87] Byles, *Bills* (4th edn, 1843), 116.

[88] *Edie* v. *East India Co* (1761) 2 Burr. 1216 at 1226–7. See also *Snee* v. *Prescot* (1743) 1 Atk. 245 at 249; *Ancher* v. *Governor and Co of Bank of England* (1781) 2 Doug. 637.

[89] *Lloyd* v. *Sigourney* (1829) 5 Bing. 525 at 531, affirming *Sigourney* v. *Lloyd* (1828) 8 B. & C. 622.

[90] *Robertson* v. *Kensington* (1811) 4 Taunt. 30. See also *Adams* v. *Jones* (1840) 12 Ad. & El. 455 and *Bell* v. *Ingestre* (1848) 12 Q.B. 310, where the condition was not indorsed on the bill, but still bound the indorsee.

[91] See *Soares* v. *Glyn* (1845) 8 Q.B. 24.

[92] Chitty, *Bills* (8th edn, 1833), 261. This had been the case in *Robertson* v. *Kensington* (1811) 4 Taunt. 30.

the very nature of a bill of exchange that a drawer could not draw conditionally on the acceptor.[93] That being so, it made no sense to allow an indorser—a stranger to the drawee—to impose conditions which the drawer could not. It was also essential to a bill that the payee be certain, yet a conditional indorsement rendered it uncertain whether the indorsee was entitled to payment. For Chalmers, the solution was to treat the indorsement as if it were restrictive. The holder would be entitled to recover on the bill from those liable to pay irrespective of whether the conditions had been fulfilled, but he would hold the funds in trust for his indorser if they had not.[94] When he came to draft the 1882 Code, Chalmers thus altered the law, section 33 enacting that '[w]here a bill purports to be indorsed conditionally the condition may be disregarded by the payer, and payment to the indorsee is valid whether the condition has been fulfilled or not'.

Indorsers could also give *qualified* indorsements, passing the property in the bill to the indorsee, but without accepting liability on it. This occurred primarily where bills were bought by an agent for a customer, where the agent did not want to assume any responsibility on the bill.[95] To make such an indorsement, the agent would have to put the words 'sans recours' on the bill.[96] If the words were not used, the agent would be liable, since any person who signed his own name on a bill made himself liable, even if he was acting as the agent of another.[97] Nevertheless, the courts and jurists were unhappy with any suggestion that a principal could recover from an agent omitting to insert the words 'sans recours',[98] particularly since the words were often omitted so as not to diminish the credit of the bill. Where the agency relationship was continuing—as where an agent was regularly employed abroad to buy and remit bills to the principal at home at a lower rate of commission—the courts considered that there was a broader contractual understanding between these parties that the agent should not be liable on the bill.[99]

Consideration and Passing the Property in Bills

For those holding them, bills and notes represented a species of property. Since a bill or note represented a debt, it was a chose in action; but since it could be

---

[93] See *Dawkes* v. *Earl of Deloraine* (1771) 2 W. Bl. 782.

[94] Chalmers, *Digest* (2nd edn, 1881), 110. He showed that the draft Indian code provided for conditional liability for the indorser.

[95] Consequentially, he obtained a smaller commission that would be the case if liability was accepted.

[96] See also s 16 of the Bills of Exchange Act 1882.

[97] See *Goupy* v. *Harden* (1816) 7 Taunt. 159; *Leadbitter* v. *Farrow* (1816) 5 M. & S. 345.

[98] See e.g. *Kidson* v. *Dilworth* (1818) 5 Price 564; *Pike* v. *Street* (1828) M. & M. 226.

[99] *Castrique* v. *Buttigieg* (1855) 10 Moore P.C. 94 at 108. See also Chitty, *Bills* (8th edn, 1833), 39.

assigned, some judges observed that it 'is to be considered rather as a chattel personal than a chose in action'.[100] It did in many ways resemble a chattel,[101] since it could be passed on by way of sale, gift, or will, or deposited with bailees[102] as other chattels could.[103] At the same time, property in bills and notes passed more easily than was the case with chattels, since any holder of a bill or note who had obtained possession of it *bona fide* acquired property in it, regardless of the title of the person from whom he had obtained it.

If bills and notes constituted a form of property in the hands of the holder, his rights were grounded in a contractual obligation on the part of the ultimate debtor (the acceptor or maker) or his sureties (the drawer or indorsers) to pay. *Prima facie*, this meant that there had to have been consideration given for the bill or note. Late eighteenth-century courts, influenced by Lord Mansfield's attempts to reform the doctrine of consideration,[104] were prepared to uphold promissory notes given by way of gift.[105] But by the early nineteenth century, judges were beginning to turn against Mansfield's views, and the question was once more debated whether donees of bills and notes had to show that they had given consideration for them before they could recover from the donor.[106] The matter was resolved in 1835, in *Easton* v. *Pratchett*. In Lord Abinger's view, a person making a gift of a bill of exchange by indorsing it to another gratuitously would not be liable to the donee.[107] For since an indorsement was a promise to the indorsee to accept liability, it could not be binding if it was a gratuitous promise. However, in contrast to the general rule in contract law, it was for the defendant to show that no consideration had been given[108] and not for the plaintiff to show that it

---

[100] *M'Neilage* v. *Holloway* (1818) 1 B. & Ald. 218. This meant that a husband could sue in his own name on a bill payable to his wife while *feme sole*. This decision was controversial, however, given that it suggested that bills in the wife's name would vest in her husband's executors on his death. It was later criticized: see *Richards* v. *Richards* (1831) 2 B. & Ad. 447, where a promissory note to a wife from a husband was held a chose in action and not a chattel. See also *Gaters* v. *Madeley* (1840) 6 M. & W. 423; *Hart* v. *Stephens* (1845) 6 Q.B. 937.

[101] Cf. *Milnes* v. *Dawson* (1850) 5 Exch. 948 at 950. See also *Hornblower* v. *Proud* (1819) 2 B. & Ald. 327.

[102] It could be deposited with bailees, as chattels were. *Ex p Flint* (1818) 1 Swans. 30.

[103] But it was unlike a chattel in other respects. E.g. they could not be described as chattels in indictments. Byles, *Bills* (4th edn, 1843), 2.

[104] *Pillans* v. *Van Mierop* (1765) 3 Burr. 1663.

[105] See e.g. *Seton* v. *Seton* (1789) 2 Bro. C.C. 610. See also the argument of counsel in *Tate* v. *Hilbert* (1793) 2 Ves. Jun. 111 at 117.

[106] There was some debate over whether natural affection counted as consideration for a promissory note: see *Holliday* v. *Atkinson* (1826) 5 B. & C. 501; *Easton* v. *Pratchett* (1835) 1 C. M. & R. 798 at 808; *Nash* v. *Brown* (1817) in Chitty, *Bills* (8th edn, 1833), 85n.

[107] *Easton* v. *Pratchett* (1835) 1 C. M. & R. 798 at 808–9. The case involved an indorsor and indorsee, rather than the original parties. See also *Milnes* v. *Dawson* (1850) 5 Exch. 948.

[108] *Guichard* v. *Roberts* (1763) 1 W. Bl. 445.

had,[109] since there was a presumption in the case of such instruments that value had been received.[110]

Easton v. *Pratchett* settled the position between all *immediate* parties—not only between indorser and indorsee, but also between the original parties. However, the fact that there had been no consideration in the original transaction did not bar subsequent *bona fide* holders from suing the original donor of the bill. In litigation between 'remote' parties, as when an indorsee sued the acceptor, the plaintiff could recover, unless it was shown *both* that the defendant had received nothing for his liability, *and* that neither the plaintiff, nor any party from whom he had obtained the bill, had given value for it.[111] As long as value had been given at some stage, the holder could sue. The fact that the original acceptor received no value did not vitiate the instrument,[112] since (as Chitty put it), '[i]t is but just, that if one of two innocent persons must sustain a loss, he who has suffered a negotiable security with his name attached to it, to get it into circulation, ought to bear the loss, and seek his remedy against the person who improperly passed the instrument'.[113]

If the defendant showed that no consideration had passed between the original parties to the bill, the subsequent holder had to show that it had been obtained for good consideration.[114] Where the instrument was founded in fraud,[115] or the plaintiff's title derived from a fraudulent holder,[116] or where the original consideration was illegal,[117] the onus was on the plaintiff to show that value had been given.[118] In such cases, the holder had to prove not only that he had given value for the instrument, but also that he had done so in good faith, without knowledge

---

[109] See e.g. *Philliskirk* v. *Pluckwell* (1814) 2 M. & S. 393 at 395–6; *Ridout* v. *Brislow* (1830) 1 C. & J. 231.

[110] *Josceline* v. *Lassere* (1714) Fortescue 281; *Poplewell* v. *Wilson* (1720) 1 Stra. 264. Nor was it necessary in litigation to declare that the bill or note had been given for value, since that was implied in it: *Hatch* v. *Trayes* (1840) Ad. & El. 702.

[111] Byles, *Bills* (4th edn, 1843), 93. As Parke B. put it in *Edwards* v. *Jones* (1837) 2 M. & W. 414 at 418, 'the title of an indorsee is the title of all the prior parties to the note'. See also *Thomas* v. *Newton* (1827) 2 C. & P. 606; *Heath* v. *Sansom* (1831) 2 B. & Ad. 291; *Masters* v. *Ibberson* (1849) 8 C.B. 100 at 112.

[112] *Robinson* v. *Reynolds* (1841) 2 Q.B. 196. See also *Thiedemann* v. *Goldschmidt* (1859) 1 De G. F. & J. 4.

[113] Chitty, *Bills* (8th edn, 1833), 90.

[114] The acceptor could not challenge the validity of the bill solely on the grounds that later parties had not given value. He had first to show lack of consideration between the original parties: *Whitaker* v. *Edmunds* (1834) 1 Ad. & El. 638.

[115] *Bailey* v. *Bidwell* (1844) 13 M. & W. 73; *Harvey* v. *Towers* (1851) 6 Exch. 656.

[116] *Smith* v. *Braine* (1851) 16 Q.B. 244.   [117] *Bingham* v. *Stanley* (1841) 2 Q.B. 117.

[118] As Lord Blackburn pointed out in *Jones* v. *Gordon* (1877) 2 App. Cas. 616 at 627, in cases of fraud or illegality, it was assumed that the holder who could himself not sue on the instrument would pass it on to another to recover for him. The onus was therefore shifted to that person to show he had given value.

of the fraud.[119] Before 1836, the courts also took the view that where the original transaction was an accommodation bill, given without consideration, the onus was on the holder to show value had been given. However, it was settled in *Mills* v. *Barber* that there was no such onus on the holder, since it might be presumed that money had been raised on instruments such as these whose very purpose was to generate credit.[120] In such cases, the onus henceforth lay on the defendant to show that the plaintiff had given no value. Given that this was a rather more difficult burden of proof, it was a decision which made accommodation bills secure.[121] Moreover, when it came to accommodation bills, the fact that the holder knew that the original transaction lacked consideration did not prevent his recovering, since to do so would frustrate the very object of such bills.[122]

Courts dealing with bills of exchange took a broader view of the nature of consideration than was taken in cases involving the general law of contract. First, it was accepted that a bill could be given for an existing or antecedent debt, without falling foul of the rule against past consideration. The rule was in place by the end of the eighteenth century,[123] but the reasons for it continued to be debated. Some judges argued that where a bill of exchange was given for an antecedent debt, consideration could only be found in a promise by the creditor to suspend taking action on any remedy he might have to recover the debt until the bill was due.[124] Other judges felt that the payment of the debt by a bill or note constituted a conditional payment of the debt.[125] In 1875, it was held by the Exchequer Chamber in *Currie* v. *Misa* that the second view was the correct one.[126] If these doctrinal explanations

[119] The position was clarified by s 30(2) of the Bills of Exchange Act 1882, which stipulated that where a bill was affected with fraud or illegality, it had to be shown that the holder had to show that 'value has in good faith been given'. The fact that the holder had to prove both that he gave value and acted in good faith was confirmed in *Tatam* v. *Haslar* (1889) 23 QBD 345.

[120] *Mills* v. *Barber* (1836) 1 M. & W. 425 at 432. See also his comments in *Simpson* v. *Clarke* (1835) 2 C. M. & R. 342 and the view of the court in *Percival* v. *Frampton* (1835) 2 C. M. & R. 180.

[121] See also *Sturtevant* v. *Ford* (1842) 4 M. & G. 101.

[122] Story, *Bills*, § 191, pp. 213–14; *Smith* v. *Knox* (1799) 3 Esp. 46; *Charles* v. *Marsden* (1808) 1 Taunt. 224; *Fentum* v. *Pocock* (1813) 5 Taunt. 192 at 196.

[123] In *Stedman* v. *Gooch* (1793) 1 Esp. 3 at 6, Lord Kenyon noted 'the law was clear, that if in payment of a debt the creditor is content to take a bill or note payable at a future day, that he cannot legally commence an action on his original debt, until such bill or note becomes payable, or default is made'. See also Story, *Bills*, § 183, p. 204. See also *Brix* v. *Braham* (1823) 1 Bing. 281.

[124] See *Baker* v. *Walker* (1845) 14 M. & W. 465. See also *Price* v. *Price* (1847) 16 M. & W. 232 at 241–2. See also Byles, *Bills* (4th edn, 1843), 91.

[125] This position was taken in cases where those who had been given negotiable instruments sought to recover in actions of assumpsit or debt for the money owed; and they were held unable to do so until the payment of the bill or note had been defeated. See *Kearslake* v. *Morgan* (1794) 5 T.R. 513; *Griffiths* v. *Owen* (1844) 13 M. & W. 58 at 64; *Belshaw* v. *Bush* (1851) 11 C.B. 191.

[126] *Currie* v. *Misa* (1875) LR 10 Ex 153 at 163. This view was endorsed by the House of Lords in *M'Lean* v. *The Clydesdale Banking Co* (1883) 9 App. Cas. 95.

were ways of avoiding the admission that there was no fresh consideration, the matter was settled by section 27(1)(b) of the Bills of Exchange Act 1882, which simply declared that an antecedent debt or liability constituted consideration.

Secondly, it was accepted that a bill or note could be given for the debt of a third party.[127] Early nineteenth-century courts felt that the same kind of consideration which was required for simple contracts was not necessary in the case of bills and notes, though they did not explore precisely what kind was needed.[128] By mid-century, judges and jurists located the consideration in the donee's forbearance to sue the debtor, an idea to be found in texts such as Byles's.[129] According to this view, if the bill or note was payable at a future date, then consideration could be found in the forbearance; whereas if it was payable on demand, and the credit had not originally been given to the debtor at the maker's request, the courts would accept pleas that there was no consideration.[130] By the later nineteenth century, commentators agreed that a promise in consideration of a third party debt had to be supported by the kind of consideration which would support a promise on a simple contract.[131]

In theory, the 'value' given for the bill was the face value of the bill. Where bills were drawn 'in the regular course of business'—that is, where consideration had originally been given—the holder could 'recover the whole' of the face value.[132] But if the original transaction lacked consideration—as where accommodation bills were given—then early nineteenth-century courts held that the holder could only recover the value which he (or the person from whom he acquired it) had given for the bill.[133] Thus, in *Simpson* v. *Clarke* in 1835, where the second indorsee of an accommodation bill drawn for £98-5-3 (on which no prior parties have given value) proved that he obtained the bill in consideration of a £20-18 debt due to him, he was held entitled only to the money he had paid out.[134] In practice,

---

[127] *Parish of Poplewell* v. *Wilson* (1720) 1 Stra. 264.

[128] See e.g. *Sowerby* v. *Butcher* (1834) 2 C. & M. 368 at 372; *Ridout* v. *Bristow* (1830) 1 C. & J. 231 at 234.

[129] Byles, *Bills* (4th edn, 1843), 92, note k. This point was also stressed in *Nelson* v. *Serle* (1839) 4 M. & W. 795.

[130] *Crofts* v. *Beale* (1851) 11 C.B. 172, where Jervis CJ drew his arguments from Byles. See also *Balfour* v. *Sea Fire Life Assurance Co* (1857) 3 C.B. N.S. 300.

[131] See Chalmers, *Digest* (1878), 67. In the twentieth century, it was held that s 27(1)(b) of the 1882 Act did not extend to existing debts of third parties: *Oliver* v. *Davis* [1949] 2 KB 727.

[132] *Wiffen* v. *Roberts* (1795) 1 Esp. 261. Lord Kenyon suggested here that if the indorsee had obtained the bill cheaply from the indorser, he might be regarded as trustee for the latter of the surplus.

[133] See *Jones* v. *Hibbert* (1817) 2 Stark. 304 and *Nash* v. *Brown* (1817) in Chitty, *Bills* (8th edn, 1833), 85n, where Lord Ellenborough ruled at *nisi prius* that a bill of exchange, which had been accepted by the defendant as a present to the payee, and then indorsed to the plaintiff for a small sum, only entitled the latter to the small sum he had paid for it, rather than the face value of the bill.

[134] *Simpson* v. *Clarke* (1835) 2 C. M. & R. 342.

where a party discounted an accommodation bill, he could sue on its face value, for by discounting it he gave the holder its full value, making his profit on a collateral commission and interest. But if, instead of discounting it, he merely bought it for half its face value, he could only recover the sum paid.[135] But by the end of the nineteenth century, the notion that the holder of an accommodation bill with notice could only recover what he had paid had gone,[136] thanks to the provision in the 1882 Act (s 28(2)) that accommodation parties were liable to holders for value, whether or not they knew of the accommodating nature of the bill.

The Subsequent Holder's Property

It was a general rule that a holder's right to a bill was not affected by any infirmity in the title of the person who transferred it to him, provided that he took it *bona fide* and for value. This meant that if a bill originated in a fraudulent transaction between two parties, a third party indorsee could have no action on it, if he knew of the fraud, even if it had been given for a *bona fide* debt to him.[137] However, the title of a holder was not vitiated by the fact of his knowledge of the original fraud, if the bill had passed through the hands of another *bona fide* holder who had no knowledge of the fraud.[138] To succeed, a defendant had to show that the holder was somehow party to the fraud.[139]

In the 1820s, the King's Bench and Common Pleas sought to impose a tougher test of *bona fides*, holding that where a holder for value had obtained the bill in circumstances which should have raised his suspicions, he could not recover unless he used due diligence to check that the person holding the bill had come by it honestly. Earlier courts had been of opinion that to impose such a duty would paralyse commerce.[140] But in *Gill* v. *Cubitt*, where a stolen bill of exchange was discounted by a bill broker who failed to make any inquiries about the person who brought it to him, Abbott CJ declared it to be 'for the interest of commerce, that no person should take a security of this kind from another without using reasonable caution'.[141] The judges in the 1820s were especially concerned to curb the theft of notes payable to bearer; and they felt that people were experienced enough with them to know how much care was needed to be taken with

---

[135] See Chalmers's illustrations, *Digest* (2nd edn, 1881), 86.

[136] See Byles, *Bills* (17th edn by W. B. Byles and E. R. Watson, 1911), 152 note e. *Simpson* v. *Clarke* was not mentioned in this work. See also *Ex p Newton* (1880) 16 Ch D 330, which held that the holder of an accommodation bill could prove in bankruptcy for the full amount of he bill, but only receive dividends to the sum he was really owed.

[137] *Whistler* v. *Forster* (1863) 14 C.B. N.S. 248.   [138] *May* v. *Chapman* (1847) 16 M. & W. 355.

[139] *Masters* v. *Ibberson* (1849) 18 L.J. C.P. 348. See also Bills of Exchange Act 1882, s 29(3).

[140] *Miller* v. *Race* (1758) 1 Burr. 452; *Lawson* v. *Weston* (1801) 4 Esp. 56 at 57.

[141] *Gill* v. *Cubitt* (1824) 3 B. & C. 466 at 471. See also *Down* v. *Halling* (1825) 4 B. & C. 330.

them. According to Best CJ, 'the neglect of such caution could not fail to encourage the robbery of coaches, and the stealing of notes by clerks and servants'.[142] But the next generation of judges reverted to the rule established in the era of Mansfield. The rule rejected by Best CJ—that gross negligence itself did not vitiate the holder's rights, but was at most evidence of *mala fides*—was endorsed by Lord Denman CJ in 1836;[143] and in 1849, Lord Brougham could declare that 'the negligence of the party taking a negotiable instrument, does not fix him with the defective title of the party passing it to him'.[144] The Bill of Exchange Act 1882 (section 90) confirmed that the fact that a holder had been negligent did not prevent him being a *bona fide* holder.

Nonetheless, the courts continued to hold that wilful abstaining from inquiry—as opposed to mere negligence—could constitute constructive notice of a fraud.[145] In *Jones* v. *Gordon* in 1877, the plaintiff sought to recover from the estate of two bankrupts the face value of bills which he had purchased from them. The value of the bills was £1727, and the plaintiff (who had previously discounted bills) had bought them for £200. The two men in question had drawn accommodation bills, while insolvent and contemplating bankruptcy, and had disposed of them in fraud of their creditors. Although the plaintiff was not a direct party to the fraud, it was held in the House of Lords that the evidence showed that he was sufficiently aware of the suspicious circumstances surrounding the transaction to make his failure to inquire further amount to dishonesty.[146] In so doing, the Lords endorsed the comment in *Byles on Bills* that '[a] wilful and fraudulent absence of inquiry into the circumstances, when they are known to be such as to invite inquiry, will (if a jury think that the abstinence from inquiry arose from a suspicion or belief that inquiry would disclose a vice in the bills) amount to general or implied notice'.[147] Lord Blackburn suggested that had he only been 'honestly blundering and careless', he would have recovered the full face value, despite only paying £200.[148]

---

[142] *Snow* v. *Peacock* (1826) 3 Bing. 406 at 413.

[143] *Goodman* v. *Harvey* (1836) 4 Ad. & El. 870. See also his working towards this conclusion in *Backhouse* v. *Harrison* (1834) 5 B. & Ad. 1098 and *Crook* v. *Jadis* (1834) 5 B. & Ad. 909, and his later comments in *Uther* v. *Rich* (1839) 10 Ad. & El. 784. See also *Foster* v. *Pearson* (1835) 1 C. M. & R. 849.

[144] *Bank of Bengal* v. *Fagan* (1849) 7 Moo. P.C. 61 at 72. See also *Raphael* v. *Governor of Bank of England* (1855) 17 C.B. 161.

[145] *May* v. *Chapman* (1847) 16 M. & W. 355 at 361; *Oakeley* v. *Ooddeen* (1861) 2 F. & F. 656; *The London Joint Stock Bank* v. *Charles James Simmons* [1892] AC 201 at 231.

[146] *Jones* v. *Gordon* (1877) 2 App Cas 616.   [147] *Ibid.*, at 625.

[148] Brett LJ had also said in the Court of Appeal that if Jones had not known of the fraud, he could have recovered in full, despite only paying a small sum. *In re Gomersall* (1875) 1 Ch D 137 at 149. Jones was allowed to prove for £200, which represented the sum which he had advanced to the drawers of the bill. See *ibid.*, p. 146.

Forgers and Fictitious Parties

Since those who had acquired bills payable to bearer *bona fide* and for value could recover on them regardless of flaws in the title of earlier holders, they had a valid title to bills which had been lost or stolen from their original holders,[149] and could sue all those whose names were on the bill. However, no holder could acquire title to property in a bill or note through any forgery.[150] *Bona fide* holders of bills which bore forged indorsements could not sue the acceptor on them,[151] since he had done nothing to give credit to the forged signature, through which the holder had to trace his title.[152] Equally, if the maker or acceptor of a bill paid out on a forged indorsement, he remained liable to those defrauded by the forgery.[153] If bills or notes themselves were forged, the purported 'maker', 'drawer' or 'acceptor' was not liable on them.

However, since courts from Mansfield's era were keen to maintain the credit of negotiable instruments which had been allowed to circulate, it was held that if a party accepted a bill which had been forged, and thereby gave it currency, he was estopped from disputing the capacity or signature of the drawer, since it was incumbent on him to satisfy himself that the drawer's signature was genuine.[154] On the same principle, it was held that bankers who paid on the forged acceptance of their customers were liable.[155] Similarly, if a person whose acceptance had been forged induced others to assume the acceptance was genuine, he was held liable on it.[156] However, in 1843, in *Beeman* v. *Duck*, the Exchequer held that where a forger drew a bill in the name of an existing firm, payable to their order, which was accepted by the drawee, and the forger then indorsed it to a third party, the drawee was not liable to that party; for while he admitted 'that the bill was drawn by the parties by whom it purports to be drawn, [he] does not admit the indorsement by the same parties'.[157]

---

[149]   *Miller* v. *Race* (1758) 1 Burr. 452; *Peacock* v. *Rhodes* (1781) 2 Doug. 633.

[150]   See s 24 of the Bills of Exchange Act 1882.

[151]   They could be obliged to deliver them up to be cancelled: *Esdaile* v. *La Nauze* (1835) 1 You. & Coll. 394; *Johnson* v. *Windle* (1836) 3 Bing. N.C. 225. In *Burchfield* v. *Moore* (1854) 3 E. & B. 683, Lord Campbell CJ observed (at 687) that 'the plaintiff's remedy is confined to a right to recover the consideration for the bill, as between himself and the party from whom he received it: a similar remedy may be resorted to till the party is reached through whose fraud or laches the alteration was made.'

[152]   See *Smith* v. *Chester* (1787) 1 T.R. 654; *Johnson* v. *Windle* (1836) 3 Bing. N.C. 225.

[153]   *Cheap* v. *Harley*, cited in *Allen* v. *Dundas* (1789) 3 T.R. 125 at 127.

[154]   *Jenys* v. *Fawler* (1733) 2 Stra. 946; *Price* v. *Neal* (1762) 3 Burr. 1354. Cf. *Porthouse* v. *Parker* (1807) 1 Camp. 81; *Mather* v. *Lord Maidstone* (1856) 18 C.B. 273.

[155]   *Smith* v. *Mercer* (1815) 6 Taunt. 76.

[156]   *Leach* v. *Buchanan* (1802) 4 Esp. 226; *Phillips* v. *Im Thurn* (1866) LR 1 CP 463.

[157]   *Beeman* v. *Duck* (1843) 11 M. & W. 251. The fact that all was done in the name of the firm was not conclusive, since it was perfectly possible that the bill might have been drawn by an agent who had authority to draw, but not to indorse. See *Robinson* v. *Yarrow* (1817) 7 Taunt. 455.

The question whether an indorser was precluded from resisting an action by the holder, by showing that prior indorsements had been forged, took longer to settle. In *Critchlow* v. *Parry*, Lord Ellenborough accepted that a holder did not have to prove the genuineness of earlier indorsements, as the indorser he sued was to be considered as a new drawer.[158] But in 1824, Bayley J. was not prepared to rule that every indorser warranted the genuineness of prior indorsements.[159] The question remained moot,[160] but in 1856 it was settled that the indorser was estopped by his indorsement from traversing earlier ones,[161] a position confirmed in section 55(2) of the 1882 Act. To promote the negotiability and security of bills, it was considered important to prevent acceptors and indorsers from disputing their liability on the grounds that they had passed on a forged bill.

If a forged note had been discounted, the discounter could recover the sums paid, since the payment had been made under a mistake of fact (that the bill was genuine) and since there had been a total failure of consideration.[162] This was so even if the person selling the bill was unaware of the forgery and did not indorse it.[163] Where one firm of brokers which had discounted a bill presented by a forger sold it in turn to another firm without an indorsement, it had to restore the money received, since the bill sold was not what it purported to be.[164] Since dealings in financial instruments were often conducted via agents, courts also had to explore when those who had paid money on forged instruments could recover from the agents of the fraudsters. Where it was shown that the defendant had acted solely as an agent, was ignorant of the falsehood, and had none of the money remaining in his hands, he was not to be held liable.[165]

The party paying under a mistake could not recover, however, if he was at fault, or failed to act quickly, before the recipient altered his position. If the mistake was discovered before the receiver lost his remedy against any prior indorsers, then the party paying could recover;[166] but if the receiver lost his remedy against

---

[158] *Critchlow* v. *Parry* (1809) 2 Camp. 182.

[159] *East India Co* v. *Tritton* (1824) 3 B. & C. 280 at 289.

[160] Contrast the positions of Story, *Bills*, § 110, p. 125n; Chitty, *Bills* (8th edn, 1833), 266 and Bayley, *Bills* (5th edn by F. Bayley, 1833) 170. Cf. Byles, *Bills* (4th edn, 1843), 113.

[161] *Macgregor* v. *Rhodes* (1856) 6 E. & B. 266 at 270–1.

[162] Similarly, where bankers in ignorance paid an illegal cheque to a holder, who knew of the relevant facts, they were able to recover in an action for money had and received: *Martin* v. *Morgan* (1819) 1 B. & B. 289.

[163] *Jones* v. *Ryde* (1814) 5 Taunt. 488 at 492–3. See also *Wilkinson* v. *Johnson* (1824) 3 B. & C. 428.

[164] *Gurney* v. *Womersley* (1854) 4 E. & B. 133 at 141.

[165] *Ex p Bird, In re Bourne* (1851) 4 De Gex. & Sm. 273. It was settled that an agent could only be required to pay back money paid by mistake where he retained it in his hands: *Buller* v. *Harrison* (1777) 2 Cowp. 565.

[166] *Wilkinson* v. *Johnson* (1824) 3 B. & C. 428.

others by delay, then he could not.[167] In 1827, it was therefore held in *Cocks* v. *Masterman* that a bank which paid a forged bill presented for payment on its due date, but which did not discover the forgery for another day, could not recover the money.[168] This was because the holder of the forged bill was entitled to know on the day that it was due whether it was dishonoured or not, so that he could take immediate steps against any prior parties. The rule derived from this case was a stringent one, but was (according to Mathew J.) 'indispensable for the conduct of business'.[169] Because of its stringency, it was held in 1903 only to apply to negotiable instruments with indorsers to whom notice of dishonour had to be given. In other cases (such as where cheques were forged without indorsements), money could be recovered if 'notice of the mistake is given in reasonable time, and no loss has been occasioned by the delay in giving it'.[170]

If merchants regarded forgery as a constant danger which undermined credit, they habitually drew bills which were made payable to fictitious persons, as a way of promoting credit.[171] They were commonly used to accommodate the trader in need of credit. Bills would be drawn by a firm, payable to a fictitious party, which would then be accepted by their bankers. The fictitious 'payee' would then indorse the bill to the firm, which could then negotiate it to raise funds. The practice caused problems when firms drawing such bills failed, and were unable to pay their debts. The question was raised in a number of cases arising from such failures whether the bill had to be regarded as one transferrable by delivery, or by indorsement. If the latter view were taken, a subsequent holder would not be able to recover from the acceptor, for a holder of a bill payable to order had to trace his title through that of the person from whom he obtained it; and he could get no title on a forged or falsely indorsed bill. The question came to the House of Lords in 1791 in *Gibson* v. *Minet*, where the failed firm's bankers—who were fully aware of the fiction—sought to resist the claims of the holders of the bill. In their advice to the Lords, a majority of the judges felt that the bill should be given effect, as one payable to bearer.[172] For Baron Hotham, the case was ruled by the principle that no one should take advantage of his own wrong. Having knowingly accepted a bill incapable of being sued on as the 'order' bill it purported to be, they were to be held

---

[167] *See Smith* v. *Mercer* (1815) 6 Taunt. 76.   [168] *Cocks* v. *Masterman* (1829) 9 B. & C. 902.

[169] *The London and River Plate Bank* v. *The Bank of Liverpool* [1896] 1 QB 7 at 10–11.

[170] *Imperial Bank of Canada* v. *Bank of Hamilton* [1903] AC 49 at 58. For another case involving laches (but not forgery), see *Pooley* v. *Brown* (1862) 11 C.B. N.S. 566.

[171] The use of these bills first came to the courts' attention after the failure in 1788 of the cotton firm of Livesey, Hargreaves & Co, with huge debts. See J. S. Rogers, *The Early History of the Law of Bills and Notes: A Study in the Origins of Anglo-American Commercial Law* (Cambridge, 1995), 226 *et seq.*

[172] For earlier litigation involving this failure, see *Vere* v. *Lewis* (1789) 3 T.R. 182; *Minet* v. *Gibson* (1789) 3 T.R. 481; *Collis* v. *Emett* (1790) 1 H. Bl. 313.

to have accepted it in a form on which it could be sued. To do otherwise would leave this as 'mere waste paper'.[173] Since they intended it not to be such, but rather to be an instrument on which money was to be raised, they were to be held to have intended it to bear the form on which it could be sued. This view was clearly aimed at protecting subsequent holders who gave value on the faith of these bills.

Not all late eighteenth-century judges were happy with this view. Eyre CJ criticized the use of accommodation bills for encouraging 'a spirit of rash adventure, a spirit of monopoly, a spirit of gaming in commerce, luxury, extravagance and fraud of every kind'. In his view, since a bill payable to a fictitious person was payable to no one, it was 'impossible ever to animate it, or give it motion or transmissibility'.[174] Other judges were also hostile to the use of fictitious names in accommodation bills.[175] But the House of Lords had settled that, provided the acceptor knew that the payee was fictitious, such a bill was to be treated as one to bearer.[176] The rule was also soon settled that where the drawer's name was fictitious—the bill having in reality been drawn by 'his' indorsee—the acceptor was liable to subsequent holders. As Lord Tenterden put it in 1830, where there was no person who was the drawer, 'the fair construction of the acceptor's undertaking is, that he will pay to the signature of the same person that signed for the drawer'.[177]

Where the original parties to them were aware of the fiction, they were estopped from denying that the bills were payable to bearer. The requirement for the parties to have knowledge of the fiction was abandoned in 1882, when section 7(3) of the Bills of Exchange Act stipulated that where a payee was ficititous or non-existing, the bill was to be treated as payable to bearer.[178] Earlier case law had shown courts prepared to throw the risk on acceptors who had not been aware of the full facts. In *Phillips* v. *Im Thurn*, a rogue forged a bill drawn in the name of an existing company. He made it payable to a fictitious person, and indorsed it to himself. The original drawees (who normally dealt with the company) having stopped payment, the bill was accepted for the honour of the drawers by the defendant; whereupon the rogue had the bill discounted by the plaintiffs. Having accepted the bill, the defendant was unable to deny liability for the original

---

[173] *Gibson* v. *Minet* (1791) 1 H. Bl. 569 at 585. See also *Gibson* v. *Hunter* (1794) 2 H. Bl. 288.

[174] *Gibson* v. *Minet* (1791) 1 H. Bl. 569 at 619, 609.

[175] *Hunter* v. *Jeffery* (1797) Peake Add. Cas. 146.

[176] *Bennett* v. *Farnell* (1807) 1 Camp. 130 explained at 180c; *Ex p Royal Bank of Scotland* (1815) 19 Vesey Junior 310 at 311.

[177] *Cooper* v. *Meyer* (1830) 10 B. & C. 468 at 471.

[178] Until 1882, textbooks continued to hold that bills in the names of fictitious parties were only to be held to be bearer bills if the fact was known to the acceptor. Chitty, *Bills* (11th edn by J. A. Russell, 1878), 113, citing *Phillips* v. *Im Thurn* for the proposition. See also the judgment of Bowen LJ in *Vagliano Brothers* v. *Bank of England* (1889) 23 QBD 243 (CA) at 260.

forgery, having in effect vouched the signature of the forgers. The Common Pleas also rejected his attempt to dispute the liability to pay on the indorsement by a fictitious person, by ruling that the bill was to be regarded as a bearer bill; for 'he must be taken to have had all the knowledge that [the company] would be assumed to have if they had really been the drawers of the bill'.[179] Even though he had himself no knowledge of the fiction, the defendant was estopped from saying that the fictitious party did not exist.

After 1882, some judges continued to urge that fictitious bills should only be treated as bearer bills where the acceptor was aware of the fiction. But this view was rejected by the House of Lords in *Vagliano Brothers* v. *Bank of England*. In this case, a rogue, who was a clerk in the plaintiff's office, which regularly accepted bills drawn by a merchant in Odessa made payable to another in Constantinople, forged bills involving these parties, and obtained payment from his employer's account to the tune of £71,500. He did this by forging indorsements from the 'real' payee to a fictitious person, and then indorsing them to himself. The plaintiff succeeded in the divisional court and the Court of Appeal, on the grounds that the bills could not be regarded as bearer bills, since the original payees were real people, and the acceptors had no knowledge of the fiction.[180] However, the House of Lords (agreeing with Lord Esher's dissent in the Court of Appeal) held that the effect of the 1882 Act was to remove the need for knowledge. The Lords took a self-consciously business-minded approach, holding that it was more efficient to cast the risk in these cases on the acceptor than on the bank, which was equally innocent. As Lord Halsbury LC put it, if the Bank had to make inquiries in cases like these, then the delay might involve the bills being dishonoured, which would affect the plaintiff's credit. '[N]o banker could hesitate to pay such bills as came to him, so accredited as they were by Mr Vagliano's acceptance', he held 'without throwing the whole mercantile world into confusion'.[181] The Lords equally held that the new code of law was not to be interpreted through the lenses of the earlier law it had effectively replaced, but according to the sense of its own wording.

2. LETTERS OF CREDIT

Letters of credit were another form of paper credit given to merchants. Letters of credit took two forms. They could firstly take the form of unsealed letters sent to a named correspondent, requesting him to furnish the bearer with a certain sum,

---

[179] *Phillips and Another* v. *Im Thurn* (1866) LR 1 CP 463 at 471; cf. *Phillips* v. *Im Thurn* (1865) 18 C.B. N.S. 694.

[180] *Vagliano Brothers* v. *Governor and Co of the Bank of England* (1889) 22 QBD 103, (1889) 23 QBD 243 (CA).

[181] *The Governor and Co of the Bank of England* v. *Vagliano* [1891] AC 107 at 117.

or sums up to a specified amount. In return, the recipient of the money would draw a bill of exchange on the writer of the letter, who in his letter of credit bound himself to accept the bill. Besides such 'special' letters, there were also 'general' letters of credit, addressed to all merchants, and stating that the writer authorized the bearer to draw bills on him up to a certain amount, which the writer would honour. Letters of credit had been used throughout Europe since the middle ages by merchants who sent agents to buy commodities in foreign markets on credit, for they avoided the need either to carry sufficient cash for purchases, or to buy more bills than might turn out to be needed.[182] They were also a means used by banks to remit money from one place to another. For example, if a customer in London wished to send money to a correspondent in Bristol, he would pay the sum to his bank in London. This bank would then give him a letter of credit, addressed to a bank in Bristol, requesting it to honour the drafts of the correspondent, up to the sum which had been paid into the bank. The customer would send the correspondent the letter of credit, and he would draw money on it accordingly.

As the nineteenth century wore on, such documents were increasingly used to finance trade. An importer who wished to buy goods in a foreign market would seek a letter of credit from his bank to finance the transaction, paying a commission for the privilege. The letter of credit would be used to purchase goods from a seller, who would receive a bill drawn by the merchant, to be accepted by the bank, at (for instance) 90 days after sight. The seller would be required to note on the letter of credit how much credit had been given (for such a letter could continue to be used), and the merchant would be required to deposit with the bank's agent any documents of title to the goods being sold, as well as insurance documents, which would operate as security for the acceptances.[183] The bills would be honoured when the documents of title had arrived, with payment being arranged between the bankers of the trading parties. Bankers and traders often had running accounts, with the merchants sending remittances to cover letters of credit given, sometimes being in credit to the bank, and sometimes in debt.[184]

Although letters of credit were a widespread feature of commercial life, and were often defined as 'a species of bill of exchange',[185] treatise writers on bills of exchange largely ignored them in the early nineteenth century. For unlike bills

---

[182] See e.g. Pothier, *Traité du Contrat de Change*, § 236.

[183] See e.g. the transaction in *In re Agra Bank Ex p Tondeur* (1867) LR 5 Eq 160; *In Re Suse Ex p Dever* (1884) 13 QBD 766.

[184] See the practice described in *In Re Suse (No. 2) Ex p Dever* (1885) 14 QBD 611.

[185] Beawes, *Lex mercatoria* (6th edn by J. Chitty, 1813), i, 606; cf. J. Montefiore, *Commercial and Notarial Precedents* (2nd edn, 1813), 369.

of exchange, they were not negotiable instruments.[186] When a bank sold a letter of credit to a merchant, it agreed in the instrument to honour drafts drawn by the recipient of the letter on those giving him credit. If the bank paid the wrong person, who happened to have got hold of the letter, but had given no credit, it would have to repay the purchaser, since it had not done what it had promised.[187] Moreover, if the bank which sold the letter of credit failed to honour it, the purchaser could recover general damages to cover his losses, since a letter of credit was brought 'on a special contract, the incidents of which differ materially from those which belong to the contract constituted by becoming a party to a negotiable instrument, and which are strictly limited by the law merchant'.[188]

Although the party obtaining a letter of credit could not negotiate it, he did use it as authority to draw bills of exchange which were given to payees who could negotiate them. What, then, was the relationship between this payee and the acceptor at whose request he gave credit? Writers from the seventeenth century argued that the person writing the letter was bound to repay the person who gave credit at his request. As Beawes put it, if any money were advanced on the faith of these letters, and bills given for the sum mentioned, then the writer of the letter was obliged to accept. If he did not, then he could be compelled to pay, 'rather than the drawer, as the remitter of the loan of cash had more regard to his correspondent's sufficiency than the drawer's whom it is probable he knew nothing of'.[189] Unlike in the case of a guarantee, it was not the recipient of the money who was primarily liable, but the person who had requested the credit.

If it was clear enough that the writer of a special letter of credit was liable to the person who had advanced money on the faith of it, since the writer of the letter had requested him to pay, nineteenth century jurists felt that it was less clear whether the writer of a letter of credit addressed generally was liable to any person who had advanced money on the faith of it. Joseph Story felt that the letter could be treated as 'as a floating contract, designed to circulate as a direct promise, in the nature of a negotiable security, for the benefit of any party, advancing funds on the faith thereof'.[190] In the view of one American judge cited by Story,

---

[186] *Orr & Barber* v. *Union Bank of Scotland* (1854) 1 Macq. H.L. 513 at 523 (per Lord Cranworth). Cf. *The Conflans Stone Quarry Co* v. *Parker, Public Officer of the National Bank* (1867) LR 3 CP 1 at 8.

[187] For the position regarding lost letters, see *The Conflans Stone Quarry Co* v. *Parker, Public Officer of the National Bank* (1867) LR 3 CP 1.

[188] *Prehn and Another* v. *The Royal Bank of Liverpool* (1870) LR 5 Ex 92 at 97. In actions on bills of exchange, only the amount of the bill and interest could be recovered.

[189] Beawes, *Lex mercatoria* (6th edn, by J. Chitty), 607. Merchants were duly advised—given the extensive liability which could be incurred—to take great care in choosing the bearers entrusted with them. Savary advised merchants to describe minutely the person who was to be given credit, in case the bill was lost: W. Glen, *A Treatise on the Law of Bills of Exchange, Promissory Notes and Letters of Credit in Scotland* (Edinburgh, 1807), 312.

[190] Story, *Bills*, § 461, p. 544.

unless these letters were regarded as 'negotiable' in this way, they would never possess any credit in the commercial world, since money was never advanced on the mere credit of the recipient, but on the promise of the writer of the letter to accept any bill drawn.[191]

English courts resolved the problem in the second half of the nineteenth century by invoking the notion of the unilateral contract. The crucial decision was *In re Agra and Masterman's Bank, Ex p Asiatic Banking Corporation*, where the first named bank gave a letter of credit to a company, Dickson, Tatham & Co, authorizing them to draw bills on the bank, and to negotiate them. Although Sir George Turner LJ appeared to doubt whether there was a remedy at law under a letter of credit (since the contract in question was between the bearer of the letter and the writer, and not between the writer and the person giving credit), he felt that the recipient did have a remedy in equity.[192] But Sir Hugh Cairns LJ accepted the argument of counsel that at common law, that 'an open offer of this kind constitutes a contract with anyone who complies with its terms',[193] which would overcome the problem of privity which had worried jurists earlier in the century.[194] Even if it were assumed, he added, that the contract was only made with Dickson, Tatham & Co, he ruled that the contract was assignable in equity. Although a chose in action was ordinarily only assignable subject to existing equities between the original parties, it was clear here that the parties intended it to be assignable without such equities. 'The essence of the letter is', he said, 'that the person taking bills on the faith of it is to have the absolute benefit of the undertaking in the letter, and to have it in order to obtain the acceptance of the bills which are negotiable instruments payable according to their tenor, and without reference to any collateral or cross claims'.[195] Two years later, James VC felt it was clearly settled that an indorsee for value of a bill of exchange drawn under the authority of a letter of credit could sue the acceptor, even though the drawer had violated the terms of their agreement with the writers of the letter, by failing to remit shipping documents to them. In his view, the letter of credit 'was intended to be a representation or a promise to any person who should become in due course the holder

---

[191] This view was expressed in an unreported case set out in Story, *Bills*, p. 546n.

[192] *In re Agra and Masterman's Bank, Ex p Asiatic Banking Corporation* (1867) LR 2 Ch App 391 at 395–6.

[193] Giffard's argument in *In re Agra and Masterman's Bank, Ex p Asiatic Banking Corporation* (1867) LR 2 Ch App 391 at 393. Cairns cited *Williams* v. *Carwardine* (1833) 4 B. & Ad. 621; *Denton* v. *Great Northern Railway Co* (1856) 5 E. & B. 860; *Warlow* v. *Harrison* (1858) 1 E. & E. 295, 309; and *Scott* v. *Pilkington* (1862) 2 B. & S. 11 to show there had been privity.

[194] It had still to be shown that there was a contract between the creditor and the writer. Thus, it had to be clear that a letter of credit was intended to be shown to third parties: see *Nicholson* v. *Ricketts* (1860) 2 El. & El. 497. Contrast *Withington* v. *Herring* (1829) 5 Bing. 442.

[195] *In re Agra and Masterman's Bank, Ex p Asiatic Banking Corporation* (1867) LR 2 Ch App 391 at 397.

of that bill of exchange, that the bill would be duly honoured'.[196] All the holders
had to do was to show that they gave value for the bills. Drafters of letters of credit
soon took the hint by specifying in them that they included not merely an agreement with the addressees of the letters, but also 'a separate engagement with the
bonâ fide holders of the bills drawn in compliance with the terms of this credit,
that the same shall be duly accepted on presentation and paid at maturity'.[197]

3. BILLS OF LADING

Where bills of exchange were negotiable instruments which passed property in
a debt, bills of lading were used to transfer property in goods. The bill of lading
performed a double function, being at the same time the contract of carriage with
the master of the ship (made on behalf of the shipowner) and a document of title
to the goods.[198] As a contractual document, it contained stipulations as to the
amount of freight which would be charged, as well as any exemptions from liability which the carrier sought to include. As a document of title, it could transfer
property in the goods carried to any indorsee for value.[199]

Bills of lading were issued by the shipowner carrying the cargo. When the
goods were put on board, a mate's receipt would be given, from which point the
shipowner would be considered in possession of the goods, and liable for them.[200]
The mate's receipt would then be exchanged for a bill of lading. The normal practice was to make out three copies of the bill of lading, one of which was sent to
the consignee who was to receive the goods, one of which was kept by the shipper,
and one of which was kept by the master of the ship.[201] Once the ship reached its
port of destination, the consignee would give the master his copy of the bill of
lading, and receive the goods.

The fact that there were three copies of the bill issued did not normally raise
problems, since the consignee was generally given the first numbered copy, and

[196] *Maitland v. The Chartered Mercantile Bank of India, London and China* (1869) 38 LJ Ch 363
at 368.

[197] This was the form used in *In Re Suse Ex p Dever* (1884) 13 QBD 766

[198] Where the consignor had chartered the whole ship, the contract of carriage was contained in
the charterparty rather than in the bill of lading, which only acted as a receipt for goods shipped.
However, if the consignor sold goods on board, through the bill of lading, the buyer was only bound
by such terms of carriage as were contained in the bill of lading. See T. E. Scrutton, *The Elements of
Mercantile Law* (1891), 96–101.

[199] Scrutton, *Elements of Mercantile Law*, 87–9.

[200] See *Cobban v. Downe* (1803) 5 Esp. 41 (on the effect of delivery to the mate); and *The British
Columbia and Vancouver's Island Spar, Lumber and Saw-Mill Co v. Nettleship* (1868) LR 3 CP 499.

[201] The first two needed to have stamps: Beawes, *Lex mercatoria* (6th edn by J. Chitty, 1813), i, 196;
J. Montefiore, *A Commercial Dictionary: Containing the Present State of Mercantile Law, Practice,
and Custom* (1803), Tit. Bill of Lading.

each copy of the bill stated that once it was accomplished, the other copies should be void. But since there were multiple copies of the bill, there was always the chance that more than one person might claim the goods, having had a copy of the bill indorsed to him. It was decided in the eighteenth century that where the master was presented with two rival claims, he was under no duty to check which holder had the better title, but could deliver the goods to either party.[202] This rule was confirmed *obiter* by Dr Lushington in 1863, but treatise writers throughout the century regarded it as doubtful law. For Charles Abbott, the rule put too much power into the hands of the master; for Judah Benjamin, the master should be seen as in the same position as bailees who had to decide at their peril between rival claimants or interplead.[203] The matter did not lead to litigation, since masters may have declined to make a choice in such circumstances. However, in 1882, in *Glyn Mills, Currie & Co* v. *The East and West India Dock Company*, the House of Lords held that if the master had notice, or even knowledge of rival claims, he delivered the goods at his peril.[204] But if he acted *bona fide* and with no grounds for suspicion when giving goods to the first person to present a bill of lading, he was not liable, even if property in them had already been assigned to another.[205] The fact that the master delivered the goods to the party who did not have the best title did not, of course, give him a better title.[206]

It had been recognized in the eighteenth century, in the leading case of *Lickbarrow* v. *Mason*, that property in goods passed with the transfer of the bill of lading.[207] Bills of lading could be indorsed specially or in blank, the latter kind of indorsement having the same effect as if it had been indorsed to the holder by name. Nonetheless, they were not negotiable in the same way that bills of exchange were.[208] The hallmark of a bill of exchange was that the *bona fide* holder

[202] *Fearon* v. *Bowers* (1753) 1 H. Bl. 364 n.

[203] *In re 'Tigress'* (1863) Brow & Lush 38 at 43; C. Abbott, *A Treatise of the Law Relative to Merchant Ships and Seamen* (2nd edn, 1804), 353; J. P. Benjamin, *A Treatise on the Law of Sale of Personal Property* (1868), 656 citing in support C. Blackburn, *A Treatise on the Effect of the Contract of Sale* (1845), 266. The master's remedy was to take an indemnity or file a bill of interpleader in Chancery. For the position of bailees, see *Wilson* v. *Anderton* (1830) 1 B. & Ad. 450. See also Willes J.'s comments in *Meyerstein* v. *Barber* (1866) LR 2 CP 38 at 55.

[204] *Glyn Mills, Currie & Co* v. *The East and West India Dock Co* (1882) 7 App Cas 591 at 611, 613 (Lord Blackburn). See also T. E. Scrutton, *The Contract of Affreightment, as expressed in Charterparties and Bills of Lading* (5th edn by T. E. Scrutton and F. D. Mackinnon (1904), 245.

[205] See also *Townsend* v. *Inglis* (1816) Holt 278; *Knowles* v. *Horsfall* (1821) 5 B. & Ald. 13. In practice, the risk to the master was small, since he generally took an indemnity from legal proceedings from the person to whom he gave the goods.

[206] *Barber* v. *Meyerstein* (1870) LR 4 HL 317.

[207] *Lickbarrow* v. *Mason* (1787) 2 T.R. 63; (1793) 5 T.R. 367; (1793) 4 Brown P.C. 57. See also Buller J.'s advice to the Lords, reported in 6 East 20n.

[208] See W.P. Bennett, *The History and Present Position of the Bill of Lading as a Document of Title to Goods* (Cambridge, 1914), 19.

for value acquired property in the instrument, even though the person transfer-ring it did not have a good title. They constituted an exception to the maxim *nemo dat quod non habet*. By contrast, the holder of a bill of lading could not obtain a better title than the transferor from whom he obtained it. Thus, if a bill of lading for a consignment of goods was fraudulently obtained and indorsed, no property passed in them, and a *bona fide* assignee of the bill would be liable on them in an action of trover from their true owner.[209] Transferees of bills of lading also held them subject to the equities between prior parties, such as carriers' liens for the goods shipped.[210]

Bills of lading were thus transferable rather than fully negotiable.[211] Furthermore, at common law, the indorsement of a bill of lading transferred only the property in the goods shipped: it did not transfer any contractual rights. This meant that while consignees of goods could sue carriers for non-delivery, since they were parties to the contract under which the goods were shipped,[212] indorsees could not bring such actions, since they were not privy to the original contract, and the contractual rights were not assigned by the indorsement.[213] Given the difficulties this created for commercial parties, legislation was passed in 1855 to allow indor-sees of bills of lading to sue on them.[214]

A bill of lading only passed property if it were transferred *bona fide* and for good consideration. This meant that an indorsee who had given nothing for the bill had no property in the goods it represented.[215] Equally, an indorsee who knew that the consignee was insolvent, and who took the bill of lading to pre-vent a stoppage *in transitu* had no greater title than the consignee, since he had not acted *bona fide*.[216] Moreover, property only passed with the document if the transferor intended it to.[217] In contrast to bills of exchange, which embodied the

[209] *Schuster* v. *McKellar* (1857) 7 E. & B. 704; *Finlay* v. *Liverpool and Great Western Steamship Co* (1870) 23 LT 251 at 255. Similarly, if a shipper indorsed a bill of lading in blank, and it was then stolen or transferred without his authority, he could still recover the goods: *Gurney* v. *Behrend* (1852) 3 E. & B. 622 at 633–4. By contrast, if the indorsee had acquired the bill through a valid indorsement, he could pass the property to a *bona fide* holder for value, even when he acted fraudulently. See *Pease* v. *Gloahec, The Marie Joseph* (1866) LR 1 PC 219.

[210] *Small* v. *Moates* (1833) 9 Bing. 574; *Kern* v. *Deslandes* (1861) 10 C.B. N.S. 205.

[211] In this way, they were like cheques marked 'not negotiable' (for which, see below). T. E. Scrutton, *The Contract of Affreightment* (7th edn by Scrutton and F. E. D. Mackinnon, 1914), p. 155.

[212] *Tronson* v. *Dent* (1853) 8 Moore P.C. 419 at 436.

[213] *Thompson* v. *Dominy* (1845) 14 M. & W. 403 at 407–8; cf. *Sanders* v. *Vanzeller* (1843) 4 Q.B. 260 at 297; *Howard* v. *Shepherd* (1850) 9 C.B. 297.

[214] Bills of Lading Act 1855, 18 & 19 Vict. c. 111.

[215] *Waring* v. *Cox* (1808) 1 Camp. 369 at 370; *Newsom* v. *Thornton* (1805) 6 East 17 at 40, *Sewell* v. *Burdick* (1884) 10 App Cas 74 at 80.

[216] See Lord Ellenborough's comments in *Cumming* v. *Brown* (1808) 9 East 506 at 514. See also *Gilbert* v. *Guignon* (1872) LR 8 Ch 16.

[217] See *Hibbert* v. *Carter* (1787) 1 T.R. 745.

holder's right to the debt, a bill of lading was only evidence of the holder's title to the goods.[218] In fact, shippers often indorsed bills of lading to a party to whom they did not wish to give property, such as factors.[219] Property did not simply pass when an indorsed bill was handed to the buyer. Vendors often made conditional indorsements of bills of lading. For instance, the shipper might send the buyer a bill of exchange with the bill of lading, making the indorsement of the bill of lading conditional on his acceptance of the bill of exchange. If the buyer retained the bill of lading, but did not accept the bill of exchange sent to cover the payment, then no property passed.[220] In such cases, the condition did not appear on the face of the bill of lading; rather, it was for a jury to decide whether the contract of sale was that property was only to vest when payment had been received.[221]

Although bills of lading were not negotiable in the way bills of exchange were, their transfer could nevertheless confer property on *bona fide* holders for value against the wishes of the consignor in some situations. First, if a factor sold goods while exceeding his authority, or embezzled the proceeds of the sale, the purchaser acquired a good title, and the loss fell on the principal. For having intrusted the factor with the goods (or the bill of lading which symbolized them), he was bound by the apparent authority he had given the factor to sell them.[222] At common law, the factor was held not to have any power to pledge the goods, and the principal could recover from a party who had lent on the security of a bill of lading, even if he did not know that he was dealing with a factor.[223] However, a number of Factors Acts between 1823 and 1889 enacted that a factor who was intrusted with documents of title to goods was to be taken to be their true owner so far as to give validity to any sale or pledge of them.[224] Secondly, a seller's right to stop the goods he had sold to a purchaser while they remained in transit[225]

---

[218] This also meant that property could pass without the buyer needing to produce the bill: see *Coxe* v. *Harden* (1803) 4 East 211.

[219] An agent, to whom a bill of lading was indorsed by his principal without consideration was not held to have property in the goods himself: *Waring* v. *Cox* (1808) 1 Camp. 369 at 370–1; *Patten* v. *Thompson* (1816) 5 M. & S. 350. Factors who raised money to pay for the cargo might also hold the bill of lading as a pledge for the moneys raised. See e.g. *Anderson* v. *Clark* (1824) 2 Bing. 20.

[220] *Shepherd* v. *Harrison* (1871) LR 5 HL 116. Cf. Sale of Goods Act 1893, s 19(3).

[221] *Moakes* v. *Nicolson* (1865) 19 C.B. N.S. 290.

[222] F. L. Holt, *A System of the Shipping and Navigation Laws of Great Britain*, 2 vols (1820), ii, 60; *Pickering* v. *Busk* (1812) 15 East 38 at 43.

[223] *Paterson* v. *Tash* (1743) 2 Stra. 1178; *Daubigny* v. *Duval* (1794) 5 T.R. 604; *Newsom* v. *Thornton* (1805) 6 East 17 at 41–2; *Martini* v. *Coles* (1813) 1 M. & S. 140.

[224] See pp. 1122–4.

[225] While the purchaser obtained property by having the bill of lading indorsed to him, the courts did not hold the passing of the bill of lading to amount to such a possession as ended the shipper's right to stop the goods in transit. See *Patten* v. *Thompson* (1816) 5 M. & S. 350 at 356–7; *Pease* v. *Gloahec, The Marie Joseph* (1866) LR 1 PC 219; *Berndtson* v. *Strang* (1867) LR 4 Eq 481 at 489–90; *Bethell & Co* v. *Clark & Co* (1888) 20 QBD 615 (CA); *Lyons* v. *Hoffnung* (1890) 15 App Cas 391. The

could be lost if the buyer indorsed the bill of lading to a *bona fide* purchaser;[226] though the right would not be lost if the bill of lading was not transferred.[227] Similarly, if the buyer in possession of the bill of lading failed to accept the bill of exchange (so that property did not pass to him), but sold the goods on to a *bona fide* third party, that third party could retain the goods by virtue of the Factors Act 1889 and section 25(2) of the Sale of Goods Act 1893.[228]

Bills of lading were commonly pledged by buyers, who wished to raise money on the faith of goods yet to arrive. This practice posed the problem of the relative rights regarding the property of the lender holding the bill, and the unpaid consignor of the goods. It was determined in the early nineteenth century that where a bill of lading was pledged by the consignee for a loan, the property and right to possession passed to the lender, with the consignor retaining an equitable claim to the surplus. As Lord Denman saw it, the transfer by the holder would be treated in equity as 'a pledge, or mortgage, only', and the consignor would 'be considered as having resumed his former interest in the goods, subject to that pledge or mortgage; in analogy to the common case of a mortgage of a real estate, which is considered as a mere security, and the mortgagor as the owner of the land'.[229] In 1843, Lord Langdale confirmed that where a bill of lading was indorsed and delivered only as a security for the repayment of money, the unpaid vendor had a right to stop the goods *in transitu*, subject to the lien for the advance.[230]

Nonetheless, it long remained unclear whether the security represented by the bill of lading was in the nature of a mortgage, with legal property in the goods passing to the lender, and the borrower retaining an equity of redemption; or whether it was in the nature of a pledge of goods at common law, with the pledgee acquiring an exclusive right of possession during the time of the pledge, but only a special property in the goods.[231] Judges were often ambiguous in their answer to

shipper could exercise the right of stoppage by demanding the bills of lading: *Ex p Watson* (1877) 5 Ch D 35. In this case, James LJ noted that the bills of lading remained in the hands of the carrier.

[226] 'If the goods are actually delivered to an agent of the vendee, employed by him to receive delivery, the vendor is divested of his right of stoppage *in transitu*' (Lord Chelmsford LC): *Schotsmans v. Lancashire and Yorkshire Railway Co* (1867) LR 2 Ch 332 at 335. The mere fact that the goods were delivered to a carrier (even on an fob contract where the bill of lading had not been given) did not mean that they had entered the buyer's possession. *Ex p Rosevear China Clay Co* (1879) LR 3 Ch 560.

[227] *Akerman v. Humphery* (1823) 1 Car. & P. 53 at 56–7. This was confirmed in s 47 of the Sale of Goods Act 1893.

[228] *Cahn v. Pockett's Bristol Channel Steam Packet Co* [1899] 1 QB 643.

[229] *In re Westzinthus* (1833) 5 B. & Ad. 817 at 834.

[230] *Spalding v. Ruding* (1843) 6 Beav. 376 at 380. See also *Kemp v. Falk* (1882) 7 App Cas 573.

[231] Common law courts treated the deposit of goods as security for loans as contracts under which the lender was obliged to restore the goods on being paid, but that he had the right to sell them if not. See *Pothonier v. Dawson* (1816) Holt N.P. 383 at 385; see also *Pigot v. Cubley* (1864) 15 C.B. N.S. 701;

this question,[232] but its resolution was crucial in two cases heard in the 1880s. In the first, *Glyn, Mills, Currie & Co* v. *The East and West India Dock Company*, the issue was whether a warehouse keeper who had delivered goods on the order of their owner (who had retained one of the copies of the bill of lading), was liable to the bank to which he had previously indorsed another copy of the bill, as security for a loan. The answer to this turned on whether the lender had a general legal property in the goods, or only special property. In the second, *Burdick* v. *Sewell*, the court had to consider whether a party who lent on the security of an indorsed bill of lading was liable as owner of 'the' property for freight charges. In both cases, Brett in the Court of Appeal took the view that the pledgee acquired full legal property, in the manner of a mortgagee, subject to an equity in the pledgor to recover the goods or their surplus. In his view, the courts were not to look at whether the parties intended to pass a general or only a special property, since any *bona fide* indorsement of a bill of lading for an advance passed all the legal property by the custom of merchants, as effectively as if it had been done by a bill of sale.[233] This view was not shared by the majority of the Court of Appeal in the first case, or by the House of Lords in the second. In the view of the Lords, the court had to consider the original agreement between the parties in determining what property passed.[234] This confirmed that where a shipper indorsed bills of lading and deposited them with a lender as security for an advance, only a qualified property passed.

Besides bills of lading, merchants also used other documents to transfer the interest in goods. In particular, they made use of dock warrants and delivery orders. Once goods were landed, and were housed at a dock, the dock company gave a warrant to the owner of the goods (whose title to them had been evidenced by the bill of lading). Delivery orders required the warehouse keeper to deliver the owner's goods to the person named. They were given by the warehouse keeper to the owner of goods kept in his warehouse, making the goods deliverable to him, or to his assigns. Merchants treated such documents as if they were negotiable, seeking to transfer interests in the property with the documents. However,

Martin v. *Reid* (1862) 11 C.B. N.S. 730. This 'special property' in goods pledged entitled the pledgee to recover the goods from anyone who took them. He could recover damages for their full value, and not merely for the sums advanced, though he remained liable to the pledgor to hand over the surplus. See the pawnbroking case of *Swire* v. *Leach* (1865) 18 C.B. N.S. 479.

[232] See the treatment of the question in *Meyerstein* v. *Barber* (1866) LR 2 CP 38 at 45, 49; (1866) LR 2 CP 38 at 53; (1870) LR 4 HL 317 at 326, 335–7.

[233] *Burdick* v. *Sewell* (1884) 13 QBD 159 at 163, 167. See also his views in *Glyn, Mills, Currie & Co* v. *The East and West India Dock Co* (1880) 6 QBD 475 at 480.

[234] *Burdick* v. *Sewell* (1884) 13 QBD 159 at 173–4 (Bowen LJ); *Sewell* v. *Burdick* (1884) 10 App Cas 74 at 100–3. For an earlier example suggesting that the nature of the transfer was determined by the agreement, see *Haille* v. *Smith* (1796) 1 B. & P. 563 at 570–1.

judges consistently denied that they were negotiable in the way that bills of lading were. As Blackburn explained, dock warrants and delivery orders differed from a bill of lading; for while the purchaser who took a bill of lading had done all he could to take possession of the goods which were at sea, a merchant on dry land had the power to take possession of them.[235] In 1846, the Exchequer confirmed that a delivery warrant was no more than an engagement by the wharfinger to deliver the goods to the consignee. Notwithstanding the passing of a delivery order, the wharfinger continued to hold the goods as agent of the consignor until such time as he had accepted that he held them for the consignee.[236] Until the holder of the delivery warrant acted on it, he was not held to have acquired property in the goods.[237]

The fact that dock warrants and delivery orders were not negotiable created risks for traders; for *bona fide* holders for value did not acquire any title to them. For it was held that the seller did not intend to pass property and possession via these documents.[238] This rule, which was confirmed by the Exchequer Chamber in 1856, was controversial since it appeared to undermine the security of these instruments; but despite protests by the commercial community, the rule remained in place.

4. BANKS AND CHEQUES

By the mid-nineteenth century, cheques drawn on a bank were beginning to replace bills of exchange and promissory notes as the preferred domestic method for payment. Cheques were bills of exchange drawn on bankers, with some particular rules governing their use. As bills payable at sight, they were only presented once for 'acceptance', which was when they were paid.[239] Bankers did not give credit to the bills drawn on them, by accepting them prior to their being negotiated, as acceptors of other bills did. For if this were done, cheques would be able to circulate as banknotes, in a way forbidden by the Bank Charter Act 1844. The banker's obligation to pay came therefore not from his acceptance of the bill, but by virtue of his contract with his customer, to honour the latter's cheques.[240] According to this contract, the banker was obliged to pay any cheques presented to him, provided that the customer had sufficient money in his account to cover them.[241]

---

[235] Blackburn, *Sale* (1845), 297–8.   [236] *Farina* v. *Home* (1846) 16 M. & W. 119.

[237] See *M'Ewan* v. *Smith* (1849) 2 H.L.C. 309; *Griffiths* v. *Perry* (1859) 1 El. & El. 680.

[238] *Kingsford* v. *Merry* (1856) 1 H. & N. 503; *Pease* v. *Gloahec, The Marie Joseph* (1866) LR 1 PC 219.

[239] J. R. Paget, *The Law of Banking* (1904), 72; cf. *Grant* v. *Vaughan* (1764) 3 Burr. 1516 at 1517. See also the observations of Parke B. in *Ramchurn Mullick* v. *Luchmeechund Radakissen* (1854) 9 Moore 46 at 69–70.

[240] See *Foley* v. *Hill* (1848) 2 H.L.C. 28.   [241] *Marzetti* v. *Williams* (1830) 1 B. & Ad. 415.

Payments by Cheque

In contrast to bills, which were continuing securities, a cheque was intended for prompt payment to the banker. This did not mean that the debt it represented was lost if time were taken in presenting the cheque, since the claim of a holder of a cheque against the drawer could remain alive for up to six years. As observed in 1841, between drawer and payee, 'the question of reasonable time for presentment can scarcely arise unless some damage has arisen in consequence of the non-presentment'.[242] A solvent drawer who had an account with a solvent banker would therefore remain liable for the full limitation period, and could not instruct his banker not to pay. Moreover, since cheques, like bills of exchange, were regarded as conditional or qualified payments of debts, merely issuing a cheque did not extinguish the debt. The drawer would therefore have to pay the debt if the cheque was not paid, just as the drawer of a bill had to pay if the bill was dishonoured.[243] But as with bills, if the holder of the bill had negotiated it or were guilty of laches, he lost his remedy. In practice, this meant that if the drawer was prejudiced by the holder's delay in presenting the cheque—as he might be, if the bank failed in the meantime—the latter lost his right.[244] If the payee did not present the cheque for payment promptly, he would lose his remedy if the bank failed. Cases in the mid-century laid down stringent rules on the timing. In *Alexander* v. *Burchfield*, it was held that the holder of a cheque had to present it for payment at the latest on the day after he had received it, whether he presented it himself or via another bank.[245] Where the holder of the cheque and the bank on which it was drawn were in different places, both parties had to take action at the latest on the day after receipt of the cheque.[246] If the bank failed within the time allowed for presenting the cheque, the drawer of the cheque remained liable; but if the holder presented it too late, he could no longer recover on the cheque. This was because it was assumed that the funds which the drawer had appropriated for paying the cheque would no longer be available, so that he would be prejudiced by the delay.

Equally, if the payee of a cheque lost it, he could not recover on the debt it was issued to settle. It was clear that if a creditor took a negotiable instrument in payment of a debt, he could not sue on the debt until there had been default

---

[242] *Serle* v. *Norton* (1841) 2 Moo. & Rob. 401 at 405n.

[243] As Lord Eldon put it, 'I take it to be now clearly settled, that, if there is an antecedent debt, and a bill is taken, without taking an indorsement, which bill turns out to be bad, the demand for the antecedent debt may be resorted to': *Ex p Blackburne* 10 Ves. (1804) 205 at 206. See also *Cohen* v. *Hale* (1878) 3 QBD 371.

[244] *Robinson* v. *Hawksford* (1846) 9 Q.B. 52; *Laws* v. *Rand* (1857) 3 C.B. N.S. 441.

[245] *Alexander* v. *Burchfield* (1842) 7 Man. & G. 1061. Cf. *Heywood* v. *Pickering* (1874) LR 9 QB 428 at 432.

[246] *Hare* v. *Henty* (1861) 10 C.B. N.S. 65. See also *Rickford* v. *Ridge* (1810) 2 Camp. 537.

in payment of the instrument.[247] Case law involving bills of exchange payable to the bearer also made it clear that the acceptor who paid the bearer was taken to have discharged the debt due on the bill. Since the acceptor was liable to any *bona fide* holder, a holder who lost a bill payable to bearer could not recover the debt it represented from the acceptor.[248] What of instruments payable to order? In 1854, the Exchequer Chamber held that where the holder of a bill of exchange payable to order, which had been given to pay for a debt, lost it, he could not recover in an action of debt. Coleridge J. made the principles clear: 'A bill given "for and on account" of money due on simple contract operates as a conditional payment, which may be defeated at the option of the creditor, if the bill is unpaid at maturity in his hands; in which case he may rescind the transaction of payment and sue on the original demand.' If the bill were lost, the condition on which the payment could be defeated would simply not arise (while the acceptor might be compelled to pay another on the bill), for the creditor would not be able to produce the instrument to be dishonoured.[249]

These principles were applied to cheques in *Charles* v. *Blackwell* in 1877. Here, the defendants bought goods from the plaintiff's business, paying for them by a cheque which was fraudulently endorsed by the plaintiff's agent. In Cockburn CJ's judgment, the receipt of a cheque by the payee or his agent extinguished the debt, 'subject only to the condition that, if upon due presentment the cheque is not paid, the original debt revives'.[250] If, after receipt, the holder of the cheque lost it, and failed to stop the cheque in time, the loss fell on him. For having taken the cheque in payment, he could not call for a second payment as long as there had not been a default in payment on due presentation.

The Banker and its Customer

The general relationship between a banker and the customer who held cash with the bank was held to be that of a debtor and creditor.[251] This meant that customers were unable to recover money which they had left untouched in an account for a period of six years, since the claim (in debt) would be barred by the statute

---

[247] See *Stedman* v. *Gooch* (1793) 1 Esp. 3.

[248] Not even if he offered an indemnity: see *Hansard* v. *Robinson* (1827) 7 B. & C. 90, where it was held that the acceptor only had to pay on delivery of the bill, which was his security against having to pay it a second time. The same rule applied to bills payable to order: *Ramuz* v. *Crowe* (1847) 1 Exch. 167.

[249] *Crowe* v. *Clay* (1854) 9 Exch. 604 at 608. Cf. *Woodford* v. *Whiteley* (1830) M. & M. 517.

[250] *Charles* v. *Blackwell* (1877) 2 CPD 151 at 158.

[251] See *Carr* v. *Carr* (1811) 1 Mer. 541, n; *Devaynes* v. *Noble, Sleech's case* (1816) 1 Mer. 529 at 568; *Parker* v. *Marchant* (1843) 1 Phillips 356; cf. *Sims* v. *Bond* (1833) 5 B. & Ad. 389. See also *In re Agra bank, Ex p Waring* (1866) 36 LJ Ch 151.

of limitations.[252] In 1848, a plaintiff sought to challenge this rule, by arguing (in equity) that the relationship between a banker and his client was a fiduciary one, rendering the statute of limitations inapplicable and permitting him to obtain an account in equity. Admitting that an agent or factor was to be regarded as a quasi-trustee when dealing with his principal's property, Lyndhurst LC ruled that the analogy could not be applied to a banker. Money paid to a banker became the property of the banker, and he was only bound to return an equivalent when demanded. However he employed the money, a banker was not liable for a breach of trust; nor was he 'answerable to the principal if he puts it into jeopardy, if he engages in a hazardous speculation'.[253]

This meant that if a bank failed, each customer became merely another creditor claiming a proportion of its assets. It also meant that a customer whose personal account with a bankrupt firm was in credit could not set off the surplus against his partnership account with the same bank, which was in deficit.[254] Once a customer had paid his money to a bank,[255] he could only recover it if he could show that it had not been mixed in any way with the money of the bank. Thus, in *Sadler* v. *Belcher* (1843), plaintiffs who paid a banknote into their bank on the evening when it stopped payment could recover it, since it was paid in after the accounts of the day had been made up and had been placed in a separate deposit.[256]

Customers who deposited bills of exchange with the bank could find themselves in a better position in case of its failure. It was held in the eighteenth century that if bills were deposited with a banker without being discounted, or credit being given for them, property in them remained with the customer.[257] In such cases, the banker only had a lien on the bill for the balance of his account, similar to the position of a factor in possession of his principal's goods.[258] Cases in the early nineteenth century confirmed that the customer could recover his bills, unless the banker had advanced money on the credit of them,[259] or they had been treated by the parties as cash.[260] In 1824, Bayley J. declared that, unless there was an agreement between the bank and its customer that property was

---

[252] *Pott* v. *Clegg* (1847) 16 M. & W. 321.   [253] *Foley* v. *Hill* (1848) 2 H.L.C. 28 at 36.

[254] *Watts* v. *Christie* (1849) 11 Beav. 546 at 552.

[255] *In re Agra and Masterman's Bank, Ex p Waring* (1866) 36 LJ Ch 151.

[256] *Sadler* v. *Belcher* (1843) 2 M. & R. 489. Cf. *Threffall* v. *Giles* (1822), cited in this case.

[257] See *Ex p Dumas* (1754) 2 Ves. Sr. 582; *Zinck* v. *Walker* (1777) 2 W. Bl. 1154. See also *Brown* v. *Kewley* (1801) 2 B. & P. 518 at 524 (another case arising from the failure of Caldwell & Co): 'it is admitted on all sides that while the bill remained entered short, nothing but an assent of the respective parties could bind either to accept the bill as a payment of money'.

[258] *Bolton* v. *Puller* (1796) 1 Bos. & Pul. 539 at 546.   [259] *Giles* v. *Perkins* (1807) 9 East 12 at 14.

[260] See *Ex p Sargeant* (1810) 1 Rose's Bank. Cases 153; *Ex p Sollers* (1811) 18 Ves. 230. In *Ex p Pease* (1812) 19 Ves. 25 at 32–3, Sir Samuel Romilly noted that a short bill 'is a bill, remitted by the customer to the banker, to be held in trust; and as evidence of that, it ought to be written short in the book; and the customer does not draw upon the credit of that bill'.

to pass when the bills were deposited, the customer could recover them.[261] The position was thus settled that unless it was clear that property was intended to pass, the customer retained property in a bill left with the bank,[262] and could recover it in bankruptcy.[263] If the bank had passed on the bills, however, the merchant lost his security. Unlike a factor, bankers holding a bill of exchange which had been indorsed to them had property in the instrument, and could sell or pledge it.[264] This could generate risks where merchants made payments through their bankers, using bills.[265] But since courts did not wish to do anything which might restrict the negotiability of these instruments, merchants who paid their bills over to their bankers were held to run the risk of their bankers abusing their positions.

Bankers were held to have a duty to honour their customer's drafts, where there were funds in his account. It was the bank's duty to know what funds were in the client's account; and if the banker did not pay when there were funds, he was liable to the customer in damages. This was settled in 1830 in *Marzetti* v. *Williams*. The plaintiff, who was a London merchant, paid a bank note into his account at the defendants' bank in the morning. Two-and-a-half hours later, a cheque drawn by him was presented to the bank by the holder for payment. The clerk, who was unaware that there were sufficient funds to pay the cheque as a result of the earlier deposit, refused to pay the cheque until the following day. The plaintiff sued for a tort, even though no actual damage was suffered, and the King's Bench found for him.[266] The court also accepted the jury's view that it was reasonable for a customer to expect to have his account credited within 2½ hours.[267] Where a customer paid a cheque into his account, and it was credited to him, the onus was on the bank to show that the cheque had not been cleared in order to justify any refusal to honour the customer's cheques for lack of funds.[268]

Equally, where a bank acted without due care in handling cheques, it would have to bear the loss. Thus, if the collecting bank delayed in presenting a bill for payment to the drawer's bank, it would be liable to its customer for the loss.[269] Similarly, where one customer paid into his account a cheque drawn by another

---

[261] *Thompson* v. *Giles* (1824) 2 B. and C. 422 at 429.

[262] See the endorsement of this view in *Gaden* v. *The Newfoundland Savings Bank* [1899] AC 281.

[263] Where property had not passed, the banker was regarded as a trustee, so that the bill of exchange would not be regarded as under the banker's reputed ownership. See *Ex p Pease and Others* (1812) 1 Rose 232; *Hornblower* v. *Proud* (1819) 2 B. & Ald. 327.

[264] See Eyre CJ's comments in *Collins* v. *Martin* (1797) 1 B. & P. 648 at 651–2.

[265] See the litigation in *Bolton* v. *Puller* (1796) 1 B. & P. 539 and *Bent* v. *Puller* (1794) 5 T.R. 494.

[266] *Marzetti* v. *Williams* (1830) 1 B. & Ad. 415 at 424.

[267] *Whitaker* v. *Bank of England* (1834) 6 Car. & P. 700.

[268] See *Bransby* v. *East London Bank* (1866) 14 LT 403.

[269] *Hare* v. *Henty* (1861) 10 C.B. N.S. 65.

customer of the same bank (who subsequently went bankrupt), the bank was liable to the first customer if it did not transfer such funds as it had of the second customer to pay the cheque.[270] There were other risks for bankers. In *Lubbock* v. *Tribe* (1835), the plaintiff bank lost a cheque for £100 drawn by the defendant, as a deposit for shares in the Kellewerris Consolidated Mining Company, who were customers of the bank. Tribe's debt to the company was not extinguished, but the bank reimbursed the company for the money it should have collected. It then entered into a correspondence with Tribe, to recover the sum from him, on promising to indemnify him if the cheque reappeared. Tribe initially agreed, but—having lost much money in speculating in mining shares—later declined to pay. The Court of Exchequer held that the loss had to fall on the bank. As Lord Abinger put it, 'when [the bank] failed to present the cheque in due time, they made it their own, and they are bound to pay the company, and cannot recover from the plaintiff'.[271] Parke B. held that in paying the company, the bank had not exonerated the defendant from his liability, and so it was not money paid to his use. The decision in effect penalized banks which lost cheques; for while they were liable to their customers for their loss, they would not be able to recover from the parties issuing the cheques.

Forged Cheques

While banks were under a duty to pay the cheques of their customers, they ran a risk in paying on forged cheques. It was settled that where banks paid a bill of exchange which had been accepted as payable at their house, they had to satisfy themselves of the genuineness of any indorsement, or they would be liable for the sums paid.[272] This meant that where the drawer's signature, or any indorsement, was forged, the bank which had paid the cheque had to bear the loss.[273] Equally, it was decided in 1824 that if the holder of a cheque fraudulently altered it, by adding in words and figures, the bank could only debit the customer for the sum he had originally drawn.[274] This was clearly a matter of some risk for bankers, since they had a duty to pay any cheque properly signed, regardless of the handwriting on the rest of the instrument.

The liability of a banker in such a position was debated in the institutional literature. The seventeenth century commercial writer Sigismundus Scaccia stated

---

[270] *Kilsby* v. *Williams* (1822) 5 B. & Ald. 815. It was held that had the two been customers of different banks, the plaintiff could have demanded immediate payment and default thereof sought a remedy against the drawer.

[271] *Lubbock* v. *Tribe* (1838) 3 M. & W. 607 at 612.

[272] See *Forster* v. *Clements* (1809) 2 Camp. 17.   [273] See *Smith* v. *Mercer* (1815) 6 Taunt. 76.

[274] *Hall* v. *Fuller* (1826) 5 B. & C. 750.

that the drawer of a bill later falsified had to bear the loss, since the banker who was mandated by the drawer to pay had to be recompensed under his contract of mandate, provided he acted without fault.[275] Pothier, by contrast, held that the banker had to bear the loss, since the loss was not mandated, unless the drawer had been at fault in the way in which he drew the bill.[276] Pothier's view was followed by Best CJ in *Young* v. *Grote* in 1827. In this case, the drawer had left blank cheques for his inexperienced wife to fill in, and she had drawn one so carelessly as to make it easy for a later holder to insert additional words. In Best's view, the bank should not be liable since they were induced to pay by the drawer's 'neglect of […] ordinary precautions'.[277] This suggested that if the customer was careless, he could not recover; though if the bank carelessly paid out on an instrument which had obviously been tampered with, he could.[278] Park J. agreed with the result, but rested his decision on different grounds: since the drawer left blank cheques to be filled out by his inexperienced wife, they were to be regarded as his genuine orders once filled out.

Mid-century judges had some difficulty in articulating the principle on which *Young* v. *Grote* was based. Some followed Park J.'s view that a person who signed a blank cheque gave authority to anyone to fill it out to any amount.[279] Others felt that the doctrine which best explained the case was that the customer whose negligence induced his bankers to pay on a forged order was estopped from denying the genuineness of the document.[280] Although the latter view gained the wider currency in the second half of the century, judges were troubled by the potential reach of such a doctrine, which might make a person liable for remote consequences of his carelessness. It was admitted that a customer had a duty to his banker to fill out cheques carefully, and that he would be liable for losses proximately caused by the negligence.[281] But judges were less prepared to apply the doctrine when the causal connection between the carelessness and the loss was more remote.

---

[275] S. Scaccia, *Tractatus de Commerciis et cambio* (Cologne, 1620), sect. 2, gl. 5, queat. 1.

[276] Pothier, *Traité du Change*, part I, c. 4, § 99.   [277] *Young* v. *Grote* (1827) 4 Bing. 253 at 259.

[278] See Lord Brougham's observations in *Kennedy* v. *Green* (1834) 3 Myl. & K. 699 at 721. For a case where a forger added a 'y' to a cheque, and the court found there was no negligence by the drawer of the cheque on leaving a space for this, see *Société Générale* v. *Metropolitan Bank* (1873) 27 LT 849.

[279] See *Robarts* v. *Tucker* (1851) 16 Q.B. 560; *Swan* v. *North British Australasian Co* (1863) 2 H. & C. 175 at 183 (per Blackburn J.); *Ingham* v. *Primrose* (1859) 7 C.B. N.S. 82. Cf. *Russel* v. *Langstaffe* (1780) 2 Doug. 514; *Schultz* v. *Astley* (1836) 2 Bing. N.C. 544 at 553.

[280] *Orr* v. *Union Bank of Scotland* (1854) 1 Macq. 513; *Bank of Ireland* v. *Trustees of Evans's Charities* (1855) 5 H.L.C. 389 at 413–14; *Arnold v The Cheque Bank* (1876) 1 CPD 578 at 587. See also pp. 929–30.

[281] See Brett's comments in *Baxendale* v. *Bennett* (1878) 3 QBD 525 at 533 and *Mayor &c of Merchants of the Staple of England* v. *the Bank of England* (1887) 21 QBD 160 at 172. See also *The Guardians of Halifax Union* v. *Wheelwright* (1875) LR 10 Ex 183.

The authority of *Young* v. *Grote* continued to be debated into the 1890s.[282] At issue was the question whether a person who signed a negotiable instrument intending that it should be delivered to a series of holders owed them a duty of care to take reasonable precautions against forgery. In *Scholfield* v. *The Earl of Londesborough*, a majority of the Court of Appeal, and the House of Lords, held that neither drawers of cheques nor acceptors of bills had a duty 'to consider generally the possibility of a fraud being committed, and to take precautions accordingly'.[283] Judges in both courts felt that Best (and those who followed him) had misapplied Pothier's comments on the contract of mandate. They also felt that a rule which imposed such a duty of care would create unnecessary uncertainty in the commercial world, since acceptors might be compelled to reject bills whenever they saw something which looked like blank space. In Lord Watson's view, 'it is not consistent with the general spirit of the law to hold innocent persons responsible for not taking measures to prevent the commission of a crime which they may have no reason to anticipate'.[284] *Young* v. *Grote* remained an authority for the proposition that if a customer gave a signed blank cheque to another to fill in, the bank was justified in paying whatever amount was filled in;[285] but it was not authority to estop one whose cheque had been fraudulently altered from denying the holder's title to the sum written on the cheque.[286] The only duty of care which might exist in drawing a cheque was one owed by the customer to his banker arising on the contract between them.[287] This duty could come into play if an account holder knew that his signature had been forged, but omitted to inform the bank.[288]

Who was to bear the loss if a bank paid out on one of its customers' cheques after an indorsement had been forged? This question was raised in *Robarts* v. *Tucker* in 1851, a case involving a claim by Elizabeth Isherwood on a life insurance policy with the Pelican Life Insurance Company. According to its practice, when country customers made claims, the company met them by accepting drafts in London, drawn by country agents to the order of the customer, after they had been indorsed by the payee. After Mrs Isherwood had apparently indorsed the draft, and made it payable to a bank in London, the company accepted it. However, it later transpired that the solicitor had forged the signature. Having

---

[282] It was, however, endorsed in *Bank of England* v. *Vagliano Brothers* [1891] AC 107 at 170.

[283] *Scholfield* v. *The Earl of Londesborough* [1895] 1 QB 536 (CA) at 556 (Rigby LJ).

[284] *Scholfield* v. *The Earl of Londesborough* [1896] AC 514 at 537.

[285] *Union Credit Bank* v. *Mersey Docks and Harbour Board* [1899] 2 QB 205 at 211.

[286] *Imperial Bank of Canada* v. *Bank of Hamilton* [1903] AC 49 at 54.

[287] See also *Marcussen* v. *Birkbeck Bank* (1889) 5 TLR 179, 463, 646.

[288] See *M'Kenzie* v. *British Linen Co* (1881) 6 App Cas 82. But contrast *Ogilvie* v. *West Australian Mortgage and Agency Corporation* [1896] AC 257.

paid Mrs Isherwood her claim, the company successfully recovered the money paid by their bank to that of the fraudulent solicitor. As Parke B. put it, an acceptance made payable at a bank was an order to the bank to pay anyone 'who is according to the law merchant capable of giving a good discharge for the bill',[289] which a forger clearly was not. Where a bill was payable to order, they only had authority to pay those who had received the bill by way of a genuine indorsement. Where a bank paid on a forged indorsement, the bank, rather than the customer, bore the risk.

Given the risk this ruling imposed on bankers who paid cheques payable to order, when the Stamp Act 1853 opened the way for the widespread use of cheques payable to order, it was decided to transfer the risk onto the account holder. Since the customer obtained the advantage of being able to use cheques payable to order, it was considered reasonable to put the risk of forged indorsements on the drawer, since the banker could not be expected to know the signatures of the indorsers. Section 19 of the Act stated that any draft or order drawn on a bank payable to order on demand, which purported to be indorsed by the party to whom it was drawn payable, was to be regarded as sufficient authority to the bank to pay. The bank was not to bear the risk of forged indorsements on drafts. The legislation did not give banks comprehensive coverage, however. The section only applied to drafts drawn on the bank which were payable to order, and did not protect banks which paid their customers' acceptance of bills domiciled at the bank.[290]

If this seemed to give good protection to the bank on which the cheque was drawn, its reach was narrowed in 1874 in *Ogden* v. *Benas*. Ogden, a London merchant, had sent a crossed cheque to a supplier in Liverpool, Vincent Willis. The cheque was payable at his London bank, but it was cashed at a Liverpool bank on a forged indorsement. The Common Pleas Division held that the collecting bank in Liverpool was not protected by section 19. As Keating J. saw it, the plaintiff's own bank—which had paid the money to the defendant bank—was protected by the section; but the defendant bank was in the position of a party which had obtained money by means of a forged indorsement, and which could not retain it. Nor was the judge moved by the fact that the bank had only paid the cheque after it had forwarded it to London for presentment. The decision came as something of a surprise,[291] but it was accepted as a correct interpretation of section 19.[292] Legislation followed which qualified this. Section 12 of the Crossed Cheques Act 1876 enacted that a banker, who in good faith and without negligence received payment for a customer of a crossed cheque, would not incur any liability to the

---

[289] *Robarts* v. *Tucker* (1851) 16 Q.B. 560 at 579.   [290] That is to say, made payable at the bank.
[291] *Matthiessen and Another* v. *The London and County Bank* (1879) 5 CPD 7 at 15.
[292] *Arnold and Others* v. *The Cheque Bank* (1876) 1 CPD 578 at 585.

true owner in case the title proved defective. Section 12 was re-enacted as section 82 of the Bills of Exchange Act 1882.

Negotiating and Crossing Cheques

Those who issued cheques were naturally keen to ensure that only the right payee would obtain them. Since cheques were negotiable, there was a risk that the cheque might not reach the intended payee, but might be cashed or passed on by a rogue. Since bankers could hardly be expected to know anyone who was a payee, the practice emerged of making cheques payable through bankers who would be known and reputable. This was done by crossing cheques. There were two ways in which a cheque could be crossed. Where it was 'specially' crossed (or 'doubly' crossed), the name of a banker would be written across the face of the cheque, the effect of which was to inform the drawees only to pay *that* banker. Where the cheque was 'generally' crossed, the words '& Co' were written on the face of the cheque, indicating that the cheque was to be paid through *any* bank. The practice of crossing cheques originated for the purpose of facilitating the clearing process.[293] It was extended as a means of protection against fraud. Rather than simply paying the person who presented the cheque (on his signing the back of it), payment would go through a bank to ensure the funds reached the right payee. The use of the practice was limited until mid-century by the fact that joint stock banks were not given access to the London Clearing House.

Those who gave cheques to agents to bank often crossed them to guard against the agent misappropriating the funds. If the intention of parties who did this was to restrict the negotiability of the cheques, they were frustrated by the courts. For instance, in 1828, in *Stewart* v. *Lee*, where one of the assignees of a bankrupt paid a cheque into his own account, rather than into the account of the assignees, the other assignee attempted to recover the money from the bank. His argument that since the cheque had been crossed, it should only have been paid into the assignees' account was rejected.[294] As Lord Tenterden CJ put it, the object of crossing was only 'to ensure the presentment by a banker for the purpose of making it easier to trace the checks, not to secure the payment to a particular party, or to restrict the circulation'.[295]

---

[293] Writing the name of the bank to whom it was paid on the cheque helped the process of cancelling out debts to and from banks at the end of the day. See the discussion in *Boddington* v. *Schlencker* (1833) 4 B. & Ad. 752.

[294] *Stewart* v. *Lee* (1828) M. & M. 157. Although the dishonest assignee was one of the payees of the cheque, and had his own account with the same bank, it was argued that the case was to be treated as if the two accounts were kept with separate bankers, and that the crossing meant that the cheque had to be paid to the assignees' bankers (and hence their account) only.

[295] *Stewart* v. *Lee* (1828) M. & M. 157 at 161.

The notion that crossing a cheque did not restrict its negotiability was confirmed in 1852 in *Bellamy* v. *Marjoribanks*, where a solicitor in a Chancery suit,
who had received a cheque specially crossed for payment to the Bank of England,
struck out that name, substituted the name of his own bank, and obtained payment for the cheque. Ordering a new trial (after a verdict for the plaintiffs), the
Exchequer barons held that crossing a cheque could not be seen as an indorsement to the banker since it was not done with the intention to transfer property,
nor was the instrument delivered to the banker. Nor could the crossing be seen
as a direction to pay a particular person only, rendering the bank contractually
liable for ignoring the direction, since if that were the case, a bearer cheque
specially crossed would become an instrument payable to order, subject to the
stamp duty which did not then apply to bearer cheques. The barons conceded
that if a cheque which had been generally crossed was not paid via a bank, this
would be evidence of negligence in the paying banker which might make him
liable; but since the money here had been paid to a bank, there had been no
negligence.[296]

The fact that crossing a cheque did nothing to restrain its negotiability also
meant that if the holder of a crossed cheque cashed it with someone who was
not a banker, there was no remedy. Thus, where a clerk who was instructed to
cash a cheque for his employers cashed it with a tavern keeper, they were unable
to recover, since the tavern keeper had it *bona fide* and for value. As the Queen's
Bench put it in *Carlon* v. *Ireland* in 1856, while the crossing of a cheque might be
relevant for a jury in deciding whether a banker had been negligent in paying a
sum, it did not impose on the party taking the cheque any duty to look into the
title of the holder. To decide otherwise would be to deny its negotiability while
claiming the cheque was negotiable.[297]

These decisions provoked disquiet and much debate over how to increase the
security of cheques, since they seemed to show that 'any one of acuteness and
apparent respectability can get change for a crossed check nearly as readily as for
a large banknote'.[298] In 1856, legislation was proposed to make specially crossed
cheques payable only to the named banker, and generally crossed cheques payable
only via a bank.[299] The bill was watered down, however, and the ensuing Crossed
Cheques Act merely enacted that crossed cheques had to be paid through a banker.[300] Judges soon decided that its effect was to make the crossing of a cheque a
direction to the banker only to pay via a bank, so that he could be held liable for

[296] *Bellamy* v. *Marjoribanks* (1852) 7 Exch. 389.
[297] *Carlton and Another* v. *Ireland* (1856) 25 L.J. N.S. Q.B. 113.
[298] *The Times*, 14 December 1855, col. 5a. See also 19 December 1855, col. 7b.
[299] *The Times*, 5 March 1856, col. 11a. It was also proposed that cheques could only be crossed
once.   [300] 19 & 20 Vict. c. 25.

paying it in any other way, even absent negligence.[301] However, since the Act did not restrict the negotiability of crossed cheques, it did not mean that crossed cheques could only be paid via bankers, for that would be to render a draft which on the face of it was payable to bearer *not* payable to bearer.[302]

In *Simmons* v. *Taylor*, it was further held that crossing a cheque was only a direction to the banker at the moment it was presented to him, and not when it was drawn. Since later holders could add a crossing, there was no reason why later holders could not remove one. This meant that where a fraudster had got hold of a crossed cheque and obtained payment by obliterating the crossing, the bank paying would not be liable. Moreover, since a crossing was not part of the instrument, obliterating it did not (according to the court) constitute a forgery, which would throw the risk on the bank.[303] This decision generated renewed alarm in the commercial community, since it seemed to suggest that crossings could effectively be ignored. It was followed by renewed legislation. The Crossed Cheques Act 1858 enacted that a crossing was to be deemed a material part of the instrument, and that its fraudulent obliteration or alteration was to constitute a felony.[304] It also put into law the proposal lost two years earlier, that where a cheque was specially crossed, it was only to be paid to that bank. At the same time, bankers succeeded in including a controversial clause to protect them in cases of forgery.[305] A banker paying a cheque which did not appear to have been crossed or altered, would not be liable, if he had acted in good faith and without negligence.[306]

The effect of this legislation was to allow the drawer of a crossed cheque to seek a remedy against his banker who had not paid according to the crossing; although if the crossing had been obliterated by a forger, the banker was protected.[307] Nonetheless, although the crossing was now deemed to be a part of the

[301] *Simmons* v. *Taylor* (1857) 2 C.B. N.S. 528 at 538.

[302] See *Simmons* v. *Taylor* (1857) 2 C.B. N.S. 528 at 536 (Cresswell J.) and *Simmons* v. *Taylor* (1858) 4 C.B. N.S. 463 at 468 (Bramwell B.).

[303] See *Simmons* v. *Taylor* (1857) 2 C.B. N.S. 528 at 539–40 (Cresswell J.) and *Simmons* v. *Taylor* (1858) 4 C.B. N.S. 463 at 467 (Wightman J.).

[304] 21 & 22 Vict. c. 79.

[305] It was pointed out that the loss was to fall on the customer, even though the bank supplied the crossed cheques and might be able to make them more secure: *The Times*, 20 August 1858, col. 4f. It was argued for the bankers that a crossing could only be erased or altered if the original drawer had been careless (in which case he should take the risk), or if the payee had been careless; though customers protested that cheques might be lost in the post without carelessness and that the banks were rich enough to bear the risk: *The Times*, 26 August 1858, col. 6a.

[306] It was opposed by 600 London firms, and passed despite an assurance from the government that no such clause would be included. For the controversy, see *The Times*, 31 July 1858, col. 10a.

[307] However, where a crossed cheque bore a forged indorsement, the bank remained liable. Although a drawee banker was protected by s 19 of the Stamp Act 1853 where he paid someone whose title came via a forgery, because of the Crossed Cheques Act 1856, this protection did not extend to

instrument, the fact that its negotiability was not restrained was reiterated in 1875, in *Smith* v. *Union Bank of London*. Here, a cheque drawn on the defendant bank, payable to the plaintiff's order, was indorsed by the latter, and crossed with the name of his bankers. It was subsequently stolen and sold for value to a *bona fide* purchaser, who obtained payment on the cheque through his bank. Since the cheque had not been paid according to the crossing, the plaintiff sued the drawee bank. However, both the Queen's Bench Division and Court of Appeal held that the 1858 Act did not restrain the negotiability of the cheque. Since the plaintiff had indorsed the cheque, property in it passed to a *bona fide* holder for value. Since property had passed, and the owner had been paid and no one had been damnified, it did not matter that the cheque was not paid according to the plaintiff's crossing.[308] If a holder of a crossed cheque wanted security, Blackburn noted, he should either indorse it specially to his bankers, or leave it unindorsed; since in such cases, a thief would have to forge an indorsement, which would deny a subsequent holder property.[309]

This decision provoked considerable disquiet in the commercial community.[310] The *Economist* declared that legislation was needed to make the crossing to a particular banker imperative, and to restrict the negotiability of such cheques.[311] A bill was introduced by J. G. Hubbard to restore the law to what bankers thought it was. In Hubbard's view, cheques should be regarded as private arrangements enabling payment to be made by one party to another, and not be universally negotiable as banknotes or bills of exchange. He wanted to restrict the payment of crossed cheques to the banker named; and he also wanted the title of the holder of a crossed cheque to depend on that of the person from whom he obtained it; so that a *bona fide* holder who acquired the cheque from a thief would get no title to it. At the same time, Cairns LC introduced another bill for the government, leading Hubbard to withdraw his. However, Cairns's bill only proposed that cheques specially crossed with a particular name should not be negotiable.[312] The government's bill maintained the essential negotiability of cheques, to Hubbard's consternation. Since most cheques—notably dividend cheques—were not specially crossed, and since the payee could not specially cross a cheque until it came into his hands, the risk of cheques being appropriated by thieves remained in place. But the government remained firm that negotiability was the essence of a cheque. Nor was this merely a doctrinal matter. As Sir John Holker AG put it, '[i]t would

---

cases where the payment was not made according to the crossing. See *Smith* v. *Union Bank of London* (1875) LR 10 QB 291 at 296.

[308] *Smith* v. *Union Bank of London* (1875) LR 10 QB 291 at 295–6.   [309] *Ibid.*
[310] *The Times*, 17 December 1875, col. 8b.   [311] *The Times*, 6 December 1875, col. 5g.
[312] See *The Times*, 28 February 1876, col. 9e.

be most disastrous to trade if within six years somebody could come down on a firm which had received a cheque as so much money, and had applied it to the benefit of a customer, and require them to refund'.[313] He proposed to leave general and special crossings as they were, but to introduce a new form of crossing. According to his proposal (which became section 12 of the Act), only if the cheque was marked 'not negotiable' did the person taking it have no better title than the person from whom he took it.[314] This meant that if a cheque was not so marked, then any *bona fide* holder for value could recover, as in *Smith*.[315] The effect of marking a crossed cheque 'not negotiable' was not to impede its transferability, but to give greater security to the instrument by preventing later holders getting a better title to the cheque than that of the transferor.[316] If a cheque so crossed were stolen and sold on to a third party, that party would have to refund the true owner.

The rules protecting bankers were codified in the Bills of Exchange Act 1882, which extended the protection given by section 19 of the Stamp Act 1853. Section 60 of the 1882 Act stipulated that where a banker paid a cheque bearing a forged or invalid indorsement 'in good faith and in the ordinary course of business', he would be deemed to have paid it in due course.[317] The stipulation of good faith was an innovation on the provisions of 1853, and reflected the notion imported into the Crossed Cheques Act 1858. But the need to act without negligence was omitted from the section, and section 90 made it clear that one could still act in 'good faith' while being negligent.

Banks were also protected by ss 80 and 82, which consolidated the Crossed Cheques Act 1876. Section 80 reproduced section 9 of the 1876 Act, which gave protection to the drawee bank which paid a crossed cheque in good faith and without negligence. Section 82 reproduced the second paragraph of section 12, which enacted that where the banker in good faith and without negligence received payment of a crossed cheque for a customer who had no title to it, he should not incur liability to the true owner.[318] Subsequent courts interpreted the

---

[313] *PD* 1876 (s3) 231: 1216.   [314] 39 & 40 Vict. c. 81, s 10.

[315] Section 10 of the Act did say that a banker who did not pay according to the crossing of a cheque would be liable to the true owner. This in effect consolidated the existing law, but did not overturn *Smith*, since the holder in that case was held to be the 'true owner'.

[316] See *Great Western Railway Co* v. *London and County Banking Co* [1901] AC 414 at 422. As Chalmers pointed out, the words meant in effect 'not fully negotiable', and such a bill was of the same effect as an overdue bill, with holders being deemed to have notice of all facts relating to it. M. D. Chalmers, *A Digest of the Law of Bills of Exchange* (1878), 215.

[317] Section 19 of the 1853 Act was not repealed since, unlike the 1882 Act, it was not confined to bills of exchange.

[318] Hubbard had argued that this protected a bank paying a thief who cashed a crossed cheque. This seemed to him entirely to undermine the protection promised by s 10 (reproduced in s 79(2) of

section restrictively. To begin with, it was clear that the section did not protect a bank which acted negligently.[319] Equally, the Act was held only to protect the bank which collected money for a regular customer.[320] If the bank did more than merely receiving the cheque for its customer—such as when it gave the holder cash before the cheque was cleared, becoming the indorsee of the cheque itself—it became liable. For as Lord Macnaghten put it in 1903, '[i]t is well settled that if a banker before collection credits a customer with the face value of a cheque paid into his account, the banker becomes holder for value of the cheque',[321] rather than being merely an agent for collection. This was a problematic interpretation of the law: if the bank gave credit at once to the customer for the cheque, it was not protected by the Act; but if instead it allowed the customer to overdraw his account to an equivalent amount prior to the clearing, it was protected. Moreover, it was recognized that if a banker could not immediately credit a cheque as cash on his customer's account, then commerce might be impeded. There was particular concern about the effect of the decision on the Stock Exchange, since a vast number of cheques were paid into banks on settlement days, which were immediately credited so that stock could be delivered.[322] Given this anomaly, amending legislation was passed in 1906, stating that bankers were protected by section 82 of the 1882 Act, if they credited customers' accounts before receiving payment of the cheque.[323]

---

the 1882 Act), which made the banker liable for paying on a crossed cheque: *The Times*, 29 August 1876, col. 7f.

[319] *Bissell* v. *Fox, Brothers & Co* (1885) 51 LT 663, 53 LT 193 (CA); *Bavins and Another* v. *London and South-Western Bank* (1899) 81 LT 655. See also *Hannan's Lake View Ltd* v. *Armstrong* (1900) 5 Com Cas 188.

[320] See *Matthews* v. *Brown & Co* (1894) 10 TLR 386; *Lacave & Co* v. *Crédit Lyonnais* [1897] 1 QB 148 at 154–5; *Great Western Railway Co* v. *The London and County Banking Co* [1901] AC 414.

[321] *Capital & Counties Bank* v. *Gordon* [1903] AC 240 at 244.

[322] *PD* 1906 (s4) 158: 1290 (Sir F. Dixon-Hartland).

[323] Bills of Exchange (Crossed Cheques) Act 1906, 6 Edw. 7 c. 17.

IV

Bankruptcy and Insolvency

THE spectre of bankruptcy weighed heavily on the Victorian mind.[1] It has been argued that Victorians saw as one of Parliament's greatest failures its 'inability to formulate bankruptcy laws which satisfied the business community, on the one hand, while upholding conventional moral standards, on the other'.[2] Reform of the law of bankruptcy remained on the agenda throughout our period, as commercial groups, lawyers, and politicians debated and experimented with how far such matters should be regulated by official intervention, and how far they should be left to participants in the market.[3] Reform in this area was not driven by ideology. Rather than being the stuff of high politics, it was generally the product of debates between the legal profession and the commercial world. When major changes were made to the system, they were responses to perceived failures in the preceding model. These would, in their own turn, be seen as not answering the needs of business, and invite major revision. The triumph of laissez-faire represented by the repeal of the Corn Laws in 1846 was hence not replicated in the sphere of bankruptcy, where legislation in 1849 built on and expanded an existing regulatory system, set up in 1831. It was the perceived failures of that system, rather than ideology, which lay behind the abolition in 1869 of the system of official control it had put in place.

Legislators and businessmen were also concerned with the morality of business failure. It has been argued that the mid-nineteenth century saw a shift in attitudes. According to Boyd Hilton, in the first half of the century, influential evangelicals stressed that bankruptcy was a 'moral preventive check' which controlled

---

[1] See B. Weiss, *The Hell of the English: Bankruptcy and the Victorian Novel* (Lewisburg, 1986).

[2] G. R. Searle, *Morality and the Market in Victorian Britain* (Oxford, 1998), 88–9; cf. G. R. Searle, *Entrepreneurial Politics in Mid-Victorian Britain* (Oxford, 1993), 176–81 and V. M. Batzel, 'Parliament, Businessmen and Bankruptcy, 1825–1883: A Study in Middle Class Alienation' (1983) 18 *Canadian Journal of History* 171–86.

[3] See C. Stebbings, ' "Officialism": Law, Bureaucracy and Ideology in Late Victorian England', in A. Lewis and M. Lobban, *Law and History: Current Legal Issues 6* (Oxford, 2004), 317–42 at 329–31. On the workings of the bankruptcy laws, and their reform, see I. P. H. Duffy, *Bankruptcy and Insolvency in London during the Industrial Revolution* (1985) and V. M. Lester, *Victorian Insolvency: Bankruptcy, Imprisonment for Debt and Company Winding Up in Nineteenth Century England* (Oxford, 1995).

avaricious overtrading, just as Malthusians argued that pestilence controlled overpopulation. '[I]n that evangelically conditioned climate', he writes, 'there was a tendency to regard innocent bankrupts as sacrificial offerings, beloved of God, and atoning vicariously for the sins of a commercially fallen world.'[4] By the mid-century, this pessimistic view is said to have lost its hold, and it was increasingly acknowledged that debtors were innocent victims of the trade cycle, or had simply been unlucky.[5] The new 'optimistic' view has been linked to the triumph of *laissez-faire* and the passing of the Limited Liability Act 1855.[6] However, although this legal reform has been taken as representing a turning point, the moral shifts described by historians are difficult to map onto the law.[7] For the debates discussed by these historians were not about the law, but about the market and the conduct of traders and investors in it.[8] It was the fact of failure which concerned these moralists, not the legal response to it.[9]

When we look inside the system of bankruptcy, a simple model of a punitive regime being replaced by a *laissez-faire* one does not work. From the start of our period, reformers sought to make a distinction between the unfortunate and the blameworthy, and to devise a system whereby those who were unable to pay their bills because of simple commercial misfortune would be absolved, while those who were at fault would be punished.[10] This was a project, in effect, of limiting the liability of the unfortunate. However, persistent disagreements about what constituted blameworthy commercial conduct, and about who should be the judge of this, rendered the reform process halting, complex, and often contradictory.

1. THE SYSTEM OF BANKRUPTCY IN 1820

The idea that a person's property could be seized by compulsory process, to be distributed among his creditors, was originally regarded as punitive, and was aimed at fraudulent debtors seeking to evade their creditors.[11] The foundation

---

[4] B. Hilton, *The Age of Atonement: The Influence of Evangelicalism on Social and Economic Thought, 1785–1865* (Oxford, 1988), 138, 118–20.

[5] See e.g. T. McGann, 'Literary Realism in the Wake of Business Cycle Theory: The Way We Live Now (1875)', in F. O'Gorman, *Victorian Literature and Finance* (Oxford, 2007), 133–56.

[6] Hilton, *Age of Atonement*, Ch. 7.

[7] See further M. Lobban, 'The Politics of English Law in the Nineteenth Century' (forthcoming).

[8] Moreover, it has been shown that ideas of morality in economic conduct remained relevant: see Searle, *Morality and the Market* and E. J. Garnett, 'Aspects of the Relationship between Protestant Ethics and Evangelical Activity in Mid-Victorian England' (Oxford University D. Phil., 1986).

[9] Hence, the importance of limited liability was that it offered investors the ability to avoid insolvency altogether (if only in theory).

[10] As Duffy points out, '[i]n the eighteenth century, [...] [b]ankruptcy came to be viewed as an act of mercy for the innocent victim of the uncontrollable workings of the economy': *Bankruptcy and Insolvency*, 17.

[11] 34 & 35 Hen. 8 c. 4 (1543).

of bankruptcy law was laid by Elizabethan legislation, which authorized the Lord Chancellor to act through commissioners, in taking hold of the property of traders who had committed certain 'acts' of bankruptcy.[12] Not until the eighteenth century did the idea take root that commercial activity involved particular risks, which justified giving traders a measure of protection not accorded to the general debtor. This was done by legislation in 1705, under which a trader could be discharged from liability if he was granted a certificate of conformity by the commissioners.[13] Subsequent legislation added the requirement that the creditors consent to the discharge.[14]

Only traders who had committed an act of bankruptcy, and who owed large sums,[15] were subject to the jurisdiction of the bankruptcy commissioners. A series of statutes since 1571 had laid down what occupations rendered a person liable to be made a bankrupt as a trader.[16] The basic definition, set out in the first bankruptcy statute, rendered those who sought their living by 'buying and selling' subject to the bankrupt laws. It was left to the courts to decide which occupations were covered by the statutes, and what constituted trading. Over time, a number of complex rules had emerged. Common carriers, who did not buy and sell merchandise, were regarded as not subject to the bankruptcy statutes.[17] Those engaged in making bricks on their own property, as a means of exploiting the real estate, were not subject to the bankruptcy laws, though they were if it was done 'substantially and independently as a trade'.[18] Similarly, farmers, grazers, and drovers were not covered by the bankrupt laws, though the holder of an estate who added ingredients to its produce and sold it on might be liable to the bankrupt laws.[19] To be liable to bankruptcy, the person had to be engaged in permanent, rather than merely occasional, trading.[20] This requirement also gave much scope for doubting whether a person was subject to the law: for it had to

[12] 13 Eliz. c. 7. See also Lester, *Victorian Insolvency*, 15.

[13] 4 & 5 Anne c. 17, s 19; Duffy, *Bankruptcy and Insolvency*, 11.

[14] 5 Anne c. 22; see also 5 Geo. I c. 24, s 16 and 5 Geo. II, c. 30 s 10.

[15] Under the 1825 Act, a creditor could only seek a petition if he was owed £100, or, if there were more than two creditors to the insolvent trader, that the debts amounted to more than £200, 6 Geo. IV c. 16, s 15.

[16] These included factors, scriveners, bankers, and brokers, as well as traders. See Basil Montagu, *A Digest of the Bankrupt Laws* 4 vols (1805–7), i, 14; and Duffy, *Bankruptcy and Insolvency*, 18–19.

[17] The 1825 consolidating Act extended the law to cover those who sought their living 'by buying and letting for hire, or by the workmanship of goods and commodities': 6 Geo. IV c. 16, s 2.

[18] See R. H. Eden, *A Practical Treatise on the Bankrupt Law* (2nd edn, 1826), 4. See also *Sutton* v. *Weeley* (1806) 1 East 442 and *Ex p Gallimore* (1816) 2 Rose 424.

[19] According to Montagu, *Digest*, i, 19–20, it was not settled how much had to be added to the produce to make the seller a trader subject to bankruptcy 'but it seems it is not trading when the value of the produce is greater than the value of the purchased ingredients'.

[20] It was for the jury to decide whether the trade was incidental or not: see e.g. *Gale* v. *Halfknight* (1821) 3 Stark. 56.

be determined both whether the activity was only occasional, and whether—if it was permanent—this activity was the one from which the insolvent person's subsistence derived.[21]

Before a trader could be subjected to the jurisdiction of the commissioners, he had to have committed an act of bankruptcy. The trader's bankruptcy commenced as soon as the act was committed, and once committed, it could not be explained away or 'purged'.[22] From that point, he was deprived of all power of disposing of his property. Assignees subsequently appointed under the bankruptcy proceedings obtained all rights over the property from the moment of bankruptcy, by the doctrine of relation. Seventeen acts of bankruptcy were defined by statute. Some of these were acts whereby a trader in debt sought to avoid his creditors. It was an act of bankruptcy to depart from the realm or stay in one's house, with the intention of defeating one's creditors. In such cases, it was necessary to prove the intent, for (in Lord Kenyon's words), '[t]he intent and the Act must both concur to constitute the crime' of bankruptcy.[23] It was for the jury to determine the person's intention in departing.[24] It was also an act of bankruptcy to suffer an arrest for a debt not due,[25] or to suffer one's goods to be seized, with the intent of delaying one's creditors; or to remain in prison for two months after being arrested for debt.[26]

Other acts of bankruptcy were those by which the trading debtor sought to dispose of his assets. It was an act of bankruptcy to make any fraudulent conveyance of one's property, whereby one's creditors might be delayed. Before 1825, such conveyances would only constitute an act of bankruptcy if they were effected by a deed; though an assignment of property to defeat one's creditors would be regarded as void, even if it did not itself constitute an act of bankruptcy. After 1825, any transfer of property might constitute an act of bankruptcy,

---

[21] Montagu, *Digest*, i, 25.

[22] J. S. M. Fonblanque, *Observations on a Bill now before Parliament for the Consolidation and Amendment of the Laws relating to Bankrupts* (1824), 4. See *Colkett* v. *Freeman* (1787) 2 T.R. 59; *Wood* v. *Thwaites* (1800) 3 Esp. 245.

[23] *Fowler* v. *Padget* (1798) 7 T.R. 509 at 514. See also *Ramsbottom* v. *Lewis* (1808) 1 Camp. 279, where it was held that a man who knew that the necessary consequence of his departing the realm would delay his creditors committed an act of bankruptcy by leaving.

[24] *Deffle* v. *Desanges* (1819) 8 Taunt. 671. For the intent needed in secluding oneself in one's home, away from one's creditors, see *Dudley* v. *Vaughan* (1808) 1 Camp. 271; *Harvey* v. *Ramsbottom* (1822) 1 B. & C. 55.

[25] Suffering an arrest for a just debt one had money to pay, in order to induce one's creditors into a composition was an act of bankruptcy: *Ex p Barton* (1734) Charles Viner, *A General Abridgment of Law and Equity* (Aldershot, 1757), vii, 61–2 (tit. Creditor and Bankrupt, B 15).

[26] Under Jacobean legislation, the period of lying in prison was two months: the 1825 Act reduced it to 21 days. In such cases, it was not necessary to show any intent to delay one's creditors: *Robertson* v. *Liddell* (1808) 9 East 487.

if intended to defeat the trader's creditors. Fraudulent conveyances could be of two kinds. First, there were such conveyances as were void under the common law[27] and Elizabethan legislation, which directed that no act done to defraud a creditor should be effective against the creditor.[28] It was for the court in each case to determine if a conveyance was fraudulent; the mere fact that property had been assigned to one creditor over another did not necessarily make it so.[29] The fact that a debtor had given a bill of sale, transferring property in his chattels, to a creditor, while retaining possession of them was regarded in the late eighteenth and early nineteenth century by some judges as fraudulent and the sale void.[30] But by the 1820s, the view was taken that the fact that the debtor had retained possession of the goods was not itself conclusive evidence of fraud, and that it was for the jury to consider the debtor's intent.[31] It was therefore possible to obtain loans on the security of chattels remaining in the borrower's possession.[32]

Secondly, conveyances which would not be regarded as fraudulent when made by non-traders could be regarded as fraudulent when done by traders, for being in contravention of the 'policy' of the bankrupt laws. Acts which constituted frauds on the bankruptcy laws included a trader assigning all his property to one or more creditors, since it was a fraud against any creditor omitted from the arrangement.[33] Equally, if a trader conveyed so much of his stock-in-trade to a particular creditor, as would hinder him from carrying on his business, this was regarded as an act of bankruptcy, even if he was able to carry on trading for some time thereafter.[34] Since acts of bankruptcy were seen as criminal in their nature, judges construed the law strictly. It was therefore held that a fraudulent conveyance executed abroad was not within the statute, 'upon the narrow principle that an act of bankruptcy being a crime, it could not be committed abroad'.[35]

It was also regarded as a fraud on the bankrupt laws to assign all one's property to a trustee for the benefit of all the creditors. At common law, a 'composition' agreement, whereby creditors accepted a smaller payment to extinguish a

[27] See *Twyne's case* (1601) 3 Co. 80b.

[28] 13 Eliz. c. 5. Cf. 27 Eliz. c. 4, which rendered void all conveyances intended to defeat purchasers.

[29] *Holbird* v. *Anderson* (1793) 5 T.R. 235; *Estwick* v. *Caillaud* (1793) 5 T.R. 420; *Meux* v. *Howell* (1803) 4 East 1.

[30] *Edwards* v. *Harben* (1788) 2 T.R. 587; *Wordall* v. *Smith* (1808) 1 Camp. 332.

[31] *Hoffman* v. *Pitt* (1803) 5 Esp. 22 at 24; *Lady Arundell* v. *Phipps* (1804) 10 Ves. 139 at 145; *Leonard* v. *Baker* (1813) 1 M. & S. 251; *Eastwood* v. *Brown* (1825) Ry. & Moo. 312; *Latimer* v. *Batson* (1825) 4 B. & C. 652.

[32] *Martindale* v. *Booth* (1832) 3 B. & Ad. 498.

[33] See *Worseley* v. *De Mattos* (1758) 1 Burr. 467; *Hooper* v. *Smith* (1763) 1 W. Bl. 441 at 442.

[34] *Pulling* v. *Tucker* (1821) 4 B. & Ald. 382; cf. *Smith* v. *Cannan* (1853) 2 E. & B. 35; *Ex p Bailey* (1853) 3 De G. M. & G. 534.

[35] Eden, *Practical Treatise*, 26. This rule was overturned by the Bankruptcy Act 1825.

larger debt, would only be valid if done by a formal deed.[36] However, making such a deed was considered an act of bankruptcy.[37] Although no creditor who was party to the agreement was permitted to challenge it on these grounds,[38] it could be challenged by any dissenting creditor, or those who had been defrauded by a secret agreement between the debtor and any particular creditor.[39] This doctrine rested on two principles. The first was that, by conveying away his property, a trader rendered himself unable to carry on trading. The second was that, by appointing trustees, he attempted to arrange for a distribution of his property on principles different from those set by the bankruptcy law.[40] It was a controversial doctrine, since composition agreements could be beneficial to all creditors.

Judges realized that it was essential for business that solvent traders should be able to use their assets as they saw fit, to obtain and discharge credit. However, if a trader was seen to prefer a chosen creditor at a time when he was contemplating bankruptcy, it was regarded as a fraud on the other creditors.[41] Whether or not a payment was made in contemplation of bankruptcy was a matter of fact to be decided by a jury.[42] A conveyance of part of one's property to a creditor would only be regarded as an act of bankruptcy if it had been voluntary: for '[i]f the goods be delivered through the urgency of the demand, or the fear of prosecution, whatever may have been in the contemplation of the bankrupt, this will not vitiate the proceeding'.[43]

Since acts of bankruptcy were seen as offences rather than as tests of insolvency, no trader could apply for his own commission. Instead, it was for the

---

[36] See pp. 384–5, on this issue.

[37] The doctrine was said to derive from Lord Mansfield's decision in *Kettle* v. *Hammond* (1767), cited in William Cooke, *The Bankrupt Laws*, 2 vols (2nd edn, 1788), i, 111, that such deeds were void unless all creditors signed. Eden, *Practical Treatise*, 29. See also *Dutton* v. *Morrison* (1809–10) 17 Ves. 193.

[38] *Bamford* v. *Baron* (1788) 2 T.R. 595n; *Back* v. *Gooch* (1815) Holt 13; *Marshall* v. *Barkworth* (1833) 4 B. & Ad. 508.

[39] See *Leicester* v. *Rose* (1803) 4 East 371, *Ex p Sadler and Jackson* (1808) 15 Ves. 52. See also *Dauglish* v. *Tenannt* (1866) LR 2 QB 49; see also in equity, *Ex p Cowen* (1867) 2 Ch Ap 563. Moreover, the fraudulent creditor was later penalized in bankruptcy, by being held barred by the release given in the composition deed from proving in bankruptcy, when other creditors were allowed so to do: *Ex p Cross* (1848) 4 De G. & S. 364n.

[40] *Dutton* v. *Morrison* (1809–10) 17 Ves. 193 at 199. As Eldon pointed out, early eighteenth-century judges had taken a different view: *Small* v. *Oudley* (1727) 2 P. Wms. 427.

[41] *Harman* v. *Fishar* (1774) 1 Cowp. 117; *Hartshorn* v. *Slodden* (1801) 2 B. & P. 582 at 584; *Morgan* v. *Horseman* (1810) 3 Taunt. 241.

[42] See *Smith* v. *Payne* (1795) 6 T.R. 152; *Hartshorn* v. *Slodden* (1801) 2 B. & P. 582; *Fidgeon* v. *Sharpe* (1814) 5 Taunt. 539.

[43] *Hartshorn* v. *Slodden* (1801) 2 B. & P. 582 at 584 (per Lord Alvanley CJ). See also *Crosby* v. *Crouch* (1809) 11 East 256. Where all the bankrupt's property was conveyed, even under pressure, this was regarded as an act of bankruptcy: *Thornton* v. *Hargreaves* (1806) 7 East 544.

creditor to obtain a commission by *ex parte* proceedings, on showing that an act of bankruptcy had been committed.[44] A trader could be proclaimed a bankrupt in the *London Gazette*, have his possessions seized and be summoned to court without having been given any opportunity to answer the evidence brought before the commissioners by the petitioning creditor.[45] If the trader disputed committing an act of bankruptcy, his only remedy was to petition the Lord Chancellor to supersede the commission or to bring an action at common law against the assignees who took his property, both of which took such time that he might be ruined.[46] By the time a superior court judge heard his case, the bankrupt trader would have been examined before the bankruptcy commissions, where 'his most secret transactions may be exposed to the scrutiny of his enemy'.[47] The bankrupt had little choice: if he did not surrender to the examination, or if he concealed property, he committed a capital felony.[48]

Disputed bankruptcies might drag on for years, and lead to ruin. The banker A. M. Chambers, who was declared bankrupt in 1825 owing some £300,000, disputed the adjudication against him, the issue turning on whether or not he had requested his servant to deny that he was at home, in order to defeat his creditors.[49] The case went on for over a decade. Although the assignees of the estate collected £170,000, they were unable to distribute any money to Chambers' creditors while the dispute dragged on. Meanwhile, £50,000 was swallowed up in costs and legal fees. Chambers himself ended in the Fleet debtors' prison, and

---

[44] Eden, *Practical Treatise*, 12; R. H. Eden, *Observations on the Bill now Depending in Parliament for the Consolidation and Amendment of the Bankrupt Laws* (1824), 11. See also C. Fane, *Bankruptcy Reform; in a series of letters addressed to Sir Robert Peel, Bart* (1838), 27–8.

[45] Sir James Bland Lamb, *An Enquiry into the Causes of the Procrastination and Delay Attributed to the Judicial Proceedings of the House of Lords and the Court of Chancery* (1824), 70. This was a revised edition of Part II of the author's 1785 *Considerations on the Law of Insolvency with a Proposal for Reform* (published under the name Sir James Bland Burgess). The commissioners, according to Cecil Fane, had an interest in making an adjudication of bankruptcy, 'for, if they acquit him, their fees cease, and if they condemn him, their fees continue, and *may* amount to any sum!' Fane, *Bankruptcy Reform*, 27.

[46] See Eldon's comments on how little protection the law might offer in *Ex p Stokes* (1802) 7 Ves. 405 at 407–9.

[47] Fonblanque, *Observations*, 4.

[48] This penalty was introduced by the 4 & 5 Anne c. 17, but was replaced by a penalty of life transportation by 1 Geo. IV c. 115, re-enacted in 6 Geo. IV c. 16, s 112.

[49] See *The Times*, 29 November 1825, col. 3a. For the petition to supersede the bankruptcy, see *ibid.*, 25 June 1835, col. 4b. After much discussion in court (see *ibid.*, 26 June 1835, col. 6b; 11 August 1835, col. 6d; 12 August 1835, col. 4c; 13 August 1835, col. 6f; 14 August 1835, col. 4a; 15 August 1835, col. 7d; 17 August 1835, col. 4b; 18 August 1835, col. 7b), the parties decided to come to an arrangement, but they were once more seeking the Chancellor's assistance within the year: 11 July 1836, col. 6f. The question of the commission's validity had also been debated in some ten legal suits. See also the comments of the Attorney General on this case in *PD* 1831 (s3) 7: 906.

all his properties were sold off.[50] The fact that the act of bankruptcy could be challenged in different courts contributed to delay and uncertainty, since different views might be taken as to whether an act of bankruptcy had occurred. Commenting on the case of Bartholomew Thomas, whose bankruptcy had been confirmed in various legal actions, only to have the commission superseded in equity, the Attorney General observed in 1831 that '[i]t never could be right, that one jurisdiction should have the power of sanctioning the debt as perfectly good, and all that had been done as legal; yet that another Court should be able to deal differently with the very same subject matter, and undo all that had been effected by an equally competent authority'.[51]

Under these circumstances, it was not surprising that most bankruptcies were concerted between the trader and his creditor. It was claimed by John Smith that the commonest act of bankruptcy—whereby the debtor denied himself to the creditor to avoid the debt—could only practically be committed when done in concert with the creditor, whose servant would prove the denial.[52] According to the commissioner Archibald Cullen, 'a majority of the commissions which issue, may be considered as a sort of conspiracies [sic] between the debtor and one or more of his creditors, to plunder the rest'.[53] Such proceedings were themselves risky, for concerted commissions of bankruptcy could be superseded.[54] If another creditor felt that the act had been concerted with a view to disadvantaging him— for instance to prevent him from obtaining execution of a judgment against the debtor—he would generally seek to have it superseded. According to Smith, if the debtor chose not to cooperate with his creditors, the only effective way for them to proceed was to arrest him for debt, and keep him in prison for two months, which would constitute an indisputable act of bankruptcy. During those two months, however, the debtor was able to 'pay the debts of his own family or friends, and only go into the Gazette when all his property was disposed of or dissipated'.[55]

If there were objections to the procedure, there were equally strong objections to the organization of the jurisdiction. In London, there were 14 lists of five commissioners, nominated by the Lord Chancellor. Commissions were issued in rotation to these lists. According to Basil Montagu, one of the London commissioners, this was 'the worst constituted tribunal in the country'. The large

[50] Fane, *Bankruptcy Reform*, 34–5.

[51] See *PD* 1831 (s3) 7: 905–6.

[52] *PD* 1818 (s1) 38: 983.

[53] Select Committee on the Bankrupt Laws: Minutes of Evidence, *PP* 1818 (127), vi, 23 (cited henceforth as 1818 Bankruptcy Committee), at p. 81. For a less conspiratorial view, see also the evidence of J. F. Vandercom and G. Lavie at pp. 40, 47.

[54] 4. *Ex p Moule* (1808) 14 Ves. 602; *Ex p Binmer* (1816) 1 Madd. 250.

[55] 5. *PD* 1818 (s1) 38: 983.

number of commissioners resulted in divergences in the administration of both procedural and substantive law.[56] Since only three out of five commissioners in each list were required to attend a meeting, 'the suitor is exposed, even in the same court, to a perpetual change of the judge' even in the course of the same meeting.[57] The decisions made by bankruptcy commissioners were often unsatisfactory, and proceedings before them could be slow, costly, and uncertain. They could also be oppressive, for commissioners had extensive powers to commit people examined before them, and this power was sometimes used at the behest of creditors keen to pressure relatives of the debtor to pay.[58] Outside London, the system was even worse, for there were no settled lists. Instead, the petitioning creditor's solicitor generally nominated commissioners of his own choice.[59] In the country, where meetings were held 'in the back parlour of some obscure inn, a few illiterate tradesmen, their own tenants or clients, the only audience', corruption was notorious.[60]

Appeals from these commissioners could be made to the Lord Chancellor. By the 1820s, according to Basil Montagu, such appeals took up a quarter of the time of the Chancery.[61] Lord Eldon was frequently criticized for devoting time to bankruptcy, in the expectation of getting fees from such business; but he was also clearly concerned with the need for speed. Where possible, he determined contentious questions without sending them to be settled at common law, since 'promptness, in cases of paper credit, is life itself to commercial men'.[62] The need for speed also meant that bankruptcy litigants effectively jumped the Chancery queue, which angered those who desired a more effective court of equity. Yet while a bankruptcy petition was supposed to be a *festinum remedium* which saved time and money,[63] by the 1820s it was 'a very dilatory, and very often a very expensive

<hr/>

[56] Basil Montagu, *Inquiries Respecting the Courts of Commissioners of Bankrupts and Lord Chancellor's Court* (1825), 93ff.

[57] Royal Commission on the Practice of the Chancery, *PP* 1826 (143), xv, 1 (cited henceforth as Chancery Commission), Minutes of Evidence, p. 394.

[58] On this power, see *Ex p Vogel* (1818) 2 B. & Ald. 219 at 224. Commissioners using these powers were not liable for false imprisonment: *Doswell v. Impey* (1823) 1 B. & C. 172. Basil Montagu in his evidence to the Chancery Commission (p. 403) showed that from 1810 to 1822, the fourteenth list of London commissioners committed 35 people to prison, with the other 13 lists committing only 31. See also his evidence to the 1818 Bankruptcy Committee, p. 26.

[59] B. Montagu, *Inquiries*, 7.

[60] Fonblanque, *Observations*, 34–5, see also Lord Eldon's comments in *Ex p Story* (1817) Buck 70 and his criticisms of the system in 6 Ves. 1. See also B. Montagu, *Letters on the Report of the Chancery Commissioners to the Rt Hon Robert Peel* (1826), 41–2.

[61] Montagu, *Letters on the Report*, 1–17.

[62] *Ex p The Leeds Bank* (1812) 1 Rose 254 at 255, quoted in Montagu, *Letters on the Report*, 23.

[63] *Ex p John Cowan* (1819) 3 B. & Ald. 123 at 127, where (refusing a writ of prohibition) Abbott CJ added, 'The proceeding under the commission operates by way of sudden seizure of property

proceeding'.[64] When cases came to the Chancellor, issues of fact were again presented to the court in long and contradictory affidavits, often on new evidence, which made the appeal in effect a rehearing,[65] while doubtful questions of law and fact could be remitted to common law courts and juries for determination.

Once a trader was pronounced bankrupt, his creditors obtained control over his assets. Under legislation dating from 1732, a majority in value of creditors who had proved debts of £10 could elect unpaid trustees to whom the commissioners were bound to assign the bankrupt's property. The system was premised on the assumption that creditors, who were the parties most interested in maximizing the dividend, would put themselves forward and do the work with the minimum cost. In fact, as Basil Montagu noted in 1811, few *bona fide* creditors were keen to devote much valuable business time in gathering assets they would only receive part of. Becoming an assignee was, however, attractive to less scrupulous creditors, who might hope to benefit from the bankrupt's property, 'by obtaining his customers, or by trading with his property; or by purchasing his estates either directly or in collusion with the bankrupt; or by retaining unclaimed dividends; or by retaining the undivided residue of the estate; or by obtaining total dominion over his property'.[66] Assignees might speculate with the bankrupt's money, and in turn become bankrupt at a time when the bankrupt's assets were mingled with their own. Sir James Bland Lamb in 1824 argued that 'the right of the creditors to nominate the assignees is become the main foundation of the complicated and iniquitous system of fraudulent bankruptcies'.[67] The control exerted over assignees was limited. They could be sued by other creditors, but since the latter ran the risk of costs (while the former could seek costs from the estate), this was an imperfect remedy. Sir Samuel Romilly's Act of 1809 aimed to curb the practice of assignees trading with the goods of bankrupts by charging an annual interest of 20 per cent on money wilfully retained, and by continuing the liability of an assignee after his bankruptcy to an estate to which he owed £100.[68] Nonetheless, the effect this Act was limited, when it was ruled that the interest could not be

---

belonging or supposed to belong to bankrupt. A process so summary and speedy requires to be controuled by a speedy and summary course of relief.'

[64] Montagu, Chancery Commission, Evidence, p. 409.

[65] Chancery Commission, Report, p. 36. See also the comments of T. C. Glyn in Chancery Commission, Evidence, p. 436. See also the comments of Cullen to the 1818 Bankruptcy Committee.

[66] B. Montagu, *Enquiries Respecting the Administration of Bankrupts' Estates by Assignees* (1811), 6–10. See also Montagu's evidence to the 1818 Bankruptcy Committee, 5–8; and see Duffy, *Bankruptcy and Insolvency*, 26–31.

[67] Lamb, *Enquiry*, 75–6.

[68] 46 Geo. III c. 135, s 1; see also 56 Geo. III c. 137, s 1, protecting the delivery of goods without notice of an act of bankruptcy.

levied on bankrupt assignees, since this would penalize their creditors and not themselves.[69]

Once the commission had been issued, the bankrupt's assets had to be calculated and collected. The property which could be taken by the assignees extended beyond that which was owned by the bankrupt. According to a rule established in 1623, where at the time of a trader's bankruptcy he had in his 'possession, order and disposition' any property belong to another person, with that person's consent, then that property would fall into the bankrupt's estate.[70] The rule was designed to ensure that secret creditors would not keep the trader afloat, deceiving others to give credit to someone who appeared to have many more assets than in fact he had. Under this provision, if a trader sold his goods to another, by a bill of sale, but retained possession of them, then the property would be considered part of the insolvent's property, and be available to his creditors. It was held in the eighteenth century that the same rule applied to conditional sales, where the chattels had been mortgaged. Burnet J. then observed that while it might be inconvenient for traders to be unable to mortgage their stock, it would be far more dangerous to allow a man's friends to secure themselves by secret mortgages and allow him to carry on trade. In his view, the easy solution was for the trader to 'take in partners, when he is not equal to the carrying on the whole'.[71] Applying this rule, it was held in 1805 that where the publisher of a newspaper had mortgaged his interest to a creditor, but carried on as publisher, the interest in the newspaper passed to the publisher's assignees, when he became bankrupt.[72] The rule generated risks for *bona fide* traders, who often needed to raise credit by loans secured on their stock-in-trade. In such cases, the lenders had to ensure that they took possession of the goods (or demanded their return) before any act of bankruptcy was committed by the borrower.[73] Traders sometimes gave their creditors the security of choses in action, such as debts owed to them by court judgments or mortgages, or life assurance policies. In such cases, to avoid the effects of the statute, the trader had to assign his interest in the security fully to his creditors to avoid the security going to his assignees.

The rules relating to reputed ownership affected any owner who by consent left his property in the order and disposition of the insolvent trader.[74] The doctrine

[69] See the evidence of T. C. Glyn to the Chancery Commission, Evidence, p. 437.

[70] 21 Jac. I c. 19.

[71] *Ryall* v. *Rowles* (1749) 9 Bligh. N.S. 377 at 394. See also the reports in 1 Ves. 369 and (*sub nom.* *Ryall* v. *Rolle*) in 1 Atk. 165.

[72] *Longman* v. *Tripp* (1805) 2 B. & P. N.R. 67; cf. *Ex p Foss* (1858) 2 De G. & J. 230.

[73] See R. Gregory and P. Walton, 'Fixed and Floating Charges—A Revelation' [2001] *Lloyd's Maritime and Commercial Law Quarterly*, 123–49 at 129. See also *Jones* v. *Dwyer* (1811) 15 East 21; *Arbouin* v. *Williams* (1824) R. & M. 72; *Smith* v. *Topping* (1833) 5 B. & Ad. 674.

[74] See e.g. *Mace* v. *Cadell* (1774) 1 Cowp. 232.

generated risks for many traders who had not made secret loans to the insolvent trader, but had merely dealt with him. If an importer, who had bought goods from another merchant, allowed them to remain with a wharfinger in the name of the seller, he would lose them to the assignees in the case of the latter's bankruptcy. Equally, if a merchant regularly gave another goods on a sale-or-return basis, such property would also go to assignees.[75] But not every possession gave the holder the 'order and disposition' of the goods. If a factor became bankrupt, his assignees would not obtain goods belonging to his principal, unless they had been sold and their proceeds had become so mixed with that of the factor that they could no longer be identified.[76] Similarly, property held by trustees would not go to their assignees.[77]

When a merchant failed, those who dealt with him sought to protect their own financial position by disputing whether the insolvent merchant had become owner of the property in question. Much litigation in the early nineteenth century on the passing of property when goods were sold arose out of bankruptcies. Unlike the law of several European countries at this time, English law did not permit a seller on credit to recover his goods from buyers who were insolvent.[78] Nor did it allow an insolvent trader who had received the goods to rescind the contract, on discovering that he could not pay, and return them; since to do so would be to prefer a particular creditor.[79] However, it did allow those who had consigned goods on credit to stop them coming into the possession of an insolvent trader (and thence into his estate). This was done through the doctrine, established in the eighteenth century, of stoppage *in transitu*. The consignor could exercise this right as soon as he suspected that the purchaser would be insolvent and unable to pay for the goods; but if it turned out that the trader was not insolvent before the goods were to arrive, he would be bound to deliver them and indemnify for the delay.[80] The consignor did not have to regain actual possession of the goods himself: it was sufficient for him to countermand the delivery. There were, however, limits to the protection this doctrine gave. For instance, if the consignee had sold his interest in the goods to a third party prior to delivery—as by the delivery of a bill of lading to another merchant for valuable consideration and without notice

---

[75] *Livesay* v. *Hood* (1809) 2 Camp. 83. Contrast *Gibson* v. *Bray* (1817) 8 Taunt. 76; *Delauney* v. *Barker* (1819) 2 Stark. 539 (where the sale-and-return arrangement was not a regular one).

[76] See *Whitecomb* v. *Jacob* (1711) 1 Salk. 160; *Scott* v. *Surman* (1743) Willes 400; *Zinck* v. *Walker* (1777) 2 W. Bl. 1154; *Taylor* v. *Plumer* (1815) 3 M. & S. 562. See also p. 572.

[77] *Ex p Martin* (1815) 2 Rose 381.

[78] This was regretted by Lord Kenyon: *Inglis* v. *Usherwood* (1801) 1 East 515 at 523.

[79] *Barnes* v. *Freeland* (1794) 6 T.R. 80. Contrast *Bartram* v. *Farebrother* (1828) 4 Bing. 579, where the court held that the goods had not yet arrived.

[80] *The Constantia* (1807) 6 C. Rob. Adm. 321 at 326–7.

of the insolvency—the consignor lost his ability to stop them.[81] This could present particular problems in a commercial world where goods which were stored in warehouses and wharves were bought and sold by various merchants exchanging documents giving a right to property and possession.[82] Much litigation also followed to establish what constituted a delivery of goods, sufficient to end the right to stop *in transitu*.

To entitle themselves to a share of the assets, the creditors had to prove their debts before the commissioners. There were three reasons for a creditor to prove his debt: it allowed him a vote in the choice of assignees; it gave him a voice in determining whether the bankrupt would be discharged; and it permitted him to obtain a dividend.[83] If the loan given by the creditor was secured, he could obtain full payment out of those securities, if they were sufficient. If the value of the security was greater than the sum secured—as where property was mortgaged—the assignees could only redeem it from the creditor on paying interest up to the time of redemption. Besides raising loans on the security of title deeds, traders often raised money from pledges. In such cases, the lender held the property pledged as security only for the sum originally lent: he was not permitted to use it as a security for advances made subsequently, against the claims of other creditors in bankruptcy.[84] If a secured debt could not be satisfied by the security, the creditor was not permitted both to retain the security, and prove the residue of his debt in the bankruptcy. Instead, he had first to realize the asset, or give it up to the court.[85] Unsecured creditors had to prove their debts before the commissioners. Once the claims were made, it was for the commissioners to declare a dividend from the assets collected, paying each creditor however much money per pound of debt which was available for distribution.

The decision whether to release the bankrupt from future liability, by granting a certificate of conformity, was left largely in the creditors' hands. Legislation dating from 1732 had left it to four-fifths of the creditors in number

[81] *Lickbarrow* v. *Mason* (1793) 4 Brown P.C. 57; *Vertue* v. *Jewell* (1814) 4 Camp. 31.

[82] See e.g. *Harman* v. *Anderson* (1809) 2 Camp. 243; *Stoveld* v. *Hughes* (1811) 14 East 308; *Hawes* v. *Watson* (1824) 2 B. & C. 539; *Spear* v. *Travers* (1815) 4 Camp. 251.

[83] B. Montagu, *Digest*, i, 442. Creditors could, however, elect not to prove their debt to obtain a dividend, but rather to proceed against the debtor at common law. They were still permitted to prove to obtain a vote regarding the discharge, since any discharge would end his right at common law: Cooke, *Bankrupt Laws*, 174.

[84] *Adams* v. *Claxton* (1801) 6 Ves. 226 at 229.

[85] Since it might be uncertain how much the security would realize, or even if it was valid, the holder was not to be 'enabled in a contest with the rest of the creditors to sustain his disputed title in a situation of predominant advantage': *Ex p Smith* (1813) 2 Rose 63 at 64 (per Lord Eldon).

and value to determine whether there should be a discharge.[86] Although there might be a moral obligation on creditors to sign, the law left the decision entirely to their caprice.[87] Creditors thereby had the power of 'imprisoning the bankrupt until his debts are paid: which, as the whole of his property is distributed amongst his creditors, may be imprisonment for life'.[88] In the decades around the turn of the nineteenth century, over 40 per cent of bankrupts did not receive a certificate.[89] While some creditors withheld their consent when they thought the debtor's conduct was criminal, others could do so in the hope of receiving a bribe from the debtor's relatives, or to ensure that the debtor, as an undischarged bankrupt, would be disqualified as a witness in any subsequent proceedings to uncover the location of money.[90] Given these concerns, Sir Samuel Romilly in 1809 brought a bill to take away the creditors' control over the certificate, but his bill was watered down in the Lords by Lords Eldon and Redesdale, who amended it so that the assent of three-fifths would still be required.[91]

The bankruptcy commissioners had to sign the certificate, which had also to be allowed by the Lord Chancellor. However, the power of these officials to refuse to sign or allow the certificate was limited. They could only take into account the bankrupt's conduct since his bankruptcy, to see whether he conformed to the statute.[92] A number of legal objections could be made to a certificate being granted. If the bankrupt had lost money in gaming or stock jobbing, if he concealed property above a certain value, or if he suffered false debts to be proved, his certificate would be voided. Similarly, if any creditor was induced by money to sign the certificate, it was void.[93] The bankrupt against whom a commission had issued was also liable to criminal sanctions, since it was a felony to refuse to surrender to an examination, to fail to make discovery of his property at the examination, to fail to surrender his books, or to embezzle or conceal property with intent to defraud his creditors.

---

[86] 5 Geo. II, c. 30, s 10.

[87] *Ex p Joseph* (1811) 18 Ves. Jun. 340 at 342. See also the comments of Tindal CJ in *Browne* v. *Carr* (1831) 7 Bing. 508 at 516.

[88] B. Montagu, *An Inquiry Respecting the Expediency of Limiting the Creditor's Power to Refuse a Bankrupt's Certificate* (1809), 1.

[89] *Ibid.*, 17.

[90] *Ibid.*, 40–52.

[91] 49 Geo. III c. 121, s 28.

[92] *Ex p Gardner* (1812) 1 V. & B. 45 at 47–8; *Ex p King* (1805) 11 Ves. Jun. 417 at 420. Nevertheless, the discretion of the commissioners was absolute: they could not be forced to sign the certificate. *Ex p King* (1806) 13 Ves. 181; *Ex p King* (1808) 15 Ves. 126.

[93] *Robson* v. *Calze* (1779) 1 Doug. 228.

2. REFORMING THE LAW OF BANKRUPTCY, 1825–1831

In the first two decades of the nineteenth century, there was widespread dissatisfaction with the law of bankruptcy, both from the mercantile and legal communities. The system was slow and expensive, and came under increasing pressure in the early nineteenth century, when the number of bankruptcies rose sharply.[94] A select committee of the House of Commons investigated the matter in 1817 and 1818, revealing many problems both with the substantive law and its procedure.[95] The substantive law was reformed first. In 1825, a consolidating and reforming Act was passed, after seven years during which various attempts had been made to amend the law in accordance with the recommendations of the select committee.[96]

Reformers sought to take away the criminal associations of bankruptcy by facilitating the voluntary insolvency of the trader, which would allow him to distribute his remaining assets as early as possible.[97] Implementing a recommendation of the 1818 committee, the 1825 Act permitted debtors to declare themselves insolvent at the Bankrupt Office.[98] It remained for the creditors, rather than the trader himself, to initiate bankruptcy proceedings, since the declaration constituted an act of bankruptcy. To shorten the time during which an imprisoned insolvent might dispose of his property, the Act specified that remaining in prison for 21 days constituted an act of bankruptcy. The Act also clarified other conduct which constituted acts of bankruptcy.[99]

The Act also permitted parties to enter into composition deeds, 'the most beneficial mode of distributing insolvents' estates'.[100] Reformers were aware that composition deeds might be secretly entered into, with the creditors who were party to the agreement being paid by a new set of creditors.[101] There was also the danger that not all the insolvent's creditors had signed, and that those who had been omitted might later challenge the arrangement. The 1825 Act sought to overcome these problems, and give protection to the omitted creditor, by enacting that entering into a composition deed would not be considered as an act of

---

[94] Duffy, *Bankruptcy and Insolvency*, 40–4, 168.

[95] Lamb, *Enquiry*, 75–6.

[96] 6 Geo. IV c. 16. The Act was prepared by Robert Henley Eden under the supervision of Lord Eldon. For the debt of the legislation to the 1817 select committee, see Eden, *Observations*, 5.

[97] See the comments of W. Courtenay on seeking leave for the bill: *PD* 1824 (s2) 10: 213.

[98] Eden, *Practical Treatise*, 37. The provision was 6 Geo. IV c. 16, s 6.

[99] It enacted that remaining abroad, with the intention of delaying one's creditors, was an act of bankruptcy, as was any fraudulent transfer of property not by deed.

[100] Eden, *Practical Treatise*, 31. 6 Geo. IV c. 16, s 4.

[101] Eden, *Observations*, 13.

bankruptcy, unless a commission of bankruptcy had issued within six months of its being made. Notice of the composition deed had to be Gazetted within two months of its execution. Following the example of Scots law, the Act allowed for the bankruptcy to be terminated by a composition contract. This was premised on the notion that 'the bankrupt can commonly make more from the wreck of his estate than any one else can'.[102] Under this proceeding, an offer of a composition could be made after the last examination of the bankrupt, and the agreement would then be voted on at a second meeting of creditors. If nine out of ten creditors in number and value consented, the commission of bankruptcy would be superseded.

As if to confirm that bankruptcy was not to be equated with crime, the statute also allowed the bankrupt to be given maintenance from his estate during the period of his examination.[103] However, it did not address the problem of how to deal with the immoral debtor, which had long been a subject of concern.[104] Following the recommendations of the select committee, John Smith's bill in 1818 required the commissioners to investigate the previous conduct of the bankrupt in contracting his debts. However, objections were soon raised to the imposition of new duties on the commissioners, and it was felt that 'judicializing' the issuing of the certificate could not be contemplated until there had been reform of the bankruptcy commissions.[105] Absent such reform, the 1825 Act therefore merely amended the law relating to certificates. The failure to reform the jurisdiction also prevented any attempts to change the *ex parte* nature of the proceedings. While Robert Eden felt that this procedure was unjust to the debtor, he thought that no form of preliminary inquiry—as on the Scottish model—could work as long as commissioners in bankruptcy continued.[106]

It was evident, after the passing of the 1825 Act, that 'a complete alteration [...] in the *Tribunal* by which Bankrupt Law is *primarily* administered' was still needed.[107] The issue had not been addressed in the reforms of that year, since the problem of the jurisdiction was closely connected with the wider problem of whether to remove bankruptcy from the Chancellor's jurisdiction.[108] The

---

[102] Eden, *Practical Treatise*, 443. 6 Geo. IV c. 16, ss 133–134.

[103] Section 114. Under the old law, an allowance (on statutory percentages) was only granted after the examination, and depended on the dividend produced: see *Thompson v. Councell* (1786) 1 T.R. 157.

[104] See the comments of Lockhart in *PD* 1818 (s1) 37: 88.

[105] For the abandonment of these ideas in 1819, see *PD* 1819 (s1) 39: 1388, 40: 252.

[106] Eden, *Observations*, 20–1.

[107] Eden, *Practical Treatise*, lx.

[108] See e.g. M .A. Taylor's speeches of 30 March 1819: *PD* 1818 (s1) 39: 1261, 1821 (s2) 5: 1025. See also M. Lobban, 'Preparing for Fusion: Reforming the Nineteenth Century Court of Chancery, Part I' (2004) 22 *Law and Hist. Rev.* 389–427 at 404–9.

Chancery Commission which investigated the issue felt that the Lord Chancellor should retain the final jurisdiction in bankruptcy.[109] Their proposed remedy for the heavy bankruptcy workload imposed on the Chancellor was to create an intermediate court of appeal between the commissioners and the Chancery, made up of ten commissioners from the London lists.[110] However, this proposal was not acted on, and reform had to wait until 1831, when Brougham LC created a new structure of bankruptcy courts to replace the London (but not the country) commissioners.[111]

There had long been proposals to reduce the number of commissioners to between six and eight. Commissioners such as Montagu and Glyn wanted a system where single commissioners would deal with cases, subject to an appeal to a board of commissioners, from whom an appeal would lie to the Chancellor.[112] Brougham, however, had his own ideas. In place of the 14 London lists, he created ten commissioners, four of whom were also to be judges on a new Court of Review, which would take over most of the workload which had hitherto gone to the Chancery. Montagu was horrified when he heard of the proposal for the Court of Review, describing the measure as 'an eighteen pounder to kill a fly',[113] premised on the incorrect assumption that there was a great deal of pressure of business in bankruptcy which required the attention of four judges. Despite much opposition, Brougham pressed ahead with this plan, claiming that it was the legal profession which insisted on the need for so many judges.[114] Brougham also thought that the Court of Review would be faced with issues to be tried according to defined rules of evidence, and determined by a jury, in the manner of a common law court. In practice, there were no issues to try, and little work for the court.[115] As the four judges initially appointed either died or found promotion elsewhere, they were therefore not replaced.[116] In 1842, the work of the Court of

[109] Chancery Commission Report, 35.

[110] Chancery Commission Report, Propositions, 166–73.

[111] Brougham consulted bankruptcy experts, was advised by a committee of London bankers and merchants. See B. Montagu, *Letters to Sir Edward Sugden on the Court of Commissioners and Court of Review* (1834), 7–9. See also Montagu's evidence to the 1840 Royal Commission on Bankruptcy and Insolvency, *PP* 1840 [274], xvi, 1 (henceforth cited as 1840 Bankruptcy Commission), 77. See also Lester, *Victorian Insolvency*, 53–9.

[112] Montagu, Chancery Commission, Evidence, 395. Glyn, Chancery Commission, Evidence, 437–40. For another proposal to reduce the number of commissioners, see C. S. Cullen, *Reform of the Bankrupt Court* (2nd edn, 1830), 47 et seq.

[113] Montagu, *Letters to Sugden*, 20.

[114] *PD* 1831 (s3) 3: 389 et seq, defeating a motion by Lord Wynford.

[115] See Montagu, *Letters to Sugden*, 24 and *The New Bankrupt Court Act* (1831), xii. See also his evidence to the 1840 Bankruptcy Commission, 78.

[116] The Act 5 & 6 Will. 4 c. 29, s 21 enacted (after Sir Albert Pell's death) that there should only be two judges in the court besides the chief justice. The first Chief Judge, Erskine, was appointed to

Review was delegated to one of the newly created Vice Chancellors. Five years later, the court was formally abolished, its jurisdiction formally transferred back to the Chancery to be exercised by a Vice Chancellor.[117] The six remaining bankruptcy commissioners found themselves frustrated in their expectation that rank and promotion would follow their appointments.[118]

Under the reform of 1831, bankruptcy proceedings commenced with the issuing of a *fiat* by the Chancellor, which was granted as of course after the petitioning creditor had made an affidavit of his debt. However, it remained an *ex parte* proceeding. Brougham had initially contemplated reform here, but changed his mind when fears were raised that since proceedings were based on a rule *nisi*, the insolvent trader might in the interim tamper with his creditors or dispose of his property.[119] It was felt that *ex parte* proceedings should be retained, both because of the need for dispatch in securing both the person and the property, and because it was argued that the proceedings were only in the nature of indictments rather than final judgments.[120] In this area, Brougham felt it better to act cautiously.

The Act also transformed the management of the bankrupt's estate, for it created a system of official assignees, attached to the court, who replaced the creditors' assignees. Such a proposal had long been in the air.[121] While a number of lawyers (including Sir Edward Sugden) continued to argue that assignees should be under the control of the creditors and not the court,[122] official assignees seemed to others to promise greater efficiency. Though he was highly critical of much of Brougham's bankruptcy measure, Montagu praised the official assignees, having been initially sceptical.[123] While there was much political criticism over the fact that the Chancellor would have the patronage to appoint official assignees, who

the Common Pleas in 1839. The other original judges were Sir George Rose, who became a master in Chancery in 1840, and Sir John Cross, who died in 1842.

[117] 5 & 6 Vict. c. 122, s 64; 10 & 11 Vict. c. 102, ss 1–2. Knight Bruce VC had already (since 1842) been doing the work, as Chief Judge of the Court of Review. See his evidence to the 1849 Select Committee on the Bankrupt Law Consolidation Bill (henceforth cited as 1849 Bankruptcy Committee), PP 1849 (551), viii, 159, at pp. 70 *et seq.*

[118] See especially the grumbles of C. Fane, as in his *A Letter Addressed to His Majesty's Attorney General* (1837) and *Copy of a Letter Addressed to the Lord High Chancellor of England* (1861).

[119] *PD* 1831 (s3) 2: 930; *ibid.*, 7: 509.

[120] See the evidence of Montagu to the 1840 Bankruptcy Commission, 75–6.

[121] See e.g. B. Montagu, *Enquiries Respecting the Administration of Bankrupts' Estates*, 14n., Lamb, *Enquiry*, 110–15.

[122] See *PD* 1831 (s3) 8: 32–4.

[123] Montagu, *Letters*, 12–13. For his earlier sceptical view, see Montagu, *The New Bankrupt Court Act*, xix.

would themselves reap high rewards from the office,[124] Brougham in fact delegated the power of drawing up a short list to a committee of merchants.[125]

3. THE LAW OF INSOLVENCY, 1810–1838

In 1820, civil imprisonment remained a key element in debt recovery.[126] Parties could be arrested both at the beginning of the legal process, and at its end.[127] Those whose debts exceeded £15 could be arrested on mesne process,[128] in theory to secure their attendance in court. They were released on giving bail, which was usually double the amount of the debt claimed.[129] Arrest and imprisonment was also available on final process, in order to induce payment. This remedy was available to those who had received judgments for damages or debts, since they were unable to get at all the defendant's property. Though a plaintiff could obtain execution of judgment against the goods and chattels of the debtor, by a *fieri facias*, this did not reach intangible property such as bank notes, bills, or annuities.[130] Nor could he obtain satisfaction from the defendant's landed property easily, since the writ of *elegit* only enabled him to obtain the profits of half of the debtor's lands until his debt was satisfied. Imprisoning the debtor under a *capias ad satisfaciendum* did not give the plaintiff his money, since it was considered a satisfaction of the debt. Debtors with assets which had not been reached by their creditors were therefore able to remain in debtors' prisons, living on their remaining fortune.[131]

By the early nineteenth century, the system of imprisoning for debt, which was premised on the assumption that solvent debtors had to be coerced into

---

[124] Freshfield was unhappy that such assignees would be paid 5% of sums recovered: *PD* 1831 (s3) 8: 659. See also Sugden's comments *ibid.*, col. 34, and Wetherell's at *ibid.*, 665–6.

[125] See Lyndhurst's comments in *PD* 1833 (s3) 19: 315 and Brougham's reply at cols 363–4 and see his comments to the 1849 Bankruptcy Committee, 65. Brougham claimed subsequent Lord Chancellors had exercised the jurisdiction themselves.

[126] Imprisonment for debt derived from medieval legislation, dating from 1283 and 1352 which authorized creditors to arrest and imprison their debtors pending the settling of their accounts. See R. Pugh, *Imprisonment in Medieval England* (Cambridge, 1979), 46 and M. C. Finn, *The Character of Credit: Personal Debt in English Culture, 1740–1914* (Cambridge, 2003), 109–10.

[127] The procedural aspects are discussed in XI, Pt 3, Ch. III.

[128] 12 Geo. I c. 29 of 1725 enacted that there could be no arrest where the debt was under £10. This was extended to inferior courts in 1779 by 19 Geo. III c. 70. 51 Geo. III c. 124 (1811) increased the sum to £15.

[129] W. Tidd, *The Practice of the Courts of King's Bench and Common Pleas in Personal Actions*, 2 vols (1817), i, 22. This was despite the rule in 12 Geo. I c. 29 that the bail should be taken only for the sum named.

[130] See Tidd, *Practice*, 1039 *et seq.*

[131] Imprisonment for debt was also a key feature of debt recovery for the small debtor in the Courts of Requests. See Finn, *Character of Credit*, 207–8.

paying, had come in for increasing criticism. 'Whilst we are tender of the creditor's *property*', James Neild wrote, 'we ought equally to be tender of the debtor's *liberty*'.[132] Charitable institutions such as the Thatched House Society (dating from 1772) were set up to secure the discharge of debtors.[133] In the late eighteenth century, periodic legislation was also passed to liberate insolvent debtors from gaol.[134] But this approach treated the profligate and fraudulent in the same way that it treated the innocent. Since these statutes freed the debtor from future liability, there was concern that fraudulent debtors could remain in (often comfortable) debtors' prisons awaiting their amnesty, or that they would arrange to be arrested when an insolvent debtors' act was in the offing, to profit from it.[135] In this context, there was increasing agreement on the need for a permanent system which would avoid the dangers to commercial credit caused by these periodic amnesties,[136] and which would distinguish the fraudulent from the honest debtor. It came to be accepted that the unfortunate debtor who could not pay his way should not be kept imprisoned, but that imprisonment was appropriate for the fraudulent.

This principle lay behind the Insolvent Debtor's Court, which was created in 1813 on Lord Redesdale's initiative, and reformed in 1820. Under the original statute, any person imprisoned by process of court could petition this court after three months' confinement,[137] on surrendering his possessions (save clothing and tools up to £20 in value) and giving details of his creditors and assets. The creditors would be notified of his petition and schedule of effects. If there was no evidence of fraudulent conduct when he was examined, the debtor would be discharged from gaol, and his property would be put in the hands of assignees for his creditors. He was not discharged from liability for his debts, however, and his future property remained liable. Not all debtors could make use of its provisions: uncertificated bankrupts; those who wantonly wasted their effects while in gaol; those who obtained credit by false pretences or by fraudulent means; those who were charged in execution for damages obtained in certain torts; or those who

---

[132] J. Neild, *An Account of the Rise, Progress, and Present State of the Society for the Discharge and Relief of Persons Imprisoned for Small Debts throughout England and Wales* (1802), 11. Nor was the criticism only an eighteenth-century matter: in *The Second Part of the Institutes of the Laws of England* (1642), 394, Sir Edward Coke had argued that there should be execution against the goods prior to any execution against the body.

[133] See Finn, *Character of Credit*, 161–3, who shows that from 1772 to 1831 it secured the release of over 50,000 debtors.

[134] Acts were passed in 1764, 1766, 1768, 1772, 1774, 1776, 1778 and 1781.

[135] See Althorp's comments in *PD* 1819 (s1) 40: 587.

[136] See Eldon's comments *PD* 1806 (s1) 7: 141.

[137] Further legislation reduced the time which the debtor had to spend in prison before applying for his release to 14 days after arrest (in 1820), and then to none (in 1826). 1 Geo. IV c. 119; 7 Geo. IV c. 57.

ran up gambling debts were not permitted the benefit of the legislation unless their creditors consented to their discharge.[138] Moreover, the costs of an application were such as to prevent the poor debtor from applying to the court.

The system was designed to prevent a debtor obtaining a discharge who had been guilty of fraud, or who failed to give up money which he had. In 1816, the commissioner Charles Runnington agreed that the Act should be extended, with the court being given power to inquire into 'the conduct of the insolvent, for some time previous to his going into actual custody, as to the management or mis-management of his property'.[139] The Act was amended to empower the commissioner to refuse a discharge where the debtor had entered 'into any Engagements, without any fair Prospect or probable Means of paying such Debts'.[140] This was to acknowledge that imprisonment for debt should constitute a punishment for extravagance as well as fraudulent concealment. Where the question was whether the debtor had a reasonable expectation of being able to pay, the court looked at his situation in life, at the nature of the goods, and the regularity of the debtor's income. This promised to give the Insolvent Debtors Court a far greater power to police the moral conduct of the insolvent than the bankruptcy commissioners had. Where large traders, able to use bankruptcy procedures, might escape without a thorough investigation of their conduct or censure for it,[141] the small trader or private individual who had been imprisoned for debt was to be subjected to an examination into his conduct.

In practice, however, the system was not effective at rooting out fraud. So draconian was the penalty for contracting debts rashly—continued incarceration for five years—that Runnington was loathe to apply it.[142] Moreover, although the court could examine the debtor and refuse a discharge without any creditors opposing,[143] the active opposition of creditors was generally needed to prevent

---

[138] Further legislation in the 1820s modified the structure and practice of the court. See 3 Geo. IV c. 123 (1822) which allowed the court to specify that the detained debtor was to be kept within the walls of the prison, rather than within the liberties; and 5 Geo. IV c. 61 (1824) which empowered the insolvency commissioners to go on circuit, and enacted that petitioning the Insolvent Debtor's Court constituted an act of bankruptcy. See also 7 Geo. IV c. 57 (1826).

[139] Report from the Select Committee on the Insolvent Debtors Acts, PP 1816 (472), iv, 345, at p. 90.

[140] 56 Geo. III c. 102, s 1. When the legislation was renewed in 1820, the court was empowered to refuse a discharge for three years where the debtor was guilty of destroying his books or concealing his debts, and for two years where he had contracted debts fraudulently or without any reasonable expectation of paying them: 1 Geo. IV c. 119, ss 17–18.

[141] Cooke, *Treatise*, xii.

[142] Duffy, *Bankruptcy and Insolvency*, 90.

[143] For instance, if the debtor had given an undue preference to a creditor: Report from the Select Committee on the Insolvent Debtors Acts, PP 1816 (472), iv, 345, at p. 90 (Sjt Runnington).

a discharge.[144] When the court was reconstituted in 1820, provision was made for the creditors to meet to examine the debtor's assets before his final examination, to enable them more effectively to oppose the discharge. However, the court remained very inefficient at rooting out fraud. In 1827, William Jones, marshal of the King's Bench, claimed that the 'facility with which people get out of gaol' made them anxious to get into it.[145] Many debtors arranged collusive arrests to be able to take the benefit of the Act. It served them well: under the regime set up in 1820, the 'innocent' debtor generally remained in gaol for approximately eight weeks before his release. Moreover, it generated paltry dividends. Joseph Hume pointed out in 1827, that since its formation, the court had freed 11,617 debtors, whose debts amounted to more than £8.8 million; but it had distributed only £4,788, or 8 shillings per debtor.[146] Nor was the court cheap, with the cost of a discharge ranging between £10 and £20.[147] By the late 1830s, it was widely agreed that compared with the new bankruptcy court, with its system of official assignees managing the bankrupt's affairs, the Insolvent Debtors Court lacked an adequate mechanism either to uncover fraud or collect property.[148]

The system created by Redesdale's Act of 1813 was premised on the existence of arrest for debt, regardless of fraud, since it was designed to secure release and not to prevent arrest. But by the 1820s,[149] reformers attacked this premise, regarding *any* imprisonment of the debtor as a punishment, which should only be imposed for a crime.[150] In 1829, Henry Dance, the provisional assignee of the Insolvent Debtors Court, complained that

at present we commence by imprisoning a debtor, and make the proof of his honesty the condition of his discharge, instead of making the proof of his fraud the condition of his imprisonment. It is not until after this has been done, that he should receive the sentence

---

[144] 'The Court at all times cheerfully lends its utmost assistance to the vigilant and active creditors; but it cannot be expected to act without their concurrence': E. Cooke, *A Treatise upon the Law and Practice of the Court for the Relief of Insolvent Debtors* (1827), xvi.

[145] W. Jones, *Observations on the Insolvent Debtors' Act; Miscalled 'an act for the relief of insolvent debtors'* (1827), 16.

[146] This gave a dividend, as Waithman had pointed out in 1817, of half of a quarter of a penny in the pound (0.05%): *PD* 1819 (s1) 39: 180. But where Waithman used this argument as a reason for abolishing the insolvent debtors jurisdiction, Hume used it to argue against imprisonment for debt.

[147] These figures are from Jones, *Observations*, 8. Cooke, *Treatise*, xiiin.

[148] 1840 Bankruptcy Commission, Report, viii, xxi. In his dissenting report, however, W. Law argued that the court was indeed efficient at rooting out fraud. For other commentators who accused the court as being unable to root out fraud see Hume in *PD* 1729 (s2) 20: 371 and Peel in *ibid.*, 433 (19 February 1829).

[149] As early as 1823, the Solicitor General had argued in support of Insolvent Debtor legislation that imprisonment should be used only for crimes (such as fraud) and not for debt: *PD* 1823 (s2) 8: 612.

[150] *PD* 1827 (s2) 17: 234.

of the Court, which should then be really carried into effect, and not remain subject to the caprice or the collusion of a creditor, who may enforce or abandon it without control.[151]

Reformers wanted to separate out the criminal and civil processes. Where a debt was owed, instead of seeking a remedy from the body of the debtor, it was argued that the law should target the defendant's property, with attachment of property prior to judgment (as happened by the custom of the City of London), and with judgments executed against all forms of property hitherto exempted.[152] Where conduct was fraudulent, the miscreant should be incarcerated as a result of the judgment of a court, and not at the whim of a creditor.

Reformers sought firstly to end arrest on mesne process, and replace it with a power to attach the debtor's property. The law was criticized for allowing a purported creditor to have someone groundlessly arrested at very little cost,[153] leaving the alleged debtor to have to find bail. This lent itself to extortion.[154] A bill brought by Joseph Hume in 1827 to abolish such arrests failed in the face of those who argued that such arrests were useful, since they provided a test of a debtor's solvency (since a solvent debtor could always find bail), and since they induced debtors to settle their debts promptly.[155] Although Hume's initiative was defeated, Sir Nicholas Tindal did pilot legislation to prevent arrest on mesne process for any debt under £20.[156] In the government's view, arrest on mesne process was only suitable for larger debtors, and the Attorney General admitted he would be happy to have no arrest on mesne process for any debt under £100. In 1832, the Common Law Commissioners called for an ending of arrest on mesne process, and by 1837, a general consensus had been reached that arrest on mesne process should be abolished. Legislation passed in 1838 brought an end to it, save where the debtor was about to abscond.

There was less success in achieving the second aim of abolishing arrest on final process. Critics (such as the members of the Common Law Commission, who reported in 1832) argued that it generated a false sense of security: imprisoning the body did not satisfy the debt, and it allowed the debtor to defraud his creditors by remaining in gaol. It also had the potential to ruin the insolvent: while Redesdale's Act prevented a creditor detaining an innocent debtor indefinitely,

---

[151] H. Dance, *Remarks on the Practical Effect of Imprisonment for Debt and on the Law of Insolvency* (1829), 3, 12.

[152] *PD* 1828 (s2) 18: 125. See also Brougham's view in *PD* 1828 (s2) 18: 192–4, 234.

[153] According to Hume, 4s 10d would pay the cost of an affidavit; while bail was £3 10s for a £10 debt: *PD* 1827 (s2) 17: 225.

[154] See Fourth Report of the Common Law Commissioners (henceforth cited as Common Law Commission, Fourth Report), *PP* 1831–2 (239), xxv, 1, at p. 19.

[155] *PD* 1827 (s2) 17: 231. It was also objected that much of a debtor's property (such as his landed property) was not liable to attachment: *PD* 1827 (s2) 17: 384.

[156] *PD* 1827 (s2) 17: 981, leading to 7 & 8 Geo. IV c. 71.

by being gaoled for three months, his credit and character were ruined.[157] The system also seemed to give a preference to the first creditor who sued, since any debtor who wished to distribute his money equally to his creditors had to wait at least two months before doing this in the Insolvent Debtors Court, where any creditor could oppose him. In the view of the Common Law Commissioners, all debtors should, on surrendering their property, have the benefit of the cession, unless they could be shown to have been fraudulent. They also wanted more effective provisions for the punishment of fraudulent debtors, and criticized the Insolvent Debtors Court, where 'the detaining creditor has at any time the power of causing the prisoner's liberation, even after an adjudication by the Court that he has been guilty of fraud, and remanded to prison, in pursuance of a judgment of the Court'.[158] It recommended a better defined set of offences, and also proposed reforms to facilitate criminal prosecution. Thus, a blueprint was set out which would demarcate criminal fraud from debt recovery, and accomplish the end of imprisonment for debt.

A series of bills followed in the 1830s which provoked widespread debate.[159] In 1834, Sir John Campbell AG brought a bill to allow a *cessio bonorum* for both traders and non-traders, without the debtor being previously gaoled; and to give creditors the power to compel the debtor to yield up all property.[160] The bankruptcy system would be opened to all, and the Insolvent Debtors Court would be closed. Campbell's bill aimed to relieve the innocent—whose future property would not be liable for the debts—while punishing the fraudulent. Under his proposals, those refusing to pay were to be treated as criminals. Those who incurred debts under false pretences or without a reasonable expectation of being able to pay them, and those who failed to disclose their property would be liable to punishment by the court for misdemeanour.[161] This attempt at legislation—and ones brought in the following years—failed in the face of determined opposition from commercial interests, from those worried by the impact of the criminal provisions, and from those who feared the damage to landed families, if judgment could be obtained against their property.[162]

---

[157] In an oft-quoted phrase, they wrote, 'His habits of honest industry are interrupted, his connections in business, profession or trade broken off, his family left destitute; he is compelled to associate in idleness with the dissolute and depraved': Common Law Commission, Fourth Report, 37.

[158] Common Law Commission, Fourth Report, 43.

[159] A detailed discussion can be found in B. Kercher, 'The Transformation of Imprisonment for Debt in England, 1828 to 1838,' (1984) 2 *Australian Journal of Law and Society*, 60–109 at 79ff.

[160] This would be to extend the provisions of the Lords' Act beyond the £300 limit and prevent wealthy debtors remaining within the rules: PD 1834 (s3) 24: 414–15.

[161] *PD* 1834 (s3) 24: 412.

[162] In 1838, legislation (1 & 2 Vict. c. 110, s 11) was passed to allow all the land of a debtor to be taken under a writ of *elegit*.

Reformers in the early 1830s wanted an efficient system of procedure in reformed courts, which would permit the ending of imprisonment for debt as part of debt recovery, while retaining criminal sanctions for fraud. This was to apply to small debtors as well as large ones. Sir Robert Peel's local courts bills in 1827 and 1828 accordingly proposed execution only against property, not against the person.[163] In Peel's view, efficient small debt courts would replace the need for imprisonment.[164] However, in the 1830s, under pressure from mercantile interests, political opinion turned back in favour of the principle established by small debts Acts which allowed execution on the body, on the assumption that the non-paying small debtor was guilty of fraud.[165] When Lord John Russell's local courts measure was referred to a select committee in 1839, it therefore endorsed the established principle that small debtors needed to be coerced to pay by execution on final judgment.[166]

The tide also turned against abolishing imprisonment for debt on final process in the superior courts, save in cases of fraud. Provisions for its abolition were dropped from the measure in 1838 which ended arrest on mesne process. In Lord Cottenham's view, imprisonment after judgment, at the behest of the creditor, had to be retained for three reasons. First, the debtor would always have some property which he would attempt to hide or dispose of, and the only way ultimately to pressure him into paying was by gaol. Secondly, imprisonment for debt could not be removed because of 'the necessity of giving effect to the jurisdiction of courts for the recovery of small debts';[167] for it was inevitably the case that people sued in these courts would have no property to be subject to execution. Thirdly, he felt it would be impossible to root out fraud without imprisonment for debt. This reason betrayed a sentiment, commonly repeated in the mid-nineteenth century, that the criminal law relating to fraud was too weak. Instead of abolishing the Insolvent Debtors Court and legislating for more cases of misdemeanour, the 1838 Act reformed the court, allowing creditors to set its procedures in motion, to prevent debtors remaining in gaol and defying their creditors.

---

[163] Peel still favoured this policy two years later, when Brougham brought his own bill to reform local courts: *PD* 1830 (s2) 24: 281–2.

[164] Arrest on mesne process was not available for small debts. Eighteenth-century legislation to prevent frivolous and vexatious arrests enacted that parties could only be arrested for debts over £10; and legislation in 1827 extended this to £20. See 12 Geo. I c. 29; 19 Geo. III c. 70; 43 Geo. III c. 46; 7 & 8 Geo. IV c. 71.

[165] See Finn, *Character of Credit*, 206–7. At 217–19 she shows failed attempts in 1780 to replace execution on the body with execution on goods.

[166] See the principle adopted in the County Courts bills of 1839: *PP* 1839 (387), ii, 465, 497. The bill was reintroduced in 1841, when Campbell AG opposed the provisions allowing imprisonment on execution: see *PD* 1841 (s3) 57: 177.

[167] *PD* 1838 (n.s.) 43: 657.

4. REFORMING BANKRUPTCY AND INSOLVENCY, 1838–1849

The debates over the reform of 1838 focused attention on the need for a wider examination of the law of insolvency and its relationship with bankruptcy, and in the following year, a royal commission was appointed to look at both bankruptcy and insolvency. It was recognized that although in theory, bankruptcy was a system for traders whose failure was due to commercial cycles they could not control, whereas insolvency law was for improvident non-traders living beyond their means, such distinctions broke down in practice. Almost two-thirds of the 3,691 who petitioned the Insolvent Debtors' Court in 1839 were small traders unable to get into bankruptcy. At the same time, it was noted that reform of arrest for debt had an impact on the working of bankruptcy. Since an arrest on mesne process followed by three weeks in gaol constituted an act of bankruptcy, its abolition removed the easiest involuntary test of insolvency. The 1838 bill sought to provide an alternative compulsory act of bankruptcy, which was committed if a debtor failed to pay a debt or provide a bond to pay any sum recovered in an action against him, after being served by an affidavit by his creditors.[168] However, this was a less effective device, given that fear of arrest on mesne process had often provoked other (voluntary) acts of bankruptcy—such as departing from one's house.[169] In addition, the failure in 1838 to effect a wider institutional reform which would abolish the Insolvent Debtors Court and reformulate the Court of Bankruptcy made it more pressing to address the problem of the country bankruptcy commissioners.[170]

The Royal Commission of 1840 sought to address these problems by proposing reforms to unite bankruptcy and insolvency; to allow the debtor to make a *cessio bonorum*; and to give judges the jurisdiction to punish fraud. In the commissioners' view, 'the just and only effectual mode of checking frauds is, by giving a simple, speedy, and cheap mode of recovering debts; by holding out relief and benefit to the honest but unfortunate debtor; and by subjecting the dishonest and fraudulent to searching inquiry, and certain punishment'. They proposed that the insolvent debtor should be able to make a voluntary cession of property. This would solve the problem of individual creditors using common law to obtain a preference over other creditors, which only served to encourage debtors to make unjust defences and to buy time during which they settled with other creditors. To reach those who attempted to avoid an early voluntary distribution

---

[168] 1 & 2 Vict. c. 110, s 8.
[169] 1840 Bankruptcy Commission, xiv–xvi.
[170] See PD 1838 (s3) 43: 1250.

of property, they proposed that creditors be able to come to court and demand payment. If the debtor did not swear that he had a just answer to the demand (in which case the case would be remitted to the ordinary legal process) or failed to pay or give security for payment, this was to be taken as an act of insolvency, to be followed by an equitable distribution of his assets.[171] There should also be a searching inquiry into the debtor's conduct, with a view to punishing fraud. Criminal sanctions would be imposed on debtors who obtained credit by false pretences, or who concealed their property or books.[172] In the commissioners' view, all imprisonment for debt should be ended: where a person was imprisoned, it should be as a punishment for dishonesty.

The commissioners accepted that only traders should obtain relief from future liability. However, they felt that the law regarding who counted as a 'trader' needed to be clarified, so that it would reach all those who were engaged in trade, or business requiring capital and credit. They also suggested procedural reforms which would close the loopholes which still permitted friendly creditors to initiate proceedings in a way which might create sufficient delay to prejudice rivals. They favoured changes which would allow the bankrupt to challenge the *ex parte* proceedings before his bankruptcy had been advertised to the world. They were also critical of the fact that creditors retained the power over the bankrupt's certificate, arguing that the decision to grant or withhold it should be a judicial one. The proposed reforms would distinguish commercial misfortune from dishonesty, and give the power of discriminating between them to the court.

By the 1840s, it was generally agreed that the innocent debtor should be left at liberty, while only the fraudulent should be punished. However, reformers disagreed over how this was to be achieved. Lord Cottenham felt that all issues of criminality should be left to the criminal courts, with imprisonment for debt forming no part of insolvency law. He therefore attempted to pass bills in 1842 and 1844 to implement the commissioners' proposals, and to abolish all imprisonment for debt.[173] They did not pass, however, for they were opposed by Lords Lyndhurst and Brougham, who felt that imprisonment on final process needed to be retained. They piloted rival bills which aimed to prevent innocent debtors being gaoled in the first place but to keep the guilty in gaol.[174] Though they had ambitious plans to unite the bankruptcy and insolvency systems,[175] the legislation

---

[171] 1840 Bankruptcy Commission, ix–xii.

[172] *Ibid.*, xx.

[173] The bill was introduced on 21 February 1842 (*PD* 1842 (s3) 60: 530), and sought to unite bankruptcy and insolvency, and abolish imprisonment on execution of judgment.

[174] See *PD* 1842 (s3) 65: 225 *et seq.*

[175] Lyndhurst had asked Sjt Manning to investigate the law of bankruptcy of other countries with a view to reforming the English law. Manning produced a report in May, which proposed uniting the

they passed (in 1842 and 1844) was piecemeal, and dealt separately with insolvency and bankruptcy.

Legislation in 1842 created a system of country commissioners recommended by the 1840 report, and gave creditors power to summon their debtors to court to acknowledge the debt.[176] In order to root out fraud more effectively, control of the bankrupt's certificate was taken away from the creditors and given to the commissioners. In coming to their decision, they were to 'judge of any objection against allowing such a certificate' and to consider the bankrupt's conduct as a trader before as well as after his bankruptcy.[177] The statute made it a misdemeanour to obtain goods on credit with intent to defraud the owner of them, within three months of the bankruptcy. However, no direct power was given to the court to punish the bankrupt. Instead, imprisonment on execution of judgment continued, as a by-product of a decision to withhold the certificate. In the view of Lyndhurst and Brougham, the law had to be self-executing, to prevent debtors escaping.[178] In adopting this approach, they accepted the views of Bankruptcy Commissioner Cecil Fane, who argued that if the decision to imprison were left to a criminal process, the debtor could simply challenge his adversaries to prove misconduct. Since he could not be forced to incriminate himself, no one would ever be convicted.[179] In fact, while the ultimate power of punishment remained with the creditors, it was a weak power; for no creditor who had proved his debt before the court could subsequently seek his debtor's arrest.[180]

courts of bankruptcy and insolvency, and making provision for six different classes of debtor, which formed the basis of a bill drawn up by him. See *Statement submitted to the Bankruptcy Committee of the Society for Promoting the Amendment of the Law by Mr Sjt Manning* (London 1860; reprinted from the *Law Amendment Journal*, 17th session No. 17). Manning's proposal sought (following the continental model) to distinguish the treatment accorded to the unfortunate, the improvident, the culpable, and the fraudulent debtor. See also Brougham's comments in *PD* 1844 (s3) 74: 459. A bill based on Manning's principles was introduced in May, but dropped: see Cottenham's comments in *PD* [1844] (s3) 76: 1394.

[176] *PD* 1842 (s3) 65: 225, *ibid.*,1086 (5 August 1842). 5 & 6 Vict. c. 122, ss 11–14 duly enacted that a creditor making an affidavit of debt could summon the debtor into court; and that a debtor who made no appearance or failed to claim that he had a defence would thereby commit an act of bankruptcy.

[177] 5 & 6 Vict. c. 122, s 39. The court could suspend the certificate or impose conditions. Legislation in 1844 gave the commissioners greater discretionary power to look into the bankrupt's conduct. Brougham explained that in place of the provisions of 1842, which merely refused a discharge where the bankrupt had been guilty of one of five offences, this bill sought to give the court power to limit the imprisonment according to the circumstances of the case: *PD* 1844 (s3) 75: 1175.

[178] *PD* 1844 (s3) 75: 1175–8. Cottenham felt Brougham's proposals were potentially draconian: *PD* 1844 (s3) 76: 1397.

[179] Fane, *Bankruptcy Reform*, ix. Fane also supported arrest on mesne process as a test of insolvency.

[180] See W. J. Law, *Comments on the New Scheme of Insolvency, with some remarks on the change in the law of certificate of bankruptcy* (1843), 48.

Lyndhurst and Brougham also piloted an Insolvent Debtors Act in 1842, which empowered insolvent debtors to petition the Court of Bankruptcy prior to being arrested. Provided that the debt had not been contracted in a fraudulent way, or without 'reasonable assurance' of being able to be paid, the insolvent would be given protection from arrest.[181] In 1844, a Debtor's Arrangement Act passed, which allowed non-traders to enter into amicable trust deeds to settle their debts. Under this Act, a debtor who had obtained the consent of one-third of his creditors could apply to the Bankruptcy Court to sanction the appointment of trustees to collect and distribute his assets. To encourage the use of such deeds, the insolvent was given a certificate which had the same operation as one obtained in bankruptcy, and all the proceedings were to be carried out in private.[182] Since these Acts encouraged poorer debtors—and the 'inferior practitioners' who advised them—to use the Bankruptcy Court, commercial groups protested that it had the effect of deterring 'the higher classes of practitioners and creditors' from using the court.[183] In 1847, jurisdiction over the petitions against imprisonment was transferred to the Insolvent Debtors Court.[184]

This was not the only area in which Brougham's tinkering legislation irritated commercial groups. Although he had wished to retain imprisonment on final process for those guilty of misconduct, Brougham was so moved by the poor conditions in small debtors' prisons which he learned about before a select committee, that in 1844 he introduced a measure which abolished imprisonment on final process in all actions for less than £20.[185] This measure undercut the principle of Sir James Graham's county courts bill, then in progress, which included imprisonment on execution, as a 'self-executing' way to punish fraud in small debt cases.[186] It also outraged commercial groups,[187] and a committee of London

[181] 5 & 6 Vict. c. 166, s 4. The petitioner sought redress from the Court of Bankruptcy since the Insolvent Debtor's Court's jurisdiction was premised on an existing imprisonment.

[182] 7 & 8 Vict. c. 70. See also P. Polden, *A History of the County Court, 1846–1971* (Cambridge, 1999), 31–4.

[183] 1854 Royal Commission to inquire into the fees, funds and establishments of courts of bankruptcy, *PP* 1854 [1770], xxiii, 1 (henceforth cited as 1854 Bankruptcy Commission), App. B, pp. 221–2. He attributed the decline in the court's business to this cause. The 1844 Debtors Arrangement Act was not much used.

[184] *PD* 1847 (s3) 91: 256. 10 & 11 Vict. c. 102 transferred the insolvency business handled by the Court to Bankruptcy to the Insolvent Debtors Court and to the county courts.

[185] 7 & 8 Vict. c. 96, s 57. After the passing of this Act, the courts wondered whether the order granted by the court only protected the person, so that a creditor could still bring a suit for debt, but in the end it was decided that the creditor could take no action: see *Toomer* v. *Gingell* (1846) 3 C.B. 322; *Jacobs* v. *Hyde* (1848) 2 Exch. 508; *Markin* v. *Aldrich* (1862) 11 C.B. N.S. 599.

[186] See (1844) 3 *LT* 9, 144. It may be noted that members of the government were still clearly uncertain about maintaining imprisonment for debt for small debtors. See the views expressed by Thesiger Sol.-Gen. and Graham in *PD* 1844 (s3) 76: 1706 and *ibid.*, 80: 1019 (29 May 1845).

[187] (1845) 4 *LT* 406.

merchants met to call for its abolition. An amending Act was rapidly passed in 1845, which allowed execution debtors owing up to £20 to be gaoled for a period of up to 40 days on the grounds of fraud, which was broadly defined.[188] The principle was reiterated in the following year in the County Courts Act, which imprisoned in a common gaol those who were fraudulent and contracted debts without the means to pay them.[189] The principle was significant, for the debtor was to be gaoled not for debt, but for fraud, on the judgment of a judge, and not on arrest by a creditor.

5. BANKRUPTCY LAW, 1849–1861

Reform of the system of bankruptcy returned to the parliamentary agenda in 1848 when Brougham introduced another bill, which was referred to a parliamentary select committee, which was attended daily by both bankruptcy commissioners and members of the London committee of merchants. The deliberations of the committee revealed that after a decade of debate, disagreements persisted on the most fundamental matters. Although much legal opinion favoured uniting the bankruptcy and insolvency codes, the insistence by commercial interests that the extensive machinery of the Bankruptcy Court was inappropriate for collecting the small debts of non-traders[190] led to the confirmation that the bankruptcy system was to be used only by larger traders. Under the Bankruptcy Consolidation Act 1849, the law remained one for larger traders. Petitioning creditors had to be owed in excess of £50 by persons falling within one of the categories of trader defined by the Act. As in 1825, the insolvent trader could himself petition for an adjudication of bankruptcy against himself, but only if he could pay a dividend of at least five shillings in the pound.[191]

Legal and commercial interests also disagreed over how to reform the law of bankruptcy. Lawyers stressed the need for more stringent punishment of fraudulent and improvident traders, calling for more graduated punishments and greater supervision by judicial officers.[192] By contrast, commercial opinion favoured giving greater facilities to creditors to make their own arrangements

---

[188] 8 & 9 Vict. c. 127.

[189] 9 & 10 Vict. c. 95, ss 98–99.

[190] See J. Nicholls and E. Doyle, *Practice in Insolvency in the Courts of Bankruptcy*, (2nd edn, 1845), xx–xxi.

[191] This was amended in 1854, to allow only those who could pay £150 to petition for themselves. 17 & 18 Vict. c. 119, s 20.

[192] The *Law Times* thus noted that current punishments 'are not proportioned to the different degrees of offence, and they are not of a kind to deter by the terror of example' (1847) 8 *LT* 456. In particular, it was felt that the fraudulent contracting of debts should be made a criminal offence.

with minimal curial supervision. Commercial groups argued that bankruptcy commissioners lacked the necessary business knowledge to judge whether or not a certificate should be granted.[193] They felt that the Bankruptcy Court was essentially an administrative court, rather than a criminal one, and that 'what is the best advantage to the Creditors in each particular case can be better decided by the Creditors than by Commissioners'.[194] Since their own credit might be damaged if it became known that they had lent to insolvent traders, they looked for better mechanisms to secure private arrangements, rather than a public punishment of fraud. The principal obstacle they faced under the regime established in 1825 was the threat from dissenting creditors to treat the deed of assignment as an act of bankruptcy. To counter this, commercial interests called for provisions to allow the majority of an insolvent's creditors to be able to bind the minority. Against this, bankruptcy officials feared that leaving everything to a majority of creditors might permit impositions on dissenting creditors, and might open the way to fraud.

In the end, the 1849 Act provided two methods for coming to arrangements. First, the Act provided for arrangements to be entered into under the supervision of the court. It allowed a debtor to apply to the court for protection while he sought to negotiate an arrangement with his creditors.[195] If three-fifths of the creditors proving their debts at a first meeting agreed, a second meeting would be called, at which the arrangement could be confirmed by three-fifths of the creditors and (if it was felt to be reasonable) by the court. Much thus remained in the hands of the court, which was jealous to guard against abuse by the petitioner. Not only did the arrangement require the court's assent, but the estate of the petitioner vested in the official assignee.[196] Secondly, it provided for deeds of arrangement not under the control of the court. Any deed entered into by six-sevenths of an insolvent's creditors in value and number would bind the minority; though dissenting creditors were given three months in which to challenge the arrangement.[197] The Act also allowed for compositions to be entered

---

[193] (1848) 37 *Legal Observer* 162. Freshfield said that while creditors could oppose the grant of a certificate, most were reluctant to 'take the prominent and obnoxious part of being opposers'.

[194] Paper from the Incorporated Law Society, quoted in (1849) 38 *LO* 46–7.

[195] Bankruptcy Act 1849, 12 & 13 Vict. c. 106, s 211. This section also allowed a petitioner to be discharged from prison. The petition itself constituted an act of bankruptcy, if the petition for an arrangement was dismissed within two months.

[196] Such arrangements were rarely used: judicial statistics beginning in 1858 give 240 for 1858, 31, 56 and 49 for the subsequent three years.

[197] Bankruptcy Act, s 224. Brougham wanted to have 9/10ths to be the proportion, feeling generally suspicious of such arrangements: see 1849 Bankruptcy Committee, 70. By 1852, it was ruled that such deeds could not be used to impose a composition agreement on the minority, but could only be used to distribute all the insolvent's assets: *Tetley* v. *Taylor* (1853) 1 E. & B. 521.

into after bankruptcy. Unlike those entered into under the 1825 Act, these bound all creditors, provided that nine-tenths agreed.[198]

If commercial groups sought to increase their power to deal with insolvency outside the court, legal reformers were keen to increase the punitive powers of the court. When the matter was considered by Brougham's select committee, it was agreed that the bankruptcy commissioners should be given a direct power to imprison for fraud or misconduct.[199] The bill which was initially presented to Parliament included a very broad discretionary clause, which gave the power to punish any bankrupt who 'wilfully committed or suffered any act which, [...] shall appear to the Court to have been committed or suffered by the bankrupt in violation of good faith, or with intent to defraud or injure some one or more of his creditors'. The clause was controversial, since (as the *Legal Observer* noted), there was 'a very substantial distinction between refusing to discharge a person already in custody under the operation of a well-understood law, and sentencing a party to imprisonment for a lengthened period who has never before, perhaps, seen the inside of a gaol'.[200] Many were worried by the thought that a trader might be gaoled by a jury-less tribunal. Brougham himself was more concerned that debtors might be made to incriminate themselves. To overcome this, it was decided to leave it to the creditor to cause the bankrupt to be gaoled (for a period of 12 months) where his certificate was refused or suspended.[201] To effect this, creditors who had proved their debts were to be deemed judgment creditors, entitled to issue and enforce execution against the body of the unprotected bankrupt.[202] In addition to the general discretion given to the court to refuse or suspend a certificate, the Act defined a number of 'offences' which required the court to withhold a certificate or protection from arrest.[203] The offences identified had initially been included as punishable crimes.[204] While the decision to cause imprisonment for

---

[198] Bankruptcy Act, s 230. Unlike the 1825 Act, the 1849 Act made composition deeds binding on non-assenting creditors, provided 9/10ths agreed. See *Tuck* v. *Tooke* (1829) 9 B. & C. 437.

[199] (1848) 37 *LO* 81, 161.

[200] (1849) 37 *LO* 446.

[201] 1849 Bankruptcy Committee, 67–8. Bankruptcy Consolidation Act 1849, ss 257–259.

[202] Under the earlier regime, a creditor who had proved his debt was prevented from prosecuting his debtor, having made use of the bankruptcy provisions: see the comments of the court in the case of Samuel Halfhide: *The Times*, 17 March 1849, col. 8a, drawing attention to 6 Geo. IV, c. 16, s 59. The provision was re-enacted in 12 & 13 Vict. c. 106, s 182, but where the certificate was denied, was qualified by s 257.

[203] The court had the power to deprive the bankrupt of protection from arrest for a shorter period than that during which his certificate (and hence his absolution from liability for his debts) was suspended. See e.g. *Ex p Manico* (1853) 3 De G. M. & G. 502.

[204] Section 256 of the Bankruptcy Act 1849 enumerated nine offences for which the certificate would be withheld and protection from arrest removed: these included keeping false books, contracting debts fraudulently, and giving undue preferences. Sections 251–254 enumerated offences

these 'offences' remained in the hands of the creditors, the legislation empowered the court to direct a criminal prosecution for the existing offences against the law of bankruptcy (defined in earlier legislation) without needing the assent of any creditors.[205]

While the power to cause the unprotected bankrupt debtor to be imprisoned was left to the creditors, bankruptcy judges were given a power to pronounce on the commercial morality of the trader, for the Act introduced a new three-fold classification of certificates to distinguish degrees of blameworthiness in the trader's conduct prior to bankruptcy.[206] This provision was introduced at the suggestion of the merchant John Howell, who felt that imprisonment was not working, and that this kind of branding would better inform the trading community of the conduct of the bankrupt.[207] Many lawyers were unsure of the desirability 'of importing into the administration of the Bankrupt Laws the distinctions of railway travelling',[208] particularly since the classifications had no legal effect.

In 1850, Commissioner Goulburn described the job of the bankruptcy judge:

it was no part of the duty of the Court [of Bankruptcy] to punish the bankrupt for having been engaged in a foul conspiracy to defraud the credulous, even if he were guilty. Other courts possessed abundant powers for that purpose. His duty was to determine upon the conduct of the bankrupt as a trader.[209]

In doing this, he was to consider (as the authors of one text stated) whether the bankrupt trader was 'an unfortunate but honest man entitled to the consideration and sympathies of his fellow citizens' or 'a cheat and vagabond wholly unworthy of the confidence hitherto reposed in him'.[210] If a trader had engaged in reckless trading and desperate speculation, or obtained money by false pretences, his certificate would be withheld.[211] If his assets had been inadequate to meet his liabilities for three years, he had to provide an explanation before he obtained a

(such as refusing to deliver his books or embezzling his estate) which carried terms of imprisonment, and s 255 empowered the court to direct a prosecution. Section 201 repeated the provisions of 6 Geo. IV c. 16, s 130, according to which certificates were denied to those who lost money by gaming or stock jobbing, or who destroyed their books.

[205] Under 5 & 6 Vict. c. 122, s 36, the assent of three creditors of £50 or more was needed.

[206] Bankruptcy Act, s 199. The form of the certificate was given in Sch. Z.

[207] See Howell's evidence in the Select Committee on the Working of the Bankruptcy Act (1861), PP 1864 (512), v, 1 (cited henceforth as 1864 Bankruptcy Committee).

[208] (1849) LO 38, 298.

[209] The case of William Thomas Ferris, The Times, 8 January 1850, col. 7c. Since he had acted most fraudulently, his certificate was denied.

[210] A. A. Doria and D.C. Macrae, The Law and Practice in Bankruptcy, 2 vols (1861–3), ii, 676.

[211] For the meaning of these rules, see e.g. Ex p Wakefield (1850) 4 De G. & S. 18 and Ex p and Re Staner (1852) 2 De G. M. & G. 263.

certificate.[212] Similarly, an explanation would be required if the court felt that his conduct had been 'unfair, untradesmanlike and disreputable'.[213] Only if the trader had acted in a *bona fide* way would he obtain a first-class certificate.

In practice, this system proved problematic. First, bankrupt traders were permitted to appeal to the Vice Chancellor against the decisions of the commissioners. In the 1850s, 'an unfortunate difference' developed between the appellate and bankruptcy judges, with the former 'almost invariably reducing the quantum of punishment' imposed by the latter.[214] In 1855, for instance, Commissioner Ayrton had ordered that the flax spinner Samuel Hammond should be given a third-class certificate, which was to be suspended for two years. Hammond had started business in 1852 with capital of £10,000, but had given £60,000 worth of accommodation bills in two years, using some of the money to speculate in purchasing paintings. In Ayrton's view, although he was not guilty under the penal clauses, his 'style of living, considering his means, has been in the highest degree extravagant, and so reckless as to be divided from absolute fraud by a very thin partition'. On appeal, however, the penalty was reduced, with Knight Bruce VC finding Hammond merely guilty of 'a certain degree of imprudence'.[215] This was taken up in the press as indicative of 'the morals of bankruptcy', and led also to a campaign to take a tougher line against those who failed to pay their debts.[216] At the same time, a feeling persisted that the system of appeals benefited bankrupts who had wealthy friends.[217] Secondly, the system of awarding different classes of certificate caused difficulties, since the commissioners did not have the same view of commercial morality.[218] Even those who supported the system admitted that merchants needed to be familiar with the particular commissioner's approach to make sense of the decision.[219] Even Cecil Fane, who supported the system, began

---

[212] *In re Dornford* (1851) 4 De G. and Sm. 29.

[213] *In re Curties* (1852) 2 De G. M. and G. 255 at 256.

[214] *The Authorised Report of the Mercantile Law Conference 1857* (1857), 17 (Commissioner Ayrton). For the judges' approach, see e.g. the remarks of Turner LJ in *Ex p Brown* (1858) 3 De G. & J. 369 at 373. In *Ex p Manico* (1853) 3 De G. M. & G. 502, the court suspended a third-class certificate for two years and gave protection after six months: but the commercial community felt this was a case of reckless trade: see J. P. Gassiot's evidence to the 1854 Bankruptcy Commission, p. 142. *Ex p and Re Hodgson* (1853) 3 De G. M. & G. 547.

[215] (1855) 24 *LT* 213. See also *Ex p Hammond* (1855) 6 D. M. & G. 699 at 729. Knight Bruce reduced the period of suspension to one year whereupon a second-class certificate would be given.

[216] (1855) 24 *LT* 170, 230.

[217] See J. P. Gassiot's evidence to the 1854 Bankruptcy Commission, at 142.

[218] 1854 Bankruptcy Commission, App. C: of the 310 cases Fane heard annually in the early 1850s, 23% were given first-class certificates, 26% were given second-class certificates, 34% were given third-class, and 17% were given suspensions. Of the 372 cases before Fonblanque, 5% were given first class, 37% second, 25% third, and 32% were suspended, while the respective proportions for Evans' 334 cases were 5%, 60%, 4%, and 31%.

[219] 1854 Bankruptcy Commission, 127.

to suspect that it had the effect of deterring insolvents from coming to the court, fearing the investigation of their past conduct and the stigma which a third-class certificate entailed.[220]

When the matter was discussed by another royal commission in 1854, doubts were raised once more about a system which imprisoned debtors for general commercial misbehaviour. The report stated that the provisions which obliged the court to withhold or suspend a certificate (under section 256) were too severe and noted that commercial delinquencies should be dealt with under the general discretionary power of the court (in section 198) subject to appeal.[221] The report also criticized section 257 of the Act which made the creditor a judgment debtor, able to take the body of the bankrupt at pleasure: 'for the punishment inflicted will seldom operate by way of example, as it may be procured at the suit of a private person for private purposes'.[222] They wanted any criminal offence to be clearly defined and left to criminal courts.[223] They recommended that punishment should be by a distinct tribunal: 'defined legal offences should be punished only after trial by jury before regularly constituted Courts of penal judicature'.[224] However, further reform in this area had to await the following decade.

Mid-century reformers also turned their minds to the law relating to fraudulent disposals of property prior to bankruptcy. In 1849, Lord Brougham was concerned that the law generated uncertainty, since a preference had to be both voluntary and made in contemplation of bankruptcy to count as fraudulent.[225] He sought to cut the Gordian knot by deeming as fraudulent any payments, not made in the ordinary course of business, to a creditor within two months of bankruptcy, regardless of whether they were voluntary or in contemplation of bankruptcy. He also wanted to reform the rules regarding bills of sale, which (he argued) were a prime means by which frauds in bankruptcy were committed.[226] He proposed that it should be an act of bankruptcy to give any bill of sale, while retaining possession of the goods. These proposals were

---

[220] *Ibid.*, 192.

[221] *Ibid.*, xviii. The commissioners wanted to enumerate only offences which had the effect of defeating the law of bankruptcy, rather than aiming at wider commercial abuses.

[222] *Ibid.*, xix.

[223] By contrast, some witnesses felt that the current regime, which allowed the creditor to cause the debtor to be gaoled without a criminal prosecution acted as a kind of 'safety valve' which satisfied the creditor's ire without sending the bankrupt to the more severe criminal trial. *Ibid.*, 136 (evidence of F. J. Reed).

[224] *Ibid.*, xx.

[225] Therefore, 'a man may be insolvent, but yet not contemplate bankruptcy', *Morgan* v. *Brundrett* (1833) 5 B. & Ad. 289 at 297.

[226] 1849 Bankruptcy Committee, 65–6 (Brougham).

regarded with alarm in both the legal and commercial communities. The Wolverhampton Law Society declared that the measure would affect all credit and undermine the commercial enterprise on which the country depended.[227] Knight Bruce VC, who felt the current law was not ineffective, argued that the only effect of the proposed articles would be 'to cut down honest transactions, for no good purpose of which I am aware'.[228] In the face of such opposition, Brougham dropped both his proposals regarding fraudulent preferences and bills of sale.[229]

Bills of sale continued to cause concern. In 1854, the *Law Times* wrote, '[o]f all securities experience tells us that none have ever proved so frail as bills of sale'.[230] Such instruments were very useful for raising money on the security of tools or stock-in-trade retained by the trader. Given their usefulness, they were widely used by those who needed an injection of cash to sustain businesses in tough times. But those who raised money in this way faced three problems: the bill of sale given might be held void for being a fraudulent preference; giving it might itself be regarded as an act of bankruptcy; and, where possession of the goods remained with the person giving the bill, the property would pass to the assignees in event of his bankruptcy. Great care had to be taken in drafting such securities, though practitioners often failed to do this since they were 'generally prepared on an emergency'. To avoid the risk that the bill would be seen as a fraudulent preference, lenders were advised to specify in their deed that the borrower was permitted to retain possession until he defaulted in payment, since 'possession consistently with the terms of the mortgage-deed will rebut the presumption of fraud'.[231] In addition, drafters of bills had to take care how they described the goods which were charged. This was important where traders borrowed on the security not merely of their present property, but on the security of property to be acquired in future. It was clearly settled law that one could not simply assign future acquired property by deed.[232] However, a donor could 'give a donee such a power over his after-acquired property as will justify the latter in converting it to

---

[227] (1849) 38 *LO* 22.

[228] 1849 Bankruptcy Committee, 72, 75.

[229] To overcome objections, Brougham in committee proposed that if a trader registered his bill of sale, then it would not be an act of bankruptcy: but it was felt that even this might undermine the credit of traders registering (being seen as an admission of insolvency) and so might affect trade: 1849 Bankruptcy Committee, 66–7.

[230] (1854) 24 *LT* 215.

[231] (1854) 24 *LT* 96; *Martindale* v. *Booth* (1832) 3 B. & Ad. 498.

[232] According to *Lunn* v. *Thornton* (1845) 1 C.B. 379, for the holder to obtain the security of later-acquired goods, the grantor had to perform some act which ratified the grant after he obtained the goods.

the purpose of his bill of sale'.[233] To allow this, the bill had to show that it charged goods which were substituted for those originally assigned.[234]

Care also had to be taken in setting out what property was liable for the debt, to avoid the giving of the bill of sale being seen as an act of bankruptcy. It had long been held that the assignment by such a bill of all the trader's property, to satisfy a pre-existing debt, was an act of bankruptcy.[235] By contrast, it was not considered to be an act of bankruptcy for a trader to sell all his goods for a valuable consideration, or for a future advance.[236] However, in 1852, in *Graham* v. *Chapman*, the Common Pleas held that it was an act of bankruptcy for a trader to give a bill of sale, giving the right to seize future-acquired as well as current property, to a lender in consideration both of a past debt and a present advance. In the view of Jervis CJ, since the bill assigned future-acquired property, 'the trader [...] gets no equivalent for any part of the stock transferred; and such a transfer necessarily defeats and delays his creditors'. The courts would consider this to be an act of bankruptcy even where the loan had been made *bona fide*, with the intention of allowing a trader to carry on in business.[237] In the light of this decision, practitioners were advised not to prepare bills of sale assigning the whole of a trader's stock and effects or even so much as might deprive him of the power to trade ordinarily 'as a security for a pre-existing or unsecured debt': 'if a client should require a security for a debt and the debtor has nothing but personal goods and chattels to offer, the safer plan will be to take an assignment of a part of his goods' only.[238] Many judges were unhappy with the decision in *Graham* v. *Chapman*, preferring the court to ask whether the transaction was *bona fide*, and in 1883, the Court of Appeal held that granting a bill of sale which allowed the seizure of all future property was not an act of bankruptcy.[239]

Legislators continued to be suspicious that bills of sale would be drawn up secretly, to allow traders to continue on false and preferred credit. Revisiting the issue of bills of sale, the royal commission on bankruptcy in 1854 reported

---

[233] 24 *LT* (1854) 170.

[234] *Chidell* v. *Galsworthy* (1859) 6 C.B. N.S. 471; *Carr* v. *Allatt* (1858) 27 LJ Exch. 385; *Congreve* v. *Evetts* (1854) 10 Exch. 298.

[235] *Siebert* v. *Spooner* (1836) 1 M. & W. 714 at 717; *Lindon* v. *Sharp* (1843) 6 M. & G. 895; 7 Scott. N.R. 730. Where a trader wished to assign all his property as security for a past debt owed to the lender, the latter was advised to obtain 'an absolute bill of sale, with delivery and retention of possession': (1854) 24 *LT* 159. The writer felt (at p. 114) that provided no prior act of bankruptcy had been committed, the lender would be protected by s 133 of the 1849 Act.

[236] *Baxter* v. *Pritchard* (1834) 1 Ad. & El. 456.

[237] *Graham* v. *Chapman* (1852) 12 C.B. 85 at 104. Contrast *Hutton* v. *Cruttwell* (1852) 1 E. & B. 15, where such a deed was not held an act of bankruptcy.

[238] (1854) 24 *LT* 171.

[239] *Ex p Hauxwell* (1883) 23 Ch D 626; Gregory and Walton, 'Fixed and Floating Charges', 132–3.

that their harmful effect could be checked by 'providing for the registration of such instruments, within a certain period after their execution, and at least two months before the bankruptcy, and by giving to registered instruments complete protection against acts of bankruptcy subsequent to their registration'.[240] A bill was by then already before Parliament, brought on the initiative of a trade protection society, to prevent traders obtaining credit by giving secret bills of sale of chattels. The Act which followed enacted that such bills of sale had to be registered within 21 days of being made in order to be valid as against assignees in bankruptcy or insolvency.[241] Further legislation in 1882 outlawed bills of sale which were not in a statutory form.[242]

Although the 1854 Act added a further requirement for those drafting bills to bear in mind, it did not confer any new protection on bills which complied with the requirement. As Crompton J. put it, '[a]ll that the Act does is to take away the validity of bills of sale unless its provisions are complied with; it does not give them extra validity'.[243] Those who allowed goods to remain in the borrower's possession continued to run the risk that their goods would be regarded as within the reputed ownership of the borrower.[244] Under section 125 of the 1849 Act (which repeated earlier provisions), the assignees obtained the right to goods in the reputed ownership of the trader at the time he became bankrupt. Since this referred to the moment of the act of bankruptcy, rather than from the time that bankruptcy proceeding commenced,[245] any lender who took the goods when aware that an act of bankruptcy had occurred was liable to lose them.[246] To be safe, the lender had to recover his goods before he knew that an act of bankruptcy had been committed.

---

[240] 1854 Bankruptcy Commission, xxxvi.

[241] *PD* 1854 (s3) 133: 474; 17 & 18 Vict. c. 36: which also made unregistered bills void against those claiming under any assignment for the benefit of creditors, or against seizure by legal process.

[242] The Bills of Sale Act (1878) Amendment Act did not allow bills of sale to be taken for future property, save in certain circumstances, including where it was necessary for the maintenance of the security.

[243] *Badger* v. *Shaw* (1860) 2 El. & El. 472 at 482. See also *Stansfeld* v. *Cubitt* (1858) 2 De G. & Jo. 222; *Ex p Harding, In re Fairbrother* (1873) LR 15 Eq 223.

[244] It remained a question of fact for a jury to consider whether the goods had been within the reputed ownership of the insolvent trader, allowing him to obtain false credit. Where it was 'notorious' that the goods did not belong to the party retaining possession, or where it was known to be the custom of the trade for manufacturers to use machinery which they did not own, the doctrine would not apply: *Muller* v. *Moss* (1813) 1 M. & S. 335; *Horn* v. *Baker* (1808) 9 East 215.

[245] *Fawcett* v. *Fearne* (1844) 6 Q.B. 20.

[246] *Ex p Heslop* (1852) 1 De G. M. & G. 477; *Ex p Lucas* (1858) 3 De G. & J. 113.

6. REFORMING BANKRUPTCY AND INSOLVENCY, 1861–1883

The bankruptcy regime created in 1849 was one characterized by a high degree of official administration, via official assignees, by the attempt to make bankruptcy and insolvency courts regulate commercial morality, and by a reluctance to allow private arrangements beyond the control of the courts. In the 1860s, thanks to pressure from commercial interests, channelled through Chambers of Commerce and the Social Science Association, this policy was reversed by two pieces of legislation which recast the law, in 1861 and 1869.

In 1861, the Insolvent Debtors Court was abolished, and the jurisdiction over bankruptcy and insolvency was united in the Court of Bankruptcy. By now, there was a general consensus in favour of putting the law relating to traders and non-traders on the same footing. It was argued that in the age of shareholder capitalism, it was increasingly difficult to draw a line between commercial and non-commercial people.[247] There was also increasing concern in the 1850s that traders managed to be 'whitewashed' in the insolvency courts by means of friendly arrests. By this time, the vast majority of petitions to the insolvency court came from traders.[248] Although the commissioners had the power to look into the insolvent's conduct, refusing relief to those contracting debts without a reasonable expectation of payment,[249] unless the case was a very plain one, they would not refuse relief unless it was opposed by a creditor. If a trader obtained a collusive arrest in a distant place, it could therefore be easy for him to be released.[250]

The Court of Bankruptcy was now made available to everyone. The legislation distinguished between those acts which made a trader liable to bankruptcy from those which made a non-trader liable. This preserved something of the old distinctions, and avoided the risk that gentlemen would be caught by provisions aimed at testing a trader's solvency and dragged before the bankruptcy courts.[251] The rule which limited the amount which a bankrupt had to be able to pay before he could petition was duly removed. The effect of these changes was to open a flood of people petitioning the court for relief. Between 1858 and 1861, an average

[247] Thus, a shareholder in a joint stock company with unlimited liability would be liable to insolvency, while an investor in a partnership would be treated as a bankrupt trader: (1861) 36 LT 502.

[248] According to (1860) 35 LT 123, in 1858, of 1024 protection petitions presented in London's Insolvency Court, 816 came from traders.

[249] D. C. Macrae, The Law and Practice of the Court for Relief of Insolvent Debtors (1857), 357–8.

[250] See the discussion in The Authorised Report of the Mercantile Law Conference 1857, p. 32.

[251] See (1860) 36 LT 78.

of 389 bankrupt traders had petitioned the court annually (compared with 780 petitions by their creditors), while an average of 3041 debtors had petitioned the Insolvent Debtors Court. From the passing of the 1861 Act to its replacement in 1869, 8082 debtors petitioned the court annually, compared with 766 petitions from creditors.

Reformers also addressed the question of punishment. The 1861 Act reversed the policy of 1849, by leaving it to businessmen to judge of the commercial morality of traders, and giving the courts a power of punishment. The Act abolished the classification system, which Sir Richard Bethell regarded as 'of little more use than if the certificates were written on so many pieces of white, or red, or pink paper'.[252] The bankruptcy commissioners were given a criminal jurisdiction, though the bankrupt was to be allowed a jury trial in a criminal court if he chose.[253] Section 221 listed the misdemeanours for which a debtor could be imprisoned for up to three years; and section 159 enumerated six kinds of conduct which were not misdemeanours, but for which a certificate could be withheld or imprisonment (up to one year) imposed. They included some which came from insolvency law, including contracting debts without any reasonable expectation of being able to pay them, and 'rash and hazardous speculation'.

In practice, these punitive provisions proved largely ineffective. Section 221 was little used, since the bankrupt had to consent to be tried in this court for misdemeanour, which he almost never did. In any case, to be convicted under the clause, the court had to be satisfied of a criminal intent, which was hard to establish.[254] Judges also read their powers under section 159 narrowly, feeling that their discretionary power to look at issues of general misconduct had been removed.[255] In the view of one of the most experienced practitioners, the Act resulted in a 'lamentable failure in the judicial power of suppressing fraud', since 'two-thirds of the usual and ordinary fraudulent and dishonest modes of contracting debts are omitted'.[256] Many felt that debtors had been given an easy time of it under the new regime.[257]

Reformers also considered the wider question of imprisonment for debt on final process. In piloting the 1861 legislation, Sir Richard Bethell hoped that imprisonment for debt could be abolished with the union of jurisdictions. In

---

[252] (1861) 36 *LT* 582; *PD* 1861 (s3) 161: 294.

[253] *PD* 1861 (s3) 161: 296.

[254] See the evidence of S. S. Lloyds to the 1864 Bankruptcy Committee at pp. 162–3.

[255] *Ex p Dell* (1862) 5 LT 725; *Re Curtis* (1862) 5 LT 724; *Ex p Udall, re Mew & Thorne* (1862) 6 LT 732.

[256] (1862) 37 *LT* 199.

[257] Holroyd told the 1864 Bankruptcy Committee (p. 65) that 'nothing but a discretionary power can overtake frauds and delinquencies of every description'. See also the view of C. E. Lewis at p. 20.

the face of loud voices from the mercantile community insisting on retaining imprisonment,[258] the Act did not end imprisonment for debt, but Bethell did put in place a mechanism to ensure that the gaols would be emptied. Under the new legislation, paupers were to be able to petition for their release. In addition, monthly returns were to be made of people gaoled for debt, who would then be examined by a registrar from the Bankruptcy Court. No debtor would remain in gaol beyond two to three weeks unless he had been guilty of fraud; 'but whether he will or no, will be discharged, and his property, if he has any, taken from him and made available for the benefit of his creditors at large'.[259] Significantly, however, Bethell exempted those imprisoned by county courts for their debts, since he noted their incarceration was a criminal punishment for a kind of fraud. With the prisons being systematically cleared of those gaoled for large debts, the system of putting them there in the first place began to be questioned. As Edward Lawrance told a select committee of the Commons in 1864, sending 'a man to prison for the mere form of petitioning *in forma pauperis* is an absurdity'.[260]

When the matter was considered in a select committee in 1864, the tide of commercial opinion was also turning against imprisonment for debt. George Moffat, chairman of the committee, noted that over two-thirds of debtors who came to court had no assets available for creditors, and were simply freed from their liabilities at public cost. 'The proper remedy for this abuse', he opined, 'would seem to be the abolition of imprisonment for debt, a penalty which has already lost its terrors'.[261] In the view of commercial men, the procedure of imprisonment followed by release continued to allow traders to be 'whitewashed'. Instead of improving commercial morality, it cost them money. The 1864 committee preferred a system under which, if a bankrupt paid 6s 8d in the pound, he should be freed from all future claims. By contrast, if any wilful act was committed to delay or injure his creditors, the debtor should be prosecuted for it in the criminal courts. Imprisonment for debt on final process was finally abolished for the larger debtor in 1869. Since it was argued that working-class credit depended on the sanction of imprisonment, the Debtors Act permitted the imprisonment for up to six weeks of any person who defaulted in payment of money due by court order.[262] Larger debtors would only be gaoled in criminal cases, for offences which

[258] See the evidence of S. S. Lloyd to the 1864 Bankruptcy Committee, at p.165. While it was true that the Mercantile Law Conference of 1857 had stated that no debtor should be imprisoned who had not been examined by a court which had come to a judgment on it, this reflected their fears of traders being whitewashed: *The Authorised Report of the Mercantile Law Conference 1857*, 64.

[259] *PD* 1861 (s3) 161: 304.

[260] 1864 Bankruptcy Committee, at p. 43. See also the evidence of E. Holroyd at *ibid.*, pp. 64, 69. Holroyd also felt imprisonment for debt was objectionable on principle: p. 78.

[261] *Ibid.*, xi–xii.   [262] See p. 837.

were to be indicted and prosecuted at the quarter sessions, and which carried a penalty of two years' imprisonment.[263]

In a system designed to maximize returns rather than to minimize immorality, debtors were no longer to be permitted to petition for their own bankruptcy. If the debtor paid 10s in the pound, he would be entitled to a discharge. If he paid less, then a majority of his creditors could recommend a discharge if they were satisfied his failure arose from circumstances beyond his control.[264] The abolition of imprisonment also had profound effects on the structure of the court. Since the refusal of a discharge was no longer linked to imprisonment, it was no longer necessary to have bankruptcy commissioners exerting a judicial control and in effect policing commercial morality. The Act thus transferred the country bankruptcy jurisdiction to county courts, and created a new Court of Bankruptcy in London, with four registrars and a chief judge, who was also to be a superior court judge. At the same time, while judicial control was reduced, the legislation created a Comptroller in Bankruptcy to keep a register of every gazetted notice (open to the public) and to make annual reports to Parliament.

Reformers in the 1860s also revisited the question of voluntary arrangements. The 1861 Act aimed to give greater powers to allow arrangements to be made between debtors and creditors.[265] In practice, there were far more private arrangements than formal bankruptcies in the mid-nineteenth century, and commercial parties constantly repeated their preference for these forms.[266] Yet they remained problematic. As the 1854 commissioners pointed out, there was no mechanism for informing the minority of creditors that a deed had been entered into. Equally, deeds could be challenged within three months by any dissenting creditor; and arrangements which did not distribute all assets were not protected by the law.[267] In 1861, Bethell hoped that his amendments would address these problems and ensure that bankruptcy proceedings would be the exception, and deeds of arrangement the norm.[268] Borrowing from the Scottish model,[269] section 185 enacted that three-quarters of the creditors could resolve that the estate should be wound up under a deed of arrangement. If the court found the resolution had been duly carried and was reasonable, it would be confirmed, and

[263] Debtors Act, 32 & 33 Vict. c. 62, ss 11–20.
[264] See 32 & 33 Vict. c. 71, s 48.
[265] The word 'composition' was generally used in legislation to refer to settlements after a declaration of bankruptcy, under which not all the bankrupt's property needed to be distributed; while 'arrangements by deed' referred to agreements not under court control. But in the debates of the later 1850s, the word 'composition' was often used to indicate the latter.
[266] See Lester, *Victorian Insolvency*, 79.
[267] The 1854 commissioners proposed registering deeds: 1854 Bankruptcy Commission, xxi–xxii.
[268] *PD* 1861 (s3) 161: 304.
[269] 19 & 20 Vict. c. 79, ss 35–40 which allowed sequestration to be superseded by arrangement.

registered with the court. It would bind creditors who had not signed it, and it would not require a *cessio bonorum* of all the debtor's property.

The Act also sought to deal with the problem that, hitherto, the only way to enforce a deed of arrangement was by a suit in Chancery against the default-ing trustee. In place of this, section 188 enacted that parties could apply to the Bankruptcy Court, which would decide according to the law of bankruptcy. The effect of this provision was to encourage many more deeds of arrangements and compositions to be registered: the annual average between 1861 and 1869 was 4946. Nonetheless, there remained some disquiet over how the interests of the dissenting minority were sacrificed. There was a widespread feeling that, under the new regime, creditors were being compelled to accept less than the estate could pay, as a result of secret agreements between the debtor and favoured credi-tors, sometimes effected by way of fictitious credit.[270] With such fears in mind, the 1864 select committee thus recommended that no deed should bind the minority which did not distribute all the assets of the debtor, nor should such a deed dis-charge debts unless 6s 8d were paid in the pound.[271] Moreover, in 1868, legislation was passed to prevent debtors using the voices of sham creditors to secure deeds of arrangement in the face of opposition from substantial creditors.[272]

Further reforms followed in 1869 to facilitate voluntary arrangements. A new regime of liquidation by arrangement was introduced, described by one writer as being 'bankruptcy without a bankruptcy petition being presented, or an order of adjudication made'.[273] Under section 125, a debtor could summon a meeting of his creditors, a majority of whom (in person or by proxy) could vote that the affairs of the debtor were to be liquidated by arrangement.[274] A trustee was then to be appointed, in whom the property of the debtor would vest. Section 126 allowed the creditors, without any bankruptcy proceedings, to vote to accept a composition. In both cases, all resolutions had to be registered in the Court of Bankruptcy. A trustee in liquidation had the same powers and duties as a trustee in bankruptcy; but where the latter was under the control of the court with respect to his release and the auditing of his accounts, the former was wholly subject to the control of the creditors.[275] The creditors similarly had control over the discharge. Under this system, while an insolvent could not apply for his own formal bankruptcy,

---

[270] G. Y. Robson, *A Treatise on the Law of Bankruptcy*, (4th edn, 1881), 741.

[271] Select Committee on Working of Bankruptcy Act (1861), Report: *PP* 1865, xii, (144) 589, at p. 5.

[272] 31 & 32 Vict. c. 104. See Lester, *Victorian Insolvency*, 153–4.

[273] Robson, *Bankruptcy*, 742.

[274] However, no deed was required.

[275] Robson felt this was the main cause of the failure of these provisions: Robson, *Bankruptcy*, 742n. M. Parkyns observed that 'the procedure after the choice of trustees is the same [in liquidation] as in bankruptcy, except that by Part 9 the protection which (in case of need) the Court might have afforded to creditors is taken from them': Report to the Lord Chancellor of a committee appointed

he could initiate these voluntary arrangements, thereby avoiding such control as the court still had. Between 1870 and the next major reform in 1883, the number of annual bankruptcy petitions (now only available to creditors) thus fell back to 1040 per annum (slightly above the annual average of 771 creditors' petitions per annum brought between 1858 and 1869), while the number of compositions and arrangements rose to 7704 each year, compared with 4946 under the 1861 regime.

At the same time that the court was reformed, so increased powers were given to the creditors to control the distribution of the estate. By the 1860s, there was a widespread view in the mercantile community that the whole system of bankruptcy was inefficient and wasteful. The court was considered costly, and the system of using official assignees who were unfamiliar with the bankrupt's business was widely criticised. The 1854 Bankruptcy Commission reported that the expense of the court was 'disproportionate to the benefits derived', and that administering an estate in bankruptcy could be as costly as in Chancery.[276] From the late 1850s, Chambers of Commerce and the Social Science Association began to urge a return to a system of control by creditors' assignees. This proposal was resisted by the legal profession, which pointed out that the earlier system of creditors' assignees had manifestly failed, descending into a system of jobbery, delay, and expense.[277] Bethell's bill of 1861 aimed at a compromise: creditors were to be given the power to appoint assignees to receive money and administer the estate, though all debts under £10 would be collected by the official assignee.[278] The compromise did not convince the commercial community. As Sampson Lloyd told a select committee in 1864, since it was often hard to tell whether a debt was for more or less than £10, it was difficult to demarcate the role of the official and creditors' assignees. Since the latter was unpaid, it was hard to get commercial men to do the work; and given that the legislation imposed duties on them (such as making accounts), it often proved easier to use a costly solicitor.[279] Like many commercial men, he looked north of the border for his example of a bankruptcy system which ran without any official assignee to meddle. The select committee, having received (misleading) information about the cheapness and efficiency of the Scottish system, proposed abolishing official assignees, and leaving all in the hands of the creditors, who could appoint and supervise their own trustee. By now, the government supported the idea of a system of bankruptcy

to consider the working of the Bankruptcy Act 1869: *PP* 1877 (152), lxix, 41 (henceforth cited as 1877 Report to the Lord Chancellor), p. 15. See also the criticisms in Lester, *Victorian Insolvency*, 178.

[276] 1854 Bankruptcy Commission, xiv–xv.
[277] (1859) 34 *LT* 145.
[278] *PD* 1861 (s3) 161: 292. This was enacted in 24 & 25 Vict. c. 134, ss 116–117, 127–128.
[279] 1864 Bankruptcy Committee, 152 *et seq.*

administration which would be completely run by creditors,[280] and in 1869, the system of official assignees created by Brougham's 1831 measure was abolished.

7. THE LAW OF BANKRUPTCY, 1883–1914

There were soon worries that the new system was no more effective in ensuring a high return to creditors than the old. According to Mansfield Parkyns, the Comptroller in Bankruptcy, who was highly sceptical about the efficiency of the Scottish system and who delighted in pointing out the statistical errors of those who had endorsed it, the system was open to great manipulation by debtors. While those who paid 10s in the pound were none too worried about obtaining a formal discharge, being protected by section 54, those who did not were able to manipulate the system to obtain their discharge.[281] Whether in bankruptcy or by liquidation, creditors were allowed to act by proxies, which were bought and sold, and used by debtors and their friends to secure discharges. The end of official control led to abuse: Parkyns noted that liquidation trustees were often the debtor's agents, effectively doing the debtor's bidding. Moreover, being effectively unsupervised, these trustees could appropriate unclaimed dividends and make use of money for themselves. In his view, it was the parasites who profited, as creditors tended to write off losses, regarding any dividend as a profit.

Criticism of the system increased. In 1879, a committee of London merchants petitioned the prime minister, attacking the facility which private arrangements gave to the debtor to escape his liabilities. Having previously desired greater creditor control, they now looked once more to a court to control commercial morality. They claimed

that the present law is rendered nugatory by leaving to those who have already incurred losses the investigation of the bankrupt's affairs, and has laid upon them the obligation of exposing the misconduct of bankrupts, which in the plain interests of public morality and commercial policy should be dealt with not as a private matter, but by a public Court or Judge.[282]

There was outrage at the 'scandalous collusion' which allowed 'fraudulent bankrupts to evade their liabilities'.[283] As Parkyns later recalled, the system 'withdrew

---

[280] Lester, *Victorian Insolvency*, 150–2.

[281] General Report by the Comptroller in Bankruptcy for the year 1876: *PP* 1877 (314), lxix, 23.

[282] Quoted in *PD* 1883 (s3) 277: 837.

[283] Quoted in (1883) 74 *LT* 391.

from those engaged in private enterprise the chief safeguards of honesty and prudence, and virtually placed a premium on recklessness and fraud'.[284]

Reformers began to see the need for more supervision of the procedure. A committee appointed by the Lord Chancellor in 1874 proposed restricting the use of
proxies, and reforming the use of liquidations to ensure the bankrupt's conduct
was properly investigated. This committee set out a blueprint which was to be put
forward on a number of occasions in the late 1870s, before becoming the basis of
legislation in 1883. To prevent the problem of frauds allowed by the current system
of compositions and arrangements, all proceedings were to be commenced by an
application to the court—by either the debtor or the creditors—which would take
control of the assets until a decision was made by the creditors whether to accept
a composition or proceed to bankruptcy. However, if no positive decision was
taken, the case would proceed to bankruptcy.[285] In this process, the examination
of the bankrupt's conduct by the court was to be a crucial element.

The 1883 reform was piloted by Joseph Chamberlain, who stated that the system of 'voluntaryism' introduced in 1869 had 'led to absolute chaos and gave general dissatisfaction'.[286] Introducing the measure, he stressed the need for a system
of bankruptcy which would secure both the honest administration of bankrupt
estates and an improved tone of commercial morality. The 1869 regime failed to
achieve this since it left all the investigation (and in cases of crime, prosecution)
in the hands of creditors. In his view, bankruptcy was not merely a private concern between debtors and creditors. It was something of interest to the public, in
which there needed to be public representation. If it was not a crime to go bankrupt, it nonetheless needed explanation and inquiry. Since experience had shown
that creditors refused to act, a public official should investigate, as was done in
rail and sea accidents. At the heart of Chamberlain's project stood the new official receiver, who would investigate the conduct of the bankrupt and report to
the court when asked to consider the bankrupt's discharge. The official receiver
would both have a private preliminary interview with the bankrupt to establish
the causes of his failure, and he would conduct a public examination. The official
receiver would be responsible to the Board of Trade. But he was not to be akin to
the old official assignees. In Chamberlain's view, the state had no duty to 'save the
pockets of the creditors': all the state should do was to supervise the procedure
so that the minority of creditors would be protected and honest dealing would
be secured.[287]

---

[284] Fourth Report under s 131 of the Bankruptcy Act 1883 by the Board of Trade: *PP* 1887 [C. 5194],
lxxv, 1 (henceforth cited as 1887 Bankruptcy Report), p. 17.

[285] 1877 Report to the Lord Chancellor.

[286] *PD* 1883 (s3) 277: 825. See Lester, *Victorian Insolvency*, 190–3.

[287] *PD* 1883 (s3) 277: 827.

Under the new regime, both the debtor and the creditor could petition for bankruptcy. Although the 1881 bill had sought to enact that, in every case, the debtor would be declared bankrupt, by 1883 this had been modified, since it was considered to be too harsh to stigmatize every insolvent as a bankrupt prior to the investigation of his conduct.[288] Instead, proceedings would begin with a receiving order, which would stay all other proceedings, and which might or might not ripen into bankruptcy. After it was made, a meeting of creditors would be called to consider proposals for composition, which would only bind if they were agreed by a three-quarter majority at a second meeting. Meanwhile, the bankrupt would be subject to an examination, so that the official receiver would be able to report on his conduct at the second meeting. Moreover, unlike earlier liquidations, the composition had to be approved by the court, which could refuse its sanction if its terms were not reasonable or calculated to benefit the general body of creditors, or if any fact were proved about the debtor which would justify the court in withholding a discharge. Where a composition was agreed upon, the trustee was to be treated as if he were a trustee in bankruptcy, and would be subject to the same supervision by the Board of Trade as trustees in bankruptcy (s 18(12)). If no trustee was appointed, then the official receiver was to act in that capacity.

The Board of Trade could object to the appointment of trustees if they felt the person chosen would not be fit or impartial. Those who had themselves to render accounts to the estate or those who were trustees for other bankrupts with claims against the estate could be rejected as being likely to be partial.[289] Trustees were also to be supervised by the Board, which could summon a meeting of creditors if it was felt to be necessary to draw any matter of the trustee's conduct to their investigation. Trustees were to give annual accounts to the Board, and those guilty of misconduct could be removed. Under this legislation, there was far greater power to control the conduct of trustees than had been the case under the 1869 Act.[290] Moreover, the transfer of powers of control to a bureaucratic body rather than a court was designed to increase their efficiency.

Where the debtor was declared bankrupt—either by the decision of the creditors or on his own petition—the discharge was once more put into the hands of the court, rather than being left to the creditors. Having heard the report of the official receiver, the court could give or refuse an absolute order of discharge, or suspend it, or impose conditions (including those relating to after-acquired income). The regime of 1883 thus sought to import back into the law some of the

[288] This had also been the view of the 1877 Report to the Lord Chancellor.
[289] *Ex p Board of Trade, Re Martin* (1888) 21 QBD 29; *Ex p Board of Trade, Re Stovold* (1889) 37 WR 511; *Ex p Board of Trade, Re Lamb* [1894] 2 QB 805.
[290] See e.g. *Ex p Brown, re Maltby* (1880) 16 Ch D 497, holding that a receiver had no *locus standi* to complain of conduct of the trustee in the administration of assets.

considerations removed in 1869. The court was always to refuse a discharge where an offence had been committed against the bankruptcy laws, while it had a discretion in other areas, as where the bankrupt had failed to keep adequate books, had traded when knowing himself to be insolvent, had contracted a debt without having a reasonable expectation of being able to pay it, or had been engaged in hazardous speculations or unjustifiable extravagance (section 28). The legislation further sought to ensure that those who had committed criminal offences would be punished, for the court was given the powers of a stipendiary magistrate to commit to trial anyone suspected of such offences. The subsequent prosecution was to be conducted by the Director of Public Prosecutions.

Those administering the system soon proclaimed the effectiveness of the new controls. In 1887, the Inspector General in Bankruptcy, John Smith, declared that the 'full publicity and exposure of commercial irregularities' secured by the examination of the bankrupt 'and the certainty with which *criminal* fraud is followed up and punished on the other, have both had a powerful effect in repressing the grosser forms of misconduct, and in promoting a healthier tone of commercial morality'.[291] Nevertheless, Smith felt that the law was far from perfect. He felt that stricter provisions were needed to deal with trading misconduct such as failing to keep proper books, trading without capital when aware of one's insolvency, and reckless or fraudulent disposition of assets on the eve of bankruptcy. He also considered the penalties imposed by the courts—which often only involved short suspensions of the discharge—were not sufficiently effective at deterring frauds.

Smith was not the only one concerned. By the mid-1880s, it was apparent that the courts were not being as severe as some commercial groups wanted. Concern was raised that the county courts were too lenient in dealing with discharges. To combat this, in 1886, a new bankruptcy rule allowed the Board of Trade to appeal from an order of discharge where the official receiver had reported facts which would justify the refusal of an unconditional discharge.[292] Even the superior judges were not above suspicion. Though judges approved of their power to reject unreasonable compositions, there were complaints that compositions were only refused when creditors raised complaints.[293] Judges endorsed composition deeds which were felt to be for the benefit of the creditors, even if there had been

---

[291] 1887 Bankruptcy Report, 18.

[292] See *In re Stainton, Ex p Board of Trade* (1887) 19 QBD 182, where at 185 Cave J. spoke of the need 'to regard the interest of society and commercial morality'. The case was also discussed in 1887 Bankruptcy Report, 19.

[293] See Third Report by the Board of Trade under section 131 of the Bankruptcy Act 1883, *PP* 1886 (C. 4815), lx, 1 (henceforth cited as 1886 Bankruptcy Report), p. 19.

an offence committed by the debtor.[294] Insolvents seemed able to use deeds of composition offering small returns to avoid being investigated.

Commercial men once more urged that the law should be used more actively to control fraud. Sir Albert Rollit brought a number of bills in the late 1880s supported by the Associated Chambers of Commerce to strengthen the law. To begin with, he wanted tougher criminal provisions. He aimed to make it a misdemeanour to engage in hazardous speculation or unjustifiable extravagance, to give undue preference to a creditor within three months of insolvency, or to commit any fraud or fraudulent breach of trust. In addition, he sought to repeal section 85 of the Larceny Act, to ensure that the disclosure of offences of fraud or embezzlement during a bankruptcy examination would no longer be a bar to a prosecution. He also wanted to deal with an anomaly under the 1883 Act, under which those who petitioned for their own bankruptcy were not amenable to prosecution under the Debtors Act, thanks to clumsy wording borrowed from a regime when the bankrupt could not himself petition.[295]

The commercial community was also concerned about the ineffectiveness of the suspension of the discharge. The only sanction provided was that if an undischarged bankrupt incurred a debt of more than £20 without disclosing his bankruptcy to his creditor, he committed a misdemeanour. This was said to encourage hopeless trading, as bankrupts whose discharges were suspended for short periods found it easy to resume trade. Rollit aimed to reform the provisions regarding the discharge: it was proposed to have a minimum period of suspension of five years. If the debtor had been guilty of any felony or misdemeanour, no discharge would be allowed. Alongside the problem of fraud, the commercial community worried about the inability of the bankruptcy system to produce assets. Rollit pointed out that, in 1887, 80 per cent of bankruptcies produced less than 2/6s in the pound; 37 per cent produced nothing. He therefore proposed that there should be a minimum dividend of 10s in the pound before a discharge was given, and (in composition cases) a minimum payment of 7/6s.[296]

The proposals were certainly draconian: under them, no shareholder in a bankrupt unlimited liability company would have any prospect of a discharge. During the course of its passing, the bill which became the Bankruptcy Act 1890 was therefore watered down, with many of the criminal parts omitted. The new

[294] See the comments of the court in *In re Genese, Ex p Kearsley & Co* (1886) 56 LJ Rep n.s. 220 (where the agreement was not upheld).

[295] See Rollit's explanation in *PD* 1890 (s3) 342: 1169.

[296] The idea of minimum payments was not new, having been considered in the early 1880s. It was struck out of the 1883 bill by the 'grand committee', or Standing Committee on Trade, Shipping and Manufacturers: *PD* 1890 (s3) 342: 1212. For a similar proposal, see Special Report from the Select Committee on Bankruptcy Act Amendment Bill 1880 (324 – Sess. 2), viii, 211, iii–iv.

Act did, however, require a minimum composition of 7/6s in the pound; and required the bankrupt to pay 10s in the pound to obtain a discharge unless his inability to pay arose from 'circumstances for which he cannot justly be held responsible'. Moreover, on proof of any other misconduct, the minimum period of suspension was to be two years, or the court could suspend it until 10s in the pound had been paid. While reproducing the provisions relating to misconduct from the 1883 Act, the new legislation tightened them. Thus, where under the old Act, the discharge might be withheld if the bankrupt engaged in hazardous speculation which 'brought on' his bankruptcy, the new Act allowed it to be withheld where such conduct had only 'contributed' to it.

Despite these reforms, there was still continuing disquiet. In 1891, Smith reported that the law still failed to punish frauds disclosed in the public examination. He still felt that the criminal sanctions were inadequate. While the Debtors Act and Bankruptcy Act empowered the court to order a prosecution for offences under these Acts, there was no such power regarding related crimes, such as perjury, forgery, or fraudulent breaches of trust, whose prosecution was still left to private individuals. Moreover, Smith complained that juries who were not in full possession of the facts often acquitted, or light sentences were imposed by the court. To make the law more efficient, Smith returned to an old theme, suggesting that bankruptcy judges should have the power summarily to imprison debtors where they were satisfied crimes had been committed.[297] In putting this forward, he reflected an opinion widely held in commercial communities.

The matter was considered by a committee on bankruptcy appointed by the Board of Trade in 1906, chaired by Montague Muir Mackenzie. Realizing that the judges were unenthusiastic about being given a criminal jurisdiction, the committee did not recommend imposing criminal sanctions for the forms of conduct justifying the withholding of a discharge, with some exceptions. Where the bankrupt had failed to keep proper books, where a trader failed because of unjustifiable speculations unconnected with trade, or where he failed to supply a reasonable explanation of the loss of a substantial part of his estate within a year of his bankruptcy, he should (it recommended) be liable to summary punishment by the court. The committee was also concerned about the slow procedure by which criminal cases arising from bankruptcies came to court. To resolve this, it recommended that the official receiver should be able to initiate prosecutions directly before magistrates (without going through the Director of Public Prosecutions). It also wanted to reverse the burden of proof, so that 'on proof of the facts constituting an offence (such for instance as destruction of books

---

[297] Ninth Report by the Board of Trade under s 131 of the Bankruptcy Act 1883, *PP* 1892 (c. 6825), lxxii, 1, 9.

or papers) the whole burthen of proving absence of dishonesty and intention to defraud or excusable circumstances shall lie upon the accused debtor'.[298]

The committee was also concerned about the position of the undischarged bankrupt, who (it was felt) was often able to carry on trade unhindered. The effectiveness of the 1883 regime in policing commercial morality was largely undermined by the fact that many bankrupts did not apply for their discharge. Those whose examination went badly often preferred not to apply for a discharge, but continued to trade, often under assumed names. Between 1884 and 1890, only 24 per cent of bankrupts sought a discharge, while from 1891 to 1910, the proportion fell further to 19 per cent.[299] The only sanction against this was that it was a misdemeanour for an undischarged bankrupt to incur a debt of £20 without disclosing his status. This was regarded as a weak sanction. By 1906, it was widely felt that not all should not be left to the trader, and the committee agreed that after the final examination of the bankrupt, a day should be set for the presentation of the official receiver's report, whereupon the court would decide on the question of discharge. In addition, the committee recommended that it should be a misdemeanour both to incur a £10 debt without disclosing one's bankruptcy, and to trade under an assumed name.[300]

These proposals were largely implemented in 1913. All offences under the Act were now to be dealt with in summary courts, rather than at assize or quarter sessions, and were to carry a maximum six-month penalty.[301] The onus of disproving a criminal intent was thrown on the debtor. Where the Debtors Act had imposed a criminal liability on acts committed within four months of the bankruptcy, the 1913 Act extended it to six months. The statute made it a criminal offence to fail to keep proper accounts and to engage in gambling and hazardous speculation; and the penalty for undischarged bankrupts obtaining credit was increased from one year to two years in prison, while the amount of debt for which the penalty was imposed was reduced from £20 to £10.[302] At the same time, following the 1908 report, the legislation removed the requirement that 10s in the pound had

---

[298] Report of the Committee appointed by the Board of Trade to inquire into the Bankruptcy Law and its administration: *PP* 1908 [Cd 4068], xxxiv, 1 (henceforth cited as 1908 Bankruptcy Committee), p. 6.

[299] Throughout the period 1884–1910, roughly 1% of bankrupts (or 3% of those seeking a discharge) were refused; 14% (or 69% of those seeking a discharge) had suspended discharges; and 3% (14% of those seeking a discharge) were given conditional discharges. In the period overall, 1.8% of bankrupts were given an unconditional discharge (or 9% of those who applied), though the proportion was higher in the first period than in the second.

[300] 1908 Bankruptcy Committee, p. 12.

[301] Bankruptcy and Deeds of Arrangement Act 1913, 3 & 4 Geo. V c. 34, s 1.

[302] Although the 1883 Act made this an offence under the Debtors Act, it was unclear whether it fell under s 11 or s 13 of the Act, and it was only settled in *Re Turner* [1904] 1 KB 181 that the shorter penalty applied.

to be paid before a discharge would be granted. It was felt that where the only fault in the debtor was his inability to pay that sum, the court should have greater discretion to give a discharge. Moreover, as the 7/6s minimum for composition agreements was deemed to have decreased the number of feasible compositions, the sum was lowered to 5s in the pound. Thus, on the eve of war, legislation was still experimenting with how best to punish fraudulent bankrupts, but without being unduly harsh on honest failures.

Besides being concerned with the problem of the discharge, reformers sought to impose greater controls on voluntary arrangements. The 1883 Act effectively put an end to the light-handed approach to composition agreements which had existed in the 1870s. Accordingly, the number of compositions taken out under the provisions of the Act plummeted.[303] But arrangements did not disappear; rather, they continued to be conducted without any court supervision. Indeed, there was a perception that the number of private arrangements was increasing in the 1880s, made by those who disliked the 'officialism' of the 1883 Act.

Such deeds were not popular either with the Board of Trade, the Law Officers, or the Associated Chambers of Commerce, for it was feared that they left too much room for abuse. It was too easy for some creditors to make such arrangements which were then forced at the last minute on other creditors, who would not have agreed, but who were not in a position by then to challenge. Debtors might choose incompetent or biased trustees. Although such trustees were liable for breaches of trust, this was a far less effective way to ensure probity than the more extensive controls offered in the Bankruptcy Court, since it was left to the creditors to investigate and take action in respect of the breach of trust.[304] A final disadvantage—though one which was perhaps of more interest to public officials than private creditors—was that there was no mechanism in this system to investigate the conduct of the debtor and his trustees and to verify that debt had not been recklessly incurred and to ensure that there were no fraudulent preferences.[305]

The Law Officers looked for ways to restrict the use of such arrangements. In 1887, the Solicitor General gave an opinion that where a deed of arrangement was challenged by a non-assenting creditor, bringing the case into bankruptcy, none of the assenting creditors could be permitted to prove their debts, having released the debtor by an instrument under seal. The effect of this would be to prevent any recovery of their debts by creditors who had sought to enter an arrangement out

---

[303] The first three years of the new regime saw only 314 compositions per annum, the next three years an average of 131, the annual number thereafter remaining in double figures in each year until the outbreak of the First World War.

[304] See *Cooper* v. *Adams* (1894) 2 Ch 557.

[305] 1886 Bankruptcy Report, p. 12.

of court. While ruffling some feathers, few lawyers took the opinion too seriously, pointing out that such deeds made the payment of the composition a condition, and noting that any potential problem could easily be overcome by redrafting the form of deeds.[306] When the Board of Trade sought to clamp down on such deeds in a test case, the Divisional Court rejected the Law Officers' views, observing that such a position might lend itself to worse frauds, as unscrupulous creditors refusing to sign might recover all their debts at the expense of those who, by signing, would have debarred themselves from proving.[307]

In early 1887, Sir Albert Rollit, on behalf of the Associated Chambers of Commerce, brought a bill to make compulsory the registration of such deeds at the Supreme Court. The Chambers of Commerce were worried that those who avoided publicity were too often able to settle privately with their creditors, and then immediately obtain credit once more. The promoters of the bill had initially sought a much tougher measure, under which any debtor obtaining £20 of credit within two years of making an unregistered deed would be guilty of a misdemeanour. This was opposed by the government, which felt it was too 'too severe a step to make it a criminal offence when credit is obtained simply because some legal step has been omitted'.[308] The Deeds of Arrangement Act only provided that any deed which was not registered would be void. Under the Act, the deed had to be registered within seven days of being made, and be accompanied with an affidavit stating the debtor's assets and liabilities. This provision it was assumed, would 'make it necessary, before the deed is executed, to have a thorough investigation of the debtor's affairs, and to ascertain how far the creditors are likely to accede to the proposed arrangement'.[309] Moreover, while unregistered deeds were voided, the Act did not give any additional protection to registered deeds: to make a private deed of arrangement continued to constitute an act of bankruptcy.

The legislation provided for recording of the number of deeds made outside the Act. Between 1888 and 1913, the average number of such deeds annually was 3391, compared with the number of receiving orders of 4272. In John Smith's view, one reason for the popularity of deeds of arrangement was that creditors were not vindictive, and did not push people into bankruptcy unless their conduct was seriously objectionable. Equally, he added, since many creditors were owed debts of under £50, they were unable to complain that the deed constituted an act of bankruptcy.[310] Smith was not wholly hostile to such deeds, feeling

---

[306] (1887) 31 *Sol. J.* 312.

[307] *In Re Stephenson* (1888) 20 QBD 540. See also (1888) 33 *Sol. J.* 215.

[308] *PD* 1887 (s3) 315: 1340 (Sir Richard Webster AG).

[309] G. Y. Robson, *A Treatise on the Law of Private Arrangements with Creditors* (1888), 12.

[310] Eleventh General Annual Report of the Board of Trade under section 131 of the Bankruptcy Act 1883, *PP* 1894 (304), lxxvii, 1, at p. 19.

that if the debtor had not been guilty of any misconduct, it would be wasteful to require him to come to court and be examined if his creditors were happy with an arrangement.[311] But he felt that allowing a majority to condone the offences condemned by the Act would 'degrade commercial morality into a question of barter, and to undo much of the benefit which the Act has conferred upon honest and prudent trade'. The dissenting creditor should thus have the power to bring a deed of arrangement before the court. Nevertheless, he also felt that the court should be able to make the deed bind all creditors, if it felt there had been no misconduct.[312]

Continuing concern led to a provision in the Bankruptcy Act 1890 (s 25), which enacted that all trustees acting under such deeds had to send annual accounts to the Board of Trade. However, this was a weak mechanism of control for the Board was given no power to call the trustee to account. These matters were raised before the 1906 bankruptcy committee. It found that, in some trades, the system of deeds of arrangements worked well, as professional trustees were appointed who worked efficiently. In such trades, the principal objection was to the power of dissenting creditors to take the case to bankruptcy, often after the trust had been partly executed. The risk of this, in turn, often put trustees off acting for the first three months. On the other hand, there were also complaints about unscrupulous trustees who used the debtor's assets without distributing to the creditors. There were particular problems caused by people who offered themselves as trustees under deeds to any debtor against whom a judgment was entered in the county courts. Drawing on evidence given to the Inspector General, the committee published evidence of many such unscrupulous operators. In one case, two partners had by this means been appointed trustees in 230 deeds of arrangement since 1892. Such operators absorbed all the money of the debtor, so that creditors obtained no dividends.[313]

The committee therefore sought much more stringent measures. First, it was proposed that no deed of arrangement should be valid unless it had received the assent of a majority in value and in number of the creditors within 21 days of its execution. The aim of this recommendation (which was enacted in the Bankruptcy and Deeds of Arrangement Act 1913) was that creditors would be given greater control over assignments, and to prevent them being made without

---

[311] It has been argued that the use of deeds rendered the English system of bankruptcy more efficient that those of its continental neighbours: P. Di Martino, 'Approaching Disaster: Personal Bankruptcy Legislation in England and Italy, c 1880–1939' (2005) 47 Business History 23–43 at 32.

[312] Eighth Report by the Board of Trade under section 131 of the Bankruptcy Act 1883: PP 1890–1 [C 6462], lxxvii, 1, at p. 15.

[313] Report of the Committee appointed by the Board of Trade to inquire into the Bankruptcy Law and its administration: vol. II Evidence, PP 1908 [Cd 4069], xxxiv, 49, at p. 390.

their knowledge. Secondly, it recommended that dissenting creditors should only be able to claim an act of bankruptcy had been committed within one month. The ensuing legislation duly enacted that if the trustee served on a dissenting creditor a notice of the deed, he would have to present any petition for bankruptcy within one month. Thirdly, the committee sought to strengthen the control of trustees. All questions relating to the enforcement of such trusts were to be dealt with in the Bankruptcy Court. Furthermore, trustees should give security, equal to the available assets, unless a majority of the creditors dispensed with this provision. If no such security were given, the court would be able to declare the trust void, or appoint another trustee. If the first one continued to act, he would be guilty of a misdemeanour. The creditors could further request an audit by the Board of Trade, while any money undistributed after two years was to be put into an account at the Bank of England.[314]

---

[314] 1908 Bankruptcy Committee, at 25–9.

V

Consumer Credit and Debt

THROUGHOUT the nineteenth century, access to credit was essential to the maintenance of the domestic economy, for working-class as well as middle-class households. Over our period, the disposable income of the working poor increased, and with it their use of formal credit agreements grew. While historians have long debated the standard of living among the working poor in the period before 1850,[1] it seems clear that wage earners' average real incomes were at best largely stagnant in the early nineteenth century.[2] It was only in the second half of the century that substantial gains were achieved.[3] However, incomes could fluctuate significantly. Since work was seasonal and irregular in many occupations, and since there were cyclical downturns which led to periods of high unemployment, workers and their families needed access to flexible credit mechanisms to keep afloat in bad times.

Credit was used not merely for day-to-day living expenses, but for the acquisition of consumer goods. A working-class market for consumer goods drawing on credit mechanisms, such as pawnbroking, was not new to the second half of the nineteenth century. But this era did see a significant expansion in the number of pawnbrokers, and the development (after the ending of the prohibition on usury in 1854) of money lenders, who lent without security. This era also saw the beginning of a system of hire-purchase, which by the early twentieth century would supplant pawnbroking as the most important credit mechanism for the poorer consumer. Behind each of these mechanisms stood the county

[1] See e.g. P. H. Lindert and J. G. Williamson, 'English Workers' Living Standards during the Industrial Revolution: A New Look' (1983) 36 *Econ. Hist. Rev.* 1–25; N. F. R. Crafts, 'English Workers' Living Standards During the Industrial Revolution: Some Remaining Problems' (1985) 45 *JEH* 139–44; P. H. Lindert and J. G. Williamson, 'English Workers Real Wages: A Reply to Crafts' (1985) 45 *JEH* 145–53; J. Mokyr, 'Is There Still Life in the Pessimist Case? Consumption During the Industrial Revolution, 1790–1850' (1988) 48 *JEH* 69–92.

[2] C. H. Feinstein, 'Pessimism Perpetuated: Real Wages and the Standard of Living in Britain During and After the Industrial Revolution' (1998) 58 *JEH* 625–58 at 649.

[3] See G. R. Boyer, 'Living Standards, 1860–1939', in R. Floud and P. Johnson (eds), *The Cambridge Economic History of Modern Britain. Volume II: Economic Maturity 1860–1939* (Cambridge, 2004), 280–313 at 284–6.

courts, created by legislation in 1846, which acted as an efficient forum of debt recovery.

Throughout the nineteenth century, jurists and legislators remained aware of the need to maintain a special regime to maintain working-class credit, both by protecting their creditors, and by regulating the terms of credit. At the heart of the system was the continuation of the sanction of imprisonment for debtors who failed to pay their debts. County court judges and legislators generally agreed that, without this sanction, poor debtors would simply refuse to pay, and poor people would be unable to get credit. The policy contradicted the general view which emerged in the mid-century that criminal sanctions should not be used for civil debt recovery, but should be imposed by criminal courts in cases of fraud. Defenders of the system claimed that it aimed not to gaol the debtor, but to make him repay affordable instalments. This would sustain the credit mechanism, of which opponents of imprisonment for debt were often suspicious. In practice, imprisonment was generally used simply as the sanction in a debt collection system, although the practice of individual county court judges varied significantly, with many using their discretion to protect the poor from harsh creditors.[4]

While imprisonment remained the crucial underpinning of credit, policymakers were also determined to maintain a regulatory framework which would prevent creditors from exploiting their debtors, through charging high rates of interest or imposing harsh terms. Just as a special regime existed for the recovery of debts, so throughout the nineteenth century a regulatory regime—often imperfect in practice—existed for pawnbrokers which aimed to give some protection to the poor. In the later nineteenth century, the legislature also intervened to protect poor borrowers from money lenders. At the same time, judges and jurists sought to apply equitable notions to ensure fairness and equality in the contract, and to prevent the lender from making his own terms.

In practice, the degree of regulation reflected public perceptions of the nature of the creditor. On the one hand, by the late nineteenth century, there was widespread hostility to money lenders. Perceived as exploitative and fraudulent, these traders were subjected to the strongest controls. On the other hand, pawnbrokers and Hire Traders, with their own professional organizations, were better placed to seek reforms in their favour, though the former, faced with competition from unlicensed 'dolly shops', sought to maintain their own respectability through a form of protectionism.

---

[4] See M. Finn, 'Working Class Women and the Contest for Consumer Control in Victorian County Courts' (1998) 161 *P&P* 116–54.

1. IMPRISONMENT FOR DEBT

Execution against the body had long been part of the process of small debt recovery. The power to imprison debtors who failed to pay was routinely included in statutes creating summary Courts of Requests from the late eighteenth century.[5] In the 1820s, when attempts were made to revive county courts, reformers sought to end imprisonment on final process, as part of a wider move to abolish imprisonment for debt.[6] But opinion turned away from this again in the 1830s, when (under pressure from mercantile interests) reformers opted to endorse the execution on the body used in the Courts of Request, on the assumption that the non-paying small debtor was guilty of fraud. When Lord John Russell's local courts measure was referred to a select committee in 1839, it thus endorsed the established principle that small debtors needed to be coerced to pay by execution on final judgment.[7]

Governments in the 1840s were uncertain on whether to retain imprisonment for small debts. Sir James Graham's 1844 county courts bill endorsed it as essential for the maintenance of working-class credit;[8] but some of his colleagues remained unsure.[9] The continuation of imprisonment for the small debtor was assured when the commercial community reacted with fury to Lord Brougham's 'Rogues Indemnity Act', which abolished imprisonment for debts under £20.[10] An amending Act was rapidly passed in 1845, which allowed execution debtors owing up to £20 to be gaoled for up to 40 days on the grounds of fraud, which was broadly defined.[11] The principle was reiterated in the following year in the County Courts Act, under which those who were fraudulent and contracted debts without the means to pay them could be imprisoned in a common gaol.[12]

Henceforth, the small debtor was excepted from the more general reforms in insolvency law. Those gaoled by the county courts were thus excluded from the

[5] M. C. Finn, *The Character of Credit: Personal Debt in English Culture, 1740–1914* (Cambridge, 2003), 215–19; P. Polden, *A History of the County Court, 1846–1971* (Cambridge, 1999), 10–12. See also XI, Pt 3, pp. 855–7.

[6] See pp. 801–03.

[7] See the principle adopted in the County Courts bills of 1839: *PP* 1839 (387) II 465, 497. The bill was reintroduced in 1841, when Campbell AG opposed the provisions allowing imprisonment on execution: see *PD* 1841 (s3) 57: 177.

[8] See (1844) 3 *LT* 9, 144.

[9] See the views expressed by Thesiger SG and Graham in *PD* 1844 (s3) 76: 1706 and *ibid.*, 80: 1019 (29 May 1845). Lyndhurst opposed imprisonment in small debt cases, feeling that it undermined the ability of the poor to work and pay off their debts: *ibid.*, 76: 1410 (25 July 1844).

[10] 7 & 8 Vict. c. 96 ss 57–58. See also (1845) 4 *LT* 406; (1844) 29 *LO* 2.

[11] 8 & 9 Vict. c. 127. The debtor could be gaoled if he was guilty of fraud in contracting the debt, ir if he wilfully contracted it without having the reasonable prospect of being able to pay it.

[12] 9 & 10 Vict. c. 95, ss 98–99.

1861 Act, which allowed the release of debtors from gaols;[13] for (in Sir Richard Bethell's view), they had been punished for contracting debts by fraud or with no reasonable means to pay, and 'it would be very wrong to interfere with that description of criminal imprisonment'.[14] The 1869 Debtors Act similarly permitted six weeks' imprisonment by order of a county court judge or where the judgment was for under £50.[15] Protests were raised at this time against the continued incarceration of small debtors, as creating one law for the rich, and another for the poor. Against arguments which stressed that no one should be gaoled unless for fraud or crime,[16] Sir R. P. Collier noted that it was necessary to keep imprisonment, since many debtors refused to pay until faced with gaol.[17] In the end, the statute provided imprisonment not for the fraud of contracting a debt which could not be paid, but for failing to pay the instalments ordered by a court, when the judge was satisfied the debtor could pay. This system was to remain in place until 1971.

As a proportion of debtors, the number imprisoned was not high. Although many debtors who lost their cases in the county courts did not pay up at once, most did before they were gaoled. During the 1870s, in 36 per cent of the 308,000 average annual number of contested cases in which judgment was given for the plaintiff, a judgment summons had to be issued. Just over half of these (53 per cent) proceeded to a hearing. Of the hearings, just under half (46 per cent) resulted in a committal order against the debtor. One in five of those against whom such an order was issued were finally gaoled, amounting to less than 2 per cent of the number of those who had lost their case. By the first decade of the twentieth century, although plaintiffs were having a harder time getting their debtors to pay up,[18] the proportion of those losing their case who wound up in prison remained at 2.3 per cent. Nonetheless, the number incarcerated was not small, running to more than 5600 a year on average in the 1860s and over 9800 in the 1900s.[19]

The system operated imperfectly. Although only debtors who refused to pay when able to do so were to be imprisoned, the judges had very inadequate means of discovering what could be afforded. Since workers usually remained at work rather than risk the loss of their job—and since there was no power to commit

---

[13] Bankruptcy Act 1861, 24 & 25 Vict. c. 134, s 104.

[14] *PD* 1861 (s3) 161: 304.   [15] Debtors Act 1869, 32 & 33 Vict. c. 62, s 5.

[16] *PD* 1869 (s3) 195: 177.   [17] *Ibid.*, 180.

[18] In this decade, 84% of the 432,776 contested cases which ended in judgments for the plaintiff were followed by a judgment summons, 63% of which went to a hearing. 61% of those heard resulted in committal orders, though only 7% of these ended in imprisonment.

[19] Figures taken from Polden, *History of the County Court*, tables 4–5. The proportions were similar in the previous decade, save that the number who were gaoled was slightly higher, with 30% of those against whom a committal order was issued being gaoled; representing almost 3% of those who had lost their case.

a debtor who did not appear[20]—the debtor was generally not in court to answer questions about his assets. Courts were therefore left to conjecture on the basis of evidence given by the creditor as to what could be paid,[21] and it was often assumed that anyone in work could pay.[22] Many judges did attempt to overcome this problem by estimating what would be reasonable for a man in the debtor's position to pay, and reducing payments in times of slump or in cases of strikes.[23] Nevertheless, practices which may have been intended to show lenience to the debtor could prove oppressive in practice. For instance, it was common practice to suspend the warrant and order the payment of instalments, on failure of which the warrant would become effective.[24] Although this appeared to be generous to the debtor—allowing him time to pay—it could easily become oppressive, since a suspended warrant of commitment could be activated by any subsequent failure to pay an instalment.

Since it was held that the judge's order of committal related only to the failed instalment, rather than the entire debt, a debtor could be imprisoned for every default in paying an instalment. In the words of Judge Henry Tindal-Atkinson, this created a 'legal thumbscrew' against the debtor.[25] For a debtor who had been ordered to pay an affordable sum by the judge could be peremptorily gaoled when the payments were no longer affordable for him. Equally, since many judges only considered judgment debts in looking at the debtor's liabilities, they were often unable to make an accurate assessment of the debtor's ability to pay.[26] If the judge

---

[20] This was the result of the Act 22 & 23 Vict. c. 57.

[21] Report from the Select Committee on Imprisonment for Debt (henceforth cited as 1873 Select Committee on Imprisonment for Debt), *PP* 1873 (348), xv, 1 at p. vi. The Committee of County Court Judges in 1859 reported that 'in nearly all cases where the party summoned does not appear sufficient evidence can be obtained to enable the judge to decide upon the question of committal': Return addressed by the Committee of the County Court Judges to the Judges of those Courts on County Court Commitments (henceforth cited as Return Relating to County Court Commitments 1867), *PP* 1867 (209), lvii, 61 at p. 1.

[22] Evidence of Judge Selfe, Report from the Select Committee of the House of Lords on the Debtors Act (cited henceforth as 1893 Select Committee on the Debtors Act), *PP* 1893–4 (HL 156), ix, q. 242.

[23] 1893 Select Committee on the Debtors Act, q. 936 (Evidence of Judge Bedwell).

[24] e.g. evidence of William Raine, Return Relating to County Court Commitments 1867, p. 23, q. 5. This practice was confirmed as lawful by *Stonor* v. *Fowle* (1887) 13 App Cas 20, which held that such an order would be an order for commitment in respect of a past default, and not an unlawful anticipatory order in respect of future defaults: cf. G. R. Rubin, 'Law, Poverty and Imprisonment for Debt, 1869–1914', in G. R. Rubin and D. Sugarman, *Law, Economy and Society: Essays in the History of English Law 1750–1914* (Abingdon, 1984), 241–99 at 256.

[25] *Horsnail* v. *Bruce* (1872) LR 8 CP 172. See the explanation of Judge Henry Tindal-Atkinson, in Report from the Select Committee on Debtors (Imprisonment) (henceforth cited as 1909 Select Committee on Debtors), *PP* 1909 (239), vii, 281, p. 111, q. 1957, discussed in Rubin, 'Imprisonment for Debt', 256.

[26] See the evidence of Daniel in 1873 Select Committee on Imprisonment for Debt, at p. 218, qq. 5084–85. Judge Bedwell told the 1893 select committee that he did not look at general indebtedness

subsequently discovered that the debtor was unable to pay, his discretion to stay execution was limited. For it was settled by 1895 that although he could do so if the debtor was unable to pay from 'sickness or other sufficient cause', he could not do so merely on the grounds of the debtor's lack of means.[27] In any event, the mechanics of the system militated against care. Judge Dodd (whose circuit included Hull and Whitby) told the 1909 select committee that he had dealt with 600 applications for imprisonment in a single afternoon and without (for the most part) the presence of the debtor.[28] In West Hartlepool, judgments were made in less than a minute and a half, which hardly left time for any consideration of means.[29] For all the theoretical talk that the law aimed to imprison only those who wilfully defied the court when able to pay—the principle which underlay the notion that they were being punished for a contempt—many judges admitted their job was essentially that of a debt collector, acting 'on the "screw" principle, of endeavouring to get payment for the creditor, and at the same time, not really unduly harassing the debtor'.[30]

In fact, judges had a good deal of scope to exercise discretion, and there was a great deal of variation in practice between the different courts, some judges being more doveish than others.[31] Numerous judges endorsed a freedom-of-contract approach, but many others exhibited a view of the 'moral economy'. Judge Tindal-Atkinson, ever conscious of the hardships imposed by poverty, made the practice of ordering minimal instalment payments, or adjourning hearings. His judgments 'were designed to infuse common-law conceptions of contract with more equitable understandings of status, misfortune and obligation'.[32] Some judges were clearly keener to imprison than others: in 1902, the North Riding circuit had slightly fewer plaints than its Durham neighbour, but imprisoned three-and-a-half times more debtors.[33] Equally, different judges imprisoned for different periods, as they strove to find the shortest sentence which would secure

outside of the court in estimating how much was to be paid, since after 1883 a man who wanted these taken into account could use administration orders if he chooses to: 1893 Select Committee on the Debtors Act, q. 945.

[27] *Attenborough* v. *Henschel* [1895] 1 QB 833.

[28] 1909 Select Committee on Debtors, pp. 22–4, qq. 295, 287–90.

[29] P. Johnson, 'Class Law in Victorian England' (1993) 141 *P & P* 146–69 at 159.

[30] 1893 Select Committee on the Debtors Act, q. 1400 (evidence of Judge J. B. Edge). See also the ambiguous answers of Judge Bedwell to the questions of Lord Thring, *ibid.*, q. 1056.

[31] In 1906, warrants of distress were ordered in 25% of cases brought to county courts, and orders of commitment were made in 16.46% of cases. But in Yorkshire, orders of commitment were made in 30.7% of cases; while in the London metropolitan area the figure was only 4%. Figures from 1909 Select Committee on Debtors, 339. The lowest percentage was that of the City of London (1.47%), the highest the East Riding of Yorkshire (38.04%).

[32] Finn, *Character of Credit*, 263.

[33] Rubin, 'Law, Poverty and Imprisonment for Debt', 295.

the payment of the debt. Judge Bedwell of the Hull County Court found that 28 days was the ideal period: if a shorter period was given, the man would elect to stay in prison and not pay, while a longer period served no useful purpose.[34] But other judges took a different approach, with some imprisoning for short periods and others for the maximum of 42 days. Periods of imprisonment could also vary according to the size of the debt, and whether the debtor had acted in a fraudulent way.[35]

Throughout our period, protests were regularly raised against the system. In 1872, at the suggestion of the county court judge George Russell—the only judge who opposed imprisonment—Michael Bass brought a bill to abolish imprisonment for debt. Denouncing the fact that there was one law for the rich and another for the poor, he stressed its high cost both to the country, and to the debtor, who never recovered the position he had lost.[36] He candidly admitted his view that the system of credit, supported by imprisonment for debt, was bad for the poor. Bass, whose own fortune came from brewing, put forward a familiar argument that while the poor could not get drink on credit, they could get food: hence the law encouraged the reckless giving of credit which enabled men to drink.[37] The bill was lost, but in the following year a select committee was appointed, which endorsed the ending of imprisonment for debt, and putting in its place a kind of poor man's bankruptcy system.[38]

In 1874, Bass tried once more to introduce legislation to abolish imprisonment for debt, though without including the wider provisions proposed by the select committee. This time, he was supported by Sir Henry James, who denounced the whole county court system as 'a great debt-collecting office' which was 'used entirely by creditors who were traders, as against the honest portion of the community, on a reckless system of credit'.[39] If imprisonment for debt were abolished, James noted, the workman 'would find ready money for the draper as well as for the publican, and would get goods at a lower price without incurring fees or imprisonment'.[40] Although this bill only aimed to abolish imprisonment for

---

[34] 1893 Select Committee on the Debtors Act, q. 1034–6.

[35] Judge Hamilton told the 1909 committee that he always committed for 20 days, though some judges only committed for five, which he felt cost the country money without deterring the debtor: 1909 Select Committee on Debtors, p. 18, q. 218. Both the 1893 and 1909 committees favoured reducing the maximum period of imprisonment to 21 days, and promoting a more uniform approach by the judges, something which it was felt could be done under orders from the Lord Chancellor.

[36] PD 1872 (s3) 211: 1978.   [37] Ibid., 1980.

[38] 1873 Select Committee on Imprisonment for Debt, at p. xi.

[39] PD 1874 (s3) 218: 555.

[40] Ibid., 557. See also the letter of Judge Eardley Wilmot (a supporter of abolishing imprisonment for debt) to the The Times: 'Our labouring classes are, as a rule, absolutely thriftless, and chiefly because they have never learnt their first lesson—namely, to pay ready money for what they want,

debts under £5, strong mercantile opposition led to its failure. Bass continued to keep up the pressure for reform, and bills were introduced on a yearly basis in the late 1870s. Nonetheless, governments continued to oppose abolition, since it would allow debtors to escape their obligations. Moreover, Joseph Chamberlain, having passed his bankruptcy reform of 1883 which introduced a form of poor person's bankruptcy without abolishing imprisonment, claimed that henceforth imprisonment 'would only remain *in terrorem* over the heads of absolutely dishonest debtors'.[41]

The issue continued to be debated in the decades around the turn of the twentieth century. In December 1892, a 'county court judge'—W. T. Greenhow—wrote a long letter defending the system to the *The Times*.[42] By this era, there was concern at the oppressive use of the county courts both by tallymen who sold goods to workmen's wives on credit, and by money lenders.[43] The question was referred by Lord Herschell LC to a select committee of the House of Lords, but its findings did not result in legislation.[44] The matter was raised in Parliament once more in 1907, when E. H. Pickersgill pointed to a recent increase in the number of people committed—which had grown from 7867 in 1899 to 11,096 in 1904—and to the variation in judicial practice. Pickersgill argued that the main beneficiaries of the system were 'tallymen, money-lenders, and that class of sharks to whom certain tradesmen sold their debts at about a shilling in the £'.[45] He was dismayed that a County Courts bill in the previous year had not addressed the issue of imprisonment, and sought a restriction of the power to imprison to fraudulent transactions. Although cautious on the subject of reform, Sir W. Robson SG felt that a select committee would be the best way to proceed, and in 1908 the government resolved to appoint one.[46]

A committee was duly appointed. Although it was unconvinced by 'humanitarian' arguments in favour of abolishing imprisonment for debt, the 1909 select committee was convinced that the poor needed protection from money lenders and jewellers who abused the power given by the Debtors Act. On the suggestion of three county court judges, it proposed allowing the procedure only to be used

---

and, in homely language, to cut their coat according to their cloth' (*The Times*, 5 January 1893, col. 8c, *sub nom.* Judex, reprinted in 1893 Select Committee on the Debtors Act, pp. 196–7).

[41] *PD* 1883 (s3) 280: 1626.   [42] *The Times*, 27 December 1892, col. 11e.

[43] See 1893 Select Committee on the Debtors Act, 191ff. On tallymen, see G. R. Rubin, 'The County Courts and the Tally Trade, 1846–1914', in G. R. Rubin and D. Sugarman (eds), *Law, Economy and Society, 1750–1914: Essays in the History of English Law* (Abingdon, 1984), 321–48; idem., 'From Packmen, Tallymen and "Perambulating Scotchmen" to Credit Drapers' Associations, c. 1840–1914' (1986) 28 *Business History* 206–25.

[44] *PD* 1893 (s4) 8: 1343. Herschell noted that although committals were designed to force the fraudulent (and solvent) to pay, the law often acted so as to put pressure on relatives and friends to pay.

[45] *PD* 1907 (s4) 171: 937.   [46] *PD* 1908 (s4) 183: 1079.

where the judgment debt had been obtained either for necessaries or where there was a tort judgment. Judges were already well used to deciding what constituted necessities (in cases of infants and where wives made purchases), and by refusing incarceration where the goods were luxuries, it was felt illegitimate credit could be controlled.[47] But nothing came of this proposal.[48] In the event, there was no reform of the system at the eve of the First World War.

Reform initiatives failed not least because imprisonment for debt was consistently defended. Those favouring its retention argued, first, that poor debtors could afford to pay their debts, but that they had to be coerced to do so. 'Treating the power of imprisonment not as a punishment, but as a power of coercion, to be exercised against a man who can at any time relieve himself from the pressure', the Bradford judge W. T. S. Daniel said, 'I think it would be like taking the linch-pin out of the wheel, or taking the nut from the screw, to take that power away from the county court judge.'[49] Daniel claimed that debtors who were happy enough to serve 10-day sentences for failing to pay what was owed managed to produce the money when they were faced with a 40-day penalty.[50] In his view, when debtors wound up in prison, it was because of fecklessness and drink rather than poverty. Defenders of the system also denied that this was class legislation. The 1909 committee reported abundant evidence that the richer classes were also compelled to pay by this means.[51]

It was argued, secondly, that without imprisonment for debt as a security to lenders, working-class credit would dry up.[52] In 1859, Judge D. D. Heath stated that, failing a direct attachment of the workman's wages, any system of credit for the working classes had necessarily to rest ultimately on punishment. Judge Bagshawe observed that 'modern lovers of humanity' should bear in mind that 'refusal of credit would mean the workhouse or starvation'.[53] Judge Greenhow wrote to the *The Times* in 1893 that the system was 'just, merciful, and necessary' since it permitted poor traders to grant credit with 'extraordinary forbearance and kindness' to poor customers.[54] It was also argued that imprisonment for debt might be less harsh than execution against goods. Judge Heath noted in

---

[47] 1909 Select Committee on Debtors, ix.

[48] Rubin, 'Law, Poverty and Imprisonment for Debt', 278.

[49] 1873 Select Committee on Imprisonment for Debt, p. 219, q. 5106.

[50] *Ibid.*, pp. 216–17, qq. 5068–73.   [51] 1909 Select Committee on Debtors, vi.

[52] See also Return Relating to County Court Commitments 1867, at p. 1: 'any alteration of the law…would produce great misery among the working classes, who, forced to buy on credit, would hereafter only obtain it on terms which would cause those who paid their debts to pay for those who did not'.

[53] *Law Gazette*, 13 January 1893, reprinted in 1893 Select Committee on the Debtors Act, at 187.

[54] Letter reproduced in 1893 Select Committee on the Debtors Act, 191–2. See also the memorandum by Judge Sir William Selfe in 1909 Select Committee on Debtors, pp. 373–4.

1859 that labouring men could have warrants against them suspended, either by paying an instalment or asking relatives to pay. Even if the debtor were gaoled, he was not necessarily in a worse position than if his goods were seized: for in that case, he would have to pay the costs of execution, his goods would be sold for a small value, and he would live in misery until he had saved enough to recover. In Heath's view, 'the debt is seldom much reduced by the process, and the creditor is at liberty, without control, to pounce down upon him again, if he does scrape together some comforts again'.[55]

Against these arguments in favour of the system, there were protests that the law was essentially class legislation. In 1873, Judge J. A. Russell, of the Manchester and Salford court, denied that it was only the feckless who were gaoled, but he observed 'that even supposing that were the fact, we have no right to punish people for being thriftless, improvident, and drunken'.[56] He pointed out the inequality whereby the small debtor could not be discharged of his debt unless he paid 20s in the pound, whereas larger debtors were able to make use of bankruptcy proceedings. Similarly, in his draft report presented to the 1909 select committee, E. H. Pickergill noted that in practice only the working classes were gaoled under the Debtors Act. He pointed to the evidence of H. B. Simpson, the Governor of Worcester prison, who was moved to lend a gaoled debtor the 5s 9d debt run up by his late wife.[57] He argued that the system was designed to screw money out of the poor, by a kind of blackmail. Faced with gaol, the poor either borrowed from others to pay the debt, or were rescued by their relatives.[58] Looking back at the end of our period, Judge Parry noted that, since 1869, over 300,000 had been gaoled without being guilty of any crime: they had been imprisoned for poverty or improvidence—'that blessed word that so insidiously describes in the poor that failure in economic asceticism, that lack of cold self-denial of luxury and extravagance, that absence of patient thrift and simplicity of life—characteristic features which are never wanting in the beautiful lives of those social classes above them that the poor must learn to look up to and to imitate'.[59]

The view that execution on the body was kinder than taking the goods was also challenged. Russell noted that if a man's goods were taken, he could buy new ones in good time: 'but if he goes to prison it throws him out of employment, and it

[55] Return Relating to County Court Commitments 1867, p. 52 (qq. 2–3).

[56] 1873 Select Committee on Imprisonment for Debt, p. 210, q. 2926.

[57] 1909 Select Committee on Debtors, xii and 371–2.

[58] For a judicial recognition of the practice, see Lord Bramwell in *Stonor* v. *Fowle* [1888] AC 20 at 29.

[59] E. A. Parry, *The Law and the Poor* (1914), 57.

may throw those who depend upon him out of employment'.[60] He endorsed the view of the early nineteenth-century Common Law Commissioners that imprisonment for debt perverted a civil offence into a criminal one. The result of this was to encourage the reckless giving of credit. To deter this, he required traders to present clear evidence of the debtor's ability to pay, a demand which had the effect of diminishing the lax granting of credit in his area, and of reducing the number of plaints in his court. While admitting that the number gaoled in his court was very small, he doubted whether they 'were not the very persons who ought not to have been imprisoned, for this reason, that I can hardly imagine anyone going to prison who had the means of paying his debts'.[61] Russell's successor in Manchester and Salford, E. A. Parry, agreed that the system encouraged reckless credit, not only tempting a man to mortgage his future earnings to buy useless consumer goods, but tempting his wife to run up extravagant debts and himself 'to spend his wages in drink and leave his wife to obtain credit at the grocer's for food'.[62] Pickersgill, writing in 1909, was as scathing, describing as a 'social canker' the 'grossly excessive' credit which was encouraged by the system.[63] For these witnesses, credit was clearly a bad thing. The MP J. A. Seddon told the 1909 committee that 'whenever a working man or his wife begins to get credit they get to that extent demoralised, and they see things that they do not really require, but they get them'.[64]

2. THE POOR MAN'S BANKRUPTCY

Critics of imprisonment for debt generally contrasted the rich debtor's ability to relieve himself of his obligations through bankruptcy with the poor man's continuing liability. In 1873, the select committee on imprisonment for debt proposed a system akin to bankruptcy, without the sanction of imprisonment. It proposed

That upon hearing of any judgment summons, the judge should inquire whether there are any other debts, and the debtor should be required within such time as the court may direct, to deliver in a full and true account of all the debts due from him, and of his means of payment, and the judge should make such order for payment of the same, either

---

[60] 1873 Select Committee on Imprisonment for Debt, p. 215, q. 5006. See his evidence in general at 205–16.

[61] *Ibid.*, p. 210, q. 4924.

[62] 1909 Select Committee on Debtors, p. 95, q. 1680.

[63] *Ibid.*, xiii.

[64] *Ibid.*, p. 216, q. 3867.

in full or by way of instalment, or by an execution against the goods of the debtor, as to him should seem just.[65]

Although the committee's ideas on abolishing imprisonment for debt did not gain ground, section 122 of Chamberlain's 1883 Bankruptcy Act did introduce a system of bankruptcy for the small debtor, albeit backed by imprisonment. Under this legislation, where a judgment had been obtained in a county court against a debtor whose debts amounted to less than £50, the court was empowered to make an order for the administration of his estate. It could then order the payment of his debts by instalment 'either in full or to such extent as to the County Court under the circumstances of the case appears practicable, and subject to any conditions as to his future earnings or income which the Court may think just'.[66] If the debtor's property exceeded £10, there could be execution against his goods at the request of any creditor. The system promised to give a good measure of protection for the debtor, particularly after the 1906 decision in the Court of Appeal in the case of *Pearson* v. *Wilcock*, which ruled that once an administration order was issued, all proceedings not only by existing but also by future creditors was stayed. This meant that a debtor for whom an order had been issued was protected against imprisonment for debts later acquired.[67] The money paid by the debtor went first to pay the plaintiff's legal costs, and secondly to pay Treasury fees,[68] and only thereafter to pay the creditors rateably. The debtor's first creditors were paid out first, and his later creditors—who might have lent while unaware than an administration order had been taken out—were only paid subsequently.

The system allowed any debtor against whom a judgment summons had been issued to tell the court that he would not be able to pay that sum and the costs of the suit, and to seek an administration order. Practically, it had the same effect as a county court judgment to pay off debts by instalments, since the composition payments could be ordered to be paid over a period up to six years. In contrast to proper bankruptcy proceedings, where the property was vested in trustees, in this system payment went through the court, and was handled by the chief clerk

---

[65] 1873 Select Committee on Imprisonment for Debt, xi.

[66] Bankruptcy Act 1883, s 122(1).

[67] *Pearson* v. *Wilcock* (1906) 2 KB 440. The first set of creditors were given priority. The previous practice had allowed subsequent creditors to sue: see Rendall's evidence to the 1908 Departmental Committee on bankruptcy: Report of the Committee appointed by the Board of Trade to inquire into the Bankruptcy Law and its administration: vol II Evidence (henceforth cited as 1908 Bankruptcy Committee, Evidence), PP 1908 [Cd 4069], xxxiv, 49, p. 345, q. 7984. See also the comments of Judge Smyly at p. 168, qq. 3993–5. Smyly's practice was to supersede the first order with a second, taking into account the changed conditions.

[68] These were two shillings in the pound, a rate criticized as excessive: see Parry's comments in 1909 Select Committee on Debtors, p. 100, q. 1745.

of the relevant county court. The procedure was used mainly by debtors against whom a number of judgments had been issued, in order to make a composition of the various debts.[69] Moreover, its use depended in many ways on the enthusiasm of the county court judge before whom the case came for, as Judge Parry observed, the working-class debtors did not understand the system unless it was explained to them by a registrar.[70]

Like the system of debt recovery in the county courts, the system itself rested on the continued power to imprison the debtor for default of payment. Since the defendant had to make a declaration about his income and his family before an order was granted, the court was better able to ascertain a reasonable rate of payment than in the case of other judgments against small debtors, where the defendant was generally absent. But this declaration generated a legal presumption that the debtor had the means to pay the amount ordered, not only at the time of making the declaration, but subsequently as well.[71] Any failure to pay any instalment thus resulted in imprisonment, unless the debtor could prove that he did not have the means to pay, in which case the court could direct the order to have been suspended at that time. This power to imprison was found to be less controversial in these cases than in ordinary county court judgments. For instance, Judge Wightman Wood who wanted the abolition of imprisonment in cases of ordinary debt, argued that 'it should be maintained with regard to debtors under administration orders, because they have time given to them, as a rule they are let off a large part of their debts, and they make themselves bankrupt, and come under a different system'.[72]

Between 1884 and 1912, an average of 4268 administration orders were issued annually, made on an average of 4954 applications. The average after 1902 was higher than before, since the right of a majority in number and value of the creditors to oppose it was removed and the judges were given full discretion.[73] Over the same period, an average of 207 were imprisoned each year for failing to pay the instalments due, far fewer than were gaoled by the county courts for failing

---

[69] See the explanation of the system given by Judge Smyly, in 1908 Bankruptcy Committee, Evidence, at pp. 166–7, qq. 3982 et seq.

[70] In Parry's court, where he found a man had several debts, he sent him upstairs to fill out the forms with the registrar: 1909 Select Committee on Debtors, p. 99, q. 1741. See also Judge Selfe's comments at p. 276, q. 4981.

[71] In contrast, in an ordinary judgment summons, the means had to be proved on oath: see Smyly's evidence, 1908 Bankruptcy Committee, Evidence, p. 167, q. 3988.

[72] 1909 Select Committee on Debtors, p. 309, q. 5620.

[73] Figures from Thirty-First General Annual Report by the Board of Trade under section 131 of the Bankruptcy Act, 1883, PP 1914 (413), lxvii, 5, at p. 11. See also the evidence of Athelstan Rendall (who wanted the old power restored) in 1908 Bankruptcy Committee, Evidence, pp. 344–5, q. 7971, 7982. For the order, see E. T. Baldwin, The Law of Bankruptcy and Bills of Sale, (11th edn, 1915), 1044.

to pay their debts.[74] The poor man's bankruptcy system thus played a relatively minor role in debt recovery.[75]

Although the system came in for criticism from those who opposed the ultimate sanction of imprisonment on which it was based,[76] it was regarded as a good system for the poor debtor, even though a good deal of effort was required to encourage him to seek an administration order before he had fallen hopelessly into debt. Judge Smyly argued that those who were too poor to afford the £12 to £14 it would cost to make themselves bankrupt, but whose debts were larger than the £50 for which an administration order was available, were in the most hopeless position.[77] He argued that the level of debt which would allow a debtor to seek an administration order should be increased.[78] This view was also taken by the Departmental Committee on Bankruptcy Law, which in 1908, proposed raising the sums for which an administration order could be had to £100.

The system was also praised for being more efficient than other parts of the bankruptcy system in recovering money. Thomas Marshall, registrar of the Leeds County Court, told the Departmental Committee on Bankruptcy Law that whereas the small bankruptcies administered by official receivers under section 121 of the Act produced a ½ per cent return,[79] the rate of return under section 122 was 21.45 per cent. This was due to the sanction of imprisonment, for under section 122 the debtor was made to pay for the protection given to his person and property, whereas in bankruptcy he was not.[80] Nonetheless, there were some criticisms. Many were critical of *Pearson* v. *Wilcock*, for giving too much protection to the debtor against the claims of subsequent creditors. The Departmental Committee on Bankruptcy Law therefore recommended that an administration order should only be effective against those creditors whose debts existed at the time of the order, or those who voluntarily came under the order and took advantage of it.[81] The committee also felt it should not be necessary for the debtor to have to await a judgment against him before making an application, for this was felt to be expensive and wasteful.[82]

---

[74] *PP* 1914 [Cd. 7267], c, 187, at p. 27.

[75] However, the number of applications under s 122 was similar to the number of bankruptcy receiving orders, which between 1888 and 1913 averaged 4272 annually.

[76] Report of a Committee appointed by the Lord Chancellor and the Board of Trade to inquire into the Working of Section 122 of the Bankruptcy Act 1883, *PP* 1887 [C. 5139], lxxv, 63.

[77] 1908 Bankruptcy Committee, Evidence, p. 169, q. 4009.

[78] A special committee appointed by the Law Society recommended in 1906 that the level of debts it covered might safely be increased to £200. 1908 Bankruptcy Committee, Evidence, p. 392.

[79] These were bankruptcies under £300.

[80] 1908 Bankruptcy Committee, Evidence, p. 70 (evidence of Thomas Marshall).

[81] Report of the Committee appointed by the Board of Trade to inquire into the Bankruptcy Law and its administration, *PP* 1908 [Cd. 4068], xxxiv, 1, at p. 35.

[82] See the evidence of Judge Smyly, 1908 Bankruptcy Committee, Evidence, p. 169, q. 4007.

There were also criticisms of how the system affected the debtor. Judge Gent told the 1909 select committee that the orders were onerous on the debtor, since they lasted a long time and attached his future earnings. If a debtor could raise the £10 fee to make himself bankrupt, he pointed out, he freed himself from future liability; but if he was unable to find this sum, then his future was mortgaged.[83] In Gent's view, the law was unequal, and what was needed was some machinery for relieving the poor from the constant burden of debt.[84] He also felt that under this system, debtors who were genuinely unable to pay were gaoled thanks to the operation of the legal presumption that the man could pay.[85] Judge Bedwell also found administration orders unsatisfactory, arguing that the main problem was the lack of elasticity in the system, insofar as the judge having made one order for repayment was not able to revise it later. 'Now the fluctuations in these poor fellows' lives are remarkable', he noted, 'and I would give anything in many of these cases to be able to reduce my old order'.[86] In consequence, he noted, many merely absconded.

But despite the criticisms from both sides, section 122 of the 1883 Act remained in force when the First World War broke out. Writing on its eve, Judge E. A. Parry noted that while the Act had not been wholly a failure, it had failed to meet Chamberlain's hopes. In part, this was because the 'brutal method of the judgment summons' was preferred to the complicated bankruptcy proceeding; in part because it was limited to £50 debts; and in part because the Treasury set such high fees.[87] More broadly, though, Parry observed that bankruptcy proceedings were premised on the assumption that the debtor had been solvent once; an assumption which was not true for most of the poor, who lived in a constant state of insolvency.[88] The continuance of imprisonment for debt after 1869 was thus widely perceived by contemporaries—as it has been by historians—as class legislation.[89]

---

[83] 1909 Select Committee on Debtors, p. 243, q. 4335. Parry agreed that the £10 needed to seek bankruptcy excluded the poor: 'Bankruptcy is like divorce, it is a rich man's luxury' (p. 100, q. 1749).

[84] By contrast, Parry argued that since the initial investigation of the man's condition was more thorough, a smaller number wound up gaoled. 1909 Select Committee on Debtors, p. 100, q. 1744. This was endorsed by Judge Bray at p. 132, q. 2284.

[85] Evidence of Judge Gent, 1909 Select Committee on Debtors, p. 242, qq. 4316–18.

[86] 1893 Select Committee on the Debtors Act, p. 62, q. 1006.

[87] Parry, The Law and the Poor, 121.

[88] Ibid., 107.

[89] Johnson, 'Class Law', 161. See also P. Johnson, 'Creditors, Debtors and the Law in Victorian and Edwardian England', in W. Steinmetz (ed.), Private Law and Social Inequality in the Industrial Age (Oxford, 2000), 485–504 at 504, explaining the contrasting attitudes to debt of small debt and bankruptcy courts in terms of 'a deeply rooted belief among a majority of judges that the working classes were morally inferior'.

3. PAWNBROKING

If it was true that many middle-class commentators criticized poor consumers for buying goods perceived to be luxuries, there remained a concern to preserve the credit mechanisms available to the poor, and to protect the poor consumer from exploitation. Nowhere was this more apparent than in the treatment of pawnbroking. Throughout the nineteenth century, working-class households depended heavily on pawnbrokers for loans on the security of pledged goods. The business was large, and the number of pawnbrokers significant. The number of licences granted to pawnbrokers grew from 1945 in 1852 to 3537 in 1872.[90] The industry was well organized. Professional associations of pawnbrokers evolved in the Midlands and the North West from the late eighteenth century, while the first regular trade association for pawnbrokers in London was formed in 1821.[91] From the 1830s, sporadic attempts were made to create a national association to lobby Parliament for their interests, which by the 1860s was able to exert considerable influence on policy-makers. Opposition from the pawnbrokers also helped defeat attempts in the 1840s to introduce a system in England in imitation of the continental *monts de piété*, under which the poor could obtain loans at fixed rates of profit from publicly run institutions.[92] Pawnbrokers engaged in lucrative private enterprise were always keen to defend their interests.

At the 'top' end of the pawnbroking market were the dealers who lent large sums of money on the security of jewellery and plate to professional people; while at the 'lower' end were the 'industrial' dealers who lent small sums to the working classes, often on the security of soft goods, such as clothing or bedding, which could be redeemed on a weekly basis. The distinction between the two was marked. Robert Attenborough, who employed more than 100,000 people in his business, and who lent thousands of pounds on the security of expensive jewels, saw his role as akin to that of a banker.[93] He felt that the higher class of pawnbroker should be given the title 'silverbroker', and he found it objectionable to have to identify himself as a pawnbroker at his premises.[94] The goods received by such pawnbrokers could be grand. The firm of the Honourable Secretary of the

---

[90] Return of Number of Pawnbrokers Licences taken out in Great Britain 1848–71, *PP* 1872 (250), liv, 525.

[91] A. Hardaker, A Brief History of Pawnbroking (1892), Ch. 12; M. Tebbutt, Making Ends Meet: Pawnbroking and Working Class Credit (Leicester, 1983), 103.

[92] See F. Turner, *The Contract of Pawn* (1866), 16. In the 1830s, a number of *monts de piété* were formed in Ireland, and attempts were made to bring bills in England in 1843 and 1844: Hardaker, *History*, Ch. 14. See also *PD* 1843 (s3) 70: 86; *PD* 1844 (s3) 74: 92.

[93] Report from the Select Committee on Pawnbrokers (henceforth cited as 1870 Select Committee on Pawnbrokers), *PP* 1870 VIII (377) 391, at pp. 158–9, qq. 3345, 3363.

[94] 1870 Select Committee on Pawnbrokers, p. 153, qq. 3243, 3253.

Metropolitan Pawnbrokers' Protection Society, George Attenborough, who took in both kinds of business, was sued in 1896 by the executors of the Maharajah Duleep Singh for the return of a brilliant emerald ornament, two single stone rings, a waist buckle, an emerald pendant, and a pair of pearl and emerald earrings which had been pledged by the Maharajah's banker, the corrupt and bankrupt Lawrence Wynne.[95]

The lower end of the market provided an essential credit mechanism for the working classes. Those most in need of the credit it offered were workers whose earnings were irregular and seasonal, and who ran up debts at slack times of the year which would be paid off in good times. The period from 1820–40, which saw much instability in the labour market, therefore saw the most significant expansion of pawnbroking.[96] While middle-class opinion generally saw the pledging of one's goods as a sign of fecklessness and indiscipline, the poor often regarded 'luxurious' objects as investments which could be used as a means to obtain credit in lean times. A worker might buy an expensive item in good times as a form of insurance against bad times, when it might be pawned. In times of depression, more goods were pawned, but fewer redeemed, which served to put pressure on the pawnbrokers. There was also much short-term pledging. Sunday-best clothing might be pawned on a Monday morning, and redeemed on the following Saturday, not merely because this enabled the owner to raise money on it, but because the clothes would be kept cleaner and safer in the pawnbroker's store.

Although pawning goods was an essential part of working-class finances, it remained a subject of shame. Resort to the pawnbroker allowed a family to maintain a public face of respectability, for at Christmas, or on a Sunday, appearances would be maintained. This aim for respectability required families to keep their visits to the pawn shop secret. Discretion was thus essential to the success of the pawnbroker, and often clients used false names and addresses when making pledges. Within families, pawning might remain a secret, as when women, who were in control of the family budget, kept from their husbands the extent of credit which was keeping the household afloat. Piece workers were known to pawn the materials they were given to work on for part of the week, and washer women would redeem one set of pledged washing with another, before returning the first set to its owner.[97] Such behaviour could generate risks for the pawnbroker dealing with property whose ownership was often at best uncertain.

---

[95] *Singh* v. *Attenborough*, *The Times*, 14 July 1896, col. 13d. The Maharajah had given the jewels to his banker as security for a loan he needed to pay his bookmaker.

[96] Tebbutt, *Making Ends Meet*, 13.

[97] *Ibid.*, 73.

The dual nature of pawnbroking was reflected in the legal regime which governed it. Under legislation passed in 1800,[98] pawnbrokers accepting pledges for loans up to £10 were exempted from the usury laws, which set a maximum 5 per cent rate of interest. In exchange, the brokers were licensed and the rates they charged were regulated by law. The annual rates of interest under the statute ran at 20 per cent for loans under 42s and 15 per cent on higher sums; but given that pledges would be redeemed and repledged within the year, often on a weekly basis, the amount which the borrower paid for credit was often very much higher, for the interest would be paid afresh every week, along with fees for issuing the ticket given to the pawnor. Pawnbrokers were subject to further regulations: their premises could be searched if they were suspected of receiving stolen property and they were required to give into custody any person suspected of dealing in stolen goods. In addition to these regulations, the Act also regulated the opening times of the brokers' shops and provided penalties for infringements of the Act. Larger loans were not regulated by the statute. Until 1839, any loans on pledges above £10 were subject to the usury laws.[99] From then on, there was complete freedom of contract for the lucrative higher class of pledges.

The law setting the rates of interest for the small loans was notoriously complex. It regulated everything down to the payment of the last farthing.[100] According to the author of the main legal text on the topic, Francis Turner, an uneducated pledger could not read the regulations and make any sense of them.[101] This was an understatement: with a system which calculated rates of interest according to fractions and half months, even magistrates found themselves unclear as to whether a pawnbroker had overcharged. English pawnbrokers constantly claimed that they made no profit on small loans, since the interest they received did not cover their incidental charges. It was claimed that this sent business to unrespectable unlicensed brokers. They looked with envy to Ireland, where legislation dating from the late eighteenth century tabulated the interest which could be charged per sum lent, at higher rates than applied in England and without the complexity of fractional payments.[102]

Under the legislation, the pledger was allowed a week's grace from interest at the end of the month if he wished to redeem, and to pay only half the month's

[98] 39 & 40 Geo. III c. 99.

[99] 2 & 3 Vict. c. 37 exempted contracts for loans above £10 from the usury laws.

[100] The rate on loans up to 2s 6d was ½d per month, the rate increasing with the size of the loan up to £10: 39 & 40 Geo. III c. 99, s 2.

[101] 1870 Select Committee on Pawnbrokers, p. 139, q. 2938.

[102] 26 Geo. III c. 43, 28 Geo. III c. 49. Where the English rate for a loan of 2s was ½d, the Irish was 1d; where the English rate for 10s was 2d, the Irish charged 3d. See the table in J. O. Byrne, *Irish Pawnbroking Law* (Dublin, 1886), 8. For English attitudes, see Turner, *Contract of Pawn*, 17.

interest if he redeemed within two weeks. The Act also provided an elaborate system of book keeping. Pawns were to be entered into a book kept 'in a fair and regular manner', describing the goods pledged and the money given, and providing the name and address of the pledger, taking note of whether he was a lodger or householder.[103] The pawnbroker gave a ticket to the pledger with the same information, which carried a fee depending on the amount of money advanced.[104] When the ticket was returned, the pawnbroker had to note his profit on it, and retain the record for a year. If the ticket had been lost, the pledger could obtain a duplicate.[105]

After one year, any goods pledged which were worth less than 10s became the absolute property of the pawnbroker. If the goods were worth over 10s (and up to £10), they were to be sold at a public auction. Before this was done, the pledger was able to give notice to the pawnbroker not to sell the goods for a further three months, during which period of grace he was allowed to redeem them. The pawnbroker had to keep records of any sales, and if the auction raised more than the principal money and profit advanced on the pledge, he had to return the 'overplus' to the pledger. The pawnbroker was not himself allowed to buy the goods in his custody.

As bailees, pawnbrokers were liable for losses to the goods in their custody which arose from their negligence, which meant a failure to take such care as a man would take of his own goods. They could be sued at common law[106] or under section 24 of the 1800 Act, which allowed magistrates to award compensation where goods were lost through the fault of the pawnbroker.[107] Unsurprisingly, those who lost their goods preferred to use the cheaper summary method to obtain compensation than to sue at common law. Provided that he had not been careless, a pawnbroker was not liable if cloth he had stored for a long period was eaten by moths, or if goods deposited were stolen,[108] or if they were damaged by fire.[109] This could create problems. Since the pawnbroker only insured his own interest in the goods, if his shop was destroyed by fire, he was covered, but the

---

[103] The pawnbroker was not liable, however, if the pledger gave false information: see *Attenborough* v. *London* (1853) 8 Exch. 661, a case where a pawnbroker sued a borrower to make good the excess losses he suffered after selling the forfeited pledge. However, it was held in *Fergusson* v. *Norman* (1838) 5 Bing. N.C. 76 that a pawnbroker could not recover where he had only inserted a general location for the address.

[104] 39 & 40 Geo. III c. 99 s 6.   [105] 39 & 40 Geo. III, c. 99, s 16.

[106] *Coggs* v. *Bernard* (1703) 2 Ld. Raym. 909 at 911–12.

[107] *Shackell* v. *West* (1859) 2 El. & El 326. However, magistrates did not have the power under the Act to commit those who failed to pay the compensation: *Ex p Cording* (1832) 4 B. & Ad. 198.

[108] Turner, *Contract of Pawn*, 97–9.

[109] *Syred* v. *Carruthers* (1858) E. B. & E. 469.

uninsured owner of the goods would be uncompensated.[110] To redress this, and protect the poor pawnors, the Pawnbroking Act 1872, which replaced the 1800 Act, made the pawnbroker liable to pawnors if their goods were lost in a fire, and entitled him to insure for the loss.

Goods could be redeemed by presenting the pawnbroker with the ticket, issued on the deposit of the goods. Since section 15 of the 1800 Act provided that the goods had to be handed over to anyone who produced a valid ticket, the tickets could be traded. The system generated a number of risks for pawnbrokers. To begin with, there was the risk that the goods might have been pledged by someone who had no property in them, having either stolen them or obtained them fraudulently. In such cases, the true owner was able to recover the goods in trover, without tendering the ticket.[111] A pawnor with no title to the goods had no right to recover from the pawnbroker, despite his holding a ticket.[112] If the pawnor was apprehended on a criminal charge, the police would usually simply recover the stolen goods from the pawnbroker, leaving him to bear the loss.[113] A pawnbroker who was complicit in receiving stolen goods was himself liable to prosecution. Although liable in trover to the original owner, a pawnbroker who innocently sold goods in which the pawnor had no property was protected from actions by the purchaser. For mid-nineteenth-century judges, aware of the need to give some protection to pawnbrokers, held that in such a sale the pawnbroker only warranted such title as he had.[114]

Pawnbrokers also faced problems when there were rival ticket holders claiming the goods. The original holder of the ticket often lost it. With this in mind, section 16 of the 1800 Act gave him the power to obtain a copy of the original ticket and a declaration of his title to them from the pawnbroker, which then had to be authenticated by a magistrate. This gave the holder the right to redeem the goods.[115] Meanwhile, another person might have obtained the original. An

---

[110] 1870 Select Committee on Pawnbrokers, p. 187, q. 3944 (evidence of Francis Turner).

[111] *Packer* v. *Gillies* (1806) 2 Camp. 336; *Peet* v. *Baxter* (1816) 1 Stark. 472; *Singer Manufacturing Co* v. *Clark* (1879) 5 Exch. D. 37. See also Martin B.'s comments in *Cheesman* v. *Exall* (1851) 6 Exch. 341 at 343. In *Parker* v. *Patrick* (1793) 5 T.R. 175, the King's Bench held that a pawnbroker who had received goods obtained by the pawnor by fraud could recover them: but later courts held that no property passed in such cases of fraud. For the rules on fraud, see pp. 457–8; for trover, see pp. 1114–22.

[112] See counsel's comments in *Crawshay* v. *Thornton* (1836–7) 2 Myl. and Cr. 1 at 11. In *Cheesman* v. *Exall* (1851) 6 Exch. 341 at 343, Martin B. said, 'It may be, that a person with whom property is pledged may contract absolutely, and at all events, to deliver back the property to the pledgor; in which case I agree that the former would be answerable in damages for the breach of such a contract, though the damages might be nominal only'.

[113] e.g. *R* v. *Trebilcock* (1858) Dearsly and Bell 453.

[114] *Morley* v. *Attenborough* (1849) 3 Exch. 500; *Eicholz* v. *Bannister* (1864) 17 C.B. N.S. 708 at 722.

[115] Those who stole such duplicates could therefore be prosecuted for larceny: *R* v. *Morrison* (1859) Bell 158.

indemnity given in section 16 provided some protection to pawnbrokers who refused to hand over goods to their real owners, doubting their right to them. In *Vaughan* v. *Watt* in 1840, where goods were claimed by the true owner in possession of the original ticket, after a duplicate had been issued, the Exchequer overturned Rolfe B.'s holding that the pawnbroker's refusal to return the goods itself amounted to a conversion. According to its view of the law, under the legislation the pawnbroker had to be given a reasonable time to satisfy himself that the claimant was *bona fide*, by finding out whether the magistrate had given his authentication.[116] In 1873, in *Burslem* v. *Attenborough*, the Common Pleas similarly held that the true owner who had obtained a duplicate could maintain an action for conversion against the pawnbroker only if the latter had received notice through the authenticated declaration that the holder of the original ticket was not the true owner. For, as Keating J. ruled, '[t]he legislature could not have intended to place the pawnbroker in the difficulty of not knowing what had been done with respect to the declaration and yet being liable to be affected by it'.[117]

There were some doubts over whether the pawnbroker was protected by the statutory indemnity if a false declaration had been made and another party in fact had a right to the goods. This problem was likely to arise, since magistrates, who were supposed to take care to establish that the property was that of the claimant, often simply signed the document without seeing the applicant.[118] Opinion was divided over the pawnbroker's liability. On the one hand, it was argued that section 16 gave a complete indemnity where goods were returned on the duplicate ticket.[119] On the other hand, it was argued the position of the pawnbroker was analogous to that of a banker who paid a forged cheque. Addressing this question, Francis Turner argued in 1866 that the law was best understood as giving an indemnity to the pawnbroker who gave the goods either to the holder of the ticket or to the holder of the duplicate, whenever he had no notice that the goods had been fraudulently obtained or had not been instructed by the true owner not to hand them over. In his view, '[t]he pawnor's liability to lose his property by a wrongful declaration is as much an incident of his contract, as the liability to lose

---

[116] *Vaughan* v. *Watt* (1840) 6 M. & W. 492.

[117] *Burslem* v. *Attenborough* (1873) LR 8 CP 122 at 127.

[118] In F. Turner's view, the legislation of 1800 was ambiguous, seeming to suggest that the magistrate was in any event duty bound to authenticate the declaration: 1870 Select Committee on Pawnbrokers, p. 141, q. 2988. Sir Thomas Henry, the chief magistrate of the metropolitan police courts, said that each court had up to 50 applications per day in respect of lost ticket, very few of which were fraudulent: p. 171, q. 3629.

[119] See *Mack* v. *Walter* in *Pawnbrokers Gazette*, 19 June 1865, discussed in Turner, *Contract of Pawn*, 128.

it by losing it or being robbed of the duplicate'.[120] The matter was clarified and settled by the 1872 Act.[121]

The complicated system rooted in the 1800 Act proved troublesome for the pawnbroking interest, which lobbied hard in the middle of the nineteenth century for its reform. They complained that a regime which allowed a pawnbroker to be fined whenever his shop assistant omitted to record whether a pledger was a lodger, or charged a farthing too much, was too harsh. A repeated objection to it was that it encouraged professional informers to entrap brokers into a technical overcharging of interest, and to prosecute them for it.[122] A pawnbroker could be fined up to £10 for any infraction of the Act, half of which was given to the informer. To address this problem, legislation in 1839 empowered London magistrates not to award any fee to the informer,[123] and similar provisions were extended to other towns. But it was only in 1859 that it was extended nationally, which made such informing unprofitable.[124]

The pawnbroking lobby was also keen to reform the complicated system of the rates of interest charged. By 1854, when the usury laws were finally repealed, pawnbrokers were in an anomalous position. For nearly a century, their exemption from these laws had been regarded as a privilege, which justified their regulation. With the ending of the prohibition on usury, many pawnbrokers argued that they should be free to set their own rates. William Neilson Hancock, the Irish lawyer, economist and government adviser, took a determinately laissez-faire view.[125] He argued 'that when the trade in money was set free the pawnbrokers ought to have been set free'.[126] Ever confident of the merits of competition, Hancock (who wrote a report in 1868 for the Irish government on the subject) told a select committee on pawnbroking in 1870 that poor people would benefit from freedom of contract.[127] He felt that there should be implied contractual terms regarding both the rate of interest and the time to redeem pledges, but that the parties should be free to vary them.

---

[120] Turner, *Contract of Pawn*, 125–6.

[121] A person obtaining a declaration made before a justice had to present it within three days to the pawnbroker, who would be indemnified if he handed over the goods, provided he had no notice, actual or constructive, of its being false: Pawnbrokers Act, 35 & 35 Vict. c. 93, s 29.

[122] One informer, Charles O'Callaghan, who had been dismissed from the police in 1840, made a living by employing a woman to pledge goods for him with various pawnbrokers, allowing him to prosecute them for alleged overcharging of interest: Hardaker, *History*, 51.

[123] 2 & 3 Vict. c. 71, s 34.

[124] 22 & 23 Vict. c. 14.

[125] For Hancock, see J. F. McEldowney, 'William Neilson Hancock (1820–1888)' (1985) 20 *Irish Jurist* 378–402.

[126] 1870 Select Committee on Pawnbrokers, p. 103, q. 2235.

[127] *Ibid.*, p. 104, q. 2240.

Hancock's arguments provided a focus for discussion among English pawn-brokers, but there was no consensus among them in favour of freedom of contract. Some were keenly in favour of it, arguing that it was unfair that pawn-broking should be the only commercial activity whose profits were capped.[128] It was also argued that allowing pawnbrokers to charge higher rates for smaller loans would benefit the poor borrower as much as the lender. Evidence was given to the 1870 select committee that it was not cost-effective for pawnbrokers to take on pledge large goods of low value (such as furniture), since the cost of storing them was disproportionately high.[129] Poor people unable to pawn their furni-ture were therefore (it was argued) driven to sell it to dealers, who drove much harder bargains.[130] It was also argued that the rules which required the pawnbro-ker to retain goods for up to 15 months was a deterrent to good business practice. J. F. May of the Manchester and Salford Pawnbrokers Association argued that he should be able to accept as a pledge entirely perishable commodities, such as a bag of mussels which could be pledged in the morning and redeemed by the end of the day.[131] He made a common comparison in drawing attention to the fact that a railway passenger was perfectly free to leave luggage at the station on the terms he pleased: if the passenger could, why not the pledger? For such traders, there was no need to protect the working class. When it came to dealing with creditors, it was argued, they were quite capable of looking after themselves.[132]

At the same time, many pawnbrokers felt that their profession would be damaged by freedom of contract. Where advocates of free trade endorsed the principle of competition, its opponents urged that competition would take the form of unscrupulous and hitherto unlicensed pawnbrokers—the Dolly Shops, which respectable pawnbrokers had long searched to eradicate.[133] If many respect-able pawnbrokers were wary of free trade, those outside the profession were even more solicitous of the needs of the poor. As the magistrate Sir Thomas Henry put it, if freedom of contract were allowed, 'the pawnbroker would take advantage of the necessities of the poor people and charge an exorbitant rate of interest'.[134] Given these divisions on the principle of freedom of contract, the Pawnbrokers' Reform Association settled on a compromise reflecting Hancock's views: legisla-tion should be passed which would set a rate of interest to be implied in all con-tracts of pawn, unless modified by a special contract.

---

[128] See Hardaker, *History*, 126 *et seq.*
[129] 1870 Select Committee on Pawnbrokers, p. 32, q. 706 (evidence of George Attenborough).
[130] *Ibid.*, p. 188, q. 3956.   [131] *Ibid.*, p. 44, q. 927.
[132] *Ibid.*, p. 32, q. 708 (evidence of George Attenborough).
[133] *Ibid.*, p. 157, q. 3311 (evidence of Robert Attenborough).
[134] *Ibid.*, p. 169, q. 3579 (evidence of Sir Thomas Henry).

Reporting in 1871, the select committee recommended that restraints on pawn-broking should be kept within 'the narrowest limits' possible. It acknowledged that some statutory control was necessary, to protect needy people, and those with 'reckless and improvident habits' who might borrow money on pledges with-out understanding the conditions. It therefore proposed to maintain a system whereby rates were fixed by law, albeit one which was simpler than the one being replaced. But it also sought to draw a line 'at which free contract should take the place of statutory regulation'. In its view, wherever a loan was for a sum over £2, its terms should be left to the parties. However, since people had been used to a system of regulation, it recommended that where no special contract was made, the terms which applied to loans under £2 should be implied into the contract of pawn.[135] This recommendation was implemented by the Pawnbrokers Act 1872,[136] which also simplified the rates charged, charging ½d per shilling interest.

The Act also reformed the law relating to the redeeming of pledges. When this question was investigated, pawnbrokers rejected the widely held view that they profited from selling forfeited pledges, claiming that their profits came from customers who regularly redeemed their goods, rather than leaving them to be sold off.[137] Accepting the arguments of the pawnbroking lobby, which disliked the inconvenience of having to keep possession of pawned stock, the select commit-tee recommended reducing the time required for redeeming pledges (from one year to six months). It also proposed allowing the pawnor only one week's grace to redeem the goods at the expiry of this period, rather than the three months allowed under the old law. But the Act which passed did not give the pawnbrokers everything they wanted on this matter. Although it reduced the period of grace to seven days, it maintained the one-year period of redemption. However, the Act did address another grievance of the pawnbroker who sold unredeemed goods. Under the old law, while they were liable to pay back any surplus on any sales of individual items, they were unable to set-off any losses made on sales of other goods pledged by the pawnor. The 1872 Act altered the rule, giving pawnbrokers the power to set off losses.[138]

---

[135] Report from the Select Committee on Pawnbrokers; with the proceedings of the Committee, *PP* 1871 (419), xi, 377, at p. v.

[136] 35 & 36 Vict. c. 93, s 24. An attempt during the passage of the bill to ban all pledges under 2s was stoutly resisted by the Pawnbrokers Protection Association, which retorted that pawning sup-plied the finance needs of families: *Pawnbrokers Gazette*, 15 July 1872, p. 244; P. Johnson, *Saving and Spending: The Working Class Economy in Britain, 1870–1939* (Oxford, 1985), 167.

[137] George Attenborough told the 1871 committee that 95% of goods were redeemed at his shops, and that he did not make any profit on the 5% sold off. Pawnbrokers also drew attention to the prac-tice of 'duffing', where fake items were pawned for high sums and left unredeemed, causing them loss. 1870 Select Committee on Pawnbrokers, p. 32, qq. 696–9.

[138] Section 22.

The pawnbroking lobby had another success in this era. Throughout the nineteenth century, they were suspected of acting as outlets for stolen property, and in 1869 a Habitual Criminals bill was introduced, including three sections aimed at pawnbrokers. Under these sections, a pawnbroker who kept goods which were stolen was deemed to have knowledge of the theft and liable to be convicted as a receiver of stolen goods if he had been given information about the theft. The pawnbroking interest reacted swiftly to this threat, and lobbied the Home Office for the clauses to be dropped. They argued that rather than being receivers of stolen property, pawnbrokers were often instrumental in detecting theft. They claimed that there were 28 million pledges in London alone in 1866, and that they could positively account for the ownership of the goods in 99 per cent of cases. They also resented the proposal that their premises could be searched by ordinary police officers, which would put many clients off depositing their goods.[139] Finally, a profession with over 3000 licensed members resented the slur of being included in a Habitual Criminals Bill. Under strong pressure from the lobby, Lord Kimberley dropped the clauses. Although there remained much suspicion that pawnbrokers' shops received stolen goods,[140] the 1870 select committee did not recommend any toughening of the law.[141]

The reform of 1872 thus put the law of pawnbroking on a new foundation. For the most part, the legislation addressed the concerns of the brokers rather than their clients and the wider public. Pawnbroking remained regulated, with concern being shown to limit the freedom of contract available. If this looked to protect the poor, it was an artificial form of protection, since the real cost of loans to the poor on pledge remained extremely high. In practice, regulation remained a way of attempting to keep the unrespectable, unlicensed traders at bay.

4. MONEY LENDERS

Besides borrowing on the security of their property given to pawnbrokers, the needy were also able to borrow from money lenders without giving away their possessions. Money lenders were prepared to give loans to the poor either on the security of a promissory note, or else on a bill of sale, which transferred the property in the borrower's chattels to the lender, but allowed him to retain possession.

---

[139] See Lord Lyveden's speech in *PD* 1869 (s3) 194: 1344.

[140] Evidence of Sir Thomas Henry, 1870 Select Committee on Pawnbrokers, pp. 169–70, qq. 3593 *et seq.*

[141] The Act extended the discretion given by the Metropolitan Police Act 2 & 3 Vict. c. 71 to the police magistrate to award payment to the pawnbroker of the sum advanced by him: 35 & 36 Vict. c. 93, s 34.

The rise of money lending was linked to the repeal of the usury laws in 1854. Since money was now treated as a commodity which was allowed to find its own price in the market, it was now possible to lend money to rich and poor at any rate of interest. The repeal of the usury laws saw the triumph of the notion of freedom of contract when it came to money. It was a freedom, however, that not all approved of. J. B. Byles, writing in 1845, warned against removing the protection given to the poor borrower by controlled rates of interest, saying that the poor man was not in a position to bargain equally.[142]

The reforms of 1854 did nothing to protect the poor borrower. Legislation was passed in that year requiring the registration of bills of sale, but this statute was designed to protect creditors of bankrupts who were liable to be defrauded, rather than protecting borrowers. Although the Act required bills of sale to be registered within 21 days of being made in order to make them valid as against assignees in bankruptcy, their non-registration did not invalidate them as between the parties.[143] According to the Bristol money lender, Abraham Collins, who dealt mainly with farmers, much business was done before 1878 with unregistered bills of sale. Indeed, many customers refused to register bills of sale, wishing to avoid the extra cost as well as the stigma—and possible ruin—of being listed in a trade gazette as having such a debt.[144] Many money lenders also preferred not to register, since the publicity would encourage rival lenders to contact the client. Lenders protected themselves by seizing the goods before an act of bankruptcy had been committed, and by notifying county court bailiffs of the bill of sale to forestall any distress on goods comprised in it. In any event, money lenders were often not much bothered about legal niceties. Henry Buer told a select committee in 1882 that when a group of farmers came to claim livestock which had been pledged to him by another farmer, 'I and my men armed ourselves with a stick, and I said "Now you take your pigs and it is all up with you"'. In the end, they 'were glad to get rid of me, by giving me the money'.[145]

In 1878, legislation was passed which paved the way for much more widespread registration of bills of sale. The Bills of Sale Act was the fruit of an initiative by the Associated Chambers of Commerce, which wanted to prevent fraudulent lending by means of unregistered bills of sale.[146] Under the Act, bills

---

[142] J. B. Byles, *Observations on the Usury Laws* (1845), 31.

[143] See pp. 813–16. Since the Act did not dislodge the doctrine of reputed ownership, many lenders did not bother to register them.

[144] Report from the Select Committee on Bills of Sale Act (1878) Amendment Bill (Henceforth cited as 1881 Bills of Sale Committee), PP 1881 (341), viii, 1, at p. 21, q. 513.

[145] 1881 Bills of Sale Committee, p. 12, q. 251. See his evidence in general: pp. 8–18.

[146] See letter of S. S. Lloyd, *The Times*, 18 March 1882, col. 5b.

of sale were to be attested to and explained to the grantor by a solicitor, and registered within seven days.[147] In fact, the Act protected the lender more than the borrower. First, it removed the doctrine of reputed ownership.[148] Secondly, many considered that the attestation and explanation given by the solicitor protected the grantee against the grantor disputing the bill. As a result, Buer explained, '[w]e look upon a bill of sale attested and registered as like a judgment in the county court, there is no upsetting it'.[149] Nonetheless, failure to register a bill did not render it void: such bills remained valid as between grantor and grantee.[150] It was widely believed that the effect of the Act was not to increase the number of bills given, but only to increase the number registered,[151] as lenders sought to gain the benefit of the protection it offered. The increase was striking: the total number of bills registered grew from 11,844 in 1875 to 55,513 in 1880; while the number for sums under £10 grew from 36 in 1875 to 8872 in 1880.[152]

The flood of registrations drew judicial attention to the harsh use of such bills, which were often drawn in such a way as to allow seizure for any act which might prejudice the security.[153] Although many of these could be set aside, most debtors did not have the means to challenge them.[154] Many began to call for reform to protect the poor who used them. For instance, the county court judge James Motteram wanted the interest which could be charged on bills of sale to be limited. Faced with the questionable use of bills of sale by money-lenders, the Chambers of Commerce supported the idea of limiting the use of bills to transactions over £100, and to have a standard form which would protect the borrower.[155] In 1881, a bill was presented to Parliament on behalf of the Associated Chambers of Commerce, to provide that each bill of sale should specify the chattels covered (so that future acquired assets could not be included); to render wholly invalid an unregistered bill of sale; and to forbid bills of sale under £50, which by 1880 comprised the majority in number of

[147] 41 & 42 Vict. c. 31, s 10. Under the Act, the consideration for the bill had to be stated on it. The bill was to be filed with a registrar (a Master of the Supreme Court), as warrants of attorney were under 3 Geo. IV c. 39 and 6 & 7 Vict. C. 36. Registration had to be renewed every five years.

[148] Section 20 stated that chattels in a registered bill were not to be deemed to be in the possession, order, or disposition of the grantor.

[149] 1881 Bills of Sale Committee, p. 13, q. 292, p. 10, q. 225,.

[150] *Davies* v. *Goodman* (1880) 5 CPD 128 which held that the failure to have the bill explained to the grantor and be attested by a solicitor did not render it void as between grantor and grantee.

[151] 1881 Bills of Sale Committee, p.21, qq. 502–13 (evidence of Abraham Collins).

[152] Return of Number of Bills of Sale 1881: PP 1882 (319), lxiv, 1.

[153] 1881 Bills of Sale Committee, pp. 2–3, qq. 22–5 (evidence of Charles Ford).

[154] *Ibid.*, pp. 63–5, qq. 1567–82 (evidence of James Motteram).

[155] *Ibid.*, p. 61, qq. 1511–26 (evidence of James Hole).

such bills.[156] This was a direct attack on the use of these instruments by money lenders.[157]

The bill was referred to a select committee, which heard evidence from money lenders which was described as more sensational than anything to be found in Dickens.[158] The committee considered whether to abolish bills of sale altogether, but came to the conclusion that since money could be raised on the security of real property, it was only right to allow money also to be raised on personal property. However, it wanted strict controls to prevent fraud.[159] When the bill was reintroduced in 1882, it obtained the support of Sir Henry James AG, who felt that the poor should seek their credit from pawnbrokers rather than money lenders, who were sure to seize 'on some small pretence, and for a much larger sum than was really due'.[160] The 1882 Act sought to protect the poor borrower, while permitting bills of sale to continue to be used commercially. Bills of sale under £30 were rendered void. Unregistered bills of sale were also rendered void, even between the parties.[161] The Act restored the rule as to reputed ownership where the bill of sale was given by way of security,[162] and restricted credit being obtained on future goods. The bill had to include a schedule of the chattels secured, specifically described, which had to be the property of the grantor at the time of the bill of sale.[163] To prevent contracts being drawn which would enable lenders to seize goods at very short notice for very minor breaches, the legislation specified the conditions permitting a seizure of the goods. A five-day period was given for the grantor to apply to the High Court to restrain the seizure. The resulting regime was complex, since it amended but did not entirely replace the 1878 Act.

By the 1890s, there was renewed concern at the activities of money lenders. It was evident that, despite the 1882 Act, money lenders continued to use bills of sale. They managed to evade the £30 limit and to extract extortionate rates of interest.[164] If someone wanted to borrow £10, he would give the money lender a bill of sale for £30; £20 of this sum would immediately be returned, which was a

---

[156] In 1880, 38,177 out of 55,513 bills of sale were for such small sums: *The Times*,16 March 1882, col. 9f.

[157] *The Times*, 9 March 1882, col. 9a.   [158] *PD* 1882 (s3) 267: 395.

[159] *Ibid.*, 398 (8 March 1882) (Simon Sjt).

[160] *Ibid.*, 1401–2 (20 March 1882).

[161] Indeed, if any provision of the Act were not complied with, the entire bill would be void, though the lender could recover in an action for money had and received. *Davies* v. *Rees* (1886) 17 QBD 408 held that such a bill was not merely void as regarded the personal chattels comprised in it, but that a covenant for repayment contained in it was also avoided.

[162] See *Swift* v. *Pannell* (1883) 24 Ch D 210; *Heseltine* v. *Simmons* (1892) 2 QB 547 at 552.

[163] With the exception of growing crops and trade machinery and fixtures: 45 & 46 Vịct. c. 43, ss 5–6.

[164] Eighth Report by the Board of Trade under section 131 of the Bankruptcy Act 1883, *PP* 1890–1 [C. 6462], lxxvii, 1, at p. 10.

condition of the loan. Meanwhile the money lender would charge £1 10s as a fee for his expenses, so that for a secured £30 debt, the borrower would receive £8 10s.[165] Borrowers were also deceived into giving bills, by being told they were signing an insurance form or a receipt for goods.[166] Since an amendment of the Bills of Sale Act removed the need for the person attesting to be a solicitor, many such bills were attested by the lender's clerk, which removed all protection. Though bearing an appearance of legality, many of these devices were plainly unlawful. However, as Thomas Farrow pointed out, 'people are too ignorant to appreciate it [...] and if it is found out by them they are too poor to prosecute, or they are afraid of exposure'.[167]

If the use of bills of sale was popular among money lenders, they more frequently made use of promissory notes, which could not be impeached. These lacked the security of a valid bill of sale—since the lender trusted to the creditworthiness of the giver—but large profits could be made on them. Borrowers often assumed that the quoted interest rate was an annual one, only to find that it was in fact monthly. This meant that instead of diminishing as the borrower repaid what he thought was due, the debt in fact grew. Failure to pay punctually might also permit the lender to charge a default rate interest on the whole sum due.[168] As a result, the sums which money lenders extracted could vastly exceed the money lent. For instance, John Kirkwood lent one man £20 in exchange for a promissory note for £36 15s. The borrower failed in a payment, incurring default interest, and subsequently borrowed another £40, but again made a default in his payments. Having repaid £58 15s of the £60 lent, the borrower found himself owing £689, for which Kirkwood sued him.[169] The borrower's predicament of having to find more money at the end of the loan period, to repay the loan, was shared by many. Numerous money lenders— including Henry Trowbridge Pockett and Isaac Gordon—took advantage of this by using a variety of aliases, which allowed them to give new loans in one name to permit their debtors to pay off loans contracted in another name, but at a higher rate of interest.[170]

Such practices were exposed in the 1890s, when a campaign against money lenders was started by R. A. Yerburgh MP and Thomas Farrow, who were both

[165] Report from the Select Committee on Money Lending (henceforth cited as 1897 Money Lending Committee Evidence), *PP* 1897 (364), xi, 405, pp. 8, 26, qq. 91, 320.

[166] 1897 Money Lending Committee Evidence, p. 8, q. 84.

[167] *Ibid.*, p. 8, q. 88.   [168] T. Farrow, *Money Lender Unmasked* (1895), 34.

[169] 1897 Money Lending Committee Evidence, p. 11, qq. 111 *et seq.* (Farrow); p. 202, qq. 4381 *et seq.* (Kirkwood). Kirkwood traded under the name of the Provincial Union Bank, a limited company, whose shareholders included only members of his own family (p. 192, q. 4056).

[170] Gordon also operated in Scotland: see e.g. *Kerr* v. *Kerr and Another* (1896) 4 SLT 158.

advocates of cooperative credit arrangements for the working classes.[171] In a series
of publications,[172] Farrow revealed the techniques by which lenders entrapped
the poor and named the worst culprits. One of the money lenders exposed—
Lewis Simmons—brought a defamation action against *The Truth* (where Farrow
published his exposé) but won only a farthing in damages.[173] In the meantime,
Farrow and Yerburgh initiated prosecutions against the money lenders.[174]
Although it was difficult to get cases against such men, since there had to be sufficient evidence of systematic practice to show a criminal intent, they had some
success. Pockett was prosecuted in 1895 for obtaining money under false pretences, when extracting preliminary fees from potential clients he had no intention of lending money to.[175] He was sentenced to six months' imprisonment with
hard labour and a £500 fine, but managed to resume trading as a money lender
when he got out of prison.[176] Isaac Gordon was also imprisoned for obtaining
money by false pretences, after giving a borrower only £60 in return for a promissory note for £100.[177] Gordon was sentenced to 18 months' imprisonment, but
was released after eight months because of his ill health.[178] He also resumed his
career.

Bad practices by money lenders could also result in their failure to recover in
civil courts. For instance, in *Gordon* v. *Street* in 1899, a borrower successfully
rescinded a contract of loan with Gordon on the grounds that he had misrepre-
sented his identity, after using multiple identities in money lending.[179] But lenders
were as often able to make the law serve their own ends. Thus, Simmons obtained
a judgment in the House of Lords in 1892 which confirmed that a bill of sale
which described the grantee as the Discount Bank of London, and only once

[171] Yerburgh, who was president of the Urban Co-operative Banks Association and chairman
of the Agricultural Banks Association, advocated the Raiffeisen system which had developed in
Germany: *The Times*, 20 May 1896, col. 12f.

[172] He wrote extensively in the *Pall Mall Gazette*, *The Councillor* (the organ of the Agricultural
Bank Association), and *The Truth*, as well as being the author of *The Money Lender Unmasked*.

[173] 1897 Money Lending Committee Evidence, p. 198, q. 4268.

[174] Thomas Farrow was disappointed in the Money Lenders Act of 1900, and in 1904 set up a bank
to give cheap credit to the poor. It made losses, however, and ceased trading in 1920. The following
year, he was sentenced to four years' penal servitude for having made false accounts: *The Times*, 30
August 1934, col. 14d.

[175] *The Times*, 7 November 1895, col. 14b. The ruse of 'fee snatching' entailed asking potential
borrowers to send small sums (often repeatedly) to the lender purportedly to cover the cost of investigating the borrower's creditworthiness, and ultimately to refuse the loan.

[176] 1897 Money Lending Committee Evidence, p. 6, q. 62 (Farrow), p. 156, qq. 3432 *et seq.* (Cuffe).

[177] Gordon was convicted by a jury after the judge ruled that he would be guilty if they felt he
had obtained the promissory note from him by falsely promising to pay £100. *The Queen* v. *Gordon*
(1889) 23 QBD 35.

[178] *The Times*, 9 July 1897, col. 13e.

[179] *Gordon* v. *Street* [1899] 2 QB 641.

mentioned Simmons as its sole proprietor, was valid. 'I do not care whether the person who is intended to enforce his rights under it is a money lender or not', Lord Halsbury ruled, 'I do not care whether the person who is borrowing is an ignorant person or not.'[180] The decision was a good one for money lenders who masked their trade with the names of banks.

Money lenders also made profitable use of court procedure, by 'snapping judgments'. When an instalment on a promissory note was in arrear, the lender would obtain a writ from the High Court. He would at the same time tell the borrower that there was no need to enter an appearance, and that nothing would happen if the next instalment were paid. Meanwhile, a judgment would be signed against the ignorant borrower, and since the writ had come from the High Court (rather than the county court), the borrower would know nothing of the judgment.[181] Kirkwood claimed that the device was only used to get around section 23 of the Bankruptcy Act 1890, which restricted the interest paid on debts to 5 per cent until all other creditors had been paid.[182] But Farrow felt the device was designed to obtain a conclusive hold over the borrower, akin to that given by warrants of attorney.

Money lenders also benefited from the Bills of Exchange Act, which stated that in actions on bills, notes, and cheques, a defendant would not have leave to appear, unless he filed an affidavit asserting that he had a defence on the merits.[183] Since in many cases, there was no defence on the merits—for the default in payment had resulted from other matters such as illness—the debtor was bound.[184] Another legal device resorted to was the use of the Scottish law of summary diligence. If bills were dated from Scotland, proceedings could be taken in that country, with an execution on goods being levied by an English sheriff before the debtor—who may never have visited Scotland—even knew of the case against him.[185] Faced with debtors with no substantive defence, there was little scope for county court judges to offer them protection. The main device in the hands of

---

[180] *Simmons* v. *Woodward* [1892] AC 101 at 106. See also *Heseltine v. Simmons* [1892] 2 QB 547, where the Court of Appeal held that a covenant to repay a loan secured by a bill of sale was not defeated by the fact that the consideration of the bill was falsely stated, although that vitiated the security of the chattels included in it.

[181] Farrow, *Money Lender Unmasked*, 66.

[182] 1897 Money Lending Committee Evidence, pp. 232–3, q. 4895. Other methods used by money-lenders to avoid the Act was to state that all payments made by the borrower would comprise only interest, and not pay off the principal.

[183] In *Kirkwood* v. *Smith and Another* [1896] 1 QB 582 the Queen's Bench Division took a restrictive view of what constituted a promissory note under the Act; but its decision was later overruled in *Kirkwood* v. *Carroll and Another* [1903] 1 KB 531: both cases involved John Kirkwood, and both used the same phrase in the note.

[184] 1897 Money Lending Committee Evidence, p.13, q. 144 (evidence of Farrow).

[185] See *ibid.*, p. 136, qq. 2784 *et seq.*, for Isaac Gordon's use of the procedure.

these judges was to use their power to order instalment payments in an equitable way. For instance, when called on to enforce one £90 debt, Judge Owen ordered repayments at the rate of a shilling a month, and joked to the defendant, 'I hope you will live until you pay it'.[186]

Yerburgh and Farrow's exposures led to the appointment of a parliamentary select committee in 1897 which aimed to reform the law. A number of witnesses before it argued in favour of applying equity's approach to unconscionable bargains to such loans of money.[187] The idea was not new. Since the 1860s, some Chancery judges had tried to expand the doctrine of undue influence which had long been applied to expectant heirs. In 1866, in *Barrett* v. *Hartley*, Sir John Stuart observed that the abolition of the usury laws brought 'into operation, to a greater extent than formerly [...] that principle of the Court which prevented any oppressive bargain, or any advantage exacted from a man under grievous necessity and want of money, from prevailing against him'.[188] In his view, if assent to an agreement was not given by parties on an equal footing, 'perfectly free from any influence or pressure', it would be vitiated. A number of equity judges followed this approach to ensure fairer contracts between money lenders and their clients.[189] Moreover, in 1888, *Fry* v. *Lane* confirmed a line of cases which suggested that the court would set aside purchases at considerable undervalue from a poor and ignorant vendor, acting in the absence of independent advice.[190] If such cases seemed to promise an expansion of equitable doctrine to ensure contractual fairness and qualify the principle of freedom of contract,[191] county court judges remained hamstrung by their lack of equitable powers. While they could make equitable adjustments while handling bankruptcy matters,[192] under the County Courts Act 1888 they could only set aside deeds where there had

---

[186] *Ibid.*, p.211, q. 4508. At the rate ordered, it would take 150 years to repay the loan.

[187] The equitable doctrine was set out by H. H. L. Bellot and R. J. Willis in *The Law Relating to Unconscionable Bargains with Money-lenders* (1897). It was published in an expanded second edition: H. H. L. Bellot, *The Legal Principles and Practice of Bargains with Money Lenders* (1906).

[188] *Barrett* v. *Hartley* (1866) LR 2 Eq 789 at 794–5.

[189] See *Helsham* v. *Barnett* (1873) 21 WR 309, where Malins VC stated that 10% interest was a reasonable rate, and ruled that he would not allow money lenders 'to entrap persons by offers of easy terms and then charge exorbitant ones'; *Neville* v. *Snelling* (1880) 15 Ch D 679; *Howley* v. *Cook* (1873) Ir R 8 Eq 570 at 589.

[190] *Fry* v. *Lane* (1888) 40 Ch D 312: the precedent cases were ones where the same solicitor had acted for both sides: *Longmate* v. *Ledger* (1860) 2 Giff. 157; *Clark* v. *Malpas* (1862) 4 D. F. & J. 401; *Baker* v. *Monk* (1864) 4 D. J. & S. 388.

[191] The Scottish courts also took this 'equitable' approach (although the English doctrine of expectant heir did not apply there): see *Gordon* (*Gordon's Administrator*) v. *Stephen* (1902) 9 SLT 397.

[192] 1897 Money Lending Committee Evidence, p.204, qq.4407–9 (Judge Owen).

been fraud or mistake: their powers did not extend to matters of duress or undue influence.[193]

A number of judicial witnesses before the 1897 select committee therefore urged an expansion of these equitable powers, to allow the court to examine the entire history of a transaction, and to allow relief where lenders' terms were particularly punitive.[194] But not all were convinced by the proposal. Judge Collier observed that working people knew what they were doing when they went to a money lender, and he felt that passing such a law would result in endless litigation as every loan was challenged. In his view, if county court judges were given the discretion to set aside money lending contracts as unconscionable, there would be no reason not to allow them to interfere in all contracts.[195] Mathew J. worried that judges given such powers might come to different conclusions, which would undermine the certainty of the law. Judge Lumley Smith had a different concern. He pointed out that since judgments often went by default, judges would not be called on in most cases to consider the fairness of the transaction.[196] A rival proposal was therefore made that there should be a maximum rate of interest set by law.

In its recommendations, the select committee opted for giving judges an unfettered discretion. Cases involving money lenders 'should be open to complete judicial review', with judges awarding such rates of interest as seemed reasonable to them. It also wanted the minimum amount for which a bill of sale could be given to be raised to £50, and that it should no longer be possible to use warrants of attorney in connection with money lending. The committee recommended that money lenders be registered, and that it should be an offence for a money lender to use a misleading name, such as that of a bank. It also recommended that the Scottish summary diligence procedure should no longer be available, and that official receivers should be able to examine the whole history of a transaction, to prevent the evasion of section 23 of the Bankruptcy Act.[197]

The report was followed by the introduction of bills in Parliament in 1899 and 1900, to control money lenders. Although they ran into opposition from those who disliked any interference with freedom of contract,[198] the bills were supported by

---

[193] *Ibid.*, pp. 206 *et seq.* (qq. 4431ff), pp. 213 *et seq.* (qq. 4547ff) (Judge Owen), referring to s 67 of the 1888 County Courts Act. Judge Lumley Smith also felt that legislation was needed: p. 223, q. 4661.

[194] *Ibid.*, p. 223, q. 4664 (Lumley Smith); see also the evidence of Sir Henry Hawkins, pp. 41–2.

[195] Report from the Select Committee on Money Lending (henceforth cited as 1898 Money Lending Committee Report), PP 1898 (260), x, 101, p. 26, qq. 301–3.

[196] 1897 Money Lending Committee Evidence, p. 224, q. 4669 (Lumley Smith).

[197] 1898 Money Lending Committee Report, vi, x–xi.

[198] *PD* 1900 (s4) 84: 693 (Birrell) and 698 (Maclean).

many who felt that the principle was inappropriate where borrowers were poor.[199] The resulting Money Lenders Act 1900 abandoned the idea (included in the bill of 1899) that there should be a legislated maximum rate of interest, but gave courts the power to reopen any transaction with a money lender, where the rate of interest charged had been excessive or the transaction was 'harsh and unconscionable or is otherwise such that a court of equity would give relief'. In such cases, the court could relieve the borrower from paying more than a reasonable sum.[200] It was left to the judge, rather than a jury, to determine whether the bargain was unconscionable, a policy which reflected both the fear that juries would always find for the borrower and also the realization that juries were almost never used in debt cases in the county courts.[201] The Act also required money lenders to register and to use only their own name in trade.

As soon as the Act passed, judges began to disagree as to its ambit. In *Wilton & Co* v. *Osborne* (1901), a money lender repeatedly renewed a promissory note, increasing the debt, and charged default interest when an instalment was not paid. According to Ridley J., the rate of interest charged (160%) was harsh and unconscionable. But he held that statute only gave him power to relieve if a court of equity would, and he felt that such a court would not grant relief merely on the ground that the charges were excessive. In this case, where no coercion or oppression had been used which would vitiate the bargain on grounds of undue influence, the borrower had simply made an improvident bargain.[202] This tough-minded approach was also taken by Channell J. in the following year, in a case in which he rejected an interpretation of the Act which (in his opinion) would 'revolutionize the law' and 'give power to the judge to act according to his own fancy'.[203] However, in 1903, the Court of Appeal confirmed that a contract might be set aside under the Act merely for including an excessive rate of interest.[204] This view was confirmed in 1906 by the House of Lords which held that the policy of the Act was to allow the court to prevent oppression by looking behind the

---

[199] Bellot, *Legal Principles*, 85–6. The Bettings and Loans (Infants) Act 1892, 55 & 56 Vict. c. 4, s 2 made it a criminal offence to send a circular offering to lend money to an infant. If the circular inviting applications for a loan were sent to a place of education, including a university, the lender was presumed to know that the borrower was under age.

[200] 63 & 64 Vict. c. 51, s 1(1).

[201] For an affirmation of the point that the question was one for the judge and not the jury, see *Abraham* v. *Dimmock* 1914 WN 37.

[202] *Wilton & Co* v. *Osborne* [1901] 2 KB 110.

[203] *Barnett* v. *Coronna, The Times*, 16 June 1902, col. 5c.

[204] In *Poncione* v. *Higgins* (1904) 21 TLR 11 at 12; Cozens-Hardy LJ noted, 'it was possible that the interest might be deemed so extravagantly excessive as alone to satisfy the Court that the transaction was harsh and unconscionable'. See also his comments in *Wells* v. *Allott* [1904] 2 KB 848 (where the court held that the summary procedure under Order XIV could not be used where the rate of interest was excessive), and *In re a debtor* [1903] 1 KB 705.

contract to see if there was an abuse of power. For the Lords, excessive interest alone could be evidence of harshness and unconscionability.[205]

Judges had difficulty in determining what was such an excessive rate of interest, particularly where the loan was unsecured.[206] Since there was no normal rate of interest for unsecured loans, some judges felt there was no way of judging whether it was excessive.[207] Some judges sought to overcome this problem by considering the risk incurred by the lender.[208] However, this approach was criticized by those who felt that risk calculation was a commercial matter, and who felt that the court should focus on whether the borrower had been imposed upon.[209] A number of judges therefore took the view that a high rate of interest alone could not vitiate a contract, but that it could throw the onus on the lender to show that the transaction had been fair.[210] In practice, the crucial question was whether the court felt that undue advantage had been taken of the borrower.[211] Channell J., who continued to maintain that no court should impose its own view of reasonableness in the absence of evidence of ignorance or need,[212] accordingly refused to apply default clauses, whose real effect borrowers clearly did not appreciate.[213] Similarly, where the lender set out to tempt borrowers, the transaction could be set aside.[214]

The Act also required money lenders to register, and failure to do this constituted a criminal offence. In practice, the Commissioners of Inland Revenue failed to prosecute unregistered money lenders, and so (as Bellot put it in 1906), 'this

[205] *Samuel* v. *Newbold* [1906] AC 461.

[206] Where the loan was secured, it was not too difficult to determine a fair rate of interest. See *Part* v. *Bond* (1905) 21 TLR 553 at 554, where Joyce J. held, 'As to the rate of interest, […] if it were much above 10 per cent upon a reasonably safe security that would be excessive'. Channell J. in *Carrington Ltd* v. *Smith* [1905] 1 KB 79 sought to distinguish between secured and unsecured loans, seeing 10% as a fair rate for the former. This approach was approved of by J. B. Matthews, *The Law of Money-Lending Past and Present* (1906), 37 *et seq.*, but disapproved of by Bellot, *Legal Principles*, 148.

[207] Darling clearly endorsed a principle of freedom of contract, for he said the borrower here 'is apparently quite sane, and therefore it is a contract, like any other contract, by which he is bound, because he has chosen to enter into it'. *Samuel* v. *Miles* (1903), reported in Bellot, *Legal Principles*, 271; and Matthews, *Law of Money-Lending*, 130.

[208] *In re a debtor* [1903] 1 KB 705. See also *Saunders* v. *Newbold* [1905] 1 Ch 260 at 274 affirmed in [1906] AC 461.

[209] (1905) LQR 21, 103; cf. Bellot, *Legal Principles*, 152. In *Bonnard* v. *Dott* (1905) 21 TLR 491 at 494, Kekewich accepted Pollock's criticism.

[210] See *Poncione* v. *Higgins* (1904) 21 TLR 11 at 12.

[211] See e.g. *Bonnard* v. *Dott* (1905) 21 TLR 491 at 494.

[212] *Carrington's Ltd* v. *Smith* [1905] 1 KB 79 at 85–6.

[213] *Levene* v. *Greenwood* (1904) 20 TLR 389; cf. *Wells* v. *Joyce* [1905] 2 Ir Rep 134; *Carrington's Ltd* v. *Smith* [1906] 1 KB 79. Levene was prosecuted in 1913 for sending a circular offering a loan to a minor; *The Times*, 30 May 1913, col. 3d.

[214] See *King* v. *Osborne*, *The Times*, 22 May 1905, col. 3f, where the lender twice lent to an army officer, trusting that his father would pay the high rates of interest to save his son from exposure. See also *Samuel* v. *Bell*, *The Times*, 6 December 1905, col. 4a.

part of the Act has hitherto been largely inoperative'.[215] Money lenders remained confident that their clients would not prosecute them, as this would involve them in social embarrassment and exposure. The registration provisions did offer some protection to borrowers, for it was held in *Victorian Daylesford Syndicate Ltd* v. *Dodd* that a contract entered into with an unregistered money lender was illegal and could not be sued on.[216] Nonetheless, in 1910 the House of Lords proved to be less strict in its treatment of money lenders than the Court of Appeal, holding that where a money lender had registered in a name which was not his usual trading name, the contract would not be considered void, even though the money lender could be fined for a violation of the statute.[217] Borrowers were still liable to be misled by the names used by money lenders, and so in the following year legislation was passed which forbad money lenders from using names which implied that they carried on banking businesses.[218]

The Money Lenders Act was perceived as paternalistic legislation. The money lender remained an object of suspicion, but the practice remained widespread, from street loans given by women to each other to larger-scale commercial enterprises. The effect of the legislation on the market was unclear. In 1906, *The Times* suspected that, now that the money lender ran the additional risk that his transactions would be set aside by a judge, interest rates were increased to cover these losses.[219] Four years later, it considered the working of the Act to be haphazard, as different judges made their respective guesses over what was a fair rate of interest.[220] Nonetheless, this newspaper remained suspicious of money lenders, who on the eve of the First World War seemed as active and as solicitous of business as ever.[221]

5. HIRE PURCHASE

In the second half of the nineteenth century, an increasingly large number of consumers began to purchase goods through hire purchase agreements. Middle-class consumers used such agreements to buy expensive items such as pianos.[222]

---

[215] Bellot, *Legal Principles*, p. 157. However, he said the policy had been modified with the prosecution of Abraham Lazarus—though this prosecution was dropped when he was convicted of another offence.

[216] *Victorian Daylesford Syndicate Ltd* v. *Dodd* [1905] 2 Ch 624. This was affirmed in the Court of Appeal, and was followed in *Bonnard* v. *Dott* [1906] 1 Ch 740.

[217] In *Whiteman* v. *Sadler* [1910] AC 514. See also *Kirkwood* v. *Gadd* [1910] AC 422, overruling *Gadd* v. *Provincial Union Bank* [1909] 2 KB 353.

[218] Money Lenders Act 1911, 1 & 2 Geo. V c. 38.

[219] *The Times*, 20 July 1906, col. 9d.

[220] *The Times*, 1 March 1910, col. 11d.

[221] *The Times*, 2 December 1913, col. 9f.

[222] The Bishopsgate piano maker Henry Moore claimed to have invented the system (though for an earlier case of hire purchase see *Hickenbotham* v. *Groves* (1826) 2 C. & P. 492): R. M. Goode,

As the century went on, working-class consumers increasingly resorted to such credit arrangements. When in 1890 a Hire Traders Protection Association was set up, the largest number of its members dealt in sewing machines and furniture; by 1908, they also dealt in washing machines, bicycles, motor cars, musical instruments, and electrical goods.[223] By then, it was estimated that there were 2 million hire purchase agreements made annually, with 30 trades (and 40,000 traders) using the system. One of the most important, Singer, the sewing machine manufacturer, had 5000 people employed in sales at this time.[224] The Hire Purchase system enjoyed considerable expansion in the first decade of the twentieth century, though its more important growth would be in the interwar period.[225] Hire purchase was not merely used for consumer goods. In a number of trades, such as printing, it was common for plant and machinery to be hired in this manner.[226] A system of hire purchase existed even in the largest industries, such as the railways.[227]

Although there was some suspicion about the system of hire purchase, and numerous calls for either the regulation or even the prohibition of hire purchase,[228] there was to be no legislative control until the eve of the Second World War. In this context, the courts were happy to apply the principles of freedom of contract, upholding agreements even when the contract included clauses excluding warranties, and imposing heavy charges should the hirer not wish to proceed with the purchase.[229] Moreover, if the hirer failed to make the instalment payments as stipulated, the owner had the right to recover the goods. Thus, in 1884, the piano dealers Cramer & Co recovered a piano from a hirer who had paid £50 of the £60 to be paid in regular instalments, and had offered to pay the outstanding £10 for the piano, which had not been paid on time. The Court of Appeal held that the hirer was not entitled to the piano. As Fry LJ put it, 'The agreement was

---

Hire-Purchase Law and Practice (2nd edn, 1970), 2. For examples, see *Kirkman* v. *Keast, The Times*, 17 January 1862 col. 11f; *Cramer & Co (Ltd)* v. *Barre, The Times*, 20 November 1866, col. 11a; *Cramer and Others* v. *Aylen, The Times*, 7 May 1868, col. 11a; *Cramer and Others* v. *Amsler, The Times*, 7 May 1868, col. 11a; *Cramer & Co (Ltd)* v. *Mott, The Times*, 11 May 1869, col. 11b.

[223] Johnson, *Saving and Spending*, 156; 1908 Bankruptcy Committee, Evidence, p. 227 q. 5371 (evidence of Henry Edmund Tudor).

[224] 1908 Bankruptcy Committee, Evidence, p. 274, qq. 6570–7 (Samuel James Sewell). This was to claim there were 8 million agreements in force at any time. But contrast the lower figures in P. Scott, 'The Twilight World of Inter-War Hire Purchase' (2002) 177 *P & P* 196–225 at 197.

[225] Johnson shows that in 1921 there were 16 million hire purchase agreements, and 24 million in 1935: *Saving and Spending*, 157.

[226] *Ex p Hughes and Kimber (Ltd), Re Thackrah* (1888) 5 Morr. 235, *The Times*, 4 July 1888, col. 4a.

[227] See e.g. *Yorkshire Railway Wagon Co* v. *Maclure* (1882) 21 Ch D 309 (CA).

[228] 25 *PD* 1912 (s5) 25: 196 (question of Baron de Forest).

[229] Goode, *Hire-Purchase*, 9.

primarily one for the hire of the piano, but in the event of the instalments being paid punctually they were to be treated as purchase money'.[230]

The major problem faced by hire purchase companies was that the hirer would pass the goods on to third parties, by selling or pledging them. In the 1860s and 1870s, hire purchase dealers were able to recover their goods on the principle that the hirer was a bailee who could not pass property in them.[231] Moreover, in *Singer Manufacturing Company* v. *Clark* in 1879, the Exchequer Division allowed an action of conversion against a pawnbroker, who had delivered the sewing machine to a person who produced the ticket for it. Prior to the delivery, the company—who had not received any hire payment from their client—had demanded the return of their machine. The pawnbroker sought to rely on section 25 of the Pawnbrokers Act 1872, claiming that the company had not given proper statutory notification; and that they were protected by an indemnity. However, the court ruled that the section only protected the pawnbroker from claims by the real pawnor, where another person obtained the goods using the ticket. The section 'in no degree affects an owner whose property has been pledged against his will'.[232]

Such decisions seemed to protect hire traders. However, in 1893, in *Lee* v. *Butler*, the Court of Appeal held that a hirer was a person who had 'agreed to buy' goods and had a good title to them under section 9 of the Factors Act 1889. This meant that the hire trader could not recover the goods which had been sold to a third party. This decision alarmed the hire purchase trade. Things were made worse for them when in the summer of 1893, the Pawnbrokers' Society informed the Hire Traders Protection Association that henceforth no hired goods which had been taken in by pawnshops would be returned to the hire trader.[233] The Hire Traders Protection Society resolved on bringing a test case, *Helby* v. *Matthews*, which ended with the House of Lords putting their minds at rest. Overturning the Court of Appeal,[234] the Lords held that since the hirer had an option to buy the goods or return them, he had not 'agreed to buy' under the Factors Act. Property had therefore not passed, and the owners could recover the goods from the pawnbroker. *Lee* v. *Butler* was distinguished on the ground that the purchaser of the furniture in that case had bound herself absolutely to pay the two instalments

---

[230] *Cramer & Co* v. *Carlton*, *The Times*, 9 May 1884, col. 3d.

[231] e.g. *Cramer & Co (Ltd)* v. *Barre: The Times*, 20 November 1866, col. 11a. A bailee who fraudulently converted bailed goods to his own use—as by pledging them—was guilty of larceny: *R* v. *Wynn* (1887) 16 Cox C.C. 231.

[232] *Singer Manufacturing Co* v. *Clark* (1879) 5 Exch D 37 at 45. In *Burrows* v. *Barnes* (1900) 82 LT 721, the Queen's Bench Division held that the owner of a bicycle, which had been pledged by its hirer, and sold on by a pawnbroker to a third party after the pawnor failed to keep up his payments, could be returned to the original owner.

[233] (1895) 5 *The Hire Traders Guide and Record* 47.

[234] *Helby* v. *Matthews* [1894] 2 QB 262.

on the furniture, whereas in this case the piano could always be returned.[235] The hire trade was delighted by its victory, and one enthusiastic piano dealer declared that 'the House of Lords have granted us a charter'.[236] If this was an exaggeration, nonetheless the *Hire Traders Record* continued regularly to publicize cases where the rule in *Helby* v. *Matthews* had been applied. If the decision was a triumph for the trade, it did cause disquiet among those who felt that it undermined the policy of the Factors Act, that where the owner of goods had invested another with the appearance of ownership, he should not later be allowed to deny it. The decision was clearly bad for third party purchasers. In 1912, attempts were made to pass a Sale of Goods Bill to protect such third party purchasers, but the bill made little progress.[237]

Hire traders were equally concerned by the law of distraint. At common law, landlords could seize property in the possession of their tenants in arrears, and hold them in the nature of a pledge; and by a seventeenth century statute they were allowed to sell the goods to cover their charges.[238] This meant that the goods of a hire trading company could be seized in distraint and sold, although there had to be a valid sale by the landlord, who was not entitled simply to buy the goods himself.[239] This right to seize the property of another could lead to injustices, notably where the property of lodgers was seized for rent due to a superior landlord from the lodger's landlord, and in 1871, legislation was passed to enable lodgers to serve notice of their property and secure its protection.[240] However, no protection was given to hire traders, whose property remained subject to seizure. Throughout the first years of the twentieth century, the Hire Traders Protection Association sought to obtain legislation to address this question; and cases continued to be brought winning small victories for them.[241] In 1908, legislation was passed to amend the 1871 Act and give more protection to tenants, but without giving full protection to hire traders. Under the Act, lodgers, under-tenants and other persons who were not tenants could inform the landlord of their property and protect it from distraint; but section 4 of the Act exempted from its

---

[235] *Helby* v. *Matthews* [1895] AC 471 at 477–8.

[236] (1895) 5 *Hire Traders Guide and Record* 47. Although this trade journal saw this as an exaggeration, modern authority agrees in seeing it as a charter: Goode, *Hire-Purchase*, 5.

[237] Goode, *Hire-Purchase*, 8. In the same year, there was an effort to legislate to protect the hirer, which also failed.

[238] 2 W. & M. s 1, c. 5 s 2: this authorized a sale of goods after five days: see *Wallace* v. *King* (1788) 1 H. Bl. 13; *Robinson* v. *Waddington* (1849) 13 Q.B. 753. The period was extended to 15 days by the Law of Distress Amendment Act 1888, 51 & 52 Vict. c. 21, s 6.

[239] *Mary Ann King* v. *Younger* (1864) 4 B. & S. 782; *Moore, Nettlefold & Co* v. *Singer Manufacturing Co* [1904] 1 KB 820 (CA).

[240] Lodgers Goods Protection Act, 34 & 35 Vict. c. 79.

[241] e.g. *Perring & Co* v. *Emerson* [1906] 1 KB 1, where it was held that an uncertificated bailiff who seized the furniture owned by a hire trader was not permitted to seize his goods under a distress.

provisions goods comprised 'in any bill of sale, hire purchase agreement, or settlement made by such tenant'.[242]

Although on the face of it, the legislation gave no protection to the trade, in practice the hire traders were able to win some victories. Where goods were let on hire purchase to the tenant's wife, and an appropriate declaration was made, it was held that the goods did not fall within the section 4 exemption.[243] In 1912, in *The London Furnishing Company* v. *Solomon*, the King's Bench Division refused to allow the landlord to distrain even when the Hire Purchase agreement was in the name of the tenant, in a case where the company gave notice of the termination of the agreement before being notified of the arrear of rent.[244] But not all judges were so friendly to the Hire Traders Protection Association: in *Hackney Furnishing* v. *Watts*, Bray J. refused to follow the earlier case, and held that where a tenant had goods on hire purchase, he could not get the statute's protection. The owners of the goods voluntarily put the goods in the tenant's possession for their own gain, he said, and by so doing induced the landlord to give credit to the tenant. If a demand by the owners was all it took to end the Hire Purchase agreement, he said, there would be no point in having section 4 of the Act.[245]

Hire traders obtained greater sympathy from judges when seeking to protect their assets, when the hirer became bankrupt. Bankruptcy generated the risk that any goods in the bankrupt's possession would be available to his creditors under the doctrine of reputed ownership. However, where there was an established custom in a trade to leave certain goods in the possession of one who was not their owner, the doctrine did not apply.[246] In 1875, the Court of Appeal held that a custom among hoteliers to hold furniture on hire purchase was established by slight, but uncontradicted, evidence;[247] six years later, the Court of Appeal ruled that the custom was so well established that it should be noticed judicially.[248] Similarly, in 1888, Cave J. ruled in a bankruptcy case that it had been proved to be the custom in the print trade to let printing machinery on hire, but not type, so that while the latter was within the reputed ownership of the bankrupt, the

---

[242] Law of Distress Amendment Act, 8 Edw. 7 c. 53, s 4.

[243] *Shenstone & Co* v. *Freeman* [1910] 2 KB 84; *Rogers, Eungblut & Co* v. *Martin* [1911] 1 KB 19.

[244] *The London Furnishing Co* v. *Solomon* (1912) 28 TLR 265. As Darling J. put it, once the plaintiffs had put an end to the agreement, the goods were no longer those of the tenant, but were the same as the goods of any stranger left on the premises; and so the exemption in s 4 could not apply.

[245] *Hackney Furnishing* v. *Watts* [1912] 3 KB 225, followed in *Jay's Furnishing Co* v. *Brand & Co* [1914] 2 KB 132.

[246] e.g. *Priestley* v. *Pratt* (1867) LR 2 Ex 101 (the custom to leave farm stock on the seller's premises after sale was recognised); *Ex p Watkins, in re Couston* (1873) LR 8 Ch App 520 (the custom of leaving whisky under the control of the vendors).

[247] *Ex p Powell, In re Matthews* (1875) 1 Ch D 501 (CA).

[248] *Crawcour* v. *Salter* (1881) 18 Ch D 30.

former was not.[249] It was similarly held by the Irish Court of Appeal in 1894 that there was a custom to rent out gas engines on hire purchase, taking them out of the reputed ownership law.[250] Hire traders had greater difficulty persuading judges that there was a custom for consumer goods, such as furniture, to be left in the possession of someone who did not own them. In 1883, Jessel MR dismissed as extravagant the proposition that 'the habits of English society have become so changed by furniture dealers occasionally letting out furniture on a three years' hiring agreement that the public at large no longer attribute the ownership of the furniture to the person who is in possession of it'.[251] But where the professional hire trader was able to show the court that a custom existed, then he could be protected from the reputed ownership doctrine, even for items such as pianos.[252]

Through litigation brought by the Hire Traders Protection Association, the courts gradually moved towards greater protection for the hire purchase trade. There remained, however, some suspicion on the part of both the judiciary and the wider public of a system which was suspected of encouraging fraud,[253] and thriftlessness.[254] Given these concerns, the 1908 Departmental Committee on Bankruptcy Law discussed whether Hire Purchase agreements should be compulsorily registered, as bills of sale were. The proposals faced determined opposition from the Hire Traders, who could see no practical way to register and check millions of agreements,[255] and who argued that there was a key distinction between bills of sale and hire purchase. In the words of S. J. Sewell, secretary of the association, 'a hire agreement is evidence of improved financial condition, whereas the other is evidence of an impaired financial condition'.[256]

In fact, the line between the respectable hire purchase trade and unrespectable money lenders could be a thin one. For it was a common practice for money lenders to use the hire purchase system, by buying the goods of the borrower and letting them back on a hire purchase basis. This was a way of lending money at high rates of interest on the security of property, while attempting to evade the

[249] *Ex p Hughes and Kimber* (Limited), *Re Thackrah* (1888) 4 TLR 659.

[250] *Ex p Crossley Brothers Ltd* [1894] 1 IR 235. In *Hobson* v. *Gorringe* [1897] 1 Ch 182 (CA) at 186, Lord Russell CJ expressed surprise that the court felt there was evidence to come to this conclusion. The point was not raised on appeal to the Lords, which held that such a hire purchase agreement did not constitute a sale, which would require a bill of sale to protect it from the trustees in bankruptcy: *McEntire* v. *Crossley Brothers* [1895] AC 457.

[251] *Ex p Brooks, In re Fowler* (1883) 23 Ch D 261 at 266, following *Ex p Lovering, In re Jones (No. 2)* (1874) 9 Ch App 621. The real owner in both cases was not a professional hire trader.

[252] *In re Blanshard, Ex p Hattersley* (1878) 8 Ch D 601; *Chappell & Co* v. *Harrison* (1910) 103 LT 594.

[253] (1900) 9 *Hire Traders Record* 219; (1905) 14 *Hire Traders Record* 3.

[254] See the view of the Registrar of Leeds County Court in *The Times*, 8 December 1904, col. 15c.

[255] See PP 1893–4 (280) I 171. Cf. letter from M. R. Brandreth, *The Times*, 4 April 1893, col. 2f.

[256] 1908 Bankruptcy Committee, Evidence, p. 276, q. 6588.

provisions of the Bills of Sale Acts.[257] On the face of it, it seemed a valid way of proceeding. It had been accepted in 1878 by the Court of Appeal that a hire purchase
agreement was not a bill of sale which required registration, since the property
in the goods did not pass until the payment of the final instalment.[258] But courts
became more wary where the hirer was in fact buying what had been his own
goods on hire purchase. This can be seen from judicial reaction to the practices of
the Tower Furnishing and Finance Company. Where a potential borrower was in
arrear of rent, he would be advised to allow his landlord to distrain his furniture
for the arrears, which would then be sold to a broker. The broker would arrange
the sale of the furniture to the company (which paid a commission), and its lease
back to the borrower, or frequently his wife. When these transactions found their
way into the courts in the late 1880s, they were regarded as assurances regulated
by the Bills of Sale Acts.[259] In 1891, in *Beckett* v. *Tower Assets Company*,[260] the
Court of Appeal overruled the decision of Cave J. (who held that the hire purchase agreement was not a bill of sale, and hence did not need registration),[261]
holding that it had to look at the facts to see if the money was given by way of
security for the payment of money.[262] Everything hinged on whether the hire
traders had an independent title to the goods (in which case no bill of sale was
needed) or whether they did not. This was determined not by legal Chinese walls,
but by looking at the parties' intentions, which showed that there was no intent
to pass an absolute title, despite the form of the transaction.[263] Where money was
loaned on the security of a hire purchase agreement, with the lender's interest
in the property being merely as a security for the loan, he could not recover the

---

[257] The property would be sold under an absolute bill of sale, which was not covered by the 1882
Bills of Sale Act (so that the reputed ownership doctrine remained abolished regarding them): see
Swift v. *Pannell* (1883) 24 Ch D 210. See also 1897 Money Lending Committee Evidence, pp. 9–10, q.
109 (Farrow); 1898 Money Lending Committee Report, viii.

[258] *Ex p Crawcour, In re Robertson* (1878) 9 Ch D 419 (CA); *McEntire* v. *Crossley Brothers* [1895]
AC 457.

[259] See *French* v. *Bombernard* (*Tower Furnishing and Finance Co, Claimants*) (1888) 5 TLR 55 For
the company's workings, see also *The Tower Assets Co* v. *Weigall and Wife, The Times*, 31 October
1890, col. 5c.

[260] *Beckett* v. *Tower Assets Co* [1891] 1 QB 638.

[261] *Beckett* v. *Tower Assets Co Ltd* [1891] 1 QB 1.

[262] The Court of Appeal had taken that position in *In re Watson, Ex p Official Receiver in
Bankruptcy* (1890) 25 QBD 27 (CA) and *Madell* v. *Thomas & Co* [1891] 1 QB 230 (CA).

[263] As Fry LJ put it, 'it was the intention of both parties that the legal estate in the goods
should pass by the sale, but, nevertheless, that it should pass subject to a trust, until a repurchase
agreement was executed': *Beckett* v. *Tower Assets Co* [1891] 1 QB 638 at 646. However, where it
appeared that there was an intention to effect a bona fide sale, registration was not needed, even
when there was an agreement to repurchase: *The Victoria Dairy Co (of Worthing)* v. *West* (1895)
11 TLR 233.

property unless it had been registered as a bill of sale.[264] In a similar same way, the courts held that the reputed ownership clause of the Bankruptcy Act applied in cases where the bankrupt had re-purchased his own property on hire purchase.[265] In this way, the courts were able to control the use of hire purchase agreements by money lenders.

---

[264] See also *Trustee of G. Mellor* v. *Maas* [1903] KB 226, affirmed in *Maas* v. *Pepper* [1905] AC 102; *Wheatley's Trustee* v. *H. Wheatley Ltd* (1901) 85 LT 491.

[265] *Ex p Lovering, In re Jones (No. 2)* (1874) 9 LR Ch App 621; *Ex p Brooks, In re Fowler* (1883) 23 Ch D 261 (CA). There was authority for this which long antedated the rise of large-scale hire purchase: *Lingham* v. *Biggs* (1797) 1 B. & P. 82.

Part Four

TORT

I

The Development of Tort law

ENGLISH society was transformed in the era between 1820 and 1914. By the eve of the First World War, a society which had been largely rural and agricultural was predominantly urban and industrial. Just as the scale of economic activity increased, so a society of mass communication, brought by the railway and the telegraph, looked beyond the narrow horizons of the locality to a wider national stage. In this world, the number of economic and social problems which needed coordination on a national scale was unimaginably larger than at the start of the nineteenth century. The new world of industrial Britain generated a host of new risks and harms. Travellers on rapid new railways faced the risk of being injured or killed in a train crash. Factory workers and miners, whose labour generated much of the wealth of the world's first industrial nation, worked in dangerous conditions, which posed daily threats to their well-being. The rapid and often uncontrolled expansion of industrial towns generated a raft of risks to public health, both from industrial pollution, and from the by-products of mass human habitation. If Victorian England enjoyed unprecedented prosperity, it was also a society which was often uncomfortable and unhealthy.[1]

The most important legal responses to these new dangers did not come from the common law courts, but from the legislature. In an age of reform, those who worried about factory conditions or sanitary problems or the risks presented by mass transport did not look first to the courtroom for solutions. Rather, they debated how far the state should intervene to control activities which were hazardous to health, and in what way it should do so. Although statutory regulation of hazardous activities was not new, the nineteenth-century 'revolution in government' initiated a transformation in both its nature and scale. But this 'revolution' was often a painfully slow and cautious one. In many areas, effective national regulation had to await the 1870s, when governments keen to please the new electorate enfranchised in 1867 put new reforms on the agenda. In this world, tort law played an important, if subsidiary, role in regulating social and economic

---

[1] See XI, Pt 1, Ch. VI, and XIII, Pt 2, Ch. IV.

activity. In the absence of clear rules from the legislature, parties had necessarily to look first to the courts.

In contrast to contract law, nineteenth-century tort law was a body of disparate rules, which did not add up to a coherent, well-defined whole. In the first half of the nineteenth century, those seeking for information on torts had to look to abridgments, practitioners' manuals on evidence or pleading, or to works on 'the law of *nisi prius*'.[2] Treatises were available which discussed particular kinds of civil wrong, notably libel.[3] Remedies in tort were also discussed in treatises on property rights, such as C.J. Gale's treatise on easements.[4] But there was no general treatise on the topic until the publication in America of Francis Hilliard's *The Law of Torts* in 1859, and C. G. Addison's *Wrongs and their Remedies* in England in 1860. Early nineteenth-century legal literature, Hilliard complained, treated wrongs as merely incidental to remedies, concentrating on the actions available at law rather than the injuries they redressed. This was to treat the law as a 'system of forms rather than principles'.[5] Addison also wished to search for broader principles than the forms of action. After the reforms in civil procedure of 1852, he wrote, 'the pathway to legal science and to the general attainment of a certain amount of useful legal knowledge has been rendered comparatively easy and inviting'. But Addison's treatise was not an attempt to place the law of torts on a new theoretical foundation. He told his readers that torts were 'infinitely various' and that, since 'it would be an endless task to enumerate all the wrongs of which the law takes cognizance', he was only going to discuss those 'as constantly occur in the ordinary intercourse of mankind, and daily occupy the attention of the lawyer'.[6] Almost 20 years later, Oliver Wendell Holmes, reviewing the latest edition of Addison's work, questioned whether the law of tort was the proper subject for a law book, and 'long[ed] for the day when we may see these subjects treated by a writer capable of dealing with them philosophically'.[7] It was only in the late nineteenth century—after Holmes had himself taken up the challenge—that jurists began to develop coherent theories of tort law.

In contrast to contract lawyers, those dealing with civil wrongs did not find a convenient set of continental texts to hand, to borrow or adapt. No single coherent vision of tort could be found to guide judges in the way they developed the

---

[2] e.g. F. Buller, *An Introduction to the Law Relative to Trials at Nisi Prius* (1767); I. Espinasse, *A Digest of the Law of Actions at Nisi Prius*, 2 vols (1789); W. Selwyn, *An Abridgment of the Law of Nisi Prius*, 2 vols (1806).

[3] F. L. Holt, *The Law of Libel* (1812); T. Starkie, *A Treatise on the Law of Slander, Libel, Scandalum Magnatum and False Rumours* (1813; 2nd edn, 1830).

[4] C. J. Gale and T. D. Whatley, *A Treatise on the Law of Easements* (1839).

[5] F. Hilliard, *The Law of Torts*, 2 vols (3rd edn, Boston, 1866), preface, vi.

[6] C. G. Addison, *Wrongs and their Remedies, Being a Treatise on the Law of Torts* (1860), preface.

[7] Quoted in G. E. White, *Tort Law in America: An Intellectual History* (Oxford, 1980), 12.

law. The growth of tort law was experimental and halting, as courts reacted to new social problems which came before them. Judges and jurists sought to develop a vision of the law of torts at the same time that the law was being developed. Their visions were often contested and contentious. Towards the end of the nineteenth century, two rival visions had emerged. The first sought to build only established, recognized categories of tort law. While these categories could be extended by analogy to new situations as they arose, many areas would be left without remedies in tort. The second sought to develop an overarching theory, whose master principle was not to be found in legal logic, but in community morality.

1. THE USES OF TORT LAW

Victorian society was famously one with a strong respect for property, and for the principles of self-help, individualism, and *caveat emptor*. The era which saw the stigmatization of those unable to provide for themselves as paupers was not fertile ground for the development of a compensation culture. The courts aimed to protect property rights from invasion, but expected those who suffered from the vagaries of ill fortune to make provision for themselves. In an age in which liability insurance was yet to develop, judges were reluctant to spread the cost of compensation beyond those whose personal faulty conduct had caused harm.

Nineteenth-century tort law provided no remedy for many kinds of harms, which came to be central to the concerns of judges and jurists in the twentieth century. The development of a doctrine of a manufacturer's liability for defective products was stunted in the 1830s by judges fearful of expanding the principles of liability. Consumer protection was not seen as one of the common law's tasks. This is not to say that consumers were wholly unprotected. Bread Acts were passed in 1822 and 1836, and concern over the adulteration of food led to the passing of the 1875 Sale of Food and Drugs Act, which made it a criminal offence both to mix injurious ingredients with any food or drug to be sold, and to sell any article which differed in nature from that demanded by the purchaser. Provision was made for public analysts to be appointed locally to check samples and to direct prosecutions where necessary.[8] Judges occasionally heard cases appealed from the decisions of police magistrates dealing with such legislation.[9] But there was no trend to develop a broader law to protect consumers from damage done by a larger range of goods. The quality of goods was regarded generally as a matter of contract.

---

[8] Legislation regulating the sale of food continued to be passed throughout the late nineteenth century. See Report from the Select Committee on Food Products Adulteration, *PP* 1894 (253), xii, 1.

[9] e.g. *Fitzpatrick* v. *Kelly* (1873) LR 8 QB 337.

The number of actions for professional negligence, such as those brought against doctors, also remained small. The nineteenth-century medical profession was fragmented, between physicians, surgeons, and apothecaries, who became general practitioners. Although the Apothecaries Act 1815 made it unlawful for members of that branch to practice without a certificate from the Society of Apothecaries, the development of a united medical profession with a common set of standards was slow. In an age where medical education was often weak, and the demand for some form of treatment high, the courts were not prepared to take a tough stance against doctors.[10] Like all persons professing particular skills, medical practitioners were expected to use the level of skill reasonably expected of men in their profession. According to Tindal CJ, a doctor did not 'undertake to use the highest possible degree of skill', but only 'a fair, reasonable, and competent degree of skill'.[11] Where a practitioner was qualified and registered, it might be presumed that he had used the requisite skill.[12] Even if he was not registered, it was not to be assumed that he was incompetent. Rather, it had to be shown that the person administering medicine had done so carelessly. As Pollock CB observed in 1859, 'it would be most fatal to the efficiency of the medical profession if no one could administer medicine without a halter round his neck'.[13] In determining whether there had been negligence, the courts often drew on the testimony of experienced practitioners, who were also likely to be sympathetic to their colleagues.[14] Moreover, doctors were held liable for the treatment they gave, rather than for expressing opinions about a person's state of health.[15] The result was that relatively few doctors found themselves sued for professional negligence.[16] There were some other actions for professional negligence. Actions were regularly brought against attorneys and solicitors in cases which helped sketch out the nature of the duties of these

---

[10] See e.g. *Perionowsky* v. *Freeman* (1866) 4 F. & F. 977.

[11] *Lanphier* v. *Phipos* (1838) 8 Car. & P. 475 at 479.

[12] In criminal cases, a presumption was raised that a registered surgeon was competent, throwing the onus on the prosecution to prove negligence. *R* v. *Spencer* (1867) 10 Cox C.C. 525. See also *Hancke* v. *Hooper* (1835) 7 Car. & P. 81 at 84: 'The plaintiff must shew that the injury was attributable to want of skill; you are not to infer it.'

[13] *R* v. *Crick* (1859) 1 F. & F. 519 at 520.

[14] Nor did judges disapprove. In the words of Erle CJ, 'it was hard for one medical man to come forward and condemn the treatment of a brother in the profession, and say that he would have done this or that, when, probably, had he been in a position to judge of the case from the first, he would have done no better': *Rich* v. *Pierpont* (1862) 3 F. & F. 35 at 40.

[15] *Pimm* v. *Roper* (1862) 2 F. & F. 783.

[16] Early twentieth-century cases also established that hospitals would not be vicariously liable for the negligence of their staff: see *Hall* v. *Lees* [1904] 2 KB 602; *Hillyer* v. *The Governors of St Bartholomew's Hospital* [1909] 2 KB 820.

professionals.[17] Similarly, actions for negligence were brought against professionals such as auctioneers, surveyors, and stockbrokers. But these cases tended to flesh out what were regarded as the contractual duties of these professionals, rather than developing a broader notion of tortious liability for carelessness.[18] The way which businessmen secured their financial expectations was regarded as a matter of private contract.

What kinds of cases did come to court? Three kinds of tort litigation dominated the caseload of the courts.[19] The largest number of tort claims heard by judges in the second half of the nineteenth century involved wrongs against the person, including personal injury claims, and claims for assault and false imprisonment. Between 300 and 500 of these cases came annually before the courts on average in this period. Roughly half were brought under Lord Campbell's Act, which gave relatives of those killed by negligence standing to sue. Torts against property—trespass to land, trover, and nuisance—were less frequent, accounting for between 200 and 300 cases annually coming in front of the superior common law judges; though property disputes—notably those raising questions of nuisance—were more likely than personal injury ones to require equitable assistance. Defamation actions, seeking to protect a person's reputation, also continued to provide the courts with a significant caseload, running on average between 100 and 200 actions annually. The number of actions brought for intentional or malicious torts which did not interfere with a person's body or his property remained small. Roughly 10 seduction cases were brought annually in the second half of the century, and there were usually between 20 and 30 malicious prosecution cases a year. In the final quarter of the century, the number of actions for deceit increased, from over 30 actions a year in the 1870s, to over 50 during the years of the last decade of the nineteenth century and the first decade of the twentieth.[20]

---

[17] e.g. *Reece* v. *Rigby* (1821) 4 B. & Ald. 202; *Godefroy* v. *Dalton* (1830) 6 Bing. 460; *Lowry* v. *Guilford* (1832) 5 Car. & P. 234; *Taylor* v. *Blacklow* (1836) 3 Bing. N.C. 235; *Stannard* v. *Ullithorne* (1834) 10 Bing. 491; *Hunter* v. *Caldwell* (1847) 10 Q.B. 69.

[18] These actions were generally contractual. By contrast, doctors who undertook to treat a patient had to use the appropriate level of skill in so doing, regardless of whether they had a contract with the patient: *Pippin* v. *Sheppard* (1822) 11 Price. (Ex.) 400; *Gladwell* v. *Steggall* (1839) 5 Bing. N.C. 733.

[19] The number of tort actions tried before the superior court judges was consistently smaller than the number of contractual actions. M. Lobban, 'The Strange Life of the English Civil Jury, 1837–1914', in J. W. Cairns and G. Mcleod (eds), *The Dearest Birthright of the People of England: The Jury in the History of the Common Law* (Oxford, 2002), 173–215 at 214.

[20] The figures in the graph (overleaf) for property torts include actions determined in the superior courts of common law for nuisance, trespass, trover, and actions for the infringement of easements, but not 'tortious' actions to try title (such as those brought via ejectment). The figures for torts against the person include actions brought under Lord Campbell's Act, actions for injuries caused by negligence, assault, and false imprisonment. The figures do not include actions for infringements of intellectual property rights.

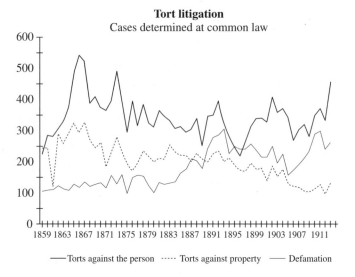

Tort litigation
Cases determined at common law

——— Torts against the person   ····· Torts against property   ——— Defamation

The aims of litigants bringing these cases, and the questions considered by the courts dealing with them, differed greatly. Most claims for personal injury arose out of transport or workplace accidents, with claimants seeking to secure financial compensation, often for the loss of a breadwinner. A subsidiary concern in bringing these actions was to punish those who had generated danger by their negligence, in the hope that the disincentive of heavy damages would sharpen their minds to removing dangers they might control. The press which commented avidly on the aftermath of railway accidents, and the trade unions which funded suits against negligent employers, were keen for decisions to be made which would deter potential future wrongdoers. These cases therefore focused the attention of the courts on questions of fault, and of how much care an employer, or transport provider, was expected to take in his business. Claims for assault, which might be brought as much where a person's dignity was offended as where he had suffered physical hurt, also raised issues of culpability, with wrong-doers held liable for intentionally harming others. In these areas, deterrence and punishment were often regarded as more important than compensating a victim. But in many areas of tort law, culpability was not an issue. Tort law was used to protect the spheres of private property; and where property rights had been violated, moral fault was irrelevant. For, besides mapping out what constituted acceptable conduct in the public world, courts in tort cases also performed the function of adjudicating between rival claims to property.

Many of the problems which judges encountered were new. Disputes over the uses of property forced judges to consider who was to bear the cost of industrial pollution. Injuries on the road or at work forced them to consider how far it was legitimate to undertake risky activity which might injure others without paying for it. How did judges go about answering these novel questions? Some scholars have argued that in seeking the factor explaining judicial responses to novel problems, we have to look outside the courtroom. According to one instrumentalist school of thought, associated with the work of Ronald Coase and Richard Posner, nineteenth-century tort law was used to promote economically efficient activity. In contrast to interventionist state regulation, the common law aimed to allow the market to determine where liability should fall. According to the view of economic analysts, the common law's task was to mimic the market, allocating rights in the most efficient way, by assigning them to those who most valued them.[21] Judges in this era (it is argued) took into account the economic implications of their decisions, asking whether the gain of preventing the harm done to the plaintiff was greater than the loss which would be suffered elsewhere if the harmful conduct were prohibited.[22] Court cases provided judges with opportunities to develop rules which would promote efficiency and wealth maximization, imposing the cost of harms on those who could reduce these costs most efficiently and most cheaply. Moreover, those who valued disputed rights most highly were likely to spend more on litigation than those who valued them least. Even if judges were not consciously developing rules promoting efficiency, the market of litigation ensured that this would occur.

A second instrumentalist school of thought lays greater stress on the ideology of the judiciary. This view holds that judges, influenced by new theories of political economy, sought to promote laissez-faire, individual responsibility and freedom of trade, in a way which benefited property-owners and businessmen at the expense of the working class. The choices they made transformed a common law which had been based on a paternalistic vision of a moral economy into a system where morality had no place, but where economic and commercial growth was to be promoted, whatever the social cost.[23] Although historians taking this view do not argue that judges were routinely motivated by crude class bias, in some areas of law, most notably the development of rules which denied workmen compensation

---

[21] R. Coase, 'The Problem of Social Cost' (1960) 3 *JLE* 1–69; R. Posner, *Economic Analysis of Law* (Boston, 1972), *passim*.

[22] Coase, 'The Problem of Social Cost', pp. 19–22. For a criticism, see A. W. B. Simpson, *Leading Cases in the Common Law* (Oxford, 1995), Ch. 7 and *ibid.*, 'Coase v Pigou Reexamined' (1996) 25 *JLS* 53–97. On the influence of economic ideas, see further XI, Pt 1, Ch. VI.

[23] This is the argument of M. J. Horwitz, *The Transformation of American Law, 1780–1860* (Cambridge, Mass., 1977) and P. S. Atiyah, *The Rise and Fall of Freedom of Contract* (Oxford, 1979). See the challenges to Horwitz's interpretation in G. T. Schwarz, 'Tort Law and the Economy in Nineteenth Century America' (1981) 90 *YLJ* 1717–75 and P. Karsten, *Heart versus Head: Judge-Made Law in Nineteenth Century America* (1997).

for industrial injuries, judges self-consciously developed rules which affected different social classes unequally. Unlike the economic analysts, these historians do not regard the outcomes as neutrally efficient: Victorian economic development came at a great social cost, disproportionally paid for by the poor.

Instrumentalist views of nineteenth-century tort law raise the question of how far judges were motivated by their visions of policy. Although some judges were enthusiastic and even partisan adherents of *laissez-faire* economic ideology, the understanding which many judges had of the business world was limited. They were more likely to see the world through the lenses of a paterfamilias than through the eyes of an entrepreneur. While the judiciary was composed of men who acquired great affluence, they were not in general men who came from the commercial or industrial classes, nor did they invest their fortunes in speculative investments.[24] The most admired, and most influential judges, were those who kept their political views quiet, but whose knowledge of and enthusiasm for legal doctrine was considerable. Since legal decisions were made collegially, and had to be justified to the wider profession with legal reasons, there were clear limits to how far individual judges with pronounced economic views could pursue a policy agenda. Moreover, the party political affiliations of the nineteenth-century bench were not monolithic: political and economic positions which were contested and contentious in the public arena could not simply be implemented in the law.

Nonetheless, judicial disavowals of the 'unruly horse' of policy[25] are not to be taken at face value. The nineteenth century judiciary—most notably in the area of tort law—was constantly faced with novel problems generated by a new industrial society, which could not simply be solved by the application of rules derived from precedent. Moreover, in many areas, where Parliament was slow to legislate, or created only imperfect regulation, it was left to the courts to develop rules to guide the public. Whether they liked it or not, judges were forced in many areas into the role of policy-makers, who developed the law with one eye on analogy and precedent, and another eye on the consequences of their decisions. The judges who developed new rules were not merely the midwives of the policy of economists or industrialists. Rather, in the forum of the various courts, the small body of English judges sought to work out the policy of the law, reacting to problems as they arose. In some areas—as in the case of workplace accidents—the policy which evolved was one which assisted enterprise, in throwing the cost of injuries on the wider community. In others—as in the protection of private property— the policy which evolved was less business-friendly. But in an age where the law

---

[24] D. Duman, *The Judicial Bench in England 1727–1875: The Reshaping of a Professional Elite* (1982).
[25] *Richardson* v. *Mellish* (1824) 2 Bing. 229 at 252.

of tort was not settled, either in its parts or in the whole, the development of the law was often inconsistent and incoherent.

Unlike legislators, judges saw the problems of modern industrial society through the prism of litigation between two parties, following a past event which had caused an injury. Their prime function was not to create rules which would impose costs on those ablest to bear them, or to create deterrents designed to prevent harmful conduct. It was to provide a remedy for a wrong inflicted by a defendant on a plaintiff. Because of the nature of the forum in which they sat, judicial attention was focused on whether a plaintiff's rights had been infringed, and whether a defendant should be held responsible for the outcome.[26] Settling these questions was often complex, and involved policy choices. But in making these choices, judges had to try to develop a doctrine which was coherent and which could generate reasons rooted in legal principle justifying the results of individual cases. Nineteenth-century judges did not merely have to apply policy: they had to make policy choices while inventing a new law of tort. Moreover, they developed this law in a forum in which the jury continued to play a major role in determining liability.

2. THE STRUCTURE OF TORT LAW

Although there was no theory of tort in England at the start of our period, lawyers did not think of torts solely in terms of the forms of action. From the later eighteenth century, English writers sought to make maps of the common law, and set out its principles in a coherent form. The task was a particularly challenging one in the law of obligations, which had been organized around the multiplicity of remedies offered for the redress of wrongs. Blackstone had made a start. His division in the *Commentaries* between the 'Rights of Things' (Book 2) and 'Private Wrongs' (Book 3) was a way of distinguishing between questions of distributive justice—the allocation of property rights—and corrective justice, or the system of remedies. In Book 3, he did not merely list the actions available to correct wrongs. Rather, he arranged his discussion around various interests, setting out remedies for the violation of rights he had set out earlier. According to his view of tort, the mere violation of the right to security, liberty, or property generated a right of action against the infringer. Blackstone's was a Lockean view, which saw a person's life, liberty, and estate as forms of property to be protected. In an era when the law was conceived of in positivist terms, and in which the

---

[26] On theories of corrective justice, see E. J. Weinrib, *The Idea of Private Law* (Cambridge, Mass., 1995); J. L. Coleman, *The Practice of Principle* (Oxford, 2001); W. Lucy, *Philosophy of Private Law* (Oxford, 2007).

legislature came to assume an increasingly prominent role, both in theory and in practice, the rights which the law of tort protected continued to be perceived to derive from nature or reason. How far these rights were to be protected, and what remedies were available, remained a matter for the reasoning of judges and jurists, and not a matter for legislative policy.

The common law of torts was shaped by the medieval distinction between trespass and the action on the case. By the late eighteenth century, it was accepted that the former was used for direct harms, and the latter for consequential ones. The action on the case was a particularly broad form, and was used for a large variety of wrongs, including slander and libel, trover, nuisance, and negligence. While it was essential for the pleader to choose the correct form of action in commencing litigation, legal thinking was shaped by the causes of action which lay behind the procedural forms, rather than the forms themselves. The fact that nuisance and negligence were both pleaded as actions on the case did not induce lawyers to imagine that the rules of liability were the same for both. Not only did judges think of the substance beyond the procedure, in a number of contexts, early nineteenth-century judges made it clear that pleaders could use either trespass or case when bringing certain cases to court. Judges who were sure of the cause of action might be less sure about which form was to be used (and therefore which kinds of counts could be combined).[27]

According to Frederick Pollock, writing in 1887, 'the really scientific treatment of principles' of tort only began after the passing of the Common Law Procedure Act in 1852.[28] The mid-century reforms which led to the dismantling of the forms of action certainly impelled jurists on both sides of the Atlantic to attempt to articulate the principles on which the law of torts stood, since once the forms of action were removed, the common law needed to be explained by a new theoretical structure. But these jurists were not starting afresh: their theories sought to explain and make sense of the inherited substantive rules, and to develop them further. It was not the forms of action which continued to rule the late nineteenth century from their graves, but rather the causes of action which lay behind them. Most of these causes of action were well established by 1820. Well-settled rules relating to nuisance, trespass, slander, libel, or trover, which protected a person's property, person, or reputation, were familiar enough to practitioners by 1820. The early nineteenth century did, however, see the evolution of a new understanding of negligence. The development of this new category did not await the abolition of the forms of action. Rather, it developed in the first half of the century, in response to new problems generated by modern society. Beginning as

---

[27] It will be seen that judges allowed trespass or case to be used in cases brought for negligent driving, or for actions *per quod servitium amisit*.

[28] F. Pollock, *The Law of Torts: A Treatise on the Principles of Obligation arising from Civil Wrongs in the Common Law* (1st edn, 1887), vii.

a qualification of the liability imposed in a range of different wrongs, it developed in the twentieth century into a tort of its own.

The development of negligence helped to reorientate thinking about torts, for it put the notion of fault at the heart of thinking about tort. In the eighteenth century, those who had infringed the rights of others were in general held liable for the harm so caused, unless they could show that it had been an inevitable accident. The question of whether the defendant had taken a proper amount of care was only normally raised where a duty to take such care had been undertaken (as with attorneys or surgeons dealing with their clients and patients) or imposed by law (as upon innkeepers). The paradigm problem in this world was that of the Englishman in his home, whose private domain was invaded by the unauthorized intrusion of another. Since his neighbour had no right to walk across his land, or let his cattle stray there, or interfere with his easements, the fact that he was careful counted for nothing. By the early nineteenth century, the courts were much more aware of the problems faced by the Englishman in the world, who was injured in the bustle of the modern town by others who were conducting their business in the same place that he was. There was far less room for strict liabilities and strict rights in this world. Courts had to figure out how much care was expected in this world of social interaction, and how far one's duty of care to others extended. The problem of social interaction was hardly new, of course. But two developments made it much more pressing for the courts. The first was the sheer scale of the change, which came with the transport revolution and the expansion of urban England. The second was the early nineteenth century rise in litigation rates, after the mid-eighteenth century era of slumber.

In the mid-nineteenth century, judges experimented with new remedies, exploring how far to impose liabilities. The approach which was taken was a cautious one. Rather than developing an open-ended general tort of negligence, judges preferred to anchor liability in settled categories of doctrine. Liability was not to be strict where harms occurred in the world at large, but the defendant had to be shown to have been at fault. But the notion of fault invoked was a narrow one, which did not impose a general requirement to take care of others. This notion of fault acted in many ways to limit the liability of those whose actions impacted adversely on others in the world at large. Towards the end of the nineteenth century, this view was challenged by those who wished to develop a broader vision for tort law as a whole, which would expand liability by imposing a more general duty to take care. This new theory was championed both by judges and jurists.

By 1881, commentators were able to identify two trends in judicial thinking. The *Solicitor's Journal* noted that some judges strove to define the limits of tortious liability very clearly 'on the principle that it is better on the whole for the community that *fas* and *nefas* should be separated by plain, clearly distinguishable lines, about which there can be no doubt or fluctuation'. This was to identify the traditional approach, which linked remedies to the traditional causes of action recognized at common law. But there were also others who 'tend rather to think that such hard and fast lines are not really suited to the exigencies of civilization, but only serve as charts to the tortiously minded, advertising them how they may pursue their wrongful enterprises without running onto legal rocks or shoals'.[29] Like many of its contemporaries, the journal worried about the potential open-endedness of the latter approach.

The author of this article had in mind W. B. Brett, later Lord Esher, who tried in a number of areas in the 1880s to introduce broad principles which would impose general notions of liability in place of the more particular established rules. A conservative in politics, Brett took a very moralistic view of law; 'every general proposition laid down by judges, as a principle of law', he once held, 'is the statement of some ethical principle of right and wrong applied to circumstances arising in real life'.[30] This judge wished to make the law of torts into a system which would ensure good moral conduct by citizens. Instead of imposing particular duties on defendants, Brett looked for a broader conception. In his view, those who damaged others by any conduct which could foreseeably harm them were to be held liable for it; those who inflicted any damage on others with the intention of harming them were to be held liable for their immoral behaviour. Brett blazed the path of reform in a number of important and significant judgments. But his formulations were often controversial, and his peers often remained unconvinced.

At the same time that Brett was experimenting from the bench with new ways of thinking about tort, Frederick Pollock became the first writer to develop a theoretical vision of tort law in England. Pollock's ambition was 'to fix the contents and boundaries of the subject' by searching for the principle which united the various different torts.[31] Pollock's treatise was written at the same time that he was engaged in drafting a civil wrongs bill for the Government of India, which he completed in 1886, the year before the first edition of his *Torts* was published. Although there were some variations to suit Indian conditions, the draft bill was largely a codification of the law of tort. The very enterprise of drafting a bill for India required Pollock to think broadly and to set out principles, since the particular historical or procedural explanations which might make sense of the common law for the English lawyer would mean nothing to Indian practitioners.

In a preface addressed to Oliver Wendell Holmes, Pollock stated that in this work he had 'endeavoured to turn to practical account the lessons of what I saw and heard' at Harvard.[32] It was Holmes who inspired Pollock's thinking. In *The*

---

[29] (1881) 25 *Sol. J.* 738.
[30] *Blackburn, Low & Co* v. *Vigors* (1886) 17 QBD 553 at 558.
[31] Pollock, *Torts* (1st edn, 1887), 1.
[32] *Ibid.*, vi.

Common Law, Holmes had sought to find a general principle of civil liability from the material of common law cases. At the heart of this book stood an attempt to develop a theory of tort law, something no Anglophone writer had attempted before. Holmes argued that the common law did not invite people to act at their peril by imposing a strict liability, except in particular situations determined by policy. Instead, a notion of fault was central to Holmes's view of the common law. In general, he argued, the policy of the common law was to let losses lie where they fell. A person was only to be liable for harms caused by his actions if he had been in a position to choose to avoid the harm, and had failed to do so. While this was a moral vision of the law of tort, it did not rest on the personal morality of each individual. Rather, the morality of the common law was that of the community at large: the citizen was held strictly liable to conform to the standards expected of the ordinary prudent man. These standards would initially be set by the good sense of the jury, but with the repetition of cases would be translated into law. The centrality of an objective idea of fault was seen both in his understanding of negligence and of intentional wrongdoing. In neither case were the motivations of the defendant important. Rather, the law set up a moral standard to which people had to conform their actions, to give them a fair chance of avoiding inflicting harm before they were held liable. It was 'intended to reconcile the policy of letting accidents lie where they fall, and the reasonable freedom of others with the protection of the individual from injury'.[33]

Pollock took his cue from Holmes's theory, seeking a general principle. Pollock stated baldly 'that it is a wrong to do wilful harm to one's neighbour without lawful justification or excuse'.[34] This principle was not to be found in any express authority, since law began with an enumeration of particular remedies, rather than with general principles. But the general principles of tort law could be inferred from the particular remedies, just as the general principles of contract law could be inferred from the old contractual actions. Pollock's new theory was driven by modern developments. He began by pointing out that '[t]he whole modern law of negligence [. . .] enforces the duty of fellow-citizens to observe in varying circumstances an appropriate measure of prudence to avoid causing harm to one another'. If this positive duty to avoid harm existed, Pollock reasoned, there had to be as a corollary a negative duty of not doing wilful harm.[35]

Like Holmes, Pollock sought a theory based on a moral conception of wrongdoing. For him, the key principle of the law was to be found in Ulpian's statement, *alterum non laedere*: 'Thou shalt do no hurt to thy neighbour'. The English law of tort—'with all its irregularities'—had for its main purpose 'nothing else than the

---

[33] O. W. Holmes, *The Common Law* (1881), 144.
[34] Pollock, *Torts* (1st edn, 1887), 21.
[35] *Ibid.*, 22.

development of this precept'. This involved 'the technical working out of a moral idea by positive law, rather than the systematic application of any distinctly legal conception'.[36] In Pollock's view, the material of English tort law could be divided into 'three main heads of duty [...] to abstain from wilful injury, to respect the property of others, and to use due diligence to avoid causing harm to others'. Two of the three heads could be clearly related to notions of moral blameworthiness. The first head, which comprised personal wrongs such as assault, seduction, or defamation, involved conduct which was 'the object of strong moral condemnation'.[37] The last head, which embraced nuisance and negligence, involved wrongs which may not have been wilful, but which were not 'morally indifferent'. A person who engaged in conduct which generated certain risks to others was held both morally and legally blameworthy if he did not take care to avoid foreseeable risks. However, Pollock had to admit that not all of the law of torts could be related to moral precepts so clearly. The last head also included some cases (such as those involving dangerous goods or bursting reservoirs) where the law imposed a strict liability; so that the legal duty went beyond the moral one. In Pollock's view, it was unnecessary to impose such strict liabilities, but he noted that courts had opted to create a strict duty to insure safety where particularly dangerous things were involved. The remaining class of torts, those involving wrongs to property (such as trespass to land) also challenged his moral view, since they were 'apparently unconnected with moral blame'.[38] Instead, they imposed a strict liability on the tortfeasor, expecting him at his peril to know the boundaries of another man's property. Pollock felt that the existence of this group of torts, and 'their want of intelligible relation to any moral conception', made it difficult to ascribe any rational unity to the English law of torts. His solution to this problem was to describe them as historical anomalies, and to suggest that it was possible to rethink their rationalizations in moral terms.[39]

Like Holmes, Pollock sought to diminish the role of strict liability, and find a unity in negligent and intentional torts. Just as all people were under a duty to take care not to harm others, so they were to be held liable in his view for all harms intentionally inflicted which could not be justified. Pollock and his followers felt that the law of tort was not limited by fixed, inherited categories, but could develop in response to new problems. His theory laid far less emphasis on the notion of duty than those theorists wedded to a more traditional view of torts; indeed, some argued that the very notion of duty was an unnecessary fifth wheel

---

[36] *Ibid.*, 12.   [37] *Ibid.*, 9.   [38] *Ibid.*

[39] *Ibid.*,12, 15–16. In Pollock's view, if it was 'morally unreasonable' to expect a man at his peril to know what land or goods belonged to his neighbour, 'it is not so evidently unreasonable to expect him to know what is his own, which is only the statement of the same rule from the other side'.

to the coach.[40] Instead, the focus of attention was on the excuse or justification offered by the person inflicting harm. In the view of Pollock and his followers, it was a matter for the courts to decide whether the defendant had a justification, whether his conduct was merely the lawful exercise of his own common rights, or was an actionable wrong. In effect, this would enable the judiciary to develop the law of torts in accordance with its own view of policy or the public good. If this was to echo Holmes's view of the function of the common law courts in setting standards—rather than Brett's rather more subjective and intangible notion of right and wrong—Pollock did not follow the path charted by his American friend, in turning his mind to how judges were to make policy. For Pollock, this remained a matter of unproblematic common sense.

Pollock's description of tort law was as much prescriptive as descriptive, and invited a reaction from those who took a narrower view of liability in tort. The late nineteenth-century editions of Addison's textbook, edited by L.W. Cave (5th edn, 1879), Horace Smith and A. P. P. Keep (6th edn, 1887, 7th edn, 1893) described a tort as 'the infringement without lawful excuse of a right vested in some determinate person'. The fact that an action directly harmed a person's interests adversely was not enough.[41] The editors of the 8th edition were blunter still, stating at the outset 'that there is no scientific definition of a tort'. Considering that the indefinable nature of legal rights and duties made it impossible to define a tort, the editors contended that the most which could be said was that the law recognized certain rights relating to person, property, and reputation, and imposed certain duties to protect these rights.[42] Shortly after this edition was published, the most important rival text to Pollock's was published by John Salmond. Salmond's heart was in the same place as Pollock's, for he also felt that tort law should reflect the community morality, and that the principle of fault should lie at its heart. Like Pollock, he had read and been influenced by Holmes's theory. But Salmond was conscious of the fact that Pollock's view did not describe the law as administered in the courts. In his view, the law of torts did not consist of a fundamental general principle that it was wrongful to cause harm to others without excuse, but was instead made up of 'a number of specific rules prohibiting certain kinds of harmful activity, and leaving all the residue outside the sphere of legal responsibility'.[43] Like the editors of Addison, Salmond stressed the existence of *damna sine injuria*, where the common law offered no remedy.

---

[40] W. W. Buckland, 'The Duty to Take Care' (1935) 51 *LQR* 637–49 at 639.
[41] Addison, *Torts* (7th edn by H. Smith and A. P. P. Keep, 1893), 1–2.
[42] Addison, *Torts* (8th edn by W. E. Gordon and W. H. Griffith, 1906), 2.
[43] J. W. Salmond, *The Law of Torts: a Treatise on the English Law of Liability for Civil Injuries* (2nd edn, 1910), 9.

The two rival schools of thought continued to debate the foundations of tortious liability, with the followers of Pollock holding that there was a single principle, and the followers of Salmond taking the view that there was a finite number of distinct duties in tort.[44] The view of the latter school was more conservative, seeking to root all tortious remedies in causes of action which had an established pedigree at common law, and leaving it to the legislature to develop new ones. At the end of our period, it was Salmond's view which better described the law. The general principle urged by Pollock to unify the tort of negligence was not articulated by the House of Lords until 1932; the general principle urged by Pollock to unify intentional torts was rejected by the House of Lords in 1898. Moreover, thanks to *Rylands* v. *Fletcher*, strict liability torts remained rooted in the textbooks, even if they were rare interlopers in the twentieth-century courtroom.

3. THE PROBLEM OF VICARIOUS LIABILITY

The moral language of fault which lay behind new theories of responsibility centred on the notion of negligence was focused on the culpability of the individual. Yet the harms which generated the bulk of the litigation in the industrial era resulted from the careless actions of relatively impecunious employees who were not worth taking to court. The question was therefore raised as to how far one person should be held vicariously responsible for harms generated by the carelessness of another.

Judges developing the rules of vicarious liability were aware of the policy implications of the choices they made. It was evident that to leave plaintiffs with only the option of suing the immediate instrument of harm would give them no effective remedy at all: there was no point in a train passenger attempting to sue the engine driver. On the other hand, to allow plaintiffs to sue the party who was ultimately benefited by the action which caused the harm might impose huge liabilities on the richest business for harms caused by subcontractors over whom it had no control. Judicial policy-making was most evident in their refusal to hold employers vicariously liable for the careless acts of one employee injuring another. In developing the rules regulating workplace accidents, judges often had an old-fashioned view of economic enterprise, seeing matters from the perspective of the small entrepreneur or householder, rather than the large enterprise. Even where they were aware that the defendant was a large enterprise with capacity to control a large workforce, and internalize the costs of its activities, judges stressed that

---

[44] See P. H. Winfield, 'The Foundation of Liability in Tort' (1927) 27 *Columbia LR* 1–11; A. L. Goodhart, 'The Foundations of Tortious Liability' (1938) 2 *MLR* 1–13; G. L. Williams, 'The Foundation of Tortious Liability' (1939) 7 *CLJ* (1939) 111–32.

they had to make the common law for a wider public. Regretting the outcome in one case, Pollock CB observed that 'we must administer the law, not merely as between the public and a Railway Company, but upon the broad principles which govern the relation between principal and agent, and master and servant. ... The rule is the same between a private individual and a Railway Company, as it is where the same matter is in dispute between two private individuals'.[45]

In the early nineteenth century, a number of judges associated the principle of vicarious liability with the maxim *sic utere tuo ut alienum non laedas*. This made a party liable for all harms emanating from the use of his property, whether or not he was the agent of the harm. Where the harm resulted from work done on his property, or from its use, he was to be liable. This rule of liability made him responsible for agents working for him, as well as for his servants. Wherever work was done for his benefit, the maxim *qui facit per alium facit per se* applied. According to this notion, one person's vicarious liability for the harm caused by another was not founded in any moral notion of his responsibility for that other person's actions.

This theory was consistently applied in the nineteenth century in cases of nuisance. Where a nuisance emanated from the defendant's land—or, after *Rylands* v. *Fletcher*, when something liable to do harm escaped from it—the landowner was held liable, regardless of whether the harm resulted from his actions or those of an agent or servant.[46] In the late eighteenth and early nineteenth centuries, this strict view of vicarious liability was also used to hold those who hired agents to do work on their property responsible for nuisances created by those agents. In *Bush* v. *Steinman*, the employer of a builder was therefore held liable for an accident caused by the builder's leaving lime in the road.[47] In 1824, Best CJ explained the principle behind this decision to be 'that he who expects to derive advantage from an act which is done by another for him, must answer for any injury which a third person may sustain from it'.[48]

Nonetheless, from the beginning of our period, judges were unhappy with this extensive application of the principle of vicarious liability. Doubts were first raised in cases where the harm resulted not from the defendant's use of his real property, but from accidents involving his chattels. In *Laugher* v. *Pointer*, where the judges had to consider whether the owner of a carriage who had hired horses

---

[45] *Roe* v. *Birkenhead Lancashire and Cheshire Junction Railway Co* (1851) 7 Exch. 36 at 40.

[46] See *Littedale* v. *Lonsdale* (1793). The case is reported on a point of pleading in 2 H. Bl. 267, 299; but the substantive decision was mentioned by Eyre CJ in *Bush* v. *Steinman* (1799) 1 B. & P. 404 at 407.

[47] *Bush* v. *Steinman* (1799) 1 B. & P. 404 at 408. See also *Matthews* v. *West London Water Works Co* (1813) 3 Camp. 403.

[48] *Hall* v. *Smith* (1824) 2 Bing. 156 at 160. In this case, paving commissioners were held exonerated since they were undertaking an unremunerated public service.

and a driver for the day was liable for the driver's carelessness, Littledale J. distinguished between two kinds of liability. Since houses and land were 'under the fixed use and enjoyment of a man for his regular occupation and enjoyment in life', he was compelled 'to take care that no persons come about his premises who occasion injury to others'. By contrast, '[m]oveable property is sent out into the world by the owner to be conducted by other persons: the common intercourse of mankind does not make a man or his own servants always accompany his own property; he must in many cases confide the care of it to others who are not his own servants, but whose employment it is to attend to it'.[49] This was to endorse the developing view that the strict liabilities of the home were not to be replicated in the world. A man should only be held liable insofar as he could control the risk. Littledale was persuaded by the argument, taken from Pothier, that masters were held liable for the acts of his servants in order to make them 'careful in the choice of whom they employ'.[50] Aided by the theoretical discussion of vicarious liability to be found in Joseph Story's treatise on agency, English courts subsequently rejected the broad notion that a person was liable for all injuries caused by the acts of those carrying out work for his benefit, in favour of the narrower one which imposed liability only where the defendant had chosen or exerted control over the agent occasioning harm.[51]

By the 1840s, Littledale's view regarding the liabilities attaching to the use of fixed property was being challenged by those who felt that a property owner should not be liable for harms caused by the carelessness of contractors working for him. Littledale's distinction was abandoned in 1849 in *Reedie* v. *The London and North Western Railway Company*. The plaintiff's husband had been killed when workmen employed in constructing a railway bridge negligently dropped a stone onto the highway below. The workmen were employed by an independent contractor, though the railway company had the power to dismiss any of them for incompetence. For Rolfe B., the maxim *qui facit per alium facit per se* could only apply where the master had the choice of the party employed. It was reasonable to hold the person who chose a careless person liable for harms occasioned by his lack of care: but otherwise not. Overruling *Bush* v. *Steinman*, he noted that there was no distinction between real and personal property cases, unless the act complained of was itself such as amounted to a nuisance.[52] Where the contractor

---

[49] *Laugher* v. *Pointer* (1826) 5 B. & C. 547 at 562.

[50] R. J. Pothier, *A Treatise on the Law of Obligations or Contracts*, 2 vols (trans. W. D. Evans, 1806), i, 72.

[51] *Quarman* v. *Burnett* (1840) 6 M. & W. 499, *Milligan* v. *Wedge* (1840) 12 A. & E. 737, *M'Laughlin* v. *Pryor* (1842) 4 M. & G. 48.

[52] *Reedie* v. *The London and North Western Railway Co* (1849) 4 Exch. 244 at 256. In a case of nuisance, he added, 'his liability must be founded on the principle, that he has not taken due care to prevent the doing of acts which it was his duty to prevent, whether done by his servants or others'.

created something which amounted to a public nuisance—as where he left rubble in the street—the owner would only be liable if the work contracted for could not be done without generating a nuisance.[53] An employer was liable for nuisances he directly authorized; he was not liable for the collateral negligence of contractors, which might generate public nuisances.[54]

The courts' attitude towards contractors reveals a narrowing of the scope of vicarious liability. In place of a broad liability based on the *sic utere* maxim, judges began to favour a narrower construction of the maxim *respondeat superior*, which made a man liable for the acts of his servants, who were part of his household, but not of his agents, who were not similarly placed. According to this approach, a master was liable for the harmful acts of his servants, since he had chosen them, and could control them. This view suggested a narrower vision of liability: for it raised the question whether the person inflicting the harm was in fact a servant, rather than an independent agent, and whether he was acting in the course of his employment.

In many respects, judges who developed the notion that a defendant was to be liable for harms caused by negligence were very uncomfortable with the notion of vicarious liability. In the commonest cases—those where railways were held liable for harms done to passengers from their employees' negligence, or where employers were exonerated from liability for harms inflicted by one of their workers on another—the courts justified the outcome by invoking implied terms of a contract between the employer and the person suffering the harm, terms which reflected judicial policy choices over where liability should fall. But in those cases where no contract could be found, the courts explored the nature of the relationship of master and servant, and the scope of the servant's employment.

It was not every act of the servant which rendered the master liable. Masters were not to be held liable for the wilful, illegal acts of their servants,[55] nor where the servant went 'on a frolic of his own, without being at all on his master's business'.[56] Where an employee was doing his job, but did so dangerously, or in breach of company rules, the courts allowed the public to recover, seeking to induce

[53] *Peachey* v. *Rowland and Evans* (1853) 13 C.B. 182; *Ellis* v. *The Sheffield Gas Consumer's Co* (1853) 2 El. & Bl. 767. See further the discussion at p. 973.

[54] *Pickard* v. *Smth* (1861) 10 C.B. N.S. 470 at 480. See also the rule that contractors were not liable for their subcontractors: *Rapson* v. *Cubitt* (1842) 9 M. & W. 711; *Knight* v. *Fox* (1850) 5 Exch. 721; *Overton* v. *Freeman* (1852) 11 C.B. 867.

[55] *Lyons* v. *Martin* (1838) 8 Ad. & El. 512 at 515.

[56] *Joel* v. *Morison* (1834) 6 Car. & P. 501 at 503. This principle was endorsed by Jervis CJ in *Mitchell* v. *Crassweller* (1853) 13 C.B. 237. A broad interpretation of what constituted the master's business was made in *Patten* v. *Rea* (1857) 2 C.B. N.S. 606.

companies 'to take care that they employ proper persons'.[57] For instance, where bus drivers caused accidents, by racing each other, or obstructing each other, plaintiffs were able to recover.[58] Similarly, since a conductor's job permitted him to deal with troublesome customers, his employer would be liable even if he acted wrongly, as when a guard violently ejected a passenger from a bus mistakenly assuming him to be drunk.[59] But if an employee exceeded the powers he had in his employment, the injured plaintiff might find himself without a remedy. For while judges were aware that injured members of the public would get no satisfaction from a driver or guard, they also avoided making large companies insurers against harms caused by those in their employ. There was some judicial sympathy for railway companies' desires to limit their liability for overzealous railwaymen who claimed to be acting in the interest of the company, particularly if there were signs that the employee was pursuing his own grudges. In 1870, Blackburn J. held that a clerk in the ticket office had no authority to summon a constable to arrest a customer. He was clearly concerned about the ramifications of a contrary decision: 'if the law were that the defendants are responsible for the act of their booking-clerk in giving the plaintiff into custody on an unfounded charge', he ruled, 'every shopkeeper in London would be answerable for any act done by a shopman left in his shop who chose to accuse a person of having attempted to plunder the shop, every merchant would be responsible for a similar act of his clerk, and every gentleman for the act of his butler or coachman'.[60]

In the later nineteenth century, judges began to take a more expansive view of vicarious liability, showing greater sensitivity to the need to hold corporations liable for the wrongs of those acting for them. Judges began to develop the notion that non-delegable duties of care might exist, which would render a property owner liable for the acts of his agents. It was settled in the mid-nineteenth century that where a person was bound by statute to do a particular act, he could not avoid the responsibility of doing it by contracting with another person to do it for him.[61] In 1876, in a case involving harm done by a building contractor, Cockburn CJ ruled that where a man employed someone to undertake work

---

[57] Sleath v. Wilson (1839) 9 Car. & P. 607 at 611.

[58] Green v. The London General Omnibus Co (1859) 7 C.B. N.S. 290 at 303; Limpus v. London General Omnibus Co (1862) 1 H. & C. 526 at 539.

[59] Seymour v. Greenwood (1861) 7 H. & N. 355.

[60] Allen v. The London and South Western Railway Co (1870) LR 6 QB 65 at 69. By contrast, in Moore v. the Metropolitan Railway Co (1872) LR 8 QB 36, Blackburn held it within an inspector's authority to make an arrest. See also Poulton v. The London and South Western Railway Co (1867) LR 2 QB 534; Walker v. South Eastern Railway Co (1870) LR 5 CP 640; Edwards v. The London and North Western Railway Co (1870) LR 5 CP 445.

[61] Hole v. Sittingbourne and Sheerness Railway Co (1861) 6 H. & N. 488; Gray v. Pullen (1864) 5 B. & S. 970.

on his own premises which was lawful, but from which harmful consequences might ordinarily be expected unless care was taken, he would be liable for not averting the mischief. Where injurious consequences were to be expected, the employer should be liable 'no matter through whose default the omission to take the necessary measures for such prevention may arise'.[62] In the same year, the Queen's Bench Division held a proprietor liable for the negligence of a gasfitter in repairing his lamp, on the grounds that a man who allowed a heavy lamp to project over the highway was bound to maintain it. There were thus certain duties to which were proprietors were strictly held. As Lush J. put it, a man who put the public safety in peril by hanging such a lamp was bound 'to keep it in such a state as not to be dangerous; and he cannot get rid of the liability for not having so kept it by saying he employed a proper person to put it in repair'.[63]

At the same time that the courts imposed broader duties on property owners to prevent harm to others, so companies were increasingly held liable for the wrongs of their employees. Mid-century judges were willing to countenance arguments that corporations could never be sued for malicious torts, or for fraud, having no mental capacity to intend to do a wrong.[64] In the second half of the century, judges began to allow actions for torts such as libel to be brought against companies, since 'great injustice would be suffered by individuals if their remedy for wrongs authorized by corporations aggregate were to be confined to the agents employed'.[65] Moreover, by 1867, it was accepted that a company could be sued for the fraud of its employees, while acting in the course of their business.[66]

4. THE JURY AND DAMAGES

Judges and jurists who developed the law of tort in the nineteenth century worried constantly about the role which should be left to juries. After new rules of procedure were introduced in 1883, the number of contract cases which were decided with a jury declined dramatically. However, juries were still generally used in tort cases to the end of our period.[67] In an area of law where outcomes often depended on an evaluation of whether a defendant acted reasonably, litigants in tort proved unwilling to leave the determination of facts to judges. While judges narrowed the room left to juries to exercise their discretion by defining duties and defences more clearly, they were often content for the jury to be seen to

[62] *Bower* v. *Peate* (1876) 1 QBD 321 at 327.
[63] *Tarry* v. *Ashton* (1876) 1 QBD 315 at 320.
[64] *Stevens* v. *The Midland Counties Railway Co and Lander* (1854) 10 Exch. 352 at 356.
[65] *Whitfield* v. *The South Eastern Railway Co* (1858) E. B. & E. 115 at 121–2.
[66] *Barwick* v. *English Joint Stock Bank* (1867) LR 2 Ex 259.
[67] Lobban, 'Strange Life', 214–15.

be making the difficult decision. Furthermore, in contrast to contract law, where damages were largely a matter of calculation, in tort law, juries continued to have a good deal of discretion in awarding damages.

In some actions in tort, juries were constrained in the damages which could be awarded. Where the plaintiff's property was wrongfully acquired, judges laid down rules of assessment. For instance, in actions for injuries to land, the jury was to measure the diminution in value of the property in question, rather than awarding the sum which would be required to restore the property.[68] Where a defendant wrongfully extracted coal from the plaintiff's mines, mid-century courts developed a rule which took into account the good or bad faith of the tortfeasor. This rule was that if the defendant had acted inadvertently in mining the coal (as where he mistakenly assumed it to be his), then he would be liable for its value at the coalface; but if he had intentionally or negligently violated his neighbour's property right, then he was liable for the full value of the chattel, even if he had increased its value in taking it to market.[69] In actions of trover, the plaintiff was similarly awarded the value of the goods taken. Normally, this would be the market price of the goods at the moment when they were demanded by the plaintiff.[70] In trover, it was for the plaintiff to prove the value of the goods taken. As Patteson J. put it in 1838, '[t]he injury done to the plaintiff is by the conversion of those articles which are proved to have been converted, and the value of such as have never been returned, is the proper measure of damages'.[71] Plaintiffs in trover were able to make claims for additional special damage, as where the taking of the plaintiff's tools of trade deprived him of the chance to work; but even here, the jury would award the sum which had been shown to have been lost.[72] Mid-nineteenth century judges who developed rules to guide juries on how to value property which had been wrongfully taken nonetheless often remained content to give juries considerable leeway in awarding sums. 'Juries have not much compassion for trespassers', Alderson B. noted in 1841, where a sheriff was sued for wrongfully taking and selling the plaintiff's goods, 'and I do not think they are bound to weigh in golden scales how much injury a party has sustained by a trespass.'[73]

---

[68] *Jones* v. *Gooday* (1841) 8 M. & W. 146; *Hosking* v. *Phillips* (1848) 3 Exch. 168 at 182; *Whitham* v. *Kershaw* (1885) 16 QBD 613 (CA).

[69] See *Martin* v. *Porter* (1839) 5 M. & W. 351; *Wild* v. *Holt* (1842) 9 M. & W. 672; *Morgan* v. *Powell* (1842) 3 Q.B. 278, explained in *Hilton* v. *Woods* (1867) LR 4 Eq 432 and *Mayne's Treatise on Damages* (7th edn, by J. D. Mayne and L. Smith, 1903), 416–17. See also *Wood* v. *Morewood* (1841) 3 Q.B. 440. In all of these cases, plaintiffs were also entitled to additional damages for injuries done to the property, and for way-leave.

[70] *Henderson & Co* v. *Williams* [1895] 1 QB 521 (CA).

[71] *Cook* v. *Hartle* (1838) 8 Car. & P. 568 at 570.

[72] *Bodley* v. *Reynolds* (1846) 8 Q.B. 779; *Davis* v. *Oswell* (1837) 7 Car. & P. 804.

[73] *Lockley* v. *Pye* (1841) 8 M. & W. 133 at 135.

Where the wrong done did not involve depriving the plaintiff of his property, but consisted of a personal injury, or injury to his reputation, juries had far greater latitude in awarding damages. Judges were reluctant to order new trials on the grounds that excessive damages had been awarded, unless the damages were 'enormous and disproportionate'[74] or the jury acted under error or the influence of undue motives.[75] The fact that high damages were given was not itself taken as a sign of error by the jury.[76] Only if the damages were so high that no reasonable jury could have awarded them would a new trial be ordered.[77] Where a plaintiff had suffered personal injury, or an insult to his reputation, the courts were loath to intervene, since calculating the cost of the injury was a tricky matter, depending on all the circumstances of the case.[78] It would not be until the second half of the twentieth century that the courts sought to achieve consistency in damages awards in personal injury cases, by drawing analogies with damages determinations in previous cases.[79]

Judges were also content to allow the law of torts to be used as an instrument of punishment, rather than compensation. In some areas of tort law, it was regarded by judges as particularly appropriate for juries to condemn immoral conduct through the award of damages. Where fathers brought actions for the debauching of their daughters, *per quod servitium amisit*, it was held that the measure of damages was not calculated by the value of her service to her father, since '[a]ctions of this sort are brought for example's sake'.[80] In other areas, where questions of family honour were at stake—notably in actions for criminal conversation—large damages were often expected to be awarded.[81] In other torts, evidence of the defendant's state of mind was admitted in mitigation or aggravation of damages, to allow the jury to punish tortfeasors for malice or wilful misconduct.[82] In dealing with damages of trespass to land, where the slightest incursion rendered the defendant liable at least to nominal damages, juries were asked to consider the defendant's intentions. If the defendant had acted with the intention of insulting or injuring the plaintiff, then larger sums might be awarded

---

[74] *Price* v. *Severn* (1831) 7 Bing. 316 at 318; cf. *Sharpe* v. *Brice* (1774) 2 W. Bl. 942; *Leith* v. *Pope* (1779) 2 W. Bl. 1327; *Williams* v. *Currie* (1845) 1 C.B. 841.

[75] *Chambers* v. *Caulfield* (1805) 6 East 244.

[76] e.g. *Lambkin* v. *South Eastern Railway Co* (1880) 5 App Cas 353 PC.

[77] *Praed* v. *Graham* (1889) 24 QBD 53 (CA).

[78] Where the tort consisted of a minor affront to a person of lower status, the courts more readily intervened to order new trials: *Jones* v. *Sparrow* (1793) 5 T.R. 257; *Price* v. *Severn* (1831) 7 Bing. 316.

[79] See P. Mitchell, *The Making of the Modern Law of Defamation* (Oxford, 2005), 57–9. See also XIII, Pt 5, Ch. I.

[80] *Tullidge* v. *Wade* (1768) 3 Wils. K.B. 18 at 19; *Bennett* v. *Allcott* (1787) 2 T.R. 166; *Irwin* v. *Dearman* (1809) 11 East 23.

[81] See XIII, Pt 4, Ch. IV.

[82] *Doe* v. *Filliter* (1844) 13 M. & W. 47 at 51.

as a punishment.[83] In 1814, a verdict of £500 awarded against a banker who had trespassed on the plaintiff's land was upheld by the Common Pleas, which found that the defendant's drunken conduct was unbecoming of a gentleman. In Heath J.'s judgment, allowing heavy damages against gentlemen who misconducted themselves was a good way to prevent offended parties from resorting to duels.[84] In the mid-century, it was confirmed that juries could take into consideration the defendant's motives, in actions for harms caused by negligence. It was universally felt, Pollock CB observed in 1860, 'that there is a difference between an injury which is the mere result of such negligence as amounts to little more than accident, and an injury, wilful or negligent, which is accompanied with expressions of insolence'.[85] Where the tort was one charging malice, as in malicious prosecutions, judges allowed very high awards of damages to remain unimpeached. In 1813, for instance, the Common Pleas refused to set aside an award of £2000 to an attorney's clerk who had been wrongfully indicted for embezzlement by his employer.[86] Similarly, in defamation, juries were left with a wide discretion in awarding damages, and were expected to award larger sums where the defendant's motive had been malicious.[87]

The bottom line in tort cases—the sums to be recovered by the plaintiff—therefore remained largely a matter for determination by the voice of the community's morality—the 12 jurymen. Judicial control of the jury in tort cases did not take the form of elaborating rules for the calculation of damages. Instead, judges sought to control juries by controlling the evidence which they were permitted to consider, and by specifying to them what constituted a duty, and what counted as a breach of duty. In the mid-nineteenth century, when juries were eager to give high damages awards against railway companies, and when those companies were eager to defend cases which threatened to expand their liability, some judges did try to rein in the scope for juries to determine liability. But towards the end of our period, judges and jurists began to develop broader notions of duty, which would reflect a broader notion of community morality, which might derive from the sense of the jury.

---

[83] *Sears* v. *Lyons* (1818) 2 Stark. 317.

[84] *Merest* v. *Harvey* (1814) 5 Taunt. 442 at 444.

[85] *Emblen* v. *Myers* (1860) 6 H. & N. 54 at 58. See also *Bell* v. *Midland Railway Co* (1861) 10 C.B. N.S. 287.

[86] *Hewlett* v. *Cruchley* (1813) 5 Taunt. 277. He had spent £100 in clearing his name.

[87] *Pearson* v. *Lemaitre* (1843) 5 M. & G. 700.

II
Negligence

1. THE BIRTH OF NEGLIGENCE

THE eighteenth-century structure of pleading left relatively little room to explore questions of fault.[1] When the action of trespass was used, it was not necessary for plaintiffs to show that their adversaries had been at fault when harming them by their actions, but only that the act—such as firing a gun—had caused the harm. Liability was not strict, for the defendant could avoid liability by showing that the harm was the result of an 'inevitable accident', or 'utterly without his fault'.[2] But few defendants sought to explore precisely what this meant, since to do so required them to admit the facts charged.[3] The question of fault was more likely to arise where harms had resulted from the defendant's 'neglect'. For the most part, when defendants were charged with 'negligence', the gist of the action was that they had 'neglected' to perform a duty, such as keeping their fire or their cattle from harming others;[4] although it had been recognized, by the start of the eighteenth century, that a defendant could be held liable for harms resulting from his negligence, even absent such a duty.[5] At the start of the eighteenth century, liability for harms caused by neglect was often spoken of in the same terms as harms caused by direct actions. As one lawyer expressed it, 'a man shall be answerable for all mischief proceeding from his neglect or his actions, unless they were of unavoidable necessity'.[6] However, by the middle of

[1] I am grateful to Mark Lunney for his helpful comments on the subject of this chapter.

[2] *Weaver* v. *Ward* (1616) Hob. 134. For a discussion, See S. G. Gilles, 'Inevitable Accident in Classical English Tort Law' (1994) 43 *Emory Law J.l* 575–646 at 589 *et seq*; R. J. Kaczorowski, 'The Common-Law Background of Nineteenth Century Tort Law' (1990) 51 *Ohio State Law J.* 1127–99 at 1170–1; D. J. Ibbetson, *A Historical Introduction to the Law of Obligations* (Oxford, 1999), Ch. 8.

[3] Ibbetson, *Historical Introduction*, 158.

[4] See J. Comyns, *A Digest of the Laws of England*, 6 vols (1800), i, 279 *et seq.* (tit. Action upon the case for Negligence).

[5] *Mitchell* v. *Allestry* (1676) in J. H. Baker and S. F. C. Milsom, *Sources of English Legal History: Private Law to 1750* (1986), 572.

[6] *Mason* v. *Keeling* (1700) 1 Ld. Raym. 606 at 607.

the century, a broader notion of fault was beginning to gain ground. A treatise attributed to Francis Buller began its chapter on 'injuries arising from negligence or folly' with the statement that '[e]very man ought to take reasonable care that he does not injure his neighbour'.[7]

The principle proclaimed in this text remained largely undeveloped at the start of our period, but by its end it had come to be central to many jurists' conception of the law of torts, and negligence was coming to be recognized as an independent tort.[8] In this chapter, the development of the concept of negligence and its place in the law of torts will be explored. In the following chapters, the substantive law relating to personal injuries will be examined.

Road Accidents

It was in the context of the road transport revolution, and the rapid expansion of towns in the early nineteenth century, that the concept of fault took hold in English law. Thanks to the late eighteenth-century transformation in road building, by the 1830s there were 15 times as many road passengers as 40 years before.[9] The need to combine speed with numbers of passengers inevitably led to a high number of accidents. Statutes were passed to regulate the construction of vehicles and limit passenger numbers.[10] Proprietors were fined for breaking these rules. Drivers were frequently fined for furious driving, particularly when drunk, and prosecuted for manslaughter when fatalities followed.[11] Much to the regret of some judges, the coach-owners could not be reached by this law,[12] though some magistrates did bend the law to prosecute them for the furious driving of their servants.[13]

---

[7] F. Buller (ed.), *An Introduction to the Law Relative to Trials at Nisi Prius* (1772), 25.

[8] P. H. Winfield, 'The Foundation of Liability in Tort' (1927) 27 *Columbia Law Rev.*, 1–11. The House of Lords would give expression to its foundational principle in *Donoghue* v. *Stevenson* [1932] AC 562. For further discussions of the history of tort in our period, see M. J. Prichard, '*Scott* v. *Shepherd* (1773) and the Emergence of the Tort of Negligence', *The Selden Society Lectures, 1952–2001* (Buffalo, 2003), 415–57. D. J. Ibbetson, '"The Law of Business Rome": Foundations of the Anglo-American Tort of Negligence' (1999) 52 *Current Legal Problems*, 74–109; D. J. Ibbetson, 'The Tort of Negligence in the Common Law in the Nineteenth and Twentieth Centuries' in E. J. H. Schrage (ed.), *Negligence* (Berlin, 2001), 220–71; D. Kretzmer, 'Transformation of Tort Liability in the Nineteenth Century: The Visible Hand' (1984) 4 *OJLS* 46–87.

[9] P. S. Bagwell, *The Transport Revolution* (2nd edn, 1988), 27–31.

[10] 28 Geo. III c. 57; 30 Geo. III c. 36; 46 Geo. III c. 136; 50 Geo. III c. 48. See also Third Report from the Committee on the Highways of the Kingdom, *PP* 1808 (315), ii, 527, at pp. 197–9, 205.

[11] The law relating to manslaughter was stiffened in 1823 (3 Geo. IV c. 38): see the prosecution of Joseph Hodgkiss in *The Times*, 10 March 1826, col. 3f.

[12] *The Times*, 4 August 1827, col. 3d.

[13] See the prosecution of William Pool in *The Times*, 20 July 1824, col. 4c. He was convicted under 3 Geo. IV c. 95, s 11, which extended liability to beyond the driver and guard to any 'other Person having care of' the coach; though its wording made them liable only if they were intoxicated.

Coach passengers and bystanders who had been injured in accidents regularly sued coach proprietors for damages. There was a great incentive to do so, given that the coach firms were large, highly capitalized concerns, involving large partnerships.[14] For the most part, proprietors were prepared to settle claims, often generously.[15] They resisted payment only when they felt that the plaintiff was seeking excessive damages.[16] Rather than disputing genuine claims, they preferred to try to make their drivers pay.[17] So determined were some coach owners to recover from their drivers that they refused to release them from liability,[18] thereby disqualifying them from testifying on their master's behalf in actions brought by the victim.[19] Although owners took such positions to reassure the public of their concerns for safety, it was nevertheless well known that they encouraged speed.

The litigation which emerged from these accidents played a significant part in developing the law of negligence.[20] Two kinds of litigant came to court. The first was the victim who had not been a passenger in the defendant's coach, but who was a bystander or traveller in another vehicle which was hit. When coach accident litigation had first come to court around the turn of the nineteenth century, the question had been raised whether trespass or case was the correct form of action to use in such cases. According to *Scott* v. *Shepherd*,[21] trespass was to be used where the harm was direct, while case was to be used for consequential harms. This distinction suggested that if a coach driven by the defendant directly struck the plaintiff's vehicle, as a result of his furious driving, trespass

---

[14] D. Gerhold, *Road Transport Before the Railways: Russell's London Flying Waggons* (Cambridge, 1993), Ch. 3.

[15] e.g. *Tapley* v. *Willan*, *The Times*, 5 July 1815, col. 3e. In another case, Abbott J. observed that 'Mr Willan acts with great propriety on questions of this kind.' *Kickson* v. *Willan*, *The Times* 2 July 1817, col. 3d.

[16] e.g. *Vazie* v. *Bretherton*, *The Times*, 22 August 1825, col. 2f; *Hughes* v. *Eames*, *The Times*, 23 July 1823, col. 3c; *Culverwell* v. *Eames and Billett*, *The Times*, 29 May 1823, col. 4a.

[17] For instance, the Leeds coach proprietor Peter Brotherton recovered the compensation he had agreed to pay a victim of a coach crash from the driver of his coach: *Waterhouse and Brotherton* v. *Boswood*, *The Times*, 8 January 1825, col. 3e. In 1827, he unsuccessfully sought to deduct the value of a horse from the wages of a driver involved in an accident—amounting to 47 weeks' wages: *Scott* v. *Brotherton*, *The Times*, 15 September 1827, col. 3b.

[18] Contrast *Vazie* v. *Bretherton*, *The Times*, 22 August 1825, col. 2f with *Bretherton* v. *Davies*, *The Times*, 3 September 1830, col. 4a.

[19] On the rule requiring a release, see *Morish* v. *Foote* (1818) 8 Taunt. 454; cf. the comments of Lord Kenyon in *Green* v. *New River Company* (1792) 4 T.R. 589 and the comments of Lord Ellenborough in *Cuthbert* v. *Gostling* (1814) 3 Camp. 515. See also *Kerrison* v. *Coatsworth* (1825) 1 Car. & P. 645 ; *Wake* v. *Lock* (1833) 5 Car. & P. 454.

[20] See esp. M. J. Prichard, '*Scott* v. *Shepherd*' and *idem*. 'Trespass, Case and the Rule in *Williams v Holland*' (1964) *CLJ* 234–53.

[21] *Scott* v. *Shepherd* (1773) 2 W. Bl. 892.

was the correct form to use,[22] whereas if the harm resulted consequentially from nonfeasance (such as where ships had collided as a result of the defendant's 'negligent and improvident management'), an action on the case lay. Some lawyers had attempted in the late eighteenth century to develop the distinction, arguing that trespass was the proper form where the act was 'wilful', and case was the proper form where the injury resulted from negligence.[23] But in 1803, the King's Bench held that where there was 'an immediate injury from an immediate act of force by the defendant, the proper remedy is trespass; and wilfulness is not necessary to constitute trespass'.[24] At the start of our period, the view of the King's Bench judges was that trespass was the correct form to use in road accident cases against negligent drivers, while the Common Pleas judges felt that the action on the case was the appropriate form.[25] Pleaders choosing the form of action to use faced the further difficulty that, in most road accident cases (though not all),[26] it was not the coach proprietor, but his servants, who had been holding the reins. Despite some doubts, by the start of our period, the King's Bench and Common Pleas agreed that an action on the case was the correct form to use against the master,[27] who would be sued for 'compensation for the damage consequential from his employing of an unskilful or negligent servant'.[28]

In practice, given that most accidents involved coaches driven by servants, case was the form which came predominantly to be used. The use of this form encouraged a greater focus on the substantive issue of negligence. Judges gradually began to allow its use where the harm had been directly inflicted by the defendant.[29] When, in 1825, three coach proprietors objected that the plaintiff should have sued in trespass rather than case, after it was found that one of the defendants had himself been driving the coach, the King's Bench rejected the argument. Bayley J. noted that although trespass was necessary where the harm

---

[22] *Day* v. *Edwards* (1794) 5 T.R. 648. In Lord Kenyon's view, it was essential to keep the forms distinct, since nominal damages carried costs in case but not in trespass: *Savignac* v. *Roome* (1794) 6 T.R. 125.

[23] *Ogle* v. *Barnes* (1799) 8 T.R. 188 at 192; *Turner* v. *Hawkins* (1796) 1 B. & P. 472.

[24] *Leame* v. *Bray* (1803) 3 East 593 at 600. In this case, where the defendant had been driving a carriage, and through his lack of skill crashed into another, trespass was the correct form to use.

[25] *Rogers* v. *Imbleton* (1806) 2 B. & P. N.R. 117. Here the declaration was in case for negligently driving a cart against the plaintiff's horse with force and violence.

[26] In 1823, the proprietor Peter Brotherton was acquitted of manslaughter for having himself run over a deaf man collecting weeds by the roadside, *The Times*, 19 August 1823, col. 3a.

[27] *Morley* v. *Gaisford* (1795) 2 H. Bl. 441. See Kenyon's earlier view (that trespass should be used) in *Savignac* v. *Roome* (1794) 6 T.R. 125 at 130.

[28] *M'manus* v. *Crickett* (1800) 1 East 106 at 108. See also the comments of Chambre J. in *Huggett* v. *Montgomery* (1807) 2 B. & P. N.R. 446 at 448 and also *Bowcher* v. *Noidstrom* (1809) 1 Taunt. 568.

[29] *Lloyd* v. *Needham* (1823) 11 Price 608.

was 'wilful', case could be used for negligence.[30] Since '[t]he real ground of action is the negligence of Hardern', Holroyd J. held that the remedy in trespass could be waived and the action in case substituted.[31] In 1833, the Common Pleas in *Williams* v. *Holland* confirmed that trespass did not have to be used, where the ground of action was an injury occasioned by the defendant's own careless driving. For, as Tindal CJ put it, 'carelessness and negligence is, strictly and properly in itself, the subject of an action on the case'.[32] Provided that the act was not 'wilful', case could be brought.

In road accident cases, the focus of attention was therefore increasingly on whether the driver had been negligent. Judges were already very familiar with the idea that liability depended on carelessness from their handling of criminal cases involving road accidents. 'The lives of those who travel in stage-coaches are, for the time, placed in the hands of the individuals who drive them', Bayley J. told one jury in 1821, 'and it is only by the punishment of negligence that protection can be ensured to them'.[33] Two years later he told a jury that

In driving along a public road, the caution and care of the driver must be regulated by a variety of local circumstances, according as the road may be situate, according as it may be frequented by the old and infirm, the feeble and the young, who cannot be expected to get out of the way of a coach driven at a quick pace, as smartly as stronger people could, and under such circumstances proportionate caution was required on the part of the driver.[34]

Judges were also aware from other kinds of litigation that when accidents occurred in the world at large, liability should not be strict, but depend on whether reasonable care had been taken. In *Daniels* v. *Potter*, for instance, where a cellar flap which had been left open fell onto the plaintiff's leg, Tindal CJ ruled that tradesmen were not bound to use the strictest care, but were 'bound to use such care as any reasonable man, looking at it, would say was sufficient'.[35]

The fact that careful conduct in the public domain could prevent accidents made judges increasingly aware that plaintiffs might be to blame for the harm themselves. It was argued that if the plaintiff had contributed to an accident by his

---

[30] 'No doubt that action lies when an injury is incited by the wilful act of the defendant, but it is also clear that case will lie where the act is negligent, and not wilful:' *Moreton* v. *Hardern* (1825) 4 B. & C. 223 at 227.

[31] *Moreton* v. *Hardern* (1825) 4 B. & C. 223 at 228.

[32] *Williams* v. *Holland* (1833) 10 Bing. 112 at 115.

[33] *The Times*, 25 August 1821, col. 4a

[34] *The Times*, 19 August 1823, col. 3a.

[35] *Daniels* v. *Potter* (1830) 4 Car. & P. 262. Cf. his ruling in *Proctor* v. *Harris* (1830) 4 Car. & P. 337 (where a cellar flap was left open) that the defendant 'was not bound to resort to every mode of security that could be surmised, but he was bound to use such a degree of care as would prevent a reasonable person, acting with an ordinary degree of care, from receiving an injury'.

own negligence, 'it was but fair that they should both swim in the same boat'.[36] In this context, the courts began to develop rules of contributory negligence, in order to establish who had caused the harm. In *Butterfield* v. *Forrester*, where the defendant had left a pole in the street which the plaintiff had ridden into, Bayley J. told a jury that they should find for the defendant 'if a person riding with reasonable and ordinary care could have seen and avoided the obstruction'. Lord Ellenborough agreed: 'One person being in fault will not dispense with another's using ordinary care for himself.'[37] Similarly in *Flower* v. *Adam*, where the plaintiff's horse was frightened by dust blown from a heap of rubbish left by the defendant in front of his house, leading to his chaise being damaged, the defendant succeeded. In the court's view, the proximate cause of the accident was the driver's unskilfulness, not the negligence of the defendant.[38] In public spaces, care was expected to be taken by both sides. Only if the accident was entirely attributable to the defendant would he lose.[39] Plaintiffs had a duty to take ordinary care to avoid accidents, even if (for instance) it meant going onto the wrong side of the road to avoid an accident.[40] As Abinger CB put it in one case, '[t]he negligence of the plaintiff, in order to preclude him from recovering, must be such as that he could by ordinary care have avoided the consequences of the defendants' negligence'.[41]

Victims of road accidents were still able, after *Williams* v. *Holland*, to sue in trespass. This did not mean that liability was necessarily stricter in that form.[42] It was certainly easier to deny fault in case than in trespass. Since the declaration in case alleged negligence (in the performance of an otherwise lawful activity), defendants were permitted to provide evidence on the general issue that the

---

[36] *Meux and Co* v. *Poole, The Times*, 18 November 1820, col. 3e (Sir James Scarlett).

[37] *Butterfield* v. *Forrester* (1809) 11 East 60 at 61.

[38] *Flower* v. *Adam* (1810) 2 Taunt. 314. Sir James Mansfield told the trial jury that if the mishap was the result of pure accident or the lack of the plaintiff's skill as a horseman, he could not recover: only if there was 'blameable negligence' by the defendant could he succeed.

[39] e.g. *Vanderplanck* v. *Miller* (1828) M. & M. 169 at 170. Cf. *Vennall* v. *Garner* (1832) 1 Car. & M. 22; *Luxford* v. *Large* (1833) 5 Car. & P. 421; *Sills* v. *Brown* (1840) 9 Car. & P. 601. See also *Drew* v. *The New River Company* (1834) 6 Car. & P. 754 at 756; *Hawkins* v. *Cooper* (1838) 8 Car. & P. 473 at 474.

[40] *Turley* v. *Thomas* (1837) 8 Car. & P. 103. Cf. *Hawkins* v. *Cooper* (1838) 8 Car. & P. 473, where Tindal CJ spoke of the need for 'common caution'; and *Woolf* v. *Beard* (1838) 8 Car. & P. 373 where Coleridge J. spoke of 'ordinary care', in *Marriott* v. *Stanley* (1840) 1 M. & G. 568, Bosanquet spoke of reasonable and ordinary care by the plaintiff. The courts, however, were sometimes more charitably disposed to foot passengers: see *Cotterill* v. *Starkey* (1839) 8 Car. & P. 691.

[41] *Bridge* v. *Grand Junction Railway Co* (1838) 3 M. & W. 244 at 247.

[42] In 1841, Tindal CJ intimated that the liability regimes in trespass and case differed, with the former being stricter than the latter. 'Where a servant drives his master's carriage against the carriage of another, trespass might be brought against the servant, and inevitable necessity would form the only excuse', he noted, 'But if an action on the case be brought against the master, the inquiry has always been, not whether the injury was the result of inevitable necessity, but of negligence on the part of the servant': *Aldridge* v. *The Great Western Railway Co* (1841) 3 M. & G. 515 at 521.

collision had been purely accidental, or had been the fault of the victim.[43] By contrast, in trespass, where the declaration put in issue the wrongful act of the defendant in striking the plaintiff, questions of fault could not be raised as easily. Evidence of accidental harm could be given under a plea of not guilty only if the harm had been caused by some other intervening force, rather than the defendant's own act.[44] If the harm had resulted from the defendant's own act, any justification had to be put on the record by a special plea.[45] If the defendant failed to make the necessary plea—such as, that the plaintiff had been paralytic and walking in the middle of the street when he was hit—the jury would only be asked if the defendant had run over the plaintiff.[46] In practice, where the requisite pleas were made, it may be doubted whether the courts treated the plea of inevitable accident when used in road accident cases brought in trespass very differently from how they treated denials of negligence. Given that defendants in trespass were permitted to enter a special plea alleging contributory negligence by the plaintiff, which raised issues of blame, there is reason to assume that courts would have allowed the jury to consider a defendant's plea of inevitable accident, if it was supported by sufficient evidence of lack of fault as to deny negligence.[47]

The second kind of litigation to arise from road accidents concerned passengers suing proprietors of the coaches in which they were travelling. Although the relationship between the parties in such cases was generally contractual, early nineteenth-century litigants were permitted to sue coach proprietors in tort, as common carriers sued on the custom of the realm.[48] Since it was not necessary to join all tortfeasors as defendants in such an action (whereas it was necessary to join all contractors), this proved advantageous to plaintiffs, who were generally ignorant of the complex business partnerships of the coach proprietors.[49] Litigation between coach owners and their passengers raised the question of

[43] *The Times*, 5 December 1805, col 3c. Cf. *Pluckwell* v. *Wilson* (1832) 5 Car. & P. 375.

[44] See *Gibbons* v. *Pepper* (1695) 1 Ld. Raym. 38; 4 Mod. 405; 2 Salk. 638. See also *Goodman* v. *Taylor* (1832) 5 Car. & P. 410, where the court allowed evidence on a not guilty plea to trespass that a pony and chaise had collided with a horse after the pony was frightened by a showman. As a result of this, the defendant's wife, who was standing with the horse, could no longer hold the reins.

[45] See e.g. *Milman* v. *Dolwell* (1810) 2 Camp. 378; *Knapp* v. *Salsbury* (1810) 2 Camp. 500; *Pearcy* v. *Walter* (1834) 6 C. & P. 232; *Hall* v. *Fearnley* (1842) 3 Q.B. 919.

[46] However, defendants might 'give evidence in mitigation of damages anything that does not amount to a defence'. *Boss* v. *Litton* (1832) 5 Car. & P. 407 at 409. Cf. *James* v. *Campbell* (1832) 5 Car. & P. 372.

[47] See *Wakeman* v. *Robinson* (1823) 1 Bing. 213.

[48] *Ansell* v. *Waterhouse* (1817) 6 M. & S. 385; *Bretherton* v. *Wood* (1821) 3 B. & B. 54 at 62; cf. *Wood* v. *Brotherton*, *The Times*, 11 November 1820, col. 4a.

[49] The courts nevertheless did allow defendants in such cases to recover a contribution from their fellow proprietors, against the normal rule that joint tortfeasors could not recover from each other: *Wooley* v. *Batte* (1826) 2 Car. & P. 417.

what standard of care was required. In 1791, in the first reported decision on the subject, Lord Kenyon ruled that the proprietors of mail coaches were bound to carry passengers 'safely and properly'.[50] This led some litigants to argue that just as common carriers were regarded as insurers of the goods they carried, so they were to be held strictly liable for the safety of their passengers. This idea was rejected by Eyre CJ in *Aston* v. *Heaven*, when he declared that this 'action stands on the ground of negligence alone'.[51] There were good policy reasons for this, for (as James Scarlett pointed out), if coach proprietors were to become insurers for the safety of passengers, 'no one would undertake a responsibility the extent of which was so doubtful'.[52] The level of care needed was in effect that which would contractually have been required of someone providing a service. As Best CJ put it:

The coachman must have competent skill, and must use that skill with diligence; he must be well acquainted with the road he undertakes to drive; he must be provided with steady horses; a coach and harness of sufficient strength, and properly made; and also with lights by night. If there be the least failure in any one of these things, the duty of the coach proprietors is not fulfilled, and they are answerable for any injury or damage that happens. But [...] It is not his fault, if having exerted proper skill and care, he from accident gets off the road.[53]

Coach drivers, like other professionals, were expected to have competent diligence and skill.[54]

Where the vehicle was itself faulty, the courts tended to take a stricter view. In 1809, Sir James Mansfield held that it was *prima facie* evidence of negligence if a coach broke and injured the plaintiff. When this occurred, the onus was on the defendant to prove 'that the coach was as good a coach as could be made, and that the driver was as skilful a driver as could anywhere be found'.[55] Six years earlier, Lord Ellenborough held that proprietors 'were bound by law to provide a sufficient carriage for the safe conveyance of the public who had occasion to travel by them'.[56] In 1824, Best CJ similarly observed that 'every coach-proprietor warrants to the public that his stage-coach is equal to the journey it undertakes', though in

---

[50]   *White* v. *Boulton* (1791) Peake N.P. 113.

[51]   *Aston* v. *Heaven* (1797) 2 Esp. 533 at 535. Nevertheless, he held that 'a driver is answerable for the smallest negligence'.

[52]   *Culverwell* v. *Eames and Billett, The Times*, 29 May 1823, col. 4a.

[53]   *Crofts* v. *Waterhouse* (1825) 3 Bing. 319 at 320–1.

[54]   See *Hughes* v. *Eames, The Times*, 23 July 1823, col. 3c; *Vazie* v. *Bretherton, The Times*, 22 August 1825, col. 2f. Cf. *Lack* v. *Seward* (1829) 4 Car. & P. 106; *Pluckwell* v. *Wilson* (1832) 5 Car. & P. 375.

[55]   *Christie* v. *Griggs* (1809) 2 Camp. 79 at 81. In this case the axletree had been inspected and appeared to be sound, as far as the human eye could see.

[56]   *Israel* v. *Clark and Clinch* (1803) 4 Esp. 259.

the case before him he felt there was also clear proof of negligence.[57] Similarly, in 1833, Alderson J. ruled that 'a coach proprietor is liable for all defects in his vehicle which can be seen at the time of construction, as well as for such as may exist afterwards and be discovered on investigation'.[58]

Lost Goods

In road accident cases, the courts did not explore the meaning of negligence in great detail, preferring to leave it to the common sense of the jury to find fault. Its meaning was explored more fully in another kind of litigation brought with great frequency against common carriers, who had a duty (by the common custom of the realm) to carry any goods offered for a reasonable charge. Although a number of eighteenth-century judges regarded actions against common carriers who lost or damaged goods as contractual, whether declared on the custom of the realm or in assumpsit,[59] by the early nineteenth century it was agreed that the action could be laid either in tort or contract.[60] Like coach passengers, those who sent goods by carrier generally found it more convenient to sue in case.

At common law, carriers were strictly liable as insurers for any goods carried.[61] They were only exempted from liability if goods were destroyed by an act of God or the king's enemies, or in accidents 'such as could not happen by the intervention of man, as storms, lightning, and tempests'. The fact that the damage could not have been prevented by human care or foresight provided no defence.[62] Carriers were, however, allowed to limit their liability for valuable goods by making a special acceptance (charging a higher price),[63] and they were relieved of liability if they had been defrauded by the customer.[64]

---

[57] Bremner v. Williams (1824) 1 Car. & P. 414 at 416.

[58] Sharp v. Grey (1833) 9 Bing. 457 at 459–60. This case, and Bremner v. Williams, were pleaded in assumpsit. On these cases, see P. Karsten, Heart versus Head: Judge-Made Law in Nineteenth Century America (1997), 89–90.

[59] Dale v. Hall (1750) 1 Wils. K.B. 281. The matter may have been regarded as contractual since carriers tended to set their own prices and terms, rather than having them set by magistrates (as provided by a number of statutes): see Lord Kenyon's comments in Anon v. Jackson (1800) Peake Add. Cas. 185 at 186. Kenyon himself insisted that all contracting parties therefore had to be joined: see Buddle v. Wilson (1795) 6 T.R. 369; cf. Max v. Roberts (1807) 2 B. & P. N.R. 454.

[60] Govett v. Radnidge (1802) 3 East 62.

[61] This liability was founded on considerations of convenience. See Proprietors of the Trent Navigation v. Ward (1785) 3 Esp. 128 at 131 (Ashhurst J.).

[62] Dale v. Hall (1750) 1 Wils. K.B. 281; Forward v. Pittard (1785) 1 T.R. 27 at 33 (Lord Mansfield).

[63] See Titchburne v. White (1618) 1 Stra. 145; Morse v. Slue (1673) 1 Vent. 238.

[64] Kenrig v. Eggleston (1648) Aleyn 93; Gibbon v. Paynton (1769) 4 Burr. 2298 (where the customer hid £100 in an old nail bag containing hay).

By the early nineteenth century, carriers also limited their liability for valuable goods by notice. Judges in the first decade of the nineteenth century found this practice acceptable.[65] But by the second decade doubts had crept in.[66] Many judges and legal commentators felt that the ability of carriers to limit their liability had been carried to its utmost extent and should be curtailed.[67] In 1815, Lord Ellenborough regretted that the law allowed carriers to make their own terms, commenting that 'it leads to very great negligence'.[68] He struck a blow against the carriers in 1817 in *Kerr* v. *Willan*, finding against a proprietor who had failed to inform an illiterate porter of the contents of a notice.[69] The decision sent shock waves among the carriers, who argued that henceforth any customer would be able to avoid paying the higher rate chargeable for valuable goods simply by sending a deaf or blind man to deliver them. A raft of cases against proprietors followed.[70]

The judicial hostility to carriers[71] demonstrated a clear lack of business sense. Ellenborough's suggestion that carriers should give receipts and read them out to the illiterate was hardly workable at a coaching inn such as John Willan's *Bull and Mouth*, where seven clerks received 1000 parcels daily, one-third of them in the rush to catch the mail coaches.[72] Judges often overlooked the fact that carriers' clients were not simply vulnerable individuals, but large commercial enterprises which were fully aware of the effect of notices, but which sought to save money by not insuring the goods transported.[73] The carriers' publicists retorted to the

---

[65] *Nicholson* v. *Willan* (1804) 5 East 507. See also *Clay* v. *Willan* (1789) 1 H. Bl. 298; *Bignold* v. *Waterhouse* (1813) 1 M. & S. 255. Contrast Kenyon's earlier approach in *Hide* v. *Proprietors of the Trent and Mersey Navigation* (1793) 1 Esp. 36 and in *Kirkman* v. *Shawcross* (1796) 6 T.R. 14.

[66] *Down* v. *Fromont* (1814) 4 Camp. 40 at 41.

[67] See the reporter's comments in *Gouger* v. *Jolly* (1816) Holt 317 and Burrough J.'s lament in *Smith* v. *Horne* (1818) 8 Taunt. 144.

[68] *Maving* v. *Todd* (1815) 4 Camp. 225; cf. his comments in *Leeson* v. *Holt* (1816) 1 Stark. 186.

[69] *Kerr* v. *Willan* (1817) 2 Stark. 53; *The Times*, 28 April 1817, col. 3c; Holt 645n, aff'd in (1817) 6 M. & S. 150.

[70] See e.g. *Davies* v. *Willan and Others* (1817) 2 Stark. 279; *The Times*, 23 December 1817, col. 3c; *Currey* v. *Willan* (1818) *The Times*, 3 July 1818, col. 3e; *Baldock* v. *Waterhouse*, *The Times*, 19 July 1819, col. 3d; *Wood* v. *Waterhouse*, *The Times*, 21 December 1819, col. 4c.

[71] Burrough J. 'complained of the dictatorial and irresponsible manner in which carriers undertake the conveyance of goods to the entire alteration and subversion of the old law of the land': *Lea* v. *Pickford & Co*, *The Times*, 5 November 1823, col. 3c. Cf. Best CJ in *Brooke* v. *Pickwick* (1827) 4 Bing. 218; *Gill* v. *Waterhouse*, *The Times*, 29 April 1830, col. 3d.

[72] *Riley* v. *Horne* (1828) 5 Bing. 217 at 221, Best CJ acknowledged the difficulties of issuing receipts.

[73] The carriers' policy was aimed, among others, at country banks who remitted large quantities of negotiable instruments and notes by coach. Willan's publicist noted that a bank sending £1000 of notes weekly would save £4 a week by not insuring: J. Knipe, *A Letter to the Right Hon N Vansittart, Chancellor of the Exchequer &c &c and to Common Carriers in General tracing the Insecurity of Property while in the hands of carriers to the present state of the law and suggesting a remedy* (1819), 7–8.

THE BIRTH OF NEGLIGENCE

suggestion by judges that they could cover their own risks by putting up their prices by arguing that it revealed how 'unskilled in the minor matter of ordinary trade' the judiciary was,[74] unaware that increased charges might have an adverse effect on the transporters of bulky cheap goods, who might not be able to bear them as well.

If judicial hostility to the carriers was bad for business, it was good for the development of the law of negligence. The judges' suspicion of the carriers' desire to limit their liability made them construe the effect of notices in a way more friendly to the customer. They did this by exploring the carriers' liability for negligence. This question had already been examined in Sir William Jones's *Essay on the Law of Bailments*, first published in 1781. Jones distinguished between three degrees of care which the law imposed on bailees. Where a bailment benefited both the bailor and bailee (as in contracts of sale or hire), the bailee was liable for ordinary negligence. Where only the bailee was benefited (as where he borrowed for his own use), he was liable for the slightest negligence. Where it benefited only the bailor (as in a deposit), the bailee was liable only for 'gross' negligence, which tended towards fraud.[75] Although under this scheme, carriers should only have been liable for 'ordinary negligence', Jones pointed out that for policy reasons they were given an insurer's liability,[76] stricter even than that imposed where the bailment was for the bailor's sole benefit.

Where a notice was used, carriers attempted to contract out of this strict rule. Courts at the start of the century permitted them to contract not merely out of the strict liability, but also out of liability for ordinary negligence.[77] Only if the defendant had been guilty of such a tortious misfeasance as amounted to a renunciation of his duty as a common carrier was the limitation held void. Early nineteenth-century judges referred to this kind of misfeasance as 'gross' negligence. Examples of it were found where a waggoner who was told of a leaking cask of brandy failed to take any steps to stop the leak,[78] or where the goods were delivered to the wrong person.[79] Similarly, if the carrier of goods by a wrongful

---

[74] Knipe, *Letter*, 16.

[75] W. Jones, *An Essay on the Law of Bailments* (3rd edn, 1823, ed. W. Nichols), 6, 9. In the late eighteenth and early nineteenth centuries, the phrase 'gross negligence' was used by judges in numerous cases which did not involve bailments. Equity judges often spoke of gross negligence as akin to fraud. See e.g. *Tourle* v. *Rand* (1789) 2 Bro. C.C. 650; *Hughes* v. *Williams* (1806) 2 Ves. Jr. Supp. 311. Cf. *Moore* v. *Mourgue* (1776) 2 Cowp. 479; *Hope* v. *Cust*, cited in *Shirreff* v. *Wilks* (1800) 1 East 48. See also the discussion in Ibbetson, 'Law of Business Rome', 93–9, and 'Tort of 'Negligence', 231.

[76] Jones, *Bailments*, 100.

[77] *Nicholson* v. *Willan* (1804) 5 East 507.

[78] *Beck* v. *Evans* (1812) 16 East 244.

[79] *Birkett* v. *Willan* (1819) 2 B. & Ald. 356 (for the same litigation see also *Logan* v. *Willan*, *The Times*, 7 July 1818, col. 3e; *Basker* v. *Willan*, *The Times*, 9 November 1818, col. 3c; *Burkit* v. *Willan*, *The Times*, 11 November 1819, col. 3c; *Duff* v. *Budd* (1822) 1 B. & B. 177.

act divested himself of the charge of the goods, he lost the benefit of his notice, for this was not mere negligent performance of a contract, but the refusal to perform it.[80] In effect, the courts in the first decade of the century treated the notice as converting a strict liability into one where there was only liability for *culpa lata*.

As their hostility to carriers grew, however, judges began to hold that liability for ordinary negligence could not be excluded by notice. In *Bodenham* v. *Bennett*, the carriers were thus held unable to rely on the notice, when uninsured banknotes went missing on a stage coach whose driver was drunk. Garrow B. explained that the decision would teach owners 'that it is in their interest to employ persons capable of attending to their duty'.[81] The courts still used the language of 'gross' negligence, but in 1820 Best J. protested against using the phrase in a way as to require the jury to look for special blameworthiness. As with all bailees for reward, he said, they had to take the care that 'a prudent man would take of his own property'.[82] Judges continued to use the epithet 'gross', but did not expect juries to find for the plaintiff only where the carrier had been guilty of bad faith. Rather, the courts felt that while carriers should be allowed to contract out of the strict liability imposed on them by law (which in practice would have forced carriers to take very exacting precautions to prevent losses), they should not be allowed to contract out of their duty to take the ordinary degree of care which (by Jones's criteria) should be expected of a carrier. In practice, when judges asked juries whether the carrier had been guilty of 'gross' negligence, what they now meant was whether the carrier had failed to take ordinary care.[83]

Judges may have continued to use the epithet 'gross' in such cases out of an awareness that the plaintiff was often himself not blameless, in order to focus attention on which party was the more blameworthy. For instance, when Dallas J. asked a jury to consider whether the defendants had been guilty of 'gross' negligence, he drew their attention to the fact that the plaintiff had been culpable in delivering to them a valuable package without declaring its value: 'He lulls the defendants into a false security; for they would probably have taken more care, if they had known the value of the parcel.'[84] Using the epithet 'gross' for such judges may have been a way of telling a jury that they should consider that the level of

---

[80] *Garnett* v. *Willan* (1821) 5 B. & Ald. 53; *Sleat* v. *Fagg* (1822) 5 B. & Ald. 342.

[81] *Bodenham* v. *Bennett* (1817) 4 Price 31 at 34. Not all judges were as hostile to carriers: see *Smith* v. *Horne* (1817) Holt 643.

[82] *Batson* v. *Donovan* (1820) 4 B. & Ald. 21 at 30.

[83] See *Duff* v. *Budd* (1822) 1 B. & B. 177; *Riley* v. *Horne* (1828) 5 Bing. 217 at 225; Ibbetson, 'Law of Business Rome', 95.

[84] *Smith* v. *Horne* (1817) Holt N.P. 643 at 644–5. The jury found for the plaintiff, and the Common Pleas, manifesting a sense of hostility to such notices, confirmed that they regarded this as gross negligence: 8 Taunt. 144. See also *Batson* v. *Donovan* (1820) 4 B. & Ald. 21.

care needed to be proportionate to the level of known risk: but the level of care they expected was the care any ordinary informed carrier should be expected to take. As Abbott CJ told a jury in another case, the jury was to consider whether by negligence 'the plaintiff's property had been exposed to a greater degree of risk than [was] usually sustained in the carriage of such property'.[85] Asking juries if the carrier had simply been negligent would have been an invitation to juries to find for the plaintiff in each case.

In 1830, the carriers obtained legislation to protect them from liability in respect of parcels whose real value had been concealed. Under the Carriers Act, no land carrier was liable for the loss or injury to articles in parcels where their value exceeded £10, unless at the time of delivery, their nature and value was declared and a higher charge paid (s 1). Parties were also allowed to make their own special contracts, albeit not by general notice (section 6).[86] In 1834, the Exchequer ruled that a carrier was protected by the legislation when the plaintiff failed to declare the value of an expensive mirror, though he would not have been protected had he been guilty of a misfeasance, such as 'dashing the window to the ground'. In so ruling, Bayley B. commented that 'gross' negligence was the equivalent to such a misfeasance, implying that the statute protected carriers from negligence but not misfeasance. This was in effect to restate the early nineteenth-century rule.[87] In 1842, a customer whose silk had been lost (but who had failed to make the declaration) argued that the carrier was not protected by the Act where his servants had been 'grossly' negligent. Since the plaintiff dropped his accusation of misfeasance, Lord Denman CJ found the carriers were protected. Rejecting the contention that there was any distinction between gross and ordinary negligence, he observed that since the carrier would not lose items without some degree of negligence, he would be given no protection by the statute if he could be liable in such a case.[88]

---

[85] *Lambert* v. *Eames*, *The Times*, 3 March 1827, col. 4b. See also his comments in *Bradley* v. *Waterhouse*, *The Times*, 5 March 1828, col. 3f.

[86] 11 G. 4 and 1 W. 4 c. 68. However, statute did not protect the carrier from liability arising from the felonious act of his servants (s 9). Regarding thefts by one's servants, it had been established by *Finucane* v. *Small* (1795) 1 Esp. 315 that the bailee was only liable for the theft of his servants if he had been shown to be grossly negligent. In *Butt* v. *Great Western Railway* (1851) 11 C.B. 140, it was held that to succeed, a plaintiff who claimed his goods had been stolen by the defendant's servants had to show evidence of gross negligence: though the court seems to have considered that this need only require showing due caution by the defendant. See also J. Story, *Commentaries on the Law of Bailments* (4th edn, 1846), 336, § 335 and 401–2, § 407.

[87] *Owen* v. *Burnett* (1834) 1 C. & M. 353.

[88] *Hinton* v. *Dibbin* (1842) 2 Q.B. 646.

By 1843, 'gross' negligence was regarded as 'the same thing' as negligence 'with the addition of a vituperative epithet'.[89] The phrase began to fall out of fashion in a number of areas where judges had previously used it, as in cases of gratuitous bailments (following Holt and Jones) and in those of professional negligence. For example, in cases brought against negligent attorneys, judges had sometimes said that defendants could only be liable for *crassa negligentia*.[90] This only meant that the attorney had failed to live up to the standard expected of a professional in his position: *'gross'* negligence defined the borderline of actionability.[91] By the mid-century, judges preferred to ask whether a reasonable or ordinary degree of skill and care had been used. This did not mean that they lost sight of the need to instruct juries that a different degree of care was required from a professional than from a gratuitous bailee. However, each defendant was required to live up to the ordinary standard of care required of a person in his position.[92]

Expanding the Reach of Negligence

Just as judges used the concept of negligence to allow them to reimpose a duty which defendants had attempted to contract out of, so they began to use it to restore liability in cases where it had been removed by statute. This can be seen particularly from cases where damage was done by fire. At common law, by the common custom of the realm, a person had a duty to keep his fire safe, and the only defence available if it spread was inevitable accident, such as that the fire had spread by some external factor such as a sudden gust of wind.[93] As Lord Tenterden explained the old law, 'if a fire began on a man's own premises, by

[89] *Wilson* v. *Brett* (1843) 11 M. & W. 113 at 116 (Rolfe B.). This comment came in a case against a defendant who had ridden the plaintiff's horse to Peckham on his behalf, to show it to a potential buyer. The horse had fallen when ridden on slippery ground. The defendant argued that since he was a gratuitous bailee, the plaintiff had to show gross negligence; but the court held that all that had to be shown was that he failed to use the care reasonably to be expected of one in his position.

[90] *Godefroy* v. *Dalton* (1830) 6 Bing. 460 at 468. In *Lowry* v. *Guilford* (1832) 5 Car. & P. 234 at 235 Taunton J. contrasted 'gross negligence' and 'due diligence'. Similar language was used in a case against a parliamentary agent: *Godefroy* v. *Dalton* (1830) 6 Bing. 460. For a discussion, see J. Getzler, 'Duty of Care', in P. Birks and A. Pretto, *Breach of Trust* (Oxford, 2002), 41–74.

[91] Nonetheless, their use of this terminology was not consistent. In numerous cases involving 'professional' negligence, judges felt it unnecessary to use the epithet of 'gross' negligence, but rather asked whether the defendant had used reasonable and proper care: e.g. *Reece* v. *Rigby* (1821) 4 B. & Ald. 202; *Stannard* v. *Ullithorne* (1834) 10 Bing. 491 (attorneys); *Seare* v. *Prentice* (1807) 8 East 348; *Lanphier* v. *Phipos* (1838) 8 C. & P. 475 (medical); *Chapman* v. *Walton* (1833) 10 Bing. 57 (broker).

[92] See *Giblin* v. *M'Mullen* (1868) 5 Moore NS 434 and *Moffat* v. *Bateman* (1869) 6 Moore NS 369. As Getzler shows ('Duty of Care', 55–8), this meant (in cases of gratuitous bailment), a shift away from Holt's emphasis on subjective carelessness by the defendant.

[93] *Turberville* v. *Stamp* (1697) 3 Ld. Raym. 375. See also Comyns, *Digest*, i, 284 (tit. Action upon the case for Negligence, A 6); cf. J. I. Foote, 'Liability for fire before 1880' (1969) 20 *NILQ* 141–60;

which those of his neighbour were injured, the latter, in an action brought for such an injury, would not be bound in the first instance to show how the fire began, but the presumption would be (unless it were shown to have originated from some external cause) that it arose from the neglect of some person in the house'.[94] However, eighteenth-century statutes provided that no action could be brought against anyone on whose property a fire had accidentally begun.[95] In Blackstone's view, the legislation removed liability not only for accidental fires, but also for those negligently started.[96] This was a view which came to be challenged in the 1830s and 1840s.

In 1837, in *Vaughan* v. *Menlove*, an action on the case was brought against a defendant for so negligently constructing a hayrick on the edge of his land, that it spontaneously ignited, and set fire to two cottages on the plaintiff's land. The hayrick, which had stood for six weeks and become wet, had begun to smoulder, and the defendant was warned about its dangerous condition. However, he decided to 'chance it', as a result of which a fire broke out. When the case came to trial, attention centred on whether the damage resulted from the defendant's negligence or carelessness in managing his hayrick. Summing up at the Shrewsbury *assizes*, Patteson J. asked the jury whether the defendant 'had acted with such a reasonable degree of caution as a prudent and careful man might have been expected to exercise'. It was not enough if he had done what he himself felt was sufficient, for 'he might be a rash and imprudent person, and therefore his neighbour's property was not to be endangered by his injudicious conduct'.[97] Although the jury only awarded £5 damages, the defendant sought a new trial on the grounds of misdirection, claiming that it should have been asked whether he had acted *bona fide* according to his best judgment.

In the Common Pleas, the defendant argued that the principle underlying his liability was to be compared with that governing dangerous animals, where a *scienter* had to be alleged and proved. According to this view, the plaintiff would have to show that the defendant had subjectively been aware of the risk. This argument was countered by the plaintiff's view that where the danger was objectively apparent, the defendant was liable for neglecting to control it. Pointing out that the declaration stated that the defendant knew of the danger, yet negligently allowed

---

J. Oldham, *The Mansfield Manuscripts and the Growth of English Law in the Eighteenth Century*, 2 vols (1992), ii, 1117.

[94] *Becquet* v. *MacCarthy* (1831) 2 B. & Ad. 951, 958.

[95] 6 Ann. c. 31, 14 Geo. III c. 78. Fines were imposed on servants by whose negligence fires began. However, Lord Denman observed in *Filiter* v. *Phippard* (1847) 11 Q.B. 347 at 356 that 'making servants punishable for fires resulting from their negligence is no exemption of masters from responsibility for the same fault; for fires which accidentally begin are not fires produced by negligence'.

[96] *Comms*, i, 419.

[97] *Vaughan* v. *Menlove* (1836) 7 Car. & P. 525; *Ipswich J.*, 20 August 1836.

it to remain, Talfourd Sjt contended that 'there were no means of estimating the defendant's negligence, except by taking as a standard, the conduct of a man of ordinary prudence'. He added that, 'though new in specie, [the action] is founded on a principle fully established, that a man must so use his own property as not to injure that of others'.[98] This argument was accepted by the court, which endorsed the objective principle of liability in negligence. Instead 'of saying that the liability for negligence should be co-extensive with the judgment of each individual, which would be as variable as the length of the foot of each individual', Tindal CJ ruled, 'we ought rather to adhere to the rule which requires in all cases a regard to caution such as a man of ordinary prudence would observe'.[99]

The decision significantly applied the concept of ordinary prudence to the principle, *sic utere tuo ut alienum non laedas*. As Tindal CJ put it:

the case falls within the general rule of law which requires that a man shall so use his own property as not to injure or destroy that of his neighbour, and which renders him liable for all the consequences resulting from the want of due care and caution in the mode of enjoying his own.[100]

The *sic utere* principle was not usually discussed in such terms. Instead, where actions of trespass or nuisance were brought, it was generally noted that the invasion of established rights *per se* constituted an injury for which damages would lie, regardless of intent.[101] However, in this case, where no act of trespass had been committed by the defendant, and where the hayrick was not itself a nuisance, bringing an action on the case for negligence raised the question of the nature of the defendant's fault.

During argument in the case, Bosanquet J. made the observation that '[t]he course that a reasonably prudent and careful man would adopt is the criterion [of liability] in the case of a fire kept in a house'.[102] This comment was later taken by Lord Lyndhurst LC to identify a judicial feeling that while the liability for purely accidental fires may have been removed by statute, it remained for fires

---

[98] Although this was the first reported case on fires since *Turberville* v. *Stamp*, it was not quite a case of first impression, for there had been at least one other action on the case for negligently keeping a fire in the 1830s. This was a case before Alderson J. at the Berkshire Assizes, mentioned by Talfourd Sjt in argument: *Vaughan* v. *Menlove* (1837) 4 Scott 244 at 248.

[99] *Vaughan* v. *Menlove* (1837) 3 Bing. N.C. 468 at 475.

[100] *Vaughan* v. *Menlove* (1837) 4 Scott 244 at 251.

[101] See e.g. H. Broom, *A Selection of Legal Maxims* (2nd edn, 1848), 274–5. The same can be said of the cases where defendants were held liable for damage done by dangerous animals, of whose dangerous tendency they were aware: e.g. *Card* v. *Case* (1848) 5 C.B. 622. Both counsel in this case drew parallels with the case of dangerous animals.

[102] He added 'the same principle must govern this case': *Vaughan* v. *Menlove* (1837) 4 Scott 244 at 248.

negligently started.[103] A decade after *Vaughan* v. *Menlove*, it was confirmed that liability for negligently started fires was not excluded by statute.[104] As with carriers' notices, judges were keen to establish that liability could be reimposed where conduct was negligent.

Courts encountering statutes authorizing public works similarly began to interpret them as not authorizing harms occasioned by negligence. By 1830, it was clear that a body was justified in causing harm in the exercise of its statutory powers,[105] provided it did not exceed them, or act negligently.[106] In the following decade, an era of railway expansion saw a rise in litigation centred on the negligent execution of statutory powers, as sparks flying from railway locomotives driven under statutory powers caused fires on neighbouring property. The first case involving a fire caused by sparks from a railway engine was *Aldridge* v. *The Great Western Railway*, which came before the Common Pleas judges on a case stated for its opinion. For the plaintiff, Channell Sjt argued that the railway's statute gave it no authority to cause harms, but only to run engines. Though the declaration was in case for negligence, he argued that the defendant's liability did not turn on any weighing of fault, but fell within the *sic utere* principle, under which liability was strict. Arguing that the driver would have been liable in trespass—where his only defence could have been inevitable accident on *Weaver* v. *Ward* principles—he contended that his master had to be held vicariously liable in case, without any need to show negligence on his part. Drawing on the approach taken to faulty coaches in *Christie* v. *Griggs*,[107] he argued that the facts alleged (that the engine emitted sparks) showed *prima facie* that there had been negligence. In reply, Bompas Sjt contended that the statute authorized the use of the engines: so that the plaintiff had to show not merely a harm, but negligence, which could not be presumed merely from the fact that sparks flew. The court agreed with Bompas that negligence could not be presumed. However, it felt that the question had to be sent to a jury, to hear evidence which would reveal whether engines frequently set fire to

---

[103] *Viscount Canterbury* v. *Attorney General* (1843) 1 Ph. 306 at 320. The statutes were not mentioned in *Vaughan* v. *Menlove*, perhaps because the fire started spontaneously.

[104] In *Filliter* v. *Phippard* (1847) 11 Q.B. 347 at 357, Lord Denman CJ observed that the statute was overlooked in *Vaughan* v. *Menlove* because of the 'universal impression of eminent lawyers … that the clause in the Building Act respecting accidental fires cannot apply to such as are produced by negligence'. Foote, 'Liability for Fire' at 150–2 argues that the statute had no application to *Vaughan* since the latter case dealt with the unprecedented problem of a spontaneous combustion, rather than the defendant's fire which had got out of control.

[105] *The King* v. *Pease* (1832) 4 B. & Ad. 30, holding that a railway authorized by statute was not a nuisance.

[106] See *The Governor and Co of the British Cast Plate Manufacturers* v. *Meredith* (1792) 4 T.R. 794; *Sutton* v. *Clarke* (1815) 6 Taunt. 29 at 42; *Jones* v. *Bird* (1822) 5 B. & Ald. 837; *Hall* v. *Smith* (1824) 2 Bing. 156 at 159.

[107] *Christie* v. *Griggs* (1809) 2 Camp. 79.

stacks. This case is significant in a number of respects. First, the court rejected the notion that there was a strict liability for railway fires. This is not surprising, given the existence of the statute authorizing the use of engines, and the fact that Tindal himself had decided *Vaughan* v. *Menlove* only four years earlier. Secondly, the court imposed liability based on the idea of negligence, which involved notions of fault. When counsel sought to draw parallels with road accident cases to argue for a strict liability, Tindal CJ noted that, in case, the heart of the issue was negligence. But where in road cases the negligence at issue was that of the driver, it was evident here that the relevant negligence was that of the owner.[108]

By 1846, when the problem of fires caused by trains was no longer a novel one, Tindal CJ's attitude towards the railway companies had hardened, in a way to make things easier for plaintiffs. He no longer felt that he needed a jury to tell him that locomotives had a tendency to set hayricks on fire. In *Piggot* v. *The Eastern Counties Railway Company*, he invoked medieval precedents on the negligent keeping of fires,[109] and declared:

The defendants are a company intrusted by the legislature with an agent of an extremely dangerous and unruly character, for their own private and particular advantage: and the law requires of them that they shall, in the exercise of the rights and powers so conferred upon them, adopt such precautions as may reasonably prevent damage to the property of third persons through or near which their railway passes.[110]

Coltman J. agreed: the mere fact that the plaintiff's building were set on fire by sparks from the defendant's engine created a *prima facie* case of negligence.

In later cases involving fires caused by sparks, judges were similarly keen to impose a high level of liability on railways. Some were happy to ignore the question of statutory authorization altogether. In a case in 1853, Martin B. told a Liverpool jury that 'if locomotives are sent through the country emitting sparks, the persons doing so incur all the responsibilities of insurers', and he invited counsel to tender a bill of exceptions.[111] Bramwell B. took a similar view. However, in 1860 the Exchequer Chamber (following *R* v. *Pease*) ruled that while it was true that at common law anyone keeping a dangerous instrument was strictly liable for the harm it did, where an activity was permitted by statute, the party using the instrument was not liable 'if damage results from the use of such a thing independently of negligence'.[112] Nonetheless, the threshold for negligence might

---

[108] *Aldridge* v. *Great Western Railway Co* (1841) 3 M. & G. 515 at 523.

[109] *Beaulieu* v. *Fingham* (1401) Y.B. 2 Hen. 4, p.18, pl. 6.

[110] *Piggot* v. *The Eastern Counties Railway Co* (1846) 3 C.B. 229 at 240.

[111] See *Blyth* v. *Birmingham Waterworks Co* (1856) 11 Exch. 781 at 783.

[112] *Vaughan* v. *The Taff Vale Railway Co* (1860) 5 H. & N. 679 at 685. Bramwell continued to be of the view that *Pease* (and *Vaughan*) were wrong: see *Powell* v. *Fall* (1880) 5 QBD 597 (CA) at 601. However, the Exchequer Chamber did not doubt its view: *Smith* v. *The London and South Western*

be low. Williams J. told a jury on the Norfolk circuit in 1860 that railway companies were not merely bound to use all due care and skill, but 'were bound to avail themselves of all the discoveries which science had put within their reach for that purpose'.[113] Moreover, it was ruled by Blackburn J. in 1868 that where locomotive engines were used without statutory authorization, they were strictly liable for any harm done, regardless of negligence.[114]

In a number of other cases where statutory powers had been given, the courts elaborated the rule that it did not justify interference with the rights of others through negligence. In *Lawrence* v. *Great Northern Railway Co*, a railway company which was authorized by statute to build an embankment constructed it in such a way as to cause the plaintiff's land to flood, and was held liable in an action. As Patteson J. expressed it, 'the company might, by executing their words with proper caution, have avoided the injury which the plaintiff has sustained: and we think that the want of such caution is sufficient to sustain the action'.[115] The principle was reiterated throughout the century that an action lay for negligently doing what the legislature had authorised.[116]

2. DEFINING NEGLIGENCE

The 1820s and 1830s saw a significant expansion in liability for negligence. By 1840, the courts were often prepared to impose liability where defendants had generated risks in public places which had resulted in harms which could have been foreseen. For instance, in *Illidge* v. *Goodwin*, the owner of a cart, which had been left unguarded in the street, was held liable when the horse backed into the window of a china shop, after being whipped by a stranger. Tindal CJ observed that if a man left a cart in the street, he ran the risk of any mischief which it might run.[117] Similarly, in *Lynch* v. *Nurdin* in 1840, a seven-year-old child succeeded in an action, after he was thrown from a cart left unattended in the street. He had climbed onto the cart while his friend had led the horse.[118] The case was

---

Railway Co (1870) LR 6 CP 14. Bramwell B. repeated his dissenting view in *Hammersmith Railway Co* v. *Brand* (1869) LR 4 HL 171.

[113] *Fremantle* v. *The London and North-Western Railway Co* (1860) 2 F. & F. 337 at 340.

[114] *Jones* v. *The Festiniog Railway Co* (1868) LR 3 QB 733.

[115] *Lawrence* v. *Great Northern Railway Co* (1851) 16 Q.B. 654.

[116] *Geddis* v. *Proprietors of Bann Reservoir* (1878) 3 App Cas 430, 455. See also *The Mersey Docks and Harbour Board Trustees* v. *William Gibbs* (1864) LR 1 HL 93 at 112; *Brine* v. *Great Western Railway* 2 B. & S. 402. See also the comments of Truro LC in *London & North-Western Railway Co* v. *Bradley* (1851) 3 Mac. & G. 341; *Biscoe* v. *Great Eastern Railway Co* (1873) 16 Eq 636.

[117] *Illidge* v. *Goodwin* (1831) 5 Car. & P. 190.

[118] *Lynch* v. *Nurdin* (1840) 1 Q.B. 29.

problematic, since leaving a horse and cart in a street was not of itself wrong, while the plaintiff was clearly a trespasser who had contributed to the mischief by climbing onto the cart. However, Denman CJ noted that if the jury found that children were likely to resort to the spot, it would be gross negligence to leave the cart there.

In the years around the mid-century, judges began to rein in the scope of the growing tort of negligence. The developments of the 1820s and 1830s seemed to leave the law of negligence open-ended, and judges were now keen to set boundaries to its operation. They began to seek to define the nature of defend-ant's duty more precisely, and to take a narrow view of what constituted breach of duty, and causation of damages. In this way, they sought to develop a more mechanical view of liability for negligence, which would reduce the discretion of juries to award large damages against defendants with deep pockets, such as railway companies. By defining duties more precisely, judges could remove some cases from the jury altogether by holding that no duty had been breached. They could also remove cases from the jury by holding that the evidence pre-sented did not disclose such negligence as would amount to a breach of the duty.[119]

The narrower approach adopted can be seen from the 1863 case of *Cox* v. *Burbidge*, where a horse left in the street kicked and badly injured a child. In contrast to *Lynch*, the plaintiff here failed to recover. To entitle him to do so, Erle CJ ruled, there had to be 'some affirmative proof of negligence in the defendant in respect of a duty owing to the plaintiff'. In the court's view, no such duty had been shown. Even if the horse had been on the street unlawfully and the owner liable to be prosecuted under the Highway Act, this was no wrong to the child. Nor had it been shown that the owner knew of the animal's vicious tendency, which might have made him liable under a *scienter*. Even if there was negli-gence in the defendant, the court did not see how it had caused the damage, for '[i]t appears that the horse was on the highway, and that, without anything to account for it, he struck out and injured the plaintiff'.[120] Three years later, in *Mangan* v. *Atterton*, the Exchequer also took a narrow view of liability, in a case where a boy of four had his fingers crushed by a machine for grinding oilcake, which the plaintiff had exhibited unfenced and unguarded in a public place. The harm was done when the boy's brother turned the handle which operated it. Bramwell B. felt that there was no negligence in thus exposing the machine; while Martin B. said that even if there was negligence, this was too remote a

---

[119] See further, Ibbetson, *Historical Introduction*, 170–4.
[120] *Cox* v. *Burbidge* (1863) 13 C.B. N.S. 431 at 436.

cause of the harm to make him liable: 'The accident was directly caused by the act of the boy himself.'[121]

Defining Duties and their Breach

The first means by which the scope of negligence was narrowed was by defining duties more closely. Lamenting the 'undefined latitude of meaning in which the word "negligence" has been used', Erle J. in 1860 declared 'it essential to ascertain that there was a legal duty, and a breach thereof, before a party is made liable by reason of negligence'.[122] Six years later, Willes J. noted that '[c]onfusion has arisen from regarding negligence as a positive instead of a negative word. It is really the absence of such care as it was the duty of the defendant to use'.[123] Judges were clearly worried by the fact that juries were willing to give damages on the merest suggestion that defendants—particularly railway companies—had been negligent. This was made clear by the Common Pleas in 1866, in *Smith* v. *Great Eastern Railway Company*, where the plaintiff had been bitten by a stray dog on a station platform while waiting for a train. Evidence was given that the dog had pounced at a woman at 9 pm, attacked a cat at 10.30 pm (when it was driven away by the porter) and had then bitten the plaintiff at 10.40 pm. The jury's verdict for the plaintiff for £50 was overturned in the Common Pleas, where Willes J. ruled that it was not enough to show damage might have occurred through the negligence of the railway staff: 'The plaintiff must show something which the defendants might have done, and which they omitted to do, before they can be held responsible for the misfortune which has happened to her.'[124]

Instead of attempting to develop a broad independent tort of negligence, judges now sought to identify duties of care which could be linked to the interests protected by the old forms of action. They were aware that the strict liabilities associated with trespass and nuisance could not appropriately be applied to accidental harms occurring in the world at large. But they did not wish to develop an open-ended tort of negligence. As a result, liability in negligence was linked to specific, recognized common law duties. A duty to ensure passenger safety was recognized, which was analogous to contractual duties, or to duties imposed by those exercising a 'common calling'. The duty to take care to avoid collisions was seen

---

[121] *Mangan* v. *Atterton* (1866) LR 1 Ex 239.

[122] *Marfell* v. *The South Wales Railway Co* (1860) 8 C.B. N.S. 525 at 534. Erle dissented in this case, holding there was no duty imposed by a statute to fence a railway from an adjoining tramway.

[123] *Grill* v. *The General Iron Screw Collier Co* (1866) LR 1 CP 600 at 612. Cf. the comments of Bowen LJ in *Thomas* v. *Quartermaine* (1887) 18 QBD 685 at 694.

[124] *Smith* v. *Great Eastern Railway Co* (1866) LR 2 CP 4 at 10. Cf. his remarks in *Gautret* v. *Egerton* (1867) LR 2 CP 371 at 374–5.

as analogous to the interests protected by the action of trespass. A duty not to leave hazardous items in public places was recognized, and analogized to nuisance. A duty not to sell dangerous goods was recognized, which was a version of the duty not to deceive.[125]

The narrowing of negligence by linking it to specific duties can be seen in two cases involving personal injuries. In the first, *Langridge* v. *Levy*, the plaintiff was injured when a gun purchased by his father exploded on use. '[W]e should pause', Parke B. commented, 'before we made a precedent by our decision which would be an authority for an action against vendors, even of such instruments and articles which are dangerous in themselves, at the suit of any person whomsoever into whose hands they might happen to pass, and who should be injured thereby.'[126] The plaintiff could not succeed in a contractual action, for want of privity. However, he found for him on the ground of deceit. Since the defendant had warranted the gun to be sound, he had made a false representation, which was intended to be acted on by the plaintiff. That being so, he was liable for the consequences.[127] This was to root the liability not in a duty of care to those who could foreseeably be harmed, but in the tort of deceit. Fourteen years later, in another case involving defective goods sold which harmed a third party, Parke B. denied that (in the absence of any awareness of the defect which might permit an action for deceit) shopkeepers owed a (non-contractual) duty of care to consumers:

it would be going much too far to say, that so much care is required in the ordinary intercourse of life between one individual and another, that, if a machine not in its nature dangerous—a carriage, for instance—but which might become so by a latent defect entirely unknown, although discoverable by the exercise of ordinary care, should be lent or given by one person, even by the person who manufactured it, to another, the former should be answerable to the latter for a subsequent damage accruing by the use of it.[128]

In the second case, *Winterbottom* v. *Wright* in 1842, the Exchequer denied a remedy to the driver of the Holyhead mail coach, who was injured when he was thrown from a faulty vehicle, since he had no contract with the defendant. The coach itself

---

[125] These duties are discussed in the following chapter.

[126] *Langridge* v. *Levy* (1837) 2 M. & W. 519 at 530. Ironically, Lord Abinger CB in *Winterbottom* v. *Wright* noted that 'the plaintiff in that action, who could not make the bargain himself, [...] was really and substantially the party contracting': 10 M. & W. 114.

[127] Citing *Pasley* v. *Freeman* (1789) 3 T.R. 51, he ruled that the principle applied equally where the instrument which was the subject of a misrepresentation had been placed in the hands of a third party for the purpose of being delivered to the plaintiff. Indeed, he said the principle applied even if it was not shown that the defendant intended the false statement to be communicated to the ultimate user.

[128] *Longmeid* v. *Holliday* (1851) 6 Exch. 761 at 768.

was supplied to the Post Master General by the defendant, whose contractual duty it was to keep the coach in good repair. Winterbottom was unable to sue the Post Master General, since he was an officer of the Crown; nor, thanks to the recent decision of *Priestley* v. *Fowler*,[129] could he sue his immediate employer, Nathaniel Atkinson. He therefore brought an action in negligence against the defendant. Lord Abinger, whose anxiety about the scope of negligence had already been evident in his judgment in *Priestley*, was concerned about the possible consequences of finding for the plaintiff. If the plaintiff won, 'every passenger, or even any person passing along the road, who was injured by the upsetting of the coach, might bring a similar action'. For Abinger, the duty undertaken here was essentially contractual, and its operation had to be limited to the parties to the contract. More extensive duties could exist, as '[w]here a party becomes responsible to the public, by undertaking a public duty' or 'in cases of public nuisance' where 'you are liable to an action at the suit of any person who suffers'.[130] But absent these factors, there was no duty owed to the public to take care.

At the same time that judges began to narrow the reach of negligence by specifying duties, so the jurists who wrote the earliest English treatises on negligence began to stress the centrality of duty. Their formulations may have been influenced by John Austin's *Lectures on Jurisprudence*, published in 1863, which related all legal rights to sovereign commands imposing duties. Austin also discussed negligence in terms of breaches of duty: 'the term *"negligent"*', he wrote, 'applies exclusively to injurious omissions:– to breaches by omission of positive duties'.[131] The notion of duty was also central to the American Francis Wharton's treatment in his *Treatise on the Law of Negligence*, first published in 1874. In Wharton's view, the concept of duty was central, for it helped distinguish between perfect and imperfect obligations. Wharton was critical of the definition which had been given by Alderson B. in 1856 in *Blyth* v. *The Company of Proprietors of the Birmingham Waterworks*, according to which '[n]egligence is the omission to do something which a reasonable man, guided upon those considerations which ordinarily regulate the conduct of human affairs, would do, or doing something which a prudent and reasonable man would not do'.[132] The definition seemed problematic for losing sight of the notion of duty. In the absence

---

[129] *Priestley* v. *Fowler* (1837) 3 M. & W. 1, discussed at pp. 1002–3.

[130] *Winterbottom* v. *Wright* (1842) 10 M. & W. 109 at 115. For a discussion, see V. Palmer 'Why Privity Entered Tort—An Historical Reexamination of *Winterbottom* v. *Wright*' (1983) 27 *AJLH* 85–98.

[131] J. Austin, *Lectures on Jurisprudence or the Philosophy of Positive Law* (4th edn, 1873, ed. R. Campbell), 439. Cf. 440: 'The party who is negligent *omits* an act, and breaks a *positive* duty.'

[132] *Blyth* v. *The Company of Proprietors of the Birmingham Waterworks* (1856) 11 Exch. 781 at 784.

of a duty, he noted, no omission could be actionable: 'for if the law undertook to compel men to perform toward each other offices of mere charity, then the practical and beneficent duty of supporting self would be lost in the visionary and illusory duty of supporting every one else'.[133]

Wharton's criticism of Alderson B.'s formulation in *Blyth* v. *Birmingham Waterworks* was perhaps misplaced, for the judge had not been concerned with the question of whether a duty of care was owed to the plaintiff, but rather with the question of whether there was any evidence of negligence. The litigation raised the question whether the defendant company had been negligent in the exercise of its statutory powers. Its statute required the company to instal and maintain fire plugs in each street. In the severe winter of 1854–5, the plugs—which normally acted as safety valves for the main drains—froze, and the plaintiff's house was flooded by rising water. Since the company acted under statutory powers in constructing its main, it could only be liable for negligence. After a finding for the plaintiff by a jury in Birmingham County Court, the Exchequer held that there had been no evidence of negligence to go before them, since the 'defendants had provided against such frosts as experience would have led men, acting prudently, to provide against'.[134]

Jurists in this era took the view that negligence was one of the ways in which a wrong could be committed, rather than an independent tort. It was a way of breaching distinct duties, which had distinct standards of liability, some being more strict, some less. In his treatise of 1871, Austin's editor, Robert Campbell, invoked the threefold distinction used by Sir William Jones between *culpa lata*, *culpa levis*, and *culpa levissima* to describe the level of care required by different duties. In his typology, the *sic utere* principle imposed a duty to take great care, or use exact diligence.[135] The higher standard of care was also imposed by common custom on common carriers and innkeepers, and it could be imposed by contract in other cases. A lower standard, that of ordinary care, of simple *culpa*, was imposed 'in ordinary cases of contract',[136] as well as 'where persons are thrown

---

[133] F. Wharton, *A Treatise on the Law of Negligence* (2nd edn, Philadelphia, 1878), § 82, p. 71.

[134] *Blyth* v. *The Company of Proprietors of the Birmingham Waterworks* (1856) 11 Exch. 781 at 784. Although the plaintiffs argued that there was evidence for the jury, since a 'scientific man' could have foreseen the danger, the court did not discuss whether higher standards of care were required by water companies. However, Bramwell B.'s comment—'that it would be monstrous to hold the defendants responsible because they did not foresee and prevent an accident, the cause of which was so obscure, that it was not discovered until many months after the accident had happened'— suggests that the court was not convinced that there was evidence that an expert would have foreseen the harm.

[135] R. Campbell *The Law of Negligence* (2nd edn, 1878), 25, 28–9.

[136] *Ibid.*, 25–6.

into collision in the ordinary transactions of life'.[137] The lowest level—attracting liability for *culpa lata*—was limited to those such as gratuitous bailees.[138]

Horace Smith also divided his analysis into the neglect of duties[139] requiring ordinary care, and those requiring more or less than ordinary care,[140] though, he rejected the Romanist language as 'vague and misleading'.[141] His rejection of this language was influenced by his reading of Wharton's treatise. Following the research of Hasse,[142] Wharton rejected Jones's tripartite model, arguing that the concept of *culpa levissima* was a medieval fiction which should have no place in law. In his view, there were only two standards. Non-specialists were held to use the diligence an ordinary man of common sense used. By contrast, the specialist was held to a different standard, that of the good businessman. This was a standard which depended 'upon the qualifications of the party discharging the duty, taken into connection with the duty to be discharged'.[143] This was to acknowledge that the degree of diligence required in any situation was proportionate to the duty imposed.[144] Following Wharton, Smith noted that '[p]ersons coming into collision in their ordinary avocations are liable for ordinary negligence, for it is their duty to take ordinary care'.[145] By contrast, those holding out a special skill were held to a higher standard of care. For Smith, the standard of care also changed when rights were not equal. This meant, on the one hand, that a landowner had no duty of care to an intruder who had no right to be on his land, so that he could not complain if he fell into a trap. It also meant, on the other, that a man who had violated a neighbour's right to support of his land could not be relieved by showing he had taken care.[146]

[137] *Ibid.*, 97. Campbell gave as examples mere licensees on premises; and of railway accidents where the harm was, in Campbell's view, collateral to the contract of carriage—as where a passenger was hurt when alighting from a train.

[138] *Ibid.*, 163.

[139] His articulation of the concept of duty was much clearer than Campbell's: 'It cannot be predicated of any particular act that it is *per se* negligent; it is only so because it is a breach of duty, so that an act done by one man may be negligent which, done by another, would not be so, because he had no duty with respect to it': H. Smith, *A Treatise on the Law of Negligence* (1880), 2.

[140] Ibid., 11–12.

[141] *Ibid.*, 11.

[142] J. C. Hasse, *Die Culpa des Römischen Rechts* (Bonn, 1838). See Ibbetson, 'Law of Business Rome', 100–1.

[143] Wharton, *Negligence* (2nd edn, 1878), § 53, p. 38.

[144] *Ibid.*, § 47, p. 28.

[145] Smith, *Negligence*, 22.

[146] *Ibid.*, 73. The reason for this was evident in cases where the owner of property charged for admission, but it also applied to invitees. Here, Smith said, the occupier had a greater liability both because the invitee came for his (the owner's) benefit, and because 'he has taken upon him[self] a duty of a high degree' (80).

Causation and Damages

At the same time that judges began to look at the question of duty more closely, so they began to devote more attention to questions of causation. If a defendant had breached a duty by his negligence, it had further to be established that the breach had caused the harm. Judges in the mid-century took a narrow view of causation, using Francis Bacon's maxim that *in jure non remota causa sed proxima spectatur*. The meaning of this maxim was discussed in the first half of the century primarily in insurance and defamation cases. In both areas, a narrow approach was taken. Insurers were only held liable to pay for losses if the last event in the chain of causation leading to the loss was a peril insured against. According to this rule, if a ship caught fire because of the negligence of the crew, the shipowners could recover under a policy for losses caused by fire.[147] The courts were reluctant to take such a narrow approach outside the insurance context,[148] refusing to permit defendants to evade liability for harm consequent on their wrongful acts by invoking subsequent natural events. However, a narrow view was taken if a third party intervened. In the first half of the century, the law on this seemed settled by the defamation case of *Vicars* v. *Wilcocks*,[149] where it was held that if the defendant's slanderous words had provoked a third party into committing an act against the plaintiff for which he might be sued, he was not liable for the resulting damage, since it was not the 'legal and natural consequence of the words spoken'. Although the decision came in for academic criticism from writers like Thomas Starkie, who argued that the 'natural and immediate consequences' of a wrongful act might well include a wrongful act by a third party,[150] tort lawyers continued to argue that the chain of causation was broken by the intervention of third parties. 'It is very important that when we negligently set natural forces in action we should be liable for the damage these misdirected

---

[147] *Busk* v. *The Royal Exchange Assurance Co* (1818) 2 B. & Ald. 73 at 80; *Walker* v. *Maitland* (1821) 5 B. & Ald. 171 at 174. See further the discussion at pp. 712–13.

[148] See *Davis* v. *Garrett* (1830) 6 Bing. 716 at 723–4, holding that the proximate cause of damage to goods which caught fire in a storm was the wrongful deviation of a vessel, rather than the fire. See also Brett's arguments in *Lloyd* v. *The General Iron Screw Co* (1864) 3 H. & C. 284, which he applied as a judge in *The Chartered Mercantile Bank of India, London, and China* v. *The Netherlands India Steam Navigation Co* (1883) 10 QBD 521 at 531. T. Beven, *Principles of the Law of Negligence* (1889), 76 saw *Davis v. Garrett* as the first case to lay down a general rule of causation in negligence. In fact, the court was concerned with whether a carrier could invoke a limitation of liability clause for harms caused by accident when the vessel had deviated. See the comments on the case in *Lilley* v. *Doubleday* (1881) 7 QBD 510 at 511; *Taylor* v. *The Great Northern Railway Co* (1866) LR 1 CP 385 at 388.

[149] *Vicars* v. *Wilcocks* (1806) 8 East 1 at 3–4.

[150] T. Starkie, *A Treatise on the Law of Slander and Libel and Incidentally of Malicious Prosecutions*, 2 vols (2nd edn, 1830), i, 206n. See also J. W. Smith, *A Selection of Leading Cases on Various Branches of the Law*, 2 vols (4th edn, 1856, by J. S. Willes and H. S. Keating), ii, 429–32, which preferred a 'common sense' view of causation.

forces produce', Wharton wrote, 'But if another person comes in, and of his own free will takes a new departure, how can we be made liable without extending our liability indefinitely?'[151]

The question of how third party interventions affected the issue of causation was further explored in a number of mid-century cases, in which it was held that a victim of fraud might be estopped by his own negligence from recovering against those who had wrongfully disposed of his property. The roots of this doctrine lay in the 1827 decision in *Young* v. *Grote*, where the Common Pleas held that the strict liability of a bank which had paid out on a forged cheque was displaced where the instrument had been filled out in such a way as to make it easy to write in additional sums.[152] A bank paying out on the basis of fraudulent instruments was also relieved from liability in *Coles* v. *Governor of the Bank of England* in 1839, when a jury found that the plaintiff had been grossly negligent.[153] In the mid-century, these cases were identified as establishing a doctrine of estoppel by negligence, and it was at this point that judges began to look more closely at the problems of causation they raised. They were particularly concerned with the question of whether a claimant, who had been negligent, should bear the losses resulting from the fraud of a rogue. This can be seen from *Bank of Ireland* v. *Trustees of Evans' Charities*, where the trustees' secretary fraudulently transferred stock registered with the bank to himself.[154] At the trial, Lord Chief Justice Blackburne told a Dublin jury that if the trustees had contributed to the loss by their negligence, they should find for the bank. The House of Lords, however, found the direction faulty. As Parke B. told the Lords, the

---

[151] Wharton, *Negligence* (2nd edn, 1878), § 139, p. 114. He added: 'when there is intervening negligence, or *casus*, diverting, varying, or continuing the injurious element, the party originally negligent ceases to be liable for the final damage, unless such intervening negligence was such a natural incident of the original negligence that it ought to have been foreseen as probable by the party to whom such original negligence is imputable': § 155, p. 136.

[152] *Young* v. *Grote* (1827) 4 Bing. 253. The grounds of the decision were open to debate, Best CJ (at 258) cited Pothier's *Traité du Contrat de Change* for the proposition that where the customer was at fault, he was to bear the loss. But in 1851, Parke B. interpreted it as a judgment that one who signed a blank cheque thereby gave authority to anyone into whose hands it came to fill it up: *Robarts* v. *Tucker* (1851) 16 Q.B. 560 at 580. By the mid-1850s, it was taken to establish that the customer should be held liable for the loss because of the negligent manner in which the cheque had been drawn: *Governor and Co of the Bank of Ireland* v. *The Trustees of Evans' Charities* (1855) 5 H.L.C. 398 at 410. See also the comments of Cleasby B. and counsel in *The Guardians of Halifax Union* v. *Wheelwright* (1875) LR 10 Ex 183 at 188, 192; and Brett LJ's interpretation in *Baxendale* v. *Bennett* (1878) 3 QBD 525.

[153] *Coles* v. *Governor of Bank of England* (1839) 10 Ad. & El. 437 at 451 (where the plaintiff's nephew had forged her signature and used an impersonator while selling her stock. The aunt was negligent in signing warrants for the reduced dividends).

[154] *Governor and Co of the Bank of Ireland* v. *The Trustees of Evans' Charities* (1855) 5 H.L.C. 389. See the remarks of Cranworth LC at 414 and Parke B. at 411.

trustees' negligence in leaving their seal with the secretary was only remotely connected with the transfer of the stock. It was in effect a *causa sine qua non*, not a *causa proxima*. '[T]he negligence which would deprive the Plaintiff of his right to insist that the transfer was invalid', Parke ruled, 'must be negligence in or immediately connected with the transfer itself.'[155] This narrower view of causation made the courts less sympathetic to the defendant banker than the earlier cases suggested they should be.[156]

This narrow view of causation was reiterated in *Swan* v. *The North British Australasian Co*, which centred on the acts of the plaintiff's broker, who had fraudulently filled out blank share transfer deeds he had been given. The case raised important questions about the nature of estoppel, negligence, and causation, and divided the judges. In the Exchequer, Wilde B. held the plaintiff estopped by his own negligence from disputing the transfer of property, since he had 'led others into a belief of a certain state of facts by conduct of culpable neglect'.[157] He rejected the contention of some of his brethren that an estoppel could only be raised if an action for negligence could be maintained on similar facts, by making a distinction between them. 'The doctrine of estoppel, as applied to these cases of negligence', he held 'is based on the injustice of allowing a plaintiff to be the author of his own misfortune, and then charging the consequences on others.' By contrast, '[t]he action for negligence proceeds from the idea of an obligation towards the plaintiff to use care, and a breach of that obligation to the plaintiff's injury'. This comment has been described as 'a classic definition' of the general principle of negligence. In fact, Wilde was aware that no action lay for a negligent misrepresentation, and his aim was to distinguish the doctrines, to show that the estoppel might apply where the action would not.[158]

His views did not persuade the majority of the Exchequer Chamber. Blackburn J. endorsed the views of Parke B. in *Freeman* v. *Cooke* that, for an estoppel to exist, one party must have induced the other so to alter his position

---

[155] (1855) 5 H.L.C. 409–10. He added (at 410–11): 'If a man should lose his cheque-book, or neglect to lock the desk in which it is kept, and a servant or stranger should take it up, it is impossible in our opinion to contend that a banker paying his forged cheque would be entitled to charge his customer with that payment.'

[156] According to Field QC in *The Guardians of Halifax Union* v. *Wheelwright* (1875) LR 10 Ex 183 at 188, the copy of the report of this case in the court of Exchequer contained the following MS note by Pollock CB: 'Whatever doubt may seem to be thrown upon the case of *Young* v. *Grote* and *Coles* v. *Bank of England*, as to the result in each case, no doubt whatever is thrown upon the principles on which those cases were avowedly decided. This case is an authority for the correctness of those principles, though it professes to doubt the propriety of their application'.

[157] *Swan* v. *The North British Australasian Co* (1862) 7 H. & N. 603 at 633.

[158] *Swan* v. *The North British Australasian Co* (1862) 7 H. & N. 603 at 636. Ibbetson, *Historical Introduction*, 170, 'Tort of Negligence', 235.

that he would be answerable in an action for it.[159] He proceeded with a narrower view:

the neglect must be in the transaction itself, and be the proximate cause of leading the party into that mistake; and also [...] it must be the neglect of some duty that is owing to the person led into that belief, or, what comes to the same thing, to the general public of whom the person is one, and not merely the neglect of what would be prudent in respect to the party himself.[160]

Cockburn CJ agreed. In his view, even if the defendants had been negligent, it was too remote, for '[t]he proximate cause of the fraud perpetrated was the forgery and felony of the agent'.[161]

Just as a plaintiff could not succeed if the proximate cause of the harm had been the act of a third party, so he could not succeed if it resulted from his own wrongful act or negligence. The mid-nineteenth century saw courts elaborate the rules regarding contributory negligence which had been developed earlier in the century. In determining whether the plaintiff was responsible for his own loss, the first question to consider was whether he had been negligent in the first place. Not all risk-taking was considered negligent. It was settled early in the century that if someone was harmed as a result of taking risky action to save himself from a danger generated by the defendant—as by jumping off a stage coach in danger of crashing—he could recover as long as the action he took was one a reasonable man would take in that situation.[162] The fact that the plaintiff might have made a bad decision when trying to avoid danger did not remove his remedy, if the defendant's wrong impelled him to take the action.[163] Similarly, in *Clayards* v. *Dethick* in 1848, a cabman successfully sued the Holborn and Finsbury commissioners of sewers for negligence, after his horse fell fatally into a dangerous trench dug by their labourers. The Queen's Bench felt that he was within his rights in running the risk of using the passage in question, which led to his mews. Patteson J.

---

[159] As Parke B. had put it, to have the effect of estopping a party, the negligence had to be 'neglect of some duty cast upon the person who is guilty of it'. Alderson B. said 'A person cannot be said to be culpable in not doing a particular thing, unless it is his duty to do it': *Freeman* v. *Cooke* (1848) 2 Exch. 654 at 657.

[160] *Swan* v. *North British Australasian Co* (1863) 2 H. & C. 175 at 182.

[161] Cockburn added, using the words of Parke B. in *The Bank of Ireland* v. *The Trustees of Evans's Charities*, ' "but for the occurrence of a very extraordinary event", namely, the forgery and felony of the plaintiff's agent, the act of the plaintiff could not have had any effect on the shares now in question': *Swan* v. *North British Australasian Co* (1863) 2 H. & C. 191.

[162] *Jones* v. *Boyce* (1816) 1 Stark. 493, where a man jumped from a stage coach which he feared was about to overturn.

[163] See *The George and Richard* (1871) LR 3 A & E 466.

felt that the defendants could succeed only if 'the danger was so great that no sensible man would have incurred it'.[164]

By contrast, if the harm resulted from the plaintiff's own wrongful act or risk-taking, he could not recover.[165] In *Lygo* v. *Newbold* in 1854, a woman who had contracted with the defendant to transport her furniture across London was held not to be entitled to damages for the broken leg she sustained when the cart collapsed, since she had ridden on it without his authority, and was therefore a trespasser. As Pollock CB put it, she 'brought the accident wholly upon herself' and so had to 'take all the consequences of her own culpable conduct'.[166] Similarly, in *Wyatt* v. *Great Western Railway Company* in 1865, the plaintiff failed to recover, when a divided Queen's Bench held that he had no right to open the gate of an unmanned level crossing, to be able to cross the line, even though the railway had no right to obstruct the highway. Instead of opening it (and running the risk that his horse would be startled and overturn his carriage when the gate shut), he should have sued the company for its failure to open the gate.[167] The harm he suffered was hence not the natural consequence of the defendant's wrong, but the result of his own wrongful act.

If the plaintiff had been negligent, the defendant had to show a causal link between that negligence and the harm, in order to evade liability himself. Although some judges continued to hold that a plaintiff could not succeed if he had 'been guilty of such negligence or want of due care as to have contributed or conduced to the injury',[168] in the mid-nineteenth century, the view was generally adopted that the plaintiff would only fail if his negligence had been the 'immediate and proximate cause' of the damage.[169] This approach can be seen from *Davies* v. *Mann* in 1842, where the defendant's servant had negligently driven his horse and waggon against the plaintiff's ass, which was grazing on the edge of a highway, with its feet fettered. Counsel for the defendant contended that where there was fault on both sides, the plaintiff could not recover. But the Exchequer judges upheld the jury's

---

[164] *Clayards* v. *Dethick* (1848) 12 Q.B. 439. See also *Thompson* v. *North Eastern Railway Co* (1860) 2 B. & S. 106.

[165] Some judges took a tougher line on risk taking, see especially Bramwell B.'s approach in *Lax and Bainbridge* v. *Borough of Darlington* (1879) 5 Ex D 28 at 35. See also Appendix B to Smith, *Negligence* (2nd edn, 1884), which gives Bramwell's judgment and Smith's observations.

[166] *Lygo* v. *Newbold* (1854) 9 Exch. 302 at 306. In effect, the court's view was that the defendant owed her no duty since she was a trespasser running her own risk.

[167] *Wyatt* v. *The Great Western Railway Co* (1865) 6 B. & S. 709.

[168] e.g. *Thorogood* v. *Bryan* (1849) 8 C.B. 115 at 130; *Martin* v. *Great Northern Railway Co* (1855) 16 C.B. 179 at 192. Brett J. also took the view that any contributory negligence by the plaintiff disentitled him: *Bridges* v. *North London Railway* (1874) LR 7 HL 213 at 232; *Radley* v. *London & North Western Railway Co* (1883) 12 QBD 70; *Davey* v. *London & South Western Railway Co* (1883) 12 QBD 70 at 71.

[169] C. G. Addison, *Wrongs and their Remedies* (2nd edn, 1864), 16. See also Pollock CB's charge of heart on the approach to take in *Greenland* v. *Chaplin* (1850) 5 Exch. 243 at 248.

verdict for the plaintiff. The mere fact that the donkey was negligently left on the highway was no answer to the action, Parke B. held, 'unless the donkey's being there was the immediate cause of the injury'.[170] The rule was restated in 1855, in *Dowell v. General Steam Navigation Company*,[171] where two vessels had collided at night. Lord Campbell held that if the defendant could have avoided the accident, notwithstanding the plaintiff's negligence, then the latter would not 'have contributed to the accident within the rule upon this subject'. But since the jury had found that the plaintiff's negligence had 'directly contributed to the accident', he could not recover, even though the defendant was more at fault.

This case was drawn on three years later in *Tuff* v. *Warman*, another marine collision case. Here, the defendant's negligently navigated steamer collided with the plaintiff's barge on the Thames. There was no look-out on the plaintiff's barge, although if there had been one, the accident could have been avoided. At the trial, it had been left to the jury whether the plaintiff had 'directly' contributed to the accident, and a verdict was found for the plaintiff. Seeking a new trial in the Common Pleas, the defendant argued that the plaintiff could not recover if his negligence contributed in any way to the accident, directly or indirectly. However, the court found for the plaintiff. As Williams J. put it:

if the negligence or default of the plaintiff was in any degree the proximate cause of the damage, he cannot recover, however great may have been the negligence of the defendant; but […], if the negligence of the plaintiff was only remotely connected with the accident, then the question is, whether the defendant might not, by the exercise of ordinary care, have avoided it.[172]

The need for proximity was reiterated in the Exchequer Chamber by Wightman J.: '[m]ere negligence or want of ordinary care or caution' would not disentitle a plaintiff 'unless it were such, that, but for that negligence or want of ordinary care and caution, the misfortune [would] not have happened'.[173] Similarly, in 1866, Willes J. held that the jury was to be asked not only whether the plaintiff had been negligent, but also whether this negligence was the proximate or direct cause of

---

[170] *Davies* v. *Mann* (1842) 10 M. & W. 546 at 548–9. He restated the rule from *Bridge* v. *Grand Junction Railway Co* (1838) 3 M. & W. 244 at 247 that 'the negligence which is to preclude a plaintiff from recovering in an action of this nature, must be such as that he could, by ordinary care, have avoided the consequences of the defendant's negligence'.

[171] *Dowell* v. *General Steam Navigation Co* (1855) 5 E. & B. 195.

[172] *Tuff* v. *Warman* (1857) 2 C.B. N.S. 740 at 757.

[173] *Tuff* v. *Warman* (1858) 5 C.B. N.S. 573 at 585. See also *Radley* v. *London and North Western Railway Co* (1876) 1 App Cas 754. The report uses the word 'could', but later judges quoted the words as 'would': see Beven, *Negligence* (1889), 132n: 'common sense satisfies us that what the Court intended to negative, was not *possibility*, what could have happened, but *probability*, what would have happened'.

the harm.[174] Finally, in 1876, the House of Lords confirmed that even if the plaintiff had contributed to an accident by his negligence, 'yet if the Defendant could in the result, by the exercise of ordinary care and diligence, have avoided the mischief which happened, the Plaintiff's negligence will not excuse him'.[175] This was to take a view of causation which attributed liability to the last person whose actions had caused the harm.

Once it had been established that the defendant's acts had been the proximate cause of the harm, he was held liable for all the damage which followed, however remote. Stating the rule to be found from such cases, C. G. Addison wrote:

whoever does an illegal or wrongful act is answerable for all the consequences that ensue in the ordinary and natural course of events, though those consequences be immediately and directly brought about by the intervening agency of others, provided the intervening agents were set in motion by the primary wrong-doer, or provided their acts, causing the damage, were the necessary or legal and natural consequences of the original wrongful act.[176]

As Lefroy CJ observed in the Irish case of *Byrne* v. *Wilson* in 1862, 'any party is liable, not only for the immediate consequences of the negligence, but also for the resulting consequences'.[177] Commenting on the doctrine of the common law courts in 1871, Sir Robert Phillimore observed 'that the inclination of the Courts in cases of tort seems to be to render the wrongdoer liable for the injurious consequences of his illegal tortious act, although very remote'.[178] He may have had in mind the case of *Smith* v. *The London and South Western Railway Company* in 1870, where both the Common Pleas and the Exchequer Chamber endorsed the rule that where a defendant was found guilty of negligence, he was liable for all the harms flowing therefrom, regardless of whether he had foreseen the extent of the damages. In this case, sparks from the defendants' train had set fire to grass trimmings left by the side of the line, and the fire had been blown by a gust of

---

[174] *Walton* v. *London, Brighton and South Coast Railway* (1866) H. & R. 424.

[175] *Radley* v. *London and North Western Railway Co* (1876) 1 App Cas 754 at 759. For the earlier litigation, see LR 9 Ex 71, LR 10 Ex 100.

[176] Addison, *Wrongs and their Remedies* (2nd edn, 1864), 5. This reflected not only the approach found in the English case of *Scott* v. *Shepherd* (1773) 2 W. Bl. 892 at 899 ('[e]very one who does an unlawful act is considered as the doer of all that follows'), but also the American cases of *Guille* v. *Swan* (1822) 19 Johns 381, 10 Am. Dec. 234; *Vandenburgh* v. *Truax* (1847) 4 Denio 464, 47 Am. Dec. 268.

[177] *Byrne* v. *Wilson* (1862) 15 Ir. L.R. 332. In this case, a woman fell into the lock of a canal as a result of the defendant's negligence, and drowned when the lock was opened and water flowed into it. The court said that although the death 'was not caused immediately by the act of the defendant, nor was the immediate and instantaneous result of his negligence, yet it was the consequential result of the defendant's act, and enables her representative to maintain this action'.

[178] *The George and Richard* (1871) LR 3 A & E 466 at 476.

wind and burned down cottages 200 yards away. It was argued for the defendants that there was no evidence to be left to the jury of negligence, since the damage done was not foreseeable. However, in the view of both courts, the fact that sparks might set fire to the trimmings was reasonably foreseeable. Having breached the duty to take care to avoid the risk of fire, the company could not limit its liability by claiming it could not foresee the extensive consequences of a fire breaking out.[179] In the judgment of Channell B.: '[w]here there is no direct evidence of negligence, the question what a reasonable man might foresee is of importance in considering the question whether there is evidence for the jury of negligence or not [...] but when it has been once determined that there is evidence of negligence, the person guilty of it is equally liable for its consequences, whether he could have foreseen them or not'.[180] This was to hold that if a type of harm could be foreseen, defendants should be held liable even if they could not foresee the consequences of that harm.

Just as there were doubts about the narrow, mechanical view of causation, so doubts were raised about this view to the question of damages. In 1850, in two cases where the majority of the Exchequer judges applied the rule 'that, generally speaking, where an injury arises from the misconduct of another, the party who is injured has a right to recover from the injuring party for all the consequences of his injury',[181] Pollock CB raised a doubt 'whether a person who is guilty of negligence is responsible for all the consequences which may under any circumstances arise, and in respect of mischief which could by no possibility have been foreseen, and which no reasonable person would have anticipated'. In his opinion, the proper rule should be 'that a person is expected to anticipate and guard against all reasonable consequences, but that he is not, by the law of England, expected to anticipate and guard against that which no reasonable man would expect to occur'.[182] Pollock's doubts were in part explained by his unease that, where there was evidence of contributory negligence by the plaintiff—as in both cases before the court—the defendant would be liable for all losses, if the jury found against him.

Controlling the Jury

Since the assessment of damages was a matter for the jury, it was in practice very difficult for judges to set limits to it. This was exacerbated by the fact that tort

---

[179] *Smith* v. *The London and South Western Railway Coy* (1870) LR 5 CP 98; (1870) LR 6 CP 14. See also *Bailiffs of Romney Marsh* v. *Trinity House* (1870) LR 5 Ex 204 at 208 (aff'd in (1872) LR 7 Ex 247).
[180] *Smith* v. *The London and South Western Railway Co* (1870) LR 6 CP 14 at 21.
[181] *Rigby* v. *Hewitt* (1850) 5 Exch. 240 at 243.
[182] *Greenland* v. *Chaplin* (1850) 5 Exch. 243 at 248.

damages were not the subject of calculation (like contract damages), which made it difficult to seek a new trial on the grounds that excessive damages had been awarded. Once the court had decided that there was evidence both of a breach of duty and of causation—as it did in *Smith* v. *London and South Western Railway*—it effectively no longer had any control over what damages were awarded. Where the defendant was a railway company, however, it was a safe bet that juries would be generous in their damages awards.

Judges in the second half of the century therefore attempted to control the power of the jury, not only by defining more strictly which duties existed, but also in determining whether there was sufficient evidence of breach of duty and causation for the case to be put to the decision of the 12 laymen. As Pollock B. put it in 1874:

although the question of negligence or no negligence is one of pure fact, and therefore for the jury, it is the duty of the Judge to keep in view a distinct legal definition of negligence as applicable to the particular case; and if the facts proved by the Plaintiff do not, whatever view can reasonably be taken of them, or inference drawn from them by the jurors, present an hypothesis which comes within that legal definition, then to withdraw them from their consideration.[183]

The problem was particularly acute in cases of railway accidents. In such cases (the *Solicitor's Journal* noted in 1873), 'the Courts have very largely taken upon themselves the functions of juries, in consequence of the absolute necessity for the exercise of supervision over the verdicts arising from the tendency of juries to favour the private individual at the expense of the company'.[184] Many judges felt that the case should only be submitted to them if evidence existed on the basis of which a reasonable jury could find for the plaintiff. If there was only a mere 'scintilla' of evidence, a nonsuit should be entered.[185]

Judges were given the opportunity to hold that there was no evidence to submit to the jury when considering three questions. The first question was whether the defendant company (or its agents) had been negligent at all, and thereby in breach of duty. If there was no evidence of negligence at all, there would be nothing for the jury to decide upon. Much turned on the judges' view of the facts.[186] The issue

---

[183] *Bridges* v. *The Directors &c of the North London Railway Co* (1874) LR 7 HL 213 at 221–2.

[184] 'Contributory Negligence' (1873) 17 *Sol. J.* 609 at 610.

[185] The phrase was used by Williams J. in *Toomey* v. *The London, Brighton and South Coast Railway Co* (1857) 3 C.B. N.S. 146 and was adopted in *Cornman* v. *The Eastern Counties Railway Co* (1859) 4 H. & N. 781 and *Cotton* v. *Wood* (1860) 8 C.B. N.S. 568.

[186] See the contrasting approaches in *Bilbee* v. *London, Brighton and South Coast Railway* (1865) 18 C.B. N.S. 584; *Stubley* v. *The London and North Western Railway Co* (1865) LR 1 Ex 13 at 18; *Stapley* v. *The London, Brighton and South Coast Railway Co* (1865) LR 1 Ex 21; and *Skelton* v. *London and North Western Railway Co* (1867) LR 2 CP 631.

whether there was evidence of negligence for a jury was explored in numerous cases where passengers had been injured while alighting from trains which had not yet stopped at a station.[187] Where there was no evidence that the victim had been invited to alight,[188] judges leaned to the view that there was nothing to be left to the jury. As Pigott B. put it in *Siner* v. *The Great Western Railway*, 'people with ordinary ability and common sense travelling upon a railway must be taken to know what is dangerous, and what not'.[189] Where trains overshot stations in daylight, judges were also willing to remove the case from the jury. Even if the guard had called out the name of the station, this was not to be taken as an invitation to descend.[190] The trend to remove questions of negligence from the jury was checked in 1874, however, by the Lords' decision in *Bridges* v. *The Directors of the North London Railway Company* that there was evidence for the jury to consider, in a case where the plaintiff's husband died after alighting from a train in a dark tunnel.[191] This seemed a significant reaffirmation of the role of the jury. As Brett JA later observed, before this case, some judges felt that the court should say what was reasonable for the passenger to do, removing the issue from the jury as much as possible; but '[t]he House of Lords held, that as the carrying of railway passengers was conduct in the ordinary affairs of life the jury was the proper tribunal to decide'.[192]

If there was evidence of negligence by the company, a second question was raised whether the negligence—as opposed to some other factor—had occasioned the accident. In *Adams* v. *The Lancashire and Yorkshire Railway Company* in 1869, a plaintiff who fell from a train while trying to close a door which kept flying open was denied the damages a jury had awarded when it was held by the Common Pleas that there had been no evidence to submit to them, since the company's negligence respecting the door was 'neither the immediate nor the efficient cause of the accident'.[193] As with the cases where passengers fell from

---

[187] There was little dispute that where a passenger fell into a gap between the train and the platform while alighting, this was in itself evidence of negligence by the company. See *Praeger* v. *Bristol and Exeter Railway* (1871) 24 LT 105; *Cockle* v. *London and South Eastern Railway Co* (1871) 24 LT 105.

[188] *Foy* v. *London, Brighton and South Coast Railway* (1865) 18 CB NS 225; *Weller* v. *London, Brighton and South Coast Railway Co* (1874) LR 9 CP 126.

[189] *Siner* v. *The Great Western Railway* (1868) LR 3 Ex 150 at 152–3. See also *Harrold* v. *Great Western Railway* (1866) 14 LT 440.

[190] *Lewis* v. *The London, Chatham, and Dover Railway Company* (1873) LR 9 QB 66.

[191] As Pollock B. told the Lords, 'it cannot be correctly affirmed that under no circumstances could the jury have reasonably drawn the two inferences that there was negligence of the company's servants and no contributory negligence on the part of the deceased': *Bridges* v. *The Directors of the North London Railway Co* (1874) LR 7 HL 213 at 224.

[192] *Robson* v. *North-Eastern Railway Co* (1876) 2 QBD 85 at 89.

[193] *Adams* v. *The Lancashire and Yorkshire Railway Co* (1869) LR 4 CP 739 at 741 (per Byles J.)

trains, different nuances of fact determined whether cases should be left the jury.[194] Its role was discussed once more by the Lords in 1877 in *Metropolitan Railway Company* v. *Jackson*,[195] where the plaintiff's thumb had been crushed when a porter slammed the door on it. The train on which he was travelling had been overcrowded, and he had stood up to prevent more people attempting to board. When the train began to move, he put his hand on the door frame to prevent himself from falling, and it was at this point that the door closed. The trial judge left it to the jury to decide whether the company's negligence had caused the harm, and it awarded the plaintiff £50. The Court of Appeal was divided on the issue, Amphlett LJ holding that *Bridges* v. *The North London Railway Company* had settled that it was a question of fact for the jury, and not one of law, 'whether, in cases of this sort, negligence can be inferred from a given state of facts'.[196] But the Lords disagreed. In Lord Cairns LC's view, although the company's servants might have been negligent in allowing too many people on the train, it was not shown that this had made the plaintiff any less the master of his acts. The negligence of the company in allowing the train to be overcrowded was not connected with the injury, for it was perfectly reasonable for the porter to close the door to prevent others getting on.

The Lords saw this ruling as clarifying, rather than undermining, the role of the jury.[197] For Lord Blackburn, while the decision in *Bridges* prevented judges removing the case from a jury simply where they felt a verdict for the plaintiff would be unsatisfactory, it did not (as some lower judges seemed to think) mean that everything was to be left to the jury. As Lord Cairns explained, it was for the judge to say whether any facts existed from which negligence *might* be inferred, while the role of the jury was to say whether the evidence was such that negligence *ought* to be inferred. Juries were not to be allowed to infer negligence from any facts whatever, though if there were facts from which 'negligence may reasonably be inferred', it should be left to the jury.

If the company's negligence had caused harm, a third question arose as to contributory negligence by the plaintiff. There was some disagreement among judges over whether the case could be withdrawn from a jury if there was any evidence

---

[194] Contrast *Richardson* v. *The Metropolitan Railway Co* (1868) LR 3 CP 374n and *Fordham* v. *The London, Brighton and South Coast Railway Co* (1868) LR 3 CP 368.

[195] *Metropolitan Railway Co* v. *Jackson* (1877) 3 App Cas 193.

[196] *Jackson* v. *Metropolitan Railway Co* (1877) 2 CPD 125 at 127.

[197] Indeed, Lord O'Hagan felt the 'legitimate authority' of juries often furnished the only protection the public had against the mismanagement of railways: 'They are potent monopolies, comparatively little subject to the various forms of control which law and opinion exercise upon individuals, and but for the action of juries in preventing negligence and disregard of the general comfort and safety, the want of that control would be a great mischief to society': *Metropolitan Railway Co* v. *Jackson* (1877) 3 App Cas 193 at 204.

of contributory negligence. In *Gee* v. *Metropolitan Railway Company*, where the plaintiff sued after falling from an underground train, when a door gave way as he leaned to look out of the window, the Exchequer Chamber held that the evidence of his contributory negligence did not disqualify a jury from considering the company's liability. Brett J., ever a friend to juries, ruled that while the plaintiff had to show that the defendants' negligence was the sole cause of the accident in order to succeed, the court could nonsuit only if an act was proved which was 'so clearly contributory to the accident that it would be unreasonable for any reasonable men to find to the contrary'.[198]

The role of the contributory negligence was examined further by the House of Lords in 1878 in *Dublin, Wicklow and Wexford Railway Company* v. *Slattery*.[199] The plaintiff's husband was killed one night at a station, when crossing the railway track without looking to see if it was safe to do so. Although the company never prevented anyone crossing the line at that point, there were notice boards telling people not to cross, and the company had a rule requiring express trains to whistle on approaching the station. At the trial, the engine driver testified that he had whistled, and his evidence was confirmed by several other witnesses. However, since one witness (who heard the rumble of the train) claimed not to have heard a whistle, the trial judge left it to the jury to decide whether the engine driver had whistled, and whether there had been any contributory negligence by the deceased in walking across the line. The jury, characteristically sympathetic to the victim, found for the plaintiff, awarding £1205 damages. The company appealed, arguing that there had been no evidence of any negligence by the company for the jury, and contending that the death had been caused solely by the deceased's carelessness. The question divided the Lords. Lords Hatherley, Coleridge, and Blackburn felt the case had not been properly left to the jury. As Coleridge saw it, if at the end of the plaintiff's case, there was evidence which would convince reasonable men either that no negligence by the defendant had caused the injury or that the plaintiff had been negligent, then the case should be removed from the jury.[200] Hatherley felt that a nonsuit was appropriate since, 'assuming that [the plaintiff] had proved negligence on the part of the Defendant in not whistling, she had likewise proved negligence on the part of the deceased' in crossing the line without looking to see if it was clear.[201]

But the majority of the Lords felt that the question of negligence had been rightly left to the jury, even though it resulted in the company being made to

[198] *Gee* v. *Metropolitan Railway Co* (1873) LR 8 QB 161 at 175.
[199] *Dublin, Wicklow and Wexford Railway Co* v. *Slattery* (1878) 3 App Cas 1155.
[200] *Dublin, Wicklow and Wexford Railway Co* v. *Slattery* (1878) 3 App Cas 1155 at 1197.
[201] *Ibid.*, at 1170.

pay a very large sum for an accident for which (in Lord Cairns LC's view) they
should not have been made liable. As Cairns saw it, had the accident occurred
by day, there would have been no evidence for the jury: for even if the driver had
failed to whistle, the jury could not 'be allowed to connect the carelessness in
not whistling, with the accident to the man who rushed, with his eyes open, to
his own destruction'. However, as the accident happened in the dark, it was for
the jury to say 'whether the absence of whistling on the part of the train, or the
want of reasonable care on the part of the deceased, was the *causa causans* of the
accident'.[202] For Lord Penzance, once it was established that there was any negligence by the defendant which was connected with the harm, it was for the jury
to weigh its effect. He also rejected the notion that where there was unanswered
prima facie evidence of contributory negligence by the plaintiff, the matter could
be removed from the jury. As Penzance saw it, this would have the effect of shifting the burden of disproving contributory negligence onto the plaintiff, and
leaving it to the judge to decide matters of fact if he failed to take up the challenge. This Penzance saw as 'an unconstitutional innovation of a serious if not an
alarming character'.[203] For this judge, the first question in such cases was always
whether the defendant had been negligent. Only when this was established did
the question arise whether the plaintiff had contributed to it: but when there was
such conflicting evidence, the matter had to be sent to the jury. The effect of the
decision was to give juries considerable power in determining issues of contributory negligence.

3. RETHINKING NEGLIGENCE

For much of the mid-nineteenth century the language of duty, breach, and causation in negligence was developed by judges, such as Blackburn, who sought
to restrict the role of the jury in determining questions of liability. But not all
judges were so sceptical about the jury. In the later nineteenth century, judges,
like Brett, who had great confidence in the role of the jury,[204] began to move away
from the narrow approach adopted by many in the mid-century. Looking for a
more embracing principle, they began to take a much broader view both of the
scope of duty in negligence, and of the nature of causation. At the same time, they
accepted the idea that there should be a limitation in the damages which could

---

[202] *Ibid.*, at 1166–7.   [203] *Ibid.*, at 1176.

[204] 'In my opinion, and according to my experience, they have hardly ever gone wrong as to the
question of liability': Report from the Select Committee on Employers Liability for Injuries to their
Servants, *PP* 1877 (285), x, 551, at p. 114.

be awarded in cases of negligence. In place of the largely mechanical view of the scope of negligence taken by many judges in the mid-century, according to which a defendant was liable for all harms which followed as a proximate consequence of his breach of a defined duty, judges like Brett and jurists like Frederick Pollock took a moral view of the scope of the tort. The law of negligence was to reflect a notion of responsibility which reflected the moral values of the community. This reorientation of the law of negligence began in the courtroom, with Brett's attempts to formulate a broad definition of the duty in negligence. However, he did not persuade his fellow judges that there was a unifying principle to the tort, and it would not be until 1932 that his efforts were endorsed by the House of Lords. In the meantime, jurists led by Pollock continued to urge the need to put the law on a new basis.

Those who sought a reorientation of the law of negligence were particularly influenced by the work of Oliver Wendell Holmes, the first common lawyer to seek to develop a theory of tort. Holmes began his quest in 1873 from Austinian premises, viewing tort through the language of duty.[205] But by the time his *Common Law* was published in 1881, he was much more sceptical about Austin's approach and looked more for the principles which could explain the case law to be found in English history. According to Holmes, the common law did not require men to act at their peril, save in particular situations determined by policy. Liability was only imposed where harms could be foreseen and avoided: '[u]nless my act is of a nature to threaten others, unless under the circumstances a prudent man would have foreseen the possibility of harm, it is no more justifiable to make me indemnify my neighbour against the consequences, than to make me do the same thing if I had fallen upon him in a fit, or to compel me to insure him against lightning'.[206] A person was only held liable for those consequences which could be foreseen since '[a] choice which entails a concealed consequence is as to that consequence no choice'.[207] Holmes also rejected Austin's view that a person was only to be held liable if he was subjectively at fault. Rather, the law considered 'what would be blameworthy in the average man, the man of ordinary intelligence and prudence, and determines liability by that'. For Holmes, the jury was to be taken as the equivalent to the 'ideal

---

[205] In his early view, enumerating all successful tort actions, he said, would reveal the 'primary duties' imposed by law. Tort law thus consisted of 'duties of all the world to all the world' as well as duties to particular individuals. O. W. Holmes, 'The Theory of Torts', in S. M. Novick, *The Collected Works of Justice Holmes*, 3 vols (Chicago, 1995), i: 326–35 at 331.

[206] O. W. Holmes, *The Common Law* (1881), 96.

[207] *Ibid.*, 94.

average prudent man'.[208] It was the jury, reflecting community morality, which determined the standard of liability; though once the standard had been set, it could be treated as a settled rule.

Holmes's thinking was particularly influential on Frederick Pollock. Like Holmes, Pollock felt that no one could be held responsible for mere accidents. However, '[a] man who fails to take order, in things within his control, against risk to others which he actually foresees, or which a man of common sense and competence would in his place foresee, will scarcely be held blameless by the moral judgment of his fellows'.[209] Just as men were liable for their intentional wrongs, so they were to be held liable for harms inflicted by their negligence. A 'general rule' could be formulated: 'that every one is bound to exercise due care towards his neighbours in his acts and conduct, or rather omits or falls short of it at his peril; the peril, namely, of being able to make good whatever harm may be a proved consequence of the default'. This general duty to take care arose whenever any voluntary act was undertaken.[210] Following Alderson B.'s definition in Blyth v. Birmingham Waterworks, Pollock noted that the standard of care required was that of the 'average prudent man'.[211] Pollock spent less time than Holmes in discussing how the court was to establish this standard, but in his correspondence with his American friend, he showed that he concurred with the view that it had a significant role to play: 'The jury, aided & moderately controlled by the judge, play the part of Aristotle's φρόνιμος and I don't think the frankness and practical wisdom of his appeal to the judgment of reasonable men on concrete questions of duty [...] has ever met with full justice from later philosophers'.[212]

Pollock was aware that his view of the law of negligence ran ahead of what was settled by the cases. Nonetheless, he was keen to see the scope of the tort of negligence expand. He argued that the law of torts should recognize a liability for negligent misrepresentations,[213] and was appalled by the House of Lords' decision in Derry v. Peek, which he felt 'ought to be disregarded by every tribunal which

---

[208] Ibid., 108, 111.

[209] F. Pollock, The Law of Torts: A Treatise on the Principles of Obligations arising from Civil Wrongs in the Common Law (1887), 10–12, 117.

[210] 'One who enters on the doing of anything attended with risk to the persons or property of others is held answerable for the use of a certain measure of caution to guard against the risk': Pollock, Torts (1st edn, 1887), 353.

[211] Ibid., 357.

[212] M. D. Howe (ed.), The Pollock Holmes Letters, 2 vols (Cambridge, 1942), i, 13; cf i, 92. See also Pollock, Torts (1st edn, 1887), 357n.

[213] See the notes to Firbank v. Humphreys (1886) 18 QBD 54 (CA) and Seton v. Lafone (1886) 18 QBD 139 in (1887) 3 LQR 251–2, where Pollock spoke of 'the inherent capacity of the Common Law for developing equitable conclusions'. See also his comment on Peek v. Derry (1888) 37 Ch Div 54 in (1888) 4 LQR 369.

is at liberty' to do so.[214] In his treatise, he also went out of his way to deny that *Winterbottom* v. *Wright* settled that a person who had been injured as a result of another person's negligent performance of his contract had no action.[215] Pollock continued to argue that there was a single tort of negligence. In the 1920 edition of his book, he wrote that '[t]he whole modern law of negligence, with its many developments, enforces the duty of fellow-citizens to observe in varying circumstances an appropriate measure of prudence to avoid causing harm to one another'. He added that the situations in which people were not under such a duty were exceptional.[216]

Not all scholars agreed that there was a general principle of liability in negligence. The leading voice among those who doubted it was that of Sir John Salmond, whose treatise on torts was first published in 1907. For Salmond, just as the criminal law was merely a catalogue of proscribed wrongs, so was tort. 'Whether I am prosecuted for an alleged offence, or sued for an alleged tort', Salmond wrote, 'it is for my adversary to prove that the case falls within some specific and established rule of liability, and not for me to defend myself by proving that it is within some specific and established rule of justification or excuse.'[217] Salmond's view of the law of torts was influenced by his conviction that the decisions taken by English courts—many since the appearance of the first edition of Pollock's work—did not justify the view that there was a single principle. Not all harms were actionable: the law offered no remedy for harms done by trade competition, or for causing mental suffering, or for negligent misstatements. Moreover, the fact of the courts' continued adherence to strict liability in some areas—such as the rule in *Rylands* v. *Fletcher*—meant that there was not even a coherent view of liability where it was imposed. This was a matter of some regret for Salmond. 'Had the law been content to adopt the uniform principle that liability for accidental harm depended in all cases on the existence of negligence', he wrote, 'most of the serious difficulties and complexities which now exist would have been eliminated.'[218] For like Pollock, Salmond felt that a moral principle of liability for fault should be regarded as the foundation for the law of torts. Echoing Holmes, he wrote, '[i]f I am not in fault, there is no more reason why I should insure other persons against the harmful issues of my own activity, than why I should insure them against lightning or earthquakes'.[219]

---

[214] 'Derry v. Peek in the House of Lords', (1889) 5 *LQR* 410–23 at 210; cf. *Torts* (10th edn, 1916), 301.

[215] Pollock, *Torts* (1st edn, 1887), 448–9.

[216] Pollock, *Torts* (11th edn, 1920), 21.

[217] J. W. Salmond, *The Law of Torts: A Treatise on the English Law of Liability for Civil Injuries* (2nd edn, 1910), 9.

[218] Salmond, *Torts* (4th edn, 1916), v.

[219] J. W. Salmond, *The First Principles of Jurisprudence* (2nd edn, 1907), § 145, p. 373.

Pollock's view would ultimately triumph.[220] In *Donoghue* v. *Stevenson*, Lord Atkin held that there was in English law 'some general conception of relations giving rise to a duty of care, of which the particular cases found in the books are instances'. The key principle in the law of negligence was that '[y]ou must take reasonable care to avoid acts or omissions which you can reasonably foresee would be likely to injure your neighbour'.[221] In the aftermath of this decision, many jurists began to question the function of duty altogether, seeing it as an unnecessary element. As Percy Winfield argued, instead of asking a plaintiff to prove that the defendant was under a duty to behave with reasonable care, he should only be asked to show facts which indicated that there was a *prima facie* case that he had not acted with reasonable care. It was not the duty which was difficult to discuss. Rather, 'the determination of how a reasonably careful man would thus behave is one of the most difficult problems that judges have to decide'.[222]

Rethinking the Notion of Duty

By the time Pollock published the first edition of his textbook, a number of decisions had already been handed down which suggested a broader notion of duty. Where plaintiffs had been injured by things which had turned out to be dangerous, and where they had acted on misstatements negligently made by defendants, some judges appeared keen to expand the boundaries of liability.

The change of approach can be seen from two cases of the late 1860s. In *Collis* v. *Selden*, the Common Pleas followed the traditional, narrow approach to liability for accidents. In this case, the plaintiff sued the defendant for negligently hanging a chandelier in a public house, which fell on him. He contended that the defendant was liable, since the law 'casts a duty upon a man who undertakes to do something from which injury may result to another, to exercise reasonable care and skill in doing it'. However, the Common Pleas rejected his case, holding that no duty of care existed, since the defendant was neither the occupier of the premises, nor in a contractual relationship with the plaintiff. The fact that there was no liability was not a matter of regret for the court. 'There would be no end of actions', Willes J. ruled, 'if we were to hold that a person having once done a piece of work carelessly, should, independently of honesty of purpose, be fixed with liability in this way by reason of bad materials or insufficient fastening'.[223]

---

[220] Even Salmond's editor, W. T. S. Stallybrass, conceded that the law was moving towards recognizing Pollock's general principle: Salmond, *Torts* (7th edn, 1928), 67.

[221] *Donoghue* v. *Stevenson* [1932] AC 562 at 580.

[222] P. H. Winfield, 'Duty in Tortious Negligence' (1934) 34 *Columbia LR* 40–66.

[223] *Collis* v. *Selden* (1868) LR 3 CP 495 at 497–8. Contrast *Tarry* v. *Ashton* (1876) 1 QBD 315, where the owner of a lamp projecting over a pavement was held liable when it fell on the plaintiff. In the

By contrast, in the following year, in *George* v. *Skivington*, the Exchequer allowed an action for negligence to be brought against the vendor of a hair shampoo, which had injured the purchaser's wife. On the face of it, this action should have failed for want of privity between the victim and the vendor, for shampoo was not in itself dangerous, and there was no fraud in the sale. However, as Kelly CB put it, 'there was a duty on the defendant [...] to use ordinary care' in preparing the hair wash, and the duty extended not merely to the purchaser, but to the person for whose use he knew it was bought. The Exchequer in this case extended the principle of *Langridge* v. *Levy*, holding the vendor liable for harms done to third parties. While in *Langridge*, the court had based its judgment on the finding of deceit by the vendor, in Cleasby B.'s view, the analogy with that case was complete if one substituted the word 'negligence' for 'fraud'.[224]

Cleasby endorsed his decision in the following year, in *Francis* v. *Cockrell*, in which the plaintiff had been hurt when a grandstand at Cheltenham racecourse collapsed. The defendants, members of an organizing committee, denied liability, claiming that any negligence was the fault of independent contractors, for whom they were not vicariously liable. The judges in the Queen's Bench and the Exchequer Chamber felt that the plaintiff could win on the grounds of an implied warranty in the contract between the promoters of the meeting and members of the public that the stands had been erected with due care, whether by the promoters or a third party.[225] But Cleasby B. doubted whether a personal contract existed between the plaintiff and defendants, for the race going public had no idea of 'contracting with any particular person', but relied 'upon the security of the thing itself'. In his view, regardless of contract, there was a duty on those who provided the building 'to take care that the stand should be erected so as to be reasonably fit and proper for the purpose'.[226]

The broadest statements of negligence liability made in the nineteenth century were articulated by Brett MR in 1883. On 2 July, in *Cunnington* v. *The Great Northern Railway Company*, he told the Court of Appeal that,

wherever the circumstances disclosed are such that, if the person charged with negligence thought of what he was about to do, or to omit to do, he must see that, unless he used reasonable care, there must be at least a great probability of injury to the person charging

---

Queen's Bench Division, Lush and Quain JJ ruled that a person who kept a lamp projecting over a highway had a duty to maintain it so that it was not a danger, and the defendant was liable even though he had not been negligent. The lamp here was in the nature of a public nuisance.

[224] *George* v. *Skivington* (1869) LR 5 Ex 1, 39 LJ Exch 8, 21 LT 495. On the case, see Ibbetson, 'Tort of Negligence', 255, and *id*. 'George v. Skivington (1869)' in C. Mitchell and P. Mitchell, *Landmark Cases in the Law of Tort* (Oxford, forthcoming).

[225] *Francis* v. *Cockrell* (1870) LR 5 QB 184, 501.

[226] *Francis* v. *Cockrell* (1870) LR 5 QB 501 at 514, 516.

negligence against him, either as to his person or property, then there is a duty shown to use reasonable care.[227]

Brett was self-consciously seeking to expand the notion of duty in negligence beyond the categories of breach of contract, fraud, or nuisance. Later in the year, Brett restated his views in *Heaven* v. *Pender*. In this case, a workman was injured when the scaffolding which he used while painting a ship in the defendant's dock gave way. Although the majority felt the plaintiff could succeed on the principle of an occupiers' liability to an invitee,[228] Brett again sought to enunciate the wider rule. He said:

whenever one person is by circumstances placed in such a position with regard to another that every one of ordinary sense who did think would at once recognise that if he did not use ordinary care and skill in his own conduct with regard to those circumstances he would cause danger of injury to the person or property of the other, a duty arises to use ordinary care and skill to avoid such danger.[229]

Brett's judgment sought to shift attention away from the limited number of duties defined in the mid-century case law, to a broader notion of a duty to avoid foreseeable harms. In his view, the test that the harm was reasonably foreseeable had been satisfied in *George* v. *Skivington*, but not in *Winterbottom* v. *Wright*.[230] In 1887, in another case involving an injured workman, Lord Esher MR (as he had become) answered the argument that 'you cannot have liability for negligence except it is founded on a duty' by suggesting that the duty 'is that you are bound not to do anything negligently so as to hurt a person near you, and the whole duty arises from the knowledge of that proximity'.[231]

---

[227] *Cunnington* v. *The Great Northern Railway Co* (1883) 49 LT 392 at 393. This case concerned the delivery by the defendants of empty casks to the plaintiff, to be filled with ketchup. The defendants negligently delivered casks with traces of turpentine, which were then filled with ketchup which was spoiled. The Court of Appeal here held that a man in the defendant's position would not have seen that if they acted negligently there would be harm to the plaintiff's property, for it was not unreasonable to assume that empty casks would be checked.

[228] This was doubted in (1883) 27 *Sol. J.* 778, on the grounds that it was a fiction to regard the plaintiff as an invitee of the defendant.

[229] *Heaven* v. *Pender* (1883) 11 QBD 503 (CA) at 509. This has been described as 'the first step in the perception of a coherent jurisprudence of common law negligence': *Burnie Port Authority* v. *General Jones Pty* (1994) 120 *ALR* 42 at 55. Brett's position here may be contrasted with that he took in 1870 in *John* v. *Bacon*, where the plaintiff fell through a hatchway on a hulk, onto which he had been invited prior to boarding the defendant's steamer which he had contracted to take him to Liverpool. Brett here said 'I doubt whether any invitation, which does not amount to a contract or to a false and fraudulent misrepresentation, can be the foundation of a legal liability': LR 5 CP 437 at 444.

[230] In that case, it was not clear 'that the defendant, if he had thought about it, must have known, or ought to have known, that the coach would be necessarily or probably driven by the plaintiff': *Heaven* v. *Pender* (1883) 11 QBD 503 (CA) at 509 at 513.

[231] *Thomas* v. *Quartermaine* (1887) 18 QBD 685 at 688.

Brett's desire to expand the notion of duty was also evident in his approach to liability for negligent misstatements. In *Coventry, Sheppard & Co* v. *The Great Eastern Railway Company* in 1883, where the defendants had issued two delivery orders relating to only one consignment of goods, he held them estopped by their negligence from denying their liability to plaintiffs who had lent money on the faith of the orders. '[T]he documents have a certain mercantile meaning attached to them', he ruled, 'and therefore the defendants owed a duty to merchants and persons likely to deal with' them.[232] Four years later in *Seton, Laing & Co* v. *Lafone*, he observed that 'if a man in the course of business volunteers to make a statement on which it is probable that in the course of business another will act, [...] there is a duty to take reasonable care that the statement shall be correct'.[233] This was a statement which went further than any decision in a common law action for deceit had yet gone.[234]

Brett's attempt to place the law of negligence on a broad moral principle generated much discussion among jurists. Many (besides Pollock) found it attractive.[235] In the second edition of his treatise on negligence, Horace Smith referred to Brett's judgment in *Heaven* v. *Pender* as 'the true rule', and included the case in an appendix.[236] The *Solicitor's Journal* also preferred Brett's daring approach in *Heaven* v. *Pender* to the majority's attempt at 'stretching an old formula [instead of] framing a new one'. But there were also reservations about his formulation.[237] In the view of the journal, it was 'dangerously wide', for it would impose a liability on any landholder who built an unsafe bridge on his land for any injury suffered by a poacher using it. As this example showed, 'such a doctrine will not hold water when put forward as universally applicable and apart from the particular case'. Indeed, one could not summarize 'in one proposition all the conditions

[232] *Coventry, Sheppard & Co* v. *The Great Eastern Railway Co* (1883) 11 QBD 776 at 780.

[233] *Seton, Laing & Co* v. *Lafone* (1887) 19 QBD 68 at 72. See also his approach in *Firbank's Executors* v. *Humphreys* (1886) 18 QBD 54 (CA).

[234] Later in the same year, the Court of Appeal (without Lord Esher) held there was liability at common law for negligent misrepresentation in *Peek* v. *Derry* (1887) 37 Ch D 541 (CA); and in the following year Chitty J., explicitly applied the principle of *Heaven* v. *Pender* to an action for a negligent valuation: *Cann* v. *Wilson* [1888] 39 Ch Div 39 at 42–3.

[235] The American jurists T. G. Shearman and A. A. Redfield praised Brett's 'masterly opinion', and reformulated their own definition of negligence to reflect his view more closely. Shearman and Redfield, *A Treatise on the Law of Negligence* (4th edn, New York, 1888), § 116, p. 202.

[236] Smith, *Negligence* (2nd edn, 1884), 8. He summarized the principle enunciated by Brett MR to be 'that if a reasonable man must see that if he did not use care in the circumstances he might cause injury to the person or property a duty arises to use such care'. This seemed to solve Smith's problem (faced in the first edition) of defining the duty (which he felt existed) owed by a defendant who had a contract with a third party, to a plaintiff harmed by the failure properly to perform that contract.

[237] As Pollock observed in later years, '[t]he precision of a neat draftsman has never been counted among Lord Esher's accomplishments': 'The Snail in the Bottle, and Thereafter' (1933) 49 *LQR* 22–6 at 25.

which may create a duty not to be negligent'.[238] A book review of Smith's treatise similarly felt that the rule in *Heaven* v. *Pender* needed qualification, since
it appeared to render defendants potentially liable not merely for their own acts
and those of their servants, but also for those of complete strangers.[239] Brett's
principle seemed to impose unbounded liability.

Brett's formulation of the duty imposed also seemed too broad, in its failure
to distinguish between negligent acts and omissions. It seemed to overlook the
common lawyers' long-held view that '[i]f a person undertakes to perform a voluntary act he is liable if he performs it improperly, but not if he neglects to perform it'.[240] Thomas Beven, author of the most substantial treatise on negligence
published in nineteenth-century England,[241] was particularly sceptical about the
attempt to formulate one broad duty. Although a man had to exercise care where
he had the control of property, or where he personally came into contact with
others, either directly or through the intervention of others, he was not under
any duty to prevent others incurring harm in reliance on him. 'In the absence of
contract or fraud, one man is not liable to another for injury sustained by such
other from reliance on his acts or words.' Beven illustrated his point: if '[a] man
places a plank across a stream for his own purposes; another uses it and falls
into the stream because it is insecurely placed; there is no liability'. Beven therefore sought to explain the train of cases which included *George* v. *Skivington* and
Heaven v. *Pender* as cases of misfeasance, which could be covered by the following principle: 'where the act of one person or his user of his property naturally
and necessarily, if not diverted, works injury to another person', he incurred a
liability; as he did in using or leaving about a dangerous object.[242] In his view,
any person who sent goods out into the world which might cause harm was to
be held liable, if he was the last person under whose authority the goods were

---

[238] 'Duty not to be negligent: Towards Whom and Under What Circumstances it Arises' (1883)
27 *Sol. J.* 778–9.

[239] (1885) 1 *LQR* 254: 'The general rule of responsibility for oneself and one's servants, though
sometimes harsh in operation, is intelligible; when it is sought to extend responsibility to the acts
of people who are not one's servants, the extension must rest on special grounds of policy limited to
special classes of cases'.

[240] *Skelton* v. *London and North Western Railway Co* (1867) LR 2 CP 631 at 636. On the distinction
of misfeasance and nonfeasance, see also the comments of Bramwell LJ in *Hayn* v. *Culliford* (1879)
4 CPD 182 at 185.

[241] Beven's *Principles of the Law of Negligence* (1889) was rearranged and published in a two-
volume second edition in 1895 as *Negligence in Law*. Beven's was the largest English work: its 4th
(1928) edition ran to some 1849 pages, of which 175 were devoted to the table of cases.

[242] Beven, *Negligence*, 2 vols (2nd edn, 1895), i, 72. Cf. his criticisms in the 1st edition (1889), 8
and 63n.

used.[243] He therefore had his own explanation of *Heaven* v. *Pender*: the defendant was liable for the defective staging, since there was no other person subsequently dealing with it who had any duty to inspect it, or under whose authority it was used.[244] Even those sympathetic to Brett sought to qualify the rule. As Pollock put it, '[t]he law does not and cannot undertake to make men render active serv- · ice to their neighbours at all times when a good or brave man would do so'.[245]

A decade after *Heaven* v. *Pender*, Brett (now Lord Esher) qualified his definition, in *Le Lievre* v. *Gould*. In this case, the mortgagees of a builder sued a surveyor for negligent misstatements contained in certificates he had given relating to the progress of the works. In the aftermath of the decision of the House of Lords in *Derry* v. *Peek* that there was no common law liability for negligent misrepresentation,[246] he had little option but to find for the defendant. In doing so, he clarified his thoughts on duty. 'A man is entitled to be as negligent as he pleases towards the whole world if he owes no duty to them', he now stated. *Heaven* v. *Pender*, he ruled, had established that

under certain circumstances, one man may owe a duty to another, even though there is no contract between them. If one man is near to another, or is near to the property of another, a duty lies upon him not to do that which may cause personal injury to that other, or may injure his property.[247]

The earlier case was thus limited to foreseeable personal injuries and property harms, and could not embrace economic harms. Significantly, Esher also cast the duty in negative terms, *not to do* something. Three years later, in *Lane* v. *Cox*, he reiterated the point that a person could not be held liable in negligence unless he owed 'some duty' to the plaintiff which was neglected; and he listed a set of duties which were akin to the traditional ones.[248] His list seemed to suggest that he was retreating to the (still mainstream) view that a man was liable for harms which resulted from breaches of particular duties.

---

[243] In his view, 'a liability to all the world for accidents arising through the use of low-priced articles, or those repaired in a particular or makeshift way, is not to be traced back beyond the person under whose authorisation they are in use. He has a duty to examine and approve': Beven, *Negligence*, 2 vols (3rd edn, 1908), i, 57.

[244] Beven *Negligence* (2nd edn, 1895), i, 62–3

[245] Pollock, *Torts* (1st edn, 1887), 352.

[246] *Derry* v. *Peek* (1889) 14 App Cas 337. See further, pp. 430–1.

[247] *Le Lievre* v. *Gould* [1893] 1 QB 491 at 497. Cf. the formulation of Smith LJ: 'The decision of *Heaven* v. *Pender* was founded upon the principle, that a duty to take due care did arise when the person or property of one was in such proximity to the person or property of another that, if due care was not taken, damage might be done by the one to the other. *Heaven* v. *Pender* goes no further than this, though it is often cited to support all kinds of untenable propositions' (at 504).

[248] *Lane* v. *Cox* [1897] 1 QB 415 at 417.

Rethinking Breach of Duty and Damages

At the same time that judges and jurists were beginning to rethink the nature of duty, so they began to rethink the question of which consequences of negligent conduct a defendant could be held liable for. As they did so, they began to challenge the mechanical approach dominant in the mid-century, which took a narrow view of causation, but held the defendant liable for all the damage which had been caused by his negligence. The mechanical view of causation associated with Bacon's maxim came under increasing scrutiny in the second half of the century, in the aftermath of the publication of works such as J. S. Mill's *System of Logic*. Judges and jurists now began to take a broader view of what constituted factual causation. Taking a broader view allowed them to consider a defendant liable for harmful consequences he could have foreseen, even if he was not the final agent inflicting the harm. At the same time, they sought to restrict the range of consequences for which a careless person might be held liable, by holding that defendants should only be liable in damages for such consequences as could have been foreseen.

From the 1860s, judges hearing cases where more than one party had been negligent began to look not at whose negligence was the last encountered prior to the suffering of the harm, but rather at whose negligence was the main or real cause of the harm. There had been increasing doubts about the rule in *Vicars* v. *Wilcocks* since the middle of the century. It was qualified in 1853, when the Queen's Bench held in *Lumley* v. *Gye* that it did not apply where the defendant had intended to provoke the wrongful act of the third party.[249] Its application in slander was doubted further in 1861, when Lord Campbell suggested that a slanderer might be liable if the consequential wrongful act of the third party 'might fairly and reasonably have been anticipated'.[250]

The effect of acts by third parties on liability for negligence was considered in 1868 in *Hill* v. *The New River Co*, where a defective water pipe owned by the defendants spouted a jet of water four feet high on a highway. This frightened the plaintiff's horse, which fell into an unfenced excavation in the highway left by contractors constructing a sewer. It was argued for the defendants that the proximate cause of the harm was not the jet of water, but the unfenced excavation, since the water would have caused no damage but for the opening of the drain. Invoking Mill's *Logic*, Mellish argued that the court could look no further back than the excavation for the real cause of the harm, since '[e]very effect proceeds

---

[249] *Lumley* v. *Gye* (1853) 2 E. & B. 216. For a history of this case, see S. M. Waddams, 'Johanna Wagner and the Rival Opera Houses' (2001) 117 *LQR* 431–58.

[250] *Lynch* v. *Knight* [1861] 9 H.L.C. 577 at 600. Here the wrongful act of the husband was to eject his wife from the marital home, after hearing accusations of infidelity.

from a number of causes, to inquire into the origin of all of which would be infinite'. Lush J. was not convinced, for had it not been for the jet, the horse would never have fallen into the ditch. Noting that there was no authority on the point, Mellor J. said, 'on principle I think the proximate cause of the injury is the first negligent act which drove the carriage and horses into the excavation'. The spouting of the water was 'the causa causans of the mischief'.[251] Similarly, in *Burrows* v. *The March Gas and Coke Co*, where leaking gas exploded after a gasfitter negligently entered the plaintiff's shop carrying a lighted candle, the firm which had fitted the original pipe under a contract was held liable for the damage. Although the court saw the defendant's liability as contractual, Cockburn CJ used language relating to causation which was to attract the attention of tort lawyers. 'The pipe they supplied was defective', he ruled, 'and the consequence—the natural and necessary consequence—was that the gas escaped, and having so escaped, a further natural consequence was that an accident might be expected to result.'[252]

The notion that courts should look to the effective cause of the harm, rather than trace the last event, was also championed by Brett. In *Collins* v. *The Middle Level Commissioners*, where the defendants were held liable for damage done to the plaintiff's property, even though it had been increased by the action of their neighbours, he held that 'the primary and substantial cause of the injury was the negligence of the defendants' so that they could not claim 'that they are absolved from the consequence of their wrongful act by what the plaintiff or someone else did'.[253] Similarly, in *Gee* v. *Metropolitan Railway Co*, he stated that '[t]he meaning of the phrase, "that it must be solely caused by the defendants" is solely caused as between them and the plaintiff, that is to say, that it is caused by the negligence of the defendants, without being contributed to by any negligence or want of care on the part of the plaintiff'.[254] He reiterated his notion that the intervention of third parties did not indemnify the wrongdoer in 1881 in *Bowen* v. *Hall*, when he declared that an action on the case could be brought 'wherever a man does an act which in law and in fact is a wrongful act, and such an act as may, as a natural and probable consequence of it, produce injury to another, and which in the particular case does produce such an injury'. If these conditions applied, 'the

---

[251] *Hill* v. *The New River Co* (1868) 9 B. & S. 303 at 305–6.

[252] *Burrows* v. *The March Gas and Coke Co* (1872) LR 7 Ex 96 at 97. Over a decade earlier, in *Stokes* v. *Eastern Counties Railway Co* (1860) 2 F. & F. 691 at 695, he told a jury that even if the defendants had not manufactured a defective wheel which caused a train crash, if they had been negligent in failing to inspect it, 'then, even although they did not know of the latent cause of danger, yet as their negligence gave effect to it, it would be, though not the proximate, yet the efficient cause of the accident, and would be negligence for which they are liable'.

[253] *Collins* v. *The Middle Level Commissioners* (1869) LR 4 CP 279 at 288. See also *Allen* v. *Hayward* (1845) 7 Q.B. 960 at 974; *Harrison* v. *The Great Northern Railway Co* (1864) 3 H. & C. 231.

[254] *Gee* v. *Metropolitan Railway Co* (1873) LR 8 QB 161 at 174–5.

action does not the less lie because the natural and probable consequence of the act complained of is an act done by a third person: or because such act so done by the third person is a breach of duty or contract by him, or an act illegal on his part, or an act otherwise imposing an actionable liability on him'.[255]

The fact that the intervention of a third party did not break the chain of causation was confirmed in 1878 in *Clark* v. *Chambers*. In this case, the owner of a sports ground abutting a private road placed a barrier across the road, armed with spikes. Although he had no right to do so, he closed the barrier when events were in progress to prevent people from bringing their carriages up the road to watch them from the fence. One dark evening, on his way home from visiting a friend, the plaintiff walked into a spike, and lost an eye in consequence. At the time of the accident, the spike had been moved to the side of the road by an unknown third party, without the defendant's knowledge. For the defence, it was argued that he could not be held liable, as the immediate cause of the accident was that of the anonymous person moving the spiked hurdle. For the plaintiff, it was argued that there should be liability on the principle of *Scott* v. *Shepherd*. Cockburn CJ found for the plaintiffs:

a man who unlawfully places an obstruction across either a public or private way may anticipate the removal of the obstruction, by some one entitled to use the way, as a thing likely to happen; and if this should be done, the probability is that the obstruction so removed will, instead of being carried away altogether, be placed somewhere near; thus, if the obstruction be to the carriageway, it will very likely be placed, as was the case here, on the footpath. If the obstruction be a dangerous one, wheresoever placed, it may, as was the case here, become a source of damage, from which, should injury to an innocent party occur, the original author of the mischief should be held responsible.[256]

Cockburn's judgment was highly critical of the approach taken by the court in *Mangan* v. *Atterton*. For him, someone who left something dangerous in a public place was guilty of negligence: 'and not the less so because the imprudent and unauthorized act of another may be necessary to realize the mischief to which the unlawful act or negligence of the defendant has given occasion'.[257]

Addressing the question of a tortfeasor's liability when one of the links in the chain of causation had been the subsequent wrongful act of a third party, Clerk and Lindsell noted that 'if the defendant's act is wrongful, and is likely to afford

---

[255] *Bowen* v. *Hall* (1881) 6 QBD 333 at 337–8. See also his approach in *Coventry, Sheppard & Co* v. *The Great Eastern Railway Co* (1883) 11 QBD 776 at 780, holding the defendants estopped by their negligence from disputing their liability for the fraud committed by another. Brett MR held their negligence was the 'direct and immediate cause', for it 'was to the prejudice of the plaintiffs and allowed the fraud to be perpetrated upon them'.

[256] *Clark* v. *Chambers* (1878) 3 QBD 327 at 338.

[257] *Ibid.*, at 339.

an opportunity to the third party to do the act immediately producing the damage', then the defendant would be liable if the third party's act, or omission, was negligent. However, if the third party's act was a wilful wrong, the defendant would not be liable, even though his 'own act was wrongful, and the act of the third party was the natural consequence of it', unless he had either intended the consequence or led the third party to believe his act would be justified.[258]

At the same time that the idea of causation was broadened to hold defendants liable for foreseeable harms inflicted through the agency of others, so some jurists became sceptical about the workability of the rule in *Davies* v. *Mann*. As Clark and Lindsell's treatise noted, the rule suggested that where there was 'a succession of negligences in point of time', the one who was negligent last was the one to blame:

> [B]ut it may be observed that if a man places his person or property in a position of danger, or establishes a state of things which is or may be dangerous to others, his negligence in so creating a source of danger to himself or others continues as long as that source of danger remains unremedied, that is to say, continues down to the very moment of the accident.[259]

They pointed out that in a case such as *Radley* v. *London & North Western Railway Co*[260]—where the defendant company had been held liable for damaging trucks belonging to the plaintiffs, which had negligently been left in a siding—it could not be said that either party was negligent later in time than the other, since the failure to remove the trucks was a negligent omission continuing down to the time of the accident. But if this was so, the defendant's liability rested only on the fact that 'the latter being in motion was the one who actually did the damage', a principle which might lead to 'curious results'. They were also troubled by the fact that the rule did not make it clear whether the last actor's liability depended on his awareness of the preceding actor's negligence. Salmond was another author troubled by *Davies* v. *Mann*, and he raised similar objections. 'In matters such as this, in which juries have to be directed as to the law', he noted in 1920, 'it is much to be regretted that the law should be so obscure and difficult.' Instead of finding a mechanical formulation, he felt that 'the essential basis and presupposition in every case of contributory negligence is the fact that the negligence of each party was one of the causes of the accident—the fact, that is to say, that without the negligence of both of them the accident would not have happened'.[261]

---

[258] J. F. Clerk and W. H. B Lindsell, *The Law of Torts* (1889), 99.

[259] Clerk and Lindsell, *Torts*, 380.

[260] *Radley* v. *London & North Western Railway Co* (1883) 12 QBD 70.

[261] Salmond, *Torts* (5th edn, 1920), 48–9. In the 4th edn (1916), 45, he spoke of liability falling on the person who had the last opportunity to avoid the accident (simplifying his earlier definitions),

Just as concepts of causation were reviewed to focus attention on foreseeability, so some judges also sought to restrict liability for a breach of duty to only those damages which were foreseeable. In so doing, they were influenced by the rule in *Hadley* v. *Baxendale* in 1854 that damages in contract lay for losses 'as may fairly and reasonably be considered either arising naturally, i.e. according to the usual mode of things [...] or such as may reasonably be supposed to have been in the contemplation of both parties, at the time they made the contract, as the probable result of the breach if it'.[262] Alderson B.'s formulation had been influenced by Pollock CB's views in *Greenland* v. *Chaplin* and *Rigby* v. *Hewitt,* and it was in turn invoked in tort cases.[263] The idea that 'there must be some limit to the liability of a man for the consequences of a wrongful act' was raised by the Common Pleas judges in 1872.[264] In *Sharp* v. *Powell,* Bovill CJ commented:

> No doubt, one who commits a wrongful act is responsible for the ordinary consequences which are likely to result therefrom; but, generally speaking, he is not liable for damage which is not the natural or ordinary consequence of such an act, unless it be shown that he knows or has reasonable means of knowing that consequences not usually resulting from the act are by reason of some existing cause likely to intervene so as to occasion damage to a third person.[265]

In this case, the defendant's servant, in breach of a Police Act, washed his van in a public street, allowing the water to run off down a gutter. Unknown to him, the grating of the gutter had frozen, and instead of running away, the water spread over the road, creating ice on which the plaintiff's horse slipped and broke its leg. The plaintiff sued, alleging a nuisance from which he had suffered special damage. The court appeared to accept that there had been a breach of duty to the defendant, but held that he should not be held legally liable for the consequences, since they were too remote. In so deciding, it upheld the decision of the trial judge to nonsuit the plaintiff. Although questions of breach and damages were ones for the jury, it was felt that here there was no evidence on which a jury could rightly find for the plaintiff.[266]

In *Clark* v. *Chambers,* Cockburn CJ endorsed the approach taken in this case, noting that recent decisions

---

though he noted that the rules of contributory negligence were as 'rough and ready' attempt to do justice; and argued that it was impossible to formulate a rule satisfactory in all its applications.

[262] *Hadley* v. *Baxendale* (1854) 9 Exch. 341.

[263] See *Richardson* v. *Dunn* (1860) 8 C.B. N.S. 655 at 665–6 (where the notion of what was in the parties' contemplation was invoked in a case of deceit); and *The Notting Hill* (1884) 9 PD 105 at 114 where Brett MR, following Mayne's treatise on *Damages,* felt there was no distinction between the measure of damages in tort and contract.

[264] *Sharp* v. *Powell* (1872) LR 7 CP 253 at 260 (Grove J.).

[265] *Sharp* v. *Powell* (1872) LR 7 CP 253 at 258.

[266] Salmond, *Torts* (2nd edn, 1910), 112 noted it was too remote in law.

have shewn a disposition to confine the liability arising from unlawful acts, negligence, or omissions of duty within narrower limits, by holding a defendant liable for those consequences only which in the ordinary course of things were likely to arise, and which might therefore reasonably be expected to arise, or which it was contemplated by the parties might arise, from such acts, negligences, or omissions.[267]

But where in his view the injury to the horse was not foreseeable in *Sharp*, the injury to the plaintiff from something dangerous like a spike in *Clark* was foreseeable.

In the aftermath of these cases, two rival theoretical views emerged of how to approach causation and damages. The 'progressive' view was that championed by Pollock. '[T]he rule of "natural and probable consequences"', he wrote, 'is not a logical definition, but only a guide to the exercise of common sense.'[268] 'Natural and probable consequences' were those 'which a person of average competence and knowledge [...] might be expected to foresee.'[269] The principle that liability in negligence should only lie for foreseeable harms lay behind both his approach to what constituted a breach of duty, and his approach to what damages could be recovered consequent on a breach. For Pollock, the approach taken by Bovill in *Sharp* v. *Powell* was the correct one. John Salmond also rejected the position suggested by *Smith* v. *The London and South Western Railway Company* that once it was established that there was negligence, the defendant was liable for all consequences, whether foreseeable or not. In his view, such a ruling would 'eliminate the doctrine of remoteness of damage altogether'.[270] In his view, where there was evidence for the jury that the damage was the natural and probable result of the defendant's act, 'they are at liberty to find either that it was or was not such a consequence, and to determine the existence or extent of the defendant's liability accordingly'.[271]

The rival 'traditionalist' view was put forward by Thomas Beven. In discussing breach of duty, Beven drew a distinction between foreseeable consequences, the ignoring of which constituted a negligent act, and consequences which followed from a negligent act. If a person owing a duty of care to another could foresee loss and injury as a natural and probable consequence of his act, then he would be liable for his negligence. If such loss could not be foreseen, there would be no breach of duty, even if injurious consequences followed. However, if a breach of duty had occurred, the wrongdoer was liable for all the consequences 'even

---

[267] *Clark* v. *Chambers* (1878) 3 QBD 327 at 336.

[268] Pollock, *Torts* (1st edn, 1887), 33.

[269] *Ibid.*, 28.

[270] Salmond, *Torts* (2nd edn, 1910), 112n.

[271] *Ibid.*, 110. Clerk and Lindsell, *Torts*, 97, took a similar view, citing Bovill's comments in *Sharp* v. *Powell*. Unlike Salmond, however, they suggested that this was a matter of fact, which was to be decided by the court.

though antecedently, to a reasonable man, the consequences that do flow seemed neither natural nor probable'.[272] Once breach occurred, liability depended 'not on the nearness of the wrongful act, but on the absence of power to divert or avert its consequences, and continued through the various consequences till the first impulse either spends itself [...], or is diverted by some independent agency intervening'. Beven explained *Sharp* v. *Powell* by suggesting that no duty to the plaintiff had been breached. The defendant's violation of the Police Act involved no breach of duty towards the plaintiff; and while his creating a nuisance might have done so, once the water had flowed into the channel designed to receive it 'the natural and probable effects' of his act 'were exhausted' for by then 'the consequences of his wrongful act ceased'.[273] In taking this position, Beven restated the mechanical view of the relationship of causation and damages developed in the mid-nineteenth century.[274]

It was Beven's view, rather than Pollock or Salmond's, which was to prevail, at least in the short term. In *Re Polemis*, in 1921 the Court of Appeal endorsed Beven's position. As Scrutton LJ put it, while the foreseeability of damage was relevant to establishing negligence, 'if the act would or might probably cause damage, the fact that the damage it in fact causes is not the exact kind of damage one would expect is immaterial, so long as the damage is in fact directly traceable to the negligent act, and not due to the operation of independent causes having no connection with the negligent act, except that they could not avoid its results'.[275] But just as Pollock's views on the nature of the duty of care were accepted by the House of Lords in 1932, so 30 years later the Lords in *The Wagon Mound* accepted his view that defendants who had breached a duty of care should only be liable for such consequences as were foreseeable.[276]

By the middle third of the twentieth century, the era of jury trials in tort cases had more or less come to an end. In an age when judges controlled both questions of law and fact, there was no longer the same need for narrow definitions of duty and causation as a way to control the jury. At the same time,

---

[272] Beven, *Negligence* (2nd edn, 1895), i, 97.

[273] Beven, *Negligence* (2nd edn, 1895), i, 104–5.

[274] Salmond was equally sceptical of Beven's attempt to trace the chain of causation until interrupted by some new agency. In his view, the only difference between one consequence and another was a difference in probability; and 'the only practicable measure of the requisite degree of probability is to be found in the knowledge and foresight of a reasonably careful or prudent man': Salmond, *Torts* (2nd edn, 1910), 109.

[275] *In Re Polemis and Furness, Withy & Co* [1921] 3 KB 560 at 577. See Frederick Pollock 'Liability for Consequences' (1922) 38 *LQR* 165–7.

[276] *Overseas Tankship (UK) Ltd v. Morts Dock and Engineering Co (The Wagon Mound)* [1961] AC 388.

judges became much more concerned with questions about the assessment of damages in tort, which had largely been left to jury discretion in our period. In this age, for many judges, it was both safe and desirable to develop the law in the direction pointed to by judges like Brett and jurists like Pollock since the 1880s.

III

Personal Injuries

Since the age of industrialization and urbanization was also one of accidents, personal injury suits constituted a high proportion of cases heard by
common law judges. In deciding how far those who had caused accidents were
responsible for the harms which ensued, the courts did not develop a general
tort of negligence, but looked rather at the particular rights and duties of each
of the parties. If the accident occurred somewhere where the actor had a right
to do what he was doing, and the victim had no right to be, then the victim was
without remedy, however careless the actor had been. An Englishman's home
being his castle, if he engaged in dangerous activity at home, an interloper could
not complain. By contrast, if the accident occurred somewhere the victim had
a right to be, but the agent had no right to engage in the hazardous activity—as
where he created a public nuisance on the highway—then the balance tipped,
and the victim could recover, however careful the agent had been. Between these
extremes were cases where both agent and victim had the right to go about their
business in the world. Here, the question whether liability was imposed or not
generally turned on whether the agent—or the victim—had been negligent.

In dealing with personal injury cases, the courts looked at whether any duty
was owed to the victim, and if so, what kind of duty it was. The courts set limits to
the reach of liability for accidents which occurred in the world at large by limiting
such duties to a defined number, derived from the established categories, such as
trespass, nuisance, contract, or deceit. At the same time, a person's liability for
accidents which occurred in his own home expanded, not into a general duty of
care, but one determined by the nature of the rights conferred on the visitor by
the householder. In taking this narrow, technical approach, the courts were keen
to avoid opening the floodgates to litigation.

1. RAILWAY ACCIDENTS

As railway transport replaced the stage coach as the dominant means of transport across the nation, so an increasing number of passengers were killed in
railway accidents. By the 1860s, an average of 44 passengers were killed a year

in railway accidents. Though rail travel was safer than road travel, periodic catastrophic accidents ensured that the Victorian public mind thought of the railway as creating unique dangers. The public anxiety over railway safety, and the desire of victims to seek compensation ensured a steady flow of litigation. Cases against railways dominated personal injury litigation. Where passengers had been injured in a railway accident, companies were generally willing to offer compensation, and often paid out large sums after accidents had occurred; but they usually defended cases either where victim's claims for compensation were excessive, or where the company's legal liability was in doubt. In doing so, they had to face the hostility of juries who were keen to mulct the companies, backed often by the support of a wider public opinion, which was happy for jurymen to punish the pockets of railway companies, in order to induce them to take greater care to provide safe travel.[1]

Railway companies' liability for the safety of their passengers derived from their status as common carriers. Following the early nineteenth-century treatment of coach accidents, the courts held that cases brought by injured passengers could be pleaded either in contract or tort.[2] The companies were under a duty to carry safely any person whom they had permitted to be a passenger, though if the traveller intended to defraud the railway (by fare-dodging), he would be considered a trespasser, to whom no duty of care was owed. Although the duty to the passenger did not depend on his having made a contract,[3] judges saw it as deriving from a relationship which was analogous to a contractual one.[4] In 1855, Maule B. described an action of negligence against a railway company as 'an action of tort founded upon contract', distinct from 'an action purely for a tort, as

---

[1] See R. W. Kostal, *Law and Railway Capitalism, 1825–1875* (Oxford, 1994); R. Harrington, 'Railway Safety and Railway Slaughter: Railway Accidents, Government and Public in Victorian Britain' (2003) 8 *Journal of Victorian Culture* 187–207.

[2] *Marshall* v. *The York, Newcastle and Berwick Railway Co* (1851) 11 C.B. 655 at 658.

[3] *Austin* v. *The Great Western Railway Co* (1867) LR 2 QB 442 at 446. See *Collett* v. *London and North Western Railway Co* (1851) 16 Q.B. 984 at 989; *Great Northern Railway Co* v. *Harrison* (1854) 10 Exch. 376; *Meux* v. *Great Eastern Railway Co* [1895] 2 QB 387. For cases where the plaintiff had contracted with a different company, see *Foulkes* v. *The Metropolitan District Railway Co* [1879] 4 CPD 267, affirmed in Court of Appeal [1880] 5 CPD 157, and *Dalyell* v. *Tyrer* (1858) 28 LJ QB 52. Where a person was injured while being given a free ride in the vehicle of one not a common carrier, they owed no duty of care and could only be liable for gross negligence: *Moffatt* v. *Bateman* (1869) LR 3 PC 115.

[4] See *Hammack* v. *White* (1862) 11 C.B. N.S. 588 at 594; *Austin* v. *The Great Western Railway Co* (1867) LR 2 QB 442; *Foulkes* v. *The Metropolitan District Railway Co* [1879] 4 CPD 267; *O'Sullevan* v. *Dublin and Wicklow Railway Co* 2 Ir. CL rep. 124. See also the comments of Bramwell B. in Report from the Select Committee on Railway Companies, *PP* 1870 (341), x, 207 (henceforth cited as 1870 Select Committee on Railway Companies) at p. 55. By 1895, it was settled (for the purposes of costs) that the obligation was tortious: *Taylor* v. *Manchester, Sheffield and Lincolnshire Railway Co* [1895] 1 QB 134.

in the case of a collision between two vessels in a river or two vehicles on a road, where there is no special duty due from the owner of the one to the owner of the other'.[5] A railway company was hence 'under the same obligations in reference to the security of the passenger [who had no contract], as it would have been if it had directly contracted with him'.[6] This meant that the duty of care was owed only to the passenger, and only he could sue the railway in tort. A master, whose servant was injured in a train accident, could therefore not sue the company in tort for negligence, *per quod servitium amisit*.[7]

By its contract of carriage, the company warranted that its 'servants shall not be guilty of negligence'.[8] Where everything—train, line, carriages—was under the control of the defendant, and an accident occurred—as where trains came off the line[9]—negligence might be presumed under the doctrine of *res ipsa loquitur*.[10] In such cases, the onus fell on the company to show due care had been taken.[11] This rule made it easier for plaintiffs injured in train crashes to recover for the harm done,[12] but it did not translate into a strict liability for accidents. First, the plaintiff was still required to show evidence of negligence where 'the balance was even'.[13] Secondly, the company could offer evidence to disprove negligence. Thus, in *Hart v. The Lancashire and Yorkshire Railway Company*, the company showed that an accident had occurred after the driver of a locomotive being shunted from a coaling shed suffered a fit and collapsed, and argued that the circumstances under which the accident occurred were such as no precautions could have guarded against. Overturning a verdict for the plaintiffs, Kelly CB said that 'we must use our common sense in the matter'. Since no such accident had ever occurred before, it was unreasonable to suppose that the railway should have foreseen it.[14]

---

[5] *Martin* v. *Great Northern Railway Co* (1855) 16 CB 179 at 196. 1870 Select Committee on Railway Companies, iii–iv and p. 56, q. 857.

[6] *Foulkes* v. *The Metropolitan District Railway Co* (1880) 5 CPD 157 at 170 (Thesiger LJ).

[7] *Alton* v. *Midland Railway Co* (1865) 19 CB NS 213.

[8] Select Committee on Railway Companies, p. 162, q. 2218 (Willes J.).

[9] *Dawson* v. *Manchester, Sheffield and Lincolnshire Railway Co* (1862) 5 LT 682.

[10] *Scott* v. *London and St. Katherine Docks Co* (1865) 3 H. & C. 596 at 601. *Prima facie* proof was not conclusive proof: the question still had to be put to the jury whether a company had been negligent: *Bird* v. *Great Northern Railway Co* (1858) 28 LJ Exch. 3.

[11] *Carpue* v. *London and Brighton Railway Co* (1844) 5 Q.B. 747; *Skinner* v. *London, Brighton and South Coast Railway Co* (1850) 5 Exch. 787; *Great Western Railway Co of Canada* v. *Braid* (1863) 1 Moore N.S. 101.

[12] Martin B. later observed, 'it always seemed to me that that began the mischief [of high damages] which has gone on since that time'. 1870 Select Committee on Railway Companies, p. 59, q. 869.

[13] *Hanson* v. *The Lancashire & Yorkshire Railway Co* (1872) 20 WR 297 at 298, quoting W. Hodges, *A Treatise on the Law of Railways* (4th edn by C. M. Smith), 532; *Patchell* v. *Irish North Western Railway Co* (1871) Ir. Rep. 6 CL 117.

[14] *Hart* v. *The Lancashire and Yorkshire Railway Co* (1869) 21 LT 261 at 262–3; *Liverpool Mercury*, 24 March 1869, p. 5, 26 March 1869, p. 3.

The question whether an appropriate degree of care had been taken arose more usually where equipment had failed. While they were generally prepared to accept liability for accidents where their 'servant has mistaken a signal, or anything of that sort', companies tended to contest their liability for latent defects in equipment[15] seeking to show 'the public that the accident was one wholly beyond ordinary control'.[16] Despite Lord Campbell's assertion that 'if they are bound to carry, they are bound to carry safely',[17] mid-century courts followed early nineteenth-century coach precedents in holding that carriers did not warrant the safety of their equipment. This can be seen from *Stokes* v. *Eastern Counties Railway Company*, a case which arose from the 1860 Tottenham rail crash, when a train ran onto a platform and overturned, after a defectively welded tyre failed. At the trial, Cockburn asked the jury to consider firstly if the company had been responsible for the welding, and if so, whether it was done negligently.[18] If they found the company was not responsible for the flaw in the welding, the jurymen were to consider secondly whether the company had been negligent in not noticing a visible flaw. In answering this question, he added, they were not to expect the railway company to undertake minute scientific examinations of every wheel, for '[t]he business of railways and of life could not go on if this were required'.[19] Rather, they were to consider whether the flaw was visible 'not with the aid of highly scientific authorities and scientific instruments, but on an ordinary, reasonably proper and careful examination, such as all feel ought to be made before engines are used'.[20] After a six-day trial, the jury found for the company.[21]

The notion that railway companies did not guarantee the safety of their rolling stock was confirmed at the end of the decade in *Readhead* v. *The Midland Railway Company*. The plaintiff had been injured in a rail accident while travelling in a carriage which had been leased by the defendants from another railway company. The defendants denied negligence, arguing that since they had tested the tyres in the usual manner (by sounding them), they had acted with due care.[22] Having heard evidence that the failure was caused by an air bubble in the iron,

[15] 1870 Select Committee on Railway Companies, p. 2, q. 13 (evidence of James Blenkinsop).

[16] The words of Mr Johnson, counsel to the company at the inquest into the Wimbledon crash: *The Times*, 4 March 1861, col. 6d.

[17] In *Collett* v. *The London and North Western Railway Co* (1851) 16 Q.B. 984 at 990.

[18] Cockburn left five questions to the jury: see *Daily News*, 29 December 1860, p. 3.

[19] *Stokes* v. *Eastern Counties Railway Co* (1860) 2 F. & F. 691 at 693. See also Kostal, *Law and Railway Capitalism*, 300–1.

[20] Cockburn's comment regarding scientific men should be read in the light of his scepticism regarding the scientific evidence brought by the company regarding the flaw in the wheel. See *Daily News*, 29 December 1860, p. 3.

[21] See also *Ford* v. *London and South Western Railway Co* (1862) 2 F. & F. 730 at 732–3.

[22] *Newcastle Courant*, 9 March 1866, p. 2.

which could not be discovered by a reasonable inspection, the jury found for the company.[23] The plaintiff appealed, claiming that the judge should have told the jury that the company was liable for a latent defect. In the Queen's Bench, Lush J. restated the established view that a carrier of passengers did not insure their safety, but was only liable for negligence.[24] However, Blackburn J. sought to impose a higher level of liability, holding that the defendant 'is bound at his peril to supply a vehicle in fact reasonably sufficient for the purpose; and is responsible for the consequences of his failure to do so, though occasioned by a latent defect.[25] In making this argument, he was persuaded by the analogies drawn by the plaintiff with the liability of vendors selling goods.[26] Blackburn agreed that a carrier could not be regarded in general as an insurer of passengers, as he was of goods, since he did not have the same control over people which he had over objects. However, when it came to the condition of the vehicle, the passenger lost all control, and trusted entirely to the choice of the carrier. Here a higher standard needed to be imposed on the carrier. Just as sellers of goods supplied for a particular purpose were held to warrant them fit for that purpose, since the purchaser had nothing to do with making the selection, so a carrier should be held to warrant his vehicle to be 'reasonably fit for the journey'.[27]

Buoyed by this dissent, the plaintiff appealed to the Exchequer Chamber. It rejected Blackburn's view. Delivering the judgment of the whole court, Montague Smith J. ruled that to hold railways strictly liable for latent undiscoverable defects 'would be to compel a man, by implication of law and not by his own will, to promise the performance of an impossible thing, and would be directly opposed to the maxims of law'.[28] Railway companies were to be held to a 'high degree of care' with a 'duty of exercising all vigilance to see that whatever is required for the safe conveyance of their passengers is in fit and proper order'. But they were not 'compelled by law to make reparation for a disaster arising from a latent defect in the machinery which they are obliged to use, which no human skill or care could either have prevented or detected'.[29] If this was to indicate that the liability of passenger carriers was not strict, the consensus of late nineteenth-century

---

[23] *Readhead* v. *The Midland Railway Co* (1867) LR 2 QB 412.

[24] While he admitted that sea carriers were strictly liable for the seaworthiness of their vessels, the cases in which this duty was alleged all concerned the loss of goods at sea, rather than harm to passengers: *Readhead* v. *Midland Railway* (1867) LR 2 QB 418.

[25] *Readhead* v. *Midland Railway* (1867) LR 2 QB 412 at 432.

[26] Esp. *Brown* v. *Edgington* (1841) 2 M. & G. 279.

[27] *Readhead* v. *Midland Railway* (1867) LR 2 QB 412 at 433–40. Blackburn also drew analogies with implied warranties in shipping contracts. He did not, however, say that the duty to provide a safe vehicle was absolute: where there was an extraordinary peril, the carrier would be excused.

[28] *Readhead* v. *The Midland Railway Co* (1869) LR 4 QB 379 at 384–5.

[29] *Readhead* v. *The Midland Railway Co* (1869) LR 4 QB 379 at 393.

opinion was that the standard of care required of railways was nonetheless very high.[30] *Readhead* only protected companies from undiscoverable defects.

In *Readhead*, the court did not have to discuss whether a railway company would be held liable for the negligence of the manufacturers of a vehicle. However, in the following year, it was suggested that railway companies warranted that reasonable care had been taken by those who had manufactured their equipment.[31] The question was largely academic in railway cases, since the company had a duty to check the safety of their vehicles.[32] The academic point was discussed, however, by Hannen J. in *Francis* v. *Cockrell* (where the committee organizing the Cheltenham steeplechase was sued when a stand collapsed). Hannen treated the matter as purely contractual, asking whether the contract between the racegoer and the committee contained an implied term that due care had been taken by the persons employed as independent contractors to erect the stands. He sought a parallel from the railway example. Hannen pointed out that passengers were usually ignorant whether the company or another manufacturer had made the component which failed. Since the passenger could not sue the manufacturer if he had been injured (thanks to the rule in *Winterbottom* v. *Wright*),[33] the only way to give him a remedy 'is by supposing that the carrier is to be responsible to the passenger, and to look for his indemnity to the person whom he selected and whose breach of contract has caused the mischief'.[34] The carrier warranted that due care had been taken in the manufacture of the vehicle. The principle was applied in 1881, in *Hyman* v. *Nye and Sons*, where Lindley J. held that the defendant—a jobmaster who had hired out a defective carriage to the plaintiff—had a duty 'to supply a carriage as fit for the purpose for which it is hired as care and skill can render it'. If the carriage broke, the onus was on the defendant to show that 'the break down was in the proper sense of the work an accident not preventable by any care or skill'. He was 'an insurer against all defects which skill and care can

---

[30] See e.g. E. R. Thayer, 'Liability without Fault' (1916) 29 *Harvard LR* 801–15 at 805–6; T. G. Shearman and A. A. Redfield, *A Treatise on the Law of Negligence*, 2 vols (4th edn, New York, 1888), p. 50, § 43.

[31] In *Sharp* v. *Grey* (1833) 9 Bing. 457, Alderson B. did suggest a coach proprietor was liable for the state of a coach supplied by others.

[32] A similar issue had arisen in *Grote* v. *The Chester and Holyhead Railway Co* (1848) 2 Exch. 251, where an injury resulted from a defective bridge. The railway claimed they had not been negligent, as they had hired a competent engineer—Robert Stephenson—to build the bridge. However, it was held that the company would not be protected by merely hiring a competent engineer: the engineer himself had to be 'fully competent to the work', and the best method and materials had to have been used.

[33] *Winterbottom* v. *Wright* (1842) 10 M. & W. 109.

[34] *Francis* v. *Cockrell* (1870) LR 5 QB 184 at 194.

guard against'. The risk should be thrown on the owner of the goods, since it was more in his power to control the risk.[35]

In an age when a multiplicity of companies had running rights over the same lines, questions were regularly raised as to the liability of railway companies to guard against the negligence of others. A number of distinctions were developed. To begin with, companies were held to have a duty of care to ensure that the lines on which they ran their trains were in a proper condition to carry passengers.[36] 'If a railway Company chooses to contract to carry passengers not only over their own line, but also over the line of another Company', Cockburn CJ ruled in *The Great Western Railway Company* v. *Blake*, 'the Company so contracting incurs all the liability which would attach to them if they had contracted solely to carry over their own line.'[37] The company was therefore liable for a collision with a carriage negligently left on the line by employees of another company. In *Thomas* v. *The Rhymney Railway Co*, Kelly CB confirmed that carriers contracted 'not only that they will not themselves be guilty of any negligence, but that the passenger shall be carried with due and reasonable care along the whole line from one end of the journey to the other'.[38]

By contrast, railway companies were not held liable for the negligence of other railway companies using the line. As Bramwell B. pointed out in *Wright* v. *The Midland Railway Co* (where the plaintiff's train was hit by another company's train, which had ignored a signal), although the contract of carriage imported an undertaking that railway lines and equipment should be fit for the voyage, whoever managed it, companies did not contract that everyone using the railway should use diligence. For if plaintiffs could have an action in respect of accidents caused by the negligence of other companies, there was no reason why they could not sue in respect of harms suffered on their journey at the hands of a complete stranger.[39] For Bramwell, if the railway were liable here, it would be akin to holding a cab driver liable to his passenger if a bus crashed into him.

Nor were companies which allowed others to use their line held to warrant that care had been taken to ensure that their vehicles were safe. This was settled, after some hesitation, in the test case of *Richardson* v. *The Great Eastern Railway*

---

[35] *Hyman* v. *Nye and Sons* (1881) 6 QBD 685 at 688. He ruled that this was the case in *Readhead* v. *Midland Railway*. This view of the law was endorsed by Buckley LJ in *Wing* v. *London General Omnibus Co* [1909] 2 KB 652 CA at 669.

[36] *Thomas* v. *Rhymney Railway Co* (1871) LR 6 QB 266 at 273; *John* v. *Bacon* (1870) LR 5 CP 437 at 441. However, a company would not be liable for any malicious act by a third party, as when a stranger threw a log onto the line.

[37] *Great Western Railway Co* v. *Blake* (1862) 7 H. & N. 987 at 991–2. Cf. *Buxton* v. *North Eastern Railway Co* [1868] LR 3 QB 549 at 553.

[38] *Thomas* v. *Rhymney Railway Co* (1871) LR 6 QB 266 at 273.

[39] *Wright* v. *The Midland Railway Co* (1873) LR 8 Ex 137 at 140.

Company, in which the plaintiff was injured in a crash caused by the failure of an axle on a goods truck belonging to another company. The defendant company had tested the axle, in the usual manner with a hammer, and had found no defect in it. Kelly CB told the trial jury that, had the carriage belonged to the defendants, they would have been liable for the consequences of any defect discoverable by reasonable care; but since the carriages belonged to another company, whose vehicles they only had a limited right to deal with, the jury had to consider whether the examination given had been reasonable. In answer to questions put, the jury found that the defect in the axle would have been discovered by a fit and careful examination, but that it was not the duty of the company to make such an examination. The jury did find, however, that the defendants should have obtained some assurance from the owners of the truck (after earlier repairs) that it was safe. On the basis of this verdict, Kelly directed them to find for the defendants, since he considered the last issue immaterial.

The judgment was badly received. As the *Pall Mall Gazette* observed, it meant that an examination which was not 'fit or careful' might be 'reasonable', and that the company had taken reasonable care while neglecting to take a precaution which the jury felt they should have taken. On the basis of the jury's findings, the Common Pleas held that the defendants were liable for negligence in allowing a defective truck on their line. Lord Coleridge CJ admitted that it was not the defendant's duty to check all vehicles running on their tracks, for that would put a stop to all business. Nonetheless, 'it was their duty to see that someone else did it'.[40] But Coleridge's view was not shared by the Court of Appeal. Jessel MR agreed that the defendants were under a duty to ascertain that vehicles passing over their line were safe; but he felt that the jury's finding was that they had taken reasonable care, in the inspection they made. He did not take up Coleridge's notion that they had a further duty to ensure that the owners of the vehicle had done all that human care and skill could do to make it safe. Nor was he persuaded that they had a duty to inquire.[41]

Railway companies were also exonerated from liability for accidents caused by the negligence of others working off the line. This was confirmed by the House of Lords in 1871 in *Daniel* v. *Metropolitan Railway*. The case arose from an accident in 1866, when a girder used in the construction of the new Smithfield market

[40] *Pall Mall Gazette*, 1 April 1874, p. 4; *Richardson* v. *Great Eastern Railway Co* (1875) LR 10 CP 486 at 494.

[41] 'If it was the defendants' duty to inquire, it could only be because they were bound to satisfy themselves of the fitness of the trucks, and if so bound, they could not exonerate themselves by mere inquiry of the waggon company': *Richardson* v. *Great Eastern Railway Co* (1876) 1 CPD 342 at 345–6.

fell onto a train below, killing three passengers, and injuring the plaintiff.[42] After the accident, two of the employees of the Thames Ironworks Company, the construction firm working on the site, were indicted for manslaughter; though the charges were dropped, after the death of one of the workmen. During these criminal proceedings, Keating J. noted that the accident was attributable to the culpable omission of any provision of notice when the trains were approaching.[43] At the trial of Daniel's action, evidence was given that it was the usual practice for the railway to signal to building workers when a train was approaching, where dangerous work was being done. A verdict for the plaintiff was agreed, subject to the opinion of the court as to whether there was sufficient evidence of negligence by the defendants to support the plaintiff's case. The Common Pleas found that there was sufficient evidence. As Willes J. pointed out, 'if the company know that there is unusual danger from work which is in progress on or over the line and have it in their power to avert the consequences of that danger by the use of reasonable precaution, they are bound to adopt that precaution, and, not doing so, they are guilty of a breach of duty'.[44] In effect, he was ruling that the company was obliged to take precautions to protect its passengers against the foreseeably dangerous consequences of someone else's negligence. Under these circumstances a jury might reasonably have found for the plaintiff. The judges in the Exchequer Chamber (whose judgment was delivered by Blackburn) agreed with the Common Pleas' view of the duty owed.[45] They also agreed that there was evidence of a breach of duty, which might have been left to a jury. But as a matter of fact, they held that there had been no negligence, since 'they could have no reason to suppose that the persons who were doing the work would do so negligently'.[46]

The House of Lords, which also found for the company, took a different view of the duty. Lord Chelmsford held that there was no duty on the company to take precautions against the possible negligence of third parties. For Lord Hatherley, while 'those who undertake the carriage of passengers are bound to take all reasonable precaution and care with reference to any danger which may reasonably be expected upon the line of road over which they travel'—which might include taking precautions for safety on lines owned by other companies over which they

---

[42] See *The Times*, 20 December 1866, col. 10d. For the inquest see *ibid.*, 22 December 1866, col. 4e; 29 December 1866, col. 9a. The case is discussed further in M. Lobban, 'Daniel v The Metropolitan Railway Company (1871)', in C. Mitchell and P. Mitchell, *Landmark Cases in the Law of Tort* (Oxford, forthcoming).

[43] *The Times*, 31 January 1867, col. 11d.

[44] *Daniel* v. *Metropolitan Railway Co* (1868) LR 3 CP 216 at 222–3.

[45] '[R]ailway companies are bound to take reasonable care to carry their passengers safely': *Daniel* v. *Metropolitan Railway Co* (1868) LR 3 CP 591 at 593–4.

[46] *Daniel* v. *Metropolitan Railway Co* (1868) LR 3 CP 591 at 594.

ran—they were not liable 'for any mischief occasioned by any matter extraneous altogether to the work in which they were engaged, and as to which they had no reasonable ground for supposing that ordinary and proper care had not been taken by those persons whose duty it was to take such care'.[47] Lord Westbury, who agreed that the duty to take care lay on the Thames Ironworks Company, and not on the railway, concluded, 'I have much satisfaction in thinking that this decision will greatly tend ultimately to bring the liability of railway companies to a position in which it may be found to be more consistent with law, and less with feeling and excitement, than it has hitherto been.'[48]

Just as companies were held exempt from liability for the negligence of third parties not on the railway, so they were held not to be liable for the acts of other passengers.[49] In 1891, the Queen's Bench Division held that no duty to the plaintiff—whose job was to evict striking miners from their homes—was breached by a railway company's failure to protect him from being assaulted on the train by angry workers. As A. L. Smith LJ put it, '[t]here is no duty [...] to take extraordinary care of a passenger by reason of any unknown peculiarity then attaching to him'.[50] In 1901, the Privy Council revisited the question of how far the railway carrier's duty was to 'carry safely', in a case where three Indian passengers had been killed on a train by fireworks unlawfully brought on to the train. As Lord Halsbury LC explained, the train company's duty was not to carry safely, but only to use proper care and skill in carrying.[51]

Limiting Liability

Railway companies sought to restrict their liability for accidents not only by resisting legal claims, but also by inserting terms into their contracts of carriage limiting the sums for which they would be held liable. Carriers had long limited their liability for lost goods, a power which was regulated (for the railways) by the Railway and Canal Traffic Act 1854. The liability of railways for injuries suffered by passengers on cheap 'workmen's trains', which they were compelled to run under legislation passed in the 1860s, was also limited.[52] Under these Acts, the amount of compensation was determined by an arbitrator appointed

[47] *Daniel* v. *Metropolitan Railway Co* (1871) LR 5 HL 45 at 54–5.

[48] *Daniel* v. *Metropolitan Railway Co* (1871) LR 5 HL 45 at 62.

[49] They were, however, liable for foreseeable harms done by passengers: in *Hogan* v. *South Eastern Railway Co* (1873) 28 LT 271, the Common Pleas held that there was evidence of negligence for a jury when the plaintiff was thrown from an overcrowded platform by the pressure of the crowd.

[50] *Pounder* v. *North Eastern Railway Co* [1892] 1 QB 385 at 388. The decision was doubted however in *Cobb* v. *Great Western Railway Co* [1894] AC 419 at 423.

[51] *East Indian Railway* v. *Kalidas Mukerjee* [1901] AC 396 (PC) at 403.

[52] W. Hodges, *A Treatise on the Law of Railways*, 2 vols (7th edn by J. M. Lely, 1888), i, 502.

by the Board of Trade, and could not exceed £100. For other travellers, however, liability was unlimited, whether they paid the first-class fare or travelled in the third-class carriages which railways were compelled to provide under the Cheap Trains Act.[53] By the 1860s, railway companies, who felt that they were uniquely discriminated against by juries, lobbied hard for a way to limit their liability. Two inquiries recommended legislation permitting liability to be limited according to the fare paid. Doubts persisted at this time over whether at common law companies 'could legally by notice given to a passenger [...] diminish their liability'.[54] Even judges like Bramwell, who felt that companies were at liberty either to decline to carry people, or to 'take upon such terms as they think fit', nonetheless doubted whether a company could restrict its liability by mere notice, feeling no jury would consider a passenger to have assented to such a special contract.[55]

By the later nineteenth century, such doubts seem to have settled. It was accepted that, provided notice had been sufficiently brought to the passenger's attention, the company was permitted contractually to limit its liability for personal injury as well as for damage to property.[56] Although railway companies had publicly proclaimed their anxiety over their potential liability to wealthy passengers, they first sought to restrict their liability to those paying a low fare, or none at all. One such class consisted of cattle drovers, who were given free passes, which allowed them to accompany livestock which was being transported. These passes stated that the bearer travelled at his own risk. In 1872, the Queen's Bench held that a railway company was protected by such a clause, since its liability was determined by its agreement with the drover.[57] Sometimes, the drover who

---

[53] 7 & 8 Vict. c. 85.

[54] 1870 Select Committee on Railway Companies, iii–iv; Royal Commission on Railways of Great Britain and Ireland, PP 1867 [3844], xxxviii, Pt 1.1 (henceforth cited as 1867 Royal Commission on the Railways) at pp. xxx–xxxi. As an alternative, the select committee recommended that compensation be determined by a juryless tribunal. See also Kostal, Law and Railway Capitalism, 319.

[55] 1870 Select Committee on Railway Companies, pp. 53–4, q. 842 (Bramwell), p. 162, q. 2223 (Willes). Bramwell stated that they could decline to carry passengers since they were not common carriers of people, save in the case of 'government trains' (under the Cheap Trains Act), where liability could therefore not be limited.

[56] Stewart v. London and North Western Railway Co (1864) 3 H. & C. 135; Parker v. South Eastern Railway Co (1877) 2 CPD 416. This test was applied in a personal injury test in Burke v. the South Eastern Railway Co (1879) 5 CPD 1; Richardson, Spence & Co v. Rowntree [1894] AC 217. See also Johnson v. Great Southern and Western Railway Co (1874) Ir. Rep. 9 CL 108. For a case involving a cattle drover, see Duff v. Great Northern Railway Co (1878) LR 4 Ir. 178.

[57] McCawley v. Furness Railway Co (1872) LR 8 QB 57. In so doing, it rejected the plaintiff's contention that the clause could not protect the railway where it was guilty of 'gross' negligence. The Pall Mall Gazette, 19 November 1872, p. 4 approved of this result. The press reported the case as having been pleaded in contract: see also Macaulay v. The Furness Railway Co in The Times, 16 November 1872, col. 11b.

was injured was also the cattle dealer who had contracted for the carriage;[58] but on other occasions, he might be an employee of the dealer.[59] Railway companies sought to overcome any problems of privity this presented by issuing tickets to drovers, which required them either to sign the ticket (permitting free travel at their own risk) or to pay the full fare. Given this practice, the courts held drovers bound by the terms if they travelled without paying, even if they neglected to sign.[60] Colliery workers who were given free passes onto trains—paid for by their employers, in contracts made with the railway—were similarly required to sign documents exonerating the carrier from liability for injuries. Such arrangements were regarded as strictly contractual by late nineteenth century judges,[61] though in 1894 the Court of Appeal held that the agreement was so prejudicial that it could not be held to bind an infant.[62]

By the early twentieth century, judges began to set limits to the practice of limiting liability by contract. In *Clarke* v. *West Ham Corporation*, the plaintiff suffered an electric shock while travelling on a tramcar. His ticket referred to a notice on the tram which stated that passengers were being carried at less than the maximum authorized charges, and that the corporation which owned the trams was limiting its liability to £25. Despite this term, a jury awarded the plaintiff £500. In the King's Bench Division, Lord Coleridge J. held that the tramway company was a common carrier of persons. As such, it had a duty to carry passengers, and could not limit its liability by special contract, without also offering the passenger the option (at a different price) to travel at the risk of the carrier. This decision was upheld in the Court of Appeal.[63] The decision meant that a common carrier could only limit its liability by offering a concession in the fare charged. A common carrier could not limit its liability to those paying the full fare.[64]

---

[58] *Gallin* v. *London and North Western Railway Co* (1875) LR 10 QB 210. Blackburn J. compared the situation of the passenger to whom a duty was owed with an invitee; though without asking what care was owed to those 'invited to come on premises without any payment of money' (at 216).

[59] It was the cattle dealers rather than the drovers who would be prosecuted for cruelty to animals: *Jackson's Oxford Journal*, 10 July 1869, p. 7.

[60] *Hall* v. *North Eastern Railway Co* (1875) LR 10 QB 437 at 441. The court dealt with the issue of whether the liability could still be excluded, since the accident occurred not on the defendant's line, but on another company's line. Quain J. answered this by saying 'there is but one contract'.

[61] In *The Stella* [1900] P 161 at 167, Gorell Barnes J. observed that it made little difference 'whether the pass is termed a license, or whether it indicates a contract to carry upon the conditions mentioned [...] if the conditions which are on the back are terms agreed to by the passenger'. See also the contractual view taken by the Privy Council in *Grand Trunk Railway Co of Canada* v. *Robinson* [1915] AC 740.

[62] *Flower* v. *London and North Western Railway* [1894] 2 QB 65.

[63] *Clarke* v. *West Ham Corporation* [1909] 2 KB 858.

[64] It was also settled after the war that a contract limiting the liability of the tortfeasor did not limit the sum which his relatives could recover in the event of his death: *Nunan* v. *Southern Railway Co* [1924] 1 KB 223.

2. ACCIDENTS ON THE HIGHWAY

Highway Collisions

While railways faced the bulk of transport accident litigation after 1840, accidents were also frequent on the roads. The courts in the second half of the century accepted that those who caused road accidents were only liable if they had been at fault. Attempts to argue that defendants were strictly liable in trespass for direct harms failed. In *Corr* v. *Cole*, where the recital of the writ stated that it was an action of trespass, the court regarded it in substance as an action on the case for negligence. Reiterating a distinction made two decades before, Erle J. said, '[i]f I wilfully drive against a man, it is a trespass; but not, if I do so negligently only'.[65] The notion that the victim of a road accident could not use trespass to recover where the defendant had not been at fault was confirmed in 1875 in *Holmes* v. *Mather*. Explaining the turn of the century cases, Bramwell B. held that if the act causing injury was one of direct force *vi et armis*, trespass was the proper remedy; but it could only be used if 'the act is wrongful, either as being wilful or as being the result of negligence'.[66] This was a necessary approach to take in the modern world, where everyone had a right to be on the highway: 'For the convenience of mankind in carrying on the affairs of life, people as they go along roads must expect, or put up with, such mischief as reasonable care on the part of others cannot avoid.'[67]

This trend towards a fault liability did not undermine the application of a stricter liability in trespass where it was held that the defendant had no right to be on the streets in the first place. In *Sadler* v. *The South Staffordshire and Birmingham District Steam Tramways Company*, the plaintiff was injured and his wife killed, when a tramcar left its tracks and ran into them, having gone over a faulty point. Since the defendants had not been negligent, nor were they responsible for the management of the tracks, they invoked *Holmes* v. *Mather* and argued that this had been an inevitable accident. However, Lord Esher MR ruled that they were only allowed by their statute to run trams on safe rails. The rails being unsafe, 'I think that they were doing what the Act did not allow them to do. That being so, and the accident being the result of their immediate action, they are, as it seems to me, liable in trespass in respect of its consequences.' To set up a defence of inevitable accident, they would have had to show that the

---

[65] *Carr* v. *Cole* (1850) 16 LTR 148 at 149. See also *The Times*, 12 November 1850, col. 7b.

[66] *Holmes* v. *Mather* (1875) LR 10 Ex 261 at 268–9. See this point confirmed in *Stanley* v. *Powell* [1891] 1 QB 86.

[67] *Holmes* v. *Mather* (1875) LR 10 Ex 261 at 267.

accident was 'not really the result of their action at all', as if a miscreant had laid a log across the line.[68]

Those with a right to be on the streets also had to take care to avoid accidents. 'It is as much the duty of foot-passengers attempting to cross a street or road to look out for passing vehicles as it is the duty of drivers to see that they do not run over foot-passengers', Erle CJ ruled in 1860: 'Where it is a perfectly even balance upon the evidence whether the injury complained of has resulted from the want of proper care on the one side or the other, the party who founds his claim upon the imputation of negligence fails to establish his case.'[69] The mere fact that the defendant had collided with the plaintiff therefore did not generate a presumption of lack of care on his part. Mid-century courts were particularly lenient when accidents in the world at large involved non-professionals. In 1862, in *Hammack* v. *White*, the Common Pleas rejected the plaintiff's contention that the fact that a horse, being ridden by the defendant for the first time after its purchase, had run onto a pavement and killed a man was itself evidence of negligence. It had rather to be shown either that the defendant had been unskilful in handling the horse, or that he had known of its bad temper. Erle CJ rejected the plaintiff's argument that all she had to show was 'that the deceased was in a place where he might reasonably conceive himself to be safe, and that the defendant rode where he had no right to be'.[70] In his view, 'a man is not to be charged with want of caution because he buys a horse without having any previous experience of him. There must be horses without number ridden every day in London of whom the riders know nothing'.[71]

By contrast, the fact that the defendant was running a business might sway the view of the judges. Thus, where a horse belonging to the London General Omnibus Company kicked a passenger, Bovill CJ ruled that the burden of proof that the horse was not 'habitually a kicker' lay on the defendants.[72] Negligence could also be presumed from the circumstances of the accident. Where two carts collided when a shaft broke on one of the vehicles, negligence in the owner of the faulty vehicle could be presumed.[73] Where an unattended horse and cart bolted, a similar presumption could arise.[74]

---

[68] *Sadler* v. *The South Staffordshire and Birmingham District Steam Tramways Co* (1889) 23 QBD 17 at 21–2.

[69] *Cotton* v. *Wood* (1860) 8 C.B. N.S. 568 at 571. See also *Williams* v. *Richards* (1852) 3 Car. & K. 81 at 83.

[70] *Hammack* v. *White* (1862) 11 C.B. N.S. 588 at 592.

[71] *Hammack* v. *White* (1862) 11 C.B. N.S. 588 at 594–5.

[72] *Simson* v. *London General Omnibus Co* (1873) LR 8 CP 390 at 393.

[73] *Templeman* v. *Haydon* (1852) 12 C.B. 507.

[74] *Watson* v. *Weekes* (1887), cited in *Tolhausen* v. *Davies* (1888) 57 LJ QB 392 at 394.

Public Nuisances

Besides collision cases, the mid-nineteenth century also saw a number of cases where plaintiffs had been damaged by things left on the highway by the defendant, in such a way as to constitute a public nuisance. Such nuisances could be of various types. First, if a person's fixed property encroached onto the highway, creating a danger to passers-by, it was *prima facie* a public nuisance, for which he was liable to any one suffering particular damage. He was not liable for accidents, however, if he could show a right to encroach on the highway. The distinction between the two turned on whether the nuisance in question had existed prior to the dedication of a highway to the public: if it had, the dedication was held to have been accepted by the public subject to the risk. As Blackburn J. saw it, 'great injustice and hardship would often arise if, when a public right of way has been acquired under a given state of circumstances, the owner of the soil should be held bound to alter that state of circumstances to his own disadvantage and loss, and to make further concessions to the public altogether beyond the scope of his original intention'.[75] If the defendant had no right to obstruct the highway, and the obstruction was permanent, the nature of the nuisance was clear, and the defendant was strictly liable if the plaintiff had suffered special damage, without being himself negligent. By contrast, if the danger was temporary, the question of care was more prominent. For instance, many accidents occurred when plaintiffs fell into cellar flaps left open in a public street. Since opening a cellar flap was not in itself a nuisance, judges asked juries to consider both the care taken by the defendant in generating a risk, and the care taken by the plaintiff in avoiding it.[76]

Secondly, risks might be generated by a defendant excavating his land next to the highway. In 1850, Jane Barnes was killed after falling into a hole by the roadside, on unfenced land owned by the defendant, on which houses were being built. The plaintiff alleged the breach of a duty to fence the area. Maule J. held the defendant guilty of a public nuisance, even though the danger consisted in the risk of a passer-by accidentally deviating from the road, and trespassing. It was a nuisance, 'for, the danger thus created may reasonably deter prudent persons from using the way, and thus the full enjoyment of it by the public is, in effect, as much impeded as in the case of an ordinary nuisance to the highway'.[77] In such cases, the courts had to consider how far into the defendant's property the

---

[75] *Fisher* v. *Prowse, Cooper* v. *Walker* (1862) 2 B. & S. 770 at 780. See also this view endorsed in *Robbins* v. *Jones* (1863) 15 C.B. N.S. 221.

[76] *Proctor* v. *Harris* (1830) 4 C. & P. 337. Cf. *Pickard* v. *Smth* (1861) 10 C.B. N.S. 470, where the cellar flap was at a railway station, and so raised issues of occupier's liability rather than public nuisance. See also *Attorney General* v. *Sheffield Gas Consumers Co* (1853) 3 De G. M. & G. 304 at 340.

[77] *Barnes* v. *Ward* (1850) 9 C.B. 392 at 420. Cf. *Coupland* v. *Hardingham* (1813) 3 Camp. 398.

excavation had to be before it ceased to be a public nuisance, so that the interloper ran his own risk. Pollock CB's answer was that if a man could fall into the excavation when stumbling off the highway it was a nuisance, whereas if he had to be a trespasser before he reached it, it was not.[78] The liability here was strict, insofar as leaving an unfenced excavation next to the highway constituted a clear breach of a duty to the public. However, liability in any action could be disputed on the grounds that the harm had occurred not because of the breach of duty, but because of contributory negligence by the plaintiff, which served to introduce a negligence issue not seen in private nuisance cases.

Besides nuisances arising from the use of fixed property, cases were brought where builders left rubble on the highway from excavations to lay pipes,[79] or where something—like a horse—had been left on the highway which might generate a danger.[80] In the former type of case, it was clear that a nuisance had been created, but the courts faced disputes both over whether the contractor or his client should be liable, and over whether victims should have taken care to avoid the harm. In the latter kind of case, the issue looked more like one of negligence, since horses were not in themselves nuisances. Such cases were pleaded as actions on the case for consequential harms, in which the basis of the action could be seen either as negligence by the defendant in generating a risk,[81] or nuisance causing special damage to the plaintiff. Since, in either case, the question of contributory negligence could be raised,[82] by the mid-nineteenth century, the courts came to regard them as actions for negligence.[83]

Motor Vehicles

The later nineteenth century saw the arrival of a new form of self-propelled transport taking to the roads: the motor car. Although the 1830s had seen attempts to introduce steam powered vehicles on the roads, they petered out in the mid-century, faced with opposition from those who feared boiler explosions and damage to the roads. Locomotive Acts in 1861 and 1865 permitted the use

[78] *Hardcastle* v. *The South Yorkshire Railway and River Dun Co* (1859) 4 H. & N. 67 at 74–5. See also *Binks* v. *The South Yorkshire Railway and River Dun Co* (1862) 3 B. & S. 244 at 253 and *Hadley* v. *Taylor and Others* (1865) LR 1 CP 53 at 55.

[79] e.g. *Burgess* v. *Gray* (1845) 1 C.B. 578; *Peachey* v. *Rowland and Evans* (1853) 13 C.B. 182.

[80] e.g. *Lynch* v. *Nurdin* (1840) 1 Q.B. 29; *Cox* v. *Burbidge* (1863) 13 C.B. N.S. 431.

[81] See *Illidge* v. *Goodwin* (1831) 5 Car. & P. 190 (where an action for harm done by a cart was brought in negligence).

[82] See *Butterfield* v. *Forrester* (1809) 11 East 60, 'an action on the case for obstructing a highway'.

[83] *Lynch* v. *Nurdin* (1841) 1 Q.B. 29 was thus brought as an action of negligence; though by the end of the century a number of judges sought to reinterpret it as one of nuisance, in order to limit the liability of occupiers on whose land trespassing children were injured.

of such self-propelled machines, but limited their speed to 4 mph, and required a man carrying a red flag to walk in front of each vehicle. The machines which were built were used mainly as traction engines, and agricultural engines, which traveled only short distances.[84] By the 1890s, some 8000 steam traction engines were running on Britain's roads.[85] In the second half of the century, there was occasional litigation arising from harms caused by them. The cases were of two kinds. First, there were cases where locomotives had frightened horses, leading to injuries either to the animal or its owner. Secondly, there were cases where the engine had caused damage, as when sparks flew from it and caused fires. Despite the existence of legislation which permitted and regulated their use, the courts consistently found owners of the vehicles liable for the harms done in a way suggesting that liability here was strict.

In 1861, in a case where negligence was alleged, Erle CJ told a jury that an injured plaintiff was entitled to succeed if the defendant's engine 'was calculated by its noise and appearance to frighten horses, so as to make the use of the highway dangerous to persons riding or driving horses. For the defendant has clearly no right to make a profit at the expense of the security of the public.'[86] In 1880, in *Powell* v. *Fall*, when finding the owner of a traction engine liable after its sparks had set fire to a haystack, Bramwell B. similarly said, '[i]t is just and reasonable that if a person uses a dangerous machine, he should pay for the damage which it occasions'.[87] The Court of Appeal confirmed the view that the Locomotive Act only permitted the owners of traction engines to run them on the streets and it did not authorize nuisances, for which a strict common law liability remained.[88] Within ten years, the Court of Appeal applied the same analysis to cases of personal injury. 'If an engine of this sort fulfilled all the requirements of the statute, and yet was calculated to frighten horses of ordinary nerve and courage on a highway', Lord Esher ruled in *Galer* v. *Rawson*, 'the engine was a nuisance, and there was nothing in the statutes to absolve the owner from liability to pay damages to those whose person or property was injured in consequence thereof.'[89] Later

---

[84] Select Committee on Locomotives on Roads, *PP* 1873 (312), xvi, 477.

[85] P. Thorold, *The Motoring Age: The Automobile and Britain 1896–1939* (2003), 11–15; K. Richardson, *The British Motor Industry, 1896–1939* (1977), 11.

[86] *Watkins* v. *Reddin* (1861) 2 F. & F. 629 at 634. For a discussion, see J. R. Spencer, 'Motor-cars and the rule in *Rylands* v. *Fletcher*: A chapter of accidents in the history of law and motoring' (1983) 42 *CLJ* 65–84.

[87] *Powell* v. *Fall* (1880) 5 QBD 597 (CA) at 601. See also *Gunter* v. *James* (1908) 24 TLR 868; *Mansel* v. *Webb* [1919] 88 LJ KB 323.

[88] Mellor J., hearing the case, invoked the strict liability principle of *Rylands* v. *Fletcher* to dangerous things taken into a public place, which caused damage to another's property.

[89] *Galer* v. *Rawson* (1889) 6 TLR 17.

judges followed Lindley LJ's view that the question whether a traction engine was a nuisance was one for the jury.[90]

By the 1890s, the pan-European craze for horseless vehicles to transport the public had reached Britain. Legislation in 1896, permitting 'light locomotives' to travel at a maximum speed of 14 mph, paved the way for the development of the motor car, and within ten years there were more than 23,000 private cars in the country. By the end of our period, more than 13,000 vehicles were registered annually. Legislation in 1903 increased the speed limit to 20mph, and required owners of vehicles to license them. Drivers who drove too quickly were prosecuted and fined;[91] they responded by creating motoring organizations whose first task was to provide look-outs to warn drivers of speed traps.[92] Once the motor vehicle was in common use, the courts had to consider whether liability for harms done by them was to be as strict as it was for traction engines, or whether fault was required, as with horse buses.

In 1908, in a case brought against the Vanguard Motorbus Company for damage done to lamps when their bus skidded, the Divisional Court upheld (though not without some hesitation) the finding of a county court judge that the company was liable 'for placing a nuisance on the highway and for negligently using the highway', even though it was convinced the driver had not been negligent.[93] In so deciding, the court ignored the argument 'that an owner of property by the side of a highway must take the risk of that property being injured through an accident arising from the lawful use of the highway'.[94] By contrast, in 1909, in *Wing* v. *London General Omnibus Company*, where the company was accused of negligence, the Court of Appeal held that there had been no case to put to a jury, since the plaintiff had given no evidence of negligence, beyond the mere fact that the bus had skidded and hit a lamppost.[95] In Fletcher Moulton LJ's words, 'the so-called negligence of the defendants, in allowing the omnibus to run when the roads were in a greasy state, must mean that they ought not to have done so because, when so run, the omnibus constituted a nuisance'.[96] He did not deny

[90] *Bantwick* v. *Rogers* (1891) 7 TLR 542; *Jeffery* v. *St. Pancras Vestry* (1894) 63 LJ QB 619, where Collins J. held that evidence that a horse had been frightened by a steam roller would be sufficient to put the case to a jury.

[91] See e.g. *Elwes* v. *Hopkins* [1906] 2 KB 1; *Du Cros* v. *Lambourne* [1907] 1 KB 40.

[92] S. O'Connell, *The Car and British Society: Class, Gender and Motoring, 1896–1939* (Manchester, 1998), 114. For litigation arising from this practice see e.g. *Bastable* v. *Little* [1907] 1 KB 59.

[93] *Gibbons* v. *Vanguard Motorbus Co* (1908) 25 TLR 14.

[94] A point made by Dankwaerts in the accompanying case of *Isaac Walton and Co* v. *The Vanguard Motorbus Co* (1908) 25 TLR 14.

[95] Vaughan Williams LJ said, 'I do not think that an accident arising from the tendency of motor omnibuses, however well constructed and designed, to skid is any evidence of negligence or of nuisance': *Wing* v. *London General Omnibus Co* [1909] 2 KB 652 at 662.

[96] *Wing* v. *London General Omnibus Co* [1909] 2 KB 652 at 665.

that if a man placed a vehicle on the street which was so unmanageable that it constituted a danger, then he would do so at his peril, and be liable for all the consequences, however much care he had taken. But he held that it was for the plaintiff to show by evidence that a nuisance had been committed; and merely running a bus in the rain could not be a nuisance.

In practice, this language of nuisance, borrowed from the cases of traction engines, was unsuitable for modern motor accidents. Where—as in *Wing*—the plaintiff was a passenger, it was difficult to argue that the defendant had been creating a public nuisance causing her special damage. Equally, where an accident resulted from collisions between motor vehicles, the plaintiff could only succeed by showing that the other party had been at fault.[97] In such cases, the courts began to speak the language of negligence. By 1913, it could be said that '[t]he liability of owners and drivers of motor cars for negligence is neither more nor less than that of owners and drivers of other vehicles'. Though the doctrine of *res ipsa loquitur* did not apply generally to accidents on the highway, it was apparent by now that where a bus collided with a lamp post in clear daylight, it was *prima facie* evidence of negligence. As the author of an early treatise warned his readers, '[i]t behoves drivers, therefore, to be extremely careful when driving in the daytime, because if they run into, or collide with, another vehicle or with some fixed object, it would be extremely difficult to convince a jury that no blame attached to the driver'.[98]

3. OCCUPIERS' LIABILITY

General Principles

The injuries discussed so far occurred in the world of public interchange, where each person was agreed to run his own risks, and where each owed a duty to others not to generate unnecessary risks to them.[99] But injuries also occurred on the property of others, raising the question of the liability of proprietors to those on their land. The early nineteenth-century view was that if the plaintiff had no right to be on the defendant's land, he could not complain if he was harmed by anything on it liable to cause danger.[100] 'I know it is a rule of law, that I must occupy my own so as to do no harm to others; but it is their legal rights only, that

[97] See e.g. the Scottish case *Pressley* v. *Burnett* 1914 SC 874.

[98] D. Warde, *The Law of Motor Cars and Motor Accidents* (1913), 38, citing *Barnes Urban Council* v. *London General Omnibus Co* (1909) 100 LTR 115, 73 JP 68, LGR 359.

[99] See G. P. Fletcher, 'Fairness and Utility in Tort Theory' (1972) 85 *Harvard LR* 537–73.

[100] *Blyth* v. *Topham* (1608) Cro. Jac. 158. See also Dallas CJ's formulation *Deane* v. *Clayton* (1817) 7 Taunt. 489 at 522.

I am bound not to disturb', Gibbs CJ noted in *Deane* v. *Clayton* in 1817: 'It is the rights of others, and not their security against the consequences of wrongs, that I am bound to regard.'[101] So saying, he took the view that a plaintiff, whose hunting dog had died from running onto spikes placed on the defendant's land, had no cause of action.

The court in this case was divided, however, since the defendant had set spikes with the intention of killing dogs who happened to stray onto his land. The right of a proprietor to defend his land from intruders was further debated in a number of cases where spring-guns had been placed to deter poachers. Before the question had been made wholly academic by the outlawing of spring-guns,[102] it was held that a trespasser who knew that spring-guns were placed in a wood could not maintain an action for injury done to him, after he accidentally triggered one of them;[103] but that a defendant who placed spring-guns was liable to trespassers if he had failed to give notice of the danger.[104] These cases showed that although a landowner owed no duty of care to those who came without his invitation onto his land, he was not allowed intentionally to injure them.

It was soon settled that those who were invited onto property were owed a duty of care. This can be seen from *Parnaby* v. *The Lancaster Canal Company*, where the plaintiff's boat struck a vessel lying submerged in the defendants' canal. Since the company invited the public to use its property in return for tolls, Tindal CJ ruled, it had a duty 'to take reasonable care, so long as they keep it open for the public use of all who may choose to navigate it, that they may navigate without danger to their lives or property'. This was parallel to the duty of a shopkeeper who invited customers to enter his shop not to leave trap doors open without protection.[105] Their duty, in Tindal's view, was not a strict one, but was a duty to take the same kind of care he had earlier held was required of occupiers who opened cellar flap doors, through which passers-by were in danger of falling.[106]

By contrast, it was agreed in the mid-nineteenth century that members of a household, as well as their servants and visitors who were permitted onto the property, were not owed a duty of care, but were in the same position as recipients

---

[101] *Deane* v. *Clayton* (1817) 7 Taunt. 489 at 529. The other judges found for the plaintiff, Burrough holding that the defendant's intent to harm any stray dog made his act unlawful, and Park holding that no trespass had been committed by the dog.

[102] 7 & 8 Geo. IV c. 18.

[103] *Ilott* v. *Wilkes* (1820) 3 B. & Ald. 304.

[104] *Bird* v. *Holbrook* (1828) 4 Bing. 628.

[105] *Parnaby* v. *The Lancaster Canal Co* (1839) 11 Ad. & El. 223 at 242–3.

[106] *Daniels* v. *Potter* (1830) 4 Car. & P. 262; *Proctor* v. *Harris* (1830) 4 Car. & P. 337. See also *Pickard* v. *Smith* (1861) 10 C.B. N.S. 470, where Williams J. also spoke of the duty of the occupiers of cellars not to lay traps for unwary members of the public in terms of taking 'reasonable precautions'.

of a gift, who had to take it as they found it.[107] In *Hounsell* v. *Smyth*, where the plaintiff fell into an unfenced quarry on the defendant's land, while taking a short cut cross it, Williams J. ruled that those who were given a license to cross the land 'must take the permission with its concomitant conditions, and, it may be, perils'. Since he had no right to be on the land, but only permission, no duty of care was owed to him.[108] Similarly, in 1867, in *Gautret* v. *Egerton*, Willes J. held that there could be no duty to take preventive action (to protect persons crossing land from falling into an unsafe canal), even if the owner was aware of the danger. 'To create a cause of action, something like fraud must be shewn', he ruled: 'Every man is bound not wilfully to deceive others, or do any act which may place them in danger.'[109] This confirmed that the only risks from which bare licensees were protected were those presented by concealed traps. Thus, in *Corby* v. *Hill* in 1858, the Common Pleas ruled that the owner of land with a private road leading to the Hanwell Lunatic Asylum was liable for allowing building materials to be placed on the road, which caused the plaintiff damage: as the defendant had held the road out to be safe, he could not 'set a trap for the plaintiff'.[110]

From the 1860s, the courts began to expand the number of people who would be regarded as invitees. In 1862, in *Wilkinson* v. *Fairrie*, the Exchequer had taken a narrow view of an occupier's duty. In this case, a carman fetching goods from the defendant sugar refiners was sent along a passage to find the warehouseman. The passage was dark, and he fell down a staircase. The Exchequer held that there was no duty on the defendants to light the passage. '[I]t is the duty of every person to take care of his own safety.' Pollock CB ruled: 'As there was no contract, or any public or private duty on the part of the defendants that their premises should be in a different condition from that in which they were, it seems to us that the nonsuit is right.'[111] However, the decision in this case was not followed. In *Indermaur* v. *Dames* in 1866, a gasfitter who had been sent to the plaintiff's sugar refinery to check the work was injured by an unfenced shaft. Willes J. in the Common Pleas ruled that by settled law, customers were entitled to 'the exercise of reasonable care by the occupier to prevent damage from unusual danger'; and that the same

---

[107] *Southcote* v. *Stanley* (1856) 1 H. & N. 247 at 250; *Chapman* v. *Rothwell* (1858) E. B. & E. 168 at 170. The notion that members of the household and other mere visitors had to take the location as they found it was influenced by the view taken in employment cases of the liability of the masters to his servants. See pp. 1002–3.

[108] *Hounsell* v. *Smyth* (1860) 7 C.B. N.S. 732 at 743. See also *Bolch* v. *Smith* (1862) 7 H. & N. 736.

[109] *Gautret* v. *Egerton* (1867) LR 2 CP 371 at 374–5. Cf. Bramwell B.'s remarks in *Southcote* v. *Stanley* that a man was liable for acts of commission, but not omissions. See also the rule regarding licensees as expressed by Pigot CB in *Sullivan* v. *Waters* (1864) Ir. Rep. 14 CL R 460 at 475.

[110] *Corby* v. *Hill* (1858) 4 C.B. N.S. 556. This case drew on old ideas that a nuisance on one's own land was actionable as a trap if there had been an allurement to draw the plaintiff on to the land.

[111] *Wilkinson* v. *Fairrie* (1862) 1 H. & C. 633 at 635–6.

duty applied to those 'who go upon business which concerns the occupier, upon his invitation, expressed or implied'.[112]

A further step was taken in 1868, when the Common Pleas extended the duty of occupiers to invitees to those who were on the premises for the business of others. In *Smith* v. *London and Saint Katharine Docks Company*, the defendant dock company provided gangways between the shore and ships lying in their docks, and the plaintiff, who had been invited onto a ship, was injured when he returned from the ship, and stepped onto a gangway which had been moved in such a way as to make it insecure. It was argued that here there was no privity between plaintiff and defendant, and that the plaintiff ran his own risks by walking on the gangway, but Bovill CJ ruled for the plaintiffs, noting that while the defendants owed no duty to a 'mere volunteer', such as a hawker, 'the gangway being placed there as the means of access to all persons having business on board the ship it amounts to an invitation to persons having business on board the ship to go upon it'.[113] Since a duty was owed to the shipowners, a duty was equally owed to their guests. As a result of these developments, by the end of our period, a distinction was drawn between three levels of care owed by occupiers. The liability was lowest towards a trespasser, who had no right to be on the property, and who could not complain, even if he fell into hidden dangers. A licensee had to take premises as he found them, though the occupier was not permitted to expose him to hidden perils. An invitee was entitled to expect reasonable care to have been taken to prevent damage from unusual dangers of which the occupier should have been aware.[114]

The issue of an occupier's liability was most frequently litigated in the context of accidents arising on railway premises.[115] Those who entered stations lawfully had the status of invitees, to whom a duty of care was owed.[116] Those who went to part of the station where the railway could not anticipate them going lost that status, and no duty of care was owed them.[117] Attempts were made at the end of our period to argue that since intending travellers were on railway premises as a matter of right, they were owed a greater duty than invitees were. But this view was

---

[112] *Indermaur* v. *Dames* (1866) LR 1 CP 274 at 287. See also *Paddock* v. *North Eastern Railway Co* (1868) 18 LT 60.

[113] *Smith* v. *London and Saint Katharine Docks Co* (1868) LR 3 CP 326 at 332–3.

[114] *Norman* v. *Great Western Railway* [1915] 1 KB 584 at 591–2.

[115] Since those who entered railway stations were not yet passengers, they could not sue the railway alleging a breach of the carrier's duty.

[116] See *Watkins* v. *Great Western Railway* (1877) 37 LT 193 at 195; *Thatcher* v. *Great Western Railway* (1893) 10 TLR 13.

[117] *Griffiths* v. *London and North Western Railway* (1866) 14 LT 797. A person on a platform without a platform ticket was also technically a trespasser, though the fact he had been allowed onto the platform by a railway employee might be sufficient to permit him to be regarded as an invitee.

rejected. Railways were only required to take reasonable care that their premises were safe.[118] Moreover, where injuries were sustained in stations, the courts were unwilling to apply the *res ipsa loquitur* principle.[119] Thus, in 1869, it was held that the mere fact that a plank and roll of zinc had fallen on the plaintiff's head from work being done on the portico at London Bridge station, while he was checking the company's timetables, was not itself regarded as evidence of negligence to go to a jury.[120] Nor was the fact that a structure could have been made more safe evidence for the jury of negligence.[121]

Outside stations, people who entered railway property without invitation were regarded as trespassers. The only time passengers were normally permitted onto railway property outside stations was on level crossings. Where they were placed in such a way as to expose the public to greater risks than was usual, the failure by the railway to take precautions to prevent accidents (such as whistling) could be left to juries as evidence of negligence.[122] In 1858, Watson B. told a jury that where a company was aware that the public made use of an unrecognized crossing, it had a duty to take reasonable care that they were not injured.[123] But if a person crossed where no crossing was recognized, no duty of care arose.[124]

Trespassing Children

Judges developing the rules on occupiers' liability resisted developing a general duty of care to avoid foreseeable harms. Instead, the courts looked at the kind of rights visitors to the premises had before deciding what duties were owed to them. Towards the end of the century, however, this approach was challenged by some judges, when confronted with the problem of accidents to children. In these cases, some courts sought to apply a more general principle.[125]

---

[118] *Norman* v. *Great Western Railway* [1915] 1 KB 584 at 591–2.

[119] *Cornman* v. *Eastern Counties Railway Co* (1859) 4 H. & N. 781; *Blackman* v. *London, Brighton and South Coast Railway* (1869) 17 WR 770.

[120] *Welfare* v. *The London and Brighton Railway Co* (1869) LR 4 QB 693.

[121] See also *Crafter* v. *Metropolitan Railway* (1866) LR 1 CP 300.

[122] See *Bilbee* v. *London Brighton and South Coast Railway Co* (1865) 18 C.B. N.S. 584; cf. *Cliff* v. *Midland Railway Co* (1870) LR 5 QB 258 at 261 (Mellor J.) and 264 (Lush J.); *Ellis* v. *Great Western Railway Co* (1874) LR 9 CP 551.

[123] *Barrett* v. *Midland Railway Co* (1858) 1 F. & F. 361.

[124] *Harrison* v. *N E Railway* (1874) 29 LT 844.

[125] For late nineteenth-century American developments, see P. Karsten, *Heart versus Head: Judge-Made Law in Nineteenth Century America* (1997) Ch. 7; R. N. Batson, 'Trespassing Children: A Study in Expanding Liability' (1966) 20 *Vanderbilt LR* 139–69.

The concern with children was a new one, and reflected a growing sensitivity to the nature of childhood.[126] Before the 1880s, the courts did not give special protection to children who suffered accidents on the land of others. In 1859, in *Singleton* v. *The Eastern Counties Railway Company*, a 3½-year-old child whose leg was cut off by a passing train failed to recover damages, since she 'was wrongfully upon the railway'.[127] Four years later, in *Hughes* v. *Macfie*, the Exchequer held that a child who had injured himself by jumping from a cellar flap and pulling it on himself and his friend could not recover, since he voluntarily meddled with the object and caused his own injury.[128] In these cases, the injured child had no right to be on the land or meddle with the property. By contrast, in *Burchell* v. *Hickisson*, a four-year-old boy, who had accompanied his sister while visiting the defendant's house on business, and who fell through a broken railing, was no trespasser. That being the case, a duty was imposed on the occupier to ensure there was no concealed danger. Although Lindley J. admitted that the child was not capable of seeing the danger, he held that the child was only invited onto the premises on condition that he was in the care of an adult; in which case 'there was no concealed danger'.[129]

By the late 1880s, however, there were signs that the courts were seeking to protect children more. In *Jewson* v. *Gatti*, where a girl fell into a cellar in which scenery was being painted, after leaning on a bar protecting the opening, Lord Esher overturned the trial judge's finding that there was no evidence of negligence for a jury, since the child had no right to lean against the bar. In his view, the circumstances were such as to amount 'almost an invitation, certainly an inducement, to the children to lean against the bar'.[130] In 1893, he upheld a verdict against a schoolmaster, who had negligently left a stick of phosphorous in a conservatory at his school, which injured one of the boys. For Lord Esher, a schoolmaster was 'bound to take notice of the ordinary nature of young boys, their tendency to do mischievous acts, and their propensity to meddle with anything that came in their way'.[131] By the end of the century, judges were becoming much more aware

---

[126] See H. Hendrick, *Children, Childhood and English Society, 1880–1990* (Cambridge, 1997), Ch. 2; C. Steedman, *Childhood, Culture and Class in Britain: Margaret McMillan, 1860–1931* (1990).

[127] Erle CJ in *Singleton* v. *The Eastern Counties Railway Co* (1859) 7 C.B. N.S. 278 at 289. See also the same judge's approach in *Cox* v. *Burbidge* (1863) 13 C.B. N.S. 431 and Bramwell B.'s in *Mangan* v. *Atterton* (1866) LR 1 Ex 239.

[128] *Hughes* v. *Macfie* (1863) 2 H. & C. 744.

[129] *Burchell* v. *Hickisson* (1880) 50 LJ CP NS 101 at 102.

[130] *Jewson* v. *Gatti* (1886) 2 TLR 441 at 442. Contrast *Bailey* v. *Neal* (1888) 5 TLR 20, where a boy of 9½ had his fingers crushed in the works of a steam roller: the defendants had taken precautions to prevent the vehicle being set in motion, but they were tampered with by another boy, and the court found there was no negligence by them.

[131] *Williams* v. *Eady* (1893) 10 TLR 41 at 42.

that defendants should foresee the things that children might do, as well those that adults did.[132]

The question of whether special foresight was needed where children were concerned came before the House of Lords in 1909 in *Cooke* v. *Midland Great Western Railway of Ireland*. The accident—in which a child lost a leg—occurred on a railway turntable, which was kept unlocked on the defendants' land, near to a public road. The company was aware that children were in the habit of getting through a gap in the fence to play on the turntable. The company denied liability, claiming that the children were trespassers, who could not be regarded as licensees merely because they had not been turned off the land. But the Lords focused on the fact that they were children. Lord Macnaghten was more interested in the general question of negligence, than in the question of their status on the land: 'It cannot make very much difference whether the place is dedicated to the use of the public or left open by a careless owner to the invasion of children who make it their playground'. For him, the issue of foreseeability was more crucial:

Would not a private individual of common sense and ordinary intelligence, placed in the position in which the company were placed, and possessing the knowledge which must be attributed to them, have seen that there was a likelihood of some injury happening to children resorting to the place and playing with the turntable, and would he not have thought it his plain duty either to put a stop to the practice altogether, or at least to take ordinary precautions to prevent such an accident as that which occurred?[133]

Holding that the boys had not been trespassers, but were there by the licence of the defendants, Lord Atkinson noted that the doctrine that occupiers of land were only liable to licensees for concealed traps did not apply to children. 'The duty the owner of premises owes to the persons to whom he gives permission to enter upon them must', he said, 'be measured by his knowledge, actual or imputed, of the habits, capacities, and propensities of those persons.'[134]

The Lords' attempt to develop a more general duty of care, at least as regards children, did not succeed, for their decision came in for serious criticism, leading subsequent judges to revert to traditional models. In Thomas Beven's view, Lord Macnaghten's dictum was an echo of the dictum of Brett MR in *Heaven* v. *Pender*—of which he disapproved—applied to children. He felt the Lords had failed to maintain any clear distinction between trespassers, licensees, and invitees, and thus failed to perceive that different duties were imposed in each case. They had therefore muddled a moral duty—which Beven in any case felt lay

---

[132] See e.g. *Harrold* v. *Watney* [1898] 2 QB 320 at 325.

[133] *Cooke* v. *Midland Great Western Railway of Ireland* [1909] AC 229 at 234.

[134] *Cooke* v. *Midland Great Western Railway of Ireland* [1909] AC 229 at 238. Lord Collins regarded the defendants' action as amounting to an invitation.

on the parents of this 'rabble of Irish ragamuffin raiders'[135] rather than on the railway—with their legal duty. Judges also showed a keenness to distance themselves from Lord Macnaghten's broad proposition of law, and to restate the settled principles of occupier's liability. *Cooke* was interpreted as showing that where a child had been tempted to come onto the defendant's land by an allurement, he was to be regarded as a licensee who needed to be protected from concealed traps.[136] This meant that if children strayed onto land to play with things which judges did not regard as offering a temptation to children, no duty was owed to them to ensure they were not hurt. Fine distinctions could be drawn. In *Jenkins v. Great Western Railway*, for instance, the Court of Appeal held that while an injured 2½-year-old child might have been regarded as a licensee when playing on railway sleepers (to the knowledge of the company), it was a trespasser once it crawled onto the neighbouring line, where no duty was owed it.[137] In this case, the court was clearly sympathetic to the company, considering (as Beven had) that it was for parents to ensure that children did not endanger themselves.[138]

Similarly, in *Latham v. R. Johnson & Nephew*, the Court of Appeal sought to restate the established categories, Farwell LJ noting there was no case 'that imposes any greater liability on the owner towards children than towards adults'.[139] In this case (where a child's fingers were crushed by building rubble on the defendant's land), it was held that since she had not been invited onto the land, the child was either a trespasser who could only claim a remedy if she had been allured onto the land, or a licensee who could only claim in respect of a concealed trap. Hamilton LJ rejected the idea that the child had been allured onto the land, considering a heap of paving stones as insufficiently strong an object of temptation to a child.[140] He also rejected the idea that the company was liable for having a concealed trap. He admitted that children, unlike adults, were unable to judge all apparent dangers for themselves. But this did not mean that owners had to ensure that their land was 'as safe as in a nursery'.[141] Rather, as in *Burchell v. Hickisson*, he held that where there was something which might constitute a trap for a child, though not for an adult, the child was not licensed to come onto the

---

[135] This wording in Beven's 1909 pamphlet (*The House of Lords on the Law of Trespass to Realty and Children as Trespassers*, 39) was excised by Beven's editor, who pointed out that the plaintiff 'was the quite presentable little son of a respectable chemist': Beven, *Negligence* (4th edn, by W. J. Byrne and A. D. Gibb, 1928), i, 216n.

[136] *Holland v. The District Committee of the Middle Ward of Lanarkshire* (1909) 2 SLT 7 at 11; *Lowery v. Walker* [1910] 1 KB 173 (CA) at 200–1 (affirmed in *Lowery v. Walker* [1911] AC 10).

[137] *Jenkins v. Great Western Railway* [1912] 1 KB 525 at 532.

[138] Compare also *Schofield v. Mayor &c of Bolton* (1910) 26 TLR 230 at 231.

[139] *Latham v. R. Johnson & Nephew* [1913] 1 KB 398 (CA) at 407.

[140] *Latham v. R. Johnson & Nephew* [1913] 1 KB 398 (CA) at 416.

[141] *Latham v. R. Johnson & Nephew* [1913] 1 KB 398 (CA) at 414.

land unless accompanied by an adult. It was not the responsibility of the owner to ensure safety, but that of the parent.

In the view of the Court of Appeal, the children in *Cooke* had been licensees on the land, who had been allured onto it by a dangerous machine which had all the attractions of a merry-go-round. The case did not stand for a broader proposition about the duty of care owed to children who might foreseeably come onto the defendant's land. The decision was welcomed by the academic community, though the *Law Quarterly Review* noted that it was 'perhaps too much to hope that adventurous plaintiffs and practitioners will cease to misunderstand *Cooke's* case or to bring futile actions on the strength of their misunderstanding'.[142] After the end of the First World War, even one of the judges who decided *Cooke* in the House of Lords explained the case in traditional terms, regarding the children as having been on a dangerous turntable by the leave and licence of the defendants. *Cooke* was thus explained as a case involving the duty of an occupier whose land contained dangerous machinery to children who were permitted to be there. It did not, Atkinson thereby implied, apply to children who were trespassers. This meant that occupiers of land had no general duty to take care to avoid harm to those who could foreseeably be harmed.[143] Mischievous children who had no business on railway property—even stations—were to be regarded as trespassers who would have no redress against the company if they were injured.[144]

4. DANGEROUS GOODS

Outside the railways, the commonest and most dangerous accidents in the nineteenth century involved exploding boilers, which by the 1860s killed more than 75 people annually.[145] The nature of an owner's liability for boiler explosions depended on his relationship with the victim. An owner's liability for deaths caused by dangerous boilers kept on his premises was not strict, but was governed by the rules relating to the liability of occupiers. Most boiler explosions occurred in the workplace. Workmen themselves were often blamed for the explosion,[146] since it was assumed boilers only exploded if there had been

---

[142] 29 *LQR* (1913) 122.

[143] *Corporation of the City of Glasgow* v. *Taylor* [1922] 1 AC 44 at 55.

[144] *Hardy* v. *Central London Railway Co* [1920] 3 KB 459.

[145] P. W. J. Bartrip, 'The state and the steam-boiler in Nineteenth Century Britain' (1980) 25 *International Review of Social History* 77–105 at 81.

[146] Select Committee on the Cause of Steam Boiler Explosions, *PP* 1870 (370), x, 459, at q. 1323 (W. McNaught). Workmen in charge of boilers which exploded were often prosecuted for manslaughter.

negligence in their construction, working, or fitting.[147] Thanks to the doctrine
of common employment, workmen were unable to sue their employer, if the
cause of the accident could be attributed to the negligence of the workman in
control of it.[148] Only if the boiler was shown to have been unsafe to the knowledge of the employer could an action could be brought against him.[149] Few such
cases therefore came before the common law courts. Nor did concern about
boiler accidents in the workplace result in regulatory legislation until 1882.[150]
Boilers also exploded on railways and steam ships, injuring passengers. Here,
the nature of the liability was determined by the duty of a common carrier not
to insure the safety of his passengers, but to take care that they were safe.[151]
Since such explosions threatened the travelling public, greater efforts were
made by legislation to regulate railway boilers[152] and those of steam ships[153] than
those in the workplace. By contrast, where boilers exploded in the street, injuring passers-by, as where traction engines exploded, the liability of the owner
was regarded as strict, since he had no right to take something which was in
the nature of a nuisance on the street which injured others with the right to be
there.

   In cases arising from exploding boilers, the courts had to consider the liability
of an owner for accidents caused by goods in his possession, over which he had
control. But injuries were also inflicted by objects which had been sent, lent, or
sold to the victim. These raised the question of the liability of the original owner
or manufacturer for such harms. It was settled in the early nineteenth century
that a duty of care was imposed on those who sent items they knew to be dangerous out into the world. A person who gave a loaded gun to a child was guilty of
negligence;[154] a person who disguised a dangerous gun to appear safe was guilty
of deceit.[155] From the mid-century, the courts began to explore how far to extend
the liability of the owner of dangerous goods who entrusted them to others.

[147] Select Committee on the Cause of Steam Boiler Explosions, *PP* 1871 (298), xii, 267, at p. iv.
[148] The workmen blamed for the explosion were often prosecuted for manslaughter where fatalities ensued, though they were often acquitted: see e.g. *The Times*, 19 March 1851, col. 7c. On the
doctrine of common employment, see pp. 1003–5.
[149] *Mellors* v. *Shaw* (1861) 1 B. & S. 437 (a case of a dangerous mine shaft).
[150] Boiler Explosions Act 1882.
[151] The level of care required was high: Erle CJ told one jury that '[t]he company were only bound
to take all reasonable care, and nothing more'. At the same time, he told them that the boiler had
been insufficient, and criticized the company for driving up the costs of the suit by bringing a large
number of scientific witnesses: *Beattie* v. *London and North Western Railway Co* in *The Times*, 17
February 1862, col. 11c.
[152] Railway Regulation Act 1840.
[153] Steam Navigation Act 1851; Merchant Shipping Acts 1854 and 1862.
[154] *Dixon* v. *Bell* (1816) 1 Stark. 287 at 289. See also *Tessymond's case* (1828) 1 Lewin C.C. 169.
[155] *Langridge* v. *Levy* (1837) 2 M. & W. 519.

The issue was first raised in cases involving carriers. Explosions on transport ships caused by volatile chemicals could be as disastrous as boiler explosions.[156] In such cases, courts in the mid-century imposed a strict liability on the shipper. In *Brass* v. *Maitland*, a majority of the Queen's Bench held that a shipper was under a contractual duty to inform the carrier of the nature of any dangerous goods being transported. The defendants, who had received casks already packed from another supplier could not be held liable in tort, for there was no fraudulent concealment. However, since the carriers had 'no reasonable means during the loading of a general ship to ascertain the quality of the goods offered for shipment', Lord Campbell held, 'it seems much more just and expedient that, although they were ignorant of the dangerous quality of the goods or the insufficiency of the packing, the loss occasioned by the dangerous quality of the goods and the insufficient packing should be cast upon the shippers'.[157] This was done by implying a term into the contract of carriage, by which the shippers warranted that the goods had been so packed as not to be dangerous.[158]

The Common Pleas was soon prepared to extend the shipper's strict duty to disclose the dangerous nature of goods beyond other parties to the bill of lading. In *Farrant* v. *Barnes*, the defendant had a consignment of nitric acid to be transported by a railway carrier.[159] Since the railway (which had special regulations for the transport of dangerous goods) could not deliver it in time, it was handed by the railway carrier's carman to another carrier, who was not told that the carboy contained nitric acid. It burst while being transported, and severely burned the plaintiff. The defendant denied that he was liable in tort, since there had been no evidence of fraudulent concealment. He also denied contractual liability, since there was no privity between himself and the injured man. However, Erle CJ held that '[t]he defendant, knowing the dangerous character of the article, and omitting to give notice of it to the plaintiff, so that he might exercise his discretion as

---

[156] For instance, in April 1866, nearly 50 people were killed at Colon in Panama, when a cargo of nitro-glycerine exploded on board the *European*: *The Times*, 30 April 1866, col. 10g. For the litigation arising from the case, see *West India and Pacific Steamship Co* v. *Guion* in *The Times*, 22 August 1867, col. 11d; see also *Pall Mall Gazette*, 12 September 1867.

[157] *Brass* v. *Maitland* (1856) 6 E. & B. 470 at 483.

[158] Crompton J. dissented on the contractual obligation, being concerned about the insurance implications of such a decision: *Brass* v. *Maitland* (1856) 6 E. & B. 470 at 491.

[159] The transportation of dangerous goods by rail was regulated under the Railway Clauses Consolidation Act 1845 (8 Vict. c. 20, s 105), which required the consignor to identify the dangerous nature of the parcel and permitted the company to refuse to carry it. The Explosives Act 1875 required railway companies to make bye-laws for regulating the transport of dangerous substances, and a model code was drawn up by the companies: see Sir William Hodges, *A Treatise on the Law of Railways* (6th edn by J. M. Lely, 1876), 612, 978. Mid-century courts did not hold those liable who forwarded goods sent by those who had not disclosed their dangerous nature: *Hearne* v. *Garton* (1859) 2 El. & El. 66.

to whether he would take it or not, was guilty of a clear breach of duty'.[160] Willes J. also felt that the 'general principle' governing the case was 'that, wherever a person employs another to carry an article which from its dangerous character requires more than ordinary care, he must give him reasonable notice of the nature of the article, and that, if he fails to do so, he is responsible for the probable consequences of his neglect'.[161] In these transport cases, where plaintiffs were injured while doing work for the benefit of the defendant, the courts extended a contractual duty to disclose the dangerous nature of goods to all who handled them.

By contrast, when equipment was lent, which turned out to be dangerous, the courts were much less willing to find a duty of care, as the widow of James Blakemore discovered in 1858. When crossing the line at Weston-super-Mare station one day, her husband was asked by Samuel Harvey, the consignee of some blocks of stone, to help unload them from some train trucks. To do this, they used a crane which the company knew to be unsafe, and which hit Blakemore on the head, killing him. Coleridge J. found that no contractual duty was owed to Blakemore, since the railway company's only contract was with Harvey. Following Pothier and Story, he noted that where something was gratuitously lent to another to use for his own benefit, 'a duty is contracted towards the borrower not to conceal from him those defects known to the lender which may make the loan perilous or unprofitable to him'. However, this duty was only owed to the borrower, and not to a third party stranger. In taking this view, Coleridge was clearly keen to place limits on the lender's liability, in order to put limits on the reach of the duty of care:

It has always been considered that *Levy* v. *Langridge* was a case not to be extended in its application. It may be urged that the defendants must be taken, from the circumstances, to have known that some one beyond Harvey must be employed in using the crane; and that may be so: but so also, in *Winterbottom* v. *Wright* the defendant must have known that some coachman must drive the mail coach; and yet the plaintiff, happening to be that coachman on a particular occasion, could not sue for the damage sustained by the defective building of the coach.[162]

By the 1860s, the reach of the duty of care seemed narrowly settled: alongside the strict duties which existed in contract, a lender or giver had a duty not to

---

[160] *Farrant* v. *Barnes* (1862) 11 C.B. N.S. 553 at 561–2.

[161] *Farrant* v. *Barnes* (1862) 11 C.B. N.S. 553 at 564. Where Erle rested his judgment on the existence of an implied undertaking, Willes (citing *Williams* v. *The East India Co* (1802) 3 East 192 at 200–1) also considered that there might be a duty to give notice in such cases, independently of contract.

[162] *Blakemore* v. *The Bristol and Exeter Railway Co* (1858) 8 E. & B. 1035 at 1051–4. See also *MacCarthy* v. *Young* (1861) 6 H. & N. 329.

conceal dangers of which he was aware. As the cases quoted by Coleridge confirmed, the duty was drawn in such a narrow way as to exclude the liability of a seller or manufacturer of goods for injuries suffered by third party consumers. As has been seen,[163] this narrow approach to duties of care was challenged in the era of *George* v. *Skivington*[164] and *Heaven* v. *Pender*,[165] when judges and jurists sought to develop a broader notion, according to which a duty of care existed to all those who might foreseeably be harmed by a person's negligence. *George* v. *Skivington* suggested a broader duty of care might be owed to consumers, while the decision in *Heaven* v. *Pender* indicated that gratuitous lenders of chattels might incur a greater level of liability than *Blakemore* had suggested. The new approach triumphed in 1932 in *Donoghue* v. *Stevenson*,[166] when a consumer was given protection in tort for the negligence of a manufacturer. However, in the later nineteenth century, judges resisted Brett's initiative and restated the narrower view settled in the mid-century. The limits to the duty of a gratuitous lender were restated in *Coughlin* v. *Gillison* in 1899, where the Court of Appeal confirmed that a gratuitous lender only had the duty to disclose those defects in his goods of which he was aware, but had no duty to take care that the machine was safe.[167] The idea that a supplier of ordinary goods was only liable for latent defects in the goods to those with whom he had a contract was restated in *Earl* v. *Lubbock*, where the principle of *Winterbottom* v. *Wright* was applied.[168] Similarly, in *Cavalier* v. *Pope*, where the plaintiff's wife was injured by an accident, caused by her husband's landlord's failure to effect repairs as he was contractually bound to do, Lord Atkinson ruled there was 'neither fraud, misrepresentation, nor warranty, nor the handing over of a thing known to be dangerous without warning'.[169]

The courts were prepared to extend consumer protection where they considered that the thing which harmed the plaintiff was dangerous in itself. As Lord Dunedin put it, 'there is a peculiar duty to take precaution imposed upon those who send forth or install such [dangerous] articles when it is necessarily the case that other parties will come within their proximity'.[170] It was on this basis

---

[163] See pp. 945–6.

[164] *George* v. *Skivington* [1869] LR 5 Ex 1.

[165] *Heaven* v. *Pender* [1883] 11 QBD 503 (CA).

[166] *Donoghue* v. *Stevenson* [1932] AC 562.

[167] *Coughlin* v. *Gillison* [1899] 1 QB 145 (CA). The court rejected the French doctrine that the lender was liable for latent defects he of which should have known.

[168] *Earl* v. *Lubbock* [1905] 1 KB 253 (CA). See also the comments of Farwell LJ in *Latham* v. *R. Johnson & Nephew* [1913] 1 KB 398 at 408 (CA).

[169] *Cavalier* v. *Pope* (1906) AC 428 at 433. See also *Malone* v. *Laskey* [1907] 2 KB 141.

[170] *Dominion Natural Gas Co* v. *Collins and Perkins* (1909) AC 640, 646–7. Nonetheless, there were some limits to the liability: 'if the proximate cause of the accident is not the negligence of the defendant, but the conscious act of another volition, then he will not be liable. For against such conscious act of volition no precaution can really avail'.

that Collins MR in 1903 held that a vendor of chlorinated lime powder had a duty of 'of taking reasonable precautions in the way of warning the purchaser that special care will be requisite'.[171] In May 1913, in *White* v. *Steadman*, Lush J. seemed to extend the duty respecting dangerous goods further, in holding a stable keeper liable to a passenger who was injured when the nervous horse pulling the landau hired out to her husband overturned the vehicle. Where something dangerous was lent out, Lush held, the owner had a duty to inform not only those he knew would use it of its propensities, but also those he 'ought to contemplate will use it'. Since the defendant would have been liable had he known of the horse's vicious tendencies, he was not to be in a better position if, through his own carelessness, he failed to use the means of knowledge at his disposal: 'a person who has the means of knowledge and only does not know that the animal or chattel which he supplies is dangerous because he does not take ordinary care to avail himself of his opportunity of knowledge is in precisely the same position as the person who knows'.[172] The liability of the manufacturer of dangerous items, he concluded, did not arise from a contract, but sounded in tort.

At the same time, there was a reluctance to expand the categories of dangerous goods. In *Blacker* v. *Lake and Elliott*, it was held that the question whether an item was dangerous was for the judge and not the jury to define. For as Hamilton J. put it, the law recognized a defined number of specific situations where liability was imposed for injuries caused by defective things: they included the occupier's liability for traps, the common law liability for dangerous animals, and the liability for dangerous things which escaped from land. They did not include liability for a cheap welding torch which had exploded after only one year of use. In taking this view, the court expressed its disapproval of *George* v. *Skivington*, as an authority for a general duty of care to third parties. Lush J. agreed that no duty of care was owed by manufacturers to third parties. He also agreed that this item was not one of a class of dangerous goods which could not be sold without warning.[173]

Three weeks after Lush's decision in *White* v. *Steadman*, Horridge J. decided in *Bates* v. *Batey & Co* that a manufacturer of ginger beer was not liable when the bottle containing the drink exploded, putting out the eye of a boy who had

---

[171] *Clarke* v. *Army and Navy Co-operative Society* [1903] 1 KB 155 at 164–5. The reviewer of the fourth edition of Clerk and Lindsell, saw this case as an application of *Heaven* v. *Pender*: (1906) 22 LQR 335–7 at 336.

[172] *White* v. *Steadman* [1913] 3 KB 340 at 348. In making this comment, the judge had in mind cases where dangerous goods had been sold, which were intended to be used by third parties. The comment went further than the cases on the liability of gratuitous lenders suggested.

[173] *Blacker* v. *Lake and Elliott* (1912) 106 LT 533.

bought it.[174] At trial, the jury found there was a defect in the bottle which could have been discovered with reasonable care, and that the defect was caused by the negligence of the defendant, and assessed the damages at £275. Overturning this, Horridge ruled that a bottle of ginger beer was not in itself a dangerous item. Although it was dangerous in its defective state, the defendants were unaware of this. Although they had the means of discovering the defect, the court (following *Longmeid* v. *Holliday*) felt there was no duty cast on them to do so. It would take a different bottle of ginger beer to transform English tort law.

Academic commentary remained unhappy with the trend of decisions which protected vendors selling faulty goods. Sir John Salmond regretted that such a narrow view was taken of those who negligently put dangerous chattels into circulation. Clerk and Lindsell also sought to articulate a broader principle, that where goods were supplied, care had to be taken to ensure that they would not injure the person to whom they were supplied. The duty was cast on suppliers in three situations: first, where goods were supplied under contract; secondly, where the person supplying the goods had such superior knowledge that the other party was likely to rely on them; and thirdly, where the goods were dangerous. Moreover, they noted that '[t]he duty to take care will exist towards all persons to whom the original party to the contract, reasonably relying on care having been taken, may innocently deliver the thing as one fit and proper to be dealt with in the way in which the defendant intended the original contractor to deal with it himself'.[175]

5. DAMAGES FOR PERSONAL INJURY

Where a person had been injured as a result of another's negligence, the assessment of damages was left largely to the jury's discretion, for judges felt that the damages to be awarded in cases of negligence could never be subject to precise calculation. The court only intervened if the damages were unreasonably high or low.[176] In 1847 Parke B. observed that 'it would be most unjust if whenever an accident occurs, juries were to visit the unfortunate cause of it with the utmost amount which they think an equivalent for the mischief done'.[177] In 1873, Brett J. said the invariable direction to juries in his experience was 'that they must not attempt to give damages to the full amount of a perfect compensation, but must take a reasonable view of the case, and give what they consider, under all the

---

[174] *Bates* v. *Batey & Co* [1913] 3 KB 351.
[175] J. F. Clerk and W. H. B. Lindsell, *The Law of Torts* (2nd edn, 1896), 364.
[176] *Britton* v. *South Wales Railway Co* (1858) 1 F. & F. 171.
[177] *Armsworth* v. *South Eastern Railway* (1847) 11 Jur. 758.

circumstances, a fair compensation'.[178] This reflected a view that tort damages could not be calculated as exactly as contractual damages. It also reflected a view, occasionally articulated, that juries might bear in mind how blameworthy the defendants were.[179] Judges were often concerned about the conduct of juries in 'capitalising the uncertain income which a man is assumed to be prevented from making by reason of his being disabled', treating the defendant like an insurance office.[180] But if they sought to restrain juries' inclination to generosity, they also looked dimly on the attempts of railway companies to reduce their liability for injuries, when rejecting arguments that sums received by accident victims from insurance should be taken into account.[181]

The principles to be applied in assessing damages were discussed in 1879 in *Phillips* v. *The South Western Railway Company*, where a 47-year-old physician sought compensation for the injuries he had suffered in a railway accident, which rendered him unable to work. Dr Charles Phillips was unusually well-heeled, having a private income of £3500 a year and an average annual income from his medical practice of £6000–£7000. At the trial, Field J. clearly wished to discourage the jury from calculating a sum which would purchase an annuity equal to the physician's income: 'Perfect compensation is hardly possible, and would be unjust.'[182] He also indicated that the jury might take into account the fact that he had a substantial unearned income. Thus directed, the jury returned a verdict for £7000. Dissatisfied with this sum, Dr Phillips successfully sought a new trial on the grounds of inadequacy of damages. In the view of the Queen's Bench, given that he had, by the time of the trial, already suffered a 'positive pecuniary loss' of at least £7000 (by way of medical bills and lost income) as a result of the accident, the jury could not have taken into account his loss of future income and loss of health.[183] A new trial had to be ordered, since the jury failed to take all the circumstances into account.

---

[178] *Rowley* v. *London and North Western Railway Co* (1873) LR 8 Ex 221 at 231.

[179] See Lord Abinger's approach in *Rapson* v. *Cubitt* (1841) C. & M. 64 at 68 (for further proceedings, see (1842) 9 M. & W. 710). At the end of the century, Lord Coleridge instructed a jury that they were not to give the plaintiff an 'indemnity, but only a compensation': *Smith* v. *South Eastern Railway* in *The Times*, 27 February 1893, col. 13d.

[180] 1870 Select Committee on Railway Companies, p. 163, q. 2228 (J. S. Willes).

[181] *Bradburn* v. *Great Western Railway Co* (1874) LR 10 Ex 1 at 2. In Bramwell B.'s view, accident insurance was to be treated on the same principle as life assurance: the assured paid his premiums not to obtain an indemnity, but to obtain 'an equivalent for the premiums he has paid' on the happening of an event.

[182] *Phillips* v. *South Western Railway Co* (1879) 5 QBD 78 (CA) at 79, 81. *The Times*, 5 August 1879, col. 6b.

[183] *Phillips* v. *South Western Railway Co* (1879) 4 QBD 406, aff'd by the Court of Appeal in 5 QBD 78.

A second jury awarded the physician £16000. On this occasion, the railway sought to obtain a new trial, objecting that Lord Coleridge had failed to tell the jury to take into account his private income. The company was also particularly concerned at the injustice of giving large sums in compensation to physicians with lucrative practices, while poorer folk would get only smaller sums. An attempt was therefore made to persuade the judges that the rule in *Hadley* v. *Baxendale* should apply, which would absolve the company of liability for the loss of an income of which they had no notice when he bought his ticket. Although the Court of Appeal accepted that the action was contractual, it rejected the proposition that the principle of *Hadley* could apply to personal injuries.[184] The decision caused some alarm among supporters of the railway interest, who argued the injustice of holding companies potentially liable for vast claims made by wealthy passengers who had paid only a simple fare, and sought a legislative change. Liability for passenger injuries, it was felt, should reflect that for goods: all passengers should be awarded an average compensation, unless they had paid a higher price to insure themselves.[185] But if the railway interest was alarmed by high damages awards, those who worried about their safety record welcomed them. '[E]very injured person should rigidly demand compensation', *The Times* urged in 1865, 'and when a disputed case is brought before a jury the most exemplary damages, without being positively vindictive, should be awarded.'[186]

Besides claims for physical injuries sustained in the accident, in the mid-nineteenth century, plaintiffs increasingly claimed for non-visible injuries. From the 1850s, it was apparent that victims of train accidents—even those who had sustained only minor injuries—often suffered from trauma after the accident, including memory loss or pain, rendering them unable to work. Railway companies were often sceptical of such claims, contending that victims were fabricating purely mental symptoms, merely in order to obtain compensation. Moreover, it was generally accepted in the mid-nineteenth century that the law could not value mental distress caused by a tort, but that compensation could only be given for material damage.[187] However, railways soon found themselves having to pay large sums in compensation for psychological harms, after medical practitioners began to argue that these effects were caused by the physical shock of the accident, which damaged the spine and consequently the nervous system. Rather than being the result of the power of suggestion, or mental frailty, it was argued

---

[184] *Phillips* v. *South Western Railway Co* (1879) 5 CPD 280 at 289.

[185] *The Times*, 8 December 1879, col. 9c.

[186] *The Times*, 14 December 1865, col. 8g.

[187] *Lynch* v. *Knight* (1861) 9 H.L.C. 577 at 598. See also *Blake* v. *Midland Railway Co* 21 LJ QB 233, 238.

that these symptoms were the result of a physical condition caused by the crash, known as 'railway spine'. From the late 1850s, an increasing number of claims came to court, where plaintiffs called medical witnesses, whose expertise could convince juries that their claims were valid.[188] In 1865, Richard Joseland, a wine merchant from Worcester, was travelling in a train which crashed. He assisted in attending the wounded, thinking he had not suffered any injury. However, he later became seriously ill, suffering from headaches, spasms, and bad dreams. After a trial where evidence was given by J. E. Erichsen, the leading expert on railway spine, he was awarded £6000. Although the Great Western Railway sought a new trial on the grounds that the damages were excessive, they did not succeed.[189] For the rest of the century, though railway companies continued to claim that plaintiffs were exaggerating the symptoms they suffered from 'railway spine', juries continued to award damages for injuries which were by the later nineteenth century described as 'nervous shock'.[190]

Since it was difficult for companies to challenge the sums awarded by juries, they sometimes argued that victims of 'railway spine', whose symptoms appeared some time after the accident, were barred by the fact that they had already accepted compensation. Where passengers had been injured, railway companies were often keen to settle claims quickly, in order to avoid liability for later, higher claims. When Thomas Lee, a civil engineer from Macclesfield, was injured in an accident near Manchester, the doctor called in by the company at the time of the accident wrote to its medical officer recommending 'a settlement at once, for there is much scope for exacting very heavy damages for injuries (even doubtful injuries) of the spine'.[191] The simple fact that a victim had accepted compensation did not bar his subsequent claim. For instance, it was clear to Cockburn CJ, in a

---

[188] D. Mendelson, *The Interfaces of Medicine and Law: The History of the Liability for Negligently Caused Psychiatric Injury (Nervous Shock)* (Aldershot, 1998), Ch. 2; R. Harrington, 'The Railway Accident: Trains, Trauma and Technological Crises in Nineteenth Century Britain', in M. S. Micale and P. Lerner, *Traumatic Pasts: History, Psychiatry and Trauma in the Modern Age, 1870–1930* (Cambridge, 2001), 31–56; Harrington, 'Railway Safety and Railway Slaughter'; K. M. Odden, '"Able and intelligent medical men meeting together" : the Victorian railway crash, medical jurisprudence, and the rise of medical authority' (2003) 8 *Journal of Victorian Culture* 33–54. For the similar debates in America, see E. Caplan, *Mind Games: American Culture and the Birth of Psychotherapy* (Berkeley, 1998); B. Y. Welke, *Recasting American Liberty: Gender, Race, Law and the Railroad Revolution, 1865–1920* (New York, 2001).

[189] *The Times*, 13 March 1865, col. 11c; 14 April 1876, col. 11b; *Birmingham Daily Post*, 10 March 1865, p. 4. See also *Britton v. South Wales Railway Co* (1858) 1 F. & F. 171.

[190] Erichsen's theories, first set out in *On Railway and Other Injuries of the Nervous System* (1866), were challenged by the railway surgeon H. W. Page in his work *Injuries of the Spine and Spinal Cord without apparent Mechanical Lesion and Nervous Shock in their Medico-Legal Aspects* (1883).

[191] *The Times*, 17 December 1870, col. 11a.

case of 1859, that a man who thought he had been wholly uninjured in an accident, and accepted £2 as compensation for a crushed hat, could not be taken to have accepted it as satisfaction for the illness which he later suffered.[192] However, railway companies sought to bind victims to settlements, by giving receipts stating that the money had been accepted in full discharge of any claims on the company. Those who found that their condition later deteriorated began to challenge such receipts. Believing their common law claims to be barred, they turned to equity instead, seeking injunctions to prevent the company entering pleas of accord and satisfaction when the case went to law.[193] In *Stewart v. Great Western Railway Co*, the plaintiff succeeded by claiming that he had signed on the basis of false representations by the company's medical attendant that his injuries were less serious than in fact they were.[194] Thomas Lee, having consulted his own doctor, was unable to make such an argument, and simply claimed that it was inequitable for the company to rely on the receipt. He sought £3000 compensation, claiming that his health was quite broken, until he suddenly recovered his powers in April 1867. The company resisted, arguing that his illness was a sham, that his claim was a 'nefarious attempt to swindle the company' and that he was barred by the receipt. Finding for the plaintiff, Malins VC strongly criticized the company, which had 'caught him in this state; and, doubtless, the officials went home chuckling over their bargain'.[195] The Lord Justices dismissed his bill, but pointed out to Lee (and all other litigants) that a receipt such as this was 'merely evidence of satisfaction, and liable to be rebutted by contrary evidence'.[196] It was, in other words, an appropriate question for a common law jury. On the common law side, judges in the later 1860s also began to view receipts with some suspicion.[197] At the end of the century, by which time the practice was in decline, Lord Coleridge could still observe that a company doctor who 'turned himself into a sort of accident broker' was to be regarded as a 'dirty chafferer in damages' who had abandoned the duties of a noble profession.[198]

The question whether a plaintiff could recover for nervous shock was also discussed at the end of the century in cases where the victim had not been hurt in a railway accident, but had suffered trauma as a result of what she had seen or heard. It came before the Judicial Committee of the Privy Council in 1888, in an

[192] *Roberts v. Eastern Counties Railway Co* (1859) 1 F. & F. 460.
[193] Some litigants also sued the doctor giving the receipt for fraud: Mendelson, *Interfaces*, 46.
[194] *Stewart v. Great Western Railway Co* (1865) 2 De G J & S 319.
[195] *The Times*, 17 December 1870, col. 11a.
[196] *Lee v. Lancashire & Yorkshire Rail Co* (1871) LR 6 Ch App 527.
[197] See also *Baker v. London and South Western Railway Co* (1867) LR 3 QB 91 (a case under Lord Campbell's Act).
[198] *Smith v. South Eastern Railway* in *The Times*, 27 February 1893, col. 13d.

appeal from the Supreme Court of Victoria. Mary Coultas had suffered a severe fright, after a gate keeper had invited her husband to drive their buggy across a level crossing, narrowly missing a passing train. As a result of her nervous shock, she suffered a miscarriage. The Supreme Court of Victoria held that Mrs Coultas could maintain an action for this damage, but the Privy Council reversed the decision. The judges held that the Victorian court had erred in finding that the damages awarded were not too remote. In Sir Richard Couch's view, damages arising from 'mere sudden terror unaccompanied by any actual physical injury' could not be a consequence which 'in the ordinary course of things, would flow from the negligence of the gate-keeper'.[199] The court's decision was informed by the fear that to allow the plaintiff to succeed would open the floodgates 'for imaginary claims'. This decision was not well received by jurists. Thomas Beven argued that '[w]here nervous shock is produced, the terror is merely another expression for a direct effect on the nervous system—a portion of the physical organisation'. Where the terror was followed by physical consequences, an action should lie.[200]

Two years later, the Irish Exchequer Division heard Bell v. Great Northern Railway, in which the plaintiff suffered a nervous shock when the carriage she was in reversed at high speed down an incline, generating panic in the carriage. Although she was thrown over when the train stopped, there was no collision. The trial judge, Andrews J., told the jury that if her fright was a reasonable and natural consequence of the circumstances in which the company had placed Mrs Bell, she could recover. Conceding that there was evidence of negligence and of injury for the jury to consider, the defendant argued that the damages awarded for her nervous shock were too remote, since it had not been occasioned by any physical injury occasioned at the time of the company's negligence. The court rejected this, holding that physical symptoms occasioned by a nervous shock could manifest themselves subsequently. In his judgment, Palles CB drew on Beven's critical discussion of Coultas, denying the assumption of the Privy Council that 'injuries, other than mental, cannot result from nervous shock' and that such injuries could not be palpable.[201] By the turn of the century, English courts also followed the jurists in doubting the Privy Council's reasoning. In Wilkinson v. Downton, the Queen's Bench held that a plaintiff could

---

[199] Victorian Railway Commissioners v. Coultas (1888) 13 App Cas 222 at 225. On the case, see Mendelson, Interfaces, Ch. 3.

[200] Beven, Negligence in Law (2nd edn, 1895), i, 79. See also Pollock, Torts (6th edn, 1901), 50–2.

[201] Bell v. Great Northern Railway Co (1890) LR 26 Ir. 426 at 440–1. He also referred to an unreported case, Byrne v. Great Southern and Western Railway Co (1884), where a plaintiff who was himself frightened, though untouched, when a train ran into the building in which he was working, could recover.

recover who suffered a nervous shock having been told—as a practical joke—
that her husband's legs had been broken in a serious accident.[202] In *Wilkinson*,
the defendant's tort had been intentional; in *Dulieu* v. *White & Sons*, where the
plaintiff gave birth prematurely to a disabled child, having witnessed the defendant's van crash into the public house where she was working, the defendants
were sued for negligence.[203] Having surveyed the literature critical of *Coultas*,
and considered American decisions, the divisional court held the damages not
to be too remote.

Where the victim of an accident had been killed, no action could be brought
against the tortfeasor until 1846, thanks to the rule *actio personalis moritur
cum persona* and the principle that 'the death of a human being could not be
complained of as an injury' for which anyone else could sue.[204] Victims' families were not wholly without remedy in such cases, for coroners' courts had
the power to levy a deodand. This was a fine on the owner of the instrument
which had caused the death, paid in lieu of its forfeiture to the king. Deodands
were frequently levied after coach accidents, with sums of between £40 and £50
awarded to the families of victims.[205] Large deodands could also be imposed
where coroners' juries felt that the owner of the thing causing the death had
been particularly negligent.[206] In the late 1830s, coroners' juries began to take a
tough approach where deaths resulted from dangerous machinery. After nine
people were killed when a boiler exploded on the *Victoria* steam ship in June
1838, the jury levied a deodand of £1500 on it.[207] Juries also now began to levy
deodands on the property of railway companies. They responded with a number
of successful challenges to the coroner's jurisdiction,[208] which resulted in the
emasculation of the deodand as an effective remedy. As Lord Campbell observed
in 1846, 'it was hardly possible that an inquiry before the coroner could be so
conducted as afterwards to stand fire in the Court of Queen's Bench'.[209] The legal
profession was also unhappy at the use of deodands, finding them not merely

---

[202] *Wilkinson* v. *Downton* [1897] 2 QB 57. See also 41 *Sol. J.* 539.

[203] *Dulieu* v. *White & Sons* [1901] 2 KB 669.

[204] *Baker* v. *Bolton* (1808) 1 Camp. 493.

[205] See *The Times*, 25 April 1820, col. 2d (coroner's inquest on pregnant woman); 18 December 1821,
col. 3e (coroner's inquest on Abraham Slade); 11 March 1825, col. 3d.

[206] See E. Cawthorn, 'New Life for the Deodand: Coroners' Inquests and Occupational Death in
England, 1830–1846' (1989) 33 *AJLH* 137–47 at 141.

[207] *The Times*, 15 August 1838, col. 7a. The Queen's Bench later quashed this on a technicality: *The
Queen v. Brownlow* (1839) 11 Ad. & El. 119.

[208] See *The Queen* v. *Grand Junction Railway Co* (1839) 11 Ad. & El. 128n; *R.* v. *West* (1841) 1 Q.B.
826; (1842) 3 Q.B. 333; *R.* v. *Midland Railway Co* (1846) 8 Q.B. 587.

[209] *Parl. Debs.*, 3rd ser., 85: 968 (1846). His view was supported by Thomas Wakley, who as coroner
had encouraged the use of deodands: (1846) 7 *LT* 372.

outdated, and difficult to use, but also inappropriate. Since deodands were granted in case of death by misadventure, it seemed inappropriate where the death has resulted from someone's fault.[210] By the mid-1840s, it was felt that, in such cases, an action of negligence was more suitable. As the The Times noted in 1845, approving the abolition of deodands, it was desirable to 'provide a remedy against negligence' which 'while it punishes the guilty [...] relieves the innocent and the afflicted'.[211]

Deodands were abolished in 1846, at the same time that Lord Campbell's Fatal Accidents Act was passed.[212] Campbell's Act was aimed specifically to hold railway companies liable when death occurred as a result of their negligence. Lord Campbell's Act significantly increased the financial liability of railway companies for accidents. After an accident at Lewisham station in June 1857, in which 12 were killed and 62 injured, for instance, the South Eastern Railway company paid out £25,000 in compensation.[213] However, the proportion of a company's expenses taken up by compensation remained small, and '[t]he pressure put upon the shareholders by the fear of having to make compensation, although no doubt advantageous, does not [...] appear invariably to act so as to make those in whom the management is vested work the lines with safety'.[214] It could not be left to the disincentive of litigation to make railways safer: that required the publicity of regular reports on accidents, and an active inspectorate from the Board of Trade.[215]

---

[210] In R. v. Polwart (1841) 1 Q.B. 818, it was held that no deodand could be levied where the jury had entered a finding of manslaughter, since the death had to be by misadventure. In The Queen v. Grand Junction Railway Co (1839) 11 Ad. & El. 128n, the railway company sought to argue that where a fatality caused by negligence, the deodand could not be levied: but in fact the jury in this case had specified that those operating the train had been blameless. See also Cawthorn, 'New Life for the Deodand', 145. The Legal Observer (vol. 29, 1845, p. 337) pointed out that 'In recent cases, juries have given large damages where the accident is the result of wilful negligence—but this is as much a violation of their oath as assessing a nominal sum'.

[211] The Times, 23 April 1845, col. 5e.

[212] 9 & 10 Vict. c. 93. A similar attempt to reform the law had failed in 1845, due to opposition from the government.

[213] Report to the Lords of the Committee of Privy Council for Trade upon the Accidents which have occurred on Railways during the year 1857, PP 1857–8 [2338], li, 183 at pp. 20, 82–99. See also H. Parris, Government and the Railways in Nineteenth-Century Britain (1965), 169. According to the figures in PP 1857–8 [2437], li, 1 at pp. 70–1, the South Eastern Railway spent £23,350 in 1857 in accident compensation of a total expenditure of £617,954 (or 3.8% of its budget). All English railway companies in that year spent £100,514 in accident compensation, of a total of £12,861,306 spent (0.8%). As Kostal has shown, the proportion of costs incurred by accidents was thus not high.

[214] Report to the Lords Committee of Privy Council for Trade upon the Accidents which have occurred on Railways during the year 1854, PP 1856 [0.7], liv, 297 at p. 14.

[215] See Parris, Government and the Railways, Ch. 6.

The Act permitted an action to be brought against anyone causing death by a wrongful act or negligence, on behalf of the deceased's spouse, parent, or child. The action had to be brought by an executor or administrator, a requirement which made the legislation difficult for the poor to use.[216] The action only lay under the statute if the deceased could have sued the defendant. This meant that if the deceased had settled with the railway company, his relatives were unable to sue, being bound by his accord and satisfaction.[217] According to the Act, the jury 'may give such damages as they may think proportioned to the injury resulting from such death to the parties [...] for whose benefit such action shall be brought'. Damages were therefore assessed according to what financial benefits the deceased's dependent relatives could have reasonably expected had he not died.[218] The Queen's Bench held in 1852 that the wording of the statute meant that juries should not consider the incalculable mental anguish of the various relatives, or give damage for loss of solatium: they should only award the more readily calculable pecuniary losses.[219] From the first cases on the statute, judges were keen to discourage juries from giving such sums as they felt would fully compensate the victim for his loss.[220] By the 1870s, most judges were content to ask juries to calculate the loss as an actuary would.[221] In awarding damages, moreover, juries before 1908 were told to deduct any sums received from accident insurance, as the Act was interpreted to compensate plaintiffs for actual pecuniary losses sustained by their relative's death.[222] Similarly, juries were told not to take into account losses which had been incurred as a result of the death, such as funeral expenses.[223]

The restrictive approach taken by the judiciary in the aftermath of the passing of the Act can be seen from Alderson B.'s approach in the case arising from

---

[216] P. W. J. Bartrip and S. B. Burman, *The Wounded Soldiers of Industry: Industrial Compensation Policy, 1833–1897* (Oxford, 1983), 101. The legislation was accordingly amended in 1864.

[217] *Read* v. *The Great Eastern Railway Co* (1868) LR 3 QB 555. It was held further in *Williams* v. *Mersey Docks and Harbour Board* [1905] 1 KB 804 that where the right of the deceased was barred by statute, his relatives could not bring an action.

[218] See *Franklin* v. *South Eastern Railway Co* (1858) 3 H. & N. 211.

[219] *Blake* v. *Midland Railway Co* (1852) 18 Q.B. 93. See also *Taff Vale Railway* v. *Jenkins* [1913] AC 1.

[220] *Armsworth* v. *South Eastern Railway* (1847) 11 Jur. 758.

[221] *Rowley* v. *London and North Western Railway Co* (1873) LR 8 Ex 221.

[222] *Hicks* v. *The Newport, Abergavenny and Hereford Railway Co* (1857) 4 B. & S. 403n. This rule was altered by the Fatal Accidents (Damages) Act 1908. However, if the deceased had a life assurance policy, the only deductions should be in respect of premiums which the deceased would have had to pay, had he lived. See also *Grand Trunk Railway Co of Canada* v. *Jennings* (1888) 13 App Cas 800.

[223] *Dalton* v. *The South Eastern Railway Co* (1858) 4 C.B. N.S. 296; *Clark* v. *London General Omnibus Co Ltd* [1906] 2 KB 648.

the death of Anne Langston, whose mother claimed compensation both for herself and Anne's illegitimate child. Alderson took the view that the Act did not entitle illegitimate children to compensation, since only 'lawful' children had a legal right to support. This view was endorsed by other judges, and remained in place until 1934.[224] Alderson also held that Anne's mother could not recover since her daughter had not been legally obliged to support her. 'It may be that the deceased acted very kindly and meritoriously in supporting her mother, and that [the] mother may in fact have suffered greatly by her daughter's death', he said, 'but the jury ought not to act upon motives of compassion.' This view was not adopted by later judges, however. By the late 1850s, it was accepted that there was no need for the deceased to be under a legal liability to support his relative. It was enough if the surviving relative had a reasonable expectation of financial benefit from the continuance of the life, as where a parent was shown to receive regular sums of money from a deceased child.[225] At the same time, it had to be clear that the expectation derived from the relationship: where the survivor's expectation derived from a contractual relationship with his deceased relative, no claim could be made.[226]

These restrictive interpretations of the Act often made it difficult for poorer families to obtain substantial compensation.[227] However, more affluent families were able to obtain large sums. This can be seen from *Pym* v. *Great Northern Railway Company*. Francis Pym, the plaintiff's husband, was a 41-year-old magistrate whose income, under a family settlement, was £3869 a year. On his death (resulting from a rail crash), the estate descended to his eldest son in fee, with his widow receiving £1000 annually for life, and his other eight children £100 a year for life. In June 1861, a special jury in Westminster awarded £13,000 damages, £1000 for the widow and £1500 each for the children. The verdict generated alarm among railway proprietors who looked for means to reform the law.[228] However, the verdict was upheld by the Queen's Bench and Exchequer Chamber. While each of his heirs received what they were entitled to under the family settlement, the court accepted that the children's father (who died intestate) would have spent more on their upbringing, and that he might have

---

[224] (1850) 15 LT 521 at 522; *Dickinson* v. *North Eastern Railway Co* (1863) 2 H. & C. 735.

[225] *Franklin* v. *South Eastern Railway Co* (1858) 3 H. & N. 211; *Dalton* v. *South Eastern Railway Co* (1858) 4 C.B. N.S. 296.

[226] *Sykes* v. *The North Eastern Railway Co* (1875) 44 LJ CP 191.

[227] Report to the Lords of the Committee of Privy Council for Trade upon the Accidents which have occurred on Railways during the year 1857, *PP* 1857–8 [2338], li, 183 at p. 20. *Dalton* v. *The South Eastern Railway Co* (1858) 4 C.B. N.S. 296.

[228] *Leeds Mercury*, 6 July 1861, p. 5. Suggestions included the introduction of provisions similar to those under the Merchant Shipping Act, which limited liability to the value of the vessel.

increased the sums they would each receive on his death by savings effected in his life.[229] Erle CJ in the Exchequer Chamber rejected the company's argument that the relatives as a whole lost nothing, since they received his entire estate, by pointing out that the statutory remedy was given to individuals, not to a class.[230]

[229] It was pointed out by a number of commentators that had he left a will, specifying the money each was to obtain from him, they would not have suffered any pecuniary loss by his death and the company would have been protected: 1870 Select Committee on Railway Companies, p 161, q. 2218 (Willes).

[230] *Pym* v. *Great Northern Railway Co* (1862) 2 B. & S. 759; (1863) 4 B. & S. 396. *The Times* spoke approvingly of the result: 19 June 1862, col. 10f. The damages were reduced by the Queen's Bench to £9000, which the company paid: *Daily News*, 18 June 1863, p. 7.

IV

Workplace Injuries

Most accidents and injuries in the nineteenth century occurred at work. In the decade after 1871, almost five times as many railwaymen were killed in rail accidents than passengers. Even more mineworkers were killed than railwaymen, though since the industry was a far larger employer, mining was a less risky occupation.[1] The problem of workplace accidents first came into the public consciousness in the 1830s and 1840s, when a number of parliamentary inquiries, motivated by a concern to protect women and children, revealed that a large number of preventable accidents took place in factories and mines. Although proposals to hold employers strictly liable for industrial accidents were put forward in this era by Edwin Chadwick, they were not taken up by the legislature. It was not until 1844 that legislation was passed offering limited compensation for factory workers injured in industrial accidents, and not until 1850 that miners obtained legislation. In both cases, the compensation offered was limited and ineffective.[2]

Factory and mines legislation aimed to improve safety at work through regulating the conduct of employers, rather than offering remedies to victims for harms suffered. Safety was to be promoted by setting rules, policing them by inspections, and fining employers who violated them. In an era when there was a limited number of inspectors, who generally tried to avoid confrontation, victims of workplace accidents were left to use the common law. Since deodands had been used in the early 1840s to compensate the victims of workplace accidents,[3] it may have been presumed at the time of the passing of the Factory Act that the families of workmen killed as a result of negligence would succeed under Lord Campbell's

---

[1] Between 1872 (when the Railways Regulation Act introduced a more reliable reporting of accidents) and 1881, there were on average 339 fatalities in factories, 1123 in mines, and 684 fatalities involving railway employees. In that era on average 143 railway passengers died annually. Statistics taken from P. W. J. Bartrip and S. B. Burman, *The Wounded Soldiers of Industry: Industrial Compensation Policy, 1833–1897* (Oxford, 1983), 43–6.

[2] Bartrip and Burman, *Wounded Soldiers*, 16–21, 89. See further Vol. XIII, Pt 2, Ch. V.

[3] For deodands, see pp. 996–7.

Act. In fact, the common lawyers in the mid-century made it almost impossible for workmen to succeed.

1. WORKMEN AND THE COMMON LAW

In the mid-nineteenth-century, workmen were prevented from recovering at common law by courts which held that they had voluntarily assumed the risks of their employment, including the risk of being injured by the negligence of their fellow workmen. This doctrine was rooted in the 1837 case of *Priestley* v. *Fowler.*[4] The plaintiff was a butcher's servant, whose thigh was broken when a cart which he was accompanying collapsed. His claim was premised on the assumption that his employer owed him the same duty of care which a stage coach proprietor owed to a passenger. In rejecting his claim, the Exchequer aimed to restrict the scope of the newly developed remedy in negligence, being worried by the potential consequences of a finding for the plaintiff.[5] In Lord Abinger CB's view, a master did not contract with his servant to take care to provide safe equipment, in the way that a coach proprietor did with his passengers. Unlike passengers, employees were in a position to make their own judgments about the condition of equipment they used.[6] They would generally understand the risk better than the master, and could decline any dangerous tasks. For Abinger, it would be bad policy to allow the action, since the servant would be encouraged to 'omit that diligence and caution which he is in duty bound to exercise on behalf of his master, to protect him against the misconduct or negligence of others who serve him'.[7] It would also carry liability 'to an alarming extent', for if an employer were 'responsible for the sufficiency of his carriage to his servant', he would be 'responsible for the negligence of his coach-maker, or his harness-maker, or his coachman'.[8] This case suggested that the employer's duties to his workers would be similar to those which determined occupiers' liabilities.[9] Like the master himself—or any other

---

[4] On this case, see esp. A. W. B. Simpson, *Leading Cases in the Common Law* (Oxford, 1995), Ch. 5; R. W. Kostal, *Law and English Railway Capitalism, 1825–1875* (Oxford, 1994), 259–70; M. A. Stein, 'Priestley v. Fowler (1837) and the Emerging Tort of Negligence' (2002–3) 44 *Boston College Law Review* 689–731. For general surveys, see Bartrip and Burman, *Wounded Soldiers*; E. A. Cawthorn, *Job Accidents and the Law in England's Early Railway Age: Origins of Employer Liability and Workmen's Compensation* (Lampeter, 1997), and M. A. Stein, 'Victorian Tort Liability for Workplace Injuries' (2008) *Illinois Law Review* 933–84.

[5] *Priestley* v. *Fowler* (1837) 3 M. & W. 1 at 5.

[6] *Priestley* v. *Fowler* (1837) 3 Murph. & H. 305 at 306.

[7] *Priestley* v. *Fowler* (1837) 3 M. & W. 1 at 7.

[8] *Priestley* v. *Fowler* (1837) 3 M. & W. 1 at 6.

[9] Abinger's judgment in this case was drawn on in *Southcote* v. *Stanley* (1856) H. & N. 247.

resident of the household—the servant was expected to run the ordinary risks of the workplace.

Priestley v. *Fowler* did not directly raise the question of the employer's vicarious liability to an injured employee for harms caused by the negligence of other employees. This question was first raised in 1850, in *Hutchinson* v. *York, Newcastle and Berwick Railway Co*, in which a railwayman had been killed in a crash while travelling on his employer's train. In contrast to *Priestley*, where the court found that the plaintiff had not been injured as a consequence of any breach of duty owed to him, in *Hutchinson* it was admitted that the plaintiff's husband had been killed as a result of the negligence of the defendants' servants. The question was raised whether the vicarious liability which attached to railway companies when members of the public were hurt also applied when employees suffered injuries. Seeking to distinguish the approach taken in *Priestley*, counsel for the plaintiff argued that where an injury did not result from 'danger so connected with the employment that servant would be necessarily exposed to it', the master should be held liable. It was pointed out that no care on the workman's part could have saved him. However, influenced by Lord Abinger's analogies, Alderson B. found for the company. In so doing, he introduced the common employment rule into English law. Hutchinson had known, he held, 'when he engaged in the service, that he was exposed to the risk of injury, not only from his own want of skill or care, but also from the want of it on the part of his fellow servant; and he must be supposed to have contracted on the terms that, as between himself and his master, he would run this risk'. The master's duty was only to take 'due care not to expose his servant to unreasonable risks' and to 'associat[e] him only with persons of ordinary skill and care',[10] but this duty had been discharged.

The principle behind the doctrine was further discussed in *Bartonshill Coal Co* v. *Reid* and *Bartonshill Coal Co* v. *McGuire*,[11] in which the House of Lords imposed the tougher English rule onto Scots law, which had hitherto taken a more generous approach to the claims of injured workers. Lord Cranworth explained that the two reasons which explained why employers were liable to members of the public for their servants' negligence could not apply to fellow-servants. The first reason was that strangers could not tell whether the harm had been done by a servant or his master, a reason which self-evidently could not

---

[10] *Hutchinson* v. *York, Newcastle and Berwick Railway Co* (1850) 5 Exch. 343 at 351, 353. See also *Wigmore* v. *Jay* (1850) 5 Exch. 354. This view had already been taken in Massachusetts by Shaw CJ in *Farwell* v. *Boston and Worcester Railroad* (1842) 45 Mass. 49.

[11] *Bartonshill Coal Co* v. *Reid* (1856) 3 Macq. (HL Sc.) 266; *Bartonshill Coal Co* v. *McGuire* (1858) 3 Macq. (HL Sc.) 300.

apply to employees. The second reason was that people who chose to engage in action which generated risks were liable to those who suffered harms from them. In Cranworth's judgment, this reason could not apply to a servant, since he could not 'say the master need not have engaged in the work at all, for he was party to its being undertaken'. Unlike a stranger, a workman entering employment knew what risks he was running, and knew that his employer could not prevent harms from other workers' carelessness.

A series of mid-century cases explored what constituted 'common employment'. In deciding this question, Lord Chelmsford noted in *McGuire*, the courts should consider 'what the servant must have known or expected to have been involved in the service which he undertakes'.[12] In practice, judges interpreted this very broadly, and thereby continued to reduce the scope for the injured worker to recover. For instance, in *Morgan v. Vale of Neath Railway Co*, a carpenter working on the roof of an engine shed was held to be in common employment with porters below turning a train on a turntable who dislodged his scaffold, since they were all engaged in the 'common object of their masters, viz., fitting the line for traffic'. Although their tasks were dissimilar, 'the risk of injury from the negligence of the one is so much a natural and necessary consequence of the employment which the other accepts, that it must be included in the risks which are to be considered in his wages'.[13] Attempts to distinguish between grades of employees, distinguishing between fellow-workers and those who might be regarded as surrogates for the master, also failed. In 1868, the House of Lords confirmed that a foreman or manager—whose orders had to be obeyed by the worker—could not be regarded as a representative of the master, but had to be seen as another fellow servant.[14] Nor did it make any difference, if the injury was caused by the negligence of a worker who had left his job before the victim was hired. In such cases, Lord Cairns held, 'the master is […] not liable, although the two workmen cannot technically be described as fellow-workmen'.[15] What mattered was not

---

[12] *Bartonshill Coal Co v. McGuire* (1858) 3 Macq. (HL Sc.) 300 at 308. In this case, the operator of a cage lowering miners into the mine was held in common employment with them.

[13] *Morgan v. The Vale of Neath Railway Co* (1865) LR 1 QB 149 at 154–5, following *Morgan v. The Vale of Neath Railway* (1864) 5 B. & S. 570 at 580. This expansion of the doctrine of common employment was not universally supported (see *Holmes v. Clarke* (1861) 6 H. & N. 349 at 357) though most judgments found workers in common employment: see *Searle v. Lindsay* (1861) 11 C.B. N.S. 429; *Waller v. South Eastern Railway Co* (1863) 2 H. & C. 102; *Lovegrove v. London Brighton and South Coast Railway Co* (1864) 16 C.B. N.S. 669; *Hall v. Johnson* (1865) 3 H. & C. 589, *Murphy v. Smith* (1865) 19 C.B. N.S. 362; *Tunney v. Midland Railway Co* (1865) LR 1 CP 291.

[14] *Wilson v. Merry & Cunningham* (1868) LR 1 Sc 326. See also *Gallagher v. Piper* (1864) 16 C.B. N.S. 669; *Feltham v. England* (1866) LR 2 QB 33. That the same rule applied where the defendant was a corporation was confirmed in *Howells v. Landore Siemens Steel Co* (1874) LR 10 QB 62.

[15] *Wilson v. Merry & Cunningham* (1868) LR 1 Sc 326 at 332.

whether a workman was factually in common employment with the negligent workman, but whether he was to be regarded as having contracted to run the risk which ensued.[16]

If employers were not liable for the negligence of a victim's fellow workman, they did have a duty to take care to provide proper equipment and to hire competent workmen. In *Paterson* v. *Wallace*, a Scottish appeal, the House of Lords held that the employer had a duty 'to be careful that his servant is not induced to work under a notion that tackle or machinery is staunch and secure, when in fact the master knows, or ought to know, that it is not so'. In this case, the pursuer's husband had been killed in a mining accident, when working in an unsafe chamber. It was held to be the master's duty to ensure the working environment was reasonably safe, and that he was liable in negligence for breach of this duty.[17] However, if the workman's injury was caused by his own rashness, the employer could invoke the defence of contributory negligence.

Although the master's duty to provide suitable equipment was non-delegable,[18] employers were not held to warrant the safety of their equipment. In Crompton J.'s words, 'it is negligence for which the master is liable, if he knows that the machinery or tackle to be used by the persons employed by him is improper or unsafe, and notwithstanding that knowledge sanctions its use'.[19] If employers had no reason to know or suspect that machinery was unsafe, they were not held liable. In *Hall* v. *Johnson*, the Exchequer Chamber accordingly acquitted an employer of liability for an injury sustained in a mining rock fall. Since the mine had operated safely for six years, the negligence which led to the plaintiff's injury was held to be that of the person employed to check the roof of the mine, who was a fellow servant, rather than the mineowner.[20] Similarly, if equipment became unsafe because of the negligence of another workman, the employer, who was ignorant of the defect, was not held liable.[21] In such cases, the injured worker could only recover if he could show that the master had been careless in appointing the negligent servant.

The employer's liability was also removed 'where the servant is aware of the defective state of the machinery, and so may be presumed to have taken upon

---

[16] See C. P. Ilbert's comments, in Report from the Select Committee on Employers Liability for Injuries to their Servants, *PP* 1876 (372), ix, 669, q. 296.

[17] *Paterson* v. *Wallace* (1854) 1 Macq. 748. See also *Brydon* v. *Stewart* (1855) 2 Macq. 30.

[18] T. Beven, *Negligence in Law*, 2 vols (4th edn by W. J. Byrne and A. D. Gibb, 1928), i, 764.

[19] *Mellors* v. *Shaw* (1861) 1 B. & S. 437 at 444. See also *Ogden* v. *Rummens* (1862) 3 F. & F. 751 at 755.

[20] *Hall* v. *Johnson* (1865) 3 H & C 589. Cf. *Ogden* v. *Rummens* (1862) 3 F. & F. 751 at 755. See also *Smith* v. *Dowell* (1862) 3 F. & F. 238.

[21] *Searle* v. *Lindsay* (1861) 11 C.B. N.S. 429.

himself the extra risk for the sake of extra wages'.[22] Judges who were aware of the propensity of juries to award damages nonsuited plaintiffs if they felt that there was evidence that a risk had been voluntarily run, since, as a matter of law, *volenti non fit injuria*. In such cases, any duty of care owed by the master was annulled. In *Skipp* v. *Eastern Counties Railway Co*, Martin B. accordingly rejected evidence that an accident which injured the plaintiff had occurred because the company had not employed enough staff to perform the task, since the plaintiff had done the work for three months without complaining: '[t]he plaintiff brought the accident upon himself, for, if he found that he could not do the work which was set him, he ought to have declined it in the first instance'.[23] Similarly, in *Dynen* v. *Leach* in 1857, where a worker was killed when an unusually cheap clip, securing a heavy sugar mould, gave way, Channell B. held that since the man had continued to work, 'with full knowledge of all the circumstances, [...] he directly contributed to the accident'.[24]

But where dangerous equipment deteriorated after the workman had commenced his employment, he was not held to have run the additional risks, even if he continued working with it. In these cases, the employer was under a duty either to inform the workman of dangers of which he was (or should have been) aware or to remove them.[25] In *Clarke* v. *Holmes*, a plaintiff who lost his arm when his clothing was caught in unfenced machinery therefore recovered, even though he had carried on working at a machine he knew to be dangerous. The machine had been fenced when he started work, and, after it had been left unfenced for some time, he complained to his employer, who promised to repair it. Under these circumstances, Pollock CB held that the employer who failed to effect the repairs had to be taken to have run the risk.[26] In the Exchequer Chamber, Cockburn CJ confirmed that while a servant could not complain of the risks of a job he had undertaken, his master would be liable if he permitted the danger to be aggravated by failing to keep the machinery in the condition in which the employee had a right to expect it to be.

---

[22] *Mellors* v. *Shaw* (1861) 1 B. & S. 437 at 444. See also *Saxton* v. *Hawkesworth* (1872) 26 LT 851 at 853.

[23] *Skipp* v. *Eastern Counties Railway Co* (1853) 9 Exch. 223 at 226.

[24] *Dynen* v. *Leach* (1857) 26 LJ Ex. 221 at 223. Pollock CB had observed (at 222) that every worker was bound to know the nature of the instrument he used, and that if the work was more than ordinarily dangerous, he should have declined to continue.

[25] *Vaughan* v. *Cork and Youghal Railway Co* (1860) 12 Ir. Rep. 297 at 303.

[26] *Holmes* v. *Clarke* (1861) 6 H. & N. 349 at 358. Although this was an action for breach of statutory duty, only Willes and Wightman JJ in the Exchequer Chamber considered the defendant's liability to rest on the statute. *Holmes* v. *Clarke* (1862) 31 LJ Ex. 359, 360.

Besides their liabilities at common law, employers could also be sued for breaches of statutory duties, such as those imposed by the Factory Act 1844.[27] In 1852, Lord Campbell ruled in *Couch* v. *Steel* that an action could be maintained in tort for the breach of any duty, whether imposed by the common law or by statute, as long as this right of action had not been taken away by the statute. In this case, the Queen's Bench had to interpret the meaning of legislation which required shipowners to keep certain medicines on board, and which imposed penalties for non-compliance, which could be recovered by a common informer. In Campbell's judgment, an injured sailor could recover here in tort: since the penalty was imposed only for the breach of the public duty, and was recoverable by anyone, it did not remove the common law rights of a victim who had suffered special damage.[28] Although Campbell's view was later questioned as a general proposition regarding breaches of statutory duty,[29] the principle was applied in cases where there were breaches of duties to provide safe workplaces.

In response, employers attempted to persuade the courts to interpret their duties under the statutes narrowly.[30] They also invoked the *volenti non fit injuria* defence. In *Caswell* v. *Worth*, Lord Campbell held that a plaintiff, who was injured after he set in motion unfenced machinery against the order of the defendant, could not recover, since the Act was 'clearly not intended to protect persons employed in factories from the consequences of their own misconduct'.[31] Not all judges were happy with this approach. In 1872, in *Britton* v. *Great Western Cotton Co*, Pigott B. observed that the master in *Caswell* should have been 'held liable, as he had been clearly guilty of a breach of his statutory duty'. Nonetheless, he admitted that even where a statutory duty was imposed, the workman had to be careful of his own safety. In Bramwell B.'s view, where a statutory duty had been breached, the employers 'are in default to begin with, and the mere circumstance that the deceased entered on a dangerous employment does not exonerate them, unless he knew the nature of the risk to which, in consequence of that default, he was exposed'.[32] But if the workman 'dispensed with the performance of [the

---

[27] However, a failure to do what the statute required was not regarded as itself evidence of negligence at common law. See *Coe* v. *Platt* (1852) 7 Exch. 923 at 926, where the victim was a child. For a contrasting view of the care owed to children, see *Grizzle* v. *Frost* (1863) 3 F. & F. 622.

[28] *Couch* v. *Steel* (1852) 3 E. & B. 402.

[29] *Atkinson* v. *Newcastle Waterworks Co* (1877) 2 Ex D 448; *Clegg, Parkinson & Co* v. *Earley Gas Co* [1896] 1 QB 594, *Groves* v. *Wimborne* [1898] 2 QB 402.

[30] See esp. *Coe* v. *Platt* (1852) 7 Exch. 923. Some counsel sought to argue that the act only protected children, an argument which Cockburn CJ found persuasive in *Clarke* v. *Holmes* (1861) 7 H. & N. 937.

[31] *Caswell* v. *Worth* (1856) 5 E. & B. 849 at 855.

[32] *Britton* v. *Great Western Cotton Co* (1872) LR 7 Ex 130 at 137–8; 41 LJ Ex 99.

statutory duty] knowing the duty and knowing the danger, I think he would be *volens*'.[33] This suggested that where a statutory duty had been breached, a greater onus lay on the employer to show that the workman had consented to the risk than was the case at common law.

By the 1860s, some common law judges were increasingly conscious that the workman could not be expected to understand risks posed by dangerous machinery. In *Clarke* v. *Holmes*, Byles J. sought to restrict the ambit of the *volenti* doctrine, by suggesting that the principle of *Priestley* v. *Fowler* was limited to 'the casualties of ordinary domestic life', and did not extend to dangerous things, the risks of which could not be judged by ordinary workmen:

> It is, in most cases, impossible that a workman can judge of the condition of a complex and dangerous machine, wielding irresistible mechanical power, and, if he could, he is quite incapable of estimating the degree of risk involved in different conditions of the machine; but the master may be able, and generally is able, to estimate both. The master again is a volunteer, the workman ordinarily has no choice.[34]

He concluded that 'the owner of dangerous machinery is bound to exercise due care that it is in a safe and proper condition'. In the late nineteenth century, other judges also began to move away from a presumption that workmen had consented to assume all the risks of dangerous equipment. In 1887, in *Thomas* v. *Quartermaine*, the workman's position was treated as analogous to that of an invitee. As Bowen LJ explained, where dangers were apparent to an invitee, the occupier owed no duty of care to protect him from them; but the less apparent the danger, the greater the duty on the master. He added that 'mere knowledge' by the workman might not be a conclusive defence, since there could be 'a perception of the existence of the danger without comprehension of the risk, as where the workman is of imperfect intelligence'.[35]

Where dangerous equipment failed, the employer was regarded as being *prima facie* in breach of his duty to take reasonable care to protect workmen by monitoring the safety of equipment.[36] The mere fact that a workman had continued to work with it was not considered as sufficient to establish that he had consented to run the risk. Whether he had in fact done so was a question of fact to be determined

---

[33] *Britton* v. *Great Western Cotton Co* (1872) 41 LJ Ex. 99, 101. This passage is not found in the report in LR 7 Ex 130.

[34] *Clarke* v. *Holmes* (1862) 7 H. & N. 937 at 947–8.

[35] *Thomas* v. *Quartermaine* (1887) 18 QBD 685 at 692–3, 695–6. For parallels with occupiers' liability, see also *Woodley* v. *The Metropolitan District Railway Co* (1877) 2 Ex D 384 at 390.

[36] *Webb* v. *Rennie* (1865) 4 F. & F. 608 at 612, *Murphy* v. *Phillips* (1876) 35 LT 477. The master could discharge this duty by appointing a competent person to inspect the equipment. If he did so, he would not be liable for that person's negligence.

in each case.[37] By the end of the century, it was clear that for the defence of *volenti non fit injuria* to be raised, the plaintiff had to prove the consent of the victim, and not merely his knowledge.[38] Where the danger was inherent in the employee's own tasks, the courts were more willing to find an assumption of risk; but where the danger was generated in another department of the work, or where the risk was generated by the organization of work over which the employer had control, then the courts held the victim could recover from the master.[39]

Despite this increasing willingness to hold employers accountable for the state of their premises, for most of the Victorian era, the judiciary placed great obstacles before those injured workmen who attempted to obtain compensation in tort though the expensive and costly procedure of litigation. Historians have noted the striking contrast between their judicial willingness to hold railway companies accountable for injuries to passengers caused by their employees, and their unwillingness to provide remedies for workmen injured in the same way.[40] This has sometimes been attributed to simple class bias, with judges feeling sympathy for middle-class travellers, but not for working-class victims. In an age when freedom of contract became a political mantra, judges interpreted employees' contracts very differently from those contained in passengers' tickets. Where the contract of carriage was interpreted to contain an implied warranty that none of the carrier's employees would be negligent,[41] mid-century judges raised a legal presumption—one which was seriously out of kilter with economic reality—that the workman had freely contracted to run all the risks of his employment. The simple fact that the worker had accepted the job at the price offered was taken to mean that he must have factored the risk into the price. Although it would be simplistic to portray the body of the judiciary as wedded to promoting free enterprise at the expense of the working man, many judges did express concern to limit the reach of employers' liability.[42]

One reason why judges took this view was that they shared the common perception that most industrial accidents were caused by the negligence of workmen. In judicial eyes, it was the workers, rather than the employers, who needed a deterrent to give them an incentive to create a safe workplace. The

---

[37] In *Yarmouth* v. *France* (1887) 19 QBD 647; *Thrussell* v. *Handyside & Co* (1888) 20 QBD 359, the victim was shown to have been compelled by his employer to continue to work in an unsafe environment.

[38] *Williams* v. *Birmingham Battery and Metal Co* [1899] 2 QB 338.

[39] *Smith* v. *Charles Baker and Sons* [1891] AC 325, following *Bartonshill Coal Co* v. *McGuire* (1858) 3 Macq. 300 at 310.

[40] Kostal, *Law and Railway Capitalism*, Ch. 7.

[41] Report from the Select Committee on Railway Companies, *PP* 1870 (341), x, 207, q. 2218 (Willes J.).

[42] *Wiggett* v. *Fox* (1856) 11 Exch. 832 at 839.

model on which they drew to develop this approach was the household. They regarded employers as equivalent to the master of the household, rather than seeing them as large abstract corporations, who should be held to internalize their costs. This made it very difficult to bring successful actions against railway companies, where the person whose negligence injured the workman would almost always be another employee, rather than a master. The paradigm of the householder hardly fitted the world of railway enterprise. However, in an age when the legislature intervened regularly in railway matters, the judges remained aware that they were not developing the common law specifically for this sector. Vast and imposing as they were, railways were atypical: as late as 1871, the average manufacturing establishment employed fewer than 20.[43] Made up as it was of a generation reaching middle age before the arrival of the railways, the mid-century judiciary focused their attention on the individual tortfeasor. Rather than considering how to allocate losses in a corporate economy, they developed a law which would hold employers liable only for the kind of personal fault which they would find blameworthy in the master of a household or small workshop.

Since judges refused to develop the law of torts into a system of compensation for industrial accidents, injured workmen had to look to other means of support. In the aftermath of major accidents, public subscriptions were generally raised to compensate the injured and their families.[44] Those hurt in isolated incidents had to look to the parish. Injured workers were likely to be given out-door relief, rather than being confined to the workhouse, though the relief they obtained was generally reduced if they obtained funds from a charity.[45] Workmen also insured themselves, through Friendly Societies. In contrast to trade unions, these societies were encouraged by middle-class reformers, who felt they would inculcate the kind of thrift which would ease the burden of the poor laws.[46] The

[43] P. Hudson, 'Industrial Organisation and Structure' in R. Floud and P. Johnson (ed). *The Cambridge Economic History of Modern Britain. Volume I: Industrialisation, 1700–1860* (Cambridge, 2004), 28–56 at 37.

[44] Thus, over £56,000 was raised after 500 miners were killed in an explosion at the Oaks colliery near Barnsley in 1866: *The Times*, 19 December 1866, col. 5f; 28 December 1866, col. 9e; 4 January 1867, col. 8d; 26 November 1867, col. 4f. In this case, the union decided not to litigate: J. Benson and R. Sykes, 'Trade Unionism and the Use of the Law: English Coalminers' Unions and Legal Redress for Industrial Accidents, 1860–97' (1997) 3 *Historical Studies in Industrial Relations* 27–48.

[45] See Twenty Second Annual Report of the Poor Law Board, 1869–70: *PP* 1870 (c. 123), xxxv,1 at xxxii and 108–11. This was endorsed by the Friendly Societies' Commission: Fourth Report of the Commissioners appointed to inquire into Friendly and Benefit Building Societies (henceforth cited as Friendly Societies Commission, Fourth Report), *PP* 1874 (c. 961), xxiii.1 1 at clxxxix.

[46] See S. Cordery, 'Friendly Societies and the Discourse of Respectability in Britain 1825–1875', (1995) 34 *Journal of British Studies* 35–58; P. H. J. H. Gosden, *The Friendly Societies in England, 1815–1875* (Manchester, 1961); S. Cordery, *British Friendly Societies, 1750–1914* (Basingstoke, 2003).

mid-nineteenth century saw an expansion in the number of such societies, and by 1880 roughly 2.2 million people, accounting for about 30 per cent of adult males, were members of a Friendly Society.[47] However, they were not always a reliable source of income, and if funds ran out either because too little had been collected or too much paid out, or if the society became insolvent, benefits might not be forthcoming.[48] In the second half of the nineteenth century, working people also began to take out commercial insurance.[49] The most important firm was the Prudential, which started its industrial insurance business in 1854, and had over a million policy-holders by the early 1870s.[50] Workmen also made savings through institutions created by the state designed to encourage thrift and self-help, such as the Post Office Savings Bank (created in 1861 and backed by government guarantee), and trustee savings banks, which together held more than a million accounts in 1870.

Besides commercial insurance and voluntary membership of Friendly Societies, from the 1860s, workers were sometimes given cover by assurance schemes run by their employers, which collected contributions from both workers and employers. Such schemes were common on the railways, where it became a condition of employment to join.[51] Miners' Permanent Relief Funds were also set up from the 1860s, covering half the country's miners by 1890, and offering similar benefits to the railway schemes.[52] Although associated with employers, these societies were not guaranteed by them, and their financial position was often unsound, as the societies promised more than they could pay. The fact that employers contributed generated a false sense of security, and encouraged lax administration by

[47] E. Hopkins, *Working Class Self Help in Nineteenth Century England* (London, 1995), 31, 51; B. B. Gilbert, *The Evolution of National Insurance in Great Britain: The Origins of the Welfare State* (1966), 165; J. Benson, 'The Thrift of English Coal-Miners, 1860–95' (1978) 31 *Econ. Hist. Rev.*, ns 410–18. For levels of benefits given, see also Evidence of H. Hughes, Second Report of the Commissioners appointed to inquire into Friendly and Benefit Societies, *PP* 1872 (c. 514), xxvi.1, at qq. 23,865–6.

[48] Gosden, *Friendly Societies*, 95.

[49] Tidd Pratt told the 1853 Select Committee on Assurance Associations that Friendly Societies were in effect insurers, but who were forbidden by law to insure above £200. Some associations acted as Friendly Societies for smaller amounts and as Joint Stock Companies for larger amounts: Report from the Select Committee on Insurance Associations: *PP* 1852–3 (965), xxi.1, qq. 502–11.

[50] Benson, 'Thrift', 414.

[51] They paid between £20 and £40 in case of death, and a weekly payment in case of disablement. On the Midland Railway Friendly Society, see Friendly and Benefit Societies Commission: Reports of the Assistant Commissioners: *PP* 1874 (c . 996) at 193, xxiii.2, at p. 77; on London and North Western Railway's scheme, see Report from the Select Committee on Employers Liability for Injuries to their Servants (henceforth cited as 1877 Select Committee on Employers Liability), *PP* 1877 (285), x, 551, p. 74, q. 1297–8 (George Findlay).

[52] G. L. Campbell, *Miners' Insurance Funds: Their Origin and Extent* (1880); Benson, 'Thrift', 415–16; A. Wilson and H. Levy, *Workmen's Compensation*, 2 vols, Vol I: Social and Political Development (1939), 55.

the workers; but the employers themselves, by making membership compulsory, encouraged this false sense of confidence.[53]

2. THE EMPLOYERS' LIABILITY ACT 1880

By the 1870s, trade unions began to agitate for reform of the law. They were less motivated by a desire to obtain compensation for the victims of accidents than by the need to improve industrial safety.[54] Improved statistics in the 1870s revealed a much higher number of railway injuries and fatalities, and led to the appointment of a royal commission on railway accidents. In the view of the unions, abolishing the doctrines of common employment and *volenti non fit injuria* would compel employers to improve workplace safety. In face of calls for reform, supporters of the employers' interest argued that it was unfair to make them liable to injured workers for harms done by other workers, and that instead, a system of compulsory insurance for all industrial accidents should be introduced, contributed to equally by employer and workman.[55] The idea of insurance was opposed strongly by the trade unions, who felt that it would make employers reckless.[56]

After a bill had been introduced in Parliament to abolish the doctrines of common employment and assumption of risk, sponsored by the TUC's parliamentary committee, the matter was referred to a select committee. Given official concerns about the effect on employers of so great a change, the committee was asked to consider only whether the doctrine of common employment should be better defined and whether the master should held be liable for the negligence of those in a position of superiority. The committee heard evidence from members of the judiciary, whose views diverged. On one side stood Sir George Bramwell, who defended the doctrine of common employment and doubted the entire doctrine of vicarious liability. While it made sense in his view to hold a carrier vicariously liable for the negligence of his servants—since he had contracted with passengers for their care—there was no reason to hold any employer vicariously liable for the negligence of his servant, if he had no contract with the victim. In his view of the law, it was an error to assume that employers contracted out of a *prima facie* liability. Instead, (unlike carriers) they never contracted into a liability.[57] This

---

[53] The commissioners were also concerned that the employers' agreement to contribute was not legally binding and might be *ultra vires*. Friendly Societies Commission, Fourth Report, lxxi–lxxii.

[54] See Bartrip and Burman, *Wounded Soldiers*, 93.

[55] See the letter of Lord Shand in *The Times*, 24 August 1880, col. 6c. See also the views of Joseph Brown QC in *The Times*, 30 April 1879, col. 9f.

[56] Bartrip and Burman, *Wounded Soldiers*, 150–1.

[57] 1877 Select Committee on Employers Liability, p. 59 q. 1100–02.

was as it should be, since masters needed protection from the negligence of their men.[58]

On the other side stood Sir William Baliol Brett, who showed greater sensitivity to the vulnerability of the workman. He pointed to the fact that 'the condition of the master and the servant is not equal', and that a fellow servant would never have any assets to compensate a workman. Accepting that the current law was premised on an implied term in the contract of employment, he argued that the premise was based on an incorrect understanding of the doctrine of implied terms. In his view, it was an error to imply a term into the contract that the worker assumed the risk of the negligence of fellow workers 'of whom he knows nothing, and never will, probably know anything until the accident happens'.[59] Brett urged reform. He felt that, even though large damages might be awarded against an employer if the law were changed, he would suffer no greater misfortune than (for instance) the members of a racecourse committee, who were held liable when a grandstand collapsed:

He may be ruined; it is a thing that cannot be helped. He is ruined if he accident happens to strangers; I see no logical reason why he should not be liable even to ruin when it happens to his servants.[60]

In its report, the committee endorsed the dominant judicial view that the good running of an enterprise depended on workers being vigilant, and noted the serious consequences for the economy if masters were made liable. However, it recommended that 'where the actual employers cannot personally discharge the duties of masters, or where they deliberately abdicate their functions, and delegate them to agents', they should be liable for the acts of these agents.[61] It also recommended that the doctrine of common employment should be limited to those situations where one workman was in a position to observe the other, and report any misconduct on his part to the employer.

The ensuing Employers' Liability Act 1880 was seen as a symbolic triumph for the labour interest, though it was limited in scope. The Act gave a workman the right to damages where he was injured as a result of defective machinery. It also

---

[58] Contrast the view of Frederick Pollock, defending the common employment rule in 'Employers' Liability', in his *Essays in Jurisprudence and Ethics* (1882), 114–43.

[59] 1877 Select Committee on Employers Liability, p. 116, q. 1926. He felt that it could not be implied, as a matter of contract law, since ordinary people would not assume that both parties had this in mind when the contract was made.

[60] 1877 Select Committee on Employers Liability, q. 1926. His allusion was to *Francis* v. *Cockrell* (1870) LR 5 QB 184. Brett's disillusionment with the doctrine was not new. In 1876, he said he could not understand the principle on which the immunity rested: *Lovell* v. *Howell* (1876) 1 CPD 161 at 167. See also his argument in *Potter* v. *Faulkner* (1861) 1 B. & S. 800.

[61] 1877 Select Committee on Employers Liability, v.

gave him a remedy where he was injured by the negligence of 'any person in the service of the employer who has any superintendence entrusted to him, whilst in the exercise of such superintendence'; or by the negligence of anyone whose orders the workman was bound to follow at the time. The employer was also liable if a workman was injured by a fellow servant failing to obey the rules of the workplace. However, there were limits to the remedy offered. Damages under the Act were limited to three years' wages. Furthermore, notice of the accident had to be given within six weeks, and litigation had to commence within six months (or 12, if death ensued).

After the passing of the Act, employers feared that the Act would see an explosion of litigation against them. So great was the fear that factory inspectors in 1881 reported a new enthusiasm among employers for fencing machinery.[62] After the introduction of the Act, two judicial approaches were to be found, one of which 'construed the Act as narrowly as possible with a view to preventing what they conceived to be injustice to masters' and the other construing it 'liberally in favour of the workman'.[63] Brett, who had by now become Lord Esher, was in the forefront of the latter camp. In 1887, in *Thomas* v. *Quartermaine*, he held that the Act 'recognized' a duty on the master not to have his machinery in a defective condition, and removed the master's defence that the employee had undertaken all ordinary risks of the employment. For Esher, the master was liable in an action of negligence, founded on the broad principle which he had developed in *Heaven* v. *Pender*,[64] 'that you are bound not to do anything negligently so as to hurt a person near you' and that 'the duty arises from the knowledge of that proximity'.[65] One year later, he held that a master should be held liable wherever a machine could be regarded as dangerous, 'even although that machine could not be improved upon'.[66] But Esher's view was not taken up by his brethren and, in both cases, he was in the minority. In *Thomas*, Bowen LJ retorted that the legislation had not generated any new duties of the kind Esher had in mind.[67] Its effect was simply to put the workman in the position of any member of the public, in respect of the matters covered. Where the workman covered by the Act encountered hazardous equipment in the workplace, he was in the same position as a licensee visiting the master's property. The Act, therefore, did not remove the defences

---

[62] Wilson and Levy, *Workmen's Compensation*, 47.

[63] *Walsh* v. *Whiteley* (1888) 21 QBD 371 at 375 (Lord Esher).

[64] *Heaven* v. *Pender* (1883) 11 QBD 503.

[65] *Thomas* v. *Quartermaine* (1887) 18 QBD 685 at 688.

[66] *Walsh* v. *Whiteley* (1881) 21 QBD 371 at 376.

[67] 'What sort of duty could that be which does not exist at law, and which is not defined by statute? It would be a duty that had no limits except the benevolence of a jury exercised at the expense of the pockets of other people': *Thomas* v. *Quartermaine* (1887) 18 QBD 685 at 692–3.

of contributory negligence[68] and voluntary assumption of risk. Similarly, when considering the effect of the Act on the liability for defective machinery, Esher's colleagues insisted that the negligence of the employer was a necessary element to his liability.[69] Injured workmen making use of the statute still had to prove fault, which meant that they could not recover for pure accidents.[70]

According to the Act, where injuries were caused by a defect in the ways, works, machinery, or plant, workmen could recover if the defect was caused by the negligence of the employer or of those of his staff responsible for the equipment. Although this clause gave increased protection to workmen who had been injured by faulty equipment, counsel for the employers persuaded many courts not to read the provisions too broadly. For instance, a majority in the Court of Appeal confirmed in *Walsh* v. *Whiteley* that the plaintiff had to show that the equipment was defective, and not merely that it was dangerous. It had to be shown that the equipment was 'not in a proper condition for the purpose for which it was applied'. Where equipment had long been used without injury, and the court felt that the accident was caused by the workman's carelessness, he would get no remedy.[71] However, if the equipment, while not intrinsically defective, generated a risk of injury to a careful worker, it was held to fall within the Act.[72] Similarly, when dealing with defective 'ways', along which workmen were injured, the courts held that it was not enough that the way had become dangerous as a result of a temporary obstruction or from the effects of bad weather: the defect had to be something which permanently altered its condition.[73]

A narrow approach was also taken in a number of cases in interpreting the provision permitting the worker to sue his employer if he had been injured by the negligence of someone supervising him. This provision had been designed to remove the common employment rule from cases where the accident had been caused by the negligence of someone to whom the master had delegated his authority. If it was clear enough that this provision covered general managers, it was less clear how far it covered foremen. To fall within this rule, the courts held that the negligent person had to be in a position of supervision. Where the foreman was engaged in manual work with the other labourers, and an accident occurred when he did that work negligently, it was held that the victim could not

---

[68] See e.g. *Bunker* v. *Midland Railway Co* (1882) 47 LT 476; *Callender* v. *Carlton Iron Co* (1893) 9 TLR 646 (CA); *Hooper* v. *Holme* (1896) 12 TLR 537.

[69] *Walsh* v. *Whiteley* (1881) 21 QBD 371 at 378.

[70] *Harris* v. *Tinn* (1888) 5 TLR 221.   [71] *Walsh* v. *Whiteley* (1888) 21 QBD 371 at 378.

[72] See *Heske* v. *Samuelson* (1883) 12 QBD 30 at 31; *Paley* v. *Garnett* (1885) 16 QBD 52; *Morgan* v. *Hutchins* (1890) 6 TLR 219.

[73] *McGiffin* v. *Palmer's Shipbuilding Co* (1882) 10 QBD 5 at 9 (Field J.). See also *Willetts* v. *Watt* [1892] 2 QB 92.

rely on the Act.[74] Furthermore, even if the negligent workman was considered to be in the position of a supervisor, he was only liable if the injury occurred because of his negligence as a supervisor, rather than because of his negligence as a workman.[75] The distinctions could be very fine, and the courts were prepared to find for the worker if the accident occurred after a foreman engaged in manual labour with the others told the victim to do something.[76] Nonetheless, the approach taken by the courts created a degree of uncertainty which acted as a disincentive to litigate, which was compounded by the fact that the workman could not recover if he had followed instructions to do something which he could see was dangerous,[77] or if he had been negligent himself.

The Act also allowed the injured worker to recover if he was harmed by the negligence of someone whose orders he was bound to obey. Such a person did not have to be a superior, but could be a worker of equal rank, who had control over machinery or a particular task. Once more, some judges read the legislation in a way which limited the right of injured workmen to recover. If the order given was one which the injured worker was not bound to obey—as where an order was given which violated company rules—he could not recover for his injury.[78] According to this rule, the family of a labourer killed when he obeyed his foreman's instructions to work on part of a railway line where no look-out was posted was held unable to recover: for the foreman had no mandate to give such an order, and the worker had no duty to obey it.[79] Employers also sought to argue that if the order given by the fellow worker had not been negligent, the victim could not recover if he was injured by negligence in the performance of the Act. This argument succeeded in *Howard* v. *Bennett*, where the defendant was held not to be liable for an injury to a worker, who had put his hands into a calico printing machine, after he was asked to do so by a fellow worker who had control over the machine, and who had negligently started the machine. For, in Lord Coleridge's judgment, the proximate cause of the injury was not the order which was given, but the subsequent negligence.[80] By 1892, however, the Court of Appeal rejected

---

[74] *Kellard* v. *Rooke* (1887) 19 QBD 585; (1888) 21 QBD 367; *Allmarch* v. *Walker* (1898) 78 LT 391; *Hall* v. *North Eastern Railway Co* (1885) 1 TLR 359.

[75] See *Shaffers* v. *The General Steam Navigation Co* (1883) 10 QBD 356, discussed in A. H. Ruegg, *The Employers' Liability Act 1880* (2nd edn, 1892), 79. See also *Harris* v. *Tinn* (1888) 5 TLR 221.

[76] *Osborne* v. *Jackson and Todd* (1883) 11 QBD 619.

[77] *Booker* v. *Higgs* (1887) 3 TLR 618.

[78] *Bunker* v. *Midland Railway Co* (1882) 47 LT 476 (where the foreman gave the employee extra money to break the rule). Contrast the approach of Cave J. in *Marley* v. *Osborn* (1894) 10 TLR 388 at 389, where he said that 'The Legislature did not intend to leave it to the workman to go into the question whether the order given was right if it was an order he was bound to obey'.

[79] *Hooper* v. *Holme* (1896) 12 TLR 537, 13 TLR 6.

[80] *Howard* v. *Bennett* (1888) 58 LJ (QB) 129; 60 LT 152. See also *Martin* v. *Connah's Quay Alkali Co* (1885) 33 WR 216.

this kind of argument. Provided the injury resulted from the negligence of the person giving the orders, and the victim's conforming to those orders, he could recover, even if the order itself had not been negligent.[81]

Thanks to the restrictive approach to the legislation taken by many judges, levels of litigation remained small,[82] and in 1904 a Departmental Committee reported that the Act had failed 'as a means of obtaining compensation for injury by accident with a reasonable degree of certainty'.[83] According to one observer in 1905, under the Act, 5 per cent of injured workers recovered, compared with 2 per cent at common law.[84] Employers used a number of tactics to limit their liability.[85] Many followed the practice of the Earl of Dudley, who put up a notice at his collieries that anyone who worked there agreed only to seek compensation for accidents from the colliery club fund. The Earl's policy was challenged in 1881, in a case brought by the widow of a miner killed in a pit accident, with the support of trade union funding. The judge in the Dudley county court held that the contract made by the notice was void, for being against public policy. But the Queen's Bench Division found for the Earl. In Field J.'s view, the contract was valid. 'There is no suggestion that the contract was induced by fraud, or by force, or made under duress', he ruled, 'and it was not a naked bargain made without consideration, for the defendant contributed an amount to the club equal to the whole amount of contributions from the workmen'. Nor was it against public policy, since it affected only the interests of the workmen, who were perfectly able to make their own contracts.[86] The decision was controversial, and aroused strong opposition from the unions.[87] While only a minority of workers were subjected

[81] *Wild* v. *Waygood* [1892] 1 QB 783 (CA).

[82] In the first decade of its operation, an average of 133 cases a year came before the County Courts under the Statute, with an average of under six being removed to the High Court: PP 1884 (151), lxiii, 139; PP 1884–5 (320), lxiv, 195; PP 1886 (226 sess. 1), liii, 99; PP 1888 (290), lxxxii, 147; 1888–91 PP 1892 (357 sess. 1), lxxii, 129. See Bartrip and Burman, *Wounded Soldiers*, 187–8.

[83] Report of the Departmental Committee appointed to inquire into the Law relating to Compensation for Injuries to Workmen (henceforth cited as 1904 Departmental Committee Report), PP 1904 (Cd. 2208), lxxxviii, 743, p. 11.

[84] Departmental Committee appointed to inquire into the Law relating to Compensation for injuries to Workmen: Vol II Minutes of Evidence (henceforth cited as 1905 Departmental Committee Evidence), PP 1905 (Cd. 2334), lxxv, 487, q. 7923 (Stanley Brown).

[85] Employers attempted to use the notice requirements to their advantage. Some sought to lull workers into a false sense of security by paying them in full until the six-week period had expired. They also sought to hold workers to strict requirements for giving notice, with varying degrees of success: see *Keen* v. *The Millwall Dock Co* (1882) 8 QBD 482; *Clarkson* v. *Musgrave and Sons* (1882) 9 QBD 386 at 390; *Stone* v. *Hyde* (1889) 9 QBD 76; *Prevesi* v. *Gatti* (1888) 4 TLR 487.

[86] *Griffiths* v. *The Earl of Dudley* (1882) 9 QBD 357 at 362–3.

[87] See *The Times*, 5 October 1882, col. 7d. In 1883, the Social Science Association also debated whether to forbid both contracting out, and the employers insuring themselves: *The Times*, 9 October 1883, col. 7a.

to contracting-out provisions—up to perhaps 25 per cent—the system was used predominantly in areas with weak trade unions, or where the work was especially dangerous.[88]

3. THE WORKMEN'S COMPENSATION ACT 1897

By the 1890s, it was apparent that the law needed reform. Two positions emerged. The first was that traditionally espoused by trade unionists and liberals, that the common law doctrines of common employment and assumption of risk needed to be abolished, since they made the employers careless of safety. The second view was announced by Joseph Chamberlain during debates on the Liberals' unsuccessful 1893 bill to reform the law. Chamberlain felt that since most industrial accidents were not the product of negligence, reform of the common law would not be sufficient.[89] Instead, a system needed to be devised to compensate workmen for industrial injuries, regardless of fault. Chamberlain's approach appealed to those conservatives who had argued in 1893 that, rather than unleashing a flood of litigation against employers, more encouragement should be given to joint accident funds. When his Liberal Unionists joined the Conservatives, and won the 1895 election, he was given the chance to put his ideas into practice.

Under the Conservative scheme, employers alone were to be the insurers of the safety of workers in dangerous industries, and not merely contributors to joint benefit funds with their workers. Behind this project lay an awareness of the role of insurance. Employers had, since 1880, already been protecting themselves from liability through insurance. In 1880, an Employers Liability Insurance Corporation was set up, which had 13,000 policies by 1886.[90] Mutual insurance societies were also set up in particular industries.[91] In this context, it came to be argued that a system of insuring workmen could be created which would neither require large state intervention, nor impose an excessive burden on industry.[92] Policy was also informed by overseas models, most notably the 1884 German law

---

[88] Bartrip and Burman, *Wounded Soldiers*, 172–3.

[89] J. Chamberlain, 'The Labour Question' (1892) 32 *Nineteenth Century* 677–710. On the passing and working of the Act, see also D. G. Hanes, *The First British Workmen's Compensation Act, 1897* (1968). See also W. C. Mallalie, 'Joseph Chamberlain and Workmen's Compensation' (1950) 10 *JEH* 45–57.

[90] H. P. Robinson, *The Employers' Liability Assurance Corporation Ltd, 1880–1930* (1930), 15–16, 22.

[91] See *The Times*, 1 September 1881, col. 4a.

[92] A. D. Provand, 'Employers' Liability' (1894) 66 *Contemporary Review* 137–52. See also his article, 'Compensation to Workmen' (1898) 46 *Journal of the Society of Arts* 277–85.

on compulsory accident insurance.[93] British trade unions were not keen on the project, however. Besides being suspicious of a system of insurance outside their control, which might undermine their benefit funds, they feared that a system insulating employers from liability might increase accidents.[94] Chamberlain admitted that insured employers might have few incentives to improve safety; but he felt the question of safety could be left to other forms of regulation.[95]

The principle behind the 1897 Act was that workers in industries covered by statutory safety regulations—such as railways, factories, and mines—were to be given no-fault protection, because of the dangerous nature of the work they did. The worker was not strictly speaking compensated for the accident. Instead, he would be given sufficient benefit to take him out of the poor law. Compensation was to be paid according to the rate of wages the worker received before the accident. In case of death, the worker's dependants would receive a lump sum equivalent to three years' wages, up to a maximum of £300 (and a minimum of £150). In cases of incapacity to work, the worker would get a weekly payment of half of his wages, up to a maximum of £1 a week; but (in order to guard against the danger of 'malingering'), the worker would only get this sum after two weeks. Where a worker was 'partially' incapable of working, the statute stipulated that, in awarding the rate of compensation, 'regard shall be had' to the difference in wages which he could obtain before and after the accident. This meant that where an injured worker had recovered sufficiently to work, his payments could be cut.

In 1900, the legislation was extended to cover agricultural workers. This reform was motivated not by concern that one million agricultural workers were exposed to particular dangers,[96] but by political concerns.[97] Its effect was to unsettle the principle on which the legislation was based. For it raised the question why other more dangerous trades remained excluded from the scheme. In 1903, a Departmental Committee considering the question rejected the proposal that all employees (including domestic servants) should be included, but recommended a modest piecemeal extension of the Act to industries which had

[93] See E. P. Hennock, *British Social Reform and German Precedents: The Case of Social Insurance 1880–1914* (Oxford, 1987), 52.

[94] See Hennock, *Social Reform*, 63–4; V. M. Lester, 'The Employers' Liability/Workmen's Compensation Debate of the 1890s revisited' (2001) 44 *Hist. Jnl.* 471–95.

[95] *PD* 1893 (s4) 8: 1963–4.

[96] Figures collected by the Registrar General suggested a mortality rate among all males of 56/1000. The rate among farm labourers was below the average (42), while bargemen and lightermen (223) and seamen (202)—both excluded from the Act—had the highest rates: 1904 Departmental Committee Report, App. VIII(1).

[97] P. W. J. Bartrip, *Workmen's Compensation in Twentieth Century Britain: Law, History and Social Policy* (Aldershot, 1987), 27 *et seq.*

high rates of accidents, and where the change would not impose high costs.[98] In 1906, the new Liberal government abandoned the original notion that the legislation was designed to cover dangerous trades, and extended it to all occupations, unless specifically excluded. The Act thus almost doubled the working population covered by the scheme, taking it to 13 million. The new Act covered manual workers, and all non-manual workers (including domestic workers), whose incomes were less than £250 per annum (on the assumption that those earning more would provide for themselves). Equally importantly, the Act provided for compensation for those industrial diseases which were itemized in the legislation.[99] It also reduced the period of waiting before compensation was paid to a week. 'If your clerk, crossing the Strand from the Temple to the Law Courts in the course of his employment, is run over by a bus and killed, you will have to compensate his dependants', the *Solicitors Journal* told its readers at the start of 1907: 'it is obvious, therefore that [...] every wise employer will protect himself by insurance'.[100]

The new Act did not create a German style state-administered system of compulsory insurance, but imposed the liability to pay on the employer, who was expected (but not compelled) to insure himself. In an effort to avoid litigation, the legislation provided for a system of joint committees of employers and workmen, and subsequent arbitration to settle disputes.[101] Employers were only permitted to contract out of the legislation if they subscribed to a scheme which the Chief Registrar of Friendly Societies considered as not less favourable to the workman than the statutory scheme. Few took this option.[102] In some industries, such as mining and building, employers relied on mutual insurance associations, considering commercial rates too high.[103] But most resorted to commercial firms, such as the Employers Liability Assurance Corporation, which grew rapidly after 1880.[104] Such firms were initially hampered by the lack of accurate actuarial

---

[98] 1905 Departmental Committee Evidence, qq. 154, 1427–39, 624.

[99] Bartrip, *Workmen's Compensation*, 47–58.

[100] (1907) 51 *Sol. J.* 166. Frederick Pollock wrote, 'In practice the real defendant is almost always the insurance company': *The Law of Torts* (10th edn, 1916), 113n.

[101] The use of joint committees was rare. For one example, see the 1904 Departmental Committee Report, p. 42.

[102] 1905 Departmental Committee Evidence, q. 502; 1904 Departmental Committee Report, pp. 103–4. Report of the Departmental Committee appointed to inquire into the System of Compensation for Injuries to Workmen, *PP* 1920 (Cd. 816), xxvi, 1, at p. 63.

[103] 1905 Departmental Committee Evidence, qq. 4182–7 (Ratcliffe Ellis); q. 5428 (Stanley George Bird). In 1910, 38 mutual associations paid out one-third of the compensation given in the seven industries required by statute to provide returns. Figures from the Holman Gregory report, *PP* 1920 (Cd. 816), xxvi, 1 at p. 14 and *PP* 1911 (Cd. 5896), lxxv, 743 at 3, and *PP* 1911 (121), lxxv, 539, at p. 204.

[104] There was some rivalry between commercial firms and mutual societies: see (1898) 42 *Sol. J.* 384.

information,[105] and attempts were made from the late nineteenth century to set an agreed tariff. By 1920, 48 companies operated on an agreed tariff under the umbrella of the Accident Offices Association (originally formed in 1898, and refounded in 1906), while 17 companies operated outside.[106]

Many trade unionists as well as some liberals argued for a system of compulsory insurance, given the risks to workmen whose employers had failed to take out insurance.[107] When the matter was considered in 1906, insurance companies proved uneasy at the idea of state supervision of their business, while the government shied away from a full state system.[108] In 1907, a Departmental Committee considered whether the Post Office should provide insurance under the Act for the very small employers now liable under it, who might otherwise remain uninsured. However, it rejected the idea as impractical and unprofitable,[109] recommending only that Post Offices should be used to publicize the liabilities under the Act, to advise people of the need to insure, and to publicize insurance companies. The question of whether to impose compulsory insurance on small employers was considered again in 1920, but was once more rejected.[110]

While many worried about the small employer who failed to insure, the insurance companies themselves were more concerned by the practices of small, under-capitalized firms which might undercut their business, and then become insolvent. To meet this concern, the 1904 Committee recommended that accident insurance companies should be required to make annual returns disclosing their liabilities and the assets they had to meet them. In 1907, an Employers Liability Insurance Companies Act was passed, which required these companies to deposit £20,000 with the Board of Trade and to give annual statistics to the Board. The effect of this legislation was to protect the interests of the larger insurers and to remove the risk of smaller insolvent ones.

In an era when Liberal legislators were turning their minds towards a system of national health and unemployment insurance, the workmen's compensation legislation thus became a form of welfare benefit outside the state structure, rather than a vehicle to improve workplace safety. The 1904 Departmental Committee reported that the Act had made no significant impact on safety. Indeed, magistrates had begun imposing nominal fines for infringements of factory legislation,

[105] Robinson, *Employers' Liability Assurance Corporation*, 26–8.

[106] *PP* 1920 (Cd. 816), xxvi, 1, at p. 12.

[107] 1904 Departmental Committee Report, p. 123.

[108] Hennock, *Social Reform*, 80 *et seq.*

[109] Report of the Departmental Committee appointed to consider whether the Post Office should provide facilities for Insurance under the Workmen's Compensation Acts: *PP* 1907 (Cd. 3568), lxviii, 163, at pp. 6–7.

[110] Compulsory insurance by employers was only introduced by the Employers' Liability (Compulsory Insurance) Act 1969.

since fines would simply be set off against compensation claims.[111] Although some claims were made that employers were induced to improve safety though the level of insurance premiums, the Holman Gregory report of 1920 showed that insurers in Britain largely relied on factory legislation to ensure safety, and did not look to the steps taken by the employer to improve safety in setting their rates.[112]

Workmen's Compensation legislation generated very little litigation, compared with the number of claims made.[113] Most cases were settled between trade unions and employers (or employers' associations), with resort to county court judges only being made where disputes over liability could not be resolved.[114] John Taylor of the Cotton Trade Assurance Association reported that, in 1903, only 17 out of 1605 cases he dealt with ended in court. 'I am in touch with the trade union secretaries all round', he noted, 'and we agree pretty well in settling these cases.'[115] The most prominent barrister in this field advised that employers should only litigate claims if the claim involved a new principle of liability, or if the claim was extortionate.[116] If the proportion of claimants who went to court was small, the numbers using this Act grew significantly in the first decade of the twentieth century, and by 1911 there were over 8000 cases arising from the Act in the county courts.[117] Few workers now resorted to the common law remedy offered by the Employer's Liability Act.[118] It was only worth suing for negligence if the aim was to punish a particularly negligent employer.[119] Moreover, once a

---

[111] *PP* 1904 Departmental Committee Report, at 21ff.

[112] *PP* 1920 (Cd. 816), xxvi, 1, at p. 65.

[113] Peter Bartrip has estimated that fewer than 1% of cases in which compensation was payable resulted in litigation: Bartrip, *Workmen's Compensation*, 24. This figure was that quoted to the 1904 Departmental Committee by C. E. Troup of the Home Office: 1905 Departmental Committee Evidence, q. 462. Published statistics are unreliable, for agreements between employers and workmen settling claims did not have to be registered and the Act made no provision for the collection of statistics.

[114] See 1905 Departmental Committee Evidence, qq. 456–99 (Richard Bell), q. 2332 (David Cummings).

[115] 1905 Departmental Committee Evidence, q. 4871. Cf. Evidence taken before the Holman Gregory Committee: *PP* 1920 (Cd. 908), xxvi, 87 at q. 5018 (H. E. Gray).

[116] Ruegg, *The Employers' Liability Act*, 25. As he put elsewhere, it was always worthwhile for a worker to claim compensation since he would be unable to pay costs if he lost—whereas even if the insurer won, it would be out of pocket. *Butterworth's Workmen's Compensation Cases*, vol. 3 (A. H. Ruess and D. Knocker, eds, 1910), v–vi.

[117] For the figures, see Bartrip *Workmen's Compensation*, pp. 20–5, 68–71.

[118] For the figures, see *ibid.*, 220.

[119] 1904 Departmental Committee Report, at 93; *PP* 1920 [Cd. 816], xxvi, 1 at p. 409. A workman who failed in an action of negligence also had to pay the costs out of any money later received as workmen's compensation. He had to apply at once to the judge trying the action: *Edwards* v. *Godfrey* [1899] 2 QB 333. Even if the workman's compensation claim failed, having made this election, he could not later commence an action under the Act: *Cribb* v. *Kynoch Ltd (No. 2)* [1908] 2 KB 551.

worker had sought compensation under the Workmen's Compensation Act, he could not (unless he was a minor)[120] sue for negligence.

The employer's liability to compensate his injured worker under the new legislation derived from the statute, rather than from the law of tort or contract.[121] Judges who had interpreted the 1880 Act restrictively, out of concern that the kind of broad approach favoured by Esher might have adverse effects on the wider common law of torts, were often happy to take a generous approach when dealing with a self-contained statutory regime. Common law rules were still applied, however, when employers sought indemnities from those they felt had been negligent in causing the accident. Thus, in *Cory & Son* v. *France, Fenwick & Co*, the Court of Appeal refused to allow an action of indemnity under s 6 of the 1906 Act to plaintiffs who had paid compensation to an workman injured in the course of his employment thanks to the negligence of the defendants' employee, since there was contributory negligence by the plaintiffs' employees.[122] More worrying for workmen was the decision in *Lees* v. *Dunkerley Brothers*, where the House of Lords ruled that an employer could seek indemnity for compensation paid to a worker from his fellow employee, whose breach of statutory factory regulations had caused the accident.[123]

'Accident'

The Act itself was poorly drafted, and insurers, keen to keep down their claims, were prepared to litigate over the precise degree of their liability where it was unclear. Since the compensation system was founded on the legal liability of employers as defined by a statute, which was interpreted by county court judges supervised by the Court of Appeal, rather than by an administrative system of tribunals, litigation over the meaning of the legislation remained plentiful. Disputes arose firstly over whether the workman had been injured in an industrial 'accident'. Despite the efforts of insurers to obtain narrow interpretations of the meaning of the legislation, the early twentieth century proved willing to apply the policy of the statute. For instance, in determining whether something was an accident, it was held in 1905 that courts should look 'from the standpoint of the person who suffered through it'.[124] This meant that compensation was not denied when the harm had been intentionally inflicted. Families of victims

---

[120] *Stephens* v. *Dudbridge Iron Works Co* [1904] 2 KB 225.

[121] See *Cooper & Crane* v. *Wright* [1902] AC 302 at 307–8, 20 *LQR* (1904) 117.

[122] *Cory & Son* v. *France, Fenwick & Co* [1911] 1 KB 114. Vaughan Williams LJ on the facts in any case found the defendant's employee's negligence was not a proximate cause of the accident.

[123] *Lees* v. *Dunkerley Brothers* [1911] AC 5 at 8.

[124] *Challis* v. *London and South Western Railway Co* [1905] 2 KB 154 at 156–7.

murdered at work were consequently able to claim compensation for their 'accidental' deaths.[125]

Many disputes arose when workers suffered physical injuries as a result of overexertion. At the turn of the century the courts, guided by the approach taken in cases arising from accident insurance claims, took the view that, for a worker to recover, the proximate cause of his injury had to have been a 'fortuitous event'. According to this view, no claim could be brought where a fatal rupture was triggered by a workman straining to turn a wheel.[126] But courts soon strained themselves to find a fortuitous element in an accident[127] and in 1903, in *Fenton* v. *Thorley*, the House of Lords held that the word 'accident' was to be read in its ordinary usage, to mean a mishap not expected or designed. It thereby granted a remedy to a plaintiff who ruptured himself by overexertion when turning a wheel. Lord Macnaghten also confirmed that the Act covered all physiological injuries sustained as a result of the work engaged in.[128] The fact that the victim's health might be fragile did not disentitle him to compensation. As Lord Loreburn ruled in 1910 (in awarding compensation where a worker had died after suffering an aneurism while tightening a nut), it was sufficient 'if it appears that the employment is one of the contributing causes' of the death.[129] Compensation could therefore be given if a workman died of a heart attack at work, provided that the death was connected with the work he was doing.[130] This generosity soon attracted criticism. In 1910, *The Times* accused the House of Lords of exhibiting

[125] *Nisbet* v. *Rayne and Burn* [1910] 2 KB 689; *Board of Management of Trim Joint District School* v. *Kelly* [1914] AC 667 (overruling *Murray* v. *John Denholm & Co* (1911) 2 SLT 125 where the Court of Session held that a strike breaker who was hurt when attacked by one of the strikers was not injured by an accident). But contrast *Blake* v. *Head* (1912) 5 BWCC 303.

[126] *Hensey* v. *White* [1901] 1 QB 481 (CA). The judgment of Collins LJ followed *Hamilton, Fraser & Co* v. *Pandorf & Co* (1887) 12 App Cas 518 (where the Lords held that rats gnawing through a pipe was an accident and peril of the sea) and *Winspear* v. *Accident Insurance Co* (1880) 6 QBD 42 (where a person who drowned while having an epileptic fit was held covered by an insurance policy which excluded liability for injuries caused by natural disease).

[127] In *Roper* v. *Greenwood & Sons* (1900) 83 LT 471, a woman who suffered a prolapse of the womb while lifting boxes could not recover as there had been no fortuitous event, but in *Timmins* v. *Leeds Forge Co* (1900) 83 LT 120, where a man ruptured himself while attempting to lift planks which had frozen together, the court found a fortuitous event in the freezing. Similarly, in *Boardman* v. *Scott and Whitworth* [1902] 1 KB 73, the Court of Appeal found that where a worker gave a heave to straighten an unevenly balanced weight he was carrying on his shoulders, there was a fortuitous event.

[128] *Fenton* v. *Thorley* [1903] AC 443 at 449, endorsing *Stewart* v. *Wilsons and Clyde Coal Co*, (1902) 5 F 120.

[129] *Clover, Clayton & Co* v. *Hughes* [1910] AC 242 at 245, 247.

[130] See *Barnabas* v. *Bersham Colliery Co* (1910) 103 LT 513; 4 BWCC 119; *Hawkins* v. *Powell's Tillery Steam Co Ltd* [1911] 1 KB 988.

'a subtly operating temptation to slide into a vein of uncritical generosity'.[131] Like many contemporaries, this newspaper felt that the House of Lords took a distinctly more liberal approach to the claims of injured workmen than the Court of Appeal,[132] though the difference in approaches may have been exaggerated.[133]

Judges did not limit compensation to physical injuries. In 1910, the Court of Appeal held that nervous shock which had resulted from witnessing a fatal accident to another miner was a 'personal injury by accident'. Cozens-Hardy MR ruled that '[i]t created such a shock that it produced a physiological effect, although there was no abrasion, or cut, or wound visible to the eye'.[134] Morever, despite the concerns in the legislation about potential malingering, judges were prepared to continue to give support where the worker was found to have a *bona fide* nervous disposition.[135] Judges in this era also began to consider that compensation might be awarded under the Act where workmen had committed suicide as a result of depression consequent on accidents.[136]

The broad view of what constituted an 'accident' taken by the House of Lords in *Fenton* v. *Thorley* led the Court of Appeal in 1903 to hold that it included 'the accidental catching of infection arising out of the work';[137] though two years later the same court held that where a disease was progressive and could not be associated with a single moment of causation, the worker was not covered by the Act.[138] In the same year, the Lords confirmed that the Act applied where anthrax was caught by a bacillus from wool alighting on the worker's body,[139] a decision which helped convince the government to include provisions in the 1906 Act giving compensation for six industrial diseases, including anthrax and lead and

[131] *The Times*, 20 July 1910, col. 11e. See also *The Times*, 18 March 1910, col. 15d (reproduced in 26 *LQR* (1910) 110. A medical examiner to the London and North Western Railway responded to the decision by pointing out that it would lead to corporations taking greater care to examine the health of those they employed. *The Times*, 29 March 1910, col. 5b. See also the leading article of 22 March 1910, col. 11f.

[132] See R. Stevens, *Law and Politics: The House of Lords as a Judicial Body* (1979), 164–70.

[133] Bartrip, *Workmen's Compensation*, 63 notes that the statistics of the Lords' decisions 'calls into question' the view that they were 'pro-employee', for only 46% of appeals were won by workmen.

[134] *Yates* v. *South Kirkby, &c. Collieries* [1910] 2 KB 538 at 540. The court followed the view taken in the insurance case of *Pugh* v. *The London, Brighton and South Coast Railway Co* [1896] 2 QB 248 (CA), which had also been discussed in *Clover, Clayton & Co* v. *Hughes* [1910] AC 242 at 248–9.

[135] *Eaves* v. *Blaenclydach Colliery Co* [1909] 2 KB 73 at 75.

[136] *Malone* v. *Cayzer, Irvine & Co* (1908) 1 BWCC 27; *Withers* v. *London, Brighton, and South Coast Railway Co* [1916] 2 KB 772 at 775, 778.

[137] *Higgins* v. *Campbell & Harrison; Turvey* v. *Brintons* [1904] 1 KB 328 at 335 (Collins MR).

[138] *Steel* v. *Cammell, Laird & Co* [1905] 2 KB 232. Cozens-Hardy LJ observed (at 237–8), 'The doctor called as a witness by the workman said that the paralysis was an "occupation" disease, which he should expect in a certain number of cases to follow on the work on which the workman was engaged. It was not unforeseen; it was not unexpected'.

[139] *Brintons* v. *Turvey* [1905] AC 230.

mercury poisoning.[140] However, the courts remained cautious when dealing with industrial diseases.[141] The onus still lay on the claimant to show that the disease he contracted was accidental: thus, the fact that a workman who had been asked to clean a mortuary at a fever hospital became ill within several hours with scarlet fever did not of itself prove that he contracted the illness by an accident.[142]

In defining accidents arising from employment, the courts thus often proved themselves generous, in ways which excited much popular comment. Thus, it was held that a seaman who contracted sunstroke while painting a ship had suffered an accident,[143] as had a trimmer on a steamer who contracted heat stroke.[144] Similarly, compensation was given where a workman got inflamed fingers from washing up for 12 hours in hot water with soda,[145] and where a worker died having caught an acute inflammation of the kidneys after spending 14 days in water cleaning a mill race.[146] At the same time, however, the very fact that it was unclear how the words of the Act would apply to particular fact situations meant that there was room to dispute liability, so that employers also had the chance to succeed. Thus, a baker's assistant who contracted frostbite from collecting accounts on a very cold day was not held entitled to compensation;[147] nor was a worker who developed eczema when employed to dip rings into a basin of bisulphide;[148] nor was a worker who spent five days inspecting cess pools, which resulted in his suffering ptomaine poisoning and death.[149] For as Lord Loreburn put it in 1912, 'these cases are difficult enough, and we are apt sometimes to forget that what is decided in the county court is much more often a question of fact than a question of law; and if it is a question of fact, then it is for the county court judge to decide it'.[150]

'Course of Employment'

Given that the defences of contributory negligence and voluntary assumption of risk were not available, employers sought to limit their liability by claiming that

---

[140] The 1903–4 departmental committee had opposed including diseases in the legislation, feeling that a separate system of sickness insurance was preferable: 1904 Departmental Committee Report, p. 45; but its recommendations were made after the decision of the Court of Appeal.

[141] See *Broderick* v. *The London County Council* [1908] 2 KB 807.

[142] *Martin* v. *Manchester Corporation* (1912) 106 LT 741 (CA). See also the rule in *Eke* v. *Hart-Dyke* [1910] 2 KB 677, that the applicant had to be able to indicate the time, day, circumstance, and place in which the accident occurred which occasioned the disease, by means of some definite event.

[143] *Morgan* v. *Owners of Steamship Zenaida* (1909) 25 TLR 446.

[144] *Ismay, Imrie & Co* v. *Williamson* [1908] AC 437.

[145] *Dotzauer* v. *Strand Palace Hotel* (1910) 3 BWCC 387.

[146] *Sheerin* v. *Clayton & Co* [1910] 2 IR 105.   [147] *Warner* v. *Couchman* [1912] AC 35.

[148] *Evans* v. *Dodd* (1912) 5 BWCC 305 (CA).   [149] *Eke* v. *Hart-Dyke* [1910] 2 KB 677.

[150] *Warner* v. *Couchman* [1912] AC 35 at 37.

the worker had acted outside his employment. The first question this raised was when work actually began and ended. The courts rejected employers' claims that a worker was only covered when actually at work.[151] Miners who were injured on trains provided by their employers to take them to work were given compensation.[152] In *Gane* v. *Norton Hill Colliery Co* (1909), a miner was seriously injured when, having ended his shift in the pit, he crossed some mine railway tracks, taking a short cut under some trucks which began to move. The Court of Appeal held he was entitled to compensation, since the course of a workman's employment did not end the moment he came up from the pit and since it was customary for workers to use this short cut.[153] By contrast, a strike-breaker who was attacked by strikers in a street on his way home from work was not covered by the Act.[154] The courts were often (though not always) generous to seamen returning from shore visits. In 1910, a majority of the House of Lords held in favour of the dependants of a seaman who had died when he had fallen from an insecure ladder while returning onto the ship at midnight, having gone ashore after work to buy some goods for himself and to drink. According to Loreburn LC, if a man went ashore with leave, he was protected, 'for the employment is continuous and implies leisure as well as labour'.[155]

A second question was whether the workman was doing something which was part of his employment in an improper way, or whether his improper conduct meant that he was acting outside his employment. In these cases, the courts were notably less generous to workers, since they were keen to ensure that they did not take careless risks while at work which the employer could not control. Thus,

---

[151] Workers who were injured during lunch breaks could thus claim compensation: *Blovelt* v. *Sawyer* [1904] 1 KB 271.

[152] See *Cremins* v. *Guest, Keen & Nettlefolds* [1908] 1 KB 469 (CA), holding that miners' employment began when they boarded a train provided on behalf of their employers to take them to work. See also *Holmes* v. *Great Northern Railway Co* (1900) 2 QB 409. By contrast, where miners had the choice whether to use a train, it was held that they were not covered: *Davies* v. *Rhymney Iron Co Ltd* (1900) 16 TLR 329. Nor was a worker covered who rode on a tram in defiance of orders, on his way home from a colliery: *Pope* v. *Hill's Plymouth Co* (1911) 5 BWCC 175. See also the pro-worker Irish decisions of *Nelson* v. *Belfast Corporation* (1908) 1 BWCC 158; *M'Kee* v. *Great Northern Railway Co* (1908) 42 Ir. LT 132.

[153] *Gane* v. *Norton Hill Colliery Co* [1909] 2 KB 539. The case was distinguished by the Lords which found for the employer in *Lancashire and Yorkshire Railway Co* v. *Highley* [1917] AC 352.

[154] *Poulton* v. *Kelsall* [1912] 2 KB 131: this worker, however, had a special contract with the employer to compensate him for any injury.

[155] *Moore (Pauper)* v. *Manchester Liners* [1910] AC 498 at 500. See also *Canavan* v. *Owners of the SS Universal* (1910) 3 BWCC 355 (CA); *Robertson* v. *Allan Brothers & Co (Liverpool and London)* (1908) 1 BWCC 172 (CA). Nevertheless, the question of whether the seaman was still acting in the course of employment was a matter of fact which could go against the claimant: see *McDonald* v. *Owners of SS Banana* [1908] 2 KB 926 (CA); *Biggart* v. *SS Minnesota (Owners of)* (1911) 5 BWCC 68 (CA); *Dixon* v. *SS Ambient (Owners of)* (1912) 5 BWCC 428 (CA).

in 1912, the Lords held that a boy employed at a colliery, who (in defiance of a prohibition) rode in a tub to get to his place of work instead of walking, and was killed when his head hit the roof of the mine, did not suffer an accident arising from his employment. As Lord Atkinson put it, while a peril which arose from the reckless or negligent manner in which an employee did his work could be said to be a risk incidental to his employment, this could not be said where a worker exposed himself to a risk unconnected with his work.[156] This approach was applied in 1913 by the Lords to a case where workers who were meant to stack sacks by hand decided to make use of a revolving shaft running near the ceiling to make their work easier. For Lord Dunedin, the men here had generated the peril themselves.[157] In general, the courts attempted to distinguish cases where workers violated their employers' orders while acting within the scope of employment, and when they engaged in conduct which they knew was well beyond their authority.[158] It could be a fine line to draw, and the House of Lords by the end of our period leaned towards a tough view.[159] Even where a worker thought that something was part of her job, if she had no reasonable grounds for this view, then she was not entitled to compensation,[160] unless the worker was helping the employer in the case of an emergency.[161]

Workers injured at work while engaged in their own purposes were denied compensation. Thus, an engine driver, who was killed when he crossed a siding to borrow a book, was not covered by the Act.[162] The Court of Appeal also took a narrow approach when accidents arose from the misbehaviour of fellow workers. Where the injury was caused by the tortious act of fellow workers, injured workmen could not recover.[163] It was argued that '[a]s it is no part of the sphere of the employment of workmen to indulge in "larking" or "fooling", an accident which

[156] *Barnes* v. *Nunnery Colliery Co* [1912] AC 44 at 49–50.

[157] *Plumb* v. *Cobden Flour Mills Co* [1914] AC 63.

[158] Contrast *Mawdsely* v. *West Leigh Colliery Co* (1911) 5 BWCC 80 (CA); *Whitehead* v. *Reader* [1901] 2 KB 48; and *Harding* v. *Brybddu Colliery Co* [1911] 2 KB 747 with *Lowe* v. *Pearson* [1899] 1 QB 261. See also *Marriott* v. *Brett and Beney* (1911) 5 BWCC 145 and *Smith* v. *Morrison* (1911) 5 BWCC 161 (CA).

[159] Contrast the Court of Appeal's more generous approach in *Watkins* v. *Guest, Keen and Nettlefolds* (1912) 5 BWCC 307 with the Lords' approach in *Herbert* v. *Samuel Fox & Co* [1916] AC 405 at 410–11.

[160] *Losh* v. *Richard Evans & Co* (1903) 19 TLR 142; discussed by Ruegg in 1905 Departmental Committee Evidence, qq. 693–7.

[161] *Rees* v. *Thomas* [1899] 1 QB 1015.

[162] *Reed* v. *Great Western Railway Co* [1909] AC 31. See also *Smith* v. *Lancashire and Yorkshire Railway* [1899] 1 QB 141.

[163] *Armitage* v. *Lancashire and Yorkshire Railway Co* [1902] 2 KB 178 (CA), where the plaintiff was injured when hit by a piece of iron thrown by one worker at another; *Fitzgerald* v. *Clarke & Son* [1908] 2 KB 796 (CA), where some workmen as a practical joke, hooked the plaintiff onto a crane, from which he fell, crippling him.

occurs through doing so does not arise out of the employment, even though the sufferer was not participating in it'.[164] Compensation was accordingly denied to a worker who lost an eye when he was accidentally hit by another worker who was defending himself from an assault by a third.[165] However, in 1915 the House of Lords (overturning the Court of Appeal) held that a boy, who was employed with others to pick stones out of coal running past on a belt and lost an eye when other boys began to throw stones at each other, could recover as the nature of the work was such as to impose a special risk of such harm.[166]

If the accident which hurt the worker did not result from any risk associated with the employment, compensation was not given. In *Craske* v. *Wigan*, a county court judge held that a seamstress who had injured her eye while sewing, when alarmed by a cockchafer which flew into the room, was not entitled to compensation, since the risk could not have been in the contemplation of the master or servant. Confirming this, Cozens-Hardy said that, in order to succeed, a plaintiff had to be able to say, '[t]he accident arose because of something I was doing in the course of my employment or because I was exposed by the nature of my employment to some peculiar danger'.[167] The Court of Appeal accordingly took a narrow approach in cases where employees were injured on bicycles, requiring the plaintiff to prove a greater risk was thrown on them than on other cyclists,[168] though in 1917 the Lords adopted the broader Scottish approach, which accepted that merely riding a bicycle at work generated risks.[169]

Compensation

Between 1899 and 1905, the average sum given in cases of death was £177–3s, some £14–3s more on average than was paid in informal settlements. The legislation provided for payment to dependants, and much litigation turned on who constituted a dependant. Prior to 1906, illegitimate children were excluded as a matter of law. Where spouses no longer cohabited, it was a question of fact whether the survivor was a dependant. In the first decade of the century, the courts were often

---

[164] A. Elliott, *The Workmen's Compensation Act 1906* (7th edn, 1915), 85.

[165] *Shaw* v. *The Wigan Coal and Iron Co Ltd* (1909) 3 BWCC 81 (CA).

[166] *Clayton* v. *Hardwick Coilliery* (1915) 9 BWCC 136.

[167] *Craske* v. *Wigan* [1909] 2 KB 635 at 638. See the criticism of the narrowness of this formulation in *Mrs Margaret Thom or Simpson (Pauper)* v. *Sinclair* [1917] AC 127 at 141–2 (Sc).

[168] See *Pierce* v. *Provident Clothing and Supply Co* [1911] 1 KB 997; *Dennis* v. *A. J. White & Co* [1916] 2 KB 1; *Read* v. *Baker* [1916] 1 KB 927; *Ince* v. *Reigate Education Committee* [1916] 2 KB 671.

[169] *Dennis* v. *A. J. White and Co* [1917] AC 479 adopting the views of *M'Neice* v. *Singer Sewing Machine Co* 1911 SC 12.

generous to claimants who had not seen their husbands for some time.[170] Where a family member—such as a child—contributed to a common fund, the family could be seen as dependants, entitled to a claim, even though they did not rely on this money.[171] The fact that the family could maintain itself without the child's help was not considered relevant, provided that the child had made a net payment into the family fund.[172]

The average weekly amount paid in case of total incapacity was 11s 9d, and the average for partial incapacity was 10s 2d.[173] Employers and insurers seeking to keep down costs were keen to seek restrictive interpretations of the law. In determining who was entitled to payment, the Court of Appeal was initially persuaded that only workers who had been in a job for two weeks were covered by the Act, since only in such cases could an 'average' wage be calculated on the basis of which to award compensation.[174] However, in 1902, the House of Lords overturned this.[175] Employers also challenged the policy of county court judges who routinely gave the injured workman the maximum compensation, to give a sum as close to his wages as possible. In 1904, the House of Lords held that judges were not entitled to do this, but had to exercise their discretion.[176] In the same year, the Departmental Committee criticized the generosity of some county court judges, taking the view that the loss should be shared between worker and employer, to avoid an unfair share of the burden falling on the employer.[177] In 1911, the Court of Appeal upheld Judge Lumley Smith's view, that in calculating the sums to be paid, the court should award half the difference between the rates of pay the workman had been 'able to earn' before and after the accident.[178]

The rate of compensation paid could also be revised as the injured worker began to recover. Insurers were worried that workers continued to be paid for many weeks

[170]   *Coulthard* v. *Consett Iron Co* [1905] 2 KB 869; *Stanland* v. *North-Eastern Steel Co (No. 2)* [1907] 2 KB 425 n; *Williams* v. *Ocean Coal Co* [1907] 2 KB 422. In *New Monckton Colliery Co* v. *Davies* [1900] AC 358, the House of Lords held a 20-year absence too long; and it led to a less generous approach being taken: see *Lee* v. *SS Bessie (Owners of)* [1912] 1 KB 83.

[171]   See *Main Colliery Co* v. *Davies* [1900] AC 358. But in *Tamworth Colliery Co* v. *Hall* [1911] AC 665, it was held that a father did not depend on the income of his son whose income was only sufficient to cover his own costs. See also the optimistic argument attempted in *Rees* v. *Penrikyber Navigation Colliery Co* [1903] 1 KB 259.

[172]   *Howells* v. *Vivian & Sons* (1901) 85 LT 529 (CA); 18 TLR 36; *French* v. *Underwood* (1903) 19 TLR 416 (CA).

[173]   Bartrip, *Workmen's Compensation*, 20.

[174]   *Lysons* v. *Andrew Knowles & Sons* [1900] 1 QB 780 (CA) and *Stuart* v. *Nixon & Bruce* [1900] 2 QB 95 (CA).

[175]   *Lysons* v. *Andrew Knowles & Sons* [1901] AC 79.

[176]   *Webster* v. *Sharp & Co* [1904] 1 KB 219, [1905] AC 284.

[177]   1904 Departmental Committee Report, p. 83.

[178]   *Humphreys* v. *City of London Electric Lighting Co* (1911) 4 BWCC 275 at 276.

after they had recovered.[179] Against this, workers' representatives alleged sharp practice by insurers, such as pestering injured workers to see if they were recovering, and cutting payments to workers still incapacitated.[180] Employers were also accused of rehiring disabled workers at their old rate, to prove that they had the capacity to earn their full able-bodied wage, in order to evade payments when the term of work was over; and to dispute compensation claims if the injured worker refused the job. The Court of Appeal was unsympathetic to these attempts.[181]

There was also concern about employers who wanted disabled workers to settle for lump sums rather than weekly payments. Employers were given the option under the legislation to redeem their weekly payments after six months by paying a lump sum to the worker.[182] Few chose to do this, since the courts were bound to calculate the sum due on an actuarial basis, which meant that the sum awarded might exceed the maximum awarded in cases of death.[183] Insurers were active, however, in sending agents to persuade workers to sign away their claims for a small sum.[184] While county court judges were unhappy at the practice, the Court of Appeal confirmed its validity. Thus, in 1912, a bricklayer who earned 35s a week accepted a payment of 35s compensation, although without signing the receipt offered. The worker claimed that he refused to sign this since he did not want to accept the money as a final settlement. The county court judge felt that he had intended to take the money on the employer's terms and had omitted his signature to trick the employer. In the Court of Appeal, Cozens-Hardy MR held that there was nothing to prevent an adult worker coming to any agreement with his employer before the entering a claim, and so the case was dismissed.[185]

Insurers also sought to reduce the payments to workmen on the grounds that they were capable of getting work. If a worker was considered capable of doing light work, but admitted not to having looked for it, judges might reduce compensation.[186] The courts were also prepared to support the employers' viewpoint

---

[179] 1905 Departmental Committee Evidence, q. 1345 (A. H. Ruegg).

[180] *Ibid.*, q. 3416 (J. N. Bell), q. 2345 (D. C. Cummings).

[181] *Warwick Steamship Co* v. *Callaghan* (1912) 5 BWCC 283; *Eyre* v. *Houghton Main Colliery* (1910) 3 BWCC 250.

[182] Schedule 1, para 17. It was held in *Calico Printers Association* v. *Higham* [1912] 1 KB 93 that this payment was only to be made where the disability was proven to be permanent.

[183] Insurers therefore wanted a maximum sum imposed and opposed any idea that the worker should be able to compel redemption: 1904 Departmental Committee Report, at pp. 86ff. In *Victor Mills Ltd* v. *Shackleton* [1912] 1 KB 22, the Court of Appeal held that where a lump sum was awarded, the county court judge could not deduct moneys paid to the worker before the award.

[184] 1905 Departmental Committee Evidence, q. 1372 (Ruegg); q. 2986 (G. H. Copley).

[185] *Ryan* v. *Hartley* [1912] 2 KB 150.

[186] *Anglo-Australian Steam Navigation Co* v. *Richards* (1911) 4 BWCC 247. Cozens-Hardy MR observed of the plaintiff (at 249) that 'he seems to have taken the view that he is entitled for the rest of his life to do no work'.

when they laid off disabled men owing to slackness of work, since (as Cozens-Hardy MR put it) 'the employer does not guarantee the state of the labour market'.[187] For the court, the incapacity to get work had to result from the accident, and not from slackness of trade. The Court of Appeal also held that where a worker stopped working, following a doctor's advice after suffering a rupture in an accident, the county court judge was not to consider whether he had acted reasonably in following the advice, but whether he would be able to earn money at any other work.[188]

---

[187] *Dobby* v. *Wilson Pease & Co* (1909) 2 BWCC 370. Similarly, a disabled worker dismissed by his employer for misconduct could not claim higher compensation, since his incapacity to work now was his own fault: *Hill* v. *Ocean Coal Co* (1909) 3 BWCC 29. But in *W. White & Sons* v. *Harris* (1910) 4 BWCC 39, it was held that one act of misconduct did not justify dismissal and so the worker could claim higher compensation.

[188] *Evans* v. *Cory Brothers & Co* (1912) 5 BWCC 272.

V

Intentional and Economic Torts

TRADITIONAL tort doctrine taught that a person who intentionally performed an unlawful act which harmed another was liable for the damage suffered. In the second half of the nineteenth century, judges and jurists sought to extend this law, to hold those who performed otherwise lawful acts liable if they had done so with the intention of harming others, and with no justification. This development was part of the late nineteenth-century attempt to put the law of tort on a set of broad, theoretical principles.

As with the development of the tort of negligence, W. B. Brett was the leading judge who sought to develop a broad theory. Brett, whose approach to law was informed by a strong sense of morality, focused primarily on the intentions of the person inflicting harm. He took the view that any act of malice should be held actionable, if it resulted in harm, whether that harm was physical or economic. But Brett's view of malice was worryingly wide, and seemed to give the courts great discretion to determine what conduct was fair or unfair. Frederick Pollock, the first treatise writer to handle this question, found the concept of malice increasingly troubling, and focused his attention more on the notion of justification. For Pollock, every harm intentionally inflicted was *prima facie* a tort. But it could be justified if it was inflicted in the course of the defendant's exercise of his common rights. In determining liability, the courts would not look at the defendant's motives, but would follow rules which had established the ambit of common rights.

The debates over the nature and scope of intentional torts were largely conducted in the 1890s and 1900s in a series of cases dealing with harms inflicted by the use of economic power. Both Brett's and Pollock's vision promised to give the courts a far greater role in policing economic activity, Brett's at trial level, and Pollock's in letting the courts set out the contours of justification. But neither view was adopted by the judiciary. In a highly political area of law, early twentieth-century judges wished at the same time to avoid interfering in business competition and to prevent trade unions from exerting their economic power. This led them to develop doctrines of economic tort which were often inconsistent, and where the outcome of cases often depended on whether the judges approved or disapproved of the economic activity in question.

1. MALICE AND INTENT IN EARLY
NINETEENTH-CENTURY LAW

In determining whether a tort had been committed, the common law courts generally regarded motives as irrelevant. Defendants were liable in trespass for every unauthorized intentional interference with a man's person or his property, regardless of motive.[1] For instance, in cases of false imprisonment, it was only necessary to show that the defendant had done something which was intended to deprive the plaintiff completely of his liberty of movement.[2] If this was done, it was for the defendant to show that he had good legal grounds for his actions. The fact that he acted in good faith was no justification. A constable who arrested and detained a person in good faith on an unfounded charge was hence liable, as was a constable who took charge of a plaintiff wrongfully arrested by another.[3] An innkeeper who refused to allow a guest to leave was not held to have a justification in the fact that the guest had refused to pay his bill.[4] Similarly, where a person had been assaulted, either by being hit or handled roughly, the defendant had to justify his action, by claiming that it had been done in self-defence, in defence of his property, or in execution of some lawful authority, such as making an arrest. It was no assault to lay hands on a person who had been requested to leave, and who had refused to do so, unless excessive force was used.[5] In determining whether a justification existed in such cases, the defendant's motive was irrelevant.[6]

The question of motive became relevant if it was unclear whether a plaintiff's rights had been infringed. For example, it was not always clear whether an assault had taken place. At common law, '[e]very laying of hands on the person of another, and every blow or push, constitutes an assault and trespass, in respect of which an action for damages is maintainable, unless the act can be justified'.[7] Even a threat—or 'attempt or offer' to do a person corporal harm—could amount

---

[1] As has been seen, in early nineteenth-century road accident cases, the courts did not require the defendant to show an intention to harm the plaintiff, but merely that the harm had flowed from his deliberate act. However, from the 1820s to *Holmes* v. *Mather* (1875) LR 10 Ex 261, judges leaned to the view that liability in trespass required a 'wilful' act, intended to interfere with the plaintiff's rights. See pp. 906, 970.

[2] The action required a 'restraint within some limits defined by a will or power exterior to our own', it was not enough simply to stop someone from going where they wanted to: *Bird* v. *Jones* (1845) 7 Q.B. 742 at 744.

[3] *Griffin* v. *Coleman* (1859) 4 H. & N. 265. See also *Cobbett* v. *Grey* (1850) 4 Exch. 729.

[4] *Sunbolf* v. *Alford* (1838) 3 M. & W. 248 at 254. See also *Warner* v. *Riddiford* (1858) 4 C.B. N.S. 180; *Grainger* v. *Hill* (1838) 4 Bing. N.C. 212.

[5] *Wheeler* v. *Whiting* (1840) 9 Car. & P. 262 at 265.

[6] *Oakes* v. *Wood* (1837) 2 M. & W. 791.

[7] C. G. Addison, *Wrongs and their Remedies* (2nd edn, 1864), 481.

to assault.[8] But not every touch or threat amounted to trespass. It was not an assault to push one's way through a crowd, or to tap a person on his shoulder to attract his attention.[9] Whether a touch constituted an assault or not depended on the defendant's intentions.[10] Where the defendant was someone purporting to exercise authority over the plaintiff, juries were asked whether the act was done with the intention of exerting that authority. If it was, the next question would be whether the defendant had a right so to act. By these criteria, a tap on the shoulder to effect an arrest or a haircut given to a pauper by a parish officer could constitute an assault, if unauthorized.[11] Where the defendant was not purporting to exert authority over the plaintiff, juries looked more closely at his state of mind. Where no physical contact had taken place, they had to be persuaded that the defendant had offered a 'threat of violence exhibiting an intention to assault'.[12] Where contact had taken place, juries were to consider whether the defendant's act was 'hostile'.[13] By these definitions, a tap on the shoulder to gain attention was not an assault; but rushing towards a man, with a fist poised to punch, was.

Towards the end of our period, some jurists preferred to focus not on the defendant's state of mind, but on the plaintiff's, asking whether he had consented, expressly or impliedly, to the act.[14] For they were aware that assaults could be committed where the act performed had not been intended to be hostile, but which had nevertheless not been consented to, as where a surgeon vaccinated a patient without consent. This was not the approach taken for most of our period, however. Defendants in the first half of the nineteenth century were unable to raise the plea that the plaintiff had consented to the assault, for the view was taken that 'it is a manifest contradiction in terms to say that the defendant assaulted the plaintiff by his permission'.[15] For most courts, it was the

---

[8] Eighteenth-century jurists distinguished between assault and battery by holding the former to require only a threat and the latter 'any injury, however small, actually inflicted'. M. Bacon, *A New Abridgment of the Law*, 7 vols (6th edn, Dublin, 1793), i: 154. Nineteenth-century writers distinguished between them by concentrating of the degree of force used: battery was where 'a man is actually struck or touched in a violent, angry, rude or insolent manner': Addison, *Wrongs and their Remedies* (2nd edn, 1864), 483.

[9] *Cole* v. *Turner* (1704) 6 Mod. 149; *Wiffin* v. *Kincard* (1807) 2 B. & P. N.R. 471.

[10] '[A] Man's Intention must operate with his Act in constituting an Assault': Bacon, *Abridgment* (6th edn, 1793), i: 154.

[11] *Forde* v. *Skinner* (1830) 4 Car. & P. 239.

[12] *Read* v. *Coker* (1853) 13 C.B. 850 at 860. See also *Stephens* v. *Myers* (1830) 4 Car. & P. 349; *Blake* v. *Barnard* (1840) 9 Car. & P. 626.

[13] *Coward* v. *Baddeley* (1859) 4 H. & N. 478.

[14] See J. F. Clerk & W. H. B. Lindsell, *The Law of Torts* (1889), 131.

[15] *Christopherson* v. *Bare* (1848) 11 Q.B. 473 at 477 (Lord Denman J.). In trespass to land cases, defendants did confess and avoid by a plea of consent.

defendant's improper motive—his malicious state of mind—which rendered a mere touch an assault.

The question of motive was also relevant in a number of other areas where the defendant had exercised his rights in a malicious way, and thereby interfered with the plaintiff's rights. The first was where returning officers denied the plaintiff his right to vote.[16] In 1819, Abbott CJ told a jury that they were to consider whether the High Bailiff's conduct in denying the plaintiff his vote in a parliamentary election 'proceeded from an improper motive, or from an honest intention to discharge his duty acting under professional advice'. He explained that returning officers had to exercise judgment and discretion in the admission or rejection of votes, and if they were held liable for an honest mistake, no officer could 'discharge his duty without great peril and apprehension'.[17] Abbott's view was acted on in 1857 in *Tozer* v. *Child*, a case concerning a parish election. At the trial, Campbell CJ told the jury that the plaintiff had to show the act to have been malicious. This could be proved 'not only by evidence of personal hostility or spite, but by evidence of any other corrupt or improper motive'.[18] Parallel to these cases were those where officers acted beyond the scope of their authority, or exercised the authority they had in a malicious way.[19]

A second area where motive was relevant was in cases of malicious prosecution and abuse of legal process.[20] An action could be brought against a defendant who had instituted legal proceedings maliciously and without reasonable cause in a criminal court or in bankruptcy or liquidation proceedings. It could also be brought against a defendant who had issued execution against a judgment debtor after the debt had been satisfied.[21] Besides showing that the proceedings had failed, the plaintiff had to show firstly that the facts known to the defendant when instituting the proceedings did not provide him with a probable cause[22]

---

[16] The remedy derived from *Ashby* v. *White* (1703) 2 Ld. Raym. 938.

[17] *Cullen* v. *Morris* (1819) 2 Stark. 577 at 587–8. Cf. *Williams* v. *Lewis* (1797) Peake Add. Cas. 157 at 164 and Erle CJ's comments in *Kemp* v. *Neville* (1861) 10 C.B. N.S. 523 at 551.

[18] *Tozer* v. *Child* (1857) 7 E. & B. 377 at 379. See also *Pryce* v. *Belcher* (1847) 4 C.B. 866; cf. Blackburn J.'s observations during argument in *Pease* v. *Chaytor* (1863) 3 B. & S. 620 at 628.

[19] e.g. *Sutherland* v. *Murray* (1783), described in *Johnstone* v. *Sutton* (1785) 1 T.R. 510 at 538. The latter case, however, determined that an inferior officer could not sue his superior for imprisoning him for disobeying an order. Cf. also *Warden* v. *Bailey* (1811) 4 Taunt. 67.

[20] See J. Getzler, 'The Fate of the Civil Jury in Late Victorian England: Malicious Prosecution as a Test case', in J. W. Cairns and G. McLeod, *The Dearest Birth Right of the People of England: The Jury in the History of the Common Law* (Oxford, 2002), 217–37.

[21] *Churchill* v. *Siggers* (1852) 3 E. & B. 929; cf. *Gilding* v. *Eyre* (1861) 10 C.B. N.S. 592. It could not, however, be brought against those who commenced ordinary civil proceedings, for it was felt that unsuccessful civil litigation would not damage a person's standing: *Quartz Hill Gold Mining Co* v. *Eyre* (1883) 11 QBD 674 at 689 (Bowen LJ).

[22] A probable cause was equivalent to a *prima facie* case, rather than sufficient evidence as would secure a conviction. Mere suspicion was not regarded as a probable cause: see *Clements* v. *Ohrly* (1848) 2 Car. & K. 686.

for taking legal action.[23] The crucial question was what the defendant knew and believed. It was not sufficient to show that the true facts showed that no probable cause existed, unless it was also shown that the defendant himself knew those facts.[24] By contrast, if the true facts showed that a probable cause existed, a plaintiff could still succeed, if he showed that the defendant did not believe that he had a probable cause to sue.[25] Determining whether the defendant had a probable cause for instituting proceedings was partly a question of fact, and partly one of law. It was for the jury to find the facts which the defendant knew, but for the judge to rule whether they amounted to a probable cause to prosecute.[26] The line between the function of the judge and that of the jury was a fine one to draw, and many judges preferred to leave such questions as far as possible to the jury.[27]

Secondly, the plaintiff had to persuade the jury that the defendant's motive in prosecuting had been malicious.[28] This was wholly a question of fact. The jury was not bound to infer that the defendant's conduct had been malicious from the determination that he had no probable cause to institute proceedings.[29] If a person believed that he had a probable cause, when as a matter of law he did not, the jury could acquit him, since he lacked a malicious motive. Conversely, it was not necessary for the jury to be convinced that the defendant had been motivated by spite, for a malicious motive was defined simply as an 'improper' one. As Alderson B. put it in 1854, '[a]ny motive other than that of simply instituting a prosecution for the purpose of bringing a person to justice, is a malicious motive

---

[23] Hawkins J. defined 'reasonable and probable cause to be, an honest belief in the guilt of the accused based upon a full conviction, founded upon reasonable grounds, of the existence of a state of circumstances, which, assuming them to be true, would reasonably lead any ordinarily prudent and cautious man, placed in the position of the accuser, to the conclusion that the person charged was probably guilty of the crime imputed': *Hicks* v. *Faulkner* (1878) 8 QBD 167 at 171. Equally, if the defendant did not at the time of the charge know of facts which would have constituted a probable cause, he could not avail himself of them later: *Delegal* v. *Highley* (1837) 3 Bing. N.C. 950.

[24] The onus of showing what the defendant knew could be a difficult one to discharge: see *Abrath* v. *The North Eastern Railway Co* (1883) 11 QBD 79, 11 QBD 440 (CA).

[25] See *Broad* v. *Ham* (1839) 5 Bing. N.C. 722.

[26] *Johnstone* v. *Sutton* (1785) 1 T.R. 510 at 545, Lords Mansfield and Loughborough had held that the question of probable cause was a mixed matter of law and fact: for 'whether the circumstances alleged to shew it probable, or not probable, are true and existed, is a matter of fact; but whether, supposing them true, they amount to a probable cause, is a question of law'. See also *Davis* v. *Russell* (1829) 5 Bing. 354 at 365; *Willans* v. *Taylor* (1829) 6 Bing. 183; *Mitchell* v. *Jenkins* (1833) 5 B. & Ad. 588; *Turner* v. *Ambler* (1847) 10 Q.B. 252.

[27] The doctrine that the question of probable cause was one for the judge to decide was regretted by the House of Lords in *Lister* v. *Perryman* (1870) LR 4 HL 521, which saw this issue as one too closely bound into matters of fact to be appropriate for judicial decision. For a case showing the court's desire to leave much to the jury, see *Quartz Hill Consolidated Gold Mining Co* v. *Eyre* (1883) 11 QBD 674.

[28] 'Malice alone is not sufficient, because a person actuated by the plainest malice may nevertheless have a justifiable reason for prosecution': *Willans* v. *Taylor* (1829) 6 Bing. 183 at 186 (Tindal CJ).

[29] *Mitchell* v. *Jenkins* (1833) 5 B. & Ad. 588.

on the part of the person who acts in that way'. This meant that 'the prosecution of a person for the purpose of frightening others' might be regarded as malicious, even if brought for probable cause.[30] Often, however, the inference of malice was easy to make, once the jury had found that the defendant had no grounds to believe he had a probable cause of action.[31]

The third area where malice was relevant was in defamation. Although malice appeared here to be the gist of the action, and was always charged in the pleadings,[32] it was confirmed in 1825 that in ordinary actions for uttering defamatory words, the allegation of malice was a formality which needed no proof. 'Malice in common acceptation means ill will against a person', Bayley J. explained, 'but in its legal sense it means a wrongful act, done intentionally, without just cause or excuse.'[33] It was only necessary to prove malice 'in fact' where the defamatory words were spoken or published in privileged communications. Where a communication was made 'in the discharge of some public or private duty, whether legal or moral, or in the conduct of [a person's] own affairs, in matters where his interest is concerned', then 'the occasion prevents the inference of malice, which the law draws from unauthorized communications, and affords a qualified defence depending upon the absence of actual malice'.[34] It was for the defendant to show that his communication was a privileged one;[35] but if he did so, the onus was put on the plaintiff to prove actual malice.[36] As in malicious prosecution cases, judges stressed that malice need not mean spite, but could mean 'any indirect motive, other than a sense of duty'.[37] If a defendant used a privileged communication to gratify his anger, 'he uses the occasion not for the reason which makes the occasion privileged, but for an indirect and wrong motive'.[38]

[30] *Stevens* v. *Midland Counties Railway Co* (1854) 10 Exch. 352 at 356. See also Cave J.'s definition quoted in *Abrath* v. *The North Eastern Railway Co* (1883) 11 QBD 440 at 444. In *Brown* v. *Hawkes* [1891] 2 QB 718 at 722, Cave J. ruled, 'malice, in its widest and vaguest sense, has been said to mean any wrong or indirect motive; and malice can be proved, either by shewing what the motive was and that it was wrong, or by shewing that the circumstances were such that the prosecution can only be accounted for by imputing some wrong or indirect motive to the prosecutor'.

[31] *Haddrick* v. *Heslop* (1848) 12 Q.B. 267.

[32] See *Smith* v. *Richardson* (1737) Willes 20 at 24.

[33] *Bromage* v. *Prosser* (1825) 4 B. & C. 247 at 256. For the case and its importance, see P. Mitchell, 'Malice in Defamation' (1998) 114 *LQR* 638–64. For the difficulties in determining the extent of malice in law, see Vol. XIII, Pt 5, Ch. I.

[34] Parke B. in *Toogood* v. *Spyring* (1834) 1 C. M. & R. 181 at 193.

[35] *Huntley* v. *Ward* (1859) 6 C.B. N.S. 514. For nineteenth-century debates about the scope of privilege, see Vol. XIII, Pt 5, Ch. I.

[36] *Somerville* v. *Hawkins* (1851) 10 C.B. 583. See also *Spill* v. *Maule* (1869) LR 4 Ex 232.

[37] *Dickson* v. *The Earl of Wilton* (1859) 1 F. & F. 419 at 427. See also *Wright* v. *Woodgate* (1835) 2 C. M. & R. 573 at 577.

[38] *Clark* v. *Molyneux* (1877) 3 QBD 237 at 246–7. See also *Laughton* v. *The Lord Bishop of Sodor and Man* (1872) LR 4 PC 495 at 505; *Royal Aquarium and Summer and Winter Garden Society* v. *Parkinson* [1892] 1 QB 431.

The fourth area where malice mattered was where the defendant had slandered the plaintiff's title to property, or had otherwise spoken words intending to influence a person dealing with the plaintiff to his detriment. In such cases, the plaintiff had to prove both that he had suffered special damage from the statement, and that the defendant had acted with malice, intending to injure him.[39] Such actions were sometimes brought against people intervening at auctions, passing information to purchasers which had the effect of diminishing the price which the plaintiff's property would fetch. Where the intervention was made by someone exercising an office, such as a surveyor of highways, the jury had to consider 'whether the defendant was actuated by a malicious intention to injure the plaintiff, and was not acting under mere misconception of the power and authority vested in him by the statute'.[40] The courts dealing with slander of title cases sometimes invoked the language used in malicious prosecution cases, asking the jury to consider whether the defendant had any probable cause for claiming an infirmity in the plaintiff's title, and if he did, whether his statement had been made with malice.[41] This same language was used in cases where the plaintiff's title to property had not been slandered, but where false words were spoken which damaged him. In *Green* v. *Button*, for instance, the defendant falsely told the plaintiff's supplier not to deliver goods, as he claimed to have a lien on them. Parke B. categorized the claim as one 'for a false and malicious representation', and held 'that the action is maintainable, though the defendant makes a claim of right, if it be made maliciously, and without reasonable or probable cause, and the special damage accrues from the claim so made'.[42]

2. ECONOMIC TORTS

The cases just discussed show that the question whether the defendant's actions had been malicious was raised only in a limited number of areas of tort law. The question was primarily relevant in the four classes of cases where non-physical damage had been suffered as a consequence of behaviour by the defendant, which would not have been actionable absent malice. The common law also offered protection to the plaintiff's economic interests in a number of other areas, where harms had been inflicted. Here, the question of the defendant's motives was not seen as relevant. However, where the harm was a purely economic one, the courts took the view that the defendant's conduct had to have been intentional.

[39] *Hargrave* v. *Le Breton* (1769) 4 Burr. 2422; *Smith* v. *Spooner* (1810) 3 Taunt. 246, *Pitt* v. *Donovan* (1813) 1 M. & S. 639; *Pater* v. *Baker* (1847) 3 C.B. 831; *Brook* v. *Rawl* (1849) 4 Exch. 521.
[40] *Pater* v. *Baker* (1847) 3 C.B. 831 at 861.
[41] *Ibid.* at 868–9.
[42] *Green* v. *Button* (1835) 2 C. M. & R. 707 at 715.

The first remedy by which economic interests were protected was the action of deceit, which developed out of the 1789 decision of *Pasley* v. *Freeman*.[43] The action of deceit had long been used in cases where the defendant had induced the plaintiff to enter into a contract with him, by making false assertions. *Pasley* extended the remedy to situations where the defendant had induced the plaintiff to enter into a contract with, or give credit to, a third person, who turned out to be uncreditworthy. The doctrine was controversial from the outset, since it enabled 'a man to do that indirectly, which the statute of frauds expressly forbids to be done in direct terms, to guarantee the debt of another'.[44] To prevent this, legislation was passed in 1829, stating that no action could be brought on misrepresentations of a person's creditworthiness unless they had been put in writing.[45]

To succeed in this action, it had to be shown that the defendant had knowingly made a false statement of fact, which he intended the plaintiff to act upon. The comments did not have to be addressed directly to the plaintiff to be actionable, provided it was within the defendant's contemplation that they would be communicated to and acted on by him.[46] Since the gist of the action was fraud, it also had to be shown that the person making the statement knew (or believed) that it was false. The central issue in deceit was the honesty of the speaker's belief. If he honestly believed his statement to be true, he was not liable, however unreasonable his belief may have been. On the other hand, if he did not believe in the truth of his statement, he was liable, even if the statement was one about his own intentions.[47] The speaker's motive was irrelevant. For as Tindal CJ put it in 1830, '[t]he law will infer an improper motive if what the defendant says is false within his own knowledge, and is the occasion of damage to the plaintiff'. A person who made a false statement without in any way intending the recipient to be damnified by it was therefore fully liable for damage which ensued.[48] Although some judges and jurists sought to hold that liability could attach to negligent misrepresentations, or 'legal'—as opposed to 'moral'—fraud, it was confirmed

[43] *Pasley* v. *Freeman* (1789) 3 T.R. 51.

[44] *Hutchinson* v. *Bell* (1809) 1 Taunt. 558 at 564 (Mansfield CJ); cf. *Tapp* v. *Lee* (1803) 3 B. & P. 367 at 370. See also Lord Eldon's criticism in *Evans* v. *Bicknell* (1801) 6 Ves. 174 at 186–7.

[45] 9 Geo. IV c. 14, c. 6.

[46] *Langridge* v. *Levy* (1837) 2 M. & W. 519; *Pilmore* v. *Hood* (1838) 5 Bing. N.C. 97. See also the comments of Quain J. in *Swift* v. *Winterbotham* (1873) LR 8 QB 244 at 253, citing *Bedford* v. *Bagshaw* (1859) 29 LJ Ex 59.

[47] As Bowen LJ put it in *Edgington* v. *Fitzmaurice* (1885) 29 Ch D 459 at 483, '[t]he state of a man's mind is as much a fact as the state of his digestion'.

[48] *Foster* v. *Charles* (1830) 6 Bing. 396 at 403. See also *Polhill* v. *Walter* (1832) 3 B. & Ad. 114 at 123; *Corbett* v. *Brown* (1831) 8 Bing. 33.

in *Derry* v. *Peek*[49] that there could be no action at common law for negligent misstatements.[50]

The common law recognized a second kind of economic tort through the action of trespass *per quod servitium amisit*,[51] which allowed a master to recover for financial losses arising from wrongs depriving him of his servant's work. This remedy was used in three situations: where the defendant had debauched the plaintiff's daughter, leaving her pregnant; where he had physically harmed the plaintiff's servant, rendering him unfit for work; and where he had enticed a servant to leave his employment. The first kind of these actions was an 'an action *sui generis*'[52] to compensate parents for the corruption of their daughters,[53] masquerading as an economic tort. The legal foundation of this action was loss of the service provided by the daughter, and not the fact that the family was financially harmed by the arrival of an illegitimate child.[54] A parent could only recover if the daughter was 'in some way or another his servant'.[55] Nevertheless, the courts took a broad interpretation of what constituted service;[56] and held it unnecessary to show that the seducer had been aware of the service on which the plaintiff's action depended.[57] Moreover, the courts allowed juries to give damages for the distress caused to the parent as well as the economic loss.[58] However, since it was necessary to show that the daughter was a member of the household, providing service there,[59] the remedy could be partial. As Manning Sjt put it, 'the quasi fiction of *servitium amisit* affords protection to the rich man, whose daughter

---

[49] *Derry* v. *Peek* (1889) 14 App Cas 337.

[50] See pp. 412–14, 429–31.

[51] The action was seen as one in trespass in *Woodward* v. *Walton* (1807) 2 B. & P. N.R. 476 and *Ditcham* v. *Bond* (1814) 2 M. & S. 436. In *Chamberlain* v. *Hazlewood* (1839) 5 M. & W. 515, however, it was confirmed that the action could also be pleaded in case, as had often been done. When pleaders used trespass, it was to allow them to join counts for breaking the plaintiff's close. On the action, see G. Jones, 'Per Quod Servitium Amisit' (1958) 74 *LQR* (1958) 39.

[52] *Irwin* v. *Dearman* (1809) 11 East 23 at 24.

[53] The action was brought against those thought to have fathered the daughter's child: *Dodd* v. *Norris* (1814) 3 Camp. 519; *Eager* v. *Grimwood* (1847) 1 Exch. 61.

[54] See *Grinnell* v. *Wells* (1844) 14 LJ CP 19.

[55] *Bennett* v. *Allcott* (1787) 2 T.R. 166 at 168. Cf. *Postlethwaite* v. *Parkes* (1766) 3 Burr. 1878. By contrast, actions could be maintained for enticing away a wife, without any allegation of service: *Winsmore* v. *Greenbank* (1745) Willes 577; *Philp* v. *Squire* (1791) Peake 114; *Berthon* v. *Cartwright* (1796) 2 Esp. 480.

[56] *Fores* v. *Wilson* (1791) Peake 77; *Manvell* v. *Thomson* (1826) 2 Car. & P. 303.

[57] *Fores* v. *Wilson* (1791) Peake 77.

[58] *Andrews* v. *Askey* (1837) 8 Car. & P. 7. See also *Irwin* v. *Dearman* (1809) 11 East 23, and Lord Ellenborough's comments in *Dodd* v. *Norris* (1814) 3 Camp. 519.

[59] *Dean* v. *Peel* (1804) 5 East 45; *Harris* v. *Butler* (1837) 2 M. & W. 539; *Grinnell* v. *Wells* (1844) 7 M. & G. 1033; *Davies* v. *Williams* (1847) 10 Q.B. 725; *Manley* v. *Field* (1859) 7 C.B. N.S. 96; contrast *Mann* v. *Barrett* (1806) 6 Esp. 32.

occasionally makes his tea, but leaves without redress the poor man, whose child, as here, is sent, unprotected, to earn her bread amongst strangers'.[60]

The second kind of action *per quod servitium amisit* was used where the master was deprived of his servant's labour, as a result of the defendant's tort in injuring that servant. In such cases, it was not necessary to show that the tortfeasor knew that the injured man was the plaintiff's servant: the plaintiff was simply able to recover his own special damages suffered from the defendant's wrongful act. He recovered the economic value of the service which he had lost,[61] but could not recover non-pecuniary damages.[62] The commonest cases using this form were those where a workman had been beaten by the defendant, rendering him unfit for work, or where the servant had been attacked by an animal which the owner was bound to keep from harming. However, it was not necessary for the wrong done to the servant to have been one for which only an action of trespass lay. In the first half of the century, masters were able to recover for loss of service where servants were injured in road accidents, resulting from the defendant's negligence.[63] However, judges in the second half of the century were less keen to permit this action in cases arising from negligence, and interpreted the law in a restrictive way, making it harder for masters to recover when their servants had been injured through negligence.[64]

Where the first two uses of the action *per quod servitium amisit* permitted plaintiffs to recover damages for economic losses suffered as a result of the defendant's physical interference with those in their service, the third use was for a purely economic wrong: interfering with the master's interest in his servant's labour, by enticing him to leave his job.[65] Although the pleadings charged the defendant with 'contriving and intending to injure the plaintiff',[66] it was not necessary to show malice. It was only necessary to show that the defendant knew that the workman was another's servant. Showing this knowledge was enough to establish an intention to interfere with the plaintiff's rights. Since it was not necessary

---

[60] *Grinnell* v. *Wells* (1844) 7 M. & G. 1033 at 1044n.

[61] *Hodsoll* v. *Stallebrass* (1840) Ad. & El. 301.

[62] *Flemington* v. *Smithers* (1826) 2 Car. & P. 292.

[63] *Flemington* v. *Smithers* (1826) 2 Car. & P. 292; *Martinez* v. *Gerber* (1841) 3 M. & G. 88. See also *Hall* v. *Hollander* (1825) 4 B. & C. 660, an action brought in trespass.

[64] In *Alton* v. *Midland Railway Co* (1865) 19 C.B. N.S. 213, the Common Pleas held that a master could not sue for an injury suffered by a servant while travelling on the defendant's train, since the company's obligation was a contractual one. In *Osborn* v. *Gillett* (1873) LR 8 Ex 88, the Exchequer held a master could not recover where his servant had been killed by the plaintiff's negligent driving, since *actio personalis moritur cum persona*. But contrast *Berringer* v. *Great Eastern Railway Co* (1879) 4 CPD 163 where Lopes J. allowed an action in tort against a railway company, *per quod servitium amisit*.

[65] *Hart* v. *Aldridge* (1774) 1 Cowp. 54.

[66] Clerk & Lindsell, *Torts* (2nd edn, 1896), 185.

for the defendant to have enticed the servant into his own employment, a number of slave owners in the late eighteenth and early nineteenth centuries attempted to use this action against those who encouraged slaves to leave their master.[67] More usually, the action was brought against rival employers, who could be held liable even if they had employed the plaintiff's servant without knowing of his previous engagement, provided that they harboured the workman after having been given notice of the plaintiff's interest.[68] Since the master's interest in the workman was economically quantifiable, he was permitted to waive the tort of seduction, and bring an action for work and labour against the new employer for the work done by his servant.[69] Those accused of seducing servants could defend themselves by showing that the plaintiff's contract of employment with the servant was void, for being so one-sided as to lack mutuality, or for being in restraint of trade.[70] In practice, such actions were not common. Given the power masters exerted over servants under the Master and Servants Act 1823, it was generally unnecessary to seek a remedy from a rival.

3. EXPANDING ECONOMIC TORTS, 1853–1887

The second half of the nineteenth century saw the creation of a new economic tort, as well as an attempt to develop a broader theory of intentional torts. The root of these developments was the case of *Lumley* v. *Gye*, which arose from the fierce rivalry of Benjamin Lumley, proprietor of Her Majesty's Theatre, Haymarket, and Frederick Guy of the new Royal Italian Opera Covent Garden for the services of Johanna Wagner, the prima donna of the Royal Theatre at Berlin.[71] It was not the first time these men had squabbled over a singer. In 1847, Lumley had induced Jenny Lind to break her contract with Gye, in order to perform at his theatre. Since his takings for the season ran to nearly £46,000, Lumley was easily able to pay the £2000 awarded against Miss Lind for breaching her contract, as well as her £5,600 fee.[72] When his own artiste, Miss Wagner, was poached by Gye, Lumley obtained an injunction to prevent her from singing,[73] and sought

---

[67] *Keane* v. *Boycott* (1795) 2 H. Bl. 511; *Forbes* v. *Cochrane* (1824) 2 B. & C. 448.

[68] *Blake* v. *Lanyon* (1795) 6 T.R. 221. A rival trader would not be guilty of seducing a servant, however, if he tried to persuade him to leave his master at the end of his term of employment: *Nichol* v. *Martyn* (1799) 2 Esp. 732.

[69] *Lightly* v. *Clouston* (1808) 1 Taunt. 112; *Foster* v. *Stewart* (1814) 3 M. & S. 191.

[70] *Sykes* v. *Dixon* (1839) 9 Ad. & El. 693; *Hartley* v. *Cummings* (1847) 5 C.B. 247; *Pilkington* v. *Scott* (1846) 15 M. & W. 657.

[71] For a history of the case, see S. M. Waddams, 'Johanna Wagner and the Rival Opera Houses' (2001) 117 *LQR* 431–58.

[72] Waddams, 'Johanna Wagner', 433 & n.

[73] *Lumley* v. *Wagner* (1852) 5 De G. & Sm. 485, 1 De G. M. & G. 604, 19 LT 264.

£30,000 damages in a tort action which accused Gye of maliciously procuring her to break her contract.

Gye demurred the declaration, claiming that the remedy could only be sought in contract. However, a majority of the Queen's Bench found against him. The reasons given by the judgments were varied. In Crompton J.'s view, Lumley could recover on the grounds of seduction.[74] Although it had been held in 1795 that an action *per quod servitium amisit* could not be brought for the loss of service of a singer at an Opera House, since 'he was not a servant at all',[75] Crompton felt the remedy should be available for enticing away 'any person employed to give his personal labour or service for a given time', not only for particular kinds of service.[76] Liability on these grounds did not require Gye to have acted with any malice, provided he had notice of Miss Wagner's contract. Crompton also took the opportunity to comment favourably on the broader argument put forward for the plaintiff, 'that the malicious and intentional procurement of a breach of contract was a wrong':[77]

Suppose a trader, with a malicious intent to ruin a rival trader, goes to a banker or other party who owes money to his rival, and begs him not to pay the money which he owes him, and by that means ruins or greatly prejudices the party: I am by no means prepared to say that an action could not be maintained, and that damages, beyond the amount of the debt if the injury were great, or much less than such an amount if the injury were less serious, might not be recovered.[78]

Erle and Wightman JJ felt that Gye was liable for having procured the breach of contract. In Erle's view, 'the procurement of the violation of a right is a cause of action in all instances where the violation is an actionable wrong [...] he who procures the wrong is a joint wrong-doer'.[79] For Wightman, '[i]t was undoubtedly prima facie an unlawful act on the part of Miss Wagner to break her contract, and therefore a tortious act of the defendant maliciously to procure her to do so'.[80] In taking this view, these judges mixed together two different doctrines. The first was the doctrine which regarded those who procured the commission of a tort as joint tortfeasors.[81] The second was the doctrine that those who induced third

---

[74] *Lumley* v. *Gye* (1853) 2 E. & B. 216 at 224–5.

[75] *Taylor* v. *Neri* (1795) 1 Esp. 386 at 387.

[76] Wightman J. agreed: *Lumley* v. *Gye* (1853) 2 E. & B. 216 at 240.

[77] *Lumley* v. *Gye* (1853) 2 E. & B. 216 at 220 (Cowling).

[78] *Ibid.* at 230.

[79] *Ibid.* at 232–3. In *Bowen* v. *Hall*, Lord Coleridge noted that Erle felt that inducing a breach of contract was actionable without malice.

[80] *Lumley* v. *Gye* (1853) 2 E. & B. 216 at 238.

[81] J. Comyns, *A Digest of the Laws of England*, 6 vols (London, 1800), vi, 380: trespass lay 'against all whom procure or command it' (tit. Trespass C. 1.). See also the comments of Alderson in *Robinson* v. *Vaughton* (1838) 8 C. & P. 252 at 255.

parties not to deal with the plaintiff, by making false statements, were liable to an action for the malicious falsehood.[82] Neither of these doctrines applied separately to the case: for the 'wrong' committed by Gye was clearly distinct from that committed by Miss Wagner; and he had made no false statements. But put together, they seemed to open the way to a new tort.

Coleridge J. dissented. In his view, where a contract had been broken, only the contracting parties could sue for damages caused by its breach. Gye could only be liable in tort, in his view, if he had committed a wrongful act whose direct and natural consequence was a loss to the plaintiff. In this case, the act which caused the damage to Lumley was Miss Wagner's breach of contract. Gye's action in procuring her to break her contract was 'too remote from the damage to make him answerable for it'. For Coleridge, Gye's bad motives were not relevant, since malice could 'neither supply the want of the act itself, or its hurtful consequence'. Referring approvingly to Abinger's judgment in *Winterbottom* v. *Wright*,[83] Coleridge worried about the consequences of relaxing the rules of remoteness of damage which the majority judgment entailed, and spoke of the 'manifest absurdity in attempting to trace up the act of a free agent breaking a contract to all the advisers who may have influenced his mind, more or less honestly, more or less powerfully, and to make them responsible civilly for the consequences of what after all is his own act'. He also felt that it would be impossible to draw a clear line between advice, persuasion, and procurement. To allow this unprecedented action would also, in his view, transform the law, since 'important contracts are more commonly broken with than without persuaders or procurers, and these often responsible persons when the principals may not be so'.[84] Coleridge also rejected the argument that Gye could be liable for procuring Lumley's servant to leave her master. In his view, this action was an exceptional one, derived from the Edwardian Statute of Labourers, and did not apply to theatrical performers.

Although Lumley won on the demurrer, he lost his case before a jury, after Lord Campbell told them that he could not win, if Gye *bona fide* believed that Miss Wagner had no binding contract with his rival.[85] Despite Coleridge's fears, *Lumley* v. *Gye* was not followed by a rush of cases for inducing breach of contract. It took almost three decades for the next significant case, *Bowen* v. *Hall*,[86]

---

[82] In his judgment, Erle J. made particular mention of *Green* v. *Button* (1835) 2 C. M. & R. 707 and *Sheperd* v. *Wakeman* (1662) Sid. 79, where the defendant had written a letter to the plaintiff's suitor falsely claiming to be her husband, which lost her a potential marriage.

[83] *Winterbottom* v. *Wright* (1842) 10 M. & W. 109.

[84] *Lumley* v. *Gye* (1853) 2 E. & B. 216 at 247–50.

[85] Waddams, 'Johanna Wagner', 456. Such a defence would not have been available in the cases of harbouring servants.

[86] *Bowen* v. *Hall* (1881) 6 QBD 333 (CA).

to come to court. The defendant was the proprietor of a brick making company who had persuaded a brick maker, George Pearson, to break his contract with Edward Bowen, in which he had promised to produce a particular kind of glazed brick exclusively for Bowen for five years.[87] Litigation which began in 1878 finally arrived at the Court of Appeal in 1881, when the court had to decide whether or not to endorse the broad principle derived from *Lumley* v. *Gye*.

The majority decision was given by Brett LJ, a judge with clear ambitions to set the law of tort on a broad moral basis. *Bowen* v. *Hall* gave him the chance to set forth some of his views. He began with a broad statement of principle: 'wherever a man does an act which in law and in fact is a wrongful act, and such an act as may, as a natural and probable consequence of it, produce injury to another, and which in the particular case does produce such an injury, an action on the case will lie'.[88] He added his own view of remoteness, stating that the action lay even where the natural and probable consequence was an actionable or wrongful act of a third party.[89] In Brett's view, merely persuading someone to break his contract was not an actionable wrong; but if it was done 'for the indirect purpose of injuring the plaintiff, or of benefiting the defendant at the expense of the plaintiff, it is a malicious act which is in law and in fact a wrong act, and therefore a wrongful act, and therefore an actionable act if injury ensues from it'.[90] A malicious intent could make an otherwise innocent act wrongful.

Like his father before him, Lord Coleridge CJ argued against this doctrine:

I do not know, except in the case of *Lumley* v. *Gye*, that it has ever been held that the same person for doing the same thing under the same circumstances with the same result is actionable or not actionable according to whether his inward motive was selfish or unselfish for what he did. I think the inquiries to which this view of the law would lead are dangerous and inexpedient inquiries for courts of justice; judges are not very fit for them, and juries are very unfit.[91]

Some legal commentators shared this disquiet. The *Solicitor's Journal* was concerned that Brett's broad invocation of the principle of *Ashby* v. *White*—that a remedy was given for every wrong—failed to give a distinct definition of 'the

---

[87] For earlier litigation, see *The Times*, 4 November 1889, col. 4b; 7 February 1881, col. 11a.

[88] *Bowen* v. *Hall* (1881) 6 QBD 333 (CA) at 337. Although Brett said this was derived from *Ashby* v. *White* (1703) 2 Ld. Raym. 938, and endorsed in *Lumley* v. *Gye* (1853) 2 E. & B. 216 at 219, his formulation was broader. The formulation quoted in *Lumley* was taken from J. Comyns, *A Digest of the Laws of England*, 5 vols (1780), i, 128 (tit. 'Action on the Case for Misfeasance A'): 'In all cases, where a man has a temporal loss, or damage by the wrong of another, he may have an action on the case.'

[89] He therefore held that the doctrine of *Vicars* v. *Wilcocks* (1806) 8 East 1 was wrong.

[90] *Bowen* v. *Hall* (1881) 6 QBD 333 (CA) at 338.

[91] *Ibid.* at 344.

exact nature of the duty' which would mark out the limits of the doctrine. It was also unhappy at the idea that the defendant's malice should be the crucial factor in determining liability, for this would leave too much power to juries to determine what was wrongful and what was not. It therefore advised against any 'endeavour to extract any very sweeping principle' from *Lumley* and *Bowen*.[92]

In fact, it did not take long for a new principle to be set forth by an academic lawyer. In the year after the decision in *Bowen* v. *Hall* was made, Frederick Pollock began work on his draft Indian Civil Wrongs Bill, which was completed at the same time that he published the first edition of his textbook on *Torts*. In this textbook, he posited a new theory of intentional torts.[93] He began with a general principle, which was not found in any express authority, but had to be inferred by a process of generalization from the variety of actionable injuries recognized at common law. The principle was that 'it is a wrong to do wilful harm to one's neighbour without lawful justification or excuse'.[94] It was the corollary of the principle underlying negligence that there was a duty to avoid harming others.[95] Not every harm suffered was actionable, for life could not go on unless things were done which were likely to cause loss to others. A person had an excuse where harms were suffered 'in consequence of any act done for a lawful purpose and in a lawful manner in the exercise of ordinary rights'.[96] By 1887, Pollock had set out a theory of *prima facie* torts.

In his textbook, Pollock also addressed the role of malice in three areas. First, he discussed whether a person was liable who had exercised his rights maliciously, and with the sole purpose of damaging his enemy. He pointed out that Roman law gave a remedy in such cases, by its doctrine of *animo vicino nocendi*. The Roman doctrine had been mentioned by some mid-century judges, in cases where malice was not an issue.[97] In 1859, in *Chasemore* v. *Richards*, Lord Wensleydale observed

---

[92] (1881) 25 *Sol. J.* 738.

[93] See K. J. Vandevelde, 'A History of Prima Facie Tort: the Origins of a General Theory of Intentional Tort' (1990) 19 *Hofstra LR* (1990) 447–97 at 471, which states that Pollock was the first writer to develop such a theory.

[94] F. Pollock, *The Law of Torts: A Treatise on the Principles of Obligations arising from Civil Wrongs in the Common Law* (1887), 21. See also clauses 8 and 22 of his Indian bill, in *The Law of Torts* (2nd edn, 1890), 522, 535.

[95] *The Law of Torts* (1st edn, 1887), 22. See also N. Duxbury, *Frederick Pollock and the English Juristic Tradition* (Oxford, 2004), 270–2.

[96] *The Law of Torts* (2nd edn, 1890), 535; cf. *Torts* (1st edn, 1887), 129–32.

[97] In *Acton* v. *Blundell* (1843) 12 M. & W. 324 at 336, Maule J. quoted Marcellus's comment that 'if a man digs a well in his own field, and thereby drains his neighbour's, he may do so, unless he does so maliciously'. See the passage in D.39.3.1.12 discussed in M. Taggart, *Private Property and Abuse of Rights in Victorian England: The Story of Edward Pickles and the Bradford Water Supply* (Oxford, 2002), 124–5. Cf. Cresswell J.'s comments in *Smith* v. *Kenrick* (1849) 7 CB 515 at 566.

that the Roman rule 'has not found a place in our law'.[98] While Pollock agreed that Wensleydale had expressed the general view of English lawyers, he felt that in principle there was much to recommend the Roman doctrine.[99] Rejecting the objection that the law regarded only intentions, and not motives, he observed that the law already did regard motives as important, in malicious prosecution and defamation cases. In his draft Indian code, he therefore stated that a landowner who dug a deep well on his land, with the sole intention of cutting off the water to his neighbour's well, should be liable for a wrong done to his neighbour, since 'he has used his own land not for any lawful purpose, but only for the unlawful purpose of doing wilful harm'.[100]

Secondly, Pollock argued that the question of malice might be relevant where the defendant interfered with another person's trade or occupation. Pollock had in mind cases such as *Keeble* v. *Hickeringill*, where the defendant was held liable for shooting at the plaintiff's decoys to scare off ducks,[101] and *Tarleton* v. *M'Gawley*, where the defendant was held liable for maliciously contriving to hinder Africans from trading with the plaintiff's ship, by shooting at them.[102] Although Holt CJ had observed in *Keeble* that 'he that hinders another in his trade or livelihood is liable to an action for so hindering him', Pollock noted that these were 'in a kind of obscure middle region' for they did not involve 'the breach of an absolute specific duty', nor were they 'exempt from search into their motives as being done in the exercise of common right'.[103] Pollock also pointed to the case of *Gregory* v. *The Duke of Brunswick*, where the plaintiff failed in an action against the defendant for conspiring to hiss him off stage, since he had been unable to show there had been malice, which Pollock saw as the gist of the action.[104]

The third area discussed was the doctrine of *Lumley* v. *Gye*. In the early editions of his textbook, Pollock saw this case as illustrating the same principle as cases such as *Keeble* and *Tarleton*, and argued that the difficulties which commentators felt about *Lumley* and *Bowen* 'either disappear or are greatly reduced when the cause of action is considered as belonging to the class in which malice, in the

---

[98] *Chasemore* v. *Richards* (1859) 7 H.L.C. 349 at 388. See Taggart's explanation of Wensleydale's position in *Private Property*, 54–5.

[99] Pollock, *Torts* (1st edn, 1887), 137.

[100] Pollock, *Torts* (2nd edn, 1890), 536.

[101] *Keeble* v. *Hickeringill* (1706) 11 East 575–6n; Holt K. B. 14, 17, 19, 11 Mod. 130; 3 Salk. 9. The decision was followed in *Carrington* v. *Taylor* (1809) 11 East 571.

[102] *Tarleton* v. *M'Gawley* (1794) 1 Peake N.P.C. 270. See also *Garret* v. *Taylor* (1620) Cro. Jac. 567, where the defendant was held liable for threatening the plaintiff stonemason's workmen and customers so that they desisted from coming.

[103] Pollock, *Torts* (1st edn, 1887), 269.

[104] *Gregory* v. *Duke of Brunswick* (1843) 6 M. & G. 205, 953.

sense of actual ill-will, is a necessary element'.[105] In these cases, the act 'must be malicious, in the sense of being aimed at obtaining some advantage for himself at the plaintiff's expense, or at any rate causing loss or damage to the plaintiff'.[106] Like Brett, Pollock felt that where special damage and malice were both present, the damage done to the plaintiff could not be held too remote.[107]

In his textbook, Pollock set out the framework of a general principle for intentional torts. In the 15 years following the publication of this work, Pollock would refine his theory in response to a number of cases in which the House of Lords sought to establish how far one person should be held liable for economic damage intentionally inflicted on another. In these cases, Lord Esher, who as Brett LJ had first sought to generalize the rule from *Lumley* v. *Gye*, attempted to develop the doctrine in a way which would make the justifiability of the defendant's motives central, and which would leave it largely in the hands of jurymen to evaluate these motives. This was an approach Pollock felt increasingly uncomfortable with, and he gradually diminished the role of malice in his discussion.

4. RETHINKING MALICE AND INTENT, 1887–1901

The fact that Pollock's chosen examples of cases successfully brought for interfering with a person's occupation were pre-nineteenth-century ones was not insignificant. For nineteenth-century judges had hitherto been largely untroubled with such litigation. When rare cases involving complaints about anti-competitive business did come to court, complainants generally found the judiciary unsympathetic. In 1860, for instance, the Privy Council had in *Rogers* v. *Rajendro Dutt* overturned a judgment of the Calcutta Supreme Court, which had held the defendant Superintendant of Marine liable in damages after he had ordered all pilots in the government service to cease using the respondent's tugs. 'It is essential to an action in tort', Dr Lushington ruled, 'that the act complained of should, under the circumstances, be legally wrongful as regards the party complaining; that is, it must prejudicially affect him in some legal right.'[108] Since Dutt had no right to the government's business, and since Rogers was using a lawful discretion, he had no right to complain. Nor were mid-century judges troubled by anti-competitive behaviour by those forming cartels. Common lawyers accepted that agreements between traders not to compete with each other were not void for

---

[105] Pollock, *Torts* (1st edn, 1887), 270.   [106] *Ibid.*, 452.

[107] Where the defendant intended the consequence, 'it would [...] be contrary to the facts to hold that the interposition of B's voluntary agency necessarily breaks the chain of proximate cause and probable consequence': Pollock, *Torts* (1st edn, 1887), 453–4.

[108] *Rogers* v. *Rajendro Dutt* (1860) 8 Moo. I.A. 103 at 135–6.

being in restraint of trade or against public policy.[109] Only when trade unions were involved did judges take a different view. In 1855, an agreement between employers which fixed the wages and conditions of labour for their workers was held unlawful and unenforceable, with the Queen's Bench majority taking the view that it was in the nature of a conspiracy.[110] For the judges realized that if a lock-out agreement could be legally upheld, so could a strike agreement.

The issue of whether there were limits set by the common law to the legitimate use of economic muscle was revisited in the 1890s, in a series of cases raising very different economic issues. Most of the litigation in this era arose from the activities of trade unions, whose economic power had increased significantly in the age of New Unionism. As they had been for much of the century, judges were generally more hostile to trade unions than political opinion was, and doctrinal developments fashioned with an eye to curbing the power of collective action needed legislative correction. At the same time, the judiciary was much less hostile to businessmen or property owners using their economic power or assets in an aggressive way.

The question of the legality of a cartel was raised in *Mogul Steamship Company* v. *McGregor, Gow & Co.* The plaintiff company was a freighter operating steamers on the Yangtze River, transporting tea in season. The defendants were members of a shipping cartel, which wished to secure the tea trade on this river for themselves, and to maintain remunerative rates of freight. In 1885, the cartel informed tea exporters that they would lose a rebate if they used the plaintiffs' vessels. It also told its agents that they would be dismissed if they dealt with owners of vessels who were not members of the cartel, and dismissed those who did so. Since no contract had been broken, and no positive act had been done to interfere with their right to trade, the plaintiffs claimed a conspiracy in restraint of trade, invoking the precedent of *Hilton* v. *Eckersley.* The plaintiffs lost at every stage.[111] In the Court of Appeal, Bowen LJ gave a judgment which particularly pleased Pollock. For Bowen, the question of conspiracy was not the key issue: the gist of the action was the damage done, not the conspiracy.[112] Had an actionable wrong been done? To answer this question, Bowen gave the following definition:

intentionally to do that which is calculated in the ordinary course of events to damage, and which does, in fact, damage another in that other person's property or trade,

---

[109] *Wickens* v. *Evans* (1829) 3 Y. & J. 318; *Jones* v. *North* (1875) LR 19 Eq 426; cf. *Collins* v. *Locke* (1879) 4 App Cas 674 (PC).

[110] *Hilton* v. *Eckersley* (1855) 6 E. & B. 47.

[111] For the early stages of the litigation, see *Mogul Steamship Co* v. *McGregor, Gow & Co* (1885) 15 QBD 476 and (1888) 21 QBD 544.

[112] *Mogul Steamship Co* v. *McGregor, Gow & Co* (1889) 23 QBD 598 at 616.

is actionable if done without just cause or excuse. Such intentional action, when done without just cause or excuse, is what the law calls a malicious wrong.[113]

In Bowen's view, a trader would be justified if he made *bona fide* use of his own property, even if his act had been selfish. He would not be justified if the act was done merely with the intention of causing harm 'without reference to one's own lawful gain, or the lawful enjoyment of one's own rights'. Deciding which side of the line conduct fell was to be left to the 'good sense of the tribunal which had to decide'.[114] Since the members of this cartel had simply wanted to benefit themselves, by attracting all the tea freights, and had been guilty of none of the acts (such as fraud, intimidation, or inducing breaches of contract) which were forbidden in trade, they were justified.[115] Since the action taken was not itself unlawful, the fact that it had been done by a cartel of traders did not make it a conspiracy.

The truth is, that the combination of capital for the purposes of trade and competition is a very different thing from such a combination of several persons against one, with a view to harm him, as falls under the head of an indictable conspiracy. There is no just cause or excuse in the latter class of cases. There is such a just cause or excuse in the former.[116]

Bowen did not see the need to regulate the economic activity of businessmen seeking to profit themselves.

Lord Esher MR dissented, wanting a much tougher approach to be taken to the cartel. Esher's view of malice was much broader than Bowen (or Pollock) had in mind. Referring to his decision in *Bowen* v. *Hall*, he argued that '"malice" is satisfied by the thing being done with the knowledge of the plaintiff's right and with intent to interfere with it [...] "with notice"'.[117] Drawing on Sir William Erle's memorandum on *The Law Relating to Trade Unions*, written for the 1867 Royal Commission on Trade Unions,[118] he stated 'that every trader has a legal right to a free course of trade, meaning thereby a legal right to be left free to exercise his trade according to his own will and judgment'. While '[f]air trade competition' was lawful, even though it damaged a rival, any unfair action in Esher's view 'leads to an almost irresistible inference of an indirect motive, and is therefore—unless, as may be possible, the motive is negatived—a wrongful act'.[119]

---

[113] *Ibid.* at 613. For Pollock's reaction, praising Bowen's 'masterly judgment', see (1890) 6 *LQR* 113; and F. Pollock, 'The Merger Case and Restraint of Trade' (1904) 17 *Harvard LR* 151–5 at 151–2.

[114] *Mogul Steamship Co* v. *McGregor, Gow & Co* (1889) 23 QBD 598 at 617–18.

[115] Some found Bowen's stress on motive troubling: see W. E. Ormsby, 'Malice in the Law of Torts' (1892) 8 *LQR* 140–50 at 149.

[116] *Mogul Steamship Co* v. *McGregor, Gow & Co* (1889) 23 QBD 598 at 617.

[117] *Ibid.* at 608–9.

[118] W. Erle, *The Law Relating to Trade Unions* (1868), 6, quoted in *Mogul Steamship* v. *McGregor & Gow*, 23 QBD 607–8.

[119] *Mogul Steamship Co* v. *McGregor, Gow, & Co* (1889) 23 QBD 598 at 609.

Drawing on Crompton J.'s judgment in *Hilton* v. *Eckersley*, he added that if two or more traders agreed to interfere with another's trade, this was also an indictable conspiracy.

The majority view was upheld in the House of Lords in 1892. The Lords agreed with Bowen LJ that the defendants' actions had not been actuated by malice, since it was part of the ordinary course of trade to undercut one's rivals and seek to monopolize. In Lord Field's judgment, acts done by a trader 'in the lawful way of his business' were not the subject of any action, even though 'by the necessary result of effective competition' they interfered 'injuriously with the trade of another'. They would only be actionable 'if the acts complained of, although done in the way and under the guise of competition or other lawful right, are in themselves violent or purely malicious, or have for their ultimate object injury to another from ill-will to him, and not the pursuit of lawful rights'.[120] Bramwell dismissed Esher's idea that the courts should determine what was fair competition. Lowering one's prices was not to be seen as an interference with another's trade, but as an exercise of one's own right to trade. The only interference with trade which was actionable, in Bramwell's view, was molestation or obstruction. The Lords also rejected the argument that the cartel had been a conspiracy. Dismissing Crompton J.'s comments in *Hilton*—that an agreement between employers in restraint of their trade could be regarded as a criminal conspiracy—as wrong, the Lords held that an agreement in restraint of trade among traders might be unenforceable *inter se*, but it was not actionable. While a conspiracy to violate a private right might be actionable, it was agreed that in the case before them, no private right had been violated.[121] As Pollock explained, the case decided that the courts would not undertake to regulate the competition of traders and that '[t]hey will not found new heads of "public policy" on disputed economic propositions'.[122] He clearly approved of the approach of this court in finding a justification in the pursuit of economic competition, and was uncomfortable with Lord Esher's very broad notion of malice. The decision in *Mogul* was not uncontroversial, as there had been concern expressed about the rise of cartels.[123] For *The Times*, the case 'forces us to realize that we are left with no defence against the monopoly or "trust", except such as the Legislature chooses to give us'.[124]

---

[120] *Mogul Steamship Co* v. *McGregor, Gow & Co* [1892] AC 25 at 52.

[121] Field J. noted that for an action of conspiracy to lie, there had to be either 'an ultimate object of malice' or 'wrongful means of execution': *Mogul Steamship Co* v. *McGregor, Gow & Co* [1892] AC 25 at 52.

[122] (1892) 8 *LQR* 101.

[123] See e.g. *The Times*, 12 January 1889, col. 9 d.

[124] *The Times*, 15 July 1889, col. 9e. In the United States, the Sherman Act of 1890 rendered illegal 'every contract, combination, in the form of a trust or otherwise, or conspiracy in restraint of trade'. See T. Freyer, *Regulating Big Business: Antitrust in Great Britain and America, 1880–1990*

Commentators had other concerns besides the threat of cartels. For some, the decision threatened to justify the practice of boycotting in Ireland.[125] There was also concern about the activity of trade unions, which sought to enforce closed shops by the use of blacklists against non-union members and those who employed them. It was in this context that a number of judges held trade union-ists liable, on the ground that they had acted with malice. This was done in 1893, in *Temperton* v. *Russell*, when the defendants—members of a joint committee of three trade unions who had called a boycott of the plaintiff's business—were sued for maliciously procuring breaches of contract, and for conspiring to injure the plaintiff by persuading people not to enter into contracts with him. In his judgment, Lord Esher—whose hostility to trade unions was well known[126]—held that the defendants were liable on both counts. In a controversial judgment, he ruled that the principle of *Bowen* v. *Hall* applied not only where breaches of con-tract were induced, but also where people were induced not to enter contracts, since '[t]here was the same wrongful intent in both cases'.[127] At the same time, he restated his opinion that personal malice was not a precondition of liability: it was sufficient that the defendants desired to injure him in his business in order 'to force him not to do what he had a perfect right to do'.[128] Other judges dealing with trade union cases at this time similarly encouraged juries to find malice where there was no evidence of personal spite. For instance, in *Trollope and Sons* v. *The London Building Trades Federation*, Kekewich J. held that although the 'final cause' of the actions of trade unionists who had posted a blacklist was no doubt to benefit themselves, their 'principal and primary motive' was to injure the plaintiff.[129] Hawkins J. similarly told a jury that a man was allowed to open

(Cambridge, 1992); E. T. Sullivan, *The Political Economy of the Sherman Act* (Oxford, 1991). See also pp. 670–3.

[125] *The Times*, December 19 1891, col. 9c.

[126] Lord Esher had shown his own hostility to collective action by trade unions in the famous Gas Stokers case, *R* v. *Bunn* (1872) 12 Cox CC 316, where his interpretation of the common law doctrine of conspiracy effectively undermined the Liberal legislation of union 1871. For a wider discussion of labour law, see Vol. XIII, Pt 3, Ch. III.

[127] *Temperton* v. *Russell* [1893] 1 QB 715 (CA) at 728. At least, he said, this could be actionable if done in combination. Citing *Gregory* v. *Duke of Brunswick* (1843) 6 M. & G. 953, he ruled that a conspiracy maliciously to injure the plaintiff by preventing others entering a contract with him was actionable.

[128] *Temperton* v. *Russell* [1893] 1 QB 715 (CA) at 726. Although the union officials intended to appeal to the House of Lords, it was never heard, for Temperton successfully took bankruptcy pro-ceedings against the three officials, in order to recover his judgment debt and costs prior to the hearing. See *In re Russell, Ex p Temperton*, *The Times*, 18 December 1893, col. 13d.

[129] When the case went to the Court of Appeal, Lord Halsbury interjected, '[i]f you want to for-ward your own interests by destroying the rights of others, it seems to me that that is express malice': *Trollope and Sons* v. *The London Building Trades Federation* (1895) 72 LT 342 at 343–4.

a shop which undercut that of his neighbour, but if he opened one solely for the purpose of ruining that of his neighbour, that would be a malicious act.[130]

Lord Esher reiterated his views in 1895 in *Flood* v. *Jackson*. The plaintiffs were shipwrights, members of one trade union, who were denied work after the local delegate of a rival union, Thomas Allen, told their employer that his members would leave their work if these men were re-hired. The facts of the case made it particularly significant. Unlike *Temperton*, this case did not raise any questions of conspiracy, since Allen had full discretion under the union rules to deal with the matter himself. Equally, since the plaintiffs were on daily contracts, there was no question that he had induced any breach of contract. Nor had there been any intimidation. The question for the court was therefore solely that of Allen's liability for persuading employers not to hire someone. At trial, the jury found him liable, on the grounds that he had maliciously induced the company to discharge the men and not to re-engage them. Lord Esher confirmed the decision, and expressed himself content with the jury's finding of malice. 'One person has a perfect right to advise another not to make a particular contract, and that other is at perfect liberty to follow that advice', Esher held, '[b]ut if the first person uses that persuasion with intent to injure the other, or to injure the person with whom he is going to make the contract, then the act is malicious, and the malice makes that unlawful which would otherwise be lawful.'

At the very same time that Lord Esher sought to develop his notion of malice, to allow courts to hold those liable for actions which were aimed to inflict economic damage on others, the Court of Appeal and House of Lords in *Bradford* v. *Pickles* held that questions of malice were irrelevant when the harm was consequent on the defendant's exercise of his proprietorial rights.[131] The defendant in this case was Edward Pickles, the owner of a farm near Bradford, whose underground water had fed the town's reservoirs for 40 years. He had hatched a plan to drain his land, specifically to force the corporation to buy his mineral and water rights at an extortionate price. The corporation was in no mood to give in to what was perceived to be his blackmail, and chose to litigate, thereby squarely raising the question discussed in Pollock's Indian bill of whether a landowner's use of his right to extract water on his own land with the intention of damaging his neighbour was actionable.

Rejecting the Roman position, the Law Lords held that English law gave the corporation of Bradford no cause of action. Thanks to the decision in *Chasemore*

---

[130] *Trollope and Sons* v. *The London Building Trades Federation* (1895) *The Times*, 1 May 1896, col. 13d; 2 May 1896, col. 18f; 5 May 1896, cols 13b–c. See also *Wright* v. *Hennessey* in *The Times*, 27 July 1895, col. 7d.

[131] On this case, see esp. Taggart, *Private Property* and A. W. B. Simpson, *Victorian Law and the Industrial Spirit* (Selden Society, 1995).

v. *Richards*,[132] the town had no right to the flow of water which percolated through undefined underground channels. A landowner on higher ground was fully within his rights to extract all the water which flowed through his land, if he chose to. The fact that he did so with the intention of harming the corporation's interests was irrelevant. 'If the act, apart from motive, gives rise merely to damage without legal injury,' Lord Macnaghten ruled, 'the motive, however reprehensible it may be, will not supply that element.'[133] Although some felt that moral objections could be raised to one man preferring his private interest to the public good,[134] a selfish approach to the use of one's own economic assets was not regarded as a matter for the courts.[135] Indeed, some of the conservative members of the bench—whose hostility to the economic muscle used by trade unions would later become apparent—felt that there was little wrong with a landowner seeking to use his own property to his best advantage. As Lord Macnaghten saw it, Pickles had something to sell: 'Why should he, he may think, without fee or reward, keep his land as a store-room for a commodity which the corporation dispense, probably not gratuitously, to the inhabitants of Bradford?'[136] For judges like Macnaghten and Halsbury, the defence of property rights was as important as the defence of freedom of contract. In the event Pickles's victory was pyrrhic: the corporation never purchased his asset, and after the turn of the century, he emigrated to obscurity in Canada.[137]

As Pollock pointed out, when viewed together, the cases of *Flood* v. *Jackson* and *Bradford* v. *Pickles* seemed paradoxical. They showed that a malicious use of one's property was not illegal, 'but the malicious use of a right which has not reference to property is, or may be, an abuse [...] As regards the exercise of the one class of rights, motive is irrelevant; as regards the exercise of the other class of rights, motive is, or may be, material.'[138] In light of the decision in *Bradford* v. *Pickles*, Pollock modified his textbook, abandoning his earlier suggestion that a malicious exercise of one's rights was actionable. He continued to maintain that parties could be held liable for actions which maliciously interfered with another person's trade, and that *Lumley* v. *Gye* was to be explained as a case resting on malice, but was highly critical of the approach taken to these doctrines by Lord Esher. In the edition produced after *Temperton*, he told his readers that the

---

[132] *Chasemore* v. *Richards* (1859) 7 H.L.C. 349.

[133] *Bradford* v. *Pickles* [1895] AC 587 at 601.

[134] *Ibid.* at 600–1. See also Lindley LJ's comments regarding Pickles's morality [1895] 1 Ch at 159.

[135] Lord Macnaghten thus asked 'where is the malice?' *Bradford* v. *Pickles* [1895] AC at 601; while Lord Herschell LC in the Court of Appeal noted that his actions could not be seen as malicious: [1895] 1 Ch 158.

[136] *Bradford* v. *Pickles* [1895] AC 587 at 600.

[137] Simpson, *Victorian Law and the Industrial Spirit*, 17.

[138] [F. Pollock] Case note on *Bradford* v. *Pickles* and *Flood* v. *Allen* (1896) 12 *LQR* 5.

Court of Appeal was incorrect to hold it actionable maliciously to procure people not to enter into contracts, where it was done without using unlawful means.[139] In Pollock's view, since in that case, the unionists were persuading employers to do something which it was in their lawful discretion to do, no wrongful act could have been committed, however malicious the motives of the person using their powers of persuasion. In the edition after *Flood*, Pollock criticized Esher's treatment of 'malice' as simply equivalent to the intent to injure the plaintiff, an approach which gave an unlimited discretion to juries to find against plaintiffs.[140] It would take 'only one step more to applying the supposed principle to business competition, and putting enterprise at the mercy of juries of rival tradesmen'.[141] If this doctrine were upheld, he warned, no 'prudent man could advise another in any kind of business involving contentious matter without requiring an indemnity'.[142]

Jackson v. *Flood* went on appeal to the House of Lords, where the decision was handed down in December 1897. Lord Halsbury, who was hostile to trade unions and keen to ensure that the Court of Appeal's decision would be upheld, asked for the advice of eight judges, without consulting his brethren. Their answers were made public in September, with six favouring the plaintiff.[143] Given the decision in *Bradford* v. *Pickles*, Lord Halsbury accepted that where none of the plaintiff's rights had been infringed by the defendant, he could not succeed. However, he held that the plaintiffs' 'right to employ their labour as they will is a right both recognised by the law and sufficiently guarded by its provisions to make any undue interference with that right an actionable wrong'.[144] In his advice, Hawkins J. had similarly spoken of the plaintiffs' right to follow a lawful calling.[145] Both he and Halsbury found authority for the idea that it was actionable to interfere with a man's right to trade in *Keeble* v. *Hickeringill*, *Tarleton* v. *M'Gawley*, and *Garret* v. *Taylor*.

According to these judges, since the right to trade had been interfered with, it was for the defendant to show he had a lawful excuse, such as the exercise of a privilege or the defence of a right. For Halsbury, where there was malice, there could be no just excuse. Endorsing Lord Field's comments in *Mogul* that when

---

[139] Pollock, *Torts* (4th edn, 1895), 295, 500.

[140] For other expressions of concern at leaving such questions to the jury, see *The Times*, 29 July 1895, col. 9e.

[141] [F. Pollock] Case note on *Bradford* v. *Pickles* and *Flood* v. *Allen* (1896) 12 *LQR* 5 at 6.

[142] Pollock, *Torts* (5th edn, 1897), 308.

[143] R. F. V. Heuston, 'Judicial Prosopography' (1986) 102 *LQR* 90–113 at 97–8; see also *The Times*, 4 September 1897, col. 5a.

[144] *Allen* v. *Flood* [1898] AC 1 at 71.

[145] *Ibid.* at 16. Since this was not a vested right, he called it a 'probable expectation'. Lord Morris also spoke of a right to trade (at 155).

'the purposed infliction of loss and injury upon another cannot be attributed to any legitimate cause', malice was to be presumed, he held that if Allen's object had merely been to point to the inconvenience of having men from different unions working together, he would have had a just excuse; but if his object was to 'punish the men belonging to another union', then it would be malicious.[146] In Hawkins's view, where a trade unionist sought to force an employer to discharge workmen obnoxious to his union, he was not acting within his rights.[147] The position taken by these judges was in effect that Allen had inflicted a harm on Flood through his intentional act, and that there was no justification to be found in the fact that he had acted to promote the interests of his trade union.[148]

Halsbury failed to convince the Lords to uphold the Court of Appeal's view. The majority in the Lords felt that for an action to lie, the plaintiff's rights had to have been interfered with by an act which was legally wrong. They were unhappy with Lord Esher's attempts to expand the doctrine of *Lumley* v. *Gye* into a general doctrine of liability for intentionally inflicted harms. As Lord James of Hereford put it, if Esher's principles were applied 'to the ordinary affairs of life, great inconvenience as well as injustice would ensue': for any competitor for business, seeking to advance his own interests, might be liable for persuading a client not to hire a rival.[149] There was, moreover, in Lord Herschell's view, a 'chasm' between procuring a breach of contract—the gist of the action in *Lumley*—and persuading someone not to enter a contract.[150] For only in the first was a legal right violated. Herschell was worried by Esher's attempt to give a remedy for what he considered morally wrongful actions. Indeed, he did not agree that using persuasion to benefit oneself at another's expense was morally wrong.

In taking this view, the majority rejected the minority's view (borrowed from Erle's memorandum) that a legal right to trade existed, which could not be violated without an excuse. The right to trade was not a specifically legal right, but was only an example of the broader idea that 'everyone has a right to do any lawful act he pleases without molestation or obstruction'.[151] For an action to be brought for violating this kind of right, it had first to be shown that the defendant's act was itself wrongful. This had been done in each of the older cases cited by the minority in favour of the proposition, where violence or the threat of violence had been

---

[146] *Ibid.* at 77, 85.

[147] *Ibid.* at 23, drawing on *Walsby* v. *Anley* (1861) 3 El. & El. 516 at 522.

[148] Though hardly a friend to unions, Pollock himself preferred Holmes's dissenting approach in *Vegelahn* v. *Guntner* 167 Mass 92, 44 NE 1077 (1896), finding trade union activities justified on the same grounds that the cartel in *Mogul* was. See 'Allen v. Flood' (1898) 14 *LQR* 129–32 at 129.

[149] *Allen* v. *Flood* [1898] AC 1 at 179.

[150] *Ibid.* at 121.   [151] *Ibid.* at 138.

used.[152] Nor did the majority think that a malicious intent could make a lawful act unlawful. Malice was only relevant where the initial act had been wrongful—as where a defamatory statement was made or a prosecution was brought without probable cause—but the defendant claimed to be acting under a privilege.[153]

The majority of judges in the Lords were concerned about the consequences which would follow from allowing a remedy for malicious acts. 'I can imagine no greater danger', Lord Herschell said, than to allow a jury to penalize actions which were otherwise lawful 'because they choose, without any legal definition of the term, to say that they are malicious. No one would know what his rights were. The result would be to put all our actions at the mercy of a particular tribunal whose view of their propriety might differ from our own.'[154] He equally rejected the idea (suggested by Wills J.) that it could be left to a jury to decide whether the means used in advancing one's self-interest were fair, since there would be widely differing opinions as to what a right-minded man should be allowed or not be allowed to do. Herschell's concern was with the potential open-endedness of the doctrine which would make actionable any lawful act committed with the intent to benefit oneself at another's expense. He thus rejected not only Esher's formulation, but Bowen LJ's words in *Mogul*. If Bowen's proposition meant 'that a man is bound in law to justify or excuse every wilful act which may damage another in his property or trade, then I say, with all respect, the proposition is far too wide'.[155]

The decision in *Allen* v. *Flood* was a politically important—though short-lived—victory for a trade union. It was also doctrinally important, for curbing the development of the *prima facie* tort theory. The case settled that a person was free intentionally to cause another economic harm provided that illegal means were not used,[156] and consequently limited the development of a tort of intent in England.[157] The decision was welcomed by those who were troubled by the potential ambit of the doctrine. Even *The Times*, which regarded Allen's conduct as cruel, and the decision as potentially legalizing a dangerous kind of pressure, was doubtful of a doctrine which might be used against a member of a club who threatened to blackball a rival, and which opened up the prospect of 'an alarming vista of litigation'.[158]

---

[152] *Ibid.* at 139.   [153] *Ibid.* at 126 (Herschell).

[154] *Ibid.* at 118. Lord Macnaghten at 153 also spoke of the 'probability of injustice being done by juries in a class of cases in which there would be ample room for speculation and wide scope for prejudice'.

[155] *Ibid.* at 139.

[156] See (1897) 42 *Sol. J.* 109; T. Weir, *Economic Torts* (Oxford, 1997), 21.

[157] See J. Salmond and R. F. V. Heuston, *The Law of Torts* (21st edn, 1996), 346 for a criticism of the case as placing an arbitrary and illogical limit on a rational general principle of law.

[158] *The Times*, 16 December 1897, col. 9d.

The decision in *Allen* v. *Flood* made Pollock recast his theory. He welcomed the fact that the Lords had rejected the view of malice taken in the Court of Appeal, which threatened to 'let loose a disastrous flood of speculative actions, which before long would have had to be restrained either by legislation, by the laying down of elaborate and obscure judicial exceptions to the new rule, or by assuming much greater power of interfering with the verdicts of juries than the judges have habitually claimed of late years'.[159] Pollock now rewrote his treatise, to remove the previous stress on malice. Where he had hitherto spoken of cases such as *Keeble* and *Tarleton* as examples of a tort liability for maliciously interfering with trade, he now said that liability in those cases rested on the fact that distinct torts had been committed.[160] Moreover, he now argued for the first time that the ground of the decision in *Lumley* v. *Gye* was not the presence of malice, but that the wilful procuring of a breach of contract was itself a wrong. A defendant could justify himself by claiming to have given disinterested advice, but such a defence would be one claiming a privilege. Pollock pointed out that *Allen* v. *Flood* confirmed that it was not a wrong to persuade a third party not to employ someone, whatever their motives. Having stated the rule from *Bradford* v. *Pickles*, he now added that 'it is generally true that "an act which does not amount to a legal injury cannot be actionable because it is done with a bad intent"'.[161] Moreover, he added some new passages to his general discussion. 'If there is a general duty not to do wilful harm', he now noted, 'it would seem on principle that the law need not regard the motive, in the sense of personal disposition, from which such an act proceeds [...] Again, it is a settled general rule in our law that when an act is done in the exercise of a common right, the motive is immaterial.' Malice could only ever be relevant, he now argued, where (as in defamation) a person who had committed a wrong claimed to have acted under a privilege.[162] *Allen* v. *Flood* had shown, Pollock noted shortly after the decision, that ordinary acts or words which were not themselves wrongs (such as deceit or defamation) were 'matters of common and equal right, not of privilege'.[163] At the same time, he made clear his view that the question of what was to be regarded as a matter of common right was not fixed and that it would be for the courts, in developing rules on matters such as unfair competition, to decide what activity fell within this justification.

---

[159] F. Pollock, '*Allen* v. *Flood*' (1898) 14 *LQR* 129–32 at 129. For Pollock's criticism of Esher's reasoning, see M. D. Howe (ed.), *The Pollock-Holmes Letters* (Cambridge, 1942), i, 72, 84.

[160] Similarly, he now argued that the wrong which the court was concerned with in *Gregory* v. *Duke of Brunswick* was not the malice of the audience: it was the act of hissing itself which would have constituted a tort: Pollock, *Torts* (6th edn, 1901), 314n.

[161] Pollock, *Torts* (6th edn, 1901), 154.

[162] *Ibid.*, 23–4.   [163] F. Pollock, '*Allen* v. *Flood*' (1898) 14 *LQR* 129–32 at 131.

5. RETHINKING CONSPIRACY, 1901–1914

Shortly after closing the door to the development of a doctrine which would have given a remedy for intentionally inflicted economic harms, the House of Lords confirmed that a civil action of conspiracy was available for those who suffered economic harms at the hands of a trade union. The criminal law of conspiracy had been used against trade unions throughout the mid-nineteenth century. Under this law, an offence had been committed if a person agreed with others to perform an act which was itself unlawful, or to perform a lawful act by criminal means.[164] An indictment could be brought as soon as the agreement had been made, for its criminality did not depend on its execution. However, in 1875, the Conspiracy and Protection of Property Act curbed the use of the charge of criminal conspiracy against unions, by enacting that nothing done by a trade union should be held criminal unless it would be regarded as criminal if done by an individual.

Civil actions could also be brought where plaintiffs had suffered special damage from a criminal conspiracy.[165] However, doubts existed whether a distinct tort of conspiracy existed, which would allow a civil action to be brought for collective actions which were neither criminal conspiracies nor torts themselves.[166] The ancient writ of conspiracy only lay for procuring an indictment of felony or treason; it was brought against at least two and could be brought without the conspiracy being put into execution. Although writs of conspiracy could be found in older law books for other kinds of cases, they were (according to Sjt Williams) 'in truth nothing else but action[s] upon the case, and not properly writs of conspiracy'. They were actions in tort, which 'might be brought against one person only'.[167] The view that plaintiffs recovered in civil actions of conspiracy for the damage suffered from the defendant's legal wrong, rather than for damage suffered as a result of the collective action, was also put forward in Pollock's treatise, where he suggested that 'the conspiracy or "confederation" is not in any case the gist of the action, but is only matter of inducement or evidence'.[168]

---

[164] See Second and Final Report of the Commissions appointed to inquire into the Working of the Master and Servant Act 1867, the Criminal Law Amendment Act, 34 & 35 Vict. c. 32 and for other purposes, *PP* 1875 XXX (c. 1157) 1 at pp. 24–5. See also R. S. Wright, *The Law of Criminal Conspiracies and Agreements* (1873). See further, Vol. XIII, Pt 1, pp. 314–20.

[165] *Mulcahy* v. *Reg* (1868) LR 3 HL 317.

[166] This was the view of Arthur Cohen QC in Report of the Royal Commission on Trade Disputes and Trade Combinations (henceforth cited as Royal Commission on Trade Disputes), *PP* 1906 LVI (c. 2825) 1 at p. 22.

[167] *Skinner* v. *Gunton* (1670) 1 Wms. Saund. 228 at 230(b)(4). See also *Savile* v. *Roberts* (1699)1 Ld. Raym. 374 at 378–9; and Sir Godfrey Lushington's dissenting report in 1905 to the Royal Commission on Trade Disputes.

[168] Pollock, *Torts* (1st edn, 1887), 267.

This view of the law was endorsed in 1890 by the Irish Exchequer Division in *Kearney* v. *Lloyd*, where the incumbent of a Protestant living sued members of the vestry for conspiracy, in persuading people not to contribute to his voluntary sustentation fund. Palles CB held that 'the *gist* of the action is not the conspiracy itself, but the wrongful acts done in pursuance of it', which meant that '[t]he cause of action must exist, although the allegation of conspiracy be struck out'.[169] Palles CB's view was followed at the end of 1897 in *Huttley* v. *Simmons*, where a trade union had taken action to prevent a cabman getting work. Following the rule in *Allen* v. *Flood*, Darling J. held that since nothing had been done which would have constituted a civil wrong without malice, no tort had been committed; and following Palles CB's approach, he held that as the acts were all in themselves legal, conspiring to effect them was not actionable.[170]

In the 1890s, employers seeking compensation in the civil courts from trade unions frequently accused them of conspiracy. But the judges in this decade who held unionists civilly liable for conspiracy—as Esher did in *Temperton* v. *Russell*— were also convinced that the 'malicious' actions were themselves actionable.[171] Where conduct which did economic damage was not regarded as malicious or criminal, such judges did not feel an action of conspiracy could be brought. This can be seen from Lord Esher's approach in *Salaman* v. *Warner*, where the defendants published a prospectus stating that the bulk of the company's shares were to be issued to the public, only to allocate the shares to themselves, to make a profit on the stock market. The plaintiff, a stockbroker, sued when he found that he was unable at the time of allotment to buy shares which he had already contracted to sell. Esher held that he had no cause of action, since the prospectus was not addressed to him. While the promoters might have been criminally indicted if they had conspired to do an illegal act or use illegal means, the plaintiff could bring no civil action for a conspiracy unless they had 'conspired to do something against the rights of the plaintiff, and had effected their purpose and committed a breach of those rights'.[172]

It was in the context of this general doctrinal scepticism about the existence of a tort of conspiracy that the decision in *Quinn* v. *Leathem* was made. This was another case brought by a trader who had been blacklisted by a union. The facts

[169] *Kearney* v. *Lloyd* (1890) 26 LR Ir. 268 at 280.

[170] *Huttley* v. *Simmons and Others* [1898] 1 QB 181. Darling J. also followed the dictum in *R* v. *Warburton* (1870) LR 1 CC 274, at 276.

[171] In *Mogul Steamship Co* v. *McGregor* [1892] AC 25 at 45, Lord Bramwell did defend the notion that actions which were not individually wrongful could collectively amount to a criminal conspiracy; though in this case (as in the trade union cases), the court looked at the questions of intentional wrong and conspiracy together, and found the acts neither to amount to a conspiracy nor to be wrongs.

[172] *Salaman* v. *Warner and Others* (1891) 7 TLR 484 at 485.

were very similar to those in *Temperton* v. *Russell*, and the House of Lords had to determine whether the doctrine laid down in that case had survived its decision in *Allen* v. *Flood*. The case reached the Lords in August 1901: with Lords Herschell and Watson now dead, and Lord James of Hereford (who as Attorney General in 1873 had favoured reforms which would protect trade unions from conspiracy charges)[173] absent, and with Henry Hawkins (as Lord Brampton) now on the panel, the anti-union Lord Halsbury got his way.[174] In Lord Macnaghten's view, all the Lords had done in *Allen* was to confirm that the unfortunate expressions used by Esher in *Bowen* v. *Hall* and *Temperton* v. *Russell* suggesting that malice was the gist of the action were wrong. It did not overrule these cases. The decision in *Temperton* was correct: the defendants were liable firstly for having knowingly induced a breach of contract; and secondly for a conspiracy to induce people not to contract with the plaintiff. In his view, all the 1875 Act had done was to remove the criminal liability for such a conspiracy. He felt there was good sense and authority for the proposition that a conspiracy to injure, which resulted in damage, should give rise to civil liability. 'A man may resist without much difficulty the wrongful act of an individual [...] but it is a very different thing [...] when one man has to defend himself against many combined to do him wrong.'[175] This was to take it for granted that a collective exercise of a union's economic rights was itself a wrong.

Lord Lindley's judgment made it clear that he supported the notion that the law should recognize intentional torts, for he praised Bowen's 'admirable judgment' in *Mogul* and stated that the principle behind *Lumley* v. *Gye* 'reaches all wrongful acts done intentionally to damage a particular individual'. He did not 'understand the decision in *Allen* v. *Flood* to be opposed to' this position.[176] In fact, Lindley's arguments were of the same stripe as the minority's in *Allen*, for he asserted that every person had a right recognized by law to earn his own living in his own way, which could only be interfered with where the 'interference is justifiable in point of law'. In his view, the union's actions here were not justifiable. In this case, '[t]he intention to injure the plaintiff negatives all excuses and disposes of any question of remoteness of damage'.[177] For Lindley, it was the union's coercion of the plaintiff through the use of numbers which made the action wrongful. Significantly, he felt that even a single trade union official, such as Thomas Allen,

---

[173] M. Curthoys, *Governments, Labour and the Law in Mid-Victorian Britain* (Oxford, 2004), 193.

[174] He observed that if the plaintiff had no remedy, 'it could hardly be said that our jurisprudence was that of a civilized community': *Quinn* v. *Leathem* [1901] AC 495 at 506.

[175] *Quinn* v. *Leathem* [1901] AC 495 at 511.

[176] *Ibid.* at 534–5.   [177] *Ibid.* at 537.

could be held liable for his acts, if he had and used the power to control a mass membership:

not to work oneself is lawful so long as one keeps off the poor-rates, but to order men not to work when they are willing to work is another thing. A threat to call men out given by a trade union official to an employer of men belonging to the union and willing to work with him is a form of coercion, intimidation, molestation, or annoyance to them and to him very difficult to resist, and, to say the least, requiring justification. None was offered in this case.[178]

This seemed to suggest that he did not feel that the defendants' liability turned on their having been part of a conspiracy. However, he did confirm that the 1875 Act did not remove the plaintiff's remedy in tort, and rejected the view that the civil liability depended on the criminal.[179]

The fullest discussion of conspiracy in this case was given by Brampton. It had already been clearly established that those who entered agreements to harm others could be prosecuted for conspiracy. It was also established that prosecutions for conspiracy could be brought even though none of the individual overt acts which evidenced the conspiracy were in themselves wrongs. The question for Brampton was

whether, assuming the existence of a conspiracy to do a wrongful and harmful act towards another and to carry it out by a number of overt acts, none of which taken singly and alone would, if done by an individual acting alone and apart from conspiracy, constitute a cause of action, such acts would become unlawful or actionable if done by the conspirators acting jointly or severally in pursuance of their conspiracy, and if by those acts substantial damage was caused to the person against whom the conspiracy was directed.[180]

Brampton's opinion was that they would. For it was the conspiracy which was the wrong, and not the overt acts manifesting it. This was as it should be: for just as a grain of gunpowder, harmless in itself, could become highly dangerous, so things which were not actionable if done separately could become dangerous when done in a conspiracy.[181]

Quinn v. *Leathem* appeared to establish that, although it was lawful for a single individual intentionally to inflict economic damage on another, provided he committed no other tort while doing so, it was an unlawful conspiracy for a group of people to do so. The pressure of collective action made the activity unlawful,

---

[178] *Ibid.* at 538.

[179] For a critique of Lindley's doctrinal reasoning, see also M. H. Kramer, N.E. Simmonds, and H. Steiner, *A Debate over Rights* (Oxford, 1998), 168–82, 187–90.

[180] *Quinn* v. *Leathem* [1901] AC 495 at 529.

[181] Brampton cited as authority the case of *Gregory* v. *The Duke of Brunswick* (1843) 6 M. & G. 205, 953.

where it was exercised with the intention of coercing a third party, rather than with the sole intention of promoting the interest of the group.[182] The Lords' recognition of a tort of conspiracy and its endorsement of *Lumley* v. *Gye* reopened the path for employers to sue trade unions for using their economic power against them, and to win enormous damages.[183] In such actions, juries were not asked if the union was actuated by malice. Where a unionist was accused of knowingly inducing a breach of contract, it was held to be no justification to show 'that he acted on a wrong understanding of his own rights, or without malice, or bona fide, or in the best interests of himself, nor even that he acted as an altruist, seeking only the good of another and careless of his own advantage'. He had rather to show 'an equal or superior right' to that of the plaintiff.[184] Where the focus of attention was on conspiracy, good intentions were equally irrelevant.[185] As Romer LJ put it in 1903, 'a combination of two or more persons, without justification, to injure a workman by inducing employers not to employ him or continue to employ him, is, if it results in damage to him, actionable'.[186]

Since any trade union official—and after *Taff Vale* any union itself—was liable at common law for any damages caused when strikers left their work in breach of their contracts, reform of the law became a priority for trade unionists and, in 1906, their liability was removed by s 3 of the Trade Disputes Act.[187] The Act did not affect the common law, however, but only created an immunity for actions done in furtherance of a trade dispute. It left in place the economic torts of inducing breaches of contract and conspiracy. The former remained important in three areas. First, it continued to be applicable in cases against trade unionists, in cases where courts found that the 1906 Act did not apply. In 1909, the House of Lords held that no

[182] As Scrutton J. put it: 'combinations intended to secure the interests of the confederates in their trade by reasonable and legitimate means are not actionable', *Ware and De Freville Ltd* v. *Motor Trade Association* [1920] 3 KB 40 at 71.

[183] See M. J. Klarman, 'Judges versus the Unions: The Development of British Labor Law, 1867–1913', (1989) 75 *Virginia LR* 1487–1602 at 1519; J. V. Orth, *Combination and Conspiracy: A Legal History of Trade Unionism, 1721–1906* (Oxford, 1991). See also Vol. XIII, Pt 3, pp. 698–701.

[184] *Read* v. *The Friendly Society of Operative Stonemasons of England, Ireland and Wales and Others* [1902] 2 KB 88 at 97. Cf. *South Wales Miners' Federation and Others* v. *Glamorgan Coal Co and Others* [1905] AC 239 at 245–6 and *Pratt and Others* v. *British Medical Association and Others* [1919] 1 KB 244 at 266.

[185] *Read* v. *The Friendly Society of Operative Stonemasons of England, Ireland and Wales and Others* [1902] 2 KB 732 at 736 (Collins MR).

[186] *Giblan* v. *National Amalgamated Labourers' Union of Great Britain and Ireland* [1903] 2 KB 600 at 618. See also the Lords' decision in *Larkin and Others* v. *Long* [1915] AC 814, which was a dispute held not covered by the 1906 Act.

[187] On the passing of this Act, see J. Thompson, 'The Genesis of the 1906 Trades Disputes Act: Liberalism, Trade Unions and the Law' (1998) 9 *Twentieth Century History* 175–200.

protection was given if threats had been used,[188] and in the decade which followed this decision, judges sought to draw a line between unlawful threats—which might include 'moral intimidation'—and lawful warnings.[189] Secondly, it continued to be used where one employer poached the employee of another, inducing a breach of contract—cases covered by the older actions for seduction or harbouring.[190] Thirdly, it was used in cases where a commercial party used underhand means to obtain access to the goods or services of his rival, by inducing intermediaries— often inadvertently—to break contracts of exclusive dealing.[191]

The question at the heart of *Allen* v. *Flood*—whether it was actionable, in the absence of violence or breach of contract, to induce someone not to employ a workman—was soon regarded as still unsettled. In 1903, Romer LJ said that it was unnecessary to prove a conspiracy in such a case. An individual who, 'by virtue of his position or influence, has power to carry out his design' could be held liable for unlawful molestation of a plaintiff, if he used his power to prevent others dealing with him.[192] In 1909, Lord Loreburn held that if 'some meddler sought to use the trade dispute as a cloak beneath which to interfere with impunity in other people's work or business' for 'sectarian, political, or purely mischievous', ends, he could be held liable for his intentional wrong.[193] A person could be held liable for using 'unlawful means' in furthering his interests, even in the absence of conspiracy. In 1918, McCardie J. therefore ruled that

a single person, or a body of persons, will commit an actionable wrong if he or they inflict actual pecuniary damage upon another by the intentional employment of unlawful means to injure that person's business, even though the unlawful means may not comprise any specific act which is per se actionable.[194]

Whether the means used were lawful or not depended on whether they could be justified; and where the defendant's motive was an 'indirect' one, or one not approved of by the law, there was no justification.[195] The question whether the means used to promote one's self-interest were legitimate or not was invariably one

---

[188] *Conway* v. *Wade* [1909] AC 506.

[189] Contrast the post-war cases of *Valentine* v. *Hyde* [1919] 2 Ch 129 at 146–7; *Hodges* v. *Webb* [1920] 2 Ch 70 at 88.

[190] See *Fred Wilkins and Brothers* v. *Weaver* [1915] 2 Ch 322; *Rose Street Foundry and Engineering Co* v. *John Lewis & Sons* 1917 1 SLT 153.

[191] See *Exchange Telegraph Co* v. *Gregory & Co* [1896] 1 QB 147; *National Phonograph Co* v. *Edison-Bell Consolidated Phonograph Co* [1908] 1 Ch 335.

[192] *Giblan* v. *National Amalgamated Labourers' Union of Great Britain and Ireland* [1903] 2 KB 600 at 619–20.

[193] *Conway* v. *Wade* [1909] AC 506 at 511. Such activity, Loreburn held, would not be protected by the Trade Disputes Act.

[194] *Pratt and Others* v. *British Medical Association and Others* [1919] 1 KB 244 at 260.

[195] The judgment was well received in (1919) 35 *LQR* 116.

of policy, which turned on the court's understanding of whether the defendant's real intentions were to benefit themselves, or to harm another.[196]

In the decade following the decision in *Quinn* v. *Leathem*, jurists were also uncertain about its meaning. Frederick Pollock continued to argue that conspiracy could not itself be a cause of action, and could not understand why the Lords had spent so much time discussing the issue. In his view, 'the cause of action was, in effect, ruining the plaintiff's business by coercing his customers not to deal with him, which is well within a line of old authorities'. He questioned Brampton's opinion that actions which were in themselves not actionable could become so when done by numbers. If this meant that acts which were 'positively lawful when done by one person alone, and not merely insignificant', became actionable when done in numbers, then no authority could be found to support it. It was true that an actionable wrong—such as nuisance—could be made up of numerous acts not in themselves actionable. It was true that a wrong could be made up of the otherwise indifferent acts of many individuals. But in such cases, it was the joint wrongful act, and not the conspiracy, which was actionable.[197] For Pollock, the wrong which was committed when unions coerced employers was that of intimidation. In his view, exercising the 'common right' of giving advice and speaking freely might become actionable when unlawful means were used, 'such as intimidation (whether open or disguised as persuasion)'. He worried that parties who had difficulty proving intimidation would rather try 'to persuade a jury to find that there has been a "malicious conspiracy" than to prove what really happened, and persuade the Court that it amounts to a good cause of action'.[198] While critical of the discussion of conspiracy in this case, Pollock nonetheless felt that his view of wilful harms had been given support by the decision in *Quinn*. Welcoming the fact that the Lords shared his view of *Lumley* v. *Gye*, he pointed out that Lord Lindley had said that this principle reached all wrongful acts done with the intention of inflicting damage. Pollock was still striving for a *prima facie* tort doctrine, and in his next edition in 1908, argued for it more strongly than ever.

John Salmond's view was similar view to Pollock's. He felt that where a trade unionist compelled an employer's customers to cease dealing with him, he could be held liable for the 'wrong of intimidation'. Such compulsion occurred both where individuals threatened illegal action against the customers, or where 'the intimidation assumes the form of a conspiracy'.[199] But (like Pollock), Salmond did not feel that combination was essential to the cause of action: it was sufficient

[196] *Sorrell* v. *Smith* [1925] AC 700; *Crofter Hand Woven Harris Tweed Co* v. *Veitch* [1942] AC 435.

[197] Pollock, *Torts* (7th edn, 1904), 318–19.

[198] *Ibid.*, 326–7.

[199] J. W. Salmond, *The Law of Torts: A Treatise on the English Law of Liability for Civil Injuries* (2nd edn, 1910), 466.

'for *one* person intentionally and without lawful justification to do harm to the plaintiff by threatening other persons with harm'.[200] Absence of ill-will, Salmond added, could not constitute a justification. What could was a matter of law, for the judges to develop.

By the early 1960s, some academic commentators and judges accepted a broader tort of intimidation, where the intimidation could consist of a threat to procure an illegal act or where it was the act of two or more acting in the pursuance of a common intention.[201] But there continued to be discomfort with the civil tort of conspiracy, which 'attracted more controversy among academic writers than success in practical application' and which at least one judge regarded as 'a highly anomalous cause of action'.[202] In an age of economic regulation, judges could not always resist the temptation to make controversial policy judgments, under the guise of applying pure legal principle.

---

[200] *Ibid.*, 471.

[201] *Salmond on Torts* (13th edn, 1961 by R. F. Heuston), 697 endorsed by the House of Lords in *Rookes* v. *Barnard* [1964] AC 1129, which held that the tort of intimidation included a threat to break contracts.

[202] Per Lord Diplock in *Lonrho* v. *Shell Petroleum (No. 2)* [1982] AC 173 at 188. See also the discussion in *Metall und Rohstoff AG* v. *Donaldson Lufkin & Jenrette Inc* [1990] 1 QB 391 at 451–67. For a general discussion, see P. Sales, 'The Tort of Conspiracy and civil secondary liability' (1990) 49 *CLJ* 491–514.

VI

Nuisance

WHILE there had always been problems caused by smoke, or polluted water, noise or overcrowding, they were significantly magnified in the nineteenth century as a result of rapid industrialization and urbanization. All cities suffered severely from coal smoke emitted by domestic fires and steam engines.[1] Many also suffered from poisonous chemical fumes emitted by new industries such as alkali production[2] and copper smelting.[3] Rivers were rendered foul from industrial effluents, and (after 1840) from the draining of water closets via sewage pipes. Urban development also brought other irritants, as when brick kilns filled residential areas with smoke when new houses were built, or when new buildings blocked the light of established householders.

Although the major environmental problems caused by urbanization could ultimately only be dealt with by legislation and regulation,[4] the common law continued to play an important role.[5] To begin with, those responsible for

---

[1] P. Thorsheim, *Inventing Pollution: Coal, Smoke and Culture in Britain since 1800* (Athens, Ohio, 2006).

[2] See A. E. Dingle, '"The Monster Nuisance of All": Landowners, Alkali Manufacturers, and Air Pollution, 1828–64' (1982) 35 *Econ. Hist. Rev.* (2nd ser) 529–48; R. Hawes, 'The Control of Alkali Pollution in St Helens, 1862–1890' (1995) 1 *Environment and History* 159–71; A. W. B. Simpson, *Leading Cases in the Common Law* (Oxford, 1995), 176–9. Royal Commission on Working and Management of Works and Manufactures from which Sulphuric Acid, Sulphuretted Hydrogen, and Ammoniacal and Other Vapours and Gases are given off, and effect on Animal and Vegetable Life, *PP* 1878 [c. 2159] [c. 2159-I], xlvi, 1, at p. 43 (henceforth cited as 1878 Royal Commission on Noxious Vapours), 363.

[3] R. Rees 'The South Wales Copper-Smoke Dispute, 1833–95' (1980–1) 10 *Welsh History Review* 480–96.

[4] On the history of regulation, see XIII, Pt 2, Ch. IV. See also A. S. Wohl, *Endangered Lives: Public Health in Victorian Britain* (1983); C. Hamlin, *Public Health and Social Justice in the Age of Chadwick: Britain, 1800–54* (Cambridge, 1998); idem, 'Public Sphere to Public Health: The Transformation of "Nuisance"', in S. Sturdy, *Medicine, Health and the Public Sphere in Britain, 1600–2000* (2002), 189–204; S. Halliday, *The Great Stink of London: Sir Joseph Bazalgette and the Cleansing of the Victorian Capital* (Stroud, 1999).

[5] The subject has been given detailed treatment in J. P. S. McLaren, 'Nuisance Law and the Industrial Revolution—Some Lessons from Social History' (1983) 3 *OJLS* 155–221. See also J. F. Brenner, 'Nuisance Law and the Industrial Revolution' (1974) 3 *JLS* 403–31; B. Pontin, 'Tort Law and Victorian Government Growth: The Historiographical Significance of Tort in the Shadow of Chemical Pollution and Factory Safety Regulation (1998)' 18 *OJLS* 661–80.

nuisances could be indicted. To be subject to prosecution, the nuisance had to be a general annoyance to the public, rather than a harm to particular individuals only.[6] Where the defendant's conduct constituted a public nuisance, a private action was only available if the plaintiff suffered special damage of a different kind from that suffered by the general public.[7] Nuisances subject to indictment included infringements of public rights, such as the obstruction of highways (including by non-repair), the pollution of public (navigable) rivers, or the interference with public health by polluting the air or creating noise. Besides such environmental nuisances, offences against public morals, such as the keeping of bawdy houses or indecent exposure, could be prosecuted as public nuisances; while a number of other matters were defined as public nuisances by statute. They were punishable by fines or imprisonment; and the nuisance could be abated, or prohibited by a mandatory writ from the King's Bench.

Besides affecting the public in general, nuisances could constitute infringements of private rights. The prime common law remedy was the action on the case for nuisance, in which the plaintiff usually complained that the defendant's wrongful act disturbed his possession of property. The common law action was used either to compensate for past damage or to establish the legal fact of nuisance, as a preliminary step to obtaining injunctive relief in Chancery, which only gave relief if it was convinced that a common law right had been infringed. The law of nuisance offered a remedy in two distinct situations. The first was where the defendant's use of his property interfered directly with the plaintiff's property rights, as where his prescriptive right to light was blocked or where his natural right as a riparian owner to clean water was interfered with. Where nuisances were seen to injure property, and could be seen as in the nature of a trespass, nineteenth-century courts tended to take a strict view of the defendant's liability. In such cases, the courts tended to see their role as that of protecting established property rights, rather than balancing rival interests, which might entail sacrificing individuals for the greater economic good.

The second was where the defendant's activity did not harm the property itself or interfere with any easement, but rather interfered with the comfort of the occupants, as where loud noise or unpleasant smells were generated.[8] In such cases, the focus was less on the nature of the plaintiff's right than on the nature of the

---

[6] *R* v. *Lloyd* (1802) 2 Esp. 200.

[7] See *Rose* v. *Miles* (1815) 4 M. & S. 101; *Greasley* v. *Codling* (1824) 2 Bing. 263; *Wilkes* v. *Hungerford Market Co* (1835) 2 Bing. N.C. 281; *Winterbottom* v. *Lord Derby* (1867) LR 2 Ex 316; *Fritz* v. *Hobson* (1880) 14 Ch D 542; E. W. Garrett, *The Law of Nuisances* (1890), 17–20. Thus, if a man owned a colliery, access to which was blocked by the obstruction of a public highway, he could bring a private action: *Iveson* v. *Moore* (1699) 1 Ld. Raym. 486; 1 Salk. 15; Holt 10; Com. 58; 12 Mod. 262; Carth. 451; Comb. 480; Willes, 74n. See also *Chichester* v. *Lethbridge* (1738) Willes 71.

[8] A third use of the action was to offer a remedy for plaintiffs harmed in accidents occurring in public places, as a result of the creation of a public nuisance by the defendant. The third kind of

defendant's activity. As Lord Westbury put it in 1865, where the nuisance did not produce any 'material injury to the property' but was only 'productive of sensible personal discomfort', a different standard applied. While proprietors were not expected to accept inconveniences which diminished the value of their property, those living in towns had to put up with 'that amount of discomfort which may be necessary for the legitimate and free exercise of the trade of their neighbours'.[9] In such cases, the courts were to ask not whether the proprietary interest of the plaintiff was being interfered with, but whether the defendant was making more noise than was acceptable in the context of the location.[10] In such cases, those with reversionary rights to the property often found themselves unable to sue for the nuisance caused by noise or smells, after their tenants quit, since they could only maintain actions for damage to the reversion as was either permanent or might harm their title to the property, by allowing the development of rights adverse to his title.[11]

Plaintiffs complaining of nuisance had to have some kind of interest in the property, since it was only in the context of a right to peace and quiet in a specific place that any nuisance was a wrong. Nineteenth-century courts did not spend much time exploring exactly what legal interest the plaintiff had to have. In 1906, however, the Court of Appeal suggested that where a plaintiff was in *de facto* occupation of property—as in this case, where an oyster merchant had occupied oyster beds on a foreshore belonging to the lord of the manor—he could maintain an action of nuisance against a polluter.[12] However, in the following year, in *Malone* v. *Laskey*, the Court of Appeal held that 'a person who is merely present in the house cannot complain of a nuisance which has in it no element of a public nuisance'. The case was an untypical nuisance case, however. It was brought by a man who was permitted by his employers to occupy a house which they had let, after his wife was injured when a bracket fell on her, having been dislodged by vibrations from an engine on the defendants' adjoining premises. Having ruled

---

case generally raised questions of negligence, both by plaintiff and defendant, and thus an overlap developed in the mid-nineteenth century with the emerging tort of negligence.

⁹ *St Helen's Smelting Co* v. *Tipping* (1865) 11 HLC 642 at 650.

¹⁰ 10 See *Robinson* v. *Kilvert* (1889) 41 Ch D 88 at 96, qualifying the position taken in *Cooke* v. *Forbes* (1867) LR 5 Eq 166 at 173.

¹¹ *Jesser* v. *Gifford* (1767) 4 Burr. 2141; *Dobson* v. *Blackmore* (1847) 9 Q.B. 991; *Kidgill* v. *Moor* (1850) 9 C.B. 364, 19 LJ CP 177; *Mumford* v. *Oxford, Worcester and Wolverhampton Railway Co* (1856) 1 H. & N. 34; *Simpson* v. *Savage* (1856) 1 C.B. N.S. 347; *Mott* v. *Shoolbred* (1875) LR 20 Eq 22. See also T. J. Bullen and C. Dodd, *Bullen and Leake's Precedents of Pleadings*, 2 vols (4th edn, 1882), 486n; C. G. Addison, *A Treatise on the Law of Torts, or wrongs and their remedies* (7th edn by H. Smith and A. P. P. Keep, 1893), 409; *Jones* v. *Chappell* (1875) LR 20 Eq 539.

¹² *Foster* v. *Urban District Council of Warblington* [1906] 1 KB 648. On this case, see *Motherwell* v. *Motherwell* (1976) 73 DLR (3d) 62.

against the plaintiff's claim in negligence, the Court of Appeal was keen to prevent the action of nuisance being used as a substitute. With this in mind, Sir Gorell Barnes P. held that the injured woman had 'no right of occupation in the proper sense of the term'.[13]

1. THE RIGHT TO LIGHT

Throughout the nineteenth century, urban householders resorted to the common law to prevent their neighbours constructing tall buildings which would darken their light. Building construction was subjected to some control throughout the century, through local legislation allowing by-laws to be made to control street widths and the height of buildings.[14] In an era when many builders sought to erect increasingly tall structures, notably in London, by-laws were introduced to limit permissible heights.[15] However, these regulatory controls on construction were often not particularly effective, and individual parties disturbed by new buildings continued to go to law. For instance, the speculative, luxurious development of Queen Anne's Mansions, built near St James's Park in the later 1870s, caused considerable concern because of its height, and its developers found themselves before the Westminster Police Court on a number of occasions for infringements of the Building Act.[16] But since developers could negotiate and come to terms with the district surveyor, the law of nuisance offered a last resort to those whose concerns escaped officialdom. When the company owning Queen Anne's Mansions projected to extend the development, the Secretary of State for War obtained an injunction on the grounds that the new development would deprive the Guards Chapel of light. The press welcomed the decision which prevented this 'eyesore [...] spreading westwards'.[17]

[13] *Malone* v. *Laskey* [1907] 2 KB 141 at 154 (per Fletcher Moulton LJ), 154 (per Barnes P.). *Malone* v. *Laskey* was followed in *Cunard* v. *Antifyre* [1933] 1 KB 551 and *Oldham* v. *Lawson (No. 1)* [1976] VR 654; but was challenged in *Khorasandjian* v. *Bush* [1993] QB 727, which was overruled in this respect in *Hunter* v. *Canary Wharf* [1997] AC 655.

[14] W. Ashworth, *The Genesis of Modern British Town Planning: A Study in Economic and Social History of the Nineteenth and Twentieth Centuries* (1954). London had seen statutory controls of building since the eighteenth century. See also 7 & 8 Vict. c. 84, 18 & 19 Vict. c. 122.

[15] In 1875, the Public Health Act allowed sanitary authorities to make building by-laws, to be confirmed by the Local Government Board. In 1877, this body issued a series of model by-laws for the use of sanitary authorities, to regulate (among other things) the layout of new streets and buildings: *The Times*, 20 December 1877, col. 3c; Eighth Annual Report of the Local Government Board, *PP* 1878–9 [c. 2372], xxviii, 1 at p. cxxxix.

[16] *The Graphic*, 22 December 1877; *Pall Mall Gazette*, 10 January 1878.

[17] *AG* v. *The Queen Anne and Garden Mansions Co* (1889) 60 LT 759; *The Times*, 18 April 1889, col. 9c. Cf. *Knowles* v. *Queen Anne and Garden Mansions*, *The Times*, 15 December 1888, col. 16a.

All property owners had a natural right to the light which 'falls perpendicu-larly on his land'.[18] Any right to light from lateral sources could derive only from prescription, for the right to such light was not an ordinary incident of property. A plaintiff could claim a negative easement after 20 years' uninterrupted enjoy-ment of the light, this being seen as long enough to 'induce a presumption that there was originally some agreement between the parties'.[19] The person having such a right whose light was blocked could remove the obstruction, and defend any claim of trespass brought against him by stating his right to abate the nui-sance.[20] He could also sue in an action on the case for nuisance,[21] or seek an injunction.

The number of cases involving the deprivation of light rose in the mid-cen-tury, thanks both to the legislative ending (in 1832) of the custom of the city of London that owners could rebuild houses on ancient foundations to any height,[22] and to the ensuing increase in the number of large commercial build-ings and warehouses.[23] Disputes typically arose between property owners, each of whom sought to extend his own building, while restricting his neighbour's ability to build. Particular problems were caused when a dominant tenant (the party enjoying a prescriptive right) rebuilt his building, enlarging his windows and adding a new storey. Since he had no greater right than came from the grant implied by continuous user, it was settled that the servient tenant could block up any new windows, although he could not interfere with the old.[24] But since the windows on the top floor could not be blocked without also blocking the ancient ones, did this mean that the dominant tenant could obtain new rights, and prevent his neighbour building? This question was addressed in 1852 in *Renshaw* v. *Bean*, when the Queen's Bench held that by enlarging his

---

[18] C. J. Gale, *Treatise on the Law of Easements* (5th edn by D. Gibbons, 1876), 319. For the prescrip-tive nature of the right to light from lateral sources, see *Aldred's Case* (1610) 9 Co. Rep. 57b; *Moore* v. *Rawson* (1824) 3 B. & C. 322 at 341.

[19] See Wilmot J.'s comments in *Lewis* v. *Price* (1761) and *Dougal* v. *Wilson* (1769), as reported by Williams' notes to *Yard* v. *Ford*, in 2 Wms. Saund. 175n. In *Moore* v. *Rawson* (1824) 3 B. & C. 322 at 340, Littledale J. commented that the right was better described as derived from a covenant implied by law not to interrupt the free use of light and air, rather than from a grant, since it was not 'a privi-lege of something positive to be done or used in the soil of' another man's land.

[20] *R* v. *Rosewell* (1699) 2 Salk. 459; and see *Penwarden* v. *Ching* (1829) M. & M. 400 and *Roberts* v. *Macord* (1832) 1 M. & Rob. 230.

[21] See J. Wentworth, *A Complete System of Pleading*, 10 vols (1797–9), viii, 548.

[22] See W. Bohun, *Privilegia Londini* (1702), 54. See also *Plummer* v. *Bentham* (1757) 1 Burr. 248.

[23] See Wood VC's comments in *Dent* v. *Auction Mart Company* (1866) LR 2 Eq 238, 244–5. On the building history, see M. Daunton, 'Introduction', in M. Daunton (ed.), *The Cambridge Urban History of Britain, III: 1840–1950* (Cambridge, 2000), 1–56 at 37; J. Summerson, *The London Building World of the 1860s* (1973).

[24] *Chandler* v. *Thompson* (1811) 3 Camp. 80 at 81; *Blanchard* v. *Bridges* (1835) 4 Ad. & El. 176.

windows, and thereby exceeding his rights, the dominant tenant lost his rights until such time as 'he shall, by himself doing away with the excess and restoring his windows to their former state, throw upon the defendant the necessity of so arranging his buildings as not to interfere with the admitted right'.[25] Other judges agreed that since the dominant tenant's right derived from his neighbour's consent, and since he could not impose new obligations without consent, he must be taken to have lost his anterior right if he so 'confused and mixed up [the old light] with the new lights that the latter cannot be blocked up without obstructing the former'.[26]

Renshaw v. Bean proved controversial,[27] and was overruled in *Tapling* v. *Jones*. Tapling, a silk mercer in Wood Street, demolished a set of buildings in 1852 and erected a warehouse in their place. Four years later, Jones did the same, building a warehouse which obstructed Tapling's light. Following the guidelines in *Renshaw v. Bean*, Tapling restored his ancient windows, and sued for an obstruction of his light. Jones argued that, having exceeded his old right, Tapling must be taken to have abandoned it, and that he could not simply resume it by rebuilding. The judges in the Exchequer Chamber were divided on the case. Blackburn J. and Bramwell B. felt that Jones's original obstruction of the ancient lights—when building his warehouse—was unjustified. The mere fact that new lights were opened did not in their view justify the obstruction of old ones, notwithstanding *Renshaw v. Bean*. For, as Blackburn put it, '[i]f it were the law that a person opening any new window, however small, in such a position that it could not be obstructed without obstructing an antient one, forfeited his antient light, it might lead to very inconvenient results'.[28] Wightman J. and Crompton J. felt that the original obstruction was justifiable, since the plaintiff had exceeded his rights, but that now he had blocked up the excess, the defendant was bound to remove his obstruction. Pollock CB and Martin B. felt that both the original and continued obstructions were lawful. Martin B. did 'not at all regret that a man having a house in the city of London, who increases the height of his building, and thereby compels his neighbour to build up a wall at an expense in order to protect himself, is found to have difficulties from having so done'.[29]

The House of Lords found for Tapling. In Lord Westbury LC's view, section 3 of the Prescription Act 1832 was a positive enactment, and made the right to light acquired after 20 years' enjoyment absolute and indefeasible. It could only be lost

[25] *Renshaw* v. *Bean* (1852) 18 Q.B. 112 at 130. See also *Cooper* v. *Hubbuck* (1860) 30 Beav. 160.
[26] *Hutchinson* v. *Copestake* (1861) 9 C.B. N.S. 863 at 870.
[27] See the comments of Kindersley VC in *Wilson* v. *Townend* (1860) 1 Dr. & Sm. 324 at 331–2.
[28] *Jones* v. *Tapling* (1862) 12 C.B. N.S. 826 at 838.
[29] *Ibid* at 862.

by a clear act of abandonment, and not by a merely temporary interruption of enjoyment. Once the right was acquired, the dominant tenant could open new windows as he liked, and the owner of the servient tenant might attempt to block the new ones, but he could not interfere with the established ones. This interpretation of the statute gave a more fixed view of the right to light than was to be found in some of the earlier cases.[30]

While *Tapling* v. *Jones* established that the dominant tenant had a right to receive damages from the servient tenant who obstructed his ancient lights, it was not immediately clear that he would obtain equitable relief. Lord Romilly MR was particularly sceptical. In *Heath* v. *Bucknall*, he held that where the owner of ancient lights so dealt with it 'as essentially to alter its character, to convert it into a different easement', then 'the owner of the servient tenement is not debarred from the enjoyment of his land as heretofore', though he would have to pay damages.[31] Romilly was concerned that by granting an injunction, the court might allow the plaintiff in effect to acquire new rights. Romilly's views were not shared by other equity judges, however. Giffard LJ denied 'that a Plaintiff who, according to *Tapling* v. *Jones*, has clear legal rights, cannot come to this Court and get protection for those rights'. In his view, 'when there is a material injury to that which is a clear legal right, and it appears that damages, from the nature of the case, would not be a complete compensation, this Court will interfere by injunction'.[32] The Lord Justices also disagreed with Romilly's view in *Durell* v. *Pritchard* that a mandatory injunction could not be granted to have buildings pulled down, where works were completed before the filing of the bill,[33] although they did hold that a mandatory injunction would only be granted 'in cases in which extreme, or at all events very serious, damage will ensue from its interference being withheld'.[34] While injunctions would be granted to prevent work being done, courts of equity remained reluctant to grant mandatory injunctions to take down buildings which had been put up, granting damages instead.[35]

---

[30] e.g. in *Moore* v. *Rawson* (1824) 3 B. & C. 322 where Littledale J. ruled (at 340–1) that '[t]he right, therefore, is acquired by mere occupancy, and ought to cease when the person who so acquired it discontinues the occupancy'.

[31] *Heath* v. *Bucknall* (1869) LR 8 Eq 1 at 5–6.

[32] *Staight* v. *Burn* (1869) 5 Ch App 163 at 167. See also *Aynsley* v. *Glover* (1874) LR 18 Eq 544.

[33] *Durell* v. *Pritchard* (1865) LR 1 Ch 244. He added that where such an injunction were refused, the court could award no damages under Lord Cairns's Act, having only power to award damages in lieu of an equitable remedy.

[34] *Durell* v. *Pritchard* (1865) LR 1 Ch App 244, 250. The appeal was dismissed as the court held that there was not a sufficiently serious nuisance to warrant the court's intervention.

[35] *Isenberg* v. *East India House Estate Company* (1863) 33 LJ (Ch) 392 at 393; *The Curriers Co* v. *Corbett* (1865) 2 Dr. & Sm. 355; (1865) 4 De G. J. & S. 764 at 769; *Aynsley* v. *Glover* (1874) LR 18 Eq 544 at 553–4; *City of London Brewery Co* v. *Tennant* (1873) LR 9 Ch App 212 at 218. See also Wood VC's view in *Senior* v. *Pawson* (1866) LR 3 Eq. 330, 334.

Nineteenth-century courts also debated the quantity of light to which a dominant tenant had a prescriptive right. Two rival views emerged. The first view was that the plaintiff was only entitled to the quantity needed for ordinary purposes. This view derived from two early nineteenth-century authorities. The first was Lord Eldon's comment in *Attorney General* v. *Nichol* that there were 'many obvious cases' of new buildings depriving those opposite of light 'but not in such a degree that an injunction could be maintained, or an action upon the case'.[36] This meant that there had to be a a serious obstruction of light before an action could be brought.[37] The second was Macdonald CB's decision in *Martin* v. *Goble* in 1808, that where a malt house with ancient windows had been converted into a workhouse, the occupiers only had the right to such light as was necessary for a malt house, not for a dwelling-house, since '[n]o man could by any act of his suddenly impose a new restriction upon his neighbour'.[38]

Eldon's words were drawn on by Lord Westbury in 1864 in *Jackson* v. *The Duke of Newcastle*, when holding that the foundation of Chancery's jurisdiction was 'injury to property which renders it in a material degree unsuitable for the purposes to which it is now applied, or lessens considerably the enjoyment which the owner now has of it'.[39] In the following year, Lord Cranworth considered that the crucial question was whether the plaintiff was deprived of such light and air 'as he might reasonably calculate on enjoying', and whether it caused material inconvenience to the occupiers of the house in their ordinary occupations. 'Persons who live in towns, and more especially in large cities', he observed, 'cannot expect to enjoy continually the same unobstructed volumes of light and air as fall to the lot of those who live in the country'.[40] Six years later in *Kelk* v. *Pearson*, the Lord Justices rejected the plaintiff's argument that the Prescription Act conferred an absolute and indefeasible right to all the light and air which came through his windows. In their view, the legislation had not altered the nature of the right, which was 'to have that amount of light through the windows of a house which was sufficient, according to the ordinary notions of mankind, for the comfortable use and enjoyment of that house as a dwelling-house, if it were a dwelling-house, or for the beneficial use and occupation of the house, if it were a warehouse, a shop, or other place of business'.[41]

---

[36] *Attorney-General* v. *Nichol* (1809) 16 Ves. 338 at 342–3.

[37] See also *Back* v. *Stacey* (1826) 2 Car. & P. 465 at 466; *Parker* v. *Smith* (1832) 5 Car. & P. 438 at 439; *Wells* v. *Ody* (1836) 7 Car. & P. 410; *Pringle* v. *Wernham* (1836) 7 Car. & P. 377 at 378–9.

[38] *Martin* v. *Goble* (1808) 1 Camp. 320.

[39] *Jackson* v. *The Duke of Newcastle* (1864) 3 De G. J. & S. 275 at 284.

[40] *Clarke* v. *Clark* (1865) LR 1 Ch App 16, at 17–18.

[41] *Kelk* v. *Pearson* (1871) LR 6 Ch App 809 at 811, per James LJ. See also *City of London Brewery Co* v. *Tennant* (1873) LR 9 Ch App 212 at 216–17; *Dickinson* v. *Harbottle* (1873) 28 LT 186.

Macdonald's words were drawn on by Malins VC in *Lanfranchi* v. *Mackenzie*, when refusing to grant an injunction to silk merchants seeking to protect the light entering a cellar they had used as a sample room for 14 years. It was agreed that while the new building did darken the cellar at some times of the day, there would be more light at other times, owing to the reflection of light from the windows of the new building. In Malins's view, this was not such an interference with light as would induce the court to act, were the building used for ordinary business purposes. In his view, in order to acquire a right to the particular quantity of light claimed, the plaintiff would have to have shown a continual 20-year enjoyment of that amount of light, which 'would establish the right against all persons who had reasonable knowledge of it'.[42]

The second stricter view of the dominant tenant's rights developed after *Tapling* v. *Jones*. Once attention was focused on the Prescription Act, Cranworth's suggestion that there were different rules for the town and country, which had been initially followed,[43] was abandoned. In *Yates* v. *Jack*, where Smithfield merchants sought an injunction to prevent the doubling in height of a building opposite their premises, Wood VC said that since the custom of the city of London regarding rebuilding had been abolished, he was precluded from considering 'any point which might be urged as to the necessity of making a difference between the circumstances of buildings in towns and in other places'.[44] Although still doubting the policy of giving such protection to urban lights,[45] Lord Cranworth admitted that the effect of the Prescription Act was to recognize that the right to light enjoyed for 20 years 'is an absolute indefeasible right to the enjoyment of the light without reference to the purpose for which it has been used'.[46]

According to this approach, the owner of a dominant tenement did not have to be content with such a quantity of light which other traders would find sufficient.[47] Rather, 'the plaintiff was entitled to the same quantum of light as he had theretofore enjoyed, irrespective of the purpose for which he had

---

[42] *Lanfranchi* v. *Mackenzie* (1867) LR 4 Eq 421 at 430. See also *Herz* v. *The Union Bank of London* (1859) 2 Giff. 686 at 691; *Hutchinson* v. *Copestake* (1861) 9 C.B. N.S. 863 at 869.

[43] *Robson* v. *Whittingham* (1866) 12 Jur. N.S. 40 at 41.

[44] *Yates* v. *Jack* (1866) LR 1 Ch App 295 at 296n. See also his comments in *Dent* v. *Auction Mart Co* (1866) LR 2 Eq 238, 249–50.

[45] Even Wood VC (who arguably had prompted Cranworth's reconsideration of the matter) observed that the decision went 'a little beyond what, as far as I am aware, any previous case has decided': *Dent* v. *Auction Mart Co* (1866) LR 2 Eq 238 at 249.

[46] *Yates* v. *Jack* (1866) LR 1 Ch App 295 at 298, 300. Section 3 of the Act read, 'When the access and use of light to and for any dwelling-house, workshop, or other buildings shall have been actually enjoyed therewith for the full period of twenty years without interruption, the right thereto shall be deemed absolute and indefeasible'.

[47] See *Dent* v. *Auction Mart Co* (1866) LR 2 Eq 238 at 250–1.

enjoyed it'.[48] The fact that the use made of premises changed did not alter the plaintiff's right to light.[49] Rather, the plaintiff obtained an 'absolute right' to that 'cone of light' which for 20 years passed over the servient tenant's property and through the dominant tenant's aperture.[50] In Jessel MR's view, *Jackson* v. *Duke of Newcastle* had been overruled by *Yates* v. *Jack*.[51] Kekewich J. was another judge who rejected the view that the nature of the plaintiff's actual use of the light was relevant. In *Attorney General* v. *The Queen Anne and Gardens Mansions*, he held the plaintiff was entitled to an injunction to protect light entering the Guards Chapel, even though it had already been darkened by the installation of stained glass.[52] In *Lazarus* v. *Artistic Photographic Co*, he declined to follow *Lanfranchi* v. *Mackenzie*, upholding a plaintiff's right to the enjoyment of extraordinary light for photographic purposes, even though he had not made such use of the light for 20 years.[53]

Other judges held that the right to light claimed under the Prescription Act did not depend on its actual uninterrupted use for 20 years. Provided the owner of a building had the amenity of using the access of light which came through a fixed aperture for 20 years,[54] he had 'enjoyed' it within the meaning of section 3 of the Prescription Act without actually needing to show continuous user. Thus, in *Cooper* v. *Straker* in 1888, wool merchants in Bishopsgate who had shuttered windows which were occasionally opened to allow them to display their wares obtained a perpetual injunction to prevent the darkening of their lights.[55] As Lord Chemsford put it in *Calcraft* v. *Thompson*, '[t]he right which is gradually ripening—and which after twenty years' enjoyment, is absolutely acquired—is a right to have the light freely admitted to the house through an aperture of certain dimensions. The particular use to which the house is applied during the period in which the right is thus growing never enters at all into consideration. When the full statutory time is accomplished, the measure of the right is exactly that (neither more nor less) which has been uniformly enjoyed previously.'[56]

---

[48] *Moore* v. *Hall* (1878) 3 QBD 178 at 179–80 (per Manisty J.). See also *Aynsley* v. *Glover* (1874) LR 18 Eq 545 at 548, affirmed in (1875) 10 Ch D 283.

[49] See *Ecclesiastical Commissioners* v. *Kino* (1880) 14 Ch D 213.

[50] *Scott* v. *Pape* (1886) 31 Ch D 554 at 569.

[51] *Aynsley* v. *Glover* (1874) LR 8 Eq 544. In his view, equity should grant an injunction whenever the common law awarded substantial damages, which he felt should always be done unless the action was only brought by the reversioner to try the right.

[52] *Attorney General* v. *The Queen Anne and Gardens Mansions* (1889) 5 TLR 430.

[53] *Lazarus* v. *Artistic Photographic Co* [1897] 2 Ch 214.

[54] *Harris* v. *De Pinna* (1886) 33 Ch D 238. The right was not lost if new windows were put in the place of the ancient ones: *Scott* v. *Pape* (1886) 31 Ch D 554; *Ecclesiastical Commissioners* v. *Kino* (1880) 14 Ch D 213.

[55] *Cooper* v. *Straker* [1888] 40 Ch D 21. See also *Courtauld* v. *Legh* (1869) LR 4 Ex 126.

[56] *Calcraft* v. *Thompson* (1867) 15 WR 387 at 388.

The strict view permitted owners of property to use their right to light as a means to prevent property developments they found undesirable, regardless of whether they interfered with the actual use of their own property. For example, in *Dyers' Co* v. *King*, an injunction was granted preventing the defendants erecting a building which would interfere with light which had reached the plaintiffs' property over the defendant's land for 20 years, despite the fact that, thanks to the widening of streets in the area and the demolition of other buildings, the plaintiffs would have more light than hitherto, even if the new building was put up. 'The right is a right as between the owner of the dominant tenement and the owner of every servient tenement', James VC ruled, and the latter could not deprive the former of the light which passed over his property merely 'because the owner of the dominant tenement has, either by purchase from, or by the free gift of, any other person, or by the operation of any Act of Parliament, obtained other light in addition to that which he had a prescriptive right to'.[57]

Judges continued to hold rival views of the doctrine into the twentieth century. In 1900, in *Warren* v. *Brown*, Wright J. held that a plaintiff who required an unusual degree of light for the manufacture of hosiery (which had been carried on at the premises for 14 years) had no cause of action, since there was enough light for the ordinary purposes of business. In his view, a stricter view of the right to light would unduly impede urban development.[58] His decision was reversed by the Court of Appeal, which at the same time overruled *Lanfranchi* v. *Mackenzie* and *Dickinson* v. *Harbottle*,[59] taking the strict view. However, three years later the 'strict' view was overturned by the House of Lords in *Colls* v. *Home and Colonial Stores*, when it held that to constitute an actionable obstruction of ancient lights, there had to be not merely a diminution of light, but a substantial privation, enough to render the house uncomfortable according to the ordinary notions of mankind or to prevent the plaintiff from carrying on his business as beneficially as before. As Lord Halsbury LC saw it, it was better to regard the matter as being in the nature of a nuisance—by which he meant, akin to 'smoke, smell, and noise' nuisances—than to consider the plaintiff to have a sort of proprietary right in the air. Like Wright, he felt that granting the dominant tenant the right to all the light enjoyed for 20 years 'would render it almost impossible for towns to grow'.[60] Instead, the test was whether the interference amounted to a nuisance, which was a more elastic test. Lord Davey noted that section 3 of the Prescription Act had not altered the nature of the right, but only

[57] *Dyers' Company* v. *King* (1870) LR 9 Eq 438 at 442.
[58] *Warren and Others* v. *Brown*. [1900] 2 QB 722 at 734.
[59] *Warren* v. *Brown* [1902] 1 KB 15.
[60] *Colls* v. *Home and Colonial Stores* [1904] AC 179 at 182.

the conditions by which the right could be acquired. The right itself was to light which was sufficient according to the ordinary notions of mankind: 'it is impossible to assert that any man has a right to a fixed amount of light ascertainable by metes and bounds'.[61]

The effect of this decision was to rule that the correct approach was not to consider the right to light as being a property right, but rather to consider it as a negative easement 'being a right to prevent some landowner from using his land so as to constitute a nuisance to the owner or occupier of a house upon adjoining land'.[62] In *Kine* v. *Jolly* in 1904, the majority in a divided Court of Appeal reiterated the view that the deprivation of light was in the nature of nuisance. As Vaughan Williams LJ put it, the action of nuisance was not limited to cases where the plaintiff had acquired a legal right, let alone by way of prescription. It lay where a defendant had used his land so as to injure his neighbour's land. Whether the rights at issue were common law ones or prescriptive ones, the action was one of nuisance. However, to succeed in that action, there had to be a substantial interference with the plaintiff's comfort. In this judge's view, 'no man should be allowed to enforce rights to such an extent as to interfere with the good and the progress of the community'. Moreover, 'citizens are not to be allowed to enforce rights which limit the user by others of property, unless the facts relied upon as constituting a nuisance are such as interfere with the ordinary rights which according to the ordinary notions of mankind they are entitled to exercise in relation to one another and in relation to their property'.[63] The Court of Appeal's judgment was upheld by the Lords in 1906, where Lord Atkinson noted that *Colls*' case had declared the view that the owner of the dominant tenement had a proprietary right to continued access to all the light he had enjoyed for 20 years 'an erroneous doctrine'.[64] Moreover, the view that interference with light had to be seen as being in the nature of a nuisance was endorsed in the King's Bench Division by Bray J., who ruled that—contrary to the view of Malins VC in *Lanfranchi*—even 20 years' continued user of an unusually large amount of light, to the knowledge of the defendant, would not establish a prescriptive right to a certain quantity of light.[65]

---

[61] *Colls* v. *Home and Colonial Stores* [1904] AC 179 at 200.

[62] Per Vaughan Williams LJ in *Kine* v. *Jolly* [1905] 1 Ch 480 at 487.

[63] *Kine* v. *Jolly* [1905] 1 Ch 480 at 489. Interference with light was treated as a nuisance in *Litchfield-Speer* v. *Queen Anne's Gate Syndicate (No. 2)* [1919] 1 Ch 407, and in *Charles Semon & Co* v. *Bradford Corporation* [1922] 2 Ch 737, where (at 747–8) Eve J. discussed evidence of 'the point whereat ordinary common sense people would begin to grumble at the quantum of light'.

[64] *Jolly* v. *Kine* [1907] AC 1 at 8.

[65] *Ambler and Fawcett* v. *Gordon* [1905] 1 KB 417. 'If one turns to the nuisance cases, do we find any trace of a doctrine that a person in bad health or carrying on a delicate trade is entitled to more comfort or freedom from annoyance than ordinary people because for twenty years his neighbours

2. WATER RIGHTS

Industrialization and urbanization generated serious water pollution problems. The principal causes of water pollution were sewage and industrial effluent. Although river conservators had always been concerned to take action against river polluters, by the 1840s, local sanitary authorities sometimes regarded water pollution as a price worth paying for the removal of sewage,[66] particularly if it was deposited downstream. Not until the mid-1870s did it become an offence to discharge untreated sewage into any stream,[67] though polluters were still permitted (under the Rivers Pollution Prevention Act 1876) to continue to pour effluent down channels whose construction had begun before the Act was passed. Moreover, proceedings under the Act required the consent of the Local Government Board, which would be withheld if they would injure manufacturing industry. Given the difficulty of tracing and suing polluters, many argued from the 1860s for a regulatory authority 'having the means and the power to deal with nuisances throughout an entire drainage area'.[68] Yet in an age when there was little enthusiasm for centralization, responsibility for pollution control remained in the hands of local authorities, which were themselves often the worst polluters (as with sewage), or which were dominated by powerful industrial concerns which polluted. It was only in the last decade of the nineteenth century that river-wide authorities were set up, in 1892 by Cheshire and Lancashire for the Irwell and Mersey; in the following year for the West Riding.[69]

Given this weak regulatory regime, litigants still made regular resort to the common law. Water pollution generated suits from three kinds of plaintiff. First, local authorities were often impelled to bring actions against other local authorities to prevent the nuisance created by sewage,[70] often creating a merry-go-round of litigation between different authorities on the same river.[71] Secondly,

---

have been aware of his state of health or the trade he was carrying on and have left him undisturbed?' This approach was disapproved by the Court of Appeal in *Allen* v. *Greenwood* [1980] 1 Ch 119.

[66] Report from the Select Committee on Sewage (Metropolis), *PP* 1864 (487), xiv, 1 (henceforth cited as 1864 Select Committee on Sewage), p. 129, q. 3137 (evidence of S. H. Gael).

[67] Rivers Pollution Prevention Act 1876, s 3. The Public Health Act 1875, ss 15–17 permitted local authorities to dispose of treated sewage into watercourses.

[68] Second Report of the Commissioners appointed to inquire into the Best Means of Preventing the Pollution of Rivers (River Lee), *PP* 1867 [3835] [3835-I], xxxiii, 1 (henceforth cited as 1867 River Lee Commission Report), p. xv.

[69] B. Luckin, *Pollution and Control: A Social History of the Thames in the Nineteenth Century* (Bristol, 1986) 172.

[70] See *Attorney General at the Relation of the Trustees of the River Lee* v. *The Metropolitan Board of Works* (1863) 1 H. & M. 298; see also 1867 River Lee Commission Report, p. 142, q. 4469 (evidence of J. Marchant).

[71] Peter Marshall, surveyor to Local Board of Tottenham, said in 1867: 'We have now an action pending against us by the river Lee trustees, and we have commenced an action against Hornsey,

manufacturers who required clean water for industrial processes sued other manufacturers who drew on the same source of water for polluting it.[72] Thirdly, proprietors of valuable rural estates whose banks and lakes were rendered pestilent often resorted to law against either sewage or industrial polluters. Such parties could be actuated by mercenary motives, such as a desire to induce the authority to buy their land, or by public-spirited ones, such as a desire to compel the local authority to spend money on sewage works.[73]

In the absence of regulation, litigation by private individuals or rival boards could have some effect in provoking improvements.[74] For instance, after four years of fruitless negotiations with the Birmingham Council, in 1858 Sir Charles Adderley, the owner of an estate on the river Tame, obtained an injunction against the town to force it to take steps to prevent the pollution of the river by its sewage. Despite grim warnings that stopping the drains would lead to an overflow of sewage in the town and the creation of a plague which would engulf the entire country, an injunction was granted, forcing the council to turn its attention to the treatment of the sewage. This did not solve the problem or end the litigation, for (having introduced a new system of intercepting tanks) the council found itself sued by riparian users who found their quantity of water diminished. Nor was Adderley himself satisfied with the progress made by the council, and he continued to seek injunctive relief. For nearly 40 years, this prominent litigant kept returning to Chancery to cajole the council into taking the best measures it could to abate the nuisance.[75] Similarly, in Croydon, a celebrated sewage irrigation scheme was set up after members of the local board had been threatened with imprisonment if they continued to violate an injunction not to pollute the River Wardle.[76]

---

and Colney Hatch has an action against Edmonton, and Edmonton has an action against us': 1867 River Lee Commission Report p. 112, q. 3543. In the case between Edmonton's local board and the Colney Hatch Lunatic Asylum, E. T. Busk, the chairman of the local board was in fact seeking an injunction against himself as visitor of the asylum: *ibid.*, pp. 117–18, q. 3717.

[72] For litigation arising from competing use of Bradford's Bowling Beck, see *Wood* v. *Waud* (1849) 3 Exch. 748; *Wood* v. *Sutcliffe* (1851) 2 Sim. N.S. 163.

[73] See C. Hamlin, 'Muddling in Bumbledom: On the Enormity of Large Sanitary Improvements in Four British Towns, 1855–1885' (1988–9) 32 *Vict. St.* 55–83.

[74] *Ibid*, 61.

[75] L. Rosenthal, 'Economic Efficiency, Nuisance and Sewage: New Lessons from *Attorney General* v. *Council of the Borough of Birmingham* 1858–95' (2007) 36 *JLS* 27–62; E. P. Hennock, *Fit and Proper Persons: Ideal and Reality in Nineteenth-Century Urban Government* (1973), 107–11. See also XIII, Pt 2, pp. 554–6.

[76] N. Goddard, '"A mine of wealth"? The Victorians and the agricultural value of sewage', (1996) 22 *Journal of Historical Geography* 274–90 at 284. According to Tom Taylor, the Secretary of the Local Government Board, the result of six or seven injunctions in Croydon 'was to embarrass the Local Board in dealing with the sewage, so that they had to give up the practice of sending it into

However, litigation was often a poor substitute for regulation. Local boards finding their rivers polluted often found it cheaper to seek a remedy in Chancery than to attempt to deal with the problem caused by the sewage itself, or even to cooperate with neighbouring boards in finding a common solution. Nor did litigation invariably spur a solution. For instance, Nantwich's local board, which was subjected to an injunction in 1870 to prevent it from polluting the river, found itself unable to buy any land on which to make a sewage farm, since local landowners feared the potential impact of such a development. Consequently, the town was hit by smallpox epidemics in 1871 and 1873.[77] In the previous decade, when an injunction was obtained against Hitchin's local board, its members were 'so afraid to go on with their functions, in consequence of their liability to proceedings, that they resigned *en masse*' and no one could be found to stand in their place.[78]

Industrial Water Pollution, 1820–70

The right to clean water was an incident of the right to property. This meant that a propertyless individual poisoned by foul water could not sue privately for nuisance, though if the pollution of the water was great enough to cause a public nuisance, the polluter could be indicted at the suit of the Attorney General, whether the river was private or a navigable one.[79] Although there was some disagreement in the early nineteenth century over whether riparian owners had a natural right to the flow of water, or whether upstream owners had the right to appropriate as much water as they chose, it was agreed that upstream owners had no right to pollute the water which came downstream.[80] Where the watercourse was artificial, no natural right could arise, but by mid-century it was accepted, after some hesitation, that there could be a prescriptive right to the flow.[81] After

the river. They first attempted to free it from noxious matters, but they found that insufficient, and they have lately leased land for the purpose of taking the sewage on to the land and deriving a profit therefrom': 1864 Select Committee on Sewage, p. 165, q. 3817.

[77] Luckin, *Pollution and Control*, 158–63.

[78] 1864 Select Committee on Sewage, p. 165, q 3829 (evidence of T. Taylor). Similarly, Tottenham's action against Hornsey mentioned above failed 'because there was no public body at Hornsey to be made amenable': 1867 River Lee Commission Report, xiv.

[79] *The Attorney General* v. *The Mayor, Aldermen, and Burgesses of the Borough of Kingston-upon-Thames* (1865) Jur. N.S. 11, 596 at 601; cf. *The Attorney General* v. *The Luton Local Board of Health* (1856) 2 Jur. N.S. 180.

[80] *Mason* v. *Hill* (1833) 5 B. & Ad. 1 at 18. By the mid-century, judges agreed that riparian owners had a natural right to the flow of natural watercourses. The natural right to water was held to be subject to the right of other riparian proprietors to a reasonable enjoyment of the flow through their land: *Embrey* v. *Owen* (1851) 6 Exch. 353. See in general J. Getzler, *A History of Water Rights at Common Law* (Oxford, 2004).

[81] In *Arkwright* v. *Gell* (1839) 5 M. & W. 203, Lord Abinger CB held that no prescriptive right could be applied to water drained from a mine, but his position was questioned by Lord Denman

initially considering that the right to clean water in an artificial watercourse also depended on a prescriptive right,[82] it was accepted by mid-century that the right not to have water in an artificial watercourse polluted existed absent a prescriptive right to the water.[83]

A third source of water was that which flowed underground. By the mid-century, it was agreed that there was no natural right to underground water akin to the right to surface streams, but that the owner through whose land underground water flowed in undefined channels had an unlimited right to extract as much water as he chose.[84] By contrast, where underground water ran in defined channels, a natural right attached to it, since its existence could be known. The question whether a proprietor entitled to extract all subterranean percolating water was permitted to pollute it was debated in a number of cases after mid-century. In 1863, in *Hodgkinson* v. *Ennor*, where the plaintiff's paper mill used water from a pool fed by percolations which were polluted by the defendant's factory, the Queen's Bench applied the rule of *Tenant* v. *Goldwin* that 'he whose dirt it is, must keep it that it may not trespass'.[85] As Blackburn J. put it, it was correct that 'the defendant had a right to use the water on his own land, but then in doing so he had to dispose of the poisoned and corrupted water'.[86]

If it was settled by mid-century that landowners had no general right to pollute water, it was also accepted that they could acquire prescriptive rights to pollute. This was recognised in 1836 in *Wright* v. *Williams*, which upheld the Marquis of Anglesea's right to discharge water impregnated with metal as a result of a process of copper precipitation into a watercourse on his land.[87] Similarly, in 1857, Watson B. ruled that there was no reason why a privilege to pollute, 'although injurious to the plaintiff to a great extent, might not be granted'.[88] Nonetheless, if the right claimed could not be the subject of a valid grant, 20 years' user did not avail the plaintiff. In *The Company of Proprietors of the Rochdale Canal* v. *Radcliffe*, the defendant, who was by statute entitled to draw off water from a canal to condense into steam, returning the water to the canal, claimed a prescriptive right to take

in *Magor* v. *Chadwick* (1840) 11 Ad. & El. 571 at 586. By 1850, it was agreed that such a prescriptive right to water from an artificial watercourse could arise, where it was intended to be permanent: see *Wood* v. *Waud* (1849) 3 Exch. 748; *Gaved* v. *Martyn* (1865) 34 LJ CP 353; *Ivimey* v. *Stocker* (1866) LR 1 Ch App 396 at 409.

[82] *Magor* v. *Chadwick* (1840) 11 Ad. & El. 571.

[83] *Wood* v. *Waud* (1849) 3 Exch. 748 at 779.

[84] *Acton* v. *Blundell* (1843) 12 M. & W. 324; *Chasemore* v. *Richards* (1859) 7 H.L.C. 349. See Getzler, *Water Rights*, 261–7.

[85] *Tenant* v. *Goldwin* (1704) 1 Salk. 360 at 361; cf. Holt KB 500 at 501; 2 Ld. Raym. 1089 at 1093.

[86] *Hodgkinson* v. *Ennor* (1863) 4 B. & S. 229 at 241. See also *Turner* v. *Mirfield* (1865) 34 Beav. 390; *Womersley* v. *Church* (1867) 17 LT 190.

[87] *Wright* v. *Williams* (1836) 1 M. & W. 77.

[88] *Carlyon* v. *Lovering* (1857) 1 H. & N. 784 at 798.

larger quantities of water, after 20 years' use, when sued by the canal company. The argument failed, since the company had no power to make any such grant under its statute.[89] The courts were also not keen in the mid-century to allow Boards of Health to claim prescriptive rights to pollute.[90] In 1856, Wood VC held that the Luton Board of Health could not claim a prescriptive right to pollute the Lee, since it had only been created as a corporate body in 1848.[91] If boards tried to argue that they were merely exercising as a collective the rights which all individual householders had exercised, by draining sewage into a river, they were told that when individual householders previously drained into the river, they did it without causing a nuisance; but when the town did it on a larger scale, it was productive of a nuisance.[92]

In 1867, the Rivers Pollution Commissioners denounced prescriptive rights to pollute as 'privileged abuses'. Since the law encouraged polluters to continue to deposit waste in the river in order to establish a prescriptive right, it acted as a disincentive to 'those who are well disposed, and renders ineffectual voluntary combination, even upon a large scale, amongst manufacturers, to preserve the river'.[93] They drew particular attention to *Baxendale* v. *McMurray*, where the Lord Justices ruled that a paper mill owner had an easement to pour 'refuse liquor and foul washings' produced by his manufacturing process into a river, and that his right extended to any new materials he might use 'which are proper for the purpose'.[94] In fact, despite the anxiety of the commissioners, judges were never keen to see prescriptive polluting rights extend. For instance, in *Murgatroyd* v. *Robinson*, in 1857, a downstream mill owner on the Calder brought an action of nuisance against an upstream mill owner for polluting the river with cinders. The latter claimed a prescriptive right to deposit the waste, but the court ruled against him since he failed to show that the cinders had for the requisite period polluted the water which reached the plaintiff's land.[95] The prescriptive right was to be measured by the nuisance to the plaintiff, not the upstream user by the polluter.

A similarly restrictive view of the right to pollute was taken in *Crossley & Sons* v. *Lightowler* in 1866, where the owners of a carpet manufactory sought to restrain the owners of dyeing works from polluting the Hebble. The defendants

---

[89] *The Company of Proprietors of the Rochdale Canal* v. *Radcliffe* (1852) 18 Q.B. 287.

[90] There could be no prescriptive right to a public nuisance: See *R* v. *Cross* (1812) 3 Camp. 224 at 227.

[91] *The Attorney General* v. *The Luton Local Board of Health* (1856) 2 Jur. N.S. 180.

[92] *Attorney-General* v. *The Council of the Borough of Birmingham* (1858) 4 K. & J. 528 at 542.

[93] Third Report of the Commissioners appointed to inquire into the best means of preventing the pollution of rivers (Rivers Aire and Calder etc), PP 1867 [3850] [3850-I], xxxiii, (henceforth cited as 1867 Aire and Calder Commission Report), 231, 329 at p. lii.

[94] *Baxendale* v. *McMurray* (1867) 2 Ch App 790 at 794.

[95] *Murgatroyd* v. *Robinson* (1857) 7 E. & B. 391 at 398.

had since 1864 occupied premises which been used for dyeing until 1839. They therefore claimed a prescriptive right to pollute. However, Wood VC ruled that right to pollute had been abandoned. While non-user was not conclusive of an abandonment of the right—which was a question of fact—where someone by non-user encouraged others to invest on the presumption that the right would not be exerted, he should not be allowed to resume his right. If it were otherwise, there could be no development along rivers, 'for I suppose there is hardly a river in the kingdom where there has not been, at some time or other, a work which might be detrimental to a riparian proprietor lower down'.[96] The Lord Justices affirmed the decision, Lord Chelmsford LC drawing attention to the fact that the quantity of pollution had increased: 'The user which originated the right must also be its measure, and it cannot be enlarged to the prejudice of any other person.'[97] This view was also applied to sewage pollution: in *Goldsmid* v. *Tunbridge Wells Improvement Commissioners*, in 1865, Sir John Romilly MR ruled 'that when the pollution is increasing, and gradually increasing, from time to time, by the additional quantity of sewage poured into it, the persons who allow the polluted matter to flow into the stream are not at liberty to claim any right or prescription'.[98]

Thus, in an era of industrial development and the transformation of techniques, industrialists could neither increase the amount of pollution they deposited in rivers, nor purchase the sites of old polluters and expect to be able to use the old easement for fresh waste. The courts were not keen to establish rights to pollute, but rather restricted them. Moreover, by 1888, in a case which seemed to contract the view taken in *Baxendale* v. *McMurray*, the Queen's Bench Division held that if the type of waste produced by a factory changed, the easement to pollute was lost. As Field J. put it, '[i]t cannot be supposed that a man who has carried on business for a number of years, which has entitled him to certain easements, can suddenly change his business, and yet claim the same right to easement in respect of it that he enjoyed in his former condition'.[99] Riparian users with a natural right to clean water could thus take action against fellow industrialists who were polluters.

The question whether a polluter was strictly liable for harming the property rights of other proprietors, or whether he could claim that he was making a reasonable use of his own property was debated in a number of cases. Some litigants invoked a principle raised in smoke pollution cases that no remedy should be given where the polluting activity was carried on in a reasonable and proper

---

[96] *Crossley & Sons* v. *Lightowler* (1866) LR 3 Eq 279 at 293.

[97] *Crossley & Sons* v. *Lightowler* (1867) LR 2 Ch App 478 at 481.

[98] *Goldsmid* v. *Tunbridge Wells Improvement Commissioners* (1865) LR 1 Eq 161 at 169. Cf. *Goldsmid* v. *The Tunbridge Wells Improvement Commissioners* (1866) LR 1 Ch App 349 at 352.

[99] *Clarke* v. *The Somersetshire Drainage Commissioners* (1888) 57 LJ NS MC 96 at 100.

manner in a proper place.[100] But such arguments cut little ice. In *Attorney-General v. The Council of the Borough of Birmingham*, Wood VC rejected the council's argument that the plaintiff's 'private interests must bend to those of the country at large', given the potentially dire consequences for the city's health were its sewage system unable to function: 'in the case of an individual claiming certain private rights, and seeking to have those rights protected against an infraction of the law, the question is simply whether he has those rights'.[101] In this case, the plaintiff had previously enjoyed an unpolluted river, which had been polluted by the defendant's acts. Similarly, in *Stockport Waterworks Co v. Potter*, where the plaintiffs' reservoirs were polluted by traces of arsenic from the defendants' calico printing works which flowed into the Mersey, the court rejected arguments based on the reasonableness of the defendants' activity, after a Chester jury had found that the defendants, although exceeding their prescriptive rights to pollute, had conducted a lawful trade in a reasonable place. As Martin B. put it, 'what answer is that to an action by persons whose drinking water is affected by arsenic poured into it by persons carrying on such a trade?'[102] These cases suggested that downstream owners would only have to put up with inconveniences arising from the natural use of property (such as the water which 'descends in the natural course of drainage' in mines[103]) or from pollution for which there was a prescriptive right.

The fact that the right to clean water was seen as a strict property right, rather than one which (like the right to clean air or peace and quiet) depended on the reasonable user of the polluter, was confirmed in *Ballard v. Tomlinson* in 1885. In this case, the Court of Appeal granted an injunction to the plaintiff to prevent the defendant polluting his own well, as a consequence of which dirty water percolated through and poisoned the plaintiff's well. It overturned Pearson J.'s decision that since the plaintiff had no right to receive any quantity of underground water percolating from the defendant's land, he had no right to any particular quality of water which arrived, but had to take it as it came.[104] '[A]lthough nobody has any property in the common source' of percolating water, Brett MR ruled 'everybody has a right to appropriate it [...] in its natural state'.[105] For Lindley LJ, 'if any contends that he has a right to pollute the natural supply he must establish such right'.[106] The court distinguished between a man's right to

---

[100] *Hole* v. *Barlow* (1858) 4 C.B. N.S. 334.

[101] *Attorney-General* v. *The Council of the Borough of Birmingham* (1858) 4 K. & J. 528 at 539.

[102] *Stockport Waterworks Co* v. *Potter* (1861) 7 H. & N. 160 at 169. For later litigation, see *Stockport Waterworks Co* v. *Potter* (1864) 3 H. & C. 300.

[103] *Attorney-General* v. *The Council of the Borough of Birmingham* (1858) 4 K. & J. 528 at 542.

[104] *Ballard* v. *Tomlinson* (1884) 26 Ch D 194.

[105] *Ballard* v. *Tomlinson* (1885) 29 Ch D 115 at 121.   [106] *Ibid.* at 127.

the ordinary use of his land and his duty not to commit a nuisance. As Cotton LJ put it, '[n]o one can say that putting filth on your land in such a position and with such little care that it gets down to the stratum where the water is common to you and to your neighbour is a natural use of the land'.[107] In Lindley's view, 'if a man chooses to poison his own well he must take care not to poison waters which other persons have a right to use as much as himself'.[108] This was to suggest—as Wood VC had in 1858—that neighbours had to put up with what nature threw at them, but they did not have to put up with anything which went beyond the natural use of land, absent a prescriptive right; a view which had also been found in *Rylands* v. *Fletcher*.[109] Nineteenth-century judges dealing with cases involving interferences with water rights thus did not look at the nature of the defendant's conduct, asking whether the harm was foreseeable or the use of his property was reasonable. Rather, they looked at whether the plaintiff's rights had been infringed.

Nor were common law courts swayed by the apparent injustice that 'one manufacturer should be proceeded against and mulcted for doing that which hundreds of others, who do not happen to offend a powerful neighbour, are doing with impunity.[110] The fact that there were other polluters did not provide a defence, for judges were aware that a party who continued to pollute for 20 years might establish an easement, giving a right to pollute even if all the other polluters disappeared.[111] Equally, the courts were concerned to prevent public authorities acquiring rights without paying for them. Thus, in *Cator* v. *The Board of Works for the Lewisham District*, the Exchequer Chamber upheld the plaintiff's right to an action against a Board of Works for fouling a waterway when they built a new drainage system, since if the defendants had a right to pollute the stream, 'they would permanently deteriorate the value and enjoyment of the plaintiff's property for residential and agricultural purposes, and would in effect produce a sale by compulsion which the[ir] statute has expressly excluded'.[112]

---

[107] *Ibid.* at 124.

[108] *Ibid.*at 126. Lindley held further that 'the law of nuisance is not based exclusively on rights of property' and drew an analogy between the right to clean percolating water and to clean air. Noting that no man had property in the air, he said, 'a man who poisons the air which another has a right to breathe commits an actionable wrong'. Despite this analogy, Lindley's argument did not suggest that water rights should be subjected to the kinds of questions of reasonable user which had developed in respect to urban air and noise pollution. See the comments about this case in *Cambridge Water Co* v. *Eastern Counties plc* [1994] 2 AC 264.

[109] *Rylands* v. *Fletcher* (1868) LR 3 HL 330.

[110] 1867 Aire and Calder Commission Report, lii.

[111] *Wood* v. *Waud* (1849) 3 Ex. 748 at 772–3; *Crossley & Sons* v. *Lightowler* (1867) LR 2 Ch App 478 at 481–2.

[112] *Cator* v. *The Board of Works for the Lewisham District* (1864) 5 B. & S. 115 at 147. The statute was the Metropolis Local Management Act, 18 & 19 Vict. c. 120.

The willingness of judges to hold individual users to account for major pollution can be seen clearly in *The Queen* v. *The Bradford Navigation Co.* The Bradford canal had been fed (since 1798) by water from the Bradford Beck. As the town grew, and its local Board of Health was empowered to develop a sewage system, the canal became increasingly foul, becoming a channel for the waste of Bradford. Not only was the company not responsible for creating this nuisance, but under their statute, they were not empowered to take water from any source save that which was now polluted. Aware that their sewage system polluted the canal, the Board of Health failed to take action against the company. Instead, a number of local residents indicted the company for a public nuisance. The Queen's Bench found that since they were only permitted to operate the canal so long as they did not cause a nuisance, once the water was foul, they could no longer legally use it. This did not necessarily mean they had to close the canal, but it threw on them the 'the necessity of taking legal steps to compel the Local Board of Health to do their duty in cleansing the beck, or, if that be found an inefficient remedy, to obtain a private Act of Parliament for the purpose'.[113] Litigation such as this was a blunt instrument to use to get at the root causes of pollution, as the Rivers Pollution Commissioners of the 1860s were all too aware. Nevertheless, in the absence of a coordinated policy by government, judges were prepared to find against polluters, even if the consequences for them were severe, in order to cajole local authorities into action.

Public Authorities and the Problem of Sewage, 1870–1914

By the 1870s, the problem of sewage pollution was increasingly subject to statutory regulation, and under the control of local Boards of Health. The Public Health Act 1875 vested sewers in the local authority (section 13), and enacted that they had to be constructed without being a nuisance. If the authority was in default, an order could be issued by the Local Government Board, enforced by a mandamus (section 299). Householders were entitled (section 21) to connect their sewers with those of the authority, with its sanction, whereupon the sewers vested in the latter.[114] Under section 3 of the Rivers Pollution Prevention Act 1876,[115] it was an offence to allow untreated sewage to pass into a stream. However, if it was carried by channels already existing or being built at the time of the legislation, no

---

[113] *The Queen* v. *The Bradford Navigation Company* (1865) 6 B. & S. 631 at 652. The action was followed by an injunction issued in Chancery, and the canal faced closure. See evidence of John Rust Jeffery in 1867 Aire and Calder Commission Report, p. 295, qq. 9684 *et seq.*

[114] Public Health Act, 38 & 39 Vict. c. 55.

[115] 39 & 40 Vict. c. 75.

offence would be deemed to have been committed, if the polluter was using 'the best practicable and available means' to make it harmless.

The existence of this regime led the courts to take a more sympathetic approach to urban authorities. By this stage, it was evident that many boards were genuinely seeking to address the sanitary problems caused by sewage pollution, and that coordination was required between different authorities. In *Glossop* v. *Heston and Isleworth Local Board*,[116] where the plaintiff sought an injunction to prevent the defendants' sewers polluting the River Crane, the Court of Appeal agreed that there was a substantial grievance to be addressed, but showed much sympathy to the local board. The judges were aware both that such works needed cooperation between local boards, and that any board which took steps to improve the sewage system might find itself creating new nuisances. '[A]nybody who has to deal with them,' Brett LJ noted, 'is bound to look to their conduct with the greatest indulgence.'[117] Nor did it approve of the plaintiff's attempt to use the means of an injunction to force the board to act. If plaintiffs could succeed in such cases, 'it would be a very serious matter indeed for every ratepayer in England', since any proprietor might be able to compel a local authority to make improvements in the area to increase the value of his property. The prospect of litigious persons seeking profit was 'a far more formidable nuisance' than the nuisances sought to be removed by it.[118] In *Attorney-General* v. *Guardians of Poor of Union of Dorking*, the appeal court judges were similarly sympathetic to the plight of the authority. In contrast to Wood VC's tough-minded approach in *Attorney-General* v. *The Council of the Borough of Birmingham*, Jessel MR said the court could not grant an injunction 'to prevent a certain state of things being allowed to continue without being aware of any means by which it can be stopped'. He was reluctant to force the authority to stop the sewer 'and thereby cause a most frightful nuisance to the inhabitants of the district whose drainage it is their business to protect and perfect'.[119]

In denying injunctions, the Court of Appeal in these cases developed a new distinction, according to which a defendant would be liable for misfeasance, by causing the pollution, but not for nonfeasance.[120] In both *Glossop* and *Dorking*, the amount of sewage passing through sewers which vested in the defendant authorities after their creation had steadily increased over the years. Some of it came from landowners who had prescriptive rights to send their drainage down the sewer, and some came from drainage by townspeople who had no prescriptive

---

[116] *Glossop* v. *Heston and Isleworth Local Board* (1879) LR 12 Ch D 102.

[117] *Ibid.* at 119.   [118] *Ibid.* at 115.

[119] *Attorney-General* v. *Guardians of Poor of Union of Dorking* (1882) 20 Ch D 595 at 605–6.

[120] See also *Earl of Harrington* v. *Corporation of Derby* [1905] 1 Ch 205 at 224. Cf. *Charles* v. *Finchley Local Board* (1883) 23 Ch D 767.

rights. None was generated by the defendants.[121] In *Dorking*, Jessel MR ruled that the authority could not be liable for the nuisance, since it 'had not done anything as regards that particular sewer', but merely endeavoured to carry out its statutory powers. In his view, since some landowners had a prescriptive right to use the sewer, it could not be blocked up. As for those landowners who fouled the stream without a prescriptive right, the only way for the authority to stop them was to take legal action against them. But in Jessel's view, this could not make the authority liable to the plaintiff: 'did any one ever hear of an action against a man because he did not bring an action against his neighbour?'[122] Both courts also rejected arguments that the authority was liable under statute. In *Glossop*, the court rejected the argument that the board was liable under section 17 of the Public Health Act, which stated that nothing in the Act authorized local authorities to 'make or use any sewer' for the purpose of conveying sewage until it had been freed from noxious matter. For this was read as a proviso relating only to the opening of new sewers, rather than to the use of old ones. In *Dorking*, the court rejected the argument that the authority was liable under section 3 of the Rivers Pollution Prevention Act, for 'knowingly permit[ting] to fall or flow or to be carried, into any stream any solid or liquid sewage matter'. As Jessel saw it, since the plaintiff's rights under the statute were only 'to prevent the authority from committing a nuisance', it could not apply where the authority had done nothing. In the aftermath of *Glossop* and *Dorking*, injunctions were not granted against sanitary authorities which would interfere with prescriptive rights to pollute. Moreover, since under section 21 of the Public Health Act householders had a right to connect their drains to sewers,[123] injunctions were not granted whose effect would be to interfere with these rights. They were only granted to restrain authorities from increasing the nuisance in future, by 'directing or authorizing' sewage into streams.[124] If the authority carried out new works which caused a nuisance, they were liable; but if their existing ones were lawfully used by others in a way which caused a nuisance, no injunction would be issued.

This did not mean that sanitary authorities were free to do nothing. Rather, it was felt that public law procedures needed to be used. In both *Glossop* and

---

[121] James LJ pointed out that in previous cases, such as *Goldsmid* v. *Tunbridge Wells Improvement Commissioners* (1865) LR 1 Eq 161, local authorities found themselves liable for nuisance when they created new sewers: *Glossop* v. *Heston and Isleworth Local Board* (1879) LR 12 Ch D 128. Cf. per Brett LJ at 120.

[122] *Attorney-General* v. *Guardians of Poor of Union of Dorking* (1882) 20 Ch D 595 at 602.

[123] *Ainley* v. *Kirkheaton Local Board* (1891) 60 LJ Ch 734.

[124] However, the courts did not restrain sanitary boards from 'permitting' sewage to flow, given householders' rights under s 21 of the Public Health Act. See *Attorney General* v. *Acton Local Board* (1883) 22 Ch D 221; *Attorney General* v. *Clerkenwell Vestry* [1891] 3 Ch 527; *Brown* v. *Mayor, Aldermen and Burgesses of Dunstable* [1899] 2 Ch 378.

Dorking, the judges felt that the basis of the plaintiffs' complaint was not that the local board was creating a nuisance, but that it failed in its statutory duty to cure the problem of the filthy river. They were unsympathetic to plaintiffs' attempts to obtain damages and injunctions as a method to force public bodies to exercise their statutory powers. As the court put it in *Glossop*, the aim of compelling the authority to act could not be effected by a mandatory injunction in Chancery, but only by a mandamus from the Queen's Bench Division. Such a remedy could only be given in cases such as this under the conditions prescribed by section 299, acting through the Local Government Board. Subsequent courts reiterated the point that decisions on urban drainage had to be made by public authorities, and that private litigants should not be permitted to compel authorities to act.[125] Although this demonstrated a sympathy to the difficulties of sanitary authorities, in cases where the courts felt the authority had no excuse for its failure to act, they were often content to hold the authority liable for the nuisance,[126] or prevent it from passing on its obligations to householders who had not strictly complied with the law.[127]

The new statutory regime also served to protect private polluters using the stream. The shelter given to polluters by section 3 of the Rivers Pollution Prevention Act—which enacted that no person who discharged sewage into a drain communicating with any sewer under the control of any sanitary authority, with its sanction, would be guilty of an offence—was in effect extended to private actions. In *Ferrand* v. *Hallas Land and Building Co*, a riparian owner failed to obtain an injunction against a building society, whose development of 69 cottages polluted the stream. The Court of Appeal held that no injunction could be granted, since householders whose homes were drained into the local authority's sewer with its permission had no control over how the sewage was subsequently dealt with. Once any sewer was vested in the local authority, it was to be regarded as the body liable for harms caused by its effluent.[128] Since householders had a statutory right to discharge waste into the sewers vested in the authority, it was considered absurd to hold them liable if the authority subsequently failed to deodorize the waste, as it was obliged to do.[129] However, if householders connected their drains

---

[125] The courts were aware that large industrial polluters might settle in new areas, and seek to impose high waste disposal costs on local ratepayers by attempting to use mandamus. See *Pasmore* v. *The Oswaldtwistle Urban District Council* [1898] AC 387. See also *Robinson* v. *Mayor and Corporation of Workington* [1897] 1 QB 619.

[126] See the approach of the Court of Appeal to s 3 of the Rivers Pollution Prevention Act in *Yorkshire West Riding Council* v. *Holmfirth Urban Sanitary Authority* [1894] 2 QB 842.

[127] *Kirkheaton District Local Board* v. *Ainley, Sons & Co* [1892] 2 QB 274.

[128] *Ferrand* v. *Hallas Land and Building Co* [1893] 2 QB 135 at 143.

[129] See the comments of Lord Loreburn LC in *Butterworth and Another* v. *West Riding of Yorkshire Rivers Board* [1909] AC 45 at 49.

to public sewers without permission, they lost the protection of section 3 of the 1876 Act, and could be held accountable for the nuisance.[130]

After the turn of the twentieth century, a tougher approach was taken to claims that prescriptive rights to pollute could not be interfered with. In *Butterworth and Another* v. *West Riding of Yorkshire Rivers Board* in 1909, the House of Lords rejected the appellants' claim to a 50-year prescriptive right to pollute, while holding that they had committed an offence under the 1876 Act by polluting a stream with industrial effluent. As Lord Macnaghten noted, a prescriptive right to foul a stream could not avail against a statute which forbad fouling. The 1876 Act only preserved prescriptive rights to deposit industrial pollutants insofar as the user showed he had used the best practicable and available means to render them harmless, which had not been shown here. Contrary to the 'erroneous opinion which prevailed at one time', Macnaghten ruled, the Public Health Act did not give manufacturers 'the right of pouring their refuse into the sewers of the local sanitary authority'.[131] Nor was this tough approach limited to industrial polluters. Two years later, in *Jones* v. *Llanrwst Urban District Council*, Parker J. held that '[a] prescriptive right to turn sewage into sewers belonging to a corporation cannot be a defence to an action against them for nuisance; they are not thereby absolved from the duty of seeing that it does not become a nuisance'.[132]

From the turn of the century, the courts began to take a tougher approach towards public bodies. In *Foster* v. *Urban District Council of Warblington*, the Court of Appeal upheld a plaintiff's right to damages after his oyster beds had been polluted by sewage from the sanitary authority's drains. The sanitary authority sought to resist the claim by invoking arguments from *Glossop*: that prescriptive rights existed; that householders had rights under the Public Health Act to use the sewer, which the authority could not refuse; that this was not a case of misfeasance, but nonfeasance; that the plaintiff was seeking to use a private law remedy to compel the authority to improve its sewage system. These arguments were unsuccessful. 'No doubt the deposit of this sewage [...] was a nuisance', Stirling LJ ruled, 'but it is a nuisance in respect of which an action for trespass lies'.[133] In his view, had the action been brought against a private individual, the

---

[130] *Kirkheaton District Local Board* v. *Ainley, Sons & Co* [1892] 2 QB 274.

[131] *Butterworth and Another* v. *West Riding of Yorkshire Rivers Board* [1909] AC 45 at 54.

[132] *Jones* v. *Llanrwst Urban District Council* [1911] 1 Ch 393 at 398–9. See also *Hulley* v. *Silversprings Bleaching and Dyeing Company* [1922] 2 Ch. 268, where it was held that there could be no prescriptive easement claimed which was contrary to ss 3–4 of the Rivers Pollution Prevention Act, since no lost grant could be presumed. Eve J. ruled (at 282), 'A lost grant cannot be presumed where such a grant would have been in contravention of a statute, and as title by prescription is founded upon the presumption of a grant, if no grant could lawfully have been made, no presumption of the kind can arise.'

[133] *Foster* v. *Urban District Council of Warblington* [1906] 1 KB 648 at 672.

plaintiff would have succeeded, on the principles laid down in *Rylands* v. *Fletcher*. He conceded that, on the authority of *Glossop*, the local board would not have been liable if they had done nothing themselves; but he held that in this case, the authority had made additional sewers, taking themselves out of the rule. In *Jones* v. *Llanrwst Urban District Council*, Parker J. took up the suggestion that a polluting sanitary authority was guilty of trespass, holding that anyone who allowed 'faecal matter [...] under his control to escape into a river, [...] under such conditions that it is carried, whether by the current or the wind, on to his neighbour's land is guilty of a trespass'.[134] Invoking the principle of *Rylands* v. *Fletcher*, he noted that the owner's 'duty at common law would be to see that the sewage in his sewer did not escape to the injury of others, and mere neglect of this duty would give any person injured a good cause of action'.[135] For Parker J., private individuals were entitled to injunctions to restrain authorities from allowing sewage to escape, even though local inhabitants had a statutory right to send sewage into their sewers. The fact that they had the right to turn their waste into the authority's sewers did not give it the right to pass it on. Despite Parker's attempt to undo the distinction of misfeasance and nonfeasance introduced in *Glossop*, by invoking a principle of strict liability associated with *Rylands* v. *Fletcher*, twentieth-century courts continued to endorse the distinction. In 1924, Scrutton LJ observed (in a sewage case) that 'the general rule is that a local authority is liable for misfeasance but not for non-feasance'.[136] Where towns grew so that the existing sewage system was inadequate, plaintiffs found themselves unable to bring claims in nuisance, unless they could convince the court there was misfeasance or a continuation of a nuisance by its adoption.[137]

3. SMOKE AND NOISE

For much of the nineteenth century, nuisances from noise and smoke were not regarded as causing the same serious damage as those which could be seen to interfere with prescriptive property rights. As a result, historians have often seen the wealth of nineteenth-century industry as having been paid for by the health of its workers, who were forced to breathe dangerous and noxious fumes. For much of the century, however, the impact of industrial smoke on

---

[134] *Jones* v. *Llanrwst Urban District Council* [1911] 1 Ch 393 at 402–3.

[135] *Ibid.*, at 405. Though Parker J. felt bound by *Glossop*, he felt the *ratio decidendi* of the case was unclear, and that whichever view was taken of it, it did not apply to the case before him. For a detailed discussion of *Rylands* v. *Fletcher* (1868) LR 3 HL 330, see pp. 1140–44.

[136] *Hesketh* v. *Birmingham Corporation* [1924] 1 KB 260 at 271.

[137] Contrast *Pride of Derby and Derby Angling Association* v. *British Celanese* [1953] 1 Ch 149 and *Smeaton* v. *Ilford Corporation* [1954] 1 Ch 450.

human health was hotly disputed. When polluters were sued for nuisance, they generally produced expert medical evidence to show that the smoke in question was not merely harmless, but even beneficial to the health of the population.[138] Moreover, for working men, unhealthy employment was preferable to unemployment. In this context, the question was often raised how far a certain level of personal discomfort had to be put up with in modern urban environments, as part of the give-and-take of life, and how far urban dwellers were protected from nuisances.

Some attempts were made to regulate smoke pollution in the first half of the century. They included M. A. Taylor's 1821 Act to control smoke emissions from steam engines;[139] Palmerston's Smoke Nuisance Abatement (Metropolis) Act of 1853;[140] and the Nuisances Removal Act 1855.[141] The first of these imposed summary penalties on 'any trade or business which shall occasion any noxious or offensive effluvia'; and the second empowered local authorities to send inspectors to examine premises suspected of creating nuisances and to prosecute summarily any trader certified by two medical officers.[142] In practice, these statutes delivered less than they promised. Prosecutions under Palmerston's Act had declined by 1862; while doubts arose over how many trades the 1855 Act covered.[143] Other statutes controlling smoke emissions also omitted important polluters, leaving them unregulated.[144] In any case, polluters who fell foul of rules set by a town corporation could always move outside its borders, as occurred when Swansea's copper smelters moved into the valley beyond the town's boundary, turning

[138] Rees, 'The South Wales Copper-Smoke Dispute', 488–9.

[139] 1& 2 Geo. IV c. 41. See also Report from the Select Committee on Steam Engines and Furnaces, *PP* 1819 (574), viii, 271 and 1820 (244), ii, 235. For prosecutions see e.g. *Barnard* v. *Austin*, *The Times*, 30 March 1820, col. 3c; *Salmon* v. *Bensley*, *The Times*, 21 January 1825, col. 3b.

[140] 16 & 17 Vict. c. 128. See also 7 & 8 Vict. c. 84, ss 55–56 regulating offensive trades. For criticism, see the Report of the Select Committee on Noxious Businesses, *PP* 1873 (284), x, 431.

[141] 18 & 19 Vict. c. 121. There had been earlier Nuisance Removal legislation, which this Act consolidated: 9 & 10 Vict. c. 96 (1846) was passed in the wake of a cholera epidemic and was renewed and amended in 11 & 12 Vict. c. 123 (1848), 12 & 13 Vict. c. 111 (1849). The 1855 Act was amended in 1860 and incorporated into general legislation in 1875. The 1847 Towns Improvement Clauses Act also included model smoke clauses: 10 & 11 Vict. c. 34.

[142] 18 & 19 Vict. c. 121, amended by 23 & 24 Vict. c. 77.

[143] The legislation referred to 'any trade, business, process, or manufacture causing effluvia', but this was interpreted to have reference to the trades specified in the Act. In any event, if the offender took reasonable steps to abate the nuisance, the magistrates could suspend their final determination: Report of the Select Committee on Injury from Noxious Vapours, *PP* 1862 (486), xiv, 1 (henceforth cited as 1862 Select Committee on Noxious Vapours), v. The permissive Public Health Act 1848 also forbad the introduction of such trades without the consent of the Local Board of Health: 11 & 12 Vict. c. 64, s 64.

[144] For instance, the Local Government Act 1858 excluded smoke produced in the burning of bricks, or in the smelting of iron ores or the manufacture of glass: 21 & 22 Vict. c. 98, s 108. See also Dingle, 'Monster Nuisance of All'.

the area into a desert by the mid-nineteenth century.[145] With growing concern over noxious vapours, a select committee in 1862 recommended the consolidation of existing nuisance legislation. Among its recommendations were that the provisions of Palmerston's Act be made universal; that 'gases evolved in manufacturing processes from furnaces or chimnies should be placed on the same footing as smoke from furnaces'; that there should be greater powers for medical inspectors to enter premises; and that there be an inspection regime for alkali manufacturers.[146] However, although the latter idea was taken up in the Alkali Act 1863, its recommendations for general nuisance legislation were ignored.

Despite the increase in legislation—notably the passing of mandatory Acts such as the Sanitary Act 1866 and the Public Health Act 1875—legislative regulation had little effect in controlling smoke for two reasons. First, there was continued opposition to industrial smoke control, both from manufacturers and from local populations in industrial areas. When Swansea's first Medical Officer of Health urged the Board of Health to make use of anti-smoke legislation, a number of influential inhabitants petitioned that nothing be done to harm the town's industry. When a local landowner obtained an injunction in 1890 against the owners of the Cwmavon works, 3000 inhabitants petitioned against it.[147] Smoke pollution was often equated with wealth and jobs. 'Noxious as are the vapours', a local paper wrote in 1862, 'St Helens cannot be said to be unhealthy.'[148] The industrial interest was thus often able to dilute the strength of legislation, and to ensure that local administrators were not overly hostile to polluters. Secondly, the prime smoke polluter in most nineteenth-century towns was not the factory, but the domestic chimney. By 1880, there were over 3½ million fireplaces in London, producing smoke which made London famous—and deadly—for its fogs.[149] Despite much agitation for the introduction of cleaner stoves, notably by the National Smoke Abatement Institution, the English proudly resisted giving up their hearths, and it would take the Great London Smog of 1952 to pave the way for effective legislation.[150] Meanwhile, litigating against the domestic fireplace at common law was both legally and socially unthinkable.

Unlike rights to light and to clean water, the right of a landowner to unpolluted air was not a property right. While polluters could be prosecuted if they created nuisances which rendered 'the enjoyment of life and property uncomfortable'

---

[145] Rees, 'The South Wales Copper-Smoke Dispute'.
[146] 1862 Select Committee on Noxious Vapours, viii–ix.
[147] Rees, 'The South Wales Copper-Smoke Dispute', 491–6.
[148] Quoted in Wohl, *Endangered Lives*, 216.
[149] E. Ashby and M. Anderson, *The Politics of Clean Air* (Oxford, 1981), 56.
[150] See B. Luckin, 'Pollution in the City', in M. Daunton (ed.), *The Cambridge Urban History of Britain, III: 1840–1950* (Cambridge, 2000), 207–28.

and dwellings 'untenable',[151] their neighbours had no absolute right to clean air. As John Comyns expressed it, an action for nuisance 'does not lie for a reasonable use of my right, though it be to the annoyance of another; as, if a butcher, brewer, etc, use his trade in a convenient place, though it be to the annoyance of his neighbour'.[152] Comyns referred to *Jones* v. *Powell*, a case of 1627 where the King's Bench ruled that erecting a private brewhouse was not a nuisance, unless it was built so close to another's house as to damage his goods and make the house uninhabitable. 'A tan-house is necessary, for all men wear shoes', Hyde J. ruled, 'and nevertheless it may be pulled down if it be erected to the nuisance of another', for such buildings 'ought to be erected in places convenient for them'.[153] This appeared to suggest that in deciding whether a nuisance had occurred, the courts should take the locality of the activity into consideration.[154]

Early nineteenth-century judges accordingly held that where the plaintiff had 'come to a nuisance', he had no right of action. In Dallas CJ's view, if plaintiffs moved near to a manufactory, they could not complain of the nuisance it caused, for otherwise 'traders might be precluded from advancing themselves in their several callings; a man coming to live near a blacksmith who worked one forge might afterwards say to that blacksmith "you shall not work two"'.[155] Besides such considerations of convenience, the theory behind this doctrine was akin to the riparian doctrine of prior appropriation: the first appropriator of a site was able to make such pollution in the air as he chose, and later occupiers took subject to his use. By contrast, the courts were not well disposed to those who made noise or smells in settled areas. In *Salmon* v. *Bensley* in 1825, counsel for the defendant, a printer who had installed a new steam engine, argued that the jury should take into account that this noise was being made in what was already one of the busiest parts of London, and urged on them the danger of a finding that might force the closure of many useful businesses using steam. But Abbott CJ observed that even if a verdict for the plaintiff 'would render property, which had been completed at a large expense, of no value [...], the party who so conducted his property as to annoy his neighbours had no right to complain'.[156]

---

[151] *R* v. *White* (1757) 1 Burr. 333 at 334, 337; *The King* v. *Davey* (1805) 5 Esp. 217 at 218–19. Cf. J. Oldham, *The Mansfield Manuscripts and the Growth of English Law in the Eighteenth Century*, 2 vols (1992), ii, 887–9.

[152] J. Comyns, *A Digest of the Laws of England*, 5 vols (1780), i, 215 (tit. Action upon the Case for a Nuisance, (C))

[153] *Jones* v. *Powell* (1627) Palm. 536 at 539.

[154] Noxious activities should not be conducted in 'the principal parts of the city, but in the outskirts': *The King* v. *Jordan*, cited in *The King against Pierce* (1683) 2 Show. K.B. 327.

[155] Quoted in *Rankin* v. *Acraman*, *The Times*, 22 August 1822, col. 3e. See also *R* v. *Cross* (1826) 2 Car. & P. 484.

[156] *The Times*, 21 January 1825, col. 3b.

The doctrine of 'coming to a nuisance' was overturned in the 1830s, when it was held that a neighbour was only precluded from complaining about nuisance from a neighbour if the latter had a prescriptive right, the time of prescription running from when the nuisance affected the complainant. '[T]he Plaintiff came to the house he occupies with all the rights which the common law affords, and one of them is, a right to wholesome air', Tindal CJ ruled in *Bliss* v. *Hall*. 'Unless the Defendant shews a prescriptive right to carry on his business in the particular place, the Plaintiff is entitled to judgment.'[157] In 1839, moreover, the Queen's Bench found a plea bad which alleged a 20-year right in the defendant to keep a mixen on his land, which generated foul smells, for it was not shown that the smells had for 20 years reached the plaintiff's land.[158]

In determining whether smoke or noise coming from neighbouring property constituted a nuisance, the courts had to strike a balance. As Erle J. told the jury in *Rich* v. *Basterfield* in 1847, 'every man is bound so to use his property as not to injure his neighbour's rights—with this qualification, that he may make a reasonable use of his own rights, exercising them in a reasonable place'.[159] However, mid-century judges did not agree over whether the main focus of attention was to be on the invasion of the plaintiff's rights, or the reasonableness of the defendant's use of his property. The divergent approaches can be seen in a number of cases involving smoke caused by brick kilns erected on suburban plots where new housing was being developed. This question was particularly prominent in the 1850s and 1860s, an era of significant urban development.[160] While earlier judges had often opined that brick kilns set up to build homes could not be regarded as nuisances,[161] by the mid-century a number of judges had come to think that they could. In 1851, in *Walter* v. *Selfe*, Knight Bruce VC issued an injunction to prevent the defendant burning bricks in Surbiton 'so as to occasion damage or annoyance' to the plaintiff. Although the plaintiff did not necessarily have the right to air 'as fresh, free and pure' as when his own house was first put up, he had a right to air quality which was not incompatible with 'the physical comfort of human existence'. The defendant had no right to 'diminish seriously and materially the ordinary comfort of existence' of the occupier and inmates of the plaintiff's house, 'whatever their rank or station, whatever their age, whatever their state of health'.[162]

---

[157] *Bliss* v. *Hall* (1838) 4 Bing. N.C. 183 at 186. Cf *Elliotson* v. *Feetham* (1835) 2 Bing. N.C. 134.

[158] *Flight* v. *Thomas* (1839) 10 Ad. & El. 590.

[159] *Rich* v. *Basterfield* (1847) 4 C.B. 783 at 787

[160] London (where much of the brick-burning litigation arose) saw a boom in house building from the mid-1850s to 1868, followed by another boom in the 1870s, which peaked in 1881. J. Parry Lewis, *Building Cycles and Britain's Growth* (1965), 129.

[161] *Rudge* v. *New*, *The Times*, 5 May 1825, col. 3e; *Attorney General* v. *Cleaver* (1811) 18 Ves. 211 at 220.

[162] *Walter* v. *Selfe* (1851) 4 De G. & Sm. 315 at 321, 323.

Other judges laid more stress on the notion that whether something was a nuisance depended on its context, such as how far the clamp was from the plaintiff's property. This was to focus more on whether the defendant's activity was reasonable. 'Every trade and occupation called into existence to supply the wants of civilised life, whether in the construction of dwellings or otherwise, must be lawfully carried on somewhere', Wood VC observed in 1853, 'and therefore, irrespective of the circumstances by which it was surrounded, it could not be pronounced a nuisance.'[163] In 1858, in *Hole* v. *Barlow*, Byles J.—bearing in mind Comyns's definition—asked the jury to consider firstly whether the place where the bricks were burned was a proper and convenient one; and only if their answer was in the negative to consider whether the nuisance was such as to make the enjoyment of life in the house uncomfortable. As he saw it, 'it is not everybody whose enjoyment of life and property is rendered uncomfortable by the carrying on of an offensive or noxious trade in the neighbourhood, that can bring an action'. If that were so, there would be countless suits in areas such as Birmingham or Wolverhampton, which would harm the manufacturing interests of the country. In this judge's view, while placing brick burning clamps in the immediate vicinity of Berkeley Square would not be justifiable, the temporary burning of bricks from clay dug on the spot in new neighbourhoods on the outskirts of London—in this case on Brunswick Road, near Highgate Hill—could not be seen in the same way.

Byles's direction was held to be correct by the Common Pleas. Crowder J. noted that what Comyns wrote about trades applied equally to activities such as brick burning, and that it was for the jury to decide what was a suitable area. Willes J. went further, by raising a policy argument: 'The common-law right which every proprietor of a dwelling-house has to have the air uncontaminated and unpolluted', he ruled, 'is subject to this qualification, that necessities may arise for an interference with that right pro bono publico, to this extent, that such interference be in respect of a matter essential to the business of life, and be conducted in a reasonable and proper manner, and in a reasonable and proper place.'[164] Byles's remark that he 'rather expected that the jury would find for the plaintiff'[165] suggests that he felt the clamp was too close to the plaintiff's property, and hence not a convenient place. Nevertheless, his wide formulation, as endorsed by his brethren, implied a kind of zoning which would permit brick burning in some locations, and not in others. It was this which was to prove controversial, for as a result of the decision (as Bramwell B. put it in 1862) many 'claims have been made

---

[163] *Pollock* v. *Lester* (1853) 11 Hare 266 at 275.
[164] *Hole* v. *Barlow* (1858) 4 C.B. N.S. 334 at 335, 345.
[165] *Ibid.*, at 335, 337.

to poison and foul rivers, and to burn up and devastate land, on the ground of public benefit'.[166]

Hole v. Barlow was soon criticized in another brick burning case, Bamford v. Turnley. At trial, Cockburn CJ felt bound by Hole v. Barlow to direct the jury that if they felt the brick burning was done in a convenient place, then it constituted a reasonable use by the defendant of his land, which would entitle him to a verdict. The Queen's Bench accepted Cockburn's ruling,[167] but it was overruled in the Exchequer Chamber, which held that where a defendant caused such annoyance to another man as to constitute prima facie a cause of action, it was no defence to say that the defendant had made a reasonable use of his own land in a convenient place. Its judgment was strongly influenced by W. H. Willes's notes to Gale on Easements, which had examined the meaning of the passage in Comyns relied on by the court in Hole v. Barlow. Giving the judgment of the majority, Williams J. pointed out that while the Common Pleas in Hole interpreted Comyns's word 'convenient' to mean 'proper and convenient for the purpose of carrying on the trade', it could equally be read as meaning 'a place where nuisance will not be caused to another'.[168] The latter meaning would allow trades to be carried on which might annoy residents, but only provided they were not an actionable nuisance. '[T]he true doctrine', he ruled, 'is, that whenever, taking all the circumstances into consideration, including the nature and extent of the plaintiff's enjoyment before the acts complained of, the annoyance is sufficiently great to amount to a nuisance according to the ordinary rule of law, an action will lie whatever the locality may be.'[169] Where this was established, 'the jury cannot properly be asked whether the causing of the nuisance was a reasonable use of the land'.[170] The majority's approach was thus to look at the plaintiff's viewpoint to see if the interference with his right to clean air constituted a nuisance, rather than considering whether the defendant had a right to pollute.[171] Agreeing with the majority, Bramwell B. dismissed the notion that private rights had to be sacrificed to the public good, holding that the cost of pollution could be financially quantified, and that it had to be paid by the polluter. He also offered a test to determine whether an activity was a nuisance: 'those acts necessary for the common and ordinary use and occupation of land and houses may be done, if conveniently done, without subjecting those who do

---

[166] Bamford v. Turnley (1858) 3 B. & S. 66 at 86.
[167] Ibid., 62.   [168] Ibid., 66 at 75.
[169] Ibid., at 77.   [170] Ibid., 77–8.
[171] As Willes pointed out in his notes to Gale on Easements, if it was a defence to say that the polluter had acted in a reasonable way or in a spot convenient to him, why had the court in Bliss v. Hall and Elliotson v. Feetham required polluters to show a prescriptive right? C. J. Gale, Treatise on the Law of Easements, with the notes of W. H. Willes (4th edn by D. Gibbons, 1868), 453n.

them to an action', he suggested, while unnatural or extraordinary uses might be nuisances.[172] Only Pollock CB dissented. In his view, all social life involved compromises, in which some natural rights were invaded 'for the more general convenience or necessities of the whole community'. Juries should be asked whether the defendant's conduct was reasonable, and 'it cannot be supposed that a jury would find that to be a reasonable act by a person which produces any ruinous effect upon his neighbours'.[173]

Despite this decision, there remained some uncertainty among the judges as to how to handle intangible nuisances such as smoke pollution in urban areas, with Willes J.'s view in *Hole* v. *Barlow* still receiving some support.[174] The matter was reconsidered in 1865 in *St Helen's Smelting Co* v. *Tipping*. In contrast to the cases discussed hitherto, this did not concern brick clamps, but the rather more serious pollution from a copper factory,[175] which had caused permanent damage to property. Mellor J. instructed the Liverpool jury hearing this case that no man could use his own property to injure that of his neighbour, unless he had a prescriptive right to do so. In an action for nuisance from noxious vapours, 'the injury to be actionable must be such as visibly to diminish the value of the property and the comfort and enjoyment of it'. He added that the law 'does not regard trifling inconveniences' and that 'every thing must be looked at from a reasonable point of view'. In determining whether there was a nuisance, the jury was to take into account the location of the works, for 'in counties where great works have been erected and carried on, which are the means of developing the national wealth, persons must not stand on extreme rights and bring actions in respect of every matter of annoyance, as, if that were so, business could not be carried on in those places'.[176] After the jury awarded damages of £361, the company sought a new trial on the grounds of a misdirection. The direction was upheld both in the Exchequer Chamber and the House of Lords, which distinguished between nuisances causing sensible personal discomfort and those causing physical harms to property. 'If a man lives in a town', Lord Westbury LC stated, 'it is necessary that he should subject himself to the consequences of those operations of a trade which may be carried on in his immediate locality.' As long as his neighbour conducted his business in a fair and reasonable way, he could not complain. By contrast, if his property were injured, the fact that the defendant was acting reasonably in a reasonable place

---

[172] *Bamford* v. *Turnley* (1858) 3 B. & S. 66 at 83.   [173] *Ibid.*, at 80–1.

[174] See *Wanstead Local Board of Health* v. *William Hill* (1863) 13 C.B. N.S. 479 at 484; Erle CJ's comments in *Cavey* v. *Ledbitter* (1863) 13 C.B. N.S. 47 at 477; *Scott* v. *Firth* (1864) 10 LT 240.

[175] See also the litigation in *Bankart* v. *Houghton* (1859–60) 27 Beav. 425 and *Houghton* v. *Bankart* (1861) 3 De G. F. & J. 16.

[176] *Tipping* v. *St Helen's Smelting Co* (1863) 4 B. & S. 608 at 610.

would offer no defence.[177] Since Tipping's property was damaged, he succeeded, and was ultimately able to have the factory closed.[178]

The decision suggested that those who lived in an industrial area would have to put up with the sensory irritations which came with it.[179] For instance, in *Salvin* v. *North Brancepeth Coal Co*, in 1874, Jessel MR dismissed a claim for an injunction from a Durham landholder to restrain the defendants from working a coal mine and coking ovens within 400 yards of his plantations, since no serious damage had been done to the property, and since most of the smoke which interfered with the enjoyment of the premises came from other collieries. His decision was upheld by the Chancery Court of Appeal. As James LJ put it, 'If some picturesque haven opens its arms to invite the commerce of the world, it is not for this Court to forbid the embrace'. Indeed, the 'man to whom Providence has given an estate, under which there are veins of coal worth perhaps hundreds or thousands of pounds per acre, must take the gift with the consequences and concomitants of the mineral wealth in which he is a participant'.[180] However, those who found industry invading their locality could complain. In *Crump* v. *Lambert*, in 1867, an injunction was granted to restrain iron manufacturers who had opened a factory next to the plaintiff's houses, situated on the other side of a ridge from the manufacturing part of Walsall. In Romilly MR's view, the smoke from the factory produced 'a completely new state of things as regards the plaintiff's house and grounds' which materially interfered with human comfort.[181]

The question whether the court should focus more on whether the defendant's use of his property was reasonable than on its effect on the plaintiff continued to be debated to the end of our period. In *Reinhardt* v. *Menasti*, for instance, Kekewich J. observed that in nuisance, the question was not whether the defendant acted reasonably in using his property, but '[t]he real question is, does he injure his neighbour?'[182] His view was criticized by Buckley J. in *Sanders-Clark* v. *Grosvenor Mansions Co and G. D'Allessandri*, who held that where a defendant was using his property reasonably, 'there is nothing at law which can be considered a nuisance; but if he is not using it reasonably, if he is using it for purposes for which the building was not constructed, then the plaintiff is entitled to

---

[177] *St Helen's Smelting Co* v. *Tipping* (1865) 11 HLC 642 at 650.

[178] *Tipping* v. *St Helen's Smelting Co* (1865) LR 1 Ch App 66; see Simpson, *Leading Cases*, 191.

[179] Over a decade after the decision, the Royal Commission on Noxious Vapours observed that '[p]ersons whose houses are rendered almost uninhabitable by the stench of sulphuretted hydrogen from Widnes or St Helens waste heaps appear to be practically without any remedy whatever': 1878 Royal Commission on Noxious Vapours, p. 34.

[180] *Salvin* v. *North Brancepeth Coal Co* (1874) LR 9 Ch App 705 at 709–10.

[181] *Crump* v. *Lambert* (1867) LR 3 Eq 409 at 414. Romilly followed the approach of Knight Bruce in *Walter* v. *Selfe*.

[182] *Reinhardt* v. *Menasti* (1889) 42 Ch D 685 at 690.

relief'.[183] In the following year, Kekewich replied that even if a defendant was running his business in a reasonable manner, he might create a nuisance. Once it was established that a nuisance was created, 'the fact that [the defendant] was doing what was reasonable from his point of view was no defence', for if a man created a nuisance, it was contradictory to say that he was acting reasonably.[184] The debate was perhaps not all that important. For in practice, the courts took the view that in determining whether the defendant's conduct was unreasonable, they had to consider its effect on the plaintiff; and in determining whether its effect on the latter was such as to constitute a nuisance, they took into account the context in which the activity occurred.

For instance, in the 1870s, the courts considering whether to give a remedy to complainants whose residences were disturbed by noisy neighbours looked at whether the defendant's conduct was unusual. In *Ball* v. *Ray*, the Court of Appeal granted an injunction to a plaintiff, whose neighbour made alterations to stables in the ground floor of his house, which so increased the noise as to make the house unlettable. In Lord Selborne's view, if adjoining houses were used for the 'ordinary purposes' for which they were constructed, then as long as they were so used, there could be no nuisance. But if a house was converted 'to unusual purposes in such a manner as to produce a substantial injury to his neighbour, it appears to me that that is not according to principle or authority a reasonable use of his own property'.[185] While some noises—such as pianos—had to be endured from neighbours, others—such as the noise of horses clanking their chains against party walls—did not. Three years later, Jessel MR dismissed the defendant's claim that he was making a reasonable use of his property in having noisy stables on a damp artificial mound. Although, he said, there were 'many trades and many occupations which are not only reasonable, but necessary to be followed', this did not mean they could 'be allowed to be followed in the proximity of dwelling-houses, so as to interfere with the comfort of their inhabitants'.[186]

As the Court of Appeal confirmed in 1906, plaintiffs were entitled to enjoy the 'ordinary comfort of human existence' which was enjoyed in the particular area in which they lived. This meant that although someone who chose to live in an area where noisy trades were conducted could not complain of the noise, if his neighbour introduced new machinery which made a substantial addition to the disturbance, he could obtain relief.[187] It also meant that a business which made an

---

[183] *Sanders-Clark* v. *Grosvenor Mansions Co and G. D'Allessandri* [1900] 2 Ch 373 at 375–6.

[184] *Attorney-General* v. *Cole & Son* [1901] 1 Ch 205 at 206.

[185] *Ball* v. *Ray* (1873) LR 8 Ch App 467 at 469–70.

[186] *Broder* v. *Saillard* (1876) 2 Ch D 692 at 701.

[187] *Rushmer* v. *Polsue & Alfieri* [1906] 1 Ch 234, 250–1. The decision was affirmed by the Lords: [1907] AC 121.

unusual level of noise in a quiet area could not resist an action of nuisance merely because they had done it for a long time. In *Sturges* v. *Bridgman* in 1879, the Court of Appeal granted an injunction to a physician who had 14 years earlier purchased the lease of a house in Wimpole Street in London. In 1873, he built a consulting room at the end of his garden, which shared a party wall with the kitchen of a confectioner. Large pestles and mortars were used in the kitchen to break up and pound loaf sugar, creating noise and vibration which interfered with the quiet of the consulting room. The confectioner claimed a prescriptive right to make the noise, having used such equipment for over 20 years, but this argument was rejected by both Jessel MR and the Lord Justices, since the noise had not been a nuisance to the plaintiff for such a period. The court also rejected the argument that if the plaintiff could stop an established business by building a consulting room next to it, then he might also stop 'all the tanneries of Bermondsey' by building his home there. As Thesiger LJ put it, whether something was a nuisance was not to be determined in the abstract but according to circumstances. Where there were trades established, he noted, juries would be justified in finding that such trades would not constitute nuisances, so that what would be a nuisance in Belgrave Square would not necessarily be so in Bermondsey.[188] 'Unfortunately', *The Graphic* commented on this case, 'it is only the rich who can resort to such methods of obtaining relief; the poor must put up with noises and evil odours, unless the nuisance reaches such a pitch as to warrant the interference of some official authority'.[189]

If it was relatively easy to bring cases against noisy neighbours, it continued to be difficult to take nuisance proceedings against large industrial polluters, for the courts took the view that individual polluters could only be liable for the damage their smoke actually produced. Where there were many polluters, litigants faced insuperable difficulties in apportioning blame.[190] Litigants also faced difficulties where nuisances were committed by those acting under statutory authority. This was confirmed by the Lords in *Hammersmith and City Railway Co* v. *Brand*, when rejecting the appellants' claim for compensation for the effect of noise, vibration, and smoke from the working of the railway, which resulted in the value of their property falling. In advising the Lords, Bramwell B. took the view that earlier cases, which held that statutes authorizing the creation of railway lines legalized the accompanying nuisance,[191] were wrongly decided. Since railway statutes

---

[188] *Sturges* v. *Bridgman* (1879) LR 11 Ch D 852 at 865.

[189] *The Graphic*, 5 July 1879. On the case see A. W. B. Simpson, 'Coase v Pigou Reexamined', (1996) 25 *JLS* 53–97.

[190] 1878 Royal Commission on Noxious Vapours, pp. 56 (evidence of J. E. Pardey), 107 (evidence of William Keates).

[191] *Rex* v. *Pease* (1832) 4 B. & Ad. 30; *Vaughan* v. *Taff Vale Railway Co* (1860) 5 H. & N. 679.

included extensive compensation schemes for land taken or injuriously affected by the construction of such works,[192] he felt it would be a gross injustice for the courts to construe the legislation as removing a common law action for nuisance, when no statutory compensation was given. In his view, this would involve unfairly passing the economic cost of the railway onto private individuals. Only Blackburn J. among the judges felt the appellants had no remedy, on the grounds that 'no Court can treat that as a wrong which the Legislature has authorized'.[193] However, the Lords agreed with his position.

The question of statutory authorization of nuisances was revisited by the Lords in 1881 in *Metropolitan Asylum District* v. *Hill*, when they upheld an injunction against a smallpox hospital. In doing so, they distinguished between compulsory and permissive powers granted by statute. According to Lord Blackburn, *Hammersmith and City Railway Co* v. *Brand* only settled that where the legislature directed something to be done, any right of action in respect of doing it was removed: for it was absurd to suppose one might have an injunction to prevent what the legislature intended to be done. But where the statute was only an enabling one, the fact that no compensation clauses were included afforded a reason to think that the legislature intended that the act should only be done, if it could be done without causing injury to others.[194] In 1885, the Court of Appeal held further that where a gas company was given power to lay pipes under a street, it did not have the power to use such heavy steam rollers as would injure the plaintiffs' pipes, absent specific statutory authority to do so.[195] Although much depended on the court's interpretation of the relevant statute,[196] if the court was persuaded that the powers were only permissive, then injunctions could be awarded.

In cases involving the use of statutory powers, the courts generally considered the question of negligence, as well as whether any nuisance committed by

---

[192] Earlier cases had given compensation under the 1845 Railway Clauses Consolidation Act for damage to property rights occasioned by the construction: see *R* v. *Eastern Counties Railway Co* (1841) 2 Q.B. 347; *Glover* v. *North Staffordshire Railway Co* (1851) 16 Q.B. 912; *Reg* v. *Great Northern Railway Co* (1849) 14 Q.B. 25. Mid-century courts were less certain whether plaintiffs could succeed who had lost business as a result of roads being blocked: see *Chamberlain* v. *West End of London and Crystal Palace Railway* (1845) 2 B. & S. 605; *Senior* v. *Metropolitan Railway Co* (1863) 2 H. & C. 258 (in favour of compensation); *Rex* v. *London Dock Co* (1836) 5 Ad. & El. 163; *Cameron* v. *Charing-Cross Railway Co* (1865) 19 C.B. N.S. 764; *Ricket* v. *Metropolitan Railway Co* (1865) 5 B & S 156 (against compensation). The House of Lords attempted to reconcile the cases in *Ricket* v. *Metropolitan Railway Co* (1867) LR 2 HL 175, holding that no compensation could be given as the damage to the claimant was too remote.

[193] *Hammersmith and City Railway Co* v. *Brand* (1869–70) LR 4 HL 171 at 196.

[194] *Metropolitan Asylum District* v. *Frederick* (1881) 6 App Cas 193 at 203.

[195] *The Gas Light and Coke Company* v. *The Vestry of St. Mary* (1885) 15 QBD 1.

[196] See *London, Brighton, and South Coast Railway Co* v. *Truman and Others* (1885) 11 App Cas 45.

the defendant had been legalized, for where the defendant had acted negligently, no statutory authorization could justify him. However, the fact that negligent conduct might remove a statutory defence did not mean that negligence was an element of nuisance. In *Rapier* v. *London Tramways Co*, the Court of Appeal took the occasion to make it clear that, if the defendant's nuisance was not permitted by statute, the fact that he had not acted negligently did not avail him. In this case, the defendant company had built stables in Tooting which could hold up to 400 horses. 'If the Defendants are right in saying that they cannot concentrate their stables to such an extent as is desirable without committing a nuisance to the neighbourhood', Lindley LJ ruled, 'then they must not concentrate their horses to such an extent.'[197] The law of nuisance was not to be assimilated to the law of negligence: for it was the effect of the defendant's conduct on his neighbour which mattered, not simply the reasonableness of his conduct or the care which he took in his business.

4. REMEDIES

Although the question of whether a right had been invaded or a nuisance committed was one for the common law, many litigants had to resort to the Chancery to prevent nuisances being committed. Sometimes, a decision of a common law court might resolve the dispute without the need for further litigation. For example, in 1824, Mr Ogilvy, a gentleman with a residence at Sunbury, sued a pea farmer who lodged between 20 and 30 seasonal pickers 'from distant parts' in a barn opposite the plaintiff's home: 'Their conversation was loud, and often of a nature unsuited to female ears; their habits were uncleanly; and their whole establishment unprovided with suitable accommodations, and extremely disagreeable to the inmates of Mr Ogilvy's house.' Ogilvy had commenced an action two years earlier, but suspended it, to allow the defendant to abate. When he did not, Ogilvy returned to court, where he sought nominal damages, provided the defendant entered into a rule to stop lodging his labourers in the barn. This was duly agreed to.[198]

But more frequently, the mere decision of a common law action did not induce the parties to come to an agreement. Since nuisances were likely to continue, and since the cost of bringing an action might swallow up any sum recovered, injunctive relief was often the only effective remedy,[199] and the common law

---

[197] *Rapier* v. *London Tramways Company* [1893] 2 Ch 588 at 602.

[198] *Ogilvy* v. *Collins*, *The Times*, 23 February 1824, col. 4a.

[199] See e.g. the experience of Sir John Gerard's experience of common law litigation in the 1830s and 1840s: 1862 Select Committee on Noxious Vapours, p. 7, q. 60 (evidence of Adolphus Moubert);

action was therefore only the preliminary step to seeking an injunction. In the early nineteenth century, Chancery's intervention in nuisance cases was rare and confined,[200] but from 1810s and 1820s, more litigants sought Chancery's help, and its use continued to grow in the following decades.[201] Where the nuisance was private, the plaintiff might obtain an injunction where the harm could not be repaired by damages.[202] Where there was a public nuisance, an information lay in equity to stop the nuisance and restrain its continuance, without any damage having to be shown.[203]

Before the courts of equity would intervene, they had to be certain that a legal right had been infringed. This did not always necessitate a prior action at law, for in some cases it was self-evident, and in others it might be admitted by the defendant's answer to the plaintiff's bill. But where there was any doubt, Chancery judges were not prepared to give final relief on conflicting evidence, but referred the issue to a common law court.[204] Interlocutory injunctions were granted to restrain nuisances pending the decision of a court of law,[205] provided the plaintiff could show a *prima facie* case in support of his title. In such cases, the court would balance the question between the two sides, refusing an injunction if the inconvenience to the defendant, should he be proved to be in the right, would be greater than that to the plaintiff, should he be right.[206] However, where the nuisance was clear, Chancery did not weigh convenience even in interim injunctions.[207]

1878 Royal Commission on Noxious Vapours, pp. 41 *et seq.*, qq. 1415 *et seq.* (evidence of Moubert); cf. Simpson, *Leading Cases*, 177.

[200] The Exchequer intervened more frequently to prevent public nuisances obstructing highways.

[201] See Eldon's observations in *Attorney General* v. *Cleaver* (1811) 18 Ves. 211. See also McLaren, 'Nuisance Law', 186. See also the notes to *Baines* v. *Baker* (1752) Amb. 158, for the use of the injunction.

[202] See E. R Daniel, *The Practice of the High Court of Chancery* (2nd edn, 1845, with additions by T. E. Headlam), 1507.

[203] See *Mayor of London* v. *Bolt* (1799) 5 Ves. 129; *Attorney General* v. *Nichol* (1809) 16 Ves. 338. In such cases, the Attorney General was to be a party to the suit, as representing the public, though private individuals could also seek the court's assistance where they had suffered particular damage. See *Attorney General* v. *Forbes* (1836) 2 M. & C. 123. If the plaintiff had suffered special damage from a public nuisance, it was held that he did not have to join the Attorney General: *Soltau* v. *De Held* (1851) 2 Sim. N.S. 133.

[204] It was held in *Broadbent* v. *The Imperial Gas Co* (1857) 7 De G. M. & G. 436 (upheld in *The Directors etc of the Imperial Gas Light and Coke Co* v. *Samuel Broadbent* (1859) 7 H.L.C. 600) that the finding of an arbitrator was equivalent to a common law decision.

[205] *Harman* v. *Jones* (1841) Cr. & Ph. 299.

[206] *Hilton* v. *Earl of Granville* (1841) Cr. & Ph. 283 at 297. See also *Elmhirst* v. *Spencer* (1849) 2 M. & G. 45 at 51.

[207] *Attorney-General* v. *Council of Borough of Birmingham* (1858) 4 K. & J. 528.

After Sir John Rolt's Act of 1862 enacted that equity judges should determine all questions of law on which equitable relief depended, there should have been no further need to send litigants to common law courts to establish the nuisance. Nevertheless, defendants continued to be permitted a jury trial at common law if the judge doubted whether there was a legal right, or where evidence was contradictory.[208] Judges were also uncomfortable with assessing damages. The 1860s also saw judges debate whether plaintiffs who had been refused an injunction were forbidden from seeking damages at law. Although it was argued that under Rolt's Act, a plaintiff would be estopped as the legal matter had already been settled, Chancery judges often argued that if legislation *allowed* them to consider the question of damages and the right at law, they were not *obliged* to do so, and so they reserved to plaintiffs the right to proceed at law.[209] But by the time of fusion, equity judges were comfortably handling questions concerning legal rights and damages.[210]

The fact that a plaintiff had established a right at law did not necessarily entitle him to a perpetual injunction.[211] If the damage to the plaintiff was trivial, no injunction would be given. According to Kindersley VC in 1851, the 'mere dry fact' that a plaintiff had an 'abstract right' to clean water did not entitle him to an injunction for any slight infringement. He refused an injunction to restrain the defendant from polluting a river near Bradford, noting that the plaintiff had waited for five years before bringing his action. He had also previously obtained financial compensation from another polluter by threatening an action at common law.[212] In 1867, in another water pollution case, Malins VC held that although private rights had to prevail over public convenience, the court would not intervene unless the nuisance materially diminished the enjoyment of health or the value of property. '[I]f the extent of the inconvenience sustained by the plaintiff is

---

[208] *Eaden* v. *Firth* (1863) 1 H. & M. 573; *Inchbald* v. *Robinson; Inchbald* v. *Barrington* (1869) LR 4 Ch App 388 at 397. See also the comments in *Roskell* v. *Whitworth* (1870) LR 5 Ch App 459 at 463; *Broadbent* v. *Imperial Gas Company* (1857) 7 De G. M. & G. 436; *Swaine* v. *Great Northern Railway* (1864) 33 L.J. Ch. 399.

[209] *Langmeid* v. *Maple* (1865) 18 C.B. N.S. 255; *Swaine* v. *Great Northern Railway* (1864) 33 LJ Ch 399. Judges left the question open when they refused injunctions because the plaintiff had delayed, or because there was not a sufficiently continuing nuisance to justify and injunction: but when an injunction was refused because the harm was trivial, equity judges were willing to consider damages. See e.g. *Johnson* v. *Wyatt* (1863) 33 LJ NS Rep. 394, where no damages were awarded.

[210] See e.g. *Fritz* v. *Hobson* (1880) 14 Ch D 542; *City of London Brewery Company* v. *Tennant* (1873) LR 9 Ch App 212 at 216.

[211] *Attorney General* v. *Nichol* (1809) 6 Ves. 338 at 341–2.

[212] *Wood* v. *Sutcliffe* (1851) 2 Sim. N.S. 163, 167. The Vice Chancellor noted that (given the growth of the town), no injunction would restore pure water, for all the courts in England could not 'remove the mass of human beings who are congregated on the banks of the stream'. All an injunction would do would be to ruin the defendant.

of a trifling nature, such as may be readily compensated for in money, you cannot and ought not to interfere with the rights of others in a matter of so much
importance as this [...] namely, the drainage of a not inconsiderable town.'[213] It
was not unknown for parties to seek injunctions as bargaining chips in disputes
with urban authorities, and judges may have been aware in cases involving isolated litigious downstream landowners of the need for some scepticism when it
came to their claims.

But where the court was convinced that the nuisance was substantial, plaintiffs obtained injunctions.[214] Once a plaintiff had established his right at law,
and showed that damages were inadequate, he was held entitled as of right to an
injunction.[215] Damages would be inadequate where the harm was continuing—
which would require repeated actions by a plaintiff—or where the calculation
of damages would prove impossible. In cases concerning deprivation of light,
equity judges gave injunctions where substantial damages would be given at law,
'as distinguished from some small sum of £5, £10, or £20', for otherwise 'those
who are minded to erect a building that will inflict an injury upon their neighbour [would] have a right to purchase him out without any Act of Parliament for
that purpose having been obtained'.[216]

After the passing of Cairns's and Rolt's Acts, the question was raised in a
number of cases whether the Chancery judges, armed with the power to award
damages, should give them in lieu of injunctions where public convenience was
at stake. In 1894, in *Shelfer* v. *City of London Electric Lighting Co*, where the plaintiff's public house suffered from noise and vibration coming from the Bankside
power station, Kekewich J. refused an injunction and directed an assessment of
damages, in view of the inconvenience which would result from closing a power
station. However, his decision was overturned by the Court of Appeal. According
to Lord Halsbury, Cairns's Act had not intended to revolutionize the principles
on which equity jurisprudence worked. In his view, to allow compensation by
damages in cases such as this would simply encourage companies who could
afford it to drive out their neighbours by paying for the continuing nuisance.[217]
A. L. Smith LJ confirmed that where rights were invaded, the plaintiff was *prima
facie* entitled to an injunction. In his view, the rule could be relaxed in four

---

[213] *Lillywhite* v. *Trimmer* (1867) 36 LJ NS Ch 525 at 529–30. Cf. *Attorney-General* v. *Gee* (1870) LR 10
Eq 131 and *Attorney-General* v. *Guardians of Poor of Union of Dorking* (1882) 20 Ch D 595 at 607.

[214] Rolt LJ attributed this view (which he doubted) to St Leonards in *Walter* v. *Selfe*: see *Luscombe*
v. *Steer* (1867) 17 LT 229, 231.

[215] *Imperial Gas Light and Coke Co* v. *Samuel Broadbent* (1859) 7 H.L.C. 600.

[216] *Dent* v. *Auction Mart Co* (1866) LR 2 Eq 238 at 246. See also Jessel MR in *Aynsley* v. *Glover* (1874)
LR 18 Eq 544 at 552.

[217] *Shelfer* v. *City of London Electric Lighting Co* [1895] 1 Ch 287 at 311. See also *Wood* v. *Conway
Corp* [1914] 2 Ch 47 at 57; *Martin* v. *Price* [1894] 1 Ch 276.

circumstances: where the injury to the plaintiff's rights was small; where the injury was one which could be estimated in money; where it could be adequately compensated by a small financial payment; and where it would be oppressive to the defendant to grant an injunction.[218] The courts also rejected arguments that they should (following *St Helens* v. *Tipping*) distinguish between cases involving harms to property (where the nuisance was in the character of a trespass) and those involving mere personal discomfort.[219] The distinction might have been relevant when establishing whether the activity constituted a nuisance or not, but it was not relevant for the determination of whether an injunction was to be given.

The fact that the granting of an injunction would create serious difficulties was not in itself a reason to refuse one. Thus, in *Attorney General* v. *Birmingham*, Page Wood VC dismissed the objection that the council had done their best to find a solution, but had run out of money. 'If, after all possible experiments, they cannot drain Birmingham without invading the plaintiff's private rights, they must apply to Parliament for power to invade his rights', he said, 'and if the case be one of such magnitude as it is represented to be, Parliament, no doubt, will take measures accordingly, and the Plaintiff will protect himself as best he may.'[220] Similarly, in 1868 granting an injunction to prevent an asylum from polluting a stream, he noted that an injunction would only be refused in cases where it would be impossible to obey,[221] as where one was sought to restrain the destruction of a sea wall already taken down. It was not, in his view, impossible to restore things to how they were before the erection of the asylum: 'It is only a question of expense, and this Court is not in the habit of listening to any argument on the ground of expense when it restrains the doing of a wrong.'[222]

Plaintiffs occasionally sought injunctive relief to prevent the future occurrence of harms. The Chancery's general approach was that a plaintiff had to wait until a right had been interfered with before coming to court.[223] Injunctions to prevent future harms—*quia timet* injunctions—would only be granted in very

---

[218] *Shelfer* v. *City of London Electric Lighting Co* [1895] 1 Ch 287, 322–3, followed in *Jordeson* v. *Sutton, Southcoates and Drypool Gas Co* [1899] 2 Ch. 217; *Kine* v. *Jolly* [1905] 1 Ch 480. A. L. Smith LJ added that the right was lost where there had been laches by the plaintiff.

[219] Thus, in 1889, Kekewich J. wondered whether injunctions were to be issued where the nuisance was in the character of a trespass, but otherwise not: *Reinhardt* v. *Menasti* (1889) 42 Ch D 685 at 686.

[220] *Attorney-General* v. *The Council of the Borough of Birmingham* (1858) 4 K. & J. 528 at 541.

[221] It was on the grounds of impossibility of compliance that some judges refused to issue injunctions against authorities in whom sewage pipes were vested which others had a prescriptive right to use. See *Attorney-General* v. *Guardians of Poor of Union of Dorking* (1882) 20 Ch D 595; *Earl of Harrington* v. *Corporation of Derby* [1905] 1 Ch 205.

[222] *Attorney-General* v. *Colney Hatch Lunatic Asylum* (1868) LR 4 Ch App 146 at 158.

[223] *The Manchester, Sheffield &c Railway Co* v. *The Worksop Board of Health* (1856–7) 23 Beav. 198.

rare circumstances of apprehended danger which would do irreparable harm to property.[224] More usually, they were refused. For instance, in 1865, the conservators of the Thames failed to obtain an injunction against the construction of a new sewage system by the corporation of Kingston-upon-Thames, which would flow into the Thames. Wood VC noted that this was the first case involving a large river, and in an area where there were no prescriptive rights. The same Vice Chancellor who was so keen to maintain the cleanliness of rivers where private rights were harmed noted here that '[r]unning water is one of the means provided by Providence for getting rid readily of that which must be got rid of for the benefit of health, and, *de facto*, it has been used for that purpose'. If it could be shown that there was a nuisance to the public, or that there was any special private nuisance, an injunction could be awarded, but 'the nuisance must actually exist, you cannot stop it *quia timet*'.[225] The Chancery Division again considered *quia timet* injunctions in 1893 when the Withington District Local Board sought to restrain the building of a smallpox hospital, which they claimed would be dangerous to the community. Chitty J. noted that the court would intervene where it was certain that injury would arise, or even where it was extremely probable. However, in the case before him, where there was contradictory evidence as to the danger the hospital would pose, the plaintiffs had not made out a sufficiently cogent case for the remedy to be given.[226]

When injunctions were granted, however, they were often suspended, to allow defendants to take steps to resolve the problem. In *Attorney General* v. *The Metropolitan Board of Works* in 1863, another case concerning pollution of the Lee, Lord Hatherley (as Page Wood had become) repeated his view that 'a mere question of expense' could not be taken into account, but instead of granting an injunction to stop the works, he required the defendants to make certain undertakings.[227] In another case, while Hatherley felt that a nuisance had been created, he sent a reference to determine in what way the sewage could be carried off, leaving liberty to the parties to apply to him again.[228] This was to make the

---

[224] *Hepburn* v. *Lordan* (1865) 2 H & M 345, where there was apprehended danger by fire by the spontaneous combustion of damp jute; and *Crowder* v. *Tinkler* (1816) 19 Ves. 617, where the defendants were manufacturers of gunpowder. See also the approach to such injunctions in *Earl of Ripon* v. *Hobart* (1834) 3 My. & K. 169 at 176 and *Haines* v. *Taylor* (1847) 2 Ph. 209.

[225] *The Attorney General* v. *The Mayor, Aldermen, and Burgesses of the Borough of Kingston-upon-Thames* (1865) Jur. NS 11: 596, 600.

[226] *Attorney-General* v. *Corporation of Manchester* [1893] 2 Ch 87. Cf. *Fleet* v. *Metropolitan Asylums Board* (1886) 2 TLR 361 at 362.

[227] *Attorney General* v. *The Metropolitan Board of Works* (1863) 1 H. & M. 298.

[228] The case was the unreported case of *Heath* v. *Wallingford*, mentioned in *Attorney General* v. *Colney Hatch* (1868) LR 4 Ch App 146 at 162. Wood VC took a similar approach in a case concerning the diminution of light, *Yates* v. *Jack* (1866) LR 1 Ch App 295, where he directed an inquiry into the modification of building plans, an approach disapproved of by Lord Cranworth.

judge a kind of regulator, in effect supervising the works from the Chancery. By 1868, Hatherley had come to the conclusion that this approach was wrong both in principle and in practice, for the result was that '[t]here were repeated steps taken at Chambers, great expense occasioned, and the parties were driven to compromise in a great measure by the terms in which I originally framed the order'.[229] Nonetheless, if they did not wish to intervene in such a close manner, equity judges (including Hatherley in the *Colney Hatch* case) continued to suspend the implementation of injunctions, to allow time for solutions to be found.[230] As a result, injunctions might prove ineffective, as local authorities returned time and again to court to explain their failure to act and buy more time from the judge.

[229] *Attorney General* v. *Colney Hatch* (1868) LR 4 Ch App 146 at 162.
[230] See also *Goldsmid* v. *Tunbridge Wells Improvement Commissioners* (1865) LR 1 Eq 161 at 170 for a similar example.

VII
Property Torts

THE common law was highly protective of property. In an age when concepts of fault were beginning to gain primacy in personal injury cases, judges remained keen to protect property interests strictly. Those who interfered with other people's goods through their deliberate actions did so at their own risk. As Frederick Pollock put it, 'we touch the property of others at our peril, and honest mistake in acting for our own interest, or even an honest intention to act for the benefit of the true owner, will avail us nothing if we transgress'.[1] When it came to such wrongs, he noted, neither the intention to violate another's rights, nor even a knowledge that one was doing so, was necessary. Pollock, who had developed a theory in which moral fault stood at the centre of the law of tort, was troubled by the common law's strict approach to property wrongs. In his view, it was to be explained by an accident of history, whereby the law of wrongful injuries had been used, for procedural reasons, to try property rights. Arguing that 'a rational exposition' of law could 'get rid of the extraneous matter' introduced under 'conditions that no longer exist',[2] Pollock duly attempted to reconcile these rules as far as possible with his moral view of fault, suggesting that in most cases where someone's property rights were violated, the perpetrator would have been at least negligent. While there were exceptional cases (which 'may be of real hardship'), they were too rare to determine the 'general rule of law'. Following Holmes's view, he explained the strict liability which attached in particular situations in policy terms, arguing that it was imposed 'to avoid the difficulty of proving negligence, or [...] to sharpen men's precaution in hazardous matters'.[3] This could explain cases such as *Rylands* v. *Fletcher*, which imposed a strict liability on landowners whose reservoirs burst and flooded their neighbours' land.

Pollock's contemporary Sir John Salmond also agreed with Holmes's view that '[t]here is no more reason why I should insure other persons against the harmful results of my own activities, in the absence of any *mens rea* on my part,

---

[1] F. Pollock, *The Law of Torts: A Treatise on the Principles of Obligation Arising from Civil Wrongs in the Common Law* (1887), 272.

[2] Pollock, *Torts* (1887 edn), 15.

[3] *Ibid.*, 16, 18.

than I should insure them against [any other] inevitable accidents'.[4] Salmond
explained that in cases where the common law exceptionally imposed absolute liability, it was either the product of historical accident, or was justified on
the grounds that a conclusive presumption of negligence was needed in cases
where requiring proof of *mens rea* would be too burdensome and would undermine the efficiency and certainty of justice.[5] Salmond also pointed out that it
was never a defence to argue that one had acted under an inevitable mistake.
That is, any wilful interference with another's rights 'on a supposed justification is done at the doer's peril; and if the justification does not in truth exist, a
belief in its existence, however honest and reasonable, is no defence'. The rule
that a mistaken belief could not justify an invasion of another's right, Salmond
suggested, had its reason 'in the evidential difficulties' which would ensue if the
courts had to inquire into the honesty and reasonableness of the defendant's
mistake.[6]

Both Pollock and Salmond were striving to find a single unifying moral principle for the law of tort. For Salmond, it was the decision in *Rylands* v. *Fletcher*,
and its revival and reworking of an ancient rule regarding liability for animals,
which had done most 'to prevent the establishment of a simple and uniform system of civil responsibility'.[7] Yet throughout our period, when it came to dealing
with wrongs to property, the courts showed themselves keen to give maximum
protection to those with property rights, and to cast the risk on those who
interfered with them. As has been seen, when personal property was damaged
by accidents occurring in the world at large—as where coaches collided on the
road—the common law did not impose strict liability. By contrast, where one
person acquired another's property without having the right to it, his liability
was strict. This meant that those who dealt in good faith with property which
belonged to another were liable to the true owner, even if they acted carefully
throughout, when the real owner had not. This strict approach to the protection
of property was often regarded as commercially inconvenient, for it gave little
protection to *bona fide* purchasers in the market. Where fixed property was accidentally damaged, liability also remained strict. In this area, the courts in the
mid-century began to explore whether liability should be based on negligence;
but finally opted to reiterate the view that a man's property rights, in his own
domain, were to be strictly protected.

---

[4] Sir John Salmond, *The Law of Torts* (2nd edn, 1910), 13.

[5] Salmond was uncomfortable with the decision in *Rylands* v. *Fletcher*, seeing it as an unwar-
ranted reaffirmation of a strict rule of liability for cattle trespass which Salmond felt should have
waned away with other strict trespass liabilities: see *Torts* (2nd edn, 1910), 197n.

[6] Salmond, *Torts* (2nd edn, 1910), 15.

[7] Salmond, *Torts* (4th edn, 1916), vi.

1. WRONGS TO CHATTELS

Any direct physical interference with a chattel in the plaintiff's possession constituted the wrong of trespass.[8] Jurists agreed, on an analogy with trespass to land,
that the action lay even though no damage was done to the chattel.[9] Although, by
the 1870s, trespass could not be brought where harm had been caused uninten-
tionally or without negligence,[10] it could be maintained for anything done purposely, even if by mistake, or without any moral fault.[11] In 1876, a defendant was
accordingly held liable in trespass for having moved jewellery from an unlocked
drawer in the room in which her brother-in-law had died, to a box in a cupboard in the neighbouring room. Her motives were honourable, for she sought
to safeguard the jewellery.[12] The action could also be used against employers who
wrote disparaging comments on documents which were the property of their
employees—such as driving licences—even though the words themselves might
have been written *bona fide* and were not defamatory.[13] However, this action was
only usually resorted to when the plaintiff's property was damaged—as where his
dogs or horses had been beaten,[14] or where other goods had been damaged[15]—or
where it was taken away by the defendant.

The commonest disputes over personal property in our period arose not
when it was damaged while in the plaintiff's possession, but when it found its
way into another's hands. In the commercial society of Victorian England, disputes constantly arose over who had the right to goods, between parties who

---

[8] 'Scratching the panel of a carriage would be a trespass': *Fouldes* v. *Willoughby* (1841) 8 M. & W.
540 at 549 (per Alderson B.).

[9] Pollock, *Torts* (1st edn, 1887), 283; Salmond, *Torts* (2nd edn, 1910), 340–1. Cf. T. A. Street, *The
Foundations of Legal Liability*, 3 vols (Northport, New York, 1906), i, 16. This, it was argued, was
required to ensure the protection of certain kinds of property, 'as where valuable objects are exhibited' in public: Pollock, *Torts* (8th edn, 1908), 350.

[10] *Holmes* v. *Mather* (1875) LR 10 Ex 261 at 268, referring to liability for personal injury.

[11] See *Basely* v. *Clarkson* (1681) 3 Lev. 37.

[12] *Kirk* v. *Gregory* (1876) 1 Ex D 55. She was sued by the executors when the jewels later went missing from the box. The Exchequer Division only awarded nominal damages, however, rather that the
value of the jewels.

[13] *Rogers* v. *Macnamara* (1853) 14 C.B. 27; *Wennhak* v. *Morgan* (1888) 20 QBD 635. It was even held
in 1905 that an action of trespass (but not libel) lay against the chairman of the Barrow-in-Furness
health committee for showing a letter belonging to the plaintiff, which impugned her moral character, to the mayor of the town: *Thurston* v. *Charles* (1905) 21 TLR 659.

[14] See e.g. *Grant* v. *Hulton* (1817) 1 B. & Ald. 134; *Hanway* v. *Boultbee* (1830) 1 M. & R. 15; *Walley* v.
Holt, *The Times*, 11 November 1876, col. 11d; *Morris* v. *Nugent* (1836) 7 Car. & P. 572. Although a man
could justify beating, or killing a dog, if he had been attacked, the mere fact that a ferocious dog was
at large did not justify a person in shooting it.

[15] Such cases were often brought against others who had damaged or interfered with the plaintiff's property, while claiming to exercise a right: e.g. *Drewell* v. *Towler* (1832) 3 B. & Ad. 735; *Smith*
v. *Pritchard* (1849) 8 C.B. 565.

acted in equal good faith. Creditors who seized the goods of their debtors often found themselves in court, facing either the debtor (who disputed the defendant's right to take the goods) or a third party, whose property had been seized in error. Sheriffs or assignees in bankruptcy were especially vulnerable to suits, since they often seized property in error, or exceeded their powers in taking the debtor's property.[16] In a world where fraudulent transactions were rife, disputes often arose between the original owners of property, who had been defrauded of the property by rogues, and those who had later bought it from the rogue in good faith. Disputes also arose outside the world of commerce, between finders of goods and those who claimed them, or between family members over who was to have property.[17]

Where goods were removed, the common law gave four rights of action: trespass *de bonis asportatis*, trover, detinue, and replevin (which was used to recover goods which had been distrained).[18] Detinue and replevin were actions to recover the property itself, while trespass and trover were actions for damages.[19] In trespass, mere asportation (regardless of any moral fault) rendered the defendant liable.[20] This action offered some advantages to debtors whose premises were broken into by creditors in search of goods to be taken in satisfaction of a debt. For under this form, damages could be obtained for the unlawful entry (even if it turned out that the defendant had the right to the goods), or for the special loss the plaintiff suffered if his customers deserted him out of the belief that he was insolvent.[21] However, if the plaintiff sought only to recover for the goods, he was better advised to use a form (such as trover) which required him only to

---

[16] e.g. *Palmer* v. *Baker* (1813) 1 M. & S. 1; *Leonard* v. *Baker* (1813) 1 M. & S. 251; *Goode* v. *Langley* (1827) 7 B. & C. 26; *Glasspoole* v. *Young* (1829) 9 B. & C. 696; *Vaughan* v. *Wilkins* (1830) 1 B. & Ad. 370; *Dillon* v. *Langley* (1831) 2 B. & Ad. 131; *Manders* v. *Williams* (1849) 4 Exch. 339; *Fawcett* v. *Fearne* (1844) 6 Q.B. 20.

[17] e.g. *Elliott* v. *Kemp* (1840) 7 M. & W. 306.

[18] See *Burroughes* v. *Bayne* (1860) 5 H. & N. 296 at 301 (per Martin B.).

[19] See *Kettle* v. *Bromsall* (1738) Willes 118 at 120. However, until 1854 (Common Law Procedure Act, s 78), the defendant had the option of retaining the property, on paying the plaintiff the sum on which the jury assessed the value of the goods: see Second Report made to His Majesty by the Commissioners appointed to Inquire into the Practice and Proceedings of the Superior Courts of Common Law, *PP* 1830 (123), xi, 547, at p. 10.

[20] There was nonetheless considerable overlap with trover, for 'the declaration usually alleges a conversion, but the defendant need not specifically justify it': *Weeding* v. *Aldrich* (1839) 9 Ad. & El. 861 at 865 (per Littledale J.). In *Norman* v. *Bell* (1831) 2 B. & Ad. 190 at 192, Parke J. held 'a plaintiff may always bring an action of trover where an action trespass de bonis asportatis would lie'.

[21] *Brewer* v. *Dew* (1843) 11 M. & W. 625, holding that the right of the plaintiff to sue for special damages did not pass to his assignees in bankruptcy: see also *Rose* v. *Buckett* [1901] 2 KB 449. Such cases also often involved issues of trespass to land, by breaking the plaintiff's close: see also *Rogers* v. *Spence* (1844) 13 M. & W. 571, (1846) 12 Cl. & F. 700.

prove their value,[22] rather than the damage he had suffered from the interference, which might be nominal only.

The gist of the action of detinue was the unlawful detention of particular goods to which the plaintiff had the right of possession.[23] It could be used both when the original obtaining of the property by the defendant was lawful, as where it was obtained through a bailment (where the declaration was for *detinue sur bailment*) and where it had been acquired tortiously[24] (where the declaration was for *detinue sur trover*).[25] Detinue offered some advantages over the 'tortious' counts, since there was no need to show that the defendant committed any wrong beyond the wrongful detainer of the goods. In contrast to trespass, there was no need to show any damage to property or any asportation; in contrast to trover, no conversion to the defendant's use had to be shown.[26] There were, however, some disadvantages in using this form of action. Until 1833, wager of law was available in detinue, and until 1852, counts in detinue could not be joined with counts in trover, though they could be joined with counts in debt.[27] Where goods had been tortiously acquired, early nineteenth-century pleaders generally preferred to use trover.[28]

---

[22] The value of the goods was recoverable in trover even though the loss was not the natural and probable result of the defendant's act: see Salmond, *Torts* (2nd edn, 1910), 302–4. Plaintiffs could not in trover recover damages for the tortious taking, but only the value of the property: *Wilbraham* v. *Snow* (1670) 1 Mod. 30.

[23] If the finder of goods parted with them before the plaintiff acquired a right to possession, then he would not be liable in detinue: *Crossfield* v. *Such* (1853) 8 Exch. 825.

[24] An averment that the defendant had obtained the goods by a bailment was not traversable, and the plaintiff 'is at liberty, notwithstanding the averment of bailment, to shew any other mode by which the goods came into the hands of the defendant': *Whitehead* v. *Harrison* (1844) 6 Q.B. 423 at 432; cf. *Gledstane* v. *Hewitt* (1831) 1 C. & J. 565 at 570; *Clements* v. *Flight* (1846) 16 M. & W. 42 at 50.

[25] J. F. Clerk and W. H. B. Lindsell, *The Law of Torts* (5th edn by W. Paine, 1909), 262. See e.g. *Kernot* v. *Pittis* (1852) 2 E. & B. 406; *Mason* v. *Farnell* (1844) 12 M. & W. 674. These forms were abolished by the 1852 Common Law Procedure Act , 15 & 16 Vict. c. 76, s 49. See also J. Chitty *Treatise on Pleading*, 3 vols (7th edn, by H. Greening, 1844), i: 137–8; ii, 428.

[26] C. G. Addison, *A Treatise on the Law of Torts* (8th edn, by W. E. Gordon and W. H. Griffith, 1906), 593.

[27] Although substantively an action for the tort of detaining property, detinue was procedurally regarded as one of the 'contractual' actions. See *Walker* v. *Needham* (1841) 3 M. & G. 557; *Danby* v. *Lamb* (1861) 11 C.B. N.S. 423 at 426. See also *Broadbent* v. *Ledward* (1839) Ad. & El. 209. By 1878, the Court of Appeal recognized the essentially tortious nature of the action: *Bryant* v. *Herbert* (1878) 3 CPD 389 (CA). However, since the refusal by a bailee to return bailed goods might be a contractual breach, late nineteenth-century courts (considering the procedural question whether the action was contractual or tortuous) looked at whether the plaintiff, to succeed, had to rely on a contract or not: per A. L. Smith LJ in *Turner* v. *Stallibrass* [1898] 1 QB 56 at 58 (CA).

[28] This may also be because of the view, repeated well into the nineteenth century in books for practitioners, that detinue could not be brought if the goods had been tortiously acquired: see J. Comyns, *A Digest of the Laws of England*, 5 vols (1780), ii, 633 (tit. Trover D.); W. Selwyn, *An Abridgment of the Law of Nisi Prius*, 2 vols (12th edn, by D. Power, 1861), i, 660. The view was challenged: see J. Chitty, *A Treatise on the Parties to Actions, the Forms of Action and on Pleading*, 3 vols (1819), i, 119.

Detinue was the appropriate form to use where a bailee refused to return goods. In such cases, the plaintiff had to show he had requested and been refused the goods, since the defendant's possession had to be adverse, to support the action.[29] Bailees were not strictly liable for the loss or destruction of goods in their possession, since the nature of their liability depended on the nature of the bailment. Thus, where an attorney lost deeds entrusted to him by a client, he was only liable in detinue if the loss could have been prevented by the exercise of ordinary care.[30] But where the defendant was not a bailee—as where an auctioneer mistakenly delivered the plaintiff's goods to another purchaser—the courts did not ask whether the defendant had acted without due care, but regarded the parting with the possession as a fault for which the defendant was liable.[31]

Since detinue could be brought against those who had wrongfully disposed of the goods as well as those who merely detained them, it overlapped with the action of trover, usually leaving the plaintiff with a choice over which remedy to use. Trover had borrowed its terminology in the early modern period from the action of detinue sur trover, but had been regarded as preferable owing to the availability of a jury.[32] The wrong committed in this action was not the 'finding' (or taking) of the goods, but their 'conversion' to the defendant's use.[33] According to Martin B., 'conversion' meant 'detaining goods so as to deprive the person entitled to the possession of them of his dominion over them'.[34] The mere fact of taking was not enough to constitute conversion; but '[a]ny asportation of a chattel *for the use of the defendant*, or a third person, amounts to a conversion' since it was 'an act inconsistent with the general right of dominion which the owner of the chattel has in it, who is entitled to the use of it at all times and in all places'.[35] If the goods had been lost or destroyed accidentally while in his possession, trover could not be brought (though trespass could), since the defendant could not

---

[29] *Clements* v. *Flight* (1846) 16 M. & W. 42.

[30] *Reeve* v. *Palmer* (1858) 5 C.B. N.S. 84. Bailees were not liable in trover for goods lost by accident or carelessness when in their possession since conversion required a voluntary act.

[31] *Jones* v. *Dowle* (1841) 9 M. & W. 19. See also the distinction between cases where property was intrusted for safe keeping, and other cases in *Wilkinson* v. *Verity* (1871) LR 6 CP 206.

[32] Salmond, *Torts* (2nd edn, 1910), 295–6. J. H. Baker, *The Oxford History of the Laws of England* (Oxford, 2003), vi, 804–5.

[33] *Cooper* v. *Chitty* (1756) 1 W. Bl. 65 at 68. The allegation of a fictitious loss and finding was immaterial and not traversable; and it was abolished by s 49 of the Common Law Procedure Act 1852. As Blackburn J. pointed out in *Hollins* v. *Fowler* (1874) LR 7 HL 757 at 765, the form assumed that the possession had been obtained lawfully, but that the 'conversion' was the tort.

[34] *Burroughes* v. *Bayne* (1860) 5 H. & N. 296 at 302. See also *Heald* v. *Carey* (1852) 11 C.B. 977.

[35] *Fouldes* v. *Willoughby* (1841) 8 M. & W. 540 at 548–9 (emphasis added). In this case, where a ferry owner removed horses from his boat, belonging to an unruly customer, and lodged them at an hotel, he was not liable in trover to the owner after the horses had been sold to pay for their board and lodging in the stables.

'convert' goods he no longer had.[36] A bailee who lost goods could not be held liable in trover, having done nothing to deny the owner's right of dominion, though he could be liable for negligence or be sued for detinue or on the bailment.[37]

For trover to lie, there had to have been some wilful act by the defendant demonstrating an intention to exercise dominion over the goods. There was no requirement for any intention to harm the plaintiff, or for any moral fault to be shown. Nor need the defendant have personally benefited. Commission agents or auctioneers who sold goods in the belief that they belonged to a particular consignor would therefore be liable to the real owner for their deliberate acts, even if they had passed on the proceeds of the sale.[38] Servants were liable in trover, even when acting *bona fide* under instructions from their masters.[39] Bankers who cashed cheques for customers dealing wrongfully with them would themselves be liable for conversion.[40] An exception was made for those following the ordinary course of a public employment, such as carriers, who acted as a mere 'conduit pipe' for property. In 1824, Abbott CJ accordingly held that a packer who merely shipped goods could not be liable in trover.[41] But where a servant not in public employment relied on the title of his master, and repudiated the title of the owner, he would be liable.

Since trover was a wrong against the right of possession, rather than against the rights of an owner, owners without the right of possession could not sue. The action could be brought by those with an undisputed right of possession, such as bailees or agents. Moreover, anyone in *de facto* possession of goods could sue anyone, except the true owner, in trover; for 'a person possessed of goods as his property has a good title as against every stranger'.[42] Those who found property could therefore recover its value from those who took it from them,[43] even though, as against the original owner, they had no title and might even be considered to have committed larceny.[44] In 1851, in *Bridges* v. *Hawkesworth*, a traveling salesman was therefore held entitled to recover the value of banknotes which he had found on the floor of a shop from the shopkeeper, with whom he had left them

[36] See *Smith* v. *Young* (1808) 1 Camp. 439 at 441.

[37] *Williams* v. *Gesse* (1837) 3 Bing. N.C. 849.

[38] *Featherstonhaugh* v. *Johnston* (1818) 8 Taunt. 237.

[39] *Perkins* v. *Smith* (1752) 1 Wils. K.B. 328, Sayer, 40; *Stephens* v. *Elwall* (1815) 4 M. & S. 259; *Cranch* v. *White* (1835) 1 Bing. N.C. 414.

[40] *Fine Art Society* v. *Union Bank* (1886) 17 QBD 705, 712; *Kleinwort* v. *Comptoir d'Escompte* [1894] 2 QB 157. See also pp. 768–73.

[41] *Greenway* v. *Fisher* (1824) 1 Car. & P. 190. See also *Lee* v. *Bayes* (1856) 18 C.B. 599.

[42] *Jeffries* v. *The Great Western Railway Co* (1856) 5 E. & B. 802 at 805, following the view set out in note (1) to *Wilbraham* v. *Snow* (1670) 2 Wms. Saund. 47.

[43] *Armory* v. *Delamirie* (1721) 1 Stra. 505.

[44] *Merry* v. *Green* (1841) 7 M. & W. 623; *R.* v. *Rowe* (1859) Bell C.C. 93.

pending the discovery (which never occurred) of their true owner.[45] However, in 1896, in a case where workmen discovered two rings while draining the plaintiff's pool, the Queen's Bench Division held that the rule in *Bridges* was to be explained by the fact that the notes had been found in a place open to the public, and that they had never been under the shopkeeper's control. Where goods were found on private property, they belonged to the party in possession of that property, rather than the finder.[46]

In seeking to protect original property holders, judges threw great risks on those who dealt with the property of others, even when they had acquired it in good faith. Recipients were bound to check the title to the goods they took.[47] Those who dealt with rogues ran particular risks, for no property passed to a buyer where goods had been stolen, or (after *Hardman* v. *Booth*[48] and *Cundy* v. *Lindsay*[49]) where the rogue had induced the seller into a mistake as to his identity, unless the sale was in market overt.[50] The morally innocent buyer of the goods of another might therefore be liable in trover if he sold the goods on, or dealt with them as his property.[51] This occurred in *Hollins* v. *Fowler*, where a firm of brokers bought some bales of cotton from a rogue, and sold them on to a buyer, receiving only a broker's commission. The case was considered to be of considerable importance to brokers, warehousemen, and wharfingers who habitually dealt with the goods of others, for it raised the question whether they should share the immunity which carriers had. Brett J. felt that to hold such brokers liable would greatly inconvenience the cotton trade of cities such as Liverpool.[52] He held that 'a possession or detention, which is a mere custody or mere asportation made without reference to question of property [...] is not a conversion'.[53] However, the House of Lords disagreed with his view, and held the brokers liable. 'However hard it may be on those who deal innocently and in the ordinary course of business

---

[45] *Bridges* v. *Hawkesworth* (1851) 21 L.J. Q.B. 75; 15 Jur. 1079.

[46] *South Staffordshire Water Co* v. *Sharman* [1896] 2 QB 44. See also the sceptical approach to a claim of trover by a finder in *Buckley* v. *Gross* (1853) 3 B. & S. 566.

[47] See *Jackson* v. *Anderson* (1811) 4 Taunt. 24 at 29.

[48] *Hardman* v. *Booth* (1863) 1 H. & C. 803.

[49] *Cundy* v. *Lindsay* (1878) 3 App Cas 459. On the doctrine of mistake of identity, see pp. 450–70.

[50] The courts did not take an extensive view of what constituted a market overt: it had to be an open, public, and legally constituted market. This meant that shops (outside the City of London), or horse repositories, or commodity markets did not constitute markets overt.

[51] See *Hilbery* v. *Hatton* (1864) 2 H. & C. 822, where a principal was liable in trover for ratifying the act of his agent, in purchasing a stranded vessel from one without title, which was subsequently let at a profit.

[52] *Hollins* v. *Fowler* (1874) LR 7 HL 757 at 780. Brett was of the view that to sustain an action of trover, there had to be an 'intention to interfere with the property in the chattel', which he felt was absent here.

[53] *Fowler* v. *Hollins* (1872) LR 7 QB 616 at 630.

with a person in possession of goods', Blackburn J. ruled, 'yet, as long as the law, as laid down in *Hardman* v. *Booth* is unimpeached, I think it is clear law, that if there has been what amounts in law to a conversion of the Plaintiffs' goods, by any one, however innocent, that person must pay the value of the goods to the real owners.'[54] A similarly strict view was taken in *Hiort* v. *Bott*. Here, the plaintiff firm of corn merchants, after receiving an order from their broker, sent a delivery order and invoice to the defendant brewer, and dispatched 83 quarters of barley to him via the London and North Western Railway. In fact, Bott had ordered no barley. Rather, the whole project was a fraud by the broker, who told Bott that the goods had been dispatched to him by mistake, and that expense would be saved if he simply indorsed the delivery order to him. On obtaining this document, the rogue broker sold the goods, and made off with the money. Although Bott never had any intention to convert the goods for his own use, he was held liable in trover for their full value.[55]

It was not merely the existence of rogues which caused commercial difficulties. Since any refusal to return goods when requested was regarded as evidence of a conversion,[56] a defendant who refused to hand goods back when requested could be liable, since the very act of denying the plaintiff his property on request showed his intention to hold the goods in defiance of the plaintiff's rights.[57] In the commercial world, those who refused to hand over other people's property therefore ran a high risk.[58] Trover was often brought against wharfingers or innkeepers who withheld the property of others, when they had been presented with a rival claim from assignees in bankruptcy or sheriffs. While such parties could legitimately refuse to hand over goods pending an inquiry whether they were the plaintiff's property, they had to take care in the way they proceeded. As Best CJ put it, '[a]n unqualified refusal is almost always conclusive evidence of a conversion; but if there be a qualification annexed to it, the question then is, whether it be a reasonable one'.[59] If the

---

[54] *Hollins* v. *Fowler* (1874) LR 7 HL 757 at 764. Blackburn J. pointed out that the Liverpool cotton market was not a market overt: had it been so, the loss would have fallen on the plaintiff. For a critical comment, see *Pall Mall Gazette*, 18 June 1872, p. 10.

[55] *Hiort* v. *Bott* (1874) LR 9 Ex 86 at 89. Grimmett was convicted of embezzlement: see *Hurt* v. *Bott* in *Birmingham Daily Post*, 29 July 1873.

[56] This occurred often where an innocent buyer acquired property from a rogue: see e.g. *Cooper* v. *Willomatt* (1845) 1 C.B. 672; *Lee* v. *Bayes* (1856) 18 C.B. 599. See also Salmond's criticism of the idea that detention after a demand was merely evidence of a conversion, rather than conversion itself: Salmond, *Torts* (2nd edn, 1910), 298.

[57] *Alexander* v. *Southey* (1821) 5 B. & Ald. 247. However, the plaintiff had to have demanded the specific goods due: *Abington* v. *Lipscomb* (1841) 1 Q.B. 776.

[58] See *Wilson* v. *Anderton* (1830) 1 B. & Ad. 450.

[59] *Alexander* v. *Southey* (1821) 5 B. & Ald. 247 at 251; cf. *Gunton* v. *Nurse* (1821) 2 B. & B. 447 at 449, where 'a reasonable hesitation in a doubtful matter was permitted'; *Vaughan* v. *Watt* (1840) 6 M. & W. 492.

defendant refused to hand the goods over without any qualification, merely relying on the title of another, '[h]e asserts a title adverse to the title of the real owner of the goods, and so is guilty of a conversion'.[60] Indeed, in Martin B.'s view, 'where one person detains from another goods, which he either actually knows or has the means of knowing, and which, by instituting proper inquiries, he might have ascertained to be that person's property, that detention the law deems a "conversion" '.[61] The holder of the goods was thus obliged to return them to the real owner, whose title to them he could invoke if sued by the bailor for breach of the bailment. [62]

Holders of goods might have genuine doubts as to their right to hand them over, particularly if they were claimed under process of law. A sympathetic approach to this problem was taken by the Exchequer in 1835. In *Verrall* v. *Robinson*, a coach manufacturer failed in an action brought against a livery stable keeper, who refused to return a coach hired by a customer named Banks, after the coach had been attached in a process out of the sheriff's court in an action against Banks. In the court's view there was nothing to show the defendant intended to convert it to his use, since it was in the 'custody of the law' when the demand was refused.[63] However, later judges sought to distinguish this case. In 1842, an innkeeper and his wife were held liable for refusing to hand over cattle wrongfully taken by bailiffs under an execution and lodged with them, when the court held the goods were not held under an attachment.[64] In 1864, it was held that the mere fact that an attachment was issued did not prevent there being a conversion, provided the goods had not actually come into the custody of an officer.[65]

The fact that those without property rights ran significant risks in refusing to hand over property can be seen from the case of *Burroughes* v. *Bayne* in 1860. Burroughes had rented a billiard table to Thomas Filmer on hire-purchase, which the latter subsequently assigned (along with all his household goods) by a bill of sale to Bayne. When Burroughes wished to remove it from Filmer's Harley Street hotel, Bayne refused to permit him to do so until he had seen the agreement. Burroughes later gave notice that he would come to remove the billiard table, but when he arrived to take the table, the man in charge of the house—who had been told by Bayne to give up the table—could not find the key to the billiard

---

[60] *Lee* v. *Bayes* (1856) 18 C.B. 599 at 607.

[61] *Pillot* v. *Wilkinson* (1863) 2 H. & C. 72 at 82.

[62] *Biddle* v. *Bond* (1865) 6 B & S 225.

[63] *Verrall* v. *Robinson* (1835) 2 C. M. & R. 495.

[64] *Catterall* v. *Kenyon* (1842) 3 Q.B. 310.

[65] *Pillot* v. *Wilkinson* (1863) 2 H. & C. 72; *Pillott* v. *Wilkinson* (1864) 3 H. & C. 345, where a wharfinger was held liable for not handing over champagne to the holder of a warrant.

room. The table was later seized by Filmer's landlord for rent; and Burroughes succeeded in an action of trover against Bayne.[66]

The law's enthusiasm to protect the rights of original proprietors, and the commercial inconvenience this could cause, can also be seen in the approach taken to factors who dealt with the goods of their principals. It was established at common law that factors had authority to sell but not to pledge the goods of their principals.[67] It was a rule of which early nineteenth-century merchants were often unaware. In 1811, when the price of colonial produce was low, London factors borrowed large sums by pledging goods in their possession. This allowed them to postpone sales of commodities until prices rose, an arrangement which was generally beneficial to the owners. However, when some factors failed, their principals succeeded in recovering the value of their goods from the lenders in trover. This was controversial. As Lord Ellenborough saw it, although it might have been preferable to hold 'that where it was equivocal whether a person was authorized to act as principal or factor, a pledge made by such person free from any circumstances of fraud was valid', the law on factors' pledges was settled differently.[68] As traders became aware of the rule, they urged its reform.[69] A select committee in 1823 considered that the current law rendered it impossible for a capitalist safely to lend on the security of goods. Taking the view that it was unfair to make the loss fall on an innocent party, when it was the original owner who had entrusted his goods to a rogue, it recommended that pawnees and innocent purchasers of pledged goods should be protected, and that there should be strict penalties against factors who breached their duty.[70] A cautious Act followed in 1823, which gave protection to the lender where pledges were taken from factors on the faith of goods in their possession. Further legislation in 1825 enacted that a lender could take a pledge of goods from a factor known to be only an agent, to the extent of the factor's interest in the goods. It also stipulated that persons 'intrusted with' documents of title could deal with the goods as if they were

[66] *Burroughes* v. *Bayne* (1860) 5 H. & N. 296. See also the views of Bramwell B. in this case, that there was no conversion. By contrast, Martin B. suspected that merely taking the bill of sale would constitute conversion.

[67] *Paterson* v. *Tash* (1743) 2 Stra. 1178; *M'Combe* v. *Davies* (1805) 7 East 6.

[68] *Martini* v. *Coles* (1813) 1 M. & S. 140 at 146. See also *Graham* v. *Dyster* (1816) 2 Stark. 21. In *De Leira* v. *Edwards* (unreported) he did hold that where a factor by the assent of the principal exhibited himself to the world as owner, then the principal was liable: 1 M. & S. at 147. See also his comments in *Whitehead* v. *Tuckett* (1812) 15 East 400.

[69] *The Times*, 16 May 1823, col. 1d.

[70] Select Committee on the State of the Law relating to Goods, Wares and Merchandises intrusted to Merchants, Agents or Factors, *PP* 1823 (452), iv, 265.

the owner, which allowed them to pledge such goods to lenders who had no notice that they were only agents and not owners.[71]

Despite the desire of the commercial community to protect those dealing *bona fide* with factors in possession of goods, the courts throughout the mid-nineteenth century interpreted the factors legislation restrictively, seeking to protect the original owner, rather than the innocent lender.[72] This can be seen in *Phillips* v. *Huth*. A factor in possession of a bill of lading had entered the goods in question at the Custom House, obtained a dock warrant in his own name, and used it as security for an advance of £20,000 to his firm, Warwick & Claggett. The firm was in serious difficulties, as a result of over-speculation in tobacco, and the credit was needed to attempt to keep the business afloat. However, the endeavour failed and Warwick became bankrupt in 1837. The Exchequer allowed the owner of the goods to recover their proceeds, on the ground that the factor had not been 'intrusted' with the dock warrant for the purposes of the Act. As Parke B. put it, '[p]rincipals can never be deemed to have intrusted the agents with a document which the agents obtained in breach of their trust'.[73] The decisions arising from the frauds of Warwick & Claggett alarmed the commercial community, and an amending Act was passed in 1843, which, recognizing that pledges on the security of goods were a standard feature of the factor's business for the principal, provided that the factor was to have the same power to pledge as he had to sell. [74]

If this seemed to promise greater security to lenders, the courts continued to interpret the legislation restrictively, to protect the original owner of the property.[75] In 1863, Blackburn J. held that the mere fact that a factor had been put in possession of goods by an owner did not mean he was 'intrusted' with them for the purpose of the Act, though it was for the person seeking to recover

---

[71] 6 Geo. IV c. 94.

[72] It was held in *Fletcher* v. *Heath* (1827) 7 B. & C. 517, that a lender giving money on a pledge of goods by the factor known to be an agent could not retain them against the principal, if at the time of the pledge the principal no longer owed money to the factor. It was further held in *Taylor* v. *Kymer* (1832) 3 B. & Ad. 320 at 337 that where a factor exchanged one set of dock warrants (the property of his plaintiff) for another, replacing one security for another, this was not protected by the Act, since it was not a pledge for money or a negotiable instrument given on the faith of the documents. See also *Bonzi* v. *Stewart* (1842) 4 M. & G. 295.

[73] *Phillips* v. *Huth* (1840) 6 M. & W. 572 at 598. See also *Hatfield* v. *Phillips* (1842) 9 M. & W. 647, confirmed by the House of Lords in *Hatfield* v. *Phillips* (1845) 14 M. & W. 665; 12 Cl. & F. 343.

[74] The Act also reversed the rule applied in *Phillips* v. *Huth* (1840) 6 M. & W. 572.

[75] However, in 1862, the Exchequer confirmed that the buyer or lender was protected even where the factor had obtained goods from his principal through a fraud: '[i]f the agent was in fact intrusted with the goods, it is immaterial in what way that was effected': *Sheppard* v. *Union Bank of London* (1862) 7 H. & N. 661 at 665.

the goods to prove that they had not been so 'intrusted'.[76] In 1868, the Common Pleas held that where a factor's authority had been revoked by his principal— even where this was unknown to the lender—he could no longer be considered to be 'intrusted' with goods under the legislation. In Willes J.'s view, the Factors Acts were not intended 'to provide a remedy for all the hardships which may occur to innocent persons dealing with one in the apparent ownership of the goods', but only to provide one where the agent was intrusted with them with the assent of the owner.[77] The restrictive view taken by the courts to the Factors Acts can be seen again in the 1877 decision in *Johnson* v. *Credit Lyonnais*. Here, a tobacco agent, who—following the custom of the trade—was permitted to retain the documents of title to the goods after his principal had become their absolute owner, pledged the property as security for a loan, before absconding and becoming bankrupt. Denman J. held that the agent was not 'intrusted with' the goods as a factor to sell, but only to clear the goods and forward them to the plaintiff. The mere fact that the plaintiff had given his agent the indicia of property in the goods, enabling him to commit a fraud, was not in itself such conduct as should prevent the plaintiff from recovering his property.[78] The decision was immediately followed by legislation, after merchants urged that it was essential that they should be able to deal confidently with factors. The Factors Act 1877 enacted that an innocent lender or purchaser would not be affected if the agency had been secretly revoked, without his knowledge, and that he would equally be protected where the owner permitted the factor to retain the documents of title.[79] Further legislation followed in 1889, when an Act was passed largely consolidating the earlier statutes, but in some respects altering its language. The Act was perceived to make it safe to buy or lend to a 'mercantile agent' who was in possession of goods or documents of title to goods, with the consent of the owner. Consent was to be assumed unless the contrary was shown, and the innocent party was not to be affected by any secret revocations of authority. The Act removed the troublesome words 'intrusted with' and replaced them with the concept of consent. The Act came at the end of over half a century when the courts continued to take restrictive views of the legislation, seeking to uphold the protection given by the common law to the original owner of goods, and where the mercantile community argued for greater protection to the merchant dealing with factors.

---

[76] *Baines* v. *Swainson* (1863) 4 B. & S. 270 at 285–6.

[77] *Fuentes* v. *Montis* (1868) LR 3 CP 268 at 276, 282. The case was affirmed by the Exchequer Chamber in (1868) LR 4 CP 93.

[78] *Johnson* v. *Credit Lyonnais* (1877) 2 CPD 224.

[79] *The Times*, 17 May 1877, col. 6a; 40 & 41 Vict. c. 39. *Johnson* v. *Credit Lyonnais* went to the Court of Appeal after the Act was passed (1877) 3 CPD 32, where the judges confirmed that the law prior to 1877 was that the owner could recover his property.

2. WRONGS TO REAL PROPERTY

The common law also aimed to give strong protection to real property. As Lord Camden put it, '[e]very invasion of private property, be it ever so minute, is a trespass'.[80] Actions of trespass lay for wrongfully entering the plaintiff's house or land without his consent, regardless of whether any damage was done.[81] Trespass was used both where the defendant had broken the plaintiff's close and done damage, and where there was a dispute over whether the defendant had a right of access to the land;[82] and it was used whether the trespasser was a man or his beast.[83]

By the time Pollock and Salmond were composing principled treatises, jurists were beginning to question whether trespass lay when the act had been neither intentional nor negligent. In Salmond's view, the approach taken in the personal injury cases of *Holmes* v. *Mather* and *Stanley* v. *Powell*[84] applied generally to all forms of trespass, which suggested that '[a]n accidental, as opposed to a mistaken entry [...] is not actionable unless due to negligence'.[85] Clerk and Lindsell agreed with this interpretation, citing Bacon's comment that if a man 'who is assaulted and in danger of his life, run through the ground of another without keeping in the footpath, an action of trespass *vi et armis* does not lie'.[86] Pollock seemed less certain and seemed to acknowledge a stricter liability in trespass to land.[87] In fact, judicial dicta suggested that strict liabilities were only displaced where human intercourse in the world at large generated particular risks. Blackburn J.'s comment in *Fletcher* v. *Rylands* that 'those who go on the highway, or have their property adjacent to it' had to accept that they held their property subject to the risk of accidental injury indicated that property not so situated was more strictly protected.[88]

Unsurprisingly, the question of whether a person was liable for his wholly unintentional, non-negligent trespass on another's land did not arise in our period. However, the courts did deal with trespasses by a person's animals.

[80] *Entick* v. *Carrington* (1765) 19 *State Trials* 1066.

[81] Comyns, *Digest* (1780), v, 575.

[82] e.g. *Parker* v. *Mitchell* (1840) Ad. & El. 788; *Hollins* v. *Verney* (1884) 13 QBD 304.

[83] See e.g. *Ellis* v. *The Loftus Iron Co* (1874) LR 10 CP 10.

[84] *Holmes* v. *Mather* (1875) LR 10 Ex 261; *Stanley* v. *Powell* [1891] 1 QB 86.

[85] Salmond, *Torts* (2nd edn, 1910), 162.

[86] Clerk & Lindsell, *Torts* (4th edn, by W. Paine, 1906), 43, quoting M. Bacon, *A New Abridgment of the Law*, 5 vols (1736–66), v, 173. Bacon's comment merely reiterated the point that inevitable accident (as opposed to absence of negligence) was a defence in trespass.

[87] Pollock, *Torts* (1887 edn), 280–2.

[88] *Fletcher* v. *Rylands* (1866) LR 1 Ex 265 at 286–7; cf. his comment in *River Wear Commissioners* v. *Adamson* (1877) 2 App Cas 743 at 767. See McCardie J.'s endorsement of the principle relating to property adjoining a highway in *Gayler and Pope* v. *B. Davies and Son* [1924] 2 KB 75.

It had long been settled that owners of cattle had to prevent their cattle from straying onto their neighbour's land.[89] As Sjt Williams's notes to Saunders' reports expressed it, 'I am bound to take care that my beasts do not trespass'.[90] This language of care was repeated elsewhere,[91] but in 1863, Williams J. pointed out that '[w]hether or not the escape of the animal is due to my negligence, is altogether immaterial'.[92] Since beasts were likely to do damage if they escaped, liability was imposed on their owner for not penning them. Where the animal was not of a nature liable to do mischief—such as a dog—a plaintiff had to include a *scienter*, to aver that the defendant knew the animal's propensity to do mischief.[93] Provided this was averred, it was unnecessary to aver any negligence by the defendant. As Lord Denman put it, 'a person keeping a mischievous animal with knowledge of its propensities is bound to keep it secure at his peril', and 'if it does mischief, negligence is presumed, without express averment'.[94] Where the defendant's animals strayed, the gist of the action was their trespass on the plaintiff's land; where the animal caused an injury (as a dog biting), liability lay in case for the injury.[95]

The strictness of an owner's liability to prevent his animals straying was seen in the case law as parallel to a landowner's duty to keep his filth to himself,[96] and hence part of a general property principle of *sic utere tuo ut alienum non laedas*. Treatise writers did not share this view. Salmond deplored the fact that at the time that the old rule of absolute liability in trespass was eroded in the nineteenth century, it was preserved in cattle trespass cases. Pollock saw it as an anomalous rule imposed for policy reasons.[97] Yet, in fact, the judges' endorsement of strict liability for animals, and their extension of this principle in *Rylands* v. *Fletcher*, was not a perverse swim against the tide of doctrinal development. It was a reflection of their desire to preserve property rights.

---

[89] The defendant might be liable for failure to maintain a fence which he had a duty to maintain; where no such duty existed, he could be liable for allowing his cattle to stray.

[90] *Pomfret* v. *Ricroft* (1669) 1 Wms. Saund. 321, note c.

[91] C. G. Addison, *Wrongs and their Remedies* (1860), 141–2; *Churchill* v. *Evans* (1809) 1 Taunt. 529; *Boyle* v. *Tamlyn* (1827) 6 B. & C. 329 at 337.

[92] *Cox* v. *Burbidge* (1863) 13 C.B. N.S. 430 at 438. See also *Lee* v. *Riley* (1865) 18 C.B. N.S. 722, where the defendant was liable for the trespass of his horse, having failed in his duty to repair a fence.

[93] *Mason* v. *Keeling* (1699) 12 Mod. 332.

[94] *May* v. *Burdett* (1846) 9 Q.B. 101 at 112. See also *Jackson* v. *Smithson* (1846) 15 M. & W. 563; *Card* v. *Case* (1848) 5 C.B. 622; *Read* v. *Edwards* (1864) 17 C.B. N.S. 245.

[95] Chitty, *Pleading* (7th edn, 1844), i, 202. Where a duty to fence the land existed, the action could be brought either in case or trespass: *Star* v. *Rookesby* (1710) 1 Salk. 335. But where no such duty existed, the action was pleaded in trespass. Salmond pointed out the anomalous nature of the rule: *Torts* (2nd edn, 1910), 164n.

[96] See *Tenant* v. *Goldwin* (1704) 6 Mod. 311.

[97] Salmond, *Torts* (2nd edn, 1910), 197n. Pollock, *Torts* (1887 edn), 282.

Accidental Damage to Real Property

Disputes over straying cattle were as likely to be about rights to graze, or about land boundaries, as about the actual damage done by the beasts. Real property was much more likely to be damaged when land or buildings were harmed from mining activity conducted underground, or from support being removed by neighbours. A number of different doctrines were relevant to such accidents. The strictest liability was imposed where the plaintiff enjoyed an easement imposing on the servient tenant an obligation not to remove support. In such cases, while the owner of the servient tenement would not be liable for nonfeasances, such as the failure to repair a building supporting another, he would be strictly liable for the misfeasance of removing support.[98] Where there was no easement, trespass could arguably be maintained if one person's building damaged another, as where '[t]he lateral pressure of a heavy building on soft ground [...] causes an ascertainable physical disturbance in a neighbour's soil'.[99] If work was done negligently in such a way as to damage the plaintiff's property, an action of negligence could be maintained for the misfeasance. Finally, if the damage was done by something harmful coming from the defendant's land, such as polluted water, an action for nuisance could be maintained.[100] These doctrines imposed different standards of duty on defendants, and in a number of cases mid-century, courts had difficulties in deciding which to apply. Solutions were not dictated by the forms of action.[101] Rather, it was left to the courts to figure out substantive distinctions which may have owed their origins to older forms, but which were adapted in the short term by judges to novel situations.

Fixed property was commonly damaged when it was undermined by excavations by a neighbour. Property was often damaged by mining operations conducted by those with mining rights to the soil below. Just as a neighbour had a natural right to have his land supported by that of his neighbour, so the courts confirmed that the owner of land on the surface had a natural right to have it supported from beneath. Mineowners were accordingly held liable for subsidence, without the plaintiff having to show either a prescriptive right or negligence. As Lord Campbell CJ put it in *Humphries* v. *Brogden*, there was no need to show a prescriptive right, since 'the plaintiff claims no greater degree of support for his

---

[98] See *Pomfret* v. *Ricroft* (1670) 1 Wms. Saund. 321 at 322 and *Colebeck* v. *Girdlers Co* (1876) 1 QBD 234 at 243.

[99] *Charles Dalton* v. *Henry Angus & Co* (1881) 6 App Cas 740 at 775. Similarly, taking down a party wall could constitute a trespass: *Cubitt* v. *Porter* (1828) 8 B. & C. 257.

[100] This is discussed at pp. 1082–8.

[101] Cases which generated novel problems sometimes originated in the county courts, where the parties did not set out whether the case was one of negligence, nuisance, or trespass. E.g. *In re Williams* v. *Groucott* (1863) 4 B. & S. 149; *Ross* v. *Fedden* (1872) LR 7 QB 661.

lands than they must have required and enjoyed since the globe subsisted in its present form'.[102] Nor was negligence necessary. The owner of the surface did not merely have a right to reasonable support, for 'we cannot measure out degrees to which the right may extend; and the only reasonable support is that which will protect the surface from subsidence, and keep it securely at its ancient and natural level'.[103] Campbell continued in later cases to reiterate that where a natural right of support existed, the question negligence was irrelevant.[104]

A landowner could grant away his right of support. If the grant made it explicitly clear that the surface might be 'rendered uneven and less commodious to the occupiers thereof', then the owner of the surface soil could not complain if damage occurred.[105] But the courts rejected the view that any surface owner granting a right to mine must be presumed to have granted away his right to support since any limitation of the right to mine would derogate from the grant. In *Harris* v. *Ryding*, a defendant who mined without putting in any support claimed that he had no obligation to support the surface, since his grant gave him the right to minerals under the plaintiff's land and to enter onto this land in order to gain access to them. Interpreting the intention of the parties to the grant, the Exchequer ruled that the grant only reserved 'so much of the mines and minerals as could be got, leaving a reasonable support to the surface'.[106] Endorsing this approach to the interpretation of grants, Lord Campbell observed that, 'generally speaking, mines may be profitably worked, leaving a support to the surface by pillars or ribs of the minerals, although not so profitably as if the whole of the minerals be removed; and a man must so use his own as not to injure his neighbour'.[107]

The nature of the plaintiff's right to the support of land and its violation was considered once more in 1861 by the House of Lords in *Bonomi* v. *Backhouse*. The judges deciding this case agreed that the defendant's liability was strict, for he had violated a right naturally pertaining to property. But they disagreed over whether the action was barred by the Statute of Limitations, for while the mining

---

[102] *Humphries* v. *Brogden* (1850) 12 Q.B. 739 at 742. See also *Earl of Lonsdale* v. *Littledale* (1793) 2 H. Bl. 267.

[103] *Humphries* v. *Brogden* (1850) 12 Q.B. 739 at 745. The jury in this case had found that the mine was worked carefully and according to the customary mode.

[104] *Roberts, Fereday and Smith* v. *Haines* (1856) 6 E. & B. 643 at 652–3.

[105] *Rowbotham* v. *Wilson* (1857) 8 E. & B. 123; (1860) 8 H.L.C. 348. In this case, the mining had been conducted without any negligence.

[106] *Harris* v. *Ryding* (1839) 5 M. & W. 60 at 70–1 (per Parke B.). The grant also contained a compensation clause, in respect of any damage done to the surface by the mining, but the court held it did not apply. As Parke B. put it, at p. 63: 'The clause as to compensation means for damage done by exercising the power reserved. This is case for working the mines in an unreasonable manner. If you work the mines in an unreasonable manner, it is not within the clause'.

[107] *Humphries* v. *Brogden* (1850) 12 Q.B. 747, 753. See also *Smart* v. *Morton* (1855) 5 E. & B. 30.

which caused the damage had been done more than six years previously, the actual damage to the land had occurred within six years of the commencement of the action. A majority in the Queen's Bench took the view that the cause of action arose when the natural right was violated, which occurred when the support was originally removed.[108] Erle J. felt there were policy justifications for this view as well as doctrinal ones: while it was true that landowners who did not know that mining operations were conducted under their land might suffer, it would impose a hardship on mine owners if they were liable for damage occurring long after they ceased mining. Wightman J. dissented, arguing that the cause of action arose not from a violation of the plaintiff's right of support, but from 'a breach of duty on the part of the defendant, by so using his own property as to injure that of his neighbour'.[109] His view was endorsed by the Exchequer Chamber and the Lords, where Lord Wensleydale ruled that the right 'was not in the nature of an easement', but was a right to the enjoyment of property, which the owner of neighbouring property should not interrupt.[110] Policy considerations also stood behind the final judgment, since the rival view might require landowners to litigate against mine owners before any actual harm was done, which would both encourage litigiousness and interfere with a mine owner's right to use his property. The decision confirmed that there could be strict liability, on the *sic utere* principle, for harms to property, without that liability being founded on a natural or prescriptive right in the plaintiff. Following the decision in *Bonomi* v. *Backhouse*, the House of Lords in *Darley Main Colliery Co* v. *Mitchell*[111] held that a defendant who had ceased mining in 1868, and then paid compensation for damage done to houses on the surface, had to pay compensation again in 1882 for further subsidence caused by his earlier operations. Each subsidence generated a fresh cause of action, for, as Lord Halsbury saw it, the defendant 'originally created a state of things which renders him responsible if damage accrues; if by the hypothesis the cause of action is the damage resulting from the defendant's

---

[108] *Bonomi* v. *Backhouse* (1858) E. B. & E. 622 at 642–3. See also the position taken by Parke B. in *Nicklin* v. *Williams* (1854) 10 Exch. 259 at 267–8. Parke ruled 'We think this action is for an injury to a right; and, consequently, there was a complete cause of action when the wrong was done, and not a new cause of action when damage was sustained by reason of the original wrong. When so much of the land coal, or substratum was taken away as to deprive the plaintiff's land and house &c of the support to which the plaintiffs were entitled, a cause of action accrued, though no actual damage occurred by the sinking of the land or the falling of the house, or any part of it, or even by part of the structure being cracked and displaced; although it would not be easy to prove that an essential part of the support was withdrawn, unless some actual effect upon the land or structure was produced.' The latter comment was apposite, given that Parke did not intend to interfere with established mining rights.

[109] *Bonomi* v. *Backhouse* (1858) E. B. & E. 622 at 637.

[110] *Backhouse* v. *Bonomi* (1861) 11 H.L.C. 503 at 513.

[111] *The Darley Main Colliery Co* v. *Mitchell* (1886) 11 App Cas 127.

act, or an omission to alter the state of things he has created, why may not a fresh action be brought?'[112]

The doctrine that the cause of action arose at the time the damage was suffered, rather than at the time when the support was removed, raised the question whether a proprietor was liable for omitting to maintain support when he had not been the original miner. The question whether new lessees were liable for failing to shore up the excavations of a previous owner, or for continuing an existing nuisance,[113] was addressed in 1897 in *Greenwell* v. *Low Beechburn Coal Co.* Bruce J. ruled that the defendants were not liable. First, there was no nuisance until the damage occurred:

At no moment prior to the subsidence can it be said that there was any duty upon any one to provide artificial support; and, therefore, it seems to me that it cannot be said that the defendants are guilty of a default of duty in allowing a state of things to continue which was a perfectly lawful state of things.[114]

Nor was the defendant liable for the subsidence. While it was true that the owner of land had to use it so as not to hurt the property of another, here the defendant had committed no *act* on his property to harm the plaintiff's: 'unless they are under an obligation to prevent the consequences of an act done by their predecessor in title, they have not been guilty of any omission of duty for which they can be held liable'.[115] This case showed that the courts were not prepared to impose strict liability on landowners for harms which did not result from their own use of their property. Where a proprietor had excavated, or engaged contractors to tear down walls, he would be liable for failing to prevent harmful consequences to his neighbours: but where he had inherited something in the nature of a nuisance, he was not liable.[116]

In contrast to land, there was no natural right to the support of buildings from neighbouring lands or buildings. It had been held in the seventeenth century

---

[112] *Ibid.*, at 133.

[113] It was established that the occupier of premises was liable for continuing nuisances, which he had the power to prevent: *Broder* v. *Saillard* (1876) 2 Ch D 692 at 700.

[114] *Greenwell* v. *The Low Beechburn Coal Co* [1897] 2 QB 165 at 178. Contrast the dissenting approach of Lord Blackburn in *Darley Main Colliery Co* v. *Mitchell*, where he held that the original act of digging and failing to provide support was wrongful, but only actionable when damage resulted, just as where 'a man in breach of the duty to take reasonable care in the management of a horse in a public street gallops along it, no action lies except at the instance of a person who has suffered damage': *The Darley Main Colliery Co* v. *Mitchell* (1886) 11 App Cas 127 at 142.

[115] *Greenwell and Others* v. *The Low Beechburn Coal Co* [1897] 2 QB 165 at 178–9. See also *Hall* v. *Duke of Norfolk* [1900] 2 Ch 493. Cf. Salmond, *Tort* (2nd edn, 1910), 244–6.

[116] This approach echoed that in nuisance, where an occupier was only liable if he adopted or continued an existing nuisance: see *Saxby* v. *Manchester and Sheffield Railway Co* (1869) LR 4 CP 198; *Barker* v. *Herbert* [1911] 2 KB 633.

that no action lay where a man built a house on the very edge of his land, and his neighbour undermined it by digging foundations for a building of his own, 'inasmuch as it was the fault of A himself that he built his house so near the land of B, for he cannot by his own act prevent B from making the best use of his land that he can'.[117] However, it was accepted that a right to support from land could be acquired as an easement.[118] In 1803, Lord Ellenborough ruled that where a man had 'built to the extremity of his soil and had enjoyed his building above twenty years, upon analogy to the rule as to lights, &c., he had acquired a right to support, or as it were of leaning to his neighbour's soil, so that his neighbour could not dig so near as to remove the support; but that it was otherwise of a house, &c. newly built'.[119] Where such an easement existed, liability was strict.

Where a prescriptive right could not be shown, plaintiffs could sue using an action on the case for negligence. This action was used against those who were not neighbouring property owners, including public bodies. In cases brought against those negligently exercising statutory powers—as in 1822, when the Westminster commissioners of sewers were sued for causing five houses to collapse while rebuilding the arch of a sewer—judges required proof of 'a want of due care and diligence on the part of the defendants'.[120] Only negligence could render liable those acting under statutory powers.[121] However, in cases not involving such powers, plaintiffs suing on allegations of negligence succeeded without having to show any fault. Thus, in 1850, in *Jeffries* v. *Williams*, the Exchequer allowed a plaintiff without a prescriptive right to recover for damage done to his cottages by the mining activities of a defendant, who had failed to show his right to mine the soil and was therefore *prima facie* a wrongdoer. 'If a house is *de facto* supported by the soil of a neighbour, that appears to us to be sufficient title against any one but that neighbour, or one claiming under him', Parke B. ruled. In his view, anyone who 'prop[ped] up his house by a shore resting on his neighbour's ground, would have a right of action against a stranger, who, by removing it, causes the house to fall; but none against his neighbour, or one authorised by the neighbour to do so, if he took it away and caused the same damage'.[122] Although the case

---

[117] *Wilde* v. *Minsterley* (1640) 2 Rolle Abr. 564, 565 [Trespass I pl. 1b].

[118] See *Palmer* v. *Fleshees* (1663) 1 Sid. 167.

[119] *Stansell* v. *Jollard* (1803) in W. Selwyn, *Abridgment* (8th edn, 1831), i, 444.

[120] *Jones* v. *Bird* (1822) 5 B. & Ald. 837 at 844.

[121] See also *Sutton* v. *Clarke* (1815) 6 Taunt. 29.

[122] *Jeffries* v. *Williams* (1850) 5 Exch. 792 at 800. See also *Bibby* v. *Carter* (1859) 4 H. & N. 153, where the Exchequer upheld a count against a defendant not alleged to be owner of the neighbouring property, which failed to state that the plaintiff had a prescriptive right to support, but stated that she received support from her neighbour's land, which the defendant 'wrongfully and negligently' undermined.

was pleaded in negligence, liability was assumed from the mere fact that damage was done.

In cases brought against neighbouring householders with a *prima facie* right to dig their own soil, pleaders generally included counts for negligence as well as counts for 'wrongful and injurious' digging. This raised the question whether neighbours could be liable for negligence, absent any prescriptive right. In a case at *nisi prius* in 1829, the question whether a prescriptive right existed was not put to the jury. Rather, Tindal CJ asked them whether the injury to the plaintiff's house was caused by the defendant's digging; whether any notice was given to the plaintiff of the work to be done, and whether the defendants had used reasonable and ordinary care in doing the work.[123] Similarly, in *Brown* v. *Windsor* in 1830, Goulburn J. asked the jury firstly whether the defendant's excavation caused the injury to the wall; and secondly, if it did, whether the work had been done with that care and skill which every man was bound to exercise when doing any act which could harm his neighbour. The jury found the work carelessly done and awarded £50 damages. This appeared to suggest that negligence was at the heart of the issue. But when the case went before the Exchequer Barons, they emphasized (in refusing a rule for a new trial) that the plaintiff had shown that he had enjoyed an easement since 1803.

The idea that a plaintiff without a prescriptive right could succeed against a negligent neighbour was endorsed by the Common Pleas in 1836 in *Trower* v. *Chadwick*. In this case, the plaintiff wine merchant's cellar was badly damaged when his neighbour pulled down the walls of his adjoining cellar without shoring up the plaintiff's side. The first count of the plaintiff's declaration mentioned his prescriptive right, but the second only stated that the defendant had negligently taken down his wall, without giving notice to the plaintiff to enable him to shore up his wall. Nonetheless, Tindal CJ held that there was a substantial ground of action on both counts, 'viz., that of negligence and carelessness in the exercise of the Defendant's rights, by reason whereof the Plaintiff's rights were injured'.[124] The court's decision to uphold the second count, which made no allegation of any easement, suggested that even if a man had no right to support from neighbour's building, if the latter chose to withdraw it, he had to use reasonable care in doing so, in effect by shoring.[125]

---

[123] *Massey* v. *Goyder* (1829) 4 Car. & P. 161.

[124] *Trower* v. *Chadwick* (1836) 3 Bing. N.C. 334 at 354. Tindal CJ doubted that the defendant had a duty to give notice, but felt the second count was supported by the allegation that the defendant injured the vault by failing to use care and skill in pulling his wall down.

[125] C. J. Gale, *Treatise on the Law of Easement* (4th edn by D. Gibbons, 1868), 392.

However, this decision was soon disapproved, confirming that a plaintiff could not succeed against his neighbour without showing an easement.[126] When Trower went to the Exchequer Chamber, the second count was held bad.[127] In Parke B.'s view, absent an easement, the law did not impose a duty to take care when pulling down his wall, because of the proximity of the premises:

Supposing that to be so where the party is cognisant of the existence of the vault, we are all of opinion that no such obligation can arise where there is no averment that the Defendant had notice of its existence: for, one degree of care would be required where no vault exists, but the soil is left in its natural and solid state; another, where there is a vault; and another and still greater degree of care would be required where the adjoining vault is of a weak and fragile construction. How is the Defendant to ascertain the precise degree of care and caution the law requires of him, if he has no notice of the existence or of the nature of the structure?[128]

Parke took the same view in later cases. In 1854, in *Gayford* v. *Nicholls*, while overturning a county court ruling that a defendant could be liable for the negligence of his contractors in removing the support from his neighbour's house regardless of any easement, he reiterated the point that a house owner had no recourse against a neighbour who did damage in the proper exercise of his rights, unless he had a right established by prescription or grant. Although a defendant might have been 'liable for improperly building on his own soil'—a negligent misfeasance—the obligation to support a neighbour's house could only arise from an easement.[129]

This view was also applied to buildings which were damaged by those with mining rights. This can be seen from *Partridge* v. *Scott* in 1838, where the plaintiff's houses, built on land over some excavated mines, were damaged by subsidence caused by the defendant mining on his own land. A Staffordshire jury found for the plaintiff, subject to the opinion of the court on a case stated. In their view, the defendant was negligent in not leaving a rib of sufficient thickness while mining, 'if the plaintiff was entitled to support from the defendants' land and substrata'. The Exchequer found for the defendant. As Alderson B. noted, rights to the support of houses could only be founded on a grant, for a man 'has no right to load his own soil so as to make it require the support of that of his neighbour,

---

[126] See also *Wyatt* v. *Harrison* (1832) 3 B. & Ad. 871. See also the comments of Martin B. on this in *Bibby* v. *Carter* (1859) 4 H. & N. 153 at 156.

[127] A new trial was ordered, since the jury had not specified on which count the verdict was given: *Chadwick* v. *Trower* (1839) 6 Bing. N.C. 1.

[128] *Chadwick* v. *Trower* (1839) 6 Bing. N.C. 1 at 10.

[129] *Gayford* v. *Nicholls* (1854) 9 Exch. 702 at 708. Where a neighbour had a prescriptive right to support, defendants were liable for the acts of their contractors in weakening foundations: *Bower* v. *Peate* (1876) 1 QBD 321.

unless he has some grant to that effect'. By building on land which was itself insufficiently supported, the plaintiff 'caused the injury to himself, without any fault on the part of the defendants; unless, at the time, by some grant, he was entitled to additional support from the land of the defendants'. Here, no such grant could be presumed, since there was nothing to show that the excavations which undermined the plaintiff's house were not less than 20 years old.[130]

After *Humphries* v. *Brogden*, some judges began to wonder whether the right to the support of land with houses on it might itself also be a natural right,[131] but this view was not adopted. The question was made largely academic for mining cases by *Brown* v. *Robins* in 1859, in which it was held that a plaintiff whose house was damaged by subsidence could recover for the damage to the house, provided that the weight of the buildings had not caused the subsidence. Since in any case where mining operations caused subsidence, the surface land would be affected, as well as the buildings, plaintiffs could now recover damages regardless of whether the buildings had stood for 20 years or more.[132] Urban householders whose buildings fell when neighbouring land was excavated did not benefit from this rule.

If an easement had been established, was the defendant's liability strict? In *Brown* v. *Windsor*, Garrow B. suggested that it was not. 'There may be cases where a man, altering his own premises, cannot support his neighbour's, and the support if necessary must be supplied elsewhere', he observed. 'In such case, he must give notice, and then, if any injury occur, it would not be occasioned by the party pulling down, but by the other party neglecting to take due precaution.'[133] The relevance of negligence was also raised in 1834, in *Dodd* v. *Holme*, where the plaintiffs' ancient house was damaged when the defendants 'carelessly and negligently' dug foundations on their land. At the Lancaster summer *assizes*, it was shown that, having dug excavations, the defendants tried to shore up the plaintiffs' gable wall, which had begun to bulge; but that they had failed to take action beforehand. The defendants denied liability, contending that the wall was in such a rotten state that it could not effectively be shored up. Bolland B. told the jury that if the fall was caused by the defendants' negligence, they would be liable but if it fell because of its own infirmity, the plaintiffs would be responsible. 'If I have a building on my own land, which I leave in the same state, and my neighbour digs in his land adjacent, so as to pull down my wall, he is liable to an action', he

---

[130] *Partridge* v. *Scott* (1838) 3 M. & W. 220 at 229. See also *Hunt* v. *Peake* (1860) Johns 705.
[131] Watson B. in *Rogers* v. *Taylor* (1858) 2 H. & N. 828 at 834–5.
[132] *Brown* v. *Robins* (1859) 4 H. & N. 186 at 193. See also *Stroyan* v. *Knowles* (1861) 6 H. & N. 454.
[133] *Brown* v. *Windsor* (1830) 1 C. & J. 20 at 26–7.

ruled: 'If, however, I have loaded my wall, so that it had more than it could well bear, he would not be liable.'

After the jury found for the plaintiffs, the defendants sought a rule for a new trial. In the King's Bench, their counsel, Pollock, treated the jury's verdict as if it had been an endorsement of a strict liability where an easement existed. He argued that the only neglect shown in this case was the simple failure to shore up the plaintiffs' house, whereas the plaintiffs should have proved 'actual negligence' by the defendants. In his view, there could be no strict duty to maintain a wall where the condition of the building was unclear. As he put it, if a man opened new windows, or a new path, his neighbour would have notice of such acts sufficient to allow him to act in a way to prevent a prescriptive right arising. But if he built 'a crazy house at the extremity of his land', his neighbour would not be aware of possible consequences: 'He cannot ascertain how the building is constructed; nor, if he could, can he interfere by action or otherwise.'[134] In his view, a person who chose to build on the edge of his land had to build in a way that it would bear the exercise by others of their rights on their own land. By contrast, counsel for the plaintiffs argued that regardless of any prescriptive rights, a man digging on his land had to take care not to harm buildings already erected by his neighbour, which had not been done here.[135] Upholding the verdict, Lord Denman ruled that since the jury had found that the negligent act of the defendants in digging caused the fall, the verdict was safe. He admitted that the condition of a house might be a relevant matter in determining causation: but even if a house were weak, '[a] man has no right to accelerate the fall of his neighbour's house'.[136] Although the plaintiffs' house had stood for more than 20 years, the court was clearly uneasy about using this as a peremptory reason for holding the defendants liable, given the dispute over the state of the building. Under these circumstances, the finding of negligence was all that was necessary to settle the case, without determining whether a defendant was liable without negligence for undermining any building standing for 20 years.

If these cases suggested a defendant's liability was not strict, mid-century judges generally asked juries simply to consider whether the easement had been established, and did not consider negligence relevant. In *Hide* v. *Thornborough*, Parke B. instructed a jury that where a plaintiff's house had for 20 years been supported by the land of his neighbour, and both parties knew of the support, 'the plaintiff had a right to it as an easement, and the defendant could not withdraw that support without being liable in damages for any injury that might

---

[134] *Dodd* v. *Holme* (1834) 1 Ad. & El. 493 at 495, 502.
[135] They cited *Turberville* v. *Stamp* (1697) 1 Salk. 13.
[136] *Dodd* v. *Holme* (1834) 1 Ad. & El. 493 at 504–5.

accrue to the plaintiff thereby'.[137] Similarly, in *Brown* v. *Robins*, the court rejected the defendants' contention that they had mined carefully, according to the custom of mining; for, as Martin B. put it, 'if the plaintiff was entitled to the support of the defendant's land, and was deprived of it, the absence of negligence is immaterial'.[138]

Early nineteenth-century judges were generally more sceptical of the notion that there could be a prescriptive right to support from neighbouring houses (as opposed to neighbouring soil), though there were suggestions that a neighbour could be held liable for negligence in pulling down his house. In 1829 in *Peyton* v. *The Mayor of London*, part of the plaintiffs' old and decayed house collapsed when the defendants pulled down a neighbouring—and equally old and decayed—house, giving notice. Their action on the case for negligently pulling down a house failed. Lord Tenterden pointed out that the plaintiffs had neither alleged a title to the support, nor was there any allegation from which a title could be inferred as a matter of law.[139] Doubting whether a neighbour had any duty to give notice of works, he held that even if such duty existed, its breach here would not have caused the accident, since the defective state of the houses was known to both parties, and all the activity was done in open daylight. Shortly after the King's Bench decided this case, Lord Tenterden told a Guildhall jury that the owner of premises adjoining those being pulled down had to shore them up, and that a plaintiff whose house fell when his neighbour's building was taken down could only complain if the latter acted in 'a wasteful, negligent, and improvident manner, so as to occasion greater risk to the plaintiffs than in the ordinary course of doing the work they would have incurred'. Where 'a fair and proper caution was exercised', the jury should find for the defendant.[140]

The question whether a proprietor could acquire a prescriptive right to support from a neighbouring building was discussed again in a number of mid-century cases. In 1853, the Exchequer ruled that where several houses were built together, belonging to the same owner, each of which required support from the neighbouring house, the right of support was retained when individual houses were sold. For the law presumed that the owner reserved to himself the right of support, and granted to the new owner a similar right. This was to see the right of

---

[137] *Hide* v. *Thornborough* (1846) 2 Car. & K. 250 at 255.

[138] *Brown* v. *Robins* (1859) 4 H. & N. 186 at 193. See also *Stroyan* v. *Knowles* (1861) 6 H. & N. 454.

[139] *Peyton* v. *Mayor and Commonality of London as Governors of St Thomas' Hospital* (1829) 9 B. & C. 725. Counsel for the defendants argued strongly (at 729–30) against the recognition of an easement in such cases, which might generate a right to support from a building which could no longer support itself, and which might force neighbours to take action to prevent an easement arising, whenever a building shifted.

[140] *Walters* v. *Pfeil* (1829) M. & M. 362.

support as derived from the grant of the original proprietor. While such a right could be acquired by an implied grant in the case of terraces constructed together, the courts were less sure as to whether a right of support could be acquired by prescription. This can be seen from *Solomon* v. *Vintners Co*, where the plaintiff's house in the City of London was supported by a neighbouring house, which was itself supported by a third house, owned by the defendants. The houses, which were old and out of repair, were built on a slope, and each leaned westwards. The defendants granted a lease of their house to one Robins, who agreed to pull it down and rebuild it. Robins did the work in a negligent manner, and the plaintiff's house fell down. However, the Exchequer ruled that the plaintiff had no cause of action. The defendants were not (according to the by-then established rules on vicarious liability) liable for the negligence of the contractor;[141] and since the houses did not adjoin each other, the plaintiff had no separate right to support. In his judgment, Pollock CB looked more generally at the right of neighbouring houses to support, reiterating the scepticism he had shown as counsel in *Dodd* v. *Holme*. He rejected the idea that such a right could be natural, but also doubted the proposition, for which there was authority, that the right to support could be acquired by 20 years' user. '[I]t seems contrary to justice and reason,' he noted,

> that a man, by building a weak house adjoining to the house of his neighbour, can, if the weak house gets out of the perpendicular and leans upon the adjoining house, thereby compel his neighbour either to pull down his own house within twenty years or to bring some action at law, the precise nature of which is not very clear; otherwise it is said, an adverse right would be acquired against him.[142]

These cases showed the discomfort felt by judges in allowing prescriptive rights to arise to protect weak buildings.

The general question of prescriptive rights to support from neighbouring land was revisited once more in *Angus* v. *Dalton*, which reached the House of Lords in 1881. In this case, a coach factory in Newcastle belonging to the plaintiffs collapsed after the owners of the neighbouring building (the commissioners for public buildings) employed a contractor to pull it down and dig new foundations. The plaintiffs' building had been converted in 1849 into a coach factory, with the internal walls being removed and girders inserted into a stack of brickwork in such a way as to increase the lateral pressure on the defendants' building. The work was done by the contractors without any negligence on their part, and in accordance with plans which might reasonably have been assumed to have

---

[141] See also *Butler* v. *Hunter* (1862) 7 H. & N. 826 at 832–3.

[142] *Solomon* v. *Master, Wardens and Freemen and Commonality of the Mystery of Vintners in the City of London* (1859) 4 H. & N. 585 at 598–9.

been sufficient to prevent damage. At issue was whether the plaintiffs, who had enjoyed the support of the defendants' building for 20 years, had a right of action when the latter took away the lateral support afforded by the land. At the trial at Newcastle in 1876, Lush J. directed the jury to find a verdict for the plaintiffs, but this was overturned in the Queen's Bench Division,[143] whose decision was in turn overturned by the Court of Appeal.[144] At the trial, Lush told the jury that the right to support from a building was not a natural right, but that a building which had stood for 20 years acquired an absolute prescriptive right to support. He reiterated his view while dissenting in the Queen's Bench Division, where his brethren repeated the sceptical views mid-century judges had articulated regarding permitting this kind of easement for the support of buildings.[145]

When the case came to the Lords, the judges were consulted on the question whether any prescriptive right acquired by the plaintiffs arose from an implied grant—whose existence might depend on the level of the defendants' knowledge or power to prevent the user—or whether it was a matter of positive law that 20 years' enjoyment secured the right. They agreed that a building which had *de facto* enjoyed support for more than 20 years acquired the same right to support that an ancient house would have had, though they did not agree in their reasoning towards this result. Fry J. felt that principle and authority were in direct opposition to each other on this question. He felt 'unable to find any principle upon which to justify the acquisition of the right to support by a house independently of express covenant or grant'. Such a right could only be acquired by acquiescence, and as no man could prevent his neighbour from building, he could never be said to acquiesce in giving support.[146] Moreover, in his view, it was very difficult for a neighbour to know what amount of support would be required; which also served to counter the notion of acquiescence. Nonetheless, he admitted that precedents had established that such a right could be acquired independently of express covenant. Pollock B. and Field J. felt that the case law established that the plaintiffs' right was acquired after 20 years as a matter of positive law, rather than being based on an easement.[147] The right being established, each 'owner has the right given to him by implication of law to use his property as best he likes,

---

[143] *Angus* v. *Dalton* (1877) 3 QBD 85.

[144] *Angus* v. *Dalton* (1878) 4 QBD 162.

[145] See the comments of Cockburn CJ in *Angus* v. *Dalton* (1877) 3 QBD 85 at 117, self-consciously following the wording of Pollock CB in *Solomon* v. *Master &c of Vintners' Co* (1859) 4 H. & N. 585 at 599.

[146] Fry said that the only way a neighbour could prevent such a right from being acquired might be by excavating his own land to undermine his neighbour's house within 20 years, but he felt it would be churlish to require a man to destroy his own property to prevent a right being acquired: *Dalton* v. *Angus* (1881) 6 App Cas 740 at 775.

[147] See the view of Pollock B.: *Dalton* v. *Angus* (1881) 6 App Cas 740 at 748.

provided that he does not by such user injure the rights of his neighbour'.[148] As Field J. pointed out, the question had to be looked at not from the viewpoint of an easement enjoyed by the plaintiffs, but in terms of the defendants not having the right so to use their property to harm another.

Lord Blackburn followed a similar approach. Citing *Backhouse* v. *Bonomi*, he noted that just as the right to the support of land was a property right enjoyed by the proprietor, rather than an easement restricting the neighbour's use of his land, so the owner of a building could acquire a similar right by 20 years' enjoyment. He rejected the notion that the right derived from a grant or acquiescence, and that it could only arise where the neighbour knew the nature of the support enjoyed and was in a position to prevent its exercise. Prescriptive rights, he said, were not derived from natural justice, but were positive rules founded on ideas of expediency particular to each country. For reasons of public convenience, 'it irresistibly follows that the owner of a house, who has enjoyed the house with a *de facto* support for the period and under the conditions prescribed by law, ought to be protected in the enjoyment of that support, and should not be deprived of it by shewing that it was not originally given to him'.[149] It was expedient to give the owner of a house 'the right to forbid digging near the foundations of a house without taking proper precautions to avoid injuring it', and it was not onerous to a neighbour to give such a right. While there could be no right where the enjoyment was concealed, Blackburn said, 'I do not see that more can be requisite than to let the enjoyment be so open that it is known that some support is being enjoyed by the building.'[150] Thus, where it was known that the owner of a neighbouring building had been enjoying some support for 20 years, this was enough to give him the right to support. It was only where the enjoyment of support was concealed or secret that the neighbour gained no right. In 1902, Vaughan Williams LJ similarly pointed out that the neighbour had to have some knowledge of the support required. But the amount of knowledge needed was not great, for 'the interest of the community, and especially of the inhabitants of large towns, requires that those who occupy adjacent buildings or structures should be taken to be warned of the inherent probability of one building or structure being connected with and supported by some adjacent structure or building'.[151]

Dalton v. *Angus* settled not only that a plaintiff could have the right to support offered by his neighbour's soil, but also that there could be a prescriptive right to support from his buildings.[152] Where such a right existed, the servient tenant was

[148] Per Field J.: *Dalton* v. *Angus* (1881) 6 App Cas 740 at 752.
[149] *Dalton* v. *Angus* (1881) 6 App Cas 740 at 827. For the principle of convenience, see D. 41.3.1.
[150] *Ibid.*, at 828.
[151] *Union Lighterage Co* v. *London Graving Dock Co* [1902] 2 Ch. 557 at 568–9.
[152] *Lemaitre* v. *Davis* (1881) 19 Ch D 281; *Waddington* v. *Naylor* (1889) 60 LT 480.

not permitted to do anything which would diminish support, however much care he took in doing this.[153] Where there was no such right, late nineteenth-century judges nevertheless held a duty of care to exist. Thus, in *Hughes* v. *Percival* in 1883, the House of Lords confirmed that householders could not contract out of their duty to their neighbours by employing contractors. Although the householder's duty of care did not go 'so far as to require him absolutely to provide that no damage should come to the plaintiff's wall from the use he thus made of it', Lord Blackburn held, it did go 'as far as to require him to see that reasonable skill and care were exercised in those operations which involved the use of a party-wall, exposing it to this risk'.[154]

The Rule in Rylands v. Fletcher

In *Rylands* v. *Fletcher*, the judges were presented with a novel problem: whether a defendant was liable for damage caused when a natural substance—water—accidentally escaped from a reservoir flooding the plaintiff's land. Fletcher's colliery was flooded when water from a reservoir built by Rylands burst through disused mine shafts which had been inadequately filled with soil, and which proved unable to bear the weight of the volume of water. This was a case of first impression: unlike earlier cases of flooded mines, there was here no continuing nuisance taking the form of seeping water. The accident itself was minor: the reservoir was small and its bursting caused no fatalities. However, as Brian Simpson has shown, it occurred in an era which had seen a number of major accidents involving the bursting of reservoirs. In 1864, two years after Fletcher's case was heard at the Liverpool *assizes*, Sheffield saw 238 killed when the Bradfield reservoir cracked, and a parliamentary inquiry recommended a permanent inspectorate for reservoirs and strict liability for those responsible for accidents. Simpson argues that the case was sent to the Exchequer in 1865, after the Sheffield disaster, in order to establish what the common law position was, in anticipation of the passing of legislation. He suggests that the court sought to impose a uniform principle of strict liability on waterworks, at a time when their common law liability was unclear, but when their liability when constructed under statute was strict. This is to argue that the court was responding to a particular problem.[155]

A number of remedies were already available where things liable to do harm escaped from a defendant's land. At common law, a man was liable if fire

---

[153] At the same time, there was no obligation on the servient tenant to repair his own building in order to maintain support for his neighbour: *Colebeck* v. *Girdlers Co* (1876) 1 QBD 234 at 242–3.

[154] *Hughes* v. *Percival* (1883) 8 App Cas 443 at 446.

[155] A. W. B. Simpson, 'Bursting Reservoirs and Victorian Tort Law: *Rylands and Horrocks* v. *Fletcher* (1868)' in his *Leading Cases in the Common Law* (Oxford, 1995), 195–226.

accidentally spread from his property to another's, unless the accident was 'inevitable', as by an act of God.[156] He was strictly liable if his cattle strayed onto his neighbour's land. He was strictly liable if filth from his privy escaped onto his neighbour's land.[157] Where the harm had been directly caused by the act of the defendant, an action of trespass lay, as it did (anomalously) where his cattle trespassed. Where the harm was indirect—as where fire or filth spread—the form of action was case. But neither negligence nor a continuing nuisance was necessary to sustain the action, even where the harm had not resulted from the direct act of the defendant. Nor were judicial conceptions of the substantive law simply determined by the forms of action, even in the early modern period. Thus, in *Tenant* v. *Goldwin*, which was pleaded in case, Holt spoke of the escape of the filth as 'a trespass on his neighbour'. Later jurists would think of the case as one of nuisance,[158] liability for which (at common law) did not require any continuation of the harm over time.

If allowing the escape of fire or filth was actionable at common law, was it a tort to allow water to escape? This question was raised in a number of mid-century mining cases. In *Smith* v. *Kenrick*, where water from the defendant's mine flooded the plaintiff's (when it passed through holes wrongfully bored by a previous tenant in the plaintiff's seams), the court rejected counsel's argument that '[t]he law does not permit a man to transmit fire, *or water*, or impure air, or to allow his cattle to stray, beyond his own boundaries, so as to injure or annoy his neighbours'.[159] In the court's view, the defendant had done nothing wrong, for water was a 'common enemy against which each man must defend himself'.[160] During argument at trial, Maule J. observed that '[a] man may very well justify the consequences resulting from the legitimate use of his own land. But, if he acts negligently, or capriciously, and injury results, no doubt he is liable'. This view was echoed by Cresswell J. who gave the judgment of the court. As he pointed out, in a case such as this, where there were no servitudes, each mine owner had a natural right 'to work his own in the manner most convenient and beneficial to himself, although the natural consequence may be, that some prejudice will accrue to the owner of the adjoining mine'. Liability could hence only attach if the harm arose from 'negligent or malicious conduct'.[161]

---

[156] Addison, *Wrongs and their Remedies* (1st edn, 1860), 129: see *Turberville* v. *Stamp* (1697) 1 Comyns 32; 1 Ld. Raym. 264; 12 Mod. 152; Bacon, *Abridgment*, i, 55. The strict liability was modified by statute: 6 Ann. c. 31, ss 6–7; 12 Geo. III c. 73, s 37; 14 Geo. III c. 78, s 86.

[157] *Tenant* v. *Goldwin* (1704) 1 Salk. 360, Holt K B 500, 6 Mod. 311, 2 Ld. Raym. 1089.

[158] e.g. Clerk and Lindsell, *Torts* (4th edn, by W. Payne, 1906), 344.

[159] *Smith* v. *Kenrick* (1849) 7 C.B. 515 at 545 (emphasis added).

[160] *Ibid.* at 566.

[161] *Ibid.* at 559, 564. In Cresswell's view, the cases establishing liability for fires required evidence of negligence; while *Tenant* v. *Goldwin* rested on the defendant's duty to maintain a wall.

By contrast, 14 years later in *Baird* v. *Williamson*, the Common Pleas held a mine owner liable for actively pumping water into an adjoining mine. Although neighbouring mine owners had to put up with ordinary percolations of nature, the defendants had no right to add to the ordinary percolations of nature, unless the plaintiffs were subject to a servitude of receiving it.[162] Although the defendants had worked the mine according to the usual and approved course of mining in the area, and had not been negligent, they were held strictly liable, for they had no right to pump water on to the plaintiffs' land. The liability was rooted in the fact that they had been 'active agents in sending water into the lower mine'. No malice, or intent to harm, was needed.

In *Fletcher* v. *Rylands*, the defendants had not been active agents in pumping the water into the plaintiff's mine; but neither was the flow of water merely the result of the percolations of nature. It resulted from water being artificially brought there. However, Manisty for the plaintiff argued that the case was covered by the maxim, *sic utere tuo ut alienum non laedas*, claiming that the 'plaintiff has a right to enjoy his land free from the injury resulting from an act, not in the ordinary course, done by the defendants on their land'.[163] If it escaped, he added, 'it is a trespass', echoing the terminology used in the earlier cases where counsel argued for liability for escaping water.[164] But this raised the question of which category of tort the case fell into. Finding for the defendants, Martin B. in the Exchequer made use of old and new arguments. Invoking a traditional argument, he held that the act could not constitute trespass, since—as all early nineteenth-century pleaders knew—the harm had to be direct and not consequential for such an action to lie. Invoking a modern argument, he held that there could be no liability for the consequential harm unless the defendant had been negligent. Invoking the recently settled rule 'that when damage is done to personal property, and even to the person, by collision either upon the road or at sea, there must be negligence in the party doing the damage to render him legally responsible', he saw no reason why damage to real property should be governed by a different rule.[165] Nor could the case be seen as one of nuisance, since here there was nothing 'hurtful or injurious to the senses'. The dissenting Bramwell B. disagreed. In his view, the facts could be seen to constitute either trespass—for

---

[162] *Baird* v. *Williamson* (1863) 15 C.B. N.S. 376 at 391.

[163] *Fletcher* v. *Rylands* (1865) 3 H. & C. 774 at 781.

[164] The judgment of Erle J. was not cast in these terms. See the comments of Byles J. in *Baird* v. *Williamson* (1863) 15 C.B. N.S. 376 at 391. In *Smith* v. *Kenrick*, Cresswell J. noted that the natural percolation of water 'cannot be considered as a trespass': 7 C.B. at 562.

[165] *Fletcher* v. *Rylands* (1865) 3 H. & C. 774 at 793. Where the law made a defendant an insurer, as with innkeepers or carriers, it was (he said) exceptional. He also seemed to suggest, on the authority of *Chadwick* v. *Trower*, that absent a servitude, there was no duty on the defendant to take care when building on his own property.

which wilfulness was not requisite—or nuisance. But in any event, *Backhouse* v. *Bonomi* showed that there did not have to be a trespass, nuisance, or negligence for liability to attach, for one could be liable for the mischievous consequences of a lawful act. What mattered in his mind was 'that the defendants have caused water to flow into the plaintiff's mines, which, but for their [...] act would not have gone there'.[166] As *Backhouse* had shown, a landowner whose use of his land caused harm to another could be liable absent a servitude or negligence, simply by virtue of the *sic utere* principle.

In 1866, the Exchequer Chamber overturned the decision of the Exchequer. In his judgment, Blackburn J said,

the true rule of law is, that the person who for his own purposes brings on to his lands and collects and keeps there anything likely to do mischief if it escapes, must keep it in at his peril, and, if he does not do so, is prima facie answerable for all the damage which is the natural consequence of its escape. He can excuse himself by showing that the escape was owing to the plaintiff's default; or, perhaps, that the escape was the consequence of vis major, or the act of God; but as nothing of the sort exists here, it is unnecessary to inquire what excuse would be sufficient.[167]

Blackburn felt this interpretation of law was just in principle—since the victim was 'damnified without any fault of his own'—and was consistent with the case law. He gave a number of examples of strict liabilities, including cattle trespass, the escape of filth from a privy (as in *Tenant* v. *Goldwin*), or damage to the health of one's habitation 'by the fumes and noisome vapours' from alkali works.[168] He invoked *Tenant* v. *Goldwin* 'in support of the position that he who brings and keeps anything, no matter whether beasts, or filth, or clean water, or a heap of earth or dung, on his premises, must at his peril prevent it from getting on his neighbour's, or make good all the damage which is the natural consequence of its doing so'.[169] He also rejected Martin's contention that the law relating to accidents on real property should be assimilated with the law of personal injury:

Traffic on the highways, whether by land or sea, cannot be conducted without exposing those whose persons or property are near it to some inevitable risk; and that being so, they who go on the highway, or have their property adjacent to it, may well be held to do so subject to their taking upon themselves the risk of injury from that inevitable danger; and persons who by the licence of the owner pass near to warehouses where goods are being

---

[166] *Fletcher* v. *Rylands* (1865) 3 H. & C. 774 at 790.

[167] *Fletcher* v. *Rylands* (1866) LR 1 Exch 265 at 279–80.

[168] Referring to the recent alkali suits in Liverpool, he noted that questions of negligence or fault were not considered relevant in such nuisance actions. He did not mention *St Helen's Smelting Co* v. *Tipping* (1865) 11 H.L.C. 642 at 650, where the Lords had distinguished between strict liabilities where property was harmed, and less strict ones where physical comfort was affected.

[169] *Fletcher* v. *Rylands* (1866) LR 1 Exch 265 at 285.

raised or lowered, certainly do so subject to the inevitable risk of accident. In neither case, therefore, can they recover without proof of want of care or skill occasioning the accident; and it is believed that all the cases in which inevitable accident has been held an excuse for what prima facie was a trespass, can be explained on the same principle, viz., that the circumstances were such as to shew that the plaintiff had taken that risk upon himself. But there is no ground for saying that the plaintiff here took upon himself any risk arising from the uses to which the defendants should choose to apply their land.[170]

This ruling was reaffirmed in the House of Lords in 1868, where Lord Cairns LC modified Blackburn's formulation. Cairns ruled that the defendants were within their rights to make use of their own property 'for any purpose for which it might in the ordinary course of the enjoyment of land be used'. If 'in what I may term the natural user of that land' water had accumulated, and then flowed onto the plaintiff's land 'by the operation of the laws of nature', the plaintiff could not have complained. But if the defendants, 'not stopping at the natural use of their close, had desired to use it for any purpose which I may term a non-natural use, for the purpose of introducing into the close that which in its natural condition was not in or upon it', they acted at their peril.[171] In making these comments, Cairns clearly had in mind the distinction between the approaches in *Smith* v. *Kenrick* and *Baird* v. *Williamson*, according to which a landowner was not liable for the ordinary course of nature. This reformulation opened the way for courts to reconsider what was an 'ordinary' or 'natural' use of land, and thereby to qualify the rule.[172]

The decision in *Rylands* v. *Fletcher* reflected the view that, outside the public space of the highway, where risks were shared, one person's rights were not to be interfered with by the voluntary action of another. Although the latter was not to be held liable for harms resulting from the ordinary exercise of his own rights, if harm resulted from any 'non-natural' activity, it was actionable. Although *Rylands* was a case about harm to real property done by a substance liable to do damage, Blackburn's judgment—which spoke the language of trespass rather than nuisance—was cast in a way which suggested that it applied to damage to chattels, as well as personal injuries.[173] But if the case demonstrated a judicial desire to limit the ambit of negligence to accidents in the public sphere, the scope of the decision was limited in the later nineteenth century.

---

[170] *Fletcher* v. *Rylands* (1866) LR 1 Exch 265, at 286–7.

[171] *Rylands* v. *Fletcher* (1868) LR 3 HL 330 at 339.

[172] See F. H. Newark, 'Non-Natural User and *Rylands* v. *Fletcher*' (1961) 24 *MLR* 557–71.

[173] Blackburn invoked cases where dangerous animals had caused personal injuries, and spoke of the risk caused by water as being that of drowning. He also observed that 'he whose stuff it is must keep it that it may not trespass': *Fletcher* v. *Rylands* (1866) LR 1 Exch 265 at 286. For its application to personal property, see the comments of Blackburn J. in *Cattle* v. *Stockton Waterworks* (1875) LR 10 QB 453 at 457 and *Jones* v. *Festiniog Railway Co* (1868) LR 3 QB 733.

Within a generation, jurists came to describe *Rylands* v. *Fletcher* as an effort to impose a strict liability in respect of unusually hazardous things, making the owner an insurer of the safety of the public in exceptional circumstances. In 1886, Frederick Pollock argued that while the general policy of the law was to require people to conduct their undertakings 'with diligence proportioned to the apparent risk', a duty to insure safety was imposed were a man by his conduct exposed his neighbour to extraordinary risk.[174] His friend Oliver Wendell Holmes agreed that where there was an unusually high degree of risk of harm, the law as a matter of policy departed from its more usual imposition of a fault liability. In cases of danger, he observed, 'the safest way to secure care is to throw the risk upon the person who decides what precautions shall be taken'.[175] Jurists treated *Rylands* v. *Fletcher* as a policy-driven anomaly to the general approach whereby liability only attached to intentional or negligent wrongs.

However, the rule was not generalized by jurists to cover all harms caused by dangerous substances. Although Pollock discussed *Rylands* in a chapter on 'duties of insuring safety', its content showed that the common law did not impose strict liabilities for harms done by dangerous goods. If liability for harms done by dangerous animals remained strict, liability for harm done by explosives which were transported, or for badly fitted gas pipes, was governed by the principles of negligence.[176] Some judges continued to invoke the principle from *Rylands* v. *Fletcher* as covering personal injuries. Thus, in *Filburn* v. *The People's Palace and Aquarium Co*, an action for personal injury caused by an elephant not known to the defendants to be dangerous, Bowen LJ ruled that '[t]he broad principle that governs this case is that laid down in *Fletcher* v. *Rylands*, that a person who brings upon his land anything that would not naturally come upon it, and which is in itself dangerous, must take care that it is kept under proper control'.[177] However, by the turn of the twentieth century, judges and jurists tended to treat *Rylands* v. *Fletcher* as articulating a principle of the law of nuisance.[178] In this context, in 1907 the Court of Appeal dismissed a case brought on behalf of a woman injured

---

[174] F. Pollock, 'Duties of Insuring Safety: The Rule in *Rylands* v. *Fletcher*' (1886) 2 *LQR* 52–65 at 52.

[175] O. W. Holmes, *The Common Law* (1881), 117.

[176] See *Farrant* v. *Barnes* (1862) 11 C.B. N.S. 553; *Parry* v. *Smith* (1879) 4 CPD 325.

[177] *Filburn* v. *The People's Palace and Aquarium Co* (1890) 25 QBD 258 at 261. Here the elephant in question had been on the defendant's property (*Leeds Mercury*, 17 March 1890, p. 7). The notion that the principle applied to personal injuries is also to be found in *Eastern & South African Telegraph Co* v. *Cape Town Tramways* [1902] AC 381 at 392 and *Hoare & Co* v. *McAlpine* [1923] 1 Ch 167 at 174; though the House of Lords took a dim view of arguments that there could be recovery for personal injury under the *Rylands* principle in *Read* v. *J. Lyons & Co* [1947] AC 156 at 170–1, 178, 180–1.

[178] Salmond therefore treated *Rylands* v. *Fletcher* in his chapter on nuisance: *Torts* (2nd edn, 1910), 195 *et seq*. As he saw, it was harder, after *Holmes* v. *Mather*, to argue for a strict liability in trespass, at least outside established categories, such as dangerous animals.

when a water tank collapsed on her as a result of vibrations caused by her neighbour's machinery, in which *Rylands* had been invoked. The court took the view that the cause of action here was one of nuisance, for which the defendant must be shown to have a proprietary interest.[179] Isolated accidents caused by dangerous things were also now described as nuisances.[180] *Rylands* v. *Fletcher* was also invoked in numerous cases of nuisance, notably where damage was done by leaking sewage, where defendants were held strictly liable for the harm done to the plaintiff's land.[181]

At the same time, judges considering whether harms emanating from the defendant's land constituted nuisances began to refine Lord Cairns's notion of 'natural' user. Where judges in the 1870s seemed content to say that nuisance liability resulted from any annoyance which was not 'the result of the natural user by a neighbour of his land' but was in any way artificial,[182] by the 1890s, the language had modified. In *National Telephone Co* v. *Baker*, Kekewich J. held, following *Rylands*, that a tramway company, whose lines caused electrical interference with the equipment of a licensed telephone company, would have been liable for the damage caused, were it not for the statutory protection it enjoyed.[183] An owner was liable under the *Rylands* principle if he made 'extraordinary' use of his land, rather than merely 'non-natural' use. In the sources from which Kekewich drew, 'extraordinary' uses were to be contrasted with 'reasonable' ones. [184]

---

[179] *Malone* v. *Laskey* [1907] 2 KB 141. She failed in her claim of negligence, since she could show no duty of care owed to her.

[180] Thus, in 1905 Collins MR held, 'It cannot [...] seriously be contended that, where the premises of an adjoining owner are blown up by an explosion brought about through the agency of the defendants' system of electric lighting, there is not a nuisance': *Midwood & Co* v. *Manchester Corporation* [1905] 2 KB 597 at 604–5.

[181] e.g. *Humphries* v. *Cousins* (1877) 2 CPD 239 at 243–4; *Hobart* v. *Southend Corporation* (1906) 75 LJ KB 305 at 308; *Foster* v. *Urban District Council of Warblington* [1906] 1 KB 648 at 671–2; *Jones* v. *Llanrwst Urban District Council* [1911] 1 Ch 393 at 402–3.

[182] *Hurdman* v. *North Eastern Railway* (1878) 3 CPD 168 at 174. See also *Broder* v. *Saillard* (1876) 2 Ch D 692.

[183] Following the latter case, Kekewich J. ruled that a man who 'called into special existence, an electric current for his own purposes, and who discharges it into the earth beyond his control' was as liable as if he had discharged a stream of water: *National Telephone Co* v. *Baker* [1893] 2 Ch. 186 at 201. The plaintiffs treated the case as one of nuisance, citing the smoke pollution cases of *Crump* v. *Lambert* (1867) LR 3 Eq 409 and *Fleming* v. *Hislop* (1886) 11 App Cas 686 as well as *Hurdman* v. *North Eastern Railway* (1878) 3 CPD 168.

[184] E. W. Garrett's formulation of the rule, which Kekewich drew on and for which he suggested modifications, referred to *Farrer* v. *Nelson* (1885) 15 QBD 258, 52 LT 766, a case dealing with the overstocking of the plaintiff's farm by a defendant who had shooting rights on it, in which Pollock B. contrasted reasonable user with 'unnatural or extraordinary user'. *The Law of Nuisances* (1890), 117 (modified in the second edition (1897, p. 130) in response to Kekewich with the addition of the word 'extraordinary'). Kekewich himself seems to have taken the phrase from Lord Kingsdown's phrase in *Miner* v. *Gilmour* (1858) 12 Moo. P.C. 131 at 156. See also Newark,

By the 1890s, judges and jurists were rethinking the language of the *Rylands* principle, converting the contrast between nature and artifice which stood at the heart of *Rylands* v. *Fletcher* into one between usual and unusual uses. This can be seen particularly in cases involving shared buildings. In *Carstairs* v. *Taylor* in 1871, the plaintiffs failed to recover for damage done to their goods—stored on the bottom floor of the defendant's warehouse—after storm water which was gathered on the roof leaked through the building. In Bramwell B.'s view, since the collection of the water by the drains was done for the plaintiffs' benefit as well as the defendant's—unlike the accumulation of water in *Rylands*—they had to be taken to have consented to it 'and the defendant can only be liable if he was guilty of negligence'.[185] Similarly, in *Ross* v. *Fedden*, where the plaintiff's goods were harmed after water leaked from a blocked water closet, the county court judge hearing the case doubted whether *Rylands* applied to houses jointly occupied, since all occupants consented to the state of the premises. Since a house was 'a thing wholly artificial', he observed, 'it is rather a straining of language to speak of any one state of things as more natural than another'. In the Queen's Bench, it was noted that all the tenants in the building knew that there were water pipes in it, which supplied water for the common benefit. Blackburn J. noted that 'there is a very great difference between two tenants, one occupying an upper and another a lower storey of a house, held under the same landlord, and two holders of adjacent land'.[186] He rejected the proposition that 'occupiers of the upper storey of a house in which there is a water-closet, with a pipe which had been demised to them along with the rest', were under an obligation, 'at their peril, to keep that pipe from giving way'.[187] The courts continued to reject the application of *Rylands* to jointly occupied properties, where the water was supplied for the use of all tenants.[188] This was generally on the ground that those who drew water from pipes in a building assented to the storage of that water on the premises by the defendant.[189] But when the question was raised in 1898 in *Blake* v. *Woolf*, Wright J. held that, under the principle of *Rylands* v. *Fletcher*, no liability attached 'where a person is using his land in the ordinary way and

---

'Non-natural user', 566 and n. Modern scholars have pointed to the differences between the notion of reasonable user in nuisance and non-natural use in *Rylands*. See e.g. J. Murphy, 'The Merits of *Rylands* v. *Fletcher*' 24 *OJLS* (2004), 643–69; D. Nolan, 'The Distinctiveness of *Rylands* v. *Fletcher*' (2005) 121 *LQR* 421–51. Kekewich himself was sceptical of the idea of reasonable user in nuisance: see pp. 1101–02.

[185] *Carstairs* v. *Taylor* (1871) LR 6 Ex 217 at 221.

[186] *Ross* v. *Fedden* (1872) 26 LT 968.

[187] *Ibid.* Cf. LR 7 QB 661 at 663, 665.

[188] See *Anderson* v. *Oppenheimer* (1880) 5 QBD 602 at 607 and *Stevens* v. *Woodward* (1881) 6 QBD 318, where *Rylands* was not even mentioned.

[189] e.g. *Gill* v. *Edouin* (1895) 72 LT 579.

damage happens to the adjoining property without any default or negligence on his part'.[190] Bringing water into a building through a cistern was in his view an ordinary use of land. Similarly, in 1913, in *Rickards* v. *Lothian*, an Australian appeal where the plaintiff's stock of schoolbooks was damaged when the building owned by the defendant was flooded due to the actions of an intruder, the Privy Council endorsed the view that strict liability only attached to particularly dangerous uses. In Lord Moulton's judgment, not every use of land rendered the proprietor liable on *Rylands* principles: 'It must be some special use bringing with it increased danger to others, and must not merely be the ordinary use of the land or such a use as is proper for the general benefit of the community.'[191] The provision of a proper water supply in houses was not merely reasonable, but was 'an almost necessary feature of town life'. Such a supply could not be installed without creating some danger of leakage, he ruled; but '[i]t would be unreasonable for the law to regard those who instal or maintain such a system of supply as doing so at their own peril, with an absolute liability for any damage resulting from its presence even when there has been no negligence'.[192]

The rule in *Rylands* was also qualified in two other respects. First, in the 1870s, the courts took a broad view of the defence of inevitable accident. In *Carstairs* v. *Taylor* in 1871, where a leak had occurred after a rat had gnawed through the box collecting rainwater, Kelly CB stated that 'the accident was due to vis major, as much as if a thief had broken the hole in attempting to enter the house, or a flash of lightning or a hurricane had caused the rent'.[193] In 1876, in *Nichols* v. *Marsland*, the Court of Appeal regarded a storm which caused the defendant's artificially created ornamental pools to burst their banks and sweep away four county bridges to be an act of God which removed the defendant's liability.[194] The case was controversial, and some judges found it hard to accept that an unusually heavy rainfall was an unforeseeable act of God.[195] Significantly, Mellish LJ's judgment focused on whether the defendant was at fault, and he held that since she could not have been expected to anticipate the result, she was

---

[190] *Blake* v. *Woolf* [1898] 2 QB 426 at 428.
[191] *Rickards* v. *Lothian* [1913] AC 263 at 280.
[192] *Ibid.*, at 281–2.
[193] *Carstairs* v. *Taylor* (1871) LR 6 Ex 217 at 220–1.
[194] *Nichols* v. *Marsland* (1876) 2 Ex D 1 at 5.
[195] In *Dixon* v. *The Metropolitan Board of Works* [1881] 7 QBD 418 at 422, Lord Coleridge CJ expressed himself confused by claims that there was a distinction in principle (as opposed to one on the facts) between this case and *Rylands*. In the case before him, he did not regard a heavy storm (followed by the opening of sluice gates) as an act of God. See also *Greenock Corp.* v. *Caledonian Railway Co* [1917] AC 556 at 572, where it was considered that extraordinary storms must be anticipated from time to time; and *Attorney General* v. *Cory Bros* [1921] AC 521. See also the discussion in C. G. Hall, 'An Unsearchable Providence: The Lawyer's Concept of an Act of God' (1993) 13 *OJLS* 227–48 at 234–5.

not liable. His approach may have been influenced by the same court's decision earlier in the year in *Nugent* v. *Smith*, where it sought to widen the defence of inevitable accident in a way as to dilute the strict liability of a common carrier, by raising questions of fault.[196] This attempt to expand the notion of what constituted an act of God remained controversial.[197]

Secondly, it was held that a proprietor could not be held strictly liable for harms caused by the acts of third parties.[198] In *Nichols* v. *Marsland*, Bramwell B. had opined that it was unthinkable that if a 'mischievous boy bored a hole in a cistern in any London house, and the water did mischief to a neighbour, the occupier of the house would be liable'.[199] Taking a similar view, Kelly CB held in *Box* v. *Jubb* that the law did not require defendants 'to construct their reservoir and the sluices and gates leading to it to meet any amount of pressure which the wrongful act of a third person may impose'.[200] These views were endorsed in *Rickards* v. *Lothian*, where the Privy Council held that the proprietor could not be held liable for the wrongful act of an unknown trespasser.

Rylands v. *Fletcher* was decided in an era where judges committed to the sanctity of private property felt that remedies should be given to those whose private property was harmed by the risk-generating activity of others. It was also decided in an era when the forms of action were giving way to more substantive categories. In the modern era, scholars have debated the relationship between the rule in *Rylands* v. *Fletcher* and the law of private nuisance, as well as asking whether the strict liability generated by the rule should be replaced by ordinary negligence liability. Commentators today make a clear distinction between nuisance and the rule in *Rylands* v. *Fletcher*. They point out that nuisance is concerned with continuing interferences with the enjoyment of land in which the plaintiff must have a proprietary interest, and that liability depends on whether, from the plaintiff's viewpoint, the defendant's use of his land is reasonable. By contrast, the strict liability rule in *Rylands* is concerned with accidental damage done to a plaintiff, who need have no proprietary interest in the land affected, when the defendant has generated risks by the unnatural use of his land. Despite some calls for its reform, the rule in *Rylands* remains in place as a rule of strict liability,

---

[196] *Nugent* v. *Smith* (1876) 1 CPD 423.

[197] Contrast Lord Westbury's view in an earlier Scottish case that 'it is undoubtedly the duty of that individual so to construct the work as to provide in an efficient manner, not only against usual occurrences and ordinary state of things, but also to provide against things which are unusual and extraordinary': *Tennent* v. *Earl of Glasgow* (1864) 2 M. (HL) 22, 25–7, cited in *Greenock Corp.* v. *Caledonian Railway* [1917] AC 556 at 576.

[198] In *Ross* v. *Fedden* (1872) 26 LT 966 at 968, Blackburn J. observed that in cases involving the right to support, the defendant would not be liable for the acts of strangers.

[199] *Nichols* v. *Marsland* (1875) LR 10 Ex 255 at 259.

[200] *Box* v. *Jubb* (1879) LR 4 Ex 76 at 79.

distinct from both negligence and nuisance, where the basis of liability is either the unreasonableness of the defendant's conduct, or its unreasonable effect on the claimant.

If in the early twenty-first century, the boundaries seem clear (if contestable), in the later nineteenth century, the boundaries of the categories used by judges and jurists were in some flux. As *St Helens* v. *Tipping* showed, the courts took two approaches in cases involving nuisance. Where property was physically damaged (by sewage, vibrations, or airborne poisons), liability tended to be strict. In such cases, the courts often described the nuisance (following *Tenant* v. *Goldwin*) as a 'trespass'. Nor did the damage have to be continuing. By contrast, where something offended the senses, causing an annoyance, the courts asked whether the level of annoyance was unreasonable. In answering this question, some judges were prepared to take locality into account. The issue raised by *Rylands* looked in many ways like the first branch of nuisance, raising a question about physical harm done to the plaintiff's property by the defendants' use of their property. The judges who found for the plaintiff saw the issue as analogous to the 'trespassory' nuisances, which were regarded as raising strict liabilities. In seeking to draw a distinction between harms in the home and harms in the world, judges like Blackburn went so far as to express the rule in a way suggesting that—unlike nuisance—it would extend to personal injuries. By this formulation, a defendant would be liable for any unnatural risks he had generated which injured the plaintiff in his own domain. In the aftermath of *Holmes* v. *Mather*, judges showed no appetite for such an extension. At the same time, judges—notably those dealing with the cases arising from the joint occupation of buildings—realized that the borderline between the home and the world was not as clear cut as Blackburn assumed. In deciding whether an activity was in effect a nuisance attracting strict liability, judges therefore began to look more closely at whether it was an abnormally risky one. In the modern world of risks, the backward-looking strict liability which Blackburn sought to repackage was therefore reined in. But the doctrine of *Rylands* v. *Fletcher* remained in place, as an anomaly which jurists who wanted to build a law of tort around a concept of fault had difficulty in explaining.

Further Reading

Part One: Property

Wills and trusts

Alexander, G., 'The Dead Hand and the Law of Trusts in the Nineteenth Century' (1985) 37 *Stanford Law Rev.* 1189–266.

Alexander, G., 'The Transformation of Trusts as a Legal Category, 1800–1914' (1987) 5 *LHR* 303–50.

Chesterman, M. R., 'Family Settlements on Trust', in G. R. Rubin and D. Sugarman (eds), *Law, Economy and Society, 1750–1914* (Abingdon, 1984), 124–67 plus xii pages of notes.

Green, D. R. and Owens, A., 'Metropolitan Estates of the Middle Class, 1800–50' (1997) 70 *BIHR* 294–311.

Keeton, G. W., 'The Changing Conception of Trusteeship' [1950] *CLP* 14–29.

Kerridge, R. and Rivers, J., 'The Construction of Wills' (2000) 116 *LQR* 287–317.

Marsh, D. R., *Corporate Trustees* (1952).

Morris, R. J., *Men, Women and Property in England 1780–1870* (Cambridge, 2005).

Owens, A., 'Property, Gender and the Life-course' (2001) 26 *Social History* 299–317.

Polden, P., *Peter Thelluson's Will of 1797 and its Consequences on Chancery Law* (Lewiston, NY 2002).

Polden, P., 'The Public Trustee in England 1906–86' (1989) 10 *JLH* 229–55.

Stebbings, C., *The Private Trustee in Victorian England* (Cambridge, 2002).

Land

Anderson, J. S., *Lawyers and the Making of English Land Law 1832–1940* (Oxford, 1992).

Englander, D., *Landlord and Tenant in Urban Britain 1838–1918* (1983).

English, B. and Saville, J., *Strict Settlement: A Guide for Historians* (Hull, 1983).

Habakkuk, J., *Marriage, Debt and the Estates System* (Oxford, 1994).

Howell, J., 'Deeds Registration in England: A Complete Failure?' (1999) 58 *CLJ* 366–98.

Getzler, J., *A History of Water Rights at Common Law* (Oxford, 2004).

Martin, D., 'Land Reform', in P. Hollis (ed.), *Pressure from Without in Early Victorian England* (1974), 131–58

Offer, A., 'The Origins of the Law of Property Acts 1910–1925' (1977) 40 *MLR* 505–22.

Offer, A., *Property and Politics 1870–1914* (Cambridge, 1981).

Perkin, H. J., 'Land Reform and Class Conflict in Victorian Britain', in *The Victorians and Social Protest*, ed. J. Butt and I. F. Clark (1973) 177–217, 235–9.

Pottage, A., 'The Originality of Registration' (1995) 15 *OJLS* 371–401.

Pottage, A., 'Evidencing Ownership', in S. Bright and J. Dewar (eds), *Land Law* (Oxford, 1998), 129–50.

Reynolds, J., 'Statutory Covenants of Fitness and Repair: Social Legislation and the Judges' (1974) 37 *MLR* 377–98.

Rudden, B., 'A Code Too Soon', in *Essays in Memory of Professor F H Lawson*, ed. P. Wallington and R. M. Merkin (London, 1986), 101–16.

Simpson, A. W. B., *A History of the Land Law* (2nd edn, Oxford, 1986).

Spring, D., *The English Landed Estate* (Baltimore, 1963).

Thompson, F. M. L., *Hampstead: Building a Borough, 1650–1964* (1974).

Part Two: Contract

Books

Atiyah, P. S., *The Rise and Fall of Freedom of Contract* (Oxford, 1979).

Baker, J. H., *Introduction to English Legal History* (4th edn, 2002).

Baker, J. H. and Milsom, S. F. C., *Sources of English Legal History: Private Law to 1750* (1986).

Baloch, T. A., *Unjust Enrichment and Contract* (Oxford, 2009).

Birks, P., *An Introduction to the Law of Restitution* (Oxford, 1989).

Bristow, E. J., *Individualism versus Socialism in Britain, 1880–1914* (New York and London, 1987).

Brooks, C. W., *Lawyers, Litigation and English Society since 1450* (1998).

Burrows, A. S., *The Law of Restitution* (2nd edn, 2002).

Cornish, W. R. and de N. Clark, G., *Law and Society in England 1750–1950* (1989).

Cox, H., *The Global Cigarette: Origins and Evolution of British American Tobacco, 1880–1945* (Oxford, 2000).

Devine, T. M., *The Tobacco Lords: A Study of the Tobacco Merchants of Glasgow and their Trading Activities, c.1740–1790* (Edinburgh, 1975).

Duxbury, N., *Frederick Pollock and the English Juristic Tradition* (Oxford, 2004).

Finn, M. C., *The Character of Credit: Personal Debt in English Culture, 1740–1914* (Cambridge, 2003).

Fraser, W. H., *The Coming of the Mass Market, 1850–1914* (1981).

Goff, R. and Jones, G., *The Law of Restitution* (7th edn by G. Jones, 2007).

Gordley, J., *The Philosophical Origins of Modern Contract Doctrine* (Oxford, 1991).

Gordley, J., *Foundations of Private Law: Property, Tort, Contract, Unjust Enrishment* (Oxford, 2006).

Hindley, D. and Hindley, G., *Advertising in Victorian England, 1837–1901* (1972).

Howe, M. D. (ed.), *The Pollock-Holmes Letters: Correspondence of Sir Frederick Pollock and Mr Justice Holmes 1874–1932*, 2 vols (Cambridge, 1942).

Horwitz, M., *The Transformation of American Law, 1780–1860* (Cambridge, MA, 1977).

Ibbetson, D. J., *Historical Introduction to the Law of Obligations* (Oxford, 1999).

Jackson, R. M., *The History of Quasi-Contract in English Law* (Cambridge, 1936).

Karsten, P., *Head versus Heart Judge-Made Law in Nineteenth Century America* (1997).

Kreitner, R., *Calculating Promises: The Emergence of Modern American Contract Doctrine* (Palo Alto, 2006).

Kynaston, D., *The City of London*, Vol. 1 (1994).

MacMillan, C., *Mistakes in English Law* (forthcoming, Oxford, 2010).

Nevett, T. R., *Advertising in Britain: A History* (1982).

Morgan, K., *Bristol and the Atlantic Trade in the Eighteenth Century* (Cambridge, 1993).

Oldham, J., *The Mansfield Manuscripts and the Growth of English Law in the Eighteenth Century*, 2 vols (1992).

Palmer, V. V., *The Paths to Privity: The History of Third Party Beneficiary Contracts at English Law* (San Francisco, 1992).

Polden, P., *A History of the County Court, 1846–1971* (Cambridge, 1999).

Searle, G. R., *Morality and the Market in Victorian Britain* (Oxford, 1998).

Simpson, A. W. B., *A History of the Common Law of Contract* (Oxford, 1975).

Simpson, A. W. B., *Leading Cases in the Common Law* (Oxford, 1995).

Steinfeld, R. J., *Coercion, Contract and Free Labour in the Nineteenth Century* (Cambridge, 2001).

Stoljar, S. J., *A History of Contract at Common Law* (Canberra, 1975).

Stoljar, S. J., *The Law of Quasi-Contract* (2nd edn, Sydney, 1989).

Treitel, G., *The Law of Contract* (1962, with 12 edns to 2007).

Treitel, G. H., *Frustration and Force Majeure* (2nd edn, 2004).

Waddams, S. M., *Dimensions of Private Law* (Cambridge, 2003).

Winfield, P. H., *The Province of the Law of Tort* (Cambridge, 1931).

Zimmermann, P., *The Law of Obligations: Roman Foundations of the Civilian Tradition* (Oxford, 1996).

Articles

Adams, J. N., 'The Standardization of Commercial Contracts, or the Contractualization of Standard Forms' (1978) 7 *Anglo-Am. Law Rev.* 136–54

Baker, J. H., 'From Sanctity of Contract to Reasonable Expectation?' (1979) 32 *Current Legal Problems* 17–39.

Baker, J. H., 'The History of Quasi-Contract in English Law', in W. R. Cornish, R. Nolan, J. O'Sullivan, and G. Virgo, *Restitution: Past, Present and Future*, (Oxford 1998), 37–56.

Baker, J. H., 'The Use of Assumpsit for Restitutionary Money Claims 1600–1800', in E. J. H. Schrage, *Unjust Enrichment* (2nd edn, Berlin, 1999), 31–57.

Barton, J. L., 'Contractual Damages and the Rise of Industry' (1987) 7 *OJLS* 40–59.

Barton, J. L., 'Cutter v. Powell and Quantum Meruit' (1987) 8 *JLH* 48–63.

Barton, J. L., 'Redhibition, Error and Implied Warranty in English Law' (1994) 62 *Tijdschrift voor Rechtsgeschiedenis* 317–29.

Birks, P. B. H., 'English and Roman Learning in *Moses v. Macferlan*' [1984] *Current Legal Problems* 1–28.

Bristow, E., 'The Liberty and Property Defence League and Individualism' (1974) 18 *Historical Journal* 761–89.

Bronaugh, R., 'A Secret Paradox of the Common Law' (1983) 2 *Law and Philosophy* 193–232.

Cranston, R., 'The Rise and Rise of Standard Form Contracts: International Commodity Sales 1800–1970', in R. Cranston, J. Ramberg, and J. Ziegler (eds), *Commercial Law Challenges in the 21st Century: Jan Hellner in Memoriam* (Stockholm, 2007), 11–71.

Danzig, R., 'Hadley v. Baxendale: A Study in the Industrialization of the Law', (1975) *JLS* 249–84.

Daunton, M., 'The Material Politics of Natural Monopoly: Consuming Gas in Victorian Britain', in M. Daunton and M. Hilton (eds), *The Politics of Consumption: Material Culture and Citizenship in Britain and America* (Oxford, 2001), 69–88.

Dawson, F., 'Metaphors and Anticipatory Breach of Contract' (1981) 40 *CLJ* 83–107.

Faust, F., '*Hadley v. Baxendale*—an Understandable Miscarriage of Justice' (1994) *JLH* 41–71.

Finn, M., 'Working-Class Women and the Contest for Consumer Control in Victorian County Courts' (1998) 161 *P & P* 116–54.

Ferguson, R. B., 'The Horwitz Thesis and Common Law Discourse in England', (1983) 3 *OJLS* 34–58.

Flannigan, R., 'Privity—the End of an Era (Error)' (1987) 103 *LQR* 564–93.

Francis, C. W., 'Practice, Strategy, and Institution: Debt Collection in the English Common Law Courts, 1740–1840' (1986) 80 *Northwestern University Law Rev.* 807–954.

Gardner, S., 'Trashing with Trollope: A Deconstruction of the Postal Rules in Contract' (1992) 12 *OJLS* 170–94.

Getzler, J., 'Equitable Compensation and the Regulation of Fiduciary Relationships', in *Restitution and Equity: Vol. I. Resulting Trusts and Equitable Compensation*, ed. P. Birks and F. Rose (2000), 235–57.

Graziadei, M., 'Changing Images of the Law in Nineteenth Century English Thought (the Continental Impulse)', in M. Reimann (ed.), *The Reception of Continental Ideas in the Common Law World, 1820–1920* (Berlin, 1993), 115–63.

Hamburger, P. A., 'The Development of the Nineteenth-Century Consensus Theory of Contract' (1989) 7 *Law and History Review* 265–9.

Hanbury, H. G., 'The Recovery of Money' (1924) 40 *LQR* 31–42.

Harley, C. K., 'Trade: Discovery, Mercantilism, and Technology', in R. Floud and P. Johnson (eds), *The Cambridge Economic History of Modern Britain: Vol. I: Industrialisation, 1700–1860* (Cambridge, 2004), 175–203.

Hedley, S., 'From Individualism to Communitarianism? The Case of Standard Forms', in T. G. Watkin (ed.), *Legal Record and Historical Reality: Proceedings of the Eighth British Legal History Conference, Cardiff, 1987* (Cardiff., 1989), 229–42.

Horwitz H. and Polden, P., 'Continuity or Change in the Court of Chancery in the Seventeenth and Eighteenth Centuries?' (1995) 34 *JBS* 24–57.

Hudson, A. H., 'Gibbons v. Proctor Revisited' (1968) 84 *LQR* 502–12.

Hutchison, T. W., 'Economists and Economic Policy in Britain after 1870' (1969) 1 *History of Political Economy* 231–55.

Ibbetson, D., 'Implied Contracts and Restitution: History in the High Court of Australia' (1988) 8 *OJLS* 312–327.

Ibbetson, D., 'Absolute Liability in Contract: The Antecedents of *Paradine v. Jayne*', in F. D. Rose (ed.), *Consensus ad Idem: Essays in the Law of Contract in Honour of Guenter Treitel* (1996), 3–37.

Ilbert, C., 'Sir James Stephen as a Legislator' (1894) 10 *LQR* 222–7.

Jolowicz, J. A., 'Damages in Equity—A Study of Lord Cairns's Act' (1975) 34 *CLJ* 224–52.

Jones, G., 'The Role of Equity in the English Law of Restitution', in E. J. H. Schrage, *Unjust Enrichment* (2nd edn, Berlin, 1999).

Kull, K., 'Restitution as Remedy for Breach of Contract' (1993–4) 67 *Southern California Law Rev.* 1456–1518.

Kull, K., 'James Barr Ames and the Early Modern History of Unjust Enrichment' (2005) 25 *OJLS* 297–319.

Liu, Q., 'Claiming Damages Upon an Anticipatory Breach: Why Should an Acceptance be Necessary?' (2005) 25 *Legal Studies* 559–77.

Lobban, M., 'Contractual Fraud in Law and Equity, c.1750–c.1850' (1997) 17 *OJLS* 441–76.

Lobban, M., 'The Strange Life of the English Civil Jury, 1837–1914', in *The Dearest Birthright of the People of England: The Jury in the History of the Common Law,* ed. J. W. Cairns and G. McLeod (Oxford, 2002), 173–215.

Lobban, M., 'Erlanger v New Sombrero Phosphate Co (1878)', in C. Mitchell and P. Mitchell (eds), *Landmark Cases in the Law of Restitution* (Oxford, 2006), 123–62.

Lobban, M., 'Foakes v. Beer', in C. Mitchell and P. Mitchell (eds), *Landmark Cases in the Law of Contract* (Oxford, 2008), 223–67.

McDermott, P. M., 'Jurisdiction of the Court of Chancery to Award Damages' 108 (1992) *LQR* 652–73.

MacMillan, C., 'How Temptation Led to Mistake: An Explanation of *Bell v. Lever Bros Ltd*', (2003) 119 *LQR* 625–59.

MacMillan, C., 'Mistaken Arguments: The Role of Argument in the Development of a Doctrine of Contractual Mistake in Nineteenth Century England', in A. Lewis and M. Lobban (eds), *Law and History* (Oxford, 2004), 285–315.

MacMillan, C., 'Rogues, Swindlers and Cheats: The Development of Mistake of Identity in English Contract Law' (2005) 64 *CLJ* 711–44.

MacMillan, C., 'Solle v Butcher', in C. Mitchell and P. Mitchell, *Landmark Cases in the Law of Restitution* (Oxford, 2006), 325–60.

MacMillan, C., 'Taylor v Caldwell (1863)', in C. Mitchell and P. Mitchell (eds), *Landmark Cases in the Law of Contract* (Oxford, 2008), 167–203.

Mason, J. W., 'Political Economy and the Response to Socialism in Britain, 1870–1914' (1980) 23 *Historical Journal* 565–87.

Mitchell, C. and Mitchell, C., '*Planché v. Colburn* (1831)', in C. Mitchell and P. Mitchell (eds), *Landmark Cases in the Law of Restitution* (Oxford, 2006), 65–95.

Mitchell, P., 'The Development of Quality Obligations in Sale of Goods' (2001) 117 *LQR* 643–63.

Mitchell, P., 'Hochster v De La Tour (1853)', in C. Mitchell and P. Mitchell (eds), *Landmark Cases in the Law of Contract* (Oxford, 2008), 135–66.

Mitchell, P. and Phillips, J., 'The Contractual Nexus: Is Reliance Necessary?' (2002) 22 *OJLS* 115–34.

Mokyr, J., 'Accounting for the Industrial Revolution', in R. Floud and P. Johnson (eds), *The Cambridge Economic History of Modern Britain: Vol. I: Industrialisation, 1700–1860* (Cambridge, 2004), 1–27.

Morris, R. J., 'Men, Women and Property: The Reform of the Married Women's Property Act, 1870', in F. M. L. Thompson, (ed.), *Landowners, Capitalists, and Entrepreneurs: Essays for Sir John Habakkuk* (Oxford, 1994), 171–91.

Mustill, M., 'Anticipatory Breach of Contract: The Common Law at Work', *Butterworth Lectures 1989–1990* (1990).

O'Sullivan, J., 'In defence of *Foakes v. Beer*' (1996) 55 *CLJ* 219–28.

Palmer, G. E., 'History of Restitution in Anglo-American Law', in *International Encyclopedia of Comparative Law*, vol. X (Tübingen, 1989).

Perillo, J. M., 'Robert J. Pothier's Influence on the Common Law of Contract' (2004–5) 11 *Texas Wesleyan Law Rev.* 267–90.

Phillips J. and French, M., 'Adulteration and Food Law, 1899–1939' (1998) 9 *Twentieth Century History*, 350–69.

Rodger, A., 'The Codification of Commercial Law in Victorian Britain' (1992) 108 *LQR* 570–90.

Simmons, J., 'Railways, Hotels and Tourism in Great Britain 1839–1914' (1984) 19 *Journal of Contemporary History* 201–22.

Simpson, A. W. B., 'Quackery and Contract Law: The Case of the Carbolic Smoke Ball' (1985) 14 *JLS* 344–89.

Simpson, A. W. B., 'Innovation in Nineteenth Century Contract Law', in his *Legal Theory and Legal History: Essays on the Common Law* (1987), 171–202.

Smith, C., 'Allcard v Skinner (1887)', in C. Mitchell and P. Mitchell (eds), *Landmark Cases in the Law of Restitution* (Oxford, 2006), 183–211.

Smith, J. S. and Thomas, J. A. C., 'Pothier and the Three Dots' (1957) 20 *MLR* 38–43.

Smith, L. D., 'Tracing in *Taylor v. Plumer*: Equity in the Court of King's Bench' [1995] *Lloyds Maritime and Commercial Law Quarterly* 240–68.

Soldon, N., 'Laissez-faire as Dogma: The Liberty and Property Defence League, 1882–1914', in K. D. Brown, *Essays in Anti-Labour History* (1974), 208–33.

Stoljar, S. J., 'Conditions, Warranties and Descriptions of Quality in Sale of Goods' (1952) 15 *MLR* 425–45, (1953) 16 *MLR* 174–97.

Stoljar, S. J., 'The Transformations of Account' (1964) 80 *LQR* 203–24 at 215–18.

Swadling, W., 'The Myth of *Phillips v. Homfray*', in W. Swadling and G. Jones (eds), *The Search for Principle: Essays in Honour of Lord Goff of Chieveley* (Oxford, 1999), 277–94.

Swain, W., '*Cutter v Powell* and the Pleading of Claims of Unjust Enrichment', *Restitution Law Review* 11 (2003), 46–56.

Swain, W., 'The Changing Nature of the Doctrine of Consideration, 1750–1850' (2005) 26 *JLH* 55–72.

Swain, W., 'The Will Theory of Contract in the Nineteenth Century: Its Influence and its Limitations', in A. Lewis, P. Brand, and P. Mitchell, *Law in the City: Proceedings of the Seventeenth British Legal History Conference* (Dublin, 2007), 162–80.

Swain, W., 'Third Party Beneficiaries in English Law, 1880–2004', in E. J. H. Schrage (ed.), *Ius Quaesitum Tertio* (Berlin, 2008), 331–56.

Swain W. and Ibbetson, D., 'Third Party Beneficiaries in English Law: From *Dutton v Poole* to *Tweddle v Atkinson*', in E. J. H. Schrage (ed.), *Ius Quaesitum Tertio* (Berlin, 2008), 191–213.

Treitel, G., 'Conditions and Conditions precedent' (1990) 106 *LQR* 185–92.

Waddams, S., 'What *Were* the Principles of Nineteenth-Century Contract Law?', in A. Lewis, P. Brand, and P. Mitchell, *Law in the City: Proceedings of the Seventeenth British Legal History Conference* (Dublin, 2007), 304–18.

Washington, G. T., 'Damages in Contract at Common Law I' (1931) 47 *LQR* 345–79.

Washington, G. T., 'Damages in Contract at Common Law II' (1932) 48 *LQR* 90–108.

Wladis, J. D., 'Common Law and Uncommon Events: The Development of the Doctrine of Impossibility of Performance in English Contract Law' (1986–7) 75 *Georgetown Law Journal* 1575–1631.

Wright, R. A. (Lord), 'Ought the Doctrine of Consideration to be Abolished from the Common Law?' (1936) 49 *Harvard Law Rev.* 1225–53.

Wright, R. A. (Lord), 'Sinclair v. Brougham' (1938) 6 *CLJ* 305–26.

Part Three: Commercial Law

Books

Alborn, T. L., *Conceiving Companies: Joint Stock Politics in Victorian England* (1998).

Alborn, T. L., *Regulated Lives: Life Assurance and British Society, 1800–1914* (Toronto, 2009).

Atiyah, P.S., *The Rise and Fall of Freedom of Contract* (Oxford, 1979).

Boyson, R., *The Ashworth Cotton Enterprise: The Rise and Fall of a Family Firm 1818–80* (Oxford, 1970).

Cato Carter, E. F., *Order out of Chaos: A History of the Loss Adjusting Profession. Part I: Evolution and Early Developments* (1984).

Clark, G., *Betting on Lives: The Culture of Life Insurance in England, 1695–1775* (Manchester, 1999).

Collins, M., *Money and Banking in the UK: A History* (1988).

Cooke, C. A., *Corporation, Trust and Company: An Essay in Legal History* (Manchester, 1950).

Cornish W. R. and de N. Clark, G., *Law and Society in England 1750–1950* (1989).

Cottrell, P. L., *Industrial Finance 1830–1914: The Finance and Organization of English Manufacturing Industry* (1980).

Crouzet F., *The Victorian Economy*, trans. A Forster (1982).

Dickson, P. G. M., *The Sun Insurance Office, 1710–1960* (Oxford, 1960).

Dubois, A. B., *The English Business Company after the Bubble Act* (New York, 1938).

Duffy, I. P. H., *Bankruptcy and Insolvency in London during the Industrial Revolution* (1985).

Farnie, D. A., *The English Cotton Industry and the World Market 1815–1896* (Oxford, 1979).

Finn, M. C., *The Character of Credit: Personal Debt in English Culture, 1740–1914* (Cambridge, 2003).

Freyer, T., *Regulating Big Business: Antitrust in Great Britain and America, 1880–1990* (Cambridge, 1992).

Goode, R. M., *Hire-Purchase Law and Practice* (1962, with 2 edns to 1970).

Hannah, L., *The Rise of the Corporate Economy* (1976).

Hardaker, A., *A Brief History of Pawnbroking* (1892).

Harris, R., *Industrializing English Law: Entrepreneurship and Business Organization, 1720–1844* (Cambridge, 2000).

Hilton, B., *Corn Cash Commerce: The Economic Policies of the Tory Governments 1815–1830* (Oxford, 1977).

Hilton, B., *The Age of Atonement: The Influence of Evangelicalism on Social and Economic Thought, 1785–1865* (Oxford, 1988).

Holden, J. M., *The History of Negotiable Instruments in English Law* (1955).

Hunt, B. C., *The Development of the Business Corporation in England 1800–1867* (Cambridge, MA, 1936).

Jefferys, J. B., *Business Organisation in Great Britain, 1856–1914* (New York, 1977).

Johnson, P., *Saving and Spending: The Working Class Economy in Britain, 1870–1939* (Oxford, 1985).

King, W. T. C., *History of the London Discount Market* (1936).

Kostal, R. W., *Law and English Railway Capitalism, 1825–1875* (Oxford, 1994).

Kynaston, D., *The City of London. Vol. I: A World of its Own 1815–1890* (1994).

Lester, V. M., *Victorian Insolvency: Bankruptcy, Imprisonment for Debt and Company Winding Up in Nineteenth Century England* (Oxford, 1995).

Mitchell, C., *The Law of Subrogation* (Oxford, 1994).

Mitchell, C., *The Law of Contribution and Reimbursement* (Oxford, 2003).

Mitchell C. and Watterson, S., *Subrogation: Law and Practice* (Oxford, 2007).

Michie, R. C., *The London and New York Stock Exchanges, 1850–1914* (1987).

Michie, R. C., *The London Stock Exchange: A History* (Oxford, 1999).

Morgan E. V. and Thomas, W. A., *The Stock Exchange: Its History and Principles* (1962).

Nishimura, S., *The Decline of Inland Bills of Exchange in the London Money Market, 1855–1913* (Cambridge, 1971).

Oldham, J. *The Mansfield Manuscripts and the Growth of English Law in the Eighteenth Century*, 2 vols (1992).

Pearson, R., *Insuring the Industrial Revolution: Fire Insurance in Great Britain, 1700–1850* (Aldershot, 2004).

Polden, P., *A History of the County Court, 1846–1971* (Cambridge, 1999).

Raynes, H., *A History of British Insurance* (1948).

Robb, G., *White Collar Crime in Modern England: Financial Fraud and Business Morality, 1845–1929* (Cambridge, 1992).

Rogers, J. S., *The Early History of the Law of Bills and Notes: A Study in the Origins of Anglo-American Commercial Law* (Cambridge, 1995).

Searle, G. R., *Entrepreneurial Politics in Mid-Victorian Britain* (Oxford, 1993).

Searle, G. R., *Morality and the Market in Victorian Britain* (Oxford, 1998).

Shapiro, S., *Capital and the Cotton Industry in the Industrial Revolution* (Ithaca NY, 1967).

Supple, B., *The Royal Exchange Assurance: A History of British Insurance 1720–1970* (Cambridge, 1970).

Taylor, J., *Creating Capitalism: Joint Stock Enterprise in British Politics and Culture, 1800–1870* (Woodbridge, 2006).

Tebbutt, M., *Making Ends Meet: Pawnbroking and Working Class Credit* (Leicester, 1983).

Thomas, S. E., *The Rise and Growth of Joint Stock Banking* (1934).

Trebilcock, C., *Phoenix Assurance and the Development of British Insurance, Vol. 1: 1782–1870* (Cambridge, 1985).

Westall O. M. (ed.), *The Historian and the Business of Insurance* (Manchester, 1984).

Wright C. and Fayle, C. E., *A History of Lloyds* (1928).

Jenkins D. and Yoneyama, T., *History of Insurance*, 8 vols (2000)

Weiss, B., *The Hell of the English: Bankruptcy and the Victorian Novel* (Lewisburg, 1986).

Ziegler, D., *Central Bank, Peripheral Industry: The Bank of England in the Provinces, 1826– 1913* (Leicester, 1990).

Secondary sources: articles

Alborn, T. L., 'A Calculating Profession: Victorian Actuaries among the Statisticians', in M. Power (ed.), *Accounting and Science: Natural Enquiry and Commercial Reason* (Cambridge, 1994), 81–119.

Alborn, T. L., 'The First Fund Managers: Life Insurance Bonuses in Victorian Britain' (2002) 45 *Victorian Studies* 65–92.

Alborn, T. L., 'Dirty Laundry: Exposing Bad Behavior in Life Insurance Trials, 1830–1890', in M. Finn, M. Lobban, and J. B. Taylor (eds), *Legitimacy and Illegitimacy in Law, Literature and History* (Basingstoke, 2009).

Anderson, M., Edwards J. R., and Matthews D., 'A Study of the Quoted Company Audit Market in 1886' (1996) 6 *Accounting, Business and Financial History* 363–87.

Anderson, M., Edwards J. R., and Chandler, R. A. ' "A Public Expert in Matters of Account": Defining the Chartered Accountant in England and Wales' (2007) 17 *Accounting, Business and Financial History* 381–423.

Armour, J., 'The Chequered History of the Floating Charge' (2004) 13 *Griffith Law Rev.* 25–56.

Armstrong, J., 'The Rise and Fall of the Company Promoter and the Financing of British Industry', in J. J. Van Helten and Y. Cassis (eds), *Capitalism in a Mature Economy: Financial Institutions, Capital Exports and British Industry 1870–1939* (Aldershot, 1990), 115–38.

Batzel, V. M., 'Parliament, Businessmen and Bankruptcy, 1825–1883: A Study in Middle Class Alienation' (1983) 18 *Canadian Journal of History* 171–86.

Boyer, G. R., 'Living Standards, 1860–1939', in R. Floud and P. Johnson (eds), *The Cambridge Economic History of Modern Britain, Vol. II: Economic Maturity 1860–1939* (Cambridge, 2004), 280–313.

Boyns T. and Edwards, J. R., 'The Construction of Cost Accounting Systems on Britain to 1900: The Case of the Coal, Iron and Steel Industries' (1997) 39 *Business History* 1–29.

Cassis, Y., 'The Emergence of a New Financial Institution: Investment Trusts in Britain, 1870–1939', in J. J. Van Helten and Y. Cassis (ed.), *Capitalism in a Mature Economy: Financial Institutions, Capital Exports and British Industry, 1870–1939* (Aldershot, 1990).

Cornish, W. R. 'Legal Control over Cartels and Monopolization, 1880–1914: A Comparison', in N. Horn, and J. Kocka, *Law and the Formation of the Big Enterprises in the 19th and early 20th Centuries* (Göttingen, 1979), 280–305.

Crafts, N. F. R., 'English Workers' Living Standards During the Industrial Revolution: Some Remaining Problems' (1985) 45 *JEH* 139–44.

Di Martino, P., 'Approaching Disaster: Personal Bankruptcy Legislation in England and Italy, c.1880–1939' (2005) 47 *Business History* 23–43.

Edey H. C. and Panitpakdi, P., 'British Company Accounting and the Law, 1844–1900', in A. C. Littleton and B. S. Yamey (eds), *Studies in the History of Accounting* (1956), 356–79.

Edwards J. R. and Webb, K. M., 'The Influence of Company Law on Corporate Reporting Procedures, 1865–1929: An Exemplification' (1982) 24 *Business History* 259–79.

Edwards J. R. and Webb, K. M., 'Use of Table A by Companies Registering under the Companies Act 1862' (1985) 15 *Accounting and Business Research* 177–97.

Feinstein, C. H., 'Pessimism Perpetuated: Real Wages and the Standard of Living in Britain During and After the Industrial Revolution' (1998) 58 *JEH* 625–58.

Ferguson, R. B., 'Legal Ideology and Commercial Interests: The Social Origins of the Commercial Law Codes' (1977) 4 *British Journal of Law and Society* 18–38.

Finn, M. C., 'Being in Debt in Dickens' London: Fact, Fictional Representation and the Nineteenth-century Prison' (1996) 1 *Journal of Victorian Culture* 203–26.

Finn, M. C., 'Working Class Women and the Contest for Consumer Control in Victorian County Courts' (1998) 161 *P & P* 116–54.

French, E. A., 'The Evolution of Dividend Law in England', in W. T. Baxter and S. Davidson, *Studies in Accounting* (1977), 306–31.

Getzler, J., 'Duty of Care', in P. Birks and A. Pretto (eds), *Breach of Trust* (Oxford, 2002), 41–74.

Getzler, J., 'The Role of Security over Future and Circulating Capital: Evidence from the British Economy circa 1850–1920', in J. Getzler and J. Payne (eds), *Company Charges:* Spectrum *and Beyond* (Oxford, 2006), 227–51.

Getzler J. and Macnair, M., 'The Firm as an Entity before the Companies Acts', in P. Brand, K. Costello, and W. N. Osborough (eds), *Adventures of the Law: Proceedings of the Sixteenth British Legal History Conference, Dublin* (Dublin, 2005), 267–88.

Gregory R. and Walton, P., 'Fixed Charges over Changing Assets—The Possession and Control Heresy' [1998] *Company Financial and Insolvency Law Rev.* 68–87.

Gregory R. and Walton, P., 'Fixed and Floating Charges—A Revelation' [2001] *Lloyds Maritime and Commercial Law Quarterly* 123–49.

Harris, R., 'Government and the Economy, 1688–1850', in R. Floud and P. Johnson (eds), *The Cambridge Economic History of Modern Britain, Vol. I: Industrialisation 1700–1860* (Cambridge, 2004), 204–37.

Hudson, P., 'Industrial Organisation and Structure', in R. Floud and P. Johnson (eds), *The Cambridge Economic History of Modern Britain, Vol. I: Industrialisation 1700–1860* (Cambridge, 2004), 28–56.

Ireland, P., 'The Triumph of the Company Legal Form, 1856–1914', in J. Adams (ed.), *Essays for Clive Schmitthoff* (Abingdon, 1983), 29–58.

Ireland, P., 'Capitalism without the Capitalist: The Joint Stock Company Share and the Emergence of the Modern Doctrine of Separate Corporate Personality' (1996) 17 *Journal of Legal History* 40–72.

Itzkowitz, D. C., 'Fair Enterprise or Extravagant Speculation: Investment, Speculation, and Gambling in Victorian England' (2002) 45 *Victorian Studies* 121–47.

Jefferys, J. B., 'The Denomination and Character of Shares, 1855–85' (1946) 16 *EHR* 45–55.

Johnson, P., 'Class Law in Victorian England' (1993) 141 *P & P* 146–69.

Johnson, P., 'Creditors, Debtors and the Law in Victorian and Edwardian England', in W. Steinmetz (ed.), *Private Law and Social Inequality in the Industrial Age* (Oxford, 2000), 485–504.

Jones, S., 'A Cross-sectional Analysis of Recommendations for Company Financial Disclosure and Auditing by Nineteenth Century Parliamentary Witnesses' (1995) 5 *Accounting, Business and Financial History* 159–86.

Jones, S., 'The Professional Background of Company Law Pressure Groups' (1997) 7 *Accounting, Business & Financial History* 233–42.

Kercher, B., 'The Transformation of Imprisonment for Debt in England, 1828 to 1838' (1984) 2 *Australian Journal of Law and Society* 60–109.

Kingston, C., 'Marine Insurance in Britain and America, 1720–1844: A Comparative Institutional Analysis' (2007) 67 *JEH* 379–409.

Lindert P. H. and Williamson, J. G., 'English Workers' Living Standards During the Industrial Revolution: A New Look' (1983) 36 *EHR* (2 s) 1–25.

Lindert P. H. and Williamson, J. G., 'English Workers Real Wages: A Reply to Crafts' (1985) 45 *JEH* 145–53.

Lobban, M., 'Corporate Identity and Limited Liability in France and England, 1825–67' (1996) 25 *Anglo-Am. Law Rev.* 397–440.

Lobban, M., 'Nineteenth Century Frauds in Company Formation: *Derry* v. *Peek* in Context' (1996) 112 *LQR* 287–334.

Lobban, M., 'Erlanger v New Sombrero Phosphate Company', in C. Mitchell and P. Mitchell (eds), *Landmark Cases in the Law of Restitution* (Oxford, 2006).

Lobban, M., 'Preparing for Fusion: Reforming the Nineteenth Century Court of Chancery' (2004) 22 *LHR* 389–427, 565–600.

McEldowney, J. F., 'William Neilson Hancock (1820–1888)', (1985) 20 *Irish Jurist.* 378–402.

Mokyr, J., 'Is There Still Life in the Pessimist Case? Consumption During the Industrial Revolution, 1790–1850' (1988) 48 *JEH* 69–92.

Newton L. and Cottrell, P. L., 'Joint Stock Banking in the English Provinces 1826–1857: To Branch or Not To Branch' (1998) 27 *Business and Economic History* 115–28.

Nolan, R.C., 'Property in a Fund' (2004) 120 *LQR* 108–36.

Pearson, R., 'Thrift or Dissipation? The Business of Life Assurance in the Early Nineteenth Century' (1990) 43 *EHR* 236–54.

Pearson, R., 'Taking Risks and Containing Competition: Diversification and Oligopoly in the Fire Insurance Markets of the North of England During the Early Nineteenth Century' (1993) 46 *EHR* 39–64.

Pearson, R., 'Towards an Historical Model of Services Innovation: The Case of the Insurance Industry, 1700–1014' (1997) 50 *EHR* 235–56.

Pennington, R. R., 'The Genesis of the Floating Charge' (1960) 23 *MLR* 630–46.

Poovey, M., 'Writing about Finance in Victorian England: Disclosure and Secrecy in the Culture of Investment' (2002) 45 *Victorian Studies* 17–41.

Reid, J. M., 'Judicial Views on Accounting in Britain before 1889' (1987)17 *Accounting and Business Research* 247–58.

Robb, G., 'The English Dreyfus Case: Florence Maybrick and the Sexual Double Standard', in G. Robb and N. Erber, *Disorder in the Court: Trials and Sexual Conflict at the Turn of the Century* (Basingstoke, 1999), 57–77.

Rodger, A., 'The Codification of Commercial Law in Victorian Britain' (1992) 108 *LQR* 570–90.

Rubin, G. R., 'Aron Salomon and his Circle', in J. Adams (ed.), *Essays for Clive Schmitthoff* (Abingdon, 1983), 99–120.

Rubin, G. R., 'Law, Poverty and Imprisonment for Debt, 1869–1914', in G. R. Rubin and D. Sugarman, *Law, Economy and Society: Essays in the History of English Law 1750–1914* (Abingdon, 1984), 241–99.

Rubin, G. R., 'The County Courts and the Tally Trade, 1846–1914', in G. R. Rubin and D. Sugarman (eds), *Law, Economy and Society, 1750–1914: Essays in the History of English Law* (Abingdon, 1984), 321–48.

Rubin, G. R., 'From Packmen, Tallymen and "Perambulating Scotchmen" to Credit Drapers' Associations, c. 1840–1914' (1986) 28 *Business History* 206–25.

Saville, J., 'Sleeping Partnerships and Limited Liability, 1850–1856' (1956) 8 *EHR* (2 s) 418–33.

Scott, P., 'The Twilight World of Inter-War Hire Purchase' (2002) 177 *P & P* 196–225.

Shannon, H. A., 'The First Five Thousand Limited Companies and their Duration',(1932) 3 *Economic History* 396–424.

Shannon, H. A., 'The Limited Companies of 1866–83' (1933) 4 *EHR* 290–316.

Stebbings, C., 'Statutory Railway Mortgage Debentures and the Courts in the Nineteenth Century' (1987) 8 *JLH* 36–47.

Stebbings, C., 'The Legal Nature of Shares in Landowning Joint-stock Companies in the Nineteenth Century' (1987) 8 *JLH* 25–35.

Stebbings, C., "'Officialism': Law, Bureaucracy and Ideology in Late Victorian England', in A. Lewis and M. Lobban, *Law and History: Current Legal Issues 6* (Oxford, 2004), 317–42.

Taylor, J., 'Commercial Fraud and Public Men in Victorian Britain' (2005) *Historical Research* 230–52.

Taylor, J., 'Company Fraud in Victorian Britain: The Royal British Bank Scandal of 1856' (2007) *English Historical Review* 700–24.

Yamey, B. S., 'The Case Law Relating to Company Dividends', in W. T. Baxter and S. Davidson (eds), *Studies in Accounting Theory* (1962), 428–42.

Part Four: Tort

Books

Ashby E. and Anderson, M., *The Politics of Clean Air* (Oxford, 1981).

Ashworth, W., *The Genesis of Modern British Town Planning: A Study in Economic and Social History of the Nineteenth and Twentieth Centuries* (1954).

Atiyah, P. S., *The Rise and Fall of Freedom of Contract* (Oxford, 1979).

Bagwell, P. S., *The Transport Revolution* (2nd edn, 1988) (1st edn, 1974).

Baker, J. H., *The Oxford History of the Laws of England*, Vol. 6 (Oxford, 2003).

Baker J. H. and Milsom, S. F. C., *Sources of English Legal History: Private Law to 1750* (1986)

Bartrip P. W. J. and Burman, S. B., *The Wounded Soldiers of Industry: Industrial Compensation Policy, 1833–1897* (Oxford, 1983).

Bartrip, P. W. J., *Workmen's Compensation in Twentieth Century Britain: Law, History and Social Policy* (Aldershot, 1987).

Cawthorn, E. A., *Job Accidents and the Law in England's Early Railway Age: Origins of Employer Liability and Workmen's Compensation* (Lampeter, 1997).

Coleman, J. L., *The Practice of Principle* (Oxford, 2001).

Cordery, S., *British Friendly Societies, 1750–1914* (Basingstoke, 2003).

Cornish W. R. and de N. Clark, G., *Law and Society in England 1750–1950* (1989).

Curthoys, M., *Governments, Labour and the Law in Mid-Victorian Britain* (Oxford, 2004).

Daunton M. (ed.), *The Cambridge Urban History of Britain, Vol. III: 1840–1950* (Cambridge, 2000).

Duman, D., *The Judicial Bench in England 1727–1875: The Reshaping of a Professional Elite* (1982).

Duxbury, N., *Frederick Pollock and the English Juristic Tradition* (Oxford, 2004).

Freyer, T., *Regulating Big Business: Antitrust in Great Britain and America, 1880–1990* (Cambridge, 1992).

Gerhold, D., *Road Transport Before the Railways: Russell's London Flying Waggons* (Cambridge, 1993).

Getzler, J., *A History of Water Rights at Common Law* (Oxford, 2004).

Gilbert, B. B., *The Evolution of National Insurance in Great Britain: The Origins of the Welfare State* (1966).

Gordley, J., *Foundations of Private Law: Property, Tort, Contract, Unjust Enrichment* (Oxford, 2006).

Gosden, P. H. J. H., *The Friendly Societies in England, 1815–1875* (Manchester, 1961).

Halliday, S., *The Great Stink of London: Sir Joseph Bazalgette and the Cleansing of the Victorian Capital* (Stroud, 1999).

Hamlin, C., *Public Health and Social Justice in the Age of Chadwick: Britain, 1800–54* (Cambridge, 1998).

Hanes, D. G., *The First British Workmen's Compensation Act, 1897* (1968).

Hendrick, H., *Children, Childhood and English Society, 1880–1990* (Cambridge, 1997).

Hennock, E. P., *Fit and Proper Persons: Ideal and Reality in Nineteenth-Century Urban Government* (1973).

Hennock, E. P., *British Social Reform and German Precedents: The Case of Social Insurance 1880–1914* (Oxford, 1987).

Hopkins, E., *Working Class Self Help in Nineteenth Century England* (1995).

Horwitz, M. J., *The Transformation of American Law, 1780–1860* (Cambridge MA, 1977).

Howe, M. D. (ed.), *The Pollock Holmes Letters*, 2 vols (Cambridge, 1942).

Ibbetson, D. J., *A Historical Introduction to the Law of Obligations* (Oxford, 1999).

Karsten, P., *Heart versus Head: Judge-Made Law in Nineteenth Century America* (1997).

Kostal, R. W., *Law and Railway Capitalism, 1825–1875* (Oxford, 1994).

Kramer, M. H., Simmonds, N. E. and Steiner, H., *A Debate over Rights* (Oxford, 1998).

Lewis, J. P., *Building Cycles and Britain's Growth* (1965).

Luckin, B., *Pollution and Control: A Social History of the Thames in the Nineteenth Century* (Bristol, 1986).

Lucy, W., *Philosophy of Private Law* (Oxford, 2007).

Mendelson, D., *The Interfaces of Medicine and Law: The History of the Liability for Negligently Caused Psychiatric Injury (Nervous Shock)* (Aldershot, 1998).

Mitchell, P., *The Making of the Modern Law of Defamation* (Oxford, 2005).

O'Connell, S., *The Car and British Society: Class, Gender and Motoring, 1896–1939* (Manchester, 1998).

Oldham, J., *The Mansfield Manuscripts and the Growth of English Law in the Eighteenth Century*, 2 vols (1992).

Orth, J. V., *Combination and Conspiracy: A Legal History of Trade Unionism, 1721–1906* (Oxford, 1991).

Parris, H., *Government and the Railways in Nineteenth-Century Britain* (1965).

Posner, R., *Economic Analysis of Law* (Boston, 1972, with 7 edns to 2007).

Richardson, K., *The British Motor Industry, 1896–1939* (1977)

Simpson, A. W. B., *Leading Cases in the Common Law* (Oxford, 1995).

Steedman, C., *Childhood, Culture and Class in Britain: Margaret McMillan, 1860–1931* (1990).

Sullivan, E. T., *The Political Economy of the Sherman Act* (Oxford, 1991).

Summerson, J., *The London Building World of the 1860s* (1973).

Taggart, M., *Private Property and Abuse of Rights in Victorian England: The Story of Edward Pickles and the Bradford Water Supply* (Oxford, 2002).

Thorold, P., *The Motoring Age: The Automobile and Britain 1896–1939* (2003).

Thorsheim, P., *Inventing Pollution: Coal, Smoke and Culture in Britain since 1800*, (Athens, Ohio, 2006).

Weinrib, E. J., *The Idea of Private Law* (Cambridge MA, 1995).

Weir, T., *Economic Torts* (Oxford, 1997).

White, G. E., *Tort Law in America: An Intellectual History* (Oxford, 1980, with 2 edns to 2003).

Wohl, A. S., *Endangered Lives: Public Health in Victorian Britain* (1983).

Secondary sources: articles

Bartrip, P. W. J., 'The State and the Steam-boiler in Nineteenth Century Britain' (1980) 25 *International Review of Social History* 77–105.

Batson, R. N., 'Trespassing Children: A Study in Expanding Liability' (1966) 20 *Vanderbilt Law Rev.* 139–69.

Benson, J., 'The Thrift of English Coal-Miners, 1860–95' (1978) 31 *EHR* n.s. 410–18.

Benson J. and Sykes, R., 'Trade Unionism and the Use of the Law: English Coalminers' Unions and Legal Redress for Industrial Accidents, 1860–97' (1997) 3 *Historical Studies in Industrial Relations* 27–48.

Brenner, J. F., 'Nuisance Law and the Industrial Revolution' (1974) 3 *JLS* 403–31.

Buckland, W. W., 'The Duty to Take Care' (1935) 51 *LQR* 637–49 at 639.

Cawthorn, E., 'New Life for the Deodand: Coroners' Inquests and Occupational Death in England, 1830–1846' (1989) 33 *AJLH* 137–47 at 141.

Coase, R., The Problem of Social Cost' (1960) 3 *JLE* 1–69.

Cordery, S., 'Friendly Societies and the Discourse of Respectability in Britain 1825–1875' (1995) 34 *Journal of British Studies* 35–58.

Dingle, A. E., ' "The Monster Nuisance of All": Landowners, Alkali Manufacturers, and Air Pollution, 1828–64' (1982) 35 *EHR* (2 s) 529–48.

Fletcher, G. P., 'Fairness and Utility in Tort Theory' (1972) 85 *Harvard Law Rev.* 537–73.

Getzler, J., 'The Fate of the Civil Jury in Late Victorian England: Malicious Prosecution as a Test Case', in J. W. Cairns and G. McLeod, *The Dearest Birth*

Right of the People of England: The Jury in the History of the Common Law (Oxford, 2002), 217–37.

Gilles, S. G., 'Inevitable Accident in Classical English Tort Law' (1994) 43 *Emory Law Journal* 575.

Goddard, N., ' "A Mine of Wealth"? The Victorians and the Agricultural Value of Sewage', (1996) 22 *J. Hist. Geography* 274–90.

Goodhart, A. L., 'The Foundations of Tortious Liability' (1938) 2 *MLR* 1–13.

Hall, C. G., 'An Unsearchable Providence: The Lawyer's Concept of an Act of God' (1993) 13 *OJLS* 227–48.

Hamlin, C., 'Muddling in Bumbledon: On the Enormity of Large Sanitary Improvements in Four British Towns, 1855–1885' (1988–9) 32 *Victorian Studies* 55–83.

Hamlin, C., 'Public Sphere to Public Health: The Transformation of "Nuisance"', in S. Sturdy, *Medicine, Health and the Public Sphere in Britain, 1600–2000* (2002), 189–204.

Harrington, R., 'The Railway Accident: Trains, Trauma and Technological Crises in Nineteenth Century Britain', in M. S. Micale and P. Lerner, *Traumatic Pasts: History, Psychiatry and Trauma in the Modern Age, 1870–1930* (Cambridge, 2001), 31–56.

Harrington, R., 'Railway Safety and Railway Slaughter: Railway Accidents, Government and Public in Victorian Britain' (2003) 8 *Journal of Victorian Culture* 187–207.

Hawes, R., 'The Control of Alkali Pollution in St Helens, 1862–1890' (1995) 1 *Environment and History* 159–71.

Hudson, P., 'Industrial Organisation and Structure', in R. Floud and P. Johnson (eds), *The Cambridge Economic History of Modern Britain. Volume I: Industrialisation, 1700–1860* (Cambridge, 2004), 28–56.

Ibbetson, D. J., ' "The Law of Business Rome": Foundations of the Anglo-American Tort of Negligence' (1999) 52 *CLP* 74–109.

Ibbetson, D. J., 'The Tort of Negligence in the Common Law in the Nineteenth and Twentieth Centuries', in E. J. H. Schrage (ed.), *Negligence* (Berlin, 2001), 229–71.

Jones, G., 'Per Quod Servitium Amisit' (1958) 74 *LQR* (1958), 39.

Kaczorowski, R. J., 'The Common-Law Background of Nineteenth Century Tort Law' (1990) 51 *Ohio State LJ* 1127–99.

Kidner, R., 'A History of the Fatal Accidents Acts' (1999) 50 *Northern Ireland Legal Quarterly* 318–35.

Klarman, M. J., 'Judges versus the Unions: The Development of British Labor Law, 1867–1913' (1989) 75 *Virginia Law Rev.* 1487–1602.

Kretzmer, D., 'Transformation of Tort Liability in the Nineteenth Century: The Visible Hand' (1984) 4 *OJLS* 46–87.

Lester, V. M., 'The Employers' Liability/Workmen's Compensation Debate of the 1890s revisited' (2001) 44 *Historical Journal* 471–95.

Lobban, M., 'The Strange Life of the English Civil Jury, 1837–1914', in J. W. Cairns and G. Mcleod (eds), *The Dearest Birthright of the People of England: The Jury in the History of the Common Law* (Oxford, 2002), 173–215.

Luckin, Bill, 'Pollution in the City', in M. Daunton (ed.), *The Cambridge Urban History of Britain, III: 1840–1950* (Cambridge, 2000), 207–28.

McLaren, J. P. S., 'Nuisance Law and the Industrial Revolution—Some Lessons from Social History' (1983) 3 *OJLS* 155–221.

Mallalie, W. C., 'Joseph Chamberlain and Workmen's Compensation' (1950) 10 *JEH* 45–57.

Mitchell, P., 'Malice in Defamation' (1998) 114 *LQR* 638–64.

Murphy, J., 'The Merits of *Rylands v Fletcher*' 24 *OJLS* (2004), 643–69.

Newark, F. H., 'The Boundaries of Nuisance' (1949) 65 *LQR* 480–90.

Newark, F. H., 'Non-Natural User and Rylands v Fletcher' (1961) 24 *MLR* 557–71.

Nolan, D., 'The Distinctiveness of *Rylands v Fletcher*' (2005) 121 *LQR* 421–51.

Odden, K. M., '"Able and intelligent medical men meeting together": The Victorian Railway Crash, Medical Jurisprudence, and the Rise of Medical Authority' (2003) 8 *Journal of Victorian Culture* 33–54.

Palmer V., 'Why Privity Entered Tort—An Historical Reexamination of *Winterbottom* v. *Wright*' (1983) 27 *AJLH* 85–98.

Pagan, J. R., 'English Carriers' Common-Law Right to Reject Undeclared Cargo: The Myth of the Closed Container Conundrum' (1981–2) 23 *William & Mary Law Rev.* 791–833.

Pollock, F., 'The Snail in the Bottle, and Thereafter' (1933) 49 *LQR* (1933), 22–6.

Pontin, B., 'Tort Law and Victorian Government Growth: The Historiographical Significance of Tort in the Shadow of Chemical Pollution and Factory Safety Regulation (1998) 18 *OJLS* 661–80.

Prichard, M. J., 'Trespass, Case and the Rule in *Williams v Holland*' (1964) *CLJ* 234–53.

Prichard, M. J., '*Scott v Shepherd* (1773) and the Emergence of the Tort of Negligence', *The Selden Society Lectures, 1952–2001* (Buffalo, 2003), 415–57.

Rabin, R. L., 'The Historical Development of the Fault Principle: A Reinterpretation' (1980–1) 15 *Georgia Law Rev.* 925–61.

Reed, C. M., '*Derry v. Peek* and Negligence' (1987) 8 *JLH* 64–78.

Rees R., 'The South Wales Copper-Smoke Dispute, 1833–95' (1980–1) 10 *Welsh History Review* 480–96.

Rosenthal, L., 'Economic Efficiency, Nuisance and Sewage: New Lessons from *Attorney General* v. *Council of the Borough of Birmingham* 1858–95' (2007) 36 *JLS* 27–62.

Sales, P., 'The Tort of Conspiracy and Civil Secondary Liability' (1990) 49 *CLJ* 491–514.

Schwarz, G. T., 'Tort Law and the Economy in Nineteenth Century America' (1981) 90 *YLJ* 1717–75.

Simpson, A. W. B., *Victorian Law and the Industrial Spirit* (1995).

Simpson, A. W. B., 'Coase v Pigou Reexamined' (1996) 25 *JLS* 53–97.

Spencer, J. R., 'Motor-cars and the Rule in *Rylands v. Fletcher*: A Chapter of Accidents in the History of Law and Motoring' (1983) 42 *CLJ* 65–84.

Stein, M. A., '*Priestley* v. *Fowler* (1837) and the Emerging Tort of Negligence' (2002–3) 44 *Boston College Law Rev.* 689–731.

Stein, M. A., 'Victorian Tort Liability for Workplace Injuries' (2008) *Illinois Law Rev.* 933–84.

Thompson, J., 'The Genesis of the 1906 Trades Disputes Act: Liberalism, Trade Unions and the Law' (1998) 9 *Twentieth Century History* 175–200.

Vandevelde, K. J., 'A History of Prima Facie Tort: The Origins of a General Theory of Intentional Tort' (1990) 19 *Hofstra Law Rev.* 447–97.

Waddams, S. M., 'Johanna Wagner and the Rival Opera Houses' (2001) 117 *LQR* 431–58.

Williams, G. L., 'The Foundation of Tortious Liability' (1939) 7 *CLJ* 111–32.

Winfield, P. H., 'The History of Negligence in the Law of Torts' (1926) 42 *LQR* 184–201.

Winfield, P. H., 'The Foundation of Liability in Tort'(1927) 27 *Columbia Law Rev.* 1–11.

Winfield, P. H., 'Duty in Tortious Negligence' (1934) 34 *Columbia Law Rev.* 40–66.

INDEX OF NAMES

This index relates mainly to persons who were active in the period 1820–1914. Double surnames are given under the first of the names. Peers with titles differing from their family name are given under the family name, with a cross-reference from the title.
* indicates a person who served as a superior court judge in Britain and/or as a judicial member of the House of Lords. The same indication is given to persons of equivalent status in other jurisdictions.
** indicates a person who served as a County Court judge.
*** indicates a person who served as a Stipendiary Magistrate or Recorder, or in other judicial office not mentioned above.

Abbott, C. (Lord Tenterden) * 99, 115, 169, 364, 447, 496, 498, 527, 534, 573, 586, 589, 617, 713, 748, 753, 759, 773, 915, 916, 1036, 1096, 1118, 1136

Abinger (Lord) *see* Scarlett, J.

Adderley, Sir Charles 1081

Addison, C.G. 302, 313, 337, 374, 389, 398, 505, 508, 880, 893, 934

Alderson, Sir E.H. * 99, 143, 446, 533, 536, 541, 544, 900, 911, 925–6, 942, 954, 998–9, 1003, 1037, 1133

Alvanley (Lord) *see* Arden, R.P. *

Ames, J.B. 310, 313

Amphlett, Sir R.P. * 938

Andrews, W.D. * 995

Anson, Sir W.R., Bt 308, 310–11, 313, 351, 355 365, 376, 380–2, 387, 390, 395–6, 433, 469, 505 517, 520
    on 'quasi-contract', 569

Arden, R.P. (Lord Alvanley) * 21, 519

Arnould, J. 699

Ashley, C. 356, 397

Ashurst (or Ashhurst), Sir W.H.* 133, 491, 532

Atiyah, P.S. 297–8, 315

Atkin, J.R. (Lord Atkin of Aberdovey) * 944

Atkinson, J. (Lord) * 982, 988, 1028

Attenborough, R. 849

Austin, J. 242, 306, 568, 925–6

Ayrton, W.S. *** 812

Bacon, F. (Viscount St Alban) 928, 950

Bacon, Sir J. * 147–8, 345, 443–4

Bacon, M. 1125

Baggallay, Sir R. * 119, 583

Bagshawe, W.H.G. ** 842

Bass, M. 840–1

Bayley, Sir J. * 331, 498, 540, 574, 585, 586, 587, 708, 731, 751, 767, 906–8, 1038

Beale, J.H. 382

Beawes, W. 756

Bedwell, F.A. ** 840

Bellenden Ker, C.H. 23, 49, 51–2, 60–1, 63, 78, 181, 191, 620–1, 626

Bellot, H.H. 868

Benjamin, J.P. 308, 345, 433, 466, 484–5, 510–11, 759

Bentham, J. 50–1

Best, W.D. (Lord Wynford) * 38, 481, 527–8, 577, 712, 742, 749, 770–1, 895, 910, 914, 1120

Bethell, R. (Lord Westbury) * 8, 89, 194, 198, 211, 368, 422–3, 528, 650–1, 818–20, 822, 837, 1070, 1073, 1075, 1100

Beven, T. 948–9, 955–6, 982–3, 995

Bickersteth, H. (Lord Langdale) * 24, 35, 236, 248, 261, 275, 437, 762

Blackburn, C. (Lord) * 34, 45, 99–100, 302, 304, 308, 339, 341–3, 386–7, 424, 449–50, 452, 465–6, 483, 488, 493, 503, 514–15, 517, 519–20, 539, 658, 708, 749, 764, 776, 898, 921, 930–1, 938–40, 962, 966, 972, 1073, 1083, 1104, 1120, 1123, 1125, 1139–40, 1143–4, 1147, 1150

Blackburne, F. * 929

Blackstone, Sir W. * 98, 316, 887, 917

Bolland, W. * 1134

Bompas, C.C. 919

Bosanquet, Sir J.B. * 362, 364–5, 918

Bovill, Sir W. * 581, 954–5, 971, 979

Bowen, C.S.C. (Lord) * 354–5, 366, 490–1, 580, 582, 604, 695, 1008, 1014, 1050–2, 1058, 1062, 1145

Bramwell, G.W. (Lord)* 44, 299, 341–2, 344, 353, 410, 429–31, 455, 464, 489, 513, 517, 525, 546, 548, 592–3, 625–6, 920, 922, 964, 968, 974, 1007, 1012, 1052, 1073, 1098–9, 1103–4, 1142–3, 1147, 1149

Bray, R.M. * 873

Brett, W.B. (Viscount Esher) * 342, 348–9, 376, 483, 494, 505–6, 516, 548, 660, 671, 687, 700, 724–5, 763, 890, 893, 937, 939–41, 945–6, 948–9, 951–2, 957, 970, 974,

981, 988, 990, 1013–15, 1033, 1046, 1049,
    1051–8, 1061–2, 1086, 1089, 1119
Brodie, P.B. 60, 73
Brougham, H.P. (Lord Brougham and
    Vaux) * 28, 39, 71–2, 145–6, 159–60,
    248, 288, 405–6, 415, 749, 795–7, 805–8,
    810, 813–14, 836
Bruce, G. * 1130
Bryan, Sir T. * 342
Buckley, H.B. (Lord Wrenbury) * 156, 661,
    667, 1101
Buer, H. 859–60
Bullen, E. 595
Buller, Sir F.* 525–6, 592, 904
Burnet, T. * 789
Burrough, Sir J. * 337
Byles, Sir J.B. * 379, 731, 738, 747, 859,
    1008, 1098

Cairns, H.C. (Earl Cairns) * 29, 91–3, 107, 197,
    200, 208, 211, 340, 424, 466, 603, 648,
    650–1, 757, 776, 938, 940, 1004, 1144, 1146
Campbell, J. (Lord) * 39, 51, 54, 59–61, 73,
    100, 150, 185–6, 352, 417, 419–21, 448,
    500–3, 543, 545, 600, 702, 706, 710, 713,
    740, 802, 933, 950, 961, 986, 996–7, 1007,
    1036, 1045, 1127–8
Campbell, R. 926
Cave, L.W. * 873, 875, 893
Chadwick, D. 640
Chadwick, E. 1001
Chalmers, Sir M.D.** 307, 308, 326, 483,
    485, 679, 688, 731–2, 742–3
Chamberlain, J. 824, 841, 848, 1018–19
Chambers, A.M. 785–6
Chambre, A. * 526, 587, 709
Channell, Sir A.N.* 519, 867–8
Channell, Sir W.F. * 919, 935, 1006
Chelmsford (Lord) see Thesiger, F.
Cherry, Sir B.L. 203, 224, 226, 228–30
Chitty, J. (the elder) 316, 731, 745
Chitty, J. (the younger) 301, 303, 313, 317, 336,
    364, 378, 389, 396, 398, 508, 541
Chitty, Sir J.W. * 93, 293, 646, 725, 1110
Christie, J.H. 61, 63, 72n, 77, 181, 193
Churchill, Sir W. 680
Cleasby, Sir A. * 944
Clerk, J.F. 952–3, 1125
Coase, R.H. 885
Cockburn, Sir A.J.E. Bt * 341–2, 489–90, 504,
    510, 547, 593, 603, 687, 695, 766, 898, 931,
    951–2, 954, 961, 964, 993, 1006, 1099
Coke, Sir E. * 386, 401
Colebrooke, H. 301
Coleridge, B.S.J. (Lord) * 969
Coleridge, J.D. (Lord) * 528, 939, 965,
    994, 1016, 1046

Coleridge, Sir J.T. * 371, 461, 527, 766,
    987–8, 1045
Collier, J.F. ** 866
Collier, R.P. (Lord Monkswell) * 837
Collins, A. 859
Collins, R.H. (Lord) * 519, 705, 989
Coltman, T. * 920
Comyns, J. 302, 1096, 1098–9
Cook, T. 327
Copley, J.S. (Lord Lyndhurst) * 39, 60, 159,
    181, 252, 368, 436, 454, 708, 767,
    805–6, 918
Cottenham (Lord) see Pepys, C.C.
Cotton, Sir H. * 393, 425, 428–30, 570, 1087
Cozens-Hardy, H.H. (Lord) * 176, 1025,
    1029, 1031–2
Cranworth (Lord) see Rolfe, B.
Cresswell, Sir C. * 337, 459, 704, 1141
Crompton, Sir C. * 6, 352, 390, 496, 501,
    512, 541, 545, 1005, 1044, 1052, 1073
Crouch, Sir R. 995
Crowder, Sir R.B. * 1098
Cullen, A. 786

Dallas, Sir R. * 497, 574, 914, 1096
Dance, H. 800
Daniel, W.T.S. ** 842
Darling, Sir C.J. * 518, 1061
Davey, H. (Lord) * 155, 214, 216, 641,
    647, 653, 1078
Davidson, C. 11, 72–3, 81, 86, 89–91, 101–3,
    105, 137, 140, 150, 209
Day, Sir J.C.F.S. * 351
Denman, G. * 1124
Denman, T. (Lord) * 28, 112, 350, 364–5, 375,
    377, 402, 413, 459, 492, 498–9, 574, 577,
    593, 706, 749, 762, 915, 922, 1126, 1135
Denning, A.T. (Lord) * 444
Dicey, A.V. 47–8
Dodd, C. ** 839
Domat, J. 537
Duer, J. 699–700
Dunedin (Viscount) see Murray, A.G.
Duval, L. 69, 74

Eden, R. 794
Edward VII, King 518
Eldon, (Earl) see Scott, J.
Ellenborough (Lord) see Law, E.
Elphinstone, Sir H. 220, 222, 224
Émérigon, B.M. 677
Erichsen, J. E. 993
Erle, Sir W. * 306, 355–6, 379, 474, 484, 502,
    512, 702, 720, 922–3, 970–1, 974, 986,
    1000, 1044, 1051, 1057, 1097, 1129
Erskine, T. (Lord) * 441
Esher, Viscount see Brett, W.B.

Evans, Sir W.D.   301, 360, 567
Eyre, Sir J. *   753, 910

Fane, R.G.C. ***   806, 812
Farrow, T.   862–5
Farwell, Sir G. *   983
Field, D.D.   306–7
Field, Sir W.V. *   991, 1017, 1052, 1056, 1085,
    1138–9
Fletcher Moulton, H.F. (Lord
    Moulton)   975, 1148
Fortescue Brickdale, Sir C.   202, 219,
    222, 224–5
Fox, W.   302
Fry, Sir E. *   100, 162, 394, 425, 428–9, 467,
    550, 559, 870, 1138

Gale, C.J.   880
Garrow, Sir W. *   914, 1134
Gent, J. **   848
Gibbs, Sir V. *   455, 511, 532, 587, 977
Giffard, Sir G.M. *   1074
Giffard, H.S. (Earl of Halsbury) *   33, 37,
    43, 214–7, 529, 665, 754, 864, 1055–7,
    1062, 1078, 1108, 1129
Gladstone, Sir W.E.   620
Gloag, R.   326
Glyn, T.C.   795
Gordon, I.   469, 862–3
Gordon, W.E.   313
Goulburn, E. ***   811, 1132
Graham, Sir J.   807, 836
Grant, A.   642, 661
Grant, Sir W. *   22, 24, 41, 135–6, 257,
    391, 417, 439
Green, T.H.   299
Greenhow, W.T.   841–2
Grove, Sir W.R. *   680
Gutteridge, H.C.   609

Hadfield, G.   188, 285
Haldane, R.B. (Viscount Haldane) *   157–8,
    220, 228–9, 607–8
Hall, Sir C. *   7, 237, 261
Halsbury, Earl of see Giffard, H.S.
Hamilton, J.A. (Viscount Sumner) *   609,
    983, 989
Hanbury, H.G.   609–10
Hancock, W.N.   855–6
Hanworth (Viscount) see Pollock, E.M.
Hannen, J. (Lord) *   963
Harcourt, W.V.   378
Hardwicke, (Lord) see Yorke, P.
Hasse, J.C.   927
Hatherley, Lord see Page Wood, W.
Hawkins, H. (Lord Brampton) *   354, 1053,
    1056–7, 1062–3

Heath, D.D. **   842–3
Heath, Sir J. *   526–8, 579, 590
Henry, Sir T.   856
Herschell, F. (Lord) *   217, 252, 430–1, 683,
    841, 1057–8, 1062
Hilliard, F.   880
Hilton, B.   779–80
Hobbes, T.   372
Hogg, J.E.   190, 223–4
Holker, Sir J. *   776
Holland, Sir T.E.   310–12
Holmes, O.W. *   311–13, 372, 394–5, 548,
    880, 890–1, 893, 941–3, 1145
Holroyd, Sir G.S. *   740, 907
Holt, J. (Lord) *   731, 916, 1048, 1141
Honyman, Sir G.E. *   341
Hooley, E.T.   644
Horridge, Sir T.G. *   989–90
Hotham, Sir B. *   752
Howell, J.   811
Hubbard, J.G.   776
Hume, J.   800–01
Humphreys, J.   49–53
Hyde, Sir N.*   1096

James, H. (Lord James of Hereford) *   204, 840,
    861, 1057, 1062
James, Sir W.M. *   28, 30, 36, 38, 40–4, 46,
    126, 170, 261, 276, 344, 428, 648, 650,
    757, 1078, 1101
Jarman, T.   14, 22, 25–6, 83, 112, 242, 273
Jervis, Sir J. *   474, 815
Jessel, Sir G. *   15, 26, 34, 38, 41–2, 45, 139, 171–2,
    176, 205, 260–1, 267, 273, 276, 280, 392, 425,
    427–8, 528, 570, 582, 603–5, 607, 664–5,
    694, 874, 965, 1077, 1089–90, 1101–3
Jones, Sir W.   913–14, 916, 926–7
Jones, W. (Marshal of the King's Bench)   800

Kay, Sir E.E. *   34, 40, 42, 46, 147,
    404, 406, 646
Keating, Sir H.S. *   305, 379, 772, 854, 966
Keep, A.P.P.   893
Kekewich, Sir A. *   283, 1053, 1077, 1101–2,
    1108, 1146
Kelly, Sir F.E. *   343–4, 504, 720, 944, 960,
    964–5, 1148–9
Kenyon, L. (Lord) *   20–1, 27, 45, 118, 412,
    413, 457, 459, 594, 782, 910
Ker, H.B.   23, 49, 51–2, 60–1, 63, 78, 181, 193,
    620–1, 626
Kimberley (Lord) see Wodehouse, John
Kindersley, Sir R. *   42, 106, 147, 234,
    420–1, 554–5, 1107
Kirkwood, J.   862, 864
Knight Bruce, Sir J.L. *   39, 105, 138, 257–9,
    420, 556, 558, 812, 814, 1097

Lamb, Sir J.B. 788
Langdale, (Lord) *see* Bickersteth, H.
Langdell, C.C. 308, 310–11, 313, 346, 365,
    380–1, 386, 398
Law, E. (Lord Ellenborough) * 118, 177, 304,
    315, 330, 384, 480, 487, 492, 495–6, 511,
    579, 587, 604–5, 617, 712, 751, 908, 910,
    912, 1122, 1131
Lawrence, E. 819
Lawrence, N.T. 91, 208–9
Lawrence, Sir S. * 491, 684–5, 688
Le Blanc, Sir S. * 579–80
Leach, Sir J. * 46, 247, 454, 553
Leake, S.M. 307, 338–9, 345, 398, 434, 441,
    466–7, 471, 504, 519, 568–9, 595
Lefroy, T.L. * 934
Lewin, T. 238–9, 242
Lindley, N. (Lord) * 148, 154–5, 175, 292–3, 346,
    355, 408, 429, 560, 597, 605, 644, 666, 668,
    963, 975, 981, 1062, 1066, 1086–7
Lindley, W.B. 641
Lindsell, W.H.B. 952–3, 1125
Littledale, Sir J. * 592, 594, 896
Lloyd, S. 822
Locke, J. 887
Loreburn (Earl) *see* Reid, R.T.
Lowe, R. (Lord Sherbrooke) 197, 462, 625–8
Ludlow, J.M.F. 299, 627
Lush, Sir R. * 359, 393, 899, 951, 962, 989, 1138
Lushington, Sir S. * 759, 1049
Lyndhurst (Lord) *see* Copley, J.S.

Macaulay, T.B. (Lord) 306
Macdonald, Sir A. * 117, 1075–6
Mackenzie, M.M. 828
Macnaghten, E. (Lord) * 152, 155, 778,
    982–3, 1024, 1055, 1062, 1092
Macpherson, W. 433
Maine, Sir H.J.S. 298, 394, 568
McCardie, Sir H.A. * 470, 1065
McGovney, D.O. 357
Malins, Sir R. * 33–4, 36–7, 39–42, 44, 170,
    176, 259, 261, 267, 276, 285, 558, 560, 603,
    994, 1076, 1107
Mansfield (Lord) *see* Murray, Sir W.
Mansfield, Sir J. * 579, 702, 910
Marshall, T. 847
Martin, Sir S.* 379–80, 385, 455, 512, 543,
    545–7, 570, 575, 625, 654, 920, 922, 1006,
    1073, 1086, 1117, 1121, 1136, 1142–3
Mathew, Sir J.C. * 205, 752, 866
Maule, Sir W.H. * 600, 959, 972, 1141
May, J.F. 856
Mayne, J.D. 536–7
Mellish, Sir G. * 344–5, 450, 593, 653, 950, 1148
Mellor, Sir J. * 483, 694, 951, 1100
Mill, J.S. 298, 950

Mitford, J.F. (Lord Redesdale) * 28, 31–2, 35, 38,
    145, 792, 798
Moffat, G. 819
Monkswell (Lord) *see* Collier, R.P.
Montagu, B. 786–8, 795–6
Morgan, Sir G.O. 203–4, 207
Motteram, J. ** 860
Moulton, H. Fletcher (Lord) * *see* Fletcher
    Moulton, H.F.
Murray, A.G. (Viscount Dunedin of
    Stenton) * 988, 1028
Murray, W. (Earl of Mansfield) * 359, 361–2,
    364, 366, 374, 395, 525, 566–7, 576–7, 583,
    593, 609–10, 686, 731, 733, 744, 749–50

Neild. J. 798
Nelson, S. * 537
Northcote, Sir S. 184

Owen, D. 688
Owen, W.S. ** 865

Page Wood, W. (Lord Hatherley) * 24, 249,
    258–9, 285, 391–2, 426, 439–40, 466,
    551, 555, 557, 560, 603, 606, 665, 939,
    966, 1076, 1084–7, 1089, 1098, 1109–11
Paine, W. 313
Palles, C. * 995, 1061
Palmer, R. (Lord Selborne) * 40, 45, 199, 208,
    387, 403, 1102
Palmerston, Vis *see* Temple, H.J. (Viscount
    Palmerston)
Pardessus, J.-M. 304
Park, Sir J.A. * 458, 573, 770
Park, J.J. 698
Parke, J. (Lord Wensleydale) * 27, 32, 116–7, 129,
    162, 350, 363, 371, 384, 401–2, 412–13, 459,
    474, 481, 484, 496, 499, 526–8, 575, 584–6,
    599–600, 625, 697, 704, 727, 769, 772, 924,
    929–30, 933, 990, 1039, 1047, 1123, 1129, 1131,
    1133, 1135
Parker, R.J. (Lord) * 158, 176, 277,
    556, 1092–3
Parker, T. (Lord Macclesfield) * 552
Parkyns, M. 823
Parry, Sir E.A. ** 843–4, 846, 848
Parsons, T. 356
Patteson, Sir J. * 125, 371, 374, 900, 917, 921, 931
Pearson, Sir J. * 583, 1086
Peel, Sir R. 50–1, 803
Penzance, (Lord) *see* Wilde, J.P.B.
Pepys, C.C. (Earl of Cottenham) * 30, 106, 130,
    138–9, 159, 170–3, 197, 235, 242, 248, 252,
    255, 257, 337, 368–9, 391–2, 406, 537, 559,
    653, 803, 805
Phillimore, Sir R.J. * 934
Pickersgill, E.H. 841, 843–4

Pigott, Sir G. * 937, 1007
Pitt, W., the Younger 689
Plumer, Sir T. * 24, 146, 440
Pockett, H.T. 862–3
Pollock, Sir C.E. * 936, 1138
Pollock, Sir F. 307, 308–13, 322, 339, 345,
    347–8, 351, 353–4, 355, 357, 360, 365–6, 370,
    371–2, 374, 380–3, 386–7, 390, 394–9,
    430–1, 433–4, 449, 452, 467, 469, 471, 548,
    609, 731, 888, 890–4, 941–4, 947, 949,
    954, 955–7, 1033, 1047–52, 1055–6,
    1059, 1060, 1066, 1112–13, 1125, 1145
Pollock, Sir J.F., Bt * 160, 371, 456, 461, 465, 482,
    487, 509, 543–4, 546, 567, 575, 597,
    882, 895, 932, 935, 973, 978, 1006, 1073,
    1100, 1135, 1137
Posner, R. 885
Pothier, R.J. 301–4, 336, 343, 345–6, 433, 450,
    452, 466–7, 469–70, 513–14, 537–8, 541,
    543, 587, 677, 742, 770–1, 896, 987
Powell, J.J. 89n, 135, 338, 360
Pratt, C. (Earl Camden) * 383, 385, 1125
Price, R. 676
Puller, C. 362, 364–5

Reid, R.T. (Earl Loreburn) * 228, 522, 1024,
    1026–7, 1065
Richards, Sir R. * 35, 97, 134, 436, 553
Ridley, Sir E. * 867
Ritchie, J. 313
Robson, W. 841
Rolfe, R.M. * (Lord Cranworth) 28, 32, 39,
    87–8, 90, 150, 152, 162, 257–9, 276, 289,
    368–9, 391, 410, 420–1, 423, 448, 585, 854,
    896, 1003–4, 1075–6
Rolle, H. * 509
Rollit, Sir A. 827, 831
Rolt, Sir J. * 340
Romer, Sir R. * 642, 666–7, 1064–5
Romilly, J. (Lord) * 8, 38, 86, 131, 140, 147,
    176, 182, 259–60, 285, 306, 340, 406,
    418, 426–7, 435, 438, 440, 442–4,
    549–50, 554–5, 557–8, 651, 663, 665,
    1074, 1085, 1101
Romilly, Sir S. 182, 407, 788, 792
Runnington, C. 799
Russell, G.L. ** 840
Russell, Lord J. 803, 836
Russell, J.A. 843–4

Salmond, Sir J.* 893–4, 943, 953, 955–6,
    1066–7, 1112–13, 1125–6
Savigny, F.C. von 308–10, 339, 346, 353,
    371–2, 390, 399, 433, 449, 453, 467, 471
Scaccia, S. 769
Scarlett, J. (Lord Abinger) * 116, 375, 412–13,
    459, 477, 536, 578–9, 584, 589, 593, 744,
    769, 908, 910, 925, 1002–3, 1045

Scott, J. (Earl of Eldon) * 13, 24–5, 31, 35, 38, 116,
    126, 134–6, 138, 145, 239, 249, 253, 255, 262,
    332, 360, 373, 416–17, 558, 560, 599, 617–18,
    684–5, 787, 792, 1075
Scrutton, Sir T.E. * 956, 1093
Seddon, J.A. 844
Sedgwick, T. 305, 536–8, 541
Selborne (Lord) see Palmer, R.
Selwyn, Sir C.J. * 666
Senior, N.W. 225
Sewell, S.J. 874
Shadwell, Sir L. * 42, 131, 175, 255, 273, 281, 283,
    406, 553, 558–9, 691–2
Shaw, T. (Lord Shaw of Dunfermline) * 681
Shaw-Lefevre G. J. (Baron Eversley) 204
Sheppard, W. 401, 508
Simmons, L. 863, 864
Simpson, A.W.B. 1140
Simpson, H.B. 843
Smith, A. 324
Smith, A.L. * 205, 468–9, 1108
Smith, H. 893, 927, 947–8
Smith, J. (Inspector General in
    Bankruptcy) 637, 668, 826, 831–2
Smith, J. (MP) 786, 794
Smith, J.W. 305
Smith, L. ** 866, 1030
Smith, Sir M.E. * 962
Smyly, W.C. ** 847
St Leonards (Lord) see Sugden, E.B.
Starkie, T. 928
Stephen, Sir J.F. * 225–6, 307,
    370, 731
Stewart, J. 60, 71, 73, 75, 77
Stirling, Sir J. * 430, 605, 1092
Story, J. * 305, 359, 374, 435–6, 699, 731,
    737, 756, 896, 987
Story, W.W. 336
Stuart, Sir J. * 39, 41, 139, 148–9, 205, 235–6,
    262, 276, 404, 422, 865
Sugden, E.B. (Lord St Leonards) * 29, 33, 51,
    70, 73, 76, 89–90, 100, 107, 124–5, 138, 150,
    152, 181, 183–6, 188, 235, 255, 258, 276, 285,
    288–90, 302, 441, 559–61, 796

Talfourd, Sir T.N. * 918
Taylor, J. 1022
Taylor, M.A. 1094
Temple, H.J. (Viscount Palmerston) 1094
Tenterden, (Lord) see Abbott, C.
Thesiger, A. * 308, 344, 605
Thesiger, F. (Lord Chelmsford) * 89, 150,
    407, 420–1, 540, 561, 608, 966, 1004,
    1077, 1085, 1103
Thurlow, E. (Lord) * 130, 133, 247, 438, 441
Tindal, Sir N.C. * 330, 481, 526, 533, 566, 577,
    600, 685, 706, 801, 882, 907, 918, 920–1,
    977, 1040, 1097, 1132

Tindal-Atkinson, H. ** 838–9
Torrens, Sir R.R. 215
Truro (Lord) *see* Wilde, T.
Turner, F. 851, 854
Turner, Sir G.J. * 16, 86, 275, 407, 419, 421–4, 552, 757
Turquand, W. 648

Underhill, Sir A. 226, 230, 240

Vangerow, K.A. von 353
Vaughan Williams, Sir R.B. * 516, 518–19, 668, 1139
Vesey, F. 332, 414–15

Watson, W. (Lord Watson, then Thankerton) * 669, 671–2, 771, 980, 1062
Watson, W. (2nd Lord Thankerton) * 1083
Wedderburn, A. (Lord Loughborough) * 133
Wensleydale (Lord) *see* Parke, J.
Westbury, (Lord) *see* Bethell, R.
Wharton, F. 925, 927, 929
Wightman, Sir W. * 590, 933, 1044, 1073, 1129
Wigram, Sir J. * 33, 255, 257, 557, 652
Wilde, J.P.B. (Lord Penzance) * 45, 940
Wilde, T. (Lord Truro) * 36, 379–80, 528, 545, 559, 930
Willes, Sir J.S. * 305–6, 338, 353, 537, 539, 547, 585, 597, 660, 687, 705, 710, 720, 923, 933, 944, 966, 978, 987, 1098, 1100, 1124

Willes, Sir J. * 572, 686
Willes, W.H. 1099
Williams, E.E. 670
Williams, Sir E.V. * 145, 355, 371, 445, 488, 511, 921, 933, 978, 1099, 1126
Williams, Sir J. * 496
Williams, J. [John] 305, 596, 1060, 1126
Williams, J. [Joshua] 74, 149, 225–6, 233
Williams, T.C. 47, 220, 224, 226, 228–9, 231
Williams, Sir R.V. *see* Vaughan Williams
Williston, S. 310, 313, 356, 372, 381–3, 398, 505–7
Wills, Sir A. * 1058
Wilson, R. 190, 194, 199
Winfield, Sir P.H. 610, 944
Wodehouse, John (Lord Kimberley) 858
Wolstenholme, E.P. 91, 195–6, 208, 212, 223, 236
Wood, W. ** 846
Woolley, C. 670
Wrenbury (Lord) *see* Buckley, H.
Wright, R.A. (Lord Wright of Durley) * 399
Wright, Sir R.S. * 408, 1078, 1147
Wright, Whittaker 644, 661–2
Wynford (Lord) *see* Best, W.D.

Yerburgh, R.A. 862–3, 865
Yorke, P. (Earl Hardwicke) * 25, 403, 552–3, 555

INDEX OF SUBJECTS

This index is for the contents of Vol. XII only. The reader may also consult the full Index for Volumes XI–XIII, to be found in Vol. XIII.

accidents,
    see tort, personal injury
account
    action of 563
    in equity 564–5, 601–3, 645–6, 663, 692
accumulations, rule against 21n, 215, 250
administration of estates,
    see succession
Admiralty Court Act 1840 687
advertising 327–8, 352–5
agents and agency 305–6, 324–5, 454,
        456, 595, 657
    account for profits 602–5, 645–6, 662–3
    agent contracting for non-existent
        principals 462, 469
    apparent authority of 761
    bills of exchange, and 743
    company directors as 421–3, 657–60,
        662–4, 738–9
    company promoters as 392, 420, 645–6
    del credere 324, 448
    factors 324, 742, 761, 790, 1122–4
    Factors Act 1889 762, 871–2, 1124
    fiduciary aspects 404–5, 663
    frauds and misrepresentations of
        agents 412–13, 419–21, 423, 659–60
    general and particular 657
    principal's liability for 419–21, 423,
        659–60, 699–701, 894–9
    purchases from principal 662–3
    warranty of authority 463
animals,
    see tort
annuities 591
    commercial
        for life 142–4, 153
        judicial control 143–4, 147
        registration 143–4, 185
    settlements, in 10
    see also mortgages, settlement of
        property generally
arrest,
    see debtor and creditor
assignment
    insurance policies 688–9, 691–3
    of choses in action 691–3, 733, 757
    of liabilities 595n
    of negotiable instruments 733, 757

assumpsit, action of 314–20, 326, 396, 447, 454,
        498, 524–5, 527, 530, 563–6, 569, 587
    indebitatus assumpsit 314–15, 319,
        495–6 530–34, 575
    see also contract

bailment 305–6, 1116–18
    bailees 514
        duty of care 913–16, 1118
        hire purchasers as 871,
        insurance by 695
        pawnbrokers as 852
    gratuitous 374, 927
Bank of England 275, 728–31
banking 728–31, 764–78
    Bank Charter Act 1844 729, 764
    banknotes 728–9
    banks
        duties to customers 766–9
        incorporation of 619, 728–9
        limited liability of 629–30, 633
        winding up of 630
    Institute of Bankers 307
bankruptcy 68, 121, 182, 265, 326, 578–9,
        779–97, 804–33
    acts of bankruptcy 781–6, 793, 804,
        813–15, 817, 831
    fraudulent conveyances 782–3, 813–14
    Bankruptcy Act 1825 793–4
    Bankruptcy Act 1861 818, 820, 821, 837,
    Bankruptcy Act 1869 647
    Bankruptcy Act 1883 561, 824–6, 825–8, 830,
    Bankruptcy Act 1890 827, 832, 864
    Bankruptcy Consolidation Act 1849
        808–9, 816,
    Bankruptcy and Deeds of Arrangement
        Act 1913 829, 832
    commissioners 781, 786–8, 792, 795,
        806, 809, 812
    composition agreements 384–5, 783–4,
        793–4, 809–10, 820–2, 824–6, 828, 830–3
    Deeds of Arrangement Act 1887 831
    creditors' assignees 788–9, 822
    Departmental Committee (1906–8) 828–9,
        832–3, 847, 874
    discharge of 823, 825–9
        certificate of conformity 781, 791–2, 794,
        805–6, 810–13, 818

bankruptcy (cont.)
    examination of 824–5, 827–8,
    fraudulent 798–9, 801–2, 804–8, 810, 813,
      818–20, 823–4, 826, 828–30
    official assignees 796, 809, 817, 822
    official receiver 824–6
    'poor man's' 840–1, 844–8
    reputed ownership, doctrine 692, 789–90,
      817, 860–1, 873–4
    reform of courts 795–6, 817, 820,
    Royal Commission (1839–40) 804–5
    Royal Commission (1854) 813, 815, 820, 822
    Select Committee (1864) 821–1
    see also insolvency
bills of exchange 144–5, 303, 305, 307,
    325, 729–54, 766
    acceptance 733–7
    accommodation bills 732, 736, 746, 752–3
    Bills of Exchange Act 1882 731, 739, 741,
      743, 747, 749, 751, 753–4, 773, 777, 864
    consideration 743–8
    deposited with bank 767–8
    dishonour 337, 735–7
    fictitious payees 752–4
    foreign 729, 734, 736, 740
    forged 749–52
    indorsement 732–3, 740–3
    inland 729–30, 734, 736, 740
    joint stock companies' use of 738
    negligence, and 748–9
    payable to bearer 732, 739–40
    payable to order 740
    Regulation of Acceptances Act 1821 734
    see also cheques
bills of lading 324, 758–64, 790
    Bills of Lading Act 1855 760
    indorsement of 759–61
bills of sale 121, 152, 154, 156, 783, 789,
    813–16, 859–62, 874–6
    Bills of Sale Act 1854 816
    Bills of Sale Act 1878 859–60
    Bills of Sale Act 1882 861
    see also mortgages
Birmingham Law Society 105, 108, 227n
bonds 314, 393, 524–5
    conditional 497, 524–5
Board of Trade 619, 626, 630, 683,
    824–6, 830–3, 968, 997, 1021

cartels 670–3
carriers 904–16, 926, 958–69
    Carriers Act 1830 458, 473, 543, 915
    liability for goods 458, 474, 909–16, 1118
      use of exemption clauses 472–5, 543,
      911–16, 967–9
      shippers' duties to disclose dangers 986–7,
    railways 959–67, 985

road 904–11
Chancery Commission (1824) 795
Chancery, Court of 321–2, 414, 434–5,
    564–5, 624,
    bankruptcy appeals 787–8, 795, 812
    business 7, 85, 87–8, 235–7, 323,
    equity jurisprudence in 171–2
    fusion of jurisdictions 321–22
      preference for equity, in Judicature
      Act 1873 161, 178, 425
    injunctions
      to prevent breaches of
      charterparties 561–2
      to prevent breach of personal
      service contracts 559–61
      to prevent nuisances 1071–8, 1081–2,
      1089–91, 1101–11
    reforms of 1850s 194, 271
      Cairns's Act 1858 540, 551–2, 1108
      Rolt's Act 1862 1107–8
    see also contract
      specific performance 161, 173–4, 253–4,
      312, 321, 548–59
      building works 556–8
      denied where fraud, surprise or
      mistake 373, 414, 439–41
      personal services 558–9
      sale of goods 552–6
      sale of land 103–4, 438, 550–2
      sale of shares 553–4
Chancery Division (1876)
    business 236–7
charity 4, 241
charterparties 324, 489–90, 495–6, 503,
    511–12, 561
cheques 730–1, 764–78
see also bills of exchange
    Bills of Exchange (Crossed Cheques)
      Act 1906 778
    Crossed Cheques Act 1856 774
    Crossed Cheques Act 1858 775, 777
    Crossed Cheques Act 1876 772, 777
    crossing cheques 773–8
    forged 769–73, 775
    Stamp Act 1853 772, 777
    see also bills of exchange
children
    guardianship and wardship 12–13, 244
    occupiers' liability for 980–4
choses in action 615, 743–4
    assignment of 691–3, 733, 757, 789
Church of England 113, 169
    see also religion
Code Civil (France) 301, 304, 541
codification 306–8, 679, 731–2
    Society for the Reform and Codification of
      the Law of Nations 715

commercial law,
    see agents and agency, banking, bills of
        exchange, bills of lading, companies,
        debtors and creditors, insurance, sale
        of goods
Common Law Commission (1828) and judges
    of local courts 317–18, 801–2,
Common Law Commission (1850) 319
Common Law Procedure Acts 1854 321, 556
Common Pleas, Court of, Office of 185–7
companies 613–73
    accounts 621–3, 628, 641, 653–57
    auditors 621, 628
    bills of exchange given by 737–9
    Bubble Act 617–18
    cartels 670–3, 1050–2
    Davey Committee 638, 641, 656, 667–70
    debentures 155–7, 287, 636–8
    dividends, paid from capital 654–6, 664
    directors 621, 623, 738
        as agents 420–3, 657–60, 662–4
        breach of fiduciary duties 604, 662–5
        criminal liability of 661–2
        liability for misconduct 422, 426–30,
            654–5
        liability for negligence 666–7
        liability for *ultra vires* acts 663–4
    floating charges 157–8, 636–8
    formation of 620, 638–47
    Gladstone Committee 620–2
    incorporation 613, 620–3, 628
    investors, protection of 618, 623–5, 648–9
        rescission of share purchases 418, 420–6,
            648–9
    limited liability 298, 620–1, 625–30, 633
    Loreburn Committee 638, 657, 667
    management of 652–67
        rule in *Foss* v. *Harbottle* 652–3
    private 633, 667–70
    promoters
        fiduciary duties of 603, 643–6
        flotation of companies 638–9, 643–6
        rescission of contracts with 643, 645–6
    prospectuses 641–2, 644, 670
    shareholders
        disputes over company
            membership 339–40, 343–4, 648–9
        liability of 622–3, 649–50
    shares 120, 287
        Founders' Shares 635
        preference 634–6
        scrip 623–4, 638
        underwriting of issue 646–7
    Trading Companies Act 1834 619
    ultra vires doctrine 392, 421, 606–10, 657–61
        payment of dividends from capital 654–5
    unincorporated 616–21
    winding up 628–30, 647–52
company legislation
    Companies Act 1862 630, 647, 652, 656, 659
    Companies Act 1867 640
        s 38 428, 640–2, 643
    Companies (Memorandum of Association)
        Act 1890 659
    Companies Act 1900 638, 641, 647, 656, 670
    Companies Act 1907 657, 667, 670
    Companies Clauses Consolidation
        Act 1845 622, 636, 662
    Companies (Winding Up) Act 1890 651–2
    Directors' Liability Act 1890 644, 651
    Joint Stock Companies Act 1844 621–2, 625,
        627–8, 738
    Joint Stock Companies Act 1856 627–8, 738
    Limited Liability Act 1855 627, 780
    Winding Up Act 1844 624, 630
    Winding Up Act 1848 624–5, 630
compensation,
    see tort, workmen's compensation
        acts, workplace injuries
Conservative party, property law, and 119, 197,
        199, 204, 206, 208–9, 211, 213–7,
        224, 228
conspiracy, tort of 1048 1050–3, 1060–7
    Pollock's view on 1060
construction,
    see statute, will, contract
consumers 326–8, 352, 355, 473, 522, 834–76,
        881, 924, 988–90
    railway tickets 327–8, 967–71
contingent remainders,
    see estates in land
contract
    accord and satisfaction 383–4, 492, 740,
        994, 998
    breach
        anticipatory 494–508
        marine insurance policies 702–3
        termination for 487–90
        waiver of 491, 494
    caveat emptor 98, 400, 409, 414, 451,
        479–81, 483–4, 641
    conditions 305, 485, 488–91
        dependent and independent 485–7
    consideration 301, 310, 313, 315–17, 358–90,
        394, 486–7
        adequacy of 360, 372–4
        Ames's views on 382–3, 387–8, 396–8
        Anson's views on 365, 376, 380–2,
            387, 390, 395–6
        bills of exchange 743–8,
        causa and 394
        forbearance to sue 375–6
        gratuitous promises 333–4, 358
        Langdell's theory of 380–1

contract (*cont.*)
  meritorious consideration 233–5, 265, 361, 388
  moral consideration 361–6, 567
  motive and 370–1
  part-payment of debts, and 383–7,
  past consideration 362, 364–6
  performance of existing
    duties 376–83, 386
  Pollock's views on 360, 365–6, 371–2,
    374, 380–3, 386–7, 394–9
  promise as consideration 396–7
  sufficiency of 372, 374–5
  theories of 380–1, 394–9
  total failure of 436, 448, 450, 588–95
  treatment in equity 233–5, 265, 359, 372
contractual intention 309–10, 355,
    369–72, 399
  intention to create legal
    relations 309–10, 371–2
deed 253–4, 360
duress 148, 322, 400–2,
  duress of goods 401–2, 576
  duress to the person 400–1
entire contract rule 515, 532
executed and executory 315–16, 319, 331, 592
fraud,
  see fraud
freedom of contract 120, 147–8
frustration 508–21
  of commercial purpose 516–19
  notion of implied condition 514–15
  leases 509, 513
  Pollock's views on 522
  in sale of goods 509–11
good faith 148, 312, 409, 415, 418
  insurance contracts 697–701
guarantee 306, 349, 355
illegal 508, 591–5
  wagers 594–5
implied in fact 531–3, 600, 986, 963, 1013
implied in law 568–9, 580
indemnities 425–7
Indian Law Commission 306–7, 369, 386
Indian Contract Act 1872 307–9, 345n
infants 363
  Infants Relief Act 1874 363
Lord Tenterden's Act 1828 331, 363, 1040
misrepresentation: *see* misrepresentation
mistake: *see* mistake
offer and acceptance 301, 303, 309–57
  acceptance by conduct 342, 473–4
  Anson's view on 351, 355
  auctions 333
  communication of acceptance 336–45
  Langdell's view on 347–8
  'mirror-image' rule 334–5
  'objective' view of contract
    formation 310, 332–3, 338–9, 451

  Pollock's view on 339, 345, 347–8,
    351, 353–4, 355, 357
  postal rule 335–7, 343–5
  revocation of offer 345–6, 355–7
  'subjective' view of contract
    formation 336–7, 343, 346
  theories of 347–8
  unilateral contracts 348–57, 757
parol evidence rule 411, 446, 699
personal service: *see* employment
pleading and procedure 313–22
privity of contract 360, 388–94, 969
  Pollock's views on 390
rectification 435, 437–9, 442–3, 446
rescission
  for fraud 411, 415–16
  loss of right to 408, 411, 460
  for mistake 436–7, 441, 590
  for non-fraudulent
    misrepresentation 418–25, 431–2, 649
  for undue influence 408
  in sale of goods 478, 589
  on terms 416, 645
restraint of trade 371, 527, 671–2, 1050–2
retail price agreements 672–3
Roman law influence 306, 309, 434,
    449, 450, 505, 514–15, 518, 566
sale *see* sale of goods, sale of land
seamen's contracts 377–8, 532
specific performance *see* Chancery
Statute of Frauds *see* Statute of Frauds
termination 494–521
terms
  exemption clauses 473–5, 870, 911–16, 967–9
  incorporation of 474–5, 968
  standard terms 327, 473, 476–7
  waiver of performance 491–4
theories of contract 94, 98
  bargain theory 360, 371–2, 387, 395–6
  reliance theory 311–12, 366–70
  will theory 297, 301–3, 306, 308–13, 315,
    346, 360, 370, 433, 452
see treatises
variation 492
void and voidable 400, 408, 434, 436–7, 444,
    448–9, 452–4, 458–60, 462, 465, 468–72
warranty
  express 479–80
  implied 117, 409, 473, 475, 480–5, 510
see also damages, forms of action
contract misrepresentation, effect of, *see also*
  see misrepresentation
contributory negligence,
  see negligence
conversion 121, 401–2, 464–6, 1115–22
  damages in 900
  hire traders and 871
  pawnbrokers and 853–4, 871

conveyances
    covenants for title in 101–2, 209
    deed, by 60–1, 90
    lease and release, by 49, 60
    recitals in 64
    short forms of 72, 77, 203
        statutory 71–2, 90, 209, 211
    stamp duty on 57, 59–61, 72
    see also conveyancing, sale of land
conveyancing 48, 86, 107, 140, 186, 202–3
    attendant terms 62, 65–8, 72–3, 77
    barristers, and 52, 66, 75, 96–7, 101, 196, 202,
        220, 222–5, 227, 230
    conditions of sale, and 76–7, 96, 102–9
    costs of 67, 77, 98, 211–2
        fee scales 207, 211–12
    judgment debts, and 61, 184–90
    land and succession taxes, and 183–4
    Landed Estates Courts, and 197–8
    Real Property Commissioners, and 56–8
    registers of charges, and
        annuities 143, 185
        Crown debts 185–6, 188
        consolidated 213
        judgments 185–90
        land improvement loans 185–7
        Land Registry, and 187, 213, 219
        lites pendentes 185
        local authority charges 227
        official searches 210–11
        searching 187, 210–11
    simplifying 176, 208–13
    solicitors, and 65–6, 68, 70–1, 187–9, 208, 211
    see also conveyances, registration of deeds,
        sale of land
copyhold 53n, 55–6, 59n, 82, 230
Corn Laws 229, 779
corporation,
    see company
Council of Legal Education, composition of 306
County Councils 220
County Courts 123, 327, 522, 803, 807–8,
        819–20, 826, 832
courts of requests 803, 836
Court of Review 795–6
covenant, action of 314, 316, 495, 599
creditors,
    see debtors and creditors, judgment debt
Crown, debts to 57, 183, 185–6, 188

damages
    contractual
        anticipatory breach of contract 505–6
        in equity 322, 540
        expectation 99–100, 501, 534–39
        land sales 98–100, 539–40
        loaned stock 535–6
        lost profits 537–8

    mitigation of 534–6
    penalties and liquidated damages 523–9
    Pollock's views on 548
    quantum meruit 530–4
    remoteness 305, 541–8
    tort 899–902, 905, 934–5, 954–6,
        990–1000, 1041–2, 1107–8
    misrepresentation 426–30
    writs of inquiry 524
debt
    imprisonment for 185
        Debtors Act 1869 819–20, 827–9, 837
        on final process 797–803, 805–8, 813,
            818–20, 835–44
        on mesne process 400–01, 797–803
        Select Committee on (1873) 840, 844
        Select Committee on (1893) 841
        Select Committee on (1909) 841–3, 848
    see also insolvency
debt, action of 314, 320, 565
    on bond 314, 316, 523–5
    on simple contract 314, 320, 530
    see also forms of action
debtors and creditors 834–76;
    see also judgment debt
deceit 320, 322, 411–14, 428–30, 462,
        540, 924, 947, 1040
    see also fraud
defamation, 'malice' 1038, 1058–9
deodand 996–7, 1001
detinue, action of 577n, 1116–18
dissenters 55
distress
    hire traders and 872–3
    see landlord and tenant
District Councils 164
dock warrants 324, 753–4
dower 9, 56–8, 129
    see also married women's property

easements and profits 159–71
    acquiescence, and 161–2, 177
    air 168
    contracts, in equity 161
    deeds, at law 160–1
        non-derogation 165, 167–8
    equity, and 161
    implied 167–8
    in gross 163
    licences, and 160–2, 165, 167
    light 168–70, 1071–9
    lists of permissible 162
    mining and quarrying 166–7, 200,
        1127–34, 1136, 1141–2
        subsidence 166–7, 1129–40
    negative 171
    nuisance, permitting 163, 167, 1083–6,
        1089–92

easements and profits (*cont.*)
  prescription 58, 160, 163, 168–71
    Prescription Act 1832 169–70, 1073, 1076–8
    Real Property Commission, and 58, 168
  profits 159, 177
  statutory alternatives 163–6, 177–8
  title registration 222, 226
  water and watercourses 159, 162–6, 1082–88
  see also nuisance, restrictive covenants
employer and employee
  Master and Servant Acts 1823 and 1867
    299, 1043
  wrongful dismissal 496–7, 501
employers' liability
  Employers Liability Act 1880 677
  Employers Liability Insurance Corporation
    1018 1020–1
  see also workmen's compensation
enclosure
  Inclosure Commissioners 86–7, 90, 187
equity,
  see Chancery, fiduciary duties, trusts
estates in land 186, 223
  abolition of 225, 230
  contingent remainders 19–20, 22, 31–2, 49,
    53, 62–4, 215
  fee simple 190–4, 196, 198, 246
  fee tail (entail) 14, 16, 29, 31, 45, 79–80, 93,
    214–15, 217, 246
  life estate 19, 29, 80, 83, 90, 92, 112,
    142, 196, 215
  life tenant 54–5, 85, 92–3, 233–4
  reduction of 196, 229
  remainders and reversions 10, 16, 18–19, 38,
    103, 148, 191, 258
  see also land
estoppel 129–30, 338, 451, 456, 750–1, 754, 770
  by negligence 929–30
  by representation 366, 371, 416
  promissory 367
evidence, of parties 321, 433
executors 7, 22–3, 54, 130, 180, 189n, 194, 214,
    216–17, 278, 290n, 293
  restitutionary actions against 575–6
  trustees, as 242–3
  see also wills, probate

factors,
  see agents and agency
  false pretences, obtaining goods by 457
    fraudulent purchasers 457–69
  'long firm' frauds 463–69
  see also deceit
fiduciary duties
  breach of 404, 564–5, 601–5
  company directors 604, 662–3
  company promoters 643–5

undue influence and 402–9
fines and recoveries 49, 58, 103
fire,
  see insurance
forms of action 310, 314–15, 317, 319–20, 565,
    569, 582, 880, 887–8, 923, 1127, 1141, 1149
  see also superior courts
fraud 100–1, 117, 301, 321, 326, 409–32, 434–5,
    453, 457–60, 899, 924, 929–31, 978
  'legal' and 'moral' fraud 412–14,
    417–19, 429, 431
  rescission for 414–15
freedom of contract, theory of 297–9, 385, 400,
    473, 528, 625, 672, 839, 855–7, 859, 865–7,
    870, 1009, 1055
friendly societies 1010–11

gambling
  Gaming Act 1845 594–5, 632–3, 680

hire and hire purchase 121, 123, 835, 869–76
  Hire Traders Protection Association 870–4
housing
  private development
    building leases 54, 82–3, 88–9,
      112, 142, 172
    covenants 171–7
  private renting 116–7
    eviction of tenants 124–7
    powers of JPs 122, 124
  public regulation
    lodging houses 122
  see also landlord and tenant, leases

imprisonment for debt,
  see debt
incorporeal things,
  see debtor and creditor, easements and
    profits, intellectual property
indebitatus assumpsit,
  see assumpsit
independent contractor 896–7, 945, 963, 973
Indian Law Commission 306–7, 369, 386, 485
  Indian Contract Act 1872 307–9, 345n
insanity 244
  see also lunacy, criminal defences
insolvency 797–805, 808–7, 817–33
  Debtors' Arrangement Act 1844 807
  Insolvent Debtors Act 1842 807
  Insolvent Debtors Court 798–804, 807, 817
  see also bankruptcy
insurance 304, 674–727
  accident 677, 991n, 1011–12, 1018–22, 1024,
  Average Clause Act 1828 721
  duties to disclose 697–9, 705–11
  fire 675, 693–6, 703–4, 706–7, 719–26
    'average' policies 721–2

Fire Prevention (Metropolis)
  Act 1774 694
Employers Liability Insurance Companies
  Act 1907 1021
Gambling Act 1774 676, 679, 691, 694
insurable interest 679–80, 684–96
law of insurance companies 629–30
  winding up 650–1
life assurance 449, 676–7, 689–93,
  703–11, 726–7
  assignment of policies 691–3
  Life Insurance Companies Act 1870 630
  Life Assurance Companies
    (Payment into Court) Act 1896 693
  premiums 703–6, 711
  suicides 692, 726–7
marine insurance 674, 679–89,
  696–703, 711–19
  abandonment 716–7
  assignment of policies 688–9
  'c.f.i.' policies 683
  general average 714–16
  'lost or not lost' policies 700
  Marine Insurance Act 1906 679,
    681–2, 688, 700, 703, 717
  Marine Insurance (Gambling Policies) Act
    1909 681
  particular average 716–19
  payment of premiums 697
  policy 711–14, 716–19
  'p.p.i.' policies 678–81, 683
  professional average adjusters 678, 715
  time policies 701–2
  valued policies 681–4, 717
  York-Antwerp Rules 715
Policies of Assurance Act 1867 692
principle of indemnity 678, 682–4, 686,
  689–90, 693–5, 725
reinsurance 675, 679, 704–5
rules as to causation of loss 712–14,
  719–20
subrogation 694, 723–6
Ireland 145, 197–8, 851, 1053

judgment debts 386, 838, 813, 841–2
  conveyancing, and 61, 184–90
  Crown, to 57, 183–6
  enforcement against land 61, 184–90
  equitable execution 189
  receivers, and 189
  security, as 144–5
  see also debtors and creditors,
    mortgages
Judicature Acts 1873–75 320, 322, 393, 425,
  439n, 636n, 693,
  preference for equity, in
    Judicature Act 1873 161, 178, 425

Juridical Society 307
juries
  in contract cases 316–18,
    320, 530–2
  in tort cases 899–901, 936–40
Justices of the Peace 122

land
  creditors' remedies against 57, 180–90
    deceased debtor 54, 180–3
    living debtor 184–90
  devises 7–8, 180–3
    interpretation 19–22, 25–6, 28–9, 31–3,
      38–9, 43–6
  executory trusts of 14–18
  partition 86–7
  real property, law of 47, 49, 53, 61, 225
    assimilation with personalty 54, 56, 77,
      179–201, 207, 214, 225–31
    codes and digests 49–54, 225, 230
    simplification 195–6, 204, 224–31
  taxation of 183–4, 228
  trusts of 4, 80, 82, 92, 94, 106, 110,
    192–4, 201, 203, 232–5, 243–4,
    256, 263–6, 268
  see also estates in land, perpetuities,
    sale of land, settlements, strict
    settlement, succession, tenure
Land Registry 187, 198–9, 213, 219
  finances of 205, 219
  land brokers at 218, 220
  Middlesex Deeds Registry, and 205, 219
  officials at 219, 228
  registrar 203, 219, 226
    rule-making 214, 217, 222
  solicitors, and 220, 225–8
  workload of 198, 205
  see also registration of title
land, sale of
  see sale of land, vendor
    and purchaser
landlord and tenant
  distress 120–4, 401–2, 596, 598–9,
    872–3, 875, 1115
    remedies for unlawful 121
    statutory limitation 122–3
  eviction 124–7
  fixtures 117–8
  forfeiture 114, 124–7
    relief against 124–6, 209n
  notice 113, 119
  obligations, implied 116
    fitness for habitation 116–7
  penal rents 115, 119
  tenant right 118–19
  waste 114, 116
  see also housing, leases

Larceny
    Larceny Act 1827 463–4
    Larceny Act 1861 463, 467–8,
        661, 827
Law Amendment Society
    real property law, and 58, 60,
        71, 75, 194
law officers
    role in government and Parliament 221
law reform 49–64, 220–1, 276,
        290, 306, 308
    bankruptcy law 779–80, 793–7,
        800–08, 810, 813, 817–33
    company law 619–27
    procedural reform 317–20, 569–70
Law Society 141
    conveyancing, and 107, 196, 208,
        211–12, 227n
    law reform 208, 212–13, 276
    title registration, and 196, 222, 226
    trusts law, and 213, 276, 291, 293
law societies 70, 96, 108, 207, 211–12,
        220, 291
leases 54, 71, 97, 104, 107, 185, 234
    agricultural 88, 111–15, 119
    building and repairing 54, 82–3, 88–9,
        112, 142, 172
    Church and 113
    covenants in 112–17, 124–32, 172, 174
        equity and 115, 127, 130–2, 173
        mortgagees, and 128–31
        Real Property Commissioners and 110–11
        running of 127–32, 177
        usual 174
    drafting of 110
        short forms 71–2
    houses, of 116–17, see also housing
    lives, for 111–13, 196
    private statutes, under 54, 112–13
    settlements, under 54, 81–4, 87–90, 112–13
    title registration, and 220
    universities and 113
    yearly tenancies 113, 118–19
    years, for 111–12
    see also landlord and tenant
legacies 7, 25, 181, 242–3, 246, 249, 258
legislation (local and private) 85, 163–5, 177–8
    Clauses Acts 1845 85, 163, 622, 629, 636, 654
    interpretation of 165–6
legislation (personal)
    estate acts 54, 83–4, 87, 112–13
legislation (public general)
    parliamentary process 207
letters of credit 754–8
Liberal party
    land law, and 119, 123, 198–9, 204–5,
        208–9, 214, 217, 225, 228

Liberty and Property Defence League 299
lien 69, 121, 123n, 685, 695, 760, 762, 767
life assurance,
    see insurance
life estate,
    see estates in land
life tenant,
    see estates in land, strict settlement
light, easement of,
    see easements and profits, nuisance
limitation of actions 56, 58, 102, 362, 427, 604,
        766–7, 1128–9
Liverpool 122
    solicitors in 96, 108
local government
    borrowing 284, 286–7
    spending by
        Borough Fund Act 1872 164
London 68, 70, 82, 89, 110, 134, 187, 324–5, 467,
        475–6, 807–8, 823, 849, 855, 858, 1071,
        1072, 1076, 1095
    banking in 728, 730, 773
    bankruptcy commissions 786–7, 795
    solicitors in 96, 205
London Stock Exchange 631–4, 638–40
    speculative booms on 617, 623, 631, 728
Lord Chancellor 220–1
    bankruptcy jurisdiction 781, 786–9, 795–6
Lord Chancellor's Office 220, 230
Lords, House of 221
    functions of 220

Manchester
    Law Society 227n
    solicitors in 108
marine insurance,
    see insurance
maritime law,
    see bills of lading, charter parties
marriage 7
    breach of promise action 498, 504, 512–13
marriage settlements 9, 66, 232–5, 257, 264,
        283, 323–4, 330, 436–7, 443
    articles for 13–15
    covenants in 260–1, 265–6
    marriage consideration 254, 260, 264–5,
        368–70
    usual form of 11, 14, 132, 262–3, 283
    volunteers under 264–6
    see also married women, trusts
married women's property
    property brought into marriage by
        wife 264–5
    reforms in 1870 8
    reforms in 1882 8
    rights on death of partner 215
    separate use 8, 159, 178, 247–52

see also dower, marital breakdown, marriage
    settlements, private international law,
    settlement (of property generally)
Mercantile Law Commission 556
Metropolitan and Provincial Law
    Association 141
misrepresentation 400, 409–32, 924
  change of circumstances 410
  damages for 426–31
  in equity
    indemnity 425–7
    making representations good 338, 367–9,
      416–19, 425, 428
  fraudulent 412–4
  in insurance law 698–9, 706–7
  negligent misrepresentations 418–20, 942,
    944, 947, 949
  rescission for 419–25, 649
  Pollock's views on 370, 430–1
mistake in contract law 301, 303, 307, 309, 313,
    319, 321, 433–72, 588
  common mistake 437, 448
  common law 445–52, 445–70
  cross-purpose 446
  in equity 434–45
    rectification 435, 437–9, 442–3, 446
    rescission for mistake 436–8, 441–5, 590
  of identity 434–5, 452–70, 1119
    in equity 452–4
  of law 441–2, 587–8,
  of quality 440–1, 445, 449–52
  of rights 442
  of subject-matter 435, 448
  Pollock's views on 433–4, 449, 452, 467,
    469, 471–2
  unilateral mistake 439–43, 447, 451–2
mistaken payments, recovery for 583–8
  bills of exchange 751–2
  change of position 586
money had and received, action for,
  see restitution
moneylenders 835, 841, 858–69, 874–5
  Money Lenders Act 1900 867–9
  Select Committee (1897) 865–6
  summary diligence procedure,
    use of 864, 866
monopolies,
  see cartels
mortgages 47, 81, 85, 92, 94–5, 132–58
  annuities, and 142–4, 147, 153, 156
  chattels, of 152
  collateral advantages 142, 145–8, 153
  contracts, as 139–41, 147–50
  conveyancing, and 65–7, 132–3, 137–40
    Real Property Commissioners 134
  debentures 155–8
  deeds registration, and 65, 69, 71, 133, 206–7

devolution of 137
equity of redemption
  clogs and fetters on 135, 138, 150–9
  forms of 153
    by charge 200–1, 203, 207, 222–3, 229
    by deposit of deeds 69, 71, 133–5, 206, 222
    by term of years 136
    by transfer 136, 196, 229
    by trust for sale 135–6
    with power of sale 135–41, 151, 158, 194
  foreclosure 61, 135–6, 141
  further advances 133, 149–50, 207
  investment in 132, 283, 285
  judgment debts, and 61, 144–5
  leases, of 128–31, 142
  mortgagees
    oppression by 138–40, 145–9
    in possession 145–6
    sale by 137–40, 149
  powers in 137–41, 208–9
  priorities of 149–50
    consolidation 133, 209
    tacking 133, 136, 149–50, 206, 208
  sale 61, 106
    purchaser protection 139–41
  substance of 152–4
  title registration, and 200–1, 222–3
  usury laws, and 142–6, 152
  see also annuities, bills of sale, judgment
    debts, pawnbroking

negligence 888–91, 894, 903–57, 1014, 1118,
    1127, 1131–2, 1134, 1136
  causation of harm 922, 928–34, 937–8, 950–3
  cheques, drawing of 770–1, 929–30
  common carriers 911–16
  contributory negligence 908, 931–2,
    938–40, 953, 973, 1005, 1014–15
  damages in 934–6, 990–1000
  duty of care 922–8, 944–50, 982–3, 985,
    987–90
    breach of duty 936–7, 954–7
  estoppel by 929–30, 947
  faulty vehicles 910, 961–4
  fire, keeping of 916–20
  foreseeability 890, 935, 946, 950–7, 966, 988
  'gross' 913–16
  misrepresentation 418–32
  Pollock's views on 941–4, 947, 949, 954, 955–7
  professional 882–3, 916
  railways 919–21, 958–67, 985
  'reasonable man' standard 917–18, 925–7,
    942, 944
  res ipsa loquitur 960, 976, 980
  road accidents 904–911, 970–1, 973–6
  Salmond's views on 943, 953,
    955, 990

negotiable instruments,
  see bills of exchange, bills of lading,
    cheques, promissory notes
notice 67, 97, 128, 171, 174–6, 210
  charges registration, and 181–6, 189
  deeds registration, and 69, 205–7
  mortgages, and 133, 139–41, 206–7
  restrictive covenants, and 171, 174 6
  trusts, and 181–2, 201
nuisance 163, 895, 1068–1111, 1127, 1130,
    1141–2, 1145–6, 1149–50
  common law actions 1069
  injunctions against 1105–11
  interference with light 169–70, 1071–9
  noise 1102–3
  Nuisances Removal Act 1855 1094
  public nuisances 972–6, 985, 1069, 1082
    indictment 1069
  'reasonable user' 1079
  remedies 1105–11
  smoke pollution 1085–6, 1093–1101, 1104
    Smoke Nuisance Abatement (Metropolis)
      Act 1853 1094
  strict liability in 1069
  water pollution 1080–93
    percolating underground water 164–6,
      1083, 1086–7
    prescriptive rights to pollute 1083–5, 1090,
      1092
    Rivers Pollution Commission 1867 1084
    Rivers Pollution Prevention Act
      1876 1080, 1088, 1090–2
    statutory regulation 1088–93

Overend, Gurney & Co 426, 640, 661,
    666, 729–30

pandectists 306, 309, 311
partnership 153, 306, 613–16
  en commandite 626–7
  liability of partners for each other's acts 665
  Pollock's Digest 731
  use of bills of exchange by 737
  see also companies
patents for invention 590–1
pawnbrokers 146, 401, 836, 849–58, 871
  calculation of interest 851, 855–6
  Pawnbroking Act 1872 853, 855, 857
  Pawnbrokers' Reform Association 856
  Select Committee on Pawnbroking
    (1870) 855–7
penalties 115, 523–9
perpetuities 9, 48, 55
  modern rule against 19–22, 62–4, 247, 249
  'old' rule against 18–20
    cy-près 20–1, 25–6, 28
pleadings

Common Law Courts 313–5, 317, 319, 905–6
  equitable pleas 321–2, 446–8
  general issue 316–18
  Hilary Rules 1834 318, 320
  joinder of parties 315
  special pleading 314, 317–18, 320
pledges 761–3, 791
  see also debtors and creditors
Post Office 226, 336–7
  Post Office Savings Bank 1011
powers (proprietary) 80–1, 262, 266–7, 271
  appointment, of 8, 30, 243, 262–3
  literature on 89
  theory of 89–92
prize law 685
probate 5, 8, 10, 57, 67, 191
promissory notes 144–5, 728–9, 732–3, 862
  see also bills of exchange
public health controls
  Alkali Act 1863 1095
  Board of Health 74
  Public Health Act 1875 1088, 1090, 1095
  Sale of Food and Drugs Act 1875 881
  Sanitary Act 1866 1095
  see also nuisance

railway companies 76, 84, 90, 235, 287
railways 327, 402, 870, 879, 897, 1010–11, 1103
  accident litigation 958–69, 992
    attempts to limit liability 474–5, 967–9
    liability for fires 920–1
    liability for stations 979–80
  investment in 631
  Railway and Canal Traffic Act 1854 474, 967
  railway mania 328
real property,
  see land
Real Property Commission 3, 5–6, 9, 22,
    48, 50–78, 96, 102, 110–11, 134, 171,
    178, 185, 193, 196, 206–7
registration of births, deaths and
    marriages 55, 59
registration of charges,
  see conveyancing
registration of deeds 49, 64–71, 73–8, 134,
    192, 196, 203–8
  bills for 70–1, 73–4
  caveats, and 206, 210, 226
  conveyancing costs, and 64, 75, 77–8, 196
  forgery, and 203
  indexing 69–70, 74
  Land Registry, and 205
  Middlesex, in 69, 204–6
  notice, and 69, 205–7
  Real Property Commissioners, and 52–3, 57,
    64–71, 134, 206
  Select Committee on (1852–3) 192

Select Committee on (1878–9) 203–4,
   207, 215, 226
solicitors, and 70, 74–5
Yorkshire, in 206–7
see also conveyancing
registration of title 69, 106–7, 194–202, 214–25
   absolute title 194, 215, 222, 226
   boundaries, and 199, 214, 217
   centralization, and 200, 216, 228
   compulsory 199, 203, 216–28
   consols, analogy with 190–7, 200, 203
   costs of 222, 226
   fee simple ownership, and 192–7
   insurance fund 214, 216
   land taxes, and 228
   landed estates courts, and 197–8
   leases, and 200
   London, in 204, 218
   mortgages, and 200–1, 222–3, 226
   obstacles to 93, 195
   possessory title 194, 211, 222
   real representatives, and 193, 199, 201,
      214, 216–8
   Royal Commission (1857) 192, 194, 196–9, 216
   Royal Commission (1870) 106, 198–9
   Royal Commission (1909–11) 201, 218,
      223, 225, 226–8
   servitudes, and 222, 226
   simplification of title, and 195–6, 204,
      224–5, 229–31
   solicitors and 199, 202, 215–20, 222, 225–7
   strict settlement, and 193
      Westbury's Act 1862 194, 198–9
   theories of 192–5, 198, 200, 202–3, 223–4
   Torrens system 215–6, 218, 224
   see also land registry
remainders 10, 16, 19–23, 32, 38, 45, 49, 62–4,
   80, 92, 103, 183, 233, 243n, 245
   see also estates in land
rent,
   see landlord and tenant
rentcharges 9, 142–3, 172, 200
replevin, action of 121, 124, 1115
restitution,
   account 564–5, 601–3, 645–6, 663, 692
   action for money had and
      received 401–2, 562–3, 566–7, 570–95
   action for money paid 563, 595–601
   common counts, use of 578–80
   failure of consideration 588–95
   mistaken payments 583–8
      bills of exchange 751–2
      change of position 586
   quantum meruit 530–4
   theories about 565–70, 601, 608–10
      Anson's views 569
      'quasi-contract' 566–70, 607–10

tracing 570, 604, 608
waiver of tort 562, 573–83
restrictive covenants 159, 171–8
   Brougham, Lord, and 171
   building schemes, in 173, 175–6
   Cottenham, Lord, and 171–5
   early uses of 172
   in gross 176–7
   Jessel MR, and 176–7
   notice 171, 174–6
      tenants, and 174–5
   positive obligations, and 173–4
   property interest, as 176–8
   see also easements
reversions 103, 148, 191, 258
   see also estates in land
Roman law 306, 309, 434, 449, 450, 505,
   514–15, 518, 566, 1047–8
rule against perpetuities,
   see perpetuities

sale of goods 304, 306, 330, 409, 415,
   475–85, 509–10
   arbitration and 476–7
   damages in 534–9,
   by description 477
   duties of disclosure 409–10, 479
   express warranties 479–80
   fraudulent purchasers 457–69
   implied warranties 986
      of quality 409, 473, 475, 480–4
      of title 484–5, 510
   liens 762
   market overt, sales in 457, 459
   nemo dat quod non habet, rule 760
   passing of property in 478, 509–10, 761
   quality obligations 475–85
   rescission in 478, 589
   Sale of Goods Act 1893
      s 11 490, 494
      s 14 483–4
      s 24 468
      s 25 762
      s 31 488
      s 51 535
      s 52 556
   by sample 476, 483
   specific performance of 554–6
   stoppage *in transitu* 760, 762, 790–1
sale of land 94–109
   auction, by 95–6, 107
   buyer's remedies 98–102
   conditions of sale 47, 76, 96, 102–9
      common forms 96, 102–6
      criticisms of 103
      deeds registration, and 76–7
      enforcement of 103–4

sale of land (*cont.*)
    law societies and 105, 107–8
    statutory 107
    uses of 96, 102
    contract for 94–108
        exchange of 108
        interpretation of 101, 104
        open 97, 107–9
    conveyancing counsel 96–7
    leasehold, of 97, 104
    particulars of sale 95
    private treaty, by 96, 107–8
    process of 95, 107–9, 168
        costs of 98, 105–8
    solicitors and 95–6, 107–8
    title registration, and 106–7
    see also conveyancing, vendor
            and purchaser
salvage 721–2
    see also insurance
set-off 455
settlement (of property generally) 3, 5, 67,
        77, 110, 232–5
    common forms of 10–12, 234–5
    executory 13–18, 83
    land, of (*see also* strict settlement) 12, 112–14,
        116, 192, 196, 203, 263–6
    married women's equity to 12–13, 18
    personalty, of 11, 13–18, 21, 25–6, 39,
        41, 43–4, 220–4
    testamentary 233–4
    usual powers 54
    see also marriage settlements, strict
            settlements, trusts, wills
ships and shipping 179, 190–1, 197
    Royal Commission on Unseaworthy
            Ships 682
    see also charterparties
Social science, National Association for
        the Promotion of 817, 822
société en commandite,
    see partnership
solicitors
    conveyancing, and 53, 65–6, 68, 70, 74–5,
        95–6, 105, 107–8, 187–89, 199, 203, 207
    Liverpool 96, 108
    London 96, 205
    Manchester 108
    title registration, and 215–20, 222, 225–8
    trustees, as 235, 237, 269, 288
specific performance,
    see Chancery
Statute of Frauds 329, 333, 337–8, 368–70, 389,
        447, 476, 492–3, 533, 565
    s 4, 329–30
    s 17, 329–31
    part-performance rule 329

statutory duty, breach of
    see tort
Stock Exchange
    see London Stock Exchange
stoppage *in transitu*,
    see sale of goods
strict settlements 11, 16, 48, 79–94, 233
    borrowing under 81, 85, 185
    estate acts 83–4, 112
    Enclosure Commissioners, and 86–7
        exchange and partition 86–7, 92
    leasing under 81–4, 88–9, 112, 114, 116
    life tenant 53–4, 82–3, 85, 92
        owner, as 85
    mortgages, and 81–2, 92
    politics of 92–3, 208–9, 214–5
    powers in 81–4, 112–13
        sale 82, 87–8, 92
    reform of 87–94, 112, 196, 199, 208–9
    Settled Estates Acts 1856 87–90, 193
        Chancery approvals 87–8, 193
    Settled Land Acts 1882 91–4, 112, 208–9,
        214–15, 287
    title registration, and 93, 193, 198–9, 204, 226
    trustees in 67, 82, 92, 233
    usual forms 80, 112
subrogation 694, 723–6
succession 5–46, 67, 180, 182
    heir 5–6, 8, 23, 54, 65, 137, 180–2, 193,
        214, 216, 264n, 272–4, 277
    intestate 214, 217
        personalty 5
        realty 5–6, 207, 214
    partible inheritance 10, 214, 233
    primogeniture 11–12, 48, 54, 93,
        214, 217, 233
    Real Property Commissioners, and 5–6, 54
    real representatives 23, 54, 192–3, 199, 210,
        207, 214, 216–8
    taxation on 183–4, 217
    see also wills
succession and estate duties 183–4, 217
superior courts of common law, jurisdiction
        and business
    joinder of parties 315
    pleadings 313–5, 317, 319, 905–6
    special pleadings 314, 317–18, 320
        general issue 316–18
        variances 314, 317–18
    rules of 1834 318, 320
sureties 599–600

tenure and tenures 56, 186, 230
    abolition of 53, 55, 225
    Borough English 55
    copyhold 53n, 55–6, 59n, 82, 230
        commissioners 59, 86

gavelkind 55
Real Property Commissioners, and 55
title (to land) 37, 56, 66, 75, 86, 96–100, 102–4,
        106, 108, 199, 203, 229
    abstracts 97, 109
    covenants for 101, 209
tort
    *actio personalis moritur cum
        persona* 576, 582, 996
    action on the case 888, 905–9, 970
    animals, liability for 917, 922, 1126
    assault 1034–6
        consent to 1035–6
    breach of statutory duty 1007–8
    conspiracy 1048 1050–3, 1060–7
    damages 544, 899–902
    defective products 881, 988–90
    economic torts 1033 1039–67
        procuring breach of contract 1043–7, 1057,
        1059, 1064–5
        seduction 579–80, 1041–4
    false imprisonment 1034
    inevitable accident, defence of 889, 903, 909,
        916, 970–1, 1148–9
    intentional torts: *see* malice, prima facie torts
    litigation rates 883–4
    Lord Campbell's Act 1844 883, 997–1001
    malice 1033–9, 1044–59
        Pollock's views on 1033, 1047–52, 1055–6,
        1059, 1066
        Salmond's views on 1066–7
    malicious prosecution 1036–8
    negligence *see* negligence
    non-delegable duties 898–9, 1005
    nuisance *see* nuisance
    occupiers' liability 976–84
        children 980–4
        railway companies' 979–80
    personal injuries
        boiler explosions 984–6
        damages for 990–1000
        dangerous goods 985–90
        nervous shock 991–6, 1025
        railway accidents 936–40, 958–69, 985
        road accidents 904–11, 970–6
        workplace injuries, *see* workplace
            injuries
    'prima facie' torts 1047 1050–1, 1054–9, 1066
    property torts 1112–50,
        Pollock's views on 1112–13, 1125–6
        see also conversion, trespass
    Rylands v. *Fletcher*, rule in 1093 1140–50
    sic utere tuo ut alienum non laedas 895–7,
        918–19, 926, 1097, 1126, 1129, 1142–3
    slander of title 1039
    strict liability 894, 896, 943
        Pollock's views on 1112 1145

    Salmond's views on 1112–13
    theories of 880, 885–94, 941–4
        Holmes's 891, 941–2
        Pollock's 890–4, 942–3
        Salmond's 893–4
    trespass *see* trespass
trade unions
    conspiracy 1050–4, 1060–7
    Conspiracy and Protection of Property
        Act 1875 1060, 1062–3
    Trade Disputes Act 1906 1064
transport,
    see carriers, railways
Treasury
    Land Registry, and 205, 219
treatises, legal
    'civilian' 300–01, 305, 336, 433,
        450–2, 466, 541, 677
    contract law 300–13, 340, 346,
        433, 452, 466
    insurance 677–8
    negotiable instruments 731
    tort 880
trespass
    to goods 1114–17
    to land 121, 972–3, 980–4, 1125–6, 1141–3
    Salmond's views on 1125–6
    vi et armis 888, 903, 905–8, 970
trover *see* conversion
trustee 235–8, 268–94
    apportionment and conversion 245, 278–9
    Chancery as 235–7
        investment by 236, 279–82, 284
    corporate 235, 237, 290
    court advice to 290, 293
    death of 271–4
    delegation by 269–70, 288–94
    executors as 242, 278
    fraud by 288
        Fraudulent Trustees Act 1857 288, 661
    investment by 132, 232–4, 268–9, 278–87
        Chancery practice 279–84
        clauses regulating 234, 279,
            282–4, 287
        legislation on 284–7
        standards for 279–80
    liability 207, 288–94
        defences against 289–91
        restitutionary remedies against 564–5,
            601–2
        standards for 238, 289–94
    powers of 82, 87n, 90–2, 106, 137, 213
    precatory, duties of 244–6
    public trustee 235, 237, 290–1, 293
    receipts 181–2, 201
    retirement and replacement 90, 201,
        210, 269–78

trustee *(cont.)*
  discretions, transmission of 201, 269,
    273–5
  property, transmission of 270–5
  solicitors as 235, 237, 269, 288, 290–1
  see also trusts, settlement (of property
    generally), strict settlements
trusts
  charitable 241
  common forms of 232–5
  constitution of 253–62
  constructive 240, 565, 601
  debts, for payment of 240–1
  discretionary 250–1
  Eldon, Lord, and 239, 249, 253, 255,
    258–60, 262, 267
  enforcement of
    by volunteers 255–8, 263–8
  executory 13–18, 22–6, 283
  inter vivos 242–4
  land, of 4, 80, 82, 92, 94, 106, 110, 192–4, 201,
    203, 232–5, 243–4, 256, 263–6, 268
  literature on 238–40
  marriage settlements, in 254, 257, 260–1
  married women, for 246–8
  powers of appointment, and 262–3, 271, 273
  precatory 5, 35–7, 244–6
  property relation, as 239–44, 246–52
  protective 249–52
  purposes, for 241
  revocability of 262–8
    by creditors 256, 258, 267
  sale, for 135–6, 143, 180–1, 194, 233–4, 243
  secret 4
  termination of 242–4, 252–3
  testamentary 10–11, 231, 233–4, 242–4, 252,
    257
  see also settlement (of property generally),
    trustees

undue influence 148, 321–22, 400, 402–9
  expectant heirs 148, 403
  money lenders 865–6
  presumption of 403–8
United States 170, 251–2
universities 113
unjust enrichment,
  see restitution
usury 535, 626, 729n, 876, 851, 855, 859, 865
  see also annuities, mortgages

vendor and purchaser
  damages 539–40
  misrepresentations 414–16

rescission 436–8, 441,
specific performance of 373, 438–41, 550–1
  see also sale of land
vicarious liability 894–99, 964–7,
  1003–4, 1012–13

wager of law 1116
warranty 432, 473, 478–9
  implied 409, 473, 475, 480–5
  insurance 698, 701–03, 706, 708–10
  see also contract
warrants of attorney 401, 523, 866
water,
  see easements and profits, nuisance
wills 3, 68, 227n
  common uses 4, 10–11, 39, 242
  conveyance, as 23
  debts, directions to pay, in 180–2
  formalities 3–4, 56
  interpretation of 19, 22–46,
    278–9, 282–4
    class gifts 22, 30, 39–41, 44–5
    executory trusts 13–18,
      20, 24–6
    'general intention' 21, 26–3, 45, 262
    Malins VC, and 33–4, 37, 39–42, 44
    'ordinary meaning' 31–46, 261
    precatory words 35–7, 45
    purpose of 33, 44–6
    rules of construction 27–8, 37–46
    standards for 26–46
    'technical words' 31–2
  land, of 6–7, 16, 18–24, 29, 31–2
  numbers of 9–10
  Real Property Commissioners, and 22–3
  testamentary freedom 6–9, 48
    restraints on marriage 7–8
  see also executors, probate, settlement
    (of property generally), succession
Wills Act 1837 3, 19, 22–3, 58–9
women 8, 37, 57, 266–7
Workmen's Compensation Acts 1897 1018–32
  accident, definition of 1023–6
  compensation 1019 1029–32
  course of employment,
    definition of 1026–9
workplace injuries 1001–32
  common employment rule 894–5, 985,
    1003–5, 1012–13, 1015, 1018
  contributory negligence 1005 1014–15
  Employers Liability Act 1880 677,
    1012–18, 1022,
  volenti non fit injuria 1006–9, 1012,
    1014–15, 1018

The Oxford History of the Laws of England

THE OXFORD HISTORY OF THE LAWS OF ENGLAND

General Editor: Sir John Baker, Q.C., LL.D., F.B.A., Downing Professor of the Laws of England, and Fellow of St Catharine's College, Cambridge

The Oxford History of the Laws of England will provide a detailed survey of the development of English law and its institutions from the earliest times until the twentieth century, drawing heavily upon recent research using unpublished materials.

Volume I: The Canon Law and Ecclesiastical
Jurisdiction from 597 to the 1640s   Helmholz
ISBN 0–19–825897–6

Volume II: *c.* 900–1216   Hudson
ISBN 0–19–826030–x

Volume III: 1216–1307   Brand
ISBN 0–19–826866–6

Volume IV: 1307–1377   Donahue
ISBN 0–19–926951–3

Volume V: 1399–1483
ISBN 0–19–926599–2

Volume VI: 1483–1558   Baker
ISBN 0–19–825817–8

Volume VII: 1558–1625   Ibbetson
ISBN 0–19–825802–x

Volume VIII: 1625–1689   Brooks
ISBN 0–19–826031–8

Volume IX: 1689–1760
ISBN 0–19–826100–4

Volume X: 1760–1820   Oldham
ISBN 0–19–826494–1

Volume XI: 1820–1914   English Legal System
Cornish, Anderson, Cocks, Lobban, Polden, and Smith
ISBN 978–0–19–9258819

Volume XII: 1820–1914   Private Law
Cornish, Anderson, Cocks, Lobban, Polden, and Smith
ISBN 978–0–19–9258826

Volume XIII: 1820–1914   Fields of Development
Cornish, Anderson, Cocks, Lobban, Polden, and Smith
ISBN 978–0–19–9239757

(Three volume set of Volumes XI, XII, and XIII: ISBN 978–0–19–9258833)

The Oxford History
of the
Laws of England

VOLUME XII
1820–1914

Private Law

OXFORD
UNIVERSITY PRESS

OXFORD
UNIVERSITY PRESS

Great Clarendon Street, Oxford OX2 6DP

Oxford University Press is a department of the University of Oxford.
It furthers the University's objective of excellence in research, scholarship,
and education by publishing worldwide in

Oxford New York

Auckland Cape Town Dar es Salaam Hong Kong Karachi
Kuala Lumpur Madrid Melbourne Mexico City Nairobi
New Delhi Shanghai Taipei Toronto

With offices in

Argentina Austria Brazil Chile Czech Republic France Greece
Guatemala Hungary Italy Japan Poland Portugal Singapore
South Korea Switzerland Thailand Turkey Ukraine Vietnam

Oxford is a registered trade mark of Oxford University Press
in the UK and in certain other countries

Published in the United States
by Oxford University Press Inc., New York

British Library Cataloguing in Publication Data

Data available

Library of Congress Cataloging in Publication Data

Data available

Typeset by Newgen Imaging Systems Pvt Ltd., Chennai, India
Printed in Great Britain
on acid-free paper by
Antony Rowe, Chippenham, Wiltshire

ISBN 978-0-19-9258826

1 3 5 7 9 10 8 6 4 2